The
ENCYCLOPEDIA
of
POPULAR
MUSIC

First edition published 1992
Reprinted 1994
Second edition published 1995
Reprinted 1997
Third edition published November 1998
Reprinted with minor corrections 2000
Fourth edition published 2006 by Oxford University Press

MUZE UK Ltd
email: colinl@muze.com

MUZE UK Ltd is a wholly owned subsidiary of MUZE Inc.
304 Hudson Street, New York, NY 10013, USA
www.muze.com

Oxford University Press, Inc., publishes works that further
Oxford University's objective of excellence
in research, scholarship, and education.

Oxford New York
Auckland Cape Town Dar es Salaam Hong Kong Karachi
Kuala Lumpur Madrid Melbourne Mexico City Nairobi
New Delhi Shanghai Taipei Toronto

With offices in
Argentina Austria Brazil Chile Czech Republic France Greece
Guatemala Hungary Italy Japan Poland Portugal Singapore
South Korea Switzerland Thailand Turkey Ukraine Vietnam

Library of Congress Cataloging-in-Publication Data
Encyclopedia of popular music (London, England)
The encyclopedia of popular music / compiled & edited by Colin Larkin. – 4th ed.
p. cm.
Rev. ed. of: The Guinness encyclopedia of popular music. 2nd ed. 1995.
Includes bibliographical references and index.
ISBN-13: 978-0-19-531373-4
ISBN-10: 0-19-531373-9
1. Popular music–Encyclopedias. I. Larkin, Colin. II. Guinness encyclopedia of popular music. III. Title.
ML102.P66G84 2006
781.6403–dc22
2006018335

Conceived, compiled and edited by Colin Larkin for MUZE UK Ltd
to whom all editorial enquiries should be sent

Editor In Chief: Colin Larkin
Assistant Editor: Nic Oliver
Production Editor: Susan Pipe
Senior Contributor: Bruce Crowther
Production team MUZE USA: Scott Lehr, Paul Brennan and Paul Parreira

CONTENTS

Volume 1
Preface   vii
Notes On Style   ix
Acknowledgements   xiii
Popular Music: An Introduction   xv

A–Brown, Lloyd

Volume 2
Brown, Marion–Dilated Peoples

Volume 3
Dill, Danny–Grenadine

Volume 4
Grenfell, Joyce–Koller, Hans

Volume 5
Kollington–Morphine

Volume 6
Morricone, Ennio–Rich Kids

Volume 7
Rich, Young And Pretty–Swift, Richard

Volume 8
Swift, Rob–ZZ Top

Volume 9
Selected Albums   3
Bibliography by Artist   699
Bibliography by Subject   859

Volume 10
Indexes

ALBUM RATINGS

★★★★★
Outstanding
Magnificent, even with one or two less than outstanding tracks.
A classic and therefore strongly recommended.
No comprehensive record collection should be without this album.

★★★★
Excellent
A high standard album from this artist and therefore highly recommended.
Usually with three or four absolute gems.

★★★
Good
Good by the artist's usual standards and therefore recommended.
Maybe with only one or two classics but still highly listenable.

★★
Disappointing
Flawed or lacking in some way. Not recommended.
Usually filed away after two or three listens and rarely played thereafter.
Nevertheless a useful addition to the artist's catalogue.

★
Poor
Terrible and often excruciating; however, quite useful to break the ice at parties.
An album to avoid unless you are a wealthy completist or tonally challenged.

The
ENCYCLOPEDIA
— *of* —
POPULAR
MUSIC

—— *Edited by* ——
COLIN LARKIN
—— *4th Edition* ——

3
DILL, DANNY–GRENADINE

muze

OXFORD
UNIVERSITY PRESS

D

(CONTINUED)

Dill, Danny

b. Horace Eldred Dill, 19 September 1924, Carroll County, Tennessee, USA. Although Dill became famous as a country music songwriter, he began his career in 1943, on WTJS Jackson as a performer. He played local venues, often as a country comedian with red wig and blacked out teeth. In 1944, he worked on the *Mid-Day Merry-Go-Round*, on WNOX Knoxville, before returning to Jackson and marrying his first wife, Annie Lou. In December 1945, they relocated to Nashville, where as Annie Lou And Danny, The Sweethearts of the Grand Ole Opry, they played on WLS for 11 years. In 1949, they recorded for Bullet and began touring with the various package shows. Dill not only sang with Annie Lou but also compered the shows, soon acquiring a reputation for his ability to keep shows going smoothly. He and Annie Lou toured with **Hank Williams** and **Eddy Arnold** but in 1952, soon after the birth of daughter Ava, they divorced. (He later married Carolyn Penick.) When he was offered a writer's contract with Cedarwood Music, Dill cut back on his performing and for a time, he concentrated on songwriting. He gained no major hits, but **Carl Smith** recorded 'If You Saw Her Through My Eyes'. In 1953, he joined **Ernest Tubb** as rhythm guitarist and compere and also wrote 'Partners', which later became a country number 5 for **Jim Reeves**. In 1954, he worked as a radio announcer in Georgia, before returning to Nashville, where he achieved a major breakthrough as a songwriter. In 1959, he wrote the lyrics to 'The Long Black Veil'; Marijohn Wilkin added the melody and **Lefty Frizzell** recorded it. The recording reached number 6 and the song went on to become a much recorded country standard. During the 60s, various songs he wrote or co-wrote became major hits including 'The Comeback' (**Faron Young** 1962), 'Detroit City' (**Billy Grammer** as 'I Want To Go Home' and **Bobby Bare**, both 1963) and 'Old Courthouse' (Faron Young 1964). He spent some time, during the 60s, in California working as a session musician before leaving the music for some years. He became addicted to alcohol, which finally resulted in a serious car crash that put him in intensive care for over three weeks. During his convalescence, he decided it was time to change his ways and he managed to break the alcohol addiction. He returned to Nashville, where he made appearances on major shows including with Annie Lou on a *Grand Ole Opry Reunion* show. Dill was elected into the Nashville Songwriters Association International Hall Of Fame in 1975, and he has several BMI awards. He was never a prolific recording artist, but he did record two albums, which mainly included his own songs. His 1957 rockabilly recording of 'Hungry For Your Lovin'' for **ABC** Paramount is rated a very collectable disc. In 1993, he made a considerable impression by an appearance on the NSAI Songwriters Concert—an event for those classed as 'superwriters'.

● ALBUMS: *Folk Songs Of The Wild West* (MGM 1960) ★★, *Folk Songs From The Country* (Liberty 1963) ★★.

Dillard And Clark

Refugees from the **Dillards** and the **Byrds**, respectively, Doug Dillard (b. 6 March 1937, East St. Louis, Illinois, USA) and **Gene Clark** (b. Harold Eugene Clark, 17 November 1941, Tipton, Missouri, USA, d. 24 May 1991) joined forces in 1968 to form one of the first country rock groups. Backed by the Expedition, featuring **Bernie Leadon** (banjo/guitar), Don Beck (dobro/mandolin) and David Jackson (string bass), they recorded two albums for **A&M Records**, which confirmed their standing among the best of the early country rock exponents. *The Fantastic Expedition Of Dillard And Clark* featured several strong compositions by Clark and Leadon including 'The Radio Song', 'Out On The Side', 'Something's Wrong' and 'Train Leaves Here This Mornin''. Leadon later took the latter to his next band, the **Eagles**, who included the song on their debut album. By the time of their second album, Dillard and Clark displayed a stronger country influence with the induction of **Flying Burrito Brothers** drummer Jon Corneal, champion fiddle player **Byron Berline** and additional vocalist Donna Washburn. *Through The Morning, Through The Night* combined country standards with Clark originals and featured some sumptuous duets between Clark and Washburn that pre-empted the work of **Gram Parsons** and **Emmylou Harris**. Although the Expedition experiment showed considerable promise, the group scattered in various directions at the end of the 60s, with Clark reverting to a solo career. Both albums were issued together on one CD in 1999.

● ALBUMS: *The Fantastic Expedition Of Dillard And Clark* (A&M 1968) ★★★★, *Through The Morning, Through The Night* (A&M 1969) ★★★★.

● FURTHER READING: *The Byrds: Timeless Flight Revisited*, Johnny Rogan.

Dillard, Bill

b. 20 July 1911, Philadelphia, Pennsylvania, USA, d. 1995, Hollywood, California, USA. Initially self-taught on trumpet, Dillard received some tuition in high school, but by the age of 18 he was working professionally in New York City. His name band experience began with **Jelly Roll Morton** and he also worked with **King Oliver**. In 1933 he was with **Benny Carter** and appeared on important recording sessions with the band. Throughout the 30s Dillard worked in a succession of different sized units including those of **Lucky Millinder**, **Teddy Hill** and **Coleman Hawkins**. In the early 40s he was in **Louis Armstrong**'s band and also worked with **Red Norvo**. In 1943 Dillard diversified into acting and thereafter concentrated on this aspect of his career, although his acting roles sometimes called for him to play trumpet and/or sing. Among the shows in which he appeared over the next four decades were *Carmen Jones* on Broadway in 1943, *Anna Lucasta* (1945), *Green Pastures* (1951), *One Mo' Time* (1981). During these years Dillard made occasional appearances on recording sessions, but acting had clearly taken over as the driving force in his life.

● FILMS: *The Fight Never Ends* (1949).

Dillard, Doug And Rodney

Brothers Douglas (b. 6 March 1937, East St. Louis, Illinois, USA; banjo) and Rodney (b. 18 May 1942, East St. Louis, Illinois, USA; guitar) were the founders of the pioneering bluegrass outfit the **Dillards**. In 1968, Doug left after six reasonably successful years, and joined the **Gram Parsons**–era **Byrds** for a few months, before Parsons himself departed. This association led to the formation of the groundbreaking **Dillard And Clark**, with ex-Byrd **Gene Clark**, and **Bernie Leadon** (later with the **Eagles**), Michael Clarke (another former Byrd) and fiddle champion **Byron Berline**. Their two albums for **A&M Records**, *The Fantastic Expedition Of Dillard & Clark* (1968) and *Through The Morning, Through The Night* (1969), produced an unusual, but highly successful, blend of bluegrass and southern soul, but internal disputes caused the group to disband soon afterwards. During this time he also released *The Banjo Album*, which has subsequently become a cult classic.

Doug Dillard released several disjointed solo albums in the 70s and occasionally recorded with his brother Rodney and long-time friend **John Hartford**. Together, they recorded the promising *Dillard Hartford Dillard* in 1975, a bluegrass-folk hybrid that mixed some good picking with light-hearted tunes. Subsequently, Doug Dillard fronted his own band with vocalist **Ginger Boatwright** and played the US festival circuit with the Dillards. Never a prolific writer, he nevertheless contributed several memorable 'character' songs to the Dillards' repertoire, such as 'Dooley' and 'Ebo Walker'. After the Dillards split in the early 80s, he spent a couple of years with country music star **Earl Scruggs**' band. In 1985 **Flying Fish Records** released the misleadingly titled *Rodney Dillard At Silver Dollar City*, a low-budget recording that featured Rodney on two tracks. In the early 90s, Rodney followed the excellent *Let It Fly*, by the re-formed Dillards, with his own *Let The Rough Side Drag*, a mixture of bluegrass and folk.

● ALBUMS: as Douglas Dillard *The Banjo Album* (Together 1969) ★★★★, *Duelling Banjos* (20th Century 1973) ★★★, *Douglas Flint Dillard* (20th Century 1974) ★★★, *Heaven* (Flying Fish 1979) ★★★, *Jackrabbit!* (Flying Fish 1980) ★★★, *What's That?* (Flying Fish 1986) ★★, *Heartbreak Hotel* (Flying Fish 1988) ★★★. Rodney Dillard *At Silver Dollar City* (Flying Fish 1985) ★★★, *Let The Rough Side Drag* (1992) ★★★. As Dillard Hartford Dillard *Dillard-Hartford-Dillard* (Sonet 1975) ★★★, *Permanent Wave* (Flying Fish 1980) ★★★.

Dillard, Moses

b. 30 September 1946, Greenville, South Carolina, USA, d. 14 July 1993, Nashville, Tennessee, USA. Dillard was a southern-based performer who was best recalled for 'My Elusive Dreams', his powerful soul-styled interpretation of a C&W favourite. Credited to Moses And Joshua Dillard, this irresistible single was a minor hit in 1966 and later became a **Northern Soul** favourite in the UK. The fictitious brother was in fact James Moore, a member of Dillard's backing group, the Tex-Town Display, which included future singing star **Peabo Bryson**. Dillard's session guitar work was heard throughout the 60s on many soul artists' recordings including those of **James And Bobby Purify** and **Mighty Sam McClain**. In later years, Dillard pursued more of a backroom role and was featured songwriter, guitarist and producer on **Al Green**'s 1984 gospel album *Precious Lord*, for which he won

a Grammy and received a Dove award. At the age of 47 Dillard died of a heart attack.

● ALBUMS: *Moses Dillard & The Tex-Town Display* (Tex-Town 1969) ★★★, with Jesse Boyce *Dillard & Boyce* (Mercury 1980) ★★★.

Dillard, Varetta

b. 3 February 1933, Harlem, New York City, USA, d. 4 October 1993, Brooklyn, New York City, USA. Dillard was known for several hits of poppish R&B in a style very reminiscent of **Ruth Brown**. As the result of a bone deficiency she spent most of her childhood years in a hospital, where she discovered singing as a therapy. Encouraged and inspired by Carl Feaster, lead singer with the **Chords**, Dillard began entering talent shows, which led to two consecutive wins at the **Apollo**'s amateur show. Signed to Savoy Records in 1951, she made her own records and duetted with **H-Bomb Ferguson**, enjoying success with 'Easy, Easy Baby' (number 8 R&B) in 1952, 'Mercy Mr. Percy' (number 6 R&B) in 1953 and, after **Johnny Ace**'s untimely demise, 'Johnny Has Gone' (number 6 R&B) in 1955. In 1956 Dillard switched to the **RCA Records** subsidiary label Groove, where, much to her distaste, she was coerced into capitalizing on James Dean's death with 'I Miss You Jimmy'. Later recordings for Triumph and **MGM**'s Cub subsidiary failed to match her Savoy successes, and she ended her solo recording career in 1961, although she continued singing into the late 60s by joining her husband's group, the Tri-Odds, who were active in the Civil Rights movement, performing jazz, a cappella, and black-centric poetry.

● COMPILATIONS: *Double Crossing Daddy* (Mr. R&B 1984) ★★★, *Mercy Mr. Percy* (Savoy Jazz 1988) ★★★, *Got You On My Mind* (Bear Family 1989) ★★★, *The Lovin' Bird* (Bear Family 1989) ★★★.

Dillards

Brothers **Rodney** (b. 18 May 1942, East St. Louis, Illinois, USA; guitar/vocals) and **Doug Dillard** (b. 6 March 1937, East St. Louis, Illinois, USA; banjo/vocals) formed this seminal bluegrass group in Salem, Missouri, USA. Roy Dean Webb (b. 28 March 1937, Independence, Missouri, USA; mandolin/vocals) and former radio announcer Mitch Jayne (b. 7 May 1930, Hammond, Indiana, USA; bass) completed the original line-up which, having enjoyed popularity throughout their home state, travelled to Los Angeles in 1962 where they secured a recording contract with the renowned **Elektra Records** label. *Back Porch Bluegrass* and *The Dillards Live! Almost!* established the unit as one of America's leading traditional acts, although purists denigrated the band's sometimes irreverent attitude. *Pickin' & Fiddlin'*, a collaboration with violinist **Byron Berline**, was recorded to placate such critics. The Dillards shared management with the **Byrds** and, whereas their distinctive harmonies proved influential to the latter band's development, the former act then began embracing a pop-based perspective. Dewey Martin (b. 30 September 1942, Chesterville, Ontario, Canada), later of **Buffalo Springfield**, added drums on a folk rock demo that in turn led to a brace of singles recorded for the **Capitol Records** label.

Doug Dillard was unhappy with this new direction and left to form a duo with ex-Byrd **Gene Clark**. Herb Peterson joined the Dillards in 1968 and, having resigned from Elektra, the reshaped quartet completed two exceptional country rock sets, *Wheatstraw Suite* and *Copperfields*. The newcomer was in turn replaced by Billy Rae Latham for *Roots And Branches*, on which the unit's transformation to full-scale electric instruments was complete. A full-time drummer, Paul York, was now featured in the line-up, but further changes were wrought when founder member Jayne dropped out following *Tribute To The American Duck*. Rodney Dillard has since remained at the helm of a capricious act, which by the end of the 70s returned to the traditional music circuit through the auspices of the respected **Flying Fish Records** label. He was also reunited with his prodigal brother in Dillard-Hartford-Dillard, an occasional sideline, which also featured the wonderfully talented multi-instrumentalist **John Hartford**.

● ALBUMS: *Back Porch Bluegrass* (Elektra 1963) ★★★, *The Dillards Live! Almost!* (Elektra 1964) ★★★, with Byron Berline *Pickin' & Fiddlin'* (Elektra 1965) ★★★, *Wheatstraw Suite* (Elektra 1968) ★★★★, *Copperfields* (Elektra 1970) ★★★, *Roots And Branches* (Anthem 1972) ★★, *Tribute To The American Duck* (Poppy 1973) ★★★★, *The Dillards Versus The Incredible LA Time Machine* (Sonet 1977) ★★, *Glitter-Grass From The Nashwood Hollyville Strings* (1977) ★★★, *Decade Waltz* (Flying Fish 1979) ★★, *Homecoming & Family Reunion* (Flying Fish 1980) ★★★, *Mountain Rock* (Flying Fish 1980) ★★★, *Let It Fly* (Vanguard 1990) ★★★, *A Long Time Ago: The First Time Live!* (Varèse Sarabande 1999) ★★★.

● COMPILATIONS: *Country Tracks* (Elektra 1974) ★★★, *I'll Fly Away* (Edsel 1988) ★★★, *There Is A Time (1963–1970)* (Vanguard 1991) ★★★★, *Let The Music Flow: The Best Of 1963–79* (Raven 2005) ★★★★.

● DVD/VIDEOS: *A Night In The Ozarks* (Hendring Music Video 1991).

● FURTHER READING: *Everybody On The Truck*, Lee Grant.

Dillinger

b. Lester Bullocks, 25 June 1953, Kingston, Jamaica, West Indies. In 1971, Dillinger commenced his career as a DJ, working on the **sound systems** of Prince Jackie and El Brasso, where he initially imitated **U-Roy**, **Dennis Alcapone** and **Big Youth** before forging his own style. In 1974, he recorded the excellent 'Freshly' for **Yabby You** and the following year had a glut of material released, including 'Brace A Boy' for **Augustus Pablo**, 'CB 200' for **Joseph 'Joe Joe' Hookim** and 'Killer Man Jaro' for **Coxsone Dodd**. It was Dodd who released Dillinger's stunning first album, *Ready Natty Dreadie*, on which he effortlessly delivered 10 strong toasts over a selection of **Studio One**'s classic **rocksteady** and reggae rhythms. It is only the first pressing of the album that contains the brilliant title track, as it was subsequently replaced by 'Natty Kung Fu'. Hookim released Dillinger's second album, *CB 200*, which features several singles including the title track, 'Plantation Heights', 'Cocaine In My Brain' and 'Crank Face'. In late 1976, he made an album (*Clash*) in the UK with **Trinity** for producer **Clement Bushay**, which suffered from hurried recording sessions. Hookim released a further album, *Bionic Dread*, which was far less compelling than its predecessor. 'Cocaine In My Brain' had proven to be so popular in Europe and the USA that he recorded a follow-up, 'Marijuana In My Brain' (1979), which became a number 1 hit in Holland, and an album of the same name quickly followed. Unfortunately, most of his material from this time did not match his earlier work, although he was still brave enough to attempt one of the first reggae electro recordings with 1980's *Badder Than Them*. He was inactive for

most of the 80s, but in 1990, he returned to the recording scene.

● ALBUMS: *Ready Natty Dreadie* (Studio One 1975) ★★★★, *CB 200* (Island 1976) ★★★★, *Bionic Dread* (Black Swan 1976) ★★★, with Trinity *Clash* (Burning Sounds 1976) ★★, *Talkin' Blues* (Magnum 1977) ★★★, *Top Ranking* (Third World 1978) ★★★, *Answer My Questions* (Third World 1979) ★★★, *Marijuana In My Brain* (Jamaica Sound 1979) ★★★, *Badder Than Them* (A&M 1980) ★★★, *Corn Bread* (Vista Sounds 1983) ★★★, with Clint Eastwood *Live At London* (Vista Sounds 1983) ★★★, *King Pharaoh* (Blue Moon 1984) ★★★, *Best Of Live* (Vista Sounds 1984) ★★, *Cocaine* (New Cross 1984) ★★★, *Tribal War* (New Cross 1986) ★★★, *Say No To Drugs* (Lagoon 1993) ★★★.

● COMPILATIONS: *Cocaine In My Brain* (Trojan 2000) ★★★★, *Under Heavy Manners: The Best Of Dillinger* (Fuel 2000, 2001) ★★★★, *The Prime Of Dillinger: Gangster Prankster And Rasta* (Music Club 2002) ★★★★, *Cocaine In My Brain: The Anthology* (Trojan 2004) ★★★★.

Dillinger Escape Plan

Perhaps the best way to describe the sound and approach of Dillinger Escape Plan is as an all-out assault on the senses. Formed in New Jersey, USA, during 1997, the band was formed from the remnants of hardcore band Arcane. Dimitri Minakakis (vocals), Ben Weinman (guitar), Derrick Brantley (guitar), Chris Pennie (drums) and Adam Doll (bass) played two shows together before the exit of Brantley reduced the line-up to a quartet. Mixing the aggression of hardcore metal with pure cacophony separated the band from the rest of the pack almost immediately, as they issued a self-titled debut the same year as their formation (the album would be reissued several years later). Second guitarist John Fulton was added to the line-up on the subsequent tour, following which the band signed a new recording contract with Relapse Records. Fulton departed shortly before the release of the EP, *Under The Running Board*, and further disruption ensued when Doll was partially paralyzed in a car accident and was forced to leave. Guitarist Brian Benoit was added to the line-up during this period. The band's highly anticipated major label release, *Calculating Infinity*, received excellent reviews and was supported by a US tour opening for **Mr. Bungle**. During the tour, they made a major fan out of Mr. Bungle vocalist Mike Patton, who in turn lent his vocal talents to the *Irony Is A Dead Scene* EP after Minakakis was ousted from the band. The other members used their website to search for a replacement vocalist, uploading an instrumental track which their fans were encouraged to download and add their vocals to. The successful applicant proved to be Greg Puciato, who made his debut live appearance at the 2001 CMJ Music Festival in New York.

The band kept up a busy touring schedule during 2002/3 and also began compiling new material for future release. Their first studio release with Puciato on vocals was released in summer 2004. *Miss Machine* saw the Dillinger Escape Plan attempting to break away from their hardcore roots, toning down the heavier edges of their sound and demonstrating a greater willingness to experiment with melody and grooves.

● ALBUMS: *Dillinger Escape Plan* (Now Or Never 1997) ★★★, *Calculating Infinity* (Hydrahead/Relapse 1999) ★★★★, *Miss Machine* (Relapse 2004) ★★★.

● DVD/VIDEOS: *Miss Machine* (Relapse 2004).

Dillingham, Charles B.

b. Charles Bancroft Dillingham, 30 May 1868, Hartford, Connecticut, USA, d. 30 August 1934, New York City, New York, USA. Dillingham's connection with the turn-of-the-century theatre began as a reviewer for *The New York Evening Post* and he subsequently became an artists' manager. By the early years of the twentieth century he had taken a big and unusual step, becoming a Broadway producer. Among his important collaborations were those he enjoyed with **Victor Herbert** and **Jerome Kern**. With Herbert he produced *Mlle. Modiste* (1905), *The Red Mill* (1906) and several others. With Kern, he produced nine musical comedies. In addition to producing his own shows, he also co-produced with **Florenz Ziegfeld**. During these years, Dillingham worked with many leading singers, dancers and comedians of the day. In addition to producing shows, in the years immediately following World War I, Dillingham also operated New York's Hippodrome Theatre and built The Globe Theatre, which is still in existence as The Lunt-Fontanne Theatre. Like so many others, Dillingham was ruined by the reversal of America's fortunes in the late 20s and early 30s. Recovering from bankruptcy, Dillingham tried again and in the last year of his life had one more hit with the 1934 revue *New Faces*.

● FILMS: *Glorifying The American Girl* (1929).

Dillon, Cara

b. 1975, Dungiven, Co. Derry, Eire. The sister of Mary Dillon, former singer with the group **Déanta**, Cara demonstrated the same vocal talents in winning the All Ireland Singing Trophy at the age of 14. She went on to sing with Óige and then the folk supergroup **Equation**, joining the latter in 1995 as the replacement for **Kate Rusby**. Dillon left Equation before the release of their Blanco y Negro debut and began working with another previous member, Sam Lakeman (of the **Lakeman Brothers**). A new contract was signed with Blanco y Negro and material recorded with a number of collaborators, but after four years of sessions, Dillon and Lakeman, who were now personal partners as well, parted company with the Warners organization. They recorded an album of largely traditional material, which was released (under Dillon's name) by the newly revived **Rough Trade Records** label in 2001. Dillon's expressive vocals and Lakeman's piano work squeezed new life into the well-worn traditional material, while the two Dillon/Lakeman originals ('Blue Mountain River' and 'I Wish I Was') gave evidence of a fully-formed songwriting talent. The album placed Dillon firmly in the new folk tradition blazed by singers such as Rusby, **Eliza Carthy** and **Bill Jones**. She received two awards (Best Traditional Track for 'Black Is The Colour' and Best Newcomer) at the following year's BBC Folk Awards. Dillon and Lakeman added more of their own material on the follow-up album *Sweet Liberty*, attracting further praise for the way their arrangements fluently bridged the divide between pop and folk. The album also featured a beautiful reading of **Tommy Sands**' 'There Were Roses'. Dillon's third album, *After The Morning*, was released at the start of 2006.

● ALBUMS: *Cara Dillon* (Rough Trade 2001) ★★★★, *Sweet Liberty* (Rough Trade 2003) ★★★, *After The Morning* (Rough Trade 2006) ★★★.

Dillon, Clifton 'Specialist'

b. July 1960, Montego Bay, Jamaica, West Indies. Dillon initially set up his own Specialist **sound system** and, inspired by the efforts of **Coxsone Dodd**, resolved to set up his own record label. He found employment at the Music Works studios where he studied record production under the tutelage of **Gussie Clarke**. Initially Dillon released a few local hits on his Pioneer Muzik label before he relocated to Chicago, Illinois, USA. He soon established his career when he set up the Solid Gold sound system that subsequently won the Chicago International Reggae Award for Best Discotheque. Dillon maintained his Jamaican **dancehall** connection by recruiting artists such as **Shabba Ranks**, **Patra** and **Mad Cobra** to his newly formed Shang enterprise. The partnership proved beneficial to all parties. In his role as the executive producer of Ranks' *X-Tra Naked*, Dillon was directly involved in the DJ winning two Grammys and his subsequent international chart success. The market leaders included a remake of 'Mr Loverman' and the combination hit with **Maxi Priest**, 'Housecall'. Curiously the original 'Mr Loverman' had been recorded at Music Works with Clarke, while the remake was a joint production with his old alumni Mikey Bennett. Dillon continued to enjoy a high profile when he was involved in the production of international hits for Patra ('Worker Man'), Mad Cobra ('Flex'), Eddie Murphy ('I Was A King') and **Buju Banton**'s controversial 'Boom Bye Bye'. As a result of their success, Shang opened offices in Miami and Kingston, where Dillon released tracks from artists such as **Trinity**, **Dillinger**, **Ghost**, **Red Dragon**, **Bounty Killer** and **Terror Fabulous**. While successful in the music industry, Dillon harboured further aspirations, setting his sights on the movie industry. He secured contracts for **Ky-mani** to feature on a number of soundtracks including *Money Talks* and *Senseless*. Ky-mani then obtained the role of Biggs in the movie *Shottas*, a story of two youths struggling to survive in the streets of Kingston. Shang produced the soundtrack with performances from **Elephant Man**, **Baby Cham**, **Wyclef Jean** and **Spragga Benz**, who played Ky-mani's sparring partner, Wayne. In 2001 Dillon repeated his success at the Grammys when Ky-mani was accredited for *Many More Roads*. Dillon is acknowledged as the man who brought dancehall music to the international market and is regarded as an inspiration to all Jamaican hopefuls.

Dillon, Dean

b. 26 March 1955, Lake City, Knoxville, Tennessee, USA. Dillon, a self-confessed victim of alcohol and substance abuse, started writing songs in the early 70s, when he appeared on a local television show. He subsequently moved to Nashville and eventually worked at Opryland Theme Park for four years as a member of the Mac Magaha quartet (Magaha had previously worked as **Porter Wagoner**'s fiddle player for many years) with Barry Moore (bass) and Mark Barnett (banjo). This group made an obscure independent label album, *Rise And Shine*, primarily for sale at gigs. By the mid-70s, Dillon had been signed to a songwriting contract. His first big hit as a writer came in 1979 with 'Lying In Love With You', which he co-wrote with Gary Harrison and which was a Top 3 US country hit for **Jim Ed Brown** and **Helen Cornelius**. He enjoyed eight minor US country hits between 1979 and 1983 and continued to write hits for others such as 'Tennessee Whisky' for **George Jones** (Top 3 country, 1983) and 'Leave Them Boys Alone' for **Hank Williams Jnr.** (Top 10, 1983). In 1982 Dillon teamed up with singer-songwriter **Gary Stewart** (both were signed to **RCA Records** at the time), and the duo recorded two albums—one of which was titled

Brotherly Love—and a handful of minor hit singles; Dillon later described the partnership as 'the biggest mistake either of us could ever have made'.

However, by the time the duo dissolved, Dillon had written a number of hits in partnership with other Nashville writers such as **Paul Overstreet**, Buzz Rabin, **Randy Scruggs** and especially **Hank Cochran** and Frank Dyeas. Many of these songs became big hits for country superstar **George Strait**, including such country chart-toppers as 'The Chair' (1985), 'Nobody In His Right Mind Would've Left Her' and 'It Ain't Cool To Be Crazy About You' (both 1986), 'Ocean Front Property' (1987) and 'Famous Last Words Of A Fool' (1988). These successes led to a new recording contract for Dillon with **Capitol Records**, which resulted in two albums produced by Scruggs, *Slick Nickel* and *I've Learned To Live*, which included a duet with **Tanya Tucker**. By 1993, he had released another two albums, but he remains more successful as a songwriter than as an artist. In the 90s Dillon's days as a rowdy honky-tonker appeared to be over, and he is a contented family man. 'I had the **Hank Williams** syndrome,' he says, 'and I almost killed myself by drinking and taking drugs.' He still looks very distinctive in performances, with his long-flowing hair and handlebar moustache. Dillon was inducted into the Nashville Songwriters Hall of Fame in 2002.

● ALBUMS: with Gary Stewart *Brotherly Love* (RCA 1982) ★★★, with Stewart *Those Were The Days* (RCA 1983) ★★, *Slick Nickel* (Capitol 1988) ★★★, *I've Learned To Live* (Capitol 1989) ★★★, *Out Of Your Ever Lovin' Mind* (Atlantic 1991) ★★, *Hot, Country And Single* (Atlantic 1993) ★★★.

Dillon, Phylis

b. 1945, Linstead, St. Catherine, Jamaica, West Indies, d. 15 April 2004, Long Island, New York, USA. Dillon was a greatly underrated **rocksteady** vocalist who had been recording in Jamaica for a number of years before her first hit. In the mid-60s, she released 'Perfidia' and 'Don't Stay Away' with **Tommy McCook** And The Supersonics, which was produced by **Duke Reid** at Treasure Isle studios in Bond Street. She emigrated to New York late in 1967 but periodically returned to Jamaica where she recorded at the Bond Street studio. In 1970, Reid produced 'Right Track', a duet with **Hopeton Lewis**, which demonstrated Dillon's sweet vocals and impeccable talent. She also recorded a number of duets with **Alton Ellis**.

When rocksteady evolved into reggae, Dillon was able to adapt to the new beat with dexterity. The turning point in her career came on one of her reappearances at Treasure Isle when the Duke Reid–produced 'One Life To Live, One Love To Give' reached the Jamaican Top 10. Reid licensed *One Life To Live* to **Trojan Records** in the UK, which featured her hits along with 'Long Time No Nice Time', 'The Love That A Woman Should Give A Man', 'Love The One You're With', 'I Can't Forget About You Baby' and 'Close To You'. A bizarre interpretation of the latter was used by Dennis Al Capone for a wedding ceremony, appropriately entitled 'The Wedding Song', on his album *DJ's Choice*. He also chanted over Dillon's 'Woman Of The Ghetto' and 'Picture On The Wall'. Trojan lifted her cover version of **George Harrison**'s 'Something' from the album, which proved a moderate success. By the mid-70s Dillon was devoting her time to raising a family, although she made a moderately successful comeback in the 90s. She succumbed to cancer in April 2004.

● ALBUMS: *One Life To Live* (Trojan 1972) ★★★.
● COMPILATIONS: *Love Is All I Had* (Treasure Isle 1995) ★★★, *Midnight Confessions: Classic Rocksteady And Reggae 1967–71* (Westside 2000) ★★★★.

Dils

Formed in San Diego, California, USA, in 1977, the Dils' most stable line-up comprised Chip Kinman (guitar/vocals), Tony 'Nineteen' Kinman (guitar/vocals) and Endre Alquover (drums), who had replaced Pat Garrett. The trio was an integral part of the Los Angeles punk movement, completing two powerful singles in 'I Hate The Rich' and 'Class War' (both 1977). Drummers Rand McNally and John Silvers later passed through the line-up, but the band's only other release was 1980's *Made In Canada* EP. The Dils then evolved into **Rank And File**, where the Kinmans were joined by ex-**Nuns** guitarist **Alejandro Escovedo**. The new act revived 'Sound Of The Rain' on their *Long Gone Dead* album. The Dils broke up in 1980, with only the three singles documenting their existence until the advent of two posthumous live albums.

● ALBUMS: *Live* (Iloki/Triple X 1987) ★★★, *The Dils* (Lost 1990) ★★★.

Dim Stars

Formed in New York in 1991, Dim Stars is an occasional project featuring **Richard Hell** (b. Richard Myers, 2 October 1949, Lexington, Kentucky, USA; vocals/bass), Don Fleming (ex-**Velvet Monkeys**; **B.A.L.L.**; guitar/vocals) and two members of **Sonic Youth**, Thurston Moore (guitar/vocals) and Steve Shelley (drums). A live three-single pack, *Dim Stars*, was issued that year on Sonic Youth's Ecstatic Peace! label. It included a lengthy version of 'You've Got To Lose', first featured on Richard Hell And The Voidoid's classic *Blank Generation*. *Three Songs*, an EP credited to 'Richard Hell', ensued, although this featured the Dim Stars' line-up. The quartet's eponymous album was an informal, but exciting, set, combining Hell's visionary lyrics with the debauched ease of the **Rolling Stones**' *circa Exile On Main Street*. Guitarist Robert Quine, formerly of the Voidoids, and **Jad Fair** assisted the proceedings, the highlight of which was a memorable take of **Howlin' Wolf**'s 'The Natchez Burning'. Prior commitments to Sonic Youth preclude Dim Stars from becoming a permanent fixture, but the album proved to be an excellent reiteration of Richard Hell's talent.

● ALBUMS: *Dim Stars* (Ecstatic Peace! 1993) ★★★.

Dimensión Latina

Dimensión Latina was Venezuela's premier band at the height of salsa's popularity in the country during the 70s. Originally formed in the early 70s, a band bearing their name continued to exist into the 90s. They began as a sextet, initially called Oscar Y Sus Estrellas, performing in a bar named La Distinción in Venezuela's capital, Caracas. After a couple of changes of pianist and a joint album with Clan De Victor, the personnel that appeared on their 1973 debut *¡Triunfadores!* comprised: composer/arrangers **Oscar D'León** (b. Oscar Emilio León Samoza, 11 July 1943, Antímano, Caracas, Venezuela; lead vocals/bass) and César Monje aka César Monge (trombone/vocals), José Antonio 'Rojitas' Rojas (trombone/vocals), Jesús 'Chuíto' Narváez (piano), Elio Pacheco (congas) and José 'Joseíto' Rodríguez (timbales). On their second release, *En La Dimensión Latina*, they were joined by co-lead singer Wladimir Lozano (b. 2 March 1950,

Venezuela), who specialized in boleros. A third trombone, played by Carlos Guerra Jnr., was added on *Dimensión Latina '76/Salsa Brava.*

D'León left in 1976 to front his own band, Salsa Mayor, and Monje took on the mantle of musical director. The bass playing slot was filled by Gustavo Carmona. Veteran singer Argenis Carruyo was brought in as co-lead vocalist just for *Dimensión Latina 77/Internaciónal.* Shortly afterwards, the band pulled off a considerable coup when they managed to lure **Andy Montañez** (b. Puerto Rico) away from **El Gran Combo** with a better contract. For the previous 15 years, Montañez had been one of Latin music's most popular singers. He made his recording debut with Dimensión Latina on *Los Generales De La Salsa.* Sharing lead vocals with Montañez and Lozano on this album was Rodrigo Mendoza (ex–Los Satélites), who possessed a powerful voice with a high-pitched timbre. The same trio of lead singers appeared on *780 Kilos De Salsa.*

Lozano departed in 1978, teaming up with D'León to record the double album *Oscar D'León Y Su Salsa Mayor Con Wladimir*, then recording with his own short-lived band, La Constelación. Conga player Elio Pacheco left to form the charanga band La Magnifica and later directed La Mafia Latina. He was replaced by Carlos Jesús 'Pacuso' Guillen. **Luis 'Perico' Ortiz** arranged and directed three tracks, including his own composition 'Cantante Errante', on *. . . Tremenda Dimensión!* (1978). In 1979, pianist Jesús 'Chuíto' Narváez and Mendoza left to form the band La Amistad. Argenis Carruyo returned to replace Mendoza and Samuel Del Real took over on piano.

In November 1980, Oscar D'León reunited with Dimensión Latina for *Dos Colosos En Concierto*, recorded in concert at the Poliedro Stadium in Caracas. Montañez went solo in 1980, while Del Real formed his own band and recorded two albums in Venezuela before relocating to the USA. Narváez, Pacheco and Lozano re-grouped for Dimensión Latina's *Producto De Exportación* in 1984. César Monje went on to work as a freelance arranger, musical director, session musician and producer, collaborating with his old band from time to time. The only 70s members in the early 90s version of Dimensión Latina were Mendoza, Lozano and timbales player Joseíto Rodríguez, who had assumed the role of musical director. Rodríguez, Monjes, Pacheco and Narváez and Rodrigo Mendoza reunited in 2002 under the name Los Generales De La Salsa.

● ALBUMS: *Clan De Victor Y Dimensión Latina* (Top Hits 1972) ★★★, *¡Triunfadores!* (Top Hits 1973) ★★★★, *En La Dimensión Latina* (Top Hits 1974) ★★★★, *Dimensión Latina '75* (Top Hits 1974) ★★★, *Dimensión Latina '76/ Salsa Brava* (Top Hits 1975) ★★★★, *En Nueva York '76 1/2* (Top Hits 1977) ★★★, *Dimensión Latina '77/Internaciónal* (Top Hits 1977) ★★★, *Los Generales De La Salsa* (Top Hits 1977) ★★★★, *780 Kilos De Salsa* (Top Hits 1977) ★★★, *. . . Tremenda Dimensión!* (Velvet 1978) ★★★, *Dimensión Latina '79* (Color 1978) ★★, *Inconquistable* (Color 1978) ★★, *Dimensión Latina* (Velvet 1979) ★★★, *Combinación Latina No. 4* (Top Hits 1979) ★★★, *. . . Para Siémpre!* (Velvet 1980) ★★★, *Dos Colosos En Concierto* (Top Hits 1980) ★★★, *El Número Uno Con La Número Uno* (Velvet 1980) ★★★, *Cuerda Para Rato* (Velvet 1981) ★★, *10 Años Repartiendo Salsa . . .* (Velvet 1982) ★★★, *Producto De Exportación* (Guantanamera 1984) ★★, *Canto Para Ti* (Velvet 1989) ★★, *Los Dueños Del Caribe* (Velvet 1990) ★★.

● COMPILATIONS: *Oro Salsero* (PolyGram 1995) ★★★, *Sus Grandes Exitos Vol. 1* (Top Hits 1996) ★★★★, *Sus Grandes Exitos Vol. 2* (Top Hits 1996) ★★★, *Una Dimensión De Exitos* (Top Hits 1996) ★★★★.

Dimension Records

The Dimension label was founded in New York, USA, in 1962 by music publishers **Don Kirshner** and Al Nevins. Aldon Music, their pioneering independent company, boasted staff songwriters **Neil Sedaka**, **Barry Mann** and Cynthia Weil, but Dimension was initially envisaged as an outlet for the skills of Aldon's brightest protégés, **Gerry Goffin** and **Carole King**. The pair wrote, arranged or produced virtually all of the label's output during its first year of existence. Such releases included King's 'It Might As Well Rain Until September', originally issued on Companion, a previous Kirshner/Nevis outlet, and 'The Loco-motion', an international million-seller for **Little Eva**. The **Cookies**' 'Chains', later popularized by the **Beatles**, was another early Dimension release, and the label's early success inspired the founding of three short-lived subsidiaries, Motion, Chairman and Plateau. However, in April 1963 Kirshner opted to sell Dimension, and indeed the Aldon empire, to Screen Gems/**Columbia Records**. The involvement of Goffin and King waned considerably after this point as other budding entrepreneurs from the parent company stepped in. **Lou Adler** produced the novelty disc, 'A Beatle I Want To Be', for ex-**Crickets** member, **Sonny Curtis**, while the Storytellers' 'Time Will Tell' featured the talents of **Steve Barri** and **Carol Connors**. However, further commercial success proved elusive and Dimension folded in June 1965. Its last release was 'Bye Bye Baby' by future **Love** guitarist, Nooney Rickett.

● COMPILATIONS: *The Dimension Dolls* (Dimension 1963) ★★★.

Dimitri

Publicity-shy DJ (b. Amsterdam, Holland) who regularly hosts the Hi-Tech Soul Movement nights at the Roxy and also plays the Richter club, both in his home-town. He began his DJ career on the radio in the early 80s, before graduating to clubs. Famed for his mix tapes and CDs, he has latterly hooked up with **Carl Craig** and Rhythim Is Rhythim (**Derrick May**) to set up a new record label. He is the part owner of the Outland shop and label and has founded two further labels, Spiritual and BeST. Some of this roster's better-known releases include Super Jazz's 'Hi-Tech Soul Anthem' and MDMA's 'Cerebral Ascendence'. He has also worked with fellow-Amsterdam talent Eric Nouhan ('Tecnobility', etc.) and released his own material in conjunction with Jaimy ('Don't Be A Prisoner Of Your Own Style', which neatly encapsulates his own DJing principles). In 1994, he established the Outland imprint in the UK, commemorating the occasion with the release of a compilation, *The Best Of Outland And Spiritual*. He also licensed recordings such as Two Men Will Love You's 'Goodbye Thing' and remixed for Chanelle ('Work That Body').

Dimitri From Paris

b. October 1963, Istanbul, Turkey. Dimitri is a founding father of the late 90s wave of French **house** DJs, producers and artists, such as **Etienne De Crécy**, **Cassius** and **Bob Sinclar**, who take their influences from diverse sources such as 50s lounge music, 60s film scores, disco, hip-hop and New York house music. These styles are all blended into a kitsch, funky, mid-tempo sound that has had a broad appeal on the European club scene. Dimitri was born to hippie intellectual parents, whose travels took them to Paris. Growing up there, he was enchanted by disco at its peak and later, hip-hop and **electro**. He began mixing his collection of US import 12-inches on a pair of decks in his bedroom. Instead of the usual teenage activities, Dimitri spent hours honing his turntable skills and this led to a series of jobs at various European radio stations. At NRJ, in 1985, he presented *Megamix*, Europe's first house music radio programme. In the same year, he began producing and remixing, working on tracks by artists including **Björk**, **Brand New Heavies**, **New Order**, **James Brown**, Etienne Daho and **Mory Kanté**.

At the time remixes were a rare phenomenon in France, and Dimitri's skills helped to pioneer the remix in France. During the early 90s Dimitri's mixing skills were used by famous fashion designers to accompany their models down the catwalk. In order to avoid copyright problems, Dimitri was asked to provide original music. The mixes were recorded onto tape and used in boutiques around the world. Eventually, Dimitri signed a contract with underground label, Yellow Productions, who released two EPs and a mini-LP. His long-playing debut, 1996's *Sacrebleu*, was voted Best Dance Album Of The Year by *Mixmag*. The album sold 50,000 copies worldwide before Dimitri was signed to EastWest Records, although his mix albums continued to be released on independent labels. Idiosyncratic and uncompromising, Dimitri From Paris' witty eclecticism continues to win new fans.

● ALBUMS: *Sacrebleu* (Yellow 1996) ★★★★, *Cruising Attitude* (Discograph 2004) ★★★.
● COMPILATIONS: *Monsieur Dimitri's De-Luxe House Of Funk* (Mixmag 1997) ★★★, *ICU Session: Three* (Max 1999) ★★★★, *A Night At The Playboy Mansion* (Virgin/Astralwerks 2000) ★★★, *After The Playboy Mansion* (Virgin/Astralwerks 2002) ★★★, *In The House Of Love* (In The House 2006) ★★★.

Dimmu Borgir

Probably the most overblown of the Norwegian black metal bands, Dimmu Borgir ('black castle' or 'dark fortress' in Icelandic) envelop their riffs and screams in layers of warm keyboards, adding classical instrumentation and ambient elements to create music that is a long way from the rawness of other contemporaries such as Immortal. The band has seen so many players from the incestuous Scandinavian black metal scene come and go that it has almost achieved the status of a collective.

The band first formed in 1993 around Erkekjetter Silenoz (guitar/vocals), Shagrath (guitar, drums, vocals) and Tjodalv (drums/guitar), with Brynjard Tristan (bass), and Stian Aarstad (keyboards) added to the line-up shortly afterwards. A single, 'Inn I Evightens Morke', appeared in 1994 on the Necromantic Gallery Productions label, following which a contract was signed with No Colours and the now-classic *For All Tid* was released. *Stormblåst* appeared on the Cacophonous label, following which Nagash was brought in to replace Tristan and the band signed a new recording contract with Nuclear Blast Records. The band debuted for the label with the classic *Enthrone Darkness Triumpant*. Further personnel change saw them recruiting guitarist Astennu (b. Australia) and new keyboard player Mustis. Following the release of

1999's *Spiritual Black Dimensions* Nagash also left to found a band called Covenant with ex-**Mayhem** drummer Hellhammer—this became the Norwegian Grammy-winning **Kovenant**. He was replaced by sometime **Borknagar** member Simen Hestnaes aka I.C.S. Vortex. Tjodalv left during the tour to promote the album and was replaced by ex-**Cradle Of Filth** drummer Nicholas Barker. New guitarist Galder (b. Tom Rune Anderson) was brought in to replace Astennu on the highly acclaimed *Puritanical Euphoric Misanthropia*. By now the band's sound was both harsher (Barker having added a certain power) and more melodic (Mustis bringing a definite classical edge to their songs). Barker left the band in January 2004, and the remaining members decided to use session drummers on future releases.

Dimmu Borgir remain the most musically proficient of the Norwegian crop, although the more their music develops, the less they can be said to practising true black metal. However, they can boast one of the most loyal audiences of any band of this type.

● ALBUMS: *For All Tid* (No Colours 1994) ★★★★, *Stormblåst* (Cacophonous 1996) ★★★, *Devil's Path* mini-album (Hot 1996) ★★★, *Enthrone Darkness Triumphant* (Nuclear Blast 1997) ★★★★, *Godless Savage Garden* (Nuclear Blast 1998) ★★★, *Spiritual Black Dimensions* (Nuclear Blast 1999) ★★★, *Puritanical Euphoric Misanthropia* (Nuclear Blast 2001) ★★★★, *Alive In Torment* (Nuclear Blast 2001) ★★★, *Death Cult Armageddon* (Nuclear Blast 2003) ★★★.
● DVD/VIDEOS: *World Misanthropy* (Nuclear Blast 2002).

Dimond, Mark 'Markolino'
(see **Canales, Angel**)

DiMucci, Dion
(see **Dion And The Belmonts**)

Dingoes

Working out of Melbourne's inner suburban pubs in 1973, the Dingoes soon became Australia's premier country-influenced rock band, using the popular American west coast sound of the time, but with Australian imagery in their lyrics, and featuring the fine talents of lead singer Broderick Smith and Kerryn Tolhurst and Chris Stockley (ex-**Axiom**) on guitars. The original line-up also featured John Du Bois (bass) and John Lee (drums), but the latter was replaced by Ray Arnott before the release of their debut album. The band's initial success was due to the hard work of all the members over a long period in previous bands. After some commercial success with the first single and album in 1974, the band was keen to go overseas. Rather than tackling the American market directly, they established themselves in Canada in 1976. By this point, Lee had returned to the line-up. Despite sharing management with the **Rolling Stones**, under Peter Rudge the band was not able to break into the market. Their second album, recorded in California in 1977, included several re-recordings of songs off their first album, in an attempt to appeal to the USA market. The album and subsequent singles failed to make much impact, and Stockley departed early in 1978. The band took on an American as replacement and a third album was recorded amid growing despondency. The band broke up as 1979's *Orphans Of The Storm* was released, and gradually all the members returned home to Australia.

● ALBUMS: *The Dingoes* (Mushroom 1974) ★★★, *Five Times The Sun* (A&M 1977) ★★★, *Orphans Of The Storm* (A&M 1979) ★★.
● COMPILATIONS: *Way Out West* (Mushroom 1992) ★★★.

Dinning Sisters

This versatile close harmony vocal trio, popular in the late 40s and 50s, comprised Lou (b. Lucille Dinning, 29 September 1922, Kentucky, USA; alto) and twins Ginger (b. Virginia Dinning; lead) and Jean (b. Eugenia Dinning; soprano—both b. 29 March 1924, Oklahoma, USA). The trio, from a family of five daughters and four sons, were blessed with perfect pitch and sang together in their church choir from an early age. In their teens, the girls had their own 15-minute local radio show and later toured clubs and theatres in the Midwest with Herbie Holmes' orchestra. After moving to Chicago in 1939, they won a five-year contract with NBC and during the early 40s were regulars on programmes such as the *Bowman Musical Milkwagon*, *Gary Moore's Club Matinee* and the **National Barn Dance**, and they headlined at venues such as the Chez Paree, the Chicago Theatre and the Latin Quarter.

A trip to Hollywood led to an appearance with **Ozzie Nelson**'s band in the movie *Strictly In The Groove*. They also provided vocals for two **Walt Disney** films, *Fun And Fancy Free* and *Melody Time*, in the latter of which they sang 'Blame It On The Samba', accompanied by organist Ethel Smith. While on the west coast they signed for **Capitol Records** and had several hits in the late 40s, including 'My Adobe Haçienda', 'I Wonder Who's Kissing Her Now', 'Beg Your Pardon' and the million-seller 'Buttons And Bows' (1948), accompanied by accordionist Art Van Damme's Quintet. Lou Dinning also made some solo records, including 'The Little White Cloud That Cried', 'Trust In Me', 'Just Friends' and 'Nobody Else But Me', with **Paul Weston**'s Orchestra. By the mid-50s the Dinning Sisters' appeal had waned, and they subsequently retired. In 1960 their brother, **Mark Dinning**, topped the US chart in a very different style, with 'Teen Angel'.
● ALBUMS: *Songs By The Dinning Sisters* (Capitol 1957) ★★★.
● COMPILATIONS: *The Dinning Sisters, Volume 1* (Capitol 1984) ★★★, *The Dinning Sisters, Volume 2* (Capitol 1986) ★★★.

Dinning, Mark

b. 17 August 1933, Grant County, Oklahoma, USA, d. 22 March 1986. Mark Dinning was the younger brother of Lou, Ginger and Jean, the well-known 40s vocal trio the **Dinning Sisters**. He learnt to play the electric guitar when he was aged 17, and in 1957 he auditioned for publisher **Wesley Rose** in Nashville, who helped him get a recording contract with **MGM Records**. Two years later his sister Jean wrote 'Teen Angel', and Mark's tragic storyline vocal took the ballad to number 1 in the US charts in early 1960. It also reached number 37 in the UK, despite being banned and classified as a 'death disc' by the radio stations because of its morbid lyrics. He died of a heart attack aged 52.

Dino

b. Dino Kartsonakis, 1946, Manhattan, New York City, USA. The son of Helen and John Kartsonakis, Dino began to play the piano when he was three years old and has gone on to become contemporary Christian music's most prolific pianist. Indeed, some consider his technique to be 'flashy' enough to warrant the title Christian Liberace. His studies continued through high school, Kings College in Braircliff Manor, New York, and the Juilliard School Of Music in Manhattan. He then joined Arthur Rubinstein on several tours of Europe. His first album was recorded in 1963 for Diadem Records when he was just 17 years old. After serving in the army, he moved to California where he formed his own record label and released a further five albums of devotional piano compositions. He also played as the concert pianist for Kathryn Kuhlman for three years and was the musical director on her syndicated television programme *I Believe In Miracles*. In 1974 he signed with Light Records for whom he has now recorded over 20 albums. In 1978 he won sections in both the Dove and Grammy Awards. By now Dino was frequently to be seen in concert with his wife Debby, who formerly attended the Oral Roberts University in Tulsa and sang with the World Action And Television Singers. Together they hosted a religious television show and continued to record light, almost classically-themed music into the 90s.
● ALBUMS: *Dino Plays Folk Musical Themes* (Light 1974) ★★★, *My Tribute* (Light 1974) ★★★, *Dino-Patriotic* (Light 1974) ★★★, *Dino On Tour . . .With Debby* (Light 1975) ★★★, *Miracle* (Light 1976) ★★★, *Alleluia* (Light 1976) ★★★, *He Touched Me* (Light 1977) ★★★, *Playing Your Favorite Christmas Carols* (Light 1977) ★★★, *Classic Country* (Light 1978) ★★★, *Love Song* (Light 1979) ★★★, *Peace In The Midst Of The Storm* (Heartwarming 1987) ★★★.

Dino, Desi And Billy

The trio comprised the son of actor/singer **Dean Martin**, Dino (b. Dean Paul Anthony Martin Jnr., 12 November 1951, Los Angeles, California, USA, d. 21 March 1987), the son of actors **Desi Arnaz** and **Lucille Ball**, Desi (b. Desiderio Alberto Arnaz IV, 19 January 1953, Los Angeles, California, USA) and Billy (b. William Ernest Joseph Hinsche, 29 June 1951, Manilla, The Philippines), a friend from school. The trio met while playing Little League baseball in Beverly Hills in 1965 and decided to form a pop group. With their connections, they were easily signed to **Frank Sinatra**'s **Reprise** label. Their first single, the easy listening 'I'm A Fool', was their biggest hit, reaching number 17 in the summer of 1965, and they placed five other singles and two albums on the charts before breaking up in 1970. Although Martin and Arnaz joined a blues band in the 70s, Hinsche kept the highest musical profile, as a session musician and briefly a member of the **Beach Boys**' stage back-up band. Martin was killed in 1987 when his Air National Guard jet crashed.
● ALBUMS: *I'm A Fool* (Reprise 1965) ★★★, *Our Times Are Coming* (Reprise 1966) ★★, *Memories Are Made Of This* (Reprise 1966) ★★, *Souvenir* (Reprise 1966) ★★★, *Follow Me* (1969) ★★.
● COMPILATIONS: *The Rebel Kind* (Sundazed 1996) ★★★.

Dino, Kenny

b. 12 July 1939, Astoria, New York City, USA. Dino placed one single in the US pop Top 30 in 1961, 'Your Ma Said You Cried In Your Sleep Last Night' (covered in the UK by Doug Sheldon). He grew up in Hicksville, New York, and enlisted in the navy in 1957. Stationed in Iceland, he entered a music contest, which inspired him to pursue a career in music upon his discharge. Moving first to the state of Maine and then to Texas, Dino joined a band that played Tex-Mex and R&B music. He recorded his first single, 'On My Mind', in Texas for Arrow Records in 1958 but nothing happened. Moving back to New York, he signed with **Dot Records** and then with Musicor Records, for which he recorded his only hit. Subsequent singles for Musicor and several other labels failed before he turned to acting, appearing in the film *The Valley Of The Dolls*. He started recording again in 1980 but did not have any commercial success. Dino's name made some news in 1990 when **Robert Plant** covered 'Your Ma Said You Cried In Your Sleep Last Night' on *Manic Nirvana*.

Dinosaur Jr

This uncompromising alternative rock band from the university town of Amherst, Massachusetts, USA, was originally called simply Dinosaur. Their musical onslaught eventually dragged them, alongside the **Pixies**, into the rock mainstream of the late 80s. Both J. Mascis (b. 10 December 1965, Amherst, Massachusetts, USA; vocals/guitar) and Lou Barlow (bass) were formerly in the hardcore band Deep Wound, along with a singer called Charlie. The latter recruited his best friend Murph (b. Patrick Murphy; ex–All White Jury) from Connecticut and was rewarded by the first line-up of Dinosaur ejecting him and thus becoming a trio. Mascis had by this time switched from drums to guitar to accommodate the new arrival. Mascis, apparently a huge fan of **Sham 69** and the UK Oi! movement, had actually known Murphy at high school but they had never been friends. He formed Deep Wound as a response to seeing **999** play live when he was 14 years old.

During Dinosaur Jr's career, internal rifts never seemed far from the surface, while their leader's monosyllabic press interviews and general disinterest in rock 'n' roll machinations gave the impression of 'genius anchored by lethargy'. SST Records saw them establish their name as a credible underground rock act—*You're Living All Over Me* featured backing vocals from **Sonic Youth**'s Lee Ranaldo. However, their debut album for Homestead had brought them to the attention of ageing hippie group Dinosaur, who insisted the band change their name. Mascis elected to add the suffix Junior. Real recognition came with the release of the huge underground anthem 'Freak Scene', which more than one journalist called the perfect pop single. Its sound was constructed on swathes of guitar and Mascis' laconic vocals, which were reminiscent of **Neil Young**. However, the parent album (*Bug*) and tour saw Barlow depart (to **Sebadoh**) and Donna became a temporary replacement. This line-up recorded a version of the **Cure**'s 'Just Like Heaven', which so impressed Robert Smith that it led to joint touring engagements. Soon afterwards they signed to **Warner Brothers Records** subsidiary Blanco y Negro, remixing their **Sub Pop Records** track 'The Wagon' as their debut major label release. Subsequent members included Don Fleming (Gumball, etc.), Jay Spiegel and Van Conner (**Screaming Trees**), while Mascis himself flirted with other bands such as Gobblehoof, **Velvet Monkeys** and satanic metal band Upside Down Cross, principally as a drummer.

By the advent of *Green Mind*, Dinosaur Jr had effectively become the J. Mascis show, with him playing almost all the instruments. Although critically acclaimed, *Where You Been* did not manage to build on the commercial inroads originally made by *Green Mind*. *Without A Sound* included several strong compositions such as 'Feel The Pain' and 'On The Brink', with the bass now played by **Mike Johnson** (b. 27

August 1965, Grant's Pass, Oregon, USA). Mascis also produced other artists including the **Breeders** and **Buffalo Tom** and wrote the soundtrack for and appeared in Allison Anders' movie *Gas Food Lodging*. A new album, *Hand It Over*, was released in March 1997, and proved a full-bodied Dinosaur Jr recording that sounded like Mascis was once more committed to his music. While the lyrics were often muddied, Mascis' melodic grunge was very much intact. However, Mascis formally announced the end of Dinosaur Jr in December 1997. He subsequently collaborated with Kevin Shields (**My Bloody Valentine**) and Bob Pollard (**Guided By Voices**) on his next project, J Mascis And The Fog, releasing the excellent *More Light* in September 2000.

● ALBUMS: as Dinosaur *Dinosaur* (Homestead 1985) ★★★, *You're Living All Over Me* (SST 1987) ★★★, *Bug* (SST 1988) ★★★★, *Green Mind* (Blanco y Negro/Sire 1991) ★★★, *Whatever's Cool With Me* mini-album (Blanco y Negro/Sire 1993) ★★, *Where You Been* (Blanco y Negro 1993) ★★★★, *Without A Sound* (Blanco y Negro 1994) ★★★, *Hand It Over* (Blanco y Negro 1997) ★★★, *In Session* 1988 recording (Strange Fruit 1999) ★★★.
Solo: J Mascis *Martin + Me* (Baked Goods/Reprise 1996) ★★★, as J Mascis + The Fog *More Light* (Ultimatum/City Slang 2000) ★★★★, as J Mascis + The Fog *Free So Free* (Ultimatum/City Slang 2002) ★★★, *The John Peel Sessions* (Strange Fruit 2003) ★★.
● COMPILATIONS: *Ear Bleeding Country: The Best Of Dinosaur Jr* (Rhino 2001) ★★★★.

Dinosaurs

Formed in 1982 in San Francisco, California, USA, the Dinosaurs comprised former members of the popular San Francisco rock bands of the 60s. The initial line-up comprised guitarist **Barry Melton** (ex–**Country Joe And The Fish**), guitarist **John Cipollina** (ex–**Quicksilver Messenger Service**), bass player Peter Albin (formerly of **Big Brother And The Holding Company**), drummer Spencer Dryden (**Jefferson Airplane**) and songwriter/vocalist **Robert Hunter** (**Grateful Dead**). The band came together with the intent of recreating the sound and ambience of the era from which the members sprang. Long, winding improvisations were the norm whether the group performed new, original material or songs associated with the 60s. They played locally in the San Francisco area. In 1985, Hunter left and was replaced by keyboard player **Merl Saunders**, who worked with the Grateful Dead's **Jerry Garcia** in a number of extra-curricular bands during the 70s. They recorded their only album in 1988. After Cipollina's death in 1989, the group went on a hiatus, but by the mid-90s had replaced him with violinist **Papa John Creach**, formerly of Jefferson Airplane/Starship and **Hot Tuna**. Creach died in February 1994.
● ALBUMS: *Dinosaurs* (Big Beat 1988) ★★★.

DiNovi, Gene

b. 26 May 1928, New York City, New York, USA. DiNovi began playing piano seriously at the age of 12, when his brother arranged for piano lessons from a teacher who owed money for a painting job. Soon, more important lessons took place, again on piano, but this time from guitarist **Chuck Wayne**, followed by professional work with the Henry Jerome band. Amongst his fellow sidemen were **Al Cohn** and **Zoot Sims**. DiNovi's influences at this stage in his career (he was still only 16) were largely boppers, but then, as he entered his twenties, he worked with **Joe Marsala**, with whom he made his first records, and then with **Lester Young**. He also played with **Tiny Kahn**, **Don Fagerquist** and **Anita O'Day**. In the early 50s he gigged mostly in New York and in 1956 became **Lena Horne**'s regular accompanist. He had previously accompanied **Peggy Lee**, that and a later job with **Tony Bennett** established a reputation for working with singers stood him in good stead for a spell in west coast film and television studios.

In the 70s DiNovi moved to Canada where he remained for some years re-emerging on the international jazz scene in the late 80s after successful recording sessions with **Ruby Braff**. In the early 90s he visited Japan, the UK and also played with classical clarinettist James Campbell. Although his early influences amongst pianists included **Art Tatum** and **Teddy Wilson**, he was particularly affected by hearing **Bud Powell** and for a time, still in his teens, was used by proto-boppers such as **Dizzy Gillespie** along with other emerging bop pianists who included Powell, **Joe Albany**, **George Wallington** and **Al Haig**. The heady influence of these early days and associations has indelibly marked DiNovi's playing and he remains one of the very few keepers of that particular flame still demonstrating his art around the world.

● ALBUMS: *Scandinavian Route* (Roulette 1960) ★★★★, *Softly As I Leave You* (Pedimega 1977) ★★★, with Ruby Braff *My Funny Valentine* (Pedimega 1985) ★★★★, *Precious Moments* (Marshmallow 1990) ★★★, *How Beautiful Is Night* (Marshmallow 1991) ★★★, *Remembrance* (Marshmallow 1991) ★★★, *Renaissance Of A Jazz Master* (Candid 1993) ★★★, *Live At The Montréal Bistro, Toronto* (Candid 1996) ★★★, with Spike Robinson *At The Stables* (Hep 1996) ★★★, *Plays The Music Of Benny Carter* (Hep 1999) ★★★, *Plays Duke Ellington & Billy Strayhorn Live With Dave Young* (Baldwin Street 2003) ★★★.

Dio
(see **Dio, Ronnie James**)

Dio, Ronnie James

b. Ronald Padavona, 10 July 1940, Portsmouth, New Hampshire, USA. Dio was raised in New York, USA, and served his musical apprenticeship in the late 50s with school-based bands such as the Vegas Kings, Ronnie And The Rumblers and Ronnie And the Redcaps (one single, 'Lover'/'Conquest', in 1958). From 1961–67 he led Ronnie Dio And the Prophets, not solely as a vocalist, but also playing the piano, bass guitar, and even trumpet. A multi-talented musician, he also acted as a record producer. During that time, the Prophets released at least seven singles, including a gimmick version of 'Love Potion No. 9' that featured the same song on both sides, plus an album. In 1967, with his cousin, David Feinstein, he formed the Electric Elves, who, in 1970, changed their name to **Elf**. The same year, the entire band was involved in a car crash, in which guitarist Nick Pantas died. Dio took over lead vocals in Elf and played the bass. Elf were discovered by **Roger Glover** and Ian Paice of **Deep Purple** in 1972, and they went on to support Deep Purple on two American tours as well as signing to their Purple label in the UK.

In 1975, Glover gave Dio the opportunity to appear on his *The Butterfly Ball*, and the widespread recognition that ensued helped to persuade **Ritchie Blackmore**, who had already recorded one track, 'Black Sheep Of The Family', with Elf and had recently left Deep Purple himself, to link up with Dio. The remnants of Elf, with the exception of the ousted Steve Edwards, became **Rainbow**. This saw Dio develop from the honky-tonk influence of his former band to the harder rock of Blackmore and Rainbow. Dio's penchant for writing about supernatural events, thoughts and fantasies also began to emerge at this stage, combining with the succession of often excellent musicians in Rainbow (the former members of Elf had been rapidly discarded) to produce four albums of high quality and enduring appeal. In 1978, Dio left Rainbow, taking his gift for singing and songwriting to **Black Sabbath**, where he built on the previously phenomenal, but now waning, success of the band, doing much to rejuvenate the flagging supergroup. *Heaven And Hell* arrived alongside the **New Wave Of British Heavy Metal**, outclassing most of its rivals with its tight, solid, bass-dominated sound and science fiction-themed lyrics.

After an acrimonious disagreement over the mixing of *Live Evil*, Dio left in November 1982 to form his own band, Dio, which comprised Vinnie Appice (drums), Jimmy Bain (former bass player with Rainbow and **Wild Horses**) Vivian Campbell (b. 25 August 1962, Belfast, Northern Ireland; guitar) and Claude Schnell (keyboards). Together, they recorded four albums, with Dio taking on all the lyrics and songwriting himself, allowing his creative muse a completely free rein. While the subject matter remained other worlds, times and beings, the style ranged from anthemic to epic. A lack of direction led to stagnation, and by 1987, when Craig Goldie replaced Campbell, the band was failing. In 1991, Dio renewed his acquaintance with Black Sabbath, joining them for a UK tour and recording *Dehumanizer* with them the following year. However, November saw **Judas Priest**'s Rob Halford stand in for Dio when he refused to appear with the band in California after hearing of **Ozzy Osbourne**'s intention to re-form the original Sabbath line-up as part of his solo farewell tour. Dio, whom some commentators had described as 'the Cliff Richard of heavy metal', simply returned to the studio with yet another incarnation of his eponymous band. He has continued to release further albums and tour extensively.

● ALBUMS: as Ronnie Dio And The Prophets *Dio At Dominos* (Lawn 1963) ★★, *Holy Diver* (Vertigo 1983) ★★★★, *The Last In Line* (Vertigo 1984) ★★★, *Sacred Heart* (Vertigo 1985) ★★★, *Intermission* (Vertigo 1986) ★★★, *Dream Evil* (Vertigo 1987) ★★★, *Hey Angel* (Vertigo 1990) ★★★, *Lock Up The Wolves* (Vertigo 1990) ★★★, *Strange Highways* (Reprise 1994) ★★, *Angry Machines* (Mayhem 1996) ★★, *Dio's Inferno—Live In Line* (SPV 1998) ★★★, *Magica* (Spitfire 2000) ★★, *Killing The Dragon* (Spitfire 2002) ★★★, *Master Of The Moon* (Sanctuary 2004) ★★.

● COMPILATIONS: *Diamonds: The Best Of Dio* (Vertigo 1992) ★★★, *Anthology* (Connoisseur 1997) ★★★, *The Very Beast Of Dio* (Rhino 2000) ★★★, *Anthology Volume Two* (Connoisseur 2001) ★★★, *Stand Up And Shout: The Anthology* (Rhino 2003) ★★★.

● DVD/VIDEOS: *Live In Concert* (Channel 5 1986), *Special From The Spectrum* (PolyGram Music Video 1986), *Evil Or Divine* (Eagle Vision 2003).

Dion

During his peak, from 1958–63, Dion (b. Dion DiMucci, 18 July 1939, Bronx, New York City, USA) was the quintessential Italian-American New York City rocker and was, perhaps, the first major white rock singer who was not from a southern city. The career of one of America's legendary artists has spanned six decades, during which time he has made numerous musical style changes. Between 1958 and 1960 **Dion And The Belmonts** were one of the leading doo-wop groups.

The **Belmonts** comprised Angelo D'Aleo (b. 3 February 1940, Bronx, New York City, USA), Carlo Mastrangelo (b. 5 October 1938, Bronx, New York City, USA) and Freddie Milano (b. 22 August 1939, Bronx, New York City, USA). The slick besuited Italian look rivalled the black harmony groups that dominated the era. They had nine hits in two years, including two of the all-time great examples of white doo-wop, 'I Wonder Why' and 'No One Knows'. Their classic reading of the **Doc Pomus** and **Mort Shuman** song 'A Teenager In Love' with the memorable line of teenage despair 'each night I ask, the stars up above, (bom, bom, bom, bom), why must I be a teenager in love?' It poignantly articulated growing pains in an era when conservative values were being challenged by a new moral climate. In 1960 they attempted a version of 'When You Wish Upon A Star' from **Walt Disney**'s *Pinocchio* and followed with a worthy, but slushy, cover of **Cole Porter**'s 'In The Still Of The Night'. Dion left for a solo career in 1960 and had immediate success in the USA with 'Lonely Teenager'. The following year he had two consecutive hits that made him one of America's biggest artists. Both 'Runaround Sue' and 'The Wanderer' are rock classics; the former, warning everybody to keep away from Sue, while the latter warns Flo, Jane and Mary to steer clear of the wanderer. The similarity of the theme can be forgiven as they are both wonderfully uplifting songs, great dance records and two of the finest of the era. Dion sustained an incredible output of hits, including another classic 'Lovers Who Wander'. In 1963 with seven major singles he was in the US charts for the entire year. The following year Dion disappeared from the scene to fight a serious addiction to heroin, a drug to which he had fallen victim in 1960. Although he and the Belmonts reunited briefly in 1967, little was heard of him until December 1968. He returned during a turbulent year in American history; the escalation of the Vietnam War had received strong opposition, particularly from the music world, and the assassinations of Robert Kennedy and Martin Luther King were fresh in people's minds. The emotional Dick Holler song, 'Abraham, Martin And John' was a perfectly timed stroke of genius. This lilting folksy ballad barely left a dry eye as it climbed to number 4 in the US charts. The following year a heroin-free Dion delighted festival and concert audiences with a striking solo act, accompanied on acoustic guitar. That same year the excellent *Dion* was released, including sensitive covers of songs by **Bob Dylan**, **Joni Mitchell**, **Leonard Cohen** and a brave attempt at **Jimi Hendrix**'s 'Purple Haze'.

Dion's critical ranking was high but his commercial standing dwindled, and two acoustic-based albums were commercial disasters. Wily entrepreneurs encouraged another reunion with the Belmonts in 1973, and in 1975 **Phil Spector** produced 'Born To Be With You'. An excellent album of the same name (on Spector's own label) failed, and another underrated album, *The Return Of The Wanderer*, appeared in 1978 on Lifesong Records. For the next few years Dion became a devout born-again Christian and recorded sporadically, releasing Christian albums including *Inside Job* and *Kingdom Of The Street*. He returned to rock 'n' roll in 1988 playing with **Bruce Springsteen** and released the **Dave Edmunds**–produced *Yo Frankie*; and toured the UK where he has always found an enthusiastic cult following. Dion is one of the few survivors from a school of American vocalists who had genuine talent, and he should be credited for a series of uplifting songs that still sound remarkably fresh. He was elected to

the **Rock And Roll Hall Of Fame** in 1989. A surprisingly fresh new album was released in 2000.

● ALBUMS: with the Belmonts *Presenting Dion And The Belmonts* (Laurie 1959) ★★★, with the Belmonts *Wish Upon A Star* (Laurie 1960) ★★, *Alone With Dion* (Laurie 1961) ★★★, *Runaround Sue* (Laurie 1961) ★★★, *Lovers Who Wander* (Laurie 1962) ★★★★, *Dion Sings His Greatest Hits* (Laurie 1962) ★★★, *Love Came To Me* (Laurie 1963) ★★★, *Ruby Baby* (Columbia 1963) ★★★, *Dion Sings The 15 Million Sellers* (Laurie 1963) ★★★★, *Donna The Prima Donna* (Columbia 1963) ★★★★, *Dion Sings To Sandy* (Laurie 1963) ★★★, with the Belmonts *Together* (Laurie 1963) ★★★, with the Belmonts *Together Again* (ABC 1967) ★★★, *Dion* (Laurie 1968) ★★★★, *Sit Down Old Friend* (Warners 1969) ★★★, *You're Not Alone* (Warners 1971) ★★★, *Sanctuary* (Warners 1971) ★★★, *Suite For Late Summer* (Warners 1972) ★★★, with the Belmonts *Reunion: Live 1972* (Reprise 1973) ★★, *Born To Be With You* (Spector 1975) ★★★★, *Streetheart* (Warners 1976) ★★★, *The Return Of The Wanderer* (Lifesong 1978) ★★★, *Inside Job* (Dayspring 1980) ★★, *Only Jesus* (Dayspring 1981) ★★, *I Put Away My Idols* (Dayspring 1983) ★★★, *Seasons* (Dayspring 1984) ★★★, *Kingdom In The Streets* (Myrrh 1985) ★★, *Velvet And Steel* (Dayspring 1986) ★★★, *Yo Frankie!* (Arista 1989) ★★★, *Dream On Fire* (Vision 1992) ★★★, *Déjà Nu* (Collectables 2000) ★★★★, *New Masters* (Collectables 2003) ★★★.

● COMPILATIONS: *Dion's Greatest Hits* (Columbia 1973) ★★★, *20 Golden Greats* (K-Tel 1980) ★★★★, *24 Original Classics* (Arista 1984) ★★★★, *So Why Didn't You Do That The First Time?* (Ace 1985) ★★★★, *Runaround Sue: The Best Of The Rest* (Ace 1988) ★★★, *Bronx Blues: The Columbia Recordings (1962–1965)* (Columbia 1990) ★★★★, *The Road I'm On: A Retrospective* (Columbia Legacy 1997) ★★★, *The Best Of The Gospel Years* (Ace 1997) ★★★, *Bronx Blues: The Columbia Recordings (1962–1965)* (Columbia 1999) ★★★, *King Of The New York Streets* 3-CD box set (The Right Stuff 2000) ★★★★, *Dion: The EP Collection* (See For Miles 2001) ★★★, *70s: From Acoustic To The Wall Of Sound* (Ace 2004) ★★★.

● DVD/VIDEOS: *Live* (BMG 2004).

● FURTHER READING: *The Wanderer*, Dion DiMucci with Davin Seay.

Dion And The Belmonts
(see **Dion**; **Belmonts**)

Dion, Celine

b. 30 March 1968, Charlemagne, Montreal, Quebec, Canada. The youngest of 14 children, Celine Dion was a vastly popular artist at home long before her success in the US and European charts as the 'new **Whitney Houston** or **Mariah Carey**'. Her parents and large family had a singing group and toured playing folk music, the influence of which was soon felt. It was Dion's mother who wrote the first song for her, which she recorded with her brother at the age of 12. Together with Mrs. Dion, the two siblings were sent to the office of René Angélil, then a local rock manager, who took over the young star's guidance (later, in December 1994, he married Dion, despite a 26-year age gap). Following a series of albums addressed to her French Canadian audience she made her English language debut in 1990 with *Unison*, an impressive achievement as she had only learned English in

1989. Although this produced four hit singles, her true international breakthrough arrived with the soundtrack of the **Walt Disney** movie, **Beauty And The Beast**. Her duet with **Peabo Bryson** on the title track reached the US Top 10 and earned an Academy Award for Best Song and a Grammy. Following a tribute collection comprising Dion's interpretations of the songs of Canadian writer Luc Lamondon, she concentrated on developing an international audience.

'Beauty And The Beast' formed the centrepiece of her second English language album, which also produced the hit singles 'Love Can Move Mountains', 'Water From The Moon', 'If You Asked Me To' and 'Did You Give Enough Love'. In its wake Dion became a veritable staple of awards ceremonies, making a second appearance at the Grammys, becoming a personal favourite of *The Tonight Show*'s Jay Leno and herself hosting Canada's Juno Awards where in 1993 she won the Female Vocalist Of The Year Award for the third time in succession. Before the release of a third English language set, Dion recorded 'When I Fall In Love', the theme tune to the hit movie *Sleepless In Seattle*. This was included on **The Colour Of My Love** alongside a cover of **Jennifer Rush**'s AOR classic, 'The Power Of Love', also released as a single. It saw her work with songwriters including **David Foster**, **Diane Warren**, Phil Goldstone, **Albert Hammond**, **Charlie Dore** and Ric Wake. A similarly impressive cast of producers added Guy Roche, **Aldo Nova** and many others to a project seemingly without budget restrictions. Regardless, Epic Records' investment was repaid multi-fold by the astonishing singles success of 'Think Twice', which spent several weeks on top of the UK charts and also charted strongly in the US during 1995.

The album, and its follow-up *Falling Into You*, simultaneously topped both UK and US charts in 1994 and 1996, and 'Because You Loved Me' became the bestselling adult contemporary single ever. Dion was chosen to sing (in front of billions of television viewers) at the opening of the 1996 Olympic Games in Atlanta, Georgia, USA. In 1997, she released *Let's Talk About Love* and achieved another huge worldwide hit with 'My Heart Will Go On' from the soundtrack of the blockbuster movie, *Titanic*. She also collaborated with the **Bee Gees** on 'Immortality' and **R. Kelly** on 'I'm Your Angel', both of which were predictably international hit singles.

The singer took a break from performing in the late 90s to concentrate on conceiving a child. She gave birth to a son, Rene Charles, in January 2001 and announced that her music career would remain on hold while she tried a new career as a mother. The lure of singing meant Dion was not away for long, returning in March 2002 with *A New Day Has Come*. The album went straight to the top of the US charts. Two years later she collaborated with children's photographer Anne Geddes on the CD/book project, *Miracle*.

● ALBUMS: *La Voix Du Bon Dieu* (Disques Super Etoiles 1981) ★★, *Celine Dion Chante Noël* (Disques Super Etoiles 1981) ★★, *Tellement J'ai D'amour* (Saisons 1982) ★★, *Les Chemins De Ma Maison* (Saisons 1983) ★★, *Du Soleil Au Coeur* (Pathe Marconi 1983) ★★, *Chants Et Contes De Noël* (1983) ★★, *Mélanie* (TBS 1984) ★★, *Les Oiseaux Du Bonheur* (Pathe Marconi 1984) ★★, *C'est Pour Toi* (TBS 1985) ★★, *Celine Dion En Concert* (TBS 1985) ★★, *Incognito* (Columbia 1987) ★★, *Unison* (Epic 1990) ★★, *Dion Chante Plamondon/Des Mots Qui Sonnent* (Epic 1991) ★★★, *Celine Dion* (Epic 1992) ★★★★, *The Colour Of My Love* (Epic 1993) ★★★★, *Celine Dion À L'Olympia* (Columbia 1994) ★★★, *D'Eux/The French Album* (Epic

1995) ★★★, *Falling Into You* (Epic 1996) ★★★★, *Live À Paris* (Epic 1996) ★★★, *Let's Talk About Love* (Epic 1997) ★★★, *S'Il Suffisait D'Aimer* (Epic 1998) ★★, with Mariah Carey, Gloria Estefan, Aretha Franklin, Shania Twain *Divas Live* (Epic 1998) ★★, *These Are Special Times* (Epic 1998) ★★★, *A New Day Has Come* (Epic 2002) ★★★, *One Heart* (Epic 2003) ★★★, *A New Day . . . Live In Las Vegas* (Epic 2004) ★★, with Anne Geddes *Miracle* (Epic 2004) ★★.

● COMPILATIONS: *Les Plus Grands Succès De Celine Dion* (TBS 1984) ★★★, *Les Chansons En Or* (TBS 1986) ★★, *Vivre: The Best Of Celine Dion* (Carrere 1988) ★★, *Les Premières Années* (Versailles 1993) ★★, *Celine Dion Gold* (Versailles 1995) ★★★, *Celine Dion Gold Volume 2* (Versailles 1995) ★★★, *C'est Pour Vivre* (Eureka 1997) ★★★, *All The Way . . . A Decade Of Song* (Epic 1999) ★★★, *The Collector's Series Volume One* (Epic 2000) ★★★.

● DVD/VIDEOS: *Unison* (1991), *The Colour Of My Love Concert* (Epic Music Video 1995), *Live À Paris* (1996), with Mariah Carey, Gloria Estefan, Aretha Franklin, Shania Twain *Divas Live* (Sony Music Video 1998), *Live In Memphis—The Concert* (Sony Music Video 1998), *All The Way . . . A Decade Of Song* (Epic Music Video 2001), *Au Coeur Du Stade* (Sony Music Video 2002), *A New Day Has Come* (Epic Music Video 2002), *Miracle* (Epic Music Video 2004).

● FURTHER READING: *Celine Dion: Behind The Fairytale*, Ian Halperin. *Celine Dion: Falling Into You*, Barry Grills. *A Voice And A Dream: The Celine Dion Story*, Richard Crouse. *Celine: The Authorized Biography*, Georges-Hébert Germain. *Celine Dion*, Marianne McKay. *Celine Dion: The Complete Biography*, Lisa Peters with Della Druick. *My Story, My Dream*, Celine Dion. *Miracle: A Celebration Of New Life*, Anne Geddes and Celine Dion.

● FILMS: *Quest For Camelot* voice only (1998), *Passionnément* (1999).

Diop, Wasis

b. c.1952, Dakar, Senegal. Diop moved to Paris at the age of 20 and co-founded the West African Cosmos, a pioneering Afro-Parisian band. Travelling to Jamaica in the late 70s, he worked at **Lee Perry**'s Black Ark studio before moving to China and then England, where he recorded tracks with Robin Millar, **Sade**'s producer, that were never released. Returning to Paris, he co-wrote Amina Annabi's Eurovision Song Contest winner 'C'est Le Dernier Qui A Parlé Qui A Raison' and, in 1993, supplied the soundtrack music to *Hyènes*, a film directed by his brother Djibril Diop Mambéty. 1995's *No Sant* entered the UK album chart and 'African Dream', a single taken from it featuring **Lena Fiagbe**, made the UK Top 50. Polished and diverse (one track featured African drumming, bagpipes and a Japanese opera singer!), *No Saint* was one of the most popular world music albums of the year. *Toxu*, the follow-up, was released three years later. Produced by **Wally Badarou**, it was even glossier-sounding than its predecessor. The most interesting track on the album was an inventive vocal/percussion-based version of **Talking Heads**' 'Once In A Lifetime'.

● ALBUMS: *Hyènes* film soundtrack (Verve 1993) ★★★, *No Sant* (Mercury 1995) ★★★★, *Toxu* (Mercury 1998) ★★★.

● COMPILATIONS: *Everything Is Never Quite Enough* (Triloka/Artemis 2003) ★★★★.

Diorio, Joe

b. Joseph Louis Diorio, 6 August 1936, Waterbury, Connecticut, USA. Following in the footsteps of an uncle, Diorio took up the guitar, studying formally in the early 50s at a local music school. He worked for a while with local bands but in the early 60s he ventured into New York City where he quickly established a reputation. He played with many bop musicians, such as **Eddie Harris**, **Sonny Stitt** and **Ira Sullivan**. He also played in mainstream groups fronted by noted jazzmen including **Conte Candoli** and **Stan Getz**. From the 60s to the 80s he worked in various centres, including Florida, where he played on television and radio and also taught at the University of Miami. He also played in the Netherlands, France, Brazil and Australia and recorded as a leader for the Spitball label during the 70s. Among musicians with whom he has recorded are guitarists **Mick Goodrick** and John Pisano, **Anita O'Day** and Sullivan. In addition to performing and teaching, Diorio has also written textbooks, including the praised *21st Century Intervallic Designs*, and is a painter and sculptor. Gradually, as the new century began, he was gaining a much-deserved audience.

● ALBUMS: *Solo Guitar* (Spitball 1973) ★★★★, with Wally Cirillo *Rapport* (Spitball 1974) ★★★, with Cirillo *Solo-Duo* (Spitball 1976) ★★★, with Steve Bagby *Straight Ahead To The Light* (Spitball 1976) ★★★, *Peaceful Journey* (Spitball 1977) ★★★, *Bonita* (Zdenek 1980) ★★★, with Jeff Berlin, Vinnie Colaiuta *20th Century Impressions* (J Disc 1981) ★★★★, *Earth Moon Earth* (Nocturne 1987) ★★★, *Italy* (MGI 1989) ★★★, with Robben Ford *Minor Elegance* (MGI 1990) ★★★, with Riccardo Del Fra *Double Take* (Ram 1992) ★★★, *We Will Meet Again* (Ram 1992) ★★★, with Mick Goodrick *Rare Birds* (Ram 1993) ★★★, with Ira Sullivan *The Breeze And I* (Ram 1993) ★★★★, with Hal Crook Quartet *Nārāyāni* (Ram 1994) ★★★, with Steve La Spina, Steve Bagby *More Than Friends* (Ram 1994) ★★★, *To Jobim With Love* (Ram 1995) ★★★, *I Remember You: A Tribute To Wes Montgomery* (Ram 1998) ★★★, *Stateside* (Diorio Jazz 2000) ★★★, *Live* (Diorio Jazz 2002) ★★★.

Dioubate, Oumou

b. *c.*1964, Kankan, Guinea. Born into a family of 'jelis' (hereditary praise singers), Dioubate started singing at the age of seven. Six years later her mother, Gnamakoro Kante, died and Oumou replaced her as the singer with the traditional Kankan Regional Ensemble. She married her cousin, a musician and teacher, with whom she moved to Conakry (the Guinean capital) and formed Les Messagers De Morifing Diabate in 1983. She began to develop a modern style with outspokenly feminist lyrics. Moving to Paris in the mid-80s, she was spotted in 1987 by the renowned producer **Ibrahima Sylla** while singing backing vocals on **Ismaël Lo**'s *N'Diawar*. Dioubate and Sylla worked on her debut solo album for three years, finally completing *Lancey* in 1990. Even then Sylla considered the album, with its high-tech funky sound and controversial lyrics, as too daring for release. Dioubate returned to Guinea in the early 90s to discover that she had become even more controversial than ever and her husband had left her. At this point Sylla decided to release *Lancey*, which became an instant hit in Guinea and across West Africa. The album was subsequently picked up by **Stern's Records** and released internationally. The success of *Lancey* gave Dioubate celebrity status in her home country where she remains a controversial figure. *Wambara* was an even more daring and varied set than its predecessor, with Sylla again producing and Dioubate's voice soaring over a mix of funk, jazz, reggae, salsa and West African sounds. To promote the album Dioubate toured internationally as a part of the Griot Groove tour alongside fellow West African artists **Sékouba Bambino** and **Kandia Kouyaté**.

● ALBUMS: *Lancey* (Stern's 1993) ★★★, *Wambara* (Stern's 1999) ★★★★.

DiPasqua, Michael

b. 4 May 1953, Orlando, Florida, USA. Born into a highly musical family, DiPasqua began his professional career very early, gigging on drums with a band co-led by **Zoot Sims** and **Al Cohn** when still only in his mid-teens. During the next few years DiPasqua played with several other musicians of note, including Don Elliott and **Gerry Mulligan** and he also accompanied singers **Jackie Cain** and **Roy Kral**. Towards the end of the 70s, DiPasqua was for a number of years co-leader of Double Image. He then co-led Gallery and followed that with a spell in Later That Evening, a band led by **Eberhard Weber**, before joining **Jan Garbarek**. DiPasqua has consistently proved himself to be a sleekly inventive percussionist with the ability to comfortably co-exist in a range of musical styles, from the modern end of the mainstream through jazz rock to the cutting edge of improvisational music.

● ALBUMS: *Double Image* (Enja 1977) ★★★, *Gallery* (ACM 1981) ★★★, *It's OK To Listen To The Grey Voice* (ECM 1984) ★★★.

DiPiero, Bob

Bob DiPiero played in rock 'n' roll bands in Ohio and used the income to fund his university education. He moved to Nashville in the late 70s to concentrate on songwriting. His first success was with 'Forever In Your Eyes' for **Reba McEntire** and he also wrote 'Little Rock' for her. He himself is either a talented Nashville songwriter or his collaborators are, as he rarely writes on his own. His songs include 'American Made' (**Oak Ridge Boys**), 'Cleopatra, Queen Of Denial' (**Pam Tillis**), '(Do You Love Me) Just Say Yes' (**Highway 101**), 'Sentimental Ol' You' (**Charly McClain**) and 'That Rock Won't Roll' (**Restless Heart**). DiPiero was married to Tillis from 1991–98 and is a former president of the Nashville Songwriters' Association. He is also part of a goodtime band of session men and songwriters, **Billy Hill**, who have been on the US country charts with 'Too Much Month At The End Of The Money' and a revival of the **Four Tops**' 'I Can't Help Myself'. Recent songs include 'Ancient History' (**Prairie Oyster**), 'Forgiveness' (**Victoria Shaw**), ' I Am Just A Rebel' (**Confederate Railroad**), 'Let Me Drive' (Greg Holland), 'Take Me As I Am' (**Faith Hill**), 'Take That' (Lisa Brokop), 'Wink' (**Neal McCoy**) and, best of all, 'Wild Love' (**Joy Lynn White**).

● ALBUMS: *Laugh: Live At The Bluebird Cafe* (American Originals 2001) ★★★.

Diplomats

Although they are considered a group, the focus of the US rap outfit the Diplomats aka Dipset is undoubtedly **Cam'ron** (b. Cameron Giles, 4 February 1976, Harlem, New York City, USA) who scored several hits on his own before an album from the aforementioned unit was issued. Originating from the streets of Harlem, New York City, USA, the Diplomats officially formed during the late 90s. Even though locals **Jim**

Jones (b. Joseph Agurmella Jones, 1976, the Bronx, New York City, USA) and Freekey Zeekey grew up with Cam'ron, it was not until newcomer (and the youngest member of the group) Juelz Santana signed on that the Diplomats were complete. A buzz was instantly built when **Juelz Santana** (b. LaRon Louis James, 18 February 1982, Harlem, New York City, USA) made a guest appearance on Cam'ron's hit single 'Oh Boy' (off 2002's *Come Home With Me*), which resulted in the quartet being granted their very own label, Diplomat Records, a subsidiary of the same label that served as Cam'ron's home, Roc-A-Fella. In 2003, the Diplomats released their debut, *Diplomatic Immunity*, which expectedly charted high in the US *Billboard* mainstream album chart. A Jim Jones solo album preceded the recording of the Diplomats' far superior follow-up album, which introduced new members Jha Jha, Hell Rell, J.R. Writer and 40 Cal, but was recorded without the recently incarcerated Freekey Zeekey. The group also recorded a series of highly popular mixtapes for the underground scene, several of which received an official release through Koch Entertainment. (NB: Not to be confused with the 60s soul group of the same name.)

● ALBUMS: *Diplomatic Immunity* (Diplomat/Roc-A-Fella 2003) ★★★, *Diplomatic Immunity 2* (Diplomat/Koch 2004) ★★★★, as Dipset *More Than Music, Vol. 1* (Diplomat/Koch 2005) ★★★.

Dipset
(see **Diplomats**)

Dire Straits
Few groups can claim to be synonymous with a lifestyle, but Dire Straits are an exception, whether they like it or not. *Brothers In Arms*, released in 1985, established them as the first real darlings of the compact disc 20-something generation that grew out of the boom years of the 80s. Their accessible, traditional blues-based music made them perfect for the massive, mature, relatively wealthy strata of the public that likes its music tightly performed and readily digestible. The album was number 1 in the US charts for nine weeks and spent three years in the UK chart.

Surprisingly, Dire Straits first surfaced during a period that was the antipathy of what they were to become—the London punk scene of 1976/7. **Mark Knopfler** (b. 12 August 1949, Glasgow, Scotland) and his brother **David Knopfler** (b. 27 December 1952, Glasgow, Scotland) were the sons of an architect who moved to Newcastle-upon-Tyne, England, when the boys were young. Mark Knopfler studied English literature at Leeds University, and for a short while worked as a junior reporter with the *Yorkshire Evening Post* and with an Essex local newspaper. After university he played in a part-time pub band called **Brewer's Droop**, but his main income was drawn from teaching. The Knopflers moved to London during the early 70s and Mark met bass player John Illsley (b. 24 June 1949, Leicester, England) and drummer Pick Withers. Illsley, a sociology graduate, was working in a record shop and Withers had been a session drummer for many years. The climate was not right for the group as punk took a grip on music and almost every UK record label passed on the offer to press up Dire Straits' polished music. One song began to stand out from their repertoire: a basic blues progression with dry, affectionate lyrics, entitled 'Sultans Of Swing', it contained the line, 'check out guitar

George, he knows all the chords', allegedly referring to jobbing guitarist George Borowski. It was picked up by Radio London DJ and Oval Records proprietor, **Charlie Gillett**, and by the end of 1977 the group was recording their debut, *Dire Straits*, for **Vertigo Records** with producer **Muff Winwood**. 'Sultans Of Swing' was a hit first in Holland and later made the UK Top 10. The powerful **Warner Brothers Records** took over distribution in the USA and aggressively backed the album until in March 1979 it had reached number 2 in the *Billboard* chart. 'Sultans Of Swing' also reached the US Top 5. Their second single, 'Lady Writer', was a relative failure but it did not impair their attraction as an 'albums band'.

Dire Straits' second album *Communiqué*, produced by **Jerry Wexler** and **Barry Beckett**, sold three million copies worldwide. It missed the commercial edge of the debut but developed Knopfler's trademark incisive, cynical lyricism. Before the recording of *Making Movies*, David Knopfler opted out to begin a solo career and has since released acclaimed records with various small independent labels. He was replaced by Hal Lindes (b. 30 June 1953; ex-Darling), with Alan Clark (b. 5 March 1952) joining on keyboards at the same time. Knopfler was heavily criticized for not varying his songwriting formula but the album still spawned a UK Top 10 single with the poignant love ballad, 'Romeo And Juliet'. *Love Over Gold* fared better than its predecessor in the USA and the single from it, 'Private Investigations', reached number 2 in the UK during September 1982.

Following the *Love Over Gold* album, Knopfler took time off to produce **Bob Dylan**'s *Infidels* (1983) and wrote **Tina Turner**'s comeback hit, 'Private Dancer'. Now respected as both a songwriter and an exceptionally gifted guitarist, it looked for a while as if Dire Straits might not record again because of Knopfler's other production commitments with artists as diverse as **Aztec Camera**, **Randy Newman** and **Willy DeVille**. They reassembled, however, in 1983 with ex-**Man** drummer Terry Williams replacing Withers, and completed an arduous world tour. The *Twisting By The Pool* EP and a live double album, *Alchemy*, filled the gap before the band's next studio album release, *Brothers In Arms*. Like many others, Dire Straits' appearance at the **Live Aid** concert boosted sales and their own 200-date tour helped it become one of the decade's biggest-selling albums. Many die-hard fans would shake their head and ask, why? It was an album that by no means could justify such huge sales, especially in view of the fact that the debut and *Making Movies* were superior collections. Knopfler used *Brothers In Arms* to make several wry observations on his own position as a rock star, laughing at the folly of videos and the **MTV** channel on 'Money For Nothing'—a number 1 in the USA, thanks in no small part to constant rotation on MTV, an ironic turn of events later acknowledged by Knopfler. Three other songs from the record, 'Walk Of Life', 'So Far Away' and the title track, also charted on both sides of the Atlantic, with 'Walk Of Life' reaching number 2 in the UK.

With *Brothers In Arms* still riding high in the charts, Knopfler turned once again to other projects. Having already written three film scores in 1983 and 1984 (for *Local Hero*, *Cal* and *Comfort And Joy*), he wrote the music for the fantasy comedy film, *The Princess Bride*, in 1987. With Dire Straits on extended sabbatical, bass player John Illsley also took the chance to release two solo albums, *Never Told A Soul* in 1984 and *Glass* in 1988, neither of which sold in significant quantities. In 1990, Knopfler formed an *ad hoc* and low-key pub band with **Brendan Croker** and **Steve Phillips**, called the **Notting Hillbillies**. Their self-titled debut album was a disappointing, soporific release, and the group disbanded after one UK tour.

During the summer of 1991 Dire Straits announced a massive 'comeback' tour and the release of a new album, *On Every Street*. The line-up now comprised Knopfler, Illsley, Clark and guitarist/keyboard player Guy Fletcher. The latter had been appearing with the band since the mid-80s. While Knopfler strived to find new challenges in various other music-related spheres, his group was able to leave a six-year gap between album releases and still maintain their incredible popularity. This was owing, in no small measure, to masterful global marketing and the unflinching mainstream appeal of their music. Their world tour, taking two years to complete, marked their first concerts since their 1988 appearance as part of the Nelson Mandela birthday concert at London's Wembley Stadium, and it was captured on their second live album, *On The Night*. With Dire Straits on indefinite hold, Mark Knopfler embarked on a solo career in 1996.

● ALBUMS: *Dire Straits* (Vertigo/Warners 1978) ★★★★, *Communiqué* (Vertigo/Warners 1979) ★★★, *Making Movies* (Vertigo/Warners 1980) ★★★★, *Love Over Gold* (Vertigo/Warners 1982) ★★★, *Alchemy* (Vertigo/Warners 1984) ★★, *Brothers In Arms* (Vertigo/Warners 1985) ★★★, *On Every Street* (Vertigo/Warners 1991) ★★★, *On The Night* (Vertigo/Warners 1993) ★★, *Live At The BBC* (Windsong 1995) ★★★.

● COMPILATIONS: *Money For Nothing* (Vertigo/Warners 1988) ★★★, *Sultans Of Swing: The Very Best Of Dire Straits* (Mercury 1998) ★★★★, *Private Investigations: The Very Best Of Dire Straits & Mark Knopfler* (Vertigo 2005) ★★★.

● DVD/VIDEOS: *Brothers In Arms* (PolyGram Music Video 1988), *Alchemy Live* (Channel 5 1988), *The Videos* (PolyGram Music Video 1992), *Sultans Of Swing: The Very Best Of Dire Straits* (Universal 2004).

● FURTHER READING: *Dire Straits*, Michael Oldfield. *Mark Knopfler: An Unauthorised Biography*, Myles Palmer.

Dirt Nation

New York rap trio comprising JB (b. Brooklyn, New York City, USA), KD (b. Jamaica, West Indies) and E Depp (b. New Jersey, USA). Specializing in smooth, easily palatable (at least musically) goods, Dirt Nation's debut 45, 'Khadijah', became a summer 1993 hit throughout urban America. Quoting **Curtis Mayfield**, **Jimmy McGriff** and **Marvin Gaye**, and alluding to the golden age of soul in its mellow rhythms too, 'Khadijah' was a tribute to the womenfolk often degraded as 'bitches' and 'ho's' in gangsta rhymes. The group met at school in Maryland, relocating to Manhattan in search of a record contract. There they recorded their debut single, plus a track with rapper Biggie Smalls (**Mary J. Blige**). Their debut album's title was lifted from the movie of the same name, while a collaboration with Guru of **Gang Starr** was also mooted.

● ALBUMS: *Three The Hard Way* (1994) ★★★.

Dirtbombs

A garage rock revival was in full force during the early twenty-first century, and it is fitting that the Dirtbombs come from a town most associated with the genre, Detroit, Michigan, USA, the same locale that spawned the **Stooges**, the **MC5** and the more recent **White Stripes**. The mastermind

behind the Dirtbombs is Mick Collins (b. 18 December 1965; vocals/guitar), who has previously appeared in similarly styled outfits such as Blacktop, King Sound Quartet, the Screws and the **Gories**. Rumours of Collins' Dirtbombs project first surfaced when he was still part of the Gories, but after years of speculation and no product, many assumed the band was just a fabrication. This proved not to be the case, as a single appeared in 1997 that led to further releases shows. The line-up includes Collins, bass player Jim Diamond (b. James Andrew Diamond, 12 February 1965), plus drummers Ben Blackwell (b. Benjamin Jesse Blackwell, 12 June 1982) and Patrick Pantano. Additionally, Ghetto Records owner Jim Diamond has been known to supply additional bass from time to time.

After several other singles appeared, the Dirtbomb's debut was issued in 1998, *Horndog Fest*. In 2001, the quartet released their follow-up, *Ultraglide In Black*, a recording that paid tribute to the soul masters of the 60s and 70s by including cover versions of **Smokey Robinson**, **Stevie Wonder**, **Marvin Gaye**, **Sly And The Family Stone** and even an obscure **Phil Lynott** solo track. The Dirtbombs returned to straight ahead garage rock, however, with 2003's *Dangerous Magical Noise*. In addition to his aforementioned projects, Collins has also guested on recordings by **Rocket From The Crypt** and **Andre Williams** and has either mixed or produced tracks for the **Jon Spencer Blues Explosion** and the **Demolition Doll Rods**.

● ALBUMS: *Horndog Fest* (In The Red 1998) ★★★, *Ultraglide In Black* (In The Red 2001) ★★★, *Dangerous Magical Noise* (In the Red 2003) ★★★★.

● COMPILATIONS: *If You Don't Already Have A Look* (In The Red 2005) ★★★★.

Dirtsman

b. Patrick Thompson, 1966, Spanish Town, Jamaica, West Indies, d. 21 December 1993. The brother of **Papa San**, Dirtsman was a similarly inclined **dancehall** DJ until his brutal death. His father was the owner of the Black Universe **sound system**, but he subsequently moved on to the Creation Rock Tower Sound, based in Willowdene. His first chart appearance came with 'Thank You' in 1990, preceding 'Borrow Man' on **Steely And Clevie**'s label. Later, he teamed up with Phillip Smart in New York City, USA, achieving further success with 'Hot This Year'. On the cusp of mainstream success, he signed to BMG, but his career was cut short in 1993 when he was shot on his veranda by four gunmen, being pronounced dead on arrival at Spanish Town Hospital.

● ALBUMS: *Acid* (VP 1988) ★★★.

Dirty Beatniks

Dirty Beatniks originally comprised Irishmen Neil Higgins and Rory Carlile, and Justin Underhill from Leeds, Yorkshire, England. Inspired by **acid house** and the nascent **dance music** scene, Higgins and Carlile visited London in 1988 to buy their first sampler. They stayed, and while working in a variety of second-hand record shops and recording studios, they met Underhill, a studio engineer, in 1993. They released the EP *Mental Spiritual* on the **Wall Of Sound** label in 1994 under the name Rootless. In 1995, they released the Rootless mini-album, *Rotten Wood For Smoking Bees*, and the Dirty Beatniks EP *Bridgin' The Gap*, prompting the UK's *Muzik* magazine to comment on 'an explosion of instrumental collages which will have you scratching your head while shaking your booty'. Their debut album, *One One*

Seven In The Shade, was released in 1996 to a positive critical reception. The Dirty Beatniks sound combines Detroit **techno**-inspired basslines, breakbeats and samples but does not fit comfortably into either the trip-hop or **big beat** categories. They have also assembled a band for live performances that involves live bass, drums and scratching. In 1997, their performances at the Back To Basics club in Leeds, on the Wall Of Sound Back To Mono tour and at the Essential and Reading Festivals won them many admirers. In the same year, they remixed tracks for **INXS**, **Space** and **James**. After a quiet period Higgins resurfaced in 2000 with ex-**Earthling** vocalist Mau with the single 'The New Adventures Of Sandy And Bud'. *Feedback* followed three months later.

● ALBUMS: *One One Seven In The Shade* (Wall Of Sound 1996) ★★★★, *Feedback* (Wall Of Sound 2000) ★★★★.

Dirty Blues Band

Formed in Riverside, California, USA, in 1967, the Dirty Blues Band evolved out of several groups active in the region. **Rod Piazza** (b. 18 December 1947, Riverside, California, USA; vocals/harmonica) led the Mystics, whereas Glenn 'Ross' Campbell (steel guitar) was previously a member of the innovative **Misunderstood**. Taking their cue from the **Butterfield Blues Band**, the Dirty Blues Band offered a mixture of classic songs from **Albert King**, **Sonny Boy Williamson** and **Willie Dixon**, sprinkled with stylized originals. Robert Sandell (guitar), Pat Malone (organ), Les Morrison (bass) and John Milliken (drums) completed the line-up featured on the band's debut album. Although promising, the set failed to exploit Campbell's original playing style and he left the band soon afterwards. The guitarist later played with **Juicy Lucy**. By the release of *Stone Dirt* only Piazza and Malone remained from the founding line-up. Rick Lunetta (steel guitar), Greg Anderson (bass) and Dave Miter (drums) joined them but the album lacked direction and the Dirty Blues Band broke up soon after its release. Piazza subsequently embarked on a solo career and formed the popular **Mighty Flyers**.

● ALBUMS: *Dirty Blues Band* (ABC/Bluesway 1967) ★★★, *Stone Dirt* (ABC/Bluesway 1968) ★★.

Dirty Dancing

If films that adhered to a conventional musical formula could be counted on the fingers of one hand in the 80s, the excitement of dance never ceased to attract enthusiastic audiences. Following in the dance steps of the success of Footloose and Flashdance, *Dirty Dancing*, released in 1987, caught the imagination of many with its combination of raunchy dancing, romance and upbeat soundtrack. Directed by Emile Ardolino, with a screenplay by Eleanor Bergstein, it tells the story of Baby (Jennifer Grey), her father's favourite daughter, who suffers the ups-and-downs of growing up while on a family holiday at a Catskills resort in the summer of 1963. Baby is an idealistic girl, soon to begin at college, who thinks she can right any problem, and help anyone, whatever the situation. These are all characteristics which one of the resort's leading dancers, Johnny (Patrick Swayze), finds refreshing and attractive. When someone is desperately needed to fill the shoes of Johnny's dancing partner, Penny (Cynthia Rhodes), it's hardly surprising that Baby is chosen to substitute, learning all the steps from scratch—almost a mild modern variation of the chorus girl becomes star routine. It's at this point that Baby and Johnny begin to fall

in love, and despite the protestations of most of the adults around them—particularly Baby's father (**Jerry Orbach**)—the young lovers are isolated for a time before the inevitable happy ending. The uplifting finalé features the film's biggest song hit, '(I've Had) The Time Of My Life' sung by **Bill Medley** and **Jennifer Warnes**, which won an Oscar and a Grammy, and topped the US chart. Many of the other tracks reflect the film's theme of 60s nostalgia with contributions from **Frankie Valli**, the **Four Seasons**, **Otis Redding**, the **Shirelles** and **Mickey And Sylvia**. There is even one song on the soundtrack, 'She's Like The Wind', performed and written by Swayze (with Stacy Widelitz). *Dirty Dancing* was the first feature release for the home video company Vestron Pictures. While its plot is simplistic, it is a sensitive and original portrayal of a young girl's coming of age, helped along by fine performances and some great frenetic and exciting dancing.

Dirty Dozen Brass Band

Originally formed in 1977 to recreate the traditional sounds of the New Orleans marching bands, but with an overlay of contemporary music such as funk and latter-day R&B, the Dirt Dozen Brass Band has attained considerable popularity. Using a fluid line-up often featuring two trumpets, trombone, sousaphone, tenor and soprano (doubling baritone) saxophones, snare drum and two bass drummers, the band has worked at festivals and parades around the world and has also made club appearances and records. It has collaborated with a wide range of artists, including **Dizzy Gillespie**, **Branford Marsalis**, **Manhattan Transfer**, **Elvis Costello**, **Neville Brothers**, **David Bowie**, **Dr. John**, the **Black Crowes**, **Modest Mouse** and **Widespread Panic**. A lively, high-spirited unit, all but one of whom originate from New Orleans, the Dirty Dozen Brass Band has undoubtedly helped draw into jazz an audience which might otherwise have sought entertainment elsewhere. Founding members Roger Lewis (baritone/soprano saxophone), Kevin Harris (tenor saxophone) and Efrem Towns (trumpet) remain at the helm of the band in the new millennium. Another founding member, Tuba Fats (b. Anthony Lacen, 15 September 1950, New Orleans, Louisiana, USA, d. 11 January 2003, USA), died shortly after the recording of *Funeral For A Friend*.

● ALBUMS: *My Feet Can't Fail Me Now* (Concord Jazz 1984) ★★★★, *Live: Mardi Gras In Montreux* (Rounder 1985) ★★★, *Voodoo* (Columbia 1987) ★★★, *The New Orleans Album* (Columbia 1989) ★★★, *Open Up: Watcha Gonna Do For The Rest Of Your Life?* (Columbia 1991) ★★★, *Jelly* (Columbia 1992) ★★★, as the Dirty Dozen *Ears To The Wall* (Mammoth 1998) ★★★, *Buck Jump* (Mammoth 1999) ★★★, with Widespread Panic *Another Joyous Occasion* (Widespread/Sanctuary 2000) ★★★, *Medicated Magic* (Ropeadope 2002) ★★★, *We Got Robbed! Live In New Orleans* (Own Label 2003) ★★★, *Funeral For A Friend* (Ropeadope 2004) ★★★.

● COMPILATIONS: *This Is The Dirty Dozen Brass Band Collection* (Shout! Factory 2005) ★★★★.

Dirty Looks

Founded in the early 80s by Dutch-born Hendrik Ostergaard, Dirty Looks released three albums on three different independent labels before achieving a major contract with **Atlantic Records** in 1987. Ostergaard handled both vocals and guitar, ably supported by Paul Lidel (guitar), Jack Pyers (bass) and Gene Barnett (drums). Their major label debut,

Cool From The Wire, showed the band to be purveyors of straight-ahead, no-nonsense power metal very much in the **AC/DC** mould. Both the crushing style of guitar riffing and the vocal delivery of Ostergaard made comparisons with the Australian supremos inevitable. However, such was the energy and commitment the band brought to recording and live performances that their indebtness quickly became forgivable. The follow-up, *Turn Of The Screw*, was not as successful, despite critical acclaim. *Bootlegs* saw the band presenting the same style of relentless power boogie, albeit with a return to a smaller label.

● ALBUMS: *Dirty Looks* (Axe Killer 1985) ★★, *I Want More* (Storm 1986) ★★★, *In Your Face* (Mirroe 1987) ★★★, *Cool From The Wire* (Atlantic 1987) ★★★, *Turn Of The Screw* (Atlantic 1988) ★★, *Bootlegs* (Shrapnel 1991) ★★★, *One Bad Leg* (Rockworld/Music For Nations 1995) ★★★.

Dirty Three

Founded in Melbourne, Australia, in 1992, instrumental trio Dirty Three was formed as an offshoot of various established local bands, including Busload Of Faith, Fungus Brains, Venom P. Stinger and the Blackeyed Susans. During breaks from these bands, Warren Ellis (electric violin), Mick Turner (guitar, ex-Moodists) and Jim White (drums) worked together on a high-energy bar room set, which eventually made them one of the area's top live attractions. They soon picked up impressive support slots to touring acts including **Pavement** and **Jon Spencer Blues Explosion**, before their debut album *Sad & Dangerous* was released on the small Boston label Poon Village Records. Essentially a repackaging of their homemade demo tape, its release was followed by an extensive north American tour.

The trio's meteoric rise was confirmed by a place on the 1995 **Lollapalooza** mobile festival, before arriving in England to provide a live soundtrack to Carl Dreyer's silent film *La Passion De Jeanne d'Arc*, shown at the National Film Theatre. They were joined in this performance by fellow expatriate **Nick Cave** on piano, who had been enraptured by the trio's furious performances in Australia in 1994, often appearing onstage for impromptu jam sessions. Ellis later joined Cave's backing band the Bad Seeds and, with Dirty Three, Cave performed two unbilled songs on *Songs In The Key Of X*, a soundtrack album to the hit television show *The X-Files*. The trio also collaborated with **Will Oldham** of **Palace** prior to the release of their third album, 1996's *Horse Stories*. Their most restrained effort thus far, it nevertheless sustained the trio's reputation for lyrical instrumental work that transcends expectations and offers a genuine alternative to contemporary rock sounds. *Ocean Songs* (1998) and *Whatever You Love, You Are* (2000) were further collections of quietly evocative and atmospheric music.

The trio put Dirty Three on hold after scrapping the follow-up to *Whatever You Love, You Are*, with Ellis concentrating on his Bad Seeds commitments and Turner starting up the King Crab label. They reunited in 2003 to begin afresh, teaming with producer Fabrice Lor to complete *She Has No Strings Apollo*. The follow-up *Cinder* featured vocal input from **Cat Power** ('Great Waves') and Sally Timms ('Feral').

● ALBUMS: *The Dirty Three* cassette (Scuzz 1992) ★★★, *Sad & Dangerous* (Poon Village 1994) ★★★, *Dirty Three* (Big Cat/Touch & Go 1995) ★★★, *Horse Stories* (Big Cat/Touch & Go 1996) ★★★★, *Ocean Songs* (Bella Union/Touch & Go 1998) ★★★★, *Whatever You Love, You Are* (Bella Union/Touch & Go 2000) ★★★★, *She Has No Strings Apollo* (Bella Union/Touch & Go 2003) ★★★, *Cinder* (Bella Union/Touch & Go 2005) ★★★.

Solo: Warren Ellis *3 Pieces For Violin* (King Crab 2002) ★★★. Mick Turner *Tren Phantasma* (Drag City 1997) ★★★, *Marlan Rosa* (Drag City 1999) ★★★★, *Moth* (Drag CIty 2002) ★★★.

● COMPILATIONS: *Lowlands* (Anchor & Hope 2000) ★★★.

Dirty Tricks

This blues-based UK heavy rock outfit was formed in 1974 by vocalist Kenny Stewart and guitarist John Fraser Binnie. With bass player Terry Horbury and drummer John Lee completing the line-up, they drew inspiration from **Bad Company**, the **Faces**, **Black Sabbath** and **Deep Purple**. However, they never graduated from support status, as their attempt to bridge the divide between hard rock and heavy metal was handicapped by weak material. They released three albums on **Polydor Records** during the mid-70s that failed to reflect the energy they generated in a live setting. In 1976 Andy Beirne took over as drummer, but the band was soon overwhelmed by the growing punk movement. Beirne later joined **Grand Prix**, Terry Horbury teamed up with speed metal outfit **Vardis** and guitarist John Fraser Binnie was recruited by **Rogue Male** in 1984.

● ALBUMS: *Dirty Tricks* (Polydor 1975) ★★★, *Night Man* (Polydor 1976) ★★, *Hit And Run* (Polydor 1977) ★★.

Dirty Vegas

UK electronica trio comprising Paul Harris (b. London, England; keyboards/production), Ben Harris (b. Kent, England; guitar/production) and Steve Smith (b. London, England; vocals, guitar, percussion). Paul Harris started DJing at an early age, and by his late teens had a residency at Nicky Holloway's London club The Milk Bar. Ben Harris (no relation) played with indie band Fluid before setting up a specialist dance shop with his brother and producing **house** music as Bullit. He teamed up with Paul Harris in early 2000, working under the moniker Hydrogen Rockers. Paul then brought in Smith, an experienced session percussionist and former vocalist with the band Higher Ground. Renaming themselves Dirty Vegas, they set about recording a song written by Smith, 'Days Go By'. This hypnotic, bass-driven track was championed by UK DJ **Pete Tong** and led to a recording contract with **Parlophone Records**. Released as a single, 'Days Go By' broke into the UK Top 30 in May 2001, but ultimately proved more successful in America owing to its prominent use in a Mitsubishi car commercial. Their album met with a particularly favourable response in the USA.

● ALBUMS: *Dirty Vegas* (Parlophone/Capitol 2002) ★★★, *One* (Parlophone 2004) ★★.

● COMPILATIONS: *A Night At The Tables* (Ultra 2003) ★★★, *The Trip* (Family 2003) ★★.

Dirty White Boy

This 'supergroup' was put together by **Earl Slick** (ex-guitarist with **David Bowie**, **John Waite** and **John Lennon** bands) and David Glen Eisley, former vocalist of **Giuffria**. Adding ex-**Autograph** drummer Keni Richards and bass player F. Kirk Alley to the line-up, their style and approach was the antithesis of what one might expect from their collective pedigrees. Throwing caution to the wind, they went for a no-holds-barred, down-and-dirty rock 'n' roll attack with their debut album. Produced by Beau Hill (of **Ratt**), *Bad Reputation* found these seasoned musicians rediscovering their roots and enjoying themselves in the process. 'Let's Spend Momma's Money', released as a single, also attracted approving glances.

● ALBUMS: *Bad Reputation* (PolyGram 1990) ★★★.

Disc Jockey Jamboree

Considered the most anodyne film of the rock 'n' roll era, this 1957 feature starred Kay Medford and Robert Pastine as two theatrical agents. Once married, now separated, they individually represent 'Pete' and 'Honey', two singers who begin to work together and become 'America's Sweethearts'. During the course of this, the Medford and Pastine characters are reconciled. Amid this sugary plot are performances by rock 'n' roll and rockabilly stars **Jerry Lee Lewis** ('Great Balls Of Fire'), **Buddy Knox** ('Hula Love'), **Charlie Gracie** ('Cool Baby') and **Carl Perkins** ('Glad All Over'). **Fats Domino**, **Connie Francis** and **Frankie Avalon**—later the star of innumerable 'beach' films—are also featured in this film that at best showcases acts rarely enshrined on celluloid.

Discharge

Many fans would argue that UK band Discharge were the most influential punk band after the **Sex Pistols**. Certainly, their caustic wall of sound (a million miles away from anything **Phil Spector** could ever have envisaged when he invented the term) has inspired both punk and metal bands throughout the UK and USA. Discharge was formed in 1978 in Birmingham, England. In Keeping with many of the early 80s punk bands, Discharge's line-up was fluid and comprised people who refused to offer anything other than nicknames to the press—but the nucleus of the band has always been demonic singer Cal (b. Kevin Morris) and long-serving bass player Rainy. Other early members of the band included Bones (guitar) and Rainy's brother Tezz (drums), who was subsequently replaced by Bambi and then Gary. Their debut EP, released in 1980 as the first record on Stoke-On-Trent label Clay Records, preceded their participation on the renowned Apocalypse Now tour, on which they joined such punk luminaries as the **Exploited**, **Chron Gen** and **Anti-Pasti**. In common with each of these bands, Cal's lyrics decried the horrors of war, but they eschewed the melodies pursued, to varying degrees, by the others. They were also closest of these bands to **Crass'** ideals about cheaply priced records, vegetarianism and suspicion of the press. Gary Bushell (later a newspaper critic for *The Sun*), whose *Sounds* music paper was alone in documenting the emerging scene, railed at their methodology: 'Umpteen versions of the same pneumatic drill solo . . . awful . . . no tunes, no talent, no fun . . . dull, boring and monotonous . . . the musical equivalent of glue-sniffing.' However, others did not agree, and the band soon built up a considerable following through EPs such as *Realities Of War*, *Why?* and *Fight Back*. Over a full album Discharge could be a uniquely intimidating experience, and their impact dwindled as the 80s progressed. However, the impact of their sonic assaults can still be heard in a thousand or more bands, including practically everything on Earache Records through to mainstream metal bands **Guns N'Roses** and **Metallica**. The original band re-formed and released a new album in 2002.

● ALBUMS: *Hear Nothing, See Nothing, Say Nothing* (Clay 1982) ★★★★, *Never Again* (Clay 1984) ★★★, *Brave New World* (Clay 1986) ★★★, *The Nightmare Continues* (Clay 1988) ★★★, *Live At City Garden* (Clay 1990) ★★, *Shootin' Up The World* (Clay 1994) ★★★, *Discharge* (Sanctuary 2002) ★★★.

● COMPILATIONS: *Discharge 1980–1986* (Clay 1987) ★★★, *Why* (Receiver 1998) ★★★, *Anthology: Free Speech For The Dumb* (Castle 1999) ★★★, *Decontrol: The Singles* (Castle 2002) ★★★, *Society's Victims* (Castle 2004) ★★★.

Disco Citizens
(see **Chicane**)

Disco Droids
(see **Corsten, Ferry**)

Disco Evangelists

The Disco Evangelists comprised **Ashley Beedle** (b. London, England), **David Holmes** (b. Belfast, Northern Ireland) and Lyndsay Edwards (b. London, England; ex-**If?**). Originally released on Beedle's Black Sunshine label before **Positiva Records** picked it up, their 'De Niro' hit referred to the namesake actor's movie, *Once Upon A Time In America*. The follow-up, 'A New Dawn', also found a home on Positiva's release schedule. Beedle worked alongside the **Stereo MCs'** Nick and Rob as Axis ('Rollin' With Rai'), and as part of Workshy, **X-Press 2**, Black Science Orchestra and Marden Hill. In 1994 he formed Delta House Of Blues, which signed to **Go! Discs**. He has also undertaken remixes for **Jodeci** and **East 17** ('Deep'). Holmes is one of the most interesting and prolific of England's DJ fraternity, working as part of Scubadevils (with ex-members of **Dub Federation**) and running the Sugarsweet/Exploding Plastic Inevitable club/label empire in Belfast. He has also enjoyed critical acclaim for his solo album *Let's Get Killed*.

Disco Four

The Disco Four, who included in their number the son of **Enjoy Records'** president Bobby Robinson, were probably most famous for their 'Country Rock Rap' recording for that label. Produced by early hip-hop innovator Pumpkin, it used cow horns and hoe-down instrumentation to arrive at a sound that inspired **Malcolm McLaren's** 'Buffalo Gals' novelty. The Disco Four, whose origins were in the Bronx **sound system** days (Troy B was in an early incarnation of the **Fearless Four**), didn't last much longer, though they did switch to **Profile Records** for a hit and miss mini-career.

Disco Magic Records

Italian label Disco Magic was the original home to **Black Box**'s groundbreaking 'Ride On Time'. They also introduced artists such as rapper Tony Carrasco, who released a cover version of **Adamski**'s 'NRG'. Disco Magic's popularity continued with Pierre Fieroldi's 'Moving Now', Hoomba Hoomba's 'Voice Of Africa' and Rhythm Orchestra's 'Such A Good Feeling', a revision of Dave Seaman and Steve Anderson's **Brothers In Rhythm** original, orchestrated by DJ Oliver. Marmalade contributed 'Mi Piace' in 1992.

Disco Tex And The Sex-O-Lettes

Led by Sir Monti Rock III (b. Joseph Montanez Jnr.), whose camp posturings in an extravagant white pimp suit made him a favourite in the gay and straight disco clubs in the USA and UK during the 70s, the group was put together by producer **Bob Crewe**. They had two highly influential hits on the Chelsea label with the irresistible 'Get Dancin'' (1974) hitting the US and UK Top 10, and 'I Wanna Dance Wit' Choo (Doo Dat Dance), Part One' (1975) making the UK Top 10 and US Top 30.

● ALBUMS: *Disco Tex And The Sex-O-Lettes* (Chelsea 1975) ★★.

● COMPILATIONS: *Get Dancin'* (Start 1989) ★★, *The Story Of Disco Tex And His Sex-O-Lettes* (Chelsea/Sequel 1999) ★★.

Dishwalla

US alternative rock band Dishwalla made something of a startling entry into the recording industry when they appeared alongside much more celebrated acts on the **Carpenters**' 1994 tribute album, *If I Were A Carpenter*, before they had even released a single. Their contribution, a version of 'It's Going To Take Some Time', alerted several record labels to their presence, but unbeknownst to them Dishwalla were already signed to **A&M Records**. Originally comprising George Pendergast (b. Santa Barbara, California, USA; drums), Scot Alexander (b. 10 December 1971, Santa Barbara, California, USA; bass), J.R. Richards (b. 30 April 1972, Santa Barbara, California, USA; vocals/guitar) and Rodney Browning (b. Santa Barbara, California, USA; guitar), the band formed in Santa Barbara in 1991 and spent three years locked together in a tiny rehearsal space before hitting the Los Angeles club scene. Keyboard player Jim Wood (b. Santa Barbara, California, USA) was added to the line-up during this period. Originally titled simply Dish, they were forced to extend that name when they discovered the rights to it were already held by a group from the east coast of America. They switched instead to Dishwalla, a name taken from a magazine article about satellite-dish pirates in rural India.

After Dishwalla toured with **Better Than Ezra**, A&M released debut album in 1995 the band's; it comprised 11 selections produced by the Butcher Brothers. While songs such as the US Top 20 hit single 'Counting Blue Cars' and 'Explode' revealed the influence of the **Cure**, others owed more to the sustained riffing of heavy metal and hard rock bands. Another unusual feature was the predominance of sampling within the basic rock framework; while this was not a wholly original idea it had rarely been practised so extensively. *Pet Your Friends* went to sell over a million copies as the band embarked on an extensive touring schedule to promote the album. The promotion of the follow-up *And You Think You Know What Life's About* was hampered by record company politics, with A&M caught up in the fallout from the PolyGram/Universal merger.

Dishwalla parted company with A&M at the start of the new millennium and signed to the independent Immergent label. Pendergast was replaced by Pete Maloney during this time, with the new drummer making his debut on the band's 2002 release *Opaline*. This collection marked a return to form after the disappointing reception of their second album. The following year's live release captured some of the energy of the band's live shows and was well received by their devoted fans. 2005's self-titled album was another strong outing and was released on manager Leo Rossi's The Orphanage label.

● ALBUMS: *Pet Your Friends* (A&M 1995) ★★★★, *And You Think You Know What Life's About* (A&M 1998) ★★★, *Opaline* (Immergent 2002) ★★★, *Live .... Greetings From The Flow State* (Immergent 2003) ★★★, *Dishwalla* (The Orphanage 2005) ★★★.

Disk-O-Tek Holiday

This 1966 film was a US adaptation of *Just For You*, a UK feature from 1964. In the latter DJ Sam Costa lay in bed watching pop acts perform on television. Among those he saw were **Peter And Gordon**, the **Applejacks**, the **Merseybeats**, **Freddie And The Dreamers**, Louise Cordet and **A Band Of Angels** (with **Mike D'Abo**). For *Disk-O-Tek Holiday* Costa was replaced by US disc jockeys Arnie Ginsburg and Bob Foster. A few lesser-known UK acts were also axed in favour of the **Chiffons**, **Freddie Cannon**, the Rockin' Ramrods and the **Vagrants**, the last-named of which featured future **Mountain** guitarist, **Leslie West**.

Disley, Diz

b. William C. Disley, 27 May 1931, Winnipeg, Manitoba, Canada. Disley grew up in Wales and the north of England, where he learned to play banjo, switching to guitar at the age of 14 when he heard **Django Reinhardt**. Among his earliest jazz gigs was a period with the Yorkshire Jazz Band. In the 50s he lived in London, working as a newspaper cartoonist and playing in a variety of bands. Although many of Disley's engagements in the 50s and 60s were with traditional bands, he also played skiffle and folk music. Eager to restore the place of the acoustic guitar in the face of the pop-scene successes of its electric counterpart, he gradually developed a substantial reputation as a leading mainstream guitarist.

In the early 70s Disley began a fruitful association with **Stéphane Grappelli**, persuading the organizers of the **Cambridge Folk Festival** to book the violinist. With the group rounded out by guitarist **Denny Wright**, who had worked with Grappelli in 1944, they were a huge success and Grappelli's resurgence was assured. Later, Disley added **Len Skeat** and continued to accompany the violinist on some of the most memorable moments of his career comeback. On and off, Disley was with Grappelli for about a decade, a period which also saw record sessions with **Teresa Brewer** and others, and tours of Australia, Europe and the USA. Undoubtedly, Disley's acute business sense, allied to his impeccable musical taste and dedication to Reinhardt was a significant factor in the renewal of Grappelli's career. Subsequently, Disley formed his own group that worked mostly in London through the 80s. He continues to play, bringing wit and invention allied to an urgent unflagging swing to all his sessions.

● ALBUMS: *Zing Went The Strings* (Waterfront 1986) ★★★, with Johnny Silvo *Blues In The Backyard* (Fellside 1999) ★★★.

Dislocation Dance

Quirky jazz-pop was the speciality of Manchester group Dislocation Dance. Signed to the **Buzzcocks**' New Hormones label after forming in late 1978, the band comprised Ian Runacres (vocals/guitar), Dick Harrison (drums), Paul Emmerson (bass) and Andy Diagram (trumpet/vocals). An EP, *It's So Difficult* (1980), was a co-release with the band's Delicate Issues label. The EP *Slip That Disc* (1981) included an offbeat version of the **Beatles**' 'We Can Work It Out' and was followed by what was for the group a transitional album, *Music Music Music*. Having now been joined by Kath Way (vocals/saxophone), Dislocation Dance then issued the comparatively poppy 'Rosemary' (1982), but left New Hormones after the fashionably bossa-nova-tinged 'You'll Never Never Know' (both 1982). In 1983 a one-off single, 'Violette', for the Music Label, passed the time before the band signed to **Rough Trade** later that year, releasing 'Show Me'. A second album, *Midnight Shift*, also appeared, but they left the label soon afterwards. A final 12-inch single, 'What's Going On', on the Slipped Discs label, signalled the end of Dislocation Dance in late 1985. Andy Diagram also fronted the Diagram Brothers and later appeared with the **Pale Fountains**.

● ALBUMS: *Music Music Music* (New Hormones 1981) ★★★, *Midnight Shift* (Rough Trade 1984) ★★.

● COMPILATIONS: *BBC Sessions* (Vinyl Japan 1999) ★★★.

Dismember

Swedish band Dismember is a product of the increasingly active Scandinavian death metal scene. Like most of their peers, Dismember are rather short on subtlety and originality, but in terms of musical vitriol and intensity, they are a force with which to be reckoned. They have also developed a talent for attracting controversy and outrage, a valuable asset in the shock-hungry death metal genre. Most notably, upon the release of *Like An Ever Flowing Stream*, several hundred copies were seized at UK customs, as the track 'Skin Her Alive' was deemed obscene. The song dealt with a murder that had taken place in the flat beneath that of vocalist Matti Karki, and the lyrics attempted to explore the thoughts of the killer. Despite widespread mainstream consensus that death metal did not deserve freedom of speech, the album was acquitted of obscenity in court. Dismember continued to flout good taste, dressing their drummer, Fred Estby, as Jesus Christ in a demonic parody of the crucifixion on video shoots and album artwork. *Indecent And Obscene* refers to the attempted prosecution of their debut and comes complete with a track designed to provoke similar outrage, entitled 'Eviscerated (Bitch)'. The band's third album employed a more considered production from Thomas Skogsberg at Sunlight Studios in Sweden, but their lyrical concerns survived intact.

● ALBUMS: *Like An Ever Flowing Stream* (Nuclear Blast 1991) ★★, *Indecent And Obscene* (Nuclear Blast 1993) ★★, *Massive Killing Capacity* (Nuclear Blast 1995) ★★★, *Death Metal* (Nuclear Blast 1997) ★★★, *Hate Campaign* (Nuclear Blast 1999) ★★★.

Dismemberment Plan

Alternating between angst and cool melody, the Dismemberment Plan was one of the shining examples of the strength of the emo (emotional hardcore) genre. Hailing from Washington, DC, USA, the band was formed on New Year's Day 1993 by Joe Easley (drums), Travis Morrison (vocals/guitar), Jason Caddell (guitar) and Eric Axelson (bass)—the latter three of which also split keyboard duties. The band's first release was the four-track single, 'Can We Be Mature?', during spring 1994. The quartet signed to the indie label DeSoto soon after, resulting in the release of their debut, *!*, in 1995. The album was more punk-based than any of their subsequent efforts, but it still did a fine job of introducing the band to the then-burgeoning emo scene. Their follow-up, *Dismemberment Plan Is Terrified*, came in 1997 before the quartet discovered bands such as **Talking Heads** and let funky, quirky sounds filter into their style. This became especially evident on their next two more stylistically varied albums, 1999's *Emergency & I* (during which time the band opened up a string of European dates for newly anointed fans **Pearl Jam**) and especially 2001's *Change*. The latter proved to be the band's swansong, with lead singer Travis Morrison subsequently embarking on a solo career.

● ALBUMS: *!* (DeSoto 1995) ★★★, *Dismemberment Plan Is Terrified* (DeSoto 1997) ★★★, *Emergency & I* (DeSoto 1999) ★★★★, *Change* (DeSoto 2001) ★★★.

Disney, Walt

b. 23 August 1901, Chicago, Illinois, USA, d. 15 December 1966, New York, USA. Apart from creating legendary cartoon characters such as Mickey and Minnie Mouse, Donald Duck, Goofy and Pluto, the Walt Disney Studio was responsible for a series of phenomenally successful full-length animated feature films, the first of which, *Snow White And The Seven Dwarfs*, was released in December 1937. It was three years in the making, with 600 artists producing more than two million Technicolor drawings, only about an eighth of which were used. The ravishing fairy story by the brothers Grimm was adapted for the screen by Ted Sears, Dorothy Ann Blank, Otto Englander, Earl Hurd, Richard Creedon, Dick Richard, Merrill de Maris and Webb Smith. All the dwarfs, Grumpy, Doc, Sleepy, Happy, Sneezy, Bashful and Dopey (who Charlie Chaplin said was one of the greatest comedians of all time), were given their own delightful personalities, and the soundtrack voices of Andriana Caselotti, Harry Stockwell, Lucille LaVerne, Roy Atwell, Pinto Colvig, Otis Harlan, Billy Gilbert, Scot Mattraw and Moroni Olsen were perfectly matched to them and the rest of the characters including the handsome Prince whose kiss brings Snow White back to life after the evil Queen has tried to get rid of her. All this was supplemented by some marvellous songs by Frank Churchill (music) and Larry Morey (lyrics), which included 'Whistle While You Work', 'Heigh-Ho', 'Someday My Prince Will Come', 'With A Smile And A Song', 'I'm Wishing', 'One Song' and 'Isn't This A Silly Song?'. David Hand was the supervising editor, and, although *Snow White And The Seven Dwarfs* was released late in the 30s, it went on to take more money than any other film at the US box office during the decade, with the exception of *Gone With The Wind*.

In 1938, Walt Disney received a special Academy Award 'in recognition of a significant screen innovation which has charmed millions and pioneered a great new entertainment field for the motion picture cartoon' (one statuette and seven miniature statuettes). More than 50 years later, in 1993, the picture's overall earnings were estimated at £92 million, a record for any animated film until Disney's own *Aladdin* overtook it (with the help of inflation) after being screened for just 11 incredible weeks in the world's cinemas. As just one more example of the enduring interest in this historic picture, in 1992 an original production cel (a hand-painted celluloid still) from the film fetched £115,000 at Sotheby's auction house in New York, three times its estimated price. A digitally restored version of *Snow White* was released in 1994, and in the same year the film appeared in the USA on home-video for the first time. Most of Disney's other full-length animated features have already been made available in that form, although usually only for a strictly limited period of time before being withdrawn. In May 1994 it was reported that nine out of 10 of all home-videos sold had been Disney films. These included:

Pinocchio (1940). Inspired by the stories of nineteenth-century author Carlo Collodi, this film concerns a wilful puppet whose habitual 'economy with the truth' results in his nose growing longer and longer. However, by listening to his conscience, in the shape of the loveable character Jiminy Cricket, he mends his ways, bravely rescues his personal Svengali, Geppetto the wood-carver, from inside Monstro the whale, and eventually achieves his ambition and is turned into a real live boy by the Blue Fairy. **Cliff Edwards**, the puckish entertainer, provided the voice for Jiminy Cricket, and he had two of Leigh Harline and **Ned Washington**'s most endearing and enduring songs, 'Give A Little Whistle' and 'When You Wish Upon A Star'. The latter number won an Academy Award, and the two songwriters, together with P.J. Smith, won another Oscar for their original score. The remaining songs were 'Hi-Diddle-Dee-Dee (An Actor's Life For Me)', 'I've Got No Strings', 'Three Cheers For Anything', 'As I Was Say'n' To The Duchess' and 'Turn On The Old Music Box'. Some of the other voices which, together with the brilliant animation, brought the various characters to life with startling effect, were provided by Dickie Jones (Pinocchio), Christian Rub (Geppetto), Evelyn Venable (the Blue Fairy), **Walter Catlett** (J. Worthington Foulfellow), Charles Judels (Stromboli) and Frankie Darrow (Lampwick). Ben Sharpsteen and Hamilton Luske were the supervising editors, and the film, which was photographed in Technicolor, took over $40 million in the USA and Canada, becoming the fourth-highest-grossing film of the decade.

Fantasia (1940). This was an astonishingly successful blending of cartoon characters and classical music that featured Leopold Stokowski and the Philadelphia Orchestra. It was narrated by Deems Taylor and contained eight pieces, 'Toccata And Fugue In D Minor' (Bach), 'The Nutcracker Suite' (Tchaikovsky), 'The Sorcerer's Apprentice' (Dukas), 'The Rite Of Spring' (Stravinsky), 'Pastoral Symphony' (Beethoven), 'Dance Of The Hours' (Ponchielli), 'Night On The Bald Mountain' (Mussorgsky) and 'Ave Maria' (Schubert). Amidst all this wonderful music, there cavorted Mickey Mouse and any number of other animals, including hippopotami, dinosaurs, alligators, elephants and ostriches, along with nymphs, satyrs, the Goddess of Night and many more strange and fantastic creations. Ben Sharpsteen was the production supervisor, and this incredible piece of entertainment was filmed in Technicolor and Fantasound. It was the second-highest-grossing 40s picture in the USA. Fifty years after it burst gloriously upon the scene, *Fantasia* was subjected to the currently fashionable desire for 'political correctness' which prevailed in the early 90s. Prior to its video release, and at a reputed cost of hundreds of thousands of pounds, a black 'piccaninny centaurette' seen polishing the hooves of a preening blonde figure was removed from all prints.

Bambi (1942). The general consensus of opinion seems to be that this is the most naturalistic of all Walt Disney's full-length animated features. The animators' skill in their drawing of the animals' graceful movements and charming facial expressions gave the tender, exquisite story of a young deer growing up in a world of changing seasons an exceptional sense of reality. Apart from Bambi himself, another star to emerge was Thumper the rabbit, whose amusing voice was dubbed by Peter Behn. Frank Churchill and Larry Morey wrote the score, which included 'Love Is A Song', 'The Thumper Song', 'Let's Sing A Gay Little Spring Song', 'Twitterpated' and 'Little April Showers'. David Hand was the production supervisor, and the screenplay was adapted from a book by Felix Salten. By 1993, according to the *Variety* trade newspaper, *Bambi* was at the head of the US money-earning list of films made in the 40s.

Cinderella (1950). Based on Charles Perrault's traditional fairytale, this was another triumph for the Disney Studio. Once again, as in previous features, the animators came up with some more endearing creatures. This time they were two resourceful rodents, Jaq and Gus, who enlist the help of their friends to make a gorgeous gown so that Cinderella can finally go to the Ball. The dynamic duo were dubbed by James Mcdonald, and the rest of the soundtrack voices were just about perfect, including Ilene Woods as the lovely Cinderella, William Phipps (Prince Charming), Eleanor Audley (wicked stepmother), Verna Felton (fairy godmother) and Luis Van Ruten (King and Grand Duke). Rhoda Williams and Lucille Bliss voiced the ugly stepsisters and were suitably disagreeable on the incongruously titled 'Sing Sweet Nightingale'. The remainder of **Mack Gordon**, Jerry Livingston and **Al Hoffman**'s score was first-rate, and included 'A Dream Is A Wish Your Heart Makes', 'Bibbidi-Bobbidi-Boo', 'The Work Song', 'So This Is Love' and 'Cinderella'. The Technicolor production was supervised by Ben Sharpsteen and directed by Wilfred Jackson, Hamilton Luske, and Clyde Geronomi. Some sources, including *Variety*, regard *Cinderella* as a 1949 film because it is said to have been released in December of that year. The newspaper places it third in domestic rental earners during that decade.

Peter Pan (1953). Not regarded as one of the best of Disney's animated features at the time, although it was still an outstanding piece of work. John M. Barrie's classic story was ideal material from which the studio's artists crafted a magical picture. All the much-loved characters were on hand, including Peter himself (dubbed by Bobby Driscoll), Wendy (Kathy Beaumont), the deliciously evil Captain Hook (Hans Conreid), Mrs. Darling (Heather Angel), Mr. Darling (Paul Collins), Smee (Bill Thompson), John (Tommy Luske) and Tom Conway (narrator)—not forgetting Tinkerbell and the animal that Frank Churchill and Jack Lawrence warned about in their amusing song, 'Never Smile At A Crocodile'. **Sammy Cahn** and **Sammy Fain** wrote most of the remaining numbers, including the popular 'You Can Fly', 'Your Mother And Mine', 'The Elegant Captain Hook' and 'What Makes The Red Man Red?', and there were also contributions from Oliver Wallace and Erdman Penner ('A Pirate's Life') and Wallace also collaborated with Winston Hibler and Ted Sears on 'Tee Dum-Tee Dee'. The production and direction credits were the same as *Cinderella*. *Peter Pan* is third in the line of 50s top money-spinners in the USA, just behind the next listed film.

Lady And The Tramp (1955). The first of these full-length animated features to be photographed in Cinemascope was based on Ward Green's waggish tale about a mongrel called Tramp who falls in a big way for Lady, a spoilt pedigree cocker spaniel, while he is helping her to come to terms with the changes that are taking place (such as the arrival of a new baby) in her owners' family. Getting in on the act are Trusty the bloodhound, Lady's owners Jim Dear and Darling, and a sundry collection of hounds such as Toughy, Bull, Boris,

Pedro and an ex-show dog called Peg. Erdman Penner, Joe Rinaldi, Ralph White and Donald Da Gradi wrote the screenplay, while **Sonny Burke** and **Peggy Lee** came up with some charming songs that included 'He's A Tramp', 'The Siamese Cat Song', 'Bella Notte', 'Peace On Earth' and 'La La Lu'. Lee herself provided the voices for Peg (an ex-show dog), two naughty Siamese cats, and Darling, and other characters were dubbed by Barbara Luddy (Lady), Larry Roberts (Tramp), George Givot, Bill Thompson, **Stan Freberg**, Bill Baucon, Verna Felton and Alan Reed. Production and direction credits as for *Cinderella* and *Peter Pan*. A sad aspect of this production is that, nearly 40 years after it was made, Peggy Lee was locked in litigation with the Disney organization over disputed amounts of home-video royalties. *Sleeping Beauty* (1959). The Disney Studio's preoccupation with live-action feature films, beginning with *Treasure Island* in 1950 and leading to 60s classics such as Mary Poppins, meant that this was one of their last animated fairytales—for some time, at least. Extremely expensive to make, it was a box-office failure following its original release, although subsequent re-valuation of the film's outstanding qualities has resulted in substantial earnings from reissues, pushing it into the 50s US Top 6 in more recent times. Like *Cinderella*, the film was based on a Charles Perrault fairytale in which the three good fairies, Flaura, Fauna and Merryweather, care for the Princess Aurora after the wicked fairy, Maleficent, has put a spell on her. After many exciting adventures involving some superb animation and special effects, the seriously handsome Prince Philip ensures that, as always with Disney, good triumphs over evil. Opera singer Mary Costa voiced the Princess, with Bill Shirley (Prince), Eleanor Audley (Maleficent), Verna Felton, Barbara Luddy, Candy Candido and Bill Thompson as the other main characters. The songs included 'Once Upon A Dream' (Sammy Fain–Jack Lawrence), 'Hail The Princess Aurora' and 'The Sleeping Beauty Song' (both Tom Adair–George Bruns), 'I Wonder' (Winston Hibler–Ted Sears–Bruns), 'The Skump Song' (Adair–Erdman Penner–Bruns) and excerpts from Tchaikovsky's *Sleeping Beauty*. This production, which was supervised by Don da Gradi and Ken Anderson and directed by Clyde Geronomi, was shot in Technicolor and the wide-screen process Super Technirama 70, a combination that enhanced the proceedings for some viewers but was a disturbing influence for others.

The Jungle Book (1967). After a lean spell—and Walt Disney's death the year before—the Studio was back on top form with this captivating film which was inspired by Rudyard Kipling's *Mowgli* stories. It tells of the boy Mowgli, who was raised by wolves in the jungle until he was 10 years old. After it is learned that Shere Khan the tiger intends to kill him, Bagheera the panther undertakes to return the youngster to the safety of the man village. After some scrapes along the way involving Baloo the bear, a band of monkeys led by King Louie of the Apes, and Shere Khan himself, the youngster reaches the village where he really belongs. Major features of this production are the inspired choice of actors to voice these marvellous characters, such as **Phil Harris** (Baloo), **Louis Prima** (King Louie), Sebastion Cabot (Bagheera), George Sanders (Shere Khan) and Sterling Holloway (Kaa the Snake), and the jazzy score, which comprised 'Colonel Hathi's March', 'Trust In Me', 'I Wan'na Be Like You', 'That's What Friends Are For' and 'My Own Home' (all by **Richard M. Sherman** and **Robert B. Sherman**),

and 'The Bare Necessities' (Terry Gilkyson). This joyous and immensely entertaining Technicolor film had a screenplay by Larry Clemmons, Ralph Wright, Ken Anderson and Vance Gerry, and was directed by Wolfgang Reitherman. Since then, there have been two further attempts to bring the story to the screen: Disney's *Rudyard Kipling's The Jungle Book* (1994) starring Jason Scott Lee, and *The Second Jungle Book: Mowgli & Baloo* (1997, TriStar-MDP).

In the 70s Disney released further full-length animated features, *The Aristocats*, *Robin Hood*, and *The Rescuers*, which, although fine in their way, were not in the same class as many of the Studio's earlier efforts. It was not until 1989 that the great Disney comeback began with **The Little Mermaid** and continued via **Beauty And The Beast**, *Aladdin* and **The Lion King**. That money-spinning quartet was soon joined by other major features such as **Pocahontas** (1995), with its strong plea for tolerance, *Toy Story* (1995), *The Hunchback Of Notre Dame* (1996), *Hercules* (1997) and *Mulan* (1998). In 1994, the 'Disneyfication' of Broadway began with an extravagant stage adaptation of *Beauty And The Beast*. This was followed three years later by *King David*, the first Disney musical conceived for the stage. It had a limited run at the re-opened New Amsterdam Theatre on 42nd Street, former home of the **Ziegfeld Follies**, which been derelict for some years before Disney spent an estimated £21 million restoring it to its former Art Nouveau glory. Also in 1997, the New Amsterdam hosted Disney's spectacular stage version of *The Lion King*, which most critics agreed was a 'roaring sensation'. Not so well received was **Elaborate Lives: The Legend Of Aida**, which had its premiere on 7 October 1998 well away from Broadway in Atlanta, Georgia.

● FURTHER READING: *The Story Of Walt Disney*, Diane Disney Miller. *The Disney Version*, Richard Schickel. *The Art Of Walt Disney*, Christopher Finch. *Walt Disney: Hollywood's Dark Prince*, Marc Eliot. *Walt Disney's Snow White And The Seven Dwarfs*, Jack Solomon. *Disney Animation: The Illusion Of Life*, Frank Thomas and Ollie Johnston. *The Disney Studio Story*, Richard Hollis and Brian Sibley.

Disorder

This punk band from Bristol, England, blended breakneck thrash with tales of gargantuan cider consumption. The first incarnation dated from 1980, comprising Mick (bass), Steve (guitar), Virus (drums) and Dean (vocals). They produced a demo tape that was sent to Riot City Records, but after being turned down they formed their own Disorder Records instead. After the release of 'Complete Disorder', Mick left and was replaced by Steve Robinson. The *Distortion Till Deafness* EP was subsequently released, before bizarre developments followed. Robinson split from girlfriend Beki Bondage (of **Vice Squad**, the band who had vetoed Disorder joining Riot City) and took up glue-sniffing as a hobby. Then the CID caught up with Virus concerning the ownership of his new drumkit. Dean left too, going on to salubrious employment as a toilet cleaner in Taunton. He was replaced by Taff (ex–X-Certs Review), who took up bass, and the group persuaded Boobs, their roadie, to take over vocals. Luckily he had almost completed his then-current prison sentence for defrauding his electricity company. After the recording of 'Perdition', they set about a short touring stint with the Varukers, but their first foreign tour was sabotaged by a typical series of farcical miscalculations concerning European geography and train timetables. Virus felt enough was enough and was replaced by Glenn (ex–Dead Popstars), while the band moved into a shared squat with friends **Amebix**. Later releases were somewhat more restrained, daring to flirt with melody on occasion.

● ALBUMS: *Perdition* (Disorder 1982) ★★, *Under The Scalpel Blade* (Disorder 1984) ★★, *Live In Oslo* (Disorder 1985) ★★, *One Day Son, All This Will Be Yours* (Disorder 1986) ★★, *Violent World* (Disorder 1989) ★★.

● COMPILATIONS: *The Singles Collection* (Riot City 1984) ★★★.

Disposable Heroes Of Hiphoprisy

A hugely innovative contemporary hip-hop crew formed by Rono Tse (percussion) and **Michael Franti** (b. 21 April 1966, Oakland, California, USA; vocals). Both residents of the Bay area of San Francisco, California, USA, the duo worked together for several years, most notably in *avant garde* industrial jazz band the Beatnigs. Following their inception as the Disposable Heroes Of Hiphoprisy they won significant allies amongst press and peers, support slots to **Billy Bragg**, **U2**, **Public Enemy**, **Arrested Development** and **Nirvana** demonstrating the range of their appeal. Their sound recalled some of the experimental edge of their former incarnation, while Franti's raps were considered the most articulate and challenging of his generation. Typically he broke down his subject matter beyond the black/white rhetoric of much urban rap and was willing to place his own inadequacies as a person at the forefront of his manifesto. When he called himself a 'Jerk' in the intensely personal 'Music And Politics', Franti took rap into a whole new dimension. Examples of his skilled deployment of words litter the band's debut album: 'Imagination is sucked out of children by a cathode-ray nipple, Television is the only wet-nurse/that would create a cripple' (from 'Television, The Drug Of The Nation', which also bemoans the amount of violence visited upon an average American child through his television set). 'Language Of Violence' took to task rap's penchant for homophobia, forging a link between a wider circle of prejudice. Franti was more effective still when dealing with subjects on a personal level: 'I was adopted by parents who loved me/they were the same color as the kids who called me nigger on the way home from school' (from 'Socio-Genetic Experiment'). One unfortunate consequence of Franti's eloquence was that the Disposable Heroes Of Hiphoprisy became the token rap band that it was 'safe for white liberals to like'. Otherwise there was precious little to fault in them. In 1993, they recorded an album with *Naked Lunch* author, **William Burroughs**. However, as the year closed they informed the press that the Disposable Heroes Of Hiphoprisy were no longer a going concern, with both parties going on to solo careers. The first result of which was Franti's 1994 album *Home*, as **Spearhead**, with producer Joe 'The Butcher' Nicolo. There were also liaisons with the Disposables' live guitarist **Charlie Hunter** and a projected dub album with **Adrian Sherwood**. Rono, meanwhile, has worked with Oakland rappers Mystic Journeymen.

● ALBUMS: *Hypocrisy Is The Greatest Luxury* (4th & Broadway 1992) ★★★★, with William Burroughs *Spare Ass Annie & Other Tales* (4th & Broadway 1993) ★★★.

Dissidenten

The group Dissidenten was originally conceived of by Friedemann Josch and Uve Müllrich (b. Baltic Islands) in 1980 after they broke from their previous multi-cultural Berlin, Germany art rock band, Embryo, who would continue without them. Josch and Müllrich travelled to India, where they had previously toured with Embryo and made field recordings between September 1978 and May 1979. Returning to the friends and acquaintances they had made there, Dissidenten would use India as an occasional base (alongside spells in Africa, Spain and Portugal). The core of the group was augmented in 1983 when Josch (woodwinds, keyboards, vocals) and Müllrich (guitar, bass, strings, keyboards, vocals) were joined by former Pili Pili percussionist Marlon Klein. This trio has been joined by several itinerant musicians as the moment and mode of music demanded. For example, their 1982 debut album, *Germanistan*, featured the Karnataka College Of Percussion from India. They moved to Tangier for *Sahara Elektrik* in 1984 (featuring Lem Chaheb, whose albums would later be produced by Klein). Taken from it, 'Fata Morgana' sold over a million copies in Brazil as well as becoming an enormous hit in Spain (reaching number 1) and Canada. This was followed by *Life At The Pyramids* (1986), with a lyric/short story written by author Paul Bowles ('The Hyena') and *Out Of This World* (1989). These albums melded influences drawn from Arabic, Scandinavian and Celtic as well as Germanic traditions. Rather than write their own lyrics they would also use these sources, often heavily adopted, to provide the subject matter. On each occasion local musicians would be deployed to enhance the authenticity of the project, though these were rarely retained for live shows, leading to a distinct lack of quantifiable image for the group (they still refuse to have their photographs taken unless they are disguised by esoteric garb). For *The Jungle Book* they returned to India in 1992, employing 'found sound' to emboss and supplement their own playing of truly multi-cultural songs, combining Northern European folk with the sounds of the natural and man-made environment of the subcontinent as well as contemporary dance themes. Once again it featured singer Ramamani and the Karnataka College of Percussion.

● ALBUMS: *Germanistan* (Globestyle 1982) ★★★, *Sahara Elektrik* (Globestyle 1984) ★★★, *Life At The Pyramids* (Exil 1986) ★★★, *Out Of This World* (Exil 1989) ★★★, *The Jungle Book* (Exil 1993) ★★★, *Mixed Up Jungle* (Exil 1996) ★★★, *Instinctive Traveler* (Exil 1997) ★★★.

Distel, Sacha

b. Alexandre Distel, 29 January 1933, Paris, France, d. 22 July 2004, Rayol-Canadel-sur-Mer, France. The scion of a well-heeled showbusiness family, Distel's mother was the sister of Ray Ventura, who, with his group Les Collégiens, was one of the top band leaders in France during the pre-war period. Distel studied piano at the Marguerite Long–Jacques Thibaud School and was a professional jazz guitarist at the age of 16, often sitting in with distinguished Americans visiting Parisian clubland. Distel was recognized as one of his country's foremost jazz instrumentalists by the mid-50s. He played with the **Martial Solal** Trio and recorded with pianist Raymond Le Senechal, vibraphonist Sadi and the **Modern Jazz Quartet**. He also gained publicity for his liaisons with Brigitte Bardot and beatnik icon **Juliette Gréco**, while becoming a businessman with interests in music publishing. Having been a **Frank Sinatra** fan for many years, Distel started singing in the late 50s with the encouragement of the arranger Bill Byers. In 1959, his debut single 'Scoubidou' made the French hit parade. His marriage to skiing champion Francine Bréaud in 1963, and the birth of their son, Laurent, did not affect the growth of a following that had extended beyond France to North America, where he starred in his own television spectacular. He recorded a French-language version (with cover girl Johanna Shimus) of **Frank Sinatra** and **Nancy Sinatra**'s 'Somethin' Stupid' in 1967. Distel's prolific songwriting talent gave birth to such standards as 'La Belle Vie' aka 'The Good Life', but his biggest moment on disc remains 'Raindrops Keep Fallin' On My Head'. This Oscar-winning number from the movie *Butch Cassidy And The Sundance Kid*, which outsold the **B.J. Thomas** original in the UK chart, peaked at number 10 in January 1970, making no less than three re-entries throughout that year. An attendant album sold well in Britain and the USA, and set Distel up as a top cabaret draw throughout the world.

The multi-lingual singer hosted many television and radio shows throughout the world and also appeared in several movies. During the 80s he returned to guitar playing with a series of albums including *Ma Premiere Guitare* and *Ma Guitare And All That Jazz*. In 1985 he was involved in a car crash with soap opera star Chantal Nobel, an accident that resulted in the actress becoming a wheelchair-bound recluse. Distel's popularity in his native country was affected by the scandal, but by the end of the decade he had managed to reassert his star status. In 1993, he co-starred with the television hostess and compère, Rosemarie Ford, on the UK tour of *Golden Songs Of The Silver Screen*. The same year he set up the 18-piece dance band, Les Collégiens, to record an album of jazz classics by his uncle Ray Ventura. In 1995, Distel and Les Collégiens recorded a set of new songs in the Ventura style. Two years later Distel was awarded the Chevalier de la Légion d'Honneur for his contribution to French music. In October 2000, he joined the London cast of the hit musical *Chicago*, playing the role of slippery lawyer Billy Flynn. Distel died after a long illness in July 2004. He had successfully battled thyroid and skin cancer in previous decades.

● ALBUMS: with John Lewis *Afternoon In Paris* (Atlantic 1957) ★★★★, *Everybody Loves The Lover Sacha Distel* (Philips 1961) ★★★, *From Paris With Love* (RCA 1963) ★★★, *The Good Life* (MCA 1968) ★★★, with Slide Hampton *Slide Hampton And Sacha Distel* (Pathe-Marconi 1968) ★★★, *Sacha Distel* (Warners 1970) ★★★★, *Close To You* (Warners 1970) ★★★, *More And More* (Warners 1971) ★★★, *Love Music* (Polydor 1973) ★★★, *Love Is All* (Pye 1976) ★★★, *From Sacha With Love: Sacha Distel's 20 Favourite Love Songs* (Mercury 1979) ★★★, *Move Closer* (Towerbell 1985) ★★, *More And More* (Warners 1987) ★★★, *Dédicaces* aka *Dedications* (Carrere 1992) ★★★, *Sacha Distel Et Ses Collégiens Jouent Ray Ventura* (Carrere 1993) ★★★★, *Swinguer La Vie* (Carrere 1995) ★★★, *En Vers Et Contre Vous* (Universal France 2003) ★★★.

● COMPILATIONS: *Golden Hour Of Sacha Distel* (Golden Hour 1978) ★★, *The Sacha Distel Collection* (Pickwick 1980) ★★★, *The Very Best Of Sacha Distel* (Telstar 1997) ★★★★.

● FILMS: *Femmes De Paris* (1953), *Les Mordus* aka *The Fanatics* (1960), *Zazie Dans Le Métro* (1960), *Goodbye Again* (1961), *Nous Irons À Deauville* aka *We Will Go To Deauville* (1962), *La Bonne Soupe* aka *Careless Love* (1963), *La Bonne Occase* aka *The Real Bargain* (1965), *Viale Della Canzone* (1965), *Le Voyou* aka *The Crook* (1970), *Sans Mobile Apparent* aka *Without Apparent Motive* (1971).

Distillers

Guitarist/vocalist Brody Dalle (b. Melbourne, Australia) paid her dues on the local punk rock circuit with an obscure band, Sourpuss, before relocating to America in 1998. Shortly after arriving, she found a kindred spirit in Detroit, Michigan–based guitarist Rose Casper. Soon thereafter, the other pieces to the Distillers puzzle neatly fell into place, as Kim 'Chi' Fuelleman (bass) and Matt Young (drums) signed on. A recording contract with the **Epitaph Records** imprint Hellcat followed shortly thereafter (a label run by **Rancid**'s Tim Armstrong, who later married Dalle), resulting in the release of the band's debut album in 2000. Despite the disc becoming a favourite among punk revivalists, the entire Distillers line-up then split-up, with two previous members (Fuelleman and Young) signing on with former **X** singer **Exene Cervenka**'s new band, the Original Sinners.

New members Ryan Sinn (bass) and Andy Outbreak (drums) joined Brody Armstrong and Casper for the recording of the Distillers' second album *Sing Sing Death House*, released in 2002. The album featured the live favourite 'Seneca Falls' and helped attract the attention of the major labels. With Brody's marriage to Tim Armstrong falling apart, the band parted company with Hellcat and signed a new recording contract with **Sire Records**. The excellent *Coral Fang* was released in October 2003.

● ALBUMS: *The Distillers* (Hellcat 2000) ★★★, *Sing Sing Death House* (Hellcat 2002) ★★★, *Coral Fang* (Sire 2003) ★★★★.

Distractions

This Manchester, England, new wave band was first formed in 1975 by college friends Mike Finney (vocals) and Steve Perrin-Brown (guitar), together with Lawrence Tickle (bass) and Tony Trap (drums). Restructured under the influence of the **Buzzcocks** towards the end of 1977, Finney and Brown stabilized the line-up with the addition of Pip Nicholls (bass), Adrian Wright (guitar) and Alec Sidebottom (drums), who had previously played with the **Purple Gang** in the 60s. Their live set included 'Doesn't Bother Me', 'Pillow Talk', 'Valerie' and 'Paracetomol Paralysis', mixing the spirit of punk with a taste of the 60s.

After supporting most of the main bands in the Manchester area, they made their recording debut in January 1979 with 'You're Not Going Out Dressed Like That'. This resulted in a contract with Tony Wilson's **Factory Records** label and the release of 'Time Goes By So Slow'. Originally, the b-side, 'Pillow Fight', was to be the main track, but was flipped over at the last minute. Both good pop songs, they had the potential to climb the national charts, but failed through lack of radio play and promotion. At the end of September they signed to **Island Records** and released a re-recorded version of 'It Doesn't Bother Me'. In 1980 *Nobody's Perfect* was issued, a mixture of new and old songs from their early live set, followed by the singles 'Boys Cry'—a remake of the old **Eden Kane** hit 'Something For The Weekend'—and the EP *And Then There's*. All received favourable reviews, but commercial success remained elusive, causing the inevitable split in 1981.

● ALBUMS: *Nobody's Perfect* (Island 1980) ★★★★.

Disturbed

This Chicago, Illinois, USA–based nu metal outfit attracted a great deal of media attention with their March 2000 debut, *The Sickness*. The band was formed by Dan Donegan (b. Oak Lawn, Illinois, USA; guitar), Fuzz (b. Covington, Kentucky, USA; bass), Mike Wengren (b. Chicago, Illinois, USA; drums) and the charismatic Dave Draiman (b. Brooklyn, New York City, USA; vocals). Draiman, who also suggested the band's name, provided an immediate focal point when he joined the three other members in 1997. The quartet soon built up a sizeable following on the Chicago rock scene, but national success beckoned when their demo caught the attention of the major Giant Records. *The Sickness* polished off the rough edges of their demo, leaving a fairly traditional metal sound with the occasional nod to electronica in the style of **White Zombie** or **System Of A Down**. In common with most of their nu metal contemporaries the band also rattled out a desultory but interesting cover version of an 80s classic, in this case **Tears For Fears**' 'Shout'.

Steady touring in support of their debut album helped propel Disturbed to multi-platinum status. The band's status as one of nu metal's most commercially successful acts was confirmed when their second album, *Believe*, debuted at number 1 on the *Billboard* chart in October 2002. Bass player Fuzz left the band the following November. The band's third album, *Ten Thousand Fists*, debuted at the top of the US charts in October 2005.

● ALBUMS: *The Sickness* (Giant 2000) ★★★, *Believe* (Giant 2002) ★★★, *Ten Thousand Fists* (Giant 2005) ★★★.

● DVD/VIDEOS: *M.O.L.* (Warner Music Vision 2002).

Disturbing Tha Peace

Rap crew affiliated with leading 'dirty south' hip-hop star **Ludacris** (b. Chris Bridges, 11 September 1977, Atlanta, Georgia, USA). Buoyed by the success of his national radio hit 'Southern Hospitality' and the albums *Back For The First Time* and *Word Of Mouf*, on which members of Disturbing Tha Peace made cameo appearances, Ludacris teamed up with Shawnna, Jay Cee, Tity Boi, I-20 and Lil' Fate to record the collective's debut, *Golden Grain*. Released in September 2002, the album included some notable raps from Ludacris but was let down by some hackneyed beats and mediocre performances from the other rappers. A second collection limped out in 2005.

● ALBUMS: *Golden Grain* (Def Jam South 2002) ★★, *Disturbing Tha Peace* (Def Jam South 2005) ★★.

Dittman, Kyat-Hend

b. Zaire. A genuine character in African music, Dittman made his name as drummer to top stars such as **Sam Mangwana**, **Kanda Bongo Man** and Aurlus Mabele. His debut solo album was recorded in Berlin, Germany, in a fervent, vivid soukous style (despite the complete absence of guitars). An airline pilot by profession, Dittman based the album on research conducted into soukous throughout Africa. The nature of that research soon became obvious. The sleeve boasted the following effusive, autobiographical quote: 'Dittman counts 67 children of his own, and of all colours, and he is in command of 42 women in love; I have all types of woman except a German police woman, which I am currently looking for to fill my pockets for the future, in this world of modern love.'

● ALBUMS: *Le Premier Cosmonaute* (Shauva 1995) ★★★.

Divine

This female R&B vocal trio enjoyed immediate success when their 1998 debut, 'Lately', rose to the top of the US singles charts barely weeks after the members had graduated from high school. Nikki Bratcher (b. 10 August 1980, Newark, New Jersey, USA), Kia Thornton (b. 15 July 1981, Inglewood, New Jersey, USA) and Tonia Tash (b. 3 July 1979, Brooklyn, New York City, USA) were brought together in 1995 by their management team and were swiftly signed to Pendulum Records. While the trio were in the studio recording their debut album, Pendulum merged with Red Ant Entertainment. The success of 'Lately' was not matched by subsequent singles drawn from *Fairy Tales*, although 'One More Try' did break into Top 30 in spring 1999.

● ALBUMS: *Fairy Tales* (Red Ant 1998) ★★★.

Divine Comedy

This Irish band has been led from its inception by Neil Hannon (b. 7 November 1970, Londonderry, Northern Ireland), the son of the Bishop of Clogher. Hannon originally formed the band in 1989 with John McCullagh (vocals) and drummer Kevin Traynor and signed to Setanta Records (a spiritual home for wayward pop stars such as **Frank And Walters** and **A House**). The band's opening salvo was 1990's *Fanfare For The Comic Muse*. Filled with elegant, resourceful observations on the perversities of Irish and British life, this proved the most pop-orientated of Hannon's 90s work. Of his ensuing albums he would confess: 'I was very interested in the purity of three chords and all that but I was lured away by polyphonic harmony.' Following the album's release, McCullagh and Traynor elected to return to their studies with Hannon candidly pointing out that the decision was partially due to the band members 'realising Neil's an arrogant, egocentric bastard'.

The prevailing influences on the ensuing *Liberation* (1993) and *Promenade* (1994) included **Michael Nyman**, European art and **Scott Walker**. *Promenade* included 'The Booklovers', in which Hannon recounted the names of some 60 authors, leaving a gap for them to answer (many of the replying voices were provided by the Irish comedian Sean Hughes). Hannon also struck up a fruitful working partnership with Joby Talbot, who was named BBC Young Composer Of The Year in 1996. Critics were full of praise for both albums, partly because of Hannon's ability to provide self-conscious but highly amusing interview copy.

A breakthrough beyond critical success came in 1996 with the highly accessible, yet bleak, *Casanova*, which put Hannon in the UK Top 20 courtesy of the singles 'Something For The Weekend' (number 14) and 'The Frog Princess' (number 15). He returned a few months later with the wondrous mini-album *A Short Album About Love*, featuring seven heavily orchestrated new songs including another Top 20 single, 'Everybody Knows (Except You)'. Hannon, by now working with an expanded Divine Comedy line-up, also collaborated with composer **Michael Nyman**. The Divine Comedy's final album for Setanta, *Fin De Siècle*, provided Hannon with his first Top 10 album placing in September 1998. The jaunty 'National Express' entered the UK charts at number 8 in January 1999. A re-recorded version of 'The Pop Singer's Fear Of The Pollen Count', a track originally featured on *Liberation*, was released to promote the following year's compilation set, *A Secret History*. A limited edition version of this album came with an additional disc of rarities.

The Divine Comedy's first album for new label **Parlophone Records** was released in March 2001. *Regeneration* was overseen by noted producer Nigel Godrich, and it eschewed the orchestral pop leanings of Hannon's previous work in favour of a more understated and rock-orientated sound, with the other band members more involved in the creative process. The album proved to be the last by the expanded line-up of the Divine Comedy, although Hannon confirmed he would continue to record for Parlophone. He returned to the arch, orchestral style of his earlier albums on the warmly received *Absent Friends*.

● ALBUMS: *Fanfare For The Comic Muse* (Setanta 1990) ★★, *Liberation* (Setanta 1993) ★★★, *Promenade* (Setanta 1994) ★★★★★, *Casanova* (Setanta 1996) ★★★★, *A Short Album About Love* mini-album (Setanta 1997) ★★★★, *Fin De Siècle* (Setanta 1998) ★★★, *Regeneration* (Parlophone/Nettwerk 2001) ★★★, *Absent Friends* (Parlophone/Nettwerk 2004) ★★★.

● COMPILATIONS: *A Secret History* (Setanta/Red Ink 1999) ★★★★, *Rarities* (Divine Comedy 2005) ★★★.

● DVD/VIDEOS: *Live At The Palladium* (Parlophone 2004).

Divine Horsemen

Formed in 1984 in Los Angeles, California, USA, the Divine Horsemen revolved around the talents of Chris D(esjardins) (guitar/vocals), formerly of the **Flesheaters**. He produced the acclaimed *Days Of Wine And Roses* for the **Dream Syndicate** before embarking on this new venture. The virtually acoustic *Time Stands Still* gave full rein to Desjardins' chilling lyricism which explored the darker side of the human psyche. Members of **X**, the **Gun Club** and **Blasters** provided sympathetic accompaniment. On *Devil's River* Desjardins shared vocals with long-time partner Julie C(hristensen). Herein the emphasis was on cowboy/Western imagery, but the prevailing atmosphere of doom remained intact. *Middle Of The Night*, the bulk of which was recorded at the same time as its predecessor, was largely lighter in tone, the two singers performing many of the tracks as a harmony duo. It included versions of **David Allen Coe**'s 'Fields Of Stone', the **Rolling Stones**' 'Gimme Shelter' and the **Cramps**' 'Voodoo Idol', choices that suggested Desjardins' concurrent musical influences. Pete Andrus (guitar) joined the Divine Horsemen for *Snake Handler*, resulting in a tighter, more rock-based sound. The results were generally less satisfying, although the terrifying 'Fire Kiss' was one of the group's finest recordings. The personal relationship between Desjardins and Christensen ended soon after this album was issued and the Divine Horsemen broke up. In 1989 Desjardins recorded *I Pass For Human* with Stone By Stone. It documented the end of an era, notably through a new, embittered version of 'Time Stands Still'. Following this release, Desjardins re-formed the Flesheaters.

● ALBUMS: *Time Stands Still* (Enigma 1984) ★★★, *Devil's River* (SST 1986) ★★★, *Middle Of The Night* (SST 1986) ★★★, *Snake Handler* (SST 1987) ★★, as Stone By Stone *I Pass For Human* (SST 1989) ★★★.

Divine Styler

b. Brooklyn, New York City, USA. Unusually, Divine Styler says he has a responsibility to take profanity out of hip-hop. The Orthodox Muslim MC was introduced to **Ice-T** by DJ and long-term collaborator Bilal Bashir and became a member of the former's Rhyme Syndicate in the mid-80s. According to

Divine Styler, his early rhymes were 'all about killing MCs—I was from Brooklyn, there wasn't nothing else', and these early recordings coincided with a period of what the rapper now describes as 'bad illegal business'. The Divine Styler was jailed on violation of probation, serving four months although he had faced a five-year sentence. The experience apparently put things in perspective for the rapper. His debut album, 1989's *Word Power*, subsequently eschewed the expected thugged-out lyrics in favour of Black awareness, politics and culture. The curiously named follow-up *Spiral Walls Containing Autumns Of Light* featured rock, speed metal, jazz, folk and hip-hop, prompting the MC to be simultaneously dubbed 'the **Jimi Hendrix** of hip-hop' by critics but dropped by his record label. After an extended break, Divine Styler's career was legendarily re-triggered by the chance discovery of a London-based fanzine called *In Search Of . . . The Divine Styler*. The rapper hooked up with the **Mo' Wax Records** label via **DJ Shadow** to release an album that echoed the title of his debut. Many of the album's samples were lifted from cassettes in an attempt to emphasize the dirt, noise and hiss of the format, while the album itself is apparently intended to explore the balance between good and evil within Divine Styler himself.

● ALBUMS: *Word Power* (Rhyme Syndicate/Epic 1989) ★★★, *Spiral Walls Containing Autumns Of Light* (Rhyme Syndicate/Giant 1992) ★★★★, *Word Power 2: Directrix* (Mo' Wax 1999) ★★★.

Diving For Pearls

This cult AOR quintet was formed in New York in 1988, when ex-Urgent guitarist Yul Vazquez joined Danny Malone (vocals), Jack Moran (keyboards), David Weeks (bass) and ex–Jean Beauvoir drummer Peter Clemente, taking their unusual name from an **Elvis Costello** lyric ('Shipbuilding'). The band signed within nine months to Epic Records on a development contract and were subsequently able to record their full debut. *Diving For Pearls*, produced by David Prater, was received with a wave of acclaim in AOR circles, prompting comparisons to a diverse array of acts for their classy blend of keyboard-flavoured, commercial hard rock, also featuring superb vocals and melancholy lyrics from Malone. However, given minimal promotion, the album simply failed to sell, and Diving For Pearls broke up when they lost their contract. Malone later reappeared in Band Of Angels.

● ALBUMS: *Diving For Pearls* (Epic 1989) ★★★.

Divinyls

Led by the provocative Chrissie Amphlett (b. Christina Amphlett, 25 October 1960, Geelong, Australia), whose songwriting with guitarist Mark McEntee (b. Australia) formed the basis of the band, this Australian unit recorded some excellent work in a career spanning over 15 years. Amphlett's sexy image complemented the mesmerizing urgency of the music, and the band was guaranteed the audience's undivided attention. Amphlett, who had previously worked with country rock band One Ton Gypsy, met McEntee in Sydney in early 1980, and the duo began working as the Divinyls shortly afterwards. They were joined by a number of local musicians, including former **Air Supply** bass player Jeremy Paul. Their first mini-album was written for the 1982 movie *Monkey Grip*; it produced the Australian Top 10 single 'Boys In Town' as well as the excellent ballad

'Only The Lonely'. The former was promoted by a striking video featuring Amphlett cavorting provocatively in a school uniform and fishnet stockings. Signing with the UK label **Chrysalis Records**, the Divinyls' first album *Desperate* was a hit in Australia. Several hit singles and extensive touring bridged the gap to *What A Life!* (1985), which was greeted enthusiastically; however, the sales did not match the reviews. Later material, with the exception of the next single 'Pleasure And Pain', did not compare well with their earliest work.

The Divinyls became a duo when bass player Rick Grossman left in 1988 to join **Hoodoo Gurus**, with musicians added whenever a tour was undertaken. They underwent a mini-revival with the controversial single 'I Touch Myself', a deliberately blatant reference to masturbation, which reached the US Top 5 and UK Top 10 in 1991. Following one further recording in the mid-90s (the muted *Underworld*) the Amphlett/McEntee duo drifted apart to work on solo projects. In recent years, Amphlett has established herself as a stage actor, appearing in Australian productions of *Blood Brothers* and *The Boy From Oz*. She still performs from her base in Woodstock, New York, USA. McEntee continues to write songs but his main career is working in the family clothes business.

● ALBUMS: *Desperate* (Chrysalis 1983) ★★★, *What A Life!* (Chrysalis 1985) ★★, *Temperamental* (Chrysalis 1988) ★★★, *Divinyls* (Virgin America 1991) ★★★, *Underworld* (RCA 1996) ★★★.

● COMPILATIONS: *Essential* (Chrysalis 1987) ★★★, *The Collection* (Alex 1994) ★★★, *Make You Happy 1981–1993: Hits, Rarities & Essential Moments Of An Incendiary Australian Band* (Raven 1997) ★★★★, *Pleasure & Pain* (Disky 2003) ★★★.

Divorce Me, Darling!

Following upon his immensely successful 20s musical comedy spoof, **The Boy Friend** (1953), **Sandy Wilson** (b. Alexander Galbraith Wilson, 19 May 1924, Sale, Cheshire, England) had something similar in mind when he wrote the libretto, music and lyrics for this two-act show. First produced in 1964 at London's Players Theatre, the show enjoyed a good run, transferring the following year to the Globe Theatre. A comedy of marital errors and misunderstanding, *Divorce Me, Darling!* affectionately parodies 30s musical comedies, especially those of **Noël Coward**. The story follows the fortunes of a group of bright young things who were, 10 years ago, pupils of Madame Dubonnet's finishing school for girls. Now married but dissatisfied, their reunion at the Hotel du Paradis in the south of France leads to flirtations and promises and an innocent interchange of partners. When Madame Dubonnet, who moonlights as cabaret singer Madame K, is so transparently happy at the return of her husband Percy, the young women realize that they have all along had the partner they really love. This, allied to revelations that the patter of numerous tiny feet will soon be heard, leads to a happy ending. The cast included Patricia Michael (Polly), Cy Young (Bobby), Irlin Hall (Bobby's sister) and Joan Sterndale Bennett (Madam Dubonnet). Among Wilson's songs are 'Back Where We Started', 'Blondes For Danger', 'Divorce Me, Darling', 'Here We Are In Nice Again', 'No Harm Done', 'On The Loose', 'Someone To Dance With', 'Together Again' and 'Whatever Happened To Love?'.

In 1979, a revised version of *Divorce Me, Darling!* was presented at London's Tower Theatre by the Tavistock Repertory Company, and the show was produced at the Houston, Texas Theatre Under The Stars in 1984 where it was paired with the original short version of *The Boy Friend*. There was a London revival in 1997. The original London cast recording of the show has been reissued by Must Close Saturday Records and the 1997 cast recording is on CDJay Records.

Dixie Chicks

This female trio's beguiling mixture of bluegrass, straight country and pop shook up the contemporary country scene in the late 90s. Raised in Texas, USA, sisters Martie Maguire (b. Martie Erwin, 12 October 1969; mandolin/fiddle) and Emily Robison (b. Emily Erwin, 16 August 1972; banjo/dobro) were playing their instruments from an early age. When they were still only teenagers they toured throughout the USA with the bluegrass group Blue Night Express. Taking their name from the **Little Feat** song 'Dixie Chicken', the Dixie Chicks were founded in 1989 when the sisters, with two other original members Laura Lynch and Robin Lynn Macy (ex–Danger In The Air) began busking on street corners in Dallas. They performed at clubs and dance halls and released two bluegrass-orientated independent label albums and a Christmas single before Macy left to form the Domestic Social Club with Sara Hickman and Patty Lege. The more contemporary sounding *Shouldn't A Told You That* was the last recording to feature Lynch, who was replaced by new lead vocalist Natalie Maines (b. 14 October 1974, Texas, USA; daughter of steel guitarist **Lloyd Maines**) in 1995.

The new look Dixie Chicks were considered the perfect flagship act for the 1997 relaunch of Monument Records, home to **Roy Orbison** and **Dolly Parton** in the 60s prior to its closure. Released in January 1998, **Wide Open Spaces** quickly became the bestselling country album released by a group in that year, and it eventually climbed to number 4 on the *Billboard* Hot 200 and achieved multi-platinum sales. Its success was buoyed by the release of the singles 'I Can Love You Better' and 'There's Your Trouble' (a US Country number 1), both examples of the group's spirited, original take on traditional Nashville musical values. They also made a name for themselves in the press, Maines making statements opposing the legalization of marijuana on the *Politically Incorrect* television show. At September's **Country Music Association** Awards they completed a fine year by winning the Vocal Group and Horizon trophies. At the following year's Grammy Awards, *Wide Open Spaces* was voted Best Country Album.

The Dixie Chicks next studio album, *Fly*, introduced a more pop-orientated style, but still shot to number 1 on the US album chart in September 1999 and spent many months at the top. The Top 10 single 'Goodbye Earl', a *Thelma And Louise*–style tale of two women exacting the ultimate revenge on a violent husband, became a *cause celebre* after it was banned by several male radio programmers and DJs. The group went on to win four awards at October 2000's CMA ceremony, including one for 'Goodbye Earl'. They subsequently entered into major litigation with their record company, Sony Music. In September 2002, with the legal wrangles finally sorted out, the trio returned to the top of the US charts with their new studio album, *Home*.

America's love affair with the Dixie Chicks was soured the following March after Maines made derogatory statements about President George W. Bush at a concert in London, England. With the second Gulf War against Iraq still being fought, several sectors of the American media reacted furiously, resulting in *Home* being struck from playlists and copies of the CD being destroyed in certain states.

● ALBUMS: *Thank Heavens For Dale Evans* (Crystal Clear 1990) ★★★, *Little Ol' Cowgirl* (Crystal Clear 1992) ★★★, *Shouldn't A Told You That* (Crystal Clear 1993) ★★★, *Wide Open Spaces* (Monument 1998) ★★★★, *Fly* (Monument 1999) ★★★★, *Home* (Monument 2002) ★★★, *Top Of The World Tour Live* (Monumetn/Columbia 2003) ★★★.

● DVD/VIDEOS: *An Evening With The Dixie Chicks* (Columbia Music Video 2003), *Top Of The World Tour Live* (Columbia Music Video 2003).

● FURTHER READING: *Chicks Rule: The Story Of The Dixie Chicks*, Scott Gray. *Dixiechicks: The New Photo Biog*, Kathleen Tracy. *All About The Dixie Chicks*, Ace Collins.

Dixie Cups

Formed in New Orleans, Louisiana, USA, in 1963, the Dixie Cups were a female trio best known for the original recording of the hit 'Chapel Of Love' in the early 60s. The group comprised sisters Barbara Ann Hawkins (b. 23 October 1943) and Rosa Lee Hawkins (b. 24 September 1944) and their cousin Joan Marie Johnson (b. January 1945, New Orleans, Louisiana, USA). Having sung together in church and at school, the girls formed a group called the Meltones for a high school talent contest in 1963. There they were discovered by **Joe Jones**, a New Orleans singer who had secured a hit himself with 'You Talk Too Much' in 1960. He became their manager and signed the trio with producers/songwriters Jerry Leiber and Mike Stoller, who were then starting their own record label, Red Bird, with industry veteran **George Goldner**.

The Dixie Cups recorded **Jeff Barry** and **Ellie Greenwich**'s 'Chapel Of Love' despite the fact that both the **Ronettes** and the **Crystals** had failed to have hits with the song, which was described by co-producer Mike Leiber as 'a record I hated with a passion'. Released as the debut Red Bird single, the trio's first single reached number 1 in the USA during the summer of 1964 (the trio later claimed that they received only a few hundred dollars for their part in the recording). Following that hit, the Dixie Cups toured the USA and released a number of follow-up singles for Red Bird, four of which charted. 'People Say', the second, made number 12, and the last, 'Iko Iko', a traditional New Orleans chant, reached number 20. The song was subsequently used in soundtracks for a number of films, in common with 'Chapel Of Love'. After Red Bird closed down in 1966, the Dixie Cups signed with ABC-Paramount Records. No hits resulted from the association, and the trio have not recorded since, although they continue to perform (the two sisters are the only originals still in the act).

● ALBUMS: *Chapel Of Love* aka *Iko Iko* (Red Bird 1964) ★★★, *Ridin' High* (ABC-Paramount 1965) ★★.

● COMPILATIONS: *The Best Of The Dixie Cups* (Delta 1997) ★★★, *Chapel Of Love: The Very Best Of The Dixie Cups* (Collectables 1999) ★★★, *The Complete Red Bird Recordings* (Varèse Vintage 2002) ★★★.

Dixie Dregs

Formed in 1973, the instrumental Dixie Dregs fused rock, jazz, classical and bluegrass with seamless musicianship, and one of their alumni, guitarist **Steve Morse** (b. 28 July 1954, Hamilton, Ohio, USA) is regarded as one of the most technically proficient players of that instrument. The band was formed by Morse, electric violinist Allen Sloan, bass player Andy West (b. 6 February 1954, Newport, Rhode Island, USA) and drummer Rod Morgenstein. Morse and West had played in the Augusta band Dixie Grit. They met Sloan, from Miami, and Morgenstein, from Plainview, New York, at the University of Miami School of Music in Florida, adding Frank Josephs on keyboards. For college credit, the quintet, now calling itself the Dixie Dregs, produced and recorded an album called *The Great Spectacular*, later privately issued in 1976. After graduating from college, the band moved to Augusta and began playing live dates. They were signed by Capricorn Records in December 1976 and moved to Atlanta, Georgia. Their debut album for the label, *Free Fall*, was released in spring 1977 and featured keyboard player Steve Davidowski. He was replaced by Mark Parrish later that autumn. Their next two albums, *What If* and *Night Of The Living Dregs*, received critical acclaim and broke into the US charts. The latter included one side of live performances recorded on 23 July 1978 at the **Montreux Jazz Festival**. After completing *Night Of The Living Dregs*, T Lavitz replaced Parrish. The band switched to **Arista Records** for *Dregs Of The Earth* and remained there for the subsequent *Unsung Heroes* and *Industry Standard*, both of which were released under the shortened Dregs moniker. The latter, in addition to featuring two tracks with vocals, saw Sloan (who went on to become a doctor) replaced by violinist **Mark O'Connor** (b. 4 August 1962, Seattle, Washington, USA). O'Connor stayed for a year before leaving to record several solo albums of virtuoso bluegrass and jazz. The Dregs carried on as a quartet for several months before disbanding in 1983. Morse's highly acclaimed solo career began with the 1984 release of the Steve Morse Band's *The Introduction*. Morgenstein played on the band's first two albums before joining soft rockers **Winger**. The original Dregs and O'Connor teamed up in 1988 on a promotional 3-track mini-CD for the Ensoniq company. Minus West, the Dixie Dregs reunited on a more permanent basis in 1992 for live appearances, which ultimately led to the release of a brand new studio album, *Full Circle*, in 1994. The line-up on this album comprised Morse, Morgenstein, Lavitz, Dave LaRue (bass; also a member of the Steve Morse Band) and Jerry Goodman (violin; ex–**Mahavishnu Orchestra**), who replaced the departing Sloan. In 1999, the Dixie Dregs reunited once more, with West and Sloan returning to the line-up. Both were featured on the new live set *California Screamin'*.

● ALBUMS: *The Great Spectacular* (Dixie Dregs 1976) ★★★, *Free Fall* (Capricorn 1977) ★★★, *What If* (Capricorn 1978) ★★★, *Night Of The Living Dregs* (Capricorn 1979) ★★★★, *Sex, Dregs & Rock 'n' Roll* (Minotauro 1979), *Dregs Of The Earth* (Arista 1980) ★★★★, *Live In New York 1981* (Four Aces 1981) ★★★, as The Dregs *Unsung Heroes* (Arista 1981) ★★★, as The Dregs *Industry Standard* (Arista 1982) ★★, *Bring 'Em Back Alive* (Capricorn 1992) ★★★, *Full Circle* (Capricorn 1994) ★★★, *Live On The King Biscuit Flower Hour* 1979 recording (King Biscuit Flower Hour 1998) ★★★, *California Screamin'* (Zebra 2000) ★★★.

● COMPILATIONS: *The Best Of The Dixie Dregs* (Grand Slamm 1987) ★★★, as The Dregs *Divided We Stand: The Best Of The Dregs* (Arista 1989) ★★★, *The Millennium Collection* (Mercury 2002) ★★★★.

Dixie Echoes

Originating from Pensacola, Florida, USA, gospel vocal group the Dixie Echoes was formed in 1960 by Dale Shelnut. The ever-changing line-ups of this enduring southern gospel unit have featured his sons Randy Shelnut Snr. (lead) and Randy Shelnut Jnr. (baritone), Randy Harper (piano), Jimmy Holmes (drums), Billy Hodges (tenor) and Billy Todd (bass). From 1960 onwards the group became a popular attraction at church and community gatherings for their authentic renditions of southern spirituals, alongside hymns and country gospel songs. In addition to standards, the group also wrote a large number of original compositions. They were effectively led by lead singer and manager Dale Shelnut, an energetic and active member of the southern gospel community. His son Randy Shelnut Snr. took over the leadership of the group in later years. Best known nationally for their performances on *The Gospel Singing Jubilee* television show, by the end of the 70s the Dixie Echoes had recorded over 20 albums including many for Supreme. In the 80s and 90s they were less prolific, though they remained active on the Florida scene.

● ALBUMS: *Turn Your Radio On* (Supreme 1971) ★★★, *I Want To See Jesus* (Supreme 1972) ★★★, *Live* (Supreme 1973) ★★★, *My Real Home* (Supreme 1974) ★★★, *Today* (Supreme 1975) ★★★, *Get On Board* (Supreme 1975) ★★★, *Come On In* (Supreme 1976) ★★★, *Heavenly Echoes* (Supreme 1977) ★★★, *Coast To Coast* (Supreme 1978) ★★★.

● COMPILATIONS: *The Best Of* (Supreme 1977) ★★★★.

Dixie Flyers

The Dixie Flyers were the house band at Miami's Criteria Studio, purchased in 1970 by **Atlantic Records**. Their name derived from a literary reference to writer William Faulkner that likened him to a south-bound train, in the phrase 'When the Dixie Flyer comes down the track you'd better get out of the way'. Prior to their work for Atlantic at Criteria, the Flyers had performed on **Tony Joe White**'s *Continued* 1969 album for Monument and then behind **Betty LaVette** on her remarkable 'He Made A Woman Out Of Me' for Lelan Roger's Silver Fox label, recorded the same year in Memphis. The group was assembled by pianist **Jim Dickinson**, who had previously worked with producer **Sam Phillips**. Mike Utley (keyboards), Tommy McClure (bass) and Sammy Creason (drums) were joined by ex–**Mar-Kay** Charlie Freeman (guitar) in what was one of the last great house rhythm sections. Their finest sessions included those for **Aretha Franklin**'s *Spirit In The Dark* and **Brook Benton**'s 'Rainy Night In Georgia' (both 1970). However, the studio could not support a full-time group, as much of its work came from self-contained units, including the **Allman Brothers Band** and **Derek And The Dominos**. The group left their Miami enclave at the end of 1970, touring North America and Europe with **Rita Coolidge**. They disbanded in March 1972, leaving Dickinson's eclectic solo album *Dixie Fried* as a fitting testament to their skills. The pianist later returned to Memphis, where he has worked with such disparate acts as **Big Star**, **Ry Cooder** and **Green On Red**. Charlie Freeman died as a result of pulmonary oedema on 31 January 1973 following years of narcotics abuse.

Dixie Gentlemen

An Alabama band that was founded in 1956 and tended to specialize in the bluegrass music of the 60s rather than the early style of the pioneers of the genre. The original three founder members were **Jake Landers** (b. Jacob Landers, 14 August 1938, Lawrence County, Alabama, USA; guitar/vocals), Herschel Sizemore (b. Herschel Lee Sizemore, 8 August 1935, Sheffield, Alabama, USA; mandolin/vocals) and Rual Yarborough (b. 13 January 1930, Lawrence County, Alabama, USA; banjo/vocals). Originally Sizemore and Yarborough were playing in a country group when they met Landers, who had just been released from military service. They formed a group, calling themselves the Dixie Gentlemen. They readily found work and until the late 60s, they proved a competent and popular act at bluegrass venues and on various radio stations including WMSL Decatur. During the years they were joined by various other musicians including fiddler **Vassar Clements**. In 1959, they made their first recordings (two gospel numbers) for a small Florida label and were offered the chance to provide bluegrass backing on an album with **Tommy Jackson**. They also recorded a selection of popular bluegrass tunes for two albums on Time Records billed as the Blue Ridge Mountain Boys. In 1963, they recorded an album for **United Artists Records** that was almost completely comprised of songs written by Landers. In 1966, they recorded their final album as the Dixie Gentlemen for an album on Yarborough's Tune label. They were joined on it by both Clements and dobroist Tut Taylor. (Yarborough also recorded a banjo album on which he received backing from his colleagues.)

In 1967, the Dixie Gentlemen disbanded not because they were not popular but because the members had the opportunity to join better-known acts. Sizemore played first with **Jimmy Martin** and then, in 1969, settled in Virginia, where he played with several major groups including the Shenandoah Cutups and the Bluegrass Cardinals. Yarborough also joined Martin, but in 1969 he became a member of **Bill Monroe**'s band until 1971. He then reunited with Landers to form the Dixiemen with whom he recorded several albums. Landers made recordings with several units but for a time concentrated on his songwriting. In December 1972, the original Dixie Gentlemen plus Clements recorded a reunion album for Old Homestead, and in 1992 they repeated the event to record on Rutabaga. Apart from their group recordings, Landers, Sizemore and Yarborough also recorded albums under their own name.

● ALBUMS: as Blue Ridge Mountain Boys *Hootenanny N'Blue Grass* (Time 1963) ★★★, as Blue Ridge Mountain Boys *Blue Grass Down Home* (Time 1963) ★★★, *The Country Style Of The Dixie Gentlemen* (United Artists 1967) ★★★, *Blues And Bluegrass* (Tune 1967) ★★★, *Together Once More* (Old Homestead 1973) ★★★, *Take Me Back To Dixie* (Rutabaga 1992) ★★★.

Dixie Hummingbirds

This gospel group, originally fronted by baritone James Davis, was formed in 1928 in Greenville, South Carolina, USA. In the 30s and 40s they sang hymns, spirituals and jubilees with little accompaniment except for their precise and warm harmonies. Baritone Ira Tucker (b. 17 May 1925, Spartanburg, North Carolina, USA) joined the line-up in 1938 and was later established as the flamboyant showman of the group, introducing a dramatic live act that had a lasting influence on many soul singers. Their 1939–49 recordings for labels including Apollo and Gotham are best heard on the *In The Storm Too Long* compilation, which captures the intricate vocal interplay of Tucker and Paul Owens. From 1952 onwards, the Dixie Hummingbirds recorded a series of compelling albums for **Don Robey**'s Peacock Records, the compassion and emotive timbre of which matched the power of **Mahalia Jackson** and **Rev. James Cleveland**, with outstanding teamwork rather than individual flair their greatest asset. The line-up on such classics as 'Wading Through Blood And Water', 'Let's Go Out To The Program', 'Christian Testimonial', 'Nobody Knows The Trouble I See' and 'Our Prayer For Peace' comprised Tucker, Davis, Beachey Thompson (b. 1915, d. 1994), William Bobo (d. 1976) and Owens' replacement, the honey-throated James Walker (b. 1926, d. 1992).

With the advent of the 60s the Dixie Hummingbirds began to embrace secular music, fusing their traditional gospel with jazz, blues and even rock, and appearing at the 1966 Newport Folk Festival. Their most famous appearance outside of the church circuit came in 1973 when they backed **Paul Simon** at the Muscle Shoals Studio on his recording of 'Loves Me Like A Rock' (featured on the singer-songwriter's *There Goes Rhymin' Simon*). The death of bass vocalist Bobo in 1976 brought an end to the classic line-up of the Dixie Hummingbirds. Two years later the group was inducted into the Philadelphia Hall Of Fame. Founder member James Davis retired in 1984, while Walker and Thompson died in 1992 and 1994 respectively. In the late 90s, Tucker was still performing with a line-up comprising Paul Owens, Howard Carroll and Carl Davis, he and celebrated the group's 70th anniversary with the *Music In The Air* album. The Dixie Hummingbirds' natural market has always been within the gospel community, where recordings such as 'Somebody Is Lying', 'You Don't Have Nothing If You Don't Have Jesus' and 'The Devil Can't Harm A Praying Man' are still venerated.

● ALBUMS: *A Christian Testimonial* (Peacock 1959) ★★★★, *In The Morning* (Peacock 1962) ★★★, *Prayer For Peace* (Peacock 1964) ★★★, *Every Day And Every Hour* (Peacock 1966) ★★★, *Live* (Mobile Fidelity 1976) ★★, *Dixie Hummingbirds* (Gospel Heritage 1988) ★★★, *Music In The Air: The 70th Anniversary All-Star Tribute* (House Of Blues 1999) ★★★, *Diamond Jubilation: 75th Anniversary* (Rounder 2003) ★★★★.
● COMPILATIONS: *In The Storm Too Long* 1939–1949 recordings (Golden Jubilee 1985) ★★★, *The Best Of The Dixie Hummingbirds* (MCA 1988) ★★★★, *Dixie Hummingbirds 1939–47* (Document 1996) ★★★, *Thank You For One More Day: The 70th Anniversary Of The Dixie Hummingbirds* (MCA 1998) ★★★★, *Looking Back: A Retrospective* (Platinum 1998) ★★★, *Up In Heaven: The Very Best Of The Dixie Hummingbirds & The Angelics* (Collectables 1998) ★★★, *The Best Of The Dixie Hummingbirds: The Millennium Collection* (MCA 2002) ★★★.
● DVD/VIDEOS: *Live In Atlanta* (Atlanta 1995).
● FURTHER READING: *Great God A' Mighty! The Dixie Hummingbirds Celebrating The Rise Of Soul Gospel Music*, Jerry Zolten.

Dixie Melody Boys

A US gospel octet who comprise four singers and a four-piece band, the Dixie Melody Boys formed in Cincinnati in 1960. Ed O'Neal (bass), Henry Daniels (baritone), David Kimbrell (lead) and Jamey Ragle (first tenor) are the singing part of the group, accompanied by Greg Simpkins (piano), Allen O'Neal (guitar), Reb Lancaster (bass) and Ron Well (steel guitar). Appearing regularly at church and community gatherings, they subsequently appeared on a number of local radio and television programmes as well as issuing a sequence of albums for their local record label, QCA Records.

● ALBUMS: *Are You Ready?* (QCA 1972) ★★★, *Lord Don't Move That Mountain* (QCA 1978) ★★★.

Dixies

One of the most flamboyant, exciting and popular of Irish showbands, the Dixies was a strong live attraction and enjoyed considerable chart success in Eire during the 60s. They had first come together as the Dixielanders and, in 1954, played in a jazz band led by clarinettist Sean Lucey and featured trombonist Theo Cahill and the outrageous drummer Joe McCarthy. They soon became a five-piece with the addition of pianist Mick Murphy and trumpeter Larry Neville. Inspired by the **Clipper Carlton**, they played a varied set and by the end of the 50s had added bass player Chris O'Mahony, second saxophonist Jimmy Mintern and guitarist Steve Lynch. Neville, meanwhile, had been replaced by John Sheenan and Murphy by Finbarr O'Leary. In 1961, after an exceptional performance at the Olympia Ballroom in Waterford (where they rivalled the **Royal Showband**), the unit turned professional. Determined to magnify their appeal, they recruited vocalist Brendan O'Brien, who rapidly became one of the most popular singers on the showband circuit. A record contract with **Decca Records** saw the release of the Cahill-composed instrumental 'Cyclone' in 1963. Soon afterwards, the Dixies were in the Irish charts with 'Christmas Time', followed by 'I'm Counting On You' and 'It's Only Make Believe'. During 1964, they appeared at Carnegie Hall and returned home as conquering heroes. O'Brien was enamoured with **Buddy Holly** and introduced his music to a new generation of listeners with chart hits including 'Oh Boy', 'Peggy Sue' and 'It Doesn't Matter Anymore'. With O'Brien's strong vocal talents and McCarthy's acrobatic, zany comedy, the band were a marvellously complementary unit. With over 20 hits to their credit, including the engaging 'Katie's Kisses' and a chart-topping cover of **Leapy Lee**'s 'Little Arrows', they ended the 60s by transferring their attentions to Las Vegas. Lucrative bookings followed, but, as with many of the top showbands of the era, they split in the early 70s. The mainstays of the band, O'Brien and McCarthy, formed the aptly named Stage Two, while the remainder of the group continued with new vocalist Sandie Jones. Their 'Ceolan Ghra' represented Ireland in the 1972 Eurovision Song Contest and reached number 1 in the Irish charts. By the mid-70s, the remaining members of the original line-up had moved on, but in the early 80s they reunited for a series of shows.

Dixon Brothers

Brothers Dorsey Murdock Dixon (b. 14 October 1897, Darlington, South Carolina, USA, d. 16 April 1968, Florida, USA) and Howard Britten Dixon (b. 19 June 1903, Darlington, South Carolina, USA, d. 24 March 1961) were two of seven Dixon children. At the age of 12, Dorsey left school and like his father, William McQuiller Dixon, he worked in the mill of the Darlington Cotton Manufacturing Company. Dorsey, who was playing the guitar at 14, later taught himself to play fiddle and when Howard also learned guitar, they began playing fiddle and guitar duets in the East Rockingham film theatre. In 1929, Dorsey wrote a poem called 'The Cleveland Schoolhouse Fire', which he based on the true story of a school fire that, in May 1923, had led to the deaths of 76 children. His mother and Howard, using the tune of 'Life's Railway To Heaven', first popularized the number by singing it at local venues. In 1932, inspired by Jimmie Tarlton (of **Darby And Tarlton**), the brothers began to play together at local venues and two years later appeared regularly on the *Saturday Night Jamboree* on WBT Charlotte, North Carolina. Between February 1936 and 1938, they recorded 60 songs (most were written or co-written by Dorsey) for **RCA-Victor Records**, which were released on the **Bluebird** or Montgomery Ward labels. Without doubt the most famous of these songs was 'I Didn't Hear Anybody Pray', which must rank as the genre's first 'don't drink and drive song'. It was later recorded as 'The Wreck On The Highway' by **Roy Acuff**, who subsequently attempted to claim the song as his own. Dorsey opposed Acuff's claim and after some acrimony, the matter was eventually settled amicably. They eventually gave up hopes of a full-time musical career in the early 40s but continued to play locally. Howard worked for a time with **Wade Mainer**, with whom he co-wrote several songs including 'Intoxicated Rat' and 'Two Little Rosebuds'. He also recorded a classic version of 'Barbara Allen' with Mainer for the Library of Congress. Dorsey continued to work in various mills until 1951, when his fading sight forced him to quit. He had married Beatrice Moody, a fellow mill worker, in 1927 and they had raised four sons before divorcing in 1953. Howard continued to work in the mills and died suddenly, while at work, in March 1961. Dorsey, who appeared at the Newport Folk Festival in 1963, died in April 1968. Old Homestead released a series of albums in the 80s, which contained most of the Dixons' recorded work.

● COMPILATIONS: *The Dixon Brothers, (Howard And Dorsey), Volume 1, Early Recordings & Transcriptions* (Old Homestead 1983) ★★★★, *The Dixon Brothers, (Howard And Dorsey), Volume 2* (Old Homestead 1984) ★★★, *The Dixon Brothers, Volume 3—Early Sacred Songs* (Old Homestead 1986) ★★★, *The Dixon Brothers, Volume 4—Fisherman's Luck* (Old Homestead 1986) ★★★, *Complete Recorded Works Volumes 1–4 (1936–38)* (Document 1999) ★★★.

Dixon, Adele

b. Adela Helena Dixon, 3 June 1908, Newington, London, England, d. 11 April 1992, Wythenshawe, Greater Manchester, England. A versatile actress with a pleasing soprano voice who was equally at home in dramatic roles and musical comedies. Her trim figure, attractive red-brown hair and commanding appearance also made an ideal pantomime Principal Boy. Dixon attended the Italia Conti stage school and made her London stage debut in 1921 at the age of 13 as the First Elf in *Where The Rainbow Ends*. After studying at the Royal Academy of Dramatic Art, she toured in various Shakespearean roles before joining the Old Vic Company where she impressed opposite John Gielgud in *Romeo And Juliet* and *Hamlet*. In 1928 she attracted attention in her first singing role as Princess Beauty in *Adam's Opera*. The music for that production was composed by **Richard Addinsell**, and

three years later, when he wrote the songs for the stage adaptation of J.B. Priestley's novel, *The Good Companions*, Dixon was cast—again opposite Gielgud—in the important role of Susie Dean, the young and enterprising soubrette. Shortly after appearing alongside the high-kicking **Charlotte Greenwood** in Robert Stoltz's *Wild Violets* (1932), Dixon took over from **Evelyn Laye** in *Give Me A Ring* (1933), combining with **John Mills** (who had replaced Ernest Verebes) on the attractive 'A Couple Of Fools In Love'. She survived the farcical goings-on in the **Leslie Henson** vehicle *Lucky Break* (1934) to co-star later in the year with **Stanley Holloway**, and again with Greenwood, in *Three Sisters*. **Jerome Kern** and **Oscar Hammerstein**'s lovely score for this original musical, which was presented at Drury Lane, contained the future standard, 'I Won't Dance', on which Dixon duetted with Richard Dolman. The song's lyric was subsequently revised, and the new version featured in several films, including *Roberta* (1935) with **Fred Astaire** and **Ginger Rogers**, and the 1952 remake, *Lovely To Look At*. In 1935 Dixon played Hope Harcourt in **Cole Porter**'s *Anything Goes*, an American import full of good songs, and in the following year she introduced, with Eric Fawcett, the delightful 'I Breathe On Windows' in **Charles B. Cochran**'s production of *Over She Goes*, which also starred **Stanley Lupino** and **Laddie Cliff**. By this time Dixon was one of the West End's best-loved leading ladies, and in November 1936 she became the first female performer to be seen in Britain on the new medium of television, being chosen to sing the specially composed 'Television' ('Bringing Television To You') when the BBC launched the world's first regular service from Alexandra Palace on 2 November 1936. Her Broadway debut with **Jack Buchanan** and Evelyn Laye in *Between The Devil* (1937) was not so successful, in spite of a score by **Arthur Schwartz** and **Howard Dietz** containing the superior ballad, 'I See Your Face Before Me', which was introduced by Laye, and reprised by Dixon and Buchanan. A further trip to New York in 1948 with Buchanan, to appear in the comedy *Don't Listen Ladies!* also proved a disappointment. Back home in 1938, Dixon continued to triumph in the 'musical frolic' *The Fleet's Lit Up*, which had a **Vivian Ellis** score, plus **Frances Day**, Lupino and Ralph Reader, with whom she combined on 'Hide And Seek'; and the revue, *All Clear*, in company with **Bobby Howes**, **Beatrice Lillie**, and Fred Emney. In December 1940 at the Sheffield Empire, Dixon made the first of more than a dozen appearances as Principal Boy in Christmas pantomime, playing Prince Charming to Jack Buchanan's Buttons in *Cinderella*. Constantly mixing roles in both the straight and musical theatre, Dixon joined **Sonnie Hale** in the short-lived (10 performances at the Piccadilly Theatre) *The Knight Was Bold* in 1943, and she said farewell to the London musical stage in an old fashioned romantic piece, with a score by **Eric Maschwitz** and **Jack Strachey**, entitled *Belinda Fair* (1949). Two years earlier, she had also concluded her occasional film career, which had included the musical *Calling The Tune* (1936), featuring guest artists Sir Henry Wood and Reginald Forsyth. West End audiences saw Dixon for the last time as Prince Charming in the 1953 production of *Cinderella*, which starred **Julie Andrews** just prior to her ascendancy to superstardom on Broadway via *The Boy Friend* and *My Fair Lady*. Thereafter Dixon made several forays into the provincial theatre before retiring in the late 50s. Her husband of nearly 50 years, jewel expert Ernest Schwaiger, died in 1976, and some 10 years later Dixon moved from London to a retirement home in Sale, Greater Manchester.

● FILMS: *Uneasy Virtue* (1931), *The Happy Husband* (1932), *Calling The Tune* (1936), *Banana Ridge* (1941), *Woman To Woman* (1947).

Dixon, Bill

b. William Robert Dixon, 5 October 1925, Nantucket Island, Massachusetts, USA. Though born of the generation that brought bebop to fruition, Dixon did not rise to prominence until the early 60s, when he emerged as one of the leading pioneers of the new music. He grew up in New York, started on trumpet at the age of 18, studied painting at Boston University and then attended the Hartnott School of Music (1946-51). In the 50s he freelanced in the New York area as a trumpeter and arranger, and struck up friendships with **Cecil Taylor** and, later, **Archie Shepp**, with whom he co-led a quartet and helped to found the New York Contemporary Five (which also featured **Don Cherry**, **John Tchicai** and **J.C. Moses**; Dixon himself never actually played with the group). In 1964 he organized the October Revolution—six nights of concerts by young *avant gardists* such as Taylor, Shepp, **Roswell Rudd**, **Paul Bley**, **Milford Graves** and the not-so-young **Sun Ra**—which is generally acknowledged as the event that gave the New Thing its identity as a movement. Its success led him to form the short-lived Jazz Composers Guild, one of the first musicians' self-help organizations (its history is recounted in Val Wilmer's *As Serious As Your Life*).

In 1965 Dixon met dancer/choreographer Judith Dunn, with whom he worked for many years, their first notable collaboration being at the **Newport Jazz Festival** in 1966. That same year Dixon played on Taylor's *Conquistidor*, his tersely lyrical style a rare counterweight to the pianist's volcanic energy, and also recorded his own *Intents And Purposes*, with tracks by a 10-piece orchestra, a quintet and two brief, overdubbed solo pieces. Dixon's insistence on total artistic control over his music and its presentation meant that *Intents And Purposes* (on **RCA Records**) remained the only recording he was able to release on a major USA label. Already known as a teacher of art history, he became involved in music education, helping to initiate New York's University of the Streets community programme and, in 1968, taking up a teaching post at Bennington College in Vermont, where he set up a Black Music department (and where he continues to work). In 1976 he was invited to perform at the Paris Autumn Festival, where he premiered his 'Autumn Sequences From A Paris Diary' over five days with regular associates Stephen Horenstein (saxophones) and bass player **Alan Silva**. Throughout the 70s and 80s, Dixon continued to recording his music himself, a little of which has appeared on European labels such as **Soul Note Records** and Fore, while a limited-edition two-album box-set of his solo music was released by the independent USA Cadence label in 1985.

A painter too, who has exhibited widely in Europe and the USA, Dixon's music could be described as painterly, though its attention to form, line, texture and colour is as much the mark of a composer (and of a superb instrumental technique). His musical evocations of times, seasons, moods etc. are more abstract than representational, and record titles such as *Considerations* and *Thoughts* indicate the essentially reflective quality of his music. In his small-group recordings he has often shown a preference for darker sonorities,

sometimes using two or three bass players, and the results are remarkable for their balance of intellectual freight, sensitivity to nuance and implicit structural coherence. One of America's most original, and neglected, instrumentalist/composers, Dixon published *L'Opera* in 1986, a collection of letters, writings, musical scores and drawings.

● ALBUMS: with Archie Shepp *The Archie Shepp-Bill Dixon Quartet* (Savoy Jazz 1962) ★★★★, with Shepp *Archie Shepp & The New York Contemporary 5/The Bill Dixon 7-Tette* (Savoy Jazz 1964) ★★★, *Intents And Purposes* (RCA Victor 1967) ★★★★, with Franz Koglmann *Opium/For Franz* (Pipe 1976) ★★★, *In Italy—Volume One* (Soul Note 1980) ★★★★, *In Italy—Volume Two* (Soul Note 1981) ★★★, *Considerations 1* 1972-76 recordings (Raretone 1981) ★★★, *Considerations 2* 1972-76 recordings (Raretone 1981) ★★★, *November 1981* (Soul Note 1982) ★★★★, *Collection* box set (Cadence 1985) ★★★★, *Thoughts* 1985 recording (Soul Note 1987) ★★★, *Son Of Sisyphus* 1988 recording (Soul Note 1990) ★★★, *Vade Mecum* 1993 recording (Soul Note 1995) ★★★★, with the Tony Oxley Celebration Orchestra *The Enchanted Messenger: Live From The Berlin Jazz Festival* (Soul Note 1997) ★★★, *Vade Mecum II* 1993 recording (Soul Note 1997) ★★★★, with Tony Oxley *Papyrus Volume 1* (Soul Note 2000) ★★★★, *Papyrus Volume 2* (Soul Note 2000) ★★★, *Berlin Abbozzi* (FMP 2001) ★★★.

● FURTHER READING: *L'Opera*, Bill Dixon.

Dixon, Charlie

b. *c*.1898, Jersey City, New Jersey, USA, d. 6 December 1940, New York City, New York, USA. In 1922, banjo player Dixon joined the orchestra of **Sam Wooding** before moving on to play with **Fletcher Henderson**. Although often overlooked in potted accounts of the development of big band music, Dixon was a skilled arranger and provided many musical scores for the Henderson band, which helped establish it as the forerunner of the commercial successes of the swing era. After leaving the band he continued in music mostly as an arranger. During the next few years he wrote for Henderson and, notably, **Chick Webb**, for whom he arranged 'That Naughty Waltz' and 'Harlem Congo'.

Dixon, Don

Better known as producer to a generation of influential US pop rock bands (**R.E.M.**, **Smithereens**, **Let's Active**), Dixon toiled for 14 years as part of North Carolina's Arrogance before releasing his solo album in 1985. This wonderfully titled debut consisted partly of leftover Arrogance tracks, as well as several other cast-offs and demos from Dixon's recent history. Clearly evident, as with all his recordings, was his abiding affection for clean-cut 60s pop. Guests included Mitch Easter on a version of **Nick Lowe**'s 'Skin Deep'. Indeed, if Dixon has a UK equivalent then it is probably Lowe, whose wry sense of humour is possibly an influence on the ironic nostalgia of the title track. Spongetones guitarist Jamie Hoover, Dixon's wife Marti Jones and Easter all played on *Romeo At Juilliard*, an album that fulfilled the promise of the debut with a more fully realized and better-produced collection of pop songs. Picking from a vast canon of songs, Dixon used this set to reassert his credentials as a fine singer-songwriter, rather than merely as the highly regarded right-hand man of better-known artists. The strength of these and previous compositions allowed them to work well live, and this was confirmed by the release of *Chi-Town Budget Show* in 1988. Both this and the subsequent studio album were illuminated by powerful duets with Marti Jones, with *EEE* featuring more forceful instrumentation (notably brass) as Dixon pursued a commercially appetizing pop-soul direction. That he did so without sacrificing the quality, added further to his growing reputation.

● ALBUMS: *Most Of The Girls Like To Dance But Only Some Of The Boys Like To* (Enigma 1985) ★★★, *Romeo At Juilliard* (Enigma 1987) ★★★★, *Chi-Town Budget Show* (Restless 1989) ★★★, *EEE* (Enigma 1989) ★★★, *Romantic Depressive* (Sugar Hill 1995) ★★★.

● COMPILATIONS: *I'm A Ham, Well You're A Sausage* (Mau Mau 1992) ★★★.

Dixon, Eric

b. 28 March 1930, New York City, New York, USA, d. 19 October 1989, New York, USA. Through his early teens Dixon studied the tenor saxophone, then gained practical experience in a military band. After leaving the army he began working as a professional musician in New York, playing tenor in bands led by **Cootie Williams** and **Johnny Hodges**. During the late 50s he played in theatre orchestras and also toured Europe, working with various bands including one led by **Quincy Jones**. In 1961 he joined **Count Basie**, playing tenor and flute, remaining with the band for a decade. During this period he appeared often on record with the band, including *On My Way And Shoutin' Again*, and also in small group recordings with **Roy Eldridge**, including 1966's *The Nifty Cat Strikes West*. After a three-year retirement, Dixon rejoined Basie in 1975 and was still there in 1984 when the leader died. Subsequently, he played in the posthumous Count Basie Band. A sound section player and a fluent improviser, Dixon contributed numerous striking solos during his long periods with Basie.

● ALBUMS: *Eric's Edge* (Master Jazz 1974) ★★.

Dixon, Floyd

b. 8 February 1929, Marshall, Texas, USA. Dixon, aka J. Riggins Jnr., began playing piano and singing as a child, absorbing every influence from gospel and blues to jazz, and even hillbilly. In 1942 his family moved to Los Angeles and he came into contact with fellow ex-Texan **Charles Brown** who, sensing Dixon's potential, introduced him to his brand of cool, jazzy nightclub blues as singer and pianist with **Johnny Moore**'s Three Blazers. When the Blazers split up, Dixon was the natural choice for a substitute Charles Brown, and he made early recordings in the Brown style with both Eddie Williams (the Blazers' bass player) for Supreme and with Johnny Moore's new Blazers for **Aladdin** and Combo. His own trio recorded extensively for **Modern**, Peacock and Aladdin labels between 1947 and 1952; later, they played in a harder R&B style for **Specialty Records**, Cat and **Checker Records**, and in the late 50s and 60s for a host of tiny west coast and Texas independent labels. In 1975 Dixon made a comeback, beginning with a tour of Sweden and became the first artist to be featured on Jonas Bernholm's celebrated Route 66 reissue label. Dixon was commissioned to write 'Olympic Blues' for the 1984 Los Angeles games. In the 90s he surfaced on the **Alligator Records** label.

● ALBUMS: *Opportunity Blues* (Route 66 1980) ★★★, *Houston Jump* (Route 66 1980) ★★★, *Empty Stocking Blues* (Route 66 1985) ★★★★, *Hitsville Look Out, Here's Mr.*

Magnificent (1986) ★★★, *Wake Up And Live* (Alligator 1996) ★★★.

● COMPILATIONS: *Marshall Texas Is My Home* (Ace 1991) ★★★, *Cowtown Blues* (Ace 2000) ★★★.

Dixon, Fostina

b. c.1953, Delaware, USA. Taking her early musical inspiration from the church, Dixon began playing clarinet at school, later adding the baritone saxophone. After leaving school, she studied medicine but a year later changed track and began studying at **Berklee College Of Music**. There she added bass clarinet and flute to her instrumental range, eventually becoming adept also on alto and soprano saxophones. As a child she had listened to pop music, much of it **Motown Records**, and while still at Berklee she was hired to play in the band backing **Marvin Gaye** where she stayed for the next two years. Settling in Los Angeles, Dixon found work with several bands, backing artists such as **Sammy Davis Jnr.** and **Nancy Wilson**. She also formed a group of her own, named Collage, in which she pursued her own musical identity. She was also discovering jazz and gradually incorporating this into her work.

In addition to her considerable instrumental ability, Dixon is also a composer of distinction and a vocalist. With a broad appreciation of many varied musical forms, Dixon's commitment is total, and she is also eager to extend her audience by finding a style in both playing and composing that appeals beyond the merely intellectual. She is acutely aware of the strictures placed upon her as a woman in jazz, which, added to her being black, has placed unwarranted pressures upon her. Although she often works in groups with other women, including **Melba Liston** and Company, her band, Collage, happened to be all male. This was not from deliberate choice but occurred because the musicians whose sounds she felt to be compatible with her aural image of how the group should play were men.

Dixon, Jesse

b. San Antonio, Texas, USA. As a child, Dixon regularly attended church, though he admits this was more for the music he heard there than the sermons. He then attended St. Mary's College as a music major and met gospel legend **Rev. James Cleveland**. Cleveland invited him to travel to Chicago to join him as a vocalist and composer, working with the Cleveland Gospel Chimes Singers. From there he organized his own group, the Jesse Dixon Singers, who secured a recording contract with Savoy Records. Numerous gospel hit albums followed, including one, *He Ain't Heavy*, which was a Grammy nominee. Among the group's more successful singles were 'Sit At His Feet And Be Blessed', 'God Never Fails' and 'These Old Heavy Burdens'. However, it was only later in 1972 that he became what he terms 'a true convert to Christianity'. Since then he has appeared at many college concerts, as well as performing in such venues as Carnegie Hall, Madison Square Garden and Harlem's **Apollo** Theatre.

● ALBUMS: *He Ain't Heavy* (Savoy 60s) ★★★, *It's All Right Now* (Light 1978) ★★★.

Dixon, Lucille

b. 27 February 1923, New York City, New York, USA, d. 23 September 2004, New York City, New York, USA. Raised in Harlem where her father was a Baptist minister, Dixon was taught by her mother to play piano. Studying classical music, she at first wanted to play clarinet but switched to bass. Tutored by Frederick Zimmerman of the New York Philharmonic, she was selected for the All-City High School Orchestra and for the National Youth Association's Orchestra. Having studied at Brooklyn College she then attended Iona College and in 1942, while still a student, spent three months playing with the **International Sweethearts Of Rhythm**. Her colour restricted career options; symphony orchestras were out and she was unable even to audition for **Phil Spitalny**'s popular all-female orchestra. Opting for jazz, she joined the **Earl 'Fatha' Hines** band in 1943, remaining until 1945 when she settled in New York with her husband, trombonist Gus Chappell, and began raising a family. The following year, she formed a six-piece band she named the Starliners, becoming very successful in the city. Among several extended engagements was a 12-year residency at Club Savannah in Greenwich Village. Divorced and remarried, Dixon continued to lead bands in New York and among leading jazzmen of the day she employed were **Tyree Glenn**, **Taft Jordan**, **George Kelly**, **Fats Navarro**, **Sonny Payne** and **Buddy Tate**.

In addition to jazz, Dixon also played Latin and classical music. Her many classical orchestra affiliations include being a founder member, in 1964, and manager of the Symphony Of The New World. As a studio musician, she played in support of artists such as **Tony Bennett**, **Ella Fitzgerald**, **Frank Sinatra**, **Sarah Vaughan** and **Dinah Washington**, and for almost two decades was in pit bands for dozens of Broadway shows. In 1981 she was a member of an all-female quintet that played at Carnegie Hall as part of a presentation entitled 'Women Blow Their Own Horns'. She retired in 1996, but following the death of her second husband she played again, now as a member of a trio led by pianist Carli Muñoz. In addition to her busy playing schedule, Dixon was also active in social and cultural affairs and in particular with matters relating to racial prejudice in the music industry.

Dixon, Mary

A native of Texas, Dixon is otherwise a biographical blank. Her five records, made in New York in 1929, include a pop coupling, 'Dusky Stevedore' and 'I Can't Give You Anything But Love', but otherwise are exclusively blues, with interesting lyrics about sex, violence and superstition. They are distinguished by first-class jazz accompaniments. Her powerful singing voice has the distinctive nasal tone of many women from her native state, and her imitation of **Bubber Miley**'s growling trumpet is an arresting gimmick.

● COMPILATIONS: *The Complete Blues Sessions Of Gladys Bentley & Mary Dixon* (Collectors Classics 1988) ★★★.

Dixon, Mort

b. 20 March 1892, New York, USA, d. 23 March 1956, Bronxville, New York, USA. A leading lyricist for popular songs during the 20s and 30s, as a young man Dixon became an actor in vaudeville, and then served in France during World War I. After the war he directed the famous army show *Whiz Bang*, in France. He began to write songs in the early 20s, and in 1923 collaborated with **Ray Henderson** on 'That Old Gang Of Mine', which became a big hit for Billy Murray and Ed Smalle, and **Benny Krueger**, amongst others. Throughout the decade Dixon had more success with 'Wonder Who's Kissing Her Tonight?' and 'If I Had A Girl Like You' (both Krueger), 'Follow The Swallow' (**Al Jolson**),

'Bam, Bam, Bamy Shore' (**Ted Lewis**), 'Bye Bye Blackbird' (written with Henderson, and one of Dixon's biggest hits, for **Nick Lucas** and **Gene Austin**, and revived later by **Helen Merrill**), 'I'm Looking Over A Four Leaf Clover' (written with **Harry Woods**, and another of Dixon's most enduring numbers, especially in the Al Jolson version), 'Just Like A Butterfly' (Ipana Troubadors), 'Nagasaki' (written with Warren, and a song which epitomized the whole 20s flappers scene) and 'Where The Wild Flowers Grow'.

In 1928, 'If You Want A Rainbow (You Must Have The Rain)' (written by Dixon, **Billy Rose** and **Oscar Levant**) was included in the early talkie, *My Man*. This was followed by Billy Rose's Broadway revue *Sweet And Low* (1930), for which Dixon, **Harry Warren** and Rose wrote 'Would You Like To Take A Walk?'. When the show was re-staged the following year under the title of *Crazy Quilt*, 'I Found A Million-Dollar Baby (In A Five-And-Ten-Cent Store)' was added. Later the number was associated mostly with **Nat 'King' Cole** and was featured in the **Barbra Streisand** vehicle, *Funny Girl* (1975). Also in 1931, Morton, together with **Joe Young** and Warren, wrote 'Ooh! That Kiss', 'The Torch Song' and 'You're My Everything'. The latter became the title song of the 1949 movie starring **Dan Dailey** and **Anne Baxter** and was used even later by the popular UK entertainer, **Max Bygraves**, as the signature tune for his *Sing-Along-A-Max* television series. In the early 30s, Dixon collaborated with composer **Allie Wrubel** on the songs for several Warner Brothers movies.

For the spectacular *Dames* (1934), they merely added 'Try To See It My Way' to the existing Warren-Dubin score, but for *Flirtation Walk* they wrote 'Mr And Mrs Is The Name', 'I See Two Lovers', 'When Do We Eat?' and the title song. Other Dixon-Wrubel scores included *Happiness Ahead* ('Pop! Goes Your Heart', 'All On Account Of A Strawberry Sundae' and the title song), *Sweet Music*, starring **Rudy Vallee** ('Fare Thee Well, Annabelle', 'The Snake Charmer'), *In Caliente* ('To Call You My Own', the title song and 'The Lady In Red'), *I Live For Love* ('Mine Alone', 'Silver Wings', 'I Wanna Play House', 'A Man Must Shave', and the title song) and *Broadway Hostess* ('He Was Her Man', 'Let It Be Me', 'Weary', 'Who But You' and 'Playboy Of Paris'). His other songs included 'Under The Ukelele Tree', 'I'm In Love With You, That's Why', 'Is It Possible?', 'Moonbeam', 'In The Sing Song Sycamore Tree', 'Where The Forget-Me-Nots Remember', 'River, Stay 'Way From My Door' (a hit in 1931 for **Ethel Waters** and **Kate Smith**, and revived by **Frank Sinatra** over 20 years later), 'Pink Elephants' (George Olsen and **Guy Lombardo**), 'I Raised My Hat', 'Marching Along Together', 'So Nice Seeing You Again', 'Toddlin' Along With You', 'Did You Mean It?', 'Every Once In A While' and 'Tears From My Inkwell'. In the late 30s, Dixon's output declined, and he retired early to live in Westchester County, New York.

Dixon, Reginald

b. 1905, Sheffield, England, d. 9 May 1985, Blackpool, Lancashire, England. The son of a craftsman in the local Sheffield steel industry, as a teenager Dixon played the organ in a Methodist church and provided the accompaniment for silent films. In 1930 he accepted the position of organist at the Tower Ballroom in Blackpool and stayed there—except for a spell in the RAF during World War II—for 40 years, until his retirement. Heralded by his much-loved signature tune 'Oh, I Do Like To Be Beside The Seaside', he came to be known as 'Mr. Blackpool' and was almost as famous as the Tower itself. However, his reputation also reached other areas of the UK through his frequent broadcasts and recordings of medleys of familiar popular tunes and light classical pieces.

● ALBUMS: *Presenting Reginald Dixon* (Columbia 1963) ★★★★, *Happy Memories Of Blackpool* (Encore 1964) ★★★, *Mr. Blackpool* (Columbia 1964) ★★★★, *Sing Along At The Tower* (Columbia 1966) ★★★, *Gala Night At The Tower* (Encore 1966) ★★★, *Great Organ Favourites* (Columbia 1967) ★★★, *At Your Request* (Columbia 1967) ★★★, *Meet Mr. Blackpool* (Columbia 1968) ★★★, *Beside The Seaside* (Columbia 1969) ★★★★, *Farewell Mr. Blackpool* (Columbia 1970) ★★★, *At The Movies* (One-Up 1976) ★★★, *Isn't This A Lovely Day* (EMI 1980) ★★★, *At The Wurlitzer Organ* (Ideal 1981) ★★★★, *Over The Waves* (EMI 1981) ★★★, *Blackpool Nights* (EMI 1985) ★★★★, *Fascinating Rhythm* (Burlington Records 1988) ★★★, *At The Organ Of The Tower Ballroom, Blackpool* (Ideal 1991) ★★★.

● COMPILATIONS: *World Of Reginald Dixon* (Decca 1969) ★★★★, *Magic Of Reginald Dixon* (MFP 1987) ★★★.

● FURTHER READING: *Mr Blackpool: Reginald Dixon MBE*, Peter Ashman.

Dixon, Willie

b. 1 July 1915, Vicksburg, Mississippi, USA, d. 29 January 1992, Burbank, California, USA. At an early age Dixon was interested in both words and music, writing lyrics and admiring the playing of **Little Brother Montgomery**. As an adolescent, Dixon sang bass with local gospel groups, had some confrontation with the law and hoboed his way to Chicago, where he became a boxer. He entered music professionally after meeting **Baby Doo Caston**, and together they formed the **Five Breezes**, whose 1940 recordings blend blues, jazz, pop and the vocal group harmonies of the **Inkspots** and the **Mills Brothers**. During World War II, Dixon resisted the draft and was imprisoned for 10 months. After the war, he formed the Four Jumps Of Jive before reuniting with Caston in the **Big Three Trio**, who toured the Midwest and recorded for **Columbia Records**. The trio featured vocal harmonies and the jazz-influenced guitar work of Ollie Crawford.

Dixon's performing activities lessened as his involvement with **Chess Records** increased. By 1951 he was a full-time employee, as producer, A&R representative, session musician, talent scout, songwriter and occasionally, name artist. Apart from an interlude when he worked for Cobra in a similar capacity, Dixon remained with Chess until 1971. The relationship, however, was ultimately complex; he was forced to regain control of his copyrights by legal action. Meanwhile, Dixon was largely responsible for the sound of Chicago blues on Chess and Cobra, and of the black rock 'n' roll of **Chuck Berry** and **Bo Diddley**. He was also used on gospel sessions by Duke/Peacock, and his bass playing was excellent behind Rev. Robert Ballinger. Dixon's productions of his own songs included **Muddy Waters**' 'Hoochie Coochie Man', **Howlin' Wolf**'s 'Spoonful', Diddley's 'You Can't Judge A Book By The Cover', **Otis Rush**'s 'I Can't Quit You Baby' (a triumph for Dixon's and Rush's taste for minor chords) and **Koko Taylor**'s 'Wang Dang Doodle', among many others.

In the early 60s, Dixon teamed up with **Memphis Slim** to play the folk revival's notion of blues and operated as a booking agent and manager, in which role he was crucial to the American Folk Blues Festival Tours of Europe. Many British R&B bands recorded his songs, including the **Rolling Stones** and **Led Zeppelin**, who adapted 'You Need Love'. After leaving Chess, Dixon went into independent production with his own labels, Yambo and Spoonful, and resumed a recording and performing career. He also administered the Blues Heaven Foundation, a charity that aimed to promote awareness of the blues and to rectify the financial injustices of the past. Willie Dixon claimed, 'I am the blues'; and he was, certainly, hugely important in its history, not only as a great songwriter, but also as a producer, performer and mediator between artists and record companies.

● ALBUMS: *Willie's Blues* (Bluesville 1959) ★★★, *Memphis Slim & Willie Dixon At The Village Gate* (Folkways 1962) ★★★★, *I Am The Blues* (Columbia 1970) ★★★, *Peace* (Yambo 1971) ★★★, *Catalyst* (Ovation 1973) ★★★, *Mighty Earthquake And Hurricane* (Chase 1983) ★★★, *Hidden Charms* (Bug 1988) ★★★, with Hubert Sumlin, Sunnyland Slim *Blues Anytime!* 1964 recording (Evidence 1994) ★★★.

● COMPILATIONS: *Collection* (Deja Vu 1987) ★★★, *The Chess Box* box set (Chess 1988) ★★★★, *The Original Wang Dang Doodle: The Chess Recordings & More* (MCA/Chess 1995) ★★★★, *Poet Of The Blues* (Columbia/Legacy 1998) ★★★★, *The Songs Of Willie Dixon* tribute album (Telarc 1999) ★★, *Mr. Dixon's Workshop* (Fuel 2000 2001) ★★★.

● FURTHER READING: *I Am The Blues*, Willie Dixon.

DIY

Nottingham, England–based party collective, populated by numerous contributors, the best known of which are Harry, Damien, Digs and Woosh. 'Our main intention from the start was really to be able to do our own thing . . . rather than having to pander to club owners, record labels, managers or whoever.' Their releases include the *Duster* EP and the acclaimed 'Shock Disco Invasion'. Their debut album numbered some 14 assorted DJs, remixers and musicians working in a spirit of collective adventure. The title of *Strictly 4 Groovers* also doubled as the name of their record company. In 1994 the group recorded a split single with **Chumbawamba** to protest at the Criminal Justice Bill, and launched a second imprint, Spacehopper, for hip-hop/funk projects.

● ALBUMS: *Strictly 4 Groovers* (Warp 1993) ★★★.

Dizzee Rascal

b. Dylan Mills, 1984, London, England. In September 2003, Dizzee Rascal's stunning debut, *Boy In Da Corner*, was the surprise (but deserving) winner of the UK's Mercury Music Prize, the second consecutive album (following the success of **Ms. Dynamite**'s debut, *A Little Deeper*) to receive the accolade to have originated from the UK urban music scene.

Mills is reported to have admitted that prior to music making he was 'a bit of a naughty boy' at Langdown Park School in Bow, east London. He was excluded from every class at school with the exception of music, where the teacher Mr. Smith saw his potential and encouraged him to create music on a school computer (Smith was thanked on the sleeve of *Boy In Da Corner* with the words 'I'll never forget da way you kept your faith in me, even when things looked grim.'). 'Music was the only option available to me,' Mills has recalled, 'I put all my energies into it. [Otherwise] I'd have ended up carrying on a life of crime.'

Although Mills distances himself from any genre ('It ain't UK garage so get used to it', he declares on b-side 'Vexed'), the sometime Roll Deep Crew member undoubtedly comes from a garage-inspired UK MC tradition. Mills himself credits his mutated take on garage to the simple fact that in the context of pirate radio, his panicked yelp sounded ineffective over blaring garage music: he had to create a new music to suit his voice. Looking beyond garage's aspirational aesthetic, however, *Boy In Da Corner* frequently sounded like a lament for a prematurely finished childhood: 'We used to fight with kids from other estates/Now eight millimetres settle debates' ('Brand New Day'). Rascal's remarkable first single, 'I Luv U', meanwhile, hung on a duet/argument (with Jeanine Jacques) about whether he was the father of a 15-year-old's child. Elsewhere, as on opening track 'Sittin' Here', Mills frequently sounds on the verge of tears.

Mills' voice and music have been compared to artists as implausible as **David Sylvian** and Kurt Cobain. His voice shares a similar sense of vulnerability and desperation to the **Nirvana** front man. 'There was something rugged and rebellious about them,' says Mills of the latter's surprisingly acknowledged influence, in *The Guardian* newspaper, 'Kurt Cobain, he was just heavy.' The melodies of tracks such as 'Sittin' Here', meanwhile, seemed to echo Sylvian/**Ryûichi Sakamoto** compositions, albeit juxtaposed with the sounds of police sirens and distant gunshots. A more apt comparison point might be trip-hop pioneer **Tricky**. Dizzee Rascal's grimy and dystopian debut shared the latter's sense of paranoia, claustrophobia and ability to unsettle.

In the same week *Boy In Da Corner* was released, Mills was stabbed five times in the popular Cyprian summer clubbing resort of Ayia Napa. Despite rumours that his follow-up album would take a more US-friendly approach, there was little on *Showtime* that indicated a willingness to pander to a commercial market. Recorded quickly and released barely a year after *Boy In Da Corner*, Dizzee Rascal's new album confirmed his standing as one of the most important of the new generation of UK rappers.

● ALBUMS: *Boy In Da Corner* (Dirty Stank/XL Recordings 2003) ★★★★, *Showtime* (XL Recordings 2004) ★★★.

Dizzy Miss Lizzy

Danish hard rock band Dizzy Miss Lizzy made a huge domestic impact with the release of their self-titled debut album in 1994. Sales of 180,000 units (equivalent to triple platinum status in Denmark) made it the biggest-selling debut of all time in that country. It later won two Danish Grammy Awards. The group were also hugely successful in Japan, touring there in 1995 and recording a live album in Osaka, the modestly titled *One Guitar, One Bass And One Drummer—That's Really All It Takes*, for release in that territory. Guitarist/vocalist Tim Christensen took the group back to the studio in November 1996—this time Abbey Road, London, with producer Nick Foss. On this occasion there were more rough edges left in the final mix, though the album again took the Danish charts by storm, while reaching a mainstream European audience outside of Scandinavia for the first time.

● ALBUMS: *Dizzy Miss Lizzy* (EMI-Medley 1994) ★★★, *One Guitar, One Bass And One Drummer—That's Really All*

It Takes (EMI Japan 1995) ★★★, *Rotator* (EMI-Medley 1996) ★★★.

DJ Assault

Drawing inspiration from the Miami music makers of the 80s (such as **2 Live Crew**) and the Chicago ghetto **house** scene of the 90s, Detroit, Michigan, USA–based DJ Assault—production team Ade Mainor alias Mr De and Craig Adams aka DJ Assault—create a bass heavy hybrid of **techno**, **electro**, R&B, funk and soul dubbed 'booty bass', 'ghetto tech' or 'Detroit bass'. Track titles include 'Ass N Titties', 'Drop Dem Panties', 'Big Bootie Hoes And Sluts Too' and 'Asses Jigglin'', but this speaker-quaking party music is as sonically thrilling as it is morally remiss. There is an overtly sexual motivation behind DJ Assault's music and, accordingly, De and Assault eulogize their local strip joints: 'Strip clubs are different in Detroit,' claims De, 'Our strip club DJs are real DJs not just guys with two CD mixers.' Although their lyrics are generally permutations of 'ass', 'titties', 'clit', 'dick' and 'bitch', the duo surprisingly point to women as their core audience: 'If it wasn't for women none of the guys would come to the club,' reasons Adams, 'and women like to be naughty too'. De and Assault celebrated their local 'booty' through the creation of their groundbreaking *Straight Up Detroit Shit (SUDS)* series of mix-albums and their duo of labels, Assault Rifle and Electrofunk. Amusingly, however, Ade has admitted his mother is a preacher and the DJ himself claims to be deeply religious. 'As long as we're making money and it ain't illegal, our parents don't mind . . . well, my mother likes the music, not the words.' The duo dissolved their partnership in summer 2000, with Adams going on to launch his own Jefferson Ave. imprint.

● ALBUMS: *Jefferson Ave* (Intuit-Solar 2003) ★★★.
● COMPILATIONS: *Straight Up Detroit Shit* (Electrofunk 1996) ★★★, *Straight Up Detroit Sh*t Vol. 2* (Electrofunk 1996) ★★★, *Straight Up Detroit Shit Volume 3* (Electrofunk 1997) ★★★, *Belle Isle Tech* (Assault Rifle 1997) ★★★, *Straight Up Detroit Shit Volume 4* (Electrofunk 1997) ★★★, *Straight Up Detroit Shit Volume 5* (Electrofunk 1998) ★★★, *Off The Chain For The Y2K* (Intuit 2000) ★★★.

DJ Biznizz

b. Billy Ntimih. Alongside the **Underdog** DJ Biznizz is the UK's leading rap producer, with most of the important UK artists (**Cookie Crew**, **London Posse**, **Caveman**, **Monie Love**, **MC Mell 'O'** and **Cash Crew**) having sought his favours. He has also remixed for the Cookie Crew ('Love Will Bring Us Back Together') and **House Of Pain** ('Jump Around') and established his PD3 and Points Proven collectives. The floating personnel involved in these two rallying groups are fascinating in themselves. Byron the Greek is co-owner of the Hitt Recording Studio and had previously worked as a rock guitarist. Cutch is a session drummer, and Dego has worked with DJ Silk Worm of **Digable Planets** and is now part of the production team. Female vocalist Face has provided backing to **Don-E** and **Gabrielle** as well as rap artists **Son Of Noise**, MC Mell 'O' and **London Posse**. Fly was once in rap group Rap Conscious, while Niles Hailstones had previously worked with reggae artists such as **Misty In Roots**, **Mad Professor** and **Delroy Wilson**. Ola The Soul Controller is an expatriate Canadian rapper. Together with DJ Biznizz this personnel has been responsible for a number of releases.

● ALBUMS: *Does Anybody Really Know What Time It Is?* (Syncopated Productions 1993) ★★★.

DJ Cam

b. Laurent Daumail, Paris, France. Daumail is a respected artist who has done much to raise the profile of the French hip-hop scene and is a one-man embodiment of beathead and turntablist culture, pushing artistic boundaries of hip-hop as far as he can. Daumail grew up with the influence of a jazz aficionado father and a mother who was a fan of classical music. These influences, along with Daumail's extensive knowledge of 70s US funk, can be heard in his eclectic, beat-driven sound, which has drawn comparisons to the established sound of the UK's **Mo' Wax Records**. Daumail developed a passion for rap as a teenager in the early 90s, and he immersed himself in hip-hop culture, forming the Les Erotic Warriors crew with his high school friends and naming himself 'Cam'—meaning 'already'. He also became a prolific graffiti artist and became a fan of US artists such as **Eric B And Rakim** and **Public Enemy**. It was the jazz-inflected breaks of **DJ Premier** and **Gang Starr** that proved to be his most powerful source of inspiration. His 1995 debut, *Underground Vibes* (on his own label, Street Jazz, later renamed Inflamable) was praised by the critics, but it was his groundbreaking set, *Underground Live Act* that was acclaimed as one of the most important live mix albums ever made. The set melds **Miles Davis**' trumpet sounds with slamming breakbeats and improvised reconstructions of his own studio tracks. The French revolution in **dance music** that occurred in the second half of the 90s boosted Cam's profile and career, his name being associated with other credible French acts such as **Air**, **Motorbass**, La Funk Mob and Mighty Bop. *Substances* from 1996 was something of a departure, experimenting as it did with **house**, **jungle** and ambient styles.

The ensuing *The Beat Assassinated* introduced some new influences to Cam's sound, namely **ragga** and drum 'n' bass and MCs from New York, the UK and France. *Loa Project*, his 2000 album demonstrated a return to his first love, instrumental, jazzy hip-hop but was also partly inspired by the positive aspects of voodoo, the African religion. Cam studied the religion for two years, visiting Mauritius and the island of Réunion and the Haitian community in Canada. He made recordings of live percussion and steel bands and incorporated the sounds into *Loa Project*. His remix credits include Air, **DJ Vadim**, Tek 9 and **Jean-Michel Jarre**.

● ALBUMS: *Underground Vibes* (Street Jazz 1995) ★★★, *Underground Live Act* (Inflamable 1996) ★★★★, *Substances* (Inflamable/Columbia 1996) ★★★, *The Beat Assassinated* (Inflamable/Columbia 1998) ★★★★, *Loa Project* (Six Degrees 2000) ★★★★.

● COMPILATIONS: *Mad Blunted Jazz* (Shadow 1996) ★★★★, *DJ-Kicks* (Studio !K7 1997) ★★★★, *The French Connection* (Shadow 2000) ★★★★.

DJ Cheb I Sabbah

b. 7 August 1947, Constantine, Algeria. Born into a family of classical Algerian musicians, Sabbah moved to Paris as a teenager and took up DJing, playing soul and R&B in Parisian nightclubs in the early 60s. Subsequently he alternated between DJing and working in the theatre, including a stint in the 70s with the experimental Living Theater Company, through which he met beat poet and artist Brion Gysin, whose experiments with 'cut up' were a strong influence on the way in which Sabbah worked. The beginning of the 80s saw a move back to DJing in Paris, playing predominantly Brazilian music. Towards the end of the decade he moved to California, USA, where he found a receptive audience for his favoured mixture of Arabic, African and Indian music. In the 90s he hooked up with the trumpeter **Don Cherry** (who he had first met 20 years earlier while with the Living Theater Company). Initially, Sabbah developed a theatrical element to compliment Cherry's music, then played records between the live sets and subsequently played tunes over which the musicians improvised. Leaving Cherry, Sabbah produced a number of remixes for other artists and an album which blended poetry, free jazz and Sufi trance music from Morocco. He also performed in numerous live shows with musicians from around the world, where he would DJ before and after the live sets and mix videos and dancers with the live performance. These were based around wherever the musicians were from. *Shri Durga*, his international debut, featured a group of highly respected Northern Indian and Pakistani classical musicians and singers performing traditional ragas over understated and sympathetic backing, with the emphasis on allowing the live performers space to shine. *Maha Maya* was a remix album with tracks from *Shri Durga* remodelled by Anglo-Asian producers including State Of Bengal, **T.J. Rhemi**, **Bally Sagoo** and **Fun-Da-Mental**.

● ALBUMS: *Shri Durga* (Nation 1999) ★★★★, *Maha Maya* (Nation 2000) ★★★, *Krishna Lila* (Six Degrees 2002) ★★★.

DJ Clue?

b. Queens, New York City, USA. Alongside his peer **Funkmaster Flex** one of New York's most prominent hip-hop DJs, Clue? made his national breakthrough in the late 90s with the platinum-selling, star-studded mix set, *The Professional*. He started off selling mix tapes on the streets of Queens, earning a hot reputation with his 1990 debut *Clue #24*. A relentless series of bestselling tapes followed, characterized by his ear for digging out unreleased material. He graduated to radio in the mid-90s as host of Hot 97's nationally syndicated show. In 1998, he signed a recording contract with **Jay-Z**'s Roc-A-Fella imprint and was employed as in-house DJ. His major label debut *The Professional* called on a highly impressive cast of east coast MCs, including **DMX**, **Nas**, **Method Man**, **Foxy Brown**, **Cam'ron** and **Ma$e** among others, and featured several exclusive tracks. A DJing slot on Jay-Z's *Hard Knock Life* tour followed, captured for posterity on the *Backstage Mixtape* set. Released in late 2000, *The Professional 2* was an equally star-studded follow-up.

● ALBUMS: *The Professional* (Roc-A-Fella/Def Jam 1998) ★★★★, *Backstage Mixtape* (Roc-A-Fella/Def Jam 1999) ★★★, *The Professional 2* (Roc-A-Fella/Def Jam 2000) ★★★★.

● FILMS: *Backstage* (2000).

DJ Dag

This Frankfurt, Germany–based DJ/producer's many classic **dance music** releases include 'Sun Down' (released on **Eye Q** and credited to the Volunteer). One of the pre-eminent forces in the development of **trance**, he was originally based at the Dorian Gray club in Frankfurt before moving to **Sven Vath**'s Omen club in 1993. Dag was behind the chart success of Dance 2 Trance, a collaboration with Jam El Mar (of **Jam**

And Spoon) and vocalist Tony Clark, breaking the Top 40 with 'Power Of American Natives' and 'Take A Free Fall'. He worked with Jam El Mar on Peyote's 'Alcatraz' for **R&S Records** and in 1994 was purportedly purchasing land in Dakota in order to give it back to the indigenous population.

DJ Duke

An underground **dance music** DJ talent who exploded as a crossover proposition in the early 90s when 'Blow Your Whistle' became a chart fixture. Duke had served a long apprenticeship, however. He made his first record in 1990 on a white label, selling out of its first five hundred records shortly after. Faced with rejection from every record company he approached, he set up his own label. These have eventually expanded to include four separate imprints: Power Music Records (vocal tracks), Power Music Trax (**techno**), Sex Mania (sexually inspired **trance** themes, such as Erotic Moments' 'Touch Me') and DJ Exclusive (for other artists)—housed under the collective Power Music umbrella. Group names exercised have included Inner Soul, Club People, The Music Choir, Tribal Liberation and The Pleasure Dome. As DJ Duke the follow-up to 'Blow Your Whistle' was 'Turn It Up', which again followed the route from club to chart.

DJ Flowers

One of the pioneering forces in the early 80s of the Brooklyn, New York City, USA, rap scene, DJ Flowers never progressed like peers such as **Grandmaster Flash** to recorded status. He was nevertheless an important presence in hip-hop's development as it grew from its base in warehouse club 'jams' and street-corner gatherings to an international pop medium. As legend has it, he would frequently perform live by hiring a friend to pedal a bicycle attached to his sound system, thereby acting as a generator, while he 'scratch mixed' old soul and R&B records on the record decks.

DJ Food

As part of **Coldcut**'s DJing angle on creating music, Jonathon Moore and Matt Black released a series of albums entitled *Jazz Brakes*, beginning in 1990 when they formed **Ninja Tune Records**, under the name DJ Food. Containing mainly funk and hip-hop instrumentals, often cut up with samples of bizarre dialogue, it was partly intended as material for mixing, remixing and producing. Volumes 4 and 5 (1993, 1994) were co-written with the producer PC (Patrick Carpenter) and developed the abstract hip-hop sound by incorporating shades of Latin, **dub**, **techno**, ambient, **jungle** and non-Western music. The two 12-inch records, *Refried Food*, in 1995, contained mixes by **Autechre**, **Fila Brazilia** and **Ashley Beedle**, among others, and were collected onto one album the following year. PC and Strictly (Kevin Foakes) became more involved on *A Recipe For Disaster* (1995), and later took over the reins, still with the assistance of Coldcut. DJ Food present live sets during which PC works with Strictly on four decks.
● ALBUMS: *Jazz Brakes Vols. 1–5* (Ninja Tune 1990–94) ★★★★, *A Recipe For Disaster* (Ninja Tune 1995) ★★★, *Refried Food* (Ninja Tune 1996) ★★★, *Kaleidoscope* (Ninja Tune 2000) ★★★, *Quadraplex* (Ninja Tune 2001) ★★★.
● COMPILATIONS: with DK *Solid Steel Presents . . .* (Ninja Tune 2001) ★★★★.

DJ Format

b. Southampton, Hampshire, England. Although his first official release was not until 1997, DJ Format had already had seven years to refine his art. As he put it, 'I started sampling stuff around 1990 or 1991 when I got my equipment. When we were first trying to sample stuff, we were just going through our parents' record collections, just finding little bits and pieces.' During 1995 he played with Suspekt but the project proved to be shortlived. DJ Format then teamed up with Dave Paul at Bomb Hip Hop Records in the USA, which culminated in his first release, the underground favourite 'English Lesson'. In 1999, DJ Format became friendly with Pablo from the **Psychonauts** who put him in contact with **Mo' Wax Records**. The result of this was 'Last Bongo In Brighton' and a further two remixes, Nigo's 'March Of The General' and Major Forces' 'Re-Return To The Original Artform'. While working on his debut album in 2002 Format supported **DJ Shadow** on his UK tour, bringing him to the attention of his largest audience to date. DJ Format's *Music For The Mature B-Boy* was released to rave reviews in 2003. Featuring vocals from Chali 2na and Akil of **Jurassic 5**, Aspects, Abdominal and Fatski, the album earned comparisons to the work of fêted US turntablist Cut Chemist.
● ALBUMS: *Music For The Mature B-Boy* (Genuine 2003) ★★★★, *Presents A Right Earful* (Antidote 2004) ★★★, *If You Can't Join 'Em . . . Beat 'Em* (Genuine 2005) ★★★.

DJ Gusto

b. 28 July 1971, Trenton, New Jersey, USA. After initially working as a care assistant for the elderly and disabled, Gusto secured his first DJing job at the Funhouse in Trenton in 1990, abandoning plans to become a rapper. By the mid-90s he had launched his career as a recording artist, with singles including 'Disco's Revenge' (Manifesto Records) and 'Move The Drum' (Bullet Records). His remixes include **Shara Nelson**'s 'I Feel' for **Chrysalis Records**, and he also produced Roz White's 'Bad For Me'. In 1996 he began work on a full studio album for Manifesto and played a number of European dates at venues including Amsterdam's Escape Club. His preferred medium is contemporary funk and soul, with his set list regularly including classics from **Stevie Wonder** and **Diana Ross**.

DJ Hell

b. Helmut Geier, 1962, Traunstein, Bavaria, Germany. Producer, label boss and icon DJ Hell has been photographed by Karl Lagerfeld and has produced catwalk soundtracks for Paris Fashion Week. Deliberately inverting the idea that **techno** should be 'faceless' because he believes that he should share his musical knowledge and influence, DJ Hell has cultivated an image of a flashy international DJ gigolo (to appropriate the name of his record label) with a taste for the highlife.
Apparently spending his money on records in preference to food, the young Geier had initially begun playing punk, rock 'n' roll, pop, ska, hip-hop, new wave and disco and rapidly became a renowned DJ. In 1992, Hell was offered a recording contract by Belgium label **R&S Records** after ending a set at Berlin's Love Parade with his own track, 'My Definition Of House', that is based on a cello sample from a **David Byrne** and **Brian Eno** theatre production. Hell subsequently launched Disko B, the label that released most of his 90s recordings. Initially entitled Disko Bombs, the label was

originally intended as a **dance music** counterpart to Munich punk label Optimal Records, an association that echoed Hell's childhood fascination with the **Damned**'s *Damned Damned Damned*. In 1995, Hell launched International Deejay Gigolos, the iconic label mixing modern retro, flash, trash, glamour and sex and drawing from disco, Detroit techno, Chicago **house** and punk. By the new millennium, the roster of artists had expanded to include **Fischerspooner**, **Tuxedomoon**, **Miss Kittin**, **Jeff Mills** and **Dave Clarke**. Having released hits such as Mills' *Shifty Disco* EP, Christopher Just's 'I'm A Disco Dancer', Miss Kittin And The Hacker's *Champagne!* EP and Zombie Nation's 'Kernkraft 400', the label celebrated its 100th release by issuing a pair of knickers by the lingerie company, Agent Provocateur, in preference to the more usual anniversary retrospective.

Hell's Detroit-inspired 1994 debut, *Geteert & Gefedert*, was recorded with Mijk Van Dyk and Disko B labelmate Richard Bartz. His second release *Munich Machine* was preceded by a mix compilation *Wildstyle* that asserted the DJ Hell aesthetic with tracks by Random Noise Generator, **Surgeon** and **Bobby Konders**. Deriving its name (as well as its most overt sonic influence) from the title of a **Giorgio Moroder** project from the 70s, *Munich Machine*, it featured covers of the Normal's 'Warm Leatherette' and No More's 'Suicide Commando', as well as a beefy cover version of **Barry Manilow**'s 'Copacabana (At The Copa)'. Rejecting techno's penchant for minimal artwork, the album sleeve featured Hell posing with bikini-clad women. The single, 'This Is For You', notably featured the voice of **Chicks On Speed**'s Melissa Logan as well as references to Slim-Fast, bathrobes and Wall Street.

Hell's 2002 mix compilation *Electronicbody-Housemusic* seemed to be a deliberate reaction to the electroclash scene he had become associated with, eschewing such electro pop in favour of electronic house from the Kompakt and Playhouse labels as well as brutal electronic body music from the likes of **Nitzer Ebb**, **Front 242** and Terrence Fixmer.

● ALBUMS: *Geteert & Gefedert* (Disko B 1994) ★★★, *Munich Machine* (Disko B 1998) ★★★, *NY Muscle* (International Deejay Gigolos 2004) ★★★.

● COMPILATIONS: *X-Mix, Vol. 5: Wildstyle* (!K7 1996) ★★★★, *Fuse Presents Hell* (Music Man 2000) ★★★, *Presents International Deejay Gigolos* (International Deejay Gigolos 2001) ★★★★, *Electronicbody-Housemusic* (React 2002) ★★★.

DJ Hollywood

Just like **DJ Flowers** and **Kool Herc**, Hollywood was one of the earliest DJ/MC rap artists, yet one whose legacy does not confer his true status because his performances predated rap recordings (the posthumous 'Um Tang Tum Tang' aside). His background was as a compere at the Apollo Theatre in Harlem, where he chatted over disco records between performers. **Grandmaster Flash** remembers him as 'one of the greatest solo rappers that ever there was' for his later performances at venues including Club 371.

DJ Hurricane

b. Wendell Fite, USA. The **Beastie Boys**' long-standing musical collaborator, DJ Hurricane finally made his solo debut in 1995 but boasted a much longer history in hip-hop. Before joining the Beastie Boys in 1986, Hurricane had been part of the Solo Sounds—the first ever rap group in Hollis, Queens, New York City, (even pre-dating **Run DMC**). While with the Beasties he was also a component of the entertaining **Afros** sideshow. His debut solo album used more up-to-date moves, however, with the strong rhythmic influence being **Cypress Hill** (Sen Dog guested on one track, 'Feel The Blast'). Other guests included **MC Breed** ('What's Really Going On' and newcomer Tye Bud ('Comin' O-F-F'). The Beastie Boys themselves turned in a strong performance for the agenda-setting 'Four Fly Guys', while Beastie associate Mario Caldato Jnr. provided production. Hurricane returned in 1997 with the harder-hitting *Severe Damage*.

● ALBUMS: *The Hurra* (Wiija 1995) ★★★★, *Severe Damage* (Wiija 1997) ★★★, *Don't Sleep* (TVT 2000) ★★★.

DJ Hype
(see **Ganja Kru**)

DJ Hyper

b. Guy Hatfield, Lincoln, Lincolnshire, England. A contemporary of **Adam Freeland** and **Tayo**, Hatfield is also a rising star of the progressive breakbeat or nu-skool breaks scene. Hatfield left his home town of Lincoln and a job making garden sheds to relocate to London and take up a position with Sony Music. He also established his own promotions company at this time, Waxworks, working with the PuSH and TCR labels and artists such as **Hybrid** who were part of the emergent progressive breakbeat scene of the time. Hatfield began DJing with the Tyrant **sound system** and continues a relationship with Lee Burridge and Craig Richards. Hatfield's sound caught the attention of progressive **house** godfather, **John Digweed**, who engaged him as a resident in the backroom of his highly successful 'Bedrock' night at London's Heaven. Hatfield's mission to educate club audiences on the delights of breakbeat was embodied on his mix album *Y3K > Deep Progressive Breaks* for Distinctive Breaks. The mix was very well received by the **dance music** press and was given the Album Of The Month accolade by many of the leading industry magazines. The mix featured breakbeat tracks and mixes by progressive luminaries such as **BT**, **Sasha**, **Way Out West** and Hybrid. Hatfield can be found remixing for other artists, producing his own tracks, DJing and reviewing singles for several magazines.

● COMPILATIONS: *Y3K > Deep Progressive Breaks* (Distinctive Breaks 2000) ★★★★, *Bedrock Breaks* (Bedrock 2002) ★★★.

DJ International

Alongside **Trax Records**, DJ International was the pivotal label in documenting the rise of Chicago **house** music (priding itself on never releasing anything in a different musical category). The imprint was founded in the late 80s by DJ Rocky Jones and picked up on DJ artists such as **Mr. Fingers** ('Mystery Of Love', 'You're Mine'), **Tyree** ('Tyree's Got A Brand New House' and, with Kool Rock Steady, 'Turn Up The Bass'), **Joe Smooth** ('Promised Land'), Sterling Void ('It's Alright'), Pete Black ('How Far I Go') and Fast Eddie ('Hip House', 'Get On Up', 'Let's Go', 'Yo Yo Get Funky'). On the ground floor of the label's premises was the Chicago Music Pool where promotional releases were distributed to DJs, thereby ensuring that the label kept its ear to the ground for new talent. The backroom stalwarts included Frankie 'Hollywood' Rodriguez, who produced much of the label's output as well as his own solo projects (including the jokey

Lincoln Boys). He also mixed for house radio show B96. Other prominent names were Julian Perez and Martin 'Boogieman' Luna, who recorded 'House Express'/'Pump It Up Homeboy', the latter forming the backbone of **D-Mob**'s 'Come And Get My Love'. Like many of the label's releases, it became sample-fodder to the European masses.

DJ Jazzy Jeff And The Fresh Prince

The Fresh Prince, aka **Will Smith** (b. Willard Christopher Smith Jnr., 25 September 1968, Philadelphia, Pennsylvania, USA) is now just as famous for his acting career, which started when he played the streetwise tough suffering culture shock when transplanted into the affluent Beverley Hills household of television series *The Fresh Prince of Bel Air*. However, this was initially very much a second career for Smith. Together with DJ Jazzy Jeff (b. Jeffrey Townes, 22 January 1965, Philadelphia, Pennsylvania, USA), this young duo had already recorded a highly successful debut album in 1987 and charted with the hit single 'Girls Ain't Nothing But Trouble'. Musically the duo operated in familiar territory, working a variety of inoffensive, borrowed styles to good effect and in marked contrast to the threatening 'street style' of other rap artists.

Jazzy Jeff started DJing in the mid-70s when he was a mere 10 years old (though he is not to be confused with the similarly titled **Jazzy Jeff** who recorded an album, also for **Jive Records**, in 1985). He was frequently referred to in those early days as the 'bathroom' DJ, because, hanging out with better-known elders, he would only be allowed to spin the decks when they took a toilet break. He met the Fresh Prince at a party, the two securing a recording contract after entering the 1986 New Music Seminar, where Jeff won the coveted Battle Of The Deejays. Embarking on a recording career, the obligatory **James Brown** lifts were placed next to steals from cartoon characters like Bugs Bunny, which gave some indication of their debut album's scope.

In the late 80s, DJ Jazzy Jeff And The Fresh Prince cemented their reputation with million-selling teen anthems such as 'Girls Ain't Nothing But Trouble', which sampled the *I Dream Of Jeannie* theme and was released three weeks before Smith graduated from high school. They became the first rap act to receive a Grammy Award for their second album's 'Parents Just Don't Understand', even though the ceremony was boycotted by most of the prominent hip-hop crews because it was not slated to be 'screened' as part of the television transmission. In its wake, the duo launched the world's first pop star 900 number (the pay-phone equivalent of the UK's 0898 system). By January 1989, 3 million calls had been logged. The duo's second album, *He's The DJ, I'm The Rapper*, contained more accessible pop fare, the sample of *Nightmare On Elm Street* being the closest they came to street-level hip-hop. The raps were made interesting, however, by the Fresh Prince's appropriation of a variety of personas. This is doubtless what encouraged the television bosses to make him an offer he could not refuse, and *The Fresh Prince Of Bel Air*'s enormous success certainly augmented his profile.

The duo picked up a second Grammy for 'Summertime' in 1991, before scoring a surprise UK number 1 in 1993 with 'Boom! Shake The Room', the first rap record (**Vanilla Ice** and **MC Hammer** aside) to top the British singles chart. The same year's *Code Red* was the duo's final album, with Smith electing to concentrate on his acting career. He moved seamlessly into dramatic film roles, beginning with *Where The Day Takes You* and *Six Degrees Of Separation* (1993), and reaching a peak with *Independence Day* (1996) and *Men In Black* (1997), two of the highest-grossing movies of all time. In 1997, Smith also released his debut solo album, the hugely successful *Big Willie Style*. Townes, meanwhile, formed A Touch Of Jazz Inc., a stable of producers working on rap/ R&B projects. His own production duties included **Jill Scott**'s debut, *Who Is Jill Scott?* He released his solo debut, *The Magnificent*, in August 2002.

● ALBUMS: *Rock The House* (Word Up 1987) ★★, *He's The DJ, I'm The Rapper* (Jive 1988) ★★★, *And In This Corner* (Jive 1990) ★★★, *Homebase* (Jive 1991) ★★★, *Code Red* (Jive 1993) ★★★.

● COMPILATIONS: *Greatest Hits* (Jive 1998) ★★★★, *Before The Willennium* (BMG 2000) ★★★.

DJ Jean

b. Jan Engelaar, 1971, Netherlands. DJ Jean is Holland's number one DJ/producer and initially became famous for his Friday night residency at the 'Madhouse' night at Amsterdam's It! Club. He also DJs across Europe, in Tel Aviv and in clubland's headquarters, **Ibiza**. Engelaar also has his own record label, It Records, and is an in-demand remixer for **Masters At Work**, Airscape and Full Intention. He also releases his own productions with recording partner, Peran, and hosts a Saturday night mix show on the Dutch national radio station, 538. His mix albums such as *Around The World With DJ Jean* and *Strictly DJ Jean* have reached number 1 in the Dutch charts. Engelaar's first two hit singles, 'U Got My Love' and 'The Launch' appeared on the Mo Bizz label, owned by his Dutch compatriots, the Klubbheads. It was the UK DJ, **'Tall' Paul Newman** who popularized 'The Launch' in UK clubs in March 1999, when it was only available as an import. Before long, other powerful figures in the UK **dance music** scene such as **Pete Tong** and **Judge Jules** were including it in their club sets and national radio shows. Almost laughably simple, the track was also enormously crowd-pleasing on the dancefloor and its distinctive horn fanfare became part of the soundtrack to a thousand Saturday nights all over Europe. Having already created a wave of interest through the clubs and radio during the summer, 'The Launch' was finally given a full UK release on the **Island**/ Universal dance imprint AM:PM in August 1999. DJ Jean made several appearances on UK television and at clubs and the record climbed to number 2 in the national charts in September 1999. It also appeared on numerous club-based mix compilations, retrospectives of the year and millennium dance music 'cash-ins'.

● COMPILATIONS: *Madhouse* (Visio 1999) ★★.

DJ Krush

b. Hideaki Ishii, Tokyo, Japan. DJ Krush is a leading figure on the Japanese hip-hop scene and one of **Mo' Wax Records**' most influential artists. As a result of seeing a Tokyo screening of the rap film *Wild Style*, he began DJing to accompany breakdancers and in 1987 formed the Krush Posse. Several releases in the early 90s passed with little recognition until he met **James Lavelle**, who signed Krush to Mo' Wax. His first release for that label was the track 'Kemuri', which appeared on a double a-side with **DJ Shadow**'s 'Lost And Found' in September 1994. This was followed the next month by the eagerly awaited *Strictly*

Turntablized. A collection of laid-back hip-hop beats with abstract jazz inflections, it received an enthusiastic response from both the public and the press. At the same time, Krush was also featured on Mo' Wax's *Headz* compilation (1994), helping to establish the label's unique sound. Since this time he has collaborated on a number of projects. The album *Meiso* featured a number of American rappers, including C.L. Smooth and Malika B (The Roots), and the stark texture of *Strictly Turntablized* was replaced by a more accessible, vocal-orientated sound. On *MiLight* Krush worked with the Japanese singer Eri Ohno, Deborah Anderson and others, producing a set of contemplative and positive tracks quite unlike much 'gangsta rap' of the time. *Ki-Oku* was an interesting collaboration with Japanese trumpeter Toshinori Kondo and included a version of **Bob Marley**'s 'Sun Is Shining'. Krush released *Holonic*, a mixed compilation of some of his previous work, in 1998. *Jaku* employed the use of Japanese instrumentation but failed to set the critics alight.

● ALBUMS: *Krush* (Chance 1993) ★★★, *Strictly Turntablized* (Mo' Wax 1994) ★★★★, *Meiso* (Mo' Wax 1995) ★★★, *MiLight* (Mo' Wax 1997) ★★★★, with Toshinori Kondo *Ki-Oku* (R&S 1998) ★★★, *Kakusei* (Sony 1998) ★★★, *Zen* (Red Ink/Sony 2001) ★★★★, *Shinsou: The Message At The Depth* (Red Ink/Sony 2003) ★★★, *Jaku* (Columbia 2004) ★★.

● COMPILATIONS: *Holonic* (Mo' Wax 1998) ★★★, *Code4109* (Sony 2000) ★★★.

DJ Luck And MC Neat

This production duo was one of the first recognized UK **garage** acts. Luck (b. Joel Samuels, Hackney, London, England) had already found a niche as a drum 'n' bass DJ, whereas Neat (b. Michael Anthony Rose, Hammersmith, London, England) gained experience as an MC on London pirate radio stations. It was at one of these stations that the two were introduced, and they began collaborating in 1998. The following year they completed 'A Little Bit Of Luck', an underground garage recording with cool strings and rapid MCing from Neat. Played incessantly in UK clubs, the instantly recognizable track grew to become a national Top 10 hit, selling over a quarter of a million copies and spawning a fresh wave of tracks in the relatively new UK garage genre. Vocalist J.J. featured on their second release, 'Masterblaster 2000', a take on **Stevie Wonder**'s 'Masterblaster (Jamming)', and originally issued as the b-side to 'A Little Bit Of Luck'. The third single, 'Ain't No Stoppin' Us', was a slightly more chilled recording. Samuels and Rose have compiled several mix albums for London-based radio station Kiss FM and signed an album contract with Universal Island at the end of 2000. Their frenzied activity on the UK live circuit has garnered them a considerable following.

● COMPILATIONS: *Presented By . . . DJ Luck & MC Neat* (Universal 2000) ★★★★, *DJ Luck & MC Neat Present . . . II* (Universal 2000) ★★★.

DJ Mark The 45 King

b. Mark James, 16 October 1961, USA. Rap DJ Mark The 45 King broke through in the late 80s with the breakbeat classic 'The 900 Number' but remains primarily known for his extensive work as a producer.

Raised in New York, the young Mark James got his first break working as a 'record boy' for DJ Breakout of the Funky Four, locating and passing records up to the decks as the DJ requested them. He worked as a DJ and producer during the mid-80s and gained notoriety though his involvement with Latee's 1987 track, 'This Cut's Got Flava'. The cut 'The 900 Number' was another tribute, in this case to the Akai 900 sampler. Based around a horn line sampled from Marva Whitney's 'Unwind Yourself', the track was a huge club smash and remains an enduring old school classic. He worked on releases by his own Flavor Unit crew and contributed heavily to Queen Latifah's acclaimed debut album, *All Hail The Queen*.

In the 90s, DJ Mark The 45 King went on to become a hip-hop backroom guru ranking alongside **Marley Marl** and Hank Shocklee. He recorded several solo releases for the Tuff City label and produced numerous breakbeat albums, including 1991's classic *The Lost Breakbeats Volume 1 & 2*. Despite ongoing personal problems, the producer bounced back at the end of the decade with high-profile work for **Jay-Z** ('Hard Knock Life') and **Eminem** ('Stan').

● ALBUMS: *Master Of The Game* (Tuff City 1988) ★★★★, *Rhythmical Madness* (Tuff City 1989) ★★★, *The 45 King Presents The Original Flavor Unit* (Tuff City 1990) ★★★, *The Lost Breakbeats Volume 1 & 2* (45 King 1991) ★★★★, *Tuff Ass Jazz* (Tuff City 1995) ★★★, *Zig*A*Zig*A*ZZ* (Tuff City 1995) ★★★, *Champain* (Tuff City 1997) ★★★, *Beats For The New Millennium* (45 King 2000) ★★★, with XR5 *In Rotation* (Innerground 2004) ★★★.

● COMPILATIONS: *45 Kingdom* (Tuff City 1990) ★★★★.

DJ Pete Jones

One of the earliest US hip-hop DJs, enjoying a residency at the 371 club in the late 70s and taking **Grandmaster Flash** under his wing, he also introduced **Afrika Bambaataa** by allowing him to play on his system. The latter adapted his 'switch' mechanism for changing channels on the decks to great effect, to all intents and purposes inventing 'scratch' DJing in the process.

DJ Pierre

b. Pierre Feroldi, USA. Beginning his DJing career in 1983, Pierre was his second choice of name after hosting a disastrous set under his original title. He would play at several early **Lil' Louis** parties before he was credited with developing **acid house**, alongside his collaborators Spanky and Herb J, in a Chicago basement in 1985. They had just purchased a bass machine, the Roland TB 303. Through a process of experimentation the 'acid squelch' sound came forth, which was recorded and passed on to DJ **Ron Hardy** to play at his Warehouse club. These quickly became known as Hardy's 'Acid Tracks' and the term stuck. The trio then re-recorded the track (now known as 'Acid Trax') with **Marshall Jefferson** on production duties. Released under the Phuture moniker in 1987, it became a huge club hit and an anthem of the burgeoning **acid house** scene in the UK.

Pierre went on to form Phuture Records, started in 1987, which consolidated on his invention with the hugely influential *Acid Trax* series. From there, his name first became synonymous with the Acid House movement, before he tired of Chicago and moved to New York to help establish the **Strictly Rhythm** empire. His work there in the capacity of A&R head, producer and artist was pivotal. Pierre's discography is a varied and prolific one, beginning with singles such as 'Annihilating Rhythm' (as Darkman), 'Masterblaster', 'Rise From Your Grave', 'Musik' and

'Generate Power'. In New York he perfected the 'Wyld Pitch' musical style, and in later years operated more as a free agent (releasing material like 'More Than Just A Chance' on the UK's **Vinyl Solution**, and 'I Might Be Leaving U' for Moving, which featured a vocal from LaVette), though he maintained links with Strictly Rhythm. He also remixed widely, his clients including Yo You Honey, Midi Rain and **DIY**. Not to be confused with the similarly titled DJ Pierre (Pierre Fieroldi) from Italy, who, along with **Gianfranco Bortolotti** was responsible for Euro hits by the 49ers, **Cappella** and others, plus his own tracks such as 'We Gonna Funk'. Various heated letters were exchanged between the two as confusion increased.

DJ Pogo

One of UK hip-hop's prime spinners of the early 90s, Pogo made his name through the World DJ Championships. From there he took on remix and production work for UK rap troupes such as **London Posse**, **Demon Boyz**, **MC Mell 'O'** and **Monie Love**, as well as US imports like **House Of Pain** and **Cypress Hill** and even the **Fine Young Cannibals**. This was in addition to his regular stints on London's Kiss FM Radio Station. He was also the prime mover behind PLZ (Party A La Mazon), together with Brooklyn born and bred duo Regi and Fredi, who had been operating out of London since 1987. Regi is a former dancer while Fredi is a business student turned rapper. They met Pogo in 1990, releasing their first record as PLZ two years later ('If It Ain't PLZ . . .'/'Bad Person' on Go For The Juggler Records). Producing positive industry reaction, it was followed by the *Build A Wall Around Your Dreams* EP and a debut long-playing set.
● ALBUMS: as PLZ *Parables And Linguistic Zlang, Volume One* (Go For The Juggler 1993) ★★★.

DJ Premier

The musical foundation of **Gang Starr**, DJ Premier (b. Chris Martin, 3 May 1969, Brooklyn, New York City, USA) also became one of hip-hop's most respected producers and remixers in his own right during the 80s. As a child his interest in music was demonstrated by the fact that he collected records from the age of four. Unlike many of the original producers, Premier learned his craft through technology and experimentation rather than the manual dexterity ethos of scratching ('I believe that sampling is an art form if you don't abuse it'). He recorded his first demos with Boston rapper MC Topski, and after Gang Starr's success there was no stopping him. Those artists who have benefited from the Premier production tradition include **Jeru The Damaja**, **Nas**, **KRS-One**, **Branford Marsalis**, **Da Youngstas**, **Neneh Cherry**, **Heavy D**, **Subsonic 2**, **Cookie Crew**, **K-Solo** and **Lady Of Rage**. His remix roster includes **Shyheim**, **Boss**, **Loose Ends**, **MC Solaar**, **Fat Joe** and **MOP**.

DJ Quik

b. David Blake, 18 January 1970, Compton, California, USA. Rap artist whose deification of his home-town, where he had grown up the youngest of ten children, pervaded both his first two albums ('Born And Raised In Compton' on his 1991 debut, and minor hit single 'Jus Lyke Compton' on the follow-up set). At the age of 12 Blake began to learn the art of DJing, but it wasn't until **N.W.A.** exploded on the west coast that he actually considered these skills might provide a career. He began recording cassettes, one of which found its

way into the hands of **Profile Records** A&R man Dave Moss, head of their newly opened Los Angeles office. His debut set saw comparisons to **Prince**, though in mode of operation rather than musical terms, with Quik writing, rapping, producing and arranging the set in its entirety. Rather than repeating the gangsta stance of his near-neighbours N.W.A. (though he claimed to be a former member of the Bloods gang), Quik confirmed that 'There's a fun side to Compton, too', reflecting this in songs about sex (the rather too obvious 'Sweet Black Pussy'—I'm like Noah's Ark, My bitches come in pairs'), alcohol ('8 Ball') and marijuana ('Tha Bombudd'). His biggest hit, however, came with the Top 50-breaking 'Tonite'. He also produced widely for Compton groups including **2nd II None** and Penthouse.

DJ Quik signed a distribution contract with the influential **Death Row Records** for his 1995 set, *Safe + Sound*, which borrowed even more heavily from **George Clinton**'s G-funk sound. By now his commercial star was on the wane, and despite a new contract with **Arista Records** in the late 90s, he was dropped following the flop 2000 release *Balance & Options*. The success of productions for **2Pac**, **Janet Jackson**, **Whitney Houston**, **Jay-Z**, **Ludacris**, **Dr. Dre**, **8Ball And MJG** and **Truth Hurts** helped keep Quik's name in the media spotlight, however, as did a prominent slot on Won-G's 2001 hit single 'Nothing's Wrong'. He continued to record as a solo artist in the new millennium, releasing the independent albums *Under Tha Influence* (2002) and *Trauma* (2005). Both albums saw Quik wisely dropping his G-funk obsession and drawing inspiration from the new generation of Dirty South rappers.
● ALBUMS: *Quik Is The Name* (Profile 1991) ★★★, *Way 2 Fonky* (Profile 1992) ★★, *Safe + Sound* (Profile 1995) ★★★, *Rhythm-Al-Ism* (Arista 1998) ★★★, *Balance & Options* (Arista 2000) ★★, *Under Tha Influence* (Ark 21 2002) ★★★, *Trauma* (Mad Science 2005) ★★★.
● COMPILATIONS: *The Best Of DJ Quik: Da Finale* (Arista 2002) ★★★★, *Platinum & Gold Collection* (Arista 2004) ★★★, *Born And Raised In Compton* (BMG 2005) ★★★.
● DVD/VIDEOS: *Visualism* (Image Entertainment 2003).

DJ Rap

b. Charrissa Saverio, 1969, Singapore. DJ Rap is one of the UK's leading female DJs and certainly the most high-profile female drum 'n' bass DJ. Born to an Italian father and an Irish-Malaysian mother, Saverio was brought up in many parts of the world and learned classical piano as a child. The family relocated to Southampton, England, when she was a teenager, where she discovered pop music. After leaving school, she modelled for two years and travelled in Europe, before returning to the UK and joining a legal firm in London. Her friends took her to a **rave**, and like many others, her life changed. After meeting budding producer Jeff B, they made a track 'Ambience—The Adored'. Written by Rap, it became a hit on the rave scene and elsewhere. Rap promoted the track by appearing on a few land-based pirate radio stations, including Rave FM, where she was taught to mix by Coolhand Flex, one of the original London 'junglists'. While at a **hardcore** night at London's Astoria, Rap was asked to fill in for the DJ Fabio when he did not appear for his set. She slowly began to establish her reputation and by 1993 had played at all the major raves in the UK, such as World Dance, Dreamscape, Lydd Airport and Rezerection. Rap continued to make her own productions and scored a dancefloor hit with 'Spiritual

Aura' in 1993. Its success prompted Rap to start her own label, Proper Talent, and a subsidiary in 1995, Low Key Recordings. She continues to DJ all over the world and is known for her eclectic taste and combination of gentle, ambient dreamscapes with tough breakbeats. She released her first album, *Intelligence*, on Proper Talent. Though it proved her to be an able writer and vocalist, the album was not a significant commercial success. In 1997, she signed to the Higher Ground label, home of **Grooverider** and **Leftfield**. Her debut for them, *Learning Curve*, was released in April 1999. It demonstrated a range of styles, live instrumentation, drum 'n' bass, **techno** and **trance**, and elicited positive reviews.

● ALBUMS: *Intelligence* (Proper Talent 1996) ★★, *Learning Curve* (Higher Ground 1999) ★★★.

DJ/rupture

b. Jace Clayton, Boston, Massachusetts, USA. DJ/rupture claims to spend 98 percent of his time producing his own tracks and working on original compositions but is predominantly known for his mix releases, *Gold Teeth Thief* and *Minesweeper Suite*. On the latter 2002 release, the Madrid, Spain–based DJ utilized around 60 records, three turntables and the opportunities of post-production tweaking to juxtapose music by Jamaican MCs and provocative female rap stars, post-rockers and iconic jazz singers, MOR balladeers and violent breakbeat artists, anti-music laptop provocateurs and recently deceased R&B superstars. Although these albums mix and match other people's seemingly disparate a cappella vocals and instrumentals, DJ/rupture distances himself from the bootleg or 'bastard pop' culture which looks to nostalgia and novelty value for its kicks. Unusually, DJ/rupture's mix collections thrill for their interference and noise as much as their perfect beat matching, giving equal footing to music from African, European, American and Arabic culture. Having relocated to Madrid in 1999, Clayton formed Soot Records, because no one else would release his music. Clayton says the label is 'a strike against geography', and is excited by artists who explicitly work with more than one musical tradition, especially those fluent in digital audio and indigenous traditional music. Among Soot's discography are releases by DJ/rupture himself, Nettle and Mutamassik. The latter is an Egyptian woman living in Brooklyn, exploring the shared resonances between Egyptian classical and street music and American hip-hop.

● ALBUMS: *Gold Teeth Thief* (Negrophonic/Violent Turd 2001) ★★★★, *Minesweeper Suite* (Tigerbeat6 2002) ★★★.

DJ S The Karminsky Experience

In the mid-90s a bizarre development occurred within London, England's club scene. Eschewing the more abrasive delights of jungle and techno, several clubs sprang up to regale crowds with the delights of 'easy listening' music. Among the most popular DJ teams in this context were brothers Martin and James Karminsky, who proudly used old **K-Tel Records** and **Matt Munro**/Klaus Wunderlich albums to form the basis of their playlists at clubs including Sound Spectrum and the Bamboo Curtain. As Martin elaborated, 'Maybe there's a trend towards more relaxed music. When people get in from a techno club they want to explore other musical areas.' This underground scene was brought to the mainstream at the end of 1995 when **Mike Flowers Pops**

recorded a version of **Oasis'** 'Wonderwall', which became a huge national hit. As a result **London Records** signed the brothers as DJ S The Karminsky Experience, releasing an album of their selections and mixes titled *In Flight Entertainment* in the early months of 1996. Selections included Brigitte Bardot's 'St. Tropez', Max Gregor's 'Big Train' and a version of the **Doors'** 'Light My Fire' performed by the **Edmundo Ros** Orchestra.

● ALBUMS: *In Flight Entertainment* (London 1996) ★★★.

DJ Screw

b. Robert Earl Davis Jnr., Houston, Texas, USA, d. 16 November 2000, Houston, Texas, USA. A leading figure on Houston's underground scene, Davis' contribution to the city's rise as a force on the rap scene was unfortunately overshadowed by his tragic overdose in 2000.

Davis began recording mix tapes as DJ Screw in the early 90s and had soon developed his trademark style: well-known tracks were 'screwed down' to a funereal pace, creating an eerie atmosphere reminiscent at times of the UK's trip-hop genre. The sound was directly influenced by Screw's advocacy of 'syrup sippin'', a southern rap phenomenon based around the drinking of codeine-laced cough syrup, which induces a sluggish, hallucinatory state in the user. Other advocates of the drug included **Three 6 Mafia**, who enjoyed a minor hit with 'Sippin' On Some Syrup'.

Screw recorded hundreds of mix tapes which he sold at his own Screwed Up Records And Tapes store. A flourishing underground scene developed around the store and the DJ's home studio, the Screw Shop. What became known as the Screwed Up Click included the rappers **Lil' Keke**, **Big Pokey** and **Big Moe**, all of whom made their name performing on DJ Screw's mix tapes. The DJ was found dead in his own studio on 30 November, the victim of a fatal heart attack. Ironically, the cause was an overdose of a mixture of drugs and the 'syrup' that he had so passionately advocated during his short life.

● COMPILATIONS: *3 'N The Mornin'* (Big Time 1995) ★★★, *3 'N The Mornin': Part Two* (Big Time 1996) ★★★, *All Work No Play* (Jam Down 1999) ★★★, *The Legend* (Big Time 2001) ★★★, *Sentimental Value* (Big Time 2002) ★★★, *All Work No Play: Volume 2* (Big Time 2002) ★★★, *All Work No Play: Volume 3* (Big Time 2002) ★★★.

DJ Shadow

b. Josh Davis, 1972, Hayward, California, USA. Self-proclaimed 'vinyl-addict and beat-head', DJ Shadow was turned on to hip-hop by **Grandmaster Flash**'s 'The Message' and later began compiling his own mix tapes. His first release on **Mo' Wax Records**, 'In/Flux'/'Hindsight' (1993), was seen by some as a benchmark in instrumental hip-hop and helped to define that label's approach. His second Mo' Wax single, 'Lost & Found', was released together with **DJ Krush**'s 'Kemuri' in 1994 and was followed by 'What Does Your Soul Look Like' the next year. Towards the end of 1996 he released his first album, *Endtroducing . . .* , as well as the singles 'Midnight In A Perfect World' and 'Stem', which brought him to the mainstream consciousness through coverage in the national press. The album was widely acclaimed for the way in which Davis blended hip-hop grooves with elements of jazz, rock, ambient, **techno** and other styles to create a unique, coherent sound that never resorted to the formulae of these influences. As with some of the more melodic instrumental hip-hop, compared to the humorous abstract collages of artists such as **DJ Food**, much of the album seemed deeply introspective and rather earnest, with its mournful cello, piano and organ melodies and sequences. This feeling was further emphasized by the raw production and the tendency towards slow tempos.

In 1997 Shadow DJed at the **Verve**'s appearance at Wembley Arena, as a result of working with **Richard Ashcroft** on **James Lavelle**'s **U.N.K.L.E.** project. Later that year, he released a set of his tracks performed by DJ Q-Bert (renowned for his technical mastery) entitled *Camel Bob Sled Race*. Davis has collaborated with other Mo' Wax artists, including **Blackalicious** and DJ Krush. Recording with old friends Blackalicious and Latyrx as Quannum, he released 1999's diversely entertaining *Spectrum*. The long-awaited follow-up to *Endtroducing . . .* was finally released in 2002, but *The Private Press* prompted the first mixed reviews of DJ Shadow's illustrious career.

● ALBUMS: *Endtroducing . . .* (Mo' Wax 1996) ★★★★, with Q-Bert *Camel Bob Sled Race (Q-Bert Mega Mix)* mini-album (Mo' Wax 1997) ★★★, *Pre-emptive Strike* (Mo' Wax 1998) ★★★, with Cut Chemist *Brainfreeze* (Sixty7 1999) ★★★★, with Cut Chemist *Product Placement* (One29 2001) ★★★★, *The Private Press* (Mo' Wax 2002) ★★★.
● DVD/VIDEOS: with Cut Chemist *Freeze* (Regeneration TV 2001), *Live! In Tune And On Time* (Geffen 2004).

DJ Sneak

b. 1 January 1969, Puerto Rico. Sneak is a highly respected member of Chicago's 'second generation' of **house** music producers. Arriving in Chicago in 1983, Sneak, who could not speak English, was drawn to instrumental music and graffiti art. He was later inspired by early pioneers such as **DJ Pierre** and **Marshall Jefferson**. Several of these inspirational figures had left for New York by the late 80s, just as Sneak was entering the music business. Nevertheless, **Cajmere** had begun to revive the city's classic house sound and established Cajual Records. DJ Sneak released a series of records on Cajual's sister-label, Relief Records, which promoted a slightly harder sound. He has also worked on productions for **Strictly Rhythm Records**, Henry Street, ZYX, 83 West and Feverpitch. Several of the Feverpitch recordings featured **Armand Van Helden** as co-producer and the partnership's strong Latin influences can be heard on them. Sneak has also remixed **Sneaker Pimps** and has worked with **Roger Sanchez** and Dave Clarke. His DJing skills are in demand all over the world and he is a regular visitor to **Ibiza** during the summer clubbing season. His 1996 track 'You Can't Hide From Your Bud' was something of a masterpiece, setting a blueprint for many subsequent 'filtered disco' tracks and preceding the wave of funky, disco-influenced house that would prove massively popular during the next few years—'Music Sounds Better' by Stardust (Thomas Bangalter) being a prime example. Sneak remains committed to the original Chicago heritage of house music and feels that many current DJs and producers have lost touch with the music's roots. Sneak has a simple plan for when the 'underground' inevitably goes 'overground': 'I'll go deeper underground.'

● ALBUMS: *Blue Funk Files* (Ultra 1997) ★★★.
● COMPILATIONS: *Kinky Trax Collection* (React Music 1996) ★★★, *Buggin' Da Beats* (Moonshine Music 1997) ★★★, *Housekeepin'* (Magnetic 2004) ★★.

DJ Spooky

b. Paul Miller, Washington, DC, USA. An experimental DJ working in contemporary electronica, Spooky, aka That Subliminal Kid, is an energetic, as well as prolific, performer. His world view was partially shaped by his parents' involvement in the civil rights movement—his father was a lawyer for the Black Panthers and his mother a leading light in the Afro-Futurism fashion movement. He first became attuned to music when his father purchased a computer: 'The idea of sound becoming a way of creating text, or even code, really blew my mind.' As well as recording extensively, he exhibits his visual art, contributes articles to magazines such as *The Village Voice* and *Vibe* and writes books (covering music theory, intellectual property and, bizarrely, science fiction). He defended his billing as a modern renaissance man thus: 'We're in an aesthetic that is so linked to all these different world cultures, the music that I'm trying to create celebrates that diversity. It's all in the mix.'

Miller's DJ sets adopt his aesthetic, routinely mixing easy listening (**Esquivel!**) with reggae, drum 'n' bass and soul, a sonic collage reflected in his recorded work. His 1996 debut *Songs Of A Dead Dreamer* included the club hit 'Galactic Funk', while the follow-up, 1998's *Riddim Warfare*, included intriguing collaborations with **Dr. Octagon** and **Arto Lindsay**. DJ Spooky has also remixed tracks by **Metallica**, **Spooky Ruben** and **Nick Cave**, and he wrote the soundtrack to the 1998 movie *Slam*. In 1999, Miller collaborated with *avant garde* electronic outfit the Freight Elevator Quartet on the stunning *File Under Futurism* project. Another notable collaboration saw the DJ teaming up with jazz artists **William Parker** and **Matthew Shipp** to record his debut for the Thirsty Ear label, *Optometry*. At the start of 2004 he teamed up with Ryan Moore of dub outfit Twilight Circus to record *Riddim Clash*.

● ALBUMS: *Songs Of A Dead Dreamer* (Asphodel 1996) ★★★★, as Paul D. Miller *The Viral Sonata* (Asphodel 1997) ★★★, *Riddim Warfare* (Outpost 1998) ★★★★, as DJ Spooky vs The Freight Elevator Quartet *File Under Futurism* (Caipiranha 1999) ★★★★, *Optometry* (Thirsty Ear 2002) ★★★, as DJ Spooky vs Twilight Circus *Riddim Clash* (Play 2004) ★★★★, as DJ Spooky vs Dave Lombardo *Drums Of Death* (Thirsty Ear 2005) ★★★.
● COMPILATIONS: *Necropolis: The Dialogic Project* (Knitting Factory Works 1996) ★★★, *Under The Influence* (Six Degrees 2001) ★★★, *Modern Mantra* (Shadow 2002) ★★★, *Dubtometry* (Thirsty Ear 2003) ★★★, *Rhythm Science* (Sub Rosa 2004) ★★★★, *Celestial Mechanix: The Blue Series Mastermix* (Thirsty Ear 2004) ★★★.

DJ SS

b. Leroy Small, 1971, Leicester, Leicestershire, England. Small has been at the forefront of the UK hardcore dance movement since the early 90s. Before concentrating on building a profile as DJ SS, he had operated under a number of guises and aliases, including International Rude Boys, Rhythm For Reasons, Sounds Of The Future and MA1 and MA2. He was also the co-founder and in-house producer of **Formation Records**, the acclaimed Leicester-based imprint. This involved him in some capacity in the vast majority of the label's 60 plus releases. Small had first worked as a DJ at the age of 13, playing at school discos before specializing in commercial hip-hop nights. He soon transferred over to the nascent rave scene when his interest in rap waned with the advent of the gangsta groups. Conversely, his affection for hip-hop (the parent style of much of the hardcore phenomenon) has been rekindled since he began recording as DJ SS. Releases such as 'Hearing Is Believing', 'The Lighter', 'Smoker's Rhythm' and 'The Rollidge' in 1995 brought him to nationwide prominence as the leader of the 'hardstep' (or purist drum 'n' bass) sound. Despite being heavily rooted in jungle's rhythmic dynamism, this style eschewed the intimidatingly violent narratives of ragga-based jungle.

DJ Talla 2XLC

One of Europe's most prominent producers and DJs, Talla had listened from an early age to the electronics of **Kraftwerk** and the **Yellow Magic Orchestra**. He rebelled against the pre-eminence of guitar and rock music by opening in 1984 the Techno Club in Germany—a club dedicated to preserving and spreading electronic music. Within five years he had also started his own label, Music Research. This developed two subsidiary outlets: Zoth Ommog, for electronic and industrial based acts, and New Zone, for electro dance. In the 90s further division occurred. Suck Me Plasma was incorporated to cover hard trance and techno house releases, while Influence dealt with more melodic techno projects. Talitha pandered to electro goth fans, while Zoth Ommog continued to service the more experimental concerns. New Zone was effectively discontinued. As well as running the club and various imprints, Talla is also the creative force behind his own band, Bigod 20, who is signed to **Warner Brothers**. Other artists on his various labels include Armageddon Dildos, Leather Strip, X Marks The Pedwalk and Psychopomps.
● ALBUMS: as Bigod 20 *Steel Works* (Sire 1992) ★★★, *Supercute* (Warners 1994) ★★★.

DJ Tiësto

b. Tijs Verwest, 17 January 1969, Breda, Netherlands. Tiësto is one of a crop of Dutch and German DJs whose euphoric, melodic style of **trance** saw their stars rise with the surge in the style's popularity during 1999. Along with **Ferry Corsten**, Vincent De Moor, Armin Van Buuren, **Paul Van Dyk**, **Oliver Lieb**, **Taucher** and others, Tiësto's productions and DJing could be found on numerous compilations and in the major clubs of Europe.

Tiësto began DJing in a small club in his home-town of Breda at the end of the 80s. Since then he has steadily built an international profile, playing at major festivals, such as Berlin's Love Parade in **Ibiza** and at the UK's trance epicentre, **Gatecrasher**, where he held a monthly residency. His success as a producer was helped by a collaboration with Corsten as Gouryella, who enjoyed two UK hit singles in 1999, and by his remix of Delerium featuring **Sarah McLachlan**'s 'Silence', which was a UK Top 10 hit and club anthem in 2000. Tiësto has also recorded with Armin Van Buuren as Major League and Alibi. He has released numerous mix sets on the Guardian Angel and Black Hole Recordings labels, and made his album debut in July 2002 with the double CD *In My Memory*. On 13 August 2004, Tiësto performed at the opening ceremony of the Olympic Games in Athens, Greece.
● ALBUMS: *In My Memory* (Nebula/Virgin 2002) ★★★, *Just Be* (Nebula/Nettwerk 2004) ★★★.
● COMPILATIONS: *Forbidden Paradise 3: The Quest For Atlantis* (Guardian Angel) ★★★, *Forbidden Paradise 4: High As A Kite* (Guardian Angel) ★★★, *Forbidden*

Paradise 5: Arctic Expedition (Guardian Angel) ★★★, *Forbidden Paradise 6: Valley Of Fire* (Guardian Angel) ★★★, *Forbidden Paradise 7: Deep Forest* (Guardian Angel) ★★★, as Magik *First Flight* (Black Hole) ★★★, as Magik *Story Of The Fall* (Black Hole) ★★★, as Magik *Far From Earth* (Black Hole) ★★★, as Magik *A New Adventure* (Black Hole) ★★★, as Magik *Heaven Beyond* (Black Hole) ★★★, as Magik *Live In Amsterdam* (Black Hole) ★★★, *Space Age* (Black Hole 1999) ★★★, with DJ Montana *Space Age 2.0* (Black Hole 1999) ★★★, *In Search Of Sunrise* (Songbird 2000) ★★★★, *Summerbreeze* (Nettwerk 2000) ★★★★, *In Search Of Sunrise 2* (Songbird 2001) ★★★★, *Revolution: Uplifting Progressive Trance* (Virgin 2001) ★★★★, *In Search Of Sunrise 3* (Songbird 2002) ★★★, *Nyana* (Nettwerk 2003) ★★★.

DJ Vadim

Vadim was born in the Soviet Union but moved to London when he was three. After becoming interested in hip-hop, he began to DJ and in 1995 released his first EP, *Abstract Hallucinogenic Gases*, on his own Jazz Fudge label. Later that year he continued his abstract hip-hop experiments on the EP *Headz Ain't Ready*, after which he signed to **Ninja Tune Records**. His first release for Ninja was 'Non Lateral Hypothesis' in April 1996, and his debut album, *USSR Repertoire*, 'a crazy selection of minimal hip-hop, ansa machines, *musique concrete* and the old school', arrived towards the end of the year. His only release of 1997 was the EP *Conquest Of The Irrational*. While recording for Ninja Tune he has continued to develop 'audio research into minimal hip-hop' at Jazz Fudge, with a number of artists and collaborators such as Andre Gurov, Mark B, the Creators, **Blade** and the Bug. He also DJs around the world, with particular success in Japan, which prompted an album of remixes, *USSR Reconstrustion—Theories Explained* (1998), featuring work by the Prunes, **Kid Koala**, the **Herbaliser** and **DJ Krush**, among others.
● ALBUMS: *U.S.S.R. Repertoire* (Ninja Tune 1997) ★★★★, *U.S.S.R. Reconstrustion—Theories Explained* (Ninja Tune 1998) ★★★, *U.S.S.R. Life From The Other Side* (Ninja Tune 1999) ★★★, *U.S.S.R. The Art Of Listening* (Ninja Tune 2002) ★★★.

DJ Yoda

b. Duncan Beiny, London, England. In a UK hip-hop scene with a sometimes over-inflated sense of self-importance, DJ Yoda brings some light-hearted relief with his own sub-genre of 'comedy-hop'. With early tape releases bearing the titles *Jewbonics*, *Jews Paid* and *Jews Paid, Too!*, it comes as no surprise to learn that DJ Yoda is the alias of Jewish Londoner Duncan Beiny.

DJ Yoda hit the musical radar in a big way with the release of his debut, *DJ Yoda's How To Cut & Paste*, in 2001. The mix included some beats by Quasimoto and Edan, superbly scratched and cut into old tunes by **Parliament** and **Cymande**, with some samples from television's *Cheers* theme to the *Doctor Who* music thrown in for good measure. In 2002, *DJ Yoda's How To Cut & Paste Vol. 2* was released, which included some strong tracks by **DJ Format**, **Black Moon** and Quasimoto, and some crazy samples ranging from comic actor John Cleese to the late ukulele-playing entertainer **George Formby**. The following year the *Unthugged* mix CD, with Yoda's former DJ partner Dan Greenpeace, was released.

However, *DJ Yoda's How to Cut & Paste: The 80s Edition* took the comedy vibe a step too far (**Johnny Hates Jazz** and **Europe**), but served as good backing music for 'late 30–something' parties.

● COMPILATIONS: *DJ Yoda's How To Cut & Paste* (Antidote 2001) ★★★★, *DJ Yoda's How To Cut & Paste Vol. 2* (Antidote 2002) ★★★, with Dan Greenpeace *Unthugged* (Antidote 2003) ★★★, *DJ Yoda's How To Cut & Paste: The 80s Edition* (Antidote 2003) ★★★.

Djaimin

b. Dario Mancini. Swiss DJ whose 'Give You' recording was discovered by **Tony Humphries**, who unveiled it at 1992's New Music Seminar. It was quickly picked up by **Strictly Rhythm** and then licensed to **Cooltempo** in the UK. 'Give You' featured singers Mike Anthony and Alessandra. Djaimin himself had been a DJ since the age of 16. Born of mixed Italian and English parentage, he is based in Lusanne, the French-speaking region of Switzerland. He moved there in 1986, hooking up with Anthony, best known for his 1983 cover version of Timmy Thomas' 'Why Can't We Live Together'. Together they run a national Swiss radio show. The follow-up to 'Give You' was 'She's Ga Ga', again for Strictly Rhythm.

Django Reinhardt

This movie was a good examination of the work of the first European to achieve international status in jazz. Directed by Paul Paviot, this 1958 film features several musicians associated with Reinhardt, including his brother, Joseph, and **Stéphane Grappelli**.

Djavan

b. 27 January 1949, Maceió, Alagoas, Brazil. Djavan's marriage of traditional South American rhythms with music drawn from Africa and Europe, including rock and pop, has made him successful in North America. Indeed, his music has been named 'South American Global Pop' in some quarters, although it retains enough ethnic flavour to please its native audience too. Albums such as *Seduzir* (his third collection) illustrate his sound, with a strong melody balancing the furious backing tracks. On songs such as 'Luanda' and the title-track it can be a spectacular combination. Other recordings, including *Puzzle Of Hearts* and *Bird Of Paradise*, have seen him mix English language songs with ones sung in Portuguese, although the English ones are rarely as effective or fluent. His 1988 Epic Records single, 'Stephen's Kingdom', featured a guest appearance from **Stevie Wonder**.

● ALBUMS: *A Voz, O Violão, A Música De Djavan* (Som Livre 1976) ★★★, *Djavan* (EMI/Odeon !978) ★★★, *Alumbramento* (EMI/Odeon 1980) ★★★, *Seduzir* (EMI/Odeon 1981) ★★★★, *Luz* (CBS 1982) ★★★, with Chico Buarque, Tom Jobim *Para Viver Um Grande Amor: Trilha Sonora Do Filme* (CBS 1983) ★★★, *Lilás* (CBS 1984) ★★★, *Meu Lado* (CBS 1986) ★★★, *Não É Azul Mas É Mar* (CBS 1987) ★★★, *Bird Of Paradise* (Epic 1988) ★★★, with Ivan Lins, Patti Austin *Brazilian Knights And A Lady* (Jazzvisions 1988) ★★★, *Djavan* (CBS 1989) ★★★, *Puzzle Of Hearts* (Epic 1990) ★★★, *Flor De Lis* (WEA Latina 1991) ★★★, *Coisa De Acender* (Sony 1992) ★★★, *Novena* (Sony 1994) ★★★, *Malásia* (Epic/Sony 1996) ★★★, *Songbook Djavan* (Lumiar Discos 1997) ★★★, *Bicho Solto O XIII* (Sony 1998) ★★★, *Djavan Ao Vivo, Vols. 1 & 2* (Epic/Sony 1999) ★★★, *Milagreiro* (Epic/Sony 2001) ★★★, *Vaidade* (Luanda 2004) ★★★.

● COMPILATIONS: *Água* (EMI/Odeon 1982) ★★★, *Pétala* (CBS 1988) ★★★, *Djavan: Meus Momentos, Vols. 1 & 2* (EMI 1999) ★★★, *Novelas* (Som Livre 2001) ★★★.

● DVD/VIDEOS: *Djavan Ao Vivo* (Epic/Sony 2000).

Djax Up Beats

House label esteemed by the critics and run by the similarly garlanded Dutch DJ, Miss Djax (aka Saskia Slegers). Voted Best DJ by German magazine *Frontpage* in 1992, she started DJing in her native Eindhoven in the mid-80s, establishing the record label in 1989. Djax Up has released records by the likes of Trance Induction, Terrace (aka Stefan Robbers, *The Turning Point* EP), Mike Dearborn (*Unbalanced Frequency* EP), Planet Gong (**Dylan Hermeljin**), Edge Of Motion, Acid Junkies and Random XS, just a few of the better examples of a very strong discography. However, the one thing that singles out Djax Up among other UK and European labels is its profligate release schedule (Paul Johnson's 'Psycho Kong' being its 200th release). Despite the extensive catalogue (and the fact that over 90% of sales originate from outside of Holland) there have been relatively few lapses of taste. For example, they conquered the rise of ambient house with releases from Optic Crux, a group from Utrecht whose output was engineered by Random XS.

DJM Records

Dick James first made his name in the music business as a singer in the 50s, most notably with the theme to the UK *Robin Hood* television programme. He moved into publishing, making his biggest coup when he signed the **Beatles** as songwriters and formed Northern Songs through Dick James Music. He later sold the Beatles' catalogue for over £1 million in 1969. He was already involved with **Larry Page** at Page One Records in the late 60s, but when that folded he set up DJM Records, with his son Stephen running the business. His first major act was **Elton John**, who James had signed as a songwriter in the publishing half of the business in February 1969. Other key artists of the label's heyday in the 70s were **Jasper Carrott**, **Hookfoot**, **Blackfoot Sue**, **Philip Goodhand-Tait**, **Viv Lewis** and **Edward Woodward**. However, by 1973 Elton John had left to form his own label, Rocket. Dick James died on 1 February 1986 and son Stephen restarted the business as a publishing company now known as Dejamus.

DKV Trio

(see **Drake, Hamid**; **Kessler, Kent**; **Vandermark, Ken**)

D'León, Oscar

b. Oscar Emilio León Samoza, 11 July 1943, Antímano, Caracas, Venezuela. Charismatic singer and bass player D'León, commonly known as 'El Leon de la Salsa' (The Lion of Salsa), is one of the few contemporary salsa musicians to capitalize on the strengths of 40s and 50s Cuban big band arrangers, yet recognizably with a distinctive modern flavour. Drawing on Cuban classics and compositions by other prominent Latin composers as a vehicle for imaginative reinterpretations, he has accumulated an impressive body of work, from a country not typically associated with producing a world-class Latin artist. D'León possesses an exceptionally good voice, with a large range, very silky and playful yet emotionally impressive. The interplay of the harmonized lead vocals and nasal background singing (which is traditional to the Afro-Cuban form called son) perfectly complements and mirrors the brass arrangements, giving a rich dynamic texture. D'León's band is essentially a salsa orquesta with a line-up of the usual rhythm section of percussion, bass and piano augmented by varying numbers of brass instruments, particularly trombones. On stage, D'León is an exuberant, tongue-in-cheek showman, with an outstanding ability to involve the audience in his extended improvisations on his many hits and Latin music classics. Contrary to his reputation as a bass player, he concentrates his 'live' performances only on singing and energetic dancing, unavoidably involving the audience.

D'León was a founder member of Venezuela's leading salsa band, **Dimensión Latina**, and recorded six albums with them between 1972 and 1976. D'León departed in 1976 and organized his own two trumpet/two trombone band called La Salsa Mayor, which featured the distinguished piano playing of ex–Federico Y Su Combo Latino member, Enrique 'Culebra' Iriarte. He released three albums with La Salsa Mayor until a split occurred in 1978, retaining only Iriarte and his principal trumpeter, César Pinto (another ex-Federico accompanist), plus substantially new personnel for *Y Su Salsa Mayor Con Wladimir*. This album marked the reunion with former Dimensión Latina co-lead vocalist, Wladimir Lozano. From this point, Victor Mendoza and Humberto 'Tigre' Becerra (with D'León) comprised the crucial typically Cuban nasal style of background vocals that has remained one of D'León's trademarks to date. The other members continued concurrently as Salsa Mayor, releasing *. . . De Frente Y Luchando . . . ! La Salsa Mayor 'Nuestra Orquesta'* (1978), with Pellín Rodríguez (ex-**El Gran Combo**) sharing lead vocals, and *La Salsa Mayor* (1979). In 1978, D'León began an association with the band La Crítica, then featuring Teo Hernández, the ex-lead singer of the exciting and funky all-trombone Los Dementes, which was led by pianist, arranger and composer Ray Pérez. D'León sang the hit track 'Se Necesita Rumbero' from La Crítica's album of that year. The band on *Oscar D'León Y Su Salsa Mayor Con Wladimir* (1978) featured a frontline of three trumpets and two trombones, a combination D'León retained on his next three albums. Commencing with *El Mas Grande!* (1979), his band was just referred to as his 'orquesta'. After *Al Frente De Todos* (1980), Culebra left to pursue an undistinguished solo career and was replaced by Enrico Enriquez on *A Mí Sí Me Gusta Así!* (1981) This Puerto Rico–recorded album featured a hefty brass section, plus the novel addition of saxophone. After several undistinguished albums in the early 80s, D'León began a return to form with 1984's *Con Cariño*. Between 1985 and 1987 D'León issued a succession of albums featuring some of his strongest material, inspired playing and assured arrangements, which justified his position as one of salsa's true international stars. The definitive albums of this period were 1987's *Riquiti . . . !* and *La Salsa Soy Yo*. In June and October 1988, D'León demonstrated his live reputation by playing three sell-out concerts at London's Hackney Empire. The last was recorded and broadcast in 1989 as a programme in BBC television's *Rhythms Of The World* world music series, then released as *Oscar D'León Live*, the first salsa video to be issued in the UK.

From 1988 onwards, there followed a fallow period of unexceptional, largely salsa romántica recordings. In 1991,

D'León joined an all-star line-up of his new label RMM's top vocalists, including **José Alberto**, **Tony Vega** and **Ismael Miranda**, plus **Celia Cruz**, for **Tito Puente**'s *The Mambo King: 100th LP*. He carried on recording for the RMM subsidiary Sonero, releasing *El Rey De Los Soneros* (1992) and *Toitico Y Tuyo* (1994). The Grammy-nominated 1996 release *El Sonero Del Mundo* was recorded in Miami with Willie Chirino. The following year's live album was recorded in New York with help from guests such as **Arturo Sandoval**, trumpeter Piro Rodriguez and vocalist India. He then returned to the studio to complete another fine set, *La Formula Original*.

D'León marched on into the new millennium with neither his creativity nor popularity showing signs of faltering, and a new recording contract with Universal Latino spurred him on to record one of his finest albums for several years, *Infinito*, released to uniformly positive reviews in 2003. The same June D'León suffered three heart attacks while performing in the Caribbean island of Martinque, although he vowed to carry on touring and recording after recovering.

● ALBUMS: *Con Bajo Y Todo* (TH-Rodven 1976) ★★★, *2 Sets Con Oscar* (TH-Rodven 1977) ★★★, *El 'Oscar' De La Salsa* (TH-Rodven 1977) ★★★, *Y Su Salsa Mayor Con Wladimir* (TH-Rodven 1978) ★★★, *El Mas Grande!* (TH-Rodven 1979) ★★★, *. . . Llegó . . . Actuó . . . Y . . . Triunfó . . . !* (TH-Rodven 1979) ★★★, *La Crítica* (TH-Rodven 1979) ★★★, *Al Frente De Todos* (TH-Rodven 1980) ★★★, *A Mí Sí Me Gusta Así!* (TH-Rodven 1981) ★★★, *El Discóbola* (TH-Rodven 1982) ★★, *. . . Con Dulzura* (TH-Rodven 1983) ★★, *El Sabor De Oscar* (TH-Rodven 1983) ★★, *Con Cariño* (TH-Rodven 1984) ★★★, *Yo Soy* (TH-Rodven 1985) ★★★, *Oscar '86* (TH-Rodven 1986) ★★★, *Riquiti . . . !* (TH-Rodven 1987) ★★★★, *La Salsa Soy Yo* (TH-Rodven 1987) ★★★★, *De Aquí Pa'lla* (TH-Rodven 1988) ★★★, *Live* (TH-Rodven 1989) ★★★, *En Puerto Rico* (TH-Rodven 1990) ★★, *Autentico* (TH-Rodven 1991) ★★★, *Con Los Blanco* (Sonotone 1991) ★★★, *El Rey De Los Sonero* (Sonero 1992) ★★★, *Toitico Y Tuyo* (Sonero 1994) ★★★, *El Sonero Del Mundo* (RMM 1996) ★★★★, *En Nueva York* (RMM 1997) ★★★, *La Formula Original* (RMM 1999) ★★★★, *Mas Que Amor . . . Frenesi* (Universal Latino 2001) ★★★, *Infinito* (Universal Latino 2003) ★★★★.

● COMPILATIONS: *Esenciales: The Ultimate Collection Volume 1* (Universal Latino 2000) ★★★★, *Exitos Eternos* (Universal 2004) ★★★★.

● DVD/VIDEOS: *Live* (IVA 1989).

DMC

The hugely influential and important Dance Music Club was established by the former DJ and head of programming at **Radio Luxembourg**, Tony Prince. In 1982, Prince was impressed by one of the many 'demo' tapes he was sent by aspiring radio DJs. It featured no speech between the tracks, which were also segued into each other. Inspired, he set about establishing DMC and in 1983 released the organization's first 'megamix' cassette, featuring a sequence of hits by **Shalamar**. The notion of the megamix of one artist's material was in itself revolutionary. DMC pioneered the idea of mixing and the notion of the DJ as the star, releasing a succession of megamixes and remixes. In 1985, DMC established its now world-famous annual World DJ Mixing Championship, sponsored by electronics company Technics. The competition attracts DJing talent from all over the world and has helped to launch the career of many famous DJs, including **Chad Jackson**, **Cash Money**, **Carl Cox** and Cutmaster Swift. UK DJs **Dave Seaman** and **Guy Ornadel** were both employed by DMC in the early 90s, Seaman as an A&R man and Ornadel as manager of their US office in New York City. **Sasha** was also managed by DMC for some time. It was DMC's newsletters that, in 1989, evolved into the clubber's bible, *MixMag*. In 1990, DMC established two subsidiary imprints, **Stress Records** and FBI, to release the work of recording artists rather than mixes by DJs, including **John Digweed** (Bedrock). In June 1999, DMC launched the world's first **dance music** weekly, *7* magazine.

D'Molls

This Chicago, Illinois–based heavy metal band featured Desi Rexx (vocals/guitar), Billy Dior (drums), S.S. Priest (guitar), Nigel Itson (vocals) and Lizzy Valentine (bass). Their self-titled 1988 debut album caused a stir at the time of its release, with its self-assured **Aerosmith**-meets-**Poison** approach. However, the songwriting on the follow-up, *Warped*, was weak and rigidly formularized, lacking the cutting edge of its predecessor. They relocated to Los Angeles, but with poor reviews and sales to match, they disbanded in 1991. Rexx went on to work with former **Derringer** guitarist Danny Johnson, while Itson joined Millionaire Boys Club.
● ALBUMS: *D'Molls* (Atlantic 1988) ★★★, *Warped* (Atlantic 1990) ★★, *Beyond D'Valley Of D'Molls!* (Delinquent 1997) ★★★.

DMX

b. Earl Simmons, 18 December 1970, Baltimore, Maryland, USA. The leading hardcore rapper of the late 90s and early 00s, Earl Simmons was raised from an early age by his aunt in New York City's Yonkers district. He took his name from the DMX digital sound machine and developed a reputation as a DJ on the local projects. DMX won *Source* magazine's Unsigned Hype Award in January 1991 and released the promo single 'Born Loser' for **Columbia Records** the following year. He managed to escape from Columbia's punitive contract, but little was heard from him afterwards apart from a 1994 single, 'Make A Move'. He made a dramatic re-entry onto the hip-hop scene with a show stopping appearance on **LL Cool J**'s '4,3,2,1'. Further cameos on **Ma$e**'s '24 Hours To Live', the **LOX**'s 'Money, Power & Respect' and the remix of **Ice Cube**'s 'We Be Clubbin'' built up a highly marketable reputation. Newly signed to Ruff Ryders/**Def Jam Records**, DMX returned to recording with the powerful 'Get At Me Dog' single, a US Top 40 single built around a **B.T. Express** guitar sample.

Marketed as a return to the chaotic, raw roots of street rap, DMX became hip-hop's latest sensation during 1998 when his debut album, *It's Dark And Hell Is Hot*, entered the US *Billboard* album chart at number 1. An impressive slice of east coast hardcore rap, the album centred around DMX's ferocious rhymes and dark lyrics. The same year the rapper made his film debut in Hype Williams' *Belly*. The follow-up, *Flesh Of My Flesh, Blood Of My Blood*, stayed at number 1 in the US for three weeks during January 1999 and eventually went triple platinum like its predecessor. The album included cameo appearances from the LOX, **Jay-Z**, **Mary J. Blige** ('Coming From') and **Marilyn Manson** ('The Omen'). A string of arrest warrants threatened to upset DMX's career during 1999, the most serious of which saw the police filing weapons, drug possession and animal cruelty charges against the rapper and his wife. The charges were eventually settled by a plea-bargain leading to fines and community service. After contributing to the Ruff Ryders' chart-topping *Ryde Or Die Vol. 1* set, DMX quickly recorded tracks for his new album. Despite being his third release in the space of two years, *. . . And Then There Was X* was another quality slice of hardcore rap and a welcome antidote to the bland hip-hop product still flooding the American market. The album followed its predecessors to the top of the US charts in January 2000 and generated the R&B hit single 'Party Up (Up In Here)'. The album went on to sell over five million copies.

The following February, after a string of run-ins with the police, Simmons was ordered to serve a 15-day jail sentence for driving without a license and possession of marijuana. During this period he also co-starred in the hit movies *Romeo Must Die* and *Exit Wounds*, contributing the hit single 'No Sunshine' to the soundtrack of the latter. The albums *The Great Depression* (2001) and *Grand Champ* (2003) also debuted at the top of the US mainstream charts, making DMX the only artist in the history of the *Billboard* charts to have his first five albums debut at number 1. In 2003 he reunited with *Romeo Must Die* co-star Jet Li in *Cradle 2 The Grave*. Despite his success, at the end of 2003 Simmons announced he was taking time out from the music business to spend time with his family. His legal problems continued, however, and in October 2005 he was sentenced to 60 days in prison after pleading guilty to two traffic violations while his license was suspended. He remains one of the bestselling rap artists in the history of American music.
● ALBUMS: *It's Dark And Hell Is Hot* (Def Jam 1998) ★★★★, *Flesh Of My Flesh, Blood Of My Blood* (Def Jam 1998) ★★★, *. . . And Then There Was X* (Def Jam 1999) ★★★★, *The Great Depression* (Def Jam 2001) ★★★, *Grand Champ* (Def Jam 2003) ★★★.
● DVD/VIDEOS: *The Best Of DMX: Make It Or Break It* (MVC Video 2001), *Angel* (Universal 2001), *Smoke Out Presents DMX* (Eagle Rock 2005).
● FURTHER READING: *E.A.R.L.: The Autobiography Of DMX*, Earl Simmons and Smokey D. Fontaine.
● FILMS: *Belly* (1998), *Romeo Must Die* (2000), *Boricua's Bond* (2000), *Backstage* (2000), *Exit Wounds* (2001), *Cradle 2 The Grave* (2003), *Beef* (2003), *Never Die Alone* (2004).

DMZ

Formed in Boston, Massachusetts, USA, DMZ was one of the city's premier punk attractions. Leader/vocalist/organist Mono Mann (aka Jeff Conolly) combined a love of 60s garage bands (**Seeds**, **Music Machine**) with an equal interest in **Iggy Pop**. The group's debut EP was issued on **Bomp Records** in 1977. It revealed an urgent confidence in which Mann successfully re-created the atmosphere of his idols, notably on a version of the **Thirteenth Floor Elevators**' 'You're Gonna Miss Me'. The set, produced by Craig Leon, was later compiled with previously unissued material to create *Relics*. By contrast *DMZ* was a disappointment. Producers **Flo And Eddie** failed to translate the group's enthusiasm into a coherent sound. DMZ split up in 1979, after which Mann/Conolly formed the similarly-influenced Lyres.
● ALBUMS: *DMZ* (Sire 1978) ★★, *Relics* (Voxx 1981) ★★★, *DMZ! Live At Barnabys!! 1978!!* (Crypt 1986) ★★★.

DNA

This US band was a short-lived collaboration between guitarist **Rick Derringer** (b. Richard Zehringer, 5 August 1947, Fort Recovery, Ohio, USA) and drummer **Carmine Appice** (b. 15 December 1946, Staten Island, New York City, USA). With the assistance of Duane Hitchings (keyboards) and Jimmy Johnson (bass), they released *Party Tested* in 1983. This featured a wide range of styles that included jazz, rock, funk, blues and pop. The playing was beyond criticism, but the songs were devoid of soul, and the album as a whole lacked unity and cohesion. Failing to win support in the media, DNA disintegrated when Carmine Appice accepted an offer to join **Ozzy Osbourne**'s band. He subsequently formed **King Kobra**.

● ALBUMS: *Party Tested* (Polydor 1983) ★★.

Dntel

b. Jimmy Tamborello, Silverlake, California, USA. Assuming the enigmatic Dntel moniker because it sounded like an archetypal electronica track title, the self-confessed nervous recluse creates the most beguiling of musics at the midpoint between soporific indie pop and state-of-the-art glitch-ridden electronica. In the early 90s, Tamborello was playing hardcore but, via a love of **My Bloody Valentine** and **Tortoise**, ended up investigating the wayward electronic music of **Plaid**, **Aphex Twin** and **Autechre**. Tamborello's initial experiments in electronic music, in collaboration with David Figurine, were released under the provocative Antihouse moniker and recorded concurrently with the experimental hardcore of Strictly Ballroom. His Dntel alter ego was booted in 1994 and subsequently released a duo of instrumental recordings, *Early Works For Me If It Works For You* (a collection of tracks created between 1995 and 1997) and *Something Always Goes Wrong* (an EP recorded in 1994 but unreleased until six years later) via southern California CD-R label Phthalo. However, Tamborello's studio experiments really came to fruition with 2001's *Life Is Full Of Possibilities*. From his appositely named Dying Songs Studio, the Los Angeles–based musician coalesced electronic clicks and pulses, drum 'n' bass rim-shots, the murk of static, the tinkle of xylophone and even the sampled sound of fireworks into sublime glitch-pop suites that shared partial aesthetics with Múm and **Piano Magic**. Tamborello recruited friends and indie illuminati such as Rachel Haden (**That Dog**), Chris Gunst (**Beachwood Sparks**), Meredith Figurine (Figurine) and Benjamin Gibbard (**Death Cab For Cutie**) to provide narratives to his electronic music. Tamborello's juxtaposition of fat bass and elegiac guitar, wayward distortion and pretty vocals could sound perverse but, as it is, Dntel sounds tender, understated and perfectly poised. Tamborello is also, notably, one third of techno pop outfit Figurine, and records with Gibbard as **Postal Service**.

● ALBUMS: *Early Works For Me If It Works For You* (Phthalo 1999) ★★★, *Life Is Full Of Possibilities* (Plug Research 2001) ★★★★.

Do I Hear A Waltz?

It has been called 'a creative match made in heaven', but for some of the participants it became a living hell. Put another way, the 'dream ticket' of **Stephen Sondheim** (lyrics), **Richard Rodgers** (music) and Arthur Laurents (book), became a kind of nightmare. Apparently, Sondheim was reluctant to commit himself to the project from the start, and in the event, he and Rodgers just did not get along. *Do I Hear A Waltz?* opened at the 46th Street Theatre in New York on 18 March 1965. It was based on Laurents' own play, *The Time Of The Cuckoo*, which had also been filmed in 1955 as *Summertime*, with Katharine Hepburn. The story concerns Leona Samish (Elizabeth Allen), 'a virginal spinster lady' who travels to Venice and falls in love with Renato Di Rossi (Sergio Franchi), who she subsequently discovers is a married man. Although, for the first time in her life 'she hears a waltz', she terminates the affair and returns from her holiday a sadder but wiser woman. Sondheim and Rodgers have both expressed their unhappiness and general dissatisfaction with each other, and with the piece, but their collaboration did result in a charming and interesting score. Several of the songs are more than worthwhile, including a tourists' lament, 'What Do We Do? We Fly!' ('If it's white, it's sweet/If it's brown, it's meat/If it's grey, don't eat!'), 'Take The Moment', the ravishing 'Moon In My Window', 'Someone Woke Up', 'Stay', 'Thinking' and the title song, a typically lovely Rodgers waltz. Sondheim was forced to change the lyric to 'We're Gonna Be All Right', which was sung by a couple whose marriage was shaky, because it was considered 'not suitable for a Rodgers' musical'. The original surfaced during the 70s in the revue, *Side By Side By Sondheim*, and contained lines such as 'Sometimes she drinks in bed/Sometimes he's homosexual/But why be vicious?/They keep it out of sight/Just so we're gonna be all right'. *Do I Hear A Waltz* staggered along for only 220 performances but is fondly remembered via its fine cast album. Revivals occasionally emerge, particularly in Britain, where, in the early 90s, two concert versions and a production by the Guildhall School of Music were widely applauded.

Do Or Die

Coming from the tough west side of Chicago, Illinois, USA, Do Or Die comprises brothers AK (b. Dennis Round) and N.A.R.D. (b. Anthony Round) and their lifelong friend, Belo Zero (b. Darnell Smith). Deciding to form a rap outfit in the early 90s, the trio slowly built a following on the strength of local live performances. It was through one of these local shows that Do Or Die caught the ear of Rap-A-Lot Records head Carlton Joshua, but before the trio signed a recording contract with the label, they issued a single, 'Po Pimpin', on their own. The track, which featured fellow Chicago rapper **Twista**, immediately caused a buzz within the rap underground, and it crossed over and began scaling the US **Billboard** pop singles chart, just missing the Top 20 in 1996. Figuring if they could obtain this much commercial success on their own, a contract with an established label could only help their cause, the trio finally took the plunge and signed with Rap-A-Lot. The move paid off, as their next three albums, 1996's *Picture This* 1998's *Headz Or Tailz* and 2000's *Victory* (which included cameos by **Ja Rule**, Felony, **Irv Gotti**, and **E-40**), all crossed over onto the pop album charts, the latter two managing to creep to just outside the Top 10. The trio has gone on to issue further albums (2002's *Back 2 The Game* and 2003's *Pimpin' Ain't Dead*), but they have failed to continue in the successful path of their earlier releases.

● ALBUMS: *Picture This* (Rap-A-Lot/Noo Trybe 1996) ★★★★, *Headz Or Tailz* (Rap-A-Lot/Virgin 1998) ★★★, *Victory* (Rap-A-Lot/Virgin 2000) ★★, *Back 2 The Game*

(Rap-A-Lot/Virgin 2002) ★★★, *Pimpin' Ain't Dead* (Rap-A-Lot/Virgin 2003) ★★, *D.O.D.* (The Legion 2005) ★★★.

Do Ray Me Trio

Like many R&B groups in the immediate post–World War II era, the Do Ray Me Trio (also called Do Ray And Me Trio) were a nightclub act that played a combination of vocal harmony ballads, jive numbers, jazz and blues. The group was formed in 1942 in California, USA, as the Al 'Stomp' Russell Trio, and comprised Al Russell (tenor and piano), Joel Cowan (tenor and guitar) and William 'Doc Basso' Joseph (bass and bass fiddle). They recorded for Excelsior, Deluxe, and **Queen Records** without much success. In 1947, Joseph was replaced by Joe Davis and the group adopted the name Do Ray Me Trio. This new ensemble made their first recordings for the **Commodore Records** label and had a hit with 'Wrapped Up In A Dream' (number 2 R&B) at the end of 1947. Bass player Joe Davis was replaced in 1948 by Curtis Wilder, whose tenor made the group an all-tenor group. One of the trio's finest all-tenor recordings was the blow-harmony ballad 'Only One Dream', recorded for Ivory Records in 1949. When Cowan left in 1950 to join **Camille Howard**, the trio broke up. The Do Ray Me Trio was re-formed in 1951 with members Al Russell (piano), Al Moore (bass) and Buddy Hawkins (drums). This group recorded several singles for **OKeh Records** in 1951, then sporadically throughout the 50s for labels including **Brunswick Records**, Variety, **Coral Records**, Reet and Carlton. The trio recorded one album for the Stereophonic label in 1960, and it proved to be the group's last recording. The Do Ray Me Trio continued to play in nightclubs for several decades afterwards.

● ALBUMS: *The Do-Ray-Mi Trio* (Stereophonic 1960) ★★★.

Do Ré Mi (indies)

One of the more respected post-punk bands, Do Ré Mi achieved limited success both in Australia and overseas since its formation in Sydney in 1981. The band had success with their second single, 'Man Overboard', from the debut album in 1985, although they had previously released an obscure mini-album in 1982. Subsequent releases did not attract the mainstream listeners and the excellent album *Domestic Harmony*, while critically acclaimed, did not sell well. Lead vocalist Deborah Conway went on to pursue a solo career.

● ALBUMS: *Domestic Harmony* (Virgin 1985) ★★★, *Happiest Place In Town* (Virgin 1988) ★★★.

Do Re Mi (stage musical)

Not remotely connected with the famous song of that title written in 1959 by **Richard Rodgers** and **Oscar Hammerstein** for their smash-hit musical, **The Sound Of Music**, this show, which opened a year later on 26 December 1960 at the St. James Theatre in New York City, USA, had a much more contemporary theme—and **Phil Silvers**. He had recently been 'demobilized' from the long-running television series in which he had starred as the conniving Sergeant Bilko, and was returning to the New York musical stage after an absence of nearly 10 years. Prospects looked good for *Do Re Mi*—the book was written by the celebrated author Garson Kanin, and **Jule Styne** (music) along with **Betty Comden** and **Adolph Green** (lyrics) provided the score. **Nancy Walker**, who had made such an impact on her Broadway debut in **High Button Shoes** nearly 20 years before, was Silvers' co-star in a story

that concerned one of America's greatest gifts to the civilized world—jukeboxes. Hubie Cram (Phil Silvers) persuades some old slot machine hoodlums, Brains Berman, Fats O'Rear and Skin Demopoulos, to come out of retirement and help him to make the big time. When their singer, Tilda Mullen (Nancy Dussault), is poached by rival businessman John Henry Wheeler (John Reardon), it sparks off a bitter jukebox war. In the end, Hubie decides it is better to have his wife, Kay (Nancy Walker), by the hearth (she leaves him for a time) than a jukebox in the Zen Pancake Parlour. Nancy Dussault and John Reardon had the show's big hit, 'Make Someone Happy', and they combined again on the unconventional 'Fireworks'. The rest of the delightful score included 'All You Need Is A Quarter', 'Cry Like The Wind', 'What's New At The Zoo?', 'The Late, Late Show', 'I Know About Love', 'Asking for You', 'All Of My Life', 'Adventure' and 'Ambition'. *Do Re Mi Ran* for 400 performances on Broadway, but the 1961 production at London's Prince of Wales Theatre did not appeal, even with popular comedian/singer **Max Bygraves** and a cast which included Maggie Fitzgibbon, Jan Waters and Steve Arlen. Almost 40 years later, the show was featured in the 1999 New York City Center *Encores!* series, with a starry cast that included Nathan Lane (Hubie), Randy Graff (Kay), Stephen DeRosa, Lee Wilkof, Lewis J. Stadlen and Michael Mulheren. Brian Stokes Mitchell (**Ragtime**) and Heather Headley (**The Lion King**) sang the enduring 'Make Someone Happy'.

Dobrogosz, Steve

b. 26 January 1956, Belfont, Pennsylvania, USA. Educated at **Berklee College Of Music**, Dobrogosz moved from North Carolina to Stockholm, Sweden in 1978. His lushly textured solo playing is strongly affected by a fluent, virtuoso command of post-romantic piano. Dobrogosz has a fine lyric gift, which is most fully realized in his highly expressive accompaniments to singers such as **Radka Toneff** and Berit Andersson. He has also recorded with bass player **Arild Andersen** and saxophonist Joakim Milder.

● ALBUMS: *Songs* (Caprice 1980) ★★★, *Pianopieces* (Proprius 1982) ★★★, with Radka Toneff *Fairy Tales* (Odin 1982) ★★, with Berit Andersson *Scary Bright* (Dragon 1984) ★★★, *The Child's Gift* (Proprius 1986) ★★★, *The Final Touch* (Dragon 1990) ★★★★, *Jade* (Dragon 1990) ★★★, *Skin Baloon* (Sand Castle 1993) ★★★, with Jeanette Lindström *Feathers* (Prophone 2000) ★★★.

Dobson, Dobby

b. Highland Dobson, 1942, Kingston, Jamaica, West Indies. 'The Loving Pauper', as he has been affectionately nicknamed, has crafted an impressively individual technique, built around a voice of rich, modular tone. Dobson began singing as part of a group known as the Deltas while at the Kingston College; the group also included Howard Barrett. They recorded their first song for the Tip Top label—'Cry A Little Cry', written by Dobson and produced by **Sonia Pottinger**. Though it proved a radio hit, the group split and Dobson continued to record solo for Pottinger. His first recording session resulted in the release of a duet with Chuck Joseph, 'Baby How Can I'. Although the Tip Top release was greeted with indifference, Dobson's distinctive vocal style secured recording sessions with **Coxsone Dodd** and **Duke Reid**. With Reid, he recorded 'Loving Pauper', as well as cutting 'Seems To Me I'm Losing You' for Coxsone Dodd at roughly the same time. He enjoyed a succession of hits with both producers, although it was 'Loving Pauper' that garnered most attention and became his signature tune. He recorded it twice more after its initial release on Treasure Isle, and many other reggae stars (including **Freddie McGregor** and Ruddy Thomas) would also cover it.

Nevertheless, Dobson modestly maintained his jobs as a salesman and proofreader for the *Jamaican Gleaner*. In his spare time he was enrolled to perform with various short-term local bands, including the Sheiks alongside **Jackie Mittoo**, and the Virtues, before establishing a fruitful partnership in 1971 with **Rupie Edwards**. His initial single, 'That Wonderful Sound', sold in excess of 40,000 copies in the Caribbean and was followed by his other distinguished opus, 'Endlessly'. The song was equally successful and signalled international fame when the independent Ashanti label took the song into the lower reaches of the UK pop chart. Despite his prolific past, it was not until Edwards compiled an album directly following the success of 'Wonderful Sound' that Dobson added a long-player to his canon. Unfortunately, it failed to sell in the quantities that both parties anticipated, and was followed shortly afterwards by *Sweet Dreams* for Federal Records. This comprised big 50s and 60s ballads, delivered in Dobson's smoothest lovers tones. His bad luck was compounded, however, when a third album, for a Miami label, failed to produce any royalties. He began working as a producer and relished a notable achievement with the **Meditations**' *Wake Up*, released through Count Shelley. In 1979 Dobson emigrated to New York where he pursued a career outside of the music industry, although he occasionally returned to the studio. Instead he worked in real estate and junior management (he had previously been a marketing student at the University of West Indies). In 1982, during one of his sporadic studio sessions, he recorded 'Sweetheart', produced by **Inner Circle**, which enjoyed another brush with the UK pop chart. While pursuing other interests, he occasionally performed live and is a favourite on the 'oldies night' section at both Reggae Sunsplash and Reggae Sumfest celebrations in Jamaica. His popularity as a 'big people's' performer prompted the release of a series of mellow lovers compilations, including *Love You Through It All*, *Sweet Dreams Again Volume Two*, *Love Your Woman*, *Nothing But Love Songs Volume Three*, *At Last* and *To Lovers Everywhere*.

● ALBUMS: *Wonderful Sound* (Success 1977) ★★★, *Sweet Dreams* (Federal 1978) ★★★★, *History For Lovers* (Shelley 1990) ★★★, *Through The Years* (Studio One 1991) ★★★.

● COMPILATIONS: *Best Of Dobby Dobson* (Super Power 1997) ★★★★.

Dobson, Richard

b. 19 March 1942, Tyler, Texas, USA. Dobson planned to be a novelist and he only took up the guitar and started songwriting in 1963. He played in Texas folk clubs alongside **Guy Clark** and **Townes Van Zandt**, but a meeting with **David Allan Coe**'s band outside a Nashville recording studio led to Coe immediately recording 'Piece Of Wood And Steel'. With the money he saved from working on shrimpers and oil rigs, Dobson was able to finance his highly rated debut, *In Texas Last December*. The album included 'Baby Ride Easy', which was recorded as a duet by **Carlene Carter** and **Dave Edmunds**. Dobson wrote regularly for the UK fanzine *Omaha Rainbow*, and his novel, *The Gulf Coast Boys*, was published in 1998. **Nanci Griffith**, who recorded his song 'The Ballad Of Robin

Wintersmith', calls him 'the Hemingway of country music', but he has not been able to expand his following. His best-known song is 'Old Friends', which he wrote with Guy and Susanna Clark, and which was used as the title track of Clark's 1988 album. In the early 90s Dobson signed with the Swiss record label Brambus. He currently lives in Switzerland.

● ALBUMS: *In Texas Last December* (Buttermilk 1977) ★★★, *The Big Taste* (Rinconada 1979) ★★★, *Save The World* (RJD 1982) ★★★, *True West* (RJD 1986) ★★★, *Richard Dobson & State Of The Heart Live At The Station Inn* (RJD 1988) ★★★, *Hearts And Rivers* (RJD 1989) ★★★, *Blue Collar Blues* (Brambus 1993) ★★★, *Amigos: Richard Dobson Sings Townes Van Zandt* (Brambus 1994) ★★★, *Mankind* (Sundown 1994) ★★★, *One Bar Town* (Brambus 1995) ★★★, *Love Only Love* (Brambus 1996) ★★★, *Salty Songs* (Brambus 1998) ★★★, *Global Village Garage* (GEMA 1999) ★★★, *New York Night* (Lalo 2000) ★★★, *Hum Of The Wheels* (Brambus 2001) ★★★★, with Thomm Jutz *Doppelganger* (Brambus 2002) ★★★, *A River Will Do* (Brambus 2003) ★★★.

● COMPILATIONS: *Back Tracks: Save The World/True West* (Out Your Back Door 1990) ★★★.

Doc Holliday

Not to be confused with Frank Carillo's band from the early 70s (although both groups were American and played Southern boogie/rock), this version of Doc Holliday formed in 1980 with Bruce Brookshire (guitar/vocals), Rick Skelton (guitar), Eddie Stone (keyboards) and Robert Liggio (drums), and followed the 'heavier' style of **Blackfoot**, mixed with more obvious influences such as the **Outlaws** and the **Allman Brothers Band**. Having released two excellent albums without gaining mass acceptance, they made what fans saw as a mistake in changing musical tack, with an album in 1983 more suited to the listening tastes of **Journey** or **Styx** fans. When this, too, failed, they broke up. In 1986 they returned with a harder edge and finally gained overdue attention with *Danger Zone. Song For The Outlaw Live* also earned strong reviews, although afterwards they fell silent.

● ALBUMS: *Doc Holliday* (A&M 1981) ★★, *Doc Holliday Rides Again* (A&M 1982) ★★★, *Hell Bent And Whisky Bound* (A&M 1982) ★★★, *Modern Medicine* (A&M 1983) ★★, *Danger Zone* (Metal Masters 1986) ★★★, *Song For The Outlaw Live* (Loop 1989) ★★★.

Doctor And The Medics

This UK pop rock outfit was the most successful act to emerge from the psychedelic revival of 1981. The band was formed in the early 80s by Clive Jackson (b. 7 July 1961, Liverpool, England; vocals), Steve McGuire (guitar), Richard Searle (bass), Vom (drums) and backing vocalists Wendi West and Collette. Jackson was a part-time DJ who had formed the underground club The Clinic in 1981, and was also instrumental in running the popular nightclub Alice In Wonderland in London's Soho district. Doctor And The Medics released 'The Druids Are Here' 7-inch single on the Whaam! label before landing a major label recording contract with I.R.S. Records. The band came to prominence in 1986 with a cover version of **Norman Greenbaum**'s 1970 hit 'Spirit In The Sky'. The single was promoted by a memorable video that spotlighted the heavily made-up and eccentrically dressed Jackson (the Doctor) as the focal point of the band.

Doctor And The Medics hit number 1 in the UK, but they found it difficult to consolidate their success, with the subsequent 'Burn' and 'Waterloo' (featuring **Roy Wood**) only achieving UK chart placings of 29 and 45, respectively. The same year's *Laughing At The Pieces* peaked at number 25 in the UK album charts, primarily on the back of the band's major single success. Following this every release sunk without trace and the band was dropped by their label. Jackson and McGuire have continued to record and tour as Doctor And The Medics, joined by Wendi (Jackson's wife) and Collette from time to time. The band also run their own Madman Records label. Former bass player Richard Searle enjoyed success in the 90s as a member of acid-jazz outfit **Corduroy**.

● ALBUMS: *Laughing At The Pieces* (I.R.S. 1986) ★★★, *I Keep Thinking It's Tuesday* (I.R.S. 1987) ★★, *The Adventures Of Boadicea And The Beetle* (Castle 1993) ★★, *Instant Heaven* (Madman 1996) ★★★.

Doctor Butcher

Doctor Butcher were formed in Florida, USA, in 1992, when Jon Oliva (ex-**Savatage**; vocals) and guitarist Chris Caffery, who had previously worked together on Savatage's *Gutter Ballet* opus, began writing and recording together. Joined by John Osborn (drums) and Brian Gregory (bass), the quartet set about rehearsing songs that, unsurprisingly, attracted the attention of Savatage's many fans. However, work was put in abeyance in late 1993 when Jon's brother, Savatage guitar player Criss Oliva, was killed. Jon elected to rejoin his former band to complete their *Handful Of Rain* album in tribute to his brother. He had returned to Doctor Butcher by the summer, however, and set about working on the group's self-titled debut. Bracing classic rock against more contemporary developments (especially evident in its guitar platform), the album was completed at Morrisound Studios in Tampa, Florida. Track titles such as 'The Altar' and 'Season Of The Witch' revealed that Oliva's lyrical focus had shifted little since his Savatage heyday.

● ALBUMS: *Doctor Butcher* (Gun 1995) ★★★.

Doctor Dolittle

A disaster movie of the wrong kind—this lavish and expensive musical about one man's incredible affinity with animals was released from captivity in 1968 by 20th Century-Fox, and quietly crawled into a corner and died. **Rex Harrison**, just a few years after his triumph in the screen version of **My Fair Lady**, played the country Doctor who could talk to the animals in more than 400 different languages (courtesy of a parrot named Polynesia), and whose house in the English village Puddleby-on-the-Marsh, resembled London Zoo—only more so. Samantha Eggar and **Anthony Newley** tried hard to inject some life into the proceedings, and Richard Attenborough, as a much be-whiskered circus promoter confronted by Pushmi-Pullyu, a double-headed llama (one at each end), was suitably incredulous on 'I've Never Seen Anything Like It'. That song was part of an engaging score by **Leslie Bricusse** that also included 'My Friend The Doctor', 'Beautiful Things', 'When I Look In Your Eyes', 'After Today', 'Fabulous Places', 'I Think I Like You', 'At The Crossroads', 'The Vegetarian', 'Like Animals', 'Where Are The Words?', 'Something In Your Smile' and 'Doctor Dolittle'. Harrison's most effective number, 'Talk To The Animals', won the Academy Award for best song, and

the film picked up another Oscar for special effects (L.B. Abbott), the most impressive of these being the Great Pink Sea Snail. Other, more human, roles were taken by Peter Bull, William Dix, Geoffrey Holder, Norma Varden, Muriel Landers and Portia Nelson. Leslie Bricusse was responsible for the screenplay which was based on Hugh Lofting's much-loved stories, and Herbert Ross designed the choreography. Richard Fleischer directed, and the film was shot in DeLuxe Color and Todd AO.

It was reportedly Jim Henson, creator of the Muppets, who first suggested to Bricusse that *Doctor Dolittle* should be turned into a stage show. After Henson's sudden death in 1990, his son Brian took over the British-based Henson Creature Workshop, and in 1998, the organization fulfilled its creator's dream by taking on the £4 million stage version of *Doctor Dolittle*. It created a menagerie of some 92 animals—from an eight-inch long goldfish to an eighteen-foot-tall dinosaur. Using a system known as animatronics, the large creatures contained human operators, with remote controls for the smaller ones. The chief human being, Dr. John Dolittle, was played by **Phillip Schofield**, making a substantial leap from his comparatively undemanding role in **Joseph And The Amazing Technicolor Dreamcoat**. He is aided, abetted—and sometimes obstructed (a spell in an asylum on the charge of abducting a seal)—in his search for the pink sea snail by, among others, girlfriend Emma Fairfax (Sarah Jane Hassell), 10-year-old local boy Tommy Stubbins (James Paul Bradley/Samuel Carter-Bown/Darien Smith), circus owner Albert Blossom and his wife Gertie (John Rawnsley and Jane Stoggles), Cats fish man Matthew Mugg (Bryan Smyth), fisherman Charlie (Hadrian Delacey) and colleague Straight Arrow (Peter Gallagher). Chee-Chee the chimpanzee (Holli Hoffman) got in on the act as well, and in a real coup for the production, Broadway and West End legend **Julie Andrews** provided the recorded voice of Polynesia the parrot. Polynesia joined Dolittle, Matthew and Tommy on 'Talk To The Animals', one of several surviving songs from Bricusse's film score. Another making the trip from celluloid to stage was 'When I Look In Your Eyes' (sung by the good Doctor to Sophie the Seal), and there were three newcomers, 'You're Impossible' (Dolittle and Emma), 'Save The Animals' (Straight Arrow and Company), and 'The Voice Of Protest' (Emma and Company). The whole affair was played out on Mark Thompson's exquisite sets, and he was also responsible for the ravishing costumes. Aletta Collins designed the (minimal) choreography, and by the time Dolittle made his hair-raising descent aboard the luminescent Giant Lunar Moth, in order to sort out a pack of raging foxhunters, the evening had a definite feeling of 'Animal Lib Rules OK' about it.

A few days after the show opened, fans of Lofting's stories, who may have found it too sentimental for them, were able to catch the release of a new, non-musical film version starring Eddie Murphy. Henson's Creature Workshop provided the animatronics for this one too, although with the movie's 'lavatorial and butt humour, messages of political correctness and cultural diversity in San Francisco', along with 'an alcoholic marmoset, flatulent rodents, and a suicidal circus tiger', there were few other similarities.

Doctor Ice

b. Fred Reeves, Brooklyn, New York City, USA. Rapper thus named because he wanted to belong to the medical profession while at school. Doctor Ice was formerly a member of **U.T.F.O.**, with whom he remained for five years, and before that **Whodini**, as a live dancer (one of the first such occurrences). Striking out solo he enlisted the aid of **Full Force** member Brain 'B-Fine' Lou to write new material. The record was completed within one month. Doctor Ice toured to support it, appearing in white coat and with a medical team as part of the 'theme'. His two dancers were presented as 'patients', and his DJ 'the surgeon'. Other songs traced different 'concepts' but were similarly narrative: in the single excerpt, 'Sue Me', Doctor Ice is depicted in the accompanying video driving a white Porsche until his alter ego, Doctor Dread, crashes into him in a taxi, with riotous court scenes and accusation and counter-accusation following. 'Love Jones' featured contributions from Full Force and Cheryl 'Pepsi' Riley, while the album closed with 'True Confessions', which featured a cameo from **Lisa Lisa** and Blair Underwood of *L.A. Law* fame on a song concerning an unhappy married couple and their interceding lawyer. Renaming himself simply Doc Ice, he switched to **Ichiban Records** to set up his own Selph Records, which housed his *Rely On Selph* set. In the intervening years, rather than hanging up his stethoscope as many had assumed, he had developed a career in acting and choreography, working on several high profile commercials and the feature film, *Don't Let Your Meat Loaf*.

● ALBUMS: *The Mic Stalker* (Jive 1989) ★★★, as Doc Ice *Rely On Selph* (Selph/Ichiban 1993) ★★★.

Doctor West's Medicine Show And Jug Band

Founded in Los Angeles, California, USA, Doctor West's Medicine Show And Jug Band were led by former Boston-based folk singer, **Norman Greenbaum**. Bonnie Wallach (guitar/vocals), Jack Carrington (guitar, vocals, percussion) and Evan Engber (percussion) completed the original line-up. The group played a mixture of jug and goodtime music similar to **Sopwith Camel**. They enjoyed a minor US hit in 1967 with the novelty song, 'The Eggplant That Ate Chicago' and attracted attention for the title of its follow-up, 'Gondoliers, Overseers, Playboys And Bums'. They broke up at the end of that year after which Greenbaum formed several low-key acts before teaming with producer **Erik Jacobsen** and scoring international success with 'Spirit In The Sky'.

● ALBUMS: *The Eggplant That Ate Chicago* (Go Go 1967) ★★.

Doctors Of Madness

When punk fermented in 1976, several relatively established bands waiting in the wings were somehow dragged along with it. The Doctors Of Madness were one such group. Comprising Richard 'Kid' Strange (vocals, guitar, keyboards, percussion), Colin Stoner (bass, vocals, percussion), Peter (drums, percussion, vocals) and Urban (guitar/violin), the Doctors were already signed to **Polydor Records** and had issued two rock albums verging on the theatrical by late 1976: *Late Night Movies, All Night Brainstorms* and *Figments Of Emancipation*. Much of their momentum was lost, however, when they issued only one single in 1977, 'Bulletin', and it was not until 1978 that *Sons Of Survival* appeared. By that time, the post-punk era had arrived, awash with new ideas, and the Doctors Of Madness seemed acutely anachronistic. They broke up soon afterwards, their career later summarized on a compilation, *Revisionism*. Richard Strange, meanwhile, set

about an erratic but fascinating solo career that included such singles as 'International Language' (1980) on **Cherry Red Records**, and the narcissistically entitled album *The Phenomenal Rise Of Richard Strange*, on **Virgin Records**.

● ALBUMS: *Late Night Movies, All Night Brainstorms* (Polydor 1976) ★★★, *Figments Of Emancipation* (Polydor 1976) ★★★, *Sons Of Survival* (Polydor 1978) ★★. Solo: Richard Strange *The Live Rise Of Richard Strange* (Ze/PVC 1980) ★★★, *The Phenomenal Rise Of Richard Strange* (Virgin 1981) ★★★, as Richard Strange And The Engine Room *Going-Gone* (Side 1987) ★★★.

● COMPILATIONS: *Revisionism (1975–78)* (Polydor 1981) ★★★.

Dodd, Coxsone

b. Clement Seymour Dodd, 26 January 1932, Jamaica, West Indies, d. 4 May 2004, Kingston, Jamaica, West Indies. It is an indisputable fact that without the vision and work of Clement 'Sir Coxsone' Dodd, reggae music as we now understand it, would not exist. Always interested in music, the former automobile mechanic and farm labourer was among the first in Jamaica to run his own **sound system**—Sir Coxsone The Down Beat ('Coxsone' was inspired by a popular Yorkshire cricketer of the 50s)—a forerunner to the mobile discos of the 60s. The power and amount of amplification equipment ensured that the listener could 'feel' the music rather than merely hear it. Competition was fierce to be first with the latest and most exclusive discs. The music favoured was hard R&B, with **Shirley And Lee**, **Amos Milburn** and **Lyn Hope** being particular favourites. The 'sounds' would often play in competition with each other, drawing wild cheers and ecstatic reactions when certain tunes were played. Titles were scratched out on the records and songs were renamed to prevent rival sounds discovering their identity. For instance, 'Later For Gator' by **Willis Jackson** was known as 'Coxsone Hop' to Down Beat followers. Reportedly, Dodd had been playing 'Later For Gator' for months and his closest rival, **Duke Reid**, had been unable to find its true identity. Later, Reid managed to acquire the record for himself, and played it against Dodd at one of their 'clashes'; Dodd apparently almost passed out with shock. Small fortunes were spent on record-buying sprees in America in order to keep on top.

In the mid-50s, the supply of hard R&B records dried up as smoother productions began to find favour with the black American audience. These were not popular in Jamaica, however, and starved of American records, the sound system operators started to create their own music. Initially, these productions were intended solely for live use and were played as **dub plates** only, but their popularity proved overwhelming and the sound system owners began to offer them for sale to the public. Among the earliest sides to appear at the end of the 50s on Coxsone's Worldisc label were records by local artists such as Jackie Estick, Lascelles Perkins ('Destiny'), Bunny And Skitter ('Lumumba'), Basil Gabbidon And The Mellow Larks ('Time To Pray'), **Clue J And His Blues Blasters** ('Shuffling Jug'), Aubrey Adams and the Dewdroppers ('Marjie') and **Theophilius Beckford** ('Easy Snappin''). Other artists recorded later included organist **Monty Alexander** And The Cyclones ('Stack Is Back'), the Jiving Juniors, featuring a young **Derrick Harriott**, **Derrick Morgan**, **Clancy Eccles** ('River Jordan' and 'Freedom'), Alton And Eddie ('Muriel'), the Charmers (featuring Lloyd Tyrell aka **Lloyd Charmers**), Joe Higgs And Wilson ('How Can I Be Sure'), **Cornell Campbell** and **Owen Gray** ('On The Beach'), as well as the first sides by such legendary hornsmen as **Don Drummond** ('Don Cosmic') and **Roland Alphonso**.

Although his empire was growing rapidly, Dodd shrugged off the attention with a typical 'I didn't realize that this could be a business. I just did it for enjoyment!'. Dodd's productions caught the mood of the times, and as Jamaican R&B evolved into ska, with the accent firmly on the off-beat, he was always at the forefront with his teams of session musicians and raw young vocalists. Throughout the ska era he ruled with records such as 'Joe Liges' and 'Spit In The Sky' by **Delroy Wilson**, 'Six & Seven Books Of Moses' and 'Hallelujah' by the **Maytals**, 'Simmer Down', 'Hooligan', 'Rudie' and many more by the **Wailers**, 'Rude Boy Gone A Jail' and 'Shoo Be Do Be' by the **Clarendonians**, 'I've Got To Go Back Home' by **Bob Andy**, a brace of **Lee Perry** tunes including 'Rub & Squeeze' and 'Doctor Dick', as well as dozens of fiery instrumentals by the **Skatalites** (often released crediting only the lead instrumentalist), the crack ensemble who also provided the backing on all Dodd recordings during this time.

Dodd opened his own Jamaica Recording and Publishing Studio on Brentford Road in October 1963, known as Studio One, which became the generic title for all his productions thereafter. The advantages were numerous: multiple 'takes' to ensure that the final one was right, the opportunity to experiment without having to worry about the high costs of studio time and the capacity to attempt 'uncommercial' ventures. Dodd placed many of the island's top musicians on his payroll and the results were impressive. With accomplished arrangers and musicians supervising—such as Lee Perry, **Jackie Mittoo**, **Larry Marshall** and Leroy Sibbles—just about every top name in reggae music worked for Studio One at some stage in his or her career—usually at the beginning, because Dodd was always keen to develop new talent, holding regular Sunday auditions for aspiring artists.

During the 1967–70 period, the hits flowed out of Brentford Road in a veritable deluge of unparalleled creativity. By late 1966, ska's furious pace was beginning to give way to the slower **rocksteady** beat; the sparser instrumentation and the availability of multi-track recording equipment allowed for a greater emphasis on melody and subtlety, and although it is recognized that Duke Reid's Treasure Isle productions represent much of the finest rocksteady extant, Dodd's raw, almost organic productions from this period have since gone on to form what amounts to the foundation of reggae music in the following decades. Much of this incredible output appeared on a number of labels in the UK, notably the Coxsone and Studio One imprints handled by **Island Records**' B&C group, and, later, on the Bamboo and Banana labels. Such artists as **Ken Boothe** (a cover of **Kenny Lynch** and **Garnet Mimms**' 'Moving Away', 'Thinking', 'Without Love', 'Just Another Girl'), Bob Andy ('I've Got To Go Back Home', 'Too Experienced', 'Going Home', 'Unchained', 'Feeling Soul'), Alton Ellis ('I'm Just A Guy', 'I'm Still In Love With You', 'Can I Change My Mind', 'Still Trying'), the **Heptones** ('Fattie Fattie', 'Love Won't Come Easy', 'Heptones Gonna Fight', 'I Hold The Handle', 'Pretty Looks', 'Give Me The Right', 'Sweet Talking'), **Marcia Griffiths** ('Truly', 'Feel Like Jumping'), **John Holt** ('Strange Things', 'A Love I Can Feel', 'OK Fred'), **Slim Smith** ('Born To Love You', 'Never Let Go', 'Rougher Yet'), Delroy Wilson ('Never Conquer', 'I Don't Know Why'), **Carlton And His Shoes** ('Love Me Forever'),

Jackie Mittoo ('Ram Jam', 'Hot Milk', 'One Step Beyond', 'Drum Song', 'Peanie Wallie', 'In Cold Blood'), Ernest Wilson ('Undying Love'), Larry Marshall And Alvin ('Nanny Goat', 'Throw Me Corn', 'Mean Girl'), **Ken Parker** ('My Whole World Is Falling Down'), Roland Alphonso ('Jah Shaky'), the **Gaylads** ('Africa', 'Love Me With All Your Heart'), the Eternals featuring Cornell Campbell ('Queen Of The Minstrels', 'Stars'), the **Cables** ('Baby Why', 'What Kind Of World', 'Be A Man') and dozens of instrumental sides by the in-house session band the Soul Vendors/Sound Dimension ('Full Up', 'Swing Easy', 'Psychedelic Rock', 'Frozen Soul', 'Real Rock', 'Mojo Rocksteady') and countless others made some of their finest records at Brentford Road.

Many of these songs, arrangements and rhythm tracks in particular, are endlessly recycled by younger artists and producers. Indeed, one recent trend in the music was to sample snatches of Dodd's classic old rhythms and build new versions out of the sample. Other younger producers, some of whom—Lee Perry and **Winston 'Niney' Holness**, in particular—had learnt their trade while with Dodd, began to take over in the early 70s, leaving their mentor to take a less prominent role in the music's development. Nonetheless, throughout the decade Dodd still produced a great deal of fine music including some of the earliest material from **Horace Andy** ('Skylarking', 'Just Say Who', 'Fever', 'Every Tongue Shall Tell'), **Dennis Brown** ('No Man Is An Island', 'If I Follow My Heart', 'Easy Take It Easy'), the **Wailing Souls** ('Mr Fire Coal Man', 'Back Out With It'), **Burning Spear** ('Door Peep', 'Joe Frazier', 'Swell Headed'), **Dennis Alcapone** ('Power Version', *Forever Version*), **Dillinger** (*Ready Natty Dreadie*) and **Freddie McKay** (*Picture On The Wall*). He also re-released much of his back catalogue through the 1974–79 period, which ensured his music was heard by a new generation of reggae music lovers. As the **dancehall** style began to supersede the **rockers** and steppers forms, he was once more in full swing with artists such as Freddie McGregor, Sugar Minott, Johnny Osbourne, Judah Eskender Tafari, **Willie Williams** and DJs **Michigan And Smiley** and the **Lone Ranger** all recording fine singles and albums.

This proved to be the final golden period for Studio One, however, and in the mid-80s Dodd closed his Brentford Road studio and relocated to Brooklyn, New York. In 1991, Dodd celebrated 35 years in the business with two huge shows in Jamaica, featuring many of the people with whom he had worked over the years. The same year he received the Order of Distinction, Jamaica's third highest honour. Dodd moved back to Kingston in 1998 and reopened the Brentford Road studio. Plagued by arthritis in his later years, he succumbed to a heart attack in May 2004.

Some of the pivotal albums in reggae history have been Coxsone Dodd productions, including the Skatalites' *Ska Authentic*, Dub Specialist's *Hi-Fashion Dub Top Ten*, Roland Alphonso and Jackie Mittoo's *Macka Fat*, Cedric Brooks' *Im Flash Forward*, Dennis Brown's *If I Follow My Heart*, Bob Andy's *Song Book*, Burning Spear's *Studio One Presents*, Carlton And His Shoes' *Love Me Forever*, Alton Ellis' *Sunday Coming*, Heptones' *On Top*, Freddie McGregor's *Bobby Babylon*, Bob Marley And The Wailers' *Wailing Wailers*, Johnny Osbourne's *Truths & Rights*, Maytals' *Never Grow Old*, Sugar Minott's *Live Loving*, Wailing Souls' *Studio One Presents*, and Delroy Wilson's *Feel Good All Over*. Dodd was reluctant to talk about past glories, however, preferring to look to the future. Sadly, with the exception of the occasional gem, his newer work rarely matched his previous high standards. There is always a selection of his music available at specialist reggae shops—and, in a business controlled by the latest and the newest, they continue to sell. Despite rumours of financial and personal disagreements between Dodd and his recording artists, the majority have stated that their time was well spent at his 'musical college'. His position as the guiding light of Jamaican music is beyond question and the true extent of his influence has yet to be fully realized.

● COMPILATIONS: *All Star Top Hits* (Studio One 1961) ★★★★, *Oldies But Goodies (Volumes 1 & 2)* (Studio One 1968) ★★★★, *Best Of Studio One (Volumes 1, 2, & 3)* (Heartbeat 1983–87) ★★★★, *Respect To Studio One* (Heartbeat 1995) ★★★.

● DVD/VIDEOS: *Studio One Story* (Soul Jazz 2002).

● FURTHER READING: *A Scorcha From Studio One/More Scorcha From Studio One*, Roger Dalke.

Dodd, Deryl

b. 12 April 1964, Texas, USA. Country singer-songwriter Deryl Dodd was 32 years old when he released his **Columbia Records** debut, *One Ride In Vegas*, in October 1996. He had begun his career several years earlier on the Texas honky-tonk circuit, having first picked up a guitar while a student at Baylor University in Waco. After graduation Dodd and his band became permanent fixtures on the Dallas club scene. Eventually he moved to Nashville, backing artists including **Martina McBride** and **Tracy Lawrence**. He also worked as a songwriter, but he never felt comfortable with the process of manufacturing tunes decreed by fashion and soon returned to his own songwriting. The resultant debut album featured his own original material, though the medium was implacably that of traditional country. It positioned Deryl Dodd at the forefront of a renaissance in conservative country music values, alongside other talented newcomers such as **Gary Allen**. His self-titled second album was less successful, however, and by the release of 2002's *Pearl Snaps* Dodd had relocated to the Lucky Dog label. He also recovered from a life-threatening viral illness.

● ALBUMS: *One Ride In Vegas* (Columbia 1996) ★★★★, *Deryl Dodd* (Columbia 1998) ★★★, *Pearl Snaps* (Lucky Dog 2002) ★★★, *Live At Billy Bob's Texas* (Image 2003) ★★, *Stronger Proof* (Dualtone 2004) ★★★★.

Dodd, Ken

b. 8 November 1927, Liverpool, England. Primarily one of Britain's all-time great stand-up comedians, Dodd has also had a successful recording career singing romantic ballads in a warm mezzo-tenor voice. His only comedy record—as the Diddy Men in 1965—was a flop. He grew up in Liverpool and sang in a church choir before developing a comedy act as Professor Yaffle Chuckabutty, Operatic Tenor and Sausage Knotter, in which he sang comic versions of well-known songs. Dodd worked in sales before becoming a professional comic in 1954, playing theatres and summer shows at Blackpool's Central Pier, where he topped the bill in 1958. This led to appearances at the London Palladium and a television series in the 60s. Like other comedians of his generation, Dodd was a competent singer and frequently closed his shows with a romantic ballad. In 1960 he signed to **Decca Records** and recorded 'Love Is Like A Violin', a 20s ballad which became a Top 10 hit. This was followed by 'Once

In Every Lifetime' (1961) and 'Pianissimo' (1962). He next switched to **EMI**'s **Columbia** label, where **Geoff Love** was the musical director for the minor hits 'Still' (1963) and the exuberant 'Happiness' (1964). But the biggest hit of his career was the contrasting 'Tears' (1965), a weepie of a ballad produced by **Norman Newell**. After five weeks at number 1 in the UK, it was displaced by the **Rolling Stones**' 'Get Off Of My Cloud'. A hit for **Rudy Vallee** in 1931, 'Tears' sold nearly two million copies for Dodd and led to six more Top 20 singles in the next few years. Among these were translations of three Italian Ken Dodd hits ('The River', 'Broken Hearted' and 'When Love Comes Round Again') and 'Promises', based on Beethoven's *Pathetique Sonata*. During the 80s, Dodd had modest success with 'Hold My Hand' (1981). In 1990 he hit the headlines following a controversial High Court action brought by the Inland Revenue, which he won. Four years later, he began a six-part BBC Radio 2 series, *Ken Dodd's Comedy Club*, explaining: 'I'm an intellectual entertainer; at one time there was only me and **Noël Coward** doing this sort of stuff.'

● ALBUMS: *Tears Of Happiness* (Columbia 1965) ★★★, *Hits For Now And Always* (Columbia 1966) ★★★, *For Someone Special* (Columbia 1967) ★★★, *Now And Forever* (VIP 1983) ★★.

● COMPILATIONS: *Ken Dodd Collection* (One-Up/EMI 1975) ★★★, *20 Golden Greats* (Warwick 1980) ★★, *More Than Ever* (MFP/EMI 1981) ★★, *The Very Best Of Ken Dodd* (MFP/EMI 1983) ★★★, *Greatest Hits* (Hour Of Pleasure/ EMI 1986) ★★★, *Happiness: The Very Best Of Ken Dodd* (EMI 2001) ★★★.

Dodds, Baby

b. Warren Dodds, 24 December 1898, New Orleans, Louisiana, USA, d. 14 February 1959, Chicago, Illinois, USA. Dodds began taking drum lessons in his early teens and made appearances in street parades. Among his first professional engagements were stints in the bands of **Bunk Johnson**, Willie Hightower, **Oscar 'Papa' Celestin** and **Fate Marable**, with whom he stayed for three years until 1921. He then joined **King Oliver**, who was working in San Francisco, and travelled with the band to Chicago the following year. From 1924 he played in a succession of leading bands, mostly in Chicago, among them those of **Honore Dutrey**, **Freddie Keppard** and his older brother, **Johnny Dodds**. Throughout the 30s Dodds was still based in Chicago, playing with his brother, and recorded with many leading traditionalists. In the early 40s Dodds again worked with Bunk Johnson, now a rediscovered trumpet legend. He also played with **Mezz Mezzrow**, **Art Hodes** and **Miff Mole**. In 1950 he suffered a stroke but was soon back, playing with **Natty Dominique** and also performing in pick-up groups at various clubs in New York and Chicago. Persistent ill health eventually resulted in partial paralysis and he died in 1959. Generally held to be the master of New Orleans drumming, Dodds' style was based upon immaculate timekeeping and faultless technique. Eagerly studied by young drummers in Chicago during his many years there, he was a formative influence upon **Dave Tough**, who urged his slightly younger colleague **Gene Krupa** to listen to the same source. In practice, few of his devotees ever played like him, mainly because, in performance, Dodds did much more than merely keep time. His accompaniment, especially for soloists, was usually a display of all of his many skills and was, consequently, much fussier than many front-line players liked. Although he adhered closely to the New Orleans tradition, Dodd used his drum patterns in a manner that was in advance of his time and which was not fully exploited until the advent of bebop. In 1946 he recorded a session for Circle Records, during which he explained his technique and played several demonstration solos.

● ALBUMS: *The Baby Dodds Drum Method—Band* (American Music 1951) ★★★, *The Baby Dodds Drum Method—Trio* (American Music 1951) ★★, *The Baby Dodds Drum Method—Solo* (American Music 1951) ★★, *Footnotes To Jazz, Volume 1—Baby Dodds' Drum Solos* 10-inch album (Folkways 1951) ★★★.

● FURTHER READING: *The Baby Dodds Story*, Warren 'Baby' Dodds and Larry Gara.

Dodds, Johnny

b. 12 April 1892, New Orleans, Louisiana, USA, d. 8 August 1940, Chicago, Illinois, USA. Dodds did not begin playing clarinet until he was aged 17, but in taking lessons from **Lorenzo Tio** ensured that his late start did not hamper his career. In the years before World War I he played with **Kid Ory** and **Fate Marable**, mostly in his home-town, and also worked with a minstrel show where he met **Mutt Carey**. In 1920 he joined **King Oliver** in Chicago. After leaving Oliver at the end of 1923 he worked with among others **Honore Dutrey** and **Freddie Keppard**. During this period he appeared on the classic Hot Five and Hot Seven records with **Louis Armstrong**. In the 30s he worked mostly in Chicago, leading bands at various clubs. A heart attack in 1939 withdrew him from music for a few months. However, he returned in early 1940 but ill health persisted and he died in August that year.

A striking performer with a fluent style, Dodds made an important contribution to jazz, and to clarinet playing in particular. His death occurred when clarinettists were in the ascendancy. Not only were big band leaders **Benny Goodman** and **Artie Shaw** enjoying great commercial success, but also more traditionally inclined players such as **Sidney Bechet**, **Jimmy Noone** and **George Lewis** were benefiting from a resurgence of interest in early forms of jazz. Despite the passage of time and the wide-ranging developments in jazz, not least the decline in popularity of the clarinet as a front-line instrument, Dodds' recordings of the 20s and 30s are still highpoints in the history of jazz recording and are rarely out of print.

● ALBUMS: *The King Of New Orleans Clarinets* 10-inch album (Brunswick 1950) ★★★★, *Johnny Dodds, Volume 1* 10-inch album (Riverside 1953) ★★★, *Johnny Dodds, Volume 2* 10-inch album (Riverside 1953) ★★★, with Jimmy Noone *Battle Of Jazz, Volume 8* (Brunswick 1953) ★★★, *Johnny Dodds' Washboard Band* (X 1954) ★★★, *New Orleans Clarinet* (Riverside 1956) ★★★★, with Kid Ory *Johnny Dodds And Kid Ory* (Epic 1956) ★★★★.

● COMPILATIONS: *Sixteen Rare Recordings* (RCA Victor 1965) ★★★, *The Stomp* (Rhapsody 1983) ★★★★, *Johnny Dodds 1928–29 recordings* (Swaggie 1989) ★★★★, *Blue Clarinet Stomp 1926–29 recordings* (Bluebird 1990) ★★★★, *King Of The New Orleans Clarinet 1926–38 recordings* (Black & Blue 1992) ★★★★, *Johnny Dodds Volumes 1–2* (Village Jazz 1992) ★★★.

● FURTHER READING: *Johnny Dodds*, G.E. Lambert.

Dodge City Productions

London-based duo who filter jazz and rap into a cohesive music, usually fronted by the voice of Ghida De Palma.

Principal members Dodge (b. Roger Drakes) and I.G. also employ guest musicians such as the **Young Disciples** and jazzmen **Ronny Jordan** and **Steve Williamson**, and when the need arises, alongside rappers such as MC Bello (Of **Brothers Like Outlaw/KLF** fame) and **MCM**. Dodge and I.G. have also remixed for **Gang Starr**, **Digital Underground** and **Naughty By Nature**. Singles such as 'Unleash Your Love' led to them being viewed as the new **Soul II Soul** in some corners, particularly the way in which they operated as a collective, with live shows usually featuring no less than eight people on stage at any given time.

● ALBUMS: *Steppin' Up And Down* (4th & Broadway 1993) ★★★.

Dodgion, Dottie

b. Dorothy Giaimo, 23 September 1929, Brea, California, USA. After working as a singer, Dodgion began playing drums when she was in her early twenties, following the example of her father, Chuck Giaimo. She played drums first with a trio, gradually learning her new trade sitting in with various bands and at after-hours sessions. When she married saxophonist Jerry Dodgion in the mid-50s, she was actively encouraged to develop her skills and was soon working in Las Vegas with musicians such as **Carl Fontana**. While there, she jammed with her husband, who was playing with **Benny Goodman**, and Goodman heard her and also sat in. A short time later, in New York, she was hired by Goodman. This was in 1959 when the band included **Red Norvo**, Fontana, **Buddy Childers**, **Jimmy Rushing** and **Zoot Sims**. She became quite popular with audiences, which was a sure way to be fired, Goodman having a well-known antipathy towards drummers who might upstage him.

Dodgion continued to work throughout the 60s and 70s, mostly in and around New York, also in Lake Tahoe, Nevada, and Washington, DC. Amongst the artists with whom she has worked are **Lee Konitz**, **Randy** and **Michael Brecker**, **Ruby Braff**, **Carol Sloane**, **Mary Osborne**, **Melba Liston** and **Thad Jones**. She recorded a vocal album for the Arbors label in 1996. An instinctive timekeeper with a subtle flair for accompaniment, Dodgion is deeply conscious of the need for a drummer in jazz to support and lift soloists and ensemble. A committed professional, she has an enviable reputation amongst musicians although the general jazz public is often unaware of her subtle and much-valued skills.

● ALBUMS: *Sings* (Arbors 1996) ★★★.

Dodgy

This pop trio was based in north London, England, at the height of their Britpop success, but the roots of Dodgy can be traced to mid-80s Birmingham, where Nigel Clark (vocals/bass) joined local goth band Three Cheers For Tokyo, finding a musical ally in drummer Mathew Priest. Their shared tastes included **The The**'s *Infected* and a revulsion for their guitarist's Flying V exhibitionism. The pair relocated to London instead and placed an advert in *Loot* that simply read: 'Wanted: Jimi Hendrix'. Andy Miller (guitar) rallied to the call, and the trio moved to Hounslow. They spent a year practising the three-part harmonies that would become their trademark. Taking the name Dodgy, the band played their first gig at the John Bull pub in Chiswick. Afterwards, the 'Dodgy Club' was inaugurated. By taking over a Kingston wine bar, the band created their own weekly hangout with DJs mixing up indie and dance tracks, with the band playing as the finale. Guests included **Oasis**, **Shed Seven** and even **Ralph McTell**.

The band's first demo, featuring an early take on 'Lovebird', won BBC DJ Gary Crowley's 'Demo Clash' for several consecutive weeks, before **A&M Record**s requested their signatures. 1993's *The Dodgy Album*, filled with buoyant 60s-styled pop tunes, nevertheless failed to sell, though The Dodgy Club was now being exported as far afield as Amsterdam and Scandinavia. 1994 was the band's break-through year, with *Homegrown* producing two memorable singles in 'Staying Out For The Summer' (a hit when reissued in 1995) and 'So Let Me Go Far'. Despite lacking any discernible image aside from that of three wide-eyed and unspoilt souls with a fondness for dressing down (matching red trousers apart) and big, eminently hummable songs, Dodgy were now welcome guests in both the charts and the pop press. **Free Peace Sweet** was a solid album containing some memorable songs. 'You've Gotta Look Up' (with shades of the **Ad Libs**' 'The Boy From New York City') and 'Good Enough' (a UK number 4 single in the summer) were both outstanding, yet overall, it fell short of the greatness that many had expected. Paul Moody of the UK's **New Musical Express** summed it up well: 'A fine pop album then, but not a great Dodgy album.'

With rumours of personality clashes flying around, Clark left the band in June 1998. The trio's final single, 'Every Single Day', was released in September. Miller and Priest returned in summer 1999 with new singer David Bassey, keyboard player Chris Hallam and bass player Nick Abnett. A solid new album, funded by their fans, was released in July 2001. Miller went on to record with M.A.S.S. while Priest guested with UK indie rockers the **Electric Soft Parade**.

● ALBUMS: *The Dodgy Album* (A&M 1993) ★★★★, *Homegrown* (A&M 1994) ★★★★, *Free Peace Sweet* (A&M 1996) ★★★, *Real Estate* (Bostin' 2001) ★★★.
● COMPILATIONS: *Ace As & Killer Bs* (A&M 1998) ★★★★, *The Collection* (Spectrum 2004) ★★★.

Doe, John

b. John Nommensen Duchac, 25 February 1954, Decatur, Illinois, USA. The co-founder and bass player of one of America's original leading punk bands, **X**, John Doe has pursued an increasingly impressive but commercially unrewarding solo career. Doe formed X in 1977 with his future wife **Exene Cervenka**, and in the following decade they recorded a series of well-received albums that would also prove an enormous influence on the nascent US alternative rock scene. The mid-80s line-up of X also teamed up with **Dave Alvin** in the part-time country outfit, the **Knitters**. X embarked on an extended hiatus at the end of the 80s, with both Cervenka and Doe launching solo careers.

Doe's 1990 debut, *Meet John Doe*, featured some superb material but was over-produced and bland, despite featuring the talents of guitarist **Richard Lloyd**. He reunited with Cervenka and X three years later on *Hey Zeus!*, although their unplugged album from two years later is a more worthwhile recording. During this period Doe formed his own band, the John Doe Thing, who made their recording debut with 1995's *Kissingsohard*. The album was a far more successful attempt at recreating X's inspired fusion of punk, rockabilly and blues, and even included a reworking of his old band's 'My Goodness'. By now, Doe had established himself as a reliable character actor with appearances in *Salvador*, *Road House*

and *Great Balls Of Fire!* During the latter part of the 90s his acting career took off, with acclaimed roles in *Boogie Nights* and the television series *Roswell*. Nevertheless, he found time to make the occasional live appearance with X, and in 2000 released his third album, the excellent *Freedom Is . . . .* The 2002 follow-up *Dim Stars, Bright Light* was credited to Doe alone, and featured guest vocals from **Aimee Mann**, **Jane Wiedlin**, **Rhett Miller** and **Juliana Hatfield** among others. Doe's debut for the Yep Roc label, 2005's *Forever Hasn't Happened Yet*, was recorded with help from Alvin, **Cindy Lee Berryhill**, **Neko Case** and **Grant Lee Phillips**.

● ALBUMS: *Meet John Doe* (DGC 1990) ★★★, as the John Doe Thing *Kissingsohard* (Forward/Rhino 1995) ★★★, as the John Doe Thing *Freedom Is . . .* (spinART 2000) ★★★★, *Dim Stars, Bright Light* (iMusic 2002) ★★★, *Forever Hasn't Happened Yet* (Yep Roc 2005) ★★★.
● FILMS: *Urgh! A Music War* (1981), *The Decline Of Western Civilization* (1981), *3:15* (1986), *Salvador* (1986), *Slam Dance* (1987), *Border Radio* (1987), *Road House* (1989), *Great Balls Of Fire!* (1989), *A Matter Of Degrees* (1990), *Without You I'm Nothing* (1990), *Liquid Dreams* (1991), *Roadside Prophets* (1992), *Pure Country* (1992), *Wyatt Earp* (1994), *Georgia* (1995), *Black Circle Boys* (1997), *Touch* (1997), *The Price Of Kissing* (1997), *Scorpion Spring* (1997), *The Last Time I Committed Suicide* (1997), *Boogie Nights* (1997), *The Pass* aka *Highway Hitcher* (1998), *Odd Man* (1998), *Lone Greasers* (1998), *Sugar Town* (1999), *The Rage: Carrie 2* (1999), *Forces Of Nature* (1999), *Wildflowers* (1999), *Knocking On Death's Door* (1999), *Brokedown Palace* (1999), *Drowning On Dry Land* (1999), *The Specials* (2000), *Gypsy 83* (2001), *Jon Good's Wife* aka *The Red Right Hand* (2001), *The Employee Of The Month* aka *Under The Gun* (2002), *The Good Girl* (2002), *Bug* (2002), *Pledge Of Allegiance* aka *Red Zone* (2002) *Media Whore* (2002), *Mayor Of The Sunset Strip* (2003), *Lucky 13* (2004), *Torque* (2004), *The Sandpiper* (2005).

Dog Eat Dog

Formed in New York, USA, this metal crossover act originally comprised John Connor (vocals), Dan Nastasi (guitar/vocals), Sean Kilkenny (guitar), David Neabore (bass) and David Maltby (drums). Their earliest releases, the 1993 EP *Warrant*, and 1994 album *All Boro Kings*, were stylistically diverse, combining hip-hop, hardcore and dancehall reggae as well as more traditional rock riffing. The album featured contributions from Darryl Jenifer of **Bad Brains**, with production by Jason Corsaro. Accused in some quarters of jumping onto **Rage Against The Machine**'s rock/rap bandwagon, the band nevertheless provided an intoxicating blend of forceful music. 'No Fronts' was a caustic reply to their detractors in the press: 'No front, no tricks, no soap-box politics, no guns, just blunts, we kick this just for fun.' Comparisons to **Cypress Hill** were prompted by the introduc-tion of the Solid Ground hip-hop crew and a brass section. Playing live with both hip-hop (**Goats**, **Onyx**) and metal/ alternative acts (**Biohazard**, Bad Brains) further extended their audience. This eclecticism was confirmed by the 1995 release of a remix EP, *No Fronts—The Remixes*, with mixes from Jam Master Jay (**Run DMC**), the **Beatnuts** and Phil Greene. Nastasi left the band in 1995 and subsequently formed Number 9 with ex-Hades guitarist Dan Lorenzo, before forming the eponymous Nastasi. Subsequent Dog Eat Dog recordings have struggled unsuccessfully to produce another anthem along the lines of 'No Fronts'.

● ALBUMS: *All Boro Kings* (Roadrunner 1994) ★★★, *Play Games* (Roadrunner 1996) ★★★, *Amped* (Roadrunner 1999) ★★★.
● COMPILATIONS: *In The Dog House: The Best And The Rest* (Roadrunner 2000) ★★★.

Dog Soldier

A UK rock quintet of the mid-70s, Dog Soldier comprised **Miller Anderson** (b. 12 April 1945, Johnston, Renfrewshire, Scotland; guitar/vocals), Paul Bliss (bass), Derek Griffiths (guitar), **Keef Hartley** (drums) and Mel Simpson (keyboards). The group were very much Hartley's project after having established his reputation as a first class blues/rock drummer with **John Mayall**'s Bluesbreakers and the **Artwoods**. He had already had one attempt at forming his own group, the Keef Hartley Band, but with Dog Soldier he linked up with former Artwoods colleague Griffiths (who in the interim had worked with **Mike Cotton** Sound and Satisfaction). Anderson was one survivor from the Keef Hartley Band, having also worked with the Voice, At Last The 1958 Rock 'N' Roll Show and Hemlock. Anderson proved to be by far the most talented member of the band, both as a musician and songwriter. However, Dog Soldier's sole album for **United Artists Records** in 1975 (there was also a single, 'Pillar To Post') failed to ignite commercially and prompted Hartley to forgo his ambitions for a solo career. Largely inactive, Hartley has returned to carpentry as a career. Anderson now performs regularly as a solo acoustic artist.
● ALBUMS: *Dog Soldier* (United Artists 1975) ★★.

Dog, Tim

b. Timothy Blair, 1 January 1967, Bronx, New York City, USA. A dropout from St. John's University in Queens, Dog's 'Fuck Compton' single proved to be one of the most notorious releases in rap's chequered history. Yet this anti-**NWA** tirade (at one point he sings 'Shut up bitch/You can't sing' while simulating intercourse with **Eazy-E**'s 'girlfriend') was an undeniably forceful manifesto, for all its wanton tribalism. Indeed, legend has it that it provoked death threats from members of the west coast rap community. Dog was also a guest member of **Ultramagnetic MC's** for a period, appearing on their 'Chorus Line' anthem. Dog's second album, *Do Or Die*, was a largely discredited offering, despite the presence of **KRS-One** on 'I Get Wrecked'. Other tracks such as 'Silly Bitch' featured a refrain of 'Clean out the kitchen/And the bathroom sink', just in case listeners were unaware as to Dog's vision of women in the scheme of things. In 1994, Dog made a surprise signing to **Phonogram Records**' Talkin' Loud label, home to artists including **Incognito** and **Galliano**. The first result of this contract was the single, 'Bitch Wid A Perm', dedicated to fellow canine rapper **Snoop Doggy Dogg**.
● ALBUMS: *Penicillin On Wax* (Ruffhouse 1991) ★★★, *Do Or Die* (Ruffhouse/Columbia 1993) ★★★.

Dogbowl

b. Stephen Tunney, 1960, the Bronx, New York City, USA. Tunney is an obvious admirer of eccentric rockers **Ween** and **Frank Zappa**. Look no further than the titles of his songs ('Transforming The Eyeball', 'Michael The Human Headed Dog') and, most obviously, his knack for penning quirky ditties, whether it is as a member of **King Missile** or issuing recordings under his alias, Dogbowl.

While his earliest musical memories centred around watching the **Beatles** in films, it was not until Tunney discovered punk rock in the late 70s that he picked up the guitar and began playing with a neighbourhood friend, specializing in writing songs loose on set structures. Tunney was then invited by his friend John S. Hall to join his fledgling oddball rock band, King Missile (aka King Missile (Dog Fly Religion)), in 1984. Appearing on cult classics such as 1988's *They* and 1990's *Mystical Shit*, it appeared as though Dogbowl had found a suitable home for his bizarre musings. However, he had a taste of what being a solo artist was like, issuing his Dogbowl debut in 1989, the interestingly titled *Tit! (An Opera)*. Quitting King Missile on the eve of the band signing a major label recording contract with **Atlantic Records**, Tunney concentrated on launching his Dogbowl project, as well as working as a graphic designer (he earned a diploma as an art teacher at Parsons School of Design) and finishing a novel, *Flan*. The first post King Missile Dogbowl release was 1991's *Cyclops Nuclear Submarine Captain*, which was followed up a year later with a musical adaptation of his aforementioned novel, also going by the title of *Flan*. The relatively conventional *Project Success* followed in 1993 before Tunney opted to collaborate with **Kramer** (the main producer of Dogbowl's label, **Shimmy-Disc**) on two releases, 1994's *Hot Day In Waco* and 1995's *Gunsmoke*. Also around this time, Dogbowl issued his first live album, 1995's *Live On WFMU*, that saw Tunney joined by long-time band members Lee Ming Tah (bass) and Rage Age (drums). Subsequently, Tunney decided to carry on as a solo artist, issuing 1998's *The Zeppelin Record* and 2001's *Fantastic Carburetor Man*, and a career spanning compilation, *The Best Of Dogbowl Vol. II*.
● ALBUMS: *Tit! (An Opera)* (Shimmy-Disc 1989) ★★, *Cyclops Nuclear Submarine Captain* (Shimmy-Disc 1991) ★★★, *Flan* (Shimmy-Disc 1992) ★★★★, *Project Success* (Shimmy-Disc 1993) ★★★★, as Dogbowl And Kramer *Hot Day In Waco* (Shimmy-Disc 1994) ★★, *Live On WFMU* aka *Cigars, Guitars And Topless Bars* (Lithium 1995) ★★, as Dogbowl And Kramer *Gunsmoke* (Shimmy-Disc 1995) ★★, *The Zeppelin Record* (Lithium 1998) ★★★, *Fantastic Carburetor Man* (Eyeball Planet 2001) ★★★.
● COMPILATIONS: *The Best Of Dogbowl Vol. II* (62TV 2001) ★★★★.
● FURTHER READING: *Flan: A Novel*, Stephen Tunney.

Doggett, Bill

b. 16 February 1916, Philadelphia, Pennsylvania, USA, d. 13 November 1996, New York City, New York, USA. In 1938 pianist Doggett formed his first band, partly drawing his sidemen from the band of Jimmy Goreham, with whom he had played for the past few years. Later that year he worked with **Lucky Millinder**, with whom he also played in the early 40s—Millinder having taken over leadership of Doggett's band. During this period Doggett wrote many arrangements for various bands, including **Lionel Hampton** and **Count Basie**, and also worked as staff arranger and accompanist with the popular vocal group the **Ink Spots**. He made a number of recordings with **Buddy Tate** and **Illinois Jacquet**, then worked with **Willie Bryant**, **Johnny Otis** and **Louis Jordan**. In the mid-40s he began playing organ, and when he formed his own R&B band in 1951, concentrated on this instrument. He had big hits with 'Honky Tonk', which reached number 1 in the R&B charts and number 2 in the US charts in 1956, and was in the Top 10 for 14 weeks with 'Slow Walk'. He showed his versatility by arranging and conducting **Ella Fitzgerald**'s 1963 album *Rhythm Is Our Business*. Doggett continued leading a swinging R&B-orientated band into the 80s.

● ALBUMS: *His Organ And Combo* 10-inch album (King 1955) ★★★, *His Organ And Combo Volume 2* 10-inch album (King 1955) ★★★, *All-Time Christmas Favorites* 10-inch album (King 1955) ★, *Sentimentally Yours* 10-inch album (King 1956) ★★★, *Moondust* (King 1957) ★★, *Hot Doggett* (King 1957) ★★, with Earl Bostic *C'mon And Dance With Earl Bostic* (King 1958) ★★★★, *As You Desire* (King 1958) ★★★, *A Salute To Ellington* (King 1958) ★★★, *Goin' Doggett* (King 1958) ★★★, *The Doggett Beat For Dancing Feet* (King 1958) ★★★, *Candle Glow* (King 1958) ★★★, *Dame Dreaming* (King 1958) ★★★, *Everybody Dance To The Honky Tonk* (King 1958) ★★★, *Man With A Beat* (King 1958) ★★★, *Swingin' Easy* (King 1959) ★★★, *Dance Awhile With Doggett* (King 1959) ★★, *Hold It* (King 1959) ★★★, *High And Wide* (King 1959) ★★★, *Big City Dance Party* (King 1959) ★★★, *On Tour* (King 1959) ★★★, *Christmas* (King 1959) ★★, *For Reminiscent Lovers, Romantic Songs* (King 1960) ★★★, *Back Again With More Bill Doggett* (King 1960) ★★★, *Focus On Bill Doggett* (King 1960) ★★, *Bonanza Of 24 Songs* (King 1960) ★★★, *The Many Moods Of Bill Doggett* (King 1963) ★★, *American Songs In The Bossa Nova Style* (King 1963) ★★, *Impressions* (King 1964) ★★★, *Honky Tonk Popcorn* (King 1969) ★★★, *Midnight Slows Volume 9* (Black & Blue 1978) ★★★.

● COMPILATIONS: *The Best Of Bill Doggett* (King 1964) ★★★, *Bonanza Of 24 Hit Songs* (King 1966) ★★★, *14 Original Greatest Hits* (King 1988) ★★★, *Leaps N'Bounds* (Charly 1991) ★★★, *The EP Collection* (See For Miles 1999) ★★★.

Dogs

Formed in 2003 by Johnny Cooke (vocals), Rikki Mehta (guitar), Luciano Vargas (guitar/vocals), Duncan Timms (bass) and Rich Mitchell (drums), the Dogs tapped into the growing public fervour for new UK rock bands in the mid-00s. The quintet gained rather clichéd comparisons to **Razorlight** by virtue of sharing the same manager, but in truth rocked harder than their erstwhile compatriots with a sound that drew on the early **Clash** in its barely controlled fury. The band's frantic live performances made an immediate impact on the London indie circuit and, scarcely a year after forming, were being championed in the UK music press. The thrilling limited edition double a-side 'London Bridge'/'End Of An Era' heralded the Dogs' arrival in autumn 2004. Extensive radio play for the single helped up the band's profile considerably, and after being courted by the major labels the quintet signed a recording contract with **Island Records** and decamped to the Sawmills Studio in Cornwall to begin work on their debut album. Their first Island single, 'She's Got A Reason', was released at the start of 2005 and attracted more critical plaudits. Further singles, 'Tuned To A Different Station' and 'Selfish Ways', set the scene for the autumn release of the Dogs' debut, *Turn Against This Land*. The album lived up to the hype generated by the singles and, more importantly, managed to capture on record the energy of the band's live shows.

● ALBUMS: *Turn Against This Land* (Island 2005) ★★★★.

Dogs D'Amour

This rock outfit was originally formed in London, England, during 1983, with a line-up comprising Tyla (b. Tim Taylor, England; guitar/vocals), Ned Christie (b. Robert Stoddard; vocals), Nick Halls (guitar), Karl Watson (bass) and Bam Bam (drums). After making their London debut on 12 April 1983 and recording a track for the Flicknife compilation *Trash On Delivery*, they underwent a rapid series of personnel changes. Halls, Bam Bam and Christie departed, prompting Tyla to assume lead vocal responsibilities. He and Watson recruited replacements Dave Kusworth (guitar/vocals) and Paul Hornby (drums). They relocated to Finland after being offered a contract by the Kumibeat label. The band's hard rock style won them an underground following but a completed album was never released (material from the sessions later showed up on *The (Un)Authorised Bootleg* release).

After returning to the UK in 1985, further changes in the line-up were underway, with Bam Bam returning to replace Hornby, while Kusworth departed in favour of the elegantly named Jo-Dog (b. Jo Almeida). Later that year, the procession of changes continued with the departure of Watson in favour of **Doll By Doll** bass player Marc Duncan, and then Marc Drax who lasted until 1987 when Steve James arrived. The classic line-up of Tyla, Bam Bam, Jo-Dog and Steve James then signed a new recording contract with China Records, debuting for the label with the album *In The Dynamite Jet Saloon*. Dogs D'Amour finally broke through with the minor hit 'How Come It Never Rains', and the mini-album *A Graveyard Of Empty Bottles*. The follow-up, 'Satellite Kid', also reached the UK Top 30 in August 1989, as did their album, *Errol Flynn*. The latter met with some resistance in the USA where it was forcibly retitled *The King Of The Thieves*.

Having at last stabilized their line-up, Dogs D'Amour failed to establish themselves in the top league of hard rock acts, but continued to tour extensively. *. . . Straight??!!* was recorded in Hollywood, with ex-**Faces** keyboard player **Ian McLagan** helping out. During a lull in the early 90s, prompted by Tyla inflicting a horrific wound upon himself at a gig in Los Angeles, James formed the Last Bandits, while Bam Bam joined the **Wildhearts** and Jo-Dog played with ex-**Guns N'Roses** member Gilby Clarke. Dogs D'Amour re-formed in 1993 with Darrell Bath (ex-**Crybabys**) replacing Jo-Dog. The new line-up completed a final album for China entitled *More Unchartered Heights Of Disgrace*. However, by 1994 the band had ground to a halt, with Tyla embarking on a solo career and Steve James and Bam Bam forming Mary Jane. Tyla, Jo-Dog and Bam Bam reunited in late 1991 to record new material, eventually released on 2001's *Happy Ever After*. The album featured Bam Bam's wife Share Pedersen on bass. Further line-up changes saw sole remaining original member Tyla joined by a revolving cast of musicians, including Yella (vocals), Danny McCormack (bass; ex-**Wildhearts**) and Tom Spencer (guitar; ex–Yo-Yo's).

● ALBUMS: *The State We're In* (Kumibeat 1984) ★★, *The (Un)Authorised Bootleg* (China 1988) ★★, *In The Dynamite Jet Saloon* (China 1988) ★★★, *A Graveyard Of Empty Bottles* mini-album (China 1989) ★★★★, *Errol Flynn* (UK) *King Of The Thieves* (USA) (China 1989) ★★★★, *. . . Straight??!!* (China 1990) ★★★, *More Unchartered Heights Of Disgrace* (China 1993) ★★, *Happy Ever After* (Artful 2001) ★★, *When Bastards Go To Hell* (GMR 2004) ★★.

● COMPILATIONS: *Dogs Hits & Bootleg Album* (China 1991) ★★★, *The Best Of . . . Skeletons* (Nectar 1997) ★★★, *Heart Shaped Skulls (Best Of . . . '88–'93)* (Warners 2004) ★★★.

● DVD/VIDEOS: *Heart-Shaped Skulls: The Best Of 88–93* (WSM 2004).

Dogs Die In Hot Cars

Based in Glasgow, Scotland, the excruciatingly named Dogs Die In Hot Cars were one of a string of bands to emerge in 2004 that took direct inspiration from the UK new wave scene of the early 80s. Craig Macintosh (guitar/vocals), Gary Smith (guitar/vocals), Lee Worrall (bass) and Laurence Davey (drums) grew up in the home of Scottish golf, St. Andrews, and began playing cover versions together in their first band. They relocated to Glasgow in 2001, recruiting Ruth Quigley (keyboards/vocals) along the way and adopting their new moniker. Their first single, 'I Love You 'Cause I Have To', an upbeat ska pop song, was released on the independent label Radiate in summer 2003. A near disaster followed shortly afterwards when lead singer Macintosh was electrocuted on stage at the Cotton Club in Dundee. Macintosh and the band bounced back to sign a major label recording contract with V2 Records. They made their debut for the label in January 2004 with the limited edition *Man Bites Man* EP. The quintet recorded songs for their debut album with veteran 80s producers Clive Langer and Alan Winstanley, providing further fuel for detractors who noted the lineage of some of the band's quirky indie pop melodies and Macintosh's vocal similarities to Andy Partridge of **XTC**. The single, 'Godhopping', broke into the UK Top 30 in May 2004, serving as a taster for Dogs Die In Hot Cars' debut, *Please Describe Yourself*.

● ALBUMS: *Please Describe Yourself* (V2 2004) ★★★.

Dog's Eye View

Dog's Eye View is the 90s USA band spearheaded by noted solo performer Peter Stuart (b. New York City, New York, USA), a regular support act to artists such as **Counting Crows** and **Tori Amos**. Stuart began playing seriously while studying in Chicago, playing with a number of bands as well as spending six months in Scotland. He moved back to New York in 1993, and began to establish his reputation as a solo performer. Touring with the Counting Crows over a sustained period, he subsidized his existence with over 6,000 sales of his demo tape. On Dog's Eye View's 1995 debut for **Columbia Records**, Stuart was joined by a 'shifting ensemble' of supporting musicians, including long-term collaborator John Abbey (bass), Oren Bloedow (guitar) and Alan Bezozi (drums). The group's title was taken from the view Stuart had enjoyed while living in a cramped downtown basement in Chicago. *Happy Nowhere* was produced by Jimbo Barton alongside Stuart, and recorded in a 'haunted house' in Woodstock, New York. The self-penned songs were initially recorded as solo demos with the accompanying musicians invited to build on these foundations. Stuart's natural musicality and emotionally involved songwriting worked best on lyrics such as 'Everything Falls Apart', 'Waterline' and 'I Wish I Was Here', songs which accrued strong reviews throughout the USA press.

● ALBUMS: *Happy Nowhere* (Epic 1995) ★★★.

Dogstar

Formed in Los Angeles, California, USA, Dogstar faced immediate reservations at its formation from an incredulous music press. This, in no small measure, was due to the fact that the bass player was heartthrob actor Keanu Reeves (b. 2 September 1964, Beirut, Lebanon). Drummer Rob Mailhouse (b. New Haven, Connecticut, USA) was also a Hollywood actor, although not nearly as famous. Reeves and Mailhouse formed the band in 1990, but didn't make any significant progress until they met singer and guitarist Bret Domrose (b. 13 December 1968, Santa Clara, California, USA) in 1994. Domrose offered a significant musical pedigree as an ex-member of seminal Californian punk band the **Nuns**. Originally a quartet (second guitarist Gregg Miller left over musical differences), the band embarked on a sold-out national tour in 1994 before even signing a recording contract. A contract was subsequently negotiated with Zoo Records, Mailhouse complaining that 'we never had a chance to grow naturally. But we just wouldn't go away because we felt really strong about what we're doing.' Nevertheless, the band exploited the opportunities made available to them by Reeves' celebrity, including opening for **Bon Jovi** on only their second performance as a trio. They then recorded four songs with **Pearl Jam** producer Rick Parashar for the *Quattro Formaggi* EP, which was followed by their debut album release. Veteran producer Ed Stasium oversaw *Our Little Visionary*, which **Billboard** magazine described as 'a cohesive package of nicely ragged, tuneful guitar rock.' Aside from a cover version of **Badfinger**'s 'No Matter What', the contents were all originals. The collapse of Zoo Entertainment put the trio's musical career on hold at the end of the 90s, but they bounced back in 2000 with the release of *Happy Ending*.

● ALBUMS: *Our Little Visionary* (Zoo 1996) ★★★, *Happy Ending* (Ultimatum 2000) ★★.

Dogwood

This contemporary Christian duo was formed by childhood friends Ron Elder and Steve Chapman in their native West Virginia, USA. Both were the sons of ministers and shared common interests in gospel and country music. After parting so that Elder could go to college and Chapman join the American navy, they reunited in the early 70s and began to play concerts around the country. As a return to the Christian values of their upbringing they formed Dogwood in 1974 as what they termed 'a mobile, positive musical ministry'. A sequence of albums followed, beginning with *After The Flood, Before The Fire*. Successive releases helped introduce them to a wider Christian following, genre critics focusing on what *Campus Life* magazine described as the duo's 'crystal clear acoustics and vocals'. That reputation eventually led to noted artists such as the Imperials and **Boones** recording the duo's compositions on their own records during the 70s.

● ALBUMS: *After The Flood, Before The Fire* (Lamb/Lion 1974) ★★★, *Love Note* (Lamb/Lion 1976) ★★★, *Out In The Open* (Lamb/Lion 1978) ★★★.

Doherty, Denny

b. 29 November 1941, Halifax, Nova Scotia, Canada. Doherty established his reputation as a member of the **Halifax Three**, a clean-cut folk act modelled on the **Kingston Trio**. In 1964 he formed the **Mugwumps** with **'Mama' Cass Elliott**, before opting for the New **Journeymen**, a group including **John Phillips** and **Michelle Phillips**. The seeds were thus sewn for the **Mamas And The Papas**, a highly popular mid-60s folk rock attraction, of which Doherty's confident voice was an integral part. The quartet was disbanded in 1968 and Doherty subsequently embarked on a solo career. *What'cha Gonna Do*, an unpretentious, country-influenced set, was not a commercial success, and thus its follow-up, *Waiting For A Song*, gained only limited exposure. The artist did complete several singles for the Paramount, Columbia and Playboy labels, but achieved a higher profile following his role in Phillips' musical *Man On The Moon*. By 1978 Doherty had returned to Halifax where he hosted a television variety show, but the following year agreed to join a reconstituted Mamas And Papas. He remained in the line-up until the late 80s when, tired of touring, Doherty gave up his place to long-time associate **Scott McKenzie**.

● ALBUMS: *What'cha Gonna Do* (Dunhill 1971) ★★, *Waiting For A Song* (Ember 1974) ★★★.
● FURTHER READING: *Papa John*, John Phillips with Jim Jerome. *California Dreamin': The True Story Of The Mamas And The Papas*, Michelle Phillips. *Go Where You Wanna Go: The Oral History Of The Mamas And The Papas*, Matthew Greenwald.
● FILMS: *Oh, What A Night* (1992), *Hurt Penguins* (1992), *The Real Howard Spitz* (1998).

Dokken

This Los Angeles, USA heavy metal band was put together by vocalist Don Dokken (b. 29 June 1953). His first break came when producer Dieter Dierks recruited him to supply (eventually unused) back-up vocals on the **Scorpions'** *Blackout* in 1982. Dierks then allowed Dokken the remaining studio time to produce demos. These rough recordings impressed Carrere Records enough to secure him a contract, and he enlisted the services of guitarist George Lynch (b. 28 September 1954), drummer Mick Brown and bass player Juan Croucier (who later left to form **Ratt** and was replaced by Jeff Pilson) to form Dokken. The band's intimate fusion of hard rock, melody and atmospherics led to a major label contract with **Elektra Records**. They remixed and re-released their Carrere debut, *Breaking The Chains*, which made the lower end of the US **Billboard** album chart. Thereafter, Elektra allowed the band a substantial recording budget, with producers Michael Wagener, Geoff Workman, Tom Werman and Roy Thomas Baker being used at different times. The band recorded three excellent studio albums for Elektra (*Back For The Attack* reaching US number 13 in December 1987) before internal disputes between Lynch and Don Dokken led the band to split in 1988. A farewell live album, *Beast From The East*, followed, and provided a fitting epitaph.

Lynch went on to form **Lynch Mob**, while Don Dokken negotiated a solo contract with **Geffen Records** and released *Up From The Ashes* in 1990. Pilson fronted War And Peace, but soon began writing with Dokken once more. Having been begged by Dokken fans over the preceding years for some form of reunion, they eventually elected to make it permanent. With Brown already on board, Lynch finally settled his differences with Don Dokken and rejoined in May 1994. The original line-up released the acoustic live set *One Live Night* (from a December 1994 concert) and recorded the lacklustre studio albums *Dysfunctional* and *Shadow Life*.

Lynch left in November 1997, and was replaced by Reb Beach (ex-**Winger**). The latter appeared on 1999's *Erase The Slate* before in turn being replaced by John Norum on 2002's surprisingly sound *Long Way Home*. This album also featured new bass player Barry Sparks.

● ALBUMS: *Breaking The Chains* (Carrere/Elektra 1982) ★★★, *Tooth And Nail* (Elektra 1984) ★★★, *Under Lock And Key* (Elektra 1985) ★★★, *Back For The Attack* (Elektra 1987) ★★★★, *Beast From The East* (Elektra 1988) ★★★, *Dysfunctional* (Columbia 1995) ★★, *One Live Night* (CMC 1995) ★★★, *Shadow Life* (CMC 1997) ★★, *Erase The Slate* (CMC 1999) ★★, *Live From The Sun* (CMC 2000) ★★, *Long Way Home* (CMC 2002) ★★★, *Hell To Pay* (Sanctuary 2004) ★★★.
Solo: Don Dokken *Up From The Ashes* (Geffen 1990) ★★.
● COMPILATIONS: *The Very Best Of Dokken* (Elektra 1999) ★★★.
● DVD/VIDEOS: *One Live Night: The Concert Video* (CMC International 1996).

Doky Brothers

Brothers Niels Lan Doky (b. 3 October 1963, Copenhagen, Denmark; piano) and Chris Minh Doky (b. 7 February 1969, Copenhagen, Denmark; bass) play an intriguing mix of mainstream jazz and contemporary pop music. The Doky brothers were raised in a musical family; their physician father was a classical guitar player, and their mother was a Danish pop singer. Niels began playing the piano professionally at the age of 13, and accompanied trumpeter **Thad Jones** two years later, leading to a scholarship at Boston's **Berklee College Of Music**. Attending the college between 1981 and 1984, Niels graduated with a degree in professional music and performed with artists including **Terri Lyne Carrington**, **Cyrus Chestnut** and **Branford Marsalis**. Relocating to New York he recorded the first in a series of albums for Storyville Records, and began playing as co-leader with his brother. After an early flirtation with piano, Chris took up electric bass when he was 15, switching to acoustic two years later. He moved to New York in 1988, performing with musicians of the calibre of **John Scofield** and **Randy Brecker**, and releasing a debut set on the Storyville label.

While performing together both brothers continued to record solo sessions, and Niels worked extensively as a producer. In 1995 they finally recorded as a duo for **Blue Note Records**, with guests including the Brecker brothers, Carrington, guitarist Ulf Wakenius and MOR singer **Curtis Stigers**. A follow-up set repeated the beguiling formula of Doky originals and interpretations of contemporary pop hits, and featured guest appearances by singers **Al Jarreau**, **Dianne Reeves** and Gino Vannelli.

● ALBUMS: *Doky Brothers* (Blue Note 1996) ★★★★, *Doky Brothers 2* (Blue Note 1998) ★★★.
Solo: Chris Minh Doky *Appreciation* (Storyville 1989) ★★★, *The Sequel* (Storyville 1990) ★★★, *Letters* (Storyville 1991) ★★★, *Minh* (Hori Pro 1998) ★★★, *Listen Up!* (Hori Pro 2000) ★★★. Niels Lan Doky *Here Or There* (Storyville 1986) ★★★★, *The Target* (Storyville 1987) ★★★★, *The Truth* (Storyville 1987) ★★★, *Daybreak* (Storyville 1989) ★★★, *Close Encounter, Vol. 1* (Storyville 1989) ★★★, *Close Encounter, Vol. 2* (Storyville 1989) ★★★, *Dreams* (Milestone 1990) ★★★★, *Friendship* (Milestone 1991) ★★★, *The Toronto Concert* (DAM 1991) ★★★, *An Evening Of Standards* (DAM 1992) ★★★★,

Paris By Night (Soul Note 1992) ★★★, *Manhattan Portrait* (DAM 1993) ★★★★, *Misty Dawn* (Sony 1994) ★★★, *Niels Lan Doky* (Verve 1998) ★★★, with Gino Vannelli *Haitek Haiku (See The World As A Plum)* (Universal 2001) ★★★.

Doky, Chris Minh
(see **Doky Brothers**)

Doky, Niels Lan
(see **Doky Brothers**)

Dolan, Joe
b. 16 October 1943, Mullingar, West Meath, Eire. After appearing on local radio, Dolan began singing professionally in early 1962. His accomplished backing group, the Drifters, comprised his brother Ben Dolan (saxophone), Tommy Swarbrigg (trumpet), Jimmy Horan (bass guitar), Joey Gilheaney (trumpet), Des Doherty (keyboards) and Donal Aughey (drums). After signing a record contract with **Pye**, the band recorded a promising cover of **Burt Bacharach**'s 'The Answer To Everything', which reached the Irish Top 10 in 1964. During the mid-60s Dolan and the Drifters established themselves as one of the most successful Irish showbands of their era. At their peak they enjoyed a string of hits in Eire including 'My Own Peculiar Way', 'Aching Breaking Heart', 'Two Of A Kind', 'Pretty Brown Eyes', 'House With The Whitewashed Gable' and 'Tar And Cement'. The latter was unfortunate not to cross over into the UK charts, and it was followed by the fragmentation of the original Drifters, several of whom reappeared in the **Times**. It was not until Dolan recorded solo, with the specific intent of becoming successful in Britain, that he won through. Mike Hazelwood and **Albert Hammond** of the **Family Dogg** provided the crucial hit with 'Make Me An Island', which reached number 3 in the summer of 1969. Subsequent hits from the songwriting partnership included the plaintive 'Teresa' and the up-tempo 'You're Such A Good Looking Woman'. As late as 1976 Dolan was back at number 1 in the Irish charts with 'Sister Mercy'. The following year, 'I Need You' repeated the feat and also infiltrated the UK Top 50. Dolan remains a regular performer on the Irish dancehall circuit.
● ALBUMS: *The Answer To Everything* (Pye 1969) ★★★, *Lady In Blue* (Pye 1975) ★★★, *Crazy Woman* (Pye 1977) ★★★, *I Need You* (Pye 1977) ★★★, *Turn Out The Light* (Pye 1980) ★★★, *It's You, It's You, It's You* (Ritz 1986) ★★★, *Always On My Mind* (Harmac 1989) ★★★.
● COMPILATIONS: *At His Best* (K-Tel 1988) ★★★, *Golden Hour Of Joe Dolan, Volumes 1 & 2* (Golden Hour 1988) ★★★★, *More And More* (1993) ★★★.

Dolby, Ray, Dr.
Through his eponymous noise-reduction units, Dolby made the most important technical contribution to the success of the tape cassette. From 1949 he was employed by Ampex on noise reduction programmes and then studied physics in London, England. After working in India for some years, Dolby opened a laboratory in London in 1965, selling his initial A-type system, designed for recording studios, to **Decca Records** and others. His research on reducing tape hiss for the 8-track cartridge and the cassette resulted in the B-type system in 1971. Within 12 months almost every major cassette manufacturer was using this system, although

Philips Records held out for a few years before converting. In 1978, Dolby's invention was adapted for the cinema and *Star Wars* was the first movie to have its soundtrack enhanced by the noise-reduction method. This system was upgraded for digital sound in 1991. So jealously guarded was the Dolby name that in 1987 Dolby Laboratories sued the musician/ producer **Thomas Dolby** (b. Thomas Morgan Robertson) for copyright infringement. Robertson agreed to 'license' the name from Ray Dolby's company.

Dolby, Thomas
b. Thomas Morgan Robertson, 14 October 1958, Cairo, Egypt. Dolby is a self-taught musician/vocalist/songwriter and computer programmer. After studying meteorology and projectionism at college, he started building his own synthesizers at the age of 18. With his own hand-built PA system he acted as sound engineer on tours by the **Members**, **Fall** and the **Passions**. Afterwards, he co-founded Camera Club with Bruce Wooley in January 1979, before joining the **Lene Lovich** backing group in September 1980, for whom he wrote 'New Toy'. His first solo output was the single 'Urges' on the Armageddon label in 1981, before he scored hits the following year with 'Europa' and 'The Pirate Twins'. For a series of 1982 concerts at the Marquee he recruited ex-**Soft Boys** Matthew Seligman and Kevin Armstrong of the **Thompson Twins**, while finding time to contribute to albums by **M**, **Joan Armatrading** and **Foreigner**. Other collaborations included **Stevie Wonder**, **Herbie Hancock**, **Dusty Springfield**, **Howard Jones** and **Grace Jones**. The most visual of such appearances came when he backed **David Bowie** at **Live Aid**. A strong 'mad scientist' image proliferated in his videos, which also featured famous British eccentric Magnus Pike. These earned him a strong media profile, but, surprisingly, his best-known singles, 'She Blinded Me With Science' and 'Hyperactive', only peaked at numbers 31 and 17, respectively. The latter did, however, reach the Top 5 in the USA, and charted in the UK again when re-released in 1996. As well as production for **Prefab Sprout** and **Joni Mitchell**, Dolby scored music for several movies including *Howard: A New Breed Of Hero*. He married actress Kathleen Beller (Kirby Colby from *Dynasty*). In 1993, he founded the computer software company Headspace, an enterprise that began to take precedence over his musical activities. Dolby commands high respect in the music business, as his back-room contributions have already been considerable.
● ALBUMS: *The Golden Age Of Wireless* (Venice In Peril 1982) ★★★★, *The Flat Earth* (Parlophone 1984) ★★★, *Aliens Ate My Buick* (Manhattan 1988) ★★, *Astronauts & Heretics* (Virgin 1992) ★★★, *The Gate To The Mind's Eye* (Giant 1994) ★★★.
● COMPILATIONS: *The Best Of Thomas Dolby: Retrospectacle* (Capitol 1995) ★★★★, *Hyperactive* (EMI 1999) ★★★.
● DVD/VIDEOS: *The Gate To The Mind's Eye* (Miramar Images 1994).

Dolce, Joe
b. 1947, Painesville, Ohio, USA. Of Italian/American extraction, Dolce was supposedly a member of Headstone Circus aka Sugar Creek, an obscure country rock act which released an album *Please Tell A Friend*, on Metromedia Records in 1968. By 1974, he was touring the USA east coast, fronting a 'poetry/rock' group, but he emigrated to Australia in 1979

where he formed the Joe Dolce Music Theatre, a cabaret-style act, with Dolce himself playing a character known as Giuseppe. In this guise, he recorded a novelty single, 'Shaddap You Face', which became a major hit in Australia, and was licensed to Epic in the UK and MCA in the USA. No doubt it appealed to Italian immigrants on both sides of the Atlantic, and while it stalled just outside the US Top 50 in mid-1981, it had already topped the UK singles chart for three weeks in February 1981, supplanting 'Woman' by **John Lennon**, whose records were dominating the UK chart in the wake of his recent murder. As with many novelty acts, Dolce was unable to follow up this success, although (remarkably) an album titled after the hit spent a month in the US Top 200 album chart also in 1981. Dolce subsequently returned to performing with the Joe Dolce Music Theatre, turning his back on the comic elements of his work and staging ambitious adaptations of the writings of Sappho, Albert Schweitzer and Sylvia Plath. Much of his work has been performed with Lin Van Hek as part of the literary-music group, Difficult Women.

● ALBUMS: *Shaddap You Face* (Full Moon/Epic/MCA 1981) ★★, *Christmas Album* (Frituna 1981) ★★, *Memoirs Of A Mouth Organ* (Own Label 1997) ★★★, *Free Love Days* (Own Label 2000) ★★★.

● COMPILATIONS: with Lin Van Hek *Flower* (Own Label 2001) ★★★.

Doldinger, Klaus

b. 12 May 1936, Berlin, Germany. Doldinger studied classical piano and clarinet at the Robert Schumann Institut der Musikhochschule Rheinland, Dusseldorf. He played traditional jazz as an amateur in the early 50s before turning to the tenor saxophone and developing a more modern style. In the 60s he toured extensively in a quintet with Ingfried Hoffman: Europe, Africa, South America and Asia. Then he formed a jazz rock unit **Passport**, with which he found success in the 70s and beyond. He also began to write film scores, the best known of which are the music for *Das Boot* and *The Never Ending Story*.

● ALBUMS: *Live At The Blue Note, Berlin* (Philips 1963) ★★★★, *Doldinger Goes On* (Philips 1963) ★★★, *Blues Happening* (Liberty 1968) ★★, *Doldinger The Ambassador* (Liberty 1969) ★★★, *Das Boot* film soundtrack (WEA 1985) ★★★, *In New York: Street Of Dreams* (WEA 1994) ★★★.

● COMPILATIONS: *Works And Passion 1955–2000* 4-CD set (Warners 2002) ★★★★.

Doll

Formed in late 1977, this UK new wave group originally comprised Marion Valentine (b. 1952, Brighton, Sussex, England; vocals/guitar), Christos Yianni (b. 6 September 1954, London, England; bass), Adonis Yianni (b. 10 October 1957, London, England; keyboards) and Mario Watts (b. 1958, London, England; drums). After signing to **Beggar's Banquet**, the group issued 'Don't Tango My Heart', but it was their second single, the infectious 'Desire Me', that propelled them into the UK charts in 1978. Inter-group politics, exacerbated by the inevitable promotion of their female singer and lyricist, caused several line-up changes. By the time they came to record their sole album, *Listen To The Silence*, Dennis Hayes (keyboard), Jamie West-Oram (guitar) and Paul Turner (drums) had joined. The group split soon afterwards, and although it was expected that the feline

Valentine (complete with leopard-skin guitar and jump suit) would be launched as a solo, she concentrated instead on songwriting, eventually retiring from the music business.

● ALBUMS: *Listen To The Silence* (Beggars Banquet 1979) ★★.

Doll By Doll

Essentially a vehicle for singer-songwriter **Jackie Leven** (b. 1950, Fife, Scotland), this UK rock band was formed in 1977 and first came to the fore in 1979, riding on the coat-tails of the punk explosion, with *Remember*. An interesting debut, the work featured Leven's wide-ranging vocal work to startling effect. The other members of the band on this release were Jo Shaw (guitar), David McIntosh (drums) and Robin Spreafico (bass). A great leap forward was made with the same year's *Gypsy Blood*, which saw Leven, Shaw and McIntosh joined by Tony Waite (bass), Graham Preskett (violin/keyboards) and **B.J. Cole** (steel guitar). Despite excellent reviews the album failed to cross over into the mainstream. The adoption of an unfashionable rock style, coupled with an uneasy relationship with the music press, undoubtedly hampered progress. Signed with Magnet Records, the band released the accomplished *Doll By Doll* which provided them with a minor hit in 'Caritas' (1981). For Doll By Doll's final album *Grand Passion*, Leven teamed up with vocalist Helen Turner and a number of session musicians for his most ambitious and experimental piece, but the critical reception proved lukewarm. On the break-up of the band Leven continued under his own name before retreating from the music scene for the rest of the decade. He resurfaced in the 90s with an acclaimed series of 'celtic soul' albums.

● ALBUMS: *Remember* (Automatic 1979) ★★★, *Gypsy Blood* (Automatic 1979) ★★★★, *Doll By Doll* (Magnet/ MCA 1981) ★★★, *Grand Passion* (Magnet 1982) ★★, *Revenge Of Memory* 1980 recording (Haunted Valley 2003) ★★.

Dollar

Under the aegis of producer Trevor Horn, this UK singing duo were designed to appeal to much the same market as **Guys And Dolls** before, and **Bucks Fizz** after them. Attired in stylish but not too way-out costumes for UK television's *Top Of The Pops*, Thereze Bazaar and David Van Day (b. 28 November 1957) made a promising start with November 1978's 'Shooting Star' (number 14 in the UK). For the next four years, it was unusual for the latest Dollar single to miss the Top 20. With vocals floating effortlessly above layers of treated sounds, the team's biggest work included: 'Love's Gotta Hold On Me', a revival of the **Beatles**' 'I Wanna Hold Your Hand', 'Mirror Mirror (Mon Amour)', 'Give Me Back My Heart' and the futuristic 'Videotheque'. By 1982, however, sales had become erratic, and, coupled with failure to crack the US charts, as well as Bazaar and Van Day's growing antagonism towards each other, Dollar signed off with a 'best of' compilation harrying the album lists. While Van Day managed a small hit with 'Young Americans Talking' in 1983, overall lack of record success as individuals prompted a reunion in 1986, but only 'O L'Amour' made more than a minor impact. Van Day subsequently joined Bucks Fizz in addition to running a mobile hamburger wagon and Bazaar moved to Australia and out of the music business. She reunited with Van Day in 2002 to perform on the 80s nostalgia tour, Here And Now.

● ALBUMS: *Shooting Stars* (Carrere 1979) ★★, *The Dollar Album* (Warners 1982) ★★.
● COMPILATIONS: *The Very Best Of Dollar* (Carrere 1982) ★★, *Shooting Stars: The Dollar Collection* (Castle 2002) ★★.

Dollar Princess, The

Staged at Daly's Theatre in London, where it opened on 25 September 1909, the music for *The Dollar Princess* was by Leo Fall with lyrics by **Adrian Ross**. The libretto was adapted by **Basil Hood** from the original book by A.M. Willner and Fritz Grünbaum. Concurrently, a different version of the show, with book and lyrics by **George Grossmith Jnr.**, was staged at Broadway's Knickerbocker Theatre, opening on 6 September 1909, where it ran for 288 performances. Additional songs were written for this production by **Jerome Kern**. The story follows the adventures of Alice, daughter of coal baron John Couder, and her cousins Dick and Daisy Gray, in their encounters with British and European aristocracy. Also on hand to keep things lively is cabaret singer Olga Labinska. The songs include 'A Boat Sails On Wednesday', 'The Dollar Princess', 'Love! Love! Love!', 'A Self Made Maiden', 'Love's A Race', 'My Dream Of Love', 'Reminiscence' and 'Then You Go?'. Among the cast for Hood's London version were **Lily Elsie** (Alice), Cranston Neville (Dick), Gabrielle Ray (Daisy), Joseph Coyne (Couder) and Madeline Seymour (Olga). Among other players were Doris Stocker (Sadie von Tromp), Gertrude Glyn (Lady Gwendoline) and Robert Michaelin (Freddy Fairfax). Elsie is believed also to have appeared in some performances of the New York version.

Dollar, Johnny

b. John Washington Dollar Jnr., 8 March 1922, Kilgore, Texas, USA, d. 13 April 1986, Nashville, Tennessee, USA. In the 50s, Dollar worked on radio in Dallas and Shreveport, at one time fronting a band named the Texas Sons. During the 60s he moved away from rock 'n' roll to become a shortlived country star, recording for **Columbia Records**, **Dot Records**, Date and Chart. He registered six minor hits and a Top 15 with 'Stop The Start Of Tears In My Heart'. His last chart entry, 'Truck Driver's Lament', was a minor hit in 1970. In the early 80s, Dollar basically quit performing to work for a record company that specialized in custom recordings. It is believed he was suffering from cancer when he committed suicide in 1986. Not to be confused with the R&B/blues artist of the same name, born John Sibley.
● ALBUMS: *Johnny Dollar* (Date 1967) ★★★, *Big Rig Rolling Man* (Chart 1969) ★★★, *Country Hit Parade* (Chart 1969) ★★★, *My Soul Is Blue* (Isabel 1980) ★★.
● COMPILATIONS: *Mr. Action Packed* (Rollercoaster 1998) ★★★.

Dollface

This UK hard rock band, formed in autumn 1992, comprises Adrian Portas (b. Sheffield, Yorkshire, England; vocals/guitar), John Alexander (b. Surrey, England; bass), Rob Todd (b. Wales; guitar) and Dave Mage (b. Buckinghamshire, England; drums). Signing to Kill City Records in 1993, they made their debut with the *Methedrine EP*, followed by another four-track collection, *Rock Stars*. This, with endearing songs such as 'Dead Boyfriend' and the ironic title track, brought them to the attention of a media who admired their straightforward approach to dynamic rock. The personal confessions and character studies continued on their debut album, the critically lauded *Giant*. It saw Portas deified, a little prematurely, as 'the last great story-teller in rock 'n' roll'. Support slots with **Slash's Snakepit** on their UK tour broadened their fanbase further, while Alexander's attempts to charm Polish barmaids on their European tour saw him become a minor celebrity of the gossip columns. However, their impetus stalled in 1995 when Kill City Records collapsed. They continued to play well-received shows on the London club circuit while searching for a new recording contract. Mage was replaced in July 1996 by ex-**Blue Aeroplanes** drummer Graham Russell.
● ALBUMS: *Giant* (Kill City Records 1995) ★★★★.

Dolly Mixture

This female UK pop trio comprised Deborah Wykes (b. 21 December 1960, Hammersmith, London, England; bass, piano, vocals), Rachel Bor (b. 16 May 1963, Wales; guitar, cello, vocals) and Hester Smith (b. 28 October 1960, West Africa; drums). The band was formed by the three school friends in Cambridge, with a musical style that echoed the **Shangri-Las** and the 70s **Undertones**. Championed by influential UK disc jockey **John Peel**, the band released a cover version of the **Shirelles** hit 'Baby It's You' on **Chrysalis Records** in 1980—which at the time of issue they disowned, protesting at the label's attempted manipulation of their image. They were one of the first bands to record for **Paul Weller**'s Respond label, releasing 'Been Teen' (1981) and 'Everything And More' (1982), both of which were produced by **Captain Sensible** and Paul Gray of the **Damned**. The UK record-buying public found difficulty coming to terms with the trio's idiosyncratic mode of dress and independent attitude, something with which a portion of the music press also had problems. They proved their worth, however, with exhilarating live performances. In 1982, they released a double album on their own Dead Good Dolly Platters label, featuring demo tapes collected over the previous four years. The album has since achieved cult status among later 80s independent groups. Dolly Mixture eventually found national fame by acting as Sensible's backing vocalists on his UK number 1 single 'Happy Talk', in 1982. They also guested on his subsequent singles and albums, while Bor and the Captain formed a romantic partnership. Meanwhile, their own career floundered, despite the critical plaudits. The trio dissolved as a working band in 1984, leaving as their swansong *The Fireside* EP, released on Cordelia Records, a set consisting mainly of 'pop/chamber' music, featuring their often ignored talents on piano and cello. In 1986, Wykes and Smith resurfaced with **Coming Up Roses**.
● ALBUMS: *The Demonstration Tapes* (Dead Good Dolly 1982) ★★★.

Dolly Sisters, The

The real-life American-Hungarian twins called the Dolly Sisters (b. Janzieska (Jenny) and Roszieska Deutsch (Rosie), 25 October 1892, Hungary) started in American vaudeville before graduating to Broadway musicals and revues such as the *Ziegfeld Follies* (1911) and the *Greenwich Village Follies* of 1924. In the latter production they introduced **Cole Porter**'s 'I'm In Love Again', and they were always surrounded by good songs. There were plenty of those, too, in this 1945 film biography, which had a screenplay by John Larkin and

Marian Spitzer, based on John Kenyon Nicholson's story. **Betty Grable** and **June Haver** portray the song-and-dance sister act which, after playing small-time clubs and theatres, catch the attention of producer Oscar Hammerstein (grandfather of **Oscar Hammerstein II**) played by Frank Middlemass, and zooms right to the top. Along the way—in the film, at least—Haver falls for Frank Latimore, and Grable gets **John Payne** at last—something she failed to do in *Tin Pan Alley* (1940). Also in the cast were S.Z. Sakall, Reginald Gardiner, Gene Sheldon, **André Charlot**, Sig Ruman, Colette Lyons and Lester Allen.

As for the songs, they were a mixture of old and new. Grable, Payne and Haver all had a crack at the best of the newcomers, 'I Can't Begin To Tell You' (**Jimmy Monaco–Mack Gordon**), and the trio shared the honours on the remainder which included 'I'm Always Chasing Rainbows' (Harry Carroll-**Joseph McCarthy,** adapted from Chopin), 'Give Me The Moonlight, Give Me The Girl' (**Albert Von Tilzer–Lew Brown**), 'Darktown Strutters' Ball' (**Shelton Brooks**), 'The Sidewalks Of New York' (James Blake–Charles Lawlor), 'Powder, Lipstick And Rouge' (**Harry Revel-Mack Gordon**), 'Carolina In The Morning' (**Walter Donaldson–Gus Kahn**), 'We Have Been Around' (Gordon–Charles Henderson) and 'The Vamp' (Byron Gay). This lively, colourful and thoroughly enjoyable film—it grossed nearly $4 million and became one of the hit musicals of the 40s—was choreographed by Ernest Palmer and directed by Irving Cummings. It was photographed in Technicolor and produced by 20th Century-Fox.

Dolorean

This Portland, Oregon–based avant folk band is primarily the focal point for the songwriting of poet Al James. Originally from the small town of Silverton, Oregon, James recorded a number of home demos in the late 90s featuring his plaintive vocals and restrained acoustic guitar. Local keyboard player Jay Clarke joined him for live work and together the duo recorded the *Sudden Oak* EP. They became something of a fixture on the local art house scene, playing their own sets or accompanying at poetry readings. Drummer Ben Nugent fleshed out the line-up during this period, but the additional instrumentation did little to alter the sound of James' restrained indie folk musings. Dolorean made their album debut in November 2003 with the release of *Not Exotic*, which had actually been recorded the previous summer with the help of producer Jeff Saltzman. Occupying a space somewhere between **Low** and **Bedhead**, the pace on the album rarely got beyond a slow waltz, providing the perfect aural accompaniment for James' quasi-gothic tales of everyday despair and regret. Bass player James Adair was added to the line-up for the recording of Dolorean's follow-up, *Violence In The Snowy Fields*. A more upbeat recording than the band's debut, the album featured electric guitar, violin, vibraphones and prominent backing vocals from drummer Nugent.
● ALBUMS: *Not Exotic* (Yep Roc 2003) ★★★, *Violence In The Snowy Fields* (Yep Roc 2004) ★★★.

Dolphy, Eric

b. 20 June 1928, Los Angeles, California, USA, d. 29 June 1964, Berlin, Germany. A fluent performer on several reed instruments, Dolphy began to play clarinet while still at school. On the west coast of America in the second half of the 40s he worked with **Roy Porter**'s band, before spending a couple of years in the US army. After his discharge, he played with several leading musicians, including **Gerald Wilson**, before becoming a member of the popular **Chico Hamilton** quintet. The stint with Hamilton brought Dolphy to the attention of a wide audience and many other young musicians. In New York in 1959 Dolphy joined **Charles Mingus**, all the time freelancing at clubs and on recording sessions with such influential musicians as **George Russell** and **John Coltrane**.

In the early 60s, Dolphy began a hugely prolific and arduous period of touring and recording throughout the USA and Europe. He played in bands led by **Ornette Coleman** (on the seminal *Free Jazz* sessions), **John Lewis**, **Ron Carter**, **Mal Waldron**, **Oliver Nelson**, **Max Roach**, **Gil Evans**, **Andrew Hill**, **Booker Little**, **Abbey Lincoln**, Mingus and Coltrane, with whose quartet he toured Europe in 1961. He also recorded a series of albums as leader, perhaps most notably the *At The Five Spot* sessions, with the brilliant young trumpeter **Booker Little** (later reissued as *The Great Concert Of Eric Dolphy*), and his **Blue Note Records** debut *Out To Lunch!* The latter, with its dislocated rhythms and unusual instrumental textures (**Bobby Hutcherson**'s vibes sharing front line duties with **Freddie Hubbard**'s trumpet and Dolphy's reeds), is a landmark of modern music, and was voted best post-war jazz LP in a 1984 poll of *Wire* magazine critics. Shortly after recording *Out To Lunch!* Dolphy left the USA to live in Europe because, as he told writer A.B. Spellman, 'if you try to do anything different in this country, people put you down for it'. He was working in Germany when he suffered a complete circulatory collapse caused by too much sugar in the bloodstream (he was diabetic), and died suddenly on 29 June 1964.

A major influence on jazz, and especially on alto saxophone players, Dolphy was a remarkably gifted musician. During his short career he established himself as a significant force, playing alto, flute and bass clarinet, an instrument before and since unusual in jazz. He was comfortable in the varied idioms of the bands in which he played, from the relatively orthodox Hamilton to the forward-thinking Coltrane and the Third Stream innovations of **Gunther Schuller**. He was, however, very much his own man, creating strikingly original solo lines, frequently dashed off at breakneck tempos and encompassing wide intervallic leaps. Although he is rightly associated with the concept of free jazz, Dolphy brought to this area of music his own carefully reasoned attitude, and he is perhaps better thought of as someone who stretched bebop to its very limits. Nearly 40 years after his death, the importance of Dolphy's contribution to jazz is still being explored by musicians.
● ALBUMS: *Out There* (New Jazz 1960) ★★★★, *Outward Bound* (New Jazz 1960) ★★★★, *Candid Dolphy* (Candid 1961) ★★★, with Mal Waldron *The Quest* (New Jazz 1961) ★★★★, *At The Five Spot* (New Jazz 1961) ★★★★, *Stockholm Sessions* (Enja 1961) ★★★, *Far Cry* (New Jazz 1962) ★★★★, *Eric Dolphy Quartet* (Tempo 1962) ★★★, *Music Matador* (Affinity 1963) ★★★, *Conversations* (FM 1963) ★★★, *Naima* (West Wind 1964) ★★★, *The Memorial Album* (Vee Jay 1964) ★★★★, *Last Date* (EmArcy 1964) ★★★, *At The Five Spot Volume 2* (Prestige 1964) ★★★★, *Out To Lunch!* (Blue Note 1964) ★★★★★, *In Europe Volume 1* (Prestige 1964) ★★★, *In Europe Volume 2* (Prestige 1965) ★★, *In Europe Volume 3* (Prestige 1965) ★★, *Here And There* (Prestige 1965) ★★★★, *Eric*

Dolphy And Cannonball Adderley (Archive Of Folk And Jazz 1968) ★★★, *Iron Man* (Douglas 1969) ★★★, *The Illinois Concert* 1963 recording (Blue Note 1999) ★★★★.

● COMPILATIONS: *The Great Concert Of Eric Dolphy* 3-LP set (Prestige 1965) ★★★★, *Other Aspects* 1960–62 recordings (Blue Note 1982) ★★★, *The Complete Prestige Recordings* 9-CD box set (Prestige 1995) ★★★★, *Vintage Dolphy* 1962/1963 recordings (GM 1996) ★★★★.

● FURTHER READING: *Like A Human Voice—The Eric Dolphy Discography*, Uwe Reichardt. *Eric Dolphy: A Musical Biography & Discography*, Vladimir Simosko and Barry Tepperman. *The Importance Of Being Eric Dolphy*, Raymond Horricks.

Domain

This hard rock band was formed in Germany in 1986 by Bernie Kolbe (vocals/bass) and British expatriate Cliff Jackson (guitar; formerly the leader of UK progressive rock group **Epitaph**). Originally named Kingdom, the group added guitarist Alex Ritt, keyboard player Voker Sassenberg and drummer Thorstein Preker before releasing their self-titled 1988 debut for Teldec Records. The name-change occurred shortly afterwards, owing to confusion with the similarly named US hard rock group **Kingdom Come**. Their debut album was subsequently repackaged and credited to Domain, with its title extended to *Our Kingdom*. The following year's *Before The Storm* was produced by Albert Bockholt (previously a collaborator with **Magnum** and Treat) and saw the group continue on its path of experimental but somewhat mannered psychedelic hard rock.

● ALBUMS: *Our Kingdom* (Teldec 1988) ★★★, *Before The Storm* (Teldec 1989) ★★.

Domingo, Placido

b. 21 January 1941, Madrid, Spain. One of the world's leading tenors who, along with Luciano Pavarotti, has attempted to give opera in recent years a widespread, classless appeal. Domingo's family emigrated to Mexico in 1950, where he studied piano, conducting and singing. He debuted as a baritone in 1957, and his first major tenor role came in 1960 performing in Giuseppe Verdi's *La Traviata*. Domingo became a member of the Israel National Opera from 1962–65 and latter made acclaimed performances at the New York City Opera and Metropolitan, and at La Scala (Milan) and Covent Garden (London)—singing alongside sopranos such as Katria Ricciarelli, Rosalind Plowright and Montserrat Caballe. His first flirtation with the pop world came in 1981, when he recorded as duet with **John Denver**, 'Perhaps Love'. This Denver-penned song reached the UK Top 50 and US Top 20, consequently opening up a parallel career for Domingo in light entertainment and simultaneously introducing to the mass-market the delights of the operatic aria as well as Spanish love-songs. In 1985 he joined forces with **Sarah Brightman** and Lorin Maazel for **Andrew Lloyd Webber**'s *Requiem*, which became a UK Top 10 album. 'Till I Loved You', a duet with **Jennifer Rush**, reached the UK Top 30 in 1989. Domingo's efforts, plus those of similar promotions from Luciano Pavarotti, **Nigel Kennedy** and José Carreras, signalled the beginnings of the early 90s boom in sales of populist classical and operatic music. In particular, the 'Three Tenors' concert with Carreras and Pavarotti, promoting the 1990 soccer World Cup in Italy, gained the three men widespread media coverage and huge record sales. They

repeated the concert for the 1998 World Cup in France. The same year Domingo released *Por Amor*, an album dedicated to the work of Mexican composer **Agustín Lara**. In October 2002, Domingo received an honorary knighthood for his contributions to music and his charity work in England and around the world.

● ALBUMS: with John Denver *Perhaps Love* (Columbia 1981) ★★, *Domingo-Con Amore* (RCA 1982) ★★★, *My Life For A Song* (Columbia 1983) ★★★, *Be My Love* (DGS 1984) ★★★, *Christmas With Placido Domingo* (Columbia 1984) ★★, *Placido Domingo Sings Zarzuelas* (HMV 1988) ★★★, *Goya . . . A Life In A Song* (Columbia 1989) ★★★, with José Carreras, Luciano Pavarotti *In Concert* (Decca 1990) ★★★, *Be My Love . . . An Album Of Love* (EMI 1990) ★★★, with the London Symphony Orchestra *The Broadway I Love* (EastWest 1991) ★★★, *Domingo: Arias And Spanish Songs* (Deutsche Grammophon 1992) ★★★, with Montserrat Caballe, Carreras, Domingo *From The Official Barcelona Games Ceremony* (RCA 1992) ★★★, with Carreras, Diana Ross *Christmas In Vienna* (Sony Classical 1993) ★★★, with José Carreras, Natalie Cole *Celebration Of Christmas* (Elektra 1996) ★★★, *Por Amor* (WEA 1998) ★★★, with Carreras, Pavarotti *The 3 Tenors Live In Paris* (Decca 1998) ★★★, with Carreras, Pavarotti *A Tenors Christmas* (Sony Classical 1998) ★★★, with Carreras, Pavarotti *A Tenors Valentine* (Sony Classical 1999) ★★★, *100 Años De Mariachi* (EMI Latin 1999) ★★★, *The Three Tenors Christmas* (Sony Classical 1999) ★★★.

● COMPILATIONS: *Placido Domingo Collection* (Stylus 1986) ★★★, *Greatest Love Songs* (Columbia 1988) ★★★, *The Essential Domingo* (Deutsche Grammophon 1989) ★★★★.

● DVD/VIDEOS: *The 3 Tenors—Paris 1998* (PolyGram Music Video 1998), *The Three Tenors Christmas* (Sony 2000).

Dominique, Lisa

Dominique is a former beautician and is the sister of guitarist Marino. She started her career in the UK singing in Marino's band, but came to prominence through the pages of *Kerrang!* magazine, appearing regularly as a pin-up. With interest already generated, she decided on a career in the music business and was signed by FM Revolver/Heavy Metal Records. With the help of Marino (guitar), Pete Jupp (drums) and other session musicians, she debuted with *Rock 'N' Roll Lady* in 1989. The album was universally slated by the music media, and Dominique was subsequently dropped. Undaunted by this setback, she signed to **Castle Communications** and delivered *Lisa Dominique* in 1991. Again, this was not well received in the heavy metal fraternity, or anywhere else for that matter.

● ALBUMS: with Marino *Wanna Keep You Satisfied* (LRM 1985) ★★, *Rock 'N' Roll Lady* (FM Revolver 1989) ★, *Lisa Dominique* (Essential/Castle 1991) ★★.

Dominique, Natty

b. 2 August 1896, New Orleans, Louisiana, USA, d. 30 August 1982, Chicago, Illinois, USA. Born into a musical environment with **Barney Bigard** as a cousin, Dominique studied trumpet with **Manuel Perez** before heading north in 1913 to play in Chicago. In the early 20s he joined **Carroll Dickerson**'s band. Later that decade he played with **Johnny Dodds**, with whom he remained substantially throughout the 30s. In the early 40s ill health forced him to leave music, but he reappeared in 1949 and began leading his own band in the 50s, employing such kindred spirits as **Baby Dodds** and **Volly De Faut**. He continued playing into the mid-60s but then faded from sight.

● ALBUMS: *Natty Dominique And His New Orleans Hot Six* (Windin' Ball 1954) ★★★.

Domino

b. Shawn Ivy, *c*.1972, St. Louis, Missouri, USA. From the new school of rappers hailing from Long Beach, California, Domino typified the area's preoccupation with cool, languid, almost sexual delivery. His hybrid accent was accounted for by the fact that he spent his first seven years in St. Louis. He had begun singing professionally in nightclubs such as Marla Gibbs' Crossroads and Sir Alex in Compton before he embarked on a rap style. Just as contemporaries like **Snoop Doggy Dogg** spiced their rhymes with outbursts of actual singing, Domino repeated the feat, with slightly less contentious lyrics, with a greater degree of success. After a childhood spent listening to soul and funk standards from the **Stylistics** and **Funkadelic**, he caught the rap bug and began writing words for himself and Snoop. According to Domino, Snoop could not resist the temptation to 'go gangsta' when it was offered to him on a plate by **Dr. Dre**, and the duo split. Domino's perseverance with a more cognitive style was eventually rewarded. After several years of trying to get the major labels to listen, he signed with the small independent Outburst. 'Getto Jam' underlined his appeal: these were still tough-talking rap words, but sauntered through in an easy, inviting fashion. The buzz created by the track saw him and Outburst signed up for distribution by **Def Jam**. Samples from **Kool And The Gang** sat side by side with lines like: 'Everybody loves them dead presidents' on his debut album. This was combined with a more realistic overview of Domino's place in the scheme of things, with rhymes discussing his desire for sexual gratification ('Ass For Days') contrasting with morally tinged attitudes to safe sex ('Raincoat'), from which he even launched a condom range of the same name. Similarly, rather than the glorification of the drive-by shooting so evident in the work of others, there is a matter-of-fact discourse instead on the hassles of getting paid ('Money Is Everything'). Such platitudes saw him discussed in one magazine as 'a soft spoken businessman who will make an excellent bank manager when he gets sick of making records'. His own view: 'There's so much going on in the 'hood apart from guns and murder'. However, he did face criticism on his first British outing when misguided punters paid £10 to hear him perform three songs at a PA, when they had expected a full gig. Not to be confused with the production specialist Domino of **Del Tha Funkee Homosapien**'s Hieroglyphics crew fame, he has failed to live up to his reputation on subsequent outings *Physical Funk* and *Dominology*.

● ALBUMS: *Domino* (Outburst 1994) ★★★★, *Physical Funk* (Outburst 1996) ★★, *Dominology* (Thug 1997) ★★.

Domino, Fats

b. Antoine Domino, 26 February 1928, New Orleans, Louisiana, USA. From a large family, Domino learned piano from local musician Harrison Verrett who was also his brother-in-law. A factory worker after leaving school, Domino played in local clubs such as the Hideaway. It was there in 1949 that band leader **Dave Bartholomew** and Lew **Chudd** of **Imperial Records** heard him. His first recording, 'The Fat Man', became a Top 10 R&B hit the next year and launched his unique partnership with Bartholomew who co-wrote and arranged dozens of Domino tracks over the next two decades. As With **Professor Longhair**, Domino's playing was derived from the rich mixture of musical styles to be found in New Orleans. These included traditional jazz, Latin rhythms, boogie-woogie, Cajun and blues. Domino's personal synthesis of these influences involved lazy, rich vocals supported by rolling piano rhythms. On occasion his relaxed approach was at odds with the urgency of other R&B and rock artists and the Imperial engineers would frequently speed up the tapes before Domino's singles were released. During the early 50s, Domino gradually became one of the most successful R&B artists in America. Songs such as 'Goin' Home' and 'Going To The River', 'Please Don't Leave Me' and 'Don't You Know' were bestsellers and he also toured throughout the country. The touring group included the nucleus of the band assembled by Dave Bartholomew for recordings at Cosimo Matassa's studio. Among the musicians were Lee Allen (saxophone), Frank Field (bass) and Walter 'Papoose' Nelson (guitar).

By 1955, rock 'n' roll had arrived and young white audiences were ready for Domino's music. His first pop success came with 'Ain't That A Shame' in 1955, although **Pat Boone**'s cover version sold more copies. 'Bo Weevil' was also covered, by **Teresa Brewer**, but the catchy 'I'm In Love Again', with its incisive saxophone phrases from Allen, took Domino into the pop Top 10. The b-side was an up-tempo treatment of the 20s standard, 'My Blue Heaven', which Verrett had sung with **Papa Celestin**'s New Orleans jazz band. Domino's next big success also came with a pre-rock 'n' roll song, 'Blueberry Hill'. Inspired by **Louis Armstrong**'s 1949 version, Domino used his Creole drawl to perfection. Altogether, Fats Domino had nearly 20 US Top 20 singles between 1955 and 1960. Among the last of them was the majestic 'Walking To New Orleans', a **Bobby Charles** composition that became a string-laden tribute to the sources of his musical inspiration. His track record in the *Billboard* R&B lists, however, is impressive, with 63 records reaching the charts.

Domino continued to record prolifically for Imperial until 1963, maintaining a consistently high level of performance. There were original compositions such as the jumping 'My Girl Josephine' and 'Let the Four Winds Blow' and cover versions of country songs (**Hank Williams**' 'Jambalaya (On The Bayou)') as well as standard ballads such as 'Red Sails In The Sunset', his final hit single in 1963. The complex off-beat of 'Be My Guest' was a clear precursor of the ska rhythms of Jamaica, where Domino was popular and toured in 1961. The only unimpressive moments came when he was persuaded to jump on the twist bandwagon, recording a banal number titled 'Dance With Mr Domino'. By now, Lew Chudd had sold the Imperial company and Domino switched labels to ABC Paramount. There he recorded several albums with producers Felton Jarvis and **Bill Justis**, but his continuing importance lay in his tours of North America and Europe, which recreated the sound of the 50s for new generations of listeners. The quality of Domino's touring band was well captured on a 1965 live album for **Mercury Records** from Las Vegas with **Roy Montrell** (guitar), Cornelius Coleman (drums) and the saxophones of Herb Hardesty and Lee Allen. Domino continued this pattern of work into the 70s, breaking it slightly when he gave the **Beatles**' 'Lady Madonna' a New

Orleans treatment. He made further albums for **Reprise Records** (1968) and **Sonet Records** (1979), the Reprise sides being the results of a reunion session with Dave Bartholomew.

Official recognition of Domino's contribution to popular music came in the late 80s. In 1986 he was inducted into the **Rock And Roll Hall Of Fame**, and won Hall Of Fame and Lifetime Achievement awards at the 1987 Grammy's. In 1991 **EMI Records**, which now owned the Imperial catalogue, released a scholarly box set of Domino's remarkable recordings. Two years later, Domino was back in the studio recording his first sessions proper for 25 years, resulting in his *Christmas Is A Special Day* set. 'People don't know what they've done for me', he reflected. 'They always tell me, "Oh Fats, thanks for so many years of good music". And I'll be thankin' them before they're finished thankin' me!' He remains a giant figure of R&B and rock 'n' roll, both musically and physically.

● ALBUMS: *Carry On Rockin'* (Imperial 1955) ★★★★, *Rock And Rollin' With Fats* (Imperial 1956) ★★★★, *Rock And Rollin'* (Imperial 1956) ★★★★, *This Is Fats Domino!* (Imperial 1957) ★★★★, *Here Stands Fats Domino* (Imperial 1958) ★★★★, *Fabulous Mr D* (Imperial 1958) ★★★★, *Let's Play Fats Domino* (Imperial 1959) ★★★★, *Fats Domino Swings* (Imperial 1959) ★★★★★, *Million Record Hits* (Imperial 1960) ★★★★, *A Lot Of Dominos* (Imperial 1960) ★★★★, *I Miss You So* (Imperial 1961) ★★★, *Let The Four Winds Blow* (Imperial 1961) ★★★★, *What A Party* (Imperial 1962) ★★★, *Twistin' The Stomp* (Imperial 1962) ★★★, *Just Domino* (Imperial 1962) ★★★, *Here Comes Fats Domino* (ABC-Paramount 1963) ★★★, *Walkin' To New Orleans* (Imperial 1963) ★★★★, *Let's Dance With Domino* (Imperial 1963) ★★★, *Here He Comes Again* (Imperial 1963) ★★★, *Fats On Fire* (ABC 1964) ★★★, *Fats Domino '65* (Mercury 1965) ★★★, *Getaway With Fats Domino* (ABC 1965) ★★★, *Fats Is Back* (Reprise 1968) ★★★, *Cookin' With Fats* (United Artists 1974) ★★★, *Sleeping On The Job* (Sonet 1979) ★★, *Live At Montreux* (Atlantic 1987) ★★★, *The Domino Effect* (Charly 1989) ★★★, *Christmas Is A Special Day* (Right Stuff/EMI 1994) ★★.

● COMPILATIONS: *The Very Best Of Fats Domino* (Liberty 1970) ★★★★, *Rare Domino's* (Liberty 1970) ★★★, *Rare Domino's Volume 2* (Liberty 1971) ★★★, *Fats Domino—His Greatest Hits* (MCA 1986) ★★★, *My Blue Heaven—The Best Of Fats Domino* (EMI 1990) ★★★★, *They Call Me The Fat Man: The Legendary Imperial Recordings* 4-CD box set (EMI/Imperial 1991) ★★★★★, *Out Of Orleans* 8-CD box set (Bear Family 1993) ★★★★★, *The EP Collection Volume 1* (See For Miles 1995) ★★★★, *The Early Imperial Singles 1950–52* (Ace 1996) ★★★★, *The EP Collection Volume 2* (See For Miles 1997) ★★★★, *The Imperial Singles Volume 3* (Ace 1999) ★★★★, *Legends Of The 20th Century* (EMI 1999) ★★★, *Walking To New Orleans: 100 Legendary Imperial Recordings 1949–1962* (Capitol 2002) ★★★★★, *Fats Domino Jukebox: 20 Greatest Hits* (EMI 2002) ★★★★, *The Fat Man: The Essential Early Fats Domino* (Indigo 2002) ★★★, *The Best Of Fats Domino* (EMI 2004) ★★★★, *Sweet Patootie: The Complete Reprise Recordings* (Rhino 2005) ★★.

● DVD/VIDEOS: with Rick Nelson *Rockin' With Rick & Fats* (Fuel 2000 2003), *The Legends Of New Orleans: The Music Of Fats Domino* (Shout! Entertainment 2003).

● FILMS: *The Girl Can't Help It* (1956), *Jamboree* aka *Disc Jockey Jamboree* (1957), *The Big Beat* (1957).

Dominoes
(see **Ward, Billy, And The Dominoes**)

Domnérus, Arne
b. 20 December 1924, Stockholm, Sweden. Alto saxophonist and clarinettist Domnérus is virtually a Swedish jazz institution by himself. He led bands professionally in the 40s that included exceptionally talented players such as **Lars Gullin**, **Rolf Ericson** and **Putte Wickman**. American musicians including **Charlie Parker** had already come to know the high standard of Domnérus' playing through the Paris Jazz Fair Festival in 1949. His bands since the 60s have usually included bass player and composer Georg Riedel, pianists **Bengt Hallberg** or **Jan Johansson** and guitarist Rune Gustafsson. Although the cool manner of **Lee Konitz** and **Paul Desmond** were formative on Swedish alto players in the 50s, Domnérus' tone and phrasing are now closer to that of **Benny Carter**.

● ALBUMS: with Lars Gullin *New Sounds From Sweden, Volume 3* 10-inch album (Prestige 1952) ★★★★, *New Sounds From Sweden, Volume 4—Arne Domnérus Clarinet Solos* 10-inch album (Prestige 1952) ★★★, *Around The World In Jazz—Sweden* 10-inch album (RCA Victor 1953) ★★★, *Arne Domnérus Nalenorkester 1951–55* (Odeon 1956) ★★★, *Mobil* (Megafon 1965) ★★★, *Dedikation. En Tribut Til Johnny Hodges* (Megafon 1971) ★★, *I Let A Song Go Out* (RCA 1972) ★★★, *Jazz At The Pawnshop* (Proprius 1976) ★★★, *Ja, Vi Älskar* (Zarepta 1977) ★★★, *Downtown Meeting* (Phontastic 1978) ★★★, *Duets For Duke* (Sonet 1978) ★★★, *The Sheik: Featuring Jimmy Rowles* (Four Leaf Clover 1979) ★★★★, *Jumpin' At The Woodside* (Four Leaf Clover 1979) ★★★★, *A.D. 1980* (Phontastic 1980) ★★, *Duke's Melody* (Phontastic 1981) ★★★, *Blue And Yellow* (Phontastic 1982) ★★★, *Fragment* (Phontastic 1982) ★★★, *When Lights Are Low* (Salut 1988) ★★★, *Swedish Rhapsody 1980–1982 recordings* (Phontastic 1984) ★★★★, *Blatoner Fra Troldhaugen* (FXCD 1986) ★★, *Dompan At The Savoy* (Phontastic 1992) ★★, *Sugar Fingers* (Phontastic 1993) ★★★★, *Shall We Dance* (Proprius 1994) ★★★, *Portrait Of Arne Domnérus* (Phontastic 1994) ★★★, *Happy Together* (Ladybird 1997) ★★★★, *In Concert, Live 1996* (Caprice 1997) ★★★, with Bernt Rosengren *Face To Face* (Dragon 1999) ★★★.

Don-A-V
b. Donovan George Pinnock, 2 December 1964, Victoria Town, Manchester, Jamaica, West Indies. During his formative years Don-A-V studied mechanical engineering and the arts although his first love was music. He initially performed in church as a singer although following his education at the local Holmwood Technical college he decided to pursue a career in the **dancehall** as a DJ. He soon realized that his personal aspirations were more suited to the role of a singer. In 1986 his audition with producer **Harry J.** resulted in his first recording session. Sadly his debut remained unreleased and it was not until 1989 that his distinct vocals appeared on vinyl. His first releases were produced by the New York–based producer Jah C who released, 'Must Haffe Get You', 'Silver Bells', 'Twilight Zone' and 'Do Me Baby'. Having established his name within the

Jamaican recording industry Don-A-V began recording with a number of top producers including **King Jammy**, Jah Life, Count Shelly and Philip Smart. In the late 90s Don-A-V embarked on sessions in the UK with **Fashion Records** who released the favoured 'Prophecy Revealing'. The song led to an introduction to **Coxsone Dodd** who offered to release the singer's album debut. The sessions resulted in the release of 1999's *Cry For Tomorrow*. The album featured the classic 'What A Joy Will It Be' and featured backing vocals from **J.D. Smoothe**.

● ALBUMS: *Cry For Tomorrow* (Studio One 1999) ★★★★.

Don And Dewey
(see **Harris, Don 'Sugarcane'**)

Don And Juan
Don And Juan were a US R&B vocal duo who recorded one Top 10 ballad that has since become a doo-wop classic: 'What's Your Name' (1962). Don (b. Roland Trone) and Juan (b. Claude Johnson) were members of a vocal quartet called the **Genies** in Brooklyn, New York City, USA. In 1959 the Genies released the up-tempo single 'Who's That Knockin'', which reached number 71 in the US charts on Shad Records. Unable to follow it with another hit, the group was dropped from the label, and subsequent recordings for Hollywood Records and Warwick Records also failed to chart. Trone and Johnson left the group and became house painters in the Long Island, New York area, until they were rediscovered, this time by an agent named Peter Paul, who arranged for the pair to sign with Big Top Records. Under their new name, they recorded 'What's Your Name', which reached number 7 in the *Billboard* charts in February 1962. Only one other single, 'Magic Wand', charted, although Don And Juan continued to record until 1967. Trone died in 1983 and Johnson rekindled the act with Alexander 'Buddy' Faison, another former member of the Genies, as the new Don.

● COMPILATIONS: *What's Your Name* (Collectables 1995) ★★★.

Don And The Goodtimes
Formed in Portland, Oregon, USA, this pop attraction featured Don Gallucci (organ/vocals), previously of the **Kingsmen**. Gallucci appeared on 'Louie Louie', the latter group's smash hit, but bowed to parental pressure not to tour. Don McKinney (saxophone/vocals), Peter Outlette (guitar), Dave Childs (bass) and Bob Holden (drums) completed the line-up of an act, which was initially content to remain in Portland and record solely for regional outlets. The quintet moved to Los Angeles in 1966, having secured a major recording contract, firstly with **Dunhill Records**, then Epic. They enjoyed two minor US hits, 'I Could Be So Good To You' and 'Happy And Me' (both 1967), and procured a regular spot on ABC-TV's *Where The Action Is*, which starred northwest contemporaries **Paul Revere And The Raiders**. Two subsequent Goodtimes' alumni, Jim 'Harpo' Valley and Charlie Coe, switched to the latter group, and by 1968 Gallucci and Holden had been joined by Joey Newman (lead guitar), Jeff Hawks (rhythm guitar) and Ron Overman (bass). Newman and Hawks later remained with Gallucci in a new act, Touch, following which Don joined the staff of **Elektra Records**, where he produced **Crabby Appleton** and the **Stooges**' Fun House.

● ALBUMS: *So Good* (Epic 1967) ★★★, *Where The Action Is* (Wand 1969) ★★.

● COMPILATIONS: *Greatest Hits* (Burdette 1966) ★★★, *The Original Northwest Sound Of Don And The Goodtimes* (Beat Rocket 2000) ★★★.

Don Caballero
Originating from Pittsburgh, Pennsylvania, USA, Don Caballero is one of the few post-hardcore bands to specialize in all-instrumental fare, and additionally to have no problem showing off their affection for fusion. The band was formed in 1991 by Damon Che (drums), Mike Banfield (guitar) and Pat Morris (bass). Live shows soon beckoned, and a name was taken from a Canadian television show, *SCTV*, in which a character, whose name was usually Guy Caballero, was rechristened Don Caballero during a spoof of the movie, *The Godfather*. Eventually, second guitarist Ian Williams joined and the new-look quartet signed a recording contract with the renowned Chicago based indie label, Touch & Go. They forged a fruitful union with producer **Steve Albini** and recorded their debut, 1993's *For Respect*.

Further studio releases followed, including 1998's *What Burns Never Returns* (the last to feature Banfield) and 2000's *American Don*. A series of tours alongside equally musically challenging acts such as the **Fucking Champs**, **Trans Am** and **Atari Teenage Riot** helped promote their musical vision to a wider audience, with drummer Che's remarkable time signatures earning particular praise from fans of the cult 'math-rock' genre. Although Don Caballero called it quits shortly after the dawn of the twenty-first century, most of its former band members later turned up in other projects, including Storm & Stress (Williams) and Bellini (Che). The latter resurrected Don Caballero in 2004 with members of Pittsburgh's Creta Bourzia. The band then signed a new recording contract with Relapse Records.

● ALBUMS: *For Respect* (Touch & Go 1993) ★★★★, *2* (Touch & Go 1995) ★★★, *What Burns Never Returns* (Touch & Go 1998) ★★★★, *American Don* (Touch & Go 2000) ★★★.

● COMPILATIONS: *Singles Breaking Up Vol. 1* (Touch & Go 1999) ★★★.

Don Patrol
Comprising Dille Diedricsson (vocals), Peter Nordholm (guitar), Imre Daun (drums) and Henrik Thomson (keyboards), Don Patrol formed in Sweden in 1990. The base component of their sound was immediately obvious— drawing heavily on the blues their composite hard rock style drew comparisons with artists such as **Free**, **Bad Company** and **Grand Funk Railroad**. In the studio the group have consistently eschewed studio polish in favour of spontaneous, uninhibited performances. The best example of this was their 1990 self-titled debut, which received widespread recognition and airplay. A more complex record, 1992's *A Wire, A Deal And The Devil* was less immediate and ultimately less compelling.

● ALBUMS: *Don Patrol* (Record Station 1990) ★★★, *A Wire, A Deal And The Devil* (Record Station 1992) ★★.

Don Yute
b. Jason Andrew Williams, 9 May 1974, Kingston, Jamaica, West Indies. Don Yute is best remembered for his 1995 combination hit with **Wayne Wonder**, 'Sensi Ride'. He

performed in a style reminiscent of **Beenie Man** and **Bounty Killer**. He also recorded in combination with **Prezident Brown** on the enlightening 'African Thing'. Don Yute's success led to him working with a number of producers, including **Donovan Germain** ('All That Glitters'), **Bobby Digital** ('Funny Funny') and **Steely And Clevie** ('Hard Core'), while Colin 'Bulby' York produced 'Click Click'. He maintained a high profile with the hits 'Gal It Wouldn't Easy', 'You Own Di Man', 'La La La', 'Golden Child' and 'Livin' In A Dream'. In 1997 he released his debut album, which included the cream of his hits. In the same year he appeared at Sting 97 with newcomer **Sean Paul**, who had enjoyed a combination hit, 'Ladies Night', with **Spanner Banner**. Don Yute is considered a 'name brand' DJ, but he has yet to repeat the success of 'Sensi Ride'. In the latter half of the 90s the studios in Jamaica were delivering literally thousands of **dancehall** releases, and much of Don Yute's later work was neglected as a result; some hope emerged, however, when the Jamaican Government asked the island's producers to limit the number of releases.

● ALBUMS: *Golden Child* (Nuff Tings 1997) ★★★.

Donà, Cristina

b. Italy. This singer-songwriter and guitarist attended the Academy of Arts of Brera in Milan, beginning her performing career after graduating at the end of the 80s. She teamed up with Manuel Agnelli of the rock band Afterhours and earned early acclaim as a finalist in the 1995 award show, Premio Ciampi. Donà signed a recording contract with the Mescal label and began working with Agnelli and a number of leading Italian musicians on her 1997 debut, *Tregua*. Markedly different from anything on the Italian charts at the time, the dreamlike lyrics and sensual flow of Donà's vocals were compared by some excitable critics to **Jeff Buckley** on his acclaimed *Grace* debut. *Tregua* was well received by the Italian press and public, winning a couple of awards (including the prestigious Tenco Award) and helping push Donà into the media spotlight in her homeland. The following year Donà recorded a version of the **Robert Wyatt** track 'Maryan' for inclusion on the Italian tribute album to the cult UK singer-songwriter, *The Different You*. Wyatt returned the favour on Donà's second album, 1999's *Nido*, appearing on the sumptuous 'Goccia'. Wyatt subsequently invited Donà to perform at the 2001 Meltdown festival at London's Royal Festival Hall, a performance that helped introduce her music to a wider European audience. During this period Donà was also championed by US musician **David Byrne** and UK disc jockeys **Charlie Gillett** and Robert Elms, and the inevitable happened when she was signed to US label **Rykodisc Records**. The artist made her English-language debut in 2004 with a re-recording of her third Italian album, *Dove Sei Tu*, produced by Davey Ray Moor of UK noir pop band **Cousteau**.

● ALBUMS: *Tregua* (Mescal 1997) ★★★★, *Nido* (Mescal 1999) ★★★★, *Dove Sei Tu* (Mescal 2003) ★★★, *Cristina Donà* (Rykodisc 2004) ★★★.

Donahue, Al

b. 1903, USA, d. 20 February 1983. Al Donahue And His Orchestra played their first professional engagement at the Weber Duck Inn in Boston, Massachusetts, USA, in 1925. Donahue had learnt his musical craft on steamships for the Eastern Steamship Line, and also played for campus groups while at college. The shows in Boston were well-received and brokered further engagements at the Hollywood Beach Hotel in Florida, where the band would play annually for five years. More lucrative still was a performance at the Bermudiana Hotel. So impressed by their performance were the hotel's managers that they asked Donahue to arrange for the band to play for their whole chain, which included steamboats as well as hotels. Thus Al Donahue's orchestras could be found almost everywhere in America during the 30s, with some 37 units performing the Donahue theme song, 'Lowdown Rhythm In A Top Hat'. Some of the vocalists commissioned by the band included Lynne Stevens, **Paula Kelly** (later to join **Glenn Miller**), Phil Brito, **Snooky Lanson** and Dee Keating, all big names of the time. Donahue himself was able to choose the cream of the bookings to personally appear at, including the Rainbow Room in New York's Rockefeller Center where he filled in for **Ray Noble** (he would return annually for the next six years).

By the 40s the orchestra's sound and style had moved to swing from its more self-consciously highbrow origins, and engagements at **Frank Dailey**'s Meadowbrook, the Hollywood Palladium and other top concert halls and theatres were in abundance. After relocating to California in the 40s he continued to tour coast to coast, also appearing in a film, *Sweet Genevieve*. In the 50s Donahue and his orchestra were part of an unsuccessful west coast television series, before their band leader returned to musical direction for the Furness Bermuda Line. He also opened a music store in Bermuda with long-standing friend and band manager Frank Walsh. When that was the subject of a compulsory purchase order by the Bermudan government, they used the finance from the sale to purchase Ponzi's House Of Music in Oceanside, California. It closed in the mid-70s.

Donahue, Jerry

b. 24 September 1946, Manhattan, New York City, USA. This stylish guitarist arrived in Britain in 1961, aiming to further his academic education. He was, however, attracted to music, garnering plaudits in **Poet And The One Man Band** prior to joining **Fotheringay**, the short-lived but innovative unit formed by **Sandy Denny**. Donahue continued his exemplary work with **Head, Hands And Feet**, but is better recalled for a spell with **Fairport Convention**. He remained with this renowned folk rock group between 1972 and 1976, contributing to three of their late-period albums before opting for a career as a session musician. This did not, however, preclude solo recordings, and recent album releases show him exploring 'new age' styles. Like **Richard Thompson**, Donahue is a guitarist's guitar player whose dexterity transcends commercial opportunity.

● ALBUMS: *Telecasting* (1986) ★★★, *Meetings* (1988) ★★★, *Neck Of The Wood* (1992) ★★★, *Telecasting Recast* (Telebender 1998) ★★★.

Donahue, Sam

b. 8 March 1918, Detroit, Michigan, USA, d. 22 March 1974, Reno, Nevada, USA. Among the most respected of swing era musicians, tenor saxophonist Donahue formed his first group in the mid-30s, leaving **Sonny Burke** as leader when he later joined **Gene Krupa**'s band. In the early 40s he played with **Harry James** and **Benny Goodman**. He returned to leading his old group again but in 1942 was drafted into the US Navy. When **Artie Shaw** was discharged from military service in 1944, Donahue took over Shaw's navy band. In the next two years he built it into a first-class swinging unit, much admired by musicians and fans alike. After the war, Donahue formed a new unit, hiring many of his former service personnel, which he led during the uneasy commercial decline of big bands. He worked in other bands, including those of **Stan Kenton**, **Billy May** and **Tommy Dorsey**. In 1961, five years after the latter's death, Donahue became leader of the official Tommy Dorsey orchestra, which toured extensively, and featured **Frank Sinatra Jnr**. as singer.

A highly skilled musician and one capable of drawing the best from his musicians, whether young or his contemporaries, Donahue remained one of the lesser-known names of the swing era but to the end retained a faithful following. In later years he became musical director for the Playboy Club in New York.

● ALBUMS: *For Young Moderns In Love* (Capitol 1954) ★★★, *Classics In Jazz* (Capitol 1955) ★★★★, *Dance Date With Sam Donahue* (Capitol 1958) ★★★.

● COMPILATIONS: *Hollywood Hop* 1944–48 recordings (Hep Jazz 1983) ★★★, *Take Five: 1945–1947* (Hep 2002) ★★★.

Donahue, Tom

b. 21 May 1928, South Bend, Indiana, USA, d. 28 April 1975, USA. Affectionately known as 'Big Daddy' in deference to his massive girth, Donahue played a pivotal role in the evolution of San Franciscan music. He arrived in the city in 1961, having already established himself as a leading disc jockey with Philadelphia's top station WBIG. At KYA he befriended colleague Bob Mitchell, and together they began promoting concerts at the Cow Palace auditorium. The **Beatles** and the **Rolling Stones** were two of the acts presented there. Donahue and Mitchell founded Autumn Records in 1964. They scored a national hit with **Bobby Freeman**'s 'C'mon And Swim' before embracing nascent American rock with the **Beau Brummels**. Fellow disc jockey Sylvester Stewart, aka **Sly Stone**, produced many of the label's acts. The entrepreneurs also established a North Beach club, Mothers, which showcased some of the early acts synonymous with the San Franciscan sound, including the **Great Society**. However, they singularly failed to sign other important acts, including the **Charlatans**, the **Grateful Dead** and **Dino Valenti**, despite recording demos with them. This hesitancy was one of the factors contributing to Autumn's demise. Mitchell died in 1966, but Donahue retained his influential position. He managed several artists, including **Ron Nagle**, **Sal Valentino** and the aforementioned Valenti, and revolutionized radio at station KSAN-FM by adopting a bold 'album' format. He masterminded an ambitious touring revue, the *Medicine Ball Caravan*, which later spawned a film, and Donahue remained a fixture within the city until his premature death from a heart attack in 1975.

Donald And The Delighters

The members of this early soul vocal group from Chicago, Illinois, USA, were lead Donald Jenkins, baritone Walter Granger and tenor Ronnie Strong. The group's most famous record was 'Elephant Walk', which in 1963 was a top record in several markets, including Chicago, Pittsburgh, and Washington, DC, but inexplicably never reached the national charts. The record has retained its appeal over the decades and remains one of the most popular records among collectors. The follow-up also garnered strong sales, 'Adios (My Secret Love)' (1963), a remarkable remake of a 1954 doo-wop recorded by the **Diablos**. The third release was also outstanding, 'I've Settled Down' (1964). After a succession of releases for other labels, the group had broken up by 1970. Donald And The Delighters had a history that stretched back into Chicago's doo-wop past, when Jenkins formed a vocal group in 1955, called the Fortunes, which included, besides himself, Granger, Strong and bass William Taylor. The group recorded for **Chess** (on the **Checker** subsidiary) and **Parrot**, but only the Checker single was released. Years later, Jenkins joined up with Strong to form a duet called Rico And Ronnie, who recorded a single for Checker in 1962. The following year on the Cortland label, the pair recorded as the Starr Brothers, releasing several singles, notably 'Don Juan', before inviting Granger to join them in Donald And The Delighters. Jenkins at this time was also producing acts for Cortland, most notably the **Versalettes**.

Donald, Barbara

b. 9 February 1942, Minneapolis, Minnesota, USA. Donald began to learn trumpet at school, but when her family moved to California in 1955, a sexist teacher refused to let her join her new high school band. She formed her own group, and before long she had more gigs than the school band. After playing R&B in New York and touring the south in a big band, Donald, who had meanwhile been encouraged by **Benny Harris**, came to notice in Los Angeles bebop sessions with **Dexter Gordon** and **Stanley Cowell**. From 1962–73 she played and recorded free jazz with **Sonny Simmons**, whom she married in 1964, supplying excellent trumpet on a series of albums, including two exceptional sets for ESP Records *Staying On The Watch* and *Music From The Spheres*. In the mid-60s she also worked with **John Coltrane**, **Richard Davis**, Prince Lasha and **Rahsaan Roland Kirk**.

After a four-year break (which also saw her separate from Simmons), she returned to music in 1978, leading her own band, Unity, and other groups, which have included **Gary Peacock** and Carter Jefferson in their line-ups. In 1981, with Unity and Jefferson, Donald was finally back in a recording studio and for Cadence Records she made two outstanding albums that served notice that she had lost none of her power and passion that had marked her playing with Simmons. Despite the high quality of these Cadence sets, however, Donald's recording career once again slipped away.

● ALBUMS: *Olympia Live* (Cadence 1981) ★★★★, *The Past And Tomorrow's* (Cadence 1984) ★★★.

Donald, Duck

b. Duckworth Bruce Andrew Donald, 18 August 1951, Montreal, Quebec, Canada, d. 22 April 1984, Montreal, Quebec, Canada. A talented musician who taught himself to play guitar, mandolin, dulcimer, harmonica and Jew's Harp but never to read music. He also wrote songs and poetry and found himself attracted to bluegrass music, which he felt added something to the normal country music on which he grew up. Initially his music was a hobby and a release from his daily job in a warehouse until he was invited to join the local Bobby Cusson trio, which played for local functions. In this role he met banjo player **Cathy Fink** with whom he formed a duo that specialized in bluegrass and old timey music. Between 1974 through 1979, they toured Canada and amassed a repertoire of approximately 600 old timey duets.

In 1975, they made their first recordings for an album for Likeable Records, which proved moderately successful and led them to record for **Flying Fish Records**. A children's album on Likeable followed. Between 1981 and 1983, they toured with their own band, which included Darcy Deville (guitar/fiddle) and Dave Harvey (string bass). Later Donald played for a time with Darcy, until he suddenly died from a brain haemorrhage in 1984.

● ALBUMS: with Cathy Fink *Kissing Is A Crime* (Likeable 1975) ★★, with Fink *Cathy Fink & Duck Donald* (Flying Fish 1978) ★★★★, with Fink *I'm Going To Tell* (Likeable 1980) ★★★.

Donald, Peter

b. Peter Alexander Donald, 15 May 1945, San Francisco, California, USA. In his late teens, Donald studied at **Berklee College Of Music**, Boston and received drum tuition from **Alan Dawson**. In the early 70s he returned to California, this time taking up residence in Los Angeles, where he became noted for his sensitive accompaniment to singers who included **Carmen McRae**. He achieved notable success, however, as a member of the powerful big band co-led by **Toshiko Akiyoshi** and **Lew Tabackin**. When Akiyoshi decided to return to New York, Donald remained in Los Angeles, working in films and television studios and playing with musicians including **John Abercrombie** and **Warne Marsh**. In 1985, following the death of **Nick Ceroli**, he took his place in **Bob Florence**'s Limited Edition big band. An all-round percussionist equally at home in jazz, pop and rock, Donald is very much a part of the new generation of jazz artists, but partly through his early tutelage under Dawson retains strong links with earlier strands of jazz.

Donaldson, Eric

b. 11 June 1947, Jamaica, West Indies. Eric Donaldson, one of Jamaica's most accomplished falsetto voices, will forever be associated with the Jamaican Festival Song Competition, and in particular, with one of his five winning entries in that contest, 'Cherry Oh Baby', which won in 1971, and launched his career in reggae music. Donaldson attended school in Spanish Town before taking up a job as a house-painter, singing in his spare time. In 1964 he recorded some unreleased sides for **Studio One** in Kingston, and in the mid-60s he formed vocal group the West Indians, alongside Leslie Burke and Hector Brooks. A collection of sides for producer J.J. Johnson produced one hit, 'Right On Time', in 1968. They also recorded for **Lee Perry** ('Oh Lord') the following year, to negligible reaction. A name-change to the Killowatts and a succession of songs for J.J. Johnson and **Lloyd Daley**'s Matador label ('Slot Machine', 'Real Cool Operator') failed to ignite the fire of fame and the group split. In 1970 Donaldson recorded some sides for Alvin Ranglin's GG's label, the best of which was 'Lonely Night', and a trip to Dynamic Sounds studio for 'Never Going To Give You Up' again led nowhere, although it did bode well for the future. In 1971, apparently as a last stand, he entered the Festival Song Competition with 'Cherry Oh Baby'. By the day of the festival, he had enrolled the astute **Tommy Cowan** as manager, and the disc eventually sold an extraordinary 50,000 copies on Dynamic Records. While it has not been a smooth ride from that point, Donaldson has been periodically successful, releasing albums sporadically and recording a clutch of songs that are fondly remembered by reggae aficionados,

notably 'Miserable Woman' (1972), 'What A Festival' (1973) and 'Freedom Street' (1977). Donaldson apparently still loves the festival, winning in 1971, 1977, 1978, 1984 and 1993, and he always seems ready to give his career a shot in the arm by appearing there. He now lives in Kent Village, Jamaica, where he runs the 'Cherry Oh Baby Go-Go Bar'. The song itself is perennially popular, and both **UB40** and the **Rolling Stones** have covered it. The rhythm remained popular in 1991, with over 30 new versions issued in Jamaica, including Donaldson's own update.

● ALBUMS: *Eric Donaldson* (Trojan 1971) ★★★, *Keep On Riding* (Dynamic 1976) ★★, *Kent Village* (Dynamic 1978) ★★★, *Right On Time* (Dynamic 1985) ★★★, *Trouble In Afrika* (Blue Mountain 1992) ★★★, *Love Of The Common People* (1993) ★★★.

Donaldson, Lou

b. 1 November 1926, Badin, North Carolina, USA. Donaldson started on clarinet but, while playing in a band in the US Navy alongside **Willie Smith** and **Clark Terry**, he switched to alto saxophone. In the early 50s he was in New York, playing with **Thelonious Monk**, **Horace Silver**, **Blue Mitchell**, **Art Blakey** and other leading jazzmen. In 1954 he and **Clifford Brown** joined Blakey's **Jazz Messengers**. During the 60s and 70s Donaldson toured extensively, usually as leader of a small band, playing concerts and festivals in the USA and Europe. He recorded prolifically for **Blue Note Records**, producing a number of excellent soul jazz albums, including *Alligator Boogaloo*. During this period, Donaldson made some stylistic changes, experimenting with an R&B-inflected style, soul jazz and jazz funk; by the 80s he was back in a hard bop groove, where his striking technique and inventiveness assured him of a welcome place on the international circuit. Donaldson has often been passed over by jazz critics, as his soul-honking style was seen as too simplistic. In the new millennium, his classic Blue Note output is seen as one of the peaks of groove and riff-laden soul jazz.

● ALBUMS: *Lou Donaldson Quintet-Quartet* 10-inch album (Blue Note 1953) ★★★, *Lou Donaldson With Clifford Brown* 10-inch album (Blue Note 1953) ★★★, with Art Blakey *A Night At The Birdland* (Blue Note 1954) ★★★★★, *Lou Donaldson Sextet, Volume 2* (Blue Note 1955) ★★★, *Wailing With Lou* (Blue Note 1955) ★★★, *Lou Donaldson Quartet Quintet Sextet* (Blue Note 1957) ★★★, *Swing And Soul* (Blue Note 1957) ★★★, *Lou Takes Off* (Blue Note 1958) ★★★, *Blues Walk* (Blue Note 1958) ★★★, *LD+3* (Blue Note 1959) ★★★, *The Time Is Right* (Blue Note 1960) ★★★, *Sunny Side Up* (Blue Note 1960) ★★★★, *Light Foot* (Blue Note 1960) ★★★, *Here 'Tis* (Blue Note 1961) ★★★★, *The Natural Soul* (Blue Note 1962) ★★★★, *Gravy Train* (Blue Note 1962) ★★★, *Good Gracious* (Blue Note 1963) ★★★, *Signifyin'* (Argo 1963) ★★★, *Possum Head* (Argo 1964) ★★★, *Cole Slaw* (Argo 1964) ★★★, *Musty Rusty* (Cadet 1965) ★★★, *Rough House Blues* (Cadet 1965) ★★★, *At His Best* (1966) ★★★, *Lush Life* (Blue Note 1967) ★★★★, *Alligator Boogaloo* (Blue Note 1967) ★★★★, *Mr. Shing-A-ling* (Blue Note 1967) ★★★, *Blowin' In The Wind* (Cadet 1967) ★★★, *Fried Buzzard-Lou Donaldson Live* (Cadet 1968) ★★★, *Midnight Creeper* (Blue Note 1968) ★★★, *Say It Loud!* (Blue Note 1969) ★★★, *Hot Dog* (Blue Note 1969) ★★★, *Pretty Things* (Blue Note 1970) ★★★, *Everything I Play Is Funky* (Blue Note 1970) ★★, *Sophisticated Lou* (Blue Note 1972) ★★★,

Back Street (Muse 1972) ★★★, *Sassy Soul Strut* (Blue Note 1973) ★★★, *Sweet Lou* (Blue Note 1974) ★★★, *A Different Scene* (Cotillion 1976) ★★★, *Sweet Poppa Lou* (Muse 1981) ★★★, *Forgotten Man* (Timeless 1981) ★★★, *Life In Bologna* (Timeless 1984) ★★★, *Play The Right Thing* (Milestone 1990) ★★★, *Birdseed* (Milestone 1992) ★★★, *Caracas* (Milestone 1992) ★★★, *Relaxing At Sea: Live On The QE2* (Chiaroscuro 2000) ★★★.

● COMPILATIONS: *A Man With A Horn* 1961–1963 recordings (Blue Note 1999) ★★★, *The Complete Blue Note Lou Donaldson Sessions 1957–61* 6-CD box set (Mosaic 2002) ★★★★.

Donaldson, Walter

b. 15 February 1893, New York City, New York, USA, d. 15 July 1947. A self-taught pianist, despite his mother being a piano teacher, Donaldson began composing while still attending school. After leaving school he worked in various finance companies but also held down jobs as a song plugger and piano demonstrator. He had his first small successes in 1915 with 'Back Home In Tennessee' (lyrics by William Jerome), 'You'd Never Know The Old Town Of Mine' (**Howard Johnson**) and other songs popularizing places and regions. Donaldson's first major success was 'The Daughter Of Rosie O'Grady' in 1918, just before he began a period entertaining at US army camps. After the war he had some minor successes with songs used in Broadway shows, the best known of which was 'How Ya Gonna Keep 'Em Down On The Farm' (**Sam M. Lewis** and **Joe Young**). It was another song, written by Donaldson with Lewis and Young, that established him as a major songwriter of the 20s. This was 'My Mammy', popularized by **Al Jolson** and which ever afterwards became synonymous with the blackface entertainer. Jolson also sang other Donaldson compositions, including 'My Buddy' and 'Carolina In The Morning' (both with **Gus Kahn**). With Kahn, Donaldson also wrote 'I'll See You In My Dreams', 'Yes Sir, That's My Baby', 'I Wonder Where My Baby Is Tonight', 'That Certain Party', 'Makin' Whoopee' and 'Love Me Or Leave Me'.

These last two songs came from the Broadway show, *Whoopee!*, written by Donaldson and Kahn in 1928, where they were sung respectively by **Eddie Cantor** and **Ruth Etting**. When the Hollywood version of the show was filmed, in 1930, among additional songs Donaldson and Kahn wrote was 'My Baby Just Cares For Me'. In the 30s Donaldson also contributed numbers to films such as *Hollywood Party*, *Kid Millions*, *The Great Ziegfeld*, *Suzy*, *Sinner Take All*, *After The Thin Man*, *Saratoga* and *That's Right—You're Wrong*. Although his collaboration with Kahn was enormously successful, Donaldson sometimes worked with other lyricists, including George Whiting ('My Blue Heaven'), Howard Johnson ('Georgia'), **Cliff Friend** ('Let It Rain, Let It Pour') and **Abe Lyman** ('What Can I Say After I Say I'm Sorry'). On occasion he also wrote lyrics to his own music, notably on 'At Sundown', 'You're Driving Me Crazy' and 'Little White Lies'. In the 30s Donaldson wrote many songs for films with such collaborators as Kahn and **Howard Dietz**, and he also worked with **Johnny Mercer**.

Donato, João

b. João Donato de Oliveira Neto, 17 August 1934, Rio Branco, Acre, Brazil. Donato played the accordion from early childhood, was taught to read music by a military bandsman, and at the age of 11 he moved to Rio de Janeiro to study piano. By the time he was 15, he was performing professionally, singing in the vocal group Os Namorados Da Lua and playing accordion and piano with guitarist Ubirajara's group at Copacabana nightclubs. He attracted the attention of the popular flute virtuoso Altamiro Carrilho who invited him to appear on a recording date. For the next decade Donato was active on Rio's music scene, playing popular music and jazz, the latter form attracting his attention through records by **Stan Kenton** in particular. When he was 17, Donato became a studio musician, working at Rádio Guanabara for two years. In 1952 he played in a band led by violinist Fafá Lemos, working at many of the city's most popular nightclubs. The following year he made his own-name recording debut, releasing 'Tenderly' and 'Invitation' for Sinter Records and over the next few years made several more records. Among Donato's numerous compositions are 'Amazonas' (lyrics by Lysias Ênio) and 'A Rã' (lyrics by **Caetano Veloso**), the latter title being recorded by **Sergio Mendes** among others. He has also collaborated on compositions with **Gilberto Gil**, including 'A Paz', 'Lugar Comum', 'Bananeira', 'Emoriô' and 'Tudo Tem', and with João Gilberto, notably 'Minha Saudade'.

A highly influential figure in the bossa nova movement, Donato is less well known outside Brazil than other pioneers. It has been reported that **João Gilberto**, with whom Donato was professionally associated from in his mid-teens, admitted to taking inspiration for his violão bossa nova rhythms from Donato's piano playing. By the late 50s, Donato's style had progressed along the contemporary jazz path, making his music less acceptable to nightclub owners and audiences who wanted music they could dance to or talk over. Work became hard to find and reluctantly he left Brazil, heading for the USA where a friend, singer Elizeth Cardoso, offered him a two-week gig. Apart from a short break, he stayed in the USA for 14 years. Quickly in demand by Latin artists in the USA, Donato played and frequently recorded with musicians such as **Mongo Santamaría**, **Tito Puente**, **Astrud Gilberto**, **Bud Shank** and **Cal Tjader**. Among other artists, mostly Brazilian and American, with whom he has recorded over the years are **Johnny Alf**, **Ray Barretto**, **Randy Brecker**, **Ron Carter**, **Deodato**, **Antonio Carlos Jobim** and **Airto Moreira**. Donato also developed a long-term musical relationship with Brazilian drummer Milton Banana and the pair accompanied Gilberto on an Italian tour. The tour over, Donato returned briefly to Brazil where he resumed his recording career before heading back to the USA. In the early 70s, now back in Brazil, he made more recordings and became musical director for singer **Gal Costa**'s show, *Cantar*, in which was included some of Donato's songs.

In 1999, to celebrate his 50th anniversary in the business, Lumiar Discos released three CDs of Donato compositions, sung by artists such as Arnaldo Antunes, Costa, Gil, **Ed Motta**, Rosa Passos and Veloso. For live performances, Donato usually works in a trio format and his regular partners have included bass player Luis Alves and drummers Robertinho Silva and Claudio Slon. Donato has also worked on the production side of recording with, among others, Fernanda Abreu, **Joyce**, Rita Lee, **Marisa Monte** and Emilio Santiago. In 2000, Donato was the winner of the Shell Music Award (Prêmio Shell de Música), which celebrates distinction in Brazilian music. The following year was especially prolific with appearances in Japan, the release of six CDs and a prestigious concert at the Sala São Paulo with the city's

Orquestra Jazz Symphony, and he still found time to spend almost two weeks in isolation in the Amazon forest composing a symphonic poem. In addition to his other accomplishments, Donato also plays trombone. Although not a virtuoso pianist, Donato is highly skilled and plays with subtlety and inner fire, key characteristics of Brazilian music to which form he has made an enormous if relatively unheralded contribution over the years.

● ALBUMS: *Chá Dançante* (Odeon 1956) ★★★, *Muito À Vontade...* aka *Sambou, Sambou* (Polydor 1962) ★★★★, *A Bossa Muito Moderna* (Polydor 1963) ★★★, *Bud Shank/Donato/Rosinha De Valença* aka *Bud Shank & His Brazilian Friends* (Elenco 1965) ★★★, *Piano Of João Donato—The New Sound Of Brasil* (RCA Victor 1965) ★★★, *Donato/Deodato: Featuring João Donato Arranged And Conducted By Eumir Deodato* (Muse 1969) ★★★★, *A Bad Donato* (Blue Thumb 1970) ★★★, *Quem É Quem* (Odeon 1973) ★★★, *Lugar Comum* (Philips 1975) ★★★, with Raimundo Fagner *Beleza* (CBS 1979) ★★★, *Leilíadas: João Donato Ao Vivo No People* (Elektra Musician 1986) ★★★, *Coisas Tão Simples* (Odeon 1996) ★★★, with Eloir De Moraes *Café Com Pão* (Lumiar 1997) ★★★★, *João Donato* (32 Jazz 1999) ★★★, *Amazonas* (Elephant 2000) ★★★, *The Frog—Live With The Symphonic Jazz Orchestra Of São Paulo* (Elephant 2001) ★★★, *Ê Lalá Lay-Ê* (Deckdisk 2001) ★★★, with Palmyra & Levita *Here's That Rainy Bossa Day* (Jazz Station 2001) ★★★, *Managarroba* (Deckdisk 2002) ★★★.

● COMPILATIONS: *Songbook* (Lumair 1999) ★★★★, *Millennium* (Universal International 2000) ★★★★, *Bis Bossa Nova* (EMI 2001) ★★★★, *Gold* (Musicrama 2002) ★★★★.

Done Lying Down

Led by Jeremy Parker (b. Boston, Massachusetts, USA; vocals/guitar), Done Lying Down also comprised English musicians Ali Mac (bass), Glen Young (guitar) and James Sherry (drums). The EP *Heart Of Dirt*, released in 1993, was produced by **Membranes**/Sensurround leader and journalist John Robb. The three tracks were headed by 'Dissent', a forceful song with a stop-start construction reminiscent of **Nirvana** (a comparison that stayed with the band throughout their early career). It was awarded Single Of The Week in the **New Musical Express**. In 1994 they released three EPs (*Family Values*, *Negative One Friends* and *Just A Misdemeanor*) that brought some indie chart success, BBC radio sessions with the disc jockey **John Peel** and video appearances on the UK television show *The Chart Show*. They also toured with **Girls Against Boys**, **Compulsion**, **Ned's Atomic Dustbin** and many others. Their debut album, *John Austin Rutledge*, was named after a friend of Parker's who co-wrote some of the songs: 'All he wanted was a credit, but we decided to name it after him and put his photo on the cover!'. In 1995 the band went to America for their first live shows there before signing a new contract with Immaterial Records and recording their fifth EP, *Chronic Offender*. Their second album was issued in 1996.

● ALBUMS: *John Austin Rutledge* (Black And White Indians/Abstract 1994) ★★★, *Kontrapunkt* (Abstract 1996) ★★★.

Donegan, Dorothy

b. 6 April 1922, Chicago, Illinois, USA, d. 16 June 1998, Los Angeles, California, USA. Encouraged by her mother to learn music, Donegan studied classical piano, attending Chicago's Du Sable High School and the Chicago Conservatory of Music, but thereafter turned to jazz. A meeting with **Art Tatum** in the early 40s led to her becoming his protégée. The following year she made her first record session and became a popular figure at Chicago clubs, playing a mixture of jazz, boogie woogie and cocktail music with a strong visual appeal. She also made an appearance in the film *Sensations Of 1945*, a back stage musical featuring **Cab Calloway** and W.C. Fields, and was presented in concert at the Orchestra Hall.

Having started her jazz career as a single, she formed a trio in 1945 and continued to work in that format. Later in her career she was inclined to work as a soloist again, after being unable to appoint suitable drummers. In subsequent interviews she indicated a clear desire to return to playing classical music, a form that she used for her daily practise. A powerful performer with dazzling technique, she played with enormous swing and had a solid following. The audience at a 1980 appearance in New York's Sheraton Centre Hotel broke previous attendance records. In 1992 she was given an American Jazz Masters Award from the National Endowment of the Arts and enjoyed renewed popularity in the years before her death from cancer in 1998.

● ALBUMS: *Dorothy Donegan Piano* 10-inch album (MGM 1954) ★★★★, *Dorothy Donegan Trio* 10-inch album (Jubilee 1954) ★★★, *September Song* (Jubilee 1956) ★★★, *Dorothy Donegan At The Embers* (Roulette 1959) ★★★★, *Dorothy Donegan Live!* (Capitol 1959) ★★★★, *Donneybrook With Dorothy* (Capitol 1960) ★★★, *Swingin' Jazz In Hi-Fi* (Regina 1963) ★★★, *The Many Faces Of Dorothy Donegan* (Mahogany 1975) ★★★, *Makin' Whoopee* (Black & Blue 1979) ★★★, *Sophisticated Lady* (Ornament 1980) ★★★, *The Explosive Dorothy Donegan* (Progressive 1980) ★★★★, *Live At The Widder Bar* (Timeless 1986) ★★★, *Live At The 1990 Floating Jazz Festival* (Chiaroscuro 1990) ★★★.

● COMPILATIONS: *Dorothy Romps: A Piano Retrospective* (Rosetta 1995) ★★★★.

Donegan, Lonnie

b. Anthony James Donegan, 29 April 1931, Glasgow, Scotland, d. 4 November 2002, Peterborough, Cambridgeshire, England. Donegan, as 'The King Of Skiffle', became a more homogeneous UK equivalent to **Elvis Presley** than **Tommy Steele**. Donegan's mother was Irish and his father Scottish, and from the age of two he was raised in East Ham, London. Steeped in traditional jazz and its by-products, Donegan was a guitarist in a skiffle band before a spell in the army found him drumming in the Wolverines Jazz Band. After his discharge, he played banjo with **Ken Colyer** and then **Chris Barber**. With his very stage forename a tribute to the great black bluesman **Lonnie Johnson**, both units allowed him to sing a couple of blues-tinged American folk tunes as a 'skiffle' break. His version of **Lead Belly**'s 'Rock Island Line', issued from Barber's *New Orleans Joys* in 1954 as a single after months in the domestic hit parade, was also a US Top 10 hit. Donegan's music inspired thousands of teenagers to form amateur skiffle combos, with friends playing broomstick tea-chest bass, washboards and other instruments fashioned from household implements. The **Beatles**, playing initially as the **Quarry Men**, were the foremost example of an act traceable to such roots.

Performing with his own group and newly signed to **Pye Records**, Donegan was a prominent figure in skiffle throughout its 1957 prime; he possessed an energetic whine far removed from the gentle plumminess of other native pop vocalists. Donegan could dazzle with his virtuosity on 12-string acoustic guitar, and his string of familiar songs has rarely been surpassed: 'Don't You Rock Me Daddy-O', 'Bring A Little Water, Sylvie', 'Putting On The Style' (his second UK number 1), 'The Grand Coolie Dam', 'Tom Dooley', 'Does Your Chewing Gum Lose Its Flavour (On The Bedpost Over Night)' (a reworking of the 20s song 'Does The Spearmint Lose Its Flavor On The Bedpost Overnight?' which provided Donegan with a US Top 5 hit) and 'Jimmy Brown The Newsboy' were only a few of Donegan's gems. He successfully made the traditional 'Cumberland Gap' his own (his first UK number 1), and 1959's 'Battle Of New Orleans' was the finest ever reading of a popular song. He delved more deeply into Americana to embrace bluegrass, spirituals, Cajun and even Appalachian music, the formal opposite of jazz. However, when the skiffle boom diminished, he broadened his appeal—to much purist criticism—with old-time music hall/pub singalong favourites and a more pronounced comedy element. His final chart-topper was with the uproarious 'My Old Man's A Dustman', which sensationally entered the UK charts at number 1 in 1960. The hit was an adaptation of the ribald Liverpool folk ditty 'My Old Man's A Fireman On The Elder-Dempster Line'. He followed it with further comedy numbers including 'Lively' in 1960. Two years later, Donegan's Top 20 run ended as it had started, with a Lead Belly number ('Pick A Bale Of Cotton'), as the music scene he had inspired began to explore beyond the limitations of skiffle. However, between 1956 and 1962 he had numbered 34 hits.

Donegan finished the 60s with huge sales of two mid-price *Golden Age Of Donegan* volumes, supplementing his earnings in cabaret and occasional spots on BBC Television's *The Good Old Days*. The most interesting diversion of the next decade was **Adam Faith**'s production of *Puttin' On The Style*. Here, at **Paul McCartney**'s suggestion, Donegan remade old smashes backed by an extraordinary glut of artists who were lifelong fans, including **Rory Gallagher**, **Ringo Starr**, **Leo Sayer**, **Zoot Money**, **Albert Lee**, **Gary Brooker**, **Brian May**, **Nicky Hopkins**, **Elton John** and **Ron Wood**. While this album brushed 1978's UK charts, a 1982 single, 'Spread A Little Happiness', was also a minor success—and, as exemplified by the **Traveling Wilburys**' 'skiffle for the 90s', the impact of Donegan's earliest chart entries has continued to exert an influence on pop music.

Although no longer enjoying the best of health, having suffered a heart attack in 1976 that required open-heart surgery, Donegan continued to entertain. In the 90s, he toured occasionally with his old boss, Chris Barber, and in 1997 he was presented with a Lifetime Achievement honour at the an **Ivor Novello** Awards. The following year, Donegan recorded his first new album in 20 years. Among the highlights on *Muleskinner Blues* was a duet with **Van Morrison** and revitalized versions of several Donegan staples such as 'Rock Island Line' and 'Alabamy Bound'. His playing remained as sharp as ever, but of greater note was Donegan's voice. Not only had he maintained the power of his high treble, but also his baritone range could now shake the floor. Two years later, he received an MBE for services to British Popular Music.

Donegan, a remarkable survivor, continued to perform even after undergoing further heart surgery in May 2002, but he died a few months later while midway through a UK tour. He remains without doubt the king of British skiffle, but he is also a hugely influential figure in the development of popular music in the UK since the birth of rock 'n' roll.

● ALBUMS: *Showcase* (Nixa 1956) ★★★, *Lonnie* (Pye 1958) ★★★, *Lonnie's Skiffle Party* (Pye 1958) ★★★, *Tops With Lonnie* (Pye 1959) ★★★★, *Lonnie Rides Again* (Pye 1959) ★★★, *More Tops With Lonnie* (Pye 1961) ★★★★, *Sing Hallelujah* (Pye 1962) ★★★, *The Lonnie Donegan Folk Album* (Pye 1965) ★★★★, *Lonniepops-Lonnie Donegan Today* (Decca 1970) ★★★, *Meets Leinemann* (Philips 1974) ★★, *Meets Leinemann: Country Roads* (Philips 1975) ★★, *Puttin' On The Style* (Chrysalis 1977) ★★★, *Sundown* (Chrysalis 1978) ★★★, *Jubilee Concert* (Cube 1981) ★★, *Muleskinner Blues* (BMG 1998) ★★★★, with Van Morrison, Chris Barber *The Skiffle Sessions: Live In Belfast* (Exile 1999) ★★★, *This Yere De Story* (Upbeat Jazz 2005) ★★★.

● COMPILATIONS: *Golden Age Of Donegan* (Golden Guinea 1962) ★★★★, *Golden Age Of Donegan Volume 2* (Golden Guinea 1963) ★★★★, *Golden Hour Of Golden Hits* (Golden Hour 1973) ★★★, *Golden Hour Of Golden Hits, Volume 2* (Golden Hour 1974) ★★★, *The Lonnie Donegan File* (Pye 1977) ★★★★, *The Hits Of Lonnie Donegan* (MFP 1978) ★★★, *Greatest Hits: Lonnie Donegan* (Ditto 1983) ★★★★, *Rare And Unissued Gems* (Bear Family 1985) ★★★, *Rock Island Line* (Flashback 1985) ★★★★, *The Hit Singles Collection* (PRT 1987) ★★★★, *The Best Of Lonnie Donegan* (Pickwick 1989) ★★★★, *The Collection: Lonnie Donegan* (Castle 1989) ★★★★, *The EP Collection* (See For Miles 1992) ★★★, *More Than 'Pye In The Sky'* 8-CD box set (Bear Family 1994) ★★★★, *Talking Guitar Blues: The Very Best Of Lonnie Donegan* (Sequel 1999) ★★★★, *Meets Leinemann: The Complete Sessions 1974-1975* (Jasmine 1999) ★★★, *Rock Island Line: The Singles Anthology 1955-1967* 3-CD box set (Sequel 2002) ★★★★, *Puttin' On The Style: The Greatest Hits* (Sanctuary 2003) ★★★★, *Lonesome Traveller: An Introduction To An Inspirational Performer* (Castle 2005) ★★★★.

● FURTHER READING: *Skiffle: The Inside Story*, Chas McDevitt. *The Skiffle Craze*, Mike Dew. *Puttin' On The Style*, Spencer Leigh.

Donelly, Tanya

b. 14 July 1966, Newport, Rhode Island, USA. Tanya Donelly's career trajectory reflects a desire to have an ever-increasing level of control over her artistic output. After leaving both **Throwing Muses** and the **Breeders** because she did not want to stand back in the shadows, she eventually found the group format of **Belly** equally constrictive. Belly reached a natural death in late 1995 and Donelly began working on solo projects, using a starry roster including her husband, ex–**Juliana Hatfield** bass player Dean Fisher, **Folk Implosion** producer Wally Gagel and drummer David Lovering, formerly with the **Pixies**. She also played some gigs with Billy Coté and Mary Lorson of **Madder Rose**. While her songwriting retained its slightly left-field strengths, the new flexibility of line-up saw Donelly using less traditionally 'rock'-orientated instrumentation, such as synthesizers and drum machines, which some took as hinting at a desire to escape the indie ghetto.

The birth of her daughter in April 1999 delayed the release of Donelly's follow-up album. The following year she performed two live sets with her old band the Throwing Muses. *Beautysleep* was finally released in February 2002. The new minimalist direction hinted at on that album was fully realised on 2004's *Whiskey Tango Ghosts*, a record of quiet, understated beauty.

● ALBUMS: *Lovesongs For Underdogs* (4AD 1997) ★★★★, *Beautysleep* (4AD 2002) ★★★, *Whiskey Tango Ghosts* (4AD 2004) ★★★.

Donen, Stanley

b. 13 April 1924, Columbia, South Carolina, USA. The director and choreographer for a string of classic MGM musicals of the 50s, Donen was fascinated by film and theatre from an early age. After graduating from high school he worked on Broadway in the chorus of the **Richard Rodgers** and **Lorenz Hart** musical *Pal Joey* (1940), which starred **Gene Kelly**, and he assisted Kelly on the choreography for *Best Foot Forward* (1941) and also appeared in the chorus. Signed to MGM, during the 40s he worked as choreographer, co-choreographer and/or co-director of occasional sequences (often uncredited) on musicals such as *Cover Girl*; *Hey Rookie*; *Jam Session*; *Kansas City Kitty*; *Anchors Aweigh*; *Holiday In Mexico*; *No Leave, No Love*; *Living In A Big Way*; *This Time For Keeps*; *A Date With Judy*; *The Kissing Bandit* and *Take Me Out To The Ball Game*. In 1949 Donen made his official directorial debut as Gene Kelly's co-director on the acclaimed, groundbreaking musical *On The Town*, and they worked together on several more memorable films, including *Singin' In The Rain*, *It's Always Fair Weather* and *The Pajama Game*. Donen also brought his skill as a director of breathtakingly fresh and exuberant sequences to pictures such as *Wedding Bells*, *Give A Girl A Break* (also choreographed with **Gower Champion**), *Deep In My Heart*, *Seven Brides For Seven Brothers*, *Funny Face* and *Damn Yankees* (1958). By that time the golden age of movie musicals was over, and, with the exception of *The Little Prince* (1974), Donen concentrated on directing (and producing) dramatic and light-comedy films such as *Indiscreet*, *The Grass Is Greener*, *Arabesque*, *Two For The Road*, *Bedazzled*, *Staircase*, *Lucky Lady*, *Movie Movie*, *Saturn 3* and *Blame It On Rio* (1984). Since then, Donen has been rumoured to be trying to bring biographies of **Judy Garland** and **Marlene Dietrich** to the screen, but to date nothing has materialized. In 1988 he produced the Academy Awards show and five years later made his directorial debut on Broadway in the **Jule Styne** musical *The Red Shoes*. After the original director, Susan Schulman, bowed out in the early stages of production, Donen took over. Unfortunately, unlike those earlier MGM musicals, there was no happy ending and the show closed after three days. However, in 1998 Donen received an Honorary Academy Award 'in appreciation of a body of work marked by grace, elegance, wit and visual innovation.'

● FURTHER READING: *Dancing On The Ceiling*, Stephen M. Silverman. *Stanley Donen*, Joseph Andrew Casper.

Donington Festival

Held annually during August at the Castle Donington racetrack in north Leicestershire, England, the Donington Festival has come to represent the highlight of the UK heavy metal calendar. First staged in 1980, Donington was conceived as an alternative to the Reading Festival when the latter moved away from its hard rock roots to encompass new wave and indie acts. Donington's one-day event, billed 'Monsters Of Rock', generally features at least six top-flight rock bands, with the opening slot reserved for 'talented newcomers'. This has resulted in commercially successful acts such as **Mötley Crüe** (1984), **Cinderella** (1987), **Thunder** (1990) and the **Black Crowes** (1991) all using the spot as a platform to launch their international careers. Among the headliners, **AC/DC** have returned three times (1982, 1984, 1991), and **Iron Maiden** (1988, 1992) and **Whitesnake** (1983, 1990) twice. Although the festival has encountered fewer public disorder problems than most, in 1988 two attendees were killed during **Guns N'Roses**' performance when a video screen and supporting scaffolding collapsed at the side of the stage. Two years previously, heavy metal satirists **Bad News** were 'bottled off' as their caricatures of the heavy metal lifestyle wore thin. In 1992, BBC Radio 1 presented its first live broadcast of the festival in its entirety—with the provision of a 15-second delay before 9pm so engineers could delete any expletives. Though that year's audience fell 10,000 below the 72,500 maximum capacity imposed by safety regulators, Donington continues to be the one annual festival for heavy metal and hard rock fans that remains uncontaminated by the presence of other forms of music.

Donna Regina

Although the recording moniker suggests a solo artist, Donna Regina is actually a collaboration between Cologne, Germany–based singer Regina Janssen and sometime film/television music writer Günther Janssen, with Steffen Irlinger adding sounds and samples. The couple combines traditional songwriting with electronic production techniques to create a beguiling, soft-focus music that has been compared to **Lali Puna**, **Matthew Herbert**, **Julee Cruise**, **Nico**, **Sade** and **Saint Etienne**. Although they generally record for the Cologne-based Karaoke Kalk label, Donna Regina has released material on Herbert's Lowlife label, and the esoteric **house** producer provided assistance on the band's debut album, 1999's *A Quiet Week In The House*. Herbert seems a discrete influence, and echoing his music-making process, Donna Regina seem to delicately incorporate sampled 'found sounds' such as lapping waves alongside their acoustic and digital instruments, producing music that is pretty and classy and near-bereft of any rock impulses. Their mix of the analogue and the digital is graceful and unforced. 'Late', the title track of their third album for Karaoke Kalk, released in 2003, juxtaposes gently twanging surf guitars with computer-derived beats to curiously nostalgic effect. Donna Regina's music has been remixed by Isolée, Herbert and **Mouse On Mars**. Regina Janssen also contributed her breathy vocals to **Guitar**'s *Sunkissed*.

● ALBUMS: *A Quiet Week In The House* (Karaoke Kalk 1999) ★★★★, *Northern Classic* (Karaoke Kalk 2002) ★★★, *Late* (Karaoke Kalk 2003) ★★★.

Donnas

The adoption of a shared moniker clearly alludes to a **Ramones** influence, but this all-female four-piece band from Palo Alto, Northern California, USA, can also lay claim to influences ranging from **AC/DC**, **Kiss** and a whole host of other big-haired arena rockers. Donna A (b. Brett Anderson, 1979, California, USA; vocals), Donna C (b. Torrance

Castellano, 1979, California, USA; drums), Donna F (b. Maya Ford, 1979, California, USA; bass) and Donna R (b. Allison Robertson, 1979, California, USA; guitar) formed Ragady Anne while in high school in Palo Alto. After practising **R.E.M.**, **Shonen Knife** and **L7** covers in Castellano's garage, a 7-inch single was released by Radio Trash Records in 1994. The quartet then changed their name to the Electrocutes and played shows around the San Francisco area under this moniker. Fate struck when they were introduced to Darin Raffaelli, the owner of the local Radio X record label. Raffaelli had been writing songs for a proposed all-female act to relaunch his ailing label, and he convinced the band to work with him. Not wanting to compromise the Electrocutes, the band invented the Donnas as a side project. The band's adopted sassy bad-girl persona was in sharp contrast to the suburban, trash-rock look of the Electrocutes. The Donnas recorded 'High School Yum Yum' and 'Let's Go Mano!' for Radio X, and a cover version of the **Crystals**' 'Da Doo Ron Ron' for Raffaelli's new Super*Teem label. The cranked up 50s rock 'n' roll sound of the singles was carried over to the Donnas' long-playing debut, released on Super*Teem in 1996. The album was well received and, as a result, the band took time off school to tour Japan. By this time they had also recorded an Electrocutes album, *Steal Yer Lunch Money*, released on the Sympathy For The Record Industry label. The Donnas split from the svengali-like Raffaelli before the release of *American Teenage Rock 'N' Roll Machine*. The album featured more of their own compositions, a benefit of their newfound independence. The Donnas' Ramones tendencies were now being tempered with more of the Electrocutes' rock leanings. After graduation from high school the band had been set to attend various universities across the country, but after signing to Lookout! Records they chose to concentrate on music instead. 1999's *Get Skintight* blended the Electrocutes' tough cock-rock tendencies with the Donnas' more straight-ahead punk pop. The album included a cover version of **Mötley Crüe**'s 'Too Fast For Love', and the band completed a long held ambition by opening for **Cinderella** in Reno, Nevada. In the same year, the Donnas appeared in the movies *Jawbreaker* and *Drive Me Crazy*. They celebrated reaching the legal drinking age by releasing *Turn 21* in 2001. The following year they made their major label debut on **Atlantic Records** with *Spend The Night*.

● ALBUMS: *The Donnas* (Super*Teem 1996) ★★★, *American Teenage Rock 'N' Roll Machine* (Lookout! 1998) ★★★★, *Get Skintight* (Lookout! 1999) ★★★, *Turn 21* (Lookout! 2001) ★★★, *Spend The Night* (Atlantic 2002) ★★★, *Gold Medal* (Atlantic 2004) ★★★.

● FILMS: *Jawbreaker* (1999), *Drive Me Crazy* (1999).

Donnelly, Dorothy

b. Dorothy Agnes Donnelly, 28 January 1880, New York City, New York, USA, d. 3 January 1928, New York City, New York, USA. Donnelly's early theatrical work was as a dramatic actress, appearing in *Madame X* (1910) and other plays. Soon after this, however, she turned her considerable creative talents to writing song lyrics and librettos for musical comedies. She worked on *Flora Bella* (1916) and *Fancy Free* (1918), then teamed up for the first time with **Sigmund Romberg**. This was for **Blossom Time** (1921), which was based upon a German operetta *Das Dreimaderlhaus* that not only used original music by classical composer Franz Schubert, but was also based very loosely upon his life. The score

included 'Song Of Love', which gained lasting popularity. With *Blossom Time* a big hit on Broadway, Donnelly then worked on **Poppy** (1923), a show starring **W.C. Fields**. Following this, she again worked with Romberg; this was on a show that would be one of the greatest Broadway successes of all time. Among the lasting gems from **The Student Prince In Heidelberg** (1924), Donnelly and Romberg wrote 'Deep In My Heart', 'The Drinking Song' and 'Serenade'. Although she worked again with Romberg, they were unable to achieve a similar level of success. They wrote *My Maryland* (1927) and *My Princess* (1927) before Donnelly's death in 1928.

● FILMS: *The Thief* (1914), *Sealed Valley* (1915), *Madame X* (1916).

Donner, Ral

b. Ralph Stuart Donner, 10 February 1943, Chicago, Illinois, USA, d. 6 April 1984, Chicago, Illinois, USA. Donner had a short string of US chart singles in the early 60s, most notably the number 4 'You Don't Know What You've Got (Until You Lose It)'. He began singing in church in his teens and formed his first band at the age of 13; he began touring two years later. Building a reputation for a singing voice uncannily similar to that of **Elvis Presley**, Donner chose a Presley album track, 'Girl Of My Best Friend', for his attempt to break-through. After recording it in Florida, Donner leased the track to Gone Records and it ultimately climbed to number 19 in the US charts. His second single was his only Top 10 hit (number 25 in the UK), and Donner subsequently placed three other singles in the US chart, with 'She's Everything (I Wanted You To Be)' the most successful at number 18. His debut, *Takin' Care Of Business*, was also released on Gone in 1961, and has, in subsequent years, increased in value as a collectors' item. Donner continued to record after leaving Gone, for labels such as **Reprise Records** and several small independents. Although his commercial popularity was in the early 60s, Donner gained recognition among fans and collectors of Presley-styled rock 'n' roll, and he continued to capitalize on that association. In 1981, Donner provided the narration for the movie *This Is Elvis*, mimicking the late Presley's speaking voice with the same expertise he had applied to the sound-alike singing. Donner died of lung cancer at the age of 41.

● ALBUMS: *Takin' Care Of Business* (Gone 1961) ★★★, with Ray Smith And Bobby Dale *Ral Donner, with Ray Smith And Bobby Dale* (Crown 1963) ★★, *The Elvis Presley Sound Of Ral Donner* (Treasure 1986) ★★★, *Loneliness Of A Star* (1986) ★★★.

● COMPILATIONS: *The Complete Ral Donner* (Sequel 1991) ★★★, *You Don't Know What You've Got Until You Lose It* (Collectables 1995) ★★★, *You Don't Know What You've Got: The Anthology* (Castle 2001) ★★★.

Donohue, Jack

b. John Francis Donohue, 3 November 1908, New York City, New York, USA, d. 27 March 1984, Marina Del Rey, California, USA. An industrial worker, Donohue took up dancing as a form of physical therapy following a serious accident. He became a professional dancer in New York and from the early 30s onwards he had a dual career on Broadway, choreographing and staging shows, and in Hollywood. In the 50s he also embraced television. In the 50s Donohue choreographed *Top Banana* (1951) and **Mr.**

Wonderful (1956). Among his Hollywood musicals as dance director are **George White's Scandals** and **Music In The Air** (both 1934); **Shirley Temple**'s *The Littlest Rebel*, *The Little Colonel*, *Curly Top* and *Captain January* (all 1935); **The Fleet's In** (1942); **Girl Crazy** and **Broadway Rhythm** (both 1943); **Bathing Beauty** (1944); **It Happened In Brooklyn** (1946); and **Calamity Jane** (1953). Film credits as choreographer included 1977's **New York, New York**. He also directed some films, among them *Close-Up* (1948), *The Yellow Cab Man* (1950), *Lucky Me* (1954), **Babes In Toyland** (1961), *Marriage On The Rocks* (1965) and *Assault On A Queen* (1966).

On television from the early 50s Donohue directed numerous episodes of the shows of **Frank Sinatra**, Red Skelton and George Gobel; Donohue also directed some episodes of shows starring **Lucille Ball**, **Dean Martin** and Jim Nabors. In the 70s, he was director of **Once Upon A Mattress** (1972), *Ed Sullivan's Broadway* (1973) and *Pinocchio* (1976), as well as episodes of the series *Manhattan Transfer* (1975) and the situation comedy *Chico And The Man* (1974-78). (NB: In some credits, his name is spelled Donahue.)

● FILMS: *Our Little Girl* (1935), *Rhythm In The Air* (1936), *O.H.M.S.* aka *You're In The Army Now* (1937), *Keep Smiling* aka *Smiling Along* (1938), *Another Day At The Races* (1975).

Donovan

b. Donovan Leitch, 10 May 1946, Maryhill, Glasgow, Scotland. Uncomfortably labelled 'Britain's answer to **Bob Dylan**', Donovan did not fit in well with the folk establishment. Instead, it was the pioneering UK television show **Ready, Steady, Go!** that adopted him, and from then on success was assured. His first single, 'Catch The Wind', launched a career that lasted through the 60s with numerous hits, developing as fashions changed. The expressive 'Colours' and 'Turquoise' continued his hit folk image, although hints of other influences began to creep into his music. Donovan's finest work, however, was as an ambassador of 'flower power' with memorable singles such as 1966's 'Sunshine Superman' (UK number 2/US number 1) and 'Mellow Yellow' (UK number 8/US number 2). His subtle drug references endeared him to the hippie movement, although some critics felt his stance was too fey and insipid. He enjoyed several hits with lighter material such as the calypso influenced 'There Is A Mountain' and 'Jennifer Juniper' (written for Jenny Boyd during a much publicized sojourn with the guru, Maharishi Mahesh Yogi).

A number of the tracks on his ambitious 1967 boxed set, *A Gift From A Flower To A Garden*, displayed a jazzier feel, a style he had previously flirted with on excellent b-sides such as 'Sunny Goodge Street' and 'Preachin' Love'. Meanwhile, his drug/fairy tale imagery reached its apotheosis in 1968 with the Lewis Carroll-influenced 'Hurdy Gurdy Man' (UK number 4/US number 5). As the 60s closed, however, he fell from commercial grace, despite adopting a more gutsy approach for his collaboration with **Jeff Beck** on 'Goo Goo Barabajagal (Love Is Hot)'. Undeterred, Donovan found greater success in the USA, and many of his later records were issued only in America. *Cosmic Wheels* (1973) was an artistic and commercial success and contained the witty 'Intergalactic Laxative'. Anticipating continued success, Donovan then released the bitterly disappointing *Essence To Essence* and thereafter ceased to be a major concert attraction although he continued to release low-key studio albums on a variety of labels.

In 1990, after many inactive years, the **Happy Mondays** bought Donovan back into favour by praising his work and invited him on tour in 1991. Their irreverent tribute 'Donovan' underlined this newfound favouritism. He also appeared on UK television as part of a humorous remake of 'Jennifer Juniper' with comedians Trevor and Simon. A flood of reissues arrived as Donovan was deemed hip again, and he undertook a major UK tour in 1992. *Troubadour*, an excellent CD box set was issued the same year covering vital material from his career. The highest profile he has received in the recent past is becoming ex–Happy Monday/**Black Grape** vocalist Shaun Ryder's father-in-law. 1996's *Sutras* was released to a considerable amount of press coverage but achieved little in terms of sales. On this album he revisited whimsical and 'cosmic' territory. Instead of catchy folk songs (early period) and acid soaked rockers (late period), he opted for cloying, though sincere, material. Apart from the release of a number of reissues and a children's album, little was heard from Donovan until he made an unexpected return in 2004 with a fine new studio album, *Beat Café*.

● ALBUMS: *What's Bin Did And What's Bin Hid* (UK) *Catch The Wind* (US) (Pye/Hickory 1965) ★★★★, *Fairytale* (Pye/Hickory 1965) ★★★★, *Sunshine Superman* US only (Epic 1966) ★★★★, *Mellow Yellow* US only (Epic 1967) ★★★★, *A Gift From A Flower To A Garden* (Epic 1967) ★★★, *Wear Your Love Like Heaven* US only (Epic 1967) ★★★, *For Little Ones* US only (Epic 1967) ★★★, *In Concert* (Epic/Pye 1968) ★★★, *The Hurdy Gurdy Man* US only (Epic 1968) ★★★★, *Barabajagal* (Epic 1969) ★★★★, *Open Road* (Dawn/Epic 1970) ★★★, *HMS Donovan* (Dawn 1971) ★★★, *Brother Sun, Sister Moon* film soundtrack (EMI 1972) ★★, *Colours* (Hallmark 1972) ★★★, *Cosmic Wheels* (Epic 1973) ★★★, *Live In Japan* (Sony 1973) ★★★, *Essence To Essence* (Epic 1973) ★★, *7-Tease* (Epic 1974) ★★★, *Slow Down World* (Epic 1976) ★★, *Donovan* (RAK/Arista 1977) ★★, *Neutronica* (Barclay/RCA 1980) ★★, *Love Is Only Feeling* (RCA 1981) ★★, *Lady Of The Stars* (RCA/Allegiance 1984) ★★, *Donovan Rising* (UK) *The Classics Live* (US) (Permanent/Great Northern Arts 1993) ★★★, *Sutras* (American Recordings 1996) ★★★, *Greatest Hits Live: Vancouver 1986* (Varèse Vintage 2001) ★★★, *Celtia* (Durga 2002) ★★★, *Pied Piper* (Rhino 2002) ★★★, *Beat Café* (Appleseed 2004) ★★★.

● COMPILATIONS: *The Real Donovan* US only (Hickory 1966) ★★★, *Sunshine Superman* UK only (Pye 1967) ★★★★, *Universal Soldier* (Marble Arch 1967) ★★★★, *Like It Is, Was, And Evermore Shall Be* (Hickory 1968) ★★★, *The Best Of Donovan* (Epic/Pye 1969) ★★★★, *The Best Of Donovan* (Hickory 1969) ★★★, *The World Of Donovan* (Marble Arch 1969) ★★★, *Donovan P. Leitch* US only (Janus 1970) ★★★, *Catch The Wind* (Hallmark 1971) ★★★, *Golden Hour Of Donovan* (Golden Hour 1971) ★★★★, *Colours* (Hallmark 1972) ★★★, *The World Of Donovan* US only (Epic 1972) ★★★, *Early Treasures* US only (Bell 1973) ★★★, *Four Shades* 4-LP box set (Pye 1973) ★★★, *Hear Me Now* (Janus 1974) ★★★, *The Pye History Of British Pop Music: Donovan* US only (Pye 1975) ★★★, *The Pye History Of British Pop Music: Donovan, Vol. 2* US only (Pye 1976) ★★★, *The Donovan File* (Pye 1977) ★★★, *Spotlight On Donovan* (PRT 1981) ★★★★, *Universal*

Soldier (Spot 1983) ★★★, *Catch The Wind* (Showcase 1986) ★★★, *Colours* (PRT 1987) ★★★, *Catch The Wind* US only (Garland 1988) ★★★, *Greatest Hits . . . And More* (EMI 1989) ★★★★, *The EP Collection* (See For Miles 1990) ★★★★, *The Collection* (Castle 1991) ★★★, *The Trip* (EMI 1991) ★★★★, *Colours* (Del Rack 1991) ★★★★, *Troubadour: The Definitive Collection 1964–1976* 2-CD box set (Epic/Legacy 1992) ★★★★, *The Early Years* (Dojo 1993) ★★★, *Sunshine Superman—18 Songs Of Love And Freedom* (Remember 1993) ★★★, *Gold* (Disky 1993) ★★★, *Josie* (Castle 1994) ★★★, *Universal Soldier* (Spectrum 1995) ★★★★, *Peace And Love Songs* (Sony 1995) ★★★, *Catch The Wind: The Best Of Donovan* (Pulse 1996) ★★★, *Sunshine Troubadour* (Hallmark 1996) ★★★, *Love Is Hot, Truth Is Molten: Original Essential Recordings 1965–1973* (HMV 1998) ★★★, *Mellow* (Snapper 1997) ★★★, *Catch The Wind* (Laserlight 1998) ★★★, *Fairytales And Colours* (Select 1998) ★★★, *Summer Day Reflection Songs* (Castle 2000) ★★★★, *Sunshine Superman: The Very Best Of Donovan* (EMI 2002) ★★★★, *Sixty Four: The Donovan Archive Volume 1* (Donovan Discs 2004) ★★, *Best Of Live* (Artful 2004) ★★, *Try For The Sun: The Journey Of Donovan* 4-CD box set (Epic/Legacy 2005) ★★★.

● FURTHER READING: *Dry Songs And Scribbles*, Donovan. *She*, Donovan. *The Hurdy Gurdy Man: The Autobiography Of Donovan*, Donovan Leitch.
● FILMS: *Don't Look Back* (1967), *If It's Tuesday, This Must Be Belgium* (1969), *The Pied Piper* (1972), *Aliens From Spaceship Earth* (1977), *Sgt. Pepper's Lonely Hearts Club Band* (1978).

Donovan, Jason

b. Jason Sean Donovan, 1 June 1968, Malvern, Melbourne, Australia. Donovan appeared in the Australian television soap-opera *Neighbours*, which, when shown on British television, commanded a considerable viewing audience of pre-pubescent/teenage girls who instantly took his character, Scott Robinson, to their hearts. His co-star **Kylie Minogue** had already begun to forge a career in pop music when he also signed to the **Stock, Aitken And Waterman** label, PWL. In 1988 his first single, 'Nothing Can Divide Us Now', reached the UK Top 5. The follow-up was a collaboration with Minogue, 'Especially For You', which topped the UK charts in January the following year. Donovan consolidated his position as Britain's top teen pin-up by scoring four more Top 10 hits, including 'Too Many Broken Hearts' (a number 1 hit), 'Sealed With A Kiss', 'Every Day (I Love You More)' and 'When You Come Back To Me'. His album, *Ten Good Reasons*, reached number 1 and became one of 1989's bestsellers. His success the following year was endorsed by Top 10 hits in 'Hang On To Your Love' and a remake of the 1963 **Cascades** hit, 'Rhythm Of The Rain'. By this time Donovan had left the cast of *Neighbours*. His performances in the stage show of the **Andrew Lloyd Webber/Tim Rice** musical, **Joseph And The Amazing Technicolor Dreamcoat**, at the London Palladium, drew sell-out crowds and mostly good reviews, taking many of his regular critics by surprise. A single from the show, 'Any Dream Will Do', reached number 1 in the UK chart, scotching any notion that Donovan was wavering as a hit-maker. He was perceived by many as simply being a teen-idol, yet his obvious talent in acting and singing, and the extent of his loyal following,

echoed previous teen-idols made good as all-round entertainers (**Tommy Steele** for example).
In the spring of 1992, Donovan won a libel action he brought against *The Face* magazine. Later in the same year, his high-profile concert tour was greeted with a good deal of apathy and critical derision ('Jason's big rock dream turns sour'), and it was considered by many to be a retrograde career move when he returned to *Joseph And The Amazing Technicolor Dreamcoat* the following year. For some time he alternated with other leading performers, before taking over for the last few weeks before the show closed in February 1994. After he had collapsed several times in public during 1995, there was inevitably speculation in the press regarding drugs and alcohol abuse. However, the following year he was in London playing Mordred in the Covent Garden Festival production of Camelot, and he had his first non-singing role as a psychopath who keeps his first victim's head in a hatbox in Emlyn Williams' classic 1935 thriller, *Night Must Fall*, at the Theatre Royal Haymarket. Having also dressed in a black bin liner and Dr. Marten boots in order to host *Mr. Gay UK*, a beauty contest for men, he went one step further and donned the obligatory stockings and suspenders for the role of Frank 'N' Furter in an Australian production of **The Rocky Horror Show**. In 1998, he headed the 25th Anniversary tour of that cult show in Britain.
● ALBUMS: *Ten Good Reasons* (PWL 1989) ★★, *Between The Lines* (PWL 1990) ★★, *Joseph And The Amazing Technicolor Dreamcoat* stage show soundtrack (PolyGram 1991) ★★★, *All Around The World* (Polydor 1993) ★★.
● COMPILATIONS: *Greatest Hits* (PWL 1991) ★★★, *The Very Best Of Jason Donovan* (Music Club 1999) ★★★.
● DVD/VIDEOS: *Jason, The Videos* (PWL 1989), *The Videos 2* (PWL 1990), *Into The Nineties: Live* (Castle Music Pictures 1991), *Greatest Video Hits* (PWL 1991), *The Joseph Mega-Remix* (PolyGram Music Video 1992), *Live* (1993).
● FURTHER READING: *Jason Donovan: The Official Book*, Jason Donovan.

Dont Bother Me I Cant Cope

Conceived by director, actress, playwright Vinnette Carroll (b. 1922, New York, USA, d. 5 November 2002, Lauderhill, Florida, USA) at her Urban Arts Corps Theatre, this show, the title of which the authors are said to prefer without traditional punctuation, transferred to the Playhouse Theatre in New York on 19 April 1972. This was the first Broadway show to be directed by a black woman, and Carroll was the first to bring gospel music to the New York stage. This production was performed by an all-black cast, whose generally good-natured, self-effacing exhortations regarding their proclaimed inferior position in the scheme of things—even in the modern world—was supplemented by music and lyrics by Micki Grant that ranged through a variety of musical styles including gospel, jazz, calypso and downright joyful good-time music. The numbers included 'Dont Bother Me I Cant Cope', 'Good Vibrations', 'Fighting For Pharaoh', 'It Takes A Whole Lot Of Human Feeling' and 'Thank Heaven For You'. In the cast were Alex Bradford, Micki Grant, Hope Clarke, Bobby Hill and Arnold Wilkerson. Opinions vary as to why this particular mixture of message and music took off, but it did, and in a big way—for nearly two and half years—a total of 1,065 performances. In 1976, Micki Grant, Hope Clarke and Alex Bradford were the prime movers in another all-black production, *Your Arms Too*

Short To Box With God (without punctuation again), which was based on the Gospel according to St. Matthew and provided the 'best singing and dancing on Broadway' for a time, and it was revived twice in the early 80s. Delores Hall won a **Tony Award** for best featured actress. Another production with all-black entertainers and a book, music and lyrics by Grant, entitled *It's So Nice To Be Civilized*, closed after one week in 1980.

Don't Knock The Rock

The same production team responsible for **Rock Around The Clock** made this 1956 film. **Alan Dale** played the part of rock 'n' roll singer Arnie Haynes, accused by parents of corrupting impressionable minds when he returns to his home-town. Disc jockey **Alan Freed** enjoyed a prominent role as Haynes' agent. When a riot breaks out at a concert headlined by **Bill Haley And His Comets**, the pair stage another show to convince the adults the music is no more controversial than previous fashions. The **Treniers** and Dave Appell And His **Applejacks** make appearances, but the film's highlight comes courtesy of **Little Richard**, who contributes explosive versions of 'Long Tall Sally', 'Tutti Frutti' and 'Rip It Up'. His performances saved this hurriedly produced film from oblivion.

Don't Knock The Twist

Mindful of *Don't Knock The Rock*, a follow-up to *Rock Around The Clock*, *Don't Knock The Twist* succeeded *Twist Around The Clock*. Few could accuse its producers of possessing imagination. This 1962 feature revolved around a television executive who hurriedly stages a twisting marathon to pre-empt a similar plan by a rival station. **Chubby Checker** contributed the title song and 'Slow Twistin', the latter with the help of **Dee Dee Sharp**. Inspired by another dance craze, Ms. Sharp offered the memorable 'Mashed Potato Time', while the **Dovels** sang 'Do The New Continental' and 'Bristol Stomp'. Soul singer **Gene Chandler** provided the undoubted highlight when, replete with top hat, cape and monocle, he performed the classic 'Duke Of Earl'. Yet despite these interesting cameos, *Don't Knock The Twist* is not one of pop cinema's better features.

Don't Look Back

Probably the finest documentary in rock, *Don't Look Back* is a *cinéma vérité* film of **Bob Dylan**'s 1965 tour of England. Director D.A. Pennebaker shot the proceedings in black and white with a 16mm, hand-held camera. Indeed, the opening scene, in which 'Subterranean Homesick Blues' plays while the singer holds up placards with words from its lyric, has become a much-copied pop legend. The subsequent pace is almost relentless and, having gained access both onstage and off, Pennebaker exposes Dylan in various moods. The concert footage itself is superb, in particular because this would be Dylan's final all-acoustic tour. He performs excellent versions of 'Gates Of Eden' and 'It's Alright Ma, I'm Only Bleeding', but these are overshadowed by other events captured on film. Dylan's verbal demolition of the *Time* magazine reporter is revelatory, as is his anger when some glasses are thrown from a window at a party. Yet a sense of mischief abounds when, in the company of US companion Bobby Neuwirth, a running joke about **Donovan** only ends when Dylan finally meets his supposed 'rival'. **Joan Baez**, **Marianne Faithfull**, **Alan Price**, **John Mayall**, **Derroll**

Adams and sundry **Pretty Things** are also caught on camera, but Dylan is always the focus of attention. *Don't Look Back* was released in 1967, but screenings were generally restricted to independent cinemas. It was withdrawn on Dylan's instructions for a period during the 70s but was reactivated again in the 80s and finally released on video.

Doobie Brothers

This enduring act evolved from Pud, a San Jose–based trio formed in March 1970 by Tom Johnston (b. 15 August 1948, Visalia, California, USA; guitar/vocals) and John Hartman (b. 18 March 1950, Falls Church, Virginia, USA; drums). Original bass player Greg Murphy was quickly replaced by Dave Shogren (b. San Francisco, California, USA, d. 2000, San Jose, California, USA). **Patrick Simmons** (b. 19 October 1948, Aberdeen, Washington, USA; guitar/vocals) then expanded the line-up, and within six months the band had adopted a new name, the Doobie Brothers, in deference to a slang term for a marijuana cigarette. Their muted 1971 debut album, although promising, was commercially unsuccessful and contrasted with the unit's tougher live sound. A new bass player Tiran Porter (b. USA) and second drummer Michael Hossack (b. 17 October 1946, Paterson, New Jersey, USA) joined the line-up for *Toulouse Street*, which spawned the anthem-like (and successful) single 'Listen To The Music'. This confident selection was a marked improvement on its predecessor, while the twin-guitar and twin-percussionist format inspired comparisons with the **Allman Brothers Band**. A sparkling third set, **The Captain And Me**, contained two US hits, 'Long Train Running' and 'China Grove', which have both become standard radio classics, while *What Were Once Vices Are Now Habits*, a largely disappointing album, did feature the Doobie Brothers' first US chart-topper 'Black Water'.

By this point the band's blend of harmonies and tight rock was proving highly popular, although critics pointed to a lack of invention and a reliance on proven formula. Hossack was replaced on the drums by the previous album's guest vocalist Keith Knudsen (b. 18 February 1948, LeMars, Iowa, USA, d. 8 February 2005, Kentfield, California, USA) for *Stampede*, which also introduced ex–**Steely Dan** guitarist, Jeff 'Skunk' Baxter (b. 13 December 1948, Washington, DC, USA). In April 1975, his former colleague, **Michael McDonald**, (b. 2 December 1952, St. Louis, Missouri, USA; keyboards/vocals) also joined the band when founder member Johnston succumbed to a recurrent ulcer problem. Although the guitarist rejoined the band in 1976, he left again two years later to concentrate on a solo career, which began with the release of 1979's *Everything You've Heard Is True*. The arrival of McDonald heralded a new direction. He gradually assumed control of their sound, dominating *Takin' It To The Streets* and instilling the soul-based perspective revealed on 1978's excellent *Minute By Minute* (the band's first album without Johnston) and its attendant US number 1 single, the ebullient 'What A Fool Believes'.

Both Hartman and Baxter then left the line-up, but McDonald's impressive, distinctive voice proved a unifying factor. 1980's *One Step Closer* featured newcomers John McFee (b. 9 September 1950, Santa Cruz, California, USA; guitar, ex-**Clover**), Cornelius Bumpus (b. 13 January 1946, USA, d. 3 February 2004, USA; saxophone/keyboards) and Chet McCracken (b. 17 July 1952, Seattle, Washington, USA; drums), yet it was probably the band's most accomplished album. Willie Weeks subsequently replaced Porter, but by 1981 the Doobie Brothers' impetus was waning. They split in October the following year, with McDonald and Simmons embarking on contrasting solo careers.

A re-formed Doobie Brothers, comprising the *Toulouse Street* line-up of Johnston, Simmons, Porter, Hartman and Hossack plus long-time conga player Bobby LaKind (d. 24 December 1992) completed a 1989 release, *Cycles*, on which traces of their one-time verve were still apparent. They found a similar audience, and 'The Doctor' made the US Top 10. A second album, *Brotherhood*, was less successful with both the critics and the general public. In 1993, a remixed version of 'Long Train Running' put the Doobie Brothers back in the charts, although to many 70s fans the **Ben Liebrand** production added little to the original classic. McDonald, McFee and Knudsen returned to the fold in the mid-90s, but by 2000's new studio album, *Sibling Rivalry*, the line-up comprised Johnston, Simmons, Hossack, Knudsen and McFee.

The Doobie Brothers remain critically underrated, their track record alone making them one of the major US rock bands of the 70s. Their sizeable catalogue of hits is perfect when heard in a live environment.

● ALBUMS: *The Doobie Brothers* (Warners 1971) ★★, *Toulouse Street* (Warners 1972) ★★★, *The Captain And Me* (Warners 1973) ★★★★, *What Were Once Vices Are Now Habits* (Warners 1974) ★★★, *Stampede* (Warners 1975) ★★★, *Takin' It To The Streets* (Warners 1976) ★★★★, *Livin' On The Fault Line* (Warners 1977) ★★★, *Minute By Minute* (Warners 1978) ★★★★, *One Step Closer* (Warners 1980) ★★★, *Farewell Tour* (Warners 1983) ★★★, *Cycles* (Capitol 1989) ★★★, *Brotherhood* (Capitol 1991) ★★, *Rockin' Down The Highway: The Wildlife Concert* (Legacy 1996) ★★★, *Sibling Rivalry* (Rhino/Eagle 2000) ★★★, *Live At Wolf Trap* (Sanctuary 2004) ★★.

● COMPILATIONS: *Best Of The Doobies* (Warners 1976) ★★★, *Best Of The Doobies Volume II* (Warners 1981) ★★★, *Listen To The Music: Very Best Of The Doobie Brothers* (Warners 1993) ★★★★, *Best Of The Doobie Brothers Live* (Sony 1999) ★★★, *Long Train Runnin' 1970–2000* 4-CD box set (Warners/Rhino 1999) ★★★, *Greatest Hits* (Rhino 2002) ★★★★, *Doobies' Choice* (Rhino 2002) ★★★.

● DVD/VIDEOS: *Rockin' Down The Highway: The Wildlife Concert* (Legacy 1996), *Live At Wolf Trap* (Sanctuary 2004).

Doof

b. Nick Barber, 1968. With a background in punk, reggae, rock and Indian music, Taylor's first release, the EP *Disposable Hymn To The Infinite*, was on **Novamute Records** in 1991. He has since recorded for a number of the top **trance** labels, including the *Born Again* EP (**Matsuri Productions** 1995) and 'Double Dragons' (**Dragonfly Records**). In 1995 he released 'Let's Turn On' (a collaboration with Simon Posford aka Hallucinogen) on **TIP Records**, followed in 1996 by 'Angelina' and 'Destination Bom' (also on TIP), which all became favourites on the trance scene. Towards the end of that year, TIP released Doof's eagerly awaited debut album, *Let's Turn On*, one of the most coherent and enduring releases in the 'Goa' trance style. On tracks such as 'Mars Needs Women' and 'Destination Bom', Barber distilled the rip-roaring, four-on-the-floor/Indian mode style in careful, restrained arrangements, while presenting a more tranquil,

chilled-out trance sound on 'Sunshrine' and 'Star Over Parvati'. At the same time, the album is characterized as a whole by his focused collection of sounds. In 1997, he contributed 'The Tower And The Star' to the TIP compilation *Infinite Excursions II*; the following year 'Wormwhole' was released on TIP's *Beyond Colour*. He has also written tracks for the **dub** compilations *Dub Mashing Up Creation* and *Dubbed On Planet Skunk* for Dubmission Records. Barber frequently travels and performs around Europe and further afield. He has remixed for a number of artists including the **Green Nuns Of The Revolution**, Hallucinogen and the **Infinity Project**.

● ALBUMS: *Let's Turn On* (TIP 1996) ★★★★.

Dooley, Ray
(see **Dowling, Eddie**)

Dooleys

This family pop group from Ilford, Essex, England, was based around siblings Jim, Frank, Anne, Kathy (all b. Ilford, Essex, England) and John Dooley (b. Whitechapel, London, England). They sang as a group for their relatives, but in 1973 they decided to try to turn professional. Their musical accompaniment was provided by Frank on lead guitar, John on rhythm, plus the addition of 'outsiders' Bob Walsh (bass) and Alan Boean (b. Oldham, Lancashire, England; drums). In 1976 they created their own slice of history by becoming the first British singing group to tour the Soviet Union. However, they had to wait until 1977 for their first hit, 'Think I'm Gonna Fall In Love With You'. A series of UK hits followed, including the Top 10 entries 'Love Of My Life', 'Wanted' and 'The Chosen Few'. Preferring middle of the road ballads with a leaning towards soft disco-beats, they were one of several similar bands at the time (e.g. **Nolans, Bucks Fizz**). They left the GTO label (where they had all 10 hits) in the early 80s and put a number of singles out on smaller labels, but to no avail. They still perform on the UK club and cabaret circuit.

● ALBUMS: *The Chosen Few* (GTO 1979) ★★, *Full House* (GTO 1980) ★★, *Secrets* (GTO 1981) ★★, *Dooleys* (1983) ★★.

● COMPILATIONS: *Best Of The Dooleys* (GTO 1979) ★★★, *Greatest Hits* (Spot 1983) ★★★.

Doonan Family Band

A lively Newcastle Upon Tyne/Irish family group with main members John 'Da' Doonan (flute), Kevin Doonan (fiddle) and Mick Doonan (pipes). The trio are regularly augmented by Phil Murray (bass) and Stu Luckley (guitar/vocals), as well as a troupe of Irish step dancers. An excellent festival act, the high percentage of ex–**Hedgehog Pie** and **Jack The Lad** members ensures that their sets, though acoustic, have far more energy than some of the 'electric' bands. They frequently feature traditional arrangements of material by **Buddy Holly** and the **Beatles**, amongst others.

● ALBUMS: *Fenwick's Window* (1992) ★★★.

Doonican, Val

b. Michael Valentine Doonican, 3 February 1927, Waterford, Eire. Doonican learned to play the mandolin and guitar as a boy and later toured northern and southern Ireland in various bands before travelling to England in 1951 to join an Irish vocal quartet, the Four Ramblers. He wrote the group's vocal arrangements as well as singing and playing guitar in their BBC radio series *Riders Of The Range*. In the late 50s, on the advice of **Anthony Newley**, he went solo and appeared on television in *Beauty Box* and on radio in *Dreamy Afternoon*, later retitled *A Date With Val*. In 1963 he was recommended to impresario Val Parnell by comedian Dickie Henderson and gained a spot on ITV's top-rated television show *Sunday Night At The London Palladium*. He made an immediate impact with his friendly, easy-going style and in 1964 commenced an annual series for BBC television, which ran until the 80s. He soon became one of the most popular entertainers in the UK and was voted Television Personality Of The Year three times.

The closing sequence of his television show, in which he sang a song while seated in a rocking chair, was especially effective. The idea was later used as a self-deprecating album title, *Val Doonican Rocks, But Gently*. Later, in the age of videotape, he still preferred his shows to be transmitted 'live'. His first record hit, 'Walk Tall', in 1964, was followed by a string of chart entries through to the early 70s, including 'The Special Years', 'Elusive Butterfly', 'What Would I Be', 'Memories Are Made Of This', 'If The Whole World Stopped Loving', 'If I Knew Then What I Know Now' and 'Morning'. Equally popular, but not chart entries, were a number of novelty songs such as 'O'Rafferty's Motor Car', 'Delaney's Donkey' and 'Paddy McGinty's Goat', written by the prolific English team of Bob Weston and Bert Lee. By the early 90s Doonican was semi-retired—performing 'laps of honour', as he put it. In 1993 he released a video, 'a tribute to his favourite artists', entitled *Thank You For The Music*.

● ALBUMS: *Lucky 13 Shades Of Val Doonican* (Decca 1964) ★★★, *Gentle Shades Of Val Doonican* (Decca 1966) ★★★, *Val Doonican Rocks, But Gently* (Pye 1967) ★★★, *Val* (Pye 1968) ★★★, *Sounds Gentle* (Pye 1969) ★★★, *The Magic Of Val Doonican* (Philips 1970) ★★★, *This Is Val Doonican* (Philips 1971) ★★★, *Morning Has Broken* (Philips 1973) ★★, *Song Sung Blue* (Philips 1974) ★★★, *I Love Country Music* (Philips 1975) ★★, *Life Can Be Beautiful* (Philips 1976) ★★★, *Some Of My Best Friends Are Songs* (Philips 1977) ★★★, *Quiet Moments* (RCA 1981) ★★★, *Val Sings Bing* (RCA 1982) ★★★, *The Val Doonican Music Show* (BBC 1984) ★★, *By Request* (MFP/EMI 1987) ★★★, *Portrait Of My Love* (CRC 1989) ★★★, *Songs From My Sketch Book* (Parkfield 1990) ★★★, *Christmas With Val Doonican* (Castle 1999) ★★.

● COMPILATIONS: *The World Of Val Doonican* (Decca 1969) ★★★★, *The World Of Val Doonican, Volume Two* (Decca 1969) ★★★★, *The World Of Val Doonican, Volume Three* (Decca 1970) ★★★, *The World Of Val Doonican, Volume Four* (Decca 1971) ★★★, *The World Of Val Doonican, Volume Five* (Decca 1972) ★★★, *Spotlight On Val Doonican* (1974) ★★★, *Focus On Val Doonican* (Decca 1976) ★★★, *Mr Music Man* (Hallmark 1988) ★★★, *Memories Are Made Of This* (Elite/Decca 1981) ★★★, *Forty Shades Of Green* (MFP/EMI 1983) ★★★, *The Very Best Of Val Doonican* (MFP/EMI 1984) ★★★★, *Twenty Personal Favourites For You* (Warwick 1986) ★★★, *It's Good To See You* (K-Tel 1988) ★★★, *The Very Best Of Val Doonican* (Music Club 1998) ★★★, *His Special Years: The Very Best Of Val Doonican* (PolyGram 1999) ★★★★.

● DVD/VIDEOS: *Songs From My Sketch Book* (Parkfield 1990), *Thank You For The Music* (1993).

● FURTHER READING: *The Special Years: An Autobiography*, Val Doonican.

Doors

'If the doors of perception were cleansed, everything would appear to man as it is, infinite.' This quote from poet William Blake, via Aldous Huxley, was an inspiration to Jim Morrison (b. James Douglas Morrison, 8 December 1943, Melbourne, Florida, USA, d. 3 July 1971, Paris, France), a student of theatre arts at the University of California and an aspiring musician. His dream of a rock band entitled 'the Doors' was fulfilled in 1965 when he sang a rudimentary composition, 'Moonlight Drive', to fellow scholar Ray Manzarek (b. Raymond Daniel Manzarek, 12 February 1939, Chicago, Illinois, USA; keyboards). Impressed, he invited Morrison to join his campus R&B band, Rick And The Ravens, which also included the organist's two brothers. Ray then recruited drummer John Densmore (b. 1 December 1944, Santa Monica, California, USA), and the reshaped outfit recorded six Morrison songs at the famed World Pacific studios. The session featured several compositions that the band subsequently re-recorded, including 'Summer's Almost Gone' and 'End Of The Night'. Manzarek's brothers disliked the new material and later dropped out. They were replaced by Robbie Krieger (b. Robert Alan Krieger, 8 January 1946, Los Angeles, California, USA), an inventive guitarist whom Densmore met at a meditation centre. Morrison was now established as the vocalist and the quartet began rehearsing in earnest.

The Doors' first residency was at the London Fog on Sunset Strip, but they later found favour at the prestigious Whisky-A-Go-Go. They were, however, fired from the latter establishment, following a performance of 'The End', Morrison's chilling, oedipal composition. Improvised and partly spoken over a raga/rock framework, it proved too controversial for timid club owners, but the band's standing within the music fraternity grew. Local rivals **Love**, already signed to **Elektra Records**, recommended the Doors to the label's managing director, **Jac Holzman** who, despite initial caution, signed them in July 1966. **The Doors**, produced by **Paul Rothchild** and released the following year, unveiled many contrasting influences. Manzarek's thin-sounding organ (he also performed the part of bass player with the aid of a separate bass keyboard, although Larry Knechtel helped out on the record) recalled the garage band style omnipresent several months earlier, but Krieger's liquid guitar playing and Densmore's imaginative drumming were already clearly evident. Morrison's striking, dramatic voice added power to the exceptional compositions, which included the pulsating 'Break On Through' and an 11-minute version of 'The End'. Cover versions of material, including **Willie Dixon**'s 'Back Door Man' and **Bertolt Brecht/Kurt Weill**'s 'Alabama Song (Whiskey Bar)', exemplified the band's disparate influences. The best-known track, however, was 'Light My Fire', which, when trimmed down from its original seven minutes, became a number 1 single in the USA. Its fiery imagery combined eroticism with death, and the song has since become a standard.

The success of 'Light My Fire' created new problems and the Doors, perceived by some as underground heroes, were tarred as teenybop fodder by others. This dichotomy weighed heavily on Morrison who wished to be accepted as a serious artist. A second album, **Strange Days**, showcased 'When The Music's Over', another extended piece destined to become a *tour de force* within the band's canon. The quartet enjoyed further chart success when 'People Are Strange' broached the US Top 20, but it was 1968 before they secured another number 1 single with the infectious 'Hello, I Love You'. The song was also the band's first major UK hit, although some of this lustre was lost following legal action by **Ray Davies** of the **Kinks**, who claimed infringement of his own composition, 'All Day And All Of The Night'. The action coincided with the Doors' first European tour in September. A major television documentary, *The Doors Are Open*, was devoted to the visit and centred on their powerful performance at London's Chalk Farm Roundhouse. The band showcased several tracks from their third collection, *Waiting For The Sun*, including the declamatory 'Five To One', and a fierce protest song, 'The Unknown Soldier', for which they also completed an uncompromising promotional film. However, the follow-up album, *The Soft Parade*, on which a horn section masked several unremarkable songs, was a major disappointment, although the tongue-in-cheek 'Touch Me' became a US Top 3 single and 'Wishful Sinful' was a Top 50 hit.

Continued commercial success exacted further pressure on Morrison, whose frustration with his role as a pop idol grew more pronounced. His anti-authoritarian persona combined with a brazen sexuality and notorious alcohol and narcotics consumption to create a character bedevilled by doubt and cynicism. His confrontations with middle America reached an apogee on 1 March 1969 when, following a concert at Miami's Dinner Key Auditorium, the singer was indicted for indecent exposure, public intoxication and profane, lewd and lascivious conduct. Although Morrison was later acquitted of all but the minor charges (which went to appeal and were never resolved in his lifetime), the incident clouded the band's career when live dates for the next few months were cancelled. Paradoxically, this furore re-awoke the Doors' creativity. *Morrison Hotel*, a tough R&B-based collection, matched the best of their early releases and featured seminal performances in 'Roadhouse Blues' and 'You Make Me Real'. *Absolutely Live*, an in-concert set edited from a variety of sources, gave the impression of a single performance and exhibited the band's power and authority.

Morrison, whose poetry had been published in two volumes, *The Lords* and *The New Creatures*, now drew greater pleasure from this more personal art form. Having completed sessions at the band's workshop for a new album, the last owed to Elektra, Morrison escaped to Paris where he hoped to follow a literary career and abandon music altogether. Tragically, years of hedonistic excess had taken its toll and on 3 July 1971, Jim Morrison was found dead in his bathtub, his passing recorded officially as a heart attack. He was buried in Paris' Père Lachaise cemetery in the esteemed company of Oscar Wilde, Marcel Proust and Honore de Balzac. *L.A. Woman*, his final recording with the Doors, is one of the band's finest achievements. It was also their first album recorded without producer Paul Rothchild, with engineer Bruce Botnick tackling co-production duties. The album's simple intimacy resulted in some superb performances, including 'Riders On The Storm', whose haunting imagery and stealthy accompaniment created a timeless classic.

The survivors continued to work as the Doors, but while *Other Voices* showed some promise, *Full Circle* was severely flawed and the band soon dissolved. Densmore and Krieger formed the **Butts Band**, with whom they recorded two albums before splitting to pursue different paths. Manzarek undertook several projects as either artist, producer or manager, but

the spectre of the Doors refused to die. Interest in the band flourished throughout the decade and in 1978 the remaining trio supplied newly recorded music to a series of poetry recitations that Morrison had taped during the *LA Woman* sessions. The resultant album, *An American Prayer*, was a major success and prompted such archive excursions as *Alive, She Cried*, a compendium of several concert performances, and *Live At The Hollywood Bowl*. The evocative use of 'The End' in Francis Ford Coppola's 1979 Vietnam war movie, *Apocalypse Now*, also generated renewed interest in the Doors' legacy, and indeed, it is on those first recordings that the band's considerable reputation, and influence, rest. Since then their catalogue has never been out of print, and future generations of rock fans will almost certainly use them as a major role model. Director Oliver Stone's 1991 movie biography *The Doors*, starring Val Kilmer, helped confirm Morrison as one of the great cultural icons of the 60s.

Manzarek and Krieger reunited in the new millennium, playing live shows as the Doors with the **Cult**'s Ian Astbury on vocals and **Stewart Copeland** standing in for a temporarily indisposed Densmore. The latter then took legal action to prevent his former colleagues using the Doors name. With all respect to Astbury, a Morrison-less Doors is like building a new house without one.

● ALBUMS: *The Doors* (Elektra 1967) ★★★★, *Strange Days* (Elektra 1967) ★★★, *Waiting For The Sun* (Elektra 1968) ★★★, *The Soft Parade* (Elektra 1969) ★★, *Morrison Hotel* (Elektra 1970) ★★★★, *Absolutely Live* (Elektra 1970) ★★, *L.A. Woman* (Elektra 1971) ★★★★, *Other Voices* (Elektra 1971) ★★, *Full Circle* (Elektra 1972) ★, *An American Prayer* (Elektra 1978) ★★, *Alive, She Cried* (Elektra 1983) ★★, *Live At The Hollywood Bowl* 1968 recording (Elektra 1987) ★★, *The Doors* film soundtrack (Elektra 1991) ★★★, *Bright Midnight: Live In America* 1969/1970 recordings (Elektra 2001) ★★★, *Live In Hollywood: Highlights From The Aquarius Theatre Performances* (Elektra 2002) ★★★.

Solo: Ray Manzarek *The Golden Scarab* (Lemon 2004) ★★.

● COMPILATIONS: *13* (Elektra 1970) ★★★★, *Weird Scenes Inside The Goldmine* (Elektra 1972) ★★★, *The Best Of The Doors* (Elektra 1973) ★★★, *Greatest Hits* (Elektra 1980) ★★★★, *Classics* (Elektra 1985) ★★★★, *The Best Of The Doors* (Elektra 1985) ★★★★, *In Concert* (Elektra 1991) ★★★, *Greatest Hits* enhanced CD (Elektra 1996) ★★★★, *The Doors Box Set* 4-CD box set (Elektra 1997) ★★★, *Box Set Part One* (Elektra 1998) ★★★, *Box Set Part Two* (Elektra 1998) ★★★, *The Complete Studio Recordings* 7-CD box set (Elektra 1999) ★★★, *Essential Rarities* (Elektra 2000) ★★★, *Legacy: The Absolute Best* (Rhino 2003) ★★★★, *Boot Yer Butt! The Doors Bootlegs* 4-CD box set (Rhino 2003) ★★★★.

● DVD/VIDEOS: *Dance On Fire: Classic Performances & Greatest Hits* (Pioneer 1985), *Live At The Hollywood Bowl* (Elektra 1987), *A Tribute To Jim Morrison* (Warner Home Video 1988), *Live In Europe 1968* (Atlantic 1989), *The Soft Parade: A Retrospective* (MCA 1991), *The Doors Are Open* (Warner Home Video 1992), *The Best Of The Doors* (Universal 1997), *30 Years Commemorative Edition* (Universal 2001), *VH1 Storytellers—The Doors: A Celebration* (Aviva International 2001), *The Doors Of The 21st Century: L.A. Woman Live* (BMG 2004).

● FURTHER READING: *Jim Morrison And The Doors: An Unauthorized Book*, Mike Jahn. *An American Prayer*, Jim

Morrison. *The Lords & The New Creatures*, Jim Morrison. *Jim Morrison Au Dela Des Doors*, Herve Muller. *No One Here Gets Out Alive*, Jerry Hopkins and Danny Sugerman. *Burn Down The Night*, Craig Kee Strete. *Jim Morrison: The Story Of The Doors In Words And Pictures*, Jim Morrison. *Jim Morrison: An Hour For Magic*, Frank Lisciandro. *The Doors: The Illustrated History*, Danny Sugerman. *The Doors*, John Tobler and Andrew Doe. *Jim Morrison: Dark Star*, Dylan Jones. *Images Of Jim Morrison*, Edward Wincentsen. *The End: The Death Of Jim Morrison*, Bob Seymore. *The American Night: The Writings Of Jim Morrison*, Jim Morrison. *The American Night Volume 2*, Jim Morrison. *Morrison: A Feast Of Friends*, Frank Lisciandro. *Light My Fire*, John Densmore. *Riders On The Storm: My Life With Jim Morrison And The Doors*, John Densmore. *The Doors Complete Illustrated Lyrics*, Danny Sugerman (ed.). *Break On Through: The Life And Death Of Jim Morrison*, James Riordan and Jerry Prochnicky. *The Doors: Lyrics, 1965–71*, no author. *The Lizard King: The Essential Jim Morrison*, Jerry Hopkins. *The Doors: Dance On Fire*, Ross Clarke. *The Complete Guide To The Music Of The Doors*, Peter K. Hogan. *The Doors: Moonlight Drive*, Chuck Crisafulli. *Wild Child: Life With Jim Morrison*, Linda Ashcroft. *The Tragic Romance Of Pamela & Jim Morrison*, Patricia Butler. *Light My Fire: My Life With The Doors*, Ray Manzarek. *The Doors: When The Music's Over: The Stories Behind Every Song*, Chuck Crisafulli and Dave DiMartino. *Jim Morrison: Life, Death, Legend*, Stephen Davis. *People Are Strange: The Ultimate Guide To The Doors*, Doug Sandling.

● FILMS: *American Pop* (1981), *The Doors* (1991).

Dootones

The origins of vocal group the Dootones can be traced to Fremont High School in Los Angeles, California, USA, where singer and multi-instrumentalist H.B. Barnum played in a jazz band with his drumming friend Ronald Barrett. The Dootones were subsequently formed in 1954 when the duo added Charles Gardner and Marvin Wilkins. Their initial employment was as backing singers/musicians to the **Meadowlarks** and **Penguins**. They were titled the Dootones in 1955 by their manager, Dootsie Williams, and made their debut with 'Teller Of Fortune' in April. A pop-orientated take on R&B, it attracted local airplay, while further exposure came with Californian tours with **Etta James** and **Jackie Wilson**. Afterwards, Williams put the quartet together with Vernon Green, formerly of the **Medallions**, for a Canadian tour and made his intentions to remodel the band as the new Medallions clear. The existing Dootones were evidently unhappy with this turn of events and disbanded without issuing any further recordings. Barrett teamed up with the Meadowlarks, Gardner persevered with Green as yet another version of the Medallions, while Barnum joined the **Robins**, later working as an arranger with artists including **Ray Charles** and **Lou Rawls**. Charles Gardner became a minister in Pasadena. The Dootones recorded 'Down The Road' in 1962. Originally recorded in 1955, it backed a track entitled 'Sailor Boy' by a second, entirely different version of the Dootones assembled by Dootsie Williams. That formation had earlier released a single entitled 'Strange Love Affair'.

Dope

This self-styled post-industrial USA metal outfit is named after the Dope brothers, Edsel (b. USA; vocals/guitar) and

Simon (b. USA; keyboards). Though now based in New York, the brothers were brought up in south Florida. Edsel Dope played drums in several local punk bands before travelling around America. Simon Dope studied chemistry at the University of Florida before relocating to New York. His brother joined him there in 1997, where their shared musical influences convinced them to form their own band. They signed up three musicians, Tripp Eisen (b. Tod Rex Salvador, 29 June 1965, USA; guitar), Acey Slade (b. 15 December 1974, USA; bass) and Preston Nash (drums), who were all concurrently leading their own bands. The newly formed quintet played a handful of live dates before signing to the major label affiliate Flip Records in October 1998. They recorded their provocatively titled debut album, *Felons And Revolutionaries*, at Greene Street in Manhattan with producer John Travis (**Kid Rock**, **Sugar Ray**). Informed by the Dope brothers' own experiences, the lyrics to tracks such as the openers 'Pig Society' and 'Debonaire' railed against America's hypocritical mainstream culture, over a furious soundtrack that demonstrated the enduring influence of Trent Reznor's industrial blueprint.

Having already completed live dates with **Orgy** and **Fear Factory**, Dope landed a prime slot on a tour with **Coal Chamber** and **Slipknot**. The personnel was completely changed for the recording of the band's second album, with Slade switching to guitar and bass player Sloane 'Mosey' Jentry, guitarist Virus and drummer Racci 'Sketchy' Shay (ex-**Genitorturers**) added to the line-up. Jentry had originally played guitar with the band in their early days. Released at the end of 2001, *Life* failed to match the critical and commercial impact of their debut and marked the end of the band's tenure with Flip. They relocated to the Recon imprint for their next album. Released towards the end of 2003, *Group Therapy* was a marked improvement on the band's second album. Edsel Dope also conceived and directed videos to complement each of the album's 13 songs.

● ALBUMS: *Felons And Revolutionaries* (Flip/Epic 1999) ★★★, *Life* (Flip/Epic 2001) ★★, *Group Therapy* (Recon/Artemis 2003) ★★★, *American Apathy* (Artemis 2005) ★★.

Dope Smugglaz

A maverick trio of eccentric UK-based DJ/producers, namely Timmy Christmas (b. Tim Sheridan), Keith Binner and Chico Ijomanta. The three bearded Yorkshiremen met in the mid-80s when they DJed on the well-known Leeds student **dance music** scene where they could regularly be found behind the decks at the 'Mile High Club' nights at The Gallery, a venue that also gave rise to the **Utah Saints**. It was this same scene that was the fertile breeding ground for celebrated nights such as 'Vague' and the legendary 'Back To Basics' and 'Manumission'. Famous for marathon DJing sets, Timmy Christmas later played for 48 hours non-stop at the **Glastonbury Festival** and his average performances behind the decks continue to reach the six-hour mark. After several years in the dance music wilderness, the trio made a purposeful foray into more commercial territory with two singles featuring heavy use and sampling of old dance staples. The first was 'The Word' from the soundtrack of the 1978 hit movie *Grease*, and the second, 'Double Double Dutch', featured extensive 'recycling' of **Malcolm McLaren**'s 'Double Dutch'. Neither was well received by the UK music press but did make a slight impact on the singles chart. In the meantime, the Dope Smugglaz had negotiated a remarkable seven-album contract with **Paul Oakenfold**'s label, **Perfecto Records**. In 1999, they also began a Friday night DJing residency at the high-tech club, home, in London's west end. The trio's remix credits include those for the Utah Saints, **Finitribe**, **Moloko** and Fuzz Townsend. Their debut, *Dope Radio*, was an unusual journey through a range of styles from **dub** to pure pop, a psychedelic concept album based around the broadcasts of a fictional radio station. The first single from the album, 'Barabajagal' featured vocals from the singer Shaun Ryder and Howard Marks. The latter choice of vocalist was somewhat ironic, considering Marks' notoriety as a massively successful international marijuana trafficker. The single was also remixed by the band's old friends, Utah Saints. The Dope Smugglaz continue to DJ around the UK and Europe and at home.

● ALBUMS: *Dope Radio* (Perfecto 2000) ★★★.

Dopplereffekt

Little accurate biographical information has ever been confirmed about Dopplereffekt. The elusive duo eschew interviews and have only rarely played live. According to unsubstantiated reports, however, they are a Detroit-based, mixed-race couple who obscure their actual identities under the studio pseudonyms Rudolf Fisher and Helena Eichmann. Naming their collaboration after Austrian physicist Christian Doppler's observations about sound, Dopplereffekt create off-kilter contemporary **electro** that recalibrates **Kraftwerk**'s robotic-pop impulse with songs that merge science and sexuality. 'Pornoviewer' and 'Pornoactress' blankly state the desire to (respectively) watch and appear in licentious movies. The entire lyric of 'Scientist' reads 'Sitting in a laboratory/Conducting experiments/Analyzing data/I am a scientist', marking it out a work of succinct genius, though it remains unclear whether lines such as 'We had to sterilize the population' (from the duo's most stunning track 'Sterilization') are intended as a political/sexual philosophy, polemic or disturbing fiction.

Originally released between 1994 and 1997 on the project's own Dataphysix label, Dopplereffekt's EPs were compiled for album release by **DJ Hell**'s International Deejay Gigolos label, with the collection's title *Gesamtkunstwerk* roughly translating as 'synthesis of the arts'. In 1999, the duo adopted the pseudonym Japanese Telecom to record the *Rising Sun* mini-album.

● ALBUMS: *Linear Accelerator* (International Deejay Gigolos 2003) ★★★★.

● COMPILATIONS: *Gesamtkunstwerk* (International Deejay Gigolos/Source 1999) ★★★★.

Dorado Records

Eclectic London imprint, easily recognizable from its gold and blue sleeve designs, which has had fingers in many musical pies since its inception. Primarily, though, it has been identified as the UK's number one jazz fusion outpost, with a predilection for the club sounds of that spectrum. The label was established by Ollie Buckwell in 1992 and quickly became pre-eminent in its field, particularly in mainland Europe where much of Dorado's output is revered. It debuted with Monkey Business' 'Ain't No Fun'. The main artists on the label include Matt Cooper, a hugely talented young artist who writes, composes and arranges his own material as **Outside**, and Matt Wienevski's ambitious **D*Note**

(whom Buckwell managed). Other releases have included material by **Jhelisa Anderson** (ex–**Soul Family Sensation** and **Shamen**), Ceri Evans (former **Brand New Heavies**' keyboard player), Mesh Of Mind ('Learn The Words'), Origin ('Music Man', which featured **Jah Shaka**), Ute ('Soul Thing') and even hip-hoppers such as Dana Bryant or Brooklyn Funk Essentials ('The Revolution Was Postponed Because Of Rain'). 'I like to think of Dorado as more progressive', summarized Buckwell, 'It's almost the second wave. **Talkin' Loud** and **Acid Jazz** kind of broke the market, and we're trying to develop it—push it forward.'

● COMPILATIONS: *A Compilation Volumes 1–3* (Dorado 1992–94) ★★★★.

Dore, Charlie

b. 1956, Pinner, Middlesex, England. Dore is a respected UK songwriter who originally trained as an actress and is best known for her 1979 hit 'Pilot Of The Airwaves', which reached number 13 on the US charts. Her 1977 country-influenced band Prairie Oyster included Pick Withers on drums, who was also playing with the early **Dire Straits**, at that time playing the same UK pub circuit. The band evolved through various personnel changes into Charlie Dore's Back Pocket (guitarist Julian Littman having since become a long-time songwriting collaborator). When the band broke up, Dore started a solo career. Her 1979 debut *Where To Now* was recorded partly in Nashville and produced by the **Shadows**' **Bruce Welch** and songwriter Alan Tarney with session musicians such as **Sonny Curtis**. The first single 'Fear Of Flying' failed to make a commercial impact, although it was a major 'turntable hit', but 'Pilot Of The Airwaves' charted on both sides of the Atlantic and received extensive airplay.

Dore signed to **Chrysalis Records** in 1981 and released *Listen!*, but unable to capitalize on her early success, focused her varied talents on songwriting and acting. As well as repertory work with Michael Bogdanov, she co-starred with Jonathan Pryce in Richard Eyre's award-winning 1983 film *The Ploughman's Lunch* and appeared in several television series, including *Hard Cases* (playing in a band with former **Cockney Rebel** drummer Stuart Elliott) and *South Of The Border*. She is also a founder member of the London-based comedy improvisation team the Hurricane Club.

Dore's ability, enthusiasm and commitment have helped many others to commercial success while she remains something of a hidden talent. Her songwriting credits include many album tracks and a number of highly successful singles. 'Strut' was a worldwide hit for **Sheena Easton**, winning an **ASCAP** award in the US. She wrote a range of material for **Barbara Dickson** and in 1992 scored a UK number 1 with **Jimmy Nail**'s 'Ain't No Doubt', which she co-wrote. 'Refuse To Dance', taken from **Celine Dion**'s hugely successful *The Colour Of My Love*, was released as a single in 1995.

Following a return to the recording studio, working with Julian Littman, Danny Schogger (co-writer of 'Ain't No Doubt' and 'Refuse To Dance'), Ricky Fataar and **Paul Carrack** on a collection of new material, Dore released *Things Change* in 1995. Dore maintained her writing partnership with Littman on compositions for the television series *2000 Acres Of Sky* and *Roman Road*. The duo also collaborated on Dore's fourth album, *Sleep All Day And Other Stories*, released at the start of 2005. The cover and booklet are worth the price of the CD alone.

● ALBUMS: *Where To Now* (Island 1979) ★★★, *Listen!* (Chrysalis 1981) ★★★, *Things Change* (Grapevine 1995) ★★★, *Sleep All Day And Other Stories* (Black Ink Music 2005) ★★★.
● FILMS: *The Ploughman's Lunch* (1983), *Under The Bed* (1988).

Dørge, Pierre

b. 28 February 1946, Copenhagen, Denmark. Composer and guitarist Dørge, after brief stints as sideman, led his own bands from the mid-60s, inspired by the *avant garde* rock of **Frank Zappa**. Crucial learning years followed as participant in trumpeter Hugh Steinmetz' and **John Tchicai**'s Cadentia Nova Danica big band (1969–71), which opened Danish jazz to a broad range of styles and genres of non-Western music. Since 1980 Dørge has led the New Jungle Orchestra which plays **Duke Ellington** as reinterpreted through **Ornette Coleman**. Dørge's compositions and arrangements reinterpret the jazz tradition in a genial, yet iconoclastic manner characteristic of **Charles Mingus**' music. Dørge has brilliantly shown how jazz can be creatively transformed and developed by music outside the USA, from the Balkans, Gambia and Bali. As he stated in the magazine *Jazz Times*: 'I try not to use too much glue to make music.'
● ALBUMS: *Thermænius Live* (Pick Up 1979) ★★★, with John Tchicai *Ball At Louisiana* (SteepleChase 1981) ★★★, *Pierre Dørge And The New Jungle Orchestra* (SteepleChase 1982) ★★★★, *Brikama* (SteepleChase 1984) ★★★, *Very Hot: Even The Moon Is Dancing* (SteepleChase 1985) ★★, *Different Places, Different Bananas* (Olufsen 1986) ★★★, *Canoe* (Olufsen 1986) ★★★, *La Luna* (Olufsen 1987) ★★★★, *Live In Chicago* (Olufsen 1987) ★★★, *Johnny Lives* (SteepleChase 1987) ★★★★, *Karawane* (Olufsen 1992) ★★★, *Absurd Bird* (Olufsen 1994) ★★★, *Music From The Danish Jungle* (Dacapo 1996) ★★★, *China Jungle* (Dacapo 1998) ★★★, *Giraf* (Dacapo 1999) ★★★, with the New Jungle Orchestra *Zig Zag Zimfoni* (Stunt 2001) ★★★, *Live At Birdland* (Stunt 2003) ★★★, with John Tchicai, Lou Grassi *Hope Is Bright Green Up North* (CIMP 2003) ★★★, *Dancing Cheek To Cheek* (Stunt 2005) ★★★★.

Dorham, Kenny

b. McKinley Howard Dorham, 30 August 1924, Fairfield, Texas, USA, d. 5 December 1972, New York City, New York, USA. After learning to play trumpet while at high school, Dorham played in several late 40s big bands, including **Lionel Hampton**'s and, more significantly given his musical leanings, the bop-orientated outfits of **Dizzy Gillespie** and **Billy Eckstine**. He was originally known as Kinny (a diminutive for McKinley) and this was how his name appeared on record labels. He was persistently misspelled and eventually gave in to public ignorance and changed to Kenny. In 1948 he succeeded **Miles Davis** as trumpeter with **Charlie 'Bird' Parker**'s quintet and in 1954 joined **Horace Silver** in the first edition of what became **Art Blakey**'s long-running **Jazz Messengers**. He also worked with **Max Roach** (stepping in when Roach's co-leader, **Clifford Brown**, was killed), **Sonny Rollins** and **Charles Mingus**.

From the mid-50s onwards Dorham mostly led his own groups, which included the excellent Jazz Prophets, modelled as the name suggests, upon the Messengers. He made many fine recordings notably both as leader and with artists **Joe Henderson**, **Herb Geller** and **Jackie McLean** including several outstanding performances for **Blue Note Records**. Although rightly viewed as one of the outstanding bebop trumpeters, stylistically Dorham's playing reflected his awareness of the roots of jazz and the blues. Universally admired among his contemporaries, Dorham's death led unfairly to a decline in awareness of his stature as a fine modern musician.
● ALBUMS: *Kenny Dorham Quintet* 10-inch album (Debut 1954) ★★★★, *Afro-Cuban Holiday* 10-inch album (Blue Note 1955) ★★★★, *Kenny Dorham's Jazz Prophets Volumes 1 & 2* (ABC-Paramount 1956) ★★★, *'Round About Midnight At The Café Bohemia* (Blue Note 1956) ★★★★, *Jazz Contrasts* (Riverside 1957) ★★★, *2 Horns, 2 Rhythm* (Riverside 1957) ★★★★, *This Is The Moment! Kenny Dorham Sings And Plays* (Riverside 1958) ★★★, *Blue Spring* (Riverside 1959) ★★★, *Quiet Kenny* (New Jazz 1959) ★★★, *The Arrival Of Kenny Dorham* (Jaro 1959) ★★★, *Jazz Contemporary* (Time 1960) ★★★, *Showboat* (Time 1960) ★★★★, with Clark Terry *Top Trumpets* (Jazzland 1960) ★★★, *The Swingers* (Jazzland 1960) ★★★, *Kenny Dorham And Friends* (Jazzland 1960) ★★★, *Osmosis* (Black Lion 1961) ★★★, *Ease It* (Muse 1961) ★★★, *Whistle Stop* (Blue Note 1961) ★★★, *West 42nd Street* (Black Lion 1961) ★★★, *Hot Stuff From Brazil* (West Wind 1961) ★★★, *Inta Somethin'—Recorded 'Live' At The Jazz Workshop* (Pacific Jazz 1962) ★★★, *Matador* (United Artists 1962) ★★★, *Una Mas—One More Time* (Blue Note 1963) ★★★★, *Scandia Skies* (SteepleChase 1963) ★★★, *Trumpet Toccata* (Blue Note 1964) ★★★★, *New York 1953–56* (Landscape 1993) ★★★, *The Complete 'Round About Midnight At The Café Bohemia* (Blue Note 2002) ★★★★.
● COMPILATIONS: *The Art Of The Ballad* (Prestige 1998) ★★★★.

Dorman, Harold

b. 1926 (other sources say 1931), Sledge, Mississippi, USA. Dorman was a one-hit artist, whose 'Mountain Of Love' fared better when it was covered by **Johnny Rivers** four years later. Dorman's music career began when he left the army in 1955. His first sessions were recorded for the legendary **Sun Records** in 1957 but were never released. Two years later Dorman was signed to Rita Records, owned by former Sun artist **Billy Lee Riley** and guitarist Roland Janes, who had played with **Jerry Lee Lewis**. Dorman's first single was his own 'Mountain Of Love', one of five tracks he recorded at the **Hi Records** studio in Memphis. The record started to sell well in Georgia, at which point strings were added to the master tape and it was re-released. The single ultimately reached number 21 in 1960. Dorman continued to record for Rita for another year, then he recorded again for Sun until 1962 but failed to produce any further chart hits. In 1964 Rivers recorded 'Mountain Of Love' and took it to number 9 in the US charts. Dorman's only other notable success came when country singer **Charley Pride** recorded his 'Mississippi Cotton Picking Delta Town'. Pride also covered 'Mountain Of Love'. Although disabled by two strokes in 1984 Dorman continued writing songs.
● COMPILATIONS: *Mountain Of Love* the complete Rita recordings (Bear Family 1988) ★★★.

Dorn, Joel

b. 1942, USA. In 1961, while still a student at Temple University, a deep interest in jazz led to Dorn becoming a radio disc jockey on Philadelphia's WHAT-FM, a 24-hour jazz station later to become WWDB. His theme song was **David 'Fathead' Newman**'s 'Hard Times' and the funky nature of this particular recording set the mood for his show: soulful, good time music overlaid with a touch of class. His personal preferences in music meant that listeners to his show were assured of a diet of records by artists such as **Ray Charles**, **John Coltrane**, **Miles Davis**, **Ramsey Lewis** and **Horace Silver**. Dorn also exercised a measure of influence; for example, his frequent playing of **Betty Carter** records helped spread the message that she was a singer of merit.

In 1967, Dorn was hired by **Atlantic Records** as assistant to Nesuhi Ertegun and in this capacity during the next seven years worked on numerous recording sessions, often as producer or co-producer. Later, he worked as an independent producer. In the course of these years with Atlantic and other labels, he worked with musicians such as the **Allman Brothers**, **Oscar Brown Jnr.**, **Ray Bryant**, **Gary Burton**, **Roberta Flack**, **Eddie Harris**, **Freddie Hubbard**, **Rahsaan Roland Kirk**, **Keith Jarrett**, **Yusef Lateef**, **Les McCann**, **Don McLean** (producing *Homeless Brother*), **Junior Mance**, **Herbie Mann**, **Bette Midler** (producing her debut, *The Divine Miss M*), **Charles Mingus**, Newman, the **Neville Brothers**, **Lou Rawls**, **Leon Redbone** and **Max Roach**. Dorn was specifically instrumental in advancing the careers of Flack, and Midler, both of whom were relatively unknown, as well as **Aaron Neville** and Redbone. From these sessions, Dorn achieved a number of Grammy awards: for Jazz Album Of The Year with Burton and Jarrett, Best Original Cast Album for *The Me Nobody Knows*, Best Country And Western Instrumental for 'One O'Clock Jump' with **Asleep At The Wheel** and two Records Of The Year with Flack, for 'Killing Me Softly' and 'The First Time Ever I Saw Your Face'. For a few years in the early 80s, Dorn worked outside the record industry, promoting music for the World Wrestling Federation. Then, in the mid-80s, he returned to the recording scene, becoming deeply involved with re-issues of the back catalogues of Atlantic and Muse Records. Some of these reissues appeared on **Rhino Records**, although many appeared on one or another of his own labels, under the aegis of his Masked Announcer company: Night Music, 32 Records, Please And Thank You Music, HighNote and Savant. With these last two labels, he brought out several CDs by **Etta Jones** and **Houston Person**, the latter also being producer of many HighNote sessions. Despite his commitment to intelligently developed reissue programmes, Dorn has also continued to record new albums by contemporary artists such as **Charles Lloyd** and **Jane Monheit**, the latter demonstrating that his ability to spot talent ahead of the pack has not diminished since his early years in Philadelphia.

Dörner, Axel

b. 26 April 1964, Cologne, Germany. After studying classical piano for two years in the late 80s at a music conservatory in Arnhem, the Netherlands, Dörner moved back to Cologne. There, at the Musikhochschule, he continued with his piano studies for several more years. During this same period, he also studied trumpet for a number of years. He also began playing contemporary improvised music, often with trumpeter Bruno Leicht and various co-led bands including the Streetfighters Duo, the Streetfighters Quartet and the Streetfighters Double Quartet. He also formed the Remedy and the Axel Dörner Quartet, with Frank Gratkowski, Hans Schneider and Martin Blume. With several of these bands Dörner appeared on concert and on radio and television.

From 1994, Dörner was based largely in Berlin where he worked with many musicians from the European free improvisation scene, among them **Alex Von Schlippenbach**, **Fred Van Hove**, Sven Åke Johansson, Lines and the King Übü Örchestü. He also played with visitors, including **Sam Rivers**, Phil Minton, **Butch Morris**, **Lol Coxhill** and Chris Burns, and worked with the Berlin Contemporary Jazz Orchestra and the **London Jazz Composers Orchestra**.

Dörner has declared himself to be interested in pursuing musical sounds regardless of those pigeonholes that derive from accepted standard form and content. He has also developed a number of new devices with which to extend the trumpet's possibilities for creating sounds. Although an uncompromising free musician in performance, Dörner is also a prolific composer.

● ALBUMS: with Die Enttäuschung *Die Enttäuschung* (Two Nineteen 1995) ★★★, with the Improvisors Pool *Backgrounds For Improvisors* (FMP 1995) ★★★, with Lines *Lines* (Random Acoustics 1996), with various artists *Offline Adventures* (Leo Lab 1997) ★★★, with Fred Longberg-Holm, Michael Zerang *Claque* (Meniscus 1998) ★★★, with Sweethearts In A Drugstore *Second Edition* (Ninth World Music 1999) ★★★, *Trumpet* (A Bruit Secret 2001) ★★★★, with Sven Åke Johansson, Andrea Neumann *Barcelona Series* (hatOLOGY 2002) ★★★, *Object 1* (Locust 2003) ★★★, with von Schlippenbach, Rudi Mahall, Jan Roder, Uli Jennessen *Monk's Casino* (Intakt 2005) ★★★★.

Doro

b. Dorothee Pesch, 3 June 1964, Düsseldorf, Germany. Pesch, the leading light and vocalist of the German heavy metal band **Warlock**, dissolved the band after the release of 1987's *Triumph And Agony*. Retaining only bass player Tommy Henriksen, she embarked on a solo career under the name of Doro. To complete the new line-up she recruited guitarist John Devin and drummer Bobby Rondinelli (ex-**Rainbow**). With Joey Balin as writing partner, *Force Majeure* offered a departure from her previous heavy style, moving towards a more mainstream AOR approach in a bid for commercial success. It featured an embarrassing cover version of **Procol Harum**'s 'A Whiter Shade Of Pale' as the opening track and fared poorly. Jettisoning the entire band in favour of hired hands, she recorded *Doro* with **Gene Simmons** (of **Kiss**) as producer. Musically, this was even further away from her roots, an attempt to achieve chart success that verged on desperation, a fate that also hampered the 1991 European release *True At Heart*. The same years' *Rare Diamonds* was a compilation of older material, giving Doro time for a rethink about her next career move. When she did re-emerge in 1993 with *Angels Never Die*, interest was minimal. The 1995 follow-up *Machine II Machine* featured the producer and songwriter Jack Ponti and it managed to avoid the overt commercial overtones of its forerunners. However, tracks such as 'Tie Me Up' still offered little evidence of songwriting maturity. Doro moved to the Warners group for her next album, 1998's *Love Me In Black*, on which she finally began to embrace a new musical direction. The 2000 collection *Calling The Wild* was her first album to gain an American release in 10 years, gaining distribution through the Koch label (SPV in Europe). Following one further release for SPV/Koch, Doro switched labels again and embarked on a bold if somewhat misguided project, recording new versions of her old hits with the aid of the Classic Night Orchestra.

● ALBUMS: *Force Majeure* (Vertigo 1989) ★★★, *Doro* (Vertigo 1990) ★★, *True At Heart* (Vertigo 1991) ★★, *Angels Never Die* (Vertigo 1993) ★★★, *Live* (Vertigo 1993) ★★, *Machine II Machine* (Mercury 1995) ★★, *Love Me In Black* (WEA 1998) ★★★, *Calling The Wild . . .* (SPV/Koch 2000) ★★★, *Fight* (SPV 2002) ★★★, *Classic Diamonds* (AFM 2004) ★★.
● COMPILATIONS: as Doro/Warlock *Rare Diamonds* (Vertigo 1991) ★★, *Machine II Machine: Electric Club Mixes* (Vertigo 1995) ★★, *A Whiter Shade Of Pale* (Spectrum 1997) ★★, *Best Of* (Mercury 1998) ★★★, *Ballads* (Mercury 1998) ★★★.
● DVD/VIDEOS: *Für Immer* (SPV 2003), *Classic Diamonds* (Locomotive Music 2004).

Dorough, Bob

b. Robert Dorough, 12 December 1923, Cherry Hill, Arkansas, USA. After playing piano as a youth he studied piano and composition at college in Texas before attending Columbia University in New York. During this time he also played in New York clubs and soon began singing to his own accompaniment. In the 50s he worked in New York and Paris where he was resident for a while, playing as a solo act and also in small groups accompanying visiting American artists. He was back in the USA at the end of the decade and in the early 60s recorded with **Miles Davis**. During the 70s and 80s he combined playing clubs, usually as a solo, with work in television as a composer. He made a belated return to a major label in the 90s for the excellent *Right On My Way Home* and *Too Much Coffee Man*. Dorough's songwriting activities encompass music and lyrics. Dorough's singing style displays his appreciation of the songwriter's art and he is an especially interesting interpreter of lyrics. His sound reveals his links with the jazz world through his subtle and rhythmic phrasing.
● ALBUMS: *Devil May Care* (Bethlehem 1957) ★★★, *Oliver* (Music Minus One 1963) ★★★, *Just About Everything* (Focus 1965) ★★★, *That's The Way I Feel Now: A Tribute To Thelonious Monk* (A&M 1984) ★★★★, *Right On My Way Home* (Blue Note 1997) ★★★★, *Too Much Coffee Man* (Blue Note 2000) ★★★★, with Dave Fishberg *Who's On First* (Blue Note 2001) ★★★, *Sunday At Iridium* (Arbors 2005) ★★.

Dors, Diana

b. Diana Fluck, 23 October 1931, Swindon, Wiltshire, England, d. 4 May 1984, Windsor, Berkshire, England. Dors started out in showbusiness at the age of 13 and was in films from 1946, playing bit parts in a number of good British films of the period. Although studying at the Royal Academy of Dramatic Art and a capable straight actress, her overt sexuality, in both her physical appearance and exaggerated mannerisms, propelled her into a succession of inferior films. She was allowed to prove her acting abilities in 1956's *Yield To The Night* (US title: *Blonde Sinner*). Based upon the case of Ruth Ellis, the last woman to be executed for murder in the UK, this film took what was for its time a hard look at capital punishment and Dors delivered a striking performance. In its closing sequences no concessions were made to either the fate of or the decidedly unglamorous appearance of the central character. This was, however, a rare departure from the norm for Dors who was usually cast as a tart.

A good singer, Dors made an album for **Columbia Records**, appeared in cabaret and in stage shows and in 1959 was on television in *The Diana Dors Show*. She continued to sing in live performances throughout her later years. Among films that still stand up reasonably well, although none has relevant musical content, are *There's A Girl In My Soup* (1970), *The Amazing Mr. Blunden* (1972) and, her last film, *Steaming* (1985). A highly professional actress with a remarkable ability to swiftly learn her lines, she suffered a number of serious illnesses in her life, eventually dying of ovarian cancer in 1984.
● ALBUMS: *Swinging Dors* (Columbia 1960) ★★★.

Dorsey Brothers
(see **Dorsey, Tommy**; **Dorsey, Jimmy**)

Dorsey, Jimmy

b. 29 February 1904, Shenandoah, Pennsylvania, USA, d. 12 June 1957, New York City, New York, USA. Musically active as a small child under the tutelage of his father, who was a coal miner turned music teacher, Dorsey switched from brass to reed instruments while still in his early teens. Concentrating on clarinet and alto saxophone, he played in various bands, mostly with his brother, **Tommy Dorsey**. Their co-led group, Dorsey's Novelty Six, later renamed Dorsey's Wild Canaries, was one of the first jazz bands to broadcast on the radio. Dorsey later joined the **California Ramblers**. Sometimes with his brother, sometimes alone, Dorsey played in a number of leading bands, including those led by **Jean Goldkette**, **Paul Whiteman**, **Red Nichols** and **Ted Lewis**. He also recorded frequently, often in company with Nichols and his Goldkette/Whiteman colleague, **Bix Beiderbecke**. He continued to associate with his brother, and in 1934 they formed the Dorsey Brothers Orchestra, which became extremely popular. Unfortunately for the band, the brothers frequently disagreed, sometimes violently, and after one such argument, on the stand at the Glen Island Casino in May 1935, Tommy walked out leaving Jimmy to run the band on his own.
One of the most accomplished of the white bands of the swing era, Jimmy Dorsey's band retained a strong jazz element but also catered to popular demands. Particularly successful in this respect was a series of hit records devised by arranger Tutti Camarata. In an attempt to present all aspects of the band's work in one three-minute radio spot, Camarata made an arrangement of a song that featured first the band's male singer, **Bob Eberly**, in ballad mood, then the leader with an up-tempo jazz solo on alto, and finally, a wailing sensual vocal chorus by the band's other singer, Helen O'Connell (b. 23 May 1920, Lima, Ohio, USA, d. 9 September 1993, San Diego, California, USA). The first song treated in this manner was 'Amapola', followed by 'Yours' and then 'Green Eyes', which was a runaway hit, as was the later 'Tangerine'. Records such as these ensured Dorsey's success and, by the mid-40s, his was one of the most popular of the big bands. This ensured Dorsey's survival over the hard winter of 1946/7, a time which saw many big bands fold, but the 50s proved difficult too, and in 1953 he was reunited with his brother who promptly renamed his own still-successful band as the Dorsey Brothers Orchestra. Jimmy remained with the band until Tommy's death, by which time he too was terminally ill, dying only a few months after his brother. An outstanding technician, Jimmy Dorsey was one

of the finest jazz saxophonists of his era and a major influence on many of his contemporaries and successors.

● ALBUMS: *Latin American Favorites* 10-inch album (Decca 1950) ★★, *Contrasting Music, Volume 1* 10-inch album (Coral 1950) ★★★★, *Contrasting Music, Volume 2* 10-inch album (Coral 1950) ★★★, *Gershwin Music* 10-inch album (Coral 1950) ★★★, *Dixie By Dorsey* 10-inch album (Columbia 1950) ★★★, *Dorseyland Band* 10-inch album (Columbia 1950) ★★★, as the Dorsey Brothers *Dixieland Jazz* 10-inch album (Decca 1951) ★★★, as the Dorsey Brothers *Jazz Of The Roaring Twenties* 10-inch album (Riverside 1953) ★★★★, as the Dorsey Brothers *The Dorsey Brothers With The California Ramblers* 10-inch album (Riverside 1955) ★★★, as the Dorsey Brothers *A Backward Glance* (Riverside 1956) ★★★, as the Dorsey Brothers *The Fabulous Dorseys In Hi-Fi Volumes 1 & 2* (Columbia 1958) ★★★★.

● COMPILATIONS: *Mostly 1940* 1939–40 recordings (Circle 1984) ★★★, as the Dorsey Brothers *Spotlighting The Fabulous Dorseys* 1942–45 recordings (Giants Of Jazz 1984) ★★★★, *Contrasts* 1945 recording (Decca 1987) ★★★★, *The Early Years* 1936–41 recordings (Bandstand 1988) ★★★, *Don't Be That Way* 1935–40 recordings (Bandstand 1988) ★★★, *The Uncollected Jimmy Dorsey Volumes 1–5* 1939–50 recordings (Hindsight 1989) ★★★, *The Essential V-Discs* 1943–45 (Sandy Hook) ★★★★.

● FURTHER READING: *Tommy And Jimmy: The Dorsey Years*, Herb Sanford.

● FILMS: *The Fabulous Dorseys* (1947).

Dorsey, Lee

b. Irving Lee Dorsey, 24 December 1926, New Orleans, Louisiana, USA, d. 1 December 1986, New Orleans, Louisiana, USA. An ex-boxer (nicknamed 'Kid Chocolate') turned singer, Dorsey first recorded for Joe Banashak's Instant label. One song, 'Lottie Mo', became a regional hit and led to a contract with Fury. The infectious 'Ya Ya' (1961) was a number 1 US R&B and pop Top 10 single. A year later a version by **Petula Clark**, retitled 'Ya Ya Twist', made the US Top 10 and reached the UK Top 20. Dorsey's next release 'Do-Re-Mi' (regularly performed by **Georgie Fame** and **Dusty Springfield**) was also a hit, although this time reaching no higher than 27 in the *Billboard* pop chart, and subsequent releases on Fury Records were less successful. His career stalled temporarily when Fury collapsed, but Dorsey re-emerged in 1965 with the classic 'Ride Your Pony' on the Amy label. Written by **Allen Toussaint** and produced by Marshall Sehorn, this combination created a series of impeccable singles that blended crisp arrangements with the singer's easy delivery.

In 1966 he reached the peak of his success by gaining four Top 40 hits in the UK, including two Top 10 singles with 'Working In The Coalmine', featuring a wonderful bass riff, and 'Holy Cow', with a mix that enhances Dorsey's melancholic vocals. Both songs reached the US R&B and pop charts. The sweetly doom-laden 'Get Out Of My Life, Woman' was another excellent song that deserved a better commercial fate. 'Everything I Do Gohn Be Funky (From Now On)' became Dorsey's last substantial hit in 1969, although the title track to his 'concept' album, 'Yes We Can', did reach the US R&B Top 50. Dorsey continued to record for **Polydor Records** and **ABC Records** and remained a popular figure, so much so that he guested on the 1976 debut album

by **Southside Johnny And The Asbury Dukes** and supported the **Clash** on their 1980 tour of North America. Sadly, he died of emphysema in December 1986 and deserves to be remembered for the outstanding examples of melodic soul he recorded.

● ALBUMS: *Ya Ya* (Fury 1962) ★★★, *Ride Your Pony* (Amy/Stateside 1966) ★★★, *The New Lee Dorsey* (Amy/Stateside 1966) ★★★★, *Yes We Can* (Polydor 1970) ★★, *Night People* (ABC 1978) ★★.

● COMPILATIONS: *The Best Of Lee Dorsey* (Sue 1965) ★★, *All Ways Funky* (Charly 1982) ★★★, *Gohn Be Funky* (Charly 1985) ★★★, *Holy Cow! The Best Of Lee Dorsey* (Arista 1985) ★★★★, *Am I That Easy To Forget?* (Charly 1987) ★★★, *Can You Hear Me* (Charly 1987) ★★★, *Ya Ya* (Relic 1992) ★★★, *Freedom For The Funk* (Charly 1994) ★★★, *Wheelin' & Dealin': The Definitive Collection* (Arista 1998) ★★★★, *The EP Collection* (See For Miles 2000) ★★★, *Working In A Coalmine: The Very Best Of Lee Dorsey* (Music Club 2001) ★★★★, *Holy Cow, The Very Best Of Lee Dorsey* (Charly 2005) ★★★★.

Dorsey, Marc

A slick US R&B singer whose style is clearly modelled on **Donny Hathaway** and **Stevie Wonder**, Dorsey finally released his solo debut in 1999. The singer had already made several appearances on Spike Lee soundtracks during the 90s. He was first heard singing 'People Make The World Go Round' on 1994's *Crooklyn* and also contributed 'People In Search Of A Life' and 'Changes' to 1995's *Clockers* and 'Welcome' to 1996's *Get On The Bus*. 'Crave', the title track to his debut album, appeared on the soundtrack to Rick Famuyiwa's *The Wood*. His debut set, recorded in New York with various producers and released on **Jive Records** in August 1999, echoed his soundtrack work with its blend of contemporary beats and smooth, old-style soul grooves.

● ALBUMS: *Crave* (Jive 1999) ★★★.

Dorsey, Thomas A.

b. 1 July 1899, Villa Rica, Georgia, USA, d. 23 January 1993, Chicago, Illinois, USA. Often known as the founder of gospel music. Born into a religious family, Dorsey nevertheless shunned sacred music for many years, although it is in that idiom that he was to make the biggest impact. He learned to play piano in his youth, and when he settled in Chicago in 1916 he began to carve out a career for himself on the blues scene there. In the early 20s, he toured as a musician in the **Ma Rainey** show. Between 1928 and 1932 he recorded extensively as a blues artist under his pseudonym Georgia Tom, as partner to **Tampa Red**, as part of groups such as the **Hokum Boys** and as accompanist to many artists, from obscure figures such as Auntie Mary Bradford and Stovepipe Johnson to big names such as **'Big' Bill Broonzy**, **Memphis Minnie** and **Victoria Spivey**. Despite the comparative brevity of this period of his career, he was very influential for the quality and variety of his piano accompaniments and also for one of his best-known records, with Tampa Red, 'It's Tight Like That', a smutty, double-meaning song that was enormously popular and led to a vast number of cover versions, copies and variants.

In 1930, Dorsey began to compose and publish religious songs, and two years later, at the height of his success as a blues musician, he renounced this idiom and moved to gospel music, with which he was to stay for the rest of his long career. He joined singer Sallie Martin and developed a new career with the Gospel Choral Union. His successful blues recording career led him straight into recording gospel songs, dropping the pseudonym Georgia Tom in favour of his own full name. One of his biggest successes, however, has been as a songwriter, and it was when the Heavenly Gospel Singers recorded his song 'Precious Lord' that he really began to make his name in this respect; the song has become one of the best known, and most prolifically recorded, of all black gospel songs. Dorsey remained active into a remarkably old age, appearing in a television film as late as the 80s, still preaching and singing.

● COMPILATIONS: *Complete Recorded Works In Chronological Order Volume 1: September 1928 To 5 February 1930* (Document 1992) ★★★, *Complete Recorded Works In Chronological Order Volume 2: 5 February 1930 To 22 March 1934* (Document 1992) ★★★, various artists *Precious Lord: Recordings Of The Great Gospel Songs Of Thomas A. Dorsey* (Columbia/Legacy 1994) ★★★.

● FURTHER READING: *The Rise Of Gospel Blues: The Music Of Thomas Dorsey In The Urban Church*, Michael Harris.

Dorsey, Tommy

b. 19 November 1905, Shenandoah, Pennsylvania, USA, d. 26 November 1956, Greenwich, Connecticut, USA. Like his older brother, **Jimmy Dorsey**, Tommy was taught as a small child by his father, a music teacher. He first learned to play trumpet but switched to trombone while still very young. He played in various bands, often with his brother, their co-led group known first as Dorsey's Novelty Six, later renamed Dorsey's Wild Canaries. With his brother, Dorsey later played in a number of leading bands, including those led by **Jean Goldkette** and **Paul Whiteman**. He also recorded frequently, often in the company of leading jazzmen of the day. In 1934 he and Jimmy formed the Dorsey Brothers Orchestra, which became extremely popular. Despite, or perhaps because of, their close relationship, the brothers frequently argued, sometimes violently, and after one such disagreement, in May 1935, Tommy walked out leaving Jimmy to take over leadership of the orchestra. Tommy then took over the excellent dance band led by **Joe Haymes**.

Highly ambitious, Dorsey set about turning the band, which was already a sound and well-disciplined unit, into the finest dance orchestra of the era. Over the years he employed first-rate arrangers, including **Axel Stordahl**, **Carmen Mastren**, **Paul Weston** and, most influential of all in ensuring the band's success and musical stature, **Sy Oliver**. Dorsey also engaged the services of several strong jazz players, including **Bunny Berigan**, **Buddy Rich**, **Johnny Mince**, **Yank Lawson**, **Pee Wee Erwin**, **Buddy De Franco**, **Gene Krupa**, **Charlie Shavers** and **Bud Freeman**. Alert to the demands of audiences, Dorsey also employed some of the finest singers ever to work with the big bands. An early find was Jack Leonard, who sang on one of the band's big hits, 'Marie', and others included Edythe Wright, **Jo Stafford**, Connie Haines (b. 20 January 1922) and **Dick Haymes**. The latter was the able replacement for the best singer Dorsey hired, **Frank Sinatra**. Although Sinatra had already begun to establish a reputation with **Harry James**, it was his stint with Dorsey that made him into an international singing star and helped to make the Dorsey band one of the most popular of the swing era—in many ways the band and musical sound which most aptly epitomizes this period in American popular music.

Dorsey's popularity was enough to ensure his band's survival after the great days of the 40s were over, and he was one of the few to move into television. Nevertheless, the 50s were difficult times, and in 1953, he was happy to be reunited with his brother, whose own outfit had folded. Tommy Dorsey gave Jimmy a featured spot and renamed his band as the Dorsey Brothers Orchestra. Despite his popularity, to say nothing of his determination to succeed and his sometimes arrogant self-confidence, Dorsey was always reticent about his ability as a jazz player, although some of his early recordings display a gifted musician with a strong sense of style. Like his brother, Tommy Dorsey was an outstanding technician and brought trombone playing to new heights of perfection. His smooth playing was ideally suited to ballads and his solos on countless records were often exemplary. Even with the advent of later generations of outstanding trombone technicians, few have matched his skill and none have surpassed him in his own particular area of expertise. A noted heavy eater, Tommy Dorsey choked to death in his sleep.

● ALBUMS: *Tommy Dorsey Plays Howard Dietz* 10-inch album (Decca 1951) ★★★, *In A Sentimental Mood* 10-inch album (Decca 1951) ★★★★, as the Dorsey Brothers *Dixieland Jazz* 10-inch album (Decca 1951) ★★★, *Tenderley* 10-inch album (Decca 1952) ★★★★, *Your Invitation To Dance* 10-inch album (Decca 1952) ★★★, as the Dorsey Brothers *Jazz Of The Roaring Twenties* 10-inch album (Riverside 1953) ★★★★, *Broadcasts For The American National Guard* (Riverside 1953) ★★★, as the Dorsey Brothers *The Dorsey Brothers With The California Ramblers* 10-inch album (Riverside 1955) ★★★, *Tommy Dorsey Plays Cole Porter And Jerome Kern* (RCA Victor 1956) ★★★★, as the Dorsey Brothers *A Backward Glance* (Riverside 1956) ★★★, as the Dorsey Brothers *The Fabulous Dorseys In Hi-Fi Volumes 1 & 2* (Columbia 1958) ★★★★.

● COMPILATIONS: with Frank Sinatra *The Dorsey/Sinatra Sessions 1940-42* recordings (RCA 1972) ★★★★, *One Night Stand With Tommy Dorsey 1940* recording (Sandy Hook 1979) ★★★, *The Sentimental Gentleman 1941-42* recordings (RCA 1980) ★★★★, *At The Fat Man's 1946-48* recordings (Hep Jazz 1981) ★★★, *Solid Swing 1949-50* recordings (First Heard 1984) ★★★, as the Dorsey Brothers *Spotlighting The Fabulous Dorseys 1942-45* recordings (Giants Of Jazz 1984) ★★★★, *The Indispensable Tommy Dorsey Volumes 1/2 1935-36* recordings (RCA 1987) ★★★★, *The Indispensable Tommy Dorsey Volumes 3/4 1936-37* recordings (RCA 1987) ★★★★, *The Indispensable Tommy Dorsey Volumes 5/6 1937-38* recordings (RCA 1987) ★★★★, *The Indispensable Tommy Dorsey Volumes 7/8 1938-39* recordings (RCA 1987) ★★★★, *The Legend, Volumes 1-3* (RCA 1987) ★★★★, *Carnegie Hall V-Disc Session, April 1944* (Hep Jazz 1990) ★★★, *The Clambake Seven: The Music Goes Round And Round 1935-47* recordings (Bluebird 1991) ★★★★, with Sinatra *The Song Is You* 5-CD box set (Columbia 1994) ★★★★, *Dance With Dorsey* (Parade 1995) ★★★, *The Sky Fell Down 40s* recordings (Traditional Line 2000) ★★★, *The Early Jazz Sides 1932-1937* (Allegro 2004) ★★★.

● FURTHER READING: *Tommy And Jimmy: The Dorsey Years*, Herb Sanford. *For Once In My Life*, Connie Haines with Robert B. Stone. *Tommy Dorsey*, Robert L. Stockdale. *Tommy Dorsey: Livin' In A Great Big Way*, Peter Levinson.

● FILMS: *The Fabulous Dorseys* (1947).

Dos

Formed in Los Angeles, California, USA, in 1986, Dos comprised husband and wife bass players Mike Watt (**Minutemen**; **fIREHOSE**) and Kira Roessler (ex-**Black Flag**). Roessler had composed material for fIREHOSE, and thus much of *Dos* bears this group's eclectic imprint as the two explore contrasting atmospheres and sound textures. A 1989 EP, *Numero Dos*, saw them tackle **Billie Holiday**'s 'Don't Explain' and **Sonic Youth**'s 'Pacific Coast Highway', alongside two powerful, inventive instrumentals. Commitments to other projects ensured that Dos remained an occasional, but musically worthwhile, sideline.

● ALBUMS: *Dos* (New Alliance 1986) ★★★, *Justamente Tres* (Kill Rock Stars 1996) ★★★.

Doss, Buster

b. Marvin Earl Doss, 4 February 1925, Jefferson, Texas, USA. There can be few people in the entertainment world that have been involved in more aspects of the music than 'Colonel' Buster Doss. The Doss family was musical, and at the age of six, nicknamed Buster by his elder brother Benny, he was already playing on their shows. At 13, he ran away to join a touring Old Time Medicine Show, where he soon began to learn all about the music and entertainment business from the same people who trained **Gene Autry**, **Bob Wills** and **Roy Acuff**. He studied the acts of other members and soon set up his own Medicine Show. He became adept at all forms of entertainment that such shows promoted including the comedy, which varied from 'blackface' comedy to country hayseed characters. He also learned conjuring and ventriloquism and developed the ability to talk to his audiences. In 1942 he enlisted in the US Navy and produced shows to entertain the Armed Forces during World War II. After discharge in 1945, he moved to Hollywood and appeared in B-Western movies as both Bronco Buck Cody and the Cactus Kid. Between 1946 and 1948, he recorded for Royalty and Star Talent. In 1948, he became a member of **The Louisiana Hayride**, where he worked with several major stars including **Hank Williams** and **Johnny Horton**. He also appeared on the *Grand Ole Opry*.

Doss continued to promote shows, and during his career he has owned no less that seven major Frontier Jamboree shows at Marceline, Missouri; Harlingen, Mount Pleasant and Athens in Texas; Ashdown in Arkansas and Winchester, Tennessee. In 1950, he managed his first radio station at Hugo, Oklahoma but later owned seven other stations. From the mid-50s to the early 60s, he owned and operated country music's largest phone promotion with over 200 employees promoting the *Grand Ole Opry*, *The Louisiana Hayride*, *Cody's Helldrivers* and *Marvin The Marvellous Magician*. During this time with his Brazos Valley Ranch Hands and billed as the Country Magician, he toured internationally, presenting his comedy, magic, ventriloquism and straight country music and also appeared as Bronco Buck Cody in *The Cactus Kid* television series. In 1962 his magic act saw him voted the Number One Magician In The World by the Knights Of The Golden Wand. He also appeared at the World Fair in Seattle, and in 1962-63 he extended his business and ran Colonel Buck Cody's Pioneer Circus And Wild West Show, the world's second largest Tent Circus. Between 1963 and 1968, he based his operations in Nashville, saying 'it was then a small community where everybody helped each other and a common love of music drew us together. Kris

Kristofferson was a janitor, **Roger Miller** was a bellhop and you could always find **Willie Nelson** and **Tom T. Hall** plus a lot of others eating chilli down at Tootsie's. I never moved back until 1980 and boy had it changed'.

His Wizard label, which he had formed in 1959, became the first major independent label on Nashville's Music Row (later he also based his Stardust label there). During those years he managed several top *Grand Ole Opry* stars including **Billy Grammer** and **Billy Walker.** He relocated to Missouri in 1969 where he built a radio station and the first of seven Frontier Jamboree Theatres and Codyland Village, which he owned and operated. In 1975, a second theatre opened in Harlingen Texas with a theme park named Six Shooter Junction. In 1976 he settled in Austin, where he became involved with the 'Outlaw' movement. He formed the more contemporary group Cooder Browne, which recorded for Lone Star and **Mercury Records** and worked as opening act for Willie Nelson. In 1979 he organized the Press for Willie Nelson's *Fourth Of July Picnic* and has been regularly in demand for lecture tours based on his extensive knowledge of the entertainment business, and he also lectured on Journalism at the University of Texas. During the 80s, he continued to open his theatres—even in 1983 finding time to play the lead in the Vitonka Medicine Show at the American Place theatre on Broadway, New York City. Since 1948, he has produced several thousand recordings for numerous artists. In spite of the hectic life, he also found time to write songs; long ago he lost count of the number actually written but maintains that over 500 have been recorded.

In 1988, he returned to Tennessee and set up his home and offices at Billy Goat Hill, Winchester, on a bluff near the Elk River stating 'I am only 88 miles from Nashville but in another world.' In more recent years, the Colonel, as he is affectionately known, has devoted his experience to recording and promoting new talent which includes such fine artists as Rooster Quantrell and Troy Cook Jnr. He is dismissive of the modern country scene saying 'There are too many **Country Music Awards** shows now they have diluted its value. I'm expecting them to walk out on television and give an award for the good fried taters served that night.'

In 1990, the German Binge label released an album containing recordings made by the Doss band in 1959 and previously released on the Wizard label. Among the tracks are several vocals by Doss. Other examples of his recordings have appeared from time to time on compilations on the Stardust label. He first acquired the title of Colonel in 1964 when he was honoured by the State and made a Kentucky Colonel for his services. Since then 11 other States have also bestowed the same honour including Arkansas (when Bill Clinton was State Governor). The Buster Doss story is unique in that how one person has managed to fit so much into his life. At the beginning of the new millennium he still maintains a hectic schedule. He once said 'If you can find anyone in the music business who can come close to my track record—I'll show you a tree that a bird never lit in.'

● ALBUMS: *Bronco Buck Cody And His Brazos Valley Ranch Hands* (Binge 1990) ★★★.

Doss, Tommy

b. Lloyd Thomas Doss, 26 September 1920, Weiser, Idaho, USA. An important member of the **Sons Of the Pioneers**. The Doss family relocated to LeGrande, Oregon, in 1922 where, together with his normal schooling, Doss developed an interest in the early country sounds of **Jimmie Rodgers**, no doubt greatly encouraged by his accordion- and organ-playing father. He began singing in public at the age of 11 and in 1939, together with his brother Beek and a friend, he formed the Sons Of Grande Ronde. This trio, with a repertoire that included some of the songs of the Sons Of The Pioneers, whom he greatly admired, proved popular on local radio. During World War II, he was involved with defence work before returning to LeGrande in 1946 and forming a new trio. In 1948, for a time, he replaced **Tommy Duncan** with **Bob Wills**' Texas Playboys and appears on some of that band's Tiffany transcriptions but not on their studio recordings. He then moved to Los Angeles as vocalist with **Luke Wills**' band. He sang on some recordings including 'Shut Up And Drink Your Beer', until **RCA Records**' producer said he sounded too much like another of their artists, **Bob Nolan**. In 1949, whilst singing with Ole Rasmussen's band, he achieved a lifelong ambition when he became a member of the Sons Of The Pioneers. Nolan had wanted to retire and he and **Tim Spencer** saw Doss as the ideal replacement. He toured extensively, recorded and made films with the group, until, like Nolan, he found that he could no longer handle the pressures and in 1963, he gave up full-time connections with the group. He retired to Imnaha, Oregon, where he opened a store. He continued to record with the Pioneers and was even persuaded, on occasions, to undertake short tours until December 1967. In 1972, he appeared at a special reunion concert in Los Angeles to celebrate the Pioneers' 40th anniversary. Everyone was impressed with his performance and he was persuaded to make some solo recordings. They were planned as the first of a series of albums, but Doss had no intention of giving up his peaceful retirement. He returned home immediately after completing the session and the recordings remained unissued until 1987. The 11 songs included 'Rosa', a song he had sung on his last session with the Pioneers, 'The Memory' and perhaps the even more appropriately titled 'I Care No More'.

● ALBUMS: *Tommy Doss Of The Sons Of The Pioneers* (Bear Family 1987) ★★★.

Dot Records

Formed in 1951 in Gallatin, Tennessee, USA, by Randy Wood, proprietor of one of the region's largest mail-order record stores. Although initially an R&B outlet, Dot enjoyed a pop hit the following year with the **Hilltoppers**' 'Trying'. Group member Billy Vaughn became the company's musical director, as crooner **Pat Boone** and actor **Tab Hunter** established themselves as Dot's major signings. The former built his reputation by sanitizing material plundered from **Little Richard** and **Fats Domino**, before establishing an MOR/pop career with 'I'll Be Home', 'I Almost Lost My Mind' (1956), 'Love Letters In The Sand' and 'April Love' (1957). Thirteen of the artist's singles sold in excess of 1 million copies, and his rather languorous singing style set the tone for much of Dot's later, often conservative, output. The company did record **Nervous Norvus**, a novelty-cum-rockabilly act best recalled for the gruesome 'Transfusion', and **Gale Storm**, but was unable, or unwilling, to shake of an increasingly staid image. By the end of the 50s Wood had moved his operation to Los Angeles, and he later sold the entire company to the Gulf Western/Paramount conglomerate. The Dot catalogue was later acquired by the **ABC** group.

● COMPILATIONS: *Golden Instrumentals* (Dot 1967) ★★★.

Dotson, Big Bill

An obscure figure, Big Bill Dotson is known only for one record, made around 1952, possibly in Houston, Texas, USA, and issued on the Black & White label. Singing accompanied only by his guitar, his style on this very limited evidence was reminiscent of **Lightnin' Hopkins**, and indeed, his two tracks have appeared on a Hopkins album credited to that artist. His vocals were somewhat lighter and his guitar work more rudimentary than those of the more famous artist, but he deserves his own small place in blues history.

● COMPILATIONS: *Blues From The Deep South* (1969) ★★★.

Dotson, Jimmy

b. 19 October 1933, Ethel, Louisiana, USA. Dotson began his musical career singing blues at a local juke joint, but later developed his skills to encompass drums and guitar. He played in a band with **Lazy Lester** and later with **Silas Hogan** in a group called the Rhythm Ramblers. Although Hogan was the leader of this group, their first record was made with Dotson on vocals. Two singles were issued on **Jay Miller**'s own Rocko and Zynn labels under Dotson's name, both in an upbeat R&B vein, quite different from Hogan's down-home blues sound. Dotson lived in Memphis for several years and had another single issued on the Home Of The Blues label, but moved back to Baton Rouge in the early 80s and resumed his career at **Tabby Thomas**' Blues Box club.

● ALBUMS: *Baton Rouge Blues* (1985) ★★★, *Baton Rouge Harmonica* (1988) ★★★.

Dottsy

b. Dottsy Brodt, 6 April 1954, Sequin, near San Antonio, Texas, USA. In 1966, at the age of 12, Brodt was already singing in clubs in her local area as part of a trio. She reached the finals of a major talent competition on KBER San Antonio in 1969 and appeared on television in her own show. In 1972, she began to study special education (for teaching handicapped or subnormal children) at the University of Texas but found time to form her own band, Meadow Muffin. While singing at a convention in San Antonio, she came to the attention of Happy Shahan, who gave her the chance to appear at major events with **Johnny Rodriguez** and helped her to get a contract with **RCA Records**. Her first single, 'Storms Never Last', written by **Jessi Colter**, became a Top 20 US country chart hit in 1975 and was quickly followed by Susanna Clark's 'I'll Be Your San Antone Rose'. In the late 70s, she had further hits, including a Top 10 with '(After Sweet Memories) Play Born To Lose Again'. In 1979, **Waylon Jennings** played guitar and added harmony vocals to Dottsy's lead when she recorded his song 'Trying To Satisfy You', resulting in another Top 20 hit. When it appeared that she would go on to major stardom, she decided to cut back on her singing and concentrate on completing her college education. By the early 80s she was fully involved in working with autistic and mentally retarded children. Her last chart entry was a 1981 minor hit on Tanglewood Records with the suitably descriptive title 'Let The Little Bird Fly'.

● ALBUMS: *The Sweetest Thing* (RCA 1976) ★★★, *Trying To Satisfy You* (RCA 1979) ★★.

Double

This Swiss duo scored an unlikely transatlantic hit in 1986 with the appealing 'The Captain Of Her Heart' but had faded from view by the end of the decade. Vocalist and guitarist Kurt Maloo, a former painter and veteran of the Zurich experimental rock scene, teamed up with drummer Felix Haug (ex-**Yello**) in 1981 to form Ping Pong. Originally a trio, this unit enjoyed some notoriety as a live act before Maloo and Haug decided to go it alone as a duo. Renaming themselves Double, they released a number of under-performing singles before striking lucky with 'The Captain Of Her Heart'. This lilting jazz pop ballad was markedly different from the duo's previous experimental rock leanings, with a striking piano riff and Maloo's deadpan vocal making the track a natural for radio play. The single became a major hit in Europe, reaching number 8 in the UK, before crossing over to American radio and completing its climb up that country's charts into the Top 20. Nothing the duo subsequently released was as successful, and following the release of their second album, 1987's *Dou3le*, they parted company. Maloo, who had recorded a number of solo tracks in the late 70s, embarked on his own-name recording career with 1990's *Single*. A second solo album, *Soul & Echo*, followed in 1995.

● ALBUMS: *Blue* (Polydor 1985) ★★★, *Dou3le* (Polydor 1987) ★★.
Solo: Kurt Maloo *Single* (BMG 1990) ★★, *Soul & Echo* (Mambo 1995) ★★★.

Double Trouble (blues)

Double Trouble comprises Tommy Shannon (b. Tuscon, Arizona, USA; bass) and Chris Layton (b. 1955, Corpus Christi, Texas, USA; drums). Although veterans of the blues scene, they waited until 1999 to strike out on their own as a double act instead of acting as sidemen for better-known artists.

Shannon grew up in Dumas, Texas, before picking up a guitar and moving to Dallas. Here he received his real education in the blues from **Johnny Winter**, who not only played him his record collection but also took him on as his bass player for two years until 1969. Meanwhile, Layton studied music at Corpus Christi University and moved to Austin, Texas. His musical experience lay with jazz and funk bands, but like Shannon, he recognized the blues as his home territory as soon as he was exposed to it by **Stevie Ray Vaughan**. Vaughan had recently added vocals to his role of guitarist for blues group Triple Threat Revue. Layton joined the band which was renamed Double Trouble. In 1980, Shannon joined the line-up. Shannon and Layton were the rhythm section for Vaughan, helping the band garner four Grammy awards.

After Vaughan's death in 1990, Shannon and Layton formed a supergroup, the Arc Angels, and continued to work as session men for artists including **W.C. Clark** and **Kenny Wayne Shepherd**. Later in the decade, they joined with **Storyville** to record more albums (including *Bluest Eyes* and *Dog Years*). However, the moniker Double Trouble stuck, and they finally released their own album, *Been A Long Time*, under their own label, which was eventually taken on by Tone-Cool Records. The album featured many artists influenced by Vaughan, including Shepherd, **Lou Ann Barton** (former vocalist with Triple Threat Revue) and Reese Wynans (former Vaughan keyboard player). The album's melting pot of influences ranges from gospel/soul ('Cry Sky') and R&B ('Baby, There's No One Like You') to a cover version of **Muddy Waters**' blues classic 'She's Alright'.

● ALBUMS: *Been A Long Time* (Tone-Cool 2001) ★★★★.

Double Trouble (film)

In this 1967 feature **Elvis Presley** plays a singer on tour in Europe who falls for two girls, one in Belgium, another, a teenage heiress, in London. Of course the star did not visit Britain; location shots were handled by a second crew. In keeping with the dated air Presley's film career now epitomized, such scenes emphasised a passé 'Swinging London' image rather than concurrent psychedelia. The soundtrack material was equally lamentable, plumbing new depths with 'Old MacDonald', one of the worst songs ever recorded by an established artist. Of the nine songs featured only 'Long Legged Girl (With The Short Dress On)' showed any merit, yet when issued as a single, the song failed to reach the US Top 50 and UK Top 40. It was the first Presley a-side to do so since he joined **RCA Records** from **Sun Records** in 1956.

Double You?

European **house** group Double You? first came to prominence in the early 90s, largely through the public disagreements between their label, **ZYX Records** and **Network Records**. Network had made overtures to obtain the license for Double You?'s version of **KC And The Sunshine Band**'s 'Please Don't Go', but their approaches were rejected. Network employed **KWS** to record a version instead, earning a five-week stay at number 1 in the UK charts in 1992 in the process. Double You?'s manager Robertson Zanetti collapsed of nervous exhaustion as a result of the disagreement and subsequent litigation. Despite this, the group continued to record, achieving limited success with another cover version, 'Run To Me'. 1994's 'What's Up' was a surprise hit, many having presumed the group to have folded, while 'Hot Stuff' in 1995 was uninspired but confirmed Double You?'s continued presence in the elementary house cover version market.

Doucette

Named after the group's leader Jerry Doucette (vocals/guitar), Canadian hard rock band Doucette comprised Mark Olson (keyboards), Donnie Cummings (bass) and Dure Maxwell (drums). Doucette's skill as Canada's pre-eminent slide guitarist distinguished his group's three albums. The first of these, *Mama Let Him Play*, appeared for **Mushroom Records** in 1977 and featured eloquent original compositions alongside fluid musicianship. It was followed two years later by *Douce Is Loose*. However, following the release of *Comin' Up Roses* in 1981 the group ceased to be active, although their leader continued to work as a session musician and performed at Canadian clubs throughout the 80s.

● ALBUMS: *Mama Let Him Play* (Mushroom 1977) ★★★, *Douce Is Loose* (Mushroom 1979) ★★★, *Comin' Up Roses* (Rio 1981) ★★.

Doug E. Fresh

b. Douglas E. Davis, 17 September 1966, St. Thomas, Virgin Islands, though he grew up in the Bronx and Harlem districts of New York City, USA. Self-proclaimed as The Original Human Beatbox, i.e. being able to imitate the sound of a rhythm machine, Fresh broke through in 1985 with the release of one of rap's classic tracks 'The Show'. Joined by partner MC Ricky D (aka **Slick Rick**), the single matched rhymes with a bizarre array of human sound effects, courtesy of Fresh. It marked a notable departure in rap's development and was so distinctive it began a small flurry of similarly inclined rappers, as well as **Salt-N-Pepa**'s answer record 'Showstopper'. Despite its impact, it was a song that was hardly representative of Fresh fare: far too much of his recorded material was workmanlike and soundalike. A debut album included live contributions from Bernard Wright (synthesiser) and veteran jazz man **Jimmy Owens** (trumpet), as well as a dubious anti-abortion track. The follow-up saw him allied to **Public Enemy**'s **Bomb Squad** production team. To give him his due Fresh was very nearly rap's first superstar, but rather than capitalize on 'The Show' he would end up in court trying to sue Reality Records for non-payment of royalties on the song. He was also the first genuine rapper to appear at Jamaica's Reggae Sunsplash festival, stopping in the West Indies long enough to record alongside **Papa San** and **Cocoa Tea**. He made something of a comeback at the end of 1993 with the release of party record 'I-Right (Alright)' after he was reunited with Slick Rick (recently returned from a period of incarceration) and signed with **Gee Street Records**. Fresh has also enjoyed the distinction of seeing a 'Doug E. Fresh' switch added to the Oberheim Emulator in order to provide samples of his human beat box talents. On *Play* Fresh employed **Luther Campbell** of **2 Live Crew** to add a gangsta edge.

● ALBUMS: *Oh, My God!* (Reality 1985) ★★★, *The World's Greatest Entertainer* (Reality 1988) ★★★, *Doin' What I Gotta Do* (Bust It 1992) ★★, *Play* (Gee Street 1995) ★★, *Alright* (Gee 1996) ★★★.

● COMPILATIONS: *Greatest Hits, Volume 1* (Bust It 1996) ★★★.

Dougan, Rob

b. Sydney, Australia. Perhaps best known for his epic strings and breakbeats track, 'Clubbed To Death', that first appeared in 1995, Dougan is a literate and talented composer and producer whose music spans several genres. After abandoning his studies at the prestigious National Institute of Dramatic Arts in Sydney, he relocated to London, England, where he worked a number of odd jobs before 'Clubbed To Death' made his name on the club scene. The enormous success of that track (that later received a revival when it appeared on the soundtrack of 1999's blockbuster movie, *The Matrix*) led to remixes and production for artists including **U2**, **Pet Shop Boys**, **Moby** and **Kylie Minogue**. Initially Dougan worked with **Rollo**, the talented producer who formed **Faithless**. Together they worked as a remix team, calling themselves Dignity or **Our Tribe**. When Rollo started his own label, **Cheeky Records**, the duo released their first single, 'Understand This Groove', on it. They also recorded the club classic 'Hold That Sucka Down' as the OT Quartet. Exploring the dance genre throughout the 90s, Dougan collaborated with **Judge Jules**, continued to work with Rollo and gained remix and production credits in his own right. In 1994, Dougan produced 'Feel What You Want' for a former Miss America, Kristine W. He also produced a number of tracks on her 1996 debut, *Land Of The Living*.

During this period, Dougan began work on his solo album project, which eventually resulted in the 2002 debut, *Furious Angels*. Featuring Dougan's bluesy, rugged vocals, somewhat reminiscent of **Tom Waits** or **Matt Johnson**, the album was epic in every sense. Six years in the making, it was a labour of love and Dougan was involved in most aspects of the recording, playing many of the instruments as well as arranging and conducting the full studio orchestra and choir. The dramatic orchestral elements of *Furious Angels* demonstrated Dougan's love of classical music and film scores (the perennially influential **John Barry** is an obvious reference point), and indeed, he contributed both the track 'Furious Angels' and some original music to the score of the 2003 blockbuster, *Matrix Reloaded*.

● ALBUMS: *Furious Angels* (Cheeky/Reprise 2002) ★★★★.

Dougherty, Eddie

b. 17 July 1915, New York, USA. Dougherty first played drums as a child and quickly became highly proficient. During the 30s he was constantly on call for recording sessions in New York, playing in pick up bands fronted by artists such as **Taft Jordan**, **Mildred Bailey**, **Harry James**, **Billie Holiday**, **Frankie Newton** and boogie-woogie pianists **Pete Johnson** and **Meade 'Lux' Lewis**. In the early 40s he played with **Bud Freeman**, **Art Tatum**, **Benny Carter** and others, recording piano-drum duos with **James P. Johnson**. His round of recording sessions continued through the mid-40s, finding him accompanying **Mary Lou Williams**, **Wilbur De Paris**, **Teddy Wilson** and **Albert Nicholas**. Before the decade was out, however, Dougherty dropped out of full-time participation in music but continued to play sporadically in coming years. The quality of Dougherty's accompaniment can be measured by the company he kept, none of whom would have tolerated anyone less than a first-rate drummer. His discreetly supportive playing can be heard on many of the hundreds of recordings he made with the musicians listed.

Douglas, Blair

b. Isle of Skye, Scotland. A **Runrig** founder member who was actually in the band during two separate incarnations and graduated quite naturally to keyboards from accordion. The music he now produces solo is atmospheric, soundtrack-influenced work. He made his solo debut in 1984 with the cassette recording *Celtology*. Four years later he teamed up with Arthur Cormack, Shona MacDonald and Cailean MacLean to record *Skye: The Island*, a celebration of music and song from the Isle of Skye. The largely self-composed *Beneath The Beret* (1990) included 'Kate Martin's Waltz', which was subsequently adopted as a modern classic by traditional musicians. In 1993, Douglas joined Arthur Cormack, Eilidh MacKenzie, Alison Kinnaird and Christine Primrose in the Gaelic group Mac-talla. The quintet completed . . . *Mairidh Gaol Is Ceol* the following year. His next solo release, *A Summer In Skye*, followed in 1996. In 2001 Douglas participated in the writing and recording of Cliar's remarkable *Lasair Dhè* project. His new solo album *Angels From The Ashes* was released through Runrig's Ridge label in 2004.

● ALBUMS: *Celtology* cassette (Skye 1984) ★★★, *Beneath The Beret* (Skye 1990) ★★★★, *A Summer In Skye* (Skye 1996) ★★★, *Angels From The Ashes* (Ridge 2004) ★★★.

Douglas, Carl

Jamaican-born Carl Douglas was working with producer Biddu during 1974 when the necessity to record a b-side to 'I Want To Give You My Everything' resulted in 'Kung Fu Fighting', a song which apparently took only 10 minutes to record. When the Douglas composition was presented to the A&R department at **Pye Records**, they wisely elevated the song to an a-side. Capturing the contemporary interest in Kung Fu in films and magazines and bestowed with a catchy chorus, the song topped the charts in both the UK and USA. Douglas, gamely dressed in martial arts garb, executed his 'hoo!' and 'haaa!' grunts while performing the song and kept up the novelty long enough to chart again with 'Dance The Kung Fu'. Three years later, Douglas made a return to the UK charts with the Top 30 hit 'Run Back'. Since then little has been heard of him, though his most famous single re-entered the UK singles chart (albeit in a re-mixed form) in 1998.

● ALBUMS: *Carl Douglas* (Pye 1975) ★★, *Kung Fu Fighter* (Pye 1976) ★★, *Run Back* (Pye 1977) ★, *Keep Pleasing Me* (Pye 1978) ★.

● COMPILATIONS: *Golden Hour Of Carl Douglas* (Golden Hour 1979) ★★, *Kung Fu Fighting* (Spectrum 1995) ★★.

Douglas, Carol

b. 7 April 1948, Brooklyn, New York City, USA. Douglas was a member of US vocal group the **Chantels** in the early 70s before going solo. Her debut single, released in November 1974, was a cover of 'Doctor's Orders'—a previous UK Top 10 hit for female UK pop vocalist **Sunny**—which peaked just outside the US Top 10. After the minor hit 'A Hurricane Is Coming Tonite' further US chart success proved elusive for Douglas. Her recordings included a version of **Abba**'s 'Dancing Queen' and a mid-tempo disco remake of the **Bee Gees**' 'Night Fever'. The latter, arranged and conducted by Michael Zager, reached the lower reaches of the Top 75 in the UK in mid-1978.

Douglas, Charles

b. Dayton, Ohio, USA. Singer-songwriter Charles Douglas carved out a cult following during the late 90s with his **Lou Reed**-inspired take on US indie rock. Originally from Dayton, Ohio, Douglas enrolled on a pre-med course at Brown University before teaming up with fellow pre-med student Manish Kalvakota in Vegetarian Meat. Douglas, using the pseudonym Alex McAulay, composed a number of primitive rock 'n' roll songs that earned the duo a cult following on the New York indie circuit. Several of these were collected on two 7-inch singles and 1995's album *Let's Pet* (all released on No. 6 Records). Douglas also released his solo debut *Minor Wave* the same year. This minor classic of lo-fi indie pop, including stand-out tracks 'New Attitude' and 'King Of Industry', received some positive reviews in the independent press, but Douglas' career was effectively put on hold when he suffered a nervous breakdown. By 1998 he had regained his health and released his second vinyl-only album, *The Burdens Of Genius*, the same year. Bizarre tracks such as 'The Rabbit Never Gets The Carrot' and 'Prince' indicated the state of mind much of the album was recorded in. (Douglas' first two albums were later compiled on the *31 Flavors* CD.)

For a man so clearly inspired by the **Velvet Underground**'s music, persuading that band's former drummer **Maureen 'Mo' Tucker** to produce and play on his third album, 1999's *The Lives Of Charles Douglas*, must have seemed like a dream come true. Tucker's idiosyncratic drumming added a welcome edge to Douglas' whimsical songwriting, while the album also included notable contributions from indie stalwarts Kurt Ralske (**Ultra Vivid Scene**), Bill Whitten and Claudia Silver. Douglas worked with the **Pixies**' lead guitarist Joey Santiago on his next studio album, *Statecraft*.

● ALBUMS: *Minor Wave* (Voltage 1995) ★★★, *The Burdens Of Genius* (Voltage 1998) ★★★, *The Lives Of Charles Douglas* (No. 6 1999) ★★★★, *Statecraft* (No. 6/ Enabler 2004) ★★★.

● COMPILATIONS: *31 Flavors* (No. 6 2001) ★★★.

Douglas, Craig

b. Terence Perkins, 12 August 1941, Newport, Isle Of Wight, England. After moving to London in the mid-50s, Douglas came under the wing of agent Bunny Lewis, appeared on the television show **6.5 Special** and won a record contract with **Decca Records** before moving to **Dick Rowe**'s label Top Rank. Covering American hits was the classic route to chart success, and in 1959 Douglas scored with **Dion**'s 'A Teenager In Love' and reached number 1 with **Sam Cooke**'s 'Only Sixteen'. He co-starred with **Helen Shapiro** in the movie *It's Trad, Dad!* (1962). Several more hits followed but after four consecutive number 9s with 'A Hundred Pounds Of Clay', 'Time', 'When My Little Girl Is Smiling' and 'Our Favourite Melodies', Douglas felt the sting of the approaching beat boom. He then travelled the world, returning for a career in cabaret in the UK, where he still resides. In 1992 he joined other 60s survivors, including Helen Shapiro, on the Walkin' Back To Happiness Tour. Douglas possesses a good singing voice that should have moved into the classic pop song. His recycled past hits now sound trite and tired, although the voice is still intact.

● ALBUMS: *Craig Douglas* (Top Rank 1960) ★★★, *Bandwagon Ball* (Top Rank 1961) ★★★, *Our Favourite Melodies* (Columbia 1962) ★★★, *Oh Lonesome Me* (Jackson 1981) ★★.

● COMPILATIONS: *The Best Of The EMI Years* (EMI 1993) ★★★.

● FILMS: *It's Trad, Dad!* aka *Ring-A-Ding Rhythm* (1962).

Douglas, Dave

b. 24 March 1963, Montclair, New Jersey, USA. One of the most highly acclaimed trumpet players of the 90s *avant garde* scene, Douglas was raised in the New Jersey area and as a talented youngster learnt to play piano, trombone and trumpet at an early age. He studied music in Barcelona and Boston and then attended both the **Berklee College Of Music** and the New England Conservatory. After moving to New York City in 1984 he studied at New York University. Douglas got his first break in 1987 when he toured Europe with **Horace Silver**, but his trip to Switzerland the following year was to have a greater influence on his musical development, as Douglas incorporated Eastern European styles into his playing as part of a theatre troupe.

Douglas recorded extensively in the 90s as both leader and sideman, appearing on the hatART, Soul Note, New World and Arabesque labels. His bands include the Tiny Bell Trio with drummer Jim Black and guitarist Brad Schoeppach; his String Group with violinist Mark Feldman, cellist Erik Friedlander and bass player **Mark Dresser** and his Quartet and Sextet. He has also played with **John Zorn** in Masada and has appeared live and on record with **Don Byron**, **Myra Melford**, **Uri Caine** and **Anthony Braxton**. On all his recordings Douglas reflects a wide range of musical elements which, allied to an outstanding technique and a highly individualistic compositional style, marks him out as one of the most distinctive talents currently working in jazz. In 1999, critics in *JazzTimes* magazine chose him as Musician Of The Year, and in the same year he was signed to **RCA Records**. Similar accolades followed from the *DownBeat* critics poll in June 2000 and once again in 2003. He launched his own label Greenleaf in 2005.

● ALBUMS: *Parallel Worlds* (Soul Note 1993) ★★★★, *The Tiny Bell Trio* (Songlines 1994) ★★★, *In Our Lifetime* (New World 1995) ★★★★, *Constellations* (hatART 1995) ★★★★, *Five* (Soul Note 1995) ★★★★, *Sanctuary* (Avant 1996) ★★★, with Tiny Bell Trio *Live In Europe* (Arabesque 1997) ★★★★, *Sanctuary* (Avant 1997) ★★★, *Stargazer* (Arabesque 1998) ★★★★, *Charms Of The Night Sky* (Winter & Winter 1998) ★★★★, *Moving Portrait* (DIW 1998) ★★★★, *Magic Triangle* (Arabesque 1998) ★★★★, *Songs For Wandering Souls* (Winter & Winter 1999) ★★★★, *Convergence* (Soul Note 1999) ★★★, *Leap Of Faith* 1998 recording (Arabesque 2000) ★★★, *Leap Of Faith* (Arabesque 2000) ★★★★, *Soul On Soul: Celebrating Mary Lou Williams* (Bluebird 2000) ★★★★, with Charms Of The Night Sky *A Thousand Evenings* (Bluebird 2000) ★★★, as the Tiny Bell Trio *Constellations* (hatOLOGY 2000) ★★★, *Witness* (Bluebird 2001) ★★★★, *The Infinite* (Bluebird 2002) ★★★, *Freak In* (Bluebird 2003) ★★★, *Strange Liberation* (Bluebird 2004) ★★★, with Louis Sclavis, Peggy Lee, Dylan van der Schyff *Bow River Falls* (Koch 2004) ★★, *Mountain Passages* (Greenleaf/Koch 2005) ★★★.

Douglas, Isaac, Rev.

b. Philadelphia, pennsylvania, USA. A passionate gospel singer with his own ministry, Douglas was regularly compared to the **Rev. James Cleveland** at the inception of his career. He had grown up listening to many of the great gospel singers and sees himself as a 'guardian' of that tradition. He moved to New York from his native Philadelphia in the mid-60s and formed his first all-male singing gospel group. Named the Isaac Douglas Singers, their first release for **United Artists Records** was *Lord Have Mercy*. After this he helped to found the New York Community Choir. Among that group's notable commissions was the invitation to sing backing vocals for Nikki Giovanni's popular album *Truth Is On The Way*. Among the group's regular concert venues were New York's Museum of Modern Art, while mainstream television appearances on shows such as *Soul* ensued. Continuing to be influenced by Cleveland, in the early 70s Douglas relocated to Los Angeles to found his own ministry. At the same time he entered a new recording contract with Nashboro/Creed Records. His own band recorded with that label, as did the New York Community Choir. A move to Nashville followed, where he continued to collaborate with choirs including the Johnson Ensemble, with whom he recorded 'The Harvest Is Plentiful'.

● ALBUMS: *Faith Will Survive* (Creed 60s) ★★★, *A Little Higher* (Creed 60s) ★★★, *Rev. Isaac Douglas With The Birmingham Choir* (Creed 60s) ★★★, *You've Got A Friend* (Creed 70s) ★★, *The Harvest Is Plentiful* (Creed 70s) ★★★, *Do You Know Him* (Creed 70s) ★★★, *By The Grace Of God* (Creed 70s) ★★★, *In Times Like These*

(Creed 70s) ★★, *Beautiful Zion* (Creed 70s) ★★, *You Really Ought To Get To Know Him* (Creed 70s) ★★★, *Stand Up For Jesus* (Creed 70s) ★★★, *Special Appearance* (Creed 70s) ★★★, *You Light Up My Life* (Creed 70s) ★★★.

Douglas, Jerry

b. Gerald Calvin Douglas, 28 May 1956, Warren, Ohio, USA. A talented musician who plays guitar and lap steel guitar but is primarily now known as one of the finest dobro players ever to have played in any form of country music, he gained his initial attraction to the instrument at the age of eight, when his father, himself a bluegrass musician, took him to see **Flatt And Scruggs**. At the time, their dobro player was **Josh Graves** and his performance captivated the boy. In 1972, by then playing with his father's band, he was given the opportunity to play for a time with the **Country Gentlemen**. He later worked with **J.D. Crowe** And The New South and with **Ricky Skaggs** in Boone Creek. In 1978 his debut, *Fluxology*, was named after the nickname of 'Flux', given to him by other musicians, seemingly because of his amazing finger-picking skills. During the 80s, he worked for some years with the **Whites**, playing dobro on most of their popular recordings, but eventually he decided to follow a solo career and also to work as a session musician. In the latter capacity, he has played on numerous albums by countless artists, whose styles have varied widely from the **Nitty Gritty Dirt Band** to **Hank Williams Jnr**. In 1986 he was one of the first musicians signed to record on the new MCA Master Series. He appeared with fiddle virtuoso **Mark O'Connor** at the 1987 Wembley Festival in London and has toured various countries. His amazing talents have won him a great number of awards, including election to *Frets* Gallery Of Greats and a 1983 Grammy for Best Country Instrumental Performance. In the 80s he, **Mike Auldridge** and Josh Graves produced *Dobro Summit*, an educational video. He also featured on several albums by Irish singer **Maura O'Connell**. In the 90s Douglas turned to production, making regular appearances on the TNN channel's *American Music Shop*. He released an excellent album with **Peter Rowan** in 1996 and joined **Alison Krauss**' backing group Union Station two years later.

● ALBUMS: *Fluxology* (Rounder 1978) ★★★, *Tennessee Fluxedo* (Rounder 1981) ★★★, *Under The Wire* (MCA Master Series 1986) ★★★, *Changing Channels* (MCA Master Series 1987) ★★★, *Plant Early* (MCA Master Series 1989) ★★, *Slide Rule* (Sugar Hill 1992) ★★★, with Russ Barenberg, Edgar Meyer *Skip, Hop & Wobble* (Sugar Hill 1993) ★★, with Peter Rowan *Yonder* (Sugar Hill 1996) ★★★★, *Restless On The Farm* (Sugar Hill 1998) ★★★★, *Lookout For Hope* (Sugar Hill 2002) ★★★, *The Best Kept Secret* (Koch 2005) ★★.

● COMPILATIONS: *Everything Is Gonna Work Out Fine* (Rounder 1987) ★★★.

Douglas, Jim

b. James Douglas, 13 May 1942, Gifford, East Lothian, Scotland. Playing banjo and guitar Douglas became an important figure on the traditional jazz scene in his homeland, notably as a member of the **Clyde Valley Stompers**. From the mid-60s he was a mainstay of the **Alex Welsh** band until its dissolution in 1982, touring the UK and overseas and appearing on 1971's *In Concert*. Subsequently, Douglas played in other traditional bands but throughout his career has been at ease backing mainstream musicians. On banjo he provides an urgent thrust to the bands in which he plays, but it as a subtly inventive guitarist that he has made a valuable contribution to British jazz.

Douglas, Johnny

b. 19 June 1920, Hackney, London, England, d. 20 April 2003, Bognor Regis, West Sussex, England. A prolific composer and arranger, who composed numerous film and television scores, Douglas also recorded with many top singers and sold millions of albums, including 80 made for **RCA Records**. A talented child pianist, Douglas formed a dance band while still at school and after leaving education played with the Neville Hughes sextet. An injury during wartime service in the RAF forced him to give up piano playing for a time and concentrate on composing and arranging. After the war he was in demand from Bert **Ambrose**, **Ted Heath**, **Edmundo Ros**, **Cyril Stapleton**, **Billy Cotton**, **Joe Loss**, **Mantovani**, **Jack Parnell** and other top British bands. He also accompanied **Howard Keel**, **Shirley Jones**, **Moira Anderson**, **Shirley Bassey**, **Max Bygraves**, **Al Martino**, **John Hanson**, **Dennis Lotis**, **Barbra Streisand**, **Vera Lynn**, **Tex Ritter** (Douglas was on the 1952 hit 'High Noon'), **Harry Secombe** and **Frankie Vaughan**, among many others. He provided musical support for many international stars on television and radio and in 1955 was given the first of his several shows on BBC Radio *In The Still Of The Night*. In 1958, for the first time Douglas was given the chance to conduct a large orchestra playing his own arrangements. The RCA album *Living Strings Play Music Of The Sea* was the start of a long and successful association. Douglas scored over 30 feature films, the best known of which, 1970's *The Railway Children*, received a British Academy nomination. Others included *The Day Of The Triffids*, *The Hijackers*, *The Bay Of Saint Michel*, *Gunfighters Of Casa Grande*, *Mozambique*, *Crack In The World*, *City Of Fear*, *Kid Rodelo*, *Dateline Diamonds*, *Circus Of Fear*, *Company Of Fools*, *Run Like A Thief* and 21 films in the *Scales Of Justice* series. In 1983 Douglas formed his own record company Dulcima, taking the name from a film score he composed for an HE Bates adaptation. He continued recording into the next decade, completing his first classical composition, a symphonic poem with three movements called *The Conquest*, in 1999. Douglas, who had fought prostate cancer for several years, died in April 2003.
- ALBUMS: *Living Strings Play Music Of The Sea* (RCA Victor 1958) ★★★, *Many Sides Of Johnny Douglas And His Orchestra* (Cambra 1983) ★★★, *More Romance With The Classics* (Dulcima 1988) ★★★, *On Stage* (Dulcima 1990) ★★★★, *It's Magic* (Dulcima 1994) ★★, *In Concert* (Dulcima) ★★★.

Douglas, K.C.

b. 21 November 1913, Sharon, Mississippi, USA, d. 18 October 1975, Berkeley, California, USA. Baptized with initials only, Douglas came from a strict Baptist family, his father a minister who disapproved of blues. Although interested in the guitar, he did not acquire one until 1936, taking instruction from uncle Scott Douglas and cousin Isadore Scott. Moving to Jackson, Mississippi, in 1940, he met **Tommy Johnson**, having previously copied his style on records. In 1945 he moved to Vallejo, California, as a government recruit to work in the Kaiser shipyard. He then moved north to Richmond and met harmonica player **Sidney**

Maiden. The pair recorded for **Bob Geddins'** Down Town label in 1948, Douglas singing 'Mercury Boogie', using a guitar loaned by **Lowell Fulson**, and Maiden singing 'Eclipse Of The Sun', songs for which each man was subsequently lauded. In 1954 Douglas moved to Oakland and recorded 'K.C. Boogie' for Rhythm, another Geddins label. Two years later he was recorded at a house party, the resulting performance later released as an album on Cook, a New York label. In 1960–61 he was recorded several times by **Arhoolie Records** owner Chris Strachwitz, who leased two albums to Bluesville. He also backed Maiden and **Mercy Dee** on albums recorded at the same time and released on both labels. In the late 60s, he made further singles for Galaxy and Blues Connoisseur. His last album featured him with a band that included harmonica player Richard Riggins.
- ALBUMS: *K.C. Blues* (Bluesville 1962) ★★★, *The Country Boy* (Arhoolie 1974) ★★★, *Big Road Blues* (Ace 1988) ★★★.

Douglas, Keith

b. 7 December 1957, London, England. Douglas followed the local sounds in London, including Sir Coxsone's and the Mighty Frontline. He was inspired to perform as a DJ by his brother Tony, a member of the **Blackstones**, who topped the reggae album charts with *Take Another Look At Love*. Inspired by his love of music, Douglas embarked on a recording career, initially under the pseudonym Imperial Keith. He released his debut, 'Struggling In A Babylon', in 1976, which was well received and led to sessions with **Clement Bushay** following an introduction by **Pablo Gad** for the masterful 'Teacher Never Taught Me'. The song enhanced his notoriety as a roots singer, although this classification proved inaccurate. While pursuing his career, he learned much from his contemporaries, a notable influence being **King Sounds**, who taught Douglas basic guitar skills. The release of the classic 'Blessed Are The Meek' signalled a change of direction when he embarked on recording sessions with **Fashion Records**. Through the label he released 'I Specialise In Good Girls' and the chart-topping 'Cool Down Amina'. The success of the two singles led to him being described as Mr. Lovers Rock, and in 1982 he released 'Try Love Again' with similar success. In 1983 he began working with **Aswad**, with backing vocals provided by **Brown Sugar**'s Pauline Catilin and **Caron Wheeler** for the buoyant 'Angel', released on the band's own label. The Ladbroke Grove connection continued when he appeared with the **Sons Of Jah** for the **dancehall** favourite 'Boom', backed with the appropriately titled 'Explosive Dub'. While working with Trevor Bow and the Sons Of Jah he recorded his debut album, featuring melodies supplied by members of Aswad and the **Wailers**. Indicating a desire for independence he went into self-production for the release of 'You Move Me'. Douglas also appeared on the one rhythm *Front Line Reggae* compilation. During the 90s, Douglas maintained a low profile performing alongside **Tex Johnson**, Dennis Pinnock and Paul Dawkins as Four In A Row, releasing the single 'Love Is'.
- ALBUMS: *What The World Needs* (Natty Congo 1984) ★★, *In The Mood* (Ruff Cut 2000) ★★★.

Douglas, Mike

b. Michael Dowd Jnr., 11 August 1925, Chicago, Illinois, USA. Douglas was the host of an American television talk show in

1966, when he recorded the saccharine ballad 'The Men In My Little Girl's Life', which reached number 6 on the charts. Douglas started his career as a singer on a cruise ship outside of Chicago. In the mid-40s, after a stint in the Armed Forces and at college, he sang with **Kay Kyser** on radio and on recordings. After leaving Kyser, who had retired, Douglas' career did not go anywhere in the 50s but in 1961 he was hired by a Cleveland, Ohio, television station to host the afternoon talk show which bore his name. As his local popularity accelerated, Douglas' show became syndicated nationally, and in 1965 Epic Records signed him. He recorded four albums for the label, but only the one single was a hit and Douglas' recording career ended. He continued to host his television programme until 1980.

● ALBUMS: *It's Time For Mike Douglas* (Epic 1965) ★★, *You Don't Have To Be Irish* (Epic 1965) ★★, *The Men In My Little Girl's Life* (Epic 1966) ★★, *Dear Mike, Please Sing* (Epic 1966) ★★.

Douglas, Shirley

(see **McDevitt, Chas**)

Douglas, Tommy

b. 9 January 1906, Eskridge, Kansas, USA, d. 9 March 1965, Swiss Falls, South Dakota, USA. Douglas taught himself clarinet and saxophone while at school in Topeka before studying at the Boston Conservatory from 1924–28. While there he was friendly with the group of Boston players who were to form the core of the **Duke Ellington** saxophone section—**Johnny Hodges**, **Otto 'Toby' Hardwicke** and **Harry Carney**. He worked with a variety of bands in the south and midwest throughout the 30s and 40s but settled in Kansas City. He worked with **Jelly Roll Morton** in Chicago in 1933 and later with **Bennie Moten**. He also played briefly with Ellington in 1951 but usually led his own bands. His commercial records do not reflect what those who heard him describe as his more flowing, modern style. Certainly he was using some of the devices of modern jazz (such as extended chords and double time) in his own music as early as 1935, and he may have had some influence on **Charlie Parker**, who played with his septet in 1936 at the age of 16.

Douglas, Tony

b. 12 April 1929, Martins Mill, Texas, USA. Despite not being well known outside his native state, Douglas is one of the unsung stalwarts of Texas country music. Born on a farm on the outskirts of his native Athens, he started singing while on service with the US Army in Germany after the World War II. On his return to America Douglas landed a spot on the *Cowtown Hoedown*, a weekly live show broadcast by KCUL from Fort Worth, Texas. He recorded his first single 'Old Blue Monday' for the show's own name label and shortly afterwards was invited to join **The Louisiana Hayride** in 1957. He remained a popular live attraction until the venerable show's closure three years later. Douglas moved on to the *Big D Jamboree* and signed a recording contract with **Pappy Daily**'s new label D Records. He recorded three singles for the label with backing from his regular musicians Chuck Jennings and Orville Couch. The last of these, 'Shrimpin'', became a local hit in 1961 and earned the combo the nickname Tony Douglas And The Shrimpers. Douglas made his national breakthrough on **Vee Jay Records**, reaching the country Top 30 with 'His And Hers', but the label's

bankruptcy precluded the singer earning any royalties. An album of the same name later appeared on Sims Records, but despite further releases for Paula Records Douglas remained absent from the charts for the rest of the decade. He formed his own Cochise Records label and enjoyed a return to the country charts in 1973 with 'Thank You For Touching My Life' and 'My Last Day' (both leased to **Dot Records**). Douglas hit the charts only two more times, in 1975 with 'If I Can Make It (Through The Mornin')' and seven years later with a reworking of 'His And Hers'. Douglas, affectionately known as 'Mr. Nice Guy', remains a popular draw in his home-town of Athens, Georgia, and still releases material on his own Cochise label.

● ALBUMS: *His 'N' Hers* (Sims 1964) ★★★, *Mr Nice Guy* (Sims 1966) ★★★, *Heart* (Paula 1967) ★★, *The Versatile Tony Douglas* (Paula 1969) ★★, *Thank You For Touching My Life* (Dot 1970) ★★★.

● COMPILATIONS: *His 'N' Hers: From The Original 'Mr Nice Guy'* (Sims 2002) ★★★.

Doumbia, Nahawa

b. Mafélé, Mali. Wassoulou singer Nahawa Doumbia was orphaned at an early age. She started singing as a young child and her chosen style was very much that of the new era, as she did not share the privilege of hereditary jeli status enjoyed by **Tata Bambo Kouyaté** or Nahini Diabeté. Instead her billing is that of the Fula singer, where music is not the profession handed down from parents. In 1982 Doumbia won the first prize at the Biennalle Artistique, launching her professional career. Her fame spread further the following year when she gained another trophy at Radio France Internationale's Découverte awards. By 1984 she was part of the entertainment package for the France-Afrique Summit Meeting, illustrating her rapid rise.

After several cassette-only albums Doumbia made her debut proper in 1988 with her first European album, produced by **Boncana Maiga** for Syllart Records. Maigo brought in a team of experienced Cameroonian session players to help him perfect the follow-up, *Nyama Toutou*, released by Syllart and the **Stern's Records** label in 1990. Among many notable names on the credits was that of guitarist Rigo Star. He helped to forge a riveting collection of Bamana and Wassoulou music, updated through modern technological means into a melodic, dance-orientated whole.

The follow-up albums *Mangoni* (1993) and *Yankaw* (1997) saw Doumbia consolidating the reputation established by *Nyama Toutou*, building the bridges that led to the crossover success of *Yaala*. Released in 2000, the input of French producer **Claude Barthélémy** helped Doumbia and her band create a near perfect update of traditional Wassoulou music. During the same period, Doumbia appeared on **Frederic Galliano**'s acclaimed *Frikyiwa Collection 1*.

● ALBUMS: *Didadi* (Syllart 1988) ★★★, *Nyama Toutou* (Syllart/Stern's 1990) ★★★★, *Mangoni* (Syllart/Stern's 1993) ★★★, *Yankaw* (Cobalt 1997) ★★★, *Bougouni* (Sono 1999) ★★★, *Yaala* (Cobalt 2000) ★★★★, *Diby* (Cobalt 2004) ★★★.

Dove, Ronnie

b. 9 September 1940, Herndon, Virginia, USA. Dove intended to follow his father and be a policeman, but he somehow was sidetracked. Between 1964 and 1966, after first singing in a rock group at high school, he was a very successful pop singer. Recording for Diamond, he had six Top 20 hits out of the 11 songs that he charted. They included 'Cry' and 'Right Or Wrong'. In the early 70s, recording for **Decca Records**, he gained two Top 70 country chart hits 'Kiss The Hurt Away' and 'Lilacs In Winter'. A 1973 MCA album was described by a noted UK reviewer 'as very average, unoriginal, string sodden and a boring example of the Nashville conveyor belt at its worst'. In 1975 he recorded for Melodyland, the country subsidiary of **Motown Records**, gaining a Top 25 with his version of **Bobby Darin**'s 1962 hit 'Things'. The label soon folded and he returned to Diamond but gained no further chart success until 1987 when he had Top 80 hits with 'Heart' and 'Rise And Shine'. He was noted for his work for charities, including the mentally handicapped. Since the late 80s his name has been absent from either pop or country charts.

● ALBUMS: *One Kiss For Old Times' Sake* (Diamond 1965) ★★★, *Ronnie Dove Sings The Hits For You* (Diamond 1966) ★★★, *Cry* (Diamond 1967) ★★★, *Ronnie Dove* (MCA 1973) ★★, *Golden Classic* (Collectable 1994) ★★★, *The Love Album* (Collectables 2002) ★★★.

● COMPILATIONS: *The Collection Part 1* (Collectables 1996) ★★★, *The Collection Part 2* (Collectables 1996) ★★★, *The Collection Part 3* (Collectables 1996) ★★★, *For Collectors Only* box set (Collectables 1996) ★★★, *Best Of Ronnie Dove* (Stardust 1996) ★★★, *Rarities* (Collectables 1998) ★★★.

Dovells

Originally called the Brooktones, this Philadelphia-based R&B vocal group comprised **Len Barry** (b. Leonard Borisoff, 6 December 1942, Philadelphia, Pennsylvania, USA), Jerry Summers (b. Jerry Gross), Mike Dennis (b. Michael Freda) and Danny Brooks (b. Jim Meeley). Signed to **Parkway Records**, the group had a US number 2 hit in 1961 with 'Bristol Stomp', succeeded the following year by the Top 40 hits 'Do The Continental', 'Bristol Twistin' Annie' and 'Hully Gully Baby', all of which became dance favourites of the era. Len Barry was responsible for introducing their contemporaneous friends the **Orlons** to **Cameo Records**, and after the departure of Brooks in 1962 the Dovells achieved another major US hit with a cover of the **Phil Upchurch** Combo hit 'You Can't Sit Down'. Barry departed from the group later that year and they continued as a trio. The Dovells recorded for **MGM Records** in the late 60s under the name of the Magistrates but met with little success.

● ALBUMS: *The Bristol Stomp* (Parkway 1961) ★★★, *All The Hits Of The Teen Groups* (Parkway 1962) ★★★, *Don't Knock The Twist* film soundtrack (Parkway 1962) ★★, *For Your Hully Gully Party* (Parkway 1963) ★★, *You Can't Sit Down* (Parkway 1963) ★★★, with Len Barry *Len Barry Sings With The Dovells* (Cameo 1964) ★★★, *Discotheque* (Wyncote 1965) ★★.

● COMPILATIONS: *The Dovells' Biggest Hits* (Parkway 1965) ★★★, *Cameo/Parkway Sessions* (London 1979) ★★★, *All Their Hits And Much More* (Campary 1996) ★★★.

● FILMS: *Don't Knock The Twist* (1962).

Doves

The first great indie rock guitar album of the twenty-first century was created by a trio of Manchester, England–based musicians who, almost a decade earlier, had been synonymous with the city's then vibrant club culture. Doves

original incarnation **Sub Sub** had been conceived when a trio of former school friends became re-acquainted on the dancefloor of Manchester's **Haçienda** club. Jimi Goodwin (b. 28 May 1970, England; bass/vocals), Jez Williams (b. 18 February 1970, England; guitar/vocals) and twin Andy Williams (b. 18 February 1970, England; drums) began recording as Sub Sub. By autumn 1993, their strident **house** track 'Ain't No Love (Ain't No Use)' was omnipresent in clubs and on the radio, but when fire destroyed everything they owned, Sub Sub ceased to exist. Remarkably, the band now describe this blaze as 'a good cut-off point. It kept things interesting.'

Re-inventing themselves as Doves, eschewing the sequencers and samplers that they had previously utilized and name-checking Mark Hollis of **Talk Talk**, **Scott Walker**, **Morrissey** and **Terry Hall** as reference points, the trio ensconced themselves in a studio in north Manchester to record their inaugural *Cedar* EP and their 2000 debut album. Described by guitarist **Johnny Marr** as 'a vast 3am melancholic beauty brought to life', *Lost Souls* was saturated with beauty, intimacy and poignancy. Proof that the band was no fluke came in the shape of the glorious *The Last Broadcast* in 2002, which gave freer rein to the trio's pop instincts, most notably on the sublime single 'There Goes The Fear'.

The commercial momentum gaining force behind the Doves heightened awareness for their third album, which was completed at the end of 2004 and released at the start of the following year. Premiered by the soul-influenced single 'Black And White Town', *Some Cities* duly sped the Doves to the top of the UK charts for the first time in their career.

● ALBUMS: *Lost Souls* (Heavenly 2000) ★★★★★, *The Last Broadcast* (Heavenly 2002) ★★★★, *Some Cities* (Heavenly/Capitol 2005) ★★★★.

● COMPILATIONS: *Lost Sides* (Heavenly 2003) ★★★.

● DVD/VIDEOS: *Where We're Calling From* (Heavenly 2002).

Dowd, Johnny

b. 29 March 1948, Fort Worth, Texas, USA, but grew up in Pauls Valley, Oklahoma. Dowd's earnest, sombre take on alternative country—a category he detests—has earned comparisons to **Jimmie Rodgers** and **Townes Van Zandt**. Certainly he has little time for Nashville's glossier stars: 'There's not much country in what they call country now. Country music was people who lived in the country. They had a cow. These guys ain't even seen a cow.' Dowd's work, by contrast, is shot through with the kind of desperate loneliness and fatalism that distinguished **Johnny Cash**'s records. His lyrics are often accompanied by a sense of black humour that recalls **Nick Cave**.

Dowd grew up on a diet of blues records, admitting that at one stage he refused to listen to anything recorded after 1950. Indeed, he maintains he is a professional music fan first and an amateur musician second. He joined the army as a teenager and did not pick up an instrument until he was 30. It took him another 20 years before he released a record, during which time he concentrated on his furniture removal business, the Zolar Moving Co. At that point he put a band together in New York comprising his business partner and members of his extended family. His 1998 debut album, recorded in his spare room, was described by *Billboard* magazine as 'a homemade work of genius'. It was quickly followed by a second helping, *Pictures From Life's Other Side*, which fleshed out Dowd's acoustic guitar with a full band featuring regular collaborators Kim Sherwood-Caso (vocals), Brian Wilson (drums) and Justin Asher (keyboards).

Dedicated to his parents, the artist's third set *Temporary Shelter* was bleak and introspective even by his own standards. Regarded by critics as his 'pop' album, 2002's *The Pawnbroker's Wife* was hardly easy listening but hinted at a greater accessibility on the opening 'I Love You' and an unusual take on the classic 'Jingle Bells'. A selection of archived material recorded at the same sessions that birthed Dowd's debut was released the following year.

● ALBUMS: *Wrong Side Of Memphis* (Checkered Past 1998) ★★★★, *Pictures From Life's Other Side* (Koch 1999) ★★★★, *Temporary Shelter* (Munich 2000) ★★★, *The Pawnbroker's Wife* (Munich 2002) ★★★★, *Wire Flowers: More Songs From The Wrong Side Of Memphis* (Munich 2003) ★★★, *Cemetery Shoes* (Munich 2004) ★★★, *Cruel Words* (Munich 2006) ★★★.

Dowd, Tom

b. 1 January 1925, New York City, New York, USA, d. 27 October 2002, Aventura, Florida, USA. This much-respected engineer/producer began his career in 1947 at New York's Ampex Studio. Here he became acquainted with **Ahmet Ertegun**, co-founder of **Atlantic Records**, who invited Dowd, then still a teenager, to join the label. His early sessions included releases by **Joe Turner**, **Ray Charles** and **Ruth Brown**, to whom he brought a clarity hitherto unheard in R&B recordings. Always striving for new techniques, Dowd engineered the first stereo album, by the Wilbur De Paris Dixieland Band, which required customized equipment, including two needles, to play it. He is credited with introducing the first eight-track recording machine into a major studio in 1957. His collaborations with producers **Leiber And Stoller** brought commercial success to the **Coasters** and **Drifters**, while in the 60s Dowd engineered Atlantic's sessions at the **Stax Records** and Fame studios. His first work with **Otis Redding**, *Otis Blue*, is generally regarded as the singer's finest album and was responsible for taking the artist into the pop market. Dowd also enjoyed commercially fruitful recordings with the **(Young) Rascals**, **Dusty Springfield** and **Aretha Franklin** and later helped create the label's custom-built studio, Criteria, in Miami.

Dowd later became a fully-fledged producer and during the 70s left the Atlantic staff to pursue freelance work, notably with **Eric Clapton** on *461 Ocean Boulevard* (1974), *E.C. Was Here* and *There's One In Every Crowd* (both 1975); the **Allman Brothers** on *Live At Fillmore East* (1971) and **Rod Stewart** on *Atlantic Crossing* (1975) and *A Night On The Town* (1976). He was honoured with a National Academy of Recording Arts and Sciences Lifetime Achievement Award shortly before his death in October 2002.

● DVD/VIDEOS: *Tom Dowd & The Language Of Music* (WEA 2004).

Dowell, Joe

b. 23 January 1940, Bloomington, Indiana, USA. Pop singer-songwriter Dowell bought a $10 guitar and wrote his first song 'Tell Me' when he was 13 years old. In later years he took part in talent contests and just before his 21st birthday decided to try his luck in Nashville. He signed to Smash Records, and a version of 'Wooden Heart' (Muss I

Denn)—using bass guitar and organ instead of tuba and accordion—reached number 1 in the US charts in August 1961. The main reason for this was that **Elvis Presley**'s original was only available in Europe. After two other US hits, Joe went into advertising and had his own radio show in Illinois.

Dowlands

b. Bournemouth, England. David and Keith Dowland were late 50s **Everly Brothers** imitators. With a backing group that included guitarist Roy Phillips (b. 5 May 1943, Parkstone, Poole, Dorset, England; later of the **Peddlers**) and ex-Lonely One drummer Chris Warman, the duo were enormously successful locally. In 1962 their debut single 'Little Sue', produced by **Joe Meek**, was issued on Oriole. Later Meek recordings included 'Big Big Fella', 'Break Ups' and a 1963 arrangement of **Johnny Cash**'s 'I Walk The Line', but it was only when Meek began spicing his creations with Merseybeat that the group made chart headway. While 'Wishin' And Hopin'' and 'Don't Make Me Over' were vanquished by the **Merseybeats**' and **Swinging Blue Jeans**' respective versions, the brothers' hasty and disinclined **Beatles** cover 'All My Loving' spent seven weeks in the UK Top 50 in early 1964. They appeared on several British package tours but, via Meek's emotional disintegration and interrelated long gaps between releases, the Dowlands' decline was inevitable. Though David was still performing semi-professionally in the 80s, the two had effectively retired during 1966.

Dowling, Eddie

b. Joseph Nelson Goucher, 11 December 1895, Woonsocket, Rhode Island, USA, d. 18 February 1976, Smithfield, Rhode Island, USA. Dowling's Broadway career began as a performer and he appeared in musicals such as *The Velvet Lady* (1919) and *Ziegfeld Follies* Of 1919. He married Ray Dooley (b. Rachel Rice Dooley, 30 October 1896, Glasgow, Scotland, d. 28 January 1984, East Hampton, New York, USA) when both were in their teens. She appeared in *Ziegfeld Follies Of 1919* and also in editions of the show in 1920 and 1921. Also, she appeared in some of her husband's shows. In the 20s Dowling was in *Sally, Irene And Mary* (1922, revived 1925), for which he also wrote the book, and was a replacement cast member in **Eddie Cantor**'s long-running starring vehicle *Kid Boots*, which had opened in December 1923. He was in *Tell Me More* (1925), then wrote the book, music and lyrics for both *Honeymoon Lane* and *Sidewalks Of New York* (both 1927); his wife appeared in the latter.

From the late 20s, Dowling was more often a producer, mostly of non-musicals, such as *Stepping Out* (1929) and *Big Hearted Herbert* (1934), but also the occasional musical, such as *Thumbs Up* (1934), in which both he and his wife appeared. It was back to drama for the late 30s, including Shakespeare, *Shadow And Substance*, *Here Come The Clowns* (1938) and *The Time Of Your Life* (1939), in both of which he also appeared. He directed the revue *Sons O' Fun* (1941) and produced and/or directed other dramas, including Tennessee Williams' *The Glass Menagerie* (1945), in which he also performed, and Eugene O'Neill's *The Iceman Cometh* (1946). He supervised production of the musical *Heaven On Earth*, a one-week flop in 1948, then joined the cast of **Paint Your Wagon** during its long run that had begun on 12 November 1951. One of his last Broadway productions, which he also directed, was *The Righteous Are Bold* (1955).

Down

A US heavy metal 'supergroup', Down was formed in the early 90s by Phil Anselmo (b. 30 June 1968, New Orleans, Louisiana, USA; vocals, **Pantera**), Pepper Keenan (guitar, **Corrosion Of Conformity**), Kirk Windstein (guitar, **Crowbar**), Todd Strange (bass, Crowbar) and Jimmy Bowers (drums, Crowbar). By the time they released their self-produced debut in 1995, the members had been playing together for four years. Two demos recorded during this time were regularly traded on the underground networks. Forgoing the predicted thrash metal and hardcore influences, *Nola* ventured instead for a 70s rock 'n' roll sound on songs such as 'Lifer' and 'Stone The Crow'. Anselmo's Pantera bandmate Rex Brown replaced Strange on the belated follow-up, *II: A Bustle In Your Hedgerow*, released in March 2002.

● ALBUMS: *Nola* (Elektra 1995) ★★★, *II: A Bustle In Your Hedgerow* (Elektra 2002) ★★★.

Down Argentine Way

Don Ameche and **Betty Grable** were the headliners in this 1940 20th Century-Fox musical, but, as the opening titles gave way to the action, the first impression was made by Brazilian bombshell **Carmen Miranda** who began her American film debut with a dynamic interpretation of **Jimmy McHugh** and **Al Dubin**'s 'South American Way'—or as she insisted on singing it, 'Souse American Way'. Miranda was also involved in two other numbers, which was rather fortunate because there was not a lot to the plot. It concerned a Buenos Aires horse breeder, played by Don Ameche, who is prevented from selling one of his prized specimens to wealthy New Yorker Glenda Crawford (Betty Grable) because she is the daughter of his father's worst enemy. This is an obstacle that true romance eventually surmounts, and the two lovers, Ameche and Gable—and their respective families—settle their differences with the help of some agreeable locations and an attractive bunch of songs, most of which were written by **Harry Warren** and **Mack Gordon**. These included a lovely ballad, 'Two Dreams Met', along with 'Sing To Your Senorita', 'Nenita' and 'Down Argentina Way' which is sung by practically everyone in the film including the **Nicholas Brothers**, who use it as the setting for one of their scintillating acrobatic dance routines. The other songs were 'Mama Yo Quiero' (Jaraca and Vincente Paiva) and 'Doin' The Conga' (Gene Rose). Also in the cast were J. Carroll Naish, Henry Stephenson, Katharine Aldridge, Leonid Kinskey, Chris-Pin Martin and the ubiquitous **Charlotte Greenwood**, whose wisecracking and high kicking was a joy, as ever. Darrell Ware and Karl Tunberg's screenplay was based on a story by Rian James and Ralph Spencer, and the bright and attractive dances were staged by Nick Castle and Geneva Sawyer. Irving Cummings was the director, and this diverting and tuneful film was photographed in Technicolor.

Down By Law

This Los Angeles, California, USA, hardcore rock band were formed in the early 90s by veteran singer Dave Smalley, formerly of DYS, **Dag Nasty** and **All**. An ever-changing list of compatriots, who by the mid-90s included Tampa Bay, Florida native Sam Williams (guitar, ex-Balance; Slap Of Reality), Angry John DiMambro (bass, ex–Clay Idols; Leonards) and Danny Westman (drums, ex-Florecene; Spindle), all boasted a similar level of achievement and experience. The band's debut album featuring Smalley, Chris

Bagarozzi (guitar), Ed Urlik (bass) and Dave Nazworthy (drums), illustrated their style and outlook—uncompromising rock 'n' roll delivered with pace and a high degree of musical dexterity. It saw them signed to the influential **Epitaph Records** label. Though subsequent albums revealed steadily more complex arrangements, Down By Law's work remains thoroughly consistent with the hardcore style. *All Scratched Up!* was introduced by the typically urgent 'Independence Day', the band demonstrating its commitment to vinyl purchasers by providing them with a full side of bonus tracks unavailable on the CD. However, the simplistic nature of too many of the songs argued against the possibility of Down By Law repeating the international success of labelmates such as **Rancid** or **Offspring**. They had returned to independent label status by the time of 1999's rousing *Fly The Flag*, which featured Smalley, Williams, Keith Davies (bass) and Milo Todesco (drums). The same line-up recorded 2003's belated follow-up, *Windwardtide-sandwaywardsails*.

● ALBUMS: *Down By Law* (Epitaph 1991) ★★★, *Blue* (Epitaph 1992) ★★★, *Punkrockacademyflightsong* (Epitaph 1994) ★★★★, *All Scratched Up!* (Epitaph 1996) ★★★, *Last Of The Sharpshooters* (Epitaph 1997) ★★★, *Fly The Flag* (Go-Kart 1999) ★★★★, *Windwardtidesandwaywardsails* (Union 2003) ★★★.

● COMPILATIONS: *Punkrockdays: The Best Of DBL* (Epitaph 2002) ★★★★.

Down River Nation

Down River Nation, who comprise Shaun Atkins (vocals), Gizz Butt (guitar), Shop (bass) and Pinch (drums), were formed in Peterborough, Cambridgeshire, England, in 1994. Although they were welcomed in the pages of heavy metal magazines, there was more than a hint of third-generation UK punk rock in their fiery songwriting. This was perhaps unsurprising, as two band members had formerly been in English Dogs, who specialized in a similar brand of molten thrash. However, Down River Nation added a surly brand of funk and dance rhythms, clearly influenced by **Urban Dance Squad**. Atkins' vocals were also compared to those of Layne Staley of **Alice In Chains**. The group made their debut in 1995 with a seven-track demo, *Subworld Disciples*, before setting out on tour with **Blaggers ITA**.

Down South

Richmond, Virginia–based rappers Shawn J-Period and Soda Pop (ably assisted by DJ Myorr) combined a winning mix of jazz, funk, reggae, bluegrass and salsa on their debut recordings for **Atlantic**. The smooth, lolling rhythms proved intriguing but too insubstantial in their own right to convey the mix of reality/party themes, despite production expertise from the **Beatnuts**, T-Ray and others. However, the promotional single, 'Southern Comfort', with a guest vocal by label mates **Jomanda**, was strong. Rather than being dedicated to the alcoholic drink, it was addressed to their former locale, the trio having shipped over to New York. Down South had formed in 1990 when Pop and J-Period, who are first cousins, met Myorr at high school. Myorr had formerly worked in a lowly position at **Def Jam**, and it was his connections that led to them signing with Atlantic.

● ALBUMS: *Lost In Brooklyn* (Big Beat/Atlantic 1994) ★★★.

Downchild Blues Band

Formed in Toronto, Canada, the Downchild Blues Band is surpassed only by **Rush** in terms of name recognition within that city's musical firmament—and the Downchild Blues Band can boast of even greater longevity. Led by former pig farmer Donnie Walsh (harp, guitar), the group adopted their name from **Sonny Boy Williamson**'s recording 'Mr Downchild' when they formed in June 1969. The original participants were Donnie Walsh on guitar, brother Rick Walsh on vocals and Jim Mine on bass. Their inspiration came from seeing **Muddy Waters** play live on stage. Their first sets were 'pass-the-hat' affairs at the Grossman Tavern on Spadina Avenue in Toronto. The membership has remained fluid, with the roll-call of frontmen including Tony Flaim, John Witner and current incumbent Chuck Jackson. The present line-up also includes Mike Fonfara (keyboards), Jim Casson (drums), Gary Kendall (bass) and Pat Carey (saxophone). Estimates at the actual number of musicians involved in the band over its long existence extend to about 130. Since their inception the band has appeared at between 100 and 150 dates a year, supporting blues greats including Muddy Waters, **Buddy Guy**, **B.B. King**, **John Lee Hooker** and **Howlin' Wolf**. Their first US date, coincidentally, came in 1974 as support to Rush at Cleveland's Agora Ballroom. The group celebrated its 25th anniversary in 1994 with a 10-date return to Grossman's Tavern, with those in attendance including **Daniel Lanois** (who produced some of their 80s albums) and actor Dan Aykroyd (a long-time fan). In fact, because of this connection, two Walsh songs, 'I Have Everything I Need—Almost' and 'Shot Gun Blues', appeared on the **Blues Brothers**' 1978 number 1 album, *Briefcase Full Of Blues*.

● ALBUMS: *Bootleg* (Special 1971) ★★★, *Straight Up* (GRT 1973) ★★, *Dancing* (GRT 1974) ★★★, *Ready To Go* (GRT 1976) ★★, *We Deliver* (Attic 1980) ★★★★, *Road Fever* (Attic 1980) ★★, *Blood Run Hot* (Attic 1981) ★★★, *But I'm On The Guest List* (Attic 1982) ★★★, *It's Been So Long* (Stony Plain 1987) ★★★, *Good Time Guaranteed* (Downchild Music 1994) ★★★, *Lucky 13* (Downchild Music 1997) ★★★, *Come On In* (Downchild Music 2005) ★★.

Downes, Bob

b. Robert George Downes, 22 July 1937, Plymouth, Devon, England. It was not until he was in his late teens that Downes began to teach himself to play the saxophone. Some years later, he switched mainly to flute but also became proficient on several reed and woodwind instruments. At the end of the 60s he was briefly with **Mike Westbrook** and in the following decade he also played with the **London Jazz Composers Orchestra** and frequently led his own groups. These bands included Open Music, the Alternative Medicine Quartet and, some years later, the Flute Orchestra. With these bands, Downes played a wide range of music, including rock and free jazz, classical and ethnic. During these same decades, the 70s and 80s, he extended his reputation as a flautist of distinction, working in England and Germany. Downes has composed a great deal of music in the jazz and classical genres, including in the latter orchestral suites and music for contemporary ballet.

● ALBUMS: *Electric City* (Vertigo 1970) ★★★, *Deep Down Heavy* (Music For Pleasure 1970) ★★★, *Open Music* (Philips 1970) ★★★, *Diversions* (Ophenian 1973) ★★★, *Episodes At 4 A.M.* (Ophenian 1974) ★★★, *Hells Angels* (Ophenian 1975) ★★★.

Downing, Big Al

b. 9 January 1940, Lenapah, Oklahoma, USA, d. 4 July 2005, Leicester, Massachusetts, USA. Downing was exposed to both R&B and country music as a boy and taught himself piano on an instrument that he found in a rubbish dump. In 1958 he took the then unusual step of joining a white group, the Rhythm Rockers, led by Bobby Brant. Changing their name to the Poe-Kats, they recorded the regionally successful 'Down On The Farm' for Lelan Rogers' White Rock label in Dallas. Leased to the larger Challenge label, it narrowly missed the national charts but has become an acknowledged rock 'n' roll classic (as well as one of the shortest rock 'n' roll records, at one minute 31 seconds). Later sessions up to 1964 featured Downing's thumping piano and his deep voice, with its **Fats Domino** overtones, on such excellent rockers as 'Yes, I'm Loving You' and 'Georgia Slop'. During this period he recorded duets with **Esther Phillips** and played piano for **Wanda Jackson**, but he had to wait until 1970 for chart success when 'I'll Be Holding On' was a soul hit. The versatile Downing later reverted to his early roots and enjoyed several big US country hits between 1978 and 1989, including the Top 20 singles 'Mr. Jones', 'Touch Me (I'll Be Your Fool Once More)' and 'Bring It On Home'. He was a frequent visitor to rock 'n' roll festivals in Europe, where his broad grin and matching waistline became familiar sights. Downing died in July 2005 after suffering complications from leukaemia.

● ALBUMS: *One Of A Kind* (Hayden's Ferry 2003) ★★★.

● COMPILATIONS: *Big Al Downing And His Friends* (Collector 1971) ★★★, *Big Al Downing* (Team 1982) ★★★, *Big Al Downing And The Poe-Kats* (Jumble 1987) ★★★, *Rockin' 'N' Rollin' With Big Al Downing* (Rollercoaster 1988) ★★★★, *Back To My Roots* (Orchard 1994) ★★★★, *Rockin' Down On The Farm* (Eagle 1994) ★★★, *Rockin' Down On The Farm, Vol. 2* (Eagle 1998) ★★★, *Greatest Hits Volume #1* (Orchard 2003) ★★★.

Downing, Will

b. New York, USA. Downing was an in-demand session singer during the late 70s, appearing on recordings by artists including **Rose Royce**, **Billy Ocean**, **Jennifer Holliday** and **Nona Hendryx**. The soul singer's career was really launched when he met producer/performer **Arthur Baker** in the mid-80s. This led to him joining Baker's group Wally Jump Jnr. And The Criminal Element, whose other members included Brooklyn-bred Wally Jump, Craig Derry (ex-**Moments**; **Sugarhill Gang**), Donny Calvin and Dwight Hawkes (both ex–Rockers Revenge), Rick Sher (ex-**Warp 9**), Jeff Smith and the toasting pair **Michigan And Smiley**. After a spell with Wally Jump Jnr. recording for Baker's Criminal Records label, Downing secured a solo contract with **Island Records** and recorded his debut album in 1988 with Baker producing. The first release under Downing's own name was 'A Love Supreme', which set lyrics to one of **John Coltrane**'s most famous compositions. The single reached number 1 in the UK, while his first album, produced by Baker, was a Top 20 hit. He had further hits with 'In My Dreams' and a remake of the **Roberta Flack** and **Donny Hathaway** duet 'Where Is The Love', on which he partnered **Mica Paris**. Downing himself produced the second album, co-writing tracks with Brian Jackson, **Gil Scott-Heron**'s collaborator. Neither this nor *A Dream Fulfilled*, on which Barry J. Eastmond and Wayne Braithwaite co-produced, was able to approach the popularity of his debut. *Moods* and *Invitation Only* put Downing firmly in the smooth late-night music category, and although his exquisite vocals were suitably melancholic on both albums, they came uncomfortably close to sounding merely lethargic.

● ALBUMS: *Will Downing* (4th & Broadway 1988) ★★★★, *Come Together As One* (4th & Broadway 1989) ★★★, *A Dream Fulfilled* (4th & Broadway 1991) ★★, *Love's The Place To Be* (4th & Broadway 1993) ★★, *Moods* (4th & Broadway 1995) ★★★, *Invitation Only* (Mercury 1997) ★★★, with Gerald Albright *Pleasures Of The Night* (Verve 1998) ★★★, *All The Man You Need* (Motown 2000) ★★★, *Sensual Journey* (GRP 2002) ★★★, *Emotions* (Verve 2003) ★★★, *Christmas: Love And You* (GRP 2004) ★★.

Downliners Sect

Formed in 1962, this enduring UK act was initially known as the Downliners, but the original line-up fell apart following a brief tour of US air bases. Founder members Don Craine (b. Michael O'Donnel; vocals/rhythm guitar) and Johnny Sutton (drums) then reshaped the group around Keith Grant (b. Keith Evans; bass) and Terry Gibson (b. Terry Clemson; lead guitar) and, having added the 'Sect' suffix, the quartet secured a residency at London's Studio 51 club. A privately pressed EP, *A Nite In Great Newport Street*, captured their brash interpretation of Chicago R&B and was a contributory factor to a subsequent recording contract with **EMI Records**. A version of **Jimmy Reed**'s 'Baby What's Wrong' became the group's first single in June 1964, by which time Ray Sone (harmonica) had been added to the line-up. The Sect's brazen musical approach, redolent of the contemporaneous **Pretty Things**, was showcased on their debut album, but not only did its irreverence anger purists, Craine's ever present deerstalker hat and autoharp also did little to attract a younger, more fashion-conscious audience. The group, however, seemed unmoved by such considerations and in 1965 further confused any prospective audience with *The Country Sect*, an album of folk and country material, and *The Sect Sing Sick Songs* EP, which included the ghoulish 'I Want My Baby Back' and 'Leader Of The Sect', a riposte to the **Shangri-Las**' death-disc 'Leader Of The Pack'. Sone left the group prior to recording *The Rock Sect's In*, which neatly combined almost all of the group's diverse styles. It is now notable for the inclusion of 'Why Don't You Smile Now', which was part-composed by **Lou Reed** and **John Cale** prior to their founding the **Velvet Underground**. The Sect, however, were still struggling to find commercial success and the line-up disintegrated when two pop-orientated singles, 'Glendora' and the **Graham Gouldman**–penned 'Cost Of Living', failed to chart. Gibson and Sutton were replaced, respectively, by Bob Taylor and Kevin Flanagan, while pianist Matthew Fisher, later of **Procol Harum**, was also briefly a member. Craine abandoned his creation following the release of 'I Can't Get Away From You', after which Grant and the prodigal Sutton took the group to Sweden, where they recorded a handful of tracks before disbanding altogether. Craine and Grant revived Sect in 1976 with ex–**Black Cat Bones** singer Paul Tiller and Paul Holm (drums) joining in 1977, in the wake of the pub rock/R&B phenomenon, and the resultant *Showbiz* invoked the gutsy styles of **Dr. Feelgood** or **Count Bishops**. With further line-up changes (Holm had now departed) they continued throughout the 80s and 90s, and they are also an integral part of the British Invasion All-Stars with former

members of the **Yardbirds**, **Creation** and **Nashville Teens**. Various members teamed up with **Billy Childish** and **Thee Headcoats** to record as Thee Headcoats Sect. However, it is their 60s recordings which afford the Downliners Sect their cult-based appeal, although they continue to pack out small blues clubs with tried and tested versions of 'Got My Mojo Workin'' and 'Route 66'.

● ALBUMS: *The Sect* (Columbia 1964) ★★★, *The Country Sect* (Columbia 1965) ★★, *The Rock Sect's In* (Columbia 1966) ★★, *Showbiz* (Raw 1979) ★★★, *Sect Appeal* (Indigo 2000) ★★.

● COMPILATIONS: *I Want My Baby Back* (Charly 1978) ★★★, *Be A Sect Maniac* (Out Line 1983) ★★, *Savage Return* (1991) ★★, *The Definitive Downliners Sect—Singles A's & B's* (See For Miles 1994) ★★★, *Sectuality* (Charly 2004) ★★★.

Downs, Jason

b. 8 September 1973, Columbia, Maryland, USA. Country and folk merged with rap is not a common union of popular musical styles, but it is a fitting description for the music that singer-songwriter and actor Jason Downs specializes in. Downs (who is part Cherokee Indian) got his start in showbusiness as an actor, working in both local theatre and television at an early age. Shortly after entering his teens, he travelled to New York to do some television commercials (including spots for Sega Video Games and Shield Soap) as well as appearances in movies including John Waters' *Hairspray* and Whoopi Goldberg's *Clara's Heart*.

By the age of 17, Downs' main focus had shifted from acting to music, as he began writing his own original compositions, equally influenced by the **Beatles**, the **Everly Brothers**, **Dusty Springfield**, **Dwight Yoakam** and the **Beastie Boys**. His music career had to take a back seat to education, as he enrolled at Pepperdine University in Malibu, California, soon afterwards, and this was followed by his marriage to his long-time sweetheart. He relocated to Arkansas to live with relatives, but the marriage crumbled after only a few months, forcing Downs to move once again. This time he returned to New York City, where he attended NYU (and graduated with a BFA in drama).

Making ends meet during this period by working as a caretaker for an apartment complex, Downs struck up a friendship with **Lauryn Hill**'s manager, who also lived there. On the strength of a demo, Downs was soon put in contact with producer Mark Passy (best known for his work with **MC Lyte** and **Audio Two**). Downs began working with former Audio Two member Milk Dee, resulting in tracks that merged country and urban sounds together. A solo recording contract with **Jive Records** ensued in the early twenty-first century, which was followed by the release of Downs' debut, *White Boy With A Feather* (early working title, *Between A And B*), in late 2001. Despite spawning three singles, 'White Boy With A Feather', 'Cats In The Cradle' and 'Cherokee', the album failed to ignite the charts.

● ALBUMS: *White Boy With A Feather* (Jive 2001) ★★★.
● FILMS: *Hairspray* (1988), *Clara's Heart* (1988), *Winning Girls Through Psychic Mind Control* (2002), *Come Lovely* (2003).

Downs, Johnny

b. John Morey Downs, 10 October 1913, New York City, New York, USA, d. 6 June 1994, Coronado, California, USA. An old-styled song and dance man, Downs' contributions to the screen as a dancer and singer may not have stolen the headlines, but in their entirety they added up to a worthy body of work. The son of a navy lieutenant, Downs' family relocated to San Diego when he was eight. Encouraged by his mother to attend film auditions, he made his debut in a silent comedy alongside Charley Chase before beginning a sequence of *Our Gang* silent movies for Hal Roach. His first grounding in stage work came on the east coast, however, opposite **Jimmy Durante** in *Strike Me Pink*. Back with Roach, he took a small role in the Laurel And Hardy production of the stage musical hit, **Babes In Toyland**. His subsequent musical films of the 30s (often dubbed teen operas or college musicals) included *College Scandal* (1935—remade as *Sweater Girl* in 1942), *College Holiday*, *Pigskin Parade* (both 1936), *Turn Off The Moon* (1937) and *Hold That Co-Ed* (1938). Afterwards he switched to Universal for a further series of low-budget musical films. These began with *Swing, Sister, Swing* (1939, which saw him sing 'The Baltimore Rumble', an intended US answer to 'The Lambeth Walk'), then *Hawaiian Nights* (1939). *I Can't Give You Anything But Love, Baby* from the following year saw him sing the title-song before he moved to Republic for *Melody And Moonlight*. Another of Downs' most famous numbers, 'The Aloha Lowdown', was premiered on the cut and paste *Moonlight And Hawaii* soundtrack. The movies that Downs appeared in during the 40s included, *Mad Monster* (1942), *Harvest Melody* (1943), *Campus Rhythm*, *Trocadero* and *Twilight On The Prairie* (all 1944), **Rhapsody In Blue** (1945), *The Kid From Brooklyn* (1946) and *Square Dance Jubilee* (1949). Downs spent the early 50s in Broadway productions such as *Here Come The Girls* and *Are You With It?* He returned to Hollywood in 1953 for his last major role in *Cruisin' Down The River* before returning to his adopted San Diego home, appearing regularly on television as a host of children's programmes for nearly two decades.

Downset

These fierce and confrontational metal-rappers (usually titled downset.) from the San Fernando Valley/Sylmar area of Los Angeles, originally formed under the name Social Justice in 1986. Immersed in the 90s US independent underground scene, Rey Anthony Oropeza (b. 2 June 1970; 'Messenger'), James Morris (b. 11 April 1974; bass) and Chris Lee (b. 27 January 1975; drums) were the founder members, later joined by guitarists Rogelio 'Roy' Lozano and Brian 'Ares' Schwager (b. 12 December 1973) as they slowly evolved into downset. Typically, the band began by recording and releasing a series of singles and cassettes on a variety of labels, with 'Angel'/'Ritual' (Theologian Records) and 'Our Suffocation' (Abstract Records) being among the best known. Having established a formidable fanbase, the band inevitably attracted major label interest. By early 1993 the band had to compromise their hardcore ethics in order to reach a wider audience; adopting their current name, they opted for **Mercury Records**. In autumn 1993, they entered Silver Cloud Studios with their friend, mentor and confidant Roy Z as their producer, with the intention of recording an EP. The resultant tracks were so intensely powerful and emotionally charged that they decided to record a full album. The self-titled result was one of the most brutally heavy and intelligent albums to emerge from the Los Angeles underground, with socially aware lyrics rapped in raging hip-hop

style; their formative years in LA's violent and poverty-stricken neighbourhoods finally found full release. So impressive was their debut that they were invited to take part on a European tour with **Biohazard** and **Dog Eat Dog**, covering 42 shows in 15 countries. Unfortunately, the gruelling schedule proved too much; Lozano eventually left and the band recorded the 1996 follow-up *do we speak a dead language?* as a four-piece. Once again, the music was as uncompromising as the hip-hop, hardcore and graffiti art scenes that inspired it, mirroring their personal growth and cultivated from personal experience. By the time *Universal* was released at the end of 2004, their particular brand of rock sounded dated.

● ALBUMS: *downset.* (Mercury 1994) ★★★★, *do we speak a dead language?* (Mercury 1996) ★★★, *Check Your People* (Epitaph 2000) ★★★, *Universal* (Hawino 2004) ★★.

Downthesun

The Kansas City, USA–based nu metal outfit Downthesun features quite a few similarities to masked marauders **Slipknot**. Both bands originate from the Midwest, share the same record label, indulge in the same aggressive angst metal, and additionally, both groups are friends with each other. Bass player Lance 'Kuk' Collier and electro-specialist Church were members of a previous band that opened for Slipknot during mid-1999, which led to the duo becoming fast pals with Shawn Crahan. When the aforementioned outfit split up, Crahan suggested that Collier and Church hook up with like-minded Des Moines, Iowa, musicians such as drummer Danny Spain and vocalist Satone (the latter of whom was a former tech for Slipknot). Soon afterwards, the band was rounded out by additional members Aaron Peltz (second vocalist) and Bruce Swink (guitar), completing a line-up that Downthesun tends to refer to as 'the six'. Signed to Roadrunner Records, the sextet entered the recording studio with veteran metal producer GGGarth, with Crahan overseeing the proceedings. Downthesun's self-titled debut was issued during the autumn of 2002 as the band supported album touring alongside **Soulfly**.

● ALBUMS: *Downthesun* (Roadrunner 2002) ★★★.

Downy Mildew

This Los Angeles, California, USA, quintet comprises Jenny Homer (vocals/guitar), Charlie Baldonado (guitar/vocals), Janine Cooper (bass, ex–Pet Clark), Rob Jacobs (drums percussion) and Salvador Garze (violin). Cooper replaced original long-time bass player Nancy McCoy, who opted to devote herself to motherhood, in time for *Slow Sky*. Downy Mildew's origins can be traced to the mid-80s when renowned independent label Texas Hotel Records released their debut EP and two follow-up albums (these were later reissued on a new home, High Street Records). Recalling California's vintage 60s pop mood, with the group weaned on the sounds of the **Beach Boys** and **Mamas And The Papas**, songwriters Homer and Baldonado used these influences as a platform for their simple but affecting pop songs—often orchestrated in tandem with unexpected lyrical twists. With the duo writing both individually and collaboratively, this three-pronged approach led to considerable stylistic diversity within the band's albums, with Baldonado's enduring affection for **Burt Bacharach** (including a cover version of 'Walk On By') noted by several critics. Earlier, *Broomtree* had announced these disparate songwriting approaches, with Baldonado's writing more rooted in the folk rock tradition, contrasting with Homer's harder, up-tempo style. Comparisons to **10,000 Maniacs** were, at this stage at least, not too far wide of the mark. Another unifying factor in the band's appeal, that of accomplished musicianship and self-reliant production, was further evinced with *Mincing Steps*. A cohesive collection of songs performed in a quasi-orchestral style, it managed to balance grandeur with harmonic pop essentials. *An Oncoming Train*, Downy Mildew's acclaimed debut for High Street Records, saw them enlist the services of Mitchell Froom associate Tchad Blake, who had previously worked with **Los Lobos**, **Suzanne Vega** and **Tom Waits**. Their relationship together continued with *Slow Sky*, which refined the group's sound further. The familiar elements—lush male/female vocal interchanges overriding darker lyrical sentiments—were offered a new sheen by virtue of the group's evident self-confidence and poise.

● ALBUMS: *Broomtree* (Texas Hotel 1987) ★★★, *Mincing Steps* (Texas Hotel 1988) ★★★, *An Oncoming Train* (High Street 1992) ★★★★, *Slow Sky* (High Street 1995) ★★★.

Doyle, Charlie 'Little Buddy'

No biographical details are available for Doyle, an obscure, impoverished, blind American street blues singer who, as his name implies, was also a dwarf. He was thought to have been born in Memphis, perhaps at the turn of the twentieth century, and he recorded 10 tracks there for **Columbia Records** in July 1939, which were to be a major influence on Detroit bluesman **Baby Boy Warren**. Other Memphis-based musicians such as **Walter Horton**, **Will Shade** and **Furry Lewis** claimed to have worked with Doyle; indeed, Shade and Horton have both professed to be the harmonica player on the 1939 recordings. Informants report that Doyle probably died in early 1940 but this has never been confirmed.

Doyle, Teresa

Folk singer from Belfast, Prince Edward Island, Canada, whose repertoire is built on a strong affinity to that settlement's Celtic roots, mingling traditional songs with her own original compositions. She got her start in music in 1982 as an a cappella performer of traditional material from the Atlantic Canada region. She has subsequently gone on to appear in many folk festivals throughout her native territory and Europe. However, in the 90s such performances were confined mainly to weekends, as she concentrated on running her organic farm in partnership with her husband back in Belfast. Doyle made her recording debut in 1987 for her own Bedlam Records with *Prince Edward Isle Adieu*, which introduced her bold, slightly irreverent but always heartfelt treatment of the folk songbook. *Forerunner* took its theme from 'a symbolic event preceding a death' and actively explored the sort of amateur folklore investigated by Doyle's father in his youth. Songs such as 'Haul The Jib' concerned a ghost boat, while 'Iridescent Blue' was the colour of dress worn by the song's ghost. Recorded in Montreal, the musical cast included former Tailor's Twist members Kim Vincent on fiddle and Jon Goodman on Irish pipes. Her third album, 1993's *Stowaway*, was a collection of songs based on the experiences of the Micmac people and the early settlers. The title track derived from the story of a Scottish woman emigrating to Prince Edward Island in the early nineteenth century. Shunned by her own people, she was adopted by the local Micmacs, learning their herbal secrets until she could return to her original community as a healer. This is a fine example of the way Doyle sources her songs to written folklore, producing something quite new, rather than simply relying on folk's existing repertoire. She also spent hours of study learning Gaelic with the Rev. Gael Matheson in Caledonia so that she could sing the words to songs such as 'Eilean An Aigh (Isle Of Content)' as they were originally written. The album saw her assemble a full backing band. Produced by Oliver Schroer, who also assisted on vocals, the line-up featured the expert penny whistle and flute of Northern Ireland's Loretto Red-Tahney, guitarist Ray Montford, bass player David Woodhead (of **Stan Rogers** fame), drummer Rich Grenspon, harmonica player Carlos Del Junco, trumpet player David Travers-Smith and Keith Murphy on keyboards and accordion. Doyle also completed a tour of Japan, culminating in a performance at the Canadian Embassy in Tokyo.

● ALBUMS: *Prince Edward Isle Adieu* (Bedlam 1987) ★★★, *Forerunner* (Bedlam 1990) ★★★★, *Stowaway* (Bedlam 1993) ★★★.

Dozier, Lamont

b. 16 June 1941, Detroit, Michigan, USA. Schooled in the blossoming vocal group scene of the late 50s, Lamont Dozier sang alongside several **Motown Records** notables in the Romeos and the Voice Masters during 1957–58. He befriended local songwriter and producer **Berry Gordy** around this time and was one of Gordy's first signings when he launched the Motown label at the end of the decade. Dozier issued his debut single, 'Let's Talk It Over', under the pseudonym Lamont Anthony in 1960 and issued two further singles in the early 60s. In 1963 he recorded a one-off release with Motown songwriter **Eddie Holland** and was soon persuaded into a writing and production team with Eddie and his brother **Brian Holland**. The **Holland/Dozier/Holland** credit graced the majority of Motown's hit records for the next five years, as the trio struck up particularly successful working relationships with the **Supremes** and the **Four Tops**. Dozier contributed both lyrics and music to the partnership's creations, proving the initial impetus for hits such as 'Stop! In The Name Of Love' by the Supremes, 'Bernadette' by the Four Tops and 'Jimmy Mack' by **Martha And The Vandellas**. As a pianist, arranger and producer, Dozier was also prominent in the studio, supporting the central role of Brian Holland in the recording process.

Dozier and the Hollands left Motown in 1968, unhappy at the financial and artistic restrictions imposed by Gordy. The following year, they set up their own rival companies, Invictus and Hot Wax Records, who produced hits for artists such as **Freda Payne** and the **Chairmen Of The Board**. Dozier resumed his own recording career in 1972, registering a US hit with 'Why Can't We Be Lovers' in partnership with Brian Holland. The Holland/Dozier/Holland partnership was fragmenting, however, and in 1973 Dozier severed his ties with Invictus and signed to **ABC Records**. *Out Here On My Own* and *Black Bach* demonstrated the creative liberation Dozier felt outside the constraints of the HDH team, and he enjoyed major US hits in 1974 with 'Trying To Hold Onto My Woman', the anti-Nixon diatribe 'Fish Ain't Bitin'' and 'Let Me Start Tonite'. Dozier switched labels to **Warner Brothers Records** in 1976, issuing the highly regarded *Peddlin' Music On The Side* the following year. That album included the classic 'Going Back To My Roots', an avowal of black pride that became a big hit in the hands of **Odyssey** in the early 80s. Dozier also continued his production work, overseeing **Aretha Franklin**'s *Sweet Passion* in 1977 plus recordings by Zingara and **Al Wilson**.

In the late 70s and early 80s, Dozier's brand of soul music lost ground to the burgeoning disco scene. After several overlooked albums on Warners and A&M, he re-emerged in 1983 on his own Megaphone label, recording the muscular *Bigger Than Life* and paying tribute to his own heritage with a remarkable 18-minute hits medley 'The Motor City Scene'. He subsequently remained out of the public eye, working sporadically on production projects with the Holland brothers. After Dozier collaborated with UK artist **Phil Collins** on the Grammy award–winning 'Two Hearts', he signed a new recording contract with **Atlantic Records** and released 1991's lacklustre *Inside Seduction*. The failure of this major label release prompted Dozier and his wife Barbara to set up their own company. In the new millennium, Dozier revisited his 60s classics on the self-released *An American Original*, which earned the artist a Grammy nomination. The album was subsequently re-released as *Reflections Of . . . .*

● ALBUMS: *Out Here On My Own* (ABC 1973) ★★★, *Black Bach* (ABC 1974) ★★★, *Right There* (Warners 1976) ★★, *Peddlin' Music On The Side* (Warners 1977) ★★★★, *Bittersweet* (Warners 1979) ★★, *Working On You* (Columbia 1981) ★★, *Lamont* (A&M 1982) ★★★, *Bigger Than Life* (Megaphone 1983) ★★★, *Inside Seduction* (Atlantic 1991) ★★, *An American Original* aka *Reflections Of . . .* (D-Flawless/Jam Right 2002) ★★.

● COMPILATIONS: *Why Can't We Be Lovers: The Invictus Sessions* (Sequel 2000) ★★★, *Going Back To My Roots: The Lamont Dozier Anthology* (Castle 2000) ★★★, *The ABC Years And Lost Sessions* (Expansion 2000) ★★★, *The Legendary Lamont Dozier: Soul Master* (MCA 2002) ★★★★, *Soul Man: The Best Of* (Sanctuary 2002) ★★★, *Going Back To My Roots* (Sanctuary 2004) ★★★★.

Dr. Alban

b. Alban Nwapa, Nigeria. Swedish-based **dance music** artist who rose to prominence with his curious potpourri of styles, named 'jungle reggae hip-hop' by some commentators. Of all the artists to employ the title 'Doctor' in their names, Alban is one of the few to do so legitimately. He originally went to Stockholm, Sweden, to train as a dentist, and after qualifying, he started the Alphabet Club in the city, which eventually spawned a record and clothes shop of the same name. His attempts to 'toast' over the records he played at the venue attracted the attention of **Swemix Records**. The first result of his work with the studio was the 1990 single 'Hello Afrika', which immediately launched him in the national and international charts. With the anti-drug 'No Coke' and pro-unity 'U & Mi', Dr. Alban continued to cut himself a large slice of credibility in the European mainstream dance market. The musical style combined techno with club vocals and African rhythms. Among the most notable traits were the Nigerian percussive effects and dancehall chanting. In September 1992, he enjoyed a huge European hit with 'It's My Life', which reached number 2 in the UK pop chart. His unique Afro-Swedish patois earned praise from a variety of quarters, reinforcing the fact that rap had become a universal currency. The man behind the production on the big hits was **Denniz Pop**, who also produced **Ace Of Base**'s number 1 'All

That She Wants'. Although he failed to reproduce the crossover success of 'It's My Life', Alban continued to enjoy club success throughout the decade. He also started his own Dr. label, whose first release was the 'Alrabaiye Take Me Up' single by **Amadin**.

● ALBUMS: *Hello Afrika The Album* (Swemix 1990) ★★★, *One Love The Album* (Swemix 1992) ★★★, *It's My Life The Album* (Logic/Arista 1993) ★★★, *Look Who's Talking! The Album* (Logic/Arista 1995) ★★★, *Born In Africa* (Dr. 1996) ★★.

● COMPILATIONS: *The Very Best Of Dr. Alban 1990–1997* (Ariola 1997) ★★★.

Dr. Alimantado

The 'Ital Surgeon' Winston Thompson came to the record-buying public's attention with his DJ work for **Lee Perry** in Jamaica during the early 70s, but it was only when he started producing records for himself that he found his niche. His 'The Best Dressed Chicken In Town' (a version to 'Ain't No Sunshine'), released on Capo Records, leaned heavily on the production techniques of Lee Perry but was an unmatched assault on the senses—later to be described as two and a half minutes of **dub** lyricism. His manic approach and choice of top rhythms assured his cult status in the UK where his records on the Ital Sounds and Vital Food labels were eagerly awaited and purchased by a cult following. He was nearly killed when a downtown Kingston bus knocked him over in 1977, and his subsequent comeback single for **Channel One**, 'Born For A Purpose', and the DJ version, 'Life All Over', brought him to the fore at the same time that the punk market discovered reggae. He moved to England not long afterwards to capitalize on his new-found fame and has remained there, on and off, ever since. He still releases records on his ISDA label, none of which have matched the quality of his early recordings. He is now resident in Holland.

● ALBUMS: *Best Dressed Chicken In Town* (Greensleeves 1978) ★★★★, *Born For A Purpose/Songs Of Thunder* (Greensleeves 1981) ★★★, *Love Is* (Keyman 1983) ★★★, *In The Mix Volumes 1–5* (Keyman 1985–1990) ★★★, *King's Bread* (Ital Sounds 1986) ★★★, *King's Bread Dub* (Keyman 1989) ★★★, *The Privileged Few* (Keyman 1990) ★★★, *Wonderful Life* (Isda 1998) ★★★.

● COMPILATIONS: *Reggae Revue Part 1* (Keyman 1988) ★★.

Dr. Cosgill

An enterprising young UK band that held the torch for electric folk by playing medieval tunes as if they were the **Stranglers**. Their recorded highlight came with the 1981 single 'Benediction'/'Douce Dame'. Although they disbanded in the same year, their influence was felt a couple of years later with the 'rogue folk' movement. By then, leader Paul James had joined **Blowzabella**.

Dr. Didg

Graham Wiggins (b. 25 October 1962, New York City, New York, USA; didgeridoo, keyboards, percussion, melodica, samples), Ian Campbell (b. 4 April 1960, Ely, England; drums/percussion), Dave Motion (b. 6 July 1968, Legoa, Portugal; guitar). Formed in 1995 by Wiggins and Campbell (both previously members of Outback), the duo called themselves Dr. Didg, a nickname given to Wiggins while he was studying for his Physics PhD and learning to play the didgeridoo in the early 80s. With the addition of guitarist Mark Revell, they worked on developing a didgeridoo-based sound that combined African, Latin American, Eastern, rock, **dance music** and psychedelic influences and was built around improvisation and 'live sampling' (a process by which Wiggins created dense layers of sound by sampling and looping phrases he played on the didgeridoo). The trio quickly became popular amongst fans of world/dance, making regular appearances at festivals throughout Europe, including WOMAD and **Glastonbury**. During the recording of *Serotonality* (their second album, which featured live recordings and tracks developed from live samples), Motion replaced Mark Revell.

● ALBUMS: *Out Of The Woods* (Hannibal 1995) ★★★, *Serotonality* (Hannibal 1998) ★★★.

Dr. Dre

b. Andre Young, 18 February 1965, South Central, Los Angeles, California, USA. Widely regarded, by **Rolling Stone** magazine at least, as the chief architect of west coast gangsta rap, Dre's musical career began as a DJ at Los Angeles dance club Eve After Dark. There he would splice up a mix of new records with soul classics like **Martha And The Vandellas**. The club had a back room with a small four-track studio where he, together with future-**N.W.A.** member Yella and Lonzo Williams, would record demos. The first of these was 'Surgery', a basic **electro** track with a chorus of 'Calling Dr Dre to surgery'. These sessions, and nights at Eve After Dark, taught him the turntable techniques he would later bring to N.W.A. after forming the World Class Wreckin' Cru at the age of 17. Although other former members such as **Ice Cube** had laid the ground for rap's immersion into the mainstream, the success of Dre's 1992 solo debut, **The Chronic**, confirmed its commercial breakthrough. It also signalled a change in tack by modern gangsta rappers.

The music now took its cue from the funk of **George Clinton** and **Funkadelic**, Dre freely admitting to the influence Clinton played on his life: 'Back in the 70s that's all people were doing: getting high, wearing Afros, bell-bottoms and listening to Parliament-Funkadelic. That's why I called my album *The Chronic* and based my music and the concepts like I did: because his shit was a big influence on my music. Very big.' To this end he created a studio band for the sessions, which included the R&B talents of Tony Green (bass) and Ricky Rouse (guitar). While Dre's lyrics were just as forceful as those that had graced NWA, there was also a shift in subject matter. *The Chronic* referred heavily to the recreational use of marijuana, taking its name from a particularly virulent, and popular, brand. Together with the efforts of **Cypress Hill**, cannabis was now the drug of choice for the gangsta rapper, with crack cocaine much discussed but rarely endorsed. *The Chronic* would go on to spend eight months in the **Billboard** Top 10. At least as important was Dre's growing reputation as a producer.

As well as producing an album for one of his many girlfriends, **Michel'le**, his work with **Eazy-E**, **D.O.C.**, **Above The Law** and, most importantly, **Snoop Doggy Dogg**, broke new ground. Dogg had already rapped with Dre on the hit singles 'Deep Cover' and 'Nuthin' But A 'G' Thang'. However, the **Doggystyle** opus would break box office records, bringing gangsta rap to the top of the album charts. Many sustained the belief that Dre was the driving force behind its success,

the producer himself acknowledging: 'I can take a three year old and make a hit record with him.' At the same time he was dismissive of his own pioneering efforts for N.W.A., particularly the epoch-making **Straight Outta Compton**: 'To this day I can't stand that album, I threw that thing together in six weeks so we could have something to sell out of the trunk.' During his involvement with the NWA posse he became the house producer for Eazy-E's **Ruthless Records**. Seven out of eight albums he produced for the label between 1983 and 1991 went platinum, but he broke from Ruthless over what he alleged was under-payment. Dre's on-record sneers at Eazy-E began shortly afterwards, including the single 'Dre Day', a put-down that Eazy-E would countermand for his reply 'Muthaphukkin' Gs'.

Typical of many of rap's leading lights, Dre never strayed far from controversy, even after he bought into the comfort of a luxury home in San Fernando Valley. As if to reinstate himself as a 'true gangsta', Dre waged a war of attrition with authority. Television host Dee Barnes filed a multi-million dollar lawsuit against him for allegedly throwing her against the wall of a Hollywood nightclub in 1991. He was also convicted of breaking the jaw of a record producer (he was sentenced to house arrest and was fitted with a tracking device) and was detained by mounted police after a fracas in a New Orleans hotel lobby. Eazy-E sued him, and Dre complained bitterly about restraint of trade and moneys owed, cursed Ruthless' General Manager Jerry Heller and finally managed to find a contract with **Jimmy Iovine** at Interscope Records, who let him set up his own label, **Death Row Records**, co-founded with the controversial Marion 'Suge' Knight, **Vanilla Ice**'s ex-publicist.

The success of *The Chronic* and *Doggystyle*, and the signing of rap's biggest new star **2Pac**, briefly made Death Row one of America's most powerful labels. By 1996, however, its well-documented problems culminated in Dre acrimoniously leaving to form his own Aftermath Records label. The label's first release was a various artists compilation, whose stand-out track was Dre's declamatory hit single 'Been There Done That', a kiss-off to gangsta rap and Death Row. In 1998, Dre was back in the news again as co-producer on his protégé **Eminem**'s controversial breakthrough album *The Slim Shady LP*. The following November he released his highly anticipated second collection *Dr. Dre 2001*. Featuring collaborations with Eminem, Snoop Dogg, **Mary J. Blige** and Xzibit, the album was a highly effective reminder of Dre's pre-eminence in the world of gangsta rap.

● ALBUMS: *The Chronic* (Death Row 1992) ★★★★★, *Dr. Dre 2001* (Aftermath 1999) ★★★★, *The Wash* film soundtrack (Aftermath 2001) ★★★.

● COMPILATIONS: *Concrete Roots* (Triple X 1994) ★★, *Back 'N The Day* (Blue Dolphin 1996) ★★, *First Round Knock Out* (Triple X 1996) ★★★, *Dr. Dre Presents The Aftermath* (Aftermath 1996) ★★★★, *The Chronicle: The Best Of . . . Dr. Dre* (Death Row 2001) ★★★.

● FURTHER READING: *You Forgot About Dre!: The Unauthorized Biography Of Dr. Dre & Eminem*, Kelly Kenyatta.

● FILMS: *The Show* (1995), *Set It Off* (1996), *Rhyme & Reason* (1997), *Whiteboys* (1999).

Dr. Feelgood

The most enduring act to emerge from the UK's much touted pub-rock scene, Dr. Feelgood was formed in 1971 by a group of R&B enthusiasts who had originally played in local outfits such as the Southside Jug Band, the Fix and the Pigboy Charlie Band. The original line-up included Lee Brilleaux (b. Lee Collinson, 10 May 1952, Durban, South Africa, d. 7 April 1994, Leigh-on-Sea, Essex, England; vocals/harmonica), **Wilko Johnson** (b. John Wilkinson, 12 July 1947, Canvey Island, Essex, England; guitar), John B. Sparks (bass), John Potter (piano) and Bandsman Howarth (b. Terry Howarth; drums). When the latter pair dropped out, the remaining trio recruited a permanent drummer in The Big Figure (b. John Martin).

Originally based in Canvey Island, Essex, on the Thames estuary, Dr. Feelgood broke into the London circuit in 1974, signing a record contract with **United Artists Records** shortly afterwards. Brilleaux's menacing personality complemented Johnson's propulsive, jerky stage manner. The guitarist's staccato style, modelled on Mick Green of the **Pirates**, emphasized the band's idiosyncratic brand of rhythm and blues. Their debut album, *Down By The Jetty*, was released in 1975, but despite critical approbation it was not until the following year that the quartet secured due commercial success with their third album, the live set *Stupidity*. This raw, compulsive album, which perfectly captured the ferocity of the band's live sound, topped the UK charts and appeared to make their status assured. However, internal friction led to Johnson's departure during sessions for a projected fourth album and although his replacement, Gypie Mayo (b. John Philip Cawthra, 24 July 1951, Hammersmith, London, England), was an accomplished guitarist, he lacked the striking visual image of his predecessor.

Dr. Feelgood then embarked on a more mainstream direction which was only intermittently successful. 'Milk And Alcohol' gave them their sole UK Top 10 hit in early 1979, but they now seemed curiously anachronistic in the face of the punk upheaval. In 1981, Johnny Guitar (b. John Crippen; ex-**Count Bishops**) replaced Mayo, while the following year both Sparks and Martin decided to leave the line-up. Brilleaux disbanded Dr. Feelgood after the release of *Fast Women Slow Horses* but relaunched the band after only a few months with Gordon Russell (b. 4 June 1958, Hampstead, London, England; guitar), Kevin Morris (b. 15 May 1955, London, England; drums) and Phil Mitchell (b. Philip Henry Mitchell, 19 March 1953, Wembley, England; bass). While the new line-up could claim a loyal audience, it was an increasingly small one. However, they remained a popular live attraction in the USA where their records also achieved commercial success. They also launched their own label, Grand Records. Shortly afterwards Russell left the band for personal reasons and was replaced by Steve Walwyn (b. Stephen Martin Walwyn, 8 June 1956, Southam, Warwickshire, England). Mitchell left during the recording of 1991's *Primo*, with session musician Dave Bronze (b. David Eric Bronze, 2 April 1952, Billericay, Essex, England) taking over as bass player. In 1993 Brilleaux was diagnosed as having non-Hodgkins lymphoma and, owing to the extensive treatment he was receiving, had to break the band's often-inexorable touring schedule for the first time in over 20 years. He died the following year having completed a final album and opened the Dr. Feelgood Music Bar in Canvey Island.

Respecting Brilleaux's wish to keep the flame burning, Morris, Walwyn, Phil Mitchell and new singer Pete Gage (b. 12 February 1946, London, England) got back together a year

later to record *On The Road Again*. Robert Kane (b. 6 December 1954), latter-day vocalist for the **Animals**, replaced Gage on the solid *Chess Masters*, the band's first album of the new millennium.

● ALBUMS: *Down By The Jetty* (United Artists 1975) ★★★★, *Malpractice* (United Artists/Columbia 1975) ★★★, *Stupidity* (United Artists 1976) ★★★, *Sneakin' Suspicion* (United Artists/Columbia 1977) ★★, *Be Seeing You* (United Artists 1977) ★★★, *Private Practice* (United Artists 1978) ★★★, *As It Happens* (United Artists 1979) ★★, *Let It Roll* (United Artists 1979) ★★, *A Case Of The Shakes* (United Artists 1980) ★★, *On The Job* (Liberty 1981) ★★, *Fast Women Slow Horses* (Chiswick 1982) ★★, *Doctor's Orders* (Demon 1984) ★★, *Mad Man Blues* mini-album (ID 1985) ★★★, *Brilleaux* (Stiff 1987) ★★★, *Classic* (Stiff 1987) ★★, *Live In London* (Grand 1990) ★★★, *Primo* (Grand 1991) ★★, *The Feelgood Factor* (Grand 1993) ★★, *Down At The Doctors* (Grand 1994) ★★, *On The Road Again* (Grand 1996) ★★★, *Chess Masters* (Grand 2000) ★★★, *Speeding Thru Europe* (Grand 2003) ★★, *Going Back Home: Live At The Kursaal, Southend, 1975* (EMI 2004) ★★★.

● COMPILATIONS: *Casebook* (Liberty 1981) ★★★, *Case History: The Best Of Dr. Feelgood* (EMI 1987) ★★★, *Singles: The U.A. Years +* (Liberty 1989) ★★★★, *Stupidity + Dr. Feelgood Live 1976–1990* (Liberty 1991) ★★★, *Looking Back* 5-CD box set (EMI 1995) ★★★, *Twenty Five Years Of Dr Feelgood: 1972–1997* (Grand 1997) ★★★★, *The Best Of Dr. Feelgood: Centenary Collection* (EMI 1997) ★★★, *Live At The BBC 1974–5* (Grand 1999) ★★★, *BBC Sessions 1973–1978* (Grand 2001) ★★★, *Singled Out: U.A./Liberty A's B's & Rarities* (EMI 2001) ★★★★, *Finely Tuned: The Guitar Album* (Grand 2002) ★★★, *Wolfman Calling: The Blues Of Lee Brilleaux* (Grand 2003) ★★★, *The Complete Stiff Recordings* (Grand 2005) ★★★.

● DVD/VIDEOS: *Live Legends* (PolyGram Music Video 1990), *Going Back Home* (EMI 2005).

● FURTHER READING: *Down By The Jetty: The Dr Feelgood Story*, Tony Moon.

Dr. Hook

Sporting denims and buckskin, Dr. Hook And The Medicine Show epitomized much of the countrified and 'laid-back' style that was in vogue during the early 70s, but though their material was sung in a Dixie drawl and three members were genuine southerners, they began in 1968 as a New Jersey bar band with one-eyed Dr. Hook (b. Ray Sawyer, 1 February 1937, Chickasaw, Alabama, USA; vocals), Denis Locorriere (b. 13 June 1949, New Jersey, USA; guitar/vocals), George Cummings (b. Meridian, Mississippi, USA; lead/slide guitar), Billy Francis (b. William Francis, Ocean Springs, Mississippi, USA; keyboards) and Jay David (b. Bayonne, New Jersey, USA; drums). One evening they impressed a talent scout looking for an outfit to record *Playboy* cartoonist **Shel Silverstein**'s film score to *Who's Harry Kellerman And Why Is He Saying These Terrible Things About Me?* (1970) and later backed Silverstein's singing on record. As a result, the band was signed to **CBS Records**. Almost immediate international success (US number 5/UK number 2) followed with 'Sylvia's Mother' from their debut album. With the line-up augmented by Rik Elswit (guitar) and Jance Garfat (bass), the follow-up, *Sloppy Seconds*, was also penned entirely by Silverstein, and was attended by a US Top 10 hit that cited portrayal on

'The Cover Of 'The Rolling Stone'' (which was dogged by a BBC ban in the UK) as the zenith of the band's ambition—which they later achieved in March 1973.

The band embarked on a punishing touring schedule with a diverting act, riven with indelicate humour that came to embrace an increasing number of their own compositions. Some were included on *Belly Up!* and the US-only *Fried Face*, their last album before transferring to **Capitol Records** and the first with new drummer John Wolters, (b. John Christian Wolters, 28 April 1945, Pompton Lakes, New Jersey, USA, d. July 1997). By then, the popularity of the band—as plain Dr. Hook—on the boards gave false impressions of their standing in market terms. This was better expressed in the title of the fifth album *Bankrupt*. However, a revival of **Sam Cooke**'s 'Only Sixteen' redressed the balance financially by rocketing up the US Hot 100. A year later this feat was repeated on a global scale with the title track of *A Little Bit More*, which reached the UK number 2 slot. By this point, Cummings had left the line-up. Next came a UK number 1 in early 1979 with 'When You're In Love With A Beautiful Woman' from the million-selling *Pleasure & Pain*. With Locorriere taking the lion's share of lead vocals by then, the same year's *Sometimes You Win* was the wellspring of two more international smashes 'Better Love Next Time' and 'Sexy Eyes'.

Throughout the 80s, Dr. Hook's chart strikes were confined mainly to North America (even if a 1981 concert album was taped in London), becoming more sporadic as the decade wore on. New guitarists Bob Henke and Rod Smarr passed through the line-up, and in 1982 Sawyer left to pursue a solo career. Locorriere's efforts as a Nashville-based songwriter had all but put the tin lid on Dr. Hook by the mid-80s. In the ensuing decade, Sawyer licensed the name from Locorriere for touring purposes.

● ALBUMS: *Dr. Hook & The Medicine Show* (Columbia 1972) ★★★, *Sloppy Seconds* (Columbia 1972) ★★★, *Belly Up!* (Columbia 1973) ★★, *Fried Face* US only (Columbia 1974) ★★, *Bankrupt* (Capitol 1975) ★★, *A Little Bit More* (Capitol 1976) ★★★, *Makin' Love And Music* (Capitol 1977) ★★, *Pleasure & Pain* (Capitol 1978) ★★★, *Sometimes You Win* (Capitol 1979) ★★★, *Rising* (Casablanca 1980) ★★, *Live In The UK* (Capitol 1981) ★★, *Players In The Dark* (Casablanca 1982) ★★, *On The Run* 1976 recording (Burning Airlines 2001) ★★★.

● COMPILATIONS: *The Ballad Of Lucy Jordan* (CBS 1975) ★★★, *Greatest Hits* (Capitol 1980) ★★★, *Collection* (EMI 1983) ★★★, *Greatest Hits (And More)* (Capitol 1987) ★★★, *Completely Hooked: The Best Of Dr. Hook* (Columbia 1992) ★★★, *Pleasure & Pain: The History Of Dr. Hook* 3-CD box set (EMI 1996) ★★★, *Love Songs* (EMI 1999) ★★★, *Making Love & Music: The 1976–1979 Recordings* (EMI 2001) ★★★★, *Super Hits* (Sony 2001) ★★★, *Classic Masters* (Capitol 2002) ★★★, *The Essential Dr. Hook And The Medicine Show* (Columbia/Legacy 2003) ★★★★, *I Got Stoned And I Missed It: The Best From Shel Silverstein 1971–79* (Raven 2003) ★★★★, *Vintage Years* 3-CD set (EMI 2003) ★★★.

● DVD/VIDEOS: *Completely Hooked* (PMI 1992).

Dr. Jeckyll And Mr. Hyde

Comprising the Bronx, New York City, USA–born duo Andre Harrell aka Dr. Jeckyll (b. 26 September 1960) and Alonzo Brown aka Mr. Hyde, alongside DJ Scratch On Galaxy (b. George Llado), Dr. Jeckyll & Mr. Hyde enjoyed a steady stream of success in the early 80s. Their best-remembered song, 'Genius Rap', constructed over the **Tom Tom Club**'s 'Genius Of Love', sold over 150,000 records for **Profile Records** in 1981. Previously Brown had recorded the label's second release, and first rap record, as Lonnie Love ('Young Ladies'). 'AM:PM', backed by the **Kurtis Blow**–produced 'Fast Life', also earned the duo healthy chart placings. However, when their debut album bombed, both elected to concentrate on non-performing careers. Harrell established **Uptown Records**, scoring huge success with **Heavy D And The Boyz** as well as the New Jack Swing prime movers, notably **Teddy Riley**'s creations. He was later appointed president of **Motown Records**. Brown would work in executive posts at **Cold .Chillin' Records** and **Warner Brothers Records** before heading up A&R for **A&M Records**.

● ALBUMS: *The Champagne Of Rap* (Profile 1985) ★★★.

Dr. John

b. Malcolm John Rebennack, 21 November 1940, New Orleans, Louisiana, USA. Dr. John has built a career since the 60s as a consummate New Orleans musician, incorporating funk, rock 'n' roll, jazz and R&B into his sound. Rebennack's distinctive vocal growl and virtuoso piano playing brought him acclaim among critics and fellow artists, although his commercial successes have not equalled that recognition.

Rebennack's musical education began in the 40s when he accompanied his father to blues clubs. At the age of 14 he began frequenting recording studios and wrote his first songs at that time. By 1957 he was working as a session musician, playing guitar, keyboards and other instruments on recordings issued on such labels as Ace, Ric, Rex and Ebb. He made his first recording under his own name, 'Storm Warning', for Rex during that same year, and others followed on Ace and AFO Records with little success. In 1958 he co-wrote 'Lights Out', recorded by Jerry Byrne, and toured with Byrne and **Frankie Ford**. He had his first taste of success in 1960 when 'Lady Luck' became a big hit for **Lloyd Price**. By 1962 Rebennack had already played on countless sessions for such renowned producers as **Phil Spector**, **Harold Battiste**, H.B. Barnum and **Sonny Bono** (later of **Sonny And Cher**).

Rebennack formed his own bands during the early 60s but they did not take off. By the mid-60s he had moved to Los Angeles, where he fused his New Orleans roots with the emerging west coast psychedelic sound, and he developed the persona Dr. John Creaux, The Night Tripper. The character was based on one established by singer **Prince La La**, but Rebennack made it his own through the intoxicating brew of voodoo incantations and New Orleans heritage. In 1968 Dr. John was signed to **Atco Records** and released *Gris-Gris*, which received critical acclaim but did not chart. This exceptional collection included the classic 'I Walk On Guilded Splinters' and inspired several similarly styled successors, winning respect from fellow musicians including **Eric Clapton** and **Mick Jagger**. The same musical formula and exotic image were pursued on follow-up albums, *Babylon* and *Remedies*. Meanwhile, he toured on the rock festival and ballroom circuit and continued to do session work.

In 1971, Dr. John charted for the first time with *The Sun, Moon & Herbs*. The follow-up, *Dr. John's Gumbo*, produced by **Jerry Wexler**, charted, as did the single 'Iko Iko'. His biggest US hit came in 1973 with the single 'Right Place,

Wrong Time', which reached number 9; the accompanying album, *In The Right Place*, was also his bestselling, reaching number 24. These crafted, colourful albums featured the instrumental muscle of the **Meters**, but despite a new-found popularity, the artist parted from his record label, and subsequent work failed to achieve a similar status. During that year he toured with the Meters and recorded *Triumvirate* with **Michael Bloomfield** and **John Hammond**. He continued to record throughout the 70s and 80s for numerous labels, among them **United Artists Records**, Horizon and Clean Tracks, the latter releasing *Dr. John Plays Mac Rebennack*, a solo piano album, in 1981. In the meantime, Dr. John continued to draw sizeable audiences as a concert act across the USA, and he added radio jingle work to his live and recorded work (he continued to play on many sessions). He recorded *Bluesiana Triangle* with jazz musicians **Art Blakey** and **David 'Fathead' Newman** and released *In A Sentimental Mood*, a collection of interpretations of standards including a moody duet with **Rickie Lee Jones** on **Warner Brothers Records**.

Despite employing a low-key approach to recording, Dr. John has remained a respected figure. His live appearances are now less frequent, but this irrepressible artist continues his role as a tireless champion of Crescent City music. In 1997 he signed to **Parlophone Records** and recorded tracks with UK artists **Spiritualized**, **Supergrass**, **Paul Weller** and **Primal Scream** for the following year's *Anutha Zone*, which broke into the UK Top 40. A relaxed tribute to **Duke Ellington** followed in 1999. In between two fine collections of laid back New Orleans R&B (2001's *Creole Moon* and 2004's *New Awlinz: Dis Dat Or D'Udda*), Dr. John launched his own Skinji Brim imprint. The first of several archive live recordings, *All By Hisself: Live At The Lonestar*, was released in autumn 2003.

● ALBUMS: *Gris-Gris* (Atlantic 1968) ★★★★, *Babylon* (Atco 1969) ★★★, *Remedies* (Atco 1970) ★★★, *The Sun, Moon & Herbs* (Atco 1971) ★★★, *Dr. John's Gumbo* (Atlantic 1972) ★★★★, *In The Right Place* (Atlantic 1973) ★★★, with Mike Bloomfield, John Hammond *Triumvirate* (Columbia/CBS 1973) ★★★, *Desitively Bonnaroo* (Atlantic 1974) ★★★, *Hollywood Be Thy Name* (United Artists 1975) ★★, *City Lights* (Horizon 1978) ★★★, *Tango Palace* (Horizon 1979) ★★, with Chris Barber *Take Me Back To New Orleans* (Black Lion 1980) ★★★, *Dr. John Plays Mac Rebennack* (Clean Cuts 1982) ★★★, *The Brightest Smile In Town* (Clean Cuts 1983) ★★★, *Such A Night: Live In London* (Spindrift 1984) ★★★, with Hank Crawford *Roadhouse Symphony* (Milestone 1986) ★★★, *In A Sentimental Mood* (Warners 1989) ★★, with Art Blakey, David 'Fathead' Newman *Bluesiana Triangle* (Windham Hill 1990) ★★★, *Goin' Back To New Orleans* (Warners 1992) ★★★, *Television* (GRP 1994) ★★, *Afterglow* (GRP 1995) ★★, *Trippin' Live* (Eagle 1997) ★★★, *Anutha Zone* (Parlophone 1998) ★★★, *Duke Elegant* (Parlophone 1999) ★★★★, *Creole Moon* (Parlophone/Blue Note 2001) ★★★, *All By Hisself: Live At The Lonestar* 1986 recording (Skinji Brim 2003) ★★★, *New Awlinz: Dis Dat Or D'Udda* (Parlophone 2004) ★★★, with the Lower 911 *Sippiana Hericane* mini-album (Blue Note 2005) ★★★, *Right Place, Right Time: Live At Tipitina's—Mardi Gras '89* (Hyena 2006) ★★★.

● COMPILATIONS: *Cut Me While I'm Hot (Anytime, Anyplace)* pre-Atlantic material (DJM 1975) ★★, *I Been*

Hoodood (Edsel 1984) ★★★, *In The Night* pre-Atlantic material (Topline 1985) ★★★, *Zu Zu Man* pre-Atlantic material (Topline 1987) ★★★, *Loser For You Baby* pre-Atlantic material (Thunderbolt 1988) ★★★, *Mos' Scocious: The Dr. John Anthology* 2-CD set (Rhino 1994) ★★★★, *The Very Best Of Dr. John* (Rhino 1995) ★★★★, *The Crazy Cajun Recordings* (Edsel 1999) ★★★, *The Ear Is On Strike* (Yeaah! 2001) ★★★, *Early Prescriptions* (Snapper 2002) ★★, *Storm Warning (The Early Sessions Of Mac 'Dr. John' Rebennack)* (Edsel 2004) ★★★, *The Best Of The Parlophone Years* (Parlophone 2005) ★★★★.

● DVD/VIDEOS: *Dr. John And Chris Barber Live At The Marquee Club* (Jettisoundz 1986), *Live At The Marquee* (Hendring Music Video 1990), *New Orleans Piano* (Homespun Video 1996), *Learn From A Legend* (Homespun 2004).

● FURTHER READING: *Dr. John: Under A Hoodoo Moon*, Mac Rebennack with Jack Rummel.

Dr. Mastermind

Formed in the USA during 1986, Dr. Mastermind was part of a new wave of guitar-orientated rock bands. Comprising Kurt James (ex-**Steeler** and **Driver** guitarist), Deen Castronovo (drums) and the enigmatic Dr. Mastermind (widely believed to be Matt McCourt; ex-**Wild Dogs**) on bass and vocals, they were a power trio in every sense of the word. Frenetically paced songs, which never quite degenerated into tuneless thrash, were punctuated by high-octane and complex guitar breaks. After the release of their debut album, Castronovo joined **Cacophony**, and James left for Turbin. Rick Hosert and Pete Lachman were drafted in as replacements on drums and guitar, respectively, but this new line-up failed to find success.

● ALBUMS: *Dr. Mastermind* (Roadrunner 1986) ★★★.

Dr. Nico

b. Nicholas Kasanda Wa Mikalay, 1939, Luluaborg, Zaire, d. 1985, Kinshasa, Zaire. A member of **Le Grande Kalle**'s African Jazz in the early 60s, expert guitarist and composer Nico went on to be a founder member, with Rochereau, of African Fiesta, one of the most popular and influential Zairean bands of the mid and late 60s. He was born into a musical family but later attended the Leopold II Institute, graduating as a technical teacher in 1957. Despite the qualification, he concentrated on music from then on, inspired by his accordion-playing father and guitarist brother (Mwamba Dechaud). Kasanda soon became a virtuoso guitar player himself, leading to his induction into African Jazz. His reputation among Congolese guitarists was second to none, and during African Jazz's performance at the 1960 Zairean independence celebrations he was given his nickname Dr. Nico. After joining African Fiesta in 1963 he maintained his popularity and gift for invention, recording hundreds of singles, many of which were local and pan-African hits. He then retired from the music scene in the early 70s, infuriated by the collapse of African Fiesta's Belgian record company, feeling financially cheated. He played only a handful of shows over several quiet years before returning in 1983 with a new recording contract for Togo's Africa New Sound label. Several albums were recorded, usually alongside his brother and with the backing of Les Redoubtables De Abeti. His first American albums followed for the African Music Gallery in Washington. However, this brief period of intense activity was ended by his sudden death (suspected to be alcohol-related) in 1985. His influence on African guitar playing, acknowledged by several experts as the most pivotal of all such innovations, lives on.

● ALBUMS: *Eternal Dr Nico 1963—1965* (1963) ★★★★, *Toute L'Afrique Danse* re-released by Sonodisc 1985 (Safari Ambience 1974) ★★★, *Sanza Zomi Na Mibale* (Safari Ambience 1975) ★★★, *Afrique Tayokana* (Safari Ambience 1981) ★★★★, *Kassanda Wa Mikalaya* (LKMR 1984) ★★★, *Dieu De La Guitare* (Africa New Sound 1985) ★★★★, *Aux USA* (Africa New Sound 1985) ★★★.

Dr. Octagon

b. Keith Thornton, New York, USA. More commonly known as **Kool Keith** while a member of groundbreaking New York rap group the **Ultramagnetic MC's**, Thornton has also travelled under a variety of other pseudonyms—Dr. Dooom, Poppa Large, the Reverend Tom, Sinister 6000, Big Willie Smith and Mr. Gerbik. In the mid-90s, and now based in Los Angeles, Thornton unveiled his latest project, Dr. Octagon. In principle a band, it was effectively just his latest solo musical outlet. However, after attracting favourable reviews for his live shows, he alarmed his backers (including record label DreamWorks) by failing to appear for performances in support of **Beck** and refusing to answer messages. This all fuelled a reputation for esoteric behaviour that had been with him since his time in the Ultramagnetic MC's. For example, he was said to have spent his entire five-figure advance from DreamWorks on pornography. However, he was indulged because of a precocious talent and, when he could be persuaded to marshal it, a prolific output.

Between 1995 and 1996 he recorded tracks with **Dan The Automator**, DJ Q-Bert (of **Invisibl Skratch Piklz**), **DJ Shadow** and appeared on a track with the UK's **Prodigy**. The ensuing *Dr. Octagonecologyst* album was initially recorded for an independent label and featured a dazzling mixture of vibrant textures filled with Moog synthesizer, violin, flute, bass and even classical samples (including Pachelbel's Canon) that strove to redefine the hip-hop genre. However, the lyrics were a different matter, reflecting Thornton's obsession with pornography in lustful anatomical detail. As he told **Rolling Stone** magazine, 'I wrote that album in one day. I was like, "Fuck it. I'll write the sickest shit ever, just to bug out on it."' He followed this with *Sex Style*, released on his own Funky Ass label under the Kool Keith tag. In the meantime, Thornton was finding further time to waste on his favourite distraction by launching his own pornography magazine *All Flavors*. Thornton adopted the Dr. Dooom moniker for 1999's *First Come, First Served* before returning to his Kool Keith alias on subsequent releases.

● ALBUMS: *Dr. Octagonecologyst* (Bulk/Mo' Wax 1996) ★★★★, *Instrumentalyst: Octagon Beats* (Mo' Wax 1996) ★★★.

Dr. Phibes And The House Of Wax Equations

Formed in the late 80s at South Cheshire College of Further Education, England, where they all studied music, Dr. Phibes quickly became one of the north west's most important dance bands. The name is taken from two separate Hammer Horror films. The band comprises Howard King Jnr. (vocals/guitars), Lee Belsham (bass) and Keith York (drums). Their recording debut came with the 1990 12-inch 'Sugarblast', which preceded their long playing debut in April 1991. Topping the independent charts for two weeks, it generated

significant media coverage and critical acclaim. Their music is an eclectic, but primarily rhythmic mix, of blues, funk and psychedelia. Recording sessions for their second album were disturbed when Belsham injured a shoulder. His colleague York drove off in their van, unbeknownst to Belsham who was still lying on top of it.

● ALBUMS: *Whirlpool* (Seel 1991) ★★★, *Hypnotwister* (1993) ★★★.

Dr. Ross

b. Charles Isiah Ross, 21 October 1925, Tunica, Mississippi, USA. Ross had American Indian ancestry. He learned harmonica at the age of nine and was performing with **Willie Love** and on radio stations in Arkansas and Mississippi in the late 30s. He served in the US Army from 1943–47. His paramedical training there earned Ross the sobriquet of Doctor when he returned to music, leading his Jump And Jive Band and appearing on radio in the *King Biscuit Time Show*. Ross also developed a one-man band act, which he frequently performed in the 50s and 60s. His Memphis recordings for **Sam Phillips** in the early 50s included 'Country Clown' and 'The Boogie Disease'. In 1954 he moved to Flint, Michigan, to work in an car factory. Ross continued to perform and in 1958 set up his own DIR label. In the early 60s, he benefited from the growing white interest in blues, recording for Pete Welding's Testament label and touring Europe with the 1965 Folk Blues Festival. He returned to Europe during the 70s, recording in London and performing at the **Montreux Jazz Festival** with **Muddy Waters**' band.

● ALBUMS: *The Flying Eagle* (1966) ★★★, *Dr Ross, The Harmonica Boss* (1972) ★★★, *Jivin' The Blues* (1974) ★★★, *Live At Montreux* (1975) ★★★, *First Recordings* (Reissue 1981) ★★★, *Call The Doctor* (Testament 1994) ★★★, *One Man Band* (Takoma 1998) ★★★.

Dr. Smith's Champion Hoss-Hair Pullers

This strange sounding unit was the brainchild of a dedicated, if somewhat eccentric man namely Henry Harlin Smith (b. 16 May 1881, Spring Creek, near Calico Rock, Arkansas, USA, d. 14 October 1931). Smith, a qualified doctor, lived in Spring Creek and made his living as a surgeon for the Missouri Pacific Railroad. A keen naturalist, he was always despondent that his local area and the local musicians never received the publicity he reckoned they deserved and decided to see what he could do to help alleviate the problem. He had an idea for a musical talent contest and in January 1926, he arranged a fiddle competition at the larger community of Calico Rock, some three miles from his home. After the event he organized his Hoss-Hair Pullers from the various winners (gaining the name from the horsehair in the fiddle bows) and also formed a vocal group to support the fiddlers, which he called the Hill-Billy Quartet. After hiring a theatre at Hot Springs for several concerts, he succeeded in obtaining radio work on the powerful KTHS Hot Springs station in March 1926. This lasted until December that year when the long (180-mile) trips to Hot Springs proved too much for the members. They played nearer home for local events and dances and also for the railroad's functions and in September 1926, they recorded six sides for **Victor Records** in Memphis. The records sold well in their local area but received little distribution or publicity elsewhere. They finally disbanded in 1930. The line-up generally featured only eight members but changed regularly as and when various members were available. It is reported that in all there were 13 musicians available to Dr. Smith, who never played in the band himself. He held other contests, and winners were often given to chance to play with the Hoss-Hair Pullers. Regular musicians included fiddlers Bryan Lackey, James Duncan, Owen Hunt, W. McLeary (who also played guitar), Luther Walker and George Dillard plus Leeman Bone (guitar/vocals) and Ray Marshall (mandolin). The vocal group featured Grayton Bone, Roosevelt Garner, Hubert Simmons and Homer and Odie Goatcher. When the enthusiastic Dr. Smith was driving to Little Rock on 14 October 1931, he suffered a cerebral haemorrhage and died. Two of the band's six sides 'Where The Irish Potatoes Grow' and 'Going Down The River' were included on County Records' *Echoes Of The Ozarks Volume 2*.

Dr. Strangely Strange

This Irish trio—Ivan Pawle (vocals/bass), Tim Booth (vocals/guitar) and Tim Goulding (b. 15 May 1945, Dublin, Eire; vocals/keyboards)—made its recording debut for **Island Records** in 1969. Although *Kip Of The Serenes* betrayed an obvious debt to the **Incredible String Band** (both groups were produced by **Joe Boyd**), the album nonetheless offered a whimsical charm. The trio then moved to **Vertigo Records** and embraced a rock-based style on *Heavy Petting*, despite the assistance of traditional musicians **Andy Irvine** and Johnny Moynihan. Guitarist **Gary Moore** guested on four of the tracks, including the catchy yet subtly humorous 'Gave My Love An Apple', but this electric album lacked the purpose of its predecessor. In early 1971 Goulding left to get married and concentrate on his painting. Pawle and Booth carried on with **Gay Woods** and **Terry Woods**, newly departed from **Steeleye Span**, but this line-up disbanded in summer 1971. The original trio reunited for a brief tour of Ireland the following year. They have reunited on a number of occasions since, including the recording of 1997's *Alternative Medicine*. Goulding released his solo debut three years later.

● ALBUMS: *Kip Of The Serenes* (Island 1969) ★★★, *Heavy Petting* (Vertigo 1970) ★★, *Alternative Medicine* (Big Beat 1997) ★★.
Solo: Tim Goulding *Midnight Fry* (Sweet Ticket 2000) ★★★.

Dr. Umezu

An accomplished and versatile Japanese quartet comprising Kazutoki Umezu (saxophones, piano, percussion), Hiroaki Katayama (saxophones\percussion), Takeharu Hayakawa (bass\guitar) and Takashi Kikuchi (drums), Dr. Umezu proved equally entertaining whether exploring resonance and sound relationships in the style of **Art Ensemble Of Chicago** or in more mainstream funk-based jazz.

● ALBUMS: with Kiyoshiru *Danger* (London 1982) ★★★, *Live At Moers Festival* (Moers 1983) ★★★, *Eight Eyes And Eight Ears* (Moabi 1988) ★★★.

Drag-On

b. Mel Smalls, 1980, New York City, New York, USA. Under the tutelage of hip-hop star **DMX** and the **Ruff Ryders** crew, rapper Drag-On made a name for himself in the early years of the twenty-first century with his rapid-fire rhyming skills (incidentally where his nickname comes from). Born in the Bronx (specifically, Soundview's Bronxdale Projects), Drag-On has been a resident of several different other local boroughs, including Queens, Yonkers and Bedford Stuyvesant. Living largely on the streets, Drag-On found himself homeless at certain points before he began making ends meet by selling clothes in Harlem. During this time, Drag-On met a friend who was an acquaintance of Ruff Ryders co-CEO Darrin 'Dee' Dean. It was not long before one of Ruff Ryders' leading recording artists, DMX, became aware of Drag-On's talents and took the up-and-coming rapper under his wing, appearing on chart-topping DMX releases such as 1998's *Flesh Of My Flesh, Blood Of My Blood* and 1999's . . . *And Then There Was X*, before launching his own solo recording career. Whetting the rap world's appetite by issuing a 'street album' titled *Back From Hell* and contributing the excellent 'Down Bottom' to the Ruff Ryders' compilation *Ryde Or Die Vol. 1*, Drag-On issued his first official album, *Opposite Of H2O*, in early 2000. Despite the album clawing its way into the Top 10 of the US **Billboard** album charts, Drag-On put his promising recording career on the backburner as he turned his attention to launching an acting career. Spots in movies such as the DMX-led vehicles *Exit Wounds* and *Cradle 2 The Grave* followed, as well as *The Hustle*. However, Drag-On's desire to rap eventually returned, resulting in the release of *Hell And Back* in early 2004, a recording that included guest spots by **Jadakiss**, **Eve**, **Swizz Beats**, **Styles** and his old friend DMX.

● ALBUMS: *Opposite Of H2O* (Ruff Ryders 2000) ★★★, *Hell And Back* (Ruff Ryders 2004) ★★★.
● FILMS: *Exit Wounds* (2001), *Cradle 2 The Grave* (2003).

Dragon

Along with **Split Enz**, Dragon is considered one of New Zealand's finest rock exports. Formed in Taumarunui in 1972 and based around the brothers Marc Hunter (b. 7 September 1953, Taumarunui, New Zealand, d. 17 July 1998, Sydney, Australia) and Todd Hunter (b. 22 June 1951, Taumarunui, New Zealand), the band stayed together on-and-off for over three decades. The early line-up included Todd Hunter (bass/vocals), Graeme Collins (piano/vocals), Ray Goodwin (guitar, keyboards, vocals) and Neil Reynolds (drums), but the line-up on their 1974 debut featured Todd Hunter, Goodwin, Marc Hunter (vocals), Neil Storey (d. November 1976; drums) and Ivan Thompson (keyboards). A second album featured additional guitarist Robert Taylor (b. 27 September 1954) but minus the departed Thompson. This line-up's influences were English rock-based bands, but by the time the band emigrated to Australia in 1975, its leanings were towards silky-smooth, soul-inspired melodies, highlighting the songwriting of new keyboard player Paul Hewson (b. 25 October 1952, d. 9 January 1985, New Zealand). Hits such as 'April Sun In Cuba' and 'Are You Old Enough' were in the middle of a run of seven Australian Top 10 singles and four Top 20 albums. They were highly popular with the young teenage audience, and yet the band also had a rapport with the older generation. The band was not short of publicity, with frequent newspaper stories on the excesses indulged by the band and the arrogance of its members. Storey died from a heroin overdose in 1976 and was replaced by Kerry Jacobsen (b. 19 April 1956). The band toured extensively but eventually imploded in March 1979 when frontman Marc Hunter was fired. Dragon eventually disintegrated a few months later after recording one album (*Power Play*) without their errant frontman.

Marc Hunter recorded a solo album (*Fiji Bitter*) and enjoyed an Australian Top 20 single with 'Island Nights', which encouraged him to form his own band to tour and promote the album. Todd Hunter collaborated with his girlfriend Johanna Piggott in the bands **XL Capris** and Scribble, which received some attention. Hewson, Jacobsen and the Hunter brothers re-formed Dragon in August 1982, although Jacobson subsequently left the band prior to the recording of their slick comeback album, *Body And The Beat*. The album featured contributions from US producer Alan Mansfield (guitar/keyboards) and ex-**XTC** drummer Terry Chambers. The album included five Australian hits, of which 'Rain' also broke into the US Top 100. Hewson, previously the band's main songwriter, only contributed one track to the album and left shortly after completing a support tour. He died in January 1985 from a drug overdose.

Dragon continued as a viable commercial force in Australia but failed to build on their initial US breakthrough. They fared even worse in Europe where record company dictates saw them changing their name to Hunter. The band continued into the 90s, with the nucleus of the Hunter brothers joined by various musicians including Mansfield and long-serving guitarist Tommy Emmanuel. By this point, Marc Hunter's solo career had begun to take precedence over his work with Dragon, and the band's output was limited to singles and reworked versions of their old hits. Sadly, Marc Hunter succumbed to throat cancer in July 1998.

● ALBUMS: *Universal Radio* (Vertigo 1974) ★★★, *Scented Gardens For The Blind* (Vertigo 1975) ★★★★, *Sunshine* aka *Dragon* (CBS/Portrait 1977) ★★★, *Running Free* (CBS 1977) ★★★, *O Zambezi* (Portrait 1978) ★★★★, *Power Play* (CBS 1979) ★★, *Body And The Beat* (Polydor 1983) ★★★, *Live One* (PolyGram 1985) ★★, *Dreams Of Ordinary Men* (PolyGram 1986) ★★★, *Bondi Road* (RCA/Wheatley 1989) ★★★, *Incarnations* (Roadshow 1995) ★★.

● COMPILATIONS: *Are You Old Enough* (Portrait 1978) ★★★, *Greatest Hits Vol. 1* (CBS 1979) ★★★★, *Their Classic Collection* (J&B 1990) ★★★, *Cuts From The Tough Times* (PolyGram 1990) ★★★, *Snake Eyes On The Paradise: Greatest Hits 1976–1989* (Raven 1998) ★★★★, *Tales From The Dark Side: Greatest Hits & Choice Collectables 1974–1997* (Raven 1998) ★★★.

Dragonfly Records

The DJ and producer **Youth** and Jazz Summers set up Dragonfly and Butterfly in 1992 as a subsidiary of **Big Life Records** to develop the techno trance sound the former had heard in Goa. After **System 7**'s single, '777 Expansion', and album, *777*, in early 1993, Dragonfly released material from **Drum Club** (*Everything Is Now*), **Heather Nova** (*Glowstars*), **Spiral Tribe** (*Techno Terra*) and **The Infinity Project** ('Time And Space') over the next 12 months. At the same time the label fostered experimentation as a number of important artists worked in close collaboration in Youth's Butterfly Studios on a sound that became known as psychedelic trance (what the media termed 'Goa' trance), notably Simon Posford (Hallucinogen), Martin Freeland (Man With No Name), Nick Barber (**Doof**) as well as members of the **Green Nuns Of The Revolution**, **Slinky Wizard** and The Infinity Project. The label became associated with some of the best psy-trance around and helped to bring that style to a wider audience without entering the commercial mainstream, through releases from artists such as Doof ('Double Dragons'

and 'Youth Of The Galaxy'), Hallucinogen ('Alpha Centauri'/'LSD', 'Astral Pancakes'/'Fluoro Neuro Sponge' and *Twisted*) and Man With No Name ('Sly-ed'/'Teleport' and 'Lunar Cycle'/'Neuro Tunnel') and a number of compilations, including the *Order Odonata* series and mix albums from **Danny Rampling** and **Paul Oakenfold**. Many of these artists have played at parties and clubs organized by the label in the UK and around the world. Although many of their best-known artists have gone on to form and record for other labels, Dragonfly have continued to produce some of the best new music, notably from artists such as Genetic (*We Are ... Genetic*), Muses Rapt (*Spiritual Healing*), Oforia (*Delirious*), Pleiadians (*IFO*), **Shakta** (*Silicon Trip*), UX (*Ultimate Experience*) and Zodiac Youth (*Devil's Circus*). In 1998 the subsidiary LSD Records released material from Youth's projects Dub Trees and Hicksville (also with Simon Posford and Saul), as well as Celtic Cross.

Drain

This hard rock band (known as Drain S.T.H. in the USA) was formed by Maria Sjöholm (vocals), Flavia Canel (guitar), Anna Kjellberg (bass) and Martina Axén (drums) in Stockholm, Sweden, in 1993. Newly signed to MVG Records, they rose to prominence in the UK with a support slot to **Fear Factory**, whose grim lyrical subject matter and grating, hard-edged music was clearly an influence. Though *Kerrang!* magazine did them few favours by calling them 'the female **Alice In Chains**', they nevertheless made a strong impression with the release of their first internationally distributed single, 'I Don't Mind'. This was followed by a full album produced by Adam Kvlman. *Horror Wrestling* again drew positive press for its compelling song structures and, in particular, Maria Sjöholm's by turns melodramatic and gentle vocal delivery. The album was re-released in the USA in expanded form by **PolyGram Records**. Their second album, 1999's *Freaks Of Nature*, was another fine collection of expertly crafted post-industrial metal.

● ALBUMS: *Horror Wrestling* (MVG/The Enclave 1996) ★★★, *Freaks Of Nature* (PolyGram 1999) ★★★★.

Drake, Alfred

b. Alfredo Capurro, 7 October, 1914, New York City, New York, USA, d. 25 July 1992, New York, USA. An actor, singer, director and author, Drake will always be associated with that magical moment when the curtain rose on *Oklahoma!* at the St. James Theatre in New York on 31 March 1943, and he made his entrance singing 'Oh, What A Beautiful Mornin''. The show marked a new and exciting beginning for the American musical theatre, and Drake reigned as its leading male star for more than a decade. After singing in the Glee Club at Brooklyn College, he made his stage debut in July 1935 at the Adelphi Theatre in New York in the chorus of *The Mikado*. A year later, he was in the chorus again and also understudied one of the leading roles in a City Centre revival of **White Horse Inn**. In 1937 he introduced the title song in *Babes In Arms* and was also featured in *Two Bouquets* (1938) with Patricia Morison, an actress who would later share in one of his greatest successes. From 1939–40 Drake also appeared in three Broadway revues, *One For The Money*, *The Straw Hat Revue* (with **Danny Kaye**) and *Two For The Show*, in which, together with Frances Comstock, he introduced the future standard, 'How High The Moon'. After his magnetic performance in *Oklahoma!*, Drake co-starred

with **Burl Ives** in Walter Kerr's folk music tribute *Sing Out, Sweet Land* (1944), played Macheath in **John Latouche** and **Duke Ellington**'s contemporary version of *The Beggar's Holiday* (1946) and took the role of Larry Foreman, the union organizer, in a revival of **The Cradle Will Rock** (1947). In 1948 he enjoyed what is often considered to be his greatest personal success in **Kiss Me, Kate**. Drake gave a marvellously witty and stylish performance in the role of Fred Graham, the egocentric thespian who is tormented on and off stage by his leading lady (Patricia Morison) who also happens to be his ex-wife, Lilli. His glorious lyric tenor voice delighted audiences on numbers such as 'Where Is the Life That Late I Led?', 'I've Come To Wive It Wealthily In Padua' and 'Were Thine That Special Face'. In 1951 he turned down the leading role in **The King And I** but played it for a time in 1953 while **Yul Brynner** was on holiday. Two years later he completed a hat-trick of great roles when he played Hajj, the public poet in the musical version of **Kismet** (1955), for which he won New York Drama Critics, Donaldson and **Tony Awards**. He reprised his role in the London production and for subsequent revivals. Along with the triumphs, Drake had his flop musicals too, as a performer, director and author. They included *The Liar* (1950), *Courtin' Time* (1951), **Lock Up Your Daughters** (1960), *Kean* (1961) and *Zenda* (1963). He made his final appearance in a Broadway musical in **Gigi** (1973), a lacklustre adaptation of the classic film, which closed after three months. For most of his career he remained active in the straight, non-musical theatre and was especially applauded for his Shakespearean roles, which included Claudius to Richard Burton's Hamlet in John Gielgud's 1964 Broadway production. He bade farewell to the Broadway stage in *The Skin Of Our Teeth* in 1975. Ironically, as is often the case with Hollywood, he was not required to recreate his major stage performances for the screen; **Gordon MacRae** and **Howard Keel** took care of those. Drake made only one film, a routine musical called *Tars And Spars* (1946). He appeared on plenty of television productions, though, and there still exists a 90-minute telecast of *Kiss Me, Kate* from 1958, in which he is said to be outstanding. In 1990 Drake received his second Tony, a special award for lifetime achievement as perhaps 'the greatest singing actor the American musical theatre has ever produced.'
● ALBUMS: with Roberta Peters *Carousel* (Command 1962) ★★★.

Drake, Charlie

b. Charles Sprigall, 19 June 1925, London, England. The enormously popular actor/comedian Charlie Drake is always instantly recognizable with his shock of red hair, diminutive 5 feet 1 inch frame and distinctive cockney voice. In 1958, he hit the UK charts, outselling **Bobby Darin**, with a cover version of 'Splish Splash'. Further hits followed over the next three years, including 'Volare', 'Mr. Custer' and 'My Boomerang Won't Come Back'. The latter was co-written by Drake, in collaboration with Max Diamond. The duo also provided Drake's theme song and irritating catchphrase 'Hullo, My Darlings!'. With strong managerial backing from Colonel Bill Alexander and the producing talents of **George Martin**, Drake was in good hands and his comedy workouts translated well on to disc. Although he continued recording, acting commitments increasingly took precedence, although he did make a brief chart reappearance in 1972 with 'Puckwudgie'. His most recent appearances have been in

fellow comedian Jim Davidson's 'blue' pantomime, *Sinderella*.
● ALBUMS: *Hello My Darlings* (MFP 1967) ★★★.

Drake, Hamid

b. 3 August 1955, Monroe, Louisiana, USA. Drake studied drums extensively, including eastern and Caribbean styles. In 1974 he began what was to be a long-term musical relationship with **Fred Anderson**. In the late 70s, Anderson introduced him to **George Lewis** and **Douglas Ewart**. His most significant percussion influences, **Ed Blackwell** and **Adam Rudolph**, date from this period. The latter, who was a childhood friend, became another continuing collaborator and they appeared together in numerous contexts, including Anderson's 1979 *The Missing Link*. **Don Cherry**, who Drake first met in 1978, was another continuing collaborator. Also in the late 70s, Drake became a member of the **Mandingo Griot Society**, appearing on the group's first album. For many years Drake provided deftly inventive rhythmic support to forward-thinking musicians such as pianist **Borah Bergman** and **Peter Brötzmann**, with whom he played in a quartet alongside **William Parker** and Toshinori Kondo. Others with whom Drake has worked over the years are **Marilyn Crispell**, **Pierre Dørge**, Norwegian pianist-composer Georg Gräwe, **Herbie Hancock**, **Misha Mengelberg**, **Pharoah Sanders**, **Wayne Shorter**, **Malachi Thompson**, fellow percussionist Michael Zerang and most notably with **Kent Kessler** and **Ken Vandermark** in the DKV Trio. With these diverse artists, playing in a broad range of musical settings, Drake comfortably adapts to north and west African and Indian impulses as well as reggae and Latin.
Among drummers he has cited as being influential, aside from Blackwell and Rudolph, are **Philly Joe Jones** and **Jo Jones**. It was through the latter's broad-based concepts that Drake was impelled to explore earlier forms of drumming that had been drawn into jazz before the advent of free jazz. One result of these interests is that Drake's playing is often rather more structured and touches upon more identifiable bases than that of many of his contemporary percussionists. He also frequently plays without sticks, using his hands to develop subtly commanding undertones. His tabla playing is also notable for its subtlety and flair. Drake's questing nature and his interest in Caribbean percussion led to a deep involvement with reggae. This, too, began in the 70s and he subsequently worked with many noted names of the genre, including **Michael Rose**, **Sister Carol**, the **Heptones** and Africassa, the latter evolving into Kwame and Wan Africa. In the late 90s, he played with Dave Anderson and the I-Lites.
● ALBUMS: with Peter Brötzmann, Toshinori Kondo, William Parker *Die Like A Dog: Fragments Of Music, Life And Death Of Albert Ayler* (FMP 1993) ★★★, with Peter Brötzmann *The Dried Rat-Dog* (OkkaDisk 1994) ★★★★, with Marilyn Crispell, Brötzmann *Hyperion* 1992 recording (Music & Arts 1995) ★★★, with Crispell, Fred Anderson *Destiny* (OkkaDisk 1995) ★★★★, with Borah Bergman *Reflections On Ornette Coleman And The Stone House* (Soul Note 1995) ★★★, with Mats Gustafsson *For Don Cherry* (OkkaDisk 1995) ★★★, with Michael Zerang *Ask The Sun* (OkkaDisk 1995) ★★★, with Brötzmann, Mahmoud Gania *The WELS Concert* (OkkaDisk 1996) ★★★, with DKV Trio *Live* (OkkaDisk 1997) ★★★, with *Fred Anderson/DKV Trio* (OkkaDisk 1997) ★★★, with DKV Trio *Baraka* (OkkaDisk 1997) ★★★, with Anderson, Peter Kowald *Live At The*

Velvet Lounge (OkkaDisk 1998) ★★, with Brötzmann, Fred Hopkins *The Atlanta Concert* (OkkaDisk 1998) ★★★, with Brötzmann, Kent Kessler *Live At The Empty Bottle* (OkkaDisk 1998) ★★★, with DKV Trio *Live In Wels & Chicago* (OkkaDisk 1998) ★★★, with Joe Morris, DKV Trio *Deep Telling* (OkkaDisk 1999) ★★★, with Joe McPhee *Emancipation Proclamation: A Real Statement Of Freedom* (OkkaDisk 1999) ★★★, with Anderson, Kidd Jordan, William Parker *2 Days In April* (Eremite 2000) ★★★★, with Ken Vandermark, Nate McBride *Spaceways Incorporated: Thirteen Cosmic Standards* (Atavistic 2000) ★★★, with Adam Rudolph, Pharoah Sanders *Spirits* (Mah/Meta 2000) ★★★, with William Parker *Volume 1: Piercing The Veil* (AUM 2001) ★★★, with DKV Trio *Trigonometry* (OkkaDisk 2001) ★★★, with Marshall Allen, Edward 'Kidd' Jordan, William Parker, Alan Silva *The All-Star Game* 2000 recording (Eremite 2003) ★★★, with Anderson *Back Together Again* (Thrill Jockey 2004) ★★★.

Drake, Nick

b. Nicholas Rodney Drake, 19 June 1948, Rangoon, Burma, d. 25 November 1974, Tanworth-in-Arden, England. Born in Burma into an upper middle-class background, Drake was raised in Tanworth-in-Arden, near Birmingham. Recordings made at his parents' home in 1967 revealed a blossoming talent, indebted to **Bert Jansch** and **John Renbourn**, yet clearly a songwriter in his own right. He enrolled at Fitzwilliam College in Cambridge, and during this spell met future musical associate Robert Kirby. Drake also made several live appearances and was discovered at one such performance by **Fairport Convention** bass player **Ashley Hutchings**, who introduced the folk singer to their producer **Joe Boyd**. A series of demos were then completed, parts of which surfaced on the posthumous release *Time Of No Reply*, before Drake began work on his debut album.

Released in 1969, *Five Leaves Left* was a mature, melodic collection, which invoked the mood of **Van Morrison**'s *Astral Weeks* and **Tim Buckley**'s *Happy Sad*. Drake's languid, almost unemotional intonation contrasted with the warmth of his musical accompaniment, in particular Robert Kirby's temperate string sections. Contributions from **Richard Thompson** (guitar) and **Danny Thompson** (bass) were equally crucial, adding texture to a set of quite remarkable compositions. By contrast, the following year's *Bryter Layter* was altogether more worldly and featured support from emphatic, rather than intuitive, musicians. Lyn Dobson (flute) and **Ray Warleigh** (saxophone) provided a jazz-based perspective to parts of a selection which successfully married the artist's private and public aspirations.

Indisputably Drake's most commercial album, the singer was reportedly stunned when *Bryter Layter* failed to reap due reward and the departure of Boyd for America accentuated his growing misgivings. A bout of severe depression followed, but late in 1971 Drake resumed recording with the harrowing songs that make up his final studio album *Pink Moon*. Completed by Drake alone in two days, its stark, almost desolate atmosphere made for uncomfortable listening, yet beneath its loneliness lay a poignant beauty. Two songs, 'Parasite' and 'Place To Be' dated from 1969, while 'Things Behind The Sun' had once been considered for *Bryter Layter*. These inclusions suggested that Drake now found composing difficult, and it was 1974 before he re-entered a studio. Five tracks were completed, of which 'Black

Eyed Dog', itself a metaphor for death, seemed a portent of things to come. Four of the tracks ('Rider On The Wheel', 'Black Eyed Dog', 'Hanging On A Star' and 'Voice From The Mountain') were later released on the *Fruit Tree* box set, while 'Tow The Line' was only belatedly 'discovered' and issued on the 2004 rarities release *Made To Love Magic*.

On 25 November 1974, Nick Drake was found dead in his bedroom. Although the coroner's verdict was suicide, relatives and acquaintances feel that his overdose of a prescribed drug was accidental. Interest in this ill-fated performer has increased over the years, with a number of official and bootleg releases being released. Drake is now seen as a hugely influential artist and his catalogue contains some of the era's most accomplished music.

● ALBUMS: *Five Leaves Left* (Island 1969) ★★★★★, *Bryter Layter* (Island 1970) ★★★★★, *Pink Moon* (Island 1972) ★★★★.

● COMPILATIONS: *Nick Drake* US only (Island 1971) ★★★, *Fruit Tree: The Complete Recorded Works* 3-LP box set (Island 1979) ★★★★★, *Heaven In A Wild Flower: An Exploration Of Nick Drake* (Island 1985) ★★★★, *Fruit Tree: The Complete Works* 4-CD box set (Hannibal 1986) ★★★★★, *Time Of No Reply* (Hannibal 1987) ★★★, *Way To Blue: An Introduction To Nick Drake* (Island 1994) ★★★★, *Made To Love Magic* (Island 2004) ★★★, *A Treasury* (Island 2004) ★★★★.

● FURTHER READING: *Nick Drake*, David Housden. *Nick Drake: A Biography*, Patrick Humphries. *Darker Than The Deepest Sea: The Search For Nick Drake*, Trevor Dann.

Drake, Pete

b. Roddis Franklin Drake, 8 October 1932, Atlanta, Georgia, USA, d. 29 July 1988, Brentwood, Tennessee, USA. One of the world's leading exponents of the steel guitar, Drake arrived in Nashville in the late 50s and was quickly established as one of the city's leading session musicians. His distinctive, mellow-toned style was heard on many releases, including those by **Marty Robbins** and **Don Gibson**. Drake also recorded in his own right and while billed as Pete Drake And His Talking Steel Guitar, he secured a US Top 30 hit in 1964 with 'Forever'. However, it was for continued studio work that Drake maintained his popularity, and he crossed over into the wider rock fraternity in the wake of his contributions to three **Bob Dylan** albums, *John Wesley Harding*, *Nashville Skyline* and *Self Portrait*, and to **George Harrison**'s *All Things Must Pass*. The artist also produced **Ringo Starr**'s C&W collection *Beaucoups Of Blues*, and assembled the stellar cast supporting the former **Beatles** drummer. During the 70s Drake appeared on albums by several 'new' country acts, including **Linda Hargrove**, **Steve Young** and **Tracy Nelson**, as well as completing sessions for **Elvis Presley**. This respected musician also inaugurated his own labels, Stop Records and First Generation Records, and opened Pete's Place, a recording studio. Drake died from lung disease in July 1988.

● ALBUMS: *The Fabulous Steel Guitar Of Pete Drake* (Starday 1962) ★★★, *The Amazing And Incredible Pete Drake* (Starday 1964) ★★★ *Talking Steel And Singing Strings Forever* (Smash 1964) ★★★, *Pete Drake And His Talking Steel Guitar* (1965) ★★★, *The Hits I Played On* (1969) ★★, *Pete Drake Plays All Time Country Favourites* (1971) ★★★, *Steel Away* (1973) ★★★, *The Pete Drake Show* (Stop 1973) ★★.

Dramarama

The 80s were littered with US alt rock bands that paved the way for the genre's big commercial breakthrough in the early 90s, but they never seem to receive proper credit. Top in this category would be the **Replacements**, the **Pixies** and **Hüsker Dü**, as well as several lesser-known outfits, such as the pop art-inspired Dramarama. Comprising John Easdale (vocals), Mark Englert (guitar), Chris Carter (bass), Peter Wood (guitar), plus a revolving door of drummers, Dramarama originally formed during 1983 in Wayne, New Jersey, USA. They released an obscure single and EP, while their debut album, *Cinéma Vérité*, compiled their previous output alongside six new songs, including what would become their best-known track, 'Anything, Anything (I'll Give You)'. The album helped the band build a sizeable following among college rock devotees and became a major regional hit in Los Angeles. The excellent *Box Office Bomb* and *Stuck In Wonderamaland* failed to make any headway in a music scene still in thrall to corporate rock. Further releases continued throughout the early 90s, but despite alternative rock's emergence into the mainstream (via bands like **Nirvana**), Dramarama failed to latch onto a wider mainstream audience. They split up in 1994, with Easdale eventually launching a solo career during the latter part of the decade.

● ALBUMS: *Cinéma Vérité* (New Rose 1985) ★★★★, *Box Office Bomb* (Questionmark 1987) ★★★★, *Stuck In Wonderamaland* (Chameleon 1990) ★★★★, *Live At The China Club* mini-album (Chameleon 1990) ★★★, *Vinyl* (Chameleon/Elektra 1991) ★★★★, *Hi-Fi Sci-Fi* (Chameleon/Elektra 1993) ★★★.

● COMPILATIONS: *The Days Of Wayne And Roses* (No Label 1992) ★★★, *The Best Of Dramarama: 18 Big Ones* (Rhino 1996) ★★★★.

Dramatics

This R&B vocal group was formed in Detroit in 1964 as the Sensations. They changed their name to the Dramatics in 1965 and originally comprised lead Larry Reed, Rob Davis, Elbert Wilkins, Robert Ellington, Larry Demps (b. 23 February 1949) and Ron Banks (b. 10 May 1951, Detroit, Michigan, USA). Ellington quickly dropped out. The Dramatics were a typical 60s stand-up vocal group, specializing in romantic ballads, but ably made the transition to the disco era in the late 70s with aggressive dance numbers. They made their debut on the charts with a minor R&B hit in 1967, 'All Because Of You,' which, as with all their releases in the 60s, was issued on a small Detroit label. Around 1968, Reed and Davis were replaced by William 'Wee Gee' Howard and Willie Ford (b. 10 July 1950), respectively. The reshaped quintet's fortunes flourished when Detroit producers Don Davis and Tony Hestor took command of their career and the group signed to the Memphis-based **Stax Records** in 1971. US hits with the label included 'Whatcha See Is Whatcha Get' (R&B number 3 and pop number 9, 1971), 'In The Rain' (R&B number 1 and pop number 5, 1972) and 'Hey You! Get Off My Mountain' (R&B number 5 and pop number 43, 1973).

In 1973 Howard left to establish his solo career as 'Wee Gee', and new lead L.J. Reynolds (b. 1953, Saginaw, Michigan, USA), previously of Chocolate Syrup, was recruited by group leader Ron Banks, while Wilkins was replaced by Lenny Mayes (b. Leonard Cornell Mayes, 5 April 1951, Detroit, Michigan, USA, d. 7 November 2004, Southfield, Michigan,

USA). In 1974 the Dramatics left Stax and the following year began an association with Los Angeles–based **ABC Records** while still recording in Detroit under Davis and Hestor. US hits at ABC included the ballad 'Me And Mrs. Jones' (R&B number 4 and pop number 47, 1975), 'Be My Girl' (R&B number 3, 1976) and 'Shake It Well' (R&B number 4, 1977). Switching to MCA Records in 1979, the group secured their last Top 10 hit with 'Welcome Back Home' (R&B number 9, 1980). Shortly afterwards L.J. Reynolds left to establish a solo career, and in 1981 Craig Jones was recruited in his place, but in an age of self-contained groups the stand-up vocal group could not compete and they disbanded in 1982 after Ron Banks left to start a solo career.

The Dramatics were reunited in the late 80s and continue to the present day, keeping up a busy touring schedule and occasionally releasing a new studio album. Their grasp of superior soul remains as sure as ever.

● ALBUMS: *Whatcha See Is Whatcha Get* (Volt 1972) ★★★★, *Dramatically Yours* (Volt 1973) ★★★★, *A Dramatic Experience* (Volt 1973) ★★★★, with the Dells *The Dells vs. The Dramatics* (Cadet 1974) ★★★, *The Dramatic Jackpot* (ABC 1975) ★★★, *Drama V* (ABC 1975) ★★★, *Joy Ride* (ABC 1976) ★★★, *Shake It Well* (ABC 1977) ★★★, *Do What You Wanna Do* (ABC 1978) ★★★★, *Anytime Anyplace* (MCA 1979) ★★★, *The Dramatic Way* (MCA 1980) ★★★, *10 And A Half* (MCA 1980) ★★★, *New Dimensions* (Capitol 1982) ★★★, *Reunion* (Volt 1986) ★★★, *The Dramatics—Live* (Volt 1988) ★★, *Positive State Of Mind* (Volt 1989) ★★★, *Stone Cold* (Volt 1990) ★★★, *Look Inside* (Northcoast 2002) ★★.

Solo: L.J. Reynolds *Travellin'* (Capitol 1982) ★★★, *Lovin' Man* (Mercury 1984) ★★★, *Tell Me You Will* (Fantasy 1987) ★★★★.

● COMPILATIONS: *The Best Of The Dramatics* (Stax 1976) ★★★★, *Whatcha See Is Whatcha Get/A Dramatic Experience* (Stax 1991) ★★★★, *The ABC Years 1974–1980* (Ichiban 1996) ★★★.

Dranes, Arizona Juanita

b. c.1905, Dallas, Texas, USA. A member of the Church Of God In Christ and possibly of Mexican extraction, Arizona Dranes combined a high, forceful voice with the rocking barrelhouse piano style associated with the 'South Eastern School' to create joyful, ground-breaking gospel records that were an inspiration to many later performers. **Richard M. Jones**, who as well as being a pianist acted as a talent scout, discovered the blind singer performing in the church of Rev. Samuel Crouch in Fort Worth, Texas, and took her to Chicago to record for **OKeh Records** in 1926. In the ensuing two years she recorded 16 tracks under her own name, including some in the company of **Sara Martin**, and two piano solos, as well as possibly accompanying other singers. She was also instrumental in introducing the famous Rev. F.W. McGee to record, his first outings being in support of her third session. Dranes' opportunities to record were often restricted by the severe bouts of influenza to which she was prone. After her correspondence with the record company ceased, she disappeared back into the depression-bound south.

● COMPILATIONS: *Barrel House Piano With Sanctified Singing* (1976) ★★★, *Complete Recorded Works 1926–29* (1993) ★★★.

Dransfield, Barry

b. Harrogate, Yorkshire, England. By the age of 14 Dransfield was singing and playing blues guitar at the Harrogate folk club alongside elder brother Robin as the Dransfields. The brothers soon gravitated to the Leeds Irish music scene, where working class locals and Irish immigrants performed songs from their heritage. It influenced him profoundly and saw him drop blues in favour of exploring his own musical culture (Barry and Robin were previously part of the bluegrass band, Crimple Mountain Boys, for a period of three years). Barry continued to play the folk circuit after Robin entered college in the mid-60s, now having adapted to the fiddle as well as guitar. However, it was difficult to earn sufficient money from music, and he spent a year in London constructing harps as a secondary profession. He reunited with Robin (as **Robin And Barry Dransfield**) after his brother had completed his college studies, recording *Rout Of The Blues* in 1970. Through **Ashley Hutchings** of **Steeleye Span** Barry contributed to **Shirley Collins**' well-received 1971 album, *No Roses*. His first self-titled solo album followed the next year. A second solo set, *Bowin' And Scrapin'*, which featured Barry playing a bowed Appalachian dulcimer, was released in 1978.

By now the fraternal partnership had dissolved with both partners disillusioned with constant touring, preferring to fall back on their supplementary careers as teacher (Robin) and carpenter (Barry). While repairing violins, Barry worked as a musician for the National Theatre's production of *Translations*. He maintained links with the folk community though, playing regularly at the Islington Empress Of Russia club through the mid-80s. Afterwards he appeared as the blind fiddler, Michael Byrne, in a film version of *The Bounty* starring Mel Gibson. This involved location work in Tahiti and New Zealand, and with the money he saved he was able to set up a violin shop in Hastings, Sussex. However, this venture failed during the 80s recession. Dransfield's problems continued with the diagnosis of myalgic encephalomyelitis (M.E.), which rendered him bed-ridden for several months. However, he eventually recovered and returned to the folk circuit, recording a new album in 1994 with the help of producer Paul Dengate. Featuring versions of standards such as 'John Barleycorn' and 'Derby Ram', as well as a previously unrecorded song written by eighteenth-century Sussex composer William Mittel, it brought Barry Dransfield back into vogue within the folk community and reminded many of the depth and honesty of his earlier work with his brother. It was followed by a major tour as support to Steeleye Span and the accomplished *Wings Of The Sphinx* two years later.

● ALBUMS: *Barry Dransfield* (Polydor/Folk Mill 1972) ★★★★, *Bowin' And Scrapin'* (Topic 1978) ★★★, *Be Your Own Man* (Rhiannon 1994) ★★★, *Wings Of The Sphinx* (Rhiannon 1996) ★★★, *Unruly* (Violin Workshop 2005) ★★★.

● FILMS: *The Bounty* (1984).

Dransfield, Robin And Barry

Brothers Robin (guitar, banjo, vocals) and **Barry Dransfield** (fiddle, guitar, mandolin, gimbri, cello, vocals), both born in Harrogate, Yorkshire, England, are popular folk traditionalists who enjoyed a high profile during the 70s. They began singing and playing together in 1962, as part of a Leeds-based bluegrass band, the Crimple Mountain Boys. The group only lasted for three years, at the end of which Robin and Barry decided to concentrate on indigenous British music. Barry turned professional in 1966, having been a civil servant. Robin waited until 1969 before joining him, having performed in clubs while holding down a teaching post. *Rout Of The Blues*, its title track and the first song they had worked on together, was released by Bill Leader Records in 1970.

The duo's rising profile saw them invited to join **Steeleye Span** at this time, an offer they declined, though they did become close allies of **Ashley Hutchings**. They appeared at London's Royal Albert Hall Festival in 1971 and, in addition to Barry's fiddle tunes, contributed four tracks to the ensuing album, including 'Who's The Fool Now' and 'The Waters Of Tyne'. After touring America and participating in the *Morris On* project, the brothers then formed their own folk rock band. 1976's *The Fiddler's Dream*, with contributions from Brian Harrison, was the result, followed by the more traditional *Popular To Contrary Belief*. Although they remained popular in mainland Europe, the brothers gradually became disillusioned with the non-stop touring. 'Neither of us was stuck with music. Robin was a teacher and I was perfectly capable of making a living as a carpenter,' he recalled. Barry Dransfield resumed recording in 1994. He reunited with his brother three years later to record a number of new tracks for the compilation set *Up To Now*.

● ALBUMS: *Rout Of The Blues* (Bill Leader 1970) ★★★, *Lord Of All I Behold* (Bill Leader 1971) ★★★, *The Fiddler's Dream* (Free Reed 1976) ★★★★, *Popular To Contrary Belief* (Free Reed 1977) ★★★.

● COMPILATIONS: *Up To Now: A History Of Robin & Barry Dransfield* (Free Reed 1997) ★★★★.

Draper, Rusty

b. Farrell Draper, 25 January 1923, Kirksville, Missouri, USA, d. 28 March 2003, Bellevue, Washington, USA. Draper entered showbusiness at the age of 12, singing and playing his guitar on radio in Tulsa, Oklahoma. For the next five years, he worked on various stations including Des Moines, Iowa and Quincy, Illinois. He then became the Master of Ceremonies and vocalist at the Mel Hertz Club in San Francisco. He eventually moved to Hermie King's Rumpus Room in the same city, where he stayed for the next seven years. In 1953, his recording of 'Gambler's Guitar' reached number 6 on both the US country and pop charts and gave him his first million-seller. A second gold record followed in 1955 for his version of 'Shifting, Whispering Sands', which reached number 3 in the pop charts but surprisingly did not even make the country chart at all (a cover version by Eamonn Andrews made the UK Top 20).

During the 50s, he had further US Top 40 pop hits with 'Seventeen' (1955), 'Are You Satisfied' (1955), 'In The Middle Of The House' (1956) and a US cover version of the UK skiffle hit 'Freight Train' (1957). He did, however, have modest UK pop chart success in 1960 with his version of 'Muleskinner Blues', which peaked at number 39. In 1962 he joined **Monument Records** and reached the US pop charts with 'Night Life' in 1963. He did not achieve further US country chart successes until the late 60s, when he had very minor hits with 'My Elusive Dreams', 'California Sunshine' and 'Buffalo Nickel'. 'Two Little Boys' gave him another minor US hit in 1970, the last for 10 years, when 'Harbour Lights', an unlikely country song, became his last chart entry. Ill health severely curtailed his career during the latter stages of his life. During his career, Draper also undertook several acting roles, including appearances in some television western series such as *Rawhide* and *Laramie*, and stage musicals including **Oklahoma!** and **Annie Get Your Gun**.

● ALBUMS: *Music For A Rainy Night* (Mercury 1956) ★★★, *Encores* (Mercury 1957) ★★★, *Songs By Rusty Draper* (Mercury 1957) ★★★, *Rusty Meets Hoagy* (Mercury 1957) ★★★, *Hits That Sold A Million* (Mercury 1960) ★★★, *Country And Western Golden Greats* (Mercury 1961) ★★★, *Plays Guitar* (Monument) ★★, *Night Life* (Monument 1963) ★★★, *Something Old Something New* (Monument 1969) ★★.

● COMPILATIONS: *Greatest Hits* (Collectors' Choice 1999) ★★★★.

Dread Zeppelin

This novelty hard rock combo featured an overweight **Elvis Presley** lookalike from Pasadena, California, USA, who first attracted attention by leading the band through a succession of **Led Zeppelin** cover versions played in reggae and calypso style. The band's line-up was as bizarre as its theme and featured the aforementioned Tortelvis (b. Greg Tortell; vocals), Jah Paul Jo (b. Joe Ramsey; guitar, ex–Prime Movers), Carl Jah (b. Carl Haasis; guitar), Butt-Boy (b. Gary Putman; bass, ex–Prime Movers), Fresh Cheese (b. Paul Masselli; drums) and Ed Zeppelin (b. Bryant Fernandez; percussion), with studio input from Rasta Li-Mon. Formed in January 1989, they supposedly met when Tortelvis rammed his milkfloat into the back of the band's car, and played their first gig on 8 January, **Elvis Presley**'s birthday. They predictably attracted media curiosity and enjoyed a minor hit single with 'Your Time Is Gonna Come' from their first album and then with 'Stairway To Heaven' from the second. **Robert Plant** was reportedly highly amused at their appearance, though not so the Graceland estate of Elvis Presley. Fresh Cheese and Tortelvis left the band in 1992, forcing Butt-Boy (as Gary B.I.B.B.) to take over vocals on the disco-influenced *It's Not Unusual*. Tortelvis returned to the line-up for *Hot & Spicy Beanburger*, which was released on Jah Paul Jo's Birdcage label. Ed Zeppelin and Carl Jah were then replaced by Derf Nasna-Haj and percussionist Bruce Fernandez on 1996's *No Quarter Pounder*. On *The Fun Sessions* the band assumed the role of classic rock interpreters. A live album and rarities collection preceded their debut for the Cleopatra label, *De Jah Voodoo*.

● ALBUMS: *Un-Led-Ed* (I.R.S. 1990) ★★★, *5,000,000** (I.R.S. 1991) ★★, *It's Not Unusual* (I.R.S. 1992) ★★, *Hot & Spicy Beanburger* (Birdcage 1995) ★★★, *The First No-Elvis* (Birdcage 1996) ★★, *No Quarter Pounder* (Birdcage 1996) ★★★, *The Fun Sessions* (Imago 1996) ★★, *The Song Remains Insane* (TWA 1998) ★★, *De Jah Voodoo* (Cleopatra 2000) ★★★.

● COMPILATIONS: *Ruins* (Birdcage 1997) ★★★.

Dreadzone

This multi-faceted UK **dub** outfit is essentially a vehicle for Greg Roberts and Leo Williams (both ex–**Big Audio Dynamite**) who have been joined at various times by Dan Donovan, Tim and Chris Bran. Dreadzone's sound is particularly unique as at different times it mixes dub with elements of **techno**, **trance**, pop and folk music. Of the three albums *Second Light* captures their varied sound best, notably the folk-influenced

melodies and bouncy grooves of 'Captain Dread' and 'Little Britain' and the trancey 'One Way' and 'Zion Youth'. On 'A Canterbury Tale' they create a lush and more ambient track, blending synthesized textures with acoustic sounds such as oboe, violin, piano and a female voice. Much of their work is flavoured with samples of dialogue from cult B-movies. However their real strength seems to lie in their singles and remixes where they venture into a variety of **dance music** styles to great effect without losing their identity — 'Life, Love And Unity' (1996) included excellent dub-techno, drum 'n' bass and straight-ahead techno-trance versions of the track. Perhaps their best work is on the *Maximum EP* (1995). The first track 'Fight The Power', which was written in opposition to the Criminal Justice Bill's legislation on parties, blends the dub lines with drum 'n' bass tendencies, four-on-the-floor style techno, rock guitar and a sample from the **Beastie Boys**' 'Fight For Your Right To Party'. The energetic live drums on the final track 'Maximum', which was recorded for a **John Peel** session, highlight the band's versatility further.

● ALBUMS: *360°* (Creation 1993) ★★★, *Second Light* (Virgin 1995) ★★★★, *Biological Radio* (Virgin 1997) ★★, *Sound* (Ruff Life 2001) ★★★.

● COMPILATIONS: *The Radio One Sessions* (Strange Fruit 2001) ★★★.

D:Ream

This London-based outfit crossed over from **dance music** clubs to daytime radio and won themselves impressive chart placings in the process. D:Ream originally comprised Al Mackenzie (b. Alan Mackenzie, 31 October 1968, Edinburgh, Scotland) and Peter Cunnah (b. 30 August 1966, Derry, Northern Ireland; ex–Tie The Boy, Baby June). Their first outing came at the JFK Bar in Great Portland Street, London, in February 1992. Four months later **Rhythm King Records** released their debut 45, 'U R The Best Thing' (the **Prince**-like spellings would become a regular feature of their titles). Although they failed to score many credibility points amongst their dance music peers, they nevertheless became a sought-after remix team among mainstream pop artists (**Deborah Harry**, **EMF**, **Duran Duran**). Both 'U R The Best Thing' and, later, 'Things Can Only Get Better' were reissued in the wake of their higher profile and initial chart appearances.

Their debut album, released in August 1993, was roundly rubbished by the press. Mackenzie too appeared less than happy with its new pop direction and announced his decision to leave the band in October 1993 and return to DJ work. The revitalized 'Things Can Only Get Better' enjoyed a long stay at the top of the UK pop charts in early 1994, when there was some derision among the puritan dance community, with **Pressure Of Speech** lambasting the track for its potential to be 'the next Tory Conference song' (ironically, the song was used by the Labour Party in their triumphant 1997 election campaign). Shortly afterwards, a second remix of 'U R The Best Thing' reached UK number 4. Mackenzie, meanwhile, was embarking on a solo career as (among other things) Kitsch In Sync ('Jazz Ma Ass' for Global Grooves in 1994). The band's only other Top 10 hit came in summer 1995 when 'Shoot Me With Your Love' reached UK number 7.

● ALBUMS: *D:Ream On Vol. 1* (Rhythm King 1993) ★★★, *World* (Magnet 1995) ★★.

● COMPILATIONS: *The Best Of D:Ream* (Magnet 1997) ★★★.

Dream (pop)

This Los Angeles, California, USA–based female vocal group enjoyed their brief moment in the spotlight at the start of the new millennium. The quartet's vocal talent belied the fact that they were selected, by talent scout Judith Fontaine, from a mass audition of singers with the aim of creating a girl group to rival the all conquering **Destiny's Child** and boy band stars **Backstreet Boys** and ***NSYNC**. Formed in late 1998, the original line-up featured Ashley Poole (b. 10 May 1985), Holly Blake Arnstein (b. 3 August 1985), Melissa Schuman (b. 21 August 1984) and Alex Chester, but the latter was quickly replaced by Diana Ortiz (b. 25 September 1985). The quartet then parted company with Fontaine and was snapped up by **Sean 'Puffy' Combs'** Bad Boy Records label. They made an immediate impact on US radio with the R&B-inflected 'He Loves U Not'. The single began a steady climb up the national charts, culminating in a Top 5 slot in January 2001. By this time the quartet had completed work on their debut, *It Was All A Dream*, recorded with a cast of leading producers, musicians and songwriters. Though nothing on the album came close to matching the melodic verve of 'He Loves U Not', it was a competent enough collection of urban-lite material. The first totally pop-orientated act to be signed to Bad Boy, they also helped revive the label's fortunes.

Schuman left the group in April 2002 and was replaced by Kasey Sheridan. The new line-up returned to the studio and recorded the harder-edged single 'Crazy', which featured rapper **Loon**. The failure of the single caused Bad Boy to get cold feet over the release of a second album, and eventually they opted to drop Dream from their roster. The quartet subsequently broke up, with Poole and Schuman launching solo careers and Blake Arnstein joining rock band Whirl Magnet.

● ALBUMS: *It Was All A Dream* (Bad Boy/Arista 2001) ★★★.

Dream (stage musical)

Subtitled '*The Johnny Mercer Musical*', this revue, which was conceived by Louis Westergaard and Jack Wrangler, opened on 3 April 1997 at the Royale Theatre in New York and contained some 45 prime examples of the work of the great lyricist (and sometime composer). Lesley Ann Warren ('Goody Goody', 'Blues In The Night', 'That Old Black Magic'), **Margaret Whiting** and jazz singer/guitarist **John Pizzarelli** ('Fools Rush In', 'Jeepers Creepers', 'I Thought About You') headed a talented cast that also featured Brooks Ashmanskas, Jonathan Dokuchitz, Charles McGowan, Jessica Molaskey and Darcie Roberts. Over the years, Whiting actually introduced several of Mercer's songs, and she excelled here with 'One For My Baby', 'Day In-Day Out' and 'My Shining Hour'. Her father, **Richard Whiting**, was also one of Mercer's many collaborators, and he was represented by 'Have You Got Any Castles, Baby?', 'Hooray For Hollywood' and the enduring 'Too Marvelous For Words'. Among Mercer's other important composing colleagues were **Harold Arlen**, **Hoagy Carmichael**, **Harry Warren**, **Jerome Kern**, **Rube Bloom**, **Victor Schertzinger**, **Henry Mancini**—and of course, Mercer himself, who wrote both words and music for standards such as 'Something's Gotta Give' and the show's title number. *Dream* divided Mercer's long career into significant periods: 20s decadent Savannah (The Age of Innocence), 30s at the Rainbow nightclub (The Age of Decadence), 40s Big Band Era, and the golden, Academy Award–winning Hollywood years of the 50s, 60s, and beyond. Packed as it was with wonderful songs, *Dream* failed to register strongly when awards time came around (just one **Tony Awards** nomination, for director and choreographer Wayne Cilento), and the show closed on 6 July.

Although Broadway was not the prime source of Mercer's work over the years, he did write occasional lyrics for musical shows in the 30s, as well as providing the complete score (with Rube Bloom) for the London production of *Blackbirds Of 1936*. He subsequently collaborated on entire scores for St. Louis Woman (with Harold Arlen, 1946), *Texas, L'il Darlin'* (music: Robert Emmett Dolan, 1949), *Top Banana* (Mercer, 1951), *Li'l Abner* (**Gene De Paul**, 1956), *Saratoga* (Arlen, 1959), *Foxy* (Dolan, 1964), and *The Good Companions* (**André Previn**, London 1974). His outstanding film score for **Seven Brides For Seven Brothers** (with de Paul) was also adapted for the stage in 1982 (Broadway) and 1985 (London). Among the many revues and cabaret shows to celebrate his lyrics, was one by Peggy Herman, whose *2 Marvellous 4 Words* played at New York's Eighty Eight's in the early 90s.

Dream Academy

This 80s UK band comprised Nick Laird-Clowes (guitar/vocals; ex–the Act), Gilbert Gabriel (keyboards) and **Kate St. John** (vocals/oboe/saxophone, ex–Ravishing Beauties). Laird-Clowes, who as a child experienced the last days of the London underground movement at first hand, revived memories of that earlier era with the polished folky-pop 'Life In A Northern Town', dedicated to the memory of singer-songwriter **Nick Drake**. The single, released on the Blanco y Negro label, reached UK number 15 in 1985 (and US number 7 the following year). Hailed, or conversely, derided as one of the leading lights of the new breed of English psychedelic revivalists, the band's momentum was halted by the relative failure of 'The Love Parade'. They periodically released albums that stuck gamely to their formula, with **Pink Floyd** member **David Gilmour** contributing guitar and production work to their third album. St. John, meanwhile, found plentiful work composing incidental music for British television programmes, while Laird-Clowes later resurfaced on **Creation Records** as Trashmonk.

● ALBUMS: *The Dream Academy* (Blanco y Negro 1985) ★★★, *Remembrance Days* (Blanco y Negro 1987) ★★, *A Different Kind Of Weather* (Blanco y Negro 1990) ★★.

Dream Frequency

On the back of popular club tunes such as 'Feel So Real' and 'Take Me', Debbie Sharp and Ian Bland conquered a niche market, especially in being among the few **dance music** acts to avail themselves of the live arena. They generated several column inches when they were originally sought out by **Madonna**'s Maverick label (whose interest, they claim, dropped when it was realized that Sharp was pregnant). Further success, however, arrived with the stylish 'So Sweet', which became another club favourite. Bland has also worked with Martin Lever as Museka (The *M-Series* EP).

Dream Maker, The

(see It's All Happening)

Dream Police

Formed in Glasgow, Scotland in 1967, the Dream Police revolved around guitarist/vocalist Hamish Stuart. An early version of the group was brought to an end when Stuart briefly joined Hopscotch, but he re-formed the Dream Police in 1968. Joe Breen (guitar), Matt Irving (bass) and Charlie Smith (drums) completed the new line-up, which was signed to **Decca Records** in 1970 at the behest of Junior Campbell of **Marmalade**. The first Dream Police single, 'I'll Be Home', was more akin to Campbell's work than the group's own brand of soulful rock. Subsequent releases, 'Our Song' and 'I've Got No Choice', showed a musically competent act, but one searching for direction. In 1971 Smith was replaced by Ted McKenna, but the Dream Police split up soon afterwards. Hamish Stuart later rejoined another Hopscotch refugee, Alan Gorrie, in the **Average White Band**. Smith joined **Blue**, while McKenna found fame in the **Sensational Alex Harvey Band**.

Dream Syndicate

The early 80s were exciting times for those with a taste for American west coast rock. Several aspiring new acts appeared in the space of a few months who were obviously indebted to the late 60s but managed to offer something refreshingly vital in the process. The Dream Syndicate's self-titled debut EP and the follow-up *The Days Of Wine And Roses* (recorded in September 1982) more than justified the attention that the 'Paisley Underground' bands were attracting. Comprising songwriter **Steve Wynn** (b. 21 February 1960, Los Angeles, California, USA; guitar/vocals), Karl Precoda (guitar), Kendra Smith (bass) and Dennis Duck (drums), the band chose their finest song, 'Tell Me When It's Over', for their first UK single, issued on **Rough Trade Records** in late 1983. A contract with **A&M Records** followed, and *Medicine Show* appeared in 1984. Like their debut, there was a definite acknowledgement of the influence of both **Lou Reed** and **Neil Young**.

By this time, Kendra Smith had joined partner David Roback in **Opal** (she would also release a sumptuous solo album in 1995) and was replaced by Dave Provost (ex-**Droogs**). *This Is Not The New Dream Syndicate Album . . . Live!* featured new bass player Mark Walton, but it was to be their last engagement with A&M. Another move, this time to **Chrysalis Records** offshoot Big Time, resulted in 1987's *Out Of The Grey*. Recorded by Wynn, Walton, Duck and new guitarist Paul B. Cutler, the band's approach was now gradually shifting to the mainstream. After a 12-inch single, '50 In A 25 Zone', the Dream Syndicate moved to the Enigma Records label distributed in the UK by **Virgin Records**. *Ghost Stories* was followed by the live swan-song offering *Live At Raji's* in 1989. However, the band never surpassed the dizzy heights of their first album, leaving Wynn to go on to a similarly acclaimed but commercially unsuccessful solo career and occasional recordings with **Gutterball**. Pat Thomas' Normal Records label unearthed some excellent unreleased Dream Syndicate recordings during the 90s.

● ALBUMS: *The Dream Syndicate* mini-album (Down There 1982) ★★★★, *The Days Of Wine And Roses* (Ruby/Rough Trade 1983) ★★★★, *Medicine Show* (A&M 1984) ★★★, *This Is Not The New Dream Syndicate Album . . . Live!* mini-album (A&M 1984) ★★, *Out Of The Grey* (Big Time 1986) ★★★, *Ghost Stories* (Enigma 1988) ★★★, *Live At Raji's* (Enigma 1989) ★★★, *The Days Before Wine And Roses* 1982 live recording (Normal 1994) ★★★, *The Complete Live At Raji's* (Rykodisc 2004) ★★★.

● COMPILATIONS: *It's Too Late To Stop Now* (Another Cowboy 1989) ★★★, *The Lost Tapes: 1985–1988* (Normal 1993) ★★★.

● DVD/VIDEOS: *Weathered & Torn* (Enigma 1988).

Dream Theater

This rock band was formed in 1985 by **Berklee College Of Music** students John Petrucci (b. 12 July 1967, Long Island, New York, USA; guitar), John Myung (b. 24 January 1967, Chicago, Illinois, USA; bass) and Mike Portnoy (b. 20 April 1967, Long Island, New York, USA; drums; ex-**Inner Sanctum**). The trio subsequently enlisted old schoolfriend Kevin Moore (keyboards) and vocalist Chris Collins and began to record demos. Along with a contract with MCA Records, they also secured the services of vocalist Charlie Dominici, adopting their new name in favour of original choice Majesty. Their debut album showcased material incorporating elements of **Rush**, **Queensrÿche** and **Yngwie Malmsteen**, in addition to the English progressive tradition embodied by **King Crimson** and **Genesis**. Dynamic, multi-faceted hard rock songs, characterized by countless slick time changes and impeccable musicianship, were the band's trademarks. The album received a favourable response from the music media, but unfortunately was ignored by the record-buying public. Dismayed at the poor album sales, MCA terminated their contract and Dominici quit shortly afterwards. It took the band a year to extricate themselves from the contract, and a rigorous auditioning process began to find a new singer. The winning candidate was Canadian James LaBrie (b. Kevin James LaBrie, 5 May 1963, Penetanguishene, Ontario, Canada) formerly of Winter Rose. After their earlier label and personnel tribulations, their 90s albums for **Atco**/EastWest saw them regain their initial momentum, with both mainstream and metal critics acknowledging their fluency in meshing a variety of styles around a hard rock core. Moore left the band half way through the recording of *Awake* and was subsequently replaced by Derek Sherinian. Following the release of *Falling Into Infinity*, Sherinian was replaced by Jordan Rudess (b. 4 November 1956, New York, USA; ex-**Speedway Blvd.**), who had already played with Petrucci and Portnoy in their side-project **Liquid Tension Experiment**. A live set preceded the release of 1999's new studio album, *Scenes From A Memory*. Other projects include Playtpus (Myung) and **Transatlantic** (Portnoy).

● ALBUMS: *When Dream And Day Unite* (MCA 1989) ★★, *Images And Words* (Atco 1992) ★★★, *Awake* (Elektra 1994) ★★★, *A Change Of Seasons* mini-album (Elektra 1995) ★★★, *Falling Into Infinity* (Elektra 1997) ★★★, *Once In A LIVEtime* (Elektra 1998) ★★★, *Scenes From A Memory* (Elektra 1999) ★★★★, *Live Scenes From New York* (Elektra 2001) ★★★, *Six Degrees Of Inner Turbulence* (Elektra 2002) ★★★, *Train Of Thought* (Elektra 2003) ★★★, *Octavarium* (Atlantic 2005) ★★★.

● DVD/VIDEOS: *Images And Words* (Sony 1993), *5 Years In A LIVEtime* (Elektra 1998), *Metropolis 2000: Scenes From New York* (Warner Video 2001).

Dream Warriors

A key part of the surprisingly active Canadian rap scene, West Indian duo King Lou (b. Louis Robinson, Jamaica, West Indies) and Capital Q (b. Frank Lennon Alert, Port Of

Spain, Trinidad, West Indies—so named because his father was a **John Lennon** fan) had to go to the UK in the late 80s to secure a record contract with 4th & Broadway. Previously, they had released a single, 'Let Your Backbone Slide', on a New York independent. Their blend of hip-hop super-structure with jazz tempo arrived via arch lyrics, overflowing with obscure mystic imagery, from the pen of King Lou. The sound was big and loose, often punctuated by samples from television themes and psychedelic and African chants. They secured a hit almost immediately with 'Wash Your Face In My Sink', and the success continued in 1990 with 'My Definition Of A Boombastic Jazz Style', derived from a **Quincy Jones** television theme tune. They also charted when they moved into reggae with 'Ludi' in 1991 (Ludi is a West Indian board game), and they worked with jazz legend **Slim Gaillard** shortly before his death the same year. The follow-up album attempted the same fusion of jazz and hip-hop and also introduced some spoken word experiments. An extensive compilation set was released at the end of the decade and offers a fine overview of the duo's often underappreciated work.

● ALBUMS: *And Now The Legacy Begins* (4th & Broadway 1991) ★★★★, *Subliminal Simulation* (EMI Canada 1994) ★★★.

● COMPILATIONS: *Anthology: A Decade Of Hits 1988–1998* (Beatfactory/Priority 1998) ★★★★.

Dream Weavers

A vocal group comprising three college students, based in Miami, Florida, USA. The Dream Weavers was born out of necessity when Wade Buff and Eugene Atkinson were unable to find an artist to record their composition 'It's Almost Tomorrow'. After exposure on the college radio station, their own self-financed recording was picked up by **Decca Records** and entered the US Top 10 in 1955. It did even better in the UK, climbing to the top of the charts in the following year. Subsequently, the Dream Weavers had a minor hit with **Sammy Fain** and **Paul Francis Webster**'s 'A Little Love Can Go A Long, Long Way', from the film *Ain't Misbehavin'*, but then disappeared without a trace. 'It's Almost Tomorrow' also charted in the USA for **Jo Stafford**, **Snooky Lanson** and **David Carroll** in the 50s and was a UK hit for **Mark Wynter** in 1963.

Dreamers

R&B/doo-wop group the Dreamers formed in 1958 at a family wedding, attended by cousins Frank Cammarata (lead and tenor), Bob Malara (tenor), Luke 'Babe' Beradis (tenor and baritone) and Dominic Canzano (baritone and bass), with the only non-cousin John 'Buddy' Trancynger (baritone and bass). End Records promptly signed the band to its new offshoot, Goldisc. The sentimental ballad 'Teenagers Vow Of Love' proved popular in the New York area during 1960, when it was released as their debut recording. Afterwards Berardis and Canzano were replaced by Frank Nicholas (from the Meridians) and Frank DiGilio as the group found a new home at Cousins Records. Their first release there was a highly idiosyncratic version of **Tony Bennett**'s 'Because Of You', but when it transferred mid-release to Cousins' May Records subsidiary, the momentum was lost and with it the chance of an extended musical career. Afterwards, their opportunities to record disappeared as they concentrated on a stage show that proved particularly popular at service bases. They broke up in 1963 but re-formed briefly in the mid-80s.

● ALBUMS: *Yesterday Once More* (Dream 1987) ★★★.

● COMPILATIONS: *They Sing Like Angels* (Ace 2002) ★★★.

Dreamgirls

With a provocative book by Tom Eyen that tells of the peaks and troughs in the life of the Dreams, a black female singing group not a million miles away from the **Supremes**, *Dreamgirls* opened on Broadway at the Imperial Theatre on 20 December 1981—and stayed for nearly four years. When it is apparent that they can make it right to the top, their manager, Curtis Taylor Jnr. (Ben Harney), tells the substantially built lead singer, Effie White (**Jennifer Holliday**), who has been his lover, to move over and to the rear so that a more attractive girl can take the spotlight. The decision proves to be the right one for the group, and Effie eventually leaves and subsequently achieves her own solo stardom. **Michael Bennett**, the doyen of Broadway choreographers and directors, staged the show brilliantly, and there were some stunning moments, especially Effie's dramatic rendering of 'And I Am Telling You I'm Not Going'. That number, and the rest of the score, was the work of Henry Krieger and Tom Eyen, who succeeded in infusing the songs with a genuine **Motown** quality. They included 'When I First Saw You', 'I Am Changing', 'Fake Your Way To The Top', 'Cadillac Car', 'Hard To Say Goodbye, My Love', 'Dreamgirls' and 'Steppin' On The Bad Side'. *Dreamgirls* ran for 1,522 performances and dominated the **Tony Awards** ceremony, winning in six categories: book, choreography (Bennett and Michael Peters), best actor (Harney), best actress (Holliday), featured actor (Cleavant Derricks) and lighting (Tharon Musser). Krieger and Eyen, together with producer David Foster, also picked up Grammys for Best Cast Show Album. In 1987, after an extensive road tour, a streamlined version of the show was welcomed back on Broadway for five months. Since that time various other productions have played US regional theatres such as the Paper Mill Playhouse, Marriott's Lincolnshire Theatre and the Long Beach Civic Light Opera. A national touring company was on the road late 1997–98.

Dreamlovers

Formed as the Romances in Philadelphia, Pennsylvania, USA, in 1956, the Dreamlovers notched up two claims to fame: their own US Top 10 doo-wop ballad, 1961's 'When We Get Married', and their role as **Chubby Checker**'s back-up group on his top-selling dance hit 'The Twist'. The quintet initially comprised lead vocalist William Johnson, tenor Tommy Ricks, tenor Cleveland Hammock Jnr., baritone Conrad Dunn and bass James Ray Dunn. After Johnson was killed in a street fight, Morris Gardner was brought in as his replacement, and a new name, the Dreamlovers, was taken. In 1960 they recorded their first tracks for the Len and V-Tone labels, which failed to sell, but that same year **Cameo-Parkway Records** hired the group to provide vocals behind Chubby Checker on his future hit as well as subsequent Cameo label tracks by **Checker**, **Dee Dee Sharp** and the **Dovells**. The Dreamlovers made their mark in the pop history books with 'When We Get Married', written by Don Hogan, a part-time member of the group. One single for End Records also charted, and in 1973, after making a single under the name A Brother's Guiding Light, the group disbanded. Some of the members formed a new Dreamlovers in 1980 and were still performing in the early 90s.

● ALBUMS: *The Bird And Other Golden Dancing Grooves* (Columbia 1963) ★★★.
● COMPILATIONS: *Best Of . . .* (Collectables 1990) ★★★, *Best Of . . . Volume 2* (Collectables 1990) ★★, *The Best Of . . .* (Sequel 1994) ★★★, *The Heritage Masters Plus . . .* (Sequel 1997) ★★★.

Dreams Come True

An oddball but appealing Japanese indie pop act, observed by some to be 'an oriental **Parliament**', Dreams Come True released their first English-language album in 1997 after a decade of popularity in their native country. Masato Nakamura (bass), Miwa Yoshida (vocals/lyrics) and Takahiro Nishikawa (keyboards) formed the band in 1988, releasing nine albums in the ensuing decade and amassing a sales tally of over 25 million units. *The Swinging Star* (1992) broke all Japanese sales records to become the bestselling album in the country's history. The band enjoys unprecedented popularity as a live act and are regulars on Japanese television shows, domestic films and video game soundtracks. The band's music, built on Western influences ranging from classic soul to R&B and from rock 'n' roll to disco and funk, became omnipresent in Japanese cultural life throughout the 90s. By 1998 they had moved from long-standing label Sony to **Virgin Records**, who were keen to promote the band to an international market, especially America. The move was hailed as the first time a major Japanese band had moved from a domestic imprint to an American-owned record label. The band confessed to frustration at Sony's insular marketing regime, although Dreams Come True had previously collaborated with American star Maurice White of **Earth, Wind And Fire** (for the single 'Wherever You Are') and appeared on 'Eternity', the theme for the US animation feature *The Swan Princess*. Following the disappointing reception received by other Japanese pop acts such as **Toshi Kubota** and **Seiko Matsuda**, Virgin were taking a major gamble on their new act (who reportedly cost them $25 million to sign). They believed that Dreams Come True could follow the success of more left field or *avant garde* Asian artists such as **Pizzicato Five**, **Buffalo Daughter** and **Cornelius**.
● ALBUMS: *Dreams Come True* (Sony Japan 1989) ★★★, *Love Goes On* (Sony Japan 1989) ★★★, *Wonder 3* (Sony Japan 1990) ★★★, *Million Kisses* (Sony Japan 1991) ★★★, *The Swinging Star* (Sony Japan 1992) ★★★★, *Magic* (Sony Japan 1993) ★★★, *Delicious* (Sony Japan 1995) ★★, *Love Unlimited* (Sony Japan 1996) ★★★, *Sing Or Die* (Virgin 1997) ★★★.
Solo: Miwa Yoshida *Beauty And Harmony* (Sony Japan 1995) ★★.

Dreem Teem

The most famous sons of the UK **garage** scene, the Dreem Teem comprises Timmi Magic (b. Timmi Eugene, 23 August 1968, London, England), DJ Spoony (b. Jonathan Joseph, 27 June 1970, London, England) and Mikee B (b. Michael Bennett, 10 December 1967, Kingston, Jamaica, West Indies). The three London-based DJ-producers began their careers on pirate radio and by playing at influential garage parties in London such as La Cosa Nostra and the Arches. They are now known for their 'Twice As Nice' nights at London's Colosseum and for their shows on legitimate radio stations such as Kiss 100 and the BBC's Radio 1—where they have a

weekly show. In the late 90s, along with **Tuff Jam**, they became somewhat reluctantly associated with the 'speed garage' phenomenon—which was more of a marketing creation than a grass-roots movement. They began by playing soul, rare groove and funk before the **acid house** explosion in the UK saw them progress to **rave**, **hardcore** and drum 'n' bass. They formed the Dreem Teem after meeting on London's underground **dance music** scene in the mid-90s. They released a mix compilation based on their DJ sets, *In Session*, in 1996, which was a success, and in the following year they scored a club and UK Top 40 chart hit with their first single 'The Theme'. They have gone on to remix for high-profile artists such as **Evelyn 'Champagne' King** ('One More Time'), Amira ('My Desire'), **Shola Ama** ('Much Love') and **All Saints** ('Booty Call'). Their remix of **Neneh Cherry**'s 'Buddy X' was a huge success in the clubs and reached the UK Top 20 in 1999. Their second *In Session* album was also a commercial success. It was announced in 1999 that the Dreem Teem would join other BBC Radio 1 dance DJs such as **Judge Jules**, **Gilles Peterson** and **Grooverider** who had graduated to the BBC from the respected and influential commercial station Kiss 100 FM. This move reflected a more general surge of interest in the UK garage and 'two-step' scene. Its profile reached new heights with the commercial success of **Shanks And Bigfoot** (the chart-topping 'Sweet Like Chocolate') and the **Artful Dodger** ('Re-rewind The Crowd Say Bo Selecta' and 'Movin' Too Fast'), several compilation albums and a burgeoning scene in Ayia Napa, Cyprus, that had started to annually relocate from London during the summer months. In August 2000, they released a new mix compilation for Sony's INCredible imprint.
● COMPILATIONS: *In Session* (4 Liberty 1996) ★★★, *In Session—Volume 2* (4 Liberty 1997) ★★★, *INCredible Sound Of The Dreem Teem* (INCredible 2000) ★★★★.

Drennon, Eddie

This US musician/arranger studied violin and composition at Howard University and worked with various artists including the New Jersey Symphony and **Bo Diddley**. He recorded 20 tracks with the latter, and the electric violin sound that he invented was later 'borrowed' by the pioneering R&B band (and Diddley fans) the **Yardbirds**. As a soloist he recorded for **Chess Records** and **RCA Records** and also did a great deal of session work. In the 70s, he was based in Washington and his 12-piece string section backed acts such as the **O'Jays** and the **Stylistics** when they came to town. His sole hit came with BBS Unlimited, an eight-piece band plus female vocalists and strings, which he formed in 1971. The disco hit 'Let's Do The Latin Hustle' was originally released in the USA on Friends & Co in 1975 and just made the R&B Top 40. Combining the sounds of **MFSB** and **Barry White** with a Latin dance beat, it topped the UK soul chart and made the Top 20. The song is perhaps best remembered because of its UK cover version (Drennon called it 'the counterfeit version') by Worcestershire group the **M&O Band**, who were accused of using part of Drennon's track on their record. His follow-up was 'Let's Do It Again', but the public did not take up the offer.
● ALBUMS: *Collage* (Pye 1976) ★★.

Dresser, Mark

b. 26 September 1952, Los Angeles, California, USA. Dresser started on bass at the age of 10, played in rock groups in his early teens then studied music at Indiana University for one year, leaving because 'it was too straight for me, like a music factory'. Moving to San Diego, he studied with classical maestro Bertram turetzky and also played at weekly jam sessions in LA led by **Bobby Bradford**—other participants were **Stanley Crouch**, **David Murray** and **James Newton**. Unable to make a living playing new jazz, Dresser moved to the east coast, settling in New Haven, Connecticut, where **Leo Smith**, **Pheeroan Ak Laff**, **Gerry Hemingway**, **Anthony Davis** and **Jay Hoggard** were among his neighbours. Although he played occasional concerts in New York, often with trombonist **Ray Anderson**, when Dresser followed many of his New Haven colleagues and went to live in the city, he found work increasingly scarce and, disheartened, returned to California. He resumed his LA connection with Bradford and Newton, formed a trio that included **Diamanda Galas** (then a jazz pianist) and in 1980 toured Europe as part of the Ray Anderson Quartet (*Harrisburg Half Life*). With work still hard to find, Dresser went back to college to study music, meanwhile playing with **Charles McPherson**, recording with Bradford (*Lost In LA*) and Newton (*Binu*) and releasing his own solo cassette, *Bass Excursions*, in 1983. Later that year he moved to Italy to study, staying for two years, and in 1985 joined the **Anthony Braxton** Quartet for tours of Europe and the UK. Back in the USA, he again moved to New York and has now made his mark on the city's contemporary jazz scene.

Dresser remains a member of Braxton's quartet and plays regularly with Anderson, **Tim Berne**, the string trio Arcado (which he formed with **Hank Roberts** and violinist Mark Feldman) and the quartet Tambastics (with **Robert Dick**, Hemingway and **Denman Maroney**). He has also recorded with **John Zorn** (*Spy Vs Spy*) and **Marilyn Crispell** (*The Kitchen Concert*). A composer as well his orchestra piece *Castles For Carter* (dedicated to **John Carter**) was premiered at Amsterdam's October Meeting in 1991. Dresser's more recent work has become deeper and emotionally wandering, in particular his excellent composition 'Bosnia', featured on *Force Green*.

● ALBUMS: *Bass Excursions* (Dresser/Wolf 1983) ★★★, with Hank Roberts, Mark Feldman *Arcado* (JMT 1989) ★★★, with Arcado *Behind The Myth* (JMT 1990) ★★★, with Arcado *For Three Strings And Orchestra* (JMT 1991) ★★★, *Tambastics* (Music And Arts 1992) ★★★, *The Cabinet Of Dr. Caligari* (Knitting Factory 1994) ★★★, *Force Green* (Soul Note 1995) ★★★★, *Invocation* (Knitting Factory 1996) ★★★, *Banquet* (Tzadik 1997) ★★★★, *Eye'll Be Seeing You* (Knitting Factory 1998) ★★★★, with Eric Watson, Ed Thigpen *Silent Hearts* (Free Flight 1999) ★★★, with Eugene Chadbourne, Susie Ibarra, Joe Morris *Pain Pen* (Avant 2000) ★★★, with Fred Frith, Ikue Mori *Later . . .* (Victo 2000) ★★★, with Frances-Marie Uitti *Sonomondo* (Cryptogramaphone 2000) ★★, with Andrew Cyrille, Marty Ehrlich *C/D/E* (Jazz Magnet 2001) ★★★★, with Denman Maroney *Duologues* (Victo 2001) ★★★, *Aquifier* (Cryptogramaphone 2002) ★★★★, with Susie Ibarra *Tone Time* (Wobbly Rail 2004) ★★, with Maroney *Time Changes* (Cryptogramaphone 2005) ★★★.

Dressy Bessy

Although they could neatly be classified in the alt pop category, this Denver, Colorado, USA-based trio also exhibit elements of 60s pop. The band formed during October 1997, when Tammy Ealom (vocals/guitar) and Darren Albert

(drums) met at a local record store. Albert had recently moved to Colorado from Staten Island, New York City, along with his bass player friend, Rob Greene, who signed on soon after and completed the Dressy Bessy line-up. It was not long before the trio got to work on a number of songs that Ealom had previously written and began issuing singles straight away. By 1999 the band was signed to indie label Kindercore Records, who issued their debut, *Pink Hearts Yellow Moons*, the same year. The album was produced by **Apples In Stereo** guitarist John Hill, who also signed on as the band's lead guitarist soon after. Although only averaging about a show a month in the Denver area, Dressy Bessy received a fair amount of praise in the national music press and have appeared on a few movie soundtracks in addition to issuing further albums such as 2002's *Sound Go Round* and 2003's *Dressy Bessy*. The same year as their third album appeared, a compilation of early singles was issued, *Little Music: Singles 1997–2002*.

● ALBUMS: *Pink Hearts Yellow Moons* (Kindercore 1999) ★★★★, *Sound Go Round* (Kindercore 2002) ★★★, *Dressy Bessy* (Kindercore 2003) ★★★★.

● COMPILATIONS: *Little Music: Singles 1997–2002* (Kindercore 2003) ★★★.

Drew, Kenny

b. 28 August 1928, New York City, New York, USA, d. 4 August 1993, Copenhagen, Denmark. A child prodigy, Drew studied piano and music, making his first records in 1949 with **Howard McGhee**. In the 50s he was much in demand for recording and club sessions by mainstream and modern musicians such as **Coleman Hawkins**, **Lester Young** and **Charlie Parker**. He worked regularly with **Buddy De Franco** and appeared on **John Coltrane**'s seminal Blue Train. Towards the end of the 50s he worked with **Buddy Rich**, but by 1961 Drew was resident in Paris, relocating in 1964 to Copenhagen, where he lived until his death. In his adopted city, Drew worked mainly at composing and arranging and also ran successful companies engaged in music publishing and recording. He still found time to record his own playing and regularly accompanied local luminaries, such as **Niels-Henning Ørsted Pedersen**, and visiting American jazz artists. In performance Drew's playing was exhilaratingly complex, but he periodically exhibited his love for the dazzling simplicity of **Bud Powell**'s best work. His son, **Kenny Drew Jnr.**, is a gifted pianist who plays in a style reminiscent of his father's.

● ALBUMS: *New Faces, New Sounds: Introducing The Kenny Drew Trio* 10-inch album (Blue Note 1953) ★★★, *The Ideation Of Kenny Drew* 10-inch album (Norgran 1954) ★★★, *Progressive Piano* aka *The Modernity Of Kenny Drew* (Norgran 1954) ★★★, *Talkin' And Walkin' With The Kenny Drew Quartet* (Jazz West 1955) ★★★★, *I Love Jerome Kern* (Riverside 1956) ★★★, *Kenny Drew Trio* (Riverside 1956) ★★★, *This Is New* aka *Hard Bop* (Riverside 1957) ★★★★, *A Harry Warren Showcase* (Judson 1957) ★★★, *A Harold Arlen Showcase* (Judson 1957) ★★★, *Jazz Impressions Of The Rodgers And Hart Stage And Screen Classic 'Pal Joey'* (Riverside 1957) ★★★, *Undercurrent* (Blue Note 1961) ★★★★, with Niels-Henning Ørsted Pedersen *Duo* (SteepleChase 1973) ★★★★, *Everything I Love* (SteepleChase 1973) ★★★, with Pedersen *Duo 2* (SteepleChase 1974) ★★★, *If You Could See Me Now* (SteepleChase 1974) ★★★, with Pedersen *Duo Live In Concert* (SteepleChase 1974) ★★★, *Morning* (SteepleChase 1975) ★★★,

The Kenny Drew Trio In Concert (SteepleChase 1977) ★★★, Lite Flite (SteepleChase 1977) ★★★, Ruby My Dear (SteepleChase 1977) ★★★, Home Is Where The Soul Is (Xanadu 1978) ★★★, For Sure! (Xanadu 1978) ★★★, Afternoon In Europe (RCA 1980) ★★★, All The Things You Are (Lobster 1981) ★★★, It Might As Well Be Spring (Soul Note 1981) ★★★★, Your Soft Eyes (Soul Note 1981) ★★★, The Lullaby (Baystate 1982) ★★★, Moonlit Desert (Baystate 1982) ★★★, Swingin' Love (Baystate 1983) ★★★, And Far Away (Soul Note 1983) ★★★★, Fantasia (Baystate 1983) ★★★, By Request (RCA 1986) ★★★, Recollections (Timeless 1989) ★★★, Christmas Song (Alfa Jazz 1989) ★★★, with Karin Krog Something Borrowed . . . Something New (Century 1989) ★★★, New York Stories (Alfa Jazz 1990) ★★★, Expressions (Alfa Jazz 1990) ★★★, The Falling Leaves (Limetree 1990) ★★★, Standard Request: Live At The Keystone Korner Tokyo (Alfa Jazz 1991) ★★★, Autumn Leaves: Kenny Drew Trio Play Standards Live (Alfa Jazz 1991) ★★★, Kenny Drew: Live Key'stone (Key'stone 1992) ★★★, At The Brewhouse (Storyville 1992) ★★★, Cleopatra's Dream (Alfa Jazz 1992) ★★★, Kenny Drew's Trio Plays Standards Live At The Blue Note Osaka (Alfa Jazz 1992) ★★★.

Drew, Kenny, Jnr.

b. 14 June 1958, New York City, New York, USA. Drew was taught piano from the age of five by his grandmother who had also taught his father, the jazz pianist **Kenny Drew**. He studied the classical repertoire with an aunt and did not take an interest in jazz and pop until he was in his late teens. He then played in funk bands, moving more positively into jazz in the mid-80s. He worked steadily in Florida, playing and recording with **Charnett Moffett**, who later became a member of Drew's trio along with Cody Moffett, recording Rainbow Connection. In the meantime, Drew had toured with **Stanley Jordan**. In 1990 he won the Great American Jazz Piano Competition in Jacksonville, Florida, then played with several bands led by or featuring noted artists such as **Ronnie Cuber**, **Jon Faddis**, **Slide Hampton**, **Jimmy Heath**, **Steve Turre**, **Stanley Turrentine** and **Jack Walrath**. In Australia in 1996, he played jazz and classical music at the Barossa Festival. He also began to work intermittently in a chamber music group with David Schnyder, also playing jazz with the saxophonist. Among other musicians with whom Drew has worked on his own recording sessions are **Ravi Coltrane**, bass player Peter Washington, **Steve Wilson**, Lynn Seaton and **Marvin 'Smitty' Smith**, the last two being for a while regular members of his trio. An elegant yet forceful pianist, throughout his career Drew has managed to avoid being compared to his father. His sources are far more eclectic although, in the broadest sense there are resemblances: the elegance, lightness of touch and sheer musicality.
● ALBUMS: Rainbow Connection (Jazz City 1988) ★★★, Flame Within (Jazz City 1989) ★★★, Third Phase (Jazz City 1990) ★★★, Kenny Drew Jr. (Antilles 1991) ★★★, Live At The Maybeck Recital Hall, Vol. 39 (Concord Jazz 1995) ★★★★, Portraits Of Mingus & Monk (Claves 1995) ★★★★, Secrets (TCB 1995) ★★★, This One's For Bill (TCB 1995) ★★★★, Crystal River (TCB 1997) ★★★, Follow The Spirit (Sirocco 1998) ★★★, Passionata 1995 recording (Arkadia 1998) ★★★, Winter Flower (Milestone 1998) ★★★, Remembrance (TCB 2000) ★★★, Live At The Montreux Jazz Festival '99 (TCB 2001) ★★★★.

Drew, Martin

b. 11 February 1944, Northampton, Northamptonshire, England. Drew began playing drums as a child, studying under the well-known dance band drummer George Fierstone. Despite this early start, it was some time before he became a full-time professional musician; however, once his career was under way, he was soon one of the busiest drummers in the UK. He played on numerous club and recording sessions, accompanying many British and American musicians during tours of the UK: these include **Ronnie Scott**, **Oscar Peterson**, **Buddy Tate**, **Dizzy Gillespie**, **Gil Evans** and **Freddie Hubbard**. He has also worked effectively with singers **Ella Fitzgerald**, **Jimmy Witherspoon**, **Anita O'Day** and **Nina Simone**. An outstanding mainstream drummer who is also comfortable playing bop, Drew is one of the most sought-after session drummers playing in the UK today, and his subtly swinging skills have enhanced numerous recording sessions.
● ALBUMS: Martin Drew And His Band (Lee Lambert 1977) ★★★.

Drew, Patti

b. 29 December 1944, Charleston, South Carolina, USA, and raised in Evanston, Illinois. As lead singer of the Drew-vels, a group comprising herself, her sisters Lorraine and Erma and bass singer Carlton Black, she and the band had several local hits, notably 'Tell Him' (1963) and 'It's My Time' (1964). Drew became a solo artist two years later and achieved her biggest hits with a remake of 'Tell Him' (number 22 R&B, number 85pop), from 1967, and 'Workin' On A Groovy Thing' (number 34 R&B, number 62 pop), from 1968, a **Neil Sedaka** composition that was also a hit for the **Fifth Dimension**. After Drew's last record with **Capitol Records** in 1970 she essentially retired from the business a year later. She made one more record for Inovation in 1975. In the 80s she occasionally worked the local lounges in her home-town of Evanston with Carlton Black in a group called Front Line.
● ALBUMS: Tell Him (Capitol 1967) ★★★, Working On A Groovy Thing (Capitol 1968) ★★★, I've Been Here All The Time (Capitol 1969) ★★★, Wild Is Love (Capitol 1970) ★★★.
● COMPILATIONS: Golden Classics (Collectables 1994) ★★★.

Drewe, Anthony

(see **Stiles, George, And Anthony Drewe**)

Drexciya

The first sightings of the unidentified and enigmatic **techno/electro** outfit Drexciya occurred in 1991, but the Detroit, Michigan, USA–based act remained ultra-elusive, obscuring their biographies with myth and fiction. Despite releases on the Tresor **Warp Records**, and **Rephlex Records** labels and the Detroit triumvirate of Shockwave, Submerge and **Underground Resistance**, there are few (if any) pictures of the group. They tended to eschew interviews and their names were never officially revealed.
Though many of their Detroit contemporaries looked towards space for inspiration, Drexciya appeared fascinated by the ocean: 'Water runs free,' the mysterious duo informed UK music magazine Jockey Slut in a rare interview, 'It runs wild. It can give life and take life, and that's what we are about. We flow where we want to go. We like to keep

moving.' The Drexciya moniker refers to a fictional subcontinent inhabited by webbed, water-breathing mutants known as Drexciyans. This fiction, however, was cut-through with a political intent. In the sleeve notes to their first album-length release, *The Quest*, Drexciyans are revealed to be a marine species descended from 'pregnant America-bound African slaves [who] were thrown overboard by the thousands for being sick and disruptive cargo.' Recordings—with titles such as 'Deep Sea Dweller', 'Bubble Metropolis' and 'The Unknown Aquazone'—are intended as communications from this underwater world. The enthralling debut album *The Quest* was pronounced as the outfit's last release, but Drexciya resurfaced towards the close of 1999, asserting that, strangely, the healthy state of modern music had heralded their return. An album appeared on Berlin label Tresor, after which they pledged a complete moratorium of interviews and a steady flow of new releases. One of the outfit's central members, James Marcel Stinson (b. 7 September 1969, Detroit, Michigan, USA, d. 3 September 2002, Newnan, Georgia, USA), died from a long-term heart complaint in September 2002. The recordings he had been working on were released posthumously under the Transllusion moniker.

● ALBUMS: *The Quest* (Submerge 1997) ★★★★, *Neptune's Lair* (Tresor/EFA 1999) ★★★★, *Harnessed The Storm* (Tresor 2002) ★★★.

● FURTHER READING: *More Brilliant Than The Sun: Adventures in Sonic Fiction*, Kodwo Eshun.

Drifters

Formed in 1953 in New York, USA, at the behest of **Atlantic Records**, this influential R&B vocal group was initially envisaged as a vehicle for ex-**Dominoes** singer **Clyde McPhatter** (b. Clyde Lensley McPhatter, 15 November 1932, Durham, North Carolina, USA, d. 13 June 1972, New York City, New York, USA). Gerhart Thrasher, Andrew Thrasher and Bill Pinkney (b. 15 August 1925, Sumter, North Carolina, USA) completed the new quartet which, as Clyde McPhatter and the Drifters, achieved a million-selling number 1 R&B hit with their debut single 'Money Honey'. Follow-up releases, including 'Such A Night' (number 5 R&B), 'Lucille' (number 7 R&B) and 'Honey Love' (a second chart-topper), also proved highly successful, while the juxtaposition of McPhatter's soaring tenor against the frenzied support of the other members provided a link between gospel and rock 'n' roll styles. The leader's interplay with bass player Pinkey was revelatory, but McPhatter's induction into the armed forces in 1954 was a blow that the Drifters struggled to withstand. The vocalist opted for a solo career upon leaving the services, and although his former group did enjoy success with 'Adorable' (number 1 R&B 1955), 'Steamboat' (1955), 'Ruby Baby' (1956) and 'Fools Fall In Love' (1957), such recordings featured a variety of lead singers, most notably **Johnny Moore** (b. 1934, Selma, Alabama, USA, d. 30 December 1998, London, England). Other new members included Charlie Hughes, **Bobby Hendricks** (who came in as lead tenor when Moore was drafted in 1957), Jimmy Millender and Tommy Evans. A greater emphasis on pop material ensued, but tension between the group and their manager, George Treadwell, resulted in an irrevocable split. Having fired the extant line-up in 1958, Treadwell, who owned the copyright to the Drifters' name, invited another act, the **Five Crowns**, to adopt the appellation. Charlie Thomas (b. 7 April 1937;

tenor), Doc Green Jnr. (b. 8 November 1934, d. 10 March 1989; bass/baritone) and lead singer Ellsbury Hobbs (b. 4 August 1936, d. 31 May 1996, New York, USA; bass), plus guitarist Reggie Kimber, duly became 'the Drifters'. Hobbs was drafted and replaced by **Ben E. King** (b. Benjamin Earl Nelson, 28 September 1938, Henderson, North Carolina, USA). The new line-up declared themselves with 'There Goes My Baby'. Written and produced by **Leiber And Stoller**, this pioneering release featured a Latin rhythm and string section, the first time such embellishments had appeared on an R&B recording. The single not only topped the R&B chart, it also reached number 2 on the US pop listings and anticipated the 'symphonic' style later developed by **Phil Spector**.

Further excellent releases followed, notably 'Dance With Me' (1959), 'This Magic Moment' (1960) and 'Save The Last Dance For Me', the latter a million seller which topped the US pop chart and reached number 2 in the UK. However, King left for a solo career following 'I Count The Tears' (1960), and was replaced by Rudy Lewis (b. 27 May 1935, Chicago, Illinois, USA) who fronted the group until his premature death from drug-induced asphyxiation in 1964. The Drifters continued to enjoy hits during this period and songs such as 'Sweets For My Sweet', 'When My Little Girl Is Smiling', 'Up On The Roof' and 'On Broadway' were not only entertaining in their own right but also provided inspiration, and material, for many emergent British acts, notably the **Searchers**, who took the first-named song to the top of the UK chart. Johnny Moore, who had returned to the line-up in 1963, took over the lead vocal slot from Lewis. 'Under The Boardwalk', recorded the day after the latter's passing, was the Drifters' last US Top 10 pop hit, although the group remained a popular attraction. **Bert Berns** had taken over production from Leiber and Stoller and in doing so brought a soul-based urgency to their work, as evinced by 'One Way Love' and 'Saturday Night At The Movies' (1964).

When he left Atlantic to found the Bang label, the Drifters found themselves increasingly overshadowed by newer, more contemporary artists and, bedevilled by lesser material and frequent changes in personnel, the group began to slip from prominence. However, their career was revitalized in 1972 when two re-released singles, 'At The Club' and 'Come On Over To My Place', reached the UK Top 10. A new recording contract with Bell was then secured, and British songwriters/producers **Tony Macaulay**, **Roger Cook** and **Roger Greenaway** fashioned a series of singles redolent of the Drifters' 'classic' era. Purists poured scorn on their efforts, but, between 1973 and 1975, the group, still led by Moore, enjoyed several UK Top 10 hits, including 'Like Sister And Brother', 'Kissin' In The Back Row Of The Movies', 'Down On The Beach Tonight', 'There Goes My First Love' and 'Can I Take You Home Little Girl'. This success ultimately waned as the decade progressed, and in 1982 their stalwart lead singer Moore briefly left the line-up. He was replaced, paradoxically, by Ben E. King, who in turn brought the Drifters back to Atlantic. However, despite completing some new recordings, the group found it impossible to escape its heritage, as evinced by the numerous 'hits' repackages and corresponding live appearances on the cabaret and nostalgia circuits. They were inducted into the **Rock And Roll Hall Of Fame** in 1988, a year after McPhatter's posthumous award.

● ALBUMS: *Save The Last Dance For Me* (Atlantic 1961) ★★★★, *The Good Life With The Drifters* (Atlantic 1964)

★★★★, *The Drifters* (Clarion 1964) ★★, *I'll Take You Where The Music's Playing* (Atlantic 1965) ★★★, *Souvenirs* (Bell 1974) ★★★, *Love Games* (Bell 1975) ★★★, *There Goes My First Love* (Bell 1975) ★★★, *Every Night's A Saturday Night* (Bell 1976) ★★★, *Greatest Hits Live* (Astan 1984) ★★, *Live At Harvard University* (Showcase 1986) ★★, *Too Hot* (Columbia 1989) ★★.

● COMPILATIONS: *Up On The Roof—The Best Of The Drifters* (Atlantic 1963) ★★★★, *Under The Boardwalk* (Atlantic 1964) ★★★★, *Golden Hits* (Atlantic 1968) ★★★★, *24 Original Hits* (Atlantic 1975) ★★★★, *The Collection* (Castle 1987) ★★★, *Diamond Series: The Drifters* (RCA 1988) ★★★, *Best Of The Drifters* (Pickwick 1990) ★★★, *Let The Boogie Woogie Roll—Greatest Hits (1953–58)* (Atlantic 1993) ★★★, *All Time Greatest Hits And More (1959–65)* (Atlantic 1993) ★★★★, *Up On The Roof, On Broadway & Under The Boardwalk* (Rhino/Pickwick 1995) ★★★★, *Rockin' And Driftin': The Drifters Box* 3-CD box set (Rhino 1996) ★★★★, *Anthology One: Clyde & The Drifters* (Sequel 1996) ★★★★, *Anthology Two: Rockin' & Driftin'* (Sequel 1996) ★★★, *Anthology Three: Save The Last Dance For Me* (Sequel 1996) ★★★★, *Anthology Four: Up On The Roof* (Sequel 1996) ★★★★, *Anthology Five: Under The Boardwalk* (Sequel 1997) ★★★★, *Anthology Six: The Good Life With The Drifters* (Sequel 1997) ★★★, *Anthology Seven: I'll Take You Where The Music's Playing* (Sequel 1997) ★★★★, *The Essentials* (Atlantic 2002) ★★★★, *The Definitive Drifters* (WSM 2003) ★★★★.

● FURTHER READING: *The Drifters: The Rise And Fall Of The Black Vocal Group*, Bill Millar. *Save The Last Dance For Me: The Musical Legacy 1953–92*, Tony Allan and Faye Treadwell.

Drifting Cowboys

Country star **Hank Williams** had been using the name the Drifting Cowboys since the late 30s, and he employed an existing group, the Alabama Rhythm Boys, as the Drifting Cowboys in 1943. The line-up only became consistent after Hank Williams appeared at the *Grand Ole Opry* in 1949 and realized the need for a permanent band. He employed Jerry Rivers (b. 25 August 1928, Miami, Florida, USA, d. 4 October 1996, Hermitage, Tennessee, USA; fiddle), Bob McNett (b. 16 October 1925, Roaring Branch, Pennsylvania, USA; guitar), Hillous Butrum (b. 21 April 1928, Lafayette, Tennessee, USA, d. 27 April 2002, Nashville, Tennessee; bass) and **Don Helms** (b. 28 February 1927, New Brockton, Alabama, USA; steel guitar). There were no drums as the instrument was not favoured in country circles. In 1951 McNett and Butrum were replaced, respectively, by Sammy Pruett, who had been in the Alabama Rhythm Boys with Helms, and Howard Watts. Williams used the Drifting Cowboys on his sessions, sometimes augmenting the musicians with **Chet Atkins**. His simply chorded songs did not need elaborate embellishment, and the Drifting Cowboys' backings perfectly complemented the material. The group disbanded after Williams' death. Helms worked with the **Wilburn Brothers** and formed the powerful Wil-Helm Agency. Helms and Rivers also worked in **Hank Williams Jnr.**'s band, the Cheatin' Hearts. Rivers wrote a biography *Hank Williams—From Life To Legend* (Denver, 1967/updated in 1980). In 1976 the original line-up re-formed for radio shows with compere Grant Turner and comedian the Duke of Paducah. They had a minor success with 'Rag Mop' and recorded a tribute to Hank Williams, 'If

The Good Lord's Willing'. Hank Williams Jnr. and Don Helms recorded a duet, 'The Ballad Of Hank Williams', which was based on 'The Battle Of New Orleans' and indicated how volatile Williams was. The Drifting Cowboys first appeared in the UK in 1979, and in 1991 appeared at Wembley's country music festival with Williams' illegitimate daughter, Jett Williams.

● ALBUMS: *We Remember Hank Williams* (1969) ★★★★, with Jim Owen *A Song For Us All—A Salute To Hank Williams* (Epic 1977) ★★★, *The Drifting Cowboys' Tribute To Hank Williams* (Epic 1979) ★★★, *Best Of Hank Williams' Original Drifting Cowboys* (Epic 1979) ★★★★, *Classic Instrumentals* (1981) ★★, *One More Time Around* (1982) ★★★.

Drifting Slim

b. Elmon Mickle, 24 February 1919, Keo, Arkansas, USA, d. 17 September 1977. He was inspired to sing and play harmonica by **John Lee 'Sonny Boy' Williamson**, whose style he successfully emulated on local radio stations in the 40s. Mickle formed his first band in 1951 and recorded for the **Modern**/RPM company; he learned to play guitar and drums and worked occasionally as a one-man band. In 1957 he moved to Los Angeles where he recorded for several small labels (including Elko, E.M., J Gems, Wonder, Magnum and Styletone, using the pseudonym Model T. Slim for the latter), and in 1966 he made an album for Milestone Records. Poor health prevented him playing many club dates in the 70s; he died of cancer in September 1977.

● ALBUMS: as Model T. Slim *Somebody Done Voodoo The Hoodoo Man* (1980) ★★★.

Driftwood, Jimmy

b. James Corbett Morris, 20 June 1917, Mountain View, Arkansas, USA, d. 12 July 1998, Fayetteville, Arkansas, USA. Driftwood's name first came to prominence as a result of the **Johnny Horton** recording of Driftwood's song 'The Battle Of New Orleans' in 1959. The single made the top of both the US pop and country charts but only reached the Top 20 in the UK. **Lonnie Donegan** reached number 2 in the UK with the song in the same year. Driftwood himself had recorded a version of the song the previous year for **RCA-Victor Records**. With a strong musical heritage Driftwood learned to play guitar, banjo and fiddle while still young. Picking up old songs from his father, Neal Morris, his grandparents and other members of his family, he later travelled around collecting and recording songs. While still performing at folk festivals, Driftwood continued to teach during the 40s. With the 50s came the growing folk boom, and he found himself reaching a wider audience. RCA signed him to record *Newly Discovered Early American Folk Songs*, which included the aforementioned 'Battle Of New Orleans'. While the song's popularity grew, Driftwood was working for the *Grand Ole Opry* but left in order to work on a project to establish a cultural centre at his home in Mountain View. The aim was to preserve the Ozark Mountain people's heritage. Having later joined the Rackensack Folklore Society, he travelled the USA, speaking at universities to pass on the importance of such a project. The first Arkansas Folk Festival, held in 1963, was successful and, in 1973, a multi-million dollar cultural centre was established. He had outlived his three sons when he died from a heart attack in 1998.

● ALBUMS: *Newly Discovered Early American Folk Songs* (RCA 1958) ★★★★, *The Battle Of New Orleans* (RCA Victor 1958) ★★★, *The Wilderness Road* (RCA 1959) ★★★, *The Westward Movement* (RCA Victor 1959) ★★★, *Tall Tales In Song* (RCA Victor 1960) ★★★, *Songs Of Billy Yank And Johnny Reb* (RCA Victor 1961) ★★★★, *Driftwood At Sea—Sea Shanties* (RCA Victor 1962) ★★, *Voice Of The People* (Monument 1963) ★★, *Down In The Arkansas* (Monument 1965) ★★★, *A Lesson In Folk Music* (60s) ★★★.

● COMPILATIONS: *Famous Country Music Makers* (70s) ★★★, *Americana* box set (Bear Family 1991) ★★★.

Driscoll, Julie

b. 8 June 1947, London, England. Driscoll was employed by producer/manager **Giorgio Gomelsky** as administrator of the **Yardbirds**' fan club when the former suggested a singing career. Her singles included a cover version of the **Lovin' Spoonful**'s 'Didn't Want To Have To Do It' (1965) and an early **Randy Newman** composition 'If You Should Ever Leave Me' (1967), but this period is better recalled for Driscoll's membership of **Steam Packet**, an R&B-styled revue which also featured **Long John Baldry**, **Rod Stewart** and the **Brian Auger Trinity**. Driscoll remained with the last-named act when the larger group folded and in 1968 had a number 5 hit with **Bob Dylan**'s 'This Wheel's On Fire'. Her striking appearance engendered much publicity, and a cool, almost disinterested vocal style formed the ideal counterpoint to Auger's jazz-based ambitions.

'Jools' left the group following the release of *Streetnoise* in order to pursue a more radical direction. She contributed to **B.B. Blunder**'s *Workers Playtime* and released the excellent *1969*, which featured support from members of the **Soft Machine**, **Nucleus** and **Blossom Toes** as well as pianist **Keith Tippett**, whom the singer later married. She has since appeared on many of her husband's *avant garde* jazz creations, notably Centipede's *Septober Energy* (1971) and Ark's expansive *Frames (Music For An Imaginary Film)* (1978), as well appearing and recording with **Maggie Nicols** and the experimental vocal quartet **Voice**. Her first album in over 20 years, *Shadow Puppeteer*, was released at the end of 1999. Although challenging, it is an interesting suite of *avant garde* vocal experimentation.

● ALBUMS: with Brian Auger Trinity *Open* (Marmalade/Atco 1967) ★★★, with Auger *Streetnoise* (Polydor/Atco 1968) ★★★, *1969* (Polydor 1969) ★★, *Keith Tippett, Julie Tippetts, Harry Miller, Frank Perry* (Ogun 1975) ★★★, as Julie Tippetts *Sunset Glow* (Utopia 1976) ★★★, with Keith Tippett, Maggie Nicols *Mr Invisible And The Drunken Sheilas* (FMP 1986) ★★★, with Keith Tippett *Couple In Spirit* (Editions EG 1987) ★★★, with Keith Tippett, Willi Kellers *Twilight Etchings* (FMP 1993) ★★★, with Keith Tippett *Couple In Spirit II: Live At The Stadtgarten, Cologne* (ASC 1996) ★★★, as Julie Tippetts *Shadow Puppeteer* (Voiceprint 1999) ★★★.

● COMPILATIONS: with Brian Auger Trinity *Jools/Brian* (EMI 1968) ★★★, with Auger *London 1964-1967* (Charly 1977) ★★★, *The Best Of Julie Driscoll* (Charly 1982) ★★★, with Auger *The Road To Vauxhall 1967-1969* (Charly 1989) ★★★.

Drive

This California, USA, heavy metal group formed in the mid-80s with a line-up of David Taylor (vocals), Rich Chavez (guitar), Mercy Valdez (guitar), Michael Anthony (bass) and Valentine San Miguel (drums). Critics detected nothing startlingly original about the group's 1988 debut album, *Characters In Time*, which contained songs derived from the **Slayer** and **Anthrax** speed-metal tradition. It proved to be their sole release.

● ALBUMS: *Characters In Time* (Rampage 1988) ★★★.

Drive-By Truckers

This acclaimed US outfit is comprised of a bunch of rowdy southern rockers, who were obviously weaned on **Lynyrd Skynyrd**, **Neil Young** and the **Rolling Stones**. The band's story began in the mid-80s at the University of North Alabama, when Patterson Hood (son of renowned **Muscle Shoals** session bass player David Hood) joined forces with fellow guitarist Mike Cooley. The duo formed the post-punk outfit Adam's House Cat but failed to make much of an impact outside their local club scene. After several years apart, Hood and Cooley reunited in Athens, Georgia, in the mid-90s. They formed Drive-By Truckers in 1996, with John Neff (steel guitar), Adam Howell (bass), Matt Lane (drums) and Barry Sell (mandolin) fleshing out the line-up. The band wasted little time getting their recording career jumpstarted, releasing 1998's rollicking *Gangstabilly*, but their burgeoning popularity and increasingly demanding schedule fragmented the original line-up. Sell, Neff, Howell and Lane all left within a few months of each other, leaving Hood and Cooley to recruit Rob Malone (bass) and Brad Morgan (drums) to help record their follow-up *Pizza Deliverance*. An excellent in-concert set, *Alabama Ass Whuppin'*, confirmed the new line-up's potency.

For their first release of the new millennium, 2001's double disc *Southern Rock Opera*, Hood came up with a concept album loosely based around the career of Lynyrd Skynyrd (an idea which was reportedly being kicked around for several years by the band) and which addressed a number of Southern stereotypes. Malone switched from bass to guitar to give the Drive-By Truckers a three-prong guitar attack, with long-time band associate Earl Hicks replacing him in the rhythm section. Malone left the band following the release of the album and was replaced by another singer-songwriter and guitarist Jason Isbell. The band subsequently signed a new recording contract with Universal Records' alt country imprint, Lost Highway, who re-released *Southern Rock Opera* the following year.

Despite finishing a new set of material for a projected album, the Drive-By Truckers were dumped by Lost Highway before a release date could be sent. The New West imprint picked up the band and released the excellent *Decoration Day* in summer 2003. Shonna Tucker replaced Hicks on the following year's *The Dirty South*, an album that saw the emergence of Isbell as a songwriter of note on 'The Day John Henry Died' and the **Band** tribute 'Danko/Manuel'.

● ALBUMS: *Gangstabilly* (Soul Dump/Ghostmeat 1998) ★★★, *Pizza Deliverance* (Ghostmeat 1999) ★★★, *Alabama Ass Whuppin'* (Second Heaven 1999) ★★★★, *Southern Rock Opera* (SDR 2001) ★★★★, *Decoration Day* (New West 2003) ★★★★, *The Dirty South* (New West 2004) ★★★★, *A Blessing And A Curse* (New West 2006) ★★★.

● DVD/VIDEOS: *Live At The Watt* (New West 2005).

Drive Like Jehu

Although they were slightly more aggressive and their hardcore roots noticeably prevalent, the early 90s outfit

Drive Like Jehu is often credited as being one of a handful of bands that helped open the door for the subsequent emo (emotional hardcore) movement in the USA. Formed in San Diego, California, USA, the quartet was formed in 1990 by Eric Froberg aka Rick Farr (vocals/guitar; ex-Pitchfork), John Reis (guitar; ex-Pitchfork), Mike Kennedy (bass) and Mark Trombino (drums). With the focus of the alternative rock scene at the time being Seattle, Drive Like Jehu quietly carved their own niche and original sound with cult classic releases 1991's *Drive Like Jehu* and 1994's *Yank Crime*, the latter of which was a major label release. Disappointingly, Drive Like Jehu split up shortly thereafter before getting a shot at breaking through to a wider audience. After their break up, Reis went on to front **Rocket From The Crypt**, while Trombino became a much in demand producer/engineer for a variety of rock outfits. In 2002, *Yank Crime* was reissued with several bonus tracks not included on the original version.

● ALBUMS: *Drive Like Jehu* (Headhunter 1991) ★★★★, *Yank Crime* (Interscope 1994) ★★★★.

Drive, She Said

The band was formed in 1986 by the former **American Tears Touch** and **Michael Bolton** keyboard player Mark Mangold and previously unknown vocalist/guitarist Al Fritsch. Mangold was also a successful songwriter, co-writing **Cher**'s hit 'I've Found Someone' along with Bolton. After signing to **CBS Records** in 1988 their self-titled debut album was released a year later in the USA and featured guest appearances by artists such as multi-instrumentalist **Aldo Nova** and Bob Kulick of **Balance** and **Meat Loaf** fame. The collection of light-edged melodic rock songs, which included a reworking of the Touch classic 'Don't You Know What Love Is', was aimed directly at the American market but failed to make any significant impact. It sold well on import in the UK, however, prompting the independent Music For Nations label to sign the band for the European market (Mangold reportedly being unhappy at CBS' marketing attempts). The album was subsequently released in the UK in 1990 and was quickly followed by a club tour. *Drivin' Wheel*, a slightly harder-edged album, was released in 1991, preceded by the single 'Think About Love', both of which failed to achieve any significant success. Undeterred by the lack of chart success, they toured the UK with FM in 1992 before embarking on sessions for a third album.

● ALBUMS: *Drive, She Said* (Columbia 1989) ★★★, *Drivin' Wheel* (Music For Nations 1991) ★★★, *Exelerator* (1993) ★★★.

Driven

Irish rock band the Driven, who originally formed at the end of the 80s, began to make commercial headway in 1996 after relocating to south London and collectively abandoning their day-jobs as labourers. Signed to **Polydor Records**, the group, led by singer and acoustic guitarist Brendan Markham, made an immediate impact with the power of their debut single, 'Jesus Loves You More When You Can Drive', wherein the sharp guitar patterns and urgency resembled 70s punk more than the heavy metal fraternity the group are more usually associated with. As Markham told the press, 'The Irish rock thing was never our scene. We're from Limerick, but we've been based in London for the past five years anyway.' The other members of the quartet are Darrin Mullins (lead

guitar), Paul Power (bass) and Ned Kennedy (drums). The distinctive quality of Markham's employment of acoustic guitar was not lost on critics either, but as he elaborated, the Driven are 'not technically-minded. It feels good, that's all that matters.'

Driver

A trio of Peter Glinderman (vocals/guitar), Dennis Coats (bass) and Stephen Roxford (drums), Driver formed in Canada in the mid-70s. Signed to **A&M Records**, they recorded their debut album, *No Accidents*, in 1977. Featuring well-executed, three-minute rock songs largely composed by Glinderman, with the resourceful deployment of pop hooks, it was a critical success within Canada and also provoked good reviews in the USA. Despite this sales were poor and the group's contract was not renewed.

● ALBUMS: *No Accidents* (A&M 1977) ★★★.

Driver 67

An alias for Paul Phillips, this act had a surprise UK hit during Christmas 1978 with the novelty record 'Car 67', concerning a mini-cab driver despatched to pick up his former love of his life. The song was performed in the manner of the cabby talking to his controller over the radio. After the follow-up single 'Headlights' flopped, Phillips went on to be a successful publisher with magazines such as the highly-rated black music weekly *Echoes* and *Video Trade Weekly*. Perhaps, not surprisingly, he does not wish to be reminded of his former career.

D'Rivera, Paquito

b. 4 June 1948, Havana, Cuba. Known for a silky-smooth tone and evocative phrasing in the manner of **Dexter Gordon**, Paquito D'Rivera is one of the great jazz saxophonists of his era and is also a highly proficient clarinettist. After training in the Havana Conservatory and participating in Cuba's unique *avant garde* jazz renaissance in the 70s, D'Rivera migrated to New York, USA, to shine in the centre of the jazz world. The son of a Cuban tenor saxophonist who once played with **Benny Goodman**, D'Rivera made his professional debut on soprano when he was only six years old. At 12, he entered the same music conservatory as his future colla-borator and bandmate, pianist **Chucho Valdés**. The two men formed Orquestra De Música Moderna in 1965. By 1970, as a result of a successful showing at the Warsaw Jazz Festival, D'Rivera, Valdés and several of the younger members of the Orchestra decide to form **Irakere**, one of the most influential groups in Cuban music history. Irakere's radical exploration of the electric possibilities raised by jazz fusion groups such as **Weather Report** and the **Mahavishnu Orchestra** led to a record contract with **Columbia Records** in 1979.

In 1981, during a tour of Spain, D'Rivera defected to the USA. He was eagerly accepted into the New York jazz scene and started a group called the Havana/New York Ensemble, which produced stars such as percussionist **Daniel Ponce**, pianists **Hilton Ruiz**, **Michel Camilo** and **Danilo Pérez** and trumpeter **Claudio Roditi**. During the 80s D'Rivera also collaborated with Cuban expatriates **Israel 'Cachao' López**, the legendary bass player often credited with inventing the mambo, and **Mario Bauza**, the legendary orchestra leader who infused the basic jazz vocabulary with Cuban ideas while working as musical director for **Dizzy Gillespie**'s band in the 40s. In 1988 D'Rivera became a founder member and featured soloist with Gillespie's United Nations Orchestra (he took over the leadership following the trumpeter's death in 1993). In 1991 D'Rivera, Gillespie and **Gato Barbieri** were honoured with Grammy Lifetime Achievement awards for their contribution to Latin Music. During the 90s D'Rivera worked with Chucho's father **Bebo Valdés**, **McCoy Tyner**, **Tito Puente**, **Astor Piazzolla** and **Jerry González**, among others.

In addition to touring with his various ensembles, which include the chamber music group Triangulo, the Paquito D'Rivera Big Band and the Paquito D'Rivera Quintet, he made several recordings with his own Caribbean Jazz Project. In 1996 he released the Grammy Award–winning *Portraits Of Cuba*, a stunning collection of Cuban classics recorded with a formidable big band conducted by the premier Latin jazz arranger Carlos Franzeti. D'Rivera's work as a classical composer came to prominence during the same decade, and he regularly performs his own compositions with symphony orchestras.

● ALBUMS: *Paquito Blowin'* (CBS 1981) ★★★★, *Mariel* (CBS 1982) ★★★, *Live At The Keystone Korner* (CBS 1983) ★★★★, *Why Not!* (CBS 1984) ★★★, *Explosion* (CBS 1985) ★★★, *Manhattan Burn* (CBS 1986) ★★★★, *Celebration* (CBS 1987) ★★★★, *Return To Ipanema* (Town Cryer 1989) ★★★★, *Tico! Tico!* (Chesky 1989) ★★★★, *Who's Smokin'?!* (Candid 1991) ★★★, *Reunion* (Messidor/Rounder 1991) ★★★★, *Havana Cafe* (Chesky 1991) ★★★★, *La Habana-Rio-Conexion* (Messidor 1992) ★★★, with the United Nations Orchestra *A Night In Englewood* (Messidor 1994) ★★★, with the Caribbean Jazz Project *The Caribbean Jazz Project* (Heads Up 1995) ★★★, *Portraits Of Cuba* (Chesky 1996) ★★★★, *Paquito D'Rivera Presents Cuba Jazz* (RMM 1996) ★★★★, with the Caribbean Jazz Project *Island Stories* (Heads Up 1997) ★★★, *100 Years Of Latin Love Songs* (Heads Up 1998) ★★★, *Tropicana Nights* (Chesky 1999) ★★★★, *Live At The Blue Note* (Half Note 2000) ★★★, *Habanera* (Enja 2001) ★★★★, *The Clarinetist Volume One* (Peregrine 2001) ★★★, *Brazilian Dreams* (MCG Jazz 2002) ★★★, *The Lost Sessions* (Yemayá 2003) ★★★, *Big Band Time* (Pimienta 2003) ★★★★.

● COMPILATIONS: *A Taste Of Paquito D'Rivera* (Columbia 1981) ★★★★, *The Best Of Paquito D'Rivera* (Columbia/Legacy 2002) ★★★★.

● FURTHER READING: *My Sax Life: A Memoir*, Paquito D'Rivera.

Drivin' N' Cryin'

Guitarist/vocalist **Kevn Kinney** (b. Milwaukee, Wisconsin, USA), having relocated to Atlanta, Georgia, USA, after splitting from his old punk band the Prosecutors, met bass player Tim Nielsen in a local club, and the two formed Driving' N' Cryin'. *Scarred But Smarter* was recorded in a week and a half with a real garage rock trio sound, and the band recruited drummer Jeff Sullivan from Mr Crowe's Garden, who later became the **Black Crowes**, and began to broaden their musical style, incorporating country and R&B influences, while expanding their audience with gruelling club touring. *Whisper Tames The Lion*, by way of contrast to the debut, was rather overproduced, but *Mystery Road*, with a second guitarist in ex-**R.E.M.** roadie Buren Fowler, was more representative of the band's true sound. However, Driving' N' Cryin' had become musically somewhat schizophrenic at this stage, mixing heavy rockers with country

songs, although the latter made little impression within insular US C&W radio circles. *Fly Me Courageous* thus saw a conscious effort to focus on the rock direction of their live shows, and while it met with a mixed reception from reviewers, respectable US sales finally established the band as a force. *Smoke* refined the harder approach with a tough sound and **Ramones**-like simplicity. Kinney reserved the more acoustic-based material for his solo albums, while Nielsen (Kathleen Turner Overdrive and Toenut) and Sullivan (Kathleen Turner Overdrive) indulged their artistic whims in side projects. Fowler left after *Smoke*, and after a short break the band relocated to the DGC label for 1995's typically eclectic *Wrapped In Sky*. They returned to independent label status for the following year's self-titled effort.

● ALBUMS: *Scarred But Smarter* (Island 1986) ★★★, *Whisper Tames The Lion* (Island 1988) ★★★, *Mystery Road* (Island 1989) ★★★, *Fly Me Courageous* (Island 1990) ★★★★, *Smoke* (Island 1993) ★★★, *Wrapped In Sky* (DGC 1995) ★★★, *Drivin N Cryin* (Ichiban 1997) ★★★, *The Essential Live Drivin N Cryin* (Intersound 1999) ★★★.

● COMPILATIONS: *Ultimate Collection* (Hip-O 2001) ★★★★.

Drizabone

Club trio from the USA (named after an item of riding clothing) who made a big splash in 1991 with the 'Real Love' recording. In its aftermath many record companies sought to wave chequebooks at the group—'Real Love' having first emerged on a white label 12-inch—but they held out until they received an album offer from **Island Records**. The success of 'Real Love' had taken Drizabone too by surprise, and it would not be until 1994 that their debut album arrived. At the time of the single Drizabone were mainstays Vincent Garcia and Billy April plus vocalist Sophie Jones. She had performed the original demo versions of the song but was not really interested in a musical career. Dee Heron (b. Jamaica, West Indies) gave up her secretary's job to take over her role. However, she became the group's second casualty after a follow-up single 'Catch The Fire'. Having decided that the latter's vocal range was too limited, the backroom duo spent several months auditioning for more suitable replacements, also filling their time by performing remix duties for **Linda Layton** ('Without You (One On One)'), **Alison Limerick**, **Lisa Stansfield** ('Change') and Shanice. They eventually met Atlanta, Georgia–based singer Kymberley Peer (b. Detroit, Michigan, USA), who had formerly worked with Howard Hewitt, **Freddie Jackson** and other soul artists. She was also a partly-established actress, having appeared alongside Marvin Winans and Vanessa Bell Armstrong in the musical *Don't Get Got Started*. She was on hand to record Drizabone's first single in three years, 'Pressure', which prefaced their long-awaited debut album.

● ALBUMS: *Conspiracy* (4th & Broadway 1995) ★★★.

Droge, Pete

b. 11 March 1969, USA. Even if the world continues to ignore the talent of singer-songwriter Droge he will always have one of rock 'n' roll's most outlandish song titles to his credit: 'If You Don't Love Me (I'll Kill Myself)'. The perfect summation of adolescent, unrequited love, it was housed on his 1994 debut album and was included on the soundtrack of the 1995 movie *Dumb And Dumber*. The song was originally written in Droge's apartment in Portland, Oregon, in the summer of 1993. His mother was a music teacher and his father was a rock and folk fan, and Droge was taught to play the ukulele at the age of four. After mastering the guitar a few years later he hit the Seattle club circuit, having accumulated the songwriting influences of **Bob Dylan** and, more particularly, **Tom Petty**. However, the area was soon filled with the sound of grunge, and Droge formed his own roots band, Ramadillo, in direct opposition, although his friendship with Mike McCready of **Pearl Jam** was to prove valuable in gaining a contract with American Records.

Droge stepped out alone with an album that stressed his songwriting strength, notably with the previously mentioned gem 'If You Don't Love Me (I'll Kill Myself)'. His second album featured his backing musicians the Sinners. Produced by Brendan O' Brien (**Black Crowes**), his debut for Epic Records subsidiary 57 Records, *Spacey & Shakin'*, was a partially successful attempt to broaden Droge's roots-rock sound. In 2003 he recorded an album as part of the modern day supergroup the **Thorns**, featuring fellow songwriters **Matthew Sweet** and **Shawn Mullins**.

● ALBUMS: *Necktie Second* (Independent/American 1994) ★★★, *Find A Door* (American 1996) ★★, *Spacey & Shakin'* (57 1998) ★★★, *Skywatching* (Puzzle Tree 2003) ★★★.

Drones

Very few punk bands actually stuck to their principles and shunned the lurid advances of the major record companies. Whether the Drones from Manchester, England, were such a band, or whether they were never given the opportunity, is debatable. Either way, the band issued three singles and an ephemeral album that now seems to personify the new wave. Second division punk they may have been, but they were, nevertheless, exciting and vital. The Drones' humble recording career began with an EP on the Ohm label, *Temptations Of A White Collar Worker*, in the spring of 1977. The release of 'Bone Idol' on their own Valer label later in the year was swiftly followed by a rough but enthusiastic album entitled *Further Temptations*. The group ended the year with an inclusion on the **Beggars Banquet Records** sampler *Streets*. After that, M.J. Drone (lead vocals/rhythm guitar), Gus Callender (Gangrene to his friends; lead guitar/vocals), Pete Perfect (drums) and Steve 'Whisper' Cundall (bass) kept a low profile, turning up on the essential live punk document *Short Circuit—Live At The Electric Circus*, in mid-1978. After a final single, 'Can't See', on the Fabulous label in 1980, the band struggled on, finally breaking up in 1981.

● ALBUMS: *Further Temptations* (Valer 1977) ★★★.

Droogs

Formed in 1972, this long-serving Los Angeles, California, USA–based band initially included Rich Albin (vocals), Roger Clay (guitar/vocals), Paul Motter (bass) and Kyle Raven (drums). Unashamedly inspired by 60s garage bands, the quartet founded their own label, Plug-n-Socket, on which they recorded cover versions of favourite songs and originals inspired by their heroes. Having completed a mere six singles in the space of 10 years, during which time the group's rhythm section underwent several changes, the Droogs found themselves avatars of the then in-vogue 'Paisley Underground' scene. *Stone Cold World*, which saw Albin and Clay joined by David Provost (bass) and Jon

Gerlach (drums), was sadly obscured in the flurry to praise **Green On Red**, the **Long Ryders** and **Bangles**, but Albin and Clay doggedly pursued their chosen direction when the fashion faded. The unit's later work was issued on the German Music Maniac label. *Want Something* compiled material from previously released European albums.

● ALBUMS: *Stone Cold World* (Making Waves/Plug-n-Socket 1984) ★★★, *Kingdom Day* (PVC 1987) ★★★, *Mad Dog Dreams* (Music Maniac 1989) ★★★, *Live In Europe* (Music Maniac 1990) ★★, *Guerrilla Love-In* (Music Maniac 1991) ★★★, *Atomic Garage* (Lakota 1997) ★★★.

● COMPILATIONS: *Anthology* (Music Maniac 1987) ★★★★, *Want Something* (Skyclad 1990) ★★★.

Drootin, Buzzy

b. Benjamin Drootin, 22 April 1920, nr. Kiev, Russia, d. 21 May 2000, Englewood, New Jersey, USA. Growing up in Boston, Massachusetts, USA, Drootin and his brothers, Lewis and Al, became known locally for their lively contributions to the dixieland tradition. After working with **Ina Ray Hutton**, Drootin moved to New York where he played drums regularly with established stars and gained a solid reputation as a swinging accompanist. In the late 40s he settled into the house band at **Eddie Condon**'s club and made many records. During the 50s he worked on a long series of traditional and mainstream record sessions with artists such as **Ruby Braff** and **Bobby Hackett**. In the 60s Drootin worked in a number of bands assembled especially for festivals, concert tours and recording sessions. In the 70s he returned to Boston and worked with his brothers in the Drootin Brothers Orchestra.

Drop Nineteens

This Boston, Massachusetts, USA, quintet briefly enjoyed cult status in the 90s on the back of a fascination with all things Bostonian, a journalistic trend inspired by the breakthrough of the **Pixies** and **Throwing Muses**. Yet the Drop Nineteens, comprising Greg Ackell (guitar/vocals), Steve Zimmerman (bass/guitar), Megan Gilbert (guitar/vocals), Justin Crosby (guitar) and Pete Kosplin (drums), had an appeal in their own right. Their 1992 album debut drew its appeal from the pop savvy of 'Winona', a dedication to film star Winona Ryder also released as a single, and a cheeky cover version of **Madonna**'s 'Angel', which took them into **Sonic Youth**-styled pastiche. The beautiful 'Kick The Tragedy' had ringing wall of sound guitars and **Cocteau Twins** melody mixed with new-wave attitude. The record's cover featured an angelic looking young girl wielding a gun—a picture analogous to the record's mood swings. They pressed on with *National Coma* the following year, a more concise set highlighted by songs such as 'All Swimmers Are Brothers' and 'Moses Brown'. However, their brief flirtation as hopefuls with the music press was all but over by 1994, and the Drop Nineteens became another band whose talents never found the substantial audience they deserved.

● ALBUMS: *Delaware* (Caroline/Hut 1992) ★★★, *National Coma* (Caroline/Hut 1993) ★★★.

Dropkick Murphys

From Boston, Massachusetts, USA, the Dropkick Murphys, (their name taken from a local rehab centre) initially formed in 1996 with the sole intention of jamming punk cover versions. Original members, Mike McColgan (vocals), Ken Casey (bass), Rick Barton (guitar) and Matt Kelly (drums) soon progressed to writing original material, the future live staple 'Barroom Hero' being their earliest effort. Split singles with the **Bruisers** and the Anti-Heros, and the *Boys On The Docks* EP, brought the Dropkick Murphys to the attention of **Rancid** guitarist/vocalist and Hellcat label boss Tim 'Lint' Armstrong. Produced by Armstrong's band-mate Lars Frederiksen, January 1998's *Do Or Die* was predictably rowdy. Blending traditional folk instruments (bagpipes and tin whistle) with the ever-present guitars, the band drew heavily on both Boston's Irish heritage and the city's punk rock legacy. With songs ranging from punk singalong to sombre acoustic folk it was a compelling debut. Released to excellent reviews, tours across Europe and America followed before McColgan, unable to commit himself to constant touring, left the band. Replaced by ex-Bruisers vocalist Al Barr, 'Curse Of A Fallen Soul' confirmed Barr's suitability in time for *The Gang's All Here*. Again produced by Frederiksen, the album continued where the former had left off. Another bout of prolonged touring followed, this time including Australia and Japan, during which time Barton also quit (after picking his replacement, James Lynch of the Ducky Boys). Deciding to add some beef to the live sound the band recruited second guitarist Mark Orell, who as a self-taught accordionist could contribute to the band's more traditional leanings. The addition of Spicy McHaggis (bagpipes) and Ryan Foltz (mandolin/tin whistle) also broadened the band's live sound as well as adding a new impetus to the material. 2001's *Sing Loud, Sing Proud!*, which was produced by Casey, had more pronounced Irish leanings, exemplified by the collaboration with **Shane MacGowan** on 'Good Rats' and 'The Wild Rover'. Elsewhere Cock Sparrer vocalist Colin McFaull featured on 'The Fortunes Of War', while Barr and Casey's furious vocal trade off on 'The Rocky Road To Dublin' perfectly demonstrated the band's ability to seamlessly combine different genres.

● ALBUMS: *Do Or Die* (Hellcat 1998) ★★★★, *The Gang's All Here* (Hellcat 1999) ★★★, *Sing Loud, Sing Proud!* (Epitaph 2001) ★★★, *Live On St. Patrick's Day* (Epitaph 2002) ★★★, *Blackout* (Epitaph 2003) ★★★, *The Warrior's Code* (Hellcat/Epitaph 2005) ★★★.
● COMPILATIONS: *The Early Years* (Sidekicks 1998) ★★★★, *The Singles Collection* (Hellcat 2000) ★★★★, *Singles Collection Volume 2—1998–2004: B Sides, Covers, Comps & Other Crap* (Hellcat 2005) ★★★★.

Drowning Pool

This Dallas, Texas, USA–based quartet made an immediate impact on the rock scene with their refreshingly diverse debut, *Sinner*. Stevie Benton (bass) and Mike Luce (drums) attended high school together in Dallas but parted company when Luce moved to New Orleans. It was while in this city that he began playing music with Christian Joseph Pierce (guitar), and after several years grafting around the local circuit the two men returned to Dallas to join Benton in the nascent Drowning Pool. Naming themselves after the movie, the band spent two years establishing themselves on the Dallas music scene. In late 1998, following the departure of their original vocalist, they recruited the charismatic Dave Williams (b. 1972, USA, d. 14 August 2002, Manassas, Virginia, USA) as their new frontman. The new line-up recorded a demo, which was released in limited quantities in May 1999.

By now, the band had begun to attract attention outside of Dallas with opening slots for acts such as **Sevendust** and **Kittie**. A recording contract with Wind-Up Records followed, with producer Jay Baumgardner brought in to help the band record their debut. Released in June 2001, *Sinner* struck a fine balance between power and melody on stand-out tracks 'Bodies' and 'Tear Away'. Tragedy struck the following August when Williams was found dead in the band's tour bus. Jason 'Gong' Jones was eventually named as Drowning Pool's new vocalist. He made his debut on the band's second studio album, *Desensitized*, which was released in spring 2004.
● ALBUMS: *Sinner* (Wind-Up 2001) ★★★, *Desensitized* (Wind-Up 2004) ★★★.

DRS

Their initials an acronym for 'Dirty Rotten Scoundrels' (in itself not a million miles away from the moniker adopted by thrash band **DRI**—Dirty Rotten Imbeciles), DRS were, predictably, a gangsta soul quintet. However, when Pic, Blunt, Endo, Deuce Deuce and Jail Bait finished with the hard-nosed rhymes, they offered a surprising, and by no means unwelcome, line in close harmony a cappella. Their early inroads into the R&B charts were credited largely to this; it was something of a novelty to hear such down-and-dirty reality tales sung rather than spat out. Based in Los Angeles, their debut album took its title from the preferred burial mode of their local gangster homeboys. The production company associated with the album, Roll Wit It Entertainment, boasted **Hammer** as a silent partner.
● ALBUMS: *Gangsta Lean* (Capitol 1993) ★★★.

Dru Hill

Urban R&B outfit Dru Hill took their name from the historic Druid Hill Park complex in Baltimore, Maryland, USA, where all four members were raised. They began their rise to fame in the mid-90s, largely through the intervention of **Island Records**' Hiriam Hicks—formerly manager of **Boyz II Men**. He was looking for a group to record a song, 'Tell Me', for the soundtrack to the movie *Eddie*, to which Island held the rights. A tape of the quartet was passed to him by University Music president Haqq Islam. So impressed was Hicks after meeting the four men that, not only did he ask them to perform a version of 'Tell Me' on the spot, but he also signed them to a worldwide contract with Island. At that time the members—Jazz, Nokio (b. 21 January 1979), Woody and **Sisqo** (b. Mark Andrews, 9 November 1978, Baltimore, Maryland, USA)— were all still in their teens. Nevertheless, their self-titled debut album sounded impressively mature. The smoky jazz and R&B tracks benefited enormously from the input of producers **Keith Sweat**, Stanley Brown and Darryl Simmons, though Nokio also co-wrote and produced much of the contents.

While their syncopated vocals were one highlight, Sisqo and Jazz also contributed heavily as musicians, playing keyboards, bass and trumpet between them. By the late 90s the quartet had truly established themselves, with six consecutive American R&B Number 1 singles followed by the equally commercial follow-up *Enter The Dru*, which debuted at US number 2 on the *Billboard* 200 album chart in November 1998. The album ranged from the hard-edged urban R&B of 'How Deep Is Your Love' (US number 3/UK number 9) to the schmaltzy **Babyface** single 'These Are The Times' (US number 21/UK number 4).

In 1999, the quartet appeared on **Will Smith**'s US chart-topping soundtrack hit 'Wild Wild West' and set up their own Dru World Order production company. They also began work on separate solo projects, with Sisqo first out of the block on his **Def Jam Records** debut *Unleash The Dragon*. The various members reunited in 2002 to record *Dru World Order*, which introduced new vocalist Scola.

● ALBUMS: *Dru Hill* (Island 1996) ★★★, *Enter The Dru* (Island 1998) ★★★, *Dru World Order* (Def Soul 2002) ★★★.

Dru, Joanne

b. Joanne Letitia LaCock, 31 January 1922, Logan, West Virginia, USA, d. 10 September 1996, Beverly Hills, Los Angeles, California, USA. After moving to New York in 1940 Dru worked as a model and also danced in shows, including **Al Jolson**'s *Hold Onto Your Hats*. After marrying singer **Dick Haymes** in 1941 she relocated to Hollywood where she appeared in films from the mid-40s, several of them westerns, including *Abie's Irish Rose* (1946), *Red River* (1948), *She Wore A Yellow Ribbon* (1949), *All The King's Men* (1949), *Wagon Master* (1950), *Vengeance Valley* (1951), *Mr. Belvedere Rings The Bell* (1951), *Return Of The Texan* (1952) and *Thunder Bay* (1953). She played the title role in *Hannah Lee* (1953), although the film was subsequently retitled *Outlaw Territory*. Her co-star in this film was John Ireland, who was her second husband (the couple were together from 1949 to 1957).

Dru appeared in films from the 50s through to the 80s. During these same decades she made numerous appearances on television where her acting talents were better used, including the drama series *Pulitzer Prize Playhouse*, *Studio 57*, *The Ford Television Theatre*, *Schlitz Playhouse Of Stars*, *Lux Video Theatre*, *Matinee Theater* and *Disneyland*. Dru was also in individual episodes of many shows, among them *Climax!* (1955 and 1956), *Wagon Train* (1957), *Guestward Ho!* (1960), *Burke's Law* (1964), *The Green Hornet* (1967) and *Marcus Welby, M.D.* (1975). Her brother is actor and *Hollywood Squares* game show host Peter Marshall.

● FILMS: *Abie's Irish Rose* (1946), *Red River* (1948), *She Wore A Yellow Ribbon* (1949), *All The King's Men* (1949), *Wagon Master* (1950), *711 Ocean Drive* (1950), *Vengeance Valley* (1951), *Mr. Belvedere Rings The Bell* (1951) aka *Mr. Belvedere Blows The Whistle* (1951), *Return Of The Texan* (1952), *The Pride Of St. Louis* (1952), *My Pal Gus* (1952), *Thunder Bay* (1953), *Hannah Lee* aka *Outlaw Territory* (1953), *Forbidden* (1953), *Day Of Triumph* (1953), *Duffy Of San Quentin* aka *Men Behind Bars* (1954), *The Siege At Red River* aka *Gatling Gun* (1954), *Southwest Passage* aka *Camels West* (1954), *3 Ring Circus* aka *Jerrico, The Wonder Clown* (1954), *Hell On Frisco Bay* (1955), *The Dark Avenger* aka *The Warriors* (1955), *Sincerely Yours* (1955), *Drango* (1957), *The Light In The Forest* (1958), *The Wild And The Innocent* (1959), *September Storm* (1960), *Sylvia* (1965), *Poliziotto Superpiù* aka *Super Fuzz* (1980).

Drug Free America

Atmospheric Leeds, Yorkshire–based techno group who originally worked in a more funk-orientated vein for Blind Eye ('Throw A Crazy Shape', 'Day-Glo Pussycat', 'Heaven Ain't High Enough') and Concrete Productions ('Just Like

Daddy's Gun') between 1988 and 1990. Afterwards the group, Brian Moss and Steve Dixon, split to travel around the globe. They reunited in 1991, along with female vocalist Goochie, and signed to York's Cybersound label, releasing 'Can You Feel' and 'Loud Everybody'. Moss had formerly worked with **Soft Cell** on their debut album and was also a member of the heavily experimental Vicious Pink.

● ALBUMS: *Trip—The Dreamtime Remixes* (Dreamtime 1994) ★★★.

Drugstore

Led by Isabel Monteiro (b. São Paulo, Brazil; vocals/bass), who relocated to England in 1990, Drugstore are a London-based outfit specializing in dreamy but occasionally spiteful punk pop. The band was formed in 1992 by Monteiro, Dave Hunter (guitar) and Mike Chylinski (drums), with the singer meeting the latter, previously in a series of Los Angeles rock bands, after she had played bass in minor London bands. Hunter was replaced by Daron Robinson in November 1993. Drugstore came to nationwide prominence at the following year's Phoenix Festival, at which Monteiro took the stage in the national football strip of Brazil (this being only one of several unusual stage costumes adopted). This was enough to gain the attention of **Go! Discs**, who signed the band following the release of just one single ('Alive') on their own Honey label (just before Robinson had joined the band). Tours with **Gene**, **Tindersticks**, **Jeff Buckley** and **Echobelly** followed as did second single 'Modern Pleasure' before the advent of a debut album in 1995. With their vocalist proffering highly unusual lyrical matter with a delivery akin to **Mazzy Star**, there was delicious menace behind the seductive sound (sample lyric from *Drugstore*—'I've still got the knife that I used to get rid of that guy'—from 'Nectarine'). A complementary single, 'Solitary Party Groover', earned numerous Single Of The Week awards as Drugstore's rise continued. The band recruited a fourth member, Ian Burdge (keyboards/cello), in 1996, but the collapse of Go! Discs delayed their follow-up. A duet with Thom Yorke of **Radiohead** on the excellent single 'El President' put the band firmly back in the spotlight. While not all of *White Magic For Lovers* was able to match the high standards set by the single, tracks such as 'Say Hello' and 'Mondo Cáne' proved the band were capable of equally inspired moments. Another change of record label preceded their best album to date, *Songs For The Jet Set*.

● ALBUMS: *Drugstore* (Honey/Go! Discs 1995) ★★★, *White Magic For Lovers* (Roadrunner 1998) ★★★, *Songs For The Jet Set* (Global Warming 2001) ★★★★.

● COMPILATIONS: *Collector Number One* (Global Warming 2002) ★★★.

Drum Club

The Drum Club, named after a Sunderland nightspot that imported **Balearic** beat in 1983 and more recently Charlie Hall's own club night, comprised the duo of Lol Hammond (b. 7 January 1960, Stoke Newington, London, England) and Hall (b. 25 October 1959, Whitstable, Kent, England). The latter, self-effacing both on stage and off, and a former book reviewer for the *Catholic Herald*, was nevertheless perceived as the band's creative linchpin. Before the Drum Club he was already a well-known London club DJ, and had also played in rock/pop bands the Apaches and London Cowboys. Hammond, meanwhile, had been part of the many and varied line-ups of Spizz (Spizz Oil, Athletico Spizz, etc.). The Drum

Club's first recording arrived via the **Spiral Tribe** label in March 1992. 'U Make Me Feel So Good' was an instant club classic and was re-released a few months later on the **Guerilla Records** imprint. A follow-up, 'Alchemy', was similarly well-received. In the meantime the Drum Club were becoming a favoured remixing stable, with a variety of musicians seeking out their talents. These included **Jah Wobble**'s Invaders Of The Heart, **Meat Beat Manifesto**, **Psychick Warriors Ov Gaia** and would-be progressive indie outfits **Curve** and **Chapterhouse**. Most notable, however, was their work on **Killing Joke**'s alternative dancefloor staple 'Change'. In addition to their studio wizardry, the duo were also keen to 'play out', making their debut at the **Ministry Of Sound**, London, in October 1992. **Steve Hillage** and Emma Anderson (**Lush**) guested on their live dates. Anderson also contributed guitar to *Everything Is Now* and recorded a 1993 single, 'Stray', with the Drum Club under the name Never Never. It was Hall who came up with the idea of the MIDI circus (to rival rock's **Lollapalooza** touring phenomenon), which also featured **Orbital**, **Aphex Twin**, **Underworld**, etc. By the time of their debut album they had moved on to **Big Life Records**, signifying the very real commercial status open to their mesmeric, shimmering music. The venue, The Drum Club, closed its doors on 30 June 1994, with farewell appearances from Fabio Paris, **Justin Robertson**, Billy Nasty and others. The Drum Club themselves would finally disintegrate in the early months of 1996. Hammond had contacted Hall in advance of projected sessions in Ireland for a fourth studio album, explaining that his commitments to the Slab project with Nina Walsh of **Sabrettes** precluded him from taking part. Hall chose to concentrate on his MC Projects record label, whose releases include those by Phlex (his own pseudonym) and a remix of **Consolidated**'s *This Is Fascism*. Hammond recorded albums with Roger Eno and Nina Walsh (as Slab) in 1999.

● ALBUMS: *Everything Is Now* (Butterfly 1993) ★★★, *Drums Are Dangerous* (Butterfly 1994) ★★★.

Drum 'N' Bass
(see **Jungle**)

Drum Theatre
This cosmopolitan UK-based group comprised Kent B. (drums/keyboards), Gari Tarn (drums/vocals) and Paul Snook (drums bass guitar). Originally a very exciting visual act, they boasted six members, all of whom played the drums at some point. By the time the band were signed to a recording contract they had been slimmed down to a trio. They received attention when their first single of 1986, 'Living In The Past', made a minor impact on the UK charts, while they were supporting the **Human League** on a European tour. The reissue of their 1985 single 'Eldorado', in 1987, received plenty of radio airplay and just missed the Top 40, and their debut album was released to mixed reaction and poor sales. The same fate met their subsequent singles.

● ALBUMS: *Everyman* (Epic 1987) ★★.

Drummers Of Burundi
A percussion group from Burundi in Central Africa. They have performed in the same way for centuries, passing down traditions and techniques from father to son. Their performances were traditionally a part of particular ceremonies, such as births, funerals and the enthronement of kings. However since the 60s they have toured outside of their own country, becoming a popular attraction at concert halls and festivals throughout the world. Their massed drum sound, or the 'Burundi beat' as it became known, also caught the ear of Western rock musicians and they appeared on **Joni Mitchell**'s *The Hissing Of Summer Lawns* (1975). Their distinctive sound also influenced British rock bands of the early 80s such as **Adam And The Ants** and **Bow Wow Wow**. *The Drummers Of Burundi* features a 30-minute continuous performance, during which the 20-piece group play 41 different rhythms. However, it is for their live performances, which feature elements of dance and mime as well as percussion, that they are best known.

● ALBUMS: *The Drummers Of Burundi* (Real World 1992) ★★★.

Drummond, Bill
b. William Drummond, 29 April 1953, Butterworth, Cape Town, South Africa. After relocating to Scotland as a child, Drummond rose to fame in the music business during the late 70s rock renaissance in Liverpool. Drummond formed the Merseyside trio **Big In Japan**, which lasted from 1977–78. Drummond subsequently founded the influential Zoo Record label and backed Lori Larty in **Lori And The Chameleons**. He then enjoyed considerable success as a manager, overseeing the affairs of **Echo And The Bunnymen** and the **Teardrop Explodes**. When the Liverpool group scene saw artists moving south, Drummond left the city and during the next decade was involved in a number of bizarre projects, which testified to his imagination and love of novelty. The controversial JAMS (**Justified Ancients Of Mu Mu**), whose irreverent sampling was extremely innovative for the period, was a typical example of Drummond's pseudonymous mischief. The chart-topping **Timelords** was another spoof and, by the 90s, Drummond found himself at the heart of the creative sampling technology with the critically acclaimed and bestselling **KLF**. Along the way, the eccentric entrepreneur even managed to record a minor solo album, most notable for the track 'Julian Cope Is Dead', an answer song to the former Teardrop Explodes singer's witty 'Bill Drummond Said'.

● ALBUMS: *The Man* (Creation 1987) ★★★.
● FURTHER READING: *Bad Wisdom*, Bill Drummond and Mark Manning. *45*, Bill Drummond. *The Wild Highway*, Bill Drummond and Mark Manning.

Drummond, Billy
b. 19 June 1959, Newport News, Virginia, USA. Drummond began playing drums at the age of four, following the example of his drummer father. He played in high school and local bands and thanks to hearing his father's record collection began taking an interest in the masters of modern jazz. In his teens he attracted attention in New York and became one of several young musicians recorded by **Blue Note Records** in their series of bands named Out Of The Blue. He became a member of **Horace Silver**'s band, thereafter touring and sometimes recording with artists including **Sonny Rollins**, **Pat Metheny**, **J.J. Johnson**, **Joe Henderson**, **Freddie Hubbard**, **Tommy Smith**, **Vincent Herring**, **Jon Faddis** and **Renée Rosnes**. He has played on several records with the latter and she plays in his band, Native Colours, which also includes **Steve Wilson**. An exceptionally accomplished technician, Drummond is a highly supportive player, always

listening and eager to bring out the best in the musicians he accompanies.

● ALBUMS: *Native Colours* (Criss Cross 1994) ★★★, *The Gift* (Criss Cross 1994) ★★★, with Native Colours *One World* (Concord 1995) ★★★, *Dubai* (Criss Cross 1996) ★★★★.

Drummond, Don

b. 1943, Kingston, Jamaica, West Indies, d. 6 May 1969, Kingston, Jamaica, West Indies. One of the principal innovators in Jamaican music, Drummond tragically died before seeing the growth and success of the genre he helped to create. Don Drummond was educated at the famous Alpha Catholic Boys Home and School, in the heart of the Kingston ghetto, where he, like so many others, was allowed to develop and express his musical talents, first as a pupil and later as a teacher. By the early 50s he had established his reputation as one of the island's top jazz trombonists. His main inspiration at this stage was the American big-band sound, but as the decade wore on, the influence of R&B and **sound systems** began to be felt in Jamaica. When the sound system operators began to make their own records, they immediately turned to accomplished musicians such as Drummond, **Roland Alphonso** and **Rico Rodriguez**, who had consolidated their reputations throughout the decade with residencies at clubs such as the Glass Bucket and the Silver Slipper. Their musical knowledge and expertise were critical in determining the feel and direction of these early recordings, which were usually credited to the **Skatalites**. Drummond was also an early convert to the Rastafarian faith and his beliefs were reflected in records such as 'Addis Ababa', 'Far East' and countless uncredited recordings. His fragile mental condition was not helped by the lack both of financial rewards and recognition of his talents. Following the murder of Marguerita, his common-law wife, in 1965, he was committed to Belle Vue (Kingston's centre for Mental disorders), where he ended his days in 1969. Drummond's case was an early tragedy in Jamaican music and he was the precursor of much that was to follow. Since his death, his work has been assessed for its true worth, while one particularly perceptive critic stated that his music 'contained the hurt of his people'. Always a quiet, reserved and shy man, he let his music do the talking.

● COMPILATIONS: *Best Of* (Studio One) ★★★★, *100 Years After* (Studio One) ★★★, *Memorial* (Treasure Isle) ★★★, *In Memory Of* (Studio One) ★★★★, *Scattered Lights* (Top Deck 1985) ★★★★.

Drummond, Ray

b. 23 November 1946, Brookline, Massachusetts, USA. When Drummond started out playing music in the 50s, it was on brass instruments, but by 1961 he had switched to bass. He studied non-musical subjects for several years but in the 70s formed a jazz quartet in San Francisco, playing with **Michael White** and **Bobby Hutcherson**, then moved to New York. During the 80s, he played in bands led by others and in his own groups. Among the artists with whom he worked were **Kenny Barron**, **Johnny Griffin**, **Hank Jones**, **Wynton Marsalis**, **David Murray** and **Woody Shaw**. He also was with Mingus Dynasty and the **Thad Jones-Mel Lewis** Jazz Orchestra. For his recording sessions, Drummond regularly assembles all-star groups that might include artists of the calibre of **John Scofield**, Jones, Barron, **Renée Rosnes**, **Billy Higgins** and **Gary**

Bartz, moulding them into cogent and unified performances. A highly talented player, Drummond is especially effective when using his instrument's darker toned regions. He is also a skilled composer.

● ALBUMS: *Susanita* (Nilva 1984) ★★★, *Maya's Dance* (Nilva 1986) ★★★, *Camera In A Bag* (Criss Cross 1989) ★★★, with Bill Mays *One To One* (DMP 1990) ★★★, *The Essence* (DMP 1990) ★★★, *Excursion* (Arabesque 1992) ★★★, *Continuum* (Arabesque 1994) ★★★★, *Vignettes* (Arabesque 1995) ★★★, *1-2-3-4* (Arabesque 1999) ★★★, with Masahiro Yoshida, Allen Farnham *Uno* (DIW 2001) ★★★.

Drummond, Tim

b. Timothy Lee Drummond, 20 April 1940, Bloomington, Illinois, USA. One of the leading session players in the music business, bass player Drummond began playing R&B and rock 'n' roll when the airforce put his father on a year's transfer to Charleston, SC. Returning to Illinois, he played guitar in a local band with 'Wild Child Gibson' of **Little Richard** fame before turning his attention to the bass. Drummond toured with local attraction Eddie Cash & The Cashiers, before playing with rockabilly singer **Conway Twitty**. When Twitty began to move into straight country, Drummond relocated to Cincinnati, Ohio, where he worked the clubs with **Troy Seals**, **Lonnie Mack** and Roger Troy (**Electric Flag**) and played sessions for **Hank Ballard** and **James Brown**. He joined Brown's band, touring with great players such as **Jimmy Nolen** and **Maceo Parker** in North America Vietnam, Korea and Africa, but eventually quit. Drummond then moved to Nashville, playing sessions for blues and R&B singers including **Joe Simon**, Margie Hendricks, **Fenton Robinson** and country artists including **Ronnie Mislap**, **Jimmy Buffett**, **Doug Kershaw** and **Charlie Daniels**. A meeting with **Neil Young** resulted in Drummond playing on Young's highly successful *Harvest* and touring as part of his Straygators backing group. Drummond moved to California, where he has become an in-demand session player, working with a stellar list of artists including Young, **Bob Dylan** (*Slow Train Coming, Saved, Shot Of Love*), **Ry Cooder** (*Bop Till You Drop, The Slide Area, Borderline*), **J.J. Cale** (*Naturally, Travel Log, Anyway The Wind Blows*), **Crosby, Stills And Nash** (*CSN*), **Graham Nash** (*Wild Tales*), the **Beach Boys** (*16 Big Ones*), **John Mayall**, **Rick Danko**, **Don Henley** (*Building The Perfect Beast*) and **Jewel** (*Pieces Of You*). He is currently working with blues legend **Arthur 'Big Boy' Crudup**'s sons on the Franktown Blues project and with **Essra Mohawk** as the KillerGroove-Band. Texan guitar company Jackson Guitars are also manufacturing the Tim Drummond Signature 'BlueCollar' Bass Guitar.

Drusky, Roy

b. Roy Frank Drusky, 22 June 1930, Atlanta, Georgia, USA, d. 23 September 2004, Portland, Tennessee, USA. Drusky showed interest only in baseball during his childhood and high school days. After attending a Cleveland Indians training camp, he decided against it as a career and, in 1948, joined the navy. A country band on his ship gave him an interest in music, and when next on shore leave he bought a guitar and taught himself to play. In 1950 he left the navy, enrolled at Emory University to study veterinary medicine and sought singing work to pay for the course. He formed a country band called the Southern Ranch Boys and played daily on WEAS Decatur. He later left the university and became a disc jockey on WEAS, the resident singer in a local club and appeared on WLW-A television in Atlanta.

In 1953, Drusky began his recording career with a session for Starday Records. A year later he left his band, moved as a DJ to KEVE Minneapolis and continued with club work, but he concentrated more on songwriting. In 1958 his song 'Alone With You' became a number 1 US country hit for **Faron Young** and led to Drusky becoming a member of the **Grand Ole Opry** even though he had no hit recordings of his own at the time. He moved to Nashville, signed for **Decca Records** and between 1960 and 1962 had Top 5 country hits with his own recordings of 'Another', 'Anymore' (both self-penned), 'Three Hearts In A Tangle' (also a US pop chart hit, number 35) and 'Second Hand Rose', and further hits with 'I Can't Tell My Heart That' (with **Kitty Wells**), 'I'd Rather Loan You Out', 'I Went Out Of My Way (To Make You Happy)' and 'There's Always One (Who Loves A Lot)'.

Drusky moved to **Mercury Records** in 1963 and over the next decade charted several Top 10 country hits including 'Peel Me A Nanner', '(From Now On All My Friends Are Gonna Be) Strangers', 'The World Is Round', 'Where The Blue And Lonely Go', 'Such A Fool', 'Long Long Texas Road', 'All My Hard Times' and in 1965 achieved a country number 1 with 'Yes, Mr. Peters', a duet recording with Priscilla Mitchell. In 1966 he had Top 20 success with the original version of 'If The Whole World Stopped Lovin'', a song that gave **Val Doonican** a big number 3 pop hit in the UK the following year. In the mid-60s Drusky appeared in several country and western movies.

From the 60s to the early 80s, Drusky toured extensively, played the *Grand Ole Opry* and became involved in production and publishing work as well as hosting his own network television programmes. He moved to **Capitol Records** in 1974, having a minor hit with **Elton John**'s 'Dixie Lily' and then to Scorpion Records, attaining his last chart entry in 1977 with 'Betty's Song'. Drusky branched out into gospel music in the 90s but after a long battle against emphysema passed away in September 2004. Drusky's relaxed singing style led to him being referred to as the **Perry Como** of country music. Many felt that, had he so wished and with the right material, he may well have been the person to assume the pop country mantle left by **Jim Reeves**.

● ALBUMS: *Anymore With Roy Drusky* (Decca 1961) ★★★, *It's My Way* (Decca 1962) ★★★★, *Songs Of The Cities* (Mercury 1964) ★★★, *All Time Country Hits* (Wing 1964) ★★★, *Yesterday's Gone* (Mercury 1964) ★★★★, *The Pick Of The Country* (Mercury 1964) ★★★★, *Country Music All Around The World* (Mercury 1965) ★★, with Priscilla Mitchell *Love's Eternal Triangle* (Mercury 1965) ★★★, with Mitchell *We Belong Together* (Wing 1965) ★★★, *Country Song Express* (Mercury 1966) ★★★, with Mitchell *Together Again* (Mercury 1966) ★★★★, *In A New Dimension* (Mercury 1966) ★★★, *If The Whole World Stopped Lovin'* (Mercury 1967) ★★★, *Now Is A Lonely Time* (Mercury 1968) ★★★, *Jody And The Kid* (Mercury 1968) ★★, *Portrait Of Roy Drusky* (Mercury 1969) ★★★, *My Grass Is Green* (Mercury 1969) ★★★, *I'll Make Amends* (Mercury 1970) ★★★, *All My Hard Times* (Mercury 1970) ★★★, *I Love The Way That You've Been Lovin' Me* (Mercury 1971) ★★, *Doin' Something Right* (Mercury 1973) ★★★, *Peaceful Easy Feeling* (Capitol 1974) ★★★, *This Life Of Mine* (Capitol 1976) ★★★, *Night Flying* (Scorpion 1976) ★★★, *New Lips* (Hilltop 1976) ★★, *Ramblin' Man* (CMI 1977) ★★, *Golden Hits* (Plantation 1979) ★★, *English Gold* (Plantation 1979) ★★★, *Roy* (Big R 1980) ★★★, *Sings Willie Nelson* (Brylen 1980) ★★★, *Country Sunshine* (51 West Q 1984) ★★, with Kitty Wells *Kitty Wells And Roy Drusky* (Playback 1986) ★★★.

● COMPILATIONS: *Roy Drusky's Greatest Hits* (Mercury 1965) ★★★★, *Greatest Hits Vol. 2* (Mercury 1968) ★★★★, *The Great Roy Drusky Sings* (Harmony 1965) ★★★, *Roy Drusky* (Vocalion 1965) ★★★, *Roy Drusky's Bag Of Country Gold Hits* (Wing 1968) ★★★, *Twenty Grand Country Hits* (Wing 1969) ★★★, *El Paso* (Hilltop 1970) ★★★, *The Best Of Roy Drusky* (Mercury 1970) ★★★, *Songs Of Love And Life* (Mercury Nashville 1995) ★★★.

● FILMS: *Forty Acre Feud* (1965), *The Gold Guitar* (1966), *The Las Vegas Hillbillys* (1966).

Dry Branch Fire Squad

Formed in 1976 by Ron Thomason, Dry Branch Fire Squad started out as a bluegrass band featuring strong hints of gospel music. Thomason, who is a virtuoso mandolin player and has a rough-edged yet tuneful singing voice, brought into the band John Baker (guitar), Robert Leach (banjo) and John Carpenter (bass). The quartet made a succession of well-received albums during the late 70s, along the way adding singer Mary Jo Leet to the line-up. Over the years the band's personnel shifted and among those who contributed to its ranks are Mary Jo's husband, Charlie Leet (bass), Adam McIntosh (guitar), Dan Russell (banjo), Suzanne Thomas and **Hazel Dickens** (vocals).

From the start the band attracted a devoted following, mainly through their traditional repertoire. They maintained this albeit moving away from being solely a bluegrass group as they increasingly performed a wide range of mountain music. Thomason and his colleagues are clearly aware that the tradition they represent is a matter of importance to America's musical heritage, yet they are also refreshingly humorous. Their live shows are notable for this, with Thomason especially offering perceptively witty song lyrics as well as amusing interpolations in between songs. Fortunately, this particular aspect of Dry Branch Fire Squad's work has been captured on the 1996 release *Live! At Last*. This, then, is a band that takes its music seriously, especially the gospel material that has remained a significant element, but it can also have fun, something they readily communicate to their audiences.

● ALBUMS: *Spiritual Songs From Dry Branch* (RT 1977) ★★★, *Born To Be Lonesome* (RT 1978) ★★★, *Dry Branch Fire Squad* (RT 1978) ★★★, *On Tour* (Gordo 1979) ★★★, *Antiques & Inventions* (Rounder 1981) ★★★, *Fannin' The Flames* (Rounder 1982) ★★★, *Good Neighbours & Friends* (Rounder 1985) ★★★★, *Golgotha* (Rounder 1986) ★★, *Fertile Ground* (Rounder 1989) ★★★, *Long Journey* (Rounder 1991) ★★★, *Just For The Record* (Rounder 1993) ★★★, *Live! At Last* (Rounder 1996) ★★★★, *Memories That Bless & Burn* (Rounder 1999) ★★★★, *Hand Hewn* (Rounder 2001) ★★★, *Live At The Newburyport Firehouse* (Rounder 2005) ★★★★.

● COMPILATIONS: *Tried & True* (Rounder 1988) ★★★.

Dry Kill Logic

A hardcore metal band that came to prominence in 2001 with their successful second album, *The Darker Side Of Nonsense*, Dry Kill Logic started life in their native Westchester County, New York, USA, under the moniker Hinge. Formed in 1995 by Cliff Rigano (b. New York City, New York, USA; vocals), Dave Kowatch (b. New York City, New York, USA; bass), Louie Bravo (b. New York City, New York, USA; guitar) and Phil Arcuri (b. New York City, New York, USA; drums), the band's influences, old-school thrash such as **Sepultura** and newer, glossier acts such as **Coal Chamber**, saw them welcomed by crowds on tours with **Flotsam And Jetsam**, **Exodus** and **Pro-Pain**. The band's first EP, '*Cause Moshing Is Good Fun!*', was released on their own Psychodrama label. A debut album, *Elemental Evil*, was promoted by tours with **System Of A Down**, **Anthrax**, **Incubus** and the **Misfits**. Internal pressures saw Bravo departing in the middle of the band's 1999 summer tour. After a brief hiatus the remaining members recruited Scott Thompson (b. New York City, New York, USA) and signed a new recording contract with Roadrunner Records. Threatened by legal action from another band, the quartet briefly changed their moniker to Hinge A.D. before a lawsuit settlement in May 2001 saw them agreeing to adopt Dry Kill Logic as their new name. *Darker Side Of Nonsense* was released the following month. The album's powerful blend of riffing and atmospherics proved particularly popular with the band's audiences on the festival circuit.

● ALBUMS: as Hinge *Elemental Evil* (Psychodrama 1999) ★★★, *The Darker Side Of Nonsense* (Roadrunner 2001) ★★★★, *The Dead And Dreaming* (SPV 2004) ★★★.

Du Barry Was A Lady

Cole Porter's third show with the dynamic **Ethel Merman** as his leading lady, and the third longest-running book musical of the 30s, opened at the 46th Street Theatre in New York City, USA, on 6 December 1939. The book, by **Herbert Fields** and **Buddy De Sylva**, concerns Louis Blore (Bert Lahr), a washroom attendant at New York's Club Petite. Louis loves May Daly (Ethel Merman), the star of the club's floorshow, and feels that a windfall of $75,000 from a win on the Irish Sweepstakes puts him in with a chance. He tries to improve his odds by preparing a potent potion for May's married boyfriend, Alex Barton (Ronald Graham), but accidentally drinks it himself and passes out. After waking from the trance, during which he imagines he is Louis XV and May is Du Barry, Louis realizes that his place is really in the washroom, and leaves the field clear for Alex. The situation provides some marvellous opportunities for Lahr's inspired clowning and Raoul Péne du Bois' spectacular settings and costumes. 'Do I Love You?', sung by Merman and Graham, was the only one of Porter's songs that became popular outside the show, but his score contained several other witty and memorable numbers such as two Merman and Lahr duets, 'Friendship' (She: 'If they ever hang you, pard, send a card.' He: 'If they ever cut your throat, write a note.' She: 'If they ever make a cannibal stew of you. Invite me too.' Both: 'It's friendship, friendship . . .') and 'But In The Morning, No!'. Merman also had several excellent solo opportunities with 'When Love Beckoned (In Fifty-Second Street)', 'Give Him The Oo-La-La' and 'Katie Went To Haiti'. Another interesting item was 'Well, Did You Evah?', sung in this show by Charles Walters and the future World War II 'pin-up girl', Betty Grable, and later revised for the 1956 film,

High Society. *Du Barry Was A Lady*, the last Broadway musical of the decade, stayed on for 408 performances, and a London production, with Arthur Riscoe and Frances Day as Louis and May, ran for nearly six months. The 1943 film version starred **Gene Kelly**, **Lucille Ball**, Red Skelton and Virginia O'Brien.

Du Droppers

Although the Du Droppers formed in Harlem, New York City, USA, in 1952, each member of the vocal quartet had already sung within their local gospel communities. Indeed, while doo-wop was primarily a young man's concern, the Du Droppers—J.C. 'Junior' Caleb Ginyard (b. 15 January 1910, St. Matthews, South Carolina, USA, d. 11 August 1978; lead), Harvey Ray (tenor/baritone), Willie Ray (tenor/baritone) and Eddie Hashew (bass)—had an average age of well over 40 at formation. Ginyard's previous experience was the most extensive, having sung with the Royal Harmony Singers, Jubalaires and Dixieaires. As the Du Droppers they rehearsed in basements until Paul Kapp, manager of the **Delta Rhythm Boys**, took over. They made their debut at the end of 1952 with a single for Bobby Robinson's Red Robin Records in Harlem 'Can't Do Sixty No More'. This was an answer record to the **Dominoes**' 'Sixty Minute Man', but failed to replicate its success. After replacing Hashew with Bob Kornegay the group passed an audition for **RCA Records**, making their debut with 'I Want To Know (What You Do When You Go Round There)'. Released in March 1953, it made number 3 in the Billboard R&B charts. In retaliation Red Robin issued a single from masters that they still held, 'Come On And Love Me Baby'. However, its arrival was eclipsed by the Du Droppers' second release on RCA, 'I Found Out (What You Do When You Go Round There)', which continued firmly in the vein of their label debut. Continuing the parallels, it too hit number 3 in the R&B charts. 'Whatever You're Doin' was also an extension of the theme but failed to break the charts, nor did their first ballad 'Don't Pass Me By'. RCA then initiated a new R&B subsidiary, Groove Records, and the Du Droppers gave the label its first release 'Speed King'. For the subsequent 'How Much Longer', Prentice Moreland expanded the group to a quintet. He soon departed for spells in the Dominoes and **Cadets**, while the Du Droppers regrouped with the addition of **Ravens** singer Joe Van Loan. He did not last long and was forced to 'leave' following record company politicking between Herald Records (who wanted to sign the Du Droppers, and who had Van Loan under contract anyway) and RCA (who wished to exercise their option for another year). Harvey Ray also left the fold. From then on the lead role was handled by Charlie Hughes (later of the **Drifters**) in the studio and Van Loan live. Hughes made his debut on the April 1955 single 'Give Me Some Consideration', after which Harvey Ray rejoined for a Canadian tour. One final single emerged amid all the confusion caused by the shifting personnel, 'You're Mine Already', before Ginyard left to join the **Golden Gate Quartet**. Though the other members struggled to carry on, this signalled the death knell for the Du Droppers.

● COMPILATIONS: *Can't Do Sixty No More* (Dr. Horse 1987) ★★★.

Dual Control

The Dual Control moniker is descriptive of the recording set-up behind this stylish and classy collaboration between 'street soul' DJ Phil Styles and Grand Central Records' in-house engineer Mike Ball. The former is notable for his DJ sets on the pirate radio stations of Manchester, England, and for his inclusion in local crew the Rude Boy Assassins. The latter is a former graffiti artist who developed his music-making skills working as an engineer for **Electronic** and **M People**. Together the duo forge an assertive and hard-edged UK take on soul/hip-hop/R&B that matches big basslines, layered horns, severe beats, scratching and samples of real instruments and seems to suggest an overtly Mancunian take on a music more readily associated with sunnier (that is, American) climates. Styles and Ball have cited the influence of friend/mentor Steve Christian on their studio-birthed productions and also the acclaimed duo (**Rae And Christian**) of which Christian is half point to the impact of the sound system on their music-making. Nevertheless, Dual Control's music is undeniably borne of the studio. The duo layer sounds with a high degree of complexity, adopting a laborious and painstaking process of assembling their music. That is, rather than sampling complete basslines and looping these, Styles and Ball sample only single bass notes that they rearrange and remodel. Such a methodology partially explains Dual Control's debut album's long gestation period: Styles and Ball met in 1997 and from 1999 onwards released 'Bring It On' and 'Boogie Down Feature' at two year intervals. The album, *Left Or Right*, was not issued until 2004, preceded by the 'Stoned Mason' 12-inch. For fans of the Grand Central sound, however, *Left Or Right* was undeniably worth the wait. The album notably featured the sampling/scratching of Peter Parker aka **Fingathing**, drummer/producer Dubble D and the voice of Loretta Heywood of Bugz In The Attic.

● ALBUMS: *Left Or Right* (Grand Central 2004) ★★★.

Duarte, Chris

b. 16 February 1963, San Antonio, Texas, USA. This incredibly talented guitarist/songwriter moved to Austin, Texas, in the late 70s, where he immersed himself in the local club scene. He enjoyed a spell with **Bobby Mack** before bursting onto the blues scene in 1994 with the release of *Texas Sugar/Strat Magik*, on which he was backed by John Jordan (bass) and Brannen Temple (drums). The album brought immediate acclaim for the band's gritty, intense southern blues sound, with Duarte singled out for his technique. Indeed, in the 1995 *Guitar World* magazine Readers' Poll, he was voted fourth best blues guitarist behind the much more established and esteemed company of **Eric Clapton**, **Buddy Guy** and **B.B. King**. *Texas Sugar/Strat Magik* was additionally voted fourth best blues album. Duarte described the band's sound as 'blues based, but it has that loud aggressive edge that punk had. I liked **Dead Kennedys**, **Sex Pistols**, **Dead Boys**, anything that was hard.' The decision to employ producer Dennis Herring, the former Los Angeles session guitarist previously noted for his work with **Camper Van Beethoven** and **Throwing Muses**, was also interesting. Afterwards the album was promoted on US touring dates with Buddy Guy. *Tailspin Headwhack* built on the debut's blues edge by incorporating tape loops, wah-wah and some tasteful sampling. After a three-year hiatus, during which he moved to the Zoë label, Duarte returned with *Love Is Greater Than Me*.

● ALBUMS: with Chris Duarte Group *Texas Sugar/Strat Magik* (Silvertone 1994) ★★★★, with Chris Duarte Group *Tailspin Headwhack* (Silvertone 1997) ★★★★, *Love Is Greater Than Me* (Zoë 2000) ★★★★, with Chris Duarte Group *Romp* (Zoë 2003).

Dub

Essentially reggae in the raw, this cultish, perennially popular form strips out the majority of the music's melody at the mixing desk, leaving behind the rhythm section ('drum 'n' bass' music in reggae parlance) and the residue of other instruments, often with massive layers of echo. Reggae records with crashing effects and decidedly eccentric arrangements date back to the ska era. By 1969-70 many producers, among them **Lee Perry, Clive Chin, Joe Gibbs, Bunny Lee** and **Andy Capp**, were making largely instrumental music that was heavily dependent on the rhythm section (the **Upsetters'** 'Clint Eastwood' in 1970, for example), and it took only the addition of delay units such as the Copycat and Echoplex to create the dub boom. In 1972, encouraged by Bunny Lee, **King Tubby**, an electronics engineer and **sound system** owner, began to mix records in four-track, and by late 1973 his name graced many b-side 'versions' (the name is a corruption of instrumental version, or 'Version 2') of other people's records, notably those of Bunny Lee and Lee Perry. At the same time, engineer Sylvan Morris at **Harry J./Studio One** and **Errol Thompson** at Randy's, also experimented with the dub sound. Occasional, very limited-pressing dub albums began to appear in the shops and quickly became collectors' items. Among the best-known of these were Perry/Tubby collaborations including the ingenious stereo LP *Blackboard Jungle Dub*, which had three different mixes, one for each speaker and one for both, and *King Tubby Meets The Upsetter At The Grass Roots Of Dub*, a record that was *the* underground reggae album of 1974 in the UK. Tubby's uniquely precise, often stunningly heavy mixes also graced numerous Bunny Lee productions on his Jackpot, Justice and Attack labels.

By the mid-70s virtually no reggae singles were released without a dub version on the flip-side, and artists such as **Augustus Pablo** and **Glen Brown** had created a career from instrumental music in dub form. New engineers such as Prince (later **King**) **Jammy**, **Pat Kelly** (also a singer) and **Scientist** gradually took over from the original dub mixers, but by 1982 the original boom was pretty much finished, save a few die-hards such as UK engineer-producers **Mad Professor** and **Adrian Sherwood**. However, by 1991 a new breed of dub-inspired musicians, such as **Jah Shaka**, Sound Iration and the Disciples, had founded the 'new roots' movement and placed the music back on the map, albeit with digital equipment and modern intentions.

● COMPILATIONS: various *Blackboard Jungle Dub* (Upsetter 1974) ★★★★★, *King Tubby Meets The Upsetter At The Grass Roots Of Dub* (Fay Music 1974) ★★★★★, *Pick A Dub* (Atra 1975) ★★★, *King Tubby Meets Rockers Uptown* (Clocktower 1976) ★★★★, *King Tubby's Prophecy Of Dub* (Prophets 1976) ★★★★ *Beware* (Grove Music 1978) ★★★, *Dub Gone Crazy: The Evolution Of Dub At King Tubby's 1975-79* (Blood & Fire 1994) ★★★★.

Dub Federation

MERC recording artists whose career with that label saw the release of 'Space Funk' and 'Love Inferno'. The group, which split at the beginning of 1994, comprised Andy Ellison, Pete Latham and the surname-less Elton. After their demise,

Ellison and Latham would go on to work alongside **David Holmes** as part of the Scubadevils (who recorded a track for the *Trance Europe Express* compilation), while Elton relocated to Scotland, before guesting alongside the **Grid** on their UK television appearances on *Top Of The Pops* for 'Swamp Thing'.

Dub Pistols

Although often marketed as a group, the dance rap amalgam the Dub Pistols is truly a vehicle for leader Barry Ashworth (b. 12 November 1965, London, England). Ashworth's rise to the top was a long and winding one, as he got his start running local dance clubs in 1987 when he took over a night spot, 'Ziggy's', in Streatham previously featuring a then-unknown DJ **Paul Oakenfold**. When his residency was up, Ashworth found himself running the Monkey Drum, a locale best known at the time as a hangout for **Stone Roses** and the **Happy Mondays**, as well as his own record shop located in Covent Garden. When the shop went under, Ashworth decided it was time to launch himself as a band leader. The dance rock act Déjà Vu was formed, but despite a single that caused a bit of a stir (a cover version of the **Woodentops'** 'Why? Why? Why?'), Déjà Vu folded shortly thereafter, as Ashworth returned once more to residencies at clubs (including 'Naked Lunch' at the SW1 club and one in Kensington, where he worked alongside Charlie Chester). Ashworth also began producing and remixing tracks for a variety of other artists, including renowned names such as **Bush** and **Moby**, but it was his work on **Monkey Mafia**'s 1998 release, *Shoot The Boss*, that made dance enthusiasts the world over take note of his talents.

Ashworth decided to have another go at leading his own group, and as a result, the Dub Pistols were formed. In addition to Ashworth, other members in the Dub Pistols include songwriting collaborator and bass player Jason O'Bryan, guitarist John King and DJ Stix. **Jimmy Iovine** at Interscope Records took note of the band after hearing an early demo, and their debut *Point Blank* was released through **A&M Records** in 1998. Catching the tail end of the **big beat** craze, the Dub Pistols fashioned one of the year's finest releases to emerge from the club scene. With big beat rapidly fading from fashion, it took three years for the Dub Pistols to issue a proper follow-up, during which time they concentrated on touring their electrifying live show around the world. Ashworth also embarked on a solo US club tour and remixed tracks for a variety of artists including **Limp Bizkit**, **Korn**, **DJ Spooky** and **Banco De Gaia**. The second Dub Pistols' album, *Six Million Ways To Live*, was scheduled for release in 2001, but the band's US record company expressed concern at some of the lyrical concert in the wake of the terrorist atrocities of 11 September 2001. The album was shelved and the band parted company with their label. Distinctive Records stepped in and eventually released *Six Million Ways To Live* in 2003.

● ALBUMS: *Point Blank* (A&M 1998) ★★★★, *Six Million Ways To Live* (Distinctive 2003) ★★★.
● COMPILATIONS: *Y4K: Next Level Breaks* (Distinctive 2002) ★★★.

Dub Plate

A dub plate is simply an acetate cut onto a plastic-coated metal disc, featuring an unusual mix of a well-known record or a recording unavailable elsewhere, and used by a **sound system** to help to promote the exclusivity of the music it plays. 'Dubs' are highly prized by collectors, particularly those recorded by **King Tubby**'s or **King Jammy**'s, or those that feature famous artists offering amended renditions of classics.

Dub Poetry

Dub poetry is a style of reggae in which poets recite their works over heavy 'dubbed' rhythms, influenced by 70s DJs such as **U-Roy**, **I. Roy** and **Big Youth**. One of the originators was **Linton Kwesi Johnson**, who was born in Jamaica in 1952 and moved to England in 1963. His early poetry was in the traditional European style until he began listening to DJs and decided to set his work to music. From early on, he had found the English language too restricting and austere, and he set to work in the heavy patois in which the DJs specialized. His first album, *Dread Beat & Blood*, was released in the late 70s and proved hugely influential. Almost single-handedly it gave birth to a whole sub-genre of reggae music, where poets such as **Michael Smith**, **Benjamin Zephaniah**, **Jean Binta Breeze**, **Oku Onuora** and **Mutabaruka** performed to the accompaniment of roots reggae rhythms. Probably the most successful of all has been the Jamaican-based Mutabaruka, whose debut album in 1982 for Earl 'Chinna' Smith's High Times label was something of a classic.

In reggae music the rhythm or backing track is never completely subservient to the vocal, instrumental or DJ's contribution, but in the case of some of the dub poets, their voices became the predominant factor. Although much of the DJ output is revered in Jamaica, its Kingston patois means little to the uninitiated, and in this respect, the dub poets' clearer diction was more successful, particularly in the USA and Europe, where many have large, committed followings outside of the usual reggae audience. Most poets are well aware of the irony of their position, and Mutabaruka summarized the situation thus: 'Revolutionary poets, Have become entertainers, Babblin' out angry words'.

● ALBUMS: Linton Kwesi Johnson: *Dread Beat An' Blood* originally credited to Poet And The Roots (Front Line 1977) ★★★, *Forces of Victory* (Island 1979) ★★★★, *Bass Culture* (Island 1980) ★★★★, *In Concert With The Dub Band* (LKJ 1986) ★★★, Mutabaruka: *Check It* (High Times 1982) ★★★★, *The Mystery Unfolds* (Shanachie 1986) ★★★, *Out Cry* (Shanachie 1987) ★★★, *Any Which Way* (Greensleeves 1989) ★★★ Jean Binta Breeze *Tracks.* (LKJ 1991) ★★★★, Benjamin Zephaniah: *Dub Ranting* (Upright 1983) ★★★★, *Rasta* (Upright/Helidon 1987) ★★★, *Us And Dem* (Mango/Island 1990) ★★★, Michael Smith *Mi Cyaan Believe It* (Island 1982) ★★★.
● COMPILATIONS: Various *Dread Poets Society*.

Dub Syndicate

An On U Sound offshoot that **Roots Radics** drummer, Lincoln Valentine 'Style' Scott, and **Adrian Sherwood** have used as a flag of convenience for various collaborations, working with reggae greats such as **U-Roy**, **Lee Perry** and **Aswad**. Scott and Sherwood's exploration of **dancehall**, **dub** and reggae is an enduring project that was inaugurated in 1982 by the *Pounding System* release. Personnel are recruited as the need arises, with **Errol Holt**, **Skip McDonald** and Carlton 'Bubblers' Ogilvie the most regularly featured players. The *Classic Selection* series was given focus by the voice of poet

Andy Fairley, who also appeared on 'Lack Of Education'. Dub Syndicate's later material included ethnic chants and mantras in a nod to the global ambient school of **dance music**.

● ALBUMS: *Pounding System* (On U Sound/ROIR 1982) ★★★★, *One Way System* (On U Sound/ROIR 1983) ★★★, with Dr. Pablo *North Of The River Thames* (On U Sound 1984) ★★★, *Tunes From The Missing Channel* (On U Sound/EMI 1985) ★★★, *Strike The Balance* (On U Sound/Mango 1990) ★★★, *Stoned Immaculate* (On U Sound 1991) ★★★, *Echomania* (On U Sound 1993) ★★★★, *Ital Breakfast* (On U Sound 1996) ★★★, *Fear Of A Green Planet* (Shanachie 1998) ★★★, *Mellow & Colly* (On U Sound/EFA 1998) ★★★, *Live At The T+C 1991* (On U Sound 1999) ★★★★, *Live At The Maritime Hall* (On U Sound/Artists Only 2000) ★★★, *Acres Of Space* (Lion & Roots/EFA 2001) ★★★, *Pure Thrillseekers* (Shanachie 2005) ★★★★.

● COMPILATIONS: *Classic Selection Vol. 1* (On U Sound 1989) ★★★★, *Classic Selection Vol. 2* (On U Sound 1991) ★★★, *Research & Development* (On U Sound 1996) ★★★.

Dub Tractor

b. Anders Remmer, 19 January 1964, Denmark. Remmer creates music that is both emotional and utilitarian, such that a track named 'E47' might equally refer to a fetishized (Soundelux) microphone, as to a paean to the road that links Copenhagen and Helsingor in Remmer's native North Zealand. With laudable attention to detail, the Copenhagen-based musician merges precision-tooled programming with acoustic elements to create an initially unassuming and low-key music that necessitates (and warrants) repeated plays to yield results. Remmer appropriates electronica's usual palette of clicks, crackles and hiss but subtly deploys these alongside instruments such as (processed) acoustic guitar. Despite the inclusion of dub in his recording moniker, Remmer uses the effect discriminatingly.

On 2003's *More Or Less Mono*, the most overt nod to dub was on '50 Hz Guitar', a track that pulsed with low end noise but merged this effect with pretty guitar—tellingly, Dub Tractor's music also carries trace echoes of miserablist 80s guitar pop. For Dub Tractor, words are to be used sparingly: on 'I Don't Care' (from *More Or Less Mono*), the only lyrics utilized are those of the title, and the sentiment seems to be nonchalant rather than belligerent. On 'Hum (Part 4)' (from the same release) the words are mumbled so as to be more or less inaudible. Remmer also records as Future3 and System with Thomas Knak (aka **Björk** collaborator **Opiate**) and Jesper Skaaning (aka Acustic).

● ALBUMS: *Discrete Recordings* (Flex 1994) ★★★, *An Evening With* (Flex/Additive 1996) ★★★, *Delay* (FX 2000) ★★★, *More Or Less Mono* (City Centre Offices 2003) ★★★.

Dub War

A collision of **ragga** and punk, shot through with steely metallic guitar, Dub War emerged in 1994 as a high-octane, highly political extension of hard rock's new-found ability to merge innovative styles with the old. Formed in Newport, Wales, in 1993, the four-piece comprises Jeff Rose (guitar), Richie Glover (bass), Martin Ford (drums) and Benji (vocals), all of whom came from diverse musical backgrounds. Glover had played in several minor punk bands, while Benji's apprenticeship came in reggae dancehalls, and he had previously worked with **Mad Professor**. The band made its debut at the end of 1993 with a self-titled 12-inch EP that managed simultaneously to appear in three different **New Musical Express** charts—the 'Vibes', 'Turn Ons' and 'Hardcore' listings. Following a debut mini-album in 1994, they switched to Earache Records for the *Mental* EP, joining **Pop Will Eat Itself** and **Manic Street Preachers** on touring engagements. *Mental* featured remixes from **Senser**, **Brand New Heavies** and **Jamiroquai** and was followed by a further EP, *Gorrit*. Their first full album came in February 1995 with *Pain*, by which time the band had established a strong live following to augment their press profile. Fans were rewarded by the uniformly excellent *Wrong Side Of Beautiful*, which was later re-released in a new limited edition version with a six-track CD of remixes, *Right Side Of Beautiful*. The album failed to provide the breakthrough the band deserved, however, and ultimately led to their demise two years later. Benji teamed up with **Infectious Grooves** bass player Rob Trujillo in Mass Mental and also formed Skindred.

● ALBUMS: *Dub Warning* mini-album (Words Of Warning 1994) ★★★, *Pain* (Earache 1995) ★★★★, *Words Of Dubwarning* (Words Of Warning 1996) ★★★, *Wrong Side Of Beautiful* (Earache 1996) ★★★★.

● COMPILATIONS: *Step Ta Dis* (Earache 1998) ★★★.

Dube, Lucky

b. 3 August 1964, Ermelo, Eastern Transvaal, South Africa. The most successful African reggae artist of all time, Lucky Dube (pronounced Doobay) has taken his **Peter Tosh**-influenced music further than his hero himself managed. Guitarist-vocalist Dube formed his first group, a mbqanga combo entitled the Skyway Band, while still at school. An interest in **Rastafarianism** complemented a musical predilection for reggae, although, as a member of the Love Brothers, his first album betrayed none of these influences. His first hit single, the 'Zulu soul' of 'Baxoleleni', arrived in 1983 from his solo set *Lengane Ngeyetha*. Several albums later, he starred in a South African movie *Getting Lucky* and performed reggae tracks for its soundtrack. His first reggae album, *Rastas Never Die*, was banned in South Africa on account of its militancy, and Dube diversified into rap for *Help My Krap*. In 1986 his new band, the Slaves, recorded 'Think About The Children', and their second album, *Slave*, sold 300,000 copies.

In 1989 Lucky Dube toured France and the USA with Slaves and appeared in the movie *Voice In The Dark*. Two albums in that year, *Together As One* and *Prisoner*, sold heavily, the latter going double platinum in South Africa in only five days. In 1991 Dube became the first South African artist to play the Reggae Sunsplash festival in Jamaica, and again he issued two albums in one year, *Captured Live* (incidentally also the title of a Peter Tosh recording) and *House Of Exile*. Tours of Japan and Australia were also a success, and Dube additionally played WOMAD with **Peter Gabriel**. 1993's *Victims* again broke his own record for worldwide sales, shifting in excess of a million copies on various licensee imprints.

Although Lucky Dube's style remains too dated to achieve great success in Jamaica, he remains head and shoulders above his African reggae compatriots. Having signed a licensing contract with Shanachie Records at the start of the 90s, his records enjoyed strong sales on the North American market throughout the decade. This was no less than the artist deserved, with albums such as *Trinity* (1995), *The Way It Is* (1999) and *Soul Taker* (2002) confirming his mastery of the form. In 2003 he switched to Heartbeart Records, making his debut for the label the following year with *The Other Side*.

● ALBUMS: *Kudala Ngikucenga* (Gallo 1982) ★★★, *Lengane Ngeyetha* (Gallo 1982) ★★★, *Kukuwe* (Gallo 1984) ★★★, *Abathakathi* (Gallo 1984) ★★★, *Ngikwethembe Na?* (Gallo 1985) ★★★, *Rastas Never Die* (Gallo 1985) ★★★★, *Think About The Children* (Gallo 1986) ★★★, *Help My Krap* (Gallo 1986) ★★, *Umadakeni* (Gallo 1987) ★★★, *Slave* (Gallo/Shanachie 1987) ★★★, *Together As One* (Gallo 1988) ★★, *Prisoner* (Gallo/Shanachie 1989) ★★★★, *Captured Live* (Gallo/Shanachie 1990) ★★, *House Of Exile* (Gallo/Shanachie 1991) ★★★, *Victims* (Gallo/Shanachie 1993) ★★★, *Trinity* (Gallo/Motown 1995) ★★★★, *Taxman* (Gallo/Shanachie 1997) ★★★, *Take It To Jah* (Gallo 1998) ★★★, *The Way It Is* (Gallo/Shanachie 1999) ★★★, *Soul Taker* (Gallo/Shanachie 2001) ★★★★, *The Other Side* (Heartbeat 2004) ★★★.

● COMPILATIONS: *Serious Reggae Business* (Gallo/Shanachie 1996) ★★★★, *Africa's Reggae King* (Manteca 2001) ★★★★, *The Rough Guide To Lucky Dube—Jah In Africa: The Reggae Man* (World Music Network 2001) ★★★★.

● DVD/VIDEOS: *Live In Concert* (Shanachie 1993).

Dubin, Al

b. Alexander Dubin, 10 June 1891, Zurich, Switzerland, d. 11 February 1945. Taken by his parents to the USA when still a small child, Dubin grew up in Philadelphia. He wrote poetry and song lyrics while attending school, but his aspiration to become a professional songwriter was obstructed by parental hopes that he would follow in his father's footsteps as a surgeon. His education came to an abrupt halt in 1911 when he was expelled for neglecting his studies in favour of hanging out with musicians, gamblers and drunks, and he promptly headed for New York and a career in music. A number of moderately successful songs were published in the years before World War I. During the war Dubin was gassed while serving in France, and soon afterwards he was back in New York writing songs. His work still met with only mild success until he had the idea of writing lyrics to several popular instrumentals, some of them from the classical field. The resulting songs included 'Humoresque' (music by Anton Dvorak) and 'Song Of India' (Rimsky-Korsakov). More orthodoxically, he wrote lyrics for 'The Lonesomest Gal In Town' (**Jimmy McHugh** and **Irving Mills**). By the late 20s Dubin was in Hollywood where he was teamed with **Joe Burke**, with such popular results as 'Tip Toe Through The Tulips', 'Painting The Clouds With Sunshine', 'Sally', 'Love Will Find A Way' and 'Dancing With Tears In My Eyes'.

During the 30s, now collaborating with **Harry Warren**, Dubin enjoyed his most prolific and creative period, writing for films such as *The Crooner*, **Roman Scandals**, **42nd Street**, *Gold Diggers Of 1933*, **Footlight Parade**, **Wonder Bar**, *Moulin Rouge*, *Twenty Million Sweethearts*, **Dames**, **Go Into Your Dance**, **Gold Diggers** Of 1935, *Broadway Gondolier*, *Shipmates Forever*, *Page Miss Glory*, *Sweet Music*, *Stars Over Broadway*, *Colleen*, *Hearts Divided*, *Sing Me A Love Song*, *Cain And Mabel*, *Melody For Two*, *Gold Diggers Of 1937*, *The Singing Marine*, *Mr. Dodd Takes The Air* and *Gold Diggers In Paris* (1939). Among the many successes the duo enjoyed over a five-year period were 'You're Getting To Be A Habit

With Me', 'Young And Healthy', 'We're In The Money', 'Shanghai Lil', 'Honeymoon Hotel', 'The Boulevard Of Broken Dreams', 'I'll String Along With You', 'I Only Have Eyes For You', 'Keep Young And Beautiful', Lulu's Back In Town', 'With Plenty Of Money And You', 'Confidentially', 'Lullaby Of Broadway', which won an Oscar and 'Love Is Where You Find It' (co-lyricist with **Johnny Mercer**). Dubin's hits with other collaborators included 'Nobody Knows What A Red Headed Mama Can Do' (**Sammy Fain** and Irving Mills), 'Dancing With Tears In My Eyes' and 'For You' (Joe Burke). Despite a lifestyle in which he indulged in excesses of eating, drinking, womanizing and drug-taking, Dubin wrote with enormous flair and speed. In addition to the foregoing collaborations with Warren, Dubin also wrote 'South American Way' (with McHugh), 'Indian Summer' (**Victor Herbert**), 'Along The Santa Fe Trail' (Will Grosz) and 'I Never Felt This Way Before' (**Duke Ellington**). By the end of the 30s, Dubin's lifestyle began to catch up with him and in the early 40s he suffered severe illness, the break-up of two marriages and a final collapse brought on by a drugs overdose.

● FURTHER READING: *Lullaby Of Broadway: A Biography Of Al Dubin*, Patricia Dubin McGuire.

Dubliners

The Dubliners originally comprised Barney MacKenna (b. 16 December 1939, Donnycarney, Dublin, Eire), Luke Kelly (b. 16 November 1940, Eire, d. 30 January 1984), Ciaron Bourke (b. 18 February 1936, Dublin, Eire, d. 10 May 1988) and former teacher Ronnie Drew (b. 18 September 1935, Dun Laoghaire, Co. Dublin, Eire). They formed in 1962 in the back of O'Donoghue's bar in Merion Row, Dublin, Eire, and were originally named the Ronnie Drew Group. The members were known faces in the city's post-skiffle folk haunts before pooling their assorted singing and fretboard skills in 1962. In 1964 Kelly left the group and went to England where he continued to play on the folk scene. Two other members joined shortly after Kelly had left: Bob Lynch (b. Dublin, Eire) and ex-draughtsman John Sheahan (b. 19 May 1939, Dublin, Eire). *In Concert* was the result of a live recording on 4 December 1964 in the concert hall at Cecil Sharp House in London. The band played various theatre bars, made several albums for Transatlantic and gained a strong following on the Irish folk circuit. After an introduction by Dominic Behan, they were signed by manager **Phil Solomon** and placed on his label, Major Minor. In 1965, the group took the decision to turn professional, and Kelly wanted to return. He replaced Lynch who had wished to stay semi-professional.

Throughout their collective career, each member pursued outside projects—among them Kelly's stints as an actor and MacKenna's 'The Great Comic Genius', a solo single issued after the Irishmen transferred from Transatlantic to the Major Minor label in 1966. During this time they received incessant plugging on the Radio Caroline pirate radio station. Bigoted folk purists were unable to regard them with the same respect as the similarly motivated **Clancy Brothers** and Tommy Makem after the Dubliners were seen on **Top Of The Pops** promoting 1967's censored 'Seven Drunken Nights' and, next, 'Black Velvet Band'. 'Never Wed An Old Man' was only a minor hit, but high placings for *A Drop Of The Hard Stuff* and three of its successors in the album list were a firm foundation for the outfit's standing as a thoroughly diverting international concert attraction. A brain haemorrhage forced Bourke's retirement in 1974, and Drew's return to the ranks—after being replaced between 1975 and 1979 by Jim McCann (b. 26 October 1944, Dublin, Eire)—was delayed by injuries sustained in a road accident. Kelly's ill health (a brain tumour) saw Seán Cannon drafted into the line-up in 1980, with Nigel Warren Green also filling in on tour. Kelly passed away in January 1984.

Ronnie Drew's trademark vocal, 'like coke being crushed under a door', was heard to great effect in 1987 on the band's 25th anniversary single, 'The Irish Rover', a merger with the **Pogues** that signalled another sojourn in the UK Top 10. Eammon Campbell was added to the line-up in the late 80s, and in 1995 Drew left the band for the second time and was replaced by Paddy Reilly.

● ALBUMS: *The Dubliners* (Transatlantic 1964) ★★★★, *In Concert* (Transatlantic 1965) ★★★, *Finnegan Wakes* (Transatlantic 1966) ★★★★, *A Drop Of The Hard Stuff* aka *Seven Drunken Nights* (Major Minor/Starline 1967) ★★★★, *More Of The Hard Stuff* (Major Minor/Starline 1967) ★★★, *Drinkin' And Courtin'* (Major Minor 1968) ★★★, *At It Again* aka *Seven Deadly Sings* (Major Minor/Starline 1968) ★★★, *Live At The Albert Hall* (Major Minor 1969) ★★★, *At Home With The Dubliners* (Columbia 1969) ★★★, *Revolution* (Columbia 1970) ★★★, *Hometown!* (Columbia 1972) ★★★, *Double Dubliners* (Columbia 1972) ★★★, *Plain & Simple* (Polydor 1973) ★★★, *Live* (Polydor 1974) ★★★, *Now* (Polydor 1975) ★★★, *Parcel Of Rogues* (Polydor 1976) ★★★, *15 Years On* (Polydor 1977) ★★★, *Live At Montreux* (Intercord 1977) ★★★, *Together Again* (Polydor 1979) ★★★, *21 Years On* (RTE 1983) ★★★, *Prodigal Sons* (Polydor 1983) ★★★, *Live In Carré* (Polydor 1985) ★★, *Celebration* (Stylus 1987) ★★★, *The Dubliners' Dublin* (Baycourt 1988) ★★★, *30 Years A'Greying* (Baycourt 1992) ★★★, *Further Along* (Transatlantic 1996) ★★★, *Alive Alive O* (Baycourt 1997) ★★.

● COMPILATIONS: *The Best Of The Dubliners* (Transatlantic 1967) ★★★★, *A Drop Of The Dubliners* (Major Minor 1969) ★★★★, *Drinking And Wenching* (MFP 1969) ★★★, *It's The Dubliners* (Hallmark 1969) ★★★, *The Patriot Game* (Hallmark 1971) ★★★, *Very Best Of The Dubliners* (EMI 1975) ★★★★, *The Collection* (Castle 1987) ★★★★, *Dublin Songs* (K-TEL 1988) ★★★, *20 Greatest Hits: Dubliners* (Sound 1989) ★★★★, *20 Original Greatest Hits Volume 2* (Chyme 1989) ★★★, *The Collection, Volume 2* (Castle 1990) ★★★, *The Original Dubliners* (EMI 1993) ★★★, *The Definitive Transatlantic Collection* (Transatlantic 1997) ★★★★, *The Collection* (Camden 1999) ★★★, *Spirit Of The Irish: The Ultimate Collection* (Sanctuary 2003) ★★★★.

● DVD/VIDEOS: *Dublin* (Hendring Music Video 1990).

● FURTHER READING: *The Dubliners Scrapbook*, Mary Hardy.

Dubs

The original members of this vocal group from Harlem, New York City, USA, were lead Richard Blandon, first tenor Billy Carlisle, tenor Cleveland Still, baritone James 'Jake' Miller and bass Thomas Gardner. They came together in 1957 and were an amalgamation of members of two previous groups. Blandon and Carlisle had previously been with the Five Wings who had recorded for King (notably 'Teardrops Are Falling'), and Still, Miller and Gardner had come from the Scale-Tones, who had recorded for Jay-Dee. (Shortly after their first recordings, the Dubs replaced Gardner with former Five Wing Tommy Grate.) The Dubs never had any national hits, but several of their songs still resonate today as 'golden oldies', primarily because of their popularity on the east coast doo-wop scene. The group had five consecutive regional hits: 'Don't Ask Me To Be Lonely' (1957), 'Could This Be Magic' (1957), 'Beside (1958) and 'Chapel Of Dreams' (1958). The group broke up in 1958, but experienced sporadic reunions and break-ups in subsequent years. In the 80s there were two different Dubs groups playing the east coast oldies circuit.

● ALBUMS: *The Dubs Meet The Shells* (Josie 1962) ★★★.

● COMPILATIONS: *The Best Of The Dubs* (Collectables 1991) ★★★, *The Unavailable 24 Tracks* (Juke Box Treasures 1993) ★★.

Dubstar

This UK band was formed in 1994 when Steve Hillier (songwriting/programming) met Chris Wilkie (guitar) at a club in Newcastle where he was DJing. They auditioned for singers and eventually recruited student Sarah Blackwood (b. Halifax, Yorkshire, England) after she sang over two acoustic songs for them. They began to write and record songs together, keen to produce a sound that was authentically 'modern'. As Wilkie summarized: 'We didn't really know where we were going when we started, but it certainly wasn't backwards.' Their first demo tape, which secured a contract with **Food Records**, included a cover version of **Billy Bragg**'s 'St Swithin's Day'.

Dubstar's debut album, *Disgraceful*, mixed club-orientated beats in addition to strong hooks and pop dynamics, earning several comparisons to **Saint Etienne**. Despite critical acclaim, it failed to produce a breakthrough, although it contained the Top 40 single 'Stars'. That changed with the UK Top 20 success of 'Not So Manic Now' (a track which detailed a tower block sexual assault), which prompted a reissue of 'Stars' in early 1996. Their second album proper, *Goodbye*, contained more bittersweet songs and spawned two hit singles in 'Cathedral Park' and 'No More Talk'. One further release long-playing release followed in 2000, but with Food being swallowed up by the **EMI Records** conglomerate the band opted to call it a day. Blackwood resurfaced alongside Kate Holmes (ex–**Frazier Chorus**) in **Client**.

● ALBUMS: *Disgraceful* (Food 1995) ★★★★, *Disgraceful Remixed* (Food 1996) ★★★, *Goodbye* (Food 1997) ★★★★, *Make It Better* (Food 2000) ★★★.

● COMPILATIONS: *Stars: The Best Of* (EMI 2004) ★★★★.

Duby, Heather

b. Portland, Oregon, USA. Duby moved to nearby Seattle in 1994 and quickly immersed herself in the city's still vibrant music scene. After appearing with several acts on the local club circuit, she established a working relationship with Steve Fisk of alternative rockers **Pigeonhed**. The two recorded the tracks for her debut, *Post To Wire*, which was snapped up by Seattle's leading alternative label, **Sub Pop Records**. The album, released in October 1999, was an edgy piece of modern electronica, reminiscent of British artists such as **Beth Orton** and **Everything But The Girl**. Duby's plaintive voice added an unnerving chill to downbeat tales such as

'Judith' and 'Falter', perfectly complementing Fisk's detailed production work.
● ALBUMS: *Post To Wire* (Sub Pop 1999) ★★★.

Ducanes

Vocal group the Ducanes formed in New Jersey, USA. After sessions, the quintet—Louis Biscardi (lead), Eddie Brian (baritone), Jeff Breny (first tenor), Rick Scrofan (second tenor) and Dennis Buckley—began to harmonize popular doo-wop songs of the day, taking their main influence from the **Flamingos**. **Phil Spector** began to work with the Ducanes on 'Yes, I Love You'. Spector signed them to a production contract but later overheard them practising **Louis Lymon And The Teenchords**' 'I'm So Happy'. This became their first and only single after Spector had worked his magic with it, including adding a guitar contribution from **Jimi Hendrix**. It reached number 109 in the Billboard charts during July 1961. Spector had different priorities by this time, and the Ducanes blew their only chance to return to the studio with him. Given a country song, 'Tennessee', to record by **Liberty Records**, the Ducanes responded by savagely lampooning its sentimental lyrics and adding barnyard noises. When the head of the record company learned of what they were planning, they were ejected from the studio. With Spector concentrating on launching his own label, Philles Records, the Ducanes' recording days were over. They were still just 16 years old. Only Eddie Brian recorded again, with the Connotations and **Autumns** in the mid-80s.

Ducas, George

b. 1 August 1966, Texas City, Texas, USA. George Ducas is a Nashville singer-songwriter who eschews many of the formulaic elements that such a genre description might imply. Though clearly rooted in the country music tradition, his songs are written in a wholly different register—one that maintains the evocative narratives but plays down overt sentimentality. His debut album, which contained the singles 'Kisses Don't Lie', 'Hello Cruel World', 'Teardrops' and 'Lipstick Promises', was produced with Richard Bennett, who also helmed the 1997 follow-up. To promote it, Ducas toured major baseball stadiums, singing the national anthem at half-time. He told **Billboard** magazine in 1996 that 'It's a great time to be in country music, because the parameters of it are broader than they have ever been.' Clearly, Ducas has benefited from this situation, and he was widely tipped both inside and outside of the Nashville singer-songwriter scene although he was dropped by **Liberty Records** in 1998.
● ALBUMS: *George Ducas* (Liberty 1994) ★★★, *Where I Stand* (Liberty 1997) ★★★.

DuChaine, Kent

b. 20 April 1951, Minneapolis, Minnesota, USA. Starting on the ukulele at the age of six, it was always DuChaine's intention to be a musician. The British Invasion sparked his interest in the guitar and **Eric Clapton**'s versions of **Robert Johnson** songs drew him to the blues. As a teenager, he played in a number of groups, even playing bass in a psychedelic band, while he studied slide technique at home. In 1972 he played bass in Aces, Straights and Shuffles with **Kim Wilson** and the pair also worked as a duo. Wilson moved to Texas in 1974 and DuChaine followed soon after, with a band called Crossroads. In 1989, while living and playing in Alabama, he met **Johnny Shines** and the pair formed a fruitful

working relationship. DuChaine played on several tracks on *Back To The Country*, one of Shines' last sessions. The following year he set up his own label, which bears all the hallmarks of a cottage industry. *Take A Little Ride With Me* gives credit to his battered National steel guitar, Leadbessie, and features a song extolling his 1956 Cadillac, Marilyn, in which he lived and toured during the 80s.
● ALBUMS: with Johnny Shines, Snooky Pryor *Back To The Country* (Blind Pig 1991) ★★★, *Just Me And My Guitar* (Cadillac 1992) ★★★, *Lookin' Back* (Cadillac 1994) ★★★, *Take A Little Ride With Me* (Cadillac 1995) ★★★, *She's Irresistible* (Cadillac 1996) ★★★, *Playing The Blues Live At Les Louflats* (Cadillac 1998) ★★★★.

Duchin, Eddy

b. 1 April 1909, Cambridge, Massachusetts, USA, d. 9 February 1951, New York City, New York, USA. Immortalized by Tyrone Power, who portrayed the pianist-band leader in the movie-biography ***The Eddy Duchin Story***, with **Carmen Cavallaro** providing the soundtrack keyboard work. Though trained as a pharmacist, Duchin opted to become a professional musician during the late 20s and, after auditioning against stiff opposition for the piano chair in **Leo Reisman**'s Orchestra, eventually gained the job. Featured as part of Reisman's band at New York's Central Park Casino during the next three years, he became extremely popular owing to his suave appearance and sophisticated, flashy piano style, and in 1931 he formed his own band, taking over the residency at the Casino. With violinist **Milt Shaw** providing many of the outfit's supper-club type arrangements during the 30s, Duchin gained dates at many swanky venues, won various radio shows, appeared in films such as *Coronado* (1935) and *The Hit Parade* (1937) and won a recording contract, first with **Victor Records**, then later with **Brunswick Records** and **Columbia Records**. Following the Japanese bombing of Pearl Harbor, Duchin entered the navy, serving as a lieutenant. In 1945 he returned to civilian life and began leading one of the musical aggregations to bear his name, though his popularity was less than it had been prior to the war years. His health gradually declined and in February 1951 he died of leukaemia.

Although considered to be purely a society entertainer right to the end, the Duchin band did swing with reasonable heat on some occasions and once made a most unsociety-like record of 'Old Man Mose', which was banned by some authorities owing to an unfortunate pronunciation of the word 'bucket' which occurred frequently throughout the song's lyric. After Eddy's death, his son, **Peter Duchin**, another ultra-smooth pianist, continued to uphold the family tradition by becoming a band leader with upper-class connections.
● COMPILATIONS: *Dream Along* (Columbia 1960) ★★★, *I'll See You In My Dreams* (Columbia 1966) ★★★, *Dancing With Duchin* (Collectables 2002) ★★★.
● FILMS: *Mr. Broadway* (1933), *Eddie Duchin & Orchestra* (1933), *Coronado* (1935), *Hit Parade Of 1937* aka *I'll Pick A Star* (1937).

Duchin, Peter

b. 28 July 1937, New York City, New York, USA. The son of noted band leader **Eddy Duchin**, Peter Duchin formed his first dance band in New York City, New York, USA, in 1962. Rather than attempt to update the classic big band sound, Duchin stayed close to the music's traditions, beginning with a residency at the St. Regis Hotel in New York. He quickly became a celebrated accompaniment to high society parties and gatherings, establishing a position within the capital's upper social strata, which mirrored the achievements of his father. After three years at the St. Regis further engagements followed at the Fontainebleu Hotel in Miami and the Cocoanut Grove in Los Angeles. Such was his popularity that Duchin was then able to form several orchestras bearing his name, each of which was available for bookings throughout the country. These combos became regulars at White House functions and balls, including the inauguration of President Johnson in January 1965. A recording contract with **Decca Records** fostered several record releases, before a contract with the Universal Pictures Studio allowed him to take his band into the world of film. However, this deal collapsed before many of the contracted films were completed. Duchin concentrated instead on live performance, and continues to do so at financially lucrative venues throughout America.

Ducks Deluxe

Denizens of London's 70s' 'pub rock' circuit, Ducks Deluxe was formed in 1972 by **Sean Tyla** (b. 3 August 1947, Barlow, Yorkshire, England; guitar/vocals) and ex–**Help Yourself** member Ken Whaley (bass). The line-up was completed by former **Brinsley Schwarz** roadie, Martin Belmont (b. 21 December 1948, Grove Park, London, England; guitar) and Tim Roper (b. 9 April 1953, Hampstead, London, England; drums) before Whaley was replaced by Nick Garvey (b. 26 April 1951, Stoke-on-Trent, Staffordshire, England). The reconstituted quartet completed *Ducks Deluxe*, an exciting, emphatic set drawn from rock's traditional sources. Andy McMaster (b. 27 July 1947, Glasgow, Scotland; keyboards) expanded the band for *Taxi To The Terminal Zone*, but dissent over Tyla's autocratic rule resulted in a split. Garvey and McMasters left in October 1974 (they were later reunited in the **Motors**), while Mick Groom (bass) joined the now-ailing Ducks. Although popular in Europe, the band was all but ignored at home, and a dispirited Roper quit the following year. Brinsley Schwarz (guitar) and Billy Rankin (drums), both from the defunct Brinsley Schwarz, augmented Ducks Deluxe on a tour of France, but the band broke up on 1 July 1975 following a final appearance at London's 100 Club. Martin Belmont later resurfaced in **Graham Parker And The Rumour**, while Tyla formed the Tyla Gang with Ken Whaley.

● ALBUMS: *Ducks Deluxe* (RCA 1974) ★★★, *Taxi To The Terminal Zone* (RCA 1975) ★★★.

● COMPILATIONS: *Don't Mind Rockin' Tonite* (RCA 1978) ★★★, *Last Night Of A Pub Rock Band* (Blue Moon 1982) ★★.

Dudek, Gerd

b. Gerhard Rochus Dudek, 28 September 1938, Gross Döbern, Germany. Multi-instrumentalist Dudek emerged as a key jazz figure in the 60s with **Manfred Schoof** and **Alexander Von Schlippenbach**. He played with them over the years, as well as others, including **Joachim Kuhn** and **Albert Mangelsdorff**. In Dudek, Europe possesses probably its most convincing exponent of mid-to-late-period **John Coltrane**. Dudek has been a key partner in Schlippenbach's projects—in **Globe Unity Orchestra**, on their **Jelly Roll Morton** tribute and as one of the outstanding soloists on the *Berlin Contemporary Jazz Orchestra* session. The co-operative groups the Quartet,

the European Jazz Quartet and the European Jazz Ensemble have all benefited from his hard-driving but lyrical tenor, soprano, clarinet and flute.

● ALBUMS: with Buschi Niebergall, Edward Vesala *Open* (FMP 1977) ★★★, with Ali Haurand, Rob Van Den Broeck *After All* (Konnex 1991) ★★★, with Haurand, Van Den Broeck *Pulque* (Konnex 1993) ★★★, with Den Broeck, Haurand, Tony Levin *Crossing Level* (Konnex 1997) ★★★, *'Smatter* 1998 recording (PSI 2001) ★★★.

Dudes

Formed in 1965 in Montreal, Canada, the Dudes were a short-lived 'supergroup' led by expatriate San Franciscan, Bob Segarini (vocals/guitar). Segarini had been a member of several promising Californian groups, including **Family Tree**, **Roxy** and the **Wackers**. The Wackers' brand of exciting power pop was especially popular in Canada and the group moved there in 1973. They split up in 1974 when **Elektra Records** rejected their fourth album. Former Wackers Bill 'Kootch' Trochim (bass) and Wayne Cullen (drums) joined Segarini in the Dudes, which was completed by Brian Greenaway (ex-Mashmakan), David Henman and Richie Henman (both ex–**April Wine**). Sadly, *We're No Angels* was a marked disappointment. It offered the melodic brand of rock Segarini was renowned for, but a glossy production robbed the songs of dynamics and an air of anonymity bedevilled its content. The Dudes split up within months of its release, after which Segarini embarked on a solo career.

● ALBUMS: *We're No Angels* (Columbia 1975) ★★.

Dudgeon, Gus

b. 30 September 1942, Woking, Surrey, England, d. 22 July 2002, Berkshire, England. Dudgeon produced numerous records by UK artists, most notably **David Bowie**'s 'Space Oddity' and all of **Elton John**'s early hits. He began as a studio engineer in London, working on **Joe Brown**'s 1962 hit 'A Picture Of You' and moved to the **Decca Records** studios several years later. As assistant to **Mike Vernon**, he engineered numerous R&B recordings and gained a co-producer credit in 1967 on the first album by **Ten Years After**. Dudgeon then became a freelance producer, working with the **Strawbs** and the **Bonzo Dog Doo-Dah Band** before gaining recognition for his restrained yet imaginative special effects on Bowie's tale of an astronaut. He was next brought in to work with Elton John on the singer-songwriter's second album. His partnership with John lasted over 12 albums until 1976, when disagreements with John's manager John Reid led to Dudgeon's resignation as a director of Rocket Records. Now well-established as one of the country's top-flight producers, Dudgeon worked with a wide range of artists during the following decades including **Gilbert O'Sullivan**, **Ralph McTell**, **Joan Armatrading**, **Elkie Brooks**, **Chris Rea**, **Steeleye Span**, **Lindisfarne** and **XTC**. In 1985 Dudgeon was reunited with Elton John, producing his *Ice On Fire* and *Leather Jackets* albums. He also served as producer for the John/ **Bernie Taupin** tribute project *Two Rooms*. Dudgeon and his wife were tragically killed in July 2002 when their car veered off a motorway in Berkshire, England.

Dudley, Anne

b. England. One of five children in a London household appreciative of classical music (her parents turned the television off rather than see their children exposed to pop music), Dudley nevertheless saw the connection between the two forms when the **Beatles'** and **Smokey Robinson's** expanded orchestrations played on her transistor radio. By this time she was well on her way to a classical music career, but after leaving college in 1981 she started work as Trevor Horn's musical arranger and keyboard player. This involved working on some of 80s pop's most successful and innovative recordings, including music by **Frankie Goes To Hollywood, Wham!** and **ABC**. She then became a key member of the adventurous **Art Of Noise**, who stealthily offered the public *avant garde* compositions packaged as **dance music**. The influence of tracks such as 'Beat Box' and, in particular, 'Moments In Love' went on to reverberate around the music scene in the following decade.

After Art Of Noise disbanded at the end of the 80s, Dudley went on to enjoy a successful career in scoring soundtracks for film and television, including *Jeeves And Wooster, Kavanagh QC, Artists In Crime, The Rory Bremner Show* (theme), *Buster, The Miracle, The Pope Must Die, The Crying Game, The Grotesque* and *The Full Monty*, for which she won an Academy Award for Best Original Musical Or Comedy Score in 1998. Her non-soundtrack work includes arranging for **Pulp** and the **Pet Shop Boys** and an album of Egyptian-derived recordings made jointly with **Killing Joke's** Jaz Coleman. Dudley returned to her roots in 1995 for an album of mainly classical compositions. Titled *Ancient And Modern*, this was scored for a full orchestra and 18 singers, with the material drawn largely from historical sources. 'I'm not a pop musician who is attempting something in a style with which they're not familiar. I've always come from a classical orientation. Even the pop music I do has its classical side; the way I score it, voice it, colour it.' Dudley reunited with Horn and Paul Morley for the 1999 Art Of Noise album *The Seduction Of Claude Debussy*. In 2003 she was appointed Composer In Association by BBC Television and composed the score to the movie *Bright Young Things*. She was the producer of Alison Moyet's highly successful return *The Voice* in 2004.

● ALBUMS: with Jaz Coleman *Songs From The Victorious City* (China/TVT 1991) ★★★★, *Ancient And Modern* (Echo 1995) ★★★, *A Different Light* (Angel 2002) ★★★★, with the BBC Concert Orchestra *Seriously Chilled: New Arrangements Of Classic Chill-Out Anthems* (EMI 2003) ★★★.

Dudley, Dave

b. Darwin David Pedruska, 3 May 1928, Spencer, Wisconsin, USA, d. 22 December 2003, Danbury, Wisconsin, USA. In 1950, after an arm injury had ruined a baseball career, Dudley turned to performing country music. Following successful broadcasts in Idaho, he formed the Dave Dudley Trio in 1953. In 1960, Dudley was struck by a car while packing equipment and spent several months in hospital. He had his first US country successes, 'Maybe I Do' and 'Under The Cover Of Night', and, also in 1961, he reluctantly recorded the up-tempo 'Six Days On The Road' to please a friend. In 1963 he released it on his own Golden Wing label and it reached number 32 in the US pop charts. The song spawned a new genre of songs about truckers, usually depicting them as hard-living, hard-loving macho men. Dudley declares, 'I like my woman everywhere I go', in 'Truck Drivin' Son-Of-A-Gun'. Dudley's numerous trucking songs included 'Two Six Packs Away', 'There Ain't No Easy Run', 'One More Mile', 'The Original Travelling Man',

'Trucker's Prayer' and 'Truck Driver's Waltz', many of them being written by, and sometimes with, **Tom T. Hall**. In 1970, Dudley had a number 1 country hit with 'The Pool Shark' and recorded a duet with Hall, 'Day Drinkin''. He recorded for **Sun Records** in 1980 and had some success with 'Rolaids, Doan's Pills And Preparation H'. His comedy single, 'Where's That Truck?', with the truckers' favourite disc jockey, Charlie Douglas, did not revive his career. He died of a heart attack in December 2003.

● ALBUMS: *Six Days On The Road* (Golden Ring 1963) ★★★★, *Songs About The Working Man* (Mercury 1964) ★★★★, *Traveling With Dave Dudley* (Mercury 1964) ★★★, *Talk Of The Town* (Mercury 1964) ★★★, *Rural Route No. 1* (Mercury 1965) ★★★, *Truck Drivin' Son-Of-A-Gun* (Mercury 1965) ★★★, *Free And Easy* (Mercury 1966) ★★★, *There's A Star Spangled Banner Waving Somewhere* (Mercury 1966) ★★★, *Lonelyville* (Mercury 1966) ★★★, *My Kind Of Love* (Mercury 1967) ★★★, *Dave Dudley Country* (Mercury 1967) ★★★, *Oh Lonesome Me/Seven Lonely Days* (Mercury 1968) ★★★, *Thanks For All The Miles* (Mercury 1968) ★★★, *One More Mile* (Mercury 1969) ★★★, *George And The North Woods* (Mercury 1969) ★★★, *It's My Lazy Day* (Mercury 1969) ★★★, *The Pool Shark* (Mercury 1970) ★★★, *Will The Real Dave Dudley Please Sing?* (Mercury 1971) ★★★, *Listen, Betty, I'm Singing Your Song* (Mercury 1971) ★★, *The Original Travelling Man* (Mercury 1972) ★★★, *Keep On Truckin'* (Mercury 1973) ★★, *Uncommonly Good Country* (United Artists 1975) ★★★, *1776* (United Artists 1976) ★★, *Interstate Gold* (Sun 1980) ★★, with Charlie Douglas *Diesel Duets* (Sun 1980) ★★, *King Of The Road* (Sun 1981) ★★, *More Dudley* (Koch 1987) ★★★, *The Silver Album* (Koch 1988) ★★★, *Truck Drivin' Songs* (Intersound 1992) ★★, *Keepin' It Country* (Madroy 1998) ★★★, *Christmas Truck Stop* (Music Mill 2000) ★★★, *American Trucker* (Music Mill 2001) ★★.

● COMPILATIONS: *20 Great Truck Hits* (EMI Sweden 1983) ★★★, *Collection: Dave Dudley* (EMI 1983) ★★★, *Country Best* (Bulldog 1988) ★★★, *Trucker Classics* (Sun 1996) ★★★, *Dave Dudley Hits* (Music Mill 1999) ★★★, *Millennium Collection: The Best Of Dave Dudley* (Universal 2001) ★★★, *Truck Drivin' Son Of A Gun: The Mercury Hill Singles 1963–1973* (Westside 2004) ★★★.

Dudziak, Urszula

b. 22 October 1943, Straconka, Poland. Although Dudziak studied piano formally for some years, she began to sing in the late 50s after hearing records by **Ella Fitzgerald**. Within a few years she was one of the most popular jazz artists in her native country. She met and later married **Michal Urbaniak**, recording with him during the 60s. In the late 60s they began to travel overseas and in the 70s settled in New York. Language barriers hold no problems for her, as she customarily eschews words in favour of a wordless vocalizing that is far more adventurous than scat. Already gifted with a remarkable five-octave range, Dudziak employs electronic devices to extend still further the possibilities of her voice. She has frequently worked with leading contemporary musicians including **Archie Shepp** and **Lester Bowie** and was a member of the Vocal Summit group, with **Jay Clayton, Jeanne Lee, Bobby McFerrin, Norma Winstone**, Michelle Hendricks and Lauren Newton. Although her remarkable talent is worthy of greater exposure, Dudziak's chosen style has meant that she has remained relatively unknown except to the *cognoscenti*.

● ALBUMS: *Newborn Light* (Columbia 1972) ★★★★, *Urszula* (Arista 1975) ★★★, with Michal Urbaniak *Tribute To Komeda* (MPS 1976) ★★★, *Midnight Rain* (Arista 1977) ★★★, *Future Talk* (Inner City 1979) ★★★, *Magic Lady* (In And Out 1980) ★★★, with Fusion, Urbaniak *Heritage* 1977 recording (MPS/Pausa 1980) ★★★, with Vocal Summit *Sorrow Is Not Forever . . . But Love Is* (Keytone 1983) ★★★, *Warsaw Jazz Festival 1991* (Jazzmen 1993) ★★★, *Malowany Ptak* (Polonia 1998) ★★★.

Dufay, Rick

b. USA. Guitarist and songwriter Dufay initially earned his reputation playing on the New York, USA, club circuit, collaborating with various bar bands as well as playing his own solo slots. Word-of-mouth praise of these performances eventually led to a contract with **Polydor Records** in 1980. *Tender Loving Abuse* was recorded live in the studio under the production tutelage of Jack Douglas. Well received in the press (particularly in musicians' magazines), it served to embellish a growing reputation for Dufay's guitar virtuosity. It led to him being recruited by **Aerosmith** later that year. He contributed to that band's 1982 set, *Rock In A Hard Place*, but he left the group in 1984 following Brad Whitford's return, and he has been less in the public eye since.

● ALBUMS: *Tender Loving Abuse* (Polydor 1980) ★★★.

Duff, Arlie

b. Arleigh Elton Duff, 28 March 1924, Jack's Branch, near Warren, Texas, USA, d. 4 July 1996. Duff left the Stephan F. Austin College in Nacogdoches in 1951 with BS and MA degrees and seemingly with no thoughts of any form of career in country music. He thought he would be a teacher and/or a sport's coach but that all changed as a result of a song he wrote. (Although, he regularly used a guitar emblazoned with The Singin' Schoolteacher Arlie Duff.) One day, while staying with his grandmother, he listened to her and an old friend talking and was amused by the visitor's regular use of the phrase 'y'all come'. He reckoned there must be a song there and as he later said 'I accidentally wrote it, accidentally recorded it and it turned out to be a standard'. In 1953 he had become a disc jockey and also gained the chance to record for Starday Records. In December 1953, his own recording of 'Y'all Come' (recorded as 'You All Come') entered the **Billboard** country charts and peaked at number 7 during a 10-week stay. It won him a BMI award and gave Starday their first big record. Sadly for Duff, he never repeated the success and, even though he later recorded for **Decca Records**, he joined the ranks of one-hit-wonders. He did however pursue a successful career in music. He became a cast member of ABC-TV's **Ozark Jubilee** and made appearances on **The Louisiana Hayride** and the **Grand Ole Opry** before returning to work for many years as a disc jockey appearing on programmes such as *The Saturday Nite Shindig* on WFAA Dallas before moving to KOGT Range, Texas. Other successful songs written by Duff include 'She's Just A Housewife', 'I'll Always Wonder' and 'It's The Little Things'.

● FURTHER READING: *Y'all Come, Country Music: Jack's Branch To Nashville*, Arleigh Duff.

Duff, Hilary

b. Hilary Ann Duff, 28 September 1987, Houston, Texas, USA. The multi-talented Duff began her professional entertainment career at the tender age of six, when she landed a spot in *The Nutcracker* as part of the touring company, Columbus Ballet Met. An appearance in a US television commercial soon followed, which led to the youngster playing bit parts in several series during the later part of the 90s. Duff's hard work paid off when she obtained the lead role in the hit Disney Channel show *Lizzie McGuire*, resulting in more television appearances as well as movie roles (including, rather predictably, *The Lizzie McGuire Movie*). Shortly after the show became established, a *Lizzie McGuire Original Television Soundtrack* was assembled in summer 2002, which included a song sung by Duff, 'I Can't Wait'. A singing career soon followed, as she issued her very first solo album later the same year, the seasonal *Santa Claus Lane*. Duff's voice also graced several tracks on *The Lizzie McGuire Movie Motion Picture Soundtrack*, which became a US Top 10 hit. Already garnering comparisons to teen pop hit makers such as **Britney Spears** and **Mandy Moore**, Duff was hard at work the next year working on her second studio album. With a virtual 'who's who' list of professional teen pop songwriters and producers employed, including Chico Bennett (**Madonna**, **Usher**, **Destiny's Child**), Matthew Gerrard (**Nick Carter**), John Shanks (**Michelle Branch**) and Kara DioGuardi (**Celine Dion**, **Enrique Iglesias**), *Metamorphosis* was issued during late summer 2003. The album was an immediate hit, quickly going gold and debuting at number 2 on the **Billboard** 200 before moving into the top slot the following week.

Duff maintained her high media profile in 2004 with starring roles in the popular movies *A Cinderella Story* and *Raise Your Voice*. She was also elected as the international spokesperson of the charity organization Kids With A Cause. Her self-titled third album, which saw the singer pursuing a more rock-orientated direction, debuted at number 2 on the *Billboard* 200 in October.

● ALBUMS: *Santa Claus Lane* (Disney 2002) ★★, *Metamorphosis* (Buena Vista 2003) ★★★, *Hilary Duff* (Buena Vista/Hollywood 2004) ★★★.

● COMPILATIONS: *Most Wanted* (Hollywood 2005) ★★.

● DVD/VIDEOS: *The Concert: The Girl Can Rock* (Hollywood Music Video 2004), *Learning To Fly* (Hollywood Music Video 2004).

● FILMS: *Human Nature* (2001), *Agent Cody Banks* (2003), *The Lizzie McGuire Movie* (2003), *Cheaper By The Dozen* (2003), *A Cinderella Story* (2004), *Raise Your Voice* (2004), *The Perfect Man* (2005).

Duff, Jeff

USA born Duff (aka Duffo) possesses an excellent tenor voice that seems more suited to opera, but Duff has succeeded in recording in the rock medium. As lead singer of the **Chicago/ Blood, Sweat And Tears**–influenced big band Kush (1971–77), Duff secured plenty of attention with his antics and bizarre choice of costume. The band, limited by its size, could only work the large venues and cabarets, and despite the huge effort to maintain the band, it managed to record two albums and have two Top 40 singles. Upon its demise, Duff formed his own group and toured with a lively and varied show, which failed to relate to confused, conservative audiences. Duff moved to the UK in 1978 where he recorded and performed as Duffo, releasing several albums, touring Europe and having sporadic chart success in Holland and Italy. He also recorded under the names Ivor Biggin and Jupiter Jones. It was somewhat surprising to see him return to Australia to indifferent audiences in 1988, when he performed as a jazz singer with his Jeff Duff Orchestra, an experimental outfit. His signature song remains **Lou Reed**'s 'Walk On The Wild Side', which he has recorded at least three times. The Jeff Duff Orchestra album featured some reworking of older material, 'Pilot' and the excellent 'Killing This Affair'.

● ALBUMS: *Duffo* (1979) ★★★, *Tower Of Madness* (1979) ★★, *The Disappearing Boy* (1980) ★★★, *Bob The Birdman* (1981) ★★, *Lexicon* (1982) ★★.

Duff, Mary

b. Lobinstown, Co. Meath, Eire. Duff first sang locally at the age of 12 with her accordion-playing father. On leaving school, she worked as a school secretary and sang with a semi-professional group in the evenings around the local area and was influenced in her early days by **Patsy Cline**. Duff also began to make solo appearances at various talent contests and was seen and heard at one such event by **Daniel O'Donnell**'s manager, Sean Reilly, who signed her to his management. She toured with O'Donnell, quickly establishing a reputation as a fine singer in her own right, and soon acquired a recording contract with Ritz Records. In 1989, she won the European Gold Star Award (the country music equivalent of the Eurovision Song Contest) in Holland. Duff won the Most Popular British Female Vocalist award in 1990–91. She has appeared at various European venues, including Switzerland, and at several international shows such as the Wembley International Country Music Festival. She is also a very popular touring act throughout the British and Irish country scene and now has several popular videos. Duff has a vibrant, happy-go-lucky personality, which suggests that she lives up to her statement that 'You only live once so always do what you're happiest doing'. Her albums have varied from straight country (*Just Lovin' You*) to MOR (*Shades Of Blue*).

● ALBUMS: *Love Someone Like Me* (Ritz 1988) ★★★, *Winning Ways* (Ritz 1990) ★★★, *Silver And Gold* (Ritz 1992) ★★★, *Just Lovin' You* (Ritz 1995) ★★★, with Daniel O'Donnell *Timeless* (Ritz 1996) ★★★, *Shades Of Blue* (Ritz 1997) ★★, *Just A Country Girl: 14 Classic Country Songs* (Rosette 2004) ★★★.

● COMPILATIONS: *The Very Best Of Mary Duff* (Ritz 1999) ★★★, *The Very Best Of Mary Duff Volume II* (Rosette 2003) ★★★.

● DVD/VIDEOS: *Live In Concert* (Ritz 1990), *Give A Little Love* (Ritz 1998), *In Concert* (Rosette 2003).

Duffus, Shenley

b. 10 February 1938, Roland Field, Jamaica, West Indies. Duffus embarked on his musical career in 1950 through the legendary Vere Johns talent show. He toured the island with the showcase, although it was not until 1958 that Duffus ventured into a recording studio. As the Jamaican recording industry was still in its embryonic stage he recorded in the style of R&B singers such as **'Big' Joe Turner** and the **Drifters**' **Ben E. King**. His debut release, 'Million Dollar Baby', introduced his unique style and became a minor hit in the USA. He later recorded 'What A Disaster' and the cautionary

'Fret Man Fret' at **Studio One** with **Coxsone Dodd**. Duffus followed his initial hits with 'Lolita', which was written by producer **Lee Perry** and signalled the start of a long partnership. In the early 70s Duffus was reunited with Perry who recorded 'Bet You Didn't Know' (which utilized the rhythm from **Junior Byles**' 'Beat Down Babylon') under the guise of Shenley Duffus And The Soul Avengers. In 1972, Duffus recorded in his own name a cover version of the soul ballad 'To Be A Lover', which later surfaced on the retrospective Perry compilation *Give Me Power*. Inspired by his success covering soul classics during this period he recorded the sublime 'At The End' and 'Goodnight, My Love', both of which sadly faltered. An assortment of releases appeared in the UK credited to Duffus, notably 'Sincerely' and 'Peace Peace' recorded alongside the **Upsetters**. He also appeared on the b-side of **Dillinger**'s 'Headquarters' with a risqué variation of a classic Jamaican nursery rhyme that he re-titled 'Black Girl In My Bed'. The song that inspired him was originally sung in Jamaican playgrounds before becoming an international hit in 1978 when **Boney M** recorded and released it as 'Brown Girl In The Ring'. Duffus became disillusioned with the Jamaican recording industry and decided to concentrate on the live circuit where he was able to achieve financial stability. Twenty-five years after his initial release of 'Bet You Didn't Know' the song became a belated a hit in Egypt and assured the singer a place in the history of Jamaican music.

Duffy, Stephen

b. 30 May 1960, Birmingham, West Midlands, England. Having appeared in an early line-up of **Duran Duran**, Stephen Duffy first came to prominence in the UK under the moniker of Stephen 'Tin Tin' Duffy, with the release of his second single, 'Kiss Me', in early 1985. The track, which reached UK number 4, confirmed Duffy's power as a weaver of engaging pop melodies. His debut album, *The Ups And Downs*, divided the critics, but his formula pop was most suitable for daytime radio play. 'Icing On The Cake' restored Duffy to the UK Top 20, but his subsequent solo work proved less enticing. His second album *Because We Love You* was released under the Stephen Duffy moniker after he was forced to drop the 'Tin Tin' part of his name following legal action by lawyers representing the Belgian author Hergé.

Duffy subsequently turned his back on a solo career to form folk rock outfit the **Lilac Time** with fellow collaborators including his brother Nick (guitar), Michael Weston (piano), Bob Lamb and Michael Giri (both percussion). The Lilac Time released three excellent albums which unfortunately failed to reap the commercial rewards they deserved. Following the Lilac Time's initial demise in the early 90s, Duffy recorded an album (*Music In Colors*) with classical violinist **Nigel Kennedy** before relaunching himself as Duffy. Having been around for more than a decade, his self-depreciating quote 'it's an accident of birth, that had me a born loser' seemed to cover him against any lack of future success. His self-titled debut as Duffy, however, was a sparkling collection of guitar pop with some occasionally glorious harmonies. He had matured into a witty, perceptive songwriter, and even though there was more than a glance over his shoulder to the **Kinks**, **Beatles** and quality 60s pop, the songs (many dealing with the death of his father) stood up well. Produced by **Mitch Easter** and featuring wistful harmony vocals from **Velvet Crush**, for once the press release description of a bejewelled guitar album was accurate, but as with the majority of his work *Duffy* was ignored by the record buying public.

The 1998 follow-up *I Love My Friends*, featuring backing from **Aimee Mann** and **Blur**'s Alex James, confirmed Duffy's mastery of sweet pop music. It was, unsurprisingly, another commercial failure. The following year Duffy revived the Lilac Time as a recording unit. In 2003 Duffy's fortunes were revived when he joined **Robbie Williams**, the UK's most successful solo artist of the new millennium, as co-song-writer and touring guitarist.

● ALBUMS: as Stephen Tin Tin Duffy *The Ups And Downs* (10 1985) ★★★, *Because We Love You* (10 1986) ★★, *Music In Colors* (Parlophone 1993) ★★★, as Duffy *Duffy* (Indolent 1995) ★★★★, as Duffy *I Love My Friends* (Cooking Vinyl 1998) ★★★★.

● COMPILATIONS: *They Called Him TinTin* (Virgin 1998) ★★★.

Duffy's Nucleus

Led by **Duffy Power**, the remainder of this short-lived mid-60s group comprised Terry Cox (drums), **John McLaughlin** (guitar) and **Danny Thompson** (double bass). Their sole domestic release was a powerful, R&B-inflected version of **Elvis Presley**'s 'Hound Dog' for **Decca Records** in 1967. They also released a French-only EP in the same year (which incorporated the single, its b-side 'Mary Open The Door' and a McLaughlin/Power composition 'It's Funny'). However, with little discernible interest from press or public, Duffy's Nucleus was then put on hold while Power concentrated on a solo career under his own name.

Dufus

Although cult artists such as **Frank Zappa**, **Captain Beefheart**, and **Ween** never achieved mass commercial success, each have certainly left their mark on countless subsequent bands, including loveable New York City, USA, folk rock weirdos, Dufus. Originally formed during 1995, the multi-membered group (featuring guitars, sampler, bass, drums, plus male and female vocalists) is led by eccentric leader/multi-instrumentalist Seth Quankmeyer Faergoalzia (aka Dufu-seth). Many different members have passed through the ranks of Dufus since their inception, including alt-folk artist Jeffrey Lewis, Kimya Dawson from the **Moldy Peaches** and one-hit wonder **Imani Coppola**. Faergoalzia did not comple-tely begin focusing on Dufus until 1998, after he dropped out of college and relocated to Brooklyn, New York City. Becoming a self-described 'hermit' during this time, Faergoalzia recorded an obscure album with fellow NYC folk experimentalist Lach titled *Pip*. Several self-released, now out-of-print, recordings followed (*Our First Born*, *Eee*lai*font*, *This Revolution* and *Neuborns*) before the band signed with indie label ROIR and issued *1:3:1* in 2003. Besides performing and recording with Dufus, Faergoalzia is involved in several other projects including Dorkestra (Dufus with a variety of orchestral instruments, Doofamily comprised of previous bandmates passing through at the time) and a musical theatre 'experiment' called Fun Wearing Underwear. Despite their unpredictability, Dufus has built a large fanbase that has stretched far beyond their New York City home base.

● ALBUMS: *1:3:1* (ROIR 2003) ★★★.

Dugites

The Dugites emerged from Perth, Australia, in 1978, at the tail-end of punk and in the middle of a period heralding the arrival of several other Australian bands that featured female lead singers, such as the **Eurogliders**, **Divinyls** and **Do Ré Mi**. While their early material was naïve pop, their later work glistened with good production values and fine playing and deserved more recognition. Their first single, the plaintive 'In My Car' charted, but by the time the band gelled and matured for their last excellent album their audience had lost interest.

● ALBUMS: *The Dugites* (1980) ★★, *West Of The World* (1981) ★★★, *Cut The Talking* (1984) ★★★.

Duke Bootee

b. Edward Fletcher. Bootee was formerly a New Jersey schoolteacher in Newark until the east coast rap bug hit. As part of the **Sugarhill Records** house band/retinue, he wrote the chorus and several sections of 'The Message'. He also contributed to 'Message II', 'New York, New York' and sundry other label hits. His debut solo album comprised a rap side and a song side, with the former seeing further assistance from old Sugarhill friends. Though the song side was disappointing, he proved himself a talented rapper and maintained his reputation as an accomplished lyricist on the rest of the album.

● ALBUMS: *Bust Me Out* (Mercury 1984) ★★★.

Duke Jupiter

Formed in Rochester, New York, USA, in the late 70s, hard rock band Duke Jupiter experienced two distinct phases in their career. The first was as a generic AOR group who recorded two unexceptional albums for **Mercury Records** in 1979 and 1981. In 1982 the original line-up of Marshall James Styler (vocals/keyboards), Greg Walker (vocals/guitar), George Barajas (bass) and David Corcoran (drums) moved to Coast To Coast Records and revised their style to a much more strident, **Aerosmith**-derived hard rock sound. The songwriting had also improved, and each of the group's annual studio albums, from *Duke Jupiter 1* onwards, combined accessibility with supple musical power in an attractive manner. The most successful was *White Knuckle Ride*, which reached number 122 in the US **Billboard** charts in June 1984.

● ALBUMS: *Taste The Night* (Mercury 1979) ★★, *Band In Blue* (Mercury 1981) ★★, *Duke Jupiter 1* (Coast To Coast 1982) ★★★, *You Make It Easy* (Coast To Coast 1983) ★★★, *White Knuckle Ride* (Morocco 1984) ★★★, *The Line Of Your Fire* (Morocco 1985) ★★★.

Duke Of Paducah

b. Benjamin Francis Ford, 12 May 1901, DeSoto, Missouri, USA, d. 20 June 1986, Nashville, Tennessee, USA. Ford, in his alter-ego role as the Duke Of Paducah, became something of an American institution with his homespun humour and banjo playing. He was raised in Little Rock, Arkansas, by his grandmother but ran away to join the navy at the age of 17. He served for four years, during which time he learned to play the banjo and began to develop his comedy routines. In 1924, after playing banjo for a time in dancehalls with a dixieland band, he appeared on KTHS, Hot Springs, and fronted Benny Ford And His Arkansas Travellers. He later worked the vaudeville circuit and tent, medicine and burlesque shows, before joining **Otto Gray**'s Oklahoma Cowboys. After leaving Gray, he joined **Gene Autry** in Chicago and acted as MC of Autry's show for nine years. During this time, he became a member of the original cast of the WLS *National Barn Dance* and it was here that he acquired his stage name. He later had his own network show, *Plantation Party*, on WLW Cincinnati. In 1937 he worked with **John Lair** and **Red Foley** to establish the *Renfro Valley Barn Dance*. In the early 40s, Ford, as the Duke Of Paducah, joined the *Grand Ole Opry*, where he soon became a favourite on the *Prince Albert Show* segment. Following a disagreement with the sponsors in 1948, he was replaced on that show by **Rod Brasfield**, but he remained an *Opry* regular on other segments until 1959, although he then continued to make guest appearances for many more years. In the early 60s, he acted as ringmaster for his own circus, but in later years, he worked with **Hank Williams Jnr.**'s touring show. He appeared in various television programmes and was always popular on chat shows, where he related tales from his years in showbusiness. He played in several films, including *Country Music On Broadway*, and also delivered serious lectures at colleges. His famous closing line was 'I'm going back to the wagon, boys, these shoes are killing me.' It was, however, not the shoes but cancer that killed the Duke of Paducah, when he lost his long battle against it in 1986.

Duke Spirit

London, England–based band formed in 2002 by Liela Moss (vocals/harmonica), Luke Ford (guitar), Dan Higgins (guitar/keyboards), Toby Butler (bass) and Olly Betts (drums). The vinyl-only single 'Darling You're Mean' was released in May 2003, followed later in the year by the *Roll, Spirit, Roll* mini-album, both issued on the City Rockers imprint. The latter was co-produced by Simon Raymonde from the **Cocteau Twins** and prompted a number of positive reviews in the UK music press. The quintet's very British take on blues-laced rock 'n' roll was built around Ford's abrasive guitar work and Moss' seductive vocals, which when coupled with a smouldering stage presence began to attract a wider audience. Despite the quintet completing the majority of work on their debut album, their contract with City Rockers fell through, but James Oldham's Loog Records rescued them from contractual limbo. In 2004 Duke Spirit released two excellent singles 'Dark Is Light Enough' and 'Tracks Across The Land'.
● ALBUMS: *Roll, Spirit, Roll* mini-album (City Rockers 2003) ★★★★, *Cuts Across The Land* (Loog 2005) ★★★.

Duke Wore Jeans, The

Taking its cue from the plot of *The Prince And The Pauper*, this 1958 film starred **Tommy Steele** as the son of a Cockney pearly king who trades lifestyles with his double, the Hon. Tony Whitecliffe. Inevitably, the former falls in love with an aristocrat. *The Duke Wore Jeans* has little to commend it other than being a vehicle for Steele's chirpy personality. He contributed eight songs to the soundtrack, including 'Happy Guitar', which reached number 20 in the UK charts when issued as a single. If Steele was ever a bona fide rock 'n' roll singer, this film marked his transformation into an all-round entertainer. *The Duke Wore Jeans* was retitled *It's All Happening* for the US market. The same title was used for a British 1963 feature film starring Steele, which was known as *The Dream Maker* in America.

Duke, Andrew

b. Canada. Drawing on found sounds as his primary noise source, composer/remixer/producer Duke has been refining his approach to minimal digital composition since the late 80s. 'I enjoy the sounds of the world', he has stated, of the inspiration for his post-minimal **techno** sound design. Having initially begun constructing sounds on an increasingly damaged guitar, Duke's roots in electronic music were formed in his youth via primitive tape deck remixes of artists such as stadium rockers **Bon Jovi**. Creating music across genres, including but not limited to variations on techno, **tech-house, house, electro**, ambient, microsound and glitch, he now states his aim as to 'record challenging electronic and experimental music'. However, while Duke might abstract sounds such as water, waves, rain, thunder and vinyl hiss, he frequently underpins his sound constructions with political impetus. One of his releases in 2002, *More Destructive Than Organized*, was billed as 'an audio commentary on the effects of war and religion' and seemed to carry trace echoes of mournful bugle and helicopter whirs amidst its distressed post-techno rumbles. The same year's *Physical And Mental Health* examined 'physical and mental deterioration and disintegration, both on personal and impersonal levels'. That album's 'HRM H2o' was an aural examination (featuring samples of harbour water) of the pollution that takes place in his home-town of the fishing, oil and shipbuilding port of Halifax, Nova Scotia, the second largest natural harbour of its kind in the world. Duke's music is also intensely personal: the 2004 release *Remembering Jason Trenholm* is a tribute to a friend who he 'met when we were 5 years old; he was my best friend for the next 29 years.'

Duke has also produced other artists at his Cognition Sound studio and formed the Cognition Audioworks label in 1990 (artists include Clinker, Foal, Granny'Ark, Freiband and Formatt) after operating Incognito Musique and Digitalis Recordings between 1987 and 1990. He has contributed music journalism to *Exclaim!*, *Urb* and *XLR8R* and has notably hosted *Andrew Duke's In The Mix*, a weekly radio/Internet show. Duke is also a visual artist whose work has been exhibited internationally.
● ALBUMS: *Communion* (Cognition Audioworks 1993) ★★★, *Drowning In Oxygen* (Cognition Audioworks 1993) ★★★, *Ashes And Ceremony* (Cognition Audioworks 1994) ★★★, *Numeric* (Cognition Audioworks 1995) ★★★, *Ginga* (Cognition Audioworks 1996) ★★★, *Sit/Stand: Live Humidity* (Cognition Audioworks 2001) ★★★, *Sprung* (Bip-Hop 2002) ★★★, *More Destructive Than Organized* (Bake/Staalplaat 2002) ★★★, *Physical And Mental Health* (Folding Cassettes/Dial 2002) ★★★★, *Highest Common Denominator* (Piehead 2002) ★★★, *Take Nothing For Granted* (Cognition Audioworks/Acid Fake 2003) ★★★, *We Owe Roland* (pHinnMilk 2004) ★★★, *Remembering Jason Trenholm* (Bip-Hop 2004) ★★★, *Just Because You Can Doesn't Mean You Should* (Cognition Audioworks 2004) ★★★.

Duke, Doris

b. Doris Curry, 1945, Sandersville, Florida, USA. Duke emerged from a variety of gospel groups including the Raspberry Singers (which included **Chuck Jackson**), the David Sisters, the Evangelistic Gospel Singers and the Caravans. Between 1963 and 1967, Duke worked as a New York session singer before recording a solo single under the name Doris

Willingham. In 1968 she toured Europe with **Nina Simone** and subsequently came under the aegis of producer **Swamp Dogg**. Several superb records followed including 'I Don't Care Anymore' and 'To The Other Woman (I'm The Other Woman)' (1970), the latter reaching number 7 in the R&B charts. In spite of an excellent album, *I'm A Loser* (featuring **Duane Allman** on rhythm guitar), Duke failed to achieve mainstream success and her recording career faltered in the latter half of the 70s. Duke briefly re-emerged in 1981 with a new album, *Funky Fox*.

● ALBUMS: *I'm A Loser* (Canyon 1969) ★★★★, *Woman* (Scepter 1975) ★★★, *Funky Fox* (Manhattan 1981) ★★.

● COMPILATIONS: *A Legend In Her Own Time* (Contempo 1975) ★★★, shared with Sandra Phillips *Deep Soul Queens* (Charly 1992) ★★★, *I'm A Loser: The Swamp Dogg Sessions . . . And More* (Kent 2005) ★★★★.

Duke, George

b. 12 January 1946, San Rafael, California, USA. Duke studied the piano at school (where he ran a **Les McCann**-inspired Latin band) and emerged from the San Francisco Conservatory as a Bachelor of Music in 1967. From 1965–67 he was resident pianist at the Half Note, accompanying musicians such as **Dizzy Gillespie** and **Kenny Dorham**. This grounding served as a musical education for the rest of his life. He arranged for a vocal group, the Third Wave, and toured Mexico in 1968. In 1969, he began playing with French violinist **Jean-Luc Ponty**, using electric piano to accompany Ponty's electric violin. He played on *King Kong*, an album of music **Frank Zappa** composed for Ponty. He then joined Zappa's group in 1970, an experience that transformed his music. As he put it, previously he had been too 'musically advanced' to play rock 'n' roll piano triplets. Zappa encouraged him to sing and joke and use electronics. Together they wrote 'Uncle Remus' for *Apostrophe* (1972), a song about black attitudes to oppression. His keyboards contributed to a great edition of the **Mothers Of Invention**—captured on the outstanding *Roxy & Elsewhere* (1975)—which combined fluid jazz playing with rock and *avant garde* sonorities. In 1972 he toured with **Cannonball Adderley** (replacing **Joe Zawinul**).

Duke had always had a leaning towards soul jazz and after he left Zappa, he went for full-frontal funk. *I Love The Blues, She Heard My Cry* (1975) combined a retrospective look at black musical forms with warm good humour and freaky musical ideas; a duet with **Johnny 'Guitar' Watson** was particularly successful. Duke started duos with fusion power-drummer **Billy Cobham** and virtuoso bass player **Stanley Clarke**, playing quintessential 70s jazz rock—amplification and much attention to 'chops' being the order of the day. Duke always had a sense of humour: 'Dukey Stick' (1978) sounded like a **Funkadelic** record. The middle of the road beckoned, however, and by *Brazilian Love Affair* (1980) he was providing high-class background music. In 1982, *Dream On* showed him happily embracing west-coast hip easy listening. However, there has always been an unpredictable edge to Duke. The band he put together for the Wembley Nelson Mandela concert in London backed a stream of black singers, and his arrangement of 'Backyard Ritual' on **Miles Davis**' *Tutu* (1986) was excellent. He collaborated with Clarke again for the funk-styled *3* and in 1992 he bounced back with the jazz fusion *Snapshot*, followed by the orchestral suite *Enchanted Forest* in 1996 and *Is Love Enough?* in 1997.

Further albums have followed, showing that Duke was on a creative roll at the turn of the century and beyond.

● ALBUMS: *Jazz Workshop of San Francisco* (Saba 1966) ★★★, *The Inner Source* (MPS 1971) ★★★, *Faces In Reflection* (MPS 1974) ★★★, *Feel* (MPS/BASF 1975) ★★★, *The Aura Will Prevail* (MPS/BASF 1975) ★★★, *I Love The Blues, She Heard My Cry* (MPS/BASF 1975) ★★★, with Billy Cobham *Live—On Tour In Europe* (Atlantic 1976) ★★★, *Liberated Fantasies* (MPS/BASF 1976) ★★★, *From Me To You* (Epic 1977) ★★★, *Reach For It* (Epic 1977) ★★★, *Don't Let Go* (Epic 1978) ★★, *Follow The Rainbow* (Epic 1979) ★★, *Master Of The Game* (Epic 1979) ★★★, *Primal* (MPS 1979) ★★★, *Secret Rendezvous* (Epic 1979) ★★★, *A Brazilian Love Affair* (Epic 1980) ★★★★, with Stanley Clarke *The Clarke/Duke Project* (Epic 1981) ★★★★, *Dream On* (Epic 1982) ★★, *Guardian Of The Light* (Epic 1983) ★★★, with Clarke *The Clarke/Duke Project II* (Epic 1983) ★★★★, *1976 Solo Keyboard Album* (Epic 1983) ★★★, *Thief In The Night* (Elektra 1985) ★★★, *Night After Night* (Elektra 1989) ★★★, with Clarke *3* (Epic 1990) ★★★, *Reach For It* (Sony 1991) ★★★, *Snapshot* (Warners 1992) ★★★, *Enchanted Forest: Muir Woods Suite* (Warners 1996) ★★★, *Is Love Enough?* (Warners 1997) ★★★★, *After Hours* (Warners 1998) ★★★, *Cool* (Warners 2000) ★★★★, *Face The Music* (Bizarre Planet 2002) ★★★, *Duke* (Bizarre Planet 2005) ★★★★.

● COMPILATIONS: *The Collection* (Castle 1991) ★★★, *Greatest Hits* (Epic 1996) ★★★, *The Best Of George Duke: The Elektra Years* (Elektra 1997) ★★★★, *The Essential* (Sony 2004) ★★★★.

Duke, Patty

b. Anna Marie Duke, 14 December 1946, Elmhurst, New York, USA. A child actress, Duke first came to the fore in the 1959 Broadway play *The Miracle Worker*, in which she played Helen Keller. In 1962 she reprised the role on film, for which she became the youngest person ever to win an Academy Award. The following year she starred in her own US television situation comedy in which she played two roles as 'identical cousins'. The programme became a great success (still seen in re-runs today) and lasted until 1966.

In 1965, Duke signed a recording contract with **United Artists Records**; her first single, 'Don't Just Stand There', was a teen-orientated ballad, reminiscent of **Lesley Gore**. It hit number 8 on the US charts and her follow-up, 'Say Something Funny', reached number 22 that same year. Duke subsequently recorded several other singles and albums but never repeated her initial success. She returned to acting and built up a notable career as a television actress, most notably in the mini-series *Captains And The Kings* and the movies *Having Babies III* and *A Family Upside Down*. In 1982 she was diagnosed with manic-depressive illness but this did little to slow her workrate down. She talked about her illness in her autobiography *Call Me Anna* and a second book *A Brilliant Madness*. Today, Duke is still involved in television and film acting.

● ALBUMS: *Don't Just Stand There* (United Artists 1965) ★★★, *Billie* film soundtrack (United Artists 1965) ★★, *Patty* (United Artists 1966) ★★, *Sings Songs From Valley Of The Dolls And Other Selections* (United Artists 1967) ★★.

● COMPILATIONS: *Patty Duke's Greatest Hits* (United Artists 1966) ★★★, *TV's Teen Star* (Unart 1967) ★★, *Just*

Patty: The Best Of Patty Duke (EMI 1996) ★★★, *The Patty Duke Collection* (Teenager 2002) ★★★.

● FURTHER READING: *Call Me Anna: The Autobiography Of Patty Duke*, Patty Duke. *A Brilliant Madness: Living With Manic-Depressive Illness*, Patty Duke.

● FILMS: *Country Music Holiday* (1958), *The Goddess* (1958), *4D Man* aka *Master Of Terror* (1959), *Happy Anniversary* (1959), *The Miracle Worker* (1962), *Billie* (1965), *The Daydreamer* voice only (1966), *Valley Of The Dolls* (1967), *Me, Natalie* (1969), *You'll Like My Mother* (1972), *The Swarm* (1978), *By Design* (1982), *Willy/Milly* (1986), *The Hitch-Hikers* (1989), *Prelude To A Kiss* (1992), *Kimberly* (1999), *Wrong Turn* (2003), *Bigger Than The Sky* (2005).

Duke, Vernon

b. Vladimir Dukelsky, 10 October 1903, Parfianovka, Russia, d. 16 January 1969. A popular composer during the 30s and 40s, Duke was a child prodigy. Initially classically-trained—he studied extensively, mainly at Kiev and Odessa—in the early 20s he began experimenting with songs written in the style of such currently popular composers as **Irving Berlin** and **George Gershwin**. For these early efforts at popular song writing he used pseudonyms, a practice he continued when, in 1921, he emigrated to the USA. For the next three decades he used his real name for his classical compositions and the name Vernon Duke for his popular songs. His first songs in the New World suffered through his lack of a thorough grasp of English and his adherence to the styles of other songwriters. By the mid-20s, Duke was in Paris, pursuing his classical studies and writing music for the piano and the ballet. In London in the late 20s, he wrote for the musical stage, mostly for revues and in the field of operetta. Back in the USA before the decade was out, he was hired to write incidental music for films but still hoped to find popular success. This began with 'I Am Only Human After All', with lyrics by **E. 'Yip' Harburg** and **Ira Gershwin**, which featured in **The Garrick Gaieties** (1930). He continued to write for Broadway, with varying levels of success, and in the 1932 show *Walk A Little Faster* introduced his first standard, 'April In Paris' (with Harburg). For the 1934 show *Thumbs Up*, Duke wrote his own lyric for another song destined to become a standard, 'Autumn In New York', and in the same year contributed 'What Is There To Say?' and 'I Like The Likes Of You' to the **Ziegfeld Follies**. For the *Ziegfeld Follies Of 1936* Duke composed 'An Island In The West Indies', 'That Moment Of Moments' and the magnificent 'I Can't Get Started', which was sung in the show by **Bob Hope** and **Eve Arden**. In 1940 he wrote the music for **Cabin In The Sky**, which opened on Broadway in October and featured an all-black cast. The show's songs included 'Taking A Chance On Love' (lyrics by **John Latouche** and Ted Fetter), introduced on the stage by **Ethel Waters**, and destined to become another standard. Duke's shows of the early 40s were not so well received, and he followed his military service with a two-year sojourn in Paris. Back in the USA in the early 50s, Duke worked on a number of shows, including *Two's Company* and *The Littlest Revue* (both with **Ogden Nash**), but he was never able to recapture his earlier success. Later in his life he continued to write classical music, including oratorios and ballets. In 1994 Ben Bagley's *Vernon Duke Revisited* provided a timely reminder of several of his rarely heard, but lovely songs, such as 'Water Under The Bridge', 'Now', 'Lady', 'Roundabout', 'The Theatre Is A Lady', 'We're Having A Baby', 'I Cling To You' and 'If You Can't Get The Love You Want'.

Dukes

This British songwriting duo comprised Dominic Bugatti and Frank Musker. The pair never actually performed live and only contributed vocals to their records, and they preferred to take a **Quincy Jones** approach to their output—by producing, writing and arranging the material and letting the main vocals and music be performed by the cream of the session world. They made their name by writing many Top 20 hits including 'Modern Girl' for **Sheena Easton** and 'Woman In Love' and 'My Simple Heart' for the **Three Degrees**. In 1982 they released an album of their songs under the pseudonym of the Dukes which, aimed at the disco party market, made little impact. They have continued to write but have not enjoyed the run of success achieved during the early 80s.

● ALBUMS: *The Dukes* (1982) ★★.

Dukes Of Dixieland

Formed in 1949 by trumpeter Frank Assunto (b. 29 January 1922, New Orleans, Louisiana, USA, d. 25 February 1974, New Orleans, Louisiana, USA) and his trombonist brother Fred (b. 3 December 1929, Jennings, Louisiana, USA, d. 21 April 1966, Las Vegas, Nevada, USA), the Dukes Of Dixieland got their start with band leader **Horace Heidt** in his 'Youth Opportunity Programme', which toured the USA from 1948–53. Returning to their home-town they were resident at the Famous Door in the Crescent City for four years, building up a big reputation in person and on Roulette and **Victor Records**. At this time, when the original New Orleans musicians had either died or retired, the Dukes were hailed as authentic. True, they were capable enough, but no more so than any other revivalist band, including the British trad groups which proliferated in that era. However, they were fortunate both in having a contract with Audio-Fidelity Records, who recorded them with startling clarity on superb stereo demonstration records, and, especially, on having **Louis Armstrong** join them temporarily. They visited Japan in 1964 along with **Red Nichols** and **Gene Krupa** in a **George Wein** Dixieland To Swing package, with **Edmond Hall** as the Dukes' guest artist. The band broke up when Fred Assunto died while they were playing in Las Vegas.

● ALBUMS: *The Dukes Of Dixieland At The Jazz Band Ball* (Vik 1957) ★★★★, *You've Got To Hear It To Believe It, Vol. 1* (Audio Fidelity 1957) ★★★, *You've Got To Hear It To Believe It, Vol. 2* (Audio Fidelity 1957) ★★★, *You've Got To Hear It To Believe It, Vol. 3* (Audio Fidelity 1958) ★★, *You've Got To Hear It To Believe It, Vol. 4* (Audio Fidelity 1958) ★★★, *Mardi Gras Time* (Audio Fidelity 1958) ★★, *The Dukes Of Dixieland On Campus* (Audio Fidelity 1959) ★★★, *Up The Mississippi* (Audio Fidelity 1959) ★★, *The Dukes Of Dixieland* (RCA Victor 1960) ★★★, *Breakin' It Up On Broadway* (Columbia 1962) ★★★, *Struttin' At The World's Fair* (Columbia 1964) ★★★, *Live At Bourbon Street* (Decca 1965) ★★★, *Sunrise, Sunset* (Decca 1966) ★★★, *Come To The Cabaret* (Decca 1966) ★★.

● COMPILATIONS: *The Best Of The Dukes Of Dixieland* (Audio Fidelity 1961) ★★★, *More Best Of The Dukes Of Dixieland* (Audio Fidelity 1962) ★★★, *Greatest Songs* (Curb 1995) ★★★.

Dukes Of Stratosphear

An alter ego of **XTC**, this group was a vehicle for Andy Partridge's psychedelic frustrations of being born a decade or two out of time. Both albums the group released contained brilliant pastiches of virtually every pop band of the mid-to late 60s period. In many cases the Dukes' tongue-in-cheek parables were far superior to the songs to which they gently alluded. It was suggested that their albums actually outsold the XTC product available at the same time.

● ALBUMS: *25 O'Clock* mini-album (Virgin 1985) ★★★★★, *Psonic Psunspot* (Virgin 1987) ★★★★★.
● COMPILATIONS: *Chips From The Chocolate Fireball* (Virgin 1987) ★★★★★.

Dukes, 'Little' Laura

b. 10 June 1907, Memphis, Tennessee, USA. An early start in music led Little Laura Dukes to a lifetime of involvement with entertainment in Memphis. Her father had been a drummer with **W.C. Handy**'s band, but it was a less sophisticated idiom that Dukes chose, playing blues with the jug bands for which that city is so well known. She sang and played banjo and ukelele with the **Will Batts** Novelty Band, and although they made two recordings in the early 50s, these were not issued until 20 years later. She made some more records with the revival of interest in blues and related music in the 70s and also appeared in a BBC Television series. As late as the 80s, she was still performing in Memphis, at the Blues Alley club, set up to showcase the city's blues talent.

● ALBUMS: *South Memphis Jug Band* (1975) ★★★.

Dulcimer

Formed in 1967 as Kelpie, English progressive folk duo Dulcimer worked on projects involving poetry, books and children's stories before becoming professional musicians. They were originally discovered playing in a Cotswold, Worcestershire, restaurant by the British actor Richard Todd in 1970. Multi-instrumentalists David Eaves (guitars, harmonium, piano, keyboards, glockenspiel, Jew's Harp) and Peter Hodge (guitars, harmonica, mandolin, dulcimer, banjo, keyboards) were subsequently signed by renowned manager **Larry Page**, at that time in the process of setting up his own label, Nepentha Records. Dulcimer's self-titled debut album helped launch the label in 1971 and attracted favourable reviews for its intriguing blend of English folk (including several references to the group's local Cotswolds environment) and varied instrumentation. **Melody Maker** magazine, in particular, was effusive, comparing the duo favourably with **Simon And Garfunkel**, though *Dulcimer* also involved a third member, Hodge's cousin Jeremy North on bass. The album additionally featured Richard Todd reading poetry on two of the tracks. It sold well in the USA, Europe and Japan, and the group embarked on recording sessions for their second album, a more rock-orientated affair. Though artwork and packaging were completed, the album was never released, and Eaves and Hodge returned Dulcimer to a semi-professional footing thereafter. A further small-label album was issued in 1980, *A Land Fit For Heroes*, jointly credited to local writer Fred Archer who appeared on the recordings. Afterwards Eaves concentrated on his furniture business and Hodge on landscape gardening. 'Jem' North returned to driving lorries. However, due to residual interest in Dulcimer, the central duo re-formed the band in 1993 to enter the studio once again. *When A Child . . .* was released on President Records and returned to the group's evocative rural style. This was followed by a second 'comeback' set in 1995, *Rob's Garden*, recorded at their own 'cottage studio'. As with each of their earlier releases, there was a strong undercurrent of literature in this project: 'Creation—The Poet And The Fire Bird' concerns a meeting between Igor Stravinsky and Dylan Thomas.

● ALBUMS: *Dulcimer* (Nepentha 1971) ★★★, *A Land Fit For Heroes* (Happy Face 1980) ★★, *When A Child . . .* (President 1993) ★★★, *Rob's Garden* (President 1995) ★★★.

Dulcimer, Appalachian and Hammered

The Appalachian, or mountain, dulcimer is believed to originate from the German Scheitholt, though there are similar instruments in use in many other European countries, including the Norwegian Langeleik, the Icelandic Langspil and the French Epinette Des Vosges. The Appalachian dulcimer was so called because it found a new popularity among the early settlers in America in the Appalachian mountain region. It is essentially a three, four or six-stringed instrument, traditionally played by using a 'noter' to pick out the melody on the fingerboard, and strummed using a quill, or feather. The melody is usually played on one string, and the other strings act as 'drones', but a number of chord positions are available in each of the tuning 'modes'. There are a number of tunings for the instrument: Ionian, Aeolian, Mixolydian, Dorian, Phrygian, Lydian and Locrian. The Appalachian dulcimer has enjoyed a resurgence of interest in recent years because of its use in recordings by such performers as **Jean Ritchie**, **Richard Farina**, **Holly Tannen** and earlier albums by **Joni Mitchell**. The Hammered, or Hammer, Dulcimer is a different, and larger, instrument, usually trapezoid in shape. It contains a larger number of strings set in groups, which are struck with 'hammers' rather like a piano's strings are struck, producing a beautiful flowing sound. **Jim Couza** and **John McCutcheon** are two fine exponents of the instrument. There are also a number of books and recordings available of both the Appalachian and Hammered Dulcimer.

● ALBUMS: *The Hammered Dulcimer* (Folk Legacy Records), Roger Nicholson, Lorraine Lee *An Exultation Of Dulcimers* (1980) ★★★, *Carolan's Cup* (1984) ★★★, *Carolan's Cottage* (1986) ★★★, all Joemy Wilson *Dargason: A Dulcimer Sampler* (1982) ★★★★, *Gifts, Volume II Traditional Christmas Carols* (1987) ★★, *Beatles On Hammered Dulcimer* (1989) ★★★, *Dulcimer Lullabies* (1991) ★★★, *Celtic Dreams* (1993) ★★★, *Gifts III— Christmas Music From Around The World* (1993) ★★★, *Celtic Treasures* (1993) ★★★.
● FURTHER READING: *The Dulcimer Book*, Jean Ritchie. *Jean Ritchie's Dulcimer People*, Jean Ritchie. *Dulcimer Songbook*, Neal Hellman. *The Cripple Creek Dulcimer Book*, Bud and Donna Ford. *A Catalogue Of Pre-Revival Appalachian Dulcimers*, L. Allen Smith. *The Dulcimer Maker: The Craft Of Homer Ledford*, R. Gerald Alvey.

Dulfer, Candy

b. 19 September 1969, Amsterdam, the Netherlands. Saxophonist Dulfer was bought to prominence by **Prince**, who introduced her on the video mix of 'Party Man' with a cry of 'when I want sax, I call for Candy'. She was bought up in a family involved in the Dutch jazz scene. Her father, Hans Dulfer, a respected tenor saxophonist, exposed his daughter to the playing of **Sonny Rollins**, **Coleman Hawkins** and **Dexter Gordon**. Candy's career evolved from playing with brass bands to performing on the jazz club circuit and later fronting her own band Funky Stuff, who were invited to support **Madonna** on part of her 1987 European tour. A similar support slot with Prince was abruptly cancelled, but the singer made amends by inviting Dulfer onstage during one of his shows. The resulting recording sessions with Prince, and in particular the aforementioned 'Party Man', led to session work with **Eurythmics** guitarist, **David A. Stewart**, who gave Dulfer a joint credit on 'Lily Was Here', a UK number 6 hit in 1990. Further credits have found her working with **David Gilmour**, **Aretha Franklin** and **Van Morrison**. Her 1990 debut album was nominated for a Grammy and certified gold. Her subsequent albums have been pleasant enough but have broken no new ground, their R&B leanings similar in content to **David Sanborn**'s hard-blowing work. However, she is regarded as one of Europe's leading young saxophonists.

● ALBUMS: *Saxuality* (BMG Ariola 1990) ★★★, *Sax-a-Go-Go* (BMG Ariola 1991) ★★★, *Big Girl* (BMG Ariola 1995) ★★, *For The Love Of You* (BMG Ariola 1997) ★★★, *Girls Night Out* (N-Coded 1999) ★★★, *Live In Amsterdam* (N-Coded 2001) ★★, *Right In My Soul* (Eagle 2003) ★★.

● COMPILATIONS: *The Best Of Candy Dulfer* (N2K Encoded 1998) ★★★.

Dummer, John, Blues Band

This UK band came into being in 1965, evolving from the Muskrats and the Grebbells, and lasted until the early 70s, surviving numerous personnel changes. The line-up included prominent British blues artists such as pianist **Bob Hall**, guitarist **Dave Kelly** and his sister **Jo Ann Kelly**, **Mike Cooper** and Tony McPhee. The band backed touring American artists **John Lee Hooker** and **Howlin' Wolf** and recorded albums for **Mercury** and **Vertigo** between 1969 and 1973. Drummer John Dummer went on to work with English pop vocal group **Darts** in the mid-70s. In recent years all Dummer's albums have become much sought after items in the collectors' market and currently carry very high prices.

● ALBUMS: *Cabal* (Mercury 1969) ★★★, *John Dummer's Blues Band* (Mercury 1969) ★★★★, *Famous Music Band* (Philips 1970) ★★, *This Is John Dummer* (Philips 1972) ★★★, *Volume II, Try Me One More Time* (Philips 1973) ★★, *Blue* (Vertigo 1973) ★★, *Oobleedooblee Jubilee* (Vertigo 1973) ★★.

Dumpy's Rusty Nuts

Dumpy (b. Graham Dunnell, July 1949, London, England) had been playing with various bands since the mid-60s. His first big break came in 1977 with new wave outfit the Rivvets. Four years later he returned to his love of blues and formed Dumpy's Rusty Nuts. Taking on guitar and vocals, he was joined by Malcolm McKenzie (bass) and Chris Hussey (drums). Together they recorded the 'Biker Anthem' and 'Just For Kicks' before encountering trouble with BBC Radio 1 who objected to the band's name—for a while 'nuts' became 'bolts'. Dumpy, a natural entertainer, followed the rock traditions started by Jackie Lynton and interspersed the music with jokes, which helped to gain them a cult following in the pubs and clubs. Prior to a major tour with the **Blues**

Band, McKenzie left to join Nuthin' Fancy and was replaced by Jeff Brown. Over the next few years, the band's records sold badly, a situation exacerbated by ever-fluctuating line-ups, with transient personnel including Mark Brabbs (drums, ex-**Tank**), Alan Fish and Mick Kirton (bass and drums, both ex-**Groundhogs**), Alan Davey and Danny Thompson (bass and drums, on loan from **Hawkwind**) and guitarist Mick Grafton from **Cloven Hoof**. It was Dumpy's connections with Hawkwind that kept him in the public eye, with 1987's *Get Out On The Road* becoming his most successful release, largely owing to guest appearances by Davey, Thompson and Dave Brock from Hawkwind. The band had one last attempt at the big time in October 1990 when they entered the studio to record a cover version of the **Jo Jo Gunne** classic, 'Run Run Run', with **KimWilde** producer Steve Glenn. The single was to be released to coincide with a major support slot on the **Status Quo** tour. However, all did not go according to plan—the single only appeared as a promo copy and, under orders, they had to omit much of the humour from their live set. This undermined their unique performing style and rendered them just another blues rock band. Since that time, there have been no new records and they have returned to the pub and club circuit. McKenzie later went on to manage **Thunder** while Alan Fish formed Egypt.

● ALBUMS: *Somewhere In England* (Landslide 1984) ★★★, *Hot Lover* (Gas 1985) ★★, *Get Out On The Road* (Metal Masters 1987) ★★★, *Firkin Well Live* (Razor 1988) ★★.

● DVD/VIDEOS: *Live At The Marquee 1986* (1988), *The Vintage Video* (1990), *Live At The Hippodrome 1989* (1990).

Dunbar, Aynsley

b. 10 January 1946, Liverpool, England. This respected drummer served his musical apprenticeship in numerous Merseybeat bands including **Derry Wilkie And The Pressmen**, Freddie Starr And The Flamingos and the Excheckers. Dunbar joined Stu James' **Mojos** in March 1965, but the following year he replaced Hughie Flint in **John Mayall**'s Bluesbreakers. His skills were apparent on the band's *A Hard Road* (1967) and a later recording, 'Rubber Duck', which formed the b-side of a Bluesbreakers' single. This propulsive instrumental is memorable for its fiery drum solo. Aynsley briefly joined the **Jeff Beck** Group in April 1967 before leaving six months later to pursue a career with his own quartet the **Aynsley Dunbar Retaliation**. This compulsive, blues-based attraction was responsible for four excellent albums, but their leader left the line-up in 1969 to form a larger, brass-based unit, Aynsley Dunbar's Blue Whale. The unit's lone album included a version of **Frank Zappa**'s 'Willie The Pimp', a coincidental inclusion given that Dunbar then joined the former's group the **Mothers Of Invention**. A member between 1970 and 1972, Dunbar then defected with four other members to form **Flo And Eddie**. By this point Aynsley had become an established session musician, contributing to albums by **David Bowie** (*Pin-Ups*), **Lou Reed** (*Berlin*) and **Ian Hunter** (*All American Alien Boy*). He joined **Journey** in 1974, but left four years later in order to replace John Barbata in **Jefferson Starship**. Dunbar remained with this successful act until 1982 and subsequently maintained a lower professional profile for three years. A brief spell in **Whitesnake** was followed by work with **Alvin Lee**, **Eric Burdon** and **UFO**.

● ALBUMS: *Blue Whale* (Warners 1970) ★★.

Dunbar, Aynsley, Retaliation

This unit was formed in 1967 by ex-**John Mayall** drummer **Aynsley Dunbar** (b. 10 January 1946, Liverpool, England). Having recorded an informal version of **Buddy Guy**'s 'Stone Crazy' with an embryonic line-up of **Rod Stewart** (vocals), **Peter Green** (guitar) and **Jack Bruce** (bass), Dunbar created a permanent Retaliation around ex-**Johnny Kidd And The Pirates** and **Shotgun Express** guitarist, John Moorshead, Keith Tillman (bass) and ex-**Alexis Korner** vocalist, Victor Brox. This line-up completed a solitary single, 'Warning'/'Cobwebs', for the **Blue Horizon Records** label before Tillman was replaced by Alex Dmochowski (ex-**Neil Christian**'s Crusaders). *The Aynsley Dunbar Retaliation* showcased this superior blues act's self-assurance, with one side devoted to concise performances and the other to freer, instrumentally based workouts. Although it lacked the overall strength of its predecessor, *Doctor Dunbar's Prescription* was another worthwhile album that offered strong original songs and several judicious cover versions. However, the group is best recalled for *Retaliation* aka *To Mum From Aynsley And The Boys*, which was produced by John Mayall. Former **Grease Band** keyboard player Tommy Eyre was added for this powerful, moody collection on which the unit created some of its finest recordings, including 'Don't Take The Power Away' and 'Journey's End'. In November 1969 Dunbar and Eyre left the group to form Aynsley Dunbar's Blue Whale. A fourth set, *Remains To Be Heard*, was culled from remaining masters and newer recordings by the extant trio with singer Annette Brox, but the Retaliation broke up soon after its completion.

● ALBUMS: *The Aynsley Dunbar Retaliation* (Liberty 1968) ★★★, *Doctor Dunbar's Prescription* (Liberty 1969) ★★★, *Retaliation* aka *To Mum From Aynsley And The Boys* (Liberty 1969) ★★★, *Remains To Be Heard* (Liberty 1970) ★★.

Dunbar, Scott

b. 1904, Deer Park Plantation, Mississippi, USA, d. 4 September 1994, Centreville, Mississippi, USA. Dunbar taught himself guitar as a child, and despite some involvement with a local string band, his music was idiosyncratic and unpredictable, combining seemingly spontaneous guitar playing with a singing style that veers abruptly between normal and falsetto registers; the total performance often seems almost a free-form exploration of the song. Dunbar never travelled more than 100 miles from his rural home and was further isolated by his illiteracy, which meant that his lyrics were memorized and often startlingly fragmented. He seldom—and by the 60s, never—played for black audiences, owing to his wife's fear of possible violence. He combined work as a fisherman and guide with playing for tourists, and his repertoire reflected this, with popular tunes substantially outnumbering blues.

● ALBUMS: *From Lake Mary* (1970) ★★★.

Dunbar, Sly

b. Lowell Charles Dunbar, 10 May 1952, Kingston, Jamaica, West Indies. In 1969 Dunbar commenced his recording career with **Lee Perry**, playing drums on 'Night Doctor' by the **Upsetters**, which appears on both *The Upsetter* and *Return of Django*. The following year, he played on **Dave And Ansell Collins**' massive hit 'Double Barrel'. Around this time he also joined the Youth Professionals who had a residency at the Tit For Tat Club on Red Hills Road, Kingston. He paid frequent visits to another club further up the same road, Evil People, where he struck up a friendship with bass player Robbie Shakespeare (b. 27 September 1953, Kingston, Jamaica, West Indies). Deciding to work together, their professional relationship as **Sly And Robbie** began. In 1972/3, Dunbar joined Skin Flesh And Bones, backing **Al Brown** on his bestselling cover version of **Al Green**'s 'Here I Am Baby'. The same year, Sly and Robbie became founder members of the **Revolutionaries, Channel One** studio's house band. They recorded hit after hit, and the studio soon became the most in-demand on the island.

Dunbar's technical proficiency and relentless inventiveness drove him constantly to develop original drum patterns, and while most of the island's other drummers were copying his latest innovations, he would move on and create something new. In this way, he had an enormous influence on the direction that reggae took from the mid-70s onwards. Dunbar's inventive and entertaining playing can be heard on dub and instrumental albums such as *Vital Dub, Satta Dub* and *Revolutionary Sounds*, as well as supporting the **Mighty Diamonds** on their classic *Right Time*. He also recorded extensively with the Professionals, **Joe Gibbs**' house band, playing on classics such as *Visions* by **Dennis Brown**, *Two Sevens Clash* by **Culture** and *African Dub Chapter 3*. **Derrick Harriott** went one step further and put him on the cover of *Go Deh Wid Riddim* (1977), which was credited to Sly And The Revolutionaries. He was then signed to **Virgin Records**, who released two disappointing solo albums, *Simple Sly Man* (1978) and *Sly Wicked And Slick* (1979). Around this time, Dunbar was the first drummer successfully to integrate synthesized drums into his playing, and a little later became the first reggae drummer to use a Simmons electronic drum kit.

In 1979 Sly And Robbie moved into record production with their own Taxi label, finding success with **Black Uhuru**'s bestselling *Showcase*. Further recordings included **Gregory Isaacs**' *Showcase* and the various artists compilation *Presenting Taxi* (1981). They had their greatest commercial success with Black Uhuru, with whom they recorded four further albums. In 1984 they became official members of the group, but left later that year after the departure of **Michael Rose**. At the same time, they established **Ini Kamoze** as a major new reggae artist, released Dennis Brown's *Brown Sugar* and **Sugar Minott**'s *Sugar And Spice*, plus three groundbreaking albums with **Grace Jones** that were hugely successful and introduced their talents to the world outside of reggae. They have since recorded widely with artists such as **Mick Jagger, Carly Simon, Gwen Guthrie, Bob Dylan, Robert Palmer, James Brown, Manu Dibango** and **Herbie Hancock**. They also teamed up with **Bill Laswell** for a series of innovative soul/funk/crossover albums including *Language Barrier, Rhythm Killers, Silent Assassin* and **Material**'s *The Third Power*. They have continued to develop their own reggae sound with recordings from their new discoveries 54–46 and **Kotch**, some of which are included on the compilations *Sound Of The 90s* and *Carib Soul*. They have already changed the musical world, and their restless creativity ensures that they will continue to do so.

● ALBUMS: *Go Deh Wid Riddim* (Crystal 1977) ★★★, *Simple Sly Man* (Virgin 1978) ★★, *Sly Wicked And Slick* (Virgin 1979) ★★, *Sly-Go-Ville* (Mango/Island 1982) ★★★.

Dunbar, Ted

b. Earl Theodore Dunbar, 17 January 1937, Port Arthur, Texas, USA, d. 29 May 1998, New Brunswick, New Jersey, USA. Teaching himself to play guitar and trumpet, Dunbar played in the Lincoln High School band, continuing to play music while studying pharmacy at Texas Southern University. After graduating and receiving a license to practice pharmacy he combined working at both careers. He also extended his music studies, this time with **David Nathaniel Baker** who introduced Dunbar to **George Russell**'s Lydian Chromatic Concept of Tonal Organization that influenced his subsequent work. Concentrating on guitar, Dunbar was also influenced by the playing of **Wes Montgomery**, for whom he sometimes subbed in Indianapolis while maintaining a day job at a pharmacy across the street from the Ebony Missile Room, a club at which Montgomery was appearing. During the 60s Dunbar continued to live this double life, for a time working with his brother, also a qualified pharmacist, in their parents' drugstore and also for the Skillern drugstore chain. This job took him to Dallas where he heard and played with **David 'Fathead' Newman** and **Red Garland**. He then moved to New York together with saxophonist **Billy Harper**, and it was here that Dunbar was eventually able to concentrate on making music rather than making out prescriptions. In 1971 he followed **John McLaughlin** in **Tony Williams**' Lifetime. The year after this he became a faculty member at Livingston College, Rutgers University, and he also wrote books on music theory and several tutors concerned with guitar technique. From time to time he played on motion picture soundtracks and also played in Broadway show pit bands. Mostly, however, he played jazz, working and frequently recording with an impressive range of top-flight musicians, including **Sonny Rollins**, **McCoy Tyner**, **Gil Evans** (1973's *Svengali*), **Kenny Barron** (1974's *Peruvian Blue* and the following year's duo set *In Tandem*) and **Charles Mingus**. Dunbar's remarkable technical gifts and his fluency as soloist and improviser were never used at the expense of the form and content of his music making. He remained faithful to the core of his concept of jazz and through his work as a teacher helped pass on to a new generation his enthusiasm and knowledge.

● ALBUMS: with Kenny Barron *In Tandem* (Muse 1975) ★★★, *Opening Remarks* (Xanadu 1978) ★★★, *Jazz Guitarist* (Xanadu 1982) ★★★, *Gentle Time Alone* (SteepleChase 1992) ★★★.

● FURTHER READING: *New Approaches To Jazz Guitar*, Ted Dunbar. *A System Of Tonal Convergence For Improvisors, Composers & Arrangers*, Ted Dunbar. *The ii-V Cadence As A Creative Guitar Learning Device*, Ted Dunbar.

Duncan, Darryl

Duncan was born in Chicago, Illinois, USA, where he formed the funk group Cashmere in the mid-70s. Leaving the band prior to their chart successes on the Philly World label, he concentrated on songwriting, composing the attractive ballad 'Simply Beautiful' for **Jerry Butler** in 1982 and collaborating with artists including **Chaka Khan** and **Maurice White**. Moving to Los Angeles in 1986, he produced an album for Foxy Records and opened his own recording career with a track on **Motown**'s Police Academy IV film soundtrack. He signed a full-scale contract with Motown in 1987 and won immediate acclaim for the tribute single 'James Brown

(Part 1)' and for the mix of funk and soul styles on his self-produced debut album.

● ALBUMS: *Heaven* (Motown 1988) ★★★.

Duncan, Hank

b. Henry James Duncan, 26 October 1894, Bowling Green, Kentucky, USA, d. 7 June 1968, Long Island, New York, USA. In 1919, after studying piano at university, Duncan formed a small band in Louisville, Kentucky. A few years later he was in the northeast of the country before moving to New York, where he played in the popular band led by **Fess Williams**. He stayed with Williams for about five years, simultaneously carving out a reputation as a leading exponent of stride piano playing. After brief spells with **King Oliver**, **Sidney Bechet** and **Tommy Ladnier**, he joined **Fats Waller**, playing second piano. In the late 30s and early 40s he was a familiar figure on the New York club scene, playing with **Zutty Singleton**, **Mezz Mezzrow** and Bechet; recording with **Gene Sedric** and **Snub Mosley** and also as nominal leader of a trio with **Bingie Madison** and Goldie Lucas. From 1947–63, with only a 15-month absence on another gig with Singleton, he was house pianist at Nick's in New York. During this period he made records with **Tony Parenti**. Duncan continued to play at clubs but suffered a long period of ill health before his death in June 1968.

Duncan, Johnny

b. 5 October 1938, Dublin, Texas, USA. Duncan was born on a farm into a music-loving family. His cousins were Dan (of **England Dan And John Ford Coley**) and Jim Seals (of **Seals And Croft**). Duncan thought of himself as a guitarist, and it was not until his late teens that he appreciated his singing voice. Shortly after his marriage in 1959, Duncan moved to Clovis, New Mexico, and recorded demos for **Norman Petty**, although nothing evolved. In 1964, following a stint as a disc jockey in the southwest, he went to Nashville, working as a bricklayer while trying to break into the business. He was signed to **Columbia Records** and had his first US country chart entry with 'Hard Luck Joe' in 1967. Minor successes followed with 'To My Sorrow', 'You're Gonna Need Me' and 'When She Touches Me'. He also reached the charts with two duets with **June Stearns**, 'Jackson Ain't A Very Big Town' and 'Back To Back (We're Strangers)'. He became part of **Charley Pride**'s roadshow and wrote 'I'd Rather Lose You' for him. **Chet Atkins** recorded another of his compositions, 'Summer Sunday'. He had further success with 'There's Something About A Lady' and 'Baby's Smile, Woman's Kiss' and enjoyed his first US country Top 10 hit with 'Sweet Country Woman' in 1973. Duncan lost interest in country music, partly caused by his marriage breaking up, and he returned to Texas. **Larry Gatlin** contacted him and said, 'John, apart from **Ray Price** and myself, you're the best singer in Texas. Why aren't you making records?'. Gatlin produced Duncan on 'Jo And The Cowboy', and, on a hunch, he asked one of the Lea Jane Singers to sing a verse. **Janie Frickie** then became the 'mystery voice' on Duncan's following successes, finally sharing the billing on 'Come A Little Bit Closer'. Producer **Billy Sherrill** wanted Duncan relaxed for 'Stranger' and sent him to a bar for two hours. The bar-room song, which featured Frickie, was a number 4 country hit. Duncan's forte was plain-speaking songs about sleazy affairs such as 'Thinking Of A Rendezvous', 'It Couldn't Have Been Any Better' (both US country number 1s), 'Third Rate Romance'

and 'Cheatin' In The Key Of C'. Apart from his records with Frickie, he had country hits with 'She Can Put Her Shoes Under My Bed (Anytime)', 'Hello Mexico (And Adios Baby To You)' and 'Slow Dancing'. Duncan's luck faltered with an album called *The Best Is Yet To Come*. In the 80s he remarried and settled in Texas with his new wife and family and now records for minor labels. His most recent chart entry was in 1986 with 'Texas Moon'. He is not to be confused with skiffle pioneer **Johnny Duncan** of the Blue Grass Boys who died in 2000.
● ALBUMS: *Johnny One Time* (Columbia 1968) ★★★, with June Stearns *Back To Back* (Columbia 1969) ★★, *There's Something About A Lady* (Columbia 1971) ★★★, *Sweet Country Woman* (Columbia 1973) ★★★, *Come A Little Bit Closer* (Columbia 1977) ★★★, *The Best Is Yet To Come* (Columbia 1978) ★★★, *See You When The Sun Goes Down* (Columbia 1979) ★★★, *Straight From Texas* (Columbia 1979) ★★★, with Janie Frickie, Millie Kirkham And the Jordanaires *In My Dreams* (Columbia 1980) ★★★, *You're On My Mind* (Columbia 1980) ★★★, with Frickie *Nice 'N' Easy* (Columbia 1981) ★★.
● COMPILATIONS: *The Best Of Johnny Duncan* (Columbia 1976) ★★★★, *Greatest Hits* (Columbia 1989) ★★★★.

Duncan, Johnny, And The Blue Grass Boys

b. John Franklin Duncan, 7 September 1932, Oliver Springs, near Knoxville, Tennessee, USA, d. 15 July 2000, Taree, New South Wales, Australia. Duncan sang from an early age in a church choir and then, when aged 13, he joined a gospel quartet. At 16 he left Tennessee for Texas and while there he formed a country group. Duncan was drafted into the US army in 1952 and posted in England. He married an English woman, Betty, in 1953. After his demobilization, they went to the USA. Betty returned home for Christmas 1955 and, as she fell ill and needed an operation, Duncan worked in the UK for his father-in-law. He met jazz band leader **Chris Barber**, who was looking to replace **Lonnie Donegan**. Donegan had formed his own skiffle group, a fashion he had started with Barber's band. Barber was impressed by Duncan's nasal vocal delivery and physical resemblance to Donegan and immediately recruited him, and he joined them the following night at London's Royal Festival Hall. In 1957 Duncan left the band and called his own group the Blue Grass Boys in homage to **Bill Monroe**, but they were all British—**Denny Wright** (guitar), **Jack Fallon** (bass), Danny Levan (violin) and **Lennie Hastings** (drums). Although promoted as a skiffle artist, Duncan was a straight country performer, both in terms of arrangements and repertoire. 'Last Train To San Fernando', a Trinidad calypso he re-arranged, steamed up the UK charts, but the communication cord was pulled just before it reached the top. The b-side, 'Rock-A-Billy Baby', was equally strong. Duncan was featured on BBC Television's *6.5 Special* and hosted radio programmes for the BBC and **Radio Luxembourg**, but he only had two more Top 30 entries, 'Blue Blue Heartache' and 'Footprints In The Snow', which both reached number 27. Duncan subsequently worked as a country singer in UK clubs and encouraged local talent. In 1974 he emigrated to Melbourne, Australia, and continued to work there until his death from cancer in 2000.
● ALBUMS: *Johnny Duncan's Tennessee Songbag* (Columbia 1957) ★★★, *Johnny Duncan Salutes Hank Williams* (Columbia 1958) ★★★, *Beyond The Sunset* (1961) ★★★,

Back In Town (1970) ★★, *The World Of Country Music* (Decca 1973) ★★★.
● COMPILATIONS: *Last Train To San Fernando* 4-CD box set (Bear Family 1997) ★★★★, *Last Train, From Tennessee To Taree* (Roller Coaster 2001) ★★★.

Duncan, Lesley

b. 12 August 1943, Stockton-on-Tees, England. This singer and songwriter, who first recorded in 1963, became popular in the commercial side of the folk music field in the early 70s. Although starting out as a songwriter and married to record producer Jimmy Horowitz, she became better known for her work as a session singer, especially during the 60s and 70s. She had sung backing vocals on a number of hits including 'Goo Goo Barabajagal' (**Donovan**) and 'Back Off Boogaloo' (**Ringo Starr**) and had participated on a vast amount of albums for **Dusty Springfield**, the UK **Nirvana** and **Elton John**. It was his version of her composition 'Love Song', on *Tumbleweed Connection*, that inspired her to record *Sing Children Sing*. That and her other albums suffered from a lack of commercial success, which was at odds with her huge popularity as a backing singer on a host of albums by acts as diverse as **Long John Baldry**, **Tim Hardin**, Donovan, the **Alan Parsons Project** (*Eve*), **Pink Floyd** (*Dark Side Of The Moon*) and even Bunk Dogger. After her two releases on **CBS Records** she left the label, and subsequent releases were on GM Records. Her reluctance to perform live did not help to raise her public profile. Apart from providing backing vocals for an album by Exiled, in 1980, her name has sadly been missing from sleeve note credits. Her own recording career saw the release of a few more singles, but since 1988 she has remained relatively quiet.
● ALBUMS: *Sing Children Sing* (CBS 1971) ★★★★, *Earth Mother* (CBS 1972) ★★★, *Everything Changes* (GM 1974) ★★★, *Moonbathing* (GM 1975) ★★★, *Maybe It's Lost* (GM/MCA 1977) ★★.

Duncan, Todd

b. Robert Todd Duncan, 12 February 1903, Danville, Kentucky, USA, d. 28 February 1998, Washington, DC, USA. (Some sources give this artist's year of birth as 1900.) A splendid baritone singer, actor and teacher, Duncan is remembered particularly for creating the role of Porgy in America's most popular opera *Porgy And Bess*. After attending Butler's University and the College of Fine Arts in Indianapolis, he became a music teacher in Louisville, Kentucky. In 1931 he was appointed Professor of Voice at Howard University in Washington (a post he held until 1945) and began his operatic career three years later in a production of Mascagni's *Cavalleria Rusticana* with the Aeollian Opera. His performance was seen by *New York Times* critic Olin Downes, who put forward Duncan's name when **George Gershwin** was auditioning around 100 baritones for the role of Porgy. However, Duncan considered himself to be an opera singer and thought Gershwin rather 'Tin Pan Alley'. On their first meeting, after Duncan had sung only 12 measures of an Italian aria, Gershwin said: 'Will you be my Porgy?'. Incredibly, Duncan prevaricated, replying: 'Well, Mr. Gershwin, I've gotta hear your music first.' He soon realized the importance of the man and his music and accepted the part. Duncan stayed with *Porgy And Bess* for all 124 performances of its original 1935 Broadway run, introducing immortal numbers such as 'Bess, You Is My

Woman Now' and 'I Got Plenty O' Nuttin'". He later co-starred with his Bess (Anne Brown) on the cast album and in **Cheryl Crawford**'s 1942 revival. In 1938 Duncan joined Stewart Granger, Edna Best and **Adelaide Hall** at London's Theatre Royal, Drury Lane, in *The Sun Never Sets*, a play adapted from the West Indian stories of Edgar Wallace. Two of his numbers were the suitably atmospheric 'Drums' and 'River God'. Duncan returned to Broadway with distinguished appearances in the musicals *Cabin In The Sky* (1940, as the Lawd's General) and *Lost In The Stars* (1949, as Stephen Kumalo). In the latter, which was adapted from Alan Paton's novel *Cry, The Beloved Country*, he sang the title song and was acclaimed for his sensitive performance of a black Anglican minister whose son is sentenced to hang after killing a white man. In 1945, the same year he relinquished his post at Howard University, Duncan became the first black artist (in an otherwise all-white cast) to appear at the New York City Opera when he sang the role of Tonio in Leoncavallo's *Pagliacci*. He was then at the height of his career and continued to perform in opera and gave recitals in numerous countries as well as teaching at Howard University, the Curtis Institute of Music in Philadelphia and at his home in Washington. In 1942 Duncan was seen briefly on screen in *Syncopation*, a film tracing the history of jazz in fictional form, and in 1955 he played the part of Bill Howard in the prison drama *Unchained* and sang **Hy Zaret** and **Alex North**'s 'Unchained Melody', which has endured over the years. Duncan himself remained active for most of his life, but a few months before his death at the age of 95, he was too weak to attend a symposium on *Porgy And Bess* at the University of Michigan. Instead, he sent his good wishes and a rendition of 'Bess, You Is My Woman Now' on tape.

Duncan, Tommy

b. Thomas Elmer Duncan, 11 January 1911, Hillsboro, Texas, USA, d. 25 July 1967. Duncan grew up loving the music of **Jimmie Rodgers** and made the start of a long musical career in 1932 when he joined **Bob Wills** in the **Light Crust Doughboys**. When Wills quit in 1933 to form his own band, Duncan went with him to become one of Wills' original Texas Playboys. He stayed with Wills until 1948 when, probably tired of fronting the band in Wills' absences caused mainly by his drinking, he left to form his own band, the Western All Stars, taking with him several Texas Playboys. During his years with Wills they co-wrote several songs, and Duncan's fine baritone vocals appeared on countless recordings, including the 1940 million-selling 'New San Antonio Rose'. In 1949, recording for **Capitol Records**, he registered his only solo chart hit with his version of the Jimmie Rodgers song 'Gambling Polka Dot Blues'. In 1959 Wills and Duncan were reunited and in 1960–61 they recorded over 40 sides for **Liberty Records**. Although he made no further recordings with Wills, Duncan remained active until his death following an heart attack in July 1967. It is impossible to separate the careers of Duncan and Wills and most experts have maintained that in their solo work, neither one ever recaptured the greatness of their partnership.

● ALBUMS: with Bob Wills *Together Again* (Liberty 1960) ★★★, with Wills *Bob Wills & Tommy Duncan* (Liberty 1961) ★★★.

● COMPILATIONS: with Bob Wills *Legendary Masters—Bob Wills & Tommy Duncan* (United Artists 1971) ★★★,

Texas Moon (Bear Family 1996) ★★★, *Beneath A Neon Star In A Honky Tonk* (Bear Family 1996) ★★★.

Duncan, Trevor

b. Leonard Charles Trebilco, 27 February 1924, Camberwell, London, England. Duncan is a talented composer whose unique style has been in great demand from many publishers for their mood music libraries. At the age of 18 he joined the BBC as a sound and balance engineer, and wartime service in the RAF (allowing him to play with many different bands) increased his awareness of the needs of musicians. Back at the BBC he paid great attention to mundane matters such as microphone placings, but all this was invaluable experience for the recording career that was to follow. Encouraged by conductor **Ray Martin**, in 1949 Duncan showed his composition 'High Heels' to publishers Boosey & Hawkes, and it was immediately accepted. The next year **Sidney Torch** recorded it for **Parlophone**, and it was a great success (Duncan privately admitted the influence of **David Rose**'s 'Holiday For Strings'). A conflict arose between Duncan's BBC career (which did not allow the exploitation of his own music) and the natural wishes of his publishers to promote his undoubted composing talents. In 1956 he accepted the inevitable and decided to concentrate solely on writing. Such was his output that Boosey & Hawkes could not handle everything he wrote, so his works began to appear in the recorded music libraries of other London publishers.

In 1959 **Ron Goodwin** recorded 'The Girl From Corsica', and soon afterwards BBC Television chose Duncan's march from 'A Little Suite' as the theme music for *Dr. Finlay's Casebook*. Both pieces made a great impact on the public, and they remain popular standards of light music. Other works of note included 'Tomboy', 'Panoramic Splendour', 'Overland To Oregon', 'Twentieth Century Express', 'Enchanted April', 'Little Debbie', 'Still Waters', 'A Vision In Velvet', 'The Unwanted', 'The Challenge Of Space', 'Children In The Park', 'The House Of Tranquillity', 'The Visionaries', 'The Spirit Of Industry', 'Meadow Mist', 'The Wine Festival', 'Schooner Bay', 'Broad Horizons' and 'Passage To Windward'. Many of his pieces convey his love of sailing. 'Citizens Of The World' was used in an early ITV series *The Planemakers*, and one of Duncan's short works, 'Grand Vista', was used with great effect on Pearl and Dean advertising features in the cinema. His most serious orchestral work is 'Sinfonia Tellurica' (1970), depicting the Elements measured against mankind's endeavours and achievements. In his later career he has combined his interest in mathematics with electronic music.

● ALBUMS: *British Light Music—Trevor Duncan* (Marco Polo 1995) ★★★★.

Dundas, David

b. c.1945, Oxford, England. The son of the Marquess of Zetland, Dundas' original vocation in life was as an actor, mainly playing minor roles on stage, television and film, at one point working alongside Judy Geeson and David Niven in *Prudence And The Pill* (1968). Eschewing the actor's life, Dundas' claim to fame in the music world came when, as an advertising jingle writer, his work for the Brutus jeans advert on UK television spawned the hit single 'Jeans On'. The Dundas composition was fleshed out with help from **Roger Greenaway** and released on the Air/**Chrysalis Records** label, eventually reaching number 3 in the UK charts in the summer of 1976. The tune also reached the US Top 20 in

January the following year. His only other UK chart entry came in 1977 with 'Another Funny Honeymoon', which reached number 29. He released two, for the most part unremarkable albums for Chrysalis before taking up a career as a composer. His recent credits include the scores for *Dark City*, *Withnail And I* (with Rick Wentworth) and *How To Get Ahead In Advertising*.

● ALBUMS: *David Dundas* (Air 1977) ★★, *Vertical Hold* (Air 1978) ★★.

Dunford, Uncle Eck

b. Alex (sometimes given as Aleck) Dunford, 1878, Carroll County, West Virginia, USA, d. 1953. Dunford, who was a brilliant fiddle player and almost as good on guitar, was a very intelligent person in an area where schooling was of secondary importance. Usually fondly referred to as Uncle Eck, he could sing and had an especially commanding speaking voice, using a drawling accent totally unlike the local dialect. He surprised many with his ability to quote Shakespeare or Burns and recite monologues, and he also studied photography. In 1908 he married Callie Frost, a relative of Ernest Stoneman's future wife Hattie, and he became involved in the **Stoneman Family**'s music. A lonely figure after his wife died in 1921, he lived in a small cabin (which still stands) a mile from Galax at Ballard Branch. He concentrated more and more on his music and played fiddle for Stoneman's Dixie Mountaineers and also made solo **Victor** recordings.

In 1932, when Ernest Stoneman left the Galax area, Dunford began to play with the Ward Family and made recordings with them and with the Ballard Branch Bogtrotters for the Library of Congress. He began appearing at the Galax Fiddlers Convention from the mid-30s until his death *circa* July 1953. Sadly, in his latter years, he was regularly seen on the streets of Galax selling pencils to support himself. Examples of his work appear on many Stoneman Family albums, while he is also remembered for solo recordings such as his monologue 'My First Bicycle Ride' and his song 'Old Shoes And Leggins'', the latter being issued on a **Folkways Records** compilation. A considerable amount of information about Uncle Eck who, apart from his instrumental and vocal talents was probably one of the genre's first comedians, may be found in Ivan M. Tribe's book *The Stoneman Family*.

Dungeon Family

This rap supergroup owes its existence on record to the phenomenal sales success of **Outkast**'s 2000 recording, *Stankonia*. Andre Benjamin and Antoine Patton's label boss, **L.A. Reid**, gave them the permission to record an album with some of the leading artists on the Atlanta, Georgia rap scene, including members of **Goodie Mob** and the **Organized Noize** production team. Lesser known collaborators included Witchdoctor and Backbone. All the artists had worked with each other during the previous decade but never managed to put out a record together. Drawing inspiration from **George Clinton**'s work with the **Funkadelic** and **Parliament** collectives, *Even In Darkness* maintained a fearsome party groove over the course of its 14 tracks. The album confirmed Atlanta as one of the creative epicentres of hip-hop at the start of the new millennium.

● ALBUMS: *Even In Darkness* (Arista 2001) ★★★★.

Dunger, Nicolai

b. Sweden. It is hard to believe this eccentric Swedish singer-songwriter almost chose to be a professional soccer player, not a career readily associated with a performer who has earned favourable comparisons to maverick US alt country artist **Will Oldham**. After eschewing soccer in favour of music, Dunger signed a short-term recording contract with the Telegram label and made his album debut in 1996 with the experimental *Songs Wearing Clothes*. The follow-up *Eventide* was an even more esoteric recording, with classical flourishes provided by the string quartet Tämmelkvartetten. With sales of both albums barely registering in the thousands, Dunger was forced to carry on working as a gardener to make ends meet. His musical career was given a much-needed push by a chance meeting with Ebbot Lundberg of cult favourites **Soundtrack Of Our Lives**. The two men collaborated together on the EP *First Born Track* and 1999's *The Cloud Is Learning*. The latter, distributed through **Virgin Records**, saw Dunger eschewing some of the wayward experimentalism of his earlier work and revealed a sly, melodic touch.

True to form, Dunger announced that his next project would be a limited edition vinyl-only trilogy. The first instalment, *Blind Blemished Blues*, was recorded in collaboration with the **Esbjörn Svensson** Trio and was only made available through Dunger's online store. At the same time, Dunger teamed up with Svensson's trio to record the comparatively easy listening *Soul Rush*. The album was distributed through Virgin and provided Dunger with his international breakthrough. Many critics drew favourable comparisons to **Van Morrison**'s classic 1968 recording *Astral Weeks*, owing to Dunger's seamless fusion of jazz, rock and country. The prolific Swede then released the final two instalments of his vinyl trilogy, *A Dress Book* and *Sweat Her Kiss*, before travelling to America to record his next mainstream album, *Tranquil Isolation*, with Will and Paul Oldham.

● ALBUMS: *Songs Wearing Clothes* (Jazzbeat/Telegram 1996) ★★, *Eventide* (Atrium/Warners 1997) ★★★, *This Cloud Is Learning* (Dolores/Virgin 1999) ★★★, *Soul Rush* (Dolores/Virgin 2001) ★★★★, *Blind Blemished Blues* (Nicolai Dunger Communication/Hot Stuff 2001) ★★★, *A Dress Book* (Nicolai Dunger Communication/Hot Stuff 2001) ★★★, *Sweat Her Kiss* (Nicolai Dunger Communication/Hot Stuff 2002) ★★★, *Tranquil Isolation* (Dolores/Virgin 2002) ★★★★, *Here's My Song, You Can Have It . . . I Don't Want It Anymore/Yours 4-Ever* (Dolores/Virgin 2004) ★★★.

● COMPILATIONS: *The Vinyl Trilogy* 3-CD box set (Nicolai Dunger Communication/Virgin 2002) ★★★.

Dunham, Sonny

b. Elmer Lewis Dunham, 16 November 1914, Brockton, Massachusetts, USA, d. 1 July 1990, Miami, Florida, USA. Dunham learned to play several brass instruments and by the early 20s he was proficient enough to be hired by the popular band leader **Ben Bernie**. With Bernie he played trombone, but a later engagement with the **Paul Tremaine** Orchestra found him also playing trumpet. In the early 30s, after a brief spell leading his own band, he joined the **Casa Loma Orchestra** where his high-note solos attracted considerable attention. His feature-spot with this unit came in 'Memories Of You', a song that he adopted as his theme when he formed a new band in 1937. Like some other band leaders struggling to stand out among the many groups of the swing era, Dunham tried a gimmick—most of his sidemen doubled on trumpet—but this did not prove to be a great crowd-puller. For all his band's imperfections, Dunham employed several good musicians, among them the outstanding future lead trumpeter **Pete Candoli**. After the band folded he divided his time between studio work and occasional appearances with name outfits. From time to time, during the 50s and 60s, he assembled bands for special engagements.

● COMPILATIONS: *Sonny Dunham On The Air* 1942-44 recordings (Aircheck 1979) ★★★, *One Night Stand With Sonny Dunham* 1944-46 recordings (Golden Era 1989) ★★★.

Dunhill Records

The Dunhill label was inaugurated in Los Angeles, USA, in 1965 by **Lou Adler**, Jay Lasker and Bobby Roberts. Of the three partners, it was Adler who proved the driving force. An experienced songwriter, record producer and manager, he was the guiding light behind **Jan And Dean** and **Johnny Rivers** and already operated the successful Trousdale publishing house. Its premier compositional team, **P.F. Sloan** and **Steve Barri**, were responsible for many of Dunhill's early releases, notably 'Eve Of Destruction', a million-selling protest disc for **Barry McGuire**. In turn this singer introduced the fledgling **Mamas And The Papas** to Adler. Their sumptuous harmonies were captured in a series of memorable singles, notably 'California Dreamin'' and 'Monday Monday', and such releases established Dunhill at the vanguard of the folk rock movement. Another melodically-inclined act, the **Grass Roots**, emerged from a Sloan/Barri experiment to enjoy consistent chart success with their distinctive brand of mainstream pop. **Steppenwolf** and **Three Dog Night** were among Dunhill's bestselling acts of the late 60s, but by this point the label's character had completely altered. The Mamas and The Papas had split up, the Sloan/Barri partnership was sundered and Adler had sold his share in the company to **ABC**/Paramount. In 1967 he founded Ode, striking an international hit with **Scott McKenzie**'s 'San Francisco (Be Sure To Wear Flowers In Your Hair)'. The Dunhill name was retained until 1974, when its roster switched to the parent company.

Duning, George

b. 25 February 1908, Richmond, Indiana, USA, d. 27 February 2000, San Diego, California, USA. A composer and conductor for films from the 40s through to the 80s. Duning studied at the University of Cincinnati and the Cincinnati Conservatory Of Music, becoming a jazz and symphonic trumpet player. He was a sideman and chief arranger for the **Kay Kyser** Band in the early 40s when Kyser was one of the biggest attractions in the business. Around the same time, he began to arrange and orchestrate music for films, and in 1946 he collaborated with Irving Gertz to write the score for *The Devil's Mask*. Between then and 1950, he scored some 21 features for Columbia, a mixture of thrillers, melodramas, westerns and comedies. These included *Mysterious Intruder*; *Johnny O'Clock* and *To The Ends Of Earth*, starring **Dick Powell**; *The Guilt Of Janet James*; *I Love Trouble*; *The Man From Colorado*; *Shockproof*; *The Dark Past*; *The Undercover Man* and *And Baby Makes Three*. Duning also scored *Down To Earth* and *The Gallant Blade*, both starring Larry Parks, and Parks appeared once more in *Jolson Sings Again*, for which Duning gained the first of five Oscar nominations.

Three of the others were awarded to Duning in the 50s for his work on *From Here To Eternity*, **The Eddy Duchin Story** and *Picnic* (1955). The latter's theme music, used extremely effectively on the soundtrack in conjunction with the 1934 melody 'Moonglow', became a US number 1 for Morris Stolloff And His Orchestra and a substantial hit for pianist **George Cates**. A lyric was added by **Steve Allen**. Duning's other scores during the 50s and 60s included *Lorna Doone*; *Man In The Saddle*; *Scandal Sheet*; *Last Of The Commanches*; *Salome*; *Houseboat*; *Bell, Book And Candle*; *Cowboy*; *The World Of Suzie Wong*; *The Devil At 4 O'Clock*; *Toys In The Attic*; *My Blood Runs Cold* and *Any Wednesday*. In the 60s and 70s, apart from the occasional feature such as *Arnold* (1973), *Terror In The Wax Museum* (1976) and *The Man With Bogart's Face* (1980), which was George Raft's last film, Duning concentrated on writing for television. He scored several films such as *Then Came Bronson*, *Quarantined*, *But I Don't Want To Get Married!*, *Yuma*, *Black Noon*, *Climb An Angry Mountain*, *The Woman Hunter*, *Honour Thy Father*, *The Abduction Of Saint Anne*, *The Top Of The Hill*, *The Dream Merchants* and *Goliath Waits* (1981). He also contributed music to numerous television series, including *Star Trek*, *The Partridge Family* and *Houseboat*.

Dunkley, Errol

b. 1951, Kingston, Jamaica, West Indies. Dunkley had already recorded his first records, a duet with **Roy Shirley** entitled 'Gypsy' for Lindel Pottinger's Gaydisc label, 'My Queen' with **Junior English** for **Prince Buster** and 'Love Me Forever', issued on the Rio label in 1965, all by the ripe old age of 14. Between 1967 and 1968 he recorded 'Please Stop Your Lying', 'I'm Going Home', 'I'm Not Your Man' and 'You're Gonna Need Me' for **Joe Gibbs** before switching to **Coxsone Dodd** in 1969 where he recorded 'Satisfaction' and 'Get Up Now', among others.

In 1971 he recorded a medley of his Joe Gibbs hits entitled 'Three In One', 'Deep Meditation' and 'Darling Ooh' for **Rupie Edwards**. In an attempt to achieve musical and financial autonomy he teamed up with fellow singer **Gregory Isaacs** to form the African Museum label, achieving a local success with a version of **Delroy Wilson**'s 'I Don't Know Why', retitled 'Movie Star'. However, the partnership collapsed and Dunkley went on to form his own Silver Ring label, although no hits were forthcoming. In 1972 producer Jimmy Radway recorded him on two of his best sides: 'Keep The Pressure On' and the big hit 'Black Cinderella'. An album also emerged produced by **Sonia Pottinger**, entitled *Presenting Errol Dunkley* (re-released in 1981 as *Darling Ooh*), an excellent selection of originals and cover versions, including the classic, self-penned 'A Little Way Different'.

Throughout the first half of the 70s Dunkley appeared on a variety of labels, recording a number of fine singles including 'Little Angel', 'Oh Lord', 'Where Must I Go', 'Down Below' and 'Act True To Your Man'. The second half of the decade saw Dunkley gaining successes among the UK reggae fraternity with tunes such as 'I'm Your Man' and 'Eunoch Power' for **Winston 'Niney' Holness**, 'Stop Your Gun Shooting' for **Tapper Zukie** and a new version of 'A Little Way Different' for **Dennis Bovell**. His biggest success, however, came in 1979 with his rendition of **John Holt**'s naggingly catchy 'OK Fred', which appealed to the pop sensibilities of Britain's wider record-buying public, rising to number 11 in the UK national charts in September of that year and leading to unforgettable performances on great British television institutions such as **Top Of The Pops** and *Basil Brush*. Further forays into pop chart success proved elusive, and Dunkley, now resident in the UK, had to be satisfied with the continued grassroots popularity of records such as 'Happiness Forgets', 'Rush Me No Badness', 'If I Can't Have You', 'Come Natural' and a version of the **Stylistics'** 'Betcha By Golly Wow'.

● ALBUMS: *Presenting Errol Dunkley* (Gay Feet 1972) ★★★★, *OK Fred* (Third World 1979) ★★★, *Profile* (Third World 1980) ★★★, *Special Request* (1987) ★★, *Aquarius* (1989) ★★★.

● COMPILATIONS: *OK Fred: The Best Of Errol Dunkley* (Trojan 2004) ★★★★.

Dunlap, Larry

b. 13 June 1948, Forest Grove, Oregon, USA. Raised in a very musical family, Dunlap played baritone horn in the school band and while still in high school played piano with a local dance band the Dell Herreid Orchestra. At Lewis and Clark College in Portland, Oregon, Dunlap majored in composition. After graduating he played in and wrote for various jazz groups in Portland including the Tom Albering Trio, which included vocalist **Nancy King**, and also played with **Leroy Vinnegar** and **Ralph Towner**. Since the 70s Dunlap has been based in San Francisco, playing with many artists including **Pointer Sisters** and **Country Joe McDonald**. In the late 70s, Dunlap met and later married singer **Bobbe Norris**. Around 1980 he began a musical relationship with **Cleo Laine** and **John Dankworth** that endured into the early 00s and included recording at Carnegie Hall. Among others with whom he has performed and sometimes recorded are **Ernestine Anderson**, **Larry Coryell**, **Art Farmer**, **James Moody**, **Gerry Mulligan**, **Rebecca Parris** and **Mark Murphy**.

Dunlap's many compositions and arrangements include music for big bands and classical music ensembles. In the 70s he received an NEA grant to compose 'Immersion: A Water Suite For Jazz Quartet And Chamber Orchestra'. His long and fruitful musical association with the Cape Verde-born composer Amandio Cabral has resulted in several albums including *Why Not Forever*, *Sonho Azul: Blue Dream* and *Fly With My Love*. Early influences on Dunlap as pianist include **André Previn**, **Herbie Hancock**, **Oscar Peterson** and **Chick Corea**. Influences upon him as arranger and composer include **Gerry Mulligan**, **Gil Evans**, **Antonio Carlos Jobim** and Ivan Lins, as well as many classical composers. Through the 90s and into the early 00s, Dunlap has worked as music editor with the Sher Music Company. In the early 00s, Dunlap was active as piano teacher, giving lessons both privately and with students at Mills College, Oakland, California. In the early 00s Dunlap's schedule included appearances and tours with Norris, Laine and Dankworth, Murphy, Parris, Anderson and **Ernie Watts**.

● ALBUMS: *Why Not Forever* (Coit 1994) ★★★, *Evolution: Cape Verde—USA* (Coit) ★★★, *Sonho Azul: Blue Dream* (Coit 1998) ★★★, *Fly With My Love* (Coit 2001) ★★★, *Jazz!* (Coit) ★★★.

Dunmall, Paul

b. Welling, Kent, England. Tenor and soprano saxophonist Dunmall has built a striking reputation among fellow postmodernists. After starting on the clarinet at the age of 12, Dunmall graduated to alto and then tenor and joined his first band while still at school. He toured Europe with the *avant garde* rock group Marsupilami in 1969 before moving to America in the mid-70s where he played with **Alice Coltrane** and **Johnny 'Guitar' Watson** among others. Dunmall returned to England in 1976 and three years later co-founded the excellent modern jazz quartet **Spirit Level**. In 1985 he joined **Alan Skidmore** in Tenor Tonic and the following year formed the Paul Dunmall Quartet with Tony Moore, **Alex Maguire** and **Steve Noble**. Among the other artists with whom Dunmall has subsequently worked are **Elton Dean**, **Keith Tippett**, **Annie Whitehead**, **Paul Rogers**, **Mark Sanders**, **Tony Levin** and John Adams, in addition to being a member of **Mujician** and the **London Jazz Composers Orchestra**.

An untrammelled improviser, Dunmall has a deep sense of the roots of jazz and is also able to absorb into his playing other musical forms, including classical and, perhaps surprisingly, folk. Dunmall's vigorous and adventurous improvisations area place intellectual and emotional demands upon his listeners and his uncompromising approach to his music has kept him away from widespread popular acceptance. Nevertheless, within the improvised music coterie his reputation has flourished. By the time of the late 90s set *Bebop Starburst*, his name was being recognized farther afield and his talents much more widely accepted. Additionally, and without diminishing his status as a major improviser, Dunmall has also developed as a skilled writer.

● ALBUMS: *Soliloquy* (Matchless 1986) ★★★, *Quartet And Sextet/Babu* (Slam 1993) ★★★★, with Paul Rogers *Folks* (Slam 1993) ★★★, with Tony Levin *Spiritual Empathy: Duets 1994* (Rare 1995) ★★★, with Evan Parker, Barry Guy, Levin *Birmingham Concert* 1993 recording (Rare 1996) ★★★, with John Adams, Mark Sanders *Ghostly Thoughts* (hatOLOGY 1996) ★★★★, *Desire And Liberation* (Slam 1996) ★★★, with Adams, Sanders *Totally Fried Up* (Slam 1998) ★★★, *Bebop Starburst* (Cuneiform 1999) ★★★★, with Tony Bianco, Simon Picard *Utoma Trio* (Emanem 1999) ★★★, *The Great Divide* (Cuneiform 2001) ★★★, with Tony Bianco *I You* (FMR 2002) ★★★, with Rogers, Kevin Norton *Rylickolum: For Your Pleasure* (CIMP 2004) ★★★, with Moksha Big Band *I Wish You Peace* (Cuneiform 2005) ★★★★, *Love Warmth And Compassion* (FMR 2005) ★★★, with Rogers, Norton *Go Forth Duck* (CIMP 2005) ★★★, *Bridging The Great Divide Live* (Clean Feed 2005) ★★.

Dunn, Clive

b. 9 January 1920, London, England. Dunn became a professional actor in his youth, appearing in minor stage and film roles in the 30s. His career was interrupted by military service during World War II, during which he spent four years as a prisoner of war. His career remained low key into the 60s, with film appearances, again in minor roles, in *You Must Be Joking!* (1965) and *Just Like A Woman* (1968). He also appeared on the small screen, working with several leading names in British television comedy including Tony Hancock and Dickie Henderson. It was in 1968 that he made his breakthrough into the national consciousness. In that year he again made some film appearances including *30 Is A Dangerous Age*, *Cynthia* and *The Bliss Of Mrs. Blossom*. It was, however, a television role that made him a recognizable face; this came when, despite being only 48 at the time, he was cast as the venerable veteran solider Lance-Corporal

Jones in the situation comedy *Dad's Army*. With a steady supply of reminiscences about forgotten wars where the enemy used spears and the British army bayonets, he had catch phrases such as 'They don't like it up 'em' and especially 'Don't panic! Don't panic!', the latter passing into the general public's vocabulary.

During *Dad's Army*'s long run Dunn continued to make films including 1969's *The Magic Christian* and *Crooks And Coronets* and in 1971, a film version of *Dad's Army*. He also enjoyed a novelty UK chart-topper at the start of 1971 with 'Grandad', co-written by session man **Herbie Flowers**, which was in the UK charts for 27 weeks. The song was taken from an album Dunn recorded for **Columbia Records** *Permission To Sing Sir*. After *Dad's Army* ended in 1977 Dunn played the lead in his series, *Grandad* (1979), for children's television. In the 80s he made more film appearances including *The Fiendish Plot Of Dr. Fu Manchu* (1980) and the television production *Much Ado About Nothing* (1984). Later in the decade he published his autobiography and retired to Portugal with his wife.

● ALBUMS: *Permission To Sing Sir* aka *Grandad Requests Permission To Sing Sir!* (Columbia/MFP 1970) ★★★.

● FURTHER READING: *Permission To Speak*, Clive Dunn.

● FILMS: *Boys Will Be Boys* (1935), *Good Morning, Boys* (1937), *A Yank At Oxford* (1938), *The Treasure Of San Teresa* aka *Hot Money Girl* (1959), *What A Whopper* (1961), *She'll Have To Go* aka *Maid For Murder* (1962), *The Fast Lady* (1962), *The Mouse On The Moon* (1963), *You Must Be Joking!* (1965), *The Mini-Affair* aka *The Mini-Mob* (1967), *Just Like A Woman* (1968), *30 Is A Dangerous Age, Cynthia* (1968), *The Bliss Of Mrs. Blossom* (1968), *Crooks And Coronets* aka *Sophia's Place* (1969), *The Magic Christian* (1969), *Dad's Army* (1971), *The Fiendish Plot Of Dr. Fu Manchu* (1980).

Dunn, Holly

b. Holly Suzette Dunn, 22 August 1957, San Antonio, Texas, USA. Dunn's father was a preacher and her mother a professional artist, but they encouraged their children to sing and entertain. Dunn learned guitar and became a lead vocalist with the Freedom Folk Singers, representing Texas in the White House bicentennial celebrations. After university she joined her brother, Chris Waters (Chris Waters Dunn), who had moved to Nashville as a songwriter (he wrote 'Sexy Eyes' for **Dr. Hook**). Together they wrote 'Out Of Sight, Not Out Of Mind' for **Cristy Lane**. Among her other songs are 'An Old Friend' (**Terri Gibbs**), 'Love Someone Like Me' (**New Grass Revival**), 'Mixed Emotions' (Bruce Murray, brother of **Anne Murray**) and 'That Old Devil Moon' (**Marie Osmond**). Dunn sang on numerous demos in Nashville. Her self-named album for the MTM label in 1986, and her own composition 'Daddy's Hands', drew considerable attention. *Across The Rio Grande* was a traditional yet contemporary country album featuring **Vince Gill** and **Sam Bush** and it won much acclaim. However, MTM went into liquidation and Dunn moved to **Warner Brothers Records**. Her up-tempo 'You Really Had Me Going' was a country number 1 and other country hits include 'Only When I Love', 'Strangers Again' and 'That's What Your Love Does To Me'. Her 'greatest hits' set, *Milestones*, aroused some controversy when she issued one of its tracks, the newly recorded 'Maybe I Mean Yes' as a single. The song was accused of downplaying the trauma of date rape, and Dunn was sufficiently upset to ask radio stations not to play the record.

Her career was restored to equilibrium with the low-key but impressive *Getting It Dunn* in 1992. This was her last album for Warner, and she subsequently signed to the independent label River North.

● ALBUMS: *Holly Dunn* (MTM 1986) ★★★, *Cornerstone* (MTM 1987) ★★★, *Across The Rio Grande* (MTM 1988) ★★★, *The Blue Rose Of Texas* (Warners 1989) ★★★, *Heart Full Of Love* (Warners 1990) ★★★, *Getting It Dunn* (Warners 1992) ★★★, *Life And Love And All The Stages* (River North 1995) ★★, *Leave One Bridge Standing* (River North 1997) ★★, *Daddy's Hands* (Platinum Disc 2005) ★★★.

● COMPILATIONS: *Milestones: Greatest Hits* (Warners 1991) ★★★.

● DVD/VIDEOS: *Cowboys Are My Weakness* (River North 1995).

Dunn, Johnny

b. 19 February 1897, Memphis, Tennessee, USA, d. 20 August 1937, Paris, France. Starting out in midwest theatres, Dunn played trumpet as a solo act before joining **W.C. Handy**'s band with which he travelled to New York in 1917. He also played with singers such as **Mamie Smith** and **Edith Wilson**, recording in the early 20s. In 1923 he went to Europe with a band led by Will Vodery and returned there three years later when he recorded in London with the Plantation Orchestra. He also played with **Noble Sissle**'s band in France. During the early and mid-30s he worked steadily in Europe, being resident for some time in the Netherlands. Dunn was among the best of the musicians playing in the immediate pre-jazz years and he influenced many of his contemporaries. Overshadowed though he was by the arrival of **Louis Armstrong**, Dunn was still an able and gifted player, showing subtle power and using complex patterns that never descended into mere showmanship. His stylistic roots became outmoded during the 30s, but his decision to remain in Europe and his early death meant that his reputation never suffered, except, perhaps, by neglect, and today he can be recognized as having been a highly accomplished trumpeter.

● COMPILATIONS: with Edith Wilson *Complete Recorded Works In Chronological Order: Volume 1 1921–1922* (RST 2000) ★★★, *Complete Recorded Works In Chronological Order: Volume 2 1922–1928* (RST 2000) ★★★, *Cornet Blues* (Frog 2000) ★★★.

Dunn, Ronnie
(see **Brooks And Dunn**)

Dunn, Roy

b. 13 April 1922, Eatonton, Georgia, USA, d. 2 March 1988, Atlanta, Georgia, USA. Dunn was a blues guitarist and singer who had learned from and played with Georgia artists such as **Curley Weaver**, **Buddy Moss** and **'Blind' Willie McTell** in the 30s, although he was of a younger generation. This meant that he missed out on recording at a time when his style of music was at its most commercially popular. In his younger days he sang in a family gospel quartet, the Dunn Brothers, then between the late 30s and early 40s he toured with a series of other gospel groups. In the early 70s he recorded an album and appeared at a number of blues festivals. He was also credited as a major source of information and contacts by researchers into the blues of the east coast states.

● ALBUMS: *Know'd Them All* (1974) ★★★.

Dunne, Irene

b. Irene Marie Dunn, 20 December 1898, Louisville, Kentucky, USA, d. 4 September 1990, Los Angeles, California, USA. After studying at the Chicago Musical College, Dunne tried unsuccessfully to become an opera singer. Instead, her long and hugely successful career began in musical comedies. She played in a touring company version of *Irene* (1920) and then in New York productions of *The Clinging Vine* (1922) and *The City Chap* (1925). She was in a **Florenz Ziegfeld** touring company production of **Jerome Kern**'s *Show Boat* (1929), playing Magnolia, when she attracted the composer's attention. It was through his insistence that she gained the title role in the film version of his *Sweet Adeline* (1935) with lyrics by **Oscar Hammerstein II**, which was followed quickly by more films with Kern music: *Roberta* (1935), *Show Boat* (1936) and *High, Wide And Handsome* (1937), the latter two with lyrics by Hammerstein.

Dunne made more appearances in screen musicals, notably *Joy Of Living* (1938) and *Love Affair* (1939), but then turned almost exclusively to straight dramatic roles, becoming in the process one of Hollywood's most respected actresses. She was nominated unsuccessfully five times as Best Actress. Among her non-musical films are *Cimarron* (1931), *The Awful Truth* (1937), *Anna And The King Of Siam* (1946), *Life With Father* (1947), *I Remember Mama* (1948) and *The Mudlark* (1950). Also in 1950 Dunne made her only return to a musical film, co-starring with **Fred MacMurray** in *Never A Dull Moment*. Following her retirement from films in 1952 she worked in politics, being appointed by President Eisenhower in 1957 as an alternate delegate to the United Nations, and in commerce, being on the board of Technicolor Inc. In 1985 Dunne was honoured by the Kennedy Center for her achievements in the performing arts.

● FILMS: *Leathernecking* aka *Present Arms* (1930), *Cimarron* (1931), *Bachelor Apartment* (1931), *The Great Lover* (1931), *Consolation Marriage* aka *Married In Haste* (1931), *The Slippery Pearls* (1951), *Symphony Of Six Million* aka *Melody Of Life* (1932), *Back Street* (1932), *Thirteen Women* (1932), *No Other Woman* (1933), *The Secret Of Madame Blanche* (1933), *The Silver Cord* (1933), *Ann Vickers* (1933), *Only Yesterday* (1933), *If I Were Free* aka *Behold We Live* (1933), *This Man Is Mine* (1934), *Stingaree* (1934), *The Age Of Innocence* (1934), *Sweet Adeline* (1934), *Roberta* (1935), *Magnificent Obsession* (1935), *Show Boat* (1936), *Theodora Goes Wild* (1936), *High, Wide And Handsome* (1937), *The Awful Truth* (1937), *Joy Of Living* (1938), *Love Affair* (1939), *Invitation To Happiness* (1939), *When Tomorrow Comes* (1939), *My Favorite Wife* (1940), *Penny Serenade* (1941), *Unfinished Business* (1941), *Lady In A Jam* (1942), *A Guy Named Joe* (1943), *The White Cliffs Of Dover* (1944), *Together Again* (1944), *Over 21* (1945), *Anna And The King Of Siam* (1946), *Life With Father* (1947), *I Remember Mama* (1948), *Never A Dull Moment* (1950), *The Mudlark* (1950), *You Can Change The World* (1951), *It Grows On Trees* (1952).

Dunnery, Francis

b. 25 December 1962, Egremont, Cumbria, England. A founder member of UK rock band **It Bites**, in the 90s Dunnery relocated to New York, USA, to start a career as a singer-songwriter. His gruff, honest approach to songcraft occasionally recalls **Neil Young**. He is also a student of metaphysics and astrology (at one point writing an astrology column for *Billboard* Online). He made his debut for **Atlantic Records** in 1994 with *Fearless*, after releasing a single, abortive solo effort for **Virgin Records** (which was released in Japan). At the same time he toured with **Robert Plant** on his Fate Of Nations tour, contributing guitar to two tracks on the album of similar title. However, neither *Fearless* nor the follow-up *Tall Blonde Helicopter* made much of an impression beyond the critics, who have been enthusiastic about Dunnery's work throughout his career, and a clutch of loyal followers won over by the artist's engrossing live shows. His relationship with Atlantic ended after a sales tally of just 28,000 copies for both albums combined, leading the famously sober Dunnery to comment: 'That's what happens. If you're the shopkeeper and you're not selling any goods, they'll shut you down. It's just like that.'

In 1995 Dunnery released *One Night In Sauchiehall Street*, a live acoustic recording of his then current show with comedian Ashley Reekes. For 1998's *Let's Go Do What Happens*, Dunnery elected to sign with the New York independent label Razor & Tie, who promised to give him the one-to-one support he lacked at Atlantic. The independent's efforts resulted in increased airplay for his fourth solo effort, especially for stand-out tracks 'Riding On The Back', 'Jonah' and 'Sunflowers'. Following the release of this album, however, Dunnery elected to turn his back on the music industry and concentrate on training horses in Vermont. He made the odd session appearance, working with **Lauryn Hill**, **Santana** and **Ian Brown** among others, and in 2001 recorded a new solo album. *Man* was released on his own Aquarian Nation label. In 2002, Dunnery began a full-time psychology course at Touro College in New York City. He managed to find the time to write and record new solo material, however, returning to the music scene in 2005 with the double disc *The Gulley Flat Boys*.

● ALBUMS: *Welcome To The Wild Country* (Virgin Japan 1991) ★★, *Fearless* (Atlantic 1994) ★★★, *Tall Blonde Helicopter* (Atlantic 1995) ★★★, *One Night In Sauchiehall Street* (Cottage Industry 1995) ★★★★, *Let's Go Do What Happens* (Razor & Tie 1998) ★★★, *Man* (Aquarian Nation 2001) ★★★, *Hometown* (Aquarian Nation 2001) ★★★, *The Gulley Flat Boys* (Aquarian Nation 2005) ★★★★.

● DVD/VIDEOS: *Live At The Union Chapel* (Aquarian Nation 2003).

Dunwich Records

Launched in Chicago, Illinois, USA, in 1966, the Dunwich label was an offshoot of the Dunwich Production Company, which had been set up the previous year. It was founded by producer Bill Traut, arranger/producer Eddie Higgins and former **Atlantic Records** sales director George Badonsky. The name Dunwich was taken from the work of the horror writer H.P. Lovecraft, whom both Traut and Badonsky admired. This led to further references to Lovecraft's work in the names of the publishing company Yuggoth Music, the agency Arkham Artists and, of course, the group called **H.P. Lovecraft**. The label enjoyed immediate success with white R&B act the **Shadows Of Knight**, who took a version of **Them**'s 'Gloria' into the US Top 10. Inspired by this success, Dunwich signed the cream of Chicago's punk/garage acts including the Del-vetts, Saturday's Children and the Rovin' Kind. Sadly, none of these emulated the success of 'Gloria' and, by 1967, the Shadows Of Knight themselves had fallen out of favour. A growing rift between Badonsky and Traut resulted in the former taking away two leading acts, H.P.

Lovecraft and the Mauds, while the Dunwich label itself folded when **Jerry Wexler** axed a distribution contract because he was unhappy at the style of music Traut and Higgins were promoting. Paradoxically, the group he rejected, the Light Nites, scored instant success under a new name, the **American Breed**. Although winding up their label, Traut and Higgins continued with Dunwich Productions throughout the 60s with the added weight of new partners Jim Golden and Bob Monaco. The **Cryan' Shames** and **Crow** gave Dunwich its last success before Traut dissolved the company early the following decade. Having founded Wooden Nickel Records with Golden and Monaco, he helped launch **Styx** before abandoning production in favour of artist representation. Badonsky meanwhile formed a successful career outside the music business as a restaurateur. However, Traut's affection for Dunwich Records has remained undiminished as his active participation in its reissue programme testifies.

● COMPILATIONS: *Oh Yeah! The Best Of Dunwich Records* (Sundazed 1991) ★★★, *If You're Ready . . . The Best Of Dunwich Records Volume 2* (Sundazed 1994) ★★★.

Dupree, Big Al

b. 1923, Dallas, Texas, USA, d. 4 August 2003. By the time Dupree started to attend Booker T. Washington High School in Dallas in the 30s, he was already an accomplished tenor saxophonist. He had also taken part in impromptu sessions in the infamous Deep Ellum area of the city, renowned as much for its crime rate as for being the breeding ground of blues musicians such as **Blind Lemon Jefferson** and **Buster Smith**. Through these sessions he became acquainted with trumpeter Doug Finnell, who asked Dupree's parents if their prodigy could join his band. The group, properly titled John R. Davis And His Dallas Dandies, enjoyed a residency at the Café Drug (so-called because the café also traded as a pharmacy). Dupree continued to play with the group until he left Dallas, aged 16, to attend Xavier University in New Orleans. While there he joined a succession of touring combos.

During World War II he entered service and worked on aircraft engines. Although he professed to be semi-retired on his return to Dallas after the war, Dupree still played regularly as the frontman of the Heat Waves Of Swing, a big band blues aggregation. He also took to the road to back artists including **T-Bone Walker** and **Pee Wee Crayton**. However, when he tired of the organizational hazards of Walker's touring schedule, Dupree opted for a more comfortable existence working as a singer/pianist in cocktail lounges. He finally released his debut CD in 1995, a year after making his first festival appearance at the Texas Blues/Soul Barbecue.

● ALBUMS: *Big Al Dupree Swings The Blues* (Dallas Blues Society 1995) ★★★, *Positive Thinking* (Fedora 2000) ★★★.

Dupree, Champion Jack

b. William Thomas Dupree, 4 July 1910, New Orleans, Louisiana, USA, d. 21 January 1992, Hanover, Germany. (Dupree's birth date is the matter of some conjecture and is sometimes listed as 23 July 1909). Orphaned in infancy, Dupree was raised in the Colored Waifs Home for Boys until the age of 14. After leaving, he led a marginal existence, singing for tips and learning piano from musicians such as

Willie 'Drive-'em-down' Hall. Dupree also became a professional boxer and blended fighting with hoboing throughout the 30s, before retiring from the ring in 1940 and heading for New York. Initially, he travelled only as far as Indianapolis, where he joined with musicians who had been associates of **Leroy Carr**. Dupree rapidly became a star of the local black entertainment scene as a comedian and dancer as well as a musician. He acquired a residency at the local Cotton Club and partnered comedienne Ophelia Hoy. In 1940 Dupree made his recording debut with music that blended the forceful, barrelhouse playing and rich, Creole-accented singing of New Orleans with the more suave style of Leroy Carr. Not surprisingly, a number of titles were piano/guitar duets, although on some, Jesse Ellery's use of amplification pointed the way forward. A few songs covered unusual topics, such as the distribution of grapefruit juice by relief agencies or the effects of drugs.

Dupree's musical career was interrupted when he was drafted into the US Navy as a cook; even so he managed to become one of the first blues singers to record for the folk revival market while on leave in New York in 1943. Dupree's first wife died while he was in the navy and he took his discharge in New York, where he worked as a club pianist and formed a close musical association with **Sonny Terry** and **Brownie McGhee**. His own post-war recording career commenced with a splendid series of solo recordings for Joe Davis, on some of which the influence of **Peetie Wheatstraw** is very evident. More typical were the many tracks with small groups recorded thereafter for a number of labels from 1946–53 and for **King Records** between April 1953 and late 1955. As ever, these recordings blend the serious with the comic, the latter somewhat tastelessly on songs such as 'Tongue Tied Blues' and 'Harelip Blues'. 'Walking The Blues', a comic dialogue with **Teddy 'Mr Bear' McRae**, was a hit on King, and the format was repeated on a number of titles recorded for **RCA Records**' Vik and Groove. In 1958 Dupree made his last American recordings until 1990; 'Blues From The Gutter' appears to have been aimed at white audiences, as was Dupree's career thereafter. In 1959 he moved to Europe and lived in Switzerland, England, Sweden and Germany, touring extensively and recording prolifically, with results that varied from the excellent to the mediocre. This served both as a stamp of authenticity and as a licensed jester to the European blues scene. The tracks on the 1993 release *One Last Time* were drawn from Dupree's final recording session before his death the previous year.

● ALBUMS: *Blues From The Gutter* (Atlantic 1959) ★★★★, *Champion Jack's Natural & Soulful Blues* (Atlantic 1961) ★★★, *Champion Of The Blues* (Atlantic/Storyville 1961) ★★★, featuring Brownie McGhee *Low Down Blues* 1945 recordings (Continental 1961) ★★★, *The Women Blues Of Champion Jack Dupree* (Folkways 1961) ★★★, *Sings The Blues* (King 1961) ★★★★, *Trouble, Trouble: Champion Jack Dupree Plays And Sings The Blues* (Storyville 1962) ★★★, *The Best Of The Blues* (Storyville 1963) ★★★, *Portraits In Blues Vol. 5* (Storyville 1963) ★★★, *Cabbage Greens* (OKeh 1963) ★★★★, *From New Orleans To Chicago* (Decca 1966) ★★★, featuring Mickey Baker *Champion Jack Dupree And His Blues Band* (Decca 1967) ★★★, *When You Feel The Feeling You Was Feeling* (Blue Horizon 1968) ★★★, *Anthologie Du Blues Vol. 1* (Vogue 1968) ★★★, *Scoobydoobydoo* (Blue Horizon 1969) ★★★, *The Heart Of The Blues Is Sound* (BYG 1969) ★★★, featuring Mickey

Baker, Hal Singer *I'm Happy To Be Free* (Vogue 1971) ★★★, *The Legacy Of The Blues Vol. 3* (Sonet 1972) ★★, with King Curtis *Blues From Montreux* (Atlantic 1972) ★★, *The Hamburg Session* (Happy Bird 1974) ★★, *Shakespeare Says* 1971 recording (Saravah 1976) ★★★, *Alive, Live And Well* 1972 recording (Chrischaa Blues 1976) ★★, with Monty Sunshine Band *Freedom* (Pinorrekk 1980) ★★★, with Kenn Lending *An Evening With Champion Jack Dupree* (Gallo 1981) ★★★, with Kenn Lending *Still Fighting The Blues* (Gallo 1981) ★★, *I Had That Dream* (Pinorrekk 1982) ★★, *Get You An Ol' Man* (Paris 1984) ★★, with Axel Zwingenberger & The Mojo Blues Band *Axel Zwingenberger And The Friends Of Boogie Woogie Vol. 5: Champ's House-warming* (Vagabond 1988) ★★★, with Zwingenberger *Axel Zwingenberger And The Friends Of Boogie Woogie Vol. 6: On Stage With Champion Jack Dupree* (Vagabond 1988) ★★★, *Jubilee Album* (Blue Moon 1989) ★★★, with Zwingenberger *Axel Zwingenberger And The Friends Of Boogie Woogie Vol. 7: Champion Jack Dupree Sings Blues Classics* (Vagabond 1990) ★★★, *Back Home In New Orleans* (Bullseye Blues 1990) ★★★★, *Forever And Ever* (Bullseye Blues 1991) ★★★, *Piano Blues 1960* (Magpie 1992) ★★★, *One Last Time* (Bullseye Blues 1993) ★★★, *Jivin' With Jack: Live In Manchester, May 1966* (Jasmine 2002) ★★★, with Freeway 75 *Bad Luck Blues* 1974 recording (Blue Nose 2003) ★★★.
● COMPILATIONS: shared with Jimmy Rushing *Two Shades Of Blue* (Audio Lab 1958) ★★★, *Incredible* (Sonet 1970) ★★★, *The Blues Of Champion Jack Dupree 1962/1963* recordings (Storyville 1975), *Blues For Everybody* (King 1976) ★★★, *Boogie Woogie, Booze And Wild Wild Women 1959/1963* recordings (Storyville 1977) ★★★, *Blues Roots Vol. 8: Two Fisted Piano From New Orleans* (Storyville 1979) ★★★, *The First 16 Sides From Joe Davis: 1944-1945* (Red Pepper 1982) ★★★, *Rub A Little Boogie: 1943-1953* (Krazy Kat 1982) ★★★, *1944-45: The Other Takes* (Krazy Kat 1985) ★★, *Shake Baby Shake* (Detour 1987) ★★★, *1940-1950* (Best Of Blues 1989) ★★★, *New Orleans Barrelhouse Boogie* (Columbia 1993) ★★★★, *Home* (Charly 1993) ★★★, *Truckin' On Down* (Storyville 1998) ★★★, shared with Muddy Waters *Me And My Mule* (Magnum 1999) ★★, *Get Back Jack, Do It Again* (Catfish 1999) ★★★, *Rum Cola Blues* (Arpeggio Blues 2000) ★★★, *St. Claude And Dumaine* (Fuel 2000 2002) ★★★, *Walkin' The Blues: The Very Best Of Champion Jack Dupree* (Collectables 2003) ★★★★, *The Best Of Champion Jack Dupree: Dupree Shake Dance* (Blues Forever 2005) ★★★, *The Complete Blue Horizon Sessions* (Sony 2005) ★★★.
● DVD/VIDEOS: *The Blues Of Champion Jack Dupree* (Storyville 2001).

Dupree, Cornell

b. 19 December 1942, Fort Worth, Texas, USA. A self-taught guitarist, Dupree became a professional musician in his home-town while still in his mid-teens. Soon thereafter he joined **King Curtis'** band in New York City where he worked with **Jimi Hendrix**. Dupree developed a solid reputation as a gifted R&B player, appearing in the backing groups of numerous artists for concerts and recording sessions. These have included **Billy Cobham**, **Gene 'Mighty Flea' Connors**, **Carla Bley**, **Aretha Franklin** (with whom he toured 1967–76), **Grant Green**, **Elvin Jones**, **Rahsaan Roland Kirk**, **Yusef Lateef**, **Herbie Mann** (in the 70s and again in the 90s), **Richard Twardzik**, saxophonist Steen Vig, the funk band **Stuff**, **Grover**

Washington Jnr., bluesman **Champion Jack Dupree** (unrelated) and **Steve Gadd**'s band, the Gadd Gang, in the late 80s.

Dupree's own-name recording sessions have seen him in company with **David 'Fathead' Newman** and **Ellis Marsalis** (both appearing on 1988's Grammy nominated *Coast To Coast*), **Hank Crawford** (having recording under the saxophonist's leadership in 1986 and again in 1998), **Jimmy Smith** (on 1978's *Shadow Dancing*), **Bobby Watson**, **Terell Stafford** and **Ronnie Cuber**. Although best known for his rousing R&B work and his soulful backing, Dupree's range is considerably wider than this might suggest. On the 1994 session that produced *Bop 'N' Blues*, he does exactly what the title suggests and digs into a bop mode with considerable aplomb.
● ALBUMS: *Teasin'* (Atlantic 1974) ★★★, *Saturday Night Fever* aka *Guitar Groove* (Versatile 1977) ★★★, *Shadow Dancing* aka *Unstuffed* (Versatile 1978) ★★★, with Who It Is *Coast To Coast* (Antilles 1988) ★★★★, *Can't Get Through* (Amazing 1991) ★★★, *Child's Play* (Amazing 1993) ★★★, *Bop 'N' Blues* (Kokopelli 1994) ★★★★, *Uncle Funky* 1992 recording (Kokopelli 1998) ★★★, *Double Clutch* (Meteor 1998) ★★★.

Dupree, Simon, And The Big Sound

Formed in Portsmouth, England, by the Shulman brothers, Derek (b. 11 February 1947, Glasgow, Scotland; lead vocals), Ray (b. 3 December 1949, Portsmouth, Hampshire, England; lead guitar) and Phil (b. 27 August 1937, Glasgow, Scotland; saxophone/ trumpet). The siblings had led several local groups, including the Howlin' Wolves and Roadrunners, before a newly acquired manager suggested the above appellation in 1966. Eric Hine (keyboards), Pete O'Flaherty (bass) and Tony Ransley (drums) completed the line-up, which then became a regular attraction in London's soul and R&B clubs. 'I See The Light', 'Reservations' and 'Daytime Nightime' (penned by **Manfred Mann** drummer **Mike Hugg**) were all radio hits and a *de rigueur* compendium of dance-floor favourites, *Without Reservations*, preceded the sextet's switch to 'flower-power' with 'Kites'. The group disliked the song's overt trappings—gongs, finger cymbals and Jackie Chan's Chinese narration—but it became their biggest hit, rising to number 9 in 1967. Subsequent singles failed to emulate this success, but the band achieved a measure of notoriety the following year when their psychoactive single, 'We Are The Moles', credited pseudonymously to the Moles, was assumed to be the **Beatles** in disguise. The unit was disbanded in 1969 when Derek Shulman, tired of being 'Simon Dupree', suffered a nervous breakdown. Upon recovery he joined his brothers in **Gentle Giant**.
● ALBUMS: *Without Reservations* (Parlophone 1967) ★★.
● COMPILATIONS: *Amen* (EMI 1982) ★★, *Kites* (See For Miles 1987) ★★, *Part Of My Past: The Simon Dupree And The Big Sound Anthology* (EMI 2004) ★★.

Duprees

A rock 'n' roll vocal group from Jersey City, New Jersey, USA. One of the most pop-sounding of the Italian-American groups that were in abundance during the late 50s and early 60s, the Duprees specialized in recording updated versions of old pop hits in a smooth style with a slight rock 'n' roll feel. The group was formed as the Parisiens in 1960 from the remnants of two Jersey City–based groups, the Utopians and the Elgins. The original line-up featured lead vocalist Joey

Vann (b. Joseph Canzano, 3 April 1943, USA, d. 28 February 1984), Mike Arnone (b. Michael Arnone, 19 September 1942, Jersey City, New Jersey, USA, d. 27 October 2005, Brick, New Jersey, USA), John Salvato (b. 19 July 1940, USA), Tom Bialoglow (b. 5 November 1940, USA) and Joe Santollo (b. Joseph Santollo, 23 July 1943, USA, d. 4 June 1981). They recorded several demos between 1960 and 1962, although Vann was temporarily replaced by Michael Kelly (b. 19 April 1943, USA) during this period. After adopting their new name the group signed with Coed in 1962, who with their other acts, notably the **Rivieras**, revived old pop hits using teenage vocal harmony groups to convey them to the new rock 'n' roll audience. The Duprees' biggest hit was their 1962 remake of the old **Jo Stafford** hit, 'You Belong To Me' (number 7 pop). The best of their other seven chart entries were 'My Own True Love' (number 13 pop, a vocal version of 'Tara's Theme' from *Gone With The Wind*) and 'Have You Heard' (number 18 pop). Tom Bialoglow left the group during the recording of their second album.

Vann was replaced by the returning Michael Kelly in 1964 and the following year the Duprees signed a two-year recording contract with **Columbia Records**. They explored a new upbeat sound on 'Around The Corner', their last national hit record in 1965. Recording for Jerry Ross' Heritage/Colossus label complex during 1968/9, the Duprees failed to chart with the same formula of updating old pop hits such as **Bobby Helms**' 'My Special Angel' and Don Rondo's 'Two Different Worlds'. The group's last major recording was 'Delicious', a disco hit for **RCA Records** in 1975 featuring Jesus Alvarez standing in for Kelly. Larry Cassanova replaced Salvato in the mid-70s and Tommy Petillo took over as lead singer in 1978. Santollo died in 1981 but remnants of the Duprees subsequently built a successful career playing the oldies doo-wop circuit in the New York and New Jersey area. A line-up of the group led by Petillo but featuring no original members released a number of studio and live albums in the new millennium.

● ALBUMS: *You Belong To Me* (Coed 1962) ★★★, *Have You Heard* (Coed 1963) ★★★, *Total Recall* aka *Gold* (Heritage/Colossus 1968) ★★, *Take Me As I Am* (1st Choice 1984) ★★, *Live From The Copa Room* (Label) ★★★, *Live From The Copa Room II* (Label) ★★, *Go To The Movies* (Label) ★★, *A Duprees Family Christmas* (Label) ★★, . . . *As Time Goes By* (Label) ★★★.

● COMPILATIONS: *Sing* (Post 1968) ★★★, *The Best Of The Duprees* i (Rhino 1990) ★★★★, *The Best Of The Duprees* ii (Collectables 1990) ★★★, *The Best Of The Duprees* iii (Sequel 1993) ★★★, *Delicious—The Heritage Years* (Sequel 1994) ★★★, *Their Complete Coed Masters* (Ace 1996) ★★★, *For Collectors Only* (Collectables 1996) ★★★, *All-Time Greatest Hits* (Varèse Sarabande 2002) ★★★★.

Dupri, Jermaine

b. Jermaine Dupri Mauldin, 23 September 1973, Atlanta, Georgia, USA. Dupri has established a reputation as one of the leading contemporary US producers. He grew up in Atlanta where his father, Michael Mauldin, acted as road manager for local groups. His father's connections led to breakdancing slots for artists such as **Diana Ross** and **Cameo**. He also performed as the opening act at New York's Fresh Festival, on a bill featuring **Whodini**, **Run-DMC** and **Grandmaster Flash**. Although he was barely in his teens, Dupri

knew that he wanted to establish a career in record production. He gained early experience promoting and producing the anodyne female trio Silk Tymes Leather, who released one flop album, 1989's *It Ain't Where Ya From . . . It's Where Ya At*, on **Geffen Records**. Shortly afterwards, Dupri established So So Def Recordings. The company's big break came about when Dupri saw Chris Kelly and Chris Smith performing in Greenbriar's shopping mall in Atlanta. He transformed the two 13 year olds into **Kriss Kross**, enjoying massive success in 1991 with a US chart-topping single ('Jump') and album (*Totally Krossed Out*). Dupri subsequently established the careers of gospel-rooted **swingbeat** quartet **Xscape** (*Hummin' Comin' At 'Cha, Off The Hook*), female rapper **Da Brat** (*Funkdafied*), **Jagged Edge** and Trina Broussard.

So So Def's client list grew rapidly, serving established artists such as **Dru Hill** (the hit remix of 'In My Bed'), **TLC**, **Mariah Carey**, **Aretha Franklin**, **Lil' Kim**, **MC Lyte** and Whodini among others. The company also signed a lucrative distribution contract with **Columbia Records**. Dupri enjoyed his biggest commercial success since Kriss Kross' debut when he co-produced and contributed tracks to **Usher**'s multi-platinum *My Way*, including the huge transatlantic hits 'You Make Me Wanna' and 'Nice 'N' Slow'. During 1998, Dupri concentrated on establishing himself as a solo artist, releasing *The Party Continues* EP. The ambitious *Presents Life In 1472: The Original Soundtrack* followed, with stand-out tracks including collaborations with **Nas** ('Turn It Out'), **Slick Rick** ('Fresh') and **Jay-Z** ('Money Ain't A Thang'). The stellar guest list also included appearances by **Snoop Doggy Dogg**, **DMX**, Usher, Mariah Carey and Da Brat. The album debuted at US number 3 in August. A follow-up set was released in 2001, shortly before So So Def ended its decade-long association with Columbia. They signed a new distribution contract with **Arista Records** in January 2003, with Dupri taking a senior vice president role at the company. The following year he moved So So Def over to **Virgin Records** after accepting a new post at the label.

● ALBUMS: *Presents Life In 1472: The Original Soundtrack* (So So Def/Columbia 1998) ★★★, *Instructions* (So So Def/Columbia 2001) ★★★.

● COMPILATIONS: *Presents . . . Young, Fly & Flashy Vol. 1* (Virgin 2005) ★★★.

Duran Duran

Borrowing their name from a character in the cult 60s science fiction movie *Barbarella*, this UK pop band achieved global fame in the early 80s thanks to a series of catchy synthpop tunes, a strong visual image and expensively produced promotional videos which enjoyed endless rotation on the nascent **MTV** music channel.

The band's classic line-up featured vocalist Simon Le Bon (b. 27 October 1958, Bushey, Hertfordshire, England), keyboard player Nick Rhodes (b. Nicholas James Bates, 8 June 1962, Moseley, Birmingham, West Midlands, England), guitarist Andy Taylor (b. 16 February 1961, Wolverhampton, England), bass player John Taylor (b. Nigel John Taylor, 20 June 1960, Birmingham, West Midlands, England) and drummer Roger Taylor (b. 26 April 1960, Castle Bromwich, Birmingham, West Midlands, England). Formed by Rhodes and John Taylor in 1978, the early line-ups of the band included Simon Colley (bass/clarinet), Stephen 'Tin Tin' **Duffy** (b. 30 May 1960, Birmingham, West Midlands, England; vocals), Andy

Wickett (vocals), Alan Curtis (guitar) and Jeff Thompson. They established a residency at the Rum Runner in Birmingham, and the club's owners Michael and Paul Berrow became the band's first managers. Duran Duran came to prominence in late 1980 when they toured with **Hazel O'Connor** and won a recording contract with **EMI Records**. Firmly in the new romantic bracket, they enjoyed early publicity and reached the UK Top 20 the following year with their debut single 'Planet Earth'. The follow-up 'Careless Memories' barely scraped into the UK Top 40, but this proved merely a minor setback. 'Girls On Film', which was accompanied by a risqué **Godley And Creme** video that featured nude models, brought them their first UK Top 5 hit. Two albums quickly followed and hits such as 'Hungry Like The Wolf', 'Save A Prayer' and 'Rio' revealed that there was considerable songwriting substance behind the hype.

By 1983 Duran Duran was in the ascendant, having broken into the US Top 10 three times. 'Is There Something I Should Know?', a gloriously catchy pop song, entered the UK charts at number 1, thereby underlining the strength of their fanbase. They were now, unquestionably, the most popular teen idols in the country. An impressive run of transatlantic Top 10 hits followed over the next two years, including 'Union Of The Snake', 'New Moon On Monday', 'The Reflex' (a UK/US number 1), 'The Wild Boys' and 'A View To A Kill', the latter a James Bond movie theme which gave the band their second US chart-topper. At the peak of their success, the band members decided to wind down and venture into other projects, such as the **Power Station** and **Arcadia**, while Le Bon caused many a teenage heart to flutter when he was almost killed in a yachting accident in 1986. The same year the band regrouped, minus Roger and Andy Taylor, to record *Notorious* with producer **Nile Rodgers**. Although the title track was a big hit, the band had by now lost many of their original fans, and excellent follow-up singles such as 'Skin Trade' and 'Meet El Presidente' failed to break into the Top 20 either side of the Atlantic.

The trio of Le Bon, Rhodes and John Taylor continued recording, knowing that they had already secured a place in pop history. Pointlessly tinkering with their name (to DuranDuran) failed to restore the band's commercial fortunes, and the release of a singles compilation raised question marks about their future. Guitarist Warren Cuccurullo (b. 8 December 1956, Brooklyn, New York City, USA; ex-**Missing Persons**), who first featured on *Notorious*, and Sterling Campbell became permanent members in June 1989, although the latter left two years later, going on to play with **Cyndi Lauper** and **David Bowie** among others.

Renewed interest in Duran Duran came about in 1993 when 'Ordinary World' became a major transatlantic hit (USA number 3/UK number 6). It was followed by 'Come Undone', which reached number 7 in America. Both tracks were taken from *Duran Duran*, which caused critics who had written them off to amend their opinions. In 1995 they released *Thank You*, a covers album that paid tribute to the band's influences, although they attracted hostile criticism for versions of rap classics 'White Lines (Don't Do It)' and '911 Is A Joke'. Two years later John Taylor left the band, leaving Le Bon and Rhodes to carry on with the long-serving Cuccurullo. Their contract with EMI ended following the record company's refusal to release *Medazzaland* in the UK, although *Greatest* sold well on the back of an 80s revival. *Pop Trash*, released on the Hollywood label in 2000, was a

deliberate attempt to escape the pop tag with which Rhodes and Le Bon will forever be associated.

In May 2001, the five original members announced they intended to play together for the first time in over 15 years. They eventually performed a series of US dates in 2003 and carried on playing throughout the rest of the year and into 2004. During this time they returned to the studio to complete the first album by the original line-up since 1983's *Seven And The Ragged Tiger*. The resulting *Astronaut* was released to polite reviews in October.

● ALBUMS: *Duran Duran* (EMI/Harvest 1981) ★★★, *Rio* (EMI/Harvest 1982) ★★★★, *Seven And The Ragged Tiger* (EMI/Capitol 1983) ★★, *Arena* (Parlophone/Capitol 1984) ★★, *Notorious* (EMI/Capitol 1986) ★★★, as DuranDuran *Big Thing* (EMI/Capitol 1988) ★★, *Liberty* (Parlophone/Capitol 1990) ★, *Duran Duran* aka *The Wedding Album* (Parlophone/Capitol 1993) ★★★, *Thank You* (Parlophone/Capitol 1995) ★★, *Medazzaland* (Capitol 1997) ★★★, *Pop Trash* (Hollywood 2000) ★★★, *Astronaut* (Epic 2004) ★★★.

● COMPILATIONS: *Decade* (EMI/Capitol 1989) ★★★★, *Essential Duran Duran (Night Versions)* (EMI 1998) ★★★, *Greatest* (EMI/Capitol 1998) ★★★★, *Strange Behaviour* (EMI 1999) ★★, *Girls On Film: 'The Collection'* (EMI 2000) ★★★, *Classic Masters* (EMD 2002) ★★★, *The Singles '81-'85* box set (EMI 2003) ★★★, *The Singles 1986–1995* 14-CD box set (EMI 2004) ★★★.

● DVD/VIDEOS: *The First 11 Videos* (PMI 1983), *Dancing On The Valentine* (PMI 1984), *Sing Blue Silver* (PMI 1984), *Arena: An Absurd Notion* (PMI 1984), *The Making Of Arena* (PMI 1985), *Working For The Skin Trade* (PMI 1987), *Three To Get Ready* (BMG/Aurora 1987), *6ix By 3hree* (PMI 1988), *Decade* (PMI 1989), *Extraordinary World* (PMI 1993), *Greatest: The Videos* (EMI 1998), *Greatest: The DVD* (EMI 2003), *Astronaut* (Epic Music Video 2004), *Live From London* (Coming Home Studios 2005)

● FURTHER READING: *Duran Duran: Their Story*, Kasper deGraff and Malcolm Garrett. *Duran Duran: An Independent Story In Words And Pictures*, John Carver. *Duran Duran*, Maria David. *Duran Duran: A Behind-The-Scenes Biography Of The Supergroup Of The Eighties*, Cynthia C. Kent. *Everything You Want To Know About Duran Duran*, Toby Goldstein. *Duran Duran*, Susan Martin. *Duran Duran Live*, Peter Goddard and Philip Kamin. *Inside Duran Duran*, Robyn Flans. *Duran Duran*, Annette Weidner.

Durante, Jimmy

b. James Francis Durante, 10 February 1893, New York City, New York, USA, d. 29 January 1980, Santa Monica, California, USA. A unique entertainer: a comedian, actor and singer whose straight-legged strut, outsize nose (which brought him the nickname 'Schnozzola') and a penchant for mangling the English language ('Da hours I worked were eight to unconscious') made him a much-loved character throughout the world. The son of immigrant French-Italian parents, Durante taught himself to play ragtime on a piano his father bought him when he was 12. While in his teens he played in New York clubs and gangster hangouts and later had his own six-piece jazz band in New Orleans.

In the early 20s Durante ran his own speakeasy, the Club Durant, with his partners, dancer and businessman Lou Clayton and song-and-dance-man Eddie Jackson. When the trio began to receive 'offers that they couldn't refuse' from certain shady characters, they gave up the club and toured as a vaudeville act. They also appeared in the Broadway musicals *Show Girl* and *The New Yorkers* (1930). In 1931 the partnership split up and Durante signed a contract with MGM, going on to make nearly 40 films. In the 30s these included musicals such as *Roadhouse Nights*; *The Cuban Love Song*; **The Phantom President**; **Blondie Of The Follies**; *Broadway To Hollywood*; **George White's Scandals**; *Palooka*; *Strictly Dynamite*; *Hollywood Party*; *She Learned About Sailors*; *Sally, Irene And Mary*; *Little Miss Broadway*; and *Start Cheering* (1938). During that period Durante also starred in several Broadway musicals, *Strike Me Pink*, **Jumbo**, **Red, Hot And Blue!**, *Stars In Your Eyes* and *Keep Off the Grass* (1940), as well as performing his comedy act at the London Palladium. He was successful on radio, too, and was teamed with straight man Garry Moore in *The Camel Comedy Hour* from 1943–47. After that Durante had his own show for three years before he moved into television with the comedy-variety *All Star Revue* (they called him 'TV's newest and freshest face'—he was 57), and later, *The Jimmy Durante Show* in a nightclub setting similar to the old Club Durant with his old friend Eddie Jackson. In 1952 he was back at the London Palladium and played other theatres and important clubs. Throughout the 40s and 50s he continued to appear in film musicals such as *Melody Ranch*, *This Time For Keeps*, **Two Girls And A Sailor**, **Music For Millions**, **Two Sisters From Boston**, **It Happened In Brooklyn** and *On An Island With You*.

In 1960 Durante was one of the guest stars in *Pepe*, and, two years later, co-starred with **Doris Day** in Billy Rose's Jumbo. His final film appearance was a cameo role in that orgy of slapstick (or slapschtik), *It's A Mad Mad Mad Mad World* (1963), but he remained popular on US television shows in such as *Jimmy Durante Meets The Seven Lively Arts*, *Jimmy Durante Presents The Lennon Sisters* and *The Hollywood Palace*. In 1960, at the age of 67, he was married for the second time (his first wife died in 1943) to the actress Margaret Alice Little, whom he had been dating for 16 years. Four years later he was honoured for his 50 years in showbusiness with a lavish ceremony at the Hollywood Roosevelt Hotel. His other awards included Best TV Performer (Motion Picture Daily 1951), George Foster Peabody Award (1951), and Citation Of Merit, City Of New York (1956) and Special Page One Award (1962).

Durante was the composer or co-composer of several of his most popular numbers, including his trademark 'Inka Dinka Doo' and others such as 'Umbriago', 'So I Ups To Him', 'Start Off Each Day With A Song', 'Can Broadway Do Without Me?' and 'Jimmy, The Well Dressed Man'. Several of these, and others that he did not write but are indelibly associated with him such as 'September Song', were featured in two tribute shows, both entitled *Durante*, which played in Hollywood and San Francisco in 1982 and 1989. No doubt Durante's immortal protest 'Everybody wants to get into the act' and his closing message 'Goodnight, Mrs. Calabash, wherever you are', also cropped up in these celebrations of this loveable clown who was much-missed after he died in 1980 following several years of ill health.

● ALBUMS: *In Person* (Lion 1959) ★★★, *Club Durante* (Decca 1959) ★★★, *At The Copacabana* (Roulette 1961) ★★★, *September Song* (Warners 1963) ★★★★, *Hello Young Lovers* (Warners 1964) ★★★, *Jimmy Durante's Way Of Life* (Warners 1965) ★★★, *On the Radio* (Silva Screen 1989) ★★★, *September Song* expanded edition (Collectors 2001) ★★★★.

● COMPILATIONS: *Inka Dinka Doo* (Universal 1986) ★★★, *As Time Goes By: The Best Of Jimmy Durante* (Warners 1993) ★★★★, *The Great Schnozzle* (ASV 1998) ★★★, *The Ultimate Collection* (Prism 1999) ★★★★.

● FURTHER READING: *I Remember Jimmy: The Life And Times Of Jimmy Durante*, Irene Alder. *Schnozzola*, Gene Fowler. *Goodnight Mrs. Calabash: The Secret Life Of Jimmy Durante*, William Cahn. *Inka Dinka Doo: The Life Of Jimmy Durante*, Jhan Robbins.

● FILMS: *Roadhouse Nights* (1930), *The Cuban Love Song* (1931), *New Adventures Of Get-Rich-Quick Wallingford* (1931), *Blondie Of The Follies* (1932), *The Passionate Plumber* (1932), *The Phantom President* (1932), *Speak Easily* (1932), *The Wet Parade* (1932), *Meet The Baron* (1933), *Broadway To Hollywood* (1933), *The Lost Stooges* (1933), *What! No Beer?* (1933), *Hell Below* (1933), *She Learned About Sailors* (1934), *Student Tour* (1934), *Strictly Dynamite* (1934), *Palooka* (1934), *Hollywood Party* (1934), *George White's Scandals* (1934), *Carnival* (1935), *Land Without Music* (1936), *Little Miss Broadway* (1938), *Sally, Irene And Mary* (1938), *Start Cheering* (1938), *Melody Ranch* (1940), *The Man Who Came To Dinner* (1941), *You're In The Army Now* (1941), *Two Girls And A Sailor* (1944), *Music For Millions* (1945), *Two Sisters From Boston* (1946), *It Happened In Brooklyn* (1947), *This Time For Keeps* (1947), *On An Island With You* (1948), *The Milkman* (1950), *The Great Rupert* (1950), *Beau James* (1957), *Pepe* (1960), *Billy Rose's Jumbo* (1962), *It's A Mad Mad Mad Mad World* (1963).

Durbin, Deanna

b. Edna Mae Durbin, 4 December 1921, Winnipeg, Canada. A refreshingly natural and spirited actress and singer, with a clear, thrilling soprano voice, who was one of the top box-office stars in film musicals of the late 30s and 40s. The Durbin family moved to Los Angeles, California, when Deanna was a baby, and she received voice training from the age of eight. After being spotted by an MGM agent singing at a recital, she was set to portray the opera singer Eva Schumann-Heink as a child in a picture based on the diva's life, but that fell through and instead she co-starred with **Judy Garland** in the musical short film **Every Sunday** (1936). When MGM boss Louis B. Mayer decided to drop Durbin and keep Garland, she was immediately snapped up for Universal by producer Joe Pasternak. The public's response to her performance in *Three Smart Girls* (1936) was rapturous, and the film's receipts of $2 million saved the studio from bankruptcy. Just before it was released she had made several highly impressive appearances on the **Eddie Cantor** Radio Hour, so a great many Americans were already familiar with this enchanting 15-year-old with the mature voice and style. During the rest of the 30s, with Pasternak's guidance and skill, audiences were able to follow her gradual evolving from a precocious teenager into a lovely woman in films such as **100 Men And A Girl**, **Mad About Music**, **That Certain Age**, **Three Smart Girls Grow Up**, *First Love*, (in which she had her first screen kiss with Robert Stack), *It's A Date* and *Spring Parade* (1940). In 1938 she and that other fine young star, **Mickey Rooney**, were awarded special Oscars 'for their significant contribution in bringing to the screen the spirit and personification of youth, and as juvenile players setting a high standard of ability and achievement.'

For most of the 40s she was still Hollywood's top female attraction, via the musicals *Nice Girl?*, *It Started With Eve*, *Hers To Hold*, **Can't Help Singing** (her only film in colour), *I'll Be Yours*, *Something In The Wind* and *Up In Central Park* (1948). She tried to change her girl-next-door image by accepting straight parts in pictures such as *Christmas Holiday* and *Lady In A Train*, but Universal, who made all her 22 pictures, were not interested in grooming her for sophisticated dramatic roles, so in 1948 she quit Hollywood for good.

With two failed marriages behind her (to producer Vaughn Paul when she was 19, and German-born producer Felix Jackson in 1945), she retired with her third husband, French film director Charles David, to the French village of Neauphle-le-Château near Paris. Despite the repeated efforts of Pasternak she refused to return, saying 'I can't run around being a Little Miss Fix-it who bursts into song—the highest paid star with the poorest material.' She did have the pick of the leading men, though, including Robert Cummings, Walter Pidgeon, Franchot Tone and Melvyn Douglas. While refusing to make public appearances, she apparently works tirelessly for UNICEF and remains particularly popular in the UK where the BBC still receives more requests for her films than for any other film star of the 30s and 40s.

● COMPILATIONS: *Movie Songs* (Coral 1982) ★★★, *Best Of Deanna Durbin* (MCA 1981) ★★★★, *Can't Help Singing* (MFP/EMI 1982) ★★★, *Best Of Deanna Durbin Volume 2* (MCA 1983) ★★★, *Songs Of The Silver Screen* (MCA 1986) ★★★, *20 Golden Greats* (Deja Vu 1987) ★★★, *Favourites* (Memoir 1989) ★★★, *The Legendary* (Silva Screen 1990) ★★★, *With A Song In My Heart* (1993) ★★★, *Original Film Soundtracks* (1994) ★★★.

Durham, Eddie

b. 19 August 1906, San Marcos, Texas, USA, d. 6 March 1987, New York City, New York, USA. As a child Durham worked in travelling shows with other musical members of his large family. In the mid-20s he worked in a number of southwest **territory bands** including **Walter Page**'s Blue Devils from where he, and several others, moved to the **Bennie Moten** band. Up to this point Durham had been playing both guitar and trombone and now added arranging to his arsenal of skills. During the 30s he played in, and arranged for, the bands of **Willie Bryant**, **Jimmie Lunceford** and **Count Basie**. In the following decade he arranged for several noted swing bands including **Artie Shaw**'s and also worked closely with one of the outstanding but neglected bands of the late 40s the **International Sweethearts Of Rhythm**. Later in his career Durham arranged more and played less but did return to the stage in the 70s and 80s with **Eddie Barefield**, **Buddy Tate** and other comrades from his Basie days. Durham's contributions to jazz are extensive and include helping develop and refine the electrically amplified guitar. More important still were his loosely swinging arrangements exemplified by such Basie classics as 'Moten Swing' and the popular 'In The Mood' for **Glenn Miller**. He was also co-composer of 'Topsy', which became an unexpected hit for **William 'Cozy' Cole** in 1958.

● ALBUMS: *Eddie Durham* (RCA 1973) ★★★, *Blue Bone* (JSP 1981) ★★★.

Durham, Judith

(see **Seekers**)

Durkin, Kathy

b. Katherine Leddy, Butlersbridge, Co. Cavan, Eire. Durkin's father, Eugene Leddy (d. January 2002), was a noted dance band leader in the 50s. She learned piano accordion and enjoyed singing but did not seek a professional career. In the late 70s she married Andrew Durkin and had two children. She starred in the Cavan ladies football team, which won All Ireland honours in 1977. In the early 80s, she sang with a local band, Cavan, around the clubs, and an appearance on RTE television gained her a recording contract with Harmac Records. Her 1988 recording of 'Midnight To Moonlight' proved very successful. She appeared at the Wembley International Country Music Festival in 1990 and a year later she scored a big hit in Ireland with her version of **Rita MacNeill**'s 'Working Man'. In recent years she has worked to consolidate her position as one of the top female vocalists not only in her native Eire but also by touring country clubs in the UK.

● ALBUMS: *Memories* (Harmac 1989) ★★★, *Moonlight Reflections* (Harmac 1990) ★★★, *Kathy's Favourites* (Harmac 1991) ★★★, *Kathy's Gold* (Harmac 1992) ★★★★, *My Own Native Land* (Ceol 2000) ★★★.

Durocs

Formed in 1979, this San Francisco–based act was comprised of **Ron Nagle** (vocals/keyboards) and Scott Mathews (guitar/drums). Both musicians brought considerable experience to the project. Nagle, who founded the pioneering **Mystery Trend**, composed incidental music to several horror movies, notably *The Exorcist* and co-wrote 'Don't Touch Me There', a bestseller for the **Tubes**. Mathews, meanwhile, was an ex-member of several groups, including the **Elvin Bishop** Band and the **Hoodoo Rhythm Devils**. The duo's songs were recorded by **Michelle Phillips** and **Barbra Streisand**, and having built a recording studio, the Pen, they completed *The Durocs*, which took its name from a breed of pig noted for its large ears and genitals. The album was a strong effort but sold poorly, and the project was abandoned when **Capitol Records** refused to release a second set. Undeterred, the duo continued to compose and record together and later released a single under a new name the Profits. Their version of 'I'm A Hog For You' continued the porcine metaphor, as did its Proud Pork Productions credit. Music notwithstanding, Nagle has since become one of the USA's leading exponents of ceramic art.

● ALBUMS: *The Durocs* (Capitol 1979) ★★★.

Durst, Lavada 'Dr. Hepcat'

b. 9 January 1913, Austin, Texas, USA, d. 31 October 1995, Austin, Texas. As a 12-year-old, Durst learned to play the piano in the church opposite his home. He later claimed his left hand was influenced by **Albert Ammons** and Meade 'Lux' Lewis and his right by renowned Texas bluesman **Robert Shaw**, whom he met eight years later. Durst continued to play in an amateur capacity at house-rent parties and suppers while running recreation facilities in East Austin. His talent for jive talk landed him a job as an announcer at baseball games at Disch Field, which in turn brought him to the attention of the local radio station KVET. As 'Dr. Hepcat', in 1948 he became the first black disc jockey in Texas, broadcasting six days a week. Programme director Fred Caldwell also owned Uptown Records, for whom Durst recorded 'Hattie Green' and 'Hepcat's Boogie' in 1949.

Shortly afterwards he re-recorded the first title for **Don Robey**'s Peacock label. In the late 50s, Durst managed the Chariottes spiritual group, who also recorded for Peacock. He gave up playing music in 1965 when he was ordained as a minister at the Mt. Olive Baptist Church but returned to the piano a decade later. Durst was unusual for a Texas blues pianist by maintaining a strong left-hand pulse to his blues and boogie improvisations that accompanied his semi-improvised monologues.

● CoMPILATIONS: *Deep Ellum Blues* (Documentary Arts 1986) ★★★, *Piano Professors* (Catfish 1987) ★★★.

Durutti Column

One of the more eclectic bands to emerge from Manchester, England's punk scene, Vini Reilly (b. Vincent Gerard Reilly, August 1953, Manchester, England) and his Durutti Column have combined elements of jazz, electronic and even folk in their multitude of releases. However, Reilly's musical beginnings were as guitarist in more standard 1977 hopefuls **Ed Banger And The Nosebleeds**. Two other units from 1977— Fastbreeder and Flashback—had since merged into a new band, who were being managed by Manchester television presenter and **Factory Records** founder Tony Wilson. Wilson invited Reilly to join guitarist Dave Rowbotham and drummer Chris Joyce in January 1978, and together they became the Durutti Column (after a political cartoon strip used by the Situationist Internatiside in Strasbourg during the 60s). They were joined by vocalist Phil Rainford and bass player Tony Bowers and recorded for the famous 'A Factory Sampler EP' with the late **Martin Hannett** producing. These were the only recordings made by this line-up and the band broke up. Reilly carried on with the Durutti Column alone, while the others (except Rainford) formed the Moth Men. The debut, *The Return Of The Durutti Column*, appeared on Factory in 1980 and was largely recorded by Reilly, although Hannett, Pete Crooks (bass) and Toby (drums) also contributed.

Durutti Column soon established a solid cult following, particularly abroad, where Reilly's moving instrumental work was widely appreciated. Live appearances had been sporadic, however, as Reilly suffered from an eating disorder and was frequently too ill to play. The album was notable for its sandpaper sleeve, inspired by the anarchist movement Situationist Internatiside. Reilly and producer Hannett helped out on **Pauline Murray**'s first solo album later in 1980. The Durutti Column's own recordings over the next few years were a mixed batch recorded by Reilly with assistance from drummers Donald Johnson, then Bruce Mitchell (ex–**Alberto Y Lost Trios Paranoias**), Maunagh Flemin and Simon Topping on horns, and much later, further brass players Richard Henry, Tim Kellett and Mervyn Fletcher, plus violinist Blaine Reininger and cellist **Caroline Lavelle**.

Dozens of other musicians have joined the nucleus of Reilly and Mitchell over the years and the band is still active today. A striking example of mid-period Durutti Column was captured on *Vini Reilly*, released in 1989. The guitarist cleverly incorporated the sampled voices of Joan Sutherland, **Tracy Chapman**, **Otis Redding** and **Annie Lennox** into a moving world of acoustic/electric ballads. Reilly also lent some mesmerizing guitar to a host of recordings by artists such as Anne Clarke and **Richard Jobson** and fellow Mancunian and friend **Morrissey**. On 8 November 1991, former Durutti Column guitarist Dave Rowbotham was discovered axed to death at his Manchester home, leading to a murder hunt. Following Factory's bankruptcy in 1992, Reilly released the excellent *Sex And Death* on their new label Factory Too. Although *Fidelity* saw him on yet another label, the Durutti Column sound was still the same. In the late 90s and on into the new millennium, Reilly found a more permanent home for the Durutti Column on the Artful label.

● ALBUMS: *The Return Of The Durutti Column* (Factory 1980) ★★★, *LC* (Factory 1981) ★★★, *Another Setting* (Factory 1983) ★★★, *Live At The Venue, London* (VU 1983) ★★★, *Amigos En Portugal* (Fundacao Atlantica 1983) ★★, *Without Mercy* (Factory 1984) ★★★, *Domo Arigato* (Factory 1985) ★★★, *Circuses And Bread* (Factory 1985) ★★★, *Live At The Bottom Line New York* cassette (ROIR 1987) ★★★, *The Guitar And Other Machines* (Factory 1987) ★★★, *Vini Reilly* (Factory 1989) ★★★★, *Obey The Time* (Factory 1991) ★★★, *Lips That Would Kiss Form Prayers To Broken Stone* (Factory Benelux 1991) ★★★, *Dry* (Materiali Sonori 1991) ★★★, *Sex & Death* (Factory Too 1994) ★★★, *Fidelity* (Les Disques Du Crepuscule 1996) ★★★, *Time Was GIGANTIC . . . When We Were Kids* (Factory Too 1998) ★★★, *A Night In New York* (Shellshock 1999) ★★★, *Rebellion* (Artful 2001) ★★★, *Someone Else's Party* (Artful 2003) ★★★, *Tempus Fugit* (Kooky 2004) ★★★.

Solo: Vini Reilly *The Sporadic Recordings* (Spore 1990) ★★★.

● COMPILATIONS: *Valuable Passages* (Factory 1986) ★★★, *The First Four Albums* (Factory 1988) ★★★, *The Return Of The Sporadic Recordings* (Kooky 2002) ★★★, *The Best Of The Durutti Column* (WSM 2004) ★★★.

Dury, Baxter

b. 18 December 1971, Wingrave, Buckinghamshire, England. The son of UK singer-songwriter **Ian Dury** made an impressive start to his own recording career with *Len Parrott's Memorial Lift*, a statement of artistic intent that sadly his father did not live to see receive the accolades it so richly deserved. Baxter was born while his father was still struggling to make an impact with **Kilburn And The High Roads**, and he later appeared on the cover of Ian's 1977 classic **New Boots And Panties!!** By the time Baxter reached his teenage years Ian had largely abandoned music to pursue a fitful acting career. After kicking around in a series of stopgap jobs throughout his 20s, Baxter began writing songs with ex-Blockhead Mickey Gallagher's son, Ben, but a projected contract with **Island Records** fell through. A recording contract with the independent label **Rough Trade Records** ensued, but by this time Ian Dury was severely ill with cancer. Baxter made his singing debut at his father's wake, singing the entirely appropriate 'My Old Man'. He decamped to Austin, Texas, to record his debut album, recruiting **Richard Hawley** and members of **Portishead** to complete the work. The first output from the sessions, the *Oscar Brown* EP, was released in 2001. The lush indie pop of the title track provided a perfect introduction to the otherworldly *Len Parrott's Memorial Lift*, with Baxter's whispered vocals a far cry from his father's cockney growl. Despite the surface differences, elements of Ian's lyrical zest still shone through on the album, most notably on the tracks 'Gingham Smalls 2' and 'Boneyard Dogs'. Dury returned in 2005 with another excellent album, *Floor Show*.

● ALBUMS: *Len Parrott's Memorial Lift* (Rough Trade 2002) ★★★★, *Floor Show* (Rough Trade 2005) ★★★.

Dury, Ian

b. 12 May 1942, Harrow, Middlesex, England, d. 27 March 2000, London, England. The long held claim of being born in Upminster, Essex has been ruined by the thorough research of his biographer Richard Balls. Dury moved around a lot in his early years, from Donegal in Ireland to Mevagissey in Cornwall. He settled in Cranham, Essex, a village at the posh end of Upminster, moving there with his mother at the age of 4. In 1949 the young Dury contracted polio, a crippling disease that was particularly common between 1947 and 1954. He spent two years in hospital in East Sussex, during which time he was never to be found without a sketch pad. He attended art college and eventually received a scholarship to the Royal College Of Art. His polio had left him badly crippled but Dury turned his disability into a positive advantage. Much of his strength of character and great sense of humour was formed from these times.

Although music was a big part of his life, especially early rock 'n' roll, he decided to pursue a career in art and until his 28th birthday taught the subject at Canterbury School of Art. He began playing pubs and clubs in London with **Kilburn And The High Roads**, reinterpreting R&B numbers and later adding his own wry lyrics in a semi-spoken cockney rhyming slang. The band dissolved and the remnants formed into a new line-up called the Blockheads. The initial line-up briefly included **Wreckless Eric**, but the most stable unit comprised Dury, Chaz Jankel (guitar/keyboards), John Turnbull (guitar), Mickey Gallagher (keyboards), Davey Payne (saxophone), Charley Charles (drums) and Norman Watt-Roy (b. 1951, Bombay, India; bass). In 1975, **Stiff Records** signed them and considered Dury's aggressive but honest stance the perfect summary of the contemporary mood at that time. The first single, 'Sex & Drugs & Rock 'n' Roll', became their signature tune at every gig. The song lampooned the music business, which Dury had already experienced and had cleverly observed. The Blockheads' debut album and finest moment, **New Boots And Panties**, received superlative reviews and spent more than a year in the UK album chart. Dury's dry wit, sensitivity and brilliant lyrical caricatures were evident in songs such as 'Clever Trevor', 'Billericay Dickie', 'Wake Up And Make Love To Me', the beautifully poignant 'My Old Man' and the tribute song 'Sweet Gene Vincent'.

The success of the album was partly due to the fact that these songs had been written over a period of some years. By the time they were finally recorded, no rearranging was needed; they were already perfect. Dury became front-page tabloid news and briefly crossed over from critical acclaim to commercial acceptance with the UK number 1 'Hit Me With Your Rhythm Stick' in December 1979. *Do It Yourself* and *Laughter* were similarly inspired, although lacking the impact of the debut, and by his third album he had teamed up with ex-**Dr. Feelgood** guitarist **Wilko Johnson** and lost the co-writing partnership of the talented Jankel. He continued to work towards a stronger jazz/funk context and employed the masterful rhythm section of **Sly And Robbie** on *Lord Upminster*, which also featured the celebrated jazz trumpeter **Don Cherry**.

Dury continued to make thoughtful, polemic records in the 80s and audaciously suggested that his excellent song 'Spasticus Autisticus' should be adopted as the musical emblem of the Year Of The Disabled. He wrote 'Profoundly In Love With Pandora' for the television adaptation of Sue Townsend's *The Secret Diary Of Adrian Mole*. He recorded *4,000 Weeks Holiday* with a support band known as the Music Students, the nucleus of which included Michael McEvoy (bass/keyboards), Merlin Rhys-Jones (guitar), Jamie Talbot (saxophone) and Tag Lamche (drums). One excellent single ('Very Personal') resulted from this collaboration, although it failed to chart. Like many before him, he turned to acting and appeared in several television plays and films in the mid-to-late 80s. Among those were the movies *Red Ants, The Raggedy Rawney, Brennende Betten, The Cook The Thief His Wife & Her Lover, Judge Dredd, The Crow: City Of Angels* and **Hearts Of Fire**, and the plays *A Jovial Crew, The Country Wife* and *The Queen And I: A Play With Songs*. In 1989, Dury wrote the excellent musical *Apples* with another former member of the Blockheads, Mickey Gallagher. In the 90s Dury was seen hosting the late-night UK television show *Metro*. He continued to tour, being able to dictate his own pace. Although *The Bus Driver's Prayer And Other Stories* was a welcome return to recording Dury was now happier varying his professional interests.

Dury developed bowel cancer in 1996 but responded well to chemotherapy. He was well enough to travel to third world countries as UNICEF's goodwill ambassador. The cancer returned with a vengeance at the end of 1997, and Dury reunited with the Blockheads in 1998 for the warmly received *Mr. Love Pants*. Many of the songs had been written for a number of years, and once again the fact that they had evolved into their own arrangements over a period of time made the songs stronger. One song in particular showed the soft side of Dury, 'You're My Baby', written for one of his young sons. The saddest thing of his illness, Dury said, was that he would never be able to see his young children growing up. Although very unwell he continued to make live appearances with the Blockheads and was seen and heard discussing his illness throughout this time, right until a month before his death in March 2000. His son **Baxter Dury** released his debut album *Len Parrot's Memorial Lift* in 2002. Dury was no angel but was and is still loved, as can be gleaned from Richard Balls' well-researched book, but he was an amazing character and a man of many different talents. The way he dealt with his terminal illness was remarkable, but ultimately he will be remembered for the cockney rhyming slang and humour of his highly original catalogue of songs.

● ALBUMS: *New Boots And Panties* (Stiff 1977) ★★★★, *Do It Yourself* (Stiff 1979) ★★★, *Laughter* (Stiff 1980) ★★, *Lord Upminster* (Polydor 1981) ★★, *4,000 Weeks Holiday* (Polydor 1984) ★★★, *Warts 'N' Audience* (Demon 1991) ★★★, *The Bus Driver's Prayer And Other Stories* (Demon 1992) ★★★, *Mr. Love Pants* (RH 1998) ★★★★, *Straight From The Desk* 1978 recording (East Central One 2002) ★★★, *Ten More Turnips From The Tip* (Ronnie Harris 2002) ★★★. The Blockheads *Where's The Party?* (Blockheads Music 2004) ★★.

● COMPILATIONS: *Juke Box Dury* (Stiff 1981) ★★★★, *Greatest Hits* (Fame 1981) ★★★, *Sex & Drugs & Rock 'n' Roll* (Demon 1987) ★★★★, *Reasons To Be Cheerful* (Repertoire 1996) ★★★★.

● FURTHER READING: *Hard Lines: New Poetry And Prose*, Ian Dury. *Sex & Drugs & Rock 'N' Roll: The Life Of Ian Dury*,

Richard Balls. *Ian Dury & The Blockheads: Song By Song*, Jim Drury.

● FILMS: *Pirates* (1986), *Rocinante* (1987), *O Paradissos Anigi Me Antiklidi* aka *Red Ants* (1987), *Hearts Of Fire* (1987), *The Raggedy Rawney* (1988), *Brennende Betten* (1988), *The Cook The Thief His Wife & Her Lover* (1989), *The Rainbow Thief* (1990), *After Midnight* (1990), *Split Second* (1992), *Boswell & Johnson's Tour Of The Western Islands* (1993), *Skallagrigg* (1994), *Judge Dredd* (1995), *The Crow: City Of Angels* (1996), *Different For Girls* (1996), *Underground* (1998), *Middleton's Changeling* (1998).

Duskin, 'Big' Joe

b. 10 February 1921, Birmingham, Alabama, USA. In the 30s Duskin moved with his family to Cincinnati, Ohio, where he began playing piano, inspired by the records of **Roosevelt Sykes**, **Albert Ammons** and **Pete Johnson**. During World War II he was drafted into the army and met Ammons, Johnson and **Meade 'Lux' Lewis** on USO shows. After demobilization Joe promised his preacher father that he would not play 'the devil's music' while the old man (in his 80s) was still alive; however, he lived to be 104! Duskin's debut album was finally released by **Arhoolie Records** in 1979 and revealed him as a worthy bearer of the boogie-woogie tradition. Later albums have appeared on the Special Delivery and Wolf labels, and Duskin has also recorded with **Dave Peabody** and the **Blues Band**.

● ALBUMS: *Cincinnati Stomp* (Arhoolie 1979) ★★★, *Don't Mess With The Boogie Man* (Special Delivery 1988) ★★★, with Axel Zwingenberger, Jay McShann, Sammy Price *Axel Zwingenberger And The Friends Of Boogie Woogie Vol. 10: Kansas City Boogie Jam* (Vagabond) ★★★, *Boogie Woogie Is My Religion* (Back To Blues 1995) ★★★, *Down The Road Apiece* 1982 recording (Wolf 1996) ★★, *Big Joe Jumps Again! Cincinnati Blues Session* (Yellow Dog 2004) ★★★.

Dussault, Nancy

b. 30 June 1936, Pensacola, Florida, USA. After studying dancing and singing she appeared in several stage productions before making her Broadway debut as a replacement in the long-running *The Sound Of Music* (1959). Dussault attracted considerable attention when she appeared in *Do Re Mi* (1960), which starred **Phil Silvers** and **Nancy Walker**. With book by Garson Kanin, music by **Jule Styne** and lyrics by **Betty Comden** and **Adolph Green**, the show ran for 400 performances and brought Dussault a Theatre World Award and a nomination for a **Tony Award** as Best Featured Actress In A Musical. Dussault was next in *Bajour* (1964), which opened at the Shubert Theatre before transferring to the Lunt-Fontanne Theatre, running for a total of 232 performances. The book, by Ernest Kinoy, was based upon Joseph Mitchell's stories published in *New Yorker* magazine. Music and lyrics were by Walter Marks and choreography by **Peter Gennaro**. The show featured Herschel Bernardi, as Cockeye Johnny Dembo, and **Chita Rivera**, as Anyanka. Also in the cast, in minor roles, were Herbert Edelman (The King of Newark) and Paul Sorvino (a policeman). For her performance, as Emily Kirsten, Dussault received her second Tony Award nomination as Best Actress In A Musical. Later Broadway appearances included replacement cast member in the musicals *Side By Side By Sondheim* (1977) and *Into The Woods* (1987).

From the early 60s, Dussault had also appeared in cabaret, notably at Julius Monk's club, Upstairs At The Downstairs, on New York's West 56th Street. Also from this time, she was often on television in plays, individual episodes of series and situation comedies and in television films. Among these appearances are *The Many Facets Of Cole Porter* and *Salute To Jerome Kern* (both 1965); *The Song And The Dance Man* (1966); *The New Dick Van Dyke Show* (1971); *The In-Laws* (1979); *Too Close For Comfort* (*The Ted Knight Show*) (1980); *The Love Boat* (1981–82); *Murder, She Wrote*; *Matlock* and *Hotel* (all 1987); *Mad About You* (1992) and *Judging Amy* (2001). Dussault was also co-host of *Good Morning America* (1975–77).

● FILMS: *The In-Laws* (1979), *The Nurse* (1997).

Dust

A hard rock band formed in the USA in the early 70s, Dust comprised Richie Wise (vocals/ guitar), Kenny Aaronson (bass) and Marc Bell (drums). They launched their career in 1971 with *Dust*, a seamless exposition of standard hard rock traditions (the debt to **Led Zeppelin** and **Jimi Hendrix** was clearly audible) with the occasional unusual arrangement. For 1972's *Hard Attack* the group extended the more experimental aspects of their sound, incorporating strings on several songs. However, it was not enough to push the group into the mainstream, and they collapsed shortly after its release. Aaronson subsequently joined **Derringer** and played with several other rock bands, while Bell worked with the **Ramones**.

● ALBUMS: *Dust* (Kama Sutra 1971) ★★★, *Hard Attack* (Kama Sutra 1972) ★★★.

Dust Brothers

One of the pre-eminent remix/production teams of the 90s, the Dust Brothers comprise radio disc jockeys Mike Simpson and John King, who first came to prominence with Matt Dike of the **Delicious Vinyl** label. In addition to fostering the career of Delicious Vinyl's major acts (**Tone Loc**, **Young MC**, etc.), they also afforded **Mellow Man Ace** and the **Beastie Boys** (1989's groundbreaking *Paul's Boutique*), among others, their skills and expertise. The Beasties Boys album introduced their pioneering cut-and-paste sampling technique, which in time saw them become among the most sought after producers/remixers in music. There was some confusion when a UK-based duo sought to use the same name for their recordings, but when Dike and his colleagues objected, the other group became the **Chemical Brothers**. The original Dust Brothers subsequently worked with acts as diverse as **Technotronic**, **Shonen Knife**, **Hanson** (1997's UK/US chart-topping single 'MMMBop'), **Beck** (1996's highly acclaimed *Odelay*) and the **Rolling Stones** (tracks on *Bridges To Babylon*). They set up their own label, Nickel Bag, in 1996. In 1999 they composed the soundtrack to the controversial Brad Pitt movie *Fight Club*.

● ALBUMS: *Fight Club: Original Motion Picture Soundtrack* (BMG 1999) ★★★.

Dust Junkys

Manchester, England's Dust Junkys initially faced both press and industry scepticism when it was revealed that singer Nicholas Lockett was none other than **MC Tunes**—the much-derided white Mancunian rapper who had appeared on a series of records with **808 State** in the late 80s/early 90s as well as releasing his own UK Top 20 solo album. However, **Polydor Records** looked beyond the cynicism and hostility and liked what they saw in the five-piece, which also featured Steve Oliver Jones (bass), Mykey Wilson (drums), Sam Brox (guitar) and Ganiyu Pierre Gasper (DJ), in addition to Lockett. The Dust Junkys combine his pointed, sociological raps with sharp, furious blasts of rock music, Brox's guitar-playing winning particular praise from the cognoscenti (his father had played with **Jimi Hendrix**). Their first release was a white label three-track EP featuring 'Fever', 'Got The Funk Up' and 'Nothing Personal'—the latter featuring a Lockett rap over a deconstructed version of **Fleetwood Mac**'s 'Oh Well'. The band made its first public appearance at the In The City Festival in Dublin, Eire, at the end of 1996, quickly building a reputation as an intense and extremely loud live act. Their debut single, 'Living In The Pocket Of A Drug Queen', was released in August 1997. Further singles followed before they released the groove-heavy *Done And . . . Dusted* in early 1998.

● ALBUMS: *Done And . . . Dusted* (Polydor 1998) ★★★.

Dutch Swing College Band

This outfit's polished, cleverly arranged repertoire was still being heard in concert more than half a century after its formation by Peter Schilperoort (b. the Netherlands, d. 18 November 1990; clarinet/ saxophones) in 1945. Among musicians that have passed through its ranks are Wout Steenhuis (guitar), Jan Morks (clarinet), Kees Van Dorser (trumpet), Oscar Klein (trumpet) and **Rod Mason** (cornet). Famous US musicians visiting Europe proudly 'sat in' with the band. Schilperoort became established as the Netherlands' foremost ambassador of trad jazz following the foundation of his long-standing partnership with Arie Ligthart (banjo/guitar) in 1952. Yet, after embracing saxophonists and even amplification, the combo were to deviate further from the prescribed New Orleans precedent, via adaptations of rock 'n' roll, country' and military marches, to achieve acceptance in the generalized pop field. By the 70s, Schilperoort had started his own DSC Productions record company and was knighted by Queen Juliana of the Netherlands. The Dutch Swing College Band has survived their leader's death in 1990.

● ALBUMS: *Dixieland Goes Dutch* (Epic 1955) ★★★★, *Dixie Gone Dutch* (Philips 1962) ★★★★, *On Tour* (Philips 1981) ★★, *Digital Dixie* (Philips 1982) ★★★, *Music For The Millions* (Philips 1983) ★★★, *The Bands Best* (Verve 1984) ★★★, *Swing Studio Sessions* (Philips 1985) ★★★, *When The Swing Comes Marching In* (Philips 1985) ★★★, *40 Years 1945–1985, At Its Best* (Timeless 1986) ★★★★, *Digital Anniversary* (Philips 1986) ★★★, *With Guests Volume 1* (Polydor 1987) ★★, *Digital Date* (Philips 1988) ★★★, *Dutch Samba* (Timeless 1989) ★★, *1960* (Philips 1990) ★★★, *Jubilee Concert* (Philips 1991) ★★★, *The Old Fashioned Way* (Jazz Hour 1993) ★★★.

Dutrey, Honore

b. 1894, New Orleans, Louisiana, USA, d. 21 July 1935, Chicago, Illinois, USA. In the years preceding World War I, trombonist Dutrey worked in several New Orleans bands but during military service suffered lung damage in a shipboard accident. In the early 20s he worked with **King Oliver** in Chicago then joined **Carroll Dickerson**'s band. During the mid-20s he led his own unit and also worked in the bands of **Louis Armstrong** and **Johnny Dodds**, but his career was truncated and he retired from active playing at the end of the decade. A sound ensemble player, Dutrey appeared on many records by his exceptional contemporaries, always lending solid support to their performances.

Dutronc, Jacques

b. 28 April 1943, Paris, France. Dutronc learnt to play piano and violin during his childhood, but by the late 50s had immersed himself in the local rock 'n' roll culture. In 1959 he left Lycée Condorcet to become the guitarist in Les Tritons, who quickly established themselves as a major attraction at Paris' Golf Drouot club. The following year the group began backing Daniel Dray and changed their name to El Toro Et Les Cyclones. They were signed to Vogue Records at the end of 1961 and released their first EP the following January. Their second EP contained the domestic hit 'Le Vagabond', but Dutronc's career was put on hold when he was called up for National Service. After his discharge he played with Eddy Mitchell, **Vince Taylor** and **Gene Vincent** but chose to concentrate on songwriting. Appointed Assistant Artistic Director at Vogue, his principal clients were Zou-Zou (a twist exponent), Les Mods and **Françoise Hardy**—for whom he penned 'Le Temps De L'Amour' and 'Va Pas Prendre Un Tambour'. Dutronc may have been content to remain a backroom composer had he and Jacques Lanzmann, editor of *Lui*, not had a similar sense of humour. Setting simple melodies and maddeningly catchy hook-lines to Lanzmann's rapid-fire lyrics—mostly of topical, satiric nature—a career as a pop comedian began Dutronc's Vogue record contract and hit its stride with a series of EPs, including his first number 1, 'Et Moi Et Moi Et Moi', which became a national catch phrase. 'Mini Mini Mini'—the skirt not the car—was better known outside France but album tracks such as 'Hippy Hippy Hourrah' and 'Les Cactus' (with a nonsensical chorus) were more typical Dutronc/Lanzmann fare. In the later 60s the team reached a wider age group with 'Playboys' and 'J'Aime Les Filles'. These harked back musically to the 20s, in the same style as songs such as 'Winchester Cathedral' and 'When I'm 64'. When his records no longer charted automatically, Dutronc settled down as a 'personality' on television chat shows and panel games. Though he still records, he is more widely known for his acting. Since 1973 he has been acclaimed for his appearances in films by leading directors such as Jean-Luc Godard, Claude Lelouch and Barbet Schroeder, and he won the French César for his performance as Van Gogh in 1991's *Vincent*.

● ALBUMS: *Jacques Dutronc* (Vogue 1966) ★★★, *Jacques Dutronc* (Vogue 1967) ★★★, *Jacques Dutronc* (Vogue 1968) ★★★, *Jacques Dutronc* (Vogue 1969) ★★★, *Dutronc Au Casino Live 1992* (1993) ★★★.

● COMPILATIONS: *Greatest Hits* (Vogue 1988) ★★★★.

Duty Free Recordings

Duty Free is the label established and owned by well-known UK DJ **Tall Paul** (b. Paul Newman) with his brother Danny and his friend and manager Steffan Chandler. The label opened for business in January 1998 and is based at the London club Turnmills (home of **Trade** and 'The Gallery' nights) in Farringdon, where the team also have an 'in-house' studio. The first release on the label came in August 1998 and was signed from Dutch label Native Dance Records. Already a popular feature of Newman's sets, JS:16's 'Stomping

System' became a national club hit, owing in part to a remix by Camisra, a pseudonym for 'Tall' Paul. The label has had notable successes with the Radical Playaz' 'The Hook' and Robbie Rivera's 'The Ultimate Disco Groove'. The following year began with a collaboration between Newman and fellow DJ **Brandon Block** as the Grifters for 'Flash', which was well received by the dance music press. Subsequent releases included the debut single from DJ Lottie and a return for JS:16 with 'Love Supreme'. The label looks set to become not only a commercial success but, more importantly, an influential force in shaping the sounds of the UK and Europe's dancefloors with its no-nonsense approach to unpretentious, crowd-pleasing dance music.

● COMPILATIONS: *Keep Duty Free* (Duty Free 1999) ★★★.

Duval, Dominic

b. USA. Active on the New York free jazz scene since the 60s, bass player Duval swiftly established a high reputation among his peers. By the new millennium, owing to several well-received albums, his name had become much better known to international audiences. He has worked notably with **Cecil Taylor** and **Joe McPhee**, as well as with musicians such as pianists Matthew Goodheart, **Mark Whitecage** and **Adam Makowicz** drummers John Heward and Jay Rosen, the latter being a particular favourite collaborator of Duval's saxophonists **Ivo Perelman**, Glenn Spearman and Chris Kelsey violinist Jason Hwang and the Amici String Quartet. He performed with the semi-classical group, the Manhattan Improvisational Chamber Ensemble, which included Rosen, **Dom Minasi** (guitar), Eleanor Amlin (vocals), John Gunther (reeds) and Rod Thomas (violin). Immensely talented and possessing a formidable technique, Duval has also recorded solo bass albums, *Nightbird Inventions* and *Anniversary*. His bands include the C.T. String Quartet (named for Taylor); the Equinox Trio, an experimental improvisatory group in which he is joined by Hwang, Ron Lawrence (viola) and Tomas Ulrich (cello) and he is particularly striking in his numerous appearances in duos, with, for example, Hwang and Goodheart. For some of his work, Duval draws upon concepts outside music. *Under The Pyramid* is a paean to the people of Mexico, and Duval has also expressed through his music his solidarity with Native Americans.

Demanding of audiences, intellectually unsettling and emotionally profound, Duval's often unpredictable music is always close to, and at times is beyond, the cutting edge of jazz. Throughout his recorded work, and notwithstanding his remarkable technical gifts, it is clear that his playing is always subservient to the needs of the group and the music they perform. Among the instruments Duval plays is a Hutchings bass, designed and built by Carleen Hutchings. These instruments have electronically tuned top and back plates, a device that creates the sonority of a vintage, seasoned instrument although they are newly made. This richness of sound is a decided asset to Duval's playing because, throughout his recorded canon, he constantly and consistently demonstrates the brooding intensity that is a hallmark of his approach to jazz.

● ALBUMS: with Michael Jefry Stevens *Elements* (Leo 1995) ★★★, *Nightbird Inventions* (Cadence 1997) ★★★★, with Jay Rosen *Wedding Band* (CIMP 1997) ★★★, *Equinox* (Leo 1997) ★★★, *State Of The Art* (CIMP 1997) ★★★, *The Navigator* (Leo 1998) ★★★★, *Live In Concert* (Cadence 1998) ★★★, with Joe McPhee, Jay Rosen *The Watermelon Suite* (CIMP 1998) ★★★★, with McPhee, Rosen, Rosi Hertlein *Rapture* (Cadence 1998) ★★★, with Jason Hwang *The Experiment* (Blue Jackal 1999) ★★★, *Anniversary* (CIMP 1999) ★★★, *Under The Pyramid* (Leo 1999) ★★★, with McPhee *The Dream Book* (Cadence 1999) ★★★, with McPhee, Mike Bisio, Joe Giardullo *In The Spirit* (CIMP 1999) ★★★, with McPhee, Giardullo, Bisio *No Greater Love* (CIMP 2000) ★★★, with John Heward, Joe McPhee *Undersound* (Leo 2000) ★★★, with Matthew Goodheart *Crossings* (Cadence 2000) ★★★, *Asylum* (Leo 2001) ★★★, *Cries And Whispers* (Cadence 2001) ★★★, *American Scrapbook* (CIMP 2002) ★★★, with Mark Hewins *Bar Torque* (Moonjune 2002) ★★, with Heward, McPhee *Undersound II* 1990 recording (Leo 2003) ★★★, with Jay Rosen, Mark Whitecage *No Respect* (Acoustics 2003) ★★★★, with Devorah Day *Standard* (CIMP 2004) ★★★, with Jimmy Halperin, Jay Rosen *Joy & Gravitas* (CIMP 2004) ★★★.

Duvivier, George

b. 17 August 1920, New York City, New York, USA, d. 11 July 1985, New York City, New York, USA. After formal musical education, mostly on violin, Duvivier worked with a New York symphony orchestra but soon entered the jazz world where, having recognized the limitations of the violin in that area, he switched to bass. In the early 40s he worked with several leading artists in small and large group settings, among them **Coleman Hawkins** and **Lucky Millinder**. He also began arranging and contributing many musical scores for the later **Jimmie Lunceford** band and the elegant but short-lived **Sy Oliver** big band. In the 50s he worked extensively in the studios, often accompanying singers on record, with some of whom he also collaborated on tours at home and overseas. Among these were demanding performers such as **Lena Horne** and **Pearl Bailey**. He also played with small groups, an activity he continued alongside his writing into the 60s. During this period Duvivier was with bands led by **Terry Gibbs**, **Bud Powell**, **Shelly Manne**, **Eric Dolphy**, **Benny Goodman** and **Ben Webster**. A dominant force in any rhythm section, Duvivier played with great precision and attack. He continued to play jazz dates around the world through the 70s and into the 80s, working with musicians such as **Zoot Sims**, **Joe Venuti**, **Hank Jones** and **Warren Vaché Jnr.**

● ALBUMS: *In Paris* (Coronet 1956) ★★★, *Max Roach, Sonny Clark, George Duvivier* (Time 1962) ★★★★.

DVC

Formed in the USA in 1980, DVC comprised Bob Forest (guitar/ vocals), John Bartle (guitar/ vocals), Max Padilla (bass) and John Bollin (drums). Their energetic brand of hard rock encompassed excellent dual guitar interplay and harmonies from Forest and Bartle, but more attention focused on the fact that John Bollin was the brother of the late **Tommy Bolin**. The group's 1981 self-titled debut for Alfa Records thus attracted substantial press coverage (not least due to the presence of a cover version of Bolin's 'Teaser'), but once the novelty had worn off rock journalists looked elsewhere. In retrospect, this was a minor travesty considering the strength of the group's own compositions.

● ALBUMS: *DVC* (Alfa 1981) ★★★.

Dvorkin, Judith

b. 1928, USA, d. 24 July 1995, New York, USA. A composer, lyricist and songwriter, Dvorkin published most of her music under the pseudonym Judy Spencer. She enjoyed a varied and prolific career, which started as one of the songwriters for the children's television programme *Captain Kangaroo*. Probably her best known song was 'Soft Summer Breeze', which established itself as a radio standard that achieved more than one million plays in her lifetime. She wrote a musical play, *Cyrano*, which was performed at the Brooklyn Academy Of Music and off-Broadway. As well as her one-act opera for children, *What's In A Name*, she also wrote commercially available classical pieces such as *Three Letters*, *John Keats To Fanny Brawne*, and *Maurice: A Madrigal* and *Suite For Violin And Clarinet*. Before dying of cancer at the age of 67, she guided the careers of several young composers, while her work has been included in two American song anthologies: J.T. Howard's *Our American Music* and M. Stewart-Green's *Women Composers' Work*.

Dwarves

Though never quite matching **G.G. Allin**'s ability for outraging moral decency, this Chicago, Illinois, USA–based outfit has managed to continually offend and confuse throughout their career. Originally formed by frontman Blag Dahlia as Suburban Nightmare, the band's earliest incarnation was as a garage outfit, and the first full Dwarves album, 1986's *Horror Stories*, continued this sound. When the Dwarves took their volatile show on the road across America, stories of 15-minute shows, onstage sex acts and audiences soaked in bodily fluids only heightened the buzz around the band. Their preference for pseudonyms and a rotating door policy for band members helped to sustain the band's already unsavoury reputation. *Toolin' For A Warm Teabag* documented the band's scatological approach and also saw the debut of their skull and crossbones motif. With a relatively settled line-up comprising Blag Dahlia aka Blag Jesus (vocals), Vadge Moore (drums), He Who Cannot Be Named (guitar) and Salt Peter (bass), the band signed for the burgeoning **Sub Pop Records** label that was enjoying the fruits of the grunge revolution. The first release for the new label, *Blood, Guts, And Pussy*, saw the band refine their sound into a streamlined punk approach. Lyrically uncompromising, a glance at the song titles gave a clue to the band's primary obsessions. *Thank Heaven For Little Girls* followed soon after, and despite the typically distasteful subject matter the band demonstrated a new-found musicality. *Sugar Fix* was the band's last effort for Sub Pop, with 'Smack City' a thinly veiled attack on the label and Seattle's ongoing heroin problem. The highly publicized faked death of He Who Cannot Be Named ended the band's relationship with the label (*Sugar Fix* even carried a tribute to the guitarist).

It was to be three years before the band returned to the studio, and *The Dwarves Are Young And Good Looking* was their best work for some time. The equally likely Wholly Smokes replaced him Who Cannot Be Named, and at this point Nick Oliveri of **Kyuss** was playing with the band under the moniker Rex Everything. Likened by fans to the **Ramones**, this latest release ranked alongside *Blood, Guts, And Pussy* as the definitive Dwarves album. A contract with **Epitaph Records** followed, which saw the band release its most melodic and diverse album so far, incorporating samples and electronic beats. More line-up changes followed,

with Vadge Moore leaving the band subject to rumours that he had severed a hand in a chainsaw accident, while He Who Cannot Be Named was miraculously raised from the dead to fill the vacant bass and guitar spots. Epitaph, perhaps having glimpsed what was to come, subsequently dropped the band just as they crossed the gender barrier and recruited female bass player Tazzie Bushweed.

● ALBUMS: *Horror Stories* (Voxx 1986) ★★, *Toolin' For A Warm Teabag* (Nasty Gash 1989) ★★, *Blood, Guts, And Pussy* (Sub Pop 1990) ★★★★, *Thank Heaven For Little Girls* (Sub Pop 1991) ★★★, *Sugar Fix* (Sub Pop 1993) ★★, *The Dwarves Are Young And Good Looking* (Greedy/Recess 1997) ★★★★, *Come Clean* (Epitaph 2000) ★★★.

● COMPILATIONS: *Toolin' For Lucifer's Crank* (Recess 1996) ★★★, *Free Cocaine* (Recess 1999) ★★★, *Lick It* (Recess 2000) ★★★.

● DVD/VIDEOS: *Fuck You Up And Get Live* (Music Video Distributors 2005).

Dweeb

Lo-fi indie band Dweeb, formed in Watford, Hertfordshire, England, launched their career with three singles for acclaimed independent labels—Fierce Panda, Che and Damaged Goods. Afterwards, they surprised many by signing to a major, **WEA Records**, through their Blanco y Negro affiliate. The group, which comprises leader Kris Dweeb, his sister Lara and the similarly surnameless John Dweeb, formed after seeing a London gig by teenage lo-fi band **Bis**. They came to the attention of Blanco y Negro managing director Geoff Travis (formerly of **Rough Trade Records**) after he heard the demo that won them appearances on BBC Radio 1's *Evening Session* and the **John Peel** show. Their first two singles for Blanco, 'Scooby Doo' and 'Oh Yeah, Baby', highlighted the group's energetic pop style, with guitars allied to electronic elements including samples, drum machines and tape loops. Surprisingly, their debut album was recorded with Pete Woodroffe, best known for his work with **Def Leppard** and (more in keeping with the group's sound) **Tiger**.

● ALBUMS: *Turn You On* (Blanco y Negro 1997) ★★★.

Dwele

b. Andwele Gardner, Detroit, Michigan, USA. That this innovative nu soul artist's full first name means 'God has brought me' in Swahili is frequently cited as fitting for a man considered as an outstanding talent. This may be overstating the case but, nevertheless, the former rapper's juxtaposition of R&B, spoken word, jazz and the swagger of underground hip-hop essays an easy charm and confidence.

Dwele was brought up in Detroit in a highly musical family that was tragically reduced to his mother and younger brother after the fatal shooting of his father outside his home when Dwele was 10. The musician has subsequently acknowledged the loss of his father as impacting on his 'creative side'. Self-described as an 'old soul', Dwele has recalled that at the schools of his childhood he seemed to have different tastes in music to everybody around him, citing **Stevie Wonder**, **Donny Hathaway**, **Roy Ayers**, **Miles Davis** and **Freddie Hubbard** as particular favourites. Dwele studied piano from the age of six, was a trumpeter in the schools marching and jazz bands and was to later learn bass and guitar. Inspired by hip-hop innovators **A Tribe Called Quest**, he became an MC, the catalyst for hooking up with Jay Dee,

T3 and Muhammed Baatin aka underground hip-hop savants **Slum Village**. He appeared on their 2002 **MTV** hit 'Tainted' and the favour was returned via a guest appearance on Dwele's major label debut *Subject*. Having sold his 1998 demo *The Rize* out of the boot of his car—there were only 100 copies and they sold out in a week—Dwele subsequently signed a recording contract with **Virgin Records** and released *Subject* in 2003. Taking his cues from soul masters past and present, Dwele sprinkled his nu soul with the self-assurance of hip-hop to create an album that seemed reverent to its predecessors but (equally) remained free from the deadening hand of nostalgia. His second major label release, *Some Kinda . . .*, followed at the end of 2005.

● ALBUMS: *The Rize* (Own Label 1998) ★★★, *Subject* (Virgin 2003) ★★★★, *Some Kinda . . .* (Virgin 2005) ★★★.

Dyani, Johnny Mbizo

b. 30 November 1945, East London, South Africa, d. 25 October 1986, Berlin, Germany. Dyani was a vital, emotional bass player who earned immense respect from musicians everywhere, yet, not unusually for such artists, never achieved the recognition he deserved. At the 1962 Johannesburg Jazz Festival **Chris McGregor** invited him and four more of the best players at the Festival to form a band, and the legendary Blue Notes were created. As a mixed-race band it was impossible for them to work under apartheid and so, in 1964, while touring Europe, they decided to settle in London, where, evolving into the Chris McGregor Group, they made a huge impact on the UK jazz scene. As well as playing in the six-piece McGregor Group and the Brotherhood Of Breath (the big band that McGregor set up after disbanding the sextet), Dyani toured South America in 1966 with **Steve Lacy**, **Enrico Rava** and **Louis Moholo** (the quartet recording *The Forest And The Zoo* under Lacy's name in 1967), and he then worked with the **Spontaneous Music Ensemble** (1969) and the Musicians Co-Operative (1971). In 1969, at the Actuel Festival organized by the French record company BYG, he took part in a jam that included **Frank Zappa**, **Archie Shepp** and **Philly Joe Jones**.

Dyani had been growing unhappy with the direction that McGregor's band was taking, feeling that it was moving too close to free jazz and away from its African roots so, in the early 70s, he moved to Denmark, where he worked with **John Tchicai**, **Don Cherry** and **Abdullah Ibrahim**. He also worked with **David Murray**, **Joseph Jarman** and in the trio **Detail** with **John Stevens** and saxophonist **Frode Gjerstad** (they became Detail Plus when **Bobby Bradford** and others guested with them). After Dyani's death in 1986 several albums were dedicated to his memory including Tchicai's *Put Up The Fight*, Steven's and **Dudu Pukwana**'s *Radebe* (*They Shoot To Kill*) and *Blue Notes For Johnny*, a searingly emotional tribute by McGregor, Pukwana and Moholo. His son, Thomas, is establishing a reputation as a percussionist with his own band.

● ALBUMS: *Blues Notes For Mongezi* (Ogun 1976) ★★★, *Blue Notes In Concert* (Ogun 1978) ★★★, *Witchdoctor's Son* (SteepleChase 1978) ★★★★, *Song For Biko* (SteepleChase 1978) ★★★, *Mbizo* (SteepleChase 1981) ★★★★, *Born Under The Heat* (Dragon 1983) ★★★, *Okhela* (Affinity 1984) ★★★, *Angolian Cry* (SteepleChase 1985) ★★★★.

● FURTHER READING: *Mbizo: A Book About Johnny Dyani*, Lars Rasmussen.

Dyble, Judy

b. 13 February 1949, London, England. Singer-songwriter Dyble took her first steps in the music business with north London folk band Judy And The Folkmen. In 1967 she joined **Ashley Hutchings**, **Simon Nicol**, **Richard Thompson** and Martin Lamble in **Fairport Convention**. Dyble left library school to tour with the future giants of English folk rock, singing lead and harmony vocals and playing autoharp, and she was present for the recording of their debut single, 'If I Had A Ribbon Bow', and the same year's self-titled album. She parted company with Fairport Convention a year later and immediately joined her boyfriend Ian McDonald in Giles, Giles, Fripp, McDonald And Dyble. She recorded a number of tracks with this unit (later compiled on the 2001 release *The Brondesbury Tapes*) but departed before it evolved into **King Crimson**. Her next move was to collaborate with Irish singer-songwriter **Jackie McAuley** in **Trader Horne**, a short-lived unit that released the neglected UK psych-folk classic *Morning Way* in 1970. Dyble played briefly with Dyble Coxhill And The MB's (featuring **Lol Coxhill**, Steve Miller and Phil Miller) before 'retiring' from the music world to concentrate on her family. She worked in a library and helped her husband Simon Stable run his cassette duplicating business, briefly coming out of retirement to guest at Fairport Convention's Cropredy festival in 1981 and 1982. Fifteen years elapsed before she reunited with the band to sing at the 30th Anniversary Cropredy.

After appearing at the 35th Anniversary Cropredy in 2002, Dyble was contacted by producer Marc Swordfish of UK **trance** band **Astralasia** with a view to collaborating. Dyble and Swordfish spent the next two years writing and recording the singer's debut album, *Enchanted Garden*, which was released by the Talking Elephant label in 2004. The blending of Dyble's quintessentially English vocals and songwriting with Swordfish's contemporary production techniques, replete with samples and electronic effects, was a bold and impressive statement of musical intent, although it did raise the eyebrows of some folk fans. The title track set to music a Brian Patten poem originally written for Dyble in the late 60s.

● ALBUMS: *Enchanted Garden* (Talking Elephant 2004) ★★★, *Spindle* (Talking Elephant 2006) ★★★.

Dycus, Frank

b. Marion Franklin Dycus, 5 December 1939, Hardmoney, Kentucky, USA. Dycus initially had no thoughts of pursuing a career as a songwriter. At school he was reckoned to be studious and was writing poems to his mother when he was 14. He relocated to California in 1955 and soon afterwards he enlisted in the US Air Force. He learned to play guitar and with his friend, singer Don Gonsalez, formed a duo called Don And Frank. They attempted to be soundalike **Everly Brothers** and found regular bookings over two or three States sometimes opening for touring stars such as **Jim Reeves** and **Buck Owens**, and for a time they were regulars on KPEG Spokane. After discharge in 1962, Dycus spent a short time in Nashville but failed to find work and eventually settled in Wichita, where he worked for Boeing in the aircraft industry and also hosted a radio show on KATE. In 1967 he returned to Nashville and worked as a songwriter in **Pete Drake**'s music publishing company. In 1970 Dycus formed his own company, Empher Music, in partnership with Larry Kingston and Roger Fox. They achieved several minor hits including **Wynn Stewart**'s Top 50 with 'Paint Me A Rainbow'. In 1972 they sold their company to **Dolly Parton** and **Porter Wagoner,** and Dycus joined Parton's Owpar Publishing. He also managed Parton and Wagoner's Fireside Recording Studios. At Wagoner's instigation, Dycus made some recordings of a skiffle nature as Lonesome Frank And The Kitchen Band, with Wagoner helping out with backing vocal on some tracks. In 1979 he worked in Sweden with **Abba**'s drummer and other local musicians before returning to the USA to record an album that gained Swedish release on **Sonet Records**. In 1981 **George Strait** gained his first two *Billboard* chart hits with Dycus' songs namely 'Unwound' (number 6) and 'Down And Out' (number 16) and the following year Strait gained another number 6 hit with the Dycus song 'Marina Del Rey'. In 1987 Dycus, who had been in failing health for sometime, had heart bypass surgery and was inactive for more than two years. In 1990, after initially deciding to retire from the music business, he formed a new publishing company in Nashville and gained further success with **George Jones**' recordings of 'I Don't Need Your Rocking Chair' and 'Walls Can Fall', songs he co-wrote with **Billy Yates**.

Dyer, Ada

b. USA. Dyer first recorded as a backing vocalist for soul performer **Norman Connors** in the early 80s before joining the dance-rock group **Warp 9**. They scored several US hits under the aegis of producer **Jellybean** Benitez, first on the Prism label and later for **Motown**. After recording *Fade In, Fade Out* in 1985, the group dissolved, and Dyer was signed to a solo contract with Motown, where she was teamed with producer James Anthony Carmichael. This partnership produced *Meant To Be* in 1988, which enjoyed some acclaim in dance music circles, and the USA disco hit 'I'll Bet Ya, I'll Let Ya'.

● ALBUMS: *Meant To Be* (Motown 1988) ★★★.

Dyer, Bob

b. Robert Dies, 22 May 1909, Nashville, Tennessee, USA, d. 1984. Dyer arrived in Australia in 1937 as a hillbilly singer-comedian with a travelling show. A talented musician, he played banjo-ukulele, guitar and harmonica, but his musical talent was never really featured on his recordings. His first two recordings were made for **Columbia Records** in the UK in 1939, but he recorded nine further sides for **Regal Zonophone Records** in Sydney, Australia, in August 1940. The material was perhaps more vaudeville than country and included 'The Martins And The Coys' and 'I Never See Maggie Alone'. In the same year Dyer married Australian showgirl Dolly Mack (b. 1921, Australia, d. 25 December 2004, Gympie, Queensland, Australia). He was popular on the Australian country scene for some years before he later became a radio and television personality, as well as the presenter, with his wife, of the quiz show *Pick-A-Box*, that ran from 1957–71. Bob and Dolly were awarded a special Gold Logie to mark their contribution to the Australian television industry. After the show ended the Dyers retired to Queensland and concentrated on their love of deep-sea fishing.

● COMPILATIONS: *Pick-A-Box Hillbilly Heaven* 1939–40 recordings (Rouseabout 1996) ★★★.

Dyer, Johnny

b. 1938, Rolling Fork, Mississippi, USA. Dyer took up the harmonica when he was seven and as a teenager sat in with **Smokey Wilson** in a local club. He moved to Los Angeles California, in January 1958 and formed his own band, the Blue Notes, backing visitors such as **J.B. Hutto**, **Jimmy Reed** and **Jimmy Rogers**. He later formed a duo with George Smith, at that time still working as Little Walter Jnr. He recorded a couple of singles for **Shakey Jake**'s Good Time label before cutting an album, *Johnny Dyer And The LA Dukes*, for Murray Brothers in 1983. Some of the tracks were later issued in Japan by Mina Records. In 1991 William Clarke included him on *Hard Times*, an anthology of contemporary LA bluesmen. Soon afterwards, he formed the Houserockers with guitarist Rick 'LA Holmes' Holstrom, who had previously recorded with Clarke, **Billy Boy Arnold**, **Rod Piazza** and Smokey Wilson. *Listen Up* managed to combine Holstrom's **Pee Wee Crayton**-influenced technique with Dyer's more down-home harmonica playing, including an effective version of **Little Walter**'s 'Blue Midnight'. *Shake It!* added pianist Tom Mahon on a set of original songs that encapsulate the hybrid west coast-Chicago style.

● ALBUMS: *Johnny Dyer And The L.A. Jukes* aka *Jukin'* (Murray Brothers 1983) ★★★★, with Shakey Jake *Straight Ahead* (Mina 1985) ★★★, *Hard Times—LA Blues Authority* (Black Magic 1991) ★★★, *Listen Up* (Black Top 1994) ★★★, with Rick Holmstrom *Shake It!* (Black Top 1995) ★★★, with Mark Hummel *Rolling Folk Revisited* (Mountaintop 2004) ★★★★.

Dyke And The Blazers

This Los Angeles–based unit evolved when Dyke (b. Arlester Christian, 13 June 1943, Buffalo, New York, USA, d. 13 March 1971, USA) teamed with the Blazers, formerly the **O'Jays**' backing group. 'Funky Broadway', Dyke's own composition, gave his band its debut hit in 1967, but their performance was overshadowed by **Wilson Pickett**'s more successful remade version. Dyke And The Blazers secured two minor chart places with 'So Sharp' (1967) and 'Funky Walk' (1968) before 'We Got More Soul' and 'Let A Woman Be A Woman—Let A Man Be A Man' reached the US R&B Top 10/pop Top 40 in 1969. The group's raw and energetic dancefloor style continued with three singles on the R&B charts in 1970. Christian was shot dead the following year.

● ALBUMS: *The Funky Broadway* (Original Sound 1967) ★★★.

● COMPILATIONS: *Dyke's Greatest Hits* (Original Sound 1969) ★★★, *So Sharp* i (Kent 1983) ★★★, *So Sharp* ii (Kent 1991) ★★★.

Dykes, Omar

b. Kent Dykes, 1950, McComb, Mississippi, USA. The 12-year-old Kent wanted a baseball glove for Christmas and was not impressed by the guitar he received instead. However, he changed his mind, aided by his father's purchase of a **Jimmy Reed** album. Soon, he was crossing the road to sit in at his local juke-joint, commemorated in the title of his 1993 album *Courts Of Lulu*. At high school he played **Chuck Berry** and **Bo Diddley** songs and listened to the **Beatles**, the **Rolling Stones** and the **Animals**. His band, the Howlers, was formed in Hattiesburg, Mississippi, in 1973; three years later they moved to Austin, Texas, and Dykes turned professional. The band's basic three-pronged approach to music, one part

Creedence Clearwater Revival to two parts Theodore 'Hound Dog' Taylor, allied to Dykes' Howlin' Wolf–like vocals, was established with their second album *I Told You So*. Two albums for Columbia Records in the late 80s flirted with added instrumentation, but that ended with 1990's *Monkey Land*. Subsequent albums *Blues Bag* and *Muddy Springs Road* carry a solo credit and refine the sound. Content to work the southern club circuit and enhance his burgeoning European reputation with regular tours (*Live At Paradiso* was recorded in Amsterdam in September 1991), Dykes has taken pride in being able to survive without overt commercial success.

● ALBUMS: *Big Leg Beat* (Amazing 1980) ★★★, *I Told You So* (Austin 1984) ★★★, *Hard Times In The Land Of Plenty* (Columbia 1987) ★★★, *Wall Of Pride* (Columbia 1988) ★★, *Monkey Land* (Antone's 1990) ★★★, *Blues Bag* (Provogue 1991) ★★★, *Live At Paradiso* (Provogue 1992) ★★, *Courts Of Lulu* (Provogue 1993) ★★★, *Muddy Springs Road* (Provogue 1994) ★★★.

Dylan, Bob

b. Robert Allen Zimmerman, 24 May 1941, Duluth, Minnesota, USA. Bob Dylan is without doubt one of the most influential figures in the history of popular music. He is the writer of scores of classic songs and is generally regarded as the man who brought literacy to rock lyrics.

The son of the middle-class proprietor of an electrical and furniture store, as a teenager living in Hibbing, Minnesota, Robert Zimmerman was always intrigued by the romanticism of the outsider. He loved James Dean movies, liked riding motorcycles and wearing biker gear and listened to R&B music on radio stations transmitting from the south. A keen fan of folk singer Odetta and country legend Hank Williams, he was also captivated by early rock 'n' roll. When he began playing music himself, with school friends in bands such as the Golden Chords and Elston Gunn And The Rock Boppers, it was as a clumsy but enthusiastic piano player, and it was at this time that he declared his ambition in a high school yearbook 'to join Little Richard'. In 1959 he began visiting Minneapolis at weekends, and on his graduation from high school enrolled at the University of Minnesota there, although he spent most of his time hanging around with local musicians in the beatnik coffee-houses of the Dinkytown area. It was in Minneapolis that he first discovered blues music, and he began to incorporate occasional blues tunes into the primarily traditional material that made up his repertoire as an apprentice folk singer. Zimmerman, who by this time had changed his name to Dylan in honour of one of his favourite poets, Dylan Thomas, played occasionally at local clubs but was by most accounts a confident but, at best, unremarkable performer. In the summer of 1960, however, Dylan spent some time in Denver, Colorado, and developed as an artist in several extraordinary and important ways. First, he adopted a persona based upon the Woody Guthrie romantic hobo figure in the movie *Bound For Glory*. Dylan had learned about Guthrie in Minnesota and had quickly devoured and memorized as many Guthrie songs as he could. In Denver he assumed a new voice, began speaking with an Okie twang and adopted a new 'hard travellin'' appearance. Second, in Denver Dylan had met Jesse Fuller, a blues performer who played guitar and harmonica simultaneously by using a harp rack. Dylan was intrigued and soon afterwards began to teach himself to do

the same. By the time he returned to Minneapolis, he had developed remarkably as a performer. By now sure that he intended to make a living as a professional musician, he returned briefly to Hibbing, Minnesota, then set out, via Madison, Wisconsin, and Chicago, Illinois, for New York City, where he arrived on 24 January 1961.

For a completely unknown and still very raw performer, Dylan's impact on the folk scene of Greenwich Village was immediate and enormous. He captivated anyone who saw him with his energy, his charisma and his rough-edged authenticity. He spun stories about his background and family history, weaving a tangled web of tall tales and myths about who he was and where he was from. He played in the coffeehouses of the Village, including Cafe Wha?, The Commons, The Gaslight and, most importantly, Gerde's Folk City, where he made his first professional appearance, supporting John Lee Hooker, in April 1961. He was also paid for playing harmonica on records by Harry Belafonte and Carolyn Hester, as a result of which he came the attention of producer John Hammond, who signed him to Columbia Records in Autumn 1961. At the same time, a gig at Gerde's was reviewed favourably in the *New York Times* by Robert Shelton, who declared that Bob Dylan was clearly destined for fortune and fame.

His first album, called simply *Bob Dylan*, was released in March 1962. It presented a collection of folk and blues standards, often about death and sorrows and the trials of life, songs that had been included in Dylan's repertoire over the past year or so, performed with gusto and an impressive degree of sensitivity for a 20-year-old. However, it was the inclusion of two of his own compositions, most notably the mature and affectionate tribute 'Song To Woody' that pointed the way forward. Over the next few months, Dylan wrote dozens of songs, many of them 'topical' songs. Encouraged by his girlfriend, Suze Rotolo, Dylan became interested in, and was subsequently adopted by, the Civil Rights movement. His song 'Blowin' In The Wind', written in April 1962, was to be the most famous of his protest songs and was included on his second album, *The Freewheelin' Bob Dylan*, released in May 1963. In the meantime, Dylan had written and recorded several other noteworthy early political songs, including 'Masters Of War' and 'A Hard Rain's A-Gonna Fall', and, during a nine-month separation from Rotolo, one of his greatest early love songs 'Don't Think Twice, It's All Right'.

At the end of 1962 he recorded a single, a rock 'n' roll song called 'Mixed Up Confusion', with backing musicians. The record was quickly deleted, apparently because Dylan's manager, Albert Grossman, saw that the way forward for his charge was not as a rocker but as an earnest acoustic folky. Similarly, tracks that had been recorded for Dylan's second album with backing musicians were scrapped, although the liner notes which commented on them and identified the players remained carelessly unrevised. The *Freewheelin'* record was so long in coming that four original song choices were substituted at the last moment by other, more newly composed songs. One of the tracks omitted was 'Talking John Birch Society Blues', which Dylan had been controversially banned from singing on the *Ed Sullivan Show* in May 1963. The attendant publicity did no harm whatsoever to Dylan's stature as a radical new 'anti-establishment' voice. At the same time, Grossman's shrewd decision to have a somewhat saccharine version of 'Blowin' In The Wind' recorded by Peter, Paul And Mary also paid off, the record becoming a huge hit in the USA and bringing Dylan's name to national, and indeed international, attention for the first time.

At the end of 1962, Dylan flew to London to appear in the long-lost BBC Television play *The Madhouse On Castle Street*. The experience did little to further his career as an actor, but while he was in London he learned many English folk songs, particularly from musician **Martin Carthy**, whose tunes he subsequently 'adapted'. Thus, 'Scarborough Fair' was reworked as 'Girl From The North Country', 'Lord Franklin' as 'Bob Dylan's 'Dream' and 'Nottamun Town' as 'Masters Of War'. The songs continued to pour out and singers began to queue up to record them. It was at this time that **Joan Baez** first began to play a prominent part in Dylan's life. Already a successful folk singer, Baez covered Dylan songs at a rapid rate and proclaimed his genius at every opportunity. Soon she was introducing him to her audience, and the two became lovers, the King and Queen of folk music. Dylan's songwriting became more astute and wordy as the months passed. Biblical and other literary imagery began to be pressed into service in songs such as 'When The Ship Comes In' and the anthemic 'Times They Are A-Changin'', this last written a day or two after Dylan had sung 'Only A Pawn In Their Game' in front of 400,000 people at the March On Washington, 28 August 1963. Indeed, the very next day, Dylan read in the local newspaper of the death of black waitress Hattie Carroll, which inspired the best, and possibly the last, of his protest songs, 'The Lonesome Death Of Hattie Carroll', included on his third album, *The Times They Are A-Changin'*, released in January 1964.

Dylan's songwriting perspectives underwent a huge change in 1964. Now finally separated from Suze Rotolo, disenchanted with much of the petty politics of the Village and becoming increasingly frustrated with the 'spokesman of a generation' tag that had been hung around his neck, the ever-restless Dylan sloughed off the expectations of the old folky crowd, and, influenced by his reading the poetry of John Keats and French symbolist Arthur Rimbaud, began to expand his own poetic consciousness. He then wrote the songs that made up his fourth record, *Another Side Of Bob Dylan*—including the disavowal of his past, 'My Back Pages', and the Illuminations-inspired 'Chimes Of Freedom'—while yet newer songs such as 'Mr Tambourine Man' (which he recorded for but did not include on *Another Side*), 'Gates Of Eden' and 'It's Alright Ma, I'm Only Bleeding', which he began to include in concert performances over the next few weeks, dazzled with their lyrical complexity and literary sophistication.

Here, then, was Dylan the poet, and here the arguments about the relative merits of high art and popular art began. The years 1964–66 were unquestionably Dylan's greatest as a writer and as a performer; they were also his most influential years and many artists today still cite the three albums that followed, *Bringing It All Back Home* and *Highway 61 Revisited* from 1965 and 1966's double album *Blonde On Blonde* as being seminal in their own musical development. *Another Side Of Bob Dylan* was to be Dylan's last solo acoustic album for almost 30 years. Intrigued by what the **Beatles** were doing—he had visited London again to play one concert at the Royal Festival Hall in May 1964—and particularly excited by the **Animals**' 'folk rock' cover version of 'House Of The Rising Sun', a track Dylan himself had included on his debut album, he and producer Tom Wilson

fleshed out some of the *Bringing It All Back Home* songs with rock 'n' roll backings—the proto-rap 'Subterranean Homesick Blues' and 'Maggie's Farm', for instance. However, the song that was perhaps Dylan's most important mid-60s composition, 'Like A Rolling Stone', was written immediately after the final series of acoustic concerts played in the UK in April and May 1965 and is commemorated in D.A. Pennebaker's famous documentary film *Don't Look Back*. Dylan said that he began to write 'Like A Rolling Stone' having decided to 'quit' singing and playing. The lyrics to the song emerged from six pages of stream-of-consciousness 'vomit'; the sound of the single emerged from the immortal combination of Chicago blues guitarist **Michael Bloomfield**, bass man **Harvey Brooks** and fledgling organ-player **Al Kooper**. 'Like A Rolling Stone' was producer Tom Wilson's last, and greatest, Dylan track. At six minutes, it destroyed the formula of the sub-three-minute single forever. It was a huge hit and was played, alongside the **Byrds**' equally momentous version of 'Mr Tambourine Man', all over the radio in the summer of 1965.

Consequently, it should have come as no surprise to those who went to see Dylan at the **Newport Folk Festival** on July 25 that he was now a fully-fledged folk rocker; but, apparently, it did. Backed by the **Paul Butterfield** Blues Band, Dylan's supposedly 'new sound'—although admittedly it was his first concert with supporting musicians—was met with a storm of bewilderment and hostility. Stories vary as to how much Dylan was booed that night, and why, but Dylan seemed to find the experience both exhilarating and liberating. If, after the UK tour, he had felt ready to quit, now he was ready to start again, to tour the world with a band and to take his music, and himself, to the farthest reaches of experience, just like Rimbaud. Dylan's discovery of the Hawks, a Canadian group who had been playing roadhouses and funky bars until introductions were made via **John Hammond Jnr.** and Albert Grossman's secretary Mary Martin, was one of those pieces of alchemical magic that happen hermetically. The Hawks, later to become the **Band**, comprised **Robbie Robertson**, Richard Manuel, Garth Hudson, **Rick Danko** and **Levon Helm**. Dylan's songs and the Hawks' sound were made for each other. After a couple of stormy warm-up gigs, they took to the road in the autumn of 1965 and travelled through the USA, then, via Hawaii, to Australia, on to Scandinavia and finally to Britain, with a hop over to Paris for a birthday show, in May 1966. Dylan was deranged and dynamic, the group wild and mercurial. Their set, the second half of a show that opened with Dylan playing acoustically to a reverentially silent house, was provocative and perplexing for many. It was certainly the loudest thing anyone had ever heard, and, almost inevitably, the electric set was greeted with anger and dismay. Drummer Levon Helm was so disheartened by the ferocity of the booing that he quit before the turn of the year—drummers Sandy Konikoff and Mickey Jones completed the tour. The most infamous date took place at the Manchester Free Trade Hall in England; known erroneously as the 'Royal Albert Hall' concert for many years, the recording was officially released in 1998. After an angry folk fan shouts out 'Judas' from the audience, Dylan responds 'I don't believe you! You're a liar!' and turns round to the band and instructs them to 'play fuckin' loud!' as they begin playing the last song of the night, 'Like A Rolling Stone'.

Offstage, Dylan was spinning out of control, not sleeping, not eating, looking wasted and apparently heading rapidly for rock 'n' roll oblivion. Pennebaker again filmed the tour, this time in Dylan's employ. The 'official' record of the tour was the rarely seen *Eat The Document*, a film originally commissioned by ABC-TV. The unofficial version compiled by Pennebaker himself was *You Know Something Is Happening*. 'What was happening,' says Pennebaker, 'was drugs . . .'. Dylan was physically exhausted when he returned to America in June 1966 but had to complete the film and finish *Tarantula*, the book that was overdue for Macmillan. He owed Columbia two more albums before his contract expired, and he was booked to play a series of concerts right up to the end of the year in increasingly bigger venues, including Shea Stadium. Then, on 29 July 1966, Dylan was injured in a motorcycle accident near his home in Bearsville, near Woodstock, upper New York State. Was there really a motorcycle accident? Dylan still claims there was. He hurt his neck and had treatment. More importantly, the accident allowed him to shrug off the responsibilities that had been lined up on his behalf by manager Grossman. By now, the relationship between Dylan and Grossman was less than cordial and litigation between the two of them was ongoing until Grossman's death almost 20 years later.

Dylan was nursed through his convalescence by his wife, Sara—they had been married privately in November 1965—and was visited only rarely. Rumours spread that Dylan would never perform again. Journalists began to prowl around the estate, looking for some answers but finding no one to ask. After several months of doing little but feeding cats, bringing up young children and cutting off his hair, Dylan was joined in the Bearsville area by the Hawks, who rented a house called Big Pink in West Saugerties. Every day they met and played music. It was the final therapy that Dylan needed. A huge amount of material was recorded in the basement of Big Pink—old folk songs, old pop songs, old country songs—and, eventually, from these sessions came a clutch of new compositions, which came to be known generically as **The Basement Tapes**. Some of the songs were surreally comic—'Please Mrs Henry', 'Quinn The Eskimo', 'Million Dollar Bash'; others were soul-searchingly introspective musings on fame, guilt, responsibility and redemption—'Tears Of Rage', 'Too Much Of Nothing', 'I Shall Be Released'. Distributed by Dylan's music publisher on what became a widely bootlegged tape, many of these songs were covered by, and became hits for, other artists and groups. Dylan's own recordings of some of the songs were not issued until 1975.

In January 1968, Dylan appeared with the Hawks, at this time renamed the Crackers, at the Woody Guthrie Memorial Concert at Carnegie Hall in New York. The following month **John Wesley Harding** was released, a stark, heavily moralistic collection of deceptively simple songs such as 'All Along The Watchtower' (the subject of a memorable cover version by **Jimi Hendrix**), 'The Ballad Of Frankie Lee And Judas Priest', 'Dear Landlord' and 'Drifter's Escape', many of which can be heard as allegorical reflections on the events of the previous couple of years. The record's final song, however, 'I'll Be Your Baby Tonight', was unambivalently simple and presaged the warmer love songs of the frustratingly brief **Nashville Skyline**, released in April 1969. After the chilly monochrome of *John Wesley Harding*, here was Dylan in full colour, smiling, apparently at ease at last, and singing in a deep, rich voice, which, oddly, some of his oldest acquaintances maintained was how 'Bobby' used to

sound back in Minnesota when he was first learning how to sing. 'Lay Lady Lay', 'Tonight I'll Be Staying Here With You', a duet with **Johnny Cash** on 'Girl From The North Country'—it was all easy on the ear, lyrically unsophisticated and, for some, far too twee. Nevertheless, *Nashville Skyline* was an extraordinarily influential record. It brought a new hipness to the hopelessly out-of-fashion Nashville (where, incidentally and incongruously, *Blonde On Blonde* had also been recorded) and it heralded a new genre of music—country rock—and a new movement that coincided with, or perhaps helped to spawn, the **Woodstock Festival** of the same summer. A return to simplicity and a love that was, in truth, only a distant relation of that psychedelically celebrated by the hippies in San Francisco a couple of years earlier, to whom Dylan paid no heed whatsoever. There are, therefore, no photographs of Bob Dylan in kaftan, beads and flowers or paisley bell-bottoms.

Dylan chose to avoid the Woodstock Festival (though the Band—the newly rechristened Crackers, who by now had two of their own albums, **Music From Big Pink** and **The Band**, to their credit—did play there), but he did play at the **Isle Of Wight Festival** on 31 August 1969. In a baggy Hank Williams–style white suit, it was a completely different Bob Dylan from the fright-haired, rabbit-suited marionette who had howled and screamed in the face of audience hostility at the Albert Hall more than three years earlier. This newly humble Dylan cooed and crooned an ever-so-polite, if ever-so-unexciting, set of songs and in doing so left the audience just as bewildered as those who had booed back in 1966. However, that bewilderment was as nothing compared with the puzzlement that greeted the release, in June 1970, of *Self Portrait*. This new record most closely resembled the Dylan album that preceded it—the bootleg collection *Great White Wonder*. Both were double albums; both offered mish-mash mix-ups of undistinguished live tracks, alternate takes, odd cover versions, botched beginnings and endings. Some even heard *Self Portrait*'s opening track, 'All The Tired Horses', as a caustic comment on the bootleggers' exploitation of ages-old material—was Dylan complaining 'How'm I supposed to get any ridin' done?' or 'writin' done?' There was little new material on *Self Portrait*, but there was 'Blue Moon'. The critics howled. Old fans were (yes, once again) dismayed. **Rolling Stone** magazine was vicious: 'What is this shit?', the review by Greil Marcus began.

'We've Got Dylan Back Again', wrote Ralph Gleason in the same magazine just four months later, heralding the hastily released *New Morning* as a 'return to form'. There was Al Kooper; there was the Dylan drawl; there were some slightly surreal lyrics; there was a bunch of new songs; but these were restless times for Dylan. He had left Woodstock and returned to New York City, to the heart of Greenwich Village, having bought a townhouse on MacDougal Street. It was, he later realized, an error, especially when A.J. Weberman, the world's first Dylanologist, turned up on his doorstep to rifle through his garbage in search of clues to unlocking the secret code of his poetry and (unintentionally) scaring his kids. Weberman saw it as his duty to shake Dylan out of his mid-life lethargy and reanimate him into embracing political and moral causes, and remarkably, he met with some success. On 1 August 1971, Dylan appeared at **The Concert For Bangla Desh** benefit, his only live performance between 1970 and 1974, and in November of the same year released 'George Jackson', a stridently powerful protest song, as a single. Little else happened for some time. Dylan cropped up so frequently as a guest on other people's albums that it ceased to be seen as a coup. He began to explore his Jewishness and was famously pictured at the Wailing Wall in Jerusalem. In 1973 he played, with some aplomb, the enigmatic Alias in Sam Peckinpah's brilliant **Pat Garrett & Billy The Kid**, for which movie he also supplied the soundtrack music, including the plaintive hit single 'Knockin' On Heaven's Door'.

Also in 1973, in a move that confounded industry-watchers, Dylan left Columbia Records, having been persuaded by **David Geffen** of the advantages of signing to his **Asylum Records** label. The disadvantage, some might say, was the cruelly spurned Columbia's misguided desire to exact a kind of revenge. They put out the shambolic *Dylan*, an album of out-takes and warm-ups, presumably intending either to embarrass Dylan beyond endurance or to steal some of the thunder from his first Asylum album, *Planet Waves*, newly recorded with the Band. In terms of the records' merits, there was no contest, although a few of the *Dylan* tracks were actually quite interesting, and the only embarrassment suffered was by Columbia, who were widely condemned for their petty-minded peevishness.

A US tour followed. Tickets were sold by post and attracted six million applications. Everybody who went to the shows agreed that Dylan and the Band were fantastic. The recorded evidence, *Before The Flood*, also released by Asylum, certainly oozes energy, but it lacks subtlety: Dylan seemed to be trying too hard, pushing everything too fast. It is good, but not that good. What is *that* good, indisputably and incontestably, is **Blood On The Tracks**. Originally recorded (for Columbia, no hard feelings, etc.) in late 1974, Dylan substituted some of the songs with versions reworked in Minnesota over the Christmas period. They were his finest compositions since the *Blonde On Blonde* material. 'Tangled Up In Blue', 'Idiot Wind', 'If You See Her, Say Hello', 'Shelter From The Storm', 'Simple Twist Of Fate', 'You're A Big Girl Now' . . . one masterpiece followed another. It was not so much a divorce album as a separation album (Dylan's divorce from Sara wasn't completed until 1977), but it was certainly a diary of despair. 'Pain sure brings out the best in people, doesn't it?' Dylan sang in 1966's 'She's Your Lover Now'; *Blood On The Tracks* gave the lie to all those who had argued that Dylan was a spent force.

If Dylan the writer was reborn with *Blood On The Tracks*, Dylan the performer re-emerged on the Rolling Thunder Revue. A travelling medicine show, moving from small town to small town, playing just about unannounced, the line-up extensive and variable, but basically comprising Dylan, Joan Baez, **Roger McGuinn**, **Rambling Jack Elliott**, **Allen Ginsberg**, **Mick Ronson**, Bobby Neuwirth and **Ronee Blakley**, the Revue was conceived in the Village in the summer of 1975 and hit the road in New England, in Plymouth, Massachusetts, on 31 October. It was a long wished-for dream, and Dylan, face painted white, hat festooned with flowers, was inspired, delirious, imbued with a new vitality and singing like a demon. Some of those great performances are preserved in the four-hour movie **Renaldo And Clara**, the self-examination through charade and music that Dylan edited through 1977 and defended staunchly and passionately on its release to the almost inevitable uncomprehending or downright hostile barrage of criticism that greeted it. The Revue reconvened for a 1976 tour of the south, musical glimpses of

its excitement being issued on the live album *Hard Rain*. A focal point of the Revue had been the case of wrongly imprisoned boxer Hurricane Carter, to whose cause Dylan had been recruited after having read his book *The Sixteenth Round*. Dylan's song 'Hurricane' was included just about every night in the 1975 Revue and also on the follow-up album to *Blood On The Tracks*, **Desire**, which also offered several songs co-written with **Jacques Levy**. *Desire* was an understandably popular record; 'Isis', 'Black Diamond Bay' and 'Romance In Durango' represented some of Dylan's strongest narrative ballads.

This was further borne out by the songs on **Street Legal**, the 1978 album that was released in the middle of a year-long stint with the biggest touring band with which Dylan ever played. Some critics dubbed it the alimony tour, but considerably more funds could have been generated if Dylan had gone out with a four-piece. Many of the old songs were imaginatively reworked in dramatic new arrangements, although the recording is of poor quality. At Budokan, released in 1979, documents the tour at its outset; the Earls Court and Blackbushe concerts caught it memorably mid-stream; while an exhausting trip around the USA in the latter part of the year seemed to bring equal amounts of acclaim and disapproval. 'Dylan's gone Vegas', some reviewers moaned. True, he wore trousers with lightening flashes while behind him flutes and bongos competed for attention with synthesizers and keyboards, but some of the performances were quite wonderful and the new songs, 'Senor (Tales Of Yankee Power)', 'Changing Of The Guard', 'Where Are You Tonight? (Journey Through Dark Heat)', 'True Love Tends To Forget', sounded terrific.

In 1979, Dylan became a born-again Christian and released an album of fervently evangelical songs, *Slow Train Coming*, recorded in **Muscle Shoals**, Alabama, with **Jerry Wexler** and **Barry Beckett**, and featuring **Mark Knopfler** and Pick Withers from **Dire Straits**, and in November and December he played a series of powerful concerts featuring nothing but his new Christian material. Cries of disbelief? Howls of protest? Well, naturally; but the record was crisp and contemporary-sounding, the songs strong, the performances admirable (Dylan was to win a Grammy for best rock vocal performance on 'Gotta Serve Somebody') and the concerts, which continued in 1980, among the most powerful and spine-tingling as any in his entire career. The second Christian album, *Saved*, was less impressive, however, and the fervour of the earlier months was more muted by the end of the year. Gradually, old songs began to be reworked into the live set and by the time of 1981's *Shot Of Love*, it was no longer clear whether or not—or to what extent—Dylan's faith remained firm. The sarcastic 'Property Of Jesus' and the thumping 'Dead Man, Dead Man' suggested that not much had changed, but the retrospective 'In The Summertime' and the prevaricating 'Every Grain Of Sand' hinted otherwise.

After three turbulent years, it was hardly surprising that Dylan dropped from sight for most of 1982, but the following year he was back in the studio, again with Mark Knopfler, having, it was subsequently established, written a prolific amount of new material. The album that resulted, *Infidels*, released in October 1983, received a mixed reception. Some songs were strong—'I&I' and 'Jokerman' among them—others relatively unimpressive. Dylan entered the video age by making promos for 'Sweetheart Like You' and 'Jokerman', but he did not seem too excited about it. Rumours persisted about his having abandoned Christianity and re-embraced the Jewish faith. His name began to be linked with the ultra-orthodox Lubavitcher sect: the inner sleeve of *Infidels* pictured him touching the soil of a hill above Jerusalem, while 'Neighbourhood Bully' was a fairly transparent defence of Israel's policies towards its neighbours. Dylan, as ever, refused to confirm or deny his state of spiritual health.

In 1984 he appeared live on the David Letterman television show, giving one of his most extraordinary and thrilling performances, backed by a ragged and raw Los Angeles trio the Cruzados. However, when, a few weeks later, he played his first concert tour for three years, visiting Europe on a package with **Santana** put together by impresario **Bill Graham**, Dylan's band was disappointingly longer in the tooth (with **Mick Taylor** on guitar and **Ian McLagan** on organ). An unimpressive souvenir album, *Real Live*, released in December, was most notable for its inclusion of a substantially rewritten version of 'Tangled Up In Blue'.

The following year opened with Dylan contributing to the 'We Are The World' USA For Africa single, and in the summer, after the release of *Empire Burlesque*, a patchy record somewhat over-produced by remix specialist **Arthur Baker** but boasting the beautiful acoustic closer 'Dark Eyes', he was the top-of-the-bill act at **Live Aid**. Initially, Dylan had been supposed to play with a band, but he was asked to perform solo to aid the logistics of the grande finale. In the event, he recruited **Ron Wood** and **Keith Richards** from the **Rolling Stones** to help him out. The results were disastrous. Hopelessly under-rehearsed and hampered both by the lack of monitors and the racket of the stage being set up behind the curtain in front of which they were performing, the trio were a shambles. Dylan, it was muttered later, must have been the only artist to appear in front of a billion television viewers worldwide and end up with fewer fans than he had when he started. Matters were redeemed a little, however, at the Farm Aid concert in September, an event set up as a result of Dylan's somewhat gauche onstage 'charity begins at home' appeal at Live Aid. Backed by **Tom Petty And The Heartbreakers**, it was immediately apparent that Dylan had found his most sympathetic and adaptable backing band since the Hawks. The year ended positively, too, with the release of the five album (3-CD) retrospective feast, *Biograph*, featuring many previously unreleased tracks.

The collaboration with Tom Petty having gone so well, it was decided that the partnership should continue, and a tour was announced to begin in New Zealand, Australia and Japan with more shows to follow in the USA. It was the summer's hottest ticket and the Petty/Dylan partnership thrived for a further year with a European tour, the first shows of which saw Dylan appearing in Israel for the very first time. Israel, Unfortunately, the opening show in Tel Aviv, Israel, was not well received either by the audience or by the press, whose reviews were vitriolic. The second show in Jerusalem was altogether more enjoyable until the explosion of the PA system brought the concert to an abrupt end.

Between the two tours Dylan appeared in his second feature, the Richard Marquand-directed **Hearts Of Fire**, made in England and Canada and co-starring Rupert Everett and Fiona Flanagan. Dylan played Billy Parker, a washed-up one-time superstar who in all but one respect (the washed-up bit) bore an uncanny resemblance to Dylan himself. Despite Dylan's best efforts—and he was probably the best thing in the movie—the film was a clunker. Hoots of derision marred

the premiere in October 1987 and its theatrical release was limited to one week in the UK. The poor movie was preceded by a poor album, *Knocked Out Loaded*, which only had the epic song 'Brownsville Girl', co-written with playwright Sam Shepard, to recommend it.

Increasingly, it appeared that Dylan's best attentions were being devoted to his concerts. The shows with Tom Petty had been triumphant. Dylan also shared the bill with the **Grateful Dead** at several stadium venues and learned from the experience. He envied their ability to keep on playing shows year in, year out, commanding a following wherever and whenever they played. He liked their two drummers and also admired the way they varied their set each night, playing different songs as and when they felt like it. These peculiarly Deadian aspects of live performance were soon incorporated into Dylan's own concert philosophy. *Down In The Groove*, an album of mostly cover versions of old songs, was released in the same month, June 1988, as Dylan played the first shows of what was to become known as the Never-Ending Tour. Backed by a three-piece band led by **G.E. Smith**, Dylan had stripped down his sound and his songs and was, once again, seemingly re-energized. His appetite for work had never been greater, and this same year he found himself in the unlikely company of **George Harrison**, **Jeff Lynne**, Tom Petty and **Roy Orbison** as one of the **Traveling Wilburys**, a jokey rock band assembled on a whim in the spring. Their album, *Volume 1*, on which Dylan's voice was as prominent as anyone's, was, unexpectedly, a huge commercial success.

With his Traveling Wilbury star in the ascendancy, and fresh from his induction into the **Rock And Roll Hall Of Fame**, Dylan's next album emerged as his best of the 80s. **Oh Mercy**, recorded informally in New Orleans and idiosyncratically produced by **Daniel Lanois**, sounded fresh and good, and the songs were as strong a bunch as Dylan had come up with in a long time. However, for reasons best known only to himself, it transpired from bootleg tapes that Dylan had been excluding many excellent songs from the albums he had been releasing in the 80s, most notably the masterpiece 'Blind Willie McTell', which was recorded for, but not included on, *Infidels*. Indeed, despite the evident quality of the songs on *Oh Mercy*—'Shooting Star' and 'Most Of The Time' were, for once, both songs of experience, evidence of a maturity that many fans had long been wishing for in Dylan's song-writing—it turned out that Dylan was still holding back. The crashing, turbulent 'Series Of Dreams' and the powerful 'Dignity' were products of the Lanois sessions but were not used on *Oh Mercy*. Instead, both later appeared on compilation albums.

Not without its merits (the title track and 'God Knows' are still live staples, while 'Born In Time' is a particularly emotional love song), the nursery-rhyme-style *Under The Red Sky*, released in September 1990, was for most a relative, probably inevitable, disappointment, as was the Roy-Orbison–bereft Traveling Wilburys follow-up, *Volume 3*. However, the touring continued, with Dylan's performances becoming increasingly erratic—sometimes splendid, often shambolic. It was one thing being spontaneous and improvisatory, but it was quite another being slapdash and incompetent. Dylan could be either and was sometimes both. His audiences began to dwindle; his reputation started to suffer. The three-volume collection of out-takes and rarities, *The Bootleg Series, Volumes 1–3 (Rare And Unreleased) 1961–1991*, redeemed him somewhat, as did the

30th Anniversary Celebration concert in Madison Square Garden in 1992, in which some of rock music's greats and not-so-greats paid tribute to Dylan's past achievements as a songwriter. The previous year he received a Lifetime Achievement Award at the Grammies.

There was, however, precious little present songwriting to celebrate. Both *Good As I Been To You* (1992) and *World Gone Wrong* (1993), although admirable, were collections of old folk and blues material, performed, for the first time since 1964, solo and acoustically. *Greatest Hits Volume 3* (1994) threw together a clump of old non-hits, and *Unplugged* (1995) saw Dylan revisiting a set of predominantly 60s songs in desultory fashion. Even the most ambitious CD-ROM so far, *Highway 61 Interactive*, while seemingly pointing to a Dylan-full future, wallowed nostalgically in, and was marketed on the strength of, past glories. Although Dylan's live performances became more coherent and controlled, his choice of material grew less imaginative through 1994, while many shows in 1995, which saw continued improvement in form, comprised almost entirely of songs written some 30 years earlier.

In 1997 it was rumoured that Dylan was knocking on heaven's door. Although he had suffered a serious inflammation of the heart muscles (pericarditis brought on by histoplasmosis) he was discharged from hospital after a short time, eliciting his priceless quote to the press: 'I really thought I'd be seeing Elvis soon'. It was time, perhaps, for doubters to begin to consign Dylan to the pages of history. However, as time has often proved, you can never write off Bob Dylan. He is a devil for hopping out of the hearse on the way to the cemetery. The Lanois-produced **Time Out Of Mind** was a dark and sombre recording, with Dylan reflecting over lost love and hints of death. It was his best work for many years, and although his voice had continued to decline, the strength of melody and lyric were remarkable. One outstanding example of Dylan's continuing ability to write a tender love song was 'To Make You Feel My Love'. Both **Garth Brooks** and **Trisha Yearwood** recorded excellent versions for the movie soundtrack *Hope Floats* in 1998 (Brooks took it to number 1 on the US country chart). That same year, the official release of the legendary bootleg, recorded at the Manchester Free Trade Hall in 1966, received a staggering amount of praise from the press. This was completely justified because the concert of familiar songs reminded and confirmed his towering importance as a songwriter.

Dylan's first recording of the new millennium was 'Things Have Changed', the Grammy-Award winning main and end-title theme for Curtis Hanson's movie *Wonder Boys*. His new studio album *Love And Theft* received generous praise, far in excess of its overall quality. Only 'Mississippi' could be classed as a great Dylan song. The quality of the material was thrown into sharp relief by two further superb releases in the *Bootleg Series*, a compilation of live recordings of the Rolling Thunder Revue from 1975, and a 1964 concert from the Philharmonic Hall in New York. Dylan, meanwhile, was concentrating on completing the script for his next venture into the world of film. The star-studded **Masked And Anonymous** was greeted with resounding indifference when it was first shown in 2003, with reviewers either puzzled or openly repulsed by the cryptic screenplay. Dylan fans took another view; it was weird but brilliant. A various artists soundtrack album, featuring several radical reworkings of classic Dylan material, was released at the same time.

The following October Dylan published the first volume of his memoirs, *Chronicles: Volume One*. While retaining hints of his trademark opacity, Dylan's prose evinced a clarity and generosity absent from his previous written output. In September 2005, the Martin Scorsese television film *No Direction Home: Bob Dylan* was broadcast on public television channels in the USA and UK. This remarkable film focused on Dylan's life and music from 1961–66.

Whatever the quality of his musical output will be in the future, Bob Dylan is unquestionably the greatest musical poet of the twentieth century.

● ALBUMS: *Bob Dylan* (Columbia 1962) ★★★★, *The Freewheelin' Bob Dylan* (Columbia 1963) ★★★★★, *The Times They Are A-Changin'* (Columbia 1964) ★★★★, *Another Side Of Bob Dylan* (Columbia 1964) ★★★★, *Bringing It All Back Home* (Columbia 1965) ★★★★★, *Highway 61 Revisited* (Columbia 1965) ★★★★★, *Blonde On Blonde* (Columbia 1966) ★★★★★, *John Wesley Harding* (Columbia 1968) ★★★★, *Nashville Skyline* (Columbia 1969) ★★★★, *Self Portrait* (Columbia 1970) ★, *New Morning* (Columbia 1970) ★★★, *Pat Garrett & Billy The Kid* film soundtrack (Columbia 1973) ★★, *Dylan (A Fool Such As I)* (Columbia 1973) ★, *Planet Waves* (Island 1974) ★★★, with The Band *Before The Flood* (Asylum 1974) ★★★, *Blood On The Tracks* (Columbia 1975) ★★★★★, with the Band *The Basement Tapes* (Columbia 1975) ★★★★, *Desire* (Columbia 1976) ★★★★★, *Hard Rain* (Columbia 1976) ★★, *Street Legal* (Columbia 1978) ★★★, *Slow Train Coming* (Columbia 1979) ★★★, *At Budokan* (Columbia 1979) ★★★, *Saved* (Columbia 1980) ★, *Shot Of Love* (Columbia 1981) ★★, *Infidels* (Columbia 1983) ★★★★, *Real Live* (Columbia 1984) ★★, *Empire Burlesque* (Columbia 1985) ★★, *Knocked Out Loaded* (Columbia 1986) ★★, *Down In The Groove* (Columbia 1988) ★★, with the Grateful Dead *Dylan And The Dead* (Columbia 1989) ★, *Oh Mercy* (Columbia 1989) ★★★★★, *Under The Red Sky* (Columbia 1990) ★★★, *Good As I Been To You* (Columbia 1992) ★★★, *World Gone Wrong* (Columbia 1993) ★★, with various artists *The 30th Anniversary Concert Celebration* (Columbia 1993) ★★★, *MTV Unplugged* (Columbia 1995) ★★★, *Time Out Of Mind* (Columbia 1997) ★★★★, *The Bootleg Series Vol. 4: Bob Dylan Live 1966: The Royal Albert Hall Concert* (Columbia/Legacy 1998) ★★★★★, *Love And Theft* (Columbia 2001) ★★★, *The Bootleg Series Volume 5: Bob Dylan Live 1975: The Rolling Thunder Revue* (Columbia/Legacy 2002) ★★★★, with various artists *Masked And Anonymous* film soundtrack (Sony 2003) ★★★, *The Bootleg Series Volume 6: Bob Dylan Live 1964: Concert At Philharmonic Hall* (Columbia/Legacy 2004) ★★★★, *Live At The Gaslight 1962* (Hear 2005) ★★★.

● COMPILATIONS: *Bob Dylan's Greatest Hits* (Columbia 1967) ★★★★★, *More Bob Dylan Greatest Hits* (Columbia 1972) ★★★★, *Biograph* 5-LP box set (Columbia 1985) ★★★★★, *The Bootleg Series Volumes 1–3: Rare And Unreleased 1961–1991* 3-LP box set (Columbia/Legacy 1991) ★★★★★, *Greatest Hits Volume 3* (Columbia 1994) ★★★, *The Best Of Bob Dylan Volume 2* (Columbia 2000) ★★★, *The Essential Bob Dylan* (Columbia 2000) ★★★★, *Live 1961/2000* (Columbia 2001) ★★★, *No Direction Home: The Soundtrack—The Bootleg Series Vol. 7* (Columbia 2005) ★★★★.

● DVD/VIDEOS: *Hard To Handle* (Virgin Vision 1987), *Don't Look Back* (Virgin Vision 1988), *30th Anniversary*

Concert Celebration (Sony Music Video 1993), MTV Unplugged (Sony Music Video 1995), World Tour 1966: The Home Movies (Wienerworld 2004), Tales From A Golden Age: Bob Dylan 1941-1966 (Chrome Dreams 2004), World Tours 1966-1974: Through The Camera Of Barry Feinstein (Music Video Distributors 2005), No Direction Home: Bob Dylan (Paramount Home Entertainment 2005), After The Crash: Bob Dylan 1966-1978 (Chrome Dreams 2005), Broadcasting Live: The First 30 Years (Classic Rock Legends 2005), 1975-1981: Rolling Thunder And The Gospel Years (Wienerworld 2006).

● FURTHER READING: As with all major artists there are many books available. The editor's recommendation would contain three essential works: No Direction Home, Robert Shelton. Song & Dance Man III, Michael Gray. Wanted Man: In Search Of Bob Dylan, John Bauldie.

Others: Bob Dylan In His Own Write, Bob Dylan. Eleven Outlined Epitaphs & Off The Top Of My Head, Bob Dylan. Folk-Rock: The Bob Dylan Story, Sy and Barbra Ribakove. Don't Look Back, D.A. Pennebaker. Bob Dylan: An Intimate Biography, Anthony Scaduto. Positively Main Street: An Unorthodox View Of Bob Dylan, Toby Thompson. Bob Dylan: A Retrospective, Craig McGregor. Song And Dance Man: The Art Of Bob Dylan, Michael Gray. Bob Dylan: Writings And Drawings, Bob Dylan. Knocking On Dylan's Door, Rolling Stone editors. Rolling Thunder Logbook, Sam Shepard. On The Road With Bob Dylan: Rolling With The Thunder, Larry Sloman. Bob Dylan: The Illustrated Record, Alan Rinzler. Bob Dylan In His Own Words, Miles. Bob Dylan: An Illustrated Discography, Stuart Hoggard and Jim Shields. Bob Dylan: An Illustrated History, Michael Gross. Bob Dylan: His Unreleased Recordings, Paul Cable. Dylan: What Happened?, Paul Williams. Conclusions On The Wall: New Essays On Bob Dylan, Liz Thomson. Twenty Years Of Recording: The Bob Dylan Reference Book, Michael Krogsgaard. Voice Without Restraint: A Study Of Bob Dylan's Lyrics And Their Background, John Herdman. Bob Dylan: From A Hard Rain To A Slow Train, Tim Dowley and Barry Dunnage. No Direction Home: The Life And Music Of Bob Dylan, Robert Shelton. Bringing It All Back Home, Robbie Woliver. All Across The Telegraph: A Bob Dylan Handbook, Michael Gray and John Bauldie (eds.). Raging Glory, Dennis R. Liff. Bob Dylan: Stolen Moments, Clinton Heylin. Jokerman: Reading The Lyrics Of Bob Dylan, Aidan Day. Dylan: A Biography, Bob Spitz. Performing Artist: The Music Of Bob Dylan Volume 1, 1960-1973, Paul Williams. Dylan Companion, Elizabeth M. Thomson and David Gutman. Lyrics: 1962-1985, Bob Dylan. Bob Dylan: Performing Artist, Paul Williams. Oh No! Not Another Bob Dylan Book, Patrick Humphries and John Bauldie. Absolutely Dylan, Patrick Humphries and John Bauldie. Dylan: Behind The Shades, Clinton Heylin. Bob Dylan: A Portrait Of the Artist's Early Years, Daniel Kramer. Wanted Man: In Search Of Bob Dylan, John Bauldie (ed.). Bob Dylan: In His Own Words, Chris Williams. Tangled Up In Tapes, Glen Dundas. Hard Rain: A Dylan Commentary, Tim Riley. Complete Guide To The Music Of Bob Dylan, Patrick Humphries. Bob Dylan Drawn Blank (Folio of drawings), Bob Dylan. Watching The River Flow (1966-1995), Paul Williams. Like The Night: Bob Dylan And The Road To The Manchester Free Trade Hall, C.P. Lee. Classic Bob Dylan 1962-69, Andy Gill. Touched By The Hand Of Bob: Epiphanal Bob Dylan Experiences From A Buick Six, Dave Henderson. Song & Dance Man III: The Art Of Bob Dylan, Michael Gray. Like A Bullet Of Light: The Films Of Bob Dylan, C.P. Lee. Encounters With Bob Dylan: If You See Him, Say Hello, Tracy Johnson (ed.). The Bob Dylan Companion: Four Decades Of Commentary, Carl Benson (ed.). Down The Highway: The Life Of Bob Dylan, Howard Sounes. Razor's Edge: Bob Dylan And The Never Ending Tour, Andrew Muir. Positively 4th Street: The Lives And Times Of Joan Baez, Bob Dylan, Mimi Baez Fariña And Richard Fariña, David Hadju. The Nightingale's Code: A Poetic Study Of Bob Dylan, John Gibbens. Isis: A Bob Dylan Anthology, Derek Barker (ed.). The Formative Dylan: Transmission And Stylistic Influences, 61-63, Todd Harvey. Troubadour: Early & Late Songs Of Bob Dylan, Andrew Muir. Do You Mr Jones?: Bob Dylan With The Poets And Professors, Neil Corcoran. Dylan's Visions Of Sin, Christopher Ricks. Bob Dylan: The Life And Times Of An American Icon, Michael A. Schuman. Chimes Of Freedom: The Politics Of Bob Dylan's Art, Mike Marqusee. Young Bob: John Cohen's Early Photographs Of Bob Dylan, John Cohen. Dylan & Cohen: Poets Of Rock And Roll, David Boucher. Chronicles: Volume One, Bob Dylan. Lyrics: 1962-2001, Bob Dylan. A Simple Twist Of Fate: Bob Dylan And The Making Of Blood On The Tracks, Andy Gill and Kevin Odegard. Bob Dylan: Performing Artist 1986*1990 & Beyond: Mind Out Of Time, Paul Williams. The Rough Guide To Bob Dylan, Nigel Williamson. Bob Dylan: Voice Of A Generation, Jeremy Roberts. Like A Rolling Stone: Bob Dylan At The Crossroads, Greil Marcus. The Bob Dylan Scrapbook: 1956-1966, Robert Sandelli. Anthology Volume 2: 20 Years Of Isis, Derek Barker (ed.). Forever Young: Photographs Of Bob Dylan, Douglas R. Gilbert.

● FILMS: Don't Look Back (1967), Festival (1967), Eat The Document (1971), The Concert For Bangla Desh (1972), Pat Garrett & Billy The Kid (1973), Renaldo And Clara (1978), The Last Waltz (1978), Hearts Of Fire (1987), Catchfire (1990), Paradise Cove (1999), Masked And Anonymous (2003).

Dylans

Formed in Sheffield, England, by Colin Gregory (bass/vocals), Andy Curtis (guitar) and Jim Rodger (guitar) in 1989, this trio recorded a rough demo that led to a contract with **Beggars Banquet** before they had ever appeared live. With the addition of Garry Jones (drums) and Quentin Jennings (keyboards) they began touring, attracting comparisons with bands such as the **Charlatans** and the **Stone Roses** because of their 60s-styled jangly guitars and strong harmonies. The Dylans took the retro theme even further, however, displaying a fondness for wearing love beads around their necks and writing wide-eyed hippy lyrics. The debut single 'Godlike', released in early 1991, was widely praised and reached the UK indie Top 10, but shortly afterwards tensions in the band led to Curtis being replaced by Andy Cook. They continued to achieve indie hits with 'Lemon Afternoon' and the sublime 'Planet Love' before releasing a self-titled debut album in October. Though this also proved popular, their limited lyrical concerns were prone to become stale over the course of a whole album. After tours of the USA and Japan in 1992 the band began to fall apart, with Jones being replaced by guitarist Craig Scott and Jennings by Ike Glover. The new line-up recorded two further singles and Spirit Finger, but by now their style of indie pop was becoming increasingly dated, and with the album's lack of success the band folded.

● ALBUMS: *The Dylans* (Situation Two 1991) ★★★, *Spirit Finger* (Situation Two 1993) ★★.

Dynametrix

This London, England–based hip-hop trio comprised producer Ace Shazamme and rappers 0026 and the Phantom. Formed in the early 90s, their central appeal was the intoxicating beats and rhythms designed by Shazamme, including both 70s funk grooves and samples drawn from television and radio as well as the **Doors**. However, for many critics this served as scant compensation for misogynist lyrics conveyed by the group's MCs. Signed by emergent London rap label **Kold Sweat**, they released their debut album, *A Measure Of Force*, in 1994.
● ALBUMS: *A Measure Of Force* (Kold Sweat 1994) ★★.

Dynamic Superiors

Joining forces in Washington, DC, in 1963, Tony Washington, George Spann, George Wesley Peterbank Jnr., Michael McCalpin and Maurice Washington had to wait a decade to win a recording contract. **Motown Records** president **Ewart Abner** saw them performing at a talent show in Atlanta, Georgia, and signed them to the label in 1974. They were teamed with the **Ashford And Simpson** writing and production team, and their debut album was a collection of romantic soul ballads that produced two hits, 'Shoe Shoe Shine' and 'Leave It Alone'. Their second album, *Pure Pleasure*, added a disco feel to the Superiors' sound and spawned two further chart entries. In 1977 the group enjoyed some success with a disco rearrangement of the **Martha And The Vandellas**' hit, 'Nowhere To Run', but they subsequently left Motown and attempts to secure a major label recording contract elsewhere proved unsuccessful.
● ALBUMS: *The Dynamic Superiors* (Motown 1975) ★★★, *Pure Pleasure* (Motown 1975) ★★★, *You Name It* (Motown 1976) ★★, *Give And Take* (Motown 1977) ★★.

Dynamites

The Jamaican house band for producer **Clancy Eccles** during the early reggae years of the late 60s and early 70s, the Dynamites backed numerous Clan Disc artists such as Eccles himself, Cynthia Richards and pioneer DJ **King Stitt**. Their line-up fluctuated, though its nucleus was **Winston Wright** (organ/ piano), Hux Brown (guitar), Jackie Jackson (bass), Gladstone Anderson (piano) and Paul Douglas (drums). This combo, with added saxophones, recorded *Fire Corner* in 1969, a unique set of moody reggae instrumentals that also included King Stitt on the title track and 'Vigorton 2'.
● ALBUMS: with King Stitt *Fire Corner* (Trojan/Clandisc 1969) ★★★★, with Clancy Eccles *Herbsman Reggae* (Trojan 1970) ★★★★.
● COMPILATIONS: *The Wild Reggae Bunch* (Jamaican Gold 1997) ★★★.

Dyson, Ronnie

b. 5 June 1950, Washington, DC, USA, d. 10 November 1990. Having played a leading role in the Broadway production of *Hair*, Dyson pursued his thespian ambitions in *Salvation*, a less infamous musical, from 1970. One of its songs, '(If You Let Me Make Love To You Then) Why Can't I Touch You?', was a US Top 10 hit, while the singer reached the R&B chart with several subsequent singles including 'I Don't Wanna Cry' (1970) and 'The More You Do It (The More I Like It Done To Me)' (1976). In 1971 'When You Get Right Down To It' reached the UK Top 40. Despite switching labels from **Columbia Records** to Cotillion, Dyson was unable to achieve another major success, and 'All Over Your Face' (1983) was his last chart entry. He died of heart failure in 1990.
● ALBUMS: *(If You Let Me Make Love To You Then) Why Can't I Touch You?* (Columbia 1970) ★★, *One Man Band* (Columbia 1973) ★★, *The More You Do It* (Columbia 1977) ★★, *If The Shoe Fits* (Cotillion 1979) ★★.

Dzadzeloi

As with the better-known **Wulomei**, Dzadzeloi were part of the early to mid-70s acoustic **highlife** revival which briefly swept Ghana. Typically, their sound was characterized by sweet female harmonies and powerful Ga drumming. An exciting floorshow featuring dancers and cabaret made them suitable to both village and hotel audiences. However, their international fame was brief and had all but expired by the advent of the 80s.
● ALBUMS: *Two Paddy Follow One Girl* (1975) ★★★.

E-40

b. Earl Stevens, 15 November 1967, San Francisco, California, USA. Considered a natural successor to **Too $hort**'s reductionist thematic with his glorification of the 'player' hip-hop lifestyle, E-40 started his own independent label, Sick Wid It Records, in the Bay area of San Francisco in 1990. Working with his brothers and sisters as part of the Click, an underground sensation on the streets of Vallejo. E-40 released records with the Click, including 1993's *Down And Dirty* and 1995's *Game Related*, and as a solo artist. He enjoyed immediate success with records such as 'Captain Save-a-Ho', 'Sprinkle Me' and 'Ballin' Out Of Control', which all featured his trademark stop-start delivery and the inclusion of heavy regional slang such as 'scrilla' (money) and 'broccoli' (marijuana). By 1995, and *In A Major Way* (which included 'Sprinkle Me'), he had signed a major distribution contract with **Jive Records**.

Having sold over half a million copies of this record, the subsequent *The Hall Of Game* set was given a major international push. With producers including Studio Tone, Ant Banks and Rick Rock of the Cosmic Shop, the musical climate was more relaxed and smoother than had previously been the case. The first single from the album, 'Rapper's Ball', was a typical example, being an updated version of Too $hort's 1987 single 'Playboy Short'. This new version featured Too $hort as well as **Jodeci**'s K-Ci. Other highlights included 'On The One', featuring **Digital Underground**'s Money B and Da Funk Mob's G-Note, and 'Things'll Never Change'. This reinterpreted **Bruce Hornsby**'s 'That's The Way It Is' with a contribution from E-40's eight-year-old son, Li'l E. *The Element Of Surprise* debuted at number 13 on the **Billboard** Top 200 in August 1998. The rapper celebrated 10 years in the business with the following year's semi-autobiographical *Charlie Hu$tle—The BluePrint Of A Self-Made Millionaire.*

● ALBUMS: *Federal* (Sick Wid It 1992) ★★★, *The Mail Man* (Sick Wid It 1994) ★★★, *In A Major Way* (Sick Wid It/Jive 1995) ★★★★, *The Hall Of Game* (Sick Wid It/Jive 1996) ★★★, *The Element Of Surprise* (Sick Wid It/Jive 1998) ★★★★, *Charlie Hu$tle—The BluePrint Of A Self-Made Millionaire* (Sick Wid It/Jive 1999) ★★★, *Loyalty And Betrayal* (Sick Wid It/Jive 2000) ★★★, *The Ballatician: Grit & Grind* (Sick Wid It/Jive 2002) ★★, *Breakin News* (Sick Wid It/Jive 2003) ★★★, *My Ghetto Report Card* (Warners 2006) ★★★.

● COMPILATIONS: *The Best Of E-40: Yesterday, Today And Tomorrow* (Sick Wid It/Jive 2004) ★★★★.

● FILMS: *Rhyme & Reason* (1997), *Obstacles* (2000).

E-Lustrious

E-Lustrious comprises the Manchester duo Mike 'E-Bloc' Kirwin (nicknamed after the famed **Eastern Bloc** record shop at which he works) and Danny 'Hybrid' Bennett. Kirwin is among the north of England's most popular DJs, though his profile has been lessened by his refusal to attend events in the nation's capital. After learning the tuba at school he progressed to sundry hopeful punk bands like Bastard Antelopes. Bennett, meanwhile, grew up on breakdancing and breakbeats, and was an early scratch DJ. They began working together at the end of the 80s, when Kirwin and then fellow Eastern Bloc co-worker **Justin Robertson** planned to record a single. Bennett was hauled in owing to his having access to rudimentary recording equipment. Though the track was never completed, Bennett and Kirwin continued as a duo. Their first major success came as the men behind the Direckt single 'I Got The Feeling', which enjoyed a curious germination. *Mixmag Update* magazine invented a white label record entitled 'I Got Ya' by Direckt, giving it a magnificent review in order to gauge the reaction. As thousands assailed their local dance counters in the hope of finding this invisible disc, few noticed that Direckt was an anagram of 'Tricked'. When the scam was revealed the enterprising E-Lustrious made the most of the furore by hijacking the name for 'I Got The Feeling', enjoying instant record sales and notoriety. They have gone on to establish their own record label, UFG, which has subsequently housed tunes from the **Luvdup Twins** ('Good Time') and material from DJ **EFX And Digit** and DJ Tandoori. Under their principal name, E-Lustrious, they have established themselves with the success of 'Dance No More'. Just as notable was their second single as Direckt, 'Two Fatt Guitars', a fabulous piece of digifunk that became a party standard in 1993. They also record as Rolling Gear ('I've Got It').

E.S.G.

b. Houston, Texas, USA. Not to be confused with the heavily sampled funk group who share the same name, this Houston, Texas, USA–based gangsta rapper has been at the forefront of the city's underground hip-hop scene since the mid-90s without ever crossing over into the mainstream charts. Born and raised in Houston's southside district, the rapper adopted the moniker E.S.G. (Everyday Street Gangsta) while cutting his first tracks as a member of **DJ Screw**'s Screwed Up Click. He established his reputation as a solo artist with 1994's underground hit 'Swangin' & Bangin'', which established E.S.G.'s rapid-fire delivery and hard-hitting street lyrics. Albums of varying quality followed for the Perrion, Blackhearted and Wreckshop labels, generating the local hits 'Braids And Fades' and 'Grippin' Grain'. Following the release of 2000's *City Under Siege*, E.S.G. set up the SES label with fellow rapper **Slim Thug** and producer Sinclair 'Big Sin' Ridley. E.S.G. and Slim Thug's debut for the label, *Boss Hog Outlaws*, sold 30,000 units in its first week of release.

● ALBUMS: *Sailin' Da South* (Perrion 1995) ★★★, *Ocean Of Funk* (Perrion 1995) ★★★, *Return Of The Living Dead* (Blackhearted 1998) ★★, *Shinin' N' Grindin'* (Wreckshop 1999) ★★, *City Under Siege* (Wreckshop 2000) ★★★, with Slim Thug *Boss Hog Outlaws* (SES 2001) ★★★.

E., Sheila

b. Sheila Escovedo, 12 December 1959, Oakland, California, USA. Sheila E. came to prominence as a solo artist in 1984 but had been playing conga drums since the age of three. Her father, **Pete Escovedo**, worked briefly with **Santana** and led the Latin-jazz fusion band **Azteca**, with which Sheila sat in while in high school. She briefly gave up the idea of a musical career but eventually left school to join her father's band, appearing on two of his albums for **Fantasy Records**. She was discovered by **Prince** in 1984 and appeared as a vocalist on his 'Erotic City', the b-side of the US number 1 'Let's Go Crazy'. With that exposure she was able to sign a solo record contract with **Warner Brothers Records**; her debut was *Sheila E. In The Glamorous Life*. The album yielded the US Top 10 single of the same name and the UK Top 20 hit 'The Belle Of St. Mark'. Her follow-up, *Sheila E. In Romance 1600*, appeared on Prince's Paisley Park label in 1985 and featured the US hit single 'A Love Bizarre', with Prince himself on backing vocals. Her third solo album, self-titled, was released in 1987 but failed to garner the attention or sales of the first two. That same year she joined Prince's touring group as drummer, also appearing in the movie *Sign O' The Times*.

After a four-year lapse in recording, she returned in 1991 with the dance-orientated *Sex Cymbal*, which was self-written and produced with assistance from her brother, Peter Michael, and David Gamson. Escovedo subsequently retreated behind the scenes, writing and recording with other artists and working as music director on Magic Johnson's television show *The Magic Hour*. She also worked extensively with charitable organizations. In 2000, she produced and co-composed the music for the first Latin Grammy Awards and returned to recording with the stylish Latin jazz album *Writes Of Passage*.

● ALBUMS: *Sheila E. In The Glamorous Life* (Warners 1984) ★★★, *Sheila E. In Romance 1600* (Paisley Park 1985) ★★★, *Sheila E.* (Paisley Park 1987) ★★★, *Sex Cymbal* (Warners 1991) ★★★, with Pete Escovedo *Solo Two/Happy Together* 80s recordings (Fantasy 1997) ★★★, with the E. Train *Writes Of Passage* (Concord Vista 2000) ★★★, with the E. Train *Heaven* (Concord Vista 2001) ★★★.
● FILMS: *Krush Groove* (1985), *Sign O' The Times* (1987), *The Adventures Of Ford Fairlane* (1990).

Eade, Dominique

b. Dominique Frances Eade, 16 June 1959, Ruislip, Middlesex, England. Although born in England, Eade is an American citizen. At the time of her birth, her father was an American serviceman stationed in the UK (her mother was a Swiss national). Raised in a musical environment, Eade was educated at Vassar, where she sang with a jazz group, attended **Berklee College Of Music** in Boston in the late 70s, studying jazz exclusively, then completed her bachelor's degree at the New England Conservatory in 1982. At the NEC she studied classical theory and composition, ethnic/world musics and jazz and in addition to her degree also received an Artist Diploma. In 1984 she was appointed to the faculty of the NEC and since then has continued to teach voice, composition and improvisation there. In addition, she has also taught and coached in various parts of the USA and in Norway and Italy. Meanwhile, she performed with various jazz groups and appeared on radio and television. In the mid-80s she worked with the **Ran Blake** Quartet and in 1985 and 1986 was featured at the Boston Globe Jazz Festival. She also led her own quartet which included, at different times, **Alan Dawson** and **Bob Moses**. In the late 80s she also studied privately with Blake, Moses, **Dave Holland** and **Stanley Cowell** and with soprano Nancy Armstrong. Among other musicians with whom she worked during this time were **Stan Getz**, **Bill Frisell**, **Anthony Braxton**, **Mick Goodrick**, **Peter Leitch**, **Fred Hersch** and **Butch Morris**.

In the mid-80s Eade had begun recording, at first on albums led by others, including Gunnar Wenneborg, in Sweden, and later with Claire Ritter. She continued to perform in and around New York and Boston and in 1991 recorded her self-produced debut album for which she composed and arranged all the music and on which her accompanists included Cowell and Dawson. She continued to perform and visited France, singing at the Toulon Jazz Festival, and also performed regularly at New York's Village Gate. Her second album was voted by *Billboard* magazine as one of the Top 10 releases of 1995. Her qualities as a teacher may be determined from the fact that of the 11 finalists of the 1994 **Thelonious Monk** Jazz Vocal Competition 3, including the winner, were her students. *When The Wind Was Cool*, released in 1997, paid tribute to 50s singers **June Christy** and **Chris Connor**. Eade sings with a pure tone and although she favours the lower register, in which she is especially pleasing, her vocal range is wide. Her flawless technique and polished assurance allows her to deliver with flair a repertoire that is both imaginative and demanding.

● ALBUMS: *The Ruby And The Pearl* (Accurate 1991) ★★★, *My Resistance Is Low* (Accurate 1995) ★★★★, *When The Wind Was Cool: The Songs Of Chris Connor & June Christy* (RCA Victor 1997) ★★★★, *The Long Way Home* (RCA Victor 1999) ★★★.

Eadey, Irene

(see **Kitchings, Irene**)

Eager, Allen

b. 10 January 1927, New York City, USA, d. 13 April 2003, Daytona Beach, Florida, USA. Eager had formal tuition on clarinet but in 1943 received lessons on tenor saxophone from **Ben Webster**, a switch that marked the start of his professional career. His early experience was gained in big bands on the more lightweight side of the swing era, including those led by **Bobby Sherwood** and **Hal McIntyre**. Towards the end of 1943 he joined **Woody Herman** and later worked with **Tommy Dorsey**. In Los Angeles he played in Vine Street clubs with **Barney Kessel** and **Zoot Sims**, whom he followed into the small group led by **'Big' Sid Catlett**. Around this time he heard **Lester Young** on records by the **Count Basie** band and thereafter remodelled his playing in the style of the 'Pres'. In the mid-40s Eager was mostly to be found at 52nd Street clubs, playing with **Coleman Hawkins**, **Pete Brown** and many beboppers, including **Red Rodney**, **Stan Levey**, **Max Roach**, **Al Haig** and **Serge Chaloff**, and sometimes leading his own small groups. He also met **Charlie Parker** and, although initially unimpressed, he soon became a devotee and they often worked together. In 1948 he recorded with **Fats Navarro**, **Wardell Gray** and **Ernie Henry** as a member of **Tadd Dameron**'s band, taking part in the important sessions that produced 'Our Delight', 'Dameronia' and 'Early Bird'.

Eager continued playing into the 50s, recording with **Tony Fruscella** and **Danny Bank**, and touring with **Oscar Pettiford**. In the mid-50s he spent some time living in Paris and led his own band but gradually drifted out of music, preferring to spend his time pursuing other, mainly sporting, activities, which included racing sports cars with his partner Denise McCluggage. He also struck up a friendship with LSD guru Timothy Leary, visiting the chemist regularly at his Harvard laboratory. In 1982 Eager returned to music, recording and touring both at home and overseas, including a stint with **Dizzy Gillespie**. He died in April 2003 of liver cancer.

● ALBUMS: *New Trends In Modern Music, Volume 2* 10-inch album (Savoy Jazz 1952) ★★★, *Tenor Sax* 10-inch album (Savoy Jazz 1954) ★★★, *Renaissance* (Uptown 1982) ★★★.

● COMPILATIONS: *In The Land Of Oo-Bla-Dee 1947–1953* (Tower 2003) ★★★.

Eager, Vince

One of the many UK rock/pop artists of the late 50s, Eager was one of the more promising singers in the **Larry Parnes** stable of stars. Launched in the spring of 1958 and christened Eager because of his enthusiastic personality, the vocalist was featured on several prestigious television shows, most notably **Jack Good**'s pioneering *Oh Boy*. He seemed a strong bet to follow Parnes' other acts, **Tommy Steele** and **Marty Wilde**, into the UK charts but, despite a series of singles written by such name writers as **Floyd Robinson**, **Marty Robbins**, **Conway Twitty** and **Gene Pitney**, chart success proved elusive. Eager also received regular star billing on the BBC Television series *Drumbeat*, but his career prospects receded when he split with Parnes. In later years, he featured in the stage production of the musical *Elvis*.

● ALBUMS: *Vince Eager Plays Tribute To Elvis Presley* (Avenue 1972) ★.

Eagles

Formed in Los Angeles, California, USA, in 1971, this highly successful unit was formed by musicians drawn from singer **Linda Ronstadt**'s backing group. Of the original quartet, **Bernie Leadon** (b. 19 July 1947, Minneapolis, Minnesota, USA; guitar/vocals) boasted the most prodigious pedigree, having embraced traditional country music with the Scottsville Squirrel Barkers, before gaining significant rock experience as a member of **Hearts And Flowers**, **Dillard And Clark** and the **Flying Burrito Brothers**. **Randy Meisner** (b. 8 March 1946, Scottsbluff, Nebraska, USA; bass/vocals) was formerly of **Poco** and **Rick Nelson**'s Stone Canyon Band; **Glenn Frey** (b. 6 November 1948, Detroit, Michigan, USA; guitar/vocals) had recorded as half of **Longbranch Pennywhistle**; while **Don Henley** (b. 22 July 1947, Gilmer, Texas, USA; drums/vocals) had led Texas-based aspirants Shiloh. Such pedigrees ensured interest in the new venture, which was immediately signed to **David Geffen**'s nascent **Asylum Records** label.

The band's debut album **The Eagles**, recorded in London under the aegis of producer **Glyn Johns**, contained 'Take It Easy', co-written by Frey and **Jackson Browne**, and 'Witchy Woman', both of which reached the US Top 20 and established the quartet's meticulous harmonies and relaxed, but purposeful, country rock sound. Critical reaction to **Desperado**, an ambitious concept album based on a western theme, firmly established the band as leaders in their field and contained several of their most enduring compositions, including the pleadingly emotional title track. The follow-up, *On The Border*, reasserted the unit's commerciality. 'Best Of My Love' became their first US number 1 while new member

Don Felder (b. 21 September 1947, Topanga, California, USA; guitar/vocals), drafted from **David Blue**'s backing group in March 1974, considerably bolstered the Eagles' sound. The reshaped quintet attained superstar status with **One Of These Nights**, the title track from which also topped the US charts. This platinum-selling album included 'Lyin' Eyes', now considered a standard on Gold format radio, and the anthemic 'Take It To The Limit'. The album also established the Eagles as an international act; each of these tracks had reached the UK Top 30, but the new-found pressure proved too great for Leadon who left the line-up in December 1975. He subsequently pursued a low-key career with the Leadon-Georgiades band.

Leadon's replacement was **Joe Walsh** (b. 20 November 1947, Wichita, Kansas, USA), former lead guitarist with the **James Gang** and a successful solo artist in his own right. His somewhat surprising induction was tempered by the knowledge that he shared the same manager as his new colleagues. The choice was ratified by the powerful **Hotel California**, which topped the US album charts for eight weeks and spawned two number 1 singles in the title track and 'New Kid In Town'. The set has become the Eagles' most popular collection, selling nine million copies worldwide in its year of release alone, as well as appearing in many 'all-time classic' albums listings. A seasonal recording, 'Please Come Home For Christmas', was the quintet's sole recorded offering for 1978 and internal ructions the following year resulted in Meisner's departure. His replacement, Timothy B. Schmit (b. 30 October 1947, Oakland, California, USA), was another former member of Poco, but by this point the Eagles' impetus was waning. *The Long Run* was generally regarded as disappointing, despite containing a fifth US number 1 in 'Heartache Tonight', and a temporary hiatus taken at the end of the decade became a fully fledged break in 1982 when long-standing disagreements could not be resolved. Henley, Frey and Felder began solo careers with contrasting results, while Walsh resumed the path he had followed prior to joining the band.

Although latterly denigrated as representing 70s musical conservatism and torpidity, the Eagles' quest for perfection and committed musical skills rightly led to their becoming one of the era's leading acts. It was no surprise that the final line-up of the band eventually re-formed in the mid-90s, after months of speculation. The resulting album proved that they were still one of the world's most popular acts, even though it was a hastily assembled live collection. Their 1994/5 tour of the USA was (apart from the **Rolling Stones**' parallel tour) the largest-grossing on record. With the over indulgences of the 70s behind them, it is an exciting prospect to look forward to an album of new Eagles songs, written with the patina of age. In the meantime, the public is happy to continue to purchase their greatest hits packages. *Their Greatest Hits 1971–1975* now competes with **Michael Jackson**'s **Thriller** as the biggest-selling album of all time, with 25 million units in the US alone.

● ALBUMS: *The Eagles* (Asylum 1972) ★★★, *Desperado* (Asylum 1973) ★★★★, *On The Border* (Asylum 1974) ★★★★, *One Of These Nights* (Asylum 1975) ★★★, *Hotel California* (Asylum 1976) ★★★★, *The Long Run* (Asylum 1979) ★★, *Live* (Asylum 1980) ★★, *Hell Freezes Over* (Geffen 1994) ★★★.

● COMPILATIONS: *Their Greatest Hits 1971–1975* (Asylum 1976) ★★★★, *Greatest Hits Volume 2* (Asylum 1982)

★★★, *Best Of The Eagles* (Asylum 1985) ★★★★, *1972–1999: Selected Works* 4-CD box set (Elektra 2000) ★★★★, *The Very Best Of The Eagles* (Elektra 2001) ★★★★, *The Very Best Of* (US) *The Complete Greatest Hits* (UK) (WSM 2003) ★★★★.

● DVD/VIDEOS: *Hell Freezes Over* (Geffen Home Video 1994), *Farewell Tour: Live From Melbourne* (WSM 2005).

● FURTHER READING: *The Eagles*, John Swenson. *The Long Run: The Story Of The Eagles*, Marc Shapiro. *To The Limit: The Untold Story Of The Eagles*, Marc Eliot.

Eaglin, Snooks

b. Fird Eaglin, 21 January 1936, New Orleans, Louisiana, USA. Eaglin was left blind after a childhood illness and was given the nickname Snooks after a character in a radio series. He played guitar and sang in Baptist churches before winning a local talent contest in 1947. During the 50s he was a street singer in New Orleans, performing a variety of pop, blues and folk material. However, his first recordings, made by Harry Oster for **Folkways** and Folk-Lyric in 1958, emphasized the country blues side of his repertoire. He was equally at home in R&B, however, and his 1960 records for Imperial were in this format. During the 60s, Eaglin was a popular artist in New Orleans, where he frequently accompanied **Professor Longhair** on guitar. Eaglin returned to a 'songster' mix of folk and pop when recorded in 1972 by Quint Davis, and his later records showed a versatility ranging from flamenco to swamp-pop. Eaglin's 80s albums for Black Top were produced by Hammond Scott and included accompaniments from **Anson Funderburgh** (guitar), **Grady Gaines** (saxophones) and **Sammy Myers** (harmonica). He continued recording into the 90s.

● ALBUMS: *Blues From New Orleans Volume 1* (Storyville 1958) ★★★★, *New Orleans Street Singer* (Folkways 1958) ★★★★, *Snooks Eaglin* (Heritage 1961) ★★★, *That's All Right* (Bluesville 1962) ★★★★, *Possum Up A Simmon Tree* (Arhoolie 1971) ★★★, *Legacy Of The Blues* (1971) ★★★, *Down Yonder* (Sonet 1978) ★★★, *Baby You Can Get Your Gun!* (Black Top 1987) ★★★, *Out Of Nowhere* (Black Top 1989) ★★★, *Teasin' You* (Black Top 1992) ★★, *Soul's Edge* (Black Top 1995) ★★★, *Live In Japan* (Black Top 1997) ★★★.

● COMPILATIONS: *The Legacy Of The Blues Volume 2* (Sonet 1988) ★★★★, *Country Boy Down In New Orleans* (Arhoolie 1993) ★★★, *The Complete Imperial Recordings* (Capitol 1996) ★★★★, *The Crescent City Collection* (Fuel 2001) ★★★★.

Ealey, Robert

b. 6 December 1925, Texarkana, Texas, USA, d. 7 March 2001, Fort Worth, Texas, USA. With each parent belonging to a different church, it was inevitable that Ealey's first singing experience was with a gospel quartet. However, he favoured the music of **Frankie Lee Sims**, **Lightnin' Hopkins** and **Lil' Son Jackson**. He moved to Dallas in 1951, where he could witness artists such as **T-Bone Walker** first-hand. He had drummed for Lightnin' Hopkins and sung in clubs by the time he moved to Fort Worth, where he worked with 'Cat Man' Fleming and teamed up with guitarist **U.P. Wilson** to form the Boogie Chillen. In 1967, he formed a band with guitarist Sumter Bruton, Johnny B and Ralph Owens. The following year, Ealey, Bruton and Owens, along with Mike Buck and Freddie Cisneros, formed the 5 Careless Lovers, which on

occasions also included **Lou Ann Barton**. The band's residency was the Blue Bird, where Ealey remained for two decades before putting his name to two clubs, Robert Ealey's Underground and Robert Ealey's Thunderbird Lounge, both of which quickly folded. His later recordings featured him with some of the guitarists who passed through his bands, Hash Brown, Sumter Bruton, Jim Suhler, **Mike Morgan** and **Coco Montoya** among them. Ealey's talent as a live performer translated fitfully to record, where the inconsistencies of his technique could be hidden.

● ALBUMS: with the 5 Careless Lovers *Live At The New Blue Bird Nightclub* (Blue Royal 1973) ★★★, with the Juke Jumpers *Bluebird Open* (Amazing 1981) ★★★, with Curly 'Barefoot' Miller, Joe Jonas *Texas Bluesmen* (Topcat 1993) ★★★, *If You Need Me* aka *Turn Out The Lights* (Topcat/Black Top 1994) ★★★, *You Don't Get This Every Day* (Stark 1995) ★★★, with Tone Sommer *I Like Music When I Party* (Black Top 1997) ★★★, *Electric Ealey* (Own Label 2000).

Eamon

b. Eamon Doyle, 1984, Staten Island, New York City, USA. Foul language and misogynistic lyrics is nothing new to hip-hop, but Eamon somehow manages to take it all to a whole new extreme. Raised in New York City, Eamon first developed an interest in music via his father, who sang with a doo-wop group on the side, and would let his young son sometimes sit in and vocalize. Soon afterwards, Eamon became interested in rap and it did not take long for him to start work with other musicians on projects that did not always reflect hip-hop interests (namely, a **Hanson**-like pop group that he briefly found himself a member of). Deciding to blend the smoothness of R&B with hip-hop, Eamon created a style that he referred to as ho wop, even though artists such as **R. Kelly** had been specializing in a similar style for years beforehand. A recording contract with **Jive Records** followed, which led to the release of his brazen debut single, 'Fuck It (I Don't Want You Back)', in 2003. An obviously edited version of the track went on to become a favourite on hip-hop radio, and latterly broke through into the upper reaches of the mainstream chart. Eamon's debut, *I Don't Want You Back*, was released early the following year. The album proved to be an immediate hit in the USA, as it quickly reached the Top 10 on the **Billboard** Hot 200. In April, 'Fuck It (I Don't Want You Back)' topped the UK singles chart. New York–based artist Frankee, who claimed to be Eamon's ex-girlfriend and the subject matter of his hit, recorded the witty answer record 'F.U.R.B. (F U Right Back)'. The track knocked 'Fuck It (I Don't Want You Back)' from the top of the UK singles chart.

● ALBUMS: *I Don't Want You Back* (Jive 2004) ★★★.

Eanes, Jim

b. Homer Robert Eanes Jnr., 6 December 1923, Mountain Valley, Henry County, Virginia, USA, d. 21 November 1995, Martinsville, Virginia, USA. His early musical interest came from his father, a talented banjo player, who ran a local band. When only six months old, he suffered severe burns to his left hand that left the fingers twisted, but as a boy he developed a style of playing that, after an operation in 1937, enabled him to become a fine guitarist. He played in his father's band, appeared on local radio, where he acquired the name of Smilin' Jim Eanes (Homer seemed unsuitable) and in 1939, became the vocalist for **Roy Hall**'s Blue Ridge Entertainers, until Hall's death in a car crash in 1943. Between 1945 and 1949, he worked with the Blue Mountain Boys on the *Tennessee Barn Dance* on WNOX Knoxville and recorded with them in New York. He briefly joined **Lester Flatt** and **Earl Scruggs**, when they formed their first Foggy Mountain Boys, before finally moving to Nashville to join **Bill Monroe**. He began to write songs during his time at Knoxville, the first being his now well-known 'Baby Blue Eyes', and when, in 1949, he won a **Capitol** talent competition, it was one of the first songs he recorded. Another song, co-written at the same time with Arthur Q. Smith, was 'Wedding Bells', which Eanes first sang on the *Barn Dance* in 1947. The song's ownership moved to Claude Boone; when it failed to raise interest with the listeners, he subsequently passed it on to **Hank Williams**, for whom it became a number 2 country hit. (Arthur Q. Smith, real name James Arthur Pritchett, wrote several songs which he sold to artists and Eanes assisted with some of them. Smith, who died in 1963, should not be confused with either **Fiddlin' Arthur Smith** or **Arthur 'Guitar Boogie' Smith**.) In 1951, Eanes formed his famous Shenandoah Valley Boys and recorded for Blue Ridge. He achieved considerable success with the war song 'Missing In Action' (again co-written with Arthur Q. Smith), which sold in excess of 400,000 copies and led to him signing for **Decca**, where he recorded his popular 'I Cried Again', 'Rose Garden Waltz' and 'Little Brown Hand' (the next year, **Ernest Tubb**'s Decca recording of 'Missing In Action' reached number 3 in the US country charts). He moved to Starday in 1956, finding success with his own songs 'Your Old Standby' (recorded by **George Jones** on several occasions) and 'I Wouldn't Change You If I Could' (a number 1 US country hit for **Ricky Skaggs** in 1983). He also made a recording of 'The Little Old Log Cabin In The Lane', which is rated by some as the best recorded version of this old song. Throughout the 60s and 70s, Eanes was occupied with performing, recording, songwriting and work on various radio stations, including, in 1967, a spell on the *Wheeling Jamboree*. During the 70s, he was also much in demand as an MC for festivals and shows. In 1978, he suffered a severe heart attack but a year later embarked on a European tour (these tours were a regular occurrence and by 1990, he had completed nine, and during one recorded an album with a Dutch country band). He formed an outfit in 1984, underwent heart surgery in 1986, but as soon as possible was back entertaining and singing, as always, a mixture of bluegrass, gospel and country material. In the early 90s, emphysema caused Eanes major problems but, in spite of a general deterioration in his health, he continued to make some local appearances and even completed an album with his old friend **Bobby Atkins**. He finally died of congestive heart failure in the Blue Ridge Center, Martinsville, Virginia, on 21 November 1995, and is buried at Martinsville's Roselawn Burial Park. His fine vocals and songwriting over the years earned Jim Eanes the universal nickname of The Bluegrass Balladeer.

● ALBUMS: *Your Old Standby* (Zap 1967) ★★★, *Jim Eanes With Red Smiley & The Bluegrass Cut-Ups* (Rural Rhythm 1968) ★★★, *Rural Rhythm Presents Jim Eanes* (Rural Rhythm 1969) ★★★, *Blue Grass Special BS2* (BS 1970) ★★★, *The New World Of Bluegrass* (Folly 1973) ★★★, *The Shenandoah Valley Quartet With Jim Eanes* (County 1975) ★★★, *Jim Eanes* (Original 1976) ★★★, *Shenandoah Valley Quartet* (Outlet 1977) ★★★, *A States-*

man Of Bluegrass Music (Jessup 1977) ★★★, *Where The Cool Waters Flow* (Leather 1978) ★★★, *Jim Eanes & The Shenandoah Valley Boys (Early Days Of Bluegrass)* (Rounder 1979) ★★★★, with Smoketown Strut *Ridin' The Roads* (Racoon 1981) ★★★, *Shenandoah Grass Yesterday And Today* (Webco 1983) ★★★, *Bluegrass Ballads* (Rebel 1986) ★★★, with Bobby Atkins *Jim Eanes, Bobby Atkins And The Countrymen* (Old Homestead 1986) ★★★, *Reminiscing* (Rebel 1987) ★★★, *Log Cabin In The Lane* (Highland 1988) ★★★, *Let Him Lead You* (Rebel 1989) ★★, *50th Anniversary Album* (Rebel 1990) ★★★, *Hillbilly Sounds At Its Best* (CowgirlBoy 1990) ★★★, with Atkins *Heart Of The South* (Rural Rhythm 1991) ★★★.

● COMPILATIONS: *Jim Eanes And The Shenandoah Valley Boys* (Bear Family 2000) ★★★★.

Eardley, Jon

b. 30 September 1928, Altoona, Pennsylvania, USA, d. 4 April 1997, Cologne, Germany. Eardley began playing trumpet when he was a child, encouraged by his musician father. His early interest in jazz came from records made by his father's generation of musicians but he soon became influenced by bop. After military service he formed his own small band, playing bop, and in the early 50s settled in New York. Here he played with **Phil Woods**, **Gerry Mulligan** and others, touring Europe with Mulligan in 1956. He recorded with Woods, Mulligan and **Chet Baker**. After a spell playing in his home state he relocated to Europe, playing thereafter in studios, on radio and in clubs in Belgium and Germany. In Europe he found a high level of admiration and recognition, and was recorded by Spotlite Records under his own name and in partnership with **Al Haig**. In 1989 he soloed on some tracks for **Carmen McRae**'s *Dream Of Life*, recorded with the West German Radio Orchestra. Eardley played both trumpet and flügelhorn with a rich, burnished sound, and was always a very melodic player all of which made his ballad playing especially attractive.

● ALBUMS: *In Hollywood* 10-inch album (New Jazz 1954) ★★★, *Hey, There* 10-inch album (Prestige 1955) ★★★, *Jon Eardley Seven* (Prestige 1956) ★★★, *Namely Me* (Spotlite 1977) ★★★, with Al Haig *Stablemates* (Spotlite 1977) ★★, *From Hollywood To New York* 1954/1955 recordings (Prestige 1990) ★★★★.

Earforce

A German heavy metal band featuring Mandy Van Baaren (vocals), Burkhard Lipps (vocals), Paco Saval (keyboards, vocals), Tato Gomez (guitar) and Willi Ketzer (drums), Earforce formed in the early 80s. Their debut album, 1982's *Hot Line*, featured an eclectic mix of styles, from **Fleetwood Mac**–styled folk/blues rock to more assertive hard rock. Many critics suggested that the songs lost something in translation (they relied almost exclusively on English language lyrics), but otherwise the album was a fairly impressive achievement. Despite this, there was never a follow-up, as the band members dispersed to other projects.

● ALBUMS: *Hot Line* (Xenophone 1982) ★★★.

Earl Brutus

'Let's have none of that bollocks about great songwriters and their craft', declared singer Nick Sanderson. 'Let's have a trucker's beat and some big, bold sounds.' Sanderson, former drummer with **World Of Twist**, was describing as well as anyone can the sound of British cabaret situationists Earl Brutus. In 1996, the band, also including Jamie Fry (vocals, brother of **ABC**'s Martin Fry), Rob Marche (guitar) and Gordon King (keyboards/drum machine), financed their first single, the **Gary Glitter**-tinged 'Life's Too Long', with donations to a sperm bank, and further band exploits seemed to pander to the UK music press' hunger for sordid stories of debauchery and drunkenness. However, the sound on the band's debut album was worth the hype. The rhythms and gruff vocals were offset by crunching glam rock guitars and bizarre synth doodles reminiscent of early 80s synth eccentrics such as the Passage and **Landscape**. Their live shows went beyond mere gigs, encompassing a Crimplene-clad dancer, neon light shows, radio samples, cheese-throwing and a revolving garage-forecourt sign reading 'PISS' on one side and 'OFF' on the other. Their closest neighbour in terms of attitude is probably the **Creation**, in that they combine primeval riffs with a sense of visual theatre, but Earl Brutus have an extra 30 years of pop tradition on which to draw. 'Great' songwriters may have looked on aghast, but any band with the iconoclastic chutzpah to announce 'I'm like James Brown/I like boys' must have something very special. Sadly, despite the release of another excellent album (1998's *Tonight, You Are The Special One*) the band has largely fallen back into cult status, although they remain a highly entertaining live act.

● ALBUMS: *Your Majesty . . . We Are Here* (Deceptive 1996) ★★★★, *Tonight, You Are The Special One* (Island Fruition 1998) ★★★.

Earl Carroll Vanities
(see **Carroll, Earl**)

Earl-Jean
b. Earl-Jean McCrea, USA. McCrea followed the example set by her sister Darlene McCrea by replacing her in the moderately successful R&B vocal trio the **Cookies**, joining original member Dorothy Jones and Margaret Ross in a new line-up. The trio signed to **Goffin And King**'s Dimension label in 1962 as both artists and session singers. They had US Top 20 hits with 'Chains' (later recorded by the **Beatles**) and 'Don't Say Nothin' Bad (About My Baby)'. In 1964 Earl-Jean went solo on Colpix and her first single, 'I'm Into Something Good', another Goffin and King composition, became her only US hit, reaching the bottom of the Top 40. A year later, the song became a UK number 1 hit for **Herman's Hermits**. Earl-Jean's follow-up single, 'Randy', failed to chart, and although she continued to record she was unable to achieve consistent success.

Earl Preston And The TTs
(see **Preston, Earl, And The TTs**)

Earl Royce And The Olympics
(see **Royce, Earl, And The Olympics**)

Earl Sixteen
b. Earl Daley, 1958, Kingston, Jamaica, West Indies. After winning local talent shows, Daley joined the group Flaming Phonics as lead vocalist before voicing the self-penned 'Malcolm X' for **Joe Gibbs** in 1975, later covered by **Dennis Brown**. In 1977 Daley became a member of the **Boris Gardiner** Happening who introduced him to **Lee Perry** at the Black Ark. There he recorded four tracks in 1978/9 and met Earl Morgan of the **Heptones**, who produced his debut album, *Singing Star*. His next collection was for the radio disc jockey and DATC producer **Mikey Dread**, although there were singles for **Augustus Pablo** ('Changing World'), **Linval Thompson**, **Derrick Harriott** and others, released throughout the early 80s, including an excellent set for former Stur-Gav duo **Ranking Joe** and **Jah Screw**. By 1982/3 he was at **Studio One** where his third version of 'Love Is A Feeling' was recorded. The previous two versions were for **Aston 'Familyman' Barrett** and Stafford Douglas; to date, it remains Earl Sixteen's most popular song. The Brentford Road sessions resulted in **Coxsone Dodd**'s *Showcase* album of 1985. Shortly afterwards, he switched allegiance to former **Royals** founder **Roy Cousins**, then Skengdon and Blacka Dread ('Batman And Robin') and Bert Douglas ('Problems'). In 1988 after a two-year break, he resurfaced in England, covering **Simply Red**'s 'Holding Back The Years' and making a short-lived attempt to produce himself. During 1991/2 he was at **Ariwa Sounds**, recording *Babylon Walls* and several fine singles for the Mad Professor. Since then he has voiced for a growing number of UK producers with varying degrees of success, and appeared on tracks by **Dread Zone** and **Leftfield**. He made his major label debut in 1997 with *Steppin' Out* for **WEA Records**.

● ALBUMS: *Shining Star* (Vista 1980) ★★★, *Reggae Sounds* (DATC 1981) ★★★, *Julie* (Roy Cousins 1982) ★★★, *Special Request* (Roy Cousins 1983) ★★★, *Super Duper* (Time 1986) ★★★, *Showcase* (Studio One 1985) ★★★★, *Babylon Walls* (Ariwa 1991) ★★★, *Boss Man* (Carib Sounds 1992) ★★★, *Not For Sale* (Next Step 1993) ★★, *Phoenix Of Peace* (1993) ★★, *Steppin' Out* (Warners 1997) ★★★, *Cyber Roots* (Epark 2001) ★★★★.

Earl Zinger
b. Rob Gallagher, 1966, England. Earl Zinger is one of several recording monikers employed by UK-based DJ Rob Gallagher, who has traversed a number of different music styles during his lengthy career. He began in the mid-80s as a new age rapper and jazz poet, appearing at **Gilles Peterson**'s Babylon club in London and playing an instrumental part in the rise of the **Acid Jazz Records** label. Gallagher's iconic presence on the late 80s acid jazz scene was permanently etched onto vinyl with the formation of **Galliano**. This sprawling outfit released a number of acclaimed albums during the early 90s before disintegrating following the release of 1996's *4*.

Gallagher maintained his healthy work rate in the late 90s and new millennium, working clubs with Peterson and recording under a variety of monikers including Earl Zinger, Two Banks Of Four (with Dill Harris) and the Red Egyptians (also the name of his record label). Earl Zinger's debut album, the wonderfully-titled *Put Your Phazers On Stun Throw Your Health Food Skyward*, was released by the Stud!o !K7 label in 2002. Flitting manically between dancehall, dub, hip-hop, ragga and rare groove, the album barely paused for breath with Gallagher's gravelly vocals holding it all together. The follow-up, *Speaker Stack Commandments*, repeated the feat, even diverting into a fantastic lovers rock section at one point.

● ALBUMS: *Put Your Phazers On Stun Throw Your Health Food Skyward* (!K7 2002) ★★★★, *Speaker Stack Commandments* (!K7 2004) ★★★.

Earl, Robert

b. 17 November 1926, England. This popular ballad singer enjoyed several UK hits in the late 50s. After becoming a semi-professional with the dance bands of **Sydney Lipton** and Nat Temple, he turned full-time professional in 1950, and appeared frequently on radio and television programmes such as the *Jack Jackson Show* and *Off The Record*. In 1958, he narrowly beat **Perry Como** to the UK chart with his version of 'I May Never Pass This Way Again'. Later that year, however, his 'More Than Ever (Come Prima)' was kept out of the Top 10 by **Malcolm Vaughan**. Earl's last hit was 'Wonderful Secret Of Love' in 1959. During the 60s, he retained a small but faithful audience. Subsequently, Earl's occasional releases, such as *Robert Earl Showcase* and *Shalom*, often featured Jewish favourites, including 'Yaas', 'My Son, My Son' and 'Mom-e-le'. Favourably reviewed in a London cabaret appearance in 1991, the 'veteran song stylist' maintained the Hebrew connection by including 'If I Was A Rich Man' from *Fiddler On The Roof*, among a selection of other nostalgic items. Earl's son, also named Robert, is listed among the UK's Top 100 richest people. He heads the **Hard Rock Café** chain, and co-owns Planet Hollywood, 'New York's newest eating experience', and its London subsidiary, along with **Bruce Willis**, Sylvester Stallone and Arnold Schwarzenegger.
● ALBUMS: *Robert Earl Showcase* (Philips 1960) ★★★.

Earl, Ronnie

b. Ronald Earl Horvath, 10 March 1953, Queens, New York City, USA. Ronald Horvath was inspired to play blues guitar after seeing **Muddy Waters** at a club in Boston, Massachusetts. Listing his influences as **Robert Lockwood**, **B.B. King**, **Magic Sam** and **T-Bone Walker**, among others, he made some records with Guitar Johnny And The Rhythm Rockers and Sugar Ray And The Bluetones (alongside harmonica player/vocalist Sugar Ray Norcia), but adopted the name Earl because, 'When I used to sit in with Muddy and all those old guys, they couldn't pronounce my last name.'
Earl quickly graduated to playing clubs around the Boston area, and he also spent some time in Chicago and Texas, backing many touring blues artists. He replaced **Duke Robillard** in **Roomful Of Blues** and stayed with them for almost eight years, leaving in the late 80s to pursue a successful solo career. He had already formed the original version of his backing band the Broadcasters, recording several albums for the Black Top label while still playing with Roomful Of Blues. Earl left that band in 1987 and debuted the new line-up of the Broadcasters (featuring vocalist Darrell Nulisch) on the following year's *Soul Searching*. Of the subsequent recordings by Earl and the Broadcasters, 1991's *Surrounded By Love* was of particular note for the work of Norcia and guitarist **Robert Lockwood Jnr.** on several tracks.
Earl's next version of the Broadcasters featured Bruce Katz (organ), Rod Carey (bass) and Per Hanson (drums), but no vocalist. The all-instrumental line-up made their debut for the AudioQuest label with 1993's *Still River*, but graduated to Bullseye Blues for a string of highly accomplished and critically well-received albums. A major label contract with **Verve Records** ensued, reflecting the increasing influence of jazz on Earl's work. *The Colour Of Love* was a critical and commercial success and coincided with Earl winning a **W.C.**

Handy award for Best Blues Instrumentalist. However, the guitarist succumbed to manic depression at a crucial stage in his career and effectively retired from performing for several years. He returned at the start of the new millennium, signing a new recording contract with Telarc Records and enlisted the help of soul jazz organist **Jimmy McGriff** to record *Healing Time*. The following year's *Ronnie Earl And Friends* featured a stellar guest list of artists including **Levon Helm**, **Irma Thomas** and **Kim Wilson**. Two further albums of largely instrumental material for the Stony Plain label have confirmed Earl's return to the top of his profession. He also remains an in-demand session guitarist. Often referred to as 'Mr Intensity', Earl is rated as one of the finest living blues guitarists.
● ALBUMS: *Smokin'* cassette (Black Top 1982) ★★★, with the Broadcasters *They Call Me Mr. Earl* (Black Top 1984) ★★★, with the Broadcasters *Soul Searching* (Black Top 1988) ★★★★, with the Broadcasters *Peace Of Mind* (Black Top 1990) ★★★, *I Like It When It Rains* 1986 recording (Antone's 1990) ★★★, with the Broadcasters *Surrounded By Love* (Black Top 1991) ★★★, with the Broadcasters *Still River* (AudioQuest 1993) ★★★, with the Broadcasters *Blues And Forgiveness* aka *Blues Guitar Virtuoso Live In Europe* (Crosscut/Bullseye Blues 1993) ★★★, with the Broadcasters *Language Of The Soul* (Bullseye Blues 1994) ★★★, with the Broadcasters *Grateful Heart: Blues & Ballads* (Bullseye Blues 1996) ★★★★, with Pinetop Perkins, Calvin 'Fuzz' Jones, Willie 'Big Eyes' Smith *Eye To Eye* (AudioQuest 1996) ★★★★, with the Broadcasters *The Colour Of Love* (Verve 1997) ★★★★, *Healing Time* (Telarc 2000) ★★★★, *Ronnie Earl And Friends* (Telarc 2001) ★★★, *I Feel Like Goin' On* (Stony Plain 2003) ★★★, with the Broadcasters *Now My Soul* (Stony Plain 2004) ★★★★, with Duke Robillard *The Duke Meets The Earl* (Stony Plain 2005) ★★★★.
● COMPILATIONS: with the Broadcasters *Deep Blues* (Black Top 1988) ★★★, with the Broadcasters *Test Of Time: A Retrospective* (Black Top 1992) ★★★★.

Earl, Vince

b. Vincent Earl, 11 June 1944, Birkenhead, England. Earl was among the first Merseybeat musicians to start playing as he formed the Teenage Rebels when only 11 years old. They performed tunes such as 'Giddy-Up-A-Ding-Dong' at the Birkenhead Boys Club, with the drummer playing an empty Shell-Mex oil-drum turned upside down and the guitarist using a metal pipe as a bridge on his guitar. By 1961 he was the smooth-voiced lead singer for Vince Earl And The Zeros, performing hits by **Cliff Richard** and **Bobby Vee**, and then he moved onto the more Merseybeat-sounding Vince Earl And The Talismen. Turning fully professional, Earl, normally a front man, played bass for **Rory Storm** And The Hurricanes. He then had a spell with the harmony band, the Connoisseurs, which included a tour of Germany. Cabaret was becoming popular so he added gags to the act and led the Vince Earl Attraction until 1977. He had acting roles in *Boys From The Black Stuff* and *No Surrender* and from 1990, he played the shopkeeper Ron Dixon in the television soap *Brookside*. Considering the soap stars who have made hit records, irrespective as to whether they can sing, it seems extraordinary that the highly competent Earl has not made records.

Earland, Charles

b. 24 May 1941, Philadelphia, Pennsylvania, USA, d. 11 December 1999, Kansas City, Missouri, USA. Earland began his musical career, playing saxophone, while still at school. First on alto and then tenor, he played with a number of bands and soon after graduation joined the small band led by organist **Jimmy McGriff**. Later, he formed a band of his own using the currently popular organ/saxophone/rhythm section format. Intent on pursuing this concept but experiencing problems with organists, he began playing the organ himself. He was hired as organist for a band led by **Lou Donaldson** before he resumed as a leader. Throughout the 70s, Earland's group was in great demand and he proved popular both in live performances, in clubs and at festivals, and also as a recording artist. His first album for **Prestige Records**, 1969's *Black Talk!*, has proved to have an enduring appeal for aficionados of the soul jazz genre. Earland recorded extensively for Prestige and Muse, before releasing albums for **Columbia Records** and **Mercury Records**. He experimented with disco in collaboration with his wife, singer-songwriter Sheryl Kendrick, but her death from sickle-cell anaemia in 1985 resulted in Earland's retreat from the music scene. He returned in the late 80s with two traditional soul jazz albums for Milestone Records. In the 90s he could be heard playing not only in an updated hard bop mode but also in an earthy heavily riff-laden manner, his solidly traditional B3 sound helping him retain much of his earlier popularity. A 1995 album featured the powerhouse modern trumpet playing of **Lew Soloff**, contrasting vividly with the album's musical leaning towards R&B, and was well received by audiences geared to contemporary sounds. He recorded two superb albums with **Irene Reid** shortly before his death from heart failure in December 1999.

● ALBUMS: *Black Talk!* (Prestige 1969) ★★★★, *Black Drops* (Prestige 1970) ★★★, *Living Black* (Prestige 1970) ★★★, *Charles 3* (Prestige 1971) ★★★, *The Dynamite Brothers* film soundtrack (Prestige 1973) ★★★, *Leaving This Planet* (Prestige 1974) ★★★★, *Smokin'* (Muse 1977) ★★★, *Pleasant Afternoon* (Muse 1978) ★★★, *Infant Eyes* (Muse 1978) ★★★, *Coming To You Live* (Columbia 1979) ★★★, *In The Pocket* (Muse 1982) ★★★, *Front Burner* (Milestone 1988) ★★★★, *Third Degree Burn* (Milestone 1989) ★★★★, *Whip Appeal* (Muse 1990) ★★★, *Unforgettable* (Muse 1992) ★★★★, *I Ain't Jivin', I'm Jammin'* (Muse 1993) ★★★, *Ready 'n' Able* (Muse 1995) ★★★, *Slammin' And Jammin'* (Savant/City Hall 1996) ★★★, *Blowing The Blues Away* (High Note 1997) ★★★, *Charles Earland's Jazz Organ Summit* (Cannonball 1997) ★★★, *Stomp!* 1999 recording (HighNote 2001) ★★, *If Only For One Night* (HighNote 2002) ★★.

● COMPILATIONS: *Anthology* (Soul Brother 2001) ★★★, *The Mighty Burner: The Best Of His HighNote Recordings* (HighNote 2004) ★★★.

Earle, Stacey

b. San Antonio, Texas, USA. The younger sister of **Steve Earle**, Stacey grew up in an affluent middle-class home in southern Texas, the daughter of an air traffic controller father and property administrator mother. Often the siblings would run away together, although Stacey insists they would always call home to ensure their parents knew they were safe. While Steve set out on his personal odyssey of inspired nouveau country songwriting and scrapes with the law and substance abuse, Stacey contented herself with early motherhood. In fact, she made no serious move to take up singing until she travelled to see one of Steve's Nashville shows when she was 29 (ostensibly to baby-sit one of his children). Stacey ended up staying for several months as Steve went through his divorce, and he eventually asked his sister to contribute backing vocals to his records and join him on tour. She began to work on her own songs, and took them around Nashville publishers. She waited tables and hosted the weekly writer's night at Jack's Guitar Bar over six years in an abortive quest for a contract, although she married songwriter Mark Stuart in 1993.

Eventually, in 1998, Earle took out a bank loan for $4,000 to record *Simple Gearle*, her debut album. This was promoted to radio via the Internet, and featured strong self-compositions including 'Next Door Down', which chronicled her reception on Music Row when she first tried to finance the album. Earle's second album, *Dancin' With Them That Brung Me*, was a more upbeat collection of songs that came close to matching the quality of her debut. The double live CD *Must Be Live* was collected from over 40 concerts performed by Earle and Stuart. The latter was again credited as co-leader on the superb studio follow-ups, *Never Gonna Let You Go* (2003) and *S&M Communion Bread* (2005).

● ALBUMS: *Simple Gearle* (Gearle/E-Squared 1998) ★★★★, *Dancin' With Them That Brung Me* (Gearle/E-Squared 2000) ★★★, with Mark Stuart *Must Be Live* (Gearle/Evolver 2002) ★★★, with Stuart *Never Gonna Let You Go* (Gearle/Evolver 2003) ★★★★, with Stuart *S&M Communion Bread* (Gearle/Funzalo 2005) ★★★★.

Earle, Steve

b. 17 January 1955, Fort Monroe, Virginia, USA. Earle's father was an air-traffic controller and the family was raised in Schertz, near San Antonio, Texas. Earle played an acoustic guitar from the age of 11, but he also terrorized his school friends with a sawn-off shotgun. He left home many times and sang 'Help Me Make It Through The Night' and 'all that shit' in bars and coffee houses. He befriended **Townes Van Zandt**, whom he describes as a 'a real bad role model'. Earle married at the age of 19 but when his wife went with her parents to Mexico, he moved to Nashville, playing for tips and deciding to stay. He took several jobs to pay his way but they often ended in arguments and violence. He appeared as a backing vocalist on **Guy Clark**'s 1975 classic *Old No. 1*, before signing a publishing contract with Sunbury Dunbar. **Elvis Presley** almost recorded 'Mustang Wine', and **Johnny Lee** had a Top 10 hit in 1982 with 'When You Fall In Love'. His second marriage was based, he says, 'on a mutual interest in drug abuse'.

Earle formed a back-up band in Texas, the Dukes, and was signed to Epic Records, who subsequently released the rockabilly influenced *Early Tracks*. Recognition came when he and the Dukes signed to MCA and made 1986's famed 'New Country' album, *Guitar Town*, the term being the CB handle for Nashville. The title track, with its **Duane Eddy**-styled guitar riff, was a potent blend of country and rock 'n' roll. 'Good Ol' Boy (Gettin' Tough)' was Earle's response to President Reagan's firing of the striking air-traffic controllers, including Earle's brother. Like **Bruce Springsteen**, his songs often told of the restlessness of blue-collar workers. 'Someday' is a cheerless example—'There ain't a lot you can do in this town/You drive down to the lake and then you turn back around.' Earle wrote 'The Rain Came Down' for the Farm Aid II benefit, and 'Nothing But A Child' was for an organization to provide for homeless children. **Waylon Jennings** recorded 'The Devil's Right Hand' and **Janie Fricke**, 'My Old Friend The Blues'. Although some of Earle's compositions are often regarded as redneck anthems, the views are not necessarily his own: during this period he often wrote from the perspective of his creation, Bubba, the archetypal redneck. Another is The Beast: 'It's that unexplainable force that causes you to be depressed. As long as The Beast is there, I know I'll always write.'

Earle saw in the 1988 New Year in a Dallas jail for punching a policeman and during that year, he married his fifth wife and released an album with a hard rock feel, **Copperhead Road**, which included the Vietnam saga 'Johnny Come Lately' which he recorded with the **Pogues**. *The Hard Way* and a live album followed, before Earle's contract expired with MCA. His drug problems escalated and at one point the singer was living in crack houses or sleeping rough. Everything came to a grinding halt in 1994 when he was imprisoned for narcotics possession.

Following a successful detox program, Earle returned in 1995 with a fine album. *Train A Comin'* was mellow, acoustic and emotional, and featured some exceptional playing from **Peter Rowan** and harmony vocals from **Emmylou Harris**. In the mid-90s, fired by the acclaim for *Train A Comin'*, a cleaned-up Earle started his own label, E Squared, and contributed to the soundtrack of *Dead Man Walking*. Earle is determined never to return to drugs. He stated in January 1996, 'I am real, real active and that is how I stay clean. It's a matter of survival to me. My life's pretty together right now. I got my family back.' Earle continued his creative renaissance with *I Feel Alright* and *El Corazón*, and recorded a superb bluegrass album with the **Del McCoury** Band. His work during this period became increasingly political in nature, marking this former junkie out as a contemporary successor to one of his songwriting heroes, **Woody Guthrie**. Of particular note was the closing track on 2000's *Transcendental Blues*, 'Over Yonder (Jonathan's Song)', a searing indictment of the death penalty in America. The track was sung from the point of view of Jonathan Nobles, a convicted double-murderer who invited Earle (a passionate opponent of the death penalty) to attend his execution.

Earle's second studio album of the new millennium, *Jerusalem*, proved to be one of the best and most controversial recordings of his career. A complex exploration of the artist's emotions following the terrorist attacks of 11 September 2001, the material cast a jaundiced eye over modern America's ills with the only hint of redemption offered by the closing title track. The song that attracted most attention was 'John Walker's Blues', an attempt to explore the story of the 'American Taliban' that triggered all sorts of opprobrium from America's moral majority. During this period, Earle also published the short stories collection, *Doghouse Roses*. The compilation set *Sidetracks* collected a number of his cover versions, including a particularly powerful version of Dylan's 'My Back Pages'. The 2003 release *Just An American Boy: The Audio Documentary* was Earle's first official live release since 1991's *Shut Up And Die Like An Aviator*. He married **Alison Moorer** on 11 August 2005.

● ALBUMS: *Guitar Town* (MCA 1986) ★★★★, with the Dukes *Exit O* (MCA 1987) ★★★, *Copperhead Road* (MCA 1988) ★★★★, with the Dukes *The Hard Way* (MCA 1990) ★★★, with the Dukes *Shut Up And Die Like An Aviator* (MCA 1991) ★★★★, *BBC Radio 1 Live In Concert* (Windsong 1992) ★★★, *Train A Comin'* (Winter Harvest/ Transatlantic 1995) ★★★★, *I Feel Alright* (E-Squared/ Transatlantic 1996) ★★★, *El Corazón* (E-Squared/Warners 1997) ★★★★, with the Del McCoury Band *The Mountain* (E-Squared/Grapevine 1999) ★★★★, *Transcendental Blues* (E Squared 2000) ★★★, with Townes Van Zandt, Guy Clark *Together At The Bluebird* (Catfish 2001) ★★★★, *Jerusalem* (Sheridan Square/Artemis 2002) ★★★★, *Just An American Boy: The Audio Documentary* (Artemis 2003) ★★★, *The Revolution Starts . . . Now* (Artemis 2004) ★★★.

● COMPILATIONS: *Early Tracks* (Epic 1987) ★★★, *We Ain't Ever Satisfied: Essential Steve Earle* (MCA 1992) ★★★★, *Essential Steve Earle* (MCA 1993) ★★★★, *This Highway's Mine* (Pickwick 1993) ★★★, with the Dukes *Fearless Heart* (MCA 1995) ★★★, *The Very Best Of Steve Earle: Angry Young Man* (Nectar 1996) ★★★, *Ain't Ever Satisfied: The Steve Earle Collection* (Hip-O 1996) ★★★★, *The Devil's Right Hand: An Introduction To Steve Earle* (MCA 2000) ★★★★, *Sidetracks* (E-Squared/Artemis 2002) ★★★, *The Collection* (Spectrum 2002) ★★★, *The Best Of Steve Earle: The Millennium Collection* (MCA 2003) ★★★, *Early Tracks* (Acadia 2004) ★★.

● DVD/VIDEOS: *Live From Austin Tx* (New West 2004).

● FURTHER READING: *Doghouse Roses*, Steve Earle. *Hardcore Troubadour: The Life And Near Death Of Steve Earle*, Lauren St. John.

● FILMS: *Just An American Boy* (2003).

Earlies

Part English, part American, this quartet's style of music is as difficult to categorize as their origin. The band was originally formed in the early years of the new millennium with the four members, Giles Hatton (b. Manchester, England), Christian Madden (b. Burnley, Lancashire, England; keyboards), John Mark Lapham (b. Abilene, Texas, USA; vocals) and Brandon Carr (b. Dallas, Texas, USA; vocals), all acknowledging a shared love of the **Beach Boys**, the **Beatles** and the **Byrds**. The quartet composed songs by swapping ideas via e-mail and had not even met each other when they made their recording debut in 2001 with the limited edition 7-inch single 'Song For #3'. This beautiful, piano-led track was followed by another vinyl single '25 Easy Pieces', by which time interest in the Earlies was growing apace. 2003's 'The First Sound Of The Earlies' featured the glorious, harmony-laden 'Morning Wonder'. The single was followed in December by the Earlies' first release for the London, England-based Names label, the 10-inch *EP4*. The four tracks on the EP, 'Wayward Song', 'Slow Man's Dream', 'Bring It Back Again' and 'Sunday Morning', were the quartet's most musically adventurous to date, combining samples and electronic flourishes with layers of strings, keyboards and woodwind in a manner reminiscent of fellow psychedelic indie rock travellers **Mercury Rev**. The 10-inch *The Devil's Country* EP marked a move into country-laced psychedelia on the title track, and preceded the release of their album debut *These Were The Earlies*. Released in summer 2004, this set compiled most of the material from the vinyl releases and added a couple of new tracks.

● ALBUMS: *These Were The Earlies* (Names 2004) ★★★★.

Earls

Although 'Remember Then' was their only hit, the Earls were one of the most accomplished white doo-wop groups of the early 60s. The lead singer Larry Chance (b. Larry Figueiredo, 19 October 1940, Philadelphia, Pennsylvania, USA) formed the group in New York City's Bronx area in the late 50s. The other members were first tenor Robert Del Din (b. 1942), second tenor Eddie Harder (b. 1942), baritone Larry Palumbo (b. 1941) and bass John Wray (b. 1939). For their first single, the group revived the **Harptones**' 1954 R&B hit 'Life Is But A Dream', released by the local Rome label in 1961. The following year, the group moved to another New York label, Old Town, and made 'Remember Then', which reached the Top 30. The Earls continued to release singles on Old Town until 1965, but the only record to make an impact was a maudlin version of 'I Believe', dedicated to Palumbo, who had died in a parachute accident. With various personnel changes, including the addition of Hank DiScuillo on guitar, Chance continued to lead the group on occasional records for Mr G and **ABC Records**. With their big hit on numerous oldies compilations during the 70s, the Earls appeared on rock revival shows. 'Remember Then' was a UK Top 20 hit in 1979 for revivalist band **Showaddywaddy**.

● ALBUMS: *Remember Me Baby* (Old Town 1963) ★★★.

● COMPILATIONS: *Remember Rome: The Early Years* (Crystal Ball 1982) ★★, *Remember Then! The Best Of The Earls* (Ace 1992) ★★★, *Remember Then!* (Collectables 1999) ★★★.

Early Day Miners

Few bands nowadays can elicit such a calming effect from their music as Early Day Miners can. Coming from Bloomington, Indiana, USA (and supposedly taking their name from a vacation pamphlet taken from a town in nearby Yellowstone National Park in Montana), the band was formed during 1996 when former Ativin members Daniel Burton and Rory Leitch decided to start a new outfit together. An interesting method of writing songs was developed early on, with Burton and Leitch visualizing images from movies and pictures in their minds while constructing compositions, obviously a major catalyst for their expansive sound. Other full-time members include Joseph Brumley and Matt Lindblom, who are often joined by special guests including Dave Fischoff, Molly Kien, Maggie Polk, Kenny Childers, Pete Skafish, Tom Hoff and Darin Gray. Essentially a studio band (they play live shows only on a very sporadic basis), Early Day Miners released several albums at the start of the new millennium, including *Placer Found*, *Let Us Garlands Bring* and *Jefferson At Rest*. The latter release experimented with a more focused, rock-orientated sound.

● ALBUMS: *Placer Found* (Western Vinyl 2001) ★★★, *Let Us Garlands Bring* (Secretly 2002) ★★★★, *Jefferson At Rest* (Secretly 2003) ★★★, *All Harm Ends Here* (Secretly Canadian 2005) ★★★.

Earth

Never the most prolific of bands, Earth's brand of ambient metal is ostensibly the ongoing project of Dylan Carlson (guitar, percussion, vocals). Formed in Olympia, Washing-ton, USA, in 1990 by Carlson, Slim Moon (guitar) and Greg Babior (vocals), the band then moved to Seattle where Babior and Moon were replaced by Dave Harwell (bass) and Joe Preston (vocals/percussion). After several strong performances, initial recordings were made with Mike Lastra (later of the Kill Rock Stars label) and after opening for **L7** in Seattle the band signed to **Sub Pop Records**. Their debut, the 35-minute, three-song EP *Extra—Capsular Extraction*, featured contributions from Carlson's friend Kurt Cobain. Shortly after this release Preston left to join the **Melvins** and the band was reduced to a two-piece. *Earth 2: Special Low Frequency Version*, a 75-minute song in three movements, continued the band's obsession with repetitious, riff heavy drone rock. Soon after this release Harwell left leaving Carlson to continue alone. After several aborted attempts in the studio and amid deteriorating relations with Sub Pop, *Phase 3: Thrones And Dominions* was finally completed with the addition of Tommy Hansen (guitar) for the recording sessions. The subsequent *Sunn Amps And Smashed Guitars Live* comprised a live set recorded in London.

In 1996, Sub Pop inexplicably re-signed the band, which now featured its most stable line-up to date, including Carlson, former producer Ian Dickson (bass), Shawn McElligot (lead guitar) and Mike McDaniels (drums). *Pentastar: In The Style Of Demons* was accompanied by a video for the single 'Tallahassee' and despite being considered by many to be a more accessible affair, it still maintained Carlson's trademark colossal hypnotic sound. Carlson has maintained a low profile since, although he did make a brief appearance in the 1998 movie *Kurt & Courtney*. He returned to the music scene in 2005 with a new album for the Southern Lord label.

● ALBUMS: *Extra—Capsular Extraction* (Sub Pop 1991) ★★★, *Earth 2: Special Low Frequency Version* (Sub Pop 1993) ★★★, *Phase 3: Thrones And Dominions* (Sub Pop 1995) ★★★★, *Sunn Amps And Smashed Guitars Live* (Blast First 1995) ★★, *Pentastar: In The Style Of Demons* (Sub Pop 1996) ★★★, *Living In The Gleam Of An Unsheathed Sword* (Mega Blade 2005) ★★★, *Hex: Or Printing In The Infernal Method* (Southern Lord 2005) ★★★.

● COMPILATIONS: *Legacy Of Dissolution* (No Quarter 2005) ★★★★.

● DVD/VIDEOS: *A Bureaucratic Desire For Revenge* (Sub Pop 1996).

● FILMS: *Kurt & Courtney* (1998).

Earth And Stone

Vocal duo comprising Albert Bailey and Clifton Howell. In 1972, Howell and Bailey attended one of the weekly auditions at **Studio One**. They worked at the celebrated Brentford Road studio for a year but decided to abscond as they were disillusioned with the lack of progress with **Coxsone Dodd**. In 1973, the duo began working with brothers Ernest and **Joseph 'Joe Joe' Hookim** at the Channel One studio. Earth And Stone recorded a mix of lovers and roots orientated tunes, including the classic 'Jah Will Cut You Down' and 'Three Wise Men'. Channel One released the duo's output on the Hitbound label, but came under criticism from purists that they were simply copying old Studio One rhythms. The producers made no secret that they were reviving earlier rhythms and have since proved to have been innovators as the practice continues to the present. Bailey and Howell took turns to perform lead vocals while the other provided harmonies. Their style proved particularly popular and inspired the Hookims to compile *Kool Roots* in 1978. The compilation featured the duo's singles recorded at the Maxfield Avenue studio from 1973 onward and topped the specialist charts worldwide. Notable inclusions were 'Jail House Set Me Free', 'Free Black Man' and 'Once Bitten Twice Shy'. By 1980 the Hookims had relocated to New York and Earth And Stone consequently languished in obscurity. In 1997, the revival label Pressure Sounds reissued the duo's album, duplicating the earlier release by including the **dub** versions. While Earth And Stone were unable to achieve the success of the **Mighty Diamonds** and the Jays, their contribution to Channel One's success is considered equally as important.

● COMPILATIONS: *Kool Roots* (Cha Cha 1978) ★★★★.

Earth Crisis

This US hardcore band helped to revitalize the genre in the early 90s with their strident political message and an aggressive blend of hardcore and metal, an approach that continues to win new converts. The band was formed by Karl Buechner (vocals) after he graduated from high school in Syracuse, New York, in 1989. By 1992 a stable line-up had been established with the addition of Scott Crouse (guitar), Kris Weichman (guitar), Ian Edwards (bass) and Dennis Merrick (drums). Their 1992 debut for the Conviction label, 'All Out War', was well received and after strong live showings they signed to Victory Records. 'Firestorm', a reissue of 'All Out War' and their 1995 debut *Destroy The Machines* brought the band to the notice of the mass media, resulting in features on CNN, CBS and in *The New York Times*. Their ideologically charged lyrics, concerning environmental activism, animal liberation and straight edge principles, coupled with their electrifying live shows and fervent sound continued to be a potent mix, helping *Destroy The Machines* to become one of Victory's biggest selling releases. *Gomorrah's Season Ends* furthered their reputation, and with their profile growing they performed at the inaugural Ozzfest. They also performed a sell-out show in April at the Whisky A-Go-Go in Los Angeles with label-mates **Strife** and **Snapcase**, captured on *The California Takeover . . . Live*. Their final release for Victory, 1998's *The Oath That Keeps Me Free*, was a collection of rare and live tracks, including a crushing cover version of **Cream**'s 'Sunshine Of Your Love'. Shortly afterwards, Weichman was replaced by Ian Edward's brother Eric. In an attempt to convey their message to as many people as possible the band moved to Roadrunner in 1998. Despite a high volume of sales for that year's *Breed The Killers* and successful tours with **Sepultura**, **Fear Factory** and **GWAR**, Roadrunner dropped the band and they returned to Victory. In 1999, they played in front of 200,000 people in Colombia. The following year's *Slither* was considered a breakthrough album, with Buechner emerging as a more potent vocalist than previously expected while the album's more diverse and eclectic style, though still intense and powerful, gave them a more potent weapon with which to spread their message. The charismatic Buechner has also spoken for the US congress on youth issues.

● ALBUMS: *Destroy The Machines* (Victory 1995) ★★, *Gomorrah's Season Ends* (Victory 1996) ★★★, *The Oath That Keeps Me Free* (Victory 1998) ★★, *Breed The Killers* (Roadrunner 1998) ★★★, *Slither* (Victory 2000) ★★★★.

● COMPILATIONS: *Last Of The Sane* (Victory 2001) ★★★, *Forever True: 1991–2001* (Victory 2001) ★★★★.

Earth Messengers

Back in the mid-70s, Vincent 'Vinnie' Taylor (b. *c.*1960, St. Anns, Jamaica, West Indies) was a Rasta youth seeking an outlet for his singing talents. That outlet arrived in 1976 when Taylor formed Vinnie Taylor And The Revealers, a roots vocal trio modelled along the lines of local heroes **Burning Spear**. The Revealers went to Spear's producer, **Jack Ruby**, who recorded their single 'Hard Times'. When it flopped, Taylor returned to grass roots, changing the group's name to Earth Messengers and acting as a channel for frustrated Ocho Rios youth talent. Among those who passed through Earth Messengers were Donovan Francis, later to sign to **Island Records** as a solo singer, and Errol Douglas, who later appeared in **Foundation**. In 1988 Ruby picked up on Earth Messengers, now comprising Vinnie Taylor, his brother Milton, and Bedster Henry, and they recorded *Ivory Towers*, which was critically well received but commercially unsuccessful. Persistence did not pay off for Taylor: further recordings were stymied when Ruby died of a heart attack in the spring of 1989, and Earth Messengers' current activities are unknown. They remain yet another unlucky reggae act.

● ALBUMS: *Ivory Towers* (Mango/Island 1989) ★★★.

Earth Nation

This German ambient/new age rock project, masterminded by studio experts Markus Deml and Ralf Hildenbeutel, was released in 1994 on the Eye Q Records label. Hildenbeutel had already earned his reputation in the ambient dance community as co-producer to Eye Q founder, **Sven Vath**. Deml was a guitarist and had worked with a number of rock bands. These diverse influences were channelled into their debut album, featuring meshed guitar and voices underpinned by a hypnotic, shifting backbeat. Their debut single, 'Alienated', quickly established an audience in the **trance** clubs of Europe.

● ALBUMS: *Thoughts In Past Future* (Eye Q/Warners 1994) ★★★.

Earth Opera

Formed in Boston, Massachusetts, USA, in 1967, Earth Opera revolved around **Peter Rowan** (b. 4 July 1942, Boston, Massachusetts, USA; vocals/guitar) and **David Grisman** (b. 1945, Hackensack, New Jersey, USA; mandocello/mandolin). Both were veterans of the bluegrass and old-time circuit, Rowan with **Bill Monroe**'s Blue Grass Boys and the Mother State Bay Entertainers, and Grisman as leader of the New York Ramblers and a member of the **Even Dozen Jug Band**. The two musicians worked as a duo, performing Rowan's original songs, before adding John Nagy (bass) and Bill Stevenson (keyboards/vibes). *Earth Opera* was produced by fellow folk music associate Peter Siegel, who shared an unerring empathy with the material. Rowan's lyrical, highly visual compositions were enhanced by his unusual, expressive tenor, particularly on the graphic 'Death By Fire' and 'The Child Bride'. Elsewhere the material reflected the questioning rootlessness prevalent in the immediate post-1967 era. Drummer Paul Dillon was then added to the line-up, but Bill Stevenson left the group prior to recording a second album.

Although worthy, *The Great American Eagle Tragedy* featured a roughshod horn section that altered the tone of several songs, with only one track, 'Mad Lydia's Waltz', retaining the delicacy of the previous set. The collection was marked by its uncompromising title -track, a lengthy impassioned attack on the Vietnam War. A compulsive example of the genre, replete with images of terror and madness, this accomplished piece overshadowed much of the remaining content, although Rowan's talent was equally obvious on 'Home To You' and 'Sanctuary From The Law'. The former contained the memorably quirky lyric 'It's tired and I'm getting late'. Earth Opera broke up soon after the set was issued. Rowan later joined **Seatrain**, before enjoying a successful solo career, while Grisman became a leading figure in traditional music circles.

● ALBUMS: *Earth Opera* (Elektra 1968) ★★, *The Great American Eagle Tragedy* (Elektra 1969) ★★★.

Earth Quake

Formed in 1966 as Purple Earthquake, this San Francisco, California, USA, group comprised Gary Boykin, Ronnie Boykin, John Sargent, Mike Jones and Stan Miller (bass). The last-named subsequently retained the Earth Quake name for an act that, by 1971, was completed by John Doukas (vocals), Robbie Dunbar (lead guitar) and Steve Nelson (drums). The quartet recorded their first two albums while domiciled in Los Angeles, before returning to the Bay Area where they signed with the fledgling Berserkley label. Several singles, including 'Mr. Security', 'Friday On My Mind' (**Easybeats**) and 'Kicks' ensued, as well as a live album, all of which engendered considerable cult interest. Having accompanied **Tommy James** on his 1976 'comeback' album, Earth Quake were buoyed by the addition of guitarist/vocalist Gary Phillips (aka Phillipet), formerly of **Copperhead**. Three energetic albums followed, but the band was unable to attain a widespread appeal and its momentum faltered when Phillips opted to join **Greg Kihn**. *Two Years In A Padded Cell* featured the 1971 line-up, but Dunbar's subsequent defection signalled the end of this act. By 1983 Doukas had moved permanently to the UK, while Miller formed a new band.

● ALBUMS: *Earth Quake* (Berserkley 1971) ★★★, *Why Don't You Try Me* (Berserkley 1972) ★★★, *Earth Quake Live* (Berserkley 1975) ★★★, *Rockin' The World* (1975) ★★★, *8.5* (1976) ★★★, *Leveled* (1977) ★★★, *Two Years In A Padded Cell* (1979) ★★.

● COMPILATIONS: *Purple: The A&M Recordings* (Acadia 2003) ★★★.

Earth, Wind And Fire

The origins of this imaginative US group date back to the 60s and Chicago's black music session circle. Drummer Maurice White (b. 19 December 1941, Memphis, Tennessee, USA) appeared on sessions for **Etta James**, **Fontella Bass**, **Billy Stewart** and more, before joining the **Ramsey Lewis** Trio in 1965. He left four years later to form the Salty Peppers, which prepared the way for an early version of Earth, Wind And Fire. The new band—Verdine White (b. 25 July 1951, Illinois, USA; bass), Michael Beale (guitar), Wade Flemmons (vocals), Sherry Scott (vocals), Alex Thomas (trombone), Chet Washington (tenor saxophone), Don Whitehead (keyboards) and Yackov Ben Israel (percussion)—embarked on a diffuse direction, embracing jazz, R&B and funk, as well as elements of Latin and ballad styles. The extended jam 'Energy', from their second album for **Warner Brothers Records**, was artistically brave, but showed a lack of cohesion within the band.

White then abandoned the line-up, save his brother, and pieced together a second group around **Ronnie Laws** (b. 3 October 1950, Houston, Texas, USA; saxophone/guitar), **Philip Bailey** (b. 8 May 1951, Denver, Colorado, USA; vocals), Ralph Johnson (b. 4 July 1951, Los Angeles, California, USA; drums/percussion), Larry Dunn (b. Lawrence Dunhill, 19 June 1953, Colorado, USA; keyboards), Roland Battista (guitar) and Jessica Cleaves (vocals). He retained the mystic air of the original band but tightened the sound immeasurably, blending the disparate elements into an intoxicating 'fire'. Two 1974 releases, *Head To The Sky* and *Open Our Eyes*, established Earth, Wind And Fire as an album act, while the following year 'Shining Star' was a number 1 hit in both the US R&B and pop charts. Their eclectic mixture of soul and jazz was now fused to an irresistible rhythmic pulse, while the songs themselves grew ever more memorable. By the end of the decade they had regular successes with such infectious, melodious singles as 'Fantasy', 'September', 'After The Love Has Gone' and 'Boogie Wonderland', the latter an energetic collaboration with the **Emotions**. A further recording, 'Got To Get You Into My Life', transformed the song into the soul classic composer **Paul McCartney** had originally envisaged.

The line-up of Earth, Wind And Fire remained unstable. Philip Bailey and Ronnie Laws both embarked on solo careers as new saxophonists, guitarists and percussionists were added. White's interest in Egyptology and mysticism provided a visual platform for the expanded group, particularly in their striking live performances. However, following 11 gold albums, 1983's *Electric Universe* was an unexpected commercial flop, and prompted a four-year break. A slimline core quintet, comprising the White brothers, Andrew Woolfolk (b. 11 October 1950), Sheldon Reynolds and Philip Bailey, recorded *Touch The World* in 1987 but they failed to reclaim their erstwhile standing. *Heritage* (1990) featured cameos from rapper **M.C. Hammer** and **Sly Stone**, in an attempt to shift White's vision into the new decade.

Since 1987 Maurice White has no longer toured with the band, making only the occasional live appearance. He seemed to regain his enthusiasm in the studio with 1997's *In The Name Of Love*, a back-to-basics album recorded for new label Pyramid, with brother Verdine and Bailey also in the line-up (the album had originally been released in Japan in a slightly different form under the title *Avatar*). In March 2000, the band was inducted into the **Rock And Roll Hall Of Fame**. Despite Maurice White announcing he is suffering from Parkinson's Disease, Earth, Wind And Fire has continued to remain active in the recording studio, releasing albums on their own Kalimba label.

● ALBUMS: *Earth, Wind And Fire* (Warners 1971) ★★, *The Need Of Love* (Warners 1971) ★★, *Last Days And Time* (Columbia 1972) ★★, *Head To The Sky* (Columbia 1973) ★★★, *Open Our Eyes* (Columbia 1974) ★★★★, *That's The Way Of The World* (Columbia 1975) ★★★★, *Gratitude* (Columbia 1975) ★★★, *Spirit* (Columbia 1976) ★★★, *All 'N All* (Columbia 1977) ★★★, *I Am* (ARC 1979) ★★★, *Faces* (ARC 1980) ★★★, *Raise!* (ARC 1981) ★★★, *Powerlight* (Columbia 1983) ★★★, *Electric Universe* (Columbia 1983) ★★, *Touch The World* (Columbia 1987) ★★★, *Heritage* (Columbia 1990) ★★, *Millennium* (Columbia 1993) ★★★, *Greatest Hits Live, Tokyo Japan* (Rhino 1996) ★★, *Avatar* Japan only (Kalimba 1996)

★★★, *In The Name Of Love* (Pyramid/Eagle 1997) ★★★, *That's The Way Of The World: Alive In '75* (Columbia/Legacy 2002) ★★★, *Live In Rio* 1980 recording (Kalimba 2002) ★★, *The Promise* (Kalimba/Snapper 2003) ★★★, *Illumination* (Sanctuary 2005) ★★★.

● COMPILATIONS: *The Best Of Earth, Wind And Fire Vol. 1* (ARC 1978) ★★★★, *The Collection* (K-Tel 1986) ★★★, *The Best Of Earth, Wind And Fire Vol. II* (Columbia 1988) ★★★★, *The Eternal Dance* 3-CD box set (Sony 1993) ★★★, *The Very Best Of Earth, Wind And Fire* (Sony 1993) ★★★, *Ultimate Collection* (Sony 1999) ★★★★, *The Essential Earth Wind & Fire* (Sony 2002) ★★★★, *Love Songs* (Columbia/Legacy 2004) ★★★.

● DVD/VIDEOS: *In Concert* (Channel 5 1981), *The Eternal Vision* (Columbia 1992), *Live (The Millennium Concert)* (Sony 1994), *Live In Japan* (Pioneer Artists 1998), *The Ultimate Collection* (Sony Music Video 1999), *Live* (Image 2001), *Shining Stars: The Official Story Of Earth, Wind & Fire* (Evergreen Entertainment 2001), *Live By Request* (Sony 2002), *Live At Montreux 1997* (Eagle Vision 2004), with Chicago *Live At The Greek Theatre* (Image Entertainment 2005).

● FILMS: *That's The Way Of The World* (1975).

Earthling

Originating in London, England, in late 1994, Earthling, along with the **Mo' Wax Records** roster, **Portishead** and **Tricky**, were a core element of the new wave of trip-hop cross-genre experimentation. Led by rapper Mau (b. Ilford, Essex, England), the band's '1st Transmission' single for **Cooltempo Records** married the requisite **dub** rhythms with languid, occasionally inspired lyrics. It followed on from their debut white label 12-inch, 'Nothing', which won them their recording contract. The resultant album featured extended dub/jazz passages, courtesy of musical collaborator and former BBC kitchen staffer Tim Saul. Mau employed these as an anchor for his highly imaginative lyrics, which he stated are influenced as much by **Leonard Cohen** as conventional rap sources. The subject matter included issues as diverse as alcohol, news trivia, psychedelia and space travel, all related in cut and paste, stream of consciousness narratives. The release of 'Nefisa' later in the year provided the second great single to be associated with the album, but some rather savage critical comparisons to Portishead prompted Earthling's early demise. Mau later resurfaced in the **Dirty Beatniks**.

● ALBUMS: *Radar* (Cooltempo 1995) ★★★.

Earthshaker

This Japanese heavy metal band was modelled on the styles of **Y&T**, **Deep Purple** and **Van Halen**. Formed by guitarist Shinichiro Ishihara in 1981, even its name was taken from Y&T's third album. After a series of false starts, the band was completed with the addition of Masafumi Nishida (vocals), Takayuki Kai (bass) and Yoshihiro Kudo (drums). Relocating to San Francisco in 1983, they utilized the talents of ex-**Gamma** keyboard player Mitchell Froom on the following year's *Fugitive* opus. As a consequence the band's sound became less aggressive, which only served to highlight their obvious limitations. They continued to release albums as a four-piece, but made little impact outside their native Japan.

● ALBUMS: *Earthshaker* (Music For Nations 1983) ★★, *Fugitive* (Music For Nations 1984) ★★★, *Midnight Flight* (Music For Nations 1984) ★★★, *Live* (Nexus 1985) ★★, *Over The Run* (Eastworld 1986) ★★★, *Treachery* (Eastworld 1989) ★★★, *Live Best* (Eastworld 1990) ★★.

Earthtone9

A band that appeared to receive as much press attention for their lavish facial hair as their brand of skewed virulent metal, Earthtone9's arrival was something of a revelation for the UK metal scene. Taking their name from lyrics in the **Helmet** song 'In The Meantime', the band was formed in Nottingham in 1998 by former members of Blastcage, Karl Middleton (b. 19 March 1974; vocals), Owen Packard (b. 7 July 1972; guitar), Joe Roberts (b. 9 April 1969; guitar), Graeme Watts (bass) and **Iron Monkey** member Justin Greaves (drums). Several line-up changes and two demos followed before Earthtone9 issued 1998's *Lo-Def(Inition) Discord*. Produced by Andy Sneap and Dave Chang, the debut was a maelstrom of feedback drenched riffing, shuffling rhythms and Middleton's feral vocals. Winning eager praise, the band then set out on tour in support before issuing *Off Kilter Enhancement* a mere 12 months later (by now having settled with permanent drummer Simon Hutchby). Similar in style to its forerunner, the aptly-titled opener 'Grind And Click' set the scene, seeing the band rivalling luminaries such as **Will Haven** for levels of intensity and recalling **Alice In Chains** in the more restrained moments. Keeping up a relentless pace *Arc'tan'gent* followed soon after, with Packard filling in for the departed Watts (in turn replaced by Jamie Floate then Dave Anderson (b. 14 September 1974). With a typically clear production from Sneap, it was a confident display, including contributions by Ishmael Lewis of Liberty37 on 'P.R.D Chaos' and 'Yellow Fever'. Earthtone9 was edging into ever more melodic territory without sacrificing their dark metallic edge.

The *Hi-Point* EP preceded a slot on the Evolution tour with fellow British bands **Stampin' Ground**, **Lostprophets** and Defenestration before European supports with **Fear Factory** and **Soulfly**. Ex-Blastcage and Sunna drummer Richie Mills replaced the departing Hutchby in late 2001 before the band recorded *I Hate Corn Nuts* for **Island Records**, although the songs were only available in MP3 format from their website. An ambitious set, it saw Earthtone9 moving more in a mainstream direction, yet with no loss of quality or complexity.

● ALBUMS: *Lo-Def(Inition) Discord* (Copra 1998) ★★★★, *Off Kilter Enhancement* (Copra 1999) ★★★, *Arc'tan'gent* (Copra 2000) ★★★★, *Omega* (Copra 2002) ★★★.

East End

A UK-based remix team of the mid-90s who have closely protected their identity. However, it is known that they are a 'UK record company boss', 'an engineer who's worked on **Eric Clapton** and **Phil Collins** albums' and two A&R men. Their client list includes artists such as **Dina Carroll**, **Judy Cheeks**, **Eternal** and **Pauline Henry**. East End was unfortunately set up to remix dance music in a commercial manner, with the participants tired of the esoteric and wholly unmarketable remixes offered to their clients by 'name' producers.

East Of Eden

Formed in 1967, this versatile Bristol, England –based outfit's best known line-up comprised Dave Arbus (violin), Ron Caines (alto saxophone), Geoff Nicholson (lead guitar), Andy

Sneddon (bass) and Geoff Britton (drums). Their debut, *Mercator Projected*, offered an imaginative brew of progressive rock, jazz and neo-eastern predilections, but this robust, *avant garde* direction contrasted with the novelty tag placed on the band in the wake of their surprise hit single, 'Jig A Jig'. This lightweight, fiddle-based instrumental reached number 7 in the UK in April 1971, and in the process confused prospective audiences. East Of Eden was plagued by personnel problems and by 1972 had shed every original member. Joe O'Donnell (violin), Martin Fisher (bass) and Jeff Allen (drums, ex-**Beatstalkers**) then maintained the band's name in Europe before their demise later in the decade. Meanwhile, Arbus gained further acclaim for his contributions to the **Who**'s *Who's Next* while Britton later joined **Wings**. Arbus, Caines and Nicholson reunited in 1999 to record *Kalipse* and have since pursued a more *avant garde* direction.

● ALBUMS: *Mercator Projected* (Deram 1969) ★★★★, *Snafu* (Deram 1970) ★★★, *East Of Eden* (Harvest 1971) ★★, *New Leaf* (Harvest 1971) ★★★, *Another Eden* (EMI 1975) ★★, *It's The Climate* (EMI 1976) ★★, *Silver Park* (EMI 1978) ★★, *Kalipse* (Castle 1999) ★★★, *Armadillo* (HTD 2001) ★★★.

● COMPILATIONS: *The World Of East Of Eden* (Deram 1971) ★★★, *Masters Of Rock* (EMI 1975) ★★★, *Things* (Nova 1976) ★★★.

East Orange

A quartet formed in Columbus, Georgia, USA, in 1991, East Orange comprise Chad Etchison (guitar/vocals), Mark Skinner (guitar), John Skinner (drums) and Alex Johnston (bass). The Skinner brothers and Johnston had previously played together in several unrecorded bands. In 1993 the group relocated to a rented house in Atlanta, after their youngest member had graduated. East Orange made their debut in 1994 with the *Navigation Without Numbers* EP. This received widespread local airplay and earned comparisons to both the **Replacements** and **Elvis Costello**. Showcases in Nashville and Memphis followed in 1995, at which time the group's melodic pop demos earned them columns in mainstream magazines such as *Billboard*.

East River Pipe

The creation of Fred M. Cornog (b. USA), a home studio – based auteur who crafts elegant songs that belie their lo-fi origins. His unusual recording name was inspired by the tawdry sight of raw sewage emptying out of a pipe into the East River, a fitting symbol for Cornog's downbeat songs about human detritus.

Although he was born in Norfolk, Virginia, USA, Cornog grew up in Summit, New Jersey. After leaving high school he held down several menial positions before alcoholism left him unemployed and homeless, sleeping rough in a Hoboken train station. His saviour was a woman called Barbara Powers who, impressed by one of Cornog's self-recorded cassettes, took him in and helped set up a home studio in their Astoria, Queens apartment. Employing a Tascam 388 home recorder to great effect, Cornog and Powers issued several singles and cassettes on their own Hell Gate label. Elegant, cracked gems such as 'Make A Deal With The City', 'My Life Is Wrong' and 'Axl Or Iggy' evoke early 70s-era **Brian Wilson** by virtue of their deceptively simple construction and an aura of lush melancholia. This early work is collected on the excellent 1994 compilation, *Shining Hours In A Can*.

Cornog's two albums for UK independent **Sarah Records** again belie their lo-fi, urban origins, creating a spacious, pastoral sound to complement the cryptically personal lyrics. In 1995 Cornog signed a recording contract with Merge Records, the label set up by Ralph 'Mac' McCaughan of **Superchunk**. The following year's *Mel* was one of the year's finest independent releases, although at times ('I Am A Small Mistake', 'Kill The Action') Cornog's self-obsession reached genuinely disturbing levels. His work reached a wider audience when Kurt Wagner's sprawling ensemble **Lambchop** recorded several of his songs, although a contract with EMI-America fell through when the company closed down. Relocating to suburban New Jersey spurred Cornog's songwriting to new heights on 1999's *The Gasoline Age*. Despite viewing American society through a jaundiced eye, tracks such as 'Atlantic City (Gonna Make A Million Tonight)', 'Party Drive' and 'Shiny, Shiny Pimpmobile' held out for its ultimate redemption with a guarded optimism.

By the start of the new millennium Cornog had quietly established himself as one of the most impressive songwriters on the US alternative scene. New albums for Merge included *Garbageheads On Endless Stun* (2003) and *What Are You On?* (2006).

● ALBUMS: *Point Of Memory* cassette (Hell Gate 1990) ★★★, *I Used To Be Kid Colgate* cassette (Hell Gate 1991) ★★★, *Goodbye California* mini-album (Sarah 1993) ★★★, *Poor Fricky* (Sarah/Merge 1994) ★★★, *Mel* (Merge 1996) ★★★★, *The Gasoline Age* (Merge 1999) ★★★★, *Garbageheads On Endless Stun* (Merge 2003) ★★★, *What Are You On?* (Merge 2006) ★★★★.

● COMPILATIONS: *Shining Hours In A Can* (Ajax 1994) ★★★★.

East 17

Tony Mortimer (b. Anthony Michael Mortimer, 21 October 1970, Stepney, London, England), Brian Harvey (b. 8 August 1974, London, Barking, London, England), John Hendy (b. Jonathan Darren Hendy, 26 March 1971, England) and Terry Coldwell (b. Terence Mark Coldwell, 21 July 1974, London, England), the founding members of East 17, met while attending school in Walthamstow, London. Their name was taken from the London postal district from which they originate, and they even named their debut album after their home town.

Critics initially scoffed at their attempts to imitate hardcore Bronx rap crews. With former **Bros** svengali Tom Watkins as their manager, they cultivated an image of youthful arrogance and 'street style' in obvious opposition to the then prevalent UK teenage craze, **Take That**. Indeed, in early interviews they made a point of behaving badly, with incidents including pinching female journalists' bottoms and revelling in flatulence. Their debut single, 'House Of Love', became a major hit in August 1992, peaking at number 10 in the UK charts. The subsequent 'Gold' proved disappointing, but 'Deep' brought them to the Top 5. Both 'Slow It Down' and a lacklustre cover version of the **Pet Shop Boys**' 'West End Girls' also made the UK Top 20, accompanying the album *Walthamstow*. December 1993's 'It's Alright' was their bestselling single so far, reaching number 3 and staying in the UK charts for 14 weeks. Their first two 1994 singles, 'Around The World' and 'Steam', continued their commercial ascendancy. They finally hit the UK number 1 spot in December with 'Stay Another Day', a lush ballad with memorable harmonies and orchestration, which was 1994's Christmas number 1.

During preparations for their 1995 tour Mortimer, who had recently been awarded an **Ivor Novello** Award for his songwriting, was rushed to hospital suffering from exhaustion. Harvey was sacked in January 1997 after some ill-chosen comments about the drug Ecstasy. Fearing that his pro-drug statement could damage their reputation with a younger audience, it appears that they were faced with no alternative. However, Mortimer himself left in 1997 to embark on a solo career. Harvey subsequently returned, and plans to relaunch the group (now known as E-17) as an urban R&B trio met with initial success when 'Each Time' debuted at number 2 in the UK charts in November 1998. The commercial failure of follow-up singles and the attendant *Resurrection*, however, demonstrated just how vital Mortimer was to East 17. The remaining members subsequently called it a day not long afterwards, with Harvey attempting to launch himself as a solo artist.

● ALBUMS: *Walthamstow* (London 1993) ★★★★, *Steam* (London 1994) ★★★, *Up All Night* (London 1995) ★★★, as E-17 *Resurrection* (Telstar 1998) ★★.
● COMPILATIONS: *Around The World—The Journey So Far* (London 1996) ★★★.
● DVD/VIDEOS: *Up All Night* (PolyGram Music Video 1995), *Letting Off Steam: Live* (PolyGram Music Video 1995), *Greatest Hits* (PolyGram Music Video 1996).
● FURTHER READING: *East 17: Talk Back*, Carl Jenkins.

East Texas Serenaders

A string band of part-time musicians that was formed in Lindale, Texas, USA, in the late 20s. The original members were Cloet Hammen (guitar), Huggins Williams (b. Daniel Williams, 13 September 1900; fiddle), Henry Bogan (cello/string bass) and John Munnerlyn (tenor banjo) but a second fiddle played by Henry Lester was soon added. Hammen's family were all musical, his father was a noted Texas fiddler and as a boy, Cloet played guitar accompaniment for his father at fiddle contests. Williams' father also played fiddle and taught Huggins as a child, although the fact that Huggins was left-handed caused initial problems until a suitable instrument was obtained. Bogan was noted for his ability to play, by bow or by plucking the strings, his three-stringed cello. Munnerlyn, who played on their early recordings, was later replaced by banjoist Shorty Lester. They played a mixture of fiddle dance tunes, ragtime and tunes of the day and may, by their example, have influenced later Texas bands. Although they became popular enough to play at numerous Texas venues, including a residency in Tyler, and on some occasions in Oklahoma, they never completely gave up their daytime occupations. Hammen drove a truck, Bogan worked for the post office and Williams worked for a florist and undertaker. They first recorded for **Columbia Records** in 1927, but in the early 30s, they also recorded for **Brunswick Records**. Their final recordings were made for **Decca Records** in February 1937, when Hammen, Bogan, Williams and the two Lesters recorded 10 sides, which included their popular 'East Texas Drag', 'Arizona Stomp' and 'Sweetest Flower Waltz'. When they finally ceased playing local venues is unknown, but a compilation album of some of their recordings was issued in 1977.

● COMPILATIONS: *The East Texas Serenaders, Early Western Swing 1927–36* recordings (County 1977) ★★★★, *Complete Recorded Works 1927–37* (Document 1998) ★★★★.

Easter Brothers

A country and gospel group formed in 1953, comprising Russell Easter (b. Russell Lee Easter, 22 April 1930, Mount Airy, North Carolina, USA; banjo, guitar, vocals), James Easter (b. James Madison Easter, 24 April 1933, Mount Airy, North Carolina, USA; guitar, mandolin, vocals) and Ed Easter (b. Edward Franklin Easter, 28 March 1934, Mount Airy, North Carolina, USA; mandolin, banjo, vocals). They grew up greatly influenced by bluegrass music, in particular that of a gospel nature. Russell Easter first formed a band in 1947, and was later joined by his siblings. In 1953, with one other musician, they began to perform as the Green Valley Quartet and regularly played stations in Mount Airy and Danville. Turning more and more to bluegrass gospel music, they built their reputation throughout the 60s, playing various radio and television programmes. In 1960, they recorded for both Commandant and King. In 1968, when they recorded an acoustic album for County, the group (by then the Easter Brothers And The Green Valley Quartet) also included Russell Jnr. (banjo, dobro, guitar). During the 70s and 80s, they recorded albums for Old Homestead, Life Line and Morningstar. James' son Jeff played harmonica with the group for a time but eventually left to work as a duo with his wife Sheri (a relative of the Lewis Family) and in more recent years, a third generation Easter, namely Russell's grandson Jason, has played bass with the group.

● ALBUMS: as the Easter Brothers *I've Been Touched* (Commandment 60s) ★★★★, as the Easter Brothers And The Green Valley Quartet *The Bible On The Table* (Troy 60s) ★★, *Let Me Stand Lord* (Commandment 1965) ★★★, *Lord I Will* (Commandment 1966) ★★★, *14 Songs Of Faith* (Commandment 1967) ★★★, *Bluegrass & Country Hymns* (Stark 1967) ★★★, *Country Hymn Time* (Commandment 1967) ★★★, *The Easter Brothers & The Green Valley Quartet* (County 1968) ★★★, *From Earth To Gloryland* (Commandment 1969) ★★★, *He's Everything I Need* (Commandment 1970) ★★★, *Just Another Hill* (Commandment 1972) ★★★, *Don't Overlook Your Blessings* (Mission 1974) ★★★, *Hold On* (Old Homestead 1976) ★★★, *The Easter Brothers In Nashville* (Mission 70s) ★★★, *Coming Home* (Mayberry 70s) ★★★, *I'm Holding To His Hand* (QCA 70s) ★★★, *We're Going Home* (QCA 70s) ★★★, *He's The Rock I'm Leaning On* (Morningstar 1981) ★★★, *I Feel Like Travelling On* (Rebel 1981) ★★★, *Songs About Mama* (Life Line 1981) ★★★, *Almost Home* (Rebel 1982) ★★★, *The Easter Brothers* (Life Line 1983) ★★★, *Hereafter* (Life Line 1984) ★★, *Tribute To Reno & Smiley* (Rebel 1985) ★★★.
● COMPILATIONS: *Early Sessions 1960–1961* (Rebel 1984) ★★★★, *They're Holding Up The Ladder* (Rebel 2004) ★★★.

Easter Parade

It is fascinating to think how it would all have turned out if **Gene Kelly** had not broken his ankle and therefore been able to partner **Judy Garland** in this 1948 musical. As it was, MGM tempted **Fred Astaire** out of retirement—and the rest is history. Astaire played Don Hewes, whose partner in a successful dance act, Nadine (**Ann Miller**), gets the urge to go solo and leaves him in the lurch. More than slightly miffed, especially as he had hoped to marry the lady, Don plucks Hannah Brown (Judy Garland) from the chorus of a small club, and together they form a happy and prosperous relationship—on stage and off. **Irving Berlin**'s wonderful songs—a mixture of the old and the new—revealed the incredible range of his writing as one musical highlight followed another. Astaire, at nearly twice the age of Garland, was singing and dancing as well as ever in numbers such as 'Drum Crazy', 'Steppin' Out With My Baby' and 'It Only Happens When I Dance With You' (with Ann Miller). His moments with Garland were a joy, and included a ragtime vaudeville medley, 'When The Midnight Choo-Choo Leaves For Alabam', 'Snooky Ookums', 'Ragtime Violin', 'I Love A Piano' and, of course 'Easter Parade'. However, their most memorable number was surely 'A Couple Of Swells', in which, dressed as two social-climbing tramps, they mused: 'The Vanderbilts have asked us out to tea/We don't know how to get there, no siree.' Garland had the poignant 'Better Luck Next Time' and 'I Want To Go Back To Michigan', and Miller was scintillating and sizzling on 'Shaking The Blues Away'. **Peter Lawford** too, as Astaire's best friend, 'The Professor', displayed a pleasant light vocal touch with 'A Fella With An Umbrella'. The supporting cast was particularly fine, and included Clinton Sundberg as Mike, the philosophical barman, and **Jules Munshin** in the role of the frustrated head waiter. All in all, a triumph for all concerned, including producer **Arthur Freed**, director **Charles Walters**, dance director Robert Alton and screenwriters Sidney Sheldon, Frances Goodrich and Albert Hackett. **Roger Edens** and **Johnny Green** won Academy Awards for 'scoring of a musical picture'. In 1992, *Easter Parade* was issued on a laserdisc in a 'Technicolor restoration' from the original nitrate camera negative, with improved digital sound. The disc also included Judy Garland's performance of 'Mr. Monotony', a number that was cut from the original release. In 1998, **Tommy Tune**'s stage version of *Easter Parade* was out of town, eyeing Broadway.

Easterhouse

Formed in Manchester, England, by the Perry brothers, singer Andy and guitarist Ivor, during the mid-80s, Easterhouse first came to prominence after being championed by **Morrissey** of the **Smiths**. Taking their name from a working-class area of Glasgow, they signed to **Rough Trade Records** and were widely praised for early singles 'Inspiration' and 'Whistling In The Dark', which merged Andy's left-wing political rhetoric with Ivor's echo-laden guitar patterns. *Contenders*, a confident debut, also featured Peter Vanden (bass), Gary Rostock (drums) and Mike Murray (rhythm guitar). Contained within were entirely convincing accommodations between music and politics—the hard line of Andy Perry's lyrics exemplified by the compelling 'Nineteen Sixty Nine', a bitter assault on the betrayal of the working classes by Britain's Labour Party. Arguments broke out soon after its release and Ivor Perry went on to form the short-lived Cradle. Andy Perry kept the name Easterhouse, but by the time of 1989's *Waiting For The Red Bird* he was the only remaining original band member. He was joined on this disappointing, over ambitious record by David Verner (drums), Neil Taylor (lead guitar), Lance Sabin (rhythm guitar) and Steve Lovell (lead guitar). 'Come Out Fighting',

with its anthemic rock pretensions, failed to make the singles chart and the new Easterhouse, with all songs written solely by Perry, was heavily criticized: the political content was still high with tracks such as 'Stay With Me (Death On The Dole)', but the soul and subtle melodies were no longer present. Easterhouse's impact was, aside from one great album, probably minimal, but along with other Manchester guitar groups like the **Chameleons**, they laid the foundations for the explosion of interest in the city in the late 80s.

● ALBUMS: *Contenders* (Rough Trade 1986) ★★★, *Waiting For The Red Bird* (Rough Trade 1989) ★★.

Eastern Bloc

Famed as the north of England's premier record shop, Eastern Bloc's in-house Creed imprint launched **808 State**, **K Klass**, **Ariel** and **Justin Robertson**, The latter and Mike E-Bloc (see **E-Lustrious**) worked together on the counter before pursuing their own musical careers. Creed was brought under the generic MOS label banner in 1991 (MOS standing for More O' Same). Eastern Bloc inaugurated its own brand label in 1993. Peter Waterman (of **Stock, Aitken And Waterman** fame) was the unlikely purchaser of the establishment when it ran into financial difficulties. He then placed DJ and club owner Peter Taylor in charge of proceedings, with a brief to record strong, commercial dance music. Taylor had formerly worked with Waterman as part of the **PWL** set-up, notably remixing **Kylie Minogue**'s 'Keep It Pumping'. He also runs the Angels club in Burnley, Lancashire. The label's first release was a licensed track, 'Waterfall', by Atlantic Ocean, the second, 'She', by Ideal—Manchester DJs Jon Dasilva and A.G. Scott. However, it was the 'Loveland Saga' that earned their biggest headlines. A band of that title, affiliated to Eastern Bloc, released their version of **Darlene Lewis**' 'Let The Music (Lift You Up)' without obtaining sample clearance. A legal tussle ensued, until both parties agreed to release a joint version, performing together on *Top Of The Pops*.

Eastern Standard Time

The celebrated US-based DJ 'Two Tone' Ted Morris formed Eastern Standard Time in October 1995. The line-up featured James McDonald (drums, guitar, harmonica), Eric Schwarz (bass guitar, piano, keyboards), Franklin Wade (trumpet flügelhorn), Philip Cooper (trombone) and Matt Simms (saxophone). The name of the band was inspired by the legendary **Don Drummond**'s **Studio One** hit of the same name. The song also has the sad distinction as being the last song performed by the late **Roland Alphonso**, who collapsed on stage in 1998 shortly after completing the solo section of the ska classic. Having recruited the band members from various Washington-based ska bands, Morris and the group released their debut *Take 5* in the spring of 1996. Following the release of the EP, Eastern Standard Time embarked on a dynamic North American tour. Morris and the band also released the single 'Oh No', which clearly echoed the archetypal Jamaican ska releases of the early 60s. By December the band began working on their debut album which included appearances from a host of top musicians. **Chuck Brown** and Ele Jai lent their vocal talents to the band's reworking of **Derrick Morgan** and Patsy Todd's 'Housewives Choice', while Sledge from the Toasters and Sam Turner, of **James Brown** and **Lionel Hampton** fame, featured on a number of tracks. The release of *Second Hand* was met with critical acclaim. Some critics compared the release to **Jazz Jamaica** (who correspondingly

covered **Charlie Parker**'s, 'Barbados', which had been featured on both bands' albums) and the New York Ska Jazz Ensemble. Eastern Standard Time embarked on a European tour where they played alongside **Laurel Aitken**, the **Skatalites**, Hep Cat, **Bad Manners** and the **Specials**. The band is regarded as a precursor of the third wave of ska alongside the **Mighty Mighty Bosstones**, Bim Skala Bim, the Gangsters and the Graduates. The band was also featured on an **MTV** segment relating to the popularity of ska in the USA leading to wider exposure and rekindled interest in the band's debut.
● ALBUMS: *Second Hand* (Beatville 1997) ★★★★.

Eastman, Madeline

b. 27 June 1954, San Francisco, California, USA. An exceptionally gifted singer, much admired among her fellow professionals for her brilliant use of scat, Eastman works mainly on the west coast where she first attracted attention singing with the Full Faith And Credit Big Band. Although originally inspired by hearing **Billie Holiday** on record, Eastman's principal role models were **Miles Davis**, **Carmen McRae** and **Mark Murphy**. With **Kitty Margolis** she is co-owner of Mad-Kat Records.
● ALBUMS: *Point Of Departure* (Mad-Kat 1991) ★★★★, *Mad About Madeline* (Mad-Kat 1993) ★★★, *Art Attack* (Mad-Kat 1994) ★★★, with Tom Garvin *Bare: A Collection Of Ballads* (Mad-Kat 2001) ★★★, *The Speed Of Life* (Mad-Kat 2004) ★★★★.
● DVD/VIDEOS: with others *Saying It With Jazz* (Merrill Video 1995).

Eastmountainsouth

The folk rock duo Eastmountainsouth comprises singers Kat Maslich (b. Roanoke, Virginia, USA) and Peter Adams (b. Birmingham, Alabama, USA), who share songwriting and instrumental duties. Both come from musical families, and travelled throughout the USA (and in Adams' case, Europe, as well) to pursue careers in music. Their paths crossed in Los Angeles, California, when Maslich auditioned as a singer for a television spot Adams was producing music for. Their initial meeting did not amount to much, but when a friend of Adams' brought to his attention that Maslich was performing her music at a nearby venue, he attended. As a result, she sang on a country demo Adams was working on, and the two realized they shared similar musical tastes and songwriting styles. Additionally, there was no denying how exceptionally well their vocals blended together when they performed live, resulting in the abandonment of their solo careers, and the founding of Eastmountainsouth. One of their demos caught the attention of **Robbie Robertson**, who signed the duo to a recording contract with DreamWorks Records in autumn 2001. The duo's debut, *eastmountainsouth*, was issued in 2003. A sweet blend of folk and country, the album received a warm critical reception.
● ALBUMS: *eastmountainsouth* (DreamWorks 2003) ★★★.

Easton, Elliot

(see **Cars**)

Easton, Sheena

b. Sheena Shirley Orr, 27 April 1959, Bellshill, Scotland. Orr began performing while studying speech and drama at the Royal Scottish Academy of Music And Drama, studying by day and singing with the band Something Else in the evenings. Her short-lived marriage to actor Sandi Easton gave Orr her new name, and as Sheena Easton she was signed to **EMI Records** in 1979 following an audition for a planned documentary following a budding pop star. The resulting television film, *The Big Time*, about the creation of her chic image helped her debut single 'Modern Girl' into the UK charts. This was followed by the chirpy '9 To 5', which reached number 3 and propelled a reissued 'Modern Girl' into the Top 10. The former sold over a million copies in the USA (there known as 'Morning Train (Nine To Five)') and topped the singles chart for two weeks.

Extraordinary success followed in America where she spent most of her time. Now established as an easy-listening rock singer, Easton was offered the theme to the 1981 James Bond movie *For Your Eyes Only*, which became a US Top 5 hit. Further hits followed from her second album, including 'When He Shines' and the title track, 'You Could Have Been With Me'. In 1983, Easton, who by now had emigrated to California, joined the trend towards celebrity duets, recording the country chart-topper 'We've Got Tonight' with **Kenny Rogers**. The Top 10 hit 'Telefone (Long Distance Love Affair)' was in a funkier dance mode and her career took a controversial turn in 1984 with attacks by moralists on the sexual implications of 'Sugar Walls', a **Prince** song that became one of her biggest hits. Easton also sang on Prince's 1987 single, 'U Got The Look', and appeared in *Sign 'O' The Times*. The same year she starred as Sonny Crockett's wife in several episodes of *Miami Vice*.

Easton's later albums for EMI included *Do You*, produced by **Nile Rodgers**, and the Japan-only release *No Sound But A Heart*. In 1988, she switched labels to MCA, releasing *The Lover In Me*. When the title track was issued as a single, it soared to number 2 on the US charts. The album's list of producers read like the Who's Who of contemporary soul music, with **L.A. And Babyface**, Prince, **Jellybean** and **Angela Winbush** among the credits. *What Comes Naturally*, released in 1991, was a hard and fast dance record produced to the highest technical standards but lacking the charm of her earlier work. The same year she starred in the revival of *Man Of La Mancha*, which reached Broadway a year later. The same year Easton finally became a US citizen, but during the 90s she enjoyed most success in Japan, with several of her new albums only released in that territory. By now her focus had switched towards her acting career, and in 1996 she appeared as Rizzo in the Broadway production of *Grease*. She signed a new recording contract with Universal International in 2000, and appeared opposite **David Cassidy** in the Las Vegas production, *At The Copa*.
● ALBUMS: *Take My Time* aka *Sheena Easton* (EMI 1981) ★★, *You Could Have Been With Me* (EMI 1981) ★★, *Madness, Money And Music* (EMI 1982) ★★, *Best Kept Secret* (EMI 1983) ★★, *Todo Me Recuerda A Ti* (EMI 1984) ★★★, *A Private Heaven* (EMI 1984) ★★★★, *Do You* (EMI 1985) ★★, *No Sound But A Heart* (EMI 1987) ★★, *The Lover In Me* (MCA 1988) ★★★, *What Comes Naturally* (MCA 1991) ★★★, *No Strings* (MCA 1993) ★★★, *My Cherie* (MCA 1995) ★★★, *Freedom* (SkyJay Trax/MCA 1997) ★★★, *Home* (Universal Japan 1999) ★★★, *Fabulous* (Universal International 2000) ★★★.
● COMPILATIONS: *The Best Of Sheena Easton* (EMI America 1989) ★★★, *For Your Eyes Only: The Best Of Sheena Easton* (EMI 1989) ★★★, *The World Of Sheena*

Easton: The Singles Collection (EMI America 1993) ★★★★, *Greatest Hits* (CEMA 1995) ★★★, *The Best Of Sheena Easton* (Disky 1996) ★★★, *The Gold Collection* (EMI 1996) ★★★, *Body & Soul* (Universal 1997) ★★★, *20 Great Love Songs* (Disky 1998) ★★★, *Classic Masters* (Capitol 2002) ★★★.
● DVD/VIDEOS: *Live At The Palace, Hollywood* (Sony 1982), *Sheena Easton* (Sony 1983), *A Private Heaven* (Sony 1984), *Sheena Easton Act 1* (Prism 1986), *Star Portraits* (Gemini Vision 1992).
● FILMS: *Sign 'O' The Times* (1987), *Indecent Proposal* (1993), *All Dogs Go To Heaven 2* voice only (1996), *An All Dogs Christmas Carol* (1998).

Easton, Tim

b. Akron, Ohio, USA. This roots rock singer-songwriter remained on the fringes of the alt country scene for much of the 90s, although by the start of the new millennium he was beginning to be talked about alongside Jeff Tweedy of **Wilco** and **Jay Farrar** of **Son Volt** as one of the genre's leading talents. Raised in Akron, Ohio, Easton made his first forays into music at college with the roots rock band Kosher Spears. In the mid-90s, following a spell busking around Europe, he joined the widely tipped, Columbus-based Haynes Boys. Easton appeared on the band's solitary album, 1996's terrific *Guardian Angel*, before embarking on a solo career following their split. He made his debut in 1998 with *Special 20*, released on his own Heathen Records label. The album lurched indecisively between honky-tonk ('Just Like Home'), rock 'n' roll ('Torture Comes To Mind'), and folk rock ('Troublesome Kind', 'All The Pretty Girls Leave Town'), but served notice of a prodigious songwriting talent.
Easton subsequently relocated to Los Angeles where he signed a publishing contract with **EMI Records** and a recording contract with New West Records. He worked with Wilco multi-instrumentalist Jay Bennett on his debut for the label, 2001's *The Truth About Us*, a more cohesive, downbeat set than his debut that helped impart greater resonance to Easton's literate songwriting. The follow-up, *Break Your Mother's Heart*, was recorded with a clutch of west California session veterans, including guitarist Mike Campbell and drummer Jim Keltner.
● ALBUMS: *Special 20* (Heathen 1998) ★★★, *The Truth About Us* (New West 2001) ★★★★, *Break Your Mother's Heart* (New West 2003) ★★★.

Eastwood, Kyle

b. 19 May 1968, Santa Monica, California, USA. Raised in a home environment where jazz records were often played, he regularly accompanied his actor-director father, Clint Eastwood, to jazz concerts and also the **Monterey Jazz Festival**. As a child, Kyle Eastwood played guitar for fun but in his late teens began seriously playing the electric bass. This led to formal tuition with French bass player **Bunny Brunel** and after a brief flirtation with thoughts of a career in movies, he formed his own jazz group, West Quintet. Eastwood developed his technique on electric and acoustic instruments and was soon earning his living playing in studio bands for movies and also backing pop singers. However, Eastwood played jazz whenever the opportunity allowed. Owing to extensive exposure on the west coast his reputation spread and he appeared at venues across the country and also played in Europe. In the late 90s, Eastwood relocated to New

York City where he was able to extend still further his skills and reputation. During the same period he recorded his debut album *From There To Here*, featuring **Vince Mendoza**, Steve Tavagione, Doug Webb and **Joni Mitchell**.
In the new millennium, Eastwood provided the music for his father's acclaimed directorial feature *Mystic River*. He also began dividing his time between France (where his wife and daughter live) and England, where he played with established musicians such as Mark Mondesir (drums) and **Dave O'Higgins** (tenor saxophone). His second album *Paris Blue* was released at the end of 2004 by the hip Candid Records label.
Eastwood's playing echoes idols such as **Paul Chambers** and **Ron Carter** but also demonstrates his eclectic musical tastes. His enthusiasm for the form allied to his playing skills have allowed him to capitalize upon his early success and become a respected instrumentalist and leader.
● ALBUMS: *From There To Here* (Sony 1998) ★★★, *Paris Blue* (Candid 2004) ★★★.
● FILMS: *The Outlaw Josey Wales* (1976), *Bronco Billy* (1980), *Honkytonk Man* (1982), *The Bridges Of Madison County* (1995).

Easy

Formerly known as TV Pop Crisis, Easy was formed in 1990 with Johan Holmlund (b. 13 July 1965, Jonkoping, Sweden; vocals), Tommy Ericson (b. 23 March 1966, Umea, Sweden; guitar), Anders Peterson (b. 12 November 1965, Jonkoping, Sweden; guitar/keyboards), Rikard Jormin (b. 2 August 1965, Jonkoping, Sweden; bass/vocals) and Tommy Jonsson (b. 15 June 1966, Vastervik, Sweden; drums). Heavily influenced by the more abrasive British acts such as the **Jesus And Mary Chain**, it was a logical move for the quintet to sign to the UK arm of Blast First Records. Similarly, Easy relished the opportunity to tour the British mainland and, thanks to support slots with **Lush**, the **Charlatans** and **House Of Love**, the group's mood-dominated guitar work earned them a significant reputation and strong press support. *Magic Seed* proved to be the group's lone album for Blast First, however, which was subject to financial difficulties due to its distributor's collapse and the exodus of its main acts **Sonic Youth** and **Dinosaur Jr**. Easy were thus forced to return to Sweden without ever making good their initial promise. They negotiated a new contract with Snap Records, leading to the release of two singles, 'Never Seen A Star' and 'In Black & White', in 1993, but it proved impossible to reclaim their original impetus.
● ALBUMS: *Magic Seed* (Blast First 1990) ★★★.

Easy Action

Swedish hard rock act Easy Action formed in the early 80s and comprised Zinny Zan (vocals), Chris Lynn (guitar), Kee Marcello (guitar), Alex Tyrome (bass) and Freddy Van Gerber (drums). They made their major label recording debut in 1984 with a powerful self-titled collection that predominantly looked to US radio rock for its inspiration. However, they were dropped by **Sire Records** because of disappointing sales, and they moved to the independent KGR Records three years later for *That Makes One*. This saw them adopt more contemporary elements such as the 'sleaze rock' of **Hanoi Rocks**, but overall, the record failed to gel as effectively as their debut. When Marcello left the band to join platinum-sellers **Europe**, Easy Action foundered.

● ALBUMS: *Easy Action* (Sire 1984) ★★★★, *That Makes One* (KGR 1987) ★★★.

Easy Baby

b. Alex Randall, 3 August 1934, Memphis, Tennessee, USA. Easy Baby is an accomplished blues singer/harmonica player who was already involved in the west Memphis blues scene before he moved to Chicago in 1956, where he worked with local groups and led his own band for a time. He gave up music for many years, then began singing and playing again in the mid-70s, when he recorded for the Barrelhouse and Mr. Blues labels (with further material recorded for these companies issued by Rooster and JSP). He rarely plays in Chicago clubs nowadays.
● ALBUMS: *Sweet Home Chicago Blues* (1977) ★★★.

Easy Come, Easy Go

Elvis Presley starred as a frogman operating off the Californian coast, who discovers treasure in a sunken wreck. The plight of that ship is a perfect metaphor for the singer's career at this point. Eight songs were recorded for *Easy Come, Easy Go*, two of which, 'The Love Machine' and 'Leave My Woman Alone', were omitted from the film and subsequent soundtrack EP, the last such release under Presley's name. The rejected material could not have been much worse than those retained, notably the awful 'Yoga Is As Yoga Does'. However, the sessions were of interest for one reason. They were the first to feature bass player Jerry Scheff, who remained associated with the singer until the latter's death in 1977.

Easy Mo

(see **Badmarsh**)

Easy Rider

Released in 1969, *Easy Rider* is one of the lynchpin films of the 60s, encapsulating the mood of its time upon release. Co-stars Peter Fonda and Dennis Hopper, who also directed, play two bikers who, having finalized a drugs deal, ride to New Orleans to celebrate the Mardi Gras. En route they encounter friendship and animosity in equal doses but as the film progresses, the 'American Dream'—and indeed the idealism of the central characters—gradually sours. 'We blew it', states Fonda in the scene preceding the still numbing finale, referring both to his immediate circle and society in general. Fonda and Hopper apart, *Easy Rider* features a superb performance from Jack Nicholson playing drunken lawyer George Hansen, and the normally reclusive **Phil Spector** has a small role as the Connection. *Easy Rider* is also a technical triumph. The usually profligate Hopper is remarkably disciplined, although he would later claim 'his' film was cut to ribbons. Laszlo Kovak's photography is breathtaking and Terry Southern's script is suitably economic. *Easy Rider* also boasted a superb soundtrack and two songs in particular, **Steppenwolf**'s 'Born To Be Wild' and the **Byrds**' 'I Wasn't Born To Follow', are forever linked to the imagery they accompany. Material by the **Smith**, **Bob Dylan**, **Jimi Hendrix**, **Roger McGuinn**, the **Holy Modal Rounders**, **Fraternity Of Man** and **Electric Prunes** also is well selected, creating a new standard for the cinematic use of rock music. Indeed the whole style and content of *Easy Rider* became much copied, but few films came close to emulating it.

Easybeats

Formed in Sydney, Australia, in 1964, this beat group comprised Harry Vanda (b. Johannes Jacob Hendrickus Vandenberg, 22 March 1947, The Hague, the Netherlands; guitar), Dick Diamonde (b. Dingeman Van Der Sluys, 28 December 1947, Hilversum, the Netherlands; bass), Steve Wright (b. 20 December 1948, Leeds, Yorkshire, England; vocals), George Young (b. 6 November 1947, Glasgow, Scotland; guitar) and Gordon 'Snowy' Fleet (b. 16 August 1946, Bootle, Lancashire, England; drums). Originally known as the Starfighters, they changed their name after the arrival of Fleet, who modelled their new style on that of the Liverpool beat groups of the period. After a series of hits in their homeland, including six number 1 singles, the group relocated to England in the summer of 1966 and were offered the opportunity to work with top pop producer **Shel Talmy**. The combination resulted in one of the all-time great beat group singles of the 60s: 'Friday On My Mind'. Strident guitars, clever counter-harmonies and a super-strong beat were the ingredients that provided the disc with its power. Following a solid push on pirate radio, it peaked at number 6 in the UK. Unfortunately, the group found it difficult to follow up their hit and their prospects were not helped after splitting with Talmy during the recording of their first UK-released album. When they finally returned to the UK charts in 1968, it was with the ballad 'Hello, How Are You', the mood of which contrasted sharply with that of their first hit. Lack of morale and gradual line-up changes, including new drummer Tony Cahil, subtly transformed the group into a vehicle for key members Vanda and Young, who were already writing material for other artists. In 1969, after an Australian tour, the Easybeats split up. Ironically, they enjoyed a US hit some months later with 'St. Louis'.

In the wake of their demise, Vanda/Young went into production, released records under a variety of pseudonyms and were largely responsible for the Australian success of such artists as John Paul Jones and William Shakespeare. George Young and his two brothers, Angus and Malcolm, were part of the original line-up of **AC/DC**, while Vanda/Young found success in their own right during the early 80s as Flash In The Pan. Wright enjoyed brief solo success in Australia with tracks such as Vanda and Young's 'Evie', but his career was blighted by addiction. The Easybeats undertook a national reunion tour in 1986, the flavour of which can be sampled on the final five tracks of 1995's *Live Studio And Stage* release.
● ALBUMS: *Easy* (Parlophone 1965) ★★, *It's 2 Easy* (Parlophone 1966) ★★, *Volume 3* (Parlophone 1966) ★★★, *Good Friday* (United Artists 1967) ★★★, *Vigil* (United Artists 1968) ★★, *Friends* (Polydor 1969) ★★, *Live Studio And Stage* (Raven 1995) ★★.
● COMPILATIONS: *The Shame Just Drained* (Alberts 1977), *Absolute Anthology* (Alberts 1980) ★★★, *Best Of The Easybeats* (Rhino 1986) ★★★, *The Best Of The Easybeats* (Repertoire 1995) ★★★, *Aussie Beat That Shook The World* (Repertoire 1996) ★★★, *Gonna Have A Good Time* (Sin-Drome 1999) ★★★, *The Definitive Anthology* (Repertoire 2000) ★★★, *The Singles A's & B's* (Repertoire 2005) ★★★★.

● FURTHER READING: *Sorry: The Wretched Life Of Little Stevie Wright*, Jack Marx.

Eat

Based in King's Cross, London, England, Eat first formed in 1986, though their roots were in the picturesque location of Bath, Avon, rather than the squats of the capital. With music described as 'Louisiana swamp mindfuck blues', they signed to Fiction Records, initially on a one-off contract for the *Autogift* EP. The band, comprising brothers Paul and Max Nobel (guitars), Ange Dolittle (vocals), Tim Sewell (bass) and Pete Howard (drums), soon ingratiated themselves with their north London following by playing frequently at the underground Mutoid Waste events, while both Paul Nobel and Sewell could be found DJing at warehouse parties during the rise of **acid house**. There was always an endearing quality to the band; at a gig at London's Borderline club in its opening week they handed cash out to the audience after deciding the entrance fee was 'a rip off'. Influential disc jockey **John Peel** regularly played the track 'Skin', leading to a full five-album recording contract with Fiction Records and a second EP, *The Plastic Bag Tour*. Pinned around the anti-yuppie anthem 'Babyboom', it further revealed the depth of the band, with Dolittle's vocals distinctively cast through a Bullit harmonica microphone.

Always a somewhat fractious band, after their 1989 debut album *Sell Me A God* there was a split between the Nobel brothers and the rest of Eat in November 1990 (the second album was consequently delayed). Paul and Max Nobel went on to form TV Eye. In 1991 the band was re-formed with Dolittle joined by former members Sewell and Howard, plus guitarists Jem Moorshead and Maz Lavilla. The cover of 1992's *Gold Egg* EP showed Dolittle naked with his genitals airbrushed out, causing complaints from various councils who vowed not to put up the posters. The singer also exposed himself on stage with the **Wonder Stuff**, a band rarely outdone in onstage excess. However, despite generally positive reviews for 1993's *Epicure*, much of the momentum earned on tours with the aforementioned band and **James** had evidently elapsed, and Eat eventually ground to a halt during a US tour. In 1995, Dolittle joined with former members of the Wonder Stuff to become Weknowhereyou-live, while Howard resurfaced in **Vent 414**.

● ALBUMS: *Sell Me A God* (Fiction 1989) ★★★★, *Epicure* (Fiction/November 1993) ★★★.

Eat Static

During the 80s, while they were performing with the **Ozric Tentacles**, Merv Peplar and Joie Hinton were inspired to start writing **dance music** after coming into contact with acts such as the Mutoid Waste Company at festivals and parties. They began by recording three weird **acid house** tracks with the engineer Steve Everitt and were soon performing live at Ozrics gigs. During the early 90s they developed their live shows at many of the legendary 'orbital' **raves** and free parties, as well as releasing three singles and a cassette album, *Prepare Your Spirit*, on their own Alien Records. In 1993, as a result of their connection with the **Megadog** parties, Eat Static signed to **Planet Dog Records** and released the *Lost In Time* EP, followed by the albums *Abduction* and *Implant*. These albums featured their unique brand of psychedelic electronic music, which, while showing the influence of **techno**, **trance**, ambient and other dance styles, never simply regurgitated established formulae. They were as happy with straight four-on-the-floor beats (e.g., 'Prana' and 'Implant') as they were with more breakbeat-like grooves ('Abnormal Interference' and 'Dzhopa Dream'). Many of their titles were sci-fi and space-orientated, about which they commented, 'We can't take techno as seriously as some purists do so we've coated it in this sci-fi motif. And we're mad for all that anyway.' Over the next few years they performed live and released a number of EPs that pursued their eclectic sound, notably 'Dionysiac' (on the *Epsylon* EP), which combined an Eastern-influenced string melody with elements of **dub** and drum 'n' bass. 'Bony Incus' (1996) included collaborations with **Andy Guthrie** and a remix by Man With No Name, while 'Hybrid' (1997) featured remixes by Yum Yum and **Dave Angel**. Towards the end of 1997, Eat Static released the single 'Intercepter' and the album *Science Of The Gods*, which proved to be their most focused and adventurous work to date. While presenting a kind of psychedelic drum 'n' bass on such tracks as 'Interceptor', 'Dissection' and 'Bodystealers', Peplar and Hinton often vary the grooves and textures throughout a track, notably 'Science Of The Gods' and 'Kryll' (a collaboration with **Tangerine Dream**'s Steve Joliffe), thereby structuring and developing their music in a manner unlike the variations-on-a-groove approach of much dance music. With their unique, eclectic sound, attention to detail and outrageous production skills, Eat Static have gained the respect of a number of different camps in an increasingly fickle and narrow-minded dance music community. Their broad-minded attitude predicted the trend towards mixing styles that developed in the late 90s.

● ALBUMS: *Abduction* (Planet Dog 1993) ★★★, *Implant* (Planet Dog 1994) ★★★, *Science Of The Gods* (Planet Dog 1997) ★★★★, *Crash And Burn!* (Mesmobeat 2000) ★★★, *In The Nude!* (Mesmobeat 2001) ★★★.

● COMPILATIONS: *Decadance* (Mesmobeat 1999) ★★★, *The Alien EPs* (Mesmobeat 1999) ★★★.

Eat The Document

A documentary account of **Bob Dylan**'s controversial 1966 tour of Europe with the **Band**, this film, released in 1972, started out as a concert film intended for screening on ABC-TV. The tour itself was less than triumphant, audiences reacting badly to Dylan's decision to 'go electric'. This reaction might well have contributed to the abandonment of a concert format in favour of a documentary approach; except it is not quite that either. It is feasible that the finished film is Dylan's response to audience negativity. He appears to have chosen to justify his musical decisions by presenting a sometimes anarchic view of off-stage events. Directed, and ultimately re-edited from the concert footage, by Dylan himself as a fast-moving sequence of frequently unrelated off-stage home movie–style happenings, most of which are barely in context, the result is a hard-to-follow (there is no narration) 54-minute film that does no credit at all to Dylan as film-maker. The musical numbers that are seen and heard (almost none is complete) are more effective than contemporary live audiences believed and largely justify Dylan's musical choices. While hardcore Dylan fans might well find much to relish here, detached comparison to *Don't Look Back*, 1965's documentary of his UK tour, leaves this film severely wanting. In addition to Dylan and his musicians, **John Lennon** and **Johnny Cash** make token appearances.

Eater

This UK punk rock band formed in 1976 while the band members were still at school. Comprising Andy Blade (vocals), Dee Generate (drums), Brian Chevette (guitar) and Ian Woodcock (bass), they made their vinyl debut with '15' (a bastardized version of **Alice Cooper**'s 'Eighteen'), on *The Roxy, London W.C.2.* compilation, recorded during the spring of 1977. With equipment purchased from Woolworths, they were picked up by The Label, which released five singles including 'Outside View' and 'Lock It Up', with the latter featuring a dire version of **T. Rex**'s 'Jeepster' on the b-side. An album followed later the same year, but it only served to further highlight the band's obvious musical limitations. For all that, Eater are fondly remembered by many for being the epitome of punk's original 'get up and go' ethos.

● ALBUMS: *The Album* (The Label 1977) ★★, *Live 1977* (Anagram 2004) ★★.
● COMPILATIONS: *The History Of Eater Volume 1* (DeLorean 1985) ★★.
● DVD/VIDEOS: *Live: Outside View* (Cherry Red 2005).

Eaton, Connie

b. 1 March 1950, Nashville, Tennessee, USA, d. 20 September 1999, Nashville, Tennessee, USA. Eaton's father Bob sang on the **Grand Ole Opry** and in 1950, he achieved some success with 'Second Hand Heart', before he quit the business. After some experience and success as a child actor, she was signed to Chart Records and, working with producer Cliff Williamson (whom she subsequently married), she made her first recordings in 1968. Her first **Billboard** country chart entry came in 1970, when 'Angel Of The Morning' (a 1968 Top 10 pop hit for **Merrilee Rush**) peaked at number 34. By 1975, she added six more minor hits, two being duet recordings with Dave Peel, namely a cover version of **Ray Charles**' 1961 pop number 1, 'Hit The Road Jack', and 'It Takes Two'. In 1975, she recorded for **Dunhill Records** and gained her highest career chart placement with 'Lonely Men, Lonely Women' (number 23). Her final chart entry came the same year on **ABC Records** when 'If I Knew Enough To Come Out Of The Rain' became a very minor hit.

● ALBUMS: with Dave Peel *Hit The Road Jack* (Chart 1970) ★★★, *Something Special* (Chart 1971) ★★, *Connie Eaton* (ABC/Dot 1975) ★★.

Eaton, John

b. John Livingston Eaton, 29 May 1934, Washington, DC, USA. A self-taught pianist, Eaton was raised in a musical home environment. His great-grandfather was the operatic baritone William Carleton, who helped establish the US version of the D'Oyly Carte Opera Company. Eaton studied English Literature at Yale University in the early 50s, graduating in 1956. That same year, he played his first professional gig as a pianist in a band led by Wild Bill Whelan. In the late 50s he served in the military. It had been his intention to teach but after his military service he changed direction and opted instead for a career as a professional musician. He was encouraged in this endeavour by **Ralph Sutton**, **Teddy Wilson** and **George Shearing**. He rejoined Whelan in 1959, then played with various bands, including those led by Buck Hill, **Stuff Smith** (with whom he made his recording debut), **Jay Leonhart**, **Billy Taylor**, **Georg Brunis** and **Tommy Gwaltney**.

Meanwhile, from 1960, Eaton had begun studying with Alexander Lipsky, something that continued through into the mid-80s, and from 1965 onwards was himself a teacher of both jazz and classical piano. In 1968, he began a four-year stint as leader of the house band at Blues Alley in his hometown. There, he supported numerous important visiting jazzmen, including **Don Byas**, **Buck Clayton**, **Benny Carter**, **Wild Bill Davison**, **Roy Eldridge**, **Cliff Leeman**, **Ray Nance**, **Zoot Sims** and **Clark Terry**. In the 80s, Eaton played in nightclubs in New York and other east coast locations and in 1988 performed a solo concert for President Ronald Reagan. Back in Washington, he regularly appeared as a performer at the Smithsonian Institute where he was also involved in education. An elegant, witty and accomplished player, in much of Eaton's work can be heard echoes of two of his early mentors, Sutton and Wilson.

● ALBUMS: *Indiana On Our Minds: The Music Of Cole Porter & Hoagy Carmichael* (Chiaroscuro 1989) ★★★, *Made In America* (Chiaroscuro 1996) ★★★, *Live At Steinway Hall* (Chiaroscuro 2000) ★★★.

Eavis, Michael

b. 17 October 1935, England. Dairy farmer Michael Eavis will forever be synonymous with rock 'n' roll via the use of his land at Worthy Farm, in the Vale of Avalon, for the UK's premier rock event, the **Glastonbury Festival**. The idea originally came to him while watching the two-day Bath Blues Festival with **Led Zeppelin** and **Frank Zappa** in a field in Shepton Mallet in the summer of 1970: 'I fell in love with the idea of organizing my own festival. It seemed romantic and a great way to spend mid-summer.' The first Glastonbury Festival took place weeks later, with **T. Rex** headlining. 1,500 fans attended. From the start Eavis remained committed to the 60s ideals that he had developed in his youth, and to this day continues to contribute 10% of Glastonbury's gross receipts to charity. He has also limited music to 50% of activities on offer, which generally also include comedy, cabaret, theatre and environmental activism. The festival only became an annual event in 1982, with an eight-year gap between June 1971's Glastonbury Fayre with **David Bowie** and **Fairport Convention** and 1979's Year Of The Child benefit. It continued to grow in prestige in the 80s and 90s, with many stellar artists agreeing to appear at a fraction of their usual fees in sympathy with the broadly philanthropic ethos of the festival. In keeping with this, and contrary to rumours, Eavis has profited little from the exercise, running the entire event from his farmhouse and, in the early 90s, a small office space in Glastonbury. In 1995 the Festival sold out its 80,000 ticket allocation within a week of going on sale, a tribute to both a unique event in the British music calendar and to Eavis' continued enthusiasm and professionalism in organizing it. In 1996 Eavis announced that there would be no festival that year, stating that he wished to spend more time on his farm. He was back in the foreground in 1997 with what turned out to be the wettest and muddiest festival since **Woodstock** in 1969. Eavis managed to pursuade the local authorities not to cancel the three-day event, but many name bands were unable to perform. Eavis' wife, Jean, who co-founded the festival, died from cancer on 16 May 1999.

Eazy-E

b. Eric Wright, 7 September 1963 (1964 is also cited), Compton, California, USA, d. 26 March 1995, Los Angeles,

California, USA. There are those critics who did not take well to Eazy-E's 'whine', but his debut kept up **N.W.A.**'s momentum by managing to offend just about every imaginable faction, right and left. Attending a fund-raising dinner for the Republican Party and having lunch with police officer Tim Coon, one of the LAPD's finest charged with the beating of Rodney King, hardly helped to re-establish his hardcore credentials. His work as part of N.W.A., and as head of **Ruthless Records** (which he founded in 1985 allegedly with funds obtained from drug dealing) had already made him a household name. However, as a solo performer his raps lacked penetration, even if the musical backdrop was just as intense as that which distinguished N.W.A. His debut solo album contained a clean and dirty side. The first was accomplished with very little merit, cuts such as 'We Want Eazy' being self-centred and pointless.

The 'street' side, however, offered something much more provocative and nasty. His ongoing bitter rivalry against former N.W.A. member **Dr. Dre** provided much of his lyrical subject matter, including his 1994 single, 'Real Muhaphukkin' G's', which was essentially a rewrite of Dre's 'Dre Day'. Ruthless also released an EP, *It's On (Dr. Dre) 187um Killa*, in the same year. Eazy-E subsequently moved on to production for artists including **Tairrie B** and **Blood Of Abraham**. Having been a pivotal figure of gangsta rap, he succumbed to AIDS and died through complications following a collapsed lung after having been hospitalized for some time. The material he had been working on prior to his death was released posthumously on *Str.8 Off Tha Streetz Of Muthaphukkin' Compton*.

● ALBUMS: *Eazy-Duz-It* (Ruthless/Priority 1988) ★★★, *It's On (Dr. Dre) 187um Killa* mini-album (Ruthless 1993) ★★, *Str.8 Off Tha Streetz Of Muthaphukkin' Compton* (Ruthless 1995) ★★★, *The Godfather Of Gangsta Rap* mini-album (Ruthless 2002) ★★★.
● COMPILATIONS: *Eternal E* (Ruthless/Priority 1995) ★★★.
● DVD/VIDEOS: *Impact Of A Legend* (Ruthless 2002), *Eternal E:- The Best Of Eazy-E: Gangsta Memorial Edition* (Ruthless 2005).

Ebb, Fred
(see **Kander, John**)

Eberly, Bob
b. Robert Eberle, 24 July 1916, Mechanicsville, New York, USA, d. 17 November 1981, Glen Burnie, Maryland, USA. One of the most popular dance band vocalists of the 40s, Eberly's success was linked with that of **Helen O'Connell**, with whom he recorded a number of tempo-switching hit records. Eberly changed his surname early in his career to avoid confusion with his younger brother **Ray Eberle**, who sang with the **Glenn Miller** civilian band. He worked around New York, winning an *Amateur Hour* contest hosted by Fred Allen. On joining the Dorsey Brothers' Band in 1935, Eberly remained with **Jimmy Dorsey** after the brothers split, appearing with the band on the Kraft Music Hall radio shows, often vocalizing on arrangements penned for **Bing Crosby**. In 1939 Helen O'Connell joined the band and she and Eberly struck up a productive partnership that resulted in Dorsey's version of 'Amapola' becoming a US number 1 hit in early 1941. The record, which featured Eberly taking the opening chorus in ballad fashion, followed by a swing-tempo instrumental

passage and then a third time change as O'Connell took the song out in grand style, set a pattern that was followed by similar productions, such as 'Green Eyes', 'Yours' and 'Tangerine'.

The ensuing acclaim meant that Eberly was offered several lucrative contracts but he declined to go solo and remained with the Dorsey band until December 1943, when he entered the army, spending some time as vocalist with **Wayne King**'s army band. During the two years that Eberly was in the forces, his popularity took a tumble and though he returned to a singing career as a solo act, he never attained previous heights. After earlier film appearances in **The Fleet's In** and *I Dood It*, he guested in the screen biography **The Fabulous Dorseys**, which was released in 1947. In the 50s and 60s he featured regularly on US television, and sometimes toured with Helen O'Connell in nostalgia package shows. He was still singing occasionally in nightclubs during the 70s. Following his death from a heart attack in 1981, his son Bob Eberly Jnr. carried on the family tradition.

● COMPILATIONS: *Best Of Bob Eberly With Jimmy Dorsey* (Collector's Choice 2001) ★★★.
● FILMS: *The Fleet's In* (1942), *I Dood It* aka *By Hook Or By Crook* (1943), *The Fabulous Dorseys* (1947).

Ebonys
Formed in Camden, New Jersey, USA, and comprising Jenny Holmes, David Beasley, James Tuten and Clarence Vaughan, the Ebonys had minor success in the early 70s with a **Dells**-styled approach of baritone lead with answering falsetto second lead. The group was discovered by **Gamble And Huff** and recorded consistently for their **Philadelphia International Records** label in the early 70s, but achieved only two sizeable hits on the R&B charts, 'You're The Reason Why' (number 10 R&B, number 51 pop) from 1971, and 'It's Forever' (number 14 R&B, number 68 pop) from 1973. The group recorded for **Buddah** in 1976 with little success, with only a minor single, 'Making Love Ain't No Fun (Without The One You Love)' (number 83 R&B), making the charts. It was their last chart record.

● COMPILATIONS: *The Ebonys* (Philadelphia International 1971) ★★★, *The Ebonys* (Soul From The Vaults 1991) ★★★.

Ebsen, Buddy
b. Christian Rudolph Ebsen, 2 April 1908, Belleville, Illinois, USA, d. 6 July 2003, Torrance, California, USA. Ebsen trained as a dancer with his father, then formed a double act with his sister, Vilma. He appeared in the **Ziegfeld Follies** but from the mid-30s was mainly in films, often dancing. He was in **Broadway Melody** *Of 1936* (1935), *Captain January* (1936, singing 'At The Codfish Ball'), *Born To Dance* and *Banjo On My Knee* (both 1936), *Broadway Melody Of 1938* (1937), *The Girl Of The Golden West* and *My Lucky Star* (both 1938). In 1939 Ebsen was cast as The Tin Man in **The Wizard Of Oz**. Allergic to the metallic paint used in the make-up, he abandoned the role, which was taken by **Jack Haley**, although Ebsen sings, uncredited, 'We're Off To See The Wizard'. In the 40s and 50s Ebsen made *They Met In Argentina* (1941), *Sing Your Worries Away* (1942), *Under Mexicali Stars* (1950), *Thunder In God's Country* (1951), *Red Garters* and *Davy Crockett, King Of The Wild Frontier* (both 1954), and *Attack* (1956). He also composed the title song for 1951's, *Behave Yourself!*

In the 60s Ebsen made *Breakfast At Tiffany's* (1961), *The Interns* (1962), *Mail Order Bride* (1964) and *The One And Only, Genuine, Original Family Band* (1968). He appeared on television in the series *Climax!* (1957), *Maverick* and *Bonanza* (both 1959), *Rawhide*, *Bronco* and *Gunsmoke* (all 1960), *77 Sunset Strip*, *The Twilight Zone*, *Gunslinger*, *Have Gun—Will Travel* and *Bus Stop* (all 1961), *Tales Of Wells Fargo* (1962), *Hawaii Five-O* (1971), *Alias Smith And Jones* (1972), *Burke's Law* (1994), and the situation comedy *King Of The Hill* (1999). Most significant were his leading roles in *Northwest Passage* (1958), *The Beverly Hillbillies* (1962, as Jed Clampett), *Barnaby Jones* (1973) and *Matt Houston* (1982). He also appeared in television films including *The Andersonville Trial* (1970), *The Daughters Of Joshua Cabe* (1972), *Tom Sawyer* (1973), *Leave Yesterday Behind* (1978), *The Return Of The Beverly Hillbillies* (1981), *Stone Fox* (1987), and *Working Tra$h* (1990). He produced the 1979 television film *The Paradise Connection*. Ebsen's last big-screen role combined the two television series for which he was famous, playing Barnaby Jones in *The Beverly Hillbillies* (1993).

● FILMS: *Broadway Melody Of 1936* (1935), *Captain January* (1936), *Born To Dance* (1936), *Banjo On My Knee* (1936), *Broadway Melody Of 1938* (1937), *The Girl Of The Golden West* (1938), *Yellow Jack* (1938), *My Lucky Star* (1938), *Four Girls In White* (1939), *The Kid From Texas* (1939), *They Met In Argentina* (1941), *Parachute Battalion* (1941), *Sing Your Worries Away* (1942), *Under Mexicali Stars* (1950), *Silver City Bonanza* (1951), *Thunder In God's Country* (1951), *Rodeo King And The Senorita* (1951), *Utah Wagon Train* (1951), *Night People* (1954), *Red Garters* (1954), *Davy Crockett, King Of The Wild Frontier* (1954), *Davy Crockett And The River Pirates* (1956), *Attack* (1956), *Between Heaven And Hell* (1956), *Mission Of Danger* (1959), *Frontier Rangers* (1959), *Fury River* (1961), *Breakfast At Tiffany's* (1961), *The Interns* (1962), *Mail Order Bride* aka *West Of Montana* (1964), *The One And Only, Genuine, Original Family Band* (1968), *The Beverly Hillbillies* (1993).

Eccles, Clancy

b. 19 December 1940, St. Mary, Jamaica, West Indies, d. 30 June 2005, Spanish Town, Jamaica, West Indies. One of the most loved and respected personalities in the history of Jamaican music, Clancy Eccles started making records for **Coxsone Dodd** in 1959, recording 'Freedom', initially as an acetate that was featured on Dodd's **sound system** for nearly two years before its official release in 1961. For the same producer he also recorded the local hits 'River Jordan' and 'Glory Hallelujah'. He then provided 'Judgement' for **Leslie Kong**'s business mentor Charlie Moo in late 1962. By the mid-60s he had completed three other records, 'Miss Ida' and 'Roam Jerusalem'/'Sammy No Dead' for **Sonia Pottinger** and 'I'm The Greatest' for Mike Shadeen. By 1967 he had started his own label, his first release being **Eric Morris**' local hit, 'Say What You're Saying'. During the next few years Eccles was one of reggae's leading producers. He was instrumental in helping **Lee Perry** to set up his own operation when that producer left Coxsone, arranging Perry's huge local hit, 'People Funny Boy', in 1968.

From 1969 **Trojan Records** released Eccles' productions on UK Clandisc. Records such as 'Fire Corner' by DJ **King Stitt** and the bawdy 'Fatty Fatty' by Eccles were very popular, not only with audiences in Jamaica and the Afro-Caribbean commu-

nities in North America and the UK, but also appealing to the British skinheads who followed Jamaican music at that time. In this period, utilizing his studio band the **Dynamites**, Eccles produced records by such artists as **Alton Ellis**, **Lord Creator**, the Fabulous Flames, Lee Perry, **Larry Marshall**, **Joe Higgs**, the Beltones, Busty Brown, **Carl Dawkins** and **Cynthia Richards**. He issued many records featuring his own vocals, singing either heartfelt love songs or stinging social comment. A lifelong socialist, Eccles continued to record material on this theme right up to 1985, when he issued 'Mash Up We Country', a song that took its place alongside such classics as the pro-PNP (People's National Party) anthem 'Rod Of Correction' (1972) and 'Generation Belly' (1976). Eccles was also an adviser to Michael Manley's PNP Government from 1972 on matters relating to the music business. He continued to release compilations of oldies, as well as the occasional new production, into the new millennium. Eccles was the quintessential Jamaican producer, particularly in the attention he devoted to his craft and his awareness of his audience's tastes.

● ALBUMS: *Freedom* (Trojan 1969) ★★★, with the Dynamites *Herbsman Reggae* (Trojan 1970) ★★★★, *Top Of The Ladder* (Top Of The Ladder 1973) ★★★.

● COMPILATIONS: *Fatty Fatty 1967-1970* (Trojan 1988) ★★★★, *Joshua's Rod Of Correction* (Jamaican Gold 1997) ★★★, *Clancy Eccles' Rock Steady & Reggae Revue At The Sombrero Club 1967-1969* (Jamaican Gold 2001) ★★★, *Clancy Eccles' Reggae Revue At The Ward Theatre 1969-1970* (Jamaican Gold 2001) ★★★, *Clancy Eccles' Reggae Revue At The V.I.P. Club 1970-1973* (Jamaican Gold 2001) ★★★, *Clancy Eccles' Reggae Revue At The Carib Theatre 1973-1986* (Jamaican Gold 2001) ★★★.

Echo And The Bunnymen

The origins of this renowned Liverpool, England–based band can be traced back to the spring of 1977 when vocalist **Ian McCulloch** (b. 5 May 1959, Liverpool, England) was a member of the short-lived Crucial Three with **Julian Cope** and Pete Wylie. While the latter two later emerged in the **Teardrop Explodes** and **Wah!**, respectively, McCulloch put together his major band at the end of 1978. Initially the trio of McCulloch, Will Sergeant (b. 12 April 1958, Liverpool, England; guitar) and Les Pattinson (b. 18 April 1958, Ormskirk, Merseyside, England; bass) was joined by a drum machine that they named 'Echo'. After making their first appearance at the famous Liverpool club Eric's, they made their vinyl debut in March 1979 with 'Pictures On My Wall'/'Read It In Books', produced by whiz kid entrepreneurs **Bill Drummond** and David Balfe. The production was sparse but intriguing and helped the band to establish a sizeable cult following. McCulloch's brooding live performance and vocal inflections were already drawing comparisons with the **Doors**' Jim Morrison.

After signing to Korova Records (distributed by **Warner Brothers Records**), they replaced 'Echo' with a human being—Pete De Freitas (b. 2 August 1961, Port Of Spain, Trinidad, West Indies, d. 14 June 1989). The second single, 'Rescue', was a considerable improvement on its predecessor, with a confident driving sound that augured well for their forthcoming album. *Crocodiles* proved impressive with a wealth of strong arrangements and compulsive guitar work. After the less melodic single 'The Puppet', the band toured extensively and issued an EP, *Shine So Hard*, which crept into the UK Top 40. The next album, **Heaven Up Here**, saw them regaled by the music press. Although a less accessible and melodic work than its predecessor, it sold well and topped numerous polls. *Porcupine* reinforced the band's appeal, while 'The Cutter' gave them their biggest UK hit so far, reaching number 8 in January 1983. The same year Sergeant released a solo set, *Themes For Grind*. In January 1984 they reached UK number 9 with 'The Killing Moon', an excellent example of McCulloch's ability to summon lazy melodrama out of primary lyrical colours. The epic quality of his writing remained perfectly in keeping with the band's grandiloquent musical character. The accompanying 1984 album, *Ocean Rain*, broadened their appeal further and brought them into the US Top 100 album charts.

In February 1986 De Freitas left to be replaced by former **Haircut 100** drummer Mark Fox, but he returned the following September. However, it now seemed the band's best days were behind them. The uninspired title *Echo And The Bunnymen* drew matching lacklustre performances, while a cover version of the Doors' 'People Are Strange' left both fans and critics perplexed. This new recording was produced by Ray Manzarek, who also played on the track, and it was used as the haunting theme for the cult movie *The Lost Boys*. Yet, as many noted, there were simply dozens of better Echo And The Bunnymen compositions that could have benefited from that type of exposure.

In 1988, McCulloch made the announcement that he was henceforth pursuing a solo career. While he completed the well-received *Candleland*, his bandmates made the unexpected decision to carry on. Large numbers of audition tapes were listened to before they chose McCulloch's successor, Noel Burke, a Belfast boy who had previously recorded with St Vitus Dance. Just as they were beginning rehearsals, De Freitas was killed in a road accident. The band struggled on, recruiting new drummer Damon Reece and adding road manager Jake Brockman on guitar/synthesizer. In 1992, they entered the next phase of Bunnymen history with *Reverberation*, but public expectations were not high and the critics unkind. The Bunnymen Mark II broke up in the summer of the same year, with Pattinson going on to work with **Terry Hall**, while Sergeant conducted work on his ambient side project, B*O*M, and formed Glide. McCulloch, whose solo career had stalled after a bright start, and Sergeant eventually reunited in 1993 as **Electrafixion**, also pulling in Reece from the second Bunnymen incarnation.

In 1996, an announcement was made that the three remaining original members would go out as Echo And The Bunnymen once again. McCulloch, Pattinson and Sergeant completed a remarkable comeback when 'Nothing Lasts Forever' reached number 8 in the UK charts, and their new album, *Evergreen*, was released to widespread acclaim. Pattinson left before the recording of their second new album, a remarkably mellow set from a band not normally associated with such a concept. McCulloch and Sergeant parted company with **London Records** later in the year, and the following year's mini-album *Avalanche* was an Internet-only release. The full-length *Flowers*, picked up for release in 2001 by **Cooking Vinyl Records**, marked a return to the trademark Echo And The Bunnymen sound, with Sergeant's guitar work to the fore. Following the release of a live collection in 2002, McCulloch and Sergeant teamed up with *Heaven Up Here* producer Hugh Jones to work on a new studio album. *Siberia*, released by Cooking Vinyl at the end

of 2005, earned the band their most positive reviews since their early 80s glory years.

● ALBUMS: *Crocodiles* (Korova/Sire 1980) ★★★★, *Heaven Up Here* (Korova/Sire 1981) ★★★, *Porcupine* (Korova/Sire 1983) ★★★★, *Ocean Rain* (Korova/Sire 1984) ★★★, *Echo And The Bunnymen* (Warners/Sire 1987) ★★, *Reverberation* (Korova/Sire 1990) ★★, *Evergreen* (London 1997) ★★★, *What Are You Going To Do With Your Life?* (London 1999) ★★★, *Avalanche* mini-album (Gimmemusic 2000) ★★★, *Flowers* (Cooking Vinyl 2001) ★★★, *Live In Liverpool* (Cooking Vinyl/spinART 2002) ★★★, *Siberia* (Cooking Vinyl 2005) ★★★★.

● COMPILATIONS: *Songs To Learn And Sing* (Korova/Sire 1985) ★★★★, *Live In Concert* (Windsong 1991) ★★★, *The Cutter* (Warners 1993) ★★★, *The Peel Sessions* (Strange Fruit 1995) ★★★, *Ballyhoo: The Best Of Echo And The Bunnymen* (Korova/WEA International 1997) ★★★★, *Crystal Days (1979–1999)* 4-CD box set (Rhino 2001) ★★★★, *Seven Seas: The Platinum Collection* (WEA International 2005) ★★★★.

● DVD/VIDEOS: *Porcupine* (Virgin Video 1983), *Live In Liverpool* (Cooking Vinyl 2002).

● FURTHER READING: *Liverpool Explodes: The Teardrop Explodes, Echo And The Bunnymen*, Mark Cooper. *Never Stop: The Echo & The Bunnymen Story*, Tony Fletcher. *Ian McCulloch: King Of Cool*, Mick Middles. *Turquoise Days: The Weird World Of Echo & The Bunnymen*, Chris Adams.

Echobelly

This UK indie pop band was formed in 1992 by the Anglo-Asian singer Sonya Aurora Madan, along with Glenn Johansson (b. Sweden; guitar), Debbie Smith (guitar, ex-**Curve**), Andy Henderson (drums) and Alex Keyser (bass). Echobelly were put together when Madan met Johansson at a gig. After breaking the UK Top 40 in 1994 with the momentous 'I Can't Imagine The World Without Me', the band became the darlings of the British music press. The original, rejected title of their debut album was taken from a Suffragette's reply when asked when women would obtain the vote: 'Today, Tomorrow, Sometime, Never', leading Madan to comment: 'I feel led by similar frustrations, politically and morally, encompassing feminism and gender. Things are made much more obvious coming from a coloured background.' This last point was made clear by her Union Jack T-shirt smeared with the legend: 'My Home Too'. However, she was also keen to point out that locating Echobelly solely in the world of gender and race politics dismissed their importance as a pop band.

The band also began to win support in the USA by appearing at New York's New Music Seminar, leading to an American contract with Sony Records. Personnel problems began to surface, with Keyser being replaced by James Harris shortly after the recording of the band's second album. *On* advanced the strengths of its predecessor, with notable songs including the hit single 'Great Things', and 'Pantyhose And Roses' about the UK Conservative MP Stephen Milligan, who died of asphyxiation during a sexual incident. Debbie Smith left the band in August 1997, and was replaced by new guitarist Julian Cooper. *Lustra* was a poorly received follow-up that saw the band struggling to establish their musical direction, and also feel the effect of the commercial backlash against 'Britpop' bands. The band returned three years later with the *Digit* EP and *People Are Expensive*, both released on their own Fry Up label. By this point the departure of Harris had reduced the band to a trio.

● ALBUMS: *Everyone's Got One* (Rhythm King 1994) ★★★, *On* (Rhythm King 1995) ★★★★, *Lustra* (Epic 1997) ★★, *People Are Expensive* (Fry Up 2001) ★★★, *Gravity Pulls* (Takeout 2004) ★★.

● COMPILATIONS: *I Can't Imagine The World Without Me* (Epic 2001) ★★★.

Echoboy

The *nom de plume* adopted by guitarist Richard Warren (ex-**Hybirds**), who as a solo artist has eschewed the traditional guitar rock of his former band in favour of a dazzling synthesis of indie pop and electronica. Unfortunately, Warren gained more headlines by turning down an offer to become **Oasis**' new rhythm guitarist in 1999 than he has for his music. The influence of pioneering electronic duo **Suicide** shone through on Echoboy's debut single 'Flashlegs (Suite)', released in July 1998 on the Point Blank label shortly before the demise of the Hybirds. His self-titled debut followed in January 1999, prompting a bemused music press to attempt to pigeonhole Warren's atmospheric mixture of styles. A recording contract with **Mute Records** followed limited edition releases for Earworm and **Rough Trade Records**. The multi-faceted *Volume 1* veered unevenly between the self-indulgent ('Constantinople'), the pastoral ('Walking'), and pop genius ('Kit And Holly'). Warren returned barely six months later with *Volume 2*, a more coherent collection of material illuminated by stand-out track 'Telstar Recovery'.

● ALBUMS: *Echoboy* (Point Blank 1999) ★★★, *Volume 1* (Mute 2000) ★★★, *Volume 2* (Mute 2000) ★★★★, *Giraffe* (Mute 2003) ★★★★.

Echobrain

Although the initial media attention around Echobrain centred on the fact that it was the first post-**Metallica** project of bass player Jason Newsted (b. 4 March 1963, Battle Creek, Michigan, USA), the band's main musical focal point soon became vocalist/guitarist Dylan Donkin (b. 16 May 1977, USA). Donkin and drummer Brian Sagrafena (b. 8 August 1978, USA) grew up together in the town of Millbrae, California, USA, and were both members of their school's jazz band. Sagrafena met Newsted in 1995 at a Super Bowl party thrown at the Metallica bass player's house, after Newsted heard the drummer (who was only 16 at the time) playing in a jam session. Sagrafena told Newsted about his friend Donkin, and over the next few years, the trio jammed regularly on a variety of musical styles at Newsted's home studio, the Chophouse; but it was not until a road trip to Baja, Mexico, during 1999 that the trio decided to form a serious band. Taking the name Echobrain (which Donkin said originated from 'the voices in my head'), the trio recorded an album's worth of songs penned around the time of the aforementioned Mexico trip.

Early in 2001, Newsted left Metallica, whose members were allegedly none too pleased with the bass player's extracurricular recording activities. The move allowed Newsted to concentrate full-time on Echobrain, which issued their self-titled debut on his Chophouse label (distributed via Hollywood Records). Although the album received favourable reviews, it failed to leave an impression on the charts (perhaps owing to Metallica fans' expecting a heavier sound, instead of the album's spacey alt rock). Just a few months after the album's release, Newsted left Echobrain, to play bass in the Canadian sci-fi prog metal outfit **Voivod**. He was credited as executive producer on his former colleagues' new album under the Echobrain moniker, 2004's *Glean*. Dylan Donkin's brother Adam took over the bass duties at the recording sessions, while Andrew Gomez (guitar/keyboards) was also added to the line-up.

● ALBUMS: *EchoBrain* (Chophouse 2002) ★★★★, *Glean* (Surfdog 2004) ★★★.

Echoes

The Echoes were a white doo-wop group from Brooklyn, New York, USA, that logged one Top 20 hit, 'Baby Blue', in 1961. The group consisted of Harry Boyle (b. 1943, Brooklyn, New York, USA), Thomas Duffy (b. 1944, Brooklyn, New York, USA), and Tom Morrissey (b. 1943, Brooklyn, New York, USA). Originally called the Laurels, the group was given 'Baby Blue', written by teachers Sam Guilino and Val Lagueux, by a member of another group who had decided not to record it. The Laurels changed their name to the Echoes and financed their own demo recording of the song, and Jack Gold, owner of Paris Records, decided to release it on another label he was starting, SRG Records. The record was picked up by another label, Seg-Way, and it went up to number 12. The Echoes were unable to follow up their one hit, despite several fine subsequent recordings, and the group split up. When a revival scene for white doo-wop emerged in the New York area in the 80s, an album of the Echoes' best material was released.

● COMPILATIONS: *The Echoes Greatest Hits* (Crystal Ball 1984) ★★.

Echols, Charlie

b. *c.*1908, USA. What little is known about this trumpet player depends largely upon interviews conducted by jazz writer Albert McCarthy with various former sidemen. In the spring of·1931 Echols formed a nine-piece band in Los Angeles, California. The band included saxophonists Babe Carter and Herman Pettis, pianist Lorenzo Flennoy and drummer Preston 'Peppy' Prince. Later that year, the band also included trumpeter McClure 'Red Mack' Morris and contemporary newspaper reports indicated that none of the band's members was over 23. By 1932 the personnel of the band had been radically altered, although Prince remained. Among new members were **Bumps Myers** and **Kid Ory**. The band continued to appear in southern California during the next two years and among sidemen were **Jack McVea**, saxophonist Buddy Banks and drummer Alton Redd. A short time later, Flennoy took over leadership of the band. Echols then formed a new band, which included Morris, **Andy Blakeney**, saxophonist Paul Howard, bass player Johnny Miller and **Lionel Hampton**. Among the venues at which this band played was the Los Angeles New Cotton Club. In 1935, Echols resumed leadership of his old band, which now included **Buck Clayton**, **Tyree Glenn**, **Don Byas**, **Herschel Evans** and McVea. A later band led by Echols included **Ernie Royal**, Myers, Howard, **Al Morgan** and **Lee Young**. In 1939, Echols led a band with a similar personnel in San Francisco. Thereafter, Echols drifted into obscurity and appears to have given up band leading sometime in the 40s. Although many of the musicians who played in bands led by Echols recalled it with great affection and admiration, the band appears never to have recorded and its reputation must therefore depend upon this (admittedly well-informed) hearsay.

Eckstine, Billy

b. William Clarence Eckstein, 8 July 1914, Pittsburgh, Pennsylvania, USA, d. 8 March 1993, Pittsburgh, Pennsylvania, USA. Eckstine possessed one of the most distinctive voices in popular music, a deep tone with a highly personal vibrato. He began singing at the age of 11 but until his late teens was undecided between a career as a singer or football player. He won a sporting scholarship but soon afterwards broke his collarbone and decided that singing was less dangerous. He worked mostly in the north-eastern states in the early 30s and towards the end of the decade joined the **Earl 'Fatha' Hines** band in Chicago. Although far from being a jazz singer, opting instead for a highly sophisticated form of balladry, Eckstine clearly loved working with jazz musicians and in particular the young experimenters who drifted into the Hines band in the early 40s, among them **Wardell Gray**, **Dizzy Gillespie** and **Charlie 'Bird' Parker**. While with Hines he developed into a competent trumpeter and, later, valve trombonist, having first mimed as a trumpet player in order to circumvent union rules.

In 1943, acting on the advice and encouragement of **Budd Johnson**, Eckstine formed his own band. Although his original intention was to have a band merely to back his vocals, Eckstine gathered together an exciting group of young bebop musicians and thus found himself leader of what constituted the first true bebop big band. During the band's four-year existence its ranks were graced by Gray, Parker, Gillespie, **Gene Ammons**, **Dexter Gordon**, **Miles Davis**, **Kenny Dorham**, **Fats Navarro** and **Art Blakey**, playing arrangements by Gillespie, Johnson, **Tadd Dameron**, **Gil Fuller** and Jerry Valentine. Eckstine also hired the Hines band's other singer, **Sarah Vaughan**. In 1947 the band folded but had already served as an inspiration to Gillespie, who formed his own bebop big band that year.

Eckstine's commercial recordings during the life of the big band were mostly ballads that he wrapped in his deep, liquid baritone voice, and with his bandleading days behind him he continued his career as a successful solo singer. He gained a huge international reputation as a stylish balladeer. During his long career Eckstine had many hit records, including 'Jelly, Jelly', recorded in 1940 with Hines, 'Skylark', 'Everything I Have Is Yours', 'I Apologize' (stylistically covered by **P.J. Proby** to great success), 'Prisoner Of Love', 'A Cottage For Sale', 'No One But You' (number 3 in the UK charts in 1954), 'Gigi' (number 8 in 1959), and several duets with Vaughan, the best-known being 'Passing Strangers', which, although recorded a dozen years earlier, reached number 17 in the 1969 charts. He went on to record for **Motown Records**, **Stax Records** and **A&M Records**. In later years Eckstine recorded a new single with Ian Levine as part of his Motown revival project on the Motor City label.

● ALBUMS: *Together: Live At Club Plantation, Los Angeles* (Spotlite 1945) ★★★, *Sings* (National 1949) ★★★, *Songs By Billy Eckstine* (MGM 1951) ★★★, *Favorites* (MGM 1951) ★★★, *Sings Rodgers And Hammerstein* (MGM 1952) ★★★★, *The Great Mr B* (King 1953) ★★★, *Tenderly* (MGM 1953) ★★★★, *Earl Hines With Billy Eckstine* 10-inch album (RCA Victor 1953) ★★★, *I Let A Song Go Out Of My Heart* (MGM 1954) ★★★, *Blues For Sale* (EmArcy 1955) ★★★★, *The Love Songs Of Mr B* (EmArcy 1955)

★★★, *Mr B With A Beat* (MGM 1955) ★★★, *Rendezvous* (MGM 1955) ★★★, *I Surrender Dear* (EmArcy 1955) ★★★★, *That Old Feeling* (MGM 1955) ★★★★, *Prisoner Of Love* (Regent 1957) ★★★, *The Duke The Blues And Me* (Regent 1957) ★★★, *My Deep Blue Dream* (Regent 1957) ★★★★, *You Call It Madness* (Regent 1957) ★★★, *Billy Eckstine's Imagination* (EmArcy 1958) ★★★★, *Billy's Best* (Mercury 1958) ★★★, *Sarah Vaughan And Billy Eckstine Sing The Best Of Irving Berlin* (Mercury 1958) ★★★★, with Sarah Vaughan *Billy And Sarah* (Lion 1959) ★★★★, with Count Basie *Basie/Eckstine Inc.* (Roulette 1959) ★★★★, *Golden Saxophones* (London 1960) ★★★, *I Apologize* (Polydor 1960) ★★★★, *Mr B* (Audio Lab 1960) ★★★, *Broadway Bongos And Mr B* (Mercury 1961) ★★★, *No Cover No Minimum* (Mercury 1961) ★★★, *Billy Eckstine & Quincy Jones At Basin St. East* (Mercury 1962) ★★★, *Don't Worry 'Bout Me* (Mercury 1962) ★★★, *Once More With Feeling* (Mercury 1962) ★★★, *Everything I Have Is Yours* (Metro 1965) ★★★, *Prime Of My Life* (Motown 1965) ★★, *My Way* (Motown 1966) ★★, *For Love Of Ivy* (Motown 1969) ★★★, *Gentle On My Mind* (Motown 1969) ★★, *Feel The Warm* (Enterprise 1971) ★★, *Stormy* (Stax 1971) ★★, *If She Walked Into My Life* (Stax 1974) ★★, *Something More* (Stax 1981) ★★, *Sings With Benny Carter* (Mercury 1986) ★★★, *I'm A Singer* (Kim 1987) ★★.

● COMPILATIONS: *The Best Of Billy Eckstine* (Lion 1958) ★★★, *The Golden Hits Of Billy Eckstine* (Mercury 1963) ★★★★, *Golden Hour: Billy Eckstine* (Golden Hour 1975) ★★★★, with Sarah Vaughan (coupled with a Dinah Washington and Brook Benton collection) *Passing Strangers* (Mercury 1978) ★★★, *Greatest Hits* (Polydor 1984) ★★★★, *Orchestra 1945* (Alamac 1985) ★★★, *Mister B. And The Band: The Savoy Sessions* (Savoy Jazz 1986) ★★★, *Everything I Have Is Yours: The Best Of The M-G-M Years* (Verve 1991) ★★★★, *The Cool Mr. B* (Collectors 2001) ★★★, *Complete Savoy Recordings* (Jazz Factory 2001) ★★★, *Timeless* (Savoy Jazz 2001) ★★★, *The Legendary Big Band* (Savoy Jazz 2002) ★★★★, *The Motown Years* (Motown 2004) ★★.

Eclection

Formed in London, England, in 1967, Eclection took its name from the contrasting backgrounds of its original line-up. Although Mike Rosen (guitar), Kerilee Male (vocals), Georg Hultgren (bass) and Gerry Conway (b. 11 September 1947, Kings Lynn, Norfolk, England; drums) were not well-known figures, guitarist **Trevor Lucas** (b. 25 December 1943, Bungaree, Victoria, Australia, d. 4 February 1989, Sydney, Australia) had established himself on the folk circuit following his arrival from Australia. The quintet used his undoubted talent to forge an imaginative folk rock style that used influences from both British and American sources. Male left the band in October 1968, following the release of Eclection's debut album. Her replacement was **Dorris Henderson** (b. 2 February 1933, Lakeland, Florida, USA, d. 3 March 2005, London, England), a black American singer who had previously recorded folk-influenced albums with guitarist **John Renbourn**. A further change occurred when Poli Palmer (b. John Michael Palmer, 25 May 1943, England) succeeded Rosen, but the band was sadly unable to fulfil its obvious potential. In October 1969 Palmer left to join **Family**, and Eclection simply folded. Lucas and Conway soon resurfaced in **Fotheringay**, while Hultgren later changed his surname to Kajanus and found fame with the pop group **Sailor**. Rosen joined the early line-up of the **Average White Band**. In the 70s Henderson attempted to revive Eclection with different musicians, but she was largely unsuccessful.

● ALBUMS: *Eclection* (Elektra 1968) ★★★.

ECM Records

ECM Records—the letters stand for Edition for Contemporary Music—was launched in Munich, Germany, in 1969 with **Mal Waldron**'s *Free At Last* and, over 1,000 recording sessions later, is secure in its status as Europe's pre-eminent independent jazz label, despite a sometimes troubled relationship with the jazz mainstream and an open contempt for the music business. The company's musical direction reflects the taste and personality of its founder, producer **Manfred Eicher** (b. 1943, Lindau, Germany), who has said, 'I regard the music industry, including concert life, as a kind of environmental pollution'. Formerly a bass player, Eicher was a member of the Berlin Philharmonic Orchestra, but also played free music with **Marion Brown** and **Leo Smith** (both of whom later recorded for ECM). Experiences as a production assistant at Deutsche Grammophon prompted him to ask whether it were possible to approach jazz recording with the care that the classical companies expended. Norwegian engineer Jan Erik Kongshaug, a partner now for two decades, became an important ally.

Eicher's meticulous recordings of solo piano albums by **Paul Bley**, **Keith Jarrett** and **Chick Corea** were hailed by critic Allan Offstein as 'the most beautiful sound next to silence'—and a trading slogan and *leit-motif* was born. Though the audio quality of the recordings has endeared the label to two generations of hi-fi enthusiasts (and helped to sell more than two million copies of Jarrett's **The Köln Concert**), Eicher feels that technical excellence ought to be a given, and is much more interested in the music. Detractors who rail against the 'ECM sound' conveniently overlook the range of the label's catalogue, which has embraced the burning, outgoing energy music of the **Art Ensemble Of Chicago**, **Sam Rivers** and **Hal Russell**; the rock-influenced guitars of **Terje Rypdal**, **Steve Tibbetts** and **Pat Metheny**; the straighter jazz of **John Abercrombie**, **Kenny Wheeler** and **Dave Holland**; and the eclectic and folklore-rooted improvisations of **Egberto Gismonti**, **Jan Garbarek** and **Collin Walcott**.

A classical line, the ECM New Series, provides access to the entire art music tradition from Gesualdo to Stockhausen and has introduced Estonian composer **Arvo Pärt**, whose pure, concentrated music at the edge of silence has proved a major influence in new composition. A New Series anthology in 1989 bore the inscription 'You wish to see; Listen. Hearing is a step towards vision', and the formula works in reverse as well. ECM album sleeve photography—landscapes, seascapes, cloudscapes, mountainscapes—has provided a powerful visual corollary for the music and gives evidence of Eicher's abiding passion for film. He has released two volumes of Eleni Karaindrou's music for the films of Theo Angelopoulos, and in 1992 issued Jean-Luc Godard's *Nouvelle Vague* on laser disc. In 1991, Eicher scripted and co-directed his first film, *Holocene*, based on a Max Frisch novel. An interest in theatre is evidenced in albums of Heiner Goebbels' music for the plays of Heiner Müller, and **David Byrne**'s music for Robert Wilson's *Civil Wars*. ECM has also issued recordings of actor Bruno Ganz reading German poetry, and of Peter Rühmkorf's jazz and poetry fusions.

It seems likely that ECM will continue to move further away from 'jazz' in the years to come. Having now passed its quarter century the label has avoided ever forsaking itself for commercialism, and artists such as Metheny who moved on to bigger sales with **Geffen Records** can never dispute the faith the label had in him as he developed. ECM's honesty and uncompromising route makes it one of the truly great record labels.

● COMPILATIONS: *Selected Signs I: An ECM Anthology* (ECM 1997) ★★★★.

● FURTHER READING: *ECM: Sleeves Of Desire*, Lars Müller (ed.).

Ed.Og And Da Bulldogs

Boston, Massachusetts–based hip-hop duo who debuted with the singles 'Be A Father To Your Child' and 'I Got To Have It'. The latter, with its engaging horn lick, was quickly pilfered as a sample by many other artists, becoming the number 1 hit in *Billboard*'s Hot Rap chart. 'Be A Father To Your Child' was also widely revered for its strong moral sentiments. DJ Cruz and Ed.Og (b. Edward Anderson, Roxbury, Massachusetts, USA) are the main cogs in Da Bulldogs, who followed up the singles by cutting a well-regarded debut album. Samples from the set have been repeatedly recycled by other hip-hop artists, notably **Heavy D**. Anderson's lyrics span tales of the street and take on his own sexual chemistry, as advertized on the promotional singles for their second long-playing set, 'Skinny Dip (Got It Goin' On)' and 'Love Comes And Goes'. The latter was dedicated to those lost in street violence, who include Anderson's father. With production expertise thrown in by Joe 'Rhythm Nigga' Mansfield, **Diamond D** and the Awesome 2 (Special K and Teddy Tedd), it proved a certain east coast hit. The Ed.Og acronym stands for Everyday Day, Other Girls, while the Bulldogs suffix represents Black United Leaders Living Directly On Groovin' Sounds.

● ALBUMS: *Life Of A Kid In The Ghetto* (Chemistry/Mercury 1991) ★★★, *Roxbury 02119* (Chemistry/Mercury 1994) ★★★.

Edan

b. Baltimore, Maryland, USA. Although this US rapper resembles a young Woody Allen and dresses like a bank clerk, he merges the vitality of old school hip-hop with an attention to detail comparable to contemporary electronica artists such as **Autechre**. Unusually, Edan has name-checked artists including **Pink Floyd** and **Led Zeppelin** alongside hip-hop luminaries **Rakim**, **Slick Rick**, **KRS-One** and **Marley Marl**, and has listed *The Kinks Are The Village Green Preservation Society* as among his favourite albums. Although Edan says he listened to **N.W.A.**'s *Straight Outta Compton* for its vulgarity, the rapper eschews any urge to rap about drive-by shootings. On 'Let's Be Friends', the self-described 'ex-nerd' raps about walking in the park with other MCs and discussing personal problems. The single's b-side, 'Beautiful Food', meanwhile, was a curiously impassioned inventory of culinary delights. The album track 'Ultra '88', meanwhile, was presented as a (surprisingly accurate) lost track from **Ultramagnetic MC's**, in homage to/parody of **Kool Keith**. The title of Edan's first widely available album, 2002's *Primitive Plus*, was intended to represent the past and the future. Strangely, the album was released via a UK-based micro label Lewis Recordings. Edan claims to also make folk rock music and says he has recorded a concept album about the decline of Roman civilization.

● ALBUMS: *Primitive Plus* (Lewis Recordings/Solid 2002) ★★★★.

● COMPILATIONS: *The DJ Fast Rap* (Lewis Recordings 2001) ★★★.

Eddie And The Cruisers

The premise for this 1983 film is not uncommon: Whatever happened to that old rock band? In this case, the band is Eddie And The Cruisers, which folded back in the 60s when after two albums, one a huge hit the other a failure, the leader, Eddie Wilson (Michael Paré) vanished, presumed drowned after his car left the road. Now, the band's music is attracting a new generation of listeners and journalist Maggie Foley (Ellen Barkin) decides to interview the surviving Cruisers members. Chief among them is Frank Ridgeway (Tom Berenger), now a teacher. The film's McGuffin is the possible existence of the band's last recording *A Season In Hell*, the tapes of which were lost. Someone is hunting for the tapes, breaking into and searching the homes of former Cruisers. Suspicion grows that this could be the supposedly dead Eddie. Directed by Martin Davidson, who co-wrote the screenplay with Arlene Davidson, the story is developed effectively. With so many real-life rock legends who died young, leaving many fans in desolation and denial, the core idea has verisimilitude and owing to good performances from Paré, whose debut this is, Berenger and Barkin, together with strong soundtrack music, by **John Cafferty**, this 95-minute film did well.

So well, in fact, that a sequel came with 1989's *Eddie And The Cruisers II: Eddie Lives!* Directed by Jean-Claude Lord from Charles Zev Cohen's screenplay, this 104-minute film has the supposedly dead Eddie (Paré again) working as a carpenter in Montreal, Canada. He forms a new band but because of past experiences tries to keep it under wraps despite its growing popularity. Whatever legs the original concept might have had, they were not enough to carry this follow-up and neither was it helped by the lack of any verisimilitude to the real-life legends of rock, none of whom have ever come back from the dead. Even the presence of **Bo Diddley** did not help.

Eddie And The Hot Rods

Formed in 1975, this quintet from Southend, Essex, England, originally comprised Barrie Masters (vocals), Lew Lewis (harmonica), Paul Gray (bass), Dave Higgs (guitar), Steve Nicol (drums) plus 'Eddie', a short-lived dummy that Masters pummelled on stage. After one classic single, 'Writing On The Wall', Lewis left, though he appeared on the high-energy 'Horseplay', the b-side of their cover of **Sam The Sham And The Pharaohs**' 'Wooly Bully'. Generally regarded as a younger, more energetic version of **Dr. Feelgood**, the Rods pursued a tricky route between the conservatism of pub rock and the radicalism of punk. During the summer of 1976, the group broke house records at the Marquee Club with a scorching series of raucous, sweat-drenched performances. Their power was well captured on a live EP, which included a cover of **? And The Mysterians**' '96 Tears' and a clever amalgamation of the **Rolling Stones**' 'Satisfaction' and **Them**'s 'Gloria'. The arrival of guitarist Graeme Douglas from the **Kursaal Flyers** gave the group a more commercial edge and a distinctive jingle-jangle sound. A guest appearance on

former **MC5** singer Rob Tyner's 'Till The Night Is Gone' was followed by the strident 'Do Anything You Wanna Do', which provided a Top 10 hit in the UK. A fine second album, *Life On The Line*, was striking enough to suggest a long-term future, but the group fell victim to diminishing returns. Douglas left, followed by Gray, who joined the **Damned**. Masters disbanded the group for a spell but re-formed the unit for pub gigs and small label appearances. *Gasoline Days* was a depressingly retro affair.

● ALBUMS: *Teenage Depression* (Island 1976) ★★★★, *Life On The Line* (Island 1977) ★★★, *Thriller* (Island 1979) ★★, *Fish 'N' Chips* (EMI America 1980) ★★, *One Story Town* (Waterfront 1985) ★★, *Gasoline Days* (Creative Man 1996) ★★, *Better Late Than Never* (Voiceprint 2005) ★★.

● COMPILATIONS: *The Curse Of The Rods* (Hound Dog 1990) ★★★, *Live And Rare* (Receiver 1993) ★★, *The Best Of . . . The End Of The Beginning* (Island 1995) ★★★, *Do Anything You Wanna Do* (Spectrum 2001) ★★★.

Eddy And The Soul Band

b. Eddy Conrad, 1959, Gary, Indiana, USA. Conrad grew up in Indiana obsessed by the sound of **Isaac Hayes**' 'Theme From Shaft', the first record he ever purchased. Conrad would spend his pocket money continually attending reruns of the film at local cinemas. 'As a kid you always have heroes but with John Shaft [the film's protagonist] it was serious. He had that certain macho feeling that every kid wishes he had too.' In 1985 he fulfilled a long-held ambition by re-recording the track, which became a number 13 UK chart hit. It might well have charted higher had another version of 'Theme From Shaft' by Van Twist not been released at the same time. Afterwards, however, Conrad and his band disappeared from view completely.

Eddy Duchin Story, The

After gaining popularity as pianist with **Leo Reisman**'s band at New York's Central Park Casino in the late 20s, handsome and debonair **Eddy Duchin** (b. 1 April 1909, Cambridge, Massachusetts, USA, d. 9 February 1951, New York City, New York, USA) formed his own band. This band, too, reigned at the Casino for some years and also played other swanky New York venues. He appeared on radio and in films such as *Mr Broadway* (1933), *Coronado* (1935) and *Hit Parade Of 1937* (1937). His records sold well and by the time of America's entry into World War II he was hugely successful. When war was declared he joined the navy, serving as a lieutenant. After the war he resumed band leading although he never quite attained the same level of popularity, owing no doubt in great part to changing musical tastes. Soon, however, Duchin's health failed and he was diagnosed with leukaemia. He died in 1951 at the age of 41.

This 1956 film, directed by George Sidney from Samuel A. Taylor's screenplay, which was based upon Leo Katcher's original story, is predictably sentimental and glossy. In Duchin's case, the glossy is rather more true to life than usual because his milieu was New York's 'high society' where tuxedos and evening gowns were the order of the night. Playing the title role is Tyrone Power, who in Hollywood was the epitome of handsome and debonair. He does quite well as the pianist although the script is rather leaden. The piano playing is dubbed on the soundtrack by **Carmen Cavallaro**. Also in the cast are Kim Novak as Marjorie Oelrichs Duchin and Rex Thompson as their son, Peter, plus James Whitmore

(Lou Sherwood), Victoria Shaw (Chiquita), Shepperd Strud-wick (Sherman Wadsworth), Frieda Inescort (Edith Wadsworth) and Larry Keating (Leo Reisman). This 123-minute Technicolor and CinemaScope film was nominated for Oscars for Katcher, cinematographer Harry Stradling and musical director **George Duning**. In real life, **Peter Duchin** also became a successful pianist and band leader working at prestigious hotels and casinos.

Eddy, Duane

b. 26 April 1938, Corning, New York, USA. The legendary simple 'twangy' guitar sound of Duane Eddy has made him one of rock 'n' roll's most famous instrumental artists. The sound was created after hearing **Bill Justis**' famous 'Raunchy' (the song that **George Harrison** first learned to play). Together with producer **Lee Hazlewood**, Eddy co-wrote a deluge of hits mixed with versions of standards, using the bass strings of his Gretsch guitar recorded through an echo chamber. The debut 'Movin' 'N' Groovin'' made the lower end of the US chart, and for the next six years Eddy repeated this formula with greater success. His backing group, the Rebel Rousers, was a tight, experienced band with a prominent saxophone sound played by Jim Horn and Steve Douglas, completed by pianist Larry Knechtel. Among their greatest hits were 'Rebel-Rouser', 'Shazam', 'Peter Gunn', 'The Ballad Of Paladin' and 'Theme From Dixie'. The latter was a variation on the Civil War standard written in 1860. One of Eddy's most memorable hits was the superlative theme music for the film **Because They're Young**, brilliantly combining his bass notes with evocative strings. The song has been used by UK disc jockey Johnny Walker as his theme music for over 25 years and this classic still sounds fresh. Eddy's '(Dance With The) Guitar Man' was another major hit, which was unusual for the fact that the song had lyrics, sung by a female group. Eddy's albums played heavily on the use of 'twang' in the title, but that was exactly what the fans wanted.

The hits dried up in 1964 at the dawn of the **Beatles**' invasion, and for many years his sound was out of fashion. An attempt in the contemporary market was lambasted with *Duane Goes Dylan*. Apart from producing Phil Everly's excellent *Star Spangled Springer* in 1973, Eddy travelled the revival circuit, always finding a small but loyal audience in the UK. **Tony Macaulay** wrote 'Play Me Like You Play Your Guitar' for him in 1975, and after more than a decade he was back in the UK Top 10. He slipped back into relative obscurity but returned to the charts in 1986 when he was flattered to be asked to play with the electro-synthesizer band **Art Of Noise**, all the more complimentary was that it was his song, 'Peter Gunn'. The following year **Jeff Lynne** produced his first album for many years, being joined by **Paul McCartney**, George Harrison and **Ry Cooder**, all paying tribute to the man who should have legal copyright on the word 'twang'.

● ALBUMS: *Have 'Twangy' Guitar Will Travel* (Jamie 1958) ★★★, *Especially For You* (Jamie 1958) ★★★★, *The 'Twang's The 'Thang'* (Jamie 1959) ★★★★, *Songs Of Our Heritage* (Jamie 1960) ★★★, *$1,000,000 Worth Of Twang* (Jamie 1960) ★★★★, *Girls! Girls! Girls!* (Jamie 1961) ★★★, *$1,000,000 Worth Of Twang, Volume 2* (Jamie 1962) ★★★, *Twistin' And Twangin'* (RCA-Victor 1962) ★★★★, *Twisting With Duane Eddy* (Jamie 1962) ★★★, *Twangy Guitar-Silky Strings* (RCA-Victor 1962) ★★★★, *Dance With The Guitar Man* (RCA-Victor 1963) ★★★★, *Duane Eddy & The Rebels In Person* (Jamie 1963) ★★★, *Surfin'*

With Duane Eddy (Jamie 1963) ★★★, *Twang A Country Song* (RCA-Victor 1963) ★★, *Twanging Up A Storm!* (RCA-Victor 1963) ★★★, *Lonely Guitar* (RCA-Victor 1964) ★★★, *Water Skiing* (RCA-Victor 1964) ★★, *Twangsville* (RCA-Victor 1965) ★★, *Twangin' The Golden Hits* (RCA-Victor 1965) ★★★, *Duane Goes Bob Dylan* (RCA-Victor 1965) ★★, *Duane A Go Go* (RCA-Victor 1965) ★★, *Biggest Twang Of Them All* (RCA-Victor 1966) ★★, *Roaring Twangies* (RCA-Victor 1967) ★★, *Twangy Guitar* (1970) ★★★, *Duane Eddy* (Capitol 1987) ★★★.

● COMPILATIONS: *16 Greatest Hits* (Jamie 1964) ★★★★, *The Best Of Duane Eddy* (RCA-Victor 1966) ★★★★, *The Vintage Years* (Sire 1975) ★★★, *Legends Of Rock* (Deram 1975) ★★★, *Twenty Terrific Twangies* (RCA 1981) ★★★, *Greatest Hits* (Ronco 1991) ★★★★, *Twang Thang: The Duane Eddy Anthology* (Rhino 1993) ★★★★, *That Classic Twang* 2-CD set (Bear Family 1994) ★★★★, *Twangin' From Phoenix To L.A.—The Jamie Years* 5-CD box set (Bear Family 1995) ★★★★, *Boss Guitar* (Camden 1997) ★★★, *Deep In The Heart Of Twangsville: The Complete RCA Victor Recordings* 6-CD box set (Bear Family 1999) ★★★.

● FILMS: *Because They're Young* (1960).

Eddy, Nelson, And Jeanette MacDonald

Nelson Eddy (b. 29 June 1901, Providence, Rhode Island, USA, d. 6 March 1967) and Jeanette MacDonald (b. 18 June 1901, Philadelphia, Pennsylvania, USA, d. 14 January 1965, Houston, Texas, USA). Often called the most successful singing partnership in the history of the cinema, their series of eight operetta-style films vividly caught the imagination of 30s audiences. Eddy came from a musical family and learned to sing by continually listening to operatic records. After the family moved to Philadelphia, he worked at a variety of jobs including telephone operator, advertising salesman and copy-writer. He played several leading roles in Gilbert And Sullivan operettas presented by the Savoy Company of Philadelphia, before travelling to Europe for music studies. On his return in 1924, he had minor parts at the Metropolitan Opera House in New York, and other concert halls, and appeared on radio. In 1933, he made a brief appearance, singing 'In the Garden Of My Heart', in the film *Broadway To Hollywood*, which featured 10-year-old **Mickey Rooney**. This was followed by small roles in **Dancing Lady** (1933, in which **Fred Astaire** made his debut) and *Student Tour* (1934), after which he attained star status with MacDonald in 1935.

MacDonald took singing and dancing lessons as a child, before moving to New York to study, and in 1920 her tap-dancing ability gained her a place in the chorus of the Broadway show *The Night Boat*, one of the year's best musicals, with a score by **Jerome Kern**. In the same year she served as a replacement in *Irene*, a fondly remembered all-time favourite of the US theatre. **Harry Tierney** and **Joseph McCarthy** were responsible for the show's score, which contained the big hit 'Alice Blue Gown'. MacDonald's other 20s shows included *Tangerine*, *A Fantastic Fricassee*, *The Magic Ring*, *Sunny Days*, and the title roles in *Yes, Yes, Yvette* and *Angela*. However, she appeared in only one real hit, **George** and **Ira Gershwin**'s *Tip-Toes* (1925), in which she co-starred with **Queenie Smith**. In 1929 she was teamed with **Maurice Chevalier** for her film debut in director **Ernst Lubitsch**'s first sound picture, **The Love Parade**. The musical score, by **Victor Schertzinger** and **Clifford Grey**, included 'Dream Lover', 'March Of The Grenadiers' and 'My Love

Parade'. It was a great success and prompted MacDonald and Chevalier to make three more similar operetta-style films together: **One Hour With You**, (1932; the Oscar Strauss-**Richard Whiting**-**Leo Robin** songs included 'We Will Always Be Sweethearts' and the title song); **Love Me Tonight** (1932), one of the most innovative of all movie musicals, directed by **Rouben Mamoulian**, with a **Richard Rodgers** and **Lorenz Hart** score that included 'Lover', 'Isn't It Romantic?', 'Mimi'; and a lavish production of **The Merry Widow** (1934, with **Franz Lehár**'s enduring score being aided by some occasional Lorenz Hart lyrics). MacDonald's other movies during the early 30s were a mixture of musicals and comedies, including *The Lottery Bride*, **Monte Carlo** (both 1930) and *The Cat And The Fiddle* (1934). The latter was another outstanding Lubitsch musical that teamed MacDonald with UK song and dance man, **Jack Buchanan**, and included 'Beyond The Blue Horizon', one of her first hit recordings.

It was in 1935 that MGM brought Eddy and MacDonald together for the first time in **Naughty Marietta**. They were not at first sight an ideal combination, MacDonald's infectious personality and soprano voice, ideal for operetta, coupled with Eddy, whose acting occasionally lacked animation. Despite being known in some quarters as 'The Singing Capon And The Iron Butterfly', the duo's impact was immediate and enormous. *Naughty Marietta*'s score, by **Victor Herbert**, included 'Tramp! Tramp! Tramp!', 'Italian Street Song' and the big duet, 'Ah, Sweet Mystery Of Life'. **Rudolph Friml**'s **Rose Marie** (1936) followed, and was equally successful. Sometimes called the quintessential operetta, the original play's plot underwent severe changes to enable MacDonald to play a renowned Canadian opera singer, while Eddy became an extremely heroic Mountie. Two of the most popular Friml-**Oscar Hammerstein II**-Harbach songs were the evergreen 'Rose Marie', and the duet, 'Indian Love Call', which proved to be a major US record hit.

Both stars made other films during the 30s besides their mutual projects. In 1936, MGM starred MacDonald in the highly regarded melodramatic musical **San Francisco**, with Clark Gable and Spencer Tracy. The movie's earthquake climax was lampooned by **Judy Garland** in her legendary 1961 Carnegie Hall Concert, when she sang the film's title song, with a special verse that ran: 'I never will forget Jeanette MacDonald/Just to think of her, it gives my heart a pang/I never will forget, how that brave Jeanette, just stood there in the ruins, and sang—aaaand sang!' Meanwhile, Eddy was somewhat miscast as an American football hero in *Rosalie*, with **Eleanor Powell** as Princess Rosalie of Romanza. However, he did introduce a **Cole Porter** classic, 'In The Still Of The Night', the song that is supposed to have moved MGM boss Louis B. Mayer to tears the first time he heard it. **Noël Coward** is said also to have wept, albeit for a different reason, when he saw MacDonald optimistically playing a girl of 18, and Eddy as a starving Viennese singing teacher in the film version of Coward's **Bitter Sweet** (1940). Several songs from the original stage show were retained including 'Zigeuner' and 'I'll See You Again'. The MacDonald-Eddy partnership attracted much criticism for being over-romantic and far too saccharine. However, 30s audiences loved their films such as **Maytime** (1937), *The Girl Of The Golden West* (1938), **Sweethearts** (1938, MGM's first three-colour Technicolor picture) and *New Moon* (1940), one of their biggest box-office hits, with a **Sigmund Romberg**-Oscar Hammerstein II score, which included the memorable 'Lover, Come Back To Me', 'Softly, As In A Morning Sunrise' and 'Stout-Hearted Men'.

In 1941, MacDonald appeared in *Smilin' Through*, with her husband Gene Raymond, while Eddy's performance that same year in *The Chocolate Soldier* was generally thought to be his best acting on film. By 1942, the team had run out of steam. With the onset of World War II, moviegoers' tastes had changed. Their last film together, *I Married An Angel*, even with songs by Rodgers and Hart, was the least successful of the series. In 1942, MacDonald made her final film at MGM, *Cairo*, with Robert Young. This was followed, later in the 40s, by a brief appearance in *Follow The Boys* (1944) and a starring role in *Three Daring Daughters*, in which, with the trio, she sang an appealing version of 'The Dickey Bird Song', by **Sammy Fain** and **Howard Dietz**. In 1949, after a career that had teamed her with many of Hollywood's leading men, she made her last film, *The Sun Comes Up*, with another big star, the wonder dog, Lassie! For several years MacDonald also returned to the concert stage and appeared in operettas and on television, before eventually disappearing from the limelight. She died from a heart attack in January 1965. After their break-up, Nelson Eddy appeared in the horror-musical *Phantom Of The Opera* (1943) and **Knickerbocker Holiday** (1944), in which he sang 'There's Nowhere To Go But Up'. His final movie appearance was with Ilona Massey in the Rudolph Friml operetta *Northwest Outpost*, in 1947. He returned to the stage, played in nightclubs and stock musicals and on radio, and occasionally television. He was appearing at the Miami Beach Hotel in Florida when he became ill and was taken to hospital. He died shortly afterwards, in March 1967.

● COMPILATIONS: *Favourites In Hi-Fi* (RCA Victor 1958) ★★★, *Jeanette MacDonald And Nelson Eddy* (RCA 1984) ★★★, *Apple Blossoms* (Mac/Eddy 1989) ★★★, *The Christmas Album* (Mac/Eddy 1989) ★★★, *The Early Years* (Mac/Eddy 1989) ★★★, *Naughty Marietta* (Mac/Eddy 1989) ★★★, *Operatic Recital Volume 3* (Mac/Eddy 1989) ★★★, *Sing Patriotic Songs* (Mac/Eddy 1989) ★★★, *Chase And Sanborn Radio Show* (Mac/Eddy 1989) ★★★, *Tonight Or Never* (Mac/Eddy 1989) ★★★, *Irene* (Mac/Eddy 1989) ★★★, *Songs Of Faith And Inspiration* (Silva Screen 1990) ★★★, *When I'm Calling You* (1994) ★★★.

Solo: Nelson Eddy *Through Theatreland* (1955) ★★★, with Dorothy Kirsten *Rose Marie* (1955) ★★★, with Doretta Morrow and Cast *The Desert Song* (1958) ★★★, *Stout-Hearted Men* (1958) ★★★, *Because* (1959) ★★★★, *The Lord's Prayer* (1960) ★★★, *Story Of A Starry Night* (1961) ★★★, *Carols Of Christmas* (1961) ★★★, *Of Girls I Sing* (1964) ★★★, *Our Love* (1967) ★★★, *Till The End Of Time* (1967) ★★★, *Greatest Hits* (1967) ★★★, *World Favourite Love Songs* (1972) ★★★, *Isn't It Romantic?* (1974) ★★★, *Love's Own Sweet Song* (1988) ★★★, *On the Air* (1988) ★★★, *With Friends* (1990) ★★★, *Nelson Eddy And Ilona Massey* (1990) ★★★, *Phantom Of The Opera* (1990). Jeanette MacDonald *Smilin' Through* (1960) ★★★, *Sings 'San Francisco' And Other Silver Screen Favourites* (RCA 1983) ★★★, *Dream Lover* (Happy Days 1988) ★★★.

● FURTHER READING: *The Films Of Jeanette MacDonald And Nelson Eddy*, Philip Castanza. *Jeanette MacDonald: A Pictorial History*, Sharon Rich. *The Jeanette MacDonald Story*, James Robert Parish. *Jeanette MacDonald*, Lee Edward Stern. *Sweethearts: The Timeless Love Affair—On Screen And*

Off—Between Jeanette MacDonald And Nelson Eddy, Sharon Rich.

Edelhagen, Kurt

b. 5 June 1920, Herne, Germany, d. 8 February 1982, Cologne, Germany. Arranger, orchestra leader and pianist Edelhagen first came to prominence in the years immediately following World War II. Although the prompt formation of a symphony orchestra is often cited as a notable attempt to re-establish an element of culture in post-war German society, the formation of a radio big band is rather more striking. The Berlin Philharmonic Orchestra had never really stopped playing, but dance music, especially that with a jazz-orientation, had been frowned upon by the defeated regime. In these circumstances the speed with which Edelhagen, who had been playing piano in clubs for the Allied armies, formed a big band of such a high quality was quite remarkable. His first band was in operation before the end of 1946 and thereafter he developed a series of radio big bands that continued into the early 70s. He was one of the first post-war European band leaders to bring in foreign jazz musicians and among those who were featured in his bands were **Jimmy Deuchar**, **Derek Humble**, **Dusko Goykovich** and **Jiggs Whigham**. The various orchestras Edelhagen led featured a wide range of big-band music, with a bias towards a powerful, brassy ensemble playing that reflected his love for **Stan Kenton**'s style.

● ALBUMS: *Big Band Jazz From Germany* (Polydor 1955) ★★★★, *Kurt Edelhagen Presents* (Polydor 1957) ★★★, *Kurt Edelhagen And His Orchestra* i (Polydor 1959) ★★★, *Kurt Edelhagen And His Orchestra* ii (Polydor 1959) ★★★, *Kurt Edelhagen And His Orchestra* iii (Polydor 1964) ★★★, *Live At Lucerna Hall, Prague* (Supraphon 1965) ★★, *Swing Goodies* (Polydor 1965) ★★★, *Kurt Edelhagen And His Orchestra* iv (Polydor 1972) ★★★, *Heidelberger Jazztage 1972* (Polydor 1972) ★★★.

Edelman, Judith

b. 14 November 1964, New York City, USA. Edelman, whose father won a Nobel Prize for medicine in 1972, embarked on a solo career in 1996 having first made her name with the acclaimed Rocky Mountain bluegrass group Ryestraw. She began piano lessons at the age of five and continued her studies until she left for Swarthmore College in Pennsylvania. She majored in English but continued to take voice lessons and sang with various local bands. Immediately following graduation, she moved to Africa as part of her work in third world development. It was while recuperating from illness there in a friend's house that she began to teach herself the guitar. Returning to the Bay Area of San Francisco at the age of 26 she linked up with Ryestraw, with whom she spent several years touring, before deciding to pursue a solo career. Her debut, *Perfect World*, featured 11 original compositions matching bluegrass influences with contemporary themes, as well as Celtic and folkloric elements. Guests including **Jerry Douglas**, **Clive Gregson**, Alison Brown and **Randy Howard** provided the perfect backing for Edelman's sweet vocal style (not unlike **Nancy Griffith** or **Alison Krauss**), which belied the less than sunny content of her lyrics. Her subsequent albums have attracted strong praise for their musical eclecticism and lyrical acuity, although Edelman has still to reap the commercial rewards her formidable talent warrants.

● ALBUMS: *Perfect World* (Compass 1996) ★★★★, *Only Sun* (Compass 1998) ★★★, *Drama Queen* (Compass 2000) ★★★.

Edelman, Randy

b. 10 June 1947, Paterson, New Jersey, USA. This US singer-songwriter won a large European audience in the mid-70s by writing and performing some classic love songs. A former staff writer at **CBS Records**, Edelman made his debut on the Sunflower label in 1971 with a self-titled album that went largely unnoticed. During the 70s, however, he slowly built up his reputation and finally reached the big time with 1976's hit single 'Uptown, Uptempo Woman'. His highest chart entry in the UK came the same year with a revival of **Unit Four Plus Two**'s 1965 hit 'Concrete And Clay'. By 1978 his singles career had ground to a halt, but during this period one of his songs, 'Weekend In New England', was covered and made into a million-selling record by **Barry Manilow**. Other artists who have covered his material include the **Carpenters**, **Olivia Newton-John** and **Patti LaBelle**.

An attempted comeback in 1982 failed, and Edelman elected to concentrate on his burgeoning film scoring career. He had worked on movies as far back as the early 70s, but his career really took off in the late 80s when he worked on major Hollywood productions such as *Twins* and *Ghostbusters II*. Edelman has gone on to write and perform the soundtracks for countless movies. His credits include *The Chipmunk Adventure, Feds, Come See The Paradise, Kindergarten Cop, Drop Dead Fred, V.I. Warshawski, Beethoven, The Last Of The Mohicans, The Distinguished Gentlemen, Dragon: The Bruce Lee Story, Gettysburg, Beethoven's 2nd, The Mask, While You Were Sleeping, Diabolique, Dragonheart, Daylight, Anaconda, Gone Fishin', Six Days Seven Nights, Edtv, Passion Of Mind ,The Whole Nine Yards, Shanghai Noon, Head Over Heels, Black Knight, XXX* and *Connie And Carla*.

● ALBUMS: *Randy Edelman* (Sunflower 1971) ★★★, *The Laughter & The Tears* (Lion 1973) ★★★, *Prime Cuts* (20th Century 1974) ★★, *Fairwell Fairbanks* (20th Century 1975) ★★★, *If Love Is Real* (Arista 1977) ★★, *You're The One* (Arista 1979) ★★, *On Time* (Rocket 1982) ★★, *And His Piano: The Very Best Of* (Elecstar 1984) ★★.

● COMPILATIONS: *Uptown, Uptempo: The Best Of Randy Edelman* (20th Century 1979) ★★★.

● FILMS: *Sgt. Pepper's Lonely Hearts Club Band* (1978).

Eden's Crush

The female vocal group created by the US version of the globally successful 'reality TV' show *Popstars*. Screened on The WB channel in the first two months of 2001, the series documented the creation of a pop group by a panel of experts comprising Travis Payne, Jennifer Greig-Costin and Jaymes Foster-Levy. The original cast of thousands was whittled down, through a series of workshops, to the lucky five. Ana Maria Lombo (b. 8 May 1978, Medellin, Colombia), Ivette Sosa (b. 15 September 1976, Edison, New Jersey, USA), Maile Misajon (b. 17 September 1976, Long Beach, California, USA), Nicole Scherzinger (b. 29 June 1978, Honolulu, Hawaii, USA) and Rosanna Tavarez (b. 10 February 1977, New York, USA) were then relocated to a house in Los Angeles, where they trained and rehearsed and then recorded their **Sire Records**/143 Records debut, with the aid of several leading pop songwriters and producers. By this point in time, the television series had revealed the five women's identities and their name: Eden's Crush. The quintet's 'Get Over Yourself' repeated the global success of the *Popstars* format, becoming the biggest-selling debut for a new group in US chart history when it was released in March 2001. Despite their initial success the group's commercial star soon faded, and record company problems and personal differences hastened their demise. Scherzinger later performed with the **Pussycat Dolls**.

● ALBUMS: *Popstars* (143/Sire 2001) ★★★.

Edens, Roger

b. 9 November 1905, Hillsboro, Texas, USA, d. 13 July 1970, Hollywood, California, USA. An important arranger, songwriter—and later—producer, who was a close associate of MGM producer **Arthur Freed** from the 30s through to the 50s, when the legendary Freed Unit was turning out one magnificent film musical after another. Edens first came to notice on Broadway in *Girl Crazy* (1930) when he stepped out of the pit orchestra and took over as **Ethel Merman**'s pianist when her regular man became ill. He subsequently became Merman's arranger and accompanist for some time before joining MGM in 1934. After serving as musical supervisor on the Jean Harlow picture *Reckless*, he adapted Freed and **Nacio Herb Brown**'s songs for the studio's big-budget *Broadway Melody Of 1936*, which was released in 1935. In the same year, Edens arranged the music for a party to celebrate the 36th birthday of one of MGM's biggest stars, Clark Gable. The highlight of the affair was 14-year-old **Judy Garland**'s tender version of 'You Made Me Love You', which she prefaced with the 'fan letter' 'Dear Mr. Gable', written by Edens. The response was sensational and Garland reprised the sequence in *Broadway Melody Of 1938*. From then on Edens scored numerous films, winning Academy Awards for his work on *Easter Parade* (with **Johnny Green**), *On The Town* (with Lennie Hayton) and *Annie Get Your Gun* (with **Adolph Deutsch**). He also contributed songs to numerous pictures including *Love Finds Andy Hardy*, *Babes In Arms*, *Little Nellie Kelly*, *Strike Up The Band*, *Two Girls On Broadway*, *Lady, Be Good!*, *Ziegfeld Girl*, *Babes On Broadway*, *Girl Crazy*, *Thousands Cheer*, *Good News*, *On The Town*, *Take Me Out To The Ball Game*, *Singin' In The Rain*, *Funny Face* and *Billy Rose's Jumbo*. Out of these came numbers such as 'In-Between', 'It's A Great Day For The Irish', 'Our Love Affair', 'Nobody', 'Do The Conga', 'My Wonderful One', 'Minnie From Trinidad', 'Caribbean Love Song', 'Carnegie Hall', 'Hoe Down', 'Here's To The Girls', 'Pass That Peace Pipe', 'You're Awful', 'The Right Girl For Me', 'Strictly USA', 'Moses Supposes', 'Sawdust, Spangles And Dreams' and 'Think Pink', 'Bonjour Paris', 'On How To Be Loved' (the last three for *Funny Face*). For much of the time Edens wrote both words and music, but on other occasions his main collaborators were Arthur Freed, Ralph Freed, **Hugh Martin**, **Betty Comden** and **Adolph Green**, **Sigmund Romberg** and **Jimmy Monaco**. He was associate producer on *The Harvey Girls* (1946) and many other Freed musicals, but it was not until several years later that he took full producer credit on the **Sigmund Romberg** biopic *Deep In My Heart* (1954), and *Funny Face* (1957), for which MGM loaned him to Paramount. His last major assignment was as associate producer on *Hello Dolly!* for 20th Century Fox in 1967, although he was also involved in the preliminary work on **Irving Berlin**'s *Say It With Music*, which was to have been made in 1969 but never materialized owing to upheavals in Metro's top management.

One of the most important aspects of Edens' work was his ability to discover and nurture fresh talent. He gave **Lena Horne** her break in films, which led to appearances in *Cabin In The Sky* and *Stormy Weather*, and he befriended and nurtured Judy Garland through some well-documented difficult times, as well as writing special material for her concerts. According to the trade paper *Variety*, he coached Katharine Hepburn for her starring role in *Coco*, which opened on Broadway in December 1969. He died a few months later of lung cancer.

● FURTHER READING: *The Movies' Greatest Musicals Produced In Hollywood By The Freed Unit*, Hugh Fordin.

Edenton, Ray

b. Ray Quarles Edenton, 8 November 1926, Mineral, Virginia, USA. Renowned session guitarist Ray Edenton has long been recognized as one of Nashville's most prolific and reliable session musicians. Though his preference is for rhythm guitar, he is also equally adaptable to lead guitar, mandolin and bass. His grandfather was a fiddler, and his two brothers also were musicians; as a result, he found himself playing his first amateur contests from the age of six. Following his discharge from service after World War II, he earned money from truck driving while playing occasional singer-songwriter sets in the evenings. He then became a session radio player with the Old Dominion Barn Dance and **Joe Maphis**' Korn Krackers. After a major scare with his health during the late 40s, when he contracted tuberculosis, Edenton began his first round of engagements at the *Grand Ole Opry*, later travelling with artists including **Chet Atkins**, **George Morgan** and **Minnie Pearl**. His first major Nashville recording session came in March 1953, **Webb Pierce** cutting the country number 1 'There Stands The Glass'. Edenton's guitar-playing also appeared on **Kitty Wells** and **Red Foley**'s 'One By One', another chart-topper. Much more recently he has played on pop records recorded by Foley's granddaughter, **Debby Boone**. As well as working as a musician, Edenton has also branched out into record production, writing and plugging. However, he is still best known for his session work, which by the mid-90s included names ranging from the **Beach Boys** and **Henry Mancini** to **Andy Williams** and **Reba McEntire**.

Eder, Linda

b. 6 February 1961, Brainerd, Minnesota, USA. Judging from her recording output, vocalist Eder is equally at home singing 'contemporary standards' as she is tackling musical theatre. She was introduced to both classical and popular music at an early age, by her parents who were both singers, but it was not until high school that Eder discovered the singer that would inspire her vocally the most, **Barbra Streisand**. Eder soon began developing her own style, self-described as 'Broadway and popular style singing with classical influences.' Not long after her high school graduation, she began to hone her singing talent at local nightclubs, which led to a spot on the popular US television show *Star Search*, where Eder took the top spot and beat out the competition for a staggering 12 weeks. It was during her stay in Hollywood while taping the show when she met her future husband, composer Frank Wildhorn. He was working on the musical *Jekyll & Hyde* at the time, which Eder soon became involved with herself, landing the role of Lucy, a nightclub singer. Eder's first appearance on record was on 1990's *Highlights From Jekyll & Hyde*. A self-titled debut album for

RCA Records followed. By the mid-90s, *Jekyll & Hyde* had become a runaway smash on Broadway, where Eder earned rave reviews for her nightly renditions of show-stopping ballads such as 'Someone Like You', 'In His Eyes' and 'A New Life'. Despite her busy schedule with *Jekyll & Hyde*, Eder was able to sustain her solo career, issuing a string of releases for **Atlantic Records**.

● ALBUMS: *Linda Eder* (RCA 1991) ★★★, *And So Much More* (Angel 1994) ★★★, *It's Time* (Atlantic 1997) ★★★, *It's No Secret Anymore* (Atlantic 1999) ★★★★, *Christmas Stays The Same* (Atlantic 2000) ★★★, *Gold* (Atlantic 2002) ★★★★, *Broadway, My Way* (Atlantic 2003) ★★★.

Edge

This UK band was formed in 1978 by former **Damned** members Jon Moss (b. 11 September 1957, London, England; drums) and guitarist Lu Edmunds. They were joined by bass player Glyn Havard and pianist Gavin Povey. Although they gigged extensively and undertook studio work, backing **Kirsty MacColl** on the single 'They Don't Know' and touring as **Jane Aire And The Belvederes**, their own work was largely ignored. They issued three singles ('Macho Man', 'Downhill' and 'Watching You') during the late 70s, and issued the album *Square 1* in 1980 before disbanding. Moss went on to join **Culture Club**, while Edmunds teamed up with Athletico Spizz 80 and later the **Mekons**. The remaining members returned to session work.

● ALBUMS: *Square 1* (Hurricane 1980) ★★.
● COMPILATIONS: *The Moonlight Tapes* (1980) ★★, *Complete Works Of The Edge* (Preset 1987) ★★.

Edghill, Vyris

b. Marcia Vyris Edghill, 18 June 1954, Jamaica, West Indies, d. 12 July 2002, London, England. Edghill came from a religious family and was leader of the church choir. In the mid-60s her family immigrated to the UK. Her parents died at an early age and Edghill took on the parental responsibilities toward her younger siblings. After leaving school, in addition to her family commitments, she pursued a career in music. She initially performed as a backing singer for artists such as **Congo Ashanti Roy**, **Prince Lincoln** And The Royal Rasses, **Vincent Nap**, **Sanchez**, **Ruff Cut Band**, **Nerious Joseph** and **Bim Sherman**. In the early 80s Edghill joined **African Woman**, celebrated as one of the first female reggae bands in the world. Following a change in the line-up, Edghill became the lead singer and a year later the collective performed as **Akabu**. With the group she toured global festivals where the audiences were spellbound by this unique group of women who could sing and play world-class reggae while spreading messages of love, peace and humanity. By the late 90s Akabu merged with **AbbaKush**. Through the efforts of Culture Promotions the women then emerged as **Sista**, a combination of the two groups with additional members **Aisha** and **Trilla Jenna**. Edghill was a highly regarded performer and her demise led to sincere tributes throughout the reggae industry.

Edie Brickell And The New Bohemians
(see **Brickell, Edie, And The New Bohemians**)

Edison Lighthouse

This UK conglomeration was essentially a vehicle for session singer **Tony Burrows**, who also sang with **White Plains**, the

Brotherhood Of Man and the **Pipkins**. The backing musicians were originally part of a band called Greenfield Hammer before they became a studio 're-creation' and hit group. The **Tony Macaulay**/Barry Mason composition 'Love Grows (Where My Rosemary Goes)' provided the breakthrough in 1970 and zoomed to number 1 in the UK and also hit the US Top 5. While this was occurring, Burrows had already moved on to other projects, leaving his backing musicians to continue under the name Edison. Macaulay, meanwhile, still owned the name Edison Lighthouse and conjured up another line-up with that title for recording and touring purposes. The manufactured spin-off group failed to exploit their chart-topping name, although they did manage to scrape into the lower rungs of the UK Top 50 with a weak follow-up, 'It's Up To You Petula'.

● COMPILATIONS: *Love Grows: The Best Of The Edison Lighthouse* (Repertoire 1999) ★★★.

Edison, Harry 'Sweets'

b. 10 October 1915, Columbus, Ohio, USA, d. 27 July 1999, Columbus, Ohio, USA. A trumpeter who was inspired by **Louis Armstrong**, Edison gained valuable early experience with a number of **territory bands**, including the excellent **Jeter-Pillars Orchestra**. After a short spell with **Lucky Millinder**, Edison joined the **Count Basie** band in 1938, where he remained until Basie folded his big band in 1950. Edison then began a long career as leader of small groups, a solo artist and studio musician; he also worked occasionally with band leaders such as **Buddy Rich**. He toured with **Jazz At The Philharmonic** and in the 50s his work came to the attention of millions who never knew his name when he performed exquisite trumpet obligati with the **Nelson Riddle** orchestra behind the vocals of **Frank Sinatra**. In the 60s he worked occasionally with Basie again but was mostly heard as a soloist, touring extensively on the international club and festival circuit. He also recorded with the saxophonists **Jimmy Forrest** and **Eddie 'Lockjaw' Davis**.

In performance Edison often favoured playing with a Harmon mute and, while he had many imitators, few matched his laconic wit and inventiveness. Indeed, his trademark of repeated single notes is something no other trumpeter has been able to use to such good effect. On his numerous recording sessions he was teamed with most of the big names in jazz and continually defied his advancing years.

● ALBUMS: *Harry Edison Quartet* aka *The Inventive Harry Edison* (Pacific Jazz 1953) ★★★, with Buddy Rich *Buddy And Sweets* (Norgran 1955) ★★★, with Lester Young *Pres And Sweets* (Norgran 1955) ★★★★, *Sweets* (Clef 1956) ★★★★, *Blues For Basie* (Verve 1957) ★★★★, *Gee Baby, Ain't I Good To You?* (Verve 1958) ★★★, with Buck Clayton *Harry Edison Swings Buck Clayton And Vice-Versa* (Verve 1958) ★★★, *The Swinger* (Verve 1958) ★★★, with Roy Eldridge, Dizzy Gillespie *Tour De Force* (Verve 1958) ★★★, *Mr. Swing* (Verve 1959) ★★★, *Sweetenings* (Roulette 1959) ★★★, with Eldridge, Young *Going For Myself* (Verve 1959) ★★★★, with Eldridge, Young *Laughin' To Keep From Cryin'* (Verve 1959) ★★★★, *Patented By Edison* (Roulette 1960) ★★★, with Ben Webster *Ben Webster-Sweets Edison* (Columbia 1962) ★★★★, with Eddie 'Lockjaw' Davis *Jawbreakers* (Riverside 1962) ★★★★, *Sweets For The Taste Of Love* (Vee Jay 1964) ★★★, *Sweets For The Sweet* (Sue 1965) ★★★, *When Lights Are Low* (Liberty 1966) ★★★, with Davis *Sweet And Lovely* (Black & Blue 1975) ★★★, with Davis *Edison's Lights* (Pablo 1976) ★★★, *Harry 'Sweets' Edison And Eddie 'Lockjaw' Davis, Vol. 1* (Storyville 1976) ★★★, *Harry 'Sweets' Edison And Eddie 'Lockjaw' Davis, Vol. 2* (Storyville 1976) ★★★, *Simply Sweets* (Pablo 1978) ★★★, with Zoot Sims *Just Friends* (Pablo 1979) ★★★, *'S Wonderful* (Pablo 1983) ★★★, *For My Pals* (Pablo 1988) ★★★, with Spike Robinson *Jusa Bit 'O' Blues, Vol. 1* (Capri 1988) ★★★, with Robinson *Jusa Bit 'O' Blues, Vol. 2* (Capri 1988) ★★★, *Can't Get Out Of This Mood* (Orange Blue 1989) ★★★, *Swing Summit* (Candid 1990) ★★★, *Live At The Iridium* (Telarc 1998) ★★★, *There Will Never Be Another You* 1986 recording (Nagel-Heyer 2003) ★★★.

● COMPILATIONS: *Best Of Harry Edison* (Pablo 1982) ★★★★.

● FILMS: *Jammin' The Blues* (1944).

Editors

Birmingham, England–based indie rock band Editors made their mark in 2005 as potential rivals to the art-rock scene's critical favourites, the UK's **Franz Ferdinand** and US band **Interpol**. Tom Smith (vocals/guitar), Chris Urbanowicz (guitar), Russell Leetch (bass) and Geraint Owen (drums) first met while studying Music Technology at Staffordshire University. They began playing around the local area as the Pride and recorded a demo CD, releasing the music online through the Onemusic Unsigned website. An enforced personnel change saw drummer Owen replaced by Ed Lay, with the new line-up changing their name to Snowfield. The quartet continued to balance their studies with gigging around the Midlands circuit, before launching a full-time music career at the end of 2003. Within a year they had signed a recording contract with Kitchenware Records and begun work on recording their debut album. After a swift name change to Editors the quartet released their debut single, 'Bullets', at the start of 2005. Further singles, 'Munich' and 'Blood', reached the upper regions of the UK charts, paving the way for the release of *The Back Room* in the summer.

● ALBUMS: *The Back Room* (Kitchenware 2005) ★★★.

Edmonds, Kevon

b. Indianapolis, Indiana, USA. Edmonds enjoyed huge success in the 90s with the platinum-selling R&B trio **After 7**, in which he sang with his brother Melvin and Keith Mitchell. After 7 was put on indefinite hold proceeding 1996's compilation set, following which Edmonds collaborated with his other brother, the highly successful producer **Babyface**, on the one-off Milestone project created for the 1997 movie *Soul Food*. Comprising the three Edmonds brothers and **K-Ci And JoJo** from **Jodeci**, Milestone performed the hit ballad 'I Care About You'. Kevon subsequently began work on his debut solo album, enlisting the help of some of the 90s' most successful R&B songwriters and producers, including Darryl Simmons, Babyface and Tim And Bob, and leading session musicians including Nathan East and Greg Phillinganes. The album, released in October 1999, did not stray far from the successful After 7 formula, blending classic soul harmonies with modern beats on a collection divided equally between up-tempo numbers and ballads. Highlights included a duet with Babyface on the ballad 'A Girl Like You', 'Never Love You' and the title track, a US Top 10 hit single.

● ALBUMS: *24/7* (RCA 1999) ★★★.

Edmunds, Dave

b. 15 April 1944, Cardiff, South Glamorgan, Wales. The multi-talented Edmunds has sustained a career for many years by being totally in touch with modern trends while maintaining a passionate love for music of the 50s and 60s, notably rockabilly, rock 'n' roll and country music. He first came to the public eye as lead guitarist of **Love Sculpture** with an astonishing solo played at breakneck speed on their only hit, an interpretation of Khachaturian's 'Sabre Dance'. At the end of the 60s Edmunds built his own recording studio, Rockfield. The technical capabilities of Rockfield soon became apparent, as Edmunds became a masterful producer, working with **Shakin' Stevens**, the **Flamin' Groovies** and **Brinsley Schwarz**. The latter's bass player was **Nick Lowe**, and they formed a musical partnership that lasted many years. Edmunds' own recordings were few, but successful. He brilliantly reproduced the sound of his rock 'n' roll heroes and had hits with **Smiley Lewis**' 'I Hear You Knocking', the **Ronettes**' 'Baby, I Love You' and the **Chordettes**' 'Born To Be With You'. The first was a worldwide hit, selling several million copies and topping the UK charts.

In 1975 Edmunds' debut *Subtle As A Flying Mallet* was eclipsed by his credible performance in the film *Stardust*, and he wrote and sang on most of the Jim McLaine (**David Essex**) tracks. *Get It* in 1977 featured the fast-paced Nick Lowe composition 'I Knew The Bride', which gave Edmunds another hit. Lowe wrote many of the songs on *Tracks On Wax 4* in 1978, during a hectic stage in Edmunds' career when he played with **Emmylou Harris**, **Carl Perkins**, with his own band **Rockpile**, and appeared at the Knebworth Festival and the Rock For Kampuchea concert. *Repeat When Necessary* arrived in 1979 to favourable reviews; it stands as his best album. He interpreted **Elvis Costello**'s 'Girls Talk', giving it a full production with layers of guitars, and the record was a major hit. Other outstanding tracks were 'Crawling From The Wreckage' written by **Graham Parker**, 'Queen Of Hearts' and the 50s-sounding 'Sweet Little Lisa'. The latter contained possibly one of the finest rockabilly/country guitar solos ever recorded, although the perpetrator is **Albert Lee** and not Edmunds. The fickle public ignored the song and the album barely scraped into the Top 40. The following year Edmunds succeeded with **Guy Mitchell**'s 50s hit 'Singing The Blues' and the road-weary Rockpile released their only album, having been previously prevented from doing so for contractual reasons. The regular band of Edmunds, Lowe, Billy Bremner and Terry Williams was already a favourite on the UK pub-rock circuit. Their *Seconds Of Pleasure* was unable to do justice to the atmosphere they created at live shows, although it was a successful album. In 1981 Edmunds charted again, teaming up with the **Stray Cats** and recording **George Jones**' 'The Race Is On', although a compilation of Edmunds' work that year failed to sell. His style changed for the **Jeff Lynne**–produced *Information* in 1983; not surprisingly he sounded more like Lynne's **ELO**. As a producer he won many friends by crafting the **Everly Brothers**' comeback albums *EB84* and *Born Yesterday* and he wrote much of the soundtrack for *Porky's Revenge*. He was producer of the television tribute to **Carl Perkins**; both Edmunds and **George Harrison** were long-time admirers, and Edmunds cajoled the retiring Harrison to make a rare live appearance.

During the mid-80s Edmunds worked with the **Fabulous Thunderbirds**, **Jeff Beck**, **Dr. Feelgood**, **k.d. lang** and **Status**

Quo. His own music was heard during his first tour for some years, together with the live *I Hear You Rockin'*, although more attention was given to Edmunds for bringing **Dion** back into the centre stage with live gigs and an album. Although he has been in the background for a few years, Edmunds has made a major contribution to popular music in the UK, by working creatively, mostly without a fanfare, surfacing occasionally with his own product, evidence of a man who always puts the quality of music first, and never compromising his love for rockabilly and rock 'n' roll. In the late 90s and into the new millennium, Edmunds was a regular member of **Ringo Starr**'s All Starr Band. In September 2000 he became unwell and received an immediate triple heart-bypass operation. He is now resident in Los Angeles.

● ALBUMS: *Subtle As A Flying Mallet* (RCA 1975) ★★★, *Get It* (Swan Song 1977) ★★★, *Tracks On Wax 4* (Swan Song 1978) ★★★, *Repeat When Necessary* (Swan Song 1979) ★★★★, *Twangin'* (Arista 1981) ★★★, *D.E.7th* (Arista 1982) ★★★, *Information* (Arista 1983) ★★, *Riff Raff* (Arista 1984) ★★, *I Hear You Rockin'* (Arista 1987) ★★★, *Closer To The Flame* (Capitol 1990) ★★, *Plugged In* (Columbia 1994) ★★★, *Live On The King Biscuit Flower Hour* 1980/1990 recordings (King Biscuit Flower Hour 1999) ★★★, *A Pile Of Rock Live* (Essential 2000) ★★★.

● COMPILATIONS: *The Best Of Dave Edmunds* (Swan Song 1981) ★★★★, *The Complete Early Edmunds* (EMI 1991) ★★★, *The Anthology (1968–90)* (Rhino/WEA 1993) ★★★★, *Chronicles* (Connoisseur 1995) ★★★★, *Rockin'* (Camden 1997) ★★★, *From Small Things: The Best Of Dave Edmunds* (Columbia/Legacy 2004) ★★★★, *Here Comes The Weekend* (CMG 2005) ★★★.

● DVD/VIDEOS: *A Pile Of Rock: Live* (Silverline 2002).

● FILMS: *Give My Regards To Broad Street* (1985).

Ednaswap

This US rock band did not receive their biggest acclaim on their own terms, but when another artist covered one of their songs. Ednaswap was formed during 1993 in Los Angeles, California, USA, by Anne Preven (vocals), Rusty Anderson (lead guitar), Scott Cutler (rhythm guitar), Carla Azar (drums) and Paul Bushnell (bass). Shortly after forming, the band signed a recording contract with EastWest Records. Just months after their formation, Ednaswap issued a self-titled debut album, but relations with their label quickly turned sour, resulting in the quartet's signing by the end of the year with **Island Records**. Ednaswap's Island debut was an EP, 1996's *Chicken*, which was followed a year later by their second album, *Wacko Magneto*, both of which failed to attract much attention. It was around this time that a Preven original that originally appeared on Ednaswap's debut, 'Torn', was covered by Australian pop singer **Natalie Imbruglia**, becoming a substantial hit in Europe and America. Sensing that interest in the originators of the song may have perked up in the wake of Imbruglia's success, Ednaswap returned back to the studio and issued 1998's *Wonderland Park*, but like its predecessors, the album came and went without a trace, leading to the band's split the following year. Preven went on to supply backing vocals for other artists, including **Sinéad O'Connor**'s 2000 release *Faith And Courage* (as well as co-penning one of its tracks, 'No Man's Woman') and teen queen **Mandy Moore**'s 2001 self-titled offering.

● ALBUMS: *Ednaswap* (EastWest 1995) ★★★, *Wacko Magneto* (Island 1997) ★★★, *Wonderland Park* (Island 1998) ★★.

Edsels

This R&B vocal ensemble from Campbell, Ohio, USA, led by George Jones Jnr. (lead vocal), also included Marshall Sewell, James Reynolds, and brothers Harry and Larry Greene. They were named after the popular make of car. In 1959, they auditioned for a local music publisher who helped them secure a recording contract. Their debut single was the fast doo-wop outing 'Rama Lama Ding Dong' (written by Jones), originally released under the incorrect title of 'Lama Rama Ding Dong'. It was a local hit but flopped nationally. Two years later, when the **Marcels** had a big hit with the similar-sounding doo-wop version of 'Blue Moon', a disc jockey was reminded of 'Rama Lama Ding Dong' and started playing it. Demand grew and it was re-released under its correct title and became a hit in the USA. By this time the Edsels had moved on and could not capitalize on their success. Although the original failed in the UK the song was a hit in 1978 when it was covered by **Rocky Sharpe And The Replays**.

● COMPILATIONS: *Rama Lama Ding Dong* (Relic 1993) ★★.

Edward II

This UK act has been mixing the rhythms of reggae and ska with traditional English folk tunes since the mid-80s, initially under the name Edward II And The Red Hot Polkas, and latterly as e2K.

Formed in Notting Hill, London, England, in 1985, the original line-up of Edward The Second And The Red Hot Polkas featured Tom Greenhalgh (guitar/vocals), Jon Moore (guitar/vocals), Barney Stradling (guitar), John Gill (bass), Steve Goulding (drums), Danny Stradling (percussion), Rod Stradling (melodeon) and Dave Haines (melodeon). The band made their debut for Cooking Vinyl Records in 1987 with *Let's Polka Steady!*, but it was as a live act that they made their name with a series of pulsating gigs at festivals throughout the UK and Europe. Further additions to the fluid line-up during the late 80s included Neil Yates (trumpet), Lorna Bailey (vocals), John Hart (trombone), Gavin Sharp (tenor saxophone) and Alton Zebby (drums), all of who made their debut on the irresistible *Two Step To Heaven*. The album was the band's second, after their debut, to be produced by the **Mad Professor**.

At the start of the 90s the band shortened their name to Edward II, with Moore, Yates and Zebby joined by new members Tee Carthy (bass), Glen Latouche (vocals), Rees Wesson (melodeon/accordion) and rapper McKilla on 1991's *Wicked Men*. Simon Care (melodeon; ex-**Albion Band**) joined Edward II in the mid-90s, featuring on the studio albums *Zest* and *This Way Up*. Zebby, Latouche and Carthy elected to leave the band following the release of the latter, bringing the classic line-up of Edward II to an end. Moore, Yates, and Care relaunched the band in the new millennium as e2K, mining a richer African seam with the help of new member Kwame Yeboah. Other new members included Albion Band vocalist Kellie While.

● ALBUMS: as Edward The Second And The Red Hot Polkas *Let's Polka Steady!* (Cooking Vinyl 1987) ★★★, as Edward The Second And The Red Hot Polkas *Two Step To Heaven* (Cooking Vinyl 1989) ★★★★, *Wicked Men* (Zest

1991) ★★★, *Dashing Away* (Zest 1992) ★★★, *Zest* (Ock 1996) ★★★★, *This Way Up* (Ock 1998) ★★★, as e2K *Shift* (Topic 2001) ★★★, as e2K *If Not Now* (Topic 2003) ★★★.

Edwardes, George

b. 14 October 1855, Cleethorpes, Lincolnshire, England, d. 4 October 1915, London, England. One of the most important figures in the development of musical comedy in England, Edwardes began his career in the Victorian era and by the time of his death in the reign of King George V his Gaiety Theatre was practically synonymous with the new era. Inspired by changes taking place in musical theatre in the USA, Edwardes was himself innovative and far-sighted and had a good ear for new writing and performing talent. Previously a manager with Richard D'Oyly Carte's opera company, Edwardes joined the Gaiety under producer John Hollingshead. Edwardes was 30 when Hollingshead retired and he took over. At the Gaiety and also at Daly's Theatre, Edwardes presented an eager public with one escapist fantasy after another. A standard plot line had a poor young girl rising to high social station through true love. Director of many of Edwardes' shows was J.A.E. Malone, and among numerous composers and lyricists were **Ivan Caryll**, **Percy Greenbank**, **Basil Hood**, Sidney Jones, **Adrian Ross**, **Paul Rubens** and **Howard Talbot**. Male singers who appeared in Edwardes' shows included George Carvey, Hayden Coffin, J. Edward Fraser, **George Grossmith Jnr.** and Harry Welchman. Among the young women were **Phyllis Dare**, **Cicely Court-neidge** and Lilian Eldée. Most notable of Edwardes' protégés were composer **Lionel Monckton** and singer **Gertie Millar**. Although Edwardes' formulaic shows were pure fantasy, the Gaiety Girls were often besieged by upper-class 'stage door Johnnies'. A few of the girls even married into the aristocracy thus turning Edwardes' fantasies into self-fulfilling prophecies. Millar, for example, became Lady Dudley in real life. Edwardes' shows, the titles of which often pre-assured audiences of what they were about to see, included **The Shop Girl** (1894), *The Circus Girl*, *The Geisha* (both 1896), *A Country Girl* (1902), **Our Miss Gibbs** (1909), **The Arcadians** (also 1909), **The Quaker Girl** (1910) and **The Girl From Utah** (1913). Among Edwardes' shows that were staged on Broadway, usually in the year following their London opening and in collaboration with American producer **Charles Frohman**, were *The Arcadians*, *The Quaker Girl* and *The Girl From Utah*. Although principally and rightly remembered for his trademark shows, Edwardes also presented to London audiences some of the European operettas he was supplanting, among them **The Merry Widow** (1907), **The Dollar Princess** (1909) and **The Count Of Luxembourg** (1911).

Edwards, Alton

b. Zimbabwe. Edwards' first musical experience came as a percussionist with an oil-drum band before he moved to Zambia to study the flute. In the early 70s he returned to Zimbabwe to join the soul band Sabu as vocalist and bass player. He subsequently formed his own band, Unity, before travelling once more. In 1978 he moved to Zurich in Switzerland where he wrote songs for the Superlove group. His stay there was short-lived, however, and within a year he had moved to Los Angeles to work with **Motown Records** producer Clay McMurray. He finally embarked on a solo career in 1981 after moving to England. After securing a contract with **CBS Records**' subsidiary Streetwave, he recorded a number of songs that he had written over preceding years. One of these, 'I Just Wanna (Spend Some Time With You)', became a UK Top 20 hit at the beginning of 1982. However, follow-up efforts such as 'Take Me' did not repeat its success.

Edwards, Archie

b. 4 September 1918, Union Hall, Virginia, USA, d. 18 June 1998. From a musical family, Edwards' desire to be a guitar player developed out of the Saturday-night gatherings his father held at their home during his childhood. As a teenager he learned to sing and play by mimicking the 78s of **Blind Boy Fuller**, **Blind Lemon Jefferson**, **Mississippi John Hurt** and hillbilly artist **Frank Hutchison**. For most of his life he continued with his day jobs, only performing at weekends or evenings at clubs in Washington, DC. In more recent years, Edwards had become a great favourite on the festival circuit, having visited Europe in the 80s and recorded for the German L&R label. Together with **John Jackson** and **John Cephas**, Archie Edwards represented the continuation of the east coast blues tradition begun in the 30s by Blind Boy Fuller. He performed regularly at festivals until his death from cancer in 1998.
● ALBUMS: *The Road Is Rough And Rocky* (L&R 80s) ★★★, *Blues N Bones* (Mapleshade 1991) ★★★, *The Toronto Sessions* 1986 recording (Northern Blues 2002) ★★★.

Edwards, Bobby

b. Robert Moncrief, Anniston, Alabama, USA. Edwards placed one single near the US Top 10 in 1961 but was unable to follow it with another hit. He was a member of a group called the Four Young Men, which recorded non-hits for such labels as Dore, Delta and Crest. Edwards then recorded under his own name for Bluebonnet; that record, 'Jealous Heart', was also issued on Manco Records. The country-influenced 'You're The Reason' was released on Crest, and reached number 11, after which Edwards recorded a follow-up, 'What's The Reason?', for **Capitol Records**. He continued to record country songs throughout the 60s but never repeated his one brush with success.

Edwards, Clarence

b. 25 March 1933, Linsey, Louisiana, USA, d. 20 May 1993, Scotlandville, Louisiana, USA. Edwards began playing blues guitar at around the age of 12, when he moved to Baton Rouge. In the 50s and 60s, he was working the same local blues circuit as the likes of **Lightnin' Slim**, in bands with names such as the Boogie Beats and the Bluebird Kings. His first experience of recording was in a traditional setting, in sessions for folklorist Harry Oster between 1959 and 1961, with his brother Cornelius and violinist **James 'Butch' Cage**. Nine years later, he recorded again, this time with a more contemporary sound, and from the mid-80s with the blues scene revived with the help of **Tabby Thomas**' Blues Box club, he was playing regularly. In 1990, he recorded his first album, a powerful mixture of acoustic and electric sounds in the swamp blues style. After his death an excellent compilation, *I Looked Down That Railroad*, was released.
● ALBUMS: *Swamp's The Word* (Red Lightnin' 1991) ★★★★, with Henry Gray and Short Fuse *Thibodeaux's Cafe* (Sidetrack 1995) ★★★.

● COMPILATIONS: *I Looked Down That Railroad* (Last Call 1996) ★★★★.

Edwards, Cliff

b. 14 June 1895, Hannibal, Missouri, USA, d. 18 July 1972, Los Angeles, California, USA. This diminutive, soft-voiced singer became universally known as 'Ukelele Ike', and popularized that instrument during his successful vaudeville career in the early 20s. Before that he had worked in carnivals, St. Louis saloons, and in Chicago with comedian Joe Frisco. As well as vaudeville, Edwards appeared in several Broadway musicals including *Lady, Be Good!* (1924), with **Adele Astaire** and **Fred Astaire** (in which he sang 'Fascinating Rhythm'), *Sunny* (1925), *Ziegfeld Follies of 1927* and *George White's Scandals of 1931*. The beginning of his film career coincided with the transition from silents to talkies, and he is reputed to have made over 60 films, which included musicals, romantic comedies and dramas such as *Hollywood Revue Of 1929* (1929) in which he introduced the **Arthur Freed/Nacio Herb Brown** song, 'Singin' In The Rain', *Parlor, Bedroom And Bath* (1931) with Buster Keaton, *Hell Divers* (1932), *Take A Chance* (1933) in which he sang 'It's Only A Paper Moon', *George White's Scandals* (1934) and *George White's 1935 Scandals* (1935). He had a string of hits between 1924 and 1933 with songs such as 'It Had To Be You', 'All Alone', 'Who Takes Care Of The Caretaker's Daughter?', 'If You Knew Susie', 'Paddlin' Madelin' Home', 'Remember', 'Dinah', 'Sunday', 'I'm Tellin' The Birds And Bees (How I Love You)', 'Together', 'Mary Ann' and 'I Can't Give You Anything But Love'. On many records he was joined by top instrumentalists such as **Jimmy Dorsey**, **Miff Mole** and **Red Nichols**, and was credited with playing the kazoo, though it is fairly certain that it was a vocal effect, unaided by any instrument. In the early 30s Edwards' career waned, but was revived in 1940 when he provided the voice of Jiminy Cricket in **Walt Disney**'s animated classic *Pinocchio*. Two of the movie's most popular numbers, 'Give A Little Whistle' and 'When You Wish Upon A Star' (which won an Oscar for Best Song), were Edwards' first hits for seven years, and his last US chart entries. In 1941 he became the voice of another Disney cartoon character, Jim Crow, in *Dumbo*, and despite poor health and alcohol problems, continued to work for the studio, recording children's songs, and making appearances in the television series *Mickey Mouse Club*.

● COMPILATIONS: *I Want A Girl* (1978) ★★★, *Cliff Edwards And His Hot Combination* (1979) ★★, *The Hottest Man In Town* (1981) ★★★, *Fascinatin' Rhythm* (1988) ★★★, *Shakin' The Blues Away* (1988) ★★.

Edwards, David 'Honeyboy'

b. 28 June 1915, Shaw, Mississippi, USA. Born and raised in the Mississippi Delta country, Edwards played with and learned from such important blues figures as **Charley Patton**, **Robert Johnson** and **'Big' Joe Williams**. His first recordings were made for the Library of Congress in 1941, a set of typical Mississippi country blues, demonstrating a tense, emotional vocal delivery and considerable skills on harmonica and, particularly, guitar. Ten years later, his first commercial recording appeared on the obscure Texas label ARC, and in the next couple of years he also recorded for **Sun Records** in Memphis and **Chess Records** in Chicago, although nothing was issued at the time. Rediscovered in the 60s in Chicago, Edwards has made several fine albums, encompassing traditional country blues as well as more urban stylings. He has also toured widely, playing in Europe several times in recent years. A fascinating autobiography was published in 1997.

● ALBUMS: *I've Been Around* (Trix 1979) ★★★, *White Windows* (1989) ★★★, *Mississippi Blues: Library Of Congress Recordings* (1991) ★★★, *Delta Bluesman* (Indigo 1992) ★★★★, *The World Don't Owe Me Nothing* (Earwig 1997) ★★★, *Shake 'Em On Down* (Harmonia Mundi 2000) ★★★.

● COMPILATIONS: *Crawling Kingsnake* (Testament 1998) ★★★★.

● FURTHER READING: *The World Don't Owe Me Nothing: The Life And Times Of Delta Bluesman Honeyboy Edwards*, David Honeyboy Edwards with Janis Martinson and Michael Robert Frank.

Edwards, Dennis

b. 3 February 1943, Birmingham, Alabama, USA. Dennis Edwards became a member of the Fireworks vocal group in the early 60s, before joining the **Contours** in 1965. After they split in 1967, he appeared occasionally with the **Temptations**, becoming a full member of the band when he replaced **David Ruffin** as lead vocalist in 1968. He remained with them until 1977, lending his dramatic tenor voice to hits such as 'Cloud Nine', 'I Can't Get Next To You' and 'Papa Was A Rolling Stone'. When the Temptations left **Motown Records** for **Atlantic Records**, he chose to remain with the label and begin a solo career. While he was still working on his debut album, the band returned to Motown, and Edwards resumed his position as their lead singer. In 1984, he again parted company with the band, notching up a major hit single, 'Don't Look No Further', a duet with **Siedah Garrett**. Three additional chart successes followed in 1985, and Edwards also issued two well-received albums. When his solo career ran into difficulties in 1987, he accepted the invitation to rejoin the Temptations, and was featured on their 1987 release, *Together Again*.

● ALBUMS: *Don't Look Any Further* (Gordy 1984) ★★★, *Coolin' Out* (Gordy 1985) ★★★.

Edwards, Don

b. 20 March 1939, Boonton, New Jersey, USA. Although born in an unlikely state for cowboys, Edwards has become one of the leading exponents of cowboy and western music. He taught himself guitar at the age of 10 and grew up listening to his father's 78s of such singers as **Carl T. Sprague** and **Gene Autry**, and avidly read any books on cowboy life that he could find. He was impressed by cowboys on the silver screen, especially Tom Mix and **Ken Maynard**, whom he described as 'sure 'nuff cowboys without the glitz and glitter'. In 1958, he headed west to work on ranches and at rodeos in Texas and New Mexico.

Between 1961 and 1964, after painful rodeo experiences, Edwards turned to music and worked as a cowboy singer, actor, gunfighter and stuntman at the Fort Worth amusement park Six Flags Over Texas—his desire to perform, no doubt, inherited from his father who had been a vaudeville magician. A visit to Nashville in 1965 quickly convinced him that Music City was not for him, and after a short spell in Florida, he returned to Fort Worth. His residency at the prestigious White Elephant Saloon (named by *Esquire* magazine among America's 100 best bars) and personal appearances soon established him throughout Texas and Oklahoma.

Edwards is now regarded as a leading authority on all things Western, especially the songs and poems. He has presented programmes on cowboy songs and their history, not only in schools, but also at Yale and Harvard, the Smithsonian Institute and other important venues, as well as on network television and radio. An admirer of the work of song collector Nathan 'Jack' Thorp (1867-1940), he published his own book, *Songs Of The Cowboy*, in 1986. Edwards, the **Sons Of The San Joaquin** and cowboy poet **Waddie Mitchell** were the first artists signed by the new Warner Western label. He now appears with those acts in The Cowboy Jubilee, a travelling show of Western music and verse. Before joining Warner, he released five albums on his own label. He has toured Europe and Australasia but resides in Parker County, Texas, on his beloved Sevenshoux Ranch. He is a great admirer of **Marty Robbins** and his influence may be noted in Edwards' own singing. He described his dedication to promoting cowboy songs by saying, 'Usually, kids play cowboys and stuff like that, but they grow out of it. I never did. My only regret is that I was born about fifty years too late. However, I'm mighty thankful I wasn't born any later than I was.'

● ALBUMS: *Happy Cowboy* (Sevenshoux 1980) ★★★, *Songs Of The Cowboy* (Sevenshoux 1986) ★★★, *Guitars And Saddle Songs* (Sevenshoux 1987) ★★★, *Desert Nights & Cowtown Blues* (Sevenshoux 1990) ★★★, *Chant Of The Wanderer* (Sevenshoux 1992) ★★★, *Songs Of The Trail* (Warner Western 1992) ★★★★, *Goin' Back To Texas* (Warner Western 1993) ★★★, with Waddie Mitchell *The Bard And The Balladeer* (Warner Western 1994) ★★★, *West Of Yesterday* (Warner Western 1996) ★★★★, *Saddle Songs* (Western Jubilee/Shanachie 1997) ★★★★, *My Hero Gene Autry: A Tribute* (Western Jubilee/Shanachie 1998) ★★★, with Mitchell, the Fort Worth Symphony Orchestra *A Prairie Portrait* (Western Jubilee/Shanachie 2000) ★★★, *Kin To The Wind: Memories Of Marty Robbins* (Western Jubilee/Shanachie 2001) ★★★, *Last Of The Troubadours: Saddle Songs II* (Western Jubilee/Shanachie 2004) ★★★, *Moonlight And Skies* (Western Jubilee 2006) ★★★.

● COMPILATIONS: *The Best Of Don Edwards* (Warners 1998) ★★★★.

Edwards, Eddie

b. Edwin Branford Edwards, 22 May 1891, New Orleans, Louisiana, USA, d. 9 April 1963, New York City, USA. After playing violin in various local bands Edwards switched to trombone, which he played in **Papa Jack Laine**'s band. In 1916 Edwards was in a band led by **Johnny Stein** that went to Chicago. Later that year Edwards left the band and, with **Nick LaRocca**, formed a new outfit named the **Original Dixieland Jazz Band**. Although interrupted by military service in World War I, Edwards remained more or less constantly with the ODJB until 1925. For some years he worked outside music but was back in the mid-30s playing in revivals of the ODJB and with other like-minded bands. In the 50s and 60s he performed with various groups, mostly in and around New York, and was also accompanist to the Katherine Dunham dance troupe. Edwards also composed music, including 'Tiger Rag', 'Fidgety Feet' and 'The Original Dixieland One-Step'. A powerful player with a strong rhythmic sense, Edwards was ideally suited for the gutsy ensemble playing that so captivated audiences attracted by the 'new-fangled'

music of the ODJB. His legacy is best exemplified by the countless performances of his compositions that have echoed down the years.

Edwards, Frank

b. 20 March 1909, Washington, Georgia, USA, d. 22 March 2002, Greenville, South Carolina, USA. Raised in St. Petersburg, Florida, Edwards took up guitar at an early age, adding rack harmonica in 1934. He became an itinerant musician, with his home base in Atlanta, where he played with the Star Band, whose members included **Leroy Dallas**, a long-time associate. In 1941, Edwards recorded for **OKeh Records**, a session that was set up by Lester Melrose, manager of **Tommy McClennan**, with whom he was travelling at the time. Settling in Atlanta after World War II, he recorded for **Savoy Records** in 1949, but the titles remained unissued until the 60s, by which time Edwards himself had stopped playing, Nevertheless, he was rediscovered in the 70s, and proved able to recreate his old sound with little difficulty.

● ALBUMS: *Done Some Travelin'* (Trix 1972) ★★★, *Sugar Mama Blues* 1949 recordings (Biograph 1980) ★★★.

Edwards, Granville

b. Granville Mortlock Edwards, 3 February 1921, St. Anne's Parish, Brownstone, Jamaica, d. 7 August 2004, Manchester, England. Edwards' father was a bandmaster and as a boy he played trumpet under his tutelage. A lip injury prompted a change to reed instruments and he eventually settled with the tenor saxophone. A liking for jazz developed after hearing the music on radio and as a teenager he formed his own band, playing dance music. In 1940, he visited the USA, working at various jobs in several states, hoping to accumulate enough money to buy decent instruments for his musicians back home. Back in Jamaica, he lived and worked in Kingston where he heard bop, again courtesy of the radio, and was interested enough to seek to bring this form of jazz into his repertoire.

In 1948, Edwards went to Britain on the SS *Empire Windrush*, one of many West Indians forming a part of the new wave of migrants that was to have a lasting effect on British culture and in particular on music in London. Edwards lived in various parts of the UK before taking up residence in Manchester where he was to remain almost continuously for a half century. He took factory work, but formed a band that played whenever and wherever they, or it could find work. He continued with a day job, with music as a sideline that was more important to him for its intrinsic benefits than as a secondary income. His bands were usually multi-racial, with Africans, West Indians, Europeans; their music, ethnically-charged contemporary jazz with a pronounced Caribbean feel. One of his sidemen was bass player **Lord Kitchener**, better known as a calypso singer. From time to time, jazz musicians from London on visits to Manchester would seek out and sit in with Edwards, notably **Tubby Hayes** and **Joe Harriott**.

Edwards continued in this vein, day job and music by night, for the next 30 years, sometimes playing hotels, but mostly pubs and clubs. At first, he was able to cash in on the trad jazz boom although his musical interests were much more varied and flexible. Among locally-based musicians with whom he played were banjoist Martin Boorman, whom he joined in Mardi Gras, a band that also included trumpeter

Cuff Billett and bass player Mickey Ashman. Edwards also played with gospel singer Sheila Collier and a fellow Jamaican, pianist Chester Harriott. It was through his connection with the latter that Edwards began to work regularly at Granada Television's Manchester studios, chiefly off screen. The Granada band, actually trombonist Dave Donahoe's Hi-Life Band, a New Orleans–style marching band, entertained tourists visiting the studios and also played outside gigs, including performing at 1990's festival at Ascona, Switzerland.

Edwards continued playing until shortly after the 1994 Cork Jazz Festival when he was forced to abandon his instrument owing to a blood clot on the lung. A few years later, this habitually retiring artist's profile was raised a little when he became the subject of an affectionate article by Val Wilmer in the September 1998 issue of *Jazz Journal International*.

● ALBUMS: with Mardi Gras *Chant Of The Tuxedos* (All That Jazz 1985) ★★★.

Edwards, Gus

b. Gus Simon, 18 August 1879, Hohensaliza, Germany (then Prussia), d. 7 November 1945, Los Angeles, California, USA. Edwards was seven when his family settled in New York City. As a child he sang in saloons, soon going into vaudeville. In 1896 he joined the Newsboys Quintet and while on tour wrote his first song, 'All I Want Is My Black Baby Back'. Teamed with lyricist Will Cobb, he wrote 'Sunbonnet Sue', 'The Singer And The Song', 'In Zanzibar' and, in 1905, their first hit, 'I Can't Tell Why I Love You, But I Do'. His songs were performed in Broadway shows: *Hodge, Podge & Co.* (1900), *The Medal And The Maid* (1904), *When We Were Forty-One* (1905), *His Honor The Mayor*, *The Blue Moon* and *A Parisian Model* (all 1906), *Ziegfeld Follies Of 1907*, *The Hired Girl's Millions* and *Hip! Hip! Hooray!* (all 1907), *The-Merry-Go-Round* and *Miss Innocence* (both 1908), and he wrote the book for *Ziegfeld Follies Of 1910*. From 1907 he staged revues, notably *School Boys And Girls*, which continued into the late 20s. The Edwards/Cobb song 'School Days (When We Were A Couple Of Kids)' generated sheet music sales in excess of three million. Edwards collaborated on songs with Vincent Bryan, 'In My Merry Oldsmobile', a big hit, and 'He's My Pal', and with Edward Madden, 'Jimmy Valentine' and, best remembered today, 'By The Light Of The Silvery Moon'.

In the late 20s, Edwards went to Hollywood where he collaborated on some film scores, directed a few short subjects and appeared briefly on screen in films such as *The Song Writers' Revue* (1930). Films were not his métier, and by 1930 he was back in vaudeville. One of his last shows was *Broadway Sho-Window* (1936). His brother, Leo Edwards, was also a prolific songwriter. Among many artists discovered or encouraged by Edwards early in their careers are **Ray Bolger**, **Eddie Cantor**, **Hildegarde**, **Ina Ray Hutton**, **Elsie Janis**, **George Jessel**, the Lane Sisters, Groucho Marx, Mae Murray, **Eleanor Powell**, Sally Rand and future newspaper columnist Walter Winchell. Small wonder that he became known as 'The Star Maker'. Edwards retired from showbusiness in 1939 and when, in 1940, **Bing Crosby** starred in a Hollywood biopic that told Edwards' story, it was apt that it should be entitled *The Star Maker*.

● FILMS: *Wanted: A Leading Lady* (1915), *The Hollywood Revue Of 1929* (1929), *Mexicana* (1929), *The Song Writers' Revue* (1930), *School Days* (1932), *Mr. Broadway* (1933).

Edwards, Jackie

b. Wilfred Edwards, 1938, Jamaica, West Indies, d. 15 August 1992. The honeyed tones of Jackie Edwards graced hundreds of ska, R&B, soul, **rocksteady**, reggae and ballad recordings since he composed and sang 'Your Eyes Are Dreaming', a sentimental ballad, and the gentle Latin-beat 'Tell Me Darling', for future **Island Records** owner **Chris Blackwell** in 1959. Probably the most accomplished romantic singer and songwriter that Jamaica ever produced, he always had enough soul in his voice to escape the descent into schmaltz. In 1962, when Blackwell set up Island Records in London, Edwards made the trip to Britain with him. At Island in the early years, his duties included not only singing and songwriting but also delivering boxes of ska records by bus to the capital's suburban shops. His persistence paid off when, in 1966, the **Spencer Davis Group** enjoyed two consecutive UK number 1 pop hits with his now classic compositions 'Keep On Running' and 'Somebody Help Me'. In later years he continued to issue records whose standards of production were variable, but on which his crooning justified his sobriquet of 'the original cool ruler'.

● ALBUMS: *The Most Of Jackie Edwards* (Island 1963) ★★★, *Stand Up For Jesus* (Island 1964) ★★★, *Come On Home* (Island 1966) ★★★★, *By Demand* (Island 1967) ★★★, *Premature Golden Sands* (Island 1967) ★★★, with Millie Small *Pledging My Love* (Island 1967) ★★★, *I Do Love You* (Trojan 1973) ★★★, with Hortense Ellis *Let It Be Me* (Jamaica Sound 1978) ★★★, *Sincerely* (Trojan 1978) ★★, *King Of The Ghetto* (Black Music 1983) ★★, *Original Cool Ruler* (Vista Sounds 1983) ★★.

● COMPILATIONS: *The Best Of Jackie Edwards* (Island 1966) ★★★, with Millie Small *The Best Of Jackie & Millie* (Island 1968) ★★★, *20 Super Hits* (Sonic Sounds 1994) ★★★, *This Is My Story* (Trojan 2004) ★★★.

Edwards, Jonathan

b. 28 July 1946, Aitkin, Minnesota, USA. After forming the bluegrass band Sugar Creek in 1965, Edwards took up songwriting. Opting for a more commercial style, he saw his own composition, 'Sunshine', featuring a mid-tempo driving beat via an acoustic guitar, move swiftly up the US Hot 100 in late 1971, and peak at number 4. His self-titled album also included the ballad 'Emma' and the follow-up single 'Train Of Glory', which never charted. Subsequent albums moved towards a purer country sound, but with his sales falling Edwards eschewed his recording career to run a farm in Nova Scotia. He continued to feature on recordings by other performers, including **Emmylou Harris**, **Jimmy Buffett** and **Tom Chapin**, and resurfaced in the late 70s on the **Reprise Records** label. He also produced an album, *Rainbow Reign*, for his wife Carolina, a one-time backing singer for Edwards. Another lengthy recording hiatus ensued, before the singer returned with a live album on his own Chronic Records label. While Edwards' style has always veered between folk and country, his 1985 collaboration with the **Seldom Scene** bluegrass band saw him succeed in reworking earlier originals alongside more standard bluegrass material. 'We Need To Be Locked Away' from 1989's *The Natural Thing* was a big country hit. In addition to recording the occasional studio album Edwards has remained busy as a session player. He also composed the soundtrack for *The Mouse*, and provided the narration for the video series *Cruising America's Waterways*.

● ALBUMS: *Jonathan Edwards* (Atco 1971) ★★★★, *Honky-Tonk Stardust Cowboy* (Atco 1972) ★★★, *Have A Good Time For Me* (Atco 1973) ★★★, *Lucky Day* (Atco 1974) ★★★, *Rockin' Chair* (Reprise 1976) ★★★, *Sail Boat* (Reprise 1977) ★★, *Jonathan Edwards Live!* (Chronic 1982) ★★★, with Seldom Scene *Blue Ridge* (Sugar Hill 1985) ★★★, *Little Hands—Songs For And About Children* (American Melody 1987) ★★, *The Natural Thing* (MCA Curb 1989) ★★★, *One Day Closer* (Rising 1994) ★★★, *Man In The Moon* (Rising 1997) ★★★.

Edwards, Jonathan And Darlene
(see **Stafford, Jo**; **Weston, Paul**)

Edwards, Kathleen
b. Ottawa, Ontario, Canada. Singer-songwriter Edwards spent much of her childhood in South Korea or Switzerland owing to her father's work for the diplomatic corps. Trained on classical violin as a youngster, Edwards launched her musical career in the late 90s as a singer-songwriter. She established her reputation on Ottawa's downtown folk scene and in 1999 released the EP *Building 55*, a quirky collection of rootsy country pop. She moved out of the city and into the Quebec countryside to complete the writing for her debut album. Recording work on what would become *Failer* began in late 2000, with Edwards joined by many colleagues from the Ottawa scene, notably fellow singer-songwriter Jim Bryson and producer Dave Draves. Originally given an independent release in early 2002, *Failer* was remixed for distribution on the **Rounder Records**' imprint Zöe later in the year. The album drew favourable, if somewhat lazy, comparisons to the work of alt country favourite **Lucinda Williams**. Edwards' drink-sodden and love-weary tales of faltering relationships played out in honky-tonks and bars often belied her 23 years, although the bitter imagery and spiky put-downs of 'Hockey Skates', 'Six O'Clock News' and 'Westby' marked her out as an utterly contemporary writer. Edwards and her band spent the next two years touring in support of her debut, including prestigious opening slots for **Bob Dylan** and the **Rolling Stones**. At the start of 2004 she returned to the recording studio to begin work on her highly anticipated second album. Edwards and her producer Colin Cripps stuck close to the formula established on *Failer*, with guest musicians Benmont Tench and Eric Heywood adding subtle textures to the rock-solid backing of the singer's road band. Released at the start of 2005, *Back To Me* served further notice of Edwards' songwriting talents on tracks such as 'In State', 'Summerlong' and 'Away'.

● ALBUMS: *Failer* (Socan/Zöe 2002) ★★★★, *Back To Me* (Zöe 2005) ★★★★.

Edwards, Marc
b. 23 July 1949, New York City, USA. Percussionist and drummer Edwards received formal drum tuition from established players including Ted Reed and **Alan Dawson**. He played with various ensembles during his teenage years, including his local All City High School Band and the American Symphony Orchestra. He first came to notice with his notable contribution to **Cecil Taylor**'s powerful *Dark Unto Themselves* in 1976. Edwards has recorded some of his most challenging work with **David S. Ware** (*Passage To Music*, *Great Bliss*, *Flight Of i*) and **Charles Gayle** (*More Live At KF*).

Edwards debuted with his own band in 1990 and has performed at numerous festivals. He is a drummer who creates space where necessary and demonstrates his considerable percussive skills where demanded (such as on 'Bumblebees And Marigold Flowers' from *Black Queen*). His own recordings as leader have featured notable work by alto saxophonist **Rob Brown** and tenor player Sabir Mateen.

● ALBUMS: *Black Queen* (Alpha Phonics 1991) ★★★★, *Time & Space Vol. 1* (Alpha Phonics 1993) ★★, *Red Sprites & Blue Jets* (CIMP 1997) ★★★.

Edwards, Moanin' Bernice
b. *c.*1910, Houston, Texas, USA. Bernice Edwards was described by **Beulah 'Sippie' Wallace** as being 'one of the family'; the family in question was Sippie's own renowned Thomas Family of Houston, Bernice being the same age as its most gifted member, the child prodigy **Hersal Thomas**. From another member of the family, **Hociel Thomas**, she learned to play the piano and sing the blues. She remained in Houston when the family moved north and was often in the company of **Black Boy Shine** (Harold Holiday). When she recorded for Paramount in 1928 these influences were evident in her introspective 'moanin' blues and her piano style. When she attended her third and last session (for ARC in 1935) she was in the company of Holiday and one record was issued by her, Holiday and Howling Smith together. Apart from the fact that she later married and joined the church, little more is known.

● COMPILATIONS: *The Thomas Family* (1977) ★★★.

Edwards, Rupie
b. 4 July 1945, Goshen, near Brownstown, St. Anns, Jamaica, West Indies. Edwards found his first musical inspiration while attending the Anglican church school in Sergeantville as a seven-year-old. In early 1958 he moved to Kingston, where he attended Kingston Senior School and, like others of similar musical inclination, he formed a band with home-made instruments, bamboo saxophone and thumb piano, and performed at school concerts. In 1962 he had appeared on Vere John's *Opportunity Hour* and the same year he made four records, for the Hi-Lite label based at the Hi-Lite Haberdashery, and for the Little Wonder Music Store in Kingston. One title, 'Guilty Convict', was released in the UK on **Blue Beat Records**. Edwards was paid £15 for the session. He made two more records for President Bell's **sound system**, and then two further titles with Junior Menz, 'Mother's Choice' and a cover version of the **Impressions**' 'Amen'. By the mid-60s, Edwards was a member of the Virtues, again with Menz and guitarist Eric Frater.

From 1968, Edwards began to release his own productions; the first was 'Burning Love', recorded at **Studio One** and engineered by **Coxsone Dodd** and Graham Goodall. This and other early productions enabled him to devote himself full-time to music and give up his job at a local garage, where he repaired cars owned by Dodd and **Duke Reid**. By the early 70s Edwards had produced hits by himself and other artists, including **Bob Andy**, **Joe Higgs**, the **Ethiopians** and the Tellers, and had been instrumental in bringing the talents of **Johnny Clarke** and **Gregory Isaacs** to the attention of the public. He also recorded DJs such as the late **U-Roy** Junior, **Shorty** and **I. Roy**, as well as scores of excellent instrumentals by Jamaica's finest session musicians.

In December 1974 Edwards' single 'Ire Feelings (Skanga)' entered the UK charts and stayed there for the next 10 weeks, eventually reaching number 9. The follow-up, 'Leggo Skanga', charted for six weeks from February 1975. During this period Edwards issued an entire album on which all the tracks used the same backing track. This concept subsequently became an important feature of Jamaican music. The album, *Yamaha Skank*, utilized a rhythm given to Edwards by producer **Bunny Lee**, **Slim Smith**'s 'My Conversation'. Following his UK chart success, Edwards took up residence in London, continuing his operations from there up to the present day. Edwards released a series of his own oldies in both 12-inch and album form and also leased some material to Creole during the 70s, though there were no further hits. He continued to record material for the religious and sentimental love song markets, enjoying steady sales, and operating his own retail outlet.

● ALBUMS: *Yamaha Skank* (Success 1974) ★★★★, *Rupie Edwards Dub Basket* (Cactus 1976) ★★★★, *Dub Basket Chapter 2* (Cactus 1976) ★★★, *Jamaica Serenade* (Cactus 1976) ★★★, *Dub Classic* (Success 1977) ★★★★, *Hit Picks Volume 1* (Cactus 1977) ★★★, *Ire Feelings: Chapter & Version* (Trojan 1990) ★★★, *Let There Be Version* (Trojan 1990) ★★★.

Edwards, Scott

Bristol, England–based electronic musician who, though he has never DJed, became in the mid-90s a name on the dance circuit through his experimental approach. Recording for Out Of Orbit, a subsidiary of Italian label ACV (Annibaldi, Armani, etc.), his work reveals a stylistic debt to the Detroit techno godfathers: 'There's nothing pretentious about what I do, it's just that I have ideas which are a little different to most other people. I'm not making music which says "take ecstasy all the time". I'm trying to think beyond that.'

● ALBUMS: *Distant Horizons* (Out Of Orbit 1994) ★★★.

Edwards, Sherman

b. 3 April 1919, New York City, USA, d. 30 March 1981, New York, USA. After studying history at New York University, Edwards taught American history at James Monroe High School. He had other interests and performed as an actor, including appearing in **Harold Rome**'s Broadway revue *Pins And Needles*, which ran with a changing cast from 1937–40. He also played piano with noted artists of the worlds of pop and jazz. He wrote some songs, including 'Broken-Hearted Melody' (with **Hal David**), 'See You In September' (Sid Wayne) and 'Wonderful, Wonderful' (Ben Raleigh). Over the years, Edwards had worked extensively on a project that would bring together all his areas of interest. This was the book for what eventually became the Broadway show *1776* (1969). He took the book through numerous drafts and in addition composed the music and wrote the lyrics of the songs. For the final draft of the show, Edwards was in collaboration with **Peter Stone**, who was thereafter often credited with the book. The show was a huge success, running for more than 1,200 performances and winning a **Tony Award** as Best Musical, as well as Tony awards for Best Supporting Actor (Ronald Holgate) and Best Director (Peter Hunt). A 1970 London production was unsuccessful, perhaps because the subject matter, the breaking away from Britain of colonists and their formation of the United States of America, was quintessentially American. Revivals in the USA in 1991 and on Broadway in 1997 proved the show's lasting quality, which stands firmly upon its well-structured book, more a play with songs than a musical, and remains testimony to Edwards' vision and determination. Stone also wrote the screenplay for the 1972 film version of *1776*, which was directed by Hunt.

Edwards, Stoney

b. Frenchy Edwards, 24 December 1929, Seminole, Oklahoma, USA, d. 5 April 1997. Stoney grew up listening to country music, an upbringing described in his 1973 song 'Hank And Lefty Raised My Country Soul', and that honky tonk sound remained with him throughout his career. He played guitar from the age of 15. He moved to California and had several manual jobs before becoming a club singer and, like **Charley Pride** before him, he was at first something of a novelty in Nashville—a black performer working in country music. He signed with **Capitol Records** in 1971 and had 15 chart singles including 'Poor Folks Stick Together', 'She's My Rock', 'Mississippi, You're On My Mind' and 'Blackbird (Hold Your Head High)'. He was dropped by Capitol in 1977 and he recorded for several smaller labels including the Music America release *No Way To Drown A Memory*. He lost a leg in a shooting accident and retired from the business, but returned in 1991 with an acclaimed new album, *Just For Old Times Sake*, which was produced and mostly written by Billy Joe Kirk and featured many top session musicians. Edwards died of stomach cancer in April 1997.

● ALBUMS: *Stoney Edwards, A Country Singer* (Capitol 1971) ★★★, *Down Home In The Country* (Capitol 1972) ★★★, *She's My Rock* (Capitol 1973) ★★, *Mississippi, You're On My Mind* (Capitol 1975) ★★★, *Blackbird* (Capitol 1976) ★★, *No Way To Drown A Memory* (Music America 1981) ★★, *Just For Old Time's Sake* (CMP 1991) ★★★.

● COMPILATIONS: *The Best Of Stoney Edwards: Poor Folks Stick Together* (Razor & Tie 1998) ★★★★.

Edwards, Teddy

b. Theodore Marcus Edwards, 26 April 1924, Jackson, Mississippi, USA, d. 20 April 2003, Los Angeles, California, USA. As a child Edwards played alto saxophone with local bands and continued playing this instrument when he moved to Detroit in 1940. He toured with **territory bands** in Michigan and Florida including those led by **Ernie Fields** and **Stack Walton**. In the Walton band he played alongside several proto-boppers including **Howard McGhee**, **Wardell Gray** and **Al McKibbon**. In 1944, Edwards settled in California and after playing with an R&B band led by **Roy Milton** he joined McGhee, switching to tenor saxophone. The McGhee band worked sporadically over the next couple of years, recording for Ross Russell's Dial Records. The resulting four sides, 'Dilated Pupils', 'Midnight At Minton's', '52nd Street Theme' and 'Up In Dodo's Room', achieved the status of minor classics and the final title alerted fans and musicians to the possibility that the tenor saxophone could go down pathways other than those previously trod by **Coleman Hawkins** and **Lester Young**. In part, Edwards' original concept arose from his youthful experience on alto and his interest at the time in the music of **Charlie 'Bird' Parker**. This was his first recording session but he quickly made up for his late start and during the next months was regularly featured on many of the best west coast record sessions. In December 1947, he appeared on a **Dexter Gordon** session where the two tenor players duetted on 'The Duel', a fairly successful attempt to repeat the earlier success of Gordon's and Gray's 'The Chase'.

In the early 50s Edwards became a weekend regular at the Lighthouse, playing with **Shorty Rogers**, **Shelly Manne**, **Hampton Hawes** and others. In 1954, he joined the quintet co-led by **Max Roach** and **Clifford Brown**, replacing **Sonny Stitt** only to be replaced himself soon afterwards by **Harold Land**. He also worked in San Francisco during this period but periodic bouts of ill health, mostly related to dental problems, kept him out of the spotlight and also away from the recording studios. In 1960, he recorded for **Contemporary Records** as nominal leader of a co-operative quartet comprising pianist Joe Castro, **Leroy Vinnegar** and **Billy Higgins**. Their album, *Teddy's Ready!*, proved popular and the following year Edwards was reunited at Contemporary with McGhee, then recovering from a bout of drug addiction. This album, *Together Again!!!!*, was similarly successful and helped the re-establishment of Edwards as a potent voice in jazz. In the 60s he played with **Benny Goodman** and **Milt Jackson** and in the 70s worked with **Jimmy Smith** and singers **Sarah Vaughan** and **Tom Waits**. He also began touring internationally and continued doing so throughout the 80s. In 1991, he worked with **Bill Berry** and his LA Big Band for concerts at the Hollywood Bowl, having played in the band intermittently since the early 70s.

In between jazz dates, Edwards worked extensively in the studios, playing and writing for radio and television. He was the composer of many songs, including 'Sunset Eyes'. In the post-bop era, Edwards was a fluent and creative performer. His wide experience and imaginative mainstream concepts gave his music a thoroughly contemporary feel but remained deeply rooted in the great blues-influenced traditions of jazz.

● ALBUMS: *Teddy's Ready!* (Contemporary 1960) ★★★, with Howard McGhee *Together Again!!!!* (Contemporary 1961) ★★★★, *Good Gravy!* (Timeless 1961) ★★★, *Heart & Soul* (Contemporary 1962) ★★★, *Nothin' But The Truth!* (Prestige 1966) ★★★, *It's All Right* (Prestige 1967) ★★★, *Feelin's* (Muse 1974) ★★★, *The Inimitable* (Xanadu 1976) ★★★, with McGhee *Wise In Time* (Storyville 1979) ★★★, with McGhee, Benny Bailey *Home Run* (Storyville 1979) ★★★, *Out Of This World* (SteepleChase 1980) ★★★, *Mississippi Lad* (Antilles Gitanes 1991) ★★★, with Buck Hill, Von Freeman *Tenor Conclave* (Timeless 1992) ★★★, *Blue Saxophone* (Verve Gitanes/Polydor 1992) ★★★★, *La Villa, Live In Paris* (Verve Gitanes 1994) ★★, *Tango In Harlem* (Verve Gitanes 1994) ★★★, with Houston Person *Horn To Horn* (Muse 1994) ★★★, *Back To Avalon* 1960 recording (Contemporary 1995) ★★★, with James Van Buren *Live At Vartan Jazz* (Vartan Jazz 1995) ★★★, with Person *Close Encounters* (HighNote 1996) ★★★, *Midnight Creeper* (HighNote 1997) ★★★, with Saskia Laroo *Sunset Eyes 2000* (Laroo 1999) ★★★, *Ladies Man* (HighNote 2001) ★★, *The Legend Of Teddy Edwards* (Cope 2001) ★★★, *Smooth Sailing* (HighNote 2003) ★★★.

● COMPILATIONS: *Steady With Teddy* (Cool N'Blue) ★★★, with McGhee *Trumpet At Tempo* 1945-47 recordings (Spotlite 1983) ★★★★.

● DVD/VIDEOS: *The Legend Of Teddy Edwards* (Image 2002).

Edwards, Terry

b. 10 August 1960, Hornchurch, Essex, England. One of the unsung heroes of the UK music scene, multi-instrumentalist Edwards has worked with countless artists as a hired hand while also touring and recording with his own bands, most notably the Scapegoats.

Edwards learned to play the trumpet, piano and guitar at school, and received a saxophone for his 18th birthday. After leaving school he went into further education, studying for a degree in music from the University of East Anglia. During this period he formed the **Higsons** with Charlie 'Switch' Higson, Stuart McGeachin, Simon Charterton and Colin Williams. The quintet went on to enjoy a series of minor UK indie hits between 1980 and 1986. Following the break-up of the Higsons, Edwards formed **Butterfield 8** with ex-**Madness** bass player Mark Bedford. The duo released a solitary album, 1988's jazz and blues-tinged *Blow*.

Edwards began recording solo material at the start of the following decade, reinventing songs by the **Jesus And Mary Chain**, the **Fall** and **Miles Davis** for three EPs released on Jacko Boogie's Stim label and later compiled on 1993's *Plays, Salutes & Executes*. In the mid-90s Edwards formed the Scapegoats, a highly skilled ensemble whose playful approach to music making saw them tackling pop, jazz, blues and rock 'n' roll with equal aplomb. Edwards and the Scapegoats made their recording debut in 1995 with 'Girls And Boys'. The excellent *My Wife Doesn't Understand Me*, featuring the acerbic 'Margaret Thatcher, We Still Hate You', followed later in the year.

Since the late 80s onwards, Edwards has balanced his solo career with extensive time in the studio and on the live circuit as a session musician. The list of artists with whom he has performed includes **Yeah Jazz**, **Madness**, **Gallon Drunk**, **David Gray**, **PJ Harvey**, **Billy Bragg**, **Jimi Tenor**, **Lydia Lunch**, **Spiritualized**, **Nick Cave** and the **Tindersticks**. In 2002, Edwards performed with the Scapegoats at the **David Bowie**-curated Meltdown festival in London.

● ALBUMS: with the Scapegoats *My Wife Doesn't Understand Me* (Stim 1995) ★★★★, with the Scapegoats *I Didn't Get Where I Am Today* (Stim 1997) ★★★), *Yesterday's Zeitgeist: Terry Edwards In Concert* (Los 1999) ★★★, with Lydia Lunch *Memory And Madness* spoken word (Sartorial 2003) ★★★, *Terryedwards* (Sartorial 2005) ★★★.

● COMPILATIONS: *Plays, Salutes & Executes* (Stim 1993) ★★★★, *No Fish Is Too Weird For Her Aquarium* (Stim 1994) ★★★★, *Large Door* (Damaged Goods 1998) ★★★, *Birth Of The Scapegoats* (Hux 1998) ★★★, *Ontogeny: No Fish Is Too Weird For Her Aquarium Vol. II* (Sartorial 2000) ★★★, *681 At The Southbank* (Sartorial 2002) ★★★.

Edwards, Tommy

b. 17 February 1922, Richmond, Virginia, USA, d. 22 October 1969, Virginia, USA. This jazz/pop/R&B singer-songwriter began his professional career in 1931. He wrote the hit 'That Chick's Too Young To Fry' for **Louis Jordan** in 1946. A demo recording of his own 'All Over Again' later won Edwards an **MGM Records** contract. Early releases included 'It's All In The Game' (US number 18 in 1951), a tune based on a 1912 melody by future US Vice-President Charles Gates Dawes. Edwards re-recorded the song in 1958 in a 'beat-ballad' arrangement, hitting number 1 on both sides of the Atlantic and eventually selling 3.5 million. The song was an indisputable classic of its era, highlighted by Edwards' strong, masterful vocal. The song was covered many times and provided hits for **Cliff Richard** (1963–64) and the **Four Tops** (1970) and was a notable album track by **Van Morrison** (1979). Edwards himself enjoyed five more hits during the next two years, including 'Love Is All We Need' and remakes of earlier successes 'Please Mr. Sun' and 'Morning Side Of The Mountain'.

● ALBUMS: *For Young Lovers* (MGM 1958) ★★★, *Tommy Edwards Sings* (Regent 1959) ★★, *It's All In The Game* (MGM 1959) ★★★★, *Step Out Singing* (MGM 1960) ★★★★, *You Started Me Dreaming* (MGM 1960) ★★★, *Tommy Edwards In Hawaii* (MGM 1960) ★, *Golden Country Hits* (MGM 1961) ★, *Stardust* (MGM 1962) ★★★, *Soft Strings And Two Guitars* (MGM 1962) ★★★, *Tommy Edwards* (1965) ★★.

● COMPILATIONS: *Tommy Edwards' Greatest Hits* (MGM 1961) ★★★, *The Very Best Of Tommy Edwards* (MGM 1963) ★★★, *It's All In The Game: The Complete Hits* (Epic 1995) ★★★★.

Eek-A-Mouse

b. Ripton Joseph Hilton, 19 November 1957, Kingston, Jamaica, West Indies. It is not only Eek-A-Mouse's 6 feet 6 inches height that make him one of Jamaica's most individual talents. Hilton's unusual name was originally that of a racehorse upon which he frequently lost money; when the horse finally won a race, he had, of course, refused to back it. 'My Father's Land' and 'Creation', his first two releases, came out under his real name in the mid-70s. In 1980, he started recording with **Joe Gibbs** after working briefly with the Papa Roots, Black Ark, Gemini, Jah Life, Black Scorpio and Virgo **sound systems**. By 1981, he had teamed up with producer and Volcano sound owner **Henry 'Junjo' Lawes** and had achieved significant hits with 'Once A Virgin', 'Modelling Queen' and 'Virgin Girl'.

Between 1980 and 1984, Lawes and **Linval Thompson** used the **Roots Radics** at **Channel One** with **Scientist** mixing, to help record a number of hit albums and singles by the DJ. In 1981, after his debut *Wa Do Dem*, Eek-A-Mouse was the surprise star of Reggae Sunsplash. 'Ganja Smuggling', 'For Hire And Removal' and 'Do You Remember' and the album *Skidip* sustained his high profile. High profile singles 'Terrorists In The City', 'Anarexol' and 'Operation Eradication' (a response to his friend **Errol Scorcher**'s death) followed, along with *The Mouse And The Man* and *Assassinator* and several appearances on live **dancehall** albums. Nevertheless, it was not long before his characteristic 'biddy biddy bengs' started to wear thin and his popularity diminished somewhat after 1984's *Mouseketeer*, the last of his albums with Lawes.

Eek-A-Mouse made something of a comeback with 1991's major label release *U-Neek*, which included tracks produced by **Gussie Clarke**, **Daddy-O** and Matt Robinson, and a cover version of **Led Zeppelin**'s reggae pastiche 'D'Yer Maker'. He also made a cameo appearance in the movie, *New Jack City* and recorded for Wild Apache and former Channel One engineer Soljie. Following his brief exposure on a major label, Eek-A-Mouse returned to cult obscurity on a series of independent releases including 1996's *Black Cowboy* and 2004's *Mouse Gone Wild*.

● ALBUMS: *Wa-Do-Dem* (Greensleeves 1981) ★★★★, *Skidip!* (Greensleeves 1982) ★★★, with Michigan And Smiley *Live At Reggae Sunsplash* (Sunsplash 1982) ★, *The Mouse And The Man* (Greensleeves 1983) ★★★, *Assassinator* (RAS 1983) ★★★, *Mouseketeer* (Greensleeves 1984)

★★★, *King And I* (RAS 1987) ★★, *U-Neek* (Mango/Island 1991) ★★★, *Black Cowboy* (Explicit 1996) ★★★, *Eeksperience* (Coach House 2001) ★★★, *Mouse Gone Wild* (RAS 2004) ★★★.

● COMPILATIONS: *The Very Best Of Eek A Mouse* (Greensleeves 1987) ★★★, *RAS Portraits* (RAS 1997) ★★★, *The Very Best Of Eek A Mouse Vol. 2* (Shanachie 2003) ★★★.

Eels

Offering a novel twist on the post-grunge and lo-fi norms of American indie rock, Eels hatched in the bohemian Echo Park area of Los Angeles, California, USA, in 1995. The band was the brainchild of E (b. Mark Oliver Everett, 9 April 1963, McLean, Virginia, USA; vocals, guitar, keyboards), who had previously recorded two acclaimed solo albums for **Polydor Records** in the early 90s, and drummer Butch Norton. After finding bass player Tommy Walter at LA's Mint Club, the trio was picked up by Michael Simpson, half of the **Dust Brothers** and an A&R man for DreamWorks Records. 'Novocaine For The Soul' was a big US college/alternative hit in 1996, with a tension-and-release structure that seemed a throwback to the rock basics laid down by the **Pixies** and **Nirvana**, accentuated by characteristically indie themes of alienation and depression. The single and the follow-up 'Susan's House' also made the UK Top 10. Despite their apparently conventional power trio line-up, the band's music evinced a fascination with sonic experimentation. Co-producer Simpson's **dance music** background and experience of sampling expanded *Beautiful Freak*'s overall sound with hip-hop rhythm loops, and all three band members brought unexpected textures to play: Norton's cannibalized drum kit included a fire-alarm bell and part of a heating duct; Walter doubled on French horn; and E proclaimed himself a devotee of the ghostly Theremin, the only instrument the musician does not touch.

Walter left the band prior to the recording of the 1998 follow-up, *Electro-Shock Blues*, which was informed by several tragedies in E's personal life, most notably the near simultaneous suicide of his sister and his mother's terminal illness. The album's fascination with mortality found beautiful expression on compelling tracks such as 'Last Stop: This Town', 'Cancer For The Cure' and 'My Descent Into Madness'. Now effectively a vehicle for E's musical vision, the Eels returned in 2000 with the mellow *Daisies Of The Galaxy*. The album featured the stand-out tracks 'Mr E's Beautiful Blues' (another UK Top 10 hit, the riff stolen from the **McCoys**' 'I Got To Go Back') and 'It's A Motherfucker'. Everett received a rebuke from President George W. Bush for writing 'obscene' songs, which prompted the release of an 'edited' version of the album.

Following the release of an Internet-only live album documenting the ambitious 2000 tour by the Eels Orchestra, Everett took to dressing up as notorious US terrorist, the Unabomber, to promote 2001's disappointing *Souljacker*. This edgy and largely tuneless album was co-written and co-produced by John Parish. Another Internet live album and an E solo album under the guise of MC Honky paid testament to Everett's prolific work ethic and preceded the next dispatch from the Eels, *Shootenanny!* This 2003 release saw Everett largely ditching the experimental leanings of *Souljacker* and the MC Honky album in favour of old-fashioned songcraft, winning back a number of critics and fans in the process.

Everett subsequently switched labels within the Universal empire, signing a new recording contract with the Vagrant Records label. The first Eels release for Vagrant was 2005's excellent double album *Blinking Lights And Other Revelations*, a project which Everett had been working on for over eight years.

● ALBUMS: *Beautiful Freak* (DreamWorks 1996) ★★★★★, *Electro-Shock Blues* (DreamWorks 1998) ★★★★★, *Daisies Of The Galaxy* (DreamWorks 2000) ★★★★, *Oh What A Beautiful Morning* (E Works 2000) ★★★, *Souljacker* (DreamWorks 2001) ★★, *Electro-Shock Blues Show* (E Works 2002) ★★★, *Shootenanny!* (DreamWorks/spinART 2003) ★★★, *Blinking Lights And Other Revelations* (Vagrant 2005) ★★★★, *Eels With Strings: Live At Town Hall* (Vagrant 2006) ★★★.
Solo: E *A Man Called (E)* (Polydor 1992) ★★★★, *Broken Toy Shop* (Polydor 1993) ★★★, as MC Honky *I Am The Messiah* (spinART/B-Unique 2003) ★★.
● COMPILATIONS: *B-Sides & Rarities 1996–2003* (iTunes 2005) ★★★.
● DVD/VIDEOS: *Eels With Strings: Live At Town Hall* (Vagrant 2006).

Ef Band

Comprising John Rich (vocals), Par Ericson (bass, vocals, flute), Benet Fischer (guitar) and Dag Eliason (drums), Swedish hard rockers the Ef Band formed in 1978, originally as a trio. By 1980 they had added Rich to become a quartet. They made their debut one year later with *Last Laughs On You* for **Mercury Records**. With the **New Wave Of British Heavy Metal** movement gaining pace in the UK, the Ef Band found ready support for their similar back-to-basics hard rock assault, which also flirted with progressive rock elements. They were included on **EMI Records**' *Metal For Muthas Volume 1* compilation—one of the agenda-setting releases of the early 80s— and they also supported **Rainbow** on their Scandinavian tour. However, subsequent releases failed to build on this momentum. Eliason was replaced by Dave Dufort on drums (brother of Denise Dufort of **Girlschool**) and Rich was replaced by former Nevada Foxx singer Roger Marsden in 1984. The following year's *One Night Stand*, their first release for Mausoleum Records, sounded both dated and tired, and the Ef Band broke up soon after its release.
● ALBUMS: *Last Laughs On You* (Mercury 1981) ★★★, *Deep Cut* (Ewita 1983) ★★★, *One Night Stand* (Mausoleum 1985) ★★.

Efford, Bob

b. Robert T. Efford, 6 April 1928, London, England. Before becoming a highly accomplished reed player, especially on tenor saxophone, Efford played piano and trumpet. Drifting seemingly without design into a career in music, he played in some minor British provincial dance bands in the 40s. When one of the bands, Les Ayling's, became resident at the Lyceum Ballroom in London, Efford found his way into the local jazz scene and in 1949 joined **Vic Lewis**' **Stan Kenton**-styled band. In the early 50s, he joined **Ted Heath**, touring USA and receiving personal acclaim at the band's tour-opening concert at Carnegie Hall. He left Heath in the early 60s, thereafter mostly doing studio work, which included sessions under the leadership of visiting American stars such

as **Benny Goodman** and **Harry James**. In 1976 he moved to Los Angeles where he played in bands led by **Dave Pell**, **Bob Florence**, **Bill Holman** and the **Capp-Pierce Juggernaut**. In 1980 he made his debut as leader at Carmelo's, playing a bewilderingly huge range of instruments including pretty nearly the entire saxophone family as well as oboe, bassoon, flute, clarinet and cor anglais. Efford's forte remains the tenor saxophone and he is also especially adept as a baritone saxophonist, which he plays with an engagingly light tone.

EFX

'You can never keep anything longer than about 15 minutes for a Vegas audience, because their attention span is very short.' So said **Michael Crawford**, the star of this spectacular $41 million production that opened at the 1,800-seater MGM Grand Theatre in Las Vegas on 22 March 1995. He also pointed out that 'most of them are Asian, and they don't necessarily speak English, so it has to be very visual'. Well, *EFX* was certainly that. Introduced by a mysterious, disembodied voice, Crawford, the original 'Phantom of the Opera', emerged from a vast wall of fog, poised precariously on a flying saucer that zoomed to a height of some 70 feet above the stage, before streaking and strafing the front of the auditorium. At this point in the proceedings, he was wearing the 'hat' (actually, white and gold costume complete with cape) of the EFX! Master, whose task is to link a series of self-contained scenes, which transport the audience and himself (via time machine) from the Camelot world of King Arthur, to the science fiction future of H.G. Wells. Crawford himself re-appeared in the guise of historical figures Merlin, P.T. Barnum, Houdini and Wells. He was supported in this physically onerous task by leading players Tina Walsh (as Morgana, Bess Houdini), Jeffrey Polk (Master of Magic), Kevin Koelbl (Master of Spirits, Vladimir), Rick Stockwell (Master of Time), Stewart Daylida (Master of Laughter) and Lisa Geist (Arthur). They, of course, formed the human element of the show, and were constantly dwarfed by a multitude of the most extravagant special effects (EFX is NASA-speak for technical effects in sound, lighting, and pyrotechnics). Enormous dragons belching forth walls of fire, a little Chinese water torture, a manned rocket, a circus, leafy forests, an invasion of alien beings, a waterfall spurting from a rock face, the odd earthquake and so much more were miraculously conjured up, and played out for 90 heart-stopping, head-throbbing minutes (no interval) in a space that Crawford estimated as being 'three times the width of a London stage, and three times the height'. Almost 100,000 watts of stereo amplification belted out the musical numbers, which included 'Nexus', 'EFX!', 'The Magic That Surrounds You', 'The Sprite Dance', 'Morgana's Entrance', 'The Wizard's Dual', 'Arrival', 'The Intergalactic Circus Of Wonders', 'The Flying Kaganovich', 'The Greatest Showman In The Universe', 'Intergalactic Circus Finale', 'The Seance', 'Escape', 'Tonight', 'H.G. Wells' Laboratory', '3-D Adventure', 'Morlock Exterior', 'Morlock Interior/Slave Dance', 'Battle With The Morlocks' and 'To The Future'. It was created by Gary Goddard, Tony Christopher and the Landmark Entertainment Group. Goddard and Christopher also wrote the lyrics, and Don Grady was responsible for the music, musical production and musical direction. The director was Scott Faris, with co-direction and choreography by Anthony van Laast. Top of the 'just as important' list were David Mitchell (sets), Theoni V. Aldredge (costumes), Natasha Katz (lighting and special effects), Jonathan Deans (sound) and David Mendoza (illusions). After more that 600 consecutive performances, the majority of them suffering pain from an injury early on, Crawford was forced to withdraw in August 1996. He was replaced by **David Cassidy**, former 70s pop heart-throb-turned-actor in musicals such as *Blood Brothers*, and the production was tweaked accordingly, with David and **Shaun Cassidy**, along with **Andrew Gold**, revising script and songs. Proving the human body can only take so much, David Cassidy finished his stint in *EFX* at the end of December 1998, to be replaced by Broadway director, choreographer and song-and-dance man **Tommy Tune**.

EFX And Digit

San Francisco, California, USA–based EFX (b. Raul Recinos) began his career in the early 90s overseeing the decks at funk and hip-hop parties, also playing hi-NRG in gay clubs by night. His partner, Digit (b. Jeremy Cowan), took an active role in a succession of funk and ska bands, and was a DJ at Powerplant in Chicago when that city underwent its famous house revolution. After meeting at a record shop they steadily built a reputation with their releases, which kicked off on **Strictly Rhythm** with two records as Politix Of Dancing. These were followed with a solo EFX record, 'Is It Like My Dil-Doe', before they reunited as Killa Green Buds. They were gradually invited into the lucrative world of remixing (although EFX complains of several unpaid invoices), often under the name Third Floor Productions. After a breakthrough rebuilding **Rozalla**'s 'Everybody's Free', further big names followed, including **Sting** ('Demolition Man'), **Deep Forest** ('Sweet Lullaby') and even *Beavis And Butthead*, the **MTV** cartoon characters. They also produced a welter of productions for the N-Fusion label, before that was succeeded by their own operation, Freshly Squeezed. Credited with being the harbingers of musical movements such as San Trancedisco or San Frandisko, their style remains relentlessly buoyant, happy house.

Egan, Joe

b. c.1944 Scotland. The former partner of **Gerry Rafferty** in **Stealers Wheel**, Egan recorded two low-key albums after the band's final disintegration. *Out Of Nowhere* contained the charming 'Back On The Road Again', a turntable hit on UK radio. Both albums were similar in structure to the three Stealers Wheel collections and demonstrated the considerable songwriting ability of Egan, who sadly was unable to find his own 'Baker Street'. After a number of years of musical inactivity Egan worked with Rafferty by adding some backing vocals on Rafferty's 1993 album *On A Wing & A Prayer*. Egan also benefited from the use of the Rafferty/Egan composition 'Stuck In The Middle With You' in the film *Reservoir Dogs* that same year.
● ALBUMS: *Out Of Nowhere* (Ariola 1979) ★★★, *Map* (Ariola 1981) ★★.

Egan, Mark

b. Mark McDanel Egan, 14 January 1951, Brockton, Massachusetts, USA. Egan started playing the trumpet at the age of 10 and only turned to the double bass when he was 15. He studied at the University of Miami in the mid-70s and took lessons from **Jaco Pastorius**, **Dave Holland** and pianist **Andy LaVerne**. Meanwhile, he was working with **Ira Sullivan**, the **Pointer Sisters**, **Deodato** and **David Sanborn**. In 1977 he started

working with **Pat Metheny**'s group with whom he stayed for three years. Egan has since worked with a variety of musicians, including **Stan Getz**, **Gil Evans**, **Randy Brecker**, **John McLaughlin**, **Airto Moreira** and **Flora Purim**. In 1982 he formed **Elements** with drummer **Danny Gottlieb** with whom he has spent some time studying ethnic music. He is an educated musician who varies the sound of his playing through his fascination for and skill in the use of electronic devices, and for his inventive bass playing, which is both haunting and subtle.
● ALBUMS: *Elements* (Philo 1982) ★★★★, *Forward Motion* (Antilles 1984) ★★★, *Mosaic* (Hip Pocket 1984) ★★★, *A Touch Of Light* (GRP 1988) ★★★, *Beyond Words* (Blue Beacon 1992) ★★★★, *Freedom Town* (Wavetone 2001) ★★★★.

Egan, Walter

b. 12 July 1948, Jamaica, New York, USA. An accomplished singer, guitarist and songwriter, Egan first attracted attention in the early 60s playing alongside guitarist John Zambetti in surf rock band the Malibooz. The two musicians relocated to Washington, DC, where they joined a vibrant music scene that included future stars **Emmylou Harris** and **Nils Lofgren**. This association helped introduce Egan to the Los Angeles–based scene and he achieved due recognition when one of his songs, 'Hearts On Fire', was recorded by Harris and **Gram Parsons** on 1973's *Grievous Angel*. He then formed the short-lived Southpaw, which also included **Jules Shear** and Stephen Hague.
In 1976 Egan embarked on a solo career. *Fundamental Roll* was produced by **Fleetwood Mac** mainstays **Lindsey Buckingham** and **Stevie Nicks**, while the former was also responsible for overseeing a second set, 1978's *Not Shy*. This entertaining album included 'Magnet And Steel', Egan's solo hit single that reached number 8 in the US chart. His brand of countrified pop grew progressively less popular and after the release of *Wild Exhibitions* in 1983, the artist released no further albums throughout the 80s, concentrating on his work as a graphic artist and sculptor. He continued to work with Zambetti in the Malibooz and in 1999 released the solo album *Walternative*.
● ALBUMS: *Fundamental Roll* (Columbia 1977) ★★★, *Not Shy* (Columbia 1978) ★★★, *Hi-Fi* (Polydor 1979) ★★★, *The Last Stroll* (Edge 1980) ★★, *Wild Exhibitions* (Backstreet 1983) ★★, *Walternative* (We 1999) ★★★, *The Lost Album* aka *Mad Dog* 1985 recording (Renaissance/Red Steel 2000) ★★★.

Ege Bam Yasi

b. c.1958, Edinburgh, Scotland. Mr. Egg is a bald Scot and former plumber who took the name for his **techno** operation from a **Can** album. The group began as a band back in the mid-80s, touring a tacky cabaret show with on-stage S&M and a papier-mâché penis that squirted shaving foam. Despite such antics, he built his reputation with a series of increasingly successful acid tracks. These include the *Indigestion* EP (1991) and 'Highblow' (Groove Kissing 1991), though the then-group's career had first begun way back in 1986 with 'Circumstances' on Survival. His mini-album, *Ex Ovo Omnia* (meaning 'everything comes from the egg' in Latin) was released on **Finitribe**'s Finiflex imprint, and included such delights as 'The Good, The Bad And The Acid'. It was distinguished by the fact that all the effects were played live, without the use of either a sampler or DAT machine. He uses his new-found fortunes to invest in vast quantities of his chosen passion: eggs. He has continued to develop his talents as a remixer for such bands as the Fugues ('Sensityzed').

● ALBUMS: *Ex Ovo Omnia* mini album (Finiflex 1994) ★★★.

Egg (dance)

The Egg were formed in the UK from a conglomeration of various Oxford-based dub-influenced **dance music** acts. Comprising Dave Gaydon (bass), Mark Revell (guitar) and twin brothers Maff Scott (drums) and Ned Scott (keyboards), they have developed a unique sound combining hip-hop, psychedelia, ambient and **house**, resulting in what has been described as a 'fluid trance groove'. In 1995, they recorded their debut EP, *The Shopping*, through the iconoclastic Bristol-based Cup Of Tea Records. The release was greeted with critical acclaim, which resulted in the initial pressing selling out within two weeks. They maintained a high profile with notable performances at the **Glastonbury** and Phoenix festivals. By 1996, they had secured a contract with Indochina Records who endorsed the 11-track opus *Albumen*, which was co-produced by **Joe Gibb**. They continued performing on the live circuit throughout Europe and the USA, where the band made an appearance at the prestigious South X South West Festival. Beyond the music was the Egg's visual presentation, wherein the band members dressed in white and performed as human cinema screens, with films and pictures being projected onto their outfits. In a review of their show, **Melody Maker** described the event as 'instant psychedelia meets Aunt Harriet's home movies'. The band achieved further notoriety when they performed a benefit gig for the people of the remote Scottish Isle Of Eigg on Glasgow's Renfrew Ferry, to help the residents to buy the island from an apathetic proprietor. Through to 1998 the band released the underground hit 'Bend', which featured a **Steve Hillage** sample, performed with **Moby** alongside **Jah Wobble**, made a triumphant appearance at the Third Post Apartheid Festival and appeared in Todd Haynes' glam rock homage *Velvet Goldmine*. The band were also engrossed in studio work on a remix collection. A UK tour featuring their unique stage presentation was arranged to promote their 1998 follow-up, *Travelator*.

● ALBUMS: *Albumen* (Indochina 1996) ★★★, *Get Some Mixes Together* (Indochina 1997) ★★★★, *Travelator* (Indochina 1998) ★★★.

Egg (rock)

Egg was formed in July 1968 by **Dave Stewart** (b. 30 December 1950, Waterloo, London, England; keyboards), Hugh Montgomery 'Mont' Campbell (bass/vocals) and Clive Brooks (drums). The three musicians were all previous members of Uriel, a flower-power-influenced group that had featured guitarist **Steve Hillage**. Egg recorded two albums, *Egg* and *The Polite Force*, between 1970 and 1972. Stylistically similar to the early work of **Soft Machine**, these releases featured Stewart's surging keyboard work and a complex, compositional flair, bordering on the mathematical. The group's aficionados were thus stunned when Brooks abandoned this experimental path for the more orthodox, blues-based **Groundhogs**, and his departure resulted in Egg's demise. Stewart rejoined former colleague Hillage in the short-lived Khan, before replacing David Sinclair in **Hatfield**

And The North. However, the three original members of Egg were later reunited for the final album, *The Civil Surface*, on the **Virgin Records** subsidiary label Caroline, before dissolving again. Stewart and Campbell remained together in another experimental group, **National Health**, but then embarked on separate paths. The former has latterly enjoyed several hit singles by rearranging well-known 60s songs. He had a major hit with **Colin Blunstone** and a cover of 'What's Become Of The Broken Hearted'. His version of **Lesley Gore**'s 'It's My Party', a collaboration with singer **Barbara Gaskin**, topped the UK charts in 1981 but, for all their charm, such releases contrast dramatically with the left-field explorations of his earlier trio. Not to be confused with the more recent Oxford, England, band of the same name.

● ALBUMS: *Egg* (Nova 1970) ★★★, *The Polite Force* (Deram 1970) ★★★, *The Civil Surface* (Virgin 1974) ★★★.

● COMPILATIONS: *Seven Is A Jolly Good Time* (See For Miles 1988) ★★★.

Eggs

Influential US 'lo-fi' pop outfit the Eggs was formed in Richmond, Virginia, in 1990 by Andrew Beaujan (guitar/vocals) and Jonathon Rickman (guitar/vocals). Recruiting Dave Park (bass) and Marianne McGee (French horn) they recorded their debut album later that year for Teenbeat Records, the premier lo-fi label run by Mark Robinson (**Grenadine**, **Tsunami**, **Air Miami**). A succinct but musically expansive record crossing boundaries between pop, funk and indie rock, *Bruiser*, recorded in New York on a budget of $600, was a triumph of individualism, comparable to early **Syd Barrett**. However, afterwards the band were handicapped by their inability to find a regular drummer and other personnel shifts (contributors at various times included Rob Christiansen of Grenadine on trombone and guitar). The band's irreverently eclectic but ultimately pop-orientated approach survived to prosper on 1994's misnamed *Teenbeat 96 Exploder*, however. This comprised 68 minutes of the band's idiosyncratic compositions recorded at American University in Washington. A delirious cocktail of pop cadences streamlined by the band's essentialist approach, it won them further fans throughout the alternative rock community (including disc jockey **John Peel**). Lacking the ambition to break out of their close circle of friends and admirers, the Eggs broke up soon afterwards. Christiansen formed Viva Satellite!, releasing the bizarre concept album *Nishma* in 1996.

● ALBUMS: *Bruiser* (Teenbeat 1990) ★★★★, *Teenbeat 96 Exploder* (Teenbeat 1994) ★★★★.

● COMPILATIONS: *How Do You Like Your Lobster* (Teenbeat 1995) ★★★.

Eggs Over Easy

Formed in San Francisco, California, USA, in 1971, Eggs Over Easy was a popular attraction in the city's lively small club scene prior to arriving in London the following year. The quartet—Austin De Lone (guitar/vocals, ex-**Southwind**), Brien Hopkins (guitar/keyboards), Jack O'Hara (bass, ex-**David Blue**'s American Patrol) and Bill Franz (drums) took up a residency at a former jazz haunt, the Tally Ho in Kentish Town, and in doing so established the genre known as 'pub rock'. **Bees Make Honey**, **Brinsley Schwarz** and **Ducks DeLuxe** followed in their wake. Eggs Over Easy returned to San

Francisco in 1973 where they continued to forge an engaging blend of country, blues and rock styles. Sadly, their appeal as a live act did not transfer to their recordings. One-time **Grootna** vocalist Anna Rizzo often supplemented the band onstage and Hopkins subsequently forged a new group, the Reptile Brothers, with three ex-members of Rizzo's former act, Greg Dewey (ex-**Mad River**), Notcho Dewey and Vic Smith. Another member of the Reptiles, Tim Eshelman, worked in the **Moonlighters**, an offshoot of **Commander Cody And His Lost Planet Airmen**, which also featured De Lone. When Eggs Over Easy disbanded at the end of the 70s, De Lone and Eshelman made the Moonlighters a full-time project.

● ALBUMS: *Good And Cheap* (A&M 1972) ★★, *I'm Gonna Put A Bar In The Back Of My Car And Drive Myself To Drink* (Buffalo 1976) ★★.

Eggstone

A trio of Per Sundin (bass/vocals), Maurits Carlsson (drums/vocals) and Patrik Baktosch (guitar/vocals), Swedish pop band Eggstone's music has widely been described as 'extrovert' since their formation in 1986. Unlike many of their Scandinavian peers, they are also prolific, having released four albums since their 1991 debut for MNW/Snap, *Bubblebed*. Each album has showcased the group's natural sense of humour and musical experimentalism, incorporating everything from dance beats ('Ooh Ooh Ma Ma Mine') to bossa nova ('Those Words').

● ALBUMS: *Bubblebed* (MNW/Snap 1991) ★★★★, *Shooting Time* (MNW/Snap 1991) ★★, *Eggstone At Point Loma* (MNW/Snap 1992) ★★, *In Lemon Grove 1992* (MNW/Snap 1992) ★★★.

Ehrlich, Marty

b. Martin Lewis Ehrlich, 31 May 1955, St. Paul, Minnesota, USA. Ehrlich was raised in various parts of the Midwest but it was in St. Louis, Missouri, that he developed his interest in music. He started out on clarinet, gradually adding other reed instruments and also the flute. He had begun playing professionally while still a high school student, with the Human Arts Ensemble, but it was mainly through his exposure to the **Black Artists Group** of St. Louis that the young musician's concepts were formed. He studied at various colleges, including the New England Conservatory. In the 70s, he was active with many jazz musicians, predominantly those working in the field of free music that had made its first impact late in the previous decade. Among the artists with whom he worked and studied were **Muhal Richard Abrams**, **Ran Blake**, **Jaki Byard**, **George Russell**, **Gunther Schuller** and **Leo Smith**. In 1978, Ehrlich joined **Chico Hamilton**'s group and became a regular in Russell's New York Big Band.

Throughout the 80s, he played in many groups, including those led by Abrams, Byard, **Anthony Braxton**, **Julius Hemphill** and **Oliver Lake**. He also played in bands led by **John Carter**, including appearing on the series of albums that housed 'Roots And Folklore: Episodes In The Development Of American Folk Music'. Ehrlich also worked with **Wayne Horvitz**, **John Zorn** and **Butch Morris**. He led his own groups from 1988, including a trio with **Pheeroan Ak Laff** and bass player Anthony Cox, and his larger group, the Dark Woods Ensemble. He also co-led a quartet with **Bobby Previte**. In the 90s, he was active with his own bands and also appeared

in duo format, sometimes on record, with artists such as Abrams and bass players Cox and **John Lindberg**. His late 90s trio teamed him with **Michael Formanek** and **Peter Erskine**. He has recently worked and recorded with **Uri Caine**, **Mark Dresser**, **Billy Drummond** and **Andrew Cyrille**.

Although adept at all the instruments he plays, Ehrlich continued to favour the clarinet, and its darker-voiced cousin the bass clarinet, finding rich yet subtle voicings in his always interesting explorations along and across the boundaries of jazz and other forms of contemporary improvised music. Ehrlich is also a gifted composer and is especially adept at writing for contemporary big bands. Although dedicated to the advancement of music, Ehrlich's playing and writing clearly demonstrate his interest in and knowledge of the origins of jazz and beyond.

● ALBUMS: with John Lindberg *Unison* (Cecma 1981) ★★★, *The Welcome* (Sound Aspects 1984) ★★★, *Pliant Plaint* (Enja 1988) ★★★, *The Traveller's Tale* (Enja 1990) ★★★, with Anthony Cox *Falling Man* (Muse 1991) ★★★, with the Dark Woods Ensemble *Emergency Peace* (New World/CounterCurrents 1991) ★★★, *Side By Side* (Enja 1991) ★★★★, *Can You Hear A Motion?* (Enja 1994) ★★★, with the Dark Woods Ensemble *Just Before The Dawn* (New World/CounterCurrents 1995) ★★★, *New York Child* (Enja 1996) ★★★, with Muhal Richard Abrams *The Open Air Meeting* (New World/CounterCurrents 1997) ★★★, with Ben Goldberg *Light At The Crossroads* (Songlines 1997) ★★★★, with the Dark Woods Ensemble *Live Wood* (Music & Arts 1997) ★★★, with the Dark Woods Ensemble *Sojourn* (Tzadik 1999) ★★★★, with Peter Erskine, Michael Formanek *Relativity* (Enja 1999) ★★★★, with Mike Nock *The Waiting Game* (Naxos 2000) ★★★, *Malinke's Dance* (Omnitone 2000) ★★★, with Andrew Cyrille, Mark Dresser *C/D/E* (Jazz Magnet 2001) ★★★★, *Song* (Enja 2001) ★★★, *The Long View* (Enja 2003) ★★★, *Line On Love* (Palmetto 2003) ★★★.

Eicher, Manfred

b. 1943, Lindau, Germany. After studying at the Berlin Academy of Music and becoming adept as a bass player, Eicher began working as an assistant producer for a leading German record label. Towards the end of the 60s, he formed his own small independent label, Edition of Contemporary Music (**ECM Records**), releasing his first album, **Mal Waldron**'s *Free At Last*, in 1969. Although Eicher's musical training was classically based, he developed a liking for jazz and it is this genre that forms the bulk of his label's catalogue. Nevertheless, pigeon holing is not possible. For Eicher, the word 'jazz' covers an impressively wide range of musical styles, albeit strongly inclined towards that which is contemporary if not, indeed, cutting edge. Significantly, from the start, Eicher placed considerable emphasis on recording quality, achieving a distinctive studio sound that was maintained during the next three decades as the catalogue built to over 1,000 titles. Along the way, certain jazz artists became almost synonymous with ECM, notably **Jan Garbarek**, whose 1971 *Afric Pepperbird* was significant for artist and label alike, and **Chick Corea**'s 1972 *Return To Forever*. Even more striking was **Keith Jarrett**'s 1975 *The Köln Concert*, an album that sold more than four million copies during the next quarter century. Other musicians closely linked with Eicher's label include **Paul Bley**, **Jon Christensen**, **Dave Holland**, **Pat Metheny**, **Terje Rypdal**, **Ralph Towner** and **Eberhard Weber**.

Very much a hands-on producer, Eicher is deeply involved in preparation, recording and post-production. His overall vision extends to album cover design, in which striking photographic images create a visual counterpoint to the musical essence of the contents. From the mid-80s, Eicher also produced classical recordings, again leaning towards new trends and spotlighting the work of new composers. **Arvo Pärt**'s 1993 *Te Deum* was placed in the Top 5 of classical albums. In addition to his activities as a record producer, Eicher has also worked in cinema, a film he co-directed, *Holozän*, winning a special prize at the Locarno Film Festival in 1992. Eicher is a dedicated entrepreneur who is passionate about his subject.

Eiffel 65

This Turin, Italy–based trio, comprising singer Jeffrey Jey (b. 1970, Sicily, Italy), keyboard player Maurizio Lobina, and DJ Gabriele Ponte, is closely associated with Massimo Gabutti's hugely successful BlissCorporation label. The trio rose to prominence in 1999 when (helped by extensive radio airplay) they scored an enormous hit in Europe with 'Blue (Da Ba Dee)'. The cloying, infectious single was a number 1 in 16 countries across Europe as well as in Canada and Australia. In the UK, it sold more than a million copies and remained at the top of the charts for three weeks. Perhaps best described as 'bubblegum-dance', the track featured nonsense lyrics, vocals filtered through a vocoder and an unusual video. It was also a Top 10 hit in the USA. The follow-up, 'Move Your Body' was a number 1 single in their native Italy before becoming another Top 10 hit in the rest of Europe. The aptly-titled debut, *Europop*, released in February 2000, exhibited a range of dance styles but the disposability of their first hits would make it difficult to establish themselves as a credible act in **dance music**.
● ALBUMS: *Europop* (WEA/Eternal 2000) ★★.

8Ball

b. Premro Smith, Memphis, Tennessee, USA. Rapper 8Ball made his name as part of the southern duo **8Ball And MJG**, who during the 90s were the unsung heroes in the rise of the 'Dirty South' rap scene. 8Ball (also written Eightball) made his solo debut in summer 1998 with the sprawling three-disc set *Lost* (the third disc actually featured a sampler of other artists on 8Ball's Suave House label). The album deviated little from the gangsta blueprint 8Ball had laid down with MJG on earlier releases such as *Comin' Out Hard* and *On Top Of The World*, although little of the material sounded as inspired as the duo's work together (the same fate befell MJG's solo debut *No Glory*). 8Ball was far better represented on the following year's 8Ball And MJG set, *In Our Lifetime*, a classic of the southern rap genre. The duo's 'unrecognised geniuses' status was clearly beginning to rankle by the time 8Ball released *Almost Famous*, the title of which conveyed his frustration. Two other releases appeared under 8Ball's name in 2001, a collection of underground tracks from his time on the Suave House label (*"Lay It Down"*) and a compilation set premiering his 8 Ways label (*Presents The Slab*).
● ALBUMS: *Lost* (Uptown/Universal 1998) ★★★, *Almost Famous* (JCOR 2001) ★★★.
● COMPILATIONS: *Presents The Slab* (JCOR 2001) ★★★, *Lay It Down* (Draper 2001) ★★.

8Ball And MJG

US rap duo **8Ball** aka Eightball (b. Premro Smith, Memphis, Tennessee, USA) and MJG (b. Marlon Jermaine Goodwin, Memphis, Tennessee, USA) emerged from Memphis in the early 90s. One of the first 'Dirty South' rap acts to achieve a consistent level of commercial success throughout the southern states, the duo nevertheless failed to make the national breakthrough fellow Dirty South acts such as **Outkast** and **Goodie Mob** achieved in the late 90s.

8Ball and MJG grew up in the Orange Mound district of Memphis, Tennessee, a deprived area that afforded young black men little opportunity to progress. The duo's love of hip-hop prompted them to launch their own recording career on the southern underground circuit, and they succeeding in building a large audience with a series of self-released recordings, including their first big hit 'Listen To The Lyrics'. In a bid to promote their music to a wider audience they helped launch Suave House Records with Tony Draper, and released *Comin' Out Hard* in 1993. That album's underground hit 'Armed Robbery' and two further releases attracted the attention of Universal Records. The first fruits of Suave House's new distribution contract were two solo albums, 8Ball's *Lost* and MJG's *No Glory*. The duo reunited to record 1999's classic *In Our Lifetime*, but despite critical plaudits the album failed to establish 8Ball And MJG as a commercial force. The duo severed ties with Draper and Suave House and recorded a strong album for JCOR, *Space Age 4 Eva*, but the record went largely unheard. A new recording contract with **P. Diddy**'s Bad Boy label was testament to the duo's enduring status in the rap world. Their first album for Bad Boy, 2004's *Living Legends*, provided the duo with their national breakthrough, debuting in the US Top 5 in its first week of release.
● ALBUMS: *Comin' Out Hard* (Suave House 1993) ★★★★, *On The Outside Looking In* (Suave House 1994) ★★★, *On Top Of The World* (Suave House/Relativity 1995) ★★★, *In Our Lifetime* (Suave House/Universal 1999) ★★★★, *Space Age 4 Eva* (JCOR 2000) ★★★★, *Space Age 4 Eva: The Swisha House Screwed Up Version* (JCOR 2001) ★★★, *Living Legends* (Bad Boy 2004) ★★★, *Living Legends: Chopped And Screwed* (Bad Boy 2004) ★★.
● COMPILATIONS: *Lyrics Of A Pimp* (Omni 1997) ★★, *Memphis Under World* (OTS 2000) ★★★.

8 Ball Records

New York City, USA, record label famous for its mellow approach to **house** music, with offices on the 12th floor of a building in the Chelsea district of Manhattan. The label was established in 1991 by Alex Kaplan, then a video-maker, who still leads the company in association with A&R head Kevin Williams, a veteran of the New York club scene. It was Kaplan who recorded the label's debut single, Napoleon-Soul O's 'Come On Girl', a jazzy, funky house tune that set out 8 Ball's stall. Artists and producers were subsequently recruited and acquired by word of mouth. As well as stalwarts such as Williams' sister Joie Cardwell ('Goodbye', 'If We Try', 'Trouble') and Lectroluv (Fred Jorio), the label is equally famous for its T-shirt and merchandising, its emblem being among the most popular in the UK. Other prominent recordings arrived from Africa Dream, Groove Thing, Wall Of Sound, Screamin' Rachael, and Mack Vibe's 'I Can't Let You Go' (Al Mack, who had previously recorded as the Al Mack Project for **Strictly Rhythm**). 8 Ball also runs the

Empire State deep house subsidiary label, and has its own record store in Greenwich Village. Kaplan would return to video-making by launching his own compilation video series.

8 Bold Souls
(see **Wilkerson, Edward, Jnr.**)

8 Eyed Spy
Formed in New York City, USA, 8 Eyed Spy featured dramatic vocalist **Lydia Lunch**, formerly of leading 'no-wave' act **Teenage Jesus And The Jerks**. Fellow experimentalists Pat Irwin (saxophone/guitar), Michael Paumgarden (guitar), George Scott (bass) and Jim Sclavunos (drums) joined her in this short-lived venture. Both of the group's posthumous releases show a hypnotic tension between experiment/ confrontation (Lunch and Irwin) and the understanding of the rhythm section. The exciting blend of *avant garde* jazz, blues, rock and lyrical expressiveness resulted in two innovative, challenging collections. Their version of 'Diddy Wah Diddy', inspired by **Captain Beefheart**, encapsulates their chosen style. Sadly, Scott's premature death in 1980 brought the group to an end. Further evidence of their excellence is preserved on a Lydia Lunch retrospective, *Hysterie* (1986).
● ALBUMS: *Live* cassette-only (RIOR 1981) ★★, *8 Eyed Spy* (Fetish 1981) ★★★.

8 Mile
This Curtis Hanson–directed 2002 feature marked the mainstream acting debut of controversial but highly successful white rapper **Eminem**. Set in 1995, *8 Mile* tells the story of wannabe white rapper Jimmy Smith Jnr. aka B-Rabbit (Eminem in a semi-autobiographical role), a young man stuck on the wrong side of the tracks in Detroit, Michigan; the title of the movie is a reference to 8 Mile Road, which effectively acts as a dividing line between the middle-class suburbs and the inner-city ghettos. The movie opens with B-Rabbit 'stiffing' at a local freestyle battle, and we also learn that he has split up with his pregnant girlfriend and moved back in with his alcoholic, trailer park–dwelling mother (Kim Basinger). He is attempting to save enough money from his dead-end factory job to allow him to record a demo tape. Things do not go according to plan, however, and his relationship with his mother rapidly deteriorates. Things improve when he meets aspiring model Alex (Brittany Murphy) and a 'friend' promises to set up a demo recording, but further setbacks include Alex cheating on him and a brutal beating by his rivals. However, B-Rabbit pulls out the stops and triumphs at the next freestyle battle. The movie ends with B-Rabbit returning to work to earn the money to record his demo.
While there was a certain amount of revisionism involved in *8 Mile*, namely the positive handling of Eminem's alleged homophobia, the movie received generally positive reviews. Eminem's acting drew particular praise with Basinger and Murphy backing him up well in the supporting roles. Hanson and screenwriter Scott Silver skilfully evoked the inner city despair of a large US city, but the movie's strongest suit was its depiction of the freestyle rap battles, a milieu in which Eminem and the supporting MCs were totally at ease. The movie broke several US box office records when it opened in November, taking over $50 million in its opening weekend. *8 Mile* also featured several new Eminem tracks, the most notable of which, 'Lose Yourself', gave the rapper his first US number 1 hit.

808 State
Manchester, England's, finest **acid music** combo of the early 90s was founded by Martin Price (b. 26 March 1955, England), owner of the city's influential **Eastern Bloc** record shop, and Graham Massey (b. 4 August 1960, Manchester, Lancashire, England; ex-**Biting Tongues**), who had previously worked in a café opposite the shop. Together with Gerald Simpson, they began recording together as a loose **electro/ house** collective, releasing *Newbuild* in 1988. Simpson subsequently left to form his own **A Guy Called Gerald** vehicle, and was replaced by Darren Partington (b. 1 November 1969, Manchester, Lancashire, England) and Andrew Barker (b. 2 November 1969, Manchester, Lancashire, England). These two young DJs were working together as the Spin Masters and were regular visitors to Eastern Bloc, proffering a variety of tapes in the hope of securing a contract with Price's Creed label. *Quadrastate*, which included some input from Simpson, helped to establish the new line-up as premier exponents of UK **dance music**, with the attendant 'Pacific State' single becoming a massive underground hit that crossed over to the UK Top 10 at the end of 1989.
A lucrative contract with **ZTT Records** proved to be a mixed blessing for the band, however, as they were lumped in with the pervading 'Madchester' indie/dance boom. Simpson, meanwhile, began launching a series of attacks in the press concerning unpaid royalties. *Ninety*, the band's debut for ZTT, became an instant **rave** classic and established them as a commercial force. They also worked with Mancunian rapper **MC Tunes** on his debut *The North At Its Heights* and several singles, including June 1990's UK number 10 hit 'The Only Rhyme That Bites'. Further UK hits followed with 'Cubik/Olympic' (number 10, November 1990) and 'In Yer Face' (number 9, February 1991). *Ex:El* featured guest vocals from **New Order**'s Bernard Sumner on 'Spanish Heart', and **Sugarcubes** vocalist **Björk** on 'Oops' (also a single) and 'Qmart'. In October 1991, Price declined to tour the USA with the band, electing to work on solo projects instead, including managing Rochdale rappers the **Kaliphz**, and his own musical project, Switzerland.
He also established himself as a remixer, working with **David Bowie**, **Shamen**, **Primal Scream** and **Soundgarden**. 808 State persevered with another fine album, 1993's *Gorgeous*, which saw a new rash of collaborations. Featured this time were **Ian McCulloch** (**Echo And The Bunnymen**) adding vocals to 'Moses', and samples from the **Jam**'s 'Start', **UB40**'s 'One In Ten' and even *Star Wars*' Darth Vader. Massey occupied himself with co-writing Björk's 'Army Of Me' single and other material on her 1995 collection, *Post*, before 808 State regrouped for the following year's *Don Solaris*. Adopting a more experimental approach than the early 90s work, the album featured guest vocalists James Dean Bradfield (**Manic Street Preachers**) and Ragga. The *808:88:98* compilation included several new mixes. Since the release of this album, Massey, Partington and Barker have continued to work on new material while undertaking various remix projects.
● ALBUMS: *Newbuild* (Creed 1988) ★★★, *Quadrastate* (Creed 1989) ★★★★, *Ninety* (ZTT 1989) ★★★★, *Utd. State 90* US only (Tommy Boy 1990) ★★★★, *Ex:El* (ZTT/ Tommy Boy 1991) ★★★, *Gorgeous* (ZTT/Tommy Boy 1993)

★★★, *Don Solaris* (ZTT/Hypnotic 1996) ★★★, *Outpost Transmission* (Circus 2002) ★★★.
● COMPILATIONS: *Thermo Kings* (ZTT/Hypnotic 1996) ★★★, *808:88:98* (ZTT 1998) ★★★★, *Prebuild* (Rephlex 2004) ★★★.
● DVD/VIDEOS: *Opti Buk* (ZTT 2002).

801

Formed by **Roxy Music** guitarist **Phil Manzanera** (b. Philip Targett-Adams, 31 January 1951, London, England) in 1976, 801 also featured Manzanera's former colleague **Brian Eno** in addition to Lloyd Watson (guitar/vocals), Francis Monkman (keyboards), Bill MacCormick (bass) and Simon Phillips (drums). Manzanera's initial impetus was to form a band to perform material from his own 1975 set, *Diamond Head*, and his pre-Roxy Music outfit, Quiet Sun's reunion recording *Mainstream*. The band took their name from the 'True Wheel' song on Eno's *Taking Tiger Mountain (By Strategy)*—'We are the 801/We are the central shaft'. The other members were already vastly experienced musicians; Monkman had recorded three albums with **Curved Air** before turning to session work; and Bill MacCormick, who had played in Quiet Sun from 1970-71, recorded two albums as a member of **Robert Wyatt**'s **Matching Mole** in 1972 and joined **Gong** in 1973. He also appeared on various albums by Wyatt, Eno and Manzanera among others. Simon Phillips was a session drummer who had played on albums by **Roger Glover**, **Greenslade** and **Jack Bruce**.
This line-up of 801 only played three gigs, culminating in a sell-out show at the Queen Elizabeth Hall, London, on 3 September 1976, recorded for *801 Live*. Material played that evening was drawn from Manzanera's *Diamond Head* and his work with Quiet Sun, and Eno's **Here Come The Warm Jets**, *Another Green World* and *Taking Tiger Mountain (By Strategy)*, as well as performing cover versions of the **Beatles**' 'Tomorrow Never Knows' and the **Kinks**' 'You Really Got Me'. The band folded immediately following this gig but Manzanera issued one further 801 album, *Listen Now*, in 1977, using various rock luminaries and writer Ian MacDonald (Bill MacCormick's brother) as special guests before taking a revamped 801 on the road. The band finally dissolved after Roxy Music's reactivation in 1978. Manzanera has subsequently resurrected the name for sporadic album releases, including a 2001 recording with a group of Latin musicians.
● ALBUMS: *801 Live* (Island 1976) ★★★, *Listen Now* (Polydor 1977) ★★★★, *Live At Manchester University* (Expression 1998) ★★★, *Live At Hull* 1977 recording (Expression 2000) ★★★, *801 Latino* (Expression 2001) ★★★.

Eight Records

Liverpool, England, record label formed by the trio of Ian Wright, Peter Coyle and Steve Cummersome. They first started working together in 1989, originally envisioning licensing their work to the majors. Their debut, Morina Van Rooy's 'Sly One', was consequently placed on **DeConstruction Records**, but the trio soon decided to set up their own company. Since its inception, Eight Records has specialized in matching strong house tunes with unusual vocalists. Among the best examples of this have been Connie Lush, a local pub blues singer ('Shame'), Van Rooy ('Sly One') and G Love (DJ John Kelly) featuring Jayne Casey's 'You Keep The

Love', in 1991 (Casey was the former **Pink Military/Pink Industry** chanteuse). G Love is also the name of the club the trio run in association with Liverpool's other leading label, **Three Beat Records**. Coyne, formerly of **Lotus Eaters**, also records on the label as Coloursex (*Deep And Devastating* EP).
● COMPILATIONS: *Give Love* (Eight 1991) ★★★.

18 Wheeler

Formed in Scotland by Sean Jackson (guitar/vocals), Neil Halliday (drums), Alan Hake (bass) and Steven Haddow (guitar). The band released two singles, 'Nature Girl' and 'Suncrush', which bore the obvious influence of Glasgow's early 80s **Postcard Records** scene. They were followed in 1994 by 'Kum Back' and 'The Revealer'. On the debut album their familiar bubblegum pop was allied to rhythms drawn from folk, country and **dub**. Described in *The Guardian* newspaper as '1994's lost pop classic', this was not widespread opinion, as others saw the band as insubstantial and retrogressive. A more accomplished collection, *Formanka*, followed a year later, by which time the band's fortunes had been significantly outstripped by another **Creation Records** act, **Oasis**, who had once been third support to 18 Wheeler at the legendary gig in Glasgow when Alan McGee decided to sign them. *Year Zero* moved into crossover territory, further alienating their original fanbase, and they folded soon afterwards.
● ALBUMS: *Twin Action* (Creation 1994) ★★, *Formanka* (Creation 1995) ★★★, *Year Zero* (Creation 1997) ★★★.

8th Day

This multi-talented vocal and instrumental group had their biggest hit in 1971 on **Holland/Dozier/Holland**'s Invictus label with the infectious, million-selling 'She's Not Just Another Woman', even though the track had, in fact, been recorded some two years earlier with Steve Mancha on lead vocals, making the number sound very like an early **100 Proof Aged In Soul** release, a group led by Mancha. For the 1971 follow-up, 'You've Got To Crawl (Before You Walk)', lead vocalist Melvin Davis, a long-term Detroit drummer/singer, was recruited, and the rest of the regular line-up of the group became Tony Newton (bass), Carole Stallings (vocals/electric violin), Anita Sherman (vocals/vibes), Michael Anthony (lead guitar), Bruce Nazarian (rhythm guitar/keyboards), Jerry Paul (percussion), Lynn Harter (background vocals) and, somewhat later, Lymon Woodard (organ) and Larry Hutchison (vocals/guitar). Although 8th Day were always correctly regarded as a Detroit group, Stallings and Sherman were from the west coast. The group's first three releases reached the US charts and they cut a superb cover version of 100 Proof's 'Too Many Cooks'; however, they soon developed a penchant for quasi-gospel message-songs, aesthetically very good but commercially unsuccessful. When Invictus began to fall apart, the group did likewise. Paul, Nazarian and Newton formed the short-lived Deliverance, cutting one single for NCI. Founder member Newton then moved to the west coast, joining the **Tony Williams**' New Lifetime, and later playing with **Gary Moore** and **G-Force** and Thelma Hopkins. In the mid-90s Anita Sherman was providing background vocals for artists such as **Joe Cocker**.
● ALBUMS: *The 8th Day* (Invictus 1971) ★★★, *I Gotta Get Home* (Invictus 1972) ★★.

● COMPILATIONS: *The Best Of 8th Day* (1992) ★★★, *And On The 8th Day God Created Soul (The Complete Invictus Sessions)* (Sequel 1999) ★★★.

Eighth Wonder

A vehicle for singer Patsy Kensit (b. Patricia Jude Francis Kensit, 4 March 1968, Waterloo, London, England), a former child actress at one time known for her role in a UK television advertisement. She pursued a parallel career as an actress, including a role in the Royal Shakespeare Company production of *Silas Marner* in 1984, and as a pop singer in Eighth Wonder, which comprised Geoff Beauchamp (guitar), Alex Godson (keyboards) and Jamie Kensit (guitar). The band gained a minor UK hit with 'Stay With Me' in 1985. Kensit later landed the role of Crêpe Suzette in Julien Temple's 1986 film of Colin McInnes' novel *Absolute Beginners*. Surrounded by an intense media hype, the film, which also featured **David Bowie**, **Sade** and **Ray Davies** of the **Kinks**, was a critical and commercial flop. Kensit and Eighth Wonder found greater success in 1988 with the UK Top 10 single 'I'm Not Scared'. Two more chart singles followed that same year, including the Top 20 hit 'Cross My Heart' and a Top 50 album, *Fearless*. Kensit later restored her credibility as an actress in the 1991 Don Boyd film *Twenty-One*, although the subsequent *Blame It On The Bellboy* drew less favourable reviews.

Her first marriage in 1988 to Dan Donovan (of **Bad Audio Dynamite**) ended in 1991. She then married **Simple Minds** singer Jim Kerr in January 1992, which caused considerable interest in the UK tabloid press. They divorced in 1996. Since then she has been a favourite of the paparazzi lens, which reached a peak during 1996/7 when she started a relationship with Liam Gallagher of **Oasis**. Their three-year marriage ended in 2000.

● ALBUMS: *Fearless* (Columbia 1988) ★★.

Eighties Matchbox B-Line Disaster

Representing a new breed of UK guitar bands alongside outfits such as **Ikara Colt** and **British Sea Power**, this Brighton, England–based noise rock quintet was formed on the first day of the twenty-first century by Guy McKnight (vocals), Andy Huxley (lead guitar), Marc Norris (guitar), Sym Gharial (bass) and Tom Diamantepoulo (drums). The quintet's rudimentary music skills were more than compensated for by their raw energy, and they quickly built up a formidable live reputation, with gigs regularly brought to the edge of violence by the band's unhinged performance. Describing their sound as 'dark psychosis rock', and earning a string of lazy comparisons in the UK press to the **Birthday Party** and the **Make-Up**, the quintet made their recording debut in March 2002 with the single 'Morning Has Broken', released on the **Virgin Records**' affiliate Radiate Records. Their debut *Horse Of The Dog* featured 10 brief but thrilling tracks, opening with the sordid fuzz rock of 'Celebrate Your Mother' and taking in the crude but hugely enjoyable 'Whack Of Shit' and 'Psychosis Safari'.

● ALBUMS: *Horse Of The Dog* (No Death 2002) ★★★, *The Royal Society* (No Death 2004) ★★★.

Eikhard, Shirley

b. Sackville, New Brunswick, Canada. Singer-songwriter Shirley Eikhard was befriended as a child by **Anne Murray** and **Sylvia Tyson**, and studied with **Cleo Laine**. Father Cec

played bass and her mother June the fiddle in the family group, the Tantramar Ramblers. She was given her first guitar at the age of 11, writing her first songs in the basement of the family home in Oshawa, Ontario. Through her parents she discovered country music and the Canadian folk of **Joni Mitchell** and **Gordon Lightfoot**. Her first major concert appearance came at a fiddling festival in Colbourg, Ontario, at the age of 12. Afterwards she wrote a reply to an advertisement requesting new songwriters to audition for the Mariposal Folk Festival. She won, playing alongside Mitchell, Ian And Sylvia and **Bruce Cockburn**. Earl Ball of **Capitol Records** was alerted to her growing reputation by **Merle Haggard**'s rhythm guitarist, Bobby Wayne. Despite winning two RPM Weekly Gold Leaf Awards, *Shirley Eikhard* and its two accompanying singles failed to sell. After a four-year career break, during which time her songs were recorded by **Kim Carnes**, Anne Murray and **Chet Atkins**, she returned to recording, with three albums for Attic Records in 1975. Though none were big sellers, her cover versions of **Lindsey Buckingham**'s 'Don't Let Me Down' and **Christine McVie**'s 'Say You Love Me' attracted widespread approval. In 1981 **Emmylou Harris** recorded her 'Good News', later also releasing a version of Eikhard's 'Maybe Tonight'. Following a single 80s album, *Taking Charge* for **WEA Records**, the next artist to turn to her was **Alannah Myles**, who included 'Kickstart My Heart' (co-written with Chris Waters and Madeline Stone) on her 1989 debut album. In 1991 **Bonnie Raitt** chose 'Something To Talk About' as the lead-off single for her *Luck Of The Draw* album, further reinstating Eikhard's reputation as an articulate, emotive ballad writer. In 1995 she recorded a new album, *If I Had My Way*, co-produced with her long-standing keyboard player Evelyn Datl. She also contributed the theme song to a new Warner Brothers film, *Something To Talk About*.

● ALBUMS: *Shirley Eikhard* (Capitol 1971) ★★★★, *Child Of The Present* (Attic 1975) ★★★, *Let Me Down Easy* (Attic 1976) ★★★, *Horizons* (Attic 1977) ★★★, *Taking Charge* (WEA 1987) ★★★, *If I Had My Way* (Denon Canada 1995) ★★, *Coming Home* (Blue Note 1998) ★★★.

Einóma

This Icelandic recording act is a partnership between friends and studio partners Steindór Kristinsson and Bjarni Thor Gunnarsson. The duo take their name from an Icelandic word meaning 'means many audio sources that become one, or sound as one', claiming that the moniker is particularly apposite since it echoes the dynamics of their collaboration. Prior to the genesis of Einóma and their intriguing, mysterious strain of experimental electronica, Kristinsson and Gunnarsson initially collaborated on films, writing scripts and playing with sound and camera techniques. As their interest in film diminished, the duo began composing their own recordings somewhere between the experimental electronic music that they say they had been listening to for years and the ambience that they had hoped to attain with their short films. Einóma's subsequent experiments with rhythm prompted the release of their debut EP, *Floating Point By Zero*, via the frequently intriguing Icelandic label Uni:form and tracks from this release subsequently appeared on the *42 More Things To Do In Zero Gravity/Part One* compilation of Icelandic ambient music. The name of Einóma's 2002 debut album, *Undir Feilnótum*, roughly translates as 'in a tough spot' and the release seemed darker and more oppressive than much of the neo-ambient music coming out of Iceland. Kristinsson and Gunnarsson claim that their intent with the album was to continue a story begun on *Floating Point By Zero* and to be sustained with future releases.

● ALBUMS: *Undir Feilnótum* (Vertical Form 2002) ★★★★.

Einstein

Einstein, a German hard rock band formed in the late 70s, comprised Richard Schoenherz (vocals/keyboards), Christian Kolonovits (vocals/keyboards), Johan Daansen (bass/vocals) and Harmut Pfannmueller (drums). Their music was pitched somewhere between the progressive rock of **Emerson, Lake And Palmer** and the pomp AOR of **Kansas** or **Journey**, but on the evidence of their sole album, *First Principles*, released on a major label in 1979, they were less intuitive songwriters and performers than any of those acts. Greeted with disdain bordering on antipathy by reviewers, the band continued for only a few months after its release. A second release including the assistance of David Thomas (vocals), Reinhard Besser (guitar, keyboards, vocals), and Christian Felke (saxophone) was issued later.

● ALBUMS: *First Principles* (WEA 1979) ★★, *Beware Of Germans* (X Rec 1981) ★★.

Einstürzende Neubauten

Formed out of the Berlin arts conglomerate Die Geniale Dilletanten, Einstürzende Neubauten (inspired by the collapse of the Kongresshalle) made their live debut on April 1 1980 at the Moon. The line-up comprised Blixa Bargeld (b. Christian Emmerich, 12 January 1959, Berlin, Germany), N.U. Unruh (b. Andrew Chudy, 9 June 1957, New York City, USA), Beate Bartel and Gudrun Gut, the latter two from the punk band Mania D. Alexander Van Borsig (b. Alexander Hacke, 11 October 1965, Berlin, Germany), an occasional contributor, joined in time for the band's first single, 'Für Den Untergang'. When Bartel and Gut departed to form Malaria and Matador they were replaced by F.M. Einheit (b. Frank Strauss, 18 December 1958, Dortmund, Germany; ex-Abwärts). Einheit and Unruh formed the band's rhythmic backbone, experimenting with a variety of percussive effects, while Bargeld provided discordant vocals and guitar.

The band's first official album (there were previously many tapes available) was *Kollaps*, a collage of sounds created by unusual rhythmic instruments ranging from breaking glass and steel girders to pipes and canisters. Their 1982 12-inch single 'Durstiges Tier' involved contributions from the **Birthday Party**'s Rowland S. Howard and **Lydia Lunch**, at which point Hacke had joined the band permanently as guitarist alongside new bass player Marc Chung (b. 3 June 1957, Leeds, England; ex-Abwärts). A UK tour with the Birthday Party introduced them to **Some Bizzare Records**, which released 1983's *Die Zeichnungen Des Patienten O.T.* The following year's *Strategien Gegen Architekturen 80=83* was compiled with the help of Jim Thirlwell of **Foetus**, while the band performed live at the ICA in London. Joined by Genesis P. Orridge (**Psychic TV**), Frank Tovey (**Fad Gadget**) and Stevo (Some Bizzare), the gig ended violently and attracted heated debate in the press. Bargeld spent the rest of the year touring as bass player for **Nick Cave**, going on to record several studio albums as a member of Cave's backing band,

the Bad Seeds. He returned to the Einstürzende Neubauten set-up for the more structured *Halber Mensch*. Following the release of this enthralling album the band temporarily broke up, but reunited in 1987 to perform the soundtrack for *Andi*, a play at the Hamburg Schauspielhaus, and record *Fünf Auf Der Nach Oben Offenen Richterskala*. This was intended as a farewell album, but they, nevertheless, continued after its release.

Bargeld's part-time career with the Bad Seeds continued, and in 1987 he featured alongside them in Wim Wenders' movie *Der Himmel Über Berlin*. Hacke, ironically, was now contributing to the work of **Crime And The City Solution**, featuring Cave's old Birthday Party colleagues. Einheit restarted the Abwärts and inaugurated his solo project, Stein, while Chung formed Freibank, the band's own publishing company. The various members reunited, however, in time for 1989's *Haus Der Lüge*, which included the sounds of riots around the Berlin Wall as a backdrop. They also signed a contract with **Mute Records** and set up their own Ego subsidiary to house their soundtrack work, which has included the music for the radio play *Die Hamletmaschine* and *Faustmusik*. Their 1993 album *Tabula Rasa* was another politically inclined collection exploring the reunification of Germany. It also demonstrated the band's growing commitment to conventional musical structure, with their trademark industrial sound effects now used to accentuate the atmosphere of a piece rather than just being a case of art for art's sake. *Ende Neu*, with the departed Chung replaced by Andrew Chudy, completed Einstürzende Neubauten's gradual transition to atmospheric rock band. Jochen Arbeit and Rudi Moser were added to the line-up for the sparse, melodic *Silence Is Sexy*, a title that would have been untenable at the start of the band's career.

● ALBUMS: *Kollaps* (Zick Zack 1981) ★★★, *Die Zeichnungen Des Patienten O.T.* (Some Bizzare/Rough Trade 1983) ★★★★, *2x4* cassette-only (ROIR 1984) ★★, *Halber Mensch* (Some Bizzare 1985) ★★★, *Fünf Auf Der Nach Oben Offenen Richterskala* (Some Bizzare/Relativity 1987) ★★★, *Haus Der Lüge* (Some Bizzare/Rough Trade 1989) ★★★, *Die Hamletmaschine* film soundtrack (Ego 1991) ★★, *Tabula Rasa* (Mute 1993) ★★★, *Faustmusik* film soundtrack (Ego 1996) ★★, *Ende Neu* (Mute 1996) ★★★, *Ende Neu Remixes* (Mute 1997) ★★, *Silence Is Sexy* (Mute 2000) ★★★, *9-15-2000, Brussels* (Potomak 2003) ★★★, *Perpetuum Mobile* (Mute 2004) ★★★.

● COMPILATIONS: *Strategien Gegen Architekturen 80=83* (Mute 1984) ★★★, *Strategies Against Architecture II* (Ego/Mute 1991) ★★★, *Strategies Against Architecture III* (Mute 2001) ★★★, *Kalte Sterne: Early Recordings* (Mute 2004) ★★★.

● DVD/VIDEOS: *Halber Mensch* (Doublevision/Mute 1986), *Liebenslieder* (Mute 1993).

Eire Apparent

Originally known as the People, this Irish quartet—Mike Cox (lead guitar), Ernie Graham (vocals/guitar), Chris Stewart (bass) and Dave Lutton (drums)—came to prominence in 1967 when they were signed by the Mike Jeffery/**Chas Chandler** management team, which they shared with **Jimi Hendrix** and the **Soft Machine**. Hendrix produced and guested on the band's sole album, *Sunrise*. A crafted blend of pop and neo-psychedelia, this underrated collection featured several excellent performances, including the vibrant 'Yes I Need

Someone'. Eire Apparent supported Hendrix on a gruelling US tour, but split up after its completion. Ernie Graham later joined **Help Yourself**, before recording a solo album on which he was backed by **Brinsley Schwarz**. Although he did not record with them, **Henry McCullough** was another former member of Eire Apparent. This respected guitarist subsequently featured in the **Grease Band**, **Clancy** and **Wings**.

● ALBUMS: *Sunrise* (Buddah 1969) ★★★.
Solo: Ernie Graham *Ernie Graham* (Vinyl 2002) ★★.

Either/Orchestra

Based in Cambridge, Massachusetts, USA, the eclectic Either/Orchestra was founded in the mid-80s by tenor saxophonist Russ Gershon. A 10-piece, seven-horn group that crosses the sound of a big band with the adventurousness of a small combo, members have included guitarists John Dirac and Jerry Deupree, bass players Larry Roland and Bob Nieske, drummers Syd Smart and **Matt Wilson**, keyboard players John Medeski (of **Medeski, Martin And Wood**) and Ken Freundlich, and brass players John Carlson, Curtis Hasselbring, Russ Jewell, Charlie Kohlhase and Tom Halter, the only member, besides Gershon, who has played with the group since its inception. Gershon founded Accurate Records in 1987, on which the Either/Orchestra have released several wonderfully inventive albums drawing on a vast range of material, including selections from the songbooks of **Duke Ellington**, **Gigi Gryce**, **Sonny Rollins**, **Thelonious Monk**, **John Lennon** and **Burt Bacharach**, alongside band members' originals.

In 1997, the group celebrated their 10th anniversary with a celebratory concert and a two-CD retrospective. Although it disbanded shortly afterwards, Gershon, Kohlhase and Halter re-formed the outfit to record new material, starting with 2001's *More Beautiful Than Death*. New percussionists Harvey Wirht (from Surinam) and Vicente Lebron (from the Dominican Republic) introduced Afro-Cuban rhythms into the mix. This direction was maintained on the 2002 follow-up *Afro-Cubism*. Gershon eschewed his normal approach to write the majority of the material on 2003's *Neo-Modernism*, with the exception of one composition by former bass player Bob Nieske.

● ALBUMS: *Dial E For Either/Orchestra* (Accurate 1986) ★★★★, *Radium* (Accurate 1988) ★★★, *The Half-Life Of Desire* (Accurate 1989) ★★★★, *The Calculus Of Pleasure* (Accurate 1990) ★★★, *The Brunt* (Accurate 1993) ★★★★, *10th Anniversary Concert* (Accurate 1997) ★★★, *More Beautiful Than Death* (Accurate 2000) ★★★★, *Afro-Cubism* (Accurate 2002) ★★★, *Neo-Modernism* (Accurate 2003) ★★★, *Ethiopiques, Vol. 20: Either/Orchestra Live In Addis* (Buda Musique 2005) ★★★.

● COMPILATIONS: *Across The Omniverse* (Accurate 1997) ★★★★.

Eitzel, Mark

b. 30 January 1959, Walnut Creek, San Francisco, California, USA. Widely acclaimed songwriter Mark Eitzel, the leader of **American Music Club**, recorded his first solo studio album in 1996 (a live set recorded at London's Borderline had been released at the start of the decade). *60 Watt Silver Lining* departed a little from Eitzel's established reputation as a despondent writer, offering instead his most optimistic suite of lyrics in a career that has received almost universal adoration. Released on **Virgin Records**, it featured long-

standing American Music Club contributor Bruce Kaplan (pedal steel guitar/piano), drummer Simone White (of **Disposable Heroes Of Hiphoprisy** and **Spearhead** fame) and renowned soundtrack composer **Mark Isham** on trumpet. Alongside a cover version of **Carole King**'s 'There Is No Easy Way Down' were typically detailed narratives such as 'Some Bartenders Have The Gift Of Pardon' and 'Southend On Sea', a song documenting the time Eitzel spent in England during his youth. The following year's *West* was a startling departure, with Eitzel by now sounding positively upbeat. The fuller sound was enriched by the participation of **R.E.M.**'s Peter Buck and the **Screaming Trees**' Barrett Martin. The clumsily titled *Caught In A Trap And I Can't Back Out 'Cause I Love You Too Much Baby* was a largely acoustic affair, featuring material written before Eitzel's collaboration with Buck.

Eitzel returned after a three-year hiatus with the experimental *The Invisible Man*, which used a backdrop of percussion loops and electronic samples to showcase Eitzel's typically insightful lyrics. During this period he also pressed up limited quantities of a 1999 recording with ex–American Music Club guitarist Vudi. Other CDs sold only at Eitzel concerts include *Lover's Leap USA* and *Live On WFMU NYC*. The official 2002 release *Music For Courage & Confidence* featured only non-original material, with Eitzel tackling unlikely material including **Glen Campbell**'s Gentle On My Mind', **Culture Club**'s 'Do You Really Want To Hurt Me?' and **Anne Murray**'s 'Snowbird'. The follow-up *The Ugly American* was stranger still, with Eitzel decamping to Athens to re-record old American Music Club songs in Greek style with local musicians.

Eitzel subsequently reunited with his former colleagues to record the wonderful new American Music Club album, *Love Songs For Patriots*. The next Eitzel solo album, *Candy Ass*, was released at the end of 2005.

● ALBUMS: *Songs Of Love Live* (Demon 1992) ★★★, *60 Watt Silver Lining* (Virgin 1996) ★★★, *West* (Warners 1997) ★★★★, *Caught In A Trap And I Can't Back Out 'Cause I Love You Too Much Baby* (Matador 1998) ★★★, *The Invisible Man* (Matador 2001) ★★★★, *Live On WFMU NYC* (Own Label 2001) ★★★, *Superhitsinternational* 1999 recording (Own Label 2001) ★★★, *Music For Courage & Confidence* (New West 2002) ★★★, *The Ugly American* (Tongue Master/Thirsty Ear 2003) ★★, *Candy Ass* (Cooking Vinyl 2005) ★★★.

● COMPILATIONS: *Lover's Leap USA* (Own Label 1998) ★★★.

● FURTHER READING: *Wish The World Away: Mark Eitzel And The American Music Club*, Sean Body.

Ekyan, André

b. André Echkyan, 24 October 1907, Meudon, France, d. 9 August 1972, Alicante, Spain. A self-taught clarinettist and alto saxophonist, Ekyan became well known in France in the early 30s. He also played in London, with **Jack Hylton**, and made many recordings. The musicians with whom he worked included **Django Reinhardt**, recording with him in the late 30s and again in 1950. He also played with **Coleman Hawkins** and **Benny Carter**. A secure and competent player, Ekyan was important in helping spread swing-era jazz styling throughout France and other parts of Europe.

El Din, Hamza

b. 1929, Nubia, Egypt. After completing his studies at the Department of Electrical Engineering in Cairo, Egypt, Hamza El Din began working for a local railway company. With the contents of his first wage packet he purchased an oud, and saved up for a course at the Foado College of Music. After becoming versed in traditional Nubian songcraft, he began to write his own compositions, gradually gaining a reputation for his singing that spread throughout Cairo. In 1959 he was awarded a scholarship by the Italian government to study guitar at the Santa Cecillia College of Music in Rome. After graduation in 1968 he travelled to the USA, where he has remained since, taking part in a variety of ethnomusicology programmes at American universities to spread knowledge of African music and culture. He also taught part-time at the University of Washington in Seattle, while his notable concert appearances include the Newport Folk Festival in 1964 and **Woodstock Festival** in 1969. Over his career he has collaborated with a number of musicians, from **Mickey Hart** of the **Grateful Dead** to a Japanese waidaiko (drum) player. He has also composed music for a play directed by Peter Sellers, *The Persians*, which was performed by the **Kronos Quartet**. An excellent introduction to his wide-ranging musical abilities came in 1996 with the JVC Recordings release of *Muwashshah*, the title named after an Arabic classical song form used in performance and the teaching of vocal music. Its release confirmed the oft-stated perception of Hamza El Din as 'the king of modern Nubian music'.

● ALBUMS: *Muwashshah* (JVC 1996) ★★★★, *Available Sound—Darius* (Lotus 1996) ★★★.

El Dorados

This Chicago, Illinois, USA, R&B vocal group achieved fame with one of the great jump tracks of the early rock 'n' roll era, 'At My Front Door', also called 'Crazy Little Mama'. Members on that hit were Pirkle Lee Moses (lead), Louis Bradley (second tenor), Jewel Jones (first tenor), James Maddox (baritone) and Richard Nickens (d. 1991; bass). The group was formed in 1952, and signed with **Vee Jay Records** in 1954. The El Dorados achieved nothing but local hits until finding success with 'At My Front Door' in 1955, when it went to number 2 R&B and number 17 pop. The group's only other chart record was the mid-tempo 'I'll Be Forever Loving You' (number 8 R&B 1956). The group reorganized in 1958, when Pirkle Lee Moses was abandoned by the other members and recruited new singers from another Vee Jay group, the **Kool Gents**, whose lead, **Dee Clark**, had just deserted them. The new El Dorados besides Moses were Doug Brown, John McCall and Teddy Long (d. 1991), but, having no luck with further releases, this group broke up in 1959. Despite the El Dorados' meagre chart success most of their records have been cherished by doo-wop fans, who find the group not only one of the more soulful-sounding of the 50s doo-wop ensembles but equally adept at both ballads (notably 'I Began To Realize') and jumps (typically 'Bim Bam Boom'). The group took, perhaps unconsciously, a music that most observers considered nothing more than a commercial entertainment and created a profound and genuine folk art.

● ALBUMS: *Crazy Little Mama* (Vee Jay 1957) ★★★.

● COMPILATIONS: *Bim Bam Boom* (Charly 1981) ★★★, *Rock 'n' Roll's For Me* (Charly 1997) ★★★, *At My Front Door . . . Crazy Little Mama: The Very Best Of The El Dorados* (Collectables 2000) ★★★★.

El Gran Combo

In May 1962, under the leadership of pianist/arranger/composer Rafael Ithier, members of **Rafael Cortijo**'s Combo deserted to become the 11-piece El Gran Combo (EGC). The defectors were Rogelio 'Kito' Vélez (d. 1990; trumpet and arrangements); Eddie Pérez and Héctor Santos (saxophones), Martin Quiñones (conga), **Roberto Roena** (bongo and dancer), Miguel Cruz (deceased) (bass). They were joined by **Andy Montañez** and Pellín Rodríguez (b. Pedro Rodríguez de Gracia, 4 December 1926, Santurce, San Juan, Puerto Rico, d. 31 October 1984; vocals), Milton Correa (timbales) and Victor Pérez (trumpet). They became the quintessential salsa dance band, churning out hit albums for three decades. With the addition of a trombone in the late 60s and a third vocalist at the beginning of the 70s, EGC retained the resultant 13-piece format (two saxophones, two trumpets, trombone, conga, bongo, timbales, bass, piano and three singers) until the present day. The only founding members remaining in the 90s version of the band are leader Ithier and Eddie Pérez. In February 1963, members of EGC (Ithier, Cruz, Roena, Correa, Quiñones, Vélez, Eddie Pérez, Santos) comprised the backbone of an early morning Latin jam session (descarga) recording led by **Kako**, and issued under the title *Puerto Rican All-Stars Featuring Kako* in 1965. The other participants included **Charlie Palmieri** and **Mario Ortiz**.

Vélez handled arrangements until his departure in the mid-60s, and wrote their perennial hit 'Ojos Chinos' (Chinese Eyes), from *Ojos Chinos—Jala Jala* (1964). From 1965's *El Caballo Pelotero* until 1988, Ithier was the band's sole arranger. To accommodate the massively popular romantic salsa style, Ithier delegated arranging duties to two external arrangers on seven out of the eight tracks on 1989's chart-topping *Amame!* Ernesto Sánchez did the lion's share—five cuts, including the title track. Baritone saxophonist with Mario Ortiz since the mid-80s, Sánchez was responsible for arranging **Lalo Rodríguez**'s monster 1988 salsa romántica hit 'Ven Devórame Otra Vez' (Come And Devour Me Again). Ithier totally abstained from arranging on *Latin-Up!* in 1990, while Sánchez was hired again to write the charts for five of the tracks. EGC had gone 'off the rails' once before, in the second half of the 60s, when the overwhelming pressure of the boogaloo craze obliged them to record a number of songs in this R&B/Latin fusion style. After leaving, Vélez recorded with his own band, *Kito Vélez Y Sus Estrellas* and *Kito Vélez Y Sus Estrellas Vol. 2*, and worked with the Nelson Feliciano Orchestra. He wrote all the arrangements on *Nelson Feliciano/Canta: Junior Cordova* and arranged and played on *Nelson Feliciano Orch./Kito Vélez/Canta: Joe P.* (1973). Vélez and Quiñones appeared on 1967's *Los Mejores Musicos De Puerto Rico* (*The Best Musicians Of Puerto Rico*), which was directed by Ray Santos, who wrote the arrangements and played baritone saxophone. In mid-1969, Roena left Gran Combo to lead his own band.

For the first eight years of their existence, El Gran Combo recorded on the Gema Records label. In 1970, they launched their own EGC Record Corp. and released 11 albums on the label up to 1978. Also in 1970, they won the Momo De Oro award for The Best International Band at carnival in Caracas, Venezuela. Rodríguez departed after 1972's *Por El Libro*. He worked as a solo artist and as a co-lead singer with La Salsa Mayor, **Oscar D'León**'s former band. Charlie Aponte replaced Rodríguez on *El Gran Combo 5*, recorded in August 1973. The same month, EGC appeared at the **Fania All Stars** historic first concert at New York's Yankee Stadium. In August 1974, *Juntos Otra Vez* (*Back Together Again*) reunited Cortijo with his 1962 combo accompanists who broke away to become EGC, namely, Ithier, Eddie Pérez, Roena, Vélez, Santos, Cruz and Quiñones. In 1976, Gran Combo were featured in Jerry Masucci's movie *Salsa* and on the soundtrack album, performing a 'live' version of their 1972 hit 'Julia' (from *Por El Libro*). In 1977, EGC suffered a considerable blow when Andy Montañez split to join then top Venezuelan salsa band, **Dimensión Latina**. On the recommendation of Quique Lucca, leader of **Sonora Ponceña**, his vacancy was filled on 1978's *15to Aniversario* by Jerry Rivas (b. 1955, Puerto Rico). EGC celebrated their 20th anniversary with a tribute concert at New York's Madison Square Garden on 4 September 1982, and released the double album *20 Años—20 Exitos* (*20 Years—20 Hits*), which contained new recordings and remixes of their two decades of hits. That year, some ex-members of Gran Combo, including Pellín, Roena, Quiñones, Correa, Santos and Victor Pérez, re-grouped under the banner of El Combo Del Ayer (The Combo Of The Past) for *El Combo Del Ayer*, and again the following year for *Aquel Gran Encuentro*. In October 1983, Ithier collaborated with **Luis 'Perico' Ortiz**, **Rubén Blades**, singer Roberto Lugo and members of the Dominican merengue band Conjunto Quisqueya on *Entre Amigos* (*Between Friends*). The album contained 'Homenaje (Rafael Ithier)', a tribute to Ithier written by Perico and **Ramón Rodríguez**. In 1987, Gran Combo's quarter of a century was marked with the celebratory three-disc *25th Anniversary 1962–1987/Today, Tomorrow & Always*.

Prominent Puerto Rican composer Roberto Angleró wrote a number of Gran Combo's hits, including: 'Serrana' (*Smile It's El Gran Combo*, 1968), 'Dos Copas Y Un Olé' (*Este Si Que Es El Gran Combo*, 1969), 'La Salsa De Hoy' (*Disfrútelo Hasta El Cabo!*, 1974), 'La Soledad' (*Mejor Que Nunca/Better Than Ever*, 1976), 'Aquí No Pasado Nada' (*El Gran Combo En Las Vegas*, 1978). Angleró also recorded as a vocalist and band leader, i.e. *Roberto Angleró Y Su Combo* (*c.*1970), *Guaya Salsa?* (1973), *Tierra Negra* (1979), *Por El Color De Tu Piel* (1980), *Trulla Moderna* (1981), *El Apretón* (1982) and *Roberto Angleró* (1984).

EGC's frequent international tours included their UK debut in 1986 and return visits in 1989 and 1990. The band function as a co-operative, with each member receiving an equal share of the earnings. This has contributed to their continuity of personnel and tightness of sound. The 1991 line-up read: Ithier (piano and musical director), Aponte, Rivas and Papo Rosario (vocals), Taty Maldonado and Victor E. Rodríguez (trumpets), Eddie Pérez and Freddy Miranda (saxophones), Fanny Ceballo (d. 1991; trombone), Fernando 'Freddy' Rivera (bass), Miguel Torres (conga), Cuqui Santos (timbales) and José Miguel Laboy (bongo). Ceballo was replaced by Moises Nogueras, who worked previously as a 'staff' trombonist for Tony Moreno's Musical Productions label, sessioning on albums by Roberto Lugo, Willie González, Pedro Arroyo, Andy and Harold Montañez, Nino Segarra, Tito Rojas, Anthony Cruz and **Tito Gómez**. Ithier resumed total control of arranging chores on 1991's *Erupción!*, and the relaxed freshness of some of his charts clearly demonstrated that he had benefited from his respite.

● ALBUMS: *Meneame Los Mangos, El Gran Combo . . . De Siempre* (1962) ★★, *Acángana* (1963) ★★★, *Ojos Chinos—Jala Jala* (1964) ★★★★, *El Caballo Pelotero* (1965) ★★★, *El Swing Del Gran Combo* (1966) ★★★, *El Gran Combo En Navidad, Maldito Callo, Esos Ojitos Negros, Fiesta Con El Gran Combo, Boleros Románticos Con El Gran Combo, Boogaloos Con El Gran Combo, Tu Querias Boogaloo?, Pata Pata Jala Jala Boogaloo, Tangos Por El Gran Combo* (1967), *Los Nenes Sicodelicos, Latin Power, Smile It's El Gran Combo* (1968) ★★★, *Este Si Que Es El Gran Combo* (1969) ★★★, *Estamos Primeros* (1970) ★★★, *De Punta A Punta* (1971) ★★★, *Por El Libro* (1972) ★★★, *En Acción* (1973) ★★★, *El Gran Combo 5* (1973) ★★★★, *Disfrútelo Hasta El Cabo!* (1974) ★★, *El Gran Combo 7* (1975) ★★★★, *El Gran Combo* (1975) ★★★, *Mejor Que Nunca (Better Than Ever)* (1976) ★★★, *15to Aniversario* (1977) ★★★, *El Gran Combo En Las Vegas* (1978) ★★, *Aquí No Se Sienta Nadie!* (1979) ★★★, *Unity* (1980) ★★★, *Happy Days* (1981) ★★★, *Nuestro Aniversario* (1982) ★★★, *La Universidad De La Salsa* (1983) ★★★, *El Gran Combo In Alaska: Breaking The Ice* (1984) ★★★, *Innovations* (1985) ★★★★, *Nuestra Musica* (1985) ★★★, *Y Su Pueblo* (1986) ★★★, *Romántico Y . . . Sabroso* (1988) ★★, *Amame!* (1989) ★★★, *Latin-Up* (1990) ★★★, *Erupcíon!* (1991) ★★★, *40 Aniversario* (BMG Latin 2002) ★★★★.
● COMPILATIONS: *Sus 15 Grandes Hits, 15 Grandes Exitos Vol. 2*; *Historia Musical De El Gran Combo De Puerto Rico: 20 Años—20 Exitos* (1982) ★★★★, *25th Anniversary 1962–1987/Today, Tomorrow & Always* (1987) ★★★★.

El Gran Silencio

Latin alternative band El Gran Silencio (the Great Silence) have dubbed their energetic and eclectic music 'free-style norteno popular'. The project began in Monterray, Mexico, in 1992, as a means for brothers Tony Hernández (vocals/guitar) and Cano Hernández (vocals/guitar) to fuse their history in various rock bands with their love for hip-hop and norteno. The Hernández brothers plus 'El Vulgar' Hernandez (bass), Isaac Valdez (accordion) and Ezequiel Alvarado (drums) draw on elements as disparate as punk, ska, rock, hip-hop, norteno, cumbia, pagode, ragamuffin and rumba flamenco, and utilize instruments such as the African yambe and chekere, the Colombian guacharaca and the Middle Eastern darbuka alongside those more usually found in a rock band. El Gran Silencio state they 'feel like rockers' and have 'a rock 'n' roll heart', acknowledging that it is rock that allows them to mix and match genres so easily.

On 2003's *¡Super Riddim Internacional! Vol. 1*, the first release in a two-volume set initially envisaged as a double album but wisely truncated, the band were also explicitly inspired by the cumbia roots of norteno, looking to Colombian music such as merengue, puya, porro, and paseo for further inspiration. Yet alongside these traditional musics, the group's DJ Macojazz (actually, an alter-ego for Tony Hernández) also deploys overtly hip-hop/trip-hop influenced loops. However, this blend is not always successful; rather El Gran Silencio proves that eclecticism can sometimes be scrappy and wearying, however enthusiastically attempted. Strangely, the band incorporated the voices of their critics on 'Intro' (from *¡Super Riddim Internacional! Vol. 1*). El Gran Silencio notably dedicated 'Ingratos Corazones' to **George Harrison**, **Run-DMC**'s Jam Master Jay, **Joe Strummer** and Rodrigo 'Gzz'. The band take their name from a song by the latter (aka Rodrigo 'Rockrigo' Gonzalez), a socially conscious singer-songwriter who died in Mexico City's 1985 earthquake.

● ALBUMS: *Libres Y Locos* (EMI Latin 1999) ★★★, *Chuntaros Radio Poder* (EMI Latin 2001) ★★★, *¡Super Riddim Internacional! Vol. 1* (EMI Latin 2003) ★★★.

El Hula

The creation of singer-songwriter Blair Jollands, a New Zealand expatriate based in London, England. Prior to his departure from New Zealand in the mid-90s, Jollands played in a number of bands based in Auckland and also performed as a solo artist on the coffee house circuit. Shortly after recording his 1994 cassette debut, he left New Zealand to attempt to broker a music contract in New York, but ended up in London where he put together El Hula with guitarist Rhys Hughes. The debut album, *Hotel*, was recorded with a number of session musicians and released in 2001 through **Boy George**'s More Protein imprint. The record's elegant lush pop went largely unnoticed in the UK charts, although Jollands' adoption of the vocal mannerisms of **Scott Walker** and Jim Morrison was enough to attract the attention of several music critics. The follow-up, *Violent Love*, was a more coherent set, and included two contemporary classics in 'Bitter Girl' and 'Killer Landings'. Jollands was supported at live shows by a band including Hughes, Noam Halby (drums), Andrew Park (bass), Sarah Brown (vocals) and Sandy Mill (vocals).
● ALBUMS: as Blair Jollands *Fuzzhead* cassette (Glowb 1994) ★★, *Hotel* (Glowb/More Protein 2001) ★★★, *Violent Love* (Glowb/More Protein 2003) ★★★★.

El Medioni, Maurice

b. 18 September 1928, Oran, Algeria. A Jewish pianist, El Medioni first took up the piano at age nine. Following the Allied invasion of Algeria in 1942, he played the hits of the day in bars frequented by American soldiers from whom he learnt jazz, boogie woogie and Cuban rumba. After the war he worked as a tailor and also played with various western groups based in Algeria. In 1948 he discovered the **rai** music of Algeria's Arab community and formed a multi-cultural group with whom he played both at Muslim weddings and at the Café Oran in the city's Jewish Quarter. Two years later he also started to play with Jewish orchestras, performing the Andalusian music of Algeria's Jewish community. Following the outbreak of the Algerian War of Independence, El Medioni moved to Paris where he resumed tailoring and also backed many of the best known French Jewish singers. In 1967 he bought a clothing business in Marseilles and, aside from very occasional one-off performances with Jewish singers, retired from music. In the 80s, inspired by the resurgence of interest in rai, El Medioni reunited with some of the Arab musicians he had played with in the 40s and 50s, and re-created his unique cross-cultural style of Algerian music. Returning to music full time, he started to perform with young French-based Arab musicians and also Jewish singers in France and Israel. *Café Oran*, El Medioni's belated international debut release, was produced by Hijaz Mustapha (of **3 Mustaphas 3**) and featured guest appearances from **Salamat**'s Mahmoud Fadl and members of the **Klezmatics**, playing alongside musicians who had originally accompanied El Medioni nearly half a century earlier. The sound is a unique blend of influences, including Arabic, Jewish, Cuban, over which El Medioni improvises his own distinctly Algerian/Jewish variation of boogie woogie and jazz.

● ALBUMS: *Café Oran* (Piranha 1996) ★★★★, *Samaï Andalou* (Magda 2000) ★★★.

El-P

b. Jaime Meline, 1975, Brooklyn, New York City, USA. As a member of **Company Flow**, alongside Mr. Len and Bigg Jus, El-P aka El Producto created hip-hop that was gritty and paranoid and dismissive of mainstream agendas. Although the producer now says that the *Funcrusher* EP (1995) and its subsequent extension *Funcrusher Plus* became 'like monsters', Company Flow provided a potent counterpoint to mainstream hip-hop aesthetics. With Company Flow's relationship with their label, Rawkus Records, deteriorating, El-P formed his own Def Jux imprint (later renamed Definitive Jux, at the behest of **Def Jam Records**) releasing the last El-P/Bigg Jus/Mr. Len collaborative recordings alongside music by **Cannibal Ox**, **Aesop Rock**, **RJD2** and **Mr. Lif**. The debut album from Cannibal Ox, *The Cold Vein*, was possibly the most evocative and inventive debut hip-hop album since **Public Enemy**'s *Yo! Bum Rush The Show*. The record showcases grimy beats/bleeps/textures as wayward and dysfunctional as anything on **Warp Records** or Schematic, with El-P's corrupted post-electro backdrop and MCs Vast Aire and Vordul Megilah's brutal aphorisms complementing each other perfectly. El-P's contribution to the album was not diminished with its subsequent exposure in an instrumental version (credited to El-P).
The producer's *Fantastic Damage* sought to replicate the energy of early Public Enemy and drew influence from the literature of George Orwell and Philip K. Dick. The dense and disfigured album featured a fantasy about a post-apocalyptic Disney World, referenced late 80s US economic policy and imagined a corporation manufacturing mechanical abusive stepfathers. El-P has also collaborated with **Del Tha Funky Homosapien**, **Handsome Boy Modeling School**, **DJ Krush**, **Alec Empire**, **Quannum** and **Techno Animal**, and has been sampled by artists such as **Primal Scream**.
● ALBUMS: *El-P Presents Cannibal Oxtrumentals* (Definitive Jux 2001) ★★★★, *Fantastic Damage* (Definitive Jux 2002) ★★★★, *FandamPlus* (Definitive Jux 2002) ★★★, *High Water* (Thirsty Ear 2004) ★★★.

El Venos

A rare sextet in the 50s R&B scene, this Pittsburgh, Pennsylvania, USA, group's ranks featured Leon Daniels (lead), sister Anna Mae Jackson (lead), brother Joey Daniels (baritone), Daniel Jackson (first tenor), Leon Taylor (second tenor) and Bernard Palmer (bass). They began on the familiar street-corner career route in 1955, eventually signing with **RCA Records**, where they were placed on their Groove Records R&B subsidiary. A few months later 'Geraldine', written by Taylor, was released to instant favour. The song was played on **Dick Clark**'s *American Bandstand* television show, but the possibility of a live appearance was lost when the members were unable to raise the finance for the journey to Philadelphia. Instead the El Venos were forced to content themselves with local shows, often conducted with major artists such as the **Heartbeats** who were passing through Pittsburgh. They transferred to a second RCA affiliate, Vik Records, for their second single, 'You Must Be True', but this failed to match the impact of their debut. The next two years were spent raising money in order to travel to New York for auditions. However, Calico Records chose not to release the two songs the El Venos recorded with them. The same fate befell two more songs recorded for **Mercury Records**' Amp 3 subsidiary. Dispirited, the group broke up, with Anna Mae Jackson changing her name to Anne Keith and releasing a solo record, backed by the **Altairs** (the band formed by their erstwhile sponsor, Pittsburgh disc jockey Bill Powell).

Elaborate Lives: The Legend Of Aida

Apparently executives of **Walt Disney** Theatrical Productions felt the original title of Guiseppe Verdi's *Aida* was rather 'too gloomy and hard to pronounce' for the rock opera audience they wanted to reach with a $15 million spectacular. So they eventually sprawled the somewhat unwieldy *Elton John And Tim Rice's Elaborate Lives: The Legend Of Aida* on the marquee for this show, which had its world premiere performances at the Alliance Theatre Company, Atlanta, Georgia, from 7 October to 8 November 1998 (plus previews). The production was 'suggested' by Verdi's 1871 version of his great work—the most famous interpretation—and Linda Woolverton's 'simplistic' book covers familiar ground. With Egypt and Ethiopia at war, Ethiopian slave Aida (**Heather Headley**, 'outstanding in every way')—who turns out to be a princess—falls in love with the Egyptian general Radames (Hank Stratton). However, Aida's mistress, the Egyptian princess Amneris (Sherie Scott), has designs on Radames herself. Eventually sentenced to die for an act of betrayal, Radames is joined by Aida as a vast pyramid, the central feature of the $10 million laser-powered set, finally entombs the couple for ever. Nekhen (Scott Irby-Ranniar), as an Ethiopian slave boy, gave a notable performance, and the cast also included Neal Benari (Pharaoh), Roger Robinson (Aida's father, Amonasro), Mary Bentley-LaMar (Nehebka), Future Davis (Nenu), Pamela Gold (Shu), Jenny Hill (Hefnut) and Rich Herbert (Zoser).

Initial critical reaction suggested that this *Aida* was closer to contemporary television drama than the Metropolitan Opera Company, while one scribe's derision was reserved especially for the second number, 'Our Nation Holds Sway' (reprised as first act finalé), which he described this way: 'Oh-oh-ohhh. Our nation holds sway (on the word "sway", everyone, got up in gaudy Egyptian togs, wags his butt).' In fact, **Elton John** and **Tim Rice**'s 'infectious pop-rock score' came out of it far better than Woolverton's storyline, which appeared to be 'a spoof of Ancient Egypt' in the first act, but decidedly more melodramatic in the second. A blend of gospel, blues, 50s rock 'n' roll, a surfeit of love ballads and the odd amusing moment, were in there amongst 'Every Story Is A Love Story' (reprised at curtain), 'The Past Is Another Land', 'Another Pyramid', 'How I Know You' (and reprise), 'My Strongest Suit', 'Night Of Nights', 'Enchantment Passing Through', 'The Dance Of The Robe', 'Elaborate Lives', 'A Step Too Far', 'Easy As Life', 'Like Father Like Son', 'The Gods Love Nubia', 'Written In The Stars', 'I Know The Truth' (and reprise), 'The Judgement', and 'The Messenger'. Just a week after *Elaborate Lives* closed, Disney dismissed the backstage creative team of director Robert Jess Roth, choreographer Matt West, set designer Stanley Meyer, costume designer Ann Hould-Ward, and lighting designer Natasha Katz. These were the people behind Disney's first stage musical hit, **Beauty And The Beast**. Experienced theatre watchers wondered whether *Elaborate Lives* would ever reach Broadway and the commercial heights of Beauty, the far superior

The Lion King or those other two comparatively recent musicals inspired by operas, **Miss Saigon** (*Madame Butterfly*) and **Rent** (*La Boheme*). Their answer came on 23 March 2000, when the show, now under the title of *Aida*, finally opened at the Palace Theatre in New York with a cast headed by Heather Headley (Aida), Adam Pascal (Radames), Sherie Scott (Amneris), John Hickok (Zoser), Damian Perkins (Mereb), Tyrees Allen (Amonasro) and Daniel Oreskes (Pharaoh). This production had a book by Woolverton, Robert Falls and David Henry Hwang, choreography by Wayne Cilento, and was directed by Robert Falls. There were three new songs, 'Fortune Favours The Brave', 'Not Me', and 'Radames' Letter' in Rice and John's score, for which they won a **Tony Award**. Further Tonys went to Headley (Best Actress), Bob Crowley (Scenic Design) and Natasha Katz (Lighting). The show's Original Cast album also won a Grammy Award.

Earlier in 1998 a large scale, visually stunning production of the genuine *Aida*—500 extras, 1,500 costumes—was presented at the cavernous Earls Court in London. As with *Elaborate Lives*, it too utilized several banks of lasers—projecting shifting kaleidoscopic images along the vast length of the arena—and other sophisticated lighting and scenic effects. The similarities probably ended there though, judging by Tim Rice's reported comments prior to the debut of the Atlanta show: 'A bloke called Verdi had a go with *Aida*. We're slinging out the problem area—Verdi's music—and keeping the story with Elton's music and my words.'

● FURTHER READING: *Elton John And Tim Rice's Aida: The Making Of The Broadway Musical*, Michael Lassell.

Elastica

One of the most prominent bands on the UK independent scene during the 90s, Elastica's line-up coalesced around Justine Frischmann (b. 16 September 1969, Twickenham, London, England; vocals/guitar), Donna Matthews (b. 2 December 1971, Newport, Wales; bass), Justin Welch (b. 4 December 1972, Nuneaton, Warwickshire, England; drums) and Annie Holland (b. 26 August 1965, Brighton, England; guitar). Frischmann is the daughter of a prominent architect (her father built London's Centre Point skyscraper), and she attended a private school in London. Some of Elastica's original notoriety sprang from the fact that Frischmann was in an early incarnation of **Suede** and was romantically linked with that band's singer, Brett Anderson, then **Blur**'s Damon Albarn. Indeed, one of Elastica's songs, 'See That Animal'—the b-side to 'Connection'—was co-written with Anderson when both attended University College London. They lived together in a dilapidated north London house while Suede looked for a recording contract. She left in October 1991 just before they were signed by Nude Records.

There was more to Elastica than nepotism, as they demonstrated with a series of stunning singles ('Stutter', 'Line Up', 'Connection') after they formed as a result of Frischmann placing advertisements in the British music press. Wearing punk and new wave influences as diverse as **Adam And The Ants**, **Blondie** and **Bow Wow Wow** on their sleeves, they nevertheless chose to avoid the New Wave Of The New Wave bandwagon, consolidating their appeal with a place on the bill of 1994's Reading Festival. Their records were released in the UK by Steve Lamacq's Deceptive label and worldwide by **Geffen Records**. Elastica's fourth single, 'Waking Up', practically a musical rewrite of the **Stranglers**'

'No More Heroes', was, nevertheless, as exciting a single as any to hit the UK charts in early 1995 (the song reached number 13). While the chord sequences could too often be linked directly to particular antecedents—the similarities between the two UK Top 20 singles 'Line Up' and 'Connection', and *Chairs Missing*–era **Wire** being the best of several examples (and one that resulted in a royalty settlement, as did 'Waking Up' with the Stranglers' publishers)—Frischmann's lyrics on Elastica's self-titled debut album, released in March, fitted the post-feminist 90s perfectly. Critics also leaped on veiled references to her past and present paramours: 'We were sitting there waiting and I told you my plan, You were far too busy writing lines that didn't scan'.

Holland departed in August 1995 to be replaced by Sheila Chipperfield, and Dave Bush (keyboards) became the fifth member. Further changes ensued in 1999, with Matthews leaving and Chipperfield making way for the returning Holland. The line-up was augmented by guitarist Paul Jones (ex-Linoleum) and keyboard player Mew (b. Sharon Mew). A six-track EP of new material was released to mixed reviews at the end of the year. The band's long delayed second album, which by now had assumed almost mythical status, was finally released in April 2000. Ironically, the tracks on *The Menace* came from a six-week burst of activity the previous December. A collection of Radio 1 archive material, released in November 2001, proved to be a suitably patchy swansong for this erratic band. Frischmann reappeared as a television presenter on the BBC during 2003.

● ALBUMS: *Elastica* (Deceptive/Geffen 1995) ★★★★, *The Menace* (Deceptive/Atlantic 2000) ★★★.
● COMPILATIONS: *The Radio One Sessions* (Strange Fruit 2001) ★★★.
● FURTHER READING: *The Last Party: Britpop, Blair And The Demise Of English Rock*, John Harris.

Elbert, Donnie

b. 25 May 1936, New Orleans, Louisiana, USA, d. 31 January 1989. Elbert's prolific career began in the 50s as a member of the Vibraharps. His first solo hit, 'What Can I Do?', was released in 1957, but the singer's career was interrupted by a spell in the US Army. Discharged in 1961, recordings for **Parkway Records** and Checker then followed, before Elbert the labels, Gateway/Upstate, co-founded by Robert Schachner in 1964. His reputation was secured by 'Run Little Girl' and 'A Little Piece Of Leather', compulsive performances highlighting Elbert's irrepressible falsetto. The latter single became a standard in UK soul clubs when it was released on the Sue label and on the strength of this popularity Elbert went to the UK where he married and settled. The singer pursued his career with several releases, including an album of **Otis Redding** cover versions, *Tribute To A King*. Elbert returned to the USA in 1970 although his pounding version of the **Supremes**' 'Where Did Our Love Go?' (1972) was recorded in London. A hit on both sides of the Atlantic, it was followed in 1972 by 'I Can't Help Myself', another reworking of a Tamla/**Motown Records** classic. Elbert's last UK chart entry came with a new, but inferior, version of 'A Little Bit Of Leather' (1972), although he continued to appear in the US R&B listings up until 1977. Elbert later moved to Canada where he became an A&R director with **PolyGram Records**.

● ALBUMS: *The Sensational Donnie Elbert Sings* (King 1959) ★★★, *Tribute To A King* (Gateway 1968) ★★, *Where Did Our Love Go* (All Platinum 1971) ★★, *Have I Sinned* (1971) ★★, *Stop In The Name Of Love* (Avco 1972) ★★, *A Little Bit Of Leather* (1972) ★★, *Dancin' The Night Away* (All Platinum 1977) ★★.
● COMPILATIONS: *The Roots Of Donnie Elbert* (Ember 1973) ★★★★, *The Greatest Hits Of Donnie Elbert* (Collectables 1996) ★★★★.

Elbow

This Manchester, England–based quintet purveys atmospheric, epic rock music for the new millennium. Guy Garvey (vocals), Mark Potter (guitar), Craig Potter (keyboards), Pete Turner (bass) and Richard Jupp (drums) met at the start of the 90s at sixth form college in Bury. They formed the funk-fusion outfit Soft, before relocating to Manchester and fashioning a new rock-orientated sound as Elbow. The quintet signed a contract with **Island Records** in 1998, but was still in the process of recording their debut album when Island was taken over by Universal and their contract was terminated. The Manchester-based independent label Ugly Man Records released two EPs, *New Born* and *Any Day Now*, which generated renewed interest in the band. A new recording contract with V2 Records followed in late 2000. The band remixed five of the tracks from their abortive Island album and recorded six new songs for *Asleep In The Back*, which was released in May 2001. The intricate textures and slow-burn intensity of the music drew on a rich heritage, from the **Steve Miller** Band to **Talk Talk**, while the lyrics balanced the realities of urban living with an underlying optimism. Neither *Cast Of Thousands* (2003) or *Leaders Of The Free World* (2005) was able to replicate the majestic cohesiveness of Elbow's debut, although both were fine albums in their own right. Elbow remains one of the more interesting outfits to originate from Manchester in recent years.

● ALBUMS: *Asleep In The Back* (V2 2001) ★★★★, *Cast Of Thousands* (V2 2003) ★★★, *Leaders Of The Free World* (V2 2005) ★★★.

Elders, Betty

b. USA. Elders made a spectacular impression in the folk music fraternity with the release of her 1993 album *Peaceful Existence*, which garnered international acclaim and led to a major recording contract with **Flying Fish Records**. On the surface there was little to distinguish the material from that by a thousand other singer-songwriters, yet repeated listening identified her ability to plant captivating images through a screen of gentle, guitar-accompanied singing. *Crayons* (1995) did not vary the format, but added even darker tinges to her subject matter while maintaining the stark simplicity of her earlier recordings.

● ALBUMS: *Peaceful Existence* (1993) ★★★★, *Crayons* (Flying Fish 1995) ★★★.

Eldridge, Joe

b. 1908, Pittsburgh, Pennsylvania, USA, d. 5 March 1952. A competent alto saxophonist, with considerable experience in **territory bands**, Eldridge's career was eclipsed by that of his younger brother with whom he formed a band in 1936. After **Roy Eldridge** went on to greater things, Joe Eldridge continued working with 30s bands such as **McKinney's**

Cotton Pickers, Blanche Calloway, **Zutty Singleton** and others. In the 40s he worked again with Roy and Singleton and also with **Oran 'Hot Lips' Page** before spending several years in Canada. Back in the USA in 1950 he played and taught a little in New York until his death in 1952.

Eldridge, Roy

b. David Roy Eldridge, 30 January 1911, Pittsburgh, Pennsylvania, USA, d. 26 February 1989, Valley Stream, New York, USA. One of the chief figures in the established lineage of jazz trumpet playing, Eldridge paid his dues with **territory bands** in the Midwest, such as those of **Speed Webb** and **Horace Henderson**, before moving to New York in 1930. He then played with a number of bands, including that of **Teddy Hill** and one that he co-led with his brother, **Joe Eldridge**. In 1935 he joined **Fletcher Henderson**'s orchestra, then formed his own group, which was reasonably successful but not so much so that he could afford to refuse an offer to join **Gene Krupa** in 1941. The engagement brought Eldridge to great prominence thanks to extensive tours of the USA and numerous recordings, notably solo features on 'Rockin' Chair', 'After You've Gone' and 'Let Me Off Uptown' (on which he partnered **Anita O'Day**).

Despite the enormous boost to his popularity that resulted from the exposure he gained with Krupa, this was a very trying time for Eldridge who, as the only black member of the band, suffered racial harassment that brought him to the brink of a nervous breakdown. When Krupa was jailed in 1943, Eldridge briefly fronted the band before it broke up. He then formed his own band before giving a second chance to the white big band scene with **Artie Shaw** and once again he encountered discrimination and abuse. After briefly trying another big band of his own, Eldridge settled on leading a small group. In the late 40s he worked again with Krupa and also joined **Jazz At The Philharmonic**. In the 50s he played with **Benny Goodman**, spent some time in Europe and continued his association with JATP. This period coincided with a personal crisis during which Eldridge began to doubt his place in jazz as the new generation of trumpeters, led by **Dizzy Gillespie**, forged new ideas. The stay in Europe convinced him that his place was in the mainstream of jazz, and that it was a place in which he was respected by musicians and admired by fans. In the 60s, Eldridge played with **Ella Fitzgerald**, **Coleman Hawkins** and **Count Basie** and co-led a band with **Richie Kamuca**. In 1970 he began a residency at Ryans in New York City that lasted into the second half of the decade.

A fiery, combative player, Eldridge is often cited as a link between trumpeters **Louis Armstrong** and Dizzy Gillespie. Although there is an element of logic in this assessment, it overlooks the important role in jazz trumpet history of **Henry 'Red' Allen**; and it implies that Eldridge was a proto-bop trumpeter, which is far from being the truth. He was the outstanding trumpet stylist of the 40s, performing with daring aggression, his high register playing achieved with apparent ease and his verve and enthusiasm were such that he invariably brought out the best in his fellow musicians. His suggested link to bebop stems largely from a tiny handful of records that show that he was aware of the changes taking place around him and was unafraid to dabble even if he chose never to take the plunge. He was, however, undoubtedly a goad to Gillespie, with whom he played in many after-hours sessions at Minton's and other New York clubs where bebop was nurtured. In the late 50s and afterwards, having settled back into a swing-based groove, Eldridge showed his mastery of the form and of his instrument. Nicknamed 'Little Jazz', Eldridge was a giant who became an elder statesman of jazz without ever losing the fire and aggression that had always marked his playing. His career came to an end when he suffered a stroke in 1980, after which he never played again.

● ALBUMS: *In Sweden* 10-inch album (Prestige 1951) ★★★, *Collates* 10-inch album (Mercury 1952) ★★★★, with Sammy Price *Battle Of Jazz, Vol. 7* 10-inch album (Brunswick 1953) ★★★, *Little Jazz Four: Trumpet Fantasy* 10-inch album (Dial 1953) ★★★★, *Roy Eldridge With Zoot Sims* 10-inch album (Discovery 1954) ★★★, *The Roy Eldridge Quintet* 10-inch album (Clef 1954) ★★★, *Roy Eldridge Quartet* 10-inch album (London 1954) ★★★, *The Strolling Mr. Eldridge* 10-inch album (Clef 1954) ★★★, *The Art Tatum-Roy Eldridge-Alvin Stoller-John Simmons Quartet* (Clef 1955) ★★★★, with Dizzy Gillespie *Roy And Diz* (Clef 1955) ★★★★, with Gillespie *Roy And Diz, Volume 2* (Clef 1955) ★★★★, with Gillespie *Trumpet Battle* (Clef 1956) ★★★, with Gillespie *The Trumpet Kings* (Clef 1956) ★★★, *Little Jazz* (Clef 1956) ★★★★, *Rockin' Chair* 1951-52 recordings (Clef 1956) ★★★, *Dale's Wail* (Clef 1956) ★★★★, *Roy's Got Rhythm* 1951 recording (EmArcy 1956) ★★★, *Swing Goes Dixie* (American Recording Society 1956) ★★★, *The Urbane Jazz Of Roy Eldridge And Benny Carter* (American Recording Society 1957) ★★★, *That Warm Feeling* (Verve 1957) ★★★, with Coleman Hawkins *At The Opera House* (Verve 1957) ★★★★, with Harry 'Sweets' Edison, Gillespie *Tour De Force* (Verve 1958) ★★★, with Edison, Lester Young *Going For Myself* (Verve 1959) ★★★★, with Edison, Young *Laughin' To Keep From Cryin'* (Verve 1959) ★★★★, *Swingin' On The Town* (Verve 1960) ★★★, with Earl Hines *Grand Reunion, Volume 2* (Limelight 1965) ★★★★, with Gillespie *Soul Mates* (Verve 1966) ★★★★, *The Nifty Cat Strikes West* (Master Jazz 1966) ★★★, *The Nifty Cat* (Master Jazz 1970) ★★★, with Paul Gonsalves *The Mexican Bandit Meets The Pittsburgh Pirate* (Fantasy 1973) ★★★★, *Little Jazz And The Jimmy Ryan All-Stars* (Pablo 1975) ★★★, with Gillespie *Jazz Maturity . . . Where It's Coming From* (Pablo 1975) ★★★, with Gillespie *The Trumpet Kings At Montreux '75* (Pablo 1975) ★★★★, *Happy Time* (Pablo 1975) ★★★, *What It's All About* (Pablo 1976) ★★★, *Montreux 1977* (Pablo 1977) ★★★★, *Roy Eldridge & Vic Dickenson* (Storyville 1978) ★★★, *Comin' Home Baby* 1965, 1966 recordings (Pumpkin 1978) ★★★★, *Roy Eldridge At Jerry Newman's* (Xanadu 1983) ★★★, with Count Basie *Loose Walk* 1972 recording (Pablo 1992) ★★★, *Roy Eldridge In Paris* 1950 recording (Vogue 1995) ★★★★, *Decidedly* 1975 recording (Pablo 2003) ★★★.

● COMPILATIONS: *The Early Years* 1935-49 recordings (Columbia) ★★★★, *After You've Gone* 1936-46 recordings (GRP) ★★★★, with Gene Krupa, Anita O'Day *Uptown* 1941-42 recordings (Columbia) ★★★★, *All The Cats Join In* 1943-46 recordings (MCA) ★★★★, *Roy Eldridge Volume 1: Nuts* 1950 recording (Vogue 1993) ★★★, *Roy Eldridge Volume 2: French Cooking* 1950-51 recordings (Vogue 1993) ★★★, *Little Jazz: The Best Of The Verve Years* (PolyGram 1994) ★★★★, *Fiesta In Brass* (Le Jazz 1995) ★★★, *Heckler's Hop* (Hep 1995) ★★★, *Roy Eldridge 1935-1940* (Classics 1996) ★★★, *Roy Eldridge 1943-1944*

(Classics 1997) ★★★★, *An Introduction: His Best Recordings 1935–1946* (Best Of Jazz 1998) ★★★★, *The Complete Verve Roy Eldridge Studio Sessions* 7-CD box set (Mosaic 2004) ★★★★.
● FURTHER READING: *Roy Eldridge: Little Jazz Giant*, John Chilton.

Electrafixion

Electrafixion were formed in Liverpool, Merseyside, England, in 1994, by two former members of **Echo And The Bunnymen**, Will Sergeant (b. 12 April 1958, Liverpool, Merseyside, England; guitar) and **Ian McCulloch** (b. 5 May 1959, Liverpool, England; vocals/guitar). The demise of Echo And The Bunnymen had been followed by a period of bitterness between the two, but with McCulloch's solo career stalling after a good start, they started working together again. Tony McGuigan (drums) and Leon DeSilva (bass) also were in the band. Their first low-key concerts together occurred in summer 1994, and were followed by the EP *Zephyr* in November. McCulloch's voice remained distinctive, while the musical backdrop owed a great deal to the intensity of the 90s grunge movement. *Burned* was produced by Mark Stent and featured 11 McCulloch/Sergeant originals, plus two co-compositions with Johnny Marr (ex-**Smiths**). Electrafixion joined the **Boo Radleys** on tour in October 1995. Their future was curtailed by the re-formation of Echo And the Bunnymen in 1997.
● ALBUMS: *Burned* (Sire/Warners 1995) ★★★.

Electrelane

Originating from Brighton, England, this all-female indie rock outfit was formed in 1998 when Verity Susman (keyboards, guitar, vocals) and Emma Gaze (drums) began rehearsing together. An early version of Electrelane began performing locally, and it was during this time that the band developed something that eventually became one of their musical trademarks—their songs were largely instrumental, and when they did include vocals, the lyrics were sung in foreign languages. Gradually, a more set supporting cast was assembled around Susman and Gaze, including Debbie Ball (guitar) and Rachel Dalley (bass), and three promising singles followed in 2000, 'Film Music', 'Le Song', and 'Gabriel'. This led to a distribution contract with the 3MV company, which would oversee Electrelane's newly formed label, Let's Rock! Records. With a backlog of material to choose from (they had been writing and cataloguing their songs for the better part of two years), the quartet (with new guitarist Mia Clarke replacing Ball) entered the studio and recorded 2001's debut, *Rock It To The Moon*. Flitting between art-punk and **Stereolab**-inspired pop motorik, the album attracted the attention of several higher profile labels. A series of gigs opening for **Sleater-Kinney**, **Death In Vegas**, **Primal Scream** and **Le Tigre** followed, before the quartet released a stopgap EP, *I Want To Be The President*, for their new label Too Pure. The band was temporarily put on hold when Susman decided to finish her final year of college in Cambridge, but they picked up where they left off and flew over to Chicago to work with producer **Steve Albini**. Recorded and mixed in only three weeks, the highly ambitious and accomplished *The Power Out* featured lyrics sung in French, German, Spanish and English.

● ALBUMS: *Rock It To The Moon* (Let's Rock!/Mr. Lady 2001) ★★★, *The Power Out* (Too Pure/Beggars Banquet 2004) ★★★★, *Axes* (Too Pure 2005) ★★★.

Electribe 101

This electro-dance band featured the voice of vocalist **Billie Ray Martin** (b. Hamburg, Germany). She moved to Berlin in the hope of setting up an R&B band with 60s **Motown Records** influences. However, following several unsuccessful attempts she moved to London in 1985. Two years later, she met Joe Stevens, Les Fleming, Rob Cimarosti and Brian Nordhoff and formed Electribe 101. Their first two singles, 'Tell Me When The Fever Ended' and 'Talking With Myself', were instant hits with the **acid house** generation and Martin's voice drew comparisons to **Marlene Dietrich** and **Aretha Franklin**. Despite the acclaim, Electribe 101 broke up shortly afterwards, with Martin pursuing a solo career, while the others formed **Groove Corporation**. Martin's 'Your Loving Arms', taken from *Deadline For My Memories*, was a major club hit and went on to reach number 6 in the UK charts in May 1995.
● ALBUMS: *Electribal Memories* (Mercury 1990) ★★★.

Electric Angels

Comprising Jonathan Daniel (bass), John Schubert (drums), Ryan Roxie (guitar) and former Candy singer Shane (vocals), US rock band the Electric Angels formed at the end of the 80s. Their blend of guttural, sleazy rock (**Hanoi Rocks** were an obvious reference point) was premiered on their self-titled **Atlantic Records** debut in 1990. The producer was **Tony Visconti**, but even he failed to generate anything of substance from a suite of very average songs.
● ALBUMS: *Electric Angels* (Atlantic 1990) ★★.

Electric Boys

This Swedish funk-metal band was formed by vocalist/guitarist Connie Bloom and bass player Andy Christell in 1988. As a duo, the pair recorded 'All Lips 'N' Hips', and finding themselves with a domestic hit, completed the band by recruiting guitarist Franco Santunione and drummer Niclas Sigevall. The self-produced *Funk-O-Metal Carpet Ride* was a strong debut, with memorable songs delivered in a heavy punk style with a distinct psychedelic edge. The band replaced five songs on the original version of the debut with new, Bob Rock–produced efforts, and the revised *Funk-O-Metal Carpet Ride* made a considerable impact, emerging as the rock world was opening its collective mind to the likes of **Living Colour** and **Dan Reed Network**. The band's colourful image and live shows enhanced their growing reputation. However, the funk-metal bubble had burst by the time that the more heavily psychedelic *Groovus Maximus* appeared, and despite the potential of the **Beatles**-influenced 'Mary In The Mystery World' (the album was actually recorded at Abbey Road), the Electric Boys struggled, and after a US tour with **Mr. Big**, Santunione and Sigevall departed. Martin Thomander (guitar) and Thomas Broman (drums, ex-Great King Rat) replaced them on *Freewheelin'*, which abandoned funk in favour of a more 70s-inspired **Aerosmith/Led Zeppelin** groove, but this impressive comeback could not restore the band's waning fortunes, and they broke up shortly after its release. Bloom later worked with Ginger (ex-**Wildhearts**) in Silver Ginger 5.

● ALBUMS: *Funk-O-Metal Carpet Ride* (Mercury 1989) ★★★, *Groovus Maximus* (Mercury 1992) ★★, *Freewheelin'* (Music For Nations 1994) ★★★.

Electric Company

Multi-instrumentalist Brad Laner (b. 6 November 1966, Los Angeles, California, USA) has been making music since the early 80s, and has served as the leader for cult alt rock acts such as Debt Of Nature, Streaming Coils and probably his best known band, **Medicine**. Medicine issued three critically acclaimed but commercially underachieving albums during the early 90s for the Def American label, before Laner left in 1995 to form Electric Company. The project proved to be more musically varied than its predecessor, as it drew from influences such as alternative rock, hip-hop and experimental **techno**. Since the mid-90s Electric Company has issued a steady stream of releases, the most notable of which are 1998's *Studio City*, 1999's *Omakase* and 2000's *Exitos*, the latter appearing on kindred spirit **Kid 606**'s Tigerbeat label. As if Laner's schedule was not busy enough with Electric Company, he also fronts another band, Amnesia, and has guested on recordings by **Mercury Rev** and the **Tool** offshoot Lusk, among others. He revived Medicine to record a new studio album in 2003.

● ALBUMS: *A Pert Cyclic Omen* (Warners 1995) ★★★, *Electric Company Plays Amnesia* (Supreme 1997) ★★★, *Studio City* (PolyGram 1998) ★★★★, *Omakase* (Vinyl Communications 1999) ★★★★, *Exitos* (Tigerbeat 2000) ★★★, *Slow Food* (Planet Mu 2002) ★★★★.

● COMPILATIONS: *Greatest Hits* remix album (Tigerbeat6 2000) ★★★.

Electric Eels

Formed in Cleveland, Ohio, USA, this cult act made its performing debut in 1973 in a bar owned by Jamie Lyons, a one-time local teenage idol, as lead singer with the **Music Explosion**. The Electric Eels' core comprised John Morton (vocals), David E (McManus) (clarinet), Brian McMahon (guitar) and Paul Marotta (guitar), all of whom were students at Lakewood High School. Inspired by **Captain Beefheart**, the band forged a radical, experimental style of music, described by Morton as Art Terrorism. When he added new instruments to their canon, including a sheet of metal that he struck with a sledgehammer and a gas-powered lawnmower, the band lost the few live dates they had. They rehearsed studiously between 1973 and 1974, but Morton's penchant for confrontation—he had been known physically to attack band members—led to a fluctuating line-up. Nevertheless, the Electric Eels, whose repertoire included 'Agitated' and 'Anxiety', played a pivotal role in the development of Cleveland's music. In December 1974 they performed at the Viking Saloon alongside the **Mirrors** and **Rocket From The Tombs** in an event dubbed the 'Special Extermination Night'. Cleveland's subsequent punk scene evolved from these three acts. Unfortunately, Marotta, the only trained musician in the band (he had released a solo EP in 1973), grew frustrated with its direction and left to join the Mirrors. A drummer, Nick Knox, was added to the line-up in 1975. It was the first time the Electric Eels had featured this instrument. A marginally more orthodox sound ensued, but this did little to solve the internal friction. They disbanded in May 1975 following a fistfight at Case-Western Reserve University. Knox joined the **Cramps**, while Morton, McManus, McMahon

and Marotta formed the Men From UNCLE with drummer Anton Fier and two ex-members of the Mirrors, Jamie Klimek and Jim Jones. This short-lived act was succeeded by the more permanent **Styrenes**. The Electric Eels' abrasive muse has been captured on several posthumous releases. In 1978 **Rough Trade Records** issued 'Agitated'/'Cyclotron', which was followed by *Having A Philosophical Investigation With The Electric Eels*, comprising 10 tracks culled from their final recording session in 1975. An expanded edition was released on CD as *God Says Fuck You*.

● COMPILATIONS: *Having A Philosophical Investigation With The Electric Eels* (Tinnitus 1989) ★★★, *God Says Fuck You* (Homestead 1991) ★★★, shared with the Styrenes, the Mirrors *Those Were Different Times* (Scat 1997) ★★★, *The Beast 999 Presents The Electric Eels In Their Organic Majesty's Request* (Overground 1998) ★★★, *The Eyeball Of Hall* (Scat 2002) ★★★.

Electric Flag

The brief career of the much-vaunted Electric Flag was begun in 1967 by **Mike Bloomfield** (b. Michael Bernard Bloomfield, 28 July 1944, Chicago, Illinois, USA, d. 15 February 1981, San Francisco, California, USA), following his departure from the influential **Paul Butterfield** Blues Band. The original band comprised Bloomfield, **Buddy Miles** (b. George Miles, 5 September 1945, Omaha, Nebraska, USA; drums/vocals), **Nick Gravenites** (b. Chicago, Illinois, USA; vocals), **Barry Goldberg** (b. Chicago, Illinois, USA; keyboards), **Harvey Brooks** (b. Harvey Goldstein, USA; bass), Peter Strazza (tenor saxophone), Marcus Doubleday (trumpet) and Herbie Rich (baritone saxophone). All members were well-seasoned professionals coming from a variety of musical backgrounds. The group recorded the soundtrack for the 1967 movie *The Trip* before making a noble live debut at the same year's **Monterey Pop Festival**. Their excellent *A Long Time Comin'* was released in 1968 with additional members Stemziel (Stemsy) Hunter and Mike Fonfara, and was a significant hit in the USA. The tight, brassy-tinged blues numbers were laced with Bloomfield's sparse but bitingly crisp Fender Stratocaster guitar. Their cover version of 'Killing Floor' was a fine example of the sound that Bloomfield was aiming to achieve, but the band was unable to follow this release and immediately began to dissolve, with Goldberg and Bloomfield the first to go. Miles attempted to hold the band together but the second album was a pale shadow of their debut, with only 'See To Your Neighbour' showing signs of a unified performance. Miles then left to form the Buddy Miles Express, while Gravenites became a songwriting legend in San Francisco. Brooks, following years of session work that included the Bloomfield/**Al Kooper**/**Stephen Stills** *Super Session*, reappeared as a member of **Sky**. An abortive Electric Flag reunion produced 1974's lacklustre and inappropriately titled *The Band Kept Playing*.

● ALBUMS: *The Trip* film soundtrack (Sidewalk 1967) ★★, *A Long Time Comin'* (Columbia 1968) ★★★★, *The Electric Flag* (Columbia 1969) ★★, *The Band Kept Playing* (Atlantic 1974) ★.

● COMPILATIONS: *The Best Of The Electric Flag* (Columbia 1971) ★★★, *Old Glory: The Best Of Electric Flag—An American Music Band* (Columbia/Legacy 1995) ★★★★, *Small Town Blues* (Columbia River 2000) ★★.

Electric Frankenstein

Charged with the self-appointed mission of reviving the corpse of rock 'n' roll, Electric Frankenstein have gone about the task with a passion. Their raucous take on 70s rock combines elements of punk, hardcore, metal and 60s garage, and has been readily accepted by a growing audience. Cover artwork by cult artists Chris Cooper and Frank Kozic has helped cement their rock 'n' roll credentials. Few bands could match their productivity in the late 90s, as they unleashed a slew of 7-inch singles, split-singles, albums, live sets and compilation appearances on a variety of different labels. The band was formed in 1992 in New Jersey, USA, by record store owner Sal Canzonieri (rhythm guitar), his brother Dan (bass) and Jim Foster (guitar, ex-**Adrenalin OD**) and after going through a succession of vocalists and drummers, the line-up eventually settled with Steve Miller (vocals) and John Steele (drums). A string of singles on various labels including Mint Tone, Demolition Derby, Exit, Junk, Sonic Swirl, Get Hip, cemented Electric Frankenstein's ever-growing reputation. *The Time Is Now* and the singles compilation *Conquers The World!* both clearly demonstrated the band's excellent understanding of rock 'n' roll. They continued to roll out the 7-inch vinyl until Miller left to pursue his own band, the Crash Street Kids. The remaining members quickly found a replacement in Verbal Abuse singer Scott Wilkins, who took up the challenge to replace the charismatic Miller. More compilation appearances and touring were undertaken ahead of *Sick Songs*, a release that combined the finest elements of the Electric Frankenstein's swaggering musical approach. The six-track *Monster* EP, their debut for Au-Go-Go Records, featured punk legend Rik L Rik (b. 1961, d. 30 June 2000) on vocals and a cover version of the **Misfits**' 'Queen Wasp'. Four tracks were subsequently added to create the *Rock And Roll Monster* album. By 1998 Miller had returned as lead vocalist and Rob Sefcik had taken over on drums. 'Rocket In My Veins' was exactly that, and served as a taster for the *Listen Up, Baby!* EP (split with the Hookers), by which time the reunified band's great songwriting and ferocious live assault was making them many new friends. *How To Make A Monster*, their debut for Victory Records, followed in 1999. Electric Frankenstein's prolific approach showed no signs of abating, with a series of collections of rare and unreleased tracks on various albums being released, including *The Dawn Of Electric Frankenstein*, that collated early material and work from the members' earlier bands. Carl Porcaro replaced the long-serving Foster in August 1999.

● ALBUMS: *The Time Is Now* (Nitro!/Nesak 1995) ★★★, *Sick Songs* (US) *Action High* (UK) (Nesak/One Louder 1997) ★★★★, *Spare Parts* (Get Hip 1998) ★★★, *Rock And Roll Monster* (Au-Go-Go 1999) ★★★★, *How To Make A Monster* (Victory 1999) ★★★, *The Buzz Of 1000 Volts!* (Victory 2001) ★★★.

● COMPILATIONS: *Conquers The World!* (Get Hip/Nesak 1995) ★★★, *The Dawn Of Electric Frankenstein* (Triple X 2000) ★★.

Electric Hellfire Club

The name is derived from the English eighteenth-century group of Satanic society swingers known as the Hellfire Club; the band was formed in an attempt to emulate the club's devilish hedonism in a musical (thus 'Electric') form. At the core of the Electric Hellfire Club is the vocalist, synthesizer programmer and Satanist Thomas 'Thorn' Lockyear. The latter had previously been in the seminal industrial **dance music** act **My Life With The Thrill Kill Kult** under the name Buck Ryder. In 1991 he had become alienated by their increasingly commercial direction and contemptuous attitude towards darker topics. He left and formed the Electric Hellfire Club with a diverse group of musicians, including the Rev. Dr. Luv (b. Shane Lassen, 1970, d. 21 January 1996; keyboards), Ronny Valeo (guitars; ex-Screamer), Janna Flail (drums), who was later replaced on percussion by Richard Frost, and dancer Sabrina Satana. All of them brought different influences into the band's sound, from heavy metal and ethnic music, to punk and **techno**. Thorn's own fascination with 60s psychedelia adds to this cocktail to create a style that is distinctive and colourful. Frivolous and sinister in equal parts, the Electric Hellfire Club are far removed from the clichéd stamping grounds of Satanic rock. They have endured the death of Lassen in an automobile accident in 1996 and numerous personnel changes and continue to record prolifically.

● ALBUMS: *Burn, Baby, Burn!* (Cleopatra 1994) ★★★, *Kiss The Goat* (Cleopatra 1995) ★★★, *Calling Dr. Luv* (Cleopatra 1996) ★★★, *Empathy For The Devil* (Cleopatra 1999) ★★★, *Witness The Millennium* (Cleopatra 2000) ★★★, *Electronomicon* (Cleopatra 2001) ★★★.

● COMPILATIONS: *Unholy Roller* (Cleopatra 1998) ★★.

Electric Indian

A US studio group that recorded a song called 'Keem-O-Sabe' in 1969 and took it to number 16 on the US charts. The group was assembled by Bernie Binnick, who had founded Swan Records, and included musicians who later went on to form the Philadelphia group **MFSB**, as well as Frank Virtue of the instrumental group the **Virtues**. 'Keem-O-Sabe' was notable in that it was an Indian-music flavoured instrumental that made heavy use of the then-trendy sitar. An album was released under the Electric Indian name, and the group landed one other single on the charts, a cover of 'Land Of 1,000 Dances', but the project was soon abandoned.

● ALBUMS: *Keem-O-Sabe* (1969) ★★.

Electric Light Orchestra

The original Electric Light Orchestra (commonly shortened to ELO) line-up comprised **Roy Wood** (b. Roy Adrian Wood, 8 November 1946, Birmingham, England; vocals, cello, woodwind, guitars), **Jeff Lynne** (b. 30 December 1947, Birmingham, England; vocals, piano, guitar) and Bev Bevan (b. Beverley Bevan, 23 November 1945, Birmingham, England; drums). They had all been members of pop unit the **Move**, but viewed this new venture as a means of greater self-expression. Vowing to 'carry on where the **Beatles**' 'I Am The Walrus' left off', they completed an experimental self-titled set (commonly known as *No Answer*) with the aid of Bill Hunt (b. 23 May 1947, Birmingham, England; French horn) and Steve Woolam (violin). Despite their lofty ambitions, the band still showed traces of its earlier counterpart with Lynne's grasp of melody much in evidence, particularly on the startling '10538 Overture', a UK Top 10 single in 1972.

Although Woolam departed, the remaining quartet added Hugh McDowell (b. 31 July 1953, Hampstead, London, England), Andy Craig (cello), ex-**Balls** keyboard player

Richard Tandy (b. 26 March 1948, Birmingham, England; bass, piano, guitar) and Wilf Gibson (b. 28 February 1945, Dilston, Northumberland, England; violin) for a series of indifferent live appearances, following which Wood took Hunt and McDowell to form **Wizzard**. With Craig absenting himself from either party, Lynne, Bevan, Gibson and Tandy maintained the ELO name with the addition of Mike De Albuquerque (b. 24 June 1947, Wimbledon, London, England; bass/vocals) and cellists Mike Edwards (b. Michael Edwards, 31 May, Ealing, London, England) and Colin Walker (b. 8 July 1949, Minchinhampton, Gloucestershire, England). The reshaped line-up completed the transitional *Electric Light Orchestra 2* and scored a UK Top 10 single with an indulgent cover version of **Chuck Berry**'s 'Roll Over Beethoven' that included quotes from Beethoven's 5th Symphony. Gibson and Walker then made way for violinist Mik Kaminski (b. Michael Kaminski, 2 September 1951, Harrogate, Yorkshire, England) as ELO enjoyed a third UK hit with 'Showdown', but two ensuing singles, 'Ma-Ma-Ma Belle' and the sublime 'Can't Get It Out Of My Head', were surprising failures. The latter song reached the US Top 10, however, which in turn helped its attendant album, *Eldorado: A Symphony By The Electric Light Orchestra*, to achieve gold status.

By the release of 1975's *Face The Music*, the line-up had stabilized around Lynne, Bevan, Tandy, Kaminski, the returning McDowell, Kelly Groucutt (b. Michael Groucutt, 8 September 1945, Coseley, West Midlands, England; bass) and Melvyn Gale (b. 15 January 1952, London, England; cello). ELO became a star attraction on America's lucrative stadium circuit and achieved considerable commercial success with the albums *A New World Record*, **Out Of The Blue** and the UK chart-topping *Discovery*. Lynne's compositions successfully steered the line between pop and rock, inspiring commentators to compare his band with the Beatles. Between 1976 and 1981 ELO scored an unbroken run of 14 UK Top 20 singles, including 'Evil Woman' and 'Livin' Thing' (1976), 'Telephone Line' and 'Turn To Stone' (1977), 'Mr. Blue Sky', 'Wild West Hero' and 'Sweet Talkin' Woman' (1978), 'Shine A Little Love', 'The Diary Of Horace Wimp', 'Don't Bring Me Down' and 'Confusion'/'Last Train To London' (1979), and 'Xanadu', a chart-topping collaboration with **Olivia Newton-John**, taken from the movie of the same name. The line-up had now been slimmed to feature Lynne, Bevan, Tandy and Groucutt, but recurrent legal and distribution problems conspired to undermine ELO's momentum. *Time* (their second UK chart-topper) and *Secret Messages* lacked the verve of earlier work and despite further UK Top 20 hits with 'Hold On Tight' and 'Rock 'N' Roll Is King', the band's future was put in doubt by a paucity of releases and Lynne's growing disenchantment, and the guitarist's pursuit of a solo career signalled a final split. It should also be noted that ELO enjoyed 14 US Top 20 hits during their heyday, from 'Can't Get It Out Of My Head' in 1974 to 'Calling America' in 1986. In 1991, former drummer Bev Bevan emerged with ELO 2. That unit failed, owing to the fact that the Electric Light Orchestra without Lynne is like a toaster without a plug. It was therefore with considerable relief to loyal fans that Lynne resurrected the name in 2001. Featuring Richard Tandy and guest appearances from **Ringo Starr** and **George Harrison**, *Zoom* exhibited a few sparks to remind fans of the band's glory years. For some inexplicable reason, after many years of being unfashionable, it was suddenly OK to like ELO

again. Looking back over an impressive catalogue it is hard to see why they became the butt of so many jokes.

● ALBUMS: *Electric Light Orchestra* (UK) *No Answer* (USA) (Harvest/United Artists 1971) ★★, *Electric Light Orchestra 2* (Harvest/United Artists 1973) ★★, *On The Third Day* (Warners/United Artists 1973) ★★★, *The Night The Light Went On In Long Beach* (Warners 1974) ★★, *Eldorado: A Symphony By The Electric Light Orchestra* (Warners/United Artists 1975) ★★★★, *Face The Music* (Jet/United Artists 1975) ★★★★, *A New World Record* (Jet/United Artists 1976) ★★★★, *Out Of The Blue* (Jet 1977) ★★★★★, *Discovery* (Jet 1979) ★★★, with Olivia Newton-John *Xanadu* film soundtrack (Jet/MCA 1980) ★★, *Time* (Jet 1981) ★★, *Secret Messages* (Jet 1983) ★★, *Balance Of Power* (Epic/CBS Assoc. 1986) ★★, *Electric Light Orchestra Part Two* (Telstar 1991) ★, as ELO 2 *Moment Of Truth* (Edel 1994) ★, *Live At Winterland '76* (Eagle/Cleopatra 1998) ★★★, *Live At Wembley '78* (Eagle/Cleopatra 1998) ★★★, *Zoom* (Epic 2001) ★★★.

● COMPILATIONS: *Olé ELO* (Jet/United Artists 1976) ★★★, *The Light Shines On* (Harvest 1976) ★★★, *The Light Shines On Vol. 2* (Harvest 1977) ★★★, *Three Light Years* box set (Jet 1979) ★★★, *ELO's Greatest Hits* (Jet 1979) ★★★★, *A Box Of Their Best* (Jet 1980) ★★★, *First Movement* (Harvest 1986) ★★, *A Perfect World Of Music* (Jet 1988) ★★★★, *Their Greatest Hits* (Epic 1989) ★★★, *The Definitive Collection* (Jet 1993) ★★★, *Strange Magic: Best Of ELO* (Sony 1995) ★★★★, *The Gold Collection* (EMI 1996) ★★★, *Light Years* (Epic 1997) ★★★, *Friends And Relatives* (Eagle/Cleopatra 1999) ★★★, *Complete ELO Live Collection* (Cleopatra 2000) ★★★, *Flashback* 3-CD box set (Epic 2000) ★★★★, *The Early Years* (EMI 2004) ★★★, *All Over The World: The Very Best Of Electric Light Orchestra* (Sony 2005) ★★★★.

● DVD/VIDEOS: *'Out Of The Blue' Tour Live At Wembley* (Eagle Rock 1999), *Discovery* (Eagle Rock 1999), *Zoom Tour Live* (Aviva International 2001), *Live In Australia* (Direct Video Distribution 2003).

● FURTHER READING: *The Electric Light Orchestra Story*, Bev Bevan.

Electric Love Hogs

This Los Angeles, California, USA, quintet originated when vocalist John Feldmann and guitarist Donny Campion linked with drummer Bobby Fernandez in a San Diego covers band. The addition of second guitarist Dae Kushner and funk-orientated bass player Kelly LeMieux, who was recruited following a wrong-number phone call, saw the band move towards original material, incorporating LeMieux's slap bass into a trad/speed metal framework for an energetic hybrid style. The band adopted the Electric Love Hogs name as a reaction against the crop of Los Angeles glam bands on the late 80s club scene whom they felt were taking the music business too seriously. **London Records** signed the band without asking them to change their name, and *Electric Love Hogs* was a bright debut, offering a strong, punchy sound courtesy of Mark Dodson (although more interest centred on two tracks produced by **Mötley Crüe**'s **Tommy Lee**). Nevertheless, the album did not have the individuality to distinguish the band from the funk-metal pack. The band's live work remained impressive as they toured the USA with **L.A. Guns** and the UK with **Ugly Kid Joe** before returning to the studio. Bobby Fernandez, newly renamed Bobby Hewitt, later appeared with sleaze rockers **Orgy**.

● ALBUMS: *Electric Love Hogs* (London 1992) ★★★.

Electric Music AKA

London, England–based outfit formed by music journalist Tom Doyle and former **On U Sound** engineer Anth Brown. Originally known as Electric Music, the Scottish-born duo was forced to add AKA to their name following the threat of legal action from former **Kraftwerk** member Karl Bartos. They made their debut in 2000 with the grandly titled *North London Spiritualist Church*. The album juxtaposed retro electronica, indie guitar rock and Doyle's wistful vocals to notable effect, echoing the modus operandi employed by fellow UK oddballs the **Beta Band**. Following the surprise termination of the ZubiZaretta/Grand Royal alliance, the duo released their second album via Sanctuary Records. The memorable cover shot of *The Resurrection Show* placed Doyle and Brown in the Great Hall of London's Alexandra Palace. The music within just failed to match the organic warmth generated by the duo's debut, however, with 'Something Up With The Stars' and 'Some Bright Shining Future' the stand-out tracks.

● ALBUMS: *North London Spiritualist Church* (ZubiZaretta/Grand Royal 2000) ★★★★, *The Resurrection Show* (Sanctuary 2003) ★★★.

Electric Prunes

Formed in Los Angeles, California, USA, in 1965, the Electric Prunes originally consisted of Jim Lowe (b. San Luis Obispo, California, USA; vocals, guitar, autoharp), Ken Williams (b. Long Beach, California, USA; lead guitar), James 'Weasel' Spagnola (b. Cleveland, Ohio, USA; guitar), Mark Tulin (b. Philadelphia, Pennsylvania, USA; bass) and Michael Weakley aka Quint (drums), although the latter was quickly replaced by Preston Ritter (b. Stockton, California, USA). The quintet made its debut with the low-key 'Ain't It Hard', before achieving two US Top 20 hits with 'I Had Too Much To Dream (Last Night)' and 'Get Me To The World On Time'. These exciting singles blended the drive of garage/punk rock, the rhythmic pulse of the **Rolling Stones** and the experimentalism of the emerging psychedelic movement. Such performances were enhanced by Dave Hassinger's accomplished production. The Prunes' debut album was hampered by indifferent material, but the excellent follow-up, *Underground*, featured three of the group's finest achievements, 'Hideaway', 'The Great Banana Hoax' and 'Long Day's Flight'. However, the Prunes were sadly unable to sustain their hit profile and grew increasingly unhappy with the artistic restrictions placed on them by management and producer.

Ritter was replaced by the prodigal Quint before the remaining original members dropped out during sessions for *Mass In F Minor*. This acclaimed combination of Gregorian styles and acid rock was composed and arranged by David Axelrod, who fulfilled the same role on a follow-up set, *Release Of An Oath*. An entirely new line-up—Ron Morgan (guitar), Mark Kincaid (b. Topeka, Kansas, USA; guitar), Brett Wade (b. Vancouver, British Columbia, Canada; bass) and Richard Whetstone (b. Hutchinson, Kansas, USA; drums)—completed the lacklustre *Just Good Old Rock 'N' Roll*, which bore no trace of the founding line-up's sense of adventure.

The Electric Prunes name was then abandoned until 2001 when, following the release of the compilation *Lost Dreams*, members of the band were once again back in touch. Tulin, Lowe and Williams recruited help from the likes of Peter Lewis of **Moby Grape**, and released the wholly credible *Artifact*. Not content to rest on their laurels, a second album of new material followed in 2004.

● ALBUMS: *The Electric Prunes (I Had Too Much To Dream Last Night)* (Reprise 1967) ★★★, *Underground* (Reprise 1967) ★★★, *Mass In F Minor* (Reprise 1967) ★★★, *Release Of An Oath* (Reprise 1968) ★★, *Just Good Old Rock 'N' Roll* (Reprise 1969) ★, *Stockholm 67* (Heartbeat 1997) ★★, *Artifact* (Prunetwang 2002) ★★★, *California* (Prunetwang 2004) ★★★.

● COMPILATIONS: *Long Day's Flight* (Demon 1986) ★★★, *Lost Dreams* (Birdman 2001) ★★★★.

● DVD/VIDEOS: *Rewired* (Snapper 2003).

Electric Six

From Detroit, Michigan, USA, Electric Six have performed under various names since their inception as the Wildbunch (a moniker the band still prefer) in 1996. Formed by Jackson Pounder (vocals) and Martin M (drums), the Wildbunch made their recording debut on the Uchu Cult label with the 7-inch single 'I Lost Control (Of My Rock & Roll)', a frenetic blend of garage rock and new wave styles that enjoyed instant acclaim on the resurgent Detroit rock scene. Adding Disco (bass), Mojo Frezzato (guitar), Rock & Roll Indian (guitar) and Blacklips Hoffman (keyboards) to the line-up, the Wildbunch relocated to the Flying Bomb label for 1997's 'The Ballade Of MC Sucka DJ', a witty send-up of fake white rappers.

Despite building up a fearsome live reputation on the local scene, the band remained quiet on the recording front for the next few years. They returned to the studio in 2001 employing a set of new pseudonyms, namely Dick Valentine (vocals), M. Cougar Mellencamp (drums), Rock & Roll Indian (guitar), Dr. Blacklip Hoffman (keyboards), Frank Lloyd Bonnaventure (bass) and Surge Joebot (guitar). The band's new musical direction, a heady fusion of disco and rock, was beginning to attract a larger audience, and they enjoyed an underground hit in Europe when the hypnotic 'Danger! High Voltage' was featured on **Soulwax**'s excellent *2 Many DJ's* mix album.

Forced to adopt the Electric Six moniker for legal reasons, the band signed a new recording contract with the UK independent label **XL Recordings**. 'Danger! High Voltage' enjoyed great crossover success in Europe, and in January 2003 debuted at number 2 in the UK singles chart. The wonderful 'Gay Bar', complete with a highly controversial video featuring camp Abraham Lincolns, followed its predecessor into the UK Top 10 and preceded the release of their debut album, *Fire*. A major label recording contract with the Warners offshoot Rushmore Recordings ensued, although a pedestrian cover version of **Queen**'s 'Radio Ga Ga' at the end of 2004 hardly set pulses racing for the band's second album.

● ALBUMS: *Fire* (XL 2003) ★★★, *Señor Smoke* (Rushmore/WEA 2005) ★★★.

Electric Soft Parade

The second musical venture formed by Brighton, East Sussex, England–based brothers Alex White (b. Brighton, Sussex, England; vocals/guitar) and Tom White (b. Brighton,

Sussex, England; drums). The duo recorded three self-funded albums under the name Feltro Media before signing a recording contract with db Records in 2001. Opting to jettison their original moniker, the duo were briefly known as Soft Parade before the threat of legal action from a **Doors** tribute band forced a slight alteration. The Whites recorded most of the material for the Electric Soft Parade debut in their bedroom using digital mixing programmes and an iMac. *Holes In The Wall* was an impressive work by two musicians barely out of their mid-teens, and gained acclaim from all sectors of the music press. The album's endearingly retro psych-pop sound demonstrated a keen grasp of pop history, in particular echoing the work of 90s indie darlings the **Boo Radleys**. The brothers subsequently recruited Matt Thwaites (b. England; bass) and Steve Large (b. England; keyboard) for live work, and signed to major label BMG Records for their second album, *The American Adventure*.
● ALBUMS: *Holes In The Wall* (db 2002) ★★★, *The American Adventure* (BMG 2003) ★★★★.

Electric Sun

This German group was formed by Uli Jon Roth (guitar/vocals) after he left the **Scorpions** in 1978. At first he was assisted by Ule Ritgens on bass and Clive Edwards on drums. The group was quickly signed by the Brain label and released *Earthquake* in 1979. It was a highly spiritual record, with guitar work that aspired to imitate **Jimi Hendrix** and the west coast acid rock movement. This fusion of jazz and rock music, however, was let down by Roth's vocals. On *Firewind*, released in 1981, Clive Edwards was replaced by Sidhatta Gautama. The music was improved and featured pieces influenced by the oriental tradition, even though the vocals remained the same. Roth's solo album, *Beyond The Astral Skies*, took four years to complete, but when it was finally released, it revealed a great leap forward. In addition to the jazz rock pieces, there were also neo-classical movements that allowed Roth free reign to indulge his religious beliefs and demonstrate his musical ability and technique. The biggest improvement was in the vocals, with Roth still singing lead but having the support of seven other vocalists.
● ALBUMS: *Earthquake* (Brain 1979) ★★, *Firewind* (Brain 1981) ★★★.
Solo: Uli Jon Roth *Beyond The Astral Skies* (EMI 1985) ★★★.

Electric Wizard

Dealing in exactly the type of eerie monolithic doom that you would expect from a band emanating from darkest Dorset, England, Justin Oborn (vocals/guitar), Tim Bagshaw (bass) and Mark Greening (drums) first got together in 1993 after Oborn left his previous band Eternal. Drawn together by a mutual love of **Black Sabbath**, **Saint Vitus** and marijuana, the band would get stoned and crank out ponderous riffs until they had recognizable songs, the first examples being released as 'Demon Lung', a split single with Our Haunted Kingdom (an early incarnation of Orange Goblin). An expectedly heavy affair, the self-titled debut emerged soon after and included some ragged **Blue Cheer** moments among the ultra slow, dirge-like riffing. Despite a noticeable disinterest in playing live gigs in support, the trio nonetheless developed a rare momentum and *Come My Fanatics...* followed a year later. Still preposterously heavy, the release also contained a more pronounced **Hawkwind**-style space-

rock influence. A further split EP *Chrono.naut* (with Orange Goblin) extended the theme almost expanding into the Krautrock territory of **Can** and **Amon Düül**. The *Supercoven* EP was a return to bowel-quaking riffs with two torturously drawn out arrangements, complete with suitably twisted cover art by Oborn.
A series of mishaps then halted the band's progress. Oborn removed the tip of a finger in a 'flooring accident' and suffered a collapsed eardrum during a 1999 support slot with **Goatsnake**, the band's famed wall of prehistoric amps taking its toll. Using all the negative experiences generated since the last album as motivation for their next work, *Dopethrone* was a demonstration of sheer power, ultra slow and intensely heavy. Each track was preceded by a clip from a classic underground horror flick (Oborn's other love). Generating good reviews in the press the band reluctantly set out on the road in support. Predictably, things did not progress well. Problems began a mere four dates into their US tour with Warhorse, when they faced a grilling from the police department of Richmond, Virginia, over alleged 'suspicious behaviour'. Further dates were also not without incident as relations within the band became increasingly strained and performances increasingly chaotic.
● ALBUMS: *Electric Wizard* (Rise Above 1995) ★★, *Come My Fanatics...* (Rise Above 1995) ★★★, *Dopethrone* (Rise Above 2000) ★★★★, *Let Us Prey* (Rise Above 2002) ★★★.

Electro

Started by **Afrika Bambaataa**'s 'Planet Rock', electro music was first heard in the USA in the early 80s and harnessed the video game craze and attendant appetite for electronica and tied it to a computerized beat. For some time it became *the* sound of hip-hop. In the wake of 'Planet Rock', rap's journeymen, new and old alike, hitched themselves to the bandwagon, as releases such as 'Magic's Wand' (**Whodini**), 'Play At Your Own Risk' (Planet Patrol) and 'Hip-hop Be Bop (Don't Stop)' (**Man Parrish**) testify. More conventional **dance music**, too, was heavily influenced by these new techniques, notably the Peach Boys and D-Train. It took Bambaataa, however, to equal 'Planet Rock', when he unveiled 'Looking For The Perfect Beat'. Although electro held sway on the rap scene for a surprising length of time, it was blown away quickly and irrevocably with the arrival of **Run DMC** in the mid-80s and their more robust approach.

Electro Hippies

This eccentric 'grindcore' outfit formed in Liverpool, England, in 1985. Specializing in low-technology studio techniques, they went on to issue a sequence of albums for Peaceville, and, later, Necrosis. In each case, a distorted, bass-laden barrage was overridden by stomach-churning vocals that consciously lacked both finesse and cohesion. The band's initial line-up featured Simon (drums), Bruno (bass), Andy (guitar) and Jeff Walker (vocals) After recording a split single with Generic, Jeff and Bruno left the band, with the former joining **Carcass**. Bruno was replaced by Dom, with all three members assuming vocal duties. Chaotic and extreme, Electro Hippies used their platform to chastise the whole recording industry. Their mantle was upheld in the first case by Radio 1 disc jockey **John Peel**, for whom the band recorded a July 1987 session comprising nine tracks. Titles such as 'Starve The City (To

Feed The Poor)' and 'Mega-Armageddon Death Part 3' summed up both their appeal and limitations. The Electro Hippies split up in 1989.

● ALBUMS: *Peel Sessions* (Strange Fruit 1987) ★★★, *The Only Good Punk ... Is A Dead One* (Peaceville 1988) ★★★, *Live* (Peaceville 1989) ★★, *Play Fast Or Die* (Necrosis 1989) ★★.

● COMPILATIONS: *The Peaceville Recordings* (Peaceville 1989) ★★★, *The Only Good Punk . . . Is A Dead One* (Peaceville 2002) ★★★.

Electronic

This powerful UK duo comprises **Johnny Marr** (b. John Maher, 31 October 1963, Ardwick, Manchester, England) and Bernard Sumner (b. Bernard Dicken/Albrecht, 4 January 1956, Salford, Manchester, England), both formerly key members of very successful Manchester-based bands, the **Smiths** and **New Order**, respectively. Although they first worked together in 1983, Electronic was not formed until 1989. After a brief period as guitarist for Matt Johnson's **The The** and work with various well-known artists, such as **David Byrne** and the **Pretenders**, Electronic marked Marr's move into more commercial territory. His instinct for infectious, melodic pop guitar and Sumner's songwriting and programming ability proved to be an effective combination. Their first single, 'Getting Away With It', was released in 1989 on Manchester's highly respected **Factory Records** and featured the **Pet Shop Boys**' Neil Tennant as guest vocalist. This inspired move helped the record to number 12 in the UK chart. The individual track records of the three musicians immediately gave the band a high profile, arousing the interest of both the press and the public.

This attention was intensified by the excitement surrounding the 'baggy' dance scene emerging from Manchester and the city's explosion of new musical talent, sparked by bands such as **Happy Mondays** and the **Stone Roses**. Electronic capitalized on the new credibility that dance music had acquired and were influenced by the fusions that were taking place, using 'electronic' dance rhythms and indie guitar pop. In July 1991, a self-titled debut album followed two more UK Top 20 singles, 'Get The Message' and 'Feel Every Beat'. The singles were witty and distinctive and were praised by the critics. Not surprisingly, the album also was very well received, reaching number 2 in the UK chart. After a short gap, 'Disappointed' consolidated their early promise by reaching number 6 in the UK in June 1992. Intelligent, original and fashionably marrying the sounds of the guitar and the computer, much was expected but did not arrive. *Raise The Pressure* blended Pet Shop Boys harmony and structure with the occasional hint of wah-wah pedal from Marr. Six of the tracks were co-written with **Kraftwerk**'s Karl Bartos. Sumner and Marr returned in 1999 with the more guitar-orientated *Twisted Tenderness*.

● ALBUMS: *Electronic* (Parlophone 1991) ★★★★, *Raise The Pressure* (Parlophone 1996) ★★★, *Twisted Tenderness* (Parlophone/Koch 1999) ★★★.

● FURTHER READING: *True Faith: An Armchair Guide To New Order, Joy Division, Electronic, Revenge, Monaco, And The Other Two*, Dave Thompson.

Electropathics

Formed in 1979, as the Electropathic Battery Band, this ensemble played concerts and appeared at dances as essentially a music hall band, presenting a show in costume. The original line-up was Alan Rawlinson (b. 8 May 1955, Scholes, Leeds, Yorkshire, England; trombone, trumpet, cornet, flute, sousaphone, vocals), John Gregson (guitar/vocals), John Lewis (clarinet, banjo, mandolin, saxophone, vocals), Moira Hanvey (vocals/whistles), Dave Hanvey (melodeon/vocals), Nick Tamblin (mouth organ, glockenspiel, percussion, vocals, caller) and Maggie Andrew (percussion).

The group went through a number of personnel changes, with the departure of Dave and Moira Hanvey, and Nick Tamblin in 1984. Jackie Rawlinson (b. 26 May 1965, Wilmslow, Cheshire, England; fiddle/vocals), joined in 1985 with Andrew leaving the line-up in 1986. The line-up for *Batteries Not Included* comprised original members Alan Rawlinson and John Gregson, plus Pierce Butler (drums, percussion, vocals), who left at the end of 1987, Jackie Rawlinson, Howard Jones (hammer dulcimer, melodeon, anglo-concertina, guitar, vocals) who had joined in 1984, as well as **Keith Hancock** (b. 28 October 1953, Audenshaw, Lancashire, England; melodeon, hammer dulcimer, vocals). More changes occurred with the addition of Dave Manley (b. 20 February 1957, Warwickshire, England; flute, saxophone, vocals) and Tim Veitch (b. 29 May 1962; cello/vocals), who both joined in 1988, while Hancock left the same year to pursue a solo career. Tim Kenney (b. 15 August 1960; guitar/vocals) joined early in 1989. The most recent addition, Chris Bartram (b. 25 December 1946, Yorkshire, England; percussion/vocals), joined in 1991. The group, having changed its name to the Electropathics, and with Alan Rawlinson the only surviving original member, continued until 1994 when they decided to disband while still on a high. However, they do occasionally re-form for a reunion gig.

● ALBUMS: *(Batteries Not Included)* (Sticky Label 1987) ★★★.

Elegants

Formed in the mid-50s in Staten Island, New York City, USA, the Elegants were a white doo-wop group. They achieved a US number 1 single, 'Little Star', in 1958, only to disappear from the charts permanently thereafter. The group comprised lead vocalist Vito Picone (b. 17 March 1940), Carman Romano (b. 17 August 1939), James Moschella (b. 10 May 1938), Frank Tardogno (b. 18 September 1941) and Arthur Venosa (b. 3 September 1939). Picone and Romano had both recorded unsuccessfully with another group, the Crescents, before teaming with new singers as the Elegants. 'Little Star', built around the Mozart melody 'Twinkle, Twinkle, Little Star', was a favourite of audiences and the group recorded it in mid-1958. The Elegants did not follow up their success for over a year, and further releases failed to chart. Although the members went their separate ways, Picone was still leading a version of the group in the early 90s.

● COMPILATIONS: *A Knight With The Elegants* (Crystal Ball 1982) ★★★, *Back In Time* (Crystal Ball 1990) ★★★, *The Best Of . . .* (Collectables 1991) ★★★.

Elegies For Angels, Punks And Raving Queens

After arousing a good deal of interest off-Broadway and on the London Fringe, this highly emotional play-with-music opened in June 1993 at the Criterion Theatre in the heart of the West End. It tells the tale from the point of view of some

30 individuals who died as a result of contracting AIDS from a wide variety of sources—such as 'a regular Joe who dropped into a brothel, to a granny who was given an infected blood transfusion'. The actors step forward one by one and tell their stories in verse and song. **Kim Criswell**, who gave a stunning performance in the 1992/3 London revival of **Annie Get Your Gun**, was the best-known name in a cast that also featured Kwama Kwei-Armah, Lily Savage, Trudie Styler and Simon Fanshawe. The score, with music by Janet Hood and lyrics by the show's author, Bill Russell, was an intensely moving—and sometimes euphoric—blend of jazz, blues and gospel. It could not run for long at a mainstream theatre, of course, even one as tiny as the Criterion, and, after a late-night show on 23 July to enable other West End actors to experience this thought-provoking piece, *Elegies* closed the following night.

Eleison, Victoria

b. 1963, Zaire. After working for two years as a harmony vocalist with **Papa Wemba**'s Viva La Musica, Eleison went solo in 1982, scoring a big hit with 'Sans Preavis' (still accompanied by Viva La Musica), and even bigger ones the following year with the television-themed 'Dallas' and 'Dynasty'. Since then she has remained semi-active on the Kinshasa club scene, but has released little of note in recent years.
● ALBUMS: *Sango Mbala Commission* (1984) ★★★, *Cartouche* (1986) ★★★, *Manhattan* (1987) ★★★.

Elektra Records

Founded in New York City, USA, in 1950 by student and traditional music enthusiast **Jac Holzman**, this much respected label initially showcased recordings drawn from America's rich heritage. Early releases included **Jean Ritchie**'s *Songs Of Her Kentucky Mountain Family* and **Ed McCurdy**'s *Songs Of The Old West*, but the catalogue also boasted collections encompassing material from international sources. Elektra also made several notable jazz and blues recordings but, as the 50s progressed, became renowned for its interest in contemporary folk. It thus attracted many of the performers from the Greenwich Village and New England enclaves, notably **Judy Collins**, **Tom Paxton**, **Koerner**, **Ray And Glover**, **Fred Neil** and **Phil Ochs**, before embracing electric styles in 1966 with the **Paul Butterfield Blues Band** and **Love**. Elektra then became established on America's west coast and its transformation from folk to rock was confirmed the following year with the **Doors**. Subsequent signings included the **MC5**, **Rhinoceros**, the **Stooges** and **Earth Opera**, while the label achieved concurrent commercial success with **Bread**. Elektra also became an important outlet for many singer-songwriters, and its catalogue included superior releases by **David Ackles**, **Tom Rush**, **Tim Buckley**, **Harry Chapin**, **Incredible String Band** and **Carly Simon**.

In 1971 Elektra was absorbed into the **WEA Records** conglomerate and incongruous releases by the **New Seekers** and **Queen** robbed the company of its individuality. Two years later, and with the departure of Holzman, the label was amalgamated with **Asylum Records** and for much of the decade remained the junior partner. **Television**'s *Marquee Moon* rekindled memories of the outlet's classic era, while during the 80s Elektra was responsible for releases by **10,000 Maniacs**, the **Screaming Blue Messiahs** and the **Pixies** (the latter US only). The label was unwilling, or unable, to shake off its

early heritage, which was commemorated in a series of boxed sets under the umbrella title *The Jac Holzman Years*. Elektra's 40th anniversary was celebrated with *Rubaiyat*, in which representatives from the current roster performed songs drawn from the 'classic' era. A worthy reissue programme of forgotten gems was undertaken in 2001 by **Warner Brothers Records** releasing numerous albums as bargain double CD packages including those by **Judy Henske**, Tom Rush, **David Blue**, Tim Buckley and Fred Neil.
● COMPILATIONS: *What's Shakin'* (Elektra 1966) ★★★★, *Select Elektra* (Elektra 1967) ★★★★, *Begin Here* (Elektra 1969) ★★★★, *O Love Is Teasing: Anglo-American Mountain Balladry* (Elektra 1983) ★★★, *Bleecker & MacDougal: The Folk Scene Of The 60s* (Elektra 1983) ★★★, *Crossroads: White Blues In The 60s* (Elektra 1985) ★★★, *Elektrock: The Sixties* (Elektra 1985) ★★★.
● FURTHER READING: *Follow The Music: The Life And High Times Of Elektra Records*, Jac Holzman and Gavan Daws.

Elements

When **Mark Egan** left **Pat Metheny**'s group in 1981 he started playing with drummer **Danny Gottlieb** in the group that would, by 1983, become known as Elements. Egan is an educated musician and technically accomplished bass player who varies the sound of his playing through his fascination and skill in the use of electronic devices. Gottlieb is a skilful drummer who had wide experience playing with **Eberhard Weber**'s **Colours**, the **Gary Burton** Quartet and Pat Metheny's band before working with Egan in Elements. Egan was already fascinated by ethnic music and had spent some time studying music from Bali, south India, Africa and Brazil but with Gottlieb he spent time in Hawaii 'playing music in nature in valleys, during very extreme weather conditions (wind, rain, etc.)'. All of these influences are reflected in the music they produced with Elements.
● ALBUMS: *Elements* (Island 1982) ★★★★, *Forward Motion* (Island 1984) ★★★, *Blown Away* (Mess Bluemoon 1985) ★★★, *Illumination* (RCA/BMG 1987) ★★★, *Liberal Arts* (RCA/BMG 1989) ★★★, *Spirit River* (RCA/BMG 1990) ★★★, *Far East, Vol. I* (Wavetone 1992) ★★★, *Far East, Vol. II* (Wavetone 1993) ★★★, *Untold Stories* (Wavetone 1996) ★★★, *Wouldn't It Be Nice* (SoulCoast 1997) ★★★.

Elend

Led by singer and composer Alexandre Iskandar Hasnaoui, French/Australian group Elend specialize in the performance of baroque orchestral pieces in praise of Lucifer. Though their ambitions may be grand in design, Elend have nevertheless made two fine recordings that are far more musically literate than many of the dark metal bands attempting to incorporate classical elements into their work. The first, *Lecons De Ténébres*, was rooted in traditional black metal sentiments, but for *Les Ténèbres Du Dehors* the arrangements were more orchestral in tone and scope. The blend of Hasnaoui's piercing screams with the operatic sopranos of Eve Gabrielle Siskind and Nathalie Barbary certainly produced a disconcerting musical effect in this, the group's second instalment in their attempt to re-create the three masses of the Catholic Officium Tenebarum. The packaging also was distinctive, featuring engravings by Gustave Doré taken from *Paradise Lost*. The complexity of Elend's ideas and music is particularly unusual given that the group are based partially in Australia (where musician Renaud is based) and that their songs are systematically built as the result of overseas tape correspondence. Despite this, the classical training of each member involved in Elend shines through, as does their academic knowledge of the Baroque, Classical and Romantic periods.

● ALBUMS: *Lecons De Ténébres* (Holy 1994) ★★★, *Les Ténébres Du Dehors* (Holy 1996) ★★★.

Elephant Man

b. O'Neil Bryan, 11 September 1975, Seaview Gardens, Jamaica, West Indies. One of the more colourful characters on the 'glam' **dancehall** scene, Bryan was originally known as 'Dumbo the Elephant' as it was perceived that he had larger than average ears similar to the **Walt Disney** cartoon character. He was given the nickname by his soccer playing colleague Crack Skull who in 1991, through his music industry connections, arranged Bryan's studio debut. Elephant Man was still at school when he first ventured into the Seaview-based studio and practised beating out rhythms and rhymes among his school friends. He went on to became a member of **Scare Dem Crew** but following their demise, he demonstrated his individuality and pursued a solo career. He was celebrated for his trademark yellow-orange hair, his outlandish jewellery and his numerous catch-phrases. On stage he is a whirlwind of activity, launching himself high into the air, climbing monitors and running from side to side, claiming that he is attempting to express himself to his people. In 1998, he performed at the dancehall night of the annual Reggae Sumfest festival and the media went into overdrive describing his antics as he climbed onto the television crane and performed high above the audience. Elephant Man's early solo efforts included duets with **Mr. Vegas** on 'Jump Jump', 'What's Up', 'Ain't No Way' and the *avant garde* dancehall favourite 'Dainty'.

By 2000, Elephant Man had released a series of solo hits including the favoured, 'Watchi Pum', 'Replacement Killer', 'You Slacker You' and 'Pum Pum'. He was also reunited with Scare Dem Crew's **Harry Toddler** for the hit, 'War War War'. In 2001 the DJ recorded 'Bombing' following the attack on the World Trade Center in New York, which occurred on his 26th birthday. In December 2003, he made his major label debut with the VP Records/**Atlantic Records** release *Good 2 Go*, which featured the US R&B hit 'Pon De River, Pon De Bank'.

● ALBUMS: *Comin' 4 You!* (Greensleeves 2000) ★★★, *Log On* (Greensleeves 2001) ★★★, *Higher Level* (Greensleeves 2002) ★★★★, *Good 2 Go* (VP/Atlantic 2003) ★★★.

Elevate

Elevate are one of a clutch of Scandinavian bands formed to emulate the Euro house success of artists such as **Ace Of Base** and **Dr. Alban**. Comprising Yvette Palm (vocals), Stefan Bosson (vocals) and Robert Ahlin (keyboards), they made their debut in 1993 with a single, 'Easy To Believe', released on **Virgin Records**. Finding substantial popularity on the German club scene, the Stockholm, Sweden–based group was propelled to the top of many critics' tip sheets by the end of the year.

● ALBUMS: *The Architect* (Flower Shop 1996) ★★★.

Elevator Suite

This UK-based trio comprises two DJs, Andy Childs and Paul Roberts, alongside multi-instrumentalist Steve Grainger. Their sound is a blend of contemporary **dance music** production with funk and rock influences from the 60s and 70s. Childs and Roberts met in Salisbury, Wiltshire, and ran an ill-fated clothes and record shop called Boom Tunes before abandoning the project and immersing themselves in the blossoming early 90s club culture. As Funk Junky, Childs recorded a track, 'Bulldozer', for a Plymouth-based label, but it sank without a trace. Disheartened, Childs relocated to Totnes in Devon, where he met the classically trained Grainger. Their seemingly incongruous backgrounds became a creative partnership and after recording demos, they gained the interest of London-based publishers and record companies. Their debut release for Infectious Records, 'Man In A Towel', was a beguiling mixture of 60s influences and a contemporary obsession with somewhat kitsch lounge music. It was named Record Of The Week on the UK's national Radio 1 FM but problems with sampling clearances prevented the single from receiving a full commercial release. Sounding at times similar to **Black Grape**, **Mansun** and the **Charlatans**, their October 2000 debut, *Barefoot & Shitfaced*, featured more funky soundtrack sounds, rock guitar, saxophone and lo-fi percussion.

● ALBUMS: *Barefoot & Shitfaced* (Infectious 2000) ★★★.

Eleven:59

Ladbroke Grove, London, England, duo of DJ Daniel X and rapper Gian Carlo Morroco, formed when X heard Morroco chatting a reggae lyric, 'My Ambition's To Kill Mr Botha', at a blues party in 1987. Together they signed to **Virgin Records** subsidiary From A Whisper To A Scream, releasing two critically acclaimed singles, '3 A.M.' and 'Digi', the latter utilizing the **O'Jays'** 'For The Love Of Money' as the musical foundation for an anti-stardom rap. Despite the interest generated, Virgin soon pulled the plug on the label, and Eleven:59 elected to form their own Ticking Time imprint instead. Two more underground EPs followed, before the group signed a licensing contract with China Records in 1994. 'Trouble On My Mind' (1995) was inspired by poverty and its frustrations, though Daniel X did at least have some property to his name, in the shape of a part-ownership of a hairdressing salon in Soho. Live they utilized a series of loops with live trumpet to produce a sound that offered a soulful counterbalance to the trio's hard, politicized diatribes.

Eleventh Dream Day

This US band was formed in Chicago, Illinois,USA, in the mid-80s and comprised Rick Rizzo (guitar/vocals), Janet Beveridge Bean (b. 10 February 1964, Bartow, Florida, USA; drums), Douglas McCombs (bass) and Baird Figi (guitar/vocals). Its brand of college-rock, in the mould of the **Pixies** and **Dream Syndicate**, drew on music from the 60s and 70s, with the guitar histrionics of **Television**, **Neil Young** and **Crazy Horse** combined with a whiff of psychedelia. Signed to the **Atlantic Records** label, Eleventh Dream Day seemed set to break away from their cult status in the 90s. This impetus was struck a blow early in 1991 when Figi quit and was replaced by Matthew 'Wink' O'Bannon. *Lived To Tell* was recorded in a studio-converted Kentucky barn in an attempt to obtain the feeling of a live recording, but it ended up

sounding even more mannered than the previous albums. Bean, meanwhile, recorded several albums with her country/roots side-project, **Freakwater**. The downbeat *El Moodio* ended the band's relationship with Atlantic. A move to the small Atavistic label saw the release of *Ursa Major*, recorded by John McEntire of **Tortoise**, the influential *avant garde* instrumental band co-founded by McCombs. O'Bannon left in 1996 to concentrate on his other outfit, Bodeco. Rizzo, Bean and McCombs have continued to record together as Eleventh Dream Day whenever their busy schedules allow.
● ALBUMS: *Eleventh Dream Day* mini-album (Amoeba 1987) ★★, *Prairie School Freakout* (Amoeba 1988) ★★★, *Beet* (Atlantic 1989) ★★★, *Lived To Tell* (Atlantic 1991) ★★★, *El Moodio* (Atlantic 1993) ★★★, *Ursa Major* (Atavistic/City Slang 1994) ★★★, *Eighth* (Thrill Jockey/City Slang 1997) ★★★★, *Stalled Parade* (Thrill Jockey 2000) ★★★.

Elf

This US heavy rock unit was formed in 1967 by vocalist **Ronnie James Dio** (b. Ronald Padavona, 10 July 1940, Portsmouth, New Hampshire, USA) with cousin Dave Feinstein on guitar, plus Gary Driscoll (drums), Doug Thaler (keyboards) and Nick Pantas (guitar). They worked under the name Electric Elves until 1970 when the entire band was involved in a car crash, in which Pantas died and Thaler was hospitalized. Mickey Lee Soule (keyboards) was added to a reshuffled line-up, seen by **Roger Glover** and Ian Paice of **Deep Purple** in 1972. A production and recording contract was arranged, with Elf supporting Deep Purple on two American tours. However, the band's bar-room blues and boogie was always more effective live than in the studio. In 1973 Elf recruited bass player Craig Gruber, allowing Dio to concentrate on vocals. Their guitarist, Feinstein, gave up touring and was replaced first by Doug Thaler, previously keyboard player for the Elves, and then Steve Edwards. From 1974 Mark Nauseef (later **Ian Gillan** and **Thin Lizzy**) played percussion for the band. In 1975 Glover offered Dio the opportunity to appear on his project *The Butterfly Ball*, and this gave Dio the widespread recognition he desired. **Ritchie Blackmore** stepped in to co-opt Elf into his **Rainbow** project, though after five months only Dio remained as former Elf musicians Gruber, Lee Soule and Driscoll were summarily discarded.
● ALBUMS: Elf (Epic 1972) ★★★, *Carolina County Ball* (UK) *L.A./59* (USA) (Purple/MGM 1974) ★★, *Trying To Burn The Sun* (MGM 1975) ★★.

Elf Power

This Athens, Georgia, USA–based lo-fi/indie quartet was originally formed by Andrew Rieger (vocals/guitar) and Laura Carter (keyboards/vocals) in 1994. The band has been compared to similarly styled outfits such as **Olivia Tremor Control** and **Neutral Milk Hotel** over the years, and with good reason. Not only does Elf Power share the same record company (Elephant 6) with the aforementioned bands, but all three bands are friends and often guest on each other's albums. Shortly after issuing their debut album *Vainly Clutching At Phantom Limbs in 1995*, Elf Power made a fan out of Athens native and **R.E.M.** frontman Michael Stipe. With the addition of former associate Bryan Helium (b. Bryan Poole; bass/vocals) and Andrew Wegelin (percussion), they opened several dates on an R.E.M. tour. Further releases

soon followed, including 1997's *When The Red King Comes* and 2000's *The Winter Is Coming*. The follow-up, *Creatures*, was recorded without original bass player Poole who left to work on his own solo project, the Late B.P. Helium.
● ALBUMS: *Vainly Clutching At Phantom Limbs* (Andrew/Drug Racer 1995) ★★★, *When The Red King Comes* (Arena Rock/Elephant 6 1997) ★★★★, *A Dream In Sound* (Arena Rock/Elephant 6 1999) ★★★★, *The Winter Is Coming* (SugarFree 2000) ★★★, *Creatures* (spinART/Shifty Disco 2002) ★★★, *Walking With The Beggar Boys* (Orange Twin 2004) ★★★★.

Elf, Mark

b. 13 December 1949, New York City, USA. A hard-working and accomplished bop guitarist, Elf gained some long overdue recognition in the late 90s with several acclaimed recordings for his own Jen Bay label. Raised in New York, Elf attended the **Berklee College Of Music** from 1969–71. After graduation Elf built up a reputation on the jazz scene, playing and recording with a role call of jazz legends including **Lou Donaldson, Dizzy Gillespie, Benny Golson, Al Grey, Lionel Hampton, Jimmy Heath, Jon Hendricks, Freddie Hubbard, Branford Marsalis, Wynton Marsalis** and **Clark Terry**. He recorded his debut between 1986 and 1987, and later decamped to Santiago, Chile, for a set on the Alerce label. His second album, *The Eternal Triangle*, was recorded in 1988 but, following a series of rejections from established labels, Elf issued the set on his own Jen Bay imprint. Thanks to his own tireless self-promotion Elf's recent recordings have gained extensive airplay, introducing his fluid and melodic playing to a wider audience.
● ALBUMS: *Mark Elf Trio, Vol. 1* (Half Note 1987) ★★★, *Mark Elf Trio* (Alerce 1993) ★★★, *The Eternal Triangle* 1988 recording (Jen Bay 1996) ★★★★, *Minor Scramble* (Jen Bay 1997) ★★★★, *Trickynometry* (Jen Bay 1998) ★★★★, *New York Cats* (Jen Bay 1999) ★★★, *Over The Airwaves* (Jen Bay 2000) ★★, *Live At Smalls* 1995 recording (Jen Bay 2001) ★★, *Swingin'* (Jen Bay 2001) ★★★, *Dream Steppin'* (Jen Bay 2002) ★★★, *Glad To Be Back* (Jen Bay 2004) ★★★.

Elgar, Charlie

b. Charles A. Elgar, 13 June 1885, New Orleans, Louisiana, USA, d. August 1973, Chicago, Illinois, USA. As a child Elgar studied violin and later extended his studies at music colleges in Wisconsin and Illinois. He played in classical music ensembles in his home-town before settling in Chicago around 1913. There, he formed his own small band and then a big band, which was for many years resident at the Dreamland Café. He travelled to Europe as a member of Will Marion Cook's orchestra and then returned to Chicago for further long residencies as leader at several of the city's top nightclubs. During all this time he had been active as a teacher and at the beginning of the 30s he turned to that aspect of his career on a full-time basis. Although outside the jazz stream, his bands regularly included in their ranks top-flight early jazzmen including **Manuel Perez, Lorenzo Tio, Barney Bigard** and **Darnell Howard**. Elgar's name lives on through jazz histories rather than through a legacy of records, as he made only four sides despite his popularity and widespread activity in the 20s.
● COMPILATIONS: *Elgar's Creole Orchestra* 1926 recordings (Arcadia 1980) ★★★.

Elgart, Larry

b. 20 March 1922, New London, Connecticut, USA. An alto saxophonist, in the mid-40s he played in **Bobby Byrne**'s commercially unsuccessful band. It was while on the Byrne band that he met arranger Charlie Albertine, whose writing style he liked and whom he bore in mind when he formed his own band. Also in the mid-40s Elgart was one of the principal soloists in the band led by his brother, **Les Elgart**. Elgart's exuberant playing was an important feature of the orchestra and led to the brothers, deciding to part company and each lead a band of his own. For a while Larry Elgart And His Manhattan Swing Band enjoyed a measure of popularity in and around New York, usually playing top hotels and ballrooms. Business fell off in the 50s, however, and the brothers reunited in an attempt to meet current commercial demands. However, the passage of time and changes in public taste militated against their chances of survival. Larry Elgart And His Manhattan Swing Orchestra charted in the USA in 1982 with 'Hooked On Swing'.

● ALBUMS: *Band With Strings* (Decca 1954) ★★★, *Larry Elgart & His Orchestra* (Decca 1954) ★★★, *Barefoot Ballerina* (Decca 1955) ★★★, *Larry Elgart & His Orchestra* (RCA Victor 1959) ★★★, *New Sounds At The Roosevelt* (RCA Victor 1959) ★★★, *Saratoga* (RCA Victor 1960) ★★★, *Easy Goin' Swing* (RCA Camden 1960) ★★★, *Sophisticated Sixties* (MGM 1960) ★★★, *The Shape Of Sounds To Come* (MGM 1960) ★★★, *Visions* (MGM 1961) ★★★, *The City* (MGM 1961) ★★★, *Music In Motion!* (MGM 1962) ★★★, *More Music In Motion* (MGM 1962) ★★★, *Flight Of The Condor* (RCA Victor 1981) ★★★, *Hooked On Swing* (RCA Victor 1982) ★★★★, *Hooked On Swing 2* (RCA Victor 1983) ★★★.

● COMPILATIONS: *Live From The Ambassador* 80s recordings (Quicksilver 1995) ★★★, *Latin Obsession* 70s recordings (Sony 2000) ★★★.

Elgart, Les

b. 3 August 1918, New Haven, Connecticut, USA, d. 29 July 1995, Dallas, Texas, USA. Elgart was lead trumpeter in bands headed by **Bunny Berigan**, **Hal McIntyre**, **Charlie Spivak** and **Harry James**. His brother, **Larry Elgart**, played lead alto saxophone with the Charlie Spivak band at the age of 17, later moving on to work with **Woody Herman**, **Red Norvo** and **Freddie Slack**. In 1945 the brothers formed their own band, which recorded and toured under Les' name, and used arrangements by musicians such as **Nelson Riddle** and **Bill Finegan**. Their partnership was short-lived, and they split to form their own units, without much success. They reunited in 1953, launching a 'new sound' featuring the arrangements of Charles Albertine with the emphasis on ensemble playing, no piano, and hardly any solos. Jazz fans were unimpressed, but the modern, melodic approach caught the general public's imagination and the band became prolific album sellers. Larry resumed the leadership when Les moved to California but, in 1963 they were together again for a time as joint leaders of the Les And Larry Elgart Orchestra.

● ALBUMS: *Impressions Of Outer Space* (Brunswick 1953) ★★★, *Prom Date* (Columbia 1954) ★★★, *Campus Hop* (Columbia 1954) ★★★, *Just One More Dance* (Columbia 1954) ★★★, *The Band Of The Year* (Columbia 1954) ★★★, *The Dancing Sound* (Columbia 1954) ★★★, *More Of Les* (Columbia 1955) ★★★, *For Dancers Only* (Columbia 1955) ★★★, as Les Elgart And His Orchestra *The Elgart Touch* (Columbia 1956) ★★★★, *The Most Happy Fella* (Columbia 1956) ★★★, *For Dancers Also* (Columbia 1956) ★★★, *Sound Ideas* (Columbia 1958) ★★★, *Les & Larry Elgart & Their Orchestra* (Columbia 1958) ★★★, *Les Elgart On Tour* (Columbia 1959) ★★★, *The Great Sound Of Les Elgart* (Columbia 1959) ★★★, *The Band With That Sound* (Columbia 1960) ★★★, *Designs For Dancing* (Columbia 1960) ★★★, *Half Satin, Half Latin* (Columbia 1960) ★★★, *It's De-Lovely* (Columbia 1961) ★★★, *The Twist Goes To College* (Columbia 1962) ★★★, *Best Band On Campus* (Columbia 1962) ★★★, *Big Band Hootenany* (Columbia 1963) ★★★, *Command Performance! Les And Larry Play The Great Dance Hits* (Columbia 1964) ★★★, *The New Elgart Touch* (Columbia 1965) ★★★, *Elgart Au Go-Go* (Columbia 1965) ★★★, *Sound Of The Times* (Columbia 1966) ★★★, *Warm And Sensuous* (Columbia 1966) ★★★, *Girl Watchers* (Columbia 1967) ★★★★, *Wonderful World Of Today's Hits* (Columbia 1967) ★★★, *Ain't We Got Fun* (DRIVE Archive 1995) ★★★.

Elgins

US-born Johnny Dawson, Cleo Miller and Robert Fleming, later replaced by Norbert McClean, sang together in three Detroit vocal groups in the late 50s— the Sensations, the Five Emeralds and the Downbeats. Under the last of these names, they recorded two singles for **Motown Records** in 1959 and 1962. Also in 1962, Saundra Mallett (later Saundra Mallett Edwards) issued 'Camel Walk' for Tamla, backed by the Vandellas. Motown suggested that she join forces with the Downbeats, and the new unit was named the Elgins after the title originally used by the **Temptations** when they first signed with Motown. In the fiercely competitive climate of Motown in the mid-60s, the Elgins were forced to wait three years before they could issue a single, but 'Darling Baby'— written and produced by **Holland/Dozier/Holland**—reached the US R&B Top 10 early in 1966. 'Heaven Must Have Sent You', which also exhibited the traditional Motown sound of the period, matched that success, but after one further hit in 1967, the group broke up.

In 1971, the Elgins enjoyed two unexpected UK Top 20 hits when Motown reissued 'Heaven Must Have Sent You' and the former b-side 'Put Yourself In My Place'. The Elgins re-formed to tour Britain, with Yvonne Allen (a former session vocalist) taking the place of Saundra Mallett, but plans for the revitalized group to renew their recording career foundered. In 1989, Yvonne Allen, Johnny Dawson, Norman McLean and Jimmy Charles recorded a new arrangement of 'Heaven Must Have Sent You' for producer Ian Levine. They continued working for his Motor City label in the 90s, releasing *Take The Train* and *Sensational*. The original lead vocalist on all their Motown material, Saundra Edwards, was also recording for the same label.

● ALBUMS: *Darling Baby* (VIP 1966) ★★★, *Take The Train* (Motor City 1990) ★★, *Sensational* (Motor City 1991) ★★.

● COMPILATIONS: *The Very Best Of The Motorcity Recordings* (Motor City 1996) ★★.

Elias Zerole And His Zig Zag Jive Flutes

(see **Zerole, Elias, And His Zig Zag Jive Flutes**)

Elias, Eliane

b. 19 March 1960, São Paulo, Brazil. Before she reached the age of 21, Elias had attracted considerable attention, not only for her keyboard playing but also as a teacher of jazz music. In the early 80s she moved to New York, joined the **Randy Brecker** and **Michael Brecker** jazz rock group, **Steps Ahead**, with whom she remained until 1984, and thereafter recorded and toured extensively. She continued to play and record with Randy Brecker, whom she married, and has also recorded with **Jack DeJohnette**, **Nana Vasconcelos** and **Eddie Gomez** (upon whose advice she first tried her luck in the USA). Although a gifted and interesting pianist, Elias has only recently fulfilled her early promise to become a major figure on the contemporary jazz scene with the success of 2002's *Kissed By Nature*.

● ALBUMS: *Illusions* (Denon 1987) ★★★, *Crosscurrents* (Denon 1988) ★★★, *So Far So Close* (Blue Note 1988) ★★★, *Plays Jobim* (Blue Note 1989) ★★★, *A Long Story* (Manhattan 1990) ★★, *Fantasia* (Blue Note 1992) ★★★, *Paulistana* (Blue Note 1993) ★★★, *Solos And Duets* (Blue Note 1995) ★★★★, *The Three Americas* (Blue Note 1997) ★★★★, *Sings Jobim* (Blue Note 1998) ★★★, *Everything I Love* (Blue Note 2000) ★★★★, *Kissed By Nature* (Bluebird 2002) ★★★★, *Dreamer* (Bluebird 2004) ★★★.

● COMPILATIONS: *The Best Of Eliane Elias* (Denon 1995) ★★★, *The Best Of Eliane Elias, Volume 1: Originals* (Blue Note 2001) ★★★, *Timeless* (Savoy Jazz 2003) ★★★★, *Brazilian Classics* (Blue Note 2003) ★★★★.

Elio E Le Storia Tese

Elio E Le Storia Tese are a bustling six-piece group whose main ambition seems to be the relentless but affectionate parodying of Italian life and society. Located somewhere between the theatrical comedic tradition of Italians such as Dario Fo and the work of the UK's **Incredible String Band**, the group initially rose to fame through its appearances on the satirical football show *Mai Dire Goal! (Never Say Goal!)*. However, it was not until the 1995 San Remo Song Festival that the group's commercial fortunes improved and they left behind their previous cult following. Their song 'Lat Terra Dei Cacchi' ('The Land Of Khaki Fruits') won second place, despite the fact that all their activities at the festival seemed geared to making fun of the entire event. However, such ribaldry has masked the fact that the sextet are talented and creative musicians in their own right, capable of performing in any number of musical genres without sacrificing their inimitable sense of anarchy. Their 1995 album, *Eat The Phikis*, entered the Italian charts at number 1 in April and spawned a series of hit singles.

● ALBUMS: *Eat The Phikis* (Aspirine 1995) ★★★.

Eliscu, Edward

b. 2 April 1902, New York City, USA, d. 18 June 1998, Newton, Connecticut, USA. Some sources give Eliscu's year of birth as 1900. An author, songwriter, director, producer and actor, Eliscu was educated at City College in New York. While there, he became involved in various theatrical pursuits—writing lyrics, directing—and after graduation served as a director of entertainment at summer camps. He made his Broadway acting debut in the Helen Hayes comedy *Quarantine* (1924), and also appeared in *The Racket* and S. Ansky's 'dramatic legend', *The Dybbuk*. After being intro-

duced to **Vincent Youmans**, in 1928 Eliscu worked (uncredited) with the composer on the musical *Rainbow*. A year later, another collaboration between Eliscu, Youmans and **Billy Rose** resulted in the score for *Great Day!*, which included three future standards, 'More Than You Know', 'Without A Song' and the title number. Also in 1929, Eliscu wrote lyrics to **Joseph Meyer**'s music for *Lady Fingers*, and was subsequently represented on Broadway, as a lyricist and sometime librettist, by *The Third Little Show* revue ('You Forgot Your Gloves', with Ned Lehac, 1931), *A Little Racketeer* (1932), a production of **Franz Lehár**'s 1928 hit *Frederika* ('Kiss To Remind You', 'Why Did You Kiss My Heart Awake?', 'Rose In The Heather', 1937) and a tough political revue, *Meet The People* (with Jay Gorney, 'Four Freedoms' and title number, 1940), among others. There was also an off-Broadway musical, *The Banker's Daughter*, in 1962.

With the advent of talking pictures, coupled with often declining Broadway audiences as a result of the great Depression, from 1930 onwards Eliscu spent a good deal of his time in Hollywood. While there, he joined with **Nacio Herb Brown**, Bruno Granichstaedten and **Clifford Grey** for the score to the screen operetta *One Heavenly Night* (1931), starring British musical comedy star **Evelyn Laye** ('I Belong To Everybody', 'My Heart Is Beating', 'Along The Road Of Dreams', 'Goodnight Serenade', 'Heavenly Night') and the irresistible *Flying Down To Rio* (1933), which marked the beginning of the legendary partnership of **Fred Astaire** and **Ginger Rogers**. Eliscu and **Gus Kahn** provided the lyrics, and Vincent Youmans the melodies, for the memorable 'Carioca', 'Music Makes Me', 'Orchids In The Moonlight' and 'Flying Down To Rio'. Eliscu's other screen credits through the 30s into the early 40s included **Eddie Cantor**'s *Whoopee!* ('I'll Still Belong To You', with Nacio Herb Brown), *Queen High* ('It Seems To Me', 'I'm Afraid Of You', with **Arthur Schwartz** and **Ralph Rainger**), *Follow Thru* ('It Must Be You', with **Manning Sherwin**), *Rockabye*, *Paddy O'Day* (screenplay with Lou Breslo, and songs 'Keep That Twinkle In Your Eye', 'I Like A Balalaika', with **Harry Akst**), the Mae West vehicle *The Heat's On* ('Just A Stranger In Town', 'Hello, Mi Amigo', 'The White Keys', 'There Goes That Guitar', with Henry Myers and Jay Gorney) *The More The Merrier* ('The Torpedo Song', with Myers and Gorney) and *Hey, Rookie* (script by Eliscu, Myers, and Gorney, who composed the songs with J.C. Lewis). Eliscu also wrote the screenplays for, and produced or co-produced, several non-musical pictures.

In the early 50s, Eliscu was named as a subversive by Senator Joe McCarthy's Committee On Un-American Activities, and was unable to work in films or television for around 10 years. This episode in his life provoked right-wing objections to his election for the post of President of the American Guild of Authors and Composers, but they were overcome, and he served a term of five years in the post from 1968–73. He was also inducted into the Songwriters Hall of Fame, and performed a selection of his own works in the renowned *Lyrics And Lyricists* series at the 92nd Street 'Y' in New York City. His prolific output included 'Happy Because I'm In Love', 'A Fellow And A Girl', 'They Cut Down The Old Pine Tree', 'It's No Fun Eating Alone', 'Ankle Up The Altar With Me', 'It's The Same Old South', 'A Kiss To Remind You', 'The Four Rivers', 'Bird Of Paradise', 'You're Perfect!' and 'When The Clock Is Striking Twelve'. Amongst his other collaborators were **Johnny Green**, **Vernon Duke**, Richard Myers and **Billy Hill**.

● FURTHER READING: *With Or Without A Song: A Memoir*, Edward Eliscu.

Elite Swingsters
(see **Rathebe, Dolly**)

Elixir
This UK heavy metal quintet was formed in the mid-80s and featured Paul Taylor (b. Wanstead, London, England; vocals), Kevin Dobbs (bass), Phil Denton (b. *c*.1962, Luton, Bedfordshire, England; guitar), Norman Gordon (guitar) and Nigel Dobbs (drums). Their debut album, released in 1988, was preceded by a session for the Radio 1 Friday Rock show. A second album saw them joined by ex–**Iron Maiden** drummer Clive Burr (b. 8 March 1957), plus Mark White on bass, replacing the Dobbs brothers. Their stylistic origins date back to the **New Wave Of British Heavy Metal**, utilizing twin lead guitars to alternate between circular power-riffs and intricate solos. Early Iron Maiden and **Def Leppard** were strong influences, with their lyrical content split between mythology/epic struggles ('Son Of Odin', etc.) and the equally clichéd themes of sex, violence and drugs. After the band's dissolution Denton returned to playing the clubs with covers band Rough Diamond (not the 70s supergroup).
● ALBUMS: *Elixir* (Goasco 1988) ★★★, *Lethal Potion* (Sonic 1990) ★★★.

Elizalde, Fred
b. Federico Elizalde, 12 December 1907, Manila, Philippines, d. 16 January 1972. Elizalde spent his youth in the USA with his brother Manuel, and for a time led a dance band. His interest in music was a disappointment to his family, one of the richest in the Philippines, but any hopes that his education at Cambridge University in the UK might redirect his talents failed when Elizalde played his piano in a jazz-style band for the 1927 university ball. This event attracted wide media attention and he was soon in demand as a writer and composer. His work was played by Bert **Ambrose** and before long he was leading a professional dance band at London's Savoy Hotel that featured several leading American musicians, including some members of the **California Ramblers** such as **Adrian Rollini** and Chelsea Quealey. Although broadcast by the BBC from the Savoy, the band proved to be unpopular with hotel patrons and listeners who preferred the rather more sedate musical style of its predecessors. Later in the engagement Elizalde compromised by playing more accessible music and hiring the as-yet-unknown singer **Al Bowlly**, but he continued to employ American jazzmen, notably **Fud Livingston** and **Arthur Rollini**. Elizalde's policy paid off when he won the 1928 *Melody Maker* poll. Among his compositions was the unfortunately titled 'Heart Of A Nigger' (later retitled, without much improvement, 'Heart Of A Coon'), which was considered to be advanced for its time. In 1929 Elizalde folded his band after an unsuccessful tour of the UK and then led another band at a London theatre. His career changed direction in 1933 when he studied in Spain under the classical composer Manuel De Falla and thereafter he worked extensively as a symphony orchestra conductor, using his given name of Federico Elizalde.
● COMPILATIONS: *Fred Elizalde Volume 4 1927–33 recordings* (1980) ★★★.

Ella Guru
Ella Guru emerged from the fertile Liverpool, England–based music scene in the early years of the new millennium. Unlike other Liverpool bands such as the **Coral** and the **Zutons**, they eschewed psychedelic rock in favour of a delicate take on the type of lo-fi Americana performed by **Low** and Kurt Wagner's **Lambchop**. The band's one nod to the 'Cosmic Scouse' movement that spawned the Coral and the Zutons was naming themselves after a song from **Captain Beefheart**'s legendary *Trout Mask Replica*.
Singer and guitarist John Yates formed Ella Guru in 2002 with the intention of creating something different from the standard three- and four-piece set-ups. To this end, the band eventually swelled to include eight members with Yates joined by Kate Walsh (vocals), Christian Burwood (guitar), Nik Kavanagh (bass), Bren Moore (drums), Nick Kellington (ukulele/cornet), and Bob Pickin. The hushed ambience of their music meant the band was frequently to be found asking audience members to keep the noise down at live shows. Ella Guru made their recording debut in 2003 with the *3 Songs From Liverpool* EP, which opened with the spellbinding 'On A Beach'. The band's album debut, *The First Album*, followed in August 2004. Former **Mothers Of Invention** member Jimmy Carl Black contributed guest vocals to the last three tracks, including an unlisted version of 'On A Beach'.
● ALBUMS: *The First Album* (Banana 2004) ★★★.

Elledge, Jimmy
b. 8 January 1943, Nashville, Tennessee, USA. When he was 18 years old, Jimmy Elledge sent a demo tape to famed country producer **Chet Atkins**, who signed him to **RCA-Victor Records**. Elledge's debut single, the country ballad 'Funny How Time Slips Away'—produced by Atkins and written by soon-to-be country superstar **Willie Nelson**—reached the US Top 30 in early 1962 and earned him a gold disc for selling over a million copies. He later joined the Hickory label in the mid-60s but had no further US chart success.

Ellefson, Art
b. Arthur Ellefson, 17 April 1932, Moose Jaw, Canada. Ellefson began playing tenor saxophone in his mid-teens, having first played brass instruments. He played professionally in Canada but became best known after he moved to the UK in the early 50s. In London he played with a succession of leading musicians, including **Carl Barriteau** and **Harry Hayes**, then joined **Vic Lewis**. During the late 50s he played with modern small groups alongside musicians such as **Ronnie Ross** and **Allan Ganley** and was a member of **Woody Herman**'s Anglo-American Herd. He then played again with Lewis and also with **John Dankworth**, and spent some time with the **Ted Heath** band. The early and mid-60s found him again with Ross and he also played with **Maynard Ferguson**. He then based himself for some time in Bermuda, occasionally playing in the USA and the UK. By the 90s he had settled back in his native land, playing and recording. A fluent improviser with a fine sense of bop nuances, Ellefson is a good balladeer, bringing depth and understanding to his solos. He sometimes also plays soprano saxophone.
● ALBUMS: *As If To Say* (Sackville 1992) ★★★.

Ellen Allien
b. Germany. Two events in 1989 impacted heavily on the music making of German DJ/producer and label head Ellen

Allien: she became immersed in **dance music** for the first time and the Berlin Wall came down. The former occurred during a year spent in London, England, at the height of **acid house** and prompted Allien to begin DJing. The latter influenced the music scene in her home-town more generally but no less importantly. Having relocated back from London to Berlin, Allien began DJing at venues/events such as UFO, Tresor, Fischlabor and The Bunker. Working to a principle of 'don't wait for something to happen—activate oneself', Allien hosted a radio show and ran a record label, both named Braincandy, and worked at Berlin's Delerium record store. Although Braincandy folded (Allien has cited her youth and initial lack of self-confidence for this), a series of parties under the BPitch Control moniker eventually mutated into a new label. The label has released music by Autotune, Tok Tok vs Soffy O, Sascha Funk and Nora Below as well as Allien's own recordings and mix compilations. Allien also curates a 7-inch-only label, Spielplatz/Playground.

Recording under the Ellen Allien moniker (after a friend suggested that the music she played was not mixed by a girl from earth) rather than her own, never revealed name, she released two albums in the early years of the twenty-first century, both inextricably linked with her home-town. *Stadtkind* translated as City Kid and was intended as a paean to Berlin. Even more explicitly, its follow-up was named *Berlinette*. Allien's music is akin to a sampler for German electronic music, drawing on everything from **house** to new wave to glitch-tronica to Morr Music–like melodicism. Allien is equally comfortable with faux-naïve political lyrics such as 'We need a planet without cars and wars/No wars!/No cars!/No wars!/No cars!/I wish it could be true' ('Wish') or less cerebral commands such as 'Push! Push! Kick ass! Kick ass!' ('Push'). With both, Allien presents a face to a frequently faceless music.

● ALBUMS: *Stadtkind* (BPitch Control 2001) ★★★, *Berlinette* (BPitch Control 2003) ★★★★.
● COMPILATIONS: *Weiss Mix* (BPitch Control 2002) ★★★.

Elliman, Yvonne

b. 29 December 1951, Honolulu, Hawaii, USA. Singer Elliman played in the high school band in Hawaii before relocating to London in 1969. She was singing at the Pheasantry folk club in the Kings Road, Chelsea, when the rising songwriters **Tim Rice** and **Andrew Lloyd Webber** chanced upon her. They offered her the part of Mary Magdalene in their new rock opera *Jesus Christ Superstar* and this brought her to the public's attention. She subsequently recreated the role in the film and earned a nomination for a Golden Globe award by the Foreign Press Association. The role also gave her a first hit single with 'I Don't Know How To Love Him', which was also the title of her 1972 debut for **Decca Records**. Her co-star, **Ian Gillan** of **Deep Purple**, subsequently signed her to Purple's UK Label. Elliman then recorded an album for **Decca Records** in New York before returning to London to record a follow-up with the help of **Pete Townshend**. While appearing on Broadway in the American showing of *Jesus Christ Superstar* she met and married RSO president Bill Oakes. Through Oakes she was introduced to **Eric Clapton** and invited to sing backing vocals on the single he was then recording—'I Shot The Sheriff'. She remained a member of Clapton's band for his next five albums. She was also signed to RSO in her own right and recorded the solo *Rising Sun*, which was produced

by **Steve Cropper**. Her next album, *Love Me*, featured the UK Top 10 title track, written by **Barry Gibb** and **Robin Gibb**. The **Bee Gees** then wrote some of their *Saturday Night Fever* tracks with Elliman in mind and she had a US chart-topper in 1978 with 'If I Can't Have You'. She has since concentrated on session work although she recorded a duet with **Stephen Bishop** in 1980 that narrowly missed the US charts.

● ALBUMS: *I Don't Know How To Love Him* (Decca 1972) ★★, *Food Of Love* (Decca 1973) ★★, *Rising Sun* (RSO 1975) ★★, *Love Me* (RSO 1976) ★★★, *Night Flight* (RSO 1978) ★★, *Yvonne* (RSO 1979) ★★.
● COMPILATIONS: *The Very Best Of Yvonne Elliman* (Taragon 1995) ★★★, *The Best Of Yvonne Elliman* (Polydor 1997) ★★★, *If I Can't Have You* (Universal 1999) ★★★, *The Collection* (Spectrum 1999) ★★★.
● FILMS: *Jesus Christ Superstar* (1973).

Elling, Kurt

b. 2 November 1967, Chicago, Illinois, USA. While still in school, Elling began singing as a chorister but at college took a serious interest in jazz. He developed a wide-ranging repertoire including ballads, standards and original material. During his formative years he also established a commanding stage presence and attracted the attention of **Blue Note Records**. Signed to this label, his debut album was heavily promoted and a simultaneous national tour brought Elling to a larger audience than is usually the case for new jazz singers. Elling's chief influences are instrumentalists rather than singers, notably **Wayne Shorter** and **Keith Jarrett**, although, like so many younger singers, he holds the veteran jazz singer **Mark Murphy** in especially high regard. The high profile enjoyed by Elling in the 90s has placed him in a strong position to be a major jazz artist of the twenty-first century. He was voted best vocalist in the 2002 *DownBeat* readers poll and the 2003 *DownBeat* critics poll.

● ALBUMS: *Close Your Eyes* (Blue Note 1995) ★★★★, *The Messenger* (Blue Note 1997) ★★★★, *This Time It's Love* (Blue Note 1998) ★★★★, *Live In Chicago* (Blue Note 2000) ★★★★, *Flirting With Twilight* (Blue Note 2001) ★★★, *Man In The Air* (Blue Note 2003) ★★★.

Ellington, Duke

b. Edward Kennedy Ellington, 29 April 1899, Washington, DC, USA, d. 24 May 1974, New York City, New York, USA. Ellington began playing piano as a child but, despite some local success, took up a career as a sign-painter. In his teens he continued to play piano, studied harmony, composed his first tunes and was generally active in music in Washington. Among his childhood friends were **Sonny Greer**, **Artie Whetsol** and **Otto Hardwicke**; from 1919 he played with them in various bands, sometimes working outside the city. In 1923 he ventured to New York to work with **Elmer Snowden**, and the following year formed his own band, the Washingtonians. Also in 1924, in collaboration with lyricist Joe Trent, he composed the *Chocolate Kiddies* revue. By 1927, Ellington's band had become established in east coast states and at several New York nightclubs. At the end of the year he successfully auditioned for a residency at Harlem's Cotton Club. The benefits arising from this engagement were immeasurable: regular radio broadcasts from the club ensured a widespread audience and Ellington's tours and recording sessions during the period of the residency, which ended early in 1931, built upon the band's popularity. In the early 30s the band consolidated its reputation with extended tours of the USA, appearances in films and visits to Europe, which included performances in London in 1933. Towards the end of the decade the band returned for further seasons at the Cotton Club.

Throughout the 30s and early 40s the band recorded extensively and to great acclaim; they continued to tour and record with little interruption during the rest of the 40s and into the early 50s but, although the quality of the music remained high, the band became significantly less popular than had once been the case. An appearance at the 1956 **Newport Jazz Festival** revived their popularity, and during the rest of the 50s and the following decade Ellington toured ceaselessly, playing concerts around the world. Ellington had always been a prolific writer, composing thousands of tunes including 'It Don't Mean A Thing (If It Ain't Got That Swing)', 'Sophisticated Lady', 'In A Sentimental Mood', 'Prelude To A Kiss', 'Concerto For Cootie (Do Nothin' Till You Hear From Me)', 'Cotton Tail', 'In A Mellotone', 'I Got It Bad And That Ain't Good', 'Don't Get Around Much Anymore', 'I'm Beginning To See The Light' and 'Satin Doll'. In later years he also composed film scores, among them *The Asphalt Jungle* (1950), *Anatomy Of A Murder* (1959), *Paris Blues* (1960) and *Assault On A Queen* (1966). More importantly, he began to concentrate upon extended works, composing several suites and a series of sacred music concerts, the latter mostly performed in churches and cathedrals. Over the years the personnel of Ellington's orchestra proved remarkably stable, several of his sidemen remaining with him for decades. The ceaseless touring continued into the early 70s, with Ellington making few concessions to the advancing years. After his death in 1974 the orchestra continued for a time under the direction of his son, **Mercer Ellington**, but despite the continuing presence of a handful of survivors, such as **Harry Carney**, who had been in the band virtually without a break for 47 years, the spirit and guiding light was gone. From this moment, Ellington lived on through an immense recorded legacy and in the memories of musicians and an army of fans.

Ellington was born into relatively comfortable circumstances. His father had been a butler, even working for some time at the White House. The family was deeply religious and musical, and Ellington himself was very close to his parents. He reported that he was 'pampered and spoiled rotten', and of his parents he wrote: 'My mother was beautiful but my father was only handsome.' His mother was a piano player; under her influence, Ellington had music lessons from a teacher called Mrs. Clinkscales. In later life, he whimsically commented that one of the first things she taught him was never to share the stage with **Oscar Peterson**. Perhaps more influential than Mrs. Clinkscales were the piano players he heard in the pool-rooms, where, like any self-respecting, under-age, sharp-suited adolescent-about-town, he found his supplementary education among a diversity of gamblers, lawyers, pickpockets, doctors and hustlers. 'At heart,' he said, 'they were all great artists.' He paid special tribute to Oliver 'Doc' Perry, a pianist who gave him lessons of a less formal but more practical nature than those of Mrs. Clinkscales—'reading the leads and recognizing the chords'. Ellington became a professional musician in his teens. One of his first engagements was playing 'mood' music for a travelling magician and fortune teller, improvising to suit the moment, whether serious or mystical.

In 1914 he wrote his first compositions: 'Soda Fountain Rag' and 'What You Gonna Do When The Bed Breaks Down?'. By the age of 18 he was leading bands in the Washington area, having learned that the band leader, as 'Mr. Fixit', generally earned more money than the other members of the band. Thus, by the age of 20, he was pianist, composer and band leader: the essential Duke Ellington was formed, and would later blossom into one of the most influential musicians in jazz, although with characteristic perversity, he insisted that he wrote folk music, not jazz. By the time of the band's debut at the Cotton Club, in addition to Greer and Hardwicke, Ellington had recruited key players such as **Bubber Miley**, his first great 'growling' trumpet player; the trombonist **Joe 'Tricky Sam' Nanton**; the bass player **Wellman Braud** and Carney, whose baritone saxophone formed the rich and sturdy foundation of the band's reed section for its entire history. Perhaps just as crucial was Ellington's meeting with **Irving Mills**, who became his manager. For a black musician to survive, let alone prosper, in the America of the 20s and 30s, a tough white manager was an essential safeguard.

In 1927 came the first classic recordings of 'Black And Tan Fantasy' and 'Creole Love Call', the latter with the legendary vocal line by **Adelaide Hall**. In these, and in up-tempo numbers such as 'Hot And Bothered', the Ellington method was fully formed. The conventional way to praise a big band was to say that they played like one man. The quality of the Ellington bands was that they always played like a bunch of highly talented and wildly disparate individuals, recalling the 'great artists' of the pool-room. The Cotton Club provided an ideal workshop and laboratory for Ellington. Situated in Harlem, its performers were exclusively black, its clientele exclusively white and in pursuit of dusky exotic pleasures. Ellington, who enjoyed being a showman, gave the audience what it wanted: music for showgirls and boys to dance to, in every tempo from the slow and sultry to the hot and hectic, coloured with so-called 'jungle sounds'. Although this was a racial slur, Ellington had the skill and wit to transcend it, creating music that met the specification but disarmingly turned it inside-out. The music winked at the audience.

Moving into the 30s, the band's repertoire was enriched by pieces such as 'Rockin' In Rhythm', 'Old Man Blues', 'The Mooche' and, of course, 'Mood Indigo'. Its personnel now included **Juan Tizol** on trombone, **Cootie Williams**, de facto successor to Miley on trumpet, and the sublime **Johnny Hodges** on alto saxophone, whose lyricism, tempered with melancholy, became a crucial element in the Ellington palette. Hodges became the most striking example of the truism 'once an Ellingtonian, always an Ellingtonian'. Like Williams and Tizol, he would leave the band to become a leader in his own right or briefly a sideman in another band, only to return. The 30s saw the first attempts at compositions longer than the conventional three minutes (the length of a gramophone record), starting with 'Creole Rhapsody' in 1931. The period also saw, to oversimplify the situation, a move into respectability. Critics and musicians from the serious side of the tracks had begun to take notice. People as diverse as Constant Lambert, Percy Grainger, Leopold Stokowski and Igor Stravinsky recognized the extraordinary and unique gifts of Ellington. Phrases such as 'America's greatest living composer' crept into print.

Ellington continued to refer to himself, gracefully and demurely, as 'our piano player'. To be sure, his composing methods, from all accounts, were radically different from those of other title contenders. He would scribble a few notes on the back of an envelope, or memorize them, and develop the piece in rehearsal. The initial themes were often created by musicians in the band—hence the frequent shared composer credits: 'The Blues I Love To Sing' with Miley, 'Caravan' with Tizol, and 'Jeep's Blues' with Hodges. 'Bluebird Of Delhi', from the 1966 'The Far East Suite', was based on a phrase sung by a bird outside **Billy Strayhorn**'s room. Strayhorn joined the band in 1939, as arranger, composer, occasional piano player, friend and musical alter ego. A small, quiet and gentle man, he became a vital element in the Ellington success story. His arrival coincided with that of the tenor saxophone player **Ben Webster**, and the brilliant young bass player **Jimmy Blanton**, who died in 1943, aged 23. By common consent, the Webster/Blanton band produced some of the finest music in the Ellington canon, exemplified by 'Jack The Bear', with Blanton's innovative bass solo, and 'Just A-Settin' And A-Rockin'', where Webster demonstrates that the quality of jazz playing lies in discretion and timing rather than vast numbers of notes to the square inch.

Duke Ellington was elegantly dismissive of analysis; too much talk, he said, stinks up the place. However, he was more than capable of sensitive examination of his own music. Of the haunting and plaintive 'Mood Indigo', he said: 'Just a story about a little girl and a little boy. They are about eight and the girl loves the boy. They never speak of it, of course, but she just likes the way he wears his hat. Every day he comes to her house at a certain time and she sits in her window and waits. Then one day he doesn't come. "Mood Indigo" just tells how she feels.' The story, and the tune it describes, are characteristically Ellingtonian: they bear the hallmark of true sophistication, which is audacious simplicity. His music is never cluttered, and travels lightly and politely. His output as a composer was immense. The late Derek Jewell, in his indispensable biography of the man, estimated that he wrote at least 2,000 pieces but, because of his cavalier way with pieces of paper, it may have been as many as 5,000. Among them were many tunes that have become popular standards—'Sophisticated Lady', 'In A Sentimental Mood', 'Don't Get Around Much Anymore' and 'I'm Beginning To See The Light' are just a selected handful. Their significance, aside from the musical, was that their royalty income effectively subsidized the band, particularly during the post-war period when the big bands virtually disappeared under successive onslaughts from inflation, the growth of television, the decline of the dancehalls and, most significantly, the arrival of rock 'n' roll. Even Ellington was not immune to these pressures and in the early 50s, looking handsome suddenly became hard work. The turning-point came at the Newport Jazz Festival on 7 July 1956, when morale was low. The previous year had seen embarrassing attempts at cashing in on commercial trends with recordings of 'Twelfth Street Rag Mambo' and 'Bunny Hop Mambo', plus a summer season at an aqua show, with a string section and two harpists. The first set at Newport was equally embarrassing. Ellington arrived onstage to find four of his musicians missing. The band played a few numbers, then departed. They returned around midnight, at full strength, to play the 'Newport Jazz Festival Suite', composed with Strayhorn for the occasion. Then Ellington, possibly still rankled by the earlier behaviour of the band, called 'Diminuendo And Crescendo In Blue', a piece written almost 20 years earlier and by no means a regular item on their usual concert programme. In two sections, and linked by a bridge passage from, on this occasion, the tenor saxophone player **Paul Gonsalves**, the piece was a revelation. Gonsalves blew 27 choruses, the crowd went wild, the band played four encores, and the news travelled around the world on the jazz grapevine; it was also reported in detail in *Time* magazine, with a picture of the piano player on the cover.

After Newport and until his death, Ellington's life and career became a triumphal and global procession, garlanded with awards, honorary degrees, close encounters with world leaders and, more importantly, further major compositions. 'Such Sweet Thunder', his Shakespearean suite written with Strayhorn, contains gems such as 'Lady Mac'—'Though she was a lady of noble birth, we suspect there was a little ragtime in her soul'—and 'Madness In Great Ones', dedicated to Hamlet with the laconic remark 'in those days crazy didn't mean the same thing it means now'. Further collaborations with Strayhorn included an enchanting reworking of Tchaikovsky's 'The Nutcracker Suite' and 'The Far East Suite'—still adorned with dazzling contributions from various of the now-elder statesmen in the band: Hodges, Gonsalves and Carney in the reeds, **Lawrence Brown**, **Britt Woodman** and Tizol among the trombones, and **Ray Nance** and **Cat Anderson** in the trumpet section. Astonishingly, the band that recorded the *70th Birthday Concert* in England in 1969 included Carney, Hodges and Williams 40 years after they first joined Ellington, and on the record they still sounded like a group of kids having a good night on the town. The freshness and energy of the band, as it tackled material played hundreds of times before, was extraordinary. There was another side to the story. Ellington had always been a religious man, and in his later years he turned increasingly to the writing and performance of sacred music. The origins of this can be traced back to 'Come Sunday', from the 1945 suite 'Black, Brown And Beige', and beyond that to 'Reminiscing In Tempo', written 10 years earlier, following the death of his mother, of which he said: 'My mother's death was the greatest shock. I didn't do anything but brood. The music is representative of all that. It begins with pleasant thoughts. Then something awful gets you down. Then you snap out of it and it ends affirmatively.' From a man who was dismissive of analysis, this represented a very shrewd assessment not only of the piece in question, but of his entire output. Working within the framework of the conventional big band line-up—five reeds, four trumpets, three trombones, bass, drums and a remarkable piano player, he produced music of extraordinary diversity. His themes were startling in their simplicity, as if he had picked them off trees, and in a way, he did. The tonal qualities of the band—the unique Ellington sound—were based on a celebration of its individuals. The music might be lyrical or triumphant, elegiac or celebratory and the blues were never far away, yet it always ended affirmatively. To borrow a phrase from Philip Larkin, writing about **Sidney Bechet**, Duke Ellington's life and music added up to A Resounding Yes. In 1999, Ellington was awarded a Special Citation Pulitzer Prize commemorating the centenary of his birth and recognizing his 'musical genius' in the medium of jazz. Musical genius sits more comfortably on his shoulders than on almost anybody else's in the history of popular music.

● ALBUMS: *Carnegie Hall Concerts January 1943* (Prestige 1943) ★★★★, *The Hollywood Bowl Concert Volumes 1 & 2* (Unique Jazz 1947) ★★★★, *Mood Ellington* 10-inch album

(Columbia 1949) ★★★★, *Liberian Suite* 10-inch album (Columbia 1949) ★★★★, *Ellingtonia, Volume 1* 10-inch album (Brunswick 1950) ★★★★, *Ellingtonia, Volume 2* 10-inch album (Brunswick 1950) ★★★★, *Masterpieces By Ellington* (Columbia 1951) ★★★, *Ellington Uptown* (Columbia 1951) ★★★, *Duke Ellington Volumes 1–3* 10-inch albums (Jazz Panorama 1951) ★★★★, *Duke Ellington* (RCA-Victor 1951) ★★★★, *The Duke Is On The Air—From The Blue Note* (Bandstand 1952) ★★★★, *This Is Duke Ellington And His Orchestra* (RCA-Victor 1952) ★★★★, *Duke Ellington Plays the Blues* (RCA-Victor 1953) ★★★★, *Premiered By Ellington* 10-inch album (Capitol 1953) ★★★, *Ellington Plays Ellington* 10-inch album (Capitol 1953) ★★★★, *Early Ellington* (Brunswick 1954) ★★★, *The Music Of Duke Ellington* (Columbia 1954) ★★★★, *Plays* 10-inch album (Allegro 1954) ★★★, *Ellington '55* (Capitol 1954) ★★★, *The Duke Plays Ellington* (Capitol 1954) ★★★★, *Seattle Concert* (RCA-Victor 1954) ★★★, *Duke's Mixture* 10-inch album (Columbia 1955) ★★★, *Dance To The Duke* (Capitol 1955) ★★★, *Duke And His Men* (RCA-Victor 1955) ★★★, *Blue Light* (Columbia 1955) ★★★★, *Here's The Duke* 10-inch album (Columbia 1956) ★★★★, *Historically Speaking, The Duke* (Bethlehem 1956) ★★★, *Duke Ellington Presents* (Bethlehem 1956) ★★★, *Birth Of Big Band Jazz* (Riverside 1956) ★★★★, *Al Hibbler With the Duke* 10-inch album (Columbia 1956) ★★★, with Johnny Hodges *Ellington At Newport '56* (Columbia 1956) ★★★★★, *Ellington Showcase* (Capitol 1956) ★★★, *A Drum Is A Woman* (Columbia 1957) ★★★, *Such Sweet Thunder* (Columbia 1957) ★★★, *In A Mellotone* (RCA-Victor 1957) ★★★★, *Ellington Indigos* (Columbia 1958) ★★★★★, *At His Very Best* (RCA-Victor 1958) ★★★, *Newport 1958* (Columbia 1958) ★★★★★, *Black, Brown And Beige* (Columbia 1958) ★★★★, *The Cosmic Scene* (Columbia 1958) ★★★, *At The Bal Masque* (Columbia 1959) ★★★, *Jazz Party* (Columbia 1959) ★★★, with Hodges *Back To Back: Duke Ellington And Johnny Hodges Play The Blues* (Verve 1959) ★★★★, with Hodges *Side By Side* (Verve 1959) ★★★★★, *Festival Session* (Columbia 1959) ★★★, *Ellington Moods* (SeSac 1959) ★★★, *Anatomy Of A Murder* soundtrack (Columbia 1959) ★★★★, *Swinging Suites By Edward E. And Edward G. (Suite Thursday/Peer Gynt)* (Columbia 1960) ★★★, with Hodges *The Nutcracker Suite* (Columbia 1960) ★★★, *Piano In The Background* (Columbia 1960) ★★★, *Blues In Orbit* (Columbia 1960) ★★★★, *Paris Blues* (United Artists 1961) ★★★, *The Indispensable Duke Ellington* (RCA-Victor 1961) ★★★, with Count Basie *Ellington/Basie—First Time! The Count Meets The Duke* (Columbia 1962) ★★★, with Charles Mingus, Max Roach *Money Jungle* (United Artists 1962) ★★★★, *All American* (Columbia 1962) ★★★, *Midnight In Paris* (Columbia 1962) ★★★, with John Coltrane *Duke Ellington And John Coltrane* (MCA/Impulse! 1962) ★★★★, *Afro-Bossa* (Reprise 1963) ★★★★, with Coleman Hawkins *Meets Coleman Hawkins* (MCA/Impulse! 1963) ★★★★★, *The Symphonic Ellington* (Reprise 1963) ★★★, *Piano In The Foreground* (Columbia 1963) ★★★, with Svend Asmussen *Jazz Violin Session* (Reprise 1963) ★★★★, with Billy Strayhorn *Piano Duets: Great Times!* (Riverside 1963) ★★★, *Duke Ellington's Concert Of Sacred Music* (RCA-Victor 1964) ★★★, *Hit's Of The 60s* (Reprise 1964) ★★, *Daybreak Express* (RCA-Victor 1964) ★★★, *Jumpin' Pumpkins* (RCA-Victor 1965) ★★, *Johnny Come Lately*

(RCA-Victor 1965) ★★, *Mary Poppins* (Reprise 1965) ★, *Pretty Woman* (RCA-Victor 1965) ★★, *Flaming Youth* (RCA-Victor 1965) ★★, *Ellington '66* (Reprise 1965) ★★★, *Will Big Bands Ever Come Back?* (Reprise 1965) ★★★, *Concert In The Virgin Islands* (Reprise 1965) ★★★, with Boston Pops Orchestra *The Duke At Tanglewood* (RCA-Victor 1966) ★★★, with Ella Fitzgerald *Ella At Duke's Place* (Verve 1966) ★★★★★, with Fitzgerald *Ella And Duke At The Côte D'Azure* (Verve 1966) ★★★, *The Popular Duke Ellington* (RCA-Victor 1966) ★★★, *Concert Of Sacred Music* (RCA-Victor 1966) ★★★, with Hodges *The Far East Suite* (RCA-Victor 1967) ★★★★, *Soul Call* (Verve 1967) ★★★, *And His Mother Called Him Bill* (RCA-Victor 1968) ★★★★, with Frank Sinatra *Francis A. And Edward K.* (Reprise 1968) ★★★, *Second Sacred Concert* (Prestige 1968) ★★★, *70th Birthday Concert* (Solid State 1969) ★★★★, *The Latin American Suite* (Fantasy 1969) ★★★, *The New Orleans Suite* (Atlantic 1970) ★★★★, *Afro-Eurasian Eclipse* (Fantasy 1971) ★★★, with Ray Brown *This One's For Blanton* (Pablo 1972) ★★★, *Third Sacred Concert* (Prestige 1973) ★★★, *Eastbourne Performance* (RCA 1973) ★★, *Yale Concert* (Fantasy 1973) ★★★, with Teresa Brewer *It Don't Mean A Thing…* (Columbia 1973) ★★★★, *The Duke's Big 4* (Pablo 1974) ★★★★, *The Duke Ellington Carnegie Hall Concerts—January, 1943* (Prestige 1977) ★★★★, *The Duke Ellington Carnegie Hall Concerts—December, 1944* (Prestige 1977) ★★★★, *The Duke Ellington Carnegie Hall Concerts—January, 1946* (Prestige 1977) ★★★★, *The Duke Ellington Carnegie Hall Concerts—December, 1947* (Prestige 1977) ★★★★, *The Unknown Session* 1960 recording (Columbia 1979) ★★★, *In Concert At The Pleyel Paris* 1958 recording (Magic 1990) ★★★, *The Far East Suite: Special Mix* (Bluebird 1995) ★★★★, *Berlin '65/Paris '67* (Pablo 1998) ★★★, *Duke's Joint* 1945 live performances (RCA/Buddah 1999) ★★, *Ellington At Newport: The Complete Concert* (Columbia Legacy 1999) ★★★★★, *At The Alhambra* (Pablo 2002) ★★★.

● COMPILATIONS: *Ellington's Greatest* (RCA-Victor 1954) ★★★★, *Duke Ellington Volume 1—In The Beginning* (Decca 1958) ★★★★, *Duke Ellington Volume 2—Hot In Harlem* (Decca 1959) ★★★★, *Duke Ellington Volume 3—Rockin' In Rhythm* (Decca 1959) ★★★★, *The Best Of Duke Ellington* (Capitol 1961) ★★★★, *The Ellington Era Volume 1* 3-LP box set (Columbia 1963) ★★★★, *The Ellington Era Volume 2* 3-LP box set (Columbia 1964) ★★★★, *Duke Ellington's Greatest Hits* (Reprise 1966) ★★★★, *Duke Ellington—The Pianist* 1966–74 recordings (Fantasy 1974) ★★★★, *The Ellington Suites* (Pablo 1976) ★★★★, *The Intimate Ellington* (Pablo 1977) ★★★, *The All-Star Road Band, Volume 1* (Columbia 1983) ★★★★, *The All-Star Road Band, Volume 2* (Columbia 1983) ★★★★, *The Indispensable Duke Ellington Volumes 1–12* (RCA 1983–87) ★★★, *The Intimacy Of The Blues* 1970 recordings (Fantasy 1986) ★★★★, *The Blanton-Webster Band* 1940–42 recordings (RCA Bluebird 1987) ★★★★★, *Black, Brown And Beige* (RCA Bluebird 1988) ★★★★, *Four Symphonic Works* (Music Master 1989) ★★★★, *The Best Of Duke Ellington* (Columbia 1989) ★★★, *Braggin' In Brass—The Immortal 1938 Year* (Portrait 1989) ★★★★, *The Brunswick Era, Volume 1* (MCA 1990) ★★★★, with Blanton and others *Solos, Duets And Trios* 1932–67 recordings (RCA Bluebird 1990) ★★★★, *The OKeh Ellington* (Columbia 1991) ★★★★, *Small Groups, Volume 1* (Columbia/Legacy 1991)

★★★★, *The Essence Of Duke Ellington* (Columbia/Legacy 1991) ★★★★★, *The Complete Capitol Recordings Of Duke Ellington* 5-CD box set (Mosaic 1996) ★★★★★, *Jazz Profile* (Blue Note 1997) ★★★★, *1945, Vol. 2* (Classics 1998) ★★★, *The Centennial Edition: The Complete RCA Victor Recordings* 24-CD box set (RCA Victor 1999) ★★★★★, *The Essential Collection 1927–1962* (Columbia 2000) ★★★★, *Complete Columbia & RCA Studio Sessions With Ben Webster Featuring Jimmy Blanton* 40s recordings (Definitive 2000) ★★★★★, *Ken Burns Jazz: The Definitive Duke Ellington* (Columbia/Legacy 2000) ★★★★, *The Reprise Studio Recordings* 5-CD box set (Mosaic 2000) ★★★, *Live And Rare* 3-CD set (Bluebird 2002) ★★★, *Never No Lament: The Blanton-Webster Band* 3-CD set (Bluebird 2003) ★★★★★, *The Bubber Miley Era 1924–1929* (Jazz Legends 2004) ★★★, *The Centennial Collection* (Bluebird 2004) ★★★★, *Masterpieces By Ellington* (Columbia 2004) ★★★★, *The Treasury Shows Vol. II* (DETS 2005) ★★.

● DVD/VIDEOS: *Duke Ellington* (Virgin Vision 1992), *On The Road With Duke Ellington* (Direct Cinema 1995).

● FURTHER READING: *Duke Ellington: Young Music Master*, Martha E. Schaaf. *Sweet Man, The Real Duke Ellington*, Don R. George. *Duke Ellington*, Ron Franki. *Duke Ellington*, Barry Ulanov. *The World Of Duke Ellington*, Stanley Dance. *Music Is My Mistress*, Duke Ellington. *Celebrating The Duke*, Ralph J. Gleason. *Duke: A Portrait Of Duke Ellington*, Derek Jewell. *Duke Ellington In Person*, Mercer Ellington. *Duke Ellington: His Life And Music*, Peter Gammond. *Duke Ellington: Life And Times Of A Restless Genius Of Jazz*, James Lincoln Collier. *Duke Ellington: The Early Years*, Michael Tucker. *Duke Ellington: Jazz Composer*, Ken Rattenbury. *The Duke Ellington Reader*, Mark Tucker. *Beyond Category: The Life And Genius Of Duke Ellington*, John Edward Hasse. *The Duke Ellington Primer*, Dempsey J. Travis. *Reminiscing In Tempo: A Portrait Of Duke Ellington*, Stuart Nicholson. *Jump For Joy: Jazz At Lincoln Center Celebrates The Ellington Centennial*, Veronica Byrd, James Ty Cumbie, Tiffany A. Ellis and Rob Gibson (ed.). *The King Of All, Sir Duke*, Peter Lavezzoli. *Duke Ellington And His World*, A.H. Lawrence.

Ellington, Marc

b. 16 December 1945, Boston, Lincolnshire, England. This 70s singer-songwriter failed to achieve any great commercial success, despite recording with a number of highly respected musicians, including **Richard Thompson** and **Simon Nicol**. Between 1965 and 1978, Ellington made various appearances at concerts, folk clubs and in cabaret, both in the UK and abroad. During that time he released five singles, none of which made any major impact. *Marc Time* followed more of a country direction, and for this Ellington was joined by steel guitarist and dobro player **B.J. Cole**. Ellington was employed in much session work and provided back-up on albums by **Fairport Convention**, **Matthew's Southern Comfort** and **Richard And Linda Thompson**. Apart from being the Deputy Lieutenant for the County of Aberdeen, Scotland, Ellington now works in film video and record production, as well as composing music for television and film.

● ALBUMS: *Marc Ellington* (Philips 1968) ★★★★, *Rains/Reins Of Change* (Ampex 1970) ★★★, *A Question Of Roads* (Philips 1971) ★★★, *Restoration* (1972) ★★, *Border Skipping* (Philips 1976) ★★, *Marc Time* (Transatlantic 1975) ★★.

Ellington, Mercer

b. 11 March 1919, Washington, DC, USA, d. 8 February 1996, Copenhagen, Denmark. Any son following the same career as a famous father is bound to encounter problems of recognition. For Mercer Ellington the problem was magnified through the fact that his father was **Duke Ellington**, who was not only one of the two or three greatest figures in jazz history but was also an acknowledged master of twentieth-century music. For all the disadvantages of having such a parent, Mercer was determined to pursue a career in music. He studied formally in Washington and New York in the 20s and formed his own band, playing trumpet, in the late 30s. He sometimes used musicians more usually associated with his father, among them **Cat Anderson** and **Billy Strayhorn**, but also worked with men who only later joined Duke. In addition, he used musicians who were engaged in the emerging bebop movement, including **Dizzy Gillespie** and **Charles Mingus**.

In the early 40s Ellington was manager of the **Cootie Williams** band and also played briefly in Duke's band. He composed several tunes taken up by his father, of which the best known are 'Things Ain't What They Used To Be', 'Jumpin' Punkins' and 'Blue Serge'. Ellington spent the second half of the 50s with his father's band, mostly in an administrative capacity. He returned to the band in the mid-60s, remaining until Duke's death in 1974. Thereafter, he took over as leader of the Ellington orchestra and conducted the pit band for the Broadway show *Sophisticated Ladies* in the early 80s. His autobiography (written in collaboration with **Stanley Dance**) was published in 1978. Ellington continued to lead an orchestra into the 90s and, while still rooted in Duke's music, it developed a creditable musical personality of its own.

● ALBUMS: *Steppin' Into Swing Society* (Coral 1958) ★★★, *Colors In Rhythm* (Coral 1959) ★★★, *Continuum* (Fantasy 1975) ★★★, *Hot And Bothered* (Doctor Jazz 1985) ★★★, *Digital Duke* (GRP 1987) ★★★★, *Music Is My Mistress* (Limelight 1989) ★★★.

Ellington, Ray

b. Harry Brown, 1915, London, England, d. 28 February 1985. Ellington began playing drums as a teenager and by 1937 was proficient enough to replace **Joe Daniels** in **Harry Roy**'s popular band. He remained with Roy for almost five years, although his personal musical taste tended more towards the new jazz styles, and soon after the end of World War II he was playing bop in London clubs. He led his own quartet at this time and made a number of records, and sometimes accompanied visiting American jazzmen. His quartet in the late 40s comprised **Dick Katz** (piano), **Coleridge Goode** (bass) and **Lauderic Caton** guitar who was replaced by Laurie Deniz, and they were able to play swing, jumping R&B and popular jazz.

In the early 50s Ellington began to incorporate comedy and novelty material into his repertoire but the group's musical base was always strongly bop-influenced. Throughout the 50s the quartet was regularly featured on *The Goon Show* on BBC Radio, usually with Ellington singing, and he also took small acting roles in the programme. By the 60s and with the passing of *The Goon Show*, Ellington was much less in demand, but he continued playing until shortly before his death in February 1985. His son, Lance Ellington, played trombone with the **National Youth Jazz Orchestra** and also sang as a member of the pop duo Coffee And Cream.

● ALBUMS: *Goon Show Hits* (BBC 1958) ★★★★, *You're The Talk Of The Town* (Gold Star 1975) ★★.

● COMPILATIONS: *The Three Bears* 1948–49 recordings (Avid 2001) ★★★★.

Elliot, 'Mama' Cass

b. Ellen Naomi Cohen, 19 September 1941, Baltimore, Maryland, USA, d. 29 July 1974, London, England. Elliot's professional singing career began in the early 60s as a member of the Triumvirate with **Tim Rose** and John Brown. This evolved into the Big Three, a pivotal folk group comprising Rose, Elliot and her first husband, James Hendricks. When Rose embarked on a solo career, the remaining duo founded the **Mugwumps** with **Denny Doherty** and **Zalman 'Zally' Yanovsky**. Elliot later joined the former in the **Mamas And The Papas**, one of the most enduring folk rock attractions of the 60s. Her assured, soaring voice proved ideal for songwriter **John Phillips**' optimistic compositions, but internal disputes robbed the band of its momentum. In 1968, Elliot began an independent career with *Dream A Little Dream*, the title track from which reached the US and UK Top 20s (credited to Mama Cass with the Mamas And The Papas). 'It's Getting Better' from *Bubblegum, Lemonade And . . . Something For Mama* fared better still, climbing to number 8 in the UK despite competition from **Paul Jones**' cover version. Elliot's third set, *Make Your Own Kind Of Music*, preceded a temporary Mamas And The Papas reunion, after which she forged an equally short-lived partnership with ex-**Traffic** singer/guitarist **Dave Mason**. Tiring of her erstwhile image, Elliot began courting a wider MOR audience with appearances on prime time American television, but later recordings lacked the naive charm of their predecessors. Elliot nonetheless remained a popular figure and her death from a heart attack in July 1974 (apocryphally reported as the result of choking on a ham sandwich) robbed the 60s pop world of one of its most endearing characters.

● ALBUMS: *Dream A Little Dream* (Dunhill 1968) ★★★, *Bubblegum, Lemonade And . . . Something For Mama* (Dunhill 1969) ★★★, *Make Your Own Kind Of Music* (Dunhill 1969) ★★, with Dave Mason *Dave Mason And Mama Cass* (Blue Thumb 1971) ★★, *Cass Elliot* (RCA 1972) ★★, *The Road Is No Place For A Lady* (RCA 1972) ★★, *Don't Call Me Mama Anymore* (RCA 1973) ★★.

● COMPILATIONS: *Mama's Big Ones: The Best Of Mama Cass* (Dunhill 1970) ★★★, *Dream A Little Dream: The Cass Elliot Collection* (MCA 1997) ★★★, *Dedicated To The One I Love* (Spectrum 2002) ★★★, *Dream A Little Dream Of Me: The Music Of Mama Cass Elliot* (MCA 2005) ★★★.

● FURTHER READING: *Make Your Own Kind Of Music: A Career Retrospective Of Cass Elliot*, Jon Johnson. *Dream A Little Dream Of Me: The Life Of 'Mama' Cass Elliot*, Eddi Fiegel.

● FILMS: *Pufnstuf* (1970).

Elliot, Paul

b. 1971, Waterhouse, Western Kingston, Jamaica, West Indies. Elliot was raised in a ghetto area rich in a musical tradition associated with artists such as Don Carlos, **Junior Reid** and **Half Pint**. The area attracted producers such as **King**

Tubby, **King Jammy** and **Maurice Johnson**. It was with the Waterhouse producers that Elliot embarked on his recording career. In 1981, the 10-year-old singer released his debut 'Mini Van Man' with Jah Life. Elliot performed under the guise of Culture Paul but his initial foray into the Jamaican music industry was met with indifference. In spite of his unfortunate inauguration King Jammy was suitably impressed and enrolled the young singer as an errand boy. Elliot played an important role in the studio's promotional activities, although his own releases remained few and far between. However, one of the early Jammy productions, 'Brutalise A Sound Bwoy', proved an exception to the rule when it was a hit in the **dancehall**. Frustrated by the gradual progress toward stardom, Elliot decided to pursue his goal with Black Scorpio, whom he had met previously while working at Jammy's studio. Determined to break through into the mainstream Elliot financed and arranged his recording sessions assisted by Scorpio. He recorded 'Fat Belly Rat' in response to the needless violence that resulted in kindred fatalities.

In the mid-90s the singer enjoyed a series of hits such as 'Hype Roll', 'Cut And Clear', 'Seek Jah Blessing' and 'Save Me Oh Jah'. In 1998, the Jamaican football team qualified to play in the World Cup competition. The unprecedented success of the team resulted in a series of celebratory recordings from within the reggae community, and Elliot demonstrated his approval when he released 'Win Or Lose', which was featured on *A Tribute To The Reggae Boyz*. Following the soccer hit he maintained a high profile with songs such as 'True Love' and 'It's Strange'. In addition to his independent work Elliot also recorded with a variety of Jamaican producers and in 1999 released his debut, *Save Me Oh Jah*. He maintained a low profile through to 2000 when he licensed *Meaning Of Life* to a French record label. The album featured earlier works with producers such as Richard Bell and Colin McGregor, as well as Elliot's self-productions. In 2001, the singer starred in the annual Rebel Salute tour.

● ALBUMS: *Save Me Oh Jah* (Redbridge 1999) ★★★★, *Meaning Of Life* (Tabou 1 2000) ★★★, *Coming Home* (Artists Only 2002) ★★★.

Elliot, Richard

b. Glasgow, Scotland, but raised in Los Angeles, California, USA. It was perhaps inevitable, for a musician growing up in the 60s and early 70s, that Elliot's early taste would range through **Motown Records** and rock. However, he was also indelibly impressed by R&B. As a tenor saxophonist he found much that appealed to him in this form but he was also aware of jazz, in particular through the playing of **Dexter Gordon**. It was a visit to a concert by Gordon that prompted Elliot onto the jazz path, although in his case it proved to be a path with many turnings. As he honed his skills Elliot found work in the Los Angeles studios, backing artists such as **Natalie Cole**, **the Pointer Sisters** and **Melissa Manchester**. He was a member of the **Tower Of Power** horns from 1982 until 1987. He began recording under his own name in 1986, and in succeeding years produced albums that displayed growing confidence. They were also increasingly successful. Fortuitously, Elliot had found that his favourite musical forms, with their jazz-inflections, R&B-base and rock-tinges, were also popular with the record-buying public. His late 80s sessions for Manhattan Records were reissued in the early

90s by his new label, **Blue Note Records**, and proved to be just as popular as before.

By the late 90s, Elliot was sufficiently well-established to produce *Jumpin' Off* on which he played mostly within the R&B style, a deliberate reversion to a form that had been at the height of its commercial acceptability almost two decades before Elliot was born. By this time, however, Elliot's eclecticism was stretching still further and, like many musicians of his generation, he was developing a serious interest in salsa. In addition to playing tenor, on which he produces a rich and expressive sound, Elliot is also very effective on soprano saxophone.

● ALBUMS: *Trolltown* (Manhattan 1986) ★★★, *Initial Approach* (Manhattan 1987) ★★★★, *Power Of Suggestion* (Manhattan 1988) ★★★, *Take To The Skies* (Manhattan 1989) ★★★, *What's Inside* (Manhattan 1990) ★★★, *On The Town* (Manhattan 1991) ★★★, *Soul Embrace* (Manhattan 1993) ★★★★, *After Dark* (Blue Note 1994) ★★★, *City Speak* (Blue Note 1996) ★★★, *Jumpin' Off* (Metro Blue 1997) ★★★, *Chill Factor* (Blue Note 1999) ★★★★, *Crush* (GRP 2001) ★★★, *Ricochet* (GRP 2003) ★★★, *Metro Blue* (Artizen 2005) ★★★★.

● COMPILATIONS: *The Best Of Richard Elliott* (Blue Note 2000) ★★★.

Elliott, Bern, And The Fenmen

Formed in Erith, Kent, England, in 1961, Bern Elliott And The Fenmen spent many of their early years playing in German clubs. Signed to **Decca Records** in 1963, they had a UK Top 20 hit with their debut single, 'Money', possibly the finest cover version of this recurrent beat group favourite. A rendition of 'New Orleans' provided another chart entry, but the singer and backing group broke up following the release of 'Good Times'. While the Fenmen— Alan Judge (guitar), Wally Allen (guitar), Eric Willmer (bass) and Jon Povey (drums)— continued to record in an engaging, close-harmony style, Elliott formed a new group, the Klan, around Dave Cameron (organ), Tim Hamilton (guitar), John Silby-Pearce (bass) and Pete Adams (drums). Despite several excellent singles, including 'Voodoo Woman' (1965), the vocalist was unable to regain his initial success. Former colleagues Allen and Povey later found fame in the **Pretty Things**.

● COMPILATIONS: *The Beat Years* (1988) ★★.

Elliott, Jack

(see **Elliott, Ramblin' Jack**)

Elliott, Mike

b. 17 July 1946, Sunderland, England. A former teacher, Elliott started performing in a trio called the Northern Front. He then went on to teach drama, a talent that became useful in his performing career. Unable to do both, Elliott became a full-time performer in 1974. He has toured the USA on numerous occasions, in addition to the Middle East. More of a comedian than a folk performer, Elliott nevertheless learned his craft, like **Billy Connolly** and **Jasper Carrott**, by performing and singing traditional songs in folk clubs, in addition to using his own, highly original, comic material. His talent was recognized by Tyne Tees television, which, in 1981, made a series of six half-hour programmes starring Elliott. The series was promptly banned owing to a reluctance to broadcast some of the material. Later, Channel 4 television transmitted another series of shows, *At Last . . .*

It's Mike Elliott, although it was by and large the same material that Elliott had used for the former, banned, series. A one-hour television special entitled *Meet Mike Elliott* also was broadcast. Elliott later had a single released, 'Makin' Me Happy/Talkin' Crap', on Rubber Records, but this too was promptly banned because of the use of the word 'shit'. A man of obvious talent, Elliott has played at the Cambridge Folk Festival and toured with **Lindisfarne** and **Jack The Lad**. He is also credited as being the first British professional artist to appear in China, beating **Wham!** by two days!

● ALBUMS: *Out Of The Brown* (Rubber 1975) ★★★, *At Last . . . It's Mike Elliott* (Rubber 1984) ★★★.

Elliott, Missy 'Misdemeanor'

b. Melissa Elliott, 1 July 1971, Portsmouth, Virginia, USA. Hip-hop/R&B songwriter Missy 'Misdemeanor' Elliott has become one of the most esteemed figures in contemporary American music, providing material for artists including **MC Lyte**, **Adina Howard**, **Jodeci**, **Aaliyah** and **Busta Rhymes**, as well as working as an arranger, producer, talent scout and record boss.

Elliott first performed as part of a neighbourhood singing group, Sista, who were signed up by DeVante from Jodeci in 1992. Elliott was already writing with her long-time collaborator, Tim Mosley aka **Timbaland**, and with Sista's career terminally stalled (DeVante would not release any of their recordings) she concentrated on songwriting and production. Her distinctive 'hee haw' rap on **Gina Thompson**'s 'The Things You Do' brought her wider exposure, and several offers from record companies. Fiercely independent and ambitious, Elliott signed to **Elektra Records** as a solo artist on the understanding that they would subsidize her own label, Gold Mind Records. In 1997, she launched her solo career with the album *Supa Dupa Fly* and attendant single 'The Rain (Supa Dupa Fly)'. The well-connected Elliott was provided with immediate exposure for the song via rotation play of its Hype Williams–directed video on **MTV**. Co-produced with long-time collaborator Timbaland and producer DJ Magic, the album received excellent reviews, though Elliott was reluctant to commit herself fully to a career as a performer: 'I don't want to get caught up and be an artist always on the go, because once you do that, it's hard to get into the studio and do what I do.' The album also featured cameo appearances from Aaliyah and Busta Rhymes.

Despite her growing reputation and success, Elliott remained based in her hometown in Virginia. In September 1998, she collaborated with **Melanie B** from the **Spice Girls** on the one-off single, 'I Want You Back', which debuted at number 1 in the UK chart. Further writing and remixing work for **Whitney Houston** and **Janet Jackson** followed, although Elliott found time in her busy schedule to release her second set, *Da Real World*, in July 1999. Incredibly, Elliott and Timbaland managed to surpass their first two albums with 2001's *Miss E . . . So Addictive*, a stunning compendium of contemporary dance beats, urban ballads and left-field samples that was instantly hailed as one of the finest albums of the new millennium. The following year the drastically slimmed-down Elliott broke into the US Top 5 with 'Work It', the lead-off single from *Under Construction*.

● ALBUMS: *Supa Dupa Fly* (EastWest 1997) ★★★★, *Da Real World* (EastWest 1999) ★★★, *Miss E . . . So Addictive* (The Gold Mind/Elektra 2001) ★★★★, *Under Construction* (The Gold Mind/Elektra 2002) ★★★, *This Is Not A Test!*

(The Gold Mind/EastWest 2003) ★★★, *The Cookbook* (The Gold Mind/Atlantic 2005) ★★★.
● FILMS: *Pootie Tang* (2001), *Honey* (2003).

Elliott, Ramblin' Jack

b. Elliott Charles Adnopoz, 1 August 1931, Brooklyn, New York City, USA. The son of an eminent doctor, Elliott forsook his middle-class upbringing as a teenager to join a travelling rodeo. Embarrassed by his family name, he dubbed himself Buck Elliott, before adopting the less-mannered Jack. In 1949 he met and befriended **Woody Guthrie**, who in turn became his mentor and prime influence. Elliott travelled and sang with Guthrie whenever possible, before emerging as a talent in his own right. He spent a portion of the 50s in Europe, introducing America's folk heritage to a new and eager audience and recording material for **Topic Records**, often in partnership with **Derroll Adams**. By the early 60s he had resettled in New York where he became an inspirational figure to a new generation of performers, including **Bob Dylan**. *Ramblin' Jack Elliott* was an important release that saw the singer shaking off the imitator tag by embracing a diverse selection of material, including songs drawn from the American tradition, the Scottish music hall and **Ray Charles**. Further releases included the **Vanguard Records** release *Jack Elliott*, which featured Dylan playing harmonica under the pseudonym Tedham Porterhouse, and *Young Brigham* in 1967, which offered songs by **Tim Hardin** and the **Rolling Stones** as well as an adventurous use of dobro, autoharp, fiddle and tabla.

The singer also guested on albums by **Tom Rush**, **Phil Ochs** and **Johnny Cash**. In 1975 Elliott was joined by Dylan during an appearance at the Greenwich Village, New York, club, The Other End, and he then became a natural choice for Dylan's nostalgic carnival tour, the Rolling Thunder Revue. Elliott later continued his erratic, but intriguing, path, and an excellent early 80s release, *Kerouac's Last Dream*, showed his power undiminished. He was relatively prolific in the 90s. *Friends Of Mine* featured 'Bleecker Street Blues', written when Dylan fell seriously ill in 1997, and a host of celebratory guest singers including **Tom Waits**, **Emmylou Harris**, **Arlo Guthrie** and **Nanci Griffith**. In 2000, his daughter directed the documentary film *The Ballad Of Ramblin' Jack*. The accompanying soundtrack album serves as a useful career retrospective.

● ALBUMS: *Woody Guthrie's Blues* (Topic 1957) ★★★, with Derroll Adams *The Rambling Boys* 10-inch album (Topic 1957) ★★★, *Jack Takes The Floor* 10-inch album (Topic 1958) ★★★, *In London* (UK) *Monitor Presents Jack Elliott: Ramblin' Cowboy* (US) (Columbia/Monitor 1959) ★★★, *Sings Songs By Woody Guthrie And Jimmy Rogers* (Columbia/Monitor 1960) ★★★, *Sings The Songs Of Woody Guthrie* (Stateside/Prestige 1961) ★★★, *Songs To Grow On By Woody Guthrie, Sung By Jack Elliott* (Folkways 1961) ★★★, *Ramblin' Jack Elliott* (Prestige 1961) ★★★★, *Jack Elliott At The Second Fret* aka *Hootenanny With Jack Elliott* (Prestige 1962) ★★★, *Country Style* (Prestige 1962) ★★★, *Talking Woody Guthrie* (Topic 1963) ★★★, with Adams *Roll On Buddy* (Topic 1963) ★★★, *Muleskinner* (Topic/Delmark 1964) ★★★, *Jack Elliott* i (Everest Archive 1964) ★★★, *Jack Elliott* ii (Vanguard/Fontana 1964) ★★★, *Young Brigham* (Reprise 1967) ★★★, *Bill Durham Sacks & Railroad Tracks* (Reprise 1967) ★★★, with Adams *Folkland Songs* aka *America: Folk Songs-West-Ballads 1955–1961*

recordings (Joker 1969) ★★★, *Kerouac's Last Dream* (Folk Freak 1981) ★★★, with Spider John Koerner, U. Utah Phillips *Legends Of Folk* (Red House 1992) ★★★, *South Coast* (Red House 1995) ★★★, *Friends Of Mine* (HighTone 1998) ★★★, *Live In Japan* 1974 recording (Vivid/Bellwood 1998) ★★★, *The Long Ride* (HighTone 1999) ★★★, *The Ballad Of Ramblin' Jack* film soundtrack (Vanguard 2000) ★★★, *The Lost Topic Tapes: Cowes Harbour 1957* (HighTone 2004) ★★★, *The Lost Topic Tapes: Isle Of Wight 1957* (HighTone 2004) ★★★.

● COMPILATIONS: *The Essential Ramblin' Jack Elliott* (Vanguard 1976) ★★★, *Hard Travelin': Songs By Woody Guthrie And Others* (Fantasy/Big Beat 1989) ★★★★, *Talking Dust Bowl: The Best Of Ramblin' Jack Elliott* (Big Beat 1989) ★★★★, *Sings Woody Guthrie And Jimmie Rodgers & Cowboy Songs* (Monitor 1994) ★★★, *Me & Bobby McGee* (Rounder 1995) ★★★, *Ramblin' Jack: The Legendary Topic Masters* (Topic 1995) ★★★, *Country Style/Live* (Fantasy 1999) ★★★, *The Best Of The Vanguard Years* (Vanguard 2000) ★★★★.
● FILMS: *The Ballad Of Ramblin' Jack* (2000).

Elliott, Ron

b. 21 October 1943, Healdsburg, California, USA. Guitarist and vocalist Elliott was a founder member of the **Beau Brummels**, composing the bulk of this highly regarded 60s act's output. Initially influenced by the **Beatles**, Elliott quickly evolved an individual style in which haunting melodies were infused with elements drawn from folk and country. As well as maintaining his leading role in the Beau Brummels, he also contributed to two albums by **Harpers Bizarre**, providing services as arranger or composer on several tracks. Elliott arranged every track, bar one, of the **Everly Brothers**' 1968 release *Roots*, which also features two of his compositions, 'Ventura Boulevard' and 'Deep Water'. When the Beau Brummels split up in 1968 Elliott began working with Dan Levitt and Mike McClure. He produced the duo's *Living In The Country* and they reciprocated by accompanying Elliott on *The Candlestickmaker*. **Ry Cooder**, **Sal Valentino** (ex-Beau Brummels) and Chris Ethridge also appear on this haunting album that captures the artist at the height of his creative powers, notably on the lengthy title track.

Elliott then became a session musician, playing on albums by **Randy Newman**, **Little Feat** and **Van Morrison**. In 1972 he formed the disappointing Pan, but left in 1974 to join a re-formed Beau Brummels. Sadly, Elliott's diabetic condition, which forced the original band to retire from live performances, brought this incarnation to an end too. In 1976 he surfaced in the studio-based Giants and at the end of the decade he fronted the short-lived Goldrush. Recurring ill health has led to Elliott's virtual retirement, but he assisted archivist Alec Palao in compiling unissued Beau Brummels material during the 90s.
● ALBUMS: *The Candlestickmaker* (Warners 1970) ★★★.

Elliott, William

b. 1879, Boston, Massachusetts, USA, d. 1 December 1931, New York City, USA. Early appearances Elliott made on Broadway in acting roles include *That Man And I* (1904), *Beau Brummell* and *The Misanthrope* (both 1905) and *Charley's Aunt* (1906). He was in the musicals *A Grand Army Man* (1907) and *The Pink Lady* (1911). From hereon,

Elliott was mostly active as a producer, mainly of plays, including *The Governor's Lady* (1912), *Kitty Mackay* (1914) and *The Greatest Nation* (1916), which he also wrote and in which he performed. In 1917 he produced several musicals, some in collaboration with F. Ray Comstock and Morris Gest. First of these was **Oh, Boy!**, music by **Jerome Kern**, book and lyrics by **Guy Bolton** and **P.G. Wodehouse**, which ran for 467 performances at the Princess and Casino theatres. Next was **Leave It To Jane**, again by Kern, Bolton and Wodehouse, which ran for 167 performances, followed by **Chu Chin Chow** and *Kitty Darlin'*. The following year was also busy with musicals **Oh, Lady! Lady!!**, **Maid Of The Mountains** and *Oh, My Dear!* The latter, with music by Louis A. Hirsch and book and lyrics by Bolton and Wodehouse, ran for 189 performances at the Princess and 39th Street theatres. Elliott's last Broadway production was a play, *The Home Towners* (1926).

Other stage and film people with the same or a similar name include William H. Elliott, who appeared in Broadway dramas *Robert Emmet* (1904) and *A Very Good Young Man* (1918) and who might possibly be the same actor as discussed above; William 'Wild Bill' Elliott (b. Gordon Nance, 16 October 1904, d. 26 November 1965), who made westerns under this name, his real name, and as Gordon Elliott; William Elliott, who performed on Broadway in *Revenge With Music* (1934) and *The Eternal Road* (1937); William Elliott (b. 1953), who arranged music for **Ain't Misbehavin'** (1978) and other shows.

Ellis Bextor, Sophie

b. 10 April 1979, Middlesex, England. Growing up as the daughter of *Blue Peter* presenter Janet Ellis, Sophie Ellis Bextor was always likely to enjoy a spell in the limelight and so it proved, with the guitar pop of **Theaudience** propelling her to fame in 1997. Her perceived 'posh' image and distinctive looks attracted the UK press, and the band enjoyed Top 30 success with 'A Pessimist Is Never Disappointed' and 'I Know Enough (I Don't Get Enough)'. The first album turned out to be the last, however, with the lynchpin of the band Billy Reeves departing.

In retrospect this helped Ellis Bextor's career, as her next record became the choice **dance music** cut of 2000. Spiller's 'Groovejet (If This Ain't Love)' originated as an instrumental, a sunny Italian **house** track, but the addition of a vocal line co-written by Ellis Bextor gave the track an irresistible feel-good hook. The singer was able to combine this with a restatement of her 'posh' dress sense to see off the original Posh, Victoria Beckham, with her **True Steppers** collaboration 'Out Of Your Mind', to top the UK singles charts in August 2000. Solo recognition followed in the form of disco-inflected singles 'Take Me Home' and 'Murder On The Dancefloor', both of which reached the UK Top 5. Ellis Bextor's first solo album, *Read My Lips*, a polished pop, disco and soul hybrid, found the singer in deadpan, often flirtatious mood. Her vocal style, instantly recognizable, left potential consumers divided on its merits, but no one could deny the album's melodic hooklines.

● ALBUMS: *Read My Lips* (Polydor 2001) ★★★, *Shoot From The Hip* (Polydor 2003) ★★.

Ellis, Alton

b. 1944, Kingston, Jamaica, West Indies. Ellis, Jamaica's most soulful singer, celebrated 30 years in the business several years ago and yet he is still making important records. In many ways he epitomizes the story of reggae vocalists: a start in the business at a very early age, massive popularity for a limited period, and a gradual decline in prominence while continuing to make excellent records. In addition to his songwriting abilities and voice, Ellis' particular gift was his ability to take R&B or soul songs and place them in a specifically Jamaican context, and so make them 'reggae songs' rather than mere cover versions. Ellis was born into a musical family, and he first recorded in the late 50s as part of a duo with singer Eddy Perkins for Randy's and **Studio One** as Alton And Eddy. They enjoyed some success in the R&B style and 'Muriel' was a massive hit for them. Perkins departed soon afterwards for a solo career and Alton continued with Studio One at Brentford Road, as well as working with **Coxsone Dodd**'s arch-rival in the business, **Duke Reid**, at his Treasure Isle Studio in Bond Street, initially as Alton Ellis And The Flames.

Ellis came to undisputed prominence with the rise of **rocksteady** in 1965–66, when the ska beat slowed down and instrumental records became less important. This 'cool' music gave singers far greater freedom to express themselves (they no longer had to battle against the frantic ska pace and 'noisiness') and Alton Ellis reigned supreme—his 'Get Ready—Rock Steady' was one of the first records actually to use the term. Both Dodd and Reid made many classic records with Ellis as he moved between Brentford Road and Bond Street, but he recorded the definitive rocksteady album for Treasure Isle—*Mr Soul Of Jamaica*—while his Studio One output is collected on three albums, all of which have their high points.

In the late 60s and early 70s he went on to record for some of Jamaica's finest producers and he achieved two huge hit records for **Lloyd Daley**—'Deliver Us' and 'Back To Africa'— while a cover version of 'Too Late To Turn Back Now' that he made for Randy's in the early 70s, has remained a firm favourite with the reggae audience ever since. He toured the UK in the 60s as a vocalist for Studio One's Soul Vendors band, and he returned to England in 1972, where he has based himself (intermittently) ever since. However, he has now sadly admitted his disillusionment with the reggae business. He accepts its machinations with a dignified resignation, just as in the early days when his songs were covered and no royalties were forthcoming: 'I was just proud that, whoever, would do an Alton Ellis song.' He was involved in the beginnings of **Janet Kay**'s career and a cover version of one of his greatest songs, 'I'm Still In Love With You', formed the basis for **Althea And Donna**'s 'Up Town Top Ranking'—a UK number 1 in 1978—but his records and live shows are now few and far between.

● ALBUMS: *Sunday Coming* (Studio One) ★★★, *Sings Rock & Soul* (Studio One 1966) ★★★★, *Love To Share* (Third World 1979) ★★★, *Showcase* (Studio One 1980) ★★, *25th Silver Jubilee* (Skynote 1984) ★★★, *Still In Love* (Horse 1985) ★★★, *Continuation* (All Tone 1985) ★★★, *Jubilee Volume 2* (Sky Note 1985) ★★★★, *Here I Am* (Angella 1988) ★★, *My Time Is Right* (Trojan 1990) ★★★, *Sunday Coming* reissue (Heartbeat 1995) ★★★.

● COMPILATIONS: *Best Of Alton Ellis* (Studio One 60s) ★★★, with Hortense Ellis *At Studio One* (Heartbeat 1993) ★★★★, *Mr Soul Of Jamaica* (Treasure Isle) reissued as *Cry Tough* (Heartbeat 1993) ★★★★, *Reggae Max* (Jet Star 1997) ★★★★, *Get Ready For Rock Reggae Steady!*

(Jamaican Gold 1999) ★★★★, *My Time Is The Right Time* (West Side 2000) ★★★★, *Greatest Hits: Jamaica's Most Soulful Singer* (Third World 1980) ★★★★, *Be True To Yourself* (Trojan 2004) ★★★★.

Ellis, Anita

b. Anita Kert, 12 April 1920, Montreal, Canada. Born into an orthodox Jewish family, Ellis grew up surrounded by music. Her mother 'played the piano and sang everything from opera arias to popular songs to old glorious Jewish songs'. Her father was a cantor and for religious reasons the young girl was not allowed to sing in public. However, her mother was eager for her to have a showbusiness career and when, during the depths of the Depression, the family moved to Los Angeles, California, the young girl sought work in films and on radio. She enjoyed a little parochial success before winning a scholarship, at 17, to study opera at the Cincinnati Conservatory of Music. While there, she helped pay her way by singing with a local dance band. It was during this professional engagement, and even in singing classes at college, that she discovered that she was afflicted with literally paralyzing stage fright. Although unable to perform in a live music environment, she realized that she could function on radio and in 1940 began working on a popular Cincinnati-based radio show, *Moon River*. She was married in 1943 to a drama student, who later became an Air Force colonel, and even though the marriage lasted only three years she thereafter used her married name for her professional career. She sang on a series of shows recorded for US military personnel serving overseas, credited only as 'Anita, that five-foot-two bundle of brunette loveliness'. The series was also aired by CBS and she was among several broadcasters honoured by President Franklin Roosevelt for this morale-boosting work. In New York after the war, Ellis became the regular singer on Red Skelton's popular radio show on NBC and made a handful of records. Her popularity on the Skelton show led to an invitation to return to California to dub soundtrack vocals for non-singing actresses. Almost by chance, she had found the perfect job for someone with her malaise. Ellis' first, and most famous, vocal dub was for **Rita Hayworth**, singing 'Put The Blame On Mame' in *Gilda* (1946). She followed this with many others, including Hayworth again in *Down To Earth* (1947), *The Lady From Shanghai* and *The Loves Of Carmen* (both 1948), Shelley Winters in *The Gangster* (1947), **Vera-Ellen** in *Three Little Words* (1950) and *The Belle Of New York* (1952), Joan Caulfield, *The Petty Girl* (1950), and Jeanne Crain, *Gentlemen Marry Brunettes* (1955). In the 50s she recorded two complete albums, in addition to which a set of Lang-Worth transcriptions was released on one side only of an LP. During this decade, film work became less plentiful as television overtook both radio and the big screen in popularity and Ellis was forced to confront her demons and perform before a live audience in cabaret. In New York, she was warmly embraced by audiences, reviewers, artists and showbusiness figures. Despite this acclaim, however, she never defeated her problems. After recording her third album, in 1960, she remarried and happily retired from showbusiness to be with her new husband, Mortimer Shapiro, a neurologist. Apart from occasional performances for friends and a tiny handful of television appearances, she stayed out of sight until 1974 when she was persuaded to perform at Michael's Pub for a seven-week engagement. She then bowed out

again until 1977 when she recorded two radio shows with **Loonis McGlohon** and **Alec Wilder** in their National Public Radio series *The American Popular Song* (both issued on one CD by Audiophile Records in 2000). In 1979, she made a television appearance, taping *For The Record* for PBS, on which she was accompanied at the piano by **Ellis Larkins**. The soundtrack of this show was later released as *A Legend Sings*. During the 80s, Ellis was in constant demand for concert appearances, almost all of which she refused. Many of those that she did accept were abruptly cancelled and when she did appear the result, while musically astonishing, could be deeply disturbing to watch and was clearly deeply distressing to the singer. As James Gavin of the *New York Times* and *Village Voice* has observed, when writing of one such concert: 'No one who attended her now-fabled recital at Lincoln Center's Alice Tully Hall in 1979 will forget the sight of Ellis onstage: right leg shaking, arms stiff at her sides, eyes clamped shut beneath electrified ringlets of hair, face frozen in terror. For two hours she gave the sense that she was tearing her guts out to bring audiences this art.' She made her final troubled public appearance in 1987 and then retired to spend her time in the East Side apartment she shared with her husband and also travelling overseas, mostly to Africa. Ellis' vocal sound and style were ideal for the performance of the great standards. She sang with ringing clarity, interpreting lyrics with a depth of passion rarely achieved by other singers of the same repertoire. Her accounts to Whitney Balliett, in his book *American Singers*, of how she seeks and finds emotional depths in songs is very revealing, not only of the art of the performing artist but also of the sincerity and integrity of this particular singer. In 2000, now a widow, and still living in the same New York apartment overlooking Carl Schurz Park and the East River, Ellis was suffering from advanced Alzheimer's disease. Although lovingly cared for, she was no longer able to recognize her old friends and even the music was gone from her life. As McGlohon recounted in May 2000, at the time of the release of their long-ago radio show together: 'I do very much wish she could hear this CD and realize how great she was, but even when pianists go around to play for her, there is no sign of recognition that this is music she used to love.'

● ALBUMS: *I Wonder What Became Of Me* (Epic 1956) ★★★, *Him* (Epic 1957) ★★★, *The World In My Arms* (Elektra 1960) ★★★, *A Legend Sings* (Orion Masters 1979) ★★★★, *Look To The Rainbow* 1977 broadcasts (Audiophile 2000) ★★★★.

● COMPILATIONS: shared with Eugenie Baird *Ellis & Baird: Lang-Worth Transcriptions* (Audiophile 1995) ★★★.

Ellis, Don

b. 25 July 1934, Los Angeles, California, USA, d. 17 December 1978, Hollywood, California, USA. Appreciation of Ellis' work has increased since his death and he is now regarded by many as an important figure in jazz. From childhood he was fascinated with brass instruments and received a trumpet at the age of two. At junior high school he had his own quartet and at Boston university he was a member of the band. His first professional work was as a member of **Ray McKinley**'s **Glenn Miller** Orchestra. After his national service, Ellis formed a small group, playing coffee-houses in New York's Greenwich Village. By the late 50s he was playing with many name bands including those of **Woody Herman**, **Lionel Hampton**,

Charles Mingus and **Maynard Ferguson**. Ellis also worked in small groups, enjoying the greater freedom of expression this allowed. In 1961/2 he was a member of **George Russell**'s sextet. In Atlantic City, Ellis took up a teaching fellowship and it was there that he developed and explored his interest in the complexities of Indian rhythm patterns. Ellis made a triumphant appearance at the 1966 Monterey Jazz festival with his 23-piece band. His completely original themes were scored using unbelievably complex notation. Customarily, most big band music was played at four beats to the bar but Ellis confidently and successfully experimented with 5-beat bars, then 9-, 11-, 14-, 17-, 19- and even 27-beat bars. Mixing metres created difficulties for his rhythm sections so he taught himself to play drums in order that he might properly instruct his drummers. He also experimented with brass instruments, introducing the four-valve flügelhorn and superbone.

During the late 60s the Don Ellis Orchestra was promoted as part of the great **CBS Records** progressive music campaign and he found himself performing at rock festivals and concerts. His music found favour with the **Woodstock** generation, who could also recognize him as an exciting pioneer. His CBS albums were all successful, his work being produced by both **John Hammond** and **Al Kooper**. Dubbed the 'Father of the Time Revolution' in jazz, Ellis' music was much more than complex. It was also undeniably joyous. Tunes like the 7/4 romp 'Pussy Wiggle Stomp', 'Barnum's Revenge' (a reworking of 'Bill Bailey') and 'Scratt And Fluggs' (a passing nod to country music's **Flatt And Scruggs**), are played with zesty enthusiasm, extraordinary skill and enormous good humour. Ellis' trumpet playing was remarkable, combining dazzling technique with a hot jazz feeling that reflected his admiration for **Henry 'Red' Allen**. He also experimented with electronic devices, such as a Ring Modulator, which transformed his trumpet into a generator of atavistic moans and shouts. Conversely, as he showed on *Haiku*, he could play with delicate charm and often deeply moving emotion. Ellis scored the music for 10 films, including *The French Connection* (1971), for which he won a Grammy. It is, however, his brilliantly ambitious and innovative 'eastern' music, notably 'Indian Lady' and 'Turkish Bath', that makes his work as important as **John Coltrane**'s flirtation with the music of the mystic east. He is indubitably an outstanding figure destined for future reappraisal. Ellis stated, 'I am not concerned whether my music is jazz, third-stream, classical or anything else, or whether it is even called music. Let it be judged as Don Ellis noise.'

● ALBUMS: *How Time Passes* (Candid 1960) ★★, *Out Of Nowhere* (Candid 1961) ★★★, *New Ideas* (New Jazz 1961) ★★★★, *Essence* (Pacific Jazz 1962) ★★★, *Jazz Jamboree 1962, No 1* (Muza 1962) ★★★, *Live At Monterey* (Pacific Jazz 1966) ★★★★, *Live In 3/2/3/4 Time* (Pacific Jazz 1967) ★★★, *Electric Bath* (Columbia 1968) ★★★★★, *Shock Treatment* (Columbia 1968) ★★★★, *Autumn* (Columbia 1969) ★★★★, *The New Don Ellis Band Goes Underground* (Columbia 1969) ★★★, *Don Ellis At Fillmore* (Columbia 1970) ★★★, *Tears Of Joy* (Columbia 1971) ★★★, *Connection* (Columbia 1972) ★★★, *Soaring* (MPS 1973) ★★★, *Haiku* (MPS 1974) ★★★★, *Star Wars* (Atlantic 1977) ★★★, *Live At Montreux* (Atlantic 1978) ★★★.

● COMPILATIONS: *Don Ellis* (Giants Of Jazz 1998) ★★★★.

Ellis, Herb

b. Mitchell Herbert Ellis, 4 August 1921, Farmersville, Texas, USA. In 1941 Ellis attended North Texas State College, where his fellow students included **Jimmy Giuffre**. After graduation, he played guitar in a number of big bands, including the **Casa Loma Orchestra** and the **Jimmy Dorsey** outfit. He was next with Soft Winds, a trio formed from the Dorsey rhythm section with **Johnny Frigo** and Lou Carter, and in 1953 took **Barney Kessel**'s place in the **Oscar Peterson** trio, where he remained for five years alongside **Ray Brown**. After leaving Peterson he accompanied **Ella Fitzgerald** for four years and also worked with **Julie London**, then spent a decade in the Los Angeles film and television studios. In the early 70s he began a succession of marvellous associations with other guitarists, including **Joe Pass**, **Charlie Byrd** and Kessel (with the latter two as the **Great Guitars**). In his playing, Ellis constantly reveals a deep affinity for the blues and reflects a thorough awareness of the work of **Charlie Christian**. As a section player he brings an earthy quality few of his peers can match, and his time with Peterson was of such a high standard that thereafter the pianist rarely used another guitarist. As a soloist his command is outstanding and the bluesy muscularity of his playing is a constant source of delight.

● ALBUMS: *Ellis In Wonderland* (Norgran 1956) ★★★, *Nothing But The Blues* (Verve 1958) ★★★★, with Jimmy Giuffre *Herb Ellis Meets Jimmy Giuffre* (Verve 1959) ★★★★, *Thank You, Charlie Christian* (Verve 1960) ★★★, *Softly . . . But With That Feeling* (Verve 1961) ★★★, *The Midnight Roll* (Epic 1962) ★★, with Laurindo Almeida, Johnny Gray *Three Guitars In Bossa Nova Time* (Epic 1963) ★★★, *Herb Ellis & 'Stuff' Smith Together* (Epic 1963) ★★★, *Guitar* (Columbia 1965) ★★★, *Man With The Guitar* (Dot 1965) ★★★, *Hello, Herbie* (MPS 1969) ★★★★, with Joe Pass, Ray Brown, Jake Hanna *Jazz/Concord* (Concord Jazz 1973) ★★★★, with Pass *Seven, Come Eleven* (Concord Jazz 1973) ★★★★, with Barney Kessel *Poor Butterfly* (Concord Jazz 1973) ★★★, with Pass *Two For The Road* (Pablo 1974) ★★★, with Ray Brown *Soft Shoe* (Concord Jazz 1974) ★★★, *After You've Gone* (Concord Jazz 1974) ★★★, as Great Guitars *Great Guitars* (Concord Jazz 1974) ★★★, with Brown *Hot Tracks* (Concord Jazz 1975) ★★★, with Freddie Green *Rhythm Willie* (Concord Jazz 1975) ★★★, with Ross Tompkins *A Pair To Draw To* (Concord Jazz 1976) ★★★★, *Herb* (Sony Japan 1977) ★★★★, with Remo Palmier *Windflower* (Concord Jazz 1977) ★★★, *Soft & Mellow* (Concord Jazz 1978) ★★★, as Great Guitars *Great Guitars: Straight Tracks* (Concord Jazz 1978) ★★★, *At Montreux* (Concord Jazz 1979) ★★★, as Great Guitars *Great Guitars At The Winery* (Concord Jazz 1980) ★★★, with Monty Alexander, Ray Brown *Trio* (Concord Jazz 1980) ★★★, *Herb Mix* (Concord Jazz 1981) ★★★, with Cal Collins *Interplay* (Concord Jazz 1981) ★★★, as Great Guitars *Great Guitars At Charlie's, Georgetown* (Concord Jazz 1982) ★★★★, with Alexander, Brown *Triple Treat* (Concord Jazz 1982) ★★★, *Sweet And Lovely* (Atlas 1983) ★★★, *When You're Smiling* (Atlas 1983) ★★★, with Alexander, Brown, John Frigo *Triple Treat II* (Concord Jazz 1987) ★★★, with Alexander, Brown, Frigo *Triple Treat III* (Concord Jazz 1987) ★★★, with Red Mitchell *Doggin' Around* (Concord Jazz 1988) ★★★, *Roll Call* (Justice 1991) ★★★, *Texas Swings* (Justice 1992) ★★★, *Down-home* 1991 recording (Justice 1996) ★★★, as Great Guitars *The Return Of The Great Guitars* (Concord

Jazz 1996) ★★★, *An Evening With Herb Ellis* (Jazz Focus 1998) ★★★, *Burnin'* (Acoustic Music 1999) ★★★, with Duke Robillard *Conversations In Swing Guitar* (Stony Plain 1999) ★★★, with Robillard *More Conversations In Swing Guitar* (Stony Plain 2003) ★★★.
● COMPILATIONS: *The Concord Jazz Heritage Series* (Concord Jazz 1998) ★★★★, *Gravy Waltz: The Best Of Herb Ellis* (Euphoria 1999) ★★★★, with Ray Brown *In The Pocket* (Concord Jazz 2002) ★★★.
● DVD/VIDEOS: *Detour Ahead: An Afternoon With Herb Ellis* (Vestapol 1999).

Ellis, Hortense

b. 18 April 1941, Kingston, Jamaica, West Indies, d. 18 October 2000, Kingston, Jamaica, West Indies. Ellis began her career performing on Vere Johns' *Opportunity Hour*, where she appeared in six semi-finals and four finals demonstrating her vocal skills. Her own success was often overshadowed by her brother **Alton Ellis**, the man regularly referred to as the godfather of reggae. In 1962, **Byron Lee** enrolled her services to perform with his band the Dragonaires, and two years later she was awarded the honour of Jamaica's best female vocalist. She also recorded with Ken Lack, enjoying hits with 'I Shall Sing' and 'Brown Girl In The Ring', and with **Coxsone Dodd**, recording 'I'll Come Softly' and 'I'm Just A Girl', an interpretation of Alton's hit, 'I'm Just A Guy'. In 1969 she was again awarded the silver cup as the island's top female vocalist. She continued to record throughout the 70s. Much of her output was with **Bunny Lee** and in response to **Althea And Donna**'s international hit 'Up Town Top Ranking', he recorded her as Queen Tiney for 'Down Town Ting', followed by the popular 'Natty Dread Time'. She recorded a cover version of another song that her brother had recorded at **Studio One**, 'Sitting In The Park', and the popular 'Mark My Words'. A duet with her brother, 'Since I Fell For You', and 'Superstar' maintained her profile. She recorded several popular cuts for **Lee Perry** as Mahalia Saunders, the name she adopted after marrying Mikey 'Junior' Saunders in 1971. The marriage broke down five years later, and Ellis spent much of the late 70s raising her children. She found the time to record 'Unexpected Places' with **Gussie Clarke**, a classic cut that demonstrated her extensive vocal range. In combination with **Jackie Edwards** she had a hit with 'Let It Be Me', while as a soloist she released 'Got To Make It' and 'Time After Time'. Ellis proved an erratic performer who had to balance a career while raising her family. She lived in Miami, Florida, for much of the 80s, but subsequently returned to Jamaica. In 1993 she appeared with Bunny Lee in the television documentary *Stir It Up*, where she complained that slackness and gun lyrics were detrimental to the music and were a bad influence on young people. Throat cancer severely curtailed her performances during the rest of the decade.
● ALBUMS: *Jamaica's First Lady Of Song* (Third World 1977) ★★★★, with Jackie Edwards *Let It Be Me* (Jamaica Sound 1978) ★★★ *Reflections* (Ballistic 1979) ★★★, *Feelings* (1989) ★★.
● COMPILATIONS: with Alton Ellis *At Studio One* (Heartbeat 1993) ★★★★.

Ellis, Jimmy

(see **Orion**)

Ellis, Mary

b. 15 June 1900, New York City, USA, d. 30 January 2003, London, England. The date of birth given is the 'official' one, although Ellis is reported to have claimed in 1997 that she was born 100 years ago. A unique and enduring actress and singer, Ellis was an art student for three years and studied singing with the Belgian contralto Madame Freda Ashforth. From 1918-22 she was with the Metropolitan Opera, during which time she shared a stage with the legendary Caruso. She then turned to the dramatic theatre before creating the title role, opposite **Dennis King**, in the musical *Rose Marie* in 1924. After barely a year she left the cast on less than amicable terms, and the Hammersteins took out an injunction to prevent her singing in America for any other management. After settling in London, in the early 30s, Ellis played Frieda Hatzfeld in *Music In The Air*, which opened in 1933. **Ivor Novello** was so enchanted by her performance in the piece that he wrote two of his most celebrated shows, *Glamorous Night* (1933) and *The Dancing Years* (1939), especially for her. When the latter show was forced to close owing to the outbreak of World War II, Ellis became involved in hospital welfare, and spent much of the war years giving concerts for the troops. She and Novello were reunited in 1943 for *Arc De Triomphe*, but for the rest of the decade, and through to the early 50s, Ellis devoted most of her time to the straight theatre, including a notable role in Terence Ratigan's *The Browning Version*. Her association with **Noël Coward**'s *After The Ball* (1954) was, by all accounts, an unhappy one, and proved to be her last London stage musical. After watching her performance in that piece, the Master is said to have raged: 'Mary Ellis couldn't get a laugh if she pulled a kipper out of her drawers.' Ellis continued to work in theatre, although her last West End part came in the 1962 production of *Look Homeward Angel*. She also appeared in several films, both in Hollywood and Britain, and many television plays. Among her later television appearances was one with Jeremy Brett as Sherlock Holmes in the early 90s. Mary Ellis married four times, her third husband being the actor Basil Sydney. Her witty autobiography was published in 1982.
● FURTHER READING: *Those Dancing Years*, Mary Ellis.
● FILMS: *All The King's Horses* (1934), *Bella Donna* (1934), *Paris In Spring* (1935), *Fatal Lady* (1936), *Glamorous Night* (1937), *The Astonished Heart* (1949), *The Magic Box* (1951), *The 3 Worlds Of Gulliver* (1960).

Ellis, Pee Wee

b. Alfred Ellis, 1941, Florida, USA. Raised in Texas, and later in Rochester, New York, Ellis developed an early interest in music and had his first professional engagement in 1954 while still attending junior high school. He continued to perform while at school, playing mainly tenor saxophone but also developing on alto and as a keyboard player. Among his fellow students were **Ron Carter** and **Chuck Mangione**. Of great significance to his later career, Ellis also became a skilled arranger. For a while in 1957, he studied saxophone with **Sonny Rollins**. Following his graduation, Ellis went back to Florida where he formed his own band, Dynamics Incorporated, and worked in a variety of settings. In 1965 he was in New York City, playing in a trio led by **Sonny Payne**, and it was at this time that a friend, Waymon Reed, drew him to the attention of **James Brown**. With Brown, he played alto saxophone and organ and also wrote arrangements. In January 1967, Ellis took over leadership of the soul singer's backing band and his charts helped Brown attain some of his greatest successes.

After more than two years with Brown, Ellis left to settle in New York where he worked with **Brother Jack McDuff**, **Leon Thomas** (writing charts for some tracks on 1973's well-received *Blues And The Soulful Truth*) and others. He was also appointed musical director for the Kudu label, a subsidiary of **Creed Taylor**'s **CTI Records**, working with artists such as **George Benson** (for whom he also wrote some big band charts that were played on 1973's *Body Talk*), **Hank Crawford** and **Esther Phillips** (becoming the latter's musical director for five years). He also wrote charts for **Sonny Stitt**, appearing with him on 1975's *Dumpy Mama*. In 1977, Ellis relocated to San Francisco where he teamed up with **Dave Liebman**. Through one of Liebman's associates, **Mark Isham**, Ellis was introduced to **Van Morrison** with whom he forged long-lasting bonds. Another San Francisco artist with whom he worked in the 80s was singer **Kitty Margolis**.

At the end of the 80s, Ellis linked up with **Fred Wesley** and **Maceo Parker** to form the JB Horns, making several albums during the early 90s, some of which were released under Parker's name. In 1992 and the following year, Ellis' international reputation spread owing to appearances in Europe, notably a concert in Cologne, Germany, from which came *Twelve And More Blues* and *Yellin' Blue*, and a successful gig at **Ronnie Scott**'s club in London, where his musical companions included top-rank jazz artists of a younger generation, such as **Jason Rebello** and **Guy Barker**. He guested on **Karl Denson**'s 1994 set *Chunky Pecan Pie*, participating in a fiery two-tenor duel with the leader. In the UK in the mid-90s, Ellis settled in the west country, a rural area far from the madding crowd, and intensified his on-going musical links with Morrison, including 1997's *The Healing Game* and an American tour the following year.

Rousingly inventive in his playing and writing, Ellis has never lost the funkiness instilled during his tenure with Brown and even when playing demanding post-bop music, his work is awash with intense emotion and a verve only rarely matched by his contemporaries.

● ALBUMS: with Gotham *Pass The Butter* (Natural Resources 1972) ★★★, *Home In The Country* (Savoy Jazz/Arista 1976) ★★★, *Blues Mission* (Gramavision 1992) ★★★★, *Twelve And More Blues* (Minor Music 1993) ★★★, *Sepia Tonality* (Minor Music 1994) ★★★, *Yellin' Blue* (Minor Music 1995) ★★★, *A New Shift* (Minor Music 1996) ★★★, *What You Like* (Minor Music 1997) ★★★, with Horace Parlan *Gentle Men Blue* (Minor Music 1999) ★★★, *My Neighbourhood* (Horn Street 1999) ★★★★, *Ridin' Mighty High* (Skip 2000) ★★★, *Live And Funky* (Instinct 2002) ★★★, *What You Like* (Minor Music 2004) ★★★.

Ellis, Red

b. Marvin Thrushel Ellois, 21 December 1929, Arkadelphia, Arkansas, USA. Ellis learned to play both guitar and mandolin in his early teens and was twice wounded during military service in the Korean War. After his discharge, he studied sound and video engineering in Little Rock before, in 1955, he relocated to Michigan. He worked on radio stations as an engineer and from 1957, he also worked as a disc jockey presenting bluegrass gospel music. A friendship with Jimmy Williams, who had played with the **Stanley Brothers**, led to

their recording together and forming the Huron Valley Boys, a band that consisted of fellow southern musicians who were then resident in Michigan. In 1959/60, they recorded for Starday with Ellis even supervising the engineering; these sessions formed the basis of seven EPs and later albums. He formed his own Pathway label in the mid-60s, recorded with his wife Agee, and also worked on sessions with a gospel group, the Crossmen. In 1986, Old Homestead released albums of some of his Pathway material. He returned to Arkansas in 1968, where he worked as video engineer at KATV Little Rock. In 1971, he and Williams reunited to record two albums for Jessup. After this, although he and Williams have occasionally played together at some special events, Ellis virtually retired from active performing.

● ALBUMS: with Jimmy Williams *Holy Cry From The Hills* (Starday 1961) ★★★, *God Brings Bluegrass Back Together* (Jessup 1971) ★★★, *Little David's Harp* covers 1971 (Jessup 1975) ★★; as Red Ellis And The Huron Valley Boys *The Sacred Sound Of Bluegrass* (Starday 1962) ★★★, *Old Time Religion Bluegrass Style* (Starday 1963) ★★, *That Beautiful Land* (Pathway 1967) ★★★, *First Fall Of Snow* (Old Homestead 1986) ★★★.

● COMPILATIONS: *The Soldier's Dream* 60s recordings (Old Homestead 1986) ★★★.

Ellis, Shirley

b. New York City, USA. Before striking out on a solo career in 1963, Ellis served an apprenticeship singing with an unsuccessful vocal group, the Metronones. Her strong voice was used to good effect on dance-floor ravers 'The Nitty Gritty' (number 4 R&B and number 8 pop in 1963) and '(That's) What The Nitty Gritty Is' (number 14 R&B 1964), and her future looked bright. Ellis, however, soon found herself in novelty song territory with catchy ditties written by her manager Lincoln Chase, namely, 'The Name Game' (number 4 R&B and number 3 pop in 1965) and 'The Clapping Song (Clap Pat Clap Slap)' (number 16 R&B and number 8 pop in 1965). The latter was the only UK success for Ellis, amazingly hitting twice, in 1965, when it reached number 6, and on an EP in 1978. The **Belle Stars** successfully revived 'The Clapping Song' in 1982.

● ALBUMS: *In Action* (Congress 1964) ★★, *The Name Game* (Congress 1965) ★★★, *Sugar, Let's Shing A Ling* (Columbia 1967) ★★.

● COMPILATIONS: *The Very Best Of . . .* (Taragon 1995) ★★★, *The Complete Congress Recordings* (Connoisseur 2001) ★★★.

Ellis, Terry

b. August 1943, Hertfordshire, England. Ellis attended Newcastle-upon-Tyne University, where as social secretary he booked bands to appear at dances. It was during this period as a science student that he confronted **Bob Dylan** for a memorable scene captured in the film *Don't Look Back*. After graduating he formed his own agency, which became Chrysalis Artists in 1967. The name was a combination of the names of Ellis and his partner Chris Wright. The next year the duo set up **Chrysalis Records**, with **Jethro Tull** and **Ten Years After** among their early releases. The label's successes with these and other British acts led Ellis to move to New York in 1975. There he set up a US branch of Chrysalis, signing such acts as **Blondie** and **Pat Benatar**. He also became the first non-US citizen to be elected president of the

Recording Industry Association of America. After policy disagreements with Wright, he left Chrysalis in 1985 and worked outside the music business until becoming chairman of the British Phonographic Industry from 1989-91. Ellis subsequently set up Imago Records, with finance from BMG Records. With offices in London and New York, its first artists were King Of Fools, the **Henry Rollins** Band and Baby Animals.

Ellis, Tinsley

b. 4 June 1957, Atlanta, Georgia, USA. Like many American musicians of his generation, Ellis first took up the guitar at the age of seven, inspired by groups in the late 60s British blues rock invasion. While playing in rock bands, he took an increasing interest in the work of **Howlin' Wolf**, **Muddy Waters** and **John Lee Hooker** and particularly in guitarists **Freddie King**, **Buddy Guy** and **Magic Sam**. Returning from Florida in 1979, he joined the **Alley Cats**, a blues band that also featured future **Fabulous Thunderbirds** bass player Preston Hubbard. Two years later, Ellis formed the Heartfixers with veteran harmonica player Chicago Bob Nelson. Their debut album helped to make them the city's foremost blues rock band. With Nelson's departure, the band moved to Landslide and Ellis took over lead vocals. The release of a live album and 1986's *Cool On It* and their supporting role on **Nappy Brown**'s comeback set *Tore Up* brought them attention in America and Europe where they and Brown toured in 1987.

By then, Ellis had already determined on a solo career, and while recording *Georgia Blue*, his contract was acquired by **Alligator Records**. His subsequent albums sought to reinvent him in **Stevie Ray Vaughan**'s image, and though he had the talent to transcend such a limiting identification it was not until the release of *Kingpin* in 2000 that he was able to manifest it. The album was released on the Capricorn label, which went bankrupt shortly afterwards, leaving Ellis to cast around for a new contract. He signed to the Telarc label and released *Hell Or High Water* in 2002.

● ALBUMS: *The Heartfixers* (Southland 1981) ★★★, with the Heartfixers *Live At The Moon Shadow* (Landslide 1983) ★★★, with the Heartfixers *Cool On It* (Landslide/Alligator 1986) ★★★★, *Georgia Blue* (Alligator 1988) ★★, *Fanning The Flames* (Alligator 1989) ★★★, *Trouble Time* (Alligator 1992) ★★★, *Storm Warning* (Alligator 1994) ★★★, *Fire It Up* (Alligator 1997) ★★★, *Kingpin* (Capricorn 2000) ★★★★, *Hell Or High Water* (Telarc 2002) ★★★, *The Hard Way* (Telarc 2004) ★★★★, *Highwayman* (Alligator 2005) ★★★.

Ellis, Vivian

b. 29 October 1903, Hampstead, London, England, d. 19 June 1996, London, England. A highly respected composer, lyricist and author, chiefly celebrated for his fresh, witty and romantic music for revues and musicals in the UK during the period from the 20s through to the 50s. He also wrote the music for several films, including *Jack's The Boy*, starring **Jack Hulbert** and **Cicely Courtneidge** ('The Flies Crawled Up The Window'), *Piccadilly Incident* ('Piccadilly 1944'), *Public Nuisance No. 1* ('Me And My Dog') and individual pieces such as 'Coronation Scot', which became the signature tune of the popular BBC radio series *Paul Temple* in the 40s, and emerged again in the 80s in a television commercial for British Rail. As an author, he published a number of novels, and a series of humorous books entitled *How To Make Your*

Fortune On The Stock Exchange and *How To Enjoy Your Operation*, etc. Ellis' mother was an extremely talented violinist, and his grandmother, Julia Woolf, was the composer of a 1888 comic opera *Carina*. His early ambition was to be a concert pianist, and he studied the piano with Dame Myra Hess and composition at the Royal Academy of Music, later giving a number of recitals. In his late teens, he developed an interest in light music and did the rounds of London's music publishers with some of his compositions, eventually getting a job as a reader and demonstrator with Francis, Day & Hunter. In the early 20s he composed the music for several numbers in revues such as *The Curate's Egg*, *The Little Revue* and *The Punch Bowl*, and then, in 1924, wrote most of the songs (with lyrics by Graham John) for the successful Hulbert and Courtneidge revue *By The Way*. These included 'Three Little Hairs', 'By The Way' and 'Nothing Ever Happens To Me'. A year later, June (née Howard-Tripp) sang his 'Over My Shoulder' (lyric by Graham John) in *Mercenary Mary*, and she was one of several artists to perform Ellis and John's hit 'Little Boy Blues' in another Hulbert and Courtneidge revue *Clowns In Clover* (1927). In the late 20s, Ellis was represented by various compositions in several other West End shows, including *Kid Boots*, *Cochran's 1926 Revue*, *My Son John*, *Merely Molly*, *Palladium Pleasures*, *Blue Skies*, *The Girl Friend*, *Charlot Revue 1928*, *Vogue And Vanities*, *The House That Jack Built*, *A Yankee At King Arthur's Court* and *Will O' The Whispers* (1928), in which 'I Never Dreamt' (words and music by Ellis), was sung by the popular American vocalist 'Whispering' Jack Smith.

In 1929 Ellis moved on from the revue format and had his first musical comedy hit with **Mr Cinders**, which had a book and lyrics by **Clifford Grey** and Greatrex Newman, and additional music by Richard Myers. The show contained one of Ellis' most enduring numbers, 'Spread A Little Happiness', which was performed by **Binnie Hale**, and several other favourites, including 'Ev'ry Little Moment' (Hale and **Bobby Howes**), and Howes' comedy high spot, 'On The Amazon'. Despite initially cool reviews, the show was an enormous success, running for a total of 529 performances. Ellis himself was unable to attend the opening of the show—he was seriously ill in the south of France. On his return to Britain he collaborated with lyricist Desmond Carter for *Little Tommy Tucker* ('Let's Be Sentimental'), and again, for the wistful 'Wind In The Willows', which was featured in *Cochran's 1930 Revue* and became an extremely popular item in the repertoire of **Leslie 'Hutch' Hutchinson**. The show marked the beginning of an association with the impresario **C.B. Cochran** that was to prove one of the most important in Ellis' professional life. In the early 30s Ellis experienced mixed fortunes. **Follow A Star** was a financial failure despite the presence in the cast of Hulbert and **Sophie Tucker**, who sang Ellis and **Jack Yellen**'s powerful, bluesy 'If Your Kisses Can't Hold The Man You Love', which Tucker later used to close her cabaret act. *The Song Of The Drum* ('Within My Heart'), *Blue Roses* ('Dancing In My Sleep', 'If I Had Three Wishes', 'Where Have You Been Hiding?') and *Out Of The Bottle* (music by Ellis and **Oscar Levant**) were disappointing too. **Stand Up And Sing**, starring **Jack Buchanan** and **Elsie Randolph**, was much more successful, and contained numbers by Ellis, **Phil Charig** and **Douglas Furber**, such as 'There's Always Tomorrow', 'It's Not You' and 'Night Time'. By 1934, Ellis was one of the leading figures in the British musical theatre. For the revue *Streamline* (1934), Cochran teamed him with the author **A.P. Herbert**, a collaboration that produced 'Other People's Babies' (sung by Norah Howard), among others, which provided a foretaste of their fruitful partnership during the late 40s, and, briefly, in the 50s. In the meantime, Ellis turned once more to Desmond Carter for the lyrics to *Jill Darling* (1934), a charming musical comedy that starred **Frances Day**, one of Ellis' favourite leading ladies, and included 'Dancing With A Ghost', 'Nonny, Nonny, No', 'Pardon My English' 'Let's Lay Our Heads Together', 'A Flower For You' and another of the composer's all-time standards, 'I'm On A See-Saw', which was performed in vivacious fashion by Louise Browne and **John Mills**, who later became a celebrated dramatic actor. 'I'm On A See-Saw' was recorded by **Fats Waller**, in a typically ebullient version, and became successful in America for **Ambrose** and his orchestra—one of Ellis' rare transatlantic hits. In the late 30s, Ellis began to write more of his own lyrics for songs such as 'Drop In Next Time You're Passing' (*Going Places*), 'The Trees In Bloomsbury Square' and 'London In The Season' (*The Town Talks*), and the delightful 'She's My Lovely', sung by **Bobby Howes** in *Hide And Seek* (1937), and later adopted by band leader **Billy Ternent** as his signature tune. In 1938 he had three hit shows running in the West End: *The Fleet's Lit Up* ('Little Miss Go-As-You-Please', 'Guess It Must Be The Spring', 'How Do You Do, Mr. Right?', 'Hide And Seek'), *Running Riot* ('Take Your Partners For The Waltz', 'When Love Knocks At My Door', 'Doing An Irish Jig') and **Under Your Hat**, 'the funniest musical comedy for years', which ran for a total of 512 performances in London, and included Cicely Courtneidge's hilariously patriotic 'The Empire Depends On You', and other numbers such as 'Together Again', 'Keep It Under Your Hat' and 'If You Want To Dance'.

While those shows were running in London, Vivian Ellis lived for a time in Hollywood, where he wrote film songs for **Deanna Durbin**. He returned to Britain in the spring of 1939, and subsequently joined the RNVR. He attained the rank of Lieutenant-Commander, and spent most of World War II as a Command Entertainments Officer for ENSA. After his release in 1945, Ellis resumed his collaboration with A.P. Herbert (book and lyrics) in Cochran's production of a 'light opera' entitled **Big Ben** (1946). Remembered particularly for introducing the 19-year-old **Lizbeth Webb** to the London stage, the score included 'Let Us Go Down The River', 'London Town', 'I Want To See The People Happy', 'Love Me Not' and 'Who's The Lady?', among others. One critic wrote that *Big Ben* lacked distinction, something that could never be said about Ellis and Herbert's next effort, **Bless The Bride** (1947), which was probably Ellis' biggest hit, and the climax of his career. Featuring hit songs such as the 'gaily traditional French pastiche', 'Ma Belle Marguerite', 'This Is My Lovely Day' and 'I Was Never Kissed Before', *Bless The Bride* was essentially a romantic operetta set in Victorian England, and could hardly have been more different to the brash, young American import **Oklahoma!**, which opened at a nearby London theatre in the same week. Nevertheless, with **Georges Guétary** and Lizbeth Webb in the leading roles, *Bless The Bride* settled into the Adelphi Theatre, and ran for 886 performances. One of the main reasons it closed in 1949 was that Cochran wanted to replace it with Ellis and Herbert's *Tough At The Top*, a decision that proved to be an expensive mistake—the new show ran for just over four months.

In the 50s, the US invasion of the British musical theatre that had begun with *Oklahoma!* in 1947 intensified. In the face of all that Americana, Vivian Ellis' first score of the decade couldn't have been more parochial. *And So To Bed* (1951) was a musical adaptation of J.B. Fagan's renowned play about the Elizabethan diarist Samuel Pepys, for which Ellis was called upon to compose music in a variety of styles, such as madrigal, jig and saraband. A rather unconventional choice for the leading role was 'rubber-faced' comic actor **Leslie Henson**, whose idea the whole thing was, and the score included 'Gaze Not On The Swans', 'Moppety Mo', 'Love Me Little, Love Me Long', 'Amo, Amas' and 'Bartholomew Fair'. The show's musical director was **Mantovani**, later renowned for his 'cascading strings'. *And So To Bed* had a healthy run of 323 performances, and Ellis followed it, two years later, with a revue, *Over The Moon*, before renewing his partnership with Herbert for *The Water Gipsies* (1955). Ellis had written the melody for one song, 'Little Boat', in the film version of Herbert's 1930 novel, set on London's waterways, and now, over 20 years later, he contributed a complete musical score, which included **Dora Bryan**'s amusing versions of 'Why Did You Call Me Lily?', 'You Never Know With Men', 'I Should Worry' and 'It Would Cramp My Style'. Her presence ensured the show's initial success, but when she became pregnant and had to leave, *The Water Gipsies* folded after a run of 239 performances. It was Ellis' last major musical production, and he has been quoted as saying that it may have been his best score. Of his other work around that time, his children's musical *Listen To The Wind* (1954) contained several excellent songs, and he continued to contribute to productions such as *Half In Earnest, Four To The Bar, Six Of One, Mr Whatnot* and *Chaganog* (1964).

In 1973 Ellis received the **Ivor Novello** Award for outstanding services to British music, and, 10 years later, he was presented with the Ivor Novello Lifetime Achievement Award and became the President of the Performing Rights Society. In 1984, at the age of 80, he received the CBE, and, in the same year, the Vivian Ellis Prize, an annual award for the writers of new musicals, was instituted by the PRS. *Bless The Bride* was revived at London's Sadler's Wells Theatre in 1987, and Ellis' first musical comedy hit, *Mr Cinders*, also enjoyed London revivals in 1983 and 1993. The latter show was first produced in America in 1988, at the Goodspeed Opera House, and then, in 1992, it finally had its New York premiere at the Mazur Theatre. The show's hit song, 'Spread A Little Happiness', was sung in the 1982 film *Brimstone And Treacle*, by **Sting**, the ex-leader of the UK band **Police**; it gave him his first solo Top 10 entry. **Peter Skellern**'s version featured in an 80s television commercial for Lurpak butter. *Spread A Little Happiness* also became the title of a 'musical celebration of Vivian Ellis', devised by the author and critic Sheridan Morley, and presented at London's King's Head and Whitehall theatres in 1992. It meant that Vivian Ellis, a contemporary of Ivor Novello and **Noël Coward**, and one of the most important influences in the British musical theatre during the late 20s and 30s, still had his name up in lights more than 50 years later, alongside present incumbents such as **Andrew Lloyd Webber**. Up until shortly before his death, Ellis was working with Dan Crawford, artistic director of the King's Head Theatre, on a revival of his 1954 musical *Listen To The Wind*. He wrote three new songs and the production opened to excellent notices in December 1996.

● ALBUMS: *You've Never Had It So Good* (Decca 1960) ★★★, *Spread A Little Happiness* (Past 1996) ★★★★.
● FURTHER READING: *I'm On A See-Saw: An Autobiography*, Vivian Ellis and Desmond Carter.

Ellis, Wilbert 'Big Chief'

b. 10 November 1914, Birmingham, Alabama, USA, d. 20 December 1977, Birmingham, Alabama, USA. A part-time musician, Ellis also worked as a taxi driver, bartender and gambler. His blues piano was rooted in the rolling, hard-hitting styles of Birmingham, to which was added a strong influence from **Walter Davis**. Resident in New York from 1936, he made a few splendid records under his own name in the 50s, and accompanied **Tarheel Slim**, **Brownie McGhee**, **Jack Dupree** and others. Rediscovered in Washington in the 70s, he returned to performing, enthusiastically and with unimpaired skills, until his death.
● ALBUMS: *Big Chief Ellis* (1976) ★★★, *Let's Have A Ball* (1978) ★★★.

Ellison, Andy

b. England. Ellison has had a varied musical career. He began as a solo singer but later worked with **John's Children**, **Jet** and eventually late 70s quirky pop/punk band the **Radio Stars**. In all he released three solo singles for three different labels in the late 60s—'It's Been A Long Time' (Track), 'Fool From Upper Eden' (**CBS Records**) and 'You Can't Do That' (S.N.B.). None breached the charts or sold in substantial quantities, although each has become a collector's item owing to Ellison's subsequent musical activities. In the 90s Ellison was involved in a re-formation of the ever-popular John's Children.

Ellison, Lorraine

b. 1943, Philadelphia, Pennsylvania, USA, d. 17 August 1985. Although only associated with a few minor hits in the history of R&B, Ellison's intense, dramatic and highly gospelized vocal delivery helped to define deep soul as a particular style. Ellison recorded with two gospel groups, the Ellison Singers and the Golden Chords, but left the latter in 1964 to pursue a solo career in R&B music. 'I Dig You Baby' (number 22 R&B) in 1965 was her first chart entry, but it was the powerful 'Stay With Me' (number 11 R&B, number 64 pop) in 1966 that established her reputation. Written and produced by **Jerry Ragovoy**, the song, featuring Ellison's awe-inspiring vocal pleas, ultimately proved to be a spectacular one-off performance. Nothing in her subsequent recordings emulated its naked emotion, and even the excellent 'Heart Be Still' (number 43 R&B, number 89 pop), from 1967, was something of an anti-climax. Ellison never charted again, not even with the original version of 'Try Just A Little Bit Harder' (1968), which rock singer **Janis Joplin** later remade with great success. Ellison's compositions, on which she often collaborated with her manager, Sam Bell (of **Garnet Mimms And The Enchanters** fame), were recorded by **Howard Tate** and Garnet Mimms.
● ALBUMS: *Heart And Soul* (Warners 1966) ★★, *Stay With Me* (Warners 1970) ★★★, *Lorraine Ellison* (Warners 1974) ★★.
● COMPILATIONS: *The Best Of Philadelphia's Queen* (Warners 1976) ★★★, *Stay With Me* (Ichiban 1985) ★★★★.

Elman, Ziggy

b. Harry Finkelman, 26 May 1914, Philadelphia, Pennsylvania, USA, d. 26 June 1968, Los Angeles, California, USA. As a child Elman learned to play various brass and reed instruments, and his first professional engagement was on trombone, although his main instrument later became the trumpet. In 1936 he joined **Benny Goodman** and formed part of one of the best three-man trumpet sections of the swing era. With **Harry James** and **Chris Griffin**, Elman shared lead and solo duties and his dynamic, biting playing was a great asset to the band. After James left to lead his own band, Elman comfortably coped with his role as featured soloist, playing showstoppers such as 'Who'll Buy My Bublitchki' and 'And The Angels Sing', which he composed himself. After leaving Goodman, Elman worked with other big bands, including those of **Joe Venuti** and **Tommy Dorsey**.
In the late 40s, as name big bands were folding all around him, Elman tried leading his own big band and met with a measure of success especially with a re-recording of 'And The Angels Sing'. In the early 50s he worked in film studios in Los Angeles but ill health and personal problems kept him from achieving much success. In 1961 his financial situation was revealed during an alimony court hearing at which he agreed that many people thought him to be the world's greatest trumpet player, adding 'But I still can't get much work.' Six of his seven bank accounts had sums varying between $1.19 and $11.00 in them, while the seventh was overdrawn.
● ALBUMS: *Dancing With Zig* (MGM 1952) ★★★, *Sentimental Trumpet* (MGM 1956) ★★★, *Zaggin' With Zig* (Affinity 1978) ★★★.
● COMPILATIONS: *And The Angels Sing* (Sunbeam) ★★★, *1938-39* (Classics) ★★★, *Ziggy Elman And His Orchestra 1947* (Circle) ★★★.

Elmer Gantry's Velvet Opera
(see **Velvet Opera**)

ELO
(see **Electric Light Orchestra**)

Eloy

This German progressive-space rock band is essentially a vehicle for the creative talents of lead vocalist, guitarist and songwriter Frank Bornemann, with a somewhat unstable backing line-up. The band released their debut, *Inside*, in 1973, and achieved enormous success in Germany with a succession of albums in the vein of **Pink Floyd** and **Yes** but with a heavier, guitar-based approach. These usually featured instrumentally complex epics based on Bornemann's science fiction–flavoured concepts, but despite a domestic major label contract, and a consistent English language approach, their early material was not released outside their homeland. Bornemann, at this stage joined by Hannes Filberth (keyboards), Hannes Arkona (keyboards/guitar), Klaus-Peter Matziol (bass) and Fritz Randow (drums), was by now updating the Eloy sound, culminating in the excellent *Metromania*, where modern keyboard textures added colour to more compact, less indulgent songs, but this line-up crumbled as the rhythm section departed. Bornemann was subsequently less prolific as his duties as owner and manager of Hanover's Horus Sound Studios took up more of his time, but Eloy made a comeback with *Destination* and then *The*

Tide Returns Forever, with Michael Gerlach's keyboards helping Bornemann to produce an altogether more technical sound along the lines of latter-day **Rush** while retaining all of Eloy's individual character.

● ALBUMS: *Inside* (Electrola 1973) ★★★★, *Floating* (Electrola 1974) ★★★, *Power And The Passion* (Electrola 1975) ★★★★, *Dawn* (Electrola 1976) ★★★, *Oceans* (Electrola 1977) ★★★, *Silent Cries, Mighty Echoes* (Electrola 1978) ★★★, *Live* (Electrola 1978) ★★, *Colours* (Electrola 1983) ★★★, *Metromania* (Electrola 1984) ★★★★, *Ra* (Electrola 1989) ★★, *Destination* (SPV 1993) ★★★, *The Tide Returns Forever* (SPV 1995) ★★★.

Elsdon, Alan

b. 15 October 1934, London, England. Elsdon studied trumpet before turning to jazz and working with a succession of British traditional bands in the 50s. His reputation established, in the early 60s he decided to form his own band, but the musical times were changing and he failed to gain the same level of success achieved by many other traditional bands. Nevertheless, Elsdon succeeded in keeping his band afloat, working regularly at clubs and pubs and occasionally at more prestigious venues. He toured the UK with visiting American jazz and blues artists during the 60s and 70s. In the 80s, with his band still around, he also began playing with the **Midnite Follies Orchestra** and with other groups led by **Keith Nichols**. Despite his long association with the traditional jazz scene, Elsdon's virile playing style fits comfortably into the mainstream.

● ALBUMS: *Jazz Journeymen* (Black Lion 1977) ★★★, *Keepers Of The Flame* (Parrot 1994) ★★★, with Clinton Ford *Clinton Ford Sings Alan Elsdon Swings* (Lake 2001) ★★★.

Elsie, Lily

b. Elsie Hodder, 8 April 1886, Armley, Leeds, Yorkshire, England, d. 16 December 1962, Willesden, London, England. When Elsie's mother married Wilfred Cotton in 1891, the child took her stepfather's name (he would later marry musical comedy star **Ada Reeve**). The family was then living in Salford, a district of Manchester. From childhood, she performed in public houses in Salford, singing under the name Little Elsie. In 1897 she played the role of Princess Mirza in a Manchester production of *The Arabian Nights*. Eventually, her singing and especially her striking good looks brought her to the attention of the theatrical community, not only in the north of England but also in London. After moving to the capital, she was in several productions with increasing success, including appearing in **A Chinese Honeymoon** (1901), which was the first local production to surpass 1,000 performances.

Elsie continued to attract attention and was already greatly admired when **George Edwardes** persuaded her to take the lead in **The Merry Widow**. She was reluctant to do so, especially after he awed her by taking her to Vienna to see a production there. Elsie's fears were groundless and when *The Merry Widow* opened on 8 June 1907 at Edwardes' Daly's Theatre in Leicester Square, she was an overnight success, encoring her big number, the waltz son, some 25 times. The show ran for 778 performances and through her performance, Elsie attained an astonishingly high profile. Her portrait was used for advertising, while newspapers and magazines printed articles about her. Future prime minister Winston Churchill, then a young man, reportedly declared, 'It is unthinkable to see *The Merry Widow* without Lily Elsie.' She made some appearances in very early films and also made some poorly recorded but fascinating records. With a fragile beauty, graceful and elegant, she continued to perform for adoring fans, but she was by all accounts permanently stricken with acute shyness. Unable to live with the adulation and constant public attention, she retired at the age of 26 while her career was at its height and married Ian Bullough, a millionaire's son. In time the marriage ended, reportedly owing to her husband's excessive drinking, and she spent her last years in a nursing home.

● FILMS: *Comradeship* (1919).

Elstree Calling

This 'all-star vaudeville and revue entertainment', which was compèred by the popular radio comedian Tommy Handley and produced by British International Pictures (BIP) at Elstree Studios in 1930, is reputed to be the first British film musical. A variety of artists, most of whom were drawn from London shows, performed a series of sketches and musical numbers that included 'Ain't Misbehavin'' (**Fats Waller**-Harry Brooks-**Andy Razaf**) performed by Teddy Brown And His Orchestra; 'My Heart Is Singing' (**Ivor Novello**-Donovan Parsons, from the current show *The House That Jack Built*), sung by Helen Burnell with the Adelphi Girls; 'Why Am I Always The Bridesmaid' (Fred W. Leigh-Charles Collins) and 'He's Only A Working Man' sung by Lily Morris; 'The Ladies Maid Is Always In The Know' sung by the Charlot Girls; 'The Thought Never Entered My Head' (Novello-Parsons from *The House That Jack Built*) sung by Helen Burnell and **Jack Hulbert**; 'I've Fallen In Love' sung by **Cicely Courtneidge**; 'It's Twelve And A Tanner A Bottle' sung by Will Fyffe; and 'Dance Around In Your Bones', which was tap-danced by the Three Eddies dressed as skeletons. The remainder of the music was composed by **Vivian Ellis**, Reginald Casson, Jack Strachey and Chick Endor. Others taking part were Anna May Wong, Bobbie Comber, Hannah Jones, Jameson Thomas, John Longden, Ivor McLaren, Lawrence Green, the Berkoff Dancers, the Kasbeck Singers and the Balalaika Choral Orchestra. During the proceedings, funny-man Gordon Harker is constantly trying to receive the show on a home-made television set. The screenplay was written by Val Valentine, Walter Mycroft and Adrian Brunel, who, in his dual role as director, skilfully assembled the whole affair. The sketches and other interpolated items were staged by the 31-year-old Alfred Hitchcock. *Elstree Calling* was photographed by John Maxwell with some of the sequences in colour, including those featuring the Charlot Girls, the Adelphi Girls and Cicely Courtneidge.

Elvis On Tour

Pierre Adidge and Robert Abel, who had directed the enthralling **Joe Cocker** feature **Mad Dogs And Englishmen**, assumed the same role for this 1972 documentary. 'At last! The first real Elvis Presley movie,' proclaimed an ecstatic review in **Rolling Stone** and indeed the film captures the performer just before his final artistic decline. Superbly shot, *Elvis On Tour* showcases material from Presley's early recordings—'That's Alright', 'Mystery Train', 'Don't Be Cruel'—as well as presenting several songs pivotal to his late 60s rebirth. These include 'Suspicious Minds', 'Burning Love' and his powerful rendition of **Mickey Newbury**'s

'American Trilogy'. Martin Scorcese (*Taxi Driver*, **The Last Waltz**) was responsible for the inventive montage sequence and the film also contains footage from Presley's appearance on the *Ed Sullivan Show*, where he invests 'Ready Teddy' with awesome exuberance. The Elvis of 1972, replete with white cat-suit and rhinestones, was inevitably incapable of recreating such intensity, but his performances on this film still hold an enthralling magnetism.

Elvis—The Movie

Originally made for television, *Elvis—The Movie* is a three-hour hagiography starring Kurt Russell in the title role, with vocals provided by Presley impersonator **Ronnie McDowell**. This sentimental film, released in 1979, provided no insight into its subject, sugaring the tale by emphasizing his impoverished background and the death of his mother, while glossing over Presley's personal and professional traumas and his hedonistic lifestyle. Indeed, *Elvis—The Movie* closes with the singer's 1970's triumphs in Las Vegas, completely ignoring his sorry subsequent decline and death. Director John Carpenter later disowned the entire project, declaring it one of the worst films he had ever seen. That is perhaps too critical, but *Elvis—The Movie* is certainly a lost opportunity.

Ely, Brother Claude

b. 21 July 1922, near Pennington Gap, Lee County, Virginia, USA, d. 7 May 1978. Ely suffered from tuberculosis as a child and during convalescence, he taught himself to play guitar, harmonica and organ. He worked as a miner, until drafted for Army service during World War II, later returning to the mines until 1949. After he became a born-again Christian, as Brother Claude, he preached at revival meetings and churches in numerous venues in Tennessee, Virginia and Kentucky for almost 20 years. A fine singer, his renditions of country ballads and especially gospel songs, some of which he wrote himself, attracted the attention of King Records. In October 1953, his preaching and singing at a church meeting at Whitesburg, Kentucky, was recorded via a link back to the local radio station. The following year, further recordings were made by this method from a gospel gathering at a local courthouse. Several of his songs, including 'There's A Leak In This Old Building' and 'There Ain't No Grave Gonna Hold My Body Down', became popular (the complete recordings of the two King sessions, including some previously unissued material, were released by the UK **Ace Records** label in 1993). Throughout the 60s, he continued to preach and hold gospel meetings at numerous venues. He made studio recordings for King in 1962 and 1968. He finally settled in Newport, Kentucky, where he was the minister at the Charity Tabernacle. In the late 60s, he released an album on his own Gold Star label. After suffering a heart attack in 1977, he made home recordings of some of his unrecorded songs that, together with a recording of one of his sermons, were released after his death by his daughter. On 7 May 1978, while conducting a service in his church, Brother Claude suffered a further heart attack and died.
● ALBUMS: *The Gospel Ranger* (King 1962) ★★★, *At Home And At Church* (King 1968) ★★, *Child Of The King* (Gold Star 1969) ★★★, *Where Could I Go But To The Lord* (Jordan 1979) ★★.
● COMPILATIONS: *Satan Get Back* 1953-54 recordings (Ace 1993) ★★★★.

Ely, Joe

b. 9 February 1947, Amarillo, Texas, USA. Singer-songwriter and guitarist Ely is one of the most completely realized artists in contemporary country music, especially in the live situation where he excels. His work for MCA Records in the late 70s is latterly regarded as the link between country rock and so-called new country.

Ely moved with his parents in 1958 to Lubbock, the major city of the flatlands of Texas, from which such luminaries as **Buddy Holly**, **Roy Orbison** and **Waylon Jennings** had previously emerged. Ely formed his first band at the age of 13, playing a fusion of country and R&B, before dropping out of high school and following in the footsteps of **Woody Guthrie** and the writer Jack Kerouac, hopping freight trains and working at a variety of non-musical jobs before finding himself stranded in New York with nothing but his guitar. He joined a theatrical company from Austin, Texas, and travelled to Europe with his theatrical employers in the early 70s before returning to Lubbock, where he teamed up with fellow singer-songwriters **Jimmie Dale Gilmore** and **Butch Hancock** and a couple of other local musicians (including a musical saw player!) in an informal combo known as the **Flatlanders**. Although they were never immensely successful, the unit did some recording in Nashville for **Shelby Singleton**'s Plantation label, but only a couple of singles were released at the time. Later, when Ely was signed to MCA Records in the late 70s, the recordings by the Flatlanders, which had achieved legendary status, were anthologized on *One Road More*, an album that was first released by European label **Charly Records** in 1980, but did not appear in the USA until the mid-80s (the album is also available with the title *More A Legend Than A Band*).

After a spell with the Ringling Bros. Circus, Ely formed his own band, whose members included **Lloyd Maines** (steel drum), Jesse Taylor (guitar), Gregg Wright (bass) and Steve Keeton (drums), plus auxiliary picker Ponty Bone (accordion). This basic line-up recorded three albums, *Joe Ely*, *Honky Tonk Masquerade*, and *Down On The Drag*, before Keeton was replaced by Robert Marquam and Wright by Michael Robertson for 1981's *Musta Notta Gotta Lotta*, which also featured Reese Wyhans (keyboards), among others. Although these albums were artistic successes, featuring great songs mainly written by Ely, Hancock (especially) and Gilmore, the musical tide of the times was inclined far more towards punk and new wave music than towards Texan singer-songwriters. In 1980, the Ely Band had toured extensively as opening act for the **Clash**, with whom Ely became very friendly, and *Live Shots* was released that year. The album featured Taylor, Marquam, Wright, Bone and Maines and was recorded on dates with the Clash, but was no more successful than the three studio albums that preceded it. In 1984 Ely recorded *Hi-Res*, which featured a completely new band of little-known musicians, but was no more successful than the previous albums in commercial terms.

By 1987, Ely had assembled a new band: David Grissom (lead guitar), Jimmy Pettit (bass) and Davis McLarty (drums). This line-up recorded two artistically stunning albums for the US independent label HighTone, *Lord Of The Highway* and *Dig All Night*, the latter featuring for the first time a repertoire totally composed of Ely's own songs. Both albums were licensed in the UK to **Demon Records**; in the wake of this renewed interest, Sunstorm Records, a tiny London label launched by Pete O'Brien, the editor of *Omaha Rainbow* fanzine, licensed two albums worth of Ely's early material. *Milkshakes And Malts*, a compilation of Ely's recordings of songs by Butch Hancock, and *What Ever Happened To Maria?*, which similarly compiled Ely's own self-penned songs. At this point, the band had been together for three years and had achieved an incredible onstage empathy, especially between Ely and Grissom, whose R&B guitar work had moved the band's music away from country. In 1990, they recorded a powerhouse live album in Austin, *Live At Liberty Lunch*, which was sufficiently impressive for Ely's old label, MCA, to re-sign him.

Ely's extra-curricular activities during this period included contributions to the soundtrack of *Roadie*, a movie starring **Meat Loaf**, in which he could be heard playing 'Brainlock' and 'I Had My Hopes Up High', and his participation as a member of the *ad hoc* group Buzzin Cousins, in which he was joined by **John Mellencamp**, **John Prine**, **Dwight Yoakam** and James McMurtry, on the soundtrack to the Mellencamp movie *Falling From Grace*. Ely, Hancock, **Terry Allen**, **Robert Earl Keen**, **Wayne Hancock**, Jo Harvey Allen and Jo Carol Pierce composed a stage musical about a prostitute, *Chippy*, the soundtrack to which was released in 1995 by Hollywood Records.

Ely's 1995 release *Letter To Laredo* was a return to the sound of his early MCA albums and included an update of Butch Hancock's 'She Never Spoke Spanish To Me' (included on his 1977 debut) as 'She Finally Spoke Spanish To Me'. The key track was a fine version of **Tom Russell**'s song about cockfighting, 'Gallao Del Cielo'. The follow-up *Twistin' In The Wind* fleshed out the sound of the largely acoustic *Letter To Laredo*. In 1999, Ely joined a number of leading Mexican and American musicians in the Grammy–award winning Los Super Seven project. The following year he recorded another stinging live album with long-time collaborators Jesse Taylor and Lloyd Maines.

In the new millennium Ely reunited with Jimmie Dale Gilmore and Butch Hancock to record a new Flatlanders album, almost three decades after they had first begun making music together. The ensuing *Now Again* ably updated the trio's legendary status, with Ely and Hancock providing a greater artistic input than on the Gilmore-dominated 70s recordings. Further recordings followed as the trio were welcomed back into the musical fold by both old and new fans. Ely, meanwhile, made his debut for the **Rounder Records** label with the 2003 studio release *Streets Of Sin*.

● ALBUMS: *Joe Ely* (MCA 1977) ★★★★, *Honky Tonk Masquerade* (MCA 1978) ★★★★, *Down On The Drag* (MCA 1979) ★★★★, *Live Shots* (SouthCoast/MCA 1980) ★★★, *Musta Notta Gotta Lotta* (SouthCoast/MCA 1981) ★★★, *Hi-Res* (MCA 1984) ★★★, *Lord Of The Highway* (HighTone/Demon 1987) ★★★★, *Dig All Night* (High-Tone/Demon 1988) ★★★★, *Live At Liberty Lunch* (MCA 1990) ★★★★, *Love And Danger* (MCA 1993) ★★★, *Letter To Laredo* (MCA 1995) ★★★★, *Twistin' In The Wind* (MCA 1998) ★★★★, *Live At The Cambridge Folk Festival* 1990 recording (Strange Fruit 1998) ★★★, *Live @ Antone's* (Rounder 2000) ★★★★, *Streets Of Sin* (Rounder 2003) ★★★.

● COMPILATIONS: *Milkshakes And Malts* (Sunstorm 1988) ★★★, *What Ever Happened To Maria?* (Sunstorm 1988) ★★★, *No Bad Talk Or Loud Talk: '77—'81* (Edsel 1995) ★★★★, *Time For Travellin': The Best Of Joe Ely Volume Two* (Edsel 1996) ★★★★, *The Best Of Joe Ely* (MCA 2000) ★★★★, *From Lubbock To Laredo: The Best Of Joe Ely* (MCA 2002) ★★★, *The Best Of Joe Ely: The Millennium Collection* (MCA 2004) ★★★★, *Settle For Love* (HighTone 2004) ★★★★.

● FILMS: *South Of Heaven, West Of Hell* (2000), *Antone's: Home Of The Blues* (2004).

El'Zabar, Kahil

b. Clifton Blackburn, 11 November 1953, Chicago, Illinois, USA. Interested in music from early childhood, El'Zabar paid special attention to African music in general and percussion in particular. When he was 18, he joined the **AACM** (Association for the Advancement of Creative Musicians) in Chicago, and in 1975 became its chairman. Meanwhile, he had formed his own musical group, the **Ethnic Heritage Ensemble**, and in 1973, he attended the University of Ghana in order to further his studies of African music firsthand. He has cited drummer Harold Atu Murray as a significant influence and mentor, and among the wide range of percussion instruments he plays are balaphon, berimbau, bongos, congas, kalimba, marimba, sanza and shekere. In jazz, apart from AACM El'Zabar has worked with artists such as **Joseph Bowie**, **Ernest Dawkins**, **Dizzy Gillespie**, **Donny Hathaway**, **Fred Hopkins**, **David Murray** and **Henry Threadgill**. Among pop artists with whom he has played are **Paul Simon**, **Nina Simone** and **Stevie Wonder**. In addition to performing as an accompanist, El'Zabar has toured internationally as leader of his own groups, which include the Ritual Trio with **Malachi Favors** and saxophonist Ari Brown. In 1991, he was commissioned by the Leverkusen Jazz Festival in Germany to present a retrospective of his work. In 1997, he brought together several former members of the **Black Artists Group**, including **'Kalaparush' Maurice McIntyre**, Favors and **Steve Colson**, to record *Return Of The Lost Tribe* under the Bright Moments moniker.

El'Zabar's film work, which includes composing scores and on-screen appearances in acting roles, includes *Savannah* (1988), *So Low But Not Alone* (1989), *Mo' Money* (1992), *How U Like Me Now* (1993), *The Last Set* (1994) and *Love Jones* (1997). During the late 90s, El'Zabar was involved with the Traffic inter-arts programme at Chicago's Steppenwolf Theatre. Active in music education, El'Zabar has been associate professor at the University of Nebraska and the University of Illinois. Among many other activities, El'Zabar has served on the boards of the Sun Drummer (an African American drum society), the National Task Force on Arts Presenting in Education, the Chicago Blues Museum and of the National Campaign for Freedom of Expression. He is the author of a book of prose and poetry, *Mis'taken Brilliance*. As is apparent from his many activities, El'Zabar is a significant presence in contemporary African American arts and culture.

● ALBUMS: *Sacred Love* (Sound Aspects 1985) ★★★, *Another Kind Of Groove* (Sound Aspects 1986) ★★★★, *The Ritual* (Sound Aspects 1987) ★★★, with David Murray *Golden Sea* (Sound Aspects 1989) ★★★, *Alika Rising* (Sound Aspects 1990) ★★★, with Ritual Trio *Renaissance Of The Resistance* (Delmark 1994) ★★★, with Ritual Trio *Big Cliff* (Delmark 1995) ★★★, with Ritual Trio *Jitterbug Junction* (CIMP 1997) ★★★★, with Joseph Jarman, 'Kalaparush' Maurice McIntyre, Malachi Favors, Steve Colson *Return Of The Lost Tribe* (Delmark 1997) ★★★,

with Archie Shepp *Conversations* (Delmark 1999) ★★★, with Billy Bang, Hamiet Bluiett *The Power* (CIMP 2000) ★★★, with Murray *One World Family* (CIMP 2000) ★★★, with Ritual Trio, Pharoah Sanders *Africa N'Da Blues* (Delmark 2000) ★★★, with Billy Bang *Spirits Entering* (Delmark 2001) ★★★, with Murray, Fred Hopkins *Love Outside Of Dreams* (Delmark 2002) ★★★★, with Murray *We Is: Live At The Bop Shop* (Delmark 2004) ★★★★.
● FURTHER READING: *Mis'taken Brilliance*, Kahil El'Zabar.
● FILMS: *Mo' Money* (1992), *Love Jones* (1997).

Embarrassment

Though virtually unknown outside of a cult following in the USA, the Embarrassment provided one of the richest sources of guitar pop in the 80s. Formed in Wichita, Kansas, USA, in 1979, the band's patchwork discography militated against more widespread popularity, a problem that subsequent reissues only partially rectified. Comprising John Nichols (vocals/keyboards), Bill Goffrier (vocals/guitar), Brent 'Woody' Giessmann (drums) and Ron Klaus (bass), the band's debut came in 1980 with the single 'Patio Set'/'Sex Drive'. In 1981 they contributed a track to the Sub Pop fanzine (a long time before it became the label **Sub Pop Records**), then recorded the excellent EPs *The Embarrassment* (1981) and *Death Travels West* (1983). Both earned comparisons to the Scottish pop renaissance spearheaded by **Orange Juice** and **Josef K**, but Goffrier's fluent guitar work, in particular, was less brittle and more cutting than those bands. Songs such as 'Elizabeth Montgomery's Face' and 'Don't Choose The Wrong Song' from the debut EP, and the entirety of the second EP, dubbed a 'historical concept album', announced a quite singular talent. Shortly thereafter, however, Goffrier confirmed in a letter to UK fanzine *Blam!* that the band had broken up: 'Technically, the Embarrassment is no more. Effectively, this lifts a lot of pressure from us and three of the four (John is out) will begin work on new ideas and set sights for studio work this summer.'

In the event Goffrier worked with Big Dipper and Giessmann with the **Del Fuegos**, though the Embarrassment did reunite in 1988 to tour and record *God Help Us*, which gave the band's obvious songwriting strengths a better production slate on which to work. The lyrics, however, were still full of wit, and the musicianship accomplished and unhurried. An undoubted influence on **R.E.M.** and 90s US indie bands such as the **Ass Ponys** (who regularly covered their material), the Embarrassment's high profile is entirely deserved.
● ALBUMS: *The Embarrassment* mini-album (Cynykl 1981) ★★★, *Death Travels West* mini-album (Fresh Sounds 1983) ★★★, *God Help Us* (Restless/Bar/None 1990) ★★★★.
● COMPILATIONS: *Retrospective* cassette (Fresh Sounds 1984) ★★★, *The Embarrassment* (Time To Develop 1987) ★★★, *Heyday 1979–83* (Bar/None 1995) ★★★★, *Blister Pop* (MyPalGod 2001) ★★★.

Embrace

Unrelated to the early 80s US hardcore band of the same name, this Embrace is a UK-based quintet of musicians who, although latecomers to the Britpop phenomenon, proved to be one of its most promising post-**Oasis** standard-bearers. Led by brothers Danny (vocals) and Richard McNamara (guitar), the band was founded in Huddersfield, Yorkshire, England, in the late 80s. The story behind the band's inception is similar to that of Oasis, with elder brother Danny taking the reins of his younger brother's Gross Misconduct, a punk band who rehearsed in a shed at the bottom of the McNamaras' parents' garden. A new drummer, Mick Heaton (b. Michael Heaton, Bradford, Yorkshire, England), joined in 1990, with bass player Steve Firth completing the band's initial line-up in 1996. New demo tapes attracted the attention of manager Tony Perrin, who had previously handled the careers of **Pulp**, the **Mission** and **All About Eve**. Their debut single, 'All You Good Good People'/'My Weakness (Is None Of Your Business)', was released in a limited edition of 1,500 copies on the cult independent label Fierce Panda Records in late 1996. It brought rave reviews in the weekly music press and earned sporadic radio play. The result was a race among the major labels for the band's signatures, leading to a contract with the **Virgin Records** subsidiary Hut. By this point, keyboard player Mick Dale (b. Bradford, Yorkshire, England; ex-**Cud**) had been added to the line-up as a permanent member after his impressive work on the band's debut single.

Embrace's debut album for Hut was the *Fireworks EP*, which charted at number 34 in May 1997. It built on the band's good press and confidence in interviews by mining influences as diverse as the articulate soul of **Curtis Mayfield**, as well as more conventional guitar rock sources. Danny McNamara explained his band's brash approach to the press: 'It's not arrogance, it's confidence. If you don't believe in yourself, in a contest with hundreds of others, you've already shot yourself in the foot.' As evidence of this, he pointed out that three years previously he had insisted on a hiatus in the band's activities because they 'weren't ready'. This may also have been influenced by the fact that a *Melody Maker* reviewer in 1993 described their appearance at the Heineken Music Festival as akin to 'U2's Live Aid performance minus the laughs.' The band's second EP for Hut, *One Big Family*, charted at number 21 and their debut single, 'All You Good Good People', reached number 8 when it was re-released in October 1997. The band's series of excellent releases continued with the emphatic but beautiful 'Come Back To What You Know', which reached number 6 in June 1998. Their debut album was released the same month. Despite entering the UK charts at number 1, the album was regarded by many as an anticlimax in view of the previous hype surrounding the band. A reissued 'My Weakness (Is None Of Your Business)' also broke into the Top 10.

Embrace returned in late 1999 with the *Hooligan* EP, a collection of roots-orientated material that indicated they had been listening closely to the work of UK media darlings **Gomez**. This direction was continued on the attendant *Drawn From Memory*, which drew mixed reviews from a music press that had fallen out of love with any band associated with the Britpop scene. Embrace's third album *If You've Never Been*, released to little fanfare in 2001, updated the musical style established on the band's previous recordings but failed to draw in any new fans. The following year's compilation set *Fireworks* neatly covered their time on a major label.

Following the release of *Fireworks* and the termination of their recording contract, most of the band members were forced to return to paid employment. They made a notable live comeback at the 2004 V Festival and signed a new contract for the release of their fourth studio album. *Out Of Nothing* was neatly timed to coincide with the resurgence of melodic guitar pop bands (notably **Coldplay** and **Keane**) on the UK music scene. Coldplay's Chris Martin wrote the track 'Gravity', which returned Embrace to the UK Top 10 in September. The album went on to sell over half a million copies, easily eclipsing the combined sales of the band's first three albums.

● ALBUMS: *The Good Will Out* (Hut 1998) ★★★★★, *Drawn From Memory* (Hut 2000) ★★★, *If You've Never Been* (Hut 2001) ★★, *Out Of Nothing* (Independiente 2004) ★★★, *This New Day* (Independiente 2006) ★★★.
● COMPILATIONS: *Fireworks (Singles 1997–2002)* (Hut 2002) ★★★★, *Dry Kids (B-Sides 1997—2005)* (Hut 2005) ★★★.
● DVD/VIDEOS: *A Glorious Day: Live In Leeds* (Eagle Vision 2005).

Embry, 'Queen' Sylvia

b. 14 June 1941, Wabbaseka, Arkansas, USA, d. February 1992. Embry began playing piano as a child and sang in church choirs, moving to Memphis at the age of 19. In the 60s she settled in Chicago, where she met and married blues guitarist Johnny Embry, who taught her to play bass guitar. In the 70s she worked for several years with **Lefty Dizz** and she can be seen playing bass and singing one song with his band in the film *Mississippi Delta Blues*. She shared the credit with her husband on an album for Razor Records, was part of **Alligator Records**' *Living Chicago Blues* project and had an album released under the name Blues Queen Sylvia on the German L&R label. A strong singer and fine bass player, *Living Blues* magazine reported in 1985 that she had turned her back on blues and was playing gospel music.

● ALBUMS: Johnny And Sylvia Embry *After Work* (Razor 1980) ★★★, four titles only *Living Chicago Blues Volume Six* (Alligator 1980) ★★★, as Blues Queen Sylvia *Midnight Baby* (L&R 1983) ★★★.

Embryo

A German group founded in 1969, Embryo have been among Europe's greatest pioneers of world music in a career that has matched longevity with innovation. Based in Munich, they were originally considered part of what has been jingoistically called 'Kraut Rock', employing a variety of improvised jazz techniques as well as studio sound effects. Their immersion into world music was precipitated by an invitation from the German Embassy to tour North Africa. However, they were detained at the Morocco border crossing by a customs official who insisted that they would not be allowed entry if they did not cut their hair (the German ambassador had to intervene, and at first suggested a compromise—could not the band just cut their hair a *little* bit?). The different tonal scales employed by Moroccan musicians fascinated the group, and encouraged them to explore different world musics further, resulting in a nine-month sojourn in India. A two-week engagement as the musical accompaniment to an Afghanistan circus followed before their bus broke down in Tehran in the middle of a civil war. Their visit to Asia was later released as a double album and documentary. Back in Munich, their status as Germany's pre-eminent world music ambassadors attracted visitors such as **Mal Waldron**, **Charlie Mariano**, **Trilok Gurtu** and Rabi Abou-Khalil to their regular informal music sessions. The band that would become **Dissident** also visited

their house regularly. The permanent members of Embryo, Christian Buchard (vibraphone, hammer dulcimer, percussion, marimba), former leader of **Amon Düül II** Chris Karrer (oud/Arabic violin) and Dieter Serfas (drums/percussion; also a former member of Amon Düül II) refreshed their direct knowledge of and skills in foreign musics by travelling abroad regularly. In 1994, to celebrate the group's 25th anniversary, they released *Ibn Battuta*, a three-year project taking its title from the name of a medieval Moroccan philosopher.

● ALBUMS: *Steig Aus* (Brain 1972) ★★★, *Ibn Battuta* (1994) ★★★.

Emergency

German hard rock group Emergency originally comprised Englishman Pete Lovell on vocals plus Frans Limonard (guitar), Jos Anthonissen (bass), Hedwig Spijkers (drums) and Coen Van Hoof (keyboards). Both Anthonissen and Limonard had previously been part of Rancid (not the 90s Californian punk band) while Lovell was a former contributor to **Picture**. Achieving some momentum in mainland Europe with their expansive stage shows, the group signed to Ariola Records in 1989. Their debut, *Martial Law*, was a competent collection that failed adequately to translate their live popularity into the studio. After its release, Spijkers was replaced by former Highway Chile drummer Ernst Van Ee.

● ALBUMS: *Martial Law* (Ariola 1989) ★★.

Emerson Drive

Country pop outfit formed in Grande Prairie, Alberta, Canada, by school friends Brad Mates (b. Bradley Mates, 21 July 1978, Grande Prairie, Alberta, Canada; vocals/guitar), Pat Allingham (b. 9 July 1978, Ill-A-La-Cross, Saskatchewan, Canada; fiddle), and Chris Hartman (b. 2 January 1978, Grand Prairie, Alberta, Canada; keyboards). Originally called 12 Gauge, the trio added Jeff Loberg (bass) to the line-up and earned their musical spurs by touring Canada and recording two self-released albums. Along the way Danick Dupelle (b. 29 September 1973, Notre-Dame Perrot, Quebec, Canada; guitar/vocals) and Mike Melancon (b. Michel Melancon, 13 August 1978, Lac Des Ecurces, Quebec, Canada; drums) were added to the line-up and the band's name was changed to Emerson Drive. The sextet's hard work eventually paid off when they landed a recording contract with DreamWorks Records in 2001. Their self-titled debut album was a collection of inoffensive country pop material that garnered the band plenty of attention on country radio. 'I Should Be Sleeping' and 'Fall Into Me' broke into the country Top 5, with the latter also reaching the pop Top 40. A string of personnel changes then ensued, with Loberg leaving in August 2002, Hartman in March 2003 and Allingham in June 2003. The trio's replacements were David Pichette (b. 23 July 1977, Montreal, Quebec, Canada; fiddle), Patrick Bourque (b. 27 September 1977, Terrebone, Quebec, Canada; bass) and Dale Wallace (b. 1 November 1969, Vancouver, British Columbia, Canada; keyboards/vocals). The new look sextet teamed up with former chart artist **Richard Marx** for their follow-up *What If?*, which strayed even further into AOR pop territory than its predecessor.

● ALBUMS: *Emerson Drive* (DreamWorks 2002) ★★★, *What If?* (DreamWorks 2004) ★★★.

Emerson, Lake And Palmer

One the most prominent supergroups of the early 70s, ELP comprised **Keith Emerson** (b. 2 November 1944, Todmorden, Lancashire, England; keyboards), **Greg Lake** (b. 10 November 1948, Bournemouth, Dorset, England; vocals/bass) and Carl Palmer (b. Carl Frederick Kendall Palmer, 20 March 1950, Birmingham, West Midlands, England; drums/percussion). Formerly, the super-trio were, respectively, members of the **Nice**, **King Crimson** and **Atomic Rooster**. After making their debut at the Guildhall, Plymouth, they appeared at the much-publicized 1970 Isle of Wight Festival. That same year, they were signed to **Island Records** and completed their self-titled debut album. The work displayed their desire to fuse classical music influences with rock in determinedly flourishing style. Early the following year, at Newcastle's City Hall they introduced their arrangement of Mussorgsky's *Pictures At An Exhibition*. The concept album *Tarkus* followed some months later and revealed their overreaching love of musical drama to the full. The theme of the work was obscure but the mechanical armadillo, pictured on the sleeve, proved a powerful and endearing image.

Extensive tours and albums followed over the next three years including *Trilogy*, **Brain Salad Surgery** and an extravagant triple live album. Having set up their own label and established themselves as a top-grossing live act, the members branched out into various solo ventures, reuniting for part of *Works*. This double album included their memorably dramatic reading of Aaron Copland's 'Fanfare For The Common Man', which took them close to the top of the British singles charts. With solo outings becoming increasingly distracting, ELP released one final studio album, 1978's *Love Beach*, before embarking on a farewell world tour. With changes in the music industry wrought by punk and new wave bands, it was probably an opportune moment to draw a veil over their career.

It was not until 1986 that a serious re-formation was attempted but Carl Palmer (then in the highly successful **Asia**) would not be drawn. Instead, Emerson and Lake teamed up with hit drummer **Cozy Powell** (b. Colin Flooks, 29 December 1947, Cirencester, Gloucestershire, England, d. 5 April 1998, Bristol, England). The collaboration produced one chart album *Emerson, Lake And Powell*, which included the pomp of Holst among the many classical influences. When Powell quit, Palmer regrouped with his colleagues for a projected album in 1987, but the sessions proved unfruitful. Instead, Emerson recruited Hush drummer Robert Berry for *To The Power Of Three*, which sold poorly. In the early 90s the original trio re-formed and produced *Black Moon*, followed by another live album. Whilet their concert tour was well attended, no new ground was being broken and a new studio album, 1994's *In The Hot Seat*, proved to be a pale shadow of their former material. Nevertheless, the trio has continued to tour when solo commitments allow and remain a hugely popular live attraction.

● ALBUMS: *Emerson, Lake & Palmer* (Island/Cotillion 1970) ★★★, *Tarkus* (Island/Cotillion 1971) ★★★, *Pictures At An Exhibition* (Island/Cotillion 1971) ★★★★, *Trilogy* (Island/Cotillion 1972) ★★★, *Brain Salad Surgery* (Manticore 1973) ★★★, *Welcome Back, My Friends, To The Show That Never Ends: Ladies And Gentlemen . . . Emerson Lake & Palmer* (Manticore 1974) ★★, *Works: Volume 1* (Atlantic 1977) ★★, *Works: Volume 2* (Atlantic 1977) ★★, *Love Beach* (Atlantic 1978) ★★, *Emerson, Lake & Palmer In Concert* (Atlantic 1979) ★★, as Emerson, Lake And Powell *Emerson, Lake & Powell* (Polydor 1986) ★★, *Black Moon* (Victory 1992) ★★, *Live At The Royal Albert Hall* (Victory 1993) ★★, *Works Live* 1977 recording (Victory 1993) ★★, *In The Hot Seat* (Victory 1994) ★★, *King Biscuit Flower Hour* (King Biscuit Flower Hour 1997) ★★, *Live At The Isle Of Wight Festival 1970* (Castle 2002) ★★, *Live In Poland* 1997 recording (Castle 2002) ★★★, *Fanfare: 1997 World Tour* (Delta 2003) ★★, *Greatest Hits Live* (King Biscuit Flower Hour 2003) ★★★.

● COMPILATIONS: *The Best Of Emerson, Lake & Palmer* (Atlantic 1980) ★★★, *The Atlantic Years* (Atlantic 1992) ★★★★, *The Return Of The Manticore* 4-CD box set (Victory 1993) ★★★★, *Then & Now* (Eagle 1998) ★★, *Extended Versions: The Encore Collection* (BMG 2000) ★★, *Fanfare For The Common Man: The Anthology* (Sanctuary 2001) ★★★★, *The Very Best Of Emerson, Lake & Palmer* (Rhino 2001) ★★★★, *The Original Bootleg Series From The Manticore Vaults Vol. One* 7-CD box set (Castle 2001) ★★★, *The Original Bootleg Series From The Manticore Vaults Vol. Two* 8-CD box set (Castle 2001) ★★★, *The Original Bootleg Series From The Manticore Vaults Vol. Three* 5-CD box set (Castle 2002) ★★★★, *An Introduction To* (Sanctuary 2004) ★★★, *The Ultimate Collection* (Sanctuary 2004) ★★★★.

● DVD/VIDEOS: *Pictures At An Exhibition* (Hendring Music Video 1990), *Live At Montreux 1997* (Eagle Vision 2004). *Inside Emerson, Lake & Palmer 1970–1995: An Independent Critical Review* (Classic Rock 2004), *Beyond The Beginning* (Sanctuary Visual Entertainment 2005).

● FURTHER READING: *Emerson, Lake And Palmer: The Show That Never Ends, A Musical Biography*, George Forrester, Martyn Hanson and Frank Askew.

Emerson, Bill

b. William Hundley Emerson, 22 January 1938, Washington, DC, USA. Emerson first played guitar at the age of 17 but a year later, he adopted the banjo as his main instrument. In 1957, he played with **Buzz Busby** And The Bayou Boys, before he and Charlie Waller formed the **Country Gentlemen**, with whom he played until late in 1958. After spells with the **Stoneman Family** and **Bill Harrell**, he joined **Jimmy Martin**'s Sunny Mountain Boys. In 1964, he briefly played with **Red Allen**, during which time he also recorded albums as Bill Emerson And The Virginia Mountaineers, before rejoining Martin in 1965. In 1967/8, Emerson and Cliff Waldron led the Lee Highway Boys, who were later renamed New Shades Of Grass. In 1970, he replaced **Eddie Adcock** in the Country Gentlemen and recorded several successful albums with the group. In 1972, as the group were leaving a venue, shots were fired at them from a passing car and Emerson was wounded in the arm. In 1973, he joined the US Navy Band and, based in Washington, DC, mainly played guitar, although he formed a bluegrass band, the Country Current, as an offshoot from his normal service commitments. During his service career, he still managed to play on various albums, including Webco's *Shenandoah Grass—Yesterday And Today* with **Jim Eanes**, and to record two duet albums with Pete Goble for the label. In 1992, he recorded with some of the vocalists with whom he had worked, including Charlie Waller and Jimmy Martin, on his noted *Reunion*. He completed his naval service in 1993 and continues to play at reunion concerts and at special festivals, but seemingly has tired of the strain and stress of travelling.

● ALBUMS: with Jimmy Martin *This World Is Not My Home* (Decca 1963) ★★★, *Good 'n' Country* (Decca 1966) ★★★, *Big & Country Instrumentals* (Decca 1967) ★★; as Bill Emerson And His Virginia Mountaineers *Banjo Pickin' And Hot Fiddlin'* (Coronet 1963) ★★★★, *Banjo Pickin' And Hot Fiddlin' Volume 2* (Coronet 1964) ★★★, *Country Banjo* (Design 1969) ★★★, *Pickin' And Fiddlin'* (Mount Vernon 1970) ★★★★; as Emerson And Waldron And Lee Highway Boys *New Shades Of Bluegrass* (Rebel 1969) ★★★★, *Bluegrass Country* (Rebel 1970) ★★★, *Invite You To A Bluegrass Session* (Rebel 1970) ★★★; with the Country Gentlemen *One Wide River To Cross* (Rebel 1971) ★★★, *Country Gentlemen Sound Off* (Rebel 1971) ★★★, *The Award Winning Country Gentlemen* (Rebel 1972) ★★★, *The Country Gentlemen* (Vanguard 1973) ★★★; with Pete Goble *Tennessee 1949* (Webco 1987) ★★★, with Pete Goble *Home Of The Red Fox* (Rebel 1987) ★★★, *Dixie In My Eye* (Webco 1989) ★★, *Gold Plated Banjo* (Rebel 1990) ★★★, *Reunion* (Webco 1992) ★★★★.

● COMPILATIONS: *Little Healthy Thing* (Charly 1980) ★★.

Emerson, Billy 'The Kid'

b. William Robert Emerson, 21 December 1929, Tarpon Springs, Florida, USA. Emerson's father was a blues singer and the young Emerson played piano with the Billy Battle Band and other local groups before serving in the forces in 1952–54. On his return, he joined **Ike Turner**'s band in Memphis. Here, Emerson made his first records for **Sun Records**, which displayed his talent for wordplay and included 'No Teasing Around', the jive-talking 'The Wood-chuck', 'Little Fine Healthy Thing' and 'Red Hot', a song later taken up by rockabilly singer **Billy Lee Riley** and by **Bob Luman**. Emerson moved to Chicago soon afterwards, playing piano or organ on numerous recording sessions and releasing singles under his own name from 1955–57 for **Vee Jay Records** ('Every Woman I Know (Crazy 'Bout Auto-mobiles)', later revived by **Ry Cooder**) and from 1958–59 for **Chess Records** ('I'll Get You Too'). There were later records for Mad (1960), M-Pac! (the dance craze song 'The Whip', 1963) and USA (1963) before Emerson formed his own Tarpon label in the mid-60s. Among his Tarpon singles was 'I Dig The Funky Broadway'. Emerson later moved onto the lounge circuit with a jazz-orientated trio.

● COMPILATIONS: *Little Fine Healthy Thing* (Charly 1980) ★★★, *Crazy 'Bout Automobiles* 10-inch album (Charly 1982) ★★★, *Move, Baby, Move* (Charly 2004) ★★★★.

Emerson, Darren

b. 30 June 1971, Romford, Essex, England. Coming to prominence in the mid-90s dance scene as a member of **Underworld** and Lemon Interrupt, Emerson is a very active and highly visible DJ. He became a fan of **electro** as a 14-year-old, at which time he also bought his first decks. He was in place for the rise of **acid house**, spinning at clubs in Southend, Essex, England, before emerging as a real talent at venues including the Limelight and Milky Bar. Stylistically his modern tastes favour **trance** and European **hard house**. His remixes include **Simply Red**'s 'Thrill Me', Gat Décor's 'Passion', **Björk**'s 'Human Behaviour' and **Shakespear's Sis-ter**'s 'Hey You (Turn Up Your Radio)' and 'Black Sky'. He

also set up his own Underwater Records label in the late 90s, concentrating on techno and trance releases. Emerson left Underworld in mid-2000 to concentrate on his DJing career.

● COMPILATIONS: with Alex Paterson *Textures* (Volume 1996) ★★★, *Mixmag Live! Vol. 13* (DMC 1996) ★★★, *Cream Separates 01* (Deconstruction 1997) ★★★, *Global Underground 015—Uruguay* (Boxed 2000) ★★★, *Global Underground 020—Singapore* (Boxed 2001) ★★★, with Dirk Dreyer *Summer Love 2001* (Time Unlimited 2001) ★★★, with Tim Deluxe *Underwater Episode I* (Under-water/Thrive 2002) ★★★, with Mutiny *Underwater Episode II* (Underwater 2003) ★★★, with Paul Jackson *Underwater Episode III* (Underwater 2004) ★★★★, with Sharam Jey *Underwater Episode 04* (Underwater 2005) ★★★.

Emerson, Keith

b. 2 November 1944, Todmorden, Lancashire, England. Organist Emerson was briefly associated with several British club R&B attractions prior to joining soul singer **P.P. Arnold**'s backing band in 1967. Known as the **Nice**, this unit later embarked on an independent career and quickly established itself as a leading progressive rock act. Emerson's keyboard dexterity and showmanship—he used knives to sustain notes during lengthy improvisations—was undoubtedly the band's focal point, a feature continued on his subsequent venture, the 'supergroup' **Emerson, Lake And Palmer**. Although deemed pretentious by critics, the trio became highly successful and maintained a rigorous recording schedule throughout the early 70s. Emerson's solo single 'Honky Tonk Train Blues', recorded during a hiatus in the parent group's career, reached the UK Top 30 in 1976, but the artist did not pursue such ambitions full-time until ELP was dissolved in 1980. The artist scored Italian horror director Dario Argento's *The Inferno* and *Murderock*, and completed a series of musicianly collections, but this facet of his work conflicted with other projects, notably Emerson, Lake And Powell and 3, with Carl Palmer and Robert Berry. In 1992, Emerson, Lake And Palmer re-formed to record an album and tour once again. Ten years later, Emerson reunited with his colleagues from the Nice for some live dates.

Emerson has unfairly been judged by the trappings of his career and of some misguided musical forays. What is not in dispute is his prowess as a master of the keyboard, and he is one of the finest musicians of the rock era.

● ALBUMS: *The Inferno* film soundtrack (Atlantic 1980) ★★, *Nighthawks* film soundtrack (MCA 1981) ★★, *Honky* film soundtrack (Chord 1985) ★★, *Murderock* film sound-track (Chord 1986) ★★, *Best Revenge* film soundtrack (Chord 1986) ★★, *Harmageddon/ China Free Fall* (Chord 1987) ★★, *The Christmas Album* (Priority 1988) ★★, *Emerson Plays Emerson* (EMI Classics 2002) ★★★.

● COMPILATIONS: *The Emerson Collection* (Chord 1986) ★★, *Hammer It Out: The Anthology* (Sanctuary 2005) ★★★, *At The Movies* 3-CD box set (Sanctuary 2005) ★★★.

● FURTHER READING: *Pictures Of An Exhibitionist*, Keith Emerson.

Emery

US melodic hardcore band formed in 2001 by Toby Morelle (vocals/guitar), Matt Carter (guitar, keyboards, vocals), Devin Shelton (guitar/vocals), Josh Head (keyboards), Joel Green (bass) and Seth Studley (drums). The six members first met while studying in South Carolina and after completing their education opted to make music a full-time career. After forming Emery they relocated to Seattle and quickly established a foothold on the city's live circuit. Their highly commercial fusion of emocore and melodic alt pop attracted the attention of the Seattle independent Tooth & Nail label, which teamed the band up with producer Ed Rose to work on their debut album. Released at the start of 2004, *The Weak's End* proved to be something of a sleeper hit, with critical acclaim and the band's non-stop touring schedule helping boost sales over the 50,000 mark by the end of the year. The band's follow-up, *The Question*, was recorded with new drummer Dave Powell. The album confirmed Emery's critical and commercial potential, breaking into the mainstream charts shortly after its release in August 2005.

● ALBUMS: *The Weak's End* (Tooth & Nail 2004) ★★★, *The Question* (Tooth & Nail 2005) ★★★★.

Emery, James

b. 1951, Youngstown, Ohio, USA. In New York in the late 70s, guitarist Emery formed a duo with bass player **John Lindberg**. When **Billy Bang** sat in one evening they so enjoyed the new instrumental format that they decided to add a violinist on a regular basis, thus forming the **String Trio Of New York**. Following the departure of Bang in 1986 Emery and Lindberg were joined by, successively, Charles Burnham, **Regina Carter** and Diane Monroe. Emery has also worked with **Anthony Braxton**, **Henry Threadgill**, **Leroy Jenkins** and **Leo Smith**. Most often, Emery plays acoustic guitar without amplification and thus imbues the intricately shaped and wholly contemporary lines he plays with a traditional ambience. A skilled composer of modern jazz, an early influence of Emery's was **Charlie 'Bird' Parker** and there is in all of his work a sophisticated understanding of the essence of Parker.

● ALBUMS: *Artlife* (Lumina 1983) ★★★, *Exo Eso* (FMP 1987) ★★★★, with the Iliad Quartet *Turbulence* (Knitting Factory Works 1991) ★★★, *Standing On A Whale Fishing For Minnows* (Enja 1996) ★★★★, *Spectral Domains* (Enja 1997) ★★★, *Luminous Cycles* (Between The Lines 2001) ★★★, *Fourth World* (Between The Lines 2002) ★★, *Transformations* (Between The Lines 2003) ★★★.

Emery, Ralph

b. Walter Ralph Emery, 10 March 1933, McEwen, Tennessee, USA. Emery became one of America's most recognizable television celebrities owing to the 11 years that he spent as the host of the networked *Nashville Now* chat show. However, he had been involved with country music for many years before 1982, when he first appeared on that show. When aged four, he went to live with his grandparents, owing to his mother's breakdown caused seemingly by his alcoholic father. He grew up a shy boy, preferring to be alone, and found his greatest happiness in listening to the radio, especially the **Grand Ole Opry** broadcasts. He first worked as a cinema usher but eventually attended a special academy to learn broadcasting techniques. His first work was as a disc jockey at WTPR Paris, Tennessee, before moving to Nashville. He worked briefly at WMAK, prior to moving to WSM, where he presented an all-night show. Emery quickly established his programme by encouraging local artists to appear live and listeners to phone in. His show could be heard across almost 40 states and it ran for 15 years. In 1961, he achieved success

as a recording artist when his **Liberty Records** recording of 'Hello Fool' (an answer song to **Faron Young**'s hit 'Hello Walls') reached number 4 in the US country charts. Between 1966 and 1969, Emery also presented an afternoon show called *Sixteenth Avenue*. When he had the **Byrds** on his radio show in 1968, he denounced them as hippies and in-between denouncing them and playing their records, he read out truck commercials. As a result of this the Byrds developed 'Drug Store Truck Driving Man', with the line 'this one's for you Ralph', and further suggestions in the song of involvement in the Ku Klux Klan. The song appeared on their pioneering country rock album **Sweetheart Of The Rodeo** in 1968. In 1972, he relinquished his all-night show to move to television, although he began a weekly country music radio show he called *Take Five For Country Music*. His *Ralph Emery Show* soon established him as a major television host and led to his subsequent hosting of the *Nashville Now* show. Other programmes that he presented included *Pop Goes Country* (a syndicated programme, 1974–80) and *Nashville Alive* (a live country music series on WTBS television, 1981–82). At times, he added a comedy touch in his television programmes with the use of a hand puppet that he called Shotgun Red. Over the years, he has collected numerous awards, including in 1988, one by SESAC as Ambassador Of Country Music, and has made appearances in four country music films, *Country Music On Broadway* (1964), *The Road To Nashville* (1966), *Nashville* (1975) and *The Girl From Tobacco Row*. In 1990, his popularity with country music artists for his services to their music saw 70 of them appear in a television special, *Salute To Ralph Emery*. He left his early morning television programme in 1991 and worked with writer Tom Clark in producing his autobiography. This proved so popular that a follow-up volume appeared in 1993. Between 1960 and 1964, he was married to country singer **Skeeter Davis** but the marriage ended in acrimony. This was later reactivated by comments made by Emery in his books and also by Davis in her autobiography *Bus Fare To Kentucky*.

● ALBUMS: with Shotgun Red *Songs For Children* (RCA 1989) ★★, *Christmas With Ralph & Red* (RCA 1989) ★★.

● FURTHER READING: *Memories (The Autobiography Of Ralph Emery)*, Ralph Emery with Tom Carter. *More Memories*, Ralph Emery with Tom Clark. *The View From Nashville: On The Record With Country Music's Greatest Stars*, Ralph Emery. *50 Years Down A Country Road*, Ralph Emery with Patsi Bale Cox.

EMF

Formed in the Forest of Dean, Gloucestershire, England, in 1989 by James Atkin (b. 28 March 1969, Cinderford, Gloucestershire, England; vocals), Ian Dench (b. 7 August 1964, Cheltenham, Gloucestershire, England; guitar/keyboards), Derry Brownson (b. 10 November 1970, Gloucester, England; keyboards/samples), Zac Foley (b. Zachary Foley, 9 December 1970, Gloucester, England, d. 3 January 2002, London, England; bass), Mark Decloedt (b. 26 June 1969, Gloucester, England; drums) and Milf (DJ). All had previously been in local indie bands, with Dench in Apple Mosaic and Foley in the IUC's. The band claimed that EMF stood for Epsom Mad Funkers or, more controversially, and more attractive to the gutter press, Ecstasy Mother Fuckers. **Parlophone Records** countered that it stood for Every Mother's Favourites, which is hard to believe, given the band's notorious touring antics. Their record company signed them after just four gigs and without the advance warning of a demo. However, their opportunism was rewarded when the debut single 'Unbelievable' became a Top 5 UK hit. The follow-up, 'I Believe', was criticized in many quarters for being a straight rewrite, while many were also suggesting that the band had stolen **Jesus Jones**' pop/sample thunder. However, their ability to win over the teen-pop market was proved by debut album sales of over two million.

Together with the aforementioned Jesus Jones, the band proved particularly successful in breaking into the USA, where they were bracketed as part of a new 'British Invasion'. The band ran into some trouble with **Yoko Ono** over 'Lies', where a sample of the voice of **John Lennon**'s killer Mark Chapman reciting Lennon's lyric for 'Watching The Wheels' from his prison cell resulted in an out of court settlement of $15,000 and a retraction of the offending voice from subsequent pressings. Other samples proved less controversial, and included Radio 3 announcers and Kermit The Frog. *Stigma* disappointed, with sales less than one-fifth of the debut, a fact blamed by chief songwriter Dench on an over-demanding schedule and tabloid controversy: 'It was a self-conscious record and deliberately anti-commercial. At least we got everything out of our system.' Their label encouraged the band to spend their time getting new material right, leading to a three-year gap between 1992's *Unexplained* EP and 1995's *Cha Cha Cha*. Band suggestions for producer included **Jim Foetus** and **Butch Vig**, but these were eventually rejected in favour of Johnny Dollar, who had previously worked with **Youssou N'Dour** and **Neneh Cherry**. Dollar, however, walked out of the sessions, and the resulting album failed to sell. The band did return to the charts when they teamed up with comedians **Vic Reeves** and Bob Mortimer on a cover of the **Monkees**' 'I'm A Believer', but having been dropped by Parlophone they decided to split up. Brownson and Atkin both went on to play with **Bentley Rhythm Ace** before forming LK and Cooler respectively. Foley toured with Carrie, Dench recorded with acoustic outfit Whistler, and Milf released singles as Jose Sanchez for **Skint Records**. The unit re-formed for some gigs in 2001, but the following January Foley died after collapsing in Camden, London. Substantial traces of heroin, cocaine and ecstasy were found in his body.

● ALBUMS: *Schubert Dip* (Parlophone 1991) ★★★★, *Stigma* (Parlophone 1992) ★★, *Cha Cha Cha* (Parlophone 1995) ★★★.

● COMPILATIONS: *The Best Of EMF: Epsom Mad Funkers* (Parlophone 2001) ★★★★.

EMI Records

The present-day EMI company can trace its origins to 1897 when William Barry Owen sailed from New York to London to set up a European company to market Emile Berliner's gramophone. Another American, Fred Gaisberg, was in charge of recording, travelling throughout Europe and Asia making wax discs of local artists. Manufacturing was centred on Hannover in Germany before the UK factory at Hayes, west London, was opened in 1908. By 1910 the company had adopted the His Master's Voice name and logo (the famous 'dog and trumpet' painting) and during the 20s it absorbed the French Pathé label and the Lindstrom company, (which owned the **Parlophone Records** label) as well as other

branches across Latin America. In 1931, the effects of the Depression brought about a merger between the Gramophone Co. and its main European rival, Columbia (no relation to the US company), which was stronger in popular repertoire. The new Electrical & Musical Industries (EMI) company dominated the European market and operated an unofficial global cartel in conjunction with **RCA-Victor Records**. Lack of competition made EMI unreceptive to new ideas and it lost ground to rivals such as **Decca Records** and **CBS Records** by delaying its adoption of the 45 rpm single until 1952, four years after its invention. But EMI's fortunes improved when Joseph Lockwood (later knighted for his services) took over as managing director in 1954. Recognizing the importance of the US repertoire, he bought **Capitol Records** and revolutionized the distribution of records and tapes in the UK.

Much of the company's phenomenal success in the 60s was owing to one act: the **Beatles**. However, EMI made the mistake of diversifying into medical electronics and the leisure industries in the 70s. Similarly at the record company, a succession of senior executives could not provide a consistent strategy, although **Queen**, **Cockney Rebel** and **Cliff Richard** provided pop hits. However, the lack of priority given to music in EMI was epitomized by Lockwood's decision to drop the **Sex Pistols** because of adverse publicity in 1976. Losses from its newer ventures led to EMI's takeover by Thorn in 1979. The new owners' apparent lack of understanding of the music business led to constant rumours that EMI Records was for sale. These rumours were not dispelled until the appointment of another American, Jim Fifield, to run the music division in 1988. EMI had bought the Liberty/United Artists/Blue Note group in 1980, but Fifield embarked on a highly ambitious programme of acquisitions. He bought SBK Songs to make EMI the world's largest music publisher and also purchased the **Chrysalis Records**, IRS and Roulette labels. There were major hits from **MC Hammer**, **Wilson Phillips**, **Bonnie Raitt** and **Garth Brooks**, while in the UK, EMI entered the independent-pop scene through an agreement with the Food label, whose artists included **Jesus Jones** and **Blur**. By the early 90s, EMI was claiming a 12 per cent share of the world music market, and in March 1992 this dramatically increased with the purchase of **Richard Branson**'s **Virgin Records** for £510 million, adding, among others, the **Rolling Stones**, **Phil Collins** and **U2** to its roster. CEO Rupert Perry built up a healthy roster of international acts including **Pink Floyd**, **Thunder**, **Diana Ross** and **Kate Bush**. Current chairman Sir Colin Southgate recorded their highest profits in 1995/6 with multi-million-sellers such as the Beatles' *Anthology* and Queen's *Made In Heaven*. In August 1996, EMI de-merged from Thorn and became EMI plc. Some excellent reissues were made during its centenary celebrations in 1997, but the following year the company suffered an unsettling slump in sales and rejected the American giant Seagram's takeover offer. Seagram subsequently acquired **PolyGram Records**, the world's largest music company and EMI's biggest rival. In January 2000, EMI shocked the music industry by announcing that they were to merge with Warner Music in a joint venture to be called Warner EMI Music. The merger eventually came to nothing and EMI shares dropped. Following the departure of Richard Perry the company is now headed up by Tony Wadsworth, a highly respected 'music' person, who did much to bolster the fortunes of Parlophone Records when he was head of A&R there.

Emile Ford And The Checkmates
(see **Ford, Emile, And The Checkmates**)

Emilia
b. Emilia Rydberg, 5 January 1978, Sweden. A Europop singer described by her label manager as 'a nice, clean-cut girl', Emilia has enjoyed multi-platinum success in her native Scandinavia with her innocent brand of wide-eyed, bubble-gum pop. She is signed to Universal affiliate label Rodeo Records, run by Lars Anderson, the son of **Abba**'s **Stig Anderson**. He discovered Emilia, a classical music graduate of the Adolf Frederiks music school in Stockholm, when a member of her former R&B/funk group Ahunda People brought him their demo tape in 1996. He liked the voice, but thought the music was inappropriate for her. The title track of her debut album was released in September 1998 and in less than two weeks achieved platinum sales, staying on top of the Swedish charts for seven weeks. It also proved hugely successful in Norway, Denmark, Austria, England (number 5 in December) and the Low Countries. Emilia, who was studying economics, decided to leave her university course in order to capitalize on her breakthrough.
- ALBUMS: *Big Big World* (Universal 1998) ★★★.

Emilio
b Emilio Navaira, 23 August 1962, San Antonio, Texas, USA. Having established his name as a Tejano performer, Navaira dropped his surname in the mid-90s in an attempt to concentrate on a career in country music. His existing wide commercial exposure—he had been featured in advertisements for Coca-Cola, Wrangler and Stetson hats—lent itself naturally to the transition. As he told **Billboard** magazine in 1995, 'Country and Tejano are the same style, if you think about it. A good Tejano polka has a country music beat in it, so it's pretty much the same, and Latin music is involved with the girl leaving the guy, just like country.' His **Capitol Records** debut, *Life Is Good*, was his first record to feature English-language lyrics, written for him by a team of Nashville writers, whereas his Latin material is largely the province of his brother Raul. The album also included two Spanish-language 'bonus tracks'—a version of **Van Morrison**'s 'Have I Told You Lately' and a return to his first ever single, 'It's Not The End Of The World'. In 1994 he won Tejano Music awards for Best Male Vocalist, Male Entertainer, Best Show Band and Best Conjunto. In 2003, *Acuérdate* won a Grammy for Best Tejano Album.
- ALBUMS: *Emilio Y Rio* (Cara/CBS 1989) ★★★, *Sensaciones* (Cara/CBS 1990) ★★★, *Shoot It* (EMI Latin 1991) ★★★, *Unsung Highways* (EMI Latin 1991) ★★★, *Emilio Live* (EMI Latin 1992) ★★, *Shuffle Time* (EMI Latin 1992) ★★★, *Southern Exposure* (EMI Latin 1993) ★★★, *17 Super Exitos* (EMI Latin 1993) ★★★, *Soundlife* (EMI Latin 1994) ★★★, *Life Is Good* (Capitol Nashville 1995) ★★, *It's On The House* (Capitol Nashville 1997) ★★, *Quedate* (EMI Latin 1996) ★★★, *A Mi Gente* (EMI Latin 1997) ★★★, *12 Super Exitos* (EMI Latin 1997) ★★★, with Ram Herrera *Mano A Mano* (EMI Latin 1998) ★★★, *10 Aniversario* (EMI Latin 1999) ★★★, *El Rey Del Rodeo* (BMG 2000) ★★★, *Esto Es Lo Nuestro: 20 Exitos* (EMI Latin 2001) ★★★, *Acuérdate* (RCA International 2002) ★★★★, *Latin Classics* (EMI Latin 2002) ★★★, *Entre Amigos* (Song/BMG 2003) ★★★, *15 Canciones Favoritas* (BMG US Latin 2003)

★★★, *30 Exiros Insuperable* (EMI Latin 2003) ★★★, *La Historia* 2-CD set (EMI Latin 2004) ★★★.
- COMPILATIONS: *The Best Of Emilio Navaira: Ultimate Collection* (Song/BMG 2004) ★★★.
- DVD/VIDEOS: *La Historia* (EMI 2004).

Emilio, Frank
b. Francisco Emilio Flynn, 13 April 1921, Havana, Cuba, d. 23 August 2001, Havana, Cuba. His father, an American of Irish descent, and his mother, a Cuban, met in the USA and settled in Havana. Emilio suffered eye injuries during his birth, and by the time he was entering his teenage years he was blind. In the interim, his mother had died and his father had returned to the USA, leaving the child to be raised by an aunt and uncle only for them to die while he was still in his teens. Despite all of these physical and emotional traumas, Emilio had begun to play piano from the age of 10, subsequently studying classical music by means of Braille scores. He reached a high standard of musical skills, becoming a teacher and radio band leader during the 30s. He played with many noted Cuban musicians, playing in several forms including some linked to jazz, notably 'filin', which blended the bolero with jazz.

In the 40s Emilio formed Loquibambia, a group that played American popular music filtered through Cuban styles and sensibilities. Emilio's next band was Grupo Cubano De Música Moderna, which played in the currently popular Latin jazz style. In the 50s Emilio was often to be heard leading and co-leading bands and sometimes simply playing as sideman with other leaders. Among these bands was Los Amigos, led originally by pianist Pedro 'Peruchín' Jústiz. After Jústiz's death in 1977, Emilio took over as leader. As American jazz musicians began visiting Cuba in increasing numbers, Emilio's band was one of those called upon to accompany them. He also continued to play classical music and was also involved in the preparation of Braille scores, including those for important works by his fellow countryman **Ernesto Lecuona**. In this task he was aided by Armando Romeu Gonzalez, conductor of Havana's Tropicana Orchestra, who, although sighted, learned Braille so that he could collaborate with Emilio. Among linked activities, Emilio was involved not only in teaching the blind but also in developing new teaching methods for blind students. In the late 70s he became president of his country's National Association for the Blind.

Despite Emilio's advancing years, the 90s proved to be among the most rewarding, at least insofar as international recognition was concerned. In 1993 he played and recorded with saxophonist **Jane Bunnett**'s Spirits Of Havana band, appearing on her *Jane Bunnett And The Cuban Piano Masters*. He appeared at New York's Lincoln Center in 1998, leading to other concert appearances in the USA, Canada and Europe, at some of which he was joined by bass player William Rubalcaba. For the Lincoln Center engagement, Emilio's current edition of Los Amigos included **Orlando 'Cachaito' Lopez** (bass), **Alfredo 'Chocolate' Armenteros** (trumpet), Enrique Lazaga, Tata Gyines and Changuito (percussionists), Joaquin Oliveros (flute), Lazaro Jesus (violin) and Ñico Rojas (vocals). Emilio was also joined by **Chucho Valdés**, who has been one of his most vociferous proponents, for a performance of Lecuona's 'Danza Lecum', a piece written for two pianos. Emilio's dynamic playing, allied to his lifelong devotion to the music of his homeland made him a legendary figure whose late-flowering recognition outside Cuba was shamefully overdue and thoroughly well deserved.

● ALBUMS: as Frank Emilio Flynn *Barbarisimo* (Milan Latino 1996) ★★★, as Frank Emilio Flynn *Tribute To Ernesto Lecuona* (Milan Latino 1997) ★★★, as Frank Emilio Flynn *A Tiempo De Danzón* (Milan Latino 1998) ★★★, *Ancestral Reflections* (Blue Note 1999) ★★★.

Eminem

b. Marshall Bruce Mathers III, 17 October 1973 (1972 also is cited by some sources), Kansas City, Missouri, USA. This white rapper burst onto the US charts in 1999 with a controversial take on the horrorcore genre, and by the start of the new millennium was firmly established as one of America's most fêted and successful modern songwriters.

Mathers endured an itinerant childhood, living with his mother in various states before eventually ending up in Detroit at the age of 12. He took up rapping in high school before dropping out in ninth grade, joining ad hoc groups Basement Productions, the New Jacks and **D12**. The newly named Eminem released a raw debut album in 1997 through independent label FBT. *Infinite* was poorly received, however, with Eminem earning unfavourable comparisons to leading rappers such as **Nas** and **AZ**. His determination to succeed was given a boost by a prominent feature in *Source*'s Unsigned Hype column, and he gained revenge on his former critics when he won the *Wake Up Show*'s Freestyle Performer Of The Year award, and finished runner-up in Los Angeles' annual Rap Olympics. The following year's *The Slim Shady EP*, named after his sinister alter-ego, featured some vitriolic attacks on his detractors. The stand-out track, 'Just Don't Give A Fuck', became a highly popular underground hit, and led to guest appearances on MC Shabaam Sahddeq's 'Five Star Generals' single and **Kid Rock**'s *Devil Without A Cause* set.

As a result, Eminem was signed to Aftermath Records by label boss **Dr. Dre**, who adopted the young rapper as his protégé and acted as co-producer on Eminem's album debut. Dre's beats featured prominently on **The Slim Shady LP**, a provocative feast of violent, twisted lyrics, with a moral outlook partially redeemed by Eminem's claim to be only 'voicing' the thoughts of the Slim Shady character. Parody or no parody, lyrics to tracks such as '97 Bonnie & Clyde' (which contained lines about killing the mother of his child) and frequent verbal outbursts about his mother were held by many, outside even the usual Christian moral majority, to be deeply irresponsible. The album was buoyed by the commercial success of the singles 'My Name Is' and 'Guilty Conscience' (the former helped by a striking, **MTV**-friendly video), and climbed to number 2 on the US album chart in March 1999.

Eminem subsequently made high profile appearances on Rawkus Records' *Soundbombing Volume 2* compilation and **Missy 'Misdemeanor' Elliott**'s *Da Real World*. He was also in the news when his mother filed a lawsuit claiming that comments made by the rapper during interviews and on *The Slim Shady LP* had caused, amongst other things, emotional distress, damage to her reputation and loss of self-esteem. None of which harmed the sales of Eminem's follow-up album, *The Marshall Mathers LP*, which debuted at number 1 on the US album chart in May 2000 and established him as the most successful rapper since the mid-90s heyday of **2Pac** and **Snoop Doggy Dogg**. The brilliant single 'Stan' attracted strong responses from critics and detractors in equal measure, and helped introduce UK vocalist **Dido** to a wider public audience. By the end of the year, however, Eminem's troubled personal life and a serious assault charge had removed the gloss from his phenomenal commercial success. Despite criticism from gay rights groups, the rapper swept up three Grammy Awards the following February. He also reunited with his D12 colleagues to record the transatlantic chart-topping *Devil's Night*.

Eminem's new studio album, *The Eminem Show*, was premiered by single 'Without Me'. The track, which debuted at UK number 1 in May 2002, featured a sample from **Malcolm McLaren**'s 'Buffalo Girls' and was supported by a controversial video that saw the rapper dressing up as Osama Bin Laden. The album debuted at number 1 on both sides of the Atlantic. Later in the year, Eminem made his mainstream acting debut in **8 Mile**. The lead single from the soundtrack, 'Lose Yourself', gave the rapper his first US number 1 single in November and remained at the top of the charts well into 2003.

Shortly afterwards, Eminem reunited with D12 to record a new album. The crew enjoyed a transatlantic hit single in April 2004 with 'My Band'. Eminem's new studio album *Encore* was rush-released in November when illegal downloads began appearing on the Internet. One of the tracks 'leaked' before the official release date, 'Mosh', saw the rapper venting his spleen at President George W. Bush and American military involvement in Iraq. One of the other stand-out tracks, 'Like Toy Soldiers', tackled Eminem's ongoing feud with rappers **Ja Rule** and Ray 'Benzino' Scott. Eminem's lyrical dexterity remained as compelling as ever throughout the lengthy running time. The supporting tour was troubled by setbacks and the European leg was hastily cancelled when it was announced the rapper had entered rehab to cure an addiction to sleeping pills. He returned in late 2005 with 'When I'm Gone', one of several new songs featured on the greatest hits set *Curtain Call: The Hits*.

● ALBUMS: *Infinite* (FBT 1997) ★★, *The Slim Shady LP* (Aftermath/Interscope 1999) ★★★★, *The Marshall Mathers LP* (Aftermath/Interscope 2000) ★★★★, *The Eminem Show* (Aftermath/Interscope 2002) ★★★, with various artists *8 Mile* film soundtrack (Aftermath/Interscope 2002) ★★★, *Encore* (Aftermath/Interscope 2004) ★★★.

● COMPILATIONS: *Curtain Call: The Hits* (Aftermath/ Interscope 2005) ★★★★.

● DVD/VIDEOS: *E* (Interscope 2001), *Hitz & Disses: Unauthorized* (Wienerworld 2001), *The Slim Shady Show* (MIA 2001), *All Across Europe* (Universal 2002), *The Anger Management Tour* (Aftermath 2005).

● FURTHER READING: *Shady Bizness: Life As Marshall Mathers' Bodyguard In An Industry Of Paper Gangsters*, Byron 'Big Naz' Williams. *Eminem: Crossing The Line*, Martin Huxley. *Eminem: Angry Blonde*, Eminem. *The Dark Story Of Eminem*, Nick Hasted. *Whatever You Say I Am: The Life And Times Of Eminem*, Anthony Bozza. *Eminem: In My Skin*, Barnaby Legg and Jim McCarthy.

● FILMS: *The Wash* (2001), *8 Mile* (2002).

Emma

(see **Bunton, Emma**)

Emmons, Buddy

b. 27 January 1937, Mishawaka, Indiana, USA. A multi-instrumentalist and sometime singer, Emmons began playing the fiddle when he was 10 years old. Encouraged by his father, he switched to a lap-top steel guitar and then graduated to bigger models. However, he states, 'I wanted to be a boxer, but when I found out how easy it was to play and how hard it was to box, I changed my mind.' When only 18, he stepped in for Walter Haynes, steel guitarist with **Little Jimmy Dickens**, on a local date. As Haynes wanted to leave the band, Emmons took his place. In 1957, he and Shot Jackson built a steel guitar from scratch, the Sho-Bud, and Emmons subsequently gave his name to a steel guitar company. Emmons played with **Ernest Tubb**'s Texas Troubadours (1957–62) and **Ray Price**'s Cherokee Cowboys (1962–68), and he played on records by Ray Price ('Nightlife'), **George Jones** ('Seasons Of My Heart', 'Who Shot Sam?') and **Faron Young** ('Sweet Dreams'). He then moved to Los Angeles, played sessions for **Linda Ronstadt** and **Henry Mancini**, and became a king of the road with **Roger Miller**. In 1975 he returned to Nashville and established himself as a leading steel guitarist. He worked on albums by the Nashville Superpickers, and among his credits are the classic albums *G.P.* (**Gram Parsons**), *John Phillips—The Wolfking Of L.A.*, *Now And Then* (the **Carpenters**), and *Who Knows Where The Time Goes?* (**Judy Collins**). He has also worked on albums by **Sandy Denny**, **Doug Dillard**, **Annette Funicello**, **Mickey Gilley**, **Arlo Guthrie**, **John Hartford**, **Albert Lee**, **Manhattan Transfer**, **Rick Nelson**, **Willie Nelson**, **Mickey Newbury**, **Ricky Skaggs** and **John Stewart**. In 1993 Emmons was in sparkling form as a member of the **Everly Brothers**' touring band.

● ALBUMS: *Steel Guitar Jazz* (Mercury 1963) ★★★, with Shot Jackson *Steel Guitar And Dobro Sound* (Starday 1965) ★★★, *The Black Album* (Emmons 1966) ★★, *Steel Guitar* (Flying Fish 1975) ★★★, *Buddy Emmons Sings Bob Wills* (Flying Fish 1976) ★★, with Buddy Spicher *Buddies* (Flying Fish 1977) ★★, *Live From Austin City Limits* (Flying Fish 1979) ★★★, with Lenny Breau *Minors Aloud* (Flying Fish 1979) ★★, *First Flight* (1984) ★★★, *Christmas Sounds Of The Steel Guitar* (1987) ★★, *Swingin' By Request* (Step One 1992) ★★★, with Ray Pennington *It's All In The Swing* (Step One 1995) ★★★.

Emotionals

This charming but derivative pop group, much in the mould of the **Primitives** and **Darling Buds**, emerged from London, England, in the late 80s. Featuring Emma Vine (vocals), Pete Maher (guitar/vocals), Roz Laney (bass) and Kieron James (drums/percussion), the Emotionals were originally formed in Brixton in 1988. Vine and Maher had met at school, but were more interested in following **Richard Hell** And The Voidoids than attending lessons. They moved to London and, from the summer of that year, they began an exhaustive promotional campaign that barely ceased from its inception. Winning early support from US disc jockey Rodney Bingenheimer and **Blondie**'s Nigel Harrison, they signed to Native Records from where their two rather average albums emerged. When Native went down the pan the Emotionals followed quickly thereafter.

● ALBUMS: *Personal Pleasure* (Native 1990) ★★★, *In Response* (Native 1991) ★★★.

Emotions (female)

The Hutchinson sisters, Wanda (b. 17 December 1951; lead vocal), Sheila (b. 17 January 1953) and Jeanette, first worked together in Chicago, Illinois, USA, as the Heavenly Sunbeams, then as the Hutchinson Sunbeams up to 1968. They recorded for several local companies prior to arriving at **Stax Records** on the recommendation of Pervis Staples of the **Staple Singers**. Their debut release for the label, 'So I Can Love You' (1969), reached the US Top 40, and introduced a series of excellent singles, including 'Show Me How' (1971) and 'I Could Never Be Happy' (1972). Although Jeanette was briefly replaced by a cousin, Theresa Davis, she latterly returned to the line-up, while a fourth sister, Pamela, came into the group when Davis left. The Emotions moved to **Columbia Records** in 1976 and began working under the aegis of Maurice White of **Earth, Wind And Fire**. 'Best Of My Love' was a US number 1 the following year while the singers secured further success with 'Boogie Wonderland' in 1979, an energetic collaboration with White's group. The Emotions continued to record into the 80s and although their material was sometimes disappointing, their harmonies remained as vibrant as ever. They continue to perform on the live circuit.

● ALBUMS: *So I Can Love You* (Stax 1970) ★★★, *Songs Of Love* (Stax 1971) ★★★, *Untouched* (Stax 1972) ★★★, *Flowers* (Columbia 1976) ★★★, *Flowers* (Columbia 1976) ★★★, *Rejoice* (Columbia 1977) ★★★, *Sunshine* (Stax 1977) ★★★, *Sunbeam* (Columbia 1978) ★★★, *Come Into Our World* (ARC 1979) ★★★, *New Affair* (ARC 1981) ★★, *Sincerely* (Red Label 1984) ★★, *If I Only Knew* (Motown 1985) ★★, *Live In '96* (Raging Bull 1996) ★★, *Songs Of Innocence And Experience* (Ace 2004) ★★.

● COMPILATIONS: *Chronicle: Greatest Hits* (Stax/Fantasy 1979) ★★★★, *Heart Association—The Best Of The Emotions* (Columbia 1979) ★★★★, *Best Of My Love: The Best Of The Emotions* (Columbia/Legacy 1996) ★★★★, *Chronicle* (Stax 2002) ★★★★.

Emotions (male)

The members of this rock 'n' roll doo-wop group from Brooklyn, New York City, USA, were lead Joe Favale, first tenor Tony Maltese, second tenor Larry Cusimano, baritone Joe Nigro and bass Dom Colura. Although the Emotions, who formed in 1959, only scraped the bottom of the charts in 1962 with 'Echo' (number 76 pop), like many east coast, Italian-American doo-wop groups of the early 60s, they enjoyed substantial regional success. 'Echo' sold 250,000 copies in New York alone, indicating that it sold very little elsewhere in the country. Their second hit was an up-tempo version of the old **Nutmegs** hit 'Story Untold', which was successful only in New York in 1963. After many lean years, during which the group saw all their singles fail, they broke up in 1970. In 1982, Favale and Maltese formed a new group, with new members Joe Cavanna, Eddy Balen and John Van Soest, and recorded their first and only album, *Doo-Wop All Night Long*, on Marty Pekar's Ambient Sound label (for legal reasons they had to use the Blue Emotions name).

● ALBUMS: *Doo-Wop All Night Long* (Ambient Sound 1982) ★★★.

Emotive Records

New York dance label founded in January 1990 when their debut release was licensed from an Italian label. Emotive is one of the new breed of hip US imprints that emerged in the 90s. Generally the label creed has been to promote new names and talent on their schedule, while the style encompasses garage and house in its myriad forms. The first release came from Toronto artist Matt Di Mario (M1's 'Feel The Drums', the same artist going on to release 'Dynamite' and the *Then And Now* EP for the label). He was joined by Smoke Signals ('I Want Your Love'), B-Town ('Weekend'), Insomnia ('I'll Be There'), Deep Expressions (*Deep Expressions* EP), Michael Lavel ('Do Me This Way') and Michael Ayres ('Share My Love'). James Howard's 'We Can Do It (Wake Up)' was possibly the biggest Emotive tune in its early stages, though Valerie Johnson's 'Step Into My Life' and 'Inside', and Jovonn's 'Out All Nite' also were key releases. The latter was the first 'established' artist on the roster, and ran his own Goldtone imprint through the parent label. The second James Howard release would be 'Feeling Good', again created by label mainstay Charles Dockins (who also contributed to **Bobby Konders** Jus' Friends project (for 'As One'). Other 1992 releases included Producers On Wax (DJ Romain Gowe and Matt 'Keys' Echols El) with 'Feel The Piano' and Karen Pollack ('You Can't Touch Me'). Further material from Project 4007 ('It's Our Turn') appeared as Emotive continued its ascendency.

Emperor

Original members of the bizarre Norwegian Satanic club known as the Black Metal Circle, led by Euronymous of **Mayhem**, Emperor emerged as the most musically adventurous of the bands spearheading the black metal revival of the early 90s. The band was formed in 1991, in the small Norwegian town of Notodden, by Ihsahn (b. Vegard Tveiten, Notodden, Norway; vocals, guitar, keyboards), **Mortiis** (b. Håvard Ellefsen, 25 July 1975, Skien, Norway; bass) and Samoth (b. Tomas Haugen, 9 June 1974, Norway; drums). This line-up recorded the *Wrath Of The Tyrant* demo, following which drummer Faust (b. Bard G. Eithun) was recruited to allow Samoth to switch to guitar. This quartet released 1993's split EP with Scandinavian pagan heavy metal band **Enslaved**, before Mortiis left in mysterious circumstances, later surfacing in Sweden as a solo artist. New bass player Tchort was brought in to help record Emperor's acclaimed debut album, *In The Nightside Eclipse*, but by now the band members more unsavoury leanings were beginning to catch up on them. In the same year the Black Metal Circle were linked with a series of church burnings in Norway, Samoth was arrested in connection with the crimes. He was later released; however, in addition to the arson, Emperor drummer Faust was convicted of the 1992 murder of a homosexual and Tchort was sentenced for burglary, knife assault and desecration.

Despite this, and the murder of fellow black metal Satanist Euronymous, Emperor continued to fly the Scandinavian black metal banner with a series of impressive releases on the Candlelight label. Following Samoth's parole the band had regrouped, with the guitarist and Ihsahn joined by Alver (bass) and Trym Torson (b. 26 February 1974, Norway; drums, ex-Enslaved). This line-up recorded 1997's *Anthems To The Welkin At Dusk*, an excellent comeback that fine-tuned the musical style of their debut; a cacophonous storm of blistering guitars and bellowed vocals, with aggressive, devilish themes and a few strange, quasi-classical flourishes. Alver left the band following the release of the second album, leaving Ihsahn, Samoth and Torson to continue as a trio

augmented by session players. Increasing involvement in their own projects led the band members to announce that 2001's mighty *Prometheus: The Discipline Of Fire & Demise* would be Emperor's final recording. Samoth and Torson continued to work together in **Zyklon**.

● ALBUMS: *In the Nightside Eclipse* (Candlelight 1994) ★★★, *Anthems To The Welkin At Dusk* (Candlelight 1997) ★★★★, with the Thorns *Thorns Vs Emperor* (Moonfog 1998) ★★★, *IX Equilibrium* (Candlelight 1999) ★★★, *Emperial Live Ceremony* (Candlelight 2000) ★★★, *Prometheus: The Discipline Of Fire & Demise* (Candlelight 2001) ★★★★.

● COMPILATIONS: *Scattered Ashes: A Decade Of Emperial Wrath* (Candlelight 2003) ★★★★.

● DVD/VIDEOS: *Emperial Live Ceremony* (Candlelight 1999).

Empire Bakuba

Led by the top Zairean vocalist Pepe Kalle (b. Kabasele Yampanya, 1951, Kinshasa, Zaire), Empire Bakuba was one of the leading 'punk soukous' bands popular in Kinshasa during the 80s, playing a stripped-down, high-energy version of the music of longer established bands led by **Franco** and Rochereau. Kalle, nicknamed The Elephant Of Zaire, was an imposing front man, having come through a strong musical apprenticeship that began in 1968 with membership of African Jazz. In 1970 he established African Choc with Pay-Tex and Dilu. He subsequently changed the name of the band to Empire Bakuba. By the late 80s they had become possibly the most popular of all Zairean groups, establishing their fine blend of rumba across the continent. They also adapted to the latest dance crazes with ease, circumnavigating the Essombi, Oh Nager and Kwassa Kwassa dances without losing their own sound. By the 90s their regional popularity enabled them to embark on a series of international engagements in Europe, Japan and the USA.

● ALBUMS: *Cherie Ondi* (Verckys 1981) ★★★★, *Armour Propre* (Rhythmes Et Musique 1982) ★★★★, *Bonana 85* (PF 1985) ★★★, *La Belle Etoile* (Rhythmes Et Musique 1986) ★★★, *Kwassa Kwassa* (Syllart 1987) ★★★, with Nyboma *Bakuba Show* (Syllart 1987) ★★★★, *Moyibi* (Syllart 1988) ★★★, *Gigant-Afrique* (Globestyle 1990) ★★★.

En Vogue

Vocal R&B group originally comprising Dawn Robinson (b. 28 November 1968, Connecticut, USA), Terry Ellis (b. 5 September 1966, Texas, USA), Cindy Herron (b. 26 September 1965, San Francisco, California, USA) and Maxine Jones (b. 16 January 1966, Patterson, New Jersey, USA). They formed in Oakland, California, where they were auditioned by Denzil Foster and Thomas McElroy. The duo had worked together in both the Timex Social Club and **Club Nouveau** (who enjoyed big hits with 'Rumors' in 1986 and 'Lean On Me', a hip-hop version of **Bill Withers**' 70s classic, and a Grammy-winner, in 1987). Afterwards they decided to write and produce under their own steam: 'When Tommy and I bumped into each other in the early 80s, we had the same notion. Everyone was saying R&B was tired and worn out. The new era was hip-hop and rap. But we thought: why not combine the two eras? Put good songs—and the 70s were loaded with good songs—over the new grooves.' En Vogue were formed in October 1988 after Foster and McElroy auditioned to establish their own 'girl group'. Of the four selected, only Cindy Herron had previous 'showbiz' experience, winning Miss San Francisco and Miss Black California pageants, and also working as an actress.

En Vogue remained primarily responsible for their own image and songs, but they were groomed for success by joining **M.C. Hammer**'s 1990 tour, and that of **Freddie Jackson** a year later. They went on to enjoy transatlantic singles success with 'Hold On' (US number 2/UK number 5) and 'Lies' (US/UK Top 40) in 1990. The latter introduced female rapper Debbie T, and added a new, post-feminist outlook to traditional R&B concerns. Their second album *Funky Divas*, meanwhile, featured the hit **Curtis Mayfield** cover version 'Giving Him Something He Can Feel', and produced further transatlantic hits in 'My Lovin' (You're Never Gonna Get It)', 'Free Your Mind' and 'Give It Up, Turn It Loose'. Heavily influenced by **Chaka Khan**, En Vogue, in turn, helped to start the 'new jill swing' movement, which threw up the equally successful **SWV**, **Jade** and **TLC**. They were approached by Roseanne Barr and her then-husband Tom Arnold to appear in their own sitcom. These distractions did not affect their singing or their commercial appeal into the mid-90s, with further huge transatlantic Top 10 hits including the **Salt-N-Pepa** collaboration 'Whatta Man' and 'Don't Let Go (Love)' (from the movie *Set It Off*).

Following a short break from recording, during which Robinson left to pursue a solo career, En Vogue returned to a now highly competitive market with 1997's classy *EV3*. The album featured the US/UK Top 20 hit 'Whatever'. After another extended hiatus the trio released the inventive *Masterpiece Theatre*, but by now they had been commercially usurped by the new wave of urban groups led by **Destiny's Child**. Amanda Cole was added to the line-up in 2001 but shortly afterwards Maxine Jones announced she was leaving, reducing the group back to a trio. A low-key seasonal recording was released on the Discretion Entertainment label in 2002. The following summer Cole left the group to embark on a solo career. Herron and Ellis carried on regardless, recruiting new member Rhona Bennett (b. 10 May 1976, Chicago, Illinois, USA), although Herron was in turn replaced by original member Maxine Jones on 2004's *Soul Flower*.

● ALBUMS: *Born To Sing* (Atlantic 1990) ★★★, *Funky Divas* (EastWest 1992) ★★★★, *EV3* (EastWest 1997) ★★★, *Masterpiece Theatre* (Elektra 2000) ★★★★, *The Gift Of Christmas* (Discretion 2002) ★★, *Soul Flower* (33rd Street 2004) ★★★.
Solo: Terry Ellis *Southern Gal* (EastWest 1995) ★★.
● COMPILATIONS: *Remix To Sing* mini-album (EastWest 1991) ★★★, *Best Of En Vogue* (EastWest 1998) ★★★★, *The Very Best Of En Vogue* (Rhino 2001) ★★★★.

Enchantment

Five-piece vocal group formed in Detroit, Michigan, USA, in 1966 comprising Emanuel (EJ) Johnson, David Banks, Joe (Jobie) Thomas, Ed (Mickey) Clanton and Bobby Green. Their career did not take off, however, until they moved to Los Angeles in the 70s, signing to **United Artists Records** and releasing an excellent debut album and hitting the Top 30 of the pop charts with 'Gloria'. They subsequently signed with Roadshow (via **RCA Records**) and returned to the singles chart with 'It's You That I Need' and 'Sunshine'. They also performed the soundtrack to the film *Deliver Us From Evil*.

In 1983, they signed for **Columbia Records**, releasing one album before negotiating a new contract with Prelude, for whom they issued one single, 'Feel Like Dancing', in 1984.
● ALBUMS: *Enchantment* (United Artists 1978) ★★★★, *Journey To The Land Of Enchantment* (Roadshow 1979) ★★★, *Soft Lights, Sweet Music* (Roadshow 1980) ★★★, *Utopia* (Columbia 1983) ★★★.

End

Comprising Hugh Attwool (drums), Dave Brown (bass/vocals), Nick Graham (keyboards/vocals), Colin Griffin (steel guitar/vocals) and Terry Taylor (guitar), most of the initial enthusiasm surrounding this London, England, quintet was owing to the fact that they were managed by **Bill Wyman**. The group's sound was a superior blend of late 60s psychedelic elements with forthright hard rock properties, and much was expected of their 1969 **Decca Records** debut album *Introspection*. However, despite the presence of Wyman's fellow **Rolling Stone Charlie Watts** (playing tabla on the excellent 'Shades Of Orange', which was recorded during breaks from the sessions that resulted in the Stones' *Their Satanic Majesties Request*) and **Nicky Hopkins**, it proved commercially unsuccessful. Previously they had released two singles, 'I Can't Get Any Joy' and an earlier version of 'Shades Of Orange', but after the failure of their debut album the group transmuted into **Tucky Buzzard**. That group, still under the aegis of Wyman as producer, released further tracks in the 70s but again success eluded them.
● ALBUMS: *Introspection* (Decca 1969) ★★★.
● COMPILATIONS: *In The Beginning . . . The End* (Tenth Planet 1996) ★★, *Retrospection* (Tenth Planet 1997) ★★★, *The Last Word* (Tenth Planet 2002) ★★.

Endsley, Melvin

b. 30 January 1934, Heber Springs, Arkansas, USA, d. 16 August 2004, Drasco, Arkansas, USA. In 1937 Endsley was disabled by polio, which confined him to a wheelchair for life. Between 1946 and 1947, he was sent to the cruelly titled Crippled Children's Hospital in Memphis, where he became interested in country music after listening to artists such as **Wayne Raney** and the **Delmore Brothers** on the radio, and he learned to play guitar. He returned to Drasco and graduated from Concord High School in 1954, undecided whether he should seek a career in radio or become a teacher. He worked on KCON Conway and soon became a regular on Wayne Raney's show on KWCB Searcy. By this time, Endsley, influenced by the songwriting of **Hank Williams**, had already begun to write songs himself. It was on Raney's show that he first sang a song that he had originally copyrighted as 'I've Never Felt More Like Singing The Blues'. When the song attracted local attention, Endsley quickly decided to try his luck at getting his material published. Borrowing money to finance the trip and with a friend to drive for him, he made the long, painful journey to Nashville. He hoped to interest **Webb Pierce** but it was actually on the prompting of **Marty Robbins** that **Wesley Rose** signed Endsley to a writing contract with **Acuff-Rose Music** and initially acquired six of his songs. (Robbins subsequently enjoyed major hits with 'Singing The Blues' and 'Knee Deep In The Blues'. They were also major pop hits for **Guy Mitchell** both in the USA and the UK.) **Chet Atkins** signed Endsley to **RCA-Victor Records**, for whom he recorded in 1957/8 without chart success. In 1959, he recorded three singles for **MGM Records**, before joining Hickory the following year.

In 1961, Endsley ended his association with Acuff-Rose and formed his own label, Melark, which he operated from his farm at Drasco, but still failed to find that elusive hit. He recorded 'Singing The Blues' again for release as a Melark single, but RCA, whom he had contracted to undertake the production, lost his master tape. This marked the end of Endsley's career as a vocalist and he retired to his farm. Endsley songs recorded by other singers include 'It Happens Every Time' (**Don Gibson**), 'I'd Just Be Fool Enough' (**Johnny Cash**, **Faron Young**, **Jimmy C. Newman** and the **Browns**), 'Why I'm Walkin'' (**Stonewall Jackson**) and 'I Like Your Kind Of Love' (**Andy Williams**). Endsley may have failed to make his mark as a vocalist but he most certainly did so as a songwriter.

● COMPILATIONS: *I Like Your Kind Of Love* (Bear Family 1987) ★★★, *I Like Your Kind Of Love* CD release with 14 additional tracks (Bear Family 1993) ★★★.

Enemy

Formed in Auckland in 1977, the Enemy, alongside the **Clean**, were New Zealand's most influential punk ambassadors. Led by **Chris Knox** (b. 2 September 1952, Invercargill, New Zealand; vocals), the band's other members included guitarist Alec Bathgate (b. 1956, Tapanui, West Otago, New Zealand, and later a Knox collaborator in both **Toy Love** and the **Tall Dwarfs**), Mick Dawson (bass) and Mike Dooley (drums). When Dawson left in 1978 he was replaced first by Phil Judd and then Paul Kean. They never recorded, but Knox's live presence was formidable and a major influence on later developments in Antipodean new wave. Many of the Enemy's songs were subsequently revisited by Toy Love, the band into which Enemy evolved in 1979.

Energy Orchard

This pop rock sextet came from Belfast, Northern Ireland, and were built around the nucleus of singer **Bap Kennedy** (b. Martin Kennedy, 17 June 1962, Belfast, Northern Ireland) and guitarist Paul Toner. Snapped up by MCA in 1990, their first single was titled after their home-town, ironically after relocating to London. It dented the UK Top 70, paving the way for follow-ups 'Sailortown' and 'Lace Virginia'. After running the gauntlet of comparisons to **U2** that face most rock bands from Ireland, the reaction of the mainstream UK press hardened. Bombast and over-production somewhat neutered their debut album and the band's subsequent releases ploughed a similar path. They disbanded in 1996, their final release being a credible live album. Kennedy later embarked on an acclaimed solo career, debuting with the **Steve Earle**-produced *Domestic Blues* in 1999.

● ALBUMS: *Energy Orchard* (MCA 1990) ★★★, *Shinola* (MCA 1993) ★★, *Painkiller* (Transatlantic 1995) ★★★, *Orchardville* (Transatlantic 1996) ★★★.

Enevoldsen, Bob

b. Robert Martin Enevoldsen, 11 September 1920, Billings, Montana, USA, d. 19 November 2005, Los Angeles, California, USA. Enevoldsen was born into a musical family; his mother played piano, his sisters played string instruments, and his Danish immigrant father played violin and conducted the orchestra at a local silent movie theatre. At the age of five he too began playing violin, then switched to

trumpet, on which he was coached by an uncle who was also a musician. While attending the University of Montana Enevoldsen had embouchure problems and abandoned the trumpet in favour of the clarinet and tenor saxophone, acknowledging the influence of **Lester Young** on the latter instrument. Between 1942 and 1946 Enevoldsen was in the US Air Force, continuing to play in a services band. After his discharge he joined a band in Salt Lake City, Utah, playing tenor saxophone and it was during this engagement that he first took up the valve trombone. At the end of the decade, he also played clarinet with the Utah Symphony Orchestra and continued with his musical studies through the G.I. Bill.

In 1951, at the suggestion of **Gene Roland**, Enevoldsen moved to Los Angeles with his wife and two children. He was now also playing bass and sat in with various musicians at clubs, playing brass, reed or string instruments as required. It was on bass that he became a member of the **Marty Paich** trio and he also played with **Al Haig**. Recommended to **Bobby Troup**, Enevoldsen became a long-serving member of the singer-pianist's trio, remaining there, on bass, until 1959. The engagement allowed him to do many other things concurrently and during the 50s he played regularly at **Howard Rumsey**'s Lighthouse at Hermosa Beach and on several recording sessions under a range of leaders including Paich, **Shelly Manne**, **Shorty Rogers**, **Art Pepper**, **Bill Perkins**, **Bill Holman** and **Buddy Rich**. He also appeared on **Gerry Mulligan**'s 1953 Ten-tette date, and the following year made his debut as leader for Nocturne Records. Enevoldsen also worked extensively, often anonymously, in studio orchestras in Los Angeles and in hotel/casino bands in Las Vegas. Interviewed by Gordon Jack in *Jazz Journal International* in 2000, he wryly observed of the latter type of work, 'I got lucky when they fired me for swinging too much.'

To his skills on clarinet, tenor, valve trombone and bass, Enevoldsen added a talent for arranging, writing charts for **Stan Kenton**'s Neophonic Orchestra and for **Lionel Hampton**. Throughout succeeding decades he continued playing in a wide variety of settings, for television, recording sessions, club and concert work, with a dizzying array of distinguished leaders and fellow sidemen. He also toured with **Mel Tormé**, performing and recording in Japan. Although he had concentrated on valve trombone from 1980 onwards, in the early 90s, now a regular in several west coast rehearsal bands, he began studying slide trombone. For this work, he used a special instrument, describing it to Jack as 'a Holton with a slide and valve attachment.' Enevoldsen's rich musical skills enhanced the sessions on which he appeared and he invariably added lustre to the proceedings. Nevertheless, he appears to have been content to remain a backroom boy of jazz.

● ALBUMS: *Bob Enevoldsen Quintet* 10-inch album (Nocturne 1954) ★★★, *Smorgasbord* (Liberty 1956) ★★★, *Reflections In Jazz* (Tampa 1957) ★★★.

● FILMS: *The Subterraneans* (1960).

Engine

US band **Fates Warning** has been long associated with the prog metal genre, yet their offshoot Engine bears little resemblance to the 'thinking man's metal' of the parent group. Despite never breaking through commercially to a vast audience, Fates Warning amassed a large and dedicated cult following. By the late 90s, long-time member vocalist Ray Alder sought to launch a project in which he would provide the lion's share of the songwriting (since the writing in Fates Warning is largely handled by guitarist Jim Matheos), and would be more aligned musically to thriving hard rock styles such as alt metal and nu metal. As a result, Engine was formed in 1999. Joining Alder in Engine is current Fates Warning bass player Joey Vera (best known for his stint in **Armored Saint**), **Agent Steel** guitarist Bernie Versailles and **Face To Face** drummer Pete Parada.

Fates Warning's label, Metal Blade, received a four-song demo by Alder and instantly agreed to take on the band, issuing their self-titled debut in 1999. The album was well received by the metal audience, and as a result, Alder returned to Engine after wrapping up commitments to Fates Warning (their 2000 release, *Disconnected*). Engine's second album, *Superholic*, released in 2002, saw the band take even more chances musically, most notably on a cover version of the **Cure**'s 'Fascination Street'.

● ALBUMS: *Engine* (Metal Blade 1999) ★★★, *Superholic* (Metal Blade 2002) ★★★.

Engine Alley

Ireland's Engine Alley played polished pop music that included elements of the 70s glam rock era. Vocalist Canice Kennedy was backed by Brian (guitar), Eamonn (bass) and Emmaline (drums), and the line-up was formed in December 1989. They took their name from a particularly barren street in the heart of Dublin, and became known for their colourful and energetic stage shows. After signing a contract with the **U2**-backed Mother Records label, the band made their debut in August 1991 with *Flowerbox* EP, by which time the group had expanded to a five-piece. Their debut album was recorded in spring 1992 and was released only in Eire. Its songs dwelt chiefly on character sketches—'Diamond Jill And Crazy Jane', 'Telescope Girl' and 'Mrs Winder'. The band's first UK release, 'Infamy', accompanied their arrival in Britain in 1993, and was backed by 'Robin Hood', an attack on the Kevin Costner film of the same name. However, Engine Alley never had sufficient strength as songwriters to survive.

● ALBUMS: *A Sonic Holiday* (Mother 1992) ★★★.

England Dan And John Ford Coley

Dan Seals (b. 8 February 1950, McCamey, Texas, USA) comes from a family of performing Seals. His father played bass for many country stars (**Ernest Tubb**, **Bob Wills**) and his brother Jimmy was part of the **Champs** and then **Seals And Croft**. His cousins include 70s country star **Johnny Duncan** and songwriters Chuck Seals ('Crazy Arms') and **Troy Seals**. Seals formed a partnership with John Ford Coley (b. 13 October 1951) and they first worked as psych-outfit Southwest F.O.B., the initials representing 'Freight On Board'. The ridiculous name did not last, but Jimmy, not wanting them to be called Seals And Coley, suggested England Dan And John Ford Coley. Their first albums for **A&M Records** sold moderately well, but they struck gold in 1976 with a move to Big Tree Records. The single 'I'd Really Love To See You Tonight' went to number 2 in the US charts and also reached the UK Top 30, although its hook owed something to **James Taylor**'s 'Fire And Rain'. The resulting album, *Nights Are Forever*, was a big seller and the pair opted for a fuller sound that drew comparisons with the **Eagles**. The title track, 'Nights Are Forever Without You', was another Top 10 single. With their harmonies, acoustic-based songs and tuneful melodies, they

appealed to the same market as the Eagles and, naturally, Seals And Croft. They had further US hits with 'It's Sad To Belong', 'Gone Too Far', 'We'll Never Have To Say Goodbye Again' and 'Love Is The Answer'. When the duo split, Seals, after a few setbacks, became a country star. Coley found a new partner, but their 1981 album, *Kelly Leslie And John Ford Coley*, was not a success.

● ALBUMS: as Southwest F.O.B. *Smell Of Incense* (A&M 1968) ★★, *England Dan And John Ford Coley* (A&M 1971) ★★★, *Fables* (A&M 1971) ★★, *I Hear The Music* (A&M 1976) ★★, *Nights Are Forever* (Big Tree 1976) ★★, *Dowdy Ferry Road* (Big Tree 1977) ★★★, *Some Things Don't Come Easy* (Big Tree 1978) ★★, *Dr. Heckle And Mr. Jive* (Big Tree 1979) ★★, *Just Tell Me If You Love Me* (Big Tree 1980) ★★.

● COMPILATIONS: *Best Of England Dan & John Ford Coley* (Big Tree 1980) ★★★, *The Very Best Of England Dan & John Ford Coley* (Rhino 1997) ★★★.

England, Ty

b. Gary Tyrone England, 5 December 1963, Oklahoma City, Oklahoma, USA. The new country singer Ty England was first turned on to country music by his grandfather, who gave him his first guitar and taught him the basic chords. He sang with high school bands and played acoustic sets at coffee shops while at university. He befriended **Garth Brooks** in 1982 and they made a pact that if one of them found success, he would help the other along. Therefore, in 1988, Brooks, who had just signed with **Capitol Records**, asked England to be in his band. For five years England worked as a guitarist and harmony singer with Brooks. He almost signed a solo contract with **Liberty Records** but then decided to go with **RCA Records**. His first single, 'Should've Asked Her Faster', was a western swing number that made the US country Top 30. After recording two albums for RCA, England retreated from the spotlight to concentrate on his young family. He returned in 1999, now recording as Tyler England, with the Capitol Records release *Highways & Dance Halls*.

● ALBUMS: *Ty England* (RCA 1995) ★★★★, *Two Ways To Fall* (RCA 1996) ★★★, as Tyler England *Highways & Dance Halls* (Capitol 1999) ★★★.

England's Glory

England's Glory are best remembered for being the launching pad for critically acclaimed late 70s UK rock band the **Only Ones**. A quintet of **Peter Perrett** (b. 1952, South London, England; vocals/guitar), David Clarke (guitar), Harry Kakoulli (bass/vocals), Jon Newey (drums) and Michael Kemp (piano/organ), most of the band had already dabbled in other groups before joining England's Glory in the early 70s. Perrett had recorded his first solo demo in the spring of 1972, while Kakoulli had played with various bands and later worked with **Squeeze** as well as becoming a solo artist. Both Clarke and Newey had played in the acid rock group They Bite, who released one distinctively titled acetate demo single, 'I Wanna Screw With Jesus', in 1970. After writing their first songs together, England's Glory elected to self-finance their debut album, though only eight acetates and 25 vinyl copies were pressed. Comprising memorable early Perrett compositions such as 'City Of Fun', the album acquired legendary status when the Only Ones broke through. It was reissued on vinyl in Australia, then in

Europe in 1987. The 1994 CD reissue on Anagram Records is the easiest to obtain. While Perrett's subsequent solo activities have been well documented, it is a less publicized fact that Newey went on to be the publisher of Tower Records' *Top* magazine, having undertaken a career in music journalism for *Sounds* magazine.

● ALBUMS: *England's Glory* (Private Pressing 1973) ★★★, *Legendary Lost Recordings* (Five Hours Back 1987) ★★★.

Engle, Butch, And The Styx

Butch Engle And The Styx were based in Mill Valley, California, USA. They were formerly known as the Showmen, under which name they recorded 'You Know All I Want' for the local MEA label. They took their new name in 1965 with the line-up comprising Butch Engle (vocals), Bob Zamora (lead guitar), Mike Pardee (organ), Harry 'Happiness' Smith (bass) and Rich Morrison (drums). In 1966 they won the Band Bash at San Francisco's Cow Palace and secured the patronage of **Ron Elliott**, songwriter/guitarist with the **Beau Brummels**. He wrote and produced the group's 'Going Home', in 1967, which was issued on Loma, a subsidiary of **Warner Brothers Records**. The single was an ideal showcase for Engle's strong voice and the group's musical skills. Larry Gerughty replaced Mike Pardee before the band, now known simply as the Styx, completed a follow-up. Both sides of 'Hey I'm Lost'/'Puppetmaster' were co-composed by Elliott, but this 1968 single was not a success and the Styx broke up soon afterwards.

English Country Blues Band

The precursor to the better-known Tiger Moth (and Orchestre Super Moth), this loose collection of UK folk musicians originally coalesced during a workshop session. Including such noted musicians as **Ian Anderson**, **Maggie Holland** and Rod Stradling, they later turned to electric instrumentation and found a drummer in the **Albion Dance Band**'s John Maxwell. The group were vital in forging links between traditional English music and global styles, with the members allowed free reign to display their imagination. A single album, *Stereo Death Breakdown*, credited to Ian Anderson's English Country Blues Band, was released in 1969, and is widely regarded as a minor classic in the development of UK folk beyond the cloying environs of the established traditional music circuit. A further compilation, released in 1993, documented their free-flowing creativity on compact disc, while songs such as 'The Wreck Of The Northfleet' and 'England's Power And Glory' reminded critics of their powers of innovation. Given the composition of the group it was inevitable that the Country Blues Band would never achieve longevity, but it was probably better that the limited archive they left behind has aged well.

● ALBUMS: as Ian Anderson's Country Blues Band *Stereo Death Breakdown* (Liberty 1969) ★★★.

● COMPILATIONS: *Unruly* (Rogue 1993) ★★★.

English, Jon

b Jonathan James English, 26 March 1949, Hampstead, London, England. Blessed with good looks, a good rock voice and all-round musical talents, English has been one of the few artists to perform in all forms of media in his adopted Australia. English emigrated to the country in 1961, and four years later joined his first band, Zenith. He initially received attention for his performance as Judas, in the 1971

production of *Jesus Christ Superstar*, although during the late 60s he had made a minor splash with Sebastian Hardie, a progressive rock band that later recorded several interesting albums and backed legendary rocker **Johnny O'Keefe**. In addition, English occasionally filled in as lead singer with Duck (a short-lived band that released one jazz-influenced album).

His 1973 debut album indicated that his songwriting showed promise. Intermittent recording, which produced such chart entries as 'Turn The Page', 'Hollywood Seven' and 'Words Are Not Enough', continued between his stage and television commitments. However, it was his collaboration on the soundtrack of the television series *Against The Wind*, in late 1978, that drew the attention of a wider audience and age range. Subsequently, he wrote and produced most of his own albums and continued to write film and television scores. English spent the late 80s writing, in conjunction with UK/Australian producer David Mackay, the rock opera *Paris*, based on the ancient legend of Troy.

During the 90s, English starred in the television comedy *All Together Now* and toured in his own productions, *Turn The Page* and *Buskers And Angels*.

● ALBUMS: *Wine Dark Sea* (Warm And Genuine 1973) ★★, *It's All A Game* (Polydor 1974) ★★★, *Hollywood Seven* (Polydor 1976) ★★★, *Minutes To Midnight* (Polydor 1977) ★★★, *Words Are Not Enough* (Polydor 1977) ★★, *English History* (Polydor 1978) ★★★, *Calm Before The Storm* (Mercury 1980) ★★★, *InRoads* (Mercury 1981) ★★★, *Beating The Boards* (WEA 1983) ★★★, *Some People . . .* (WEA 1983) ★★, *Dark Horses* (Chase 1986) ★★★, *The Busker* aka *Busking* (BMG 1988) ★★★, *Paris* (WEA 1990) ★★★, *English History II* (Polydor 1978) ★★★.

● FILMS: *Touch And Go* (1980), *Walk The Talk* (2000).

English, Junior

b. Lindel Beresford English, 1951, Kingston, Jamaica, West Indies. English began performing in his teens and in 1965 he recorded 'Fay Is Gone' for **Prince Buster**. He arrived in the UK in the latter half of the 60s where he completed his education. He entered and won a talent contest run by the Palmer brothers, noted for their contribution to the UK reggae scene with **Pama Records** and later Jet Star, at the popular Club 31. His success led to his joining a band called the Magnets, with whom he recorded 'Somewhere'. The preference for Jamaican reggae thwarted his career and he spent the late 60s performing with the group on a European tour. On his return he joined another band, the Nighthawks, releasing 'Jasmine' and an obscure album. By 1970 he returned to the UK where he recorded 'Miss Playgirl', 'Daniel', 'I Don't Wanna Die' and the popular 'Back On The Scene'. He enjoyed a prolific run of hits with **Clement Bushay**, who produced 'Never Lose Never Win', which provided the backing to the combination hit for **Trinity** and **Dillinger**, 'Starsky And Hutch'. The song led to an album of the same name featuring accomplished versions of **Delano Stewart**'s 'Stay A Little Bit Longer', the **Chi-Lites**' 'Bet You'll Never Be Sorry', **Matumbi**'s 'After Tonight' and the **Royal Rasses**' 'Humanity'. With Bushay, he released the classic 'In Loving You', which, although released in October, had the distinction of being 1978's Christmas number 1 on the UK reggae charts. The success of the single was acknowledged when he won the Afro-Caribbean Post Golden Sunrise Award for best male vocalist in the same year. He maintained a high profile with 'Natural High', which was equally successful, lending its title to his second album for Bushay. The compilation was a self-production recorded at **Channel One** Studios with the **Revolutionaries**. In 1979 his credibility increased with the release of 'I'll Make It Up To You', securing a respectable position in the reggae charts alongside 'Love And Key' and 'I Am The One You Love'. He continued to release hit singles throughout the 80s, including 'Daddy's Home', 'Equal Love' and the popular 'Ready To Learn', which surfaced on his own International English label. In 1985 English was one of the many performers who featured on the British Reggae Artists Famine Appeal release 'Let's Make Africa Green Again'. In the 90s he maintained his profile, covering 'Queen Majesty', 'Cruising', 'Ready To Learn' and other popular standards.

● ALBUMS: with the Nighthawks *Man It's Reggae* (Saga 1969) ★★★, *The Great Junior English* (Horse 1975) ★★★, *Back On The Scene* (Trojan 1975) ★★★, *The Dynamic Junior English* (Cactus 1976) ★★★, *Never Lose Never Win* (Burning Sounds 1977) ★★★, *Naturally High* (Burning Sounds 1978) ★★, *Lovers Key* (International English 1980) ★★★, *Mr. Man* (International English 1990) ★★★.

English, Logan

b. 29 November 1928, Kentucky, USA. English was exposed to traditional music at an early age. He was drawn into the folk and coffee-house circuit of the 50s following a brief spell as an actor, and became a regular performer on the east and west coast clubs circuit. Several successful appearances at New York's Town and Carnegie halls predated the Greenwich Village boom of the early 60s. Sceptical of the newer generation of singers, English continued to work with traditional material and was subsequently surpassed by those embracing more contemporary forms. He remained a fixture on the folk scene, albeit in a lessened role, but despite enjoying the respect of his peers, commercial success proved elusive.

● ALBUMS: *Kentucky Folk Songs And Ballads* 10-inch album (Folkways 1957) ★★★, *The Days Of '49: Songs Of The Gold Rush* (Folkways 1957) ★★★★, *Gambling Songs* (Riverside 1957) ★★★★, *American Folk Ballads* (Monitor 1962) ★★★★, *Logan English Sings The Woody Guthrie Songbag* (20th Century Fox 1964) ★★★, *Woody Guthrie's Children's Songs Sung By Logan English* (Folkways 1974) ★★★.

English, Michael

b. USA. After several years' working as a contemporary Christian performer, by the mid-90s English elected to pursue a career in the mainstream pop idiom. The fact that his ensuing album for **Curb Records** was entitled *Freedom* was not incidental. Indeed, English saw it as the opportunity to break free of perceived notions of what Christian writers could or should do. As he told **Billboard** magazine, it afforded him 'the freedom to sing and not worry if this is going to offend anyone. Now I don't have to worry about saying "baby" or "girl" or whatever. I don't have to worry about saying "Jesus" either. I'm free to say whatever I feel there is to say.' English signed with Curb in 1994 following his departure from Warner Alliance, **Warner Brothers Records**' Christian label. Ironically, that move coincided with his greatest success, English having collected more awards than any other artist at that year's Dove Awards,

including one as Artist Of The Year. However, a Christian media witch hunt began when it was discovered that English was having an affair with, and had impregnated, married singer Marabeth Jordan of First Call. Since then he has distanced himself from Christian music circles, choosing to play dates with rock bands such as **Foreigner**. His first 'secular' release was a duet with **Wynonna**, 'Healing', which was included on the soundtrack to the film *Silent Fall*. However, he still produces southern gospel albums, and received a further Dove award for his work with the Martins. The first single to be released from *Freedom* was 'Your Love Amazes Me', a song previously released by **John Berry**.

● ALBUMS: *Freedom* (Curb 1996) ★★★, *Gospel* (Curb 1998) ★★★★.

Englishman

b. Erald Brisco. Raised in the UK, Englishman, despite his adopted name, has actually spent the majority of his years in Washington, DC, USA. He first recorded as a teenager with the London-based Revelation Reggae Band. By the time of his 18th birthday he was to be found touring Europe alongside **Ras Michael**. He has gone on to release a slew of albums, most backed by his own six-piece Roots Vibration Band, that have attracted a sizeable American audience. His rich delivery has often been compared to that of **Nat 'King' Cole**, while his bass guitar skills are credited to the influences of Robbie Shakespeare (of **Sly And Robbie**) and **Paul McCartney**.

● ALBUMS: *My African Sister* (1988) ★★★, *Check For The Youth* (1988) ★★★.

● COMPILATIONS: *Check For The Best* comprises selections from *My African Sister* and *Check For The Youth* (Mad Dawg 1991) ★★★★.

Enid

Influential art-rockers, formed in 1974 at experimental school Finchden Manor by keyboard player Robert John Godfrey (b. 30 July 1947, Leeds Castle, Kent, England) with guitarists Stephen Stewart and Francis Lickerish. The Enid's leader, Godfrey was educated at Finchden Manor (other alumni included **Alexis Korner** and **Tom Robinson**) and the Royal Academy Of Music. After starting a promising career as a concert pianist, Godfrey joined **Barclay James Harvest** as musical director in 1969 and moved them towards large orchestral works. He left the band in 1972, then recorded a solo album, *The Fall Of Hyperion*, for **Charisma Records** in 1973. He returned to Finchden Manor to form the Enid in 1974, taking the name from a school in-joke. The founding members were joined by Glen Tollet (bass), Chris North (drums) and Dave Storey (drums). Supported by dynamic live shows, a debut album, *In The Region Of The Summer Stars*, appeared in 1976. The simultaneous growth of punk 'put us in a cul-de-sac', according to Godfrey but, despite an ever-changing line-up, subsequent concept albums, rock operas and tours saw them increasing their cult audience and playing large venues.

A move to **Pye Records** just as the label went bankrupt in 1980 broke up the band. Godfrey formed his own label, distribution and studio with Stewart. They functioned uncredited as the backing band on all **Kim Wilde** albums up to *Cambodia*, and re-formed the Enid in 1983. Operating as independents, their following (known as 'The Stand') grew and the fifth studio album, *Something Wicked This Way*

Comes, was their biggest success yet. Simultaneously, Godfrey began a collaboration with healer Matthew Manning on meditational music albums. In 1986, the Enid presented its eighth album, *Salome*, as a ballet at London's Hammersmith Odeon. By 1988, the band's popularity appeared to have peaked, so, after two sold-out farewell gigs at London's Dominion Theatre, Godfrey split the band again. In 1990, based in an old house near Northampton, Godfrey re-emerged as manager and songwriter of a new band, Come September. He returned to the Enid format in 1994, releasing the instrumental concept album *Tripping The Light Fantastic* on the Mantella label. His well-publicized environmental concerns were given free rein on 1998's *White Goddess*, an ecological parable loosely based on the work of Robert Graves.

● ALBUMS: *In The Region Of The Summer Stars* (Buk 1976) ★★★, *Aerie Faerie Nonsense* (Honeybee 1977) ★★★, *Touch Me* (Pye 1978) ★★★, *Six Pieces* (Pye 1979) ★★★, *Live At Hammersmith Vol. 1* (Enid 1983) ★★, *Live At Hammersmith Vol. 2* (Enid 1983) ★★, *Something Wicked This Way Comes* (Enid 1983) ★★★, *The Spell* (Enid 1985) ★★★, *Fand* (Enid 1985) ★★★, *Salome* (Enid 1986) ★★★, *The Seed And The Sower* (Enid 1988) ★★★★, *Final Noise* (Enid 1989) ★★★, *Tripping The Light Fantastic* (Mantella 1994) ★★★, *Healing Hearts* (Mantella 1996) ★★★, *White Goddess* (Mantella 1998) ★★★.

● COMPILATIONS: *Lovers & Fools* (Dojo 1986) ★★★, *An Alternative History Volume 1* (Enid 1994), *An Alternative History Volume 2* (Enid 1994), *An Alternative History Volume 3* (Enid 1995), *Sundialer* (Mantella 1995) ★★★, *Anarchy On 45* (Mantella 1996) ★★★, *Members One Of Another* (Mantella 1996) ★★★, *Tears Of The Sun* (HTD 1999) ★★★★.

● DVD/VIDEOS: *Stonehenge Free Festival* (Visionary 1984), *Claret Hall Farm* (Visionary 1985).

Enigma

Ambient pop sculptors Enigma are the brainchild of Michael Cretu (b. 18 May 1957, Bucharest, Romania), who enrolled in the Lyzeum No. 2, a college for gifted young musicians, as a pianist, in 1966. After completing his studies Cretu moved to the Academy Of Music in Frankfurt, where Professor Philipp Mohler began to take an interest in him. Having passed his final exams in 1978, Cretu immediately found work as a studio musician and arranger. By 1980 he had earned his first significant success as producer, and he released his solo debut, *Legionare*, three years later for **Virgin Records**. He was then the architect behind the 1985 number 1 European success of Moti Special as writer, producer and keyboard player. Afterwards he devoted many of his efforts to the rise of Sandra, including masterminding 'Maria Magdelena', a number 1 in over 30 countries, and several successful albums. Further gold record status arrived in 1987 for his production work with **Mike Oldfield**, and in France he helped revitalize the career of Sylvie Vartan by writing and producing 'C'est Fatale'.

Cretu married Sandra Lauer in 1988 before putting together his most commercially successful project, Enigma, two years later, stating that 'old rules and habits have to be rejected and dismissed so that something new can be created.' Enigma's Gregorian chants and **dance music** rhythms subsequently enchanted nearly all who heard them, with the meditative repetition giving it universal appeal. 'Sadness

Part 1' hit the UK number 1 spot in December 1990, leading Cretu, who had now turned his back on a prospective career as a concert pianist, to remark, 'I started writing hits the day I sold my piano.' Almost every movement of the accompanying *MCMXC AD* album, which also topped the charts and spent no less than 57 weeks on the UK list, was used in some form of television or movie production. Gold or platinum status was attained in 25 countries.

With the phenomenal success of Enigma's debut, it was no surprise that the artist took a full three years to produce a follow-up. Film director Robert Evans invited Cretu to compose the title song to *Sliver*, resulting in the release of 'Age Of Loneliness (Carly's Song)', which also featured on the new album. Although it had pre-orders of 1.4 million units, **The Cross Of Changes**, which mined a wider range of influences than the debut, was hardly the expected blockbuster. The single 'Return To Innocence' reached number 9 in the UK charts in 1994, however, demonstrating the music's enduring appeal to the record-buying public. Subsequent albums have continued to mine Cretu's seamless fusion of new age, ambient and dance.

● ALBUMS: *MCMXC AD* (Virgin 1990) ★★★★, *The Cross Of Changes* (Virgin 1993) ★★★★, *Le Roi Est Mort, Vive Le Roi!* (Virgin 1996) ★★★, *The Screen Behind The Mirror* (Virgin 2000) ★★, *Voyageur* (Virgin 2003) ★★★.

● COMPILATIONS: *Love Sensuality Devotion: The Greatest Hits* (Virgin 2001) ★★★★.

Enjoy Records

One of the earliest US record labels to promote hip-hop, Enjoy Records was owned by Bobby Robinson, whose background in R&B stretched back to 1946, when he ran the Happy House Records' store. He elected to pursue a career in musical production when he realized that all the A&R men were coming to him for advice on what was marketable, and that he could cut out the middle man. Enjoy was actually inaugurated in 1963 with **King Curtis'** 'Soul Twist'. When rap arrived his Harlem-based operation was the first to record **Grandmaster Flash** And The Furious Five ('Super Rappin') before their contract was bought out by Joe Robinson (not a relation, though an old sparring partner from R&B days) of **Sugarhill Records**. Other notable Enjoy releases included the **Treacherous 3/Spoonie Gee**'s agenda-setting 'The New Rap Language'. 'Bodyrock' and 'Heartbeat' followed in 1981, before the Treacherous 3 also elected to join Sugarhill. Robinson's son was a member of the Disco Three, who also recorded on the label.

Ennis, Ethel

b. 28 November 1932, Baltimore, Maryland, USA. A child prodigy at the piano, Ennis was playing professionally at the age of 13 but then, two years later, began singing. Although this proved to be her métier, she was unable to make a living and took secretarial classes as a back-up. However, she began to establish a reputation along the east coast and her vocation quickly became her profession. Her attractive singing style proved popular in clubs and theatres alike and by the late 50s, she was sufficiently accomplished to be hired to sing at the 1958 Brussels World's Fair with **Benny Goodman** and **Jimmy Rushing**. Despite successes such as this, and some good albums, aimed mostly at the popular market, she failed to attract the attention of the big-time promoters and for the next few years, she worked regularly but in relative obscurity, while many lesser talents rose high on a wave of pop promotion.

Perseverance paid off and in the 90s Ennis began attracting respectful attention and headlining at places such as New York's Kennedy Center alongside more established jazz names. Stylistically, Ennis uses subtle shadings to create warm interpretations of well-known standards and less popular material alike. Her rhythmic drive is similarly understated and joyfully springy, avoiding unnecessary dramatics and allowing the full flavour of her material to emerge. Without doubt, hers is a career that deserves wider recognition, especially during the years of her prime when singers of her quality were rare.

● ALBUMS: *Lullabies For Losers* (Jubilee 1955) ★★★, *Have You Forgotten?* (Capitol 1958) ★★★, *This Is Ethel Ennis* (RCA 1964) ★★★, *Eyes For You* (RCA Victor 1964) ★★★, *My Kind Of Waltztime* (RCA) ★★★, *10 Sides Of Ethel Ennis* (BASF 1973) ★★★, *Live At Maryland Inn* (E&E 1980) ★★★, *If Women Ruled The World* (Savoy Jazz 1998) ★★★★.

● FURTHER READING: *Ethel Ennis: The Reluctant Jazz Star*, Sallie Kravetz.

Ennis, Séamus

b. May 1919, Dublin, Eire, d. 5 October 1982, Naul, Eire. One of Ireland's most influential musicians, Ennis played whistle and uillean pipes as well as singing in both English and Gaelic, and was considered to be one of the leading authorities on traditional Irish music. Ennis spent four years at college before leaving in 1938, and worked for five years at Three Candles Press. Four years later, in 1942, he joined the Irish Folklore Commission as a collector, travelling around Ireland and some of the Gaelic areas in Scotland. He moved on, in 1947, to work for Radio Eireann, and later, in 1951, the BBC. Ennis made a number of recordings, in 78 rpm format, for the BBC during the late 40s. He had earlier recorded a number of 78s for the Irish Gael-Linn label, in the Gaelic derivation of his name, Seosamh OhEanaigh. It was at the BBC that Ennis worked with folk collector **Peter Kennedy**, and they were involved in a weekly series *As I Roved Out*. Ennis also released an influential EP, *The Ace And Deuce Of Piping*, in 1960, which prefigured the revival of piping in the 60s. *Our Musical Heritage*, produced by RTE, was a three-album boxed set. The concept was based on a series of programmes presented by Sean O'Riada in 1962, on Radio Eireann. The post-humously released *Seamus Ennis—Master Of The Uillean Pipes*, was produced, recorded and engineered by **Patrick Sky**. The session was recorded in Dublin, at **Liam O'Flynn**'s flat.

● ALBUMS: *The Bonny Bunch Of Roses* (Traditional 1959) ★★★★, *Seamus Ennis* (1969) ★★★, *The Pure Drop* (1973) ★★★, *Forty Years Of Irish Piping* (Gael Linn 1974) ★★★★, *The Wandering Minstrel* (Topic 1974) ★★★, *Music At The Gate* (1975) ★★★, *The Fox Chase* (1977) ★★★★, *The King Of Ireland's Son* (1977) ★★★, *Seamus Ennis—Master Of The Uillean Pipes* (1985) ★★★★.

● COMPILATIONS: *The Best Of Irish Piping* (Tara 1996) ★★★, *The Return From Fingal* (RTE 1997) ★★★, *Forty Years Of Irish Piping* (Topic 2000) ★★★★.

● FURTHER READING: *The Master's Touch: A Tutor For The Uillean Pipes*, Séamus Ennis.

Ennis, Skinnay

b. Robert Ennis, 13 August 1909, Salisbury, North Carolina, USA, d. 3 June 1963, Beverley Hills, California, USA. Ennis joined the **Hal Kemp** band as a singer/drummer in the late 20s while still at the University of North Carolina. He became the band's leading attraction because of his unique 'out of breath' vocal style. Ennis left Kemp in 1938 and, after working with **Gil Evans** and **Claude Thornhill**, formed his own band with its theme song, 'Got A Date With An Angel', and gained maximum exposure with a prestigious residency on **Bob Hope**'s *Pepsodent Show*. Ennis also featured in the show's comedy routines and became a personality in his own right. After World War II, during which he led a service band, Ennis rejoined Hope until 1946, and then worked on radio with **Abbott And Costello** in the late 40s. He made several diverting appearances in films including *College Swing* (with Bob Hope), *Follow The Band*, *Swing It Soldier*, *Sleepytime Gal*, *Let's Go Steady* and *Radio Stars On Parade*. During the 50s his band toured the USA, playing the hotel circuit, including, from 1958, a five-year residency at the Statler-Hilton, Los Angeles. During the early 60s he recorded the album *Skinnay Ennis Salutes Hal Kemp*, using many of the musicians who had played in the original Kemp band. He died after choking on a bone while dining in a restaurant.

● COMPILATIONS: *Skinnay Ennis, 1947–1948* (Hindsight 1989) ★★★.

Eno, Brian

b. Brian Peter George St. Baptiste de la Salle Eno, 15 May 1948, Woodbridge, Suffolk, England. While studying at art schools in Ipswich and Winchester, Eno fell under the influence of *avant garde* composers Cornelius Cardew and **John Cage**. Although he could not play an instrument, Eno enjoyed tinkering with multi-track tape recorders and in 1968 wrote the limited edition theoretical handbook *Music For Non Musicians*. During the same period he established Merchant Taylor's Simultaneous Cabinet, which performed works by himself and various contemporary composers, including Christian Wolff, **La Monte Young**, Cornelius Cardew and George Brecht. This experiment was followed by the formation of a short-lived *avant garde* performance group the Maxwell Demon.

After moving to London, Eno lived in an art commune and played with Carden's Scratch Orchestra, the Portsmouth Sinfonia and his own band. As a result of his meeting with saxophonist **Andy Mackay**, Eno was invited to join **Roxy Music** in January 1971 as a 'technical adviser', but before long his powerful visual image began to rival that of band leader **Bryan Ferry**. It was this fact that precipitated his departure from Roxy Music on 21 June 1973. That same day, Eno began his solo career in earnest, writing the strong 'Baby's On Fire'. Shortly afterwards, he formed a temporary partnership with **Robert Fripp**, with whom he had previously worked on the second album by **Robert Wyatt**'s Matching Mole, *Little Red Record*. By November 1973, their esoteric *No Pussyfooting* was released, and a tour followed. With the entire Roxy Music line-up, bar Ferry, Eno next completed **Here Come The Warm Jets**, which was issued less than three months later in January 1974. It highlighted Eno's bizarre lyrics and quirky vocals.

A one-off punk single, 'Seven Deadly Finns', prompted a tour with the Philip Rambow-led Winkies. On the fifth date, Eno's right lung collapsed and he was confined to hospital. During his convalescence, Eno visited America, recorded some demos with **Television** and worked with **John Cale** on *Slow Dazzle* and later *Helen Of Troy*. His fraternization with former members of the **Velvet Underground** reached its apogee at London's Rainbow Theatre on 1 June 1974 when he was invited to play alongside Cale, **Kevin Ayers** and **Nico**, abetted by Robert Wyatt and **Mike Oldfield**. A souvenir album of the event was subsequently issued.

A second Eno solo album, *Taking Tiger Mountain (By Strategy)*, was followed by several production credits on albums by Robert Wyatt, **Robert Calvert** and **Phil Manzanera**. This, in turn, led to Eno's experiments with environment-conscious music. He duly formed the mid-price label Obscure Records whose third release was his own *Discreet Music*, an elongated synthesizer piece conceived during a period of convalescence from a road accident. During the same period, he completed *Another Green World*, a meticulously crafted work that displayed the continued influence of John Cage. A further album with Robert Fripp followed, called *Evening Star*.

After performing in Phil Manzanera's band **801**, Eno collaborated with painter Peter Schmidt on a concept titled 'Oblique Strategies', which was actually a series of cards designed to promote lateral thinking. During a hectic 18-month period, Eno recorded 120 tracks, the sheer bulk of which temporarily precluded the completion of his next album. In the meantime, he began a fruitful alliance with **David Bowie** on a trilogy of albums: *Low*, *Heroes* and *Lodger*. Even with that workload, however, he managed to complete his next solo work, *Before And After Science*. An unusually commercial single followed with 'King's Lead Hat'. The title was an anagram of **Talking Heads** and Eno later worked with that band as producer on three of their albums, including the innovative *Fear Of Music* and *Remain In Light*. Eno then turned his attention to soundtrack recordings before returning to ambient music. *Music For Films* was a potpourri of specific soundtrack material allied to pieces suitable for playing while watching movies. The experiment was continued with *Music For Airports*.

Throughout this period, Eno remained in demand as a producer and/or collaborator on albums by **Ultravox**, Cluster, **Harold Budd**, **Devo** and Talking Heads. In 1979, Eno moved to New York where he began making a series of vertical format video installation pieces. Numerous exhibitions of his work were shown throughout the world accompanied by his ambient soundtracks. During the same period he produced the *No New York* album by New York No Wave *avant garde* artists the **Contortions**, **DNA**, **Teenage Jesus And The Jerks** and Mars. His work with Talking Heads' **David Byrne** culminated in 1981 with the Top 30 album *My Life In The Bush Of Ghosts*, a fascinating collaboration that fused 'found voices' with African rhythms. In 1980, Eno forged an association with Canadian producer/engineer **Daniel Lanois**. Between them they produced *Voices*, by Eno's brother Roger, and a collaboration with Harold Budd, *The Plateaux Of Mirror*. This association with Lanois culminated in the highly successful U2 albums **The Unforgettable Fire**, **The Joshua Tree**, **Achtung Baby** and **Zooropa**. In critic Tim de Lisle's words, Eno's involvement 'converted' them (U2) 'from earnestness to gleeful irony'.

In 1990, Eno completed a collaborative album with John Cale, *Wrong Way Up*. The following year there was some confusion when Eno released *My Squelchy Life*, which

reached some record reviewers, but was withdrawn, revised, and re-released in 1992 as *Nerve Net*. As Eno's first album of songs for 15 years, it fused 'electronically-treated dance music, eccentric English pop, cranky funk, space jazz, and a myriad of other, often dazzling sounds.' For the same year's *The Shutov Assembly*, Eno returned to the ambient style he first introduced in 1975 with *Discreet Music*, and which was echoed 10 years later on his *Thursday Afternoon*. The album was conceived for Moscow painter Sergei Shutov, who had been in the habit of working to the accompaniment of Eno's previous music. *Neroli* was another hour's worth of similar atmospheric seclusion. In 1995, he worked with David Bowie on 1. *Outside* in addition to projects with **Jah Wobble** on *Spinner* and sharing the composing credits with U2's Bono, Adam Clayton and Larry Mullen Jnr. on *Passengers: Original Soundtracks 1*.

Eno's back-catalogue remains a testament to his love of esoterica, ever-shifting musical styles and experimentation. His recent solo work, however, has suffered because of the huge effort he puts into producing others—little time seems to be left to give his own work creative zip. The 2005 release *Another Day On Earth* was, however, a step in the right direction. Much of it echoed his past and as such, was hailed as the first 'great' solo Eno album for many years.

● ALBUMS: with Robert Fripp *No Pussyfooting* (Island/ Antilles 1973) ★★★, as Eno *Here Come The Warm Jets* (Island 1974) ★★★★, as Eno *Taking Tiger Mountain (By Strategy)* (Island 1974) ★★★★, with John Cale, Kevin Ayers, Nico *June 1st 1974* (Island 1974) ★★, as Eno *Another Green World* (Island 1975) ★★★★, *Discreet Music* (Island 1975) ★★★, with Fripp *Evening Star* (Island/Antilles 1975) ★★★, *Before And After Science* (Polydor 1977) ★★★★, with Cluster *Cluster And Eno* (Sky 1977) ★★★, *Music For Films* (Polydor 1978) ★★★, *Ambient 1: Music For Airports* (Ambient 1978) ★★★★, with Moebius, Roedelius *After The Heat* (Sky 1978) ★★★, with Harold Budd *Ambient 2: The Plateaux Of Mirror* (Editions EG/Ambient 1980) ★★★★, with Jon Hassell *Fourth World Vol. I: Possible Musics* (Polydor/Editions EG 1980) ★★★, with David Byrne *My Life In The Bush Of Ghosts* (Sire/Polydor 1981) ★★★★, *Ambient 4: On Land* (Editions EG 1982) ★★★, with Daniel Lanois, Roger Eno *Apollo: Atmospheres & Soundtracks* (Editions EG 1983) ★★★★, with Budd, Lanois *The Pearl* (Editions EG 1984) ★★★, *Thursday Afternoon* (EG 1985) ★★★, with Michael Brook, Lanois *Hybrid* (Editions 1985) ★★★, with Roger Eno *Voices* (Editions 1985) ★★★, with Cale *Wrong Way Up* (Land 1990) ★★★★, *Nerve Net* (Opal/ Warners 1992) ★★★, *The Shutov Assembly* (Opal/Warners 1992) ★★★, *Neroli* (All Saints 1993) ★★★, with Jah Wobble *Spinner* (All Saints 1995) ★★★, with various artists *Passengers: Original Soundtracks 1* (Island 1995) ★★★, *The Drop* (All Saints/Thirsty Ear 1997) ★★, *Extracts From Music For White Cube* (White Cube 1997) ★★★, *Lightness: Music For The Marble Palace* (Opal 1998) ★★★, *Kite Stories* (Opal 1999) ★★★, *I Dormienti* (Opal 1999) ★★★, with J. Peter Schwalm *Music For Onmyo-Ji* (Victor 2000) ★★★, *Music For Civic Recovery Center* (Opal 2000) ★★★, with J. Peter Schwalm *Drawn From Life* (Venture/Astralwerks 2001) ★★★, *Music For Films III* (All Saints 2003) ★★★, *January 07003: Bell Studies For The Clock Of The Long Now* (Opal 2003) ★★★, with Fripp *The Equatorial Stars* (Opal 2004) ★★★, *Another Day On Earth* (Opal 2005) ★★★★.

● COMPILATIONS: *Working Backwards 1983–1973* (Editions EG 1983) ★★★, with Moebius, Roedelius, Plank *Begegnungen* (Sky 1984) ★★★, with Moebius, Roedelius, Plank *Begegnungen II* (Sky 1985) ★★★, with Cluster *Old Land* (Sky 1985) ★★★, *Desert Island Selection* (EG 1986) ★★★★, *More Blank Than Frank* (EG 1986) ★★★★, *Box 1—Instrumental* 3-CD box set (Virgin 1993) ★★★, *Box II—Vocal* 3-CD box set (Virgin 1993) ★★★, with Robert Fripp *The Essential Fripp And Eno* (Venture 1993) ★★★, *Dali's Car* (Griffin 1994) ★★★, *Sonora Portraits* (Materiali Sonori 1999) ★★★, *Curiosities Volume 1* (Opal 2003) ★★★.

● DVD/VIDEOS: *Thursday Afternoon* (Sony 1984), *Excerpt From The Khumba Mele* (Hendring Video), *Mistaken Memories Of Medieval Manhattan* (Hendring Video), *Imaginary Landscapes* (Mystic Fire 1991), *14 Video Paintings* (All Saints 2006).

● FURTHER READING: *Music For Non-Musicians*, Brian Eno. *Roxy Music: Style With Substance—Roxy's First Ten Years*, Johnny Rogan. *More Dark Than Shark*, Brian Eno and Russell Mills. *Brian Eno: His Music And The Vertical Colour Of Sound*, Eric Tamm. *A Year With Swollen Appendices*, Brian Eno.

Enslaved

By taking the 80s Viking themes pioneered by Sweden's **Bathory** and combining them with a brutal black metal approach, Enslaved came to the forefront of the Norwegian Wotanist movement and earned much respect from the Scandinavian extreme metal scene in the process. Formed in 1991 from the ashes of Phobia by Grutle Kjellson (b. Kjetil Grutle, 24 December 1973, Haugesund, Norway; vocals/bass) and Ivar Bjørnson (b. Ivar Skontorp Peersen, 27 November 1977, Bergen, Norway; guitar/keyboards), plus the phenomenal drummer Trym Torson (ex-**Emperor**), Enslaved got their name from Demonaz of **Immortal** and recorded a demo, *Nema*. Although its production values were in line with the usual black metal studio techniques, i.e. the tinnier the better, it led to a much better recording, *Yggdrasill*, which impressed **Mayhem** guitarist and Deathlike Silence label head Euronymous enough to sign them up. *Vikingligr Veldi* was duly recorded, but its release was held up by the murder of Euronymous in August 1993 and it required some fancy legal footwork from the Voices Of Wonder label to get it released. It finally appeared in March 1994, as did the Osmose Records label funded recording *Frost*. Torson was replaced by Harald Helgeson on the subsequent *Eld*, which stuck firmly to the band's favoured mythical Norse themes. The follow-up, *Blodhemn*, featuring new drummer Dirge Rep (b. Per Arild Husebø, 18 July 1976, Stavanger, Norway) and second guitarist Roy Kronheim (b. 16 November 1973, Bergen, Norway), was a spoken-word narrative with more subtlety than the black metal fury of before.

● ALBUMS: *Vikingligr Veldi* (Voices Of Wonder 1994) ★★★, *Frost* (Osmose 1994) ★★★, *Eld* (Osmose 1997) ★★★, *Blodhemn* (Osmose 1998) ★★★★, *Mardraum: Beyond The Within* (Osmose 2000) ★★★, *Monumension* (Osmose 2001) ★★★, *Below The Lights* (Osmose 2003) ★★★.

Enter The Guardsman

This show won Denmark's first Musical Of The Year competition in September 1996, which attracted some 300 entries from around the world. *Enter The Guardsman* won for its creators, Americans Scott Wentworth (book), Marion Adler (lyrics) and Craig Bohmler (music), the substantial sum of £40,000 (approximately $60,000). It had previously attracted some attention when it won the Bernice Cohen Award for Outstanding Presentation Of 1994 by **ASCAP**, and had appeared at the National Alliance for Musical Theatre's 1995 Festival of New Musicals in the USA. After its success in Denmark, various producers expressed interest in mounting the show in England, and it was **Andrew Lloyd Webber**'s Really Useful Group that sponsored the production, which opened on 17 September 1997 at London's Donmar Warehouse. Set in the 20s, this chamber piece proved to be a sophisticated musical reworking of Ferenc Molnár's 1910 play *The Guardsman*, a comedy of manners that was once a favourite on Broadway, featuring Alfred Lunt and Lynn Fontanne; the story was also filmed in 1931. In this musical treatment, The Actor (Alexander Hanson) has recently married his leading lady, The Actress (Janie Dee). Aware that his new bride is not—by any means—inexperienced in the love department, The Actor decides to test her fidelity. He bombards her with red roses, sent anonymously at first. However, later, enter the guardsman (The Actor in disguise), who discovers, to his horror, that his wife succumbs to another's manly charms rather too easily for his taste. The proceedings are witnessed by the couple's old friend, The Playwright (Nicky Henson), a wryly debonair, but uncertain, character with notebook permanently poised, searching for a satisfying ending to their story. He is ultimately disappointed, because, in answer to his final question as to whether she knew that her soldier-count-lover was really her husband, the Actress enigmatically responds: 'On that night—he was.' Also in the fine Donmar cast were Angela Richards (The Dresser), Jeremy Finch (The Assistant Stage Manager), Walter Van Dyk (The Wigs Master) and Nicola Sloane (The Wardrobe Mistress). High points of the witty and tuneful score, which was suitably European in texture, included Angela Richards' 'Waiting In The Wings', 'My One Great Love' (Janie Dee), 'The First Night' (Company), 'Art Imitating Life' (Nicky Henson), and the title number (Company). The remaining, extremely attractive songs, were 'Chopin', 'My One Great Love', 'Language Of Flowers', 'Drama', 'Actor's Fantasy', 'You Have The Ring', 'True To Me', 'She's A Little Off', 'I Can't Go On', 'They Die' and 'In The Long Run'. Jeremy Sands directed the production, which played out its four-week season in the face of generally adverse critical reaction, ranging from 'lacked **Stephen Sondheim**'s cynicism, ironic wit or savage streak' to 'simply gentle, civilized fun'.

Enthroned

Along with **Ancient Rites**, Enthroned are the only black metal band of any significance to emerge from Belgium, and have been heard to complain about the prejudice they experience from the notoriously difficult-to-please fans and industry, simply because they are not Norwegian or Swedish. Be that as it may, they pack a fearsome punch and stick unswervingly to the grimmest of Satanic themes as well as the genre's usual fascination with warfare and mass extermination.

The band was formed in 1993 by Lord Sabathan (b. 21 August 1970, Charleroi, Belgium; vocals/bass, ex-Morbid Death) and sometime Blaspherion drummer Cernunnos, recruiting guitarist Tseboath of the death metal band Slanesh. A split EP with Ancient Rites on the Belgian Afterdark label led to

Prophecies Of Pagan Fire for Evil Omen (a subdivision of French label Osmose). Personnel changes included the addition of a second guitarist, Nornagest (b. 10 June 1977, Verviers, Belgium; ex-Heresia), while Tseboath was replaced by Nebiros. Recording for their second album was hindered by the unexpected suicide of Cernunnos in April 1997: Nornagest remarked in an interview shortly afterwards that 'this Christian world was not made for him . . . [Cernunnos wanted] to return to the kingdom below with Our Lord'. *Towards The Skullthrone Of Satan* was ultimately finished with the aid of new drummer Namroth Blackthorn and Enthroned went on tour with **Dark Funeral**. The band has remained a popular festival draw, despite more line-up changes, with Nebiros replaced by Nerath Daemon (b. 17 March 1981, Dunkerque, Belgium) in 2000, and Namroth Blackthorn by drummer Alsvid (b. 4 November 1976, St. Julien-en-Genevois, France; ex-Seth) the following year. Although Enthroned look unlikely ever to rise to the height of internationally known black metal bands such as **Cradle Of Filth** and **Dimmu Borgir**, it is for this reason that there is no better place to start for fans interested in learning about black metal. Few acts stick as rigidly to their roots, perhaps a lesson that could apply to those much envied Scandinavian scene-leaders.
● ALBUMS: *Prophecies Of Pagan Fire* (Evil Omen 1995) ★★★, *Towards The Skullthrone Of Satan* (Blackened 1997) ★★★★, *The Apocalypse Manifesto* (Blackened 1999) ★★★★, *Armoured Bestial Hell* (Blackened 2001) ★★★, *Carnage In Worlds Beyond* (Napalm 2002) ★★★.

Entombed

This Swedish death metal band was formed in Stockholm in 1987 as Nihilist, releasing four acclaimed demos: *Drowned, Premature Autopsy, But Life Goes On* and *Only Shreds Remain*. After dissolving Nihilist, the band reunited a few days later as Entombed, with a line-up of Lars-Goran Petrov (vocals), Uffe Cederlund (guitar), Alex Hellid (lead guitar) and Nicke Andersson (drums). *Left Hand Path* adequately demonstrated the band's potential with an atmospheric and individual sound and live shows were equally impressive. Lars Rosenberg was added on bass and Petrov departed shortly after the debut. Devor Safstrom only lasted for one single ('Crawl') before Johnny Dordevic (ex-Carnage) took over, although Andersson performed the vocals on the well-reviewed *Clandestine*. After an extensive US tour with **Morbid Angel**, Dordevic was ousted in favour of the returning Petrov for the Gods Of Grind UK jaunt with **Carcass, Cathedral** and Confessor. The mini-album *Hollowman* was swiftly followed by the hugely impressive *Wolverine Blues* as Entombed continued to ignore death metal convention, establishing themselves as one of the genre's leading acts, and creating more accessible material by incorporating into the fierce death metal framework traditional rock song structures and a rhythmic groove. Entombed's popularity continued to increase as they toured Europe on a frighteningly intense bill with labelmates **Napalm Death**, while an EP, *Out Of Hand*, saw high-class cover versions of material by **Kiss** ('God Of Thunder') and Repulsion ('Blackbreath'). The band left Earache Records in the mid-90s, but their tenure at major label EastWest Records was brief, and they were dropped without releasing an album. Moving to independent label Music For Nations, they sounded admirably unbowed on *To Ride, Shoot Straight And Speak The Truth!*, which featured new bass player Jörgen Sandström. Andersson left the band shortly afterwards to concentrate on his band the **Hellacopters**. He was replaced by Peter Stjärnwind, who made his first appearance on 1998's *Same Difference*.
● ALBUMS: *Left Hand Path* (Earache 1990) ★★★, *Clandestine* (Earache 1991) ★★★, *Hollowman* mini-album (Earache 1993) ★★, *Wolverine Blues* (Earache 1993) ★★★★, *To Ride, Shoot Straight And Speak The Truth!* (Music For Nations 1997) ★★★, *Monkey Puss (Live In London)* 1992 recording (Earache 1998) ★★, *Same Difference* (Earache 1998) ★★★, *Uprising* (Music For Nations 2000) ★★★, *Morning Star* (Music For Nations 2001) ★★★, *Sons Of Satan Praise The Lord* (Music For Nations 2002) ★★, *Inferno* (Music For Nations 2003) ★★★.
● COMPILATIONS: *Entombed* (Earache 1997) ★★★.
● DVD/VIDEOS: *Monkey Puss (Live In London)* (Earache 1999).

Entrance

This Chicago, Illinois, USA–based outfit is the creation of singer-songwriter Guy Blakeslee (b. USA). By the time he formed Entrance in 2001 Blakeslee was barely out of his teens but was already a veteran of the east coast alternative scene. He made his name as the bass player with Tonie Joy's Baltimore-based indie rock outfit the Convocation Of . . . , but a passion for early American folk music and blues led to his decision to go it alone. He first began using the Entrance moniker during a series of low-key gigs around his hometown. His debut, *The Kingdom Of Heaven Must Be Taken By Storm*, featured a memorable cover version of **Skip James**' pre-war blues 'I'm So Glad', alongside a number of folk and blues-influenced originals. The album was released in spring 2003 by the New York–based independent Tiger Style label. The *Honey Moan* EP, a collection of home recordings, followed later in the year. The equally stripped down *Wandering Stranger*, Blakeslee's second album, was released at the end of 2004.
● ALBUMS: *The Kingdom Of Heaven Must Be Taken By Storm* (Tiger Style 2003) ★★★, *Wandering Stranger* (Fat Possum/Sketchbook 2004) ★★★.

Entwistle, John

b. John Alec Entwistle, 9 October 1944, Chiswick, London, England, d. 27 June 2002, Las Vegas, Nevada, USA. As bass player (and occasional French horn player) in the **Who**, Entwistle provided the necessary bedrock to the band's individual sound. His immobile features and rigid stage manner provided the foil to his colleagues' impulsive pyrotechnics, yet paradoxically it was he who most enjoyed performing live. His stature as an important rock bass player was enhanced by his outstanding performance on the Who's 1973 double album, **Quadrophenia**. The sole member to undergo formal musical tuition, having played the French horn with the Middlesex Youth Orchestra, Entwistle quickly asserted his compositional talent, although such efforts were invariably confined to b-sides and occasional album tracks. His songs included 'Doctor Doctor', 'Someone's Coming' and 'My Wife', but he is generally recalled for such macabre offerings as 'Boris The Spider', 'Whiskey Man' and his two contributions to **Tommy**, 'Fiddle About' and 'Cousin Kevin'. These performances enhanced a cult popularity and several were gathered on *The Ox*, titled in deference to the bass player's nickname.

Entwistle released his first solo album, *Smash Your Head Against The Wall*, in 1971. It contained a new version of 'Heaven And Hell', a perennial in-concert favourite, and the set attracted considerable attention in the USA. *Whistle Rymes*, a pun on his often misspelled surname, confirmed his new-found independence with what is perhaps his strongest set to date, containing within such entertaining dark tales of peeping toms, isolation, suicide and nightmares. The following album, *Rigor Mortis Sets In*, paid homage to 50s rock 'n' roll and although an ambitious tour to support its release was set up, it had to be abandoned when the whole venture proved too costly. Entwistle then compiled the Who's archive set, *Odds & Sods*, before forming a new unit, Ox, but the attendant album, 1975's *Mad Dog*, was poorly received. He subsequently worked as musical director on two soundtrack sets, *Quadrophenia* and *The Kids Are Alright*, before completing his 1981 release, *Too Late The Hero*, which featured former **James Gang/Eagles** guitarist, **Joe Walsh**.

Entwistle's solo career was later deferred and he reunited with his former bandmates for a 1989 reunion tour. In the following decade Entwistle put together his own band with Godfrey Townsend (guitar) and Gordon Cotton (drums), touring and issuing the occasional album. He teamed up with the Who on several occasions to undertake lucrative reunion tours. In June 2002, Entwistle died from a heart attack in Las Vegas just as the band were about to embark on another US tour.

● ALBUMS: *Smash Your Head Against The Wall* (Track 1971) ★★★, *Whistle Rymes* (Track 1972) ★★★, *Rigor Mortis Sets In* (Track 1973) ★★, as John Entwistle's Ox *Mad Dog* (Decca 1975) ★★, *Too Late The Hero* (Warners 1981) ★★, *The Rock* 1986 recording (Whistle Rymes 1996) ★★, *King Biscuit Flower Hour* 1974 recording (King Biscuit Flower Hour 1997) ★★, *Left For Live* (J-Bird 1999) ★★.

● COMPILATIONS: *The Ox* (Track 1971) ★★★, *Anthology* (Repertoire 1996) ★★★, *Thunderfingers: The Best Of John Entwistle* (Rhino 1996) ★★★★, *So Who's The Bass Player? The Ox Anthology* (Sanctuary 2005) ★★★★.

● DVD/VIDEOS: *The John Entwistle Band Live* (BMG 2004).

● FURTHER READING: in addition to the Who books, *The John Entwistle Collection*, John Entwistle.

Enuff Z'Nuff

This Chicago, Illinois, USA, pop/metal crossover quartet was formed in 1985 by Donnie Vie (guitar/vocals), Chip Z'Nuff (bass), Gino Martino (guitar) and B.W. Boeski (drums). Line-up changes during the band's fledgling years saw Derek Frigo (b. 1968, USA, d. 28 May 2004, Beverly Hills, California, USA; guitar, ex-Le Mans) and Vikki Foxx (drums) replacing Martino and Boeski respectively. The quartet eventually landed a major label recording contract with **Atco Records** in the late 80s, and released their self-titled debut album in 1989. Influences such as **Cheap Trick** and the **Beatles** were apparent through Enuff Z'Nuff's extensive use of three-part harmonies, which carried the melody line in many of the songs. On a visual level, they initially appeared as multi-coloured fashion casualties from the early 70s, sporting an ambitious and often dazzling array of sunglasses, waistcoats, boots and accessories (regalia notably paraded on **MTV** via the video to their minor hits 'New Thing' and 'Fly High

Michelle'). This image was played down following the release of their second album *Strength*, an impressive and mature musical offering that combined infectious hooks, abrasive guitar work and a sparkling production to dramatic effect. Following Atco's internal problems with **Atlantic Records**, Enuff Z'Nuff moved to **Arista Records**, though their third album saw them lose Foxx to the **Vince Neil Band**. The replacement was Ricky Parent (ex–War And Peace), allegedly a distant relative of Arnold Schwarzenegger. Guitarist Derek Frigo decided to go his own way at this point, and the beleaguered band opted to release their original 1985 demo tape while they attempted to secure another recording contract. Original guitarist Gino Martino returned to the line-up on 1995's *Tweaked*, which was criticized for being too derivative. Further line-up changes ensued in the late 90s, with guitarist John Monaco joining Vie, Z'Nuff and Parent for 1998's *Paraphernalia*. They continued to release a steady stream of albums, taking Enuff Z'Nuff into the new millennium as a viable cult band. Former guitar player Frigo was found dead outside his girlfriend's Beverly Hills home in May 2004.

● ALBUMS: *Enuff Z'Nuff* (Atco 1989) ★★★, *Strength* (Atco 1991) ★★★★, *Animals With Human Intelligence* (Arista 1993) ★★, *1985* (Spitfire 1994) ★★, *Tweaked* (Spitfire 1995) ★★, *Peach Fuzz* (Spitfire 1996) ★★★, *Seven* (Spitfire 1997) ★★★, *Live* (Pony Canyon/Mayhem 1998) ★★, *Paraphernalia* (Pony Canyon/Spitfire 1998) ★★★★, *10* (Pony Canyon/Spitfire 2000) ★★★, *Welcome To Blue Island* (Pony Canyon/Dream Catcher 2002) ★★★.

Envy

Comprising Rhonni Stile (vocals), Gina Stile (guitar), Bill Spencer (bass) and Danny Kapps (drums), hard rock band Envy were formed on the east coast of America in the mid-80s. The group's highly accessible style, with distinctive female harmonies, drew early comparisons to **Heart**. The carefully constructed songwriting on *Ain't It A Sin* perfectly complemented the sisters' lovelorn lyrics with fluid arrangements and excellent production. However, despite **Atlantic Records**' self-evident investment in and early enthusiasm for the group, Envy broke up shortly after the album's release.

● ALBUMS: *Ain't It A Sin* (Atlantic 1987) ★★★.

Enya

b. Eithne Ní Bhraonáin, 17 May 1961, Dore, Gweedore, Co. Donegal, Eire. Enya, a classically trained pianist, was formerly a member of **Clannad** before embarking on a solo career that blossomed unexpectedly with her 1988 UK chart-topper, 'Orinoco Flow'. Daughter of noted Irish Showband leader Leo Brennan (Brennan is the non-Gaelic form of Bhraonáin) who led the Slieve Foy Band, Enya was born into a highly musical family. Her mother also was a musician, and in 1968 two of her brothers and two of her uncles formed the band An Clann As Dobhar (Gaelic for a family from the townland of Dore). The name was soon shortened to Clannad and another family member, harpist/vocalist **Máire Brennan**, added to the line-up. Enya joined the band on keyboards in 1980 and shared in some of their success as they recorded haunting themes for a variety of television programmes, giving them their first chart success. However, Enya, who has professed she has little time for conventional pop music, never quite fitted into the band and left amicably in 1982. Her first recordings appeared on the score to David Puttnam's 1985 feature, *The Frog Prince*. The following year Enya recorded the music for the BBC Television series *The Celts*, which was subsequently released as her debut album in 1987. An endearing blend of ethereal singing (in Gaelic and English) and lush synthesizers, the album was largely ignored, as was the accompanying single, 'I Want Tomorrow'. However, the following year, Enya signed to **WEA Records** and released *Watermark*. Climbing to number 5 in the UK charts, the album also generated a surprise number 1 with the hypnotic single 'Orinoco Flow (Sail Away)'. Working with her long-time collaborators, Roma Ryan (her lyric writer) and Nicky Ryan (her producer), Enya followed the chart-topper with two smaller hits—'Evening Falls' and 'Storms In Africa Part II'. The album also enjoyed a long chart run in America, eventually attaining multi-platinum status and establishing Enya as a fixture on the New Age album chart.

Enya adopted a lower profile for the next couple of years except for an appearance with **Sinéad O'Connor**. She returned in 1991 with the UK chart-topper *Shepherd Moons*, which by the mid-90s had attained world sales of 10 million copies. The album was hugely successful in America, and in 1993 won the Grammy for Best New Age Album. Her third collection, *The Memory Of Trees*, didn't alter the winning formula, but at some stage her warm, ambient music will begin to pale as listeners realize it is the same delicious cake with a different topping. The artist spent the remainder of the decade contributing soundtrack material to various projects, before returning to the studio to record *A Day Without Rain*. The album shot up the US and several European charts almost a year after its release, thanks to the use of the track 'Only Time' in news coverage of the terrorist attacks on the World Trade Center in New York.

● ALBUMS: *Enya* aka *The Celts* (BBC 1987) ★★, *Watermark* (WEA/Geffen 1988) ★★★★, *Shepherd Moons* (WEA/Reprise 1991) ★★★, *The Memory Of Trees* (WEA/Reprise 1995) ★★★, *A Day Without Rain* (WEA/Reprise 2000) ★★★, *Amarantine* (WEA 2005) ★★★.

● COMPILATIONS: *Paint The Sky With Stars: The Best Of Enya* (WEA/Reprise 1997) ★★★★, *A Box Of Dreams* 3-CD box set (WEA 1997) ★★★, *Only Time: The Collection* 4-CD box set (WEA 2002) ★★★.

● DVD/VIDEOS: *Moonshadows* (Warner Music Vision 1991), *The Video Collection* (Warner Music Vision 2001).

● FURTHER READING: *Enya: A Beginning Discography*, Matt Hargreaves.

Eon

Eon consists simply of Ian Loveday, whose interest in electronica and music was inspired by the theme to the BBC Television science-fiction programme *Dr Who*, which was created by the BBC radio workshop under the name Ray Cathode. Eon released a sequence of impressive singles: 'Light, Colour, Sound', 'Infinity' 'Inner Mind' (featured in the movie *Buffy The Vampire Slayer*) and 'Spice'. The latter was remixed by Loveday's long-standing hero, **Juan Atkins**, and featured samples taken from the science fiction epic *Dune*. He continued his association with Vinyl Solution for singles such as 1992's horror film–inspired 'Basket Case'. He has also recorded extensively with **Baby Ford** for the Trelik label.

● ALBUMS: *Void Dweller* (Vinyl Solution 1992) ★★★.

Epic House

(see **House**)

Epic Soundtracks

b. Kevin Paul Godley, 23 March 1959, d. 22 November 1997, London, England. Better known for starting art punk renegades **Swell Maps** with his brother, **Nikki Sudden**, in the mid-70s, then for collaborations with **Crime And The City Solution** and These Immortal Souls, Epic's late-starting solo career revealed more of his artistic muse than that normally associated with a jobbing drummer. However, in interviews he admitted to seeing his résumé as something of a drag, and wishing that his solo career had started about two decades earlier (there had previously been two singles, 'Jelly Babies' and 'Rain Rain Rain', released on **Rough Trade Records** under his name in 1981 and 1982). Just as he largely disowned his past, so he confessed to having little affection for the style of music pioneered by the punk years. His solo career instead concentrated on a more soulful, singer-songwriter approach—this despite the appearance of indie and punk luminaries such as Kim Gordon of **Sonic Youth**, J. Mascis of **Dinosaur Jr** and Will Pepper of **Thee Hypnotics** on his second album, *Sleeping Star* (Mascis and Gordon had also worked on the debut). He would also tour with **Evan Dando** of the **Lemonheads**, both artists sharing an abiding affection for **Gram Parsons**, which was evident in their own work. Godley was found dead of a suspected drug overdose in his London flat in November 1997.

● ALBUMS: *Rise Above* (Rough Trade 1993) ★★★, *Sleeping Star* (Rough Trade 1994) ★★★, *Change Of Life* (Bar None 1996) ★★★.

● COMPILATIONS: *Everything Is Temporary* (Interstate 1999) ★★★, *Good Things* (DBK Works/Koch 2005) ★★★.

Episode Six

This respected UK beat group evolved in 1964 when two amateur groups amalgamated. **Roger Glover** (b. 30 November 1945, Brecon, Wales; bass), Harvey Shields (drums) and Tony Lander (guitar) were former members of the Madisons; Sheila Carter-Dimmock (organ), her brother Graham (rhythm guitar) and Andy Ross (vocals) were from the Lightnings. Ross, who quickly tired of touring, left in May 1965, and was replaced by **Ian Gillan** (b. 19 August 1945, Hounslow, Middlesex, England). The sextet had already secured a recording contract with **Pye Records**; 'Put Yourself In My Place', written by the **Hollies**' team, Clarke/Hicks/Nash, duly became their debut single the following January. Episode Six specialized in releasing cover versions, bringing strong harmony work to the **Beatles**' 'Here, There And Everywhere', the **Tokens**' 'I Hear Trumpets Blow' and **Tim Rose**'s 'Morning Dew'. Lack of direction doubtlessly doomed their commercial prospects, but despite this, two solo singles, by Sheila Carter-Dimmock and Graham Carter-Dimmock, also were issued. The latter's release, credited to 'Neo Maya', was a cover version of 'I Won't Hurt You', originally recorded by the **West Coast Pop Art Experimental Band**.

Shields was replaced by former **Pirates** drummer John Kerrison in 1967. The following year the sextet switched to MGM, dropping the 'Six' suffix for one single, 'Little One'. Mick Underwood (ex-**Outlaws**) then joined in place of a disenchanted Kerrison, after which the group joined the Chapter One label for two more singles. Their final release, 'Mozart Versus The Rest', was a brazen pop/classical

workout. Plans for an album, *The Story So Far*, were mooted, but in July 1969 Ian Gillan was invited to join **Deep Purple**. Within weeks he was joined by Roger Glover, although Underwood kept Episode Six alive with the addition of John Gustafson (bass, ex–**Big Three**) and Peter Robinson (keyboards). In 1969 the three broke away to found progressive act **Quatermass**, effectively ending the career of Episode Six.
● COMPILATIONS: *Put Yourself In My Place* (PRT 1987) ★★★, *The Roots Of Deep Purple: The Complete Episode Six* (Collectables 1992) ★★★, *The Radio One Club Sessions: Live 1968/69* (RPM 1997) ★★★, *Cornflakes And Crazyfoam* (RPM 1997) ★★★, *Love, Hate, Revenge* (Castle 2005) ★★★.

Epitaph

USA band Epitaph's career comprises two distinct phases, linked together by founder member and guitarist/vocalist Cliff Jackson (b. 1 August 1943, England; guitar/vocals) and Jim McGillivray (drums). Originally, they were formed in Dortmund as Fagan's Epitaph with Bernd Kolbe (b. 10 October 1951, Germany; bass). The first two albums had little to do with their later hard rock style and featured a jazz-tinged AOR flavour. The band disintegrated in 1975, but Jackson resurrected Epitaph in 1979 with Heinz Glass (guitar), Harvey Janssen (bass), Michael Karch (keyboards) and Fritz Randow (drums). *Return From Reality* adopted an aggressive approach, characterized by the heavy-duty guitar work of Glass. Karch was fired after the album was released, and *See You In Alaska*, which followed, was surprisingly lightweight compared to its predecessor. *Live* redressed the balance and saw the band in good shape once more. However, internal disputes resulted in the departure of Glass, Randow and Janssen soon after the album's release. Klaus Walz, Norbert Lehmann and Bernie Kolbe were drafted in as replacements on guitar, drums and vocals, respectively, to record *Danger Man* in 1982. Unable to generate renewed interest, the band folded in 1983. Kolbe and Jackson went on to Kingdom (later renamed **Domain**), while Randow joined Victory.
● ALBUMS: *Outside The Law* (Billingsgate 1974) ★★★, *Stop, Look And Listen* (Polydor 1975) ★★, *Return From Reality* (Brain 1979) ★★★, *See You In Alaska* (Brain 1980) ★★, *Live* (Metronome 1981) ★★★, *Danger Man* (Metronome 1982) ★★★.

Epitaph Records

One of the longest-standing and most successful homes to the USA's constantly evolving alternative rock movement, Epitaph Records was originally started as an in-house label for Los Angeles, California, group **Bad Religion**. In common with that group, Epitaph took several years to rise to the prominence it currently enjoys. Guitarist Brett Gurewitz (b. c.1962, USA) formed Epitaph in the early 80s as an outlet for Bad Religion releases. Having recently recovered from crack cocaine addiction, the label at its inception was a long way from the 'greatest rock 'n' roll record company in the world' that Gurewitz envisaged for its future in the mid-90s. By 1993 the label was home to **Rancid, No FX**, Pennywise and **Offspring** in addition to Bad Religion, Gurewitz having recently left the band to concentrate on the label, but had sold only 1.5 million records in seven years. That situation changed dramatically with the Offspring's breakthrough early in 1994. Their song 'Come Out And Play (Keep 'Em Separated)'

became a major hit on **MTV** and propelled the accompanying album, *Smash*, to sales of over eight million. Gurewitz was even lionized with an article in *Newsweek* magazine under the headline 'Punk Is His Business'. From a team of six people working in a garage, Epitaph suddenly became a major concern, relocating to new offices in the plush Los Angeles neighbourhood of Silverlake. However, although the success allowed Epitaph to expand its roster, two of its most successful groups, Bad Religion and the Offspring, have jumped ship to a major record label, the latter publicly stating that Gurewitz's 'independent' attitude was just a smokescreen for his corporate interests. Despite this, Rancid followed up the Offspring's success with two further million-selling albums to keep Epitaph a highly profitable concern throughout 1995 and 1996. Whether or not the label will ever achieve the level of success that Gurewitz clearly intends for it is less clear-cut, particularly as his 1996 divorce required him to secure further finance for the label.

EPMD

Erick Sermon (b. 25 November 1968, Bayshore, Long Island, New York City, USA) and Parrish Smith (b. 13 May 1968, Brentwood, Long Island, New York City, USA) are two rappers who did much to revitalize a flagging rap scene with an early outburst of controlled creative energy, *Unfinished Business*. Taking samples from rock sources such as **Steve Miller**, as well as underground dance music, EPMD worked up a healthy, funk-fuelled groove. Particularly effective among their early recordings was the rap manifesto on 'So Whatcha Sayin''. Their early struggles to attract record company interest are best observed in the 1989 single 'Please Listen To My Demo', which documents their malaise. By then, however, they had recorded their first two albums. *Strictly Business* was distinguished by an idea for a new dance entitled 'The Steve Martin', while the fun continued on *Unfinished Business*, which in many ways sounded just like its title. Unrestrained anarchy in the studio appeared to be the order of the day, with improvised lines, interruptions and jokey singing forming the basis of proceedings. It included contributions from **K-Solo**, who had previously worked in a pre–EPMD band with Smith, and would go on to record a solo album under his tutelage.

They moved to **Def Jam Records** in time for their third album, a much more accomplished affair (at least musically) with tighter production and harder beats. Despite the prevailing ethos, they never felt the need to provide a direct political agenda like many rap groups, seeing music as a source of personal self-advancement. This is openly demonstrated by the titles of their LPs, and the fact that their initials stand for Erick And Parrish Making Dollars. However, the manner in which EPMD tried to accommodate new lyrical concerns was less than satisfactory. Their raps continued to chastise their peers as 'sucker MC's', which was by now little more than cliché. Ironically, one of the better cuts on *Business As Usual* was 'Rampage', a collaboration with **LL Cool J**, whose artistic fortunes had witnessed a similar decline in recent years. *Business Never Personal* simply continued in remorseless EPMD style. The duo split in 1993, Sermon being the first to embark on a solo career with 'Stay Real' and *No Pressure*. The latter's title reflected, wryly, on the fact that most considered Smith to be the talent of the band. Yet, *No Pressure* was an excellent collection that did much to lay that myth to rest. Smith released his own solo debut a year later, billing himself as PMD. Sermon and Smith reunited in the late 90s to release *Back In Business* and *Out Of Business*, before returning to their solo projects.

● ALBUMS: *Strictly Business* (Fresh 1988) ★★★★, *Unfinished Business* (Fresh 1989) ★★★★, *Business As Usual* (Def Jam 1991) ★★★, *Business Never Personal* (Def Jam 1992) ★★, *Back In Business* (Def Jam 1997) ★★, *Out Of Business* (Def Jam 1999) ★★★.

Epps, Preston

b. 1931, Oakland, California, USA. Epps may be the only musician who has had a Top 20 hit based on bongo drum playing. He learned how to play the instrument in the early 50s and, while supporting himself with odd jobs, he played his drums in then-popular coffee houses in the Los Angeles area. He was discovered by Los Angeles disc jockey Art Laboe, who also ran the Original Sound record label. They recorded Epps' self-penned 'Bongo Rock' and it was released on Laboe's label, eventually reaching number 14 in the USA in 1959. One follow-up, 'Bongo Bongo Bongo', also charted, in 1960, as did an album of the same title. Epps continued to record bongo-related music until the mid-60s but was unable to follow up his biggest hit with another. (A remake of the song by the Incredible Bongo Band did chart in 1973.) Epps later toured and recorded with **Johnny Otis** in the 70s.

● ALBUMS: *Bongo Bongo Bongo* (Original Sound 1960) ★★, *Bongola* (Original Sound 1961) ★★.

Epstein, Brian

b. Brian Samuel Epstein, 19 September 1934, Liverpool, England, d. 27 August 1967, London, England. One of the most famous pop managers in music business history, Epstein began his working life in the family business as a provincial shopkeeper, overseeing the North End Road Music Stores (NEMS) in central Liverpool. His life took a new direction on Saturday 28 October 1961 when a customer requested a record entitled 'My Bonnie' by a group called the **Beatles**. When Epstein subsequently attended one of their gigs at the **Cavern** in Mathew Street he was drawn into the alien netherworld of leather-clad beat groups and, against the advice of his friends, became a pop manager. His early efforts at promoting the Beatles proved haphazard, but using his influence with record companies he secured a number of interviews with important A&R representatives. A slew of rejections followed, but **Decca Records** at least offered the Beatles an audition before finally turning them down. Epstein took his revenge by crediting the unfortunate **Dick Rowe** with the immortal words, 'Groups of guitarists are on the way out.' Epstein's tardiness in securing a record contract did not diminish his abilities in other areas.

He transformed the Beatles into a more professional outfit, banned them from swearing or eating on stage and even encouraged the establishment of a rehearsed repertoire. Perhaps his most lasting contribution at this point was persuading them to replace their menacing, black leather garb with smart, grey lounge suits, with eye-catching matching collars. By the spring of 1962, Epstein at last won a record contract thanks to the intuitive intervention of producer **George Martin**. A near-crisis followed shortly afterwards when Epstein had to oversee the dismissal of drummer **Pete Best**, who was replaced by **Ringo Starr**. During October 1962, a management contract was belatedly finalized with the Beatles by which Epstein received 25 per cent of their earnings, a figure he maintained for all future signings. Weeks later, he struck a deal with music publisher **Dick James**, which culminated in the formation of Northern Songs, a company dealing exclusively with compositions by **John Lennon** and **Paul McCartney**. In an extremely clever and unusual contract for the period, the powers agreed on a 50/50 split: half to Dick James and his partner Charles Emmanuel Silver; 20 per cent each to Lennon and McCartney, and 10 per cent to Epstein.

Long before the Beatles became the most successful entertainers in music history, Epstein had signed his second group, **Gerry And The Pacemakers**. Scouring the Cavern for further talent he soon added **Tommy Quickly**, the **Fourmost**, **Billy J. Kramer And The Dakotas**, the **Big Three** and **Cilla Black**. The spree of NEMS signings during 1963 was the most spectacular managerial coup since **Larry Parnes'** celebrated discoveries during the late 50s. More importantly, the artists dominated the UK charts throughout the year, logging an incredible nine number 1 hits spanning 32 weeks at the top. By early 1964, Beatlemania had crossed from Britain to America and NEMS had transformed from a small family business into a multi-million-pound organization. The strength of the company ensured that the Beatles had few administrative problems during the Epstein era. Scrupulously fair, he even allowed his charges a 10 per cent interest in NEMS. One area where Epstein was deemed fallible was in the merchandising agreements that he concluded on behalf of the Beatles. Ironically, it was the result of delegating the matter to the inexperienced solicitor David Jacobs that the group found themselves receiving a mere 10 per cent of the sums received by the company set up to merchandise goods in their name.

By the mid-60s, licences had been granted for every product that the American merchandising mentality could conceive. This meant not only badges, dolls and toys, but even cans of Beatle breath. The lost revenue that Epstein had allowed to slip through his fingers was gruesomely revealed in the pages of the *Wall Street Journal*. According to their figures, Americans spent approximately $50 million on Beatles goods up to the end of 1964, while the world market was estimated at roughly £40 million. Although Epstein attempted to rectify the poor merchandising deal through litigation and even contributed massive legal expenses from his own pocket, the stigma of the unfortunate deal remained. Few pointed out that it was less Epstein's error than that of the inexperienced Jacobs, who had agreed to the arrangement without consulting his client. The merchandising dispute has all too often eclipsed Epstein's achievements in other areas. It deserves to be remembered that the Liverpudlian effectively ushered in the era of stadium rock with the Beatles' Hollywood Bowl concert, an event that changed rock economics for ever.

Even while the Beatles were conquering the New World, Epstein was expanding his empire. Although he signed a couple of unsuccessful artists, most of the NEMS stable enjoyed tremendous success. The career of Cilla Black was a tribute to Epstein's creative management. He helped her adapt to the rigours of showbusiness success with a feminine solicitude typical of a would-be dress designer. More importantly, however, he immediately recognized her lasting charm as the gauche, unpretentious girl-next-door, an image that another manager might have suppressed. Epstein's expert exploitation of her appeal paved the way for her eventual acceptance and remarkable success as a television host. When the Beatles ceased touring after the summer of 1966, Epstein's role in their day-to-day lives was minimal. For a time, he attempted to find satisfaction in other areas, purchasing the Savile Theatre in London's Shaftesbury Avenue and alternating serious drama with Sunday pop shows. Ever-puzzling, Epstein even sponsored an Anglo-Spanish bullfighter named Henry Higgins and astonished his colleagues by attempting to persuade the perpetually nervous Billy J. Kramer to pursue an acting career. NEMS, meanwhile, ceased to inspire the entrepreneur and he inexplicably offered a 51 per cent controlling interest to the Australian adventurer **Robert Stigwood**. By 1967, Epstein was losing control. Drug dependence and homosexual guilt brought him to the verge of a nervous breakdown and attempted suicide. He suffered at the hands of the press for advocating the use of the drug LSD. On August Bank Holiday 1967 the Beatles were in north Wales attending a course in transcendental meditation with their new mentor, the Maharishi Mahesh Yogi. Epstein, meanwhile, was lying dead at his London home in Chapel Street, Mayfair. The inquest subsequently established that he had died from a cumulative overdose of the sleep-inducing drug Carbatrol. Although suicide was suspected and some fanciful conspiracy theories have suggested the remote possibility of foul play, the coroner concluded with a prosaic verdict of accidental death from 'incautious self-overdoses'.

In spite of his foibles, Epstein is rightly regarded as a great manager, possibly the greatest in British pop history. Judged in the context of his era, his achievements were remarkable. Although it is often claimed that he did not exploit the Beatles' earning power to its maximum degree, he most certainly valued their reputation above all else. During his tenure as manager, he insulated them from corporate avarice and negotiated contracts that prevented **EMI Records** from marketing cheap reissues or unauthorized compilations. In this sense, he was the complete antithesis of **Elvis Presley**'s manager, **Colonel Tom Parker**, who allowed his artist to atrophy through a decade of bad movies. As the custodian of the Beatles' international reputation, Epstein's handling of their career was exemplary. For Epstein, honour meant more than profit and he brought an integrity to pop management that few of his successors have matched.

● FURTHER READING: *A Cellarful Of Noise*, Brian Epstein. *Brian Epstein: The Man Who Made The Beatles*, Ray Coleman. *In My Life: The Brian Epstein Story*, Debbie Geller.

Equals

Twins Derv and Lincoln Gordon (b. 29 June 1948, Jamaica; vocals and rhythm guitar, respectively), **Eddy Grant** (b. Edmond Montague Grant, 5 March 1948, Plaisance, Guyana, West Indies; lead guitar), Patrick Lloyd (b. 17 March 1948, Holloway, London, England; rhythm guitar) and John Hall (b. 25 October 1947, Holloway, London, England; drums) began playing together in 1965 on a council estate in Hornsey Rise, north London. Their best-remembered single, 'Baby Come Back', was recorded the following year as a b-side, but the quintet's early releases made little impression. Over the ensuing months the band became highly regarded on the continent, where they toured extensively. 'Baby Come Back' became a major hit in Germany during 1967 and later topped the charts in Holland and Belgium. This propulsive, infectious song was then reissued in Britain where it

eventually rose to number 1. Although the Equals enjoyed other hits, only 'Viva Bobby Joe' (1969) and 'Black Skinned Blue-Eyed Boys' (1970) reached the Top 10 as their reliance on a tested formula wore thin. Chief songwriter Grant left for a solo career in 1971, after which the band underwent several changes in personnel before finding security on the cabaret circuit. However, their career was resurrected in 1978 when Grant, by then a self-sufficient artist and entrepreneur, signed them to his Ice label for *Mystic Synster*.

● ALBUMS: *Unequalled Equals* (President 1967) ★★★, *Equals Explosion* aka *Equal Sensational Equals* (President 1968) ★★★, *Equals Supreme* (President 1968) ★★★, *Baby Come Back* (President 1968) ★★★★, *Equals Strike Back* (President 1969) ★★, *Equals At The Top* (President 1970) ★★, *Equals Rock Around The Clock* (1974) ★★, *Doin' The 45s* (1975) ★★★, *Born Ya* (Mercury 1976) ★★, *Mystic Synster* (Ice 1978) ★★.

● COMPILATIONS: *The Best Of The Equals* (President 1969) ★★★, *Greatest Hits* (1974) ★★★★, *The Very Best Of The Equals* (See For Miles 1996) ★★★, *Viva Equals! The Very Best Of The Equals* (Music Club 1999) ★★★.

Equation

This UK folk rock ensemble originally featured **Kate Rusby** (vocals/violin), **Kathryn Roberts** (vocals, keyboards, woodwind), and the three **Lakeman Brothers**, **Seth Lakeman** (violin), Sean Lakeman (guitar) and Sam Lakeman (keyboards). All of them were from musical families. Rusby and Roberts had appeared with numerous traditional and ceilidh bands, and had worked together previously as child dancers and on other collaborative projects. They released their first album as a duo in 1995. The Lakeman brothers also boasted a prodigious musical background, and formed their own group as teenagers, appearing on BBC Television's *Saturday Superstore*. For several years they proved popular attractions on the jazz and folk circuits throughout their native south-west England.

The Equation was formed in the spring of 1995, when none of the members was older than 21. Roberts, who had been awarded BBC Radio 2's Young Tradition Award, had sung vocals on the Lakeman Brothers' debut album, *3 Piece Suite*. She was then requested to put together a group of young musicians to play a Portuguese festival but the group, the Equation, stayed together afterwards. On their return to the UK they became so successful on the folk circuit that they had bookings until the end of 1997. They played the main stage at the 1995 **Cambridge Folk Festival**. The folk music press celebrated them as the scene's brightest new hopes for a young, traditional English folk band of the 90s. However, following the signing of a five-album contract with Warner Music, Rusby left the band. She was replaced by **Cara Dillon** (b. 1975, Dungiven, Co. Derry, Eire; ex-Oige), and various new personnel were also added to the line-up to help augment the group's sound, but their projected debut album *Return To Me* was not released at the time, and musical disagreements led to Dillon and Sam Lakeman also leaving. The remaining members (Roberts, Sean and Seth Lakeman, bass player Darren Edwards, and drummer Iain Goodall) opted to start from scratch, writing the new material that constituted the long-awaited debut album *Hazy Daze*. Poor sales of the album resulted in the termination of the band's ill-fated contract with the Warners group. Electric guitarist James Crocker was added to the line-up for the recording of the follow-up, *The Lucky Few*, which was released on **Geoff Travis**' Blackburst label. A much more satisfying release, *The Lucky Few* added some much needed grit to the band's melodic folk rock.

Equation went on to establish themselves on the North American market with a series of popular tours, but in 2001 Seth Lakeman elected to leave and concentrate on his songwriting and solo career. The same August, the remaining five members released the limited edition *The Dark Ages EP*, featuring their readings of five traditional English folk songs. The following year's *First Name Terms* album was released in the US on the I Scream label.

● ALBUMS: *Hazy Daze* (Blanco y Negro 1998) ★★★, *The Lucky Few* (Blackburst/Putumayo 1999) ★★★★, *First Name Terms* (I Scream 2002) ★★★, *Return To Me* 1995/ 96 recording (Rough Trade 2003) ★★★★.

Erase Errata

This all-female indie rock band was formed in 1999 by Jenny Hoyston (vocals/trumpet), Sara Jaffe (guitar), Bianca Sparta (drums) and Ellie Erickson (bass). Based in San Francisco, California, USA, the quartet had already completed work on a demo before choosing their unusual moniker. They made their debut on the Troubleman Unlimited label the following year, releasing a split single with the New York–based **Black Dice**. *Other Animals*, which was released in late 2001, struggled to strike a balance between the structured rhythms of 'Tongue Tied' and 'Marathon' and more experimental numbers such as 'Fault List'. The album failed to make much of an impact beyond the pages of sympathetic music magazines. A tour with the like-minded **Sonic Youth** and **Le Tigre** the following summer boosted Erase Errata's profile, as did the burgeoning popularity of similarly styled post-punk, no wave outfits such as the **Liars** and **Interpol**.

● ALBUMS: *Other Animals* (Troubleman Unlimited/Tsk! Tsk! 2001) ★★★, *At Crystal Palace* (Blast First 2003) ★★★.

Erasure

Keyboard player and arranger Vince Clarke (b. 3 July 1960, South Woodford, London, England) had already enjoyed success as a member of **Depeche Mode**, **Yazoo** and the **Assembly** when he decided to undertake a new project in 1985. The plan was to record an album with 10 different singers, but after auditioning vocalist Andy Bell (b. 25 April 1964, Peterborough, Cambridgeshire, England), the duo Erasure was formed. Erasure broke into the higher regions of the UK chart in 1986 with 'Sometimes', which reached number 2 and was followed by 'It Doesn't Have To Be Me' in 1987. The following month their second album, *The Circus*, reached the UK Top 10 and their popularity rapidly grew. In the late 80s and early 90s, memorable and infectious hits such as 'Victim Of Love', 'The Circus', 'Ship Of Fools', 'Chains Of Love', 'A Little Respect', *Crackers International* EP, 'Drama!', 'Blue Savannah', 'Chorus', 'Love To Hate You' and 'Breath Of Life' established the band as serious rivals to the **Pet Shop Boys** as the world's leading vocal/synthesizer duo. 'Chains Of Love' and 'A Little Respect' also reached the US Top 20. Their appeal lay in the unlikely pairing of the flamboyant Bell and the low-profile keyboards wizard and songwriter Clarke. Their stage-shows were spectacular events, whilst the overtly gay Bell's taste in clothes was campily outrageous.

During the early 90s, Erasure's singles and album sales continued to increase, with *The Innocents*, *Wild!*, *Chorus* and *I Say, I Say, I Say* all reaching number 1 on the UK album chart. Their excellent pastiche of **Abba**, 1992's *Abba-Esque* EP, topped the UK singles chart, while 'Who Needs Love (Like That)' (a remix of their first single from 1985), 'Always' and 'Run To The Sun' all reached the UK Top 10. Subsequent releases saw a dip in the duo's popularity, and they took a sabbatical following 1997's *Cowboy* before recording the follow-up, *Loveboat*. The duo returned to the UK Top 10 in January 2003 with a cover version of **Peter Gabriel**'s 'Solisbury Hill', the first single to be released from an album entirely dedicated to interpretations of other artists' work. An album of their own material was released in 2005, and was followed later in the year by Bell's solo debut *Electric Blue*. It is worth stressing that Clarke and Bell achieved their extraordinary success working through an independent label, **Mute Records**.

● ALBUMS: *Wonderland* (Mute 1986) ★★★, *The Circus* (Mute/Sire 1987) ★★★, *The Two Ring Circus* remix album (Mute/Sire 1988) ★★★, *The Innocents* (Mute/Sire 1988) ★★★, *Wild!* (Mute/Sire 1989) ★★★, *Chorus* (Mute/Sire 1991) ★★★, *I Say, I Say, I Say* (Mute 1994) ★★, *Erasure* (Mute 1995) ★★★, *Cowboy* (Mute/Maverick 1997) ★★★, *Loveboat* (Mute 2000) ★★★, *Other People's Songs* (Mute 2003) ★★, *Nightbird* (Mute 2005) ★★★.
Solo: Andy Bell *Electric Blue* (Sanctuary 2005) ★★★.

● COMPILATIONS: *Pop!—The First 20 Hits* (Mute/Sire 1992) ★★★★, *Hits! The Very Best Of Erasure* (Mute 2003) ★★★★.

● DVD/VIDEOS: *Pop—20 Hits* (Mute 1993), *The Tank, The Swan And The Balloon Live!* (Mute 2004).

Eric B And Rakim

This Queens, New York City, USA–based rap duo comprised Eric Barrier (b. Elmhurst, New York, USA) and William 'Rakim' Griffin (b. William Griffin Jnr., Long Island, New York, USA), using additional musicians such as Sefton the Terminator and Chad Jackson as required. **Rakim** was the lyricist, Eric B the DJ, or, as Rakim himself put it in 'I Ain't No Joke': 'I hold the microphone like a grudge, Eric B hold the record so the needle don't budge'. They met in 1985 when Eric was working for the New York radio station WBLS and was looking for the city's top MC. They started working together before emerging with the demo 'Eric B. Is President'. Released as a single on an obscure Harlem independent, Zakia Records, in the summer of 1986, it eventually led to a contract with 4th & Broadway. Their long-playing debut was preceded by a stand-out single of the same name, 'Paid In Full', which inspired over 30 remixes. When the album arrived it caused immediate waves. Representatives of **James Brown** and **Bobby Byrd** took legal action over the sampling of those artists' works. Conversely, they helped to galvanize Brown's career as a legion of rap imitators drew on his back catalogue in search of samples. They also originated the similarly coveted 'Pump Up The Volume' sample.

As well as Eric B putting the funk back into rap music, Rakim was responsible for introducing a more relaxed, intuitive delivery that was distinctly separate from the machismo of **Run-DMC** and **LL Cool J**, and was probably the biggest single influence on 90s hip-hop artists such as **Wu-Tang Clan**, **Nas** and **Dr. Dre**. The duo hit the UK charts in 1987 with 'Paid In Full (The Coldcut Remix)', though they themselves hated the version. Later hits included 'Move The Crowd', 'I Know You Got Soul', 'Follow The Leader', 'The Microphone', and 1989's US Top 10 collaboration with **Jody Watley**, 'Friends'. Label moves may have diminished their probable impact, though the duo themselves never went out of their way to cross over into the mainstream. Instead, each of their albums offered a significant musical development on the last, Rakim's raps growing in maturity without sacrificing impact. The split came in the early 90s, with Rakim staying with MCA to deliver solo material like 'Heat It Up', produced by new co-conspirator Madness 4 Real, and included on the soundtrack to the Mario van Peebles movie, *Gunmen*.

● ALBUMS: *Paid In Full* (4th & Broadway 1987) ★★★★, *Follow The Leader* (Uni 1988) ★★★, *Let The Rhythm Hit 'Em* (MCA 1990) ★★★★, *Don't Sweat The Technique* (MCA 1992) ★★★, *Paid In Full: The Platinum Edition* (Island 1998) ★★★★.

Eric Steel Band

A hard-working hard rock band from Chicago, Illinois, USA, the Eric Steel Band comprised Bruce Hansfield (vocals/guitar), Dave Anderson (guitar), Mike Hobson (bass) and Brad Wickham (drums). After coming to prominence on the local Illinois club scene they signed to Megaforce Records in 1984 for the release of *Eric Steel*. Though there was little distinguished about the songwriting on view, the group's natural energy ensured it was greeted as an above-average release. Four years passed before a follow-up collection, *Infectious*, was released by Passport Records. In the interim, the group had lost some of its impetus but, on the evidence of their new songs, none of their vivacity.

● ALBUMS: *Eric Steel* (Megaforce 1984) ★★★, *Infectious* (Passport 1988) ★★★.

Erickson, Roky

b. Roger Kynard Erickson, 15 July 1947, Dallas, Texas, USA. Erickson came to the fore in the infamous **13th Floor Elevators**. He composed 'You're Gonna Miss Me', the band's most popular single, while his feverish voice and exciting guitar work provided a distinctive edge. This influential unit broke up in disarray during 1968 as Erickson began missing gigs. Arrested on a drugs charge, he faked visions to avoid imprisonment, but was instead committed to Rusk State Hospital for the Criminally Insane. He was released in 1971 and began a low-key solo career, recording several singles with a new backing group, Bleib Alien. In 1980 the guitarist secured a recording contract with **CBS Records** but the resultant album, *Roky Erickson And The Aliens*, was a disappointment and compromised the artist's vision for a clean, clear-cut production. Erickson's subsequent releases have appeared on several minor labels. Their quality has varied, befitting a mercurial character who remains a genuine eccentric—he has persistently claimed that he is from the planet Mars. His music borrows freely from horror and science fiction films and, when inspired, he is capable of truly powerful performances.

Erickson was imprisoned in 1990 for stealing mail, but his plight inspired **Sire Records**' *Where The Pyramid Meets The Eye*, wherein 19 acts, including **R.E.M.**, **Jesus And Mary Chain**, **ZZ Top** and the **Butthole Surfers**, interpreted many of his best-known songs, the proceeds of which should ameliorate his incarceration. Following his release from a mental institution a grizzled Erickson recorded 1995's *All That May Do My Rhyme*, and against all expectations of a drug-wrecked casualty record, it was one of his better efforts. Like **Syd Barrett**, Erickson may never return to our cosy and supposedly sane world, but unlike Barrett he is at least still attempting to make new music.

● ALBUMS: with the Aliens *Roky Erickson And The Aliens* aka *I Think Of Demons* (CBS/Edsel 1980) ★★★, with the Aliens *The Evil One* (415 1981) ★★★, *Clear Night For Love* mini-album (New Rose 1985) ★★, *Don't Slander Me* (Enigma/Pink Dust 1986) ★★★, *Casting The Runes* (Five Hours Back 1987) ★★, *The Holiday Inn Tapes* (Fan Club 1987) ★★, *Openers* (Five Hours Back 1988) ★★, *Live At The Ritz 1987* (New Rose/Fan Club 1988) ★★, *Mad Dog* (Swordfish 1992) ★★, *All That May Do My Rhyme* (Trance Syndicate 1995) ★★★, *Demon Angel: A Day And Night With Roky Erickson 1984 recording* (Triple X 1995) ★★, *Roky Erickson & Evil Hook Wildlife* (Sympathy For The Record Industry 1995) ★★, with the Aliens *Don't Knock The Rok! 1978 recording* (Norton 2004) ★★.

● COMPILATIONS: *Gremlins Have Pictures* (Enigma/Pink Dust 1986) ★★, *Click Your Fingers Applauding The Play* (New Rose/Fan Club 1988) ★★★, *You're Gonna Miss Me: The Best Of Roky Erickson* (Restless 1991) ★★★★, *Never Say Goodbye* (Emperor Jones 1999) ★★★, *Hide Behind The Sun* (Aim 2000) ★★, *I Have Always Been Here Before: The Roky Erickson Anthology* (Shout Factory 2005) ★★★★.

● DVD/VIDEOS: *Demon Angel: A Day And Night With Roky Erickson* (Triple X 1999).

Eric's Trip

Drawing its personnel from the Canadian fishing village of Moncton, New Brunswick, Eric's Trip formed in 1990 because, as they were keen to point out, 'nothing much else happens there'. The band's line-up featured Julie Doiron (bass/vocals), Chris Thompson (guitar), Rick White (guitar/vocals) and Mark Gaudet (drums), the latter replacing original drummer Ed Vaughan in November 1991. Their sound, self-described as 'punk rock that isn't afraid to dream', first came to light on a series of cassette-only releases at the turn of the 90s. These transmuted into profligate 7-inch singles and compilation appearances, before landing on **Sub Pop Records** in 1993 for their long-playing debut (the first Canadian artists on the roster). Though their descriptions of their sound may have invoked notions of gentility, by their second album they were still averaging one minute per song—just enough time to crystallize a single idea around a simple riff. Lyrics concerned themselves primarily with small-town issues, unsurprising perhaps, as band members still struggled to hold down day jobs at the time, in Moncton, including working in a photo laboratory, record store and fast food outlet. After struggling on for a further two albums, Eric's Trip ground to a halt in 1996. Doiron continued performing under the Broken Girl moniker, while her bandmates went on to work with various low-key outfits including Elevator To Hell, Purple Knight, and Moonsocket. Eric's Trip re-formed in 2001 for a short tour. A compilation of live material dating from all periods of the band's career was released at the same time.

● ALBUMS: *Eric's Trip* cassette (Own Label 1990) ★★, *Warm Girl* cassette (Own Label 1992) ★★, *Love Tara* (Sub

Pop 1993) ★★★, *Forever Again* (Sub Pop 1994) ★★★★, *Purple Blue* (Sub Pop 1996) ★★.
● COMPILATIONS: *Long Day's Ride Till Tomorrow* (Sonic Unyon 1997) ★★, *The Eric's Trip Show* (Teenage USA 2001) ★★.

Ericson, Rolf

b. 29 August 1922, Stockholm, Sweden, d. 16 June 1997, Stockholm, Sweden. Ericson had already been playing trumpet for more than two years when, in 1933, he was taken to hear **Louis Armstrong** during his European tour and was suitably inspired. As a young teenager Ericson was playing professionally and during the late 40s he made a number of recordings. In 1947 he moved to New York and played in several big bands, including those of **Charlie Barnet**, **Woody Herman** and **Elliot Lawrence**. Ericson was attracted by bebop and also played with **Wardell Gray**. In the early 50s Ericson toured his homeland in company with **Charlie Parker** and also spent time in numerous big bands, often those assembled for one-off recording and television dates. Later in the decade and on into the 60s he divided his time between the USA and Scandinavia, playing with a wide range of musicians such as **Bud Powell**, **Brew Moore**, **Kenny Dorham**, **Stan Kenton**, **Benny Goodman**, **Gerry Mulligan**, **Ernestine Anderson** and **Duke Ellington**. During the second half of the 60s he became deeply involved in studio work, both in the USA and Germany, but found time to play with visiting American musicians. In the 80s he mostly worked from his base in Berlin, where his music would always find a receptive audience. In 1990 he was in Los Angeles and joined the Ellingtonian small band led by **Bill Berry**, which featured **Marshal Royal** and **Buster Cooper**. In the mid-90s he was forced to relocate from his home in the USA after his German wife failed to get a green card. He spent his last years residing in Stockholm.
● ALBUMS: *Oh Pretty Little Neida* (Four Leaf Clover 1971) ★★★, *Sincerely Ours* (Four Leaf Clover 1978) ★★★, *Stockholm Sweetenin'* (Dragon 1984) ★★★, with Lex Jasper *My Foolish Heart* (Interplay 1989) ★★★, *I Love You So* (Amigo 1996) ★★★.

Erkose Ensemble

A five-piece group of Turkish gypsy musicians based in Istanbul, the Erkose Ensemble comprises three brothers: Ali who plays the kaman (Turkish violin), Selahaddin who plays the ud (Middle Eastern lute) and clarinettist Barbaros Erkose. They are joined by their cousins, Gungor Hosses on darbuka drum and Serdar Ucal who plays the zither-like kanun. Erkose Ensemble have been playing together since they were children and members of the group are also involved in Istanbul's pop, jazz and classical music scenes. On *Tzigane—The Gypsy Music Of Turkey*, as the title suggests, they play traditional gypsy music, with passion and wild energy, mixing the musics of Anatolia, Greece, Balkans and the Middle East.
● ALBUMS: *Tzigane—The Gypsy Music Of Turkey* (CMP 1992) ★★★.

Erlanger, A.L.

b. Abraham Lincoln Erlanger, 4 May 1860, Buffalo, New York, USA, d. 7 March 1930, New York City, USA. Together with his business partner, Marc Klaw, Erlanger built an elaborate showbusiness empire of production companies and theatrical real estate. Among Erlanger's productions were **George M. Cohan**'s *Forty-Five Minutes From Broadway* (1906) and he backed **Florenz Ziegfeld** when the impresario was getting started. Erlanger and Klaw's company was also responsible for the construction of new theatres in New York, notably The New Amsterdam and The Erlanger, the latter later becoming known as The St. James. Another of their enterprises was the Theatrical Syndicate, with which they exercised ruthless control over bookings made by several hundred theatres across the nation. Setting rates and determining who could play where and when in a manner designed solely for their own financial benefit, Erlanger and Klaw made many enemies. Reviled by many for the ruthless and unnecessarily vicious manner in which he frequently did business, Erlanger sowed the seeds of his own destruction when he refused to honour agreements he had reached with Sam Shubert. This happened after the showman died in a railroad accident. Shubert's brothers began a campaign against Erlanger, eventually bringing him to ruin.

Eros

b. Eros Ramazotti, Italy. Ramazotti began his professional career in 1982, when he was spotted at the Castrocaro talent contest. Roberto Gallanti, at that time managing director at Italian independent label DDD Records, immediately signed him. In 1983 Ramazotti confirmed the wisdom of his faith in him by winning the newcomer's section of the San Remo Song Festival with the ballad, 'Adesso Tú'. He made his debut with *In Ogni Senso*, but his real breakthrough in Europe came with the runaway success of *Tutte Storie* in 1993, which sold more than 4.5 million copies. Afterwards Ramazotti attempted to convert his domestic popularity in to international success with the release of *Dove Cé Musica* in 1996. An album of pristine melodic rock and balladeering, this saw Ramazotti elect to take more control over his career, co-writing and producing the collection in its entirety. 'This is very much my own creation,' he told **Billboard** magazine; 'I feel as if it is my son. Every song on the album has been meticulously constructed step by step, each having its theme and vitality.' Typical of the contents was 'Piu Bella Cosa' (Most Beautiful Thing), a romantic mid-tempo ballad with gospel backing vocals, which was released as the first single from the album. The video was directed by Nigel Dick, best-known for his work with **Guns N'Roses**. Other tracks featured diverse styles ranging from salsa and merengue to country and pop. He retained his popularity in Italy, while becoming increasingly adopted by the American Hispanic community (the album was also released in a Spanish-language version as well as Italian). The album was promoted with appearances throughout Europe and South America.
● ALBUMS: *In Ogni Senso* (DDD 1989) ★★★, *Tutte Storie* (DDD/BMG 1993) ★★★★, *Dove Cé Musica* (DDD/BMG 1996) ★★★.

Errico, Melissa

b. 23 March 1970, New York City, USA. Raised in Manhasset, Long Island, in a close family of Italian descent, at the age of five Errico began ballet lessons and also trained as a gymnast. Plans to become a competitive gymnast foundered owing to weakness in a knee, but were swiftly superseded by a desire to take up acting. As her singing voice developed, a sparkling soprano, it swiftly became apparent that her forte would be the stage musical. She has proved this true with appearances in a Broadway revival of **My Fair Lady** (playing Eliza Doolittle), in a 2003 revival of *Aunt Dan And Lemon*, in the **Michel Legrand** musical, *Amour*, also on Broadway and for which she was nominated for a 2003 Tony award as Best Leading Actress In A Musical and in **The Threepenny Opera** at The Williamstown Theater Festival. She reprised her role of Eliza in a Hollywood Bowl staging of *My Fair Lady* that also starred John Lithgow and **Roger Daltrey**. Appearances in films, including *Frequency* (2000), *Life Or Something Like It* (2002) and *Loverboy* (2004), marked the opening of a new branch of her career. As a cabaret singer she has appeared at several prestigious venues, including the Oak Room at New York's Algonquin Hotel.

● ALBUMS: *Blue Like That* (Manhattan/Capitol/EMI 2003) ★★★.

● FILMS: *Loose Women* (1996), *Bury The Evidence* (1998), *Picture This* (1999), *Frequency* (2000), *Mockingbird Don't Sing* (2001), *Life Or Something Like It* (2002), *Loverboy* (2004).

Errol, Leon

b. 3 July 1881, Sydney, New South Wales, Australia, d. 12 October 1951, Hollywood, California, USA. Travelling to the USA as a young man, Errol worked in vaudeville as a comedian. He enjoyed considerable success on Broadway, appearing in the **Ziegfeld Follies** from 1911, including directing the editions for 1915 and 1916. He worked in other of **Florenz Ziegfeld**'s shows including **Sally** (1920), which starred **Marilyn Miller**, and also appeared in dramatic productions. He began making films, including the film version of *Sally* (1925) and appeared in other musical films, including **Paramount On Parade** (1930) and *Make A Wish* (1937). Errol found his *métier* in two-reel comedies. Balding and rubber-faced, and often rubber-legged too, Errol specialized in eccentric characters of which the bewildered (and often cuckolded) husband was evoked with masterly ease. In 1939 he co-starred with Lupe Velez in *The Girl From Mexico*, the success of which promptly led to *Mexican Spitfire* (with more or less the same cast and script), which was followed by a further six films in 'The Mexican Spitfire' series. Meanwhile, he worked on other films including *Never Give A Sucker An Even Break* (1941, with **W.C. Fields**), and *Follow The Band* (1943). The series with Velez ended in 1943 with *Mexican Spitfire's Blessed Event* and thereafter he appeared in other films including *Higher And Higher* (1943), *Mama Loves Papa* (1945), **Abbott And Costello**'s *The Noose Hangs High* (1948) and *Footlight Varieties* (1951). Many of his films were instantly forgettable, something Errol himself never was. At the time of his death he was in negotiation with television executives for his own series.

Erskine, Peter

b. 5 June 1954, Somers Point, New Jersey, USA. Erskine began playing drums while still a toddler, and at the age of six was attending the **Stan Kenton** Stage Band Camps. He studied advanced drum techniques under **Alan Dawson** and then, at the age of 18, joined Kenton. He played with Kenton for three years, touring internationally and establishing a formidable reputation as a player and teacher. In 1976 he joined **Maynard Ferguson**, then in a jazz rock phase, and two years later became a member of **Weather Report**, where he remained into the early 80s. After leaving Weather Report, Erskine worked in the studios and also made records and toured with

Michael Brecker and David Sancious in the band known as **Steps Ahead** and with **John Abercrombie**. From the late 80s onwards he was active as leader of his own group, a band that included Brecker and Abercrombie, playing in the tradition in which Erskine is an established master. A dazzling technician, Erskine is one of the outstanding jazz rock drummers, bringing inventiveness and rhythmic clarity to the form and playing with subtlety and swing.

● ALBUMS: *Peter Erskine* (Contemporary 1982) ★★★★, with John Abercrombie, Marc Johnson *Current Events* (ECM 1985) ★★★★, *Transition* (Denon 1986) ★★, *Motion Poet* (Denon 1988) ★★★, *Big Theatre* (Ah Um 1989) ★★★, *John Abercrombie, Marc Johnson & Peter Erskine* (ECM 1989) ★★★★, *Sweet Soul* (RCA 1991) ★★, with Jan Garbarek, Miroslav Vitous *Star* (ECM 1991) ★★★, with Palle Danielsson, John Taylor *You Never Know* (ECM 1993) ★★★, with Danielsson, Taylor *Time Being* (ECM 1993) ★★★, with Abercrombie, Johnson, John Surman *November* (ECM 1994) ★★★★, *History Of The Drum* (Interworld 1995) ★★★, with Danielsson, Taylor *As It Is* (ECM 1996) ★★★★, with Richard Torres *From Kenton To Now* (Fuzzy Music 1998) ★★★, *Juni* (ECM 1999) ★★★, with Marty Ehrlich, Michael Formanek *Relativity* (Enja 2000) ★★★★, with Abercrombie, Bob Mintzer, John Patitucci *The Hudson Project* (Stretch 2000) ★★★★, with Alan Pasqua *Live At Rocco* (Fuzzy Music 2000) ★★★, with Nguyên Lê, Michel Benita *ELB* (ACT 2001) ★★★, with Peter Epstein, Scott Colley *Old School* (MA 2002) ★★★, with Pasqua, Dave Carpenter *Badlands* (Fuzzy Music 2002) ★★.

● DVD/VIDEOS: *The Complete Cymbal Guide For The Drumset* (DCI Music 1995).

Ertegun, Ahmet

b. 1923, Istanbul, Turkey. The son of the Turkish ambassador to Washington, DC, USA, Ahmet Ertegun moved to New York upon his father's death in 1944. Although a philosophy graduate, he was drawn towards a musical career via his passion for jazz and blues, of which he was an inveterate collector. With friend and partner **Herb Abramson**, he founded two unsuccessful labels, Quality and Jubilee, before inaugurating **Atlantic Records** in 1947. Early releases featured recordings by jazz artists **Errol Garner** and **Tiny Grimes**, but Ertegun decided to pursue an R&B-styled policy and the label enjoyed its first notable hit with **Granville 'Stick' McGhee**'s 'Drinking Wine, Spo-Dee-O-Dee', which Ertegun produced. He continued to fulfil that role when **Jerry Wexler** arrived at Atlantic. The pair were responsible for producing early seminal releases for **Clyde McPhatter** and the **Drifters**, including 'Money Honey' and 'Such A Night'. Ahmet also proved himself a skilled composer, co-penning 'Chains Of Love' and 'Sweet Sixteen', the first two hits for 1949 signing **Big Joe Turner**. Many of his subsequent compositions were credited to the anagrammatical pseudonym, 'Nutgere'. During the 50s Atlantic established itself as a leading independent through the signings of **Ray Charles** and **Bobby Darin**. Ertegun and Wexler produced Ray Charles together, while Ahmet took sole charge for Darin, notably on his first hit, 'Splish Splash'. The label was quick to capitalize on the long-player format and Ertegun passed responsibility for transferring 78s to the new medium to his older brother, Nesuhi. The **Coasters** and a revitalized Drifters ensured Atlantic's success rate was maintained and with many contemporaries now experiencing financial difficulties,

Ertegun entered the 60s as a music industry survivor. Indeed, in 1965 he assisted producer/songwriter **Bert Berns** in establishing the **Bang Records** label. Although Jerry Wexler is credited with shaping Atlantic's mid-60s policies, in particular its arrangements with **Stax Records** and Fame, Ertegun signed white 'southern-styled' acts **Dr. John**, **Delaney And Bonnie** and **Jessie Davis** to the label. However, his greatest achievement was a deliberate decision to broaden Atlantic's R&B image with pop and rock signings. Ertegun brought **Sonny And Cher** to the company, a faith repaid immediately when 'I Got You Babe' became one of the bestselling singles of 1965. That same year he launched the (Young) **Rascals**, who gained 17 US Top 20 hits until leaving for **Columbia Records** in 1969.

Meanwhile, another Ertegun acquisition, **Vanilla Fudge**, found success with their dramatic rearrangements of popular songs, notably 'You Keep Me Hangin' On'. He introduced **Neil Young** and **Stephen Stills** to the public via **Buffalo Springfield**, who struck gold with 'For What It's Worth' and won critical acclaim for three excellent albums. Ertegun kept faith with Stills upon the quintet's disintegration, trading band member **Richie Furay** for **David Crosby** and securing a release for the **Hollies**' **Graham Nash**. The resultant 'supergroup', **Crosby, Stills And Nash**, became one of the era's leading attractions. However, **Iron Butterfly** did not receive the same critical approbation, although *In-A-Gadda-Da-Vida* was, for a spell, the biggest-selling album in history. Ertegun's vision proved equally astute with respect to UK acts. A licensing agreement with **Polydor Records** ensured Atlantic had first option on its British roster. He took up the **Bee Gees** and **Cream**, as well as the solo careers of the latter's ex-members following their split. **Eric Clapton** proved an important coup. Ertegun signed **Led Zeppelin** directly to US Atlantic; his faith was rewarded when the quartet became one of rock's most successful bands. Ahmet also took up the rights to the soundtrack of the **Woodstock Festival**, and in 1970, he persuaded the **Rolling Stones** that Atlantic was the natural home for their own record label. By this point, however, his company's autonomy had been affected.

In 1967 Ertegun and Wexler allowed **Warner Brothers Records** to purchase Atlantic stock in return for an executive position in a conglomerate known as **WEA Records** with the acquisition of **Elektra Records**. Although Ertegun has remained at his label's helm, it has since lost its distinctive qualities. He has concurrently pursued other interests and a passion for soccer led to his becoming a director of the New York Cosmos, to which he attracted such luminaries as Pele and Franz Bekenbauer. Even if his profile is less apparent than in previous years, Ahmet Ertegun has left an indelible mark on the development of popular music through his entrepreneurial and musical gifts. He was inducted into the **Rock And Roll Hall Of Fame** in 1987.

● FURTHER READING: *Music Man: Ahmet Ertegun, Atlantic Records And The Triumph Of Rock 'N' Roll*, Dorothy Wade and Justine Picardie.

Ervin, Booker

b. 31 October 1930, Denison, Texas, USA, d. 31 August 1970, New York City, USA. As a child, Ervin played trombone but switched to tenor saxophone in the early 50s during his military service. (He led his own small group when he was stationed on Okinawa.) After returning to civilian life, Ervin studied at **Berklee College Of Music** under Joe Viola, then worked with **Ernie Fields**' R&B band and several jazz groups in the south-west. A move to New York in 1958 brought him into a long-standing if irregular association with **Charles Mingus** that continued into the mid-60s. He recorded extensively with Mingus and **Randy Weston** and also with his own groups. A powerful player, Ervin's style demonstrates his awareness of such diverse tenor saxophonists as the Texas tenor school (his father played trombone with **Buddy Tate**'s band), **Lester Young**, **Dexter Gordon**, **Sonny Rollins** and **John Coltrane**, but he chose to follow a different star and remained very much his own man. His warm approach to ballads and searing attack on up-tempo numbers showed him to be a much hotter player than most of his contemporaries. His death in 1970 came while he was still very much in his prime.

● ALBUMS: with Roland Kirk *Soulful Saxes* (Affinity 1957) ★★★★, *The Book Cooks* (Bethlehem 1960) ★★★★, *Cookin'* (Savoy Jazz 1960) ★★★★, *That's It!* (Candid 1961) ★★★, *Exultation!* (Prestige 1963) ★★★★, *The Freedom Book* (Prestige 1963) ★★★★, *The Song Book* (Prestige 1964) ★★★★, *The Blues Book* (Prestige 1964) ★★★★, *The Space Book* (Prestige 1965) ★★★★, *Lament For Booker Ervin* (Enja 1966) ★★★, *Groovin' High* (Prestige 1966) ★★★★, with Dexter Gordon *Settin' The Pace* (Prestige 1967) ★★★, *The Trance* (Prestige 1967) ★★★★, *Heavy!* (Prestige 1967) ★★★, *Structurally Sound* (Pacific Jazz 1968) ★★★, *Booker 'N' Brass* (Pacific Jazz 1968) ★★, *The In Between* (Blue Note 1969) ★★★, shared with Horace Parlan *Back From The Gig* 1963, 1968 recordings (Blue Note 1976) ★★★★, with Pony Poindexter, Larry Young *Gumbo!* 1963–1964 recordings (Prestige 1999) ★★★, *Tex Book Tenor* 1968 recording (Blue Note 2005) ★★★★.

● COMPILATIONS: with Don Patterson *Legends Of Acid Jazz: Don Patterson/Booker Ervin* (Prestige 1996) ★★★★.

Ervin, DiFosco

(see **Irwin, Big Dee**)

Erwin, George 'Pee Wee'

b. 30 May 1913, Falls City, Nebraska, USA, d. 20 June 1981, Teaneck, New Jersey, USA. A child prodigy, Erwin first attracted attention playing trumpet on the radio with the **Coon-Sanders Nighthawks** when he was only eight years old. After playing trumpet in local bands, including John Whetstine, with whom he toured when he was just 15, Roland Evans, Eddie Kuhn and Erwin joined the nationally popular **Joe Haymes** band in 1931. He followed this with a spell in the **Isham Jones** orchestra, the outstanding dance band of the day, was briefly with **Freddy Martin**, and then joined **Benny Goodman** at the end of 1934. After a short stay with **Ray Noble** (in a band formed by **Glenn Miller** that previewed the Miller 'sound') Erwin returned to Goodman for most of 1936 and then flitted through various bands, including Noble's again, **Tommy Dorsey**'s, Raymond Scott's and then took temporary control of the **Bunny Berigan** band. From the mid-40s Erwin was often in the studios, but at the end of the decade he had become a regular at Nick's in New York. This engagement lasted through the 50s with other regular gigs at the Metropole and on numerous radio and television shows. An enormously popular man and a gifted musician, Erwin began teaching in the 60s and his qualities were imparted to many newcomers to the jazz scene, most notably **Warren Vaché Jnr**. In the 70s Erwin was constantly in demand for club and festival dates and in 1979 he rejoined Benny Goodman for the Playboy Jazz Festival in Hollywood. That same year his home-town of Falls City nominated a 'Pee Wee Erwin Day' and presented him with the keys to the city. He worked almost until the end of his life, playing the Breda Jazz Festival in Holland in May 1981, just a few weeks before his death.

● ALBUMS: *The Land Of Dixie* (Brunswick 1955) ★★★, *Oh, Play That Thing!* (London 1958) ★★★, with Dick Hyman *Some Rags, Some Stomps, And A Little Blues* (Columbia 1974) ★★★★, *Pee Wee In Hollywood* (Qualtro 1980) ★★★, *Memorial* (Jazz Crooner 1981) ★★★.

● FURTHER READING: *This Horn For Hire*, Pee Wee Erwin and Warren Vaché Snr.

Escape Club

A quartet of Trevor Steel (vocals), John Holliday (guitar), Johnnie Christo (bass) and Milan Zekavica (drums), the Escape Club took their central influence from the glam rock era of **T. Rex** and **David Bowie**. Formed in Essex, England, in 1983, they signed to **EMI Records** after the release of their first single, 'Breathing', for Bright Records. Afterwards they played regularly at the Marquee Club and supported **China Crisis** and the **Alarm** on tour. However, several singles and a debut album for EMI failed to provide a breakthrough. The band alleged 'under-promotion' by EMI and ended their association. That decision was rewarded when they found huge if fleeting success in the USA for **Atlantic Records**. Their single 'Wild Wild West' became a surprise *Billboard* number 1 hit in 1988, accompanying an album of the same title, which also achieved gold sales. However, that was the end of their commercial good fortune and further efforts failed to penetrate the American charts.

● ALBUMS: *White Fields* (EMI 1985) ★★★, *Wild Wild West* (Atlantic 1988) ★★★, *Dollars And Sex* (Atlantic 1991) ★★.

Escoffery, Shaun

b. London, England. This UK vocalist grew up in a musical environment with his mother and father pursuing part-time jobs as a singer and a DJ respectively. Escoffery began writing and singing in his early teens and in the late 90s played a small part in the West End musical *Mama, I Want To Sing*, which starred **Doris Troy** and **Chaka Khan**. His attempts to launch a recording career were going nowhere until, in 2001, a promo of his track 'Space Rider' attracted the attention of the independent label Oyster Music. A re-released 'Space Rider' and its follow-up 'Days Like This' enjoyed underground cult success and were promoted by influential UK DJ **Trevor Nelson**. The following year's self-titled debut album featured both tracks alongside new material that carried on the singles' successful mixture of soul, jazz, funk and R&B. Earlier in the year Escoffery's name was promoted to a wider audience when, in an unusual move, he was invited by England's heavyweight champion boxer Lennox Lewis to sing the national anthem before his title bout with Mike Tyson in Memphis, Tennessee. Remixed versions of several of the tracks on his debut album were released in 2003 on *Soulonica*.

● ALBUMS: *Shaun Escoffery* (Oyster 2002) ★★★, *Soulonica* (Oyster 2003) ★★★.

Escorts (UK)

Terry Sylvester (b. 8 January 1947, Liverpool, England; vocals/guitar), John Kinrade (lead guitar) and Mike Gregory (vocals/bass) formed the Escorts at Liverpool's Rose Lane school in 1962. They were originally augmented by drummer John Foster, aka Johnny Sticks, a cousin of **Ringo Starr**, replaced by Pete Clark in 1963. The quartet made their debut in April 1964 with a powerful interpretation of 'Dizzy Miss Lizzie', before scoring a minor hit two months later with 'The One To Cry'. Their next release, 'I Don't Want To Go On Without You', was also recorded by the **Moody Blues**, who secured the chart entry. This undermined the Escorts' confidence, and subsequent releases, although carefully crafted, proved unsuccessful. The band's line-up was also unstable. Sylvester left for the **Swinging Blue Jeans**, from where he later replaced **Graham Nash** in the **Hollies** and by mid-1966, Kinrade and Gregory were the sole original members. Paddy Chambers (b. 30 April 1944, Liverpool, England, d. 28 September 2000; guitar) and Paul Comerford (drums, ex-**Cryin' Shames**) completed the line-up featured on 'From Head To Toe', the Escorts final single. This accomplished performance featured **Paul McCartney** on tambourine, but the quartet split up within weeks of its release.

● COMPILATIONS: *From The Blue Angel* (Edsel 1982) ★★.

Escorts (USA)

An R&B vocal group formed in Rahway State Prison, New Jersey, USA. The members were lead Reginald Hayes, Laurence Franklin, Robert Arrington, William Dugger, Stephen Carter, Frank Heard and Marion Murphy. Producer George Kerr discovered them and under his supervision the group made a moderate impact on the charts with classic soul harmony singing. Kerr launched the group with an album recorded live at Rahway, *All We Need Is Another Chance* (1973). It produced two chart singles, 'Look Over Your Shoulder' (number 45 R&B) and 'I'll Be Sweeter Tomorrow (Than I Was Today)' (number 83 R&B), both songs written by Kerr and both recorded by the **O'Jays** years earlier when they were being produced by Kerr. A second album, *3 Down 4 To Go*, was a studio recording made when three of the members were out of prison. The album featured more originals and produced two more chart singles, 'Disrespect Can Wreck' (number 61 R&B) and 'Let's Make Love At Home Sometime' (number 58 R&B). The group could not sustain itself on its modest sales and soon thereafter broke up. Hayes surfaced in 1986 with a self-produced solo album that failed to return him to the public eye. The Escorts reunited in 1992 and released *Back To Love*, which only elicited interest in the UK.

● ALBUMS: *All We Need Is Another Chance* (Alithia 1973) ★★★, *3 Down 4 To Go* (Alithia 1974) ★★★, *Back To Love* (1992) ★★★.
Solo: Reginald Hayes *On Wings Of Love* (Escort 1986) ★★.

Escovedo, Alejandro

b. Alejandro Escovedo, 1951, San Antonio, Texas, USA. Singer-songwriter Escovedo is the seventh of 12 children born to a former Mexican prizefighter and musician. The family moved to Texas from the Mexican town of Saltillo when Escovedo was 12, before relocating to southern California by the late 50s. Several of his siblings subsequently became involved in the music industry—elder brothers Coke and **Pete Escovedo** becoming acclaimed Latin percussionists and Pete's daughter Sheila enjoying a successful pop career as **Sheila E**. Alejandro himself turned to music much later—only learning the guitar in the mid-70s after an abortive attempt at a film career. The band formed to make a movie about an aspiring rock star were the same ones who would become the **Nuns**—his first band. An abrasive, challenging San Franciscan punk band, they served as a major influence on later bands from the region such as the **Dead Kennedys** without ever making significant progress themselves. He joined two further outfits in the 80s, the country rockers **Rank And File** and the 'purist's guitar band', **True Believers**. In common with the Nuns, both these bands were expected to make mainstream progress, but neither did.

When the True Believers finally collapsed in 1987, Escovedo was forced to take a job at a record store. It was not until 1992 that he returned to recording. That year's album, *Gravity*, documented the break-up of his 13-year marriage. His ex-wife also presented the subtext for the following year's collection, titled after the length of their relationship, when she committed suicide. These circumstances left Escovedo, who subsequently remarried, philosophical about the rock 'n' roll treadmill. 'I want to survive playing music', he told **Rolling Stone** in 1996, 'I want that to be the way my family feeds itself and I pay the rent.' *With These Hands* documented a singer more at ease with himself, and a songwriter capable of talking unflinchingly about his own failures as well as his triumphs. 'Pissed Off 2A.M.', in particular, managed to be both emotionally convincing and darkly humorous.

During this period Escovedo toured Austin regularly with his side-band Buick MacKane, which allowed him to retreat to the intensity of some of his former bands (the unit recorded a glam punk album in 1996). He also played with the Alejandro Escovedo Orchestra, conversely a brass and string big band. Two stopgap albums preceded the release of 2001's stunning *A Man Under The Influence*, on which Escovedo fashioned a compelling collection of songs meditating on love and loss. The follow-up *By The Hand Of The Father* was equally masterful. Beginning life as a play that premiered in Los Angeles in 2000, the songs on the album explored the lives and stories of Mexican-Americans in the 20th century. The critical reaction to Escovedo's recent work was tempered by the singer's announcement that he was suffering from Hepatitis C.

● ALBUMS: *Gravity* (Watermelon 1992) ★★★, *Thirteen Years* (Watermelon 1993) ★★★, *With These Hands* (Rykodisc 1996) ★★★★, with Buick MacKane *The Pawn Shop Years* (Rykodisc 1996) ★★★, *Bourbonitis Blues* (Bloodshot 1999) ★★★, *A Man Under The Influence* (Bloodshot 2001) ★★★★, *By The Hand Of The Father* (Texas/Blue Rose 2002) ★★★★.
● COMPILATIONS: *More Miles Than Money: Live 1994–96* (Bloodshot 1998) ★★★.

Escovedo, Pete

b. 13 July 1935, Pittsburg, California, USA. Escovedo began playing saxophone in high school, but switched to vibraphone before choosing a variety of percussion instruments as his true métier. His first professional engagement found him in a band on the same bill as **Count Basie**, an event that prompted him to settle there and then on a career in music.

In 1970, together with his younger brother Coke Escovedo, he formed **Azteca**, touring the country as support to **Stevie Wonder**. Before the band was dissolved *Azteca* and *Pyramid Of The Moon* were recorded, both for **Columbia Records**. Escovedo next joined **Carlos Santana** touring internationally for three years and appearing on *Moonflower*, *Oneness* and *Inner Secrets*.

Based in northern California, Escovedo has continued to record successfully, mostly for Concord Records' Picante label. His daughter, **Sheila E.**, also is a gifted percussionist. Father and daughter have recorded together in a number of occasions, sometimes under his name and also including her *Sheila E.*; he also appeared on her video *Romance 1600* and the pair appeared on the Jazz Visions video *Latin Familia*, on which **Tito Puente** also performs. A dynamic and exhilarating percussionist, Escovedo has maintained a career-long dedication to Latin jazz and through his work has helped maintain the genre's popularity.

● ALBUMS: *Yesterday's Memories—Tomorrow's Dreams* (Concord Picante 1987) ★★★, *Mister E* (Concord Picante 1988) ★★★★, *Flying South* (Concord Picante 1995) ★★★★, with Sheila E. *Solo Two/Happy Together* 80s recordings (Fantasy 1997) ★★★, *E Street* (Concord Picante 1997) ★★★, *E Music* (Concord Picante 2000) ★★★, *Whatcha Gonna Do* (Concord Vista 2001) ★★★, *Live!* (Concord 2003) ★★★.

Escudero, Ralph

b. Rafael Escudero, 16 July 1898, Manati, Puerto Rico, d. 10 April 1970, Puerto Rico. After playing bass in his homeland he went to New York where he played regularly, including a spell at the famed Clef Club. He also performed in touring bands with popular shows including an out-of-town version of **Eubie Blake**'s and **Noble Sissle**'s *Shuffle Along*. Escudero played with bands led by **Wilbur Sweatman** and **Fletcher Henderson**, then spent around three years with **McKinney's Cotton Pickers**. After playing with various east coast bands, Escudero spent some time in California before deciding to continue his professional life back home in Puerto Rico, where he worked with dance bands and classical orchestras. A solid and workmanlike player with excellent time, Escudero also sometimes played the brass bass (tuba), swinging mightily and soloing well with Henderson.

ESG

Old school funk group formed in 1978 by the Scroggins sisters from the south Bronx, New York City, USA. Renee (guitar/vocals), Valerie (drums), Marie (congas) and Deborah (bass) built up a reputation on New York's club scene with their fluid polyrhythmic sound, but their first studio release was a limited edition 7-inch single produced by **Martin Hannett** and released on the UK label **Factory Records**. These studio tracks ('You're No Good', 'Moody', and the instrumental 'UFO') were later released in the USA as an expanded 12-inch EP on the 99 Records label, and proved highly popular on New York's club scene. The *ESG Says Dance To The Beat Of The Moody* EP and 1983's LP *Come Away With ESG* confirmed the group as one of the most interesting acts to emerge from the New York underground. Their adoption by the nascent rap scene came too late to prevent ESG'S, disbanding in the mid-80s, however, with the group beset by personal (Deborah's drug addiction) and financial problems.

Renee, Valerie and Marie Scroggins re-formed ESG in the early 90s, spurred on by their newly fêted status within the booming **dance music** scene and their struggle to earn compensation from the proliferation of dance, rap and indie acts plundering their early 80s club hits (most notably the sample of the air-raid whines from 'UFO' on **Public Enemy**'s 'Night Of The Living Baseheads'). The stark title of the *Sample Credits Don't Pay Our Bills* EP addressed these problems, and on 1995's *ESG Live!* the Scroggins incorporated contemporary urban styles into their unique sound. By the late 90s, a second generation of Scroggins had joined in the fun, with Renee's daughter Nicole on bass and Valerie's daughter Chistelle on guitar. In 2000, a long overdue compilation was released by the UK's Universal Sounds/Soul Jazz, and two years later an excellent new studio album was released by the label.

● ALBUMS: *Come Away With ESG* (99 1983) ★★★★, *ESG* (Pow Wow 1991) ★★★, *ESG Live!* (Nega Fulo 1995) ★★★, *Step Off* (Universal Sounds/Soul Jazz 2002) ★★★.

● COMPILATIONS: *ESG: A South Bronx Story* (Universal Sounds/Soul Jazz 2000) ★★★★.

Esham

b. Rashaam Smith, 1977, Long Island, New York, USA. The original acid rapper, this prolific Detroit, Michigan–based hip-hop artist has influenced a whole generation of hardcore rap artists. Esham is also known as the Unholy, an apt reflection of his penchant (tempered in later years) for themes revolving around death, drugs and decadent sex.

Esham spent time in both New York and Detroit as a youngster. His precocious talent soon became evident, as he started his own label, Reel Life Productions at the age of 11, and released his first album in 1990 at the age of 13. He followed this up with the ambitious double album *Judgement Day*, on which he first began incorporating rock samples into the mix. The same year he launched NATAS (Nation Ahead Of Time And Space, or Satan backwards, depending on your viewpoint) with fellow Detroit rappers Mastermind and TNT. The group made their debut with *Life After Death*, on which Esham's obsession with pornography was given free rein.

The mid- to late 90s saw Esham alternating solo projects with further NATAS releases, and while his music became more polished he was also replacing his sordid subject matter with more conventional lyrical concerns. By now rap-metal had begun to break through into the mainstream, and although fellow Detroit artists such as **Insane Clown Posse** and **Kid Rock** acknowledged their debt to Esham's pioneering work in the genre, he was still unable to extend his career beyond cult status. In 2000, he signed a distribution contract with TVT Records for his Overcore label (formerly Reel Life). Artists signed to the label included another cult legend, **Kool Keith**. Esham released his first studio album of the new millennium, *Tongues*, in 2001. A further four years passed before Esham finally charted (in the USA) with *A-1 Yola*. The album was his third release for Insane Clown Posse's Psychopathic label.

● ALBUMS: *Boomin' Words From Hell* (Reel Life 1990) ★★★, *Judgement Day, Vol. 1—Day* (Reel Life 1992) ★★★, *Judgement Day, Vol. 2—Night* (Reel Life 1992) ★★★, *Kkkill The Fetus* (Reel Life 1993) ★★★★, *Closed Casket* (Reel Life 1994) ★★★, *Dead Flowerz* (Reel Life 1996) ★★★, *Bruce Wayne: Gotham City 1987* (Reel Life 1997) ★★, *Mail Dominance* (Overcore 1999) ★★, *Tongues* (Overcore/TVT 2001) ★★★, *Repentance* (Psychopathic 2003) ★★★, *A-1 Yola* (Psychopathic 2005) ★★★.

● COMPILATIONS: *Detroit Dog Shit* (Reel Life 1997) ★★★★, *Bootleg (From The Lost Vault) – Vol. 1* (Overcore/TVT 2000) ★★★★, *Acid Rain* (Psychopathic 2002) ★★★★.

Eskelin, Ellery

b. Ellery Lane Eskelin, 16 August 1959, Wichita, Kansas, USA. Encouraged into music by his parents, both of whom were professional musicians in Baltimore, Maryland, where he was raised, Eskelin took up the tenor saxophone. After studying at Towson State University and also with **George Coleman** and **Dave Liebman**, he worked professionally in New York from the early 80s. Within a few years, Eskelin was deeply involved in the improvised music scene, recording with the co-operative group Joint Venture alongside **Paul Smoker** (trumpet), Drew Gress (bass) and Phil Haynes (drums). From the mid-90s onwards, Eskelin has led a regular and highly imaginative working band that includes Andrea Parkins (accordion/sampler) and Jim Black (drums). He has also worked with noted figures from the international improvised music scene, including **Han Bennink** with whom he has recorded a duo album, and as a member of both **Joey Baron**'s Barondown and **Mark Helias**' Attack The Future. A radical spirit imbues much of Eskelin's work. He has indicated his dislike of having to work within the accepted envelopes of jazz and other musical forms. As a consequence, his work is impossible to pigeonhole and often highly demanding of audiences through his frequently innovative concepts.

● ALBUMS: with Drew Gress, Phil Haynes *Setting The Standard* (Cadence 1989) ★★★★, with Gress, Haynes *Forms* (Open Minds 1991) ★★★, *Figure Of Speech* (Soul Note 1993) ★★★, *Premonition: Solo Tenor Saxophone* (Prime Source 1993) ★★★, *Jazz Trash* (Songlines 1995) ★★★★, *The Sun Died* (Soul Note 1996) ★★★★, with Andrea Parkins *Green Bermudas* (Eremite 1996) ★★★, with Parkins, Jim Black *One Great Day . . .* (hatOLOGY 1997) ★★★, with Parkins, Black *Kulak 29 & 30* (hatOLOGY 1998) ★★★, with Han Bennink *Dissonant Characters* (hatOLOGY 1999) ★★★, with Parkins, Black *Five Other Pieces (+2)* (hatOLOGY 1999) ★★★, *Ramifications* (hatOLOGY 2000) ★★★★, with Parkins, Black *The Secret Museum* (hatOLOGY 2000) ★★★★, *Vanishing Point* (hatOLOGY 2002) ★★★, with Parkins, Black *12(+1) Imaginary Views* (hatOLOGY 2002) ★★★, with Parkins, Black *Arcanum Moderne* (hatOLOGY 2003) ★★★, *Ten* (hatOLOGY 2005) ★★★★, *On The Road With Ellery Eskelin, Andrea Parkins And Jim Black* (Prime Source 2005) ★★, with Dave Liebman *Different But The Same* (hatOLOGY 2005) ★★.

Eskimos And Egypt

This mid-90s group is a highly regarded, mellow groove coalition. Their name was originally invoked as a gesture in support of the Inuit people's struggle for their own homeland. The four-piece, Salford, Manchester–based band consists of Paul Cundall (b. 5 April 1963, Manchester, Lancashire, England; keyboards/sequencer), Christopher O'Hare (b. 13 October 1966, Manchester, Lancashire, England; vocals/keyboards), Mark Compton (b. 14 October 1963, Salford, Manchester, England) and David Pryde (b. David Cameron Pryde, 1967, Dublin, Eire). They made their vinyl debut in December 1987 with 'The Cold' on Village Records, shortly after appearing live for the first time at Manchester's Cloud Nine venue. After a succession of singles that built their dancefloor credentials, including the Axl Rose–slamming 'The Power Of G N'R', their breakthrough release came with the gangland-inspired 'US:UK' single. Typically, it was awash with sweet female harmonies, furious raps and a slice of rock guitar. Other singles such as 'Fall From Grace' followed, with remixes from **Moby** and the **Beatmasters**. However, by 1994 they had been dropped by **One Little Indian Records** (though the band itself insisted that they had walked).

● ALBUMS: *Perfect Disease* (One Little Indian 1993) ★★★.

ESP

Leading Amsterdam **techno** record label with a release schedule featuring **Nico**, **Ken Ishii** (Rising Sun), Black Scorpion and **Blake Baxter**. The label was started in 1991 as the underground **rave** offshoot of Go Bang!, who had in turn scored hits with D-Shake, **GTO** and Turntable Hype. The ESP boss is Fred Berkhout, who describes the label's orientation as 'experimental'. Other artists on ESP include Orlando Voorn, who records as Format, the Nighttripper and the Ghetto Brothers (with Blake Baxter), Dr No No ('Paradise 3001') and **Jeff Mills**.

Espiritu

Latin-flavoured 90s dance duo from Brighton, Sussex, England, comprising Vanessa Quinnones and Chris Taplin (ex-**Frazier Chorus**). Quinnones, half-Peruvian and half-French, grew up in an affluent suburb of Paris under the care of a South American nanny, whose name, Francisca, was subsequently employed as the title of Espiritu's debut single in 1992. It was about her treatment at the hands of Quinnones' mother. The group's second single, 'Conquistador', was another slice of classy Latin dance. Its **Andrew Weatherall** remix had originally taken the club scene by storm, with copies reaching extravagant prices of over £100, before the stock release arrived. Signed to **Heavenly Records**, the single was a continuation of their thoughtful approach to lyrics demonstrated by their debut. This time the subject was the exploitation of South American Indians in the name of civilization. A third single, 'Bonita Monana', continued the club/chart crossover in 1994.

● ALBUMS: *Espiritu Number One* (Heavenly 1997) ★★★.

Esquire Records

Founded in 1947/8 by **Carlo Krahmer** and Peter Newbrook, the label's initial intention was to provide a canvas for UK jazz in general and the then emerging bop scene in particular. The label also made available in the UK music, often bop, recorded by small American labels that were otherwise unavailable to the British record-buying public. During the 50s and early 60s, Esquire was the conduit through which **Prestige Records** was marketed in the UK but soon thereafter Esquire declined. In 1976, following Krahmer's death, the label once more became available and with Newbrook in charge continued to actively promote British jazz during the succeeding decades.

Esquires

Formed in Milwaukee, Wisconsin, USA, in 1957 with a line-up featuring Gilbert Moorer, Alvis Moorer and Betty Moorer.

Originally conceived as a doo-wop group, the Esquires were briefly augmented by Harvey Scales before Sam Pace joined in 1961. In 1965 Betty Moorer was replaced by Shawn Taylor. The group then moved to Chicago where they signed to the Bunky label. An original song 'Get On Up' was recorded with the help of Millard Edwards, who sang its distinctive bass line. Edwards became a permanent member when this infectious single was an R&B hit in 1967. Shawn Taylor left before a similar-sounding follow-up, 'And Get Away', was issued, but rejoined in 1971. That same year, 'Girls In The City', featuring Taylor as lead, was a Top 20 US R&B hit. The opportunistic 'Get Up '76' was the Esquires' most recent hit; by the early 80s only Gilbert and Alvis Moorer remained from the group's heyday.

● ALBUMS: *Get On Up And Get Away* (Bunky 1967) ★★★, with the Marvelows *Chi-Town Showdown* (1982) ★★★.

Esquivel!

b. Juan Garcia Esquivel, 20 January 1918, Tampico, Tamaulipas, Mexico, d. 3 January 2002, Jiutepec, Morelos, Mexico. Although he was a huge inspiration for the revival of 'lounge' or 'easy listening' music in the 90s, Esquivel in fact began recording his heavily orchestrated pop muzak four decades earlier. Although none of his recordings from this period charted, he was widely recognized as an influence on Californian music of the time with his swinging pop arrangements. Indeed, in the 70s **Steely Dan** acknowledged Esquivel as the reason they introduced marimba, vibes and percussion into the recording of *Pretzel Logic*. Esquivel's intention was to realize the possibilities allowed by the development of stereo technology, and his records were thus infused with all manner of diverting intrusions, such as whistling and pinball percussion, that adorned big band Latin pop. He had been brought to America in 1957 by the **RCA Records** executive Herman Diaz Jnr. and became a prolific band leader, overseeing singers including Yvonne DeBourbon and Randy Van Horne. As 'The Sights And Sounds Of Esquivel' they toured widely in the USA, appearing in New York, Hollywood and Las Vegas. A visual as well as aural perfectionist, one anecdote from these times concerns Esquivel's development of a special 'walk' so as not to crease his shoes. The women in his band were severely and outrageously disciplined. Forced to step on scales before each performance, they would be summarily fined $5 for each pound of weight gained. By the artist's own reckoning, his music was used in over 200 television shows, including *Baywatch*. He finally returned to Mexico in the late 70s. In the 90s Esquivel was widely celebrated as 'the father of Lounge Music' with the release of compilation albums on Bar/None Records which became staples of US college radio. Contemporary groups including **Combustible Edison**, **Stereolab** and Black Velvet Flag appropriated his style, while Chicago's Vinyl Dance nightclub dedicated itself to his music. Despite being bed-ridden after a fall, he relished this new wave of attention. 'Perhaps I was too far ahead of my time,' he told *Rolling Stone* in 1995. The lounge-music icon died of a stroke in January 2002.

● ALBUMS: *Las Tandas De Juan Garcia Esquivel* (RCA Victor Mexicana 1956) ★★★, *To Love Again* (RCA Victor Mexicana 1957) ★★★, *Other Worlds, Other Sounds* (RCA Victor 1958) ★★★★, *4 Corners Of The World* (RCA Victor 1958) ★★★, *Exploring New Sounds In Hi-Fi* aka *Exploring New Sounds In Stereo* (RCA Victor 1959) ★★★, *Strings*

Aflame (RCA Victor 1959) ★★★, *Infinity In Sound* (RCA Victor 1960) ★★★, *Infinity In Sound, Volume 2* (RCA Victor 1961) ★★★★, *More Of Other Worlds, Other Sounds* (Reprise 1962) ★★★, *Latin-Esque* (RCA Victor 1962) ★★★★, *Esquivel '68* (RCA Victor Mexicana 1968) ★★★.
● COMPILATIONS: *The Best Of Esquivel* (RCA Victor 1966) ★★★, *The Genius Of Esquivel* (RCA Victor 1967) ★★★, *Space-Age Bachelor Pad Music* (Bar/None 1994) ★★★★, *Music From A Sparkling Planet* (Bar/None 1995) ★★★★, *Cabaret Mañana* (RCA 1995) ★★★★, *Merry Xmas From The Space-Age Bachelor Pad* (Bar/None 1996) ★★★, *Loungecore* (Camden 1998) ★★★, *See It In Sound* (7N 1999) ★★★, *The Best Of Esquivel* (BMG 2003) ★★★★.

Essential Logic

Formed in London, England, in 1978 by **Lora Logic**, **X-Ray Spex**'s erstwhile original saxophonist, Essential Logic's first single was 'Aerosol Burns', a punk masterpiece of brash guitar and hiccoughing rhythms. The group delighted in odd, jangling harmonies and eccentric song shapes: Lora Logic's loopy punk vocals (a strong influence on more successful female-led groups of the 80s such as **Throwing Muses** and **Fuzzbox**) and gorgeously primitive saxophone made *Beat Rhythm News* special. Her solo album, *Pedigree Charm*, had a smoother sound, but her sideline work with **Red Crayola** retained the harshness and power. Logic later joined the Hare Krishna cult, just like X-Ray Spex's **Poly Styrene** before her. She revived the Essential Logic moniker in the new millennium, teaming up with Gary Valentine (guitar), Dave Jones (bass) and Nick Pretzell (drums) to record a four-track mini-album.
● ALBUMS: *Beat Rhythm News* (Rough Trade 1979) ★★★.
● COMPILATIONS: *Essential Logic: Fanfare In The Garden* (Kill Rock Stars 2003) ★★★.

Essex

A rock 'n' roll vocal group formed in the early 60s by members of the US Marine Corps at Camp LeJeune, North Carolina, USA. Members were lead Anita Humes, Walter Vickers, Rodney Taylor, Rudolph Johnson and Billie Hill. The group exploded on the scene in 1963 with three singles, 'Easier Said Than Done' (number 1 R&B and pop) 'A Walkin' Miracle' (number 11 R&B, number 12 pop) and 'She's Got Everything' (number 56 pop). The vocal sound of the group, unlike many African-American groups of the day, featured meagre vocal harmony and concentrated on the warm engaging voice of Humes, and the group never sang R&B. After the initial hits, their company, Roulette, focused on Humes, and on their final album put only her picture on the cover, calling the artist Anita Humes With The Essex. The Essex's later soul-styled recordings, although thoroughly appealing, never found a market. In 1966 the group recorded a final single for **Bang Records** before disbanding.
● ALBUMS: *Easier Said Than Done* (Roulette 1963) ★★, *A Walkin' Miracle* (Roulette 1963) ★★, *Young And Lively* (Roulette 1964) ★★.
● COMPILATIONS: *The Best Of The Essex* (Sequel 1994) ★★.

Essex, David

b. David Albert Cook, 23 July 1947, Plaistow, London, England. Originally a drummer in the semi-professional Everons, Essex subsequently turned to singing during the mid-60s, and recorded a series of unsuccessful singles for a variety of labels. On the advice of his influential manager, Derek Bowman, he switched to acting and after a series of minor roles gained his big break upon winning the lead part in the stage musical **Godspell**. This was followed by the authentic 50s-inspired film **That'll Be The Day** and its sequel **Stardust**. The former reactivated Essex's recording career and the song he composed for the film, 'Rock On', was a transatlantic Top 10 hit in 1973. It was in Britain, however, that Essex enjoyed several years as a pin-up teen-idol. During the mid-70s, he registered two UK number 1s, 'Gonna Make You A Star' and 'Hold Me Close', plus the Top 10 hits 'Lamplight', 'Stardust' and 'Rollin' Stone'. After parting with producer **Jeff Wayne**, Essex continued to chart, though with noticeably diminishing returns. As his teen appeal waned, his serious acting commitments increased, most notably with the role of Che Guevara in **Evita**. The musical also provided another Top 5 hit with 1978's acerbic 'Oh, What A Circus'. His lead part in 1980's **Silver Dream Racer** resulted in a UK Top 5 hit of the same title. Thereafter, Essex took on a straight non-singing part in *Childe Byron*. The 1982 Christmas hit, 'A Winter's Tale' (number 2), kept his chart career alive, as did the equally successful 'Tahiti'. The latter anticipated one of his biggest projects to date, an elaborate musical, **Mutiny!** (based on *Mutiny On The Bounty*).

In 1993, after neglecting his showbusiness career while he spent two and a half years in the African region as an ambassador for Voluntary Service Overseas, Essex embarked on a UK concert tour, and issued *Cover Shot*, a collection of mostly 60s songs. In the same year he played the part of Tony Lumpkin in Oliver Goldsmith's comedy *She Stoops To Conquer*, in London's West End. In 1994 he continued to tour, and released a new album produced by Jeff Wayne. It included a duet with Catherine Zeta Jones on 'True Love Ways', and the VSO-influenced 'Africa', an old **Toto** number. Despite pursuing two careers, Essex has managed to achieve consistent success on record, in films and on stage. He was awarded an OBE in the 1999 New Year Honours list.
● ALBUMS: *Rock On* (CBS 1973) ★★★, *David Essex* (CBS 1974) ★★★, *All The Fun Of The Fair* (CBS 1975) ★★, *Out On The Street* (CBS 1976) ★★, *On Tour* (CBS 1976) ★★, *Gold And Ivory* (CBS 1977) ★★, *Hold Me Close* (CBS 1979) ★★, *The David Essex Album* (CBS 1979) ★★, *Imperial Wizard* (Mercury 1979) ★★, *Hot Love* (Mercury 1980) ★★, *Be-Bop—The Future* (Mercury 1981) ★★, *Stage-Struck* (Mercury 1982) ★★, various artists *Mutiny!* (Mercury 1983) ★★, *The Whisper* (Mercury 1983) ★★, *This One's For You* (Mercury 1984) ★★, *Live At The Royal Albert Hall* (Mercury 1984) ★★, *Centre Stage* (K-Tel 1986) ★★, *Touching The Ghost* (PolyGram TV 1989) ★★, *Cover Shot* (PolyGram TV 1993) ★★, *Back To Back* (PolyGram TV 1994) ★★, *Missing You* (PolyGram TV 1995) ★★★, *Living In England* US only (Cleveland International 1995) ★★★, *A Night At The Movies* (PolyGram TV 1997) ★★★, *Here We All Are Together* (Lamplight 1998) ★★, *I Still Believe* (Lamplight 1999) ★★, *Thank You* (Own Label 2000) ★★★.
● COMPILATIONS: *The David Essex Collection* (Pickwick 1980) ★★★, *The Very Best Of David Essex* (TV 1982) ★★★, *His Greatest Hits* (Mercury 1991), *Spotlight On David Essex* (Spotlight 1993) ★★★, *The Best Of David Essex* (Columbia 1996) ★★★, *Greatest Hits* (PolyGram TV 1998) ★★★★, *Greatest Hits* (BMG 2006) ★★★★.

● DVD/VIDEOS: *Live At The Royal Albert Hall* (PolyGram Music Video 1984).
● FURTHER READING: *The David Essex Story*, George Tremlett. *A Charmed Life: The Autobiography Of David Essex*, David Essex.
● FILMS: *Assault* (1971), *All Coppers Are . . .* (1972), *That'll Be The Day* (1973), *Stardust* (1974), *The Big Bus* (1976), *Silver Dream Racer* (1980), *Journey Of Honor* (1992).

Estefan, Gloria, And Miami Sound Machine

Formed in Miami, Florida, USA in 1973, this Latin/funk/pop group was originally a trio called the Miami Latin Boys, comprising Emilio Estefan (b. 4 March 1953, Cuba; keyboards), Juan Avila (bass) and Enrique 'Kiki' Garcia (drums), each of whom was born in Cuba and raised in Miami. The following year the group played at a friend's wedding where they were joined onstage by singer Gloria Fajardo (b. 1 September 1957, Havana, Cuba). The latter at first refused to join the group, then agreed to sing with them part-time as she pursued her studies. In 1975, the quartet changed its name to Miami Sound Machine. They recorded their first single, 'Renecer', for a local Hispanic company that year. Emilio and Gloria married in 1978. In 1979, the group recorded its first album, sung entirely in Spanish; it was picked up for distribution by **CBS Records** International. They recorded seven Spanish-language records during the next six years, becoming successful in predominantly US Hispanic areas, Central and South America, as well as in Europe. Meanwhile, the group's membership grew to nine musicians. Their first English-language single, 'Dr. Beat', was released in 1984 and became a club/Top 10 hit in the UK, where the group then flew to appear on the BBC Television programme **Top Of The Pops**. The following year the group toured Japan successfully, and was honoured by their hometown Miami, which renamed a local street Miami Sound Machine Boulevard. Signed to Epic Records, their first US chart single was 'Conga' in 1985, reaching number 10 by early 1986. That same year saw two other US Top 10 singles, 'Bad Boy' and the ballad 'Words Get In The Way', and **Billboard** named them the year's top singles act. Their first English-language album, *Primitive Love*, reached number 23 that same year.

The group officially changed its name to Gloria Estefan And Miami Sound Machine in 1987, a year that brought one Top 10 single, 'Rhythm Is Gonna Get You', and *Let it Loose*, which reached number 6 by the spring of 1988. Another Top 10 single, 'Can't Stay Away From You', and the number 1 ballad, 'Anything For You', were highlights of early 1988. The year closed with another US/UK Top 10 single, '1-2-3'. **Gloria Estefan** released a solo album, *Cuts Both Ways*, which also made the Top 10, in the summer of 1989, after which she went on to enjoy a hugely successful pop career under her own name.

● ALBUMS: *Miami Sound Machine* (Columbia 1976) ★★★, *Rio* (Columbia 1978) ★★★, *Eyes Of Innocence* (Columbia 1984) ★★★, *Primitive Love* (Epic 1986) ★★★, as Gloria Estefan And Miami Sound Machine *Let it Loose* (US) *Anything For You* (UK) (Epic 1987) ★★★★.
● COMPILATIONS: *Greatest Hits* (Epic 1992) ★★★★.
● FURTHER READING: *Gloria Estefan*, Grace Catalano.

Estefan, Gloria

b. Gloria Maria Milagrosa Fajardo, 1 September 1957, Havana, Cuba. Estefan, the most popular Latin American singer of the 80s and 90s, originally rose to prominence in the 70s by joining soon-to-be husband Emilio Estefan in Miami Sound Machine. Educated at Catholic high school in Miami after moving there from Cuba at the age of two, she first learned to play guitar and sing during her leisure hours. She met the other members of the band when Emilio came to her high school to offer advice on music. Together they played at a friend's wedding, but Gloria initially refused to join the group permanently, preferring to concentrate on her psychology degree and career as an interpreter. She eventually relented, marrying Emilio in 1978, shortly afterwards collecting her BA degree from the University of Miami.

Miami Sound Machine recorded a sequence of Spanish-language albums during the late 70s and early 80s, becoming massively successful not only in the USA and Europe but especially Latin America. By 1986 they had been named the Top Singles Act Of 1986 by **Billboard**. The group officially changed its name to **Gloria Estefan And Miami Sound Machine** the following year, and enjoyed further substantial hits with 'Rhythm Is Gonna Get You' and 'Anything For You' before Estefan launched her solo career in 1989 with *Cuts Both Ways*. Three singles taken from the album reached the US Top 10—'Get On Your Feet', 'Here We Are' and the number 1, 'Don't Wanna Lose You'.

Early in 1990 Estefan's impetus was halted when she was involved in a serious accident in Syracuse, New York. Having just met with President George Bush to discuss participation in an anti-drugs campaign, the group's bus was struck from behind, resulting in a broken vertebra and surgery for Estefan. She returned in 1991 with new material, after reportedly being awarded £5 million for loss of earnings caused by the accident. While songs on *Into The Light*, including the US chart-topper 'Coming Out Of The Dark', dealt with her recovery and rejuvenation, she embarked on an eight-month world tour in March 1991. This was followed in January 1992 with a performance at the interval of Super Bowl XXVI between the Washington Redskins and Buffalo Bills. In the summer she and Emilio purchased Miami Beach's famed art deco Cardozo Hotel from **Chris Blackwell** for $5 million.

Estefan's 1993 and 1995 albums, *Mi Tierra* and *Abriendo Puertas*, were Spanish-language efforts that distanced her somewhat from the American pop mainstream, but proved hugely popular in South America. *Destiny* was her first English-language collection for over five years (excepting the lacklustre pop covers collection, *Hold Me, Thrill Me, Kiss Me*). It featured 'Reach', the theme to the 1996 Olympic Games in Atlanta, an event at which Estefan sang during the closing ceremony. *Gloria!* marked a welcome return to the Latin sound of the Miami Sound Machine. The following year Estefan made her acting debut alongside Meryl Streep in *Music Of The Heart*. The title song featured Estefan duetting with pop sensations *NSYNC. The Spanish-language *Alma Caribeña*, meanwhile, reaped the commercial benefits of the late 90s boom in Latin music

● ALBUMS: *Cuts Both Ways* (Epic 1989) ★★★, *Exitos De Gloria Estefan* (Columbia 1990) ★★★, *Into The Light* (Epic 1991) ★★★★, *Mi Tierra* (Epic 1993) ★★★★, *Christmas Through Your Eyes* (Epic 1993) ★★, *Hold Me, Thrill Me, Kiss Me* (Epic 1994) ★★, *Abriendo Puertas* (Epic 1995) ★★★★, *Destiny* (Epic 1996) ★★★, *Gloria!* (Epic 1998) ★★★, with Mariah Carey, Celine Dion, Aretha Franklin,

Shania Twain *Divas Live* (Epic 1998) ★★, *Alma Caribeñña* (Epic 2000) ★★★, *Unwrapped* (Epic 2003) ★★★.

● COMPILATIONS: *Greatest Hits* (Epic 1992) ★★★★, *Greatest Hits Vol. II* (Epic 2001) ★★★★.

● DVD/VIDEOS: *Everlasting Gloria!* (Sony Music Video 1995), *The Evolution Tour: Live In Miami* (Epic Music Video 1996), with Mariah Carey, Celine Dion, Aretha Franklin, Shania Twain *Divas Live* (Sony Music Video 1998), *Don't Stop!* (Sony Music Video 1998), *Que Siga La Tradicion* (Sony Music Video 2001), *Live In Atlantis* (Sony Music Video 2002), *Live & Unwrapped* (Epic Music Video 2004).

● FURTHER READING: *Gloria Estefan*, Grace Catalano.

● FILMS: *Music Of The Heart* (1999).

Estelle

b. Estelle Swaray, 18 January 1980, London, England. One of the new generation of UK urban artists to emerge in the early years of the twenty-first century, Estelle established herself as a leading underground performer before launching her mainstream career in summer 2004 with the hit single '1980'. Estelle Swaray grew up in south west London and was introduced to music at an early age by her reggae-loving parents, while she later discovered hip-hop courtesy of one of her uncles. She began singing at the age of seven but did not begin performing in public until after her 18th birthday. By this time Swaray was working at the hip-hop record store Real Deal in Soho, and with the encouragement of her employers she began appearing at London clubs such as the Lyrical Lounge, The Hop, Scratch, and Subterania. With a strong R&B voice to go with her rhyming qualities, she made her recording debut in 2001 on DJ Skitz's *Countryman* album, while further appearances on albums by 57th Dynasty, Social Misfits and Against The Grain helped establish her credentials as one of the most exciting artists on the burgeoning UK scene. Her guest vocal on Blak Twang's 2002 single 'Trixstar', meanwhile, landed Estelle a nomination at the yearly MOBO awards.

The artist launched her own Stellar Ents label with a series of white label releases, including 'Excuse Me' and the *Da Heat* mix tape sessions, before signing a major label contract with Jdid/V2 Records at the end of 2003. The autobiographical '1980', which covered the singer's life story in four minutes starting with the moment her mother briefly died during the birth process, reached the UK Top 20 in July 2004. Estelle's debut album *The 18th Day*, released later in the year, was a highly impressive fusion of hip-hop and soul that firmly established the artist as a genuine star of the UK urban scene.

● ALBUMS: *The 18th Day* (Jdid/V2 2004) ★★★★.

Ester Drang

The number of shoegazing bands has steadily declined since its early 90s heyday, but by the new millennium there were still a few groups out there flying the stylistic flag, such as Ester Drang. While most bands of the aforementioned genre originated from England, Ester Drang is an exception, originally forming in 1995 in Oklahoma, USA, and listing **Philip Glass**, **My Bloody Valentine** and **Spiritualized** as their prime influences. Despite several line-up changes over the years, Bryce Chambers (guitars/vocals) has remained at the band's helm throughout, with his musical and lyrical vision earning comparisons to the work of fellow Oklahoma songwriter Wayne Coyne of the **Flaming Lips**.

Chambers was accompanied in the original line-up of Ester Drang by James McAlister (keyboards, percussion) and Kyle Winner (bass/vocals), with Sterling Williams (drums), David Motter (keyboards/samples) and Brian Brewer (guitar) joining the line-up at various stages. The band issued an EP, *That Is When He Turns Us Golden*, and a single, before their debut album surfaced in 2001. *Goldenwest* was supported with tours alongside **Pedro The Lion** and Unwed Sailor. Brewer, Williams and Motter all left the band during this period, with guitarist Jeff Shoop stepping in as an additional guitarist and keyboard player. Signing a new recording contract with the Jade Tree label, Ester Drang's follow-up, *Infinite Keys*, was released in 2003. A far more cohesive set than its predecessor, the album earned a number of glowing reviews in the US music press.

● ALBUMS: *Goldenwest* (Burnt Toast 2001) ★★★, *Infinite Keys* (Jade Tree 2003) ★★★★.

Estes, Sleepy John

b. John Adams Estes, 25 January 1899, Ripley, Tennessee, USA, d. 5 June 1977, Brownsville, Tennessee, USA. This influential blues singer first performed at local house-parties while in his early teens. In 1916 he began working with mandolin player **Yank Rachell**, a partnership that was revived several times throughout their respective careers. It was also during this formative period that Estes met **Hammie Nixon** (harmonica), another individual with whom he shared a long-standing empathy. Estes made his recording debut in September 1929. He eventually completed eight masters for the **RCA Records** company, including the original versions of 'Diving Duck Blues', 'Poor John Blues' and the seminal, often-covered 'Milk Cow Blues'. These assured compositions inspired interpretations from artists as diverse as **Taj Mahal**, **Tom Rush** and the **Kinks**. However, despite remaining an active performer throughout the 30s, Estes retired from music in 1941. A childhood accident impaired his eyesight and by 1950 he had become completely blind. The singer resumed performing with several low-key sessions for Hammie Nixon, before reasserting his own recording career in 1962. Several excellent albums for Chicago's **Delmark Records** label followed, one of which, *Broke And Hungry*, featured a young **Mike Bloomfield** on guitar. Estes, Nixon and Rachell also made a successful appearance at the 1964 Newport Folk Festival and the three veterans continued to work together until 1976 when Estes suffered a stroke.

● ALBUMS: *The Legend Of Sleepy John Estes* (Delmark 1962) ★★★, *Broke And Hungry, Ragged And Hungry Too* (Delmark 1963) ★★★, *Brownsville Blues* (Delmark 1965) ★★★, *Electric Sleep* (Delmark 1966) ★★★, *In Europe* (Delmark 1969) ★★★, *Down South Blues* (Delmark 1974) ★★★, *Newport Blues* 1964 recordings (Delmark 2003) ★★.

● COMPILATIONS: *1929–30 Sessions* (Roots 1978) ★★★, *The Blues Of Sleepy John Estes '34-'40* (Swaggie 1982) ★★★, *The Blues Of Sleepy John Estes '34-'40, Volume Two* (Swaggie 1983) ★★★, *I Ain't Gonna Be Worried No More: 1929–1941* (Yazoo/Shanachie 1992) ★★★, *Complete Recorded Works In Chronological Order Volume 1: 24 September 1929 To 2 August 1937* (Document 1994) ★★★, *Complete Recorded Works In Chronological Order Volume 2: 2 August 1937 To 24 September 1941* (Document 1994) ★★★, *Someday Baby: The Essential Recordings Of Sleepy John Estes* (Indigo 1996)

★★★★, *Goin' To Brownsville* (Testament 1998) ★★★★, *Someday Baby Blues* (Complete Blues 2004) ★★★★.

Eternal

This UK pop quartet originally comprised lead singer Easther Bennett plus sister Vernie Bennett, Louise Nurding (b. 4 November 1974, Croydon, Surrey, England) and Kéllé Bryan. Nurding and Bryan both attended London's Italia Conti stage school, and the Bennett sisters sang in a Croydon Baptist church. It was through Nurding that they came to the attention of manager Dennis Ingoldsby (co-owner of management agency and record label 1st Avenue). Their first two singles, 'Stay' and 'Save Our Love', made an immediate impact on the UK charts and launched the group as one of the teen phenomena of 1993. However, much more strident and demanding of the listener was their third single, 'Just A Step From Heaven', the accompanying video for which depicted gangs of youths in urban wastelands, before switching to a woman giving a lecture on self-awareness. It was perhaps a little disappointing, then, to learn that Eternal's songs were not of their own creation, and written instead by backroom staff. Nevertheless, *Always And Forever* spawned no less than six Top 15 UK hit singles (another record).

By the time Nurding left amicably in the summer of 1995 to forge a solo career (billed simply as **Louise**), Eternal had become Britain's most successful all-female group since **Bananarama**. *Power Of A Woman* became Ingoldsby's first serious attempt to break the group in America, writing material around a formula that drew obvious comparisons to modern R&B stars such as **EnVogue**. The title track was taken from the album as the group's first single as a trio, entering the UK Top 10 in October 1995 (joining Louise's first solo single). For the first time, too, roughly half the songs on the album were self-composed. The trio claimed their first UK number 1 in 1997 with 'I Wanna Be The Only One'. The following album, *Before The Rain*, confirmed the trio's soul credentials but suffered from a shortage of stand-out tracks. Bryan left the group in late 1998, and launched a solo career the following October with the UK Top 20 single 'Higher Than Heaven'. The Bennett sisters released the hard-hitting 'What'cha Gonna Do' the same month, which introduced the more pronounced **swingbeat** direction of their self-titled fourth album. **EMI Records** dropped the duo the following year.

● ALBUMS: *Always And Forever* (First Avenue/EMI 1994) ★★, *Power Of A Woman* (First Avenue/EMI 1995) ★★★, *Before The Rain* (First Avenue/EMI 1997) ★★, *Eternal* (EMI 1999) ★★★.

● COMPILATIONS: *Greatest Hits* (EMI 1997) ★★★, *Essential Eternal* (EMI 2001) ★★★.

● DVD/VIDEOS: *Always And Forever* (EMI 1994), *The Greatest Clips* (EMI 1997).

Ethel The Frog

Featuring P. Sheppard (vocals), Tognola (guitar), Hopkinson (bass) and Paul Conyers (drums), Ethel The Frog, taking their name from a *Monty Python* sketch, first came to the public's attention via a track on **EMI Records**' influential *Metal For Muthas Vol. I* compilation in 1980. This album was intended to introduce unsigned British heavy metal bands and is notable for boasting two early **Iron Maiden** tracks. The concept was very much to advance the **New Wave Of British Heavy Metal** of which Ethel The Frog was a part. However, their track, 'Fight Back', was disappointingly basic heavy metal. Soon afterwards, they recorded and released their own debut, *Ethel The Frog*, which failed to capture the public's interest and met with critical disdain. Disillusioned, they split in 1980, with Conyers and Tognola moving on to Salem.

● ALBUMS: *Ethel The Frog* (EMI 1980) ★★.

Ether

With Wales enjoying previously unimaginable exposure as a birthplace for rock and pop bands during the 90s, Ether emerged as the region's newest torchbearers in 1997. Their rise to notoriety was even swifter than that of the **Manic Street Preachers**, who originated from the same home-town, Blackwood, and employed the same manager, Martin Hall. Following a week of rehearsals and one gig, a media scrum ensued in order to secure their signatures. The group's personnel were already highly experienced musicians. Lead singer Rory Meredith, the possessor of a distinctive soul/R&B voice, came from a musical family, his father owning an eight-track studio. He had originally formed an earlier incarnation of Ether as a teenager, a band that included drummer Bret Sawmy, who graduated to the second version of the band. The new line-up was completed with the addition of bass player Gareth Driscoll. Their debut performance in Cardiff was watched by an A&R representative from London, and word of their highly commercial, bubblegum rock spread through the majors. After the release of their 1996 debut single, 'He Say Yeah' (on Regal Records), they signed with **Parlophone Records**, who put them into the studio with producer John Leckie. 'If You Really Want To Know' emerged in June 1997, its fresh-faced vivacity somewhat reminiscent of **Supergrass**. Touring engagements with **Mansun**, **babybird** and the **Supernaturals** helped to increase their profile before the release of *Strange*, an admirably quirky collection of power pop songs.

● ALBUMS: *Strange* (Parlophone 1998) ★★★.

Etheridge, John

b. 12 January 1948, London, England. Etheridge is a self-taught guitarist who started playing while he was at school. He went on to Essex University and then played with jazz rock groups in London in the early 70s, including Darryl Way's Wolf. In 1975 he replaced **Allan Holdsworth** in **Soft Machine**, staying with the band until their initial demise in the late 70s. He played with **Stéphane Grappelli** between 1978 and 1981, showing as much facility playing the acoustic guitar with him as he had previously done on the electric. At the same time, he formed the jazz fusion group **2nd Vision** with former **Albion Band** member **Ric Sanders**. He undertook solo concerts in Australia and toured the USA with bass player Brian Torff in 1982 before playing some live dates and recording with the re-formed Soft Machine.

Since the mid-80s Etheridge has worked with an impressive number of jazz musicians, including **Gordon Beck**, **John Marshall**, **Andy Summers**, **Pat Metheny**, **Herb Ellis**, **Didier Lockwood**, **Barney Kessel** and **Dick Heckstall-Smith**. He has also played with **Danny Thompson**, Yehudi Menuhin, **Nigel Kennedy** and classical guitarist **John Williams**. His own bands include a quartet dedicated to Grappelli and the eitht-piece Zappatistas, who perform the music of **Frank Zappa**. A technically gifted guitarist of immense talent, Etheridge is able to use guitar effects very effectively in his solos. More recently his solo acoustic work has been equally satisfying. On 2004's *I Didn't Know* he sensitively covered 'God Bless The Child' and 'Mercy, Mercy, Mercy'. Etheridge regularly teaches guitar courses at further education college.

● ALBUMS: with Dick Heckstall-Smith *Obsession Fees* (R&M 1992) ★★★, with Andy Summers *Invisible Threads* (Mesa 1993) ★★★, *Ash* (The Jazz Label 1994) ★★★★, *Sweet Chorus: A Tribute To Stéphane Grappelli* (Dyad 1998) ★★★★, *Chasing Shadows* (Dyad 2001) ★★★, *I Didn't Know* (Dyad 2004) ★★★.

Etheridge, Melissa

b. 29 May 1961, Leavenworth, Kansas, USA. Etheridge was still only a teenager when she began playing piano and guitar in various covers bands around Kansas. After this grounding she had a more formal training at the **Berklee College Of Music** before playing the club circuit around Boston, Massachusetts. However, it was after she relocated to Los Angeles and was spotted performing by **Island Records** chief **Chris Blackwell** that her career took off. Signed in 1986, her first break was writing the music for the movie *Weeds*. She had recruited one band to work with her but when this did not work out, she settled for a simple trio with Kevin McCormick on bass and Craig Kampf on drums. The first album was recorded live in the studio and spawned the single 'Bring Me Some Water'. A turntable hit, it took some time to pick up sales but ended up a Grammy nominee. Former **Iggy Pop** sideman Scott Thurston had made a guest appearance on the first album and he returned for the second, alongside artists including Waddy Weichtel and Island Records cohort Bono (**U2**). Kampf did not play on the album as he had been replaced by Maurigio Fritz Lewak.

In the early 90s Etheridge's third album, the excellent *Never Enough*, won a Grammy award. The follow-up **Yes I Am** was a similar mix of up-tempo, 'love crazy' material, showing a lyrical side of Etheridge that tolerated no fools, yet maintained the romantic tradition. 'If I Wanted To' for example: 'If I wanted to I could run as fast as a train, be as sharp as a needle that's twisting your brain, If I wanted to I could turn mountains to sand, have political leaders in the palm of my hand.' She also announced herself as a lesbian by jumping onstage to kiss Elvira at the gay and lesbian Triangle Ball during the inaugural celebrations of President Clinton's victory. The Hugh Padgham–produced *Your Little Secret* was further confirmation of her writing talents. She was able to swing from rockers such as the title track to the beautiful 'Nowhere To Go' about a clandestine lesbian relationship. Etheridge won the 1996 **ASCAP** Songwriter Of The Year award, but took a lengthy break from the music business to concentrate on her domestic arrangements. She returned in 1999 with the intimate, but low-key *Breakdown*. Far more high profile was the media's obsessive interest in unearthing the biological father of her and then partner Julie Cypher's two children. The sperm donor turned out to be **David Crosby**. Following the mediocre 2001 release *Skin*, Etheridge made an excellent return to form three years later with *Lucky*. Later in the year the artist announced she was battling breast cancer.

● ALBUMS: *Melissa Etheridge* (Island 1988) ★★★, *Brave And Crazy* (Island 1989) ★★★, *Never Enough* (Island 1991) ★★★★, *Yes I Am* (Island 1993) ★★★, *Your Little Secret* (Island 1995) ★★★, *Breakdown* (Island 1999) ★★, *Skin* (Island 2001) ★★★, *Lucky* (Island 2004) ★★★★.

● COMPILATIONS: *Greatest Hits: The Road Less Traveled* (Island 2005) ★★★★.
● DVD/VIDEOS: *Live . . . And Alone* (Island Entertainment 2002), *Lucky* (Island 2005).
● FURTHER READING: *Our Little Secret*, Joyce Luck. *The Truth Is . . . : My Life In Love And Music*, Melissa Etheridge.

Ethio Stars

Shimelis Beyene (b. 1 April 1952, Ethiopia; trumpet), Mengesha Teferi (b. 25 May 1954, Ethiopia; guitar), Frew Mengiste (26 November 1966, Ethiopia; bass), Berhane Kidane (b. 10 April 1961, Ethiopia; keyboards), Neser Awel (b. 31 December 1955, Ethiopia; drums). Formed in 1981 by Beyene, the Ethio Stars initially featured musicians who had previously been members of two of the most successful bands in Addis Ababa at the time (hence the name). Playing a mixture of Ethiopian music and classic **Stax**-style soul, they soon became one of the most in demand bands on the Addis live scene. Subsequently the bands incorporated other influences into their sound, (rock, funk, reggae) and performed with many of Ethiopia's most famous singers, including **Mahmoud Ahmed** and **Aster Aweke**. *Amharic Hits And Experimental Traditions From Ethiopia* (1992) featured tracks by both the Ethio Stars and Tukal Band (an Ethiopian experimental folk rock group). The aptly titled *Ethiopian Soul Review* was a recording of a 1994 concert featuring the group backing powerhouse vocalist **Teshome Wolde** at the Rocket Hall in London.

● ALBUMS: with Tukal Band *Amharic Hits And Experimental Traditions From Ethiopia* (Piranha 1992) ★★★, with Teshome Wolde *Ethiopian Soul Review* (Rags Productions 1998) ★★★★.

Ethiopians

The Ethiopians were originally a trio comprising Leonard 'Sparrow' Dillon (b. 9 December 1942, Portland, Jamaica, West Indies), Stephen Taylor (b. St. Mary, Jamaica, West Indies, d. 1975) and Aston Morris. Prior to their formation in 1966, Dillon had recorded a series of ska/mento titles for the seminal Jamaican producer **Coxsone Dodd** under the name of Jack Sparrow, including 'Ice Water' and 'Suffering On The Land' (1965). In late 1966 Morris left, and the duo of Dillon and Taylor began recording for Dodd as the Ethiopians, mostly in a style that bridged ska and **rocksteady**. Titles recorded during late 1966 and early 1967 included 'Free Man', 'Live Good', 'Owe Me No Pay Me', 'I'm Gonna Take Over Now' and 'Dun Dead Already'. After leaving Dodd they recorded at Dynamic Studios for the WIRL label, enjoying massive local hits with the rocksteady 'Train To Skaville' (1967), and the title track of their first album, *Engine 54*. In late 1967 they recorded for **Sonia Pottinger**'s Gayfeet label including 'Stay Loose Mama', 'The Whip' and 'Train To Glory'. They also worked with **Lee Perry** and his fledgling company, releasing 'Cut Down' and 'Not Me'.

By 1968 they had begun an association with producer **Harry J.** that turned out to be their most consistent, comprising a series of quintessential Jamaican vocal records that remain emblematic of the then new beat of reggae's first phase. As well as being great dance tunes, their lyrics had begun to reflect and criticize ghetto life. Rasta themes also received an airing. Their first big hit for Harry J., 'Everything Crash', was an incisive look at the post-colonial legacy and a classic rhythm. Many further titles were recorded for Harry J.

during 1968–71, including 'What A Fire', 'Gun Man', 'Hong Kong Flu', 'Woman Capture Man', 'The Selah' and many others. From 1969 they began to work with other producers; in that same year they had success with 'Fire A Mus' Mus' Tail' and 'Reggae Hit The Town' for H. Robinson. In 1970 they made 'Satan Girl' for **Lloyd Daley**, titles for **Derrick Harriott**—'Lot's Wife', 'No Baptism' and 'Good Ambition'—and sessions at **Duke Reid**'s Treasure Isle Studios produced 'Mother's Tender Care', 'Condition Bad A Yard' and 'Pirate' (1971). They continued recording with many other label owners, including Randy's (1971), **Winston Riley** (1972), Alvin 'GG' Ranglin (1972), **Joe Gibbs** (1971, 1975), **Rupie Edwards** (1972–73), Harry J. (1972) and Lee Perry again (1973). In 1975, Stephen Taylor died in a car crash, and Dillon continued alone, occasionally using session singers, including members of the Cordells. In 1977 **Winston 'Niney' Holness** produced a solid Rasta-based album entitled *Slave Call*. 'Open The Gate Of Zion' was recorded in 1978 at Channel One, with **Sly And Robbie** and the **Revolutionaries**. Dillon returned to Dodd for the release of *Everything Crash*. This was a mature, rootsy set with new versions of the title song and 'No Baptism', and excellent new songs based on vintage Studio One rhythms. The late 70s saw the release of more 45s for Dodd, followed by a break until a lively self-produced reissue of 'Pirate' surfaced in 1986. Since then, Dillon has worked with new members Harold Bishop and former **Burning Spear** drummer, Neville Duncan.

● ALBUMS: *Engine 54* (WIRL 1968) ★★★★, *Reggae Power* (Trojan 1969) ★★★, *Woman Capture Man* (Trojan 1970) ★★★, *Slave Call* (Observer/Third World 1977) ★★★, *Open The Gate Of Zion* (GG's 1978) ★★★, *Everything Crash* (Studio One 1979) ★★★, *Dread Prophecy* (Night Hawk 1986) ★★★, *The World Goes Ska* (Trojan 1992) ★★★.

● COMPILATIONS: *Original Reggae Hit Sound* (Trojan 1986) ★★★, *Owner Fe De Yard* (Heartbeat 1994) ★★★★, *Stay Loose: Best Of The Ethiopians* (Music Club 2001) ★★★★, *Train To Skaville: Anthology 1966 To 1975* (Trojan 2002) ★★★★, *Everything Crash: The Best Of The Ethiopians* (Trojan 2002) ★★★★.

Ethix

The Ethix were originally based in Lafayette, California, USA. In 1965 their line-up comprised Ken Metcalf, Bill Gerst, Gil Sanchez, Sandy Clifford, Wayne Ceballos and leader Cork Marchesi. Their debut single, 'Skopul'/'It's Time', is R&B-based with little hint of the change of style revealed on its successor, 'Bad Trip'/'Skins'. Whereas the b-side invites comparison with the early **Mothers Of Invention**, 'Bad Trip' is quite unlike contemporary 1967 releases with screaming vocals and random, distorted guitars underpinned by metronomic bass and percussion. The Ethix name was abandoned soon afterwards when Marchesi formed the equally eerie **Fifty Foot Hose**.

Ethnic Heritage Ensemble

The Ethnic Heritage Ensemble was formed in 1976 by **Edward Wilkerson Jnr.** (b. 27 July 1955, Terre Haute, Indiana, USA; reeds) and **Kahil El'Zabar** (b. Clifton Blackburn, 11 November 1953, Chicago, Illinois, USA; percussion). Wilkerson, one of the most versatile of the new Chicago saxophonists, also leads the octet 8 Bold Souls and a big band, Shadow Vignettes. El'Zabar studied at the Malcolm X School of Music

and worked with **Donny Hathaway** and **Paul Simon** as well as playing in the AACM with **Lester Bowie**, **Chico Freeman** and **Muhal Richard Abrams**; he has also served as the organization's chairman. He also leads his own groups, including the Ritual Trio (in association with **Malachi Favors**).

A typical second-generation **AACM** group, the Ethnic Heritage Ensemble owe much to the example of the **Art Ensemble Of Chicago**, particularly in their use of 'little instruments', and even more to the general AACM emphasis on space, sound-as-texture and detailed awareness of black music history. The duo were joined on their first two albums by saxophonist 'Light' Henry Huff. On *Welcome*, the third member was saxophonist **'Kalaparush' Maurice McIntyre**, and on *Ancestral Song* onwards it was trombonist **Joseph Bowie**. In 1997, Wilkerson was replaced by Ernest 'Khabeer' Dawkins, who made his debut alongside guest musician Fareed Haque (guitar/percussion) on the excellent *Freedom Jazz Dance*.

● ALBUMS: *Three Gentlemen From Chicago* (Moers 1980) ★★★, *Impressions* (Red 1981) ★★★, *Welcome* (Leo 1984) ★★★, *Ancestral Song* (Silkheart 1989) ★★★, *Hang Tuff* (Open Minds 1992) ★★★, *Dance With The Ancestors* (Chameleon 1993) ★★★★, *21st Century Union March* (Silkheart 1997) ★★★, *The Continuum* (Delmark 1998) ★★★★, *Freedom Jazz Dance* (Delmark 1999) ★★★★, *Ka-Real* (Silkheart 2000) ★★★.

● FURTHER READING: *Mis'taken Brilliance*, Kahil El'Zabar.

Ethos

Ethos were a mid-70s US rock band dealing in multi-layered pomp and progressive rock. Comprising Will Sharpe (guitar/vocals), Brad Stephenson (bass/vocals), Michael Ponczek (keyboards) and Mark Richards (drums), they released their self-titled debut album for **Capitol Records** in 1976, before touring as opening support for **Kiss**. Though good live reviews followed for their heavily syncopated, thematically dense songs, their second album, *Open Up*, failed to provide a commercial breakthrough—despite containing more accessible, radio-friendly material. With Capitol's patience wearing thin, Ethos had broken up by the end of the decade before a third album could be recorded.

● ALBUMS: *Ethos* (Capitol 1976) ★★★, *Open Up* (Capitol 1977) ★★.

Etting, Ruth

b. 23 November 1896, David City, Nebraska, USA, d. 24 September 1978, Colorado Springs, Colorado, USA. This famous torch singer sang on radio and in Chicago nightclubs before making her Broadway debut in *Ziegfeld Follies* Of 1927 in which she made a tremendous impact with 'Shaking The Blues Away'. In her next show, *Whoopee!* (1928), she introduced 'Love Me Or Leave Me', which was subsequently always associated with her, and titled her 1955 film biography, which starred **Doris Day**. After launching two more future standards, 'Get Happy' (*Nine-Fifteen Revue*) and 'Ten Cents A Dance' (*Simple Simon*), her sparkling rendition of an old **Nora Bayes** number 'Shine On Harvest Moon', in *Ziegfeld Follies Of 1931*, made the song a hit all over again. By then she was one of America's brightest stars with her own radio shows and string of hit records. There were more than 60 of them between 1926 and 1937, including 'Lonesome And Sorry', 'Thinking Of You', 'The Song Is

Ended', 'Back In Your Own Back Yard', 'Ramona', 'I'll Get By', 'Mean To Me', 'More Than You Know', 'Ain't Misbehavin'', 'Try A Little Tenderness', 'Love Is Like That', 'I'm Good For Nothing But Love', 'Guilty', 'Smoke Gets In Your Eyes' and 'Life Is A Song'.

In the 30s she also made three popular movies, **Roman Scandals**, *Hips, Hips, Hooray!* and *Gift Of Gab*, and in 1936 she appeared on the London stage in *Transatlantic Rhythm*. A year later she split from her husband and manager, Martin ('Moe The Gimp') Snyder, a Chicago 'hood' who had guided her career from the start. James Cagney played Snyder in the biopic *Love Me Or Leave Me*, and the story of his domination of Etting's life and his revenge wounding of her second husband—plus a great bunch of songs—made for an absorbing movie. After Ruth Etting's career faded towards the end of the 30s, she entertained at intervals during World War II and enjoyed a brief comeback in the late 40s, when club patrons and radio listeners were reminded that she was one of the outstanding vocalists of her era.

● COMPILATIONS: *Love Me Or Leave Me* (Pearl Flapper 1996) ★★★, *Glorifier Of American Song: A Collection Of Rare Recordings From 1930-1938* (Take Two 1999) ★★★.

● FILMS: *Paramount Movietone* (1928), *Melancholy Dame* (1928), *Glorifying The Popular Song* (1929), *Favorite Melodies* (1929), *The Book Of Lovers* voice only (1929), *Roseland* (1930), *One Good Turn* (1930), *Broadway's Like That* (1930), *Words & Music* (1931), *Stage Struck* (1931), *Seasons Greetings* (1931), *Radio Salutes* (1931), *Old Lace* (1931), *Freshman Love* (1931), *A Modern Cinderella* (1932), *A Regular Trouper* (1932), *A Mail Bride* (1932), *Artistic Temper* (1932), *I Know Everybody And Everybody's Racket* (1933), *Bye-Gones* (1933), *Along Came Ruth* (1933), *Crashing The Gate* (1933), *Mr. Broadway* (1933), *California Weather* (1933), *Roman Scandals* (1933), *Knee Deep In Music* (1933), *Hips, Hips, Hooray!* (1934), *The Song Of Fame* (1934), *Derby Decade* (1934), *Gift Of Gab* (1934), *No Contest* (1934), *A Torch Tango* (1934), *Southern Style* (1934), *Hollywood On Parade* (1934), *Bandits And Ballads* (1934), *Turned Out* (1935), *Ticket Or Leave It* (1935), *An Old Spanish Onion* (1935), *Melody In May* (1936), *Sleepy Time* (1936), *Aladdin From Manhattan* (1936).

Ettman, Carol

b. 20 June 1943, St. Louis, Missouri, USA. Ettman's early professional career was spent mainly in St. Louis, singing with various jazz groups, including one in which **David Sanborn** also played. Among several big bands with which she appeared were those led by Russ David, George Hudson, **George Johnson**, **Ted Weems** and **Oliver Nelson**. Her gigs with the latter gave her important exposure and were a significant breakthrough. Ettman sang and played piano in a number of lounge acts and jazz groups and was vocalist with the Frank Smith trio in Kansas City, Missouri. She has appeared at jazz clubs, particularly throughout the Midwest and in the Pacific north west; and also at numerous jazz festivals. She has also played on hotel and casino circuits. Active in jazz education, Ettman has taught Vocal Jazz Ensemble at the University of Nevada at Reno, as well as conducting clinics and master classes. She has administered the Reno Jazz Society and presented many major concerts in Reno and Portland, Oregon. Additionally, she has adjudicated several vocal jazz competitions. She has also sung and spoken many voice-overs for national advertisers. In the early 00s, she conducted vocal jazz clinics and master classes, and worked in teaching. Most of these activities took place in Florida, which is also where Ettman performed with various jazz groups.

● ALBUMS: *Experiment* (MakeWaves 1994) ★★★.

Eubanks, Duane

b. 24 January 1969, Philadelphia, Pennsylvania, USA. The youngest of three jazz-playing brothers, and a nephew of **Ray Bryant**, Duane Eubanks was raised in intensively musical surroundings. Deciding to learn the trumpet, he soon began to play effectively in the post-bop idiom. After studying for a degree in Business Administration at the University of Maryland, Eubanks enrolled as a jazz major at Temple University. During this period he also received private lessons from **Johnny Coles**. Relocating to New York, Eubanks formed his own quartet and in 1997 made his recording debut on his brother **Robin Eubanks**' *Wake Up Call*. He has also performed and recorded with musicians including, **Antonio Hart**, **Illinois Jacquet**, **Oliver Lake**, **Phyllis Hyman**, **Donald Byrd**, **James Moody** and the **Temptations**. Eubanks is always interesting when playing ballads, finding a delicately shaded and rounded sound. His liking for warm and melodic sounds has led him to compose a number of attractive songs, including 'Lonelyism', 'Can't Wait 'Til Dawn' and 'Clairvoyance', all of which appear on his debut album. With his older brothers, Robin and **Kevin Eubanks**, attracting rather more of the spotlight in jazz at the start of the new century, it might well be that it is as a songwriter that Duane Eubanks will make his most lasting mark.

● ALBUMS: *My Shining Hour* (TCB 1999) ★★★, *Second Take* (TCB 2001) ★★★.

Eubanks, Kevin

b. 15 November 1957, Philadelphia, Pennsylvania, USA. Eubanks comes from a very musical family: brother **Robin Eubanks** is a fine trombone player, **Ray Bryant** is his uncle and his mother, Vera, is a Doctor of Music. Kevin studied guitar at **Berklee College Of Music** and with **Ted Dunbar**. Throughout his teens he modelled his style largely on the fiery playing of **John McLaughlin**, but from the age of 22 he was more influenced by the gentler approach of **Wes Montgomery**. The Montgomery pedigree is evident in his work, but he also admires Segovia, **George Benson** and **Oscar Peterson**. From 1980-81 he was with **Art Blakey**'s Jazz Messengers. He has also worked with **Roy Haynes**, **Slide Hampton**, **Sam Rivers**, **Gary Thomas** (*While The Gate Is Open*) and **Mike Gibbs** (*Big Music*). He has made a reputation and a living from smooth, well-produced contemporary fusion, but is quite capable of more challenging playing, as shown by his work on **Dave Holland**'s highly acclaimed 1990 *Extensions*. Eubanks found his perfect niche as part of the **GRP Records** stable of artists, although he left the label in 1991 and signed with the illustrious **Blue Note Records**.

● ALBUMS: *Kevin Eubanks—Guitarist* (Discovery 1982) ★★★, *Sundance* (GRP 1984) ★★, *Opening Night* (GRP 1985) ★★, *Face To Face* (GRP 1986) ★★★, *The Heat Of Heat* (GRP 1988) ★★★, *Shadow Prophets* (GRP 1988) ★★, *The Searcher* (GRP 1989) ★★★, *Promise Of Tomorrow* (GRP 1990) ★★, with Eddie Higgins, Rufus Reid *Those Quiet Days* (Sunnyside 1990) ★★★, *Turning Point* (GRP 1992) ★★★, *Spirit Talk* (Blue Note 1993) ★★★, *Spiritalk 2, Revelations* (Blue Note 1995) ★★★, with Mino Cinelu,

Dave Holland *World Trio* (Intuition 1995) ★★★, *Live At Bradley's* (Blue Note 1996) ★★.

Eubanks, Robin

b. 25 October 1955, Philadelphia, Pennsylvania, USA. The son of a music teacher and nephew of **Ray Bryant**, trombonist Eubanks was raised in a musical atmosphere. He studied theory, harmony and arranging at high school and college. After graduating cum laude from the University of the Arts in Philadelphia, he moved to New York in 1980 where he attracted favourable attention playing trombone in bands led by his younger brother, guitarist **Kevin Eubanks**. Robin has played with many leading artists, happily working in hard bop and free jazz contexts. The wide-ranging spectrum of artists and groups with whom he has performed and toured, sometimes arranging, composing and recording, has included **Steve Coleman**, **Greg Osby**, **Art Blakey** and the **Jazz Messengers**, **McCoy Tyner**'s Big Band, the **Mingus Big Band**, **Slide Hampton**'s Jazz Masters, **Elvin Jones**' Jazz Machine and the **Dave Holland** Quintet. He appeared on **J.J. Johnson**'s 1997 Grammy nominated recording *The Brass Orchestra*, as composer, arranger and featured soloist. He has also appeared with many non-jazz artists, including the **Rolling Stones**, **Talking Heads** and **Barbra Streisand**.

Eubanks has worked on several television shows and specials including *The Tonight Show*, *Saturday Night Live*, and *Motown At The Apollo*. He has also worked on theatre and film projects. As leader of his own groups he has recorded and toured nationally and also in Europe and Japan. He is also very active in music education, not only teaching privately and holding seminars and clinics worldwide but also as Assistant Professor of Jazz Trombone at Oberlin College Conservatory of Music and at the University of Arts in Philadelphia. Eubanks is at the forefront of development of the 'electric' trombone. An immensely gifted musician, throughout his career Eubanks has shown himself capable of applying his formidable technique to the service of the music he plays. He is prominent among the generation of jazz musicians confidently carrying the music on into the new century.

● ALBUMS: *Different Perspectives* (JMT 1988) ★★★★, with Steve Turre *Dedications* (JMT 1989) ★★★, *Karma* (JMT 1990) ★★★, *Mental Images* (JMT 1994) ★★, *Wake Up Call* (Sirocco Jazz 1997) ★★, *4: JJ/Slide/Curtis And Al* (TCB 1998) ★★★, *Get 2 It* (Robin Eubanks 2001) ★★★.

Eubie!

Created by Julianne Boyd, this lively two-act revue was built around the compositions of **Eubie Blake**. In February 1978, the music of Blake, who that month celebrated his 95th birthday, was presented to New York audiences by way of a revival of *Shuffle Along*, which he had co-written with **Noble Sissle** and was first staged on Broadway in 1921. This revival ran for just 12 performances but when the new show *Eubie!* opened at Broadway's Ambassador Theatre on 20 September 1978 it was in a very different form. Very successful, the show ran for 439 performances. Some of the songs came from *Shuffle Along*, some from another of the duo's shows, **The Chocolate Dandies** (1924), and others not written for shows. Among the songs brought to a new audience, not all of which involved Sissle, were 'Shuffle Along', 'Gee, I Wish I Had Someone To Rock Me In The Cradle Of Love', 'Goodnight, Angeline', 'I'm Craving For That Kind Of Love', 'In Honeysuckle Time', 'Oriental Blues', 'Roll Jordan', 'There's A Million Little Cupids In The Sky', 'Weary', 'You've Got To Get The Gittin' While The Gittin's Good' and 'Daddy'. There were also two songs of Sissle and Blake's that had become a part of the musical fabric of American culture, the lovely ballad 'Memories Of You' and the high-kicking 'I'm Just Wild About Harry', the latter having achieved fame in the late 40s as the campaign song of US President Harry S. Truman.

Euge Groove

b. Steven Eugene Grove, 27 November 1962, Hagerstown, Maryland, USA. Grove studied piano before taking saxophone studies while at high school. At the University of Miami, he gradually developed an interest in jazz. Gigging locally, he played in the All American College Band at Disney World, Orlando. Graduating in 1984, he played in local bands while on a masters degree course in music performance, then dropped out to play music full time. Adept on alto and tenor saxophones and clarinet, he played in Latin and pop bands, including Exposé. In Los Angeles in 1987, together with James Slater he wrote 'Hearts On Fire', recorded by Richard Elliot on *Power Of Suggestion*. Elliot was with **Tower Of Power** and when he went solo, Grove took his place in the band, appearing on 1991's *Monster On A Leash*. He also played in the band accompanying **Huey Lewis And the News** on their Small World tour. In 1990, he toured with **Richard Marx** and later with others, including **Joe Cocker** and **Eros Ramazzotti**. He toured again with Marx in 1997. Among other artists with whom Grove has recorded are **Aaron Neville**, **Bonnie Raitt**, **Paula Abdul** and **Elton John**.

At the end of the decade, Grove halted his busy touring schedule to begin work on a solo project that would result in his first album. At this time he adopted the name Euge Groove. A track from the proposed album, 'Romeo And Juliet', which he had written in Verona while touring with Ramazzotti, was put onto the Internet for downloading and became very successful, auguring well for the CD, which eventually appeared on **Warner Brothers Records** in 2000. A further Cocker tour took place at the start of the new decade and Grove also worked with **Tina Turner**, recording her 60th birthday special video in London and touring with her in 2000. His first single, 'Vinyl', spent 27 weeks on the R&R NAC/Smooth Jazz chart and he was voted Best Breakout Artist for the year. Bringing technical expertise and inventiveness to his playing, Grove comfortably straddles the worlds of both jazz and pop.

● ALBUMS: *Euge Groove* (Warners 2000) ★★★, *Play Date* (Warners 2002) ★★★, *Livin' Large* (Narada Jazz/ Virgin 2004) ★★★★, *Just Feels Right* (Narada Jazz 2005) ★★★.

Eugenius

Formed in Glasgow, Scotland, Eugenius were led by Eugene Kelly, who had previously been part of the **Vaselines**, who were hailed as influential after their demise. On the other hand Kelly described them as 'a bunch of drunken, useless, awful idiots'. That did not stop Kurt Cobain of **Nirvana** praising the Vaselines and Kelly's subsequent bands. Two years after their break-up, a promoter invited Kelly to support the **Lemonheads**, even though he didn't have a band at that time. He borrowed Gordon Keen (guitar) from **BMX Bandits**, James from the Vaselines and Brendan O'Hare from

Teenage Fanclub to play the gig. The quartet wrote a couple of songs together and called themselves Captain America. Despite being only a half-hearted exercise, word quickly spread. Just four months after that debut performance, Captain America were invited to support Nirvana, just as 'Smells Like Teen Spirit' was taking off (Cobain was frequently spotted wearing a Captain America T-shirt). However, as soon as they made their debut with the *Wow* EP on Dangerhouse Records, *Marvel Comics* in America took legal action to prevent them using the name again.

Captain America became Eugenius as the group replaced Keen and O'Hare with Roy Lawrence and Ray Boyle, and signed to **Creation Records**. The press were still interested, but as the band admitted, 'The Nirvana connection could be a bit of a bastard at times. Through some bizarre logic, people automatically assumed that we would sound like them—just because Kurt wore our T-shirt on the cover of the *New Musical Express*.' *Oomalama* took three weeks in total to complete, though the band found themselves somewhat over-extended as it was originally intended to be a mini-album. Some of the fanfare surrounding the band had died down by the time they began recording *Mary Queen Of Scots*, a mature, reflective album, still dependent on the band's buzzsaw guitars and insistent melodies. One of the best examples of their new sound was 'Caesar's Vein', a track about the band's first US tour in 1992, and the first single to be lifted from these sessions.

● ALBUMS: *Oomalama* (Creation 1992) ★★★, *Mary Queen Of Scots* (August 1994) ★★★.

Euphoria

A typically grandiose US band from the era of progressive rock, Euphoria were formed at the end of the 60s by William D. Lincoln and Hamilton Wesley Watt Jnr. Their sole album, released on **Capitol Records** in 1969, was titled *A Gift From Euphoria* and featured a wide-ranging collection of country, psychedelic rock and folk moments, interspersed with ballads and neo-orchestral flourishes. The band, originally a quartet, was originally forged in Houston, Texas, USA, but like peers the **13th Floor Elevators** and **Big Brother And The Holding Company**, they soon migrated to California's burgeoning rock music climate. Lincoln and Watt's debut single release was actually credited to the Word, before they embarked on the sessions that produced *A Gift From Euphoria*. Recorded in Nashville, London and Hollywood, the contents were evidently religiously inspired in places. However, despite the sumptuous nature of the results, and the obvious money invested on their behalf by Capitol, the album failed to sell and no further recordings by Euphoria were ever issued. Watt and Lincoln continued to work in Los Angeles as session musicians.

● ALBUMS: *A Gift From Euphoria* (Capitol 1969) ★★★.

Eurogliders

Although beginning in Perth, Western Australia, in 1980 as a full-time permanent band, the Eurogliders eventually reverted to a duo based around songwriter Bernie Lynch and talented vocalist **Grace Knight**. The band's early work was new wave-influenced, but, as they progressed, their sound became a very competent rock/pop/soul mixture, featuring Lynch's excellent songs and tight playing. Each album provided charting singles such as 'Without You' (1982), 'Heaven' (1984), 'We Will Together', 'City Of Soul',

'Can't Wait To See You' (all from 1985). The band then hit a dry spell before re-emerging as a duo in 1988, but unable to recapture the wide popularity of the earlier days. Despite having little experience singing jazz, Grace Knight recorded a jazz album with **Vince Jones** in 1990.

● ALBUMS: *Pink Suit, Blue Day* (1982) ★★★, *This Island* (Columbia 1984) ★★★, *Absolutely* (Columbia 1985) ★★★, *Groove* (1988) ★★.

Europe

This Swedish heavy rock outfit enjoyed brief international success in the late 80s. The origins of the band can be traced back to 1978, when **Joey Tempest** (b. Joakim Larsson, 19 August 1963, Stockholm, Sweden; vocals/keyboards) **John Norum** (b. 23 February 1964, Vardö, Norway; guitar) and Tony Reno (b. Tony Niemstö; drums) joined Peter Olsson in Force. Olsson quit the band in 1981 and was replaced by John Levén (bass). After winning a national talent contest, the newly renamed Europe recorded two **Rush**-influenced albums for the Swedish market before signing to Epic Records in 1986. By this time, Reno had left the band and the new line-up featured his replacement Ian Haugland (drums) and Mic Michaeli (b. Gunnar Michaeli; keyboards). The first Epic album was produced by Kevin Elson and included three hits, 'The Final Countdown' (UK number 1/US number 8), 'Rock The Night' (UK number 12/US number 30) and 'Carrie' (UK number 22/US number 3). *The Final Countdown* went on to multi-platinum status, but also set the band a standard they subsequently failed to maintain.

Norum was replaced shortly after the release of *The Final Countdown* by Kee Marcello (b. Kjell Lövbom). The new line-up's continued success in Japan and the USA was assisted by their lengthy world tours, and later hits included 1988's 'Superstitious' from the Ron Nevison–produced second album. 1991's *Prisoners In Paradise*, with Beau Hill as producer, sold poorly, despite containing the UK Top 30 hit 'I'll Cry For You', and the band split up a year later. Joey Tempest signed a solo contract with **PolyGram Records** in 1994 and released his debut, *A Place To Call Home*, in 1995. Both Tempest and Norum maintained solo careers before teaming up with Michaeli, Levén and Haugland in 2003 to relaunch Europe. A new album followed in 2004.

● ALBUMS: *Europe* (Hot 1983) ★★, *Wings Of Tomorrow* (Hot 1984) ★★★, *The Final Countdown* (Epic 1986) ★★★, *Out Of This World* (Epic 1988) ★★, *Prisoners In Paradise* (Epic 1991) ★★★, *Start From The Dark* (Sanctuary 2004) ★★.

● COMPILATIONS: *1982–1992* (Epic 1993) ★★★, *Super Hits* (Columbia 1998) ★★★, *Simply The Best* (Sony 2001) ★★★.

Europe, James Reese

b. 22 February 1881, Mobile, Alabama, USA, d. 9 May 1919, Boston, Massachusetts, USA. After a formal musical education in Washington, DC, Europe worked in New York soon after the turn of the century. He became a prominent figure in the city's musical circles, leading bands at high society balls and other prestigious functions. He was one of the founders of the Clef Club, an association to advance the cause of black musicians. In 1914 he presented the Clef Club Orchestra at Carnegie Hall, using an astonishing 125 musicians. The music played was typical of the society orchestras of the day—marches, tangos, waltzes and, because these were black musicians, a selection of so-called plantation songs. The enormous splash this concert made established Europe as the top black band leader in the city and this led to jealousy and dissent at the Clef Club. Europe soon quit and formed a new organization, the Tempo Club. Europe became closely associated with the popular white ballroom dancers, **Vernon And Irene Castle**, and with them was largely responsible for popularizing the foxtrot, the dance craze that swept the USA. In 1917, Europe enlisted in the army and formed the 369th Infantry regiment's band, the Hellfighters. This band played to army and civilian audiences in France and by the time the war was over Europe's popularity was immense. The music he played, as documented on the handful of records he made, was an intriguing combination of Sousa-like brassiness and perky ragtime. Europe's music was by no means jazz, but it did hint at his awareness of early black vernacular music and, thanks to his unprecedented popularity with white audiences, he appeared the man most likely to make this music a crossover success. It was not to be. On 9 May 1919 an altercation with one of his musicians, drummer Herbert Wright, degenerated into a brawl and Europe was stabbed to death.

● COMPILATIONS: *Jim Europe's 369th US 'Hell Fighters' Band* (Memphis Archives 1996) ★★★★, *James Reese Europe Featuring Noble Sissle* 1919 recording (Iajrc 1996) ★★★.

● FURTHER READING: *A Life In Ragtime: A Biography Of James Reese Europe*, R. Reid Badger.

Eurovision

This 'comedy of homosexual manners set against the backdrop of the Eurovision Song Contest' was written and directed by Tim Luscombe, and made its debut in 1992 at the Drill Hall in Bloomsbury, London, England, a fringe theatre devoted to lesbian and gay writing. While at the Drill Hall, the piece was brought to the attention of **Andrew Lloyd Webber** who presented it at his Sydmonton Festival in the summer of 1993, where it was extremely well received. He then decided to finance a London production, which opened at the Vaudeville Theatre on 10 November 1993. It was immediately savaged by the critics who ridiculed the 'preposterous plot in which the ghosts of two gay lovers from ancient Rome materialise in the milieu of a thoroughly modern Eurovision Song Contest'. Anita Dobson, ex-*East-Enders* soap-star, played Katia Europa, 'who is suddenly possessed by something calling itself The Spirit of Europe', and she escaped more or less unscathed from the press hammering, as did James Dreyfus (Gary) and Charles Edwards (Kevin) as the 'two gay young things'. There was one genuine Eurovision song, a former Greek entry entitled 'Bim-Bam-Bom!', and several original songs, including 'Grazie, Macedonia', by Jason Carr. The show's author, Tim Luscombe, was generally held responsible for the 'utter bilge', and he fought back, claiming that the critics seemed to be regarding the show as 'Ibsen' instead of a 'self-mocking entertainment' that had 700 people falling off their chairs every night'. It was all to no avail. Unlike Broadway, where a show can close after only one night, most West End cripples stagger on for a few weeks, but Andrew Lloyd Webber saw the writing on the wall, and pulled out the financial plug so that *Eurovision* disappeared down the drain after only a run of only three weeks with estimated losses of £275,000.

Eurythmics

UK pop duo comprising **David A. Stewart** (b. 9 September 1952, Sunderland, Tyne and Wear, England) and **Annie Lennox** (b. 25 December 1954, Aberdeen, Scotland). The worldwide popularity and critical acclaim of one of pop music's leading duos came about by fastidious determination and Stewart's remarkably good ear in being able to write the perfect song for his musical partner Lennox. Both artists relied heavily on each other's considerable talent and, as former lovers, they knew better than most their strengths and weaknesses.

Stewart met Lennox in London while he was still a member of the folk/rock band **Longdancer**. She was supplementing her income by waitressing while a student at the Royal College of Music. Together they formed the **Tourists**, a fondly remembered band that was able to fuse new wave energy with well-crafted pop songs. Following the Tourists' split, with Lennox and Stewart now embroiled in their much-publicized doomed love affair, they formed the Eurythmics in 1980. The debut *In The Garden* was a rigidly electronic sounding album, very Germanic, haunting and cold. The record failed to sell. During one of the low points in their lives, having ended their four-year relationship, the duo persevered professionally and glanced the charts in November 1982 with the synthesizer-based 'Love Is A Stranger'. This gave them the confidence they needed, and the material on the subsequent *Sweet Dreams* (which climbed to number 3 in the albums chart) was superb, bringing deserved success. The album spawned a number of hits, all accompanied by an imaginative series of self-produced videos with the stunning Lennox in countless guises, showing incredible natural confidence in front of a camera. The spooky 'Sweet Dreams (Are Made Of This)' narrowly missed the top of the UK chart in February 1983, but made the top spot in the US in May. It was followed in quick succession by a reissued 'Love Is A Stranger' (UK number 6, April 1983) and 'Who's That Girl?' (UK number 3, July 1983). Released in November 1983, the UK chart-topping *Touch* became a huge success, containing a varied mixture of brilliantly accessible pop music, including the celebratory 'Right By Your Side' (UK number 10, November 1983) and 'Here Comes The Rain Again' (UK number 8/US number 4, January 1984). A remixed mini-LP of four tracks from *Touch* followed before they embarked upon scoring the music for the movie *1984*, starring John Hurt, which generated a UK number 4 hit in November 1984 with 'Sexcrime (Nineteen Eighty Four)'. Their lacklustre work on the soundtrack was immediately remedied by the excellent *Be Yourself Tonight*, which featured another huge transatlantic single 'Would I Lie To You?' (UK number 17, US number 5, April 1985). The album contained less synthesized pop and more rock music, with Stewart using guitar-based songs including a glorious soul duet with **Aretha Franklin** on 'Sisters Are Doin' It For Themselves' and the earthy 'Ball And Chain'.

During 1985, Lennox experienced serious throat problems, which forced the band to cancel their appearance at July's **Live Aid** charity concert. That same month, however, the duo enjoyed their sole UK chart-topper, the exuberant 'There Must Be An Angel (Playing With My Heart)'. Lennox made her big-screen debut in *Revolution* with Donald Sutherland and Al Pacino. Stewart, meanwhile, became one of the most sought-after record producers, working with **Bob Dylan, Tom Petty, Feargal Sharkey**, Daryl Hall (of **Hall And Oates**), **Bob**

Geldof and **Mick Jagger**. The following year another gem, *Revenge*, was released, which included the group's last UK Top 10 single 'Thorn In My Side' (number 5, September 1986), 'Missionary Man', and the comparatively lightweight 'The Miracle Of Love'. *Savage* in 1987 maintained the standard and featured one of Lennox's finest vocal performances with the R&B rocker 'I Need A Man'. In 1988, their performance at the televised Nelson Mandela Concert from Wembley was one of its highlights, and the acoustic 'You Have Placed A Chill In My Heart' was a triumph. Later that year Lennox duetted with **Al Green** for a rousing and soulful version of **Jackie DeShannon**'s 'Put A Little Love In Your Heart'. *We Too Are One* at the end of 1989 became their most successful album, staying at number 1 into 1990, but proved to be their last.

The Eurythmics gained a mass following during the 80s by the sheer quality of their songs and managed to stay favourites with the media. It helped that Lennox was one of the most visually striking female performers of her era, with a voice of rare quality. Following their split, Stewart stayed in the background, using his talent as a producer and songwriter, and releasing his own solo albums. In 1992, Lennox issued her successful solo debut, *Diva*, and consolidated her reputation with *Medusa* in 1995. She reunited with Stewart in June 1998 at a tribute concert for journalist Ruth Picardie, and again at the following year's BRIT awards where the duo were honoured for their 'outstanding contribution' to British music. Buoyed by the successful reunion, Stewart and Lennox returned to the studio to record *Peace*. The ability to still write well together after such a break was the most striking aspect of the album, especially in view of the duo's past romantic relationship. The most revealing lyrics featured in '17 Again', where Lennox sang, 'you in all your jewellery, and my bleeding heart, who couldn't be together, and who could not be apart'. The duo reunited in 2005 to record two new tracks for an updated greatest hits compilation.

● ALBUMS: *In The Garden* (RCA 1981) ★★, *Sweet Dreams (Are Made Of This)* (RCA 1983) ★★★★, *Touch* (RCA 1983) ★★★★, *Touch Dance* (RCA 1984) ★★, *1984 (For The Love Of Big Brother)* film soundtrack (Virgin 1984) ★★, *Be Yourself Tonight* (RCA 1985) ★★★★, *Revenge* (RCA 1986) ★★★★, *Savage* (RCA 1987) ★★★, *We Too Are One* (RCA 1989) ★★★, *Peace* (RCA 1999) ★★★.

● COMPILATIONS: *Greatest Hits* (RCA 1991) ★★★★, *Live 1983–1989* (RCA 1993) ★★★, *Ultimate Collection* (RCA 2005) ★★★★, *Boxed 8-CD box set* (RCA 2005) ★★★.

● DVD/VIDEOS: *Sweet Dreams* (Eagle Rock 2000), *Ultimate Collection* (RCA 2005).

● FURTHER READING: *Eurythmics*, Tony Jasper. *Eurythmics: Sweet Dreams: The Definitive Biography*, Johnny Waller. *Annie Lennox: The Biography*, Bryony Sutherland and Lucy Ellis.

Eusebe

One of the new wave of UK-based hip-hop acts to emerge in the mid-90s, London's Eusebe featured rapper Steven Eusebe, sister Sharon and cousin Allison Ettienn. Their debut came in 1994 with 'Pick It Up, Fuck It Up, Drop It', released on their own label, Mama's Yard. When Lee Haynes, A&R manager for **EMI Records**, signed them, he also took on board the Mama's Yard operation, a practice familiar in US rap circles but less so in Britain. Having briefly flirted with

hip-hop with the **Ruthless Rap Assassins**, EMI's employment of Haynes (formerly at **Wild Pitch Records** in New York) signified a new recognition of the genre, with Eusebe an important first staging post in its attempts to update its roster. Two summer 1995 singles, 'Captain Of Love' and 'Summertime Healing', the latter sampling **Marvin Gaye**'s 'Sexual Healing', were the first results of the partnership. Both showcased a mixed rap/singing approach in fully realized song structures, a distinct but commercial sound further refined on their debut album Tales From Mama's Yard. Sales of the album were disappointing and led to the break-up of the band. Sharon Eusebe resurfaced in the new millennium, working with **Beautiful South** frontman Paul Heaton and promoting a solo album, *24 Hour Blackout*.

● ALBUMS: *Tales From Mama's Yard* (Mama's Yard/EMI 1995) ★★★.

Evan And Jaron

This melodic US pop rock duo comprises identical twins Evan and Jaron Lowenstein (b. 18 March 1974, Atlanta, Georgia, USA). They took up performing together as teenagers, initially under the name Durable Phig Leaf, and continued to sing together through college. The brothers established a residency at KaLo's Coffee House in Atlanta, and in 1994 recorded and independently released a live album taped at the venue. They subsequently formed the Evan And Jaron Band and recorded the seven-track EP *Not From Concentrate*, released on their A Major Label imprint in March 1996. A real major label recording contract with **Island Records** was brokered by performer **Jimmy Buffett**, and their debut for the label, *We've Never Heard Of You Either*, was produced by another veteran of the American music scene, **Danny Kortchmar**. The unusual title was provided by Evan and Jaron's friends, the tennis playing brothers Luke and Murphy Jensen. After relocating to Los Angeles and signing a new contract with **Columbia Records** in March 1999, the duo received vital promotion when 'Crazy For This Girl', from their self-titled debut for the label, was featured on the *Dawson's Creek* soundtrack. The song subsequently broke into the US Top 20.

● ALBUMS: *Live At KaLo's Coffee House* (A Major Label 1994) ★★, *Not From Concentrate* mini-album (A Major Label 1996) ★★★, *We've Never Heard Of You Either* (Island 1998) ★★★, *Evan And Jaron* (Columbia 2000) ★★★, *Half Dozen* (Twelve Between Us 2004) ★★.

Evanescence

This rock band from Little Rock, Arkansas, USA, burst into the US mainstream in 2003 with the dramatic piano-driven ballad 'Bring Me To Life'. Founding members Amy Lee (b. 13 December 1981, Riverside, California, USA; vocals/keyboards) and Ben Moody (guitar) met at church camp in the mid-90s, and after realizing their shared love of artists such as **Type O Negative** and **Portishead** decided to form a band. Their initial writing efforts unleashed two distinctive tracks, 'Give Unto Me' and 'Understanding', which set the blueprint for Evanescence's fusion of metal, goth rock and electronica and began to attract the attention of local radio. The duo's debut EP was recorded with the help of William Boyd (bass), Matt Outlaw and Rocky Gray (both drums), and was released on CDR in 1998 on the BigWig Enterprises label. David Hodges (keyboards) was added to the line-up around this time, during which Evanescence released another EP and finished work on their long-playing debut and first non-CDR release, *Origin*, issued on BigWig Enterprises in November 2000.

Despite the sudden departure of Hodges, a major label contract with Wind-up Records ensued. The band's debut for the label, *Fallen*, featured three reworked tracks from *Origin* ('Whisper', 'My Immortal', and 'Imaginary'), alongside seven new songs and a cover version of Soul Embraced's 'My Tourniquet'. 'Bring Me To Life', on which Lee duetted with Paul McCoy of **12 Stones**, was featured on the soundtrack to the hit movie *Daredevil*. Bolstered by the prominence of the single on the nation's cinema screens, *Fallen* climbed into the Top 5 of the **Billboard** album chart in spring 2003. 'Bring Me To Life' also enjoyed success on the UK market, topping the singles chart for several weeks. Lee and Moody were joined by Gray and guitarist John LeCompt (b. 10 March 1973) for live shows to promote the album. Founder member Moody was replaced at the end of 2003 by ex-**Cold** guitarist Terry Balsamo.

● ALBUMS: *Origin* (BigWig 2000) ★★★, *Fallen* (Wind-up 2003) ★★★, *Anywhere But Home* (Wind-up 2004) ★★.
● DVD/VIDEOS: *Anywhere But Home* (Wind-Up 2004).

Evans, Bill (piano)

b. 16 August 1929, Plainfield, New Jersey, USA, d. 15 September 1980, New York City, New York, USA. One of the most important and influential of modern jazz pianists, Evans studied at Southeastern Louisiana University, while summer jobs with **Mundell Lowe** and **Red Mitchell** introduced him to the jazz scene. He was in the army from 1951–54; played with **Jerry Wald** in 1954–55; studied at the Mannes School of Music, New York, 1955–56; then began a full-time jazz career with clarinettist **Tony Scott**. Through Lowe he was introduced to **Riverside Records** and made his recording debut as leader (of a trio) in 1956. Evans then recorded with **Charles Mingus** and **George Russell**. In 1958 he joined **Miles Davis**, playing a central role on the album **Kind Of Blue**, which was so influential in the development of modal jazz. Evans left Davis after less than a year to form his own trio, and favoured that format thereafter. His recordings with **Scott LaFaro** and **Paul Motian** (1959–61) represent the summit of the genre (*Portrait In Jazz*, *Explorations*, and two outstanding live sessions at the Village Vanguard: *Sunday At The Village Vanguard* reissued as *Live At The Village Vanguard* and *Waltz For Debby*). The tragic loss of the brilliant LaFaro in a car accident deprived Evans of his most sympathetic partner, and the later recordings do not quite approach the level of those on Riverside; **Eddie Gomez** was the most compatible of later bass players. Evans recorded solo, most interestingly on the double-tracked *Conversations With Myself*; in duo with **Jim Hall**, **Bob Brookmeyer** and **Tony Bennett**; and in larger groups with such players as **Lee Konitz**, **Zoot Sims** and **Freddie Hubbard**. Towards the end of his life Evans was establishing a new trio with **Marc Johnson** and **Joe LaBarbera**, and playing with new-found freedom. Although he eventually kicked his heroin habit, he experienced continuing drug problems and these contributed to his early death from a stomach ulcer and other complications.

Evans' background is significant in that he matured away from the bebop scene in New York. Although his earlier playing was indebted to bopper **Bud Powell** and more strikingly to hardbop pianist **Horace Silver**, as well as to **Lennie Tristano**, he gradually developed a more lyrical, 'impressionistic' approach, with an understated strength far removed from the aggression of bebop. His ideas were influential in the development of modal jazz and hence of the **John Coltrane** school, whose major pianistic voice was **McCoy Tyner**; however, he did not pursue that direction himself, finding it insufficiently lyrical and melodic for his needs. The softer, understated, less obviously dissonant idiom of the great trio with LaFaro and Motian embodies the rival pianistic tradition to that of the eventually overbearing Tyner. Contemporary jazz piano tends towards a synthesis of the Evans and Tyner styles, but the Evans legacy is with hindsight the richer one.

Technically, Evans led the way in the development of a genuinely pianistic modern jazz style. Most important was his much-imitated but completely distinctive approach to harmony, in particular the way the notes of the chord are arranged or 'voiced'. **Red Garland**, who preceded Evans in the Miles Davis group, had moved away from Bud Powell's functional 'shell voicings', but it was Evans (and to a lesser extent **Wynton Kelly**) who first fully defined the new style of 'rootless voicings'. These retain only the essential tones of the chord (dispensing with the root itself, often played by the bass player), and form the grammatical basis of contemporary jazz piano. Evans employed a wider variety of tone-colour than is usual in jazz piano, with subtle use of the sustaining pedal and varying emphasis of notes in the chord voicing. He improvises thematically, 'rationally'; as he said, 'the science of building a line, if you can call it a science, is enough to occupy somebody for 12 lifetimes'. His influence on pianists is as considerable as that of Coltrane on saxophonists , most notably on several artists known to a wider public than he was, such as **Herbie Hancock**, **Keith Jarrett** and **Chick Corea**, but also on **Hampton Hawes**, **Paul Bley** and more recently **Michel Petrucciani**. Legions of imitators have tended to conceal from listeners the complete originality of his style as it developed in the late 50s and early 60s, and Evans' music still continues to yield new secrets.

A trio setting was Evans' ideal format, and his solo piano style is (with the exception of the double-tracked *Conversations With Myself*) less compelling. The trio with LaFaro and Motian is definitely one of the great combinations in jazz history. The 'collective improvisation' of this group involved rhythmic innovation, with the bass in particular escaping its standard timekeeping role. Evans commented that 'at that time nobody else was opening trio music in quite that way, letting the music move from an internalized beat, instead of laying it down all the time explicitly'. However, the apparent lassitude of Evans' mature style has led to much misunderstanding and criticism. **Archie Shepp** commented (incorrectly) that 'Debussy and Satie have already done those things'; **Cecil Taylor** found Evans 'so uninteresting, so predictable and so lacking in vitality'. As James Collier wrote, 'If Milton can write "Il Pensero", surely Bill Evans can produce a "Turn Out The Stars". But Milton also wrote "L'Allegro", and Evans is not often seen dancing in the chequer'd shade'. Melancholy is Evans' natural mood, and rhythm his greatest weakness; he does not swing powerfully, and is not interested enough in the 'groove'. **Cannonball Adderley** commented that when the pianist joined Davis, 'Miles changed his style from very hard to a softer approach. Bill was brilliant in other areas, but he couldn't make the real hard things come off . . . '. When Evans played in a determined up-tempo (as on *Montreux 1968*), the result can sound merely forced and frantic, and unlike Wynton Kelly or **Tommy Flanagan**, he was not a first-choice accompanist. Nonetheless, he swung effectively when pushed by a drummer such as **Philly Joe Jones** on *Everybody Digs Bill Evans* (listen to 'Minority'), and there are many powerful swinging musicians whose music has a fraction of the interest of Evans'.

In common with an unusual handful of great jazz musicians, Bill Evans was not a master of the blues. He rapidly learned to avoid straight-ahead blues settings, although his grasp of minor blues (e.g., **Johnny Carisi**'s wonderful 'Israel') was assured, partly because melodic minor harmony is the basis of the modern jazz sound that he helped to develop. Evans increasingly played his own compositions, which were unfailingly fine and inventive, often involving irregular phrase lengths and shifting metres, and many, incidentally, named after female friends ('Waltz For Debby', 'One for Helen', 'Show-Type Tune', 'Peri's Scope', 'Laurie', 'Turn Out The Stars', 'Blue In Green'). His originality was equally apparent in his transformations of standard songs ('Beautiful Love', 'Polka Dots And Moonbeams', 'Someday My Prince Will Come', 'My Romance', 'My Foolish Heart'). His recorded legacy is extensive and is being continually expanded by his son Evan, who has released several archive recordings on his E3 label. Peter Pettinger's objective biography is an essential tool in studying the life and work of Bill Evans, undoubtedly one of the five or six key figures of piano jazz.

● ALBUMS: *New Jazz Conceptions* (Riverside 1956) ★★★, *Everybody Digs Bill Evans* (Riverside 1959) ★★★★★, *Portrait In Jazz* (Riverside 1959) ★★★★★, with Bob Brookmeyer *The Ivory Hunters—Double Barrelled Piano* (United Artists 1959) ★★★, *Explorations* (Riverside 1961) ★★★★★, *Sunday At The Village Vanguard* aka *Live At The Village Vanguard* (Riverside 1961) ★★★★★, *Waltz For Debby* (Riverside 1961) ★★★★★, *Empathy* (Verve 1962) ★★★, with Cannonball Adderley *Know What I Mean?* (Riverside 1962) ★★★★, *Moonbeams* aka *Polka Dots And Moonbeams* (Riverside 1962) ★★★, with Jim Hall *Undercurrent* (United Artists 1962) ★★★★, *Interplay* (Riverside 1963) ★★★, *Conversations With Myself* (Verve 1963) ★★★★, *How My Heart Sings!* (Riverside 1964) ★★★★, *Trio '64* (Verve 1964) ★★★★, *At Shelly's Manne-Hole, Hollywood, California* (Riverside 1965) ★★★★, *Trio '65* (Verve 1965) ★★★, *Bill Evans Trio With Symphony Orchestra* (Verve 1965) ★★★, *A Simple Matter Of Conviction* (Verve 1966) ★★★, with Hall *Intermodulation* (Verve 1966) ★★★, *At Town Hall* (Verve 1966) ★★★, *Further Conversations With Myself* (Verve 1967) ★★★★, *At The Montreux Jazz Festival* (Verve 1968) ★★★, *What's New* (Verve 1969) ★★★, *Alone* (Verve 1969) ★★★, *Peace Pieces* (Riverside 1969) ★★★, *Montreux, Vol. 2* (CTI 1970) ★★★, *The Bill Evans Album* (Columbia 1971) ★★★★, with George Russell *Living Time* (Columbia 1972) ★★★, *Live In Tokyo* (Fantasy 1972) ★★★★, *Yesterday I Heard The Rain* (Bandstand 1973) ★★★, *Since We Met* (Fantasy 1974) ★★★, *Blue Is Green* (Milestone 1974) ★★★, *Intuition* (Fantasy 1974) ★★★★, *Montreux, Vol. 3* (Fantasy 1975) ★★★, *The Tony Bennett/Bill Evans Album* (Original Jazz Classics 1975) ★★★★, with Tony Bennett *Together Again* (DRG 1976) ★★★, *Alone (Again)* (Fantasy 1976) ★★★, *Quintessence* (Fantasy

1976) ★★★, with Lee Konitz, Warne Marsh *Crosscurrents* (Fantasy 1977) ★★★, *I Will Say Goodbye* (Fantasy 1977) ★★★, *You Must Believe In Spring* (Warners 1977) ★★★, *New Conversations* (Warners 1978) ★★★, with Toots Thielemans *Affinity* (Warners 1978) ★★★, *We Will Meet Again* (Warners 1979) ★★★, *Re: Person I Knew* 1974 recording (Fantasy 1981) ★★★, *Loose Blues* 1962 recordings (Milestone 1982) ★★★, *The Paris Concert: Edition One* 1979 recording (Elektra 1983) ★★★, *The Paris Concert: Edition Two* 1979 recording (Elektra 1984) ★★★, *Jazzhouse* 1969 recording (Milestone 1988) ★★★, *You're Gonna Hear From Me* 1969 recording (Milestone 1988) ★★★, *The Solo Sessions, Vol. 1* 1963 recording (Milestone) ★★★, *The Solo Sessions, Vol. 2* 1963 recording (Milestone) ★★★, *The Brilliant* 1980 recording (Timeless 1990) ★★★, *Letter To Evan: Live At Ronnie Scott's* 1980 recording (Dreyfus 1996) ★★★, with Stan Getz *But Beautiful* 1974 recordings (Milestone 1996) ★★★, *Half Moon Bay* 1973 recording (Milestone 1999) ★★, *Practice Tape No. 1* (E3 2000) ★★★, with Don Elliott *Tenderly: An Informal Session* 1956–57 recordings (Milestone 2001) ★★, *Getting Sentimental* (Milestone 2003) ★★, *Waltz For Debby: The Complete 1969 Pescara Festival* (Lonehill 2004) ★★★.

● COMPILATIONS: *The Best Of Bill Evans* (Verve 1968) ★★★★, *The Complete Fantasy Recordings* 9-CD box set (Fantasy 1980) ★★★★, *Eloquence* 1973–75 recordings (Fantasy 1982) ★★★, *From The Seventies* 1973–77 recordings (Fantasy 1983) ★★★, *The Complete Riverside Recordings* box set (Fantasy 1985) ★★★★★, *Consecration* 1980 recording (Timeless 1990) ★★★, *Turn Out The Stars: The Final Village Vanguard Recordings June, 1980* 10-LP/6-CD box set (Mosaic/Warners 1996) ★★★, *The Secret Sessions, Recorded At The Village Vanguard* 8-CD box set (Milestone 1996) ★★★, *The Best Of Bill Evans Live On Verve* (Verve 1997) ★★★, *The Complete Bill Evans On Verve* 18-CD box set (Verve 1998) ★★★★, *The Ultimate Bill Evans* (Verve 1998) ★★★★, *The Last Waltz: Live At Keystone Korner* 1980 recording, 8-CD set (Milestone 2000) ★★★, *Consecration* 1980 recording, 8-CD set (Milestone 2002) ★★★, *We Will Meet Again: The Bill Evans Anthology—The Warner Bros. & Elektra Years 1977–1980* (Warner Jazz 2005) ★★★★.

● DVD/VIDEOS: *In Oslo* (K-Jazz 1994), *The Bill Evans Trio* (Rhapsody 1995).

● FURTHER READING: *Bill Evans: How My Heart Sings*, Peter Pettinger. *Bill Evans: Everything Happens To Me*, Keith Shadwick.

Evans, Bill (saxophone)

b. 9 February 1958, Clarendon Hills, nr Chicago, Illinois, USA. Jazz's third famous Bill Evans (the others being the modern jazz pianist and the reedsman who changed his name to **Yusef Lateef**), this Evans is the fusion tenor and soprano saxophonist. A student of **Dave Liebman**, it was on Liebman's recommendation that he joined **Miles Davis**' jazz rock band, and was thus catapulted into the spotlight. By 1983 he was recording as a leader, and when he left Davis' band a year later, he was quickly snapped up by guitarist **John McLaughlin** for his revived **Mahavishnu Orchestra**, and also began working with **Herbie Hancock**. A lyrical, gentler voice than is common in the action packed world of fusion, he has a soft tone, and a penchant for fast, precise tonguing in place of the more common headlong, legato style. His own recordings include 1982's *Moods Unlimited*, a fine trio session, with the veteran piano and bass team of pianist **Hank Jones** and bass player **Red Mitchell**; 1985's *The Alternative Man*, a star-studded **Blue Note Records** session that should appeal to fusion enthusiasts for the presence of guitarist John McLaughlin, keyboard player Mitch Forman, bass player **Marcus Miller** and drummers **Al Foster** and **Danny Gottlieb**; and 1993's *Push*, a funky, breakbeat-orientated session with contributions by Marcus Miller, keyboard player **Bob James**, pianist **Bruce Hornsby** and assorted rappers. The 1996 release *Escape* continued Evans' flirtation with hip-hop and additionally featured **Lee Ritenour** and **Jim Beard**.

● ALBUMS: with Hank Jones, Red Mitchell *Moods Unlimited* (Evidence 1982) ★★★★, *Living In The Crest Of A Wave* (Elektra 1983) ★★★, *The Alternative Man* (Blue Note 1986) ★★★, *Summertime* (Jazz City 1989) ★★★★, *Let The Juice Loose* (Jazz City 1989) ★★★, *The Gambler* (Jazz City 1990) ★★★, *Petite Blonde* (Lipstick 1992) ★★★★, *Push* (Lipstick 1993) ★★★★, *Live In Europe* (Lipstick 1995) ★★, *Escape* (Escapade 1996) ★★★★, with Andy LaVerne, John Patitucci, Steve Davis *Modern Days & Nights: Music Of Cole Porter* (Double-Time 1996) ★★★, *Starfish & The Moon* (Escapade 1997) ★★★, *Touch* (Escapade 1999) ★★★, *Soul Insider* (Escapade 2000) ★★★, with Victor Bailey, David Gilmore, Janusz Skowron, Krzysztof Zawadzki *International Quintet* (Walk Away 2001) ★★★, *Big Fun* (Escapade 2002) ★★★.

Evans, Dale

b. Lucille Wood Smith, 31 October 1912, Uvalde, Texas, USA, d. 7 February 2001, Apple Valley, California, USA. Her name was changed to Frances Octavia during her childhood, which was spent in Texas and Arkansas. Smith's first 15 years included some major traumas, having a nervous breakdown at 11, being married at 14 (by lying about her age), becoming a mother at 15, and divorced at 17. After unsuccessfully seeking a singing career in Chicago and Memphis (with a new husband and baby to look after), she moved to WHAS Louisville. Although she auditioned as Marion Lee, she found herself named Dale Evans by the station manager and in spite of her own reservations, the name stuck. She divorced her second husband before marrying pianist Robert Dale Butts from WHAS. Still harbouring aspirations towards a singing career, she returned to Chicago as a jazz singer. She toured the Midwest as vocalist with an orchestra and sang with **Fats Waller**. Eventually, owing to a combination of circumstances, she was persuaded to try her luck in films. Her agent promoted her as being 21, and when her 13-year-old son joined her, he was quickly introduced as her kid brother. After many problems, she was chosen to play the lead in a college musical called *Campus In The Clouds*. When the Japanese bombed Pearl Harbor, America's subsequent involvement in World War II saw the 'epic' shelved. She won a few small roles but suffered by being compared to **Betty Grable**. Eventually, after further problems, she met up with a popular young singing cowboy, **Roy Rogers**, on the set of *The Cowboy And The Senorita*. Originally, Evans had no intention of playing roles in B-westerns but fate decreed otherwise and she became the leading lady to Rogers' 'King Of The Cowboys'—she even had her own horse, Buttermilk, to match his famous mount Trigger. In 1946, Rogers' first wife died and Evans divorced Butts. The couple married on 31 December 1947, and from that point Evans' film and music

career ran in parallel with that of her husband. During the 50s, most of the couple's time was devoted to Rogers' highly popular television show. Evans wrote the couple's famous theme song, 'Happy Trails', and was also instrumental in introducing Rogers to God. Her faith was instrumental in helping her cope with the death of three children before adulthood, and in later years she wrote a number of inspirational books. Her own television and recording work in later years was also in the gospel field. Evans died of congestive heart failure in February 2001, almost three years after her beloved husband.

● ALBUMS: with Roy Rogers *Hymns Of Faith* 10-inch album (RCA Victor 1954) ★★, with Rogers *Sweet Hour Of Prayer* (RCA Victor 1957) ★★, *Roy Rogers And Dale Evans' Song Wagon* (Golden 1958) ★★★, with Rogers *16 Great Songs Of The Old West* (Golden 1958) ★★★, with Rogers *Jesus Loves Me* (RCA Victor 1959) ★★, with Rogers *The Bible Tells Me So* (Capitol 1962) ★★, with Rogers *Christmas Is Always* (Capitol 1967) ★★, with Rogers *In The Sweet Bye And Bye* (Word 1973) ★★★, with Rogers *The Good Life* (Word 1977) ★★★, with Rogers, Roy Rogers Jnr. *Many Happy Trails* (1984) ★★★.

● FURTHER READING: *Angel Unaware*, Dale Evans Rogers. *Happy Trails—Our Life Story: Roy Rogers And Dale Evans*, Jane and Michael Stern. *Our Values: Stories & Wisdom*, Dale Evans Rogers with Carole C. Carlson. *Life Is A Blessing: A Heartfelt Collection Of Three Bestselling Works Complete In One Volume*, Dale Evans Rogers.

● FILMS: *Orchestra Wives* (1942), *Girl Trouble* (1942), *Swing Your Partner* (1943), *West Side Kid* (1943), *In Old Oklahoma* aka *War Of The Wildcats* (1943), *Hoosier Holiday* aka *Farmyard Follies* (1943), *Here Comes Elmer* (1943), *Casanova In Burlesque* (1943), *The Yellow Rose Of Texas* (1944), *Song Of Nevada* (1944), *San Fernando Valley* (1944), *Lights Of Old Santa Fe* (1944), *The Cowboy And The Senorita* (1944), *Utah* (1945), *Sunset In El Dorado* (1945), *The Man From Oklahoma* (1945), *Hitchhike To Happiness* (1945), *Don't Fence Me In* (1945), *The Big Showoff* (1945), *Bells Of Rosarita* (1945), *Along The Navajo Trail* (1945), *Under Nevada Skies* (1946), *Song Of Arizona* (1946), *Roll On Texas Moon* (1946), *Rainbow Over Texas* (1946), *Out California Way* (1946), *My Pal Trigger* (1946), *Home In Oklahoma* (1946), *Heldorado* (1946), *The Trespasser* (1947), *Bells Of San Angelo* (1947), *Apache Rose* (1947), *Slippy McGee* (1947), *Susanna Pass* (1949), *Down Dakota Way* (1949), *Twilight In The Sierras* (1949), *The Golden Stallion* (1949), *Trigger, Jr.* (1950), *Bells Of Coronado* (1950), *South Of Caliente* (1951), *Pals Of The Golden West* (1951).

Evans, Doc

b. Paul Wesley Evans, 20 June 1907, Spring Valley, Minnesota, USA, d. 10 January 1977, Minneapolis, Minnesota, USA. While still at high school Evans played several instruments, adding cornet in the late 20s. In the early 30s, working in and around Minneapolis, he concentrated on cornet and built a good if localized reputation. During the 30s he played, composed and arranged and also worked outside music. In the 40s he played occasionally in New York and Chicago but always returned to Minneapolis. He worked with **Bunk Johnson**, **Miff Mole**, **Tony Parenti**, **Joe Sullivan** and other noted jazzmen, but mostly led his own bands. He continued an active playing career through the 50s and 60s, sometimes working with musicians like **Turk Murphy** but again preferring the musical backwaters of Minnesota to the richer but rougher possibilities of the big time. Evans was a fluent player of traditional jazz, an admirer of **Bix Beiderbecke** as evidenced by his pure tone, but with few pretensions towards originality.

● ALBUMS: *Dixieland Concert* (Soma 1953) ★★★, *Doc Evans And His Band Vol. 1* (Audiophile 1953) ★★★★, *Doc Evans And His Band Vol. 2* (Audiophile 1953) ★★★, *Classic Jazz At Carleton* (Soma 1954) ★★★★, *Dixieland Session* (Audiophile 1955) ★★★★, *Traditional Jazz* (Audiophile 1955) ★★★, *The Cornet Artistry Of Doc Evans* (Audiophile 1955) ★★★, *Classics Of The 20s* (Audiophile 1958) ★★★, *Muskrat Ramble* (Audiophile 1959) ★★★, *Doc Evans + 4 = Dixie* (Audiophile 1959) ★★★, *Reminiscing In Dixieland* (Audiophile) ★★★, *At The Gas Light* (Audiophile 1967) ★★★, *Manassas Memories '73* (Fat Cats 1975) ★★★.

● COMPILATIONS: *Jazz Heritage Volume* (Jazzology 1949) ★★★, *Jazz Heritage Volume 2: Blues In Dixieland* (Jazzology 1980) ★★★.

Evans, Don

(see **Evans, Tyrone**)

Evans, Faith

b. 10 June 1973, Lakeland, Florida, USA. Most famous for having been married to hardcore rapper the **Notorious B.I.G.**, R&B singer Faith Evans originally rose to prominence by singing background vocals and co-writing songs for **Mary J. Blige**, **Color Me Badd** and Tony Thompson. She broke through as a solo artist in the mid-90s with the release of her winning debut single, 'You Used To Love Me'. Mixing slightly lisped rap sections with soulful singing of her predominantly romantic concerns, her self-titled debut album followed expertly in the tradition of Blige, with a wide cast of producers and collaborators. Without ever demonstrating the originality to separate her from a host of urban R&B peers, *Faith* was sufficiently contemporary and lavishly executed to arouse interest throughout the R&B community. It peaked at number 2 on the **Billboard** R&B album chart, and number 22 on the Top 200.

Following Notorious B.I.G.'s murder in March 1997, Evans appeared on the international number 1 tribute single 'I'll Be Missing You' by **Sean 'Puffy' Combs**. Her own minor hit 'Love Like This' (US number 7/UK number 24) was built around a sample from **Chic**'s 'Chic Cheer', and premiered the US Top 10 album *Keep The Faith*. Evans recorded one final album for Bad Boy, the moderately successful 2001 release *Faithfully*. A low-key acting career failed to ignite despite roles in *Turn It Up* (2000) and *The Fighting Temptations* (2003), and Evans next made the headlines in 2004 when she was arrested with her husband/manager Todd Russaw for drug possession. She bounced back the following year with her first album for new label **Capitol Records**, *The First Lady*.

● ALBUMS: *Faith* (Bad Boy/Arista 1995) ★★★, *Keep The Faith* (Bad Boy/Arista 1998) ★★★★, *Faithfully* (Bad Boy/Arista 2001) ★★★, *The First Lady* (Capitol 2005) ★★★.

● FILMS: *Turn It Up* (2000), *The Fighting Temptations* (2003).

Evans, George

b. George Louis Evans, 23 January 1963, Bloomington, Indiana, USA. Evans' parents were on the faculty of the College Conservatory of Music in Cincinnati, Ohio, both teaching Voice. Inevitably, he studied in music, dance and theatre, at the School for Creative and Performing Arts in Cincinnati, and later at the CCM's Musical Theatre department. Although he had played piano and trombone as a child, it was on singing that he concentrated. He began his professional career in New York City in the 80s, but by this time opportunities were scant for work in the musical theatre. Although this was the kind of work for which he had trained, he was thus prompted towards a career as a singer on New York's cabaret circuit. Singing standards and jazz Evans found many more opportunities and established a local reputation. His career blossomed after moving to Montreal, Canada, where, throughout the 90s, he worked extensively on radio and, owing to the popularity thus gained, also appeared in films, theatre, television and on the concert stage. In 1999, he made Toronto his base, extending his broadcasting work as a television staff announcer for a satellite station. During this period, he also found a growing audience for his singing.

In addition to performing, Evans has been active in the recording industry, compiling a number of vocal albums for **Verve Records**. He owns the recording company M-Swing Records, and in 2002, *Eyes For You* was nominated for a National Jazz Award. Evans has also written on the subject of jazz singing, chiefly for *Planet Jazz Magazine*. Developing his own distinctive approach, Evans' singing is lyrical and smoothly swinging and he interprets the great standards with eloquence and skill. He is able to appeal to the jazz world and also to the much wider audience for superior popular singing.

● ALBUMS: *Moodswing* (M-Swing 1997) ★★★, *I'm All Smiles* (M-Swing 1999) ★★★, *From Moment To Moment* (M-Swing 2001) ★★★, *Eyes For You* (M-Swing 2002) ★★★★, *Bewitched* (M-Swing 2003) ★★★.

Evans, Gil

b. Ian Ernest Gilmore Green, 13 May 1912, Toronto, Canada, d. 20 March 1988, Cuernavaca, Mexico. Although self-taught, Evans became extraordinarily proficient as a pianist and composer, though his greatest talent lay in his abilities as an arranger. He formed his first band in 1933 in California, where he was raised. He wrote most of the arrangements, a duty he retained when the band was later fronted by popular singer **Skinnay Ennis**. Up to this point Evans' work had followed the orthodox line demanded of commercial dance bands, but his musical ambitions lay in other areas. A long stint as chief arranger for **Claude Thornhill** during the 40s gave him the opportunity he needed to explore different sounds and unusual textures. Thornhill's predilection for soft and slowly shifting pastel patterns as a background for his delicate piano proved to be an interesting workshop for Evans, who would always remark on this experience as being influential upon his later work. Towards the end of his stay with Thornhill, Evans was writing for very large ensembles, creating intense moody music. However, by this time, he was eager to try something new, feeling that the music he was required to write for the band was becoming too static and sombre.

During this same period, **Gerry Mulligan** was a member of the Thornhill band and was also writing arrangements. Both he and Evans had become fascinated by the developments of the radical new beboppers such as **Charlie Parker** and **Miles Davis**, and in 1948 the two men embarked upon a series of arrangements for Davis' nine-piece band. These records, subsequently released under the generic title **Birth Of The Cool**, proved very influential in the 50s. Despite the quality of the material Evans was creating at this point in his career, he did not meet with much commercial or critical success. His own recordings during the 50s were all fine albums, but they seemed to miss out on critical favour. *New Bottles, Old Wine* (featuring some blistering playing from **Cannonball Adderley**) was the best example. Towards the end of the 50s Evans again worked with Davis; together they created a batch of landmark albums such as **Miles Ahead**, **Porgy And Bess** and **Sketches Of Spain**. His arrangements for Davis were a highly effective amalgam of the concepts developed during his Thornhill period and the needs of the increasingly restrained trumpet style Davis was adopting. Evans' use in these and later arrangements for his own band of such instruments as tubas and bass trombones broadened the range of orchestral colours at his disposal and helped him to create a highly distinctive sound and style. Davis was in no doubt as to the importance of Evans in making these recordings work so well. *Out Of The Cool* was another excellent album, again under his own name, but it was further uncredited work with Davies that paid the bills. His work on **Kenny Burrell**'s *Guitar Forms* in 1964 was another important step in Evans' career.

As with many other gifted arrangers and composers, Evans' real need was for a permanent band for the expression of his ideas, but this proved difficult to achieve. Such groups as he did form were in existence for only short periods, although some, fortunately, made records of his seminal works. He continued to write throughout the 60s, composing many extended works, often uncertain if they would ever be performed. However, in the early 70s he was able to form a band that played regularly and the music showed his ready absorption of ideas and devices from the current pop music scene. After a number of international tours during the 70s, his work became more widely known and his stature rose accordingly. So too did his popularity when it became apparent to audiences that his was not esoteric music but was readily accessible and showed a marked respect for the great traditions of earlier jazz.

By the late 70s, the music Evans was writing had developed a harder edge than hitherto; he was making extensive use of electronics and once again was happily absorbing aspects of pop. In particular, he arranged and recorded several **Jimi Hendrix** compositions. He had closely followed his career since the late 60s and became hugely impressed by Hendrix the composer. Evans' creativity showed no signs of diminishing as the 80s dawned and he continued a punishing round of concert tours, record sessions, radio and television appearances, all the while writing more new material for his band. One of his final commissions was with **Sting**, arranging a fine version of Hendrix's 'Little Wing'.

One of the outstanding arrangers and composers in jazz, Evans was particularly adept at creating complex scores that held at their core a simple and readily understandable concept. Throughout his career, his writing showed his profound respect for the needs of jazz musicians to make their own musical statements within an otherwise formally conceived and structured work. Perhaps this is why so many notable musicians—including **Steve Lacy**, **Elvin Jones**, **Lew Soloff**, **George Adams**, **Ron Carter** and **David Sanborn**—were happy to play in his bands over the years. As a result Evans'

work, even at its most sophisticated, maintained an enviable feeling of freedom and spontaneity that few other arrangers of his calibre were able to achieve.

● ALBUMS: *There Comes A Time* (RCA Victor 1955) ★★★★, *Gil Evans Plus 10* aka *Big Stuff* (Prestige 1957) ★★★★, *New Bottles Old Wine* (Pacific Jazz 1958) ★★★★, *Great Jazz Standards* (World Pacific 1959) ★★★, with Johnny Coles *Out Of The Cool* (Impulse! 1960) ★★★★★, *Into The Hot* (Impulse! 1961) ★★, *America's Number 1 Arranger* (Pacific Jazz 1961) ★★★, *The Individualism Of Gil Evans* (Verve 1964) ★★★★, with Kenny Burrell *Guitar Forms* (Verve 1965) ★★★★, *Blues In Orbit* (Enja 1971) ★★★, *Svengali* (Atlantic 1973) ★★★, *The Gil Evans Orchestra Featuring Kenny Burrell And Phil Woods* 1963 recording (Verve 1973) ★★★, *The Gil Evans Orchestra Plays The Music Of Jimi Hendrix* (Bluebird 1974) ★★★★, *Synthetic Evans* (Zeta 1976) ★★★, *Live '76* (Zeta 1976) ★★★, *Priestess* (Antilles 1977) ★★★, *Tokyo Concert* (Westwind 1977) ★★★, *At The Royal Festival Hall* (Westwind 1978) ★★★, *The Rest Of Gil Evans At The Royal Festival Hall* (Westwind 1978) ★★★, *Little Wing* (DIW 1978) ★★★, *Parabola* (Horo 1979) ★★★, *Live At New York Public Theatre Volumes 1 & 2* (Blackhawk 1980) ★★★, *The British Orchestra* (Mole 1983) ★★★, *Live At Sweet Basil Volumes 1 & 2* (Electric Bird 1984) ★★★, *Farewell* (Electric Bird 1987) ★★★, with Helen Merrill *Helen Merrill/Gil Evans* (EmArcy 1988) ★★★, with Steve Lacy *Paris Blues* (Owl 1988) ★★★, *Sting And Bill Evans/ Last Session* (Jazz Door 1988) ★★★, *Lunar Eclipse* 1981 recordings (New Tone 1993) ★★★, *Live At Umbria Jazz Vol. II* (Egea 2002) ★★★.

● COMPILATIONS: with Tadd Dameron *The Arrangers Touch* 1953/1956/1957 recordings (Prestige 1975) ★★★★, *Jazz Masters* 1964/1965 recordings (Verve 1994) ★★★★, *Giants Of Jazz: The Gil Evans Orchestra* 1957–59 recordings (Sarabandas 1994) ★★★★, with Miles Davis *Miles Davis/ Gil Evans: The Complete Columbia Studio Recordings* 6-CD/ 11-LP box set (Columbia/Mosaic 1996) ★★★★★, *Gil Evans* (GRP 1998) ★★★, *The Real Birth Of The Cool: Studio Recordings* (Jazz Factory 2000) ★★★, *The Real Birth Of The Cool: Transcription Recordings* (Jazz Factory 2000) ★★★.

● FURTHER READING: *Svengali, Or The Orchestra Called Gil Evans*, Raymond Horricks. *Gil Evans: Out Of The Cool*, Stephanie Stein Crease. *Castles Made Of Sound: The Story Of Gil Evans*, Larry Hicock.

Evans, Herschel

b. 9 March 1909, Denton, Texas, USA, d. 9 February 1939, New York, USA. Tenor saxophonist Evans' early career was centred in the south-west where he worked with many of the best **territory band**s of the 20s and early 30s. Among the bands in which he advanced his considerable skills were those of **Edgar Battle**, **Terrence Holder** and Troy Floyd. In 1933 he joined **Bennie Moten**'s outstanding Kansas City–based band, remaining there until 1935. He also worked with **Oran 'Hot Lips' Page** before deciding on stretching his geographic boundaries. After playing briefly in Chicago he wound up in Los Angeles where he became involved in the bustling Central Avenue club scene, working with the bands of **Charlie Echols**, **Lionel Hampton** and **Buck Clayton**. In 1936 he joined **Count Basie** where his robust, **Coleman Hawkins**–influenced style of playing formed a dramatic contrast with the light acerbic sound of his section-mate, **Lester Young**. Evans' career ended abruptly when he became seriously ill towards the end of 1938 while still playing with the Basie band.

Evans, Joe, And Arthur McLain

'The Two Poor Boys' were black, and are reported to have come from Fairmount, in east Tennessee, USA, where whites outnumbered blacks by 12 to one. This goes some way towards explaining the eclecticism of, and the large white influence on, their music. Recorded in 1927 and 1931, they performed blues, but this only constituted about half of their issued titles; they also recorded medicine show material, coon songs, 20s pop, white fiddle pieces such as 'Sourwood Mountain' (transferred to mandolin and guitar), black ballads such as 'John Henry' and a parody of **Darby And Tarlton**'s 'Birmingham Jail'. As well as ranging widely in styles, they featured a remarkable variety of instruments: guitar, kazoo, piano, mandolin and violin. It is thought that although both men played guitar and kazoo, only Evans played the other instruments.

Evans, Lucky

b. 1 May 1937, Estabuchie, Mississippi, USA. Also known as Lucky Lopez, Evans was inspired by the singing and playing of his father and began to play the guitar at the age of eight. As a teenager he worked with a band in Milwaukee and then travelled throughout the southern states until 1964 when he settled in Chicago, having joined **Howlin' Wolf**'s band. He worked with many of the city's leading bluesmen in the 60s and made his debut recording in 1967 (only one track was released). He next recorded in 1973, financing the session himself. In 1988, he visited Britain, touring incessantly and slowly establishing a reputation as one of the great, underrated blues singers. He recorded in England for the JSP and Borderline labels.
● ALBUMS: *Chinaman's Door* (Borderline 1988) ★★★, *Evil* (Borderline 1989) ★★★, *Southside Saturday Night* (JSP 1989) ★★★.

Evans, Mal

b. 27 May 1935, England, d. 4 January 1976, Los Angeles, California, USA. 'Big Mal' Evans was a genial telephone engineer who was part of the security at the **Cavern** club. **Brian Epstein** asked him to assist the **Beatles**' road manager, **Neil Aspinall**, and so began a long friendship and association with the group. Evans was known to the fans through writing about his experiences in the monthly *Beatles Book*. He had cameo roles in *Help!*, *Magical Mystery Tour* and *Let It Be* and he played various instruments on their records including the organ ('You Won't See Me'), harmonium ('Being For The Benefit Of Mr Kite'), trumpet ('Helter Skelter'), tambourine ('Dear Prudence') and anvil ('Maxwell's Silver Hammer'). Many professional musicians would settle for that but Evans also played one of the pianos on 'A Day In The Life'. In 1968 he was made an **Apple Records** executive and he discovered the **Iveys**, who became **Badfinger**. When **Allen Klein** took over the Beatles' affairs, Evans moved to America. By 1975 he was divorced and felt cut off from his friends. He moved in with another woman, Frances Hughes, but, on 4 January 1976, when he became paranoid, she called the police. When they arrived, he waved an air rifle and they shot him dead. In 1996 Evans' former wife was prevented from auctioning a handwritten lyric by **Paul McCartney** by McCartney himself.

The song, ironically, was 'With A Little Help From My Friends'. Although written, Mal Evans' autobiography, *Living With The Beatles*, has not been published.

Evans, Marjorie Ann

b. 17 July 1940, Shreveport, Louisiana, USA. Margie Evans was largely inspired by **Billie Holiday** and **Bessie Smith**. She studied education and music at Grambling College. After moving to Los Angeles in her late teens, she began working with Billy Ward's Sextet between 1958 and 1964. She made some unissued recordings for Dore Records in Hollywood in the early 60s and began touring with **Ron Marshall**'s orchestra from the mid- to late 60s. In 1969 she joined the **Johnny Otis** band, recorded for Epic and extensively toured the USA and the Far East. In 1972 she began touring with **Willie Dixon**'s Chicago All-Stars, and made her first solo recordings for Yambo (1972), **United Artists** (1973) and **Buddah** (1974). She was particularly renowned for her powerful live performances at clubs and jazz festivals in the USA and Europe. In recent years she has released two fine albums on L&R Records.
● ALBUMS: *Mistreated Woman* (L&R 8195) ★★★★, *Another Blues Day* (L&R 1988) ★★★★.

Evans, Maureen

b. 1940, Cardiff, Wales. Evans began her singing career on the Embassy label, which made budget-priced recordings of contemporary hits for the UK's Woolworths chain-store. She later enjoyed chart success in her own right, beginning in 1960 with 'The Big Hurt', and peaking two years later with 'Like I Do'. This perky offering, more teen-orientated than Evans' normal fare, reached the UK Top 3, but later releases failed to emulate its success. Her rather dated style was quickly surpassed by younger-minded artists, although 'Never Let Him Go', one of the singer's final releases, was an excellent interpretation of a **David Gates** song.
● ALBUMS: *Like I Do* (Oriole 1963) ★★.

Evans, Maurice

b. 3 June 1901, Dorchester, Dorset, England, d. 12 March 1989, Rottingdean, East Sussex, England. Starting out as a singer, while still very young Evans performed in productions of plays written by his father, an amateur playwright. From 1926 he was a professional actor and in 1929 scored a great success with *Journey's End*. In the early 30s he made some appearances in films and also became a member of the Old Vic company. By mid-decade he was on Broadway, usually in Shakespearean roles. Through succeeding decades he made numerous stage appearances, almost always in dramatic roles, and also appeared occasionally in films. In these same years he was also seen on television, including appearing in the situation comedy *Bewitched*. Other television appearances include *Hamlet* (1953), *The Tempest* (1960), *The Canterville Ghost* (1974) and *A Caribbean Mystery* (1983). He also played in episodes of *The Man From U.N.C.L.E.*, *Batman*, *Tarzan*, *The Streets Of San Francisco*, *Fantasy Island* and *The Love Boat*. Among his films are *The Story Of Gilbert And Sullivan* (1953, in which he played Arthur Sullivan), *Rosemary's Baby* (1968) and he was Dr Zaius in *Planet Of The Apes* (1968) and *Beneath The Planet Of The Apes* (1970). His stage appearances, chiefly on Broadway, include *Romeo And* Juliet (1936), *King Richard II* (1937), *Hamlet* (1939), *Macbeth* (1941), *Dial 'M' For Murder* (1952),

The Teahouse Of The August Moon (1953, the play winning a **Tony Award**), *No Time For Sergeants* (1955), *The Apple Cart* (1956), for which he was Emmy-nominated as Best Actor In A Play, and *Tenderloin* (1960), for which he was again nominated for an Emmy, this time as Best Actor In A Musical.

● FILMS: *Should A Doctor Tell?* (1930), *Raise The Roof* (1930), *White Cargo* (1930), *Cupboard Love* (1931), *Marry Me* (1932), *Wedding Rehearsal* (1933), *The Only Girl* (1933), *Ich Und Die Kaiserin* aka *The Empress And I* (1933), *The Path Of Glory* (1934), *Checkmate* (1935), *Bypass To Happiness* (1935), *Scrooge* (1935), *Kind Lady* (1951), *Androcles And The Lion* (1952), *The Story Of Gilbert And Sullivan* (1953), *The War Lord* (1965), *One Of Our Spies Is Missing* (1966), *Los Traidores De San Ángel* (1967), *Jack Of Diamonds* (1967), *Planet Of The Apes* (1968), *The Body Stealers* (1969), *Beneath The Planet Of The Apes* (1970), *Terror In The Wax Museum* (1973), *The Jerk* (1979).

Evans, Orrin

b. Trenton, New Jersey, USA. Raised in a musical household in Philadelphia, where his mother was a classically trained singer, Evans studied piano formally for three years with Charles Pettaway at the Settlement Music School. As a young man, Evans was encouraged and guided by various musicians, including **Kenny Barron**, **Bobby Durham**, **Ralph Peterson**, **Mickey Roker** and Tim Warfield, with some of whom he has worked and recorded. He spent two years in **Bobby Watson**'s band, alongside Peterson. He also toured internationally with Watson, **Antonio Hart** and **Wallace Roney**. Evans' driving and distinctive playing style reveals intriguing echoes of bop piano masters he has assimilated, among them **Bud Powell** and **Horace Silver**, with occasional nods of appreciation towards freer forms and the work of pianists such as **Cedar Walton**. These hints of the influence are a long way from slavish imitation; indeed, Evans is one of the most original and inventive players to have appeared at the forefront of contemporary jazz in the new millennium and is clearly a master musician in the making. In addition to performing, Evans also presents master classes, workshops and clinics in the USA and Europe, and teaches privately.

● ALBUMS: *The Orrin Evans Trio* (Black Entertainment 1994) ★★★, *Justin Time* (Criss Cross 1996) ★★★, *Captain Black* (Criss Cross 1997) ★★★, *Grown Folk Bizness* (Criss Cross 1999) ★★★, *Listen To The Band* (Criss Cross 2000) ★★★★, *Blessed Ones* (Criss Cross 2001) ★★★, *Meant To Shine* (Palmetto 2002) ★★★.

Evans, Paul

b. 5 March 1958, New York City, USA. Evans had two Top 10 singles in 1959/60 and wrote hits for others before going on to record country records, jingles and to write for the Broadway theatre and for film. Evans' first successful song placement, 'When', was a Top 5 single for the **Kalin Twins** in 1958. He later wrote the first chart hit for **Bobby Vinton**, the number 1 'Roses Are Red (My Love)', in 1962, and two songs recorded by **Elvis Presley**, 'I Gotta Know' (1960) and 'The Next Step Is Love' (1970). Evans' own recording career began in 1959 with the novelty song 'Seven Little Girls Sitting In The Back Seat', which featured a female backing group called the Curls. Released on Guaranteed Records (as were Evans' other three charting pop singles), it reached

number 9 in 1959. The following year, 'Happy-Go-Lucky-Me' reached number 10.

There were two other, minor pop chart singles, but after 1960 Evans changed course in his career, recording country music. He surfaced on the country charts in 1978 with another novelty record, 'Hello, This Is Joannie (The Telephone Answering Machine Song)', on Spring Records, and the following year with 'Disneyland Daddy', also on Spring. Those and 1980's 'One Night Led To Two', on Cinnamon Records, all made the lower rungs of the US country chart. He also wrote the scores for the minor film *Live Young* and the 1972 Broadway show *Loot*. Since then, Evans has been involved in singing advertising jingles.

● ALBUMS: *Fabulous Teens* (Guaranteed 1960) ★★, *Hear Paul Evans In Your Home Tonight* (Carlton 1961) ★★★, *Folk Songs Of Many Lands* (Carlton 1961) ★★★, *21 Years In A Tennessee Jail* (Kapp 1964) ★★, *Another Town, Another Jail* (Kapp 1966) ★★★.

● COMPILATIONS: *The Fabulous Teens, And Beyond* (Ace 1995) ★★★, *Happy Go Lucky Me: The Paul Evans Songbook* (Castle 2003) ★★★.

Evans, Ray
(see **Livingston, Jay**)

Evans, Sara

b. 5 February 1971, New Franklin, Missouri, USA. Country singer Evans got her start in music by singing with her impoverished rural family from the age of four. In 1992 she married and moved to Oregon, working alongside a band entitled North Santiam. They opened shows for artists including **Tim McGraw** and **Willie Nelson**. However, Evans elected to launch a solo career instead, relocating to Nashville to improve her prospects. It was her rendition of the **Buck Owens** standard 'I've Got A Tiger By The Tail' that triggered her breakthrough. Her version so impressed the song's writer, **Harlan Howard**, that he secured her a recording contract with **RCA Records** in 1996. She achieved a strong critical following with her 1997 debut album, *Three Chords And The Truth*, with several writers noting her flair for composition as well as her self-evident vocal skill. The project was orchestrated by **Dwight Yoakam** producer **Pete Anderson**.

The songs on the follow-up, *No Place That Far*, were written in consort with Music Row veterans **Tom Shapiro**, Tony Martin, **Billy Yates** and **Matraca Berg**. However, the album failed to produce sales figures to match the critical expectations of the artist. In an attempt to reverse this trend, Evans employed Paul Worley as co-producer on her third collection. Worley, the man who helped the **Dixie Chicks**' fashion their highly successful late 90s sound, attempted the same crossover magic on 2000's distinctly pop-orientated *Born To Fly*. Worley was back in the seat for the 2003 follow-up *Restless*, but this time around the formula was beginning to wear thin. 2005's *Real Fine Place* was a move back towards Evans' more familiar country style.

● ALBUMS: *Three Chords And The Truth* (RCA 1997) ★★★, *No Place That Far* (RCA 1998) ★★, with Martina McBride, Mindy McCready, Lorrie Morgan *Girls' Night Out* (BNA 1999) ★★★, *Born To Fly* (BNA 2000) ★★★★, *Restless* (RCA 2003) ★★★, *Real Fine Place* (RCA 2005) ★★★.

● COMPILATIONS: *Feels Like Home* (Cracker Barrel/Sony 2005) ★★★.

Evans, Stump

b. Paul A. Evans, 18 October 1904, Lawrence, Kansas, USA, d. 29 August 1928, Douglas, Kansas, USA. As a child Evans displayed proficiency on a variety of brass and reed instruments, finally choosing saxophones. In Chicago in the early 20s he played in bands led by **Erskine Tate**, **Earl Hines**, **King Oliver** and **Carroll Dickerson** and was thus regularly associated with **Louis Armstrong**. He recorded with several other important musicians, including **Jelly Roll Morton**. By the mid-20s Evans was often playing tenor saxophone, an instrument that was yet to achieve its dominant role in jazz, and was cited by **Coleman Hawkins** as an early influence. Evans developed tuberculosis and died in August 1928.

Evans, Sue

b. 7 July 1951, New York City, USA. Evans studied percussion with Warren Smith and Sonny Igoe before graduating from the High School of Music and Art in 1969. She worked with singer **Judy Collins**' backing group (1969–73) and then with **Steve Kuhn**; recorded with the **Jazz Composers Orchestra** (when it was directed by **Roswell Rudd**) and had a long association with **Gil Evans** (1969–82). She also recorded with singers **James Brown**, **Morgana King** and **Tony Bennett**, and with **Blood, Sweat And Tears**. She played with pop singer **Suzanne Vega** in the late 80s. Evans' skilful, responsive playing both as percussionist and drummer has been ideal accompanying vocalists and in satisfying the very particular requirements of music as diverse as that of the Jazz Composers Orchestra and Gil Evans. She has said she does not see herself as 'a timekeeper *per se* . . . I use percussion for melody and colours.'

Evans, Terry

b. Vicksburg, Mississippi, USA. Having spent more than a decade as one of Los Angeles' foremost session singers, in recent years Evans has taken firm steps towards a solo career. As a teenager, he sang with a high-school vocal group, the Knights, who from time to time sang with the Red Tops, a big band popular in Clarksdale and Jackson and around the Delta. Evans was 22 when he moved to Los Angeles. For several years, he held a day job and at weekends sang in small clubs around South Central LA, including the Cotton Club and the Road Runner. He met Bobby King through a mutual friend and the pair rehearsed together. In 1976, King secured a contract with **Warner Brothers Records** and called Evans when **Ry Cooder** asked for backing singers while recording *Chicken Skin Music*. Both men worked on further Cooder albums and toured with him. When not on tour, Evans gigged locally with his own five-piece group, which formed the basis of the studio band for their two albums. During that time, he also sang on albums by **Boz Scaggs**, **Maria Muldaur**, **John Fogerty** and **John Lee Hooker**. Evans' debut album came about through one of his songs being used on **Pops Staples**' debut solo album. Produced by Cooder, it drew on a studio band that included Frankie Ford, **Robert Ward**, Jim Keltner, the Paramount Singers and Cooder himself. Evans has subsequently built up an impressive catalogue with releases on AudioQuest and Telarc.

● ALBUMS: with Bobby King *Live And Let Live* (Rounder/ Special Delivery 1988) ★★★, with King *Rhythm, Blues, Soul & Grooves* (Rounder/Special Delivery 1990) ★★★, *Blues For Thought* (PointBlank 1993) ★★★, *Puttin' It Down* (AudioQuest 1995) ★★★, *Come To The River* (AudioQuest 1997) ★★★, *Walk That Walk* (Telarc 2000) ★★★, *Mississippi Magic* (AudioQuest 2001) ★★★★.

Evans, Tolchard

b. 1901, Harringay, London, England, d. 12 March 1978, London, England. Responsible for one of the biggest, international song hits of the 30s—'Lady Of Spain' (1931)— Evans also had considerable success with 'If' and 'My September Love'. Other notable works included 'Ballet Romantique', 'I'll Sing To You' and 'There's A Lovely Lake In London'.

Evans, Tyrone

b. Garth Evans, *c.*1944, Jamaica, West Indies, d. 19 October 2000, New York City, USA. While vocalist Evans was enjoying success with the **Paragons** he also recorded the little known solo side 'I Don't Care', at **Coxsone Dodd**'s Studio One alongside his early collaborator **Bob Andy**. In spite of their immense popularity the Paragons were unable to sustain a living from the Jamaican recording industry and disbanded in 1970. Evans then emigrated to the USA with his family. He embarked on a solo career recording sporadic hits, notably with **Lloyd Barnes**, although by the late 70s Evans was back at Studio One. Dodd released the sublime 'How Sweet It Is', which revitalized the singer's career. The song proved a false start following the success of **Blondie**'s cover version of the Paragons' 'The Tide Is High' that resulted in the re-formation of the group for the release of *Sly & Robbie Meet The Paragons* and *Now*. In spite of the distinctive style of the albums the group failed to achieve the success they deserved and Evans returned to New York. It was at this time that he released the classic *Sings Bullwackies Style*, which is regarded as his definitive album. In 1983, he returned to Jamaica where he formed an allegiance with **Winston Riley** who recorded and released *Don Evans* (that also became his stage name). A series of releases maintained Evans' profile, including *The Dynamic Duo* with **Audrey Hall** and *Satisfaction*, as well as the notable singles 'Lonesome Lad' and the **dancehall** hit alongside DJ John Wayne, 'War International'. Evans' untimely demise from cancer resulted in a revived interest in the Paragons and his classic Wackies release.

● ALBUMS: *Sings Bullwackies Style* (Wackies 1982) ★★★★, *Don Evans* (Techniques 1983) ★★★, with Audrey Hall *The Dynamic Duo* (Trojan 1984) ★★.

Eve

b. Eve Jihan Jeffers, 10 November 1978, Philadelphia, Pennsylvania, USA. The only female MC on the New York–based Ruff Ryders label, this bleach blonde self-styled 'pit bull in a skirt' emerged in the late 90s as a genuine rival to **Foxy Brown** and **Lil' Kim**. Jeffers first began rapping in a high school rap group under the name Gangsta. A spell as a go-go dancer followed before she changed her name to Eve Of Destruction and began creating a stir as a warm-up MC at local talent shows. Her first break came when **Dr. Dre** signed her to his Aftermath label, and helped produce her demo tape. One of the tracks on the demo, 'Eve Of Destruction', gained widespread exposure when it was featured on 1998's

Bulworth soundtrack. Unfortunately, Eve's contract with Aftermath lapsed and she was left without a label.

A chance meeting with the up-and-coming rapper **DMX** in Los Angeles resulted in her signing up with the fledgling Ruff Ryders label. 'What Ya Want', featured on the bestselling *Ryde Or Die Vol. 1* compilation, set out her stall, and guest appearances on the **Roots**' *Things Fall Apart* and **BLACKstreet**'s 'Girlfriend/Boyfriend' helped raise her profile. Her debut album, which debuted at US number 1 in September 1999, featured the in-house production work of **Swizz Beats** and guest appearances by label mates DMX and the **LOX**, as well as a cameo from **Missy 'Misdemeanor' Elliott**. The assertive declaration of independence 'Gotta Man' made it clear that the star of the show was undoubtedly Eve. Her follow-up, *Scorpion*, upped the ante even further with assertive declarations of independence on tracks such as 'Who's That Girl?' and 'You Had Me, You Lost Me', and included the hit collaboration with **No Doubt** singer Gwen Stefani, 'Let Me Blow Ya Mind'.

Eve's 2002 release *Eve-Olution* was premiered by the US Top 5 collaboration with **Alicia Keys**, 'Gangsta Lovin''. During the same year, she appeared in the high-grossing movies *Barbershop* and *XXX*.

● ALBUMS: *Ruff Ryders' First Lady* (Ruff Ryders/Interscope 1999) ★★★★, *Scorpion* (Ruff Ryders/Interscope 2001) ★★★★, *Eve-Olution* (Ruff Ryders/Interscope 2002) ★★★.

● FILMS: *Barbershop* (2002), *XXX* (2002), *The Woodsman* (2004), *Barbershop 2: Back In Business* (2004), *The Cookout* (2004).

Eve6

This US rock band was formed and subsequently signed by **RCA Records** while guitarist Jon Siebels (b. 27 August 1979, La Crescenta, California, USA) and bass player Max Collins (b. 28 August 1978, La Crescenta, California, USA) were still at high school. Originally known as Eleventeen, the line-up was completed by drummer Tony Fagenson (b. 18 July 1978, Detroit, Michigan, USA), son of producer **Don Was**. They took their unusual new name from an episode of the popular US sci-fi thriller series *The X Files*. The single 'Inside Out' announced their pop punk style, compared by some critics to **Green Day**. Their 1998 self-titled debut album was promoted by extensive touring with **Third Eye Blind**, and within a few months of release had risen to number 33 on the *Billboard* Top 200. Their second single, 'Leech', was written by Siebels and Collins about a problematic work relationship. It was typical of material dubbed by critics as 'superior brat rock'. The trio played the same card again with 2000's *Horroscope*, which peaked at one position lower in the US chart. The mellow single 'Here's To The Night' was a major pop hit, reaching the US Top 20 the following year.

The trio's experimental third album *It's All In Your Head*, released in 2003, was a notable critical and commercial failure. RCA lost faith in the band and released them from their recording contract, a decision that prompted Siebels, Collins and Fagenson to call it a day. They played their last show together on 15 July 2004 in St. Louis. Collins later worked with Brotherhood Of Lost Dogs before reuniting with Fagenson to work on a new project.

● ALBUMS: *Eve6* (RCA 1998) ★★★, *Horrorscope* (RCA 2000) ★★★, *It's All In Your Head* (RCA 2003) ★★.

Even Dozen Jug Band

Formed in 1963 by guitarists Peter Siegel and **Stefan Grossman**. Renowned in their respective fields, namely bluegrass and blues, the two musicians brought several colleagues into the line-up to create a mutually satisfying style once punningly referred to as 'jug-grass'. *The Even Dozen Jug Band*, released in January 1964, was their sole recorded legacy, but the ensemble is better recalled as an important meeting point for several influential figures. Grossman and Siegel aside, the line-up also included harmonica player John Benson, better known as **John Sebastian**, singer Maria D'Amato, later **Maria Muldaur**, mandolin player **David Grisman**, washboard player Steve Katz, a future member of the **Blues Project** and **Blood, Sweat And Tears**, and **Joshua Rifkin**, who subsequently acquired fame for his interpretations of **Scott Joplin**'s piano rags. It should be noted, however, that not all of these artists appear on all of the songs. The Even Dozen Jug Band's brief tenure ended in disagreement between those who wished to maintain the band's 'fun' status and those who wished to assume a more professional approach. The split allowed the above individuals to pursue a more independent path.

● ALBUMS: *The Even Dozen Jug Band* (Elektra 1964) ★★★.

Evensong

Evelyn Laye, who was one of the most enchanting leading ladies of the London musical theatre, especially during the 20s, only made a few films, and this was probably the best of them. In the poignant and tragic story she plays the young and lovely Maggie O'Neil who leaves her home in England, against her parents' wishes, and runs away to Paris in the hope of becoming a famous opera star. Changing her name to Mm. Irela, she is warned by her manager, Kober (Fritz Kortner), that she cannot have both romance and career. She chooses the latter course, and so loses her first love, George Murray (Emlyn Williams), who is killed in World War I. Many years later she realizes that it was the wrong decision, but by then her constant admirer, Archduke Theodore (Carl Esmond), is an old man, and she herself is embittered. After being upstaged by the young pretender Baba (Conchita Supervia), she dies in her dressing room while listening to an early recording of her voice on a gramophone record. A particularly fine supporting cast included Muriel Aked, Patrick O'Moore, Dennis Van Norton, Arthur Sinclair and Browning Mummary. The film was full of music, with both Evelyn Laye and Supervia in superb voice with operatic excerpts such as 'Mimi's Song' and 'Musetta's Song' (from *La Boheme*), the 'Drinking Song' (from *La Traviata*) and 'Carceleras' (from *Las Hijas Del Zebado*). Laye also sings a medley of old favourites that were popular during the 1914–18 war years, such as 'A Perfect Day' (Carrie Jacobs-Bond), 'There's A Long, Long Trail' (Stoddard King-Joe Elliot), 'Keep The Home Fires Burning' (**Ivor Novello**-Lena Guilbert-Ford), 'I Love The Moon' (**Paul Rubens**) and 'Love's Old Sweet Song' (G. Clifton Bingham-James L. Molloy). In addition there were two new numbers by Mischa Spoliansky and Edward Knoblock, 'Irela Valse' and 'I'll Wait For You'. In the final analysis, however, as one critic pointed out at the time, this is a tensely dramatic picture that has drama, romance, opera, comedy, tears and all the other sure-fire ingredients that make a success in showbusiness. It also had a magnificent central performance from Evelyn Laye, whose portrayal of the prima donna from girlhood to her eventual eclipse, in dramatic terms, surpassed anything she had done previously. The screenplay, by Edward Knoblock and Dorothy Farnum, was adapted from Beverley Nichols' novel, which he and Knoblock turned into a successful West End play. This memorable film was photographed by Mutz Greenbaum and impressively directed by Victor Saville.

Ever Green

The renowned English impresario **C.B. Cochran** was taking a big risk in 1930 when he cast **Jessie Matthews**, one of the most popular stars of the London stage, in *Ever Green*. A year earlier, another of the West End's favourite leading ladies, **Evelyn Laye**, had cited Matthews as co-respondent in her petition for divorce from **Sonnie Hale**, and Jessie Matthews' co-star in *Ever Green* was to be that same Sonny Hale. Would the prim and proper English theatre-going public accept the situation? Well, they did, and the show proved to be the most successful of Matthews' career. **Richard Rodgers** and **Lorenz Hart** came up with a fine score, and it was their original idea that librettist Ben W. Levy used for his story of Harriet Green (Jessie Matthews), a young, somewhat pushy actress, who, to gain publicity for herself, purports to be a woman in her sixties whose looks have been preserved by the miracle of modern cosmetics. The problem is that the man she loves, Tommy Thompson (Sonnie Hale), does not want to marry someone more than twice his age. As usual with a Cochran show there were some spectacular effects. One of the most delightful of these was the setting for the two stars' big number, 'Dancing On The Ceiling', when an enormous inverted chandelier was mounted on the revolving stage. The song had been cut from a previous Rodgers and Hart show, *Simple Simon*, and went on to become a much-admired standard, particularly in the version by **Frank Sinatra** on his *In The Wee Small Hours*. *Ever Green*'s pleasing score also contained 'If I Give In To You', 'In The Cool Of The Evening', 'Dear, Dear' and 'No Place Like Home', and the show ran for 254 performances. Jessie Matthews and Sonnie Hale married in 1931, and starred in the 1934 film version of *Evergreen* (one word), which had some different songs and a modified storyline.

Everclear

Formed in Portland, Oregon, USA, in 1991, by Art Alexakis (b. 12 April 1962, Los Angeles, California, USA; vocals/guitar), Craig Montoya (b. 14 September 1970; bass/vocals) and Scott Cuthbert (drums), although the latter was replaced by Greg Eklund (b. 18 April 1970) in 1994. Alexakis had previously worked as a roadie for a succession of north west punk bands. Indulging himself in copious quantities of drugs, he only decided to start his own band when a cocaine overdose temporarily stopped his heart. Early comparisons to **Nirvana** (exacerbated by the singer's blonde hair) went into overdrive when Kurt Cobain publicly stated his approval. Everclear made their debut in 1994 with *World Of Noise*, which included the intriguing 'Sparkle' ('Fire pulls the spirit from the corporate whore/I'm embarrassed by the plaid you wear/If I were you I'd hide behind that stupid bleached blond hair'). Critics were left unsure as to whom the reference concerned, Alexakis or Cobain.

The mini-album *White Trash Hell*, again on Fire Records, was released in 1995. The band was subsequently offered a major label recording contract with **Capitol Records**. They were signed by Gary Gersh, who had previously taken both Nirvana and **Sonic Youth** to **Geffen Records**. During the same year the band released their first album for the new label, the critically lauded and commercially successful *Sparkle And Fade*. They repeated this success two years later with the release of the infectious and highly melodic *So Much For The Afterglow*. The clumsily titled *Songs From An American Movie Vol. One: Learning How To Smile* (2000) toned down the neo-grunge guitar rock in favour of a more eclectic approach, embracing tight harmonies, strings, and a cover version of **Van Morrison**'s 'Brown Eyed Girl'. The vitriolic pop punk collection *Songs From An American Movie Vol. Two: Good Time For A Bad Attitude*, released only four months later, helped restore the band's alternative rock credibility. The band's commercial peak had long since passed by the time of 2003's *Slow Motion Daydream*, and following the album's release Montoya and Eklund both announced they were leaving. Alexakis announced he would continue recording under the Everclear name, combining music with a burgeoning political career.

● ALBUMS: *World Of Noise* (Fire 1994) ★★★, *White Trash Hell* mini-album (Fire 1995) ★★★★, *Sparkle And Fade* (Capitol 1995) ★★★★, *So Much For The Afterglow* (Capitol 1997) ★★★★, *Songs From An American Movie Vol. One: Learning How To Smile* (Capitol 2000) ★★★, *Songs From An American Movie Vol. Two: Good Time For A Bad Attitude* (Capitol 2000) ★★★★, *Slow Motion Daydream* (Capitol 2003) ★★★.
● COMPILATIONS: *Ten Years Gone: The Best Of Everclear 1994–2004* (Capitol 2004) ★★★★.

Everett, Betty

b. 23 November 1939, Greenwood, Mississippi, USA, d. 19 August 2001, Beloit, Wisconsin, USA. Having moved to Chicago in the late 50s, R&B/soul singer Everett recorded unsuccessfully for several local labels, including Cobra, C.J. and One-derful, and briefly sang lead with the all-male group the **Daylighters**. Her hits came on signing to **Vee Jay Records** where 'You're No Good' (1963) and 'The Shoop Shoop Song (It's In His Kiss)' (1964) established her pop/soul style. A duet with **Jerry Butler**, 'Let It Be Me' (1964), consolidated this position, but her finest moment came with 'Getting Mighty Crowded', a punchy **Van McCoy** song. Her career faltered on Vee Jay's collapse in 1966, and an ensuing interlude at **ABC Records** was unproductive, despite producing classic tracks such as 'Love Comes Tumbling Down'. However, in 1969, 'There'll Come A Time' reached number 2 in the R&B charts, a momentum that continued into the early 70s with further releases on Uni and **Fantasy Records**. Everett's last chart entry was in 1978 with 'True Love (You Took My Heart)', on the **United Artists Records** label. **Cher** took her version of 'The Shoop Shoop Song (It's In His Kiss)' to the top of the UK chart in 1991.

● ALBUMS: *You're No Good* (Vee Jay 1964) ★★★, *It's In His Kiss* (Vee Jay/Fontana 1964) ★★★, with Jerry Butler *Delicious Together* (Vee Jay 1964) ★★★★, *There'll Come A Time* (Uni 1969) ★★, *Love Rhymes* (Fantasy 1974) ★★, *Black Girl* (Fantasy 1974) ★★, *Happy Endings* (Fantasy 1975) ★★.
● COMPILATIONS: *The Very Best Of Betty Everett* (Vee Jay 1965) ★★★, *Getting Mighty Crowded* (Charly 1980) ★★★★, *Hot To Hold* (Charly 1982) ★★★, *The Real Thing* (Charly 1987) ★★★★, *The Fantasy Years* (Fantasy

1995) ★★★, *The Best Of Betty Everett: Let It Be Me* (Aim 1998) ★★★★, *The Shoop Shoop Song: 20 Greatest Hits* (Collectables 2000) ★★★.

Everett, Kenny

b. Maurice James Christopher Cole, 25 December 1944, Liverpool, England, d. 4 April 1995, London, England. Everett was a maverick disc jockey and comedian whose headlong broadcasting style broke established rules and outraged establishment figures. His sense of humour was a reaction to the stress of being an introverted and delicate child in Liverpool's dockside area. His first tapes earned him brief exposure on BBC Radio's Home Service, but his personal audition with Derek Chinnery (later controller of Radio 1) was a disaster. He sent the tapes to pirate station Radio London, and was immediately taken on as a disc jockey. Since pirate radio was 'of unproven legality' in the UK, all the disc jockeys adopted pseudonyms, thus did Maurice Cole become Kenny Everett. It was at Radio London that the Kenny And Cash broadcasting partnership with Dave Cash was born, later reprised on London's Capital Radio. He was sacked from Radio London for insulting behaviour on air. He then worked for a short time on BBC Light Programme's *Where It's At*. When the Marine Offences Act finished off the pirates, the BBC filled the void with the creation of Radio 1 in September 1967. A number of ex-pirate disc jockeys were taken on, including Everett. He hosted various shows and gained a loyal following for his anarchic style before being dismissed in 1970 for a remark about the wife of the Minister of Transport. Two years later he was taken back into the BBC fold, with the proviso that the show be pre-recorded (at his home studio in Wales) so that it could be vetted before broadcast.

He found a new outlet in 1973 at London's Capital Radio, the first independent commercial music station. Initially pre-recording his shows in Wales, he moved to London to revive 'Kenny And Cash' on Capital's breakfast show. His progress faltered when, 18 months after joining Capital, he took an overdose of sleeping pills. Although it was probably an accident, Everett had a history of fast living in the music business, and was under severe psychological pressure. Mixing the high life with daily breakfast broadcasting took its toll, and his marriage (at the age of 21) to Lee Middleton was under severe strain as Everett faced up to and made public his homosexuality. He switched to weekend shows, and started developing some of the characters later made famous by television. His shows were a breathless whirlwind of music, gags, jingles and vignettes, and they earned him a break on television in 1978 with Thames Television's *The Kenny Everett Video Show*. Everett's imagination and character expanded to fill every inch of the medium, frequently working on adrenalin rather than using a script. Surprisingly, the show transferred to the BBC in 1982 as *The Kenny Everett Television Show*, and also earned him a following in the USA and Australia. The show lasted until 1988. Meanwhile, he had also been sacked again from BBC Radio (Radio 2 this time) for telling a rude joke about Margaret Thatcher. He went back to Capital as part of their new Capital Gold oldies station, which became his broadcasting home for the rest of his life. He died from an AIDS-related illness in April 1995. His work inspired many of today's disc jockeys and broadcasters.

● ALBUMS: *Captain Kremmen (Greatest Adventure Yet)* (Columbia 1980) ★★, *Kenny Everett Naughty Joke Box* (Relax 1984) ★★.
● FILMS: *Dateline Diamonds* (1965).

Everette, Jack

b. Jack Everette Jackson, Cedar Rapids, Iowa, USA, d. 19 June 1972. Everette was a band leader whose career started in Cedar Rapids in the mid-20s. He was forced to adopt his middle name professionally owing to the presence of another troupe billed as Jack Jackson And His Orchestra who were then active in the Midwest region. With weekly airplay on the KWCR radio station, Jack Everette And His Orchestra soon found themselves the most popular touring dance band in Iowa. By the mid-30s the group, which included Eddie Rommers, Bill Williams, Vern Scollon, Early Hulen, Lock Lohman, Kelly Christensen, Skeets Evans, George Mull and Al Knorr, had secured engagements at the Mayfair Club (Des Moines) and the Kansas City Pla-Mor Ballroom. However, as with so many other big bands of the period, their momentum was fatally interrupted by the advent of World War II. With his ranks depleted, Everette chose to open a restaurant in Springfield, Missouri, also operating a dance hall. With the war over he reconvened the band, with essentially the same line-up. The group remained active, again principally in the Midwest, until 1956, at which time their leader founded a booking agency, Jackson Artist Corporation, with his son David.

Everette, Leon

b. Leon Everette Baughman, 21 June 1948, Aiken, South Carolina, USA. Everette was raised in New York and had no particular interest in country music as a child. In the US Navy, he worked on an aircraft carrier in the Philippines. The servicemen passed the time by singing so he bought a guitar, learned by watching others and won a talent contest. Returning to South Carolina, he married, started a family and worked at the South Carolina Power and Gas Company. After an argument at work, Everette became a professional musician, working clubs in South Carolina and Georgia. He wanted success in Nashville and, in an extraordinary act of dedication, worked in the postal rooms of record companies while still playing in his home clubs. This involved commuting 500 miles a day! On top of this, he had to sleep and maintain a family life with his wife and three children. In 1977 the small True label gave Everette a chance—though not in the way he wanted. Within hours of **Elvis Presley**'s death, Everette had recorded 'Goodbye King Of Rock And Roll'. Although True then wanted him to record some Elvis soundalikes, he was determined that he wanted to sing country and to be himself. After a small US country hit with 'I Love That Woman (Like The Devil Loves Sin)', a Florida businessman, Carroll Fulmer, formed a record label, Orlando, around him. He made the country charts with 'Giving Up Easy', 'Don't Feel like The Lone Ranger' and 'I Don't Want To Lose'. When Everette moved to **RCA Records** in 1980, he became more involved in the production of his own records. 'If I Keep On Going Crazy', with its distinctive harmonica, made the US country Top 20 and it was followed by the pile-driving 'Hurricane', which prompted him to change his band's name from Tender Loving Care to Hurricane. Everette himself is a hurricane on stage and is prone to leaping into the audience, occasionally injuring himself; at one memorable concert, he put his arm through a glass panel. **Hank Williams Jnr.** remarked, 'No doubt about it. Leon Everette is a hard act to follow'. Among other successful singles were 'I Could'a Had You', 'Midnight Rodeo' and 'Soul Searchin'. His affection for old-time country music was evident in 'Shadows Of My Mind' and he revived **Stonewall Jackson**'s 'Don't Be Angry'. In a peculiar marketing exercise, RCA issued a six-track mini-album called *Doin' What I Feel* in 1983 and reissued it in 1984 with the same packaging but three different titles. He then moved to **Mercury** and recorded *Where's The Fire?*, but rejoined Orlando soon afterwards. He retired from country music in 1988.

● ALBUMS: *Goodbye King Of Rock & Roll* (True 1977) ★★★, *I Don't Want To Lose* (Orlando 1980) ★★★, *If I Keep On Going Crazy* (RCA 1981) ★★★, *Hurricane* (RCA 1981) ★★★, *Maverick* (RCA 1982) ★★★★, *Doin' What I Feel* (RCA 1983) ★★★, *Where's The Fire?* (Mercury 1985) ★★★.

● COMPILATIONS: *Leon Everette's Greatest Hits* (RCA 1987) ★★★.

Evergreen

After delighting West End audiences with her scintillating singing and dancing in the stage musical *Ever Green* (1930), **Jessie Matthews** re-created her role for this film version (with its slightly different title) in 1934. In the screenplay, which was written by the celebrated actor and playwright Emlyn Williams and Marjorie Gaffney, Miss Matthews plays Harriet Green, the daughter of an Edwardian music-hall singing star, who secretly takes her mother's place after she has gone missing, and triumphs in her own right. Most of the songs from the stage show were dispensed with, but three survived the trip to the Gaumont British Studios at Shepherd's Bush: 'Dear, Dear', 'If I Give In To You' and the big hit 'Dancing On The Ceiling', which gave Jessie Matthews a wonderful opportunity for a fine solo dance that she is reputed to have choreographed herself. **Harry Woods** contributed two songs that the leading lady immediately made her own: 'When You've Got A Little Springtime In Your Heart' and the lively 'Over My Shoulder', which accompanied a spectacular production number atop a 'wedding cake'. Jessie's husband, **Sonnie Hale**, played stage director Leslie Benn, and also in the cast were Betty Balfour, Barry Mackay, Ivor McLaren, Hartley Power, Patrick Ludlow, Betty Shale and Marjorie Brooks. Buddy Bradley staged the imaginative dance sequences, and *Evergreen*, which was its leading lady's most successful film, was produced by Michael Balcon and directed by Victor Saville.

Evergreen Blueshoes

This quintet was formed in Los Angeles, California, USA, in 1969, by **Skip Battin** (b. Clyde Battin, 2 February 1934, Galipolis, Ohio, USA, d. 6 July 2003, Palm Springs, California, USA; bass/vocals, ex-**Skip And Flip**), Jimmy Ibbotson (drums, ex-Stone Country), Lanny Mathijson (lead guitar), Alan Rosenberg (guitar) and Ken Kleist (organ). They recorded a single, 'Maybe Someday'/'Silver Shadow' on **Kim Fowley**'s Living Legend label prior to the departure of Ibbotson for the **Nitty Gritty Dirt Band**. Chester McKracken took his place for the band's remaining recordings which were not released until after their demise. *The Ballad Of The Evergreen Blueshoes* appeared to cash in on Battin's new-

found profile as a member of the **Byrds**. Despite moments of interest, the greater part of the material on offer showed a band struggling to find its musical identity.

● ALBUMS: *The Ballad Of The Evergreen Blueshoes* (Amos 1971) ★★.

Everlast

b. Erik Schrody, 18 August 1969, USA. A former graffiti artist and protégé of **Ice-T**, US rapper Everlast was one of the few white members in the Rhyme Syndicate posse. Everything on his debut album was as might have been expected: hardcore visions of violence, extensive use of expletives, and puerile, anatomical descriptions of women. There was, at least, room for an anti-PMRC rap, and samples drawn from the diverse tangents of **Sly And Robbie**, **Sly Stone** and even **Bananarama** and the **Knack**. Everlast was introduced to hip-hop while at summer camp, a friend there teaching him both graffiti and elementary street rap. Everlast laid down a couple of tracks with the help of his friend's DJ partner, Bahal, and Ice-T liked what he heard. He released his first single as far back as 1988. Everlast toured the UK supporting Ice-T, but abandoned his solo career when he joined Irish American hip-hoppers **House Of Pain**, who enjoyed a US Top 10 smash in June 1992 with the addictive 'Jump Around'. He quit the music business in 1996, but returned to recording two years later with *Whitey Ford Sings The Blues*, an impressive slow-mo fusion of hip-hop beats and folk stylings that climbed into the US Top 10. In an eventful year, Everlast had already suffered a near fatal cardiac arrest and converted to Islam. The following year he contributed one of the stand-out tracks ('Put Your Lights On') to **Santana**'s phenomenally successful *Supernatural*. His own *Eat At Whitey's* built on the successful acoustic blues/hip-hop template of its predecessor, achieving real beauty on tracks such as 'Black Coffee' and 'Black Jesus'.

● ALBUMS: *Forever Everlasting* (Warners 1990) ★★, *Whitey Ford Sings The Blues* (Tommy Boy 1998) ★★★★, *Eat At Whitey's* (Tommy Boy 2000) ★★★★, *White Trash Beautiful* (Mercury 2004) ★★★.

● COMPILATIONS: *Shamrocks & Shenanigans: The Best Of House Of Pain And Everlast* (Rhino 2004) ★★★★.

Everly Brothers (country)

Don (b. Isaac Donald Everly, 1 February 1937, Brownie, Kentucky, USA, and Phil (b. Phillip Everly, 19 January 1939, Chicago, Illinois, USA) Everly's father, Ike Everly, was an accomplished guitarist, working with country music celebrities and developing his style with his neighbour **Merle Travis**. Ike and his wife Margaret hosted long-running family radio shows and the Everly Brothers' 1968 album, *Roots*, includes some early work. When they became a duo, Ike approached his friend **Chet Atkins** in Nashville for contacts. Don sold some songs, one of them, 'Thou Shalt Not Steal', making the charts for **Kitty Wells**. Although the Everly Brothers became the leading rock 'n' roll vocal group, their records were close to country and their harmonies are derived from the **Blue Sky Boys**, **Delmore Brothers** and **Louvin Brothers**. They used country musicians and songwriters, notably **Boudleaux and Felice Bryant** and **John D. Loudermilk**. Their own compositions, including 'Cathy's Clown', 'So Sad' and 'When Will I Be Loved?', have been recorded by country artists. In 1958, they surprised their fans with what can be seen as the first 'unplugged' album, ***Songs Our Daddy***

Taught Us, but in retrospect it is more easy to see how old-time country music fitted into their thinking. With top-flight Nashville sessionmen, they recorded the more contemporary *The Everly Brothers Sing Great Country Hits* in 1963. Ten years later, they returned to Nashville for *Pass The Chicken And Listen*, an out-and-out country record produced by Chet Atkins. It included **John Prine**'s 'Paradise', which is a town close to where they were raised in Kentucky. Splitting up after the album, Don Everly became a country performer, working at festivals with the Dead Cowboy Band and recording a highly rated album, *Brother Jukebox*. He also sang the Louvin Brothers' 'Everytime You Leave', with **Emmylou Harris**. They settled their differences in 1983 with some much publicized reunion concerts and they have been on the road ever since. Their guest appearances include joining **Johnny Cash** on a remake of 'Ballad Of A Teenage Queen'. The duo was inducted into the **Country Music Hall Of Fame** in 2001.

Everly Brothers

Don (b. Isaac Donald Everly, 1 February 1937, Brownie, Kentucky, USA) and Phil (b. Phillip Everly, 19 January 1939, Chicago, Illinois, USA), the world's most famous rock 'n' roll duo, had already experienced a full career before their first record, 'Bye Bye Love', was released. As sons of popular country artists Ike and Margaret, they were pushed into the limelight from an early age. They regularly appeared on their parents' radio shows throughout the 40s and accompanied them on many tours. In the mid-50s, as rockabilly was evolving into rock 'n' roll, the boys moved to Nashville, the mecca for such music. Don had a minor hit when **Kitty Wells** recorded his composition 'Thou Shalt Not Steal' in 1954. In 1957 they were given a **Felice** and **Boudleaux Bryant** song that was finding difficulty being placed. They took 'Bye Bye Love' and made it their own; it narrowly missed the US number 1 position and reached number 6 in the UK. The brothers then embarked on a career that made them second only to **Elvis Presley** in the rock 'n' roll popularity stakes. Their blend of country and folk did much to sanitize and make respectable a phenomenon towards which many parents still showed hostility. America, then a racially segregated country, was not ready for its white teenagers to listen to black-based rock music. The brothers' clean looks and even cleaner harmonies did much to change people's attitudes.

They quickly followed this initial success with more irresistible Bryant songs, 'Wake Up Little Susie', 'All I Have To Do Is Dream', 'Bird Dog', 'Problems', 'So Sad' and the beautiful 'Devoted To You'. The brothers were supremely confident live performers, both with their trademark Gibson Dove and later, black J50 guitars. By the end of the 50s they were the world's number 1 vocal group. Amazingly, their career gained further momentum when, after signing with the newly formed **Warner Brothers Records** for $1 million, they delivered a song that was catalogued WB1. This historical debut was the superlative 'Cathy's Clown', written by Don. No Everly record had sounded like this before; the echo-laden production and the treble-loaded harmonies ensured that it stayed at number 1 in the USA for five weeks. In the UK it stayed on top for over two months, selling several million and making it one of the most successful records of all time. The brothers continued to release immaculate records; many of them reached the US Top 10, although in England their success was even greater,

with two further number 1 hits during 1961. Again the echo and treble dominated in two more classics, 'Walk Right Back' and a fast-paced reworking of the former **Bing Crosby** hit 'Temptation'. At the end of 1961 they were drafted into the US Marines, albeit for only six months, and resumed by embarking on a European tour. Don became dependent on drugs, and the pressures from constant touring and recording began to show; during one historic night at London's East Ham Granada, England, a nervous Phil performed solo. The standard 'food poisoning/exhaustion' excuse was used. What was not known by the doting fans was that Don had attempted a suicidal drug overdose twice in 48 hours. Phil completed the tour solo. Don's addiction continued for another three years, although they were able to work during part of this time.

The advent of the beat boom pushed the brothers out of the spotlight and while they continued to make hit records, none approached their previous achievements. The decline was briefly halted in 1965 with two excellent major UK hits, 'The Price Of Love' and 'Love Is Strange'. The former, a striking chart-topper, recalled their early Warner sound, while the latter harked back even earlier, with a naïve but infectious call-and-answer spoken segment. In 1966 they released *Two Yanks In England*, a strong album that contained eight songs by Nash/Clarke/Hicks of the **Hollies**; surprisingly, the album failed to chart. The duo were recognized only for their superb singles, and many of their albums were less well-received. *Stories We Could Tell*, recorded with an array of guest players, threatened to extend their market into the rock mainstream, but it was not to be.

After a few years of declining fortunes and arrival at the supper-club circuit, the brothers parted acrimoniously. Following a show at Knotts Berry Farm, California, in 1973, during which a drunken Don had insulted Phil, the latter walked off, smashed one of his beloved Gibsons and vowed, 'I will never get on a stage with that man again'. The only time they met over the next 10 years was at their father's funeral. Both embarked on solo careers with varying degrees of accomplishment. Their country-flavoured albums found more favour with the Nashville audience of their roots. Don and his band, the Dead Cowboys, regularly played in Nashville, while Phil released the critically acclaimed *Star Spangled Springer*. Inexplicably, the album was a relatively poor seller, as were several follow-ups. Phil made a cameo appearance in the movie *Every Which Way But Lose*, performing with actress Sondra Locke. While Don maintained a steady career, playing with ex-**Heads, Hands And Feet** maestro **Albert Lee**, Phil concentrated on writing songs. 'She Means Nothing To Me' was a striking duet with **Cliff Richard** that put the Everly name back in the UK Top 10.

Rumours began to circulate of a reunion, which was further fuelled by an UK television advertisement for an Everly Brothers compilation. In June 1983 they hugged and made up and their emotional reconciliation was made before an ecstatic, wet-eyed audience at London's Royal Albert Hall. The following year *EB84* was released and gave them another major hit with **Paul McCartney**'s 'Wings Of A Nightingale'. In 1986 they were inducted into the **Rock And Roll Hall Of Fame**, and the following year Phil gave Don a pound of gold and a handmade guitar for his 50th birthday. They now perform regularly together, with no pressure from record companies. Don lives quietly in Nashville and tours with his brother for a few months every year. They still have a loyal following in

Europe. A major reissue programme, with alternative takes, was undertaken by Warners in 2001, the same year the duo was inducted into the **Country Music Hall Of Fame**.

The Everly Brothers' influence on a generation of pop and rock artists is inestimable; they set a standard for close harmony singing that has rarely been bettered, and, consciously or unconsciously, it is still used as a blueprint for many of today's harmony vocalists and groups. Their catalogue of hit singles remains one of the most emotional and uplifting in the entire history of popular music. No decent record collection should be without it.

● ALBUMS: *The Everly Brothers* (Cadence 1958) ★★★★, *Songs Our Daddy Taught Us* (Cadence 1959) ★★★★, *The Everly Brothers' Best* (Cadence 1959) ★★★, *It's Everly Time* (Warners 1960) ★★★, *The Fabulous Style Of The Everly Brothers* (Cadence 1960) ★★★★, *A Date With The Everly Brothers* (Warners 1960) ★★★★, *Both Sides Of An Evening* (Warners 1961) ★★★, *Folk Songs Of the Everly Brothers* (Cadence 1962) ★★★, *Instant Party* (Warners 1962) ★★★, *Christmas With The Everly Brothers And The Boys Town Choir* (Warners 1962) ★★, *Sing Great Country Hits* (Warners 1963) ★★★, *Gone Gone Gone* (Warners 1965) ★★★★, *Rock 'N' Soul* (Warners 1965) ★★★, *Beat 'N' Soul* (Warners 1965) ★★★, *In Our Image* (Warners 1966) ★★★, *Two Yanks In England* (Warners 1966) ★★★, *The Hit Sound Of The Everly Brothers* (Warners 1967) ★★★, *Sing* (Warners 1967) ★★★, *Roots* (Warners 1968) ★★★★, *Show* (Warners 1970) ★★★, *End Of An Era* (Barnaby/Columbia 1971) ★★★, *Stories We Could Tell* (RCA-Victor 1972) ★★★, *Pass The Chicken And Listen* (RCA-Victor 1973) ★★, *The Exciting Everly Brothers* (RCA 1975) ★★★, *Living Legends* (Warwick 1977) ★★★, *The New Album* previously unissued Warners material (Warners 1977) ★★★, *The Reunion Concert* (Impression 1983) ★★★★, *Nice Guys* previously unissued Warners material (Magnum Force 1984) ★★, *EB84* (Mercury 1984) ★★★, *In The Studio* previously unissued Cadence material (Ace 1985) ★★★, *Born Yesterday* (Mercury 1985) ★★★, *Some Hearts* (Mercury 1988) ★★★, *Live In Paris* 1963 recording (Big Beat 1997) ★★★, *Live At The Olympia* 10-inch album (Big Beat 1997) ★★★.

Solo: Don Everly *Don Everly* (A&M 1971) ★★, *Sunset Towers* (Ode 1974) ★★, *Brother Juke Box* (Hickory 1976) ★★★. Phil Everly *Star Spangled Springer* (RCA 1973) ★★★, *Phil's Diner (There's Nothing Too Good For My Baby)* (Pye 1974) ★★, *Mystic Line* (Pye 1975) ★★, *Living Alone* (Elektra 1979) ★★, *Phil Everly* (Capitol 1983) ★★.

● COMPILATIONS: *The Golden Hits Of The Everly Brothers* (Warners 1962) ★★★★, *15 Everly Hits* (Cadence 1963) ★★★, *The Very Best Of The Everly Brothers* (Warners 1964) ★★★★, *The Everly Brothers' Original Greatest Hits* (Columbia 1970) ★★★★★, *The Most Beautiful Songs Of The Everly Brothers* (Warners 1973) ★★★, *Don's And Phil's Fabulous Fifties Treasury* (Janus 1974) ★★★, *Walk Right Back With The Everlys* (Warners 1975) ★★★★, *Greatest Hits Collection* (Pickwick 1979) ★★★, *The Sensational Everly Brothers* (Reader Digest 1979) ★★, *Cathy's Clown* (Pickwick 1980) ★★★, *The Very Best Of The Everly Brothers* (Marks & Spencer 1980) ★★, *The Everly Brothers* (Warners 1981) ★★★, *Rock 'N' Roll Forever* (Warners 1981) ★★★, *Love Hurts* (K-Tel 1982) ★★, *Rip It Up* (Ace 1983) ★★★, *Cadence Classics (Their 20 Greatest Hits)* (Rhino 1985) ★★★★, *The Best Of The Everly Brothers* (Rhino 1985) ★★★, *All They Had To Do Is Dream* US only (Rhino 1985) ★★★, *Great Recordings* (Ace 1986) ★★★, *The Everly Brothers Collection* (Castle 1988) ★★★, *The Very Best Of The Everly Brothers* (Pickwick 1988) ★★★, *Hidden Gems* Warners material (Ace 1989) ★★★, *The Very Best Of The Everly Brothers Volume 2* (Pickwick 1990) ★★, *Perfect Harmony* box set (Knight 1990) ★★★, *Classic Everly Brothers* 3-CD box set (Bear Family 1992) ★★★★, *The Golden Years Of The Everly Brothers* (Warners 1993) ★★★★, *Heartaches And Harmonies* 4-CD box set (Rhino 1995) ★★★★★, *Walk Right Back: On Warner Bros. 1960 To 1969* 2-CD set (Warners 1996) ★★★★, *All I Have To Do Is Dream* (Carlton 1997) ★★★, *The EP Collection* (See For Miles 1998) ★★★, *The Masters* (Eagle 1998) ★★★, *The Very Best Of The Cadence Era* (Repertoire 1999) ★★★, *Devoted To You: Love Songs* (Varèse Sarabande 2000) ★★★★, *The Complete Cadence Recordings: 1957–1960* (Varèse Sarabande 2001) ★★★★, *The Definitive Everly Brothers* (WEA 2002) ★★★★★, *Stories We Could Tell: The RCA Recordings* (BMG 2003) ★★★, *The Best Of The Everly Brothers: The Millennium Collection* (Hip-O 2003) ★★★★, *Too Good To Be True* (Varèse Sarabande 2005) ★★★, *Give Me A Future* (Varèse Sarabande 2005) ★★★.

● DVD/VIDEOS: *Rock 'N' Roll Odyssey* (MGM 1984).

● FURTHER READING: *Everly Brothers: An Illustrated Discography*, John Hosum. *The Everly Brothers: Walk Right Back*, Roger White. *Ike's Boys*, Phyllis Karpp. *The Everly Brothers: Ladies Love Outlaws*, Consuelo Dodge. *For-Everly Yours*, Peter Aarts and Martin Alberts.

Everpresent Fullness

Formed in 1965 in Redondo Beach, California, USA, the folk rock band the Everpresent Fullness line-up included Jack Ryan (vocals), Paul Johnson (guitar), Tom Carvey (guitar) and Steve Pugh (bass). They began performing in a local coffee-house prior to signing with White Whale Records, home of the **Turtles**. Everpresent Fullness made their recording debut in 1966 with a version of 'Wild About My Lovin', a traditional song popularized by the **Lovin' Spoonful**. It offered an engaging blend of jug band music and pop. 'Darlin' You Can Count On Me' revealed a greater emphasis on rock, an element apparent on the group's only album. It was not a commercial success, and they split up soon after its release.

● ALBUMS: *Everpresent Fullness* (White Whale 1967) ★★★.

Every Mother's Nightmare

This US 'sleaze-rock' heavy metal band, originating (surprisingly) from the home of country music, Nashville, was formed in 1989 by vocalist Rick Ruhl and guitarist Steve Malone. With the addition of bass player Mark McMurty and drummer Jim Phipps, they signed a contract with **Arista Records** in 1990. Their self-titled debut, released the same year, combined **Kiss**, **Aerosmith**, **Tesla** and **Bon Jovi** influences to powerful effect. Their dynamism and musical palate gave the songs a cutting edge that elevated the resultant collection above mere plagiarism.

● ALBUMS: *Every Mother's Nightmare* (Arista 1990) ★★★.

Every Mother's Son

Formed in New York City, USA, in 1967, where each of its members was born, Every Mother's Son is best remembered for that year's Top 10 single 'Come On Down To My Boat', on **MGM Records**. The group consisted of guitar-playing brothers Dennis (b. 22 November 1948) and Larry Larden (b. 10 August 1945) who began their career as a folk duo. They were joined by pianist Bruce Milner (b. 9 May 1943), drummer Christopher Augustine (b. 25 August 1941) and bass player Schuyler Larsen (b. 19 February 1947). The group recorded the **Wes Farrell**–Jerry Goldstein song 'Come On Down To My Boat', a pop rock confection, and signed with MGM, who released the single and the group's self-titled album quickly, perhaps seeing their clean-cut image as an antidote to the summer of 1967's hippie influx. Although the debut single made the Top 10, and three later singles and the debut album reached the charts, the group could not sustain its initial success and folded in 1969. Dennis Larden later joined **Rick Nelson**'s Stone Canyon Band.

● ALBUMS: *Every Mother's Son* (MGM 1967) ★★★, *Every Mother's Son's Back* (MGM 1967) ★★.

Every Sunday

Although only 11 minutes long, this 1936 two-reel musical short is a historically interesting film. Directed by Felix E. Feist from a screenplay by Mauri Grashin, the story follows the efforts of two friends, Edna (**Deanna Durbin**) and Judy (**Judy Garland**), to help out Edna's grandfather who conducts an orchestra in the park on Sundays. Poor attendance is forcing cancellation of their concerts so Edna and Judy persuade an audience to come to the park the following Sunday where they sing with the orchestra. Edna performs a classical aria and Judy sings 'Americana'. This was the first film appearance for both young girls; Durbin, was aged 14 at the time, Garland was a year younger. When this black and white film was made, Garland had already been signed by MGM without having a screen test, so impressed with her abilities had been Louis B. Mayer. For Durbin, though, it was a test and MGM decided against signing her. In retrospect, it was a decision that greatly benefited Universal who did sign her and her ensuing films saved the studio from bankruptcy. A small but valuable and entertaining piece of film history, *Every Sunday* was added to the DVD release of Garland's 1942 film *For Me And My Gal*.

Every Which Way

This short-lived act was formed by ex-**Nice** drummer **Brian 'Blinky' Davidson** (b. 25 May 1942, Leicester, England) in May 1970. The line-up initially comprised Graham Bell (vocals, previously of **Skip Bifferty**), Geoff Peach (flute) and Alan Cartwright (bass), before being expanded to accommodate guitarist John Hedley. Bell provided much of the material featured on *Every Which Way*, which combined elements of fantasy with jazz rock. However, in spite of an acclaimed debut at London's Marquee club and the best efforts of manager **Tony Stratton-Smith**, the quintet failed to attract commercial favour. In 1971, Bell left to join Arc while Cartwright switched to **Procol Harum**. Davidson subsequently resurfaced in **Refugee**.

● ALBUMS: *Every Which Way* (Charisma 1970) ★★.

Everybody's Cheering

(see *Take Me Out To The Ball Game*)

Everyday's A Holiday

Retitled *Seaside Swingers* for US audiences, *Everyday's A Holiday* revolved around several teenagers who take seasonal work at a holiday camp, before entering a television talent contest. The film starred former **Joe Meek** protégé, **John Leyton**, famed for the ghostly 'Johnny Remember Me', and light-hearted singer **Mike Sarne**, creator of early 60s novelty hits 'Come Outside' and 'Will I What?' Pantomime beat group **Freddie And The Dreamers** were featured in a cast that also included the far superior **Mojos**. This forgettable feature was billed as including '16 smash hit numbers', a fact that was patently untrue. *Everyday's A Holiday* did contain some good photographic sequences, courtesy of Nicolas Roeg, but offered little for the pop fan. Coincidentally, both Leyton and Sarne would later abandon music for 'serious' acting roles.

Everyone Says I Love You

Woody Allen's tribute to the romantic musicals of the 30s, and subsequently, deals with a year in the life of Steffi (Goldie Hawn) and her second husband Bob (Alan Alda), a comfortably liberal, wealthy married couple residing on New York's Upper East Side. Their children and step-children include Skylar (Drew Barrymore), who is engaged to Holden (Edward Norton), Laura (Natalie Portman), Lane (Gaby Hoffman), Scott (Lukas Haas), who unfortunately has a nasty streak of political conservatism, and DJ (Natasha Lyonne), the film's narrator. Steffi's first husband, Joe (Woody Allen), lives in Paris and is mixed up and not very good with women (no surprise there), although (having been given 'inside information'), he manages to woo and win Von (Julia Roberts). Steffi meanwhile, as part of her good deed for the day, invites paroled felon Charles Ferry (Tim Roth) to dinner, only for Skylar to have a brief fling with him. All this plot—and more—is enhanced by a clutch of wonderful standard songs, sung by actors who, so it is said, signed their contracts before they knew the movie was going to be a musical. So there are varying degrees of vocal expertise here, with Goldie Hawn and Alan Alda emerging with the greatest credit, and only Barrymore having to be dubbed (in this film, even the spirits down at the funeral parlour leap out of their coffins and sing). Among the many highlights are the mood-setting 'Just You, Just Me', Alda's neat reading of **Cole Porter**'s 'Looking At You', Norton's hilarious spoofing of **Walter Donaldson** and **Gus Kahn**'s 'My Baby Just Cares For Me', 'I'm A Dreamer, Aren't We All?', 'Makin' Whoopee', 'Cuddle Up a Little Closer', 'What A Little Moonlight Can Do' and the final number, 'Hooray For Captain Spalding', sung in French by a group of Groucho Marx imitators (actually by the Helen Miles Singers). That last item was written by **Bert Kalmar** and **Harry Ruby** for the Marx Brothers' show *Animal Crackers*, and, coincidentally, the song from which this picture takes its title, 'Everyone Says I Love You', is also a Kalmar and Ruby composition that featured in another zany Marx Brothers vehicle, *Horse Feathers*. But the best of the lot—the top of the heap—is Hawn's computer-enhanced song and dance scene with Allen on the banks of the Seine. An homage to those **Fred Astaire–Cyd Charisse** and **Gene Kelly–Lesley Caron** numbers from MGM's golden age of movie musicals. Arranged and conducted by **Dick Hyman**, choreographed by Graciela Daniele, with Carlo DiPalma's stunning Technicolor photography, this film was scripted and directed by Woody Allen. It was produced by Mirimax and released in 1996.

Everything But The Girl

Tracey Thorn (b. 26 September 1962, Hertfordshire, England) and Ben Watt (b. 6 December 1962, Barnes, London, England) first began performing together when they were students at Hull University, taking their unusual name coming from a local furniture shop. Thorn was a member of the **Marine Girls**, and released the acoustic mini-album *A Distant Shore*, which was a strong seller in the UK independent charts during 1982. Watt released the critically acclaimed *North Marine Drive* the following year, by which time the duo had made their recording debut as Everything But The Girl with a gentle and simply produced version of **Cole Porter**'s 'Night And Day'.

The duo subsequently left **Cherry Red Records** and signed to the major-distributed Blanco y Negro label. In 1984, they made the national Top 30 with 'Each And Everyone', which preceded the superb *Eden*. This jazz-flavoured pop collection hallmarked the duo's understated compositional skills, displaying a great leap from the comparative naïveté of their previous offerings. Subsequent albums revealed a much more gradual growth in songwriting, though many of their older fans contend they have never surpassed that debut. Their biggest single breakthrough, meanwhile, came when a cover version of Danny Whitten's 'I Don't Want To Talk About It' reached UK number 3 in 1988. The attendant *Idlewild* enjoyed critical and commercial success. *The Language Of Life*, a collection more firmly fixated with jazz stylings, found further critical acclaim; one track, 'The Road', featured **Stan Getz** on saxophone. However, a more pop-orientated follow-up, *World-wide*, was released to mediocre reviews in 1991.

Watt's increasingly busy DJing schedule and Thorn's vocal contributions to trip-hop pioneers **Massive Attack**'s 1994 opus, *Protection*, demonstrated their increasing interest in the UK's **dance music** scene. This was reflected in the textures of *Amplified Heart*, which featured contributions from **Danny Thompson**, **Dave Mattacks**, **Richard Thompson** and arranger Harry Robinson. The album was recorded following Watt's recovery from a life-threatening illness (chronicled in the quirky *Patient: The History Of A Rare Illness*). **Todd Terry**'s remix of the track 'Missing' provided their big breakthrough, becoming a huge club hit and reaching the UK and US Top 5 in 1995. The duo's new approach was confirmed on *Walking Wounded*, their **Virgin Records** debut, which embellished their acoustic songs with drum 'n' bass and trip-hop rhythms to stunning effect. The title track and 'Wrong' both reached the UK Top 10.

Watt's involvement in the club scene meant that Everything But The Girl's new album did not appear until 1999. *Temperamental* retained some of the low-key charm of *Walking Wounded*, although three years on, the duo's work sounded less groundbreaking.

● ALBUMS: *Eden* (Blanco y Negro 1984) ★★★★, *Love Not Money* (Blanco y Negro 1985) ★★, *Baby The Stars Shine Bright* (Blanco y Negro 1986) ★★, *Idlewild* (Blanco y Negro 1988) ★★★★, *The Language Of Life* (Blanco y Negro 1990) ★★★, *World-wide* (Blanco y Negro 1991) ★★, *Amplified Heart* (Blanco y Negro 1994) ★★★★, *Walking Wounded* (Virgin 1996) ★★★★, *Temperamental* (Virgin 1999) ★★★.
Solo: Tracey Thorn *A Distant Shore* mini-album (Cherry Red 1982) ★★★. Ben Watt *North Marine Drive* (Cherry Red 1983) ★★★, *Buzzin' Fly Volume Vol. 2: Replenishing Music For The Modern Soul* (Astralwerks 2005) ★★.

● COMPILATIONS: *Home Movies: The Best Of Everything But The Girl* (Blanco y Negro 1993) ★★★★, *The Best Of Everything But The Girl* (Blanco y Negro 1997) ★★★★, *Back To Mine* (DMC/Ultra 2001) ★★★, *Like The Deserts Miss The Rain* (Virgin 2002) ★★★★, *Adapt Or Die: Ten Years Of Remixes* (Virgin 2005) ★★★.
● DVD/VIDEOS: *Like The Deserts Miss The Rain* (EMI 2002).
● FURTHER READING: *Patient: The History Of A Rare Illness*, Ben Watt.

Evil Dead

After his split with the eccentric **Agent Steel** in 1988, guitarist Juan Garcia (also ex-**Abattoir**) went on to form Evil Dead featuring a line-up of Albert Gonzalez (guitar), Phil Fiores (vocals) and Rob Ailinz (drums, ex-Necrophilia). A strong and professional thrash metal act, Evil Dead nevertheless lacked identity or the kind of individuality Agent Steel frontman John Cyriis was able to give his volatile five-piece. In the increasingly crowded thrash and death metal genres, Garcia's act struggled to hold the attention of the young, and somewhat fickle, extreme metal audiences.

● ALBUMS: *Rise Above* (Steamhammer 1988) ★★★, *Annihilation Of Civilisation* (Steamhammer 1990) ★★.

Evil Superstars

Belgium's Evil Superstars, who comprise Mauro Pawlowski (vocals/guitar), Dave Schroyen (drums), Marc Requile (keyboards), Bert Vandebroek (bass) and Tim Vanhamel (guitar), became one of a number of mainland European groups alongside **Whale**, **Bettie Serveert** and the **Cardigans** to procure UK and US audiences in the mid-90s. They recorded their debut EP, *Hairfacts*, in 1995, before touring with **Placebo** and achieving notoriety for their 'Satan Is In My Ass' single. Encompassing several traditions of music such as jazz, reggae and hard rock, the impression of eclecticism was confirmed by the 1996 release of *Love Is Okay*, which shaped these diverse influences into pop songs of genuine merit and accessibility. *Boogie-Children-R-Us* repeated the formula to lesser effect.

● ALBUMS: *Love Is Okay* (Paradox 1996) ★★★, *Boogie-Children-R-Us* (Paradox 1998) ★★.

Evingson, Connie

b. 1962, Hibbing, Minnesota, USA. Growing up in a musical household, Evingson began singing in public at the age of five, mostly in school and church choirs. Later, she attended the University of Minnesota, studying music and anthropology and attaining her Bachelor of Arts degree. Drawn to jazz and popular music, her first professional gig as a singer came in 1980 when she appeared at The Night Train, a small club in St. Paul, Minnesota. She has also appeared in clubs and concert halls nationwide and in Europe and Japan. As a member since 1986 of the vocal jazz ensemble Moore By Four (also comprising Yolande Bruce, Ginger Commodore and David Fischer), she has toured internationally. Her theatre credits include appearances in **Lady In The Dark**, **The King And I**, **South Pacific**, and *The Pearl Fishers*, with the Minnesota Opera Company. On radio, she has been host of *Singers And Standards* on KBEM, a noted jazz radio station in the twin cities of Minneapolis and St. Paul, and was featured on the Smithsonian's Jazz Singers production. In 1999, she was featured in a concert of music by **Duke Ellington** with the Minnesota Orchestra, conducted on this occasion by **Doc Severinsen**. She has also appeared in concert, as guest soloist, with the Toronto Symphony Orchestra. Among artists with whom she has sung are **Ray Brown**, **Al Grey**, **Brother Jack McDuff**, **Bobby McFerrin** and **Toots Thielemans**, most of whom have appeared with her on record. In the late 90s, Evingson staged *Fever: A Tribute To Peggy Lee*, on a number of occasions, notably at Minneapolis' Illusion Theater. Another tribute project was an intriguing selection of reworked songs by **John Lennon** and **Paul McCartney**. In development from the mid-90s, this eventually became another stage presentation at the Illusion, which Evingson presented along with pianist Mary Louise Knutson. This show, *Let It Be Jazz*, was premiered during the 2002 Fringe Festival in the Twin Cities, and 13 of the songs appear on her similarly titled album. An always interesting stylist of quality material, Evingson brings a lightness of touch to her material that often transcends the approach of better-known artists. Her decision to build her career in and around Minneapolis and St. Paul has tended to keep her from the attention of the wider world of jazz and good popular singing.

● ALBUMS: *I Have Dreamed* (Minnehaha 1998) ★★★, *Fever: A Tribute To Peggy Lee* (Minnehaha 1999) ★★★★, *Some Cats Know* (Minnehaha 1999) ★★★★, *The Secret Of Christmas* (Minnehaha 2000) ★★, *Let It Be Jazz: Connie Evingson Sings The Beatles* (Minnehaha 2003) ★★★, *Let It Be Jazz* (Summit 2003) ★★★.

Evinrudes

This US indie pop band was formed in 1995 in Nashville, Tennessee, by husband-and-wife team Sherry Cothran (vocals) and Brian Reed (guitar). The Evinrudes made their debut in 1996 with the independently released *Little Red Stars*. This pleasant collection of indie pop material became a local bestseller, but a five-song EP released the following year overshadowed its success. Featuring the radio hits 'Drive Me Home' and 'Have Some Rain', the self-titled EP brought the Evinrudes to the attention of **Mercury Records** and a major label recording contract was not long in following. Cothran and Reed were joined in the Evinrudes' line-up by Troy Verges (guitar), Ethan Pilzer (bass) and Andy Hull (drums). Their self-titled debut album, released in 1998, ably demonstrated Cothran and Reed's capacity to write melodic indie pop to match the standard of their earlier releases. Nevertheless, the commercial hopes of the album were dented by Mercury's takeover by Seagram. Cothran and Reed were granted ownership of the CD masters after being dropped by Mercury. The duo spent most of the late 90s and early 00s touring and working on material for a projected follow-up. *Somebody Has To Be Pat Boone* was eventually released on the Flying Sparks label in 2002. The album was well received on both sides of the Atlantic, but shortly after its release Cothran announced she would be taking a break from the Evinrudes to work on her solo debut. *Who Let The World In*, which featured a guest appearance from Reed, was released in 2003.

● ALBUMS: *Little Red Stars* (Own Label 1996) ★★★, *The Evinrudes* (PolyGram 1998) ★★★, *Somebody Has To Be Pat Boone* (Flying Sparks 2002) ★★★★.

Evita (film musical)

Based upon the stage production by **Tim Rice** and **Andrew Lloyd Webber**, this 1996 film retells the remarkable rags-to-riches tale of Eva Maria Duarte. Rising from desperate poverty in rural Argentina, this young, illegitimate, pretty girl came from the village of Junin to Buenos Aires where she hoped to become a dancer. Helped at first by tango dancer Agustín Magaldi, and willing to sleep her way to the top, in 1944 she met Juan Perón, then a colonel in the Argentine army who became the country's fascist dictator. After becoming his mistress Eva married her lover and as the First Lady of Argentina, Eva Perón, Evita as she was known to all, raised strong passions in just about everyone in her country. Some, especially the poor, adored her; others, the already rich and powerful, detested her. Few were indifferent to this strong-willed woman. Not surprisingly, her death from cancer in 1952 at the age of 33 brought outpourings of grief from her beloved *descamisados* (shirtless ones) and hidden delight to those who had derided her in life. As so often happens with high profile figures, her early death also turned her into a legend.

Following the example of the stage version, the screenplay by director Alan Parker employs a narrator, Ché (Antonio Banderas). The role of Perón went to British stage and screen actor Jonathan Pryce with television actor and singer **Jimmy Nail** as Magaldi. The announcement that **Madonna** had been chosen to play the title role raised some eyebrows. Her enormous popularity as a singer contrasted sharply with inadequacies she displayed as an actress in her previous films. In the event, her songs fared best although the music as a whole suffered from the repetitiveness of themes. Apart from the well-known songs, among them 'Don't Cry For Me Argentina', 'Another Suitcase In Another Hall', 'I'd Be Surprisingly Good For You', Rice and Lloyd Webber added 'You Must Love Me' to the film version's score, for which song they were awarded an Oscar. At two and a quarter hours, the film might have benefited from some judicious editing but the performances of Pryce and Banderas, allied to the sweep of the story and the undoubted and largely still unplumbed depths of the life of Eva Perón, carried the audience over the occasional *longueur*.

Evita (stage musical)

In the period following their success with **Jesus Christ Superstar**, **Andrew Lloyd Webber** and **Tim Rice** went their different ways for a time. While Lloyd Webber was involved with Alan Ayckbourn in an ill-fated attempt to bring **P.G. Wodehouse**'s **Jeeves** to the musical stage, Tim Rice spent well over a year researching the life of Eva Peron. He discovered it to be the ultimate rags-to-riches fairytale. His book tells of the illegitimate, malnourished, and barely literate young Eva Maria Duarte (**Elaine Paige**) from a poor village in Junin, arriving in Buenos Aires, helped by tango dancer Agustín Magaldi (Mark Ryan), with ambitions to be an actress. Her life changes dramatically in 1944 when she meets Colonel Juan Perón (Joss Ackland), and, after deftly ousting his young mistress (Siobhán McCarthy), becomes his First Lady two years later. Fiercely devoted to her husband, and to her *descamisados* (shirtless ones) she became Argentina's first truly international figure, the most adored—and hated—woman in Latin America, until her death from cancer in July 1952 at the age of 33.

When *Evita* opened at the Prince Edward Theatre in London on 21 June 1978, there were howls of protest from some quarters accusing Rice and Lloyd Webber of glorifying 'this wife of the Perónist regime, a loathsome fascist dictatorship', rejecting the subject as quite unsuitable for a West End musical. Many years later, Rice commented: 'You can never really know the truth about Eva Perón, and I think the best way to tell her story is through a musical because she was a larger-than-life actress on a public stage. Her life was insane, and a musical is just the sort of melodramatic document which can capture something of her—much better than a book can.' Rice and Lloyd Webber's device of utilizing the character of Che (**David Essex**) to comment on, and link, the scenes was a clever one, and he had two of the best numbers, the mocking 'Oh What A Circus' and 'High Flying, Adored'. Among the other highlights of this recitative score were Eva's 'I'd Be Surprisingly Good For You' (to Peron, that is), her 'Don't Cry For Me Argentina' on the balcony, following Peron's Presidential election victory, and the mistress-on-the-way-out's rueful 'Another Suitcase In Another Hall'. The remainder of the numbers included 'Requiem For Evita', 'On This Night Of A Thousand Stars', 'Buenos Aires', 'Goodnight And Thank You', 'A New Argentina', 'Rainbow High', 'And The Money Keeps Rolling In (And Out)', 'Waltz For Eva And Che', 'She Is A Diamond' and 'Lament'. **Harold Prince** directed, the choreographer was Larry Fuller, and *Evita* ran for nearly eight years (2,900 performances) in London. Paige received a SWET (Society Of West End Theatre) award, and the show won another for best musical. Prior to opening, just as they did with *Jesus Christ Superstar*, Rice and Lloyd Webber introduced the score via a concept album (1976), with principal singers **Julie Covington** (Eva), **Paul Jones** (Peron), Colm Wilkinson (Che), **Tony Christie** (Magaldi) and **Barbara Dickson** (Mistress). Early in 1977, Covington went to number 1 in the UK with 'Don't Cry For Me Argentina', and Barbara Dickson ('Another Suitcase In Another Hall') and David Essex ('Oh What A Circus') also had hits with songs from the show.

Evita's success in the West End was echoed in the USA where it became the forerunner of a wave of British stage musicals that helped reverse the transatlantic tide. It opened at the Broadway Theatre in New York on the 25 September 1979, with Bob Gunton (Peron), Jane Ohringer (Mistress) and Mark Syers (Magaldi). The production ran for 1,568 performances, and won **Tony Awards** for **Mandy Patinkin** (Che), **Patti LuPone** (Eva), Harold Prince, David Hersey (lighting), book, score and best musical. Since then it has been produced all round the world, although banned in Argentina, and a major revival starring **Marti Webb**, toured the UK in 1995. An acclaimed film version of *Evita*, directed by Alan Parker and produced by **Robert Stigwood**, was released in 1996. It starred **Madonna** in the title role, with Antonio Banderas (Che), Jonathan Pryce (Juan Peron) and **Jimmy Nail** (Agustín Magaldi). Madonna had hits with 'Don't Cry For Me Argentina' and a new Rice/Lloyd Webber song, the Oscar-winning 'You Must Love Me'. A new Broadway-bound production of the show began a national tour on 6 November 1998 in Detroit. It had four Latin actors in the leading roles—Natalie Toro and Ana Marie Andricain sharing the title role, Raul Esparza (Che) and Raymond Jaramillo McLeod (Perón). Coincidentally, outstanding among the rest of the cast was 16-year-old Angela Covington. The coincidence ends there. This Covington plays Perón's mistress, and scores with the highly emotional 'Another Suitcase In Another Hall'.

Evora, Cesaria

b. *c.*1944, Mindelo, San Vincente, Cape Verde (an archipelago of islands 500 miles from Africa's west coast). Evora

originates from the main port city of San Vincente, Mindelo, a base for the islands' intelligentsia and industrialists following the end of Portuguese rule in 1975. It is also home to a music named morna. Morna sounds akin to a sophisticated blend of Portuguese fado, jazz and Latin, with its name a derivation of the English word 'mourn'. Cesaria Evora is ubiquitously recognized as the pre-eminent force in the music, while her uncle, Xavier Francisco de Cruz, was the architect of many of its songs. Recognition came late in life for the singer, who had sung since her teenage years for subsistence. She eventually found fame at the turn of the 90s, with her success triggered by rave reviews in Parisian magazines (she is now partially based in the French capital). *Cosmopolitan* and *Elle*, as well as the nation's largest circulation music magazine, *Actuel*, which put her on their cover, all proclaimed her as a genuine star and original talent. Prestige dates at major French music celebrations such as the Musique Metisses (Angouleme) and Francophiles (La Rochelle) ensued.

Aided by fellow Capverdian Paulino Vieira, Evora's recordings pursue a reflective, highly melodic approach backed by acoustic instrumentation. Gentle piano, percussion, ukulele and guitar underpins the deep melancholy at the heart of morna, for which Evora's troubled life makes her the perfect cipher. The deep sadness of this music is known as 'sodade', or nostalgia without the sentiment, although a direct translation is difficult. Her emotional resonance has seen the press compare her to artists as diverse as **Edith Piaf**, **Mahalia Jackson** and **Billie Holiday**, the latter partially owing to a similarity of lifestyle (she has been married and deserted three times—on the last occasion her husband left her to join a football team in Porto—and she drinks and smokes heavily). These experiences with men have left her deeply embittered, and family aside, she has sworn that no other man shall ever again sleep under her roof. She also insists on performing barefoot, as a symbolic salute to the poverty that afflicted (and continues to afflict) her fellow Capverdians.

Evora's first stroke of good fortune came in 1985 when, after years of singing in local bars for peanuts (literally) and beer, she was invited to travel to Europe as one of four singers chosen by the Women's Organisation of Cap Vert. She made a profound impression, and was soon invited to record and to tour America by an expatriate Capverdian singer known as Bana. With her reputation established, a series of albums were issued for Melodie Records, most with the aid of producer Jose Da Silva and her aforementioned arranger, Vieira. These scaled the top of the French charts. Her growing international success led to a major label contract with **RCA Records**, for whom she has recorded several highly popular albums, including 1999's outstanding *Café Atlantico* and the equally acclaimed follow-up *São Vicente*. Evora's 2003 release *Voz D'Amor* won a Grammy Award for Best Contemporary World Music Album.

● ALBUMS: *Miss Perfumado* (Melodie 1992) ★★★, *Mar Azul* (Melodie 1993) ★★★, *Cesaria Evora* (Melodie 1995) ★★★★, *Cesaria* (RCA Victor 1996) ★★★, *Cabo Verde* (RCA Victor 1997) ★★★, *Café Atlantico* (RCA Victor 1999) ★★★★, *São Vicente* (RCA Victor 2001) ★★★★, *Voz D'Amor* (Bluebird 2003) ★★★★.

● COMPILATIONS: *The Very Best Of Cesaria Evora* (RCA 2002) ★★★★, *Club Sodade* remixes (Bluebird 2004) ★★★.

Ewans, Kai

b. Kai Peter Anthon Nielsen, 10 April 1906, Hørsholm, Denmark. After playing other instruments, Ewans chose the alto saxophone in his late teens, later also playing clarinet. He played in several bands and also formed groups under his own leadership including a big band in the mid-20s. Late in the decade he toured Europe, continuing into the 30s as a band leader. He also played with visiting Americans including, **Benny Carter**. His big band, one of the first in Denmark when it was formed in 1927, had continued sporadically over the years and eventually disbanded in 1947. After this Ewans worked mostly outside music, travelling to the USA where, in the early 60s, he was in the restaurant business with Carter in California. After picking up the threads of his musical career in Denmark in the late 60s, he eventually retired to the USA. A good player, Ewans was a potent force behind the development of interest in jazz, and in particular in big band, swing-era-style music in Denmark. His bands were always disciplined, well-rehearsed and enthusiastic outfits, reflecting the best qualities of the leader.

● COMPILATIONS: *Kai Ewans And His Swinging Sixteen* (Storyville) ★★★.

Ewart, Douglas

b. 13 September 1946, Kingston, Jamaica. Ewart moved to Chicago in June 1963 and later studied music at the **AACM**. His early influences included **Charles Mingus**, **Clifford Brown** and **Eric Dolphy**, the latter's example persuading Ewart to learn bassoon and bass clarinet in addition to alto and other saxophones and flute. He has played with many of his AACM colleagues, recording with (for example) **Roscoe Mitchell** (*Sketches From Bamboo*), **Muhal Richard Abrams** (*Lifea Blinec*), **Anthony Braxton** (*For Trio*), **Leo Smith** (*Budding Of A Rose*) and **Henry Threadgill**, in the X-75 group. In particular, Ewart formed an association with trombonist **George Lewis** in 1971 that has continued through to the present: he has played on several of Lewis' projects (*Chicago Slow Dance*, *Homage To Charles Parker*) and recorded a duo album with him. Leader of a clarinet quartet (*Red Hills*), Ewart is also an accomplished instrument-maker, particularly renowned for his beautifully crafted Ewart flutes.

● ALBUMS: with George Lewis *Jila/Save!/Mon./The Imaginary Suite* (Black Saint 1979) ★★★, *Red Hills* cassette (Aarawak 1981) ★★, *Bamboo Forest* cassette (Aarawak 1982) ★★★, *Bamboo Meditations At Banff* (Aarawak 1983) ★★★, *Douglas Ewart & Inventions Clarinet Choir* (Aarawak 1984) ★★★.

Ewell, Don

b. Donald Tyson Ewell, 14 November 1916, Baltimore, Maryland, USA, d. 9 August 1983, Pompano Beach, Florida, USA. Although classically trained on piano, Ewell was drawn to jazz and in particular to the music of the early jazz masters of New Orleans. This was despite the fact that by the mid-30s, which was when his career got under way, such forms were suffering a decline in popularity under the commercial pressures of the swing era. Undeterred, Ewell followed his bent, working with **Bunk Johnson** in the mid-40s and later in the decade with **Muggsy Spanier** and **Sidney Bechet**. Stylistically, he was influenced by pianists as different as **Jelly Roll Morton**, **Fats Waller** and **Jimmy Yancey**. In the mid-50s Ewell began a particularly rewarding association with **Jack Teagar-**

den, which lasted until the trombonist's death in 1964. Thereafter, Ewell toured extensively, sometimes in bands, sometimes in harness with fellow pianist **Willie 'The Lion' Smith**, but mostly as a soloist, until his death in 1983. Although capable of playing rousing barrelhouse style, he was also able to produce exceptionally fine and intricate playing.

● ALBUMS: *Don Ewell* 10-inch album (Windin' Ball 1953) ★★★, *Don Ewell & Mama Yancey* 10-inch album (Windin' Ball 1953) ★★★, *Plays Tunes Played By The King Oliver Band* 10-inch album (Windin' Ball 1953) ★★★, *Music To Listen To Don Ewell By* (Good Time Jazz 1955) ★★★, *The Man Here Plays Fine Piano* (Good Time Jazz 1956) ★★★★, *Free 'n Easy* (Good Time Jazz 1956) ★★★, *Jazz On A Sunday Afternoon* (Fat Cat Jazz 1969) ★★★, *Live At The 100 Club* (Solo Arts 1971) ★★★, *Don Ewell* (Chiaroscuro 1974) ★★★, *In Japan* (Jazzology 1975) ★★★★, *Chicago '57* 1957 recording (Stomp Off 1984) ★★★, *Don Ewell Quintet* 1973/74 recording (Jazzology 1986) ★★★, *In New Orleans* 1965 recording (GHB 1986) ★★★, *Yellow Dog Blues* (Jazzology 1988) ★★★, *Don Ewell And His All-Stars* 1965 recording (Jazzology 1988) ★★★★, *Don Ewell's Hot 4* 1966 recording (Center 1992) ★★★.

● FURTHER READING: *Jazz Legacy Of Don Ewell*, John Colinson and Eugene Kramer.

Ewing, Skip

b. Donald R. Ewing, 6 March 1965, Redlands, California, USA. Because he was born into a military family, Ewing travelled extensively as a child. His father bought him a guitar when he was four years old and he became hooked on country music and, in particular, **Merle Haggard**. In 1984, after graduating, he moved to Nashville as a songwriter and the first track to be recorded was 'One Hell Of A Song' by **George Jones**. **Jimmy Bowen** signed him to MCA Records and he had US country successes with 'Your Memory Wins Again' and 'Burning A Hole In My Heart'. Five hits came from his first album and his style was likened to **Randy Travis's** and **Don McLean**. Ewing continues to write songs for other artists and compositions have included 'You Leave Me Like This' (**Lorrie Morgan**), 'Who Needs You' (**Lisa Brokop**) and the superb ballad 'Still Under The Weather' (**Shania Twain**). His oddest composition is the Christmas song 'It Wasn't His Child', which has been recorded by both **Sawyer Brown** and **Trisha Yearwood**. He moved to **Capitol Records** in 1992.

● ALBUMS: *The Coast Of Colorado* (MCA 1988) ★★★★, *The Will To Love* (MCA 1989) ★★★, *A Healin' Fire* (MCA 1990) ★★★, *Following Yonder Star* (MCA 1990), *Naturally* (Capitol 1991) ★★★, *Homegrown Love* (Capitol 1993) ★★★, *Naturally* (Capitol 1994) ★★★, *Until I Found You* (Word Nashville 1997) ★★★.

● COMPILATIONS: *Greatest Hits* (MCA 1991) ★★★★.

Ex

Unconventional Dutch conglomerate formed in 1977 when punk first hit Holland and a variety of like minds came together as a politically active musical and social unit. The Ex were formed from the ashes of two small local bands, and their varied membership has included G.W. Sok (vocals), Terrie Hessels (guitar), Sabien Witteman (drums), Katrin Bornfeld (drums), Jos Kley (vocals), Han Buhrs (vocals), Yoke Laarman (bass), Luc Klaassen (bass), Wineke T. Hart (violin), Kees vanden Haak (saxophone), John van der Weert (vocals/guitar), Nicolette (guitar), Dolf Planteydt (guitar) and Tom Greene (guitar). They were strongly linked to a variety of left-field concerns in general and the Amsterdam squatting movement in particular (they also released a joint live album of a benefit tour for striking British miners). Although the sound started life as strictly agit-prop punk, they later incorporated elements such as Eastern folk music, funk and various other styles. *Scrabbling At The Lock* and *And The Weathermen Shrug Their Shoulders*, for instance, were collaborations with **Tom Cora** (cello), and they have also recorded with Iraqi Kurdish group Awara. Guests on other works have included Lee Ranaldo and Thurston Moore (**Sonic Youth**), Jon Langford (**Mekons**) and the Dog Faced Hermans (whose guitar player, Andy, joined Ex in 1990). Their attitude to the place of rebel music in the scheme of things can best be summed up by a statement on the rear of 1985's *Pokkeherrie*: 'Where have all the musicians gone? The ones who made sound disturb, who pulled down the stage, who forged music into a weapon. Where have all the musicians gone? They perform in supermarkets and have their instruments tuned. "Our ears are deaf and our strings are wrapped up in silk. We hurt nobody."' A lowlands equivalent to **Fugazi** then, but with probably more stylistic variation. In 1998 they signed to Touch & Go Records in the USA, and began recording with **Steve Albini**.

● ALBUMS: *Disturbing Domestic Peace* (Verrecords 1980) ★★★, *History Is What's Happening* (More DPM 1982) ★★★, *Dignity Of Labour* (VGZ 1983) ★★★, *Tumult* (FAI 1983) ★★★, *Blueprints For A Blackout* (Pig Brother Productions 1983) ★★★, *Pokkeherrie* (Pockabilly 1985) ★★★, *Too Many Cowboys* (Mordam 1987) ★★★, *Live In Wroclaw* cassette (Red 1987) ★★★, *Aural Guerilla* (Ex 1988) ★★★, with guests *Joggers And Smoggers* (Ex 1989) ★★★, *Dead Fish* mini-album (Ex 1990) ★★★, with Dog Faced Hermans *Treat* cassette (Demon Rage 1990) ★★, with Tom Cora *Scrabbling At The Lock* (RecRec 1991) ★★★★, with Cora *And The Weathermen Shrug Their Shoulders* (RecRec/Fist Puppet 1993) ★★★★, *Mudbird Shivers* (Ex/RecRec 1995) ★★★, with various guests *Instant* (Ex 1995) ★★★, *Starters Alternators* (Ex 1998) ★★★, with Tortoise *In The Fishtank* (Fishtank 1999) ★★★, with Sonic Youth, I.C.P. *In The Fishtank 9* (Konkurrent 2002) ★★, *Turn* (Ex 2004) ★★.

● COMPILATIONS: *Hands Up! You're Free* (Ex 1988) ★★★.

● DVD/VIDEOS: *The Ex & Guests—Live At The Bimhuis* (1992), *Terrie, Andy & Friends—Sounds Of Bells* (1995).

● FURTHER READING: *Ex-rated*, G.W. Sok.

Excalibur

This group was formed in Yorkshire, England, in 1981 by Paul McBride (vocals), Paul Solynskyj (b. 27 October 1966, England; guitar), Martin Hawthorn (bass) and Mick Dobson (drums). The band was formed while they were still schoolboys and they would reportedly fall asleep in class after a heavy night's gigging. On finishing school, Excalibur continued to tour heavily, while the members also attempted to hold down day jobs. Conquest Records signed the band in 1985 after an employee heard Excalibur by chance one night. *The Bitter End* mini-album was released in 1985, containing slightly predictable but melodic heavy metal. In 1986 Excalibur expanded to a five-piece with the addition of Steve Blades (b. 20 May 1968, Scotland; guitar/keyboards). This was followed by a session for BBC Radio 1's *Friday Rock Show*, which was broadcast in July 1986 and again in September. The four tracks that the band recorded were later released by Clay Records as the *Hot For Love EP* in 1988. That year saw Excalibur appear on a BBC television programme *On A Personal Note*, where they performed 'Hot For Love' and 'Running Scared' alongside slots from **Def Leppard** and **Little Angels**. Before the year's end, Dobson was replaced by Dave Sykes on drums, while the group supported **Uriah Heep** for most of their UK tour. In 1989 the band signed to Active Records and immediately began recording a debut album. The first taster was a track entitled 'Carole Ann', an acoustic number that drew comparisons to **Bon Jovi**. After *One Strange Night* was released to critical acclaim, Excalibur embarked on their first full headlining tour of the UK in February 1990. They supported **Saxon** on UK and European dates, though there were further personnel changes to endure. Livermore had replaced Martin Hawthorn in 1989, and he now left to make way for Dean Wilson (b. 5 March 1966, England). In 1991 Excalibur were in the studio recording their follow-up album, when Paul McBride announced that he was leaving the band, placing their career on hold.

● ALBUMS: *The Bitter End* mini-album (Conquest 1985) ★★★, *One Strange Night* (Active 1990) ★★★★.

Excellents

Formed originally as the Premiers in 1960 in New York City, USA, the Excellents consisted of John Kuse (lead), Joel Feldman (baritone), Denis Kestenbaum (falsetto), George Kuse (first tenor), Phil Sanchez (second tenor) and Chuck Epstein (bass). They signed to Mermaid Records, where their revision of **Al Jolson**'s 'When The Red, Red Robin, Comes Bob-Bob-Bobbin' Along' was coupled with another cover, the **Jesters**' 'Love No One But You', as their debut single. Encouraged by local airplay, they followed this with a second disc, their version of the **Cleftones**' 'You Baby You' on the a-side and 'Coney Island Baby' on the b-side. It was 'Coney Island Baby' (*not* the barbershop quartet standard) that attracted the attention, reaching number 51. With prominent local concerts and a rising reputation, the Excellents looked set for a promising career until record business skulduggery intervened. Booked for an appearance on *Dick Clark's American Bandstand* television programme, their record company refused to pay their travelling fees. When they learned that the group simply could not afford to travel to Philadelphia, the label instead sent an entirely different group under the same name. Justifiably devastated at this turn of events, the Excellents never recorded again, although a single, 'Helene', from their original sessions at Sinclair Records, was released in 1964 credited to the Excellons.

Excello Records

The Excello Records label was launched in August 1952 as a subsidiary of the Nashboro Record Distributing Co., which had been set up a year earlier to tap into the insatiable demand for black southern gospel music. The founder was **Ernie Young** (b. Ernest Lafayette Young, 2 December 1892, Giles County, Tennessee, USA, d. 8 June 1977, Nashville, Tennessee, USA), a jukebox operator and electronics/record retailer. He started the business from 177 Third Avenue North, Nashville, Tennessee—the home of The Record Mart (later renamed Ernie's Record Mart), a store that was to play a vital role in the Excello story.

The early Excello releases covered blues, R&B, gospel, hillbilly, even pop music. The first hits were all in the southern markets: 'Banana Split' (Kid King's Combo), 'Bus Station Blues' (Louis Brooks And His Pinetoppers) and 'Baby Let's Play House' (**Arthur Gunter**), subsequently covered by a young **Elvis Presley** as his fourth single for **Sun Records**. The flow of royalties from Presley's recording to the publishing arm Excellorec Music helped to underpin Young's business operations. In 1955 and 1956 there were further R&B chart hits: 'Rollin' Stone' (the Marigolds, led by Johnny Bragg), 'It's Love Baby (24 Hours A Day)' (Louis Brooks And His Hi-Toppers, featuring young vocalist **Earl Gaines**), and 'Pleadin' For Love' (Larry Birdsong, a protégé of local producer Ted Jarrett). Until then, most of the Excello releases had been recorded in Young's small, makeshift studio in the Ernie's Record Mart building.

Young had the foresight to sponsor nightly shows over Nashville's powerful 50,000-watt Radio WLAC, hosted by John Richbourg (John R.). Record orders started flooding into Ernie's Record Mart. Young hit upon the great idea of making up five-pack specials of 45s at a discount price (at one time $2.98). These packs contained not only the latest R&B hits, but also at least one Excello record with every order. Young applied the same principle to his gospel 'specials' by including Nashboro 45s in every pack. With good profit margins on the record packs, Young needed the assurance of regular Excello product. In 1955, he began releasing swamp blues recordings by an ambitious Crowley, Louisiana, producer, **Jay Miller**, who had already written the big country hit 'It Wasn't God Who Made Honky Tonk Angels' for **Kitty Wells**. The first Miller artist signed to Excello was **Lightnin' Slim**. By 1957, there was a string of high quality Miller swamp blues recordings from Lightnin' Slim, **Lonesome Sundown**, **Lazy Lester** and **Guitar Gable**. Miller was renowned for giving his artists colourful pseudonyms. The swamp bluesman who epitomized the laid-back Excello blues sound of mellow harmonicas and moody bass rhythms was about to make his debut record, James Moore aka **Slim Harpo**. Curiously, 'I'm A King Bee', despite its subsequent impact, never made the R&B charts of the day. With white teenagers listening to R&B records in ever increasing numbers, the cross-over from R&B to rock 'n' roll was now an established trend. Excello broke into the Top 100 charts for the first time in spring 1957 with 'Little Darlin'' by the Gladiolas (led by Maurice Williams). However, the age of white cover versions was not over and the Canadian group the **Diamonds** proceeded to spend a full half-year on the charts. Later, in 1960, with his new group, **Maurice Williams And The Zodiacs** were to make a startling comeback with 'Stay', a number 1 national hit for Herald.

In May 1957, Young had launched another subsidiary label, Nasco Records, which quickly became the pop arm of the Nashboro group. In 1958, local teen vocal group the **Crescen-dos** scored a big national hit with 'Oh Julie' at number 5 during an 18-week stay. The group could not find a follow-up record and became quintessential one-hit-wonders. The only other Nasco record to chart during a three-year lifespan was 'Prisoner's Song' by Jay Miller session drummer Warren Storm, with a Louisiana swamp pop sound. By the early 60s both Excello and Nashboro were releasing more than 20 singles per year, and were starting to issue long-playing albums by Lightnin' Slim, Slim Harpo and Nashville R&B artist **Roscoe Shelton**. Hit singles, though, were still all important. Producer Jay Miller obliged with 'Rainin' In My Heart' by Slim Harpo that peaked at number 34 on the **Billboard** Hot 100 chart in May 1961, and even higher at number 24 on the **Cash Box** chart. The gloss of the 'Rainin' In My Heart' hit quickly dissipated when Miller was unable to coax Slim Harpo to record a follow-up owing to a royalty dispute. Even so, Miller was able to step up his blues output for Excello from Lightnin' Slim, Lonesome Sundown and Lazy Lester and introduced new blues artists from the Baton Rouge area such as **Silas Hogan**, **Jimmy Anderson** and **Moses 'Whispering' Smith**.

In 1963, **EMI Records** of London licensed an album of mostly then-recent Excello singles entitled *Authentic R&B* on the Stateside label, compiled by **Guy Stevens**. The effect of this album on the British Beat-era bands and fans was considerable. Miller healed the rift with Slim Harpo and in 1966 Harpo hit the charts again with the charismatic dance record 'Baby Scratch My Back,' which made number 1 R&B and touched number 16 on the Hot 100 charts. 'Baby Scratch My Back' subsequently was voted number 3 R&B record of 1966, this in an era when **Motown Records** dominated the airwaves.

'Baby Scratch My Back' was the last hit enjoyed by Ernie Young. In summer 1966 he retired at the age of 73. He sold the Nashboro Record Company to the Crescent Company conglomerate, which installed Shannon Williams as vice-president in charge of the Nashboro Group. The new owners disposed of the Ernie's Record Mart building and developed the Woodland Sound Studios complex, in the old Woodland Theatre Building. Jack Funk and Bud Howell were also involved in the management of the new music division. Jay Miller was to sever his relationship forever when the Crescent team signed Slim Harpo direct to Excello, upon the expiration of Miller's personal contract with Harpo.

With southern soul music at its **Otis Redding**–inspired peak, Excello contracted an impressive roster of soul artists, including **Freddie North** (their promo man), **Z.Z. Hill**, **Bobby Powell**, **Kip Anderson** and **Maceo And The King's Men**. The Nashville arranger and producer Bob Holmes was brought in to oversee acts such as Slim Harpo and the **Kelly Brothers**. The soul releases were being allocated between Excello, A-Bet and a new affiliate, Mankind. Excello managed two minor soul hits with Jerry Washington from South Carolina, but the only soul hit of significance for the Nashboro Group was 'She's All I Got' by Freddie North (produced by Jerry Williams, aka **Swamp Dogg**) on Mankind in 1971. The Nashboro operation was hit badly by the change in format in WLAC Radio from R&B to Top 40 that saw the departure of old-style disc jockeys John R. and Hoss Allen (temporarily in his case). The final Excello release was in 1975. A-Bet continued until 1977 and even had modest hits by **Oliver Sain** and Skip Mahoney And The Casuals. Shannon Williams continued releasing gospel singles and albums on the Nashboro, Kenwood, Crescent and Creed labels until 1980. Meanwhile, in 1978, the Crescent Company had sold the Nashboro music complex to AVI, headed by record man Ray Harris and Ed Cobb (of the **Four Preps**).

To the world at large Excello and Nashboro were dormant throughout the 80s. The catalogues were revived in the early 90s when AVI granted licenses to **Ace Records** in England and P-Vine in Japan. The AVI stock was acquired in 1993 by former Motown executive Harry Anger, who embarked on an extensive CD reissue campaign. Then in 1997 the Excello and Nashboro masters were purchased by the Universal Music Group, and the Excellorec publishing catalogue was sold to Music Sales.

Excello Records will always be remembered as Ernie Young's brainchild. He was a smart businessman who had the vision to exploit the developing R&B and gospel record markets of the 50s and the 60s. In so doing, he has bequeathed a wealth of southern music on record. It is a tribute to him as founder, to Jay Miller as the main producer and to the artists and their music that the Excello Records story lives on.

● COMPILATIONS: *The Excello Story Volumes 1–4* (Hip-O 1999) ★★★★.

● FURTHER READING: *South To Louisiana: The Music Of The Cajun Bayous*, John Broven.

Exciter (Canada)

Formed in Ottawa, Canada, in 1979 as a three-piece outfit, the band's original line-up consisted of Dan Beehler (drums/ vocals), John Ricci (guitar) and Allan Johnson (bass), their name deriving from an old **Judas Priest** track. An impressive demo attracted the attention of Shrapnel Records, who, as well as featuring the band on an early *U.S. Metal* compilation, also released the demo as an album entitled *Heavy Metal Maniac* in 1983. This was belligerent, **Motör-head**-influenced power metal and quickly gained the band a strong following in Europe. They then changed labels and released *Violence & Force* for Roadrunner Records in 1984. Produced by ex-**Rods** drummer Carl Canedy, it was a much more stylish release, benefiting from better production and higher-quality material. By the next release, the band had changed European labels once again. Their third album, *Long Live The Loud*, appeared on the Music For Nations label in 1985. Recorded and produced in London with producer Guy Bidmead, this album did not seem as immediate as previous releases and saw them lose some of their early raw power. However, this did not deter the band from undertaking an extensive European tour in support of the release. Afterwards, Ricci left to be replaced by Brian McPhee, a friend of the band, who added a new dimension to their fourth album, *Unveiling The Wicked*. Unfortunately, even McPhee's excellent guitar work could not alleviate the sense of weariness in the music, and after a short tour of Brazil the band decided to add a vocalist/frontman to give them a stronger identity. This resulted in the recruitment of Rob Malnati. Once again they changed labels, signing to the small Canadian independent Maze Records. Their last album, *Exciter*, failed to sell and shortly after its release the band sank into obscurity, playing on the local club scene.

● ALBUMS: *Heavy Metal Maniac* (Shrapnel 1983) ★★★, *Violence & Force* (Roadrunner 1984) ★★★, *Long Live The Loud* (Music For Nations 1985) ★★★, *Unveiling The Wicked* (Music For Nations 1986) ★★, *Exciter* (Maze/Music For Nations 1988) ★★, *Better Live Than Dead* (1993) ★★.

Exciter (Netherlands)

Often confused with the Canadian **Exciter**—a band who made their breakthrough at approximately the same time and worked in the same genre—the Dutch group Exciter comprised Gert Admiral (bass), Marc Karsten (guitar), Marcel Admiral (guitar) and Walter Admiral (drums). The Admiral brothers had played music together since childhood

and formed the group in the early 80s. They immediately secured a major label contract with **WEA Records** who released their self-titled debut album in 1983. A solid but unexciting collection of stylized Euro-metal with moderate collaborative songwriting, it was their sole release. Disappointing sales resulted in WEA's dropping the group from their roster by the following year.

● ALBUMS: *Exciter* (WEA 1983) ★★.

Exciters

Formed in the Jamaica district of Queens, New York City, USA, this aptly named group, which included sole male Herb Rooney (b. New York City, USA) alongside Brenda Reid, Carol Johnson and Lillian Walker, first came to prominence with the vibrant 'Tell Him', a US Top 5 hit in 1962 (also a hit in the UK for **Billie Davis** in 1963). Produced by **Leiber And Stoller** and written by **Bert Berns** (under his pseudonym Bert Russell), the single's energy established the pattern for subsequent releases. 'Do Wah Diddy Diddy' (later a hit by **Manfred Mann**) and 'He's Got The Power' took elements from both uptown soul and the all-female group genre, but later singles failed fully to exploit this powerful combination. The group had lesser hits with 'I Want You To Be My Boy' (1965), a revival of 'A Little Bit Of Soap' (1966) and 'You Don't Know What You're Missing (Till It's Gone)' (1969), but failed to recapture the verve of those first releases. They re-entered the UK charts in 1975 with 'Reaching For The Best'. Ronnie Pace and Skip McPhee later replaced Johnson and Walker, while Rooney and Reid (his wife) had a minor 1978 hit as Brenda And Herb, releasing one album in 1979, *In Heat Again*.

● ALBUMS: *Tell Him* (United Artists 1963) ★★★, *The Exciters* (Roulette 1965) ★★★, *Caviar And Chitlins* (RCA Victor 1969) ★★, *Black Beauty* (Today 1971) ★★, *Heaven Is Wherever You Are* (20th Century 1976) ★★.

● COMPILATIONS: *Tell Him* (EMI 1991) ★★★, *Reaching For The Best* (Hot 1995) ★★★, *Something To Shout About* (Sequel 1995) ★★★.

● FILMS: *Bikini Beach* (1964).

Executives

This six-piece band had a rapid rise as a live act in Sydney, Australia, in 1966. Featuring two fine vocalists in Carole King and Gino Cunico, and backed by four musicians who could play 30 different instruments between them, they were able to produce a sophisticated, varied pop sound. Between 1967 and 1968 they recorded eight singles and three albums. Initially their set was composed entirely of cover versions, such as the hit singles 'My Aim Is To Please You', 'Sit Down I Think I Love You' and 'Windy Day', but self-penned numbers were slowly introduced. In 1969, the band moved to the USA and spent a year composing new material in California at Kama Sutra/**Buddah Records**. The name was changed to Inner Sense, more appropriate for the 'flower-power' era, but the band faded. Guitarist Ray Burton and Cunico released an unsuccessful joint album; Cunico following with two more obscure albums. Burton penned 'I Am Woman' for fellow Australian expatriate **Helen Reddy**, and then returned home to join Ayers Rock before embarking on a solo career. King and fellow Executives member, husband Brian, formed a new group, Transition. Carole King featured in the stage play *Nuclear* and its album of 1972, leading to a re-formation of the Executives with herself and several other members from the show's cast. Three singles for **Polydor Records** in the mid-70s were unsuccessful but the band soldiered on for several more years.

● ALBUMS: *The Executives* (Festival 1968) ★★, *On Bandstand* (Festival 1968) ★★★, *Now* (Summit 1968) ★★.

● COMPILATIONS: *The Happening World Of The Executives* (Festival 1989) ★★★.

Exies

This radio friendly alternative rock band originates from Los Angeles, California, USA, and draws inspiration from some of the leading US rock acts of the 90s, including the **Foo Fighters** and the **Stone Temple Pilots**. The band formed in 1997, when vocalist/guitarist Scott Stevens hooked up with bass player Freddy Herrera and drummer Thom Sullivan. Taking their name from a phrase **John Lennon** used to describe art students (abbreviated existentialists), the trio's original plan was to launch a unit sonically patterned after the 60s British Invasion. Second guitarist David Walsh was enlisted soon after to beef up the band's sound, as they adopted a more modern approach. Signed to the indie label Ultimatum, the Exies issued their self-titled album in 2000. Later in the year, Sullivan left the band and was replaced by Dennis Wolfe.

On the strength of their debut album, the Exies came to the attention of producer Matt Serletic, who took them under his wing and got them a major label recording contract with **Virgin Records**. The Exies' follow-up, *Inertia*, was boosted by the radio success of the single 'My Goddess'.

● ALBUMS: *The Exies* (Ultimatum 2000) ★★★, *Inertia* (Virgin 2003) ★★★.

Exile

Formed in Berea, Kentucky, USA, in 1963 as the Exiles, Exile first reached the pop charts in the late 70s before changing musical direction and becoming one of the most successful country bands of the 80s. They toured with the **Dick Clark** Caravan Of Stars in 1965 as back-up band for artists including **Brian Hyland** and **Tommy Roe**. In the late 60s, they recorded for Date Records and **Columbia Records**, and in the early 70s for SSS International, Date, Curb and Wooden Nickel. In 1973, they changed their name to Exile and in 1977, recording for **Atco Records**, they had their first chart single. Following a switch to **Warner Brothers Records**, Exile had a number 1 pop hit with 'Kiss You All Over', in 1978. After two more pop chart singles they switched to country. The group's membership in 1978, when they had their first hit, was J.P. Pennington (b. 22 January 1949, Berea, Kentucky, USA; guitar/vocals), Buzz Cornelison (keyboards), Les Taylor (b. 27 December 1948, Oneida, Kentucky, USA; guitar/vocals), Marlon Hargis (b. 13 May 1949, Somerset, Kentucky, USA; keyboards/vocals), Sonny LeMaire (bass/vocals) and Steve Goetzman (b. 1 September 1950, Louisville, Kentucky, USA; drums).

Exile's second, and more lucrative, career as a country group began in 1983 (by which time Cornelison had left). The first country chart single, 'High Cost Of Leaving', reached number 27, but was followed by four successive number 1 country singles in 1984: 'Woke Up In Love', 'I Don't Want To Be A Memory', 'Give Me One More Chance' and 'Crazy For Your Love'. There were six further number 1 country singles by 1987: 'She's A Miracle', 'Hang On To Your Heart', 'I Could

Get Used To You', 'It'll Be Me', 'She's Too Good To Be True' and 'I Can't Get Close Enough'. Hargis was replaced by Lee Carroll (b. 27 January 1953, Glasgow, Kentucky, USA) in 1985 and Pennington left in 1989, replaced by Paul Martin (b. 22 December 1962, Winchester, Kentucky, USA). The group signed to **Arista Records** in 1989 with a noticeable decline in commercial success. They were dropped by the label in 1993 and broke up soon afterwards, but a new version with Pennington and Taylor was on the road in 1996.

● ALBUMS: *Exile* (Wooden Nickel 1973) ★★★★, *Mixed Emotions* (Epic 1978) ★★★, *All There Is* (Epic 1979) ★★★, *Don't Leave Me This Way* (Epic 1980) ★★★, *Heart And Soul* (Epic 1981) ★★★, *Exile* (Epic 1983) ★★★, *Kentucky Hearts* (Epic 1984) ★★, *Hang On To Your Heart* (Epic 1985) ★★, *Shelter From The Night* (Epic 1987) ★★★, *Still Standing* (Arista 1990) ★★★★, *Justice* (Arista 1991) ★★★.

● COMPILATIONS: *The Best Of Exile* (Curb 1985) ★★★★, *Exile's Greatest Hits* (Epic 1986) ★★★, *The Complete Collection* (Curb 1991) ★★★★, *Super Hits* (Epic 1993) ★★★.

Exist Dance

90s Los Angeles, USA–based trance/techno label run by Tom Chasteen and Mike Kandel, covering artists like Merge (whose 'You Move Me' was their debut release), Tranquility Bass ('They Came In Peace'), High Lonesome Sound System ('Love Night', 'Were Go', 'Waiting For The Lights'), Eden Transmission ('I'm So High'), Odyssey 2000 ('The Odyssey'), Voodoo Transmission ('Voodoo Fire'), Up Above The World ('Up Above The World') and Freaky Chakra ('Freaky Chakra'). The latter was the first outside production to emerge on the label, but like the rest of their catalogue it was distinguished by an approach that cross-fertilized dance rhythms with tribal chants and environmental effects. Chasteen and Kandel met at art school, and began recording *avant garde* electronica, heavy with loops and repetition, which is again visible in their modern output.

Exit-13

This environmentally themed 'grind rock' band from Pennsylvania, USA, was launched in 1994 as a side-project for **Brutal Truth** bass player Dan Lilker. Joined by Relapse Records co-owner Bill Yurkiewicz (vocals/samples), guitarist Steve O'Donnell and former Brutal Truth drummer Scott Lewis, the band's debut fused traditional doom metal with blues and jazz. An unlikely combination, it saw the record described in one quarter as mixing '**Stevie Ray Vaughan** and early **Napalm Death**'. Yurkiewicz's lyrics continued to explore desperate themes on *Ethos Musick*—the opening track, subtly titled 'Societally Provoked Genocidal Contemplation', opened with the line 'This whole world is fucking sick', before concluding its first verse with 'Insanity frees my mind to wonder, I gleefully ponder humanity's murder.' Elsewhere the band ruminated further on the human race's capacity for self-degradation and cruelty, and the lasting effect of industrial activities on the planet. It certainly provided an intriguing contrast to hear 60s-style idealism braced against some of the 90s most fearsome noise. A follow-up set continued in 'hemp-fuelled hedonist' vein, though just as interesting was a further side-project, this time featuring Yurkiewicz, O'Donnell, Lilker, Rich Hoak (drums) and Bliss Blood (**Pain Teens**). The project, titled *Smoking Songs*, saw the ensemble re-create jazz and blues standards of the 30s and 40s.

● ALBUMS: *Ethos Musick* (Relapse/Nuclear Blast 1994) ★★★, *Didactic Grind* (Relapse/Nuclear Blast 1995) ★★, with Bliss Blood *Smoking Songs* (Relapse 1996) ★★.

Exodus

Formed in San Francisco, California, USA, in 1982, Exodus were one of the earliest thrash metal bands. Their first line-up included **Metallica** guitarist Kirk Hammett, though he did not record with the band. Their first album was a landmark in the thrash arena, with a highly aggressive musical and lyrical approach, dealing with all manner of extremes and brutalities. It was recorded by the line-up of Paul Baloff (d. 31 January 2002; vocals), Gary Holt (guitar), Rick Hunolt (guitar), Rob McKillop (bass) and Tom Hunting (drums). Vocalist Steve Sousa replaced Baloff (who formed Piranha) for *Pleasures Of The Flesh*, which was marginally more mellow, but still a daunting proposition. Even after the departure of Hunting, who was replaced by John Tempesta (b. 1964, New York City, USA), Exodus continued to record worthy material, but lacked the commercial success of contemporaries such as Metallica and **Anthrax**. They refused to compromise or waver from their straightforward thrash style, and managed to maintain a level of popularity sufficient to gain a major label record contract. However, their own exodus was confirmed in 1992 after the aptly named *Force Of Habit* saw them banging their heads against brick walls. The band briefly reunited in 1997 for a live album.

● ALBUMS: *Bonded By Blood* (Music For Nations 1985) ★★★, *Pleasures Of The Flesh* (Music For Nations 1987) ★★★, *Fabulous Disaster* (Music For Nations 1989) ★★, *Impact Is Imminent* (Capitol 1990) ★★★, *Good Friendly Violent Fun* (Roadrunner 1991) ★★★, *Force Of Habit* (Roadrunner 1992) ★★★, *Another Lesson In Violence* (Century Media 1997) ★★★.

● COMPILATIONS: *The Best Of Exodus: Lessons In Violence* (Music For Nations 1992) ★★★.

Experimental

US label based in Broadway, New York City, USA, noted for its **deep house**, **trance** and **acid house** releases. The roster included the dark, Euro-flavoured house of Big Dreams, the hard house of The Rising Sons and the effusive deep groove of Symphony Of Love. The operation was masterminded by Damon Wild, who names each of his releases after their catalogue number. Hence, 'EX17' by Bio Dreams, 'EX19' by the Lazer Worshippers and 'EX22' by Diffusions. He started DJing in the mid-80s, and was once half of the team behind Toxic Two's 'Rave Generator'. Experimental is part of New York's Northcott stable (run by **Tommy Musto**), which also includes the Sub-Urban imprint. However, Wild departed from Experimental, amicably, in March 1994, setting up the Synewave label with Tim Taylor, releasing material including Equinox's 'Pollox'.

Experimental Pop Band

The appropriately titled Experimental Pop Band originated from Bristol, England, and was founded in 1995 by Davey Woodward (b. Avonmouth, Bristol, Avon, England; vocals/guitar) and Chris Galvin (b. 1959, d. 22 December 1998; bass). The duo were previously members of **Brilliant Corners**, which

issued several underrated albums during the 80s. Much harder to pin down musically than its predecessor, the Experimental Pop Band was compared to artists as diverse as **Burt Bacharach**, **Beck** and the **Velvet Underground**, as they began issuing albums in the late 90s. The duo released several singles, EPs and compilation tracks, most of which were included on the 1997 compilation, *Woof*, that was proceeded by their debut, *Discgrotesque*. The following year was spent working on their second effort, *Homesick*, but before the album could be released, the Experimental Pop Band's future was thrust into doubt when Galvin was diagnosed with cancer. The bass player died in December 1998 (just as the album was completed), resulting in the bittersweet release of *Homesick* in 1999. Instead of giving up, Woodward opted to carry on with new members, including Keith Bailey (drums/percussion) and Joe Rooney (keyboards), and issued a third studio release in 2001, *Tracksuit Trilogy*.

● ALBUMS: *Discgrotesque* (Swarf Finger 1997) ★★★★, *Homesick* (Swarf Finger 1999) ★★★, *Tracksuit Trilogy* (City Slang 2001) ★★★, *Tarmac & Flames* (Cooking Vinyl 2004) ★★★.

● COMPILATIONS: *Woof* (Swarf Finger 1997) ★★★★.

Exploding White Mice

This hard-hitting guitar band was formed in Adelaide, Australia, in early 1985, and featured Jeff Stephens (lead guitar), Paul Gilchrist (vocals) and Giles Barrow (rhythm guitar). Their style drew influences from the tough Detroit sound of the early **Stooges** with just a hint of **Ramones**-style 'dumb fun'. In fact they took their name from the laboratory rodents that featured in the Ramones' movie *Rock 'N' Roll High School*. Their debut recording featured three originals and three cover versions, including 'Pipeline' and a burning version of **Bo Diddley**'s 'Let The Kids Dance', and indicated a young band with considerable talent. Exploding White Mice quickly developed a huge live reputation and their 1987 double a-sided single, **John Kongos**' 'He's Gonna Step On You Again', should have broken them to a wider audience. However, another version by the seasoned cover band Party Boys received more attention. Their first full-length album proved them to be one of the finest trash pop bands in the country. On *Exploding White Mice* the band developed their pop sensibilities to the point where commercial acceptance became a distinct possibility.

● ALBUMS: *Brute Force & Ignorance* (Festival 1988) ★★★, *Exploding White Mice* (Normal 1990) ★★★.

Exploited

This abrasive and unruly Scottish punk quartet was formed in East Kilbride in 1980 by vocalist Wattie Buchan and guitarist 'Big John' Duncan. Recruiting drummer Dru Stix (b. Drew Campbell) and bass player Gary McCormick, they signed to the Secret Records label the following year. Specializing in two-minute blasts of high-speed blue vitriol, they released their first album, *Punk's Not Dead*, in 1981. Lyrically they sketched out themes such as war, corruption, unemployment and police brutality, amid a chaotic blur of crashing drums and flailing guitar chords. The band quickly become entrenched in their own limited musical and philosophical ideology, and earned themselves a certain low-life notoriety. Songs such as 'Fuck A Mod', for example, set youth tribe against youth tribe without any true rationale.

'Sid Vicious Was Innocent', meanwhile, deserves no comment whatsoever. Nevertheless, they were the only member of the third generation punk set to make it onto BBC Television's *Top Of The Pops*, with 1981's 'Dead Cities'. Continuing to release material on a regular basis, they have retained a small, but ever-declining, cult following. The line-ups have fluctuated wildly, with Duncan going on to join **Goodbye Mr. Mackenzie** and, very nearly, **Nirvana**, while Buchan remained in place. The diminutive but thoroughly obnoxious lead singer, with a multi-coloured mohican haircut, strikes an oddly anachronistic figure today as he presides over his dubious musical curio.

● ALBUMS: *Punk's Not Dead* (Secret 1981) ★★★, *On Stage* (Superville 1981) ★★★, *Troops Of Tomorrow* (Secret 1982) ★★★, *Let's Start A War (Said Maggie One Day)* (Combat/Pax 1983) ★★★, *Horror Epics* (Combat/Konnexion 1985) ★★★, *Live At The Whitehouse* (Combat Core 1985) ★★, *Death Before Dishonour* (Rough Justice 1989) ★★, *The Massacre* (Rough Justice 1991) ★★, *Beat The Bastards* (Rough Justice 1996) ★★, *Fuck The System* (DreamCatcher 2003) ★★.

● COMPILATIONS: *Totally Exploited* (Dojo 1984) ★★, *Live On The Apocalypse Now Tour '81* (Chaos 1985) ★★★, *Live And Loud!!* (Link 1987) ★★, *Inner City Decay* (Snow 1987) ★★★, *On Stage 91/Live At The Whitehouse 1985* (Dojo 1991) ★★, *The Singles Collection* (Cleopatra 1993) ★★★, *Dead Cities* (Harry May 2000) ★★★, *Punk Singles And Rarities* (Captain Oi! 2001) ★★★, *25 Years Of Anarchy And Chaos* (Dream Catcher 2004) ★★★.

● DVD/VIDEOS: *Live At The Palm Cove* (Jettisoundz 1983), *1983–87* (Jettisoundz 1987), *Sexual Favours* (Jettisoundz 1987), *Live In Japan* (Jettisoundz 1991), *Live In Buenos Aires* (Jettisoundz 1993), *Rock & Roll Outlaws* (Jettisoundz 1995).

Explorer

New Jersey, USA, band Explorer, formed by Lennie Rizzo (vocals), Kevin Kennedy (guitar), Eddie Lavolpe (guitar), Johnny G. (bass) and Mike Moyer (drums), are symptomatic of the creative nadir experienced by heavy metal by the late 80s. The material on their two albums distilled elements from major sellers such as **Iron Maiden**, particularly that group's reliance on high-pitched vocals and virtuoso guitar, without ever stamping an original identity on any of their songs. As a result, Explorer's *Symphonies Of Steel* and *Beg, Borrowed And Steal* (a dangerous title given a series of reviews that chastised them for being too derivative) were quickly consigned to the bargain bins by record retailers.

● ALBUMS: *Symphonies Of Steel* (HHH 1984) ★★, *Beg, Borrowed And Steal* (Black Dragon 1987) ★★.

Explosions In The Sky

Emerging from Texas in the early years of the new millennium, this US quartet creates instrumental post-rock music that is the equal in ambition and scope of recordings by the more widely known **Godspeed You Black Emperor!** and **Mogwai**.

Midland, Texas, natives Michael James (bass), Munaf Rayani (guitar) and Mark Smith (guitar) first met up in Austin in the late 90s, and their plans for a band came to fruition in 1999 when they met drummer Chris Hrasky (b. Illinois, USA). The quartet initially played under the moniker Breaker Morant and made their recording debut in July 1999 for college radio station KVRX's *Local Live* show. The track 'Remember Me

As A Time Of Day' later appeared on a compilation released by the station. The quartet subsequently changed their name to Explosions In The Sky, a moniker that was allegedly inspired by a remark made by Hrasky about the noise of fireworks downtown on the night the band recorded their first track. They made their debut in 2000 with the locally distributed *How Strange, Innocence*. The quartet was also captured on film rehearsing early versions of several tracks from this album, with the footage appearing on the Austin Film Festival award-winning short *Cicadas*.

Explosions In The Sky's debut album caught the attention of Portland, Oregon–based independent Temporary Residence, who signed the band and released their second album, 2001's *Those Who Tell The Truth Shall Die, Those Who Tell The Truth Shall Live Forever*. Sharing a love of lengthy album and song titles with their Canadian counterparts Godspeed You Black Emperor!, the quartet lived up to their title with a dynamic six-track album that moved seamlessly between quiet guitar interludes and crashing squalls of hard rock. The closing 'With Tired Eyes, Tired Minds, Tired Souls, We Slept' punctuated its 12-minute running time with epic crescendos of distorted guitars. The album's artwork, featuring an angel and a bi-plane flying over a warning declaring 'This plane will crash tomorrow', prompted talk of eerie coincidences after the World Trade Center was destroyed a few days after its release. The follow-up, 2003's *Earth Is Not A Cold Dead Place*, turned down the volume a notch, making stately progress through its five-track running order with melodic guitar lines and washes of percussion to the fore.

● ALBUMS: *How Strange, Innocence* (Own Label 2000) ★★★, *Those Who Tell The Truth Shall Die, Those Who Tell The Truth Shall Live Forever* (Temporary Residence 2001) ★★★★, *Earth Is Not A Cold Dead Place* (Temporary Residence/Bella Union 2003) ★★★★, *How Strange Innocence* (Temporary Residence 2005) ★★★.

Export

This UK rock band was formed in 1980 by former **Hardstuff** vocalist Harry Shaw and guitarist Steve Morris. Enlisting the services of bass player Chris Alderman and drummer Lou Rosenthal, they specialized in Americanized AOR. Their material was characterized by note-perfect harmonies, sterling guitar work and infectious hooklines similar to that of **Kansas**, **Starz** and **REO Speedwagon**. After a well-received self-titled debut in 1981, they were picked up by Epic Records, who recognized their enormous potential. Two albums were delivered, with Lance Quinn at the production helm for 1986's *Living In Fear Of A Private Eye*. Surprisingly, the band failed to take off in the USA and Epic dropped them owing to poor sales figures. Steve Morris produced Torino's debut album in 1987, while Export continued to search for a (not forthcoming) new contract.

● ALBUMS: *Export* (His Masters Vice 1980) ★★, *Contraband* (Epic 1984) ★★, *Living In Fear Of A Private Eye* (Epic 1986) ★★.

Express

b. Simon Francis, *c.*1967, England. A bright new hip-hop talent from Northampton, England, Express has been rapping since 1981. However, his musical path took a different slant when he joined a local industrial dance unit. Eventually, following a major label débâcle, he and his partner Stuart left London to regroup. Together they elected to keep their music independent, setting up their own imprint, Expressive Records, to this end. In October 1993 Express' first record, the *Hit The Hook Heavy* EP, arrived. It quickly attained cult popularity, not least for its references to television fare like *Inspector Morse* and the absence of Chris Waddle from the England football squad. Even Ian Paisley got a namecheck, as the **New Musical Express** pronounced its verdict with a Single Of The Week award. Other songs also contained references to the footballer Andy Cole. However, if anyone had marked Express as a novelty act he brought about a quick rethink with 1994's follow-up, 'Gone To The Dogs'. This, as the title suggested, was a young black man's reflection on the election of a British National Party politician to the Isle Of Dogs (London) council.

Expresso Bongo (film musical)

This 1959 comedy feature began life as a stage play loosely based on the rise of British rock 'n' roll star **Tommy Steele**. Written by Wolf Mankowitz and directed by Val Guest, *Expresso Bongo* starred Laurence Harvey as an unscrupulous Soho agent, determined to make his protégé, ably played by **Cliff Richard**, into an international success. The film manages to convey some of the exploitative nature of early pop and the nascent teenage subculture spearheaded by the legendary 2I's coffee bar. However, the cynicism of Mankowitz meant the funny moments lacked warmth and the film now merely offers period charm. Although mild-mannered by the standards of today, *Expresso Bongo* was given an X-certificate, confirming the moody, threat-to-society image Richard initially bore. It did nothing to hinder his popularity, however, and in 1960 a soundtrack EP reached the number 14 position in the UK singles chart while the film's finest song, 'A Voice In The Wilderness', peaked at number 2.

Expresso Bongo (stage musical)

Considered by many to be 'the most important and original British musical of its time', *Expresso Bongo* opened at the Saville Theatre on 23 April 1958. The book, by Wolf Mankowitz and **Julian More**, was taken from a newspaper piece by Mankowitz, and is said to have been based on the true-life story of the young ex–merchant seaman Thomas Hicks. He had been discovered in 1956, playing the guitar and singing in a Soho coffee-bar called the 2I's, by his future manager John Kennedy. He, and the agent **Larry Parnes**, changed Hicks' name to **Tommy Steele**, and moulded him into Britain's first rock 'n' roller. In this show, Herbert Rudge (James Kenney) also is discovered at a trendy coffee-bar, but he is playing bongo drums, not guitar, hence his eventual stage name of Bongo Herbert. With the aid of a crafty agent, Johnnie (Paul Schofield), he quickly climbs the chart with 'Expresso Party', and then, just like Steele, shrewdly broadens his image, in Bongo's case with a magnificently ghastly hymn to his old mum, 'The Shrine On The Second Floor' ('There's a beautiful grey-haired Madonna/Who once taught me what life had in store'). The show was full of accurately drawn, colourful characters such as the stripper who wants to be a singer, Maisie King (**Millicent Martin**), a recording executive, Mr. Mayer (Meir Tzelniker), and a well-to-do, ageing actress, Dixie Collins (**Hy Hazell**), who gives Bongo a taste of the high life, and arranges for him to be represented by an 'establishment' agent. Johnnie cannot compete, looks around for new talent, and decides to promote Maisie as a

singer. The score, by **David Heneker** and Monty Norman, both of whom also collaborated on the lyrics with Julian More, was a match for the book. The songs were witty and satirical, including Bongo's wry 'Don't You Sell Me Down The River' and Johnnie's charting of his ups and downs with 'I've Never Had It So Good' and 'The Gravy Train', while Maisie ground her hips (and a good deal more) to 'Spoil The Child'. She also had two poignant ballads, 'Seriously' and 'I Am'. Dixie reflected on her life in and out of the theatre with the touching 'Time', and joined Johnnie and Mr. Mayer for 'Nothing Is For Nothing'. Opinions as to the show's value were mixed, and ran along the lines of 'an adult approach', 'wit, bite and topicality' and 'a raucous paeon of disgust aimed at the shoddy side of society'. It was certainly very different in style from that other British musical, **Sandy Wilson**'s *Valmouth* (set in an English spa town inhabited by centenarians), which came to the Lyric when *Expresso Bongo* closed after a run of 316 performances. Even then, the Tommy Steele connections continued: his brother, Colin Hicks, played the lead in the touring version of *Expresso Bongo*, and the show's co-composer and lyricist, Heneker, wrote the score for Steele's smash-hit musical **Half A Sixpence**, in 1963. The 1959 film of *Expresso Bongo* starred Laurence Harvey, **Cliff Richard**, Yolande Dolan and Sylvia Syms. Changes in the score resulted in the inclusion of 'A Voice In The Wilderness', written by **Norrie Paramor** and Bunny Lewis, which Richard took to number 2 in the UK chart.

Exquisites

Vocal group the Exquisites were formed in 1981 in Long Island, New York, USA, by former Gino And The Dells baritone Pete Chacona and tenor Bernie Festo, after Chacona had attended an audition for Festo's then group. Through local newspaper advertising, John O'Keefe (first tenor) and Bob Thomas (lead, ex-**Fascinations**) were recruited, while familial ties brought in bass singer George Chacona, Pete's brother. Rehearsing material by the **Moonglows**, **Flamingos** and **Harptones**, they set about performing at local shows and nostalgia rallies. When O'Keefe left to join the Teenchords in 1983, he was replaced on first tenor by Mike Paccione. Their first recording came in early 1985 when their version of the **Shirelles**' 'Dedicated To The One I Love' was released on Avenue D Records, followed by an update of the **El Dorados**' 'At My Front Door'. After sending a tape to local R&B revival disc jockey Don K. Reed's *Doo-Wop Shop* show in 1985, they found their version of the **Solitaires**' 'Walking Along' earn a regular slot as opening theme to the highly influential oldies programme. When Paccione departed in 1987, George Santiago (ex-**Eternals**) came on board, with the line-up also expanded by the arrival of Al Pretea (ex-**Dolphins**). A little later Zeke Suarez replaced Festo. The group embarked on sessions for their debut album in 1990 with Crystal Ball Records, recording versions of songs by the **Drifters**, **Jive Five** and El Dorados, as well as the doo-wop standard 'Over The Rainbow'.
● ALBUMS: *The Exquisites* (Crystal Ball 1991) ★★★.

Exterminator

The Xterminator (originally Exterminator) label is run by Philip 'Fatis' Burrell (b. Trenchtown, Kingston, Jamaica, West Indies). Burrell spent some of his early years in England before returning to Jamaica as a teenager. In 1984 he set up his Kings & Lions label. His first production, **Sugar Minott**'s 'More Dogs To The Bone', was released after encouragement from George Phang and Robbie Shakespeare. **King Tubby**'s Firehouse Crew performed on most of his recordings at either Dynamics or Music Works but **Sly And Robbie** played on *The Summit*, an early **dub** album. Burrell founded the Vena label in 1986. **Sanchez**, **Pinchers** and **Thriller U** all recorded some of their earliest works on it. Sampler albums from 1988 featured well-known artists such as **Gregory Isaacs**, **Charlie Chaplin** and **General Trees** alongside Burrell's new artists, Quench Aid, **Lukie D**, Conrad Crystal and **Daddy Freddie**, who released his debut, *Cater Fi She*, in 1989. **Frankie Paul** and **Red Dragon** also released hit tracks in that year, benefiting from the aggressive marketing of Burrell's new Exterminator imprint. Burrell's high-calibre roster in 1990/1 included artists such as **Ninjaman**, **Ini Kamoze** ('Hot Stepper'), **Cocoa Tea**, **Admiral Tibet**, **Tony Rebel** ('Real Rough'), Frankie Paul, Gregory Isaacs, **Beres Hammond** ('Emptiness Inside'), **Johnny Osbourne** and **Tiger. Capleton**'s 'Armshouse' (which spawned two version albums) marked the beginning of a run of exceptional releases during the next two years that ended with albums by Cocoa Tea, Sugar Minott, Pinchers, Sanchez, **Luciano** and Beres Hammond, whose *Full Attention* symbolized the pinnacle of a very creative period for Burrell. Between 1993 and 1994, **Dennis Brown**, **Yammie Bolo**, **Nadine Sutherland**, Cocoa Tea, **Buju Banton**, **General Degree**, **Chaka Demus And Pliers**, Singing Sweet, **Marcia Griffiths** and **Brian And Tony Gold** recorded fine material for Xterminator. The quality of Burrell's work remains immaculate, whether he is innovating with new hardcore beats or using classic rhythms.

● COMPILATIONS: various *Exterminator Volumes 1 & 2* (Exterminator 1988) ★★★★, *Turn On The Heat* (Exterminator 1989) ★★★★, *Exterminator Live Volumes 1 & 2* (Exterminator 1989) ★★★★, *Exterminator Presents* (Exterminator 1990) ★★★.

Extreme

This Boston, Massachusetts, USA, quartet comprised Gary Cherone (b. 26 July 1961, Malden, Massachusetts, USA; vocals), **Nuno Bettencourt** (b. 20 September 1966, Azores, Portugal; guitar), Pat Badger (b. 22 July 1967, Boston, Massachusetts, USA; bass) and Paul Geary (b. 24 July 1961, Medford, Massachusetts, USA; drums). The origins of the band can be traced to local act the Dream, whose sole six-track EP in 1983 featured Cherone and Geary. As Extreme, the original line-up found themselves on television in 1985 via a video clip for 'Mutha (Don't Wanna Go To School Today)', as part of an **MTV** competition, but it was the arrival of Bettencourt in 1986 and Badger the following year that boosted their career. A recording contract with **A&M Records** was quickly secured and the band made their vinyl debut with 'Play With Me' for the soundtrack to *Bill And Ted's Excellent Adventure*. The inevitable self-titled debut album followed. Encompassing elements of pop, metal, funk and blues, their songwriting powers were still in their infancy at this stage and although competent, the album met with widespread critical indifference. *Pornograffitti* was a stunning second release, being an ambitious concept affair, subtitled 'A Funked Up Fairy Tale'. 'Get The Funk Out' reached number 19 in the UK charts in June 1991, but the band had already broken through in America in March when the simple acoustic ballad 'More Than Words' topped the

charts. The song climbed to UK number 2 in July the same year. 'Hole Hearted' was their only other US success, reaching number 4 later that year, although they would continue to achieve Top 20 singles in the UK until 1995.

The band's music was now characterized by Bettencourt's innovative guitar playing, intelligent lyrics and a diverse style that transcended a variety of musical genres. Their appearance at the **Freddie Mercury** memorial concert in May 1992, which interrupted sessions for *III Sides To Every Story*, gave them considerable exposure beyond the heavy metal fraternity. Prior to the band's appearance at the **Donington Festival** in the summer of 1994, Mike Mangini (ex-**Annihilator**) replaced Paul Geary on drums. After the disappointing critical and commercial reaction to 1995's *Waiting For The Punchline*, Bettencourt announced plans to release a solo album through Colorblind, the label he formed through A&M. The band formally broke up in October 1996, with Cherone moving on to become lead singer with **Van Halen**. Cherone, Bettencourt and Geary later reunited in 2005 to play a number of live shows in Japan.

● ALBUMS: *Extreme* (A&M 1989) ★★★, *Pornograffitti* (A&M 1990) ★★★★, *III Sides To Every Story* (A&M 1992) ★★★, *Waiting For The Punchline* (A&M 1995) ★★.

● COMPILATIONS: *The Best Of Extreme: An Accidental Collication Of Atoms?* (A&M 1997) ★★★, *The Millennium Collection* (A&M 2002) ★★★, *The Collection* (Spectrum 2002) ★★★.

Extreme Noise Terror

A band whose name truly encapsulates their sound, Extreme Noise Terror formed in January 1985 and were signed by Manic Ears Records after their first ever gig. Their debut release was a split album with Chaos U.K., and although there were musical similarities, ENT, along with **Napalm Death**, were already in the process of twisting traditional punk influences into altogether different shapes. Along with the latter, they became the subject of disc jockey **John Peel**'s interest in 1987, recording a session (one of three) that would eventually see release on **Strange Fruit Records**. Afterwards, drummer Mick Harris, who had left Napalm Death to replace the band's original drummer Pig Killer, in turn departed, joining **Scorn**. His replacement was Stick (b. Tony Dickens), who joined existing members Dean Jones (vocals), Phil Vane (vocals) and Pete Hurley (guitar). Mark Bailey had by now replaced Mark Gardiner, who himself had replaced Jerry Clay, on bass. Touring in Japan preceded the release of *Phonophobia*, while continued Peel sessions brought the band to the attention of the **KLF**'s **Bill Drummond**. He asked them to record a version of the KLF's '3 A.M. Eternal', with the intention of the band's appearing on ***Top Of The Pops*** live at Christmas to perform the tune (BBC Television, however, decided this was not in the best interests of their audience), Eventually released as a limited edition single, the two bands' paths crossed again in 1992 when the KLF were invited to perform live at the 1992 BRIT Awards. This crazed event, which included the firing of blanks into the audience, has already passed into music industry legend.

Back on their own, 1993 saw Extreme Noise Terror touring widely, and the band signed to Earache Records the following year. By this time, the line-up had expanded to include Lee Barrett (bass; also Disgust) replacing Bailey, Ali Firouzbakht (lead guitar) and original member Pig Killer on drums. Together they released *Retro-bution*, ostensibly a compilation, but nevertheless featuring the new line-up on re-recorded versions of familiar material. Pig Killer was replaced by Was (ex-**Cradle Of Filth**) shortly afterwards, but a greater shock was the departure of Vane to join Napalm Death. That band's departed vocalist Mark 'Barney' Greenway was brought in to help record *Damage 381*. Bizarrely, Vane and Greenway then swapped places once more.

● ALBUMS: split with Chaos UK *Radioactive* (Manic Ears 1985) ★★, *A Holocaust In Your Head* (Hurt 1987) ★★, *The Peel Sessions* (Strange Fruit 1990) ★★★, *Phonophobia* (Vinyl Japan 1992) ★★, *Retro-bution* (Earache 1995) ★★★, *Damage 381* (Earache 1997) ★★★, *Being And Nothing* (Candlelight 2001) ★★★.

● DVD/VIDEOS: *From One Extreme To The Other* (Jettisoundz 1989).

EYC

US vocal pop band EYC, based in Los Angeles, California, comprise Damon Butler (b. Carson, California, USA), Dave Loeffler (b. Bellflower, California, USA) and Trey Parker (b. Auburn, Alabama, USA). Compressing highly commercial romantic songs with elements drawn from the hip-hop and soul traditions, EYC secured a string of single successes in the mid-90s (with most of their popularity centred on the UK). They released their first single, 'Feelin' Alright', in November 1993, and saw it rise to number 16 in the UK charts, selling over 60,000 copies. Their name is an acronym for Express Yourself Clearly, later the title of their debut album, and was chosen 'with the idea of creative self-determination in mind'. Butler and Parker first met while working as back-up dancers on a national concert tour. They were later joined by Loeffler in the triad, and began to record demos together. As a consequence the group were invited to perform their hastily arranged set at the Teen Idol Festival in Japan, one of three US bands invited. On their return they channelled their resources into recording a video clip that could show off their dance moves in preference to further demos. After a live audition the band were signed by Gasoline Alley Records. They went on to support slots with **Whitney Houston** in Europe and with **Kenny Thomas** and **Monie Love** as joint headliners in the UK. December 1993 brought the band the *Smash Hits* Roadshow's 'Best Newcomer' award, before performing live at Wembley Arena. The group's 10-track debut album was released in 1994, and included the club hit 'Get Some', produced by the **Boo-Yaa T.R.I.B.E.**, as well as promotional single 'Number One'. The album rose to number 14 in the UK charts in the week of its release, before the band set out on a European tour with **East 17**. With their fanbase constantly growing, EYC found further success with November 1994's 'One More Chance'.

● ALBUMS: *Express Yourself Clearly* (Gasoline Alley 1994) ★★★.

Eyden, Bill

b. 4 May 1930, Hounslow, Middlesex, England, d. 15 October 2004, England. Eyden first played drums as a member of an Army Cadet Corps band. Later, he began playing with local semi-professional dance and jazz groups where his abilities were first noticed. He was hired by front-rank dance bands such as those led by **Roy Fox** and **Harry Roy**, and later worked with the Ivor Kirchin band. Throughout these years, however, Eyden retained a preference for jazz, especially bop, and became a member of the house rhythm section at London's Studio 51. Among the musicians with whom he worked during this stage of his career was **Tubby Hayes**. In 1957 he was a member of the Jazz Couriers, the very highly regarded band co-led by Hayes and **Ronnie Scott**. Concurrently with his work with Hayes, which also included spells in the tenor saxophonist's quintet, Eyden was also in demand in other fields including R&B, rock and pop. Among musicians with whom he worked were **Long John Baldry**, **Georgie Fame** (for some years he was a member of the singer-organist's Blue Flames), **Wee Willie Harris** and **Alexis Korner**. Eyden also became a regular at Scott's own club, playing in the house band with **Stan Tracey**. Eyden was also active in the recording studios and in 1967 was brought in to a **Procol Harum** session. Reportedly, the session producer was unhappy with the regular drummer's playing on the date, which included what would become the band's big hit, 'A Whiter Shade Of Pale', and hired Eyden, at flat rate, to take over.

Through the late 60s and into the 70s, Eyden played drums in pit bands for several West End shows, including *Promises, Promises* and *Bubbling Brown Sugar*. He retained his jazz and roc and connections, playing with the Bebop Preservation Society and **Spike Robinson**, and he was one of the trio of drummers that worked in **Charlie Watts**' 30-something-piece big band, appearing on record and on tour in the UK and USA. In addition to his performance work, Eyden was also active as a teacher.

Eyehategod

Based in New Orleans, Louisiana, USA, Eyehategod was formed in 1988 by Jimmy Bower (guitar) and Joe LaCaze (drums). The original line-up was completed by Michael Williams (vocals) and Steve Dale (bass). Producing a sound that marries their two greatest influences, **Black Flag** and **Black Sabbath**, the most distinctive element of the band's sound is Williams' deliberately monotonous vocals, which act as a supplementary instrument rather than a singing voice in the conventional sense. The band initially perceived their job to be one of annoying people, but over the course of two full studio albums in the early 90s they refined their technique into a convincing and unremittingly intense soundtrack. The second of these, 1993's *Take As Needed For Pain*, featured additional guitarist Brian Patton and new bass player Mark Schultz. The band members also became well known for their outside activities. Williams is a former writer for US rock magazine *Metal Maniacs*, while Patton has concurrently worked with **Soilent Green** over several years. Joe LaCaze works with Japanese music and regularly releases underground cassettes of his work. Jimmy Bower is a member of **Down** and **Crowbar**.

After a three-year gap, when many presumed the band had sundered, Eyehategod returned with new bass player Vince LeBlanc and their third and best album, 1996's *Dopesick*. This was produced, without charge, by Billy Anderson (**Neurosis**, **Sleep**) and continued to mine the band's favourite subjects—alienation, pain and depression, informed by the rough neighbourhoods of New Orleans in which the members grew up. The members then concentrated on outside interests once again, but reconvened in the late 90s to record a number of 7-inch singles for independent outlets. These were later collected on the 2000 compilation *Southern Discomfort*. The same year's *Confederacy Of Ruined Lives* featured new bass player Daniel Nick.

● ALBUMS: *In The Name Of Suffering* (Century Media 1992) ★★, *Take As Needed For Pain* (Century Media 1993) ★★★, *Dopesick* (Century Media 1996) ★★★★, *Confederacy Of Ruined Lives* (Century Media 2000) ★★★.
● COMPILATIONS: *Southern Discomfort* (Century Media 2000) ★★, *10 Years Of Abuse (And Still Broke)* (Century Media 2001) ★★★, *Preaching The End-Time Message* (Emetic 2005) ★★★.
● DVD/VIDEOS: *Tokyo Japan March 19th, 2002* (Press Pause Media 2005).

Eyeless In Gaza

Taking their name from Aldous Huxley's famous novel, this UK outfit is the brainchild of vocalists/musicians **Martyn Bates** and Peter Becker. Known for their tortured vocals and impressive arranging skills, the band established a reasonable following on the independent circuit with their 1981 debut, *Photographs As Memories*. Several more albums for **Cherry Red Records** saw them alternate between a melodramatic and meandering style that increasingly veered towards improvisation.

Bates subsequently teamed up with former **Primitives** bass player Steve Gullaghan in Hungry I, also working solo. Eyeless In Gaza re-formed in 1992, releasing an album titled *Fabulous Library* the following year as a trio comprising Bates, Becker and chanteuse Elizabeth S. Reverting to the original two-piece line-up later in 1993, the two recorded and toured Europe and the USA extensively with self-styled 'performance poet' Anne Clark, also collaborating with Derek Jarman film soundtrack composer Simon Fisher Turner. In 1995, they relaunched the Ambivalent Scale imprint in co-operation with World Serpent Distribution. Their own releases on the label included *Bitter Apples* and *All Under Leaves, The Leaves Of Life*. The first Eyeless In Gaza album in almost five years, *Song Of The Beautiful Wanton*, was released by the US label Soleilmoon in 2000.

● ALBUMS: *Photographs As Memories* (Cherry Red 1981) ★★★, *Caught In Flux* (Cherry Red 1981) ★★★, *Pale Hands I Loved So Well* (Uniton 1982) ★★★, *Drumming The Beating Heart* (Cherry Red 1982) ★★★, *Rust Red September* (Cherry Red 1983) ★★★, *Back From The Rains* (Cherry Red 1986) ★★★, *Fabulous Library* (Orchid 1993) ★★★, *Saw You In Reminding Pictures* (Hive-Arc 1994) ★★★, *Bitter Apples* (A-Scale 1995) ★★★, *All Under Leaves, The Leaves Of Life* (A-Scale 1996) ★★★, *Song Of The Beautiful Wanton* (Soleilmoon 2000) ★★★.
● COMPILATIONS: *Kodak Ghosts Run Amok* (Cherry Red 1987) ★★★, *Transience Blues* (Integrity 1990) ★★★, *Orange Ice & Wax Crayons* (Cherry Red 1992) ★★★, *Voice: The Best Of Eyeless In Gaza (Recollections 1980–1986)* (Cherry Red 1993) ★★★★, *Sixth Sense: The Singles Collection* (Cherry Red 2002) ★★★★.
● DVD/VIDEOS: *Street Lamps N'Snow* (Visionary 1994).

Eyes

Formed in Ealing, London, England, in 1965, the Eyes were one of the era's most exciting 'pop-art' acts. Founders Terry Nolder (vocals), Chris Lovegrove (guitar), Phil Heatly (guitar) and Barry Allchin (bass) were all previously members of aspiring beat groups Dave Russell And The Renegades and Gerry Hart And The Hartbeats. They forged the Eyes upon securing drummer Bryan Corcoran and were signed by **Mercury Records** soon afterwards. Released in

November 1965, 'When The Night Falls' is a doomy, atmospheric single marked by a slow tempo, unorthodox, 'scratchy' guitar breaks and Holder's semi-spoken vocal. It was succeeded by 'My Immediate Pleasure', a brash composition encapsulating the concurrent Mod ethos. These singles were later combined on a much-prized EP, *The Arrival Of The Eyes*. Having failed to chart with original material, the Eyes opted to record cover versions for later releases. Meritorious interpretations of the **Everly Brothers**' 'Man With Money' and the **Beatles**' 'Good Day Sunshine' (both 1966) followed, but they lacked the innovative features of their predecessors. The Eyes were then persuaded to record *A Tribute To The Rolling Stones*, a collection of **Mick Jagger/Keith Richards**' songs and associated material issued on a budget-priced imprint and credited to the Pupils. By this point Heatly had been replaced by Steve Valentine but, sensing their career was over, the Eyes split up in 1967. Nolder then formed the Entire Sioux Nation with future **Pink Fairies/Motörhead** guitarist Larry Wallis.

● ALBUMS: as the Pupils *A Tribute To The Rolling Stones* (Wing 1967) ★★.
● COMPILATIONS: *The Eyes: Blink* (Bam Caruso 1983) ★★★, *Scene But Not Heard* (Bam Caruso 1985) ★★★.

Eyes Adrift

The early-twenty-first century rock supergroup Eyes Adrift comprises Curt Kirkwood (b. 10 January 1959, Wichita Falls, Texas, USA; guitar/vocals), Krist Novoselic (b. 16 May 1965, Croatia, Yugoslavia; bass/vocals) and Bud Gaugh (b. Floyd Gaugh; drums), previously members of renowned alt rock outfits such as the **Meat Puppets**, **Nirvana** and **Sublime** (respectively). The trio formed in 2001, after Novoselic and Gaugh caught separate solo acoustic Kirkwood gigs, which resulted in both asking the guitarist if he would be interested in a jamming session. All three members congregated at Kirkwood's home base of Austin, Texas, and by the second day of rehearsals, Eyes Adrift was officially born. Eschewing Nirvana's angst punk and Sublime's ska style largely in favour of the Meat Puppets' sun-baked country rock, the trio played a series of live shows to an enthusiastic response, before returning back to the studio to lay down tracks for a debut recording. Signed to the **spinART Records** label, Eyes Adrift issued their self-titled debut to unanimously favourable reviews in September 2002.

● ALBUMS: *Eyes Adrift* (spinART 2002) ★★★.

Eyes Of Blue

Founded in Neath, Wales, by Ritchie Francis (bass/vocals), Gary Pickford Hopkins (vocals/guitar), Phil Ryan (keyboards), Ray Williams (guitar) and Wyndham Rees (drums), Eyes Of Blue started out as a soul revival band before gradually attuning their musical sensibilities to the emergent US west coast rock scene. They initially recorded two singles for **Deram Records**, 'Heart Trouble' and 'Supermarket Full Of Cans', in 1966 and 1967, but for their debut album moved to **Mercury Records**. The band covered two **Graham Bond** songs on the album and he also wrote the sleeve notes. *The Crossroads Of Time* was a satisfying mix of diverse musical influences, ranging from psychedelic and ethnic instrumentation to jazz and classical styles. However, their own songwriting suffered in comparison to Bond's songs and their cover version of the **Beatles**' 'Yesterday'. For their second album, 1969's reincarnation-themed *In Fields Of*

Ardath), they replaced their original drummer with John 'Pugwash' Weathers (b. 2 February 1947, Carmarthen, Glamorganshire, Wales; drums). The album featured their collaboration with **Quincy Jones**, 'Merry Go Round', which was included on the soundtrack to Jones' *Toy Grabbers* movie score, and the band itself was later seen on film in *Connecting Rooms*. Other tracks revealed a debt to the UK progressive rock movement, although another Bond cover, 'Spanish Blues', was present as continuity. It was the band's final release, although they did also record 1971's *Bluebell Wood* under the moniker Big Sleep. After their eventual demise, the band members scattered. Ryan joined **Man**, Weathers worked with **Pete Brown** and **Gentle Giant**, while Francis recorded a solo album.
● ALBUMS: *The Crossroads Of Time* (Mercury 1968) ★★★, *In Fields Of Ardath* (Mercury 1969) ★★.

Eyuphuro

This Mozambique group comprises Zena Bakar (b. Illa De Mozambique, Mozambique; vocals), Gino Abdul Remane (b. Illa De Mozambique, Mozambique; vocals/guitar), Chico Ventura (guitar), Mario Fernandes (bass), Mussa Abdul (percussion) and Belarmino Godeiros (percussion). The name Eyuphuro is the Makau word meaning whirlwind. The sextet, led by songwriters Bakar and Remane, all currently live in Nampula, Mozambique. Their songs cover various aspects of personal relationships set in the context of modern-day life in their home country. Love songs and philosophical lyrics are set against precise, very melodic electric guitar playing and sympathetic, sometimes almost hypnotic, percussion. *Mama Mosambiki*, the band's only work easily available in the Western world, was recorded in 1990 in Toronto, Canada, in conjunction with the WOMAD organization.
● ALBUMS: *Mama Mosambiki* (Real World 1990) ★★★.

Ezell, Will

b. 1896, Shreveport, Louisiana, USA. Ezell had a recording career that lasted from September 1927 to September 1929, and produced a total of 17 tracks including alternative takes. His fame rests not only on his outstanding piano work but on being one of the originators of boogie-woogie. His 'Pitchin' Boogie' was one of the earliest known uses of the term. In his role as 'house pianist' for Paramount Records he supplied musical support for artists such as **Lucille Bogan**, Blind Roosevelt Graves, Side-Wheel Sallie Duffie and Bertha Henderson and he is also rumoured to have worked for **Bessie Smith**. Although Ezell was well respected by contemporaries such as **Little Brother Montgomery** and **Cripple Clarence Lofton**, he seems to have fallen foul of the great Depression as nothing is known of him after his last appearance in a recording studio in 1931.
● COMPILATIONS: *Pitchin' Boogie* (Oldie Blues 1986) ★★★.

Ezio

This acoustic band based in Cambridge, England, are fronted by talented songwriter Ezio Lunedei (b. Italy), although much of their appeal can also be attributed to his larger-than-life stage partner and fellow guitarist, Booga (b. Mark Fowell, Kenya). It took the pair four years to gain a recording contract, after playing regular sets in minor Cambridge venues such as Flambards wine bar, where their residencies eventually excited a large and vociferous audience. While Ezio himself gradually crafted a repertoire of excellent songs that fit firmly in the classical singer-songwriter tradition, his onstage partnership with Booga brought the material to life. Stripping the sometimes maudlin but more often wry lyrics of their occasional austerity, Booga would regularly bump into his partner, poke his tongue out at selected members of the audience, or adapt a beer bottle to aid his frenetic, Latin-influenced guitar style.

In 1993 the duo won the Cambridge Band Competition (Lunedei had already taken the honour once before while part of Cambridge rock band Spiritwalk, who recorded one limited edition single). Having recorded a self-financed cassette, *The Angel Song*, in 1993 with a full band, including future **Gary Numan** drummer Richard Beazley and keyboard player Martin Randle, **Arista Records** swooped for their signatures. Their debut was a seamless exposition of tried and tested songs, predominantly odes to daydreams and broken hearts, since the record company elected not to include the more humorous material with which they would frequently break up live sets. Problems with relationships remained Ezio's chief source of inspiration: 'When I have a particularly heartbreaking time, instead of consoling me, Booga just rubs his hands together and says "just think of all the songs we can get out of it!"'

Following the release of 1997's *Diesel Vanilla*, Ezio and Booga began performing as a four piece with Lidia Cascarino (bass) and Peter Van Hooke (drums). The latter musician, a seasoned session veteran, had produced *Diesel Vanilla*. The new line-up returned to Van Hooke's studio to record *Higher*, which was released through Ezio's own Salami imprint in the UK. Ezio also gained minor notoriety when Prime Minister Tony Blair chose their track 'Cancel Today' as one of his favourite songs when asked by the *Sydney Morning Herald* to name his desert island records.
● ALBUMS: *The Angel Song* (Salami 1993) ★★★, *Black Boots On Latin Feet* (Arista 1995) ★★★★, *Diesel Vanilla* (MCA 1997) ★★★, *Ezio & Booga Live At The Shepherds Bush Empire* (Salami 1999) ★★★, *Higher* (Salami/SPV 2000) ★★★, *The Making Of Mr Spoons* (Eagle 2003) ★★★.
● DVD/VIDEOS: *Ezio Live* (Salami 1996), *Ezio & Booga Live At The Shepherds Bush Empire* (Salami 1999).

Ezo

This Japanese band relocated to Los Angeles, California, USA, immediately after their formation in 1985, in a move deemed necessary in order to achieve wider international exposure. Featuring Masaki (vocals), Shoyo (guitar), Taro (bass) and Hiro (drums), they were retro-rock specialists, drawing heavily on the legacy of **Led Zeppelin**, **UFO** and **Kiss** for their inspiration. Signing to **Geffen Records** and linking with Kiss bass player **Gene Simmons** as producer seemed a promising start. However, *Ezo* was unimpressive. The follow-up, *Fire, Fire*, dropped many of the blatant reference points of its predecessor, but ultimately lacked direction, with the band struggling to find its own identity.
● ALBUMS: *Ezo* (Geffen 1987) ★★★, *Fire, Fire* (Geffen 1989) ★★.

F9s

This London, England-based duo named themselves after the highest function button available to them on their computer keyboard. The F9s are technocrats with samplers, as might be suggested by the name, but Uncle B. Nice is also a confident rapper, who won the DMC UK rap championships in 1989. His messages are backed by DJ Mr Islam, aka Rizla. They began their career with a three-track EP in May 1991, after which they earned a reputation as powerful advocates of forward-thinking Christianity. This led them into conflict with some of the advocates of the Nation Of Islam, notably **Professor Griff**. They were similarly vocal about British hip-hop crews who did not use their platform to put forward a positive message, criticizing many of their peers: 'They're not gathering any white fans. They talk about racism, but they only talk to black people. Why do you need to be taught racism if you are already black.'
● ALBUMS: *The F-9's Are A Hip Hop Band* (Kold Sweat 1992) ★★★.

F.U.S.E.

(see **Hawtin, Richie**)

Fab 5 Freddy

b. Frederick Braithwaite, Brooklyn, New York, USA. Freddy grew up with lawyer parents, his father managing jazz musicians like **Max Roach** and **Clifford Brown**. Nowadays best known for his hosting of *Yo! MTV Raps*, Freddy began life as a rap promoter and graffiti artist. He was responsible for the establishment of the Roxy, a former roller-skate rink turned hip-hop venue, alongside English-born Cool Lady Blue (he got **Afrika Bambaataa** his first gig there). After being name checked by **Blondie**'s 1981 hit 'Rapture', he was invited to make a rap record for the French Celluloid imprint, who had commissioned **Bill Laswell** and Michael Beinhorn to provide them with five 'rap' singles. 'Une Sale Histoire' duly emerged, while female rapper Beside, from California but also rapping in French, took b-side duties. Freddy also appeared on the New York City Rap Tour In Europe line-up. This consisted of break-dancers, artists and rappers, a club of which Freddy has never really counted himself a member. He has gone on to a successful career as video director to **KRS-One**, **Snoop Doggy Dogg** and others.

Fabares, Shelley

b. Michelle Fabares, 19 January 1944, Santa Monica, California, USA. Fabares, whose music career was highlighted by the 1962 US number 1 song 'Johnny Angel', was the niece of actress Nanette Fabray. Turning to acting herself, Fabares debuted as Trudy in the television series *Annie Oakley*. She subsequently landed roles in such 50s movies as *Never Say Goodbye*, *Rock, Pretty Baby* and *Summer Love* before being offered the part of Mary Stone in the US television situation comedy *The Donna Reed Show* in 1958.

As the show's popularity rose, both she and series costar Paul Petersen signed recording contracts with Colpix Records. Fabares was given the ballad 'Johnny Angel', written by Lee Pockriss and Lyn Duddy, and after its debut on the television show, the single quickly rose to number 1. Three follow-up singles did not fare nearly as well, and neither did the two albums she recorded for Colpix. In 1964 Fabares married record producer **Lou Adler**, who arranged a record contract for Fabares with **Vee Jay Records**. There were no hits, and Fabares then became the first artist signed to his new **Dunhill Records** label. Again there were no hits, and Fabares returned to acting, working with **Herman's Hermits** in their movie *Hold On!* and with **Elvis Presley** in *Girl Happy*, *Spinout* and *Clambake*. She divorced Adler in 1967 and continued to work in film and television. In the early 80s, she appeared in the series *One Day At A Time* as Francine Webster. She married actor Mike Farrell in 1984 and in the late 80s and early 90s was a member of the cast of *Coach*, a popular US television situation comedy. Her work rate slowed in the latter part of the decade, and in October 2000 she underwent a liver transplant.
● ALBUMS: *Shelley!* (Colpix 1962) ★★, *The Things We Did Last Summer* (Colpix 1962) ★★, with James Darren, Paul Petersen *Teenage Triangle* (Colpix 1963) ★★, with Darren, Petersen *More Teenage Triangle* (Colpix 1964) ★, *A Time To Sing* (MGM 1968) ★★.
● COMPILATIONS: *The Best Of Shelley Fabares* (Rhino/Sequel 1994) ★★★.
● FILMS: *The Girl Rush* (1965), *Never Say Goodbye* (1956), *Rock, Pretty Baby* (1956), *The Bad Seed* (1956), *Summer Love* (1958), *Marjorie Morningstar* (1958), *Annette* (1958), *Ride The Wild Surf* (1964), *Girl Happy* (1965), *Spinout* aka *California Holiday* (1966), *Hold On!* aka *There's No Place Like Space* (1966), *Clambake* (1967), *A Time To Sing* (1968), *Hot Pursuit* (1987), *Love Or Money* (1990).

Fabian (pop)

b. Fabiano Forte Bonaparte, 6 February 1943, Philadelphia, Pennsylvania, USA. Fabian, almost despite himself, was among the more endurable products of the late 50s when the North American charts were infested with a turnover of vapid boys next door—all hair cream, doe eyes and coy half-smiles—groomed for fleeting stardom. Fabian was 'discovered' by two local talent scouts, Peter De Angelis and Bob Marucci, in **Frankie Avalon**'s Teen And Twenty youth club in 1957. Enthralled by the youth's good looks, the pair shortened his name and contracted him to their own label, Chancellor Records, where a huge budget was allocated to project him as a tamed **Elvis Presley**. Accompanied by the Four Dates, Fabian's first two singles—'I'm In Love' and 'Lilly Lou'—were only regional hits, but a string of television performances on **Dick Clark**'s nationally broadcast *American Bandstand* plus a coast-to-coast tour had the desired effect on female teenagers, and Fabian found himself suddenly in

Billboard's Top 40 with 'I'm A Man,' composed by the top New York songwriting team **Doc Pomus/Mort Shuman**, who also delivered more lucrative hits in 'Turn Me Loose' and 'Hound Dog Man', the main theme from Fabian's silver screen debut of the same name. More substantial movie roles came Fabian's way after his recording career peaked with 1959's million-selling 'Tiger' and *Hold That Tiger*. As well as the predictable teen-pics, with their vacuous story lines and mimed musical sequences, he coped surprisingly well as John Wayne's sidekick in 1960's *North To Alaska* and with **Bing Crosby** and Tuesday Weld in *High Time*.

Fabian's decline was as rapid as his launch after Congress pinpointed him as an instance of one of the exploited puppets in the payola scandal. Questioned at the time, Fabian made matters worse by honestly outlining the considerable electronic doctoring necessary to improve his voice on record. Reverb was required to cover his limited vocal range. His first serious miss came in 1960 with 'About This Thing Called Love' and an irredeemable downward spiral mitigated by 1962's 'Kissin' And Twistin'' and other small hits. Nevertheless, he could be seen in films such as the 1962 war epic *The Longest Day*, but more commensurate with his talent were productions such as and 1964's *Ride The Wild Surf* and *Fireball 500* (a 1966 hot-rod epic with his old friend **Frankie Avalon**). Fabian's limited vocal range should not be held against him: he became a puppet and he danced; out of it he traded a doomed musical career for a credible movie career.

● ALBUMS: *Hold That Tiger* (Chancellor 1959) ★★, *The Fabulous Fabian* (Chancellor 1959) ★★, *The Good Old Summertime* (Chancellor 1960) ★★, *Fabian Facade* (Chancellor 1961) ★★, *Rockin' Hot* (Chancellor 1961) ★★, *Fabian's 16 Fabulous Hits* (Chancellor 1962) ★★.
● COMPILATIONS: *The Best Of Fabian* (Varèse Sarabande 1996) ★★★, *Turn Me Loose: Very Best Of Fabian* (Collectables 1999) ★★★.
● FILMS: *Hound-Dog Man* (1959), *North To Alaska* aka *Go North* (1960), *High Time* (1960), *Love In A Goldfish Bowl* (1961), *Mr. Hobbs Takes A Vacation* (1962), *Five Weeks In A Balloon* (1962), *The Longest Day* (1962), *Ride The Wild Surf* (1964), *Dear Brigitte* (1965), *Ten Little Indians* (1966), *Spie Vengono Dal Semifreddo* aka *Dr. Goldfoot And The Girl Bombs* (1966), *Fireball 500* (1966), *Thunder Alley* aka *Hell Drivers* (1967), *The Wild Racers* (1968), *Maryjane* (1968), *The Devil's 8* (1969), *A Bullet For Pretty Boy* (1970), *Little Laura And Big John* (1973), *The Day The Lord Got Busted* aka *Soul Hustler* (1976), *Disco Fever* (1978), *Kiss Daddy Goodbye* aka *Caution, Children At Play* (1981), *Get Crazy* aka *Flip Out* (1983), *Up Close & Personal* (1996).

Fabian (reggae)

b. Faybienne Miranda, 1952, Panama. Miranda emigrated to the USA with her parents when she was four years old, spending her formative years on the east coast before adopting a hippie lifestyle on the west coast. Inspired by the film **The Harder They Come**, she went to Jamaica, where she continually beleaguered the producer and **sound system** operator **Jack Ruby**. He finally succumbed to her pleas and agreed to produce her recording debut. The outcome of the session was the eternal 'Prophecy' that flopped owing to the lack of exposure in Jamaica. The song languished in obscurity thanks to censorship laws relating to the declared state of emergency. In the song Miranda cautioned,

'Prophecy—Prophecy—Garvey prophesied—people hear the call—our backs are now against the wall'. The Black Disciples, who graced **Burning Spear**'s magnum opus *Marcus Garvey*, provided a suitable accompaniment to the apocalyptic lyrics. The song found greater success internationally, initially surfacing on an independent UK label with **Jimmy Lindsay**'s 'Easy'. Miranda's hit surfaced on expatriate Jamaican **Lloyd Coxsone**'s Tribesman label before **Island Records** licensed both tracks for release on the Black Swan subsidiary. Miranda followed her debut with the similarly styled 'Destiny', echoing the extended words of its predecessor. The song featured the playing skills of **Leroy 'Horsemouth' Wallace** on drums and Robbie Shakespeare on bass but failed to emulate its predecessor. Following a period of anonymity, she resurfaced recording in the UK with the Mad Professor at his **Ariwa** studios. The unprecedented success of 'Prophecy' hindered her chances of greater achievements, as all subsequent works were evaluated against her initial hit. By 1989 Miranda was reputedly working with **Augustus Pablo**, although little surfaced from this collaboration.

Fabian, Lara

b. 9 January 1970, Etterbeek, Belgium. This Quebec, Canada–based singer-songwriter has established herself as a serious rival to **Celine Dion** in the pop diva market. Fabian, born to a Flemish father and a Sicilian mother, grew up in a musical household, and her guitar-playing father accompanied his teenage daughter when she first began performing in Brussels' boîtes à chanson. At the age of 18 Fabian represented Luxembourg in the 1988 Eurovision Song Contest, finishing a highly credible fourth. The song she performed, 'Croire', became a minor hit when it was subsequently released on the Tréma label. Fabian relocated to Quebec in 1991 in an attempt to establish a singing career in North America. Her self-titled debut, which had been recorded back in Belgium, was released that August. The album took off in Quebec, as did the 1994 follow-up *Carpe Diem*, but her big break came two years later when she was featured on the soundtrack to **Walt Disney**'s animated feature *The Hunchback Of Notre Dame*. Her third album, *Pure*, was nominated for two Juno Awards and rapidly achieved multiplatinum status. Fabian's phenomenal commercial success in the French-speaking market, coupled with Dion's 'retirement' from music, led to an inevitable attempt to woo the US charts. Her English-language debut, recorded in New York City and San Francisco, was released by Sony Music in summer 2000. One of the tracks, 'I Will Love Again', had already topped the US **dance music** charts.
● ALBUMS: *Lara Fabian* i (Polydor 1991) ★★★, *Carpe Diem* (Polydor 1994) ★★★, *Pure* (Polydor 1997) ★★★, *Live* (Polydor 1998) ★★, *Lara Fabian* ii (Sony 2000) ★★★.

Fabolous

b. John Jackson, Brooklyn, New York City, USA. This New York rapper shot to fame in 2001 as the poster boy of **DJ Clue?**'s new label, Desert Storm. Hired as much for his looks as his rapping ability, Fabolous was used by Clue? to cash in on the popularity of the 'bling-bling' mentality promoted by the fashionable Dirty South scene. His debut album featured a stellar list of producers and rappers, including the **Neptunes**, **Timbaland**, **Ja Rule** and **Nate Dogg**.

The last, one of the original G-funk vocalists, featured to great effect on Fabolous' breakthrough hit, 'I Can't Deny It'. Released in summer 2001, the single climbed to the upper reaches of the US pop charts. His debut album was a predictably tiresome affair, with the relentless materialism of the lyrics a fitting illustration of Fabolous' triumph of style over substance.

● ALBUMS: *Ghetto Fabolous* (Elektra 2001) ★★, *Street Dreams* (Desert Storm/Elektra 2003) ★★★, *Real Talk* (Desert Storm 2004) ★★★.

● COMPILATIONS: *More Street Dreams Pt 2: The Mixtape* (Desert Storm/Elektra 2003) ★★★.

Fabré, Candido

b. 20 September 1957, Cuba. Fabré first came to prominence on the Cuban music scene in 1983 when he became the chief vocalist, arranger and songwriter for Orquesta Original De La Manzanillo, who played son (the pure Cuban form of salsa) with a 'charanga' line-up of three violins and a flute replacing the brass section. The group was a popular live attraction and also recorded four highly successful albums for the local market. In 1993 he left this group to form his own 15-piece band, Candido Fabré Y Su Banda, again featuring the charanga line-up. The group toured throughout Cuba and proved as successful as Orquesta Original De La Manzanillo. In 1996 the group toured Europe to promote *Son De Cuba*, a passionate and uplifting collection of undiluted Cuban music. They played in Europe again a year later, this time to coincide with the release of *Paquito Poco*, the follow-up album, on which Fabré experimented with fusions of son and other musical forms, including flamenco and Colombian cumbia. Fabré's songs have been covered by numerous Latin artists, including **Celia Cruz**, **Los Van Van** and **Oscar D'Leon**. Fabré also wrote the music to the Spanish film *Las Edades De Manzanillo*.

● ALBUMS: *Son De Cuba* (Tumi 1996) ★★★★, *Paquito Poco* (Tumi 1997) ★★★.

Fabulous

This UK post-punk band was formed in the wake of the media success of the **Manic Street Preachers**. Fabulous comprised Simon Dudfield (vocals), Martin Goodacre (guitar), 'Hodge' (drums), Russell Underwood (second guitar) and Ronnie Fabulous (bass). They were managed by former **New Musical Express** assistant editor James Brown. Dudfield was a contributor, and both Goodacre and Underwood were photographers on the same paper. Live they were characterized by Dudfield's studied **Iggy Pop** impersonations, while musically and ideologically they borrowed from the situationist tack of the **Sex Pistols**. Their first single, 'Destined To Be Free', was just a small part of their stated agenda to reinvent 1977 and rid the UK music scene of the 'Ecstasy' mentality. They also made a point of exhibiting a stolen carpet from **EMI Records**' offices. As more than one journalist noted, the Sex Pistols had taken that record company for £50,000, which put Fabulous' achievements in some sort of perspective. Not to be confused with the American rap artist of the same name.

Fabulous Dorseys, The

The first jazz-related biopic, this 1947 film also has the dubious distinction of casting its subjects as themselves. Although both **Jimmy Dorsey** and **Tommy Dorsey** managed to avoid appearing too embarrassed by the shaky plot (much of which centred on pleasing Ma and Pa Dorsey), their acting was understandably wooden. Their playing was, of course, excellent as both men, then still in their prime, were amongst the outstanding technicians on their respective instruments. For jazz fans the best moment comes in a cornily contrived nightclub scene in which a jam session occurs. Apart from Jimmy and Tommy, the mismatched musicians include **Charlie Barnet**, **Ray Bauduc** and **Ziggy Elman**, all of whom get in the way of the superb **Art Tatum**.

Fabulous Five Inc.

The Fabulous Five Inc. were initially a show band supporting various singers in Jamaica. Lloyd Lovindeer and Glen Ricks both began their careers performing in the **Fabulous Flames** before enlisting in the group's line-up. The band formed in the late 60s and in the ensuing years received numerous awards in Jamaica, being voted the top band for three consecutive years by *Swing* magazine. They were the featured musicians on **Johnny Nash**'s *I Can See Clearly Now*, which introduced authentic reggae rhythms to a global audience. In 1972 they recorded 'Come Back And Stay', which was a popular hit within the reggae community, with two tracks of the same song being available. The preferred version included an introduction from **Scotty**, who stated: 'Heartbreak in the first degree'. The success of the single led to the release of *Fabulous Five Inc.*, produced by John Templar and Junior Lincoln. The album featured the hit single along with versions of **Bob Marley**'s 'Guava Jelly' and **Lloyd Parks**' 'Officially'. They also demonstrated their versatility with a version of the **Skatalites** hit, 'Lee Oswald', the DJ-styled 'Nanny Skank', and a calypso tune, 'That's The Time She Go Love You'. They were able to exhibit their musical talents when they toured the island backing performers in the 1975 Jamaican Song Festival. The winner was Roman Stewart with 'Hooray Festival', who toured alongside **Freddie McKay**, **Johnny Clarke**, **Jackie Edwards** and the **Silvertones**. In 1976 the group recorded the lewd 'Shaving Cream', which maintained their popularity. Following the release of 'My Jamaican Girl', little was heard of the group until 1982 when **Island Records** released the group's recording of 'Ooh Ah', backed with **Lee Perry**'s 'Dreadlocks In The Moonlight' from the soundtrack *Countryman*. Through to the 90s, the group provided backing for a number of performers, often touring with the Jamaica Song Festival finalists; they also notched up a number of local awards and released sporadic output through their own Stage Records. Following his departure from the group, Lloyd recorded as Lovindeer and enjoyed many hits, notably 'Man Shortage', 'Wash Wash' and, with **Shabba Ranks**, 'Manhunt'. Lovindeer's career proved the most commercially successful with a string of releases, *Government Boops*, *Bad Boy Crew*, *Your Boss DJ*, *Dirty Dancing Dollar Winds* volumes one and two, and *Snookie Nookie Nookie Sayonara*. In 1995 Lovindeer responded to **Beenie Man**'s popular 'Slam' with 'Slam Fashion' and 'Slam Of The Century'. He also wrote and produced a UK chart hit for **Pam Hall**, 'Dear Boopsie', in the 80s. Glen Ricks' solo career included *Ready For Love* and *Fall In Love*.

● ALBUMS: *Fabulous Five Inc.* (Ashanti 1973) ★★★, *My Jamaican Girl* (Trojan 1975) ★★★★, *Yu Safe* (Stage 1986) ★★★, *All Night Party* (Stage 1989) ★★.

● COMPILATIONS: *The Best Of Fab 5* (Stage 1996) ★★★.

Fabulous Flames

The Fabulous Flames were initially a dance troupe performing choreographed routines alongside **Byron Lee And The Dragonaires** on Jamaica's north coast. The group featured Lovindeer, Kirk Salmon and Oswald 'Dougie' Douglas. Their rhythmic cavorting led to deserved distinction, and they were enrolled to perform with Carlos Malcolm And His Afro Caribs, accompanying the band on a tour of the West Indies. In 1969 they were invited to demonstrate their agility at the Caribana festival in Canada, which led to further engagements. The group secured a concert in Toronto's famed Yonge Street where they met and performed alongside Glen Ricks, who was persuaded to join the group. Ricks returned to Jamaica with the Flames, where, with producer **Clancy Eccles**, they recorded **Neil Diamond**'s 'Holly Holy'. The organ-led song, driven by a creeping rhythm, was an instant hit, and the band became the mainstay of the Clandisc label. The success of the single led **Prince Buster** to utilize an identical rhythm for his lewd interpretation, 'Holy Fishey'. When released in the UK, the original song almost crossed into the pop chart and featured **Lord Creator**'s 'Kingston Town' on the b-side. 'Kingston Town' was later included on **UB40**'s multimillion-selling *Labour Of Love II* and topped the UK chart in 1990 when released as a single. Subsequent hits for the Flames included the melancholy 'Growing Up' and, conversely, the blithe 'Hi De High'. By the early 70s the members went their own separate ways. Lovindeer and Ricks joined the **Fabulous Five Inc.** before pursuing solo careers, and the remaining two members relocated to Canada. In the 80s Salmon returned to his musical career when he played guitar in a Canadian-based band, Livestock.

Fabulous Rhinestones

Formed in Woodstock, New York, USA, in 1971, the Fabulous Rhinestones revolved around Marty Grebb (b. 2 September 1946, Chicago, Illinois, USA; keyboards, saxophone, vocals; ex-**Buckinghams**), Harvey Brooks (b. Harvey Goldstein, USA; bass, ex-**Electric Flag**) and Kal David (b. 1943, Chicago, Illinois, USA; guitar/vocals; ex-**Illinois Speed Press**). Greg Thomas (drums; ex-**Mint Tattoo**) and Rainol 'Dino' Andino (congas) completed the line-up featured on the quintet's first two albums, both of which featured horn-orientated rock punctuated by Kal David's clear, jazz-based solos. Internal disputes followed, though, and by the time. *The Rhinestones* was released, only Brooks and David remained from the original membership. Artie Funaro (b. Arthur Funaro; guitar), Bob Leinback (keyboards) and Eric Parker (drums) had joined the line-up, but without Grebb's multi-instrumental talents, the Fabulous Rhinestones had lost much of their focus, and they broke up in 1976.

● ALBUMS: *The Fabulous Rhinestones* (Just Sunshine 1972) ★★★, *Freewheelin'* (Just Sunshine 1973) ★★★, *The Rhinestones* (20th Century 1975) ★★.

Fabulous Thunderbirds

Formed in Texas, USA, in 1977, the Thunderbirds originally comprised **Jimmy Vaughan** (b. 20 March 1951, Dallas, Texas, USA; guitar), **Kim Wilson** (b. 6 January 1951, Detroit, Michigan, USA; vocals/harmonica), Keith Ferguson (b. 23 July 1946, Houston, Texas, USA, d. 29 April 1997; bass) and Mike Buck (b. 17 June 1952; drums). They emerged from the post-punk vacuum with a solid, unpretentious brand of R&B. Their debut album, *The Fabulous Thunderbirds* aka *Girls Go*

Wild, offered a series of powerful original songs as well as sympathetic cover versions, including a vibrant reading of **Slim Harpo**'s 'Baby Scratch My Back'. This mixture has sustained the group throughout its career, although it took a move from **Chrysalis Records** to the Epic label to provide the success that their exciting music deserved. The Thunderbirds line-up has undergone some changes, with former **Roomful Of Blues** drummer Fran Christina (b. 1 February 1951, Westerly, Rhode Island, USA) replacing Mike Buck in 1980 and Preston Hubbard (b. 15 March 1953, Providence, Rhode Island, USA) joining after Ferguson departed.

Throughout these changes, Wilson and Vaughan, the brother of the late blues guitarist **Stevie Ray Vaughan**, remained at the helm until Vaughan jumped ship in 1995. Drummer Buck formed the **LeRoi Brothers** in 1980, while Ferguson went on to forge a new career with the Tail Gators. Although both of these groups offer similar bar band fare, the Thunderbirds remain, unquestionably, the masters. The **Danny Kortchmar**-produced *Roll Of the Dice* was the first album with Wilson leading the band in the wake of Vaughan's departure and showed the new lead guitarist, **Kid Ramos** (b. David Ramos, 13 January 1959, Fullerton, California, USA), having a difficult job to fill. The recent line-up in addition to Wilson and Ramos comprises Gene Taylor (piano), Jim Bott (drums) and Ronnie James Weber (bass).

● ALBUMS: *The Fabulous Thunderbirds* aka *Girls Go Wild* (Chrysalis 1979) ★★★★, *What's The Word* (Chrysalis 1980) ★★★, *Butt Rockin'* (Chrysalis 1981) ★★★, *T-Bird Rhythm* (Chrysalis 1982) ★★★, *Tuff Enuff* (Columbia 1986) ★★★, *Hot Number* (Columbia 1987) ★★★, *Powerful Stuff* (Columbia 1989) ★★★, *Walk That Walk, Talk That Talk* (Columbia 1991) ★★★, *Roll Of The Dice* (Private Music 1995) ★★, *High Water* (High Street 1997) ★★★★, with Al Copley *Good Understanding* 1992 recording (Bullseye Blues 1998) ★★★, *Live* (Sanctuary 2001) ★★★, *Extended Versions* (BMG 2002) ★★★★, *Painted On* (Tone-Cool 2005) ★★★.

● COMPILATIONS: *Portfolio* (Chrysalis 1987) ★★★★, *Hot Stuff: The Greatest Hits* (Columbia 1992) ★★★★, *Different Tacos* (Country Town Music 1998) ★★★★, *Tacos Deluxe* (Benchmark 2004) ★★★★.

● DVD/VIDEOS: *Tuff Enuff* (Hendring Music Video 1990).

Face The Music

Generally considered to be **Irving Berlin**'s best score for some years, it came at a time when both he and America were recovering from the Depression, and the Prohibition bootleggers were about to be put out of business by the newly elected President Franklin D. Roosevelt. *Face The Music* opened on Broadway at the New Amsterdam Theatre on 17 February 1932. The somewhat satirical book was the work of **Moss Hart**, who, in collaboration with the show's directors **Hassard Short** and **George S. Kaufman**, fashioned a contemporary story of shady deals, in which Mrs. Martin Van Buren Meshbesher (Mary Boland), the wife of a police sergeant who, in the course of his duty, has accumulated a great deal of money from undisclosed sources. She panics and tries to lose some of it by investing in a bizarre Broadway show. Unfortunately for her, the show is a big success and makes even more money. As usual Berlin captured perfectly the mood and the period—the bitterness and cynicism that prevailed in America at that time: 'Let's Have Another Cup Of Coffee' ('And let's have another piece of pie') was sung by the Rockefeller and Vanderbilt-types—the ex-swells (personified in the show by Katherine Carrington and J. Harold Murray) who are now eating at the Automat instead of the Astor. The song became widely popular through a recording by **Fred Waring** and his Pennsylvanians and was sung lustily by **Ethel Merman** in the 1954 film *There's No Business Like Show Business*. Carrington and Murray also had 'I Say It's Spinach', 'On A Roof In Manhattan', and the romantic and soothing 'Soft Lights And Sweet Music'. The latter song was also successful for Waring and his 'glee club'. *Face The Music* played for 165 performances and was revived briefly on Broadway in the following year.

Face To Face (80s)

Comprising Laurie Sargent (vocals), Stuart Kimball (lead guitar), Billy Beard (drums), Angelo Petraglia (rhythm guitar) and John Ryder (bass), US rock band Face To Face combined elements of the new wave tradition with memorable AOR hooks. The package was completed by Sargent's distinctive vocals, which were the most notable feature of the band's 1984 debut for Epic Records. This self-titled collection saw the band establish itself with a broad cross-section of contemporary rock styles. However, the songs, although professionally rendered, were a little lacking in substance. The best track, '10-9-8', broke into the US Top 40. After recording one more album for Epic Records, the quintet relocated to **Mercury Records** for 1988's *One Big Day*. By this time, however, the band's musical style was outdated, and they called it a day not long afterwards.

● ALBUMS: *Face To Face* (Epic 1984) ★★★, *Confrontation* (Epic 1985) ★★★, *One Big Day* (Mercury 1989) ★★.

Face To Face (90s)

This Southern California, USA–based trio specialized in the same tuneful punk pop as their better-known country men **Green Day** and **Blink-182**. Face To Face was formed by Trever Keith (b. 26 May 1969, USA; vocals/guitar), Matt Riddle (bass/vocals) and Rob Kurth (drums/vocals). Shortly after their formation in 1991, the trio signed with the independent label Dr. Strange Records, which issued their debut, *Don't Turn Away*, the following year. Unhappy with Dr. Strange's distribution, the band changed labels to Fat Wreck Chords, which in turn rereleased *Don't Turn Away* with different cover art (but the same track listing) a year later. Face To Face expanded for a spell to a quartet with the addition of second guitarist Chad Yaro. An EP of rerecorded b-sides, *Over It*, was issued soon afterwards, before their second album, *Big Choice*, appeared in 1995. The album generated the local radio hit 'Disconnected', which had originally appeared in a different form on *Over It*.

Opening gigs for the **Mighty Mighty Bosstones** and the **Offspring** increased the media buzz around the band, and with punk pop becoming one of the most in-demand musical styles among teenagers worldwide, Face To Face suddenly found themselves being courted by major labels. The quartet signed with **A&M Records** in 1996, around the same time that Riddle was replaced by Scott Shiflett (b. 22 August 1966, USA). The union with A&M proved to be a short-lived one, with only 1996's self-titled album emerging before the band returned to independent label status. *Live*, recorded over two nights in September 1997 at the infamous Los Angeles club The Roxy, proved to be the last album to include Kurth, who was replaced by Pete Parada.

With Keith the only original member left in attendance by this point, the band issued what many fans consider to be their finest offering 1999's *Ignorance Is Bliss*. The all-cover version collection, *Standards And Practices*, featured material by the **Psychedelic Furs**, the **Pixies**, the **Pogues** and the **Smiths** among others. The album was released to the foreign market in 1999 but was not given a domestic release until two years later. The following year's *Reactionary* was compiled by posting 16 tracks on the Internet and allowing the band's fans to choose the best ones for inclusion on the album. By the time 2002's *How To Ruin Everything* arrived, Yaro had left the band, returning Face To Face back to their original trio set up. A CD/DVD career overview, *Everything Is Everything*, was issued before the band announced their breakup in 2003. Keith teamed up with Shiflett in Viva Death in addition to launching his own label, Sound On Sound.

● ALBUMS: *Don't Turn Away* (Dr. Strange/Fat Wreck Chords 1992) ★★★★, *Big Choice* (Victory 1995) ★★★, *Face To Face* (A&M 1996) ★★★, *Live* (Lady Luck/Vagrant 1998) ★★★, *Ignorance Is Bliss* (Lady Luck/Beyond 1999) ★★★★, *Standards & Practices* (Lady Luck/Vagrant 1999) ★★★, *Reactionary* (Lady Luck/Beyond 2000) ★★★, *How To Ruin Everything* (Lady Luck/Vagrant 2002) ★★★.

● COMPILATIONS: *Over It* (Victory 1994) ★★★, *Everything Is Everything* (Lady Luck/Vagrant 2002) ★★★★.

● DVD/VIDEOS: *The First Seven Years* (BMG 1999).

Facedancer

Formed in the late 70s, US rock band Facedancer comprised Jeff Adams (guitar), Mike Milsap (keyboards), Scott McGuinn (bass) and Billy Trainor (drums). After establishing themselves on the local club circuit, they made a major impact with 1979's *This World*, their debut album for **Capitol Records**. Buoyed by strong songwriting, particularly the single 'Time Bomb', they created a good impression throughout the US rock mainstream. 1980's *About Face* fared significantly worse. An obvious attempt to expand their audience too early in their career, possibly due to record company pressure, pop hooks meekly replaced the boisterous riffs of their debut. Its critical and commercial failure signalled the end of the group.

● ALBUMS: *This World* (Capitol 1979) ★★★, *About Face* (Capitol 1980) ★★.

Facenda, Tommy

b. 10 November 1939, Norfolk, Virginia, USA. Facenda became known for one single he recorded in 1959 for **Atlantic Records**, 'High School USA'. Facenda, nicknamed 'Bubba', first gained a foothold in the music business in 1957 as a backup singer for **Gene Vincent**. He was performing at a club in 1958 when discovered by Frank Guida (who later discovered and managed **Gary 'U.S.' Bonds**). Facenda first recorded a single, 'Little Baby', for Nasco Records in 1958, but it did not reach the charts. Guida then wrote 'High School USA', which included the names of several schools in the section of Virginia in which Facenda worked. It was released on Legrand Records, and when Guida noticed that local high school students were buying the record to hear the name of their school, he had Facenda rerecord the vocals 28 times (some accounts put the number at 46), each version mentioning the names of schools in a different region of the USA. It was released on Atlantic and reached number 28, but

Facenda was unable to come up with another hit. Two volumes of the album *High School USA* were issued during the 80s on the revived Legrand, each including 14 versions of the title track. He later retired from the music business and became a firefighter.

● ALBUMS: *High School USA, Volume 1* (Legrand 1984) ★★★, *High School USA, Volume 2* (Legrand 1984) ★★.

Faces

Formed from the ashes of the defunct UK mod act the **Small Faces**, this quintet comprised **Ronnie Lane** (b. 1 April 1946, Plaistow, London, England, d. 4 June 1997, Trinidad, Colorado, USA; bass), Kenney Jones (b. 16 September 1948, Stepney, London, England; drums), **Ian McLagan** (b. 12 May 1945, Hounslow, Middlesex, England; organ/piano), **Rod Stewart** (b. Roderick David Stewart, 10 January 1945, Highgate, London, England; vocals) and **Ron Wood** (b. 1 June 1947, Hillingdon, Middlesex, England; guitar). The latter two members were originally part of **Jeff Beck**'s group. The Faces' 1970 debut *First Step* reflected their boozy, live appeal in which solid riffing and strong gutsy vocals were prominent but also found room for McLagan and Stewart's poignant 'Three Button Hand Me Down'. The excellent follow-up, *Long Player*, enhanced the band's appeal with its strong mix of staunch rock songs and well-chosen cover versions, including **Paul McCartney**'s 'Maybe I'm Amazed' and **'Big' Bill Broonzy**'s 'I Feel So Good'.

Throughout this period, Rod Stewart had been pursuing a solo career that took off in earnest in the summer of 1971 with the worldwide success of the chart-topping single 'Maggie May'. At that point, the Faces effectively became Stewart's backing unit, much to the annoyance of the other members. Although they enjoyed increasing commercial success with the album *A Nod's As Good As A Wink . . . To A Blind Horse* and *Ooh La La*, and a string of memorable good-time singles including 'Stay With Me' and 'Cindy Incidentally', there was no doubt that the focus on Stewart unbalanced the unit. Lane left in 1973 and was replaced by Tetsu Yamauchi (b. 21 October 1946, Fukuokoa, Japan; ex-**Free**). Despite further hits with 'Pool Hall Richard', 'You Can Make Me Dance, Sing, Or Anything' and a live album to commemorate their Stateside success, the Faces clearly lacked unity. In 1975 Stewart became a tax exile and by the end of the year announced that he had separated from the band.

Following the breakup of the Faces, Wood went on to join the **Rolling Stones**, while the remaining members briefly teamed up with Steve Marriott in an ill-fated reunion of the Small Faces. Jones also replaced the deceased **Keith Moon** in the **Who**. The Faces unexpectedly reunited for a one-off appearance at the BRIT Awards in February 1993. They performed with Rod Stewart and with **Bill Wyman** taking over the seriously ill Lane's role on bass.

● ALBUMS: *First Step* (Warners 1970) ★★★, *Long Player* (Warners 1971) ★★★★, *A Nod's As Good As A Wink . . . To A Blind Horse* (Warners 1971) ★★★, *Ooh La La* (Warners 1973) ★★★, *Coast To Coast: Overture And Beginners* (Mercury 1974) ★★★.

● COMPILATIONS: *Snakes And Ladders: The Best Of The Faces* (Warners 1976) ★★★, *Good Boys . . . When They're Asleep: The Best Of The Faces* (Warner Archives/Rhino 1999) ★★★★, *Changing Faces: The Very Best Of Rod Stewart &*

The Faces (UMTV 2003) ★★★★, *Five Guys Walk Into A Bar . . .* 4-CD box set (Rhino 2004) ★★★.

● DVD/VIDEOS: *Rod Stewart And The Faces: Video Biography 1969–1974* (Video Collection 1988), *Rod Stewart And Faces: The Final Concert With Keith Richards* (Music Video Distributors 2000).

● FURTHER READING: *Rock On Wood: The Origin Of A Rock & Roll Face*, Terry Rawlings. *'Last Orders, Please': Rod Stewart, The Faces . . . And The Britain We Forgot*, Jim Melly.

Factory (UK 60s)

A trio of Jack Brand (vocals/bass), Bill MacLeod (drums) and Ian Oates (guitar), UK garage rock band Factory were originally known as the Souvenir Badge Factory. After changing their name, they signed to **MGM Records** in 1968 and released their debut single, 'Path Through A Forest', backed by a version of **Paul Revere And The Raiders**' 'Gone'. The a-side's distorted vocals and complex arrangement won it minor celebrity among psychedelic rock fans (a popularity that has increased rather than abated over ensuing years) but little commercial reward. For their second single, 'Try A Little Sunshine', written by studio engineer John Pantry, the group moved to **CBS Records**. Despite the single's excellence, once again it failed to reach the charts. The group's four released songs have been compiled regularly on psychedelic compilations, including *The Perfumed Garden* and *Chocolate Soup For Diabetics Vol. 3*.

● COMPILATIONS: *Path Through The Forest* mini-album (Bri-Tone/Heads Together 1995) ★★★.

Factory (UK 70s)

The Oak Records label has long been famed for its popularity among collectors, and the Factory's sole 1971 single, 'Time Machine'/'Castle On The Hill', is no exception, regularly fetching over £100 when offered for sale to collectors. Different from the band of the same name that recorded for **MGM Records** and **CBS Records** at the end of the 60s, this UK band featured Laurie Cooksey (drums), Geoff 'Jaffa' Peckham (bass), Andy Quinta (vocals) and Tony Quinta (12-string acoustic guitar). Peckham was later replaced on bass by Steve Kinch. Before forming Factory, the Quinta brothers had been part of the school band Perfect Turkey, who also recorded an acetate single ('Stones'/'Perfect Turkey Blues') for Oak. The Factory's single was issued in a limited pressing of 99, helping to make it one of the label's most elusive releases. However, the Factory's main claim to fame came much later in their career. They persevered without issuing further records until 1976 and were supported at one of their final performances by the **Sex Pistols**. The Quinta brothers and Kinch subsequently formed Head On, after which Andy Quinta and Kinch continued the punk connection by joining **Hazel O'Connor**'s band.

Factory (USA 60s)

Formed in Los Angeles, California in 1965, the Factory were one of countless acts evolving in the wake of the **Byrds** and the **Turtles**. Lead guitarist **Lowell George**, Warren Klein (rhythm guitar) and Martin Kibbee (bass) were initially joined by drummer Dallas Taylor, but the last-named was quickly replaced by Richard Hayward. Taylor later resurfaced in **Clear Light**, **Crosby, Stills And Nash** and **Manassas**. The Factory reportedly played 'Hey Joe' louder than any local rivals, although contemporary releases 'Smile, Let Your

Life Begin' and 'No Place I'd Rather Be' show a group combining adventurism with melody. Former **Teddy Bears** member Marshall Leib produced these sessions, but following a support slot with the **Mothers Of Invention**, the Factory fell under the sway of the former's leader, **Frank Zappa**. He allowed the quartet an artistic freedom that ranged from the **Captain Beefheart**–influenced 'Lightning-Rod Man' to the fuzz-guitar folk/rock of 'The Loved One'. These recordings remained unreleased for 25 years. The Factory split up in 1967; George spent several weeks in the **Standells** before replacing Ray Collins in the Mothers, while Klein, Kibbee and Hayward formed the **Fraternity Of Man**. George and Hayward were subsequently reunited in **Little Feat**.
● COMPILATIONS: *Lightning-Rod Man* (1994) ★★★.

Factory Records

Cambridge graduate Tony Wilson (b. Anthony Wilson, 1950, Salford, Lancashire, England) was a regional television reporter working in Manchester when he started the Factory label in 1978. He was also responsible for the *So It Goes* and *What's On* television programmes, which in themselves had acted as an invaluable platform for the emerging new wave scene. Previously he had edited his university's *Shilling Paper*. From there, he joined television news company ITN as a trainee reporter, writing bulletins for current events programmes. It was on regional news programmes based in Manchester that he first encountered his future collaborators in the Factory operation; Alan Erasmus, Peter Saville, **Rob Gretton** (manager of **Joy Division**) and producer **Martin Hannett**.

Erasmus and Wilson began their operation by jointly managing the fledgling **Durutti Column**, opening the Factory Club venue soon after. The label's first catalogue number, FAC 1, was allocated to the poster promoting its opening event. This typified Wilson's approach to the whole Factory operation, the most famous assignation of which was FAC 51, the **Haçienda** nightclub. However, it was their records, and the impersonal, nondescriptive packaging accompanying them, that saw the label make its mark. Among the first releases were **OMD**'s 'Electricity' (later a hit on Dindisc) and **A Certain Ratio**'s 'All Night Party'. However, it was Joy Division, harnessing the anxieties of Manchester youth to a discordant, sombre musical landscape, that established the label in terms of public perception and financial security. With Curtis gone, **New Order** continued as the backbone of the Factory operation throughout the 80s, establishing themselves in the mainstream with the biggest-selling 12-inch up to that time, 'Blue Monday'. Other mainstays included **Section 25** and Stockholm Monsters, who steered a path too close to that of New Order and the resourceful Durutti Column. It took the brief arrival of **James** to restore a pop sensibility (their subsequent departure would be a huge body blow), while New Order, somewhat astonishingly, took the England Football Squad to number 1 in the UK charts in 1990 with 'World In Motion'. The latter-day success of **Electronic**, the most successful of various New Order offshoots, and the **Happy Mondays**, a shambolic post-punk dance conglomerate, diffused accusations of Factory being too reliant on a single band.

Reported cash flow problems in 1991 were vehemently denied by Wilson, but the label went bankrupt the following year. **London Records** bought Factory Communications and its associated trademarks, and Wilson set up the Factory Too imprint. The four-album compilation *Palatine* showcased the label's achievements, of which Wilson has never been reticent: 'In my opinion (popular art) is as valid as any other art form . . . a lot of the tracks on *Palatine* are phenomenal art. We're 35 years into pop now, and great records do not lose their power. The deference with which we treat this stuff is deserved.' In 2002 Wilson and Factory's story was made into an entertaining film, *24 Hour Party People*. Wilson maintained his presence on the UK music scene with further incarnations of the label, namely Factory Records Limited and F4.
● COMPILATIONS: *Palatine* 4-LP box set (Factory 1991) ★★★.
● FURTHER READING: *From Joy Division To New Order*, Mick Middles. *24 Hour Party People: What The Sleeve Notes Never Tell You*, Tony Wilson. *The True Story Of Anthony H. Wilson And Factory Records*, Mick Middles.
● FILMS: *24 Hour Party People* (2002).

Fad Gadget

Effectively a moniker for UK-born vocalist and synthesizer player **Frank Tovey** (b. September 1956, London, England, d. 3 April 2002, London, England), Fad Gadget enjoyed cult success with a series of bizarre releases on the **Mute Records** label during the early 80s. Tovey's background lay in his study of performance art at Leeds Art College. After moving to London, he transferred this interest into an unpredictable, often self-mutilating stage show. The first artist to sign with Daniel Miller's Mute label, Fad Gadget's 'Back To Nature' was released in 1979. 'Ricky's Hand' further combined Tovey's lyrical skill (observing the darker aspects of life) with an innovative use of electronics. Both these traits were evident on 'Fireside Favourites', a single and also the title of Fad Gadget's debut album. For the latter, Tovey was joined by Eric Radcliffe (guitar/bass), Nick Cash (drums), John Fryer (percussion/noises), Daniel Miller (drum machine/synthesizer) and Phil Wauquaire (bass synthesizer/guitar). After 'Make Room' in 1981 came *Incontinent*, which was more violent, unnerving and disturbing than before. Tovey had also recruited new staff, working with Peter Balmer (bass/rhythm guitar), David Simmons (piano/synthesizer), singers B.J. Frost and Anne Clift and drummer Robert Gotobed of **Wire**. In 1982 'Saturday Night Special' and 'King Of The Flies' preceded a third album, *Under The Flag*. Dealing with the twin themes of the Falklands conflict and Tovey's newborn child, the album featured **Alison Moyet** on saxophone and backing vocals. The following year saw new extremes as Tovey returned from a European tour with his legs in plaster, having broken them during a show. On the recording front, the year was fairly quiet, apart from 'For Whom The Bell Tolls' and 'I Discover Love', and in October the band supported **Siouxsie And The Banshees** at London's Royal Albert Hall. 'Collapsing New People' continued an impressive run of singles at the start of 1984 and was followed by Fad Gadget's final album, *Gag*. However, Tovey opted to use his real identity from this point on. In November he teamed up with American conceptualist Boyd Rice for *Easy Listening For The Hard Of Hearing* and went on to release several solo works, each of them as highly distinct and uncompromising as Fad Gadget's material.

Despite Tovey's relative inactivity during the 90s, Fad Gadget's reputation as a pioneering electronic act continued to grow. Fad Gadget's return to live performance, headlining

Elektrofest 2001 at The Mean Fiddler in London with Austrian band Temple X, demonstrated that the years had not diminished Tovey's remarkable stage energy. His artistic renaissance was cruelly curtailed by his death from heart failure the following April.

● ALBUMS: *Fireside Favourites* (Mute 1980) ★★★, *Incontinent* (Mute 1981) ★★★, *Under The Flag* (Mute 1982) ★★★★, *Gag* (Mute 1984) ★★★.

● COMPILATIONS: *The Fad Gadget Singles* (Mute 1985) ★★★★, *The Best Of Fad Gadget* (Mute 2001) ★★★★.

Faddis, Jon

b. Jonathan Faddis, 24 July 1953, Oakland, California, USA. Faddis began playing trumpet while still a small child and at the age of 11 was introduced by his trumpet teacher, Bill Catalano, to the music of **Dizzy Gillespie**. At 13 years old Faddis was playing with R&B bands and in mainstream rehearsal big bands, and two years later he met Gillespie, sitting in with him at a San Francisco workshop. In 1971 Faddis joined **Lionel Hampton**, then moved into the **Thad Jones–Mel Lewis** Jazz Orchestra. He was with this band on and off for the next few years, between times playing with **Gil Evans**, **Oscar Peterson**, **Charles Mingus** and Gillespie. It was while he was with Gillespie that Faddis first attracted widespread attention. Although he had set out deliberately to build his own playing ability through adherence to Gillespie's style, Faddis had succeeded in creating a style of his own. Nevertheless, he was deeply rooted in bebop and helped give the older man a boost at a time when he was under pressure to adapt to the current popularity of jazz rock. The concerts and recording sessions of the two trumpeters were hugely successful, both musically and commercially, and established a working pattern for Faddis for the next few years.

In the early 80s Faddis was heavily committed with studio work but found time for recording sessions and tours with **Jimmy Smith**, **Jackie McLean** and **McCoy Tyner**. In the late 80s he joined Gillespie in a big band for a world tour but was mostly active as leader of his own bands, which included the big band Carnegie Hall Jazz Band. One of the most striking of post-bop trumpeters, Faddis blends a dazzling technique with a thorough understanding of jazz tradition. His clear, bell-like tone, is well-suited to his richly emotional playing, and he has earned his place as one of the most gifted and important musicians in jazz.

● ALBUMS: *Youngblood* (Pablo 1976) ★★★, *Good And Plenty* (Dunhill 1978) ★★★, *Legacy* (Concord Jazz 1985) ★★★★, with Billy Harper *Jon And Billy* (Blackhawk 1987) ★★, *Into The Faddisphere* (Epic 1989) ★★★, *Hornucopia* (Epic 1991) ★★★, with the Carnegie Hall Jazz Band *The Carnegie Hall Jazz Band* (Blue Note 1996) ★★★, *Remembrances* (Chesky 1998) ★★★★.

Fadela, Chaba

b. Oran, Algeria. When Algerian rai singer Chaba Fadela embarked on her career in the late 70s, it was an inauspicious time for her country. Following the indenture of President Chadli in 1977, corruption had become endemic, with the youth frustrated by unemployment and a regime that was become increasingly intolerant of their entertainment mediums. Rai, Algeria's propulsive dance wave, was primed to explode, and Chaba Fadela announced its birth with her 1979 single 'Ana Mahlali Noum' ('Sleep Doesn't Matter To Me Any More'). Defiant and irreverent, it set the tone for much of what was to follow, though (Cheb **Khaled** was the one to reap the major profits of her innovation. However, alongside her husband Mohammed Sahraoui, who studied at the Conservatoire of Oran while singing in the city's night clubs, she has scored several further hits over the years. The best known of these is 'N'Sel Fik', which became a minor international success (particularly in the UK) in 1983. The duo signed to **Island Records** subsidiary label Mango in the 90s, with Fadela also releasing a solo album, *Hana Hana*. However, she is probably heard best in the company of her husband, and 1993's *You Are Mine* offered an excellent collection of their best-known songs, recorded alongside producer Rachid Baba-Ahmed, the man responsible for introducing modern studio technology to Algeria.

● ALBUMS: *Hana Hana* (Mango 1992) ★★★, with Cheb Sharaoui *You Are Mine* (Mango 1993) ★★★★.

Fagan, James

b. Australia. Multi-instrumentalist Fagan made his name in the late 90s as one of the brightest talents on the UK's modern folk scene through a series of excellent recordings with fiddle player **Nancy Kerr**. Fagan's parents were leading figures in the Australian folk revival of the 70s, and as soon as they were old enough, James and his sister Kate joined their parents in the family's four-part harmony group. In addition to his vocal talents, James learned to play a wide range of instruments, including guitar, piano, and the bouzouki. After completing a medical degree, he travelled to England in 1995 for a holiday and hooked up with Kerr and **Eliza Carthy** in the newly formed Kings Of Calicutt. He forged a duo partnership with Kerr as a side project but returned to Australia to take up a medical job. However, the partnership was renewed when Kerr went to Australia, and the duo completed a successful tour of the country. Fagan's medical career was put on hold in the late 90s as the duo signed a recording contract with **Fellside Records**. A string of albums for the label, including a recording with Nancy's mother Sandra Kerr, helped confirm Kerr and Fagan as one of the most exciting folk acts of their generation. They were duly rewarded by the folk establishment, winning BBC Radio Two's Horizon Award in 2000 and the Best Duo Award three years later.

● ALBUMS: with Nancy Kerr *Starry Gazy Pie* (Fellside 1998) ★★★★, with Sandra Kerr, Nancy Kerr *Scalene* (Fellside 1999) ★★★, with Nancy Kerr *Steely Water* (Fellside 1999) ★★★, with Nancy Kerr *Between The Dark And Light* (Fellside 2002) ★★★★, with Nancy Kerr *Strands Of Gold* (Fellside 2006) ★★★.

Fagen, Donald

b. 10 January 1948, Passaic, New Jersey, USA. A graduate of New York's Bard College, Fagen joined fellow student Walter Becker in several temporary groups, including the Leather Canary and Bad Rock Group. The duo then forged a career as songwriters—their demos were later compiled on several exploitative releases—and spent several years backing **Jay And The Americans**. Having completed the soundtrack to *You Gotta Walk It Like You Talk It (Or You'll Lose That Beat)*, a low-budget movie by Zalman King, Fagen and Becker then formed **Steely Dan**. Probably one of America's finest groups, their deft, imaginative lyrics were set into a music combining the thrill of rock with the astuteness of jazz. Although initially a sextet, the group soon became an avenue for the duo's increasingly oblique vision as band members were replaced by hirelings. Their partnership was sundered in June 1981, but two years later Fagen reemerged with **The Nightfly**. Abetted by Steely Dan producer Gary Katz, the singer simply continued the peerless perfection of his earlier outfit with a set indebted to state-of-the-art techniques yet in part invoking the aura of 50s' and early 60s' America. The cover shot, depicting the artist as a late-night jazz disc jockey, set the tone for its content wherein Fagen name-dropped **Dave Brubeck**, re-created 'Ruby Baby', a 1956 hit for the **Drifters** and, in 'Maxine', suggested the close harmony style of the **Hi Los** or **Four Freshmen**.

Fagen subsequently contributed to **Rosie Vela**'s *Zazu* (1986) and later scored the Michael J. Fox movie *Bright Lights, Big City*, from which the excellent 'Century's End' was culled as a single. In May 1990 Fagen was reunited with Becker at New York's Hit Factory studios, signalling the revival of Steely Dan. In the spring of 1993 the long-awaited second album was released to much critical acclaim. *Kamakiriad* is supposedly an album of eight related songs about the millennium (according to the sleeve notes); to lesser mortals, though, it simply sounded like another excellent Steely Dan record. Fagen and Becker are touring and recording together again as Steely Dan.

● ALBUMS: *The Nightfly* (Warners 1982) ★★★★, *Kamakiriad* (Reprise 1993) ★★★★.

● DVD/VIDEOS: *Concepts For Jazz/Rock Piano* (Homespun Video 1996).

Fagerquist, Don

b. 6 February 1927, Worcester, Massachusetts, USA, d. 24 January 1974, Los Angeles, California, USA. After working with the **Mal Hallett** band in the early 40s, Fagerquist joined **Gene Krupa** in 1944. He stayed with Krupa for several years, comfortably adjusting his trumpet playing to the boppish style the band adopted towards the end of the decade. After Krupa's band folded, Fagerquist spent a little time with **Artie Shaw** before becoming a member of **Woody Herman**'s Third Herd. He later worked with **Les Brown** and the **Dave Pell** Octet, the Brown band's small-group offshoot. A striking soloist, Fagerquist's thoughtful playing style admirably suited the west coast scene, and in the 50s he played extensively and sometimes recorded with **Shelly Manne**, **Pete Rugolo**, **Art Pepper** and others, including the popular big band assembled for record sessions by **Si Zentner** in the mid-60s.

● ALBUMS: *Music To Fill A Void* (Mode 1957) ★★★.

Fagin, Joe
(see **Strangers**)

Fahey, Brian

b. 25 April 1919, Margate, Kent, England. Fahey's father, a professional musician, taught him to play the piano and cello when he was a youngster. During World War II he served in the Royal Artillery and was captured during the retreat to Dunkirk and spent the next five years in prisoner-of-war camps. He survived the 'forgotten massacre' at Wormhoudt Concentration Camp and organized prisoners' entertainments. On his return to the UK, he played piano for Rudi Sarita's Band, where he met his future wife, vocalist Audrey Laurie. He then worked as an arranger for top UK dance bands, **Ken Mackintosh**, **Geraldo** and **Harry Roy**, and in the early 50s was a staff arranger with Chappells Music Publishing Company. Fahey made his first broadcast with his own orchestra in 1960, and from 1966–72 he was musical director for **Shirley Bassey** and conductor of the Scottish Radio Orchestra from 1972 until it disbanded in 1981. Later he appeared on radio and in concerts with his own outfits, such as the Brian Fahey Big Band, Little Band, Concert Orchestra and Little String Orchestra. His best-known compositions include 'Fanfare Boogie', written with Max Kaye, for which he received an **Ivor Novello** Award in 1955, and 'At The Sign Of The Swinging Cymbal', around which UK disc jockey **Alan Freeman** revamped BBC Radio's *Top Of The Pops* in the late 50s and later made it his life-long theme tune prefacing his opening 'Hi there pop pickers'. Fahey also collaborated with his ex-boss Ken Mackintosh and Gordon Langthorne on 'The Creep', which was a UK Top 10 chart entry for the Mackintosh Orchestra in 1954. His movie scores include *Curse Of The Simba*, *Where The Spies Are* (1965, starring David Niven) and two comedies, *Rhubarb* and *The Plank* (1967), which featured Eric Sykes, **Harry Secombe** and Jimmy Edwards.

● ALBUMS: *Time For TV* (Studio Two 1967) ★★★, with the Alan Dale Singers *Happy Anniversary* (1969) ★★★.

Fahey, John

b. John Aloysius Fahey, 28 February 1939, Takoma Park, Maryland, USA, d. 22 February 2001, Salem, Oregon, USA. Fahey learned to play country-style guitar in the footsteps of **Hank Williams** and **Eddy Arnold** at the age of 14, inspired by the recordings of **'Blind' Willie Johnson** and other blues greats. He toured during his teens with Henry Vestine (later of **Canned Heat**) and studied for several years at American University in Washington, D.C., to gain a BA in Philosophy and Religion. In 1963 he briefly attended the university of California at Berkeley before transferring to UCLA to study folklore and write his thesis on **Charley Patton**. Fahey announced himself with a style based on an original folk blues theme, encompassing blues, jazz, country and gospel music, and at times incorporating classical pieces, although retaining an almost traditional edge to his arrangements. His 12-string work, featuring intricate fingerpicking and open tunings, became a major influence on other American acoustic guitarists. Fahey was also quick to spot other talent. He persuaded **Bukka White** and **Skip James** to return to music and was the first to record **Leo Kottke**.

Fahey's early recordings appeared under the Blind Thomas moniker on the obscure Fonotone label. These 1958 recordings, pressed up as 78s and catalogued as 'authentic Negro folk music', were an elaborate joke at the expense of folk purists but also demonstrated Fahey's mastery of the blues idiom. He released only a hundred copies of his 1959 debut *Blind Joe Death*, financing the pressing with $300 raised from his job at a gas station. His satirical humour was again in evidence, with one side of the album credited to an obscure bluesman called Blind Joe Death, whom Fahey alleged to have discovered on a field trip to the South. Fahey re-recorded the album in 1964 and 1967 (*The Legend Of Blind Joe Death*, released in 1996, is a mix of all three albums), and by the late 60s it had become a cult record, one with which to be seen rather than actually play. Fahey's early recordings appeared on his own Takoma Records imprint, with his second and third albums also being rerecorded for reissue in 1967.

The masterful **The Transfiguration Of Blind Joe Death**, probably his greatest album, was originally released on the River Boat label in 1965. Fahey signed with **Vanguard Records** in 1967, although he only recorded two albums for the company, including the *musique concrete* album *Requia And Other Compositions For Guitar Solo*. Later still, after a brief sojourn with **Reprise Records**, during which he recorded two albums with an orchestra of Dixieland musicians, he was dropped due to insufficient sales. Fahey's work was heard in the counterculture classic **Zabriskie Point**, but generally his influence was greater than his own success. The ambitious *America*, which was restored to its intended double album length when reissued in the late 90s, didn't sell as well as its predecessors, and Takoma suffered in the general recession that hit the music industry in the 70s. The label was eventually sold to **Chrysalis Records**.

Fahey's personal problems intensified in the 80s as, suffering from diabetes and chronic fatigue caused by the Epstein-Barr virus, he fell upon hunting down and selling collectable records to earn money. He retained his cult following, however, and continued to release the occasional album. Fahey affiliated himself with the alternative rock community in the 90s, concentrating on the electric guitar and *musique concrete* instead of the acoustic blues/folk of his earlier albums. He cofounded the influential Revenant label, while his intent to disown his past was signalled by the dissonant soundscape of 'On The Death And Disembowelment Of The New Age', the key track on his comeback release *City Of Refuge*. The album, which included a dedication of the song 'Hope Slumbers Eternal' to **Mazzy Star**'s vocalist Hope Sandoval, received a good reception in the alternative press. In 1997 Fahey recorded an album with the *avant garde*'s figurehead **Jim O'Rourke** and teamed up with Boston-based post-rock outfit Cul De Sac on *The Epiphany Of Glenn Jones*. The following year he recorded his first solo electric guitar album, *Georgia Stomps, Atlanta Struts, And Other Contemporary Dance Favorites*. Fahey's creative renaissance was sadly cut short by his death in February 2001, two days after undergoing coronary bypass surgery.

● ALBUMS: *Blind Joe Death* (Takoma 1959) ★★★★, *Death Chants, Break Downs & Military Waltzes* i (Takoma 1963) ★★★★, *Blind Joe Death* ii (Takoma 1964) ★★★★, *Dance Of Death & Other Plantation Favorites: John Fahey Vol 3* i (Takoma 1964) ★★★, *The Transfiguration Of Blind Joe Death* (River Boat/Takoma 1965) ★★★★, *Guitar: John Fahey Vol. 4* aka *The Great San Bernardino Birthday Party And Other Excursions* (Takoma 1966) ★★★, *Volume 1: Blind Joe Death* iii (Takoma 1967) ★★★★, *Volume 2: Death Chants, Breakdowns, & Military Waltzes* ii (Takoma 1967) ★★★★, *Volume 3: The Dance Of Death & Other Plantation Favorites* ii (Takoma 1967) ★★★★, *Volume 6: Days Have Gone By* (Takoma 1967) ★★★, *Requia And Other Compositions For Guitar Solo* (Vanguard 1968) ★★★, *The Voice Of The Turtle* (Takoma 1968) ★★★★, *The New Possibility: John Fahey's Guitar Solo Christmas Album* (Takoma 1969) ★★★, *The Yellow Princess* (Vanguard 1969) ★★★★, *America* (Takoma 1971) ★★★, *Of Rivers And Religion* (Reprise 1972) ★★★★, *After The Ball* (Reprise 1973) ★★★, *Fare Forward Voyagers (Soldier's Choice)* (Takoma 1973) ★★★★, *John Fahey, Leo Kottke, Peter Lang* (Takoma 1974) ★★★, *Old Fashioned Love*

(Takoma 1975) ★★★, *Christmas With John Fahey Vol. II* (Takoma 1975) ★★, *Visits Washington, D.C.* (Takoma/Chrysalis 1979) ★★★, *Yes! Jesus Loves Me: Guitar Hymns* (Takoma/Chrysalis 1980) ★★★, *Live In Tasmania* (Takoma/Chrysalis 1981) ★★★, *Christmas Guitar: Volume One* (Varrick 1982) ★★★, with Terry Robb *Popular Songs Of Christmas & New Year's* (Varrick 1983) ★★★, *Railroad I* (Takoma 1983) ★★★★, *Let Go* (Varrick 1984) ★★★, *Rain Forests, Oceans, And Other Themes* (Varrick 1985) ★★★, *I Remember Blind Joe Death* (Varrick 1987) ★★★, *God, Time And Causality* (Shanachie 1989) ★★★, *Old Girlfriends And Other Horrible Memories* (Varrick 1992) ★★★, *City Of Refuge* (Tim/Kerr 1996) ★★★, *Womblife* (Table Of The Elements 1997) ★★★, with Cul De Sac *The Epiphany Of Glenn Jones* (Thirsty Ear 1997) ★★★, *Georgia Stomps, Atlanta Struts, And Other Contemporary Dance Favorites* (Table Of The Elements 1998) ★★★, *Hitomi* (LivHouse 2000) ★★★, *Red Cross* (Revenant 2003) ★★★, *The Great Santa Barbara Oil Slick* (Water/Revenant 2004) ★★★★, *On Air* 1978 recording (Tradition & Moderne 2005) ★★★.

● COMPILATIONS: *The Early Sessions* (Takoma) ★★★, *The Essential John Fahey* (Vanguard 1974) ★★★, *The Best Of John Fahey 1959-1977* (Takoma/Sonet 1977) ★★★★, *Return Of The Repressed: The John Fahey Anthology* (Rhino 1994) ★★★★, *The Legend Of Blind Joe Death* (Fantasy 1996) ★★★★, *Best Of The Vanguard Years* (Vanguard 1999) ★★★, *The Best Of John Fahey Vol. 2: 1964-1983* (Takoma 2004) ★★★★.

● DVD/VIDEOS: *In Concert* (Vestapol Video 1996).

● FURTHER READING: *How Bluegrass Music Destroyed My Life: Stories By John Fahey*, John Fahey. *John Fahey: La Storia, La Discografia Consigliata*, Roberto Menabò.

Fahn, Mike

b. Michael Jeff Fahn, 16 December 1960, New York City, New York, USA. Fahn's father was a jazz drummer who exerted a considerable influence upon his son's choice of career. At the age of 7, he started out playing trumpet but then switched to baritone horn until, at the age of 11, his father, an admirer of **Bob Brookmeyer**, gave him a valve trombone. While in his early teens, his family moved to Los Angeles, where, after leaving high school, he began finding work as a professional musician. Fahn has cited Dick Berk, **Maynard Ferguson** and **Don Menza** as his chief mentors, while other influences include **Tom Harrell**, **Freddie Hubbard** and **Woody Shaw** along with trombonists **J.J. Johnson**, **Frank Rosolino** and **Bill Watrous**. His experience on the west coast was enhanced through work with **Bob Cooper**, **Terry Gibbs**, **Bill Perkins** and **Jack Sheldon**, among many.

In 1987 Fahn received the Los Angeles Jazz Society's Shelly Manne New Talent Award. He met and married jazz bass player **Mary Ann McSweeney**, and in 1993 the couple moved to New York City, where Fahn continued to perform with numerous artists, among them **Randy Brecker**, **Andrew Hill**, **Donny McCaslin**, **Rick Margitza** and **Kenny Wheeler**. He made his recording debut with Bob Shepard and **John Patitucci** and has also recorded with Margitza, Berk, Harrell and Hill. Fahn has toured internationally, playing in Switzerland and France, and has played in many parts of the USA, leading his own quintet at the **Monterey Jazz Festival**. In the early 00s Fahn led his own groups for concert, club and recording dates, also appearing regularly as sideman with several leaders including his wife. Technically assured and a fluent improviser, Fahn's concentration on the relatively rare valve trombone makes him a notable instrumentalist who has, virtually single-handedly, brought back to deserved prominence an instrument that has been allowed to languish in jazz.

● ALBUMS: *Steppin' Out* (Cexton 1989) ★★★, *Close Your Eyes . . . And Listen* (Sparky 1 2002) ★★★.

Fain, Sammy

b. Samuel Feinberg, 17 June 1902, New York, USA, d. 6 December 1989, Los Angeles, California, USA. A prolific composer of Broadway shows and films for over 40 years, early in his career he worked for music publisher Jack Mills and as a singer/pianist in vaudeville and radio. His first published song, with a lyric by **Irving Mills** and **Al Dubin** in 1925, was 'Nobody Knows What A Red Haired Mama Can Do' and was recorded, appropriately, by **Sophie Tucker**. In 1926 he met **Irving Kahal**, who was to be his main collaborator until Kahal's death in 1942. Almost immediately they had hits with 'Let A Smile Be Your Umbrella' and 'I Left My Sugar Standing In The Rain'. In 1929 their song 'Wedding Bells Are Breaking Up That Old Gang Of Mine' was a hit for another singer/pianist, **Gene Austin**, and surfaced again 25 years later, sung by the **Four Aces**.

Fain contributed songs to several early musical films including *The Big Pond* (1930), in which **Maurice Chevalier** introduced 'You Brought A New Kind Of Love To Me'; the Marx Brothers' comedy *Monkey Business* (1931), 'When I Take My Sugar To Tea'; *Footlight Parade* (1933), 'By A Waterfall'; *Goin' To Town* (1935), in which **Mae West** sang 'Now I'm A Lady' and 'He's A Bad, Bad Man But He's Good Enough For Me'; and *Dames* (1934), which featured the song 'When You Were A Smile On Your Mother's Lips And A Twinkle In Your Daddy's Eye'—and in which Fain actually appeared as a songwriter. Fain's 30s Broadway credits included *Everybody's Welcome*, *Right This Way* (featuring 'I'll Be Seeing You' and 'I Can Dream, Can't I?'), *Hellzapoppin'* (reputedly the most popular musical of the 30s) and *George White's Scandals* of 1939 ('Are You Havin' Any Fun?' and 'Something I Dreamed Last Night'). During the 40s and 50s Fain collaborated with several lyricists including **Lew Brown**, **Jack Yellen**, **Mitchell Parish**, **Harold Adamson**, **E.Y. 'Yip' Harburg**, **Bob Hilliard** and **Paul Francis Webster**. In 1945 he worked with Ralph Freed, brother of the more famous lyricist and movie producer **Arthur Freed**. Fain and Freed's 'The Worry Song' was interpolated into the **Sammy Cahn/Jule Styne** score for the **Frank Sinatra/Gene Kelly** movie *Anchors Aweigh* (1945), to accompany Kelly's famous dance sequence with the animated Jerry the mouse.

Fain's greatest Hollywood success was in the 50s. He wrote the scores for two **Walt Disney** classics: *Alice In Wonderland* (1951), 'I'm Late' with Bob Hilliard, and *Peter Pan* (1953), 'Your Mother And Mine' and 'Second Star To The Right' with Sammy Cahn. Also with Cahn, Fain wrote some songs for the movie *Three Sailors And a Girl* (1953) ('The Lately Song' and 'Show Me A Happy Woman And I'll Show You A Miserable Man'). In 1953 Fain, in collaboration with Paul Francis Webster, won his first Academy Award for 'Secret Love', from their score for the **Doris Day/Howard Keel** movie *Calamity Jane*. His second Oscar, the title song for the film *Love Is A Many Splendored Thing* (1955), was also written in partnership with Webster, as were several other film title

songs including 'A Certain Smile', 'April Love', and 'Tender Is The Night', which were all nominated for Academy Awards. Other Fain/Webster movie songs included 'There's A Rising Moon (For Every Falling Star)' from **Young At Heart** (1954) and 'A Very Precious Love' from *Marjorie Morningstar* (1958), both sung by Doris Day. Fain's last four Broadway musicals were **Flahooley** (1951) written with Harburg ('Here's To Your Illusions' and 'He's Only Wonderful'), *Ankles Aweigh* (1955) with Dan Shapiro, *Christine* (1960) with Webster and *Something More* (1964) with **Alan And Marilyn Bergman**. Fain continued to write films songs to the 70s. He also made some vocal records and had a US chart entry as early as 1926 with Al Dubin and **Joe Burke**'s 'Painting The Clouds With Sunshine'. He was inducted into the Songwriters Hall Of Fame in 1971 and served on the board of directors of **ASCAP** from 1979 until his death from a heart attack in December 1989.

Faint

Few rock acts have started off playing lo-fi pop folk before transforming into a electronic-based, new wave dance outfit, but the Omaha, Nebraska, USA–based trio the Faint is one of the few exceptions. The band was formed during 1994 by Todd Baechle (vocals/synthesizer), Clark Baechle (drums) and Joel Petersen (bass/guitar) and soon began playing their folk-based tunes in local coffeehouses under the name Norman Bailer (Conor Oberst aka **Bright Eyes** was briefly a member). After releasing an obscure cassette, the trio toughened up their sound a bit and spent the next few years honing their new style. During this time, they recruited bass player Matt Bowen and changed their name to the Faint and in 1998 issued their debut release for the Saddle Creek label, the musically varied *Media*. They began focusing more on dance material for their 1999 follow-up, *Blank-Wave Arcade*, looking to 80s electronic acts such as **Depeche Mode**, **Soft Cell** and the **Human League** for guidance. The album was recorded without Bowen but with the input of important an new member, keyboard player Jacob Thiele. The Faint made the full musical transition with 2001's *Danse Macabre* and shortly thereafter welcomed new guitarist Dapose (ex-Lead) into their line-up. A remix album preceded the release of the band's new studio set, *Wet From Birth*.

● ALBUMS: *Media* (Saddle Creek 1998) ★★★, *Blank-Wave Arcade* (Saddle Creek 1999) ★★★★, *Danse Macabre* (Saddle Creek/City Slang 2001) ★★★★, *Wet From Birth* (Saddle Creek 2004) ★★★.

● COMPILATIONS: *Danse Macabre Remixes* (Astralwerks 2003) ★★★.

Fair, Jad

b. Ann Arbor, Michigan, USA. This US singer-songwriter has pursued his wildly eccentric muse for over three decades as a solo performer or with **Half Japanese**, the band he formed in the mid-70s with his brother David Fair. Drawing equal inspiration from **Jonathan Richman**'s primitive rock and classic 60s pop, Fair's recorded output has been dismissed as tuneless drivel by some and as the work of a childlike savant by others. Whatever the verdict (and his music generates such extreme responses), Fair has stuck with his rudimentary style over the years and resolutely refuses to learn how to play guitar or sing properly.

Fair began recording as a solo artist in 1980, shortly after Half Japanese released their long-playing debut, a three-record box set! His own full-length debut, *Everyone Knew . . . But Me*, chronicled Fair's problems with girls over an interminable 27 tracks (plus two **James Brown** covers). The follow-up, *Best Wishes*, comprised 42 brief instrumentals titled either 'O.K.' or 'A.O.K.'. The majority of his work since the late 80s has been 'collaborations' with other artists, including **Kramer**, **Daniel Johnston**, the **Pastels**, **Yo La Tengo** and **Teenage Fanclub**, although with Fair unwilling or unable to alter his DIY approach, the results have often been disjointed and sometimes hard to listen to. Confirming his status as a cult underground hero, in 1993 Fair and his band were recruited by Kurt Cobain as the opening act on **Nirvana**'s In Utero tour. Fair has also recorded several albums with Half Japanese guitarist Tim Foljahn and **Sonic Youth** drummer Steve Shelley as Mosquito.

● ALBUMS: *The Zombies Of Mora-Tau* mini-album (Armageddon 1980) ★★, *Everyone Knew . . . But Me* (Press 1982) ★★, as Between Meals *Oh No I Just Knocked Over A Cup Of Coffee* (Iridescence 1983) ★★, *Monarchs* (Iridescence 1984) ★★, *Best Wishes* (Iridescence 1987) ★★, with Kramer *Roll Out The Barrel* (Shimmy-Disc 1988) ★★, *Great Expectations* (Bad Alchemy 1989) ★★★, *Jad Fair And Daniel Johnston* aka *It's Spooky* (50 Skidillion Watts/Paperhouse 1989) ★★★, *Greater Expectations* (Psycho-Acoustic Sounds/T.E.C. Tones 1991) ★★★, *I Like It When You Smile* (T.E.C. Tones/Paperhouse 1992) ★★★, *Jad Fair/Jason Willett/Gilles Rieder* (Megaphone 1992) ★★★, with Nao *Half Robot* (Paperhouse 1993) ★★, with Phono-Comb *Monsters, Lullabies . . . And The Occasional Flying Saucer* (Shake 1996) ★★★, with the Shapir-O'Rama *We Are The Rage* (Avant 1996) ★★★, with David Fair *Best Friends* (Vesuvius 1996) ★★★, with Jason Willett *Honey Bee* (Dr. Jim 1997) ★★★, with Willett *Wild* (Megaphone 1997) ★★★, with Yo La Tengo *Strange But True* (Matador 1998) ★★★, with David Fair *26 Monster Songs For Children* (Kill Rock Stars 1998) ★★, with Willett *Enjoyable Songs* (Alternative Tentacles 1999) ★★★, with the Shapir-O'Rama *I Like Your Face* (Wire Monkey 1999) ★★★, as the Lucky Sperms *Somewhat Humorous* (Jagjaguwar 2001) ★★★, with Teenage Fanclub *Words Of Wisdom And Hope* (Geographic/Alternative Tentacles 2002) ★★★, *DQE And Jad Fair* (Dark Beloved Cloud 2002) ★★★, with R. Stevie Moore *Fair-Moore* (Old Gold 2002) ★★.

● FURTHER READING: *The Attack Of Everything*, Jad Fair.

Fair, Yvonne

b. 1942, Virginia, USA, d. 6 March 1994, Las Vegas, Nevada, USA. Fair joined the **Chantels** in the early 60s before touring for five years as a member of **James Brown**'s revue and recording two singles with Brown for King. After recording one unsuccessful single for **Motown Records**' Soul subsidiary in 1970, she spent three years as part of **Chuck Jackson**'s band before returning to Motown in 1974. Fair teamed up with producer **Norman Whitfield**, who brought her raucous vocal talents to his song 'Funky Music Sho' Nuff Turns Me On', a 1974 R&B hit, followed later that year by 'Walk Out The Door If You Wanna'. It was the b-side of the latter single—a fiery revival of **Gladys Knight**'s 1968 hit 'It Should've Been Me'— that brought her most attention when it belatedly charted in Britain early in 1976. Fair had already left the Motown stable and was unable to capitalize on this success. She appeared in the film *Lady Sings The Blues*, and before her untimely death in 1994, she worked with **Dionne Warwick**.

● ALBUMS: *The Bitch Is Black* (Motown 1975) ★★★.
● FILMS: *Lady Sings The Blues*.

Fairchild, Barbara

b. 12 November 1950, Knobel, Arkansas, USA. Fairchild was raised on a farm and was entertaining at every opportunity. The family moved to St. Louis when she was 12 years old, and she was soon recording for the local Norman label and working on television. In 1968 she moved to Nashville, to further her career, and among her early singles is 'Remember The Alimony' for **Kapp Records**. Her song 'This Stranger (My Little Girl)' has been recorded by **Loretta Lynn**, **Dottie West** and **Liz Anderson**. Fairchild was signed to **Columbia Records** in 1969 and immediately achieved her first US country hit with 'Love Is A Gentle Thing', followed by various minor entries, including 'A Girl Who'll Satisfy Her Man' and 'Love's Old Song'. Then the novelty 'Teddy Bear Song', written by a St. Louis policeman, topped the US country charts. She never repeated that success although she had country hits with 'Kid Stuff', 'Baby Doll', 'You've Lost That Lovin' Feelin'', 'Mississippi', 'Cheatin' Is' and 'Let Me Love You Once Before You Go'. She wrote 'Tara' for one of her daughters, and her husband and songwriting partner, steel guitarist Randy Reinhard, was part of her road band. After their divorce, she married Milton Carroll, who had recorded for **RCA Records**. In the early 80s she became a born-again Christian and left the music business for several years. In 1986 she recorded an album with production by her old friend **Don Williams**, but only a single was released. She joined the band Heirloom in 1989 and has also released solo gospel albums.

● ALBUMS: *Someone Special* (Columbia 1970) ★★, *Love's Old Song* (Columbia 1971) ★★★, *The Barbara Fairchild Way* reissued as *Love's Old Song* (Columbia 1971) ★★★, *A Sweeter Love* (Columbia 1972) ★★★, *Teddy Bear Song* (Columbia 1972) ★★, *Kid Stuff* (Columbia 1973) ★★, *Standing In Your Line* (Columbia 1974) ★★★, *Love Is A Gentle Thing* (Columbia 1974) ★★★, *Barbara Fairchild* (Columbia 1975) ★★★, *Mississippi* (Columbia 1976) ★★, *Free And Easy* (Columbia 1977) ★★★, *This Is Me!* (Columbia 1978) ★★★, with Billy Walker *The Answer Game* reissued as *It Takes Two* (RCA 1979) ★★★, *The Biggest Hurt* (1983) ★★, *The Light* (Benson 1991) ★★★, *The Son In My Eyes* (Benson 1993) ★★★, *Stories* (Chapel 1995) ★★★, *Classic Country* (Simitar 1998) ★★★, *Rocky Top* (Nashville Clan 1999) ★★★, *Then And Now* (Daywind 2000) ★★★, with Roy Morris *All Is Forgiven* (Daywind 2000) ★★★, with Morris *For God And Country* (Daywind 2001) ★★★, *Wings Of A Dove* (Daywind 2002) ★★★, with Connie Smith, Sharon White *Love Never Fails* (Daywind 2003) ★★★, *Forever Friend* (ACA 2003) ★★★.

Fairchild, Raymond

b. 5 March 1939, Cherokee, North Carolina, USA. Fairchild, who is of Cherokee Indian extraction, first played guitar, but in the late 50s, greatly impressed by the playing of an aunt, he decided to specialize in banjo. He first recorded for Sim around 1963, but in 1965, with his Maggie Valley Boys, he recorded several instrumental albums for Uncle Jim O'Neal's popular Rural Rhythm label. Some gained release at varying dates, but by 1976 his releases and reissues were attracting a great deal of attention. He quickly built his reputation and amazed his audiences by his playing, not only in his own Maggie Valley locale but also at various major bluegrass and folk festivals. Between 1975 and 1990, he worked with Wayne and Wallace Crowe, who played guitar and bass and added vocals. The trio became very popular around the bluegrass circuit and recorded albums for Skyline and Atteiram. He then re-formed his Maggie Valley Boys, which included his son Zane on lead guitar and Wallace Crowe's son Shane on bass. In 1989 he recorded with **Ralph Stanley**, singing for the first time, and in 1990 he recorded with **Chubby Wise**. He is noted for his deadpan expressions, even while executing his most speedy instrumental breaks, and also for his humorous anecdotes, such as his hints on how to keep rattlesnakes as household pets. He continued to play into the 90s, and his talents have seen him fondly dubbed the 'King of the Smoky Mountain Banjo Players'.

● ALBUMS: with Frank Buchanan *America's Most Authentic Folk Banjo* (Sim 1963) ★★★, *King Of The Smoky Mountain 5 String Banjo Players* i (Rural Rhythm 1966) ★★★★, *Raymond Fairchild & The Maggie Valley Boys* (Rural Rhythm 1967) ★★★, *Mama Likes Bluegrass Music* (Rural Rhythm 1968) ★★★★, *Honky Tonkin Country Blues* (Rural Rhythm 1971) ★★★★, *King Of The Smoky Mountain 5 String Banjo Players* ii (Rural Rhythm 1972) ★★★, *Smoky Mountain Banjo* (Paradise & Atteiram 1974) ★★★, *King Of The 5 String Banjo* 4 volumes (Rural Rhythm 1976) ★★★★, *World's Greatest Banjo Picker* (Rural Rhythm 1976) ★★★★, *The Maggie Valley Boys, Picking And Singing In Maggie Valley* (Atteiram 1978) ★★★, *The Legendary Raymond Fairchild Plays Little Zane* (Skyline 1981) ★★★, *Always True* (Skyline 1981) ★★★, *The Gospel Way* (Skyline 1984) ★★★, *The Winds Are Blowing In Maggie Valley* (Atteiram 1986) ★★★, *Plays Requests* (Skyline 1986) ★★★, *World Champion Banjo* (Skyline 1987) ★★★, *Jesus Is Coming* (Atteiram 1988) ★★, *Me And My Banjo At Home In Maggie Valley* (Atteiram 1989) ★★★, *Ralph Stanley & Raymond Fairchild* (Rebel 1989) ★★★, with Chubby Wise *Cherokee Tunes & Seminole Swing* (Rebel 1990) ★★★.

Fairfield Parlour

London, England, progressive rock band Fairfield Parlour were formed after their previous incarnation, **Kaleidoscope**, had been dropped by **Fontana Records**. After recording a single credited to I Luv Wight, Eddie Pumer (guitar), Peter Daltrey (vocals/keyboards), Dan Bridgeman (percussion) and Steve Clarke (d. 1 May 1999; bass) took the less unwieldy name Fairfield Parlour. Their debut single was 'Bordeaux Rose', issued in 1970, followed by the album *From Home To Home*. Though it failed to achieve significant sales, it drew vociferous support from BBC Radio disc jockey **Kenny Everett**. Despite this, the group disbanded within 12 months of their formation.

● ALBUMS: *From Home To Home* (Vertigo 1970) ★★.

Fairground Attraction

This jazz/folk-tinged Anglo/Scottish pop band comprised **Eddi Reader** (b. Sadenia Reader, 28 August 1959, Glasgow, Scotland; vocals), **Mark Nevin** (b. 13 August 1959, Ebbw Vale, Wales; guitar), Simon Edwards (guitaron, a Mexican acoustic guitar-shaped bass) and Roy Dodds (drums). After art school, Reader made her first musical forays as backing singer for the **Gang Of Four**. She moved to London in 1983 where session and live work with the **Eurythmics** and **Alison Moyet** kept her gainfully employed. She first linked with

Nevin for the Compact Organisation sampler album *The Compact Composers*, singing on two of his songs. Nevin and Reader began their first collaborations in 1985, after Nevin had graduated by playing in one of the numerous line-ups of **Jane Aire And The Belvederes**. He was also closely involved with **Sandie Shaw**'s mid-80s comeback. Around his songs they built Fairground Attraction, adding Edwards and Dodds, a jazz drummer of over 20 years' standing who had spent time with **Working Week** and **Terence Trent D'Arby**. They signed to **RCA Records** and quickly set about recording a debut album, as the gentle skiffle of 'Perfect' topped the UK singles charts in May 1988. They subsequently won both Best Single and Best Album categories at the BRIT awards.

A slight hiatus in the band's career followed when Reader became pregnant. They followed their natural inclinations by filming the video for their 1989 single 'Clare' in Nashville, and were supplemented on tour by Graham Henderson (accordion) and Roger Beaujolais (vibraphone). Their promise was cut short when the band split, and Reader went on to acting (appearing in a BBC drama, *Your Cheatin' Heart*, about the Scottish country and western scene) and a solo career, releasing her debut, *Mirmama*, in 1992. Nevin worked with **Brian Kennedy** in Sweetmouth before establishing a productive career as a songwriter with **Morrissey** and **Kirsty MacColl**. He launched a solo career at the end of the 90s.

● ALBUMS: *The First Of A Million Kisses* (RCA 1988) ★★★.

● COMPILATIONS: *Ay Fond Kiss* (RCA 1990) ★★★, *The Very Best Of Fairground Attraction* (Camden 1997) ★★★.

Fairhurst, Richard

b. 1974, Leicester, Leicestershire, England. Fairhurst began playing piano at the age of 15 and within a few years was displaying his mastery of the instrument. An exceptionally talented pianist and composer, he attracted serious critical attention in the mid-90s when a saxophone quartet he composed was short-listed for the Cornelius Cardew Composition Prize. Also during this period, he won the Pat Smythe Award for Young Jazz Musicians Of Outstanding Talent. In 1994 he appeared at **Ronnie Scott**'s club in London, where he played with **Iain Ballamy**, who appeared on Fairhurst's debut CD. In 1996 Fairhurst spent several months in New York City on a scholarship at the New School that allowed him to expand his playing and composition skills. His musical collaboration with drummer Tim Giles continued when they formed a duo in 1997 to appear at the Third European Tournament of Improvisation in Poitiers, Frances. Following that 1994 gig at Ronnie Scott's, Fairhurst had formed a quartet he named the Hungry Ants. In 1997 he recorded with this quartet at Senegal's St. Lois Jazz Festival, where the band appeared under the sponsorship of the British Council. In addition to performing, the group held student workshops at the Conservatoire in Dakar. Subsequently, Fairhurst collaborated with the British Council in arranging for musical instruments and other equipment to be made available to students there.

Fairhurst's late 90s commissions included a work for the Leicestershire Schools Symphonic Wind Band and Contemporary Dance Group, performed at the 1997 Edinburgh Festival and reprised in 1998 at Manchester's Opera Theatre. Among other commissions have been new scores for two restored silent films from the 20s, *Rain* and *Manhattan*, for

Phoenix Arts, Leicester, that were premiered in April 1999 by the Hungry Ants, expanded for the occasion by Chris Batchelor (trumpet) and Stuart Hall (violin/guitar). Fairhurst has also worked with saxophonists Osian Roberts and James Allsop and bass player Steve Watts. Fairhurst has performed with his quartet at the Glasgow Jazz Festival, at the Copenhagen Jazz Festival, in Cologne, Belfast, and in many venues around the UK.

In 1999 Fairhurst was made a Steinway International Artist, one of the youngest pianists to be added to a distinguished roster and only the second British jazz pianist to be so honoured. He has been one of only three composers awarded New Works commissions by Birmingham Jazz. He has also worked in the theatre, playing solo piano music composed by Huw Warren for a production of *Take The Fire* at The Lyric Theatre, Hammersmith. Fairhurst's suite, recorded on his album *Standing Tall*, was nominated as Best Work in the 2004 BBC Jazz Awards. Imaginative and fluent, Fairhurst is a growing musical talent, and his repertoire shows awareness of all that is happening in jazz.

● ALBUMS: *The Hungry Ants* (Babel 1996) ★★★, *Formic* (Babel 2000) ★★★, *Standing Tall* (Babel 2004) ★★★★.

Fairies

Formed in Colchester, Essex, England, in 1963 as Dane Stephens And The Deepbeats, this vibrant R&B group consisted of Dane Stephens (vocals), Fred Gandy (guitar), John Acutt (guitar), Mick 'Wimp' Weaver (bass) and John 'Twink' Alder (drums). In 1964 they secured a 'one-off' contract with **Decca Records**. Having opted for the more contemporary-sounding Fairies, the group completed a hurried version of **Bob Dylan**'s 'Don't Think Twice It's All Right'. Stephens left the line-up soon after its release and was replaced by Nick Wymer. Wymer had previously led another local act, Nick And The Nomads aka Nix-Nomads who had already recorded a single for **HMV Records**. 'You're Nobody ('Til Somebody Loves You)' was pedestrian, but its b-side, 'She'll Be Sweeter Than You', is an English R&B/punk classic. The Fairies were signed to HMV through Wymer's association. Having passed on an option to record 'Don't Bring Me Down', later a hit for the **Pretty Things**, the Fairies recorded 'Get Yourself Home', which the Pretty Things themselves had rejected. The result was another impressive slice of rhythmic R&B and, although not a hit, was one of the finest British discs of 1965. Sadly, the Fairies were forced to tame their image for their last release, the disappointing 'Don't Mind'. A chastened Wymer left the line-up and dropped out of professional music when plans for a projected group with **Them**'s Billy Harrison fell through. The Fairies split up soon after his departure. **Twink** joined the **In Crowd** and was later a member of a host of groups including **Tomorrow**, the Pretty Things and **Pink Fairies**.

Fairport Convention

The unchallenged inventors and high kings of British folk rock have struggled through tragedy and changes, retaining the name that now represents not so much who is in the band but what it stands for. The original 1967 line-up comprised **Iain Matthews** (b. Iain Matthews McDonald, 16 June 1946, Scunthorpe, Lincolnshire, England; vocals), **Judy Dyble** (b. 13 February 1949, London, England; autoharp/vocals), **Ashley Hutchings** (b. 26 January 1945, Southgate, Middlesex, England; bass), **Richard Thompson** (b. 3 April 1949, Totteridge & Whetstone, London, England; guitar/vocals), **Simon Nicol** (b. 13 October 1950, Muswell Hill, London, England; guitar/vocals) and Martin Lamble (b. 28 August 1949, St. Johns Wood, London, England, d. 12 May 1969, England; drums). The band originally came to the attention of the London 'underground' club scene by sounding like a cross between the **Jefferson Airplane** and the **Byrds**. As an accessible alternative, people immediately took them to their hearts. American producer **Joe Boyd** signed them, and they released the charming 'If I Had A Ribbon Bow'. On their self-titled debut album they introduced the then little-known Canadian songwriter **Joni Mitchell** to a wider audience. The album was a cult favourite, but like the single, it sold poorly.

Judy Dyble departed and was replaced by vocalist **Sandy Denny** (b. Alexandra Denny, 6 January 1948, Wimbledon, London, England, d. 21 April 1978; ex-**Strawbs**). Denny brought a traditional folk feel to their work that began to appear on the superlative *What We Did On Our Holidays*. This varied collection contained some of their finest songs: Denny's version of 'She Moved Through The Fair', her own 'Fotheringay', Matthews' lilting 'Book Song', the superb 'I'll Keep It With Mine' and Thompson's masterpiece 'Meet On The Ledge'. This joyous album was bound together by exemplary musicianship; of particular note was the guitar of the shy and wiry Thompson. Matthews left soon after its release, unhappy with the traditional direction the band was pursuing. Following the album's critical acclaim and a modest showing in the charts, they experienced tragedy a few months later when their Transit van crashed, killing Martin Lamble and their friend and noted dressmaker Jeannie Franklyn. *Unhalfbricking* was released, and although not as strong as the former, it contained two excellent readings of **Bob Dylan** songs, 'Percy's Song' and 'Si Tu Dois Partir' (If You Gotta Go, Go Now). Denny contributed two songs, 'Autopsy' and the definitive and beautiful 'Who Knows Where The Time Goes'. More significantly, *Unhalfbricking* featured guest musician **Dave Swarbrick** (b. 5 April 1941, New Malden, Surrey, England) on fiddle and mandolin. The album charted, as did the second Dylan number; by now the band had opened the door for future bands like **Steeleye Span** by creating a climate that allowed traditional music to be played in a rock context.

The songs that went on the next album were premiered on **John Peel**'s BBC radio show *Top Gear*. An excited Peel stated that their performance would 'sail them into uncharted waters'; his judgement proved correct. The live set was astonishing—they played jigs and reels and completed all 27 verses of the traditional 'Tam Lin', featuring Swarbrick, now a full-time member, plus the debut of new drummer Dave Mattacks (b. March 1948, Edgware, Middlesex, England). The subsequent album *Liege And Lief* was a milestone; they had created British folk rock in spectacular style. This, however, created problems within the band, and Hutchings left to form Steeleye Span, and Denny departed to form **Fotheringay** with future husband **Trevor Lucas** (ex-**Eclection**). Undeterred, the band recruited **Dave Pegg** (b. 2 November 1947, Birmingham, England) on bass, and Swarbrick became more prominent both as lead vocalist and as an outstanding fiddle player. From their communal home in Hertfordshire, they wrote much of the next two albums' material, although Thompson left before the release of *Angel Delight*. They made *The Guinness Book Of Records* in 1970 with the longest-ever title: 'Sir B. McKenzies' Daughter's Lament For The 77th Mounted Lancer's Retreat From The Straits Of Loch Knombe, In The Year Of Our Lord 1727, On The Occasion Of The Announcement Of Her Marriage To The Laird Of Kinleakie'. *Full House* was the first all-male Fairport Convention album and was instrumentally strong with extended tracks like 'Sloth' becoming standards.

The concept album *Babbacombe Lee*, although critically welcomed, failed to sell, and Simon Nicol left to form the **Albion Country Band** with Ashley Hutchings. Swarbrick struggled on, battling against hearing problems. With such comings and goings of personnel, it was difficult to document the exact changes. The lack of any animosity from ex-members contributed to the family atmosphere, although by this time record sales were dwindling. Denny rejoined, as did Mattacks (twice), but by the end of the 70s the name was put to rest. The family tree specialist Pete Frame has documented their incredible array of line-ups. Their swan song was at Cropredy in Oxfordshire in 1979. Since then, an annual reunion has taken place and is now a major event on the folk calendar. The band has no idea which ex-members will turn up! They have also continued to release albums, making the swan song a sham. With Swarbrick's departure, his position was taken by **Ric Sanders** (b. 8 December 1952, Birmingham, West Midlands, England) in 1985, who rapidly quietened his dissenters by stamping his own personality on the fiddler's role.

Some of the recent collections have been quite superb, including *Gladys Leap*, with Simon Nicol back on lead vocals, and the instrumental *Expletive Delighted*. With the release in 1990 of *The Five Seasons*, the band established the longest-lasting line-up in their history. The nucleus of Pegg, Nicol, Sanders, Mattacks and Allcock were responsible for *Jewel In The Crown* (named after their favourite tandoori takeaway). Nicol's voice sounded like it had been matured in a wooden cask and fuelled the suggestion that he should perhaps have been the lead vocalist right from the beginning. This was their bestselling and undoubtedly finest album in years and dispels any thought of old folkies growing outdated and staid. *Who Knows Where The Time Goes?* although a lesser album, did include an excellent live version of 'I Heard It Through The Grapevine', recorded at Cropredy in 1995. The 'Cropredy' box set is an invaluable chronicle of the history of the band, narrated by the band itself, it included the hilarious and now legendary 'April fool' telephone conversation. *The Wood & The Wire* was yet another excellent recording with the 2000 line-up of Pegg, Nicol, Sanders, Gerry Conway (b. 11 September 1947, Kings Lynn, Norfolk, England) and Chris Leslie (b. 15 December 1956, Oxford, England). Fairport Convention, in whatever shape they appear, is as much a part of the folk music tradition as the music itself.

● ALBUMS: *Fairport Convention* (Polydor 1968) ★★★, *What We Did On Our Holidays* (Island 1969) ★★★★★, *Unhalfbricking* (Island 1969) ★★★★, *Liege And Lief* (Island 1969) ★★★★★, *Full House* (Island 1970) ★★★★, *Angel Delight* (Island 1971) ★★★, *Babbacombe Lee* (Island 1971) ★★★, *Rosie* (Island 1973) ★★★, *Nine* (Island 1973) ★★, *Live Convention (A Moveable Feast)* (Island 1974) ★★, *Rising For The Moon* (Island 1975) ★★, as Fairport *Gottle O'Geer* (Island 1976) ★, *Live At The LA Troubadour* (Island 1977) ★★, *A Bonny Bunch Of Roses* (Vertigo 1977) ★★, *Tipplers Tales* (Vertigo 1978) ★★, *Farewell, Farewell* (Simons 1979) ★★★, *Moat On The Ledge: Live At Broughton Castle* (Woodworm 1981) ★★★, *Gladys' Leap* (Woodworm 1985) ★★★, *Expletive Delighted* (Woodworm 1986) ★★★, *House Full* (Hannibal 1986) ★★, *In Real Time—Live '87* (Island 1987) ★★, *Red And Gold* (New Routes 1989) ★★, *Five Seasons* (New Routes 1991) ★★, *25th Anniversary Concert* (Wormwood 1994) ★★★, *Jewel In The Crown* (Woodworm 1995) ★★★★, *Old New Borrowed Blue* (Woodworm 1996) ★★★, *Who Knows Where The Time Goes?* (Woodworm 1997) ★★★, *The Cropredy Box* 3-CD box set (Woodworm 1998) ★★★★, *Close To The Wind* (Mooncrest 1998) ★★★, *The Wood & The Wire* (Woodworm 2000) ★★★★, *XXXV* (Woodworm/ Compass 2002) ★★★, *Before The Moon* (Pilot 2002) ★★, *Cropredy 2002* (Woodworm 2003) ★★★, *The Quiet Joys Of Brotherhood: Live At The Cropredy Festivals 1986 And 1987* (Shakedown 2004) ★★★, *Over The Next Hill* (Matty Grooves 2004) ★★★, *Journeyman's Grace* (Snapper 2005) ★★★.

● COMPILATIONS: *History Of Fairport Convention* (Island 1972) ★★★★, *Heyday: The BBC Radio Sessions 1968–9* (Hannibal 1986) ★★★, *The Best Of Fairport Convention* (Island 1988) ★★★★, *The Woodworm Years* (Woodworm 1992) ★★★, *Fiddlestix: The Best Of Fairport 1972–1984* (Raven 1998) ★★★, *Rhythm Of The Time* (Delta 1999) ★★★, *Meet On The Ledge: The Classic Years (1967–1975)* (Island 2000) ★★★★, *Wishfulness Waltz* (Mooncrest 2000) ★★★★, *The Other Boot/The Third Leg* 3-CD set (Woodworm 2001) ★★★, *Heyday: The BBC Sessions 1968– 1969/Expanded* (Island 2002) ★★★, *Then And Now 1982– 1996: The Best Of The Fairport Convention* (Metro 2002) ★★, *Fairport Unconventional* 4-CD box set (Free Reed 2002) ★★★, *The Best Of Fairport Convention: The Millennium Collection* (A&M 2002) ★★★★, *The Airing Cupboard Tapes '71–'74* (Talking Elephant 2002) ★★★, *Across The Decade* (Snapper 2003) ★★★, *Chronicles* (Universal 2005) ★★★★, *A Lasting Spirit: The Collection* (Woodworm 2005) ★★★.

● DVD/VIDEOS: *Reunion Festival Broughton Castle 1981* (Videotech 1982), *Cropredy 39 August 1980* (Videotech 1982), *A Weekend In The Country* (Videotech 1983), *Cropredy Capers* (Intech Video 1986), *In Real Time* (Island Visual Arts 1987), *It All Comes Round Again* (Island Visual Arts 1987), *Live At Maidstone 1970* (Musikfolk 1991), *Beyond The Ledge* (Beckmann Visual Publishing 1999), *35th Anniversary Concert* (Secret Films 2003), *Live At The Marlow Theatre Canterbury* (Snapper 2005).

● FURTHER READING: *Meet On The Ledge: A History Of Fairport Convention*, Patrick Humphries. *The Woodworm Era: The Story Of Today's Fairport Convention*, Fred Redwood and Martin Woodward. *Richard Thompson: Strange Affair*, Patrick Humphries. *Fairportfolio*, Kingsley Abbott. *The Fairport Tour*, David Hughes. *No More Sad Refrains: The Life And Times Of Sandy Denny*, Clinton Heylin. *Ashley Hutchings: The Guv'nor & The Rise Of Folk Rock*, Brian Hinton and Geoff Wall.

Fairuz

b. 21 November 1935, Beirut, Lebanon. Fairuz began her musical career in 1947, when, having been discovered singing at a school party, she was invited to join a choir formed to perform national hymns on Lebanese radio. She studied singing and music at the Conservatoire National du Liban and, on the completion of her studies, sang solo on national radio. Through these performances she became a star in her own country. In the 50s she began working with renowned local composers and arrangers the Rahbani brothers, marrying Assi Rahbani in 1954. The combination of Fairuz's darkly passionate voice with the Rahbanis' innovative arrangements (which mixed traditional Arabic instrumentation with western-style orchestral strings) and memorable songs proved phenomenally popular throughout the Middle East and made Fairuz a cultural icon for Arabs all over the world. The partnership continued for decades, with the Rahbani brothers also writing a series of hit musical films in which Fairuz appeared. The 1997 recording *The Legendary Fairuz* features a selection of her most famous songs performed with full orchestral backing in various Arab countries.

● ALBUMS: *The Legendary Fairuz* (Hemisphere 1997) ★★★.

● COMPILATIONS: *The Lady And The Legend* (Union Square 2005) ★★★★.

Fairweather

This Welsh quintet comprising **Andy Fairweather-Low** (vocals/guitar), Neil Jones (guitar), Blue Weaver (keyboards), Clive Taylor (bass) and Dennis Bryon (drums) evolved from the ashes of the pop band **Amen Corner**. Although the new unit was determined to plough a more progressive furrow, they reached number 6 in the UK charts with 'Natural Sinner' in July 1970. Fairweather was unable to rid itself of a 'teenybopper' tag and split up on completing its lone album. Weaver later became a respected session musician, appearing with such disparate acts as the **Strawbs**, the **Bee Gees** and the **Pet Shop Boys**, while Fairweather-Low pursued a solo career.

● ALBUMS: *Beginning From An End* (RCO 1971) ★★.

Fairweather-Low, Andy

b. 2 August 1950, Ystrad Mynach, Cardiff, Wales. This Welsh guitarist and singer took over **Dave Edmunds**' sales assistant job at the music shop Barrett's Of Cardiff in the mid-60s, which enabled him to mix with the musicians on the local scene. He recruited a number of these to form the pop outfit **Amen Corner**. It was Fairweather-Low's intention to play guitar in the band, but as they had too many guitarists and no vocalists, he had to take on the singing duties and became a teen idol in Britain as the band enjoyed a run of hit singles. When Amen Corner split, Fairweather-Low and the brass section formed **Fairweather**, who signed to **RCA Records**' new progressive label Neon. They immediately blew their underground 'cool' by having a big hit single with 'Natural Sinner', but after a couple of less successful singles, they too broke up. Fairweather-Low retired to Wales to concentrate on writing and playing for his own amusement. He returned in 1975 with an album and hit single 'Reggae Tune'. Another memorable big hit with 'Wide Eyed And Legless' highlighted his characteristic voice. The artist's subsequent releases, including a 1986 single on the **Stiff Records** label, failed to chart, and he spent more time playing on sessions and live gigs, including some with **Roger Waters**. He also sang with the all-star ARMS band during 1987 to raise money for research into multiple sclerosis. In 1990 Fairweather-Low toured with **Chris Rea** and in December 1991 with **George Harrison** and **Eric Clapton** (Japanese tour). He continued to play in Clapton's band during the 90s and acted as the guitarist's

musical arranger (appearing on *Unplugged*). He also joined the **Big Town Playboys** and is regularly called upon for other prestigious gigs throughout the rock world.

● ALBUMS: *Spider Jivin'* (A&M 1974) ★★★, *La Booga Rooga* (A&M 1975) ★★★, *Be Bop 'N' Holla* (A&M 1976) ★★, *Mega-Shebang* (Warners 1980) ★★.

● COMPILATIONS: *Wide Eyed And Legless: The A&M Recordings* (Edsel 2004) ★★★.

Fairweather, Al

b. Alastair Fairweather, 12 June 1927, Edinburgh, Scotland, d. 21 June 1993. After a brief flirtation with the trombone, Fairweather settled on the trumpet and while still at school began playing jazz. Amongst his companions at Edinburgh Royal High School were pianist **Stan Greig** and clarinettist **Sandy Brown**, both of whom were to be important collaborators in later years. In 1953 Fairweather moved to London where he joined **Cy Laurie**'s band, and in 1954, when Brown also came to London, they resumed their musical partnership. Over the next few years the Brown-Fairweather band gained in quality and strength, and some of their recordings, especially *McJazz*, were widely regarded at the time to be the best to have come from a British band. Leadership of the band was at first nominally with Brown, but as his non-musical interests developed, Fairweather took charge. Later Brown returned, but in the mid-60s Fairweather joined **Acker Bilk**, and in the mid-70s he began a long association with Greig's London Jazz Big Band. In 1983 he suffered a severe heart attack, and thereafter he played a little and also painted, eventually retiring to Edinburgh in 1987.

Although his early playing recognised his admiration for **Louis Armstrong**, Fairweather's subtle, fluid and understated style suggested to the less discerning listener that he was the junior in his partnerships with the more forthright Brown. In fact, Fairweather's playing was deliberately couched as a perfect foil for his exuberant partner. His arrangements for their band, and for Greig's big band, reveal his deep understanding of the diverse forms of jazz. As Greig remarked, 'People didn't understand how good he was.'

● ALBUMS: *Fairweather Friends Made To Measure* (Lake 1957) ★★★, *Al's Pals* (Columbia 1959) ★★★, *McJazz Lives On!* (One Up 1963) ★★★.

Fairweather, Digby

b. 25 April 1946, Rochford, Essex, England. Fairweather first played trumpet semiprofessionally in and around his hometown. In 1971 he formed his own small band, later playing with numerous leaders, including **Eggy Ley**, **Dave Shepherd** and **Alex Welsh**. His reputation established, at the beginning of 1977 Fairweather took the plunge and became a full-time musician. Subsequently, he led his own bands and played in the **Midnite Follies Orchestra**. He also worked in small bands including Velvet, a co-operative band with **Len Skeat**, **Ike Isaacs** and **Denny Wright**, a trumpet-piano duo with Stan Barker, with whom Fairweather was also involved in educational work, the Pizza Express All Stars and **Brian Priestley**'s septet. An excellent mainstream trumpeter with a full, rich tone, Fairweather's graceful playing style is particularly well suited to ballads. In addition to his playing, Fairweather has also turned to writing and broadcasting; his published works include some jazz-inspired short stories, a trumpet tutor and, with Priestley and **Ian Carr**, a biographical directory, *Jazz: The Essential Companion,* which evolved into *Jazz: The Rough Guide.*

● ALBUMS: *Havin' Fun* (Black Lion 1978) ★★★★, *Going Out Steppin'* (Black Lion 1979) ★★★, *Velvet* (Black Lion 1979) ★★★, *Songs For Sandy* (Hep Jazz 1982) ★★★, with Stan Barker *Let's Duet* (Jazzology 1984) ★★★, *With Nat In Mind* (Jazzology 1994) ★★★, *Squeezin' The Blues Away* (Spirit Of Jazz 1996) ★★★, with George Melly *Singing And Swinging The Blues* (Robinwood 2002) ★★★.

● COMPILATIONS: with Barker *Something To Remember Us By: Complete Studio & Live Duets* (Jazzology 1984) ★★★, *A Portrait Of Digby Fairweather* 1979 recording (Black Lion 1994) ★★★★.

● FURTHER READING: *Notes From A Jazz Life,* Digby Fairweather.

Fairytale

Formed in Warrington, Lancashire, England, in March 1967, pop/psychedelic group the Fairytale comprised John Weston (guitar), Mally Rabbit (organ), Billy Fagg (drums) and Chaddy Penketh (bass). They made their debut in 1967 with 'Guess I Was Dreaming' for **Decca Records**, a single which married aggressive garage R&B with appealing piano runs. Only a month passed before the release of the group's second single. 'Lovely People' was more whimsical and less immediately appealing. However, with limited commercial and critical success, the group had broken up by 1968. The group's four released songs can be found on compact disc compilations such as *The British Psychedelic Trip, The Electric Crayon Set* and *The Clouds Have Groovy Faces.*

Faith Brothers

A passionate brand of rock, spiced with an old soul feel, allowed the Faith Brothers to address important political and moral issues without needing to preach. Their debut single, 'Country Of The Blind', in 1985 set the tone, an attack on a nation in the clutches of consumer fever and a decaying welfare state. 'Stranger On Home Ground' (1985) was closer to their hearts, dealing with the band's attitude towards the loss of community, not least where they grew up around West London's Fulham area. The year ended with the more optimistic 'Eventide (A Hymn For Change)', a title shared by the Faith Brothers' debut album released on the **Virgin Records** subsidiary 10. Alongside the main songwriter Billy Franks (guitar/vocals) were Lee Hirons (bass), his brother Mark (guitar), Henry Trezise (keyboards), Mark Waterman (saxophone), Will Tipper (trumpet) and Steve Howlett (drums). The immediacy of the singles seemed to be lost on *Eventide,* which sounded strained and tame in comparison. 'Whistling In The Dark' was taken as a further single in 1986 but failed to chart. The Faith Brothers returned in 1987 with *A Human Sound,* but like its two singles, 'That's Just The Way It Is To Me' and 'Consider Me', it made little impression, and they disbanded shortly thereafter.

● ALBUMS: *Eventide* (10 1985) ★★, *A Human Sound* (Siren 1987) ★★★.

Faith Hope And Charity

An R&B vocal trio from Tampa, Florida, USA, Faith Hope And Charity, with a solid background from the soul era, became a moderately successful unit during the disco period, when they married exuberant, gospel-styled vocals with a disco beat. Original members were lead Zulema Cusseaux,

Brenda Hilliard and Albert Bailey. After two hits on the Maxwell label in 1970, 'So Much Love' (number 14 R&B, number 51 pop) and 'Baby Don't Take Your Love' (number 36 R&B, number 96 pop), Cusseaux left the group in 1971 (Cusseaux built a moderately successful solo career in the early 70s under the name Zulema). A new third member, Diane Destry, was not added until 1974, and at that time the group was signed to the **RCA Records** label under the production aegis of **Van McCoy**. He gave them their biggest hit in 1975 with 'To Each His Own' (number 1 R&B, number 50 pop). Nothing they subsequently recorded came close, and their last chart record was 'Don't Pity Me' (number 20 R&B) for 20th Century in 1978. In the UK they reached the charts in 1976 with a revival of **Doris Troy**'s old hit 'Just One Look' (number 38). In 1978 Destry left, and Hilliard and Bailey carried on for another album before fading.

● ALBUMS: *Faith, Hope And Charity* (RCA 1975) ★★★, *Life Goes On* (RCA 1976) ★★, *Don't Pity Me* (20th Century 1977) ★★, *Faith, Hope & Charity* (20th Century 1978) ★★.

Faith No More

Formed in San Francisco, California, USA, in 1980, Faith No More, titled after a greyhound on which the members had placed a bet, were among the first outfits to experiment with the fusion of funk, thrash and hardcore styles that effectively became a new musical subgenre. The band initially comprised Jim Martin (b. 21 July 1961, Oakland, California, USA; guitar, ex–Vicious Hatred), Roddy Bottum (b. 1 July 1963, Los Angeles, California, USA; keyboards), Bill Gould (b. 24 April 1963, Los Angeles, California, USA; bass), Mike Bordin (b. 27 November 1962, San Francisco, California, USA; drums) and Chuck Mosley (vocals). Bottum had attended the same school as Gould, while Bordin was recruited from his course in tribal rhythm at Berkeley University. Gould had met Mosley on the Los Angeles club circuit in 1980, while Martin had been recommended by **Metallica**'s Cliff Burton.

This line-up recorded a low-budget, self-titled debut on the independent Mordam label, followed by the groundbreaking *Introduce Yourself* on Slash, a subsidiary of **Warner Brothers Records**. It encompassed a variety of styles but exuded a rare warmth and energy, mainly through Mosley's melodramatic vocals, and was well received by the critics (not least for the signature tune 'We Care A Lot'). However, internal disputes led to the firing of Mosley on the eve of widespread press coverage and favourable live reviews, although it had been reported that the band underwent a period when every single member walked out at some point. Mosley went on to gig temporarily with **Bad Brains** before putting together his own band, **Cement**. Against the odds, his replacement, Mike Patton (b. 27 January 1968, Eureka, California, USA), was even more flamboyant and actually more accomplished as a singer (it was also rumoured that **Courtney Love** of **Hole** auditioned/rehearsed with the group). *The Real Thing,* the album that followed Patton's recruitment, was a runaway success, with the single 'Epic' reaching number 9 on the **Billboard** chart in June 1990 and denting the UK Top 40. Their style was now both offbeat and unpredictable yet retained enough melody to remain a commercial proposition.

Despite the universal adulation, however, it transpired that offstage there was still a great deal of acrimony between the band members. *Live At The Brixton Academy* was released as a stopgap affair, while the band toured for nearly three years on the back of the worldwide success of their most recent studio album. After Patton temporarily defected back to his original, pre–Faith No More outfit, **Mr. Bungle**, the band finally returned with *Angel Dust*. A tougher, less accessible record, in keeping with the group's origins (despite a cover version of the **Commodores**' 'I'm Easy', which reached UK number 3 in January 1993), it made the US Top 10 and UK number 2 as their commercial ascent continued. However, in 1994, following a good deal of press speculation, the ever-volatile line-up of Faith No More switched again as Jim Martin was ousted in favour of Trey Spruance, who had formerly worked in Mr. Bungle. Martin went on to form the Behemoth. Bottum formed **Imperial Teen** as a side project in 1996. *Album Of The Year* received a mixed reaction, including one or two scathing reviews. The same year they collaborated with **Sparks** on a bizarre reworking of the latter's 'This Town Ain't Big Enough For The Both Of Us'. In April 1998 they announced that they were disbanding. Bottum continued recording with Imperial Teen, while Patton embarked on a diverse series of projects, including **Fantômas** and **Tomahawk**, and recorded an album with **Dan 'The Automator' Nakamura** under the Nathaniel Merriweather moniker. He also runs his own Ipecac Records label.

● ALBUMS: *Faith No More* (Mordam 1984) ★★, *Introduce Yourself* (Slash 1987) ★★★★, *The Real Thing* (Slash/Reprise 1989) ★★★★, *Live At The Brixton Academy* (Slash/London 1991) ★★★, *Angel Dust* (Slash/Reprise 1992) ★★, *King For A Day . . . Fool For A Lifetime* (Slash/Reprise 1995) ★★★, *Album Of The Year* (Slash/Reprise 1997) ★★.

● COMPILATIONS: *Who Cares A Lot?* (Slash/Reprise 1998) ★★★, *This Is It: The Best Of Faith No More* (Rhino 2003) ★★★★.

● DVD/VIDEOS: *Live At Brixton* (London 1990), *Who Cares A Lot?: The Greatest Videos* (London 1998).

● FURTHER READING: *Faith No More: The Real Story*, Steffan Chirazi.

Faith Over Reason

This English group emerged on the independent scene in the early 90s. Their version of **Nick Drake**'s 'Northern Sky' pigeonholed the group as one firmly planted within the pastoral sound of the British folk rock era of the 70s, although conversely, the group's sound has often been compared with that of the **Sundays** and **Smiths**. Formed in Croydon, South London, the group consists of Moira Lambert (b. 13 October 1970, Chichester, West Sussex, England; lead vocals/acoustic guitar), William Lloyd (b. 17 March 1971, London, England; bass/keyboards), Simon Roots (b. 1 September 1970; guitar) and Mark Wilsher (b. 1 May 1970, Croydon, Surrey, England; drums). The release of two EPs in 1990, *Believing In Me* ('Evangeline'/'Believing In Me'/'Northern Sky') and *Billy Blue* ('High In The Sun'/'Ice Queen'/'Billy Blue'/'Move Closer'), on the Big Cat label drew well-earned praise from the music press. Lambert, in the meantime, contributed vocals to **Saint Etienne**'s 'Only Love Can Break Your Heart', an indie-dance hit in 1990. The group's momentum was disrupted in late 1991 by the departure of Roots; the guitarist was replaced by Tebo Steele, who proceeded to take over all songwriting duties. With production duties handled by Stephen Malkmus of **Pavement**, *Easy* was marred by Steele's thrashy guitar that obscured both the songs and Lambert's voice. Support slots with Pavement and **Jeff Buckley** followed, but musical differences between Lambert and the rest of the group resulted in Lloyd, Wilsher and Steele leaving to form Soup. Lambert carried on under the Faith Over Reason name, recruiting ex-**Sundays** drummer Patch.

● ALBUMS: *Easy* (Big Cat 1993) ★★.

Faith, Adam

b. Terence Nelhams, 23 June 1940, Acton, London, England, d. 8 March 2003, Stoke-on-Trent, Staffordshire, England. During the British 'coffee bar' pop music phenomenon of the late 50s, two artists reigned supreme: **Cliff Richard** and Adam Faith. While the former has shown astonishing staying power, the young Faith had a remarkable run of hit records during the comparatively short time before he retired from singing. In 7 years between 1959 and 1966 he made the UK chart 24 times. Both his UK chart-toppers, 'What Do You Want?' and 'Poor Me', lasted barely two minutes; both featured the infectious pizzicato strings of **John Barry**'s orchestra, both were written by Les Vandyke (alias **Johnny Worth**) and both featured the hiccuping delivery with the word *baby* pronounced 'bybeee'. 'Poor Me' is also notable because the Barry arrangement contains an early glimmer of the 'James Bond Theme'. This became Faith's early 'gimmick'.

Faith's continued success rivalled that of Cliff Richards, and in a short period of time he appeared in three films, *Beat Girl*, *Never Let Go* and *What A Whopper!*, and made a surprisingly confident appearance in December 1960, being interviewed by John Freeman in a serious BBC television programme, *Face To Face*. Adults were shocked to find that, during this conversation, this lucid teenager admitted to pre-marital sex and owned up to listening to Sibelius and Dvorak. His career continued until the dawn of the **Beatles**, when Faith was assigned the Roulettes (featuring a young **Russ Ballard**). Songwriter **Chris Andrews** fed the singer with a second wave of infectious beat group hits, most notably 'The First Time' and 'We Are In Love'.

In the mid-60s, appearing outdated in comparison to the glut of exciting pop groups around, Faith gave up singing and went into repertory theatre and in 1971 became an acting star in the UK television series *Budgie*. He survived a near fatal car crash in 1973 and released *I Survive* a year later. Additionally Faith produced records for **Roger Daltrey** and **Lonnie Donegan** and managed **Leo Sayer**. His two supporting actor roles in *Stardust* and *McVicar* brought him critical success. For a number of years he was a successful financial consultant, although in the 90s he returned to the stage with *Budgie* and *Alfie* and to UK television as Frank Carver in *Love Hurts* and the situation comedy *The House That Jack Built*. He became a partner in the ill-fated satellite venture *The Money Channel* and was bankrupted in 2001. Faith also continued to work on the perimeter of the musical world, even though his final album was in 1993.

While he readily admitted that his vocal range was limited, Faith's contribution to popular music was significant in so far as he was the first British teenager to confront a hostile world of respectable parents and adults and demonstrate that pop singers were not all mindless 'layabouts and boneheads'. In a long and varied career he wrote two autobiographies. He died of a heart attack in March 2003.

● ALBUMS: *Adam* (Parlophone 1960) ★★★, *Beat Girl* film soundtrack (Columbia 1961) ★★★, *Adam Faith* (Parlophone 1962) ★★★, *From Adam With Love*

(Parlophone 1963) ★★★, *For You* (Parlophone 1963) ★★★, *On The Move* (Parlophone 1964) ★★★, *Faith Alive!* (Parlophone 1965) ★★, *I Survive* (Warners 1974) ★★, *Midnight Postcards* (PolyGram 1993) ★★.

● COMPILATIONS: *Best Of Adam Faith* (Starline 1974) ★★★, *The Two Best Sides Of Adam Faith* (EMI 1978) ★★★, *20 Golden Greats* (Warwick 1981) ★★★, *Not Just A Memory* (See For Miles 1983) ★★★★, *The Best Of Adam Faith* (MFP 1985) ★★★★, *The Adam Faith Singles Collection: His Greatest Hits* (EMI 1990) ★★★, *The EP Collection* (See For Miles 1991) ★★★★, *The Best Of The EMI Years* (EMI 1994) ★★★★, *The Very Best Of Adam Faith* (EMI Gold 1997) ★★★★, *A's B's & EP's* (EMI Gold 2003) ★★★★.

● FURTHER READING: *Adam, His Fabulous Year*, Adam Faith. *Poor Me*, Adam Faith. *Acts Of Faith*, Adam Faith.

● FILMS: *Beat Girl* aka *Wild For Kicks* (1960), *Never Let Go* (1960), *What A Whopper!* (1961), *What A Carve Up!* aka *No Place Like Homicide* (1962), *Mix Me A Person* (1962), *Stardust* (1974), *Yesterday's Hero* (1979), *Foxes* (1980), *McVicar* (1980).

Faith, George

b. Earl George Turner, 6 July 1946, Rae Town, Jamaica, West Indies, d. 16 April 2003. This reggae singer's vocal talent was identified at an early age, as he was often motivated to sing at parties and church services. The R&B performers of his teens, including **Jackie Wilson** and **Sam Cooke**, influenced his soulful style. His initial foray into the music business was as part of the Enchanters, although his unique vocal styling led to him being encouraged to perform as a soloist. When he was 16, with the unfamiliar Mr. Abraham's Saver productions, he recorded his debut 'Little Miss Mmm'. The single faltered, and little was heard from the singer until the mid-70s when he recorded several sides with **Lee 'Scratch' Perry** under the George Earl moniker, including his first attempt at **William Bell**'s soul classic 'To Be A Lover'.

In 1977, recording as George Faith, Turner embarked on sessions with Perry at the Black Ark Studios. The sessions resulted in the release of a new version of 'To Be A Lover' in discomix format. The 9.5-minute opus, 17 with the neatly segued b-side 'Rastaman Shuffle' featuring **Dillinger**, was greeted with international approval. The success of the single led to the release of an album of the same name. Other releases included cover versions of 'In The Midnight Hour' and 'I've Got The Groove' alongside his own composition 'Opportunity'. Unfortunately Faith had recorded 'Opportunity' with both Lee Perry and **Militant Barry**, which resulted in consecutive releases from **Island Records** and **Trojan Records**' Horse subsidiary. The confusion hampered any further chart success, which resulted in his second album with Perry being sadly neglected. In 1978 the singer began recording with **Alvin 'GG' Ranglin** at **Channel One** Studios. His work with Ranglin was credited to Earl George, as were the sessions with **Phil Pratt** later that same year. In 1980, drawing from his experience in the recording studios, he decided to embark on a career as an independent producer. His efforts were thwarted, which inspired his return to recording with Ranglin. In 1982 the producer released *Since I Met You Baby* under the George Faith appellation but was unable to recapture past glories.

Although he was never able to repeat the success of his Perry sessions, the singer maintained a respectable profile in Jamaica. He consistently performed as George Faith when he appeared on the hotel circuit in Jamaica's north coast and in 1990 began regularly performing in Toronto, Canada. Notable shows included a tour with **Gregory Isaacs** and **Philip Frazier** as well as the acclaimed Rock Steady Nite shows at the Skyline hotel. A notable recording session occurred in 1992 when he completed the material for *Just The Blues*. The album was produced by Doris Darlington—the mother of **Coxsone Dodd**—who in the 60s produced under the guise of D. Darling at her son's Brentford Road studio. Faith also enjoyed popularity on the Brazilian market and continued to record sporadically up until his death from cancer in 2003.

● ALBUMS: *To Be A Lover* (Island 1977) ★★★★, as Earl George *One And Only* (Burning Sounds 1978) ★★★, as Earl George *Loving Something* (GG 1978) ★★★, *Working On A Guideline* (Upsetter 1978) ★★★, *Since I Met You Baby* (GG 1979) ★★★, *Sings For Lovers Only* (Dynamics 1985) ★★, *First Class* (Top Ranking 1986) ★★★, *Happy Anniversary* (Music Track 1986) ★★★, *Bunny Lee Presents Soulful George Faith* (Hollywood 1988) ★★★★, *Like Never Before* (Virgo Stomach 1991) ★★★, *Just The Blues* (Studio One 1992) ★★★, *Soulful* (Mid Price 1997) ★★★.

Faith, Percy

b. 7 April 1908, Toronto, Ontario, Canada, d. 9 February 1976, Ericino, California, USA. During the 30s Faith worked extensively on radio in Canada and moved to the USA in 1940 to take up a post with NBC. During the 50s he was musical director for **Columbia Records**, for whom he made a number of popular albums, mostly of mood music. He worked with **Tony Bennett**, with whom he had three million-selling singles and, from 1950, also had several hits in his own right, including 'Cross My Fingers', 'All My Love', 'On Top Of Old Smoky' (vocal by **Burl Ives**), 'Delicado', 'Song From The Moulin Rouge (Where Is Your Heart)' (US number 1 in 1953), 'Return To Paradise' (1953), and 'Theme From A Summer Place', which reached number 1 in the US and number 2 in the UK charts in 1960. In Hollywood in the 50s Faith had composed several background film scores, including *Love Me Or Leave Me* (1955), the highly acclaimed biopic of singer **Ruth Etting**, which starred **Doris Day**. His film credits in the 60s included *Tammy Tell Me True* (1961), *I'd Rather Be Rich* (1964), *The Third Day* (1965) and *The Oscar* (1966). For *The Love Goddesses*, Faith wrote the title song with **Mack David**. His other compositions included 'My Heart Cries For You' (with his main collaborator Carl Sigman), which was a big hit for **Guy Mitchell**, **Dinah Shore**, **Vic Damone** and others in 1951. Faith died of cancer in February 1976. In the mid-90s there was renewed interest in his work, particularly in Japan, where many of his albums were reissued. New performances of his arrangements have been conducted by Nick Perito for a series of CDs.

● ALBUMS: *Continental Music* (Columbia 1956) ★★★, *Passport To Romance* (Columbia 1956) ★★★, *Music From My Fair Lady* (Columbia 1957) ★★★★, *Touchdown!* (Columbia 1958) ★★★, *North & South Of The Border* (Columbia 1958) ★★★, *Music Of Victor Herbert* (Columbia 1958) ★★★, *Viva!* (Columbia 1959) ★★★, *Hallelujah* (Columbia 1959) ★★★, *Porgy And Bess* (Columbia 1959) ★★★, *Music Of George Gershwin* (Columbia 1959) ★★★★, *A Night With Sigmund Romberg* (Columbia 1959) ★★★, *Malaguena* (Columbia 1959) ★★★, *Bouquet*

(Columbia 1959) ★★★★, *Music From South Pacific* (Columbia 1960) ★★, *Bon Voyage!* (Columbia 1960) ★★★, *Continental Souvenirs* (Columbia 1960) ★★★, *Jealousy* (Columbia 1960) ★★★★, *A Night With Jerome Kern* (Columbia 1960) ★★★, *Camelot* (Columbia 1961) ★★★★, *Carefree* (Columbia 1961) ★★★, *Mucho Gusto! More Music Of Mexico* (Columbia 1961) ★★, *Tara's Theme* (Columbia 1961) ★★★, *Bouquet Of Love* (Columbia 1962) ★★★★, *Subways Are For Sleeping* (Columbia 1962) ★★★, *The Music Of Brazil!* (Columbia 1962) ★★★, *Hollywood's Themes* (Columbia 1963) ★★★★, *American Serenade* (Columbia 1963) ★★★, *Exotic Strings* (Columbia 1963) ★★★, *Shangri-La!* (Columbia 1963) ★★★, *Great Folk Themes* (Columbia 1964) ★★★, *More Themes For Young Lovers* (Columbia 1964) ★★★, *Latin Themes* (Columbia 1965) ★★★, *Broadway Bouquet* (Columbia 1965) ★★★, *Themes For The 'In' Crowd* (Columbia 1966) ★★★, *The Academy Award Winner And Other Great Movie Themes* (Columbia 1967) ★★★★, *Today's Themes For Young Lovers* (Columbia 1967) ★★★, *For Those In Love* (Columbia 1968) ★★★, *Angel Of The Morning (Hit Themes For Young Lovers)* (Columbia 1968) ★★, *Those Were The Days* (Columbia 1969) ★★, *Windmills Of Your Mind* (Columbia 1969) ★★, *Love Theme From 'Romeo And Juliet'* (Columbia 1969) ★★★, *Forever Young* (Columbia 1970) ★★, *Leaving On A Jet Plane* (Columbia 1970) ★★, *Held Over! Today's Great Movie Themes* (Columbia 1970) ★★★, *The Beatles Album* (Columbia 1970) ★★, *A Time For Love* (Columbia 1971) ★★★, *I Think I Love You* (Columbia 1971) ★★, *Black Magic Woman* (Columbia 1971) ★★, *Jesus Christ, Superstar* (Columbia 1971) ★★, *Joy* (Columbia 1972) ★★★, *Day By Day* (Columbia 1972) ★★★.
● COMPILATIONS: *Moods* (Ditto 1983) ★★★, *Images* (Knight 1990) ★★★, *Music From the Movies* (Sony 1994) ★★★.

Faithful Breath

This progressive heavy metal band from Germany has a long and chequered history dating back to 1974. The initial nucleus of the band comprised Heinz Mikus (guitar\vocals), Horst Stabenow (bass) and Uwe Otto (drums). Influenced by **King Crimson** and **Deep Purple**, their debut album was *Fading Beauty* in 1974. This featured intricate arrangements and keyboards but lacked both melody and memorable hooks. After a lengthy gap and the abandonment of the keyboards, the band concentrated on guitar-orientated hard rock. Three competent albums followed, but each suffered from inexperienced self-production. Successful appearances at two Dutch rock festivals in 1983 attracted the attention of Mausoleum Records. Jurgen Dusterloh took over as drummer, and Andy Bibi Honig was added as a second guitarist for the recording of *Gold 'N' Glory*. Produced by Michael Wagener, it remains the band's finest recorded work. Further line-up changes ensued as the band moved towards the thrash end of the hard rock spectrum. In 1987 they changed their name to Risk, with only Mikus surviving from the original line-up.
● ALBUMS: *Fading Beauty* (Sky 1974) ★★, *Back On My Hill* (Sky 1980) ★★★, *Rock Lions* (Sky 1981) ★★, *Hard Breath* (Sky 1983) ★★★, *Gold 'N' Glory* (Mausoleum 1984) ★★★★, *SKOL* (Ambush 1985) ★★★, *Live* (Noise 1986) ★★.

Faithfull, Marianne

b. 29 December 1946, Hampstead, London, England. Ex-convent schoolgirl Faithfull began her singing career upon meeting producer **Andrew Loog Oldham** at a London party. She was thus introduced into the **Rolling Stones**' circle, and a plaintive **Mick Jagger/Keith Richards** song, 'As Tears Go By', became her debut single in 1964. This folksy offering reached number 9, the first of four UK Top 10 hits, which also included 'Come And Stay With Me' (penned by **Jackie DeShannon**) and the pounding 'Summer Nights'. Her albums reflected an impressive balance between folk and rock, featuring material by **Donovan**, **Bert Jansch** and **Tim Hardin**, but her doomed relationship with Jagger undermined ambitions as a performer. Faithfull also pursued her thespian aspirations, appearing on stage in Anton Chekhov's *Three Sisters* and on celluloid in the title role of *Girl On A Motorcycle*, but withdrew from the public eye following a failed suicide attempt upon her break with Jagger.

Drug problems bedevilled the singer's recovery, but Faithfull re-emerged in 1976 with *Dreamin' My Dreams*, a mild country set on which she was backed by the **Grease Band**. A further period of seclusion followed, but the singer rekindled her career three years later when **Chris Blackwell** instigated her signing to **Island Records**. Her debut for the label was the impressive *Broken English*. The once-virginal voice was now replaced by a husky drawl, particularly effective on the atmospheric title track, and her version of **Shel Silverstein**'s 'The Ballad Of Lucy Jordan' reached number 48 in the UK charts. Faithfull's later releases followed a similar pattern, with the most effective being 1987's *Strange Weather*, conceived by **Tom Waits** and produced by Hal Wilner. Nowhere was the trauma of Faithfull's personal life more evident than on 1990's *Blazing Away*, a live album on which the singer reclaimed songs from her past. Recorded live in Brooklyn's St. Ann's Cathedral, her weary intonation, although artistically effective, contravened the optimism of those early recordings.

Faithfull's autobiography, published in 1994, provided a revealing and fascinating insight into a true survivor of the 60s. The singer's first studio album of the 90s, *A Secret Life* (1995), was a return to the brooding atmosphere of *Broken English*. Although her voice was still captivating, the songs, with lyrics by Faithfull and music by **Angelo Badalamenti**, were generally uninspiring. The following year's *20th Century Blues* was a an ill-chosen live album from a Paris concert featuring songs by **Kurt Weill**, **Noël Coward** and, in **Marlene Dietrich** pose, 'Falling In Love Again'. More suitable was Faithfull's dramatic interpretation of the **Bertolt Brecht/Kurt Weill** piece, *The Seven Deadly Sins*, recorded live in Vienna.

In 2003 Faithfull starred in the acclaimed adaptation of Robert Wilson's play *The Black Rider*, which ran in London and San Francisco. The following year she teamed up with **PJ Harvey** to write and record *Before The Poison*, which also included collaborations with **Nick Cave**, Damon Albarn and Jon Brion. Noted UK writer Will Self came up with the album title and penned the sleeve notes. In December the singer was forced to cancel a European tour after she collapsed before a show in Italy. She was diagnosed as suffering from chronic exhaustion.
● ALBUMS: *Come My Way* (Decca 1965) ★★★, *Marianne Faithfull* (Decca 1965) ★★★★, *Go Away From My World* (Decca 1965) ★★★, *Faithfull Forever* (Decca 1966) ★★★,

North Country Maid (Decca 1966) ★★, *Loveinamist* (Decca 1967) ★★, *Dreamin' My Dreams* (Nems 1976) ★★, *Faithless* (Immediate 1977) ★★, *Broken English* (Island 1979) ★★★★, *Dangerous Acquaintances* (Island 1981) ★★★, *A Child's Adventure* (Island 1983) ★★★, *Strange Weather* (Island 1987) ★★★, *Blazing Away* (Island 1990) ★★★, *A Secret Life* (Island 1995) ★★, *20th Century Blues* (RCA 1996) ★★, *The Seven Deadly Sins* (RCA 1998) ★★★, *Vagabond Ways* (It Records 1999) ★★★★, *Kissin' Time* (Hut 2002) ★★★, *Rich Kid Blues* 1971 recording (Edsel 2002) ★★★, *Before The Poison* (Naïve 2004) ★★★.

● COMPILATIONS: *The World Of Marianne Faithfull* (Decca 1969) ★★★★, *Marianne Faithfull's Greatest Hits* (Abkco 1969) ★★★, *As Tears Go By* (Decca 1981) ★★★★, *Summer Nights* (Rock Echoes 1984) ★★★, *Rich Kid Blues* (Castle 1985) ★★★, *The Very Best Of Marianne Faithfull* (London 1987) ★★★, *Faithfull: A Collection Of Her Best Recordings* (Island 1994) ★★★, *A Perfect Stranger: The Island Anthology* (Island 1998) ★★★★, *A Stranger On Earth: An Introduction To Marianne Faithfull* (Decca 2001) ★★★★, *The Collection* (Spectrum 2005) ★★★.

● DVD/VIDEOS: *Dreaming My Dreams* (Image Entertainment 2002), *Sings Kurt Weill: Live In Montreal* (Universal-Island 2004), *Live From The Henry Fonda Theater, Hollywood* (Eagle Vision 2005).

● FURTHER READING: *Marianne Faithfull: As Tears Go By*, Mark Hodkinson. *Faithfull*, Marianne Faithfull and David Dalton.

● FILMS: *Made In U.S.A.* (1966), *Don't Look Back* (1967), *I'll Never Forget What's'isname* (1967), *Girl On A Motorcycle* (1968), *Hamlet* (1969), *Lucifer Rising* (1972), *Ghost Story* (1974), *Assault On Agathon* (1975), *When Pigs Fly* (1993), *The Turn Of The Screw* (1994), *Shopping* (1994), *Moondance* (1995), *Crimetime* (1996), *Intimacy* (2001), *Far From China* (2001), *A Letter To True* voice only (2004), *Nord-Plage* (2004).

Faithless

UK dance outfit formed around the nucleus of **Rollo** (b. Rollo Armstrong, England), one of the prime movers in the UK **house** scene, and **Sister Bliss** (b. Ayalah Bentovim, 30 December 1970, London, England), one of the country's most successful and respected female DJs. It is truly an eclectic collaboration, with both Sister Bliss and Rollo being innovative and highly skilled programmers and producers. They were joined in the original line-up by rapper Maxi Jazz (b. Maxwell Frazer, Hackney, London, England), singer/writer and instrumentalist Jamie Catto (who came from a folk background), and guitarist Dave Randall with occasional vocal input from Rollo's sister **Dido** (b. Dido Florian Cloud de Bounevialle Armstrong, 25 December 1971, England). This unique blend of skills and styles and the band's relentless global touring no doubt enabled Faithless' gradual but assured rise to critical and commercial success.

Faithless' debut single on Rollo's **Cheeky Records**, 'Salva Mea', was one of the decade's greatest and most influential house records. When it was first released in 1995, it made a fleeting appearance in the UK Top 30 in August before disappearing by the following week. Its grassroots popularity on the UK's dancefloors was emphatically confirmed when it shot straight into the UK's Top 10 upon its rerelease in December 1996. It went on to sell over one million copies worldwide, and its exhilarating pizzicato string sound spawned countless imitators who also achieved chart success

using the 'Faithless sound', one notable example being **Sash!**'s 'Encore Une Fois'. The attendant debut album *Reverence* was refreshingly difficult to categorize as its tracks ranged from brooding, **dub**-influenced ruminations on urban life and relationships through rap, through more traditional love songs ('Don't Leave') to storming dancefloor epics, such as 'Salva Mea' and 'Insomnia'. Maxi Jazz's melodic, semi-whispered raps added an intelligent and provocative edge to the soaring electronic sweeps created by Rollo and Sister Bliss. *Reverence*, like the earlier singles, was a slow-burning phenomenon, initially not selling well. On the back of subsequent Top 10 singles and a double album of remix material, however, the album went on to be certified gold in 22 countries.

Following the release of *Reverence*, the band was nominated for and won many awards, including a European Grammy for Best International Dance Band. Critical accolades included Michael Stipe of **R.E.M.** naming *Reverence* as his favourite album of the year. The awards, critical plaudits and commercial success formed unequivocal confirmation that integrity and hard work had eventually paid off for Faithless. Released in 1998, Faithless' second album *Sunday 8pm* saw them developing the more ambient, meditative element of their work but big-name DJ remixes (**Paul Van Dyk**, Robbie Rivera) of the singles ensured their sustained popularity in the clubs. The first single from the album, the provocatively titled 'God Is A DJ', was a UK Top 10 hit. In October they won the UK's *Muzik* magazine's award for the Best Live Act. By the turn of the new millennium, Faithless were established as mainstream stars, leading to accusations that they had lost the energy and drive that characterized their initial releases. They reasserted their club credentials with the following year's remix set, but their third studio album, *Outrospective*, despite including the striking single 'We Come 1', was a disappointingly bland collection. Catto had left by this point to work on his **I Giant Leap** project, while former guitarist Randall launched his solo vehicle **Slovo**. However, Dido, by now a huge star in her own right, continued to contribute to the band's recordings. The nucleus of Rollo, Sister Bliss and Maxi Jazz, with additional input from Dido, Randall and vocalists LSK and P*Nut, then spent the best part of two years working on the concept album *No Roots*. This ambitious but only partially successful 2004 album was broken into two suites, with the second being predominantly instrumental. *Everything Will Be Alright Tomorrow*, the instrumental accompaniment to *No Roots*, was released later in the year.

● ALBUMS: *Reverence* (Cheeky/Arista 1996) ★★★★, *Sunday 8pm* (Cheeky/Arista 1998) ★★★★, *Outrospective* (Cheeky/Arista 2001) ★★, *No Roots* (Cheeky/Arista 2004) ★★★, *Everything Will Be Alright Tomorrow* (Cheeky/Arista 2004) ★★★.

● COMPILATIONS: *Saturday 3am* remixes (Cheeky/Arista 1999) ★★★, *Back To Mine* (DMC/Ultra 2000) ★★★, *Irreverence* remixes (Cheeky 2001) ★★★, *Reperspective* remixes (Cheeky/Arista 2002) ★★, *Forever Faithless: The Greatest Hits* (Cheeky 2005) ★★★★.

● DVD/VIDEOS: *Forever Faithless: The Greatest Hits* (Sony 2005), *Live At Alexandra Palace* (Sony 2005).

Fajardo, José

b. José Antonio Fajardo, 18 October 1919, Cuba. Band leader, arranger, composer and producer Fajardo is one of the greatest Cuban flute players. He organized a flute, strings, rhythm section and voices charanga band that he called his All-Stars. In the course of his long career, he played a prominent role in the 50s' cha-cha fad, early 60s' charanga/pachanga craze and 70s' charanga revival. Prior to forming his own band, Fajardo did stints with female singer/band leader Paulina Alvarez (b. 1912, d. 1965) and Arcaño Y Sus Maravillas.

In 1956 Fajardo released *Cuba* (aka *Cuban Cha Cha Chá*) on the Tico Records label, which featured revered conga player Tata Güines (b. Federico Arístides Soto, 1926, Güines, Cuba). He signed with Panart Records and issued a string of albums on the label during the late 50s and early 60s. His early Panart releases emphasized the popular cha-cha rhythm, which was developed by violinist-composer-arranger-band leader Enrique Jorrín while he was a member of Orquesta América. Fajardo and his band appeared at the prestigious Tropicana nightclub in Havana. In 1959 he was invited by the US Democratic Party to play at New York's Waldorf Astoria hotel for John Kennedy's presidential campaign. His All-Stars caused more commotion with the Latino community than with the Democrats, and an engagement at New York's famous Palladium Ballroom quickly followed.

After the Cuban revolution, Fajardo left Cuba in 1960 to settle in Miami, Florida, USA. Violinist/composer/arranger Félix Reina inherited his band, which was renamed the Estrellas Cubanas, and the flautist's position was filled by Eddy Zervigón, who went on to cofound **Orquesta Broadway** in 1962. Meanwhile in 1960 the massive popularity of **Charlie Palmieri**'s charanga 'La Duboney', featuring **Johnny Pacheco** on flute, sparked off a charanga boom which was dominated by the fast pachanga rhythm created by Cuban composer Eduardo Davidson. Pachanga fever started in New York with the success of Afro-Cuban singer Rolando La Serie's version of Davidson's 'La Pachanga' from his *Sabor A Mi*, on which he was accompanied by the brass and saxophone-led big band of **Bebo Valdés**. The song topped the *Farándula* chart for a couple of months in 1960. In its wake, a string of other pachanga compositions appeared over the next few years. Fajardo promptly responded to this new trend by including an interpretation of the much covered 'La Pachanga' and Davidson's pachanga 'Pancho Calma' on his 1961 Panart release *Fajardo And His All-Stars Vol. 6*. The major label **Columbia Records** eventually picked up on the fad and signed him for *Mister Pachanga* in 1962. He also recorded *Sabor Guajiro* for them. However, by 1964 the charanga/pachanga craze had run out of steam.

A Fajardo accompanist for many years, Osvaldo 'Chi Hua Hua' Martínez (b. c.1920, Cuba, d. early 80s, New York, USA; güiro/timbales) went on to work with **Mongo Santamaría**, **Félix 'Pupi' Legarreta**, **Sonny Stitt**, **Ray Barretto**, **Kako**, the Alegre All-Stars, Johnny Pacheco, **Willie Bobo**, Don Gonzalo Fernández, Mike Pérez, **Israel 'Cachao' López**, Julito Collazo, Lou Pérez, and Javier Vázquez among others; he recorded the classic Latin jam sets *Descarga Cubana Vol. 1* (1966) and *Latin Cuban Session Vol. 2* (c.1967) on Fonseca Records (which were both collected on the CD *Descarga Cubana* in 1991); and coled Orquesta Metropolitana on *New Horizons* (1980). Fajardo maintained two charangas in 1963, one in New York and the other in Miami. He eventually tired of commuting and disbanded his Miami band but retained Sonny Bravo (b. Elio Osacar Jnr., 7 October 1936, New York, USA, of Cuban parentage; pianist/arranger) for his New York

outfit. In 1964 he issued the fifth and final volume in Panart's legendary *Cuban Jam Session* series. In 1965 Fajardo decided to relocate to San Juan, Puerto Rico. Bravo left at this point and later became a founder member of **Típica 73**. In 1966 Fajardo hired the young classically trained Cuban violinist **Alfredo De La Fé** and in 1974 recruited Afro-Cuban pianist **Alfredo Rodríguez** to the quintet he was leading in Miami. Fajardo signed with Harvey Averne's Coco Records and released a series of four albums on the label between 1975 and 1978. Although his quintet was pictured on the sleeve of the first, *Fajardo Y Sus Estrellas Del 75*, the Miami recorded album featured a 14-piece charanga with 5 violins, including brother Alberto. Fajardo found himself amid a resurgence of the charanga sound that occurred in the second half of the 70s. Rodríguez departed, and Sonny Bravo returned to session on 1977's *Selecciones Clasicas*, which contained remakes of earlier hits. Ray Barretto coproduced this album and handled the entire production of *El Talento Total* in 1978. Fajardo switched to Fania Records for four releases between 1980 and 1984, which included two collaborations with Johnny Pacheco. Rodríguez regards the relationship between Fajardo and Pacheco as being akin to teacher and pupil: 'Everybody knows Pacheco because of the selling of albums, and because of the Fania thing, but Fajardo is the master and Pacheco is the student'. De La Fé sessioned on all of Fajardo's releases between 1977 and 1980, and Chi Hua Hua appeared on *Las Tres Flautas* and *Pacheco Y Fajardo*. In addition to recording as a band leader, Fajardo sessioned with an impressive list of Latin names, including Israel 'Cachao' López, **Louie Ramírez**, **Fania All Stars**, Alfredo Valdés Jnr. and José Mangual Jnr.

● ALBUMS: *Cuba* (1956) ★★★★, *Cha Cha Chá In Havana*, *Una Noche En Montmartre*, *Fajardo At The Havana-Hilton* (1959) ★★★, *Ritmo De Pollos* (1959) ★★★, *Saludos From Fajardo* (1960) ★★★, *Fajardo And His All-Stars Vol. 6* (1961) ★★★, *Let's Dance With Fajardo* (1961) ★★★★, *Sabrosa Pachanga* (1961) ★★★, with the charangas of Johnny Pacheco and Charlie Palmieri *Las Charangas* (1961) ★★★, with Rosendo Ruiz Jnr. *Dance La Pachanga Con La Latino Charanga* (1962) ★★, *Mister Pachanga* (1962) ★★★, *Sabor Guajiro* (1962) ★★★, *Fajardo In Japan* (1964) ★★★★, *Cuban Jam Session* (1964) ★★★★, *Danzones Completos Para Bailar Vol. 1* (1964) ★★★, with various artists *Tico-Alegre All Stars Recorded Live At Carnegie Hall, Vol. 1* (1974) ★★★, *Fajardo Y Sus Estrellas Del 75* (1975) ★★★, *Fajardo '76: La Raiz De La Charanga 'Charanga Roots'* (1976) ★★★, *Selecciones Clasicas* (1977) ★★★★, *El Talento Total* (1978) ★★, with Pacheco, Pupi Legarreta, Javier Vázquez *Las Tres Flautas* (1980) ★★★, *Señor . . . Charanga!* (1980) ★★★, with Pacheco *Pacheco Y Fajardo* (1982) ★★★, *Hoy Y Mañana* (1984) ★★★.

Fake, Nathan

b. Necton, Swaffham, Norfolk, England. Utilizing a PC with 'some old bits of software', Fake has a beguiling, mildly bucolic take on **techno** that has seduced artists such as Superpitcher, Adam Beyer and Michael de Hey into including his tracks on mix albums and **Michael Mayer**, Steve Barnes and Dominik Eulberg into remixing him. Having grown up in Norfolk, Fake relocated to Berkshire to study music. He claims to have no real agenda beyond 'mixing up different ideas and textures' and has listed albums by the **Soft Pink Truth** and **Labradford** as ones he has bought (and adored). His own music making seems at the midpoint between the former's mutant disco and the latter's ecclesiastic atmospherica. Between 2003 and 2005, Fake released a series of excellent 12-inch singles for James Holden's Border Community, Satoshi Tommie's Saw Recordings, and the Cologne-based Traum Schallplatten imprint. The *Watlington Street* EP, released in 2004 on Saw Recordings, drew its name from the Reading street in which Fake lived at the time of the five tracks creation. The EP's opening track 'Adamedge' was named after a friend from Norfolk. The polemic 'Bored Of House', meanwhile, was a playful mutation of **Boards Of Canada**, the esoteric Scottish duo to whom Fake's music has regularly been compared. His most seductive release, 'The Sky Was Pink' (a 12-inch single for Border Community in 2004), was apparently inspired by the times Fake used to camp out in fields when he was younger. Over a quartet of versions, 'The Sky Was Pink' seemed cut through with trace elements of **My Bloody Valentine**, **M83** and Boards Of Canada but, equally, sounded like a club record. Fake completed a series of remixes for Tiefschwarz, Remy, Jack Addicts and Avus and then embarked on recording his debut album of 'late night psychedelic Casio rock' for Border Community.

● ALBUMS: *Drowning In A Sea Of Love* (Border Community 2006) ★★★.

Falco

b. Johann Hölzel, 19 February 1957, Vienna, Austria, d. 6 February 1998, Puerto Plata, Dominican Republic. Using a droll mixture of German and English lyrics, Falco had several international hits in the 80s. After completing his studies at the Vienna Conservatoire, he played bass guitar in the punk band Drahdiwaberl, composing 'Ganz Wien', which appeared on their *Psycho Terror* in 1979 and was banned because it contained the line 'all Vienna is on heroin today'. His solo career began in 1982 with the rap-style European hit 'Der Kommissar' and the controversial tale of prostitution 'Jeanny', which topped the German charts despite a complete radio ban. Falco's first impact on the English-speaking world came with 1985's 'Rock Me Amadeus'. Co-written with Dutch producers Rob and Ferdi Bolland, the song's zany mixture of speech and singing made it a US/UK chart-topper the following year at the same time as *Falco 3* broke into the US Top 10. After releasing the rock ballad 'Vienna Calling', Falco returned to the 'Amadeus' mode on 'The Sound Of Musik', which was an attack on Austrian president Kurt Waldheim. Despite his collaboration with model and film star Brigitte Nielsen on 'Body Next To Body', Falco's later records, such as 'Titanic' in 1992, were not successful outside German-speaking territories. Moving to the Dominican Republic for tax purposes, he was building his own recording studio when he was killed in a car accident in February 1998.

● ALBUMS: *Einzelhaft* (A&M 1982) ★★★, *Jung Roemer* (A&M 1984) ★★★, *Falco 3* (A&M 1986) ★★★★, *Emotional* (Sire 1986) ★★★, *Data De Groove* (ARD 1987) ★★★, *Wiener Blut* (Warners 1988) ★★.

● COMPILATIONS: *The Final Curtain: The Ultimate Best Of Falco* (EMI 1999) ★★★★, *Greatest Hits* (Buddha 1999) ★★★★.

Falcons

This R&B vocal group from Detroit, Michigan, USA, helped define soul music in the early 60s. The great legacy of music left by the Falcons has unfortunately been obscured by the group's reputation as the genesis of so many great talents. The group has at one time claimed as members **Eddie Floyd** (b. 25 June 1935, Montgomery, Alabama, USA), **Wilson Pickett** (b. 18 March 1941, Prattville, Alabama, USA, d. 19 January 2006, Reston, Virginia, USA), Joe Stubbs (b. Joseph Stubbles, 1942, USA, d. 19 January 1998, USA), brother of the **Four Tops**' Levi Stubbs and later a member of the **Contours** and then the **Originals**, Bonny 'Mack' Rice, the original singer of 'Mustang Sally', and guitarists Lance Finnie and Robert Ward successively, whose bluesy guitar work helped immeasurably to raise the reputation of the group. The Falcons' chart success was surprisingly slim, with only five releases making the chart, the best-known being 'You're So Fine', a proto-soul number led by Stubbs that went to number 2 R&B (number 17 pop) in 1959, and 'I Found A Love', the incredibly torrid secular gospel number led by Pickett that went to number 6 R&B (number 75 pop) in 1962.

The original Falcons was formed in 1955 and comprised lead Eddie Floyd, Bob Manardo (b. Robert Manardo, 1937, d. 6 March 2004, Warren, USA), Arnett Robinson, Tom Shetler and Willie Schofield. Manardo and Shetler were only present on 'Baby That's It'/'This Day' before being drafted and volunteering for the army respectively. In 1956 the group met Detroit producer Robert West, who for the next three years issued releases by the Falcons on several labels, including his own Flick label, but without achieving any national success. The group now featured Joe Stubbs, Bonny 'Mack' Rice and guitarist Lance Finnie, and this classic line-up blended gospel fervour to rhythm and blues harmony, as reflected in their 'You're So Fine' hit of 1959. They managed two more hits with Stubbs as lead with 'Just For Your Love' (number 26 R&B 1959) and 'The Teacher' (number 18 R&B 1960) before Pickett replaced Stubbs in 1960.

The memorable 'I Found A Love', and several other Falcons records, featured backing from the Dayton group the Ohio Untouchables, centred on the great guitar of Robert Ward. In the 70s the Ohio Untouchables emerged as the premier funk group the **Ohio Players** (Ward himself re-emerged from 25 years' retirement in 1991 to release a well-received blues album). The Falcons disbanded in 1963, but the name continued with another Detroit ensemble consisting of Carlis 'Sonny' Monroe, James Gibson, Johnny Alvin and Alton Hollowell. This group made the R&B chart in 1966 with 'Standing On Guard'.

● COMPILATIONS: *You're So Fine* (Relic 1985) ★★★★, *I Found A Love* (Relic 1985) ★★★★.

Falco's, Tav, Panther Burns

b. Gustavo Antonio Falco, Arkansas, USA. Guitarist/vocalist Tav Falco and his band Panther Burns came to prominence in 1981 with *Behind The Magnolia Curtain*, a rockabilly set fused with garage band sloppiness and **Elvis Presley**-influenced whoops and hollers. Suitably ragged instrumental support from **Alex Chilton** (ex–**Box Tops**; **Big Star**) ensured the album quickly became a cult classic. *Blow Your Top* and *Sugar Ditch Revisited*, two similarly-styled EPs, followed, the second of which was recorded at the fabled Sun Studios. It was here Falco became acquainted with pianist **Jim Dickinson**, formerly of the **Dixie Flyers**, who guested on several subsequent Panther Burns recordings. *Now!*, issued only on cassette, was released on Falco's own label and features seven songs culled from a 1984 concert in Memphis, Tennessee, USA.

In 1986 the band found a sympathetic label in New Rose Records, based in Paris, France. The Chilton-produced 1988 set *The World We Knew* is probably Falco's finest recording, with different sidemen supporting the singer on a range of material encompassing **Sun Records**–styled rockabilly, R&B and delta blues. The follow-up *Red Devil* invoked the rampaging style of early releases and featured compositions by **Chuck Berry** and **Lee Hazlewood** among others. Tav Falco enjoyed a small role in the **Jerry Lee Lewis** biopic *Great Balls Of Fire* before releasing the self-explanatory *10th Anniversary Live LP: Midnight In Memphis*. This two-record set featured Chilton, Dickinson and other assorted guests on material ranging from 'Goldfinger' to 'Train Kept A-Rollin''. Curiously, the set lacked overall sparkle, although the studio follow-up *Return Of The Blue Panther* put paid to the notion that Falco had calmed down. Distortion, reverb and unqualified excitement abounded in a set largely comprised of well-known R&B standards, including 'Rock Me Baby' and 'I Got Love If You Want It'.

Remaining a touring and recording entity well into the new millennium, Tav Falco's Panther Burns have issued further albums through a range of outlets including Last Call, Sympathy For The Record Industry and In The Red. Though they remain on the fringes of rock, the affection for the music they play remains undiminished.

● ALBUMS: *Behind The Magnolia Curtain* (Rough Trade 1981) ★★★, *Now!* (Frenzi 1984) ★★★, *The World We Knew* (New Rose 1988) ★★★★, *Red Devil* (New Rose 1988) ★★★, *10th Anniversary Live LP: Midnight In Memphis* (New Rose 1989) ★★, *Return Of The Blue Panther* (New Rose/Triple X 1990) ★★★, *Life Sentence* (UK) *Life Sentence In The Cathouse* (USA) (New Rose/Triple X 1992) ★★★, *Shadow Dancer* (Last Call/Upstart 1995) ★★★, *Disappearing Angels* 10-inch album (Sympathy For The Record Industry 1996) ★★★, *Panther Phobia* (In The Red 2000) ★★★, *Live At Subsonic* (Speed 2002) ★★★.

● COMPILATIONS: *Deep In The Shadows* (Marilyn 1994) ★★★★, *Love's Last Warning* (Last Call 1996) ★★★.

● FILMS: *New York Beat Movie* (1981), *Great Balls Of Fire!* (1989), *Highway 61* (1991), *Blue Box* (1993).

Falkner, Jason

b. 2 June 1970, Texas, USA. Before making his solo debut as the multi-instrumentalist and singer behind 1996's *Jason Falkner Presents Another Unknown*, Falkner had released records with three other groups. As a teenager he had answered a magazine advert to become guitarist with the cult 60s revivalists the **Three O'Clock**, contributing to their 1988 *Vermillion* set for **Prince**'s Paisley Park label. He subsequently joined **Jellyfish** for 1990's critically acclaimed *Bellybutton*. Then, as the result of impromptu jamming sessions, Falkner became a member of the Grays, alongside Dan McCarroll (drums), Buddy Judge (vocals/guitar) and Jon Brion (vocals/guitar). Formed by accident, the band quickly became the subject of a minor bidding war amongst record labels, but their sole album *Ro Sham Bo* proved a disappointment. Nevertheless, it did contain the Falkner composition and minor hit 'Very Best Years', which presaged the style and sweep of his solo work. After the release of his excellent 1996 debut, he commented: 'It's something I've always wanted to do. I would do demos playing all the instruments. The album is really just an extension of the 4-tracks. I wanted to keep the integrity and general excitement.' Falkner also worked with **Eric Matthews** on his acclaimed debut before releasing 1999's *Can You Still Feel?*, another minor masterpiece. Every pop ingredient was used, and although highly derivative and Beatlesque, tracks such as 'Revelation', 'The Plan' and 'Eloquence' delivered the 60s experience with great panache.

● ALBUMS: *Jason Falkner Presents Another Unknown* (Elektra 1996) ★★★★, *Can You Still Feel?* (Elektra 1999) ★★★★.

● COMPILATIONS: *Necessity: The 4 -Track Years* (spinART 2001) ★★★.

Fall

Formed in Manchester, England, in 1977, the Fall is the brainchild of the mercurial Mark E. Smith (b. Mark Edward Smith, 5 March 1957, Salford, Manchester, England). Over the years, Smith has ruthlessly utilized a battalion of musicians while taking the band on a personal odyssey defined by his wayward musical and lyrical excursions. His truculent press proclamations, by turns hysterically funny or sinister, also illuminated their career. Just as importantly, BBC disc jockey **John Peel** became their most consistent and fervent advocate, with the band recording a record number of sessions for his Radio 1 show.

The first Fall line-up, featuring Una Baines (electric piano), Martin Bramah (guitar), Karl Burns (drums) and Tony Friel (bass), made their debut on 'Bingo Master's Breakout', a good example of Smith's surreal vision, coloured by his relentlessly northern working-class vigil. Initially signed to the small independent label Step Forward the band recorded three singles, including the savage 'Fiery Jack', plus *Live At The Witch Trials*. In 1980 the unit signed to **Rough Trade Records** and went on to release the critically acclaimed but still wilful singles 'How I Wrote Elastic Man' and 'Totally Wired'. Meanwhile, a whole series of line-up changes saw the arrival and subsequent departures of Mike Leigh, Martin Bramah and Yvonne Pawlett. The band's most stable line-up featured **Marc Riley**, Steve Hanley, Paul Hanley and Craig Scanlon backing Smith. The Fall's convoluted career continued to produce a series of discordant yet frequently fascinating albums, from the early menace of *Dragnet* to the chaotic *Hex Enduction Hour*. At every turn Smith worked hard to stand aloof from any prevailing trend, his suspicious mind refusing to make concessions to the mainstream.

An apparent change in the band's image and philosophy occurred during 1983 with the arrival of future wife Brix (Laura Elise Smith) and the departure of Riley to form the Creepers. As well as appearing with the Fall as singer and guitarist, Brix later recorded with her own outfit, the pop-orientated **Adult Net**. She first appeared on the Fall's *Perverted By Language*, and her presence was felt more keenly when the Fall unexpectedly emerged as a potential chart act, successfully covering **R. Dean Taylor**'s 'There's A Ghost In My House' and later the **Kinks**' 'Victoria'. Despite this, Smith's deadpan voice and distinctive, accentuated vocals still dominated the band's sound, along with his backing band's ceaseless exploration of the basic rock riff.

On later albums, such as the almost flawless *This Nation's Saving Grace* and *The Frenz Experiment*, they lost none of their baffling wordplay or nagging, insistent rhythms, but the work seemed more focused and accessible. The line-up changes had slowed, although more changes were afoot with the arrival of drummer Simon Woolstenscroft and Marcia Schofield. Proof of Smith's growing stature among the popular art cognoscenti was the staging of his papal play *Hey! Luciani* and the involvement of dancer Michael Clarke in the production of *I Am Kurious Oranj*. Any suggestions that the Fall might be slowly heading for a degree of commercial acceptance underestimated Smith's restless spirit.

By the turn of the decade Brix had left the singer and the band (he maintains he 'kicked her out'), and Schofield followed soon afterwards. A succession of labels did little to impair the band's 90s output, with the Fall's leader unable to do wrong in the eyes of their hugely committed following, which now had outposts throughout America. Brix returned in time to guest on *Cerebral Caustic*, although Smith had persevered in her absence, recording four strong albums, with 1993's *The Infotainment Scan* even reaching number 9 in the UK album charts. *In The City* featured a live take recorded in 1996 and was followed by Smith's thirtieth album, *Levitate*, which experimented with dance rhythms. *Oxymoron* and *The More You Look The Less You Find* are among the glut of compilations of unreleased or alternative material to have flooded the market. Long-term bass player Steve Hanley walked out, along with two other musicians, following an onstage fight at a show in New York in April 1998. True to form, Smith assembled a new band and returned with a series of excellent, thoroughly contemporary albums, including *The Marshall Suite* (1999), *The Unutterable* (2000) and *Fall Heads Roll* (2005). Unpredictable and unique, the Fall under Smith's guidance remains one of the UK's most uncompromising bands.

● ALBUMS: *Live At The Witch Trials* (Step Forward 1979) ★★★★, *Dragnet* (Step Forward 1979) ★★★★, *Totale's Turns (It's Now Or Never) (Live)* (Rough Trade 1980) ★★, *Grotesque (After The Gramme)* (Rough Trade 1980) ★★★, *Slates* mini-album (Rough Trade 1981) ★★★, *Hex Enduction Hour* (Kamera 1982) ★★★★, *Room To Live* (Kamera 1982) ★★★, *Perverted By Language* (Rough Trade 1983) ★★★, *The Wonderful And Frightening World Of . . .* (Beggars Banquet 1984) ★★★★, *This Nation's Saving Grace* (Beggars Banquet 1985) ★★★★★, *Bend Sinister* (Beggars Banquet 1986) ★★★★, *The Frenz Experiment* (Beggars Banquet 1988) ★★★★, *I Am Kurious Oranj* (Beggars Banquet 1988) ★★★, *Seminal Live* (Beggars Banquet 1989) ★★★, *Extricate* (Cog Sinister/Fontana 1990) ★★★, *Shiftwork* (Cog Sinister/Fontana 1991) ★★★★, *Code: Selfish* (Cog Sinister/Fontana 1992) ★★★, *The Infotainment Scan* (Cog Sinister/Permanent 1993) ★★★, *BBC Live In Concert* 1987 recording (Windsong 1993) ★★★, *Middle Class Revolt* (Permanent 1994) ★★★★, *Cerebral Caustic* (Permanent 1995) ★★★★, *The Twenty-Seven Points* (Permanent 1996) ★★★, *The Light User Syndrome* (Jet 1996) ★★★, *Oxymoron* (Receiver 1997) ★★, *15 Ways To Leave Your Man* (Receiver 1997) ★★★, *Cheetham Hill* (Receiver 1997) ★★★, *In The City* (Artful 1997) ★★★, *Levitate* (Artful 1997) ★★★, *Live To Air In Melbourne '82* (Cog Sinister 1998) ★★★★, *The Marshall Suite* (Artful 1999) ★★★★, *The Unutterable* (Eagle 2000) ★★★★, *Liverpool 78* (Cog Sinister 2001) ★, *Are You Are Missing Winner* (Cog Sinister 2001) ★★, *2G + 2* (Action 2002) ★★, *Touch Sensitive: Bootleg Box Set* 5-CD box set (Castle 2003) ★★★, *Live At The Phoenix Festival* (Strange Fruit 2003) ★★, *The Real New Fall LP (Formerly Country On The Click)* (Action 2003) ★★★, *Interim* (Voiceprint 2004) ★★, *Fall Heads Roll* (Slogan 2005) ★★★★.

Solo: Mark E. Smith *The Post Nearly Man* (Artful 1998) ★★, *Pander! Panda! Panzer!* spoken word (Action 2002) ★★, *Live In London 1980: The Legendary Chaos Tape* (Castle 2004) ★★★.

● COMPILATIONS: *77—Early Years—79* (Step Forward 1981) ★★★, *Live At Acklam Hall, London, 1980* cassette (Chaos 1982) ★★★, *Hip Priests And Kamerads* (Situation 2 1985) ★★★, *In Palace Of Swords Reversed (80-83)* (Cog Sinister 1987) ★★★★, *458489 A Sides* (Beggars Banquet 1990) ★★★★, *458489-B Sides* (Beggars Banquet 1990) ★★★, *The Collection* (Castle 1993) ★★★, *Sinister Waltz* archive recordings (Receiver 1996) ★★, *Fiend With A Violin* archive recordings (Receiver 1996) ★★, *Oswald Defence Lawyer* archive recordings (Receiver 1996) ★★, *The More You Look The Less You Find* (Trojan 1998) ★★, *Slates/A Part Of America Therein, 1981* (Castle 1998) ★★★, *Smile . . . It's The Best Of The Fall* (Castle 1998) ★★★, *Northern Attitude: An Alternative Selection* (Music Club 1998) ★★, *The Peel Sessions* (Strange Fruit 1999) ★★★, *A Past Gone Mad: The Best Of The Fall 1990-2000* (Artful 2000) ★★★★, *Psykick Dance Hall: Classic Archive Recordings From The Fall 1977—1982* 3-CD set (Eagle 2000) ★★★, *A World Bewitched: Best Of 1990-2000* (Artful 2001) ★★★★, *Totally Wired: The Rough Trade Anthology* (Castle 2002) ★★★★, *The Rough Trade Singles Box* (Essential 2002) ★★★, *High Tension Line* (Recall 2002) ★★★, *Listening In: Lost Singles Tracks 1990-92* (Cog Sinister 2002) ★★★, *A Past Gone Mad* (Artful 2003) ★★★, *It's The New Thing! The Step Forward Years* (Castle 2003) ★★★★, *Time Enough At Last: The Receiver Years* 3-CD box set (Castle 2003) ★★★, *Words Of Expectation: BBC Sessions* (Castle 2003) ★★★, *The War Against Intelligence: The Fontana Years* (Universal 2003) ★★★, *Rebellious Jukebox* (Shakedown 2003) ★★★, *50,000 Fall Fans Can't Be Wrong* (Sanctuary 2004) ★★★★, *A Part Of America Therein 1981* (Castle 2004) ★★★, *The Complete Peel Sessions 1978-2004* 6-CD box set (Sanctuary 2005) ★★★.

● DVD/VIDEOS: *VHS8489* (Beggars Banquet 1991), *Perverted By Language Bis* (IKON 1992), *Perverted By Language Bis And Live At Leeds* (Cherry Red 2003), *A Touch Sensitive: Live* (Secret Films 2004), *Live At The Hacienda 1983-1985* (Cherry Red 2004).

● FURTHER READING: *Paintwork: A Portrait Of The Fall*, Brian Edge. *Hip Priest: The Story Of Mark E. Smith And The Fall*, Simon Ford. *A User's Guide To The Fall*, Dave Thompson. *The Fall*, Mick Middles with Mark E. Smith.

Fall Out Boy

Originating from Chicago, Illinois, USA, emo band Fall Out Boy began to take shape at the turn of the new millennium. Formed by Patrick Stump (b. 27 April 1984, Evanston, Illinois, USA; vocals/guitar), Joseph Trohman (b. 1 September 1984, Chicago, Illinois, USA; guitar), Peter Wentz (b. 5 June 1979, Wilmette, Illinois, USA; bass) and Andrew Hurley (b. 31 May 1980, Milwaukee, Wisconsin, USA; drums), all the members had played with different emo and metal-core units based around Chicago's insular underground hardcore scene. Wentz was most prominent as the leader of cult hardcore favourites Arma Angelus. As Fall Out Boy they embraced a more melodic direction while retaining the ferocious intensity of their hardcore roots. A demo CD emerged in 2001 and was followed by a split album with Project Rocket. The short and snappy *Fall Out Boy's Evening Out With Your Girlfriend* was released on the Uprising label at the start of 2003. The album served notice of the quartet's fast developing mastery of the pop punk style and their witty, self-referential lyrics. Released only a few months later, the quartet's debut for **Less Than Jake** drummer Vinnie Balzano's Fueled By Ramen label, *Take This To Your Grave*, was completed using money from the band's concurrent contract with major label **Island Records**. The album's strong critical reception allied to support from the band's powerful Internet-based fanbase, established Fall Out Boy's reputation at the forefront of the alternative rock scene. Confirming their popularity, the band's first album to be distributed through Island, *From Under The Cork Tree*, shot into the US Top 10 in May 2005. 'Sugar, We're Goin' Down' also reached the upper regions of the singles chart.

● ALBUMS: *Fall Out Boy's Evening Out With Your Girlfriend* (Uprising 2003) ★★★, *Take This To Your Grave* (Fueled By Ramen 2003) ★★★★, *From Under The Cork Tree* (Fueled By Ramen/Island 2005) ★★★.

Fallon, Jack

b. 13 October 1915, London, Canada. Fallon went to Britain with the Canadian airforce and settled there in 1946. He established a professional career playing bass in the bands of **Ted Heath** and **Jack Jackson** and played with **George Shearing** in 1948, with whom he accompanied **Duke Ellington**. Fallon became the staff bass player for Lansdowne Records where he recorded with a wide variety of musicians—from **Josh White** (vocal/guitar) through **Alex Welsh** and **Humphrey Lyttelton** to **Joe Harriott**. In the mid-50s Fallon had a successful sextet called In Town Tonight. It was during this period that he started his own company, Cana Agency, which later represented **Kenny Ball**. Fallon played regularly with light orchestral band leaders like **Frank Chacksfield** and **Ron Goodwin**, worked as a violinist with country musicians and even recorded with the **Beatles** in 1968. Since then Fallon has concentrated on his agency, but he did play with **Lennie Felix** (piano) in the 70s and later with **Stan Greig** (piano) and **Digby Fairweather**.

Falls, Ruby

b. 1946, Jackson, Tennessee, USA, d. 15 June 1986. One of the few black female singers to achieve success in country music. After relocating to Milwaukee, she sang with local country bands until 1974, when, no doubt encouraged by the success gained by **Charley Pride** and **Stoney Edwards**, she decided to move to Nashville. She toured with **Justin Tubb** and also impressed through her performances in Las Vegas. She recorded for the 50 States label and in 1975, she gained her first minor *Billboard* chart successes with 'Sweet Country Music' and 'He Loves Me All To Pieces'. Between 1976 and 1979, she had seven more minor hits, which included her biggest, 'You've Got To Mend This Heartache' (a number 40 in 1977), and her version of the **Fats Domino** pop hit 'Three Nights A Week'. Although she had no chart success after 1979, she remained a popular performer until her sudden death, following a brain haemorrhage, in the Vanderbilt Hospital, Nashville, on 15 June 1986.

● ALBUMS: *Ruby Falls—Sweet Country Lady* (50 States 1980) ★★★★.

False Prophets

'Our aim is to disarm the mechanics of oppression through persistent "making and doing" of words and music in an invocation of the ancient magic which empowers humankind through the massing of voices in sacred speech/song.' With this impressive philosophy in mind, the False Prophets, comprising Stephan Ielpi (vocals), Debra De Salvo (guitar/vocals), Steven Taylor (guitar/vocals), Nick Marden (bass/vocals) and Billy Atwell III (drums/vocals) burst into life in the early 80s as part of the famed US hardcore scene that also spawned **Black Flag** and **Hüsker Dü**. Their hypothesis was intelligence, intellect and knowledge as opposed to the horror-show shock tactics used by many US punk acts. This approach led to a contract with **Jello Biafra**'s Alternative Tentacles Records in 1986, from which sprang *False Prophets* and *Implosion*. These albums showed a willingness to experiment and break away from pure punk thrash-outs. *Invisible People*, on Konkurrel, saw them start the new decade in style, with an innovative fusion of hard-core punk, Latin rhythms, hard rock and polemic sculpted into a uniquely compelling record. They continued their quest for equality and freedom with this theory as their cornerstone: 'All music, particularly rock, is ecstatic activity, and ecstasy itself is revolutionary.'

● ALBUMS: *False Prophets* (Alternative Tentacles 1986) ★★★, *Implosion* (Alternative Tentacles 1987) ★★★, *Invisible People* (Konkurrel 1990) ★★★.

● COMPILATIONS: *Blind Roaches And Fat Vultures: Phantasmagoric Beasts Of The Reagan Era* (Alternative Tentacles 2000) ★★★.

Falsettoland

(see *March Of The Falsettos*)

Fältskog, Agnetha

b. 5 April 1950, Jönköping, Sweden. Fältskog started her musical career in 1965 at the age of 15, when she sang for a Swedish dance band. In 1968 she released her debut single—'Jag Var Så Kär' ('I Was So In Love'). It was a smash in Sweden and the rest of Scandinavia, and she successfully followed it up with further hits. In 1969 she appeared on a television show where she met Björn Ulvaeus, a former member of the Hootenanny Singers and a songwriting partner of Hep Star Benny Andersson. Agnetha (who was normally known as Anna) and Björn married on 7 July 1971. By this time Ulvaeus and Anderson were recording together, and Anna and Andersson's girlfriend Anni Fred Lyngstad were singing backing vocals for the boys. Eventually a permanent group was formed, and in 1974 they became **Abba** who first conquered Sweden then took the UK by storm when they won the Eurovision Song Contest.

Fältskog's relationship with Ulvaeus ended with divorce in 1979, and by 1982 Abba had worked together for the last time. Neither Lyngstad nor Fältskog wasted anytime in launching their solo careers. Fältskog opened with an album—*Wrap Your Arms Around Me*—produced by famed pop producer **Mike Chapman** and hit the singles chart three times in 1983 with 'The Heat Is On', 'Wrap Your Arms Around Me' and 'Can't Shake Loose'; the latter written by **Russ Ballard**. In 1987 Fältskog moved to **WEA Records** with ex-**Chicago** vocalist

Peter Cetera as producer. However, the album and the single 'The Last Time' made little impact, and Fältskog retired from the music business.

After publishing her autobiography in 1997, the singer began to express a renewed interest in music. By the start of the new millennium, with the Abba musical *Mamma Mia!* doing sterling business around the world and the 30th anniversary of the band's Eurovision Song Contest victory looming large, Fältskog signed a new recording contract with Warner Music Scandinavia. A pleasant collection of standards and 60s pop obscurities was released in 2004.

● ALBUMS: *Agnetha* (Embassy 1974) ★★, *Wrap Your Arms Around Me* (Epic 1983) ★★★, *Eyes Of A Woman* (Epic 1987) ★★, *I Stand Alone* (Warners 1988) ★★, *My Colouring Book* (WEA 2004) ★★★.
● COMPILATIONS: *My Love My Life* (Columbia 1996) ★★, *That's Me: Greatest Hits* (Polydor 1998) ★★★.
● FURTHER READING: *As I Am: Abba Before And Beyond*, Agnetha Fältskog with Brita Åhman. *Abbamania Volume 2: The Solo Years*, Peter Bingham and Bernadette Dolan.

Fame

Exiled British director Alan Parker (*Bugsy Malone*, *The Commitments*) took the reins for this 1980 film, which followed the lives of young showbusiness aspirants in time-honoured fashion. Set in Manhattan's High School for the Performing Arts, *Fame* charts the lives of a group of teenagers over a period of four years. Parker cast disparate characters—homosexuals, Puerto Ricans, individuals drawn from New York's uptown and downtown environments—in what turned out to be a box-office blockbuster. **Irene Cara** (b. Irene T Escalera, 18 March 1959, New York City, USA) played aspiring dancer Coco Hernandez, and her recording of Michael Gore and Dean Pitchford's title song won an Academy Award and went to number 1 in the UK. The rest of the songs included 'Red Light', 'I Sing The Body Electric', 'Dogs In The Yard', 'Hot Lunch Jam', 'Out Here On My Own' and 'Is It OK If I Call You Mine?', and there was an Oscar for Gore's exciting score. Prominent among the cast were Paul McCrane (b. 19 January 1961, Philadelphia, Pennsylvania, USA), Gene Anthony Ray (b. 24 May 1962, Harlem, New York City, USA, d. 14 November 2003, New York, USA, Lee Curreri (b. 4 January 1961, Bronx, New York City, USA) and Barry Miller (b. 6 February 1958, Los Angeles, California, USA) as a slick and hip Puerto Rican. Produced by David De Silva and Alan Marshall with a screenplay by Christopher Gore, *Fame* proved popular enough to inspire a spin-off television series, which in turn spawned more chart successes for **The Kids From Fame**. This played in more than 60 countries and prompted De Silva to conceive and develop a version for the stage. He formed a new creative team that included composer Steven Margoshes, lyricist **Jacques Levy** and librettist Jose Fernandez.

Fame: The Musical made its debut at the Coconut Grove Playhouse, Miami, on 21 October 1988. Despite positive audience reaction in Miami and later Philadelphia, a Broadway transfer fell through, but *Fame* subsequently proved a hit in Stockholm, Sweden, and other European countries. West End audiences were introduced to the show at the Cambridge Theatre on 27 June 1995. Gore and Pitchford's title song was still in there, along with numbers such as 'Hard Work', 'I Want To Make Magic', 'Dance Class'

(after Beethoven's 'Spring Sonata'), 'Can't Keep It Down', 'Tyrone's Rap', 'There She Goes', 'Let's Play A Love Scene', 'Bring On Tomorrow', 'The Teachers' Argument', 'Mabel's Prayer', 'Dancin' On The Sidewalk', 'These Are My Children' and 'In L.A.'. Loraine Velez played Carmen with dash and authority, and Sonia Swaby (Mabel) tore into the amusing 'Think Of Meryl Streep'. Also cast were Marcus D'Cruze (Joe), Scott Sherrin (Tyrone), Jonatha Aris (Schlomo), Richard Dempsey (Nick) and Gemma Wardle (Serena). Directed by Runa Borge and choreographed by Lars Bethke, *Fame* ran until 28 September 1996. The UK touring version called in on London's West End for Christmas seasons in 1997 and 1998, while elsewhere productions during 1998/9 were being forecast for Toronto, Paris, Sydney, Berlin, Chicago, Warsaw, Tokyo, Vienna, Oslo, Munich, Caracas, Milan, Budapest, Montreal and Los Angeles.

Fame, Georgie

b. Clive Powell, 26 June 1943, Leigh, Lancashire, England. Entrepreneur **Larry Parnes** gave the name to this talented organist during the early 60s following a recommendation from songwriter **Lionel Bart**. Parnes already had a Power, a Wilde, an Eager and a Fury. All he now needed was Fame. It took a number of years before Fame and his band the Blue Flames had commercial success, although he was a major force in the popularizing of early R&B, bluebeat and ska at London's famous Flamingo club. The seminal *Rhythm And Blues At The Flamingo* was released in January 1964. Chart success came later that year with a UK number 1, 'Yeh, Yeh'. Fame's jazzy nasal delivery, reminiscent of **Mose Allison**, made this record one of the decade's classic songs. He continued with another 11 hits, including 2 further UK chart toppers, 'Getaway' and 'The Ballad Of Bonnie And Clyde', the latter of which was his only US Top 10 single. Even the lesser hits, such as 'Something' (written by **John Mayall**) and 'In The Meantime' (written by John Burch), were of a high standard. They all maintained his jazz feel, which continued on such striking mood pieces as 'Sunny' and 'Sitting In The Park'. Thereafter for a few years Fame veered towards straight pop. His recent change of record labels (from **Columbia Records** to **CBS Records**) was an attempt to re-market him, and at one stage he was teamed with the **Harry South** Big Band. While his albums showed a more progressive style, his singles became lightweight, the nadir being when he teamed up with **Alan Price** to produce some catchy but dire pop songs. 'Rosetta' was the lowest point of musical credibility but the highest point in commercial terms.

During later years, Fame has played straight jazz at **Ronnie Scott**'s club, performed a tribute to **Hoagy Carmichael** with singer **Annie Ross** and sung over Esso advertisements. In the 90s he toured with **Van Morrison** as keyboard player, given a brief cameo to perform the occasional hit. During the renaissance of the Hammond B3 organ (an instrument that Fame had originally pioneered in the London clubs) during another jazz boom of the early 90s, it was announced that Fame had recorded a new album, *Cool Cat Blues*, and its subsequent release to favourable reviews and regular concert appearances indicated a new phase. The album was recorded to the highest standards and featured smooth contributions from **Steve Gadd**, **Robben Ford**, **Richard Tee**, **Jon Hendricks** and **Boz Scaggs**. A reggae reworking of 'Yeh, Yeh' and a graceful version of Carmichael's 'Georgia' were two outstanding tracks. Morrison joined Fame on the former's classic 'Moondance'. Fame followed up with *The Blues And Me*, an album of a similar high standard.

Tragedy struck the singer in 1994 when his wife committed suicide. Since then he has continued to work and record with Morrison and **Bill Wyman** as well as gigging with his latter-day version of the Blue Flames, which features two of his sons. Tristan Powell (guitar) and James Powell (drums) are both excellent young musicians, moulding well into their father's warm musical niche. Fame has reached a stage in his career where he can play what he chooses, and he has reverted to his first love, jazz. He is an exemplary musician whose early 60s and later work (post 90s) is necessary for any discerning record collection.

● ALBUMS: *Rhythm And Blues At The Flamingo* (Columbia 1964) ★★★★, *Fame At Last* (Columbia 1964) ★★★★★, *Sweet Things* (Columbia 1966) ★★★, *Sound Venture* (Columbia 1966) ★★★★, *Two Faces Of Fame* (CBS 1967) ★★★, *The Third Face Of Fame* (CBS 1968) ★★★, *Seventh Son* (CBS 1969) ★★, *Georgie Does His Thing With Strings* (CBS 1970) ★★, *Goin' Home* (CBS 1971) ★★, with Alan Price *Fame And Price, Price And Fame Together* (CBS 1971) ★★★, *All Me Own Work* (Reprise 1972) ★★, *Georgie Fame* (Island 1974) ★★, *Right Now!* (Pye 1979) ★★★, *That's What Friends Are For* (Pye 1979) ★★★, *Closing The Gap* (Piccadilly 1980) ★★, with Annie Ross *In Hoagland '81* (Bald Eagle 1981) ★★★★, *No Worries* (4 Leaf Clover 1988) ★★, *Cool Cat Blues* (Go Jazz 1991) ★★★★, *The Blues And Me* (Go Jazz 1994) ★★★, with Van Morrison *How Long Has This Been Going On* (Verve 1995) ★★★★, with Morrison, Ben Sidran, Mose Allison *Tell Me Something: The Songs Of Mose Allison* (Verve 1996) ★★, *Name Droppin': Live At Ronnie Scott's* (Go Jazz 1999) ★★★, *Poet In New York* (Go Jazz 2000) ★★★, *Walking Wounded: Live At Ronnie Scott's* (Go Jazz 2000) ★★★★, *Relationships* (Three Line Whip 2001) ★★★★, *Charlestons* (Three Line Whip 2002) ★★★★.

● COMPILATIONS: *Hall Of Fame* (Columbia 1967) ★★★★, *Georgie Fame* (Starline 1969) ★★★★, *Fame Again* (Starline 1972) ★★★★, *20 Beat Classics* (Polydor 1982) ★★★★★, *The First 30 Years* (Connoisseur 1989) ★★★, *The Very Best Of Georgie Fame And The Blue Flames* (Spectrum 1998) ★★★★, *Funny How Time Slips Away* (Castle 2001) ★★★, *The In-Crowd* 3-CD box set (Motor Music 2002) ★★★, *On The Right Track* (Raven 2004) ★★★★, *Anthology* (Go Jazz 2004) ★★★★.

● DVD/VIDEOS: *Anthology* (Go Jazz 2003).

Familia Valera Miranda

Félix Valera Miranda (b. 26 February 1939, Las Tunas, Cuba; lead vocal/guitar), Carmen Rosa Alarcón Ganboa (b. 30 August 1944, Las Tunas, Cuba; maracas/backing vocals), Rádames González Brugal (b. 14 October 1942, El Caney, Cuba; vocals, cuatro, tres, clave), Enrique Valera Alarcón (b. 2 January 1966, Santiago, Cuba; cuatro, clave, backing vocals), Raúl Félix Valera Alarcón (b. 31 December 1968, Santiago, Cuba; double bass/backing vocals) and Ernesto Valera Alarcón (b. 20 July 1970, Santiago, Cuba; bongos, sencerro, backing vocals). A family of musicians from the Oriente region of Cuba, Familia Valera Miranda comprise father Félix (the group's leader), his wife and sons plus his brother Rádames. They play a mid-tempo form of 'son', Cuba's traditional musical style, called 'Cauto son'. A

nonprofessional ensemble who only performed at the parties of family and close friends, they recorded their international debut, *Music From Oriente De Cuba: The Son*, at Salo Dolores, Santiago de Cuba in April 1994. It featured a selection of traditional 'son' standards (some by members of the Valera Miranda family and others by well-known composers, including **Compay Segundo**), which predated the revival of interest in the music which arose after the success of the **Buena Vista Social Club** three years later. *Cana Quema* and *Cuba: La Familia Valera Miranda* both featured songs in the traditional Cuban style performed with the groups customary easygoing swing. *Cuba: The Trova* featured Félix Valera Miranda alongside vocalist Joel Diez and Francisco Sablon on the 'laud' (Cuban 12-string guitar) playing a further selection of Cuban classics, this time in the 'trovador' style, i.e., without percussion.

● ALBUMS: *Music From Oriente De Cuba: The Son* (Nimbus 1994) ★★★★, *Cana Quema* (Nimbus 1997) ★★★, *Cuba: La Familia Valera Miranda* (Ocora 1997) ★★★, as Trio Yagua *Cuba: The Trova* (Nimbus 1998) ★★★.

Family

Highly respected and nostalgically revered, Family was one of Britain's most memorable progressive rock bands of the late 60s and early 70s. They were led by the wiry yet vocally demonic **Roger Chapman** (b. Roger Maxwell Chapman, 8 April 1942, Leicester, England), a man whose stage presence could both transfix and terrify his audience, who would duck from the countless supply of tambourines he destroyed and hurled into the crowd. Chapman was joined in the original line-up by **Ric Grech** (b. Richard Roman Grech, 1 November 1946, Bordeaux, France, d. 17 March 1990, Leicester, England; violin/bass), Charlie Whitney (b. Richard John Whitney, 24 June 1944, Skipton, North Yorkshire, England; guitar), Rob Townsend (b. 7 July 1947, Leicester, England; drums), and Jim King (b. 1945, Kettering, Northamptonshire, England; flute/saxophone).

Family's roots can be traced back to 1962 when Leicester Art College students Whitney and King formed the R&B-based **Farinas**, with Harry Overnall (drums) and Tim Kirchin (bass) completing the line-up. Grech replaced the latter in 1965, and when Chapman was brought in as lead vocalist the following year, the band's sound began to expand beyond their basic R&B roots. The quintet changed their name to the Roaring Sixties and developed a gangster image thanks to their preference for double-breasted suits. Further change ensued in 1967 with the arrival of Townsend in place of Overnall and the adoption of a more relaxed dress code. Producer **Kim Fowley** gave the quintet their new name, dubbing them 'the Family' because of their Mafioso image. After recording an obscure single ('Scene Through The Eye Of A Lens'/'Gypsy Woman') for **Liberty Records**, Family released their first album in 1968. **Music In A Doll's House** was given extensive exposure on **John Peel**'s influential BBC radio show, resulting in this **Dave Mason**–produced collection becoming a major cult record. Chapman's remarkable strangulated vibrato caused heads to turn. It was an extraordinary debut album, and the band's image received a further boost (of sorts) when fan/writer Jenny Fabian published the paperback *Groupie*, a salacious account of the underground club scene in London in which a barely disguised Family played a prominent part. Following the release of their second and most successful album, *Family Entertainment*, Family experienced an ever-changing personnel of high pedigree musicians. Ric Grech departed to join **Blind Faith** in 1969, being replaced by John Weider (b. 21 April 1947, England), who in turn was supplanted by **John Wetton** (b. 12 June 1949, Derby, Derbyshire, England) in 1971, then Jim Cregan (b. 9 March 1946, England) the following year. Poli Palmer (b. John Michael Palmer, 25 May 1943, England; ex-**Deep Feeling**) superseded Jim King in 1969 and was ultimately replaced by **Tony Ashton** (b. Edward Anthony Ashton, 1 March 1946, Blackburn, Lancashire, England, d. 28 May 2001, London, England) in 1972.

Throughout this turmoil Family maintained a high standard of recorded work and had UK singles success with 'No Mules Fool' (number 29, 1969), 'Strange Band' (number 11, 1970), 'In My Own Time' (number 4, 1971) and the infectious 'Burlesque' (number 13, 1972). Probably their finest single release, 'My Friend The Sun', failed to dent the charts. This was proof that the charts at that time had nothing to do with the quality of the songs therein. Their catalogue should be viewed album by album, as it still remains one of the strongest of the era. Their third album, 1970's *A Song For Me*, contained the blistering 'Hey—Let It Rock'/'The Cat And The Rat' and the excellent opening track 'Drowned In Wine'. *Anyway* was a live album, and although badly recorded it remains a vital record with stand-out performances of 'Lives And Ladies', 'Strange Band' and 'Good News Bad News'. Family were probably at their popularity peak when 1971's *Fearless* came out, and the album showed how democratic the band had become with diverse input from Poli Palmer and his stunning barbershop quartet song 'Larf And Sing'. Similarly evocative were the rowdy 'Take Your Partners' and 'Sat'D Barfly'. *Bandstand* was another commercial winner with the previously mentioned gem 'My Friend The Sun' and the hit 'Burlesque'. Other lively classics on the album included 'Broken Nose' and 'Ready To Go'.

Family disintegrated after the release of 1973's disappointing swan-song *It's Only A Movie*, although this album did contain two gems, 'Sweet Desirée' and the title track. Chapman and Whitney departed to form **Streetwalkers** before the former established a popular solo career. A long-lost live album from Family's tour in 1971, recorded at London's Rainbow Theatre, was released as part of the enterprising independent label Mystic Records' reissue program. Most of Family's catalogue was reissued by Mystic with extra tracks and outtakes in 2003.

While Family's stage performances were sometimes erratic and unpredictable, the sight of Chapman performing their anthem, 'The Weaver's Answer', on a good night was unforgettable. Chapman has a voice that can shatter a beer glass and crack ceilings.

● ALBUMS: *Music In A Doll's House* (Reprise 1968) ★★★★★, *Family Entertainment* (Reprise 1969) ★★★★, *A Song For Me* (Reprise 1970) ★★★, *Anyway* (Reprise 1970) ★★★, *Fearless* (Reprise 1971) ★★★★, *Bandstand* (Reprise 1972) ★★★★, *It's Only A Movie* (Reprise 1973) ★★, *The Peel Sessions* mini-album (Strange Fruit 1988) ★★, *BBC Radio 1 Live In Concert* (Windsong 1991) ★★★, *Live 1971* recording (Mystic 2003) ★★★★.
● COMPILATIONS: *Old Songs New Songs* (Reprise 1971) ★★★, *Best Of Family* (Reprise 1974) ★★★★, *Rise: The Best Of Family* (Rebecca 1981) ★★★, *From Past Archives* (Teldec 1981) ★★★, *As & Bs* (Castle 1992) ★★★★, *A Family Selection: The Best Of Family* (Essential 2000)

★★★★, *Family & Friends* 4-CD box set (Mystic 2003) ★★, *BBC Radio Volume 1: 1968–69* (Hux 2004) ★★★, *The Very Best Of Roger Chapman And Family* (Retro 2004) ★★★, *BBC Radio Vol 2: 1971–1973* (Hux 2004) ★★★, *Old Songs New Songs: The Definitive Box Set* 4-CD box set (Mystic 2005) ★★★.

Family Cat
Originally from Yeovil, Somerset, the Family Cat formed in 1988 and comprised Paul 'Fred' Frederick (vocals/guitar), Stephen Jelbert (guitar), Tim McVey (guitar), John (bass) and Kevin (drums). Based in south London, the group drew their influences from a variety of styles, in particular **Sonic Youth** and the **Pixies**, and found critical praise for their frenetic live appearances. A mini-album, *Tell 'Em We're Surfin'*, followed on from the unexpected success of their debut single, 1989's 'Tom Verlaine', on the Bad Girl, label. Despite the accolades from the British music press, the group found it difficult to break out of the 'independent' mould. The Family Cat's persistence eventually paid off with well-received singles in 'Remember What It Is That You Love' and 'A Place With No Name' (both 1990) and 'Colour Me Grey' (1991, with backing vocals from the then future indie star **PJ Harvey**). A new album in 1992 on the Dedicated label, *Furthest From The Sun*, surprised many with a effective display of power and confidence, generating some of their best reviews to date. However, by the advent of 1994's *Magic Happens*, the band had seemingly been forgotten by the majority of the British music press and disbanded at the end of that year.
● ALBUMS: *Tell 'Em We're Surfin'* mini-album (Bad Girl 1989) ★★★, *Furthest From The Sun* (Dedicated 1992) ★★★, *Magic Happens* (Dedicated 1994) ★★.

Family Dogg
Formed in the UK in 1969, the original line-up comprised Steve Rowland, **Albert Hammond** (b. 18 May 1944, London, England), Mike Hazelwood, Doreen De Veuve and Zooey. Rowland already had a chequered history as a filmmaker, actor and Continental recording artist before forming the Double R production company with Ronnie Oppenheimer. With the backing of Fontana A&R head Jack Baverstock, Rowland produced a string of hits for **Dave Dee, Dozy, Beaky, Mick And Tich** and the **Herd**, while his company also recorded such artists as **P.J. Proby**, the **Magic Lanterns** and **Amory Kane**. After assembling a talented backup crew, Rowland launched Family Dogg and soon scaled the charts with 'Way Of Life', written by **Roger Cook** and **Roger Greenaway**. Specializing in high harmony and classy covers, Family Dogg followed up unsuccessfully with **Paul Simon**'s 'Save The Life Of My Child' and recorded an album of hit standards with backing by several members of the newly formed **Led Zeppelin**. Although Family Dogg had considerable commercial potential, they were clearly a studio group with a tendency to lose members at short notice. In July 1969 De Veuve was replaced by the glamorous ex-*Charlie Girl* star Christine Holmes, and several months later Ireen Scheer took over Zooey's role. With Hammond and Hazelwood busy writing the 13-piece suite *Oliver In The Overworld* for **Freddie And The Dreamers**, Rowland was forced to explain that his group was a concept that only came together occasionally before dissipating into individual projects. The UK music press, unconvinced by such rhetoric, made sarcastic news item remarks such as 'No

change in Family Dogg line-up this week'. Nobody was too surprised when the band ceased operations early in the new decade.
● ALBUMS: *A Way Of Life* (Bell 1969) ★★, *The View From Rowland's Head* (Polydor 1972) ★.

Family Fodder

This independent band comprised Dominique Pearce (vocals), Alig Levillian (guitars, keyboards, saxophone, vocals), Felix Friedorowicz (keyboards, bassoon, violin), Mick Hobbs (bass/organ), Martin Frederick (bass/vocals), Rick Wilson (drums/vocals), Charles Bullen (drums, guitar, viola, vocals), Buzz Smith (drums), Mark Doffman (drums), Ian Hill (vocals/percussion) and Judy Carter and Jan Beetlestone (backing vocals). Their best-remembered contribution to modern music was the tribute single 'Debbie Harry', though other efforts such as 'Playing Golf', 'Warm', 'Savoire Faire' and 'Film Music' were entertaining for their idiosyncratic experimentalism. However, despite a reasonable line in songwriting craft from Pearce, it would have required greater commercial aptitude to sustain the legions of personnel.
● ALBUMS: *Monkey Banana Kitchen* (Fresh 1981) ★★★.
● COMPILATIONS: *Greatest Hits* (Crammed Discs 1984) ★★★, *Savoir Faire* (Dark Beloved 1999) ★★★.

Family Foundation

Manchester, England–based **techno** crew, made famous by their 'Express Yourself' white label single, which was selling for upwards of £100 to DJs in 1992. Led by producer Johnny Jay, the track was eventually given an official release a year later on Mancunian label 380. However, it was never originally intended to be a Family Foundation number. Jay had produced the track for an artist called Franschene Allea, but when BMG dropped Omen Records the title never saw the light of day. Instead he covered it when FF were doing demos, utilizing the services of Rachel (vocals) and Shine (ragga vocals). It proved a hugely winning formula. A debut album included tracks like 'Gunchester', a comment on Manchester's rising gang problems, and 'Red Hot'. This saw a guest appearance from ex-**Smiths** guitarist Craig Gannon, while over the top of the record Terry Christian and Johnny Rogan discussed the accusations of racism that had recently been directed at ex-Smiths singer **Morrissey**.
● ALBUMS: *One Blood* (380 1992) ★★★.

Family Tree

Bob Segarini (guitar/vocals), Mike Olsen (keyboards), Bill Whittington (bass) and Newman Davis (drums) formed Family Tree in 1965. This San Franciscan rock group was bedevilled by internal unrest, and by the time their debut album was released, Segarini was the only remaining original member. *Miss Butters* unveiled the Anglophile persuasion that marked his subsequent music but was deemed out of step with the prevailing musical trend. Mike Dure (guitar), Jim De Cocq (keyboards), Bill 'Kootch' Troachim (bass) and Vann Slatter (drums) completed the band's final line-up, which broke apart in 1970. Segarini and De Cocq formed Roxy, while founder member Olsen found fame as virtuoso **Lee Michaels**.
● ALBUMS: *Miss Butters* (RCA 1968) ★★.

Famous Jug Band

This UK folk quartet features Jill Johnson (vocals/guitar), Pete Berryman (guitar/vocals), **Clive Palmer** (b. Edmonton, London, England; guitar/vocals) and Henry Bartlett (b. Michael Bartlett; jug). Initial attention focused on Palmer, a former member of the **Incredible String Band**, and some of that band's quirkiness prevailed on *Sunshine Possibilities*, the Famous Jug Band's 1969 debut album. His premature departure from this fledgling venture robbed them of a pivotal member. Although a second album was completed by the remaining trio, it lacked the depth of its predecessor. The Famous Jug Band briefly recruited guitarist **John James** (b. Wales) and then organist Tim Rice but broke up soon afterwards.
Palmer subsequently formed **COB** and maintained a low-key solo career, while Berryman later recorded with John James. Palmer and Berryman reunited with Johnson (now Johnson-Sharp) and Bartlett in the new millennium to work on a new Famous Jug Band album. Recorded in a village hall in Dorset with producer Pierre Tubbs, *O For Summer* was a timely reminder of the quartet's often unsung musical talents.
● ALBUMS: *Sunshine Possibilities* (Liberty 1969) ★★★★, *Chameleon* (Liberty 1970) ★★, *O For Summer* (Market Square 2002) ★★★.

Famous Potatoes

The Famous Potatoes are a group that describe their sound as 'soil music'. The group comprises Keith Baxter (b. 19 October 1957, Rochford, Essex, England; banjo, trombone, washboard, zobstick), Richard Baxter (b. 13 August 1959, Westcliff-on-Sea, Essex, England; vocals, melodeon, saxophone, harmonica), Nigel Blackaby (b. 27 November 1958, Rochford, Essex, England; bass/vocals), Paul Collier (b. 12 February 1959, Rochford, Essex, England; drum/vocals), Melanie Johnson (b. 2 February 1961, Swindon, Wiltshire, England; recorder, clarinet, vocals), Paul 'Prof' McDowell (b. 30 September 1958, Rochford, Essex, England; accordion/vocals), Tony 'Please Sir' Littman (b. 17 July 1951, Westcliff-On-Sea, Essex, England; guitar) and Charlie Skelton (b. 8 February 1963, Enfield, Middlesex, England; fiddle). Tony Littman and Skelton replaced former members Nick Pynn (fiddle, mandolin, mandocello, banjo, viola) and Richard 'Rikki' Reynolds (guitar) who left the group. Pynn joined the re-formed **Cockney Rebel** with **Steve Harley**. The 'Potatoes' style encompasses cajun, skiffle, hillbilly, gospel western swing, and apart from concerts, they also play barn dances, and have appeared regularly at the Greenbelt Christian Arts festivals. Having formed in 1979 as the Folk Pistols to play barn dances, original members Johnson, McDowell and the Baxter brothers have stayed with the band, while Blackaby and Collier joined in 1982. As the Folk Pistols they released two albums in cassette format, *Get Your Skates On* (1981) and *Twist With Ken* (1982). Soon after this the new name was adopted. *It Was Good For My Old Mother* attracted a lot of interest on release, not least in their home territory in Essex. *The Sound Of The Ground* included the **Hank Williams** classic 'I Saw The Light'.
● ALBUMS: *Dig* cassette (Own Label 1983) ★★, *It Was Good For My Old Mother* (Waterfront 1985) ★★★, *The Sound Of The Ground* (Waterfront 1986) ★★★, *Born In A Barn* (Waterfront 1989) ★★★★, *Barndancing* (Sweet Soil Music 1999) ★★★.

Fan Fan, Mose

b. Mose Se Sengo, 16 October 1945, Kinshasa, Zaire. Master guitarist Mose 'Fan Fan' began to play music when he was sent to boarding school in Kinanga. On his return to Kinshasa he joined Rickem Jazz then Revolution for low-key evening performances as featured guitarist. **Franco** spotted him playing with Revolution and invited him to join OK Jazz, with whom he stayed for several years. Eventually, and in tandem with several fellow OK Jazz musicians including Youlou Mabiala, he left to form Orchestre Somo Somo. The name translates as 'Double Dread' and was lifted from the 1972 hit song 'Djamelasi', which Mose wrote for OK Jazz. However, the band collapsed when Mabiala was injured in a car crash. He eventually returned to Franco, while other former members of Somo Somo joined **Tabu Ley** and Orchestre Verve. Mose elected to leave Zaire and set up new incarnations of Somo Somo in Zambia, Tanzania and Kenya. During his five years in Tanzania he also worked simultaneously with **Orchestre Makassy**, writing songs such as 'Mosese' and 'Meloma' for them. In Kenya he met Robin Scott (the musician behind **M**'s 'Pop Musik'), who encouraged him to come to London and stay with him. Offered a contract by **Stern's Records**, Mose assembled an English-based version of Somo Somo. Two albums were released, the second recorded in Paris, at which time Somo Somo collapsed once more. Back in England, he produced an album with Bana OK, featuring several veterans of OK Jazz, but the project was abandoned when the group was unable to gain a visa to play live. Later, he worked for six months as a civil servant with the Royal Army Medical Corps but was inevitably drawn back to music. He re-emerged in 1995 with a new album, *Hello Hello*, recorded with members of the Quatre Etoiles—Syran Mbenza, Bopol Mansiamina, Wuta Mayi, Nyboma, Miguel Yamba, Komba Mafwala and guest stars **Sam Mangwana** and former colleague Youlou Mabilia. These sessions were again credited to Somo Somo.

● ALBUMS: *Paris* (Stern's 1986) ★★★, *Mose Se Fan Fan, Belle Epoque* (RetroAfric 1994) ★★★★, *Hello Hello* (Stern's 1995) ★★★, *The Congo Acoustic* (Triple Earth 1999) ★★★★.

Fandango (UK)

Comprising Jim Proops (vocals), Pete Parks (vocals/guitar), **Nick Simper** (b. 3 November 1945, Norwood Green, Southall, Middlesex, England; bass), Neil McArthur (keyboards) and Ron Penney (drums), much of the initial coverage surrounding UK heavy metal act Fandango concerned their employment of former **Deep Purple** and **Warhorse** bass player Simper. Otherwise there was little of note about the band's two albums. Both offered competent but uninspired blues rock, despite Parks' best efforts to lead from the front with some fluent guitar work. The band was also hampered by the ascendancy of an American band named Fandango—who held the international rights to the name. With the writing clearly on the wall, they broke up shortly after the release of *Future Times*, recorded by Parks, Proops and Simper.

● ALBUMS: *Slipstreaming* (Shark/Gull 1979) ★★, *Future Times* (Shark 1980) ★★.

Fandango (USA)

American melodic hard rock outfit formed in 1976 by vocalist **Joe Lynn Turner** (b. Joseph Linquito, 2 August 1951, Hackensack, New Jersey, USA) and guitarist Rick Blakemore.

Enlisting the services of Larry Dawson (keyboards), Bob Danyls (bass) and Abe Speller (drums), they signed to **RCA Records** the following year. They produced four albums in four years, with each successive release featuring more accomplished and memorable compositions. Influenced by **Kiss, Deep Purple, Journey** and **Styx**, their style was rigidly formularized and geared to US FM radio playlists. The band disintegrated in 1981, with Turner going on to work with **Rainbow, Yngwie Malmsteen**'s Rising Force and **Deep Purple** as well as pursuing a solo career. Blakemore was killed in a car crash in the early 80s.

● ALBUMS: *Fandango* (RCA 1977) ★★, *One Night Stand* (RCA 1978) ★★★, *Last Kiss* (RCA 1979) ★★★, *Cadillac* (RCA 1980) ★★★★.

Fania All Stars

The house band of Fania Records, comprised of the label's band leaders, top sidemen and vocalists, whose history represents the rise and promulgation of salsa as a marketing tag for Latin music. Italian-American lawyer Jerry Masucci cofounded Fania in 1964 with Dominican Republic-born band leader **Johnny Pacheco** and explained the genesis and early development of the band in 1973: 'In December 1967 . . . I was vacationing in Acapulco. I was out fishing and when I got back I received a phone call from New York from two promoters Jack Hooke and Ralph Mercado of Cheetah fame (a club on the south-west corner of 52nd Street and 8th Avenue, which Mercado co-managed in the 60s, promoting R&B acts like **James Brown** and **Aretha Franklin**). At that time they were holding concerts at the Red Garter (in Greenwich Village) Monday nights and were interested in getting the Fania All Stars together to do a jam session with invited guests **Tito Puente** of Tico Records and **Eddie Palmieri** and **Ricardo Ray And Bobby Cruz** of Alegre Records. It sounded like a good idea to me, so I flew back and got in touch with Johnny Pacheco. We put some material together and packed the place with 800 people. We also made the first two recordings of the Fania All Stars: *Live At The Red Garter* volumes 1 and 2 (1968). Although the albums were not too spectacular regarding sales.' A second Fania All Stars concert, held on 26 August 1971 at the Cheetah, was a complete sell-out. Volumes 1 and 2 of the Fania All Stars *Live At The Cheetah*, which were recorded that night, became the biggest selling Latin albums ever produced by one group from one concert. The Cheetah concert was filmed and featured in the documentary *Our Latin Thing (Nuestra Cosa)* produced by Masucci and directed by Leon Gast, which premiered in New York on 19 July 1972.

After sell-out concerts in Puerto Rico, Chicago and Panama, the Fania All Stars made their first appearance at New York's 63,000-capacity Yankee Stadium on 24 August 1973, with Fania's leading lights **Ray Barretto, Willie Colón, Larry Harlow**, Johnny Pacheco, **Roberto Roena, Bobby Valentín** and others jamming with **Manu Dibango, Mongo Santamaría** and Jorge Santana (younger brother of **Carlos Santana** and guitarist with **Malo**). Material from their August 1973 Yankee Stadium concert and a concert at the Roberto Clemente Coliseum in San Juan, Puerto Rico, made up one side of *Latin-Soul-Rock*. In 1974 the All Stars performances at the 80,000-seat Stadu du Hai in Kinshasa, Zaire, were also filmed by Gast and released as the movie *Live In Africa* (1974, issued on video in the UK under the title *Salsa Madness* in 1991). This Zairean appearance occurred along with **Stevie Wonder** and others at a music festival held in conjunction with the Mohammed Alp/George Foreman heavyweight title fight.

The Fania All Stars return to the Yankee Stadium in 1975 resulted in two volumes of *Live At Yankee Stadium*, which highlighted Fania's and stablemates Vaya Records' top vocalists **Celia Cruz, Héctor Lavoe, Cheo Feliciano, Ismael Miranda, Justo Betancourt, Ismael Quintana, Pete 'El Conde' Rodríguez**, Bobby Cruz and Santos Colón. Clips from their August 1973 and 1975 Yankee Stadium concerts, as well as from the Roberto Clemente Coliseum, were included in Masucci's movie production *Salsa* (1976), codirected by Masucci and Gast. The film was picked up by Columbia Pictures for distribution, which was regarded as a major coup in marketing salsa for the general audience.

Venezuelan salsa authority César Miguel Rondón commented on the marked stylistic contrast between the movie *Our Latin Thing (Nuestra Cosa)* and its successor *Salsa* in his 1980 book *El Libro De La Salsa*: 'The producers' intention was evident: so that the salsa industry could really become a million-dollar business, it had to go beyond an exclusively Latin market; it had to penetrate the North American public majority market, and from here become an authentic fashion for the masses and succeed in coming to affect even the European audiences. In order to succeed in this, Fania's impresarios felt an obligation to radically change salsa's image. The first film, *Our Latin Thing (Nuestra Cosa)*, was totally harmful in this sense; it spoke about the ghetto, about how salsa came up and developed in the haunts of the marginal barrios, in environments of poverty and misery in direct contrast to all the display and gaudiness of the North American enslaving pop culture. It therefore had to make a film that would radically say the contrary: that salsa was, in reality, a fundamental part of that pop culture, that it was susceptible to being enjoyed by the majority publics and that it, absolutely, had nothing to do with minority groups and their always repugnant misery. And this, without further ado, would be the fundamental characteristic under which the so-called salsa boom would be animated; a boom that, in effect, would increase the markets and sales, but equally weaken the true meaning of the *raison d'être* of salsa music.' This extract was translated by the sociologist Vernon W. Boggs for his article 'Salsa's Origins: Voices From Abroad', a survey of various texts on the source of the word salsa, published in *Latin Beat* magazine, December/January 1992. He found that various authors seemed to agree: 'The popularity of the term (salsa), as a generic term for several musical modalities, was consciously universalized and successfully popularized by the Fania All Stars, Jerry Masucci, Leon Gast and the 'Fania Machine'.'

In Masucci's pursuit of a wider market for salsa, he made a contract with **Columbia Records** in the USA for a series of crossover-orientated albums by the Fania All Stars. The first project was a coupling of **Steve Winwood** with the All Stars reduced to a rhythm section (Pacheco, Valentín, Barretto, Roena, Nicky Marrero and **Papo Lucca**) for the instantly forgettable *Delicate & Jumpy* (1976), released on Columbia in the USA and **Island Records** in the UK. Around that time, Island in the UK issued the Fania collection *Salsa!* (1975), compiled and annotated by Richard Williams, and *Live* (1976) by the Fania All Stars. In 1976 the Fania All Stars made their one and only UK appearance with a memorable sellout concert at London's Lyceum Ballroom, with Winwood guesting (his first time on a British stage since May 1974).

Prior to *Delicate & Jumpy*, the last 'regular' Fania All Stars album on Fania for a couple of years was the solid *Tribute To Tito Rodríguez* (1976), introducing **Rubén Blades** to the band. The Columbia series continued in lightweight vein with *Rhythm Machine* (1977), again with the slimmed down Fania All Stars and keyboard player **Bob James** (executive producer) and guitarist **Eric Gale** guesting and *Spanish Fever* (1978), with guests **Maynard Ferguson, Hubert Laws, David Sanborn**, Gale and others. 1978 also saw the release of *Live*, a 'regular' Fania All Stars album on Fania with a fully blown version of the band recorded in concert at New York's Madison Square Garden in September 1978. The last in the Columbia series, *Cross Over*, appeared the following year, as did *Habana Jam* (1979) on Fania, which came from an historic concert recorded on 3 March 1979 in Havana, Cuba. One track by the Fania All Stars was included on the various artists double album *Havana Jam* (1979) on Columbia, containing performance highlights from a trio of concerts at Havana's Karl Marx Theatre (2, 3 and 4 March 1979) with **Billy Joel, Rita Coolidge, Kris Kristofferson, Stephen Stills** and **Weather Report** together with Cuba's **Irakere** and Orquesta Aragón.

From 1980 Fania went into a downturn (attributed to the flop of Masucci's major movie *The Last Fight*, agitation by artists for unpaid royalties, the distribution deals with Columbia and **Atlantic Records** not catapulting salsa into the mainstream US market as expected and Masucci claiming he had tired of 'the same old thing' after 15 years), and the New York salsa scene, to which the label was inextricably linked, became eclipsed by the Dominican merengue craze in the first half of the decade and by the Puerto Rico–driven salsa romántica trend in the latter 80s and early 90s. Reflecting the company's decline, Fania All Stars' releases slowed to a trickle as the 80s drew to a close. Their albums between 1980 and 1989 included the Latin jazz outings *California Jam* (1980) and the particularly feeble *Guasasa* (1989) the crossover effort *Social Change* (1981) with guests **Steel Pulse** and **Gato Barbieri** *Bamboleo* (1988) with four salsa-fied versions of **Gipsy Kings** hits along with the sturdier *Commitment* (1980), *Latin Connection* (1981), *Lo Que Pide La Gente* (1984) and *Viva La Charanga* (1986). To mark the 20th anniversary of the band, *Live In Africa*, recorded in Zaire in 1974, and *Live In Japan 1976* were issued in 1986. Thirty years of Fania Records was commemorated in 1994 by a three-city tour (San Juan, Miami and New York) by the reconvened All Stars. Three years later they released a brand new studio album on the JMM label.

● ALBUMS: *Live At Red Garter, Volumes 1 & 2* (Fania 1968), *Live At Cheetah, Volumes 1 & 2* (Fania 1971) ★★★, *Our Latin Thing (Nuestra Cosa)* film soundtrack (Fania 1972) ★★★, *Latin-Soul-Rock* (Fania 1974) ★★★, *Live At Yankee Stadium, Volumes 1 & 2* (Fania 1975) ★★★, *Salsa* film soundtrack (Fania 1976) ★★, *Tribute To Tito Rodríguez* (Fania 1976) ★★★, *Delicate & Jumpy* (Columbia 1976) ★★★, *Rhythm Machine* aka *Fania All Stars Featuring Jan Hammer* (Columbia 1977) ★★★, *Spanish Fever* (Columbia 1978) ★★★, *Habana Jam* (Columbia 1979) ★★★, *Cross Over* (Columbia 1979) ★★★, *Commitment* (Fania 1980) ★★★, *California Jam* (Fania 1980) ★★★, *Social Change* (Fania 1981) ★★★, *Latin Connection* (Fania 1981) ★★★, *The Last Fight* soundtrack recording (Fania 1982) ★★, *Lo Que Pide La Gente* (Fania 1984) ★★★★, *Viva La Charanga* (Fania 1986) ★★★, *Live In Africa* (Fania

1986) ★★★, *Live In Japan 1976* (Fania 1986) ★★★, *Bamboleo* (Fania 1988) ★★★, *Guasasa* (Fania 1989) ★★, *Live In Puerto Rico, June 1994* (Fania 1995) ★★★, *Viva Colombia—En Concierto* (Fania 1996) ★★★, *Bravo '97* (JMM/Sony Discos 1997) ★★★.

● COMPILATIONS: *Greatest Hits* (Fania 1977) ★★★★, *The Best Of The Fania All Stars* (Fania 1997) ★★★★, *Salsa Caliente De Nu York!* (Nascente 2001) ★★★★, *Qué Pasa? The Best Of Fania All-Stars* (Columbia/Legacy 2002) ★★★★, *The Best Of Fania All Stars* (Charly 2004) ★★.

Fankhauser, Merrell

b. 23 December 1943, Louisville, Kentucky, USA. Fankhauser moved to California's Pismo Beach at the age of 16 and became immersed in the local surfing scene. Having played with the **Sentinals** and Impacts, Frankhauser then founded the Exiles, a pop-based act based in Lancaster, home of **Captain Beefheart** and **Frank Zappa**. In 1966 Fankhauser embraced psychedelia with a new act, Fapardokly, which later evolved into **HMS Bounty**. It was during this period that the artist recorded a solo version of 'Everybody's Talking', but his rendition lost out to that of Harry **Nilsson**'s. Fankhauser then founded **Mu**, a fascinating act that spent much of its career based on Hawaii, before recording *Merrell Fankhauser* on their demise. This melodic, acoustic selection captured his craft to perfection and became the first of several excellent solo releases. *Calling From A Star* featured guitarist John Cipollina, who also contributed to several later albums. During the 80s Fankhauser expanded his repertoire to include rock 'n' roll and pop, enjoyed a spell as host of a popular television show and undertook several live appearances. He also supervised judicious repackaging of previously released and archive material as well as continuing to record prolifically. Merrell Fankhauser remains one of the most fascinating figures to emerge out of California's 60s' milieu.

● ALBUMS: *Merrell Fankhauser* aka *The Maui Album* (1976) ★★★★, *Calling From A Star* (1983) ★★★, *A Day In Paradise* (Source 2 1985) ★★★, *Doctor Fankhauser* (1986) ★★★★, *Message To The Universe* (1986) ★★★, *Back This Way Again* (1989) ★★★, *Flying To Machu Picchu* (1991) ★★★, *Jungle Lo Lo Band* (Legend Music 1994) ★★★.

Fankhauser, Merrell, And HMS Bounty

Formed in Los Angeles, California, USA, in 1968, HMS Bounty featured **Merrell Fankhauser** (guitar/vocals) alongside Bill Dodd (lead guitar), Jack Jordan (bass) and Larry Meyers (drums). Dodd had previously worked with Fankhauser on several tracks released under the name Fapardokly. *Things* is a sumptuous example of west coast harmony rock, showing parallels with **Spirit**, **Moby Grape** and the **Bobby Fuller Four**. Fankhauser's gift for memorable hooklines is clear, his tenor voice is haunting and the occasional use of sitar and tablas adds depth to a set rich in melody and invention. Although the quartet supported **Canned Heat** and the **Paul Butterfield Band**, they were unable to find consistent live work. Meyers left the line-up in 1969, and after one more gig, Fankhauser folded the band. He then formed **Mu** with ex–**Captain Beefheart** guitarist Jeff Cotton aka Antenae Jimmy Semmems.

● ALBUMS: *Things* (Shamley 1967) ★★★.

Fanny (rock)

Warner Brothers Records claimed in 1970 that their recent signing Fanny were the 'first all-female rock group'. They sustained a career for four years on that basis, throwing off all rivals to the throne, including **Birtha**, whose tasteless publicity handout stated 'Birtha has balls'. Formerly Wild Honey, the name Fanny was suggested by **George Harrison** to their producer **Richard Perry**. It was only later in their career that the group realized how risqué their name was internationally. Comprising Jean Millington (b. 1950, Manila, California, USA; bass/vocals), **June Millington** (b. 1949, Manila, California, USA; guitar/vocals), Alice DeBuhr (b. 1950, Mason City, Iowa, USA; drums) and Nickey Barclay (b. 1951, Washington, DC, USA; keyboards), their blend of driving hard rock and rock 'n' roll was exciting, although they were always a second division act. They were more popular in the UK where they toured regularly, recording albums at Apple and Olympic studios. June Millington and DeBuhr were replaced in 1974 by Patti Quatro (sister of **Suzi Quatro**) from the Pleasure Seekers and Brie Brandt-Howard. None of their albums charted in the UK, and their sales in the USA were minimal. Their second album, *Charity Ball*, was their best work, giving them a US Top 40 hit with the title song. **Todd Rundgren** was brought in to produce *Mother's Pride*, but ironically it was as the band was fragmenting in 1975 that they scored their biggest hit 'Butter Boy' (US number 29). June and Jean Millington reunited to form Millington, who released their only album in 1978.

● ALBUMS: *Fanny* (Reprise 1970) ★★★, *Charity Ball* (Reprise 1971) ★★★, *Fanny Hill* (Reprise 1972) ★★★, *Mother's Pride* (Reprise 1973) ★★, *Rock 'N' Roll Survivors* (Casablanca 1974) ★★.

● COMPILATIONS: *First Time In A Long Time: The Reprise Recordings* 4-CD box set (Rhino 2002) ★★★.

Fanny (stage musical)

Based on the Frenchman Marcel Pagnol's film trilogy, *Marius, Fanny,* and *César,* made in the early 30s, this show marked the musical theatre debut of one of Broadway's most important post-war producers, **David Merrick**. *Fanny* opened in New York at the Majestic Theatre on 4 November 1954 and stayed around for over two years. **Joshua Logan**, the show's director, co-wrote the book with the celebrated author and playwright S.N. Behrman. Some critics felt that the librettists attempted too much—that it was not possible to do full justice to the complicated situations and personal relationships dealt with in the three books in the space of one musical evening. Audiences were faced with the dramatic story of the young Marius (**William Tabbert**), who goes to sea against the wishes of his father, César (**Ezio Pinza**), leaving Fanny (**Florence Henderson**) to have his child. She marries the affluent sailmaker Panisse (**Walter Slezak**), who brings up the boy, Césario, as his own. When Marius returns some years later, Césario wants to get to know his real father, but César insists that he stays with Panisse, and so Marius turns him away. Césario goes back to Panisse, who knowing that he is dying, pleads with Fanny to make a life together with Marius and the boy who means so much to them all.

Harold Rome's music and lyrics, usually so full of social conscience and comment, echoes the intense emotional and sentimental feelings present in the story with songs such as 'Restless Heart', 'Why Be Afraid To Dance?', 'Never Too Late

For Love', 'To My Wife', 'I Like You', 'Love Is A Very Light Thing', 'Welcome Home', 'I Have To Tell You' and 'Be Kind To Your Parents'. The show's title song had some success in a recording by **Eddie Fisher**. Slezak won the **Tony Award** for Best Actor, and *Fanny* ran for 888 performances on Broadway and for more than 300 in London. In 1986 a revival was presented at the Goodspeed Opera House in Connecticut, USA. The 1960 film version—without the songs—was directed by Joshua Logan and starred **Leslie Caron**, **Maurice Chevalier** and Charles Boyer.

Fannypack

This Brooklyn, New York, USA-based group are like a more lurid **Spice Girls**, with a fondness for rap rather than pop. Comprising female singers Jessibel Suthiwong (b. 1985, Brooklyn, New York, USA), Belinda Lovell, (b. 1987, Brooklyn, New York, USA) and Cat Martell (b. 1983, USA), two of its three members were still attending high school at the time of the group's formation in the early twenty-first century. Fannypack (named after an accessory that is worn around the waist *à la* a pocketbook) caught the attention of producer 'Big Black' Matt Goias (b. 1978) while the group was performing at a carnival in Brooklyn's Fulton Street Mall, with the only beats being provided by a man snapping belts (who also happened to be selling the item at the time). Soon second producer 'Fancy' came aboard, and Fannypack signed a recording contract with **Tommy Boy Records**. The trio scored a huge US novelty hit in summer 2003 with the catchy and lewd single 'Cameltoe' and followed it up with their debut, *So Stylistic*. Much of the same content was present on *See You Next Tuesday*, which included the irresistible 'Nu Nu (Yeah Yeah)'.
● ALBUMS: *So Stylistic* (Tommy Boy 2003) ★★★, *See You Next Tuesday* (Tommy Boy 2005) ★★★★.

Fantacy Hill

Formed in the USA in the late 70s, elaborate pomp rock band Fantacy Hill comprised Gerson Migilacio (vocals), Danny Mullins (guitar), George Durbin (guitars), Jose Conrado (bass) and Doug Golema (drums). Despite an inadequate production budget, the group's 1978 debut album, *First Step*, was a well-crafted blend of AOR ballads and more punchy, upbeat numbers. The single 'Unemployment Blues' was unable to attract much commercial attention. Sadly neither style allowed the group to genuinely assert their identity, and it proved to be the group's sole release.
● ALBUMS: *First Step* (Prodigal 1978) ★★★.

Fantasia (00s)

b. Fantasia Barrino, 30 June 1984, High Point, North Carolina, USA. Vocalist Fantasia owes her moment in the spotlight to her triumph in the third season of the highly rated Fox TV show *American Idol*. A real rags-to-riches story, Barrino auditioned for the show while she was unemployed and living with her 12-month-old daughter in a 1-bedroom apartment in High Point, North Carolina. Barrino's powerful gospel-tinged vocal performances and larger-than-life personality helped endear her to the viewing public, and she emerged from over 70,000 contestants to claim the *American Idol* title, beating runner-up Diana DeGarmo by over a million votes at the show's climax in May 2004. Now known simply as Fantasia, the singer followed former *American Idol* champion **Ruben Studdard** by signing a recording contract with veteran music mogul **Clive Davis**' J Records label. The singer's debut, 'I Believe', was a cover version of a track written by Tamyra Gray, a contestant from season one of the series. The song debuted at the top of the US Hot 100 in July 2004. Fantasia's debut album, *Free Yourself*, reached the US Top 10 later in the year.
● ALBUMS: *Free Yourself* (J 2004) ★★★.

Fantasia (film musical)

(see **Disney, Walt**)

Fantastic Baggys

The Fantastic Baggys was a recording outlet for songwriting team **P.F. Sloan** (herein known as 'Flip') and **Steve Barri**. The duo supplied surfing act **Jan And Dean** with several compositions, notably 'Summer Means Fun' and 'From All Over The World', and added backing harmonies on several sessions, factors which in turn inspired this concurrent career. Bob Myman (drums) and Jerry Cargman completed the nominal Baggys line-up, but the venture was, in essence, studio-based. The Sloan/Barri team wrote, arranged and produced every track on *Tell 'Em I'm Surfin'*, but the duo quickly tired of their creation and ceased using the name following the release of the **Gary Paxton**-penned 'It Was I' (1965). However, the Fantastic Baggys had proved highly popular in South Africa, and a second album, *Ride The Wild Surf*, was compiled the following year. Although five tracks, drawn from singles and outtakes, did feature Sloan and Barri, more than half the set featured anonymous musicians imitating the original group. By the release of *Surfer's Paradise*, the ruse had run its course. Here any connection was even more tenuous and the sole Sloan/Barri performance, 'Only When You're Lonely', was mistakenly drawn from another studio project, the **Grass Roots**. When the album proved commercially moribund, the Baggy's appellation was mercifully abandoned.
● ALBUMS: *Tell 'Em I'm Surfin'* (Imperial 1964) ★★★, *Ride The Wild Surf* (1964) ★★, *Surfer's Paradise* (1967) ★.
● COMPILATIONS: *Surfin' Craze* (1983) ★★★, *Anywhere The Girls Are! The Best Of Fantastic Baggys* (Sundazed 2000) ★★★.

Fantastic Four

Formed in Detroit in 1965 by 'Sweet' James Epps (b. 30 March 1947, d. 11 September 2000), Wallace Childs and Ralph and Joseph Pruitt. This excellent quartet's early releases were influenced by the hoarse, urgent style of the **Four Tops**. After three of the group's singles, 'The Whole World Is A Stage', 'You Gave Me Something' (both 1967) and 'I Love You Madly' (1968), reached the US R&B Top 20 on the Ric Tic label, the Fantastic Four were acquired by **Motown Records**, but the label was less successful in promoting them. The group, whose later members included Cleveland Horne (d. 13 April 2000) and Ernest Newsome, later moved to the Eastbound/Westbound complex, where their releases, including 'Alvin Stone (The Birth And Death Of A Gangster)' (1975) and 'I Got To Have Your Love' (1977), enjoyed intermittent success.
● ALBUMS: *Alvin Stone (The Life And Death Of A Gangster)* (Westbound 1975) ★★★, *Night People* (Westbound 1976) ★★★, *Got To Have Your Love* (Westbound 1977) ★★★, *BYOF (Bring Your Own Funk)* (Westbound 1978) ★★.

● COMPILATIONS: *Best Of The Fantastic Four* (1969) ★★★.

Fantastic Johnny C, The

b. Johnny Corley, 28 April 1943, Greenwood, South Carolina, USA. The Fantastic Johnny C hit number 7 in the US pop charts in October 1967 with the infectious soul mover 'Boogaloo Down Broadway'. His 'Wilson Pickett–like' vocal delivery, powered by a heavy percussion and a horn section similar to the Stax/Atlantic sound, took three months to make the US Top 10. It was written and produced by songwriter **Jesse James**, as was the flip-side, 'Look What Love Can Make You Do', which used the same backing track but with different lyrics. The chart performance of the follow-up, 'Got What You Need', proved disappointing, stalling at number 56 in February 1968. He recorded a sequel to **Cliff Nobles (And Co.)**'s US hit 'The Horse', titled 'Hitch It To The Horse', both written by James, which became his final US Top 40 hit in June 1968 when it peaked at number 34.
● ALBUMS: *Boogaloo Down Broadway* (Phil-L.A. 1967) ★★★.

Fantasticks, The

The longest running musical in the world opened off-Broadway at the 153-seater Sullivan Street Playhouse on 3 May 1960. Based on the 1894 play *Les Romanesques* by Edmund Rostand, the show is all about the illusions and dreams of young love. The simple story tells of Matt Hucklebee, The Boy (Kenneth Nelson) and Luisa Bellamy, The Girl (Rita Gardner), whose fathers, Hucklebee (William Larsen) and Amos Babcock Bellamy (Hugh Thomas) try to ensure that the couple fall in love by building a wall between their two properties and pretending to disapprove of the romance. Just to emphasise their point, they also hire the bandit El Gallo (**Jerry Orbach**, who also acts as the narrator) to seemingly attempt an unsuccessful rape of The Girl. The young couple discover the deception and, disillusioned with the ways of the world, go their separate ways, only to return eventually—much wiser—to each other's arms. Settings and costumes were by Ed Wittstein, and Word Baker was the director. Also in the cast was **Tom Jones**, who wrote the book and lyrics, with **Harvey Schmidt** composing a score which contained the gorgeous ballads 'Soon It's Gonna Rain' and 'Try To Remember' along with other numbers such as 'It Depends On What You Pay', 'I Can See It', 'Plant A Radish', 'Much More', 'They Were You' and 'Round And Round'.

The Fantasticks has played more than 5,000 American cities, and over 70 other countries around the world (put another way: 11,000 US and 700 foreign productions). A 1961 West End production with Terence Cooper (El Gallo), Peter Gilmore (Matt), Stephanie Voss (Luisa) and Michael Barrington and Timothy Bateson as the fathers fared badly, some critics considering that the engaging intimacy of the original was lost in a regular-sized Apollo Theatre. The Regent's Park Open Air Theatre and various fringe venues, such as the King's Head, Islington, proved more suitable settings when the show was presented in London again during the 90s. In 1992 Jones and Schmidt both participated in an English-speaking Japanese production, and three years later *The Fantasticks* was filmed, with Joseph McIntyre (Matt), Jean Louisa Kelly (Luisa), Jonathon Morris (El Gallo), Brad Sullivan (Matt's father) and **Joel Grey** (Luisa's father). What was, technically, still the original New York production clocked up 17,162 performances before closing on 13 January 2002.
● FURTHER READING: *The Fantasticks: The 30th Anniversary Edition*, Tom Jones and Harvey Schmidt. *The Amazing Story Of The Fantasticks: America's Longest Running Play*, Robert Viagas and Donald C. Farber.

Fantasy Records

Formed by brothers Max and Sol Weiss in 1949, Fantasy Records was actually designed to lose money! Instead, it became an important and influential jazz label, later taking on R&B, rock and other forms of music. The brothers, who owned a successful record-pressing plant, took over a failing record label called Coronet, intending to use the expected losses as a tax write-off. However, their first artist, jazz pianist **Dave Brubeck**, was a sales success, as were other jazz signings, **Chet Baker** and **Gerry Mulligan**. Fantasy was soon considered a leader in the emerging west coast jazz sound. Jazz vibraphonist **Cal Tjader** and poets **Allen Ginsberg**, Lawrence Ferlinghetti and Kenneth Rexroth were other early signings.

By the late 50s and early 60s Fantasy branched off into folk music and spoken word, recording comedian Lenny Bruce. As an example of the Weiss brothers' unorthodox methods, they briefly launched a line called RCA-Irving, half-seriously attempting to confuse record buyers searching for **RCA-Victor** recordings. In February 1955 Saul Zaentz joined Fantasy as a salesperson, leasing recordings from his own Debut label to Fantasy. In 1967 Zaentz bought the company from the Weiss siblings. That same year Fantasy signed a local rock group called the **Golliwogs**, who changed their name to **Creedence Clearwater Revival** became one of the most successful American rock bands during the next five years. Fantasy is based in Berkeley, California, USA, and owns and distributes such labels as **Stax Records**, Contemporary, Landmark, Pablo, Contemporary, Milestone, Riverside and Good Time Jazz.

Fantômas

Ex-**Faith No More** singer Mike Patton (b. 27 January 1968, Eureka, California, USA), a much revered figure in metal since the rise of his former band in the late 80s, embarked immediately on a series of projects on the collapse of that band in 1998. One of these was Fantômas (named after a French literary antihero), a very eccentric band based on his own lyrical ideas, with the unorthodox contributions of **Melvins** guitarist Buzz Osbourne (b. 4 July 1960, Kalamazoo, Michigan, USA) and Trevor Dunn (b. 1 April 1974, Kalamazoo, Michigan, USA; bass) and the enormous power of drummer Dave Lombardo (b. 16 February 1963, Havana, Cuba; ex-**Slayer**). Fantômas' recordings have appeared via Patton's own Ipecac label.

After a demo was recorded in 1998 to test the cohesion of the new band, a self-titled album was recorded the following year and attracted plenty of positive press from reviewers for whom the tidal wave of nu metal was no adequate substitute for Faith No More. The live set *Millennium Monsterwork* was credited to the Fantômas Melvins Big Band and was recorded on New Year's Eve 2000 in San Francisco, although the album did not gain a release until two years later. In the interim, the studio recording *The Director's Cut* enthralled and bemused listeners in equal measure before the ever-restless Patton put Fantômas on hold in order to work on a new act, **Tomahawk**. He resumed working relationships with

Osborne, Dunn and Lombardo on the ambitious concept album *Delìrum Còrdia*, released under the Fantômas name in early 2004. The follow-up *Suspended Animation* harked back to the sound of Fantômas' debut album, punctuated by a constant stream of cartoon samples. The original release of the album featured packaging in the form of a calendar for April 2005.

● ALBUMS: *Fantômas* (Ipecac 1999) ★★★, *The Director's Cut* (Ipecac 2001) ★★★★, as Fantômas Melvins Big Band *Millennium Monsterwork* (Ipecac 2002) ★★★, *Delìrum Còrdia* (Ipecac 2004) ★★★, *Suspended Animation* (Ipecac 2005) ★★★.

Farafina

Formed in 1973 in the city of Bobo-Dioulasso, Burkina Faso, by balafon (wooden xylophone) virtuoso Mahama Konaté. Originally a 4-piece, the group has since grown to a multi-generational 15-strong troupe of percussionists, singers and dancers. Farafina are strongly rooted in West African tradition and yet unafraid to experiment and collaborate with those from other cultures. They first became known outside of Burkina Faso via a 1982 European tour. They subsequently made regular visits to both Europe and Japan and in 1988 were the opening act for the Nelson Mandela Birthday Concert at Wembley Stadium in London, which was broadcast worldwide. The group also collaborated with American *avant garde* trumpeter **Jon Hassell** on the same year's *Flash Of The Spirit*. Coproduced by **Brian Eno** and **Daniel Lanois**, the album featured the group's trademark deep percussive sound overlaid with electronica and effects. The following year's *Bolomakoté* featured the Farafina sound unadorned. In the same year the group was featured on the **Rolling Stones**' *Steel Wheels*. Konaté left the group in 1991. Their next album, 1993's *Faso Denou*, was coproduced by jazz drummer **Billy Cobham** and featured a more relaxed and diverse sound than the full powered attack of *Bolomakoté* while at the same time retaining the group's essential hypnotic and trance-like quality. Appearing after a five-year break from recording, *Nemako* was more polished and produced than previous albums, with electric keyboards and bass and less emphasis on raw percussion.

● ALBUMS: with Jon Hassell *Flash Of The Spirit* (Intuition 1988) ★★★, *Bolomakoté* (Intuition 1989) ★★★, *Faso Denou* (Real World 1993) ★★★, *Nemako* (Intuition 1998) ★★.

Faraway Places

Exotic alt pop would be a fitting description of the music that the US boy/girl duo Faraway Places specializes in. Comprised of members who opt to only use their first names—Chris and Donna—the band (who are joined on stage and in the studio by additional members) formed in Boston, Massachusetts, USA, at a screening of a video by cult jazz artist **Sun Ra**. Listing everyone from **T. Rex** and **Stereolab** to **Fela Kuti** and **Can** as influences, the band originally went by the name the Solar Saturday. It was as Solar Saturday that the duo played their first shows (including performances alongside good friends **Papas Fritas**). Soon after, the trio began recording tracks with Papas Fritas members Keith Gendel and Tony Goddess lending a helpful hand, recording both in a studio as well as in Chris' bedroom. A self-titled four-track EP of the proceedings surfaced with Donna adding a personal touch to the release—supplying an original painting for the cover.

Soon after however, Solar Saturday was renamed Faraway Places. The group then set out to record their debut album in a secluded cabin (in the woods of New Hampshire), with producer Brian Hanna. Before releasing the album, Faraway Places opted for a change of scenery and relocated to Los Angeles, California. Signing with the UK's Bella Union, label, Faraway Places issued the nine-track *Unfocus On It* in August.

● ALBUMS: *Unfocus On It* (Bella Union 2003) ★★★.

Fardon, Don

b. Donald Maughn, 19 August 1943, Coventry, West Midlands, England. As the vocalist with the **Sorrows**, Maughn was featured on this cult act's most durable release, the pulsating 'Take A Heart'. A number 21 hit in September 1965, its hypnotic, throbbing beat was maintained on subsequent releases, several of which the singer cocomposed. Here, however, he preferred to use an alternative surname, Fardon, which was then retained for the artist's solo career. His cover version of **John D. Loudermilk**'s '(The Lament Of The Cherokee) Indian Reservation' gave him his first and only US hit single in 1968, reaching the Top 20. He broke into the UK Top 40 in 1970 with 'Belfast Boy', a homage to the talented but troubled Northern Irish footballer George Best. This success paved the way for the reissue of 'Indian Reservation' which, when resurrected, climbed to a respectable number 3 and became one of that year's most distinctive chart entries. Yet despite several further releases in the early 70s, some of which were remakes of former Sorrows material, Fardon was unable to secure consistent success. He went into the licensing trade, running pubs in Coventry and Eathorpe, while continuing to work on the cabaret and country circuits. He later helped run a security firm looking after pop stars. Fardon rereleased 'Belfast Boy' in December 2005 in honour of the recently deceased Best.

● ALBUMS: *Lament Of The Cherokee Indian Reservation* (GNP 1968) ★★, *I've Paid My Dues!* (Young Blood/Decca 1970) ★★, *Released* (Young Blood 1970) ★★, *The Next Chapter: All The Hits Plus More* (Prestige 1997) ★★.

● COMPILATIONS: *Indian Reservation: The Best Of* (C5 1994) ★★★, *I'm Alive* (RPM 2003) ★★★.

Farewell Performance

A young pop singer, played by David Kernan, who has made many enemies during his rise to fame, is murdered. A decoy is groomed for stardom, during which the culprit is apprehended. Iconoclast producer/composer **Joe Meek** provided all the music for this lightweight vehicle, which featured his blond-haired protégé **Heinz** as the Kernan character's replacement. His former group in real life, the **Tornados**, are also cast in this 1963 'B' feature. *Farewell Performance* has little merit, and Meek's wish to launch Heinz as a major attraction faltered at the first hurdle. A second film, *Living It Up*, was equally moribund, and the pair quickly sundered their relationship.

Fargo

This German heavy metal/hard rock band was formed by bass player Peter Khorn in Hanover in 1973. They earned their initial reputation by supporting bands such as **AC/DC** and **April Wine** on their German tours of the late 70s. By 1976 Khron had established a more solid line-up, with the inclusion of Peter Ladwig (guitar/vocals), Matthias Jabs (b.

25 October 1956, Hannover, Germany; guitar) and Franky Tolle (drums). Prior to the release of their debut album, however, Jabs accepted an invitation to join the **Scorpions** and was replaced by Hanno Grossman in 1978. The band's long-forestalled debut, *Wishing Well*, augured well for their future in its effective distillation of melodic rock laced with pop hooks. During touring to promote it, Tolle became exhausted and was replaced on drums by Rudi Kaeding. The band toured throughout Europe in support of *Front Page Lover* in 1981, but inter-band tensions remained. Tolle returned for 1982's *F*, while Tommy Newton replaced Grossman. The uncertainty of that recording suggested the band's demise was imminent, and rumours of further friction proved well founded when no further follow-ups were issued.

● ALBUMS: *Wishing Well* (Harvest 1979) ★★★, *No Limit* (Harvest 1980) ★★, *Front Page Lover* (Harvest 1981) ★★★, *F* (Harvest 1982) ★★.

Fargo, Donna

b. Yvonne Vaughn, 10 November 1949, Mount Airy, North Carolina, USA. Fargo is the daughter of a tobacco farmer, and she sang in church as a child. She became a school-teacher and was discovered by her future husband, record producer Stan Silver, singing in a club in Los Angeles. She first recorded in 1969, but her success started once she had signed with **Dot Records** in 1971. She won gold records for her compositions 'The Happiest Girl In The Whole U.S.A.' (number 11 US pop charts, number 1 country) and 'Funny Face' (number 5 pop, number 1 country), which was Silver's nickname for her (she called him 'fuzzy face' because of his beard). In 1973 she had country hits with more of her own songs—'Superman', 'You Were Always There', a tribute to her late mother (both number 1), and 'Little Girl Gone' (number 2). In 1974 she topped the country charts again, this time with Marty Cooper's gospel song 'You Can't Be A Beacon (If Your Light Don't Shine)'. The packaging of the US versions of her early albums included guitar chords as well as lyrics. She moved to **WEA Records** and went to number 1 on the country charts with a narration, 'That Was Yesterday'. For some years she was in poor health, but multiple sclerosis was not diagnosed until 1979. She has continued her career to the best of her ability, and her strong beliefs led to a gospel album, *Brotherly Love*. Her duet with **Billy Joe Royal**, 'Members Only', was a US country hit in 1987, and she topped the US country singles chart for independent labels with a revival of the **Shirelles**' 'Soldier Boy', which was aimed at US forces involved in the Gulf War. Fargo and her husband Silver were declared bankrupt in 1991.

● ALBUMS: *The Happiest Girl In The Whole U.S.A.* (US) *The Country Sounds Of Donna Fargo* (UK) (Dot 1972) ★★★★, *My Second Album* (Dot 1973) ★★★, *All About A Feeling* (Dot 1973) ★★★, *Miss Donna Fargo* (ABC/Dot 1974) ★★★★, *Whatever I Say Means I Love You* (ABC/Dot 1975) ★★★, *On The Move* (Warners 1976) ★★★, *Fargo Country* (Warners 1977) ★★★, *Shame On Me* (Warners 1977) ★★★, *Dark-Eyed Lady* (Warners 1978) ★★★, *Just For You* (Warners 1979) ★★★, *Fargo* (Warners 1980) ★★★, *Brotherly Love* (Warners 1981) ★★★.

● COMPILATIONS: *The Best Of Donna Fargo* (ABC/Dot 1977) ★★★★, *Winners* (Mercury 1986) ★★★, *Best Of Donna Fargo* (Varèse Vintage 1995) ★★★★, *The Best Of*

Donna Fargo: The Millennium Collection (MCA 2002) ★★★★.

Farian, Frank

b. Franz Reuther, 18 July 1941, Kirn, Germany. Farian created two of the world's bestselling pop groups, **Boney M** and **Milli Vanilli**. His father was killed in World War II, and Farian grew up in the 50s listening to US and UK pop music. His first group was named after the **Shadows**, but by the mid-60s he was a convert to soul music, leading a band devoted to performing cover versions of US hits. In the early 70s he switched to ballad singing for the Hansa-Ariola label. Among his successes were 'Dana My Love' (1972) and 'Rocky' which was number 1 in Germany in 1976. The same year Farian joined the disco boom by writing and producing with session singers 'Baby Do Ya Wanna Bump?'. The track's success in the Netherlands led Farian to form a recording and touring group that went on to notch up over a dozen European and UK hits during the next five years. During the late 70s he also produced a version of **Ann Peebles**' 'I Can't Stand The Rain' and other hits by the disco group Eruption. Farian's lack of US success with Boney M was rectified by his next bestselling act. In his studio near Munich during 1987, he produced tracks under the name Milli Vanilli, recruiting Rob Pilatus and Fabrice Morvan to front the group on live gigs. The group had number 1 hits in America with its first three singles in 1989 and had two bestselling albums. But Milli Vanilli's career ended suddenly when Farian admitted that Pilatus and Morvan had not sung on the band's records. He relaunched the group in 1991 as the Real Milli Vanilli, using Brad Howell, Johnny Davis and Charles Shaw, the singers from the original studio sessions.

Farina, Mark

b. Chicago, Illinois, USA. One of the leading DJs on the San Francisco, California, USA, **house** scene, Farina originally fell in love with **dance music** in the mid-80s. By 1988 Farina was searching the record bins to build his collection, and it was at the renowned Chicago DJ record shop, Imports Etc., that he bumped into another up-and-coming DJ, **Derrick Carter**. Soon after, a friendship blossomed. What began as a mere hobby for Farina soon turned far serious, however (as he was able to focus solely on building his record collection, by living rent-free with his parents). Farina later shared an apartment with Carter, as the duo began working together on tracks (often alongside another DJ, Chris Nazuka) and began to soak in the two leading US **techno** scenes, their home-town of Chicago, as well as Detroit, Michigan.

Farina and Carter made their recording debut under the moniker Symbols And Instruments in 1989. A recording that is often heralded as one of the first 'ambient' releases, *Mood* proved to be a sizeable hit in both the USA and the UK (selling close to 40,000 copies worldwide and landing in the year's Top 50 for the *Face* magazine). Farina began touring the world as well as focusing on other dance styles, eventually creating a style that would one day become his trademark, 'mushroom jazz'. The name would also be used for a cassette series that Farina would launch in 1992, by which time the DJ was making quite a name for himself on the west coast, resulting in his relocation to San Francisco, California. Along with partner/manager Patty Ryan-Smith, Farina created his own San Francisco Monday night dance club, also called Mushroom Jazz. Opened for a successful three-year stretch, Farina eventually shifted his focus towards making albums, including an interactive CD-ROM for OM Records titled *Mushroom Jazz*. Further volumes of the *Mushroom Jazz* series followed as well as other mix releases.

Farina continues to tour the world regularly (supposedly 200 shows a year) while still racking up the accolades, such as being voted one of the Top 20 DJs in the world by *Muzik* and *BPM* magazines.

● COMPILATIONS: *Seasons One* (Domestic 1996) ★★★★, *Mushroom Jazz* (OM 1996) ★★★, *United DJs Of America, Volume 9* (DMC 1998) ★★★★, *Mushroom Jazz2* (OM 1998) ★★★, *San Francisco Sessions* (OM 1999) ★★★, *Mushroom Jazz3* (OM 2001) ★★★, *Connect* (OM 2002) ★★★★, *Air Farina* (OM 2003) ★★★.

Fariña, Mimi

b. Mimi Margharita Baez, 30 April 1945, Palo Alto, California, USA, d. 18 July 2001, Mt. Tamalpais, California, USA. The younger sister of folk singer **Joan Baez**, Mimi was pursuing a solo career when she met and married **Richard Fariña**. The couple began performing together in 1964 and completed two exceptional albums, *Celebrations For A Grey Day* and *Reflections In A Crystal Wind*, before Richard was killed in a motorcycle accident on 30 April 1966. Two years later Mimi helped to compile the commemorative *Memories* as well as *Long Time Coming And A Long Time Gone*, a collection of her husband's lyrics, poetry and short stories. Unsure of direction, she later joined the Committee, a satirical theatre group, where she worked as an improvisational actor before returning to singing. Having forged a short-lived partnership with Tom Jans, which resulted in one low-key album, she resumed her solo career. The consuming passion of Fariña's later years was Bread And Roses, an organization which brought live music into convalescent homes, psychiatric wards and drug rehabilitation centres.

● ALBUMS: with Richard Fariña *Celebrations For A Grey Day* (Vanguard 1965) ★★★, with Richard Fariña *Reflections In A Crystal Wind* (Vanguard 1966) ★★★, with Tom Jans *Take Heart* (A&M 1971) ★★★, *Solo* (Philo 1985) ★★★.

● COMPILATIONS: with Richard Fariña *Memories* (Vanguard 1968) ★★, with Richard Fariña *The Best Of Mimi And Richard Fariña* (Vanguard 1970) ★★★, with Richard Fariña *Pack Up Your Sorrows: Best Of The Vanguard Years* (Vanguard 2000) ★★★, with Richard Fariña *The Complete Vanguard Recordings* (Vanguard 2002) ★★★.

● FURTHER READING: *Positively 4th Street: The Lives And Times Of Joan Baez, Bob Dylan, Mimi Baez Fariña And Richard Fariña*, David Hadju.

● FILMS: *Festival* (1967), *Fools* (1970), *Celebration At Big Sur* (1971), *Sing Sing Thanksgiving* (1974), *Massive Retaliation* (1984).

Fariña, Richard

b. 1937, Brooklyn, New York City, USA, d. 30 April 1966, Carmel, California, USA. A songwriter, novelist and political activist, Fariña was drawn into folk music following his marriage to singer **Carolyn Hester**. Their ill-starred relationship ended in 1961 when, following a European tour, Richard decided to remain 'in exile' to work on his first novel *Been Down So Long It Looks Like Up To Me*. It was during this time that Fariña's first recordings were made. *Dick Fariña & Eric Von Schmidt*, the product of a two-day session in the cellar of London's Dobell's Jazz Shop, also featured an impromptu appearance by **Bob Dylan**, masquerading under his celebrated pseudonym Blind Boy Grunt. Fariña returned to America in 1963 where he married Mimi Baez, the sister of folk singer **Joan Baez**. The couple began performing together and were latterly signed to **Vanguard Records**. Their two superb albums were released in the mid-60s, the first of which, *Celebrations For A Grey Day*, included Richard's classic song 'Pack Up Your Sorrows'. His novel was published in 1966, but its author was killed in a motorbike crash during a celebratory party. Fariña's death robbed a generation of an excellent writer and gifted musician.

● ALBUMS: *Dick Fariña & Eric Von Schmidt* (1964) ★★★, with Mimi Fariña *Celebrations For A Grey Day* (Vanguard 1966) ★★★, with Mimi Fariña *Reflections In A Crystal Wind* (Vanguard 1965) ★★★.

● COMPILATIONS: *Memories* (Vanguard 1968) ★★, with Mimi Fariña *The Best Of Mimi And Richard Fariña* (Vanguard 1970) ★★★, with Mimi Fariña *Pack Up Your Sorrows: Best Of The Vanguard Years* (Vanguard 2000) ★★★, with Mimi Fariña *The Complete Vanguard Recordings* (Vanguard 2002) ★★★.

● FURTHER READING: *Been Down So Long It Looks Like Up To Me*, Richard Fariña. *Positively 4th Street: The Lives And Times Of Joan Baez, Bob Dylan, Mimi Baez Fariña And Richard Fariña*, David Hajdu.

Farinas

Formed at Leicester Art College, Leicestershire, England, in 1962, the Farinas originally comprised Jim King (saxophone), Harry Overnall (drums), Charlie Whitney (guitar/vocals) and Tim Kirchin (bass). Their primary influence was the **Chess Records** catalogue of the 50s and blues rock 'n' rollers such as **Chuck Berry** in particular. The band recorded its solitary single, 'You'd Better Stop', backed by a cover version of **Chris Kenner**'s 'I Like It Like That', for **Fontana Records** in 1964. A year later **Ric Grech** replaced Kirchin, while **Roger Chapman** came in to take over lead vocals in 1966. Shortly thereafter they abandoned the name Farinas and became first the Roaring Sixties then **Family** at the suggestion of **Kim Fowley**.

Farjeon, Herbert

b. 5 March 1887, England, d. 3 May 1945. Farjeon was born into a noted literary family. His father was British novelist Benjamin Leopold Farjeon; his mother, Margaret, was the daughter of an American actor named Joseph Jefferson. His siblings were Eleanor, a writer for children, Harry, a composer, and Joseph Jefferson, also a writer under the name J.J. Farjeon. Becoming noted for the revues he wrote, Herbert had several successful years in London's West End. His revues included *Spread It Abroad*, *The Two Bouquets*, *Nine Sharp*, *The Little Revue*, *Diversion* (all in the late 30s), *Light And Shade* and *Big Top* (both 1942). Of these, *The Little Revue*, which starred **Hermione Baddeley** and Cyril Ritchard, was especially well received by critics and audiences. This show was one of several of Farjeon's shows staged at London's Little Theatre, where he was a member of the management. The show ran for 415 performances, and included in the cast were Bernard Miles, Betty Ann Davies, Gordon Little, Peggy Willoughby, V.C. Clinton-Baddeley, George Benson and Vida Hope, many of whom had also appeared in *Nine Sharp*. Also in *The Little Revue* was **Joyce**

Grenfell, making her first appearance on a London stage and performing her own 'Useful And Acceptable Gifts'.

During the 30s Farjeon also contributed essays, articles and theatrical reviews to various organs including newspapers, *The Daily Mirror*, magazines and journals, *Vogue*, *The Shakespeare Journal*, *The Listener* and *The Radio Times*. Farjeon was also a respected theatre historian. Years after his death, songs and sketches by Farjeon were used in Broadway revues such as **Leonard Sillman**'s *New Faces Of 1952* and **John Murray Anderson**'s *Almanac* (1953) and *From A To Z* (1960). NB: Confusingly, there appears to have been an American performer named Herbert 'Bert' Farjeon (b. 27 October 1879, San Francisco, California, USA, d. 3 November 1972, San Marcos, California, USA). He first appeared on Broadway in the play *The Bird Of Paradise* (1912). Among other dramas in which he appeared during the 20s are a revival of Edwin Milton Royle's *The Squaw Man* (1921), *Listening In* (1922), *Queen Victoria* (1923), *The Dust Heap* (1924) and *A Tale Of The Wolf* (1925). In 1927, billed as Bert Farjeon, he was in the revue *Grand Street Follies*.

Farley And Heller

Respected UK **dance music** producers and remixers, Terry Farley and Pete Heller initially found success at the forefront of the **Balearic/acid house** scene in the UK in the early 90s. Londoner Farley was a fan of **Studio One** reggae and ska before becoming involved with the London soul club scene during the 80s, DJing alongside a youthful **Paul Oakenfold**. Heller grew up on the south coast of England and began his musical career by DJing in a Brighton discotheque, playing disco, hip-hop and **house**. A visit to **Danny Rampling**'s legendary south London club, Shoom, opened a new chapter in his life. After playing warm-up sets for Rampling, Heller and **Andrew Weatherall** formed the *Boy's Own* collective, running a fanzine, Boy's Own club nights and eventually a record label—**Junior Boy's Own**. It was during this period that Farley and Heller met and began remixing. Farley had already remixed the **Happy Mondays**' 'Wrote For Luck' with Oakenfold as well as other tracks by that band and several by **Primal Scream**. His credibility as a producer-remixer was also enhanced by his work on the **Farm**'s cover version of the **Monkees**' 'Stepping Stone' and the subsequent 'Groovy Train'. The productions' funky dance-influenced sound lent the band kudos at the height of the Manchester-based 'baggy' scene and helped to make 'Groovy Train' a UK Top 10 hit. Farley and Heller's initial productions as a team with Hugo Nicholson were released as Bocca Juniors. Since then, their remixing skills have been used by many artists including **Michael Jackson**, **Jamiroquai**, **Sunscreem**, **K-Klass**, **Simply Red**, **New Order**, **U2**, **Janet Jackson**, **Boy George** and the **Pet Shop Boys**. They have also produced for **Kylie Minogue**. Their own productions have appeared under the name Fire Island and have been hugely popular on the club scene. As Fire Island, they covered Machine's 1979 classic 'There But For The Grace Of God'. Their 1997 recording 'Ultra Flava' was a huge hit in European clubs and **Ibiza** and eventually became a UK Top 40 hit when the vocals of **Ultra Naté** were added. In 1999 Heller's track 'Big Love' was signed to **Pete Tong**'s **London Records** and quickly became ubiquitous on European dancefloors (especially those in Ibiza) before entering the UK charts at number 12. Building on their reputation as excellent club DJs, they also mixed *Late Night Sessions* for the **Ministry Of Sound**. In 2000 Farley began producing a fanzine called *Faith*, which featured a mix of music, politics and satire and was given away in hip London clothes and record stores.

● COMPILATIONS: *Journeys By DJ Volume 12—Mixed By Farley And Heller* (JDJ 1997) ★★★, *Late Night Sessions III* (MOS 1999) ★★★★.

Farley And Riley

Although they came to prominence as members of a **Red McKenzie** band at the Onyx Club in 1935, neither Eddie Farley (b. 16 July 1904, Newark, New Jersey, USA; trumpet) nor Mike Riley (b. 5 January 1904, Fall River, Massachusetts, USA, d. 2 September 1984; trombone) took jazz very seriously. Their onstage antics drove away **Eddie Condon**, who was also a member of the McKenzie band, but the public loved them. Farley And Riley became especially popular when they performed and recorded a song written by Red Hodgson, 'The Music Goes Round And Round', attracting non-jazz audiences to 52nd Street. Farley And Riley later capitalized upon their popularity by forming bands of their own, but their success clearly depended less on intrinsic musical qualities than on the vagaries of public taste.

Farley Jackmaster Funk

The resident DJ at Chicago's Playground between 1981 and 1987 (often combining live drum machine with his selection of Philly soul and R&B), Farley was also one of the earliest **house** producers, with 'Yellow House' being the first record on Dance Mania Records. He was also a key component of the Hot Mix 5, the DJ group which provided Chicago's WBMX radio station with its groundbreaking mix shows. As Chicago backroom boy Mike 'Hitman' Wilson once stated: 'To me Farley started house. Because while **Frankie** [**Knuckles**] had an audience of 600, Farley reached 150,000 listeners.' He had a hit in 1986 with a cover version of 'Love Can't Turn Around', with a vocal from Greater Tabernacle Baptist Choir's Daryl Pandy (although this actually hijacked a **Steve 'Silk' Hurley** song). Other notable releases include 'Aw Shucks', 'As Always' (with Ricky Dillard) and 'Free At Last' (with the Hip House Syndicate). When WBMX went off air his career ground to a halt, an intermission he occupied by exploring rap and R&B. He returned to DJing in England in the 90s, where his reputation had not diminished, and started a new Chill-London label.

Farley, Eddie
(see **Farley And Riley**)

Farlow, Tal

b. Talmadge Holt Farlow, 7 June 1921, Greensboro, North Carolina, USA, d. 25 July 1998, Sea Bright, New Jersey, USA. Although his father was an amateur musician, Tal Farlow did not begin playing guitar until 1942, working as a professional sign painter for several years. Before the decade was out he had achieved a sufficiently high standard to be hired by cabaret singer **Dardanelle**, vibraphonist **Margie Hyams** and clarinettist **Buddy De Franco**. In 1950, by now a fleet and inventive guitarist inspired by **Charlie Christian**, he joined forces with another vibes player, **Red Norvo**, thus beginning a long-running and fruitful, if intermittent, musical partnership. The third member of this group was **Charles Mingus**. Although he initially struggled to keep up with Norvo's startling speed, Farlow developed a technique that in turn made him the fastest guitarist of his era.

In 1953 Farlow worked with **Artie Shaw** and later in the decade led his own trio on recordings for **Blue Note Records** and **Verve Records**, including work with **Eddie Costa**, but he drifted into retirement from music and concentrated on his career as a sign painter. In the late 60s he made a handful of festival appearances, returning to fairly consistent public performances in the late 70s. In the 80s he resumed his working relationship with Red Norvo, touring the USA, the UK and Europe and delighting audiences, many of whom had been alerted to this fine musician's talents through a 1981 television documentary, *Talmadge Farlow*. Farlow's breathtaking speed and fluent technique were highly influential, inspiring young guitarists such as **John McLaughlin**.

● ALBUMS: *Tal Farlow Quartet* 10-inch album (Blue Note 1954) ★★★, *The Tal Farlow Album* 10-inch album (Verve 1954) ★★★★, *The Artistry Of Tal Farlow* reissued as *Autumn In New York* (Norgran 1955) ★★★, *The Interpretations Of Tal Farlow* (Norgran 1955) ★★★, *A Recital By Tal Farlow* (Norgran 1955) ★★★, *Tal* (Norgran 1956) ★★★★, *The Swinging Guitar Of Tal Farlow* (Verve 1956) ★★★, *Fuerst Set* (Xanadu 1956) ★★★, *Second Set* (Xanadu 1956) ★★★, *This Is Tal Farlow* (Verve 1958) ★★★★, *The Guitar Artistry Of Tal Farlow* (Verve 1959) ★★★★, *Tal Farlow Plays The Music Of Harold Arlen* (Verve 1960) ★★★, *Tal Farlow Returns* (Prestige 1969) ★★★, *On Stage* (Concord Jazz 1976) ★★, *A Sign Of The Times* (Concord Jazz 1976) ★★★, *Tal Farlow 78* (Concord Jazz 1978) ★★★, *Chromatic Palette* (Concord Jazz 1981) ★★★, *Cookin' On All Burners* (Concord Jazz 1982) ★★★, *The Legendary Tal Farlow* (Concord Jazz 1984) ★★, *Standard Recital* (FD Music 1992) ★★, with Lenny Breau *Chance Meeting* 1980 recording (Guitarchives 1997) ★★★.

● COMPILATIONS: *The Complete Verve Sessions* 7-CD box set (Mosaic 2004) ★★★★.

Farlowe, Chris

b. John Henry Deighton, 13 October 1940, Essex, England. Farlowe's long career began during the 50s skiffle boom when the John Henry Skiffle Group won the all-England championship. He then formed the original Thunderbirds, which remained semiprofessional until 1962 when they embarked on a month's engagement in Frankfurt, Germany. Farlowe then met Rik Gunnell, owner of London's Ram Jam and Flamingo clubs, and the singer quickly became a stalwart of the city's R&B circuit. He made his recording debut that year on the **Decca Records** label with the pop-orientated 'Air Travel' and released a number of follow-up singles for **Columbia Records** including 'I Remember' (1963) and 'Girl Trouble' (1964). The singer and his backing band also recorded as the Beazers ('The Blue Beat') and Little Joe Cook (a terrific interpretation of the **T-Bone Walker** standard 'Stormy Monday Blues', released in 1965 by **Sue Records**). Farlowe failed to secure commercial success until 1966 when his version of the **Rolling Stones**' song 'Out Of Time', produced by **Mick Jagger**, soared to the top of the UK charts. Several minor hits, including 'Ride On Baby' (1966) and 'Handbags And Gladrags' (1967), followed as well as a brace of pop/soul albums, but Farlowe's intonation proved too craggy for popular consumption. He and the Thunderbirds—which between 1964 and 1967 featured **Albert Lee** (guitar), **Dave Greenslade** (organ), Bugs Waddell (bass), Ian Hague (drums) and Jerry Temple (congas)—remained one of the country's most impressive R&B acts, although session

musicians were increasingly employed for recording purposes.

By 1968 the Thunderbirds had been reduced to a line-up of Farlowe, Lee, Pete Solley (keyboards) and **Carl Palmer** (drums), but two years later the singer founded an all-new unit, the Hill. The venture's sole album, *From Here To Mama Rosa*, was not a commercial success and Farlowe joined ex-colleague Greenslade in **Colosseum**. This powerful jazz rock group disbanded in 1971, and having briefly switched allegiances to **Atomic Rooster**, Farlowe retired from rock to pursue an interest in military and Nazi memorabilia. He re-emerged in 1975 with *Live!* but during the rest of the decade conspicuously failed to find a satisfactory niche for his powerful, gritty voice. Cameo appearances during the 80s on sessions for **Jimmy Page** engendered the widely acclaimed *Out Of The Blue* and *Born Again*, which together served notice that the singer's feeling for the blues remained intact. Although he gigs infrequently Farlowe can still be seen performing as a support act, and he can still cause goosebumps with his sensational version of 'Stormy Monday Blues'. He rejoined his colleagues in Colosseum in 1996 for a reunion tour and album before resuming his solo career. Farlowe is blessed with a magnificent voice but has never been rewarded with the kind of commercial breakthrough achieved by **Tom Jones**.

● ALBUMS: *Chris Farlowe & The Thunderbirds* aka *Stormy Monday* (Columbia 1966) ★★★, *14 Things To Think About* (Immediate 1966) ★★★, *The Art Of Chris Farlowe* (Immediate 1966) ★★★, *The Last Goodbye* (Immediate 1969) ★★, as Chris Farlowe And The Hill *From Here To Mama Rosa* (Polydor 1970) ★★, *Live!* (Polydor 1975) ★★★, *Out Of The Blue* (Brand New 1985) ★★★, *Born Again* (Brand New 1986) ★★★, *Farlowe* aka *Waiting In The Wings* (Barsa/Line 1991) ★★★, with Roy Herrington *Live In Berlin* (Backyard 1991) ★★★, *Lonesome Road* (Indigo 1995) ★★★, *As Time Goes By* (KEG 1995) ★★, *BBC In Concert* 1969, 1976 recordings (Windsong 1996) ★★★, *The Voice* (Citadel 1998) ★★★, *Glory Bound* (Out Of Time 2001) ★★★, *Farlowe That!* (Delicious 2003) ★★★.

● COMPILATIONS: *The Best Of Chris Farlowe Volume 1* (Immediate 1967) ★★★, *Out Of Time* (Immediate 1975) ★★★★, *Out Of Time—Paint It Black* (Charly 1978) ★★★, *Greatest Hits* (Immediate 1978) ★★★★, *Mr. Soulful* (Castle 1986) ★★★, *Buzz With The Fuzz* (Decal 1987) ★★★, *I'm The Greatest* (See For Miles 1996) ★★★★, *Hits* (Repertoire 1999) ★★★, *Dig The Buzz: First Recordings '62–'65* (RPM 2001) ★★★, *The Very Best Of Chris Farlowe* (Camden 2002) ★★★, *Handbags And Gladrags: The Immediate Collection* (Castle 2004) ★★★★, *Rock 'N' Roll Soldier: Anthology 1970–2004* (Delicious 2004) ★★★.

Farm

If perseverance warrants its own unique award, the Farm could have expected the equivalent of the Nobel Prize for their incessant efforts. Formed in 1983 by former youth worker Peter Hooton (b. 28 September 1962, Liverpool, England; vocals), Steve Grimes (b. 4 June 1962, Liverpool, England; guitar), Phillip Strongman (bass) and Andy McVann (drums), the Farm were to become synonymous with so many cultural 'scenes' over the ensuing years that their music was rendered almost irrelevant. For much of the 80s the band flirted with politics, tagged 'The Soul Of

Socialism', encouraged the 'Scally' fashions of their Liverpool home-town, and maintained strong soccer interests—primarily through singer Peter Hooton's fanzine *The End*, a precursor to the explosion of football fanzines at the end of the decade. By 1984 John Melvin, George Maher, Steve Levy and Anthony Evans had joined, bringing with them a brass section and adding a northern soul influence to the Farm's unfashionable pop sound.

Two years on, the line-up changed again when McVann was killed in a police car chase. He was replaced by Roy Boulter (b. 2 July 1964, Liverpool, England), and the line-up was bolstered by Keith Mullen (b. Bootle, England; guitar) and new bass player Carl Hunter (b. 14 April 1965, Bootle, England). The horn section departed, and Ben Leach (b. 2 May 1969, Liverpool, England; keyboards) completed a new six-piece collective that was destined to change the Farm's fortunes. After the synth-pop flop of their fourth independent release, 'Body And Soul', the Farm started their own Produce label and had a fortuitous meeting with in-vogue **dance music** producer Terry Farley (of **Farley And Heller**). Consequently, a cover version of the **Monkees**' 'Stepping Stone' was augmented with fashionable club beats and samples, and come 1990, the Farm suddenly found themselves caught up in the Madchester 'baggy' boom. The anthemic 'Groovy Train' and 'All Together Now' (the latter incorporating a sample of the seventeenth-century composer Johann Pachelbel's 'Canon And Gigue') swept the band into the Top 10 of the UK charts, to be followed in 1991 by their debut album, *Spartacus*, entering the UK charts at number 1. If these placings were not proof enough of the Farm's new-found fame, the next achievement certainly was: the band's football connection was sealed when toy manufacturers Subbuteo designed a unique team kit, just for the band. Later they also had the great honour of playing, alongside frequent collaborator **Pete Wylie**, **Ian McCulloch** and **Gerry Marsden**, to 15,000 Liverpool soccer fans for the 'Last Night Of The Kop', before Liverpool FC's legendary terrace was demolished.

As the UK media tired of the 'baggy' sound, so a decline in the Farm's fortunes set in. 1992's *Love See No Colour* was bland and, indeed, colourless. Few bands can have gone with such velocity from an album that entered the UK charts at number 1 to one that failed to break the Top 75. The blame lay in some outrageous squandering of the money earned through their debut album and a total lack of direction in the songwriting. The band's new contract with Sony (which fostered their own End Product label) was over as quickly as it had started (although an ill-judged attempt in 1992 at the **Human League**'s 'Don't You Want Me Baby' reached the Top 20). Help, surprisingly, came from the USA, where Seymour Stein of **Sire Records** saw some remaining commercial potential in the band. In 1994 they adopted a more orthodox guitar/bass/drums approach for their parting shot, *Hullabaloo*.

Hooton and the Farm bounced back into the headlines in 2004 when a remixed version of 'All Together Now' was released to promote the English soccer team's Euro 2004 campaign. The single, which reached the UK Top 10, was edited by DJ Spoony and featured vocals by the St. Francis Xavier Boys Choir. The band reunited the following year to play a number of live shows with the **Happy Mondays**.

● ALBUMS: *Spartacus* (Produce 1991) ★★★★, *Love See No Colour* (End Product 1992) ★★, *Hullabaloo* (Sire 1994) ★★★.

● COMPILATIONS: *The Best Of The Farm* (Castle 1998) ★★★, *The Very Best Of The Farm* (Music Club 2001) ★★★, *All Together Now: Best Of* (Demon 2004) ★★★.
● DVD/VIDEOS: *Groovy Times* (Produce 1991).

Farmer, Addison

b. 21 August 1928, Council Bluffs, Iowa, USA, d. 20 February 1963, New York, USA. The twin brother of **Art Farmer**, he moved to Los Angeles in the mid-40s and was soon playing bass with noted contemporary musicians including **Dexter Gordon** and **Jay McShann** recording with both. He also gigged with visiting bop stars **Charlie Parker** and **Miles Davis**. In the early 50s he travelled to New York where he played with **Stan Getz**, **Gigi Gryce** and others. In 1959 he joined the Jazztet, a band formed by his brother and **Benny Golson**. The following year Farmer left the Jazztet and subsequently played with **Mose Allison**. An exceptional timekeeper, Farmer's playing also revealed a rich sonority, and his early death robbed jazz of one of its outstanding bass players.

Farmer, Art

b. Arthur Stewart Farmer, 21 August 1928, Council Bluffs, Iowa, USA, d. 4 October 1999, New York City, USA. While still a child Farmer moved first to Phoenix, Arizona, then to Los Angeles. This was in the mid-40s, and during the next few years Farmer played trumpet in various name bands, including those led by **Jay McShann** and **Benny Carter**, and worked and recorded with musicians as diverse as **Johnny Otis**, **Wardell Gray** and **Teddy Edwards**. In the early 50s he was with **Lionel Hampton**, touring Europe and recording there (against Hampton's express orders) with fellow sideman **Clifford Brown**. Back in New York, where Hampton fired pretty nearly his entire band for making those now classic records, Farmer worked with many of the leading contemporary musicians resident in the city. Amongst those artists were **Teddy Charles**, **Charles Mingus**, **Horace Silver**, **Gerry Mulligan** and **George Russell**.

At the end of the decade he and **Benny Golson** formed their own group, which they named the Jazztet. This band also included Farmer's twin brother, **Addison Farmer**, who played bass. The Jazztet folded in 1962, and thereafter Farmer worked mostly as a single occasionally forming his own small groups. From the mid-60s onwards he worked extensively in Europe, spending much time in Vienna, Austria, where he was a member of the national radio big band. He also played with the **Clarke-Boland Big Band**. By this time he had begun favouring the flügelhorn, especially when leading small groups, which he continued to do through the 70s and 80s. Farmer continued to tour extensively up until his death in October 1999.

A highly melodic soloist, with inventive turns of phase and a frequently elegiac approach to his music, Farmer's popularity was sometimes overshadowed by that of his less-talented contemporaries. Study of his work over several decades reveals an artist of considerable emotional depths, which he plumbed more and more as the years passed. In a quiet, unassuming manner, which reflected his personality, Farmer proved hard to pigeonhole. This was a quality that sometimes led observers to pay less attention to him than would be the case had he been a more assertive man and performer.

● ALBUMS: *Art Farmer Septet* aka *Work Of Art* (Prestige/ New Jazz 1953) ★★★★, *Art Farmer Quintet Featuring Sonny Rollins* 10-inch album (Prestige 1954) ★★★★, with Gigi Gryce *Art Farmer Quintet i* 10-inch album (Prestige 1954) ★★★★, *Art Farmer Quartet* 10-inch album (Prestige 1954) ★★★★, with Gryce *Art Farmer Quintet ii* 10-inch album (Prestige 1955) ★★★★, with Gryce *Art Farmer Quintet Featuring Gigi Gryce* aka *Evening In Casablanca* (Prestige/New Jazz 1956) ★★★★, *Bennie Green & Art Farmer* (Prestige 1956) ★★★★, with Donald Byrd *Two Trumpets* (Prestige 1956) ★★★, with Byrd, Idrees Sulieman *Three Trumpets* (Prestige 1957) ★★★★, with Gryce *When Farmer Met Gryce* 1954/1955 recordings (Prestige 1957) ★★★★, *Farmer's Market* (New Jazz 1958) ★★★★, *Portrait Of Art Farmer* (Contemporary 1958) ★★★★, *Last Night When We Were Young* (ABC-Paramount 1958) ★★★★, *Modern Art* (United Artists 1958) ★★★★★, *Brass Shout* (United Artists 1959) ★★★★, *Aztec Suite* (United Artists 1959) ★★★★, with Curtis Fuller, Benny Golson *Meet The Jazztet* (Argo 1960) ★★★, *Art* (United Artists 1961) ★★★, *Early Art* 1954 recordings (Prestige 1961) ★★★★, with Golson *Big City Sounds* (Argo 1961) ★★★, with Golson *The Jazztet And John Lewis* (Argo 1961) ★★★, with Golson *The Jazztet At Birdhouse* (Argo 1961) ★★★★, with Golson *Here And Now* (Mercury 1962) ★★★, with Golson *Another Git Together* (Mercury 1962) ★★★, with Eddie Costa *In Their Own Sweet Way* (Premier 1962) ★★★, *Listen To Art Farmer & The Orchestra* (Mercury 1963) ★★★★, *Interaction* (Atlantic 1963) ★★★, *Live At The Half Note* (Atlantic 1964) ★★★★, *Perception* 1962 recording (Argo 1964) ★★★, *To Sweden With Love* (Atlantic 1964) ★★★, *The Many Faces Of Art Farmer* (Scepter 1964) ★★★★, shared with Art Taylor *Hard Cookin'* (Prestige 1964) ★★★★, *Sing Me Softly Of The Blues* (Atlantic 1965) ★★★★, *Baroque Sketches* (Columbia 1966) ★★, *The Time And The Place* (Columbia 1967) ★★★, *Plays The Great Jazz Hits* (Columbia 1967) ★★★, *Art Worker* (Moon 1968) ★★★★, *Art Farmer & Phil Woods* (CAM 1968) ★★★, *From Vienna With Art* (MPS 1970) ★★★, *Homecoming* (Mainstream 1971) ★★★, *Gentle Eyes* (Mainstream 1972) ★★, *A Sleeping Bee* (Sonet 1974) ★★★, *To Duke With Love* (East Wind/Inner City 1975) ★★★★, *The Summer Knows* (East Wind/Inner City 1976) ★★★, *Art Farmer Quintet At Boomer's* (East Wind/ Inner City 1976) ★★★★, *On The Road* (Contemporary 1976) ★★★, *Crawl Space* (CTI 1977) ★★★★, *Something You Got* (CTI 1977) ★★★★, *Big Blues* (CTI 1978) ★★★, *Yama* (CTI 1979) ★★★, *Foolish Memories* (Bellaphon 1981) ★★★, *A Work Of Art* (Concord Jazz 1981) ★★★★, *Manhattan* (Soul Note 1982) ★★★, *Mirage* (Soul Note 1982) ★★★, *Warm Valley* (Concord Jazz 1982) ★★★★, *Maiden Voyage* (Denon 1983) ★★★, with Golson *The Jazztet: Moment To Moment* (Soul Note 1983) ★★★, *You Make Me Smile* (Soul Note 1985) ★★★, with Fuller, Golson *Back To The City* (Contemporary 1986) ★★★, *Real Time* (Contemporary 1986) ★★★★, *Something To Live For: The Music Of Billy Strayhorn* (Contemporary 1987) ★★★★, *Azure* (Soul Note 1988) ★★★, *Blame It On My Youth* (Contemporary 1988) ★★★★, *Ph.D.* (Contemporary 1989) ★★★, *In Concert* 1984 recording (Enja 1990) ★★★, *Central Avenue Reunion* (Contemporary 1990) ★★, *Soul Eyes* (Enja 1991) ★★, *Live At Sweet Basil* (Evidence 1992) ★★★, *The Company I Keep* (Arabesque 1995) ★★★, *Live*

At The Stanford Jazz Workshop (Monarch 1997) ★★★★, *Silk Road* (Arabesque 1997) ★★★, *Art In Wroclaw* (EmArcy 1998) ★★★, *Live In Europe* 1970 recording (Enja 1999) ★★.
● COMPILATIONS: *The Best Of Art Farmer* (Columbia 1990) ★★★★, *ARTistry* (Concord Jazz 2001) ★★★★.

Farmer, Betty

b. 15 October 1938, New Orleans, Louisiana, USA, d. 11 September 2001, New York City, USA. Farmer began singing as a child and first worked professionally in her mid-teens with Dixieland bands in her home-town, including that led by Ronnie DuPont. This was at the Bistro Club, and she later appeared at **Al Hirt**'s club where she was heard by **Duke Ellington**, who invited her to tour with him. She declined to go on the road with the band but reportedly sang with Ellington's band at Carnegie Hall in 1972. Settling in Denver, Colorado, she sang at Garbo's and The Bombay Club, and opened her own club, Bryant St. West. She also worked in other parts of the country, singing at clubs and festivals, including the **Monterey Jazz Festival** and **Newport Jazz Festival** as well as those at San Diego and Sacramento where she sang with the Bob Craven Summit Ridge Jazz Band. In Colorado she worked extensively with local and visiting musicians, including an appearance in the early 80s in Grand Junction with **Phil Urso** and Swedish drummer **Bert Dahlander**. This club date was informally recorded, thus providing a rare opportunity to hear Farmer. In 1996 she moved to New York City, taking a job with Showtime Entertainment. She continued to perform, singing at clubs in the city. She was also studying guitar and was rehearsing an act with actor-comedian David Jung. In August 2001 Farmer joined a bond trading company, Cantor Fitzgerald, as an executive assistant. Three weeks later she was working in the company's offices on the 105th floor of the North Tower of the World Trade Center when it was struck by a terrorist attack. Farmer was one of the estimated 700 Cantor Fitzgerald employees presumed dead.
Fellow performers and critics alike praised Farmer's strong personality and onstage presence. On the evidence of her recording with Dahlander, she had a husky contralto, a tough-edged way with a lyric and a pleasing use of a controlled vibrato. Farmer's decision to spend the central years of her life in Colorado contributed to the fact that she was far less known to jazz audiences than was her due.
● ALBUMS: with Bert Dahlander *Welcome To A Live Jazz Concert* 1980/1981 recording (Everyday 2002) ★★★.

Farmer's Boys

Along with the **Higsons**, the Farmer's Boys emerged from Norwich, Norfolk, England, in the early 80s with an amusing brand of wacky guitar pop. Baz, Frog, Mark and Stan (they never used surnames) issued the excellent 'Whatever Is He Like?' (on the Backs label) in the summer. On the follow-up 'More Than A Dream' (also on Backs), the band veered towards country and western, a formula successful enough to warrant its reissue as the Farmer's Boys' first single for **EMI Records**. 'Muck It Out', issued in early 1983, played on the band's rural name in the search for a novelty hit, but chart success was something that would always elude them. The band's debut album appeared in the autumn, but despite charm and melodic strength (exemplified by the catchy single 'For You') *Get Out & Walk* could not sustain the impact of their singles over two sides. 'Apparently', issued in the late spring of 1984, benefitted from the band's horn section of Andrew Hamilton (saxophone), Noel Harris (trumpet) and John Beecham (trombone), while a cover version of **Cliff Richard**'s 'In The Country' became the closest thing to a Farmer's Boys hit in August. However, after the release of the excellent 'I Built The World' early in 1985, the writing was on the wall, and the band split up soon afterwards. After a long hiatus, Baz, Mark and Stan reconvened as the Great Outdoors in the late 90s to record two singles for the Fierce Panda label. An album followed on the revived Backs label in 2001.

● ALBUMS: *Get Out & Walk* (EMI 1983) ★★★, *With These Hands* (EMI 1985) ★★★.
● COMPILATIONS: *Once Upon A Time In The East (The Early Years 1981–1982)* (Backs 2003) ★★★.

Farnham, Allen

b. 19 May 1961, Boston, Massachusetts, USA. Encouraged towards music by his home environment, Farnham's mother playing piano and organ, he first played trumpet but at the age of 12 switched to piano, taking formal lessons. He studied at Oberlin Conservatory of Music, developing classical and jazz piano skills before continuing his studies privately in Cleveland, Ohio, in the early to mid-80s. During this period Farnham also studied Indian music. Simultaneously, he was working as a studio musician and playing in a small jazz group co-led by bass player Kenny Davis and saxophonist **Ernie Krivda**. In the mid-80s Farnham moved to New York City and thereafter also toured, eventually becoming resident in California where he became closely associated with Concord Records. During these and following years he worked with several leaders, including **Marty Paich; Mel Tormé; Ken Peplowski**, the contemporary vibraphone player; Gust William Tsilis and **Frank Vignola**, and with the singers **Ernestine Anderson**, Eden Atwood, Lou Lanza and **Susannah McCorkle**. With some of these artists he also wrote arrangements and served as musical director (on McCorkle's *I'll Take Romance* and *Easy To Love: The Songs Of Cole Porter*). He appeared in similar capacities for Concord-backed groups, with which he also appeared in Japan. For the company, Farnham, who also plays keyboards, has appeared in multiple roles, including that of producer, on several recording sessions. A strikingly gifted accompanist and arranger, Farnham's occasional solo appearances also mark him as a talented post-bop pianist with eclectic taste and a wide-ranging repertoire.

● ALBUMS: *5th House* (Concord Jazz 1989) ★★★★, *Play-cation* (Concord Jazz 1992) ★★★, *Live At The Maybeck Recital Hall, Vol. 41* (Concord Jazz 1994) ★★★★, *The Common Thread 1986–94 recordings* (Concord Jazz 1995) ★★★, *Meets The RIAS Big Band* (Concord Jazz 1998) ★★★, with Masahiro Yoshida, Ray Drummond *Uno* (DIW 2001) ★★★.

Farnham, John

b 1 July 1949, Dagenham, Essex, England. The self-effacing Farnham has sustained a successful career in Australia for over three decades. He was raised in Dagenham before his family relocated to Melbourne, Australia, in 1959. The young Farnham balanced a plumbing apprenticeship with membership of the band Strings Unlimited before embarking on a solo career with **EMI Records**. Having initial success in 1967 as

Johnny Farnham with 'Sadie (The Cleaning Lady)', a throwaway pop song, his manager pushed Farnham into the pop limelight with 13 subsequent hit singles. He was voted Australia's 'King of Pop' five years in a row between 1969 and 1973 and was also active in a variety of stage shows and musicals.

However, for the second half of the 70s his career seemed dead, and it was not until mid-1980 that he re-emerged with another hit record, a unique rendition of the **Beatles**' 'Help'. Now billed as simply John Farnham, he released the acclaimed *Uncovered*, formed his own band and went back on the road until 1982 when he was asked to sing with the **Little River Band**, replacing original singer Glenn Shorrock. Despite adding some bite to its music, Farnham was unable to assist the band in repeating its earlier successes, and so he resumed his solo career. For his comeback, *Whispering Jack*, Farnham sifted through hundreds of songs from local and international writers, which proved fruitful as it became the largest-selling album in Australia's history. The record deserved its success as the songs were varied and strong, showcasing Farnham's excellent singing voice, not least on the UK Top 10 single 'You're The Voice'. Because of his earlier successes, his fans continued to support him, and unlike other performers, he was not afraid to change and move in new directions, although his next album, *Age Of Reason*, repeated the successful formula of *Whispering Jack*. In 1992 he starred as Jesus in the Australian production of **Jesus Christ Superstar**. Farnham remains highly successful in his native country, and 1996's *Romeo's Heart* became his fastest-selling album. In 1998 he toured alongside **Olivia Newton-John** and Anthony Warlow with The Main Event, on which the three singers were backed by a forty piece orchestra. His recent tours in Australia have been phenomenally successful, breaking all existing records. His most recent album was highly successful in his adopted homeland, and he remains one of the bestselling artists in Australia.

● ALBUMS: *Sadie* (EMI 1967) ★★, *Looking Through A Tear* (EMI 1970) ★★, *Christmas Is John Farnham* (EMI 1970) ★★, *Everybody Oughta Sing A Song* (EMI 1971) ★★, with Alison Durbin *Together* (EMI 1971) ★★, *Johnny Farnham Sings The Shows* (EMI 1972) ★★, *Hits, Magic & Rock 'N' Roll* (EMI 1973) ★★, *Johnny Farnham Sings The Hits Of '73* (EMI 1973) ★★, *J.P. Farnham Sings* (EMI 1975) ★★, *Uncovered* (RCA 1980) ★★★, *Whispering Jack* (RCA 1986) ★★★, *Age Of Reason* (RCA 1988) ★★★, *Chain Reaction* (RCA 1990) ★★, *Full House* (RCA 1991) ★★, *Then Again . . .* (RCA 1993) ★★, *Romeo's Heart* (BMG 1996) ★★, *The Last Time* (BMG 2002) ★★★.

● COMPILATIONS: *The Best Of John Farnham* (EMI 1971) ★★★, *Anthology 1: Greatest Hits 1986–1997* (Gotham City/BMG 1997) ★★★, *Anthology 2: Classic Hits 1967–1985 (Recorded Live)* (Gotham City/BMG 1997) ★★★, *Anthology 3: Rarities* (Gotham City/BMG 1997) ★★.

● DVD/VIDEOS: *Whispering Jack In Concert* (BMG Video 1987), *Classic Jack Live!* (BMG Video 1989), *Chain Reaction: Live In Concert* (BMG Video 1991), *Talk Of The Town Tour* (BMG Video 1994), *Jack Of Hearts Tour* (BMG Video 1996), *The Main Event* (BMG Video 1998), *Anthology 1: The Videos* (BMG Video 1999).

Farnon, Robert

b. 24 July 1917, Toronto, Ontario, Canada, d. 23 April 2005, Guernsey, Channel Islands, British Isles. Gifted with a prodigious musical talent, early in his life Farnon was accomplished on several instruments and at the age of 11 was playing with the Toronto Junior Symphony Orchestra. In 1932 he joined the Canadian Broadcasting Corporation Orchestra where the musical director, **Percy Faith**, made him responsible for many of the choral arrangements. In 1941 Farnon's First Symphony was performed by the Philadelphia Symphony Orchestra under Eugene Ormandy. At the start of World War II, Farnon enlisted in the Canadian army and was sent to Europe as leader of the Canadian Band of the American Expeditionary Force. After the war, he remained in the UK, writing arrangements for popular bands such as those of **Ted Heath** and **Geraldo**. He formed and led a studio orchestra for a long-running BBC radio series, and many of his light orchestral compositions became popular, most notably 'Jumping Bean', 'Portrait Of A Flirt', 'The Westminster Waltz' and 'The Colditz March'. His other important compositions have included 'Melody Fair', 'Peanut Polka', 'A La Claire Fontaine', 'Gateway To The West', 'Pictures In The Fire', 'A Star Is Born', 'Manhattan Playboy', Journey Into Melody', 'Lake Of The Woods', 'Derby Day' and 'State Occasion'.

In the late 40s and early 50s Farnon wrote scores for several movies such as *I Live In Grosvenor Square* (1945), *Spring In Park Lane* (1948), *Maytime In Mayfair* (1949), *Captain Horatio Hornblower R.N.* (1951), *His Majesty O'Keefe* (1954), *Gentlemen Marry Brunettes* (1955), *The Little Hut* (1957), *The Sheriff Of Fractured Jaw* (1958), *The Road To Hong Kong* (1962), *The Truth About Spring* (1964), *Shalako* (1968) and *Bear Island* (1979). In 1962 Farnon arranged and conducted for **Frank Sinatra**'s *Great Songs From Great Britain*, the first broadcast the singer had recorded in the UK. Subsequently, he worked in television, composing several television themes for top-rated programmes such as *Panorama*, *Armchair Theatre*, *Colditz*, *The Secret Army* and *Kessler* and continued to make occasional radio broadcasts and assemble orchestras for special concerts and recording dates. In 1996 Farnon received the Best Instrumental Arrangement Grammy Award for 'Lament', a track on his *Tangence* album with the famous trombonist **J.J. Johnson**. In the following year, Farnon's many admirers around the world, including the members of an extremely active British-based appreciation society, were celebrating his 80th birthday. He was awarded the Order Of Canada in 1998 and also completed a new piano concerto to be recorded by the Czechoslovakia Symphony Orchestra in Bratislava.

● ALBUMS: *A Robert Farnon Concert* (Decca 1950) ★★★, *Journey Into Melody* (Decca 1950) ★★★★, with Eugene Conley *Favourite Songs* (Decca 1950) ★★★, *Stephen Foster Melodies* (Decca 1951) ★★★, *Music Of Vincent Youmans* (Decca 1951) ★★★, *Hoagy Carmichael And Victor Schertzinger Suites* (Decca 1953) ★★★, *Songs Of Britain* (Decca 1953) ★★★★, *Presenting Robert Farnon* (Decca 1953) ★★★★, *Flirtation Walk* (Decca 1954) ★★★, *Two Cigarettes In The Dark* (Decca 1955) ★★★, *Gentleman Marry Brunettes* film soundtrack (Vogue/Coral 1955) ★★★, *Something To Remember You By—Music Of Arthur Schwartz* (Decca 1955) ★★★, *Canadian Impressions* (Decca 1956) ★★★★, *Melody Fair* (Decca 1956) ★★★★, *Pictures In The Fire* (Decca 1957) ★★★, *From The Highlands* (Decca 1958) ★★★, *From The Emerald Isle* (Decca 1959) ★★★, *Gateway To The West/Portrait Of The West* (MGM 1960) ★★★, *Captain Horatio Hornblower RN/Rhapsody For* *Violin And Orchestra* (Delyse 1960) ★★★★, *Sensuous Strings Of Robert Farnon* (Philips 1962) ★★★★, with Rawicz And Landauer *Robert Farnon And Leroy Anderson Encores* (Philips 1962) ★★★, *The Road To Hong Kong* film soundtrack (Decca 1962) ★★★, *Captain From Castile And Other Great Movie Themes* (Philips 1964) ★★★, with Sarah Vaughan *Vaughan With Voices* (Mercury 1964) ★★★, *Conducts My Fair Lady And Other Musical Bouquets* (Philips 1965) ★★★★, *Portrait Of Johnny Mathis* (Philips 1965) ★★★, *Plays The Hits Of Sinatra* (Philips 1965) ★★★, *Symphonic Suite—Porgy and Bess* (Decca 1966) ★★★, with Tony Bennett *Christmas Album* (Columbia 1969) ★★★, with Tony Coe *Pop Makes Progress* (Chapter One 1970) ★★★, with Bennett *With Love* (Columbia 1972) ★★★, with Bennett *The Good Things In Life* (Philips 1972) ★★★, with Bennett and the LPO *Get Happy* (Columbia 1972) ★★★, *Showcase For Soloists* (Invicta 1973) ★★★, *In A Dream World* (Rediffusion 1974) ★★★, with the LPO *At The Festival Hall* (Pye 1974) ★★★, with the Singers Unlimited *Sentimental Journey* (MPS 1975) ★★★, *Sketches Of Tony Bennett And Frank Sinatra* (Pye 1976) ★★★, with Lena Horne *A New Album* (RCA 1976) ★★★, *Dreaming* (Peerless 1977) ★★★, with the Singers Unlimited *Eventide* (MPS 1978) ★★★, with Ray Ellington *I Wish You Love* (Mayfair 1979) ★★★★, with George Shearing *On Target* (MPS 1982) ★★★★, with Jose Carreras *Love Is . . .* (Philips 1984) ★★★, with Pia Zadora *Pia And Phil* (Columbia 1985) ★★★, with Zadora *I Am What I Am* (Columbia 1986) ★★★, *At The Movies* (Horatio Nelson 1987) ★★★, with Eileen Farrell *This Time It's Love* (Reference 1992) ★★★, conducting the Royal Philharmonic Orchestra *Concert Music* (Reference 1992) ★★★, with Farrell *It's Over* (Reference 1992) ★★★, *British Light Music* (Marco Polo 1992) ★★★, with George Shearing *How Beautiful Is Night* (Telarc 1993) ★★★, with Farrell *Here* (Elba 1993) ★★★, with Joe Williams *Here's To Life* (Telarc 1994) ★★★, with J.J. Johnson *Tangence* (Gitanes 1994) ★★★, with Farrell *Love Is Letting Go* (DRG 1995) ★★★.

● FILMS: *This Man Is Mine* (1946).

Faron's Flamingos

Formed in Liverpool, England, in 1961, Faron's Flamingos were one of the pivotal acts of the Merseybeat era who completely missed the ferry (*sic*) with no commercial success whatsoever. Founding members Nicky Crouch (guitar/vocals), Billy Jones (guitar/vocals), Eric London (bass) and Trevor Morias (b. 16 October 1943, Liverpool, England; drums) had worked together since 1959 as the Ravens, before adding vocalist Faron (b. Bill Roughley). Cavern Club DJ Bob Wooler suggested the name Faron's Flamingos. In 1962 London and Jones left the group, which continued as a four-piece with ex-**Undertakers** bass player Mushy Cooper. Following a tour of France, Paddy Chambers (b. Patrick John Chambers, 30 April 1944, Liverpool, England, d. 28 September 2000; guitar/vocals) was added to the line-up, and when Cooper left for Lee Curtis in 1963, Faron took over on bass. This version of Faron's Flamingos recorded four tracks for *This Is Merseybeat*, before securing a contract with **Oriole Records**. Sadly, their rousing version of 'Do You Love Me' was eclipsed by **Brian Poole And The Tremeloes**' inferior reading, and an equally ebullient 'Shake Sherry' made little impression. The disillusioned group broke up in November

1963. Faron and Chambers joined the **Big Three**, while Morias later found success in the **Peddlers**.

Farr, Gary

Gary Farr began his music career playing folk and blues in English south coast pubs and clubs. He was persuaded to form an R&B band that, having adopted the name the **T-Bones**, secured the resident slot at London's Crawdaddy club, previously the home of the **Rolling Stones** and the **Yardbirds**. Farr led several versions of the T-Bones before dissolving the group in 1967. He joined former **Blossom Toes** drummer Kevin Westlake in a short-lived duo, the Lion And The Fish, before recording his debut solo album, *Take Something With You*. This excellent set featured contributions from members of **Mighty Baby** and the aforementioned Blossom Toes, while a similar line-up was responsible for the singer's second collection, *Strange Fruit*, which also featured guitarist **Richard Thompson**. In 1972 Farr moved to America where he completed a third album at the famed **Muscle Shoals** studio. He subsequently became resident in Los Angeles, but despite continuing to write material, the singer has made no subsequent recordings.

- ALBUMS: *Take Something With You* (1969) ★★★★, *Strange Fruit* (1971) ★★★, *Addressed To The Censors Of Love* (1972) ★★.
- COMPILATIONS: *London 1964/65* (1977) ★★★.

Farr, Hugh

b. Thomas Hubert Farr, 6 December 1903, Llano, Texas, USA, d. 17 March 1980. An important member of the **Sons Of The Pioneers**. His father played fiddle and his mother guitar at local venues and at the age of seven, Hugh was playing guitar with his father at such events. At nine, he was so proficient on his father's fiddle that his father took to playing guitar only. In 1925, after several moves, the Farr family relocated to Encino, California. He first worked in the construction industry but eventually became a full-time musician. Between 1929 and 1933, he and brother Karl played with Len Nash And His Country Boys on local venues and on KFOX Long Beach, where the two also acted as station staff musicians. During the time with Nash, Hugh also played on several **Brunswick Records** recordings. In 1933 the two brothers and Ira McCullough performed as the Haywire Trio and also played with Jack LeFevre And His Texas Outlaws. Soon afterwards, he became a fourth member of the Pioneer Trio (joining Leonard Slye [**Roy Rogers**], **Bob Nolan** and **Tim Spencer**) who, before long, became the Sons Of The Pioneers. His brilliant fiddle playing and deep bass vocals became an integral part of the group's sound. He stayed with the group until late in 1958, when he quit following differences of opinion. He formed his own Sons Of The Pioneers, an action that immediately led to controversy, and he quickly disbanded the group. He played with **Jimmy Wakely**'s band before, in the early 60s, he again attempted to use the old name until legally instructed to stop following objections by Rogers, Nolan and Spencer. He briefly formed a group he called the Country Gentlemen, but after recording *Songs Of The Pioneers*, the group folded. Farr's fiddle playing could receive no greater praise than that afforded by noted conductor Walter Winchell. When asked whom he believed was the greatest natural violinist of the century, his answer was: 'It is two musicians, the left hand of Fritz Kreisler and the right hand of that gentleman, who plays the violin with

the Sons Of The Pioneers, I don't recall his name.' Hugh Farr died in March 1980, but his playing may be heard on countless recordings of the Pioneers.

- COMPILATIONS: as Farr Brothers *Texas Crapshooter* (JEMF 1978) ★★★, *South In My Soul* covers 1930–1940 (Cattle 1978) ★★★, *Texas Stomp 1934-1944* (Country Routes 1993) ★★★★.

Farr, Karl

b. Karl Marx Farr, 25 April 1909, Rochele, Texas, USA, d. 20 September 1961. An important member of the **Sons Of The Pioneers**. The younger brother of **Hugh Farr**, he grew up in a musical environment and as a child played local venues with his brothers, Hugh and Glen. At the age of 13, he competently played guitar, mandolin, banjo and drums. After the family relocated to Encino, California, in 1925, he picked cotton and played some local venues before joining Hugh as a member of Len Nash And His Country Boys. Between 1929 and 1933, they played with Nash at local venues and on KFOX Long Beach, where the two also worked as station staff musicians. In 1933 the two brothers and Ira McCullough performed as the Haywire Trio and also played with Jack LeFevre And His Texas Outlaws. After Hugh joined the Sons Of The Pioneers, he soon persuaded the members that the group badly needed a guitarist of Karl's ability. Karl's style of playing was unlike that of the usual Texas guitarists—he used single note runs rather than the closed chord rhythm. There is little doubt that his guitar work was an inspiration to all members of the group and especially complemented the excellent fiddle playing of his brother. He has been classed as one of the true early guitar stylists, whose playing has been a direct influence on several later noted exponents of the instrument, including **Merle Travis** and **Joe Maphis**. In 1949 the Fender company gave him one of their earliest electric instruments, Telecast #0757, in appreciation of his contribution to guitar music. On 22 September 1961 Karl Farr appeared onstage with the group before a crowd of 4,000 in West Springfield, Massachusetts. While playing his acoustic Martin on a solo of 'Up A Lazy River', he broke a string. Fellow members noted that he appeared greatly upset by it, and while attempting to remove the broken string, he slumped to the floor. **Tommy Doss** and **Dale Warren** quickly carried him from the stage for medical attention. He was rushed to hospital, but the doctor later reported that for all practical purposes Karl Farr was dead on arrival, the victim of a heart attack.

- COMPILATIONS: as Farr Brothers *Texas Crapshooter* (JEMF 1978) ★★★, *South In My Soul* covers 1930–1940 (Cattle 1978) ★★★, *Texas Stomp 1934-1944* (Country Routes 1993) ★★★★.

Farr, Lucy

b. c.1912, Ballinakill, County Galway, Eire. An active member of the Rakes for 25 years, venerable Irish fiddler Lucy Farr worked regularly with folk artists such as **Bob Davenport**, Margaret Barry, Bobby Casey, Jimmy Power and Julia Clifford at a time when Irish traditional music was not achieving the attention it now enjoys. A founder member of the Comhaltas Ceoltiri Eireann organisation, including a span of seven years as its vice-chairman, she has contributed greatly to the advocacy of Irish tradition in music and arts. She began playing at the age of 12 at Saturday night 'house dances' at her father's residence and from then has concentrated on ceilidhs and pub sessions rather than pushing her able technique into the concert limelight. Never one to seek fortune other than enjoyment from her musical talent, she contributed four songs to the 1967 compilation *Paddy In The Smoke*. This was later used as the inspiration for Globestyle's 1994 album *In The Smoke*, which included another of her compositions, 'The Mother Reel'. Indeed, her tunes have been widely admired and documented, notably in Pete Cooper's book on fiddling, *All Around The World*. Arty McGlynn and Nollaig Casey also interpreted Farr's 'Music On The Wind' as part of their 1989 release. In 1992 an album was recorded to celebrate her 80th birthday, *Heart And Home*, which revealed her technique to be undiminished by her advanced age.

● ALBUMS: *Heart And Home* cassette (Veteran Tapes 1992) ★★★.

Farrar, Jay

b. 26 December 1966, Belleville, Illinois, USA. A leading figure in the roots rock and alt country movement of the 90s, Farrar was a founding member of two of the scene's main bands, **Uncle Tupelo** and **Son Volt**. He cofounded Uncle Tupelo during the late 80s along with longtime friend Jeff Tweedy. Although the band never scored a substantial hit and only issued a handful of recordings, a large cult following formed around them as countless new bands used Uncle Tupelo's rootsy approach as a blueprint for their own sounds. Following their split in 1994, Farrar teamed up with former Uncle Tupelo drummer Mike Heidorn to form Son Volt. Although Farrar's new group enjoyed more commercial success than its predecessor (1997's *Straightaways* narrowly missed reaching the Top 40 on the US album charts), the band was not as critically acclaimed as Uncle Tupelo, and after three album releases, Son Volt was put on hiatus at the end of the 90s.

Instead of forming another all new group, Farrar decided to launch a solo career. Signing on with the Artemis label at the start of the twenty-first century, Farrar worked at a breakneck pace, averaging a new album per year. In 2001 he released his solo debut, *Sebastopol*, on which Farrar used alternate guitar tunings to serve as songwriting inspiration. The following year's five-track EP, *ThirdShiftGrottoSlack*, was produced by **R.L. Burnside/Beck** associate Tom Rothrock, who introduced an interesting funk element to Farrar's songwriting. On 2003's *Terroir Blues*, Farrar teamed up with Eric Heywood (pedal steel guitar, ex–Son Volt), **Superchunk** member Jon Wurster (drums) and session musician John Horton (guitar/bass). The album was the first to be issued via Farrar's own record imprint, Act/Resist (distributed via Artemis). During the same period, Farrar composed the incidental music for the independent film *The Slaughter Rule*. A live album followed in 2004.

● ALBUMS: *Sebastopol* (Artemis 2001) ★★★, *The Slaughter Rule* film soundtrack (Bloodshot 2003) ★★★, *Terroir Blues* (Act/Resist 2003) ★★★★, *Stone, Steel & Bright Lights* (Transmit/Artemis 2004) ★★★.

Farrell And Farrell

A husband and wife team of Jayne and Bob Farrell, this US gospel duo have spent many years on the road spreading the Christian word through their own ministry. Although each had flirted with the faith before, Bob playing with several secular rock bands and Jayne singing on the nightclub circuit, Farrell And Farrell were inaugurated strictly as a religious group. Bob also cofounded the religious rock group Millennium in 1970 before joining pioneer contemporary Christian group Dove in 1972, who released an album for Myrrh Records. Jayne, meanwhile, was a featured vocalist on many religious crusades. They decided to form the duo in order to pool their songwriting, with Bob responsible for the majority of the composing. Several of Bob's songs have been covered by other religious groups, including Hope Of Glory ('Lifesaver') and the Pat Terry Group ('Restored'). As a duo the group made its debut with a self-titled collection for NewPax Records in the late 70s.

● ALBUMS: *Farrell And Farrell* (NewPax 1978) ★★.

Farrell, Joe

b. Joseph Carl Firrantello, 16 December 1937, Chicago Heights, Illinois, USA, d. 10 January 1986, Los Angeles, California, USA. After studying several reed instruments, Farrell concentrated on tenor saxophone from the mid-50s. At the end of the decade he joined **Maynard Ferguson** in New York, also playing and recording with **Slide Hampton**, **George Russell**, **Charles Mingus** and **Jaki Byard**. In the mid-60s he became a long-serving member of the **Thad Jones–Mel Lewis** Jazz Orchestra and also worked with **Elvin Jones**. Having been likened to major and various tenor stylists, such as **Stan Getz**, **Sonny Rollins** and **John Coltrane**, it is not surprising that Farrell's musical tastes drew him into many varied byways of jazz. He played on the **Band**'s Rock Of Ages and was a member of **Chick Corea**'s **Return To Forever** (Corea also played on several of Farrell's own albums). Later he was associated with **Woody Shaw**, **Paul Horn**, **George Benson**, **Airto Moreira**, **Louis Hayes** and **JoAnne Brackeen**. While still concentrating on his main instrument, Farrell also played effectively on soprano saxophone and flute. He died of bone cancer in January 1986.

● ALBUMS: *Joe Farrell Quartet* (CTI 1970) ★★★, *Outback* (CTI 1971) ★★★, *Moon Germs* (CTI 1972) ★★, *Penny Arcade* (CTI 1973) ★★★, *Upon This Rock* (CTI 1974) ★★★, *Canned Funk* (CTI 1975) ★★★, *La Cathedral Y El Toro* (Warners 1978) ★★★, *Night Dancing* (Warners 1978) ★★, *Skateboard Park* (Xanadu 1979) ★★★, *Sonic Text* (Contemporary 1979) ★★★★, *Vim 'N' Vigor* (Timeless 1984) ★★, with Airto Moreira, Flora Purim *Three-Way Mirror* 1985 recording (Reference 1987) ★★★★, *Darn That Dream* 1982 recording (Drive Archive) ★★★.

Farrell, Perry

b. Perry Bernstein, 29 March 1959, Queens, New York City, USA. This controversial icon of the alternative rock scene grew up in Miami, Florida, before relocating to Los Angeles, California, in time to catch the end of the punk rock movement. Changing his name Perry Bernstein to Perry Farrell (equals peripheral), he formed the art-goth band Psi Com where he developed his distinctive high-pitched vocal style and charismatic stage presence but also the first signs of his image-obsessed, messianic personality. Following the disintegration of Psi Com, Farrell formed **Jane's Addiction** with **Dave Navarro**, Stephen Perkins and Eric Avery. The band's wildly eclectic sound and controversial stage shows helped establish alternative rock as an important and viable musical form and served as a welcome antidote to the hackneyed macho posturings of the 80s rock giants then dominating the US musical scene.

Jane's Addiction eventually imploded in 1992, a year after Farrell inaugurated the highly successful **Lollapalooza** concert series. This travelling music festival was instrumental in raising the profile of alternative rock to even greater heights in the new decade. At the same time, Farrell formed **Porno For Pyros** with Perkins, guitarist Peter DiStefano and bass player Martyn LeNoble. Although the band raised Farrell's media profile, their albums failed to match the decadent grandeur that Jane's Addiction achieved at their peak. In 1997 Farrell, Navarro and Perkins re-formed Jane's Addiction for select live dates and even recorded some new material for inclusion on the compilation *Kettle Whistle*. By the end of the year, however, both Jane's Addiction and Porno For Pyros were no more, and Farrell finally began work on his solo debut. The first release under his name was the retrospective *Rev*, featuring hits and rarities from his eventful career. *Song Yet To Be Sung*, a challenging hotchpotch of psychedelia and electronica featuring an enviable guest list of alternative musicians and producers, was released in July 2001. At the same time, Farrell resumed live work with Jane's Addiction.

● ALBUMS: *Song Yet To Be Sung* (Virgin 2001) ★★★.
● COMPILATIONS: *Rev* (WEA 1999) ★★★.
● FURTHER READING: *Perry Farrell: The Saga Of A Hypester*, Dave Thompson.
● FILMS: *The Doom Generation* (1995).

Farrell, Wes

b. 21 December 1940, New York, USA, d. 29 February 1996, Fisher Island, Florida, USA. One of pop's most successful entrepreneurs, Farrell rose to prominence in the early 60s as an associate of Luther Dixon. He co-wrote several songs for the **Shirelles**, including the frenetic R&B song 'Boys', later covered by the **Beatles**, before joining Roosevelt Music in an A&R capacity. Farrell signed **Neil Diamond** and the Feldman/Gottehrer/Goldstein team and showed a flair for unashamed pop through his association with **Jay And The Americans**. The artist co-wrote two of their best-known singles, 'Come A Little Bit Closer' and 'Let's Lock The Door (And Throw Away The Key)', and these major US hits were the prelude to a highly lucrative period. His Picturetone publishing company became a feature of the 'teenybop' market, while Farrell enjoyed success as a producer with the **Cowsills** and **Every Mother's Son**, both of which he leased to **MGM Records**. He dabbled with underground rock through an association with Boston group the **Beacon Street Union** before returning to 'bubblegum' styles with the immensely popular **Partridge Family** and continued successfully with **Tony Orlando** And **Dawn**. An attendant television series helped this group secure five US Top 20 hits during 1970/1. Farrell later founded the Chelsea label, which became one of the leading labels of the disco era. He died from cancer in 1996.

Farren, Mick

b. Cheltenham, Gloucester, England. Raised in Worthing, Sussex, and educated in London, Farren first entered music as a member of the Mafia around 1962. He then passed through a couple of R&B bands before forming a **Fugs**-type outfit which evolved into the Social Deviants in 1967. After his time with the **Deviants** (from which he was kicked out and stranded in America) and a brief spell in the first line-up of the **Pink Fairies**, Farren released his debut solo album, *Mono The Carnivorous Circus* in 1970. That same year Farren

also worked on the original production of **Twink**'s first solo album *Think Pink*. Farren then retired from performing music and turned to writing. At first he wrote science fiction but later produced a number of books such as *The Feelies*, *Watch Out Kids*, and *The Tale Of Willy's Rats*. He also started the underground comic *Nasty Tales*, edited *IT*, contributed to the **New Musical Express**, organized the Phun City Festival and still found time to collect toy robots.

Farren re-entered the music world around 1976/7 when he began writing songs with Lemmy from **Motörhead**. He also recorded some tracks, including a reworking of the Deviants' anthem 'Let's Loot The Supermarket', which was released as an EP on **Stiff Records**. In 1977 he recorded a version of 'To Know Him Is To Love Him' for the **Phil Spector** tribute album *Bionic Gold*, before he eventually recorded his second solo album in 1978. *Vampires Stole My Lunch Money* featured contributions from **Wilko Johnson**, Andy Colquhoun, **Sonja Kristina**, Chrissie Hynde, **Larry Wallis** and others. To promote the album Farren assembled the Good Guys with Colquhoun and Wallis on guitars, Will Stallybrass on harmonica, Gary Tibbs on bass and Alan Powell on drums. Colquhoun and Powell were both from **Tanz Der Youth**, while Tibbs had just left the **Vibrators**.

Farren later married Betsy Volck of Ze Records and moved to New York where he released a single on Ork and inaugurated the first of many Deviants reunions. He continues to write, publishing his entertaining memoir *Give The Anarchist A Cigarette* in 2001.

● ALBUMS: *Mono The Carnivorous Circus* (Transatlantic 1970) ★★★, *Vampires Stole My Lunch Money* (Logo 1978) ★★★, *Deathray Tapes* spoken word (Alive 1995) ★★.
● COMPILATIONS: with The Deviants *Black Tracks Of Mick Farren & The Deviants 1967–96* (Total Energy 2000) ★★★, with The Deviants *On Your Knees Earthlings!!!* (Total Energy 2001) ★★★, *People Call You Crazy: The Story Of Mick Farren* (Castle 2003) ★★★.
● FURTHER READING: *The Quest Of The DNA Cowboys*, Mick Farren. *Synaptic Manhunt*, Mick Farren. *The Neural Atrocity*, Mick Farren. *Give The Anarchist A Cigarette*, Mick Farren.

Farris, Dionne

b. 1969, Bordentown, New Jersey, USA. Dionne Farris took a brave decision in 1994 to leave Grammy Award–winners **Arrested Development**, where she was an 'extended family member', choosing instead to set out on a solo trail with an album that spanned funk, rock, soul and jazz. Her first single, 'I Know', charted strongly in both the Hot 100 and Adult Contemporary **Billboard** charts. The only problem was that certain R&B stations and magazines did not respond to the presence of guitars in her work, while rock outlets thought her too 'pop'. Nevertheless, the album ended up in many critics' picks of 1994, while her marketing problems were addressed the following year by touring both alternative and urban R&B clubs on alternate nights. An appearance on the television programme *Saturday Night Live* preceded the May release of 'Don't Ever Touch Me (Again)'. Her debut album was an assured collection of highly charged songs, played with her group of musicians who include the highly original guitarist/musical arranger David Harris. The varied content underlines Farris' influences—she cites **James Taylor**, **Nancy Wilson** and **Chaka Khan**—hence the disparate yet cohesive content. From the **Beatles**' 'Blackbird' to her own gutsy 'Passion', complete with heavy metal guitar, Farris is an exciting prospect.

● ALBUMS: *Wild Seed—Wild Flower* (Columbia 1994) ★★★★.

Faryar, Cyrus

b. Teheran, Iran. Faryar left his home country in 1939 and, having spent several years domiciled in England, subsequently settled in Hawaii, Here he ran Honolulu's Greensleeves coffeehouse prior to becoming a founder member of folk act the **Whiskeyhill Singers**. Faryar later formed the Lexington Trio which, with the addition of **Jerry Yester**, evolved in the **Modern Folk Quartet**. This influential act was dissolved in 1966, following which Faryar guested on several albums, notably by the **Stone Poneys** and **'Mama' Cass Elliot**. He narrated *The Zodiac Cosmic Sounds*, a popular astrologically inspired collection issued by **Elektra Records** in 1967, and the same label was responsible for Faryar's solo albums. These adeptly blended folk and singer-songwriter styles, while the artist's sonorous voice, redolent of **Fred Neil**, added depth to already captivating compositions. He then retired from active performing and returned to Hawaii. However, he resumed his musical career in 1987 upon joining the reformed MFQ.

● ALBUMS: *Cyrus* (Elektra 1972) ★★★, *Islands* (Elektra 1973) ★★★.

Fascinación, Grupo

This exciting young New York salsa band of the 80s was characterized by good musicianship, enthusiastic attack and some great arrangements. Their 10-piece line-up comprised of vocals (lead and chorus), rhythm section and a frontline of three trumpets and baritone saxophone (with some doubling on flügelhorn and flute). They recorded only three albums between 1983 and 1986—all on Ralph Cartagena's Rico Records. The band's lead singer for four years was New York–born Johnny Rivera. His parents came from Ciales, Puerto Rico, and he is the nephew of the prominent salsa vocalist **Adalberto Santiago**, who encouraged him to pursue a musical career. Rivera worked previously with Los Rodríguez. After Fascinación's final release *Salsa Vice*, on which he shared lead vocals with Alfredo 'Tito' González, he left the band to join **Conjunto Clásico**. Following two albums with Clásico, Johnny signed with Ralph Mercado's RMM, label and made his solo debut with the successful *Y Ahora De Verdad* in 1990. In 1991 he appeared at the second part of the New York Salsa Festival. Playing bongo and cowbell with Fascinación on their debut, *Fascinating Sounds*, was Richie Bastar, the son of Puerto Rican percussionist/band leader **Kako**. He was replaced by Sammy 'Timbalón' Pagán on the 1985 follow-up *Tiburón*. Experienced accompanist Eddie Montalvo took over on conga on 1986's *Salsa Vice*.

In addition to playing baritone saxophone, founder member Vincent Vélez Jnr. wrote arrangements for Fascinación. Pianist Roberto Navarro worked previously as the musical director of the band Guarare on *Onda Típica* in 1981. Navarro teamed up with José 'Kokie' Colón, a composer and guitarist who possessed another vital ingredient: money. They organized the band Típica '88, which included Tito González, Eddie Montalvo, Sammy Pagán and three other members of Fascinación's personnel, for *En La Feria De La "Salsa"* in 1988. Colón wrote all the songs, and Navarro handled arranging, production, musical direction and keyboard chores. The outcome was an excellent album. Trombonist Joe de Jesús, who studied at the City College of New York with Navarro, was hired for the recording session, which he later described as 'swinging'. De Jesus' track record includes stints and/or sessions with **Rafael Cortijo** and Kako, **Ray Barretto**, Guarare, **Tito Puente**, Celia Cruz, Adalberto Santiago, Hansel And Raúl, Los Vecinos, **Camilo Azuquita** and **David Byrne**. Apart from Navarro, the only former Fascinación members remaining with Típica '88 on their 1989 lacklustre follow-up *It Feels So Good!* were Montalvo and trumpeter Lionel Román.

● ALBUMS: *Fascinating Sounds* (1983) ★★★★, *Tiburón* (1985) ★★★, *Salsa Vice* (1986) ★★★.

Fascinations

Formed in 1960 in Detroit, Michigan, USA, the Fascinations were a female vocal quartet who were produced by **Curtis Mayfield**. The group was originally called the Sabre-ettes and included lead singer Shirley Walker and **Martha Reeves** (b. 18 July 1941, Alabama, USA), who went on to lead **Martha And The Vandellas**. After several personnel changes, the group comprised Walker, new lead vocalist Bernadine Boswell Smith, her sister Joanne Boswell Levell and Fern Bledsoe. They moved to Chicago and were discovered there by members of the **Impressions**, who brought them to Mayfield's attention. Their first two singles were recorded for the **ABC**-Paramount Records label in 1962–63 and did not sell well. That label dropped them, but Mayfield did not forget the group and in 1966, when he started his own Mayfield label, he signed the Fascinations, eventually releasing five singles by the group. Of those, three made the US R&B charts, with the second of those, 'Girls Are Out To Get You', rising to number 13 (it also made number 92 on the pop chart). When the Fascinations' contract came up for renewal in 1969, Mayfield did not sign them again, and the Fascinations disbanded. In 1971 they reunited for a tour of England but split permanently after that tour.

● COMPILATIONS: *Out To Getcha!* (Sequel 1997) ★★★★.

Fashek, Majek

b. Majekodunmi Fasheke, Lagos, Nigeria. Fashek is one of the increasing number of African artists to be drawn to the music of the Caribbean, specifically reggae, rather than indigenous hybrids such as **fuji**, **juju** or **highlife**. Having grown up in a fervently religious and musical family, he was exposed to the imported sounds of **Bob Marley** at an early age alongside the innovations of local stars such as **Fela Kuti**. After learning to play the guitar he made his first notable appearance on a television show in the early 80s before spending the rest of the decade touring Nigeria with the **Mandators**. He left that group in 1987 and quickly fashioned a solo career that made him Nigeria's biggest reggae star. Following the receipt of no less than six awards at the annual PMAN ceremony, he was signed to CBS Nigeria in 1988. However, soon afterwards he transferred to **Island Records**' subsidiary Mango a label more accustomed to marketing reggae internationally. His first album for the company included a cover version of Marley's 'Redemption Song'. It saw him begin to rival **Alpha Blondy** as Africa's foremost reggae star.

● ALBUMS: *I & I Experience* (CBS Nigeria 1989) ★★★, *Prisoner Of Conscience* (Mango 1990) ★★★★.

Fashion

This band from Birmingham, England, blended offbeat funk with an independent spirit that seemed destined to ensure them commercial success. Originally a trio comprising John Mulligan (bass), Dix (drums) and Luke (guitar), Fashion issued three diverse singles on their own label, spurred on by the do-it-yourself attitudes in the wake of punk. After November 1978's 'Steady Eddie Steady' came 'Citinite' in June and then *Perfect Product*, an impressive debut album. 'Silver Blades' followed in March 1980, ensuring a contract with **Arista Records**. Now swelled to a six-piece with Martin Stoker (ex-Dance; **Bureau**) on drums, vocalist Tony (ex–Neon Hearts) and main songwriter De Harriss, many predicted that their resultant singles would break the band on the back of the futurist scene of the early 80s. 'Street Player—Mechanik' in March 1982, 'Love Shadow' in August and later 'Eye Talk' in January 1984 all scraped the lower reaches of the chart but failed to establish the band in the public eye. Despite this, Fashion enjoyed a strong undercurrent of support, reflected in a UK Top 10 album, *Fabrique*, in June 1982. However, interest gradually waned, the band moved to Epic, and *Twilight Of The Idols*, issued exactly two years later, was not as warmly received, despite two singles, 'Dreaming' in April 1984 and 'You In The Night' in June.

● ALBUMS: *Perfect Product* (Fashion 1979) ★★★, *Fabrique* (Arista 1982) ★★★, *Twilight Of The Idols* (Epic 1984) ★★.

● COMPILATIONS: *The Height Of Fashion* (Arista 1990) ★★.

Fashion Records

Founded in the summer of 1980, Fashion Records has been a rare success among UK-based reggae labels and, alongside rival **Ariwa**, remains the only studio-owning, domestic-producing company to have survived since the early 80s. The label is the brainchild of John MacGillivray and Chris Lane, two reggae devotees, and is essentially a spin-off from MacGillivray's Dub Vendor record store. The first Fashion release reached number 1 in the UK reggae charts in 1980— **Dee Sharp**'s 'Let's Dub It Up', with south London **lovers rock** band the **Investigators** supplying the rhythms (Lane had previously produced a couple of singles for the band as the Private I's). 'Let's Dub It Up' provided a benchmark in British reggae and set a standard that Fashion, incredibly, nearly always fulfilled: fine, classy harmonies, punchy rhythms, bright arrangements and, above all else, strong songs. In the next few years a veritable who's who of British reggae and those passing through from Jamaica appeared on the label: **Keith Douglas**, Carlton Manning (of **Carlton And His Shoes**), **Alton Ellis** and Carlton Lewis among many others. In 1982 Fashion opened a four-track studio, A-Class, in the basement of the new Dub Vendor shop at Clapham Junction. By this time, the **UK MC** explosion had begun, and Fashion were at the centre of it with chatters Papa Face, **Laurel And Hardy**, **Pato Banton**, Bionic Rhona, **Macka B** and Asher Senator. A dub-cutting service saw Paul Robinson of One Blood and **Maxi Priest**'s Caution band (Lane was also a member, as was Priest himself) as regulars at the tiny subterranean studio. Robinson soon enjoyed hits with the label as Barry Boom, and the company was rarely out of the specialist charts. Chirpy, fast-talking MC **Smiley Culture** had one of the biggest reggae hits of 1984 on the label with 'Cockney Translation' but bettered it when 'Police Officer'

went top 12 in the national charts, as several Fashion band regulars frightened Britain on *Top Of The Pops*. Their connection with the UK MC boom made the step into **ragga** in the mid-80s a comparatively natural one. Meanwhile, Fashion was also cutting lovers rock hits through **Michael Gordon** and the underrated **Nerious Joseph**, often coming out on another label, Fine Style. Two female acts were also recruited, Winsome and Shako Lee (aka **Janet Lee Davis**). Winsome's 'Am I The Same Girl', 'Born Free' and 'Super Woman' (with **Tippa Irie**) proved themselves classics of their type. Fashion also began to work with a variety of Jamaican acts, including **Junior Delgado**, **Joseph Cotton** ('No Touch The Style'), Leroy Gibbon, **Frankie Paul**, **Glen Brown** and **Augustus Pablo**.

In 1988 the label opened the new A-Class Studio, a sixteen-track set-up in Forest Hill, and began to use tracks laid at Penthouse Studios in Jamaica, voicing and mixing them in London. In 1989/90 the label produced a string of reggae chart hits, with Shako Lee's 'Two Timing Lover' and **Cutty Ranks**' 'The Stopper' both hitting number 1. Fashion also became involved in distribution of other labels, such as **Mafia And Fluxy**'s M&F, Paul Robinson's Merger, **Captain Sinbad**'s Sinbad and Gussie Prento's Gussie P. The label now stands virtually alone in British reggae as an entity capable of working with almost all of the modern strands of the music. A long-awaited second pop chart success, **Louchie Lou And Michie One**'s inspired ragga cover version of the Isley's 'Shout', licensed to **ffrr**, and the rise of **General Levy**, also leased to ffrr Records and perhaps the most accomplished UK ragga rapper yet, should ensure that the label's future remains secure into the next century.

● COMPILATIONS: various artists *Great British MCs* (Fashion 1985) ★★★, *JA To UK MC Clash Volume 2— Papa San Meets Tippa Irie* (Fashion 1988) ★★★★, *Fashion Revives Classic Lovers* (Fashion 1989) ★★★, *Fashion Revives Classic Lovers Volume 2* (Fashion 1988) ★★, *Jamaica's Finest Volume 1* (Fashion 1990) ★★★★, *Funky Punany* (Fashion 1990) ★★★.

Fast Forward

This one-off side project from former UK Stories vocalist Ian Lloyd came to fruition in 1984. With the help of producer Bruce Fairbairn (of **Loverboy** and **Bon Jovi** fame) and a series of highly regarded session musicians, the end result was *Living In Fiction*, a highly polished melodic rock album, featuring razor-sharp harmonies, swathes of keyboards and an infectious pop sensibility. Guest appearances included Mick Jones and **Lou Gramm** from **Foreigner** and Beau Hill (**Ratt** producer) on keyboards. Songwriting contributions from **Bryan Adams** and Jim Vallance added further interest to the project, yet, surprisingly, it was a commercial flop. As a result, plans to record a second album were abandoned.

● ALBUMS: *Living In Fiction* (Island 1984) ★★★★.

Fastball

Based in Austin, Texas, USA, alternative rock trio Fastball comprises Miles Zuniga (b. 10 September 1966; vocals/guitar), Tony Scalzo (b. 6 May 1964; vocals/bass) and Joey Shuffield (drums). Previously Shuffield and Zuniga had been members of pop/rock band Big Car, who released one album, *Normal*, for Giant Records in 1992. However, that band disintegrated owing to record company problems, and the duo began playing with Scalzo through their mutual membership of Austin singer-songwriter Beaver Nelson's backing band. The trio originally adopted the name Magneto U.S.A., before changing their title to Fastball. A series of local gigs brought rave reviews in *The Austin Chronicle*, leading to Fastball dead-heating for the best pop band category at the 1995/6 Austin Music Awards. Enlisting the services of joint-manager Russell Carter (also in charge of **Matthew Sweet** and the **Indigo Girls**), they then signed a contract with Hollywood Records for the release of their debut album.

Make Your Mama Proud was produced by Jerry Finn, who had previously worked with **Rancid** and **Green Day**, and faithfully recreated a stage show that matched energy with melodicism. In particular, the dual singing and writing roles of Zuniga and Scalzo drew initial comparisons with **Fugazi**, though in truth Fastball are a much more commercially orientated proposition. This was reinforced with 1998's exceptional *All The Pain Money Can Buy*. They had perfected the art of the snappy pop song, with every track bouncing along. Success came with 'The Way', a hypnotic track that created further interest when they reached the top of the alternative singles chart in the USA. The song also charted at number 21 in the UK in September 1998. *The Harsh Light Of Day* was another punchy album containing the best elements of Fastball, their chunky **Cars**-like guitar work and often glorious harmonies. It was some surprise when the album fell off the US chart after only three weeks in October 2000, as both 'This Is Not My Life' and 'You're An Ocean' were as good as anything they had previously recorded. The fickle world of pop rears its ugly head once more.

● ALBUMS: *Make Your Mama Proud* (Hollywood 1996) ★★★, *All The Pain Money Can Buy* (Hollywood 1998) ★★★★, *The Harsh Light Of Day* (Hollywood 2000) ★★★, *Keep Your Wig On* (Rykodisc 2004) ★★★.
● COMPILATIONS: *Painting The Corners: The Best Of Fastball* (Hollywood 2002) ★★★★.

Faster Pussycat

The mid-80s Los Angeles glam/sleaze scene that produced **Guns N'Roses** also saw the formation of Faster Pussycat in 1986 around vocalist Taime Downe and guitarist Mick Cripps—although Cripps later departed for **L.A. Guns** along with original bass player Kelly Nickels. Downe, formerly co-owner of the LA club The Cathouse, recruited guitarists Brent Muscat and Greg Steele, bass player Eric Stacy and drummer Mark Michals, and with their name deriving from Russ Meyer's movie *Faster, Pussycat! Kill! Kill!*, the band signed to **Elektra Records** in December 1986. *Faster Pussycat* was recorded on a low budget with **Poison** producer Ric Browde, and was an infectious collection of **Aerosmith/Rolling Stones**-influenced numbers, with the band's sense of humour shining through in 'Bathroom Wall', 'Don't Change That Song' and 'Babylon'. A UK tour with Guns N'Roses and US dates with **Alice Cooper**, **David Lee Roth** and **Motörhead** helped to build respectable album sales, and the band had matured considerably by the time they recorded *Wake Me When It's Over* with John Jansen. This buried the glam image under a heavier sound and greater lyrical depth, with 'Pulling Weeds' addressing the abortion issue, while the emotive 'House Of Pain' examined the trauma of divorce through a child's eyes. The humour still permeated through, however, on 'Slip Of The Tongue' and 'Where There's A Whip There's A Way'. Michals left in disgrace, jailed on drugs charges, on the eve of a European tour with the **Almighty** and **Dangerous**

Toys, and Frankie Banali filled in before Brett Bradshaw assumed the role as drummer for further US touring with **Kiss** and **Mötley Crüe**. *Whipped* showed further progression and a different approach but emerged into a much-changed musical climate. Despite the quality of the album, Faster Pussycat fell victim to a combination of the recession and the success of the Seattle, bands—ironically, Downe was a Seattle native—with Elektra dropping them while they toured America with Kiss. The band split shortly thereafter. Taime Downe was later seen working with Pigface.

● ALBUMS: *Faster Pussycat* (Elektra 1987) ★★★, *Wake Me When It's Over* (Elektra 1989) ★★★, *Whipped* (Elektra 1991) ★★★.

Fastest Guitar Alive, The

Roy Orbison remains one of pop's consummate voices; time has not diminished the emotional punch of his best recordings. He was not, however, conventionally photogenic, and the singer was one of the few successful chart acts of his era not courted by Hollywood. However, having secured a new recording contract with **MGM Records**, in 1966 Orbison sought to rectify that fact. *The Fastest Guitar Alive* was his sole entry into pop cinema and it was not an auspicious success. The film, set in the American Civil War, cast the singer as a Confederate agent, plotting to rob a Union mint. **Sam The Sham**, who with his group the Pharaohs created the immortal 'Wooly Bully', costarred alongside Orbison in a feature in which the star never looked comfortable. Eight songs were included on the soundtrack, none of which were particularly memorable. The same was true of this unconvincing film.

Fastway

After quitting **Motörhead** in May 1982, guitarist **'Fast' Eddie Clarke** (b. 5 October 1950, Isleworth, Middlesex, England) went into partnership with bass player Pete Way (b. 7 August 1951, Enfield, London, England) from **UFO**, drummer Jerry Shirley from **Humble Pie** and previously unknown vocalist Dave King. Way left soon afterwards to form **Waysted** and was replaced by Charlie McCracken. Within a year they had formulated a style far removed from Motörhead and soon drew comparisons to **Deep Purple** and **Led Zeppelin**, yet they won few fans despite a strong debut album and a minor hit single with 'Easy Living'. Finding a degree of fame in America boosted their confidence, and they recorded a second album with producer Eddie Kramer. Again, this was a good collection, but it remained largely ignored in Europe and unfortunately suffered a similar fate in America, prompting Shirley and McCracken to quit. After a new line-up and a third album, minor success came with the soundtrack to the rock/horror film *Trick Or Treat*, which kept them in the American charts for 11 months. However, they failed to capitalize on this opportunity. Clarke returned to the UK in 1988 and rebuilt the band with Paul Gray (bass, ex–**Eddie And The Hot Rods**; **Damned**; UFO), Steve Clarke (drums) and former **Joan Jett** lyricist Lea Hart on vocals and guitar. *On Target* failed to capture public interest, and Clarke and Hart formed a new line-up with American bass player K.B. Bren and a drummer known as Riff Raff. With the addition of members of **Girlschool**, this line-up recorded *Bad Bad Girls*, which was their last album. Once more the legacy of Motörhead overshadowed Clarke's involvement in Fastway—the failure of the press to view the band as a separate entity was always the rock on which Fastway ran aground and finally floundered. Clarke subsequently launched a solo career under his own name.

● ALBUMS: *Fastway* (Columbia 1983) ★★★, *All Fired Up* (Columbia 1984) ★★★, *Waiting For The Roar* (Columbia 1986) ★★★, *Trick Or Treat* film soundtrack (Columbia 1986) ★★★★, *On Target* (GWR 1988) ★★, *Bad Bad Girls* (Legacy 1990) ★★.

● COMPILATIONS: *The Collection* (Connoisseur 2000) ★★★.

Fat Boys

From the Bronx, New York City, USA, the Fat Boys were originally known as the Disco 3 before deciding to trade in the appellation in exchange for something more gimmicky. The bulk of their material dealt with just that, emphasising their size, and did little to avert the widely held perception of them as a novelty act. The trio consisted of Darren 'The Human Beatbox/Buff Love' Robinson (b. 1968, New York, USA, d. 10 December 1995), Mark 'Prince Markie Dee' Morales and Damon 'Kool Rockski' Wimbley. They were discovered by Charlie Stetler (later manager of **MTV**'s Dr. Dre and Ed Lover), whose interest was aroused by Robinson's amazing talent for rhythmic improvisation, effectively using his face as an instrument. It was Stetler who suggested they take the name change after winning a nationwide talent contest at Radio City Music Hall in 1983. Legend has it that this was prompted during an early European tour when Stetler was presented with a bill of $350 for 'extra breakfasts'.

The initial run of records were produced by **Kurtis Blow** and largely discussed the size of the group's appetites. All their LPs for Sutra offered a consistent diet (a phrase not otherwise within the Fat Boy lexicon) of rock, reggae and hip-hop textures, with able if uninspiring raps. Their fortunes improved significantly once they signed up with **Polydor Records**, however. *Crushin'* is probably their best album, crammed with party anecdotes that stand up to repeated listening better than most of their material. It yielded a major hit with the **Beach Boys** on 'Wipeout' in 1987. One year and one album later they scored with another collaboration, this time with **Chubby Checker** on 'The Twist (Yo' Twist)'. It peaked at number 2 in the UK chart, the highest position at the time for a rap record. In truth the Fat Boys had become more pop than hip-hop, though the process of revamping rock 'n' roll favourites had begun as far back as 1984 with 'Jailhouse Rock'. Also contained on *Coming Back Hard Again* was a strange version of 'Louie Louie' and 'Are You Ready For Freddy', used as the theme song for one of the *Nightmare On Elm Street* films. They also starred in another movie, *Disorderlies*, after appearing with Checker as part of Nelson Mandela's 70th Birthday Party at Wembley Stadium in June 1988 (they had previously been the only rap participants at **Live Aid**).

The decade closed with the release of *On And On*. It proved a hugely disappointing set, overshadowed by its 'concept' of being a 'rappera' and offering a lukewarm adaptation of gangsta concerns. News broke in the 90s of a $6 million lawsuit filed against their former record company, while Robinson was put on trial in Pennsylvania for 'sexual abuse of a minor'. Prince Markie Dee went on to a solo career, recording an album as Prince Markie Dee And The Soul Convention. He also produced and wrote for **Mary J. Blige**,

Christopher Williams, **Father**, **El DeBarge**, Trey Lorenz and others. Their career never recovered from the bad press after Robinson was found guilty, and the Fat Boys' true legacy remains firmly in the era of rap party records, Swatch television ads and cameo appearances on television's *Miami Vice*. Robinson died in 1995 after a cardiac arrest following a bout of respiratory flu.

● ALBUMS: *Fat Boys* (Sutra 1984) ★★★, *The Fat Boys Are Back!* (Sutra 1985) ★★★, *Big & Beautiful* (Sutra 1986) ★★★, *Cruisin'* (Tin Pan Apple/Polydor 1987) ★★★★, *Coming Back Hard Again* (Tin Pan Apple/Polydor 1988) ★★★, *On And On* (Tin Pan Apple/Mercury 1989) ★★. Solo: Prince Markie Dee *Free* (Columbia 1992) ★★.

● COMPILATIONS: *The Best Part Of The Fat Boys* (Sutra 1987) ★★★, *Krush On You* (Blatant 1988) ★★, *All Meat No Filler!* (Rhino 1997) ★★★.

Fat City

Fat City formed in Washington, DC, USA, and included in their line-up the husband-and-wife team Bill Danoff (b. 7 May 1946, Springfield, Massachusetts, USA; guitar/vocals) and Taffy Danoff (b. Kathleen Nivert, 25 October 1944, Washington, DC, USA; vocals) plus Jim Parker (guitar/ vocals). With their cheerful, summery vocals they released two albums, enlisting as guest musicians such notable artists as **Bob James**, Eric Weissberg, Artie Traum and **Hubert Laws**. After failing to achieve the predicted success, Fat City's ultimate demise led to the Danoffs forming a duo as Bill And Taffy which, in turn, led to the **Starland Vocal Band** and national fame. After the demise of Starland, the duo resurrected Fat City, and despite their marital split, they were still to be found performing together in the Washington, DC, area during later decades.

● ALBUMS: *Reincarnation* (ABC 1969) ★★★, *Welcome To Fat City* (Paramount 1971) ★★★, as Bill And Taffy *Pass It On* (RCA 1973) ★★, as Bill And Taffy *Aces* (RCA 1974) ★★. Solo: Bill Danoff *Souvenir* (Watch Your Head 1989) ★★★, *I Guess He'd Rather Be In Colorado* (Watch Your Head 2002) ★★★.

Fat Fantango

This short-lived act, based in San Francisco, USA, revolved around drummer/vocalist Joey Covington. His recording career began in the mid-60s with a version of the **Who**'s 'Boris The Spider', after which he formed the obscure Tsong before joining **Hot Tuna** in 1969. In 1970 Covington replaced Spencer Dryden in **Jefferson Airplane**, but he left to join Black Kangaroo in 1971. The drummer did not completely sever his relationship with Jefferson Airplane, as he recorded *Fat Fantango* for their Grunt label in 1973. Stevie Mack (guitar), Patrick Craig (keyboards)—both ex–Indian Pudding And Pipe—and Jack Prendergast accompanied him on this idiosyncratic set, which, like many of Grunt's releases, was not a commercial success. Covington subsequently retreated into session work, while Mack and Craig formed Natural Gas.

● ALBUMS: *Fat Fandango* (Grunt 1973) ★★.

Fat Joe

b. Joseph Cartagena, 19 August 1972, Bronx, New York City, USA. As a youth coming of age in the harsh atmosphere of the South Bronx, Joey Cartagena was profoundly affected by the tapes of **Zulu Nation** hip-hop parties brought home by his older brother Angel. Shortly thereafter he was making his own local reputation as a graffiti artist (he still maintains strong ties with Bronx-based TATS crew) under the *nom de guerre* of Joey Crack, and as the nickname implies, he also made a reputation in the narcotics trade. He eventually parlayed these multiple sources of street credibility into a record contract with **Relativity Records**, releasing his debut *Represent* under the new-found persona of Fat Joe Da Gangsta, and promptly scored a *Billboard* number 1 rap single in 'Flow Joe'. The debut's combination of ruthless realism and sterling production, furnished mostly by fellow Bronx residents the **D.I.T.C.** crew, garnered considerable attention and numerous fans, although a certain inconsistency of lyrical content engendered rumours that Joe was not always writing his own rhymes.

The 1995 follow-up *Jealous One's Envy* addressed these criticisms in no uncertain terms while largely maintaining the winning formula, a hustler's-eye view of reality backed by unassailable hardcore production (provided by **DJ Premier** among others). This period found Joe building alliances and broadening his appeal somewhat, appearing with **LL Cool J** on 'I Shot Ya' and with **Raekwon** on 'Firewater'. Similar power-moves resulted in the formation of his own Mystic imprint and a distribution-deal with Big Beat/**Atlantic Records** for the 1998 release of *Don Cartagena*. Although this latest incarnation of Fat Joe hardly abandoned the gangsta image, it did mark an increase in social consciousness purportedly inspired by a meeting with Nation Of Islam leader Louis Farrakhan, whose influence can be heard in the twin strains of cultural nationalism and conspiracy theory running through 'The Hidden Hand'.

Living up to the mantle of 'don' assumed with that record, Joe began grooming a right hand man of comparable stature (**Big Punisher**) and placed himself at the helm of a group of younger artists (the **Terror Squad**). Both acts reached the upper tiers of the US charts with their respective debuts. Fat Joe's commercial renaissance continued in 2001 with the highly successful *Jealous Ones Still Envy*. The following year he enjoyed a US number 2 hit single, collaborating with **Ashanti** on 'What's Luv?'. The solo albums *Loyalty* (2002) and *All Or Nothing* (2005) deviated little from the rapper's established formula.

● ALBUMS: as Fat Joe Da Gangsta *Represent* (Relativity 1993) ★★★★, *Jealous One's Envy* (Relativity 1995) ★★★, *Don Cartagena* (Big Beat/Atlantic 1998) ★★★, *Jealous Ones Still Envy* (Atlantic 2001) ★★★, *Loyalty* (Atlantic 2002) ★★★, *All Or Nothing* (Atlantic 2005) ★★★.

Fat Larry's Band

'Fat' Larry James (b. 2 August 1949, Philadelphia, Pennsylvania, USA, d. 5 December 1987; drums) formed this funk/disco outfit in Philadelphia following his spell as a backup musician for the **Delfonics** and **Blue Magic**. The group comprised Art Capehart (trumpet/flute), Jimmy Lee (trombone/saxophone), Doug Jones (saxophone), Erskine Williams (keyboards), Ted Cohen (guitar), Larry LaBes (bass) and Darryl Grant (percussion). James found success easier in the UK than in his homeland, having a Top 40 hit with 'Center City' in 1977 and in 1979 achieving a Top 50 with 'Boogie Town' under the title of FLB. That same year, one of James' other projects, the studio group Slick, had two UK hit singles with 'Space Bass' and 'Sexy Cream'. These two releases established them with the disco market. However, it was not until 1982 that the group secured a major national

hit, with a recording of the **Commodores**' song 'Zoom' taking them to number 2 in the UK charts, although it only managed to scrape into the US soul chart at 89. It proved, however, to be their last success of any note, and hope of a regeneration was cut short on their founder's death in 1987.

● ALBUMS: *Feel It* (WMOT 1977) ★★★, *Off The Wall* (Stax 1978) ★★★, *Lookin' For Love* (Fantasy 1979) ★★, *Stand Up* (Fantasy 1980) ★★, *Breakin' Out* (WMOT 1982) ★★★, *Straight From The Heart* (WMOT 1983) ★★, *Nice* (Omni 1986) ★★.

● COMPILATIONS: *Bright City Lights* (Fantasy 1980) ★★, *The Best Of Fat Larry's Band* (WMOT 1994) ★★★, *Close Encounters Of A Funky Kind* (Southbound/Ace 1995) ★★★.

Fat Mattress

Formed in 1969 by Noel Redding (b. David Redding, 25 December 1945, Folkestone, Kent, England, d. 11 May 2003, Clonakilty, Ireland), the disaffected bass player from the **Jimi Hendrix** Experience. A frustrated guitarist and songwriter, Redding established this outfit to run concurrently as an outlet for his talents. He was joined by ex-Cheetahs vocalist Neil Landon, a previous colleague from beat group the Loving Kind and latterly a member of the **Flowerpot Men**, and two long-standing friends, ex-Big Beats, Jim Leverton (keyboards/bass) and Eric Dillon (drums). Fat Mattress secured a large advance, but although their debut was an enjoyable, melodic set, in the English pop vein of the **Move** and **Small Faces**, it lacked a sense of identity. The quartet made its live debut in February 1969, but prestigious slots on Hendrix tours failed to generate public interest. Three singles were released, of which 'Naturally' was the strongest, but failed to sell in sufficient quantity. The final ignominy came when Redding was fired by the rest of the band and replaced by guitarist Steve Hammond and **Mick Weaver**. This reshaped line-up completed *Fat Mattress II* before breaking up. Redding continued gigging in low-profile bands from his base in Ireland until his untimely death in 2003.

● ALBUMS: *Fat Mattress* (Polydor 1969) ★★★, *Fat Mattress II* (Polydor 1970) ★★.

● COMPILATIONS: *The Black Sheep Of The Family: The Anthology* (Essential 2000) ★★★.

Fat Truckers

This Sheffield, England–based synth-rock trio comprises Ben Rymer (b. Hunters Bar, Sheffield, England), Mark Hudson (b. Doncaster, England; vocals) and Ross Orton (b. Southey Green, Sheffield, England) and was apparently conceived after initial attempts at making **dance music** ended in disaster. Rather, the trio create rock paeans to superbikes, anorexic robots and the joys of home computers. The debut 7-inch, 'Teenage Daughter', meanwhile, simply repeated the track title over dirty electronic riffs. On the basis of their early singles, the trio was notably invited to remix **Pulp**'s 'Sunrise' by Jarvis Cocker and were subsequently adopted as tour support. The band apparently appeared onstage wielding light sabres and generally not taking things seriously, a trait the trio claim they developed in response to the grimness of life in their home-town. The Fat Truckers have appeared on City Rockers' *Futurism* collection Sonic Mook's *Future Rock & Roll Volumes 1 + 2* compilations and International Deejay Gigolo's *Gigolo Vol. 6*. After releasing *The First Fat Truckers Album Is For Sale* via their Roadtrain

Recordings in 2003, the band began working on a follow-up for International Deejay Gigolo. Orton also records as Supafix (with Winston Hazel), releasing music via Earth Records, the label run by DJ Parrot from the **All Seeing I**.

● ALBUMS: *The First Fat Truckers Album Is For Sale* (Roadtrain Recordings/International Deejay Gigolo 2003) ★★★.

Fatback Band

There are many, including genuine authorities such as **Afrika Bambaataa**, who state that 'King Tim III (Personality Jock)' by Fatback, released on Spring Records in 1979, is the first true hip-hop record. 'King Tim' was actually the b-side to 'You're My Candy Sweet', before radio programmers and listeners made it the more popular selection. The rap was delivered by the band's master of ceremonies/warm-up act, King Tim III. After appearing solo on 'Charley Says! (Roller Boogie Baby)', backed by Fatback, he would disappear into the mists of hip-hop mythology. Archivists may like to note that 'King Tim III' is included on the Fatback XII album. Elsewhere, Fatback remained a predominantly R&B-based funk band. They were originally formed by Johnny King (guitar), Earl Shelton (saxophone), George Williams (trumpet), George Adam (flute), Johnny Flippin (bass) and Bill Curtis (drums). Later members included Saunders McCrae (keyboards) and Richard Cromwell (trombone).

● ALBUMS: *Raising Hell* (Event 1976) ★★★, *Night Fever* (Spring 1976) ★★★. As Fatback *Fired Up 'N' Kickin'* (Spring 1978) ★★★, *Fatback XII* (Spring 1979) ★★★, *Hot Box* (Spring 1980) ★★★, *14 Karat* (Spring 1980) ★★★, *Tasty Jam* (Spring 1981) ★★★, *Gigolo* (Spring 1982) ★★, *Second Generation* (Ace 2004) ★★★.

● COMPILATIONS: *Fatbackin': The Perception Sessions* (Castle 2000) ★★★, *Fatback Funky* (Ace 2002) ★★★, *Fatback Mellow* (Ace 2002) ★★★, *1972–1974* (BMG 2003) ★★★, *Essential 70s Funk Recordings* (Metro 2003) ★★★, *Hustle! The Ultimate Fatback* (Ace 2004) ★★★.

Fatboy Slim

b. Quentin Cook, 31 July 1963, Bromley, Kent, England. A man of many musical faces, UK DJ Norman Cook's Fatboy Slim is probably his most successful alter ego and one that made **big beat** music (a combination of rock and **dance music** styles) a huge crossover success in the late 90s. Cook began recording in the big beat style at the Big Beat Boutique (from which the movement took its name). Signing to Damian Harris' **Skint Records**, Fatboy Slim's debut single was 'Santa Cruz' and was followed by further hit records including 'Everybody Needs A 303' and the 1996 debut album *Better Living Through Chemistry*. 'Going Out Of My Head', the March 1997 single featuring samples of the **Who**, gained Cook a place in *The Guinness Book Of Records* for achieving the most UK Top 40 hits under different names (seven).

The irresistible 'The Rockafeller Skank' brightened up the UK singles chart the following year, reaching number 6 in June. 'Gangster Tripping' provided Cook with another hit single, reaching number 3 in October and paving the way for *You've Come A Long Way, Baby*. 'Praise You' provided Cook with his first UK number 1 single as Fatboy Slim in January 1999 and in the process dragged the album to the top of the charts. 'Right Here Right Now' was another hit, debuting at number 2 in April. *You've Come A Long Way,*

Baby also enjoyed crossover success in the USA, thanks to the prominent use of several tracks in movies including *She's All That* and *Cruel Intentions* and advertisements for Adidas. The cover of the US edition of the album was also notable, featuring a picture of the overflowing racks of vinyl LPs in Cook's house (the UK cover was equally memorable, but for all the wrong reasons). Cook was honoured with three **MTV** Video Awards in September for his collaboration with director Spike Jonze on the video for 'Praise You' (this lo-fi classic has since become a staple of music channels).

Fatboy Slim's 2000 follow-up album *Halfway Between The Gutter And The Stars* was influenced by both Cook's newly married status and the derision now accorded big beat in dance circles, with thumping big beat numbers such as 'Ya Mama' and 'Mad Flava' offset by the dark house grooves of 'Star 69', 'Retox' and the Jim Morrison–sampling 'Sunset (Bird Of Prey)'. The album trod a fine line in trying to appeal to both Cook's new pop audience and his dance fans, a balancing act the DJ was more or less successful in carrying through. Another brilliant video, directed by Spike Jonze and starring cult movie icon Christopher Walken, was used to promote the album track 'Weapon Of Choice'.

On 6 July 2001 Cook/Fatboy Slim played a gig in front of nearly 40,000 people on the beach in his home-town of Brighton. He repeated the event the following year in front of a crowd of almost 250,000. The concert was marred by two fatalities, however, and Cook was compelled to call off a planned ticket-only repeat in 2004 because of worries over public safety. A new Fatboy Slim single 'Slash Dot Dash' brought the DJ back into the headlines later in the year, when Tim Pope's striking video was banned by popular UK chart show *CD:UK* for fears it may encourage children to graffiti. The attendant *Palookaville* marked a change in direction for Cook, who eschewed the sample-based approach of his earlier work and teamed up with a number of guest musicians and vocalists.

● ALBUMS: *Better Living Through Chemistry* (Skint/Astralwerks 1996) ★★★, *You've Come A Long Way, Baby* (Skint/Astralwerks 1998) ★★★★, *Halfway Between The Gutter And The Stars* (Skint/Astralwerks 2000) ★★★, *Palookaville* (Skint/Astralwerks 2004) ★★★.

● COMPILATIONS: *On The Floor At The Boutique Mixed By Fatboy Slim* (Skint Brassic/Astralwerks 1998) ★★★, shared with Pete Tong, Paul Oakenfold *Essential Millennium* (ffrr 1999) ★★★★, *The Fatboy Slim/Norman Cook Collection* US only (Hip-O 2000) ★★★★, *Live On Brighton Beach* (Southern Fried 2002) ★★★, shared with Midfield General *Big Beach Boutique II* (Southern Fried 2002) ★★★.

● DVD/VIDEOS: *Live On Brighton Beach: Big Beach Boutique II—The Movie* (Southern Fried/Eagle Rock Entertainment 2002).

● FURTHER READING: *Fatboy Slim: Funk Soul Brother*, Martin James.

Fate

Comprising Jeff Limbo (vocals), Hank Shermann (b. Rene Krolmark, Denmark; guitar), Pete Steiner (bass) and Bob Lance (drums), Danish hard rock band Fate formed from the remains of **Mercyful Fate** in the mid-80s. Immediately, the band, ostensibly led by Shermann, moved away from Mercyful Fate's more mythology-based material to a melodic, contemporary metal sound redolent of outfits such as **Survivor**. Despite a major label recording contract with **EMI**

Records, their self-titled debut failed to impress critics. *A Matter Of Attitude*, released in 1987, signalled a refinement of their previous sound, with more upbeat lyrics and melodies akin to **Bon Jovi** or **Van Halen**. *Crusin' For A Brusin'* was a more disciplined conventional hard rock effort but again failed to achieve significant export sales outside of Scandinavia. Shermann rejoined Mercyful Fate in the early 90s.

● ALBUMS: *Fate* (EMI 1986) ★★★, *A Matter Of Attitude* (EMI 1987) ★★★, *Crusin' For A Brusin'* (EMI 1989) ★★★, *Sgt Death* (Rockadelic 1999) ★★★.

Fates Warning

Formed in Hartford, Connecticut, USA, in 1982, initially as Misfit, the original line-up of Fates Warning consisted of John Arch (vocals), Jim Matheos (guitar), Victor Arduini (guitar), Joe DiBiase (bass) and Steve Zimmerman (drums). After a couple of early demos the band was invited to contribute a track ('Soldier Boy') to the *Metal Massacre V* compilation, released on Metal Blade Records in 1984. The label immediately signed the band to a long-term recording agreement and released the debut album entitled *Night On Bröcken* in the same year. The album was very reminiscent of early **Iron Maiden**, both in the compositions and Arch's vocal style. *The Spectre Within* followed in 1985, but shortly after its release guitarist Arduini left the band to be replaced by Frank Aresti. *Awaken The Guardian* showed the band's music to be more progressive and complex than first impressions had suggested. However, vocalist John Arch was unhappy with the musical direction that Fates Warning had begun to pursue and left but was soon replaced by Ray Alder, whose voice was better suited to the material. This was most noticeable on *No Exit*. Released in 1988, it was widely recognized as the band's finest work to date, partially thanks to producer Max Norman, who strove for a clean, **Queensrÿche**-like sound. Soon after its release, Zimmerman left the band to be replaced by Mark Zonder. *Perfect Symmetry* was released in 1989 after the band had completed a couple of rather uneasy European tours. The result was an album that in some places sounded orchestral in its arrangements and featured **Dream Theater** keyboard player Kevin Moore as a guest musician. With the next album, *Parallels*, released in 1991, the band returned to their earlier techno-pomp metal influences. It was well received by the press, who were beginning to acknowledge a band who had a lot to offer and deserved more recognition than had previously been awarded them.

Matheos released a solo album in 1993, following which the band returned with *Inside Out*. By 1996 Aresti and DiBiase had left the band, with seasoned player Joey Vera (ex–**Armored Saint**) taking over on bass guitar. The following year's *A Pleasant Shade Of Grey*, eschewing the more compact style of the previous two releases, was comprised of a single 50-minute track. Alder also records with Bernie Versailles (guitar), Joey Vera (bass) and Pete Parada (drums) as **Engine**.

● ALBUMS: *Night On Bröcken* (Metal Blade 1984) ★★★, *The Spectre Within* (Metal Blade 1985) ★★, *Awaken The Guardian* (Metal Blade 1986) ★★★, *No Exit* (Metal Blade 1988) ★★★★, *Perfect Symmetry* (Metal Blade 1989) ★★, *Parallels* (Metal Blade 1991) ★★★, *Inside Out* (Metal Blade 1994) ★★★, *A Pleasant Shade Of Grey* (Metal Blade 1997) ★★★, *Still Life* (Metal Blade 1998) ★★, *Disconnected* (Metal Blade 2000) ★★★.

Solo: Jim Matheos *First Impressions* (Metal Blade 1993) ★★, *Away With Words* (Metal Blade 1999) ★★.

● COMPILATIONS: *Chasing Time* (Metal Blade 1995) ★★★.

● DVD/VIDEOS: *A Pleasant Shade Of Grey—Live* (Metal Blade 1998).

Fathead

b. Vernon Rainford, Kingston, Jamaica, West Indies. Fathead is particularly remembered for his renowned contribution to the **Yellowman** phenomenon. The fad often referred to as Yellow Fever began in 1980 and culminated in 1982 with a myriad of releases. The popularity of DJ duos such as **Michigan And Smiley** and **Clint Eastwood And General Saint** saw the pairing of Yellowman and Fathead. The duo performed regularly at the Aces discotheque in St. Thomas where they built a solid reputation. Yellowman's words of wisdom were punctuated by Fathead chanting 'ribbit' and 'oink' sounds at the end of each line, which became *en vogue* in the early 80s. In response to the success of pirated 'yard tapes', veteran producer Lloyd Campbell inaugurated the idea of recording a live **dancehall** session for release on vinyl. *Yellowman And Fathead Live At Aces* included performances from Jah Reubal and Little Harry alongside the DJ duo. The compilation featured Fathead both as a soloist and in combination. He was able to demonstrate his potential as an individual performer with 'Gi Me The Music', 'Fathead Sweet' and an interpretation of Yellowman's 'Operation Eradication' as 'Eradication Operation'. The success of the album led to a series of releases that would have previously only been heard on yard tapes. As the Yellowman phenomenon progressed Fathead featured on a number of recordings with a variety of producers, including Ruddy Thomas and **Henry 'Junjo' Lawes**. The early releases of the duo's work gave no indication as to Fathead's appearance. His appellation led to unfounded speculation that his head size was not in proportion with his body. These rumours were soon quashed when photographs revealed him to be a handsome, youthful man. By 1983 the partnership ended amicably, and Fathead enjoyed a minor hit with Lloyd Campbell with 'It's Me'/'Wha Dat'. Though not as prolific as Yellowman, Fathead released the equally popular singles 'Rat Trap', 'Come Me A Come', 'Champion' and 'Stop All The Fight'. The DJ also featured as a soloist on *Junjo Presents Two Big Sound*. Fathead performed alongside Early B, **U. Brown**, **Johnny Ringo**, **Ranking Toyan** and debutant **Beenie Man**. The compilation found Fathead representing both **sound systems**. He followed Beenie Man on Lees Unlimited, while in combination with Little Harry and Early B he closed the set for the Peoples Choice. Fathead is a highly regarded performer although he was unable to emulate the phenomenal success of his DJ partner. Not to be confused with the USA blues band of the same name.

● ALBUMS: *Yellowman And Fathead Live At Aces* (VP 1982) ★★★★, *For Your Eyes Only* (Arrival 1982) ★★★, *Yellowman, Fathead And The One Peter Metro* (Abbissa 1982) ★★★★, *Junjo Presents A Live Session With Aces International* (Greensleeves 1982) ★★★, *The Yellow, The Purple, The Nancy* (Greensleeves 1982) ★★★★, *Junjo Presents Two Big Sound* (Greensleeves 1983) ★★★, *King Sturgav Live* (Live And Love 1983/Rasslin 1998) ★★★.

Father

b. Timothy Brown, New York, USA. Father's debut album included the Top 20 US hit 'I'll Do 4 U' and a powerful scene-setter between Father and Lady Kazan. On his return in 1994 for a belated third album, *Sex Is Law*, he dropped the MC suffix he had previously employed. It tied in with a switch in image too, from lovers rock hip-hop to down and dirty gangsta pimp. Gimmicky raps such as '69' were the order of the day, as Father perved his way through a succession of saucy rhymes. There was a nod to the New Jack Swing movement with tracks produced by **Teddy Riley** and **Pete Rock**, who added an **En Vogue** sample to 'R&B Swinger'. Other samples included the **Jackson 5**'s 'I Want You Back'. The sexual lyrics were given a brief respite on his duet with Little Shawn, 'For The Brothers Who Ain't Here', a touching commemoration of loss in the ghetto.

● ALBUMS: as Father MC *Father's Day* (Uptown 1989) ★★★, *Close To You* (Uptown 1992) ★★★★, as Father *Sex Is Law* (Uptown 1994) ★★.

Father Abraham And The Smurfs

If ever popular music veers too close to being a serious topic of academic cultural discussion, one only has to remember episodes like those of the Smurfs in the late 70s. While the punk wars raged around them, Father Abraham And The Smurfs mounted their chart bid with 'The Smurf Song', released on **Decca Records** in May 1978. Conducted in a semi-duet fashion, with Father Abraham leading the assembled midget characters in call-response chants, delivered in their eminently silly, high-pitched voices, it served to introduce the concept of Smurf culture to the nation. The Smurfs, also depicted in a cartoon series, lived in forests and promoted pre-environmental awareness good while hiding from human beings. Similar to the **Wombles** concept of a few years earlier, Father Abraham And The Smurfs enjoyed two further UK charts hits, 'Dippety Day' (number 13) and 'Christmas In Smurfland' (number 19). This prompted music business maverick **Jonathan King** to release his own cash-in novelty record, 'Lick A Smurp For Christmas (All Fall Down)', credited to Father Abraphart And The Smurfs. There were also a number of albums for the more masochistic fans to buy.

● ALBUMS: *Smurfing Sing Song* (Decca 1979) ★★, *Merry Christmas With The Smurfs* (Dureco 1983) ★, *Smurfs' Party Time* (Dureco 1983) ★.

Fatima Mansions

A category-defying band formed in August 1989 by Cork singer **Cathal Coughlan** (b. Cork, Eire), fresh from his stint with the more restrained **Microdisney**, with the inspiration for the new name coming from a decrepit Dublin housing estate. They were almost immediately ensconced in a London studio by Kitchenware Records to record their debut mini-album. *Against Nature* was released in September 1989 to almost universal critical acclaim and a large degree of astonishment; 'staggering in its weight of ideas . . . never loses its capacity to suddenly stun you', stated the UK's *New Musical Express*. Its abrasive lyrics might have been anticipated given Coughlan's pedigree, but the directness of the musical attack certainly was not. Andrías O'Gruama's guitar contributed richly to the final results, although the Fatima Mansions served primarily as a vehicle for its singer and songwriter (drummer Nick Allum was the only other

mainstay). The debut was followed by 'Blues For Ceaucescu', a fire and brimstone political tirade that held prophetic warnings of East European tragedy. Its operatic tilt enabled it to be at once hysterical, comic and sinister. Coughlan was now established in the press as a delicious antihero and mischief maker.

Bugs Fucking Bunny was dropped as the title of the second album in favour of the comparatively nondescript *Viva Dead Ponies*. This time Coughlan's lyrics were totally submerged in vitriolic observations on the absurdities of living in the UK. The title track, for instance, considered the case of Jesus being reincarnated as a Jewish shopkeeper. A particular vehemence, as ever, was reserved for British imperialism. It prompted *The Guardian* newspaper to describe Coughlan as 'the most underrated lyricist in pop today', while **John Peel** confirmed he could 'listen to Cathal Coughlan sing the phone book'. Further paranoia, bile and doses of his full-bodied vocal were poured in to the mini-album *Bertie's Brochures* in 1991. Notable among its eight tracks was a full-scale assassination of **R.E.M.**'s 'Shiny Happy People'. The title track this time referred to an Irish artist wrongly imprisoned for terrorism, coinciding with highly topical, real-life events. In 1992 Coughlan managed to alienate a Milan audience ostensibly there to see headliners **U2**, by attempting to insert a Virgin Mary shampoo holder into his anus while singing 'fuck the Pope, I want to fuck your traitor Pope'.

The same year's *Valhalla Avenue* drove home its lyrical barbs with a furious hard rock backing, with 'Evil Man' and '1000%' providing particular highlights. After a sojourn in Newcastle, Coughlan returned to the Fatima Mansions format in 1994 with the release of *Lost In The Former West*, an album that identified him as the sort of left-field maverick genius who makes the broad church of pop music infinitely more entertaining than it might otherwise be. The only thing holding him back are the minuscule sales figures that have been his curse since Microdisney days. Coughlan also recorded two self-indulgent albums under the banner of Bubonique (including contributions from Irish comedian Sean Hughes) before embarking on a solo career in 1996.

● ALBUMS: *Against Nature* mini-album (Kitchenware 1989) ★★★, *Viva Dead Ponies* (Kitchenware 1990) ★★★★, *Bertie's Brochures* mini-album (Radioactive/Kitchenware 1991) ★★★, *Valhalla Avenue* (Radioactive/Kitchenware 1992) ★★★★, *Lost In The Former West* (Radioactive 1994) ★★★.

● COMPILATIONS: *Come Back My Children* (Kitchenware 1992) ★★★, *Tíma Mansió Dumps The Dead* (Radioactive 1992) ★★★.

● DVD/VIDEOS: *Y'Knaa* (1994).

Fatool, Nick

b. 2 January 1915, Milbury, Massachusetts, USA, d. 26 September 2000, Los Angeles, California, USA. After starting out with the fine 30s dance band of **Joe Haymes**, drummer Fatool swung through a succession of top-flight big bands, notably those of **Benny Goodman** (appearing on the excellent Sextet sides of the late 30s and early 40s) and **Artie Shaw**, being unusually prominent on the original recording of 'Concerto For Clarinet'. In the early 40s Fatool settled in California, where for the next two decades he worked in the film studios but found time to play his drums in numerous bands, including those led by **Les Brown**, **Billy Butterfield** and

Harry James. He also played and sometimes recorded with **Bob Crosby**, **Louis Armstrong**, **Tommy Dorsey** and many others, gradually moving into the field of latter-day Dixieland jazz, to which he brought a deftly swinging lightness that few of his contemporaries could match. Apart from Crosby, the Dixieland-style bands with whom he has played include those of **Charles LaVere**, **Matty Matlock**, **Pete Fountain**, the **Dukes Of Dixieland**, **Barney Bigard** and the **World's Greatest Jazz Band**. His career continued into the 80s, with tours of the USA and Europe with the **Yank Lawson**–**Bob Haggart** band. One of the unsung heroes of jazz drumming, Fatool's self-effacing style meant that he was often overlooked by audiences accustomed to the somewhat more bombastic playing of many of his contemporaries. Conversely, his subtlety and skill were always appreciated by musicians.

● ALBUMS: *Nick Fatool's Jazz Band* (Jazzology 1982) ★★★.

Fatso Jetson

This Palm Desert, California, USA, trio is a throwback of sorts to the early 80s west coast surf punk scene, with a dash of blues rock and heavy metal thrown in for good measure. Following in the footsteps of renowned local rockers **Kyuss**, Fatso Jetson's early shows took place in the desert at self-described 'generator parties', which took place in a secluded location and were comprised of several bands and lots of beer and were powered by a generator. Comprised of brother duo Mario (guitar/vocals) and Larry Lalli (bass), the band's line-up was completed with the arrival of Tony Tornay (drums) shortly after the Lalli brothers opened one of the desert's very first rock clubs, Rhythm & Brews, in 1994. It did not take long for Fatso Jetson to secure a recording contract, as one of their very first shows was opening for ex–**Black Flag** guitarist/SST Records head Greg Ginn, who promptly signed the trio to his label. Two albums followed on SST, 1995's *Stinky Little Gods* and 1997's *Power Of Three*, before the band's line-up was expanded with the arrival of ex-Kyuss drummer Brant Bjork briefly joining as a second guitarist (apart from shows and two singles, Bjork never appeared on any albums). Newcomer Gary Arce took Bjork's place in the line-up but only lasted for one album, 1999's *Flames For All*. Released a couple of months later by Bong Load Records, *Toasted* was actually recorded in 1998 by the Lalli brothers and Tornay with the help of Kyuss/**Queens Of The Stone Age** producer Chris Goss.

● ALBUMS: *Stinky Little Gods* (SST 1995) ★★★★, *Power Of Three* (SST 1997) ★★★★, *Flames For All* (Man's Ruin 1999) ★★★, *Toasted* (Bong Load 1999) ★★★.

Faultline

This UK act's enigmatic music has background death threats, Dennis Hopper dialogue and cover versions sung by rock stars. Faultline is the recording moniker for electronic DJ David Kosten (b. 1968, London, England), who claims to have turned to samplers and synthesizers after bursting a lung while playing clarinet for the National Youth Orchestra. On his debut album, 1999's *Closer Colder,* Kosten wrenched spectacular results from both this contemporary technology and more antiquated means of music making (strings, xylophone, trumpet). Faultline's debut single, 'Control' (originally released via the Fused & Bruised Records label but also featured on his debut album) hung around apparently genuine death threats left on Kosten's answer phone. It transpired that the vicious, intimidating messages had been left by a singer with whom Kosten had aborted a planned collaboration. Kosten appropriated the message, knowing that the singer could not claim any credit without incriminating himself, applying the threats alongside wayward noise and **Steve Reich**–inspired neoclassical music. On *Closer Colder* (released via the intriguing Leaf label), Faultline continued this approach to music making, utilizing samples in place of vocals. Most notably, the album's title track lifted Dennis Hopper's voice from *Blue Velvet*. Kosten is reported to have obtained permission to use the sample directly from Hopper and David Lynch, both of whom requested copies of the album. Upon the release of *Closer Colder*, Kosten claimed to be enamoured with broken amplifiers and malfunctioning circuits, and despite its careful construction, his music has appeared on extreme noise mix albums compiled by artists such as Speedranch and Jansky Noise. Kosten has confessed to humming along to the vicious distortion that punctuated his debut, admitting that he deluded himself that he was creating catchy, commercial pop music. His single 'Papercut' was also, notably, used as the title music to Channel 4's *onedottv*.

On the eloquent and intelligent post-dance album *Your Love Means Everything*, Kosten seemed to invert his attitude to 'voices', with vocal contributions from **Coldplay**'s Chris Martin, Jacob Golden, the **Flaming Lips**' Wayne Coyne and **R.E.M.**'s Michael Stipe. Kosten expressed incredulity about recording his favourite childhood song—**Brothers Four**'s 'Greenfields'—with the R.E.M. singer. Alongside his own music, Kosten has produced **Ben Christophers**' acclaimed albums, *My Beautiful Demon* and *Spoonface*.

● ALBUMS: *Closer Colder* (Leaf/Thirsty Ear 1999) ★★★★, *Your Love Means Everything* (Blanco y Negro 2002) ★★★★.

Faust

Producer/advisor Uwe Nettelbeck formed this pioneering rock outfit in Wümme, Germany, in 1971. The initial line-up—Werner 'Zappi' Diermaier (drums), Jean-Hervé Péron (bass), Rudolf Sosna (guitar/keyboards), Hans-Joachim Irmler (organ), Gunter Wüsthoff (synthesizer/saxophone) and Arnulf Meifert (drums)—worked from a custom-built studio, sited in a converted schoolhouse. *Faust* was a conscious attempt to forge a new western 'rock' music wherein fragments of sound were spliced together to create a radical collage. Released in a clear sleeve and clear vinyl, the album was viewed as an experimental masterpiece or grossly self-indulgent, dependent on taste. In more recent years, thanks in no small part to the relentless championing of the band by **Julian Cope**, the album is viewed as highly influential in the development of both industrial and ambient music. 1972's *So Far* proved less obtuse, and the band subsequently secured a high-profile recording contract with **Virgin Records**. *The Faust Tapes*, a collection of private recordings reassembled by a fan in the UK, retailed at the price of a single in 1973 (49p) and this inspired marketing ploy not unnaturally generated considerable interest. The label also issued *Outside The Dream Syndicate* on which the group accompanied Tony Conrad, a former colleague of **John Cale**. Faust's music remained distanced from mainstream acceptance, as evinced on *IV*, and in the mid-70s the original line-up disbanded. Rare items drawn from their back catalogue were later issued by Recommended Records, specialists in *avant garde* recordings.

Members of the band remained active throughout the 70s and 80s, often playing under the Faust moniker. In 1988 they reduced the price of admission to those persons arriving at live concerts with a musical instrument who were prepared to play it during the performance. Faust officially reunited at the start of the 90s with Irmler, Péron and Diermaier present from the original line-up. The 1995 release *Rien*, their first studio album in 20 years, moved in the direction of ambient noise with help from producer **Jim O'Rourke**. The follow-ups *Untitled* and *You Know Faust*, meanwhile, were the first official releases on the band's own Klangbad label. Péron had departed by the time of 1997's *Faust Wakes Nosferatu*, which was recorded by Diermaier, Irmler, percussionist Lars Paukstat, bass player Michael Stoll and guitarist Steven Wray Lobdell. The vinyl and CD versions of the album featured completely different track listings. Remaining active into the new millennium, Faust's recent work includes an intriguing collaboration with US underground rap unit **Dälek**, released by the Staubgold label in 2004.

● ALBUMS: *Faust* (Polydor 1971) ★★★★, *So Far* (Polydor 1972) ★★★, *The Faust Tapes* (Virgin 1973) ★★★, with Tony Conrad *Outside The Dream Syndicate* (Virgin 1973) ★★★, *IV* (Virgin 1974) ★★★, *The Faust Concerts Vol. I* 1990 recording (Table Of The Elements 1994) ★★, *The Faust Concerts Vol. II* 1992 recording (Table Of The Elements 1994) ★★, *Rien* (Table Of The Elements 1995) ★★★, *You Know Faust* (Klangbad 1997) ★★★, *Faust Wakes Nosferatu* (Klangbad 1997) ★★★, *Edinburgh 1997* (Klangbad 1998) ★★, *Ravvivando* (Klangbad 1999) ★★★, *The Land Of Ukko & Rauni* (Klangbad 2000) ★★, with Dälek *Derbe Respect, Alder* (Klangbad/Staubgold 2004) ★★★.

● COMPILATIONS: *Return Of A Legend: Munic And Elsewhere* (Recommended 1986) ★★★, *The Last LP* (Recommended 1989) ★★★, *71 Minutes Of . . .* (Recommended 1990) ★★★, *Untitled* (Klangbad 1996) ★★, *The Wümme Years 1970–73* 5-CD box set (Recommended 2000) ★★★, *BBC Sessions* (Recommended 2001) ★★★★, *Freispiel* remix album (Klangbad 2002) ★★, *Patch Work 1971–2002* (Klangbad/Staubgold 2002) ★★★, *Abzu* 4-CD box set (Faust List 2003), *Collectif Met(z) 2005–1996* 3-CD/1 DVD box set (Art-Errorist/Recommended 2005) ★★★.

● DVD/VIDEOS: *In Japan* (Klangbad 1998), *Impressions* (Klangbad 2005), *Authentic Life: Faust In Zagreb* (Zappi Diermaier 2005).

Favors, Malachi

b. 22 August 1927, Chicago, Illinois, USA, d. 30 January 2004, Chicago, Illinois, USA. Favors came from a religious family (his father preached as a pastor) who disapproved of secular music. He took up the bass at the age of 15, initially inspired by **Wilbur Ware**. He started playing professionally when he left school, accompanying **Freddie Hubbard** and **Dizzy Gillespie**. Moving to Chicago, he recorded with **Andrew Hill** in 1955, and in 1961 he played with **Muhal Richard Abrams** in the Experimental Band, becoming a member of the **AACM** at its inception in 1965. He played in groups led by **Roscoe Mitchell** and **Lester Bowie** and in 1969 joined with them and **Joseph Jarman** to found the **Art Ensemble Of Chicago**, who triumphantly carried the banner of 'Great Black Music: Ancient to the Future' into the 90s. Outside of the Art Ensemble, Favors recorded on Mitchell's and Bowie's own albums as well as

with fellow AACM member **Kalaparusha Maurice McIntyre**, drummer **Sunny Murray** and gospel group From The Root To The Source. *Sightsong*, an album of duos with Abrams, was released in 1976, and two years later the solo *Natural And The Spiritual* appeared on the Art Ensemble's own AECO label.

Favors, who took to appending Maghostut (in various spellings) to his name, typified the AACM's interest in mysticism and once gave his biography as 'into being in this universe some 43,000 years ago. Moved around and then was ordered to this Planet Earth by the higher forces, Allah De Lawd Thank You Jesus Good God A Mighty, through the precious channels of Brother Isaac and Sister Maggie Mayfield Favors; of ten. Landed in Chicago by way of Lexington, Mississippi, for the purpose of serving my duty as a Music Messenger.' Perhaps more plausibly he also claimed that his decision to play freely was a statement that cost him financial rewards. Favors was a foremost exponent of free jazz upright playing and was also adept at the electric bass, the African *balafon*, the zither and the banjo.

● ALBUMS: with Muhal Richard Abrams *Sightsong* (Black Saint 1976) ★★★★, *Natural And The Spiritual* (AECO 1978) ★★★, with Cheikh Tidiane Fall, Sunny Murray *African Magic* (Circle 1979) ★★★, with Joseph Jarman, 'Kalaparush' Maurice McIntyre, Kahil El'Zabar, Steve Colson *Return Of The Lost Tribe* (Delmark 1997) ★★★, with Tatsu Aoki *2x4* (Southport 1999) ★★★.

Favre, Pierre

b. 2 June 1937, Le Locle, near Neuchatel, Switzerland. The self-taught Favre spent his formative years drumming with **Philly Joe Jones**, **Bud Powell** and **Benny Bailey** as well as working in a cymbal factory before developing his own style in one of the key 60s free jazz trios with **Irène Schweizer** on piano and, initially, **George Mraz** on bass. The latter was replaced by **Peter Kowald** who came over from Germany. The addition of **Evan Parker** on saxophones took the group in further new directions. Favre appeared with the other three on *European Echoes* by **Manfred Schoof** but tended afterwards to avoid the more explosive areas of European new jazz.

Favre's search for new voices led to his involvement with Indian and other percussionists, with the singer **Tamia** and with the formation of his Drum Orchestra. A variety of bells, gongs and cymbals contribute to his percussive armoury, which has been heard to great effect in recent years on **ECM Records**. Favre also played with musicians such as **Peter Brötzmann**, **John Tchicai**, **Don Cherry** and **Eje Thelin**. A lasting collaboration with the French reed player **Michel Portal** began in 1972. Favre's work in the 90s included his own album *Window Steps*, on which he collaborated with **Kenny Wheeler** (trumpet), **Steve Swallow** (bass) and **David Darling** (cello).

● ALBUMS: *Santana* (PIP 1968) ★★★, *Pierre Favre Quartet* (Wergo 1970) ★★★, *Michel Portal À Chateauvallon* (Calig 1972) ★★★★, with Gunter Hampel, Joachim Kühn, Albert Mangelsdorff *Solo Now* (MPS 1976) ★★★, *Drum Converstaion* (Calligraph 1979) ★★★★, with Barre Phillips *Music By . . .* (ECM 1980) ★★★, with Tamia *De La Nuit . . . Le Jour* (ECM 1982) ★★, *Such Winters Of Memory* (ECM 1982) ★★★★, *Singing Drums* (ECM 1984) ★★★, *Window Steps* (ECM 1996) ★★★★, *Portrait* (Unit 1998) ★★★, *Soufflés* (Intakt 1998) ★★★★, *Punctus* (Splasch

409

2001) ★★★, with Irène Schweizer *Ulrichsberg* (Intakt 2004) ★★★, *Saxophones* (Intakt 2005) ★★★★, with Albert Mangelsdorff, Pierre Favre *Triplicity* 1979 recording (Skip 2005) ★★★★.

Fawkes, Wally

b. 21 June 1924, Vancouver, British Columbia, Canada. Fawkes moved to the UK while still very young and in the mid-40s was recruited by **George Webb**, leader of one of the first bands to attract popular attention during the trad-jazz boom. In 1947 he left Webb along with fellow sideman **Humphrey Lyttelton** to become a founder member of the latter's new band. This musical relationship lasted until 1956 and was rewarding for musicians and fans alike. After leaving Lyttelton, Fawkes played with several other leaders, including **Bruce Turner** and **Sandy Brown**, with whom he recorded in 1954 and 1956, respectively (both sessions being reissued on a single 1989 album), and he also led his own semi-professional band, the Troglodytes, a more loosely swinging band than many of his contemporaries in the sometimes staid UK trad scene. Later, Fawkes, a gifted, **Sidney Bechet**-influenced clarinettist, whose musical abilities have made him a major name on the trad circuit, chose to play freelance, usually showing a marked preference for obscure pubs in the London area. For several decades, Fawkes, using the byline 'Trog', drew the strip cartoon *Flook* in the *Daily Mail*, the script for which was written by singer **George Melly**. Fawkes continued his sporadic jazz career into the 80s and 90s with several excellent records, including reunions with Lyttelton and Ian Christie, another sparring partner from the heyday of British trad jazz.

● ALBUMS: *Wally Fawkes And The Neo-Troglodytes* (Dawn 1979) ★★★, with Humphrey Lyttelton *It Seems Like Yesterday* (Calligraph 1983) ★★★, *Wally Fawkes And The Rhythm Kings* (Stomp Off 1985) ★★★, *Whatever Next!* (Stomp Off 1986) ★★★, *October Song* (Calligraph 1986) ★★★, with Bruce Turner, Sandy Brown *Juicy And Full Toned* 1954-56 recordings (Lake 1989) ★★★★, *Fidgety Feet* (Stomp Off 1993) ★★★.

● COMPILATIONS: with Lyttelton *A Tribute To Humph, Volume 1* (Dormouse 1984) ★★★.

Fay, Frank

b. Francis Anthony Donner, 17 November 1897, San Francisco, California, USA, d. 25 September 1961, Santa Monica, California, USA. An actor, comedian, singer, writer and producer, Fay appeared on the stage from a young age. Three Broadway musical shows in which he appeared early in his career are *Girl O' Mine* (1918), *Oh, What A Girl!* (1919) and *Jim Jam Jems* (1920). In the 20s he appeared in several revues, including his own *Fables*, for which he also wrote the book and lyrics, Raymond Hitchcock's *Pinwheel* (both 1922), *Artists And Models* (1923) and Harry Delmar's *Revels* (1927). In the 30s he was chiefly in films but did appear on Broadway in *Tattle Tales* (1933). For this, he not only performed but also wrote sketches and song lyrics and produced, but the show closed after just three weeks. In the 40s his Broadway appearances were in *Laugh Time* (1943) and *Harvey* (1944). Fay's first screen role was as the Master of Ceremonies in *The Show Of Shows* (1929), on which he also had writing credits. He played small roles in *Under A Texas Moon*, *The Matrimonial Bed* and *Bright Lights* (all 1930), *God's Gift To Women* and *The Slippery Pearls* (in which he appeared as

himself) (both 1931), *A Fool's Advice* and *Stout Hearts And Willing Hands* (both 1932), *Stars Over Broadway* (1935, in which **Jane Froman** costarred with James Melton), *Nothing Sacred* (1937), *I Want A Divorce* (1940), *They Knew What They Wanted* (1940, a highly regarded drama costarring Charles Laughton and Carole Lombard), *Spotlight Revue* (1943), *Screen Snapshots: The Great Showman* (1950), appearing as himself in the latter two, and *Love Nest* (1951, which costarred **June Haver** and William Lundigan and in which **Marilyn Monroe** had a supporting role). Between 1928 and 1936 Fay was married to screen actress Barbara Stanwyck. He made a few television appearances, among them *Screen Directors Playhouse* (1955) and an episode of *Toast Of The Town* (1957).

● FILMS: *The Show Of Shows* (1929), *Under A Texas Moon* (1930), *The Matrimonial Bed* (1930), *Bright Lights* aka *Adventures In Africa* (1930), *God's Gift To Women* aka *Too Many Women* (1931), *The Slippery Pearls* (1931), *A Fool's Advice* aka *Meet The Mayor* (1932), *Stout Hearts And Willing Hands* (1932), *Stars Over Broadway* (1935), *Nothing Sacred* (1937), *I Want A Divorce* aka *The Tragedy Of Divorce* (1940), *They Knew What They Wanted* (1940), *Spotlight Revue* aka *Spotlight On Scandal* (1943), *Screen Snapshots: The Great Showman* (1950), *Love Nest* (1951).

Faye, Alice

b. Alice Jeanne Leppert, 5 May 1912, New York City, USA, d. 9 May 1998, Rancho Mirage, California, USA. An attractive blonde actress and singer, Alice Faye symbolized for many the glamorous 20th Century Fox movies musicals of the 30s and 40s. She was noticed by **Rudy Vallee** in the Broadway chorus of *George White's Scandals* of 1931, and after touring and recording with his Connecticut Yankees, she starred with Vallee in the movie *George White's Scandals* (1934), making a strong impression with her version of 'Nasty Man'. She was also cited in Vallee's divorce trial. Over the next 11 years she made more than 30 films, mostly very appealing musicals such as *Poor Little Rich Girl* (1936), *Sing, Baby, Sing* (1936), *Stowaway* (1936), *On The Avenue* (1937), *In Old Chicago* (1938), *Alexander's Ragtime Band* (1938), *Rose Of Washington Square* (1939), *Hollywood Cavalcade* (1939), *Tin Pan Alley* (1940), *Lillian Russell* (1940), *That Night In Rio* (1941), *The Great American Broadcast* (1941), *Weekend In Havana* (1941), *Hello, Frisco, Hello* (1943) and *The Gang's All Here* (1943). With her deep-throated, sexy voice, Faye serenaded her good-looking leading men, **Dick Powell**, Tyrone Power, **Don Ameche** and **John Payne**, with songs that included 'Goodnight My Love', 'No Love, No Nothin''', 'Sing, Baby, Sing', 'You're A Sweetheart' and 'You'll Never Know', the Academy Award-winning song for 1943.

By this time she was a major star, together with her friend **Betty Grable**, with an equally loyal following. Faye retired from movies in 1945 after starring in Otto Preminger's *Fallen Angel* and following a much-publicized rift with 20th Century Fox boss Darryl F. Zanuck, but she returned in 1962 for the second remake of *State Fair*. Following a first marriage to singer **Tony Martin** (with whom she costarred in 1938's *Silly, Irene And Mary*), she remarried in 1941 to band leader/singer/actor **Phil Harris**, famous for his delivery of novelty songs such as 'Woodman, Woodman, Spare That Tree', 'The Darktown Poker Club' and 'That's What I Like About The South'. From 1946-54 they appeared together on a top-rated US radio series, and thereafter Faye starred in her own television specials and continued to record, mostly songs forever associated with her. She returned to the stage in 1973 in a revival of *Good News*.

● ALBUMS: *Movie Hits* (Reprise 1962) ★★★, *Alice Faye And The Songs Of Harry Warren* (1979) ★★★★, *On The Air, Volume One* (1979) ★★, *On The Air, Volume Two* (1979) ★★, *In Hollywood* (1983) ★★★, *All The Gang's Here* (1988) ★★★, *This Year's Kisses* (1989) ★★★, *Music From Hollywood* (1993) ★★★, *Got My Mind On Music* (Jasmine 1997) ★★★, *Alice Faye* (Great Movie Themes 1997) ★★★.

● FURTHER READING: *Getting Older, Staying Younger*, Alice Faye. *Alice Faye*, Barry Rivadue.

● FILMS: *George White's 1935 Scandals* (1934), *365 Nights In Hollywood* (1934), *She Learned About Sailors* (1934), *Now I'll Tell* (1934), *George White's Scandals* (1934), *Music Is Magic* (1935), *Every Night At Eight* (1935), *Stowaway* (1936), *Sing, Baby, Sing* (1936), *Poor Little Rich Girl* (1936), *King Of Burlesque* (1936), *Wake Up And Live* (1937), *You're A Sweetheart* (1937), *You Can't Have Everything* (1937), *On The Avenue* (1937), *Alexander's Ragtime Band* (1938), *In Old Chicago* (1938), *Sally Irene And Mary* (1938), *Barricade* (1939), *Hollywood Cavalcade* (1939), *Rose Of Washington Square* (1939), *Tailspin* (1939), *Tin Pan Alley* (1940), *Lillian Russell* (1940), *Little Old New York* (1940), *Weekend In Havana* (1941), *The Great American Broadcast* (1941), *That Night In Rio* (1941), *The Gang's All Here* (1943), *Hello Frisco Hello* (1943), *Fallen Angel* (1945), *State Fair* (1962), *The Magic Of Lassie* (1978).

Faze Action

Faze Action is the recording name of brothers Simon and Robin Lee (b. Amersham, Buckinghamshire, England). Signed to the influential London-based label **Nuphonic**, their sound has disco as its foundation but also draws heavily on Latin, jazz, African music, funk and, notably, classical elements. Robin taught himself to play bass guitar when he was 15 and went on to study music at London's Goldsmith's College, specializing in Asian folk and classical composition. While Robin taught English in Japan, Simon worked in various London record shops, indulging his interest in early 80s New York disco. They collaborated on tracks, despite the geographical divide, by sending material via e-mail. Their first release for Nuphonic Records, the *Full Motion* EP, included the cult classic 'Original Disco Motion' and was played by many influential DJs. The second single, 1996's 'In The Trees', was noteworthy for its funky, bass-driven groove and soaring cello melody. It became an instant dancefloor classic and appeared on several compilation albums. The track's success led to remix work for artists such as Yellow Sox, Diana Brown, **D*Note** and **Saint Etienne** among others. Faze Action's debut *Plans And Designs* was highly acclaimed; its uncompromising progressiveness was compared to **Talking Heads**' art school funk and the electronic disco of **François Kevorkian** and bands such as D-Train and Dinosaur L. The album was distinctive for its use of classical instrumentation such as strings and timpani drums alongside disco and **house** rhythm sections. *Moving Cities* continued in such an eclectic vein but more obviously embraced Latin and African influences. Drummer Zeke Manyika (ex–**Orange Juice**; **Style Council**) contributed African chants and percussion to four tracks. Faze Action have

developed a live dimension to their music, appearing as a six-piece band on BBC television and at numerous clubs and festivals including Homelands and superclub **Cream**'s Creamfields in 1998 and 1999. Like **Groove Armada**, Faze Action are sophisticated musicians: reverential to their disco heritage but unafraid to find inspiration in any interesting musical form. It was a pity that it took over five years to release a new album, in 2004.

● ALBUMS: *Plans And Designs* (Nuphonic 1997) ★★★★, *Moving Cities* (Nuphonic/Warners 1999) ★★★★, *Broad Souls* (Bar De Lune 2004) ★★★.

● COMPILATIONS: *Abstract Funk Theory* (Obsessive 2002) ★★★.

Fazola, Irving

b. Irving Henry Prestopnik, 10 December 1912, New Orleans, Louisiana, USA, d. 29 March 1949, New Orleans, Louisiana, USA. In his teens and early twenties Fazola played clarinet with several noted New Orleans–based band leaders, including **Louis Prima** and **Joseph 'Sharkey' Bonano**. Although he played frequently with Dixieland-style bands, Fazola's classical training made him eligible for many of the more chart-bound big bands of the swing era. In the 30s his pugilistic nature took him on a headlong dash through numerous jobs, including work with **Ben Pollack**, **Glenn Miller**, **Jimmy McPartland**, **Claude Thornhill**, **Muggsy Spanier** and the band with which he attracted most attention, **Bob Crosby**'s. His fiery, ill-tempered nature led him into several violent fights, and he was also a heavy drinker and a womanizer. Despite his erratic private life, Fazola was a distinguished and polished performer and with a different nature might well have made the big time as a featured artist. But then, had his nature been different he might well have been a lesser musician. His wild lifestyle finally took its toll, and he died in his late thirties.

● ALBUMS: *Irving Fazola & His Dixielanders* 10-inch album (Mercury 1950) ★★★, *New Orleans Express* (EmArcy 1955) ★★★.

● COMPILATIONS: *Faz* (ASV/Living Era 1998) ★★★, *The Rarest Recordings Of Irving Fazola* (Swing Time 2000) ★★★, *Mostly Faz 1936–1946* (Jazz Band 2001) ★★★.

FC Kahuna

This UK DJing and production partnership comprises Dan Ormondroyd and Jon Kahuna. They made a name for themselves with their DJing and club nights (particularly their own 'Big Kahuna Burger' nights) in and around London, playing dirty house and an eclectic range of party music. In 2001, after a series of singles on their own Kahuna Cuts, label, they released 'Hayling' featuring the vocals of Hafdis Huld (ex–**Gus Gus**). On the subsequent, *Machine Says Yes*, other guest vocalists included Gruff Rhys of the **Super Furry Animals**, **Eileen Rose** and a collaboration with ex-**Verve** member Simon Jones. The FC Kahuna team attempt to challenge what they see as a creative stagnation that has occurred with the increasing commercialization of **dance music**.

● ALBUMS: *Machine Says Yes* (City Rockers 2002) ★★★.

● COMPILATIONS: *Another Fine Mess* (Azuli 2003) ★★★.

Fear

One of the most entertaining and influential of the punk bands that emerged in the late 70s in Los Angeles, California,

Fear consisted of Lee Ving (vocals, guitar, harmonica), Philo Cramer (guitar), Derf Scratch (bass) and Johnny Backbeat (drums). Formed in 1978, the band's sarcastic, almost nihilistic stance, captured on Penelope Spheeris' *The Decline Of Western Civilization* film, formed the basis of a recorded career that never quite captured the band's stroppy, chaotic live shows. The debut album, *The Record*, was, nevertheless, a searing document of the band's potent rock 'n' roll, despite some primitive attitudes to women and homosexuals. Animated by a musical ability far beyond many of their peers and fortified by Ving's bar blues vocal presence, it is one of only two essential Fear recordings within a limited discography. The other was the band's debut single, 'I Love Living In The City', a sneering put-down of Hollywood. Their most famous live appearance, meanwhile, came as Halloween guests on the syndicated *Saturday Night Live* television show. In true punk style, the event ended in chaos and controversy, with the station quite appalled at the 'slam dancing' generated by Fear fans that accompanied the filming. Later in 1982 Scratch was replaced by future **Red Hot Chili Peppers** bass player Flea in time for the release of 'Fuck Christmas'. Shortly afterwards, Lorenzo (formerly of the **Dickies**) became the permanent bass player. *More Beer* repeated the debut album's formula, with occasional stylistic variation but little else to recommend it. It featured drummer Spit Stix, who was formerly in the **Nina Hagen** band.

● ALBUMS: *The Record* (Slash/Warners 1982) ★★★, *More Beer* (Restless 1985) ★★, *Live . . . For The Record* (Restless 1991) ★★.

Fear Factory

This Los Angeles, California, USA–based band are one of the few truly innovative acts in death metal, mixing industrial-style electronic rhythms and samples with grinding guitars and harsh vocals to create their own brutal soundscape. Formed in late 1991 with the line-up of Burton C. Bell (b. 19 February 1969, Houston, Texas, USA; vocals), Dino Cazares (guitar, who has an additional side project, **Brujeria**), Andrew Shives (bass) and Raymond Herrera (b. 18 December 1972, Los Angeles, California, USA; drums), the band rapidly made an impact with two tracks on the *LA Death Metal* compilation, produced by **Faith No More** bass player Bill Gould, and subsequently signed to Roadrunner Records. The Colin Richardson–produced *Soul Of A New Machine* established Fear Factory as a genuine death metal force, with a good collection of songs delivered with originality and ferocity. Meanwhile, the band set about developing their live show on their debut tour with **Brutal Truth** in Europe, followed by US dates with **Sick Of It All** and **Biohazard**. *Fear Is The Mind Killer*, a mini-album of remixes by Canadian industrialists **Front Line Assembly**, demonstrated further dimensions and possibilities available to the Fear Factory sound by adding an industrial dance edge, bringing the band further acclaim. The band also found a permanent bass player with the addition of Belgian Christian Olde Wolber (b. 5 August 1972, Antwerp, Belgium).

Released in 1995, *Demanufacture* was produced by Colin Richardson, but the band was unhappy with the final mix and invited Rhys Fulbert (Front Line Assembly) and Greg Reely (Front Line Assembly, **Skinny Puppy**) to remix it to reflect the futuristic atmosphere they desired. The bonus tracks on one of the CD formats included a cover version of

Agnostic Front's 'Your Mistake', with **Madball**'s Freddy Cricien guesting on vocals. Press response ranked it alongside **Therapy?**'s *Infernal Love* and **White Zombie**'s *Astro Creep 2000* as one of the definitive noise albums of 1995. In the meantime, vocalist Bell found work as the vocalist on **Black Sabbath** bass player Geezer Butler's **G/Z/R** project.

Following a remix album in 1997, the band returned in 1998 with the brutal metal noisefest *Obsolete*. They also gained extensive US radio play for one of their b-sides, a cover version of **Gary Numan**'s 'Cars'. Their growing popularity was confirmed by the commercial success of *Digimortal*, but following its release Cazares announced he wanted to leave Fear Factory. Wolbers switched to guitar, and **Strapping Young Lad** member Byron Stroud was brought in as the band's new bass player. The new line-up made its debut on 2004's *Archetype*.

● ALBUMS: *Soul Of A New Machine* (Roadrunner 1992) ★★★, *Fear Is The Mind Killer* mini-album (Roadrunner 1993) ★★★, *Demanufacture* (Roadrunner 1995) ★★★★, *Remanufacture (Cloning Technology)* (Roadrunner 1997) ★★★, *Obsolete* (Roadrunner 1998) ★★★★, *Digimortal* (Roadrunner 2001) ★★★, *Archetype* (Liquid 8 2004) ★★, *Transgression* (Liquid 8 2005) ★★★.

● COMPILATIONS: *Concrete* (Roadrunner 2002) ★★★, *Hatefiles* (Roadrunner 2003) ★★★.

● DVD/VIDEOS: *Digital Connectivity* (Roadrunner 2002).

Fearing, Stephen

b. *c.*1962, Vancouver, British Columbia, Canada. Fearing was raised in Dublin, Eire, from 1969–81 following his parents' divorce. He has subsequently emerged as one of his home nation's most affecting contemporary singer-songwriters, despite never receiving the international acclaim afforded some of his peers. He began working on the Canadian club circuit in the mid-80s, releasing his first album for Vancouver label Aural Tradition in 1988. This and the subsequent *Blue Line*, released in the UK by **Rough Trade Records** in 1990, established a reputation for downbeat, at times mawkish songwriting. However, both contained songs of poignancy and charm and won over critics from the UK and Canada alike (he has found it more difficult, however, to make an impression on the US market). His 1993 album, *The Assassin's Apprentice*, was a more optimistic-sounding set and featured **Sarah McLachlan** on the extracted single 'Expectations'. In 1996 Fearing cofounded Blackie And The Rodeo Kings, a trio that included Colin Linden, the Canadian blues and folk producer/guitarist, and Tom Wilson of Junkhouse. Their album of that year, *High On Hurtin'*, comprised 15 songs written by Willie P. Bennett, a hugely influential Canadian folk songwriter. The sessions worked well, and as a result Linden was asked to serve as producer for *Industrial Lullaby*, which featured **Bruce Cockburn** on guitar, **Blue Rodeo** bass player Bazil Donovan, **Cowboy Junkies** singer Margo Timmins and **Band** keyboard player Richard Bell. Among the best tracks was 'Dog On A Chain', a song heavily influenced by **Nick Lowe**'s 'The Best In Me'.

● ALBUMS: *Out To Sea* (Aural Tradition 1988) ★★, *Blue Line* (Rough Trade 1990) ★★★, *The Assassin's Apprentice* (True North 1993) ★★★★, *High On Hurtin'* (True North 1996) ★★★★, *Industrial Lullaby* (True North 1997) ★★★, *So Many Miles: Stephen Fearing Live* (Red House 2000) ★★★.

Fearless Four

One of the earliest and more sartorially challenged of rap's formations, the 80s group the Fearless Four consisted of MCs the Great Peso (b. Mitchell Grant, 5 December 1959), the Devastating Tito (b. Tito Dones, 27 May 1964), Mighty Mike C (b. Michael Kevin Clee, 10 March 1963) and DLB the Microphone Wizard (b. 25 April 1965), aided by two DJs, Master O.C. (b. Oscar Rodriguez Jnr., 22 September 1962, Manhattan, New York, USA) and Krazy Eddie (b. Eddie Thompson, 25 July 1960). The band was originally started by Tito and Master O.C. when they were known as the Houserockers Crew, selling their tapes across Manhattan and the Bronx. They gradually picked up members, first Mike Ski, then the Great Peso and Troy B, who arrived fresh from the **Disco Four**. He was subsequently replaced by DLB before Mike Ski also departed for marriage and a steady job. The line-up was completed by Mighty Mike C and Krazy Eddie, a second DJ who took his name from a local record store renowned for its zany commercials. They first struck for the **Enjoy** label in 1981 with 'Rockin' It' which, hot on the trail of Afrika Bambaataa's 'Planet Rock' success, used **Kraftwerk**'s 'The Mean Machine' as well as excerpts from the horror film *Poltergeist*. The follow-up was 'It's Magic', based on a **Cat Stevens** song, before moving to **Elektra**. Their career there began with 'Just Rock', built on **Gary Numan**'s 'Cars' and remixed by Larry Levan, which flopped. 'Problems Of The World Today' (1983), produced by **Kurtis Blow**, was an improvement. Master O.C., meanwhile, produced the Fantasy Three's 'Biters In The City'. The Fearless Four continued to plough a furrow into the mid-80s, but the hits had long since dried up.

Fearon, Clinton

Clinton Fearon began his career as part of the **Gladiators** in 1965. In addition to performing as a backing vocalist he played the bass guitar on a number of sessions at **Studio One**. In 1971, with **Lloyd Daley**, he performed as the lead vocalist when the Gladiators recorded the Jamaican chart hits, 'Rock A Man Soul' and 'Freedom Train'. Fearon registered numerous hits with the band through to the late 80s. Although Albert Griffiths was regarded the lead singer of the group, Fearon provided lead vocals on a number of Gladiators recordings. His baritone vocals embellished popular songs such as 'Get Ready' (a runaway success for **Zion Train** in 1995), 'Chatty Chatty Mouth', 'Thief In The Night' and 'Let Jah Be Praised' among others. In 1988 Fearon formed the Defenders, a band comprising expatriate Jamaicans residing in Seattle, Washington, USA. The line-up featured Fearon alongside **Alric Forbes**, Winston Cathy and Charlie Morgan. Forbes and Fearon had previously worked together in Jamaica in 1980, collaborating at **Channel One** on *Jah Jah Way* with **Yabby You**, Fearon as part of the Gladiators, while Forbes appeared through his association with the Prophets. The Defenders released a series of local hits including 'Rock Your Bones', 'Mr. Cop' and 'Chant Down Babylon' and the album *Feel The Spirit* that was released by Hot Fire Records in 1990. The band weathered five years before Fearon embarked on a new project, the Boogie Brown Band, in 1993. Fearon enrolled Barbara Kennedy (keyboards/backing vocals), John Rodde (drums) and Lamar Lofton (bass guitar). Kennedy had previously recorded with Yabby You and supported the **Abyssinians**, while Rodde had performed alongside **Joe Higgs** and **Michael**

Prophet. In 1993 the band released their debut, *Disturb The Devil*. The album showcased Fearon's talent as writer, producer and arranger and led to a contract with the Canadian Peacemaker group. Their second album proved a success in Canada, being voted number one by *Reggae Vibes* listeners. Notable tracks include the peaceable 'Who Cares', a call for unity 'Wake Up (And Take a Stance)', and the assertive 'New Song Old Song'.

● ALBUMS: *Disturb The Devil* (Boogie Brown 1994) ★★★, *Mystic Whisper* (Peacemaker 1997) ★★★★, *What A System* (Kool Yu Foot 1999) ★★★.

Fearon, Phil

b. 30 July 1956, Jamaica, West Indies. This multi-instrumentalist, singer-songwriter and producer moved to Britain in 1962. After running a reggae **sound system** he joined Hott Wax, (who evolved into Brit Funk pioneers Hi-Tension after he left) and in the late 70s was a mainstay of hit group **Kandidate**. He set up a studio in his north London house and initially recorded with the group Proton on Champagne. Fearon's first recording as Galaxy (with assistance from singers Julie and Dorothy) was 'Head Over Heels' on Ensign in 1982, which became a club hit. The first success came with the Top 5 hit 'Dancing Tight' in 1983, and over the next 15 months they chalked up a further four UK Top 40 singles including Top 10s 'What Do I Do' and 'Everybody's Laughing'. Their radio-friendly pop/soul debut album *Phil Fearon & Galaxy* also made the Top 10 in 1984. After a quiet period Fearon returned to the Top 10 for the last time with a revival of Tony Etoria's 'I Can Prove It' in 1986 (also a small US R&B hit). He continued to run a production company from his home making commercial dance records.

● ALBUMS: *Phil Fearon & Galaxy* (Ensign 1984) ★★★★, *This Kind Of Love* (Ensign 1985) ★★★.

● COMPILATIONS: *Dancing Tight: The Best Of* (1992) ★★★★, *All The Hits* (EMI 2001) ★★★★.

Feather, Leonard

b. 13 September 1914, London, England, d. 22 September 1994, Los Angeles, California, USA. After studying piano, Feather advanced his musical interests by teaching himself arranging and in the early 30s produced a number of record sessions, contributing charts and scores. Among the musicians for whom he worked in such capacities was **Benny Carter**, and he was instrumental in persuading **Henry Hall** to hire Carter for the BBC Dance Orchestra. In the mid-30s Feather went to the USA, and during the next decade he continued to work in record production, sometimes supplying original material for artists such as **Louis Armstrong**, **Lionel Hampton** ('Blowtop Blues') and **Dinah Washington** ('Evil Gal Blues'). Feather also branched into concert promotion and produced numerous recording sessions. Additionally, he continued to compose songs for artists such as **Sarah Vaughan**, **Ella Fitzgerald**, **Cannonball Adderley** and **Sonny Stitt**. Despite all these endeavours, most of his considerable efforts in the cause of jazz were gradually concentrated into writing on the subject for several magazines, including *Esquire* and *DownBeat*, and he also wrote a jazz column for the *Los Angeles Times*. He was the author of several jazz books, notably *Encyclopedia Of Jazz* and his autobiography *The Jazz Years: Ear Witness To An Era*. He was also a frequent broadcaster on jazz on radio and television. His daughter **Lorraine Feather** is an accomplished singer and songwriter.

● ALBUMS: *Leonard Feather's Swinging Swedes* (Prestige 1951) ★★★, *Winter Sequence* 10-inch album (MGM 1954) ★★★, *Swingin' On The Vibories* (ABC-Paramount 1956) ★★, *Leonard Feather Presents Bop* aka *Leonard Feather Presents 52nd Street* (Mode 1957) ★★★, *Hi-Fi Suite* (MGM 1957) ★★★, *Oh, Captain!* (MGM 1958) ★★★, *Leonard Feather Presents* (VSOP 1988) ★★★, *Night Blooming* (Mainstream 1991) ★★★.

● FURTHER READING: *The Jazz Years: Ear Witness To An Era*, Leonard Feather. *The Encyclopedia Of Jazz* various editions, Leonard Feather.

Feather, Lorraine

b. Billie Jane Lee Lorraine Feather, 10 September 1948, New York City, USA. The daughter of jazz writer **Leonard Feather**, her given names reflect her godmother **Billie Holiday**, her band vocalist mother, family friend **Peggy Lee** and the song 'Sweet Lorraine'. After early teenage years in Los Angeles, she graduated from college and returned to New York to enter the theatre. While struggling for regular work, she sang with local jazz groups and as a backing singer. In Los Angeles as a single, she was heard by **Jake Hanna** who recommended her to Concord Jazz Records, which led to her solo debut. During the 80s she was a member of vocal trio Full Swing, with which she recorded, and after the group folded she concentrated on lyric writing, something she had begun during this time. In particular, Feather chose to write lyrics for jazz instrumentals such as **Duke Ellington**'s 'Rockin' In Rhythm' and **Horace Henderson**'s 'Big John Special'. Later, she devoted entire CDs to songs by **Fats Waller** (*New York City Drag*) and Ellington (*Such Sweet Thunder*). Among singers who have recorded her songs are **Patti Austin**, **Phyllis Hyman**, **Cleo Laine**, **Kenny Rankin** and **Diane Schuur**.

Feather's television credits include collaborative songwriting for *Dinosaurs*, *The Days Of Our Lives* and *Beverly Hills, 90210*. She has sung on film soundtracks, including *Dick Tracy* (1990), and her songs appeared in *Babes In Toyland* (1997), *The Jungle Book 2* (2003) and *The Princess Diaries 2: Royal Engagement* (2004), all in collaboration. A particularly fruitful collaboration has been that with Mark Watters. Although writing mainly for MGM Animation, they also wrote 'Faster, Higher, Stronger', which was performed by opera singer Jessye Norman at the opening ceremony of the 1996 Olympics in Atlanta. Feather has received several Emmy Award nominations and has worked with numerous noted instrumentalists, including pianists **David Benoit**, **Russ Freeman**, **Don Grusin** and **Dick Hyman** and her husband, drummer Tony Morales. She has also enjoyed a musically fruitful relationship with composer-arranger Eddie Arkin. Skilled, tuneful and imaginative, Feather ably demonstrates wit and intelligence in her writing and in her performance, especially of those songs to which she has brought a contemporary yet wholly respectful touch.

● ALBUMS: *Sweet Lorraine* (Concord Jazz 1978) ★★★, *The Body Remembers* (Bean Bag 1997) ★★★, *New York City Drag* (Rhombus 2001) ★★★★, *Café Society* (Sanctuary 2002) ★★★, *Such Sweet Thunder: Music Of The Duke Ellington Orchestra* (Sanctuary 2004) ★★★★, *Dooji Wooji* (Sanctuary 2005) ★★★.

Feathers, Charlie

b. Charles Arthur Feathers, 12 June 1932, Holly Springs, Mississippi, USA, d. 29 August 1998, Memphis, Tennessee,

USA. The work of rockabilly legend Feathers became more elevated during each revival of interest in the genre. Feathers was an enigmatic superstar, although in reality his influence totally overshadowed his commercial success. His upbringing on a farm, being taught guitar by a cotton-picking black bluesman and leaving home to work on an oilfield, gave Feathers a wealth of material for his compositions. In the early 50s, together with Jody Chastain (b. 1933, USA, d. 28 July 1999) and Jerry Huffman, he performed as the Musical Warriors. He was an early signing to **Sam Phillips'** **Sun Records**. He recorded his first song, 'Defrost Your Heart', in 1955 and claimed to have co-written **Elvis Presley**'s debut, 'Blue Moon Of Kentucky'. He did, however, co-write Presley's first hit, 'I Forgot To Remember To Forget'.

Over the years Feathers continued to record for a number of labels, still unable to break through the barrier between 'cult' and 'star'. Among his early rockabilly sides was 'One Hand Loose' on **King Records**, regarded by many collectors as one of the finest examples of its kind. His highly applauded performance at London's famous Rainbow Theatre in 1977 gave his career a significant boost in Europe and brought him a new audience, notably the fans who were following **Dave Edmunds** and his crusade for 'rockabilly'.

Feathers' later recordings suffered from the problem of being aided by younger musicians who were merely in awe of his work, and his best material was from the 50s. Influential but spartan, full of whoops and growls but, ultimately, irresistible country rock, Feathers' 'light comedy' style was an 'invisible influence' over many decades, from the **Big Bopper** in the 50s to **Hank Wangford** in the 80s. His self-titled 1991 album contained a reworked version of his classic 'I Forgot To Remember To Forget'. He performed with his son and daughter on guitar and vocals, respectively. A remarkable crop of unissued demos appeared in 1995 as *Tip Top Daddy* and further highlighted the originality of the man who defined country rockabilly long before **Garth Brooks** was born and yet never received widespread recognition for his contribution.

● ALBUMS: *Good Rockin' Tonight!* (Barrelhouse 1974) ★★★, *Live In Memphis, Tennessee* (Barrelhouse 1976) ★★★, *That Rock-A-Billy Cat* (Barrelhouse 1979) ★★★, *Charlie Feathers* (Elektra 1991) ★★★.

● COMPILATIONS: *Rockabilly Mainman* (Charly 1978) ★★★, *The Legendary 1956 Demo Session* (Zu Zazz 1986) ★★, *Jungle Fever* (Kay 1987) ★★★, *Wild Wild Party* (Rockstar 1987) ★★★, *The Living Legend* (Redita 1988) ★★★, *Tip Top Daddy* (Norton 1995) ★★★, *Get With It: Essential Recordings (1954–69)* (Revenant 1998) ★★★★, *Rock-A-Billy* (Bear Family 1998) ★★★★, *A Rockabilly Legend: His Complete King Recordings* (King 1999) ★★★★, *Honky Tonk Man + New Jungle Fever* (Last Call 2004) ★★★.

Featherstonhaugh, Buddy

b. Rupert Edward Lee Featherstonhaugh, 4 October 1909, Paris, France, d. 12 July 1976, London, England. Raised and educated in England, Featherstonhaugh played clarinet and tenor saxophone with dance bands from the late 20s. In the early 30s he worked with **Spike Hughes** and was a member of the band formed to back **Louis Armstrong** for his 1932 UK tour. Later in the decade, Featherstonhaugh recorded with his own bands and also with **Valaida Snow** and **Benny Carter**. During service with the Royal Air Force in World War II, he played in service bands. In the summer of 1943 he followed **Harry Parry** into the broadcasting slot on the BBC's popular *Radio Rhythm Club*. From the late 40s until the middle of the next decade, Featherstonhaugh drifted from view but in the mid-50s led a bop group, now playing baritone saxophone. Up-and-coming jazz artists in this band included **Bobby Wellins** and **Kenny Wheeler**. The bop group was short-lived, however, and in 1957 Featherstonhaugh retired from active playing. On tenor he showed the influence of **Coleman Hawkins**, while on clarinet he hinted at a liking for the Chicago-style players.

● COMPILATIONS: *The RAF HQ Bomber Command Sextet* 1943–44 recordings (Celebrity 1995) ★★★.

Fedchock, John

b. John William Fedchock, 18 September 1957, Cleveland, Ohio, USA. From the mid-70s into the mid-80s, Fedchock studied trombone and arranging extensively, both at university and privately. Overlapping his studies, he played trombone with and also wrote arrangements for **Woody Herman** during most of the 80s, for part of this time acting as the band's musical director. Towards the end of this decade, he was also with **Gerry Mulligan** and **Louie Bellson**. He was also co-leader with **Maria Schneider** of a big band and subsequently formed his own large ensemble, the New York Big Band. In this band, Fedchock uses a combination of experienced New York session musicians and forward-thinking jazz players. The results of this combination of musical talents, directed at performing the leader's skilful and frequently demanding charts, has been one of the best latter-day big bands. As a player, Fedchock's technical expertise allows him to bring to fruition all of his musical imaginings, including the small group session on *Hit The Bricks*.

● ALBUMS: *New York Big Band* (Reservoir 1992) ★★★, with the New York Big Band *On The Edge* (Reservoir 1998) ★★★, *Hit The Bricks* (Reservoir 2000) ★★★, with the New York Big Band *No Nonsense* (Reservoir 2003) ★★★★.

Feeder

This highly fêted UK alternative rock band was formed in 1995 by sound engineer Grant Nicholas (b. Newport, Wales; guitar/vocals) and Jon Lee (b. 1968, Newport, Wales, d. 7 January 2002, Miami, Florida, USA; drums), who had previously played together in Reel and Rain Dancer. They were joined by Taka Hirose (b. Nagoya, Japan; bass) and began playing under the name of Real. After signing to the Echo label later the same year, the trio changed their name to Feeder and played their first gig in Yeovil, Somerset, on 25 May. The band released their debut *Two Colours* EP in November 1995 and built up a substantial live reputation as a support act for **Terrorvision** and **Reef**. An acclaimed six-track mini-album, *Swim*, followed in June 1996, but their early singles 'Stereo World', 'Tangerine', 'Cement' and 'Crash' made little progress in the charts, with only the last two reaching the UK Top 50.

A new song, the dramatically charged 'High', gained heavy airplay on mainstream radio and entered the UK charts at number 24 in October 1997, with the band finally looking like achieving the success their highly melodic guitar rock deserved. 'High' was included on a reformatted version of their debut long-player *Polythene*, originally released in May 1997. An excellent collection of post-grunge alternative rock,

the album saw the band receiving further high praise from the music press. They returned in March 1999 with a new single, 'Day In Day Out', followed by the supercharged 'Insomnia' and *Yesterday Went Too Soon*. The band's third full-length set *Echo Park* was a disappointment to those fans anticipating great things on the strength of the sparkling 'Buck Rogers'. The UK Top 5 single proved to be the strongest track on an album that merely satisfied rather than excited. The commercial success of *Echo Park* consolidated the band's reputation as one of the UK's leading rock acts, but tragedy followed in January 2002 when Lee was found hanged at his home in Miami. Nicholas and Hirose carried on, teaming up with *Echo Park* producer Gil Norton and recruiting Mark Richardson to fill in on drums for the recording of *Comfort In Sound*.

● ALBUMS: *Swim* mini-album (Echo 1996) ★★★, *Polythene* (Echo 1997) ★★★★, *Yesterday Went Too Soon* (Echo 1999) ★★★, *Echo Park* (Echo 2001) ★★★, *Comfort In Sound* (Echo 2002) ★★★, *Pushing The Senses* (Echo 2005) ★★★.

Feelies

Formed in New Jersey, USA, in 1976, the Feelies originally comprised Glenn Mercer (b. Haledon, New Jersey, USA; lead guitar/vocals), Bill Million (b. William Clayton, Haledon, New Jersey, USA; rhythm guitar/vocals), Keith DeNunzio aka Keith Clayton (b. 27 April 1958, Reading, Pennsylvania, USA; bass) and Dave Weckerman (drums). Weckerman departed from the line-up and was replaced by Vinny DeNuzio (b. 15 August 1956), and this new line-up began making a name for themselves on New York's club circuit. DeNuzio was replaced by Anton Fier prior to the band's 1980 debut, *Crazy Rhythms*. This exceptional release brought to mind the jerky paranoia of an early **Talking Heads** and the compulsion of the **Velvet Underground**, while at the same time it established the Feelies' polyrhythmic pulsebeats and Mercer's scratchy but effective guitar work.

Despite critical acclaim, *Crazy Rhythms* was a commercial failure, and the band fizzled out. Fier subsequently formed the **Golden Palaminos**, an *ad hoc* unit featuring contributions from various musicians. Mercer and Million then embarked on several diverse projects (as well as contributing the soundtrack to *Smithereens*), which included work with three different groups: the Trypes, the Willies and **Yung Wu**. Mercer and Million reactivated the Feelies name in 1983 and were joined by a returning Weckerman and two of their Willies associates, Stanley Demeski (drums) and Brenda Sauter (bass). With Weckerman switching to percussion, the re-formation was complete. The Feelies' second album, *The Good Earth*, was produced by **R.E.M.** guitarist Peter Buck, a long-time fan of *Crazy Rhythms*. Despite the gap between the releases, the new quintet showed much of the same fire and purpose, a factor confirmed by the albums *Only Life* and *Time For A Witness* (distributed by **A&M Records**). The Feelies split up again in 1991, with Mercer and Weckerman forming Wake Ooloo and then Sunburst and Demeski going on to play with Dean Wareham's **Luna**. They remain one of America's most inventive post-punk ensembles.

● ALBUMS: *Crazy Rhythms* (Stiff 1980) ★★★★, *The Good Earth* (Coyote/Twin/Tone 1986) ★★★★, *Only Life* (Coyote/A&M 1988) ★★★, *Time For A Witness* (Coyote/A&M 1991) ★★★.

Fehlmann, Thomas

b. Zurich, Switzerland. An elder statesman of the German **techno** scene, with an intriguing history. Fehlmann originally met guitar wizard **Robert Fripp** in Hamburg in 1979, where he was studying art, and it was Fripp who inspired him to learn the synthesizer. Later he would make the acquaintance of the **Orb**'s Alex Paterson while working on Teutonic Beats, a mid-80s project. Paterson tried to sign him to management company EG, but the contract fell through. Undeterred, the two remained firm friends. Before joining the Orb as an ambient DJ and electronics consultant, he recorded as Readymade and produced the *Sun Electric* LP, joining with **Juan Atkins** for the release of 'Jazz Is The Teacher' on Belgian imprint Tresor (licensed to **Novamute Records** in the UK). This was recorded under the group name 3MB, with Morris Von Oswald, an old friend whom he had known from the time they liaised on **Palais Schaumburg**'s third album from a decade previously. They have worked together intermittently since. His contributions to the Orb also include 'Towers Of Dub' on the latter's live double, *Live 93*, and a more prominent role on the studio albums *Orbus Terrarum* and *Orblivion*. Following touring commitments, he teamed up once more with old guru Fripp to put together the *ad hoc* project FFWD (Fripp, Fehlmann, Weston and Dr Alex Paterson). According to the latter, Fehlmann had also been 'the first person to put a **house** record out in Britain in 1986'—as Readymade on **Rhythm King Records**.

● ALBUMS: *Visions Of Blah* (Kompakt 2002) ★★★.
● COMPILATIONS: *Good Fridge* (R&S 1998) ★★★, *One To Three* (R&S 1999) ★★★.

Feinstein, Michael

b. Michael Jay Feinstein, 7 September 1956, Columbus, Ohio, USA. A singer, pianist and musical archivist, Feinstein was a boy prodigy, able to play all manner of show tunes by ear. His mother was an amateur tap dancer and his father a singer and sales executive. After attending high school in Columbus he worked as a piano salesman in California, where he discovered some rare acetate recordings by **Oscar Levant**. He returned them to the actor/pianist's widow, who secured him a job as archivist and personal assistant to two of popular music's all-time great songwriters, **Ira Gershwin** and **Harry Warren**. In the late 70s and early 80s, as well as cataloguing their material, Feinstein unearthed several alternative Gershwin lyrics that had never been printed. Through Gershwin he met the lyricist's god daughter, **Liza Minnelli**, and she opened a great many showbusiness doors for him. He also served as her accompanist and played for other artists such as **Rosemary Clooney**, John Bubbles, **Jessie Matthews** and Estelle Reiner.

During the 80s and 90s Feinstein appeared in cabaret in Britain and America. He made his Broadway debut with *Michael Feinstein In Concert* (1988), which later toured major US cities and returned to New York in 1990. Some five years later he presented *An Evening With Michael Feinstein* at London's Comedy Theatre. He also filled the 18,000-seater Hollywood Bowl twice in July 1987. On television, Feinstein has hosted his own *Michael Feinstein And Friends* special as well as featuring in several tributes to legendary songwriters, including **George Gershwin**, **Irving Berlin** and **Jule Styne**. Therefore, it was entirely appropriate that he was chosen to pay homage to Gershwin in *A Capitol Fourth*, a spectacular Independence Day celebration held in Washington, DC, in

1998—the centenary of the composer's birth. As well as receiving an honorary doctorate of fine arts from California State University, Los Angeles, Feinstein was concerned with many other Gershwin tributes during that year, including performances with Rosemary Clooney and **Linda Ronstadt**. Clooney subsequently became the first star to appear at the New York supper club, Feinstein's, at the Regency Hotel.

By this time, Feinstein was becoming increasingly involved in writing and performing for television and films. He has also presented several series about the great American songwriters for BBC Radio 2. On his second album, 1987's *Live At The Algonquin*, Feinstein sang Raymond Jessel's 'I Wanna Hear A Show Song' ('Please don't bend my ear with punk or funk—it's junk'), which summed up his musical philosophy perfectly. One of the joys of his performances is that he includes rarely heard songs—and unfamiliar verses to more popular songs—and sings them as he believes the writers intended them to be sung. His voice has been called 'overly stylized—the high notes being rather faint, while the lower register is too loud'. Nevertheless, he has a good ear for phrasing and is recognized as a leading expert and exponent of the American standard popular song.

● ALBUMS: *Pure Gershwin* (Parnassus 1987) ★★★★, *Live At The Algonquin* (Elektra 1987) ★★★, *Isn't It Romantic* (Elektra 1987) ★★★, *Remember: Michael Feinstein Sings Irving Berlin Songbook* (Elektra 1987) ★★★, *The M.G.M. Album* (Elektra (Elektra 1989) ★★★★, *Over There: Songs Of War and Peace c. 1900-1920* (EMI Angel 1989) ★★★, *Sings The Burton Lane Songbook Volume One* (Elektra Nonesuch 1990) ★★★★, *Sings The Jule Styne Songbook* (Elektra Nonesuch 1991) ★★★, *Sings The Burton Lane Songbook Volume Two* (Elektra Nonesuch 1992) ★★★, *Pure Imagination* (Elektra 1992) ★★★, *Forever* (Elektra 1993) ★★, *Sings The Jerry Herman Songbook* (Elektra Nonesuch 1994) ★★★, *Sings The Hugh Martin Songbook* (Nonesuch 1995) ★★★, *Such Sweet Sorrow* (Atlantic 1995) ★★★, *Nice Work If You Can Get It* (Atlantic 1996) ★★★, *Michael & George: Feinstein Sings Gershwin* (Concord Jazz 1998) ★★★, with the Maynard Ferguson Big Band *Big City Rhythms* (Concord Jazz 1999) ★★★★, *Romance On Film, Romance On Broadway* (Concord Jazz 2000) ★★★★, *Livingston And Evans Songbook* (Concord Jazz 2002) ★★★, *Only One Life: The Songs Of Jimmy Webb* (Concord Jazz 2003) ★★★, with George Shearing *Hopeless Romantics* (Concord 2005) ★★★.
● COMPILATIONS: *The Very Best Of Michael Feinstein* (WEA 1998) ★★★★, *The Michael Feinstein Anthology* (Rhino 2002) ★★★★.
● DVD/VIDEOS: *Michael Feinstein & Friends* (Kulter Video/Image Entertainment 1994).
● FURTHER READING: *Nice Work If You Can Get It: My Life In Rhythm And Rhyme*, Michael Feinstein. *The Ira Gershwin Songbook*, Michael Feinstein (ed.).
● FILMS: *Scenes From The Class Struggle In Beverly Hills* (1989), *For Love Alone: The Ivana Trump Story* (1996).

Feist

b. Leslie Feist, 1976, Calgary, Alberta, Canada. Indie singer-songwriter Leslie Feist started her music career in her native Toronto, working with popular local punk band Placebo (not the internationally successful rock unit of the same name led by Brian Molko). She relocated to Toronto in the mid-90s and established a number of new musical acquaintances, notably playing guitar and singing with the rock band By Divine Right. During this period she also formed a close friendship with two of the Toronto scene's most provocative performers, art-rappers **Peaches** and **Gonzales**. Using her surname as her new performing moniker, Feist put together a band and made her recording debut in 1999 with *Monarch (Lay Down Your Jeweled Head)*. This collection of attractive indie pop material was augmented by a string quartet arranged by Dave Szigeti and featured guest appearances from Gonzales and By Divine Right's Jose Contreras.

Feist then spent the next couple of years in Europe, working with Peaches and Gonzales and contributing vocals to the debut album by **Broken Social Scene**. She teamed up with Gonzales to record her second solo album, *Let It Die*. The music on this set was more fully realized than that on her debut, blending chanson, jazz, folk and indie pop to highlight Feist's beguiling vocals. Among several cover versions on the album were stand-out readings of **Ron Sexsmith**'s 'Secret Heart' and the **Bee Gees**' 'Inside Out'.

● ALBUMS: *Monarch (Lay Down Your Jeweled Head)* (Bobby Dazzler 1999) ★★★, *Let It Die* (Arts & Crafts 2004) ★★★★.

Feld, Morey

b. 15 August 1915, Cleveland, Ohio, USA, d. 28 March 1971. He began playing drums in his late teens, working with **Ben Pollack** in 1936 and then with **Joe Haymes**. In the early 40s he played with many bands, some of them swing era big bands, others small groups orientated towards dixieland jazz. The leaders for whom he played in these years include **Bud Freeman**, **Benny Goodman**, **Teddy Wilson** and **Wild Bill Davison**. In 1947 Feld began a decade-long association with **Peanuts Hucko**, then worked in New York studios. During the mid-50s he also played with bop musicians, including **Charlie Parker** with whom he recorded. During the 60s he was active in recording studios, operated a drum school, toured overseas, then moved to Colorado where he was reunited with Hucko. In 1968 he was involved with the formation of the **World's Greatest Jazz Band**. Feld was killed when fire destroyed his home. Technically assured and adaptable to many styles of jazz, he was a particularly gifted dixieland drummer, bringing a lightness of touch not found by many of his contemporaries.

● ALBUMS: *Jazz Goes To Broadway* (Kapp 1956) ★★★.

Felder's Orioles

Active in London, England, between 1965 and 1967, Felder's Orioles comprised Barry Heiband (vocals/organ), Paul Hodgson (guitar), Rod Mealeston (baritone saxophone), Peter Newman (tenor saxophone), Nick O'Brien (bass) and John Halsey (drums). Signed to Piccadilly Records in 1965, this superior R&B band made its debut with a fine version of 'Down Home Girl', originally recorded by **Alvin Robinson** but popularised by the **Rolling Stones**. An excellent rendition of **Bobby Bland**'s 'Turn On Your Lovelight' ensued. Felder's Orioles completed two more singles, 'I Know You Don't Love Me No More' and 'Back Street' (both 1966) but split up when dropped by their record company. Halsey subsequently joined Timebox, then **Patto**.

Feldman, Victor

b. 7 April 1934, London, England, d. 12 May 1987, Los Angeles, California, USA. A remarkable child prodigy,

Feldman was encouraged into his professional career by his uncle, drummer Max Bacon, and was playing drums in a family trio at the age of seven, alongside his brothers Robert and Monty. When he was 10 years old he was featured at a concert with **Glenn Miller**'s AAAF band, and in his teens he worked with the bands of **Ralph Sharon**, **Roy Fox** and **Ronnie Scott** and like-minded spirits such as **John Dankworth**, **Stan Tracey**, **Tubby Hayes** and **Tony Crombie**. Feldman also played piano and, at the urging of **Carlo Krahmer** of **Esquire Records**, soon added the vibraphone to his armoury of instruments, gradually dropping drumming except for special features. By the mid-50s, when he immigrated to the USA, he was regarded primarily as a vibraphonist, nevertheless, he continued to play piano displaying an especially original and delicate touch.

Feldman's first transatlantic job was with **Woody Herman**, and he later became associated with the west coast scene, recording with **Shelly Manne**. In the late 50s Feldman extended his versatility by studying arranging with **Marty Paich**. In the 60s he played with diverse jazzmen such as **Benny Goodman**, with whom he toured Russia in 1962, and **Miles Davis**, for whom he wrote 'Seven Steps To Heaven'. Before hiring Feldman, **Cannonball Adderley** took the precaution of playing some of his records to his existing sidemen; only after they had acknowledged that here was an outstanding musical personality they would be happy to work with did he tell them that their new companion was British, Jewish and white.

Always open to new concepts, Feldman ventured into jazz rock fusion in the 70s and 80s, working with **Steely Dan** and **Tom Scott** among many others and recording with his own funk outfit the Generation Band. He continued to play in the mainstream of jazz, however, and in the 80s recorded with **Spike Robinson**, with whom he had played in London three decades earlier. He died suddenly, following an asthma attack.

● ALBUMS: *Suite Sixteen* (Contemporary 1957) ★★★★, *Victor Feldman On Vibes* aka *With Mallets A Fore Thought* (Mode/Interlude 1957) ★★★, *The Arrival Of Victor Feldman* (Contemporary 1958) ★★★★, *Love Me With All Your Heart* (Vee Jay 1960) ★★★★, *Merry Ole Soul* (Riverside 1961) ★★★, *Stop The World, I Want To Get Off* (World Pacific 1962) ★★★★, with Curtis Amy *Way Down* (Pacific Jazz 1962) ★★★★, *Latinsville 1959* recordings (Contemporary 1963) ★★★, *Soviet Jazz Themes* (Ava 1963) ★★, *It's A Wonderful World* (Vee Jay 1965) ★★, *The Venezuela Joropo* (Pacific Jazz 1967) ★★★, *Your Smile* (Choice 1973) ★★★, *The Artful Dodger* (Concord Jazz 1977) ★★★, *Rockavibabe* (DJM 1977) ★★, with the Generation Band *Soft Shoulder* (Nautilus 1981) ★★★, *Secrets Of The Andes* (Palo Alto 1982) ★★★, *To Chopin With Love* (Palo Alto 1983) ★★, with the Generation Band *Call Of The Wild* (Nautilus 1984) ★★, *Fiesta* (Nautilus 1984) ★★★, *High Visibility* (Nautilus 1985) ★★★, *In My Pocket* 1977 recording (Coherent 1988) ★★.

Feliciano, José

b. 10 September 1945, Lares, Puerto Rico. After early fame as a flamenco-style interpreter of pop and rock material, Feliciano turned more to mainstream Latin music, becoming one of the most popular artists in the Spanish-speaking world. He was born blind and as a child moved to New York's Spanish Harlem. He learned guitar and accordion and from 1962 performed a mixture of Spanish and American material in the folk clubs and coffeehouses of Greenwich Village. Signed to **RCA Records**, he released a gimmicky single 'Everybody Do The Click' before recording an impressive debut album in 1964. Its impassioned arrangements of recent hits were continued on *Feliciano!* With jazz bass player **Ray Brown** among the backing musicians, Feliciano's Latin treatment of the **Doors**' 'Light My Fire' became his first hit. It was followed by a version of **Tommy Tucker**'s R&B standard 'Hi-Heel Sneakers', and such was Feliciano's popularity that he was chosen to sing 'The Star-Spangled Banner' at the 1968 baseball World Series. However, the application of his characteristic Latin-jazz styling to the US national anthem caused controversy among traditionalists.

In the UK, where he recorded a 1969 live album, Feliciano's version of the **Bee Gees**' 'The Sun Will Shine' was a minor hit, but the 70s saw RCA promoting Feliciano's Spanish-language material throughout Latin America. He recorded albums in Argentina, Mexico and Venezuela and had a television show syndicated throughout the continent. He also sang the theme music to the television series *Chico And The Man*. In parallel with the Latin albums, Feliciano continued to record English-language songs, notably on *Compartments*, produced by **Steve Cropper**. In 1976 Feliciano switched labels to Private Stock-where producer **Jerry Wexler** was brought in to recreate the feeling of Feliciano's early work on Sweet Soul Music. When **Motown Records** set up its own Latin music label in 1981, Feliciano headed the roster, recording the Rick Jarrard–produced *Romance In The Night* as well as Grammy-winning Latin albums. In 1987 he signed a three-pronged contract with EMI Records to record classical guitar music and English pop (*I'm Never Gonna Change*) as well as further Spanish-language recordings (*Tu Immenso Amor*). He also pursued his jazz interests, and one of his more recent albums, *Steppin' Out,* was recorded for Optimism. He joined PolyGram Latino Records in 1995 and released *El Americano* the following year.

● ALBUMS: *The Voice And Guitar Of José Feliciano* (RCA 1964) ★★, *A Bag Full Of Soul* (RCA 1965) ★★★★, *Feliciano!* (RCA 1968) ★★★★, *Souled* (RCA 1969) ★★★, *Feliciano 10 To 23* (RCA 1969) ★★, *Alive Alive-O* (RCA 1969) ★★, *Fireworks* (RCA 1970) ★★, *That The Spirit Needs* (RCA 1971) ★★, *José Feliciano Sings* (RCA 1972) ★★, *Compartments* (RCA 1973) ★★, *And The Feeling's Good* (RCA 1974) ★★, *Just Wanna Rock 'N' Roll* (RCA 1975) ★★, *Sweet Soul Music* (RCA 1976) ★★★, *Jose Feliciano* (Motown 1981) ★★, *Escenas De Amor* (Latino 1982) ★★, *Romance In The Night* (Latino 1983) ★★, *Los Exitos De José Feliciano* (Latino 1984) ★★, *Sings And Plays The Beatles* (RCA 1985) ★★, *Tu Immenso Amor* (EMI 1987) ★★★, *I'm Never Gonna Change* (EMI 1989) ★★, *Steppin' Out* (Optimism 1990) ★★★, *El Americano* (PolyGram 1996) ★★★.

● COMPILATIONS: *Encore!* (RCA 1971) ★★★★, *The Best Of José Feliciano* (RCA 1985) ★★★★, *Portrait* (Telstar 1985) ★★★, *And I Love Her* (Camden 1996) ★★★★, *The Best Of* (BMG 2003) ★★★★.

Feline

The power base behind Feline is bass player and singer Grog, who first rose to prominence in 1994 when her first band, **Flinch**, won the Best Act award at that year's *In The City* festival. However, after five singles the group collapsed,

failing to deliver on their early promise. Grog enlisted former Flinch manager Drew Richards as her guitarist and set about writing a new cycle of songs. Initially envisaged as a solo project, Feline grew into a full group with the addition of guitarist Ted Garcia and drummer Steve Drew. Their demo provoked major label interest, leading to a contract with **Chrysalis Records** in 1997. Their debut single, an old-fashioned power pop song entitled 'Just As You Are', delivered further strong reviews. A 10-track debut album, *Save Your Face*, was completed in three weeks with **Cure** producer David M. Allen at the helm. By the time of the album's release, Steve Drew had been replaced on drums by Mig.

● ALBUMS: *Save Your Face* (Chrysalis 1997) ★★.

Felix

b. Essex, England. UK **house** artist and alleged former tax inspector Felix represented something of an enigma—never talking to the press or appearing in his videos. He even took the stage at the DMC awards sporting a lion suit. However, his anonymity was not helped by the massive success of singles like 'Don't You Want Me' and 'It Will Make Me Crazy', which sold nearly two million copies between them worldwide. Both predicted the rise of **trance** and hard house.

● ALBUMS: *#1* (Deconstruction 1993) ★★★.

Felix Da Housecat

b. Felix Stallings, 1972, Chicago, Illinois, USA. The childhood friend of **house** legend **DJ Pierre**, Stallings' youth was spent experimenting with electronic musical equipment. He taught himself keyboards by the age of 14 and a year later stepped into a studio for the first time. An early tape had been passed on to the elder Pierre by a mutual playground acquaintance. Intrigued, he decided to record it properly, and from those sessions 'Phantasy Girl' emerged. Based on the original keyboard motif from the demo tape, it became one of house music's biggest early cult smashes. Felix went on to release a steady stream of **dance music** vinyl, establishing his name alongside that of Pierre, who remained his mentor. Unfortunately, as school ended so did his parents' tolerance of his extracurricular pursuits, and he was ordered to attend college in Alabama. Three years later he returned to Chicago, taking up the house mantle once again. Numerous releases followed on all the major imprints: **Strictly Rhythm Records**, **Guerilla Records** ('Thee Dawn'), **Nervous Records**, D-Jax Up, Chicago Underground and Freetown. He also set up his own Radikal Fear Records imprint, which has released classic tracks by the likes of **DJ Sneak**, Armando and Mike Dunn and provided remixes for mainstream artists such as **Diana Ross** and **Kylie Minogue**. Under the title Thee Madkatt Courtship he also provided a long player for Deep Distraxion, while as Afrohead he proffered 'In The Garden', a classic cut, much revered by DJs such as **Darren Emerson**. After a lengthy break from the dance scene, Stallings returned in 1999 under his Thee Madkatt Courtship moniker with *I Know Electrikboy*. The dazzling *Kittenz And Thee Glitz* (2001) tapped into the fashionable nostalgia for 80s synth-pop but easily surpassed anything released by the movers and shakers on the glaringly shallow 'electro-clash' scene.

● ALBUMS: as Thee Madkatt Courtship *Alone In The Dark* (Deep Distraxion 1995) ★★★, *Metropolis Present Day? Thee Album* (Radikal Fear 1998) ★★★★, as Thee Madkatt Courtship III *I Know Electrikboy* (London 1999) ★★★★,

Kittenz And Thee Glitz (City Rockers/Emperor Norton 2001) ★★★★, *Devin Dazzle And The Neon Fever* (Emperor Norton 2004) ★★★.
● COMPILATIONS: *Felix Da Housecat's Clashbakk Compilation Mix* (Livewire 1999) ★★★★, shared with Justin Robertson *Bugged Out!* (Virgin 2000) ★★★, *Excursions* (Obsessive 2002) ★★★, *A Bugged Out Mix By Felix Da Housecat* (React 2003) ★★★.

Felix, Julie (60s)

b. 14 June 1938, Santa Barbara, California, USA. Felix arrived in the UK during the early 60s at a time when several US folk singers, including **Paul Simon** and **Jackson C. Frank**, had also relocated to London. Her early recordings revealed a commercial, rather than innovative talent, a fact emphasized by weekly appearances on UK television's *The Frost Report* (1967/8). She followed the liberal tradition of **Tom Paxton** or **Pete Seeger** rather than that of the radical left, although she was an early champion of the folk-styled singer-songwriter movement, notably **Leonard Cohen**, and was proclaimed as 'Britain's Leading Lady of Folk'. Her humanitarian beliefs had, however, been put to practical use by the singer's tour of the African states of Kenya and Uganda, working for the Christian Aid and Freedom From Hunger charities.

Felix enjoyed two successful British television series in her own right, *Once More With Felix* (1969/70) and *The Julie Felix Show* (1971), and enjoyed a UK Top 20 hit in 1970 with a version of 'El Condor Pasa', produced by pop svengali **Mickie Most**. The singer's 'wholesome' image was tarred by a conviction for possession of marijuana, but she continued a prolific recording career, albeit to less publicity on her low-key Remarkable Records imprint, into the new millennium, as well as performing for Women's Rights, Green and environmental benefits, and founding Britain's first 'New Age Folk Club'. She actively campaigned against the war in Iraq in 2003 and released an album of Dylan covers *Starry Eyed And Laughing*

● ALBUMS: *Julie Felix* (Decca 1964) ★★★, *2nd Album* (Decca 1965) ★★★, *3rd Album* (Decca 1966) ★★★, *Sings Dylan And Guthrie* (Decca 1966) ★★★, *Changes* (Fontana 1966) ★★★, *In Concert* (World 1967) ★★★, *Flowers* (Fontana 1967) ★★, *This World Goes Round And Round* aka *Julie Felix's World* (Fontana 1968) ★★★, *Going To The Zoo* (Fontana 1969) ★★★, *Clotho's Web* (RAK 1972) ★★, *Lightning* (EMI 1974) ★★★, *Hota Chocolata* (Monte Rosa 1977) ★★, *Colours In The Rain* (Scranta 1982) ★★, *Blowing In The Wind* (Scranta/Dingle's 1982) ★★★, *Amazing Grace* (Starburst 1987) ★★, *Bright Shadows* cassette (Remarkable 1989) ★★, *Branches In The Mist* (Remarkable 1993) ★★★, *Windy Morning* (Remarkable 1995) ★★★, *Fire—My Spirit* (Remarkable 1998) ★★★, *Starry Eyed And Laughing: Songs By Bob Dylan* (Remarkable 2002) ★★★.
● COMPILATIONS: *The World Of Julie Felix* (Decca 1969) ★★★, *The World Of Julie Felix Volume 2* (Decca 1970) ★★★, *This Is Julie Felix* (Philips 1970) ★★★, *The Most Collection* (RAK 1972) ★★★, *This Is Julie Felix Volume 2* (Philips 1974) ★★★, *El Condor Pasa* (Start 1995) ★★★, *The Rainbow Collection* (Track 2004) ★★★.

Felix, Julie (90s)

English singer-songwriter Julie Felix made her debut in 1995 with the release of *Breeches In The Mist*. A collection of deeply personal folk songs, its themes including survival ('Healing Hands') and feminism ('Magic Messenger'), it also included a cover version of Judy Small's 'Miss Alice Martin'. Having spent several months living in New Zealand, it also included an antinuclear song ('Aotearoa'), made topical by the French nuclear testing which coincided with its release. Another song, 'Child Of The Universe', was a collaboration with Marianne Segal. However, the critical reaction was one of disappointment, reviewers pointing out Felix's failure adequately to blend involved lyrics with her music. This artist is not to be confused with the folk-styled singer-songwriter **Julie Felix**, popular in the 60s.
● ALBUMS: *Breeches In The Mist* (Remarkable 1995) ★★.

Felix, Lennie

b. 16 August 1920, London, England, d. 29 December 1980. Although Felix began his career in the years immediately before World War II, it was in the early post-war period that he became an established pianist on the London jazz club scene. In the 50s he played in the UK with **Freddy Randall** and **Harry Gold** and in New York with **Henry 'Red' Allen** and **Buster Bailey**. Towards the end of the decade he was a member of **Wally Fawkes**' Troglodytes. He continued to play through the 60s and 70s, making records and radio broadcasts. At his best as a soloist or leading a trio, Felix displayed the traits of dominant musical personalities such as **Fats Waller**, **Earl Hines** and **Art Tatum**. Perhaps as a result of such mentors he was temperamentally unsuited to the role of accompanist, and some of his musical partnerships ended disastrously. One, with visiting American cornetist **Ruby Braff**, a man not known for his reticence in dealing with awkward associates, ended with the visitor declaring, 'I asked for a piano player and they gave me a disease.' During the Christmas season, 1980, Felix was struck by a car as he was leaving a London jazz club, and he died on 29 December that year.
● ALBUMS: *That Cat Felix!* (Label 1958) ★★★, *In His Stride* (Label 1966) ★★★★, *The Many Strides Of Lennie Felix Live At Nova Park, Zurich* (Label 1975) ★★★, *Boogie Train: Piano Solos* (Label 1980) ★★★.

Fell, Simon

b. 13 January 1959, Dewsbury, England. Fell grew up in Batley, West Yorkshire, receiving piano lessons from an early age. He took up double bass in 1973. Although originally inspired by R&B, he took the classical path—Kirklees Youth Orchestra and the Huddersfield Philharmonic—for a number of years. Leaving school he made contact with guitarist Paul Buckton and live electronics improviser John McMillan but then moved to Cambridge, where he studied English Literature. A marked preference for emotional involvement (as against free improvisation) led him to form a jazz band called Persuasion A in the mid-80s. A self-run record label, Bruce's Fingers, released their music to critical acclaim in England and the USA in 1986. In 1989 he formed a trio with Leeds-based drummer **Paul Hession** and saxophonist **Alan Wilkinson**, characterized as 'punkjazz' for its ferocity and monumental attack. In 1990 Fell released *Compilation II*, a collage of jazz, free improvisation, serial charts and electronics that was welcomed by writer Steve Lake (*Wire*) as 'a potential classic. Brilliant.' Fell's other collaborations include the trio Something Else (with Mick Beck), the string trio IST, the Arc (with **Orphy Robinson**) and VHF, while his own groups include SFQ and SFT. He also works with **Peter**

Brötzmann, **Butch Morris** and **Derek Bailey** on a regular basis and is a founder member of London Improvisers Orchestra. Along with Sheffield's **Martin Archer**, Fell is a leading composer of his generation, crossing boundaries and creating music of a passion and originality unusual in Britain.

● ALBUMS: *Amis And Amiloun* cassette (Bruce's Fingers 1984) ★★★, *Compilation I* (Bruce's Fingers 1985) ★★★★, *Nightfall Two (Standards I)* cassette (Bruce's Fingers 1986) ★★★, with Charles Wharf *Pride And Prejudice* (Bruce's Fingers 1987) ★★★, *The Universe* cassette (Bruce's Fingers 1988) ★★★, with Persuasion A *Two Steps To Easier Breathing* (Bruce's Fingers 1988) ★★★, *The Coral Island* cassette (Bruce's Fingers 1988) ★★★, *The House In Paris* cassette (Bruce's Fingers 1989) ★★★, with Wharf *Five On Genius* cassette (Bruce's Fingers 1989) ★★★, with Paul Hession, Wharf *Laid Back Leisure Spots* cassette (Bruce's Fingers 1990) ★★★, with Lol Coxhill, George Haslam, Paul Rutherford *Termite One* (Bruce's Fingers 1990) ★★★, with Hession, Alan Wilkinson, Paul Buckton, Ian McMillan *Termite Two* cassette (Bruce's Fingers 1990) ★★★, with Hession, Wharf, Robert Kretzschmar *Millions Of Wishes Come True In Plastic Film* cassette (Bruce's Fingers 1990) ★★★, *Compilation II* (Bruce's Fingers 1990) ★★★★, with Wharf *M.M.* cassette (Bruce's Fingers 1990) ★★★, *L'Huile Sur Le Feu* cassette (Bruce's Fingers 1990) ★★★, with Hession, Jeffrey Morgan *Eight Classic Jazz Originals You Can Play* cassette (Bruce's Fingers 1991) ★★★, *Max* cassette (Bruce's Fingers 1991) ★★★, with Hession, Alan Wilkinson *Bogey's* (Bruce's Fingers 1991) ★★★, with Hession, Wilkinson *Foom! Foom!* (Bruce's Fingers 1992) ★★★★, with Something Else *Rear Quarters* cassette (Bruce's Fingers 1992) ★★★, with Hession, Wilkinson *The Horrors Of Darmstadt* (Shock 1994) ★★★, with Something Else *Start Moving Earbuds* (Bruce's Fingers 1994) ★★★, *Music For 10(o)* (Leo 1995) ★★★, with Something Else *Playing With Tunes* (Bruce's Fingers 1997) ★★★, with IST *Consequences (Of Time And Place)* cassette (Front 1997) ★★★★, with IST *Anagrams To Avoid* (SIWA 1997) ★★★★, with Graham Halliwell *9 Points In Ascent* (Bruce's Fingers 1998) ★★★, with Wharf *Frankenstein* (Bruce's Fingers 1998) ★★★, *Composition No. 30* (Bruce's Fingers 1998) ★★★★, with IST *Ghost Notes* (Bruce's Fingers 1998) ★★★, with Martin Archer *Pure Water Construction* (Discus 1998) ★★★, with Hession, Wilkinson *Registered Firm* 1996 recording (Incus 1998) ★★★, with VHF *Extracts* (Erstwhile 1999) ★★★, *Composition No. 12.5* (Bruce's Fingers 1999) ★★★, with Hession, Wilkinson *St. John's* (Ecstatic Peace! 2000) ★★★, with Hession, Wharf *Improvabilly* (Bruce's Fingers 2002) ★★★, *Kaleidozyklen* (Bruce's Fingers 2002) ★★★.

Fell, Terry

b. 13 May 1921, Dora, Alabama, USA, d. 1998. Although Terry Fell's name appears only once in the *Billboard* country charts, he staked his claim to fame by being not only the writer of 'Truck Driving Man' but also the original recorder of the song. In 1930 he swapped his pet groundhog for a guitar, although it was to be three years before anyone showed him how to play it or the mandolin that he also acquired. At 16 he hitchhiked his way to California, spending some time with the Civilian Conservation Corps. He eventually returned home, but he and his widowed mother finally relocated to the Los Angeles area. In 1943, while working for Tru-Flex tyres, he began, to play bass with Merle Lindsey's Nightriders. Around 1945 he joined Billy Hughes, made his first recordings for Fargo and began to write songs for the American Music Company. In 1954, after further recordings for Memo, Courtney and 4-Star, he joined **RCA-Victor Records**, making his first recordings on their subsidiary 'X' label. 'Truck Driving Man' appeared as the b-side of his first 'X' single, in April 1954. The a-side, 'Don't Drop It', became a number 4 US country chart hit (his only one), and although 'Truck Driving Man' failed to chart for Fell, it went on to become a country standard. It has since been charted by both **George Hamilton IV** and **Red Steagall** and recorded by countless other artists, including **Buck Owens**. He made further recordings and worked as an artist for a few years, until the lack of further hits and throat problems saw him lose interest in performing. In 1962 he relocated to Nashville, where he wrote songs and worked for several publishing companies until he eventually retired. In 1993 **Bear Family Records** issued a CD containing all 24 of his RCA masters—two previously unissued. Fell also co-wrote 'You're The Reason', a US country and pop Top 12 hit for **Bobby Edwards** in 1961 and later successfully recorded by **Daniel O'Donnell**.

● COMPILATIONS: *Truck Driving Man* (Bear Family 1993) ★★★, *The Original Truck Driving Man* (CowgirlBoy 1994) ★★★.

Feller, Dick

b. 2 January 1943, Bronaugh, Missouri, USA. Feller grew up with a love of both country and blues music and became a proficient rock 'n' roll guitarist. In 1966, intent on becoming a professional songwriter, he moved to Nashville and found work playing sessions or going on the road with musicians including **Skeeter Davis**, **Warner Mack** and **Mel Tillis**. **Johnny Cash** had a US number 1 country hit with Feller's 'Any Old Wind That Blows' in 1972. **Jerry Reed** did the same in 1973 with 'Lord Mr. Ford', a song rejected by **Jimmy Dean**, and recorded many more of Feller's songs: 'East Bound And Down' (for the film *Smokey And The Bandit*), 'Second-Hand Satin Lady (And A Bargain Basement Boy)' and 'The Phantom Of The Opry'. In the mid-70s Feller had his own country hits with 'Biff, The Friendly Purple Bear', 'Making The Best Of A Bad Situation', 'Uncle Hiram And His Homemade Beer' and a narrative that is even more pertinent today, 'The Credit Card Song'. His tours of UK country clubs have shown that he is not just another Feller, and he can stop any show with 'Daisy Hill'.

● ALBUMS: *Dick Feller Wrote . . .* (United Artists 1973) ★★★, *No Word On Me* (Asylum 1975) ★★★★, *Some Days Are Diamonds* (Asylum 1975) ★★★, *Children In Their Wishes, Ladies In Their Dreams* (Asylum 1977) ★★★, *Audiograph Alive* (Indigo Music 1982) ★★★.

Fellside Records

This Cumbria-based UK label was formed, in 1976, by Paul Adams (b. 26 January 1948, Coventry, Warwickshire, England) and Linda Adams (b. 24 April 1954, Workington, Cumbria, England). From the start, encompassing a policy of recording all types of folk music, from traditional to contemporary, they released *Teller Of Tales* by Terry Docherty. Unfortunately, Docherty's career did not blossom, and the album failed to sell. Over the years, Fellside have gone from recording straight into stereo, up to the current 16-track set up. After their initial 'hic-cup', they have now recorded a number of successful folk artists, including **Bram Taylor**, **Steve Turner**, **Jez Lowe** and **Peter Bellamy**. In 1985 Paul and Linda set up the Lake label to concentrate on the jazz field. The first release was a reissue from the **Decca** catalogue by **Ken Colyer**. The first original release on Lake was called *Harlem*, by the Harlem Vintage Big Band, in 1985. Fellside's reputation has grown over the years, and they remain one of the few independent labels in England, specializing in the folk field. Although working and recording as a duo, Paul and Linda did not release records on their own label.

● COMPILATIONS: *Far Over The Fell* (1975) ★★★, *The Best Of Radio Cumbria's Folk Workshop* (1976) ★★★★, *Country Hirings* (1977) ★★★, *Among The Old Familiar Mountains* (1978) ★★★, *Flash Company* (1986) ★★★, *The Fellside Song Sampler, Volume 1* (1987) ★★★★, *The Fellside Instrumental Sampler, Volume 1* (1987) ★★★★, *Fellside Folk Favourites* (1987) ★★★★.

Felt

Cultivated, experimental English pop outfit formed in 1980 whose guru was the enigmatic Lawrence Hayward (b. Birmingham, West Midlands, England; vocals/guitar). Early collaborators included Maurice Deebank (guitar) and Nick Gilbert (bass), who practised together in a small village called Water Orton just outside Birmingham. By the time of their first album, released on **Cherry Red Records**, drummer Tony Race was replaced by Gary Ainge, and Gilbert departed to be replaced on bass by Mick Lloyd. Martin Duffy joined on organ for *Ignite The Seven Cannons*. Cult status had already arrived with the archetypal Felt track 'Penelope Tree'. The critical respect they were afforded continued, although they enjoyed little in the way of commercial recognition. The nearest they came was the 1985 single 'Primitive Painters', where they were joined by Elizabeth Fraser of the **Cocteau Twins** in a stirring, pristine pop song produced by fellow Cocteau Robin Guthrie.

They signed to **Creation Records** in 1985. However, as Felt's contract with Cherry Red expired, so did the tenure of Hayward's fellow guitarist and co-writer Deebank. The latter, classically trained, had been an important component of the Felt sound and was chiefly responsible for the delicate but intoxicating drama of early releases. Their stay at Creation saw high points in *Forever Breathes The Lonely Word* (1986) and *Poem Of The River* (1987). On the latter they were joined by Marco Thomas, Tony Willé and Neil Scott to add to the melodic guitar broadside. Felt bowed out with *Me And A Monkey On The Moon*, after a final move to Él Records, at which time guitar duties had switched to John Mohan.

By the end of the 80s the band was no more, having achieved their stated task of surviving 10 years, 10 singles, and 10 albums (*Bubblegum Perfume* is an archive release of their Creation material; *The Felt Box Set* compiles their Cherry Red recordings). Hayward chose to concentrate on his new project, 70s revivalists **Denim**. Duffy joined **Primal Scream**, while Ainge and Thomas formed Fly.

● ALBUMS: *Crumbling The Antiseptic Beauty* mini-album (Cherry Red 1982) ★★★, *The Splendour Of Fear* mini-album (Cherry Red 1983) ★★★, *The Strange Idols Pattern And Other Short Stories* (Cherry Red 1984) ★★★, *Ignite The Seven Cannons* (Cherry Red 1985) ★★★, *Let The Snakes Crinkle Their Heads To Death* (Creation 1986) ★★★, *Forever Breathes The Lonely Word* (Creation 1986) ★★★★, *Poem Of The River* (Creation 1987) ★★★, *The Pictorial Jackson Review* (Creation 1988) ★★★, *Train Above The City* (Creation 1988) ★★★, *Me And A Monkey On The Moon* (Él 1989) ★★.

● COMPILATIONS: *Gold Mine Trash* (Cherry Red 1987) ★★★, *Bubblegum Perfume* (Creation 1990) ★★★★, *Absolute Classic Masterpieces Volume 2* (Creation 1993) ★★★, *The Felt Box Set* 4-CD box set (Cherry Red 1993) ★★★★, *Stains On A Decade* (Cherry Red 2003) ★★★★.

● DVD/VIDEOS: *Felt: A Declaration* (Cherry Red 2003).

Felten, Eric

b. Eric Thomas Felten, 18 September 1964, Phoenix, Arizona, USA. Born into a highly musical family, among whom were several professional jazz musicians, a career in music was inevitable. Felten took up the trombone, studying from the age of nine with his grandfather, Lester Felten, who had played trombone in dance bands during the swing era. He earned a degree at Arizona State University and another at Harvard before starting work as a journalist in Washington, DC. This was in the summer of 1989, and meanwhile, he eagerly pursued an alternative career as a jazz musician. He played in various bands in the Washington area before forming his own group at the beginning of 1991. In the course of the next two years, the International Trombone Association named him as Best New Jazz Trombonist, and he released his first album for **Soul Note Records**, on which he was joined by **Jimmy Knepper** and **Joshua Redman**, having met the latter while both were students at Harvard. He continued to lead the Eric Felten Jazz Orchestra in Washington, gaining considerable critical acclaim for its performances of classic big band music of the swing era. His follow-up album continued his display of appreciation of the music of past masters; the concept for *Gratitude* was modelled upon the small groups drawn from the **Duke Ellington** band of the 30s. Once again, for his sidemen he called upon established jazz artists, among them **Joe Lovano**, **Randy Brecker** and **Bob Mintzer**.

Meanwhile, Felten had been showing a talent for singing, and in 1998 he sang with his big band during a one-hour show on Black Entertainment Television's BETonJazz cable network. He has also sung and played with the Bloomington Pops Orchestra in Indiana and the Mid-Atlantic Symphony Orchestra. At the end of the 90s, he occasionally played trombone duets with his grandfather, who was then in his nineties. As the mid-80s and onwards popularity of **new swing** bands demonstrates, Felten is not alone in referring back to music of an age that was over long before he was born. Significantly, he does it with flair, considerable musicality and with great respect for the originals.

● ALBUMS: *T-Bop* (Soul Note 1993) ★★★, *Gratitude* (Soul Note 1995) ★★★, *Nowhere Without You* (BSD 2003) ★★★, *Eric Felten Meets The Dek-Tette* (VSOP 2005) ★★.

Felton, Roy

b. USA. Although he never became widely known, Felton, who sang in a pleasing baritone voice, was the band singer for **Benny Carter** in 1934. Between the mid-30s and early 40s he made a small number of records, including some sides with the **Mills Brothers**.

Felts, Narvel

b. Albert Narvel Felts, 11 November 1938, Keiser, Arkansas, USA. Felts obtained his first guitar when aged 13 and taught himself to play. In 1956 he won a talent contest, appeared on local radio and passed an audition as a rock 'n' roll singer for **Sun Records** in Memphis, although his sessions were not released at the time. In 1957 his first record for **Mercury Records**, 'Kiss-a-me Baby', sold 20,000 copies. He made the US charts in 1959 with '3,000 Miles' and 'Honey Love', both for Pink Records. He had sporadic success for some years ('I'm Movin' On', 'Rockin' Little Angel'), and then, in 1973, he had a huge country hit for the Cinnamon label with Mentor Williams' 'Drift Away', which was followed by a string of country hits—'When Your Good Love Was Mine', 'All In The Name Of Love', 'Raindrops'. In 1975, moving to **Dot Records**, he had a number 2 US country hit with 'Reconsider Me'. He recorded the most successful version of 'Funny How Time Slips Away' and issued emotional revivals of 'Lonely Teardrops' and 'My Prayer'. In 1976 he had a US country hit with a song **Conway Twitty** had given him 16 years earlier, 'Lonely Kind Of Love'. He continued to register minor country hits into the 80s, such as the 1987 recording of 'When A Man Loves A Woman'. Looking like a haggard Omar Sharif, he tours with his band, the Driftaways, regularly visiting the UK and including songs from all periods of his career.

● ALBUMS: *Drift Away* (Cinnamon 1973) ★★★, *Live* (Cinammon 1974) ★★, *When Your Good Love Was Mine* (Cinammon 1974) ★★, *Reconsider Me* (Dot 1975) ★★★, *Narvel Felts* (Dot 1975) ★★★, *Narvel The Marvel* (Dot 1976) ★★★, *Doin' What I Like* (Dot 1976) ★★★, *This Time* (Hi 1976) ★★★, *The Touch Of Felts* (Dot 1977) ★★, *Narvel* (Dot 1977) ★★★, *Inside Love* (ABC 1978) ★★★, *One Run For The Roses* (ABC 1979) ★★, *A Teen's Way* (Bear Family 1987) ★★★, *Memphis Days* (Bear Family 1991) ★★★, *Pink and Golden Days* (Fox 1991) ★★★, *Season's Greetings* (Cone 2004) ★★.

● COMPILATIONS: *Narvel Felts' Greatest Hits* (Dot 1976) ★★★, *Drift Away: The Best Of 1973-1979* (Bear Family 1996) ★★★★, *The Very Best Of Narvel Felts* (De Luxe 1998) ★★★, *Ode To Bub* (Cone 1999) ★★★★, *The Hi Records Era 1959-73* (Demon 2001) ★★★, *Super Songs Narvelized* (Cone 2002) ★★★.

Femme Fatale

This US quintet formed in Albuquerque, New Mexico, in 1987. However, it was not long before they relocated to the bright lights of Los Angeles, in the quest for wider exposure and A&R attention from record companies. Fronted by Lorraine Lewis (b. 26 September, Albuquerque, New Mexico, USA), they were quickly snapped up by MCA Records, who assigned Jim Faraci (of **L.A. Guns** fame) as producer. Musically, they strived to corner the same market as **Bon Jovi**, relying on a pop/hard rock crossover approach. In interviews Lewis repeatedly stated her objective was to be the biggest 'pin up girl' in rock. The band, completed by Mazzi Rawd (guitar), Bill D'Angelo (d. 22 November 2005; guitar), Rick Rael (bass) and Bobby Murray (drums), recorded a self-titled debut album that played heavily on their vocalist's sexuality. This approach often overshadowed Lewis' genuine ability, and although it was received favourably by the critics, it was quickly consigned to the bargain bins, while the band disappeared without trace. Lewis went on to record solo

material before forming Mercy with ex–Black Eyed Susan bass player Erik Levy, with this unit releasing an album in 1993. She resumed solo work later in the decade.

● ALBUMS: *Femme Fatale* (MCA 1988) ★★★.

Fender, Freddy

b. Baldemar G. Huerta, 4 June 1937, San Benito, Texas, USA. Fender, a Mexican-American, comes from a family of migrant workers who were based in the San Benito Valley. A farmworker from the age of 10, Fender says he 'worked beets in Michigan, pickles in Ohio, baled hay and picked tomatoes in Indiana. When that was over, it was cotton-picking time in Arkansas.' Fender sang and played guitar along with the blues, country and Mexican records he heard on the radio, which eventually developed into his own hybrid style. He joined the US marines in 1953, spending his time in the brig and eventually being dismissed for bad conduct. Referring back to his military service, he says, 'It has taken me 35 years to have my discharge changed from bad conduct, and this means I am now eligible for a military funeral.' He began playing rockabilly in Texas honky tonks in the late 50s and he recorded a Spanish version of 'Don't Be Cruel' as well as his own composition 'Wasted Days And Wasted Nights' (1958). He recalls: 'I had a gringo manager and started recording in English. Since I was playing a Fender guitar and amplifier, I changed my name to Freddy Fender.' A fight in one club left him with a broken nose and a knife wound in his neck. Starting in 1960 Fender spent three years in Angola State Prison, Louisiana, on drug offences, and he recorded several tracks on a cassette recorder while in jail, later collected on an album. Upon his release, he secured a residency at a Bourbon Street club in New Orleans.

Despairing of ever finding real success, Fender returned to San Benito in 1969 and took regular work as a mechanic. He gained a sociology degree with a view to helping ex-convicts. He returned to performing, however, and 'Before The Next Teardrop Falls', which he performed in English and Spanish, became a number 1 US pop hit in 1975. He had further US chart success with 'Wasted Days And Wasted Nights' (number 8 and dedicated to **Doug Sahm**), 'Secret Love' (number 20), 'You'll Lose A Good Thing' and 'Vaya Con Dios'. Fender's overwrought vocals, which even added something to 'How Much Is That Doggie In The Window?', were skilfully matched by **Huey P. Meaux**'s arrangements featuring marimbas, accordion, harpsichord and steel guitar. His fuzzy hair and roly-poly body made him an unlikely pop star, but his admirers included **Elvis Presley**.

Fender succumbed to alcohol and drugs, which forced his wife, in 1985, to enter him in a clinic, which apparently cured him. Fender played a corrupted mayor in the 1987 movie *The Milagro Beanfield War*, directed by Robert Redford. In 1990 he formed an all-star Tex-Mex band, the **Texas Tornados**, with long-time friends Sahm and **Augie Meyers** (from **Sir Douglas Quintet**) and accordionist **Flaco Jiminez**. Their self-titled debut album was a critical and commercial success, but subsequent collaborations have failed to match its stylist blend of conjunto, country and R&B. Fender was signed to **Warner Brothers Records** as a soloist on the back of the group's success. *The Freddy Fender Collection*, his initial offering, was a disappointing collection of remakes of his early hits. In 2001 he was reported as being unwell with hepatitis, and the following year he underwent surgery for a kidney transplant (kindly donated by his daughter).

Nevertheless, his collection of Latin classics *La Música De Baldemar Huerta* won a Grammy Award for best Latin pop album.

● ALBUMS: *Before The Next Teardrop Falls* (ABC 1975) ★★★, *Recorded Inside Louisiana State Prison* (ABC 1975) ★★★, *Since I Met You Baby* (ABC 1975) ★★★, *Are You Ready For Freddy?* (ABC 1975) ★★★, *Rock N' Country* (ABC 1976) ★★★, *If You're Ever In Texas* (ABC 1976) ★★★, *If You Don't Love Me* (ABC 1977) ★★★, *Merry Christmas—Feliz Navidad* (ABC 1977) ★★, with Roy Clark, Hank Thompson, Don Williams *Country Comes To Carnegie Hall* (ABC/Dot 1977) ★★★★, *Swamp Gold* (ABC 1978) ★★★, *The Texas Balladeer* (Starflite 1979) ★★★, *Together We Drifted Apart* (Starflite 1980) ★★★, *Crazy Baby* (Starburst 1987) ★★★, with Texas Tornados *The Freddy Fender Collection* (Warners 1991) ★★, *Christmas Time In The Valley* (MCA 1991) ★★, *Canciones De Mi Barrio* (Arhoolie 1994) ★★★, *In Concert* (Hacienda 1995) ★★★, *Live At Gilley's* (Atlantic 1999) ★★★, *La Música De Baldemar Huerta* (Studio M/Virgin 2001) ★★★★, *Close To My Heart* (Fuel 2000 2004) ★★★.

● COMPILATIONS: *The Best Of Freddy Fender* (Dot 1977) ★★★, *20 Greatest Hits* (Astan 1984) ★★★, *Best Of Freddy Fender* (MCA 1985) ★★★, *Early Years 1959–1963* (Krazy Kat 1986) ★★★, *Greatest Hits: Freddy Fender* (Big Country 1988) ★★★, *The Crazy Cajun Recordings* (Edsel 1999) ★★★★, *The Best Of Freddy Fender: The Millennium Collection* (PolyGram 2000) ★★★★.

● FILMS: *Short Eyes* aka *Slammer* (1977), *She Came To The Valley* aka *Texas In Flames* (1977), *The Milagro Beanfield War* (1988).

Fender, Leo

b. 10 August 1909, Anaheim, California, USA, d. 21 March 1991, USA. Along with **Les Paul** and Adolph **Rickenbacker**, Leo Fender was one of the key names in the development of the electric guitar in the middle of the twentieth century. He first came to the attention of the musical instrument manufacturing industry when he was working with 'Doc' Kauffman producing guitar amplifiers in the mid-40s. He had developed a new smaller pick up and designed a solid body guitar based on the Hawaiian steel with which to demonstrate it. Although the pick up itself was quite revolutionary, local musicians were more intrigued with the guitar, and so Fender decided to concentrate his efforts in that direction. In 1946 he left Kauffman and formed the Fender Electrical Instrument Company. The idea of a solid body guitar had been in the forefront of manufacturer's minds since the advent of electrical amplification, which meant that hollow sound boxes were no longer essential. It was Fender, along with Californian neighbours Paul and Paul Bigsby, who spearheaded the forthcoming wave of electric guitars.

In 1948 Fender launched the Broadcaster (later called the Telecaster), which remained virtually unchanged for the next 30 or so years; there were a few variations such as the Esquire (1954), the Thinkline (1969), the Deluxe (1972) and the Custom (1972). Famous rock 'n' roll guitarist **James Burton** favours a Telecaster, as does **Bruce Welch** of the **Shadows**, **Steve Cropper**, **Roy Buchanan** and **Bruce Springsteen**. Fender's next major instrument was the Stratocaster, developed in 1953 with his chief engineer Leo Tavares and put into production the following year. Like the Telecaster, the Stratocaster was virtually untouched in design over the next few decades and became a favourite of **Buddy Holly**, **Hank B. Marvin**, **Eric Clapton**, **Rory Gallagher**, **Mark Knopfler** and the master, **Jimi Hendrix**, to name just a few of thousands. In 1990 a Stratocaster once owned by Hendrix was sold at auction for almost £200,000. The design, shape, feel and colour of the Stratocaster became an art form and, probably, the accepted icon for the electric guitar. In 1955 Fender contracted a virus that would dog him for the next decade.

In the mid-60s, convinced that he had little time to live, Fender decided to order his affairs. The Fender Electrical Instrument Company was sold to CBS in January 1965 for $13 million, shortly after which Fender made a complete recovery. CBS employed him as a consultant, and he continued to help design and develop new guitars. Later he formed the CLF Research Company before returning to consultancy work for Music Man guitars, started by former Fender employees Thomas Walker and Forrest White. In the 80s he formed G&L (George and Leo) Guitars with longtime associate George Fullerton. They continued to make popular instruments, although names like the F100–1 series were less appealing than their forebears. Fender died in the spring of 1991 aged 82. As well as the guitars mentioned, the Fender name is also attached to the Musicmaster (1956), the Jazzmaster (1958), the Jaguar (1961) and the Starcaster (1975). He also moved into electric basses in 1951 with the Precision and then the Jazz Bass (1960), Bass VI (1962) and the Telecaster Bass (1968).

● FURTHER READING: *The Fender Book: A Complete History Of Fender Electric Guitars*, Tony Bacon and Paul Day. *Fender Custom Shop Guitar Gallery*, Richard Smith. *50 Years Of Fender*, Tony Bacon.

Fendermen

Formed in 1959 in Milwaukee, Wisconsin, USA, the Fendermen were a trio best known for the 1960 US chart Top 5 rock 'n' roll adaptation of the **Jimmie Rodgers** country standard 'Muleskinner Blues'. The group consisted of guitarists Jim Sundquist and Phil Humphrey (both b. 26 November 1937, Sundquist in Niagara, Wisconsin, USA, and Humphrey in Stoughton, Wisconsin, USA) and drummer John Howard of LaCrosse, Wisconsin, USA. The two guitarists, who preferred the Fender brand of electric guitar, hence the name of the group, recorded 'Muleskinner Blues' initially for the small Cuca label. It was picked up by the somewhat larger Minnesota-based **Soma Records** and became a hit in May 1960. (Howard was added at that time for live appearances.) The group recorded one album for Soma, now a valued rarity in the USA, and continued together until 1966, with no other chart successes.

● ALBUMS: *Mule Skinner Blues* (Soma 1960) ★★.

Fenix TX

This Houston, Texas, USA–based pop punk band was originally known as Riverfenix when it was formed in 1995. Several personnel changes occurred over the next two years before the band settled on a steady line-up comprising Willie Salazar (guitar/vocals), Damon Delapaz (guitar/vocals), Adam Lewis (bass) and Donnie Reyes (drums). After relocating to San Diego and appearing on 1997's nationwide Mullets Across America tour, Riverfenix released their self-titled debut album on the Drive Thru Records label. The quartet earned more notoriety and radio play for their tribute album cover version of **Duran Duran**'s 'Ordinary World'. A major label recording contract with MCA Records was not long in following, although they were forced to change their name to Fenix TX for legal reasons. MCA remixed and rereleased the band's debut album under the new title *Fenix TX* and were rewarded when the singles 'All My Fault' and 'Speechless' began to gain heavy radio rotation. Prior to recording their second album, the band parted company with Reyes. Delapaz moved from guitar to drums to accommodate new guitarist James Love. *Lechuza* (2001) displayed a greater heavy metal influence than their debut.

● ALBUMS: as Riverfenix *Riverfenix* (Drive Thru 1997) ★★★, *Fenix TX* (MCA 1999) ★★★, *Lechuza* (MCA 2001) ★★★, *Purple Reign In Blood: Live* (Adrenaline 2005) ★★.

Fennelly, Michael

b. 1948, New Jersey, USA. Initially a minor figure in California's pop/protest movement, by 1967 Fennelly had secured a publishing contract with songwriter/producer **Curt Boetcher**'s Mee Moo Music. Together they assembled two studio-based attractions, the **Millennium** and **Sagittarius**, before Fennelly took control of struggling bar-band Stonehenge, later renamed **Crabby Appleton**. Despite complimentary reviews, the group's two albums proved unsuccessful and in 1973 the artist opted for a solo career. *Lane Changer*, recorded in London with the support of rock group **Argent**, highlighted Fennelly's powerful voice and guitar skills, but his second set, *Stranger's Bed*, was less rewarding and failed to substantiate early promise.

● ALBUMS: *Lane Changer* (1973) ★★★, *Stranger's Bed* (1975) ★★.

Fenton, Bernie

b. Bernard Shaw Fenton, 17 November 1921, Doncaster, Yorkshire, England, d. 17 November 2001, England. In the 30s Fenton began playing piano in and around his hometown, including playing in Bert Clegg's band in Mexborough and also in neighbouring Nottinghamshire before moving to London. Throughout the 40s, Fenton worked with several band leaders, including **Johnny Claes**, **Oscar Rabin**, Sid Millward and **Tito Burns**. Towards the end of the 40s Fenton was a charter member of London's famed Club Eleven, a hotbed of the burgeoning British bop scene. Here and elsewhere in the city, he worked with **John Dankworth**, **Laurie Morgan**, Joe Muddell and other pioneers, such as **Tony Crombie**, **Tommy Pollard**, alto saxophonist Johnny Rogers and **Ronnie Scott**. He spent some time in the bands of Paul Adams and **Harry Parry** before becoming a staff musician and arranger in the music publishing industry. With the advent of commercial television in the UK, he became a successful writer of advertising jingles.

In 1985 a BBC television documentary in the *Arena* series reunited Fenton with other Club Eleven veteran alumni, among them **Lennie Bush**, trumpeter Leon Calvert, Crombie, Dankworth, Morgan, Muddell, Rogers (by now a Yorkshire hill farmer), Scott, trumpeter Hank Shaw, pianist Norman Stenfalt and drummer Flash Winston. Fenton, who also played organ, continued to perform throughout his late years with several bands, including the **Glenn Miller** tribute band led by **Herb Miller**. Fenton's long service in the jingle mines obscured the significant role he had played as a founder of British bop.

Fenton, George

b. 19 October 1949, England. An important composer for the British theatre, films and television from the 70s through to the 90s. After working on minor films in the 70s and early 80s, such as *What Became Of Jack And Jill*, *You're A Big Girl Now* and *Hussy*, Fenton got his big break in 1982, when he collaborated with **Ravi Shankar** on the score for Richard Attenborough's *Gandhi*. It was nominated for a Grammy and an Oscar, and the theme, 'For All Mankind', won an **Ivor Novello** award. Five years later, Fenton, in association with **Jonas Gwangwa**, won another 'Ivor' and two Oscar nominations (score and title song) for his work on another Attenborough project, *Cry Freedom*. Fenton has scored several other superior British productions, such as *Runners*, *The Company Of Wolves*, *Clockwise*, *White Of The Eye*, *84 Charing Cross Road*, *High Spirits*, *The Dressmaker*, *A Handful Of Dust*, *White Mischief*, *Ladybird Ladybird* and *The Madness Of King George* (1994, adapted from the works of George Frederic Handel). In the late 80s and early 90s, Fenton worked a good deal in the USA and won another Academy Award nomination for his score to the Glenn Close–John Malkovich drama *Dangerous Liaisons* (1988). Apart from *Memphis Belle*, which told an American World War II story but was actually a UK production, Fenton's other US movies have included *We're No Angels*, *The Long Walk Home*, *White Palace*, *China Moon*, *The Fisher King*, *Hero (Accidental Hero in UK)*, *Groundhog Day*, *Born Yesterday* and *Shadowlands* (1993). The last film brought him an Ivor Novello award for the best commissioned score. In 1991, his music for the Richard Gere–Kim Basinger thriller, *Final Analysis* was compared favourably to 'nearly everything **Bernard Herrmann** and **Miklos Rozsa** ever did'. As well as feature films, the composer worked prolifically in television on some of the most popular and critically acclaimed programmes of their time. By the early 90s these totalled a staggering 80 productions and included *Shoestring*, *Fox*, *The History Man*, *Going Gently*, *No Country For Old Men*, *Bergerac*, *A Woman Of No Importance*, *Outside Edge*, *Natural World*, *An Englishman Abroad*, *Saigon—Year Of The Cat*, *Village Earth*, *Walter*, *The Ghost Writer*, *The Jewel In The Crown*, *The Monocled Mutineer*, *The Trials Of Life* and two sets of six plays and six monologues (*Talking Heads*) by Alan Bennett. He won the BAFTA Award for the best original television music in 1981, 1983 and 1986 and cornered the market in jingles for various daily news bulletins in the BBC's domestic and World Service.

From the early 70s he also worked in provincial theatres, with the Royal Shakespeare Company and at the National Theatre composing music and serving as musical director for a variety of productions including *Rosencrantz And Guildenstern Are Dead*, *A Month In The Country*, *Don Juan*, *Bengal Lancer*, *Kafka's Dick*, *High Society*, *Racing Demon*, *Saki* and many more. He also composed a children's opera, *Birthday*. Much of his music has been released on records.

Fenton, Shane

b. Bernard William Jewry, 27 September 1942, London, England. Fenton achieved his first notable success after securing a spot on *Saturday Club*, BBC Radio's influential show. Backed by the **Fentones** and sporting a distinctive silver lamé suit, the singer quickly became a part of Britain's pre-beat enclave, beside other home-grown talent including **Cliff Richard**, **Marty Wilde**, **Duffy Power** and **Billy Fury**. Fenton had a UK Top 30 hit in 1961 with the mythologizing 'I'm A Moody Guy', but despite several similarly structured releases, only 'Cindy's Birthday' (1962) broached the UK Top 20. Deemed passé on the rise of the **Beatles**, Fenton eked out a living from the rock 'n' roll/cabaret circuit until revitalizing his career in the 70s under a new guise, **Alvin Stardust**.

● ALBUMS: *Good Rockin' Tonight* (Contour 1974) ★★.
● FILMS: *It's All Happening* (1963).

Fentones

Jerry Wilcox (b. 1940; lead guitar), Mickey Eyre (b. 1942; rhythm guitar), William Walter Edward 'Bonney' Oliver (bass) and Tony Hinchcliffe (b. 1940; drums) provided the backing to singer **Shane Fenton**. They became a popular attraction in their own right, recording several instrumental singles, including 'The Mexican' and 'The Breeze And I', both of which reached the UK Top 50 in 1962. Briefly touted as possible rivals to the **Shadows**, such aspirations proved over-ambitious, and in keeping with many pre-beat contemporaries, the Fentones were later eclipsed by the **Beatles** and the new generation following in their wake.

● FILMS: *It's All Happening* (1963).

Fergie

b. Robert Ferguson, 16 November 1979, Larne, Belfast, Northern Ireland. A fresh-faced DJ star of the popular hard **house** scene, Fergie first performed behind the decks, aged 14, standing on a milk crate at the local Airport 2000 club. By the time he was 16, he had DJed at all the leading clubs on Ireland's **dance music** scene. While visiting The House club in Larne, the 'godfather' of hard house, **Tony De Vit**, was impressed with the ferocious energy of Fergie's set and introduced the fledgling DJ to the English club scene. In summer 1997 Fergie toured South Africa, playing at the major cities. The following summer he debuted in Ibiza, playing at the world-famous Privilege, Space and Bora Bora. The promoter of **Trade**, Laurence Malice was sufficiently impressed to make Fergie a regular guest at the influential London club. In November 1998 Fergie toured in Australia and on the east coast of America in early 1999. On a second visit to Australia the same year, he came second to house legend **Frankie Knuckles** in the Best International DJ Awards. His first single, a double a-side, 'People Are Still Having Sex'/ 'Ooh Sir!', had already been released on Trade's record label. A massive club hit, its success brought him remix work, beginning with the Tamperer's 'Hammer To My Heart'. He was also nominated as Best Newcomer in *Muzik* magazine's influential annual awards. In 2000 Fergie released tracks for various labels and took up residencies at the UK superclubs Godskitchen and Code. He also signed a single contract with **'Tall' Paul Newman**'s label **Duty Free Recordings**. His first single for the label 'Deception', was a major club success and reached the UK Top 40. After performing the first Essential Mix for BBC Radio 1 in 2001, Fergie signed a contract with the station in March to be the official Essential Mix DJ, broadcasting bimonthly mixes from major dance events such as those in Ibiza and the UK's festivals, Homelands and the Love Parade. He also won a televised 'Battle of the DJs' contest against **Fatboy Slim** and **Carl Cox** among others that was staged by the BBC as part of 2001's Comic Relief annual charity event.

● COMPILATIONS: *Hard House Anthems—Mixed By BK & Fergie* (Nukleuz 2000) ★★★, *Harder Faster: The Essential Hard House Mix* (DMC 2000) ★★★★, *Hard Energy— Mixed By Fergie And Yomanda* (MOS 2001) ★★★.

Fergus, Winston

UK-based Fergus began his career in 1976 as the lead singer of the Equators. The band is best remembered for 'Father Oh Father' on Joe Sinclair's Klik label. As well as performing in their own right, the band also provided musical backing for the up-and-coming vocalist, **Pablo Gad**. In 1977 Fergus, widely regarded as Gad's benefactor, introduced the young singer to Sinclair. The introduction led to the release of Gad's debut recordings 'International Dread' and 'Kunte Kinte' through the Caribbean-affiliated label. In the same year Fergus embarked on a solo career, releasing his debut 'Give Me Love', featured on *Jah Jah Bus*. Lightning Records signed Fergus and released 'African Woman'. The single failed to emulate Lightning's earlier success with **Althea And Donna**'s 'Uptown Top Ranking', although the label persevered with the singer and released 'Long Time'. As with the previous release the single failed to crossover, which signalled the end of Fergus' association with the label, although they later licensed 'Long Time' for release on **Trojan Records**. In 1979 Fergus released 'Fly Natty Dread' and a version of the classic 'Loving Pauper'. He maintained his profile throughout the 80s working with **Clement Bushay** ('Jezebel Woman' and 'Pay To Live'), Clive Stanhope ('Keep On Dancing' and 'One Day Up') and John Dread ('Hope For The World' and *I Will Sing*). In the early 90s Fergus demonstrated his independent stance when he set up his own Fergie Music label. His debut, 'Get Some Shopping', was followed by songs including 'My Love', 'Yesterday' and 'My Own Way' as well as the album *Love Is All Around Me*. In 1998 Fergus embarked on sessions with Chris Jay of Dubwise Productions, releasing 'Rough Times' and 'Praise H.I.M.'.

● ALBUMS: *Gangster Of Love* (Burning Sounds 1980) ★★★, *I Will Sing* (Hands & Heart 1988) ★★★, *Love Is All Around Me* (Fergie Music 1996) ★★★.

Ferguson, Ernest

b. 16 July 1918, Bon Aqua Post Office, near Nashville, Tennessee, USA. Ferguson moved to Nashville in his teens and was advised to learn mandolin because there were too many guitarists. He joined **Johnnie And Jack**'s Tennessee Mountain Boys on WSIX and later moved with them to Greenboro, Charleston and Bluefield. When World War II intervened, he worked in a Charleston factory during 1943, before playing with Wright and Eddie Hill at WNOX Knoxville until late in 1944. He then relocated to Nashville, where he worked on WSM with the **Bailes Brothers** until 1946. He made numerous appearances with them on the *Grand Ole Opry* and played on their King and **Columbia** recordings. In 1947 he ran a booking agency but also rejoined Johnnie And Jack on WSM but refrained from major touring with them. He also played on recordings they made as the King Sacred Quartet (**Clyde Moody** and **Ray Atkins** joining the duo for these recordings). In 1948 he rejoined the Bailes Brothers in Shreveport and remained with them until they disbanded. He then moved to Washington, DC, where he recorded with **Grandpa Jones** and for some years was a part-time musician as a member of the Blue River Boys. He eventually retired to Fairview, Tennessee, and worked outside of music for some years. However, in the mid-70s, after meeting members of the Bailes Brothers again, he began to play some fairs and festivals with them. He also played on their noted *Reunion* and with Walter Bailes on his solo album. Ferguson played on numerous albums with other artists, but it was not until 1977 that he recorded a solo album, a collection of mandolin instrumentals for Old Homestead. During his career, Ferguson, who was respected as one of the best mandolinists of the 40s and 50s, was also noted for his harmony vocals and for his ability to play comedy, which he presented in the guise of a character he called Abner Abernacky.

● ALBUMS: *Ernest Ferguson—Mandolin Album* (Old Homestead 1977) ★★★★.

Ferguson, H-Bomb

b. Robert Ferguson. In the fallout that succeeded the acquisition of his stage name, Ferguson obliterated all knowledge of his past beyond the fact that his father was a minister who disapproved of his son playing blues and boogie-woogie on the church piano. In later years, his identity has been further masked by a bewildering array of gaudy wigs. He first took the stage at the age of 16, having persuaded **Cat Anderson** to let him sing with his band. A year later Anderson hired him. He first recorded as Bob Ferguson with Jack Parker's Orchestra for Derby in 1950. Around this time, manager Chet Patterson suggested he call himself the Cobra Kid, but his 1951 records for Atlas billed him as H-Bomb, as celebrated in 'Rock H-Bomb Rock'. After a single for Prestige, he signed to Savoy and singles such as 'Good Lovin'' and 'Preachin' The Blues' (based on 'Bloodshot Eyes') were full-blown imitations of the **Wynonie Harris** shouting style. In 1953 he recorded two titles for **Specialty** that remained unissued for some 40 years. Further singles for Sunset, Finch, Big Bang and ARC failed to sell, and his 1960 session for Federal marked the end of his recording career at the time. In recent years, he has made a comeback, but his energetic live performances and outlandish headwear are insufficient compensation for a wayward talent long since spent.

● ALBUMS: *Life Is Hard* (Savoy Jazz 1987) ★★★, *Bad Times Blues* (Papa Lou Recordings 1990) ★★, *Wiggin' Out* (Earwig 1993) ★★.

● COMPILATIONS: *Roots Of Rock 'N' Roll Volume 9, The Shouters* (Savoy 1980) ★★★★, *Shouting The Blues* (Specialty 1993) ★★★★.

Ferguson, Jay

b. John Ferguson, 10 May 1947, Burbank, California, USA. The former lead singer of seminal progressive rock band **Spirit** and hard rock quartet **Jo Jo Gunne**, Ferguson's debut album was well received but sold poorly. However, two years later the sparkling 'Thunder Island' made the US Top 10. The accompanying album stands as his best work. His name often appeared as session singer on other albums amidst the occasional (and usually abortive) Spirit reunions.

● ALBUMS: *All Alone In The End Zone* (Asylum 1976) ★★★, *Thunder Island* (Asylum 1978) ★★★, *Real Life Ain't This Way* (Asylum 1979) ★★, *White Noise* (Capitol 1982) ★★.

Ferguson, Jim

b. James Warner Ferguson, 10 December 1950, Jefferson City, Missouri, USA. Ferguson's father had been a high school

music teacher, but not long after his son was born the family moved to South Carolina, where his father became music director at a large church. There Jim began singing in the children's choir at the age of four and later began taking piano lessons from the church organist. The piano lessons continued into his teens, but his principal musical interest was in singing. While in junior high school, he studied voice with a teacher from the University of South Carolina. During his senior year, he bought a bass, which he played to accompany the church choir. After graduating from high school, he entered USC's School of Music as a voice major, later starting formal acoustic bass lessons. Still unsure of his musical direction, Ferguson was moved towards jazz by George Naff, a graduate student at USC who was also a jazz pianist. As Ferguson's ability on the bass developed, he began to get offers of work and advice. Ferguson has cited guitarist Terry Rosen and trumpeter Johnny Helms as being especially valuable advisors at this stage in his career. Meanwhile, he had auditioned for the **New Christy Minstrels** who needed a male singer who could solo and play bass. Leaving school three weeks before the end of his first year, he joined the group at the Fontainbleau Hotel in Miami Beach, opening for veteran comedian Milton Berle.

During his spell with the group he also visited Los Angeles where he heard **Supersax** at Donte's jazz club. The band's bass player, **Buddy Clark**, invited Ferguson to attend Supersax's first recording, *Supersax Plays Bird*. This and hearing **Bill Evans** at an LA club were important moments in Ferguson's life, consolidating his desire for a career in music. Back at school in time for the next year, he continued to play bass at gigs with Rosen and Helms and also played with a local symphony orchestra. Another friend he made was **Loonis McGlohon**, who introduced him to Bill Kirchner, saxophonist-composer-arranger-producer and Grammy Award–winning jazz historian. Kirchner was also a recording artist for Challenge Records, which led in time to Ferguson too signing with the label. In 1978 Ferguson met **Chuck Israels**, bass player and arranger-director of the National Jazz Ensemble. Through this meeting, Ferguson was introduced to the New York music scene and the following year was introduced by Israels to **Red Mitchell**, who in turn introduced him to other bass players, including **Sam Jones** and **Rufus Reid**. He also attended the Eastman School of Music's jazz arrangers' workshop and played bass with various musicians including **Joe Locke** and Lee Musiker. Back home, he finished an undergraduate degree, then continued his music studies to earn a master's degree. Upon graduation in the autumn of 1981, Ferguson moved to Nashville, Tennessee, where he worked with a succession of visiting musicians, among them many leading names in jazz.

In the late 80s Ferguson appeared at the Main Street Jazz Festival in Columbia, South Carolina, where he worked with yet more distinguished jazz musicians, among them **Nat Adderley, Charlie Byrd, Louie Bellson, Jackie And Roy, Eddie Daniels, Jimmy Heath, Mundell Lowe, Chris Potter** (with whom Ferguson had played when the saxophonist was not yet 10 years old), **Red Rodney, Ira Sullivan, Lew Tabackin, Clark Terry** and **Bill Watrous**. In 1990 Ferguson toured with **Crystal Gayle**, continuing to make tours and recording sessions with the singer in later years. He also made the vocal arrangements for Gayle and helped out on backing vocals and in duets. A versatile and talented musician, Ferguson is highly respected by his peers even though his name remains relatively unknown to the general audience.

● ALBUMS: *Not Just Another Pretty Bass* (Challenge 1999) ★★★, *Deep Summer Music* (Challenge 2000) ★★★.

Ferguson, Johnny

b. 22 March 1937, Nashville, Tenneseee, USA. Pop/country singer who started his musical career in the late 50s as a disc jockey on a variety of small stations in and around the Nashville area. As a writer, he managed to have a couple of his songs recorded by country acts **Judy Lynn** and Pat Kelly, and it was a demo of one of his songs that persuaded Arnold Maxin, the managing director at **MGM Records**, to sign him. His first single, the catchy **John D. Loudermilk** song 'Angela Jones', gave him a transatlantic Top 30 hit in 1960, although in the UK a **Joe Meek**-produced cover version by **Michael Cox** fared even better. Later recordings, including a version of 'I Understand', failed to enhance his reputation on either side of the Atlantic, and he joined the ranks of one-hit-wonders.

Ferguson, Maynard

b. 4 May 1928, Montreal, Quebec, Canada. Already a band leader in his native land by his early teenage years, trumpeter Ferguson played in the bands of **Boyd Raeburn**, **Jimmy Dorsey** and **Charlie Barnet** in the 40s. His breakthrough into public consciousness came in 1950 when he joined **Stan Kenton**, electrifying audiences with his high-note playing. Unlike many other high-note trumpeters, Ferguson proved that it was possible to actually play music up there rather than simply make noises. However, it is possible that not all his fans appreciated the skills he was demonstrating. After leaving Kenton in 1953 Ferguson worked at Paramount studios in Los Angeles before turning to band leading, sometimes with a big band, at other times with a small group. Skilful use of arrangements often allowed the Ferguson bands to create an impression of size; the 12-piece band he led at the 1958 **Newport Jazz Festival** had all the power and impact of many groups twice its size.

Among the many fine musicians who worked with Ferguson in the 50s and 60s were **Slide Hampton**, **Don Sebesky**, **Bill Chase**, **Don Ellis** and **Bill Berry**. In the late 60s Ferguson moved to the UK, where he formed a big band with which he toured extensively. In the USA again during the 70s, he moved into jazz rock and reached a new audience who found the music and the flamboyance with which it was presented extremely attractive. During the 80s Ferguson formed the funk band High Voltage before returning to jazz with the big band–orientated Big Bop Nouveau, a unit with which he has continued to work on a regular basis into the new millennium. Ferguson also plays several other brass instruments with considerable skill, but it is as a trumpeter that he has made his greatest impact. His technical expertise on the instrument has made him a model for many of the up-and-coming young musicians.

● ALBUMS: *Maynard Ferguson's Hollywood Party* 10-inch album (EmArcy 1954) ★★★, *Dimensions* 10-inch album (EmArcy 1954) ★★★★, *Jam Session Featuring Maynard Ferguson* (EmArcy 1955) ★★★, *Maynard Ferguson Octet* (EmArcy 1955) ★★★★, *Around The Horn With Maynard Ferguson* (EmArcy 1956) ★★★★, *Conducts The Birdland Dream Band* (Bluebird 1956) ★★★★, *Boy With Lots Of Brass* (EmArcy 1957) ★★★, *A Message From Newport* (Roulette 1958) ★★★★, *A Message From Birdland* (Mercury 1959) ★★★★, *Plays Jazz For Dancing* (Roulette 1959) ★★★, *Newport Suite* (Roulette 1960) ★★★★, *Swingin' My Way Through College* (Roulette 1960) ★★★★, *Maynard '61* (Roulette 1961) ★★★★, with Chris Connor *Double Exposure* (Atlantic 1961) ★★★, with Connor *Two's Company* (Roulette 1961) ★★★, *Straightaway Jazz Themes* (Roulette 1961) ★★★, *Maynard '62* (Roulette 1962) ★★★, *Si! Si! M.F.* (Roulette 1962) ★★★, *Message From Maynard* (Roulette 1963) ★★★, *Maynard '64* (Roulette 1964) ★★★, *The New Sound Of Maynard Ferguson* (Cameo 1964) ★★★, *Color Him Wild* (Mainstream 1965) ★★★, *The Blues Roar* (Mainstream 1965) ★★★★, *Six By Six: Maynard Ferguson And Sextet* (Mainstream 1965) ★★★, *Sextet 1967* (Just A Memory 1967) ★★★, *Live At Expo '67, Montreal* (Just A Memory 1967) ★★★, *Trumpet Rhapsody* (MPS 1968) ★★★, *1969* (Prestige 1969) ★★★, *M.F. Horn* (Columbia 1970) ★★★, *M.F. Horn 2* (Columbia 1972) ★★★, *M.F. Horn 3* (Columbia 1973) ★★★, *M.F. Horn 4 + 5, Live At Jimmy's* (Columbia 1973) ★★★★, *Chameleon* (Columbia 1974) ★★★, *Primal Scream* (Columbia 1975) ★★★, *New Vintage* (Columbia 1977) ★★★, *Hot* (Columbia 1977) ★★★, *Carnival* (Columbia 1978) ★★, *Uncle Joe Shannon* (Columbia 1978) ★★, *Conquistador* (Columbia 1978) ★★, *It's My Time* (Columbia 1980) ★★, *Hollywood* (Columbia 1982) ★★, *Storm* (Palo Alto 1982) ★★, *Live From San Francisco* (Palo Alto 1983) ★★★, *Body And Soul* (Black Hawk 1986) ★★★, *High Voltage* (Intima 1988) ★★★, *High Voltage, Vol. 2* (Intima 1988) ★★★, *Live In Italy Vols. 1 & 2* (Jazz Up 1989) ★★★, *Big Bop Nouveau* (Intima 1989) ★★★, *Footpath Cafe* (Hot Shot 1993) ★★★, with Big Bop Nouveau *These Cats Can Swing* (Concord Jazz 1995) ★★★, with Big Bop Nouveau *One More Trip To Birdland* (Concord Jazz 1996) ★★★, with Tito Puente *Special Delivery* (Concord Picante 1997) ★★★★, with Big Bop Nouveau *Brass Attitude* (Concord Jazz 1998) ★★★, with Diane Schuur *Swingin' For Schuur* (Concord Jazz 2001) ★★★.

● COMPILATIONS: *Stratospheric* 1954–56 recordings (EmArcy 1976) ★★★★, *Maynard Ferguson* 1973–79 recordings (Columbia) ★★★, *The Complete Maynard Ferguson On Roulette* 10-CD box set (Mosaic) ★★★★, *Verve Jazz Masters, Vol. 52* 1951–57 recordings (Verve) ★★★★.

Fernández, Vicente

b. Vicente Fernández Gomez, 17 February 1940, Huentitán el Alto, Jalisco, Mexico. A ship lost at sea with a violent storm brewing on the horizon would be lucky to have Mexican singer Vicente Fernández aboard. His stentorian voice could probably whip those monstrous waves into submission in an instant. If nothing else, he could surely infuse the crew with uncommon valour. Fernández was a construction worker, store cashier, and dishwasher before devoting himself to music. At 21 he was already singing in a restaurant, doing serenades and performing in the television show *La Calandria Musical*. His close identification with his country and its traditions quickly made him a favourite among Mexicans, and he was catapulted to worldwide fame with the 1976 hit 'Volver, Volver'. True to his humble origins, Fernández has never forgotten his fans, always making a point of keeping ticket prices low enough for people of all social classes to see his concerts. Live, he does not stop singing as long as the audience continues to applaud him, to the distress of stage managers worldwide, who see his performances go two or three hours overtime. Fernández applies the same philosophy to his recorded output, releasing an album of high quality ranchera music every year. In 1998 he was inducted into the **Billboard** Latin Music Hall Of Fame and received a star on the Hollywood Walk Of Fame.

● ALBUMS: *La Voz Que Usted Esperaba* (CBS México 1968) ★★★, *Vicente Fernandez* (CBS México 1969) ★★★, *Soy De Abajo* (CBS México 1970) ★★★, *Ni En Defensa Propia* (CBS México 1970) ★★★, *Palabra De Rey* (CBS México 1970) ★★★, *Vol. II Toda Una Epoca* (CBS México 1970) ★★★, *Es Muy Tu Vida* (CBS México 1971) ★★★, *Me Estaba Esperando Maria* (CBS México 1971) ★★★, *Camino Inseguro* (CBS México 1971) ★★★, *Tacos Al Carbon* (CBS México 1971) ★★★, *El Jalisciense* (CBS México 1972) ★★★, *Arriba Huentitan* (CBS México 1972) ★★★, *Con Golpes De Pecho* (CBS México 1972) ★★★, *Si No Te Quisiera* (CBS México 1972) ★★★, *Entre Monjas Anda El Diablo* (CBS México 1973) ★★★, *El Idolo De Mexico* (CBS México 1974) ★★★, *El Rey* (CBS México 1974) ★★★, *El Hijo Del Pueblo* (CBS México 1975) ★★★, *La Ley Del Monte* (CBS México 1975) ★★★, *Para Recordar* (CBS México 1975) ★★★, *A Tu Salud* (CBS México 1976) ★★★★, *Variedad Musical* (CBS México 1976) ★★★, *Por Los Palenques* (CBS México 1977) ★★★, *Que Vas Hacer Sin Mi* (CBS México 1977) ★★★, *Joyas Al Estilo Ranchero* (CBS México 1977) ★★★, *La Muerte De Un Gallero* (CBS México 1977) ★★★, *Mi Amigo El Tordillo* (CBS México 1978) ★★★, *A Pesar De Todo* (CBS México 1978) ★★★, *El Gallo Negro* (CBS México 1978) ★★★, *El Tahur* (CBS México 1979) ★★★, *Desvelo De Amor* (CBS México 1979) ★★★, *De Que Manera Te Olvido* (CBS México 1980) ★★★, *Sentimental Y Ranchero* (CBS México 1980) ★★★, *A Las Madrecitas De Mexico* (CBS México 1981) ★★★, *Las Mañanitas* (CBS México 1981) ★★★, *El Numero Uno* (CBS México 1981) ★★★, *Alejandra Y Los Valses Clasicos* (CBS México 1981) ★★★, *Es La Diferencia* (CBS México 1982) ★★★, *Un Mexicano En La Mexico* (Sony Discos 1984) ★★★, *De Un Rancho A Otro* (Sony Discos 1985) ★★, *Holy Platique Con Mi Gallo* (Sony Discos 1986) ★★★, *Motivos Del Alma* (Sony Discos 1987) ★★★, *Lo Mejor De La Baraja Con El Rey* (Sony Discos 1988) ★★★★, *Tesoros Musicales* (Sony Discos 1988) ★★★, *Tesoros Musicales Vol. II* (Sony Discos 1988) ★★★, *Por Tu Maldito Amor* (Sony Discos 1989) ★★★, *Y Las Clasicas De J.A. Jimenez* (Sony Discos 1990) ★★★★, *El Charro Mexicano* (Sony Discos 1991) ★★★, *Que De Raro Tienne* (Sony Discos 1992) ★★★, *Lastima Que Seas Ajena* (Sony Discos 1993) ★★★, *Recordando A Los Panchos* (Sony Discos 1994) ★★★★, *Y Sus Canciones* (Sony Discos 1996) ★★, *Estatua De Marfil* (Sony Discos 1997) ★★★★, *Entre El Amor Y Yo* (Sony Discos 1998) ★★★, *Los Más Grandes Exitos De Los Dandy's* (Sony Discos 1999) ★★★, *Lobo Herido* (Sony Discos 2000) ★★★, *Más Con El Numero Uno* (Sony Discos 2001) ★★★, *Mis Corridos Consentidos* (Sony 2005) ★★.

● COMPILATIONS: *Los 15 Grande Exitos* (Sony Discos 1990) ★★★★, *16 Exitos* (Sony Discos 1995) ★★★★, *Historia de Un Ídolo Vol. 1* (Sony Discos 2000) ★★★★, *Historia de Un Ídolo Vol. 2* (Sony Discos 2002) ★★★★.

● FILMS: *Uno Y Medio Contra El Mundo* (1971), *Tacos Al Carbón* (1971), *Jalisco Nunca Pierde* (1972), *Entre Monjas Anda El Diablo* (1973), *Tu Camino Y El Mio* (1973), *La Loca De Los Milagros* (1973), *El Hijo Del Pueblo* (1973), *Dios Los*

Cria (1975), *Juan Armenta, El Repatriado* (1976), *Picardia Mexicana* (1977), *El Arracadas* (1977), *El Coyote Y La Bronca* (1978), *El Tahúr* aka *The Gambler* (1979), *Como México No Hay Dos* (1979), *Picardia Mexicana—Numero Dos* (1980), *Juan Charrasqueado Y Gabino Barrera, Su Verdadera Historia* (1981), *Un Hombre Llamado El Diablo* (1981), *Todo Un Hombre* aka *A Real Man* (1983), *El Sinvergüenza* (1983), *Una Pura Y Dos Con Sal* (1983), *El Embustero* (1983), *Matar O Morir* (1984), *Acorralado* (1984), *Sinvergüenza Pero Honrado* (1985), *El Diablo, El Santo Y El Tonto* (1985), *Entre Compadres Te Veas* (1986), *El Macho* (1987), *El Cuatrero* (1987), *Mí Querido Viejo* (1991).

Ferrante And Teicher

Arthur Ferrante (b. 7 September 1921, New York City, USA) and Louis Teicher (b. 24 August 1924, Wilkes-Barre, Pennsylvania, USA). Ferrante And Teicher met at the age of six while studying at the Juilliard School Of Music, Manhattan, New York. After they graduated as piano majors, they combined teaching and concert work until 1948, when they became full-time piano duettists, touring the USA and Canada with leading classical orchestras. During the next 12 years they gradually exchanged Rachmaninov for **Richard Rodgers**, **Cole Porter** and **Jerome Kern**, featuring their own arrangements for two pianos. They also adapted their pianos so that they could sound like other instruments and produce strange effects during novelty numbers and began to introduce comedy into their act. After recording for several labels during the 50s with their twin pianos, they signed for **United Artists Records** in 1960 and had their first big US chart hit with 'Theme From The Apartment' from Billy Wilder's Oscar-winning film. This was followed in the same year by 'Exodus—Main Theme' (which reached number 2) and in 1961 by 'Tonight'. All three titles sold over a million copies. In 1969 they had another Top 10 single with 'Midnight Cowboy'. At their peak, between 1960 and 1970, they apparently sold over 20 million records.

● ALBUMS: *West Side Story & Other Motion Picture And Broadway Hits* (United Artists 1961) ★★★, *Love Themes* (United Artists 1961) ★★★★, *Golden Piano Hits* (United Artists 1962) ★★★, *Tonight* (United Artists 1962) ★★★, *Golden Themes From Motion Pictures* (United Artists 1962) ★★★, *Pianos In Paradise* (United Artists 1962) ★★★, *Snowbound* (United Artists 1962) ★★★, *Love Themes From Cleopatra* (United Artists 1963) ★★★, *Concert For Lovers* (United Artists 1963) ★★★, *50 Fabulous Piano Favourites* (United Artists 1964) ★★★, *The Enchanted World Of Ferrante And Teicher* (United Artists 1964) ★★★, *My Fair Lady* (United Artists 1964) ★★★, *The People's Choice* (United Artists 1964) ★★★, *Springtime* (United Artists 1965) ★★★, *By Popular Demand* (United Artists 1965) ★★★, *Only The Best* (United Artists 1965) ★★★, *Music To Read James Bond By* (United Artists 1965) ★★★, *The Ferrante And Teicher Concert* (United Artists 1965) ★★★, *For Lovers Of All Ages* (United Artists 1966) ★★★, *You Asked For It!* (United Artists 1966) ★★★, *A Man And A Woman & Other Motion Picture Themes* (United Artists 1967) ★★★, *Our Golden Favorites* (United Artists 1967) ★★★, *A Bouquet Of Hits* (United Artists 1968) ★★★, *Midnight Cowboy* (United Artists 1969) ★★★, *Getting Together* (United Artists 1970) ★★★, *Love Is A Soft Touch* (United Artists 1970) ★★★, *The Music Lovers* (United Artists 1971) ★★★, *It's Too Late* (United Artists 1971)

★★★, *Fiddler On The Roof* (United Artists 1972) ★★★, *Fill The World With Love* (United Artists 1976) ★★★, *Nostalgic Hits* (United Artists 1977) ★★★.

● COMPILATIONS: *10th Anniversary—Golden Piano Hits* (United Artists 1969) ★★★, *The Best Of Ferrante And Teicher* (United Artists 1971) ★★★, *The Twin Pianos Of Ferrante And Teicher* (United Artists 1984) ★★★, *Collection* (Varèse Sarabande 1998) ★★★.

Ferrara, Don

b. 10 March 1928, Brooklyn, New York City, USA. Ferrara began playing trumpet at the age of 10, avidly listening to jazz and swing era giants on radio and records. In particular, he listened to **Roy Eldridge** who became and remained the single most important influence on his playing. In 1945 he was briefly with a band led by **Jerry Wald**, then moved over to **Georgie Auld**'s band before joining the US Army in mid-1946. During his time with the military, Ferrara played in a band where other members were bass player **Red Mitchell** and drummer Howie Mann, and he also met **Warne Marsh**. It was through the latter that Ferrara became interested in the work of **Lennie Tristano**, and after his discharge he began studying with Tristano, something he continued to do until the start of the 60s.

During this same period, in addition to teaching, Ferrara also played in the big band assembled by **Gene Roland** for a **Charlie Parker** recording session. Although he rehearsed with the band, Ferrara missed the recording session because of a date clash. This was for a 1950 session with **Chubby Jackson**, but instead of touring with this band after the recording, Ferrara joined **Woody Herman**'s Third Herd. After a year with Herman, Ferrara returned to New York where he gigged and taught and continued his own studies with Tristano. In New York during the mid-50s he played and sometimes recorded with various bands, including those led by **Lee Konitz** and **Gerry Mulligan**, playing with the latter in both a sextet and the Concert Jazz Band. In the early 60s Ferrara played a regular engagement with Tristano at New York's Half Note Club and during the rest of the decade continued with his teaching. In the early 70s he relocated to the west coast, joining Gary Foster's teaching studio. On through to the 90s, he continued to live and teach in California, most of his teaching work being conducted at long range through audio cassettes. A gifted and unassuming section man (his first ever interview was given to *Jazz Journal International*'s Gordon Jack in 1999), when the company was right, Ferrara readily proved himself to be also a skilled and highly individual soloist.

Ferrari, Frederick

b. 20 July 1912, Manchester, Lancashire, England, d. 19 April 1994, London, England. Usually known simply as 'the voice' because of his superb tenor, Ferrari was among the most popular of the post-war variety club and radio acts. He took his name—and his love for singing—from his Italian father. After appearing in small concert parties around the Manchester area, his career began in earnest when he joined the army in 1941. Although ultimately the army life helped to advance his singing ambitions (via the khaki entertainment troupe *Stars In Battledress*), his call-up actually scotched an engagement with the Carl Rosa Opera Company. Together with top comedian Charlie Chester, Ferrari went on to appear in over 2,000 service shows both at home and overseas, performances often highlighted by the rendering of his signature tune 'Love Descended Like An Angel', written for him by Chester. After the war, Ferrari joined Chester in his popular radio show *Stand Easy* before returning to variety (still as a huge star) in the early 50s. In addition to seaside residencies, he regularly performed at the London Palladium and made an appearance in front of the Queen. Alongside charity work he continued to be a popular attraction at functions and shows long after the variety halls closed.

Ferrell, Rachelle

b. Philadelphia, Pennsylvania, USA. Ferrell, who studied composition and arranging at the **Berklee College Of Music**, first attracted attention singing jazz in and around Philadelphia. Later, while teaching in New Jersey music colleges, she began developing a localized reputation as a session singer for leading artists including **Dizzy Gillespie** and **Quincy Jones**. Her debut album was released in Japan in 1990 (it belatedly received a US issue five years later). Determined not to be pigeonholed, with the inevitable career restrictions this brings, she extended her repertoire, which had at first been dominated by standards, to encompass R&B, and gradually developed a broader but still jazz-conscious, range. In 1992 Ferrell signed a contract that allows her to release urban-orientated material on **Capitol Records** and jazz for **Blue Note Records**. She has an astonishingly wide range, but unlike so many technically gifted singers, Ferrell uses her multi-octave potential with care and mature thought. She is also a highly respected composer and arranger and a compelling live performer. An eight-year recording hiatus was ended in autumn 2000 by the release of the superb *Individuality (Can I Be Me?)*.

● ALBUMS: *First Instrument* (Toshiba/Blue Note 1990) ★★★, *Rachelle Ferrell* (Manhattan/Capitol 1992) ★★★★, *Individuality (Can I Be Me?)* (Capitol 2000) ★★★★, *Live At Montreux 91–97* (Blue Note 2002) ★★★.

Ferrer, Ibrahim

b. 20 February 1927, San Luis, Cuba, d. 6 August 2005, Havana, Cuba. The release of the Grammy Award–winning *Buena Vista Social Club* in 1997 initiated a new era for Cuban music, propelling long-forgotten performers into the spotlight and making belated stars out of the artists such as pianist **Rubén González**, band leader Juan De Marcos Gonzalez and singer Ibrahim Ferrer. The last had actually retired from singing five years before he was contacted by producer **Ry Cooder**, who was seeking a 'softer voice' to sing boleros for the album. The success of *Buena Vista Social Club*, however, prompted the recording of a solo album, the elegant and eloquent *Buena Vista Social Club Presents Ibrahim Ferrer*, which went on to sell in excess of one-and-a-half million copies.

According to legend, Ferrer was actually born at a social club dance. He was orphaned at the age of 12, selling sweets and popcorn on the streets in order to survive. Nevertheless, a year later, he formed his first band Los Jovenes Del Son (Young Men Of Son). By 1955 he was singing with Santiago's top group Orquesta Chepín-Chóven, and for 20 years Ferrer sung with Pacho Alonso's Maravilla De Beltran (later renamed Los Bocucos). Like many Cuban musicians, however, music brought Ferrer little wealth, and by the time Cooder came calling Ferrer was—legendarily—selling lottery tickets and shining shoes to make ends meet. The recording of the Cooder-produced *Buena Vista Social Club Presents Ibrahim Ferrer* was partially documented in Wim Wenders' *Buena Vista Social Club* film, one of the top 10 highest grossing documentaries of all time. Such success allowed Ferrer to declare 'the singer who was no good has proved himself. The curse that I carried has been lifted'. In 2001 **Damon Albarn** of **Blur** coaxed Ferrer to perform on the **Gorillaz** track 'Latin Simone'.

Referencing **Michael Jackson**'s 1982 album, Cooder described Ferrer's 2003 release *Buenos Hermanos* as 'the *Thriller* of Latin music'. Ferrer stated that the songs on *Buenos Hermanos* 'make me feel younger', and tellingly, the sleeve showed Ferrer and his wife dancing together despite being septuagenarians. The album notably included performances from Cuban bass virtuoso **Orlando 'Cachaito' Lopez** and Grammy Award–winning gospel group the **Blind Boys Of Alabama**. Ferrer won a Grammy for *Buenos Hermanos*, but US anti-Cuban restrictions meant he was unable to travel to receive the award. An active performer despite his age, Ferrer had just returned from a tour of Europe in August 2005 when he was hospitalized with gastroenteritis. His condition worsened, and the singer died of multiple organ failure on 6 August.

● ALBUMS: *Buena Vista Social Club Presents Ibrahim Ferrer* (World Circuit 1999) ★★★★, *¡Que Bueno Esta!* (Blue Moon 2000) ★★★, *Buenos Hermanos* (World Circuit 2003) ★★★★.

● COMPILATIONS: *Mi Oriente: Ibrahim Ferrer Con Chepin Y Su Orquesta Oriental* (Tumbao 1999) ★★★, with Los Bocucos *Tierra Caliente* (Egrem 2000) ★★★, *Mis Tiempos Con Chepin Y Su Orquesta* (Egrem 2002) ★★★, *La Colección Cubana* (Nascente 2002) ★★★★, *Ay Candela* (Escondida 2005) ★★★.

Ferrer, José

b. José Vicente Ferrer de Otero y Cintrón, 8 January 1909 (sometimes cited as 1912), Santurce, Puerto Rico, d. 26 January 1992, Coral Gables, Florida, USA. Raised in the USA, while studying architecture, Ferrer took an interest in amateur dramatics and became a professional actor. From 1935's *A Slight Case Of Murder* he appeared often on Broadway: *Spring Dance* (1936), in the title role in **Charley's Aunt** (1940), **Let's Face It!** (1941), *Vickie* (1942, also director), *Cyrano De Bergerac* (1946, also producer) and *The Silver Whistle* (1948). He acted in Shakespeare, including playing Iago to **Paul Robeson**'s lead in *Othello* (1943). In 1948 he went to Hollywood, appearing in that year's *Joan Of Arc*, receiving an Oscar nomination as Best Supporting Actor. In 1950 he was in the film version of *Cyrano De Bergerac*. During the 50s he alternated between New York and Hollywood. His Broadway shows included *Twentieth Century* (1950, actor-director), *Stalag 17* (1951, director-producer), *The Fourposter* (1951, director), *The Shrike* (1952, actor-director-producer), the musical *Oh Captain!* (1958, librettist-director-producer) and *Juno* (1959, which he staged).

Among film roles was Ferrer's portrayal of Henri de Toulouse-Lautrec in *Moulin Rouge* (1952), receiving an Oscar nomination as Best Actor. In 1954 he played **Sigmund Romberg** in **Deep In My Heart**, a biopic of the composer's life. Ferrer acted in and directed a screen version of *The Shrike* (1955) and *The Great Man* (1956, which he also wrote) and *The High Cost Of Loving* (1958). In the 60s in Hollywood he directed *Return To Peyton Place* (1961) and in 1962 the

third and least version of **State Fair** (which starred **Pat Boone** and included **Bobby Darin** in its cast). On Broadway Ferrer was in the musical *The Girl Who Came To Supper* (1963) and also joined the cast of **Man Of La Mancha** (1965). In 1979 he directed the Broadway musical *Carmelina*. Ferrer continued to act in films in the USA and Europe through succeeding decades, making his last film appearance in *Primary Motive* (1992). His third wife was singer **Rosemary Clooney**; they divorced, remarried and divorced again. The oldest of their five children is actor Miguel Ferrer. Another of their children, Gabriel Ferrer, married singer **Debby Boone**. Ferrer received **Tony Awards** as Best Actor In A Play for *Cyrano De Bergerac* and *The Shrike* and as Best Director for *The Shrike*, *The Fourposter* and *Stalag 17*.

Ferris Wheel

A UK beat combo of the late 60s, the Ferris Wheel never managed to translate their live appeal into the studio. Originally formed by Dennis Elliot (b. 18 August 1950, Peckham, London, England; drums), **Linda Lewis** (vocals), Diana Ferris (vocals), Michael Snow (guitar, vocals, keyboards), George Sweetnam Ford (bass/vocals) and David Sweetnam Ford (saxophone), they signed to **Pye Records** in 1967 and released their first single, 'I Can't Break The Habit'. In abbreviated form this also gave them the title of their debut album, but both failed to chart and few critics were won over by the group's elaborate but somehow indistinct arrangements. When two further singles for Pye failed, 'Let It Be Me' and 'The Na Na Song', Ferris Wheel signed with **Polydor Records**. In the interim they had appeared in the 1968 film *The Touchables*. However, neither 'Can't Stop Now' nor the attendant self-titled debut album, which featured Bernie Holland on guitar in place of the woman who had given the band its name, Diana Ferris, reversed their fortunes. Linda Lewis subsequently enjoyed a successful solo career, while Holland worked with **Jody Grind** and Elliott with jazz rockers **If**.

● ALBUMS: *Can't Break The Habit* (Pye 1967) ★★, *Ferris Wheel* (Polydor 1970) ★★.

Ferris, Glenn

b. Glenn Arthur Ferris, 27 June 1950, Los Angeles, California, USA. After studying classical trombone and while still in his mid-teens, Ferris studied musical theory with **Don Ellis** before joining the Ellis band for a three-year spell. In 1970 he left Ellis, for whom he had composed some music, and then freelanced with a wide variety of bands, playing in many styles including classical, pop and rock. He played on the Grand and Petit Wazoo tours of 1972, recorded with **Bonnie Raitt**, **Billy Cobham**, **Stevie Wonder** and the **Average White Band** in the early and mid-70s and in the late 70s with **Frank Zappa** and also led his own band, Celebration. He worked in a duo with **Milcho Leviev**, and in the early 80s he played with **Martial Solal**'s big band and with **Tony Scott** and **Jack Walrath**, both in the USA and in Europe. Among the many other artists with whom Ferris has worked are **Manu Dibango**, Dave Frishberg, **Steve Lacy**, **Michel Portal** and **Louis Sclavis**. In the late 90s he was a member of Palatino. An immensely talented musician, Ferris' independent-minded approach to his work has kept him in relative obscurity, a fact that must be regretted by admirers of contemporary jazz trombone playing.

● ALBUMS: *Flesh And Stone* (Enja 1995) ★★★, *Face Lift* (Enja 1996) ★★★, *Refugees* (Enja 1997) ★★★.

Ferro, Nina

b. 6 September 1973, Melbourne, Victoria, Australia. Ferro began singing while in her early teens and soon thereafter took an interest in jazz, although her formal musical education was in the classical form. In 1991 she joined other young jazz musicians in the Hotter Than Six band. The group worked often in and around Melbourne, and meanwhile she continued studying, now with the Improvisation Department at the Victorian College of the Arts. She also joined a contemporary improvising ensemble, Ten Apples On Top, and toured Australia with Hotter Than Six. She travelled overseas to Vanuatu for the South Pacific Jazz Festival and to the USA for the 1994 and 1995 Sacramento Jazz Jubilee. In 1995 Ferro attracted the attention of the non-musical press for her appearance and style, being named as one of Australia's most eligible women. Heard by **Jim Cullum**, Ferro has appeared many times as guest on his Riverwalk concerts and radio programmes in San Antonio, Texas, and also recorded with him. She has appeared at jazz festivals in Australia, Japan, the USA and the Netherlands and at many club and concert venues throughout Europe, Scandinavia and the Americas.

Artists with whom Ferro has appeared and sometimes recorded are numerous and include **Tom Baker**, **Bob Barnard**, **Don Burrows** and pianists Joe Chindamo and **Dick Hyman**. With a wide range of musical influences, mostly in jazz, and with the vocal technique to accomplish all that her imagination suggests, Ferro has developed into one of the most popular young singers who have chosen to build into their repertoires a considerable amount of pre-60s music. To this music and to the more contemporary material she also sings she brings a vocal sound that is rich, powerful and passionate.

● ALBUMS: *Just You, Just Me* (Australia Jazz 1995) ★★★, *Out Of The Blue* (Australia Jazz 1997) ★★★, with Joe Chindamo *Tender Is The Night* (Newmarket 2001) ★★★★, *Crazy Way Of Lovin'* (Newmarket 2004) ★★★.

Ferron

b. 2 June 1952, Vancouver, British Columbia, Canada. Nineties singer Ferron grew up in a rural suburb of Vancouver, the eldest of seven children. After leaving home at the age of 15 she subsisted by working as a cab driver, waitressing and packing coffee in a factory. By 1975 she had started singing to 'political folk-type people, mixed audiences of men and women'. Her first recordings were completed in 1977 when she recorded, released and distributed her self-titled debut. Songs such as 'I Am Hungry' immediately announced Ferron as a natural communicator, fluent in documenting emotional peaks and troughs. *Ferron Backed Up* followed a year later and established a solid following for her staunchly feminist songwriting (notably 'Dear Marly' and 'Call Me Friend'). Through these two albums she came to the attention of Gayle Scott, an American then employed in film production in Vancouver. Scott became Ferron's manager and business partner, collaborating with her on the subsequent *Testimony* (1980) and *Shadows On A Dime* (1984). Although the music remained smooth, her songs continued to combine reflections on personal experience alongside directly political observations. *Testimony*'s title track later became an anthem

for the feminist movement. The receipt of a Canada Council arts grant in October 1985 allowed Ferron to consolidate her progress, enabling her to take time off for vocal lessons and to write new material. However, the grant soon expired, and not ready yet to return to performing, she worked as a carpenter's assistant and bartender. Eventually she returned to the studio for 1990's *Phantom Center*, re-energised by her time away from the stage. With instrumentalists including Barbara Higbie and Novi, *Phantom Center* comprised complex poetic narratives made instantly accessible by the dexterity of the musicianship. Following a well-received live album, *Resting With The Question* outlined a new dimension to the artist. Where previously Ferron's major talent had been ascribed to her lyric writing, this instrumental collection consisted of resonant, synthesizer produced sounds and sequences. She made her debut for **Warner Brothers Records** subsidiary EarthBeat in 1994 with *Driver*. It garnered substantial critical acclaim, in keeping with her less exposed previous recordings. In 1995 *Phantom Center* was remixed and remastered for release by EarthBeat. With the backing of a major record label, Ferron's profile was now higher than it had been at any other point in her two decade-long career.

● ALBUMS: *Ferron* (Own Label 1977) ★★★, *Ferron Backed Up* (Own Label 1978) ★★★, *Testimony* (Lucy 1980) ★★★, *Shadows On A Dime* (Lucy 1984) ★★★, *Phantom Center* (Chameleon 1990) ★★★, *Not A Still Life— Live At The Great American Music Hall* (Cherrywood Station 1992) ★★★, *Resting With The Question* (Cherrywood Station 1993) ★★★, *Driver* (EarthBeat 1994) ★★★, *Phantom Center* remixed/remastered version of 1990 album (EarthBeat 1995) ★★★.

Ferry Across The Mersey

Released in 1965, *Ferry Across The Mersey* represents the final fling of the genre dubbed 'Mersey beat'. **Gerry And The Pacemakers** star as the main contenders hoping to win an international beat group contest. Although hardly innovative in terms of plot, the film retains appeal, largely through the cheeky persona of Gerry Marsden. It also provides a platform for several lesser-known Liverpool acts, including the Blackwells, the Black Knights and Earl Royce And The Olympics, the last-named of whom perform a creditable 'Shake A Tail Feather'. *Ferry Across The Mersey* also features performers drawn from **Beatles**' manager **Brian Epstein**'s NEMS agency, including the **Fourmost**, who contribute 'I Love You Too', and **Cilla Black**, who sings 'Is It Love?'. However, the film is plainly a vehicle for Marsden's group, who provide nine songs, notably 'It's Gonna Be Alright' and the memorable title song, which reached number 8 in the UK. Disc jockey Jimmy Saville enjoys a cameo role in a film that captures something of the flavour of the times, albeit in a somewhat clichéd manner.

Ferry, Bryan

b. 26 September 1945, Washington, County Durham, England. Ferry began his musical career in local group the Banshees, following which he enrolled at Newcastle-upon-Tyne University where he formed R&B group the Gas Board, whose ranks included Graham Simpson and John Porter. After studying Fine Art under Richard Hamilton, Ferry briefly worked as a teacher before forming **Roxy Music**. During their rise to fame, he plotted a parallel solo career, beginning in 1973 with *These Foolish Things*, an album of favourite cover versions. At the time, the notion of recording an album of rock standards was both innovative and nostalgic. Ferry recorded half an album of faithful imitations, leaving the other half to more adventurous arrangements. Some of the highlights included a revival of **Ketty Lester**'s obscure 'Rivers Of Salt', a jaunty reading of **Elvis Presley**'s 'Baby I Don't Care' and a remarkable hit version of **Bob Dylan**'s 'A Hard Rain's A-Gonna Fall'. The album received mixed reviews but effectively paved the way for similar works including **David Bowie**'s *Pin Ups* and **John Lennon**'s *Rock 'N' Roll*.

Ferry continued the cover game with *Another Time Another Place*, which was generally less impressive than its predecessor. Two stylish pre-rock numbers that worked well were 'Smoke Gets In Your Eyes' and 'Funny How Time Slips Away'. A gutsy revival of **Dobie Gray**'s 'The In Crowd' brought another UK Top 20 hit. By 1976 Ferry had switched to R&B covers on *Let's Stick Together*, which, in addition to the hit **Wilbert Harrison** title track, featured a rousing rerun of the **Everly Brothers**' 'The Price Of Love'. It was not until 1977 that Ferry finally wrote an album's worth of songs for a solo work. *In Your Mind* spawned a couple of minor hits with 'This Is Tomorrow' and 'Tokyo Joe'. That same spring, Ferry appeared on the soundtrack of *All This And World War II* singing the **Beatles**' 'She's Leaving Home'. The following year, he retired to Montreux to complete the highly accomplished *The Bride Stripped Bare*. Introspective and revelatory, the album documented his sense of rejection following separation from his jet-setting girlfriend, model Jerry Hall. The splendid 'Sign Of The Times' presented a Dadaist vision of life as total bleakness: 'We live, we die . . . we know not why'. The track 'Can't Let Go', written at a time when he considered giving up music, maintained the dark mood.

It was another seven years before Ferry recorded solo again. In the meantime, he married society heiress Lucy Helmore, abandoning his lounge lizard image in the process. The 1985 comeback *Boys And Girls* was stylistically similar to his work with Roxy Music and included the hits 'Slave To Love' and 'Don't Stop The Dance'. After a further two-year break, Ferry collaborated with guitarist Johnny Marr on 'The Right Stuff' (adapted from the **Smiths**' instrumental, 'Money Changes Everything'). The album *Bête Noire* was a notable hit indicating that Ferry's muse was still very much alive, even though his solo work continues to be eclipsed by the best of Roxy Music. The covers set *Taxi* was followed by *Mamouna*, an album of originals that suffered from a lack of sparkle. Ferry seems to have become so good at what he does that he ceases to put any energy or emotion into the songs. The production is excellent, his singing is excellent but someone needs to remind him that emotion is necessary, too. Another five-year break ensued before Ferry returned with *As Time Goes By*, on which he tackled the Thirties and Forties standard songbook. Ferry reunited with Roxy Music in 2001 for a world tour, fitted in between sessions for his new studio album, *Frantic*.

● ALBUMS: *These Foolish Things* (Island 1973) ★★★★, *Another Time Another Place* (Island 1974) ★★★, *Let's Stick Together* (Island 1976) ★★★, *In Your Mind* (Polydor 1977) ★★★, *The Bride Stripped Bare* (Polydor 1978) ★★★★, *Boys And Girls* (EG 1985) ★★★, *Bête Noire* (Virgin 1987) ★★, *Taxi* (Virgin 1993) ★★, *Mamouna* (Virgin 1994) ★★, *As Time Goes By* (Virgin 1999) ★★★, *Frantic* (Virgin 2002) ★★★.

● COMPILATIONS: *The Compact Collection* 3-CD box set (Virgin 1992) ★★★★, *Slave To Love* (Virgin 2000) ★★★.
● DVD/VIDEOS: *Bryan Ferry And Roxy Music* (Virgin Video 1995).
● FURTHER READING: *The Bryan Ferry Story*, Rex Balfour. *Bryan Ferry & Roxy Music*, Barry Lazell and Dafydd Rees. *The Thrill Of It All: The Story Of Bryan Ferry And Roxy Music*, David Buckley.

Festival

Although not released until two years after the event, *Festival* is a dazzling documentary of the 1965 **Newport Folk Festival**. Director Murray Lerner captured the spirit of the proceedings, including backstage conversations and riveting in-concert footage. **Pete Seeger**, **Joan Baez**, **Judy Collins** and **Peter, Paul And Mary** lace acoustic folk music with contemporary 'protest' material, mindful of the music's role within the civil rights movement. **Donovan** introduces 'The Universal Soldier' by declaring it 'the song the BBC wouldn't let me sing', inspiring cheers from an audience weaned on conspiratorial notions. Blues singer **Howlin' Wolf** generates considerable excitement with the aid of electric instruments, and indeed the use of amplification would prove the catalyst for raging controversy. White Chicago group the **Paul Butterfield Blues Band** played a set to considerable behind-the-scenes argument. (A reputed fistfight between manager **Albert Grossman** and folklorist **Alan Lomax** over electrification was sadly not caught on camera.) Yet such discourse paled in comparison with the reaction to **Bob Dylan**'s set. Aided by **Mike Bloomfield** (guitar), Jerome Arnold (bass) and Sammy Lay (drums) (all from the Butterfield Band) plus **Al Kooper** (organ) and **Barry Goldberg** (piano), he performed three tough, rock-styled songs, one of which, 'Maggie's Farm', is enshrined in this film. Purists were outraged, and the notion of catcalling Dylan's performances was born with this appearance. However, criticism levelled at the singer's show was not necessarily over amplification per se but was equally due to a distorted sound obscuring his vocals. It is also evident from the film that many in the audience were in raptures. Dylan returned to sing two acoustic songs; both they and a workshop rendition of 'All I Really Want To Do', filmed the previous day, are preserved in *Festival*. His rendition of 'It's All Over Now, Baby Blue' is prophetic. It answers those expecting Dylan to remain encamped and simultaneously bids farewell to the acoustic muse of his past. The singer's use of an electric sound changed folk music forever—indeed the Newport Folk Festival then transformed itself into a rock event. This enduring film captures this pivotal moment forever.

Fesu

Born in Greenspoint, Texas, USA, Fesu, his name a corruption of his real name Yusef, began his career with a single on his own label, Air-Run-Boy 'Salt N Da Game'. The follow-up 'Streets Of Greenspoint' picked up a lot of local radio coverage, but it was with the lauded 'Blind, Cripple And Crazy' single that he really made headway. *The Source* magazine was particularly impressed, promoting him as a major new talent. Although born a Muslim, it was not until he encountered the teachings of Louis Farakhan that Fesu found a spiritual direction and became a member of the Nation Of Islam, a process recounted in the single. He went on to record a 1994 duet with **Bobby Womack** entitled 'Going Round N' Circles'.

Feuer, Cy

b. 15 January 1911, New York City, New York, USA. Taking up the trumpet, Feuer studied at the Juilliard School of Music before playing professionally. From 1938 he was in Hollywood, where he wrote music for films made by Republic Pictures, rising to become the studio's music department head. Towards the end of the 40s he became a producer of Broadway musicals, starting with **Frank Loesser**'s **Where's Charley?** (1948), which he coproduced with Ernest H. Martin. In 1950 the same team presented **Guys And Dolls**, winning the first of their three shared **Tony Awards**. Through into the mid-60s Feuer and Martin produced a succession of shows, many of which were hugely successful on Broadway: **Cole Porter**'s **Can-Can** (1953), **Sandy Wilson**'s **The Boy Friend** (1954) and Porter's **Silk Stockings** (1955), which Feuer also directed. In 1958 Feuer produced and directed *Whoop-Up* (1958), for which he, Martin and Dan Cushman wrote the book, which was based on the last's *Stay Away, Joe*. Music and lyrics were by Mark 'Moose' Charlap and Norman Gimbel and the reservation-set show included in its cast Ann Barry, Paul Ford, Susan Johnson and **Sylvia Syms**.

In the early 60s, Feuer and his partner produced Loesser's **How To Succeed In Business Without Really Trying** (1961) and **Neil Simon**'s **Little Me** (1962), for which Feuer was director and co-librettist. The former earned the duo two Tony Awards. Feuer also directed *Skyscraper* in 1965. The book for this show, which starred Julie Harris, was by **Peter Stone** and based on Elmer Rice's *Dream Girl*. Words and music were by **Sammy Cahn** and **Jimmy Van Heusen**, choreography by **Michael Kidd**. In 1966 came *Walking Happy*, which was adapted by Roger O. Hirson and Ketti Frings from Harold Brighouse's play *Hobson's Choice*. Feuer also directed and the songs were again provided by Cahn and Van Heusen. Feuer was producer of the film version of **Cabaret** (1972), and although less active on Broadway in the 70s, he and Martin produced *The Act* (1977) and *I Remember Mama* (1979), with music by **Richard Rodgers**, then nearing the end of his life, and lyrics by **Martin Charnin**. Feuer and Martin were meanwhile deeply involved with light opera associations on the west coast. In 1989 Feuer was appointed president of the League of American Theatres. He received a Special Lifetime Achievement Tony Award in 2003.

Fever Tree

Although a Texas, USA–based act, Fever Tree made its mark with a tribute to the Summer of Love's host city with their 1968 anthem 'San Francisco Girls (Return Of The Native)'. Comprising Rob Landes (keyboards), Dennis Keller (vocals), E.E. Wolfe (bass), John Tuttle (drums) and Michael Knust (guitar), the psychedelic band formed in Houston, Texas, in the mid-60s as Bostwick Vine. The name change came in 1967, and the band subsequently signed with the Chicago-based Mainstream Records. Two unsuccessful singles were recorded, and the unit then signed to Uni Records and recorded their self-titled debut album in 1968. 'San Francisco Girls (Return Of The Native)' was penned by Vivian Holtzman, one of the band's producers. Although only a minor chart hit, it received much airplay on the new USA FM rock stations and on **John Peel**'s *Top Gear* radio programme in the UK. Fever Tree recorded four albums, three of which

charted in the USA, before splitting up in 1970. Interest in the band was renewed in the mid-80s psychedelic revival, and compilation albums were issued in both the USA and UK.

● ALBUMS: *The Fever Tree* (Uni 1968) ★★★, *Another Time, Another Place* (Uni 1968) ★★, *Creation* (Uni 1969) ★★, *Angels Die Hard* film soundtrack (Uni 1970) ★, *For Sale* (Ampex 1970) ★★, *Live At Lake Charles 1978* (Shroom 1999) ★★.

● COMPILATIONS: *San Francisco Girls: The Best Of Fever Tree* (Era 1986) ★★★.

Fewell, Garrison

b. 14 October 1953, Charlottesville, Virginia, USA. Raised in Philadelphia, Pennsylvania, at the age of 11 Fewell began studying acoustic blues guitar, paying special attention to the music of old country blues artists such as **Mississippi John Hurt**, **Mississippi Fred McDowell** and **Rev. Gary Davis**. By 1967 he was performing professionally in the Philadelphia area with a repertoire that drew upon his transcriptions of Delta Blues guitarists and also featured his own compositions and improvised music. Following a 1972 tour of the Middle East and Pakistan, Fewell studied jazz guitar with **Lenny Breau** and **Pat Martino**, receiving a bachelor of music degree in guitar Performance from the **Berklee College Of Music** in Boston. Five years later, he returned to Berklee as professor of guitar. He formed his own jazz group in 1976 and also worked with front-rank artists such as **Larry Coryell** and **Herbie Hancock**.

In the early 80s Fewell spent some time in France, the start of an ongoing and rewarding symbiosis with Europe. Fewell's original grounding in the blues allied to the eastern rhythms he had assimilated during his 1972 tour made him a very well-rounded artist, and his knowledge of advanced jazz harmony and improvisation have made him a welcome guest at many European centres of musical education. In 1988 he was selected to take part in the first Faculty Exchange Program between Berklee and the Netherland's Rotterdam Conservatory. During his time in Rotterdam, Fewell played with pianist Cees Slinger and, at the North Sea Jazz Festival, in duo with a fellow-American, pianist Dave Frank. In 1989 he taught at the American School of Modern Music in Paris and also performed in France and Italy. With American pianist Alex Ulanowsky, former Berklee Harmony Department chair and author of the Berklee harmony textbooks, Fewell began a joint programme of teaching and performing at conservatories in the Netherlands, Belgium, Austria, Italy and Switzerland. In 1991 and again in 1992, Fewell taught in Germany, also playing with bass player **David Friesen** at the Zelt Music Festival in Freiburg. From 1994–99 Fewell taught harmony and guitar at a summer jazz course near Warsaw, sponsored by the Polish Jazz Society. Apart from the USA and Europe, Fewell has also performed in South America, Africa, the Caribbean and Canada.

Fewell's *Are You Afraid Of The Dark?* was voted Best Record Of 1996 by the editors of *Guitar Player* magazine. A 1995 live concert in Budapest with pianist Laszlo Gardony, broadcast for Hungarian National Radio, resulted in *Reflection Of A Clear Moon*, another critically acclaimed album. Other musicians with whom he has played are bass player **Steve LaSpina** and drummer Jeff Williams, both members of his regular trio for club and recording sessions. Throughout the 90s, Fewell was in demand as performer and educator, conducting Jazz Workshops at the **Montreux International Jazz Festival** and at Berklee. A gifted player, Fewell's extensive activities in jazz education make him a very important figure on the turn-of-the-century music scene.

● ALBUMS: *A Blue Deeper Than The Blue* (Accurate 1993) ★★★, *Are You Afraid Of The Dark?* (Accurate 1995) ★★★★, *Reflection Of A Clear Moon* 1995 recording (Accurate 1997) ★★★★, *Birdland Sessions* (Koch 2000) ★★★★, *City Of Dreams* 1999 recording (Splasch 2001) ★★★, *Red Door Number 11* (Splasch 2004) ★★★.

Feza, Mongezi

b. 1945, Queenstown, South Africa, d. 14 December 1975, London, England. Feza, nicknamed 'Mongs', began playing trumpet at the age of eight and was gigging regularly by the time he was 16. He took part in the 1962 Johannesburg Jazz Festival, where **Chris McGregor** invited him and four more of the best players at the festival to form a band, the legendary Blue Notes. As a mixed race band it was impossible for them to work under apartheid, and in 1964, while touring Europe, they decided to settle there. After a year in Switzerland they went to London, where, evolving into the Chris McGregor Group, they made a huge impact in the UK Jazz scene. As well as McGregor's Group and the big band Brotherhood Of Breath, Feza gigged and recorded with **Dudu Pukwana** and **Johnny Mbizo Dyani** (who were both colleagues in the McGregor group), **Robert Wyatt** (who, like Pukwana, had Mongezi's marvellous composition 'Sonia' in his repertoire), **Keith Tippett**'s Centipede and **Julian Bahula**.

Feza's stinging, restless trumpet contributed hugely to the special edge of the McGregor Group and was a kwela-inspired counterpart to **Don Cherry**'s folk-like melodies in the **Ornette Coleman** Quartet. Feza was very much affected by the lack of recognition that he and his colleagues had to contend with, but whatever his personal problems, he transformed them into an exhilarating blend of South African and free jazz traditions. His death in 1975 was a shock to his colleagues, dispiriting some of them, such as Dyani, far beyond the musical loss. The official cause of death was pneumonia, but it has been claimed that this was aggravated because Feza was left sick and unattended in a police cell after an arrest for disorderly behaviour. Shortly after his death, the remaining Blue Notes recorded the tribute *Blue Notes For Mongezi*, released in 1976.

Ffrench, Robert

Ffrench first achieved notoriety when he performed 'In My Heart There Is A Song' at the 1984 Jamaican Song Festival. In the same year he performed at the Reggae Sunsplash festival in Jarret Park, Montego Bay, where he wooed the crowds with his interpretation of the popular dance craze 'Shoulder Move'. His recording career gained momentum when he performed alongside the frequently extolled DJ Clement Irie for the hit 'Bun And Cheese'. The song proved internationally successful, leading to a one-rhythm album of the same name. Ffrench continued to record throughout the 90s, including a cover version of the R&B hit 'Earth Angel', 'Too Young' and 'Modern Girl'. Throughout the late 80s he endorsed his reputation as a writer and arranger with artists, including **Johnny P** for the popular 'Stamina', Clement Irie with 'Stop It' as well as **Pliers** and Henkel Irie. Following on from the success of his 1994 hit 'More Love' with rapper **Heavy D**, the duo signed with Doctor Dread's Washington-based RAS label for a one-album contract. By the end of 1995,

Ffrench performed with **Junior Reid** on the highly acclaimed One Blood tour of the USA alongside **Big Youth**. A year later, inspired by his earlier celebrated collaboration, he teamed up with another rapper, **Grand Puba**, who had recorded with **Shaggy**, and Jeff Redd for the R&B-styled 'Cry No More'.

● ALBUMS: with Frankie Paul *Reggae For The World* (Sonic 1990) ★★★, with various artists *Robert Ffrench, Heavy D And Friends* (RAS 1995) ★★★.

● COMPILATIONS: *Yesterday And Today* (Artists Only 2001) ★★★★.

ffrr Records

London Records' (UK) dance label is headed by Andy Thompson, although BBC Radio 1 presenter **Pete Tong** provides A&R support. Tong joined London in 1983 after leaving his job as advertising manager for *Blues And Soul* magazine. He became the label's club promotions manager and was the first to import the sound of the Chicago **house** explosion via **Farley Jackmaster Funk** and **Steve 'Silk' Hurley**. Tong 'began' ffrr in 1986. The original intention was to use the imprint to develop acts on a long-term basis, resulting in the signing of American white label house acts like **Jamie Principal**, **Lil' Louis** and **Degrees Of Motion** and major hits with clubland classics such as **DJ Duke**'s 'Blow Your Whistle', **Jamie Principal**'s 'Baby Wants To Ride', Lil' Louis' 'French Kiss', Barry K. Sharpe and Diana Brown's 'The Masterplan', **Salt-N-Pepa**'s 'Push It', **Good Men**'s 'Give It Up', **Joe Roberts**' 'Back In My Life' alongside sundry quality releases from **Frankie Knuckles**. In the late 80s and early 90s they also boasted some of the cream of the UK's acid house and dance music with artists like **D-Mob**, the **Brand New Heavies** ('Back To Love'), the **Utah Saints** (the classic 'What Can You Do For Me'), **Orbital** (who gave them a major hit in 1992 with the *Mutations EP*), **One Dove** and two pioneering jungle tracks, **Goldie**'s 'Inner City Life' and Leviticus' 'The Burial'. A second outlet, ffreedom, was launched in 1991 by Thompson, who, like Tong, had progressed through the ranks as club promotions director, with former **Hooj Choons** employee Phil Howells as his partner. The idea was to specialize in rave culture and be flexible enough to pick up on tunes as they broke in the club scene. They even took a bite out of the toytown techno cake by providing the nation with Shaft's ridiculous 'Roobarb And Custard' in 1992. A second subsidiary, **Internal Records**, was launched in late 1992 for album-based techno projects. The main label ffrr played things a little safer. As Thompson admitted during the recession of 1992, 'The doctrine of our company is that caution pays and we only believe in spending money where we think there is a reason to.' Nevertheless, ffrr's strict sense of discipline has not prevented it from being both prolific and successful, and they also picked up on commercial hip-hop with the **Cookie Crew** (since dropped). They also lost Orbital but maintained relationships with a series of female house vocalists including **Lisa B.** ffrr has gone on to become the most credible and successful dance division of a major UK label, with recent releases including **C.J. Bolland**'s 'Sugar Is Sweeter', Stretch 'N' Vern's 'I'm Alive', **All Saints**' huge mainstream hit 'Never Ever', The All Seeing I's 'The Beat Goes On' and the **Nightcrawlers**' 'Push The Feeling On'.

● COMPILATIONS: *Ffrr Classics 1988–1998* 3-CD set (Ffrr 1999) ★★★★.

Fiagbe, Lena

b. Ladbroke Grove, London, England. This talented, soul-inspired vocalist's demo cassette inspired a bidding war among the major record companies in 1993, with the **U2**-backed Mother label emerging as the victor. Fiagbe's father had been a huge fan of **Lena Horne** (hence his daughter's name), and Fiagbe's microphone performance certainly incorporates some of the dynamism of that artist. Her debut single, 'You Come From Earth' (released as Lena), which thematically shared fellow UK artist **Jamiroquai**'s wide-eyed wonder at the universe, was inspired by a documentary about space travel but flopped. In light of this, the record company insisted on some remixes. Fiagbe herself was unhappy with the **house** mixes applied to the follow-up single, 'Gotta Get It Right (One World)', which grazed the UK Top 20: 'The only thing I dislike is if by putting out dance mixes people start seeing me as a dance artist, then I can't handle it. That's not what I'm about.' After this she toured with **Lenny Kravtiz** and **Daryl Hall**, co-writing 'Borderline' on the latter's *Soul Alone* set, and earned further critical praise for her debut album *Visions* (limited editions of which contained a free seven-track acoustic CD—as if to confirm Fiagbe's status as a singer-songwriter). An aborted album project and a change of label subsequently stalled Fiagbe's career, although she did return to the UK Top 40 in 1996 as guest vocalist on **Wasis Diop**'s single 'African Dream'.

● ALBUMS: *Visions* (Mother 1994) ★★★.

Fialka, Karel

Born in Bengal of Scottish and Czechoslovakian parentage, Fialka was launched in 1980 as the street poet of the 80s. A poet, traveller, musician and actor, his music turned out to be a combination of acute observations on life and a keen sense of melodic phrases helped by the production touches of Wally Brill and Robin Langridge. Fialka's debut *Still Life* was well received, and 'The Eyes Have It' became an airplay favourite and gained a low but respectable UK chart position. However, after a promising start Fialka only released a couple of singles for the next seven years on a few minor labels. In 1987 he reappeared on Miles Copeland's IRS label and scored a UK and European Top 10 hit with a simple protest song, 'Hey Matthew'. An album containing new and old songs was released but failed to make any ripples.

● ALBUMS: *Still Life* (1980) ★★★★, *Human Animal* (IRS 1988) ★★.

Fiat Lux

This three-piece synthesizer outfit took their name from the Latin for 'Let There Be Light'. Fiat Lux formed in Wakefield, Yorkshire, England, in 1982. Vocalist Steve Wright and keyboard player David P. Crickmore had been at drama college together, and Wright went on to join the well-known Yorkshire Actors group. One of that company's patrons was the local guitarist and synthesizer wizard **Bill Nelson** (ex-**Be Bop Deluxe** and **Red Noise**), who on occasion provided music for their productions. Wright and Crickmore were writing material together, and Wright decided to use his contact with Nelson to send him a demo tape. Nelson was impressed and decided to release the song 'Feels Like Winter Again' on his own Cocteau label. The first recordings were made using local session musicians, but in April 1982 Bill's brother Ian, a saxophonist and keyboards player, was enrolled into Fiat Lux. Polydor picked up on the band, and they recorded their first album in Liverpool. Tours with **Blancmange** and **Howard Jones** followed, and their second and third Polydor singles—'Secrets' and 'Blue Emotion'—both made the charts. 'Solitary Lovers' was not a success, however, and as synthesizer pop fell out of favour the band fell by the wayside, although Ian Nelson would go on to work occasionally with his brother.

● ALBUMS: *Hired History* (Polydor 1984) ★★.

● COMPILATIONS: *Commercial Breakdown* (Hendring Video 1990) ★★.

Fiction Plane

Melodic UK pop rock band formed in 1999 by Joe Sumner (vocals/guitar), Seton Daunt (guitar), Dan Brown (bass) and Olly Taylor (drums). Although the band's press releases made little of it, music critics instantly latched on to the fact that Sumner is the son of rock legend **Sting**. Influenced by everything from ska to grunge to folk, the band's original name was Santa's Boyfriend, and they played shows in both Europe and the USA and self-released a collection of demos, *Swings And Roundabouts*, under this name. In 2002, minus the departed Taylor, the remaining trio signed a recording contract with MCA Records and changed their name to Fiction Plane (which was the title of an early song of Sumner's). Renowned rock producer David Kahne agreed to help guide the young band through the recording of their debut album. *Everything Will Never Be OK* was recorded with session player Abe Laboriel Jnr. filling in the vacant drum position before Pete Wilhoit signed on for the album's supporting tour. Sumner's lyrics eschewed the shrewd optimism of much of his father's work, with song titles including 'Hate', 'I Wish I Would Die', and 'Everything Will Never Be OK'.

● ALBUMS: *Everything Will Never Be OK* (MCA 2003) ★★★.

Fiddler On The Roof (film musical)

This generally satisfactory screen version of the record-breaking Broadway musical came to the screen in 1971. The Israeli actor Topol (b. 9 September 1935), who had enjoyed much success in the London stage production, was chosen to play the role of Tevye, the Jewish milkman in the small town of Anatevka in Russia who is forever trying to come to terms with his daughters (played by Michele Marsh, Rosalind Harris and Neva Small) and the lives they are making for themselves while also fighting to retain the traditions that have, for centuries, existed amongst his people. Topol gave a fine charismatic performance and had excellent support from Norma Crane as his wife and the celebrated American stage actress Molly Picon in the key role of the matchmaker. Also in the cast were Zvee Scooler, Michael Glaser, Paul Mann and Leonard Frey as Motel the tailor, the role he played in the original Broadway production. Swedish actor Tutte Lemkow appeared as the fiddler, and his playing was dubbed by Isaac Stern. **Jerry Bock** and **Sheldon Harnick**'s magnificent stage score was mostly retained and included 'Tradition', 'Matchmaker, Matchmaker', 'If I Were A Rich Man', 'Sabbath Prayer', 'To Life', 'Miracle Of Miracles', 'Tevye's Dream', 'Sunrise, Sunset', 'Wedding And The Bottle Dance', 'Do You Love Me', 'Far From The Home I Love', 'Chava Ballet Sequence' and 'Anatevka'. Tom Abbott based his choreography on **Jerome Robbins**' **Tony Award**-winning original work, and **Joseph Stein**'s screenplay was adapted from his Broadway libretto. Norman Jewison was the producer-director, and the film won Academy Awards for Oswald Morris' cinematography (DeLuxe Color and Panavision), sound (Gordon K. McCallum and David Hildyard) and adaptation and music scoring (**John Williams**). According to *Variety*, the film, which grossed nearly $40 million, was one of the hit movies of the decade.

● FURTHER READING: *The Making Of A Musical: Fiddler On The Roof*, Richard Altman and Mervyn Kaufman.

Fiddler On The Roof (stage musical)

In a Broadway season packed with musicals such as *Golden Boy*, *Ben Franklin In Paris*, *Baker Street*, *Do I Hear A Waltz?*, *Flora, The Red Menace* and *The Roar Of The Greasepaint—The Smell Of The Crowd*, *Fiddler On The Roof* opened at the Imperial Theatre on 22 September 1964 and topped them all. Set in 1905 on the eve of the Russian Revolution, **Joseph Stein**'s book is based on Sholom Aleichem's stories that recount episodes in the life of Tevye (**Zero Mostel**), a dairyman living in the impoverished Jewish village of Anatevka in tsarist Russia. Tevye has five daughters, and Yente (**Beatrice Arthur**), the matchmaker, brings his wife Golde (**Maria Karnilova**) the news that wealthy widower Lazar Wolf (Michael Granger) desires the hand of the eldest, Tzeitel (Joanna Merlin). This is unfortunate, because Tzeitel has already made her own arrangements with childhood sweetheart Motel (Austin Pendleton), admittedly a penniless tailor. In the meantime, Tevye enlists Perchik (Bert Convy), a young student revolutionary, to lecture his daughters in the ways of the Good Book. He does more than that, introducing the spirited Hodel (Julia Migenes) to certain Terpsichorean delights. Although it is strictly against his beloved tradition, Tevye eventually agrees to the wedding of Tzeitel and Motel and reluctantly accepts that Perchik and Hodel will also be together, but he absolutely refuses to endorse the intention of third daughter Chava (Tanya Everett) to marry outside the faith—but she goes ahead anyway. Perchik is arrested for his political activities and sent to Siberia. Hodel leaves to be with him, and as the pogroms advance ever nearer, Tevye and what is left of his family seek refuge in America. His problems in coming to terms with the changes in customs, language and religion, were reflected in **Sheldon Harnick** and **Jerry Bock**'s splendid score. The music drew upon traditional folk forms, and the lyrics were awash with cultural references that gave audiences a strong sense of social awareness while simultaneously providing high quality entertainment and a good deal of humour. Musical numbers included 'Tradition', 'Matchmaker, Matchmaker', 'If I Were A Rich Man', 'Sabbath Prayer', 'To Life', 'Miracle Of Miracles', 'The Tailor, Motel Kamzoil', 'Sunrise, Sunset', 'Wedding Dance', 'Now I Have Everything', 'Do You Love Me?', 'I Just Heard', 'Far From The Home I Love' and 'Anatevka'. *Fiddler On The Roof* ran on Broadway for 3,242 performances, winning the New York Drama Critics' Circle Award as best musical and **Tony Awards** for best musical, score, book, actor (Mostel), featured actress (Karnilova), director-choreographer (**Jerome Robbins**), producer (**Harold Prince**) and costumes (Patricia Zipprodt). In addition, the Original Cast album spent a total of 60 weeks in the US chart. Mostel's was a bravura performance, and his replacements during the record-breaking run included Luther Adler, who also headed the first US tour, which lasted over two years, Herschel Bernardi, Paul Lipson, Harry Goz and veteran operatic tenor Jan

Peerce. **Bette Midler**, the future 'Divine Miss M', played Tzeitel for three years, 1967-70. Mostel reprised his role opposite Thelma Lee (Golde) in the 1976 revival at the Winter Garden. A 1967 London production, with the Israeli actor Topol (b. 9 September 1935) as Tevye along with Miriam Karlin (Golde), Cynthia Grenville (Yente), Paul Whitsun-Jones (Lazar), Sandor Eles (Perchik), Rosemary Nicols (Tzeitel), Linda Gardner (Hodel), Jonathan Lynn (Motel) and Caryl Little (Chava), lasted for 2,030 performances. Topol enjoyed a surprise record hit with 'If I Were A Rich Man', which reached the UK Top 10. He also starred in the 1971 film version, a 1983 staging at London's Apollo Victoria Theatre, a 1990 Broadway revival with Marcia Lewis as Golde and the show's 30th anniversary world tour that called in at the London Palladium in June 1994 (Sara Kestelman as Golde).

● FURTHER READING: *The Making Of A Musical: Fiddler On The Roof*, Richard Altman and Mervyn Kaufman.

Fiel Garvie

An unusual UK indie band, Fiel Garvie was formed when Adam Green (guitar/programming) and Anne Reekie (vocals) left their previous Norwich, East Anglia, England group, Passing Clouds. They were joined in Fiel Garvie by Greg McDermott and Jude Bugden. The debut single for their own Foundling label, 1996's 'Glass Faced Warrior', brought rave reviews, as did the follow-ups 'For What I Love' (1997) and 'Colour You' (1998). Fusing influences as diverse as **Kurt Weill**, Eric Satie, **Philip Glass**, **Tricky** and the **Tindersticks**, Reekie's distinctive voice and studied intellectualism lent the band an edge wholly out of keeping with the retro-themed indie music of the mid- to late 90s. Their debut ¡*Vuka Vuka!*, recorded at an all-valve studio in Norfolk, was finally released on the Noisebox label in early 2001. Despite good reviews, the album was not widely heard, and the band vanished for a couple of years. They returned at the end of 2003 with a new member, Emma Corlett, and a new single, 'I Didn't Say'. Their second album, *Leave Me Out Of This*, was released the following summer.

● ALBUMS: ¡*Vuka Vuka!* (Noisebox 2001) ★★★★, *Leave Me Out Of This* (Foundling 2004) ★★★.

Field Mice

Formed in Surrey, England, in 1987 by principal songwriter Robert Wratten (b. 5 August 1966, Carshalton, Surrey, England; guitar/vocals) and Mark Dobson (b. 27 April 1965, Hartlepool, England; drums), the Field Mice linked up with Bristol-based **Sarah Records** for a series of records that unwittingly pigeonholed both band and label as exponents of whimsical, sensitive pop songs. The label's initial independent idealism—which manifested itself in 7-inch-only releases in the era of 12-inch singles and compact disc singles—merely added fire to cynics' vitriol. The Field Mice established a small yet fanatical following that spread as far as Japan by virtue of gently struck acoustic guitars and lyrics of the decidedly lovelorn variety. The line-up was expanded by the arrival of labelmate Harvey Williams (b. 31 December 1965, Cornwall, England; guitar), who had previously worked under the name Another Sunny Day. It was unfortunate that the prejudice of the music business ensured that the Field Mice remained condemned to the periphery even though the band was furthering their eclectic tastes by developing a penchant for danceable electronics

('Triangle') and experimental noise ('Humblebee'). This was in spite of contemporary crossover outfit **Saint Etienne** taking the Field Mice into the nation's clubs by covering the band's 'Let's Kiss And Make Up' single. In 1990 the trio became a quintet with the arrival of Michael Hiscock (b. 24 February 1966, Carshalton, Surrey, England; bass) and Annemari Davies (b. 9 February 1971, Oxfordshire, England; guitar/keyboards). Having previously only issued material on 7-inch and mini-albums (including the 10-inch *Snowball*), it was not until 1991 that the band released their first full albums. The first, *Coastal*, was a retrospective and *For Keeps*, a mature collection that promised much in the future. However, after the release of the acclaimed 'Missing The Moon', the Field Mice's frustrating reluctance to pursue a potentially rewarding higher profile and a growing estrangement with their label eventually led to the band dissolving in November 1991. Wratten resurfaced in the late-90s as part of the Trembling Blue Stars.

● ALBUMS: *Snowball* mini-album (Sarah 1989) ★★★, *Skywriting* (Sarah 1990) ★★★, *For Keeps* (Sarah 1991) ★★★.

● COMPILATIONS: *Coastal* (Sarah 1991) ★★★, *Where'd You Learn To Kiss That Way?* (Shinkansen 1998) ★★★★.

Field Mob

One of the better US hip-hop tag teams to emerge during the early twenty-first century, Field Mob was formed in Albany, Georgia, by Boondox Blax (b. Darion Crawford, Albany, Georgia, USA) and Kalage (b. Shawn Johnson, Albany, Georgia, USA). The duo first met during a high school 'freestyle' session, and Field Mob was formed soon afterwards. The duo recorded the independently issued 'Project Dreamz' and performed on the local circuit. The single proved popular in the Georgia area, as it created a loud enough buzz to grab the attention of MCA Records, who signed the duo. In 2000 the release of Field Mob's debut, *613: From Ashy To Classy*, received favourable reviews in esteemed US rap publications such as *The Source*. Although the album failed to catapult Blax and Kalage to elite status, quite a few of their contemporaries took notice, and the duo appeared on **Trick Daddy**'s *Thug Holiday* and worked with both **Outkast** and DJ Greg Street. *From Tha Roota To Tha Toota* saw Field Mob working with a variety of producers (including Jazzy Pha, Earth Tone, Ole-E and Willie Cool), while old friend Trick Daddy returned the favour by guesting on the track 'Haters'.

● ALBUMS: *613: From Ashy To Classy* (MCA 2000) ★★★, *From Tha Roota To Tha Toota* (MCA 2002) ★★★★.

Field, Frank

b. USA. After committing himself to his new-found Christian faith in the late 60s, Field forged a musical relationship with three like-minded friends—Chuck Girard, Tom Coomes and Jay Truax—to form Love Song. By 1972 he had moved on to membership of Noah, who toured throughout the European Continent and Middle East, recording in Israel and Germany. Most of their shows were at United States military bases in Germany, where they worked on behalf of military chaplains. They also did extensive work in support of drug-prevention campaigns. Field's first solo album followed his return to the USA in 1975. Maranatha Music released . . . *And Friends*, which led to a series of concert appearances throughout California as well as television showcases. As a talented

multi-instrumentalist, counting violin, mandolin, guitar and banjo among his proficiencies, he has also collaborated widely with other gospel music artists, including **Pat Boone**, **Brush Arbor**, Ray Hildebrandt, Parable and Gentle Faith.

● ALBUMS: . . . *And Friends* (Maranatha 1975) ★★★.

Field, Gregg

b. 21 February 1956, Oakland, California, USA. Field began playing drums as a child, studying and working with local bands in California. Although he first attracted widespread attention after joining **Count Basie**'s band in the early 80s, he had already built a formidable reputation amongst fellow musicians. In addition to appearing on television in shows such as *Saturday Night Live*, *The Merv Griffin Show* and *Frank Sinatra: A Man And His Music*, he has written many arrangements for the *Tonight Show* orchestra. He has toured or recorded with **Donald Byrd**, **Quincy Jones**, **George Benson**, **Harry James**, **Herbie Hancock** and **Wayne Shorter** and an impressive roster of singers, including **Frank Sinatra, Ella Fitzgerald, Ray Charles, Sarah Vaughan, Mel Tormé, Dianne Schuur, Tony Bennett** and **Joe Williams**. In addition to performing, Field is also a member of the faculty of the University of Southern California and is active as a record producer. His records with Basie included Grammy Award–winning albums, and following the leader's death, he has worked with all-star alumni bands, including the **Frank Wess-Harry Edison** all-star band that recorded at the 1989 and 1990 Fujitsu-Concord Jazz Festivals in Tokyo. In 1990 he was a member of an all-star band led by **Ray Anthony** for a recording session which Field also produced. In 1991 he worked with **Bill Berry** and his LA Big Band for concerts at the Hollywood Bowl.

A superbly accomplished drummer, equipped to play in almost any setting, Field is at his considerable best playing in a mainstream big band. The enthusiastic swing of his performances ensures that a great tradition on jazz drumming continues into the early years of the new millennium.

● ALBUMS: *The Art Of Swing* (DCC 1999) ★★★.

Field, Ron

b. 1934, New York City, USA, d. 6 February 1989, New York City, USA. As a child actor Field made his first appearance on Broadway in *Lady In The Dark* (1941). He was a member of the chorus for *Gentlemen Prefer Blondes* (1949), *Kismet* (1954) and *The Boy Friend* (1954). By the 60s Field was established as a choreographer and in this capacity worked on *Nowhere But Up* (1962), *Café Crown* (1964) and *Cabaret* (1966), winning a **Tony Award** for the latter. More success came with his choreography for *Zorba* (1968, Tony nominated) and *Applause* (1970, winning Tony Awards as director and choreographer). Through the 70s and 80s he worked in theatre, films and television, sometimes as choreographer, other times as director, occasionally as both. Among shows in these decades are *On The Town* (a 1971 revival), a television adaptation of *Once Upon A Mattress* (1972, with **Carol Burnett**), *Ed Sullivan's Broadway* (1973), the series *Manhattan Transfer* (1975), *Pinocchio* (with **Danny Kaye**), *The Entertainer* and *America Salutes Richard Rodgers: The Sound Of His Music* (all 1976), *Ben Vereen . . . His Roots* (1978), the last two winning him Emmy Awards, *Goldie And Liza Together* and *Baryshnikov On Broadway* (both 1980). His films included *New York, New York* (1977), King Of Hearts (1978) and *Perfectly Frank* (1980). Additionally, Field choreographed **Chita Rivera**'s act at the Grande Finale at New York's West 70th Street in the winter of 1974/5. Reportedly but uncredited he worked on the 1979 revival of **Peter Pan** and started but was replaced on **Merrily We Roll Along** (1981).

Over the years, Field helped create choreography for many noted dancers, among them **Fred Astaire**, **Ray Bolger**, **Cyd Charisse**, **Gene Kelly** and **Tommy Tune**. Additionally, Field staged spectaculars in Las Vegas, five Oscar presentations and three years each of Tony and Emmy presentations. He was also responsible for the elaborate opening ceremony at the 1984 Olympic Games in Los Angeles. Field produced and staged shows in Paris, Beirut and New Orleans, the latter for the 1984 World's Fair. Towards the end of the 80s, he worked on a revival in the UK of **Kiss Me, Kate** (1987) and on Broadway for **Rags** (1987), for which he was nominated for a Tony. In that same year he also worked on a revival of **Cabaret**, once more gaining critical acclaim. He died of complications arising after undergoing brain surgery.

Fielding, Harold

b. 4 December 1916, Woking, Surrey, England. A leading producer of stage musicals from the 50s through to the 80s, Fielding has presented or copresented some of the West End's favourite shows. When he was 10 years old he resisted parental pressure to play the piano and instead took up the violin, studying in Paris with virtuoso Szigeti. By the time he was 12, Fielding was himself a concert performer, touring as a supporting artist to the diva Tetrazzini. When he was in his early 20s, the impresario who was presenting him died, and Fielding took over the tour management. In a short space of time, he was presenting hundreds of concerts throughout the UK, including his Sunday Concert Series at Blackpool Opera House, which endured for many years. He also mounted a series called *Music For Millions* in collaboration with his wife Maisie. Among the artists appearing in his productions were Richard Tauber, **Grace Moore**, Benjamino Gigli, Rawicz And Landauer, **Jeanette MacDonald**, **Paul Robeson**, **Gracie Fields** and the London Philharmonic Orchestra.

Subsequent promotions in the popular music field would include **Johnnie Ray**, **Danny Kaye**, **Nat 'King' Cole** and **Frank Sinatra**. In January 1949, while returning from the USA after negotiating a contract for the Philadelphia Symphony Orchestra to visit England, Fielding was involved in the famous pickaback air crash. A light aircraft collided with the roof of his Constellation airliner, and the dead pilot fell into Fielding's lap. The Constellation made a perfect landing, and, having survived that kind of crash, from then on Fielding believed that flying was the safest form of travel. By the late 50s, with government-sponsored concerts affecting his business, Fielding turned to the legitimate theatre. He had already collaborated with **Charles B. Cochran** and **Jack Hylton**, one of his associations with Hylton resulting in the first ever arena concert festival at Harringay, London. They also promoted a classical ballet season. Just prior to Christmas 1958, Fielding launched himself as a solo producer with a spectacular presentation of **Richard Rodgers** and **Oscar Hammerstein II**'s *Cinderella* at the London Coliseum. Originally conceived for US television, Fielding blended pantomime material with the musical comedy aspect of the piece and cast rock 'n' roll star **Tommy Steele** as Buttons. *Cinderella* was followed by another coliseum extravaganza, *Aladdin*, and from then on Fielding lived a rollercoaster

existence—producing or coproducing many of the West End's biggest hits and some of its biggest disasters.

The Music Man, starring Van Johnson, and **Noël Coward**'s *Sail Away* led in 1963 to one of Fielding's most fondly remembered shows, **Half A Sixpence**, a musicalization of H.G. Wells' novel *Kipps*, starring Tommy Steele. However, the success of *Half A Sixpence* in London and New York paled in comparison with **Charlie Girl** (1965, 2,202 performances), which was followed by several more profitable productions in the shape of **Sweet Charity**, **Mame**, **The Great Waltz**, **Show Boat**, **I Love My Wife**, **Irene**, stage versions of the popular movies *Hans Andersen* and **Singin' In The Rain** (both with Tommy Steele) as well as **Barnum** (**Michael Crawford**). At the time, Fielding's 1971 *Show Boat* was the longest-running to date with 910 performances (**Hal Prince**'s 1994 production clocked up 951). Like all the great showmen since **Florenz Ziegfeld**, Fielding was fond of making extravagant gestures. When **Ginger Rogers** arrived in the UK to appear in **Mame** (1969), he ensured that the event made the front pages by transporting her from Southampton to London in a special train filled with pressmen and an orchestra playing tunes from the show. There was also a portable movie theatre showing her old films. The Ziegfeld reference would probably send a shiver up the now-venerable producer's spine, because **Ziegfeld** (1988), with a book by Ned Sherrin, was one of his shows, along with *Man Of Magic*, **You're A Good Man**, *Charlie Brown*, **Phil The Fluter**, *Gone With The Wind*, *Beyond The Rainbow*, **On The Twentieth Century**, *The Biograph Girl* and the 1986 revival of *Charlie Girl* with **Cyd Charisse**, which failed to set the London theatrical scene alight. He was reported to have lost £1.3 million on *Ziegfeld*, and that sum rose to £1.7 million four years later when **Petula Clark**'s American Civil War musical, **Someone Like You**, folded after only a month, ensuring that Harold Fielding Limited went into voluntary liquidation.

Since then, understandably, Fielding has not been a major force, partly due to ill health, although he was associated with the West End transfer of **Mack And Mabel** from the Leicester Haymarket Theatre in 1995, which resulted in the show's long-awaited London premiere. Over the years, he has presented a whole range of entertainment, including revues, plays, and variety shows featuring outstanding performers such as The Two Ronnies (Corbett and Barker), Petula Clark, **Julie Andrews**, Peter Sellers, **Benny Hill**, **Marlene Dietrich**, **Eartha Kitt** and **Shirley Bassey**, but it is for his often lavish and immensely likeable musicals that he will be remembered. In 1986 he 'passed' on the opportunity to present the UK version of **La Cage Aux Folles** because 'it wasn't a family show', yet more than 10 years previously he had been associated with the notorious 'sexual musical' *Let My People Come*. A much-loved personality, he belongs to the tradition of great British showman such as Hylton, Bernard Delfont and Lew Grade. He risked his own money rather than that of theatrical 'angels' and in 1996 received a Gold Badge from BASCA (British Academy Of Songwriters, Composers And Authors) in recognition of his special contribution to Britain's entertainment industry.

Fields Brothers

Bennie Fields (b. 22 January 1941, Kermit, Mingo County, West Virginia, USA; guitar/vocals) and his brother Clancy (b. 11 February 1950, Kermit, Mingo County, West Virginia,

USA; bass fiddle, guitar, mandolin, vocals). Inspired by a mandolin-playing uncle, Lundy Fields, Bennie began a singing career at 12 and had his own band at 18. In 1968 Clancy, the youngest of 12 Fields children, joined his brother. In 1970 the Fields Brothers bluegrass band, including Curtis Beck (fiddle/dobro) and banjoist Dave Clark, won a major bluegrass festival at Columbus, Ohio. They recorded their first album for the Jessup label in 1973, but on the second the next year, Clark was replaced by Tom Dew, and Orville Dingess joined to play bass. The material was a mixture of self-penned songs, old-time ballads and bluegrass numbers. They proved very popular, but disagreements saw the band break up in the mid-70s. Clancy later played with other groups including River Bend, a bluegrass band led by Dave Evans, which also included his uncle Lundy.

● ALBUMS: *Waiting And Wondering* (Jessup 1974) ★★★, *Sing Of Old Kentucky And West Virginia* (Jessup 1974) ★★★★.

Fields Of Ambrosia, The

Enthusiastically received during its tryout early in 1993 at the George Street Playhouse, New Jersey, USA, this 'adventurous black musical comedy' came under heavy fire from most of the London critics when it transferred to the Aldwych Theatre on 31 January 1996 complete with the original leads, Joel Higgins and Christine Andreas. Higgins also wrote the book and lyrics, and the music was composed by Martin Silvestri. Based on the 1970 Stacey Keach film *The Traveling Executioner*, the story is set in 1918 rural Louisiana in the American Deep South. Jonas Candide (Higgins), an ex-carnival hustler turned state executioner, comforts his 'victims' as he straps them down by painting a rose-coloured musical picture of their paradisaic hereafter—'The fields of ambrosia / Where everyone knows ya'. When he falls in love with his first female client, the beautiful Austrian countess Gretchen Herzallerliebst (Andreas), he craftily attempts to delay her death by accidentally 'misplacing' Old Reliable, his mobile electric chair. Whiskey-soaked Doc (Michael Fenton Stevens) is also involved in the deception, which sparks off a scene in which 'suspicious guards set on the assembled convicts, viciously beating and throttling and gouging their eyes out while Jonas has gleeful sex with Gretchen on a platform above'. Jonas' main rival for Gretchen's generous favours, Malcolm Piquant (Mark Heenehan), a burly butch warder, 'evidently consoles himself with impressionable male convicts'. Other 'highlights' include the rape of young mortician Jimmy Crawford (Marc Joseph) by two prisoners, an act that moves him to give out with the painful lament 'Alone' ('If it ain't one thing it's another'), and the appearance of Warden Brodsky (Roger Leach), who kindly advises Gretchen that 'your ass is too good to fry' before sexually assaulting her. Among the rest of the participants were Amanda Noar, Caron Skinns, Kevin Rooney, Henry Webster, Michael Neilson, Chris Andrew Mellon, Susie Fenwick and Peter Gallagher. At the end of this game of musical or, rather, electrical chairs, Jonas is 'shocked' himself, and 'the show's final image reveals its principals united happily in the sweet afterlife represented by the Ambrosian fields'. Although critics were generally either sickened or outraged by the book ('Surely something can be done to discourage the dumping of American theatrical refuse like *The Fields Of Ambrosia* in attractive London theatres?'), there were some kind words for the score, notably the rueful 'Too Bad', 'Continental Sunday', an evocative word-picture of New Orleans, the flag-waving 'All In This Together', the recitative 'My Name's Candide', 'Too Bad' and the impressive production numbers 'Nuthin' and 'Step Right Up'. Also present were 'Ball And Chain/Jonas' Theme', 'The Fields Of Ambrosia', 'Some Days/How Could This Happen?', 'Who Are You?', 'Reasonable Man', 'Hungry', 'The Card Game' and 'Do It For Me'. The sets were designed by Deborah Jasien, David Toguri handled the musical staging and the director was Gregory S. Hurst. Higgins and Andreas, both of whom have solid Broadway credits, emerged from the nightmare with some distinction, particularly in the singing department, but their stay in the West End was brief, and this £1.3 million production, which announced its closure for 17 February, was hastily withdrawn a week earlier.

Fields Of The Nephilim

This UK rock band was formed in Stevenage, Hertfordshire, in 1983. The line-up comprised Carl McCoy (vocals), Tony Pettitt (bass), Peter Yates (keyboards) and the Wright brothers, Nod (b. Alexander; drums) and Paul (guitar). Their image, that of neo-western desperados, was borrowed from movies such as *Once Upon A Time In the West* and *The Long Ryders*. They also had a bizarre habit of smothering their predominantly black clothes in flour and/or talcum powder for some of the most hysterically inept videos ever recorded. Their version of goth-rock, tempered with transatlantic overtones, found favour with those already immersed in the sounds of the **Sisters Of Mercy** and the **Mission**. Signed to the Situation Two label, Fields Of The Nephilim had two major UK independent hit singles with 'Preacher Man' and 'Blue Water', while their first album, *Dawnrazor*, made a modest showing on the UK album chart. The second set, *The Nephilim*, reached number 14, announcing the band's arrival as one of the principal rock acts of the day. Their devoted following also ensured a showing on the national singles chart, giving them minor hits with 'Moonchild' (also an independent chart number 1), 'Psychonaut' and 'Summerland (Dreamed)'. In October 1991 McCoy left the group, taking the 'Fields Of The Nephilim' name with him. The remaining members vowed to carry on. With the recruitment of a new vocalist, Alan Delaney, they began gigging under the name Rubicon in the summer of 1992, leaving McCoy to unveil his version of the Nephilim (renamed **Nefilim**). Rubicon released two albums on **Beggars Banquet Records** (1993's *What Starts, Ends* and 1995's *Room 101*) before disbanding. They joined in the goth-rock revival by re-forming in the late 90s and released a new studio album in 2002.

● ALBUMS: *Dawnrazor* (Situation 2 1987) ★★, *The Nephilim* (Situation 2 1988) ★★★, *Elizium* (Beggars Banquet 1990) ★★, *Earth Inferno* (Beggars Banquet 1991) ★★, *BBC Radio 1 In Concert* (Windsong 1992) ★★, *Revelations* (Beggars Banquet 1993) ★★, *Fallen* (Jungle 2002) ★★.

● COMPILATIONS: *From Gehenna To Here* (Jungle 2001) ★★.

● DVD/VIDEOS: *Forever Remain* (Situation 2 1988), *Morphic Fields* (Situation 2 1989), *Earth Inferno* (Beggars Banquet 1991), *Visionary Heads* (Beggars Banquet 1992), *Revelations* (Beggars Banquet 1993).

Fields, Benny

b. Benjamin Geisenfeld, 14 June 1894, Milwaukee, Wisconsin, USA, d. 16 August 1959, New York City, USA. A popular vaudeville entertainer, Fields appeared in *Greenwich Village Follies* (1928). Also in the cast was **Blossom Seeley**, a Broadway star. They were married, Fields becoming Seeley's third husband, and they often partnered one another on stage until his death. A brief glimpse of their act is seen in a 10-minute film short, *Blossom Seeley And Bennie Fields* (1929). This features Seeley and Fields (billed here as Bennie) singing to the duel piano accompaniment of Charles Bourne and Phil Ellis. Fields also made brief appearances in the films *Mr. Broadway* (1933) and *The Big Broadcast* of 1937 (1936). In the latter, Fields sings 'Here's Love In Your Eye' with **Larry Adler** and **Benny Goodman**'s orchestra. The short with Seeley apart, little sense of Fields' talent can be gained from these film appearances. The biopic *Somebody Loves Me* (1952) did not help, inaccurately tracing the life story of Seeley and Fields, played by **Betty Hutton** and Ralph Meeker. A number of times between 1954 and 1958, Fields appeared on television in *Toast Of The Town*.

Fortunately for posterity, Fields played the lead in one feature film, *Minstrel Man* (1944), which was directed by Joseph H. Lewis. In this film, which became available on DVD in the early 00s, Fields is Dixie Boy Johnson, a 'blackface' singer in a minstrel show who has Broadway in the palm of his hand. After his wife dies in childbirth, he leaves his baby daughter with friends, almost drowns at sea, then goes into hiding for decades before returning to see his daughter become a star on Broadway. Among several songs Fields sings are four written for the film by **Harry Revel** and **Paul Francis Webster**, 'I Don't Care If The World Knows About It', 'My Bamboo Cane', 'Cindy' and 'Remember Me To Carolina', the latter being nominated unsuccessfully for an Oscar. The music arranger for the film was **Ferde Grofé**. Uncomfortably for present-day audiences, the production numbers are done in 'blackface' but there is, thankfully, a nightclub sequence when Fields appears without makeup, accompanying himself at the piano in a medley of songs. Fields' singing voice is mellow and tuneful, and he presents the songs with care and restraint.

● FILMS: *Blossom Seeley And Bennie Fields* (1929), *Mr. Broadway* (1933), *The Big Broadcast Of 1937* (1936), *Minstrel Man* (1944).

Fields, Dorothy

b. 15 July 1905, Allenhurst, New Jersey, USA, d. 28 March 1974, New York City, USA. A librettist and lyricist, Fields was one of the few and probably the best and most successful female writers of 'standard' popular songs and the first woman to be elected to the Songwriters Hall of Fame. The list of her distinguished collaborators includes **Jerome Kern**, **Jimmy McHugh**, **Sigmund Romberg**, **Harry Warren**, **J. Fred Coots**, **Harold Arlen**, **Morton Gould**, **Oscar Levant**, **Arthur Schwartz**, **Albert Hague**, **Cy Coleman** and Fritz Kreisler. Dorothy Fields' parents were **Lew Fields** and Rose, better known as the famous comedy team Weber And Fields. She had one sister and two brothers: **Joseph Fields**, who became a Broadway playwright, and **Herbert Fields**, a librettist, with whom she worked frequently. Shortly after she was born (while her parents were on holiday in New Jersey), Weber and Fields terminated their partnership, and Lew Fields

became a Broadway producer and appeared in several of his own shows.

It was because of her father's showbusiness associations that Dorothy Fields, at the age of 15, took the lead in one of **Richard Rodgers** and **Lorenz Hart**'s earliest musical shows, *You'd Be Surprised*, which played for one night at the Plaza Hotel Grand Ballroom in New York. After graduating from the Benjamin Franklin High School, Fields contributed poetry to several magazines and worked with J. Fred Coots (who went on to write the music for songs such as 'Love Letters In The Sand', 'Santa Claus Is Comin' To Town' and 'You Go To My Head') before being introduced to the composer **Jimmy McHugh** at Mills Brothers Music. With McHugh, she initially wrote sundry novelty numbers and some songs for Cotton Club revues. The new team made their Broadway debut with the complete score for Lew Leslie's *Blackbirds Of 1928*, which starred **Bill 'Bojangles' Robinson**, Aida Ward and **Adelaide Hall** and ran for over 500 performances. The songs included 'Porgy', 'I Must Have That Man', 'Doin' The New Low-Down' and future standards 'I Can't Give You Anything But Love' and 'Diga Diga Doo'. In the same year, McHugh and Fields' next effort, *Hello Daddy*, proved to be a family affair, with Fields' brother Herbert as librettist and her father as the producer and leading man, although the show's comedy number, 'In A Great Big Way', was sung by Billy Taylor. In 1930 another of Lew Leslie's lavish productions, *The International Revue*, contained two of McHugh and Fields' most enduring songs: 'On The Sunny Side Of The Street', which was introduced by **Harry Richman**, and 'Exactly Like You', a duet for Richman and **Gertrude Lawrence**.

After contributing 'Button Up Your Heart' and 'Blue Again' to the unsuccessful *Vanderbilt Revue* (1930), McHugh and Fields moved to Hollywood and, during the next few years, wrote songs for movies such as *Love In The Rough* ('Go Home And Tell Your Mother', 'One More Waltz'), *Cuban Love Song* (title number), *Dancing Lady* ('My Dancing Lady'), *Hooray For Love* (title song, 'Livin' In A Great Big Way', 'I'm In Love All Over Again', 'You're An Angel'), and *The Nitwits* ('Music In My Heart'). *Every Night At Eight*, which starred **Frances Langford**, **Harry Barris**, Patsy Kelly and **Alice Faye**, included two more McHugh and Fields all-time favourites: 'I'm In The Mood For Love' and 'I Feel A Song Coming On'. Another of their standards, 'Don't Blame Me', was interpolated into the Broadway revue *Clowns In Clover* (1933). Two years later, Fields began to work with other composers, including Jerome Kern, with whom she collaborated on the score for the film *Roberta*, which included 'Lovely To Look At' and 'I Won't Dance', a song that had been in Kern's locker for a couple of years and which, for complex contractual reasons, is usually credited to five songwriters. The Kern/Fields partnership continued with *Swing Time*, the sixth **Fred Astaire/Ginger Rogers** screen musical. Often regarded as Kern's finest score, the songs included 'Pick Yourself Up', 'Bojangles Of Harlem', 'Waltz In Swing Time', 'A Fine Romance' ('You're calmer than the seals in the Arctic Ocean / At least they flap their fins to express emotion') and 'The Way You Look Tonight' ('With each word your tenderness grows / Tearing my fear apart / And that laugh that wrinkles your nose / Touches my foolish heart'), which gained Kern and Fields an Academy Award. During the remainder of the 30s they worked together again on *I Dream Too Much* ('I'm The Echo' and the title song),

When You're In Love ('Our Song', 'The Whistling Boy') and others such as One Night In The Tropics ('Remind Me') and Joy Of Living, which starred Irene Dunne and Douglas Fairbanks Jnr. and included 'Just Let Me Look At You', 'What's Good About Good-Night?' and 'You Couldn't Be Cuter' ('My ma will show you an album of me that'll bore you to tears! / And you'll attract all the relatives we have dodged for years and years').

Fields also wrote film songs with Oscar Levant ('Don't Mention Love To Me', 'Out Of Sight, Out Of Mind') and Max Steiner ('I Can't Waltz Alone') and provided new lyrics to Fritz Kreisler's music in The King Steps Out. Before the end of the decade Fields was back on Broadway, working with the composer Arthur Schwartz on Stars In Your Eyes. Their score included 'This Is It', 'A Lady Needs A Change', 'Just A Little Bit More', 'I'll Pay The Check' and the show's highlight, 'It's All Yours', a duet by the stars, Ethel Merman and Jimmy Durante.

In the early 40s, Fields turned from writing lyrics and collaborated with her brother Herbert on the books for three highly successful Cole Porter musicals: Let's Face It! (starring Danny Kaye), Something For The Boys, (Ethel Merman/Bill Johnson and Mexican Hayride (Bobby Clark/June Havoc), each of which ran for well over a year. In 1945 the Fields partnership again served as librettists, and Dorothy wrote the lyrics, to Sigmund Romberg's music, for the smashhit Up In Central Park. Not surprisingly with Romberg's participation, the score had operetta overtones and included the robust 'The Big Back Yard', two charming ballads, 'April Snow' and 'Close As Pages In A Book' and a skating ballet in the manner of a Currier and Ives print. Towards the end of 1945 she was set to collaborate again with Jerome Kern on Annie Get Your Gun, a musical loosely based on the life of sharpshooter Annie Oakley. When Kern died in November of that year, Irving Berlin was brought in to write what is generally regarded as his greatest score, while Dorothy and Herbert Fields provided the highly entertaining book for a production which ran for 1,147 performances. In contrast, Arms And The Girl (1950) closed after only 134 shows, despite Rouben Mamoulian's involvement with Dorothy and Herbert Fields in a libretto that was based on the play The Pursuit Of Happiness. The Dorothy Fields/Morton Gould score included Pearl Bailey's inimitable renderings of 'Nothin' For Nothin'' and 'There Must Be Somethin' Better Than Love', a strange attempt at a tender love song called 'A Cow, And A Plough And A Frau' and the double entendres of 'That's What I Told Him Last Night'.

During the 50s, Fields teamed up with Arthur Schwartz again for two shows. The first, A Tree Grows In Brooklyn, was a critical success but a commercial failure. Based on Dorothy Smith's bestselling novel, the witty and melodic score included 'If You Haven't Got A Sweetheart', 'I'll Buy You A Star', 'Make The Man Love Me', 'Look Who's Dancing', 'Mine Till Monday', 'I'm Like A New Broom' and 'Growing Pains'. Shirley Booth stopped the show each night with 'He Had Refinement', the story of Harry, her late spouse, who 'only used four-letter words that I didn't understand' and 'undressed with all the lights off until we was wed—a gentleman to his fingernails, was he!'. The show lasted for 270 performances, and so did the second Fields/Schwartz 50s collaboration By The Beautiful Sea (1954), mainly due to the presence, once again, of Shirley Booth. The songs included 'Alone Too Long', 'Happy Habit', 'I'd Rather Wake Up By

Myself', 'Hang Up!', 'More Love Than Your Love', 'By The Beautiful Sea' and 'Coney Island'. Far more successful was Redhead (1959), which ran for 452 performances and won the Tony Award for 'Best Musical'. Dorothy Fields and Albert Hague's score, which also won a Tony, included 'I Feel Merely Marvellous', 'I'm Back In Circulation', 'Just For Once', 'The Uncle Sam Rag', 'The Right Finger Of My Left Hand', 'Look Who's In Love', ''Erbie Fitch's Dilemma' and 'My Girl Is Just Enough Woman For Me'.

Fields' last two Broadway scores were written with Cy Coleman, a composer who was 25 years her junior. The first, Sweet Charity (1966), a musical version of Federico Fellini's movie Nights Of Cabiria, was conceived, directed and choreographed by Bob Fosse and starred Gwen Verdon as the good-hearted hostess at the Fan-Dango ballroom, who almost—but not quite—realizes her dream of being a conventional wife and mother. Fields and Coleman's score produced several popular numbers, including 'Big Spender' ('So let me get right to the point / I don't pop my cork for every guy I see!'), which quickly became associated in the UK with Shirley Bassey, and 'Baby, Dream Your Dream', 'If My Friends Could See Me Now', 'I'm A Brass Band', 'Where Am I Going?', 'There's Gotta Be Something Better Than This', 'Too Many Tomorrows' and 'I Love To Cry At Weddings' ('I walk into a chapel and get happily hysterical'). Fields' Broadway swan song came in 1973 with Seesaw. Her lyrics for this musical adaptation of William Gibson's play Two For The Seesaw are regarded as somewhat tougher than much of her previous work, although they continued to have the colloquial edge and the contemporary, witty, 'streetwise' quality that had become her trademark. The songs included 'Seesaw', 'In Tune', 'Spanglish', 'We've Got It', 'Welcome To Holiday Inn', 'Poor Everybody Else', 'I'm Way Ahead' and the two best-known numbers, 'Nobody Does It Like Me' ('If there's a problem, I duck it / I don't solve it, I just muck it up!') and Tommy Tune's show-stopper 'It's Not Where You Start (It's Where You Finish)'. The latter song closed with 'And you're gonna finish on top!'. Dorothy Fields did just that, 45 years after she had her first Broadway hit with 'I Can't Give You Anything But Love'. Shortly before her death in March 1974, she appeared in a programme in the Lyrics And Lyricists series at the Kaufmann Concert Hall of The 92nd Street 'Y' in New York City, giving her 'observations on the fine art and craft of lyric writing' and performing several of her own numbers. Her lyrics have rarely been celebrated by artists on record, but two notable exceptions are The Dorothy Fields Songbook, by Sally Mayes, and Close As Pages In A Book, by Barbara Cook.

● FURTHER READING: On The Sunny Side Of The Street: The Life And Lyrics Of Dorothy Fields, Deborah Grace Winer.

Fields, Ernie

b. 26 August 1905, Nacogdoches, Texas, USA, d. 11 November 1997. Trombonist, arranger and band leader Fields fronted his own outfit in the Tulsa, Oklahoma, area from the 30s and recorded for various labels, including Vocalion Records, Frisco, Bullet and Gotham. During the 50s he became an arranger for pop and rock sessions and ran his own R&B band. In 1958 he became cofounder of the Rendezvous label, and had a million-seller with his swinging revival of the 1939 Glenn Miller favourite 'In The Mood'. He followed that with his own individual interpretations of other standards such as 'Chattanooga Choo Choo' and 'The Charleston' but without the same success. He was also involved with the Rendezvous act, **B. Bumble And The Stingers**, who had hits with 'Bumble Boogie' and 'Nut Rocker', before Rendezvous folded in the early 60s and Fields retired from the music business in 1966.

His son, saxophonist and producer Ernie Fields Jnr., has worked with soul, R&B and funk artists including **Bobby Bland**, **Rick James**, **Marvin Gaye** and **Fred Wesley**.

● COMPILATIONS: *In The Mood* (Ace 1996) ★★★.

Fields, Gracie

b. Grace Stansfield, 9 January 1898, Rochdale, Lancashire, England, d. 27 September 1979, Capri, Italy. A singer and comedienne, she was so popular in the UK during the 30s and 40s that she was its most famous person next to royalty. Educated occasionally, in-between work in a cotton mill and playing in juvenile troupes, pierrot shows and revues, she took her first big step in 1918 when she won the part of Sally Perkins in the musical *Mr Tower Of London*, which ran for over seven years. Her career took off after she married the show's producer/comedian Archie Pitt. She started recording in 1928 and by 1933 was celebrating the sale of four million records. Guided by stage producer Basil Dean, Fields made her film debut in 1931 with **Sally In Our Alley**, from which came 'Sally', her famous theme song. In other movies such as *Looking On The Bright Side*, *This Week Of Grace*, *Love, Life And Laughter*, **Sing As We Go**, *Look Up And Laugh*, **Queen Of Hearts**, *The Show Goes On*, *We're Going To Be Rich*, *Keep Smiling*, and *Shipyard Sally* (1939), her vitality and spirit of determination, cheerfulness and courage endeared her particularly to working-class people during the dark years of the 30s.

After divorcing Pitt, she married Italian comedian/dancer Monte Banks in 1940. When she subsequently moved to the USA, taking with her substantial assets, questions were asked in Parliament. The once supportive UK press even went as far as branding her a traitor. During World War II she toured extensively, entertaining troops and appearing in USA stage shows, nightclubs, some films, including **Stage Door Canteen** (1944), and on her own radio programmes. After the war she was welcomed back to the UK and featured in a series of morale-building radio shows, *Gracie's Working Party*, but still retained her popularity in the USA during the 40s with chart hits 'Forever And Ever' and the Maori song 'Now Is The Hour'. As early as 1933 she had bought a villa on the Isle of Capri, and during the 50s she went into semi-retirement there with her third husband, Boris Alperovic, emerging only for the occasional concert or record date. She made her final London appearance at her 10th Royal Command Performance in 1978. Her song hits, sung in a fine soprano voice, varied from the comic 'In My Little Bottom Drawer', 'Walter, Walter', 'I Took My Harp To A Party', 'Fred Fannakapan' and 'The Biggest Aspidistra In The World' through the spirited 'Sing As We Go' and 'Wish Me Luck As You Wave Me Goodbye' to the ballads 'Around The World', 'Pedro The Fisherman', 'Little Donkey', 'La Vie En Rose' and 'Ave Maria'. Some of her more personalized material was studied, as social documents, by the Department of Social History at the University of Lancaster. Throughout her life she worked hard for charities, including the Gracie Fields Orphanage, and was awarded the CBE in 1938. Fields was made dame commander of the British Empire shortly before her death in September 1979.

● COMPILATIONS: *The World Of Gracie Fields* (1970) ★★★★, *Stage And Screen* (1972) ★★★★, *The Golden Years Of Gracie Fields* (1975) ★★★★, *Focus On Gracie Fields* (1977) ★★★★, *The Gracie Fields Story* (1979) ★★★★, *Amazing Gracie Fields* (1979) ★★★★, *Gracie Fields—Best Of Her BBC Broadcasts* (1980) ★★★★, *Life Is A Song* (1983) ★★★★, *The Biggest Aspidistra In The World* (1985) ★★★★, *Incomparable* (1985) ★★★★, *Isle Of Capri* (1987) ★★★★, *Laughter And Song* (1987) ★★★★, *Sally* (1988) ★★★★, *Queen Of Hearts* (1989) ★★★★, *Last Concert In America* (1989) ★★★, *That Old Feeling* (1989) ★★★★, *Classic Years In Digital Stereo* (1990) ★★★★, *Sing As We Go* (1990) ★★★★.

● FURTHER READING: *Sing As We Go, Her Autobiography*, Gracie Fields. *Gracie Fields: Her Life In Pictures*, P. Hudson. *Gracie Fields*, Joan Moules.

● FILMS: *Sally In Our Alley* (1931), *Looking On The Bright Side* (1932), *This Week Of Grace* (1933), *Sing As We Go* (1934), *Love, Life And Laughter* (1934), *Look Up And Laugh* (1935), *My Man Godfrey* (1936), *Queen Of Hearts* (1936), *The Show Goes On* (1937), *We're Going To Be Rich* (1938), *Keep Smiling* aka *Smiling Along* (1939), *Shipyard Sally* (1940), *Stage Door Canteen* (1943), *Holy Matrimony* (1943), *Paris Underground* aka *Madame Pimpernel* (1945), *Molly And Me* (1945).

Fields, Herbert

b. 26 July 1897, New York City, USA, d. 24 March 1958, New York City, USA. Fields was born into a family environment that was thoroughly immersed in showbusiness. His father was **Lew Fields**, his older brother was **Joseph Fields**, and his younger sister was **Dorothy Fields**. After graduation from Columbia University, he worked as an actor on stage and in the silent film *The Porcelain Lamp* (1921). While in his twenties, he worked as a choreographer and director but most notably as librettist on musical shows for some of which the music was written by markedly outstanding composers and lyricists such as **Cole Porter**, **Richard Rodgers** and **Lorenz Hart**. He also collaborated as librettist with his sister Dorothy through into the 50s. Among these shows were **Dearest Enemy** and **The Garrick Gaities** (1925), **Hit The Deck!** and **A Connecticut Yankee** (1927), *Present Arms* (1928), **Fifty Million Frenchmen** (1929), *The New Yorkers* (1930), *Pardon My English* (1932), **Du Barry Was A Lady** (1939), **Panama Hattie** (1940), **Let's Face It!** (1941), *Something For The Boys* (1943), **Mexican Hayride** (1944), **Annie Get Your Gun** (1946), **Up In Central Park** (1947), *Arms And The Girl* (1950) and *By The Beautiful Sea* (1954). Concurrent with his stage work, Fields also wrote several Hollywood screenplays, including *Hands Across The Table* (1935), *Fools For Scandal* (1938) and *Father Takes A Wife* (1941). Towards the end of the 50s, he and his sister were working together on another Broadway production, the **Tony Award**–winning **Redhead** (1959), which starred **Gwen Verdon**, when he died.

● FILMS: *The Porcelain Lamp* (1921).

Fields, Herbie

b. Herbert Fields, 24 May 1919, Elizabeth, New Jersey, USA, d. 17 September 1958, Miami, Florida, USA. Fields played clarinet and alto (occasionally tenor) saxophone in several bands in the mid- and late 30s and also studied formally at the Juilliard School of Music. Among the leaders for whom he worked were **George Handy**, **Raymond Scott**, **Woody**

Herman and **Oran 'Hot Lips' Page**. In military service during World War II, Fields led a service band, and after the war he joined **Lionel Hampton**. He led his own small and large groups during the late 40s, recorded with **Miles Davis**, but was unable to maintain the momentum of his career and by the following decade was mostly playing commercial music. Fields' playing was varied, perhaps even erratic at times. At his best, he could be a fluid and imaginative player, especially on clarinet. Sometimes, however, he could be undisciplined and his career appeared to lack direction.

Fields, Joseph

b. 21 February 1895, New York City, USA, d. 3 March 1966, Beverly Hills, Los Angeles, California, USA. Fields was born into a showbusiness family, his father was **Lew Fields**, vaudeville star turned impresario. His younger brother was librettist **Herbert Fields**, and his sister was songwriter **Dorothy Fields**. After graduation from university he served in the US Army during World War I and stayed on in Paris, France, until the early 20s. He had begun writing for newspapers and magazines and on his return to New York began working for **Florenz Ziegfeld**. Often in collaboration with Jerome Chodorov, he wrote musical comedies for the stage and screenplays for Hollywood films. Among his stage credits, mostly in collaboration, are the 1940 show *My Sister Eileen*, later adapting it as the musical *Wonderful Town* (1953, for which he won two **Tony Awards** with collaborator Jerome Chodorov), *Junior Miss* (1951), *Anniversary Waltz* (1954), *The Ponder Heart* (1955) and *The Tunnel Of Love* (1957). His biggest stage successes were *Gentlemen Prefer Blondes* (1949, with Anita Loos) and *Flower Drum Song* (1958, with **Joshua Logan**). His screenplay credits include *The Big Shot* (1931), *$1,000 A Minute* (1935), *Fools For Scandal* (1938), *The Girl From Mexico* (1939), *Mexican Spitfire* (1940), *Louisiana Purchase* (1942), *A Night In Casablanca* (1946) and *The Farmer Takes A Wife* (1953). He also worked on adaptations of several of his stage plays for the screen, including *My Sister Eileen* (1942), *Gentlemen Prefer Blondes* (1953), and *Flower Drum Song* (1961).

Fields, Kansas

b. Carl Donnell Fields, 5 December 1915, Chapman, Kansas, USA, d. 3 August 1995, Chicago, Illinois, USA. As a young teenager Fields moved to Chicago, where, a few years later, he began playing drums at various clubs. Among the musicians for whom he worked during the 30s were **Jimmie Noone** and **Horace Henderson**. In 1940 he joined **Roy Eldridge** and then flitted through the bands of **Benny Carter**, **Charlie Barnet**, **Mel Powell** and others until war service interrupted his career. After the war he was with **Cab Calloway**, **Sidney Bechet** and Eldridge again, and also ventured into modern waters with **Dizzy Gillespie**. Fields was, however, a mainstream drummer and was at his best in such surroundings. In the 50s and early 60s he spent much of his time in Europe working and recording with **Mezz Mezzrow**, **Lionel Hampton** and **Buck Clayton**. He continued working into the 80s.

Fields, Lew

b. Moses Schoenfeld, 1 January 1867, Poland, d. 20 July 1941, Beverly Hills, Los Angeles, California, USA. Relocating to America with his family while he was still a small child, Fields lived on the Lower East Side of Manhattan in New York City. He struck up a friendship with another boy, Joe

Weber, and they formed the comedy double act of Weber And Fields. Basing their routines on the German-accented characters who filled their childhood landscape, they became increasingly popular through their numerous appearances in vaudeville and burlesque. Over the years, Weber and Fields brought their routines into more sophisticated shows, although they retained the central core of knockabout comedy for which they were famous. They produced some of their own shows, among them *Whirl-i-gig* (1899), *Hoity-Toity* (1901) and *Hokey-Pokey* (1912), bringing in top vaudeville and musical comedy artists such as DeWolf Hopper, **Lillian Russell** and Faye Templeton. Fields and Weber made some film appearances, including *The Best Of Enemies* (both 1915), *The Worst Of Friends* (1916), *Friendly Enemies* (1925), *Blossoms On Broadway* (1937) and *Lillian Russell* (1940). The early *Mike & Meyer* was named after their knockabout stage characters.

Fields, who had adopted the name Lewis Maurice Fields, had three talented children, all of whom built successful careers in showbusiness: **Joseph Fields**, **Herbert Fields** and **Dorothy Fields**. In addition to his film appearances with Weber, Fields also made a number of appearances alone, including *The Duel* (1930) and *The Story Of Vernon And Irene Castle* (1939). He had meanwhile extended his interest in Broadway productions, including bringing to fruition several that teamed his son Herbert as librettist for **Richard Rodgers** and **Lorenz Hart**, among which were *Peggy-Ann* (1926) and *A Connecticut Yankee* (1929).

● FURTHER READING: *From The Bowery To Broadway: Lew Fields And The Roots Of American Popular Theatre*, Armond Fields and L. Marc Fields.

● FILMS: *Mike & Meyer* (1915), *Old Dutch* (1915), *The Best Of Enemies* (1915), *Fatty And The Broadway Stars* (1915), *The Worst Of Friends* (1916), *The Man Who Stood Still* (1916), *The Barker* (1917), *The Corner Grocer* (1917), *Friendly Enemies* (1925), *Two Flaming Youths* (1927), *23—Skidoo* (1930), *Beer Is Here* (1933), *Broadway To Hollywood* aka *Ring Up The Curtain* (1933), *Blossoms On Broadway* (1937), *The Story Of Vernon And Irene Castle* (1939), *Lillian Russell* (1940).

Fields, Richard 'Dimples'

b. 1942, New Orleans, Louisiana, USA, d. 12 January 2000, Los Angeles, California, USA. Fields earned the nickname 'Dimples' from a female admirer who remarked that he was always smiling. Fields began singing in the early 70s, purchasing a San Francisco cabaret, the Cold Duck Music Lounge, and installing himself as its entertainment. He began recording for his own DRK Records label during this period. Each of his three albums for DRK (Dat Richfield Kat) sold reasonably well, and Fields signed to Neil Bogart's Boardwalk Records in 1981. His first chart single was that year's 'Earth Angel', a remake of the 1954 **Penguins** ballad. His biggest hit was 1982's 'If It Ain't One Thing . . . It's Another', an R&B number 1, which became his only crossover pop chart hit. Two albums, 1981's *Dimples* and the following year's *Mr. Look So Good!*, also reached the charts, but Boardwalk folded as his third album for the company, *Give Everybody Some!*, was released in 1983, destroying any chance of success. Fields signed with **RCA Records** in 1984 and recorded two albums for that label before he was dropped. Further recordings, often under the name Dimples, followed for **CBS Records**, Life and Owch but Fields never managed to restore his commercial profile. His death in January 2000 was the result of a stroke.

● ALBUMS: *It's Finger Licking Good* (DRK) ★★★, *Ready For Anything* (DRK) ★★★, *Spoiled Rotten* (DRK) ★★★, *Dimples* (Boardwalk 1981) ★★★★, *Mr. Look So Good!* (Boardwalk 1982) ★★★, *Give Everybody Some!* (Boardwalk 1983) ★★, *Mmm . . .* (RCA 1984) ★★, *Dark Gable* (RCA 1985) ★★★, *Tellin' It Like It Is* (CBS 1987) ★★★, *Dimples* (Life 1990) ★★★, *The Man Who Loves Women!* (Owch 1995) ★★★.

Fields, Shep

b. 12 September 1910, Brooklyn, New York, USA, d. 23 February 1981, Los Angeles, California, USA. This saxophone and clarinet player was the leader of the 30s sweet band Shep Fields And His Rippling Rhythm. Fields led his first band while at university, then turned professional, gaining important engagements in Miami And New York during 1934. He toured with the Voloz And Yolanda dance team before playing an engagement at Chicago's Palmer House. During this period, he also received good radio coverage. The rippling rhythm gimmick was allegedly produced when Fields discovered the sound that could be made by blowing through a straw into a glass of water.

Signed to **Bluebird Records**, he had a major hit with 'Did I Remember' in 1936 and many others during the late 30s including 'There's Something In The Air', 'This Year's Kisses', 'Moonlight And Shadows', 'The Merry Go Round Broke Down', 'That Old Feeling', 'Thanks For The Memory', 'Whistle While You Work', 'Cathedral In The Pines' and 'South Of The Border'. During the early 40s Fields attempted to update his style and recorded as Shep Fields And His New Music, a band formed completely of reed instruments. Although the resulting sound was unique, his popularity waned, and by 1947 he had reverted to his former rippling rhythm style but without further success. He became a disc jockey in Houston, Texas, in 1955, occasionally fronting a band. Then in 1963 he linked with his brother Freddie to form a Hollywood talent agency. Fields died of a heart attack in 1981.

● COMPILATIONS: *Rippling Rhythms 1936–38* (Sunbeam 1988) ★★★, *Shep Fields And His Orchestra 1947–51* (Circle 1989) ★★★.

Fields, W.C.

b. William Claude Dukenfield, 29 January 1880, Philadelphia, Pennsylvania, USA, d. 25 December 1946, Pasadena, California, USA. At the age of 11 Fields ran away from a brutal, poverty-wracked home life and spent months on the verge of starvation before turning his juggling skills to profit. He was hired by a fairground and by the time he was out of his teens was a vaudeville headliner. He travelled to Europe where he appeared at the Folies-Bergère in Paris and at London's Palace Theatre and at Buckingham Palace where he gave a command performance. He was on Broadway in *The Ham Tree* (1905), following this with several appearances in the **Ziegfeld Follies** and in **George White's Scandals**. His biggest Broadway success came in **Poppy** (1923). He had made his first film appearance in 1915 and in 1925 made the screen version of *Poppy*, which was entitled *Sally Of The Sawdust*. Through the 20s he made several more silent films, including *Running Wild* (1927).

The coming of sound boosted Fields' film career, his off-screen cynicism and bitterness bringing an occasional savage edge to his dialogue, much of which he wrote himself.

Among classic screen performances are *The Dentist* (a startling sexy 1932 short), *Tillie And Gus* (1933), in which Fields first met his nemesis, child actor Baby LeRoy, who turns up again in *It's A Gift* (1934). In 1935 Fields portrayed Mr. Micawber in *David Copperfield*, seemingly his only straight performance. He was also in *Man On The Flying Trapeze* (1935) and in the following year was in a sound remake of *Sally Of The Sawdust*, which reverted to the original title of *Poppy*. In 1939 he was in *You Can't Cheat An Honest Man* (1939) and was memorably teamed with **Mae West** in *My Little Chickadee* (1940). Also in 1940 he made *The Bank Dick*, a comic masterpiece. His last starring role came with *Never Give A Sucker An Even Break* (1941), but he made a few cameo appearances thereafter, including performing his famed billiard sketch in Universal's all-star jamboree *Follow The Boys* (1944). The bitterness and cynicism that characterized his private life and which overflowed seamlessly into his onscreen performances were among the factors that contributed to his problems with alcohol. His often-savage one-liners have never become old-fashioned, and his following is higher today than it was in his troubled lifetime.

● DVD/VIDEOS: *Straight Up* (Label 2004), *The Great Man* (Passport Video 2005).

● FURTHER READING: *W.C. Fields And Me*, Carlotta Monti with Cy Rice. *Man On The Flying Trapeze: The Life And Times Of W.C. Fields*, Simon Louvish. *W.C. Fields: A Biography*, James Curtis.

● FILMS: *His Lordship's Dilemma* (1915), *Pool Sharks* (1915), *Janice Meredith* aka *The Beautiful Rebel* (1924), *Sally Of The Sawdust* (1925), *That Royle Girl* (1925), *It's The Old Army Game* (1926), *So's Your Old Man* (1926), *The Potters* (1927), *Running Wild* (1927), *Two Flaming Youths* (1927), *A Trip Through The Paramount Studio* (1927), *Tillie's Punctured Romance* (1928), *Fools For Luck* (1928), *The Golf Specialist* (1930), *Her Majesty, Love* (1931), *Million Dollar Legs* (1932), *If I Had A Million* (1932), *The Dentist* (1932), *The Fatal Glass Of Beer* (1933), *The Pharmacist* aka *The Druggist* (1933), *International House* (1933), *The Barber Shop* (1933), *Tillie And Gus* (1933), *Alice In Wonderland* (1933), *Hollywood On Parade No. 9* (1933), *Hip Action* (1933), *Six Of A Kind* (1934), *You're Telling Me!* (1934), *The Old Fashioned Way* (1934), *Mrs. Wiggs Of The Cabbage Patch* (1934), *It's A Gift* (1934), *David Copperfield* (1935), *Mississippi* (1935), *Man On The Flying Trapeze* aka *The Memory Expert* (1935), *Poppy* (1936), *The Big Broadcast Of 1938* (1938), *You Can't Cheat An Honest Man* (1939), *My Little Chickadee* (1940), *The Bank Dick* aka *The Bank Detective* (1940), *Never Give A Sucker An Even Break* aka *What A Man* (1941), *Tales Of Manhattan* (1942), *Show Business At War* (1943), *Follow The Boys* aka *Three Cheers For The Boys* (1944), *Song Of The Open Road* (1944), *Sensations Of 1945* (1944).

Fieldstones

This Memphis, Tennessee, USA–based electric blues band played an eclectic repertoire, mixing versions of traditional blues such as 'Dirt Road' and 'Sweet Home Chicago' with more modern material such as **Little Milton**'s 'Little Bluebird' and **Albert King**'s 'Angel Of Mercy'. Active from the mid-70s through to the early 80s, their appeal never outgrew their Memphis home. Vocals were shared by guitarist Willie Roy Sanders, formerly of the Binghampton Blues Boys, Little Applewhite and drummer Joe Hicks, with other regular members including bass player Lois Brown and keyboard player Bobby Carnes. The material varied between the older, brooding, Delta style and an intense, soul-cum-west side Chicago vein. Their enjoyable live performance talents did not always stand up to exposure on albums. However, their music did reflect the Memphis State University's need to release material illustrative of academic research. *Mud Island Blues* came out nearly 20 years after their 1983 debut. Most of the tracks were recorded in the early 80s, and although the material is not strong, the playing is highly proficient.

● ALBUMS: *Memphis Blues Today!* (High Water 1983) ★★★, *Mud Island Blues* (High Water 2001) ★★.

Fierce Heart

Fierce Heart was a studio project conceived to issue a single album of the same title in 1985. All instruments were played by the US-based duo of Larry Elkins (vocals/bass) and Rex Carroll (guitars). Carroll had previously been a member of Winterhawk, while Elkins was well-known as a session singer and musician. Attempting to create a multi-layered AOR record built on crafted songwriting and climatic vocals, *Fierce Heart* was widely considered to be one of the finer pomp rock albums of the mid-80s. However, Carroll's increasing commitment to his Christian faith ensured that it would remain a one-off project. He subsequently formed Whitecross.

● ALBUMS: *Fierce Heart* (Mirage 1985) ★★★★.

Fiery Furnaces

In the early years of the new millennium, in the wake of the massive success of the **White Stripes**, countless other garage rock bands popped up comprised of either only two members and/or a brother and sister combo. One of the most notable of these new acts was the Brooklyn, New York, USA–based Fiery Furnaces. Originally from Chicago, Illinois, the band is comprised of sister/brother duo Eleanor (vocals/guitar) and Matthew Friedberger (guitar). Honing their act by opening up NYC dates for national acts travelling along the east coast, including **Hot Hot Heat** and the **Kills**, the Fiery Furnaces began to create a buzz, eventually signing with **Rough Trade Records** (distributed by Sanctuary). Late in 2003 the band released their acclaimed debut, *Gallowsbird's Bark*. The album mixed the duo's basic garage rock style with a rich smattering of folk, blues and music hall. The follow-up *Blueberry Boat* was even more impressive, a dizzying collage of musical styles and surreal lyrics. Despite Eleanor and Matthew being the band's main focal point (and receiving the lion's share of credit), the Fiery Furnaces' line-up has been known to expand to include additional members, especially on stage, where their songs take on a life of their own.

● ALBUMS: *Gallowsbird's Bark* (Rough Trade 2003) ★★★, *Blueberry Boat* (Rough Trade 2004) ★★★★, *Rehearsing My Choir* (Rough Trade 2005) ★★★.

● COMPILATIONS: *EP* (Rough Trade 2005) ★★★.

Fiestas

Formed in Newark, New Jersey, USA, c.1958, the Fiestas were known for their R&B hit 'So Fine', released on Old Town Records the following year. The group consisted of Tommy Bullock (lead vocals), Eddie Morris (tenor), Sam Ingalls (baritone) and Preston Lane (bass). Two conflicting stories about the group's signing to Old Town have circulated throughout the years. One has the Fiestas recording a demo tape in Newark, which studio owner Jim Gribble brought to the attention of Old Town's Hy Weiss. The other simply has Weiss overhearing the group singing and liking them enough to take them on. The result was the group's only hit, a soulful dance number which reached number 11 in the US charts. Only one other single made the charts, but the Fiestas stayed with Old Town until 1965. Tommy Bullock formed a duo with Cleveland Horne, Tommy And Cleve, and they had a hit in 1966 with 'Boogaloo Baby' (Checker). Numerous personnel changes kept the Fiestas working into the 70s.

● COMPILATIONS: *The Oh So Fine Fiestas* (Ace 1993) ★★★★.

15-16-17

15-16-17 was a female vocal trio formed in 1974 in the UK, although they came from Jamaica. The line-up consisted of Sonia Williams, Christine McNabb and her sister Wraydette McNabb. They entered a talent contest at the Georgian club in Croydon, Surrey, England, performing as the Gorgon Sisters, but changed to 15-16-17 (the name reflecting the girls' ages) on the advice of the owner of the club, Castro Brown. They won the contest for two weeks in a row with a cover version of **Louisa Mark**'s **lovers rock** track 'Caught You In A Lie'. With Brown producing, the group recorded 'If You Love Me Smile' and 'Black Skin Boy', which featured **Dennis Bovell**. The singles surfaced on Castro Brown's Morpheus label, which enjoyed considerable support from his patriarchal colleague **Dennis Brown**. When the label folded in 1976, the trio suffered a setback but loyally remained with Castro Brown. In 1977 a partnership was formed with Dennis Brown and the DEB (Dennis Emmanuel Brown) label was set up. Castro produced their cover version of the **Temptations** track 'Just My Imagination' as 'Girls Imagination'. The track was also featured on a DEB showcase compilation *Black Echoes*, promoted by the weekly music journal of the same name. The single was an instant hit in the reggae charts and was followed by the equally popular 'Suddenly Happiness'. In 1978 they released 'Emotions', 'Good Times' and 'Someone Special'. Following an association with Pablo Black and Oneness, the girls changed their style for the release of 'I'm Hurt', which was closer to roots than the lovers style for which they were renowned. They also undertook several live appearances, touring Italy with the Wreckless Breed and supporting **Gregory Isaacs** on his UK tour. By the early 80s the group disbanded, although Christine went on to pursue a solo career, and Castro Brown set up his New Name Music label. In 1984 'Girls Imagination' was rereleased.

● ALBUMS: *Good Times* (DEB 1979) ★★★.

Fifth Angel

Formed in Seattle, Washington, USA, in 1985, Fifth Angel comprised Ted Pilot (vocals), Kendall Bechtel (guitar), Ed Archer (guitar), John Macko (bass) and Ken Mary (drums). On the back of promising club dates they came to the attention of Mike Varney, who signed them to his Shrapnel label. A self-titled debut album backed up with touring commitments won them many fans and brought them to the attention of Epic Records, who had the album remixed and reissued in 1988. *Time Will Tell* sold well but the band was unable to live up to expectations, and they broke up later that year, with only drummer Mary going on to a degree of success with the **Alice Cooper** Band and **House Of Lords**.

● ALBUMS: *Fifth Angel* (Shrapnel 1986) ★★★, *Fifth Angel* remix of debut (Epic 1988) ★★★, *Time Will Tell* (Epic 1989) ★★★.

Fifth Avenue Band

Singer-songwriter Peter Galloway led this engaging Los Angeles–based sextet whose good-time style invoked the carefree quality associated with the early **Lovin' Spoonful**. Jon Lind (vocals), Kenny Altman (lead guitar), Murray Weinstock (keyboards), Jerry Burnham (bass/flute) and Pete Heywood (drums) completed the line-up featured on the Fifth Avenue Band's debut album, but despite an undoubted charm, its anachronistic qualities found few commercial favours. Galloway subsequently formed Ohio Knox, a short-lived unit that also featured drummer Dallas Taylor, formerly of **Crosby, Stills, Nash And Young**. The vocalist then embarked on a solo career.

● ALBUMS: *The Fifth Avenue Band* (Reprise 1972) ★★★.

5th Dimension

Originally known as the Versatiles and later as the Vocals, **Marilyn McCoo** (b. 30 September 1943, Jersey City, New Jersey, USA), Florence LaRue (b. 4 February 1944, Philadelphia, Pennsylvania, USA), Billy Davis Jnr. (b. 26 June 1940, St. Louis, Missouri, USA), Lamont McLemore (b. 17 September 1940, St. Louis, Missouri, USA) and Ron Townson (b. 20 January 1933, St. Louis, Missouri, USA, d. 3 August 2001, Las Vegas, USA) were a soul-influenced harmony group, based in Los Angele,, and signed to **Johnny Rivers**' fledgling Soul City label. They sprang to fame in 1967 as an outlet for the then unknown talents of songwriter **Jimmy Webb**. Ebullient singles on the pop charts, including 'Go Where You Wanna', 'Up, Up And Away' and 'Carpet Man', established their fresh voices, which wrapped themselves around producer Bones Howe's dizzy arrangements.

Having completed two albums containing a number of Webb originals, the group then took to another composer, **Laura Nyro**, whose beautiful soul-styled songs 'Stoned Soul Picnic', 'Sweet Blindness' (both 1968), 'Wedding Bell Blues' (1969) and 'Save The Country' (1970) continued the Fifth Dimension's success and introduced the group to the R&B charts. These popular recordings were punctuated by 'Aquarius/Let The Sunshine In', a medley of songs from the rock musical *Hair*, which topped the US chart in 1969 and reached number 11 in Britain that same year. In 1971 the group reached number 2 in the USA with the haunting 'One Less Bell To Answer'. From then on, however, the MOR elements within their style began to take precedence, and the quintet's releases grew increasingly bland. In 1976 McCoo and Davis (who were now married) left for a successful career both as a duo and as solo artists. They had a US number 1 hit together in 1976 with 'You Don't Have To Be A Star', which was followed up in 1977 by their last Top 20 hit, 'Your Love'. McCoo went on to host the US television show *Solid Gold* for much of the early 80s. Townson, McLemore and LaRue carried on with new members, recording two albums for **Motown Records** before establishing themselves on the nightclub circuit. The original quintet briefly reunited in the early 90s for a series of concerts, touring as the Original 5th Dimension. Townson retired from the group in 1997 due to ill health and passed away four years later.

● ALBUMS: *Up Up And Away* (Soul City 1967) ★★★, *The Magic Garden* (Soul City 1967) ★★★, *Stoned Soul Picnic* (Soul City 1968) ★★★, *The Age Of Aquarius* (Soul City 1969) ★★★, *Portrait* (Bell 1970) ★★, *Love's Lines, Angles & Rhymes* (Bell 1971) ★★★, *Live!* (Bell 1971) ★★, *Individually & Collectively* (Bell 1972) ★★, *Living Together, Growing Together* (Bell 1973) ★★, *Soul & Inspiration* (Bell 1974) ★★, *Earthbound* (ABC 1975) ★★, *Star Dancing* (Motown 1978) ★★, *High On Sunshine* (Motown 1978) ★★, *In The House* (Click 1995) ★★.

● COMPILATIONS: *The Greatest Hits* (Soul City 1969) ★★★, *The July 5th Album* (Soul City 1969) ★★★, *Reflections* (Bell 1971) ★★★, *Greatest Hits On Earth* (Bell 1972) ★★★, *Anthology* (Rhino 1986) ★★★, *The Definitive Collection* (Arista 1997) ★★★, *The Very Best Of 5th Dimension* (Camden 1999) ★★★★, *The Ultimate 5th Dimension* (BMG 2004) ★★★★.

Fifth Estate

The Fifth Estate is recalled for a novelty hit, 'Ding Dong! The Witch Is Dead' (from **The Wizard Of Oz**), which reached number 11 in the US charts during the summer of 1967. The group had been formed three years earlier, and inspired by the 'British Invasion', they began a career that took them through a variety of short-lived record contracts until they secured their one-off success. The quintet—Wayne 'Wads' Wadham (vocals/keyboards), Rick Engler (vocals/guitar, kazoo, violin, clarinet, bass), D. Bill Shute (guitar/mandolin), Dick 'Duck' Ferrar (vocals, guitar, bass) and Furvus Evans (drums)—broke up when Shute was drafted. He later returned to music and has forged a successful career as a folk musician. His partner, Lisa Null, formed **Green Linnet Records** with **Patrick Sky**, and this outlet was responsible for several of Shute's subsequent recordings. Wayne Wadhams became a professor at Boston's prestigious **Berklee College Of Music** and founded the Boston Skyline label. The label releases mostly classical albums, but it did release a Fifth Estate compilation in 1993, *Ding Dong! The Witch Is Back!* , which includes tracks by their previous incarnation, the D-Men.

● ALBUMS: *Ding Dong The Witch Is Dead* (Jubilee 1967) ★★.

● COMPILATIONS: *Ding Dong! The Witch Is Back!* (Boston Skyline 1993) ★★★.

50 Cent

b. Curtis Jackson, 6 July 1975, Queens, New York City, USA. This New York–based gangsta rapper enjoyed fluctuating fortunes in his musical career and personal life prior to landing a lucrative recording contract with **Eminem**'s Shady Records label in 2002. Jackson grew up in the Queens district but managed to avoid the worst elements of the street, establishing a reputation as both a promising boxer and mix tape artist. He teamed up with the **Trackmasters** production team in 1999 to record the novelty underground hit 'How To Rob', which led to a recording contract with **Columbia Records**. The rapper completed an album with the Trackmasters and released a single with **Destiny's Child**, 'Thug Love', before a series of events conspired to derail his major label deal. Columbia began to get cold feet owing to *Power Of The Dollar* being extensively bootlegged prior to its official release, and then on 24 May 2000, 50 Cent received multiple gunshot wounds in a street shooting. As a result the rapper was released from his contract, and *Power Of The Dollar* was shelved.

50 Cent retreated to the security of his **G-Unit** clique and, teaming up with producer Money XL, bombarded the underground market with a series of mix tapes that enjoyed huge success on the street. Before too long, the major labels were showing renewed interest in the rapper, who elected to sign to Eminem and **Dr. Dre**'s Shady/Aftermath. The provocatively titled 'Wanksta' (allegedly a gangsta who gets caught in an endless cycle of committing crime and serving jail time), climbed up the charts at the end of 2002, as did his independent release *Guess Who's Back?* Unfortunately, 50 Cent's penchant for attracting trouble reared its ugly head in December, when he was arrested for gun possession. This did not stop both his Shady debut *Get Rich Or Die Tryin'* and the attendant singles 'In Da Club' and '21 Questions' from climbing to the top of the US charts and establishing 50 Cent as a powerful new voice in American music.

The rapper enjoyed further success when his G-Unit protégé the **Game** soared to the top of the US album charts at the start of 2005. Despite a well publicized dispute between the rappers, 50 Cent guested on the Game's Top 5 single 'How We Do' and followed up with two new solo singles, the raunchy chart-topper 'Candy Shop' (featuring **Olivia**) and the Top 5 hit 'Disco Inferno'. His new album, *The Massacre*, was released the same March and went straight to the top of the charts. Later in the month 50 Cent became the first artist since the **Beatles** to have four singles in the US Top 10 at the same time with the release of a second collaboration with the Game, 'Hate It Or Love It'. Later in the year he starred in the semi-autobiographical movie *Get Rich Or Die Tryin'*, directed by Jim Sheridan and costarring Joy Bryant and Terrence Howard. The soundtrack to the movie, not to be confused with the rapper's debut album, was released at the same time.

● ALBUMS: *Get Rich Or Die Tryin'* (Shady/Aftermath 2003) ★★★★, *The Massacre* (Shady/Aftermath 2005) ★★★, with various artists *Get Rich Or Die Tryin'* soundtrack (G-Unit/Interscope 2005) ★★★.
● COMPILATIONS: *Guess Who's Back?* (Full Clip 2002) ★★★.
● DVD/VIDEOS: *The New Breed* (Shady/Interscope 2003), *The Massacre* (Shady/Interscope 2005).
● FURTHER READING: *From Pieces To Weight: Once Upon A Time In Southside Queens*, Curtis Jackson with Kris Ex.
● FILMS: *Get Rich Or Die Tryin'* (2005).

Fifty Foot Hose

An experimental San Francisco-based group, Fifty Foot Hose comprised: Nancy Blossom (vocals), David Blossom (guitar/piano), Larry Evans (guitar/vocals), Terry Hansley (bass), Kim Kimsey (drums) and Cork Marcheschi (electronic effects). Their lone album offered an unusual mixture of styles, including a version of **Billie Holiday**'s 'God Bless The Child', that were treated by Marcheschi's synthesized accompaniment. The set also featured Nancy Blossom's haunting vocals and invited comparisons with another unit, **United States Of America**. However, Fifty Foot Hose provided a less scholarly perspective—Marcheschi had previously fronted the Ethix, a renowned local garage band—and thus appeared purposeful and exciting. Unfortunately the sextet failed to secure success and broke up in the early 70s. Evans later joined the **Hoodoo Rhythm Devils**, while David Blossom established Blossom Studios.

● ALBUMS: *Cauldron* (1969) ★★★, *I've Paid My Dues* (Decca 1970) ★★.

Fifty Million Frenchmen

That is an awful lot of people to see during 'A Musical Comedy Tour Of Paris'—the subtitle of **Cole Porter**'s first big hit show, which opened at New York's Lyric Theatre on 27 November 1929. Following the critical reaction to his *See America First* (one critic: 'See *See America First*—last!'), Porter switched his milieu to Europe, where he had spent several pleasurable years during the 20s, and found success with *Paris*, which ran for six months on Broadway from October 1928. This second theatrical excursion to the city he loved had a book by **Herbert Fields** that once again turned on the familiar theme—a rich man's desire to be loved for himself and not for his money. Peter Forbes (**William Gaxton**) is the tormented soul this time, and he bets a friend, Michael Cummins (Jack Thompson), that he will be engaged to an attractive tourist, Looloo Carroll (Genevieve Tobin), within a month—and without any recourse to his financial resources. Taking a job as a guide, he conducts Looloo on 'a musical comedy guide of city', which provides Norman Bel Geddes with a marvellous opportunity to display his impressive settings, which include the Longchamps Racetrack, the Eiffel Tower, and the Café de la Paix. Porter's score was a joy and contained one of his all-time standards, 'You Do Something To Me', as well as the humorous 'You've Got That Thing' ('You've got what Adam craved when he / With love for Eve was tortured / She only had an apple tree / But you, you've got an orchard'), 'Find Me A Primitive Man' ('I don't mean the kind that belongs to a club / But the kind that has a club that belongs to him'), 'The Tale Of An Oyster', 'I Worship You', 'I'm Unlucky At Gambling' and, of course, a couple of affectionate hymns to the city, 'You Don't Know Paree' and 'Paree, What Did You Do To Me?'. The show ran for 254 performances and launched Porter—who was already 38 years old when it opened—on a glittering career that lasted for another 25 years on Broadway. William Gaxton and **Helen Broderick** re-created their roles in the 1931 film version of *Fifty Million Frenchmen*, but the Hollywood interpretation was not classed as a musical.

53rd & 3rd

Founded in Edinburgh, Scotland, in 1986, this pivotal independent label was administered by **Pastels** guiding light Stephen Pastel, David Keegan of the **Shop Assistants** and Sandy McLean, director of record distribution company Fast Forward. Its name was derived from a song by the **Ramones**, Keegan's favourite group. 53rd & 3rd's first release was the Shop Assistants' 'Safety Net', but the label's catalogue also included non-Scottish acts the **Pooh Sticks**, **Beat Happening** and **Tallulah Gosh**. However, it is best recalled for recording groups from the emergent 'Bellshill scene'. The **BMX Bandits**' debut single, 'E102', was issued in May 1986 and this was succeeded by the Boy Hairdressers' 'Golden Shower' and 'You Made My Head Explode' by the Groovy Little Numbers. Members of both acts would later resurface in **Teenage Fanclub**, the **Pastels** and **Superstar**. The **Vaselines**, another group from the same Lanarkshire town, released two superb singles and an abrasive album, *Dum Dum*. Several of their songs, notably 'Molly's Lips' and 'Son Of A Gun', were later popularized by **Nirvana**, whose lead singer, Kurt Cobain, discovered them through his friendship with Calvin Johnston of Beat Happening. The Vaselines' Eugene Kelly later founded Captain America and **Eugenius**. Other releases on 53rd & 3rd included singles by the **Beat Poets** and Househunters, yet paradoxically, the Pastels did not feature on its roster. Stephen Pastel did compile a 1988 set, *Good Feeling*, made up of acts within and outside the label, but by that point 53rd & 3rd had lost momentum. The founding trio had other pressing commitments and decided to fold the company. The rights passed to another Edinburgh label, Avalanche who have issued a 'best of' selection and *All The Stuff And More*, a compendium of all the Vaselines' recordings.

● COMPILATIONS: *Fun While It Lasted: The Compilation* (Avalanche 1990) ★★★.

Fig Dish

Formed in Chicago, Illinois, USA, the core trio of contemporary pop rock band Fig Dish is Blake Smith (vocals/guitar), Rick Ness (vocals/guitar) and Mike Willison (bass). They formed at junior high school, growing up on a musical diet of stodgy 70s rock—the likes of **Styx** and **REO Speedwagon**—but also, crucially, **Cheap Trick**. The band made its debut for **Polydor Records** in 1995, but sales of *That's What Love Songs Often Do* proved disappointing. During the extensive touring that followed, the band nearly died when their van crashed in a Nebraskan blizzard. Their drummer, Andy Hamilton, promptly left to attend law school and was replaced on a temporary basis by Bill Swartz of Ultraswiss for their 1997 collection *When Shove Goes Back To Push*. This was produced by Phil Niccolo (half of production duo the Butcher Brothers). He was chosen not because of his well-publicized work on hip-hop records but because of the magic he had wrought on **Urge Overkill**'s *Saturation*. After its release, the band recruited a permanent drummer, Brian Nolan, who made his live debut on 12 July 1997 at Chicago's Double Door club, preceding a tour with fellow Chicago alternative rock acts **Veruca Salt** and **Local H**.

● ALBUMS: *That's What Love Songs Often Do* (Polydor 1995) ★★★, *When Shove Goes Back To Push* (Polydor 1997) ★★★★.

Figgis, Mike

b. 28 February 1948, Carlisle, Cumbria, England. From infancy until the age of eight Figgis was raised in Nairobi, Kenya. On his return to England, he studied classical guitar and also became adept on piano and trumpet. In the mid-60s he was a member of the R&B band Gas Board, whose lead singer was future **Roxy Music** frontman **Bryan Ferry**. Figgis was also involved with the People Show, an experimental theatre group. He then worked in the theatre in various capacities before making a mark as director of *The House* on television. This one-hour film for Channel 4, starring Stephen Rea and Nigel Hawthorne, was well received and brought him his first feature film assignment as director. This was *Stormy Monday* (1988) it and it led in turn to his first Hollywood project, directing *Internal Affairs* (1990). More than almost any other director, Figgis is deeply involved in other aspects of his films, including the role of producer, writer and composer, and he has also sometimes been his own cinematographer. In all five capacities, he made *Timecode* (2000) and *Hotel* (2001); as director, producer, writer and composer he made *One Night Stand* (1997) and *The Loss Of Sexual Innocence* (1999); as director, writer and

composer *Stormy Monday*, *Liebestraum* (1991) and *Leaving Las Vegas* (1995), also playing trumpet and keyboards on the soundtrack of the latter; as director and producer *Miss Julie* (1999) and *Cold Creek Manor* (2003); as director and composer *Internal Affairs*, on which he also played on the soundtrack; as director only *Mr. Jones* (1993), *The Browning Version* (1994), *Flamenco Women* (1997) and *The Battle Of Orgeave* (2001). Figgis appeared onscreen in bit parts in *Internal Affairs*, *Leaving Las Vegas* and *One Night Stand*. He received Oscar nominations as Best Director and for Best Adapted Screenplay for *Leaving Las Vegas*. He has also worked on television series including *The Sopranos* and *The Blues*. Figgis' deep interest in technological developments in filmmaking resulted in the DVD of *Timecode* being interactive, allowing choice of any of four individual soundtracks. Strikingly talented and deeply committed, Figgis brings to all his films an intensely personal vision.

● FILMS: *Internal Affairs* (1990), *Leaving Las Vegas* (1995), *One Night Stand* (1997).

Figgy Duff

This band from Newfoundland, Canada, comprised Pamela Morgan (vocals, guitar, whistle, keyboards), Dave Panting (vocals, mandolin, guitar), Geoff Butler (accordion, whistle), Derek Pelley (bass, vocal) and Noel Dinn (d. 26 July 1993; multi-instrumentalist). Mixing Celtic and Gaelic influences, the band essentially followed the folk rock path. Mixing traditional and contemporary tunes and songs, *Figgy Duff*, released in 1980 in the USA, was not released until 1982 in Europe. Although the follow-up, *After The Tempest*, received more attention and attracted good reviews, it still failed to give the band a higher profile. Sadly, Dinn died of throat cancer in 1993. Morgan compiled the excellent 1996 retrospective, which served as a fitting tribute to Dinn.

● ALBUMS: *Figgy Duff* (1980) ★★★★, *After The Tempest* (1984) ★★★.

● COMPILATIONS: *A Retrospective 1974–1993* (Amber 1996) ★★★★.

Fight

Inspired by the aggressive new metal sounds of the likes of **Pantera**, **Skid Row** and **Metallica**, the **Judas Priest** vocalist Rob Halford (b. 25 August 1951, Walsall, England) formed Fight as a solo project to explore material that he felt was inappropriate for Judas Priest, but it eventually led to a bitter and acrimonious split from his old band as they celebrated 20 years together. Taking drummer Scott Travis with him, Halford recruited guitarists Russ Parrish (ex–War And Peace) and Brian Tilse and bass player Jay Jay (both ex-Cyanide) for 1994's *War Of Words*. While Pantera comparisons were obvious, Fight proved themselves not to be the clone band some had feared, with the intense material given an individual character by Halford's distinctive vocal delivery, and the band delivered with powerful live shows. However, the demanding tour schedule proved too much for Parrish, who was replaced by Robbie Lockner for the **Anthrax** US tour and then permanently by Mark Chaussee as Fight performed with **Metallica** across the USA. The band then released the *Mutations* mini-album, a collection of live tracks and cover versions, including 'Freewheel Burning', before setting to work on their second album, *A Small Deadly Space*, whose lyrics ranged across subjects such as AIDS, the Holocaust, child abuse and domestic violence. This proved to be the band's last release with Halford going on to form the electronic rock outfit Two and then the more traditional **Halford**.

● ALBUMS: *War Of Words* (Epic 1993) ★★★, *Mutations* mini-album (Epic 1994) ★★★, *A Small Deadly Space* (Epic 1995) ★★★.

Fila Brazilia

This Hull, Yorkshire, England–based instrumental duo comprises Steve Cobby (guitar/keyboards) and Dave McSherry (bass). Cobby endured a short spell with the unsuccessful pop/funk outfit Ashley And Jackson, while McSherry was a veteran of punk band Puncture Tough Guy. The duo first met in 1982 at a Puncture Tough Guy gig but did not start working together on a regular basis until 1991. They retired to their home-town and helped set up **Pork Recordings** with Dave 'Porky' Brennan. The duo's 12-inch single 'Mermaids' became an underground club favourite and was followed by several instrumental albums characterized by a heady mixture of funk, acid jazz, trip-hop and **dub**. These albums, alongside Cobby's work with Heights Of Abraham and his solo project the Solid Doctor, helped establish Pork as one of the UK's leading underground labels. Cobby and McSherry are also sought after remixers, with clients including **Radiohead** ('Climbing Up The Walls'), **James** ('Tomorrow'), **Simple Minds** ('Theme For Great Cities'), **DJ Food** ('Freedom'), the **Orb** ('Toxygene'), **Black Uhuru** ('Boof N' Baff N' Biff'), **Busta Rhymes** ('Woo-Hah!! Got You All In Check'), **Lamb** ('Cotton Wool'), **U.N.K.L.E.** ('Berry Meditation') and **Moloko** ('Lotus Eaters'). Several of these remixes were collected on the excellent *Brazilification*. The remix compilation was preceded by *A Touch Of Cloth*, the duo's first release on their own Twentythree label, which they set-up with frequent collaborator Sim Lister.

● ALBUMS: *Old Codes New Chaos* (Pork 1994) ★★★★, *Maim That Tune* (Pork 1995) ★★★, *Mess* (Pork 1996) ★★★★, *Black Market Gardening* (Pork 1996) ★★★, *Luck Be A Weirdo Tonight* (Pork 1997) ★★★, *Power Clown* (Pork 1998) ★★★, *A Touch Of Cloth* (Twentythree 1999) ★★★, *Jump Leads* (Twentythree 2002) ★★★★, *Fub@V&A* (Twentythree 2003) ★★★, *Dicks* (Twentythree 2004) ★★★, *The Lime & Strimes Of Phoebus Brumal* (Twentythree 2004) ★★.

● COMPILATIONS: *Brazilification: Remixes 95–97* (Kudos 2000) ★★★★, *Anotherlatenight* (Azuli 2001) ★★★★, *Brazillification 2* (Twentythree 2003) ★★★★.

Fillmore

In 1971 US impresario **Bill Graham** opted to close his leading venues, the Fillmore East in New York and Fillmore West in San Francisco. The latter had been at the hub of the 60s' Bay Area scene, showcasing almost all the leading rock acts of the era. The final week's proceedings were filmed and *Fillmore* contains notable live performances from **Santana**, the **Grateful Dead**, **Quicksilver Messenger Service**, **Hot Tuna** and **Boz Scaggs**. The in-concert appearances are interspersed with interview material in which Graham reminisces about his past. Talkative and opinionated, he makes an interesting subject although his notorious quick temper is also apparent. One now-legendary scene shows guitarist/vocalist Mike Wilhelm asking Graham to find a slot for his group, Loose Gravel. Wilhelm, a former member of the pioneering **Charlatans**, San Francisco's first 'underground' act, argues that as

he was there at the beginning he should be there at the end. Graham refuses, citing the former band's unprofessionalism. 'Fuck you and thanks for the memories', Wilhelm states as he is about to leave, inciting Graham to have him bodily ejected from the premises, vowing to blacklist his group from all future bills. *Fillmore* is a nostalgic tribute to an important period in Graham's life. He continued to work as a leading concert promoter (c/f **Live Aid**), but this feature expresses the special nature of those early years and captures several acts in their prime. A triple-boxed set, with lavish booklet, was issued in 1972 to complement the film.

● ALBUMS: *Fillmore: The Last Days* (Warner 1972) ★★★★.

● FURTHER READING: *The Fillmore East*, Richard Kostelanetz. *The Art Of The Fillmore: 1966–1971*, Jacaeber Kastor (ed.). *Live At The Fillmore East*, Amalie R. Rothschild.

Filter

Brian Liesegang (programming, guitar, keyboards, drums) and Richard Patrick (vocals, guitar, bass, programming, drums, ex-**Nine Inch Nails**) first hatched the idea of working together during a cross-country trek when they visited the Grand Canyon. Patrick had already been experimenting on an eight-track console in his parents' basement in Cleveland, Ohio, USA. Liesegang, meanwhile, had just finished a degree in philosophy and turned his hand to music himself, experimenting in his own small electronic studio, which was adjacent to that owned by **Robert A. Moog** (originator of the Moog synthesizer). Occupying his time by investigating the world of computers and their applications to music, he found what he describes as a 'perfect musical match' in Patrick. Both were interested in producing hard electronic music. The line-up of the band was completed for touring purposes by Geno Lenardo (guitar), Matt Walker (drums) and Frank Cavanaugh (bass). *Short Bus* was coproduced by Ben Gross (**Jane's Addiction**, **Red Hot Chili Peppers**), while the single 'Hey Man Nice Shot' became a staple of college radio. Walker left the band to join the **Smashing Pumpkins** in August 1996. Liesegang also abandoned the band in September 1997 to pursue a solo career. The same year, Patrick contributed '(Can't You) Trip Like I Do', a collaboration with the **Crystal Method**, to the soundtrack of the movie *Spawn*. The second Filter album, *Title Of Record*, eventually appeared two years later, featuring a backing band comprising Cavanaugh, Lenardo and drummer Steve Gillis.

● ALBUMS: *Short Bus* (Reprise/Warners 1995) ★★★, *Title Of Record* (Reprise/Warners 1999) ★★★, *The Amalgamut* (Reprise/Warners 2002) ★★★.

Fina, Jack

b. 13 August 1913, Passaic, New Jersey, USA, d. 14 May 1970, Los Angeles, California, USA. Fina was a well-established big band sideman before he opted to become a band leader in his own right. He had spent 10 years with **Freddy Martin** in the 30s as piano player, notably contributing to Martin's famous recording of 'Bumble Boogie'. He had also played with **Clyde McCoy**. He formed his first band in California in 1946, a 16-piece aggregation which included Al King, Peppie Landeros, Jerry Kadovitz, Jimmy Morris, Bob Bates, Le Roy Crouch, John Kirchies, Lenny Leyson, Irving Geller, Tony Leonard, **Paul Desmond**, Ricky Marino, Tiny Magardo, Bob Morrison, Eddie Gangale and Joe Maita. The vocalists were Harry Prime and Gil Lewis. They made their debut at the Claremont Hotel in Berkeley in 1946, where they would return for the next seven years. Strongly supported on radio and with recordings issued by **MGM Records**, Jack Fina And His Orchestra soon became a national as well as regional attraction. Ballrooms, halls and hotels such as Elitch's Gardens (Denver), the Chase Hotel (St. Louis), the Aragon Ballroom (Chicago), the Balinese Room (Galveston, Texas) and the Waldorf-Astoria (New York) all booked the band. A contract with Columbia also saw the group appear in a series of movies. Much later Fina would also appear on a syndicated television show alongside Dick Sinclair. By the 50s Fina had decided to cut back on the size of his band and base them more permanently in San Francisco. Reduced to local engagements, Fina found time to establish his own Concerto Music & Entertainment talent agency. In 1960 he took the reduced group to Los Angeles, remaining the principle attraction at the Beverly Hills Hotel for an eight-year spell. Followed a two-year break he returned to the same establishment in 1970, but during his first run there suffered a heart attack and died.

Final Four

R&B vocal quartet the Final Four are unusual for their genre in that the contents of their independently released debut album were largely self-written and produced. Comprising Jimmy, Gee, E.J. and Rich, the group formed in Indianapolis as a result of each member meeting on the local church and club-singing scene. As Jimmy told **Billboard** magazine in 1996: 'Each of the groups we were in at the time was pretty good, but there were members in each of them that weren't as committed as they should have been. So the four of us joined forces, which made for a unit that wanted to do this more than just for a hobby.' The group began by playing local gigs and winning a series of talent contests. After signing to Our Turn Records in 1996, the group abandoned plans to release 'Swangin'', a collaboration with rapper **Tim Dog**, as their first single. They were concerned that this might give a wrong impression of the group, who were keen to be seen to represent the 'wholesome' side of R&B.
● ALBUMS: *Final Four* (Our Turn 1996) ★★★.

Final Solution

The Final Solution was formed in 1965 in San Francisco, California, USA. Ernie Fosselius (lead guitar), John Yager (rhythm guitar), Bob Knickerbocker (bass/vocals) and John Chance (drums) became one of the many groups based in the city struggling to find success. Their fiery brand of folk-inspired rock proved highly engaging, but the group failed to secure a recording contract. Mainstream Records showed initial interest but opted to sign **Big Brother And The Holding Company** instead. Jerry Slick, late of the **Great Society**, replaced John Chance in November 1966, and for a brief time, the group featured Jane Dornacker as vocalist. On these occasions they were billed as Earth Mother And The Final Solution. They split up in 1967 when Slick opted to resume his career in cinematography. Fosselius also pursued film-making interests and during the 70s contributed animations to *Sesame Street*. Knickerbocker completed the acclaimed television documentary *Where The Buffalo Roam*.

Finch (70s)

Comprising Owen Orford (vocals), Bob Spencer (guitar), Tony Strain (bass) and Peter McFarlane (drums), Finch formed in Australia in 1973 and devoted themselves to a conventional but well-observed style of feisty hard rock. Orford had previously been a member of Stillwater, while other members of Finch also included Mark Evans (bass, ex-**AC/DC**), Chris Jones (guitar), Graham Kennedy (guitar) and Sam Mallet (guitar). They made their debut in 1975 with the single 'And She Sings' for Picture Records, which was followed a year later with a studio collection for Eagle Records that pleased Australian rock critics. However, the group broke up when McFarlane and Orford joined Mark Evans in Contraband. Spencer moved on to Silverhooks. (NB: Not to be confused with the later US hardcore band of the same name.)
● ALBUMS: *Thunderbird aka Finch* (Eagle 1976) ★★★.

Finch (00s)

This Temecula, California, USA–based post-hardcore band has its roots in Numb, a late 90s outfit featuring four-fifths of Finch. Nate Barcalow (vocals), Alex Linares (guitar), Derek Doherty (bass) and Alex Pappas (drums) enjoyed little success with their sub-**Deftones** sound and were struggling for direction before being joined by second guitarist Randy Strohmeyer. A name change coupled with Strohmeyer's persistent harrying of record companies led to a contract for Finch with the Drive-Thru label. The quintet released their debut EP in October 2001. *Falling Into Place* was an excellent collection that helped define Finch's trademark sound. Their heartfelt fusion of hardcore and pop punk was honed close to perfection on the band's exceptional long-playing debut, *What Is It To Burn*. Recorded with producer Mark Trombino and featuring guest vocals from **Glassjaw**'s Daryl Palumbo on two tracks, the album helped place Finch at the forefront of the highly popular emo scene. (NB: Not to be confused with the 70s Australian hard rock band of the same name.)
● ALBUMS: *What Is It To Burn* (Drive-Thru 2002) ★★★★, *Say Hello To Sunshine* (Drive-Thru/Geffen 2005) ★★★.

Finckel, Eddie

b. Edwin Finckel, 23 December 1917, Washington, DC, USA, d. 7 May 2001, Madison, New Jersey, USA. After studying formally with classicist Otto Leuning, Finckel turned to jazz. In the early and mid-40s he worked as staff arranger for the bands of **Boyd Raeburn** and **Gene Krupa**. With Raeburn he helped create the distinctive qualities of this fine, progressive orchestra. Disagreements broke up the association with Raeburn, Finckel claiming sole authorship of several of the band's important numbers including 'Two Spoos In An Igloo', 'Boyd Meets Stravinsky' and 'March Of The Boyds', the last two having been credited to Raeburn and **George Handy**. Finckel, along with **Tadd Dameron**, also wrote modern, boppish arrangements for the first **Buddy Rich** band. In writing charts for Krupa he was faced with the unenviable task of making true the claim that the drummer's 1944 band really was 'the Band that Swings with Strings'. From this period Finckel created hits for Krupa with 'Leave Us Leap', 'Gypsy Mood', 'Starburst' and the breakneck tempoed 'Lover'. He wrote original music for the Ann Arbor Drama Festival and was founder and director of the Young Artists Chamber Orchestra of New Jersey. Finckel also wrote for the Broadway stage. In the classical field he composed a cello concerto, a clarinet concerto and a suite for cello and string orchestra. He also composed music for the ballet *Of Human Kindness*.

Findask

This early 80s Scottish duo featured Willie Lindsay (b. 24 January 1952, Glasgow, Scotland; vocals, guitar, flute, whistles, harmonica) and Stuart Campbell (b. 16 March 1951, Glasgow, Scotland; cittern, bouzouki, guitar, mandolin, vocals). The two met at the University of Strathclyde and started playing occasionally, leading to them playing support at festivals and concerts to groups such as **Fairport Convention**—who played the university and college circuit at the time. Interest shown in *Near Enough, Far Enough*, led them to release *Between The White Lines* on Temple Records. This album also included all original material performed in a traditional framework. Still performing, they released *Waiting For A Miracle*, but Campbell fell seriously ill, suffering from pernicious anaemia, and for a long time was unable to work. As a result, Findask now perform only occasionally.
● ALBUMS: *Near Enough, Far Enough* (Open Doors 1983) ★★★, *Between The White Lines* (Temple 1984) ★★★★, *Waiting For A Miracle* (1987) ★★, *No More Lies* (Open Doors 1993) ★★.

Finders Keepers

British character actors Robert Morley and Peggy Mount costarred alongside **Cliff Richard** and the **Shadows** in this poorly executed 1966 film. Based on a real event, the plot involves an atomic bomb lost off the Spanish coast. The device is washed up onshore, where it is discovered by Richard and his group. *Finders Keepers* lacks the charm of the singer's previous films, notably **Summer Holiday**. The *joie de vivre* is noticeably false, and the entire project seems to mirror the artistic fall of his early mentor, **Elvis Presley**. The soundtrack proved equally weak, although it did reach number 6 in the UK album chart, Richard's highest such placing since his previous film excursion, **Wonderful Life**. The material seemed contrived, 'Fiesta', 'Paella' and 'Oh Senorita' the obvious worst offenders, but it did yield a Top 10 single in 'Time Goes By'.

Fine And Dandy

A rather bizarre title for a show, considering that it opened in New York at the height of the Depression, on 23 September 1930. The production was a vehicle for the much-loved ex-vaudevillian Joe Cook, an extremely versatile and zany comedian whose routines included a range of highly amusing, inventive stories (particularly the one about the 'Four Hawaiians') and a consistently entertaining display of circus-style skills such as acrobatics, juggling and balancing—not to mention a degree of proficiency on the ukulele and saxophone. In Donald Ogden Stewart's plot for *Fine And Dandy*, Cook played the role of Joe Squibb, who, like the funnyman himself, was adept at keeping several balls in the air at once (metaphorically speaking). These consisted of his female boss, Mrs. Fordyce (Dora Maughan), his girlfriend, Nancy Ellis (Alice Boulden)—and his wife and children! The show's music and lyrics were by Kay Swift and Paul James (a pseudonym for Swift's husband, a banker named James P. Warburg). Kay Swift (b. 19 April 1897, New York, USA, d. 28 January 1993, Southington, Connecticut, USA) was one of the few female composers of popular songs to have a degree of success on Broadway. With her husband

she had contributed 'Can't We Be Friends?' to **The Little Show** in 1929 and was a close personal and professional associate of **George Gershwin**. For *Fine And Dandy* she and Warburg wrote the jaunty title song, which was sung by Cook and Boulden, along with 'Let's Go Eat Worms In The Garden' (Boulden and Joe Wagstaff) and 'Jig Hope', a number that was performed by **Eleanor Powell**, who subsequently tap-danced her way through several entertaining Hollywood musicals, notably *Broadway Melody Of 1940* with **Fred Astaire**. The show's big romantic ballad, 'Can This Be Love?' (Boulden), became successful through a recording by the pianistic duo Victor Arden and Ohman's Orchestra. They also made the bestsellers with 'Fine And Dandy', as did another rather more famous band led by **Tommy** and **Jimmy Dorsey**. On the strength of initial revues, such as 'pretty nearly everything you've yearned for in the way of 1930 entertainment', and Cook's renowned inspired clowning, *Fine And Dandy* ran at Erlanger's Theatre (later known as the St. James) for 255 performances. That production is not connected with the 1942 London revue of the same name, which starred **Leslie Henson**, **Stanley Holloway**, Dorothy Dickson and Douglas Byng.

Fine Young Cannibals

This sophisticated English pop trio from the Midlands appeared after the demise of the **Beat** in 1983. Former members Andy Cox (b. 25 January 1960, Birmingham, England; guitar) and David Steele (b. 8 September 1960, Isle of Wight, England; bass/keyboards) invited Roland Gift (b. 28 April 1961, Birmingham, England; vocals, ex–Acrylic Victims and actor for the Hull Community Theatre) to relinquish his tenure in a London blues combo to join them. Taking their name from the Robert Wagner movie of similar name (relinquishing the 'All The' prefix), the trio was quickly picked up by **London Records** after a video screening on the UK music television show **The Tube**. 'Johnny Come Home' was soon released on single, with the band joined on percussion by Martin Parry and on trumpet by Graeme Hamilton. Dominated by Gift's sparse and yearning vocal, it reached the UK Top 10 in June 1985 and defined the band's sound for years to come. The follow-up 'Blue' set out an early political agenda for the band, attacking Conservative government policy and its effects.

After the band's debut album rose to UK number 11, the first of a series of distinctive cover versions emerged with the UK Top 10 single 'Suspicious Minds'. Backing vocals were handled by **Jimmy Somerville**. It was followed by a surprise, and radical, rendition of 'Ever Fallen In Love', which the **Buzzcocks'** Steve Diggle claimed he preferred to his band's original. Meanwhile Gift's parallel acting career got underway with the parochial *Sammy And Rosie Get Laid*, after all three members of the band had appeared in the previous year's *Tin Men*. While Gift's commitments continued Cox and Steele became involved in the release of an opportunistic **house** cut, 'I'm Tired Of Being Pushed Around', under the title Two Men, A Drum Machine And A Trumpet. On the back of regular club airings it became a surprise Top 20 hit in February 1988. More importantly, it attracted the interest of several **dance music** acts who would seek out the duo for remixes, including **Wee Papa Girl Rappers** and **Pop Will Eat Itself**.

Before the unveiling of Gift's latest film, *Scandal*, the band scored their biggest hit to date with 'She Drives Me Crazy', a

US number 1 single. The second album duly followed, featuring cultivated soul ballads to complement further material of a politically direct nature. It would top the charts on both sides of the Atlantic. Of the five singles taken from the album 'Good Thing' was the most successful, claiming a second US number 1. In 1990 they won both Best British Group and Best Album categories at the BRIT Awards but felt compelled to return them because: 'it is wrong and inappropriate for us to be associated with what amounts to a photo opportunity for Margaret Thatcher and the Conservative Party'. It led to a predictable backlash in the right-wing tabloid press.

In 1990 Gift appeared in Hull Truck's *Romeo And Juliet* stage performance and left Cox and Steele to work on a remixed version of *The Raw And The Cooked*. Still with the ability to bounce back after long pauses, the band's 1996 compilation included new track 'The Flame'. Gift began performing solo in the late 90s and issued a solo album in 2002.

● ALBUMS: *Fine Young Cannibals* (London 1985) ★★★, *The Raw And The Cooked* (London 1989) ★★★★, *The Raw And The Remix* (London 1990) ★★★.
● COMPILATIONS: *The Finest* (London 1996) ★★★★.
● DVD/VIDEOS: *The Finest* (London 1996).
● FURTHER READING: *The Sweet And The Sour: The Fine Young Cannibals' Story*, Brian Edge.

Finegan, Bill

b. 3 April 1917, Newark, New Jersey, USA. Pianist Finegan's first successes were the arrangements he wrote for the **Tommy Dorsey** band, but his real breakthrough came in 1938 when he became a staff arranger for **Glenn Miller**. Throughout the late 30s and early 40s, Finegan wrote extensively for films but continued to provide charts for Miller, Dorsey, **Horace Heidt** and others. At the start of the 50s Finegan was studying at the Paris Conservatoire and began corresponding with fellow-arranger **Eddie Sauter**, who was then hospitalized with tuberculosis. Out of this correspondence emerged a decision to form an orchestra of their own that would play music other leaders might well regard as uncommercial. In 1952 the 21-piece Sauter-Finegan Orchestra made its appearance. With so many musicians, several of whom doubled and even trebled on other instruments, the tonal palette was huge and the two arrangers took full advantage of this. The band was hugely successful with memorable records such as 'The Doodletown Fifers' and 'Sleigh Ride' (based upon music by Sergey Prokofiev). On this latter title, the sound effect of horses' hooves on hard-packed snow was created by Finegan beating his chest. Later, he wryly remarked, 'This is probably my finest effort on wax—or snow'. In the late 50s Finegan worked mostly in radio and television but in the 70s returned to big band arranging with charts for the Glenn Miller reunion orchestra and for **Mel Lewis**, who continued to use his work into the 80s.

● ALBUMS: all by Sauter-Finegan Orchestra *New Directions In Music* 10-inch album (RCA-Victor 1953) ★★★★, *Inside Sauter-Finegan* (RCA-Victor 1954) ★★★, *The Sound Of Sauter-Finegen* (RCA-Victor 1954) ★★★, *Sons Of Sauter-Finegan* (RCA-Victor 1955) ★★★, *Concert Jazz* (RCA-Victor 1955) ★★★, *New Directions In Music* (RCA 1956) ★★★, *Adventure In Time* (RCA-Victor 1956) ★★★, *Under Analysis* (RCA-Victor 1957) ★★★★, *One Night Stand With The Sauter-Finegan Orchestra* (RCA-Victor 1957) ★★★, *Straight Down The Middle* (RCA-Victor 1957)

★★★, *Inside Sauter-Finegan Revisited* (RCA-Victor 1961) ★★★, *Sleigh Ride* (RCA-Victor 1961) ★★★★, *The Return Of The Doodletown Fifers* (Capitol 1985) ★★★.
● COMPILATIONS: *The Best Of Sauter-Finegan Orchestra* (Collectors 1999) ★★★★.

Fingathing

Originating from Manchester, England, and signed to the city's famed Grand Central Records label, Peter Parker (b. Dan Baxter) and Sneaky (b. Simon Houghton) have released two albums of downbeat hip-hop under their moniker Fingathing. Parker and Sneaky first began playing together in the backing band of Grand Central pioneers **Rae And Christian**. They inaugurated their own recording career in 2000 with the funky 'Atomic Drop' appearing on Grand Central compilation, *Central Heating 2*. Their passion for instrumental hip-hop informed the same year's debut, *The Main Event*. The concept was simple but effective, with Parker doing the scratching (and as a former **DMC** champion the quality is excellent) and the classically trained Sneaky playing the double bass.

Although fresh is a word that can be over used in the hip-hop community, Fingathing's follow-up, *Superhero Music*, certainly added a new spin to the instrumental hip-hop genre. From the comedy breaks of 'Drunken Master II' to the superb mood-driven 'Haze', the album expanded upon the blueprint of their debut to great effect. The duo perform live with recruits including Danny Ward aka Dubble D (drums/percussion), Steve Brown (keyboards) and DJ Treva Whateva, with spectacular live visuals supplied by resident artist Chris Drury. Fingathing supported one of their notable influences, **DJ Shadow** in 2002.

● ALBUMS: *The Main Event* (Grand Central 2000) ★★★, *Superhero Music* (Grand Central 2002) ★★★★, *Fingathing And The Big Red Nebula Band* (Grand Central 2004) ★★★.

Finger Eleven

Canadian alt metal band formed in 1994 in Burlington, Ontario, by school friends Scott Anderson (vocals), James Black (guitar), Rick Jackett (guitar), Sean Anderson (bass) and Rob Gommerman (drums). Initially going by the unprepossessing moniker of the Rainbow Butt Monkeys, the quintet recorded the independently released *Letters From Chutney* in 1995. They toyed with a number of new band names before settling on Finger Eleven and signing a major label contract with **Mercury Records** in Canada. Their 1997 debut as Finger Eleven, *Tip*, broke the quintet on a national level in their native Canada and was issued the following year in the USA by Wind-up Records. Rich Beddoe replaced drummer Gommerman in the line-up shortly afterwards. The band's debut proper for Wind-up, *The Greyest Of Blue Skies*, followed in 2000. The album was well-received by their loyal fanbase. They continued to earn good notices with their busy touring schedule but found the time to return to the recording studio to complete work on a new album. Released in July 2003, *Finger Eleven* marked a notable step up for the band by avoiding the shallow nu metal posturing of their earlier work in favour of well-constructed and melodic alt rock. The album included two acoustic songs alongside stand-out tracks 'Complicated Questions' and 'Stay In Shadow'.

● ALBUMS: *Tip* (Mercury/Wind-up 1997) ★★★, *The Greyest Of Blue Skies* (Wind-up 2000) ★★★, *Finger Eleven* (Wind-up 2003) ★★★★.

Fingerprintz

This quirky Scottish new wave group was led by Jimmy O'Neil. It also included drummer Dogdan Wiczling and acted as **Lene Lovich**'s backing band for a time (O'Neil wrote her hit single 'Say When'). Their own releases included the 1981 single 'Shadowed', and their second album was produced by Nick Garvey of the **Motors**. *Beat Noir* experimented with rock/funk fusion but failed to break the group commercially. O'Neil and Wiczling went on to play on Jaquie Brooke's solo album *Sob Stories*. Wiczling also toured and recorded with **Adam Ant**.
● ALBUMS: *The Very Dab* (Virgin 1979) ★★, *Distinguishing Marks* (Virgin 1980) ★★★, *Beat Noir* (Stiff 1981) ★★★.
Solo: Jacqui Brookes *Sob Stories* (MCA 1984) ★★★.

Fingers Inc.

(see **Heard, Larry**)

Fings Ain't Wot They Used T'Be

This show originally opened on 17 February 1959 at the Theatre Royal, Stratford East, London, home of the *avant garde* director Joan Littlewood and her 'repertory company'. During two separate runs there it was completely revised and remodelled and transferred to the Garrick Theatre in the West End on 11 February 1960. Set in the drab and dreary world of London's Soho district, with its prostitutes, pimps and small-time criminals, Frank Norman's book (Norman was an ex-convict) told of Fred Cochran (Glynn Edwards), one of life's losers, who runs a sleazy gambling club—a haven for the local low-life. He can only dream of owning a big-time venue, but a large win on the horses means that he can at least have his place decorated by the camp decorator Horace Seaton (Wallas Eaton). Unfortunately, the reopening night party is ruined when Fred is beaten up for not providing the police with their usual slice of payola. There is a good deal more trouble and strife before Fred ends up with a knees-up *al fresco* wedding to his girlfriend Lily Smith (Miriam Karlin). The local milieu is populated by a variety of characters such as the crooked copper Sergeant Collins (Tom Chatto) plus two more members of the constabulary, played by Yootha Joyce and George Sewell, a civilian crook, Redhot (Edward Carrick), Tosher (James Booth), the area's premier ponce and several 'ladies of the night', including Rosie (Barbara Windsor) and Betty (Toni Palmer). **Lionel Bart**, who had provided just the lyrics for **Lock Up Your Daughters** at the Mermaid Theatre in 1959, wrote both words and music for this exhilarating piece. His songs, which so accurately captured the show's spirit and atmosphere, included 'G'Night Dearie', 'Layin' Abaht', 'Where It's Hot', 'Contempery', 'Meatface', 'The Ceilin's Comin' Dahn', 'Where Do Little Birds Go?', 'The Student Ponce', 'Big Time', 'Polka Dots', 'Cop A Bit Of Pride' and 'Cochran Will Return'. The popular comedian-singer **Max Bygraves** took a cleaned-up version of the title song into the UK Top 5, and the personality pianist **Russ Conway** also had a minor hit with the tune. The critics were not enthusiastic about the show, but audiences loved it, and *Fings Ain't Wot They Used T'Be* enjoyed a two-year run of 897 performances. This established Lionel Bart as a real force in the London musical theatre and won the Evening Standard Award for best musical. Early in 1999 Bart was involved with the first major revival of 'Fings' at the Queen's Theatre, Hornchurch, England. Bob Carlton (**Return To The Forbidden Planet**) directed a cast that included Steve Edwin (Cochran), Anthony Psaila (Seaton), Diana Croft (Lily), Tony Hunt (Collins), Phil Hearne (Redhot), Richard Brightiff (Tosher), Nina Lucking (Rosie) and Liz Marsh (Betty).

Finian's Rainbow (film musical)

Some Broadway musicals defy even the most determined attempts to transform them into successful movies, and *Finian's Rainbow* falls very much in that category. Twenty-one years after the show made its debut at the 46th Street in New York E.Y. **'Yip Harburg'** and **Fred Saidy** finally adapted their whimsical stage libretto for this film, which was released by Warner Brothers in 1968. Their moralistic story told of simple Irishman Finian McLonergan (**Fred Astaire**), who travels to Rainbow Valley, Missitucky, USA, with his daughter Sonia (**Petula Clark**) and a crock of gold that he has stolen from a leprechaun (**Tommy Steele**). Finian believes that if he buries the gold in the ground it will increase in value just as it does at Fort Knox. It does not quite work out that way, and the crock causes a heap of trouble—especially to a bigoted southern senator (Keenan Wynn), who turns black after tinkering with its 'three wish factor'—before Sonia falls for the leprechaun—who gets his gold back—and Finian takes off by himself to pastures new. The principle of people over profit has by then been clearly established. Most of the engaging and melodic songs from the show, by **Burton Lane** and Harburg, were retained for the screen version. They included 'How Are Things In Glocca Morra?', 'If This Isn't Love', 'Look To The Rainbow', 'Something Sort Of Grandish', 'That Great Come-And-Get-It Day', 'Old Devil Moon', 'When The Idle Poor Become The Idle Rich', 'When I'm Not Near The Girl I Love', 'Rain Dance' and 'The Begat'. The film, which was Fred Astaire's last musical, was directed by Francis Ford Coppola with choreography by **Hermes Pan** and was photographed in Technicolor and Panavision.

Finian's Rainbow (stage musical)

Conceived by E.Y. **'Yip' Harburg**, this stage musical opened on Broadway on 10 January 1947. With book by Harburg and **Fred Saidy**, music by **Burton Lane** and lyrics by Harburg, the show was a fantasy with a strong satirical core. Central to the story was Harburg's desire to express his views on racial bigotry and political persecution. At the time he was blacklisted in Hollywood and had returned to Broadway out of necessity. Set in the Deep South, in Rainbow Valley in the mythical state of Missitucky, the story tells of Og, a leprechaun, who arrives there in search of Finian, who has stolen a pot of gold from Glocca Morra in Ireland. The leprechaun grants three wishes, one of which turns Billboard Rawkins, a land-grabbing racist white senator, into a black evangelist, humanizing him in the process, another gives the power of speech to Susan, a mute, while the third helps the local sharecroppers recover their land from Rawkins. Songs from the show included 'How Are Things In Glocca Morra?', 'When I'm Not Near The Girl I Love', 'If This Isn't Love', 'The Great Come-And-Get-It Day' and 'Look To The Rainbow'. *Finian's Rainbow* starred **David Wayne** as Og, Albert Sharp as Finian, Anita Alvarez as Susan, Ella Logan as

Sharon, Finian's sister, and Donald Richards as Woody, Sharon's boyfriend. With good songs and performances allied to **Michael Kidd**'s exhilarating choreography, the show was a critical and popular success running for 725 performances. The 1968 screen version starred **Fred Astaire**, **Petula Clark** and **Tommy Steele**.

Finitribe

Scottish **dance music** unit who shared the same **One Little Indian Records** label as their fellow countrymen the **Shamen** but failed to replicate their success. It was not through want of effort or, for that matter, talent. The band took their name from 'Finny Tribe', a name given to the entire fish species by Irish religious sect the Rosicrucians as well as by the common people of that country. Chris Connelly, Philip Pinsky (b. Philip David Pinsky, 23 March 1965, Appleton, Wisconsin, USA), David Miller (b. David Francis Ashbride Miller, 20 July 1962, Moffat, Dunfreshire, Scotland), Mr Samples (b. John William Vick, 6 November 1965, Edinburgh, Scotland), Simon McGlynn and Thomas McGregor were the members of the original six-piece formed in Edinburgh in 1984. Finitribe founded their own label, striking out with a debut EP, *Curling And Stretching*, in October. One month later they played their first gig together supporting **Danielle Dax** at London ULU. By 1986 they had acquired their first sampler and released 'DeTestimony', an influential recording in both the **acid house** and, later, **house** movements. The following year they began an ill-fated liaison with Chicago's **Wax Trax! Records**, releasing a version of **Can**'s 'I Want More'. Following problems with the label, vocalist Chris Connelly eventually elected to remain, ostensibly as part of **Ministry** and **Revolting Cocks**, but also recording solo.

Finitribe re-emerged in 1989 with the curtailed line-up of Mr Samples, Philip Pinsky and David Miller. Vick and Pinsky had previously been colleagues in Rigor Mortis, and Miller had served in Explode Your Heart. Their influences remained both traditional rock and indie giants (Dog Faced Hermans, **Magazine**) and a myriad of new and old dance innovators (**Jah Wobble**, **Tackhead**, **Sparks**, **Sub Sub**, **Orbital**). A succession of well-regarded releases on One Little Indian failed to deliver them much in the way of commercial reward. The first and most notable of these was the acidic 'Animal Farm', which sampled the 'Old McDonald' nursery rhyme and laid torrents of abuse at the door of the McDonald's hamburger chain. The ensuing fuss, hardly deflated by a 'Fuck Off McDonald's' poster campaign, brought the band significant media exposure for the first time.

Entering the 90s, Finitribe looked as though they might expand beyond cult tastes with a new, kitsch image (white boiler suits peppered with stars) and more pop-dance-orientated material. As critics pointed out, they resembled an underground version of **Pet Shop Boys**. By 1992 they had resurrected the Finiflex label and opened their own studio complex in Leith. Reduced to a nucleus of Miller and new vocalist Katy Morrison, Finitribe released a new studio album (*Sleazy Listening*) in 1998.

● ALBUMS: *Noise Lust And Fun* (Finiflex 1988) ★★★, *Grossing 10K* (One Little Indian 1990) ★★★, *An Unexpected Groovy Treat* (One Little Indian 1992) ★★★, *Sheigra* (London 1995) ★★, *Sleazy Listening* (Infectious 1998) ★★★.

Fink

b. Fin Greenall, Bristol, Avon, England. While growing up in Bristol, Greenall became a bedroom **rave** producer making tinny tunes under the influence of **Orbital** and the **Orb**. In his own words he made 'a horrible' ambient techno record as E.V.A. that was released on respected rave label **Kickin' Records**. This did impress the decision makers at **Ninja Tune Records**, and they promptly signed him to their experimental imprint Ntone. 2000 saw the release of Fink's debut, the abstract hip-ho-inspired *Fresh Produce*. The album had a somnolent, dubby quality harking back to the exploratory days of trip-hop in the early 90s, alongside several tracks experimenting with downbeat jazzy arrangements. This was to be Greenall's final solo dalliance with electronic music, although he remained in demand as a DJ and producer for artists including **Martin Taylor**, **Nitin Sawhney** and **Amy Winehouse**. After relocating to Brighton he locked himself away to perfect his guitar playing and songwriting. His tastes had changed, and he was listening to artists including **John Lee Hooker**, **John Martyn** and **Joni Mitchell**, all of whom were to inspire his second album immeasurably. He wrote the track 'Pretty Little Thing' and took it into the Ninja Tune office saying it was someone else on vocals. They liked the track so much they commissioned Fink to complete an album, the first time in their history the label had backed a guitar-playing singer-songwriter. The resulting *Biscuits For Breakfast* featured a heady mixture of smoky blues, folk and soul.

● ALBUMS: *Fresh Produce* (Ntone 2000) ★★★, *Biscuits For Breakfast* (Ninja Tune 2006) ★★★★.

Fink, Cathy

b. Cathy Ann Fink, 9 August 1953, Baltimore, Maryland, USA. Fink learned to play guitar, fiddle, banjo and accordion and the art of yodelling and first played on CBC Canada radio in 1974. Her main interest was folk music, until she became a student at McGill University, Montreal, where she became devoted to bluegrass and old-time. She formed an old-time duo with **Duck Donald**, and from 1974–79 they toured Canada and recorded. She later claimed, 'We learned every old time duet that had ever came out and had a repertoire of five or six hundred old time duets'.

Fink recorded her first solo album on the Likeable, label in 1975. They eventually parted, and she moved, as a solo artist, to Washington, DC. She played major festivals of bluegrass and old-time and at times devoted her recording and performing to the entertaining of children in hospital. During the early 80s, she was a Smithsonian Institution demonstrator and old-time revivalist at clubs and festivals. She also presented shows at the institution that featured several old-time female singers such as **Cousin Emmy**, **Alice Gerrard** and **Patsy Montana**. In 1981 she became the first woman to win the West Virginia Old Time Banjo Contest and was also the first old-time musician to research and present entire concerts of the music of country's female pioneers.

Fink writes most of her songs from the woman's view, once stating, 'It was very clear to me that in the bluegrass idiom there was very little material that women could sing with a sense of integrity'. Her feminist-bluegrass theme song is 'Little Darlin''s Not My Name'. She also became involved with record production, notably with Patsy Montana's *The Cowboy Sweetheart*, on **Flying Fish Records** and with others, including Magpie, **Si Kahn** and the Rude Girls. In 1986 she began working with Marcy Marxer (b. Detroit, Michigan,

USA; guitar, mandolin, vocals), who had been a member of the all-female group Bosom Buddies for eight years. In 1989 they recorded an album, which included her self-penned 'Names', a song that is claimed to be the first country song to address the topic of AIDS.

A major contribution in Fink's career has been her children's music. She has been described as the most important source of children's records in country music history. Her *I'm Gonna Tell*, *Grandma Slid Down The Mountain* and *When The Rains Come Down* are rated as classics and have sold in large numbers. She is quoted as saying: 'Children's records have more longevity in the market place. You know, there are new five-year-olds every day'. She has also worked on *The Runaway Bunny/Goodnight Moon* tapes of children's books for publishers, Harper & Row. In the early 90s she and Marxer started making instructional videos such as *Kids Guitar 1 & 2*, *How To Sing Harmony*, *Making And Playing Home Made Instruments* and *Learn To Yodel*. Fink has also produced radio network series, including *Women In Traditional Country Music* and *Songs Of Working Women*.

● ALBUMS: with Duck Donald *Kissing Is A Crime* (Likeable 1975) ★★★, with Donald *Cathy Fink & Duck Donald* (Flying Fish 1978) ★★★, *The Leading Role* (Rounder 1985) ★★★, *Blue Rose* (Sugar Hill 1988) ★★★, with Marcy Marxer *Cathy Fink & Marcy Marxer* (Sugar Hill 1989) ★★★, *Doggone My Time* (Sugar Hill 1991) ★★★★, with Marcy Marxer *Banjo Haiku* (Sugar Hill 1992) ★★★, with Marxer *A Parents' Home Companion* (Rounder 1995) ★★★, with Marxer *Blanket Full Of Dreams* (Rounder 1996) ★★★★, with Marxer *Voice On The Wind* (Rounder 1997) ★★★, with Marxer *Changing Channels* (Rounder 1998) ★★★★, with Marxer *Pillow Full Of Wishes* (Rounder 2000) ★★★, with Marxer *All Wound Up! A* with Marxer *Family Music Party* (Rounder 2001) ★★★, with Marxer *Pocket Full Of Stardust* (Rounder 2002) ★★★.

Finlin, Jeff

b. Cleveland, Ohio, USA. This US singer-songwriter initially made his name as a drummer, an instrument that he first took up in high school. Finlin hung around Boston's post punk scene in the early 80s, before making the decision to relocate to Nashville, Tennessee, with his long-time friend and collaborator Gwil Owen. The duo formed the Thieves, whose sole album, 1989's *Seduced By Money*, was produced by **Marshall Crenshaw**. Following the dissolution of the Thieves, Finlin abandoned the drums and reinvented himself as a guitar-playing troubadour. His self-produced debut *Lonely Light* established a healthy mid-period **Bob Dylan** songwriting influence, while Finlin's raspy vocals evoked comparisons to **Graham Parker** and **Tom Waits**. A short-lived major label recording contract with MCA Records failed to bring Finlin's name to a wider audience, and he subsequently relocated to producer **Pete Anderson**'s Little Dog Records label. His second album *Highway Diaries* was a stark blues/folk recording that saw Finlin blossoming into a startlingly mature talent. Matching a storyteller's eye for detail with catchy melodies, Finlin turned out a quiet masterpiece chronicling the travels of the spirit and featuring the modern classics 'Idaho' and 'Hammer Down'. *Original Fin*, released four years later on the NBFNY label, tackled the weighty themes of love, betrayal and redemption without sounding preachy. Tracks such as 'The Perfect Mark Of Cain' and 'Weight Of The Flame' saw Finlin's songwriting reaching new

heights of sophistication, while 'Love And Happiness' and 'Waiting On A Flood' slid along on deceptively loping beats. The album was rereleased two years later by BMG's new alt country imprint Gravity Records. The mini-album *Text Goes Here* and the in-concert *Live From Nowhere* were only made available from Finlin's official website and preceded the release of his new studio album, *Somewhere South Of Wonder*.

● ALBUMS: *Lonely Light* (Own Label 1991) ★★★, *Highway Diaries* (Little Dog 1995) ★★★, *Original Fin* (NBFNY/Gravity 1999) ★★★★, *Text Goes Here* mini-album (Own Label 2001) ★★★, *Live From Nowhere* (Own Label 2002) ★★★, *Somewhere South Of Wonder* (Gravity 2002) ★★★★.

Finn

In 1995 former **Split Enz** and **Crowded House** members **Neil Finn** (b. 27 May 1958, Te Awamutu, New Zealand) and his elder brother **Tim Finn** (b. Brian Timothy Finn, 25 June 1952, Te Awamutu, New Zealand) collaborated for the first time since Crowded House released the multimillion-selling **Woodface**. Their debut album as a duo saw them use a variety of instruments, from tea chest bass to keyboards and ukuleles, marking a change from the pop sound of their previous bands. However, the harmonies and songwriting were still extremely strong, with a folk-based sound on tracks such as 'Last Day Of June' and 'Angel Heap'. The tracks were written during Crowded House's break with **Capitol Records** in late 1994 and produced with Tchad Blake in just over a month for **Parlophone Records**. Recorded in York Street Studios in Auckland in their native New Zealand, all instruments were played by the Finn brothers with the exception of some percussion by Blake and a bass line on 'Kiss The Road Of Rarotonga' by Dave Dobbyn. The result was a less self-conscious record than either had been involved in for some time, but the sheer laid-back feel of the record left their previous audience underwhelmed and frustrated.

Both brothers resumed their respective solo careers following the release of *Finn*, maintaining their reputations for producing quality adult pop music and occasionally guesting on each other's records. The brothers returned to the studio in the new millennium to record a new duo album. The excellent *Everyone Is Here*, a record of subtle charms and hidden musical depths, was released under the Finn Brothers name in summer 2004.

● ALBUMS: *Finn* (Parlophone 1995) ★★★, as the Finn Brothers *Everyone Is Here* (Parlophone/Nettwerk 2004) ★★★★.

Finn Brothers
(see **Finn**)

Finn, Mickey

b. Michael Hearne. One of the 90s' more publicity shy UK DJ's, Finn's ambitions stretch to writing film soundtracks rather than desiring pinup pieces in the popular music press. His musical inclinations were established at blues parties before he got hooked on **Eric B & Rakim**. He purchased his own decks and starting mixing, getting his first paid engagement at the Tunnel Club, near the Blackwall Tunnel (under the River Thames in East London) run by his sister Nancy, who first used the 'Finn' nickname. From such beginnings in 1988 he progressed to the Genesis and Biology nights. He recorded a solo track, 'She's Breaking Up', for US label Focus in January 1991 before going on to remix for a multitude of labels including **Suburban Base**, **ffrr**, **Champion** and **PWL** (**Mandy Smith**'s 'I Just Can't Wait', of all things). A more representative example of his work would be his contribution to **Urban Shakedown** with friends Gavin King and Claudio Guissani on 'Some Justice', which enabled it to become a real chart contender (despite problems obtaining clearance for the sample of **Ce Ce Rogers**' 'Someday'). He remains a huge name on the UK DJ circuit.

Finn, Neil

b. 27 May 1958, Te Awamutu, New Zealand. Finn's reputation as one of New Zealand's leading songwriters was confirmed when he was awarded an OBE in 1993 in recognition of his work with **Split Enz** and **Crowded House**. Following the latter band's emotional farewell performance in Sydney on 24 November 1996, Finn set about recording his debut solo outing for **Parlophone Records**. The presence of producers Nigel Godrich (**Radiohead**, **Beck**, **Natalie Imbruglia**) and Marius De Vries (**Björk**, **Madonna**) added a richer atmosphere to Finn's tuneful pop melodies. Despite living in the UK and having to contribute his mixes by ISDN, Godrich added weight to the album's stand-out tracks 'Sinner' and 'Twisty Bass'. De Fries joined Finn in New Zealand to add his peculiar variety of computer wizardry to the sessions. Guest musicians on the album included guitarist Jim Moginie (**Midnight Oil**), bass player Sebastian Steinberg (**Soul Coughing**) and producer Mitchell Froom, with Finn's son contributing drums to two tracks. The Crowded House soundalike, 'She Will Have Her Way', dented the UK charts at number 26 in June 1998. The album enjoyed more commercial success, entering the UK chart at number 5 the same month, but follow-up singles failed to trouble the charts.

Future commercial success on the level of Crowded House seems unlikely, but Finn is able to enjoy the fruits of his previous labours and is more concerned now about writing credible music. He has survived his brush with the pop charts with honour, as 2001's experimental *One Nil* demonstrated. He supported the album with a series of live gigs, with musicians such as **Johnny Marr**, Ed O'Brien and Phil Selway (**Radiohead**), **Lisa Germano** and Eddie Vedder (**Pearl Jam**) providing all-star support. The results were later released on *7 Worlds Collide*. Finn subsequently teamed up with his brother **Tim Finn** as the Finn Brothers to record 2004's excellent *Everyone Is Here*. The duo had previously recorded a low-key album as **Finn** in 1995.

● ALBUMS: *Try Whistling This* (Parlophone 1998) ★★★★, *One Nil* (Parlophone 2001) ★★★, *7 Worlds Collide: Neil Finn & Friends Live At The St. James* (Parlophone/Nettwerk America 2001) ★★★.

● DVD/VIDEOS: *7 Worlds Collide: Neil Finn & Friends Live At The St. James* (Parlophone 2001).

● FURTHER READING: *Once Removed*, Neil Finn and Mark Smith.

Finn, Tim

b. Brian Timothy Finn, 25 June 1952, Te Awamutu, New Zealand. As lead singer of the New Zealand band **Split Enz**, Finn was soon recognized as a major songwriter and vocalist with a very distinctive singing voice. Even before the

dissolution of the band in 1985, he had recorded his first solo album, *Escapade*, distributed worldwide by **A&M Records**, which became the Top Album of 1983 in Australia. It featured the singles, 'Fraction Too Much Friction', 'Made My Day' and 'Staring At The Embers', all excellent melodic pop tunes. The set also made a minor impact on the US charts. However, despite a high budget and more emphasis on production, his follow-up albums were not internationally successful. Moving from A&M to **Virgin Records** in 1985, Finn released *Big Canoe*, but the concentration on production buried his songs under layers of sound and the melodies were lost.

A move to **Capitol Records** resulted in a critically acclaimed, self-titled third album, but commercial success continued to elude him. However, the switch to Capitol made it possible for Finn to join stablemates **Crowded House** in 1991—the band formed by his brother **Neil Finn** after the breakup of Split Enz six years earlier. After achieving international success with Crowded House following the release of *Woodface*, which had originally been mooted as a one-off project helmed by the brothers, Tim elected to return to a solo career. *Before & After*, inspired by his two-week sojourn in the Blue Mountains of Australia, utilized two tracks the Finn brothers were working on during the sessions for *Woodface* and also boasted the services of guest contributors **Andy White** and Liam O Maonlai (**Hothouse Flowers**). Tim briefly reunited with his brother on the **Finn** project in 1995 and worked with White and O Maonlai in Alt.

After appearing with Split Enz in December 1999 for two reunion concerts in Auckland, Finn self-released his fifth album, *Say It Is So*, which was recorded in Nashville and Sydney. The equally low-key *Feeding The Gods* followed in 2001 before Finn teamed up with his brother Neil and Crowded House associates Mitchell Froom and Bob Clearmountain to record a new duo album. The excellent *Everyone Is Here* was released under the Finn Brothers name in summer 2004.

● ALBUMS: *Escapade* (Mushroom/A&M 1983) ★★★★, *Big Canoe* (Virgin 1986) ★★, *Tim Finn* (Capitol 1989) ★★★, *Before & After* (Capitol 1993) ★★★, *Say It Is So* (What Are?/Hypertension 2000) ★★★, with Bic Runga, Dave Dobbyn *Together In Concert: Live* (Epic 2001) ★★★, *Feeding The Gods* (What Are? 2001) ★★★.

Finn, William

b. 28 February 1952, Boston, Massachusetts, USA. Finn attracted a small measure of attention with an off-Broadway production, *In Trousers* (1979). Two years later, **March Of The Falsettoes** was a critical and commercial success. The premise for this musical, a married man with children who discovers and gradually comes to terms with his homosexuality, appealed to audiences. Also off-Broadway was an unsuccessful production of *Romance In Hard Times* (1989). In 1990 Finn returned to his successful premise with **Falsettoland**. On these shows Finn collaborated with librettist **James Lapine**. In 1992 a further musical play, *Falsettos*, actually an adaptation of the two single-act plays *March Of The Falsettoes* and *Falsettoland* into a two-act show, was staged on Broadway and was garlanded with good notices and had good audiences. *Falsettos* was awarded two **Tony Awards** for Best Book and Best Score. During the 90s, severe illness threatened Finn's life, but he turned adversity to advantage with *A New Brain* (1998), staged at the Lincoln

Center. Although the run was limited, the show demonstrated that Finn was still capable of good writing.

Accurately finding an almost empty niche in American musical theatre, Finn writes songs that are intensely personal to him yet reach out and seize the emotions of the listener. As he explained in an interview with playwright Warren Hoffman, *Elegies* (2003) began with a single song written for a dying friend's funeral. The song 'Anytime' was followed by songs exploring unusual subjects but all are intuitive, witty, dramatic and in several instances deeply moving: 'Infinite Joy', 'When The Earth Stopped Turning', '14, Dwight Ave., Natick, Massachusetts', 'Dear Reader'. Following this show, which was more a song cycle than an orthodox musical, Finn presented *The 25th Annual Putnam County Spelling Bee* (2005). This was greeted with critical acclaim, Christopher Isherwood in *The New York Times* declaring it 'Irresistible!'. In the early 00s Finn taught a weekly master-class in the graduate program in musical theatre at New York University.

● FILMS: *Life With Mikey* (1993).

Finnegan, Larry

b. Johnny Lawrence Finnegan, 10 August 1938, New York City, USA, d. 22 July 1973. Finnegan nearly reached the Top 10 in 1962 with a single called 'Dear One' but never had another hit. Having studied several instruments in his youth, Finnegan and his brother Vinnie co-wrote the song that would put him on the charts in 1961. He recorded a demo of the song on his own and took it to Hy Weiss of Old Town Records, who then signed him. The up-tempo country song ultimately reached number 11 in early 1962, but follow-up attempts failed, and in 1966 Finnegan moved to Sweden, where he started his own record label, Svensk-American. He then moved on to Switzerland and came back to the USA in 1970, where he died of a brain tumour in 1973.

Finnegan, Mike

A much-respected figure within San Francisco's music community, pianist/organist Finnegan first attracted attention in the mid-60s leading Mike Finnegan And The Surfs. By the end of the decade he was a pivotal member of the Serfs, a jazz-influenced rock act responsible for *Early Bird Cafe*. In 1970 Finnegan teamed with former **Gary Burton** guitarist Jerry Hahn in Jerry Hahn's Brotherhood, but the group's sole, self-titled album failed properly to illustrate their talents. Finnegan then joined Nu Boogaloo Express, a group featuring former members of **Big Brother And The Holding Company**. When the latter act was re-formed in 1971, Finnegan joined the line-up on a part-time basis. He appears on their album, *Be A Brother*. The pianist also began his solo career that year. *Mike Finnegan And Friends* was completed with the help of **Muscle Shoals** studio musicians David Hood, Barry Beckett and Roger Hawkins. Three accomplished albums followed in the next seven years. In 1972 he recorded *Crazed Hipsters* with guitarist Jerry Wood and in 1978 formed Dudek, Finnegan And Krueger with **Les Dudek** (formerly with **Boz Scaggs** and **Steve Miller**). They completed *Sweet Salvation* and *The DFK Band* before Dudek and Finnegan formed Black Rose, a soft rock ensemble fronted by **Cher**. Finnegan resumed solo work when this act split up but failed to recapture the profile he enjoyed during the 70s. He has worked with members of **Crosby, Stills And Nash** for many

years and co-sang the **Stephen Stills** AOR hit 'Can't Let Go, in 1984. He continues to be sought after for session work, although he has an exceptional voice that is underused.

● ALBUMS: *Mike Finnegan And Friends* (RCA 1971) ★★★, as Finnegan And Wood *Crazed Hipsters* (Blue Thumb 1972) ★★★, *Happy Fingers* (Golden Crest 1972) ★★, *Mike Finnegan* (Warners 1976) ★★★, *Black And White* (Columbia 1978) ★★★, as Dudek, Finnegan And Krueger *Sweet Salvation* (70s) ★★★, as Dudek, Finnegan And Krueger *The DFK Band* (70s) ★★.

Fio Rito, Ted

b. 20 December 1900, Newark, New Jersey, USA, d. 22 July 1971, Scottsdale, Arizona, USA. Fio Rito began playing piano at an early age and also dabbled in songwriting when he was still in his teens. In the 20s he formed a band in collaboration with **Danny Russo**, which they named the Oriole Terrace Orchestra. Russo's best-known contribution to popular music was as co-writer of the **Al Jolson** hit 'Toot Toot Tootsie (Good-Bye)'. During the 30s Fio Rito was sole leader of a band that played engagements at prestigious venues such as the St Francis Hotel in San Francisco. Although Fio Rito employed a number of competent sidemen and he was an adequate performer on Hammond organ, the band's book was heavy with vocal numbers. His singers included **Betty Grable**, who later became a film star (and married **Harry James**), and a vocal group, Kay Swingle Windows Media Player and Her Brothers (one of whom, Ward, later formed the **Swingle Singers**). For a number of years Fio Rito had his own radio show, *Hollywood Hotel*. His compositions include 'Laugh, Clown, Laugh' and 'I Never Knew'. Although shifts in musical taste meant he was unfashionable before the end of the 40s, Fio Rito was still playing, in Las Vegas, in the 60s.

● COMPILATIONS: *Spotlighting The Ted Fio Rito Orchestra* 1943 recordings (Collector's Choice 2002) ★★★, *Never Been Blue* 1922–42 recordings (Transatlantic Radio 2003) ★★★.

Fiol, Henry

b. 16 January 1947, Manhattan, New York City, USA. Of Puerto Rican and Italian American parentage, Fiol is a painter of sound and colour. From his rich musical palette emerged some of the most engaging Latin albums to come out of New York in the late 70s and 80s. Originally a doo-wop fan, he became a Latin music convert in the early 60s after seeing the band of **Rafael Cortijo** with **Ismael Rivera** while visiting his family in Puerto Rico. The craze for charangas (flute and violins bands) in the first half of the 60s inspired Fiol to teach himself the flute. With the mid-60s swing to brass, Fiol was so drawn to **Johnny Pacheco**'s pure Cuban trumpet conjunto (group/band) sound that he sought out the original conjunto recordings by Cuban names like **Sonora Matancera**, Félix Chapottín, **Arsenio Rodríguez** and others. Fiol acquired his skills as a singer and conga player by joining in with voices and percussion jam sessions called rumbones, which often occurred in the streets of Latin neighbourhoods, on beaches or in parks.

Fiol's research into Cuban roots led to a fascination with the Afro-Cuban form called son, and he started creating his own New York version. In the development of his own smooth and entrancing vocal style, he soaked up the influence of the great Cuban soneros (singers of son) Abelardo Barroso, Cheo Marquetti, **Beny Moré**, Joseito Fernández and Miguelito Cuní.

'Nostalgia, however,' wrote Fiol in 1990, 'has never been my objective. I've tried to stay close to the rhythmic roots, while at the same time adding a contemporary touch to the lyrics and the arrangements. If I had to label or categorize my sound, I wouldn't really call it "Salsa". I'd probably call it "Montuno", "Típico", "Son Moderno", or as some have called it, "Corazón Music" (literally: Heart Music)'—from the liner notes to the compilation *Sonero*.

Fiol's childhood ambition was to be a painter. After graduating in Fine Arts from New York's Hunter College, he began a career in education in 1968 (he has since had an involvement with the artwork for most of his recordings and painted the cover illustrations for many of them.). Between 1969 and 1974, Fiol played conga and sang in the chorus with various bands, including Orquesta Capri, **Orquesta Broadway** and Orquesta Típica New York. He made his recording debut with the latter, providing the lead vocals to his composition 'Cundy Macundy' on *Mike Pérez Y Su Orq. Típica New York*. Besides Mike Pérez (band leader, violinist, arranger and composer), the album featured ace Cuban flautist Don Gonzalo Fernández (who also wrote two arrangements and coproduced with Pérez), percussionist **Osvaldo 'Chi Hua Hua' Martínez** and pianist Mike Martínez. In 1974 Fiol founded and co-led (with bass and tres player, William Millán) the young two trumpet, rhythm section and vocals conjunto Saoco. The outfit adopted a typical Cuban sound, but rather than simply imitate, Fiol's and Millán's progressive and creative arrangements infused the traditional Cuban structures with freshness and a distinctly urban feel. In 1975 Millán and another Saoco member, trumpeter Ken Fradley, performed on the notable *Tierra Va A Temblar* by former boogaloo star, Johnny Colón. Millán also assisted Colón with the album's production and arrangements.

Saoco's 1976 debut on Mericana Records, *Siempre Seré Guajiro*, was coproduced by Fiol, Millán and **Al Santiago**. The success of the album, which spawned the big hits 'Lejos Del Batey' and 'Yo No Como Camarón' (both written by Fiol, who composed three other tracks and co-wrote one with pianist Ray Santiago), took the band to the Madison Square Garden as one of the year's hottest properties. Fiol sang the lead vocals to his five self-penned songs on Saoco's follow-up, *Macho Mumba*, on Salsoul Records, a subsidiary of Mericana. Rafy Puente provided lead vocals to the album's three remaining tracks, although he was not given a credit. Puente was the lead singer with Yambú and performed on their releases *Al Santiago Presents Yambú* (1975) and *Yambú's Brew* (late 70s). Fiol split acrimoniously with Saoco, and the band continued under the name of William Millán Y Saoco, with mellow-voiced Ray Ramos and José Luis Ayala sharing lead vocals. The band issued a further three albums between 1978 and 1981, *Curare*, *Papa Montero* and *El Quinto*. Saoco disbanded and Ramos, who is also a gifted composer, turned band leader, releasing *Ray Ramos Y Su Sonora* (1983), *Salsa Tracks* (1985), *Yo Soy El Son* (1987) and *Fiesta De Besos* (1989). Ramos and his trumpet-led group specialized in a distinctive brand of subtly swinging salsa that benefitted his gently flowing voice; however, they adopted a more aggressive edge on their 1987 album.

Meanwhile, in 1980, Fiol made his solo debut with the deservedly bestselling *Fe, Esperanza Y Caridad* on SAR Records, on which the label's cofounder, **Roberto Torres**, produced and performed. On this album and his 1981 follow-up, *El Secreto*, Fiol was backed by a two-trumpet conjunto of

session musicians, including **Alfredo 'Chocolate' Armenteros** (trumpet), Alfredo Valdés Jnr. (piano), Johnny 'Dandy' Rodríguez (percussion) and Charlie Rodríguez (tres). In 1982 Fiol organized his own conjunto with a frontline of one trumpet and a tenor saxophone plus conga, bongo, güiro, acoustic bass, piano, tres and voices (his lead vocals plus chorus). 'My decision to change to the trumpet/tenor saxophone combination was based on years of listening to jazz', explained Fiol in 1986. He recorded his final album for SAR in 1983, the self-produced *La Ley De La Jungla*, with this conjunto. In 1983 Fiol formed his own Corazón Records label and named his conjunto Corazón. Between 1983 and 1986, he issued three essential albums on Corazón. In 1988 the shrinking salsa circuit forced him to disband his group, and he decided to discontinue Corazón Records. He worked on an English language 'salsa-pop' concept with a view to hooking up with a major label, but 'some American companies found the sound *too* Latin', explained Fiol in 1988, 'and there are many negative attitudes and prejudices here (in the USA) regarding anything "Latin" or "Hispanic".' So he aborted the project.

In the meantime, ex-Saoco and ex-Corazón member, Puerto Rican pianist, arranger and composer Ray Santiago (he performed on all Fiol's Corazón releases) debuted as the leader of his own conjunto on *Lluvia Con Salsa* in 1988 on El Abuelo Records. The label was founded that year by Humberto Corredor and Henry Cárdenas. Ray's former Saoco colleague, William Millán, played bass on the album and shared arranging and production chores with Santiago. Fiol signed with El Abuelo at the end of 1988 and released *Renacimiento* (*Rebirth*) the following year. On the album, Fiol and his 16-year-old blind son, Orlando, created an idiosyncratic blending of the typical Cuban sound with new musical technology. Apart from the two trumpets and tenor saxophone, everything was performed, arranged and produced by the father/son duo (Fiol: lead vocal, chorus and percussion; Orlando: piano, synthesizer and chorus). Talented Orlando, who won the Itzak Perlman Award in 1988 for his excellence on classical piano, played all bass and tres parts and other effects on the synthesizer.

In 1990, David Barton (with Trevor Herman) of the UK's Earthworks label compiled the critically acclaimed *Sonero*, which was a selection of some of Fiol's best material from his three albums on the Corazón label. Fiol, who had been using 'pickup' groups for his 'live' appearances, re-formed his band in 1991 (with a two-trumpet/tenor saxophone frontline) and took them into the studio to record *Creativo*. Orlando, who started studying music at Columbia University in 1990, performed on the album, acted as musical director and shared production and arranging chores with his father. A longtime associate of Henry's Russell 'Skee' Farnsworth carried out the task of transcription. Farnsworth, who worked with **Ricardo Ray** in the 60s and Pedro Rafael Chaparro in the 70s, assisted with arrangements and transcriptions on the majority of Fiol's solo albums and performed on both of Fiol's 1983 releases. Fiol has toured Colombia—where he is incredibly popular—Venezuela, Ecuador, Curaçao, Dominican Republic, Mexico, Canada, Switzerland and Italy.

● ALBUMS: with Mike Pérez *Mike Pérez Y Su Orq. Típica New York* (mid-70s) ★★★, with Saoco *Siempre Seré Guajiro* (1976) ★★★★, with Saoco *Macho Mumba* (1977) ★★★, *Fe, Esperanza Y Caridad* (1980) ★★★, *El Secreto*

(1981) ★★★★, *La Ley De La Jungla* (1983) ★★★, *Corazón* (1983) ★★★★, *Colorao Y Negro* (1985) ★★★, *Juega Billar!* (1986) ★★★, *Renacimiento* (1989) ★★★, *Creativo* (1991) ★★★.

● COMPILATIONS: *Sonero* (1990) ★★★★.

Fiona (reggae)

b. Fiona Reggae Robinson, May 1976, Kingston, Jamaica, West Indies. Robinson was hailed as following in the footsteps of **Marcia Griffiths**, **Judy Mowatt** and **Pam Hall**. She initially found success when she gained three nominations at the 1998 Tamika Reggae Awards in the New Artist Of The Year category. Her triumph was due to the release of 'I Could Fall In Love'. The success of the single led to the release of her long-playing debut, *Fiona's Moment*. This critically acclaimed release featured combinations with **Brian Gold**, **Merciless** and Teisha. Although the album was basically considered to be in a Jamaican **lovers rock** style, she revisited classic rhythms such as **Junior Byles**' 'Fade Away' and **Slim Smith**'s 'Rougher Yet', and with Merciless she performed the **dancehall**-styled 'Have A Nice Weekend'. Fiona maintained a credible profile when she released a series of hits including a cover version of 'Oops I Did It Again', 'Hold On', 'Yours Tonight', 'Sky', 'Every Little Bit Hurts' and 'Love Me', the last of which was recorded in combination with **Lukie D**. In 2002 Fiona released her follow-up, *Wanna Make Love*. The album continued to demonstrate her eclectic approach to music in tracks such as the inspirational 'Pray', the encouraging 'Rise Up', the romantic 'Take Your Heart' and the quirky 'Kindness For Weakness Part 2' that was recorded in response to **Glen Washington**'s similarly titled hit.

● ALBUMS: *Fiona's Moment* (VP 1999) ★★★, *Wanna Make Love* (VP 2002) ★★★.

Fiona (heavy metal)

b. Fiona Flanagan, New Jersey, USA. Fiona had always harboured ambitions to be a star since her teenage years singing in clubs with various rock bands in New York. Eventually she took the first steps towards achieving that dream by signing a contract with **Atlantic Records** in 1985. They put her in the studio with Bobby Messano (guitar; ex-**Starz**) along with session men Donnie Kisselbach (bass), Joey Franco (drums; ex–**Good Rats**, **Twisted Sister**) and Benji King (keyboards). After a false start with production problems, former Good Rats vocalist Peppi Marchello took over. The resulting self-titled album received good press and predictable comparisons to **Heart** and **Pat Benatar** ensued. The second album displayed a more mature sound thanks to producer Beau Hill (her boyfriend at the time) and guest appearances from Nile Rodgers and Kip Winger and Reb Beach from the **Alice Cooper** band (at the time forming their own unit, **Winger**). The album featured a poignant cover version of 'Thunder And Lightning' by German singer Chi Coltrane, which, if released as a single, might have provided a much needed hit. She did, however, come to the attention of producer Richard Marquand who cast her in his 1987 movie *Hearts Of Fire*, in which she sang alongside **Bob Dylan** and actor Rupert Everett. Her last album for Atlantic was greeted with a measure of indifference, and her career has remained on hold ever since, despite winning a new contract from **Geffen Records**.

● ALBUMS: *Fiona* (Atlantic 1985) ★★, *Beyond The Page* (Atlantic 1986) ★★.

● FILMS: *Hearts Of Fire* (1987).

Fiorello!

With a book by **Jerome Weidman** and **George Abbott** that was based on the true story of Fiorello La Guardia, the aggressive, extrovert US congressman and mayor of New York, *Fiorello!* opened at the Broadhurst Theatre on Broadway on 23 November 1959. The show's story began shortly before World War I when La Guardia was first a conscientious, reforming lawyer, and then a congressman who became a sworn enemy of the corruption that was endemic in the social and political life of New York. It continued through his time as a pilot during World War I, his initial unsuccessful campaign against James J. Walker, right up to the eve of his election as the mayor of New York, in 1933. Along the way, his wife, Thea (Ellen Hanley) dies, and he eventually finds happiness with his secretary Marie Fischer (Patricia Wilson). The role of the rough, tough, ebullient La Guardia was played by Tom Bosley, making his Broadway debut. The actor was subsequently best known for his work on television, as the indulgent father in the 50s spoof *Happy Days* and another long-running series, *Father Dowling Investigates*. *Fiorello!*'s score, by **Jerry Bock** (music) and **Sheldon Harnick** (lyrics), included 'On the Side Of The Angels', 'The Name's La Guardia', 'Politics And Poker', 'I Love A Cop', ''Til Tomorrow', 'When Did I Fall In Love?', 'Gentleman Jimmy', 'The Very Next Man', 'Marie's Law' and 'The Bum Won'. One of the most amusing numbers was 'Little Tin Box'. Setting aside a small sum therein each week apparently enabled certain of the city's apparently less than well-off citizens to buy yachts and Rolls Royces or, as one of them put it in court: 'I can see your Honour doesn't pull his punches / And it looks a trifle fishy, I'll admit / But for one whole week I went without my lunches / And it mounted up your honour, bit by bit.' Chorus: 'Up your Honour bit by bit. In spite of a few critical carpings *Fiorello!* was a great success and ran for 795 performances. It won **Tony Awards** for best director (George Abbott) outright, tied with **The Sound Of Music** for best musical, composer, and librettist and was also voted best musical by the New York Drama Critics. Even more prestigiously, it became only the third musical (not counting **Oklahoma!**'s special award in 1944) to be awarded the Pulitzer Prize for Drama. The 1962 London production stayed at the Princes Theatre for 56 performances. Four concert performances of *Fiorello!* were presented at the New York City Centre in 1994. The starry cast included Faith Prince, Jerry Zaks, Donna McKechnie, Liz Callaway, Philip Bosco, Greg Adelman, Marilyn Cooper and Adam Arkin.

Fire

Formed in Hounslow, Middlesex, England, in 1966, Fire were a UK progressive rock trio founded by David Lambert (vocals, guitar, keyboards), Bob Voice (drums/vocals) and Dick Dufall (bass/vocals). After signing to **Decca Records** in 1968 they released their debut single, the energetic and enduring 'Father's Name Is Dad'. A second single, 'Round The Gum Tree', followed a few months later. Without satisfactory chart returns, Decca lost patience, and no further releases were forthcoming until Fire signed a new contract with **Pye Records** in 1970. *The Magic Shoemaker* was an ambitious concept album concerning a group of children on a coach journey through a fantastic fairy-tale land. As well as most of the group's songwriting, Lambert also provided the narration. Although it sold poorly at the time of its release, it has become a major collector's item among followers of the progressive genre and was reissued by **See For Miles Records** in 1990. This interest was far too late to help Fire, however, who broke up at the end of 1970. Voice subsequently joined **Paul Brett**'s Sage, while Lambert worked with the **Strawbs** from 1972 onwards before completing his first solo album in 1979. He later worked as a ski instructor.

● ALBUMS: *The Magic Shoemaker* (Pye 1970) ★★★.
● COMPILATIONS: *Underground And Overhead: The Alternate Fire* (Tenth Planet 1997) ★★★.

Fire Engines

Alongside fellow **Postcard Records** bands such as **Orange Juice** and **Josef K**, the Fire Engines were part of a burgeoning Scottish music scene in the early 80s. Formed in Edinburgh in 1979 by Davey Henderson (vocals/guitar), Murray Slade (guitar), Russell Burn (drums/percussion) and Graham Main (bass), the band's debut surfaced on independent label Codex Communications in late 1980. 'Get Up And Use Me' was a manic burst of estranged, frenetically delivered guitar broken by sharp vocal outbursts. It also cut through the surrounding tendency for dense, synthesized sounds or second-rate punk. The band received considerable promotion in the music press and was strongly tipped for success by the **New Musical Express**. The next release, *Lubricate Your Living Room (Background Music For Action People!)*, an album's worth of near-instrumentals on the Accessory label, contained a similar barrage of awkward, angular funk guitar riffs. By spring 1981, the band had signed with aspiring Scottish label Pop: Aural, releasing the excellent 'Candy Skin'. More overtly pop (Henderson's nasal tones were to the forefront for the first time), the single was backed by 'Meat Whiplash', a superb slab of nasty, breakneck guitar work conflicting with an aggressive drum rhythm. By comparison, 'Big Gold Dream' (1981) was relatively melodic, perhaps in an attempt to reach a wider audience. It failed, although all the Fire Engines' product fared well in independent terms, and it was to be the band's last release.

Ideologically, the Fire Engines tapped a similar aesthetic to Josef K, fuelled by a vehement hatred of 'rock' in the general sense and the realization that punk's spirit of innovation had to be continued. Both bands remained true to that ethic, imploding rather than growing stale. Henderson went on to form **Win**, managed by Postcard founder Alan Horne, then **Nectarine No.9**. He reunited with his former Fire Engines colleagues in January 2004 to play a support slot for the Magic Band. The same December they played to a much larger audience as support for fellow Scots **Franz Ferdinand**, a band who had openly talked about the Fire Engines' influence on their music in interviews. To commemorate the concert a free 7-inch single was handed out to the audience, featuring Franz Ferdinand's rendition of 'Get Up And Use Me' and the Fire Engines' version of 'Jacqueline'. Later in the month the Fire Engines played a show alongside young Edinburgh bands **Aberfeldy** and **Sons And Daughters**.

● ALBUMS: *Lubricate Your Living Room (Background Music For Action People!)* (Accessory 1981) ★★★, *Aufgeladen Und Bereit Für Action Und Spass* (Fast America 1981) ★★★.
● COMPILATIONS: *Fond* (Creation 1992) ★★★, *Codex Teenage Premonition* (Domino 2005) ★★★.

Fire Merchants

This hi-tech power trio of well-seasoned session musicians was founded by ex-**Andy Summers** bass player Doug Lunn. Enlisting John Goodsall (ex-**Brand X** and **Peter Gabriel**) on guitar and keyboards, the line-up was eventually completed following a long search for the right drummer. Ex-**Frank Zappa** and **Genesis** drummer Chester Thompson was enlisted, allowing the band to stabilize in October 1987. Released two years later, their self-titled debut album was an all-instrumental affair, offering an eclectic fusion of jazz, rock and blues.

● ALBUMS: *Fire Merchants* (Roadrunner 1989) ★★★.

Fire Theft

Few alt rock bands of the 90s seemed as likely to succeed as the Seattle, Washington, USA, quartet **Sunny Day Real Estate**. Although the outfit was one of the major contributors to what would later be known as emo, bad choices and ill fortune prevented them from reaching as many people as their talent warranted. Soon after the band was finally laid to rest in 2001, Jeremy Enigk (b. 16 July 1974, Seattle, Washington, USA; vocals/guitar) and William Goldsmith (b. 4 July 1972, Seattle, Washington, USA; drums) convinced former bandmate Nate Mendel (b. 2 December 1968, Seattle, Washington, USA; bass) to join them in a new venture. It was the first time since 1995 the trio had played together, although Mendel and Goldsmith were both in the original line-up of the **Foo Fighters**. The Fire Theft turned out to be Sunny Day Real Estate without guitarist/vocalist Dan Hoerner (newcomer Nick Macri taking his place), and the new outfit was quite musically comparable to the trio's defunct previous band, as evidenced by their 2003 self-titled debut recording for **Rykodisc Records**. The Fire Theft supported their debut with a string of European dates later the same year. They parted company with Rykodisc the following December.

● ALBUMS: *The Fire Theft* (Rykodisc 2003) ★★★.

Fireballs

Formed in the autumn of 1957 in Raton, New Mexico, USA, the Fireballs originally comprised George Tomsco (b. 24 April 1940, Raton, New Mexico, USA; guitar/vocals), Chuck Tharp (b. 3 February 1941, d. 17 March 2006, Clovis, New Mexico, USA; lead vocals), Danny Trammell (b. 14 July 1940; rhythm guitar), Stan Lark (b. 27 July 1940; bass/vocals) and Eric Budd (b. 23 October 1938; drums). Their Tex-Mex instrumental rock 'n' roll was driven by Tomsco's clear and concise guitar sound, which helped the group place 11 singles in the US charts between 1959 and 1969, although they achieved their greatest success when they hooked up with singer Jimmy Gilmer. The Fireballs also attracted controversy in the 60s, when they were used to overdub music behind unfinished tapes recorded by **Buddy Holly** before his death in 1959.

Founder members Tomsco and Tharp met at Raton High School in New Mexico. After the others came in, they rehearsed and won a talent contest in January 1958 with a performance of 'Great Balls Of Fire', from which they took their name. After a shaky start that found members leaving for college and then returning, they recorded at **Norman Petty**'s studio in Clovis, New Mexico, in August 1958. Their debut single on **Kapp Records** was the instrumental 'Fireball', b/w a vocal performance by Tharp, 'I Don't Know'. A contract with the Top Rank label led to the breakthrough instrumental 'Torquay', which scraped into the US Top 40 in September 1959 and saw the band appearing on **Dick Clark**'s *American Bandstand*. Another Top Rank single, 'Bulldog', reached number 24 in January 1960 and one on Warwick, 'Quite A Party', reached number 27 the following June. Several non-charting singles also appeared on the Jaro and Hamilton labels. Tharp left the group and was replaced by Jimmy Gilmer (b. 15 September 1940, LaGrange, Illinois, USA). During 1962 the Fireballs were signed to **Dot Records**, where they recorded *Torquay*, after which Budd entered the army and was replaced by Doug Roberts (d. 18 November 1981). In early 1963, now billed as Jimmy Gilmer And The Fireballs, they recorded 'Sugar Shack', using an unusual keyboard called a Solovox to give the record a distinctive sound. The result was one of the bestselling hits of 1963— 'Sugar Shack' stayed at number 1 for five weeks late in the year. An album of the same title also charted. Although several other singles and albums were released, the group was unable to capitalize on that success, although 'Daisy Petal Pickin'' made number 15 in December. Such efforts as *Folk Beat*, a 1965 album crediting only Gilmer, were unsuccessful. By the following year, Dot was sold, and in 1967 the Fireballs, minus Gilmer, signed to **Atco Records**. Before Christmas that year they recorded a **Tom Paxton** song, 'Bottle Of Wine', which reached number 9 in late December 1967. Three other minor chart singles followed before the end of 1969, including the politically charged 'Come On, React!'. Although the latter marked the end of their chart success, the Fireballs continue as a popular live unit with a line-up now comprising Lark, Tomsco, Ron Cardenas (vocals, keyboards, guitar) and Daniel Aguilar (drums).

● ALBUMS: *The Fireballs* (Top Rank 1960) ★★★, *Vaquero* (Top Rank 1960) ★★★, *Here Are The Fireballs* (Warwick 1961) ★★★, *Torquay* (Dot 1963) ★★★, as Jimmy Gilmer And The Fireballs *Sugar Shack* (Dot 1963) ★★★, *The Sugar Shackers* (Crown 1963) ★★★, *Sensational* (Crown 1963) ★★★, as Jimmy Gilmer And The Fireballs *Buddy's Buddy* (Dot 1964) ★★★, as Jimmy Gilmer *Lucky 'Leven* (Dot 1965) ★★, as Jimmy Gilmer *Folk Beat* (Dot 1965) ★★, *Campusology* (Dot 1966) ★★, *Firewater* (Dot 1968) ★★, *Bottle Of Wine* (Atco 1968) ★★★, *Come On, React!* (Atco 1969) ★★.

● COMPILATIONS: *The Best Of The Fireballs (The Original Norman Petty Masters)* (Ace 1992) ★★★★, *Blue Fire & Rarities* (Ace 1993) ★★★, *The Best Of The Fireballs Vocals* (Ace 1994) ★★★, *The Fireballs/Fireball Country* (Calf Creek 1995) ★★★, *Sugar Shack: The Best Of Jimmy Gilmer And The Fireballs* (Varèse Sarabande 1996) ★★★, *The Tex-Mex Fireball* George Tomsco retrospective (Ace 1998) ★★★, *Best Of The Rest Of The Fireballs' Vocals* (Ace 2002) ★★.

F-IRE Collective

Formed in London in 1999, the Fellowship for Integrated Rhythmic Expression is a collective of like-minded musical innovators. They originated from the band Timeline that was formed by alto saxophonist **Barak Schmool** (b. 7 February 1969, London, England) in 1995. Even collectives need prime movers and highly motivated individuals, and in the case of F-IRE that role was filled by Schmool, who had studied in the USA with **Steve Coleman** of M-Base and was himself an educator at London's City University and Royal Academy of

Music. It is at CU that the musicians are able to gather in fully equipped rehearsal rooms, thus removing at a stroke several of the bugbears for musicians: rehearsal space, central location, permanent instrumental and audio set-ups. The musicians who formed Timeline were fellow students of African music and as members of the band they inventively mixed jazz improvisation with traditional African rhythms. In some instances, their musical connections included working together in other contexts; for instance, several of them were former members of Tomorrow's Warriors.

From the outset, music and dance of many cultures were performed by F-IRE, something that broadened the collective's base and its potential audience. A central characteristic of the collective has been its intention to give back to the community through performance, be it concert or carnival, and through education by way of schools and workshops. Timeline can be heard on the 2002 recording *Know Hope*. Among Timeline's participants have been instrumentalists, singers, dancers, composers including the core personnel of Schmool, keyboard player Nick Ramm, guitarist **David Okumu**, bass player Tom Herbert and percussionists Leo Taylor and Ivan Ormond. Additional performers have included dance group Bullies Ballerinas, vocalists Bembe Segue and Eska Mtungwazi and percussionist-singer **Nana Tsiboe**. Originally a small group, Timeline has also been extended to form F-IRE's big band, Synergy. Another Timeline development is Méta Méta, a group drawing its repertoire from a fusion form of Cuban batá music.

Gradually, F-IRE extended to substantial numbers of individuals, some 60 in all. Among them have been trumpeter **Tom Arthurs**, bass player Larry Bartley, vocalist Julia Biel, guitarists Jonathan Bratoeff and Jonny Phillips, pianists Tom Cawley, Robert Mitchell and **Justin Quinn**, cellist Ben Davis, saxophonists **Ingrid Laubrock**, Finn Peters, Pete Wareham and Jason Yarde, tuba player Oren Marshall, percussionists Tom Skinner and Volker Sträter and trumpeter **Byron Wallen**. Some of these individual artists have formed groups that remain within the collective, while others who have moved outside retain close practical and intellectual links. Among the many are Arthurs' Centripede, Okumu's Jade Fox and Thieves Without Loot, Mitchell's Panacea, Laubrock's quartet and quintet, Sebastian Rochford's **Polar Bear**, Phillips' Oriole and Wareham's Acoustic Ladyland. Additionally, there is Rhythms Of The City, a 20-piece street band that has appeared at festivals including that held in London's Notting Hill district.

Although strongly influenced by Coleman's M-Base, both musically and conceptually, F-IRE is very much the brainchild of its founding and continuing members. Additionally, through Schmool, F-IRE maintains links with like-minded collectives outside the UK and USA, including Aka Moon in Belgium and Hask in Paris, France. Many of the artists and bands within the F-IRE Collective have released albums under their own names. The compilation *Fire: Works* comprises tracks by groups led by musicians including Schmool, Mitchell, Arthurs, Laubrock and Bratoeff.

● COMPILATIONS: *Fire: Works* (F-IRE 2005) ★★★.

Firefall

Firefall were a second-generation US country rock band in the tradition of **Poco** and the **Eagles**. Formed during the genre's heyday, the initial line-up was comprised of ex–**Flying Burrito Brothers** members Rick Roberts (b. Florida, USA;

guitar/vocals) and Michael Clarke (b. Michael Dick, 3 June 1946, Spokane, Washington State, USA, d. 19 December 1993, Treasure Island, Florida, USA; drums, also ex-**Byrds**), Mark Andes (b. 19 February 1948, Philadelphia, Pennsylvania, USA; bass, ex-**Spirit**), Larry Burnett (guitar/vocals) and Jock Bartley (b. Kansas, USA; guitar/vocals). Their debut was a refreshing though laid-back affair, and in addition to three US hit singles the album contained a version of the **Stephen Stills/Chris Hillman** song 'It Doesn't Matter', with alternative lyrics by Roberts. The band's first three albums were all strong sellers, and for a brief time Firefall were one of the biggest-selling artists in their genre. *Luna Sea*, featuring new member David Muse (keyboards, saxophone, flute), contained a further major US hit with the memorable 'Just Remember I Love You'. While their instrumental prowess was faultless, their inability to progress significantly was their ultimate failing, although *Elan* demonstrated a will to change, with the sparkling hit 'Strange Way', which featured a breathy jazz-influenced flute solo. They continued to produce sharply engineered albums with Muse playing an increasingly important role adding other instruments, giving a new flavour to a guitar-dominated genre. After the original band broke up in 1981, Bartley assumed ownership of the name and has continued to tour and record with various personnel as Firefall.

● ALBUMS: *Firefall* (Atlantic 1976) ★★★, *Luna Sea* (Atlantic 1977) ★★★, *Elan* (Atlantic 1978) ★★★, *Undertow* (Atlantic 1979) ★★, *Clouds Across The Sun* (Atlantic 1981) ★★, *Break Of Dawn* (Atlantic 1982) ★★★, *Mirror Of The World* (Atlantic 1983) ★★, *Messenger* (Redstone 1994) ★★, *Colorado* 1979 recording (NMC Pilot 2002) ★.

● COMPILATIONS: *The Best Of Firefall* (Atlantic 1981) ★★★, *Greatest Hits* (Rhino 1992) ★★★, *You Are The Woman And Other Hits* (Flashback 1997) ★★★.

Fireflies

Formed in 1957 in Philadelphia, Pennsylvania, USA, the Fireflies placed two singles on the charts in 1959-60 and then disappeared from view. The group was started by **Gerry Granahan** (b. 17 June 1939, Pittston, Pennsylvania, USA), Lee Reynolds and Vinnie Rodgers, who were each on their way to separate auditions for a singing job at a resort in upstate New York. Learning that the club wanted a group, they decided to form one on the spot and were hired. The group lasted long enough to record a demo called 'The Crawl', which was released on Roulette Records in 1958 (under the spelling Fireflys) but did not chart. The group then disbanded while Granahan went on to chart as a solo artist with 'No Chemise, Please'. Granahan decided to reactivate the group in 1959 when he heard the song 'You Were Mine', written by Paul Giacalone. Granahan then recorded the song in his studio, singing lead. However, he was unsatisfied with his vocal and hired Ritchie Adams to re-do the vocal (Granahan sang all background vocals). It was released on Ribbon Records, which Granahan co-owned, and reached number 21. Granahan and Adams then teamed up with Lee Reynolds and toured. One follow-up single, 'I Can't Say Goodbye', also charted, in early 1960, but the group disbanded, with Adams going on to write the number 1 hit 'Tossin' And Turnin'' for **Bobby Lewis** and Granahan going on to record with other groups (such as Dicky Doo And The Don'ts) as well as producing for other artists.

● ALBUMS: *You Were Mine* (Taurus 1961) ★★★.

Firefly, The (film musical)

Remembered particularly for one of **Allan Jones'** finest film performances and his thrilling rendition of 'The Donkey Serenade', *The Firefly* was released by MGM in 1937. The song itself was based on **Rudolph Friml**'s 'Chanson', a solo piano piece written in 1920, which was arranged for the picture by Herbert Stothart with a lyric by **Robert Wright** and **George Forrest**. Most of the songs from the 1912 Broadway show were discarded, and Frances Goodrich and Albert Hackett came up with a new story, which was set in Spain at the time of the Napoleonic war. Jones and his costar, **Jeanette MacDonald** were both involved in espionage work during the hostilities, while their personal relationship flourished. The songs that survived from the original stage musical, with music by Rudolph Friml, were 'Giannina Mia' (lyric by **Otto Harbach**), 'When A Maid Comes Knocking At Your Heart' (lyric Harbach–Robert Wright–Chet Forrest), 'Love Is Like A Firefly' (lyric Wright-Forrest), and 'Sympathy' (lyric **Gus Kahn**–Harbach), were supplemented by several others including 'He Who Loves And Runs Away' (Friml-Kahn). Also in the cast were Henry Daniell, Warren William, Leonard Penn, Douglas Dumbrille, Billy Gilbert and George Zucco. The choreographer was **Albertina Rasch**, and the opulent and entertaining Hunt Stromberg production, which was photographed by Oliver T. Marsh in a sepia tint, was directed by Robert Z. Leonard.

Firefly, The (stage musical)

Composer **Rudolph Friml**'s first Broadway score and the beginning of his partnership with **Otto Harbach** who wrote the book and lyrics and with whom he collaborated for 10 musicals. *The Firefly* opened at the Lyric Theatre in New York, on 2 December 1912. Friml was given the job because **Victor Herbert**, the original choice of the composer, could not get along with Emma Trentini, who plays the role of Nina Corelli. As *The Firefly* begins, Geraldine Van Dare (Audrey Maple) is about to sail for Bermuda on her uncle's yacht in the company of her fiancé Jack Travers (Craig Campbell). To escape the clutches of her drunken father, Nina (Trentini), an Italian street singer who lives in New York, disguises herself as a boy and manoeuvres herself aboard. After the most elaborate and complicated plot schemes and some expert tutorage from the musician Franz (Henry Vogel), she becomes Giannina, a famous prima donna and, of course, marries Jack Travers. As usual with operetta, the score and not the story is the important item, and this score is regarded as one of the best of its kind. It included lovely songs such as 'When A Maid Comes Knocking At Your Door', 'Sympathy', 'Giannina Mia', 'Love Is Like A Firefly', 'In Sapphire Seas' and 'An American Beauty Rose'. The show ran for 120 performances—a decent total in the early part of the century—and was filmed in 1937. The Hollywood version had a different story that involved spies in Spain and starred **Jeanette MacDonald** and **Allan Jones**.

Firehose

This propulsive US hardcore trio (usually titled fIREHOSE) was formed by two ex-members of the **Minutemen**, **Mike Watt** (b. 20 March 1957, Portsmouth, Virginia, USA; vocals/bass) and George Hurley (drums), following the death of the latter band's founding guitarist, D. Boon, in 1985. Ed Crawford aka eD fROMOHIO, completed the new venture's line-up, which made its debut in 1986 with the impressive *Ragin', Full-On*.

Although undeniably powerful, the material Firehose offered was less explicit than that of its predecessor and showed a greater emphasis on melody rather than bluster. Successive releases, *If'n* and *fROMOHIO*, revealed a band that, although bedevilled by inconsistency, was nonetheless capable of inventive, exciting music. At their best, these songs merged knowing sarcasm ('For The Singer Of R.E.M.') with an unreconstructed approach to music making (as on drum solo 'Let The Drummer Have Some'). In 1989 Watt and Hurley also collaborated with Elliott Sharp on the *avant garde Bootstrappers* project. The band's variety argued against commercial fortune, but they were still picked up by a major, **Columbia Records**, in 1991, which released the slightly more disciplined *Flyin' The Flannel* that year. Following the disappointing critical and commercial response to *Mr. Machinery Operator*, the band decided to call it a day in 1995, with Watt having already begun a solo career.

● ALBUMS: *Ragin', Full-On* (SST 1986) ★★★, *If'n* (SST 1987) ★★, *fROMOHIO* (SST 1989) ★★★, *Flyin' The Flannel* (Columbia 1991) ★★★, *Live Totem Pole* mini-album (Columbia 1992) ★★, *Mr. Machinery Operator* (Columbia 1993) ★★.

Firehouse Five Plus 2

The Firehouse Five Plus 2 were formed in 1949 by trombonist Ward Kimball. It was a semi-professional band whose members were drawn from the staff of **Walt Disney**'s animation studios in Hollywood. Some members went on to full-time careers such as clarinettists Tom Sharpsteen and George Probert. The band was playing at the time of a renewal of interest in traditional jazz styles and although this was the basis of the band's music, the use of the bass saxophone, tuba and washboard encouraged their tendency towards a humorous rather frantic style, which perhaps reflected their Walt Disney cartoon origins.

● ALBUMS: *The Firehouse Five Plus Two, Volume 1* 10-inch album (Good Time Jazz 1953) ★★★, *The Firehouse Five Plus Two, Volume 2* 10-inch album (Good Time Jazz 1953) ★★★, *The Firehouse Five Plus Two, Volume 3* 10-inch album (Good Time Jazz 1953) ★★★, *The Firehouse Five Plus Two, Volume 4* 10-inch album (Good Time Jazz 1953) ★★★, *The Firehouse Five Story, Volume 1* (Good Time Jazz 1955) ★★★, *The Firehouse Five Story, Volume 2* (Good Time Jazz 1955) ★★★, *The Firehouse Five Story, Volume 3* (Good Time Jazz 1955) ★★★, *Plays For Lovers* (Good Time Jazz 1955) ★★★, *Goes South!* (Good Time Jazz 1955) ★★★, *Goes To Sea* (Good Time Jazz 1956) ★★★, *Crashes A Party* (Good Time Jazz 1957) ★★★, *Dixieland Favorites* (Good Time Jazz 1957) ★★★, *Around The World!* (Good Time Jazz 1958) ★★★, *At Disneyland* (Good Time Jazz 1962) ★★★, *Goes To A Fire* (Good Time Jazz 1964) ★★.

Fireside

This Swedish punk band was formed in 1992 by Frans Johansson (bass), Per Nordmark (drums), Kristofer Åström (vocals/guitar) and Pelle Gunnerfeldt (guitar). Based in Lulea, in the far north of Sweden above the Polar Circle, each member of the band had formerly played in sundry local punk and alternative outfits. Their first EPs were released through the small independent label A West Side Fabrication before they signed to Stockholm-based label Startracks in the spring of 1995. An international recording contract was then secured with American Recordings when Swedish native and American Recordings A&R executive Johan Kugelberg returned home on a holiday trip. With a sound compared to the more muscular end of the alternative rock spectrum (**Henry Rollins**, **Fugazi**), the band made its breakthrough with 1995's Pelle Gunnerfeldt–produced *Do Not Tailgate*. This won them several Swedish Album Of The Year awards in magazines such as *Aftonbladet*, *Slitz* and *Expressen*. They also won a 1996 Swedish Grammy for Best Hard Rock Band.

Following their brief association with American Recordings, the quartet switched US distribution to the independent label Crank! A Record Company label. They enjoyed further success with Uomini D'Onore but alienated many of their fans with the experimental *Elite*, which featured a 12-minute instrumental as its title track. Following its release the band remained quiet for a couple of years, during which time Gunnerfeldt worked as a producer with the Swedish break-through garage rock band the **Hives** and Johansson played with the **Soundtrack Of Our Lives**. Åström, meanwhile, recorded with his band Hidden Truck. The quartet reconvened in 2003 to release their new studio album, *Get Shot*.

● ALBUMS: *Fantastic Four* (A West Side Fabrication 1994) ★★★★, *Do Not Tailgate* (Startracks/American 1995) ★★★★, *Uomini D'Onore* (Startracks/Crank! A Record Company 1997) ★★★, *Elite* (Startracks 2000) ★★★, *Get Shot* (Startracks/V2 2003) ★★★.

● COMPILATIONS: *Hello Kids!* (Startracks/Crank! A Record Company 1998) ★★★.

Firesign Theatre

Formed in Los Angeles, California, USA, in 1966, this satirical comedy troupe comprises Philip Proctor, Peter Bergman, David Ossman and Philip Austin. The quartet's work drew on a multitude of disparate sources, encompassing 30s radio serials, **W.C. Fields**, **Lord Buckley**, the **Marx Brothers** and contemporary politics. Their surreal humour found favour with the late 60s' 'underground' audience, but despite punning wordplay and sharp wit, many cultural references were too obtuse for widespread appeal. Produced by **Gary Usher**, they were used to provide the spectacular gunshot effects on 'Draft Morning' on the **Byrds**' *The Notorious Byrd Brothers*. They subsequently completed the film script for *Zacharia* (1970), 'the first electric Western', but the final draft bore little relation to their original intention. A series of adventurous albums, including *How Can You Be In Two Places At Once When You're Not Anywhere At All?*, *Don't Crush That Dwarf, Hand Me The Pliers* and *I Think We're All Bozos On This Bus* are among the quartet's most popular collections, while *Dear Friends* included several highlights from their radio shows.

During the 70s the group also pursued independent projects, with Ossman recording *How Time Flies* (1973), Austin *The Roller Maidens From Outer Space* (1974) and Proctor and Bergman completing *TV Or Not TV* (1973), *What This Country Needs* (1975) and *Give Us A Break* (1978). Their prolific output slackened towards the end of the decade, but the Firesign Theatre subsequently found a sympathetic haven at **Rhino Records**. Another series of excellent albums ensued before the group began transferring their routines to video.

The Firesign Theatre reunited in 1993 for live performances captured on *Back From The Shadows*. The quartet began recording new studio albums again in the late 90s, which like much of their earlier work ranged from the inspired (*Give Me Immortality Or Give Me Death*) to the just plain unfunny (*Boom Dot Bust*).

● ALBUMS: *Waiting For The Electrician Or Someone Like Him* (Columbia 1968) ★★, *How Can You Be In Two Places At Once When You're Not Anywhere At All?* (Columbia 1969) ★★★★, *Don't Crush That Dwarf, Hand Me The Pliers* (Columbia 1970) ★★★★, *I Think We're All Bozos On This Bus* (Columbia 1971) ★★★, *Dear Friends* (Columbia 1972) ★★, *Not Insane Or Anything You Want To* (Columbia 1972) ★★, *The Tale Of The Giant Rat Of Sumatra* (Columbia 1974) ★★, *Everything You Know Is Wrong!* (Columbia 1974) ★★★★, *In The Next World You're On Your Own* (Columbia 1975) ★★★, *Just Folks . . . A Firesign Chat* (Butterfly 1977) ★★, *Nick Danger: The Case Of The Missing Shoe* (Rhino 1979) ★★★, *Fighting Clowns* (Rhino 1980) ★★★, *Anythynge You Want To (Shakespeare's Lost Comedie)* (Rhino 1980) ★★★, *Lawyer's Hospital* (Rhino 1982) ★★★, *Shakespeare's Lost Comedie* (Rhino 1982) ★★★, *Nick Danger: The Three Faces Of Al* (Rhino 1984) ★★★, *Eat Or Be Eaten* (Mercury 1985) ★★★, *Back From The Shadows* (Mobile Fidelity 1994) ★★★, *Give Me Immortality Or Give Me Death* (Rhino 1998) ★★★★, *Boom Dot Bust* (Rhino 1999) ★★, *The Bride Of Firesign* (Rhino 2001) ★★★.

● COMPILATIONS: *Forward Into The Past* (Columbia 1976) ★★★★, *Shoes For Industry! The Best Of The Firesign Theatre* (Columbia 1993) ★★★★, *Papoon For President (He's Not Insane)* (Laugh.Com 2002) ★★★, *All Things Firesign: As Heard On NPR's 'All Things Considered'* (Artemis 2003) ★★★.

● DVD/VIDEOS: *Boom Dot Bust* (Rhino 2000).

Fireworks

A Nashville, Tennessee, USA–based quintet of Marty McCall (vocals), Gary Pigg (vocals), Cindy Lipford (vocals), Lanny Avery (bass) and Chris Harris (drums). The members of Fireworks were all heavily immersed in contemporary Christian music before forming the band. McCall and Pigg had been involved in the career of **Chris Christian** as producers and featured as backing singers on David Meece's *I Just Call On You* and **B.J. Thomas'** *Home Where I Belong*. They also worked on commercial jingles together. Avery had formerly worked as a studio engineer, while Chris Harris had previously belonged to the Texas group Brazos. The idea for Fireworks came when Pigg and McCall discovered their mutual interest in spiritual music when they met at a Nashville church. After working with Christian, they began to write their own songs together. They expanded to a three-piece with the addition of Lipford, playing at fellowships and local churches. Their three voices were originally accompanied solely by piano, until the group added Avery and Harris as full-time backing musicians. The group's self-titled debut album followed for Myrrh Records.

● ALBUMS: *Fireworks* (Myrrh 1978) ★★★.

Firm (rap)

The Brooklyn, New York, USA-based rappers **Nas**, **Foxy Brown**, **AZ** and **Cormega** formed this hip-hop supergroup, although the latter was replaced by Nas associate Nature before the release of their self-titled 1997 debut. With three of the rap scene's biggest stars involved the project generated a huge amount of interest. Brown enjoyed huge success but became an instant enemy of the moral majority with the previous year's *Ill Na Na*. Nas was declared the future of the New York scene following the release of his *Illmatic* and *It Was Written* albums, while AZ scored a crossover hit single with 'Sugar Hill' from 1995's *Doe Or Die*. Their collaboration was delayed by various commitments, but the finished product, with production shared by **Dr. Dre** and the **Trackmasters**, was finally released in October 1997. Although a host of other rappers including Pretty Boy, Wizard, **Canibus**, **Noreaga** and Half-A-Mil cropped up at various points, the album's celebration of the gangster lifestyle was very much the work of its cocreators. Inspired by the Mafia, the album celebrated the twin themes of violence and blatant carnality with a provocative zeal.

● ALBUMS: *The Firm* (Aftermath 1997) ★★★.

Firm (rock)

It seemed to be a marriage made in heaven when ex–**Led Zeppelin** guitarist **Jimmy Page** (b. James Patrick Page, 9 January 1944, Heston, Middlesex, England) and former **Free/Bad Company** vocalist **Paul Rodgers** (b. 17 December 1949, Middlesbrough, Cleveland, England) began working together as the Firm in 1984. Enlisting ex–**Uriah Heep/Manfred Mann** drummer Chris Slade (b. 30 October 1946) and virtual unknown Tony Franklin on bass (an acquaintance of Page's from work with **Roy Harper**), the partnership never quite gelled in a manner that matched either protagonist's earlier achievements. However, the band was not without musical merit, with Slade's precise backbeat providing a solid base for Page and the stylish Franklin. On *The Firm*, Rodgers was in fine voice on varied material, from the lengthy and Zeppelinesque 'Midnight Moonlight' to the more commercial strains of 'Radioactive', which was a minor hit, plus a cover version of 'You've Lost That Loving Feeling'. Live dates proved successful, with Page producing his customary show-stopping solo spot, replete with laser effects, although neither Page nor Rodgers were willing to reprise their previous work. *Mean Business* continued in the warm, understated and bluesy style of the debut but failed to raise the band to new heights, and the Firm split after the subsequent world tour. Page and Rodgers returned to their respective solo careers, while Slade joined **AC/DC**, and Franklin teamed up with John Sykes in **Blue Murder**.

● ALBUMS: *The Firm* (Atlantic 1985) ★★★, *Mean Business* (Atlantic 1986) ★★★.

First Choice

Part of the Philadelphia sound of the mid-70s, this female vocal group's biggest success was 'Armed And Extremely Dangerous'. Rochelle Fleming (b. 11 February 1950, Philadelphia, Pennsylvania, USA), Joyce Jones (b. 30 July 1949) and Annette Guest (b. 19 November 1954, Chester, Pennsylvania, USA) were originally known as the Debronettes. Local DJ Georgie Woods introduced the trio to Norman Harris, guitarist with **MFSB**, to produce their debut single, 'This Is The House Where Love Died'. Although it sold poorly, the record led to a new contract with Philly Groove and 'Armed and Extremely Dangerous'. Also produced by Harris, the song was a hit first in the UK, where it reached the Top 20 on Bell. US success followed, and the later singles, 'Smarty Pants' and 'The Player', sold equally well. While producer Harris was associated with numerous hits during the disco boom of the late 70s, the only later chart entry for First Choice was 'Dr Debbie Martine', and in 1984 First Choice split up. In 1987 Fleming re-formed the group with her cousin Laconya Fleming and Lawrence Cottel to record 'Love Itch' (Prelude). In the same year a reissue of the 1977 track 'Let No Man Put Asunder' was a dancefloor hit in the UK.

● ALBUMS: *Armed And Extremely Dangerous* (Philly Groove 1973) ★★★, *Smarty Pants* (Philly Groove 1974) ★★★, *So Let Us Entertain You* (Warners 1976) ★★★, *Delusions* (Gold Mind 1977) ★★★, *Dr Love* (Gold Mind 1977) ★★★, *Hold Your Horses* (Gold Mind 1979) ★★★.

● COMPILATIONS: *Greatest Hits And Rarities* (KRL 2001) ★★★.

First Choice Records

This record label and studio is based in Greenwich Village, New York, USA, and was founded in the mid-90s by DJ/ remixer Andrew Komis in conjunction with **Network**. His intention to return **dance music** to the late 80s, when the dramatic **garage** divas like **Adeva** and **Kym Mazelle** held sway, was first attempted at the Big Shot label in Canada (see **Hi-Bias**). Among those involved are Pandella, the well-regarded **house** diva veteran, and **Dyone**, a highly-touted disco diva whose upfront personality and sexuality have endeared her to many, including actor Robert De Niro, which sent rumour mills into a frenzy of activity. A former beauty queen, dancer and college graduate, Dyone has been heralded as a sussed **Teena Marie** of the 90s. Komis himself records under the nom de plume Komix And Co. Of the opinion that the 90s US dance scene is dead, he formed First Choice primarily to reach English and European markets, linking up with Network after they had opened up a New York office in 1990.

First Class

This studio group was conceived by John Carter and Ken Lewis in 1974. **Carter And Lewis** were formerly the leaders of Carter-Lewis And The Southerners and the **Ivy League** and were prolific songwriters, session singers and hitmakers. They assembled some of the UK's finest studio musicians to record the summery 'Beach Baby' that made the UK Top 20 in the summer of 1974. The cast included singer **Tony Burrows**, previously in the Ivy League with Carter/Lewis and the man chosen to lead the touring version of their 1967 studio group, the **Flowerpot Men**. Burrows also sang on records by **White Plains**, **Edison Lighthouse**, **Pipkins**, the **Brotherhood Of Man** and others. In 1970 he made *Top Of The Pops* history by appearing on one show with three different groups. Others on the record included John Carter himself, Del John and Chas Mills completing the vocal harmonies plus Spencer James on guitar, Clive Barrett on keyboards, Robin Shaw on bass and Eddie Richards on drums. The follow-ups to 'Beach Baby'—'Dreams Are Ten A Penny' and the old Ivy League hit 'Funny How Love Can Be'—were flops, and the band was dismantled in 1976. Carter went on to form another studio group—Ice. In the early 80s the First Class name was resurrected for a cover of **Brenton Wood**'s 'Gimme Little Sign' on Sunny Records. The label suggests that the British Surf Mafia of Carter and company were involved but personnel details are not known.

● COMPILATIONS: *The First Class/SST* (See For Miles 1996) ★★★.

First Down

Comprising MCs King Arroe, Correkt, Baron Demus and DJ Hyste, UK rap group First Down originally formed in 1990. A full four years passed between the release of their debut single, 'Jawbreaker' (1990), and its follow-up, 'Let The Battle Begin' (1994). The debut single was a staple of pirate hip-hop shows, making their failure to capitalize on its success seem even stranger. Despite their US football–related name, their second release was a defiant slice of British rap fashioned on 'old school' precepts. It was released on their own Ill Gotten Gains label as a reaction to prevailing trends in American hip-hop culture. Correkt gave this verdict to the press: 'When was the last time you heard a good American rap record with cutting on it, apart from **Gang Starr** or **EPMD**. Rap's become too commercialised . . . it's become too conformist.' However, delays in the release of the group's debut album again stalled their progress. When *World Service* did emerge in 1995, it was on the German label Blitz Vinyl and the band was disappointed by its distribution and the financial details of the deal.

● ALBUMS: *World Service* (Blitz Vinyl 1995) ★★★.

First Strike

Though they only recorded a single album, 1984's *Rock Offensive* debut for Exit Records, First Strike were one of the more melodically articulate hard rock bands of the mid-80s. Comprising Tony Gunn (vocals), Tim Larkin (guitar), Pat Boylan (guitar), Chris Salmon (bass) and Johnnie Delaney (drums), the group's disciplined hard rock sound earned initial comparisons to **AC/DC** and **Coney Hatch**. Their most distinctive property was the overdriven dual guitar approach of Boylan and Larkin, who also contributed strong vocal harmonies. Despite a series of strong reviews and a limited degree of radio support, *Rock Offensive* proved to be their sole album.

● ALBUMS: *Rock Offensive* (Exit 1984) ★★★★.

Fischer-Z

A vehicle for the talents of singer-songwriter John Watts (b. 27 December 1954, Harrow, Middlesex, England), Fischer-Z was initially trumpeted as a bridge between new wave pop and the synthesizer wave of the early 80s. Watts, Steve Skolnick (keyboards), Steve Liddle (drums) and David Graham (bass) performed on their first two albums (1979's *Word Salad* and the following year's *Going Deaf For A Living*), but by the time of the third, Watts had taken over the keyboards and was also coproducing. The band's first two singles, 'Wax Dolls' and 'Remember Russia', were both well received. The latter even boasted a Ralph Steadman cartoon illustration on the sleeve. However, it was 'The Worker' in 1979 that gave Fischer-Z their sole major UK chart success.

In 1982 Watts started recording under his own name. However, singles such as 'I Smelt Roses (In The Underground)' and 'Mayday Mayday' attracted little interest, and his next project was the Cry, in which he was reunited with former Fischer-Z colleague David Graham. This unit released 'Take It Round Again' and the album *Quick Quick Slow* in 1984, but again to little public recognition. Watts restored the Fischer-Z name for 1987's *Reveal* and revealed a more acoustic-based direction than his earlier work. The revived unit enjoyed a minor European hit with 'The Perfect Day'. Fischer-Z continued to release albums on a regular basis, with Watts eclipsing his new wave roots on beautifully measured rock albums such as *Destination Paradise* (1992) and *Stream* (1995).

Following the release of *Stream*, Watts again put Fischer-Z on hold and recorded his next album, *Thirteen Stories High*, as J.M. Watts. Two further albums followed under the Watts moniker before the artist revived the Fischer-Z name for a second time on 2002's *Ether*. Like much of Watts' latter-day work, the album enjoyed a much warmer reception in Europe than in his homeland.

● ALBUMS: *Word Salad* (United Artists 1979) ★★★, *Going Deaf For A Living* (United Artists 1980) ★★★, *Red Skies Over Paradise* (Liberty 1981) ★★, *Reveal* (Ariola 1987) ★★★, *Fish's Head* (Ariola 1989) ★★★, *Destination Paradise* (Harvest/EMI 1992) ★★★★, *Kamikaze Shirt* (Harvest/EMI 1993) ★★★, *Stream* (SPV 1995) ★★★★, *Ether* (So-Real 2002) ★★★, as John Watts' Fischer-Z *Ether Remix* (So-Real 2002) ★★.

Solo: John Watts *One More Twist* (EMI 1982) ★★★, *The Iceberg Model* (EMI 1983) ★★, as J.M. Watts *Thirteen Stories High* (SPV 1997) ★★★, as Watts *BigBeatPoetry* (Motor 2000) ★★★, as Watts *Spiritual Headcase* (So-Real 2002) ★★★, *Ether Music & Film* (So-Real 2003) ★★★.

● COMPILATIONS: *Going Red For A Salad (UA Years 1979–1982)* (Capitol 1990) ★★★, *Still In Flames* (EMI 1994) ★★★, *The Best* (EMI 1995) ★★★★, *The Worker* (EMI Gold 1997) ★★★, *The Perfect Album* (BMG 1998) ★★★, *Highlights: 1979 To 2004* (EMI 2004) ★★★★.

● DVD/VIDEOS: *John Watts And The Cry* (Dubious 1988), *The Garden Party* (EMI 2004).

Fischer, Clare

b. 22 October 1928, Durand, Michigan, USA. After formal studies at Michigan State University, Fischer became arranger and accompanist to the popular singing group the **Hi-Lo's**. His arrangements, which are often in the more elaborate, left-field tradition of **Gil Evans** and **Lennie Tristano**, were also used by **Donald Byrd** and **Dizzy Gillespie**, with whom he worked on the album *A Portrait Of Duke Ellington*. In the 60s Fischer formed an occasional big band, an activity that he continued in later decades. Among the musicians attracted into his bands by his forward-thinking, swinging charts, which always leave space for soloists, were **Warne Marsh**, **Bill Perkins**, **Conte Candoli** and **Steve Hufstetter**. In recent years Fischer has worked more as a pianist, although he continues to write extensively, especially in the Latin idiom that has long been one of his chief musical interests. In 2001 he produced his first classical CD, *After The Rain*. His work has also been commissioned by a wide range of artists, including **Prince**, **Natalie Cole**, **Branford Marsalis** and **Brandy**.

● ALBUMS: *First Time Out* (Pacific Jazz 1962) ★★★★, *Surging Ahead* (Pacific Jazz 1962) ★★★★, *Easy Livin'* (Revelation 1963) ★★★, *Extension* (Pacific Jazz 1963) ★★★, *So Danco Samba* (World Pacific 1964) ★★, *One To Get Ready, Four To Go!* (Revelation 1965) ★★★, *Songs For Rainy Day Lovers* (Columbia 1966) ★★★, *Manteca!* (Pacific Jazz 1966) ★★★, *America The Beautiful* (Discovery 1967) ★★★, *'Twas Only Yesterday* (Atlantic 1968) ★★★, *Duality* (Discovery 1969) ★★★, *Thesaurus* (Atlantic 1969) ★★★★, *Great White Hope!* (Revelation 1970) ★★★, *The Reclamation Act Of 1972* (Revelation 1971) ★★★, *T'AA-A-A-A!* (Revelation 1972) ★★★, *And Ex-42* (MPS 1972) ★★★, *The State Of His Art* (Revelation 1973) ★★★, *Jazz Song* (Revelation 1973) ★★★, *Head, Heart And Hands* (Revelation 1973) ★★★, *Alone Together* (MPS 1975) ★★★★, *Clare Declares* (MPS 1975) ★★★, *Salsa Picante* (MPS 1978) ★★★, *Machacha* (MPS 1979) ★★★, *2x2 And Sometimes Voices* (Discovery 1981) ★★★★, *Whose Woods Are These?* (Discovery 1982) ★★★, *Starbright* (Discovery 1982) ★★★, with Gary Foster *Blues Trilogy* (Discovery 1982) ★★★, *Crazy Bird* (Discovery 1984) ★★★, *Free Fall* (Discovery 1985) ★★★, with Poncho Sanchez *Gaviota* (Discovery 1986) ★★★, *Plays By And With Himself* (Discovery 1986) ★★★, *Tjaderama* (Trend 1987) ★★★, *Lembranças (Remembrances)* (Concord Jazz 1989) ★★★, *Just Me: Solo Piano Excursions* (Concord Jazz 1995) ★★★★, *Rockin' In Rhythm* (JMI 1997) ★★★, *The Latin Side* (Koch 1998) ★★★, *Clare Fischer's Jazz Corps* (Clare Fischer 1998) ★★★, *After The Rain* (Clare Fischer 2001) ★★★, *On A Turqoise Cloud: The Clarinet Choir Of Clare Fischer* (Clare Fischer 2002) ★★★.

● COMPILATIONS: *Memento* (Discovery) ★★★, *Latin Patterns* (Motor 1999) ★★★★.

Fischer, John

b. USA. One of the original performers of what has been termed Jesus Music, Fischer grew up in a religious environment via his father's employment as musical director of the local church choir. As well as singing, he took lessons in piano, ukulele, trumpet and guitar, and while attending Wheaton College he began work on his own compositions. The musical doctrine was adopted from the folk singer-songwriter tradition, but albums such as *The Cold Cathedral* and *Have You Seen Jesus My Lord* were explicitly religious and spiritual in tone. He toured extensively and also formed the Discovery Art Guild in association with the Peninsula Bible Church—an organisation dedicated to developing religious music talent. In the 70s and 80s he continued to record widely for Light Records.

● ALBUMS: *Another INTERface Live At The Bim* (Rentry 1998) ★★★.

Fischer, Larry 'Wild Man'

b. 1945, USA. Fischer was a prominent fixture on Los Angeles' Sunset Strip during the late 60s. This imposing figure, part-eccentric, part-LSD casualty, was renowned for composing songs to order in return for small change. He became associated with **Frank Zappa** who produced Larry's uncompromising debut, *An Evening With Wild Man Fischer*. Contemporary opinion was divided on its merits. Some critics deemed it voyeuristic, while others proclaimed it a work of art and a valid documentary. Caught in the middle was an ecstatic performer, elated that his 50s-style compositions were finally recorded. Fischer made several live appearances with Zappa's group, the **Mothers Of Invention**, but it was seven years before he recorded again. Having completed a single, advertising the **Rhino Records** store, he was signed to their fledgling label. Three further albums continued the disquieting atmosphere of that first release before Fischer was released from his recording contract.

● ALBUMS: *An Evening With Wild Man Fischer* (Bizarre 1968) ★★, *Wildmania* (Rhino 1977) ★★, *Pronounced Normal* (Rhino 1981) ★★, *Nothing Crazy* (Rhino 1984) ★★.

● COMPILATIONS: *The Fischer King* (Rhino 1999) ★★★.

Fischerspooner

Created in the late 90s by New York, USA–based duo Warren Fischer (composer) and Casey Spooner (lyrics), this performance-art collective crossed over from underground cult status to emerge as leading figures of the briefly popular US electro-punk or 'electro-clash' musical movement. The pair, who had been working together since the beginning of the decade, were joined by a core group of collaborators, including vocalists Lizzy Yoder and Cindy Greene and several dancers and choreographers. The collective's multi-media enterprises, bridging visual and aural media, earned comparisons to the work of 80s UK renegades the **KLF**. Meanwhile, the heavy use of synthesisers, vocoders and sequencers in their music saw them fêted alongside other 80s-inspired acts such as **Crossover** and **Ladytron** on the underground electro-clash scene.

Fischerspooner's debut was released on Munich's International DeeJay Gigolo label in 2001. The album, featuring the club favourite 'Emerge', became an underground hit and prompted a lucrative recording contract with the UK's **Ministry Of Sound** label. The failure of the album to make a commercial impact on the mainstream charts, coupled with a series of badly received UK concerts, saw the duo rapidly fall from critical favour. They persevered with their career, however, enlisting the help of ubiquitous songwriter **Linda Perry**, renaissance man **David Byrne**, intellectual Susan Sontag and producer **Mirwais** to record their follow-up album, *Odyssey*.

● ALBUMS: *Best Album Ever* aka *#1* (International DeeJay Gigolo/Ministry Of Sound 2001) ★★★, *Odyssey* (Capitol 2005) ★★★.

Fish

b. Derek William Dick, 25 April 1958, Dalkeith, Edinburgh, Scotland. Fish acquired his nickname from a landlord who objected to the lengthy periods he spent in the bath. He sang for Nottingham band the Stone Dome before auditioning for progressive rockers **Marillion** by writing lyrics for their instrumental, 'The Web'. The band established a strong following through constant touring, before releasing their debut single 'Market Square Heroes'. Fish's bombastic vocals, markedly similar to **Peter Gabriel**, strengthened critics' arguments that Marillion were mere **Genesis** copyists. Despite this, Marillion went from strength to strength, with Fish structuring a series of elaborately linked concept albums that were still capable of yielding UK hit singles including 'Garden Party' and the melodic ballad 'Kayleigh', which reached number 2 in May 1985. His lyrics were strongly influenced in style and content by the work of **Peter Hammill**, former leader of progressive 70s band **Van Der Graaf Generator**, a debt he acknowledged by inviting Hammill to be special guest on Marillion's 1983 tour of Britain.

After the success of 1987's *Clutching At Straws*, he began to disagree with the rest of the band about their musical direction and left in 1988 to embark on a solo career; he was replaced by Steve Hogarth. Fish's debut solo album utilized stylistically diverse elements such as folk tunes and brass arrangements, as shown on the UK number 25 single 'Big Wedge', but he also retained a mixture of hard rockers and ballads. In 1989 he worked with Hammill on his opera, *The Fall Of The House Of Usher*, but their voices clashed, and Fish was replaced on the project by Andy Bell. A more successful collaboration was the single 'Shortcut To Somewhere',

recorded with Genesis keyboard player Tony Banks in 1986. His 1993 release was a desultory album of cover versions, including the **Kinks**' 'Apeman' and the **Moody Blues**' 'Question'. Far more satisfying was his 1995 duet with **Sam Brown** on 'Just Good Friends', and 1997's *Sunsets On Empire* helped to further restore favour. A glut of fanclub releases from this period helped to sustain the singer, but after struggling for several years with his own Dick Bros label, Fish signed to Roadrunner Records. He celebrated his new recording contract with the typically bombastic *Raingods With Zippos* but soon afterwards returned to independent label status. He undertook an acting career in 2000, one of the projects being the movie *Nine Dead Gay Guys*.

● ALBUMS: *Vigil In A Wilderness Of Mirrors* (EMI 1990) ★★, *Internal Exile* (Polydor 1991) ★★, *Songs From The Mirror* (Polydor 1993) ★★, *Suits* (Dick Bros/Renaissance 1994) ★★, *Sunsets On Empire* (Dick Bros 1997) ★★★★, *Raingods With Zippos* (Roadrunner 1999) ★★★, *Fellini Days* (Chocolate Frog 2001) ★★★, *Fellini Nights* (Chocolate Frog 2002) ★★.

● COMPILATIONS: *Yin* (Dick Bros/Renaissance 1995) ★★★, *Yang* (Dick Bros/Renaissance 1995) ★★★, *Kettle Of Fish '88–'98* (Roadrunner 1998) ★★★, *The Complete BBC Sessions* (Voiceprint 1999) ★★★.

Fishbone

Funk metal hybrid from Los Angeles, California, USA, who never managed to achieve the commercial success their critical reputation deserves. Five of the seven band members met through the Los Angeles School Bussing Program, a scheme that encouraged black and white children to visit each other's schools. Although their recorded output is sparse given their longevity, their hard political edge and high-octane rhythmic onslaught is every bit as deserving of mass attention as the **Red Hot Chili Peppers** or **Living Colour**. Their line-up included Chris 'Maverick Meat' Dowd (b. Christopher Gordon Dowd, 20 September 1965, Las Vegas, Nevada, USA; trombone/keyboards), 'Dirty' Walter Kibby (b. Walter Adam Kibby II, 13 November 1964, Columbus, Ohio, USA; trumpet, horn, vocals), 'Big' John Bigham (b. 3 March 1969, Lidsville, USA), Kendall Jones (b. Kendall Rey Jones, USA; guitar), Philip 'Fish' Fisher (b. 16 July 1967, El Camino, Los Angeles, California, USA; drums), John Fisher (b. John Norwood Fisher, 12 September 1965, El Camino, Los Angeles, California, USA; bass) and Angelo Moore (b. Angelo Christopher Moore, 5 November 1965, USA; lead vocals). Norwood was stabbed on stage early in their career when Fishbone played alongside hardcore bands such as the **Dead Kennedys** (the influence of **Bad Brains** is obvious in their output). After a debut mini-album, the production expertise of David Kahne saw them touch on a more conventional metal direction before exposing their true talents for the first time on *Truth And Soul*. This was helped in no small part by the airplay success of a cover version of **Curtis Mayfield**'s 'Freddie's Dead'. Subsequent recordings saw Fishbone branching out and working with rap artists such as the **Jungle Brothers**, although *The Reality Of My Own Surroundings* had more in common with the hard-spined funk of **Sly Stone**. 'Fight The Youth' and 'Sunless Saturday' demonstrated a serious angle with sociopolitical, antiracist and antidrug lyrics, in contrast to their lighter side on the humorous 'Naz-Tee May'en'. Fishbone's live shows continued to sell out without a hit to be seen, and Moore caused a minor sensation by ending a London show naked but for his saxophone. However, just as transatlantic commercial success beckoned with the *Give A Monkey . . .* set, bizarre press stories began to circulate concerning the activities of Jones, who, at the instigation of his father, had left the flock to join a religious cult. The band, which he had renounced, was accused of attempted kidnap in their attempts to retrieve him. Appearing on 1993's **Lollapalooza** tour failed to restore their diminishing reputation, as did a lacklustre new album in 1996, although they remained a popular live draw. A new line-up, which included Moore, Fisher and Kibby, resurfaced on the Hollywood label in March 2000 with *The Psychotic Friends Nuttwerk*. The band was dropped from the label shortly afterwards, prompting them to set up their own imprint for subsequent releases.

● ALBUMS: *Fishbone* mini-album (Columbia 1985) ★★, *In Your Face* (Columbia 1986) ★★, *Truth And Soul* (Columbia 1988) ★★★★, *The Reality Of My Surroundings* (Columbia 1991) ★★★, *Give A Monkey A Brain And He'll Swear He's The Centre Of The Universe* (Columbia 1993) ★★★, *Chim Chim's Badass Revenge* (Rowdy 1996) ★★★, *The Psychotic Friends Nuttwerx* (Hollywood 2000) ★★★, *Live At The Temple Bar And More* (Nuttsactor 5 2002) ★★.

● COMPILATIONS: *Singles* (Sony Japan 1993) ★★★, *Fishbone 101—Nuttasaurusmeg Fossil Fuelin'* (Columbia/Legacy 1996) ★★★, *The Best Of Fishbone* (Epic 2003) ★★★★.

Fisher, Cevin

b. 26 October 1963, East Orange, New Jersey, USA. Although he only made an impact in the late 90s with his club hits 'The Freaks Come Out', 'The Way We Used To' and '(You Got Me) Burning Up', Fisher has been involved with the music industry since leaving high school. He spent his formative years going to all-night parties in his native New Jersey run by **Tony Humphries**. He took to DJing and eventually picked up production work for Timmy Regisford at **Motown Records**. He was incorporated into **Arthur Baker**'s production team at Shakedown Studios, where he worked on remixes for **Chaka Khan** ('Love You All My Lifetime') and **Quincy Jones** ('I'll Be Good To You')—both of which were number 1s on the *Billboard* dance chart. As **house** music developed, Fisher was instrumental in developing the sound, writing 'Hands On Love' and 'House Is A Feeling' for the New York–based independent label, Hardtrax. In 1996 he released 'The Way We Used To' and 'Check This Out' on the Maxi label, which were dancefloor hits in the USA and UK, particularly at the Twilo and the **Ministry Of Sound**. His EPs *Shine The Light/New York, New York* and *I Want Music/Lead Me To The Mountain Top* were international club hits and played by influential DJs such as **Frankie Knuckles**, Terry Farley, **Junior Vasquez** and **David Morales** among others. It was 1998's 'The Freaks Come Out' that made Fisher's name in the UK, championed by BBC Radio 1 DJs **Pete Tong** and **Danny Rampling**, licensed by the Ministry Of Sound record label and featured on many mix compilation albums, including the Ministry's *Annual IV*. The same year Fisher provided vocals for **Danny Tenaglia**'s *Tourism*, repaying a favour to the man who had first convinced him to record his own material. In January 1999 '(You Got Me) Burning Up', sampling **Loleatta Holloway**'s 'Love Sensation' (the same track used by **Black Box** for their 1989 UK number 1 'Ride On Time'), received extensive radio airplay, notably from Radio 1's Dave Pearce,

and was yet another smash hit in the clubs. Fisher continues to DJ in Europe, Asia and the USA and holds a residency at the D! Club in Geneva, Switzerland.

● ALBUMS: *Underground 2000* (Razor & Tie 2000) ★★★.

● COMPILATIONS: *Cevin Fisher's Nervous Tracks* (Nervous 1999) ★★★, *My First CD: Dangerous Disco—The Adventures Of Double O Cevin* (DMC 1999) ★★★★.

Fisher, Cilla, And Artie Trezise

Cilla Fisher (b. 26 September 1952, Glasgow, Scotland) is the youngest of the Fisher family from Scotland. She sang on radio at the age of nine and performed with other members of her family, including Ray and Archie Fisher. Artie Trezise (b. 3 April 1947, St. Andrews, Scotland) sang with various folk groups including the Great Fife Road Show. Their albums together include *Balcanquhal*, featuring Allan Barty on fiddle and Cilla's brother Archie, and *Cilla And Artie*, a **Melody Maker** Folk Album Of The Year in 1979. They underwent a transformation to children's entertainers and changed their name to the Singing Kettle following the release of an album of the same title on their own label, Kettle Records. As a result, Fisher and Trezise, along with multi-instrumentalist Gary Coupland, began touring larger venues throughout the UK. In addition to recording a number of children's albums, they perform educational work in schools and have made four series for BBC Television. Aside from the new musical policy, Fisher continues to tour with members of her family and has toured the USA with her sibling Ray.

● ALBUMS: *Cilla Fisher And Artie Trezise* (1976) ★★, *Balcanquhal* (1977) ★★★, *For Foul Day And Fair* (1977) ★★★, *Cilla And Artie* (Topic 1979) ★★★★, *Songs Of The Fishing* (1989) ★★★, *Reaching Out* (1990) ★★★. As the Singing Kettle: *Singing Kettle 1* (Kettle 1981) ★★★, *Singing Kettle 2* (Kettle 1984) ★★★, *Scotch Broth* (Kettle 1987) ★★★, *Singing Kettle 3* (Kettle 1988) ★★★, *Singing Kettle 4* (Kettle 1990) ★★, *The Big Green Planet* (Kettle 1991) ★★★.

Fisher, Doris

(see **Fisher, Fred**)

Fisher, Eddie

b. Edwin Jack Fisher, 10 August 1928, Philadelphia, Pennsylvania, USA. Fisher was a 'bobby sox idol', one of the most popular US singers of the 50s, with a strong, melodic voice. He sang with the bands of **Buddy Morrow** and **Charlie Ventura** at the age of 18, and his nickname was 'Sonny Boy' because of his affection for **Al Jolson** songs. In 1949 he gained nationwide exposure on **Eddie Cantor**'s radio show. Signed to **RCA-Victor Records** and accompanied by Hugo Winterhalter, Fisher had a string of US Top 10 hits through to 1956, including 'Thinking Of You', 'A Man Chases A Girl (Until She Catches Him)', 'Turn Back The Hands Of Time', 'Tell Me Why', 'I'm Yours', 'Maybe'/'Watermelon Weather' (duets with **Perry Como**), 'Wish You Were Here' (number 1), 'Lady Of Spain', 'I'm Walking Behind You' (number 1), 'Oh My Pa-Pa' (number 1), 'I Need You Now' (number 1), 'Count Your Blessings', 'Heart', 'Dungaree Doll' and 'Cindy, Oh Cindy'. Five of those won gold discs. He also made the US Top 40 album charts in 1955 with *I Love You*. His career was interrupted from 1952–53 when he served in the US Armed Forces Special Services and spent some time in Korea. After his discharge he became immensely popular singing in top nightclubs and on his own television series, *Coke Time* and *The Chesterfield Supper Club*, with George Gobel. In 1956 he costarred with his first wife, **Debbie Reynolds**, in the film musical *Bundle Of Joy*, and he had a straight role in *Butterfield 8* (1960), in which his second wife, Elizabeth Taylor, won an Academy Award for Best Actress. During the 60s, beset by drug and financial problems, he switched record labels and recorded *Eddie Fisher At The Winter Garden* for his own Ramrod Records and *Eddie Fisher Today!* for **Dot Records**. He returned to RCA and had a minor singles hit in 1966 with 'Games That Lovers Play', which became the title of a bestselling album. His last album for RCA was a Jolson tribute, *You Ain't Heard Nothing Yet*. During the late 60s he married and divorced actress **Connie Stevens** and in the 70s attempted several unsuccessful comebacks. In 1990, following extended periods of treatment at the Betty Ford Centre, Fisher announced that he was finally cured of his drug problems and intended to resume work. His daughter by Debbie Reynolds, actress Carrie Fisher, appeared in the hit movies *Star Wars*, *The Empire Strikes Back*, *Return Of The Jedi* and *When Harry Met Sally*.

● ALBUMS: *Fisher Sings* 10-inch album (RCA-Victor 1952) ★★★, *I'm In The Mood For Love* (RCA-Victor 1952/55) ★★★, *Christmas With Fisher* 10-inch album (RCA-Victor 1952) ★★, *Irving Berlin Favorites* 10-inch album (RCA-Victor 1954) ★★★, *May I Sing To You?* (RCA-Victor 1954/5) ★★★, *I Love You* (RCA-Victor 1955) ★★★, *Academy Award Winners* (RCA-Victor 1955) ★★★★, *Bundle Of Joy* film soundtrack (RCA-Victor 1956) ★★, *Thinking Of You* (RCA-Victor 1957) ★★★, *As Long As There's Music* (RCA-Victor 1958) ★★★, *Scent Of Mystery* film soundtrack (Ramrod 1960) ★★, *Eddie Fisher At The Winter Garden* (Ramrod 1963) ★★, *Eddie Fisher Today!* (Dot 1965) ★★, *When I Was Young* (RCA 1965) ★★, *Games That Lovers Play* (RCA 1966) ★★, *People Like You* (RCA 1967) ★★, *You Ain't Heard Nothing Yet* (RCA 1968) ★★.

● COMPILATIONS: *The Best Of Eddie Fisher* 10-inch album (RCA-Victor 1954) ★★★, *Eddie Fisher's Greatest Hits* (RCA-Victor 1962) ★★★, *His Greatest Hits* (RCA 1965) ★★★, *The Very Best Of Eddie Fisher* (MCA 1988) ★★★.

● DVD/VIDEOS: *A Singing Legend* (1994).

● FURTHER READING: *The Eddie Fisher Story*, Myrna Greene. *My Life, My Loves*, Eddie Fisher. *Been There, Done That*, Eddie Fisher with David Fisher.

● FILMS: *All About Eve* (1950), *Bundle Of Joy* (1956), *Butterfield 8* (1960).

Fisher, Fred

b. 30 September 1875, Cologne, Germany, d. 14 January 1942. After an adventurous early life, which he happily elaborated upon in later years, Fisher emigrated to the USA in 1900. (His entry in **ASCAP**'s directory, presumably self-originated, indicates that his parents were American.) He settled in Chicago, a city he would eventually immortalize in one of his best-known compositions. Soon after his arrival in Chicago he learned to play the piano, and his first published songs appeared in 1904. Sometimes writing the music, sometimes lyrics, he brought a foreigner's ear to the minutiae of American life, and his early songs reflect this awareness. In 1912 he had his first major success with 'Peg O' My Heart' (lyrics by Alfred Bryan), which was written for the Broadway show of the same name. He continued to write briefly

popular songs but shortly after World War I achieved another lasting success with 'Dardanella' (music by Johnny S. Black or Felix Bernard). The first recording of this song, by **Ben Selvin**, sold a million copies. In 1922 Fisher wrote words and music for another hugely successful song that became a paean of praise for his adopted city, 'Chicago (That Toddlin' Town)'. Soon afterwards he moved to Los Angeles to work in films, writing theme music for silent movies, and was thus in the right place to become involved in early talkies. **Fanny Brice** sang 'I'd Rather Be Blue Over You (Than Be Happy With Somebody Else)' (lyrics by **Billy Rose**) in *My Man* (1928), and he was cocomposer of several other songs featured in early screen musicals. In 1936 he wrote 'Your Feet's Too Big' (lyrics by Ada Benson), which was recorded by **Fats Waller**, and in 1940 penned 'Whispering Grass' (music by Doris Fisher, his daughter), a record success for the **Ink Spots**. By the end of the 30s Fisher was seriously ill, and he ended his own life in January 1942. In 1949, 20th Century Fox released a film biography entitled *Oh, You Beautiful Doll*, with S.Z. Sakall in the role of Fisher. Doris Fisher (b. 2 May 1915, New York City, USA, d. 15 January 2003, Los Angeles, California, USA) wrote songs for several films, often in partnership with Allan Roberts, and also sang with **Eddie Duchin**. Apart from the songs listed above on which she collaborated with her father, she also cocomposed 'You Always Hurt The One You Love', 'Into Each Life Some Rain Must Fall', 'That Ole Devil Called Love', 'Tampico' and 'Put The Blame On Mame'. Fisher's sons Marvin and Dan have also written songs. Marvin Fisher (b. 26 September 1916, New York City, USA, d. 21 August 1993) studied at Juilliard and then played piano with the Justin Stone Orchestra. After arranging for **Tommy** and **Jimmy Dorsey**, **Glenn Miller**, **Johnny Green** and others, in the 40s he began composing and, on his father's death, took over control of Fred Fisher Music with his brother Dan. His best known songs are probably 'Destination Moon' (with Roy Alfred), which was taken up by **Nat 'King' Cole**, and 'When Sunny Gets Blue' (with Jack Segal), one of the first numbers to be recorded by **Johnny Mathis**. Fisher later formed Marvin Music to publish his own songs and those of composers.

Fisher, Mark

b. 3 December 1959, Manchester, England. Keyboard player Fisher is the son of Tony Fisher, a professional trumpet player who, in addition to working with the **Beatles** on *Sgt. Pepper's Lonely Hearts Club Band*, has also collaborated with **Frank Sinatra**, **Oscar Peterson** and **Sarah Vaughan**. Mark studied the piano from the age of seven, joining his first band, Magnet Records' recording artists Alibi, in 1978. By 1982 he had become a member of Second Image, a British soul/funk group signed to **Polydor Records** and then MCA Records who enjoyed several soul/club crossover hits including 'Special Lady', 'Don't You' and 'Starting Again'. When the Brit Funk revival dissipated, Fisher moved to a keyboard slot on **Womack And Womack**'s debut tour and on **Wham!**'s 1985/86 world tour. His debut solo single arrived in 1985 and featured Dotty Green on vocals. 'Love Situation', released on Total Control/**EMI Records**, managed a modest (number 52) UK chart placing. He returned to session work later in the year with employment offered by **Sister Sledge** and **Matt Bianco** among others. He then became, in tandem with founder member Mark Reilly, a full-time member of the latter band, helping to write and coproduce *Matt Bianco*,

Indigo and *Samba In Your Casa*. Other production credits, meanwhile, included sessions with Workshy and a female singer, Maribeth Pascua, destined for the Indo-Asian market. He has also written library music for television and radio use.

Fisher, Marvin

(see **Fisher, Fred**)

Fisher, Miss Toni

b. *c.*1929, Los Angeles, California, USA, d. February 1999. Miss Toni Fisher is best remembered for her one US Top 10 hit, 'The Big Hurt', which reached number 3 in November 1959, but little is known of her background. She was a torch singer who recorded the Wayne Shanklin–penned hit for the small Signet label, backed by **Heine Beau** And His Orchestra. The single featured a 'phasing' effect that would become popular on psychedelic recordings nearly a decade later, and Fisher's album, named after the hit single, was notable in that it was an early stereo recording. Fisher had two more chart singles, a remake of **Irving Berlin**'s 'How Deep Is The Ocean' and 'West Of The Wall', the latter a reference to the Berlin Wall, a newsworthy topic when the song was issued in 1962 on Big Top Records. Fisher went on to record for **Columbia Records**, **Capitol Records** and **Smash Records** in the 60s and then disappeared from the music scene.
● ALBUMS: *The Big Hurt* (Signet 1959) ★★★.

Fisher, Morgan

b. 1 January 1950, London, England. The career of this eccentric UK musician has embraced musical styles as diverse as 60s Britpop, glam rock, new wave and ambient. Beginning his apprenticeship with archetypal 60s UK pop band the **Love Affair**, Fisher branched out on his own at the start of the 70s with his own rock band Morgan. Joining glam rockers **Mott The Hoople** as a pianist in 1973, initially only for live appearances, Fisher went on to form the abbreviated **Mott** in May 1975 with Dale Griffin and Overend Watts. They were completed by new members Ray Major and Nigel Benjamin, becoming the **British Lions** in May 1977 with John Fiddler (ex–**Medicine Head**) replacing Benjamin. After two albums British Lions split in the late 70s.

Fisher's next move was a bizarre one, forming his own independent label Pip Records and producing new wave and punk artists including the **Dead Kennedys**, **Cherry Vanilla** and **Jayne County**. He also produced two albums for **Cherry Red Records** as Hybrid Kids (*A Collection Of Classic Mutants* and *Claws*). The first of these was supposedly filled by unknown new wave acts doing cover versions but was actually Fisher and a few cronies. The tracks included Jah Wurzel's (**Jah Wobble** meets the **Wurzels**) 'Wuthering Heights', British Standard Unit's 'Do Ya Think I'm Sexy', the Burton's 'MacArthur Park' and a new version of Mott The Hoople's 'All The Young Dudes'. Another 'concept' album, *Miniatures*, featured various artists doing songs less than a minute long. Included among the 51 tracks were Dave Vanian (the **Damned**), **John Otway**, Andy Partridge (**XTC**), **Robert Wyatt**, **George Melly**, the **Residents** and David Cunningham. The album was later reissued on micro-cassette, presumably suitable solely for playing on dictaphones.

Fisher continued to record for Cherry Red throughout the 80s, later relocating to Japan, where he changed his name to Veetdharm and began recording minimalist ambient music,

most notably on 1992's *Re-Series* of albums. Fisher returned to the *Miniatures* concept in the mid-90s, recruiting artists such as **Robert Fripp**, **Michael Nyman**, **Hugh Cornwell**, the **Levellers**, **Ottmar Liebert** and Jane Campion.
● ALBUMS: with Lol Coxhill *Slow Music* (Pipe/Cherry Red 1980) ★★★, *Miniatures: A Sequence Of Fifty-One Masterpieces* (Pipe/Cherry Red 1980) ★★★, *Seasons* (Cherry Red 1983) ★★★, as Veetdharm Morgan Fisher *Look At Life* (Omagatoki/Shinseido 1984) ★★★, *Ivories* 1972 recording (Strike Back 1984) ★★, as Veetdharm *Water Music* (LLE/Cherry Red 1985) ★★★, as Veetdharm Morgan Fisher *Inside Satie* (Metrotron 1985) ★★★, *Flow Overflow* (Metrotron 1987) ★★★, *Life Under The Floor* film soundtrack (Kitty Enterprises 1987) ★★, *Peace In The Heart Of The City* (Kitty Enterprises 1988) ★★★, *Outer Beauty, Inner Beauty* cassette (Dawn Awakening 1989) ★★, *Echoes Of Lennon* (Kitty Enterprises/Global Pacific 1990) ★★★, *Re-Lax* (Prem Promotions 1992) ★★★, *Re-Fresh* (Prem Promotions 1992) ★★★, *Re-Charge* (Prem Promotions 1992) ★★★, *Rebalance* (Prem Promotions 1994) ★★★, *Refresh* new version (Prem Promotions 1995) ★★★, *Relax* new version (Prem Promotions 1995) ★★★, *Recharge* new version (Prem Promotions 1995) ★★★, *Miniatures 2* (Cherry Red 1995) ★★★, *Flower Music* (Prem Promotions 1998) ★★★, *Remix: We Are In Jump Time* (Prem Promotions 1999) ★★.
● COMPILATIONS: *Echoes Of A City Life* (Kitty Enterprises 1998) ★★★.
● CD-ROMS: *Cats In The Sun* (Isle/Synforest 1995), *The Skies Of Biei (Sora To Kumo No Stage)* (Kinyosha 1998).
● DVD/VIDEOS: with Tadayoshi Arai *Translucence* (Kitty Enterprises 1990).

Fisher, Shug

b. George Clinton Fisher, 26 September 1907, Spring Creek, near Chickasha, Grady County, Oklahoma, USA, d. 16 March 1984. Later a member of the **Sons Of The Pioneers**, by the age of 16, Fisher was playing the fiddle and had also developed a natural talent for comedy. He moved to California, where he made a living at various jobs, including fruit picking and labouring in oil fields. He played fiddle at local dances and made his radio debut on KMS Fresno in 1927. In 1931 he worked with the Hollywood Hillbillies, where he first played bass fiddle, and the following year he became a member of the **Beverly Hillbillies**. In the mid-30s he worked with **Stuart Hamblem** and Roy Faulkner before linking up with **Hugh Cross**. They played together in West Wheeling for almost four years before moving to WLW Cincinnati to host their popular *Hugh And Shugs's Radio Pals*. In 1941 Fisher returned to Los Angeles to undertake defence work and entertained locally. Late in 1943 he became a member of the Sons Of The Pioneers when their comedian and bass player **Pat Brady** was drafted. He remained a member until Brady returned in 1946 but rejoined in 1949, when Brady left for film and television work with **Roy Rogers**. He remained a Pioneer until 1953, when he joined **Ken Curtis** to work in films and on radio and television. In 1955, when Deuce Spriggens left the Pioneers, he was persuaded to return and stayed with the group until 1959 when he retired, stating it was time he 'kinda took it easy and did a lot of hunting and fishing'. However, this was soon postponed when, until 1961, he became a regular on **Red Foley**'s *The Ozark Jubilee* at Springfield, Missouri. With retirement still on hold, he returned to Hollywood, where he played many film and television character parts, including a regular role in *Ripcord* with Ken Curtis, 19 episodes of *Beverly Hillbillies* and several roles in *Gunsmoke*. Deteriorating health finally forced him into retirement, and after a long illness, with old friend Ken Curtis at his side, Fisher died on 16 March 1984.

Fisk Jubilee Singers

Until the emergence of the Fisk Jubilee Singers, African-American church music was rarely if ever heard outside churches or the homes of black Americans. On 6 October 1871 a group of students at Fisk University, six female, five male, accompanied by a pianist, Ella Shepherd, and two university officials, a Miss Wells and George L. White, left Nashville, Tennessee, at the start of a fund-raising tour. The idea was White's, who, as treasurer of the university, was desperately seeking ways to ensure the continuation of Fisk, one of few educational establishments open to blacks. The tour was scheduled to last some weeks, possibly a few months. In fact, it was seven years before the group returned home! During this time the Singers appeared at many venues in the USA, including the World Peace Jubilee in Boston, Massachusetts, and then embarked on a visit to Europe where they sang for heads of state and royalty. In London, England, they performed for Queen Victoria, who was so impressed that she commissioned a portrait of the group. The tour raised $150,000, a huge sum for those days and enough to build the Jubilee Hall at Fisk. The impact made by the Jubilee Singers on the world of music was enormous, although, as Viv Broughton has pointed out in his study of gospel music, *Black Gospel*, almost from the outset they adapted their style to accommodate the needs and expectations of their largely white audience. For all of their enormous courage and success, these pioneers of gospel music were offering a diluted form of the real music sung in churches by African Americans, newly risen from slavery. 'Swing Low, Sweet Chariot', one of the early spirituals to achieve popular acceptance, is believed to have originated through a tale told to the Singers' first pianist, Shepherd, by her mother, a slave, who was separated from her daughter by the actions of her master.
● FURTHER READING: *Dark Midnight When I Rise: The Story Of The Fisk Jubilee Singers*, Andrew Ward.

Fisk, Charlie

After graduating from the University Of Missouri, Charlie Fisk formed his first dance band in the early 40s in America's Midwest. Led by his own trumpet playing, located in the classic **Harry James** mould, the band was also lent a distinctive edge by the vocals of his wife, Ginny Coon (the daughter of Carleton Coon of the **Coon-Sanders Nighthawks**). With their professional engagements overseen by the MCA organisation, they found regular bookings at the Tunetown Ballroom (St. Louis), the Pla-Mor (Kansas City), the River-view Park (Des Moines), the Pleasure Pier (Port Arthur, Texas), the New Casino (Fort Worth), the Indiana Roof (Indianapolis) and the Nu-Elm Ballroom (Youngstown, Ohio). Despite strong reviews in *Billboard* magazine and enthusiastic Midwest audiences, Fisk was never able to translate local popularity into national celebrity. Despite this and a dearth of recording opportunities, his band continued touring well into the 50s.

Fist (Canada)

This Canadian heavy rock quartet was formed in 1978 by vocalist/guitarist Ron Chenier. After several false starts and numerous line-up changes, the band stabilized with Chenier plus Laurie Curry (keyboards), Bob Moffat (bass) and Bob Patterson (drums). Influenced by **Triumph**, **Rush** and **Led Zeppelin**, they released five albums of generally average hard rock between 1979 and 1985, with *In The Red* from 1983 being undoubtedly the strongest. This featured the highly talented Dave McDonald on lead vocals instead of Chenier, who lacked both range and power. In order to prevent confusion with the British band **Fist**, their albums were released under the name Myofist in Europe.
● ALBUMS: *Round One* (TCD 1979) ★★★, *Hot Spikes* (A&M 1980) ★★★, *Thunder In Rock* (A&M 1982) ★★, *In The Red* (A&M 1983) ★★★★, *Danger Zone* (A&M 1985) ★★★.

Fist (UK)

Formed as Axe in Newcastle-upon-Tyne, England, in 1978, changing their name at the beginning of the following year, the band's original line-up consisted of Keith Satchfield (vocals/guitar), Dave Irwin (guitar), John Wylie (bass) and Harry Hill (drums). They released a couple of mediocre singles via Neat Records in 1979. However, recognizing potential, MCA Records signed the band and released their debut album, *Turn The Hell On*, in 1980. This was a lacklustre affair of standard hard rock and was largely overlooked by both press and public. Fist were subsequently dropped by MCA, and a new line-up formed around founder members Hill and Irwin. They recruited Glenn Coates (vocals), John Roach (guitar; ex-**Mythra**) and Canadian bass player Norman Appelby and re-signed to Neat Records. They released their second album, *Back With A Vengeance*, in 1982. Even though this was an improvement on their previous release, it still failed to attract any real interest, and Fist's end was in sight.
● ALBUMS: *Turn The Hell On* (MCA 1980) ★★, *Back With A Vengeance: The Anthology* (Neat 1982) ★★★.

Fitzgerald, Ella

b. Ella Jane Fitzgerald, 25 April 1917, Newport News, Virginia, USA, d. 15 June 1996, Beverly Hills, California, USA. Following the disappearance of her father, Fitzgerald was taken to Yonkers, New York, by her mother and her new man Joseph da Silva. At school she sang with a glee club and showed early promise but preferred dancing to singing. Even so, chronic shyness militated against her chances of succeeding as an entertainer. Nevertheless, she entered a talent contest at the famous **Apollo** Theatre in Harlem as a dancer, but owing to last-minute nerves, after discovering that the Edwards Sisters (a popular dance act) were also on the bill, she was unable to dance and decided to sing. Her unexpected success winning this talent night prompted her to enter other talent contests, and she began to win frequently enough to persevere with her singing. Eventually, she reached the top end of the talent show circuit, singing at the Harlem Opera House where she was heard by several influential people. In later years many claimed to have 'discovered' her, but among those most likely to have been involved in trying to establish her as a professional singer with the **Fletcher Henderson** band were **Benny Carter** and

Charles Linton. They were probably the house band at the Apollo the night she won.

Fitzgerald continued her round of the talent shows. Now effectively homeless and lacking in personal hygiene, she was not a pretty sight. Fortunately she was heard by Linton, who sang with the **Chick Webb** band at the Savoy Ballroom, also in Harlem. Webb took her on, at first paying her out of his own pocket, and for the fringe audience she quickly became the band's main attraction. Even at the age of 17 she showed a remarkable professionalism and ability to learn quickly; even on her debut recording with Webb ('Love And Kisses') in 1935, she demonstrated confidence that belied her experience and age. She recorded extensively with Webb, with a small group led by **Teddy Wilson**, with the **Ink Spots**, and with others. Her hits with Webb included 'Sing Me A Swing Song', 'Oh, Yes, Take Another Guess', 'The Dipsy Doodle', 'If Dreams Come True', 'A-Tisket, A-Tasket' (a song on which she collaborated on the lyric and was her first number 1 in 1938), 'F.D.R. Jones', 'Wacky Dust', 'I Found My Yellow Basket' and 'Undecided'. She also briefly recorded with **Benny Goodman** in 1936, but the records were quickly withdrawn due to legal problems. The three collector's items were 'Did You Mean It?', 'Take Another Guess' and 'Goodnight My Love'. After a period of moonlighting Fitzgerald returned to Webb and recorded 'Big Boy Blue' and 'Dedicated To You' with the **Mills Brothers**. Between 1937 and 1939 Webb's popularity was considerable, and Fitzgerald proportionately received considerable attention. As early as 1937 she was voted best female vocalist in the UK's *Melody Maker*.

After Webb's death in June 1939 Fitzgerald became the nominal leader of the band, a position she retained until 1942. Bill Beason took over on drums, and Webb's name disappeared in favour of Fitzgerald's. She had already gained a reputation as a tough and uncompromising artist, but while her popularity was high her musical credibility began to sour. The band was not discriminating between jazz and trite novelty songs; Fitzgerald would sing them all. She married Benjamin Kornegay in 1941, but the marriage was annuled six months later. Kornegay had a criminal record and appeared to have married her under false pretences. After Eddie Barefield took over the band, Fitzgerald departed and then began her solo career, recording numerous popular songs, sometimes teaming up with other artists, notably the Three Keys. Although she was signed to **Decca Records**, her popularity began to slip. It was not until 'Cow Cow Boogie ' in 1944 that she had another hit record. Her new A&R man at Decca was **Milt Gabler**, and although often overlooked, he should take much of the credit for resurrecting her flagging career at this time. Important songs such as her major scat number 'Flying Home' backed with the superb 'Lady Be Good', a duet with **Louis Jordan**, 'Stone Cold Dead In The Market' and a further duet with **Louis Armstrong**, 'You Won't Be Satisfied' backed with 'Frim Fram Sauce', helped to raise her profile with the public.

In 1947 Fitzgerald married the master bass player **Ray Brown**. In 1949 she began a long professional association with **Norman Granz**. He became a Svengali figure in her life, initially as booker for his JATP (**Jazz At The Philharmonic**) concerts, he went on to become her manager and A&R director. It was Granz's masterly and astute control of her career that helped to establish Fitzgerald as one of the world's leading vocalists. She was certainly the most popular jazz singer with non-jazz

audiences and through judicious choice of repertoire became the foremost female interpreter of the Great American Popular Song Book. With Granz she worked on the 'songbook' series, placing on record definitive performances of the work of America's leading songwriters, and she also toured extensively for many years as part of his Jazz At The Philharmonic package. She divorced Brown in 1953 (although they remained close professionally throughout her life). That same year her contract with Decca was up for renewal, and by late 1954 she had signed with Granz's new record label **Verve Records**. Gabler was sorry to lose her, but she did leave one last great album for Decca, *Ella Sings In A Mellow Mood*. This was recorded with only **Ellis Larkins**, and it remains one of her finest recordings. It was, however, a string of superlative albums for Verve for which Fitzgerald will be remembered (very much like **Frank Sinatra**'s golden age at **Capitol Records**). In addition to the magnificent songbook series she recorded excellent albums with **Duke Ellington**, **Count Basie**, **Nelson Riddle** and Frank DeVol. Her albums with Louis Armstrong are also gems. Other highlights during the 50s were her live recordings (some were not issued until Phil Schaap discovered the tapes rotting in the vaults). Granz eventually got bored with Verve and sold it to **MGM Records**. He relocated to Europe and signed Ella to his new label Pablo. She recorded many albums on Pablo from 1973 onwards, notably her duet work with **Joe Pass** and further quality recordings with Basie.

Fitzgerald had a wide vocal range, but her voice retained a youthful, light vibrancy throughout the greater part of her career, bringing a fresh and appealing quality to most of her material, especially 'scat' singing. However, it proved less suited to the blues, a genre that, for the most part, she wisely avoided. Indeed, in her early work the most apparent musical influence was **Connee Boswell**. As a jazz singer, Fitzgerald performed with elegantly swinging virtuosity, and her work with accompanists such as Brown (they had an adopted son, Ray Brown Jnr., a drummer), Pass, **Oscar Peterson** and **Tommy Flanagan** was always immaculately conceived. However, her recordings with Armstrong reveal the marked difference between Fitzgerald's approach and that of a singer for whom the material is secondary to his or her own improvisational skills.

For all the enviably high quality of her jazz work, it is as a singer of superior popular songs that Fitzgerald remains most important and influential. Her respect for her material, beautifully displayed in the 'songbook' series, helped her to establish and retain her place as the finest vocalist in her chosen area of music. Due largely to deteriorating health, by the mid-80s Fitzgerald's career was at a virtual standstill, although a 1990 appearance in the UK was well received by an ecstatic audience. In April 1994 it was reported that both her legs had been amputated because of complications caused by diabetes. She lived a reclusive existence at her Beverly Hills home until her death in 1996.

Fitzgerald's most obvious counterpart among male singers was Frank Sinatra (they were the greatest interpreters of the American songbook), and with both singers now dead, questions inevitably arise about the fate of the great popular songs of the 30s and 40s. While there are still numerous excellent interpreters in the 90s and beyond (**Diana Krall** and **Jane Monheit**) and many whose work has been strongly influenced by Fitzgerald, the social and artistic conditions that helped to create America's First Lady of Song no longer exist, and it is highly unlikely therefore that we shall ever see or hear her like again. No record collection (even a basic one) should be without Ella Fitzgerald.

● ALBUMS: *Souvenir Album* 10-inch album (Decca 1950) ★★★, with Ellis Larkins *Sings Gershwin Songs* 10-inch album (Decca 1950) ★★★★, with Larkins *Songs In A Mellow Mood* (Decca 1954) ★★★★, *Lullabies Of Birdland* (Decca 1955) ★★★, *Songs From Pete Kelly's Blues* Soundtrack (Decca 1955) ★★, *Sweet And Hot* (Decca 1955) ★★★, *Sings The Cole Porter Songbook* (Verve 1956) ★★★★★, *Sings The Rodgers And Hart Songbook* (Verve 1956) ★★★★★, with Count Basie, Joe Williams *One O' Clock Jump* (Columbia 1956) ★★★, with Louis Armstrong *Ella And Louis* (Verve 1956) ★★★★★, with Armstrong *Porgy And Bess* (Verve 1956) ★★★★, with Armstrong *Ella And Louis Again* (Verve 1956) ★★★★, *Like Someone In Love* (Verve 1957) ★★★★★, *Sings The Duke Ellington Songbook* 4-LP box set (Verve 1957) ★★★★, *Sings The Gershwin Songbook* (Verve 1957) ★★★★, *Ella Sings Gershwin* (Decca 1957) ★★★★, *Ella And Her Fellas* (Decca 1957) ★★★, *At The Opera House* (Verve 1958) ★★★★, *Sings The Irving Berlin Songbook* (Verve 1958) ★★★★★, *First Lady Of Song* (Decca 1958) ★★, *Miss Ella Fitzgerald And Mr Gordon Jenkins Invite You To Listen And Relax* (Decca 1958) ★★★, *Miss Ella Fitzgerald And Mr Nelson Riddle Invite You To Listen And Relax* (Decca 1958) ★★★, *Ella Fitzgerald, Billie Holiday And Carmen McRae At Newport* (Verve 1958) ★★★, *For Sentimental Reasons* (Decca 1959) ★★★, *Sings The George And Ira Gershwin Songbook* 5-LP box set (Verve 1959) ★★★★★, *Ella Swings Lightly* (Verve 1959) ★★★★, *Ella Sings Sweet Songs For Swingers* (Verve 1959) ★★★, *Hello Love* (Verve 1959) ★★★, *Get Happy!* (Verve 1959) ★★★★, *Mack The Knife—Ella In Berlin* (Verve 1960) ★★★★, *Ella Wishes You A Swinging Christmas* (Verve 1960) ★★★★, *The Intimate Ella* aka *Let No Man Write My Epitaph* (Decca 1960) ★★★★, *Golden Favorites* (Decca 1961) ★★★, *Ella Returns To Berlin* (Verve 1961) ★★★★, *Sings The Harold Arlen Songbook* (Verve 1961) ★★★★, *Clap Hands, Here Comes Charlie!* (Verve 1962) ★★★★, *Ella Swings Brightly With Nelson* (Verve 1962) ★★★★, *Ella Swings Gently With Nelson* (Verve 1962) ★★★★, *Rhythm Is My Business* (Verve 1962) ★★★★, *Great Ballads By Ella Fitzgerald* (Decca 1962 ★★★), *Sings The Jerome Kern Songbook* (Verve 1963) ★★★★, *On The Sunny Side Of The Street* (Verve 1963) ★★★, *Ella Sings Broadway* (Verve 1963) ★★★, with Basie *Ella And Basie!* (Verve 1963) ★★★, *Ella At Juan-Les-Pins* (Verve 1964) ★★★★, *These Are The Blues* (Verve 1963) ★★★, *Hello, Dolly!* (Verve 1964) ★★, *Stairway To The Stars* (Decca 1964) ★★★, *Early Ella* (Decca 1964) ★★★, *A Tribute To Cole Porter* (Verve 1964) ★★★, *Sings The Johnny Mercer Songbook* (Verve 1965) ★★★★★, with Duke Ellington *Ella At Duke's Place* (Verve 1966) ★★★★, with Ellington *The Stockholm Concert* (1966) ★★★, with Ellington *Ella And Duke At The Côte D'Azure* (Verve 1966) ★★★★, *Ella In Hamburg* (Verve 1966) ★★★, *The World Of Ella Fitzgerald* (Metro 1966) ★★★, *Whisper Not* (Verve 1966) ★★★, *Brighten The Corner* (Capitol 1967) ★, *Smooth Sailing* (Decca 1967) ★★★, *Misty Blue* (Columbia 1968) ★★★, *Ella Fitzgerald's Christmas* (Capitol 1968) ★★, *Ella 'Live'* (Verve 1968) ★★★, *30 By Ella* (Columbia 1968) ★, *Sunshine Of Your Love/Watch What Happens* (Prestige 1969) ★★★, *Ella* (Reprise 1969) ★, *Things Ain't What They Used To Be* (Reprise 1970) ★, *Ella In Budapest* (Pablo 1970) ★★★, *Ella A Nice* (Pablo 1971) ★★★, *Ella Loves Cole* (Atlantic 1972) ★★, *At Carnegie Hall* (Columbia 1973) ★★★★, with Joe Pass *Take Love Easy* (Pablo 1973) ★★★★, *Ella In London* (Pablo 1974) ★★★, *Fine And Mellow* (Pablo 1974) ★★★, *Ella—At The Montreux Jazz Festival 1975* (Pablo 1975) ★★★, with Oscar Peterson *Ella And Oscar* (Pablo 1975) ★★★, with Pass *Fitzgerald And Pass . . . Again* (Pablo 1976) ★★★★, *With The Tommy Flanagan Trio* (Pablo 1977) ★★★, *Lady Time* (Pablo 1978) ★★★, *Dream Dancing* (Pablo 1978) ★★★, with Basie *A Classy Pair* (Pablo 1979) ★★★, with Basie *A Perfect Match: Basie And Ella* (Pablo 1979) ★★★★, *Ella Abraca Jobim (Sings The Antonio Carlos Jobim Songbook)* (Pablo 1981) ★★★, *The Best Is Yet To Come* (Pablo 1982) ★★★, with Pass *Speak Love* (Pablo 1982) ★★★, *Nice Work If You Can Get It* (Pablo 1983) ★★★, *Easy Living* (Pablo 1986) ★★, *Ella In Rome 1958* recording (Verve 1988) ★★★★, *All That Jazz* (Pablo 1990) ★★★, *A 75th Birthday Tribute* (Pablo 1993) ★★★.

● COMPILATIONS: *The Best Of Ella* (Decca 1958) ★★★, *The Best Of Ella Fitzgerald* (Verve 1964) ★★★★, *The Best Of Ella Fitzgerald Volume 2* (Verve 1969) ★★★★, shared with Billie Holiday, Lena Horne, Sarah Vaughan *Billie, Ella, Lena, Sarah!* (Columbia 1980) ★★★★★, *The Best Of Ella Fitzgerald* (Pablo 1988) ★★★★, *The Pablo Years* 20-CD box set (Pablo 1993) ★★★★, *Oh Lady Be Good! Best Of The Gershwin Songbook* (Verve 1995) ★★★★★, *Ella: The Legendary Decca Recordings* 4-CD box set (Decca 1995) ★★★, *Ella Fitzgerald: Priceless Jazz* (GRP 1997) ★★★, *The Complete Ella Fitzgerald & Louis Armstrong On Verve* 3-CD box set (Verve 1997) ★★★★★, *Unforgettable Ella* (Carlton 1998) ★★★, *Ultimate Ella Fitzgerald* (Verve 1998) ★★★★★, *Ella Fitzgerald And Duke Ellington Côte D'Azur Concerts* 8-CD box set (Verve 1998) ★★★★, *Something To Live For* (Verve 1999) ★★★★, *The Last Decca Years: 1949–1954* (GRP 1999) ★★★, with Joe Pass *Sophisticated Lady* (Pablo 2001) ★★★★, *Gold* (Verve 2003) ★★★★★, *Ella For Lovers* (Verve 2003) ★★★★, *Jukebox Ella: The Complete Singles Volume 1* (Verve 2004) ★★★★, *Love Songs* (UCJ 2005) ★★★★.

● DVD/VIDEOS: *Something To Live For* (Winstar 1999), *Live At Montreux 1969* (Eagle 2005).

● FURTHER READING: *Ella: The Life And Times Of Ella Fitzgerald*, Sid Colin. *Ella Fitzgerald: A Life Through Jazz*, Jim Haskins. *Jazz Singer Supreme*, Carolyn Wyman. *Ella Fitzgerald*, Stuart Nicholson. *First Lady Of Song*, Geoffrey Mark Fidelman.

● FILMS: *Pete Kelly's Blues* (1955), *St. Louis Blues* (1958), *Let No Man Write My Epitaph* (1960).

Fitzgerald, Patrik

b. 19 March 1956, London, England. Best known for 'Safety Pin In My Heart', a slightly crass but enduring snapshot of the late 70s new wave UK scene, punk poet Fitzgerald was lauded in some circles on his arrival as 'the new **Bob Dylan**', praise that was rather excessive, although his performances do deserve to be elevated above the status of 'also-ran' behind the greater impact made by **John Cooper Clarke**. 'Safety Pin' was included on his debut five-track EP for Small Wonder Records in 1977. Following two further singles, 'Backstreet Boys' and 'The Paranoid Ward', he signed to **Polydor Records** in 1979. His first single for the label, 'All Sewn Up', featured John Maher of the **Buzzcocks** on drums, who was also in place for the accompanying debut album *Grubby Stories*. The subsequent *Tonight* EP was recorded with Colin Peacock (keyboards) and Lester Broad (saxophone). However, Fitzgerald's popularity dissolved quickly, and by the 80s his studio work was received by a dwindling audience. 1986's *Tunisian Twist* was a brave attempt at commercial revival, before he faded from view. Taking a job as a waiter at the House of Commons, he then relocated to Normandy in France in 1988. However, he found himself disenchanted and unable to find gainful employment and so returned to England three years later. He started playing gigs again and also launched an acting career, the most high profile engagement of which was a version of Moliere's *The Miser* at Stratford. Two albums emerged in 1995, the first (*Pillow Tension*) with the Patrik Fitzgerald Group and the second (*Room Service*) recorded solo on acoustic guitar. Fitzgerald is now resident in New Zealand where he is employed as a social worker.

● ALBUMS: *Grubby Stories* (Small Wonder/Polydor 1979) ★★★, *Gifts And Telegrams* (Red Flame 1982) ★★, *Drifting Toward Violence* (Red Flame 1983) ★★, *Tunisian Twist* (Red Flame 1986) ★★★, *Pillow Tension* (Lazy Dog 1995) ★★, *Room Service* (Beat Bedsit 1995) ★★★.

● COMPILATIONS: *Treasures From The Wax Museum* (Red Flame 1993) ★★★, *Safety-Pin Stuck In My Heart: Patrik Fitzgerald . . . The Very Best Of* (Anagram 1994) ★★★, *All The Years Of Trying* (Label 2005) ★★★★.

● DVD/VIDEOS: *Boardwalk* (Ikon 1995).

Fitzroy, Edi

b. 17 November 1955, Clarendon, Jamaica, West Indies. Fitzroy, like many teenagers, followed the **sound systems**, in particular, a sound called Anchio One. After leaving school he started a career with the Jamaican Broadcasting Corporation working as an accounts clerk. With a colleague, in his spare time he would often sing over dubs and play them back using the radio station's equipment. In 1975 **Mikey Dread** was the station's top disc jockey, playing reggae on his *Dread At The Controls Show*, and he heard Fitzroy's demos. Fitzroy's first hit, 'Miss Molly Colly', broke into the Jamaican Top 10 as the result of Dread's patronage, and the follow-up, 'Country Man', confirmed him as Dread's protégé. The hits kept coming, including 'African Religion', 'Gun' and 'Stylee', leading to a tour of the UK with Dread in 1980 supporting punk group the **Clash**. On returning to Jamaica Fitzroy began working with other producers, firstly Lloyd Norris, with whom he recorded 'Bad Boy', a minor hit when released in 1981. With Trevor Elliot of Musical Ambassador he recorded an album and enjoyed a massive hit with 'Check For You Once', followed by 'Youth Man In Penitentiary' (when interviewed on the radio in Jamaica, he stated categorically that the song was not inspired by personal experience) and 'Have You Ever'. His success led to a performance at the 1984 Sunsplash Festival, and his commitment to equality for women led to an appearance at Zinc Fence in Kingston on International Women's Day. His commitment was evident in the hit 'Princess Black', and he was also dubbed Jamaica's most socially conscious singer. His follow-up, a reworking of 'The Gun', enjoyed a prolonged stay on the chart, breaking all previous records for longevity. In the series of charity records to help the starving in Ethiopia, Fitzroy performed on Jamaica's contribution, 'Land Of Africa'. He provided the vocals alongside **Gregory Isaacs**, **Freddie McGregor**, **Mutabaruka**, **Triston Palma**, **Bunny Rugs**, David Hinds and the **I-Threes**. The artists involved were determined to help to alleviate the situation and formed the Music Is Life organization to emphasize their commitment. However, the single alone was regarded by the collective as an insufficient gesture towards relieving Africa's dilemma. Fitzroy became a codirector alongside **Rita Marley**, **Judy Mowatt**, Michael 'Ibo' Cooper and Orville Tyson, and between them, they established other projects. His recordings and Music Is Life commitments were undertaken alongside his career at JBC.

● ALBUMS: *Check For You Once* (Alligator 1986) ★★★, *Eclipse* (RAS 1987), *Coming Up Strong* (Musical Ambassador 1988) ★★, *Pollution* (VP 1990) ★★★.

● COMPILATIONS: *First Class Citizen* (Musical Ambassador 2001) ★★★.

Five

This UK pop quintet enjoyed widespread success in the late 90s with their polished, hip-hop inspired sound. Ritchie Neville (b. Richard Dobson, 23 August 1979, Birmingham, West Midlands, England), Scott Robinson (b. 22 November 1979, Basildon, Essex, England), Richard Abidin Breen (b. 29 June 1979, Enfield, Middlesex, England), Jason 'J' Brown (b. 13 June 1976, Aldershot, England) and Sean Conlon (b. 20 May 1981, Leeds, England) were handpicked from 3,000 hopefuls at an audition set up by the creators of the **Spice Girls**. The five members all boasted stage and music backgrounds. Neville and Robinson were, respectively, graduates of the National Youth Theatre and the Sylvia Young Stage School. Breen had attended the distinguished Italia Conti Stage School and built up experience as a DJ. Brown also worked as a DJ, while Conlon was a previous winner of Yamaha's Young Composer Of The Year award. Following in the footsteps of the Spice Girls, the band lived together in Surrey (later featuring unflatteringly in the ITV documentary series *Neighbours From Hell*). Intensive promotional work boosted the band's profile and resulted in a string of Top 10 UK hits. The debut single 'Slam Dunk (Da Funk)' reached number 7 in December 1997 and was followed by 'When The Lights Go Out' (number 4, March 1998), 'Got The Feelin'' (number 3, June 1998), 'Everybody Get Up' (number 2, September 1998) and 'Until The Time Is Through' (number 2, November 1998). 'When The Lights Go Out' broke the band in the US, steadily climbing the *Billboard* chart before reaching a peak position of number 10 in August 1998. The follow-up, 'It's The Things You Do', failed to reach the American Top 50. The band's self-titled debut album was co-written and produced by **Denniz Pop**, Cutfather and Joe and **Max Martin** and debuted at number 1 on the UK chart in June. It also broke into the US Top 30 the following year. They returned to the UK charts in July 1999 with the number 2 single 'If Ya Gettin' Down' and finally achieved the top slot in October with the irresistible 'Keep On Movin''. The attendant *Invincible* was another mixed bag of surprisingly durable pop songs and weak ballads. The following July they topped the UK singles chart with an energetic cover version of **Queen**'s 'We Will Rock You'. Their third album was premiered by August 2001's chart-topping single, 'Let's Dance', but shortly afterwards the quintet announced they were splitting up.

● ALBUMS: *Five* (RCA/Arista 1998) ★★★, *Invincible* (RCA 1999) ★★★, *Kingsize* (RCA 2001) ★★★.

● COMPILATIONS: *Greatest Hits* (RCA 2001) ★★★.

● DVD/VIDEOS: *Five Inside* (BMG Video 1998).
● FURTHER READING: *5 Versus The Rest Of The World*, Jane Preston. *Five On The Road*, Teresa Maughan. *Five: The Official Book*, Kate Thornton and Jane Preston.

Five Americans

The Five Americans are best recalled for their 1967 US Top 10 single 'Western Union'. The band formed at South Eastern State University in Durant, Oklahoma, USA, in the early 60s. They comprised Mike Rabon (vocals/guitar), Norman Ezell (guitar), John Durrill (keyboards), Jim Grant (b. James Grant, 29 July 1943, Hugo, Oklahoma, USA, d. 29 November 2004, Dallas, Texas, USA; bass) and Jimmy Wright (drums). They evolved out of an instrumental band called the Mutineers but decided to add vocals after hearing the **Beatles**. They moved to Dallas, Texas, in 1964 and began building a following at the clubs there. They first recorded in September 1964 for the Jetstar label. Further efforts did not see any action until their single 'I See The Light', originally recorded for Abnak, was picked up by HBR Records and made number 26. After one further single for that label, they had their biggest hit in 1967 with 'Western Union'. This was one of three singles of theirs that was produced by **Dale Hawkins** of 'Suzie-Q' fame. The band fragmented in 1968 and by the following year Rabon was the only original member left. The Five Americans broke up in 1969.
● ALBUMS: *I See The Light* (HBR 1966) ★★★, *Western Union/Sound Of Love* (Abnak 1967) ★★★, *Progressions* (Abnak 1967) ★★, as Michael Rabon & The Five Americans *Now And Then* (Abnak 1969) ★★★.
● COMPILATIONS: *Western Union* (Sundazed 1989) ★★★, *The Best Of The Five Americans* (Sundazed 2002) ★★★.

Five Blind Boys Of Alabama

Not to be confused with their arch rivals, the **Five Blind Boys Of Mississippi**, this gospel group can boast of similar longevity. The original line-up of the group featured George Scott (b. 18 March 1929, Notasulga, Alabama, USA, d. 9 March 2005, Durham, North Carolina, USA), John Fields, Olice Thomas, Velma Bozman Traylor, J.T. Hutton and Clarence Fountain, a singer whose booming voice has become something of a legend in gospel circles. All, with the exception of Hutton, were blind. They formed at the Talladega Institute For The Deaf And Blind, 30 miles from Birmingham, Alabama, in 1937, where the members were taught piano in Braille. Otherwise the group members had plenty of time on their hands and would 'just get to singing' whenever they could. Sneaking out of the school grounds, they entertained nearby soldier encampments, based there during World War II, for pocket money. Although their (white) teachers refused to countenance gospel singing, they still heard it all around them via a radio show on Birmingham's WSGN station—their early influences being the **Golden Gate Quartet**, the **Heavenly Gospel Singers** and the **Soul Stirrers**.
The first name the group chose for themselves was the Happy Land Jubilee Singers, at which time they were led by Traylor, who died as a result of an accident in 1947 when the group were playing with a gun (it was later erroneously reported that he had died in a traffic accident). The group changed their name in 1948, due to the success of the Five Blind Boys Of Mississippi. However, the blatancy of that tactic proved more troublesome than any benefit they accrued from it, and though the groups toured together and regularly co-opted each other's singers, the rivalry never quite died down. The Alabama group co-opted the Reverend Paul Exkano of the King Solomon Baptist Church in New Orleans into the line-up. He was also a member of that city's Chosen Five Quartet and, ironically given his ministry, was taken on with the strict condition that the group paid his alimony. He was resident on the group's first recordings in 1948 for the Coleman label and their first national hit, 'I Can See Everybody's Mother But Mine', from 1949. After two years he left, to be replaced by former Mississippi Blind Boys Percell Perkins then Joe Watson. Jimmy Carter finally became a permanent fifth member in the early 80s (again after an apprenticeship with the Mississippi 5).
By the start of the 90s the Five Blind Boys Of Alabama had established a mighty reputation in the gospel world, especially through their recordings for **Art Rupe**'s **Specialty Records**, then **Vee Jay Records**, Savoy, **Elektra Records** and others. Fountain became both the voice and soul of the group, delivering highly emotive spirituals and never straying from the path, despite at least one big money offer to adapt to R&B as had **Sam Cooke** of the Soul Stirrers. He did leave the group in 1969 to pursue a solo career, however, but returned at the end of the following decade. He ascribes the group's longevity to clean living and clean consciences, while each member of the group is proficient enough to alternate parts if illness or occasion demands it.
In the early 90s the group, now led by Fountain, Scott and Carter, rechristened themselves the Blind Boys Of Alabama. In 1995 they became the first to be signed to the new House Of Blues gospel label, for whom they recorded *I Brought Him With Me*, their first live album. In the new millennium they continued to display remarkably few signs of fatigue, recording several excellent albums for the Real World label. In 2004 they toured Europe with singer-songwriter **Ben Harper**, later fashioning the studio album *There Will Be A Light* from a series of rehearsal tapes. The group had just completed a new studio album before Scott passed away in March 2005.
● ALBUMS: include *Oh Lord—Stand By Me* (Specialty 1954) ★★★★, *Marching Up To Zion* (Specialty 1957) ★★★★, *I'm A Soldier In The Army Of The Lord* (Peace International 1982) ★★★, *Deep River* (Elektra 1992) ★★★★, as the Blind Boys Of Alabama *I Brought Him With Me* (House Of Blues 1995) ★★★★, as the Blind Boys Of Alabama *Spirit Of The Century* (Real World 2001) ★★★★, as the Blind Boys Of Alabama *Higher Ground* (Real World 2002) ★★★, as the Blind Boys Of Alabama *Go Tell It On The Mountain* (Real World 2003) ★★★, with Ben Harper *There Will Be A Light* (Virgin 2004) ★★★★, with Harper *Live At The Apollo* (Real World 2005) ★★★★, as the Blind Boys Of Alabama *Atom Bomb* (Real World 2005) ★★★.
● COMPILATIONS: *The Five Blind Boys Of Alabama* (Gospel Heritage 1990) ★★★, *The Sermon* (Speciality 1990) ★★★★, *Hallelujah: A Collection Of Their Finest Recordings* (Music Club 1999) ★★★★.
● DVD/VIDEOS: *Go Tell It On The Mountain* (Eagle Rock 2004).

Five Blind Boys Of Mississippi

This vocal gospel group, consisting of Archie Brownlee (d. 1960), Joseph Ford, Lawrence Abrams (d. 1982) and Lloyd

Woodard, was formed in 1936 by blind students of the Piney Woods School, Jackson, Mississippi. They began singing together in their school grounds and called themselves the Cotton Blossom Singers. By the mid-40s the group had moved to New Orleans and had added Melvin Henderson as their second lead. He was in turn replaced by (the sighted) Percell Perkins, whereupon the band became the Five Blind Boys Of Mississippi. Ford left the group in 1948 and was replaced by J.T. Clinkscales (also blind). The group moved to Houston, Texas, in the 50s and signed to Peacock Records. 'Our Father' was their biggest hit and became a gospel classic. It also reached number 10 in the R&B chart. Dozens of 45s, and at least five albums emerged on Peacock during the 60s as the group toured constantly. Perkins left in order to devote himself to the ministry and became Reverend Perkins. His replacements included Reverend Sammy Lewis, Reverend George Warren and Tiny Powell. Brownlee died in New Orleans in 1960, and Roscoe Robinson took over as lead, and Willmer 'Little Ax' Broadnax joined as second lead. Woodard died in the mid-70s and Lawrence Abrams in 1982, but the Five Blind Boys continued to tour with new members. Original lead Brownlee is one of the pivotal influences in the development of black soul music in the 50s and 60s, with both **Ray Charles** and **James Brown** taking their cue from his strident vocal performances.
● ALBUMS: *Precious Memories* (Peacock 1960) ★★★★, *Father I Stretch My Hands To Thee* (Peacock 1964) ★★★★, *My Desire* (Peacock) ★★★★, *There's A God Somewhere* (Peacock) ★★★.
● COMPILATIONS: *Best Of The Five Blind Boys Of Mississippi Volume 1* (MCA) ★★★★, *Best Of The Five Blind Boys Of Mississippi Volume 2* (MCA) ★★★.

Five Boroughs

Founded in South Florida, USA, during 1986, this vocal quartet took their name from their origins further north, namely the boroughs of Queens, Brooklyn, Manhattan, Staten Island and the Bronx in New York. The group consisted of Frank Iovino (lead/baritone), Charlie Notabartolo (first tenor), Bruce Goldie (lead/first tenor), Dave Strum (bass) and Geno Radicello (lead/second tenor). An EP was released on Telemedia Records headed by 'Gloria', backed with a version of the **Valentines**' 'Don't Say Goodnight'. With bookings on the nostalgia circuit confirmed as a result, the group returned to the studio in 1987 for 'A Sunday Kind Of Love' before a version of the **Cleftones**' 'See You Next Year' the following year. Two more singles emerged in 1990, after signing with nostalgia label Classic Artists Records—'Apart', and a cover version of the **Flamingos**' 'A Kiss From Your Lips'.

Five Breezes

The group comprised Gene Gilmore, **Leonard 'Baby Doo' Caston**, **Willie Dixon**, Joseph Bell and Willie Hawthorne. When pianist/guitarist Caston arrived in Chicago in 1939, he met up with Arthur Dixon and Gilmore, who, like him, wanted to make records. They made a test recording for Mayo Williams of **Decca Records**, but it was fruitless. In the meantime, Dixon had introduced Caston to his brother Willie, a prize fighter with a good bass voice who also played an imitation string bass. They joined with Gilmore and singers Joseph Bell and Willie Hawthorne to form the Five Breezes, performing material that added a bluesier dimension to the **Ink Spots**

repertoire. Each assumed a name: Caston was 'Evening Breeze', Dixon 'Big Breeze', Gilmore 'Midnight Breeze', Bell, 'Cool Breeze' (a name he used on post-war records for Bell and Ebony) and Hawthorne 'Morning Breeze'. The group worked every night of the week at the Pink Poodle, a mob club from which they could not escape. Both Caston and Gilmore recorded for Decca in June 1940 and five months later the Five Breezes recorded an eight-title session for Bluebird. The band continued to be successful until America's entry into World War II, when each man went his own way. Gilmore and Dixon, along with guitarists Bernardo Dennis and Ellis Hunter, recorded two singles as the Four Jumps Of Jive for **Mercury Records** in late 1945, just before Caston, Dixon and Dennis formed the **Big Three Trio**.
● ALBUMS: *Gene Gilmore & The Five Breezes* (Blues Documents 1989) ★★★.

Five Chances

From Chicago, Illinois, USA, the Five Chances were one of the city's most successful vocal ensembles during the early 50s to sing in the mournful and bluesy 'deep' R&B style. The group started under the name Travelers during the dawn of the R&B group era in 1950. In 1954 the group joined the **Chance** label, and were renamed the Five Chances. The members on their only Chance record, 'I May Be Small', were Darnell Austell (lead), John Austell, Harold Jones, Howard Pitman and Reggie Smith. By the time the group was on **Al Benson**'s Blue Lake label, recording their best-known single, 'All I Want', the members were Darnell Austell (lead), Johnny Jones, Harold Jones, Smith and Pitman. In 1956 the group moved to the States label and had notable success with the Johnny Jones–led 'Gloria'. Several more singles followed before the group broke up in 1960. Johnny Jones went on to form the **Blenders**. Pitman became a record producer and was responsible for the **Ideals**' 'The Gorilla' (1963).

Five Crowns

The Five Crowns were formed at Wadleigh Junior High School in Harlem, New York, USA, in 1952. The group comprised Wilbur 'Yunkie' Paul (lead), brothers James 'Poppa' Clark, Claudie 'Nicky' Clark and John 'Sonny Boy' Clark (all tenor) and Doc Green Jnr. (d. 10 March 1989; bass/baritone). Their distinctive sound (not least because of the presence of four tenors) brought them to the attention of Rainbow Records in July 1952. They found instant success in October when 'You're My Inspiration' became a major regional R&B hit. However, they failed to follow up this breakthrough, with successive singles such as 'Who Can Be True', 'Why Don't You Believe Me' and 'Alone Again' faring poorly. Finding themselves in dispute with an evidently disappointed Rainbow Records, they moved to the Old Town label in July 1953. However, neither 'You Could Be My Love' nor 'Lullaby Of The Bells' revived fortunes. In the aftermath they returned to Rainbow on its subsidiary label Riviera Records. A creative renaissance was witnessed by the powerful 'You Came To Me', but this again failed to translate into commercial sales. The group disbanded later that year. Green then put together a new Five Crowns who released one single, 'God Bless You', for Gee Records. He was also the only original member remaining in the reshuffled line-up who released 'I Can't Pretend' for Transworld Records. Titled simply the Crowns by 1958, the formation that recorded 'Kiss And Make Up' was ironically closer to the original Five

Crowns, with James Clark rejoining, plus the presence of Benjamin Nelson (later known as **Ben E. King**), Ellsbury Hobbs and Charlie Thomas. This was the only record ever to be released on **Doc Pomus'** R&B Records label. Afterwards, they performed at the **Apollo** Theatre and so impressed George Treadwell that he immediately sacked the members of his band the **Drifters** and replaced them in a straight swap with the Crowns.

Five Discs

The Five Discs were one of several doo-wop groups (**Carollons**, **Chips**, etc.) to trace their origins to the Bedford-Stuyvesant district of Brooklyn, New York, USA. They were formed in 1954 by Joe Brocco (lead), Joe Barsalona (baritone), Paul Albano (first tenor) and Tony Basile (second tenor). Composed of Italian-descended young men and originally titled the Flames, they subsequently shuffled the pack by adding black singers Mario deAndrade and Andrew Jackson from the Love Notes. This produced a new line-up of deAndrade (lead), Jackson (bass), Albano (first tenor), Basile (second tenor) and Barsalona (baritone), though membership remained fluid over ensuing years. After recording demos at Bell Sound studios in New York the group started to offer these to interested parties. There were no takers until songwriter Billy Martin introduced them to the proprietors of the Emge Records label. They were still titled the Flames when they recorded deAndrade's song 'I Remember', but when it was released they had chosen a new name, the Five Discs. Despite achieving strong popularity in the local New York and Boston markets, the group felt dissatisfied with the label's promotion of the single and looked elsewhere. 'My Chinese Girl', released on Dwain Records in 1959, failed to improve their standing. Jackson and deAndrade then left and were replaced by Lenny Hutter of the Chalets on lead and John Russell on bass. 'Come On Baby' emerged to little fanfare in 1961, and Hutter left immediately, to be replaced by John Carbone. Calo Records took over the promotion of Carbone's debut on 'Adios', an old deAndrade song. However, the band moved on again, this time to Cher Records, with Russell replaced by Charlie DiBella. 'Never Let You Go' was the last single to feature Carbone, as Eddie Parducci of the Delvons took his place. It was their most successful project for some time but still failed to breach the national charts. As a result the group changed tack to become the Boyfriends, releasing a solitary single on Kapp Records titled 'Let's Fall In Love'. Numerous line-up changes ensued before the group became Dawn in 1968 (not of 'Tie A Yellow Ribbon Round The Ole Oak Tree' fame), their sole release under this guise being a cover version of **Sam Cooke**'s 'Bring It On Home To Me'. Ironically, the last Five Discs record would see them return to the Schwarz brothers and Laurie Records for 1972's 'Rock & Roll Revival', though throughout the 70s several archive singles were also released as interest in 50s doo-wop escalated. A typically *ad hoc* line-up reunited in 1991 for the Doo-wop Society Show.

Five Dutones

Formed in St. Louis, Missouri, USA, around 1957, by Robert Hopkins, Leroy Joyce, Willie Guest, Oscar Watson and James West. Originally a doo-wop group, the Five Dutones moved to Chicago in the early 60s. By that time Hopkins and Watson had been replaced by Frank McCurry and Andrew Butler, respectively. Their exhilarating single 'Shake A Tail

Feather' was released in 1963. Later revived by **James And Bobby Purify** and **Mitch Ryder**, this definitive early version was a US Top 30 R&B hit. James West died of a heart attack in 1963 and was replaced by David Scott. The Five Dutones recorded a total of nine singles, most of which were based on local dance crazes, but split in 1967. The group's backup musicians, the Exciters, became a minor charting band, the South Shore Commission, which featured as vocalists McCurry and Scott, both latter-day members of the Five Dutones. Scott later joined the **Chi-Lites** in the late 70s, while Leroy Joyce changed his name to Leroy Brown and worked with the **Eddy Clearwater Blues Band**.

● COMPILATIONS: *Shake A Tail Feather* (1979) ★★★.

Five For Fighting

The Los Angeles, California, USA–based outfit Five For Fighting (an alias used by multi-instrumentalist singer-songwriter John Ondrasik) has gained comparisons to artists such as **Elton John**, **Satchel** and **Ben Folds Five** owing to its penchant for specializing in gentle and introspective lovelorn compositions. Born and raised in the San Fernando Valley section of Los Angeles, Ondrasik began piano lessons at the age of two and picked up the guitar from his older sister just as he became a teenager. He put music on hold to attend UCLA, where he earned a bachelor's degree in applied mathematics. Shortly after graduating, Ondrasik had a change of heart and secured a recording contract with **Capitol Records** in the late 90s. Five For Fighting's tenure with the label only lasted for a single release, 1997's *Message For Albert*, before Capitol and Ondrasik parted company.

By 2000 Ondrasik had once again landed on his feet, signing a recording contract with Sony Records and issuing Five For Fighting's second effort, *America Town*. The album achieved platinum status, buoyed by the radio success of the track 'Superman (It's Not Easy)'.

● ALBUMS: *Message For Albert* (Capitol 1997) ★★★, *America Town* (Aware/Sony 2000) ★★★★, *The Battle For Everything* (Aware/Sony 2004) ★★★.

Five Guys Named Moe

This show was playing a limited five-week engagement in October 1990 at the tiny Theatre Royal, Stratford East, in London when it was spotted by superstar impresario **Cameron Mackintosh** who was so impressed that he negotiated contracts on the spot, enabling the production to transfer to the Lyric Theatre in Shaftesbury Avenue in December of that year. The show, which was conceived and written by Clarke Peters, is a tribute to the jazz-bluesman **Louis Jordan**, who is sometimes cited as the 'musical father' of **Chuck Berry** and **Bill Haley** and therefore, by implication, of rock 'n' roll itself. The story concerns a lovelorn central character, Nomax (Dig Wayne), drowning his sorrows in drink and listening to the blues on an old-fashioned radio. The apparatus explodes, and he is confronted by the five Moes—these sharp-suited, fast-talking characters from a Jordan song—which set about improving his attitude and putting him straight about women and love. The group consists of Big Moe (Kenny Andrews), Little Moe (Paul J. Medford), No Moe (Peter Alex Newton), Eat Moe (Omar Okai) and Four-Eyed Moe (Clarke Peters). Nexus' education is delivered via song and dance routines, in some of which he is allowed to participate. At times during the show the story is temporarily dispensed with, and the audience is invited onstage and led in a conga around the theatre and then through the exits during the interval. The 20 or so songs from the 40s and 50s, which were either written by Jordan or are indelibly associated with him, are delivered joyously with lots of verve and attack. They include 'Saturday Night Fish Fry', 'Ain't Nobody Here But Us Chickens', 'Is You Is Or Is You Ain't Ma Baby', 'What's The Use Of Getting Sober', 'Look Out Sister', 'Brother Beware', 'Caldonia', 'It Must Be Jelly ('Cause Jam Don't Shake Like That)' and 'Dad Gum Your Hide, Boy'. *Five Guys Named Moe* won the 1991 **Laurence Olivier Award** for best entertainment and settled in for a long run. It celebrated its 1,000th performance in June 1993, proclaiming 'The Joint Never Stops Jumpin''. In fact, the London production did stop 'jumpin'' for a time in 1995 (4 March) while the show switched to the Albery Theatre, where it stayed for a further eight months. *Five Guys Named Named Moe* had become the longest-running musical at the Lyric (overtaking *Irma La Douce*) the year before. A Broadway production opened in April 1992, with Frank Rich, the most important critic in New York who has never been enamoured of Cameron Mackintosh's productions, describing the show derisively as 'a British tourist's view of a patch of black American pop music history'. However, it survived that initial onslaught and remained at the Eugene O'Neill Theatre for over a year, a total of 445 performances. Successful international tours indicate that this show is going to 'party on' for a very long time.

Five Hand Reel

This Scottish electric folk rock group formed in 1975 and were often compared with the JSD Band. Five Hand Reel included **Dick Gaughan** (b. Richard Peter Gaughan, 17 May 1948, Glasgow, Scotland; vocals/guitar), Chuck Fleming (fiddle), who soon left to be replaced by Bobby Eaglesham (vocals, fiddle, guitar, bouzouki), Tom Hickland (keyboards, violin, vocals), Barry Lyons (multi-instrumentalist, ex-**Trees**; Mr. Fox) and Dave Tulloch (drums, French horn, harmonica, vocals). Their material encompassed Irish and Scottish traditional music, with original contributions from the band. Gaughan left to pursue a solo career and was replaced by Sam Bracken (vocals/guitar, ex-**Therapy**) in 1978. The excellent fiddle player Fleming, known for his own recordings as well as his work with performers such as **Johnny Handle**, joined Syncopace, the group formed by **Alistair Anderson** in 1991.
● ALBUMS: *Five Hand Reel* (1976) ★★★★, *For A' That* (1977) ★★, *Earl O' Moray* (1978) ★★, *Bunch Of Fives* (1979) ★★★, *Nothing But The Best* (1980) ★★★.

Five Keys

This US R&B vocal group helped shape the rhythm and blues revolution of the early 50s. The ensemble was formed as the Sentimental Four in Newport News, Virginia, USA, in the late 40s and originally consisted of two sets of brothers—Rudy West (b. 25 July 1932, Newport News, Virginia, USA) and Bernie West (b. 4 February 1930, Newport News, Virginia, USA) and Ripley Ingram (b. 1930, d. 23 March 1995, Newport News, Virginia, USA) and Raphael Ingram. After Raphael Ingram left and Maryland Pierce and Dickie Smith became members in 1949, the name of the group was changed to Five Keys. With Pierce doing the lead work, the Five Keys joined Los Angeles–based **Aladdin Records** in 1951, and the same year had a hit with a remake of the old standard 'Glory Of

Love', which became a US R&B number 1. Despite recording an appealing combination of old standards and R&B originals, further chart success on Aladdin eluded the Five Keys. In 1952 Rudy West went into the army and was replaced by Ulysses K. Hicks, and in 1954 Dickie Smith left and was replaced with Ramon Loper. This new line-up of Five Keys was signed to **Capitol Records**, which brought the group to stardom, albeit with some modification in their style from a deep rhythm and blues sound to a more pop vein with greater instrumentation in support. The group's first hit for Capitol was the novelty pop jump 'Ling, Ting, Tong' (US R&B number 5 and pop Top 30 in 1955). Following the first Capitol recording session, Rudy West rejoined the Five Keys in October 1954, replacing the ailing Hicks, who died a few months later. Further hits on Capitol included some spectacular R&B ballads: the **Chuck Willis**–composed 'Close Your Eyes' (R&B number 5, 1955), 'The Verdict' (R&B number 13, 1955) and 'Out Of Sight, Out Of Mind' (R&B number 12 and pop Top 30 in 1956). The Capitol material also featured old standards, such as a marvellous remake of the **Ink Spots**' 'The Gypsy' (1957). Rudy West retired in 1958. An unsuccessful period at King Records from 1958–61 produced more personnel changes and no hits and few songs that could compete with the new rock 'n' roll sounds. Periodic sessions were recorded by various reunion groups in subsequent years, but the basic legacy of the Five Keys rests in their Aladdin, **Capitol Records** and **King Records** sessions.
● ALBUMS: *The Best Of The Five Keys* (Aladdin 1956) ★★★, *The Five Keys On The Town* (Score 1957) ★★, *The Five Keys On Stage* (Capitol 1957) ★, *The Five Keys* (King 1960) ★★★, *Rhythm And Blues Hits Past And Present* (King 1960) ★★★, *The Fantastic Five Keys* (Capitol 1962) ★★★.
● COMPILATIONS: *The Five Keys* (King 1978) ★★, *The Five Keys And The Nitecaps* (Detour 1988) ★★★, *The Five Keys: Capitol Collector's Series* (Capitol 1989) ★★★, *Dream On* (Charly 1991) ★★★, *The Five Keys: The Aladdin Years* (EMI 1991) ★★★.

Five Pennies, The

This schmaltzy biopic of 20s cornet player **Red Nichols** was released by Paramount in 1959. **Danny Kaye** plays Nichols, and Barbara Bel Geddes is the wife who, following his early success, stays with him through the emotional traumas of their daughter's illness until he re-emerges from depression and returns to his beloved world of jazz. Onscreen musicians include **Shelly Manne** (in the role of Dave Tough, the second time in the same year he played the part of the drummer), **Bobby Troup**, **Ray Anthony** (in the role of **Jimmy Dorsey**, despite his being a trumpet player) and **Louis Armstrong** and his All Stars, who at that time included **Peanuts Hucko**, **Billy Kyle** and **Trummy Young**. Kaye and Armstrong mug their way through a vocal and trumpet duet of 'When the Saints Go Marching In', with Nichols himself dubbing for Kaye. Period songs such as 'Runnin' Wild' (Joe Grey–Leo Wood–A. Harrington Gibbs), 'Out Of Nowhere' (**Edward Heyman–Johnny Green**), 'After You've Gone' (**Henry Creamer–Turner Layton**) and 'Indiana' (Ballard MacDonald–James F. Hanley) are supplemented by three new ones written by Kaye's wife, Sylvia Fine, 'The Five Pennies', 'Lullaby In Ragtime' and 'Goodnight Sleep Tight', the last two of which are presented in a charming contrapuntal setting. Leith Stevens won an Oscar nomination for his 'scoring for a musical film', and there were other nominations for Daniel L. Fapp's impressive Vistavision and Technicolor cinematography and Fine's title song. Melville Shavelson directed the picture, and he and Jack Rose wrote the script.

Five Red Caps

An African-American vocal/instrumental combo from Los Angeles, California, USA. Members were Steve Gibson (b. 17 October 1914, Lynchburg, Virginia, USA; guitar/bass singer), Emmett Matthews (b. c.1902, St. Louis, Missouri, USA; saxophone/tenor singer), Dave Patillo (b. Marshall, Texas, USA, d. 1966; bass/vocals), Jimmy Springs (b. 5 September 1911, Mattoon, Illinois, USA, d. 1987; drums/tenor singer) and Romaine Brown (d. 1986; piano). The Five Red Caps, in their long history, represent virtually every facet of black popular music from the 30s through to the 50s, from crooning ballads, rousing jumps, and humorous jive tunes to rock 'n' roll. They began as the Four Toppers in 1938 and in 1942 became the Five Red Caps. They signed with Joe Davis and his Beacon label in 1943 and gained their first and biggest hit with 'I've Learned A Lesson I'll never Forget' (number 3 R&B) in early 1944. Three other records that year made the charts, namely 'Boogie-Woogie Ball', 'Just For You' and 'No One Else Will Do'. In 1946 the group moved to **Mercury Records** and, recording under the name Steve Gibson And The Red Caps, achieved a hit in 1948 with 'Wedding Bells Are Breaking Up That Old Gang Of Mine' (number 21 pop). In 1950 the group signed with **RCA Records**, and with the addition of **Damita Jo** (b. Damita Jo DuBlanc, 5 August 1930, Austin, Texas, USA), the group had their last hit with the ballad 'I Went To Your Wedding' (number 20 pop) in 1952. The Red Caps, however, found it increasingly hard to compete during the rock 'n' roll revolution and disbanded in 1956. Damita Jo went on to pursue a highly successful career as a nightclub chanteuse. Gibson formed a new Red Caps group, recruiting brothers Peck and Joe Furness and Emmett Matthews from the original unit. They recorded more in the rock 'n' roll vein and had minor success with a cover version of the **Rays**' 'Silhouettes' (1957). Gibson kept various Red Caps ensembles together until 1966, when Dave Patillo died.
● COMPILATIONS: *You're Driving Me Crazy* (Mercury 1954) ★★★, *Blueberry Hill* (Mercury 1954) ★★★, *It's So Good* (Krazy Kat 1986) ★★★, *Boogie Woogie On A Saturday Night* (Bear Family 1990) ★★★★, *Blueberry Hill* (Dr. Horse 1990) ★★★.

5 Royales

The 5 Royales were hugely successful exponents of southern vocal R&B throughout the 50s, although they started their career in a different style as the Royal Sons Gospel Group of Winston-Salem, North Carolina, USA. This quintet variously featured Clarence Pauling (b. 19 March 1928, Winston-Salem, North Carolina, USA, d. 6 May 1995, Los Angeles, California, USA), Curtis Pauling and Lowman Pauling (d. 26 December 1973, Brooklyn, New York, USA), Otto Jeffries, Johnny Tanner (b. John L. Tanner Snr., 28 November 1926, Forsyth County, North Carolina, USA, d. 8 November 2005, Winston-Salem, North Carolina, USA), Obediah Carter (d. July 1994, Winston-Salem, North Carolina, USA), Johnny Moore and William Samuels.
The Paulings had started out supporting Lowman Pauling Snr. on local North Carolina stages, while his namesake son reputedly built his first guitar out of cigar boxes. Lowman

Pauling Jnr. was the group's musical arranger and springboard, while Tanner usually handled lead vocals. At the suggestion of local radio producer Robert Woodward, the group contacted New York label Apollo Records, headed by Bess Berman and Carl Le Bowe. There the group sang spirituals as the Royal Sons Quintet, until Le Bowe rechristened them 5 Royales for the purposes of recording R&B music. Having elected to pursue the latter style, Johnny Holmes, the final member of the Royal Sons who graced their 'Bedside Of A Neighbor' debut, departed. This left a core 5 Royales line-up of Lowman Pauling (guitar), Johnny Tanner (lead), Johnny Moore (tenor), Obediah Carter (tenor) and Otto Jeffries (baritone). Typical of their background, their first single, 'Give Me One More Chance' (coupled with 'Too Much Of A Little Bit'), was a spiritual standard energized into a raunchy R&B number. By 1953 Eugene Tanner (b. 1936, d. 29 December 1994, Winston-Salem, North Carolina, USA; baritone/bass) had replaced Jeffries, the oldest member of the group by over 10 years, who was no longer capable of performing their energetic stage routines, instead becoming manager. Together they achieved their first major success with 'Baby Don't Do It', which made number 1 in the US R&B charts in January 1953. The follow-up single, 'Help Me Somebody', stayed at number 1 on the same chart for five weeks, while the group's powerful and frequent live performances, now completely divorced from their gospel background, built them a formidable reputation. Their newfound fame also resulted in a lawsuit when they discovered that the Royals of Detroit were the first of several groups to impersonate them.
The 5 Royales made their first appearance at the **Apollo** in January 1953, performing for a week alongside **Willy Mabon** and **Gene Ammons**. 'Crazy, Crazy, Crazy' and 'Too Much Lovin'' were also sizeable R&B hits, although it was the latter's b-side, 'Laundromat Blues', with its sexually suggestive lyric, that provoked most attention. By 1954 the group had signed to **King Records**, following Le Bowe's defection to that label. However, the 5 Royales were never as successful again. Though over 40 singles were issued under their name up to 1965, usually of good quality, they seldom reached the charts. 'Tears Of Joy' and 'Think', both from 1957, were two notable exceptions. 'Think' was their first national US pop chart success, at number 66, although 'Dedicated To The One I Love', later covered by the **Shirelles** and **Mamas And The Papas**, also reached number 81 on the same chart in 1961. This was a revised version of a Chester Mayfield composition, 'I Don't Want You To Go', which Mayfield had written while a member of fellow North Carolina R&B group the Casanovas, also signed to Apollo. Their membership included William Samuels, Lowman Pauling's brother-in-law and formerly of the Royal Sons himself. However, after leaving King Records in 1960 the group failed to reach the charts again, despite recording for several labels with variable line-ups. Lowman Pauling left the group between stints at Home Of The Blues Records and Todd Records, replaced by Robert 'Pee Wee' Burris on guitar. Tanner also departed in December 1963 and was replaced by Eudell Graham. Graham, who became the focus of the touring 5 Royales, was later jailed for armed robbery. The group broke up in 1965 although various line-ups would continue to use the 5 Royales name well into the next decade.
The 5 Royales' influence on R&B proved fundamental to the music of **James Brown**, with whom the group had frequently

worked in their heyday. Lowman Pauling, whose uninhibited guitar style was also a major influence on the style of **Eric Clapton**, died in 1973 while working as a custodian at a Brooklyn synagogue. Clarence Pauling, who left the Royal Sons before they became the 5 Royales, renamed himself **Clarence Paul** and later became the A&R director at **Motown Records** where he helped shape the careers of **Stevie Wonder** and **Marvin Gaye**.

● ALBUMS: *The Rockin' 5 Royales* (Apollo 1956) ★★★, *Dedicated To You* (King 1957) ★★★★, *Sing For You* (King 1959) ★★★, *The Five Royales* (King 1960) ★★.

● COMPILATIONS: *24 All Time Hits* (King 1966) ★★★, *Sing Baby Don't Do It* (Relic 1987) ★★★, *Sing Laundromat Blues* (Relic 1987) ★★★, *Monkey Hips And Rice: The '5' Royales Anthology* (Rhino 1994) ★★★★, *The Apollo Sessions* (Collectables 1995) ★★★, *All Righty! The Apollo Recordings 1951–1955* (Westside 1999) ★★★★, *Take Me With You Baby* (Purple Pyramid 2000) ★★★, *The Very Best Of The 5 Royales* (Collectables 2004) ★★★, *It's Hard But It's Fair: The King Hits And Rarities* (Ace 2005) ★★★★.

Five Satins

This R&B vocal group was formed in New Haven, Connecticut, USA, in 1955. The Five Satins' first hit, 'In The Still Of The Nite' (US R&B number 3 and pop Top 30 in 1956), was one of the definitive songs of the early rock 'n' roll era, with its strong chanting of doo-wop riffs in the background and impassioned lead work. The group on this record consisted of lead Fred Parris, Al Denby, Ed Martin, bass Jim Freeman and pianist Jessie Murphy. Parris, who wrote the song, brought valuable experience to the Five Satins, having formed the Scarlets (Parris, Denby, Bill Powers, Sylvester Hopkins and Nate Mosely) in 1953, a group that hit regionally with 'Dear One' in 1954. The long-cherished national success for Parris was initially denied him, as he was in the army stationed in Japan when 'In The Still Of The Nite' became a hit, and the wonderful follow-up, 'To The Aisle' (US R&B number 5 and pop Top 30 in 1957), featured a reorganized group with Bill Baker (b. Auburn, Alabama, USA, d. 10 August 1994, New Haven, Connecticut, USA) as lead. Parris returned from Japan in 1958 and again reorganized the Five Satins, recruiting tenor Richie Freeman (b. December 1940), second tenor West Forbes (b. 1937), Sylvester Hopkins and Lou Peeples. This group was not able to secure another big hit, although 'Shadows' (US R&B number 27, 1959) kept their name visible. Their profile was significantly enhanced with the release of Art Laboe's first *Oldies But Goodies*, which included 'In The Still Of The Nite'. As a result, the song helped to create the doo-wop revival in the early 60s and re-entered the national pop chart in 1961. The Five Satins broke up in the early 60s but re-formed and became a perennial on the live circuit in the 70s. The new group consisted of Parris, Richie Freeman, Jimmy Curtis and Nate Marshall. Under the name Black Satin, they had a number 49 R&B hit in 1975 with 'Everybody Stand And Clap Your Hands (For The Entertainer)'. Another hit followed in 1982 with the medley 'Memories Of Days Gone By' before Parris and his various personnel returned to the oldies circuit.

● ALBUMS: *The 5 Satins Sing* (Ember 1957) ★★★, *Encore, Volume 2* (Ember 1960) ★★★.

● COMPILATIONS: *The Best Of The 5 Satins* (Celebrity Show 1971) ★★★.

Five Sharps

Formed in the early 50s in Jamaica, New York, USA, the Five Sharps were a vocal harmony group whose sole claim to fame is the fact that their only record, **Harold Arlen**'s 'Stormy Weather', is acknowledged by collectors to be the rarest in the world. The group consisted of Ronald Cuffey (lead vocals), Clarence Bassett and Robert Ward (both tenors), Mickey Owens (bass vocals) and Tom Duckett (piano). In late 1952 the group recorded the standard 'Stormy Weather' for Jubilee Records. The record failed to gain any significant airplay or sales, and the Five Sharps broke up. Virtually no one remembered their recording until a collector found a 78 rpm copy at a Brooklyn record store in 1961. When no others turned up, the value of the surviving original rose steadily; a second copy was finally located in 1977 and sold for nearly $4,000. No 45s were ever discovered, and should another 78 appear its value is now estimated by experts to be over $10,000.

5.6.7.8's

Japanese garage rock outfit formed in 1986 by sisters Yoshiko 'Ronnie' Fujiyama (guitar/vocals) and Sachiko Fujiyama (drums). Taking inspiration from **Chuck Berry** and the **Ramones**, the Fujiyamas were originally joined by Rico (guitar) and Yoshie (bass) and made their recording debut on the *Shinkankakuha Omnibus Vol. 2* compilation performing 'Horror Rocker'. The track set a template for the 5.6.7.8's subsequent career, with the quartet dishing up primitive punk rock to complement their deliberately kitsch visual image. Mikako replaced Yoshie on the band's debut cassette *Golden Hits Of The 5.6.7.8's*. Further personnel change ensued with Omo (bass) and male guitarist Eddie joining the Fujiyama sisters on the band's CD debut, *The 5.6.7.8's Can't Help It!* A stripped down line-up featuring the Fujiyamas, and Omo then recorded a number of singles and 1994's *The 5.6.7.8'*. The following year's *Bomb The Twist* mini-album represented the band's US debut, but after a number of further personnel changes the Fujiyama sisters decided to put the band on hiatus.

After re-forming in the new millennium, the 5.6.7.8's came to wider attention in 2003 when they were featured as the house band at the House Of Blue Leaves in Quentin Tarantino's martial arts homage, *Kill Bill: Vol. 1*. One of the songs they performed in the movie, the doo-wop-style 'Woo Hoo', received extensive coverage and was included on a career-spanning compilation released later in the year.

● ALBUMS: *Golden Hits Of The 5.6.7.8's* cassette (Tokyo Stiff 1988) ★★, *The 5.6.7.8's Can't Help It!* (Au-Go-Go/Rockville 1991) ★★★, *The 5.6.7.8's* (Au-Go-Go/Time Bomb 1994) ★★★, *Bomb The Twist* mini-album (Sympathy For The Record Industry 1995) ★★★, *Pin Heel Stomp* (Time Bomb 1997) ★★, *Teenage Mojo Workout* (Time Bomb 2002) ★★★.

● COMPILATIONS: *Bomb The Rocks: Early Days Singles 1989 To 1996* (Time Bomb 2003) ★★★★.

● FILMS: *Kill Bill: Vol. 1* (2003).

Five Stairsteps

A Chicago group comprised of Burke family members Clarence Jnr. (b. 1951), James (b. 1952), Aloha (b. 1950), Kenneth (b. 1954) and Dennis (b. 1953). Discovered and produced by **Curtis Mayfield**, this young quintet enjoyed a consistent run of R&B chart success, with releases on the

Windy C, **Curtom** and **Buddah** labels. The unit's material—'You Waited Too Long' (1966), 'World Of Fantasy' (1966), 'Come Back' (1966) and 'Danger, She's A Stranger' (1967)—ranged from gentle dance songs to orchestrated ballads, and their fledgling talent was recognized in 1967 with a NATRA award as that year's outstanding R&B group. For two years the group's name was expanded to include five-year-old sibling Cubie, but when the newcomer left in 1969, the line-up reverted to the 5 Stairsteps, later dropping the '5' altogether. Paradoxically, the 5 Stairsteps' biggest hit, 'O-o-h Child' (1970), a US Top 10 entry, came on parting with Mayfield. Instrumentally self-contained, the quintet pursued a direction similar to **Sly And The Family Stone**, but they were unable to capitalize on this new-found position. The group broke up in 1972, but whereas the majority entered full-time education, Clarence Jnr. and Kenneth became session musicians. In 1976 the duo resumed work with brothers Dennis and James, securing a contract with **George Harrison**'s Dark Horse label at the behest of singer **Billy Preston**. Although the Stairsteps returned to the soul Top 10 with 'From Us To You', they split up again soon afterwards. Clarence Jnr. subsequently formed the Invisible Man's Band, who recorded two albums, *The Invisible Man's Band* (1980) and *Really Wanna See You* (1981). Kenneth, latterly known as Keni Burke, enjoyed a successful career as a solo artist and producer.

● ALBUMS: *The Five Stairsteps* (Windy City 1967) ★★★, as the 5 Stairsteps And Cubie *Our Family Portrait* (Buddah 1968) ★★★, as the 5 Stairsteps And Cubie *Love's Happening* (Curtom 1969) ★★★, as the Stairsteps *Stairsteps* (Buddah 1970) ★★★, as the Stairsteps *The Stairsteps* (Buddah 1971) ★★★, *Second Resurrection* (1976) ★★.

● COMPILATIONS: *Step By Step By Step* (Buddah 1970) ★★★, *Comeback: The Best Of The 5 Stairsteps* (Sequel 1990) ★★★, *Greatest Hits, Featuring Keni Burke* (Sequel 1995) ★★★★, *The First Family Of Soul* (Buddah 2001) ★★★★.

Five Star

This commercial pop act was formed by the five siblings of the Pearson family, all of whom shared vocal duties and were born in Romford, Essex, England; Deniece (b. 13 June 1968), Doris (b. 8 June 1966), Lorraine (b. 10 August 1967), Stedman (b. 29 June 1964) and Delroy (b. 11 April 1970). Their father, Buster, had been a professional guitarist with a variety of acts including **Wilson Pickett**, **Desmond Dekker** and **Jimmy Cliff**. After his retirement from the live circuit he formed reggae label K&B, then the more commercially disposed Tent Records. His daughters persuaded him to let them record a version of his recently written composition, 'Problematic'. It showed promise, and he decided to throw his weight behind their career as manager, while the brothers elected to expand the group to a five-piece. Although 'Problematic' failed to chart, Buster secured a licensing agreement for Tent with **RCA Records**, but follow-ups 'Hide And Seek' and 'Crazy' also missed out. However, when Nick Martinelli took over production duties, 1985's 'All Fall Down' reached the charts. Heavy promotion, and the group's choreographed dance routines, ensured that next single, 'Let Me Be The One', followed it into the Top 20. By the time the band's debut album was released, they had worked through six different producers and countless studios. Despite the relative disappointment of chart placings for subsequent singles 'Love Take Over' and 'R.S.V.P.', the band departed for a major US promotional tour. The **Walt Disney** organization

immediately stepped in to offer the band their show, but Buster declined. Back in the UK, 'System Addict', the seventh single milked from *Luxury Of Life*, became the first to break the Top 10. Both 'Can't Wait Another Minute' and 'Find The Time' repeated the feat, before the band acquired the sponsorship of Crunchie Chocolate Bars for their UK tour. Their next outings would attract the sponsorship of Ultrabrite toothpaste, much to the derision of critics who were less than enamoured by their 'squeaky clean' image.

Meanwhile, *Silk And Steel*, the second album, climbed slowly to the top of the UK charts. It would eventually earn triple platinum status, unleashing another steady stream of singles. The most successful of these, 'Rain And Shine', achieved their best placing in the singles chart, at number 2. Continued success allowed the family to move from Romford, Essex, to a mansion in Sunningdale, Berkshire, where they installed a massive studio complex. Ever a favourite for media attacks, Buster was variously accused of keeping his offspring in a 'palatial prison' and of spending wanton sums of money on trivia. However, as their records proved increasingly unsuccessful, the family was the subject of several media stories concerning their financial instability. These hit a peak when the band was forced to move from their home in 1990. Attempts to resurrect their career in America on Epic failed, with their fortunes hitting an all-time low in October 1991 when Stedman Pearson was fined for public indecency. Although their chart days appear to be over, they are still performing and are now based in California, reduced to a trio (Stedman, Deniece and Lorraine) and still managed by their father.

● ALBUMS: *Luxury Of Life* (Tent 1985) ★★, *Silk And Steel* (Tent 1986) ★★★, *Between The Lines* (Tent 1987) ★★, *Rock The World* (Tent 1988) ★★, *Five Star* (Tent 1990) ★★.

● COMPILATIONS: *Greatest Hits* (Tent 1989) ★★★, *The Greatest Hits* (BMG 2003) ★★★.

Five Thirty

Based in north London, England, this briefly active indie rock trio comprised Tara Milton (vocals/bass), Paul Bassett (vocals/guitar) and Phil Hooper (drums). The name was taken as a reaction against the grind of nine to five employment: 'It's the time when everyone goes home and gets ready to go out.' A previous incarnation featuring Milton and Bassett had recorded the 1985 single 'Catcher In The Rye' shortly after they had left school. The new line-up debuted on record in 1990 with the four track CD single 'Abstain!' and performed a series of well-received, energetic live outings. The 'Air Conditioned Nightmare' single preceded 1991's album debut, *Bed*. Motivated by the **Jam** in spirit if not style, Five Thirty were one of a number of 'new mod' bands tipped to break through in 1991, and despite their haphazard songwriting they were undoubtedly among the best. The relative commercial failure of the album and three follow-up singles served to hasten the band's demise, however, with Hooper leaving for an acting career. By 1995 Milton had found a new home for his ambitions in the **Nubiles**, while Bassett moved on to Orange Deluxe.

● ALBUMS: *Bed* (EastWest 1991) ★★★.

5X

Japanese hard rock band founded in 1981 by ex–Midnight Cruiser guitarist George Azuma and former **Oz** vocalist

Carmen Maki. With Kinta Moriyama (bass) and Jun Harada (drums) completing the line-up, they adopted a style that incorporated elements of **Motörhead**, **Van Halen** and **AC/DC**, also veering towards thrash metal at times. By their third album, which saw them adopt a slightly altered name that gave their singer more prominent billing, they had moved into mainstream rock territory, and it appeared that vocalist Carmen Maki was striving to become the Japanese equivalent of **Heart**'s **Ann Wilson**.
● ALBUMS: *Human Targets* (EMI 1982) ★★★★, *Live X* (EMI 1982) ★★, *Carmen Maki's 5X* (Eastworld 1983) ★★★.

Fivepenny Piece
Originally known as the Wednesday Folks, this group from Lancashire, England, was formed in 1967. They largely performed songs tinged with their native Lancashire humour. The original line-up of Lynda Meeks (b. 3 August 1947, Stalybridge, Cheshire, England; vocals), her brother John Meeks (b. 24 March 1937, Stalybridge, Cheshire, England; vocals/guitar), Eddie Crotty (b. 24 February 1942, Stalybridge, Cheshire, England; guitar), Colin Radcliffe (b. 19 January 1934, Ashton-under-Lyne, Lancashire, England; guitar/harmonica) and his brother George Radcliffe (b. 9 August 1937, Ashton-under-Lyne, Lancashire; bass/trombone). As the Wednesday Folks, they won the television talent show *New Faces* in 1968 but changed their name to the Fivepenny Piece in 1969. The group was featured on the BBC television series *That's Life* during the late 70s and recorded almost a dozen shows. Despite being offered work all over the world, the group declined as they all had regular day jobs. In 1981 John Meeks left the line-up to be replaced by Trevor Chance (b. 1 March 1942, Gilsland, Cumbria, England; guitar/vocals). This was at the time that the group had its own series, *The Fivepenny Piece Show*, on BBC television. On records, Phil Barlow (drums) augmented the line-up. Many of the group's songs were self-composed, by Colin and George Radcliffe, but they trod the path between traditional folk and commercial acceptance and consequently did not gain sufficient appeal from either camp. However, *Makin' Tracks* made the UK Top 40 early in 1973, while *King Cotton* gained a Top 10 placing in 1976. In addition, the group achieved silver discs, in 1976, for *Songs We Like To Sing* and *The Fivepenny Piece On Stage*. When Lynda Meeks left, she was replaced by Andrea Mullen, formerly with the **Caravelles**, but the group broke up in 1985. Eventually, Chance went into artist management, and Colin Radcliffe became a full-time landscape painter.
● ALBUMS: *The Fivepenny Piece* (1972) ★★★, *Makin' Tracks* (1973) ★★★, *Songs We Like To Sing* (1973) ★★★★, *On Stage* (1974) ★★, *Wish You Were Here* (1975) ★★★, *King Cotton* (1976) ★★★, *The Fivepenny Piece On Stage Again* (1977) ★★, *Telling Tales* (1977) ★★★, *Both Sides Of Fivepenny Piece* (1978) ★★★★, with various artists *Lanky Spoken Here* (1978) ★★★, *Life Is A Game Of Chance* (1979) ★★★, *Peddlers Of Songs* (1979) ★★★, *An Evening With The Fivepenny Piece* (1980) ★★★★, *The Fivepenny Piece Live At The Coliseum* (1980) ★★★.
● COMPILATIONS: *The Very Best Of Fivepenny Piece* (1980) ★★★★, *This Is Fivepenny Piece* (1980) ★★★, *Lancashire, My Lancashire* (1980) ★★★ *The Fivepenny Piece* (1991) ★★★.

Fix, The
The process of preparing the mega-musical *Martin Guerre* for the West End is said to have taken **Cameron Mackintosh** seven years, but his more satirical and complex piece, *The Fix*, opened at London's Donmar Warehouse on 12 May 1997, only seven months after the producer became aware of it. The American team of John Dempsey (lyrics) and Dana P. Rowe (music) provided the score, and Dempsey also wrote the book, which dealt with what one critic called 'corrupt machinations of a dangerous political dynasty'—of the American kind. Presidential contender Senator Reed Chandler (David Firth) has suffered a fatal heart attack while *in flagrante* with hotel receptionist Donna (Christina Fry), and hot on the heels of his death, his not-so-grieving widow, Violet (Kathryn Evans), and her polio-stricken brother-in-law, Grahame (Philip Quast), prepare to groom Chandler's layabout son, Cal (John Barrowman), to take his place on the White House ladder. This entails an obligatory spell in the US Army, marriage to Deborah (Gael Johnson), the blonde (from a good family), and the formulation of his political creed—basically, the economy, crime and taxes. Enter the Mob, and Cal's life and career go rapidly downhill via his involvement with a voluptuous dancer, Tina McCoy (Krysten Cummings), hard drugs, corruption in high places, and a variety of sexual predilections. A cleaned-up comeback is short-lived, and his inevitable demise is marked by 'crass' Kennedy–Marilyn Monroe overtones. Also cast were Mark Frendo, Carrie Ellis, John Partridge, Bogdan Kominowski, Archie Preston and Christopher Holt. Accompanying the scheming and the rest of the shenanigans was a rock-driven score that incorporated elements of gospel, mock-vaudeville, country and rock 'n' roll, among other genres. The bluesy 'Lonely Is A Two-Way Street', 'Simple Words' and the second-act opener, 'Two Guys At Harvard', were prominent in a score that also included 'Advocate, Architect', 'The Funeral', 'One, Two, Three', 'Embrace Tomorrow', 'Army Chant', 'Control', 'Man And Wife', 'America's Son', 'I See The Future', 'Alleluia', 'Flash, Pop, Sizzle!', 'Making Sense Of Insanity', 'Clandestine Affairs', 'First Came Mercy', 'Bend The Spoon', 'Cleaning House', 'Upper Hand', 'Spin', 'The Ballad Of Bobby "Cracker" Barrel', 'Child's Play', 'Lion Hunts The Tiger' and 'Mistress Of Deception'. Director Sam Mendes ('sure and slick production'), choreographer Charles Augins, Rob Howell (sets and costumes) and Howard Harrison (fierce, yet shadowy, lighting) emerged relatively unscathed, and this £3.5 million 'Manchurian Candidate without the warmth' played out its month-long season despite a chilly critical reception. Cameron Mackintosh was reportedly furious at the panning, claiming that the critics were unable to deal with changes in musical style. *The Fix* had its US premiere at the Signature Theatre, Washington, D.C., in April 1998, with Linda Balgord, Stephen Bienskie, Sal Mistretta and Jim Walton.

Fixx
This durable UK new wave band originally comprised Cy Curnin (13 December 1957; vocals/guitar), Adam Woods (b. 8 April 1953; drums), Rupert Greenall (keyboards), Jamie West-Oram (guitar) and Charlie Barret (bass). They formed at the turn of the 80s when college friends Curnin and Woods made the decision to pursue music as a full-time vocation. After advertising in the music press for new members, the band released a 'one off' single for Ariola

Records 'Hazards In The Home' credited as 'The Portraits'. A year later with a more complete line-up, they changed their name to the Fixx and recorded the quirky 'Lost Planes' which led to the band's signing with MCA Records. Their debut album *Shuttered Room* remained on the US album chart for over a year, but UK reaction was less than enthusiastic, and the album and subsequent releases suffered the same fate in their home country. *Reach The Beach* was released in 1983 and earned platinum status in the US and marked the recording debut of Dan K. Brown (b. 4 June 1951), who had replaced Barret.

In 1984 the Fixx's contribution to the soundtrack of the movie *Streets Of Fire* was probably the most interesting. Further success followed with a string of single and album hits in America and Europe, with the band proving themselves to be musicians able to maintain credibility and longevity through a willingness to change with the times without compromising their creative vision. Their commercial fortunes had declined by the late 80s. Following the critical backlash that greeted 1991's dance-orientated *Ink* the band remained quiet for several years. They returned to the studio in the late 90s.

● ALBUMS: *Shuttered Room* (MCA 1982) ★★★, *Reach The Beach* (MCA 1983) ★★★, *Phantoms* (MCA 1984) ★★★, *Walkabout* (MCA 1986) ★★★, *React* (MCA 1987) ★★, *Calm Animals* (RCA 1988) ★★, *Ink* (MCA 1991) ★★, *Elemental* (CMC International 1998) ★★★, *1011 Woodland* (CMC International 1999) ★★.

● COMPILATIONS: *One Thing Leads To Another: Greatest Hits* (MCA 1989) ★★★★, *The Ultimate Collection* (Hip-O 1999) ★★★, *The Best Of Fixx: The Millennium Collection* (MCA 2000) ★★★★, *Happy Landings & Lost Tracks* (Beyond 2001) ★★★.

Fjellgaard, Gary

b. 14 August 1937, Rose Valley, Sasketchewan, Canada. Fjellgaard (pronounced Fell-gard) grew up on an isolated Canadian farm and learnt to play guitar through his own initiative and listening to the radio. He worked as a Canadian lumberjack for 15 years and became a country star in his homeland, performing originally under just his surname. His first UK release was gentle folk/country, highly derivative of **Gordon Lightfoot**. 'Riding On The Wind' was awarded the Canadian country Single Of The Year in 1987. In 1993 Fjellgaard was presented with the Juno award for Country Male Vocalist Of The Year.

● ALBUMS: *Me And Martin* (Royalty 1976) ★★★, *Ballads And Beers* (Royalty 1979) ★★★, *Time And Innocence* (Savannah 1983) ★★★, *No Time To Lose* (Savannah 1986) ★★★★, *Heart Of A Dream* (Savannah 1989) ★★★, *Winds Of October* (Savannah 1991) ★★★, *Believe In Forever* (Savannah 1994) ★★★, *Under Western Skies* (Stony Plain 1996) ★★★, with Valdy *Contenders* (Stony Plain 1999) ★★★, *Grande Olde Ride* (Slim Creek 2001) ★★★, *Caragana Wind* (Slim Creek 2005) ★★★.

● COMPILATIONS: *The Best Of Gary Fjellgaard* (Stony Plain 1997) ★★★.

Flack, Roberta

b. 10 February 1937, Asheville, North Carolina, USA. Born into a musical family, Flack graduated from Howard University with a BA in music. She was discovered singing and playing jazz in a Washington nightclub by pianist **Les McCann**, who recommended her talents to **Atlantic Records**. Two classy albums, *First Take* and *Chapter Two*, garnered considerable acclaim for their skilful, often introspective content before Flack achieved huge success with a poignant version of folk-singer **Ewan MacColl**'s ballad, 'First Time Ever I Saw Your Face'. Recorded in 1969, it was a major international hit three years later, following its inclusion in the movie *Play Misty For Me*. Further hits came with 'Where Is The Love' (1972), a duet with **Donny Hathaway**, and 'Killing Me Softly With His Song' (1973), where Flack's penchant for sweeter, more MOR-styled compositions gained an ascendancy. Her cool, almost unemotional style benefited from a measured use of slow material, although she seemed less comfortable on up-tempo songs. Flack's self-assurance wavered during the mid-70s, but further duets with Hathaway, 'The Closer I Get To You' (1978) and 'Back Together Again' (1980), suggested a rebirth. She was shattered when her partner committed suicide in 1979, but in the 80s Flack enjoyed a fruitful partnership with **Peabo Bryson** that reached a commercial, if sentimental, peak with 'Tonight I Celebrate My Love' in 1983. *Set The Night To Music* was produced by the highly respected Arif Mardin, but the bland duet with **Maxi Priest** on the title track was representative of this soulless collection of songs. Still, Roberta Flack remains a crafted, if precisionist, performer.

● ALBUMS: *First Take* (Atlantic 1970) ★★★★, *Chapter Two* (Atlantic 1970) ★★★, *Quiet Fire* (Atlantic 1971) ★★, *Roberta Flack And Donny Hathaway* (Atlantic 1972) ★★★, *Killing Me Softly* (Atlantic 1973) ★★, *Feel Like Making Love* (Atlantic 1975) ★★, *Blue Lights In The Basement* (Atlantic 1978) ★★, *Roberta Flack* (Atlantic 1978) ★★, *Roberta Flack Featuring Donny Hathaway* (Atlantic 1980) ★★★, with Peabo Bryson *Live And More* (Atlantic 1980) ★★, *Bustin' Loose* (MCA 1981) ★★, *I'm The One* (Atlantic 1982) ★★, with Bryson *Born To Love* (Capitol 1983) ★★★, *Oasis* (Atlantic 1989) ★★, *Set The Night To Music* (Atlantic 1991) ★★, *Roberta* (Atlantic/EastWest 1995) ★★★.

● COMPILATIONS: *The Best Of Roberta Flack* (Atlantic 1980) ★★★, *Softly With These Songs: The Best Of Roberta Flack* (Atlantic 1993) ★★★, *The Best Of Roberta Flack* (Atlantic 2004) ★★★.

● FURTHER READING: *Roberta Flack: Sound Of Velvet Melting*, Linda Jacobs.

● FILMS: *The Wiz* voice only (1978), *Renaldo And Clara* (1978).

Flahooley

Four years after **Finian's Rainbow** its authors **E.Y. 'Yip' Harburg** and **Fred Saidy** came up with another piece of whimsy called *Flahooley*, which opened on 14 May 1951 at the Broadhurst Theatre in New York, and, unlike that previous show, did not stay around for too long. The action takes place in Capsulanti, Indiana, USA, at the business premises of B.G. Bigelow, Inc., manufactures of all manner of dolls and specialists in novelty items such as exploding cigars and similar playthings. Sylvester (Jerome Courtland), one of the Company's puppet designers, is in love with Sandy (**Barbara Cook**), a fellow puppet operator. Sylvester has come up with a revolutionary new puppet, but before he can unveil it, a mission from Arabia arrives at the factory with a problem. Their Aladdin's magic lamp no longer produces a genie; can B.G. Bigelow, Inc. repair it? They can. The new puppet is revealed and named Flahooley: it chews gum, it reads comic books—and it laughs! B.G. Bigelow (**Ernest Truex**) is delighted, and puts it on the market, but disaster strikes. A competitor has already developed a cheaper version (industrial spies?), and Sylvester is dismayed—will he ever have enough money to marry Sandy? While the magic lamp is being mended, Flahooley's hand touches it, and the resulting genie, Abou Ben Atom (Irwin Corey), organizes the production of Flahooleys in such numbers that the market is saturated. The citizens of Capsulanti arrange a genie hunt, intending to burn every Flahooley they can find. The lamp is seized by Elsa Bulinger, the leader of the reactionary mob, but Abou escapes and decides to become a Santa Claus. Bigelow flies off on a magic carpet to marry Najla (**Yma Sumac**), one of the Arabian delegation. Harburg's books and lyrics always had a social and political edge, although they were never dull or boring, and As this show was written at the height of the McCarthy witch hunts in America, it was inevitable that the prevailing climate would be reflected in this work. All the usual targets such as politicians, big business—capitalism in general—were examined and satirized. The show's more conventional—and marvellous—songs were written by Harburg and composer **Sammy Fain** (a prolific film composer, this was regarded as Fain's best score for the stage). Jerome Courtland and Barbara Cook in her first Broadway role introduced 'Here's To Your Illusions', 'Who Says There Ain't No Santa Claus?', 'The World Is Your Balloon', 'He's Only Wonderful', and Cook also had the tender 'Come Back, Little Genie'. Other Harburg-Fain numbers included 'The Springtime Cometh', 'You, Too, Can Be A Puppet', 'Jump, Little Chillun!' and 'Flahooley!'. The remainder of the numbers—written especially for the four-octave range of **Yma Sumac** by Mosises Vivanco—were 'Birds/Enchantment', 'Najla's Lament' and Najla's Song Of Joy'. Flahooley was a charming piece, with an excellent cast—including the delightful Baird puppets—but commercially it failed dismally and closed after only 40 performances. A second version, entitled Jollyanna, with a cast that included Bobby Clark, **Mitzi Gaynor**, John Beal and Biff McGuire, opened on 11 September 1952 at the Curran Theatre in San Francisco but closed during the pre-Broadway tryout. In September 1998, the first major New York revival of the 1951 Flahooley was mounted off-Broadway at the Theatre at St. Clement's.

Flame

Slade were unequivocally one of the most popular acts of the early 70s. Although noted for boisterous singles, including 'Mama Weer All Crazee Now' and 'Cum On Feel The Noize', the quartet boasted a strong grasp of melody, redolent of their 60s' mentors. In this, their only feature film, Slade portray a group from that era, 'Flame', who achieve success only to disband, disillusioned with their management. Ex-**Animals** members **Chas Chandler**—Slade's manager/producer in real-life—and John Steele were executive producers in this project, which featured the latter in an acting role as a drummer in a band booked for a wedding. The Flame soundtrack album included two UK hit singles, 'Far Far Away' and 'How Does It Feel'. Although the former reached number 2, its successor failed to broach the Top 10 after 12 consecutive such entries. Released in 1974, Flame appeared just as Slade's star began to wane, yet it remains a meritorious look at British pop culture.

Flamin' Groovies

This unflinchingly self-assured act evolved from an aspiring San Francisco-based garage band, the Chosen Few. Roy Loney (b. 13 April 1946, San Francisco, California, USA; vocals), Tim Lynch (b. 18 July 1946, San Francisco, California, USA; guitar), Cyril Jordan (b. San Francisco, California, USA; guitar), George Alexander (b. 18 May 1946, San Mateo, California, USA; bass) and Ron Greco (drums) subsequently flirted with a new appellation, **Lost And Found**, before breaking up in the summer of 1966. All of the group, bar Greco reassembled several months later as the Flamin' Groovies. New drummer Danny Mihm (b. San Francisco, California, USA) joined from another local act, Group 'B', and the new line-up embarked on a direction markedly different from the city's prevalent love of extended improvisation. The Flamin' Groovies remained rooted in America's immediate beat aftermath and bore traces of the **Lovin' Spoonful** and the **Charlatans**. Having completed a promising private pressing, the group recorded their official debut, Supersnazz, which also revealed a strong debt to traditional rock 'n' roll. The group's subsequent albums, Flamingo and Teenage Head, were influenced by Detroit's **MC5** and offered a more contemporary perspective. The latter set drew complementary reviews and was compared favourably with the **Rolling Stones**' Sticky Fingers, but it marked the end of the original line-up. Loney and Lynch were replaced, respectively, by Chris Wilson and James Farrell.

Denigrated at home, the Flamin' Groovies enjoyed a cult popularity in Europe and a series of superb recordings, including the seminal antidrug song 'Slow Death', were recorded during a brief spell in Britain. Several of these performances formed the basis of **Shake Some Action**, their majestic homage to 60s pop, which remains their finest and most accomplished work. New drummer David Wright had replaced a disaffected Mihm, while the group's harmonies and reverberating instrumental work added an infectious sparkle. The group then adopted former Charlatan Mike Wilhelm in place of Farrell. However, subsequent releases relied on a tried formula where a series of cover versions disguised a lack of original songs. The Flamin' Groovies were then perceived as a mere revival band, and the resultant frustration led to the departure of Wilson, Wilhelm and Wright.

Buoyed by Europe's continuing fascination with the Flamin' Groovies, Jordan and Alexander continued relatively undeterred, adding Jack Johnson (guitar) and Paul Zahl (drums) from **Roky Erickson**'s backing band. The reconstituted line-up toured Europe, Australia and New Zealand and completed a handful of new recordings, including 1987's One Night Stand and 1992's Rock Juice. However, despite promises of a greater prolificacy, they remain unable to secure a permanent recording contract and remain perennial live performers. Paradoxically, original member Roy Loney has enjoyed a flourishing performing career, honing a style not dissimilar to that of Supersnazz and Flamingo.

● ALBUMS: Sneakers mini-album (Snazz 1968) ★★, Supersnazz (Epic 1969) ★★★, Flamingo (Kama Sutra 1970) ★★★, Teenage Head (Kama Sutra 1971) ★★★, Shake Some Action (Sire 1976) ★★★★, Flamin' Groovies Now (Sire 1978) ★★★, Jumpin' In The Night (Sire 1979) ★★★, Slow Death, Live! aka Bucketful Of Brains (Lolita/Voxx 1983) ★★★, Live At The Whiskey A Go-Go '79 (Lolita

1985) ★★, *One Night Stand* (ABC 1987) ★★, *Rock Juice* (National 1992) ★★★.
● COMPILATIONS: *Still Shakin'* (Buddah 1976) ★★, *Flamin' Groovies '68* (Eva 1983) ★★, *Flamin' Groovies '70* (Eva 1983) ★★, *The Gold Star Tapes* (Skydog 1984) ★★, *Roadhouse* (Edsel 1986) ★★★, *The Rockfield Sessions* mini-album (Aim 1989) ★★, *Groovies' Greatest Grooves* (Sire 1989) ★★★★, *A Collection Of Rare Demos & Live Recordings* (Marilyn 1993) ★★★, *Live At The Festival Of The Sun* (Aim 1995) ★★, *Yesterday's Numbers* (Camden 1998) ★★★★, *Grease: The Complete Skydog Singles Collection* (Jungle 1998) ★★★, *The Flamin' Groovies 2-CD set* (Charly 2002) ★★★, *Slow Death* (Norton 2003) ★★★.
● FURTHER READING: *A Flamin' Saga: The Flamin' Groovies Histoire & Discographie* Jea-Pierre Poncelet. *Bucketfull Of Groovies* Jon Storey.

Flaming Ember

Formed in Detroit, Michigan, USA, as the Flaming Embers, this white rock/soul unit consisted of Joe Sladich (guitar), Bill Ellis (piano), Jim Bugnel (bass) and Jerry Plunk (drums). The quartet made its debut in 1968 on the local Ric Tic label, before joining the Hot Wax stable the following year. Bolstered by a pulsating **Holland/Dozier/Holland** production, Flaming Ember scored two US Top 30 hits with 'Mind, Body And Soul' and 'Westbound #9', but the group's heterogeneous sound proved their undoing. Too soul-based for rock, too rock-based for soul, the quartet fell between two markets and split up in 1973.
● ALBUMS: *Westbound #9* (Hot Wax 1970) ★★.

Flaming Lips

Formed in Oklahoma City, Oklahoma, USA, the Flaming Lips won a deserved reputation in the 80s and 90s for their discordant, psychedelia-tinged garage rock and have recorded a fine body of off-kilter and unpredictable work. They are led by lyricist, vocalist and guitarist Wayne Coyne (b. Wayne Ruby Coyne, 17 March 1965, Pittsburgh, Pennsylvania, USA), who started playing music during his high school days. Coyne was joined in the band by his brother, Mark Coyne, who is best remembered for his vocals on the debut album's 'My Own Planet'. Taking up the microphone following his brother's departure, Wayne Coyne fronted a line-up completed by Steven Drozd (b. Steven Gregory Drozd, 6 December 1969, Houston, Texas, USA; drums/vocals, replacing Richard English and Nathan Roberts), Ron Jones (b. Ronald Lee Jones, 26 November 1970, Angeles, Philippines; guitars/vocals) and Michael Ivins (b. Michael Lee Ivins, 17 March 1965, Omaha, Nebraska, USA; bass/vocals). John 'Dingus' Donahue, of **Mercury Rev** fame, was also a member during the sessions for their first consistent release, 1990's *In A Priest Driven Ambulance*.
In 1993 the Flaming Lips played at the Reading Festival in the UK and toured with **Porno For Pyros**, **Butthole Surfers** and **Stone Temple Pilots**. They returned to Reading in 1994 to support the release of 'She Don't Use Jelly', which finally took off on **MTV** over the following year. This, combined with a storming appearance on the second stage at **Lollapalooza**, at last helped to build a substantial popular as well as critical following. A two-year break preceded the release of *Clouds Taste Metallic*, their seventh album, a typically confusing but arresting exercise in wide-eyed, skewed pop rock, akin to a

restrained **Pavement**. Song titles such as 'Guy Who Got A Headache And Accidentally Saved The World' and 'Psychiatric Explorations Of The Fetus With Needles' continued the penchant for adolescent shock value.
Guitarist Jones departed shortly after *Clouds Taste Metallic* was released. Reduced to a trio, the band returned with *Zaireeka*, a defiantly uncommercial 'experiment in listener participation, using multiple sound sources', whereby four separate CDs needed to be played simultaneously to hear the final mix. *The Soft Bulletin* (1999) and *Yoshimi Battles The Pink Robots* (2002) were far more satisfying records, representing the perfect fusion of the band's experimental urges and pop instincts. Wayne Coyne increased his reputation considerably when he voluntarily admitted plagiarism for a track on the latter album, 'Fight Test', which bore uncomfortable similarities to **Cat Stevens**' 'Father And Son'. He agreed to pay the artist, now known by his Muslim name Yusuf Islam, an undisclosed sum.
● ALBUMS: *The Flaming Lips* (Lovely Sorts Of Death 1985) ★★, *Hear It Is* (Pink Dust 1986) ★★, *Oh My Gawd!!! . . . The Flaming Lips* (Restless 1987) ★★★, *Telepathic Surgery* (Restless 1988) ★★, *Live* cassette (Lovely Sorts Of Death 1989) ★★, *In A Priest Driven Ambulance* (Restless 1990) ★★★, *Hit To Death In The Future Head* (Warners 1992) ★★★, *Transmissions From The Satellite Heart* (Warners 1993) ★★★, *Providing Needles For Your Balloons* (Warners 1995) ★★, *Clouds Taste Metallic* (Warners 1995) ★★★★, *Zaireeka* 4-CD set (Warners 1998) ★★, *The Soft Bulletin* (Warners 1999) ★★★★★, *Yoshimi Battles The Pink Robots* (Warners 2002) ★★★★, *At War With The Mystics* (Warners 2006) ★★★.
● COMPILATIONS: *A Collection Of Songs Representing An Enthusiasm For Recording . . . By Amateurs . . . Or The Accidental Career* (Restless 1998) ★★★, *Finally The Punk Rockers Are Taking Acid: 1983–1988* (Restless 2002) ★★★, *The Day They Shot A Hole In The Jesus Egg: The Priest Driven Ambulance Album, Demos And Outtakes: 1989–1991* (Restless 2002) ★★★, *LateNightTales* (Azuli 2005) ★★★.
● DVD/VIDEOS: *VOID: Video Overview In Deceleration: The Flaming Lips 1992–2005* (Warner Music Vision 2005).
● FURTHER READING: *Waking Up With A Placebo Headwound: Images Of The Flaming Lips From The Archives Of Jay Blakesberg And J. Michelle Martin-Coyne (1987–2004)*, Jay Blakesberg and J. Michelle Martin-Coyne.
● FILMS: *The Fearless Freaks* (2005).

Flaming Sideburns

The early twenty-first century has seen Europe spawn countless bands that would have fit perfectly in Detroit's high energy garage rock scene of the late 60s, as evidenced by the emergence of groups such as Sweden's the **Hives** and to a lesser degree Finland's the Flaming Sideburns. The latter outfit originally formed in 1995, with Eduardo 'Speedo' Martinez (vocals), Jeffrey Lee Burns (guitar), Ski Williamson (b. Jukka Suksi; guitar), the Punisher (bass) and Jay Burnside (drums), all notable participants on the local garage rock scene. After several singles and appearances on compilations helped build a local buzz (as well as a live album, 1997's *Bama Lama Boogaloo!*), the quintet signed a recording contract with the Danish indie label Bad Afro Records. In addition to further singles and compilations, the Flaming Sideburns issued two studio recordings, 1998's *It's Time To Testify . . . . . . Brothers And Sisters!* and 2001's

Hallelujah Rock 'N' Rollah. Johnny Volume replaced Jeffrey Lee Burns following the release of the latter, although the new guitarist was already familiar to the band's fans having played on half the tracks on the album. With garage rock sweeping across Europe and the USA by this time, the Flaming Sideburns were signed to Jetset Records, which issued the band's *Save Rock N' Roll* in 2002.

● ALBUMS: *Bama Lama Boogaloo!* (Smokin' Troll 1997) ★★, *It's Time To Testify . . . Brothers And Sisters!* (Bad Afro 1998) ★★★, *Hallelujah Rock 'N' Rollah* (Bad Afro 2001) ★★★, *Save Rock 'N' Roll* (Jetset 2002) ★★★★.

Flaming Star

The second 1960 film to star **Elvis Presley**, *Flaming Star* caused a minor furore upon release. It arrived soon after the highly successful **GI Blues**, but this particular feature was a vehicle for Presley the actor, not singer. Director Don Seigel, later famous for his 'Dirty Harry' work with Clint Eastwood, declared there would be no music at all, although the film did included the insouciant, but contextualized 'A Cane And A High-Starched Collar' as well as its popular title song. Set in the US Civil War, *Flaming Star* portrays Presley as a confused half-breed, torn between cultural loyalties and a love triangle when his family is slaughtered by Kiowa Indians. Critics praised his dramatic abilities, and indeed Elvis did excel in a part originally written for Marlon Brando. Fans, however, were a little more reserved, particularly in view of the downbeat ending in which Presley's character dies, echoing the close of his first feature, *Lovin' You*. *Flaming Star* was not a spectacular box-office success, paling in comparison with *GI Blues*. This perhaps explains the light-hearted features the singer was forced to complete over the next eight years.

Flaming Stars

A raucous quintet formed in Camden, North London, England, in November 1994, the Flaming Stars took their name from an **Elvis Presley** movie. Initial media comparisons placed them within the doomed romantic tradition of **Gallon Drunk** or the **Tindersticks**—unsurprising, given vocalist/keyboard player Max Decharne's previous employment as Gallon Drunk's drummer. He had also been a member of the Earls Of Suave, from whom Paul Dempsey (bass), Johnny Johnson (guitar/harmonica) and Joe Whitney (drums) were also drawn. Johnson and Dempsey had previously also played with **Thee Headcoats** and the Stingrays. Mark Hosking was then drafted in to provide additional guitar as the Flaming Stars took shape in order to fulfil a support slot at short notice. They made their debut on London-based Vinyl Japan with the typically moribund *Hospital, Heaven Or Hell* EP in March 1995, a record distinguished by the presence of the impressive 'Kiss Tomorrow Goodbye'—which Decharne had earlier contributed as a solo composition to a Death Cigarettes compilation. The alcohol tribute 'The Face On The Bar Room Floor' was followed by another EP, *Money To Burn*. They also recorded a succession of sessions for **John Peel**, Mark Radcliffe and Mark Lamarr. The alcohol theme was continued on the band's 1996 debut album, succinctly titled *Songs From The Bar Room Floor*. Huck Whitney was then brought in to replace Johnny Johnson, adding extra fuel to the band's chaotic live performances. Their prolific single releases were collected on *Bring Me The Rest Of Alfredo Garcia*. 'New Hope For The Dead', released in October 1997,

premiered the garage band classic, *Sell Your Soul To The Flaming Stars*. Extensive worldwide touring followed before the band set about recording their new album, *Pathway*.

● ALBUMS: *Songs From The Bar Room Floor* (Vinyl Japan 1996) ★★★, *Sell Your Soul To The Flaming Stars* (Vinyl Japan 1997) ★★★★, *Pathway* (Vinyl Japan 1999) ★★★, *A Walk On The Wired Side* (Vinyl Japan 2000) ★★★, *Ginmill Perfume* (Alternative Tentacles 2001) ★★★, *Sunset & Void* (Vinyl Japan 2002) ★★★, *Named And Shamed* (Vinyl Japan 2004) ★★★.

● COMPILATIONS: *Bring Me The Rest Of Alfredo Garcia* (Vinyl Japan 1997) ★★★, *The Six John Peel Sessions* (Vinyl Japan 2000) ★★★.

Flaming Youth

This short-lived UK act comprised of Gordon Smith (guitar), Brian Chatton (keyboards), Ronnie Caryl (bass) and **Phil Collins** (drums). Their sole recording, *Ark 2*, was an ambitiously packaged concept album, written and arranged by **Ken Howard/Alan Blakely**, a team better known for creating the unashamed pop of the **Herd** and **Dave Dee, Dozy, Beaky Mick And Tich**. The project was the subject of considerable hype, but its new musical departure proved unconvincing and prematurely doomed Flaming Youth's career. The group was effectively disbanded when Collins successfully auditioned for **Genesis** in 1970.

● ALBUMS: *Ark 2* (Fontana 1969) ★★★.

Flamingoes

Mod-inspired UK indie trio featuring identical twin brothers Jude (vocals, guitar) and James Cook (bass, vocals; both b. *c*.1970) plus lunatic drummer and ex-dustman Kevin, the Flamingoes formed in Hitchin, Hertfordshire, in April 1993 before relocating to Camden, London, with the express intention of becoming 'pop stars'. They took their name from a **Roxy Music** lyric, though central influences such as the **Jam** and **Clash** were the ones acknowledged in early singles 'Chosen Few' and 'Scenester'. Previously they had won disc jockey Gary Crowley's *Demo Clash* competition on BBC GLR radio with 'Teenage Emergency'. Caught up in the *New Musical Express*–christened New Wave Of The New Wave, they played the famed New Art Riot gig in December with **S*M*A*S*H** and **These Animal Men**, attracting positive press in both the *Evening Standard* and *News Of The World* as well as more traditional music journals. Meanwhile, Kevin was earning himself a reputation as a second generation **Keith Moon**, attacking audiences with sanitary towel bins and regularly throwing equipment about on stage. However, their intention remained rigidly one of world domination: 'We ain't competing with **Blur**. I want to move right over Blur's heads and go straight for **East 17**'. To this end they recorded a debut album with the assistance of Dick Meany after celebrated support gigs around the UK with labelmates (at the time) **Echobelly**.

● ALBUMS: *Plastic Jewels* (Pandemonium 1995) ★★★.

Flamingos

This R&B vocal group, formed in Chicago, Illinois, USA, in 1951, was renowned for producing the tightest and most gorgeous harmonies of the rock 'n' roll era. For much of their history they consisted of Zeke Carey (b. 24 January 1933, Bluefield, Virginia, USA), Jake Carey (b. 9 September 1926, Pulaski, Virginia, USA), Paul Wilson (b. 6 January 1935,

Chicago, Illinois, USA, d. May 1988) and Johnny Carter (b. 2 June 1934, Chicago, Illinois, USA). The group's first lead was Sollie McElroy (b. 16 July 1933, Gulfport, Mississippi, USA, d. 15 January 1995), who brought the group regional fame on 'Golden Teardrops' for the Chance, label in 1954. He was replaced by Nate Nelson (b. 10 April 1932, Chicago, Illinois, USA, d. 10 April 1984), who brought the group into the rock 'n' roll era with the magnificent ballad 'I'll Be Home', a number 5 R&B hit in 1956 on **Chess Records**. There then followed a period of disarray, in which Carter and Zeke Carey were lost to the draft. The Flamingos brought into the group Tommy Hunt (b. 18 June 1933, Pittsburgh, Pennsylvania, USA) and Terry Johnson (b. 12 November 1935, Baltimore, Maryland, USA) and moved to New York where they signed with End Records in 1958.

At this stage of their career the Flamingos had their biggest US hits, 'Lovers Never Say Goodbye' (R&B number 25 in 1958), 'I Only Have Eyes For You' (R&B number 3 and pop number 11 in 1959) and 'Nobody Loves Me Like You' (R&B number 23 and pop Top 30 in 1960), the last song written by **Sam Cooke**. One of the group's last outstanding records was 'I Know Better' (1962), a **Drifters**' sound-alike that captured top spots in many markets. During the early 60s the Flamingos lost the rest of their original members, except for Jake and Zeke Carey. The cousins managed to achieve some minor hits during the soul era, notably 'Boogaloo Party', which was the group's only UK chart hit when it reached number 26 in 1969 (three years earlier it was a US R&B number 22 hit). The Flamingos' last US chart record was 'Buffalo Soldier' 1970 (R&B Top 30). Nate Nelson died in 1984 and Paul Wilson in 1988. Sollie McElroy, after leaving the Flamingos in 1955, joined the Moroccos, with whom he recorded for three years, and Johnny Carter joined the **Dells** in 1960.

● ALBUMS: *The Flamingos* (Checker 1959) ★★★, *Flamingo Serenade* (End 1959) ★★★, *Flamingo Favorites* (End 1960) ★★★, *Requestfully Yours* (End 1960) ★★★, *The Sound Of The Flamingos* (End 1962) ★★★, *The Spiritual And Folk Moods Of The Flamingos* (End 1963) ★★, *Their Hits—Then And Now* (Philips 1966) ★★, *Flamingos Today* (Ronze 1971) ★★★.

● COMPILATIONS: *Collectors Showcase: The Flamingos* (Constellation 1964) ★★★, *Flamingos* (Chess 1984) ★★★★, *The Chess Sessions* (Chess 1987) ★★★, *The Doo Bop She Bop: The Best Of The Flamingos* (Rhino 1990) ★★★★, *The Flamingos: I Only Have Eyes For You* (Sequel 1991) ★★★, *The Flamingos Meet The Moonglows: 'On The Dusty Road Of Hits': The Complete 25 Chance Sides* (Vee Jay 1993) ★★★.

● FILMS: *Go Johnny Go* (1958).

Flanagan And Allen

Bud Flanagan (b. Reuben Weintrop [Robert Winthrop], 14 October 1896, Whitechapel, London, England, d. 20 October 1968, Kingston, Surrey, England) and Chesney Allen (b. William Ernest Allen, 5 April 1896, London, England, d. 13 November 1982, Midhurst, Sussex, England). One of Britain's best-loved comedy-singing duos during their heyday in the 30s and 40s. Allen was the straight man, with a neat, well tailored image complete with trilby, while comedian Flanagan wore a voluminous mangy fur coat and a battered straw hat. The son of Jewish refugees from Poland, Flanagan took a job as a call boy at the Cambridge Music Hall when he

was 10 and made his first stage appearance at the London Music Hall—as conjuror Fargo, the Boy Wizard—in 1908. After winning singing competitions sponsored by the popular musical hall artist Dora Lyric, Flanagan made up his young mind to run away to America and, at the age of 14, found himself washing dishes in the galley of the S.S. *Majestic* bound for New York. Once there, he worked as a Western Union messenger, newspaper vendor and prize-fighter (billed as 'Luke McGlook from England') before forming a vaudeville double act with Dale Burgess. They toured the USA and appeared in Australia, New Zealand and South Africa before Flanagan returned to England just after the outbreak of World War I and enlisted in the Royal Artillery. Posted to northern France, where he first met Chesney Allen briefly, he took his future stage name from a particularly obnoxious, anti-Semitic Sergeant-Major Flanagan. After his release in 1919, he worked with various stage partners and was a taxi driver for a spell in the early 20s before taking over from Stan Stanford as Chesney Allen's partner in **Florrie Forde**'s revue and pantomime company in 1924.

Allen, whose father was a master builder, had been articled to a solicitor before opting for a stage career. As well as performing in Forde's shows, he was also her manager. When Forde decided to retire, Flanagan And Allen's first inclination was to follow their main interest and start up as bookmakers, but they accepted D.J. Clarke's offer of a week in variety at the Argyle Theatre, Birkenhead, in January 1931. Their performances were so well received, especially their rendering of Flanagan's composition, 'Underneath The Arches', that they were swiftly booked for the Holborn Empire and the London Palladium. Flanagan And Allen also appeared at the Palladium in their first Royal Variety Performance in 1932. Flanagan's impulsive appeal for 'three cheers' for their majesties King George V and Queen Mary at the end of the show, marked the beginning of his long reign as an affectionately regarded 'court jester'. Also on the bill that year were the comic duo, Nervo And Knox, and that pair's subsequent appearances with Flanagan And Allen, Eddie Gray, Caryll And Mundy and Naughton And Gold in the Palladium's *Crazy Month* revues saw the birth of the legendary Crazy Gang. The team was reduced to seven after Billy Caryll lost a leg and died. In the 30s, as well as touring in variety and appearing together in their own shows such as *Give Me A Ring*, *Happy Returns*, *Life Begins At Oxford Circus* and *Swing Is In The Air*, Flanagan And Allen were part of the Crazy Gang (although in most cases the artists were each billed separately) in popular revues such as *Round About Regent Street*, *O-Kay For Sound*, *London Rhapsody*, *These Foolish Things* and *The Little Dog Laughed* (1939). During World War II, Flanagan And Allen entertained the troops with ENSA and were seen in the revues *Top Of The World*, *Black Vanities* and *Hi-Di-Hi*. They also starred in a series of comedy films—sprinkled occasionally with songs—which had begun in the 30s with *A Fire Has Been Arranged*, *Underneath The Arches*, *Okay For Sound*, *Alf's Button Afloat* and *The Frozen Limit* and continued in the early 40s with *Gasbags*, *We'll Smile Again*, *Theatre Royal*, *Here Comes The Sun* and *Dreaming* (1944).

Allen's ill health brought the illustrious partnership to an end in 1946, and in the same year Flanagan appeared in Robert Nesbitt's revue, *The Night And The Laughter*, before rejoining the re-formed Crazy Gang in 1947 for *Together*

Again at the Victoria Palace. It ran for more than two years, and similar productions such as *Knights Of Madness*, *Ring Out The Bells*, *Jokers Wild*, *These Foolish Kings* and *Clown Jewels* (1959) also enjoyed extended stays, keeping the same theatre fully occupied during the 50s. In the latter show, Flanagan introduced Ralph Reader's 'Strollin'', a perfect addition to the catalogue of songs indelibly identified with Flanagan And Allen, which included 'The Umbrella Man', 'Run, Rabbit, Run', 'Home Town', 'Hey, Neighbour', 'We're Gonna Hang Out The Washing On The Siegfried Line', 'Dreaming', 'Forget-Me-Not Lane', 'Music, Maestro, Please', 'Franklin D. Roosevelt Jones' 'On The Outside Looking In', 'The Oi Song' and, of course, 'Underneath The Arches'.

Flanagan received the OBE in 1959, and after the Crazy Gang's farewell show, *Young In Heart*, closed in 1962, he concentrated mainly on his bookmaking and other business interests. However, in 1968 he was persuaded to sing Jimmy Perry and Derek Taverner's 'Who Do You Think You Are Kidding Mr. Hitler' to be used over the opening titles of the brand new television comedy series, *Dad's Army*. Although he died just a few weeks after the first show was transmitted, his voice is still heard in reruns. Following his early retirement from the stage, Allen became the managing director of a theatrical and variety agency and was the Crazy Gang's manager for a time. He joined Flanagan for two more films, *Life Is A Circus* and *Dunkirk*, in 1958 and made a nostalgic appearance at the 1980 Royal Variety Performance. He also took part in the cast recording of *Underneath The Arches*, a celebration of Flanagan And Allen, starring Roy Hudd (as Flanagan) and Christopher Timothy (as Allen), which played at London's Prince of Wales Theatre in 1982.

● COMPILATIONS: *Favourites* (Decca 1953) ★★★★, *Successes* (Columbia 1953) ★★★★, *Down Forget-Me-Not Lane* (Decca 1962) ★★★★, *The Flanagan And Allen Story* (Encore 1963) ★★★★, *We'll Smile Again* (Ace Of Clubs 1965) ★★★★, *Best Of* (Encore 1978) ★★★★, *Yesterday's Dreams* (Decca 1981) ★★★★, *Arches and Umbrellas* (Flapper 1990) ★★★★, *Underneath The Arches* (MFP 1991) ★★★★.

● FURTHER READING: *My Crazy Life*, Bud Flanagan.

Flanagan, Bud
(see **Flanagan And Allen**)

Flanagan, Ralph
b. 7 April 1919, Loranie, Ohio, USA. Flanagan played piano with several local bands during his teen years, eventually becoming pianist-arranger with **Sammy Kaye** in 1940. He was a member of the Merchant Marines during World War II and later provided arrangements for **Charlie Barnet**, **Sammy Kaye**, **Gene Krupa**, **Blue Barron**, **Alvino Rey**, **Tony Pastor** and many other bands. He also worked with a number of singers including **Mindy Carson** and **Perry Como**. He struck lucky when Herb Hendler, who worked for a minor record label, commissioned him to provide an album devoted to cover versions of **Glenn Miller** favourites. The resulting record sold so well that when Hendler moved to a job at **RCA-Victor Records**, he persuaded that company (which owned all the original Miller masters) to release further tracks by Flanagan. This time, he grafted Miller-style arrangements onto material not formerly associated with the Miller band. The ploy paid off and the records sold prolifically, encouraging Flanagan to

form a full-time orchestra in early 1950 and to take it out on the road. The band was heavily influenced by Miller, and their vocal group, the Singing Winds, emulated the sounds of the **Pied Pipers**. Flanagan's band also boasted a good male vocalist named Harry Prime, filling the **Ray Eberle** role. As a result, the band quickly became one of the biggest crowd-pullers on the big-band circuit, hit records coming with 'Rag Mop', 'Nevertheless' and 'Harbour Lights' in 1950, followed by 'Slow Poke' and his own composition 'Hot Toddy'. The success of the Flanagan band sparked off a whole Miller revival, with such former Miller-men as **Ray Anthony** and **Jerry Gray**, plus many others who had never even met Miller, organizing bands that echoed the Miller sound. Most of these imitators gradually faded, although Flanagan was still an active leader/arranger in the early 60s.

● COMPILATIONS: the Ralph Flanagan And Buddy Morrow Orchestras *The War Of The Bands Concert* (RCA Victor 1954) ★★★, *On The Beat* (Golden Era 1989) ★★★, *Hot Toddy* (Aerospace 1995) ★★★, *Let's Dance With Ralph Flanagan* (Magic 1996) ★★★, *Dance Again With Ralph Flanagan* (Magic 1996) ★★★, *At The Hollywood Palladium* (Collector's Choice 2001) ★★★, *A Tribute To Glenn Miller* (Jasmine 2001) ★★★.

Flanagan, Tommy
b. 16 March 1930, Detroit, Michigan, USA, d. 16 November 2001, New York City, USA. Flanagan began playing piano as a child, following a brief flirtation with the clarinet. His professional career began during his teenage while he was still living in his home town, then a thriving centre for bop. He worked with numerous visiting musicians, impressing them with his eclecticism and innate supportive gifts. In his mid-twenties he relocated to New York where he played at Birdland. From the mid-50s he continued his supportive role, working with instrumentalists and singers. The former included **Miles Davis**, **Sonny Rollins** and **Coleman Hawkins**. The singers included **Tony Bennett** and, principally, **Ella Fitzgerald** for whom Flanagan was accompanist for the greater part of the 60s and 70s. In the late 70s Flanagan finally made the break from his subservient role and began to make a much-deserved impact in his own right.

Flanagan continued to gain stature and acclaim, both popular and critical and as both small group leader and soloist, through the 80s and into the 90s, perhaps as a result of his years in the background, perhaps through a natural diffidence and inclination towards subtly lyrical interpretations of both bop and popular standards. Though his playing was often deeply introspective, Flanagan's wide experience and stylistic grace helped make him a major player on the international stage. At the same time his bop roots and long-standing admiration of **Bud Powell** ensured that he remained close to the cutting edge of jazz piano.

● ALBUMS: *Trio Overseas/Tommy Flanagan In Stockholm* (Prestige 1957) ★★★★, *Jazz . . . It's Magic* (Regent 1957) ★★★, with Wilbur Harden *The Music Of Rodgers And Hammerstein* (Savoy Jazz 1958) ★★★, *Lonely Town* (Blue Note 1959) ★★★, *The Tommy Flanagan Trio* (Moodsville 1960) ★★★, *Eclypso* (Enja 1977) ★★★, with Ella Fitzgerald *Ella Fitzgerald With The Tommy Flanagan Trio* (Pablo 1977) ★★★, *I Remember Bebop* (Columbia 1977) ★★★, *They All Played Bebop* (Columbia 1977) ★★★, *Alone Too Long* (Denon 1977) ★★★, with Hank Jones *Our Delights* (Galaxy 1978) ★★★, *Something Borrowed,*

Something Blue (Galaxy 1978) ★★★, *Ballads And Blues* (Enja 1978) ★★★, *Together With Kenny Barron* (Denon 1978) ★★★★, *Communication: Live At Fat Tuesday's New York, Vols. 1 & 2* (Paddle Wheel 1979) ★★★, *Tommy Flanagan Plays The Music Of Harold Arlen* (Inner City 1980) ★★★, with Elvin Jones, Red Mitchell *Super-session* (Enja 1980) ★★★, with Mitchell *You're Me* (Phontastic 1980) ★★★, with Mitchell, Phil Woods *Three For All* (Enja 1981) ★★★, *The Magnificent Tommy Flanagan* (Progressive 1981) ★★★★, *Giant Steps* (Enja 1982) ★★★, *Thelonica* (Enja 1983) ★★★, *Blues In The Closet* (Baybridge 1983) ★★★, *Nights At The Vanguard* (Uptown 1986) ★★★, *Jazz Poet* (Timeless 1989) ★★★★, *Beyond The Bluebird* (Timeless 1990) ★★★, *Let's Play The Music Of Thad Jones* (Enja 1993) ★★★, *Lady Be Good . . . For Ella* (Verve 1994) ★★★, *Flanagan's Shenanigans* (Storyville 1996) ★★★, *Let's* (Enja 1996) ★★★, *Sea Changes* (Evidence 1997) ★★★★, *Sunset And The Mockingbird: The Birthday Concert* (Blue Note 1998) ★★★.

● COMPILATIONS: *The Best Of Tommy Flanagan* (Pablo 1975) ★★★.

Flanders And Swann

The son of an actor father and a mother who had been a concert-violinist before she married, Michael Flanders (b. 1 March 1922, London, England, d. 14 April 1975), was brought up in a musical household. He learned to play the clarinet and made his stage debut at the age of seven in a singing contest with *Uncle Mac's Minstrel Show*. At Westminster School in London, where Peter Ustinov was one of his classmates, he started to write and stage revues. His search for a pianist led him to **Donald Swann** (b. Donald Ibrahim Swann, 30 September 1923, Llanelli, Wales, d. 23 March 1994, London, England), and their first revue together was *Go To It*. At Oxford University in 1940 Flanders played in and directed several productions for the Dramatic Society and made his professional debut as Valentine in Shaw's *You Never Can Tell* at the Oxford Playhouse. In 1943, while serving in the Royal Navy Volunteer Reserve, having survived the infamous convoys to Russia, he was struck down by poliomyelitis. Three years later he was discharged from hospital, in a wheelchair and with a full beard, which he retained for the rest of his life.

Unable to resume a normal acting career, Flanders turned to writing and broadcasting. He contributed lyrics to several West End revues, in collaboration with Swann, including *Penny Plain* (1951), *Airs On A Shoestring* (1953) and *Fresh Airs* (1956). Flanders also appeared extensively on radio and later television in programmes ranging from sports commentary to poetry readings and including a spell of two years as chairman of *The Brains Trust*. His translation of Stravinsky's *Soldier's Tale* (with Kitty Black) became the standard English version, and his concert performance of it with Peter Ustinov and Sir Ralph Richardson was a surprise sell out at the Royal Festival Hall in 1956. After successfully entertaining their friends at parties with their own songs, Flanders and Swann decided to perform professionally, so on New Year's Eve 1956, they opened their own two-man show, *At The Drop Of A Hat*, at the intimate New Lindsey Theatre, Notting Hill, West London, moving three weeks later into the West End's Fortune Theatre. The show was a smash hit and ran for over two years. It was reported that Princess Margaret attended a performance and returned the following week with the Queen and the Duke of Edinburgh. With Flanders' urbane image contrasting with Swann's almost schoolboy enthusiasm, they introduced songs such as 'The Hippopotamus ('Mud, Mud, Glorious Mud')', 'Misalliance', 'A Gnu' and 'Madeira M'Dear?'. Two albums from the show were released, the earlier mono recording being preferable to the later stereo issue from the last night of the London run. In 1959 the show opened on Broadway, billed as 'An After-Dinner Farrago', and later toured the USA, Canada and the UK. In 1963 at the Haymarket Theatre, London, they presented a fully revised version entitled *At The Drop Of Another Hat*, which included songs such as 'The Gas-Man Cometh', 'First And Second Law' and 'Bedstead Men'. During 1964/5 they toured Australia, New Zealand and Hong Kong before returning to the West End in 1965 and, yet again, to New York in the following year.

Meanwhile, Flanders was still continuing with his other work, writing, broadcasting and performing theatrical speech recitals. He published *Creatures Great And Small*, a children's book of verses about animals and, together with Swann, released an album of animal songs entitled *The Bestiary Of Flanders And Swann*. Flanders was awarded the OBE in 1964. After the partnership broke up in 1967, Swann, who was born of Russian parents, continued to compose. In the 50s he had written the music for revues such as *Pay The Piper* and *Wild Thyme*, but in later years his music reflected his religious beliefs (he was a Quaker) and his love of Greece, and many other interests. He was still working right up to the time he died from cancer in 1994. In that same year, a musical celebration of the works of Michael Flanders and Donald Swann, entitled *Under Their Hats*, was presented at the King's Head Theatre in London.

● ALBUMS: *At The Drop Of A Hat* (Parlophone 1957) ★★★★, *The Bestiary Of Flanders And Swann* (Parlophone 1961) ★★★, *At The Drop Of Another Hat* (Parlophone 1964) ★★★.

● COMPILATIONS: *A Review Of Revues* (EMI 1975) ★★★, *Tried By Centre Court* (Note 1977) ★★★, *The Complete Flanders & Swann* 3-CD set (EMI 1991) ★★★★.

● DVD/VIDEOS: *The Only Flanders And Swann Video* (PMI 1992).

● FURTHER READING: all by Donald Swann, *The Space Between The Bars: A Book Of Reflections. Swann's Way Out. Swann's Way: A Life In Song* (autobiography).

Flanders, Michael

(see **Flanders And Swann**; **Swann, Donald**)

Flares

From Los Angeles, California, USA, the members of this vocal group were Aaron Collins, Willie Davis, Tommy Miller and George Hollis. The Flares were a one-hit-wonder, but they had a extensive pedigree in the music field long before their one hit. Collins and Davis had been members of the **Cadets/Jacks** during the 50s and had built the Flares on the ashes of that group. Miller and Hollis had been members of the Flairs, who were stablemates with the Cadets/Jacks on the label complex owned by the **Bihari Brothers**. The Flares signed with the small Felsted, label in 1960, and on their third release they reached the charts with 'Footstompin'' (number 20 R&B, number 25 pop) in 1961 (the song was later covered by **David Bowie** in 1975 on *Fame*). **Capitol Records** took notice and picked up the group for their Press subsidiary, releasing an album and a spate of dance-related songs. The group disbanded not long after the release of their last Press single in 1963.

● ALBUMS: *Encore Of Footstompin' Hits* (Press 1961) ★★★.

● COMPILATIONS: *Foot Stompin'* (Ace 2002) ★★★.

Flash

This UK rock outfit was formed by Pete Banks (b. Peter Brockbanks, 15 July 1947, Barnet, Hertfordshire, England; guitar) and Tony Kaye (b. Anthony John Selvidge, 11 January 1946, Leicester, England; organ), both ex-members of **Yes**. Colin Carter (vocals), Ray Bennett (bass/keyboards) and Mike Hough (drums) completed the line-up featured on 1972's *Flash*, after which Kaye left to join **Badger**. The remaining quartet completed two further progressive rock-styled albums, but were unable to make a significant commercial breakthrough, although they did reach the US Top 30 singles chart in 1972 with 'Small Beginnings'. Following a brief association with **Jan Akkerman**, guitarist with **Focus**, Banks enjoyed a moderate, albeit brief, solo career releasing *Peter Banks* and *Two Sides Of Peter Banks* in 1973. Hough meanwhile surfaced in the short-lived Fast Buck. Banks later worked with female vocalist Sydney Foxx in Empire but the project was short-lived. He returned to solo work in the 90s.

● ALBUMS: *Flash* (Sovereign 1972) ★★★, *In The Can* (Sovereign/Capitol 1972) ★★, *Out Of Our Hands* (Sovereign/Capitol 1973) ★★, *Two Sides Of Flash—Live In The USA* 1973 recording (Voiceprint 2005) ★★.

Flash And The Pan

(see **Vanda And Young**)

Flash Cadillac And The Continental Kids

Formed in Colorado, USA, in March 1969, Flash Cadillac And The Continental Kids were one of several bands to parody 50s rock in the wake of **Sha Na Na**. The original line-up comprised University of Colorado students Kris 'Angelo' Moe (keyboards/vocals), Linn 'Spike' Phillips III (d. March 1993; guitar/vocals), Mick 'Flash' Manresa (guitar/vocals), George Robinson (saxophone), Warren 'Butch' Knight (bass/vocals) and Harold 'Marty' Fielden (drums). They began to gain popularity within the music industry after moving to Los Angeles in 1971 where they met pop Svengali **Kim Fowley**. Line-up changes saw Manresa and Fielden replaced by Sam 'Flash' McFadin (d. 31 August 2001, Colorado Springs, USA; guitar/vocals) and John 'Ricco' Masino (drums). The latter was the first in a line of several drummers, including Jeff 'Wally' Stewart and Paul 'Wheaty' Wheatbread. The band went on to make successful appearances in the movies *American Graffiti* and *Apocalypse Now* and the television series *American Bandstand* and *Happy Days*. Their promising 1973 debut contained respectable readings of rock 'n' roll favourites. A second set, *No Face Like Chrome*, contained material indebted to 50s, 60s and 70s styles and was probably reminiscent of Britain's pub rock scene. Although they enjoyed three minor US hits with 'Dancin' (On A Saturday Night)', 'Good Times, Rock & Roll' and 'Did You Boogie (With Your Baby)', the band, with saxophonist Dwight 'Spider' Bement playing an increasingly important role in their sound, had faded from the national music scene by the late 70s. Now known as Flash Cadillac, they set up their own recording studio near Colorado Springs and continued to tour on the summer fair circuit, sometimes with a full symphony orchestra, as well as producing and performing music for the syndicated oldies radio show *Supergold*. Both Phillips and McFadin succumbed to heart attacks, the former in March 1993 and the latter in August 2001.

● ALBUMS: *Flash Cadillac And The Continental Kids* (Epic 1973) ★★★★, *There's No Face Like Chrome* (Epic 1974) ★★★, *Sons Of The Beaches* (Private Stock 1976) ★★★, *Souvenirs* (Resounding 1994) ★★★, *A Night With The Symphony* (Resounding 1994) ★★★, *25 Years* (Resounding 1994) ★★★, *Ghost Of Christmas Past* (Resounding 1996) ★★★, *Rock & Roll Rules* (Resounding 1997) ★★★.

Flash Faction

UK **techno** outfit comprising Matt Nelmes, Richard Johnstone and Jake Davies. The three worked as engineers at Soho's Berwick Street Studios before deciding to give it a go themselves with the help of DJ Sean Johnstone in late 1993. They began 1994 with two hard **trance** releases, 'Robot Criminal' on Labello Trax and 'Repoman' on **Andy Weatherall**'s **Sabres Of Paradise** label. The latter was envisioned as an 'alternative soundtrack' to Alex Cox's film of the same name. It was followed up with the release of 'Mad Moog Rising' for Third Mind.

Flashdance

Alex Owens (Jennifer Beals) yearns to be a ballet star and is encouraged and coached by former classical dancer, Hanna Long (Lilia Skala). However, until the real thing comes along, there is always the erotic disco dancing in the evening and a day job working as a female welder in a Pittsburg factory. Nick (Michael Nouri), the foreman, is her boyfriend, and Alex puts a brick through his window just to remind him, after he has been seen with another girl (it was his sister). Life can be tough, but Hanna's death inspires Alex to pass the audition and finally achieve her dream. With a screenplay (Tom Hedley and Joe Eszterhas) like that, no wonder the critics saw this film as a series of rock videos, especially as it is full of slick, gaudy images (choreograph, Jeffrey Hornaday) and a super-high energy score, composed mainly by **Giorgio Moroder**, one of the most successful and inventive dance music producers of the 80s. The numbers include 'Imagination' and 'Gloria' (performed by **Laura Branigan**), 'Flashdance . . . What A Feeling' (**Irene Cara**), 'I'll Be Here Where The Heart Is' (**Kim Carnes**), 'Seduce Me Tonight' (Cycle V), 'Lady, Lady, Lady' (Joe Esposito), 'Manhunt' (Karen Kamon), 'Love Theme From Flashdance' (Helen St. John), 'Maniac' (Michael Sembello), 'He's A Dream' (Shandi), 'Romeo' (**Donna Summer**), 'It's Just Begun' (**Jimmy Castor** and the Jimmy Castor Bunch), 'I Love Rock 'N' Roll' (**Joan Jett And The Blackhearts**) and somewhat incongruously, **Hoagy Carmichael** and **Ned Washington**'s oldie, 'The Nearness Of You'. Directed by Adrian Lyne and produced by **PolyGram Records** for Paramount in 1983, *Flashdance* was immensely successful worldwide, grossing over $36 million at the North American box office alone. The soundtrack album won a Grammy Award and spent 10 weeks at the top of the US chart, and there was another Grammy for Moroder's 'Love Theme From Flashdance'. Two number one singles, Irene Cara's 'Flashdance . . . What A Feeling' and 'Maniac' sung by Michael Sembello, also came from the score, with the former song (lyric by Keith Forsey) winning an Oscar and other honours. Not surprisingly, there was a Worst Screenplay Razzie nomination for Hedley and Eszterhas.

Flat Duo Jets

With origins dating back to the mid-80s, Chapel Hill, North Carolina' Flat Duo Jets finally made the leap to a major label in 1998. However, it was not coincidental that the label they moved to, Outpost Recordings, was overseen by highly esteemed alternative rock forefather and **R.E.M.** producer Scott Litt. He had seen the band develop over a 10-year period and considered the duo (vocalist/guitarist **Dexter Romweber** and drummer Crow) to be 'phenomenal'. Their energetic revival of early rockabilly had first come to prominence after featuring in the 1986 music documentary, *Athens, Georgia: Inside/Out*. They subsequently released a series of independent albums for a variety of local labels, with highpoints including 1990's self-titled long-playing debut and 1993's *White Trees*.

For Flat Duo Jets' Outpost debut, *Lucky Eye*, Litt contracted **dB's** alumnus **Chris Stamey**, who worked alongside him as co-producer. Sessions were completed at the **Muscle Shoals** Sound studios in Alabama, and over 18 tracks explored roots rock, traditional R&B and surf guitar—Romweber's distinctive playing being influenced by old rockabilly records and **Charlie Feathers** in particular. A 12-piece orchestra, arranged and conducted by Susie Katayama, contributed to songs such as 'New York Studio 1959' and 'Lonely Guy'. Other contributors included Tom Maxwell and Ken Mosher, the horn players for the **Squirrel Nut Zippers**. By 1999 the band had broken up. It was nevertheless stated that there was a 'strong possibility' that the duo would work together again in the future. Romweber carried on the Flat Duo Jets mix of rockabilly, blues and surf music on a number of well-received solo releases.

● ALBUMS: *In Stereo* mini-album (Dolphin 1984) ★★★, *Flat Duo Jets* (Doggone 1990) ★★★★, *Go Go Harlem Baby* (Sky 1991) ★★★, *White Trees* (Sky 1993) ★★★★, *Introducing The Flat Duo Jets* (Norton 1994) ★★★, *Red Tango* (Norton 1995) ★★★, *Wild Blue Yonder* (Norton 1998) ★★★, *Lucky Eye* (Outpost 1998) ★★★.
● COMPILATIONS: *Safari* (Norton 1993) ★★★.

Flatlanders

The seminal US country band the Flatlanders was formed in Lubbock, Texas, USA, in 1971. The three main members are all singer-songwriters and guitarists; **Joe Ely** (b. 9 February 1947, Amarillo, Texas, USA), **Jimmie Dale Gilmore** (b. 6 May 1945, Amarillo, Texas, USA) and **Butch Hancock** (b. George Hancock, 12 July 1945, Lubbock, Texas, USA). Ely met Gilmore in Lubbock, and realizing they shared a love of **Jimmie Rodgers**, they formed a traditional country band. They were joined by Sylvester Rice (bass), Tommy Hancock (fiddle) and Steve Wesson (musical saw). Tommy Hancock owned the Cotton Club in Lubbock, where **Buddy Holly** had played. According to Butch Hancock, the Flatlanders played 'parties, goat roasts and the Old Town pub in Lubbock'. An independent producer, Royce Clark, recorded them in February 1972 for Plantation Records in Nashville. They released one single, 'Dallas', written by Gilmore and credited to Jimmie Dale And The Flatlanders. It featured Ely's dobro and a prominent use of Wesson's musical saw. Seventeen tracks were recorded (including five by Hancock, four by Gilmore and three by the occasional member Al Strehli),

although they were not released until several years later when the three main members had become better known as solo artists.

From time to time, Ely, Gilmore and Hancock have collaborated on each other's solo recordings and various projects, including recording 'South Wind Of Summer' for the soundtrack to Robert Redford's 1998 film adaptation of *The Horse Whisperer*, while Steve Wesson has worked as a carpenter. A more permanent reunion took place in the new millennium, with Ely, Gilmore and Hancock touring together and working on new material. The trio was augmented by Gary Herman (vocals/bass), Tony Pearson (vocals) and Robbie Gjersoe (guitar/vocals) for the refreshing *Now Again* in 2002. The lesser *Wheels Of Fortune* followed in 2004.

● ALBUMS: *One More Road* 1972 recording (Charly 1980) ★★★, *More A Legend Than A Band* (Rounder 1990) ★★★, *Now Again* (New West 2002) ★★★, *Wheels Of Fortune* (New West 2004) ★★★, *Live At The One Knite, Austin, TX: June 8th 1972* (New West 2004) ★★★, *Live '72* (New West 2004) ★★★.
● COMPILATIONS: *Complete Plantation Recordings* (Varèse 2004) ★★★.
● DVD/VIDEOS: *Live From Austin Tx* (New West 2004).

Flatmates

The Flatmates were formed in Bristol, England, by Subway Organization label boss and guitarist Martin Whitehead in the summer of 1985, while he was promoting gigs. Whitehead recruited Rocker (drums) and was soon joined by Deb Haynes (vocals) and Kath Beach (bass), spurred on by the sounds of the **Velvet Underground**, **Blondie**, the **Stooges** and the **Ramones**. After Beach was replaced by Sarah Fletcher in 1986, the Flatmates issued the frothy 'I Could Be In Heaven' on Subway. 'Happy All The Time' continued the power pop vein the following year, which also saw Joel O'Bierne drafted in as the new drummer. The Flatmates' third single, 'You're Gonna Cry' (1987), was followed by 'Shimmer' (1988), the latter featuring guitarist Tim Rippington's debut. Like its predecessors, this fared well in the independent charts and justified the release of the band's BBC radio session for disc jockey Janice Long. Fletcher's departure was followed by the release of 'Heaven Knows', although this proved to be the band's last single. Rippington left in October 1988 after an onstage fight with Whitehead, and the Flatmates eventually split the following April. A retrospective singles compilation, *Love And Death*, rounded it all off, by which time ex-members were busy with other projects. Martin and Joel formed the Sweet Young Things, later member Jackie Carrera (bass) had joined the **Caretaker Race** and Rocker teamed up with the Rosehips. After Subway folded in the spring of 1990, Whitehead started up a new label and fanzine, *Blaster!* As a final aside, the Flatmates' road manager Paul Roberts has since enjoyed a higher commercial profile than the band ever did with his outfit **K-Class**.

● COMPILATIONS: *Love And Death (1986–1989)* (Subway 1989) ★★★.

Flatt And Scruggs

Lester Flatt (b. 28 June 1914, Overton County, Tennessee, USA, d. 11 May 1979, Nashville, Tennessee, USA; guitar) and **Earl Scruggs** (b. 6 January 1924, Cleveland County, North Carolina, USA; banjo). These influential musicians began working together in December 1945 as members of **Bill**

Monroe's Bluegrass Boys. In February 1948 they left to form the Foggy Mountain Boys with Jim Shumate (fiddle), Howard Watts aka Cedric Rainwater (bass fiddle)—both ex–Bill Monroe—and, latterly, **Mac Wiseman** (tenor vocals/guitar). They became an established feature of Virginia's WCYB radio station and undertook recording sessions for the **Mercury Records** label before embarking on a prolonged tour of the south. Here they forged a more powerful, ebullient sound than was associated with their chosen genre, and in November 1950 Flatt and Scruggs joined **Columbia/CBS Records**, with whom they remained throughout their career together. Three years later they signed a sponsorship agreement with Martha White Mills that engendered a regular show on Nashville's WSM and favoured slots on their patron's television shows. Josh Graves (dobro) was then added to the line-up, which in turn evolved a less frenetic sound and reduced the emphasis on Scruggs' banjo playing. Appearances on the nationally syndicated *Folk Sound USA* brought the group's modern bluegrass sound to a much wider audience, while their stature was further enhanced by an appearance at the 1960 Newport Folk Festival. Flatt and Scruggs were then adopted by the college circuit where they were seen as antecedents to a new generation of acts, including the **Kentucky Colonels**, the **Hillmen** and the **Dillards**. The Foggy Mountain Boys performed the theme song 'The Ballad Of Jed Clampett' to the popular *Beverly Hillbillies* television show in the early 60s, while their enduring instrumental, 'Foggy Mountain Breakdown', was heavily featured in the movie *Bonnie And Clyde*. Bluegrass students suggested that this version lacked the sparkle of earlier arrangements and declared that the group lacked its erstwhile vitality. By 1968 Earl Scruggs' sons, Randy and Gary, had been brought into the line-up, but the banjoist nonetheless grew dissatisfied with the constraints of a purely bluegrass setting. The partnership was dissolved the following year. While Flatt formed a new act, the Nashville Grass, his former partner added further members of his family to found the Earl Scruggs Revue. Plans for a reunion album were thwarted by Flatt's death in May 1979. They were inducted into the **Country Music Hall Of Fame** in 1985.

● ALBUMS: *Foggy Mountain Jamboree* (Columbia 1957) ★★★★, *Country Music* (Mercury 1958) ★★★, *Lester Flatt And Earl Scruggs* (Mercury 1959) ★★★★, *Songs Of Glory* (Columbia 1960) ★★★, *Flatt And Scruggs And The Foggy Mountain Boys* (Harmony 1960) ★★★, *Foggy Mountain Banjo* (Columbia 1961) ★★★★, *Songs Of The Famous Carter Family* (Columbia 1961) ★★★, *Folk Songs Of Our Land* (Columbia 1962) ★★★★, *Flatt And Scruggs At Carnegie Hall* (Columbia 1962) ★★★, *The Original Sound Of Flatt And Scruggs* (Mercury 1963) ★★★, *Hard Travelin'/The Ballad Of Jed Clampett* (Columbia 1963) ★★★★, *Recorded Live At Vanderbilt University* (Columbia 1964) ★★★, *The Fabulous Sound Of Flatt And Scruggs* (Columbia 1964) ★★★, *The Versatile Flatt And Scruggs* (Columbia 1965) ★★★, *Pickin' Strummin' And Singin'* (Columbia 1965) ★★★, one side is Jim And Jesse *Stars Of The Grand Ol' Opry* (Starday 1966) ★★, *Town & Country* (Columbia 1966) ★★★, *When The Saints Go Marching In* (Columbia 1966) ★★★, with Doc Watson *Strictly Instrumental* (Columbia 1967) ★★, *Hear The Whistle Blow* (Columbia 1967) ★★, *The Original Theme From Bonnie & Clyde* (Mercury 1968) ★★, *Bill Monroe With Lester Flatt &*

Earl Scruggs: The Original Bluegrass Band (Decca 1978) ★★★.

● COMPILATIONS: *Flatt And Scruggs Greatest Hits* (Columbia 1966) ★★★, *The Original Foggy Mountain Breakdown* (Mercury 1968) ★★★★, *World Of Flatt And Scruggs* (Columbia 1973) ★★★, *The Golden Era 1950–1955* (Rounder 1977) ★★★★, *Blue Ridge Cabin Home* (Rebel 1979) ★★★★, *Columbia Historic Edition* (Columbia 1982) ★★★, *Country And Western Classics* 3-LP box set (Time-Life 1982) ★★★, *20 All Time Great Recordings* (Columbia 1983) ★★★, *Mercury Sessions, Volume 1* (Mercury 1987) ★★★★, *Mercury Sessions, Volume 2* (Mercury 1987) ★★★, *You Can Feel It In Your Soul* (County 1988) ★★★, *Don't Get Above Your Raisin'* (Rounder 1992) ★★★, *The Complete Mercury Sessions* (Mercury 1992) ★★★★, *1949–1959* 4-CD box set (Bear Family 1992) ★★★★, *1959–1963* 5-CD box set (Bear Family 1992) ★★★★, *1964–69, Plus* 6-CD box set (Bear Family 1996) ★★★★, *Tis Sweet To Be Remembered: The Essential Flatt & Scruggs* (Legacy/Columbia 1997) ★★★★.

Flatt, Lester

b. 28 June 1914, Overton County, Tennessee, USA, d. 11 May 1979, Nashville, Tennessee, USA. Versed in the old-time country music style prevalent in his rural environment, Flatt began playing guitar during the 30s. At the end of the decade he abandoned his job in a textile mill to pursue a career as a professional musician. Having made his debut on station WDBJ, Flatt became a popular entertainer throughout the south and by 1944 was a feature of the **Grand Ole Opry**. He then joined **Bill Monroe**'s Bluegrass Boys where he later met banjoist **Earl Scruggs**. The two musicians left Monroe in 1948 and, as **Flatt And Scruggs**, redefined the modern bluegrass sound. For over 20 years the duo led various versions of their group, the Foggy Mountain Boys, which remained at the heart of America's traditional music circuit. They parted company in 1969, following which Flatt created another group, the Nashville Grass. He continued to tour and record, but his once-prolific work rate lessened considerably following open-heart surgery in 1975.

● ALBUMS: with Mac Wiseman *Lester 'N' Mac* (RCA-Victor 1971) ★★★, with Wiseman *On The South Bound* (RCA-Victor 1973) ★★★, with Wiseman *Over Hills To Poor House* (RCA-Victor 1973) ★★★, *Before You Go* (1974) ★★★, *Flatt Gospel* (1975) ★★★, with John Hartford, Benny Martin *Tennessee Jubilee* (Flying Fish 1975) ★★★, *Heaven's Bluegrass Band* (CMH 1976), ★★★, *Lester Flatt* (1977) ★★★, *Live At The Bluegrass Festival* (RCA 1986) ★★★, *The Golden Era* (Rounder 1988) ★★★★, *Lester Flatt's Greatest Performance* (CMH 1989) ★★★.

● COMPILATIONS: *Flatt On Victor Plus One* 6-CD box set (Bear Family 1999) ★★★.

Flatville Aces

From Southampton, Hampshire, England, the Flatville Aces are Britain's best exponents of Cajun-flavoured roots dance music. They formed in the late 80s and use French vocals with Louisiana styled Cajun fiddle and accordion. Originally comprising Tim Beckerleg (accordion), Dylan Clarke (acoustic bass/vocals), Jock Tyldesley (fiddle/vocals), Judi Wright (triangle, fiddle, vocals) and Dave Curtis (acoustic guitar), the group specialized in faithful but highly energized versions of Cajun standards such as 'Lacassine Special',

'Madelaine' and 'Bosco Stomp', prompting enthusiastic reviews from specialist music magazines as well as more mainstream sources. Following the band's growing success Wright branched out as a specialist Cajun fiddler, working with the Bluebird Cajun Band and the all-women Kitchen Girls. Clarke left to join his brother in local rivals **La Cucina** and was replaced by Don Oeters. Dave Curtis also left to become a carpenter, and Bob Still replaced him on guitar. An independently released cassette of the group's recordings pre-empted their debut CD release in 1994, which demonstrated the fidelity of their approach: 'It's very important if you're playing a traditional kind of music to learn it absolutely inside out before you start to change it. Then you've got more chance of changing it with a respect to that music.' Having researched legends such as the **Balfa Brothers**, Dennis McGee and **Nathan Abshire**, *Crawfishtrombones* became a key release in the unlikely resurgence of UK interest in Cajun music during the early 90s.

● ALBUMS: *Cajun Shakedown* cassette (1991) ★★, *Crawfishtrombones* (1994) ★★★.

Flavin, Mick

b. 3 August 1950, Gaigue, Ballinamuck, County Longford, Eire. After leaving school, Flavin was apprenticed as a carpenter, but his love of the recordings of **Hank Williams**, **George Jones** and **Charley Pride**, plus his ambition to be a professional country singer, saw him form a band and begin to entertain in local venues. However, he spent over 12 years as a part-time entertainer and also successfully defeated a drink problem before he finally achieved his goal. In 1986 he recorded a self-financed cassette album sold only at gigs. It was well received and the following year, his recording debut, *I'm Going To Make It After All*, proved prophetically correct and won him an award. Since then, he has worked hard to establish himself on the Irish and UK country scene and has made highly acclaimed appearances at several major shows. He made his English debut in 1988 at the Peterborough Festival and the following year proved very popular at the International Festival Of Country Music at Wembley. He joined the Ritz Records label in 1990 and the following year recorded a very popular duet album with **Philomena Begley**. However, it is his solo recordings that have helped make him one of Ritz's most popular singers and established him as a major artist.

● ALBUMS: *I'm Going To Make It After All* (Harmac 1987) ★★★, *Introducing Mick Flavin* (Prism 1988) ★★★★, *You're Only Young Once* (Harmac 1988) ★★★, *In Concert* (Ritz 1990) ★★★, *Travellin' Light* (Ritz 1990) ★★★, with Philomena Begley *In Harmony* (Ritz 1991) ★★, *Sweet Memory* (Ritz 1992) ★★★, *The Lights Of Home* (Ritz 1993) ★★★, *Echoes Of My Mind* (Ritz 1994) ★★★, *Country All The Way* (Ritz 1997) ★★★★, *Irish Giants Of Country* (Ritz 1999) ★★★, *Country Highways* (Ritz 2000) ★★★★, *Nashville Bound* (Ritz 2001) ★★★, *Try It You'll Like It* (Ritz 2004) ★★★.

● COMPILATIONS: *The Very Best Of Mick Flavin* (Ritz 1998) ★★★★.

● DVD/VIDEOS: *In Concert* (Ritz 1990), *Going Home Again* (1995).

Flavor Flav

b. William Drayton, 16 March 1959, Roosevelt, Long Island, New York City, USA. The sharp banter of **Public Enemy** was both heightened and lightened by Flavor Flav's interjections as stool pigeon to **Chuck D**. However, his personal life during Public Enemy's heyday won him some degree of infamy too. In February 1991 he was arrested at his Long Island home and charged with assault on his girlfriend and mother of his three children, Karen Ross. After pleading guilty to third degree assault he was sentenced to 30 days' imprisonment and served with an exclusion order. Just as his debut solo album was announced in the press, he again hit the headlines when he was arrested in the Bronx after allegedly trying to shoot another man in a dispute over a woman. That album has yet to see a release, as has a set recorded in the late 90s. In 2004 the rapper appeared in the third series of the reality television show *The Surreal Life*.

● FILMS: *Mo' Better Blues* (1990), *Listen Up: The Lives Of Quincy Jones* (1990), *New Jack City* (1991), *Why Colors?* (1992), *CB4* (1993), *Who's The Man?* (1993), *Private Parts* (1997), *Death Of A Dynasty* (2003).

Flaw

This Louisville, Kentucky, USA–based alt metal band was originally formed in 1996, when singer Chris Volz answered an advertisement in a local paper and hooked up with guitarist Jason Daunt. Although it took a while for the duo to share their same interest in intense practice and little extracurricular activity with other musicians, Volz and Daunt eventually found a suitable bass player in the form of Ryan Jurhs, who was fresh out of the US Marines. With other ultimately temporary musicians filling in, Flaw recorded an independently released eight-song debut in 1997, *American Arrogance*. Interestingly, the album cost the band nothing to make, as they bought all the recording equipment knowing that there was a 30-day return policy if not satisfied, which they utilized after wrapping up the sessions. Opening local shows for national acts such as **Fear Factory** and Econoline Crush helped expand their already growing fanbase. Two additional indie releases were issued as well, 1998's self-titled second effort and 2000's *Drama* EP, during which Flaw's line-up was solidified with members Chris Ballinger (drums) and Lance Arny (guitar). With Arny onboard, Flaw's sound became slightly more atmospheric, as both guitarists played seven-string instruments, *à la* **Korn** and **Limp Bizkit**.

After a successful showcase at New York's famed **CBGB's** club, Flaw finally signed with a major label, Republic in October 2000. One year later *Through The Eyes* was issued, produced by David Bottrill (who just happened to have previously worked with the band's two main influences, **Tool** and **Peter Gabriel**). The album punched quite a wallop both musically and lyrically, as Volz opted to tackle personal issues in his prose, as evidenced by the track 'Whole', which concerned his adoptive mother who committed suicide when he was 12 years old. Flaw supported the release by opening dates for **Sevendust**, **Kittie** and **Cold** and as part of the travelling road show Ozzfest.

● ALBUMS: *American Arrogance* (Own Label 1997) ★★★, *Flaw* (Own Label 1998) ★★★, *Through The Eyes* (Republic 2001) ★★★★, *Endangered Species* (Universal 2004) ★★★.

Fleagle, Brick

b. Jacob Roger Fleagle, 22 August 1906, Hanover, Pennsylvania, USA. In his teens Fleagle played banjo in the South, then moved North switching to guitar. He played with numerous bands including **Hal Kemp**'s and **Joe Haymes**' and began a long-running association with **Rex Stewart**. In the 40s he played with **Jack Teagarden**, **J.C. Higginbotham**, **Buck Clayton**, Stewart and others. In the 30s he had begun establishing a reputation as an arranger for big bands, writing charts for **Chick Webb**, **Jimmie Lunceford** and **Duke Ellington**. He continued this activity into the 40s, including writing for his own short-lived big band. In 1946 he entered fully into this aspect of music, operating his own arranging and music copying business, which continued for the rest of his working life.

● ALBUMS: *One Night Stand With Brick Fleagle And His Orchestra* (Joyce 1945) ★★★, *Brick Fleagle And Rex Stewart* (Black Panther/IAJRC 1999) ★★★.

Fleck, Bela

b. Béla Anton Leos Fleck, 10 July 1958, New York City, USA. Fleck and his Flecktones have been credited with expanding the parameters of the banjo by combining traditional bluegrass with jazz and classical music, similar to what **David Grisman** did with the mandolin. Inspired by the song 'Duelin' Banjos' in the movie *Deliverance*, Fleck took up the banjo at an early age before moving to Boston to play with the group Tasty Licks. In 1981 he relocated to Nashville, joining the influential **New Grass Revival**, with whom he stayed for eight years. In 1989 he formed the Flecktones with **Howard Levy** (keyboards/harmonica), **Victor Wooten** (bass) and Roy 'Futureman' Wooten (drumitar—a guitar wired to electric drums). The group's debut album for **Warner Brothers Records** sold over 50,000 copies and reached the Top 20 on the *Billboard* jazz charts. **Chick Corea** and **Branford Marsalis** have both guested on subsequent Flecktones' releases. Fleck has also collaborated with slide-player V.M. Bhatt and Chinese erhu player Jie-Bing Chen on the eclectic world music project *Tabula Rasa* and appeared on **Ginger Baker** and **Charlie Haden**'s *Falling Off The Roof*.

Fleck signed a new recording contract with **Columbia Records** and Sony Classical in early 2000. He released the classical selection, *Perpetual Motion*, the following year. Fleck is clearly an outstanding musician, but there seems to be difficulty in establishing him beyond a jazz audience, which would seem not to be his most comfortable category. His music is more eclectic and would appeal to both rock and folk/roots audiences.

● ALBUMS: *Crossing The Tracks* (Rounder 1979) ★★★, *Natural Bridge* (Rounder 1982) ★★★, *Double Time* (Rounder 1984) ★★★, *Drive* (Rounder 1988) ★★, *Bela Fleck And The Flecktones* (Warners 1990) ★★★, with the Flecktones *Flight Of The Cosmic Hippo* (Warners 1991) ★★★★, with Tony Trischka *Solo Banjo Works* (Rounder 1993) ★★★★, with the Flecktones *UFO TOFU* (Warners 1993) ★★★, *Tales From The Acoustic Planet* (Warners 1995) ★★★★, with Jie Bing Chen, V.M. Bhatt *Tabula Rasa* (Water Lily Acoustics 1996) ★★★, with the Flecktones *Live Art* (Warners 1997) ★★★★, with the Flecktones *Left Of Cool* (Warners 1998) ★★★, with Edgar Meyer, Mike Marshall *Uncommon Ritual* (Sony Classical 1998) ★★, *The Bluegrass Sessions: Tales From The Acoustic Planet, Volume 2* (Warners 1999) ★★★★, *Outbound* (Columbia 2000) ★★★, *Perpetual Motion* (Sony Classical 2001) ★★★, with the Flecktones *Live At The Quick* (Columbia 2002) ★★★, with the Flecktones *Little Worlds* 3-CD set

(Sony Jazz 2003) ★★★, with the Flecktones *Ten From Little Worlds* (Sony Jazz 2003) ★★★, with Edgar Meyer *Music For Two* (Sony Classical 2004) ★★★, with the Flecktones *The Hidden Land* (Columbia 2006) ★★★.

● COMPILATIONS: *Daybreak* (Rounder 1987) ★★★★, *Places* (Rounder 1987) ★★★, *Greatest Hits Of The 20th Century* (Warners 1999) ★★★★.

● DVD/VIDEOS: *Teaches Banjo Picking Styles* (Homespun Video 1996), *Live At The Quick* (Sony 2002).

Flee-Rekkers

Originally known as the Ramblers, then Statesiders, this primarily instrumental unit based in the UK was led by Peter Fleerackers, a Dutch-born tenor saxophonist. Elmy Durrant (tenor saxophone), Dave 'Tex' Cameron (lead guitar), Ronald Marion (rhythm guitar), Derek Skinner (bass) and Phil Curtis (drums) completed the line-up signed by producer **Joe Meek** in 1960. 'Green Jeans', a raucous version of the traditional 'Greensleeves', reached number 23 that year, but despite a series of competent singles reminiscent of **Johnny And The Hurricanes**, this was the group's only chart entry. 'Fireball', arranged by **Tony Hatch**, became the unit's final release in 1963, by which time Alan Monger and Mickey Waller had replaced Marion and Curtis. Cameron, Durrant and Monger later enjoyed success in Germany with the Giants, but Fleerackers failed to pursue a high profile career in music. Although Skinner joined the popular **Spotniks**, it was left to newcomer Waller to achieve greater fame with **Jeff Beck** and **Rod Stewart**.

● COMPILATIONS: *Joe Meek's Fabulous Flee-Rekkers* (Sequel 1991) ★★★★.

Fleet's In, The

Blonde bombshell **Betty Hutton** made her screen debut in this lively, amusing and typically wartime musical that was produced by Paramount in 1942. She plays the best friend of the Countess of Swingland (**Dorothy Lamour**), a nightclub singer whose methods of dealing with troublesome customers ensure that she does not meet with much aggravation. One of a bunch of visiting sailors, the shy and retiring Casey Kirby (William Holden) is urged by his friends to try to make a breakthrough on behalf of the navy, which he does—and ends up marrying her. **Victor Schertzinger** and **Johnny Mercer** provided a bunch of terrific numbers such as 'Tangerine', which was introduced by vocalists **Bob Eberly** and **Helen O'Connell** with the popular **Jimmy Dorsey** Orchestra and subsequently proved to be an enormous hit for them. The rest of the songs included 'Not Mine', 'When You Hear The Time Signal' and 'I Remember You' (all Lamour), 'The Fleet's In' (Betty Jane Rhodes), 'Not Mine' (Hutton and Lamour) and 'If You Build A Better Mousetrap' and 'Arthur Murray Taught Me Dancing In A Hurry' ('To my way of thinkin', it came out stinkin' / I don't know my left from my right') (both Hutton). The other songs were 'Tomorrow You Belong To Uncle Sam' and 'Conga From Honga'. Also in the cast were comedian Eddie Bracken (who winds up with Hutton), Leif Erickson, Cass Daley ('an osteopathic soprano-she sings in the joints'), Barbara Brittan, Gil Lamb and Rod Cameron. **Jack Donohue** staged the dances, and the director was **Victor Schertzinger**. Walter DeLeon and Sid Silvers' screenplay was the third time the original story by Walter de Leon had been filmed. Previous efforts in the 30s starred Clara Bow and Mary Carlisle, and there was yet another remake, in 1951, entitled *Sailor Beware*, with **Dean Martin** and Jerry Lewis.

Fleetwood Mac

The original Fleetwood Mac was formed in July 1967 by **Peter Green** (b. Peter Allen Greenbaum, 29 October 1946, Bethnal Green, London, England; guitar) and Mick Fleetwood (b. 24 June 1947, Redruth, Cornwall, England; drums), both of whom had recently left **John Mayall**'s Bluesbreakers. They secured a recording contract with **Blue Horizon Records** on the strength of Green's reputation as a blues guitarist before the label's overtures uncovered a second guitarist, Jeremy Spencer (b. 4 July 1948, Hartlepool, Cleveland, England), in a semi-professional group, the Levi Set. A temporary bass player, **Bob Brunning**, was recruited into the line-up until a further Mayall acolyte, **John McVie** (b. 26 November 1945, London, England; bass), was finally persuaded to join the new unit. Peter Green's Fleetwood Mac, as the group was initially billed, made its debut on 12 August 1967 at Windsor's National Jazz And Blues Festival.

Their first album, *Fleetwood Mac*, released on Blue Horizon in February the following year, reached the UK Top 5 and established a distinctive balance between Green's introspective compositions and Spencer's debt to **Elmore James**. A handful of excellent cover versions completed an album that was seminal in the development of the British blues boom of the late 60s. The group also enjoyed two minor hit singles with 'Black Magic Woman', a hypnotic Green composition later popularized by **Santana**, and a delicate reading of 'Need Your Love So Bad', first recorded by **Little Willie John**. Fleetwood Mac's second album, *Mr. Wonderful*, was another triumph, but while Spencer was content to repeat his established style, Green, the group's leader, extended his compositional boundaries with several haunting contributions, including the heartfelt 'Love That Burns'. His guitar playing, clean and sparse but always telling, was rarely better, while McVie and Fleetwood were already an instinctive rhythm section. *Mr. Wonderful* also featured contributions from **Christine Perfect** (b. 12 July 1943, Grenodd, Lancashire, England), pianist from **Chicken Shack**, and a four-piece horn section, as the group began to leave traditional blues behind. A third guitarist, Danny Kirwan (b. 13 May 1950, London, England), was added to the line-up in September 1968.

The quintet had an immediate hit when 'Albatross', a moody instrumental reminiscent of 'Sleep Walk' by **Santo And Johnny**, topped the UK charts. The single, which reached number 2 when it was reissued in 1973, was the group's first million-seller. Fleetwood Mac then left Blue Horizon, although the company subsequently issued *Blues Jam At Chess*, on which the band jammed with several mentors, including **Buddy Guy**, **Otis Spann** and **Walter Horton**. Following a brief interlude on Immediate Records, which furnished the hypnotic 'Man Of The World', the quintet made their debut on **Reprise Records** with 'Oh Well', their most ambitious single to date, and the superb *Then Play On*. This crafted album unveiled Kirwan's songwriting talents, and his romantic leanings offset the more worldly Green. Although pictured, Jeremy Spencer was notably absent from most of the sessions, although his eccentric vision was showcased on a self-titled solo album. Fleetwood Mac now enjoyed an international reputation, but it was a mantle too great for its leader to bear. Green left the band in May 1970 as his parting single, the wonderful 'The Green Manalishi (With

The Two-Prong Crown)', became another Top 10 hit. He was replaced by Christine Perfect, now married to John McVie, and while his loss was an obvious blow, Kirwan's songwriting talent and Spencer's sheer exuberance maintained a measure of continuity on a fourth album, *Kiln House*. However, in 1971 the group was rocked for a second time when Spencer disappeared midway through an American tour. It transpired that he had joined a religious sect, the Children Of God, and while Green deputized for the remainder of the tour, a permanent replacement was found in a Californian musician, **Bob Welch** (b. Robert Welch, 31 July 1946, Los Angeles, California, USA).

The new line-up was consolidated on two melodic albums, *Future Games* and *Bare Trees*. Neither release made much impression with UK audiences who continued to mourn the passing of the Green-led era, but in America the group began to assemble a strong following for their new-found transatlantic sound. However, further changes occurred when Kirwan's chronic stage fright led to his dismissal. Bob Weston, a guitarist from **Long John Baldry**'s backing band, was his immediate replacement, while the line-up was also bolstered by former **Savoy Brown** vocalist Dave Walker. The band, however, was unhappy with a defined frontman, and the singer left after only eight months, having barely completed work on *Penguin*. Although not one of the band's strongest collections, it does contain an excellent Welch composition, 'Night Watch'. The remaining quintet completed another album, *Mystery To Me*, which was released at the time of a personal nadir within the band. Weston, who had been having an affair with Fleetwood's wife, was fired midway through a prolonged US tour, and the remaining dates were cancelled. Their manager, Clifford Davis, assembled a bogus Mac to fulfil contractual obligations, thus denying the 'real' group work during the inevitable lawsuits. Yet despite the inordinate pressure, Perfect, Welch, McVie and Fleetwood returned with *Heroes Are Hard To Find*, a positive release that belied the wrangles surrounding its appearance. Nonetheless, the controversy proved too strong for Welch, who left the band in December 1974. His departure robbed Fleetwood Mac of an inventive songwriter whose American perspective had helped redefine their approach.

It was while seeking prospective recording studios that Fleetwood was introduced to **Stevie Nicks** (b. Stephanie Nicks, 26 May 1948, Phoenix, Arizona, USA) and **Lindsey Buckingham** (b. 3 October 1949, Palo Alto, California, USA) via the duo's self-named album. Now bereft of a guitarist, he recalled Buckingham's expertise and invited him to replace Welch. Buckingham accepted on condition that Nicks also join, thus cementing Fleetwood Mac's most successful line-up. *Fleetwood Mac*, released in 1975, was a promise fulfilled. The newcomers provided easy, yet memorable compositions with smooth harmonies, while the British contingent gave the group its edge and power. A succession of stellar compositions, including 'Over My Head', 'Say You Love Me' and the dramatic 'Rhiannon', confirmed a perfect balance had been struck giving the group their first in a long line of US Top 20 singles. The quintet's next release, *Rumours*, proved more remarkable still. Despite the collapse of two relationships—the McVies were divorced, Buckingham and Nicks split up—the group completed a remarkable collection that laid bare the traumas within but in a manner neither maudlin nor pitiful. Instead, the ongoing drama was charted by several exquisite songs; 'Go Your Own Way', 'Don't Stop', 'Second Hand News' and 'Dreams', which retained both melody and purpose. An enduring release, *Rumours* has sold upwards of 25 million copies and at one point was second to **Michael Jackson**'s *Thriller* as the bestselling album of all time. Having survived their emotional anguish, the band was faced with the problem of following up a phenomenon. Their response was *Tusk*, an ambitious double set that showed a group unafraid to experiment, although many critics damned the collection as self-indulgent. The title track, a fascinating instrumental, was an international hit, although its follow-up, 'Sara', a composition recalling the style of *Rumours*, was better received in the USA than the UK. An in-concert selection, *Fleetwood Mac: Live*, was released as a stopgap in 1980 as rumours of a complete break-up flourished. It was a further two years before a new collection, *Mirage*, appeared, by which point several members were pursuing independent ventures. Buckingham and Nicks, in particular, viewed their own careers with equal importance, and *Mirage*, a somewhat self-conscious attempt at creating another *Rumours*, lacked the sparkle of its illustrious predecessor. It nonetheless yielded three successful singles in 'Hold Me', 'Gypsy' and Buckingham's irrepressible 'Oh Diane'.

Five years then passed before a new Fleetwood Mac album was issued. **Tango In The Night** was a dramatic return to form, recapturing all the group's flair and invention with a succession of heartwarming performances in 'Little Lies', 'Family Man' and 'You And I (Part 2)'. Christine McVie contributed a further high point with the rhythmic singalong 'Anyway'. The collection was, however, Lindsey Buckingham's swan song, although his departure from the band was not officially confirmed until June 1988. By that point two replacement singer/guitarists, ex-Thunderbyrd Rick Vito (b. Philadelphia, Pennsylvania, USA) and **Billy Burnette** (b. William Beau Burnette III, 8 May 1953, Memphis, Tennessee, USA), had joined the remaining quartet. The new line-up's debut, *Behind The Mask*, ushered in a new decade and era for this tempestuous band that gained strength from adversity and simply refused to die. In recent years the release of *The Chain*, a box set compiled by Fleetwood, gave the band greater critical acclaim than it had received in several years. In September 1995 Fleetwood self-promoted the excellent *Peter Green's Fleetwood Mac: Live At The BBC*. This was a project that was dear to his heart, as during the promotion it became clear that Fleetwood still had great emotional nostalgia for the original band and clearly regretted the departure of Green and the subsequent turn of events.

A month later a new Fleetwood Mac album was released to muted reviews and minimal sales. The addition of ex-**Traffic** guitarist **Dave Mason** (b. 10 May 1945, Worcester, England) and Bekka Bramlett (b. 19 April 1968, USA, daughter of **Delaney Bramlett** and **Bonnie Bramlett**) for the disappointing album *Time* failed to ignite any spark. The dismal reaction to it must have prompted Fleetwood to reconsider the band's direction. He had made no secret of the fact that he longed for the days of Green and the latter-day line-up of Nicks and Buckingham. Some diplomacy must have taken place behind closed doors because in the spring of 1997 it was announced that the famous *Rumours* line-up had reunited and begun recording together. A live album was released in August on the 20th anniversary of *Rumours*. Christine McVie announced her retirement from Fleetwood Mac shortly

afterwards, leaving the remaining quartet to complete work on their first new studio album together since *Tango In The Night*. The 18-song *Say You Will* eventually saw the light of day in April 2003. By Fleetwood Mac standards it was an average collection, although the smooth vocals of Christine McVie were sorely missed.

● ALBUMS: *Fleetwood Mac* (Columbia/Blue Horizon 1968) ★★★★, *Mr. Wonderful* (Columbia/Blue Horizon 1968) ★★★, *English Rose* (Epic 1969) ★★★, *Then Play On* (Reprise 1969) ★★★★, *Blues Jam At Chess* aka *Fleetwood Mac In Chicago* (Blue Horizon 1969) ★★★, *Kiln House* (Reprise 1970) ★★★★, *Future Games* (Reprise 1971) ★★★, *Bare Trees* (Reprise 1972) ★★, *Penguin* (Reprise 1973) ★★, *Mystery To Me* (Reprise 1973) ★★, *Heroes Are Hard To Find* (Reprise 1974) ★★★, *Fleetwood Mac* (Reprise 1975) ★★★★, *Rumours* (Warners 1977) ★★★★★, *Tusk* (Warners 1979) ★★★, *Live* (Warners 1980) ★★, *Mirage* (Warners 1982) ★★★, *Live In Boston* (Shanghai 1985) ★★, *London Live '68* (Thunderbolt 1986) ★, *Tango In The Night* (Warners 1988) ★★★★, *Behind The Mask* (Warners 1989) ★★★, *Live At The Marquee* 1967 recording (Sunflower 1992) ★, *Live 1968* recording (Abracadabra 1995) ★, *Peter Green's Fleetwood Mac: Live At The BBC* (Fleetwood/Castle 1995) ★★★★, *Time* (Warners 1995) ★, *The Dance* (Reprise 1997) ★★★, *Live At The Boston Tea Party Part One* 1970 recording (Original Masters 1998) ★★★, *Live At The Boston Tea Party Part Two* 1970 recording (Original Masters 1998) ★★★★, *Shrine '69* 1969 recording (Rykodisc 1999) ★★★, *Live At The Boston Tea Party Part Three* 1970 recording (Original Masters 2000) ★★★, *The Vintage Years Live* 1970 recording (Eagle 2002) ★★★, *Say You Will* (Reprise 2003) ★★★, *Fleetwood Mac* expanded edition (Reprise 2004) ★★★★, *Rumours* expanded edition (Reprise 2004) ★★★★★, *Tusk* expanded edition (Reprise 2004) ★★★.

Solo: Mick Fleetwood *The Visitor* (RCA 1981) ★, *I'm Not Me* (RCA 1983) ★. Danny Kirwan *Second Chapter* (DJM 1976) ★★, *Midnight In San Juan* (DJM 1976) ★, *Hello There Big Boy* (DJM 1979) ★. Jeremy Spencer *Jeremy Spencer* (Reprise 1970) ★★, *Jeremy Spencer And The Children Of God* (Columbia 1973) ★, *Flee* (Atlantic 1979) ★.

● COMPILATIONS: *The Pious Bird Of Good Omen* (Columbia/Blue Horizon 1969) ★★★, *The Original Fleetwood Mac* (Columbia/Blue Horizon 1971) ★★, *Fleetwood Mac's Greatest Hits* (Columbia 1971) ★★★★, *The Vintage Years* (Sire 1975) ★★★, *Albatross* (Columbia 1977) ★★★, *Man Of The World* (Columbia 1978) ★★, *Best Of* (Reprise 1978) ★★★, *Cerulean* (Shanghai 1985) ★★, *Greatest Hits: Fleetwood Mac* (Columbia 1988) ★★★, *The Blues Years* (Essential 1991) ★★★, *The Chain* CD box set (Warners 1992) ★★★, *The Early Years* (Dojo 1992) ★★, *Fleetwood Mac Family Album* (Connoisseur 1996) ★★, *The Best Of Fleetwood Mac* (Columbia 1996) ★★★, *The Vaudeville Years Of Fleetwood Mac 1968–1970 Volume 1* (Receiver 1998) ★★★, *The Complete Blue Horizon Sessions 1967–1969* 6-CD box set (Columbia 1999) ★★★, *Show-Biz Blues 1968–1970 Volume 2* (Receiver 2001) ★★, *Jumping At Shadows: The Blues Years* (Indigo 2002) ★★★, *The Very Best Of Fleetwood Mac* (Rhino 2002) ★★★★, *The Best Of Peter Green's Fleetwood Mac* (Columbia 2002) ★★★★, *Green Shadows: Classics And Rarities Featuring Peter Green* (Metro 2003) ★★★, *Men Of The World: The Early Years* 3-CD set (Castle 2005) ★★★★.

● DVD/VIDEOS: *Fleetwood Mac* (Warners 1981), *In Concert—Mirage Tour* (Spectrum 1983), *Video Biography* (Virgin Vision 1988), *Tango In The Night* (Warner Music Video 1988), *Peter Green's Fleetwood Mac: The Early Years 1967-1970* (PNE 1995), *The Dance* (Warner Video 1997), *Live In Boston* (Warner Vision International 2004), *Destiny Rules* (Sanctuary Visual Entertainment 2004), *Unbroken Chain* (Passport 2004).

● FURTHER READING: *Fleetwood Mac: The Authorized History*, Samuel Graham. *Fleetwood Mac: Rumours 'N' Fax*, Roy Carr and Steve Clarke. *Fleetwood Mac*, Steve Clarke. *Fleetwood: My Life And Adventures With Fleetwood Mac*, Mick Fleetwood with Stephen Davis. *The Crazed Story Of Fleetwood Mac*, Stephen Davis. *Fleetwood Mac: Behind The Masks* (updated as *Fleetwood Mac: The First 30 Years*), Bob Brunning. *Peter Green: The Biography* (updated as *Peter Green: Founder Of Fleetwood Mac*), Martin Celmins. *Fleetwood Mac: The Complete Recording Sessions 1967-1997*, Peter Lewry. *Fleetwood Mac Through The Years*, Edward Wincentsen.

Fleetwoods

One of America's most popular doo-wop groups in the late 50s comprised Gary Troxell (b. 28 November 1939, Centralia, Washington, USA), Gretchen Christopher (b. 29 February 1940, Olympia, Washington, USA) and Barbara Ellis (b. 20 February 1940, Olympia, Washington, USA). They met while seniors at high school in the girls' home-town. Originally a female duo, they recruited Troxell initially to play trumpet. The girls had composed a song, while independently, Troxell had written a hook that went something like: 'Mmm Dooby Doo, Dum Dim Dum Doo Dum'; they put them together and 'Come Softly To Me' was born. Their first moniker, Two Girls And A Guy, was changed by a Seattle record distributor, Bob Reisdorff, who became their manager and founded Dolphin Records (later called Dolton), which released the single. Chart fame was instant for the distinctive trio, and the haunting and catchy song (on which the vocal was recorded a cappella) shot to the top of the US charts and made the UK Top 10 despite a hit cover version by **Frankie Vaughan** and the **Kaye Sisters**. Their third release, 'Mr. Blue', a Dwayne Blackwell song originally written for the **Platters**, was also a US number 1 (in the UK two cover versions took the honours) and made Troxell one of the leaders in the teen-idol stakes. In the midst of their success he was drafted into the navy, his place being taken when necessary by subsequent solo star **Vic Dana**. Despite Troxell's absence, the US hits continued, and they totalled nine Top 40 hits between 1959 and 1963, including the number 10 hit 'Tragedy', a revival of the **Thomas Wayne** song. The unmistakable close-harmony trio surfaced again in 1973 when they signed with the noted producer Jerry Dennon, but no hits resulted from this brief collaboration.

● ALBUMS: *Mr. Blue* (Dolton 1959) ★★★★, *The Fleetwoods* (Dolton 1960) ★★★★, *Softly* (Dolton 1961) ★★★★, *Deep In A Dream* (Dolton 1961) ★★★, *The Best Of The Oldies* (Dolton 1962) ★★★★, *Goodnight My Love* (Dalton 1963) ★★★, *The Fleetwoods Sing For Lovers By Night* (Dolton 1963) ★★★, *Before And After* (Dolton 1965) ★★, *Folk Rock* (Dolton 1966) ★★.

● COMPILATIONS: *The Fleetwoods' Greatest Hits* (Dolton 1962) ★★★★, *In A Mellow Mood* (Sunset 1966) ★★★, *The Best Of The Fleetwoods* (Rhino 1990) ★★★★, *Come Softly To Me: The Best Of The Fleetwoods* (EMI 1993) ★★★★.

Fleischman, Robert

b. USA. Fleischman originally came to prominence as the singer with **Journey** in San Francisco, California, USA. He was recruited by that group in June 1977 following the release of their debut album. However, after touring with Journey in support of **Emerson, Lake And Palmer**, he was ejected from the band in favour of **Steve Perry** before he had the chance to record. Two years later Fleischman returned with his debut solo album, a stolid AOR collection that allowed him to use several songs originally envisioned for inclusion on Journey's second album. Its lack of success halted his career until he joined first **Channel** and then **Vinnie Vincent**'s Invasion. Neither of these placements proved to be long-term commitments, however.

● ALBUMS: *Robert Fleischman* (Arista 1979) ★★.

Fleming, John 'OO'

b. John Fleming, 1969, Sunderland, England. Fleming is one of the UK's hardest working DJs, who has made a name for himself in both Europe and the USA for his driving **trance** and hard **house** sound. His distinctive moniker comes from the famous fictional spy in the books by Ian Fleming whose code name was 007. Fleming was diagnosed with lung cancer in 1989 but battled to overcome it and to continue DJing. While convalescing in Florida, USA, he played at events such as 'Unity', 'Limelight Club' and 'Obsession' and gained a following in Florida, Texas, Georgia and Minneapolis. He quickly re-established himself upon his return to the UK and has played at all the major clubs, including **Renaissance**, **Cream** and **Ministry Of Sound**. He holds residencies at UK clubs, **Trade**, The Zap Club, Naughty But Nice, The Manor, Sunny Side Up, Freedom, Mirage, The Opera House and Ultra Vegas. His remixing credits include **Mansun** ('Tax Loss' and 'Wide Open Space'), **Erasure**, **My Life Story**, **Junior Vasquez**, N-Trance, **Gloria Estefan** and **X-Cabs**. Fleming describes his two styles of set as 'beefy, chunky, energetic, uplifting house' or 'funky, nu-energy techno' depending on the club and the crowd. He has mixed many compilations, including several **Ibiza**-themed albums and *Reactivate 13* and *Reactivate 14* for **React Music**. He also mixed **Virgin Records**' *The Best Trance Anthems . . . Ever!*, released in July 1999, which entered the UK's national compilation chart at number 7. Fleming regularly appears on the radio in the UK, including **Danny Rampling**'s and **Pete Tong**'s Radio 1 FM shows. He has released his own singles in 1999, including 'Come On Baby' with Russell Floorplay (Automatic Records), 'Alpha 5' and, as S2POR, 'Make Me Feel' on his own Joof Recordings. He also has another record label, Bond-Age Records.

● COMPILATIONS: *Q-Music* (Fifty-First Recordings 1997) ★★★, *The Real Ibiza* (Telstar 1997) ★★★, *Ibiza Anthems 1998* (Concept Recordings 1998) ★★★, *Reacitvate 13* (React Music 1998) ★★★★, *Licensed To Thrill* (Automatic 1999) ★★★, *Sunny Side Up* (Passion Music 1999) ★★★, *Reactivate 14* (React Music 1999) ★★★, *The Best Trance Anthems . . . Ever!* (Virgin 1999) ★★★.

Fleming, Mike

b. Canada. Rock singer-songwriter Mike Fleming formed his own group at the end of the 70s. Led by Fleming himself on guitar, bass and keyboards, the rest of the band comprised

Jody Saullier (vocals) and Vince Santarelli (drums). They released a self-titled collection for Image Records in 1980 but, Fleming's guitar-playing aside, this was an uninspired, hackneyed collection of soft rock songs written around romantic themes. It proved to be Fleming's sole release before returning to low-key club work.

● ALBUMS: *Mike Fleming* (Image 1980) ★★.

Flemming, Herb

b. 5 April 1900, Honolulu, Hawaii, d. 3 October 1976. Growing up in South Carolina, Flemming studied music as a child, learning to play several brass instruments including the mellophone, the euphonium and the trombone and it was upon the latter that he became well known. He played in military bands following his enlistment and in 1917 went to France with the 369th Infantry Band that was led by **James Reese Europe**. After the war he returned to his studies, adding further instruments to his arsenal. In the early 20s he worked at many clubs in New York, playing with several bands including that led by **Johnny Dunn** with whom he recorded. He joined **Sam Wooding** with whom he travelled to Europe, playing in several countries and also recording while in Berlin. Having developed a taste for travel, Flemming returned to Europe as leader of his own band, then worked again with Wooding and with **Joséne Baker** before heading for South America, India, Ceylon and China. Throughout the 30s he continued to work in Europe and in 1936 acted as an interpreter for members of the US Olympic team at the Berlin games. During this period he was resident at the Sherbini Club in the city where his vocal feature, 'Summertime', customarily drew a standing ovation. During his time in Germany, as the Nazi regime systematically oppressed racial minorities, Flemming appears to have begun using the name Niccoliah El-Michelle, claiming Turkish nationality, and was thus able to continue working with a high profile, including a feature film appearance. Back in the USA at the start of the 40s, he played in **Fats Waller**'s 10-piece band, then joined **Noble Sissle** before quitting music to work for the US government. By 1950 he was back in music, playing with **Henry 'Red' Allen** in New York before the travelbug bit again and he moved to Spain, playing in Madrid in the mid-60s and also on the Costa del Sol where he played at clubs in Torremolinos and Málaga. Late in the decade he was recording in Germany and showing little sign of diminished energy or wanderlust.

● ALBUMS: *The Great Traditionalists In Europe* (MPS 1969) ★★★, with the Great Traditionalists In Europe *For My Friends And Me* (Hage 1969) ★★★.

Flemons, Wade

b. 25 September 1940, Coffeyville, Kansas, USA, d. 13 October 1993. Flemons made a brief impact on the R&B scene in the late 50s and early 60s, recording hits for the Chicago-based **Vee Jay Records**. He was raised in Wichita, Kansas, until the age of 15, when he moved with his parents to Battle Creek, Michigan. There he formed a vocal group, the Newcomers, and was discovered by Vee Jay Records in 1958. On Flemons' first hit, 'Here I Stand' (number 19 R&B, number 80 pop), the company billed the act as Wade Flemons And The Newcomers. As a solo artist, he charted again in 1960 with 'Easy Lovin'' (number 10 R&B, number 70 pop), but the b-side, 'Woops Now', received solid airplay in many areas. Flemons' remake of the **Percy Mayfield** song 'Please Send Me Someone

To Love' (number 20 R&B), in 1961, was his last chart record. Flemons deserved to chart in 1964 with his definitive version of 'I Knew You When', which **Billy Joe Royal** put high on the pop charts a year later. Flemons was a co-writer for one of the **Dells**' biggest hits, 'Stay In My Corner'. In the early 70s he played keyboards for **Earth, Wind And Fire**, who then recorded for **Warner Brothers**, but was not a part of the group after they signed with **Columbia** in 1973.

● ALBUMS: *Wade Flemons* (Vee Jay 1960) ★★★.

Flesh For Lulu

This UK rock band was the creation of singer/guitarist Nick Marsh and drummer James Mitchell and took their name from an American cult movie. They were joined by Rocco Barker (ex–Wasted Youth) on guitar and Glen Bishop, replaced by Kevin Mills (ex-Specimen) on bass after the single 'Restless'. Derek Greening (keyboards/guitar) became the fifth member shortly afterwards, although he continued to play with his other band, **Peter And The Test Tube Babies**. Previously their debut single had been 'Roman Candle', prefacing a first album that they would 'rather forget about'. *Blue Sisters Swing*, on the tiny Hybrid label, followed as a stopgap. The sleeve illustration of two nuns kissing resulted in bans in the USA and Europe. The release of *Big Fun City* was the first to do the band justice, even though it was hampered by artwork problems at **Polydor Records** and featured everything from country ballads to basic rock 'n' roll. Their succession of labels grew longer as they moved on to **Beggars Banquet Records** in 1986. *Long Live The New Flesh* followed a year later, recorded at Abbey Road Studios and produced by Mike Hedges. Their approach to the sophistication of their new surroundings was typical: 'Forget the cerebral approach—just turn up them guitars!' Their most pop-orientated album, *Plastic Fantastic*, was recorded in Australia by Mark Opitz, several titles from which were later employed for film soundtracks (*Uncle Buck* and *Flashback*). By this time, original members Marsh, Barking and Greening had been joined by Hans Perrson (drums) and Mike Steed (bass). Despite stronger songwriting than on previous recordings, the album failed and Beggars Banquet did not renew their option.

● ALBUMS: *Flesh For Lulu* (Polydor 1984) ★★, *Blue Sisters Swing* mini-album (Hybrid 1985) ★★, *Big Fun City* (Caroline 1985) ★★★, *Long Live The New Flesh* (Beggars Banquet 1987) ★★★, *Plastic Fantastic* (Beggars Banquet 1989) ★★★.

Flesh Quartet

A group who defy easy categorisation, Sweden's Flesh Quartet features the musical skills of Mattias Helldén (cello), Örjan Höjberg (viola), Jonas Lindgren (violin), Johan Söderburg (percussion), Sebastian Öberg (cello), Freddie Wadling (vocals) and Tim Wolde (vocals and raps). Their music a combination of blues, baroque, early music and classical with jazz and R&B influences, Wolde's raps gave the group a distinctive contemporary edge. The group have also experimented with Indian and Arabic styles on their albums for the MNW record label. The Flesh Quartet began in the late 80s as a four-piece (hence the name) before recruiting musicians as required. Their work also regularly features other Swedish and Scandinavian musicians and singers as guest artists, notably on 1993's acclaimed *Flow*. The Quartet have also toured throughout Europe, playing at venues in

New York and Moscow where one performance was televised live.

● ALBUMS: *What's Your Pleasure* (MNW 1990) ★★★★, *Goodbye Sweden* (MNW 1992) ★★★, *Flow* (MNW 1993) ★★★.

Flesheaters

Innovative rock outfit built around cult hero Chris 'D' Desjardins (vocals), who had been active on the Los Angeles, California, scene from the 70s, making movies and acting as well as co-ordinating the Flesheaters. Their first established line-up added Robyn Jameson (bass), Don Kirk (guitar) and Chris Wahl (drums). However, something of the nature of the band can be surmised by the frequency of its personnel shifts. Those passing through the ranks include Bill Bateman (drums), Steve Berlin (saxophone), Gene Taylor (keyboards), John Bazz (bass), **Dave Alvin** (guitar), all ex–**Blasters**; Pat Garrett (guitar, bass), Joe Ramirez (bass), Joe Nanini (drums), all ex–**Black Randy**; **John Doe** (bass), D.J. Bonebrake (drums), **Excene Cervenka** (vocals), all ex–**X. Stan Ridgway** (**Wall Of Voodoo**; guitar) and Tito Larriva (Plugz; guitar), who were also present in an early incarnation. These represent only a fraction of former members in a band that effectively operated in a 'pick up and play' mode. This did not diminish their appeal, however: 'The one thing that we do that mystifies our audience is we don't play in one category. The music that we play is real loud. Its real metallic. It could be described as heavy metal, or what was in 1977 punk.'

Desjardins split the band at the end of the 80s after the years of cut-and-paste line-ups finally took their toll. By the 90s, however, they were back on the circuit once more. 1991's *Dragstrip Riot*, with which Desjardins reinstated the band after years of inactivity, was a sprawling double album set that saw the band crashing out riotous swamp rock of a virulent, **Cramps**-type character. The intervening years had seen him operate with his own band, the **Divine Horsemen**, while Jameson also played with Alex Gibson and Passionel.

● ALBUMS: *No Questions Asked* (Upsetter 1979) ★★★, *A Minute To Pray, A Second To Die* (Ruby 1981) ★★★, *Forever Came Today* (Ruby 1982) ★★★, *A Hard Road To Follow* (Upsetter 1983) ★★★, *Dragstrip Riot* (SST 1991) ★★, *Sex Diary Of Mr. Vampire* (SST 1992) ★★★, *Ashes Of Time* (Upsetter 2001) ★★, *Miss Muerte* (Atavistic 2004) ★★★.

● COMPILATIONS: *Greatest Hits: Destroyed By Fire* (SST 1986) ★★★★, *Prehistoric Fits* (SST 1990) ★★★.

Fleshtones

Formed in 1976 in the Queens district of New York City, the Fleshtones were first heard on British shores as part of a 'package' tour in 1980 with the **dB's**, the Raybeats and the Bush Tetras. Each band was different, drawing energy from punk but ideas from a myriad of other musical forms. In the Fleshtones' case, Keith Streng (guitar), Peter Zaremba (vocals, keyboards), Jan Marek Pukulski (bass) and Bill Milhizer (drums, ex–Harry Toledo Band and Action Combo), this involved the fusion of the new wave with R&B and rockabilly. The group caught the attention of Miles Copeland's I.R.S. Records label via 'American Beat', their debut single from 1979 on the Red Star label. The 12-inch EP *Up-Front* duly surfaced in 1980 in America, although it was not until 1981 that its strongest track, 'The Girl From Baltimore', secured a British release. It was followed by 'The

World Has Changed' (though only in the USA) and 'Shadow-Line' in early 1982. This coincided not only with the band's first official long-player, *Roman Gods*, but also *Blast Off!*, a cassette of their unreleased 1978 studio album on Reach Out International (ROIR) Records.

All was comparatively quiet for over a year until the Fleshtones unleashed their best record, *Hexbreaker!*, promoted by two singles, 'Right Side Of A Good Thing' and the evocative 'Screaming Skull' (both 1983). The material shared the hard rock 'n' roll sound of *Roman Gods*, but the band soon curtailed their activities, apart from the strange *Fleshtones Vs Reality* set in 1987 and three live albums. Meanwhile, Streng collaborated with **R.E.M.**'s Peter Buck and most of the Fleshtones as the Full Time Men, and Zaremba released an album as the Love Delegation. However, the parent group was back on the case come 1996 with *Laboratory Of Sound* and further examples of how three chords can be milked to great effect. *More Than Skin Deep* and *Hitsburg Revisited* repeated the formula.

● ALBUMS: *Roman Gods* (I.R.S. 1981) ★★★, *Blast Off!* cassette (ROIR 1982) ★★, *Hexbreaker!* (I.R.S. 1983) ★★★★, *Speed Connection* (I.R.S. 1985) ★★, *Speed Connection II* (I.R.S. 1985) ★★★, *Fleshtones Vs Reality* (Emergo 1987) ★★★, *Soul Madrid* (Impossible 1989) ★★★, *Beautiful Light* (Naked Language 1994) ★★★, *Laboratory Of Sound* (Musidisc 1996) ★★★, *More Than Skin Deep* (Epitaph 1998) ★★★, *Hitsburg Revisited* (Epitaph 1999) ★★★, *Do You Swing?* (Yep Roc 2003) ★★★.

● COMPILATIONS: *Time Bomb! The Big Bang Theory* (Skyclad 1988) ★★★, *Living Legends Series* (I.R.S. 1989) ★★★, *Angry Years 84–86* (Amsterdamned 1997) ★★★.

Fletcher, Darrow

b. 23 January 1951, Inkster, Michigan, USA, and raised in Chicago, Illinois. Fletcher's only hit was 'The Pain Gets A Little Deeper' (number 23 R&B), released in early 1966 on the Groovy label, when he was still a freshman in high school. He toured with **Stevie Wonder** before recording with his stepfather, Johnny Haygood, who operated the small Jacklyn label in Chicago. No more national hits followed, but Fletcher enjoyed a big local hit with 'Sitting There That Night' (1966), a perfect example of Chicago-style, soft, mid-tempo soul, with its **Curtis Mayfield**-style lyrical guitar. Further singles were released on the Revue, UNI, Congress and Genna Records labels. His last chart record was in 1976 for **Ray Charles'** Crossover Records label, but it provoked little interest.

Fletcher, Liz

b. 26 June 1959, London, England. Although she began her professional career as a dancer Fletcher soon followed in her parents' footsteps by becoming a singer. During her early years she had studied dance, singing and drama at Corona Academy and subsequently worked in the theatre and on television as a dancer, singer and actress. She began concentrating on singing, working in backing groups behind singers such as Grace Kennedy and **David Grant**. By the mid-90s she had begun to move towards a jazz-orientated style, and a musical association with songwriter Rupert Wates proved fruitful. She has toured with the *Hot Foot From Harlem* show and confirmed her growing reputation with a very good debut album, on which she was backed by **Tony Coe**, **Matt Wates** and other artists on **Malcolm Creese**'s label.

With an appealingly mature sound and style, this is clearly a singer to watch in the twenty-first century.

● ALBUMS: *Mellow Mania* (Black Box 1997) ★★★, *Live In The Park* (Black Box 2000) ★★★, *Blue Afternoons* (Mainstem 2002) ★★★.

Fletcher, Tex

b. Jerry Bisceglia, 8 March 1910, Harrison, New York, USA, d. 1986. A fine singer/yodeller and left-handed guitarist, although little is known of his early life. He probably made his debut as an entertainer with *Buffalo Bill's Wild West Show*. He worked briefly as a cowboy and sang on radio in Yankton, South Dakota, which probably led to later claims being made that he originated from that state. He spent most of his time in New York, and between November 1936 and June 1937, he recorded 13 sides there for **Decca**, including two duets with Joe Rogers. He made 10 further recordings, this time with his Lonely Cowboys, between October 1937 and February 1938. The material varied from standard cowboy ballads ('The Zebra Dun') and family songs ('A Song For Mother') to the popular 'I Get The Blues When It Rains' and the strangely titled 'Meet Me Tonight In The Cowshed'. His Hollywood success consisted of a few musical shorts, and his claim to being a singing cowboy was confined to a single starring role, in 1939, in *Six Gun Rhythm*. Grand National Pictures closed just as it was released, and he was left to promote his film himself. He was drafted for army service during World War II, which prevented him from moving to another studio to continue his singing cowboy career. After his discharge, he returned to New York, and for many years, he was popular as the Lonely Cowboy, on WOR radio.

During the 50s and 60s, he also appeared fairly regularly on television. He published two songbooks and made countless personal appearances. Copies of his recordings, originally released on both Decca and Montgomery Ward, are rare, but 'The Yodelling Cowboy's Last Song' appears on MCA's *Cowboy Image* compilation.

Fleurine

b. The Netherlands. Singers who attracted Fleurine's early attention and who in different ways led her to develop an interest in singing included **Ella Fitzgerald**, in particular the Song Book recordings and the duets with **Louis Armstrong**. She studied at the Amsterdam School of High Arts Conservatory and following graduation relocated to New York, USA. Since the early 90s, she has lived and worked both in her homeland and in America. Choosing to sing jazz but eager to explore new ground, she began writing lyrics to jazz instrumentals. Among the composers whose work is now included in her repertoire are **Ray Bryant**, **Kenny Dorham**, **Curtis Fuller**, **Tom Harrell**, **Thad Jones**, **Thelonious Monk** and **Joshua Redman**. Interestingly, some of Fleurine's lyrics are written in English, others in Portuguese. She has appeared at leading New York and London clubs, including Birdland, Blue Note and Pizza Express, and has sung at several international festivals including those at Montreal and Edmonton in Canada, Havana, Cuba (where she appeared as guest vocalist with **Roy Hargrove** in 1996), Umbria in Italy and Istanbul in Turkey, and she has appeared on numerous occasions at the North Sea Jazz Festival in her homeland, including a 1997 guest appearance with **Brad Mehldau**. This last engagement led to her teaming up with the pianist for a New York date at the Village

Vanguard, subsequent international tours and a 1999 record date. Among other jazzmen with whom she has performed live and on record are trumpeters Harrell and **Don Sickler**, saxophonists Seamus Blake and **Ralph Moore**, accordionist Gil Goldstein, pianist **Renée Rosnes**, guitarist Jesse van Ruller, bass players **Christian McBride** and Johan Plomp and drummers Jeff Ballard and **Billy Drummond**. Plomp and van Ruller are long-standing accompanists of Fleurine. In addition to performing, Fleurine has also become involved in the production side of recording. In the early 00s, Fleurine's repertoire expanded to include pop music of the 60s onwards as well as jazz-inflected arrangements of classic French songs and contemporary Brazilian pop.

● ALBUMS: *Meant To Be!* (Bluemusic 1995) ★★★, *Close Enough For Love* (EmArcy 2000) ★★★★, *Fire* (3d 2005) ★★★.

Flickerstick

Alternative rock outfit originating from Fort Worth, Texas, USA. Brandin Lea (b. Dallas, Texas, USA; vocals/guitar) and Cory Kreig (b. Abilene, Texas, USA; guitar/keyboards) first met while they were classmates at Southwest High School in Fort Worth and began playing together in various bands after graduating in 1995. An embryonic version of Flickerstick, featuring Brandin's brother Fletcher Lea (b. Las Vegas, Nevada, USA; bass), Rex James Ewing (guitar) and Jeff Lowe (drums) struggled to gain a reputation outside of their hometown. The addition of new drummer Dominic Weir in May 1998 helped the band break into the Dallas music scene, and they had soon developed a reputation as one of the area's best live acts, with a rudimentary but highly effective multimedia show. The quintet's debut album was recorded and independently released in 2000, but their big breakthrough came about when they appeared on VH1's *Bands On The Run* reality music show. Taped at the end of the year, and first aired on national television in April 2001, the concept of the show involved four unsigned bands competing for $50,000 cash, $100,000 dollars in equipment and an industry showcase. Flickerstick's outlandish pursuit of the rock 'n' roll lifestyle ('We're gonna drink, we're gonna party, we're gonna meet chicks, and if you don't want to do that, then why . . . are you in a band') over the show's 15-week run helped endear them to a new audience, and despite not earning the most money from live shows and the sale of merchandise, they were voted the winner. A recording contract with Epic Records followed in July. An expanded and remastered version of *Welcoming Home The Astronauts* was released in October.

● ALBUMS: *Welcoming Home The Astronauts* (226/Epic 2000) ★★★.

Flight From Folly

This bright and breezy musical, one of the last films to be made at Teddington Studios in England, was released by Warner Brothers–First National in 1945. It starred one of the West End's favourite leading ladies, **Pat Kirkwood**. She plays showgirl Sue Brown who poses as a nurse in order to impress playwright Clinton Clay (Hugh Sinclair) while he is suffering from amnesia. The celebrated British composer **Michael Carr** contributed the appealing 'Never Like This Before', 'Miss Brown' and collaborated with Benjamin Frankel on the impressive 'Dream Sequence' during which Sue and Clinton 'find' each other. Frankel composed most of the film's instrumental themes such as 'Symphonic Jazz', 'Harem Dance' and 'Fiesta Dance'. Eric Spear, too, provided much of the film's music, including 'The Sultan', 'Cuban Song', and the spectacular 'The Majorca' song-and-dance finalé. Basil Woon, Lesley Storm and Katherine Strueby wrote the screenplay, which involved chubby comedian Sydney Howard (in his last film role), Marian Spencer, Tamara Desni, A.E. Matthews, Jean Gillie, Charles Goldner and dancers Halama and Konarski. Also taking part were the bands of **Edmundo Ros** and Don Marino Barreto. The director of this tuneful—and at times quite hilarious—feature was Herbert Mason.

Flightcrank

The creation of ex-**Prodigy** dancer Leeroy Thornhill (b. 8 October 1968, Essex, England), who left the band after the massive success of their third album, 1997's *Fat Of The Land*, and the subsequent world tours began to take their toll. He had already acquired a grounding in production and had begun to assemble his own studio by 1994. In the same year he even remixed **Moby**'s 'Come On Baby' for **Mute Records**, although it was never commercially released. His solo EP *Twisted*, featuring the reggae legend **Lee Perry**, appeared on the Los Angeles-based label Copasetik Records in May 2000. The Flightcrank debut (the name is taken from part of a BMX bike) *Beyond All Reasonable Doubt* featured guest appearances from **Finley Quaye** and the **Mad Professor**. Less electronic and **dance music**–based than the Prodigy's sound, the album also drew influences from folk, reggae and punk. Thornhill wrote, performed and produced most of the album and even sung lead vocals on the track 'Amazing'.
● ALBUMS: *Beyond All Reasonable Doubt* (Copasetik 2001) ★★★★.

Flinch

Formed in Camberwell, South London, England, at the close of 1993 by Grog (vocals), Paul (guitar, ex–Screaming Custard) and Dominic (drums, ex-**Cardiacs**), Flinch had released two independent singles before attracting press interest as one of the UK's most promising bands of 1994. Despite major label A&R interest, they chose instead to sign with the independent Clawfist Records after winning the Best New Band poll at September's In The City music seminar. In keeping with their self-image of 'cheapest dressed band in rock', they celebrated with a day out at Alton Towers pleasure park. The following month they released a third single, 'Faking It', which attacked the lack of sincerity in the music industry, and recorded a session for BBC disc jockey **John Peel**. This was followed in February 1995 with 'Jamie D' before a UK tour with Hopper and the **Nubiles** and a new contract with Vinyl Solution Records subsidiary !Dilo! Soon afterwards the band collapsed, with Grog going on to form the acclaimed **Feline**.

Flint

Comprising Don Brewer (b. 3 September 1948, Flint, Michigan, USA; vocals/drums), Billy Elsworthy (guitar), Mel Schacher (b. 3 April 1951, Flint, Michigan, USA; bass/guitar) and Craig Frost (b. 20 April 1948, Flint, Michigan, USA; keyboards), Flint formed in the late 70s following Brewer, Schacher (also ex–**? And The Mysterians**) and Frost's departure from **Grand Funk Railroad**. Their name taken from the city of their birth, they recorded a self-titled debut album

in 1978 but failed to secure any mainstream interest for their efforts. By the beginning of 1981 Brewer had rejoined a resurrected Grand Funk Railroad, with Frost moving on to **Bob Seger**'s Silver Bullet Band (whom Brewer would also later join). Schacher opted not to re-enlist due to his fear of flying, choosing instead to set up business restoring and renovating Jaguar cars. Not to be confused with the **Prodigy** spin-off group of the same name.
● ALBUMS: *Flint* (Columbia 1978) ★★.

Flint, Shelby

b. North Hollywood, California, USA. Flint was a pop vocalist whose 'Angel On My Shoulder' was her only big hit. In the late 50s she was signed as a songwriter by west coast publisher/writer Barry De Vorzon who took her to Cadence where 'I Will Love You' (1958) flopped. Flint then followed the folk boom, forming an acoustic trio before recording the Top 30 hit 'Angel On My Shoulder' for De Vorzon's label Valiant in 1961. The song also appeared on the first album by labelmates the **Cascades**. She continued to record for Valiant during the mid-60s when her most successful single was one of several vocal versions of Vince Guaraldi's tune 'Cast Your Fate To The Wind' (1966). During the 70s, Flint worked as a session singer for artists such as Batteau (1974), while DeVorzon found a niche composing television themes like 'Nadia's Theme' (a US Top 10 hit in 1976) and 'Simon And Simon'.

Flintlock

This UK teenybop band of the mid-70s was led by heart-throb drummer Mike Holoway, introduced to television audiences via the children's science fiction programme *The Tomorrow People*. The series told the story of several teenagers who had evolved beyond the rest of humanity and acted as guardians to its fate. Holoway appeared as Mike Bell in the fourth series of the programme, a would-be pop star both onscreen and off, with an affected cockney accent. In one serial, 'The Heart Of Sogguth', Holoway performed with Flintlock on a musical piece with a supposedly mind-controlling beat heralding the arrival of extraterrestrials. However, Flintlock's music was as cardboard as the sets and they achieved only one hit with 'Dawn' in 1976 despite considerable exposure from children's magazines such as *Look In*.
● ALBUMS: *On The Way* (Pinnacle 1975) ★★, *Hot From The Lock* (Pinnacle 1976) ★★, *Tears 'N' Cheers* (Pinnacle 1977) ★, *Stand Alone* (Pinnacle 1979) ★.

Flipper

San Francisco hardcore band Flipper formed in 1979 with original members Will Shatter (d. 1987; bass/vocals), Steve DePace (drums), both former members of Negative Trend, Bruce Lose (bass/vocals) and Ted Falconi (guitar), also of Negative Trend, on drums. Following the single 'Love Canal'/'Ha Ha' on Subterranean Records, the group released its debut and best-known album, *Generic*, in 1982. Sporting topical lyrics and both hardcore punk and noise dirges, the collection was instantly recognized as a classic of west coast punk. However, these were no stereotypical three-chord thrashes, the band experimenting instead with the wildly overblown 'Sex Bomb Baby' and the super-minimalist 'Life'. Other albums followed on Subterranean in 1984 and 1986 but failed to match their debut's impact, and the following year

Shatter died of an accidental heroin overdose. The three surviving members of Flipper reunited in 1990, resulting in the eventual release of *American Grafishy*. This was the first official release on the new label founded by **Henry Rollins** and **Rick Rubin**. Flipper are now cited as being highly influential in the development of **Nirvana**'s sound.

● ALBUMS: *Generic* (Subterranean 1982) ★★★★, *Blow 'N Chunks* (ROIR 1984) ★★, *Gone Fishin'* (Subterranean 1984) ★★★, *American Grafishy* (Def American 1992) ★★★, *Live At CBGB's* 1983 recording (Overground 1997) ★★★★.
● COMPILATIONS: *Public Flipper Limited Live 1980–1985* (Subterranean 1986) ★★★, *Sex Bomb Baby!* (Subterranean 1988) ★★★★.

Flirtations
A British-based R&B female group, who originally came from New York City, USA. The **Supremes** were extremely popular during the late 60s, and record companies were keen to record any female groups who sounded like them. The Flirtations were the beneficiaries of this phenomenon. The members were sisters Shirley and Earnestine Pearce and Viola Billups. The Pearce sisters had earlier been in the **Gypsies**, but after minor success the group broke up. Recording in England for **Deram Records**, the Flirtations had a notable US hit in 1969 with a Supremes-styled number, 'Nothing But A Heartache' (number 34 pop), which sounded rather retrograde in the soul market, where it did not chart. The track later became a favourite in northern soul clubs.
● ALBUMS: *Love Makes The World Go Round* (Deram 1969) ★★.

Flo And Eddie
Lead singers (and songwriters) of the **Turtles**, Mark Volman (b. 19 April 1947, Los Angeles, California, USA) and Howard Kaylan (b. Howard Kaplan, 22 June 1947, the Bronx, New York, USA) took their name—the Phlorescent Leech and Eddie—from two of their roadies when the group split up in 1970. The Turtles' brand of innocent folk pop could not survive in the new sex-and-drug-orientated climate of rock. As if to advertise the change, they joined countercultural master **Frank Zappa** for tours and recordings. In his role as circus-master, Zappa had the pair perform hilarious routines about backstage groupie shenanigans (*Live At The Fillmore East June '71*) and act desperate, on-the-road pop stars in the movie **200 Motels**. Zappa wrote suitably operatic lines for their strong voices, and the results—though they dismayed fans of the 'serious' **Mothers Of Invention**—are undeniably effective. The sleeve of *Just Another Band From LA* (1972)—with Zappa reduced to a puppet in Kaylan's hand—seems to imply they had taken control of the group. They certainly split amidst much animosity, leaving Zappa just as his accident at the Rainbow Theatre, London, had made him wheelchair-bound. The comedy albums they released subsequently lack the punch of their work with Zappa, nor did the pair seem capable of re-creating the catchy pop they wrote for the Turtles. However, they did enliven the rock scene with an animated satirical movie, *Dirty Duck* aka *Cheap*, and a weekly three-hour radio show, *Flo & Eddie By The Fireside*, which originated on LA's KROQ but was syndicated all over the USA by 1976. They also supplied their powerful falsettos to give **Marc Bolan**'s voice a lift on many **T. Rex** hits. Indelibly associated with 70s 'progressive' rock culture, their careers took a different path in the following decade. The duo wrote

soundtracks for kids' movies, continued their radio work, and revived the Turtles name for touring purposes. The early 90s Marc Bolan revival brought their voices back to the airwaves (albeit only as backing), and **Jason Donovan** brought the Turtles' evergreen 'Happy Together' back to the charts in 1991.

● ALBUMS: *The Phlorescent Leech And Eddie* (Reprise 1972) ★★, *Flo & Eddie* (Warners 1973) ★★, *Illegal, Immoral And Fattening* (Columbia 1974) ★★★, *Moving Targets* (Columbia 1976) ★★.
● COMPILATIONS: *The Best Of Flo & Eddie* (Rhino 1987) ★★★.
● FILMS: *200 Motels* (1971), *Dirty Duck* aka *Cheap* (1975).

Floaters
Originally from Detroit, USA, Charles Clark (Libra), Larry Cunningham (Cancer), Paul Mitchell (Leo), Ralph Mitchell (Aquarius) and latterly Jonathan 'Mighty Midget' Murray, who joined the group in 1978, were responsible for one of soul's more aberrant moments. 'Float On', with its astrological connotations and **Barry White**–influenced machismo, was saved from utter ignominy by a light, almost ethereal melody line that was effective enough to provide the group with a US number 2 and a UK number 1 hit single in 1977. The Floaters could not survive the gimmick, and although two further singles reached the R&B Top 50, this often-ridiculed performance remains their lasting testament.
● ALBUMS: *Floaters* (ABC 1977) ★★★, *Magic* (ABC 1978) ★★, *Into The Future* (ABC 1979) ★★.

Floating Bridge
The line-up of this US Seattle–based rock group included Rich Dangel, Joe Johansen, Joe Johnson and Michael Marinelli. Their sole album, released in 1969, showcased an exciting twin-lead guitar assault and mixed exciting original material with rearranged cover versions, including a rousing rendition of the **Beatles**' 'Hey Jude' and a compulsive medley of the **Byrds**' 'Eight Miles High' and the **Rolling Stones**' 'Paint It, Black'. However, despite their undoubted skills, and the approbation of then-influential English disc jockey, Simon Stable, who penned enthusiastic liner notes on the UK release, Floating Bridge made little commercial headway.
● ALBUMS: *Floating Bridge* (Liberty 1969) ★★★.

Flock
Although they were formed in 1966 (Chicago, Illinois, USA), it was not until 1969 that Flock burst upon a most receptive market. **CBS Records** had successfully taken the lion's share of the progressive boom, and for a short time Flock became one of their leading products. The original band comprised Jerry Goodman (violin), Fred Glickstein (guitar, vocals), Tom Webb and Rick Canoff (saxophones), Ron Karpman (drums), Jerry Smith (bass) and Frank Posa (trumpet). Their blend of jazz and rock improvisations soon exhausted audiences as the solos became longer and longer. Jerry Goodman was the outstanding musician, stunning fans with his furious and brilliant electric violin playing. Their version of the **Kinks**' 'Tired Of Waiting For You' was memorable if only for the fact that they managed to turn a three-minute pop song into a magnum opus lasting, on occasions, over 10 minutes. Goodman left in 1971 to team up with **John McLaughlin** in the **Mahavishnu Orchestra**.

● ALBUMS: *The Flock* (Columbia 1969) ★★★, *Dinosaur Swamps* (Columbia 1970) ★, *Inside Out* (Mercury 1975) ★, *Live In Europe* (GAB 2005) ★.

● COMPILATIONS: *Flock Rock: The Best Of The Flock* (Columbia 1993) ★★★.

Flock Of Seagulls, A
(see **A Flock Of Seagulls**)

Floetry

Before even having a record in the stores, the members of the UK-bred neo-soul duo Floetry, singers Marsha Ambrosius and Natalie Stewart, were already songwriting veterans, having penned songs for renowned figures such as **Michael Jackson**, **Glenn Lewis**, **Bilal** and **Jill Scott** among others. Ambrosius and Stewart first met as members of different London, England–based basketball teams. Mutual friends thought a rivalry would develop between the two, but soon after their initial meeting, a friendship blossomed instead. Basketball eventually took a backseat to music, as the duo discovered a hard-to-ignore chemistry. Taking the name Floetry (meaning 'poetry that flows'), Ambrosius and Stewart relocated from the UK to the USA. Basing themselves in Philadelphia, the duo was soon taken under the wing of the A Touch Of Jazz Productions crew, a group of producers who have worked in the past with artists including Jill Scott, **Will Smith**, and **Lil' Kim**. As a result, the duo signed a recording contract with the DreamWorks label, which issued Floetry's debut recording, *Floetic*, in 2002. The following year's live album featured a collaboration with **Mos Def** on the single 'Wanna B Where U R (Thisizzaluvsong)'. The duo made their debut in the US R&B charts in 2005 with the single 'Supastar' (featuring **Common**). Their third album, *Flo'ology*, was a notable breakthrough success for the duo, receiving excellent reviews and reaching the US Top 10.

● ALBUMS: *Floetic* (DreamWorks 2002) ★★★, *Floacism Live* (DreamWorks 2003) ★★★, *Flo'ology* (Ervingwonder/ Geffen 2005) ★★★★.

● DVD/VIDEOS: *Floacism Live* (DreamWorks 2003).

Flogging Molly

This Los Angeles, California, USA–based outfit has garnered numerous comparisons to Irish outfits such as the **Pogues** and **Black 47** and fellow Americans the **Dropkick Murphys**. Formed in 1997 by Dave King (vocals/guitar; ex-**Fastway**), Bridget Regan (violin), Tedd Hutt (guitar), Jeff Peters (bass), George Schwindt (drums) and Toby McCallum (mandolin), Flogging Molly built a solid following by playing regularly at a local Irish bar called Molly Malone's and issued a self-produced live disc, *Alive Behind The Green Door*, shortly thereafter. The band was subsequently augmented by Matt Hensley (accordion), Nathen Maxwell (bass), Robert Schmidt (mandolin) and Gary Schwindt (trumpet), with Hutt making way for new guitarist John Donovan. They soon caught the attention of acclaimed alternative rock producer **Steve Albini**, who engineered Flogging Molly's next two releases, 2000's *Swagger* and 2002's *Drunken Lullabies* (the latter recorded without Gary Schwindt and with Donovan making way for Dennis Casey). The band's irresistible blend of traditional Irish and punk sounds created a varied fanbase, as evidenced by their inclusion on several Warped tours. Their 2004 release *Within A Mile Of Home* featured tributes to two of the band's heroes, **Joe Strummer** ('Seven Deadly Sins') and **Johnny Cash** ('Don't Let Me Die Still Wondering').

● ALBUMS: *Alive Behind The Green Door* (Own Label 1997) ★★★, *Swagger* (SideOneDummy 2000) ★★★★, *Drunken Lullabies* (SideOneDummy 2002) ★★★, *Within A Mile Of Home* (SideOneDummy 2004) ★★★.

Flood

b. Mark Ellis, 16 August 1960, England. Although Ellis is now a world-renowned producer, he began his career as a 'runner' for a London recording studio before becoming its in-house engineer and then working as a freelancer. His unusual nickname is said to have originated from his willingness to make tea—another studio technician was christened 'Drought'. Flood is now known for his tough, **techno**-tinged production work for high-profile artists including **U2**, **Depeche Mode**, **Smashing Pumpkins** and **PJ Harvey**. His first career break came when he engineered **New Order**'s 1981 debut, *Movement*. This auspicious start was followed by work with new wave bands such as **Soft Cell**, **Psychic TV**, **Cabaret Voltaire** and the **Associates**. Flood quickly graduated to production, beginning with the **Nick Cave And The Bad Seeds**' albums *The Firstborn Is Dead*, *Kicking Against The Pricks*, *Your Funeral, My Trial* and **Erasure**'s first two albums. Flood's long association with U2 began when he worked as the engineer on 1987's bestselling *The Joshua Tree*. He developed his trademark electronic edge on productions such as **Nine Inch Nails**' *Pretty Hate Machine*, **Pop Will Eat Itself**'s *This Is The Day, This Is The Hour, This Is This!* and 1990's acclaimed *Violator* by Depeche Mode. The last recording was engineered by **François Kevorkian**, himself a highly acclaimed producer and remixer. This metallic, edgy sound was also strongly evident on the following year's U2 release, *Achtung Baby*. Although Flood engineered that album, he progressed to coproduction with **Brian Eno** for 1993's *Zooropa*. In the intervening time, however, he had produced **Nitzer Ebb**'s *Ebbhead*, the **Charlatans**' *Between 10th And 11th* and **Curve**'s *Doppelgänger*. In 1993 Flood collaborated with Depeche Mode again on *Songs Of Faith & Devotion* before working on PJ Harvey's *To Bring You My Love* and Smashing Pumpkins' *Mellon Collie And The Infinite Sadness*. More production work with U2 followed with 1997's post-modern extravaganza, *Pop*. In late 1998, Flood began to produce Smashing Pumpkins' new album, work that did not finish until November 1999. Despite the praise for his productions and the international fame of the artists with whom he has worked, Flood prefers to remain out of the limelight and in the studio where he can get on with a craft at which he clearly excels.

Flood, Dick

b. 13 November 1932, Philadelphia, Pennsylvania, USA. Pop singer-songwriter Flood performed with US singer Billy Graves as 'The Country Lads' on **Jimmy Dean**'s CBS television show in 1957. Flood achieved his only hit in 1959 when his cover version of the French-adapted 'The Three Bells (The Jimmy Brown Song)' reached number 23 in the US charts. It was released in the UK on the short-lived Felsted label in September 1959 but failed to chart due to versions from US vocal group the Browns and a rerelease of the US 1954 hit from French group **Compagnons De La Chanson**, both of which made the UK Top 30.

Floodgate

Formed in New Orleans, USA, in 1994, hard rock band Floodgate quickly earned comparisons to the previous year's 'big thing', **Machine Head**. Certainly there were similarities in the two groups' sound, Floodgate opting for a no-frills, driving musical approach, without sacrificing melody for bombast. The group comprises Kyle Thomas (vocals, guitar), Steven Fisher (guitar), Kevin Thomas (bass) and Neil Montgomery (drums). The two Thomas brothers had already won notoriety in their former groups (Kyle Thomas having penned Exhorder's 'Slaughter In The Vatican'). Indeed, much of Floodgate's material is written in a profane vein, stated by Kyle Thomas to be a reaction against the suffocating, abusive Roman Catholic school he attended. His other former bands include Armageddon and Raid, while his brother was a member of **Acid Bath** and Moon Crickets. Kevin also joined Kyle in Exhorder shortly before their early 90s demise. The lyrics on Floodgate's 1996 debut, *Penalty*, were apparently written from Kyle Thomas' memories of his nightmares. Certainly 'Black With Sin' and 'Running With Sodden Legs' spoke volumes about their author's ability to evoke dark, intoxicating imagery without falling into the sort of melodrama or cliché that is common to so many of their peers.

● ALBUMS: *Penalty* (Roadrunner 1996) ★★★.

Floorjam

This 90s UK **techno** act is the creation of one Nick Newell, a man whose records show a clear line of descent from **Kraftwerk**'s computerised pop. His 'Stone Age' has become a widely venerated track, but it was not always a life of boundless techno experimentalism. In 1993 he returned to his former occupation, that of session musician, picking up lucrative contracts with **Gary Glitter** and **Take That** tours.

Flora, The Red Menace

A curious piece in some ways, this show is mainly notable for the first appearance on Broadway of the 19-year-old **Liza Minnelli**, although she had made her first New York stage appearance two years earlier, off-Broadway, in a revival of **Best Foot Forward**. The production also marked the Broadway debut of the composer **John Kander** and his lyricist **Fred Ebb**. Their subsequent enduring relationship with Minnelli would eventually reach its peak in 1972 with the film version of *Cabaret*. *Flora, The Red Menace* opened at New York's Alvin Theatre on 11 May 1965, with a book by **George Abbott** and Robert Russell, which was based on Lester Atwell's novel *Love Is Just Around The Corner*. It was set in the early 30s when America was deep in the Depression and told of Flora (Liza Minnelli), a naïve young girl, who, because of her affection for her boy friend, Harry Toukarian (Bob Dishy), joins the Communist Party. She never becomes a totally committed comrade—Charlotte (Cathryn Damon) is far more dedicated to the Red cause and to Harry for a time—but he resists her advances, and he and Flora resume diplomatic (and affectionate) relations. The best thing about the whole production was the score. Minnelli had several outstanding numbers including the tender 'Dear Love', 'All I Need (Is One Good Break)', 'Knock Knock' and 'Sing Happy'. There was also 'Not Every Day Of The Week', 'Palamino Pal', 'Street Songs' and a few highly hilarious items such as the 'The Flame', 'Express Yourself' and 'Sign Here'. The show existed for 87 performances mainly on the strength of Minnelli, who won the **Tony Award** for best actress. Somehow it seemed out of place in a Broadway season that included *Fiddler On The Roof*, *Do I Hear A Waltz?*, *I Had A Ball* and *Golden Boy*. A revised production of *Flora, The Red Menace*, with a new book by David Thompson and several additional Kander and Ebb songs, was presented off-Broadway in 1987. That version played in the UK at the Cambridge Arts Theatre (1992) and the Orange Tree Theatre in Richmond, Surrey (1994).

Floradora

This is the kind of the show that was all the rage in London and New York as the 20th century dawned. It opened first at the Lyric Theatre in London on 11 November 1899. In Owen Hall's book, *Floradora* is an island in the Phillipines and also the name of the perfume that is manufactured there by a rich American, Cyrus Gilfain (Charles E. Stevens). The complicated romantic entanglements that take place on the island and in a castle in Wales—of all places—involve Angela Gilfain (Kate Cutler), Lady Holyrood (**Ada Reeve**), Dolores (Evie Greene), Frank Abercoed (Melville Stewart) and Arthur Donegal (Edgar Stevens). A private investigator, Arthur Tweedlepunch (Willie Edouin), is instrumental in unravelling the whole thing and making sure that all the lovers find the right and proper partners. The show's score was a collaboration between the composer **Leslie Stuart**, who also wrote some of the lyrics along with Ernest Boyd-Jones and **Paul Rubens**. Extra lyrics were provided by Alfred Murray and Frank A. Clement. The production, which ran for an incredible (for the time) 455 performances, attracted a great deal of attention mainly because of its Floradora Girls, a dainty sextette of parasol-twirling young ladies, accompanied by an equal number of straw-hatted young gentlemen. Their speciality song, 'Tell Me Pretty Maiden (Are There Any More At Home Like You?)', swept the country, and when the show reached the USA in 1900, the same number became popular all over again through recordings by Byron G. Harlan, Joe Belmont and the Floradora Girls, and Harry Macdonough with Grace Spencer. *Floradora* did even better in New York than in London, and gave 553 performances at the New Casino Theatre. The show's score contained several other popular items that became the hits of the day on both sides of the Atlantic, including 'I Want To Be A Military Man', 'The Silver Star Of Love', 'When I Leave Town, 'The Shade Of The Palm', 'Tact', 'When You're A Millionaire' and 'The Island Of Love'. There were London revivals in 1915 and 1931, and New York audiences saw the show again in 1920 when it ran for 120 performances.

Florence, Bob

b. Robert Florence, 20 May 1932, Los Angeles, California, USA. On discovering that he had perfect pitch, Florence's mother started him on piano lessons at the age of five, and two years later, he gave a piano recital. Intent on a career as a concert pianist, he later studied at Los Angeles City as a music major. In addition to courses on harmony, counterpoint and music appreciation, he took a class in arranging and orchestration from Bob McDonald, who had a jazz background. This changed Florence's direction, and he joined the college jazz band. He was still in college when he formed his first rehearsal band, a prime objective being to allow him the opportunity to hear the things he was writing.

Florence first attracted widespread attention amongst big band fans when he wrote elegantly crafted arrangements for **Si Zentner**'s popular recording band in the early 60s. After leaving Zentner, with whom he sometimes played piano too, he wrote for several west coast–based musicians, including **Bud Shank** and **Frank Capp**, but also varied his technique happily to accommodate blues singers **Jimmy Witherspoon** and **Big Miller**, **Joanie Sommers**, **Sue Raney** and **Sergio Mendes**. Although an accomplished pianist, Florence's chief talents are his arranging skills and especially his ability to write for big bands. Like many other arrangers he discovered that the only way to hear his charts (many of which were for his own compositions) played the way he wanted them was to have his own big band.

Following upon the idea behind his college rehearsal band, in the late 50s he formed a new rehearsal band that continued through succeeding decades to great acclaim, providing object lessons in big band writing and playing. In subsequent decades he called upon outstanding musicians such as **Bob Cooper**, **Nick Ceroli**, **Bob Efford**, **Steve Hufstetter**, **Bill Perkins**, Kim Richmond, **Buddy Childers**, **Pete Christlieb** and Warren Leuning. Although his roots are clearly in the post-swing era style of big band writing, Florence comfortably accommodates bebop and many latter-day fusions. In a *tour de force* on 'The Bebop Treasure Chest' (on 1986's *Trash Can City*), he demonstrated his skills by seamlessly blending phrases and quotations from 16 tunes. From 1981 his band was known as Bob Florence Limited Edition.

● ALBUMS: *Meet The Bob Florence Trio* (Era 1957) ★★★, *Bongos, Reeds And Brass* (HiFi 1958) ★★★, *Name Band 1959* (Carlton 1959) ★★★★, with Si Zentner *Up A Lazy River* (Liberty 1961) ★★★★, *Big Miller With Bob Florence And His Orchestra* (Liberty 1961) ★★★, with Zentner *Desafinado* (Liberty 1962) ★★★★, with Zentner *Waltz In Jazz Time* (Liberty 1962) ★★★, *Here And Now* (Liberty 1964) ★★★★, *Pet Project* (World Pacific 1968) ★★, *Live At Concerts By The Sea* (Trend 1979) ★★★★, with Joanie Sommers *Dream* (Discovery 1980) ★★★, *Westlake* (Discovery 1981) ★★★, *Soaring* (Sea Breeze 1982) ★★★, with Sue Raney *The Music Of Johnny Mandel* (Discovery 1982) ★★, *Magic Time* (Trend 1983) ★★★, with Raney *Ridin' High* (Discovery 1984) ★★★, with Raney *Flight Of Fancy: A Journey Of Alan And Marilyn Bergman* (Discovery 1986) ★★★, *Norwegian Radio Big Band Meets Bob Florence* (Odin 1986) ★★★, *Trash Can City* (Trend 1986) ★★★, *State Of The Art* (C5 1988) ★★★, *Funupsmanship* (MAMA 1993) ★★★, with Bobby Lamb *Trinity Fair* (Hep 1996) ★★★, *With All The Bells And Whistles* (MAMA 1997) ★★★★, *Earth* (MAMA 1997) ★★★, *Serendipity 18* (MAMA 1999) ★★★, *Another Side* (MAMA 2001) ★★.

Flores, Rosie

b. 10 September 1950, San Antonio, Texas, USA. Flores' background accounts for the strong Mexican influence in her brand of country music. When she was 12 years old, her family moved to San Diego, California, and in her mid-teens Flores became part of an all-female psychedelic band, Penelope's Children. She was then backed by a punk band, Rosie And The Screamers. Next came another all-female cow-punk band, the Screamin' Sirens. In 1985 she was part of a compilation album of new country artists, *A Town South Of Bakersfield*, on which she sang 'Heartbreak Train' with **Albert Lee**. Her first album for **Reprise Records**, *Rosie Flores*, was

produced with **Pete Anderson** and **Dwight Yoakam**, but her biggest single on the US country charts, 'Crying Over You', only reached number 51. Dropped by Reprise, she re-emerged five years later on Hightone with *After The Farm*. Flores remains one of those Texas artists more popular as a cult performer in Europe than in her home country. In 1994 she toured the UK as lead guitarist for **Butch Hancock**, but during the visit she broke her right arm, which ultimately delayed the recording of *Rockabilly Filly*. The album included duets with two of her rockabilly idols, **Wanda Jackson** and **Janis Martin**. She collaborated with cult rockabilly singer Ray Campi on her 1997 album, which featured tracks recorded over the previous seven years. Flores manages to successfully create an evocative sound of innocent rockabilly mixed and the nostalgia of **Les Paul** and **Mary Ford** together with contemporary pop with a strong country and folk influence.

● ALBUMS: with The Screamin' Sirens *Fiesta* (Enigma 1984) ★★★, *Rosie Flores* (Reprise 1987) ★★★★, *After The Farm* (Hightone 1992) ★★★, *Once More With Feeling* (Hightone 1993) ★★★, *Rockabilly Filly* (HighTone 1995) ★★★, *A Honky Tonk Reprise* (Rounder 1996) ★★★★, with Ray Campi *A Little Bit Of Heartache* (Watermelon 1997) ★★★, *Dance Hall Dreams* (Rounder 1999) ★★★, *Speed Of Sound* (Eminent 2001) ★★★, *Single Rose* (Durango Rose 2004) ★★.

● FILMS: *Vendetta* (1986), *The Thing Called Love* (1993).

Florida Boys

Comprising Len Beasley (lead), Glen Allred (baritone), Derrell Stewart (piano), Buddy Liles (bass), Jerry Trammell (tenor) and Tommy Watwood (various musical instruments), this southern gospel group was first formed in 1947 as the Gospel Melody Quartet. From the 50s onwards they have become one of the most recognizable and popular groups working within the gospel idiom. They became pioneers in the development of religious music broadcasting, hosting the nationally syndicated show *The Gospel Singing Jubilee*—on which Beasley is the regular host. In the process the Florida Boys became national celebrities, their albums for Canaan Records selling consistently well. They were the first act ever signed to Canaan following its establishment as a subsidiary of Word Records at the end of the 60s. Beasley is also a lifetime trustee of the Gospel Music Association and a lifetime trustee of the Gospel Music Hall Of Fame.

● ALBUMS: *What A Difference Jesus Makes* (Canaan 1970) ★★★★, *True Gospel* (Canaan 1971) ★★★, *First Class Gospel* (Canaan 1972) ★★★, *Here They Come* (Canaan 1973) ★★★, *He Loves You* (Canaan 1974) ★★★, *In Concert . . : Live* (Canaan 1974) ★★, *Vintage Gospel* (Canaan 1977) ★★★, *Sing About A New Day* (Canaan 1977) ★★★, *Together* (Canaan 1986) ★★, *Home Once Again* (Canaan 1988) ★★★.

● COMPILATIONS: *The Best Of* (Canaan 1977) ★★★★.

Florida

Originally comprising Gavin Atkin (fiddle/vocals), Tim Bull (melodeon), Chris Warner (bass) and Richard Blake (saxophone), Florida formed in the UK in 1990 after the first three named members of the band had deserted their previous project, Melons For Ecstasy. They were joined by trumpet player Charlie Handley, but by 1991 Blake had departed, to be replaced on saxophone by Richard Goodwin of the Seven Champions. The consciously rejected the idea of a drummer, basing their decision on their preference for early 80s **Oysterband** and **Blowzabella**. They quickly earned a formidable reputation by playing extensively throughout the UK, using traditional material such as 'The Leaves Of Life' and 'Dudley Boys' but imbuing them with abrasive arrangements—usually distinguished by the unusual presence of a brass section. Mixing dance numbers with ballads, they won many new supporters in 1993 with their self-titled debut album and appearances at both the Sidmouth and Warwick folk festivals. *Brass Roots* confirmed their stature as one of the more inventive of the modern 'ceilidh' bands, capturing something of the essence of their live show and mixing songs with polkas and jigs.

● ALBUMS: *Florida* (Florida 1993) ★★★, *Brass Roots* (Florida 1995) ★★★.

Flory, Chris

b. 13 November 1953, New York City, New York, USA. Flory first played guitar as a child. Strongly influenced by such major guitarists as **Charlie Christian** and **Django Reinhardt**, he began playing professionally in 1974. Within a few years he had become a regular associate of **Scott Hamilton**, touring internationally and making records. Although he continued his links with Hamilton throughout the 80s and 90s, he also played with other jazzmen including **Hank Jones, Bob Wilber** and **Ruby Braff** and for four years from 1979 was a regular member of the occasionally re-formed **Benny Goodman** Sextet. He also played with the Goodman big band in 1985 at what proved to be the leader's final public performance. In the 80s and 90s Flory appeared on numerous record sessions with artists such as Hamilton, Braff, Wilber, **Maxine Sullivan**, Judy Carmichael and **Rosemary Clooney**. He also became a familiar and popular figure on the international circuit, sometimes in company and other times as a single. A fluent improviser and gifted accompanist, Flory's solo work bears traces of his idols, but he has steadily become a distinctive and distinguished guitarist in his own right.

● ALBUMS: *For All We Know* (Concord 1988) ★★★★, *City Life* (Concord 1993) ★★★, *Word On The Street* (Double-Time 1997) ★★★, with Duke Robillard And Friends *Blues In My Heart* (Stony Plain 2003) ★★★.

Flory, Med

b. Meredith I. Flory, 27 August 1926, Logansport, Indiana, USA. Flory's early experience on alto saxophone was gained with the bands of **Claude Thornhill** and **Woody Herman**. In New York he worked mostly in small groups, some of which he led. After relocating to the west coast in 1954, he continued to play jazz in small and big bands (again sometimes as leader), but he also worked extensively in several fields other than jazz, notably as a screenwriter and an actor in films and television. While arranging for his big band in the late 50s, encouraged by **Art Pepper** and **Joe Maini**, Flory conceived the idea of arranging some of **Charlie Parker**'s solos for a complete saxophone section. The idea was not fully developed, however, until some years later when **Buddy Clark** revived the concept, and out of this shared interest Clark and Flory formed **Supersax** in 1972. Subsequently, Flory continued to lead Supersax and also played regularly with various west coast big bands.

● ALBUMS: *Jazz Wave* (Jubilee 1957) ★★★.

Flotsam And Jetsam

This thrash metal band was formed in Phoenix, Arizona, USA, in 1984 by drummer David Kelly Smith and bass player Jason Newsted (b. 4 March 1963). Adding vocalist Eric A.K. and guitarists Mike Gilbert and Ed Carlson, they debuted with tracks on the *Speed Metal Hell II* and *Metal Massacre IV* compilations. This led to a contract with Roadrunner Records and the release of *Doomsday For The Deceiver* in 1986. Hard, fast and punchy riffs were the band's trademarks, but their progress was hampered by the departure of Newsted to **Metallica** shortly after the album's release. Eventually, Troy Gregory was recruited as a permanent replacement, and *No Place For Disgrace* emerged in 1988. This sadly revealed that the band had progressed little in two years, and the new material lacked imagination. In an attempt to break into the singles market, they recorded a cover version of **Elton John**'s 'Saturday Night's Alright For Fighting', which failed commercially. Dropped by Roadrunner, they were eventually signed by MCA Records in 1990 and released *When The Storm Comes Down*. Produced by Alex Periallis (of **Testament** and **Anthrax** fame), it was aggressive and power-paced but suffered from an overall monotony of pace and tone.

● ALBUMS: *Doomsday For The Deceiver* (Roadrunner 1986) ★★★, *No Place For Disgrace* (Roadrunner 1988) ★★, *When The Storm Comes Down* (MCA 1990) ★★, *Cuatro* (MCA 1993) ★★, *High* (Metal Blade 1997) ★★★, *Unnatural Selection* (Metal Blade 1999) ★★.

Flourgon

b. Michael May, Kingston, Jamaica, West Indies. May began his career on the **sound system** circuit, performing with Stone Love, Small Axe, Rambo Mango and his own Sweet Love set. He often performed alongside his DJ sibling, **Red Dragon**, with whom he nurtured the careers of **Buju Banton** and **Terry Ganzie**. May released a succession of combination hits, including 'How You So Hot' with **Brian And Tony Gold**, 'Girls Just Wanna Have Fun' with **Thriller U**, 'Go Sit Down' with Clement Irie, 'Dungle Lover' and 'Madly In Love' with **Sanchez** and 'Jump And Spread Out' and 'Turn And Stab' with Daddy Lizard alongside the favoured 'Million And More' and the chart-topping 'Zig It Up', both of which featured the enigmatic **Ninjaman**. Following May's successful combination with the controversial DJ, Ninjaman curiously released the contemptuous 'Last Of The Flourgon'. The latter, however, had little impact on Flourgon's career, and his distinctive gritty voice continued to grace a profusion of vinyl releases. He enjoyed a notable partnership with Mikey Bennett and Patrick Lindsay, primarily for his version of the 'Oil Thing' rhythm, 'Bow Ting'. Other solo hits included 'Tender Touch', 'Bounce', 'Fret And Worry', 'Trophy', 'Live Good', 'Bad Boy Tune' and 'Follow Me'. In 1994 Jamaican producers, inspired by the **dancehall** trend of mixing various DJs over the same rhythm, began recording various artist singles that often featured Flourgon, including 'Can't Stop The Dance', performed by the 'Yardcore collective', which incorporated the talents of **General Degree, Tony Rebel, Papa San** and Buju Banton among others, while 'Informer' featured **Snagga Puss, Anthony Malvo, Anthony Red Rose, Frankie Paul**, Lizard and Flourgon's brother Red Dragon. By the late 90s his output was lost in the flood of dancehall releases, although his combination with **Freddie McGregor**, 'Bless My Soul', enjoyed some success. Although his career has been

overtaken by the young contenders, Flourgon is regarded as an influential DJ who inspired a wave of sonorous vocalists.
● ALBUMS: *Red Dragon Vs Flourgon* (Techniques 1989) ★★★.

Flower Drum Song (film musical)

While being perfectly agreeable—and successful—in the form of the stage musical, which opened on Broadway in 1958, this screen version, released three years later, seemed somewhat precious and quaint, particularly in comparison with the dynamic *West Side Story*, which arrived in US cinemas at around the same time. Joseph Fields and **Oscar Hammerstein II** were responsible for the stage libretto, which was based on a novel by Chin Y. Lee. Fields' screenplay for the film followed the original closely, telling the story of a mail-order bride, played by Miyoshi Umeki, who travels from Hong Kong to San Francisco for the sole purpose of marrying nightclub owner Sammy Fong (Jack Soo). Ultimately, circumstances work out differently, and she finally finds happiness with student Wang Ta (James Shigeta), while Fong stays true to his longtime girlfriend, Linda Low (Nancy Kwan). Umeki was in the original Broadway cast, and so was **Juanita Hall**, who gave a delicious performance in the role of Madam Liang. There were several memorable numbers in **Richard Rodgers** and Oscar Hammerstein's score, including 'I Enjoy Being A Girl' (Kwan), 'You Are Beautiful' (Shigeta), 'Sunday' (Kwan-Soo), 'Love, Look Away' (Sato), 'Chop Suey' (Hall), 'A Hundred Million Miracles' (Umeki-Kam Tong), 'I Am Going To Like It Here' (Umeki), 'Don't Marry Me' (Umeki-Soo), 'Grant Avenue' (Kwan) and 'The Other Generation' (Fong-Hall-Adiarte). As usual, **Hermes Pan**'s choreography was singled out for praise, as was Russell Metty's photography in Eastman Color and Panavision. Henry Koster was the director for this Universal picture, which, although pleasantly entertaining, dealt with a subject—the problems of adjustment between different generations of the Chinese-American community in the USA—that did not appeal to a wide range of cinemagoers in the early 60s.

Flower Drum Song (stage musical)

Most of **Richard Rodgers** and **Oscar Hammerstein**'s blockbuster musicals were adapted from existing works, and this show was based on a novel by Chin Y. Lee. It opened at the St. James Theatre in New York on 1 December 1958 and was the only Broadway show that **Gene Kelly** directed. Hammerstein's book, written in collaboration with Joseph Fields, is set in San Francisco's Chinatown and deals in a warmhearted way with the problems of the Chinese, the Chinese-Americans, and their Americanized children. The difficulties posed by the various generation gaps and cultures are sympathetically presented in a story of mail-order brides, marriage contracts, and fiendishly clever plotlines, resulting in the inevitable wedding ceremony. Mei Li (Miyoshi Umeki) is the lady who was delivered via by the US Mail, but she is not the bride. Linda Low (Pat Suzuki) is the lucky married lady and has one of the show's most popular numbers, 'I Enjoy Being A Girl', as well as the duet 'Sunday' with her groom Sammy Fong (Larry Blyden). The rest of Rodgers and Hammerstein's lovely score included 'You Are Beautiful', 'A Hundred Million Miracles', 'I Am Going To Like It Here', 'Like A God', 'Chop Suey', 'Don't Marry Me', 'Grant Avenue', 'Love Look Away', 'Gliding Through My Memories' and 'The

Other Generation'. **Juanita Hall** played Madame Liang, 'an enthusiastic candidate for American citizenship'. She also starred in Rodgers and Hammerstein's film of **South Pacific**, which was released in the same year as *Flower Drum Song* began its Broadway run of 600 performances. The popular vocalist **Anita Ellis** was also in the show's cast. She played a nightclub singer and had the novelty number 'Fan Tan Fannie'. That scene, and the rest of the production, was choreographed by **Carol Haney**, who introduced 'Hernado's Hideaway' in **The Pajama Game**. The 1960 London production of *Flower Drum Song* had different principal cast members, but Miyoshi Umeki re-created her role for the 1961 film version, which also starred Nancy Kwan.

Flowered Up

As cultural phenomenons go, rarely has a band mirrored their social surroundings more graphically than Flowered Up from the UK. Formed on a north London housing estate in 1989, they were immediately championed by so many disparate causes (the working classes, the drug dealer, proud southerners) that their rise to fame was virtually inevitable. Born out of the ecstasy boom that swept the musical underground at the turn of the 90s, Flowered Up's first gig at the close of 1989 was a shambolic affair that outraged as many onlookers as it excited. Within six months the line-up had settled down with Liam Maher (vocals), brother Joe Maher (guitar), Andy Jackson (bass, later replaced by Mick Leander), Tim Dorney (keyboards), John Tuvey (drums) and a man called Barry Mooncult who had taken to dancing with the band onstage, wearing a giant flower. Signed to London-based indie label **Heavenly Records**, the release of their debut single, 'It's On', encouraged the UK weekly music papers to take the unusual step of putting a brand new band on its front pages, but all the accusations of hype were drowned out by Flowered Up revellers convinced that the band was London's answer to Manchester's **Happy Mondays**. They were not, nor were they another **Clash** or another **Madness**, mainly because although Flowered Up's flowing rock/funk grooves graced the Top 40 of all the UK charts, they failed to upset the commercial apple cart, in spite of all the attention. A move to **London Records** ended inimically when the label refused to release the 13-minute single 'Weekender', which, with its accompanying 20-minute film, was a perfect snapshot of **rave** culture. *A Life With Brian* appeared to show that the band, for all their Cockney quirkiness, could make an album that stood on its own two feet without fear of falling over. It would also provide the band with their tombstone, however, and they released one more single ('Better Life') before splitting up in 1993. Tim Dorney went on to work with Clive Langer and **Republica**, while Liam Maher returned to his bootleg stall in Camden Market and further musical projects. The original line-up, minus Barry Mooncult, re-formed for live work in 2005.
● ALBUMS: *A Life With Brian* (Heavenly 1991) ★★★.

Flowerpot Men

This UK outfit was formed in 1967 by the **Carter And Lewis** songwriting team **John Carter** (b. John Shakespeare, 20 October 1942, Birmingham, England) and Ken Lewis (b. Kenneth James Hawker, 3 December 1942, Birmingham, England). They magnificently exploited the concurrent flower-power boom. The ensuing single, 'Let's Go To San Francisco', became a UK Top 5 hit and a quartet of session vocalists—**Tony Burrows**, Robin Shaw, Pete Nelson and Neil Landon—then assumed the name and proceeded to tour under the name. Burrows, Shaw and Landon went on to complete several well-sculpted releases, all masterminded and written by the prolific Carter, notably 'A Walk In The Sky'. An instrumental section, comprising Ged Peck (guitar), Jon Lord (b. 9 June 1941, Leicester, Leicestershire, England; organ), **Nick Simper** (b. 3 November 1945, Norwood Green, Southall, Middlesex, England; bass) and Carlo Little (drums), accompanied the singers on tour, but this line-up was dissolved when Lord and Simper founded **Deep Purple**. The three singers changed their name to Friends in late 1968 but were unable to revive their fortunes. In 1970 Burrows enjoyed great success as a vocalist for hire with **Edison Lighthouse**, the **Brotherhood Of Man** and **White Plains**. Landon resurfaced in **Fat Mattress**, while Shaw and Nelson played alongside Burrows in White Plains.

● COMPILATIONS: *Let's Go To San Francisco* (C5 1988) ★★★, *A Walk In The Sky* (RPM 2001) ★★★★, *Let's All Go To San Francisco* (Tenth Planet 2003) ★★★.

Flowers And Frolics

This UK group specialized in English country dance music and music-hall songs. Flowers And Frolics were formed in 1974, but at the time the group had no official name so were credited as the Graham Smith Band for a gig announced in *Melody Maker*. Their monicker was taken from the name of original member Graham Smith (b. Melbourne, Australia). Smith left to return to Australia before the group recorded its first album. The line-up on *Bees On Horseback* was Mike Bettison (b. 3 June 1951, Chiswick, London, England; melodeon), Roger Digby (b. 19 April 1949, Colchester, Essex, England; concertina), Bob King (b. 27 March 1952, Eastbourne, Sussex, England; banjo), Dan Quinn (b. 11 October 1949, Grimsby, South Humberside, England; melodeon), Ted Stevens (b. 27 September 1952, Redruth, Cornwall, England; percussion) and Alex West (b. 8 November 1954, England; brass/bass). By the time of *Sold Out*, King and West had been replaced by Trevor Bennett (b. 4 August 1945, Grantham, Lincolnshire, England; trombones, flügelhorn, helicon), Rob Gifford (b. 1 March 1955, Wanstead, London, England; percussion) and Nick Havell (b. Nicholas George Havell, 7 January 1951, Stratford, London, England; bass trombone).

The group achieved a good deal of popularity on the folk circuit, not least for keeping many traditional dances alive. Playing a variety of jigs, hornpipes, polkas and waltzes, they performed at festivals all over Britain and were in demand at ceilidhs and barn dances alike. Only two albums were recorded before the group split up in February 1985, having decided they had done enough. That same year, Quinn, Havell, Bennett and Gifford formed the dance band **Gas Mark 5**, supplemented by Chris Taylor from the **Oysterband**. Quinn then left in 1989 but continued to play on the folk circuit. Stevens is a member of the Old Hat Band, while King plays with jazz and rock bands. Bettison is a member of the Fabulous Salami Brothers, while West has left the folk scene.

● ALBUMS: *Bees On Horseback* (Free Reed 1977) ★★★, *Sold Out* (1984) ★★★.

Flowers For Algernon

Originally tried out in Ontario, Canada, this unusual musical played briefly at the Queen's Theatre in London from 14 June 1979. It was based on the novel of the same name by Daniel Keyes and had a score by **Charles Strouse** (music) and David Rogers (lyrics). Rogers also wrote the book, which took most of the blame for the show's early demise. The subject was a tricky one—especially for a musical. Having successfully raised the IQ of a mouse (Algernon), scientists turn their attention to the mentally handicapped Charlie (**Michael Crawford**). Initially, their experiments turn him into a near-genius, but as the effects of the operation wear off, he returns to his former condition—and makes friends with Algernon. Crawford's sensitive, gentle performance was applauded, and he was well supported by Cheryl Kennedy, the teacher who falls in love with him. The cast also featured Betty Benfield, Sharon Lee Hill, Jeanna L'Esty, George Harris, Ralph Nossek and Aubrey Woods. The score included several admirable songs, such as 'Whatever Time There Is', 'Reading', 'I Got A Friend' and 'No Surprises' along with 'His Name Is Charlie Gordon', 'Some Bright Morning', 'Our Boy Charlie', 'Hey, Look At Me!', 'Midnight Riding', 'Dream Safe With Me', 'I Can't Tell You', 'Now', 'Charlie And Algernon', 'The Maze', 'Charlie' and 'I Really Loved You'. Peter Coe directed, and the show attracted some good notices, but in spite of Crawford's box office appeal, *Flowers For Algernon* was withdrawn after only 28 performances. However, that was a slightly better achievement than the Broadway production, retitled *Charlie And Algernon*, which opened at the Helen Hayes Theatre on 14 September 1980, with P.J. Benjamin and Sandy Faison as the leads, and lasted for only 17 performances. Nevertheless, Strouse and Rogers' score was nominated for a **Tony Award** and is preserved in a London cast recording. Cliff Robertson's remarkable performance in the 1968 film version of Daniel Keyes' book, entitled *Charly*, won him an Academy Award.

Flowers, Herbie

b. England. As a session musician, Flowers' many performances have ensured his reputation as one of the world's most in-demand bass players (with the occasional request for trumpet playing). He found fame in the late 60s with the session players' 'supergroup' **Blue Mink**, enjoying success with the international hit 'Melting Pot'. His songwriting talents brought him fame with the novelty number 1 hit for Clive Dunn, 'Grandad', in January 1971. Flowers' performance on **Lou Reed**'s UK Top 10/US Top 20 hit 'Walk On The Wild Side' (*Transformer* 1972) produced one of rock's most distinctive bass lines. His later work with the virtuoso group **Sky**, with **John Williams**, Kevin Peek, Tristan Fry and Francis Monkman, brought him worldwide fame. Flowers also performed as part of one of the later line-ups of **T. Rex** in the late 70s. His many studio credits throughout his career have included work for **David Bowie** (*Space Oddity, Diamond Dogs* and *David Live*), **CCS** (*CCS*), **Melanie** (*Candles In The Rain*), **Elton John** (*Madman Across The Water* and *A Single Man*), **Cat Stevens** (*Foreigner*), **Ginger Baker** (*Eleven Sides Of Baker*), **Roy Harper** (*Bullinamingvase*), **Ian Gomm** (*Summer Holiday*), **Jeff Wayne** (*War Of The Worlds*), **Steve Harley** (*Hobo With A Grin*), **Roger Daltrey** (*McVicar*), **George Harrison** (*Gone Troppo*) and **Paul McCartney** (*Give My Regards To Broad Street*). Along the way he has also managed to release solo albums on Philips and EMI Note.

● ALBUMS: *Plant Life* (Philips 1975) ★★, *A Little Potty* (Note 1980) ★★.

Flowers, Mike, Pops

The debonair Mike Flowers (b. Mike Roberts) caused a brief mid-90s sensation when he rode into the UK charts on the crest of the 'easy listening' revival with a cover version of **Oasis**' 'Wonderwall'. It remained in the charts for several weeks and was only narrowly kept off the Christmas 1995 number 1 spot by **Michael Jackson**. Dressed in a suit that time had forgotten and bedecked by the most outrageous blonde wig, Flowers' version of 'Wonderwall' caused more grins than grimaces and sold nearly half a million copies. Even the song's writer, Noel Gallagher, was reportedly impressed by this, the cheekiest of cover versions (Oasis' 'Wonderwall' was still in the charts when it was released). It was followed by a version of **Engelbert Humperdinck**'s 'Please Release Me' in 1996 and the band's debut album, *A Groovy Place*. Alongside the singles this included original material—though titles such as 'Crusty Girl' and 'Freebase' demonstrated that the Mike Flowers Pops' tongues were still firmly in their collective cheek. After the hype died down Flowers moved on to soundtrack work.

● ALBUMS: *A Groovy Place* (London 1996) ★★★.

Floyd Lloyd

b. Lloyd Seivright, 3 June 1948, Browns Town, St. Ann's, Jamaica, West Indies. As a teenager Floyd attended Alpha Boys School, a Catholic run musical institution in Kingston. At this time the popular music in Jamaica consisted largely of American standards, New Orleans jazz, and popular hits of the 50s and the early 60s. His education at the school resulted in him writing his own songs, and at the age of 15 he performed on Jamaican television. Floyd wrote the hit 'Be Yourself' in 1969, which led to a relocation in England where he continued to pursue a career in music. The song resulted in him being invited by the **Beatles**' **Apple Records** to attend an audition, although with the band's demise his summons was neglected.

By the early 70s Floyd understood the value of retaining the publishing rights of his own works and founded Tropic Entertainment & Recording Enterprises. One of his earliest clients was **Justin Hinds** who was to discover the benefit of the contract 20 years later as his compositions, 'Over The River' and 'Here I Stand', were chart hits for **Bitty McClean**. The **EMI Records** and **Warner Brothers Records** organizations were impressed by Floyd's professional approach to publishing and employed him to resolve authorship and copyright disputes from within the reggae industry. At the time these were issues often neglected by labels and producers dealing with Jamaican artists who had no legal representation. In addition to employment in the peripheral side of the music industry Floyd continued working with artists such as **Derrick Morgan**, **Tommy McCook**, **Laurel Aitken** and **Rico Rodriguez**.

Also in the 70s Floyd formed the Red Cloud band in London who played a unique musical fusion regarded as rock-reggae. It was around this time that the **Mighty Diamonds** recorded the classic 'Sweet Lady', which was in fact a rewrite of Floyd's 'Be Yourself' and has remained a popular hit on the revival circuit. In 1977 Floyd released two solo songs, 'Soulful Lover Baby' and 'Slow Down', through **Trojan Records**. His solo venture followed the demise of the Red Cloud band and he later signed to the EMI/KPM Music Library who were inspired by his exceptionality. For the company he produced reggae songs for their music library that was used in film and

television programmes such as *EastEnders*, *Friends* and Twentieth Century Fox's *Strange Days*. He additionally performed with the ska revival group the Potato 5 and remained with them for several years. (It was while working with the Potato 5 that he coined the phrase 'Mash It Up'). He then relocated to the Netherlands before settling in New York, USA, in 1995 where, with his business partner Brenda Ray, he focused on releasing much of his material. A consequence of these releases was a variety of sync licenses to various film and television shows. 'Compatible Friends' and 'Rock Steady Party' taken from *Mango Blues* were featured in the HBO production *Real Sex* and Paramount's *Dead Men On Campus* respectively. Floyd has established himself as ska's keeper of the faith. He maintained the jazz/ska connection when he forged links with the New Orleans Jazz Stars.

● ALBUMS: *Better To Laugh* (Vista Echo 1982) ★★★, *Laurel Aitken Meets Floyd Lloyd & The Potato 5* (Gaz's 1987) ★★, *Tear It Up* (Tuff Gong 1997) ★★★★, *Our World* (Tropic 1999) ★★★, *Mango Blues* (Tropic 2000) ★★★, *Alchemy* (Tropic 2001) ★★★.

Floyd, Eddie

b. 25 June 1935, Montgomery, Alabama, USA. A founder member of the Detroit-based **Falcons**, Floyd was present on both their major hits, 'You're So Fine' (1959) and 'I Found A Love' (1962). He then recorded solo for Lupine in Detroit and Safice in Washington, DC, before moving to Memphis, in 1965 to join the **Stax Records** organization. He first made his mark there as a composer, penning **Wilson Pickett**'s '634-5789' among others. During Floyd's recording tenure at Stax, he enjoyed the use of the session bands **Booker T. And The MGs** and the **Mar-Keys**. He opened his account with 'Things Get Better' (1965), followed by the anthem-like 'Knock On Wood' (1966), one of soul's enduring moments, and probably the only time 'lightning' and 'frightening' have been coupled without sounding trite. Although subsequent releases failed to match its success, a series of powerful singles, including 'Love Is A Doggone Good Thing' (1967) and 'Big Bird' (1968), confirmed Floyd's stature both as a performer and songwriter. Although his compositions were recorded by several acts, his next US Top 20 pop hit came with **Sam Cooke**'s 'Bring It On Home To Me' in 1968. Floyd stayed with Stax until its bankruptcy in 1975, whereupon he moved to **Malaco Records**. His spell there was thwarted by commercial indifference, and he left the label for **Mercury Records** in 1977 but met with no better results. Briefly relocated to London, he recorded under the aegis of Mod resurrectionists **Secret Affair**. In 1988 Floyd linked up with **William Bell**'s Wilbe venture to release the *Flashback* album. In 1990 Floyd appeared live with a re-formed Booker T. And The MGs and continues to gig consistently, although new recordings are rare.

● ALBUMS: *Knock On Wood* (Stax 1967) ★★★, *I've Never Found A Girl* (Stax 1968) ★★★, *You've Got To Have Eddie* (Stax 1969) ★★★, *California Girl* (Stax 1970) ★★, *Down To Earth* (Stax 1971) ★★, *Baby Lay Your Head Down* (Stax 1973) ★★, *Soul Street* (Stax 1974) ★★, *Experience* (Malaco 1977) ★★, *Flashback* (Wilbe 1988) ★★.

● COMPILATIONS: *Rare Stamps* (Stax 1968) ★★★, *Chronicle* (Stax 1979) ★★★, *Knock On Wood: The Best Of Eddie Floyd* (Atlantic 1988) ★★★★, *Rare Stamps* (Stax 1993) ★★.

Floyd, Frank

b. 11 October 1908, Toccopola, Mississippi, USA, d. 7 August 1984, Memphis, Tennessee, USA. Having spent many of his earlier years travelling the southern states of the USA, playing in carnivals and street shows, Floyd, aka Harmonica Frank, developed a solo guitar and harmonica style much influenced by black country blues. This led to his first recordings—made by **Sam Phillips** in Memphis in 1951—being issued on the **Chess Records** label, at that time orientated entirely towards a black audience. These, along with later recordings that Phillips issued in 1954 on his own **Sun Records** label, in particular 'Rocking Chair Daddy', stand as direct precursors to the first **Elvis Presley** records, also on Sun, in their mixture of white and black styles, although Floyd enjoyed no similar commercial success. In the late 50s, he recorded again for a self-owned label, and there was also an album for Barrelhouse in 1975 and some interesting live recordings made in 1979 and finally issued in 2002.
● ALBUMS: *The Great Original Recordings Of Harmonica Frank* (Puritan 1974) ★★★, *Harmonica Frank Floyd* (Barrelhouse 1975) ★★★, *The Missing Link* (Memphis International 2002) ★★★.
● COMPILATIONS: *Harmonica Frank Floyd: The Great Medical Menagerist* (Edsel 1997) ★★★.
● FURTHER READING: *Mystery Train: Images Of America In Rock And Roll Music*, Greil Marcus.

Floyd, King

b. 13 February 1945, New Orleans, Louisiana, USA, d. 6 March 2006, California, USA. This itinerant singer first began performing at the age of 11, but his reputation was established by several mid-60s recordings produced by **Harold Battiste**. Floyd's first major hit came in 1970 with the excellent 'Groove Me', which topped the R&B charts and reached the US pop Top 10, and he enjoyed two further Top 5 R&B singles with 'Baby Let Me Kiss You' (1971) and 'Woman Don't Go Astray' (1972). He continued to enjoy limited success throughout the first half of that decade, but 'Body English', released in 1976, was his last chart entry. He died in 2006 from a stroke after suffering from ill health due to diabetes.
● ALBUMS: *A Man In Love* (Pulsar 1967) ★★★, *King Floyd* (Cotillion 1971) ★★★, *Think About It* (Atco 1973) ★★, *Well Done* (Chimneyville 1975) ★★★, *Body English* (Chimneyville 1977) ★★, *Old Skool Funk* (Malaco 2000) ★★★.

Fluffy

Dismissed in many quarters as 'the indie **Spice Girls**', UK pop punk band Fluffy were a colourful aggregate comprising Helen Storer (bass), Amanda E. Rootes (vocals), Bridget Jones (guitar) and Angie Adams (drums). The band, who adapted their name from the lesbian novel *Fluffy Butch*, soon found themselves facing a slew of accusations from the music press about their rich backgrounds, propensity for short skirts and lack of musical talent. Although the former was eventually revealed to be untrue, their enemies were widely acknowledged to have won the argument over the latter two slights. As Rootes lamented to the American music press in 1996, 'We are the Millwall of rock in England; Millwall is this bad football team here that everyone hates.' Nevertheless, Fluffy's 'Nothing' single, a eulogy to boredom (and, inadvertently, non-musicianship), brought them to national

television and the ***Top Of The Pops*** stage in September 1996. Sadly, the album it accompanied, *Blackeye*, merely confirmed the media's worst suspicions about the band despite the best efforts of **Clash** producer Bill Price. Rootes later surfaced in the Los Angeles based goth outfit Harlow, one of four unsigned bands competing on VH1's *Bands On The Run* reality music show.
● ALBUMS: *Black Eye* (Enclave/Capitol 1996) ★★.

Fluke

Purveyors of charismatic **dance music**, Fluke are both a stand-alone musical project and a mixing house for others. The combo was formed by Mike Bryant (b. Michael James Bryant, 1 May 1960, High Wycombe, Buckinghamshire, England), Michael Tournier (b. Michael James Tournier, 24 May 1963, High Wycombe, Buckinghamshire, England) and Jonathan Fugler (b. 13 October 1962, St Austell, Cornwall, England). Fugler and Bryant were both formerly in third-rate teenage punk bands, the Leaky Radiators and the Lay Figures. Tournier and Fugler had more prominently been part of Skin. They emerged as Fluke in 1988 with the white label 12-inch 'Island Life' and then the following September's 'Thumper!'. Other early pop **house** singles included 'Joni' (complete with a sample from **Joni Mitchell**'s 'Big Yellow Taxi') and 'Philly', their debut release for **Creation Records**. Their first live performance was on the lawn of a Kent country house at a **Boy's Own Records** party—a set that subsequently became their second album release, *Out (In Essence)*, in November 1991. It arrived as part of a new contract with **Virgin Records** subsidiary Circa Records, with whom they released their third album, the **trance**-dominated *Six Wheels On My Wagon*, in 1993. This was accompanied by a limited edition free vinyl copy of their long-deleted *The Techno Rose Of Blighty* debut. *Six Wheels On My Wagon* also proffered a further significant club hit, 'Groovy Feeling'.
Fluke maintain their own West London studio and remain somewhat aloof from the dance music community. This has not stopped them from earning considerable plaudits as remixers: **World Of Twist**, **JC-001**, Opik, **Tears For Fears**, **Talk Talk**, **New Order**, **Frankie Goes To Hollywood** and **Yello** numbering among their clients. Their notoriety continued in the mid-90s when **Björk** invited them to remix 'Big Time Sensuality' and was so impressed with the results she issued it in preference to the original version. This led to Fluke sharing a stage with the Icelandic singer at 1994's *Smash Hits* Poll Winners Party after their own single, 'Slid', had just failed to break the UK Top 40. 'Bubble' finally took them there in April 1994 and preceded their first national tour.
Fluke's fourth album, *Oto* (Greek for 'of ear'), was a surprisingly experimental work which embraced the jazzy rhythms of the new trip-hop genre. Released in the summer of 1995, the album was preceded by another highly praised single, 'Bullet'. Barry Andrews, veteran of **XTC** and **Shriekback**, was involved in the sessions in an informal production capacity. The following year's 'Atom Bomb', a track featured on the Wipeout 2097 Playstation game, provided Fluke with their first UK Top 20 single. The video for the single featured fourth member/mascot Arial Tetsuo, an anime figure represented in concerts by dancer Rachel Stewart. A high profile tour helped the **big beat** singles 'Absurd' and 'Squirt' dent the UK charts before Fluke lapsed into an extended period of silence, broken only by a handful of remixes and the release of the excellent compilation set, *Progressive*

History X. Interest had been generated by the use of 'Absurd' in the title credits of the *Tomb Raider* movie.

● ALBUMS: *The Techno Rose Of Blighty* (Creation 1991) ★★★, *Out (In Essence)* mini-album (Circa/Virgin 1991) ★★★, *Six Wheels On My Wagon* (Circa 1993) ★★★★, *The Peel Sessions* (Strange Fruit 1994) ★★★, *Oto* (Circa 1995) ★★★, *Risoto* (Circa/Astralwerks 1997) ★★★★, *Puppy* (One Little Indian 2003) ★★★.

● COMPILATIONS: *Progressive History X: Ten Years Of Fluke* (Circa/Astralwerks 2001) ★★★★, *Progressive History XXX* (Virgin 2002) ★★★.

Flux Of Pink Indians

This UK punk band was formed from the ashes of the Epileptics (who later changed their name to Epi-X due to letters of complaint from the British Epilepsy Association). Two surviving members were Colin Latter (vocals) and Derek Birkett (b. 18 February 1961, London, England; bass), who would go on to form Flux of Pink Indians, with guitarist Andy and drummer Sid. Their debut EP *Neu Smell* emerged on Crass Records. Alongside standard rejections of society, war and the eating of flesh lay the joyful 'Tube Disasters', the sort of humour that was in short order in the grim world of anarcho punk. Sid (later **Rubella Ballet**) was soon replaced by Bambi, formerly of **Discharge**, while Andy was replaced by Simon. However, both departed quickly for their original band, the Insane, and were replaced by old Epileptics guitarist Kevin Hunter and drummer Martin Wilson. Their debut album, 1982's *Strive To Survive Causing Least Suffering Possible*, confirmed the promise of the single and premiered the band's own Spiderleg label. Alongside standard thrash numbers were highly perceptive attacks on consumer society. The antireligious 'Is Anybody There' was a particularly effective example, using simple but jarring lyrics to emphasize its point. The follow-up, *The Fucking Cunts Treat Us Like Pricks*, was unsurprisingly banned by retailers HMV, and copies were seized by Greater Manchester police from Eastern Bloc record shop, which was charged with displaying 'obscene articles for publication for gain'. The album, ironically, concerned violence between men and women, based on the experiences of a band member who had been sexually assaulted. The music contained within was little short of a directionless cacophony, however. *Uncarved Block* was the most unexpected of the band's three studio albums, delivering more polemic allied to dance and funk rhythms that left their previous audience totally nonplussed. It was a brave effort, and one that, alongside their debut, stands up to repeated listening. Birkett, making use of his experiences with Spiderleg, has gone on to set up the highly successful **One Little Indian Records** and still uses the Flux title for occasional projects.

● ALBUMS: *Strive To Survive Causing Least Suffering Possible* (Spiderleg 1982) ★★★, *The Fucking Cunts Treat Us Like Pricks* (Spiderleg 1984) ★★, as Flux *Uncarved Block* (One Little Indian 1986) ★★★.

● COMPILATIONS: *Not So Brave* (Overground 1997) ★★★.

Fly Records

The Fly label was inaugurated in October 1970 as an outlet for the Straight Ahead productions company. Directors **Denny Cordell** and **Tony Visconti** had previously leased their work through **EMI**'s **Regal Zonophone**, formerly used for

Salvation Army recordings, which had been re-activated specifically for their work. The **Move**, **Joe Cocker**, **Procol Harum** and **Tyrannosaurus Rex** were among the acts they placed there. Seeking greater independence, they founded Fly, employing Malcolm Jones from EMI who continued to act as distributor, to act as the new venture's administrator. The label scored immediate success with the revamped **T. Rex**, which became one of the era's most popular chart acts with a string of hits including 'Ride A White Swan' (number 2), 'Hot Love', 'Get It On' (both number 1) and 'Jeepster' (number 2). However, Fly was unable to repeat this profile with other acts. The Move had a significant 'miss' with 'When Alice Comes Down To The Farm' (and the attendant *Looking On*), while Joe Cocker's 'High Time We Went' failed to re-create former glories. Both quickly switched to other outlets, and when **Marc Bolan** of T. Tex formed his own record company, Fly's tenure was almost over. It survived by repacking albums originally issued by Zonophone in 'TOOFA' sets (i.e. two-for-the-price-of-one), but the entire catalogue was switched to a new outlet, Cube, in 1972.

Flying Aces

Despite having never issued a record, this hard-working band from the British rock scene of the mid-70s won many admirers. As one of the many branches of the **Man** family tree, the band started life as the Splendid Humans in 1973 with the core members comprising Martin Ace (bass) and his wife Georgina Ace (guitar/vocals), eventually evolving into the Flying Aces with Richard Treece (guitar; ex-**Help Yourself**) and Mike Gibbins (drums; ex-**Badfinger**). A brief, live appearance on vinyl occurred with the band's inclusion on the 1973 compilation *Christmas At The Patti*. Appearing on the UK pub/club circuit throughout the mid-70s they performed a condensed version of the 'west coast' rock style favoured by the Welsh musicians, a feel for which was mastered by Treece. Earning critical acclaim the Flying Aces still found difficulty in securing a recording deal due to the prevalent punk trend and after a brief line-up change in 1977, with Steve Jordan and Clive Roberts replacing Gibbins and Treece respectively, the final split came in 1978. Gibbins later worked with **Bonnie Tyler** and **Digby Richards**, while Treece eventually relocated to the USA playing in various groups in the San Francisco Bay area. Since the early 90s, Martin Ace has been working alongside his erstwhile partners in a Man reunion.

● ALBUMS: *Seashell* (Voiceprint 2002) ★★.

Flying Burrito Brothers

The Flying Burrito Brothers initially referred to an informal group of Los Angeles, California, USA–based musicians, notably former members of the **International Submarine Band** (bass player Ian Dunlop and drummer Mickey Gauvin), the **Remains** (guitarist/vocalist Barry Tashain and keyboard player Bill Briggs), horn player Junior Markham, saxophonist Bobby Keys, **Leon Russell** and **Jesse 'Ed' Davis**. The name was appropriated in 1968 by former **Byrds** members **Gram Parsons** (b. Ingram Cecil Connor III, 5 November 1946, Winter Haven, Florida, USA; d. 19 September 1973, Joshua Tree, California, USA; guitar/vocals) and **Chris Hillman** (b. 4 December 1942, Los Angeles, California, USA; guitar/vocals) for a new venture that would integrate rock and country styles. 'Sneaky' Pete Kleinow (pedal steel), Chris Ethridge (bass) plus various drummers completed the line-up featured on *The Gilded Palace Of Sin*, where the founding duo's vision of a Pan-American music flourished freely. The material ranged from the jauntily acerbic 'Christine's Tune' to the maudlin 'Hippy Boy', but its highlights included Parsons' emotional reading of two southern soul standards, 'The Dark End Of The Street' and 'Do Right Woman—Do Right Man', and his own poignant 'Hot Burrito #1' and the impassioned 'Hot Burrito #2'. The album's sense of cultural estrangement captured a late 60s restlessness and reflected the rural traditions of antecedents the **Everly Brothers**.

This artistic triumph was never repeated. *Burrito Deluxe*, on which guitar player **Bernie Leadon** (b. 19 July 1947, Minneapolis, Minnesota, USA) replaced Ethridge (Hillman switched to bass) and Michael Clarke (b. Michael Dick, 3 June 1946, Spokane, Washington, USA, d. 19 December 1993, Treasure Island, Florida, USA, ex-Byrds) became the permanent drummer, showed a band unsure of direction as Parsons' role became increasingly questionable. After recording some classic country songs with the band at Hollywood's Sound Factory, Parsons left for a solo career in summer 1970. With the arrival of young songwriter **Rick Roberts** (b. Florida, USA) the Flying Burrito Brothers again asserted their high quality. The underrated *The Flying Burrito Bros* was a cohesive, purposeful set, marked by the inclusion of Roberts' 'Colorado', **Gene Clark**'s 'Tried So Hard' and **Merle Haggard**'s 'White Line Fever' plus several other excellent Roberts originals.

Unfortunately, the band was again bedevilled by defections. In 1971 Leadon joined the **Eagles**, while Kleinow opted for a career in session work, but Hillman, Clarke and Roberts were then buoyed by the arrival of **Al Perkins** (pedal steel), Kenny Wertz (b. 4 February 1942, Washington, DC, USA; guitar), Roger Bush (bass) and **Byron Berline** (b. 6 July 1944, Caldwell, Kansas, USA; fiddle) in March 1971. Wertz, Bush and Berline had formed the bluegrass outfit **Country Gazette** two months earlier, but were persuaded to join the Flying Burrito Brothers. *Last Of The Red Hot Burritos* captured the excitement and power of their live show, but the septet was sundered in October 1971 when Hillman and Perkins joined **Stephen Stills** in **Manassas**, and Clarke left as well. Roberts, Wertz, Berline and Bush were joined by **Alan Munde** (b. 4 November 1946, Norman, Oklahoma, USA; banjo), Erik Dalton (drums) and Don Beck (steel guitar) on a tour of Europe, highlights of which were released on the *Six Days On The Road: Live In Amsterdam* album.

After the tour finished, Wertz, Bush, Berline and Munde elected to concentrate on Country Gazette, while Roberts embarked on a solo career before founding **Firefall** with Michael Clarke. However, much to the consternation of Hillman, former manager Ed Tickner commandeered the Flying Burrito Brothers' name with Kleinow, Ethridge, **Gene Parsons** (b. Eugene Victor Parsons, 4 September 1944, Los Angeles, California, USA; guitar/vocals), Joel Scott Hill (vocals), and Gib Guilbeau (b. Floyd Guilbeau, 26 September 1937, Sunset, Louisiana, USA; fiddle). This new line-up signed a contract with **Columbia Records** and released the lacklustre *Flying Again* in October 1975. Ethridge was replaced by **Skip Battin** (b. Clyde Battin, 2 February 1934, Galipolis, Ohio, USA, d. 6 July 2003, Palm Springs, California, USA, ex-Byrds) for the following year's *Airborne*. Hill, Guilbeau and Kleinow subsequently formed Sierra with Thad Maxwell (bass) and Mickey McGee (drums). After one unsuccessful album for **Mercury Records**, Guilbeau, Kleinow and McGee reunited

with Parson and Battin to tour Europe and Japan as the Flying Burrito Brothers. Two live albums (*Flying High* and *Close Encounters To The West Coast*) document this period. Guitarist/vocalist Greg Harris was added to the line-up for further tours, but by the time the band enjoyed a surprise minor US country hit with a live version of 'White Line Fever' (included on the *Live From Tokyo* album), Parsons, Harris and McGee had gone their separate ways.

The arrival of country veteran John Beland (b. 1949, Home town, Chicago, Illinois, USA), who had played with Guilbeau in **Swampwater**, provided the band with a proven songwriter worthy of the earlier pioneering line-up. Now recording as the Burrito Brothers, the new line-up signed a contract with **Curb Records** and, in 1981, enjoyed Top 20 success on the country charts with the slick country pop of 'Does She Wish She Was Single Again' and 'She Belongs To Everyone But Me'. Battin objected to the new sound and left during the recording of *Hearts On The Line*, and Kleinow elected to stay in Los Angeles and concentrate on film work. Beland and Guilbeau relocated to Nashville in a desperate attempt to revive their flagging fortunes, but the **Randy Scruggs**-produced sessions for their third Curb album remained unreleased until several years later.

While the Burrito Brothers were on their last legs, a varying line-up of Gene Parsons, Kleinow, Battin, Harris, and drummers Ed Ponder and Jim Goodall had begun touring as the Peace Seekers. When the Burrito Brothers split up in 1985, Kleinow reclaimed the Flying Burrito Brothers and toured with Battin, Harris and Goodall, a line-up captured on the Relix Records releases *Cabin Fever* and *Encore: Live From Europe*. At the same time, Beland and Guilbeau briefly reunited to record a last Burrito Brothers album. The latter also recorded several demos with Kleinow in Memphis, later released on *Southern Tracks*.

In 1989 Beland and Guilbeau joined up with Kleinow, Larry Patton (bass, vocals) and Rick Lenow (drums) under the Flying Burrito Brothers name. Two years later, Beland, Guilbeau, Kleinow, **Brian Cadd** (b. 29 November 1949, Perth, Australia; keyboards), George Grantham (b. 20 November 1947, Cordell, Oklahoma, USA; drums, also of **Poco**) and the returning Chris Ethridge recorded an album, released two years later as *Eye Of The Hurricane*. Larry Patton and drummer Gary Kubal joined Beland, Guilbeau and Kleinow on the next album, 1997's *California Jukebox*. Guilbeau and Kleinow subsequently departed, meaning no original members participated on the recording of *Sons Of The Golden West*.

● ALBUMS: *The Gilded Palace Of Sin* (A&M 1969) ★★★★★, *Burrito Deluxe* (A&M 1970) ★★★, *The Flying Burrito Bros* (A&M 1971) ★★★, *Last Of The Red Hot Burritos* (A&M 1972) ★★★★, *Six Days On The Road: Live In Amsterdam* (Bumble 1973) ★★★, *Flying Again* (Columbia 1975) ★★, *Airborne* (Columbia 1976) ★★, *Flying High* (J.B. 1978) ★★, *Live From Tokyo* (Regency 1979) ★★, *Burrito Country* (Brian 1979) ★★, as Burrito Brothers *Hearts On The Line* (Curb 1981) ★★, as Burrito Brothers *Sunset Sundown* (Curb 1982) ★★, *Cabin Fever* (Relix 1985) ★★, *Encore: Live From Europe* (Relix 1986) ★★, *Skip & Sneeky In Italy* Italy only (Moondance 1986) ★★, as Burrito Brothers *Back To The Sweethearts Of The Rodeo* aka *The Burrito Bros. Farewell Album* (Disky 1987) ★★, *From Another Time* (Sundown 1991) ★★, *Close Encounters To The West Coast* (Relix 1991) ★★, *Sin City* (Relix 1992) ★★,

Eye Of The Hurricane (Sundown 1993) ★★★, *California Jukebox* (Ether/American Harvest 1997) ★★, *Sons Of The Golden West* (Grateful Dead 1999) ★★, *The Red Album* (Beau Town 2002) ★.

● COMPILATIONS: *Honky Tonk Heaven* (A&M 1972) ★★, *Close Up The Honky Tonks: The Flying Burrito Bros 1968–1972* (A&M 1974) ★★★★, *Bluegrass Special* (Ariola 1975) ★★, *Hot Burrito—2* (A&M 1975) ★★, with Gram Parsons *Sleepless Nights* (A&M 1976) ★★★, with Parsons *Dim Lights, Thick Smoke And Loud, Loud Music* (Edsel 1987) ★★★, *Farther Along: The Best Of The Flying Burrito Brothers* (A&M 1988) ★★★★, *Hollywood Nights 1979–1982* (Sundown 1990) ★★★, *Southern Tracks* (Voodoo 1993) ★★, *Relix Records Best Of* (Relix 1995) ★★★, *Out Of The Blue* (Edsel 1996) ★★★★, *The Masters* (Eagle 1999) ★★★, *Hot Burritos! Anthology 1969–1972* (A&M 2000) ★★★★, *Sin City: The Very Best Of The Flying Burrito Brothers* (A&M 2002) ★★★★, *The Collection* (Spectrum 2005) ★★★.

Flying Circus

In mid-1968, Doug Rowe (b. New Zealand; guitar) teamed up with several Australians, Colin Walker (vocals/percussion), Greg Grace (vocals), Terry Wilkins (bass) and James Wynne (guitar), in Sydney to form a group that played country rock. The band signed with **EMI Records** and at their behest recorded two singles in the then popular bubblegum pop style, 'Hay Ride' and 'La La' both of which were Australian hits in 1969. The band was leading a schizophrenic existence; known for its teenybopper hits but with a live set of US country rockers, with their own originals gradually being added. The first album reflected this; it was a mix of the singles, several **Byrds** songs, a couple of Rowe originals and rounded off with some oddities such as 'Hair'. Most of the second half of 1969 was a write-off for the band as they lost their equipment in a road accident and a fire.

In 1970 they had their third hit single, acquired guitarist Red McKelvie (b. New Zealand) and recorded a second album of all-originals. The band won the 1970 Australian National Battle of the Bands amid controversy. Heavy guitar music similar to **Cream** was popular at this time in Australia, and Flying Circus certainly did not fit this mould! To toughen up the sound Rowe sacked McKelvie, and the band took on Sam See from **Sherbet** and recorded their third album before departing for North America. After six months they returned for a brief visit in mid-1971, only to lose See to **Fraternity**. Back in Canada they recorded *Gypsy Road* for **Warner Brothers**. Sam See returned to the fold in 1973 for the recording of *Last Laugh*. The band toured as support for **Lighthouse**, but when See and Terry Wilkins quit to join the headliners, the rest disbanded. Rowe played with **Greg Quill**'s band (as did See) before returning to Australia to play with various Sydney country rock groups. McKelvie led several bands in Sydney before returning to New Zealand and session work.

● ALBUMS: *Flying Circus* (1969) ★★★, *Prepared In Peace* (Harvest 1970) ★★★, *Bonza Beaut And Boom Boom* (1972) ★★, *Gyspy Road* (1972) ★★, *Last Laugh* (1974) ★★.

● COMPILATIONS: *Steam Trains And Country Days* (1978) ★★★.

Flying Colors

The American Depression was on the point of ending when this revue opened at the Imperial Theatre in New York on 15 September 1932. With music by **Arthur Schwartz** and lyrics and sketches by **Howard Dietz**, who also directed, this was obviously from the same line-up that produced **The Band Wagon**, **Three's A Crowd** and **The Little Show**. The talented cast, an ideal mixture of actors, dancers, comedians, singers, (and one harmonica virtuoso) included **Clifton Webb**, Charles Butterworth, **Tamara Geva**, Patsy Kelly, Philip Loeb, Vilma and **Buddy Ebsen**, **Larry Adler**, **Imogen Coca** and Monette Moore. All the songs were of high quality, but there were three special numbers, 'Alone Together', 'Louisiana Hayride' and the exuberant 'A Shine On Your Shoes', that were destined to endure. The rest of the score included 'Two-Faced Woman', 'A Rainy Day', 'Mother Told Me So', 'Fatal Fascination', 'Meine Klein Akrobat' and 'Smokin' Reefers'. This smart, witty show, which dealt with the recent hard times in America and looked forward to better days (and politicians), was produced by Max Gordon and choreographed by **Albertina Rasch**. *Flying Colors* stayed around for a decent run of 188 performances, and Ebsen, a talented hoofer at the time, went on much later to star in the legendary television series *The Beverly Hillbillies*.

Flying Down To Rio

It is not recorded whether the earth moved, but it certainly should have done when **Fred Astaire** and **Ginger Rogers** teamed for the first time in this film which was released in 1933 by RKO. Dolores Del Rio, as the sultry Belinha De Rezende, was supposed to be the star of a story by Cyril Hume, H.W. Hanemann and Erwin Gelsey (from a play by **Anne Caldwell**), in which she has to choose between the charms of the glamorous American band leader-aviator Roger Bond (Gene Raymond) and her Brazilian boyfriend Julio Rubeire (Raul Roulien), but Astaire and Rogers stole the film away. The seven white grand pianos on which they danced 'The Carioca' proved to be the launching pad to a glittering future. That number was part of a score by **Vincent Youmans** (music) and **Edward Eliscu** and **Gus Kahn** (lyrics), which also included 'Orchids In The Moonlight' and 'Music Makes Me'. The spectacular 'Flying Down To Rio' sequence featured a bevy of beautiful girls clad in various modes of dress (and undress), performing a series of formation dances while balanced on the wings of biplanes apparently several thousand feet above the city. The choreography for that and the rest of the splendid dance scenes was by Dave Gould and **Hermes Pan**, and the film was directed by Thorton Freedland.

Flying Fish Records

This roots record label was founded by Bruce Kaplan (b. 1945, USA, d. December 1992) in Chicago, Illinois, USA, in 1974. For the previous two years he had worked as part of the **Rounder Records** 'collective', having met that company's cofounder, Bill Nowlin, while at Chicago University. Flying Fish subsequently released albums by **Sweet Honey In The Rock**, **Doc Watson**, **John Hartford**, **Chris Smither**, Austin Lounge Lizards and **Norman Blake**. However, when Kaplan died of bacterial meningitis in 1992, the company passed into the hands of his widow, Sandra Kaplan. She announced its sale but was keen to see it remain with a company sympathetic to her husband's original direction and aims. Rounder was the obvious choice and purchased the catalogue of 500 titles in 1995. While taking over its ownership, they allowed the label to continue in its Chicago base and maintain its current staff and release schedules.

Flying High

Soon after its opening at the **Apollo** Theatre in New York on 3 March 1930, the celebrated newspaper columnist Walter Winchell dubbed this show 'the Lindbergh of musical comedies'. That was a reference to its theme, which reflected the American public's fascination with the pioneering flights of the late 20s in general and Charles Lindbergh's 1927 record solo flight to Paris in particular. The creative crew for this trip, composer **Ray Henderson** and lyricists **Buddy De Sylva** and **Lew Brown**, who also wrote the book with John McGowan, had already had some mileage from other US fads and fancies in previous shows such as *Good News!* (football and dancing), *Hold Everything!* (boxing) and *Follow Thru* (golf). Apparently, the plot was not complete until the show went into rehearsal, but it eventually turned out to a story about an aeroplane mechanic, Rusty Krause (Bert Lahr), who carelessly takes to the air in a plane that was supposed to be piloted by Todd Addison (Oscar Shaw). Not only does he take off but he stays up there long enough to create a world endurance record simply because he does not know how to get down again. Todd does get airborne himself but is forced to make a parachute jump. In the interests of the show's romantic scenario he lands on a New York roof belonging to the lovely Eileen Cassidy (Grace Brinkley).

Kate Smith, the powerful singer, was also in the cast and had a show-stopper with 'Red Hot Chicago'. The rest of the typically De Sylva ballad and Henderson score—lively and entertaining, with the occasional classy ballad—included 'I'll Know Him', 'Thank Your Father', 'Good For You—Bad For Me', 'Without Love', 'Mrs. Krause's Blue-Eyed Baby Boy' and 'Wasn't It Beautiful While It Lasted?'. The show was a big hit and ran for 357 performances, mainly owing to Lahr's hilarious antics. He starred with **Charlotte Greenwood** and Pat O'Brien in the 1931 film version.

Flying Lizards

The brainchild of pianist David Cunningham, the Flying Lizards were a novelty UK act with a difference, taking and subverting classic pop songs in a unique and striking fashion. In the summer of 1979, they reached the UK Top 5 with a spoken, arrogant upper-middle class, English accent-version of the **Berry Gordy** classic, 'Money'. The changing line-up, which included **Julian Marshall**, Deborah Evans-Stickland, Patti Paladin, Peter Gordan and Steve Beresford on *Fourth Wall*, enabled Cunningham to pursue his love of electronic pop. The *Times* newspaper writer and ambient experimentalist **David Toop** was part of the line-up at one point.

After an extended retirement, the Flying Lizards re-emerged in 1984 with *Top Ten*, which included eccentric versions of the work of **Jimi Hendrix**, **Leonard Cohen** and **Little Richard**. With the Flying Lizards put to rest once more, Cunningham concentrated on running his Piano label and recording solo material. Evans-Stickland, the vocalist on 'Money', made an unexpected return to music as a guest artist on 'bootleg' pioneer **Richard X**'s 2003 debut.

● ALBUMS: *The Flying Lizards* (Virgin 1979) ★★★, *Fourth Wall* (Virgin 1981) ★★★, *Top Ten* (Statik 1984) ★★★, *The Secret Dub Life Of The Flying Lizards* 1978 recording (Piano 1996) ★★.

Flying Machine

Not to be confused with the US outfit from **James Taylor**'s pre-**Apple Records** days, this Flying Machine was the brainchild of British writers and producers **Tony Macauley** and Geoff Stephens. Recorded by session musicians, 'Smile A Little Smile For Me' failed to chart in the UK, but it soared to number 5 in the US in November 1969. For the purposes of touring, a group was assembled from the remnants of the British hit group, **Pinkerton's Assorted Colours**, wherein Anthony Newman (rhythm guitar/vocals), the sole surviving original member, was joined by Steve Jones (lead guitar), **Stuart Colman** (bass) and Paul Wilkinson (drums). A follow-up single version of 'Baby Make It Soon', first recorded by the **Marmalade**, scraped the American Hot 100 the following year, but the group, somewhat ungratefully, grew frustrated with their pop-orientated style. A final single, 'The Devil Has Possession Of Your Mind', suggested a change of direction, but the Flying Machine split up following its release. Stuart Colman later emerged as a noted radio broadcaster and producer of various rock 'n' roll-influenced acts.

● ALBUMS: *Down To Earth With The Flying Machine* (Pye 1970) ★★★.

Flying Pickets

This a cappella UK sextet were formed in 1980 with a line-up comprising actors Rick Lloyd (tenor), Brian Hibbard (tenor), Gareth Williams (bass), David Brett (tenor), Ken Gregson (baritone) and Red Stripe (baritone). Originally, they came together informally and were warmly received at the 1982 Edinburgh Festival. In keeping with their unusual group title and their background with the politically motivated 7:84 theatre company, they played at benefit concerts for the National Union of Mineworkers and subsequently performed in pubs and clubs. Their novel cover of **Yazoo**'s hit 'Only You' proved spectacularly successful, bringing them the coveted UK Christmas number 1 spot in 1983. Although their appeal seemed ephemeral, they enjoyed a second Top 10 hit with the **Marvelettes**' '(When You're) Young And In Love', and their albums included spirited reworkings of familiar vocal classics from different eras, ranging from the **Teddy Bears**' 'To Know Him Is To Love Him' through **Bob Dylan**'s 'Masters Of War' and even **Talking Heads**' 'Psycho Killer'. Their last appearance on the UK charts was a lowly 71 with a rendition of the **Eurythmics**' 'Who's That Girl' in 1984. Two years later Gary Howard and Hereward Kaye were the first new members to join, and the group lost its last original member in 1990 with the departure of Brett. Howard and Kaye carried on with various personnel, although the original group re-formed briefly in 1994 to record a new album.

● ALBUMS: *Live At The Albany Empire* (VAM 1983) ★★, *Lost Boys* (10/Moving Target 1984) ★★★, *Live* (10 1985) ★★, *Waiting For Trains* (10 1988) ★★★, *Blue Money* (Forlane 1991) ★★, *The Warning* (Hey U 1992) ★★★, *The Original Flying Pickets Volume One* (Warners 1994) ★★, *Politics Of Need* (Alora 1996) ★★★, *Vox Pop* (Alora 1998) ★★.

● COMPILATIONS: *The Best Of The Flying Pickets* (Virgin 1991) ★★★.

Flying Records

This Italian record label is also the country's biggest independent **dance music** distributor, who also have a London arm that distributes its own product and that from **Media, Ummm** and other labels. The UK operation was set up by Dean Thatcher in association with Charlie Chester and

Cooltempo. Their debut release was a Thatcher remix of 'Hit Me With Your Rhythm Stick' by **Ian Dury And The Blockheads**. The idea was taken from Glen Turner who played the original at the end of one of his 1990 sets at Ibiza. It had previously been remixed in 1985 by **Paul Hardcastle**, but it was the Flying version that got the chief Blockhead's blessing. Since its inception Flying has offered a consistent diet of quality dance for their many advocates in the media and the nation's club scene. Their signings include End ('Rebel Song'), Joy Salinas ('The Mystery Of Love'), Korda ('Move Your Body'), Ferrante & Co featuring Kay Bianco ('Breakin' Away'), Kwanzaa Posse ('Wicked Funk', which like many releases was Italian in origin), Digital Boy ('This Is Muthafucker', '1-2-3 Acid'), Nexy Lanton ('I Am'), Jamie Dee ('Memories, Memories'), Latin Blood ('Deseo', created by Italian brothers Max and Frank Minoia) and Lamott Atkins ('Communicate'). A series of background personnel, affiliates and colleagues were routinely involved, sometimes English, often Italian. For instance, Daybreak's 'Tomorrow' was created by Gino 'Woody' Bianchi and Corrardo Rizza and Dom Scuteri and sung by Karen Jones. The label's major successes include Gat Decor's 'Passion', remixed for the label by **Darren Emmerson**, and **Ami Stewart**'s 'Friends '91'.

Flying Rhino Records

This psychedelic **trance** label based in north London was formed in 1994 by the producers and DJs James Monro (of Technossomy), Dominic Lamb and George Barker (both of **Slinky Wizard**). It was initially established in collaboration with **Zoom Records** but became independent the following year. Their first release was Slinky Wizard's *Wizard* EP in December 1994, since which time they have put out work by artists including Technossomy, **Green Nuns Of The Revolution**, Kundalini, Process And **Tristan**, Blue Planet Corporation and Darshan. Flying Rhino pride themselves on the quality rather than quantity of their releases, and most of their compilations, including *First Flight*, *Boyd In The Void*, *White Rhino* and *Black Rhino*, contain brand new material written especially for the label. As well as artists, the company's agency promote a number of successful trance DJs, notably Lamb, Monro and Sally Welch, who play at parties and festivals around the globe. They have expanded to include a range of Flying Rhino clothing and in-house recording and design studios.

Flying Saucer Attack

This experimental post-rock outfit was formed in Bristol, England, by multi-instrumentalist Dave Pearce and bass player Rachel Brook. The two members had originally played in Lynda's Strange Vacation alongside Matt Elliot and Kate Wright but set up the Flying Saucer Attack project in 1992 to pursue their interest in lo-fi four-track home-recording. The duo initially released the 'Soaring High'/'Standing Stone' and 'Wish'/'Oceans' singles on their own FSA label. Their vinyl-only long-playing debut, released in November 1993, drew praise for an experimental edge which drew on the work of musical mentors **Popol Vuh** and **Can** as well as the feedback drenched psychedelia of contemporaries **Spacemen 3** and **My Bloody Valentine**. The follow-up *Distance* compiled the duo's early singles and unreleased material. The CD, released on new label Domino Records, reaffirmed their commitment to lo-fi recording by proudly declaring that 'CDs destroy music'. *Further* opted for a more overtly pastoral approach,

fusing acoustic folk with noisy drone to create a wonderfully intimate and atmosphere recording rarely found in the post-rock field. *Chorus* compiled further singles and unreleased radio sessions, with several tracks providing evidence that the notoriously technophobe duo had begun to dip their toes in the previously forbidden waters of digital recording. The album included another curious sleevenote, claiming that *Chorus* 'marks the end of FSA phase one . . . when we return with phase two, who knows where the wind blows.' The duo's new-found interest in digital recording was confirmed by their collaboration with Tom Fenn on his CD *Distant Station*, which was comprised entirely of Flying Saucer Attack samples. This project marked the end of Brook's involvement with Flying Saucer Attack. She has subsequently concentrated on **Movietone**, a project involving former bandmates Elliot and Wright. Pearce returned in 1997 with *New Lands*, on which samples now formed an integral part of his working method.

● ALBUMS: *Flying Saucer Attack* (FSA/VHF 1993) ★★★, *Further* (Domino/Drag City 1995) ★★★★, *New Lands* (Drag City 1997) ★★★, *Mirror* (Heartbeat/Drag City 1999) ★★★.
● COMPILATIONS: *Distance* (Domino/VHF 1994) ★★★★, *Chorus* (Drag City 1995) ★★★.

Flying Squad

Formed in Scotland in the mid-70s, Flying Squad were a proficient if unspectacular hard rock group in the gritty, unpretentious vein of **Tank** or **Fastway**. Comprising Ian Muir (vocals), Monty McMonagle (guitar), Alex Calder (guitar), George Crossan (bass) and Jim Kelly (drums), they recorded a self-titled debut album in 1978 which was produced by Francis Rossi of **Status Quo**. Played with agility and imbued with considerable melodic presence, it augured well for the group with Muir's stylish vocals attracting particular praise. However, it was never followed up, and Muir eventually defected to form **Waysted** (under the pseudonym Fin).

● ALBUMS: *Flying Squad* (Columbia 1978) ★★★.

Flynn, Frank Emilio

(see **Emilio, Frank**)

Flys (UK)

This Coventry, England–based outfit enjoyed a minor league role in the new wave but owed more to power pop and astute songwriting than punk. Singer and guitarist Neil O'Connor (brother of **Hazel O'Connor**) met school kids David Freeman (guitar/vocals) and Joseph Hughes (bass/vocals) in the mid-70s and formed Midnight Circus, eventually recruiting Pete King on drums. A name change to the Flys coincided with the discovery of punk's first tremors, but a demo in April 1977 brought an apathetic response from the usual channels. The band issued *Bunch Of Five*, an energetic EP, on their own Zama Records label in time for Christmas. Quick as a flash, **EMI Records** snapped them up, rushing out one of the EP tracks (and perhaps their finest ever moment), 'Love And A Molotov Cocktail', as a single. After a tour with the **Buzzcocks** and **John Otway** came 'Fun City', recorded at Pathway Studios. *Waikiki Beach Refugees* (also the title of their next single) emerged in October 1978 to an enthusiastic response, while the band toured Europe. 1979 saw a flurry of singles— 'Beverley' in February, 'Name Dropping' in April and 'We Are The Lucky Ones'—but internal quarrels led to the recruitment of a riotous new drummer Graham Deakin (ex–**Frankie Miller** and **John Entwistle**'s Ox). *Flys Own*, rawer than their debut, coincided with a tour with the **Ruts** in autumn 1979. The EP *Four From The Square* was released in February as the band transferred to **Parlophone Records**. This was followed by 'What Will Mother Say?' in May 1980. Internal pressures began to erupt, and the Flys broke up soon afterwards. O'Connor joined his sister for two years and two albums before becoming a musical arranger and then a producer and engineer. Freeman issued a cover version of the **Supremes**' 'Stop! In The Name Of Love', took a degree, published his poetry, sang on **Alison Moyet**'s *Raindancing* and later formed the short-lived the **Lover Speaks** with Hughes (after his spell with ex-**Specials** Roddy Radiation And His Tearjerkers). Pete King, meanwhile, joined **After The Fire** but sadly died aged 26. In 1990 **See For Miles Records** compiled an excellent self-titled retrospective of the band.

● ALBUMS: *Waikiki Beach Refugees* (EMI 1978) ★★★, *Flys Own* (EMI 1979) ★★★.

● COMPILATIONS: *The Flys* (See For Miles 1990) ★★★.

Flys (USA)

This Hollywood, California, USA-based alt rock band was formed in the early 90s by Adam Paskowitz (vocals), James Book (bass) Peter Perdichizzi (guitar) and Nick Lucero (drums), with additional vocalist/rapper Joshua Paskowitz (brother of Adam) completing the line-up prior to the release of their 1995 mini-album debut *25¢*. After several years spent on the college circuit, the quintet broke out of minor league status in 1998 when 'Got You (Where I Want You)', a track from their second album, *Holiday Man*, was featured prominently on the soundtrack to the movie *Disturbing Behavior*. The track's melodic grunge pop sound was not altogether indicative of the band's eclectic approach, which took in rap metal, funk and power pop, but sales of *Holiday Man* were nevertheless boosted by its success. The follow-up *Outta My Way* was a harder-edged recording that tied up the band's disparate influences in a more satisfying and coherent manner, but without a track as immediately catchy as 'Got You (Where I Want You)', the album enjoyed less commercial success. Joshua Paskowitz and Lucero were subsequently replaced by Matt Price and Holmes Jones.

● ALBUMS: *25¢* mini-album (Raid America 1995) ★★★, *Holiday Man* (Trauma/Delicious Vinyl 1998) ★★★, *Outta My Way* (Trauma 2000) ★★★★.

FM

FM Radio was pioneered in San Francisco by DJ **Tom Donahue** at stations KMPX and, later, KSAN. It represented a conscious attempt to reject a Top 40-based playlist in favour of album-orientated acts. By the early 70s, this formula had become common, and indeed, many such concerns offered as restrictive an output as their AM counterparts. Released in 1978, *FM* tells the fictional tale of a Los Angeles station, staffed by mavericks, who attempt to remain on air by hijacking a **Linda Ronstadt** concert, scheduled for their main rival. The film completely fails to question why the founding ethos of FM radio had been subverted, preferring the tiresome 'good versus bad' scenario that has plagued rock films from their inception. **Jimmy Buffett**, **REO Speedwagon** and **Tom Petty And The Heartbreakers** join Ronstadt in contributing musical interludes, while the soundtrack also features material by **Steely Dan** (who provided the title song),

Fleetwood Mac, **Boz Scaggs**, **Joe Walsh**, **Steve Miller**, the **Eagles**, **Foreigner** and **Foghat**. Despite its plot, *FM* enshrines the complacency of AOR music and provides a good explanation for the rise of punk.

Focus

A former Amsterdam Conservatory student, Thijs van Leer (keyboards, flute, vocals) with Martin Dresden (bass) and philosophy graduate Hans Cleuver (drums) backed Robin Lent, Cyril Havermans and other Dutch singers before 1969's catalytic enlistment of guitarist **Jan Akkerman** (b. 24 December 1946, Amsterdam, Netherlands), veteran of the progressive unit Brainbox. The new quartet's first collective essay as recording artists was humble—accompaniment on a Dutch version of *Hair*—but heartened by audience response to a set that included amplified arrangements of pieces by Bartók and Rodrigo, Focus released a *bona fide* album debut with a spin-off single, 'House Of The King', that sold well in Continental Europe. However, aiming always at the English-speaking forum, the band engaged **Mike Vernon** to produce *Moving Waves* which embraced vocal items (in English) and melodic if lengthy instrumentals. The album included the startling UK Top 20 hit 'Hocus Pocus'.

After reshuffles in which only van Leer and Akkerman surfaced from the original personnel, the band stole the show at British outdoor festivals, and a slot on BBC television's **The Old Grey Whistle Test** assisted the passage of the glorious 'Sylvia', into the UK Top 5; *Focus 3*, an earlier album, also reached the upper echelons of the charts. After stoking up modest interest in North America, 1973 began well with each member figuring in respective categories in the more earnest music journals' popularity polls. An in-concert album from London and *Hamburger Concerto* both marked time artistically, and, following 1975's *Mother Focus*, Akkerman left to concentrate on the solo career that he had pursued parallel to that of Focus since his *Profile* in 1973. With several solo efforts, van Leer was also well-placed to do likewise but elected instead to stick with a latter-day Focus in constant flux which engaged in a strange studio amalgamation with **P.J. Proby** before its final engagement in Terneuzen in 1978. Akkerman and van Leer guided Focus through a 1985 album before the 1972 line-up re-formed solely for a Dutch television special five years later. Another line-up, fronted by van Leer and guitarist Jan Dumée, released a comeback studio album in the new millennium.

● ALBUMS: *In And Out Of Focus* (Polydor/London 1970) ★★★, *Focus II* aka *Moving Waves* (Imperial/Blue Horizon/Sire 1971) ★★★★, *Focus 3* (Polydor/Sire 1972) ★★★, *At The Rainbow* (Polydor/Sire 1973) ★★, *Hamburger Concerto* (Polydor/Atco 1974) ★★, *Mother Focus* (Polydor/Atco 1975) ★★, with P.J. Proby *Focus Con Proby* (Harvest 1977) ★★★, *Jan Akkerman & Thijs Van Leer* (Vertigo 1985) ★★★, *Focus 8* (Musea/Rock Symphony 2002) ★★★.

● COMPILATIONS: *Masters Of Rock* (Bovema 1974) ★★★, *Focus* (Polydor 1975) ★★★, *Ship Of Memories* (Harvest/Sire 1976) ★★, *Greatest Hits* (Fame 1984) ★★★, *Hocus Pocus: The Best Of Focus* (EMI 1994) ★★★★, *Live At The BBC* (Hux 2004) ★★★.

● DVD/VIDEOS: *Masters From The Vaults* (Classic Rock 2003), *The Ultimate Anthology* (Direct Video 2004).

● FURTHER READING: *In & Out Of Focus: The Music Of Jan Akkerman & Focus*, Dave Randall.

Foetus

You've Got Foetus On Your Breath, Scraping Foetus Off The Wheel, Foetus Interruptus, Foetus Uber Alles, Foetus Inc— all these titles are actually the pseudonym of one person: Australian émigré Jim Thirlwell, alias Jim Foetus and Clint Ruin. After founding his own record company, Self Immolation, in 1980, he set about 'recording works of aggression, insight and inspiration'. Backed with evocatively descriptive musical slogans such as 'positive negativism' and 'bleed now pay later', Foetus released a series of albums, several of which appeared through **Stevo**'s **Some Bizzare Records**. With stark one-word titles such as *Deaf*, *Ache*, *Hole* and *Nail*, Thirlwell presented a harrowing aural netherworld of death, lust, disease and spiritual decay. In November 1983 Foetus undertook a rare tour, performing with **Marc Almond**, **Nick Cave** and **Lydia Lunch** in the short-lived Immaculate Consumptive. Apart from these soul mates, Foetus has also played live with the **Swans**' Roli Mossiman as Wiseblood (who released *Dirtdish* in 1986) and Lydia Lunch in Stinkfist and appeared on albums by several artists including **The The**, **Einstürzende Neubauten**, **Nurse With Wound** and Annie Hogan. Thirlwell also records instrumental work as Steroid Maximus, releasing *Quilombo* (1991) and *Gonwanaland* (1992) on the Big Cat label. In 1995 Thirlwell announced plans to release his first studio album in seven years. The result was the major-label release *Gash*, an album that led to a reappraisal of his work as one of the key figures in the development of the industrial music movement. Thirlwell subsequently returned to independent label status with his reputation and legendary status still intact.

● ALBUMS: as You've Got Foetus On Your Breath *Deaf* (Self Immolation 1981) ★★★, as You've Got Foetus On Your Breath *Ache* (Self Immolation 1982) ★★★, as Scraping Foetus Off The Wheel *Hole* (Self Immolation 1984) ★★★, as Scraping Foetus Off The Wheel *Nail* (Self Immolation/ Some Bizzare 1985) ★★★, as Foetus Interruptus *Thaw* (Self Immolation/Some Bizzare 1988) ★★★, as Foetus Corruptus *Rife* (No Label 1989) ★★★, as Foetus In Excelsis Corruptus DeLuxe *Male* recorded 1990 (Big Cat 1993) ★★★, *Gash* (Columbia 1995) ★★★, *Boil* (Cleopatra 1996) ★★★, as The Foetus Symphony Orchestra *York* mini-album (Thirsty Ear 1997) ★★★, *Flow* (Thirsty Ear 2001) ★★★, *Blow* Flow remixed (Noise-O-Lution 2002) ★★, *Love* (Birdman 2005) ★★★.

● COMPILATIONS: as Foetus Inc *Sink* (Self Immolation/ Wax Trax! 1989) ★★★.

● DVD/VIDEOS: *!Male!* (Visionary 1994).

Fog

b. Andrew Broder, Minneapolis, Minnesota, USA. Fog is the adopted stage name of Broder, a multi-instrumentalist genre-blender whose work mixes hip-hop, pop, *avant garde* art noise and almost everything else he can get his hands on. Like contemporaries **DJ Shadow**, **Four Tet** and **Prefuse 73**, Fog uses the deep beats, throbbing bass and montage methods of hip-hop as a palette on which to mix other styles, genres and sounds. His quirky sonic amalgams (which he composed and recorded in his basement) caught the attention of high-profile electronica label **Ninja Tune Records**, who released Fog's self-titled debut in 2002 and a 12-inch single entitled 'Check Fraud'. *Fog* announced the artist's aesthetic. Eclectic and surprising, a Broder composition typically features beats, turntable wizardry, scratching and samples that include everything from piano, Japanese flute, banjo and flamenco guitar to feather dusters, gum chewing and animal sounds. Additionally, Broder sings in a thin, unassuming voice, and his lyrics are reflective, witty, incisive and surreal in a way that invokes childhood reveries and dream states. 2003's *Ether Teeth* was more organic, intimate and introspective than its predecessor. On it Broder placed his pop songs within long passages of beat-saturated, electronic ambience. The *Hummer* EP followed a year later. This seven-song set was Fog's most abstract and least pop-orientated outing, with a dynamic range that included passages that were alternately delicate and explosive.

Broder also spearheaded a collaboration with **cLOUDDEAD**'s Why? (aka Yoni Wolf) on a project called *Hymie's Basement*. Named after Hymie's, a record store in Minneapolis co-owned by Broder's wife, the album offered further experiments in collage, beat-making and textures with a running surrealist commentary providing social critique and satire. In 2005 Broder released his first album on Lex Records. *10th Avenue Freakout* proved Fog's most ambitious effort, with the tension between the album's live instrumentation and its programmed embellishments creating a powerful effect. Broder's lyrics were evocative and strange, centring on apocalyptic themes, yet the album was filled with a complex, chaotic, upbeat energy. Broder's live shows feature backing musicians Mark Erickson, Jeremy Ylvisaker, Martin Dosh and Mike Lewis.

● ALBUMS: *Fog* (Ninja Tune 2002) ★★★, *Ether Teeth* (Ninja Tune 2003) ★★★, *10th Avenue Freakout* (Lex 2005) ★★★★.

Fogelberg, Dan

b. Daniel Grayling Fogelberg, 13 August 1951, Peoria, Illinois, USA. Having learned piano from the age of 14, Fogelberg moved to guitar and songwriting. Leaving the University of Illinois in 1971, he relocated to California and started playing on the folk circuit, at one point touring with **Van Morrison**. A move to Nashville brought him to the attention of producer Norbert Putnam. Fogelberg released *Home Free* for **Columbia Records** shortly afterwards. This was a highly relaxed album, notable for the backing musicians involved, including **Roger McGuinn**, **Jackson Browne**, **Joe Walsh** and **Buffy Sainte-Marie**. Despite the calibre of the other players, the album was not a success, and Fogelberg, having been dropped by Columbia, returned to session work. Producer Irv Azoff, who was managing Joe Walsh, signed Fogelberg and secured a contract with Epic. Putnam was involved in subsequent recordings by Fogelberg. In 1974 Fogelberg moved to Colorado and a year later released *Souvenirs*. This was a more positive album, and Walsh's production was evident. From here on, Fogelberg played the majority of the instruments on record, enabling him to keep tight control of the recordings, but inevitably it took longer to finish the projects. Playing support to the **Eagles** in 1975 helped to establish Fogelberg. However, in 1977, due to appear with the Eagles at Wembley, he failed to appear onstage, and it was later claimed that he had remained at home to complete recording work on *Netherlands*. Whatever the reason, the album achieved some recognition, but Fogelberg enjoyed better chart success in his native USA than in the UK. In 1980 'Longer' reached number 2 in the US singles charts, while in the UK it did not even reach the Top 50. Two other singles, 'Same Auld Lang Syne' and 'Leader Of The Band', both from *The Innocent Age*, achieved Top 10 places in the USA. The excellent *High Country Snows* saw a return to his bluegrass influences and was in marked contrast to the harder-edged *Exiles* that followed.

In the late 80s Fogelberg built a full-size studio (Mountain Bird Studio) at his ranch, enabling him to record new albums from his homebase. A steady stream of releases and reissues emerged in the following decades, but the artist's career was put on hold when he was diagnosed with advanced prostate cancer in 2004. From plaintive ballads to rock material, Fogelberg is a versatile writer and musician who continues to produce credible records and command a loyal cult following.

● ALBUMS: *Home Free* (Columbia 1972) ★★, *Souvenirs* (Full Moon 1974) ★★★, *Captured Angel* (Full Moon 1975) ★★, *Netherlands* (Full Moon 1977) ★★, with Tim Weisberg *Twin Sons Of Different Mothers* (Full Moon 1978) ★★★★, *Phoenix* (Full Moon 1979) ★★★★, *The Innocent Age* (Full Moon 1981) ★★★★, *Windows And Walls* (Full Moon 1984) ★★, *High Country Snows* (Full Moon 1985) ★★★★, *Exiles* (Full Moon 1987) ★★★, *The Wild Places* (Full Moon 1990) ★★, *Dan Fogelberg Live—Greetings From The West* (Full Moon 1991) ★★, *River Of Souls* (Full Moon 1993) ★★★, with Tim Weisberg *No Resemblance Whatsoever* (Giant 1995) ★★★, *The First Christmas Morning* (Chicago 1999) ★★, *Something Old, Something New, Something Borrowed And Some Blues* (Chicago 2000) ★★★, *Full Circle* (Morning Sky 2003) ★★★.

● COMPILATIONS: *Greatest Hits* (Full Moon 1982) ★★★, *Portrait: The Music Of Dan Fogelberg From 1972–1997* 4-CD box set (Epic 1997) ★★★★, *Super Hits* (Epic 1998) ★★★, *The Very Best Of Dan Fogelberg* (Sony 2001) ★★★, *The Essential* (Sony 2003) ★★★.

● DVD/VIDEOS: *Greetings From The West Live* (CBS Video 1991).

Fogerty, John

b. 28 May 1945, Berkeley, California, USA. As the vocalist and composer with **Creedence Clearwater Revival**, one of the most successful acts of its era, Fogerty seemed assured of a similar status when he began a solo career in 1972. Recording as the **Blue Ridge Rangers**, the album was a curiously understated affair designed to suggest the work of a group. The material consisted of country and gospel songs, two tracks from which, 'Jambalaya (On The Bayou)' and 'Hearts Of Stone', became US hit singles in 1973. Despite the exclusion of original songs and its outer anonymity, the work was clearly that of Fogerty, whose voice and instrumentation were unmistakable. The first of many legal problems arose when the singer charged that his label, **Fantasy Records**, had not promoted the record sufficiently. He demanded a release from his contract, but the company claimed the rights to a further eight albums. This situation remained at an impasse until **Asylum Records** secured Fogerty's North American contract, while Fantasy retained copyright for the rest of the world.

Fogerty made his solo debut proper in 1975 with a self-titled set. *John Fogerty* contained several classic tracks, notably 'Almost Saturday Night' and 'Rockin' All Over The World' which were successfully covered, respectively, by **Dave Edmunds** and **Status Quo**. However, Fogerty's legal entanglements still persisted and although a single, 'Comin' Down The Road', was released from a prospective third album,

Hoodoo, it was never issued. It was 1985 before the artist re-emerged with the accomplished *Centerfield*, which topped the US album chart and provided an international hit single in 'The Old Man Down The Road'. The set also included two powerful rock songs, 'Mr. Greed' and 'Zanz Kan't Danz', which Fantasy owner Saul Zaentz assumed was a personal attack. He sued Fogerty for $142 million, claiming he had been slandered by the album's lyrics, and filed for the profits from 'The Old Man Down The Road', asserting the song plagiarised Creedence Clearwater Revival's 'Run Through The Jungle'. Fogerty's riposte was a fourth album, *Eye Of The Zombie*, which, although failing to scale the heights of its predecessor, was the impetus for a series of excellent live performances.

Since the late 80s Fogerty has maintained a lower profile and successfully secured a decision against Zaentz's punitive action. The 1997 comeback album *Blue Moon Swamp* was a welcome return to form. The reviews were generally excellent, although the material on the album was not radically different from Fogerty's favoured mix of rock and country. Possibly his popularity is greater than his product. The live *Premonition* was released the following year. Fogerty returned to the headlines in October 2004 when he participated in the Vote For Change Tour, joining acts such as **Bruce Springsteen**, **Pearl Jam** and **R.E.M.** in a series of shows intended to influence voters to remove President George W. Bush from the White House. His new studio album, *Deja Vu All Over Again*, was released at the same time.

● ALBUMS: *John Fogerty* (Asylum 1975) ★★★★, *Centerfield* (Warners 1985) ★★★, *Eye Of The Zombie* (Warners 1986) ★★, *Blue Moon Swamp* (Warners 1997) ★★★★, *Premonition* (Warners 1998) ★★★, *Deja Vu All Over Again* (Geffen 2004) ★★★.

● COMPILATIONS: *The Long Road Home: The Ultimate John Fogerty Collection* (Fantasy 2005) ★★★★.

● DVD/VIDEOS: *Premonition* (Warner Video 1998).

Fogerty, Tom

b. 9 November 1941, Berkeley, California, USA, d. 6 September 1990, Scottsdale, Arizona, USA. A self-taught musician, this artist's career flourished upon joining a rock 'n' roll band founded by his younger brother, **John Fogerty**. Having completed their lone single 'Bonita' in 1963, Tom Fogerty And The Blue Velvets secured a recording contract with **Fantasy Records** but were persuaded to change their name to the **Golliwogs** in an effort to capitalize on the concurrent British beat boom. The group kept this detested appellation until 1967 when they became known as **Creedence Clearwater Revival**. As such they were one of the most successful groups of the era, but relationships between the siblings soured, and in February 1971, Tom Fogerty left for a solo career. He initially participated in an informal group that included guitarist **Jerry Garcia** and organist **Merl Saunders**, before completing four albums that, if inconsistent, contained several excellent tracks. Fogerty then formed a new act, Ruby, around Randy Oda (guitar/keyboards), Anthony Davis (bass) and Bobby Cochran (drums). The group recorded three albums, the last of which, *Precious Gems*, was preceded by Fogerty's final solo set, *Deal It Out*. Fogerty worked in real estate before moving to Flagstaff, Arizona, during the mid-80s, apparently planning to write an account of the Creedence story. However, he died prematurely of respiratory failure following tuberculosis in 1990.

● ALBUMS: *Tom Fogerty* (Fantasy 1972) ★★, *Excalibur* (Fantasy 1973) ★★, *Zephyr National* (Fantasy 1974) ★★, *Myopia* (Fantasy 1975) ★★, *Deal It Out* (1981) ★★; as Ruby *Ruby* (1977) ★★, *Rock And Roll Madness* (1977) ★★, *Precious Gems* (1985) ★★.

Foghat

Although British in origin, Foghat relocated to the USA, where this boogie-blues band built a large following during the 70s. The band originally comprised 'Lonesome' Dave Peverett (b. 16 April 1943, Dulwich, London, England, d. 7 February 2000; vocals/guitar), Tony Stevens (b. 12 September 1949, Willsden, London, England; bass/vocals), Roger Earl (b. 16 May 1946, London, England; drums) and Rod Price (b. 22 November 1947, London, England, d. 22 March 2005, Wilton, New Hampshire, USA; guitar/vocals). Peverett, Stevens and Earl had been members of **Savoy Brown**, the UK blues band. They left and immediately settled in the USA with the new unit, where Foghat signed with Bearsville Records, owned by entrepreneurial manager **Albert Grossman**. Their 1972 self-titled debut album was produced by **Dave Edmunds** and reached the US charts, as did the single, a cover version of **Willie Dixon**'s blues standard 'I Just Want To Make Love To You'. A live version of that song later charted in 1977. Foghat held on to its formula for another dozen albums, each on Bearsville and each a chart item in the USA. Of those, the 1977 live album was the most popular, reaching number 11 on the *Billboard* chart. The band underwent several personnel changes, primarily bass players, with Nick Jameson (on 1975's *Fool For The City*) and Craig MacGregor (from 1976's *Night Shift* to 1980's *Tight Shoes*) featuring in the line-up during this period.

Founding guitarist Rod Price was replaced by Erik Cartwright (b. 10 July 1950, New York City, USA) in 1980. Foghat remained active during the early 80s, regularly gigging in the USA, but in 1985 Peverett announced he was retiring to England. Earl, Cartwright and MacGregor (who had been in and out of the band over the previous five years) continued as the Kneetremblers before becoming known as Roger Earl's Foghat. Further personnel changes ensued before Peverett complicated matters by launching his own version of Foghat in 1990. Finally, in 1993 the original line-up of the band was reunited to record a new studio album, *Return Of The Boogie Men*. A live album ensued and Foghat continued to tour into the late 90s to great acclaim before the band was dealt two major blows. Price announced his departure and was replaced by Bryan Bassett (b. 11 August 1954, Pittsburgh, Pennsylvania, USA) in 1999, and the following year Peverett succumbed to cancer. He was replaced by Charlie Huhn, and this line-up continued to tour and recorded a new album, *Family Joules*. At the start of 2005, former bass player Craig MacGregor returned to the line-up in place of Stevens. Former guitarist Price suffered a fatal head trauma in March 2005.

● ALBUMS: *Foghat* i (Bearsville 1972) ★★★, *Foghat* ii (Bearsville 1973) ★★★, *Energized* (Bearsville 1974) ★★★★, *Rock And Roll Outlaws* (Bearsville 1974) ★★★, *Fool For The City* (Bearsville 1975) ★★★, *Night Shift* (Bearsville 1976) ★★★★, *Live* (Bearsville 1977) ★★★, *Stone Blue* (Bearsville 1978) ★★★, *Boogie Motel* (Bearsville 1979) ★★★, *Tight Shoes* (Bearsville 1980) ★★, *Girls To Chat & Boys To Bounce* (Bearsville 1981) ★★★, *In The Mood For Something Rude* (Bearsville 1982) ★★, *Zig-Zag Walk* (Bearsville 1983) ★★, *Return Of The Boogie Men* (Modern 1994) ★, *Road Cases* (Big F 1998) ★★★, *Extended Versions* (BMG 2001) ★★, *Family Joules* (Besh 2003) ★★.

● COMPILATIONS: *The Best Of Foghat* (Rhino 1989) ★★★, *The Best Of Foghat: Volume 2* (Rhino 1992) ★★★, *Slow Ride And Other Hits* (Flashback 1997) ★★★, *Anthology* (Castle 1999) ★★★, *Live On The King Biscuit Flower Hour 1974/1976 recordings* (Pinnacle 1999) ★★, *The Essentials* (WEA 2002) ★★★, *Decades Live* (Sanctuary 2003) ★★★.

Fol, Raymond

b. 28 April 1928, Paris, France, d. 1 May 1979, Paris, France. In the years immediately following World War II, Fol played piano in traditional jazz bands and in bebop groups. He worked with several noted European musicians, including Boris Vian, **Django Reinhardt** and his alto saxophonist older brother Hubert Fol. In the early 50s he regularly accompanied visiting Americans and also recorded with some of them, including **Roy Eldridge**, **Johnny Hodges** and **Dizzy Gillespie**. Also during the 50s Fol worked in Claude Luter's band and toured with **Sidney Bechet**, **Guy Lafitte** and **Stéphane Grappelli**. In the 60s he was also associated with **Duke Ellington**'s orchestra and with various Ellingtonians including **Paul Gonsalves**. A deft and imaginative soloist, Fol brought to his work a considerable measure of technical virtuosity that was always at the service of the music he played.

● ALBUMS: *Les Quatres Saisons 'In Jazz'* (Philips 1965) ★★★, *Echoes Of Harlem* (Blue Star 1975) ★★★, *The Sky Was Blue* (Chorus 1979) ★★★.

Folds, Ben

b. 12 September 1966, Winston-Salem, North Carolina, USA. Singer-songwriter and pianist Folds rose to cult status as leader of the oddly named trio **Ben Folds Five**, one of the most appealing acts to emerge from the US alternative scene of the 90s. Also featuring bass player Robert Sledge and drummer Darren Jessee, Ben Folds Five made their mark as a scintillating live act and purveyors of beautifully crafted power pop over the course of three excellent albums, most notably 1997's *Whatever And Ever Amen*, which featured the minor pop hits 'The Battle Of Who Could Care Less' and 'Brick'.

Shortly after the release of Ben Folds Five's third album, 1999's clumsily titled but endearingly charming *The Unauthorized Biography Of Reinhold Messner*, the trio decided to go their separate ways. Folds had already indulged his talents in a side project during the band's heyday, collaborating with producer Caleb Southern as Fear Of Pop on a 1998 release. He began work in earnest on his solo debut proper, *Rockin' The Suburbs*, which was released at the end of 2001. The album stayed close to the Ben Folds Five blueprint of piano-driven power pop and tender ballads, although pleasingly Folds played down his somewhat caustic collegiate wit, allowing a greater sense of humanity to shine through the songs. A terrific live album followed in 2002, cherry-picking the best of the Ben Folds Five catalogue with tracks from *Rockin' The Suburbs*. Between 2003 and 2004 Folds completed a trio of stopgap EPs, *Speed Graphic*, *Sunny 16* and *Super D*, featuring new material and a series of unlikely cover versions. He also worked with actor William Shatner, who had previously guested on the Fear Of Pop project, on his album *Has Been*. Folds returned in 2005 with his second studio collection proper, *Songs For Silverman*. While still boasting some lovely melodies and impressive piano work, the album betrayed the signs of Folds' growing domestic contentedness and a greater sincerity and maturity ('Bastard', 'Landed' and 'Gracie', in particular). Although lacking some of the spark and bloody-minded contrariness of his earlier work, this excellent album is destined to last.

● ALBUMS: as Fear Of Pop *Volume 1* (Epic 1998) ★★★, *Rockin' The Suburbs* (Epic 2001) ★★★★, *Live* (Epic 2002) ★★★, *Songs For Silverman* (Epic 2005) ★★★★.

● DVD/VIDEOS: *Live In Perth* (Epic 2005).

Folds, Ben, Five

(see **Ben Folds Five**)

Foley, Betty

b. 3 February 1933, Chicago, Illinois, USA, d. 1990. The daughter of country star **Red Foley**, her mother died in childbirth, and she was raised by her stepmother in Berea, Kentucky. She learned guitar as a child, and at 17 she began to appear regularly on the *Renfro Valley Barn Dance*, a show that her father had helped to create with **John Lair** around 1937. Her singing gained her a recording contract with **Decca Records**, and in 1954 she had a number 8 hit with 'As Far As I'm Concerned', followed the next year by a Top 3 with 'A Satisfied Mind', both being duets with her father. She left the *Barn Dance* in 1954, and in 1956 and 1957, she was a regular on the *Midwestern Hayride* on WLW Cincinnati and also played on the **Grand Ole Opry**. In 1958 she starred on WNOX Knoxville's *Tennessee Barndance* before moving to the **Louisiana Hayride** on KWKH Shreveport. After leaving Decca, she recorded for Bandera gaining a number 7 hit (her last) with 'Old Moon' in 1959. She eventually became a resident performer, with her father, on the ABC's networked *Jubilee USA* television show on KWTO Springfield, Missouri. After retiring as a performer, she had a business interest in Kentucky Fried Chicken.

Foley, Red

b. Clyde Julian Foley, 17 June 1910, in a log cabin between Blue Lick and Berea, Kentucky, USA, d. 19 September 1968, Fort Wayne, Indiana, USA. The son of a fiddle player, Foley learned guitar as a child and was encouraged to sing by his parents. After high school, he attended Georgetown College, Kentucky, where he was discovered by a scout for the noted WLS *National Barn Dance* in Chicago. In 1930 he joined **John Lair**'s **Cumberland Ridge Runners** and returned to Kentucky with Lair in 1937 to help him establish the now famous Renfro Valley Barn Dance. He returned to Chicago in 1941, costarred with Red Skelton in the network country radio show *Avalon Time* and signed with **Decca Records**. The first number he recorded was 'Old Shep', a song he had written in 1933 about a dog he had owned as a child (in reality, the dog, sadly poisoned by a neighbour, had been a German shepherd named Hoover). The song, later recorded by many artists including **Hank Snow** and **Elvis Presley**, has become a country classic. His first chart success came in 1944, when the patriotic wartime song 'Smoke On The Water' was a US pop chart number 7 and a 13-week occupant of the number 1 position in the country charts. On 17 January 1945

Foley had the distinction of making the first modern country records recorded in Nashville. In April 1946 he became a regular member of the **Grand Ole Opry**, replacing **Roy Acuff** as the star of NBC's prestigious *Prince Albert Show*. When he left Chicago for Nashville, he took with him a young guitar player called **Chet Atkins**, one of the many artists he helped. During the next eight years Foley established himself as one of the most respected and versatile performers in country music. He acted as master of ceremonies, the straight man for *Opry* comedians **Rod Brasfield** and **Minnie Pearl**, and proved himself a vocalist who could handle all types of material. In 1954 he moved to KWTO Springfield as the host of the **Ozark Jubilee**, which in 1956 became one of the first successful network television shows. Between 1944 and 1959, Foley charted 41 solo country entries, of which 38 were Top 10 hits. There were six more country number 1s, including his 1950 million-selling 'Chattanoogie Shoe Shine Boy', which also topped the pop charts. Several others achieved crossover pop chart success. During this time he also had many major hit duets with various artists including **Evelyn Knight**, his daughter **Betty Foley**, **Ernest Tubb** ('Goodnight Irene') and six with **Kitty Wells**, including their country number 1, 'One By One', which remained on the charts for 41 weeks. His performances of gospel numbers were so popular that recordings of 'Steal Away' (1950) (recorded by **Hank Williams** as 'The Funeral'), 'Just A Closer Walk With Thee' (1950) and 'Peace In The Valley' (1951) all became million-sellers. He also recorded with the **Andrews Sisters** and in the late 50s, even recorded some rock 'n' roll recordings such as 'Crazy Little Guitar Man'.

Although he continued to tour and appear on network television shows, Foley also moved into acting in the early 60s and costarred with **Fess Parker** in the ABC-TV series *Mr. Smith Goes To Washington*. His daughter Shirley married one-time pop and later gospel singer **Pat Boone**, and some 10 years after Foley's death, his granddaughter **Debby Boone** had both country and pop success. Foley never lost his love for country music and, unlike **Eddy Arnold**, never sought success as a pop artist, even though many of his recordings did attain pop chart status. His voice was mellow and had none of the raw or nasal style associated with many of his contemporaries; some have even likened it to **Bing Crosby**. His importance to the country music scene is often overlooked, and little has been written about him, but he was rightfully elected to the **Country Music Hall Of Fame** in 1967. He was headlining a touring *Opry* show when, after playing the matinée and evening shows, Foley suffered a heart attack and died in his sleep on 19 September 1968. This prompted Hank Jnr., seemingly the last person to speak to him, to write and record (as Luke The Drifter Jnr.) the tribute narration 'I Was With Red Foley (The Night He Passed Away)', which charted in November 1968. In the song, Hank Jnr. relates that after reminiscing about the problems faced by country singers such as himself and Hank Snr., Red's final words were: 'I'm awful tired now, Hank, I've got to go to bed'.

● ALBUMS: *Red Foley Souvenir Album* (Decca 1951) ★★★★, *Lift Up Your Voice* (Decca 1954) ★★★, with Ernest Tubb *Red & Ernie* (Decca 1956) ★★★★, *My Keepsake Album* (Decca 1958) ★★★, *Beyond The Sunset* (Decca 1958) ★★★★, *He Walks With Thee* (Decca 1958) ★★, *Red Foley's Dickies Souvenir Album* (Decca 1958) ★★★, *Let's All Sing To Him* (Decca 1959) ★★, *Let's All Sing With Red Foley* (Decca 1959) ★★★, *Company's Comin'*

(Decca 1961) ★★★, *Red Foley's Golden Favorites* (Decca 1961) ★★★★, *Songs Of Devotion* (Decca 1961) ★★★, with Kitty Wells *Kitty Wells & Red Foley's Greatest Hits* (Decca 1961) ★★★★, *Dear Hearts And Gentle People* (Decca 1962) ★★★, *The Red Foley Show* (Decca 1963) ★★★, *The Red Foley Story* (Decca 1964) ★★★★, *Songs Everybody Knows* (Decca 1965) ★★★, *I'm Bound For The Kingdom* (Vocalion 1965) ★★★, *Red Foley* (Vocalion 1966) ★★★, *Songs For The Soul* (Decca 1967) ★★★, with Kitty Wells *Together Again* (Decca 1967) ★★★, *I Believe* (Decca 1969) ★★★, *The Old Master* (Decca 1969) ★★★, *Red Foley Memories* (Decca 1971) ★★★★.
● COMPILATIONS: *Beyond The Sunset* (MCA 1981) ★★★★, *Tennessee Saturday Night* (Charly 1984) ★★★, *The Red Foley Story* (MCA 1986) ★★★★, *Red Foley: Country Music Hall Of Fame Series* (MCA 1991) ★★★★, *Chattanoogie Shoe Shine Boy: The Best Of Red Foley 1944–1958* (Edsel 2001) ★★★★, *Tennessee Saturday Night* (Proper 2002) ★★★★, *Yodeling Radio Joe* (British Archive Of Country Music 2005) ★★★★.

Foley, Sue
b. 29 March 1968, Ottawa, Ontario, Canada. Foley fields a strong sense of rhythm that puts an interesting spin on a Texas shuffle. She took up the guitar at 13, encouraged by her father and three brothers. Two years later, she saw **James Cotton** and spent the next few years sneaking into clubs to jam with blues bands. At 18 she formed a band of her own and moved to Vancouver, where she developed a guitar style that favoured **Earl Hooker**, **Freddie King** and **Magic Sam**. Her tours took her to the USA, and in Memphis, she was seen by Clifford Antone, who signed her to his label in March 1990. *Young Girl Blues* featured her regular rhythm team, supplemented by a guest list that included **Kim Wilson** and Reese Wynans, on a set in which cover versions predominated. There were fewer guests and more original songs on *Without A Warning*, an album that emphasized the confrontational nature of her talent. Despite a label change in the mid-90s, Foley has continued to push the boundaries of the blues to accommodate her sensual and frank approach to songwriting. Though Foley's forays into good-time roots rock (*Walk In The Sun*, *Ten Days In November*) are perfectly acceptable, it was a welcome to hear the singer picking over the bones of her recent divorce on 2000's excellent *Love Comin' Down*. Similarly credible was the all acoustic *Change* in 2004.
● ALBUMS: *Young Girl Blues* (Antone's 1992) ★★★★, *Without A Warning* (Antone's 1993) ★★★, *Big City Blues* (Antone's 1995) ★★★, *Walk In The Sun* (Antone's 1996) ★★★, *Ten Days In November* (Shanachie 1998) ★★★, *Love Comin' Down* (Shanachie 2000) ★★★★, *Where The Action Is* (Shanachie 2002) ★★★, *Change* (Ruf 2004) ★★★★.
● COMPILATIONS: *Antone's Women* (Antone's 1992) ★★★, *Back To The Blues* (Texas Music Group 2000) ★★★.

Folies Bergère De Paris
From the moment when the opening titles fade and **Maurice Chevalier**, complete with familiar straw boater, launches into the jaunty 'Valentine' (Herbert Reynolds–Henri Christine), all sense of belief is necessarily suspended while he plays an entertainer who is hired by a wealthy businessman to substitute for him at a swanky social occasion. He fools all the guests except for the busy executive's wife (Merle Oberon) who would know her husband anywhere, or would she? Chevalier played both leading male roles, of course, and **Ann Sothern** was his feisty mistress. Also in the cast were Walter Byron, **Eric Blore** and Lumsden Hare. Jack Stern and Jack Meskill wrote most of the songs, which included 'Rhythm Of The Rain' (with Chevalier and Sothern plus lots of girls and umbrellas), 'I Was Lucky', 'Singing A Happy Song' and 'Au Revoir, L'Amour'. The best of the rest was **Burton Lane** and **Harold Adamson**'s 'You Took The Words Right Out Of My Mouth'. Bess Meredyth and Hal Long wrote the screenplay, which was adapted from a play by Rudolph Lothar and Hans Adler by Jessie Enst, which was also used as the basis for two other movies, *That Night In Rio* (1941) and *On The Riviera* (1951). Roy Del Ruth directed *Folies Bergère De Paris*, which was released in 1935, and dance director Dave Gould won an Oscar for his staging of the spectacular 'Straw Hat' finalé.

Folk Implosion
This US alternative rock duo was originally formed by Lou Barlow of **Sebadoh** and solo artist John Davis and came to prominence in 1996 when 'Natural One', included on the soundtrack to the controversial movie *Kids*, became a major US hit. **London Records**, who issued the soundtrack, were keen to sign the band to a contract, but in the event, Barlow and Davis elected to release their new album on the tiny San Franciscan independent label Communion Records. Davis explained their choice to *Billboard* magazine: 'It will be really exciting to see where the limits are and to see if a real indie label can get played on the radio.' Barlow was also keen to emphasize that Folk Implosion was an act in its own right, with two songwriters, and not simply an extension of his activities with Sebadoh. The duo had already released a cassette debut on the UK label Chocolate Monk and *Take A Look Inside . . .* on Communion long before 'Natural One' had become a hit. By the time the endearing *Dare To Be Surprised* was released in April 1997, Davis had resigned from his previous full-time occupation as a librarian. The album also coincided with the release of Davis' solo effort, *Blue Mountain*, for Shrimper Records. The duo's major label follow-up was a more cohesive and slickly produced collection of material that attempted to emulate the electronic-flavoured sound of 'Natural One' but that ultimately lacked the lo-fi charm of their earlier work. Davis parted company with Barlow in 2001, leaving the latter to soldier on with Sebadoh drummer Russ Pollard and guitarist Imaad Wasif on the disappointing *The New Folk Implosion*.
● ALBUMS: *Folk Implosion* cassette (Chocolate Monk 1994) ★★★, *Take A Look Inside . . . The Folk Implosion* mini-album (Communion 1994) ★★★, *Dare To Be Surprised* (Communion 1997) ★★★★, *One Part Lullaby* (Interscope/Domino 1999) ★★★, *The New Folk Implosion* (iMusic/Domino 2003) ★★.

Folk Och Rackare
This Swedish-Norwegian folk group were formed in 1972 at the University of Gothenburg, Sweden, where two musicology students, Carin Kjellman (vocals, dulcimer, recorder, guitar, psalterion) and Ulf Gruvberg (vocals, guitar, bass, cittern, mandolin, crumhorn, jew's harp, percussion), started playing together and developed a repertoire of traditional

Swedish music. On both their albums as a duo they were accompanied by a variety of folk and jazz musicians, and in 1976 they were joined by two former members of the Norwegian band **Folque**, Jørn Jensen (mandolin, dulcimer, bassoon, psalterion, guitar, percussion, jew's harp, vocals), who had played on their second album, and Trond Villa (fiddle, hardingfiddle, crumhorn, mandolin, vocals), both of whom became full-time members of the band. Folk Och Rackare expanded their repertoire to include Norwegian ballads and tunes and developed their distinctive music: a compelling arrangement of vocal harmonies, electric and medieval instruments and Kjellman's magnificent voice. In the late 70s, they played several large European folk festivals, and after *Stjärnhästen*, a collection of Swedish Christmas carols, the band took a four-year break. They returned in 1985 with their final album, *Rackbag*, which featured the guitarist **Richard Thompson** and showed the influence of both the **Albion Band** and its offshoot **Home Service**. During most of the 80s Gruvberg was the presenter of the roots radio show *Trender Och Traditioner* (Trends And Traditions) on Swedish National radio (SR), and he is now the controller of the more rock-orientated third radio channel, P3. In 1985 Carin Kjellman released a solo album that included cover versions of songs by **Sandy Denny** and Richard Thompson, while both Jensen and Villa are still involved in folk music in Norway.

● ALBUMS: Carin Kjellman, Ulf Gruvberg *Med Rötter I Medeltiden* (Sonet 1974) ★★★, *Folk Och Rackare* (YTF 1976) ★★★, *Folk Och Rackare Rackarspel* (YTF 1978) ★★★★, *Anno 1979* (Sonet 1979) ★★★, *Stjärnhästen* (Sonet 1981) ★★★, *Rackbag* (Amalthea 1985) ★★★.
Solo: Carin Kjellman *Carin Kjellman* (Amalthea 1985) ★★.

Folk Stringers

The Folk Stringers were a USA studio-based instrumental act put together by Samuel Charters, a producer for **Prestige/Folklore Records**. The group featured Danny Kalb, one of the most popular guitarists in New York's Greenwich Village during the early 60s. The line-up was completed by Barry Kornfield (guitar/banjo) and Artie Rose (bass), both of whom had worked with Kalb in **Dave Van Ronk**'s Jug Stompers. *The Folk Strangers* is a showcase for the trio's virtuosity, drawing inspiration from folk and blues performers such as **Snooks Eaglin** and **Doc Watson**. Ill health meant Kalb was unable to complete the album. When he returned to music he joined Charters in the **New Strangers** before playing the electric guitar with the **Blues Project**. Kornfield later managed **Simon And Garfunkel** before becoming an official for the International Federation of Musicians.

● ALBUMS: *The Folk Stringers* (Prestige/Folklore 1964) ★★★.

Folkes Brothers

The three brothers Folkes, Michael, John and Eric, together with **Count Ossie** and his drummers, **Owen Gray** (piano) and extra vocalist Skitter went to **Prince Buster**'s studio and recorded a classic of Jamaican music. To be labelled a one-hit-wonder is generally something of an insult, but to be a one-record-wonder is an accolade. The Jamaican artists who have made one perfect recording and then vanished, leaving a reputation forever untarnished by later lapses, could be counted on the fingers of one hand. The Folkes Brothers are among that number. In 1961 or early 1962 they recorded 'Oh

Carolina', a unique and perfect single, and never appeared again. The record has Count Ossie's Rastafarian drummers thundering out complex African cross-rhythms, Gray's contrastingly American-styled on piano, and the Brothers, with a soulful lead singer Skitter and two lighter-voiced male accompanists, delivering the song. In 1993 an updated version of 'Oh Carolina' reached number 1 in the UK charts for ragga singer **Shaggy**.

Folkways Records

Founded in New York, USA, in 1948 by Moe Asch and Marion Distler, Folkways has grown from informal origins to become the embodiment of America's divergent traditions. Initial releases included square-dance tunes, Cuban music and jazz, but the venture was primarily devoted to folk styles. Recordings by **Lead Belly** established the label nationally, and his prodigious output—over 900 songs were committed to tape—included several now recognized as standards, notably 'Goodnight Irene', 'Midnight Special', 'Cottonfields' and 'Rock Island Line'. Folkways also recorded **Woody Guthrie**, **Cisco Houston** and **Pete Seeger**; the last completed over 60 albums for the label and embraced the urban folk revival of the late 50s and early 60s with releases by **Dave Van Ronk**, **Len Chandler**, **Paul Clayton**, **Logan English** and the **New Lost City Ramblers**. Asch also established several subsidiary outlets, including RBF and Broadside, the latter of which evolved out of a mimeographed publication devoted to the topical song. **Bob Dylan**, **Phil Ochs** and **Eric Andersen** were among those contributing to attendant albums. However, Folkways was not solely confined to folk, and its ever-increasing catalogue included language instruction, science, spoken-word and documentary material, of which *We Shall Overcome*, an audio-vérité recording of the 1963 civil rights march on Washington, D.C., was particularly impressive. In 1965 Asch founded Verve-Folkways, in an effort to secure national distribution for selected repackages from his extensive library. New recordings, by **Tim Hardin**, the **Blues Magoos** and **Blues Project**, were also undertaken but the label's title was altered to Verve-Forecast in 1967 as electric styles prevailed over acoustic. Excellent albums by, among others, **Richie Havens**, **Janis Ian**, **Odetta** and **James Cotton** ensued, but the venture folded when parent company **MGM Records** incurred financial difficulties. Asch continued to maintain the original Folkways, which, by retaining its small-scale origins, has avoided the trappings of commercialization. Between 1,500 and 2,000 titles remain in circulation at all times, and the company's peerless position within America was recognized in 1988 with *Folkways: A Vision Shared*, a star-studded recording undertaken to celebrate the label's 40th anniversary. **Bruce Springsteen**, **U2**, **Brian Wilson**, **Little Richard**, **Taj Mahal**, **Emmylou Harris** and Bob Dylan were among those gathering to pay tribute through interpretations of compositions by Lead Belly and Woody Guthrie.

● COMPILATIONS: *Folkways: A Vision Shared* (Folkways 1988) ★★★.

● FURTHER READING: *Making People's Music—Moe Asch And Folkways Records*, Peter D. Goldsmith. *Folkways Records: Moses Asch And His Encyclopedia Of Sound*, Anthony Olmsted.

Follies

Often cited as one of **Stephen Sondheim**'s more 'accessible' shows, *Follies* opened at the Winter Garden Theatre in New

York on 4 April 1971. James Goldman's book is set on the stage of the derelict, soon-to-be-demolished Weismann Theatre. For this first, and last, reunion party, showgirls who were part of the legendary *Weismann Follies* some 30 years ago return—as Dimitri Weismann (Arnold Moss) himself puts it—'to stumble through a song or two, and lie about ourselves . . . a little'. Two of them, Phyllis Stone (Alexis Smith) and Sally Plummer (Dorothy Collins), married young stage-door-Johnnies way back then. Benjamin Stone (John McMartin) wed Phyllis in spite of having a brief fling with Sally, who eventually ended up with Buddy Plummer (**Gene Nelson**). In the intervening years, both couples have been desperately unhappy. Although Ben has done well for himself and risen to be a wealthy diplomat, he looks upon Phyllis as an accessory to his jet-setting lifestyle. Buddy is a salesman, permanently on the road and with a girl in every town. Sally stays at home reading her Harlequin novels, convinced that she married the wrong man. Now they have returned to this theatre, with all its memories, and as the night progresses each one of them is confronted—in a series of flashbacks—with a ghost of their former selves. The reminiscences and recriminations are constantly interrupted by contributions from other ex-*Follies* performers attending this often dark, soul-searching soirée, some of them pastiche numbers which eerily re-create that half-forgotten era. Solange (Fifi D'Orsay) slinks sexily through 'Ah, Paris'; wheelchair-bound Heidi Schiller (Justine Johnston), accompanied by her younger self (Victoria Mallory), evokes memories of **Sigmund Romberg** with 'One More Kiss'; and two memorable anthems of survival, Hattie Walker (Ethel Shutta) reveals the desperation and heartbreak of the common chorus girl in the show-stopping 'Broadway Baby', while Carlotta Campion (played by 40s movie star Yvonne De Carlo) triumphantly insists 'I'm Still Here'. And then there are The Whitmans, a song-and-dance duo (Marcie Stringer and Charles Welch) who eagerly take on the tongue-twisting 'Listen To The Rain On The Roof', and veteran Stella (Mary McCarty) refusing to believe the image that cruel glass reveals in 'Who's That Woman?' ('the mirror number'). Ben, Phyllis, Buddy, and Sally share 'Don't Look At Me', 'Waiting For The Girls Upstairs', 'The Road You Didn't Take', 'In Buddy's Eyes', 'Too Many Mornings', 'The Right Girl', 'Could I Leave You' (Phyllis finally considers divorce) before having the second section of the final 'Loveland' sequence to themselves. Entitled 'The Folly Of Youth', it consisted of 'You're Gonna Love Tomorrow' (Ben and Phyllis), 'Love Will See Us Through' (Buddy and Sally), 'The God-Why-Don't-You-Love-Me Blues' ('Buddy's Folly'), 'Losing My Mind' ('Sally's Folly'), 'The Story Of Lucy And Jessie' ('Phyllis' Folly') and 'Live, Laugh, Love' ('Ben's Folly'). As dawn breaks, emotionally shattered and with no illusions left, the two couples go back to try and pick up their previous lives and find what consolation they can in each other. The bulldozers await: Roscoe (Michael Bartlett) has brought on his 'Beautiful Girls' for the very last time. *Follies* was a spectacular and glamorous production, and opinions vary widely as to why it was not successful. Sondheim himself is said to feel that there were too many pastiche numbers, while codirector (with **Hal Prince**) and choreographer **Michael Bennett** blamed the book. In any event, the show ran for 522 performances and collected the New York Drama Critics Award for best musical and **Tony Awards** for best score, director, choreographer, scenic design (Boris Aronson), costumes (Florence Klotz), lighting (Tharon Musser) and actress (Alexis Smith).

Follies In Concert with the New York Philharmonic played two nights, 6 and 7 September 1985, at the Lincoln Centre's Avery Fisher Hall in New York, with an all-star cast that included **Barbara Cook** (Sally), **George Hearn** (Ben), **Mandy Patinkin** (Buddy), Lee Remick (Phyllis), **Elaine Stritch**, Liliane Montevecchi, **Carol Burnett**, Phyllis Newman, **Betty Comden** and **Adolph Green**. Two years later, **Cameron Mackintosh**'s fully staged London production, which was streamlined, extensively rewritten, and incorporated some different numbers, starred **Julia McKenzie** (Sally), Diana Rigg (Phyllis), **Daniel Massey** (Ben), David Healy (Buddy), **Dolores Gray**, Adele Leigh, **Pearl Carr And Teddy Johnson** and ran for 18 months. Productions at the Theater Des Westens in Berlin (1991) and at Britain's Leicester Haymarket Theatre (1994) reverted to the 1971 US concept, with theatre buffs predicting (perhaps unwisely) that Mackintosh's radical revisions would never be seen again. When Julia McKenzie (Sally) and Pearl Carr and Teddy Johnson (The Whitmans) reprised their 1987 London performances for a BBC Radio 2 *Follies* that played the Theatre Royal, Drury Lane, on 8 December 1996, they were among the few artists who have appeared in both versions. Also cast in this broadcast concert were **Denis Quilley** (Ben), **Donna McKechnie** (Phyllis), **Ron Moody** (Buddy), Joan Savage, **Elizabeth Seal**, Libby Morris, Eileen Page, Shona Lindsay, David Bardsley, Lori Haley Fox, Michael Cahill, Angela Richards and Carrie Ellis. On 15 April 1998, the Paper Mill Playhouse, New Jersey, presented the first major New York–area staging of the whole show since the 1971 original. It starred as Sally (Donna McKechnie), Phyllis (Dee Hoty), Ben (Laurence Guittard), Buddy (Tony Roberts), Solange (Liliane Montevecchi), The Whitmans (Donald Saddler and Natalie Mosco), Stella (Phyllis Newman), Carlotta (**Ann Miller**) and Hattie (**Kaye Ballard**) with Eddie Bracken as Dimitri Weismann. It resulted in *Follies: The Complete Recording*, which contains every piece of music written for the show. There were some items missing on the original 1971 cast album, but this new set not only has the complete score but includes an appendix of eight numbers, including the famous 'Can That Boy Fox-Trot', that were cut from the show during the various stages of its life. All are orchestrated by Sondheim's long time collaborator Jonathan Tunick.

Follow A Star

Although the music and lyrics for this piece were by **Vivian Ellis** and **Douglas Furber**, this was by no means a typical Ellis show. The reason was the dominating presence in the cast of the American entertainer **Sophie Tucker**. It was Tucker's second appearance in the London theatre (as opposed to music halls and clubs), and her first book musical (she had played in the revue *Round In 50* in 1922). This time she brought along her two regular songwriters, **Jack Yellen** and Ted Shapiro, just in case Ellis and Furber did not come up with her particular kind of goods. Ironically, and much to Ellis' delight, the hit of the show and the number that became so popular that she had to close with it was 'If Your Kisses Can't Hold The Man You Love', which had music by Ellis and a lyric by Yellen. *Follow A Star* opened at the Winter Garden Theatre in London on 17 September 1930 with a book by Furber and Dion Titheradge. It was directed and choreographed by **Jack Hulbert** who also played a leading role. Hulbert had appeared in so many successful shows with his wife **Cicely Courtneidge**, but this time she had temporarily deserted musical comedy for the revue **Folly to Be Wise** and left Hulbert to deal with Tucker, whose role in the show was as a cabaret singer (Georgia Madison) who is elevated to better things when she inherits a title and becomes Lady Bohun. Jack Hulbert played Bobby Hilary, the lover of Georgia's daughter, Merrie Boon (Betty Davies). Ellis' music was as charming and delightful as ever in songs such as 'Don't Wear Your Heart On Your Sleeve', 'The First Weekend In June', 'The English Gentlemen' and 'You Do The Singing'. Tucker's numbers included 'Follow A Star', 'I Can Never Think Of The Words' and 'That's Where The South Begins', but they were cut when she left the show early in December ('If Your Kisses Can't Hold The Man You Love' stayed in) to be replaced by Maisie Gay when it reopened later in the month. The revised production had a disappointing run, closing after only 118 performances and losing a good deal of its investment.

Follow That Dream

This 1962 venture revealed a further reduction in the quality of **Elvis Presley**'s films. The plot revolves around a group of homesteaders whose business venture on a Florida beach is threatened by local mobsters. Naturally good triumphs over evil, during which Presley contributes seven songs, six of which were recorded on 5 July 1961. The seventh, 'On Top Of Old Smoky', was cut on the film set itself. 'What A Wonderful Life', 'I'm Not The Marrying Kind', 'Angel' and the film's title track made up the *Follow That Dream* EP which reached number 15 in the US singles' chart and also entered the UK Top 40. 'A Whistling Tune' surfaced on the subsequent *Kid Galahad* EP, while 'Sound Advice' appeared on 1965's *Elvis For Everyone*. In a rare deviation from the norm, **RCA Records** did not issue a single from the soundtrack, suggesting even they felt that nothing from the film's material was strong enough to warrant such a high-profile release.

Follow That Girl

A kind of hectic musical tour of London, this show was adapted by composer **Julian Slade** and Dorothy Reynolds from their 1952 production *Christmas In King Street*. It opened at the Vaudeville Theatre in London on 17 March 1960. The light and frothy story concerned Victoria (Susan Hampshire), whose parents, Mr. and Mrs. Gilchrist (James Cairness and **Patricia Routledge**), want her to marry one of two rich businessmen, Wilberforce (Robert MacBaine) or Tancred (Philip Guard). She gives them the slip, and after a long and hectic chase, is finally captured by a policeman, Tom (Peter Gilmore), who takes her into custody and marries her. Slade and Reynolds' score is generally regarded as among their very best work. The songs included 'Tra La La', 'Follow That Girl', 'Life Must Go On', 'Waiting For Our Daughter', 'Shopping In Kensington', 'Solitary Stranger', 'Lovely Meeting You At Last', 'I'm Away', 'Where Shall I Find My Love?', 'Three Victorian Mermaids', 'One, Two, Three, One', 'Doh Ray Me' and 'Taken For A Ride'. Gilmore and Hampshire both went on to television superstardom, he in *The Onedin Line* and she in *The Forsyte Saga* and *The Pallisers*. Grazina Frame, who was also in the cast of *Follow That Girl*, had her moment of glory when she starred in **Lionel Bart**'s *Blitz!* in 1962. In spite of its fun story and quality score, *Follow That Girl* received mixed notices but had a reasonable run of 211 performances. Hardly in the same league as the same authors' **Salad Days** (2,283), but then that sort of success usually only comes along once in a lifetime.

Follow The Boys

This 1962 film starred **Connie Francis**, one of the most popular singers of the pre-**Beatles** era. She had 16 US Top 10 entries prior to this role that succeeded her part in the previous year's *Where The Boys Are*. Paula Prentiss, Danny Robin and Russ Tamblyn (veteran of **West Side Story** and *Tom Thumb*) were also featured in a light-hearted musical wherein four girls arrange to meet their sweethearts at a port in the south of France. When the ship fails to dock, the quartet travel to its next destination in an old car they buy for the occasion. The appeal of *Follow The Boys* rests on Francis' distinctive *métier*, and she contributes six songs including 'Italian Lullaby', 'Waiting For Billy' and 'Tonight's My Night'. Her rendition of the title track provided another US Top 20 entry, the last time the singer achieved this feat. Francis' once pre-eminent position was then taken up by a new generation of acts.

Follow The Fleet

After their triumph in **Top Hat** in 1935, **Fred Astaire** and **Ginger Rogers** did it again with more or less the same artistic team a year later in *Follow The Fleet*. Mark Sandrich (director), **Hermes Pan** (dance director) and songwriter **Irving Berlin** all combined for another feast of song and dance. Apart from one number, 'Let's Face The Music And Dance', Fred traded in his top hat, white tie and tails for a sailor suit in Dwight Taylor and Allan Scott's screenplay that was based on Hubert Osborne's Broadway play *Shore Leave*. The central love story concerns spinster Connie Martin (**Harriet Hilliard**) who falls for Bilge Smith (Randolph Scott) in such a big way that she arranges for a ship to be salvaged for him after his discharge from the US Navy. Harriet reveals the depths of her love for Bilge via two beautiful but surprisingly melancholy ballads 'Get Thee Behind Me, Satan' and 'But Where Are You?', but that is where the film's heartaches began and ended. On a much brighter note, Fred and Ginger, as Bake Baker and Sherry Martin, the former dance team that split up when Bake enlisted in the navy, meet again at the Paradise Ballroom in San Francisco and rekindle the old magic in an effort to raise money to salvage the ship. They dance everybody's cares away to glorious Berlin numbers such as 'We Saw The Sea', 'I'd Rather Lead A Band', 'Let Yourself Go' and 'I'm Putting All My Eggs In One Basket'. Future stars **Tony Martin**, **Lucille Ball** and **Betty Grable** made brief but effective appearances in this RKO release, which some critics thought was too long at 110 minutes. The public did not seem to agree and flocked to see *Follow The Fleet* in great numbers.

Follow The Girls

This big wartime stage musical hit on both sides of the Atlantic, first saw the light of day at the New Century Theatre in New York on 8 April 1944. **Guy Bolton**, together with Eddie Davis and **Fred Thompson**, wrote the libretto, which concerns Bubbles LaMarr (Gertrude Niesen in her only book musical), a burlesque stripper whose career takes off in a big way at the Spotlight Club, a sanctuary for servicemen in Long Island, USA. Her boyfriend, Goofy Gale (**Jackie Gleason**), cannot get in to see her because, physically speaking, the army just does not want him. As this is a Bolton book (he wrote the jolly

Princess Theatre japes with **P.G. Wodehouse** and **Jerome Kern**), and Gleason is also involved, Goofy complicates the issue by stealing not an admiral or a colonel's uniform but one that is worn by a Wave. The show's setting gave ample opportunities for lots of singing and dancing, and some of the supporting characters had 'Damon Runyon'–type names such as Dinky Riley and Spud Doolittle. Niesen made a big impression every night with 'I Wanna Get Married', and the rest of the score, by Phil Charig (music) and Dan Shapiro and Milton Pascal (lyrics), included 'You're Perf', 'Twelve O'Clock And All's Well', 'Follow The Girls', 'I'm Gonna Hang My Hat', 'Out For No Good' and 'Tomorrow Will Be Yesterday Tomorrow'. *Follow The Girls* ran for over two years, a total of 882 performances, in New York and played 572 shows at His Majesty's Theatre in London, where the popular local comedian **Arthur Askey** starred as Goofy, with Evelyn Dall as Bubbles. Another member of the West End Cast was **Wendy Toye**, who also directed the piece. She went on to become one of the British theatre's most admired and respected directors.

Follow Thru

Opening at New York's 46th Street theatre on 9 January 1929, and subtitled 'A Musical Slice Of Country Life', this was another in a series of sporty shows (**Good News!** and **Hold Everything!** were about football and boxing) that songwriters **De Sylva, Brown And Henderson** had such success with in the 20s. *Follow Thru*'s book, by De Sylva and Laurence Schwab, turned the spotlight on golf. The show was the first big break on Broadway for comedian **Jack Haley**, who made a career out of playing shy diffident characters who are usually pursued by pretty women. This time he is the object of affection for Angie Howard (Zelma O'Neal), and when they do get together they give the evening a big lift with their version of one of the composers' all-time standards, 'Button Up Your Overcoat' ('Eat an apple ev'ry day, Get to bed by three, Take good care of yourself, You belong to me'). Meanwhile, back on the greens and in the locker room, Lora Moore (**Irene Delroy**) and Ruth Van Horn (Madeline Cameron) are locked in combat—for the country club's women's championship, and the chance to go round the course forever with the handsome, good guy, with a low-handicap, Jerry Downs (John Barker). Lora comes out top in both events. Another winner here who gave the show a big lift was 19-year-old tap-dancer Eleanor Powell in her first book musical following her Broadway debut in *The Optimists* revue in 1928. She went on to Hollywood fame in the 30s and 40s. De Sylva, Brown And Henderson's songs, which were so typical of the happy-go-lucky 20s period, included 'My Lucky Star', 'You Wouldn't Fool Me, Would You?', 'I Want To Be Bad', 'Then I'll Have Time For You' and, of course, the smash-hit 'Button Up Your Overcoat', which became all the rage through various recordings by **Helen Kane**, **Paul Whiteman**, **Fred Waring**'s Pennsylvanians and **Ruth Etting**. The show sang and danced its happy way to an impressive 403 performances in New York, and the London edition, *Follow Through*, which starred **Leslie Henson**, Ivy Tresmond and Elsie Randolph, added another 148. Jack Haley and Zelma O'Neal re-created their original roles for the 1930 film version.

Folly To Be Wise

This popular revue, devised by **Jack Hulbert** and Paul Murray, opened on 8 January 1931 at the Piccadilly Theatre in London. Hulbert did not appear in it himself—at the time he was in the **Vivian Ellis** musical comedy, *Follow A Star*. His wife, Cicely Courtneidge was present, though, and right at the top of her form. She was joined in the cast by Nelson Keys and Ivor McLaren, together with a couple of visitors from the USA, Mary Eaton and J. Albert Traherne. The music and lyrics were provided by a variety of songwriters, including Vivian Ellis, **Noel Gay**, Harry Graham, **Bert Kalmar**, **Harry Ruby**, **Herman Hupfield** and Dion Titheradge. Probably the best-known song to emerge from the show, at least as far as British audiences are concerned, was 'All The King's Horses' (Noel Gay and Harry Graham), which was given the full Courtneidge treatment and became extremely popular for artists such as **Jack Hylton** And His Orchestra, The New Mayfair Orchestra conducted by **Ray Noble**, The Big Four and, much later, **Dennis Lotis** with the **Ted Heath** Orchestra. Some of the other numbers included 'Looking For A Sunbeam', 'Three Little Words' (Kalmar-Ruby) and 'Sing Something Simple' (Hupfield). The show ran for 257 performances, which, for this kind of production in the days of general economic unrest in Britain during the early 30s, was considered to be a more than satisfactory state of affairs.

Folque

A Norwegian version of the folk rock band **Steeleye Span**, Folque had a strong, ringing sound, their music based on rich Norse folk legend. They disbanded in 1984 but later re-formed in 1992 as an acoustic four-piece unit, playing their old repertoire in a back-to-basics format.

● ALBUMS: *Fredlos* (1980) ★★★.

Fomeen, Basil

b. Wasily Fomin, 1902, Kharkoff, Russia, d. 1983. Fomeen emigrated to the USA in 1922, settling in New York City. Before embarking on a career as a band leader, Fomeen, a talented composer with credits including 'Manhattan Gypsy', had played his accordion with both **Joe Moss** and **Meyer Davis**. His own orchestra was formed in 1933 in New York City, with an initial engagement at the Savoy Plaza. Groomed as a 'society band', the group stayed at the Savoy for two years before transferring to the St. Moritz. Following two years there Fomeen moved to the prestigious Waldorf-Astoria for the first of several engagements. Following dates at the Carlton in Washington, D.C., the orchestra journeyed west to Ciro's in Hollywood, shows that endeared them to the film industry personnel who congregated there. Later they became one of the few dance bands to tour internationally, visiting Europe, Africa, India and China under the USO banner. 1941 saw them visit the Copacabana Casino in Rio De Janeiro, Brazil. However, after the end of World War II, despite a continuing itinerary of theatre and ballroom performances, Fomeen's fame diminished, and the members of his band dispersed.

Foncett, Frankie

b. England. A 90s UK disc jockey, producer and remixer, Foncett began his career by spinning hip-hop discs for the Rappatack **sound system**. In the mid-80s he switched to **house** music, playing at several of the major clubs of the period. In London he made appearances at the Black Market and Shoom clubs and was also resident disc jockey alongside Norman Jay at High On Hope. He travelled to the

USA in 1989 to play at New York's Payday, appearing alongside **Larry Levan**, before dates at Detroit's Music Institute with **Derrick May**. On his return to London he was among the original staff at the influential Black Market record shop, gradually earning his reputation by remixing several acts for major record companies, including the **Chimes** and **Regina Belle**. He made his solo debut at the end of 1995 with the *Streetfighter 2000* EP, which included one track, 'The Ride', dedicated to fellow UK disc jockey pioneer Paul Anderson. The intention was to 'represent the UK and London. We created our own vibe with house and I've always been big on individuality. We can listen to US music and let it influence us but we don't have to live or die by it. I wanted to show it's no big deal to do those kind of beats.' He followed its release with work on Lisa M's 1996 album, also writing and producing for the R&B act Sugar Tree.

Fong, Oden

b. USA. The son of an actor, gospel singer Oden Fong had spent his childhood amid the flamboyance of the Hollywood glitterati, and it was in these environs that the seeds of his faith were sewn. He first rose to prominence as lead vocalist and songwriter with the highly regarded Christian rock group Mustard Seed Faith. A definite streak of evangelism has been sustained through his work as a member of the group and in his solo pursuits ever since. As he once explained, 'I don't see myself just as a professional musician because I'm not a Christian music entertainer'. For his debut solo effort, *Come For The Children*, Fong employed a number of musical styles on songs that emphasised this didactic, almost hectoring quality.

● ALBUMS: with Mustard Seed Faith *Mustard Seed Faith* (Maranatha 1976) ★★★★, *Come For The Children* (A&S 1978) ★★★.

Fonseca, Celso

b. 15 November 1956, Rio de Janeiro, Brazil. Brazil's 'best kept secret', Fonseca is actually a keystone of his country's music scene. He has collaborated with luminaries such as **Gilberto Gil**, **Caetano Veloso**, **Marisa Monte** and **Bebel Gilberto** and is a producer of some repute, working on albums by Gil, **Gal Costa**, **Virginia Rodrigues**, **Daniela Mercury** and **Daúde**. For the latter he received the equivalent of a Brazilian Grammy, the Sharp Award, for Best Pop Rock Arranger. He has also written hit songs for Veloso, Costa, Gil, **Maria Bethânia**, **Milton Nascimento**, **Carlinhos Brown** and **Vinicius Cantuária**.

Unlike many of Brazil's younger musicians, Fonseca does not come from a musical family. Rather, having been inspired to pick up the guitar by the music of **Baden Powell** (he says the instrument felt 'quite familiar to me'), he played as a hobby until he met Gilberto Gil in 1982 and was invited to join his band. Fonseca has released four critically acclaimed albums in his home country while *Juventude*, his third collaboration with lyricist Ronaldo Bastos, was nominated in two categories at the Latin Grammies 2002. Although Fonseca has admitted that 'at the beginning of my career, I thought I was unable to compose', his first internationally available album, 2003's *Natural*, delightfully showcases the producer/arranger's gifts as a singer-songwriter. Recording in his own Geléla Geral Studio (which he runs in partnership with Gil) and drawing on the spaciousness and melodic economy of bossa nova, Fonseca deploys a minimalist approach that exudes a quiet, exquisite melancholy. Songs are stripped down to a voice, acoustic guitar, percussion and acoustic bass, aided by Robertinho Silva (percussion), Daniel Jobim (piano) and Jorge Helder (acoustic bass). Although *Natural* included bossa standards such as Baden Powell's 'Consolaç ao' and Jobim's 'She's A Carioca' (on which he duets with singer **Cibelle**), Fonseca has warned: 'It is important to add innovation for that thing to work out well. It is important to be careful for the artist not to lose his identity.' Endearingly, Fonseca plays without a hint of irony or kitsch.

● ALBUMS: *Minha Cara* (WEA 1986) ★★★, *O Sim Do Sim* (Natasha 1993) ★★★, with Ronaldo Bastos *Sorte* (Dubas Música 1994) ★★★, with Bastos *Paradiso* (Dubas Música 1997) ★★★, with Bastos *Juventude* (Universal 2002) ★★★, *Natural* (Ziriguiboom/Crammed Discs 2003) ★★★★, *Rive Gauche Rio* (Ziriguiboom/Crammed 2005) ★★★.

Fontaine, Claudia

b. 1961, London, England. Fontaine began her career in her early teens, initially providing backing vocals on various recording sessions. She joined a number of **lovers rock** trios, including Mellow Rose, One Love and True Harmony, before emerging as a soloist. In 1981 she recorded her version of **Bloodstone**'s classic R&B ballad 'Natural High' with producer Junior Boothe. The song became a popular lovers rock hit and was licensed to a major label, although with little success, and the follow-up, 'Not A Little Girl Any More', failed to make any impact. Fontaine continued in session work, providing backing vocals for **Keith Douglas**, **Tony Tuff** and **King Sounds**, and in 1982 she joined La Famile, singing lead vocals alongside **Brown Sugar** and **Soul II Soul** vocalist **Caron Wheeler**. The group recorded the 1982 disco hit 'Dancer', followed by the acclaimed 'All Night Long'. In 1983 she teamed up with Raymond Simpson as Raymond And Claudia, and the duo recorded versions of **George Benson**'s 'Turn Your Love Around' and **Jermaine Jackson**'s 'Paradise In Your Eyes'. The former was commercially successful, prompting a return to the studio for 'Is It Always Gonna Be Like This'. Fontaine maintained her connections with La Famile, provided backing vocals on the **Jam**'s farewell tour, and pursued a career in journalism on *West Indian World*.

Fontaine, Nasio

b. Dominique, West Indies. Fontaine was the youngest of seven siblings and spent his childhood immersed in the local music scene, although it was the neighbouring Jamaican sounds that had the most influence on him. In 1981 Fontaine migrated to St. Martin where he worked for five years to finance his first recording in 1987. The sessions resulted in the singer's debut, 'Born To Be Free', that proved a hit throughout the Caribbean. He promoted the release touring the islands, which led to his arrival in Jamaica. By 1992 he embarked on sessions at the Mixing Lab studios where he recorded his debut, *Reggae Power*. The album surfaced in 1994 and led to a US promotional tour where Fontaine signed with Aphelion Productions Inc. The partnership led to the album's rerelease, and it was selected as Best Reggae Album in 1996 by *Reggae Roots International Magazine*. He was recognised as Best New Artist by *Gavin Magazine* as well as receiving nominations from the Tamika Reggae Awards and the Canadian Reggae Music Awards. Fontaine also enjoyed acclaim for the promo-video that accompanied 'Wanna Go

Home' from *Rockers TV* and *The Beat Magazine*. Fontaine had embraced the Rastafarian religion, and his works demonstrated his commitment to his faith. The video was filmed on a plot of land donated to the Nyahbinghi men by **Bob Marley**, and the Dominican singer was granted permission to film in the sacred tabernacle. His second album included the classic 'Black Tuesday', a condemnation of the oppression of Rastafarians in Dominique, where the authorities tried to subdue the increased assemblage of the creed. Other notable tracks included 'Rainbow Generation', the prophetic 'Truth Will Reveal' and 'Jah Glory'.

● ALBUMS: *Reggae Power* (Aphelion 1994) ★★★, *Revolution* (Aphelion 1999) ★★★.

Fontaine, Seb

b. London, England. Fontaine is one of the UK's leading **house** DJs. Initially, Fontaine was interested in rare groove and hip-hop and would skip school in order to practise his mixing skills. While at Richmond College and Kingston Polytechnic in London, he would play warm up sets for DJs such as **Norman Jay** and **Jeremy Healy** (ex–**Haysi Fantayzee**) at clubs such as The Fridge, The Wag and Subterrania. His distinctive brand of funky hard house led to bookings at Deluxe in Nottingham and the seminal 'Back To Basics' night in Leeds. The DJ's style was also influenced by a visit to **Ibiza** in 1994. Fontaine established a higher profile running his own very successful night, 'Malibu Stacey' (the name of Barbie-type dolls in the US television cartoon show, *The Simpsons*) at London's Hanover Grand, which ran from November 1994 until July 1998. The club became renowned for its good-looking, well-dressed crowd (derided by some as 'Glam House') and thumping house, played by DJs such as Mark Moore (ex–**S'Express**), **Boy George** and **Dave Seaman**. He has DJed all over the world, including Brazil, the USA and Hong Kong for the handover party in 1997, and regularly plays at clubs during the summer clubbing season in Ibiza. In January 1999 he succeeded **Paul Oakenfold** in taking the prestigious position of resident DJ in the Annexe of Liverpool's **Cream**, staying at the club for three years. He has also been a regular guest DJ at clubs such as **Gatecrasher**, Golden, Godskitchen and The Gallery and runs Type, his own fortnightly evening at The Cross in London. He presented a radio show on London's Kiss 100 with close friend and colleague **Tall Paul** before making the transition to prime time with his own show on Radio 1.

Fontaine has been producing and remixing tracks since 1990 and releases his own material under the moniker Itchy and Scratchy (another reference to *The Simpsons*). Fontaine set up his own label, Spot On Records, in 1991 with Jules Vern (of Stretch And Vern), with whom he also records. He has also mixed 10 compilations, including those for the label Sound Dimension, and the clubs **Ministry Of Sound** and Cream. In 1999 the DJ was signed by the Boxed label to mix three compilation albums under their *Global Underground* banner. The first launched their *Prototype* series and demonstrated Fontaine's growing fondness for well-produced, thumping house and melodic, crowd-pleasing **trance**.

● COMPILATIONS: *Cream Anthems* (Virgin 1998) ★★★★, *Global Underground—Prototype* (Boxed 1999) ★★★★, *Prototype 2* (Boxed 1999) ★★★, *Prototype 3* (Boxed 2000) ★★★, *Prototype 4* (Boxed 2001) ★★★, *Horizons* (Thrive/Perfecto 2002) ★★★.

Fontana Records

Record label started originally in France in 1957, moving into the UK in 1958 as an auxiliary to **Philips Records**. It was set up to release both home-grown material and recordings licensed from **Columbia Records** in the USA. It was in the 60s that the label established its name. It had more than its fair share of the top chart acts of the day, including **Dave Dee, Dozy, Beaky, Mick And Tich**, **Unit Four Plus Two**, **Spencer Davies Group**, **Pretty Things**, **Manfred Mann** and the aptly named **Wayne Fontana**. During the early part of the decade they also had the privilege of releasing **Motown Records** product in the UK for a six-month period. As the mood of the 60s changed, Fontana updated its selection of acts with releases by **Joan Baez** and **Country Joe And The Fish**, in a contract with **Vanguard Records**. A number of records released in these days would become important footnotes in the development of pop and rock; the High Numbers' 'I'm The Face', **Jimmy Page**'s 'She Just Satisfies' and Ambrose Slade's *Beginnings* LP (pre-**Who**, **Led Zeppelin** and **Slade**, respectively). During the 70s, however, the label, now owned by **Phonogram Records**, took its place on the back burner with new rock acts being signed to the empire's **Vertigo Records** and **Mercury Records** outlets. In fact, no new acts were signed during the decade, and the only artist to remain on their roster was **Nana Mouskouri**, who shifted to Phillips itself in the middle of the 70s. An initial revival in the early 80s, for acts such as Weapon Of Peace and Sector 27, ran out of steam. However, later in the decade it was once again resuscitated for house artists, many of whom were influenced by the 60s' musical idealism, like **Tears For Fears**, **James** and the **House Of Love**.

Fontana, Carl

b. 18 July 1928, Monroe, Louisiana, USA, d. 9 October 2003, Las Vegas, Nevada, USA. As a teenager Fontana played trombone in a band led by his father, then joined **Woody Herman** in 1952. Subsequent big band stints came with **Lionel Hampton** and **Stan Kenton**. In the late 50s he worked with **Kai Winding**'s four-trombone band. He spent most of the 60s working in house bands in Las Vegas but returned briefly to Herman for a world tour. In the early and mid-70s he was in **Supersax** and was co-leader with **Jake Hanna** of the Hanna-Fontana Band. An enormously resourceful and inventive soloist, Fontana combined a phenomenal technique with a beautiful tone that he ably demonstrated on 'A Beautiful Friendship', recorded with Hanna at the 1975 Concord Jazz Festival. He was equally at home in a roaring big band and small groups with bebop or Dixieland orientation but was at his rhapsodic best in mainstream bands where he was given plenty of solo space.

● ALBUMS: with Jake Hanna *Live At Concord* (Concord Jazz 1975) ★★★, *The Great Fontana* (Uptown 1985) ★★★★, with the Bobby Shew Quintet *Heavyweights* (MAMA 1996) ★★★★, with Jiggs Whigham *Nice 'N' Easy* (TNC 1999) ★★★, with Joni Janak *The Wind* (JLE 2001) ★★★, with the Hungarian Jazz Trombone Company *First Time Together* (Budapest 2002) ★★★.

Fontana, D.J.

b. Dominic James Fontana, 15 March 1931, Shreveport, Louisiana, USA. Fontana says that his cousin's drums were the only instruments to hand when he was young, so he played them. He started in cocktail lounges and became the drummer for the country music radio show, *The Louisiana*

Hayride. He was placed behind a curtain as many country fans (and musicians!) were suspicious of the instrument. Fontana impressed **Elvis Presley** who appeared on the show with **Scotty Moore** (guitar) and **Bill Black** (double bass) on 16 October 1954, and he became a part of Presley's touring band on a regular basis the following year. The drummer on Presley's **Sun Records** recordings was Johnny Bernero, but starting with 'Heartbreak Hotel', Fontana recorded with Presley when he moved to **RCA Records** in 1956. He played on 'Hound Dog', 'Don't Be Cruel', 'Jailhouse Rock' and the majority of his early hits. On December 1968's *Elvis TV Special*, Fontana played a guitar case as there was no rooms for drums on the stage: 'Who cares?' he said, 'I'd done it before. That sound on 'All Shook Up' is the back of a guitar case, not a drum.' He played drums on **Ringo Starr**'s Nashville album, *Beaucoups Of Blues*, and also played for a stripper in the Robert Altman movie, *Nashville*. He has written his memoirs, *D.J. Fontana Remembers Elvis*, and in recent years, he has made several appearances including UK tours with Moore and **Charlie Gracie**. In 1997 Fontana linked up with Moore and guest artists including the **Band**, **Steve Earle**, **Jeff Beck** and **Keith Richards** to record *All The King's Men*.

● ALBUMS: with Scotty Moore *All The King's Men* (Sweetfish/Polydor 1997) ★★★.

● DVD/VIDEOS: *Scotty Moore & D.J. Fontana Live In Concert* (1993).

● FURTHER READING: *D.J. Fontana Remembers Elvis*, J.D. Fontana.

Fontana, Wayne

b. Glyn Ellis, 28 October 1945, Manchester, England. After changing his name in honour of **Elvis Presley**'s drummer **D.J. Fontana**, Wayne was signed to the appropriately named Fontana Records by A&R head Jack Baverstock. Wayne's backing group, the **Mindbenders** from the horror film of the same name, were as accomplished as their leader and provided a gritty accompaniment. Their first minor hit was with the unremarkable Hello Josephine' in 1963. Specializing in mild R&B covers, the group finally broke through with their fifth release, the **Major Lance** cover 'Um, Um, Um, Um, Um, Um', which reached number 5 in the UK. The 1965 follow-up, 'The Game Of Love', hit number 2 and spearheaded a Kennedy Street Enterprises Manchester invasion of the USA that lifted the group to number 1. Thereafter, the group struggled, with 'Just A Little Bit Too Late' and the below par 'She Needs Love' being their only further hits. In October 1965 Fontana decided to pursue a solo career, first recording the **Bert Berns** and **Jerry Ragovoy** ballad 'It Was Easier To Hurt Her' before finding success with **Jackie Edwards**' catchy 'Come On Home'. Erratic progress followed, with only the **Graham Gouldman** composition 'Pamela Pamela' breaking a run of misses. After giving up music during the early 70s, Fontana joined the revivalist circuit, although his progress was frequently dogged by personal problems.

● ALBUMS: *Wayne Fontana And The Mindbenders* (Fontana 1965) ★★★, *The Game Of Love* (Fontana 1965) ★★★, *Eric, Rick Wayne And Bob* (Fontana 1966) ★★★, *Wayne One* (Fontana 1966) ★★, *Wayne Fontana* (MGM 1967) ★★.

● COMPILATIONS: *Hit Single Anthology* (Fontana 1991) ★★★, *The Best Of Wayne Fontana & The Mindbenders*

(PolyGram 1994) ★★★, *The World Of Wayne Fontana & The Mindbenders* (Spectrum 1996) ★★★.

Fontane Sisters

The line-up of this close-harmony 50s US vocal group, whose initial success was achieved by making cover versions of black R&B records, comprised Marge Rosse (b. New Milford, New Jersey, USA; lead), Bea Rosse (b. New Milford, New Jersey, USA; low harmony) and Geri Rosse (b. New Milford, New Jersey, USA; harmony). Their mother was a choral director and organist. After leaving high school they joined an all-girl troupe and went on an eight-month tour. Later, they were joined by their brother Frank on guitar and appeared on radio and in theatres and clubs. After Frank was killed in World War II, the girls re-formed in 1944 as a trio and worked for several years on **Perry Como**'s radio and television shows; they also backed him on several records, including the US number 1 hits 'You're Adorable' and 'Hoop-Dee-Doo'. Signed to **RCA-Victor Records** in 1949, they had several minor hits in the early 50s, including 'Tennessee Waltz', 'Let Me In' (with Texas Jim Robertson) and 'Cold, Cold Heart'. In 1954 they switched to **Dot Records**, a label that specialized in making cover versions of established hits, and came under the influence of Dot's musical director, **Billy Vaughn**, who, with his orchestra, provided the backing for most of their successful records. Early that year, they made the US charts with 'Happy Days And Lonely Nights', a 1929 song by **Fred Fisher** and **Billy Rose**, and in December 1954 they went to number 1 with 'Hearts Of Stone'. The original version was the debut disc of the R&B Cincinnati group **Otis Williams And The Charms**. Other successful cover versions of black artists' records included 'Rock Love', 'Rollin' Stone' (original by the Marigolds) and 'Eddie My Love' (originally by the **Teen Queens**). Other 'white' cover versions included **Boyd Bennett** And His Rockets' 'Seventeen', which the Fontanes took to number 3 in the US chart, and 'Daddy-O', a song said to have been inspired by a character in the 1955 movie *Blackboard Jungle*, and which was originally a US Top 20 hit for **Bonnie Lou**. The Fontanes' 1957 version of 'Banana Boat Song' also made the Top 20 but was prevented from rising higher by a version by the **Tarriers**; another version, by **Steve Lawrence**, was his first chart entry. By the late 50s, with more and more black artists reaching the charts themselves, the Fontanes faded from their position as one of the top girl groups of the 50s. Their last two hits, 'Chanson D'Amour' and 'Jealous Heart', came in 1958.

● ALBUMS: *The Fontanes Sing* (Dot 1956) ★★★, *A Visit With The Fontane Sisters* (Dot 1957) ★★★, *Tips Of My Fingers* (1963) ★★.

● COMPILATIONS: *Rock Love* (Charly 1984) ★★★, *Rock Again Love* (Charly 1986) ★★★, *Hearts Of Stone* (Varèse Sarabande 1994) ★★★★.

Fontenot, Allen

b. 1932, Ville Platte, near Grand Prairie, Evangeline Parish, Louisiana, USA. One of many members of the Fontenot family to establish a reputation in Cajun music, Allen, who has been described as 'a squat, chain-smoking fiddler from Ville Platte', learned to play in his early teens. He became engrossed with the music, but, although playing at local dances for many years, he earned his living collecting outstanding bills for a local company. In the early 70s, he decided to form his Country Cajuns, which consisted of

Leroy Veilloa (concertina), Darrel Brasseaux (drums), Hudson Dauzat (guitar) and non-Cajun John Scott (bass). They played a mixture of old and new Cajun numbers, genuine hillbilly music and occasional swamp-pop. They had a regular radio show, played fairs and festivals and made a film appearance in 1975's *Hard Times* and played on several major television shows including *Austin City Limits*. The publicity gained with his band led Fontenot to become a very popular disc jockey on WSDL Slidell, Louisiana. Around 1977, he opened his club, the Cajun Bandstand, on Airline Highway in Kenner, which, until 1982, when he sold it, was the closest Cajun club to New Orleans. The Country Cajuns played the venue, and it was regularly packed with students, tourists and Cajun couples who delighted in using the large dancefloor and partaking of the Cajun food and drinks available at the venue, Fontenot recorded for Antilles and Delta before retiring from active playing.

● ALBUMS: *Jole Blon And Other Cajun Honky Songs* (Delta 1981) ★★★, *Old Fais Do Do Songs* (Delta 1982) ★★★, *Arrets Pas La Musique* (Ralph 1997) ★★★.

Fontenot, Canray

b. 16 October 1922, Basille, Louisiana, USA, d. 29 July 1995, Welsh, Louisiana, USA. Fontenot's musical apprenticeship came from the teachings of his father, the accordion player Adam Fontenot. His chosen instrument was the violin, and during his long career he became one of its greatest practitioners in the Acadian/Creole tradition. His first professional work came as a member of **Amadie Ardoin**'s band, one of the most famous and popular early Cajun performers. Fontenot's contribution to that success was rewarded in the early 60s when the folk community adopted him as a founding father, and he was invited to appear at the Newport Folk Festival. He was widely acknowledged by Cajun fiddlers such as Michael Doucet (**Beausoleil**) and D'Jaima Garnier during this time as a pivotal influence on the music's development. However, as in his earlier days, Fontenot never became a full-time musician, working also as a rice farmer and feed store employee. This helped finance records for **Arhoolie Records**, which in the 90s included *Louisiana Hot Sauce*, his final recording. He died of cancer after a long illness in 1995.

● ALBUMS: *Louisiana Hot Sauce, Creole Style* (Arhoolie 1993) ★★★, with Bois-Sec Ardoin *Cajun & Creole Masters* recorded 1987 (Music Of The World 1996) ★★★★.

Foo Fighters

The Foo Fighters were formed at the end of 1994 by former Scream and **Nirvana** drummer Dave Grohl (b. 14 January 1969, Warren, Ohio, USA), now switched to guitar and vocals. There was some conjecture that the Nirvana bass player Krist Novoselic would join him in this venture, but Grohl eventually recruited Pat Smear (b. 5 August 1959; guitar, ex-**Germs** and a 'fourth' member of Nirvana during their later career), Nate Mendel (b. 2 December 1968, Seattle, Washington, USA; bass) and William Goldsmith (b. 4 July 1972, Seattle, Washington, USA; drums). The latter pair had previously played with Seattle band **Sunny Day Real Estate**. Their debut single, 'This Is A Call', was released on Roswell/**Capitol Records** in June 1995. The Foo Fighters' arrival initiated intense A&R activity, but Grohl opted for Capitol through the auspices of Gary Gersh, who had been Nirvana's A&R representative at **Geffen Records**.

With media expectations weighing heavily on the project, analysis of the band's debut album focused on tracks such as 'I'll Stick Around', which some alleged was an attack on Cobain's widow, **Courtney Love**. Both the song's title and its lyrical refrain ('I don't owe you anything') seemed to pursue some form of personal exorcism, but it was hard to argue against the sheer impact of Grohl's new canon of songs. Detractors pointed at the similarity to Nirvana in the stop-start construction of several tracks, and Grohl's inability on occasion to match Cobain's evocation of mood. However, the simplicity of execution added greatly to the immediacy of the project. Grohl's original demos had simply been remixed rather than glossed over by a new production, and the result was, on the whole, enthralling. Goldsmith left the band during the recording of their second album and was replaced by Taylor Hawkins from **Alanis Morissette**'s touring band. Although the critics were waiting to pounce on *The Colour And The Shape*, it was another hard and tough album of blistering, paced songs, which were lightened by the band's great grasp of melody—songs such as 'Monkey Wrench' and 'My Poor Brain' burst into life in the middle eight. Smear left the band following the album's release and was later replaced by Franz Stahl (ex-Scream). In 1998 Grohl recorded the soundtrack to Paul Schrader's *Touch*. Stahl left in June 1999, shortly before the release of yet another strong set *There Is Nothing Left To Lose*, the band's first album for **RCA Records**. The recording of their fourth album was delayed by the various members outside interests, the most notable of which was Grohl's membership of **Queens Of The Stone Age**. Released in 2002, *One By One* proved to be another storming record full of hair-raising hooks and powerful melodies. Plans for an ambitious double album intrigued critics when it was announced that one full disc would be a gentle acoustic recording. When *In Your Honour* was finally issued in 2005, the wholly satisfying acoustic set did contain piano, drums and occasional string accompaniments. Together with the more familiar sounding second album the Foo Fighters took their career to another level; higher and even better.

● ALBUMS: *Foo Fighters* (Roswell/Capitol 1995) ★★★★, *The Colour And The Shape* (Roswell/Capitol 1997) ★★★★, *There Is Nothing Left To Lose* (Roswell/RCA 1999) ★★★, *One By One* (Roswell/RCA 2002) ★★★★, *In Your Honour* (Roswell/RCA 2005) ★★★★.

● DVD/VIDEOS: *Low* (RCA 2003), *Everywhere But Home* (RCA 2003).

● FURTHER READING: *Dave Grohl: Foo Fighters, Nirvana & Other Misadventures*, Martin James.

Food

In the late 90s, a chance meeting between British saxophonist-composer **Iain Ballamy** (b. 20 February 1964, Guildford, Surrey, England) and Norwegian drummer Thomas Strønen led to collaboration between them and two other Norwegians, trumpeter Arve Henriksen and bass player Mats Eilersten. The music the quartet creates is an intriguing blend of melodic romanticism and dramatic free jazz. Although the music created by the four is original, there is about it a hauntingly stark ambience that reflects the studied austerity of much contemporary Scandinavian music. Contributing to a sometimes ethereal atmosphere, all four musicians make regular use of electronics. Ballamy has expressed the view that the term *jazz* does not adequately describe Food's music, preferring instead to stress the broader range offered by describing the band's repertoire as 'adventurous, improvised' music. The mix includes not only elements of post-free jazz and Scandinavian folk themes but also hints of archaic religious music that underpin the soaring flights of fancy. By the time of their fourth album, 2004's *Last Supper*, Food had fully realized its early potential as a thoroughly original and consistently rewarding band.

● ALBUMS: *Food* (Feral 1999) ★★★★, *Organic And GM Food* (Feral 2001) ★★★, *Veggie* (Rune Grammofon 2002) ★★★, *Last Supper* (Rune Grammofon 2004) ★★★★.

Food Records

This UK record label was formed by David Balfe (ex-**Big In Japan**, the **Teardrop Explodes** manager) in 1984, and its first release was **Brilliant**'s single 'Soul Murder'. However, it was with the arrival of economics graduate and *Sounds* journalist Andy Ross (b. 31 January 1956) that the label was given a figurehead. Ross conducted the day-to-day running of the label, which focused on those bands linked with the 'indie' sector that had the greatest commercial potential (both Balfe and Ross would become comanagers of **Voice Of The Beehive**, an outfit they discovered playing above the Enterprise pub in Chalk Farm, London). The earliest signings to Food also included **Diesel Park West** and **Crazyhead**, on the strength of which **EMI Records** first took a stake in the label in 1988. The arrival of **Jesus Jones** the following year was instrumental in the long-term success of the label. By this time Food's second strongest outfit were **Blur**. Their number 8-peaking single 'There's No Other Way' gave the label its first significant success. By 1991 Jesus Jones' debut album had entered the chart at number 1 and the future looked bright. However, as Jesus Jones' success tailed off, Blur too found themselves unable to live up to expectations. When Balfe rejected their second album *Modern Life Is Rubbish* (correctly, in hindsight), it marred the label's relationship with the band; but for Ross' intervention, Blur was about to leave the label. Instead Balfe jumped ship, electing to return to management with Voice Of The Beehive and selling his shares to EMI (he was later the target of Blur's ire on their chart-topping single 'Country House'). Ross' belief in Blur was vindicated by the enormous subsequent success of **Parklife**, though **Shampoo** also offered huge commercial reward, going double platinum in Japan. Other bands such as Sensitize and Whirlpool proved less successful, but that did not stop the label investing in new talent, including Planet Claire, **Dubstar**, and **Idlewild**. Food Records was effectively put out to pasture following the end of the label's contract with EMI in August 2001.

● COMPILATIONS: *Food 100* (Food 1997) ★★★.

Foort, Lucien

b. 25 November 1969, Dordrecht, Netherlands. Foort is a respected DJ/producer based in Rotterdam whose 'progressive' **house** tracks have appeared on mix compilations by world-renowned DJs such as **Sasha**, **Nick Warren**, **Seb Fontaine** and **John Digweed**. Musically trained, Foort is a saxophonist as well as a DJ. He was inspired by hearing Sasha and Digweed play at London's **Ministry Of Sound** in 1994 and performed his first set at Club Carrera in Rotterdam in the same year. He has recorded numerous tracks as Funk Function, Groove Delight and Dutch Liquid. His remix work for labels such as Digweed's Bedrock, **Postiva Records**, 3 Beat, Cyber and **React Music**, in addition to two mix compilations

for the United label, have helped raise his international profile and to secure Foort regular appearances at the UK's **Gatecrasher**.

● COMPILATIONS: *Singularity 1* (United 2000) ★★★; *Singularity 2* (United 2001) ★★★.

Foot In Coldwater, A
(see **A Foot In Coldwater**)

Foote, Irene
(see **Castle, Vernon And Irene**)

Footlight Parade

Following their highly successful teaming in *42nd Street* and *Gold Diggers* of 1932, **Dick Powell** and **Ruby Keeler** were joined by a new boy to musicals—**James Cagney**—in this backstage saga which was released by Warner Brothers in 1933. Cagney plays a slick, hyperactive dance director of 'prologues', those miniature 'live' productions which were inserted between showings of main feature movies in the early days of the talkies. In Manuel Seff and James Seymour's screenplay for *Footlight Parade*, Chester Kent (Cagney) stages three of these creations, each of which has its own title song. The first, a somewhat saucy piece entitled 'Honeymoon Hotel' (**Harry Warren**-**Al Dubin**), is thought to be a follow-up from the 'Shuffle Off To Buffalo' number in *42nd Street*. Just married Powell and Keeler arrive at the hotel (where every guest's name is 'Smith'!), only to find their entire family is there to greet them. 'By A Waterfall' (**Sammy Fain**-Irving Kahal) is a dream sequence during which Powell and Keeler 'imagine' scores of beautiful girls swimming and relaxing in a gigantic pool that had glass sides so that head of photography George Barnes could shoot the scene from all angles. The 'five tier' finalé rounds off one of the most spectacular production numbers of any film musical. The final 'prologue', the dramatic 'Shanghai Lil' (Warren-Dubin), sees Cagney as a sailor, scouring Shanghai saloons and opium dens for his Lil (Keeler). When he finds her in a sleazy club, they perform a tap dance atop the bar before he is called back to his ship, accompanied by a sailor who looks remarkably like . . . Shanghai Lil. Fain and Kahal also contributed 'Sittin' On A Backyard Fence' and 'Ah, The Moon Is Here'. Among the rest of the cast were **Joan Blondell**, Guy Kibbee, Frank McHugh, Claire Dodd, Ruth Donnelly and Hugh Herbert. *Footlight Parade*, which was directed by Lloyd Bacon and choreographed by **Busby Berkeley** in his own highly innovative style, remains one of the most memorable of all movie musicals.

Footloose

Always on the lookout for deep psychological meanings, even in something as frivolous as a film musical, some critics saw this movie as an attempt to combine the frustrations of *Rebel Without A Cause* with the more recent disco-style *Flashdance*. On a less pretentious level and prefaced by an exciting opening sequence of dancing feet moving to urgent, restless rhythms, Dean Pitchford's screenplay concerns Ethel and Ren MacCormack (Frances Lee McCain and Kevin Bacon), a mother and son who arrive in the small midwestern US town of Bomont. Once there, they discover that owing to the influence of the 'hellfire' local preacher, the Reverend Shaw Moore (John Lithgow), rock 'n' roll music, dancing and certain forms of literature, are banned. Big city boy Ren not only refuses to abide by these 'unreasonable' laws, he also attracts the attention of Ariel Moore (Lori Singer), the preacher's daughter, and with friends Willard (Chris Penn) and Rusty (Sarah Jessica Parker), they go to a disco over the state line. On the return journey, it turns out that during a similar trip around five years ago, Ariel's brother—the preacher's son—was killed, thereby invoking the town disco ban. From then on, there is much burning of library books, re-examining of actions and beliefs and establishing of mutual respect before Ren is eventually allowed to organize a dance—outside the town limits. Dianne Wiest, John Laughlin, and Elizabeth Gorcey, Jim Youngs, Douglas Dirkson, Lynne Marta and Arthur Rosenberg were also amongst the cast, and most of the appealing songs, such as 'Footloose' and 'I'm Free (Heaven Helps The Man)' (performed by **Kenny Loggins**), 'The Girl Gets Around' (**Sammy Hagar**), 'Dancing In The Streets' (**Shalamar**), 'Holding Out For A Hero' (**Bonnie Tyler**), 'Never' (**Moving Pictures**), 'Somebody's Eyes' (**Karla Bonoff**), 'Let's Hear It For The Boy' (**Deniece Williams**), 'Almost Paradise . . . Love Theme From Footloose' (Mike Reno and Ann Wilson, lead singers of **Loverboy** and **Heart**, respectively), were written by lyricist Dean Pitchford, in collaboration with Loggins, Hagar, Bill Wolfer, **Jim Steinman**, Michael Gore, Tom Snow and **Eric Carmen**. The rest of the numbers included 'Waiting For A Girl Like You', by **Mick Jones** and **Lou Gramm**, performed by **Foreigner**, 'Hurts So Good', by **John Mellencamp** and George Green, performed by Mellencamp, and 'Bang Your Head (Mental Health)', by Carlos and Tony Cavazo, Kevin DuBrow and Frankie Banali, performed by **Quiet Riot**. Directed by veteran Hollywood choreographer-director Herbert Ross, choreographed by Lynne Taylor-Corbett, this likeable 1984 Paramount release was a box office hit, grossing $34 million in the USA and Canada alone. The soundtrack album spent 10 weeks at the top of the US charts, and both 'Footloose' (Loggins) and 'Let's Hear It For The Boy' (Deniece Williams) went to number 1 and were nominated for Oscars. Mike Reno and Ann Wilson's 'Almost Paradise' also charted.

On 22 October 1998 a $6.5 million stage version of *Footloose* opened at the **Richard Rodgers** Theatre in New York. Adapted by Dean Pitchford and director Walter Bobbie from Pitchford's original screenplay, it had Stephen Lee Anderson (Rev. Shaw Moore), Jeremy Kushnier (Ren McCormack), Catherine Cox (Ethel McCormack), Jennifer Laura Thompson (Ariel Moore), Dee Hoty (Vi Moore, Ariel's mother), Stacy Francis (Rusty), Billy Hartung (Chuck Cranston) and Tom Plotkin (Willard Hewitt). Several of the film songs were retained, including those three former chart entries, with Pitchford and composer Tom Snow providing some new material, 'On Any Sunday', 'I Can't Stand Still', 'Learning To Be Silent', 'Heaven Help Me', 'Still Rockin'', 'Can You Find It In Your Heart?', 'Mama Says', 'Dancing Is Not A Crime' and 'I Confess'. Initial critical reaction compared it unfavourably with the movie.

For Carnation, The
(see **The For Carnation**)

For Love Not Lisa
This guitar-based alternative rock band was formed in Oklahoma, USA, in 1990 by guitarist Miles, vocalist/guitarist Mike Lewis, bass player Doug Carrion and drummer Aaron Preston. They relocated to Los Angeles in mid-1991, although they soon moved away from the culture shock of the Hollywood scene and signed a major recording contract while steering well clear of the notorious pay-to-play clubs. *Merge* was an effective debut, mixing punk and rock influences into a varied style with good songwriting. The band backed up the record with live shows, during which they revealed an experimental side, including Lewis' unusual penchant for ad-libbing most of his lyrics. However, the question on many critics' lips was whether For Love Not Lisa could rise above the glut of major label, grunge-flavoured bands signed in **Nirvana** and **Pearl Jam**'s wake.
- ALBUMS: *Merge* (EastWest 1993) ★★★.

For Me And My Gal
If asked to name **Judy Garland**'s most famous movie partner, most people would plump for **Mickey Rooney**, but her partnership with **Gene Kelly** in films like this one, together with *Summer Stock* and *The Pirate*, were just as endearing in their way. *For Me And My Gal*, released by MGM in 1942, was Kelly's first film appearance, although he arrived on set at the age of 30 direct from his success in the title role of **Richard Rodgers** and **Lorenz Hart**'s Broadway musical *Pal Joey*. In this film, which had a screenplay by **Richard Sherman**, Fred Finklehoffe and Sid Silvers, Kelly is cast as Harry Palmer, an ambitious vaudeville song-and-dance-man who falls for Jo Hayden (Garland). They form a double act and dream of winning the ultimate prize—a chance to perform at the Palace Theatre. However, when they eventually achieve their goal, World War I looms large, and Kelly receives his draft notice. Desperate not to miss his big career chance, he deliberately cripples his hand. His actions help him to avoid the draft but appall Garland, and they split up. After suffering a crisis of conscience, Kelly travels overseas to entertain the troops, and while there becomes something of a hero. His moral transformation complete, the couple are reunited on the stage of the Palace Theatre after the war. **George Murphy** costarred, and also featured were Marta Eggerth, Ben Blue, Horace (later Stephen) McNally, Keenan Wynn and Richard Quine. Garland and Kelly sang a delightful version of 'For Me And My Gal' (**Edgar Leslie–Ray E. Goetz–George W. Meyer**), and the rest of the score—a substantial collection of memorable old numbers—included 'When You Wore A Tulip And I Wore A Big Red Rose' (Jack Mahoney–**Percy Wenrich**), 'After You've Gone' (**Turner Layton–Henry Creamer**) 'Ballin' The Jack' (Jim Burris–Chris Smith), 'Oh You Beautiful Doll' (Seymour Brown–**Nat D. Ayer**), 'How Ya Gonna Keep 'Em Down On The Farm?' (**Walter Donaldson–Sam M. Lewis–Joe Young**) and 'It's A Long, Long Way To Tipperary' (Harry Williams–Jack Judge). The many dance sequences were staged by Bobby Connelly (with uncredited assistance from Kelly), and the film, which was a product of **Arthur Freed**'s legendary MGM unit, was directed by **Busby Berkeley**.

For Squirrels
A quartet of Jack Vigliatura (vocals), Bill White (bass), Jack Greigo (drums) and Travis Tooke (bass), For Squirrels were busy making a firm impression on the US alternative rock circuit when their rise was marred by tragedy. In August 1995 the group was travelling between venues when they were involved in a road accident that killed both Vigliatura and White. Greigo also suffered a broken back in the carnage.

The incident occurred on the eve of the release of their debut album for 550 Music/Sony Records, *Example*. Despite the tragedy, the two living members of the band decided to countenance its release. They also announced their decision to continue with the band after they had recruited new members.

● ALBUMS: *Example* (550/Sony 1995) ★★★.

Foran, Dick

b. John Nicholas Foran, 18 June 1910, Flemington, New Jersey, USA, d. 10 August 1979, Panorama City, California, USA. Foran, the son of a US senator, studied geology at Princeton University. He worked briefly as a Pennsylvania Railroad investigator before a desire to sing in films led him to Hollywood. In 1934 he made his debut in *Gentlemen Are Born*, and in 1935 he appeared with **Shirley Temple** in the musical *Stand Up And Cheer*. He first appeared as a singing cowboy (complete with his palomino, Smoke) for Warner Brothers in *Moonlight On The Prairie*, late in 1935, thus becoming the second of the genre (**Gene Autry** beat him when *Tumbling Tumbleweeds* was released two months earlier). Between 1935 and 1937, Foran, Warner's only singing cowboy, starred in 12 B-westerns, including *Cowboy From Brooklyn* (1937), before moving to Universal in 1938, where he appeared in a variety of roles and two western serials, *Winners Of The West* (1940) and *Riders In Death Valley* (1941). The same year, he appeared with the **Sons Of The Pioneers** in the radio series *Ten-Two-Four Ranch*. His successes as a singing cowboy were few when compared to Autry, but his acting ability saw him in various roles in well over 100 films, the last being in 1967. During the 50s, he also appeared in many television productions. Although he had had operatic training, his singing was readily accepted by his western audiences.

Forbert, Steve

b. 15 December 1954, Meridian, Mississippi, USA. Forbert played guitar and harmonica in local rock bands before moving to New York in 1976. There he busked at Grand Central Station before making his first recordings in 1977 for Nemperor and was briefly heralded as 'the new [**Bob**] **Dylan**' because of the tough poetry of his lyrics. Forbert's biggest commercial success came when he had a Top 20 hit with 'Romeo's Tune' (1979). After four albums, his contract was terminated. For most of the 80s and 90s, Forbert was based in Nashville, songwriting and playing concerts around the South with a touring group including Danny Counts (bass), Paul Errico (keyboards) and Bobby Lloyd Hicks (drums). His 1988 album for **Geffen Records** had Garry Tallent from **Bruce Springsteen**'s E Street Band as producer. **Nils Lofgren** was a guest musician.

After a four-year gap, Forbert returned with the highly praised *The American In Me*, produced by **Pete Anderson**. He switched labels once again to record *Mission Of The Crossroad Palms* and *Rocking Horse Head*, two well-crafted collections of mature, roots rock material that confirmed Forbert as one of America's most celebrated singer-songwriters. He also began to attract the attention of the burgeoning alt country movement and responded to the challenge with 2000's excellent studio album *Evergreen Boy* and the following year's *Live At The Bottom Line*.

● ALBUMS: *Alive On Arrival* (Nemperor/Epic 1978) ★★★, *Jackrabbit Slim* (Nemperor/Epic 1979) ★★★, *Little Stevie Orbit* (Nemperor/Epic 1980) ★★★, *Steve Forbert* (Nemperor/Epic 1982) ★★, *Streets Of This Town* (Geffen 1988) ★★★, *The American In Me* (Geffen 1992) ★★★★, *Be Here Now: Solo Live* (Rolling Tide 1994) ★★★, *Mission Of The Crossroad Palms* (Giant 1995) ★★★, *In Concert* 1982 recording (King Biscuit Flower Hour 1995) ★★★, *Rocking Horse Head* (Giant 1996) ★★★, with the Rough Squirrels *Here's Your Pizza* 1987 recording (Paladin 1998) ★★★, *Be Here Again Live Solo 1998* (Rolling Tide 1998) ★★★, *Evergreen Boy* (Koch 2000) ★★★★, *Acoustic Live: The WFUV Concert* (Rolling Tide 2000) ★★★, with the Rough Squirrels *Live At The Bottom Line* (Koch 2001) ★★★, *Any Old Time: Songs Of Jimmie Rodgers* (Koch 2002) ★★★, *Just Like There's Nothin' To It* (Koch 2004) ★★★.

● COMPILATIONS: *The Best Of Steve Forbert: What Kinda Guy?* (Columbia/Legacy 1993) ★★★★, *Young, Guitar Days* (Madacy/Relentless 2001) ★★★, *More Young, Guitar Days* (Rolling Tide/Southbound 2002) ★★★, *Rock While I Can Rock: The Geffen Years* (Geffen 2003) ★★★★.

Forbes, Alric

b. 16 January 1951, Mandeville, Jamaica, West Indies, d. 19 June 1998, Seattle, Washington, USA. Forbes was educated and raised in Mandeville prior to embarking on a career as a metalsmith. His love of music led to the formation of the Divine Brothers, alongside Peter Peart and Vincent Hammond, with whom he performed prior to joining Vivian 'Yabby You' Jackson and Dada Smith in the Prophets. In 1972 the trio recorded 'Conquering Lion', which was curiously credited to Vivian Jackson And The Rolfe Brothers. The song proved especially popular amongst the Rastafarian community, although the artists' efforts were not sufficiently rewarded. A period of inactivity followed until 1974 when the trio recorded a variation on a Pocomania hymn, 'Run Come Rally', alongside the favoured 'Jah Vengeance'. The success of the singles led to the release of *Conquering Lion* in Jamaica. The album surfaced in the UK through **Dennis Harris**' Eve subsidiary, albeit with a slight variation, as *Ram A Dam*. The Prophets continued recording through to the late 70s, although it was Jackson that achieved distinctive notability. In 1979, demonstrating an individual stance, Forbes launched his own label in Jamaica. The free market condition on the island resulted in the Forbes label being an ephemeral venture, although his solo debut, the sublime 'Morning Train', made a significant impression in the pre charts. By 1984 Forbes was recruited to perform in the **Gladiators**, following **Clinton Fearon**'s departure, by virtue of his decision to pursue other interests. Forbes toured the USA and Canada with the group where he was also employed as the group's bass player on recording sessions. Forbes performed alongside Albert Griffith, Melvin Reed and Donald Sutherland until 1987, by which time Fearon had been reinstated. Forbes was reunited with the band on a US tour featuring both the Gladiators and **Ethiopians**. He joined the tour providing his skills as a lead guitarist where he providing backing for both groups. The tour culminated in the formation of the Defenders, whose line-up featured Winston Cathy, Clinton Rufus and Charlie Morgan alongside Forbes and Fearon. The band remained together for five years before Fearon left to form his own Boogie Brown Band. Forbes remained in Seattle where he had reputedly recorded two obscure solo CDs. In January 1998 Forbes checked into a medical centre where chronic leukaemia was diagnosed.

Following his untimely demise an outpouring of glowing tributes praised his genuine altruistic nature.

● ALBUMS: *World Pride* (I&I Pride-uctions 1992) ★★★, *Earth For Creation* (I&I Pride-uctions 1997) ★★★.

Forbidden

Originally travelling under the moniker Forbidden Evil, this band was formed in San Francisco, California, USA, in 1985. Its original line-up comprised Russ Anderson (vocals), Glen Alvelais (guitar), Craig Locicero (guitar), Matt Camacho (bass) and Paul Bostaph (drums), with Rob Flynn also briefly a member before joining **Violence**. They quickly gained a strong following playing numerous support slots with more established Bay Area bands such as **Testament** and **Exodus**. Through their early demos the band signed to Combat Records (product was released in Europe on the Music For Nations subsidiary label, Under One Flag). Their name was truncated to Forbidden, while the full title was saved for their debut long-player, *Forbidden Evil*. This arrived in 1988 to critical acclaim within the Bay Area thrash community and some of the mainstream metal magazines. They toured Europe in support of the release during 1989, appearing at the Dynamo Open Air Festival in Holland. This was recorded and the subsequent live album, *Raw Evil At The Dynamo*, was released the same year. During preparation for their next studio album, Glen Alvelais left the band but was replaced by ex-Militia guitarist Tim Calvert in time for the recordings. *Twisted Into Form*, released in 1990, was again received well by the media, with its blend of hard-hitting thrash metal, cleverly structured songs and excellent guitar interplay. The band's long-term impact was then dealt a blow by a split between Megaforce and **Atlantic Records**, which left them without an outlet for much of the early 90s (they later signed to German label Gun). On *Distortion* drummer Steve Jacobs joined Camacho, Locicero, Calvert and Anderson on a set that included a cover version of **King Crimson**'s '21st Century Schizoid Man' as well as powerful new originals. Following a final release, *Green*, the group disbanded. Camacho, Locicero and Jacobs formed Manmade God, Anderson worked on his Parking Lot Prophets project, and Calvert joined **Nevermore**.

● ALBUMS: *Forbidden Evil* (Combat/Under One Flag 1988) ★★★, *Raw Evil At The Dynamo* mini-album (Combat/Under One Flag 1989) ★★★, *Twisted Into Form* (Combat/Under One Flag 1990) ★★★, *Distortion* (Gun/Massacre 1994) ★★★, *Green* (Gun/Pavement 1997) ★★★.

● COMPILATIONS: *Point Of No Return: The Best Of Forbidden* (Combat/Under One Flag 1992) ★★★★.

Forbidden Broadway

An annual revue conceived by Gerard Alessandrini, who also writes his own, sometimes hilarious lyrics to popular show tunes in an effort to lampoon everything and anyone who dares to appear on the New York and London musical stage. The show was first performed as a cabaret revue at Palsson's Supper Club in New York on 15 January 1982. It moved off-Broadway in the following year and settled in the 125-seater Theatre East. Annual editions have followed. Alessandrini's early targets included **Annie** and **Evita** (**Andrew Lloyd Webber** and **Tim Rice** were like manna from heaven to this revue), along with Broadway icons such as **Ethel Merman**, **Mary Martin**, **Stephen Sondheim** and **Tommy Tune**. Later, highlights included 'The Ladies Who Screech' by 'Elaine Stritch'; 'My

Souvenir Things', sung by '**Cameron Mackintosh**' as he flogs T-shirts and coffee mugs; 'I've Strained In Vain To Train **Madonna**'s Brain' (a hint of **My Fair Lady**?); 'I Get A Kick Out Of Me' by '**Patti LuPone**'; shades of **On The Town** and a dig at the celebrated director-choreographer **Jerome Robbins** in 'Jerome, Jerome, I'm A Hell Of A Guy'; '**Julie Andrews**'' 'I Couldn't Hit That Note' (to the tune of 'I Could Have Danced All Night'); a chandelier and a helicopter, representing **The Phantom Of The Opera** and **Miss Saigon**, in the merry duet 'Anywhere You Can Fly, I Can Fly Higher' (from **Irving Berlin**'s 'Anything You Can Do, I Can Do Better'); and another stab at Lloyd Webber in which a **Michael Ball** clone converts the powerful ballad 'Love Changes Everything' (from **Aspects Of Love**) into 'I, I Sleep With Everyone'. **Michael Crawford**, **Barbra Streisand** and Broadway revivals such as **The Most Happy Fella**, **Guys And Dolls** and the more contemporary shows, especially **Les Misérables**, all get the treatment. The 1992 edition presented some of the 'Best' of the last decade, and in the following year the show won the 1993 Lucille Lortel Award for outstanding musical and was still going strong—blessed with four '**Carol Channing**s' (only two of which were female). Alessandrini's 1994 targets included **Kiss Of The Spider Woman**, **Blood Brothers**, **Sunset Boulevard** and **She Loves Me**. In 1989 a slightly Anglicized version had a brief run at London's Fortune Theatre, and a similar production, *Forbidden Pittsburgh*, which was not associated with Alessandrini, reigned in that city in the late 80s. In 1997 *Forbidden Broadway Strikes Back!* ('We shall steal a little bit of every show in our desire . . . to abuse them.') was hailed as Alessandrini's best effort and targeted the **Show Boat** (*Slow Boat*) revival, **Victor Victoria**, **Rent**, **State Fair**, **Titanic** and **Big** while 'accusing' Donna Murphy of allowing her bleak role in **Passion** to colour her later 'mumsy' one in **The King And I**. The marketing flair of Mackintosh ('the Napoleon of Broadway') still rankled, and his *Les Misérables* was still on the rack, to the tune of **Richard Rodgers**' 'My Favourite Things': 'Les Mis chocolates / Shaped like orphans / Patches for your sleeve / It costs one hundred dollars / To come see the show / And one hundred more to leave'. Delivering the goods were Bryan Batt, Donna English, Christine Pedi and David Hibbard. Batt returned for the 1998 edition, entitled *Forbidden Broadway Cleans Up Its Act!*, along with Lori Hammel, Edward Staudenmayer and Kristine Zbornik. Some of the other extremely talented cast members to have been involved with Alessandrini over the years include Tom Plotkin, Brad Ellis, Roxie Lucas, Susanne Blakeslee, Jeff Lyons, Michael McGrath, Mary Denise Bentley, Toni DiBuono, Brad Oscar, Craig Wells and Dorothy Kiara. A decade after failing to win over London audiences with its very own brand of sophisticated humour, in 1999 *Forbidden Broadway* tried again at the West End's Jermyn Street Theatre.

Force Inc

German label run by Achim Szepanski whose ethos is not timid: 'The philosophy is to play really energetic music, like punk where everything you say is squeezed into one moment'. Force Inc made its name with Exit 100's harsh 'Liquid' before Szepanski pulled the label away from the **acid house** direction with which it had become associated. Later releases invoked what the label termed 'Rauschen', or 'white noise', with a fusion of breakbeats and **techno**, the best example of which was undoubtedly Biochip C's *Hell's Bells* EP. The label's catalogue also features artists like Alec Empire, Jamin' Unit Vs Walker (whose *Egglayer* EP in 1992 was popular) and Space Cube. Force Inc set up an English office in 1993.

Force M.D.'s

Often neglected next to the adventures of **Afrika Bambaataa** or **Grandmaster Flash**, Force M.D.'s (from Staten Island, New York City) were nevertheless a vital component in the early 80s in rap's development. They were originally titled the LDs, working as a street-corner act in the manner of the **Jackson Five**, with Antoine 'TCD' Lundy, Stevie D, Trisco Pearson and Charles 'Mercury' Nelson holding the reigns. Alongside Planet Patrol, they were the first to instigate doo-wop hip-hop before changing tack to largely soul-based harmonies, which were an early influence on the **swingbeat** outfits of the late 80s and early 90s. They employed formation steps alongside breakdance routines as visual inducement, adding impersonations of television theme tunes and popular stars of the day, often performing on the Staten Island Ferry. They became Dr. Rock And The MCs when they were joined by a DJ of that title, introducing scratching into their nascent act (in his absence a DJ Shock would deputise). When they signed to **Tommy Boy Records** in 1984, they were billed simply as the Force M.D.'s (the M.D. component of the name is short for Musical Diversity). They enjoyed several R&B hits during the latter part of the decade, including the chart-topping 'Love Is A House'. Their pop career peaked with 1986's 'Tender Love', a US Top 10 ballad written by **Jimmy Jam** and **Terry Lewis**. Nelson and Pearson were replaced by Rodney 'Khalil' Lundy and Shaun Waters in 1990, but the premature death of Antoine Lundy was a sad loss.

● ALBUMS: *Love Letters* (Tommy Boy 1984) ★★★, *Chillin'* (Tommy Boy 1986) ★★★★, *Touch And Go* (Tommy Boy 1987) ★★★★, *Step To Me* (Tommy Boy 1990) ★★★.

● COMPILATIONS: *For Lovers And Others: Force M.D.'s Greatest Hits* (Tommy Boy 1992) ★★★, *Let Me Love You: The Greatest Hits* (Tommy Boy 2001) ★★★.

Ford, Anne Kerry

b. Anne Kerry, *c*.1960, Texas, USA. From the age of 12 Ford lived in Washington, DC, where she attended ballet school, then went to the Juilliard School of Drama, graduating four years later at the age of 20. She worked in classical theatre before being cast as Grace in *Annie*, appearing on Broadway for the first time in 1982. In 1984 she appeared in a play with the Olympic Arts Festival in Los Angeles and met guitarist **Robben Ford**, whom she married. Among her film appearances, usually in minor roles, are *Lovesick* (1983), *Time Bomb* (1984), *Clean And Sober* (1988) and *Fearless* (1993), while on television she appeared for several seasons on *Days Of Our Lives* and in individual episodes of several 80s series including *Hotel*, *Crazy Like A Fox*, *Mike Hammer* and *Murder, She Wrote*. Other stage work includes *Harry Chapin, Lies And Legends* in Chicago (also appearing on the cast album) and the poorly received 1990 Broadway production of *The Threepenny Opera* with **Sting**, **Maureen McGovern** and **K.T. Sullivan**.

In 1996, after a two-year break from performing, Ford made her cabaret debut at The Gardenia in Hollywood and also released her debut solo album. Early in 2000 she and her husband were featured artists with the West German Radio Orchestra in a tribute to **Kurt Weill** at the Philharmonic Hall in Cologne and other venues. The following year Ford reprised this material at the John Anson Ford Amphitheater in Los Angeles, this time with an American big band. That same venue was where she appeared in 2002 in *Blue Skies*, with her husband and pianist Russell Ferrante. A lively and entertaining artist, Ford has performed at many venues including the Cinegrill, the Jazz Bakery, and the Alex Theatre in Los Angeles, the Herbst Theatre and the Plush Room in San Francisco, New York's Town Hall, Sculler's in Boston and Blues Alley in Washington DC.

● ALBUMS: *In The Nest Of The Moon* (Illyria 1996) ★★★, *Something Wonderful—Songs Of Oscar Hammerstein And Stephen Sondheim* (LML Music 1998) ★★★.

● FILMS: *Lovesick* (1983), *Clean And Sober* (1988), *Fearless* (1993).

Ford, Benjamin Francis 'Whitey'
(see **Duke Of Paducah**)

Ford, Clinton

b. Ian George Stopford-Harrison, 4 November 1931, Salford, Lancashire, England. A popular singer in the UK during the late 50s and 60s, perhaps best known for his novelty songs, such as 'Fanlight Fanny' and 'Madame Moscovitch', but equally at home with a romantic ballad, such as 'A Little White Gardenia'. Ford entered showbusiness at the age of 24 and made his first public appearance at the Halifax Palace, Yorkshire. After the inevitable grind of small halls and theatres, his rise coincided with the beginning of the UK's 'trad jazz' boom, which suited his breezy, ebullient style. Ironically, his first hit, for Oriole Records in 1959, was exactly the opposite of that style—the somewhat maudlin 'Old Shep'. However, soon after its release, he was in great demand for concerts and radio broadcasts and made his first television appearance on the top-rated *Ken Dodd Show*. In January 1961 he attracted great attention by singing a 20s number, 'Oh! By Jingo! Oh! By Gee!', on BBC Television's top pop music programme *Easy Beat*, and he subsequently made the UK chart with 'Too Many Beautiful Girls' (1961), 'Fanlight Fanny' (1962) and 'Run To The Door' (1967). One of his most appealing albums was *The Melody Man*, which consisted of a mixture of up-tempo numbers such as 'Wild, Wild Women' and 'I Never See Maggie Alone' and the ballads 'By The Fireside' and 'A Beggar In Love'. His own compositions have included 'Crazy Horse' and 'Dream City Lullaby'. With his showbusiness flair and a reputed repertoire of several hundred songs, including perennial favourites such as 'What A Little Moonlight Can Do' and 'Everything Is Peaches Down In Georgia', Ford was well equipped to survive when the hit records dried up. Since then, he has continued to work in various aspects of the business, including variety and nostalgic re-creations of the good old days of music hall. In more recent years he is reported to have spent much of his time as an hotelier in Douglas on the Isle Of Man, although he hosted his own series of Radio 2 programmes in the early 90s.

● ALBUMS: *Clinton Ford* (Time-Oriole 1962) ★★★, *The Melody Man* (Columbia 1963) ★★★★, *Oh! By Jingo!* (Realm-Oriole 1964) ★★★, *Country Style-Ancient And Modern* (Time-Oriole 1964) ★★★, *Listen With Us* (Columbia 1965) ★★★★, *Dandy* (Pye 1966) ★★★★, *Big Willy*

Broke Jail Tonight (Pye 1966), *Give A Little-Take A Little* (Pye 1967) ★★★, *Clinton Ford Sings Fanlight Fanny* (Hallmark 1967) ★★, *Clinton The Clown* (Pye 1968) ★★, *Songs For Children Aged One To A Hundred* (Bell 1969) ★, *Let Me Sing A Jolson Song* (Chevron 1979) ★★★, with Alan Elsdon *Clinton Ford Sings Alan Elsdon Swings* (Lake 2001) ★★★.

● COMPILATIONS: *Run To The Door: The Piccadilly/Pye Anthology* (Castle 2002) ★★★★.

Ford, David

b. Kansas City, Kansas, USA. Gospel singer David Ford began his musical apprenticeship at Baylor University in Waco, Texas, where he received a bachelor of music degree. Further study took him to the Southern Baptist Theological Seminary in Louisville, Kentucky. Once these endeavours were completed, he embarked on a peripatetic musical career which saw him perform alongside the Cleveland, Dallas and Nashville Symphony Orchestras, as well as many impromptu groups working at Southern Baptist Conventions. He made his solo recording debut in the mid-70s with two albums for Triangle Records, though neither were particularly successful.

● ALBUMS: *Sings . . . Words Of Life* (Triangle 1976) ★★★, *Peace Like A River* (Triangle 1978) ★★★.

Ford, Dean, And The Gaylords

Formed in 1960 in Glasgow, Scotland, Dean Ford And The Gaylords were a musically accomplished act before the dawning of the Beat age. **Junior Campbell** (b. William Campbell, 31 May 1947, Glasgow, Scotland; lead guitar), Pat Fairley (b. 14 April 1946, Glasgow, Scotland; rhythm guitar), Bill Irving (bass) and Raymond Duffy (drums) had been fronted by various vocalists prior to the arrival of Thomas MacAleese (b. 5 September 1946, Coatbridge, Glasgow) in 1963, who assumed the Dean Ford name. The group was signed to **Columbia Records** by **Norrie Paramor** following an audition in Glasgow's Locarno Ballroom. Dean Ford And The Gaylords first single, released in 1964, was a breezy version of **Chubby Checker**'s 'Twenty Miles'. It was succeeded by the less distinguished 'Mr. Heartbreak's Here Instead', which in turn was followed by a powerhouse reading of **Shirley Ellis**' 'The Name Game'. In 1965 Graham Knight (b. 8 December 1946, Glasgow, Scotland) replaced Bill Irving as the group made plans to relocate in London, England. Upon their arrival in 1966 they dropped the Dean Ford prefix and, as the Gaylords, released their strongest single to date, 'He's A Good Face (But He's Down And Out).' Despite its mod connotations, the song was written by US team **Al Kooper** and Irwin Levine. Although not a chart hit, the single was often played on pirate radio and helped solidify the Gaylords' career. Somewhat bravely they then decided to change their name completely, rechristening themselves the **Marmalade**, who went on to top the UK charts in December 1968 with a cover version of the **Beatles**' 'Ob-La-Di, Ob-La-Da'.

Ford, Emile, And The Checkmates

b. 16 October 1937, Castries, St. Lucia, West Indies. Having arrived in Britain to study at technical college, Ford later began singing professionally in London's dancehalls and coffee bars. In 1958 he formed the Checkmates with step-brothers George and Dave Sweetman (bass and saxophone, respectively), Ken Street (guitar), Les Hart (saxophone),

Peter Carter (guitar), Alan Hawkshaw (piano) and John Cuffley (drums) and the following year secured a recording contract as first prize in a Soho talent contest. The group's debut single, 'What Do You Want To Make Those Eyes At Me For?', topped the charts that year, and this Caribbean-influenced rendition of a popular standard remains their best-known release. The octet enjoyed further success with the similarly styled 'Slow Boat To China', 'Them There Eyes' (credited solely to Ford) and 'Counting Teardrops'. A concurrent album featured material drawn from **Elvis Presley**, **Lloyd Price** and **Les Paul** and **Mary Ford**, but Ford's novelty aspect quickly faltered. Having parted from the Checkmates, who later accompanied **P.J. Proby**, the singer spent many years performing in UK clubs before emigrating to Los Angeles, California.

● ALBUMS: *New Tracks With Emile* (Pye 1960) ★★★, *Emile* (Piccadilly 1961) ★★★, *Emile Ford* (1972) ★★★.

● COMPILATIONS: *Under The Midnight Sun* (Pye Golden Guinea 1965) ★★★, *The Best Of Emile Ford And The Checkmates* (1991) ★★★, *Greatest Hits* (1993) ★★★, *The Very Best Of . . .* (Sound Waves 1994) ★★★, *Counting Teardrops: The Pye/Piccadilly Anthology* (Sequel 2000) ★★★★.

Ford, Frankie

b. Francis Guzzo, 4 August 1939, Gretna, Louisiana, USA. A rocker from a suburb of New Orleans, Frankie Ford is second cousin to that other New Orleans legend **Dr. John**. His first major appearance was on *Ted Mack's Amateur Hour Talent Show*, where he sang with **Carmen Miranda** and **Sophie Tucker**. After winning a scholarship to Southeastern College, Hammond, he started his first band with school friends. By 1958 he was singing with the Syncopators, when he was asked to audition for Ace Records. Subsequently, he released his first single, 'Cheatin' Woman', as Frankie Ford. Fellow musician **Huey 'Piano' Smith** (b. 26 January 1934, New Orleans, Louisiana, USA) had previously recorded with his group the Clowns a self-penned song called 'Sea Cruise', but Ace persuaded him to let Ford record a new vocal over Bobby Marcham's original. They also added a few extra effects such as paddle-steamer whistle blows, which altered the song enough for Ford to claim a cowriting credit. Released under the title Frankie Ford with Huey 'Piano' Smith and his Clowns, it sold over a million copies and docked in the national Top 20.

It was perceived in retrospect as a rock 'n' roll classic and was revived by **Jerry Lee Lewis**, **Herman's Hermits**, **Sha Na Na**, **John Fogerty** and **Shakin' Stevens**. Both 'Sea Cruise' and its follow-up, 'Alimony', were taken from original tapes recorded by composer Huey Smith with the Clowns; the lead vocals were then erased and Ford's singing super-imposed. As Morgus And The Ghouls, Ford and the Clowns also recorded 'Morgus The Magnificent', a novelty tribute to a local television personality. There was also an unissued homage to **Fats Domino**, written and recorded by Ford and **Dave Bartholomew**. Ford left Ace in 1960 to form his own Spinet Records and signed to **Liberty Records** in 1960 but never repeated the success of 'Sea Cruise'. He also formed a 'supergroup' with Huey Smith, **Robert Parker** (hitmaker of 'Barefootin'') and Dr. John (under various pseudonyms due to contractual problems), and they recorded various New Orleans favourites. He continued to record for obscure labels throughout the 70s. In 1971 he opened a club in New

Orleans' French Quarter where he became a cabaret fixture and tourist attraction. Moreover, he still looked youthful enough to play his younger self in the 1977 movie *American Hot Wax*, set in the late 50s. As part of a package, he toured the UK in 1985 along with **Rick Nelson**, **Bobby Vee** and **Bo Diddley**. Ford resents the term one-hit-wonder and rightly pointed out that his four recordings of 'Sea Cruise' have now sold over 30 million copies worldwide.

● ALBUMS: *Let's Take A Sea Cruise With Frankie Ford* (Ace 1959) ★★★, *Frankie Ford* (Briarmeade 1976) ★★, *Hot & Lonely* (Ace 1995) ★★, *Christmas* (Avanti 1999) ★★.

● COMPILATIONS: *New Orleans Dynamo* (Ace 1984) ★★★, *Ooh-Wee Baby! The Very Best Of Frankie Ford* (Westside 1997) ★★★, *Sea Cruise: The Very Best Of Frankie Ford* (Music Club 1998) ★★★, *Cruisin' With Frankie Ford: The Imperial Sides And London Sessions* (Ace 1998) ★★★.

● FILMS: *American Hot Wax* (1977).

Ford, Gerry

b. 25 May 1943, Athlone, County Westmeath, Eire. When he was aged 16, Ford emigrated to England as an apprentice baker, and on qualification, married and relocated to Edinburgh, where he joined the police force for 11 years. Since the late 60s he has been a country music performer, turning professional in 1976. He has recorded all his albums since 1981 in Nashville and has performed numerous times on the **Grand Ole Opry** as a guest of Opry star **Jean Shepard**. He has recorded six duets with Shepard, while **Boxcar Willie** added train whistles to Ford's tribute 'They Call Him Boxcar Willie'. Boxcar also wrote 'Jesus, I Need To Talk To You' for Ford's *All Over Again*. His easy-listening albums, which combine the new with the familiar, have helped to establish him as Scotland's 'Mr. Country'. In 1991 economy forced him to drop his band in favour of Nashville-made backing tapes, and they have been well received. *Thank God For The Radio* won an award as the UK country album of the year, and Ford has good cause to 'thank God for the radio', as he has presented country programmes on BBC Radio Scotland for 13 years.

● ALBUMS: *These Songs Are Just For You* (Emerald 1977) ★★★, *Someone To Give My Love To* (Emerald 1978) ★★★, *With Love* (Emerald 1980) ★★★, *On The Road* (Big R 1981) ★★, *Let's Hear It For The Working Man* (Big R 1982) ★★★, *Memory Machine* (Trimtop 1985) ★★★, *Thank God For The Radio* (Trimtop 1986) ★★★★, *All Over Again* (Trimtop 1988) ★★★, *Stranger Things Have Happened* (Trimtop 1989) ★★★, *Family Bible* (Trimtop 1990) ★★, *Better Man* (Trimtop 1991) ★★★, *Can I Count On You?* (Trimtop 1993) ★★★.

● COMPILATIONS: *16 Country Favourites Vols. 1, 2 & 3* (Trimtop 1990) ★★★.

Ford, Helen

b. Helen Isabel Barnett, 6 June 1897, Troy, New York, USA, d. 19 January 1982, Glendale, Los Angeles, California, USA. A charming and talented singer with an attractive stage presence, Ford was in her early twenties when she made her presence known on Broadway. This was in *Sometime* (1919) and over the next few years she appeared in a number of somewhat indifferent musical comedies, among them *Always You* (1920), *The Gingham Girl* (1922) and *Helen Of Troy* (1923). Soon after this, and owing in large part to **Richard Rodgers** and **Lorenz Hart**, Ford became one of

Broadway's rising stars. She was in their *Dearest Enemy* (1925, singing 'Here In My Arms'), *Peggy-Ann* (1926) and *Chee-Chee* (1928). Ford's success story faltered a little during the 30s, although she appeared in *Champagne Sec* (1933), an adaptation of Johann Strauss the Younger's *Die Fledermaus*, and *Great Lady* (1938). Soon after this, Ford retired from public performance.

Ford, Joy

b. 10 March 1946, Brilliant, Alabama, USA. The eldest of eight children of musical parents, Ford picked cotton as a child. The family relocated to Chicago in 1959 and two years later to Poplar Bluff, Missouri. In 1963, she joined the *Century 21 Show* (a large touring carnival that played state fairs all over the USA) as an acrobatic dancer. Here she worked with **Loretta Lynn** who encouraged her to sing. She eventually moved to New York where, for a time, she pursued a successful acting career and sang at venues. She joined Country International Records and gained her first chart success in 1978 with 'Love Isn't Love Until You Give It Away'. In 1979 she toured with the Nashville Magic Band, and during the 80s, she had four minor hits, the last coming in 1988 with 'Yesterday's Rain'. Outside of her music and acting she owns the Melody J Ranch in Dickson County, Tennessee, where she raises Appaloosa horses.

● ALBUMS: *Keep On Truckin' . . . Keep On Lovin'* (Country International 1983) ★★★, *From The Heart Of Joy* (Country International 1983) ★★★.

Ford, Lita

b. Lita Rossanna Ford, 19 September 1958, Streatham, London, England. Raised in Long Beach, California, USA, Ford was one of the original members of the **Kim Fowley**-conceived **Runaways**, first joining the band in 1975. In 1980 a disagreement within the ranks over musical direction led to the Runaways' breakup, leaving Ford to explore a solo career on the US glam-metal circuit (initially subsidized by her day job as a beautician). Her debut album was recorded for **Mercury Records** with the assistance of Neil Merryweather on bass, though it was Ford's guitar playing that took centre stage. 1984's *Dancin' On The Edge* made a minor impact on the US album charts, reaching number 66, although it was a less slick collection. Almost four years later in 1988 came *Lita*. Housed on **RCA Records** (a third album for MCA, *The Bride Wore Black*, had been abandoned), it reached the Top 30 and spawned the US number 12 hit, 'Kiss Me Deadly' (April 1988), plus a Top 10 hit with a duet with **Ozzy Osbourne**, 'Close My Eyes Forever' (March 1989). Ford later married **W.A.S.P.** guitarist Chris Holmes, although the marriage did not last. *Stiletto* continued to display Ford's commitment to the formula rock format prevalent in the USA, but she left RCA following disappointing sales for 1991's *Dangerous Curves*. Her subsequent studio album, *Black*, appeared on the ZYX label in 1995. The album featured backing vocals from her new husband, Jim Gillette, with whom Ford later formed the band Rumble Culture. The couple's son was born in May 1997, and Ford has subsequently devoted her time to motherhood, although she did record a new studio track for inclusion on the 2000 live album *Greatest Hits Live*.

● ALBUMS: *Out For Blood* (Mercury 1983) ★★★, *Dancin' On The Edge* (Mercury 1984) ★★, *Lita* (RCA 1988) ★★★, *Stiletto* (RCA 1990) ★★★, *Dangerous Curves* (RCA 1991)

★★, *Black* (ZYX 1995) ★★, *Greatest Hits Live!* (Dead Line 2000) ★★.

● COMPILATIONS: *The Best Of Lita Ford* (BMG 1992) ★★★, *Greatest Hits* (RCA 1993) ★★★, *Kiss Me Deadly* (BMG 2001) ★★★, *Platinum & Gold Collection* (RCA 2004) ★★★.

● DVD/VIDEOS: *Lita Live* (BMG Video 1988), *A Midnight Snack* (BMG Video 1990), *The Complete Video Collection* (BMG 2003).

Ford, Martyn

b. 28 April 1944, Rugby, Warwickshire, England. One of the most diverse conductors in the field, Ford studied at the Royal Academy of Music. He formed the New Sinfonia in 1970, which was renamed the Martyn Ford Orchestra. Before entering the UK Top 40 in spring 1977 as an orchestra conductor, Ford led an increasingly fuller life throughout the 70s as an arranger and session musician. Among his responsibilities were conducting and arranging the music for **Tommy**, working on the *Live And Let Die* soundtrack, supervising horn sections on albums by **Shawn Phillips**, Suntreader and Nasty Pop and plucking mandolin for Sharon Forrester and the **Spencer Davis Group** (on 1974's *Living In A Back Street*). His orchestra provided the strings on **Lou Reed**'s 'Walk On The Wild Side', with production by **Herbie Flowers**. His reputation spread like a forest fire in the 70s, and he worked with some of the decade's top acts including **Wings** (as the Black Dyke Mills Band), the **Grateful Dead**, **Barclay James Harvest**, **Blue Mink**, **Elton John** ('Blue Eyes' and 'Princess'), **Bryan Ferry**, **Cliff Richard**, **Man**, **Paul McCartney**, the **Rolling Stones**, **Kate Bush**, **Phil Collins**, **Art Garfunkel**, **Caravan**, **Jerry Lee Lewis**, **Yes**, **Toto** and **Led Zeppelin**. He arranged and conducted **Johnny Nash**'s 'I Can See Clearly Now' and conducted **Harry Nilsson**'s hit 'Without You'. He was also signed to Mountain Records, and the Martyn Ford Orchestra's 'Let Your Body Go Downtown' reached number 38 in the UK at the height of disco fever. Album spin-offs were notable for suggestive buzz word song titles (e.g. 'Horny') and duplication of previously issued tracks. However, none spawned a follow-up hit, and the versatile Ford returned to a lucrative career as a leading arranger, including a notable success with the theme music to the UK television series *Naturewatch*. He is a music advisor to the Arts Council.

● ALBUMS: Martyn Ford Orchestra *Smoovin'* (Mountain 1976) ★★, *Going To A Disco* (Mountain 1977) ★★, *Take Me To The Dance* (Mountain 1978) ★★, *Hot Shoe* (Mountain 1978) ★★.

Ford, Mary

(see **Paul, Les**)

Ford, Ricky

b. Richard Allen Ford, 4 March 1954, Boston, Massachusetts, USA. Ford started to play drums, then changed to tenor saxophone at the age of 15, inspired by **Rahsaan Roland Kirk**. **Ran Blake** heard him playing in a Boston Club and persuaded him to study music at the New England Conservatory. (Blake later invited him to play on several albums too, including *Rapport*, *Short Life Of Barbara Monk* and *That Certain Feeling*). In 1974 Ford joined the **Duke Ellington** Orchestra under the leadership of **Mercer Ellington**, and in 1976 he replaced **George Adams** in the **Charles Mingus** group,

recording on *Three Or Four Shades of Blue* and *Me Myself An Eye*. In the late 70s and early 80s he played with **Dannie Richmond**, Mingus Dynasty, **George Russell**, **Beaver Harris**, **Lionel Hampton** and **Adbullah Ibrahim**'s Ekaya group. However, following the release of his debut album in 1977 he has worked increasingly as a leader, often recording with **Jimmy Cobb** and ex-Ellington colleague **James Spaulding**. His latest releases also feature one of his New England Conservatory teachers, **Jaki Byard**. A strong, authoritative tenor player, Ford's fluency in most idioms of modern jazz has perhaps hindered the development of an individual voice.

● ALBUMS: *Loxodonta Africana* (New World 1977) ★★★, *Manhattan Plaza* (Muse 1978) ★★★, *Flying Colours* (Muse 1981) ★★★, *Interpretations* (Muse 1982) ★★★, *Future's Gold* (Muse 1984) ★★, *Shorter Ideas* (Muse 1986) ★★★, *Looking Ahead* (Muse 1987) ★★★★, *Saxotic Stomp* (Muse 1988) ★★, *Hard Groovin* (Muse 1989) ★★★, *Manhattan Blues* (Candid 1990) ★★★, *Ebony Rhapsody* (Candid 1991) ★★★, *Hot Brass* (Candid 1992) ★★, *Tenor For The Times* (Muse 1992) ★★★, *American-African Blues* (Candid 1993) ★★★, *Balaena* (Jazz Friends 1999) ★★★, *Ricky's Choice* (32 Jazz 2000) ★★★.

Ford, Robben

b. Robben Lee Ford, 16 December 1951, Woodlake, California, USA. A jazz, blues and rock guitarist, Robben is the most celebrated member of the musical Ford family. His father Charles was a country musician, and his brothers Patrick and Mark are bluesmen, playing drums and harmonica, respectively. Inspired initially by **Mike Bloomfield** and **Eric Clapton**, Ford's first professional engagement was with **Charlie Musslewhite** in 1970. He formed the Charles Ford Band with his brothers in 1971, then backed **Jimmy Witherspoon** from 1972–74. He toured and recorded with **Joni Mitchell** (as part of L.A. Express) and **George Harrison** in 1974, the resulting exposure bringing him a considerable amount of session work.

In 1978 Ford formed the **Yellowjackets** with keyboards player Russell Ferrante and found time to record a patchy solo debut, *The Inside Story*. The early 80s saw him performing with **Michael McDonald** and saxophonist **Sadao Watanabe**; in 1986 he joined the **Miles Davis** band on its tour of the USA and Europe. The solo *Talk To Your Daughter* was a triumphant return to Ford's blues roots and picked up a Grammy nomination in the Contemporary Blues category. In 1992 Ford formed a new unit, the Blue Line, featuring Roscoe Beck (bass) and Tom Brechtlein (drums), augmented by Bill Boublitz (keyboards). The unit recorded three acclaimed albums before disbanding in 1997. The same year's *Tiger Walk* was recorded with **Keith Richard**'s rhythm section but lacked the urgency of the Blue Line set-up captured on the following year's *The Authorized Bootleg*. Ford has also collaborated with his brother Patrick in the **Ford Blues Band**, releasing tribute albums to **Paul Butterfield** and Mike Bloomfield. Ford plays cleanly in an uncluttered style (like Bloomfield) but occasionally with the frantic energy of **Larry Carlton**.

● ALBUMS: with the Charles Ford Band *The Charles Ford Band* (Arhoolie 1972) ★★★, *The Inside Story* (Elektra 1978) ★★★, with the Charles Ford Band *A Reunion Live* (Blue Rockit 1982) ★★★, *Talk To Your Daughter* (Warners 1988) ★★★★, with Joe Diorio *Minor Elegance* (MGI 1990) ★★★, *Robben Ford & The Blue Line* (Stretch/Blue Thumb

1992) ★★★★, with Jimmy Witherspoon *Live At The Notodden Blues Festival* (Blue Rockit 1993) ★★★★, with the Blue Line *Mystic Mile* (Stretch/Blue Thumb 1993) ★★★, with the Blue Line *Handful Of Blues* (Blue Thumb 1995) ★★★★, with Witherspoon *Live At The Mint* (On The Spot 1996) ★★★, *Blues Connotation* 1992 recording (Pacific 1996) ★★★, *Tiger Walk* (Blue Thumb 1997) ★★, with the Blue Line *The Authorized Bootleg* (Blue Thumb 1998) ★★★, *Sunrise* 1972 recording (Rhino 1999) ★★★, *Supernatural* (Blue Thumb 1999) ★★★, with the Ford Blues Band *A Tribute To Paul Butterfield* (Blue Rock'It 2001) ★★★, *Blue Moon* (Concord Jazz 2002) ★★★, with Vinnie Colaiuta, Jimmy Haslip *Jing Chi* (Tone Center 2002) ★★★★, with the Ford Blues Band *In Memory Of Michael Bloomfield* (Blue Rock'It 2003) ★★★, *Keep On Running* (Concord Jazz 2003) ★★★.

● COMPILATIONS: *The Blues Collection* (Blue Rockit/Crosscut 1997) ★★★★, *Anthology: The Early Years* (Rhino 2001) ★★★.

● DVD/VIDEOS: *Highlights* (Warner Music Video 1995).

Ford, Tennessee Ernie

b. Ernest Jennings Ford, 13 February 1919, Bristol, Tennessee, USA, d. 17 October 1991, Reston, Virginia, USA. It is difficult to categorize a performer with so many varied achievements, but Ford can be summarized as a master interpreter of melodic songs and hymns. The fact that he was able to combine singing with his strong faith gave America's best-loved gospel singer great satisfaction. When only four years old, he was singing 'The Old Rugged Cross' at family gatherings, and from an early age, he wanted to be an entertainer. He pestered the local radio station until they made him a staff announcer in 1937, and he also took singing lessons. He subsequently worked for radio stations WATL in Atlanta and WROL in Knoxville, where he announced the attack on Pearl Harbor. He joined the US Army Air Corps in 1942 and married a secretary, Betty Heminger, whom he met at the bombardier's school. After the war, they moved to California, and he worked as an announcer and a disc jockey of hillbilly music for KXFM in San Bernardino. He rang cowbells and added bass harmonies to the records he was playing and so developed a country yokel character, Tennessee Ernie. He continued with this on KXLA Pasadena, and he became a regular on their *Hometown Jamboree*, which was hosted by band leader **Cliffie Stone**. He was also known as the Tennessee Pea-Picker, using the catchphrase 'Bless your pea-pickin' hearts' and appearing on stage in bib overalls and with a blacked-out tooth.

Lee Gillette, an A&R man for **Capitol Records**, heard Ford singing along with a record on air and asked Stone about him. His first record, in 1949, was 'Milk 'Em In The Morning Blues'. Ford began his chart success with 'Tennessee Border', 'Country Junction' and 'Smokey Mountain Boogie', a song he wrote with Stone. 'Mule Train', despite opposition from **Frankie Laine**, **Gene Autry** and **Vaughn Monroe**, was a national hit and a US country number 1. An attempt to write with **Hank Williams** did not lead to any completed songs, but Ford wrote 'Anticipation Blues' about his wife's pregnancy, and it reached the US charts in 1949. Capitol teamed him with many of their female artists including **Ella Mae Morse**, **Molly Bee** and the **Dinning Sisters**, and his most successful duets were 'Ain't Nobody's Business But My Own' and 'I'll Never Be Free', a double-sided single with **Kay Starr**. The duet just

missed gold record status, but he secured one, also in 1950, with his own song, 'Shotgun Boogie', which capitalized on the boogie craze and can be taken as a forerunner of rock 'n' roll. Its UK popularity enabled him to top a variety bill at the London Palladium in 1953. Ford recalls, 'When somebody told me that "Give Me Your Word" was number 1 in your charts, I said, "When did I record that?" because it wasn't big in America and I had forgotten about it!'. Ford also had success with 'The Cry Of The Wild Goose' and the theme for the Marilyn Monroe movie *The River Of No Return*, while the superb musicians on his records included Joe 'Fingers' Carr, who was given equal billing on 'Tailor Made Woman' in 1951, Speedy West and **Jimmy Bryant**.

Ford hosted a US daytime television show for five days a week, and in 1955 Capitol informed him that he would be in breach of contract if he did not record again soon. He chose a song he had been performing on the show, **Merle Travis'** 'Sixteen Tons'. Ford says: 'The producer, Lee Gillette, asked me what tempo I would like it in. I snapped my fingers and he said, "Leave that in." That snapping on the record is me.' 'Sixteen Tons' topped both the US and the UK charts, and Ford was also one of many who recorded 'The Ballad Of Davy Crockett', the theme of a Walt Disney western starring **Fess Parker**, which made number 3 in the UK. His half-hour US television show, *The Ford Show* (guess the sponsor), ran from 1956–61. He closed every television show with a hymn, which led to him recording over 400 gospel songs. One album, *Hymns*, made number 2 in the US album charts and was listed for over five years. He has shared his billing with the **Jordanaires** on several albums including *Great Gospel Songs*, which won a Grammy in 1964. Ford says: 'Long before I turned pro, it was a part of my life. There are many different types of gospel music, ranging from black music to the plain old Protestant hymns. I've shown that you don't have to sing them with a black robe on.' Ford had further US hits with 'That's All', 'In The Middle Of An Island' and 'Hicktown', but for many years, he concentrated on gospel. In 1961 he decided to spend more time with his family and moved to a ranch in the hills of San Francisco. He recorded albums of well-known songs, both pop and country; he rated *Country Hits—Feelin' Blue* and *Ernie Sings And Glen Picks*, an album that showcased his deep, mellow voice alongside **Glen Campbell**'s guitar, among his best work. Many collectors seek original copies of his earlier albums of Civil War songs. Ford, who was elected to the **Country Music Hall of Fame** in 1990, remarked: 'People say to me, "Why don't you record another 'Sixteen Tons'?" And I say, "There is no other 'Sixteen Tons'".'

● ALBUMS: *This Lusty Land* (Capitol 1956) ★★★, *Hymns* (Capitol 1956) ★★★, *Spirituals* (Capitol 1957) ★★★, *C-H-R-I-S-T-M-A-S* (Capitol 1957) ★★, *Tennessee Ernie Ford Favourites* (Capitol 1957) ★★★, *Ol' Rockin' 'Ern* (Capitol 1957) ★★★, *The Folk Album* (Capitol 1958) ★★★, *Nearer The Cross* (Capitol 1958) ★★★, *The Star Carol* (Capitol 1958) ★★★, with the Jordanaires *Gather 'Round* (Capitol 1959) ★★★★, with the Jordanaires *A Friend We Have In Jesus* (Capitol 1960) ★★★, *Sing A Hymn With Me* (Capitol 1960) ★★★, *Sixteen Tons* (Capitol 1960) ★★★★, *Sing A Spiritual With Me* (Capitol 1960) ★★, *Come To The Fair* (Capitol 1960) ★★★, *Sings Civil War Songs Of The North* (Capitol 1961) ★★★★, *Sings Civil War Songs Of The South* (Capitol 1961) ★★★★, *Ernie Ford Looks At Love* (Capitol 1961) ★★, *Hymns At Home* (Capitol 1961) ★★★, *Here*

Comes The Tennessee Ernie Ford Mississippi Showboat (Capitol 1962) ★★, I Love To Tell The Story (Capitol 1962) ★★★, Book Of Favourite Hymns (Capitol 1962) ★★, Long, Long Ago (Capitol 1963) ★★★, with the San Quentin Prison Choir We Gather Together (Capitol 1963) ★★★, with the Roger Wagnor Chorale The Story Of Christmas (Capitol 1963) ★★, with the Jordanaires Great Gospel Songs (Capitol 1964) ★★★★, Country Hits—Feeling Blue (Capitol 1964) ★★★★, Let Me Walk With Thee (Capitol 1965) ★★, Sing We Now Of Christmas (Capitol 1965) ★★★, My Favourite Things (Capitol 1966) ★★★, Wonderful Peace (Capitol 1966) ★★, God Lives (Capitol 1966) ★★, Aloha From Tennessee Ernie Ford (Capitol 1967) ★★★, Faith Of Our Fathers (Capitol 1967) ★★, with Marilyn Horne Our Garden Of Hymns (Capitol 1967) ★★, with Brenda Lee The Show For Christmas Seals (Decca 1968) ★★★, The World Of Pop And Country Hits (Capitol 1968) ★★★★, O Come All Ye Faithful (Capitol 1968) ★★★, Songs I Like To Sing (Capitol 1969) ★★★, New Wave (Capitol 1969) ★★★, Holy Holy Holy (Capitol 1969) ★★★, America The Beautiful (Capitol 1970) ★★★, Sweet Hour Of Prayer (Capitol 1970) ★★★, Tennessee Ernie Ford Christmas Special (Capitol 1970) ★★★, Everything Is Beautiful (Capitol 1970) ★★★, Abide With Me (Capitol 1971) ★★★, Mr. Words And Music (Capitol 1972) ★★★, It's Tennessee Ernie Ford (Capitol 1972) ★★★, Country Morning (Capitol 1973) ★★★, Ernie Ford Sings About Jesus (Capitol 1973) ★★, Precious Memories (Capitol 1975) ★★★, with Glen Campbell Glen Picks And Ernie Sings (Capitol 1975) ★★★, (Capitol 1975) ★★★, Tennessee Ernie Ford Sings His Great Love (Capitol 1976) ★★★, For The 83rd Time (Capitol 1976) ★★★, He Touched Me (Capitol 1977) ★★, with the Jordanaires Swing Wide Your Golden Gate (Capitol 1978) ★★★★, Tell The Old, Old Story (Capitol 1981) ★★★, There's A Song In My Heart (Word 1982) ★★★, Sunday's Still A Special Day (Capitol 1984) ★★★, Keep Looking Up (Word 1985) ★★★.
● COMPILATIONS: Tennessee Ernie Ford Deluxe Set (Capitol 1968) ★★★, The Very Best Of Tennessee Ernie Ford (MFP 1983) ★★★, 16 Tons Of Boogie/The Best Of Tennessee Ernie Ford (Rhino 1989) ★★★★, All Time Greatest Hymns (Curb 1990) ★★★★, Capitol Collectors Series (Capitol 1991) ★★★, Country Gospel Classics, Volumes 1 & 2 (Capitol 1991) ★★★, Sings Songs Of The Civil War (Capitol 1991) ★★★, Red, White & Blue (Capitol 1991) ★★★, Sixteen Tons (Capitol 1995) ★★★★, The Tennessee Ernie Ford Collection (1949–1965) (Razor & Tie 1997) ★★★★, The EP Collection (See For Miles 2001) ★★★★, Absolutely The Best (Fuel 2000 2002) ★★★★, Rock City Boogie: A Proper Introduction To Tennessee Ernie Ford (Proper 2004) ★★★★.

Forde, Florrie

b. Florence Flanagan, 14 August 1876, Melbourne, Australia, d. 18 April 1940, Aberdeen, Scotland. One of the greatest of all music hall artists, often described as a 'fine buxom woman', Forde, brandishing a chorus stick, was renowned for urging audiences to join in on enduring numbers such as 'Daisy Bell', 'Hold Your Hand Out, Naughty Boy', 'Oh, Oh, Antonio', 'Nellie Dean', 'A Bird In A Gilded Cage' and the song most associated with her, 'Down At The Old Bull And Bush'. Ironically, before she moved to England, Forde was billed as the Australian Marie Lloyd, although in physical terms at least (Lloyd was 5 feet tall and petite), there was

not much resemblance. After making her debut at the London Pavilion on 2 August 1897, Forde toured the halls, eventually with her own revue Flo And Co., which played on the Isle Of Man for a record-breaking 36 successive seasons. One of her special songs for audiences there incorporated her own real name in the title—'Flanagan' ('Take me to the Isle of Man again'), and another favourite on the island was 'Has Anybody Here Seen Kelly?' ('Kelly from the Isle of Man'). Her long career as a principal boy in pantomime (she is supposed to have played the role in Forty Thieves at the Lyceum in London during the 1935 Christmas season when she was 60) gave her the opportunity to sing 'male' songs such as 'She's A Lassie From Lancashire'. During World War I, she raised the nation's morale with rousing versions of 'It's A Long, Long Way To Tipperary' and 'Pack Up Your Trouble In Your Old Kit Bag' and remained popular throughout the 20s and 30s, appearing in two Royal Variety Performances in 1935 and 1938. Apart from her formidable reputation as a performer, Forde was also responsible for the formation of one of Britain's most popular double acts—**Flanagan And Allen**. In the early 20s, Chesney Allen was Forde's manager and the straight man to comic Stan Stanford in her Company. When Stanford left, Bud Flanagan replaced him until 1926 when Forde decided to take a break from touring and concentrate on her summer seasons in the Isle of Wight and Blackpool. However, she never finally retired, and it is said that her last performance was for patients in an Aberdeen Naval hospital, just a few hours before her death. Her memory is enshrined in the Florrie Forde bar at the Old Bull And Bush public house on London's Hampstead Heath.

Fordham, Julia

b. 10 August 1962, Portsmouth, Hampshire, England. Formerly one of **Mari Wilson**'s backing vocalists, the Wilsations, Fordham embarked on a solo career in 1986 as the archetypal angst-woman of the 80s. She achieved an initial UK chart hit with the Top 30 'Happy Ever After' (which also reached number 1 in Japan) in 1988, and a self-titled debut album and the follow-up both reached the UK Top 20. However, her biggest success came with the non-original '(Love Moves In) Mysterious Ways', which reached number 19 in February 1992. These releases, and the subsequent Swept, all on the Circa label, established the singer with a 'thirtysomething' audience, enabling her to perform headlining dates at venues such as London's Royal Albert Hall. Her fifth album, 1997's East West, saw Fordham teaming up with producer **Michael Brook**. Following a label change to **Atlantic Records**, 2002's Concrete Love teamed her with producer Larry Klein and keyboard player **Billy Preston**.
● ALBUMS: Julia Fordham (Circa 1988) ★★★, Porcelain (Circa 1989) ★★★, Swept (Circa 1991) ★★★, Falling Forward (Circa 1994) ★★★, East West (Virgin 1997) ★★★, Concrete Love (Atlantic 2002) ★★★, That's Life (Vanguard 2004) ★★★.
● COMPILATIONS: The Julia Fordham Collection (Circa 1998) ★★★.
● DVD/VIDEOS: Porcelain (Virgin Video 1990).

Fordyce, Elli

b. Elsa Frankl, 31 March 1937, New York City, USA. Attracted to music during her school years, vocalist Fordyce sat in as occasional singer with a high school dance band led by pianist/flutist Reese Markewich. During this same period, other high school musicians she hung out with included Bobby Cassotto and Dick Behrke. The former was then the jazz combo's non-singing drummer but later changed his name to **Bobby Darin**, with Behrke spending several years as his musical director. In 1955 Fordyce worked a summer-long gig, singing with a jazz trio at a Cape Cod, Massachusetts, club. This shaped her career for the next several years. During the mid- to late 60s, Fordyce worked regularly, singing on Caribbean cruise ships, Playboy Clubs in Miami and Jamaica and in hotels and clubs in Puerto Rico. During this same period and on into the next decade, she sang solo and with several pop cover bands although her main interest gradually focused on singing jazz. She has performed in hotels, motels, clubs, restaurants and at festivals in various parts of the USA and Canada. As leader of her own groups and as a soloist, she is adept in both small group and big band settings. In addition to her work as a jazz singer, she has also worked in cabaret.

In order to pursue other interests, Fordyce quit singing for 15 years but in the mid-90s returned to the scene. This time around, she demonstrated her seriousness by spending two years as a student of **Barry Harris**. Fordyce has also studied music theory and harmony with Hill Greene and George Perkins. In addition to performing as a singer, Fordyce is also an accomplished dramatic actress, appearing in many independent films, on television, in commercials, and on stage. She has also hosted a talk show. Fordyce appeared on writer/composer Dawn Crist's 2002 *Philly Heat Suite*, a recording made in connection with film and/or stage concept. In the early 00s Fordyce first own name CD was in production and while she was still seeking a distributor, it was actually bootlegged prior to release. A very able singer with a relaxed and mature approach to her material, Fordyce's singing voice is attractive and true.

● ALBUMS: *Something Still Cool* (No Label 2002) ★★★ .

Forehand, Edward 'Little Buster'

b. 28 September 1942, Hertford, North Carolina, USA. Born partially sighted but now totally blind, Forehand is an exceptionally talented guitar player and vocalist. He began singing gospel music on street corners before switching to the electric guitar. Moving to New York in the early 60s, he played at blues clubs with drummer **Melvin Taylor**, building up a loyal following that enabled him to gradually augment the group with other instruments, including bass, organ, saxophone and trumpet. He recorded sides for Jubilee in the 60s, the most successful of which were 'Looking For A Home' and 'Young Boy Blues', but a mooted album was cancelled. After two sides on **Minit Records** Forehand was forced to concentrate on live work, steadily building up a strong reputation throughout the 70s and 80s. Recording as Little Buster And The Soul Brothers for the **Rounder** offshoot Bullseye Blues, he released the acclaimed *Right On Time!* in 1996, earning a **W.C. Handy** nomination for Best Soul Blues Album. Apart from the seasoned originals (some of which dated to an aborted recording session in the mid-80s) the album included a track, 'Whatever It Takes', written by legendary songwriter **Dan Penn**.

● ALBUMS: *Right On Time!* (Bullseye Blues 1996) ★★★★ .

Foreigner

This AOR band derives its name from the fact that the original members were drawn from both sides of the

Atlantic, and this mixture of influences is much in evidence in their recorded legacy. Mick Jones (b. 27 December 1944, London, England; guitar/vocals) formed the band in 1976, having spent time in **Nero And The Gladiators** (two minor hits, 'Entry Of The Gladiators' and 'In The Hall Of The Mountain King', in 1961). The rest of the 60s were taken up working as a songwriter and musical director for French singer **Johnny Halliday**, alongside ex-Gladiator Tommy Brown, with whom Jones also recorded several singles and EPs. During the early 70s, he worked with ex-**Spooky Tooth** keyboard player **Gary Wright** in Wonderwheel, which led to Jones playing on three albums with the re-formed Spooky Tooth. Jones then worked with **Leslie West** and Ian Lloyd before taking a job as an A&R man, although he never actually signed anyone.

Prepared to make one final attempt on the music scene, Jones auditioned musicians, eventually forging a line-up that consisted of Ian McDonald (b. 25 June 1946, London, England; guitar, keyboards, horns, vocals, ex-**King Crimson**), **Lou Gramm** (b. Lou Grammatico, 2 May 1950, Rochester, New York, USA; vocals), who had played with **Black Sheep** in the early 70s, Dennis Elliott (b. 18 August 1950, Peckham, London, England; drums, ex-**If**), Al Greenwood (b. New York, USA; keyboards) and Edward Gagliardi (b. 13 February 1952, New York, USA; bass). In 1977 the band released *Foreigner* and, in a poll conducted by **Rolling Stone** magazine, emerged as top new artists. The album was an immediate success in America, climbing to number 4 in the **Billboard** chart. Jones and Gramm wrote most of the band's material, including classic tracks such as 'Feels Like The First Time' (US number 4, March 1977) and 'Cold As Ice' (US number 6, July 1977). Despite playing at the Reading Rock Festival in England twice in the 70s, Foreigner had more consistent success in the USA, where 'Hot Blooded' (number 3, July 1978) and 'Double Vision' (number 2, September 1978) were both million-sellers. In 1979 Rick Wills (b. England; bass) replaced Gagliardi, having served a musical apprenticeship with King Crimson and **Peter Frampton**; Gagliardi reportedly 'fell on the floor and passed out' on being told the news. *Head Games*, meanwhile, proved most notable for its 'exploitative' sleeve design, which contrasted with the subtle brand of rock it contained.

In 1980 McDonald and Greenwood departed to form **Spys**, leading to the guest appearances of **Thomas Dolby** and **Junior Walker** on the following year's US chart-topping *4*, produced by Mutt Lange. The album also broke the band in the UK, reaching number 5 in July of that year. 'Waiting For A Girl Like You' was the hit single lifted from the album, spending 10 weeks at number 2 in the US charts and providing the group with their first UK Top 10 single. Although it was representative of the band's highly musical approach, taking the form of a wistful yet melodious ballad, it pigeonholed the group as purveyors of the epic AOR song. This reputation was only endorsed in December 1984 by the release of 'I Want To Know What Love Is', which proved to be Foreigner's greatest commercial success. It topped the charts on both sides of the Atlantic and featured the New Jersey Mass Choir backing Gramm's plaintive vocal. *Agent Provocateur*, meanwhile, topped the UK album charts and reached number 4 in America.

In the mid-80s the members of Foreigner were engaged in solo projects, and the success of Gramm's *Ready Or Not* in 1987 led to widespread speculation that Foreigner were about to disband. This was not the case, as *Inside Information* proved, though in other respects it was a poor record and a portent of things to come, despite containing the US Top 10 hit singles 'Say You Will' and 'I Don't Want To Live Without You'. In 1989 Gramm enjoyed success with another solo project, *Long Hard Look*, before officially leaving the band in May 1990 to form **Shadow King**. Jones refused to face the inevitable and, amid much press sniping, recruited Johnny Edwards (ex–**King Kobra**) to provide vocals for *Unusual Heat*. In 1992 both Jones and Gramm grasped the nettle and reunited, launching a re-formed Foreigner, though both Wills and Elliott were deemed surplus to requirements. The 1994 model boasted a line-up of Bruce Turgon (bass; a former colleague of Gramm in Black Sheep and Shadow King), Jeff Jacobs (keyboards, ex–**Billy Joel** circa *Storm Front*) and Mark Schulman (drums), in addition to Jones and Gramm. The band was back on the road during the early part of 1995 to promote *Mr Moonlight*. The album was only a moderate success, even though it was a typical Foreigner record. At their well-attended gigs, however, it was still 'Cold As Ice', 'Urgent' and 'I Want To Know What Love Is' that received the biggest cheers. Gramm was successfully treated for a brain tumour before the band reconvened briefly in 1999. A more substantial reunion took place in 2002 for the band's 25th anniversary tour, with Jones, Gramm, Jacobs and Turgon joined by Tom Gimbel (guitar) and Denny Carmassi (drums).

A new Foreigner line-up was announced in 2005 with Jones, Jacobs and Gimbel joined by Kelly Hansen (vocals; ex-**Hurricane**), Jason Bonham (drums) and Jeff Pilson (bass; ex-**Dokken**). Whether or not their legacy grows further, Foreigner will continue to epitomize better than most the classic sound of 'adult orientated rock'.

● ALBUMS: *Foreigner* (Atlantic 1977) ★★★, *Double Vision* (Atlantic 1978) ★★★, *Head Games* (Atlantic 1979) ★★★, *4* (Atlantic 1981) ★★★★, *Agent Provocateur* (Atlantic 1985) ★★★, *Inside Information* (Atlantic 1987) ★★★, *Unusual Heat* (Atlantic 1991) ★★★, *Mr Moonlight* (BMG 1994) ★★★.
● COMPILATIONS: *Records* (Atlantic 1982) ★★★★, *The Very Best Of Foreigner* (Atlantic 1992) ★★★★, *The Very Best . . . And Beyond* (Atlantic 1992) ★★★★, *Classic Hits Live* (Atlantic 1993) ★★★, *Anthology: Jukebox Heroes* (Rhino/Atlantic 2000) ★★★★, *Complete Greatest Hits* (Rhino 2002) ★★★★, *The Definitive* (WEA 2002) ★★★★.
● DVD/VIDEOS: *Feels Like The First Time* (Atlantic 1991), *25 All Access Tonight* (Eagle Vision 2004).

Forest

Originally known as the Foresters Of Walesby, this Birmingham, England–based outfit comprised brothers Martin and Hadrian Welham and Dez Allensby (b. Derek Allensby); all three members were multi-instrumentalists. Formed in 1968, they enjoyed the patronage of pioneering disc jockey **John Peel**, who introduced the trio to the influential Blackhill agency and penned the liner notes to their 1969 debut. *Forest* revealed a brand of underground 'hippie folk', popularized by the **Incredible String Band** and **Dr. Strangely Strange**, but the set failed to reap a similar commercial success. *Full Circle* (1970) was a more professional and accomplished collection, but it also failed to rise above cult status. Forest split up in 1973, although all three members have continued to play music.

● ALBUMS: *Forest* (Harvest 1969) ★★★, *Full Circle* (Harvest 1970) ★★★.

Forest City Joe
(see **Pugh, Joe Bennie**)

Forester Sisters

Kathy (b. 4 January 1955), June (b. 22 September 1956), Kim (b. 4 November 1960, Oglethorpe, Georgia, USA) and Christy Forester (b. 21 December 1962) are from Lookout Mountain, Georgia, USA. Kathy and June sang in church as children, obtained their college degrees and started playing professionally. By 1982 both Kim and Christy had joined them. They formed their own band and started to explore songs and harmonies. In 1983 they recorded some demo tapes that led to a contract with **WEA Records**. Their first single, '(That's What You Do) When You're In Love', made the US country Top 10. Their glossy, professional sound (and looks) appealed to country fans, and they had three number 1 country hits from their first album—'I Fell In Love Again Last Night', 'Just In Case' and 'Mama's Never Seen Those Eyes'. In 1986 they teamed up with the **Bellamy Brothers** for another US number 1 country single, 'Too Much Is Not Enough', and they worked together on the Brothers And Sisters Tour. In 1987 they had a further chart-topper with the title track from *You Again*. Their commercial peak was over by the 90s, and 1996's *More Than I Am* was firmly aimed at the Christian market.

● ALBUMS: *The Forester Sisters* (Warners 1985) ★★★★, *Perfume, Ribbons & Pearls* (Warners 1986) ★★★, *You Again* (Warners 1987) ★★★★, *A Christmas Card* (Warners 1987) ★★, *Sincerely* (Warners 1988) ★★★, *Family Faith* (Warners 1988) ★★, *All I Need* (Warners 1989) ★★★, *Come Hold Me* (Warners 1990) ★★★, *Talkin' 'Bout Men* (Warners 1991) ★★★, *I Got A Date* (Warners 1992) ★★★, *More Than I Am* (Warner Resound 1996) ★★.
● COMPILATIONS: *Greatest Hits* (Warners 1989) ★★★.

Foresythe, Reginald

b. 28 May 1907, London, England, d. 28 December 1958. Son of a Yoruba (Nigerian) barrister and English mother, Foresythe received a public school education as well as studying piano and composition. American singer Walter Richardson, whom he accompanied in Australia, encouraged him to go to the USA. There he scored the D.W. Griffith film *Abraham Lincoln* and played with Paul Howard's Quality Seranaders, who recorded two of his compositions. In Chicago, he wrote for trumpeter **Wild Bill Davison** and pianist **Earl Hines**, his 'Deep Forest' becoming Hines' signature tune. He returned to London to lead a revolutionary 10-piece band in which two clarinets and a bassoon replaced the brass section. 'In my band each instrument has its own part to play in the rhythm,' he said, thereby anticipating a later view of jazz although he himself was not really a jazz artist. Back in the USA he guested with **Paul Whiteman**, who recorded his dramatic *Southern Holiday: A Phantasy Of Negro Moods*, the string writing far in advance of anything then current. In 1935 he recorded four compositions with a band that included **Benny Goodman**, **John Kirby** and **Gene Krupa**, one piece being the oft-recorded 'Dodging A Divorcee'. With his 'New Music' he played London's exclusive 400 Club, then broadcast as a piano soloist and duettist. His work was played and recorded by a variety of others, including **Louis Armstrong**, **Fats Waller**, **Henry Hall** and **Lew Stone**.

Foresythe, who was of mixed race, used his dignified bearing and upper-class British accent to achieve some measure of acceptance in otherwise segregated establishments. His writing, described variously as 'enigmatic', 'singular' and 'quirky', sat awkwardly amongst much of what passed for jazz in the UK dance band scene between the wars. In retrospect this can be seen as a consequence of his being ahead of his time. After World War II, during which he served in the Royal Air Force, he accompanied **Elizabeth Welch** and played in Italy before leading bands in obscure, English west country hotels. At the time of his death, which followed a fall downstairs, he was working as a solo pianist in small drinking clubs in London's Soho and Kensington, no longer causing a sensation with the witty compositions and highly individual writing that had created a permanent impact on his pre-war jazz contemporaries.

Forever Plaid

This 'Heavenly Musical Hit' was greeted with rave reviews from every quarter when it opened Off Broadway at Steve McGraw's on 20 May 1990. Written, directed and choreographed by Stuart Ross, it concerns the return to earth of four aspiring crooners, the members of a close-harmony group called Forever Plaid. The guys were on their way to collect four tartan tuxedos in time for their first big gig, when the vehicle in which they were travelling collided with a school bus full of Catholic teenagers on their way to see the **Beatles**' debut on the **Ed Sullivan** Show. No Catholic casualties, but the Plaids were killed instantly. That was back in 1964, but 26 years later (and several times a week subsequently), 'through the power of Harmony and the expanding holes in the Ozone layer combined with the positions of the Planets and all that Astro-Technical stuff, the Plaids return to perform the show they never got to do in life'. The rejuvenated quartet consisted of Jinx (Stan Chandler), Smudge (David Engel), Sparky (Jason Graae) and Frankie (Guy Stroman). Together with a bass player and pianist, they pay a joyous tribute to the close-harmony groups of the 50s, such as the **Four Lads**, the **Four Preps** and the **Four Aces**, via a string of potently nostalgic numbers such as 'Three Coins In The Fountain', 'Love Is A Many-Splendored Thing', 'Catch A Falling Star', 'Chain Gang', 'Magic Moments', 'Sixteen Tons', 'Heart And Soul' and some 20-odd more. **Perry Como** comes in for the treatment as well. There is also a witty and irreverent send-up of the Beatles (the indirect cause of the Plaids' premature retirement) in 'She Loves You—Yes Siree'. Showered with unanimously ecstatic reviews ('37 out 37') along the lines of 'A high octane tour-de-force' and 'Screamingly funny! Entirely enchanting, utterly entertaining, awesome!', *Forever Plaid* settled in for a long New York run and, during the next three years, repeated its success in 23 US cities. In September 1993 the show opened for a disappointingly short run in London complete with the original cast except for Sparky who was played by Larry Raben. At the West End Apollo Theatre, one aspect of the audience participation consisted of a minute's silence while one brave soul who went up on to the stage was rewarded with a pack of plaid dental floss.

Forever Tango

Conceived and staged by Luis Bravo, this exciting and passionate Argentinian dance revue played many sell-out seasons in Europe, the USA and Canada before sashaying sexily into the Walter Kerr Theatre in New York on 19 June 1997. During its stopover in London two years earlier, the show resided at the Strand Theatre, just a dance step away from the Savoy Hotel where they served 'Tango Teas' to the Prince of Wales and his cronies as the tango craze raged in Britain prior to World War I. On Broadway in 1997, *Forever Tango* featured a cast of 25 performers, including 6 brilliant dance couples who slithered, swayed, spun, kicked and thrust their way around the floor to the music of an 11-piece orchestra led by Lisandro Adrover. The key instrument in that ensemble was the bandoneón, similar to an accordion, which visiting German sailors introduced to Argentina in the late nineteenth century. Its unique, haunting and melancholy sound enhanced perfectly such numbers as 'El Dia Que Me Quieras', one of the most popular songs of the 30s, in which the singer tells of his romantic wish for an unachievable dream. Written by tango singer and composer *par excellence* Carlos Gardel, with his partner Alfredo Le Pera, it was performed in *Forever Tango* by Carlos Morel, along with 'Balada Para Un Loco', a toast to the 'crazy'. Each selection tells a story, and among the numerous dance and musical highlights were 'A Evaristo Carriego', the eternal fantasy of an older man obsessed with a younger woman, danced by Marcela Duran and Carlos Gavito; 'La Cumparista', an ensemble tribute to one of the most famous of all tangos; and the insinuating 'Jealousy', played by the *Forever Tango* orchestra. The remaining members of this dazzling, graceful and immensely skilful company comprised Miriam Larici, Diego DiFalco, Luis Castro and Claudia Mendoza, Jorge Torres and Karina Piazza, Guillermo Merlo and Cecilia Saia, Pedro Calveyra and Nora Robles, Carlos Vera and Laura Marcarie, Gabriel Ortega and Sandra Bootz and Carolina Zokalski. Initially set to close on 9 August, *Forever Tango* repeatedly extended its run and in April 1998 moved to the Marquis Theatre following the rapid demise of **Paul Simon**'s **The Capeman**. After running for more than a year, this lesson in Latin sensuality was finally withdrawn on 2 August 1998, having played 453 performances. Road companies subsequently proliferated.

Forman, Bruce

b. 14 May 1956, Springfield, Massachusetts, USA. After formal studies on piano, Forman switched to guitar and opted for the jazz scene. While playing in California he attracted the attention of **Richie Cole** who hired him for his small band. The spell with Cole brought Forman to the attention of a wider audience, and after leaving the band he struck out on his own. He appeared and recorded with **Stanley Turrentine**, **Freddie Hubbard**, **Ray Brown**, **Eddie Jefferson** and others. In the mid-80s he recorded a well-received album of duos with **Bobby Hutcherson** and **George Cables**. The duo format clearly appealed to Forman, and in the mid- and late 90s he was often teamed with drummer Vince Lateano. Forman's playing is always eminently attractive and subtly swinging. His great technical skills are always used to enhance his performances and never at the expense of good taste.

● ALBUMS: *Coast To Coast* (Choice 1979) ★★★, *River Journey* (Muse 1981) ★★★, *20/20* (Muse 1981) ★★★, *In Transit* (Muse 1982) ★★★, *The Bash* (Muse 1983) ★★★, *Full Circle* (Concord Jazz 1984) ★★★, with George Cables *Dynamics With George Cables* (Concord Jazz 1985) ★★★, *There Are Times* (Concord Jazz 1986) ★★★★, *Pardon Me!*

(Concord Jazz 1989) ★★, *Still Of The Night* (Kamei 1991) ★★★★, *Forman On The Job* (Kamei 1992) ★★★.

Formanek, Michael

b. 7 September 1958, San Francisco, California, USA. Formanek studied the bass privately in San Francisco and New York before playing with artists such as **Eddie Henderson**, **Joe Henderson**, **Dave Liebman** and **Tony Williams** and moving to New York in the late 70s. He worked with **Chet Baker**, **Bill Connors**, **Mark Murphy** and **Herbie Mann** before moving to Germany. There he played in the Media Band and then joined Gallery with **Paul McCandless**, **David Darling**, **David Samuels** and **Michael DiPasqua** (drums). In the 90s his collaborations with saxophonist **Tim Berne**, and his quartet Bloodcount were of particular note. During this period Formanek also worked with **Gerry Hemingway**, **Jane Ira Bloom**, **Marty Ehrlich**, the **Mingus Big Band**, **Lee Konitz** and **Jack Walrath** among others. In 2000 he launched Northern Exposure with drummer Jim Black, trumpeter Dave Ballou and saxophonist Henrik Frisk.

● ALBUMS: *Wide Open Spaces* (Enja 1990) ★★★★, *Extended Animation* (Enja 1992) ★★★, with Tim Berne, Jeff Hirshfield *Loose Cannon* (Soul Note 1993) ★★★★, *Low Profile* (Enja 1994) ★★★★, *Nature Of The Beast* (Enja 1997) ★★★, with Berne *Ornery People* (Little Brother 1998) ★★★★, *Am I Bothering You?* (Screwgun 1998) ★★★★, with Marty Ehrlich, Peter Erskine *Relativity* (Enja 2000) ★★★★.

Formation Records

This UK **dance music** record label specializes in hardcore/'darkside' **techno**. It was inaugurated by Leroy Small (aka DJ SS) and Eidris Hassam in 1992. They grew up as part of a break-dancing team before joining a DJ clique entitled Formation 5 in their native Leicester, Leicestershire, England. Formation was established as an outlet for their 5HQ shop in the city to fill a gap for the region's underground dance fans. The records were distributed by their own F Project operation, which also released records just as frequently in its own right. They also run their own **house** and rap labels. 'Our music's made underground to appeal to a commercial crowd. We've survived because we've stayed versatile. The whole feel and vibe of the scene has gone so we've had to change with the times', noted Small. In just over a year, via their various networking operations, Formation released over 40 12-inch singles for their enthusiastic following, the best of which included several items from DJ SS (including his collaborations with EQ and Tango, who record in their own right), as well as Oaysis, Mastersafe, Darkman, Bizz and **Mickey Finn**.

Formations

This Philadelphia-based soul group comprised Jerry Akines, Johnny Bellmon, Reginald Turner and Victor Drayton. Originally formed by Akines and Drayton as the Extremes, they were renamed when Bellmon replaced Ernie Brooks in 1965. They recorded for **Thom Bell** at Cameo, but nothing was released. In 1968 'At The Top Of The Stairs', produced in New York by John Madara and ex-**Danny And The Juniors** member Danny White on **MGM Records**, gave them a minor US hit. After a couple of less successful releases, they changed their name to the Corner Boys and recorded on **Gamble And Huff**'s Neptune label, with 'Gang War' making the

R&B Top 50 in 1969. In 1971 they had their biggest success as the writers of **Wilson Pickett**'s Top 20 hit 'Don't Let The Green Grass Fool You'. They then changed their name again and recorded as the Silent Majority on **Holland/Dozier/Holland**'s Hot Wax label. As recording artists they enjoyed their biggest success in 1971 when the **Motown**-influenced 'At The Top Of The Stairs' was rereleased in the UK and made the Top 30.

Formby, George

b. George Hoy Booth, 26 May 1904, Wigan, Lancashire, England, d. 6 March 1961, Penwortham, Lancashire, England. The son of George Formby, a successful Edwardian Music Hall comedian, George Hoy was an apprentice jockey before following in his father's footsteps when he died in 1921. At first he worked under his real name and offered what he believed to be an imitation of his father's act—although he had never seen him perform. He changed his name to Formby and discarded the old image when he introduced a ukulele into his act and then, just as significantly, married dancer, Beryl Ingham in September 1924. The lady was to mastermind—some would say, dominate—the remainder of his career. In the late 20s he developed a stage personality that was described variously as: 'the beloved imbecile', 'the modern minstrel' and 'with a carp-like face, a mouth outrageously full of teeth, a walk that seems normally to be that of a flustered hen and a smile of perpetual wonder at the joyous incomprehensibility of the universe'. Self-taught on the ukulele, he developed an individual style, that even years later, was difficult to copy.

Apart from a small part in a silent movie (*By The Shortest Of Heads*) in 1915, Formby's film career started in 1934 with *Boots, Boots* and continued until 1946 with such films as *No Limit* (1935), *Keep Your Seats Please* (1935), *Feather Your Nest* (1937), *Keep Fit* (1937), *It's In The Air* (1938), *Trouble Brewing* (1939), *Let George Do It* (1940), *Turned Out Nice Again* (1940), *Spare A Copper* (1941), *South American George* (1941), *Bell Bottom George* (1943) and *George In Civvy Street* (1946). As with his music hall act, the films featured a series of saucy songs such as 'With My Little Ukulele In My Hand', 'When I'm Cleaning Windows', 'Fanlight Fanny', 'Auntie Maggie's Remedy', 'She's Got Two Of Everything', 'You Don't Need A Licence For That' and 'Grandad's Flannelette Nightshirt'. His 'identity' songs include 'Leaning On A Lamp Post', 'Chinese Laundry Blues' and 'Mr. Wu's A Window Cleaner Now'. His film image was that of a little man, with a very attractive girl friend, fighting evil in the shape of crooks or the Germans and coming out on top in the end ('It's turned out nice again!') to the sheer delight of cinema audiences: 'Our George has done it again!'.

During the 30s and 40s, Formby and **Gracie Fields** were regarded as the most popular entertainers in the UK. Even in the early 30s his annual earnings were estimated at around £85,000. During World War II, Formby toured extensively with ENSA, entertaining troops in Europe, the Middle East and North Africa. In 1946 he was awarded the OBE for his war efforts. Five years later, he appeared in his first 'book' musical at the Palace Theatre in London's West End. The show was *Zip Goes A Million*, a musical adaptation of the George Barr McCutcheon novel *Brewster's Millions*. It gave Formby the biggest success of his career, but six months into the run he had to withdraw after suffering a heart attack, to be replaced by comedian Reg Dixon. A year later he returned to work in the usual round of revues and summer shows, but throughout the 50s he was plagued by recurring illness. In 1960 he made his first record for 15 years. The single, 'Happy Go Lucky Me'/'Banjo Boy', was also his first to make the UK Top 40. On Christmas Day of that year his wife and manager, Beryl, died. About two months later, his fans, and especially his family, were startled when he announced his engagement to a 36-year-old schoolteacher, Pat Howson. The marriage was arranged for May but never took place. Formby died in hospital on 6 March 1961. He left most of his fortune to his fiancée, a situation which led to a lengthy period of litigation when his relations contested the will. A musical play set in the period just before he died, entitled *Turned Out Nice Again*, which was written by Alan Randall and Vince Powell and starred Randall, had its world premiere at the Blackpool Grand Theatre in March 1992.

● COMPILATIONS: *George Formby Souvenir* (Ace Of Clubs 1961) ★★★, *The World Of George Formby* (Ace Of Clubs 1969) ★★★★, *The World Of George Formby, Volume Two* (Ace Of Clubs 1976) ★★★★, *At The Flicks* (President 1997) ★★★★, *The Ultimate Collection* (BMG 1998) ★★★★.

● FURTHER READING: *George Formby*, Alan Randall and Ray Seaton. *The Entertainer—George Formby*, John Fisher. *George Formby: A Troubled Genius*, David Bret.

● FILMS: *By The Shortest Heads* (1915), *Boots, Boots* (1934), *Off The Dole* (1935), *No Limit* (1936), *Feather Your Nest* (1937), *Keep Your Seats Please* (1937), *I See Ice* (1938), *Keep Fit* (1938), *Trouble Brewing* (1939), *It's In The Air* (1939), *Let George Do It* (1940), *Come On George* (1940), *South American George* (1941), *Turned Out Nice Again* (1941), *Spare A Copper* (1941), *Much Too Shy* (1942), *Get Cracking* (1943), *Bell Bottom George* (1944), *I Didn't Do It* (1945), *He Snoops To Conquer* (1945), *George In Civvy Street* (1946).

Formerly Fat Harry

Formed in England in 1971, Formerly Fat Harry revolved around the talents of US expatriates Gary Peterson (vocals, guitar,keyboards), Phil Greenberg (vocals/guitar) and Bruce Barthol (bass, ex–**Country Joe And The Fish**). Saxophonist George Khan (formerly of **Battered Ornaments**) and Laurie Allen (drums) completed the featured line-up on *Formerly Fat Harry*, a pleasant country rock, good time music set that anticipated the 'pub rock' boom. Unfortunately, the band failed to make commercial headway, and they split up when the core members returned to the USA. Allen subsequently worked with **Gong**, **Lol Coxhill** and **Robert Wyatt**. George Khan, also known as Nisar Ahmet Khan, played on several jazz rock features by **Annette Peacock** and **Mike Westbrook** before leading Mirage (1977).

● ALBUMS: *Formerly Fat Harry* (Harvest 1971) ★★★.

Forrest

This US soul group was based around lead singer Forrest Thomas (b. 1953, USA). Despite finding little success in the US national pop or R&B charts, in 1983 the group achieved two UK hits on **CBS Records** with 'Rock The Boat' (formerly a hit for the **Hues Corporation** in 1974), which reached number 4, and the follow-up, 'Feel The Need In Me', reached the Top 20 that same year (previously a hit for the **Detroit Emeralds** in 1973). By the end of the year, Forrest's brief chart success came to a halt when 'One Lover (Don't Stop The Show)' failed to climb higher than number 67. Subsequently, Thomas (and Forrest) faded from the scene.

● ALBUMS: *Forrest* (Columbia 1983) ★★.

Forrest, George
(see **Wright, Robert**)

Forrest, Helen

b. Helen Fogel, 12 April 1917 or 1918, Atlantic City, New Jersey, USA, d. 11 July 1999, Los Angeles, California, USA. Forrest began singing as child and by her mid-teenage was appearing regularly on radio in New York City. Many of her appearances were on CBS, with whom she held a salaried job, and this led to her being heard by **Artie Shaw** who hired her in 1937. The other band singer with Shaw was **Billie Holiday** whose colour prevented her from appearing at some venues and on some radio shows. Forrest was thus given opportunities she might well have preferred to avoid. Certainly, she held Holiday, her primary influence, in high regard, declaring later: 'Billie was just wonderful to me. Always trying to help, she used to tell Artie to let me sing some of her songs. She was really a great, caring person.'

When Shaw abruptly disbanded at the end of 1939 Forrest moved onto the **Benny Goodman** band. Here, the clear evidence of her almost-40 recordings with Shaw, that she was a singer of merit, was considerably enhanced by Goodman arranger, **Eddie Sauter**, who had previously worked with **Red Norvo**, writing charts for **Mildred Bailey**, who was Forrest's other main early influence. Sauter admirably tailored several charts to suit Forrest's fine, clear and expressive voice, among them 'Darn That Dream', 'Yours Is My Heart Alone' and 'The Man I Love'. In 1941 Forrest quit Goodman and joined **Harry James** where she recorded a succession of beautifully crafted performances including 'I Had The Craziest Dream', 'I've Heard That Song Before', 'I Don't Want To Walk Without You', 'Skylark', 'Time Waits For No One' and 'I Cried For You'. This band's other singer was **Dick Haymes**, and with him Forrest duetted on a succession of hit recordings, among them 'Long Ago And Far Away', 'It Had To Be You' and 'I'll Buy That Dream'. On all of the songs she sang with James, the direction signposted by Sauter was fully exploited and the singer is intelligently and exquisitely showcased.

Romantically linked with James, Forrest quit when he married **Betty Grable**, but her singing career continued apace. In the 50s she sang in clubs, worked in radio, recorded albums under her own name and in reunion with James and toured extensively throughout the USA. During the next decade the tours continued, including trips to the UK and Australia, and she made yet more records with James. Through the 70s she worked on as a club singer and also appeared in packages that teamed her with Haymes and others from her golden days. A stroke in 1980 barely gave her pause, and in 1983 she was back to the recording studios, this time for a jazz-slanted album with a group including **Hank Jones** and **George Duvivier**. This, together with reissues of her earlier work, helped ensure that her name stayed in the limelight albeit never in the full glare of publicity that sometimes surrounded lesser singers from the swing era.

Forrest's pure, clear and well-phrased voice, allied as it was to a fine interpretative gift with lyrics, drew the respect and admiration of many other singers, including **Dolly Dawn**, **Connie Haines** and **Frankie Laine**. She was regarded by many, including the noted historian, Gunther Schuller, as being one of the best white singers of the swing era and, Bailey apart, headed the list until the emergence of **Frank Sinatra**.

● ALBUMS: *Harry James In Hi-Fi* (Capitol 1954) ★★★, *Sunny Side Of The Street* (Stash 1983) ★★★, *1983 Studio Sessions* (Viper's Nest 1996) ★★★.

● COMPILATIONS: *Best Of The Big Bands: Benny Goodman Featuring Helen Forrest* (Sony 1992) ★★★, *I Wanna Be Loved* (Hindsight 1993) ★★★, *Them There Eyes* (Mister Music 1995) ★★★, with Dick Haymes *Together* (Revivendo 1995) ★★★, *Embraceable You* (Hindsight 1995) ★★★, *The Cream Of Helen Forrest* (Pearl Flapper 1996) ★★★, *Voice Of The Big Bands* (Jasmine 1997) ★★★, with Artie Shaw *Sweeter As The Years Go By 1937–38* recordings (Jasmine 1998) ★★★, with Haymes *The Complete Duets* (Empire Music Collection 1999) ★★★, with Trudy Richards *Voice Of The Name Bands/Crazy In Love* (EMI 1999) ★★★, with Goodman *The Original Recordings Of The 40s* (Columbia 2001) ★★★★.

Forrest, Jimmy

b. James Robert Forrest, 24 January 1920, St. Louis, Missouri, USA, d. 26 August 1980, Grand Rapids, Michigan, USA. Forrest's early experience on tenor saxophone came in **territory bands**, including the **Jeter-Pillars Orchestra**, **Don Albert**'s San Antonio–based band and the group led by **Fate Marable**. In 1940 he joined **Jay 'Hootie' McShann** in Kansas City, where one of his sectionmates was **Charlie Parker**. This was followed by a long period in New York with **Andy Kirk**, but by the end of the 40s he was back home in St. Louis. He had a huge R&B hit with 'Night Train', which actually owed more than was usually credited to a **Duke Ellington** composition, 'Happy-Go-Lucky Local'. At the end of the 50s he was back in New York, this time with **Harry 'Sweets' Edison**, after which he led his own bands for records and club dates that lasted into the early 70s. He was then with **Count Basie** for a number of years and also played with the **Clarke-Boland Big Band** before forming a partnership with **Al Grey**. Together, Forrest and Grey toured the USA and Europe, playing hard-driving mainstream jazz with contrasting overtones of both R&B and bebop. Forrest's robust style echoed the Texas tenors, and he proved enormously popular with audiences wherever he played.

● ALBUMS: *Forrest Fire* (New Jazz 1960) ★★★★, *Out Of The Forrest* (Prestige 1961) ★★★, *Most Much!* (Prestige 1961) ★★★, *Sit Down And Relax With Jimmy Forrest* (Prestige 1961) ★★, *Soul Street* (New Jazz 1962) ★★★★, *Al Grey-Jimmy Forrest Quintet Live At Rick's* (Aviva 1978) ★★★, with Al Grey *Truly Wonderful* (Stash 1979) ★★★, with Grey *Out 'Dere* (Grey-Forrest 1980) ★★★, *Heart Of The Forrest 1978* recording (Palo Alto 1982) ★★★.

● COMPILATIONS: *The Best Of Jimmy Forrest* (Prestige 1969) ★★★★, *All The Gin Is Gone* (Delmark 1970) ★★★★, *Black Forrest* (Delmark 1972) ★★★.

Forrester, Howdy

b. Howard Wilson Forrester, 31 March 1922, Vernon, Hickman County, Kentucky, d. 1 August 1987, Nashville, Tennessee, USA. In 1933, the youngest of four Forrester boys, he was struck down by rheumatic fever, and during eight months' convalescing, he learned to play a fiddle that his grandfather had acquired during service in the Civil War. Both his father (who died in an accident on an unmanned rail crossing in 1927) and an uncle were competent fiddlers,

and he learned much from his Uncle Bob. In the early 30s, he and brothers Clyde (guitar) and Joe (guitar/bass) began to play for local square dances. In 1936, after the family had relocated to Nashville, he played with a group on a local station. In 1938 he and Joe were playing on the *Grand Ole Opry*, as members of Harold Goodman's Tennessee Valley Boys. It was Goodman, a founder of the *Opry* singing trio the **Vagabonds**, who nicknamed him Howdy. Greatly influenced by *Opry* star **Fiddlin' Arthur Smith**, he left the *Opry* and played with various groups in Oklahoma and Texas where, in 1940, he met and married Billie Russell, a multi-instrumentalist and singer, who worked under the name of Sally Ann. They returned to Nashville, where between 1940 and 1943, he worked with **Bill Monroe**, until called for service with the US Navy in World War II (his wife continued to work with Monroe during the time he was away). When discharged in 1964, he moved to Texas, where he played with various bands and on WRLD Dallas. He recorded some **Mercury Records** sides and worked with fiddler Georgia Slim (b. Robert Rutland, 1916, d. 1969), whom he knew from his late 30s days on the *Opry* on the *Texas Roundup*. In 1949 he returned to Nashville, where he worked on the *Opry* with **Cowboy Copas**, until he became a member of **Roy Acuff**'s Smoky Mountain Boys in 1951. This marked the start of a long association with Acuff that lasted until his death. He continued to play the *Opry* but stopped touring with Acuff in 1963, and from 1964–67, he worked as a booking agent and, later, on other administrative duties for **Acuff-Rose Music**. In 1967 he announced that he would not play professionally again but within three months, he was once again, with Acuff on the *Opry*. In the middle of 1983, continuing chest pains gave rise for concern because of the rheumatic fever he had suffered as a boy, and he retired from all but his *Opry* appearances with Acuff. In late 1986 he had major surgery for the removal of his stomach when he was found to have cancer. To everyone's amazement, he was soon playing again and continued to play the *Opry* with Acuff until mid-June 1987, finally passing away at his home on 1 August that year. He is justifiably rated one of country music's finest fiddlers and is especially remembered for his exceptional ability to perfect twin fiddle technics, which he first played with Georgia Slim but later developed further on recordings with **Kenny Baker** and **Chubby Wise**. Apart from his countless recordings with Acuff, he made solo recordings for several labels including Hickory, Stoneway, **Capitol** and **MGM Records**.

● ALBUMS: *Fancy Fiddlin' Country Style* i (Cub 1960) ★★★, *Fancy Fiddlin' Country Style* ii (MGM 1962) ★★★, *Fiddlin' Country Style* (United Artists 1963) ★★★★, with Georgia Slim *Texas Roundup* radio transcriptions (Kanawha 1969) ★★, *Howdy's Fiddle & Howdy Too* (Stoneway 1973) ★★★, *Big Howdy* (Stoneway 1974) ★★★★, with Chubby Wise *Sincerely Yours* (Stoneway 1974) ★★★, with Wise *Fiddle Favorites* (Stoneway 1975) ★★★, *Leather Britches* (Stoneway 1975) ★★★, *Stylish Fiddling* (Stoneway 1976) ★★, with Kenny Baker *Red Apple Rag* (County 1983) ★★★.

Forrester, Sharon

b. 1956, Kingston, Jamaica, West Indies. Forrester's vocals were nurtured by singing from the age of six in church choirs. She came from a musical background: her father played guitar and sang, her brother was a gospel singer based in the USA and her sister was a vocalist in a group called the

Peter Ashburn Affair. Following a performance at her school of the **Supremes**' 'Baby Love', she was inspired to embark on a musical career, performing to tourists on the north coast of Jamaica. Her performances led to a television appearance in Jamaica alongside Richard Ace and an introduction to **Geoffrey Chung** of the band **Now Generation**. Chung had performed alongside Forrester's sister in the Peter Ashburn Affair, and she introduced him to Sharon. Impressed by her vocal range, he took her into the studio in the spring of 1973, and they covered **Valerie Simpson**'s 'Silly Wasn't I' with backing provided by the Now Generation. In November of the same year, Forrester appeared alongside the **Wailers** for the Ethiopian Benefit Concert—predating **Live Aid** by more than a decade. The single was not a big hit, but Chung remained undeterred, and in 1974, because of the musicians strike in Jamaica, he took the young singer to the UK to complete the album *Sharon*. Tracks included a cover version of **Smokey Robinson**'s 'Holly', 'Words With No Meaning' and 'Put A Little Love Away', which was lifted for release on the Vulcan label. While in the UK, she also appeared alongside **Danny Ray** in a film, *Moon Over The Alley*, made by the British Film Institute. Forrester's career was showing potential when in the autumn of 1974 she appeared alongside **Al Brown**, **Cynthia Richards**, **Dennis Brown**, the **Maytals** and **Count Prince Miller** as part of the blighted Jamaica Showcase tour. Junior Lincoln, the man behind the Ashanti label, and Chung were both enthusiastic about Forrester's capability, but she failed to achieve the commercial success expected of her. She appeared in the UK television programme *Aquarius*, performing **George Harrison**'s 'Here Comes The Sun' (her single at the time). Though the occasional recording surfaced, Forrester faded into obscurity. During this period she continued with studio session work, providing backup vocals on a variety of productions. It was not until 1994 that she resurfaced performing 'Love Inside' over a **jungle** rhythm for **ffrr Records**, which bubbled under the UK Top 40 in the spring of 1995. Other releases emerged, 'Dreams' and 'Heaven', both of which were included on the appropriately titled *This Time*. In the spring of 1996 she was managed by the newly formed Sandosa group in Jamaica. A major label contract with Zomba/BMG resulted in the release of 'Red Rose' in combination with **Papa San**. The lyrics were penned by **B.B. Seaton**, and the melody was a version of 'Telstar', a 60s hit for the **Tornados**. **Ernest Ranglin** played guitar, and the single was produced by **Steely And Clevie**. With all the credentials for a crossover hit, it was surprisingly still ignored by the mainstream media.

● ALBUMS: *Sharon* (Ashanti 1974) ★★★, *This Time* (Steely And Clevie 1996) ★★★.

Forsberg, Ebba

b. Sweden. Singer-songwriter Ebba Forsberg considered 'dying my hair and getting a tan just to look different from the US perception of Sweden's women' when she started her career, in an attempt to escape preconceptions created by Swedish music acts such as **Abba**, **Roxette** and **Ace Of Base**. She countered that her musical heritage—she had lived for periods in the West Indies and Botswana—derived its influence more from native African music and American folk than the Scandinavian pop tradition. She returned to Sweden in the late 80s with ambitions to develop a career in music, initially as a session player. At one of these sessions, for Eldkvarn's *Himmelska Dagar* album, she hooked up with

bass player and producer Tony Thoren. They began work on *Been There* together, which was released on the Swedish label MNW Records in March 1997. Forsberg subsequently picked up nominations for Newcomer Of The Year and Best Female Pop/Rock Album at the Swedish Grammi Awards (Thoren won Producer Of The Year for his work on the album). Many of the intimate songs on parade were co-written by Forsberg and sister Kajsa. *Been There* was rereleased on Maverick Records in 1998 after the original version was heard by A&R executive Guy Oseary. Forsberg returned to the studio, this time with Matts Asplen, to rerecord the songs and add a handful of new compositions.

● ALBUMS: *Been There* (MNW/Maverick 1998) ★★★.

Forster, Robert

b. 29 June 1957, Brisbane, Queensland, Australia. A member of the critically acclaimed Australian outfit the **Go-Betweens**, where he matched co-songwriter **Grant McLennan**'s epic pop narrative with epic pop narrative, Forster launched his solo career in the early 90s following the initial breakup of the Go-Betweens in December 1989. *Danger In The Past* addressed the albatross-like history that the Go-Betweens gave Forster, though it also proved he retained the ability to convey genuine melancholia in his songwriting. Produced by **Mick Harvey** (of **Nick Cave**'s Bad Seeds and **Crime And The City Solution**), it fared as well as all his previous Go-Betweens releases—achieving immediate critical acclaim but failing to sell in substantial quantities. The same fate befell the understated *Calling From A Country Phone* and Forster's offbeat collection of cover versions, *I Had A New York Girlfriend*, released in 1994. For 1996's *Warm Nights*, Forster chose to collaborate with the esteemed Scottish artist/producer **Edwyn Collins**. Promoted by the single 'Cryin' Love', the album's highlights included a reprise of the Go-Betweens' 'Rock 'N' Roll Friend' and a polka, 'The Fortress'. This collection proved to be the last recorded output from Forster for several years, as he returned to live in Germany with his wife Karin Bäumler and concentrated on spending time with his young family. He reunited with McLennan on several occasions, using the Go-Betweens banner for a well-received series of live dates, which became a more permanent reunion with the release of a new studio album, 2000's *The Friends Of Rachel Worth*. Forster and McLennan cemented their renewed songwriting union in 2003 with the excellent *Bright Yellow Bright Orange*.

● ALBUMS: *Danger In The Past* (Beggars Banquet 1990) ★★★★, *Calling From A Country Phone* (Beggars Banquet 1993) ★★★, *I Had A New York Girlfriend* (Beggars Banquet 1994) ★★★, *Warm Nights* (Beggars Banquet 1996) ★★★.

FortDax

b. Darren Durham, *c*.1971, West Yorkshire, England. FortDax is the recording moniker adopted by UK electronica artist Durham. He has imagined the project as a strange synthesis of Charles Ives and **Abba**, encompassing aspects of Ives' swing between melancholic abstraction and exuberant layering of sounds and Abba's pure pop dynamism.

FortDax's 2002's *Folly* (the 7-inch 'Like Cream Inside Your Spine' and mini-album *At Bracken* preceded the album) vaguely recalled the pretty near-pastoral electronica of **Boards Of Canada**, **Piano Magic** and **ISAN** and frequently sounded as if constructed on ancient music boxes. The album drew inspiration from themes as disparate as Richard

Scarry's picture books ('Senior Prom In Indigo [For Ole Risom]'), Japanese cherry blossoms ('Sakura') and temporal lobe structures ('Heschl's Gyri'). 'I'm fascinated with the way that the brain processes and stores sound', says Durham of the latter track, 'The way that something which enters as acoustic phenomena can be interpreted and housed as tiny electro-chemical impulses'. Durham says track titles such as 'The Child-Cat Is Crying Out Now', 'Foxglove Into Sparrow-Grass' and 'Seed Sleeps Under Eden' are entirely subjective: 'The titles often seem abstract in relation to the songs. It allows for the listener to fit their own interpretation, find their own space. Things acquire meaning and significance in retrospect, too. Something which begins as a melody, and indeed has no more significance than that for myself, can take on all these extra layers and angles when it's given air.' Three of the album's tracks featured the voice of Cotton Casino from **Acid Mothers Temple**. Durham and Casino have also collaborated under the Foxglove moniker, with songs recorded during the latter band's infrequent visits to the UK. FortDax has also remixed Piano Magic's 'Certainty'.

● ALBUMS: *At Bracken* mini-album (Static Caravan 2002) ★★★, *Folly* (Tugboat 2002) ★★★★.

● COMPILATIONS: split with Eu, Roricat *Witch Hazel Tales* (Earworm 2001) ★★★.

Fortnox

US melodic rockers Fortnox recorded one rather disappointing, **April Wine**-influenced album in 1982 before disappearing. Produced by the renowned Chris Tsangarides, the line-up of the band had coalesced to include Joel Shipp (bass/vocals), Rick Fowler (guitar/vocals) and Nathan De Foor (drums) by the time they entered the studio. Though proficient in their instrumental capacities, the group's songwriting lacked focus and direction. No further recordings were issued as Fortnox were consigned to the rock vaults.

● ALBUMS: *Fortnox* (Epic 1982) ★★.

Fortress

A quartet of Jim West (vocals), Eric Turner (guitar), Charlie Souza (bass) and Donny Vosburgh (drums), US hard rock band Fortress formed at the end of the 70s and played sophisticated melodic metal. An encouraging response to their early demo tapes eventually resulted in a major label contract with **Atlantic Records** in 1981. The group's debut album, *Hands In The Till*, won a fair critical response, but the sales reaction was less favourable. Fortress were dropped by Atlantic shortly after its release and broke up almost immediately thereafter.

● ALBUMS: *Hands In The Till* (Atlantic 1981) ★★★.

Fortune Records

Formed in 1951 by husband and wife Jack and Devora Brown, Fortune Records was an R&B record label based in Detroit, Michigan, USA. The Browns had begun a music publishing company in 1947 and decided to expand into recordings four years later. The label's top act became the soulful vocal group Nolan Strong And The Diablos, who began recording for Fortune in 1956. Their singles, including 'The Wind' and 'Mind Over Matter', are highly prized by R&B record collectors. The group placed only one single, 'Way You Dog Me Around', on the R&B charts. Another artist, Andre Williams, recorded his best-known track, 'Bacon Fat', in 1955 before it was leased to Epic Records and became a Top 10

R&B hit. Another Fortune single, 'Village Of Love' by **Nathaniel Mayer** And The Fabulous Twilights, was also leased, to United Artists, although the Top 20 R&B placing went to the Fortune version. The label stopped issuing new releases by the 70s but has survived into the 90s by reissuing its earlier recordings, which are anxiously bought by devoted R&B collectors.

Fortune, Lance

b. Chris Morris, 1940, Birkenhead, Cheshire, England. Until he received a guitar at Christmas 1956, this grammar school student had studied classical piano. Morris sacrificed a scholarship at a Welsh university to work as an odd-job man at the famous London coffee bar the 2I's, and it was there that he was heard singing by top manager and impresario **Larry Parnes** in 1959. Although he did not manage him, Parnes rechristened him Lance Fortune (a name he had previously given to Clive Powell, a singer and pianist, whom he later renamed **Georgie Fame**). Fortune recorded his first single 'Be Mine', an **Adam Faith**-styled pop song, backed by **John Barry**'s musicians, which was released by Pye and eventually climbed to number 4 in the UK. The producer/engineer was **Joe Meek** and this was his first all solo production. During the time it took to reach the charts in Britain, Fortune toured with his idol, **Gene Vincent**. He also managed to put the follow-up 'This Love I Have For You' into the Top 30, but it was his last taste of success—long-term fame was not on the cards for Mr Fortune.

Fortune, Sonny

b. Cornelius Fortune, 19 May 1939, Philadelphia, Pennsylvania, USA. An intense player on alto, tenor and soprano saxophones and flute, Fortune studied at Wurlitzers and Granoff School of Music and privately with Roland Wiggins. He started his playing career in Philadelphia R&B bands. He moved to New York in 1967 and played with **Elvin Jones** (1968), **Mongo Santamaría** (1968–70), **Leon Thomas** (1970), **McCoy Tyner** (1971–73), Roy Brooks (1973), **Buddy Rich** (1974) and **Miles Davis** (1974–75). He was with Davis when he made his highly controversial 'heavy' album *Agartha*. Despite all the electronics Fortune frequently blisters his way to the fore during this live double album and showed that he had lost none of the fire in the late 80s when he toured with the Elvin Jones Jazz Machine. He has also played with **George Benson**, **Oliver Nelson**, Horace Arnold, **Roy Ayers** and **Pharoah Sanders** but has recorded too seldom as a leader.

● ALBUMS: *Awakening* (A&M 1975) ★★★, *Waves Of Dreams* (A&M 1976) ★★★, *Serengeti Minstrel* (Atlantic 1977) ★★★, *Infinity Is* (Atlantic 1978) ★★★, *With Sound Reason* (Atlantic 1979) ★★★, *It Ain't What It Was* (Konnex 1991) ★★, *Laying It Down* (Konnex 1993) ★★★, *Four In One* (Blue Note 1993) ★★★★, *Monk's Mood* (Konnex 1994) ★★★★, with Gary Bartz *Alto Memories* (Verve 1995) ★★★, *A Better Understanding* (Blue Note 1995) ★★★, *From Now On* (Blue Note 1996) ★★★, *In The Spirit Of John Coltrane* (Shanachie 2000) ★★★, with Billy Harper, Stanley Cowell, Reggie Workman, Billy Hart *Great Friends* 1986 recording (Black & Blue 2003) ★★★, *Continuum* (Sound Reason 2004) ★★★★.

Fortunes

Originally formed in March 1963 as a trio, this UK beat group comprised Glen Dale (b. Richard Garforth, 24 April 1943,

Deal, Kent, England; guitar); Rod Allen (b. Rodney Bainbridge, 31 March 1944, Leicester, England; bass) and Barry Pritchard (b. 3 April 1944, Birmingham, England, d. 11 January 1999, Swindon, Wiltshire, England; guitar). The group had come together at Clifton Hall, the pop academy in the Midlands masterminded by their manager **Reg Calvert**. After perfecting their harmonic blend, the group recruited David Carr (b. 4 August 1943, Leyton, Essex, England; keyboards) and Andy Brown (b. 7 July 1946, Birmingham, England; drums) and toured consistently in the Midlands. Their debut single, 'Summertime Summertime' passed without notice, but the follow-up 'Caroline' was taken up as the theme song for the pirate radio station of the same name. By 1965 the group had broken into the UK and US Top 10 with 'You've Got Your Troubles' and modestly stated their ambition of recording pop ballads and harmonious standards. 'Here It Comes Again' and 'This Golden Ring' displayed their easy listening appeal and suggested the possibility of a long-term showbusiness career. Unfortunately, the group was hampered by the departure of vocalist Glen Dale who went on to pursue an unsuccessful solo career. To make matters worse, their manager was shot dead in a dispute over the ownership of the UK pirate station Radio City. The group continued and after switching record labels scored an unexpectedly belated US hit with 'Here Comes That Rainy Day Feeling Again' in 1971. Back in the UK, they also enjoyed their first hits in over five years with 'Freedom Come Freedom Go' and 'Storm In A Teacup' and have since sustained their career, albeit with changing personnel, on the cabaret circuit.

● ALBUMS: *The Fortunes* i (Decca 1965) ★★★, *That Same Old Feeling* (World Pacific 1969) ★★★, *The Fortunes* ii (Capitol 1971) ★★★, *Here Comes That Rainy Day Feeling Again* (Capitol 1971) ★★★, *Storm In A Teacup* (Capitol 1972) ★★★.

● COMPILATIONS: *Remembering* (Decca 1977) ★★★, *Best Of The Fortunes* (EMI 1983) ★★★, *Music For The Millions* (Decca 1984) ★★★, *Greatest Hits* (BR 1985) ★★★, *Here It Comes Again* (Deram 1996) ★★★, *The Singles* (BR 1999) ★★★.

Forty-Five Minutes From Broadway

You can get to New Rochelle, New York, in forty-five minutes from the 'great white way', and that's the location **George M. Cohan** had in mind when he wrote the music, book and lyrics for this show which opened at the New Amsterdam Theatre on 1 January 1906. As the curtain rises, Tom Bennet (Donald Brian) is expecting to inherit a great deal of money from his recently deceased millionaire uncle, which will enable him to marry the actress, Flora Dora Dean (Lois Ewell), and keep her in a style to which she is rapidly becoming accustomed. However, the important last will and testament is missing—until Tom's secretary, the cocky Kid Burns (**Victor Moore**), finds it and discovers that all the money has been left to the millionaire's housekeeper, Mary Jane Jenkins (Faye Templeton). Mary and the Kid fall in love, but when he shows her the will, she thinks he wants her for the money. Perish the thought: it has never crossed the Kid's mind, and he tells her so in no uncertain terms. He would never contemplate marrying someone with that much money—so Mary eventually tears up the will. Cohan's score contained three of his most successful songs: 'Mary's A Grand Old Name', 'So Long Mary' and the title number.

There was also 'Gentlemen Of The Press' and 'I Want to Be A Popular Millionaire'. Moore, who played Kid Burns in the show, played him again in the 1907 musical *Talk Of New York* before going on to a long and successful Hollywood career. When *Forty-Five Minutes From Broadway* was revived in New York 1912 (at the Cohan Theatre), Cohan himself took the lead. The show's initial run of only 90 performances gives no indication as to how innovative and different Cohan's ideas actually were. When this show was presented, America was still on a diet of European operetta, none of which had the flair or showmanship that this multitalented personality displayed.

Forty-Fives

Despite possessing a sound that is pure Motor City, the Forty-Fives come from the South, namely Atlanta, Georgia. Formed in 1998, the band started as a trio comprising Bryan Malone (guitar/vocals), Mark McMurtry (bass) and Adam Renshaw (drums). The fledgling trio found the missing ingredient in their sound with the addition of Trey Tidwell (Hammond organ). The quartet entered the recording studio shortly thereafter to make demos that eventually became the band's debut album, *Get It Together* (issued originally on the NG label in 1999, before being reissued a year later with different artwork, via Artemis Records).

The Forty-Fives soon earned a reputation as being an incredibly hard touring band, opening for a variety of artists and appearing at numerous US music festivals, including CMJ and South By Southwest. Work began on the quartet's second album in early 2002 that included a trip to one of the world's best known recording facilities, Sun Studios in Memphis, Tennessee. With **Southern Culture On The Skids** leader Rick Miller producing, the Forty-Fives issued *Fight Dirty* later the same year. Unsurprisingly, the band supported this release with extensive touring, as they sought to spread their soulful garage rock gospel to an even larger audience.

● ALBUMS: *Get It Together* (NG/Artemis 1999) ★★★, *Fight Dirty* (Yep Roc 2002) ★★★★.

44 Magnum

Japanese heavy metal outfit formed in 1977 by vocalist Tatsuya Umehara and guitarist Satoshi Hirorse. With the addition of Hironori Yoshikawa on bass and Satoshi Miyawaki on drums, they persevered for many years in the shadow of higher-profile Japanese bands such as Loudness, **Earthshaker** and **Bow Wow**. They eventually secured a record contract in 1982 and debuted with *Danger* the following year. Although the musicianship was competent, their ideas and style were too obviously influenced by British and American acts such as **Van Halen**, **Deep Purple** and **Led Zeppelin**.

● ALBUMS: *Danger* (Moon 1983) ★★★, *Street Rock 'n' Roller* (Roadrunner 1984) ★★★.

44xes

This **techno** rock/industrial band was formed in Bremen, Germany, in 1993, originally as Crashcat. By the beginning of 1995 Heiko Grien (vocals), Markus Gronostay (guitar), Raphael Kraft (guitar) and Dietmar Popke (drums) had changed their name to 44xes—pronounced 'forty-four excess'. Their first concert together came at an Amsterdam festival, performing in front of a mixed audience of punks, industrial and metal fans. After the release of their debut mini-album in 1995, boasting a punishing sound reminiscent of a more restrained **Nine Inch Nails**, they embarked on touring dates with **Shihad**.

● ALBUMS: *Banish Silence* mini-album (When! Recordings 1995) ★★★.

42nd Street (film musical)

The definitive backstage musical, starring **Ruby Keeler** as Peggy Sawyer. Warner Baxter played tough guy Julian Marsh who gives her a push into the spotlight after his has-been star, Dorothy Brock (**Bebe Daniels**), hits the bottle and accidentally descends a long flight of stairs. Tommy Lawer (**Dick Powell**) is the show's juvenile lead and Peg's biggest fan, but **Ginger Rogers**, as Anytime Annie, almost steals the film away from everyone. The screenplay was by James Seymour and Rian James and **Harry Warren** and **Al Dubin** contributed some memorable songs, including 'Young And Healthy', 'Shuffle Off To Buffalo', 'You're Getting To Be A Habit With Me', 'It Must Be June' and 'Forty-Second Street'. That score, and the sensational dance routines designed by **Busby Berkeley**, make this one of the all-time great screen musicals and are the reasons why it still sounds and looks so good more than 60 years later. Also in the cast were George Brent, Ned Sparks, Guy Kibbee, Allen Jenkins, George E. Stone and Una Merkel. Warren and Dubin also made brief appearances, as did another well-known songwriter, **Harry Akst**. *42nd Street* was produced in 1933 for Warner Brothers by Darryl F. Zanuck and directed by Lloyd Bacon. In 1980 a stage version began a run of more than eight years on Broadway, and in 1984 a successful production opened in London.

42nd Street (stage musical)

Based on one of the most popular film musicals of the 30s and the novel by Bradford Ropes, *42nd Street* was a kind of twin-edged sword. On the one hand, it was enormously successful, running for 3,486 performances, and on the other, well, perhaps it was a sign that, apart from composers such as **Stephen Sondheim** and **Jerry Herman**, there was beginning to be a shortage of homegrown original musicals written for Broadway. When it opened at the Winter Garden Theatre in New York on 24 August 1980, the British invasion had already begun and, during the next 10 years or so, would intensify until the New York theatre was dominated by 'intruders' such as **Andrew Lloyd Webber**. The book for *42nd Street*, which was written by Michael Stewart and Mark Bramble, told the old familiar story of a stagestruck chorus girl, Peggy Sawyer (Wanda Richert), from Allentown, Pennsylvania, who gets her big chance when the star, Dorothy Brock (**Tammy Grimes**), breaks her ankle during show's tryout. Broadway veteran **Jerry Orbach** plays the frantic producer, Julian Marsh, who tells Dorothy, 'You're going out a youngster, but you've got to come back a star!' **Harry Warren** and **Al Dubin**'s songs from the original film were supplemented by other numbers of theirs, and the score contained most of the familiar favourites, such as 'Young And Healthy', 'Shadow Waltz', 'Go Into Your Dance', 'You're Getting To Be A Habit With Me', 'Dames', 'We're In The Money', 'Lullaby Of Broadway', 'About A Quarter To Nine', 'Shuffle Off To Buffalo' and 'Forty-Second Street'. The show was produced by David Merrick and won **Tony Awards** for best musical and for **Gower Champion**'s sensational choreography. Sadly, Champion never experienced the public's ecstatic reaction to his work; he died on the day the show

opened in New York. In the 1984 London production at Drury Lane, the part of Julian Marsh, the producer, was originally played by James Laurenson. His surprise replacement during the run of 1,823 performances was the veteran popular singer **Frankie Vaughan**. Vaughan himself was succeeded by Kenneth Nelson, an American actor domiciled in Britain. Nelson also played Marsh in a limited-run revival at London's Dominion Theatre in 1991.

Fosse, Bob

b. Robert Louis Fosse, 23 June 1927, Chicago, Illinois, USA, d. 23 September 1987, Washington, DC, USA. A director, choreographer, dancer and actor for films and stage, Fosse was renowned particularly for his innovative and spectacular staging, with the emphasis very firmly on the exhilarating dance sequences. He studied ballet, tap and acrobatic dance from an early age and, while still a youngster, performed with a partner as the Riff Brothers in vaudeville and burlesque houses. After graduating from high school in 1945, he spent two years in the US Navy before moving to New York and studying acting at the American Theatre Wing. He then toured in the chorus of various productions before making his Broadway debut as a dancer in the revue *Dance Me A Song* (1950). He worked on television and in theatres and clubs for a time until Hollywood beckoned, and he moved to the west coast to appear in three films, *Give A Girl A Break*, *The Affairs Of Dobie Gillis* and *Kiss Me, Kate* (1953). On his return to New York, he gained his big break when author and director **George Abbott** hired him as a choreographer for *The Pajama Game* (1954). The show was a massive hit, and Fosse was much in demand—for a time at least. He met **Gwen Verdon** while working on *Damn Yankees* in 1955, and they were married in 1960.

He choreographed **Bells Are Ringing** in 1956 and worked with Verdon again on **New Girl In Town** a year later. From then on, with the exception of **How To Succeed In Business Without Really Trying** (1961), he directed his shows as well as staging the dancing. Fosse's dual role is considered by critics to be a major factor in the success of highly popular productions such as **Redhead** (1959), **Little Me** (1962), **Sweet Charity** (1966), **Pippin** (1972), **Chicago** (1975) and **Dancin'** (1978). Throughout all this time he moved back and forwards between New York and Hollywood, working on films such as *My Sister Eileen* (1955), **The Pajama Game** (1957) and *Damn Yankees* (1958), all three of which were well received. However, *Sweet Charity* (1968), which Fosse controlled completely in his role as director and choreographer, was hammered by many critics for Shirley MacLaine's over-the-top performance and particularly for the director's self-indulgent cinematography, with its looming close-ups, zooms and blurred focus effects. Fosse was in the wilderness for some time, but all was forgiven four years later when **Cabaret**, starring **Liza Minnelli** and **Joel Grey**, won eight Academy Awards, one of which went to Fosse. It was a box-office smash, and Fosse also satisfied most of the purists by confining the dance sequences to appropriate locations such as a beer garden and nightclub, rather than flooding the streets of Berlin with terpsichorean tourists.

In the early 70s Fosse was applauded for his direction of *Lenny*, a film biography of the comedian Lenny Bruce, that starred Dustin Hoffman. In the light of Fosse's recent heart problems, his record as a workaholic and his lifelong obsession with perfection, many observers thought that *All*

That Jazz (1979) was intended to be Fosse's own film autobiography, with its ghoulish, self-indulgent examination of life and death. However, no one denied the brilliance of the dance routines or the outstanding performance of Roy Scheider in the leading role. In 1983 Fosse wrote and directed his last film, *Star 80*, which also had a lurid, tragic theme. Three years later, he wrote, staged and choreographed his final Broadway musical, *Big Deal*—which was, in fact, far less than its title suggested. It represented an inappropriate end to a brilliant career, in which Fosse had created some of the most imaginative and thrilling dance routines ever seen on Broadway or in Hollywood, winning eight **Tony Awards** in the process. In 1987 he revived one of his most successful shows, *Sweet Charity*, and died shortly before the curtain went up on the night of 23 September. A fascinating documentary entitled *Bob Fosse—Steam Heat*, was made by the US company WNET/Thirteen in 1990. The source of one of his greatest triumphs, *Chicago*, was revived to great acclaim on Broadway and in the West End in 1996/7. The choreography of Ann Reinking (b. 10 November 1949) was created, with great respect and affection, 'in the style of Bob Fosse'. His incredible wit and vitality were remembered again early in 1999, when a retrospective of his dance numbers entitled *Fosse* opened on Broadway. The show was directed by **Richard Maltby Jnr.** and Reinking and choreographed by Reinking and Chet Walker.

● FURTHER READING: *Razzle Dazzle: The Life And Works Of Bob Fosse*, Kevin Boyd Grubb. *Bob Fosse's Broadway*, Margery Beddow. *All His Jazz: The Life And Death Of Bob Fosse*, Martin Gottfried.

Foster And Lloyd

During the early 80s, **Radney Foster** (b. 20 July 1959, Del Rio, Texas, USA) was playing in a local club when a producer suggested he move to Nashville. The new MTM music group employed him as a staff writer, and there he met Bill Lloyd (b. 6 December 1955, Fort Hood, Texas, USA). Lloyd had worked in New York and Kentucky before relocating to Nashville where they wrote for **Sweethearts Of The Rodeo** (Foster also co-wrote **Holly Dunn**'s US country hit single 'Love Someone Like Me'). By chance a recording contract was offered to them in preference to the songwriting agreement they were hoping to secure. A decision had to be taken quickly as they both had busy solo careers—they decided to take the risk, and their 1987 debut was a huge success, spawning three US country chart Top 10 hits, 'Crazy Over You', 'Sure Thing' and 'What Do You Want From Me This Time?'. The duo never managed to repeat the success of their debut, and they split up in 1992. Their final album, 1990's *Version Of The Truth*, included an instrumental 'Whoa', recorded with **Duane Eddy**. Foster continued with a solo recording career while Lloyd worked as a songwriter and session guitarist. He has also recorded the occasional solo album in the power pop vein.

● ALBUMS: *Foster & Lloyd* (RCA 1987) ★★★★, *Faster & Llouder* (RCA 1989) ★★★, *Version Of The Truth* (RCA 1990) ★★★.

● COMPILATIONS: *The Essential Foster And Lloyd* (RCA 1996) ★★★★.

Foster, Al

b. Aloysius Foster, 18 January 1944, Richmond, Virginia, USA. Given a drum kit when he was 10, Foster began playing around New York at 16 and was first recorded in 1964 (with Blue Mitchell). It was during his long residency at the Cellar Club, with the Earl May Quartet, that he was noticed by **Miles Davis**, resulting in three years and a worldwide tour with the Davis group (1972–75). He rejoined Davis for his comeback in 1980, staying with him for five years and recording. This highly versatile and respected drummer has also led several groups, including those with **Steve Kuhn**, **Charlie Haden** and **Joe Henderson**, and played in **Quest** with **David Liebman**. In 2002 Foster formed the loose collective known as ScoLoHoFo with **Joe Lovano**, **Dave Holland** and **John Scofield**.

● ALBUMS: with ScoLoHoFo *Oh!* (Blue Note 2003) ★★★.

Foster, Alex

b. Paul Alexander Foster, 10 May 1953, Oakland, California, USA. A strikingly gifted alto saxophonist and clarinettist, Foster first attracted attention in 1973. He became a founder member of **Jack DeJohnette**'s Directions, then worked with **McCoy Tyner**, **Nat Adderley** and **Freddie Hubbard**. In the mid-70s he entered the New York studios, playing on countless pop and jingle sessions, and he was also in the band for the Broadway show **Ain't Misbehavin'**. He continued playing jazz, appearing on record sessions with **Don Sebesky**, and then, in 1982, joined **Jaco Pastorius** for a big band tour. With Pastorius he made three world tours, appearing on two live albums with the big band, *Live In Japan* and *Live In New York*, and three studio sessions with a small group. In the mid-80s he joined the house band on television's *Saturday Night Live*. He continued to make studio sessions, including playing in bands supporting pop artists such as **Paul Simon** (playing on *Graceland*) and **Paul McCartney**. In the early 90s he recorded an album under his own name and also toured with the Gil Evans Orchestra, Mingus Dynasty and **Steps Ahead** with **Mike Mainieri** and in mid-decade was again with the *Saturday Night Live* band as featured soloist. An exhilarating player with a fiery sound, Foster's inventive playing marks him out as a musician to watch whenever he steps outside the relative anonymity of other people's bands.

● ALBUMS: *Beginnings . . . Goodbye* (Big World 1991) ★★★, with Michael Wolff *Pool Of Dreams* (Truspace 1997) ★★★.

Foster, Chris

b. 23 April 1948, Yeovil, Somerset, England. This singer and guitarist first started playing in public in 1964 at local folk clubs. His influences at the time ranged from **Cyril Tawney**, to **Davey Graham**, **'Big' Bill Broonzy** and **Louis Killen**. Foster included both traditional and contemporary material in his live performances. While still at college, he played support on the 1971 **Rev. Gary Davis** tour of the UK. The following year, he left art school and went into music in a full-time capacity until the mid-80s. *Layers* featured the fiddle of **Nic Jones**, while *All Things In Common* included the much covered **Bill Caddick** song 'Unicorns'. *Fylde Acoustic* was so named because all the artists (including **Gordon Giltrap** and **Martin Carthy**) performing on the album played Fylde instruments. After experiencing moderate success on the folk circuit, but feeling he was getting nowhere, Foster bowed out of the scene and, apart from occasional bookings, did little musically for three years. In the late 80s Foster began playing bass in a blues band and then, in 1991, started playing in folk clubs again. He returned to recording with 1999's *Traces*.

● ALBUMS: *Layers* (1977) ★★★, with various artists *Fylde Acoustic* (1977) ★★★, *All Things In Common* (1979) ★★★★, with various artists *Nuclear Power No Thanks!* (1981) ★★, *Traces* (Green Man 1999) ★★★.

Foster, Chuck

Chuck Foster And His Orchestra, formed in Los Angeles, California, USA, in 1938, were a hotel dance band whose sound was most commonly described as 'sweet'. With influences drawn across the board from the big band tradition, including **Jan Garber**, **Russ Morgan**, **Sammy Kaye** and **Kay Kyser**, their first major engagement came at the Biltmore Bowl in Los Angeles. With radio shows routinely broadcast from that location, it provided the band with an auspicious grounding and instant popularity (not least for their theme song 'Oh, You Beautiful Doll'). Foster had previously played reed instruments in the Topsy's Restaurant House Band in South Gate, California, a role he continued in his new band, which also included well-regarded pianist Hal Pruden, who would later take over leadership of the group. The vocalists were Dorothy Brandon, Jean Gordon, Dotty Dotson and Jimmy Castle. Radio exposure on programmes such as *The Coca Cola Parade Of Spotlight Bands* enabled the orchestra to pursue coast to coast tours, with one nighters in hotels throughout America. Moving base from California to the Midwest, they became a favoured attraction at the Peabody Hotel in Memphis, the Muehlbach Hotel in Kansas City, the Roosevelt in New Orleans, the Aragon Ballroom and the Blackhawk Restaurant in Chicago. The 50s also witnessed excursions to the Roseland Ballroom and New Yorker in New York, with the group's songs issued on **Philips**, **Mercury** and **OKeh Records**. With Foster making his home in the San Fernando Valley in the mid-60s, the group's activities centred on an extended booking at Myron's Valley in Los Angeles. Afterwards Foster concentrated on Midwest tours, which continued throughout the 60s and 70s, without ever recapturing his earlier popularity.

Foster, David

b. Victoria, British Columbia, Canada. Foster is one of the leading songwriters and producers of the modern rock era, a multi–Grammy Award winner who has been involved with some of the bestselling songs of all-time. His name is synonymous with AOR (Adult Orientated Rock).

The precocious Foster learned to play piano as a child and enrolled at the University of Washington at the age of 13. He left college three years later to play with **Chuck Berry**'s band, one of the most difficult initiations a fledgling musician could possibly undertake. Foster relocated to Los Angeles at the start of the 70s where he joined up with the Canadian band Skylark, which included his then wife B.J. Cook. The quartet signed a major label recording contract with **Capitol Records** and achieved a Canadian number 1 and a US Top 10 hit in 1973 with 'Wildflower'. Foster later worked with leading Los Angeles session men **Danny Kortchmar**, Paul Stallworth and Jim Keltner in the Attitudes, enjoying a minor hit in 1976 with 'Sweet Summer Music'. By now he had become a leading session keyboard player, working with **Rod Stewart**, **George Harrison** and **Barbra Streisand**, but of more note was his burgeoning production and writing career. Foster's clients included **Hall And Oates**, the **Average White Band**, **Boz Scaggs** and **Deniece Williams**, and in 1979 he earned the first of his many Grammy Awards for composing **Earth, Wind And Fire**'s 'After The Love Has Gone'.

Foster enjoyed even greater success in the 80s, writing and producing a string of massive hit singles for **Chicago** (including the US chart-topper 'Hard To Say I'm Sorry', 'Hard Habit To Break' and 'Will You Still Love Me?') and writing lead singer **Peter Cetera**'s solo chart-topper 'The Glory Of Love'. He also worked on **Lionel Richie**'s bestselling 1983 album *Can't Slow Down* and composed **John Parr**'s transatlantic hit single 'St. Elmo's Fire (Man In Motion)'. During this period, Foster enjoyed a hit single of his own with 'Love Theme From St. Elmo's Fire' reaching the US Top 20 in 1985. Minor solo hits with 'The Best Of Me' (a duet with **Olivia Newton-John**) and 'Winter Games', and a series of forgettable AOR collections for **Atlantic Records** followed during the late 80s.

In the early 90s, Foster worked with **Natalie Cole** on the multi-platinum and multi–Grammy Award winning *Unforgettable . . . With Love* and collaborated with **Whitney Houston** on the film soundtrack *The Bodyguard*. He teamed up with **Celine Dion** on her English language breakthroughs, 1990's *Unison*, 1993's *The Colour Of My Love* and 1996's *Falling Into You*, and enjoyed further hits with artists including **Madonna** ('You'll See'), **All-4-One** ('I Swear') and **Toni Braxton** ('Un-break My Heart'). During the mid-90s Foster launched his own Atlantic imprint 143 Records, one of the first signings to which was Irish band the **Corrs**. Foster later enjoyed huge transatlantic success with another 143 signing, jazz pop singer **Michael Bublé**.

● ALBUMS: *Songwriters For The Stars* (DFF 1982) ★★, *The Best Of Me* (Atlantic 1984) ★★★, *David Foster* (Atlantic 1986) ★★★, *The Symphony Sessions* (Atlantic 1988) ★★, *Time Passing* mini-album (Atlantic 1989) ★★, *River Of Love* (Atlantic 1990) ★★, *Rechordings* (Atlantic 1991) ★★★, *The Christmas Album* (Interscope 1993) ★★, *Love Lights The World* (143 1994) ★★, with Tony Smith *A Touch Of China* (Form 1996) ★★.

● COMPILATIONS: *A Touch Of David Foster* (WEA 1992) ★★★, various artists *The Best Of Me: A Collection Of David Foster's Greatest Works* (Warners 2002) ★★★, with various artists *Love Stories* (Warners Japan 2002) ★★★.

Foster, Frank

b. 23 September 1928, Cincinnati, Ohio, USA. Although he began his musical career playing alto saxophone, Foster showed commendable foresight in deciding to change to tenor saxophone and flute, declaring his intention of following his own path and not the one signposted by **Charlie Parker**. In the late 40s he played with several like-minded spirits in the Detroit area, among them **Wardell Gray** and **Snooky Young**, before serving in the armed forces. In 1953 he joined **Count Basie** and became a significant member of the band as soloist, arranger and composer ('Shiny Stockings'). After 11 years with Basie he joined **Elvin Jones**, another of the musicians with whom he had played in Detroit early in his career. In the mid-60s he formed a big band that continued to play intermittently over the next decade. He also played with the **Thad Jones–Mel Lewis** Jazz Orchestra and co-led a small group with former Basie sectionmate **Frank Wess**. In the mid-80s Foster began a long stint as frontman for the reactivated Basie band, with which he toured the USA and Europe.

Foster's arrangements have always shown his affinity with post-war big-band writing, and his work for Basie was an important factor in the success of that particular edition of the band. As a soloist, Foster's early decision to go his own way paid dividends as he developed a distinctively acerbic tone that, while reflecting an awareness of his contemporaries, was very much his own.

● ALBUMS: with James Moody *Sax Talk* (Vogue 1952) ★★★, *Frank Foster Quintet* 10-inch album (Blue Note 1954) ★★★, with Paul Quinichette *Jazz Studio 1* (Decca 1954) ★★★, with Elmo Hope *Hope Meets Foster* aka *Wail Frank Wail* (Prestige 1956) ★★★★, *Basie Is Our Boss* (Argo 1963) ★★★★, *Fearless Frank Foster* (Prestige 1967) ★★★, *Soul Outing!* (Prestige 1967) ★★★, *Manhattan Fever* (Blue Note 1968) ★★★, *The Loud Minority* (Mainstream 1974) ★★★, *Here And Now* (Catalyst 1976) ★★★, *12 Shades Of Black* (Leo 1978) ★★★, *Shiny Stockings* (Denon 1978) ★★★★, *Roots, Branches And Dances* (Bee Hive 1978) ★★★★, *The House That Love Built* (SteepleChase 1982) ★★★, *Two For The Blues* (Pablo 1983) ★★★, *Frankly Speaking* (Concord Jazz 1984) ★★, *Leo Rising* (Arabesque 1997) ★★★★, *Swing* (Challenge 1998) ★★★, with the Loud Minority Big Band *We Do It Diff'rent* (Mapleshade 2003) ★★★.

Foster, Fred

b. 26 July 1931, Fred Luther Foster, Rutherfordton, North Carolina, USA. Foster was born on a small farm that, as a boy, after his father died, he contrived to run for several years. He eventually relocated to live with a married sister in Washington, DC, and worked in various jobs until he achieved an administrative post with a restaurant chain. After meeting an entertainer called Billy Strickland, they began writing songs for a local publishing company. In 1952 Foster persuaded **Jimmy Dean** to record a demo of a song written by Pete Graves called 'Bumming Around'. Foster then presented it to 4 Star Records who saw its potential and released it in March 1953; it peaked at number 5 and gave Dean his first *Billboard* country charts hit.

After failing his medical to join the US Air Force because of an eye injury, Foster returned to writing and publishing. He soon became a regional promotions manager for **Mercury Records** and later moved to **ABC**-Paramount and later J&F Records, where he worked on a commission basis primarily involved with the sales of pop records. In 1958 he formed his Monument label although he had insufficient capital to launch the label and had to persuade **Chet Atkins** to let him use the RCA recording studios in Nashville with a promise to pay later. On 5 January 1959 **Billy Grammer**'s recording of 'Gotta Travel On' (based on an old British folk song) entered the charts. It reached number 5 and became Monument Records first country chart entry.

Foster relocated to Nashville and soon formed his second label Sound Stage 7. Between 1960 and 1965 pop singer **Roy Orbison** charted 19 Top 40 hits on Monument. They included 'Only The Lonely', 'Crying', 'Dream Baby', 'In Dreams', 'It's Over' and the million-selling 'Oh Pretty Woman'. In 1962 Foster's production saw **Grandpa Jones** take the old **Jimmie Rodgers**' blue yodel 'T For Texas' into the Top 5 in the country charts. The following year further major success in the pop music field came from 'Yakety Sax', an instrumental by saxophonist **Boots Randolph**. In 1964 Foster produced 'Dumb Blonde', the first chart entry for an up-and-coming singer-songwriter called **Dolly Parton**. The successes of the

Monument label attracted others singers such as **Billy Walker**, who between 1966 and 1970 scored 12 hits on Monument, the biggest being 'Bear With Me A Little Longer' and **Jeannie Seely**, who between 1966 and 1968 had eight chart entries including her first 'Don't Touch Me' (number 2). By 1970 **Henson Cargill** had gained his first seven hits on the label including his number 1, 'Skip A Rope'. Others included **Ray Stevens** (who, in 1969, gained chart success with 'Sunday Morning Coming Down'). The song's writer, **Kris Kristofferson**, signed to Foster's label in 1972 and gained a number 1 with 'Why Me' the following year. **Larry Gatlin** also joined in 1972 and by 1978 had registered 14 Monument hits including 'I Don't Want To Cry' and 'Broken Lady' and his first number 1'I Just Wish You Were Someone I Love'. In 1974 **Billy Swan**'s Monument recording of 'I Can Help' topped both US country and pop charts, reached number 6 in the UK pop charts and became a million-seller. In the late 70s, Foster produced seven chart hits for **Connie Smith**, whom he described as 'the essence of country music . . . the epitome of country singers'.

Foster's final single release was in 1982, but a year later his double album *The Winning Hand* featuring Parton, **Willie Nelson**, Kristofferson and **Brenda Lee** proved very popular. The release saw the end of Foster's involvement in the music, and he went into retirement. Experts rate his production as among the best Nashville has ever seen, and he is credited as coauthor with Kristofferson of 'Me And Bobby McGee', which stands as one of the most popular anthems of country music of all time. Foster also served on the board of the **Country Music Association**.

Foster, George 'Pops'

b. 18 May 1892, McCall, Louisiana, USA, d. 30 October 1969, San Francisco, California, USA. One of the pioneers of string bass playing, Foster began his musical career as a cellist and also occasionally played brass bass. After performing in New Orleans in the early years of the century with **Kid Ory**, **King Oliver** and others, he joined **Fate Marable**'s riverboat band in 1917. He was also with the unit Ory led in California in the early 20s. Foster spent the mid-20s in the St. Louis area, and by the end of the decade he was in New York working with **Luis Russell**. He stayed with Russell for several years, during which time the band became, in effect, the **Louis Armstrong** orchestra. In 1940, as the **revival movement** got under way, Foster was in great demand and moved on to freelance work, playing with many bands, including those led by **Sidney Bechet** and **Jimmy Archey**. He played on through the 50s and early 60s, touring the USA and Europe with **Sammy Price**, and he also spent time in bands led by **Earl Hines**, at San Francisco's Hangover Club, and **Elmer Snowden**. Although deeply rooted in the traditional forms of New Orleans jazz, Foster's early preference for string bass, which he played in the traditional 'slapping' manner, stood him in good stead when the inevitable musical changes occurred.

● FURTHER READING: *Pops Foster: The Autobiography Of A New Orleans Jazzman*, Pops Foster with Tom Stoddard and Ross Russell.

Foster, Joe

b. 9 August 1960, Bloomsbury, London, England. Foster was one of the less celebrated leading lights behind the **Creation Records** success story. His origins, like those of another Creation veteran, **Ed Ball**, can be traced back to the early 80s *avant garde* pop of the **Television Personalities**. He also produced the TVP's classic album *The Painted Word* before joining **Alan McGee** in the embryonic **Biff Bang Pow!** In 1983 he formed Creation with Alan McGee and Dick Green, going on to become the label's house producer. In this capacity he produced many of the early singles and albums that distinguished the label, including material by the **Loft**, **Primal Scream**, **Jesus And Mary Chain** and Biff Bang Pow! By 1987 Foster had begun a relationship with **My Bloody Valentine**, recording singles with them for the Kaleidoscope Sound label before bringing them and another artist on that label, Dave Kusworth, to Creation. Two albums with Kusworth, plus two **Felt** collections, were produced in 1988, before he moved to Holland to produce various projects for the Megadisc label. On his return to England he would use this experience to help young bands tour the low countries, and he also returned to live sound engineering (having initially taken this role with the fledgling Jesus And Mary Chain). In 1991 Foster set up a small demo studio with **Sonic Boom** (ex-**Spacemen 3**) to record the artist's new material and that of other local bands. The following year he returned to Creation to set up a subsidiary division, the Rev-Ola label, in order to license and remaster material from the 50s to 80s (including the excellent reissues from the **Millennium** and **Sagittarius**). He continued to run the label while producing albums by **18 Wheeler** and the **Creation**, the 60s psyche band who originally inspired the parent label's choice of title. After the breakup of Creation Records, Foster moved on to join the newly formed Poptones label. When Poptones hit second round financing problems in November 2001, Foster was unceremoniously dumped. He bounced back in 2002, joining forces with **Cherry Red Records**' Iain McNay in revitalizing the Rev-Ola label.

Foster, Leroy 'Baby Face'

b. 1 February 1923, Algoma, Mississippi, USA, d 26 May 1958, Chicago, Illinois, USA. A guitarist and drummer, Foster followed the black migration north in the 40s and worked Maxwell Street and the clubs. Foster's singing was indebted to **John Lee 'Sonny Boy' Williamson**, and like Williamson he was equally impressive on both up-tempo and slow, intense blues. In 1948 he made his debut on record, singing a riotous 'Locked Out Boogie' and a reflective 'Shady Grove Blues', with **Muddy Waters** providing guitar. Foster also made fine recordings for JOB with **Snooky Pryor**, **Sunnyland Slim** and **Robert Lockwood** in support. For **Parkway Records**, he participated in a magnificent session with **Little Walter** and a contract-jumping Muddy Waters, which constitutes, above all on the two-part 'Rollin' And Tumblin'' a striking manifesto for the transformation of Mississippi Delta blues in the Chicago ghetto.
● ALBUMS: *Genesis: The Beginnings Of Rock* (1972) ★★★, *Blues Is Killing Me* (1983) ★★★.

Foster, Little Willie

b. 5 April 1922, Clarksdale, Mississippi, USA. Foster came to Chicago in 1941, already playing guitar, piano and harmonica. Tutored on the latter instrument by **Walter Horton**, he played on Maxwell Street and in a band with **Homesick James**, **Floyd Jones** and **Moody Jones**. Foster recorded two singles in the mid-50s, and 'Crying The Blues', one of the titles, reflected both his emotional singing and his wailing, swooping harmonica. Shortly thereafter, he was shot and semi-paralyzed; he

improved slowly and remained able to play and sing, but only rarely in public. Floyd Jones stated that Foster fatally shot a man and was placed in a mental hospital early in 1974, but as he was photographed in Chicago in September of that year, this information is somewhat dubious. His debut album was issued in 1996 and was produced by **Bobby Mack**, who played the guitar parts. Foster represents another example of an artist who should not have had to wait until his twilight years to be 'discovered'.
● ALBUMS: *I Found Joy* (Palindrome 1996) ★★★.
● COMPILATIONS: *Chicago Blues—The Early 1950s* (1965) ★★★, *King Cobras* (1980) ★★★.

Foster, Radney

b. 20 July 1959, Del Rio, Texas, USA. His father, who was a lawyer (as had been his grandfather and father before him), played guitar and sang and Radney, the second of four Foster children, followed his father's example with regard to music. In 1979 dreams of being a country singer saw him drop out of university and move to Nashville in the hope of fulfilling his ambition. However, he was, at that time, unsuccessful in his quest to be either a singer or a songwriter. Although very disappointed, he refused to give up hope, but after a year, he decided that he would first return home and complete his course at the University of the South, Texas. In the evenings, he sang in local clubs and continued to write songs.
After Foster finally graduated, he returned to Nashville where, this time, he found work as a staff writer for MTM Publishing Company. Here he worked with songwriter Bill Lloyd, and after acquiring a recording contract with **RCA Records**, they began performing as **Foster And Lloyd**. In 1992, after three albums and nine country chart hits and much discussion about the direction of their individual careers, the duo parted amicably. Foster later cited as a reason for the breakup the fact that he felt that many of the songs he was writing were not suited to the duo; for that and other reasons, which probably included a downturn in the duo's success, Foster became a solo artist in 1992. He joined **Arista Records**, and his debut album was named after his birthplace and year of birth. He achieved immediate Top 10 success with 'Just Call Me Lonesome', and in 1993 three more songs, 'Nobody Wins' (a number 2), 'Easier Said Than Done' and 'Hammer And Nails', charted.
The bespectacled and usually well-dressed Foster is a serious man who once said, 'Being a songwriter is about being observant of your own life and the world you see around you'. Foster's songwriting and performing talents should make him remain popular with country music audiences for some time to come, although subsequent releases on the Dualtone label have not achieved the same level of commercial success as his two albums for Arista. Foster is presently happy to have artistic freedom rather than commercial constraints.
● ALBUMS: *Del Rio, TX 1959* (Arista 1992) ★★★, *Labor Of Love* (Arista 1995) ★★★, *See What You Want To See* (Arista 1999) ★★★, *Are You Ready For The Big Show?* (Dualtone 2001) ★★, *Another Way To Go* (Dualtone 2002) ★★★★.
● DVD/VIDEOS: *The Running Kind* (Arista 1994).

Foster, Stephen

b. 4 July 1826, Lawrenceville, Pennsylvania, USA, d. 13 January 1864, USA. Although Foster was a poor student academically, he had an early affinity for music and taught himself to play several instruments. He grew up in a northern middle-class family and learned spirituals and other songs from a household slave, Olivia Pise. Long before he reached his teens, Foster was performing for family and friends, his repertoire including many songs popularized by the minstrel shows of the time. Obliged to earn a living in commerce and prohibited from the formal study of music by his father, Foster's early manhood was a difficult time. However, he began writing songs and in 1841 abandoned all pretence at other activities, becoming a full-time songwriter. His first published song was a sentimental ballad, 'Open The Lattice, Love' (1844), his second a minstrel-type song, 'There's A Good Time Coming' (1846). These opening works marked the twin forms he would follow, ballads and minstrelsy, and as his work began attracting attention, his best songs were usually redolent of the imaginary joys of life in the Deep South under the shadow of slavery: 'Lou'siana Belle', 'Old Uncle Ned' and 'O Susannah'. The massive success of the last song, which he sold for $100, did not change parental disapproval, and he was briefly lured back into commerce by his father.

He returned to writing songs and in 1850 published several, two of which, 'Nelly Bly' and 'Camptown Races', were hugely popular (the latter was used as a campaign song by Abraham Lincoln in 1860). Also in 1850 he married Jane Denny McDowell, who was known as Jeanie and inspired his song 'Jeanie With The Light Brown Hair'. Despite this and other songs he wrote for his wife and the birth of a daughter, the marriage was unhappy. The chief problems were Foster's irresponsibility and his growing drink problem. His songs continued to be successes, many of them now being featured by Ed Christy, leader of the Christy Minstrels, including 'Old Folks At Home' (1851). Foster's habits meant that he was always desperately in need of money, and although he was not blind to the long-term benefits of royalties, he frequently sold songs outright or at best offered partial rights to Christy and others, in return for ready drinking money. In 1853 Foster wrote 'My Old Kentucky Home' and in 1855 'Come Where My Love Lies Dreaming'. In 1860, the year in which he and his wife and child moved to New York, he wrote 'Old Black Joe'.

The outbreak of the war between the states forced Foster to change direction as songs about the supposedly idyllic life led by slaves became justifiably unpopular. During the Civil War he produced many songs with a patriotic flavour, but the most lasting of this period was another wistful ballad, 'Beautiful Dreamer'. The shift of public taste had a detrimental effect upon Foster's career, and his drinking habits worsened. His wife left him, taking their daughter with her, and he sank into severe ill health that was exacerbated by his continued drinking. Shortly after an abortive attempt at suicide, Foster was hospitalized and died in January 1864. He was 37 years of age, and he had less than that number of cents on him when he died. There was a remarkable quality about Foster's livelier pieces, which rose above their questionable minstrel show origins. His own favourites were his ballads, and if they were frequently sung by inadequate singers who delivered them with a sugary coating of sentimentality, the songs themselves have withstood the test of time. They remain a significant milestone in the development of popular song in nineteenth-century America. In 1993 *The Stephen Foster Songbook*, a nostalgic tribute to

one of America's earliest songwriters by the Robert Shaw Chorale, was rereleased.

● FURTHER READING: *The Songs Of Stephen C. Foster From His Own Time To Ours*, William W. Austin. *Doo-Dah!: Stephen Foster And The Rise Of American Popular Culture*, Ken Emerson.

Fotheringay

The folk rock group Fotheringay was formed in 1970 by singer **Sandy Denny** (b. Alexandra Elene Maclean Denny, 6 January 1947, Wimbledon, London, England, d. 21 April 1978, London, England) upon her departure from **Fairport Convention** and drew its name from one of her compositions for that outfit. Two former members of **Eclection**, **Trevor Lucas** (b. 25 December 1943, Bungaree, Victoria, Australia, d. 4 February 1989, Sydney, Australia; guitar/vocals) and Gerry Conway (b. 11 September 1947, Kings Lynn, Norfolk, England; drums), and two former members of **Poet And The One Man Band**, **Jerry Donahue** (b. 24 September 1946, Manhattan, New York, USA; guitar) and Pat Donaldson (bass), completed the line-up responsible for the quintet's lone album. This impressive, folk-based set included several superior Denny originals, notably 'Nothing More', 'The Sea' and 'The Pond And The Stream', as well as meticulous readings of **Gordon Lightfoot**'s 'The Way I Feel' and **Bob Dylan**'s 'Too Much Of Nothing'. Although criticized contemporaneously as constrained, *Fotheringay* is now rightly viewed as a confident, accomplished work. However, the album failed to match commercial expectations, and pressures on Denny to undertake a solo career—she was voted Britain's number 1 singer in *Melody Maker*'s 1970 poll—increased. Fotheringay was disbanded in 1971 during sessions for a projected second set. Some of its songs surfaced on the vocalist's debut album, *The Northstar Grassman*, and whereas Donaldson and Conway began session work, Lucas and Donahue resurfaced in Fairport Convention.

● ALBUMS: *Fotheringay* (Island 1970) ★★★.
● FURTHER READING: *No More Sad Refrains: The Life And Times Of Sandy Denny*, Clinton Heylin.

Foucault, Jeffrey

b. Wisconsin, USA. Singer-songwriter Foucault studied history at the University of Wisconsin in Madison, during which time he began performing on the local coffee house circuit. Inspired by artists such as **Greg Brown**, **John Prine** and **Chris Smither**, Foucault immersed himself in the roots music of his country, drawing on blues, folk and country on his impressive debut, *Miles From The Lightning*. The album, warmly received by the roots rock community, was self-released in 2001. The critics were particularly impressed by the narrative drive of Foucault's material, augmented by sensitive backing from fellow songwriters **Peter Mulvey** and **Mark Olson**. The final track, 'Miles From The Lightning', was dedicated to **Townes Van Zandt**, a performer with whom Foucault was being regularly compared. Next was a loose-knit project teaming Foucault with fellow songwriters Mulvey and **Kris Delmhorst**. In 2003 the trio released an endearing, self-titled album as Redbird on the Signature Sounds label. Delmhorst and Mulvey returned to help out on the superb 2004 release *Stripping Cane*, which also featured Redbird multi-instrumentalist David Goodrich.

● ALBUMS: *Miles From The Lightning* (Own Label 2001) ★★★, *Stripping Cane* (Signature Sounds 2004) ★★★★.

Foul Play

Formed by John Morrow and Steve Bradshaw (d. 1997), Foul Play formed one of the more interesting teams in the UK's **jungle**/drum 'n' bass movement of the mid-90s. Their debut album recalled their back catalogue to date, with only four wholly new items standing next to remixes of their earlier club hits (the best known of which was probably 1993's 'Open Your Mind'). The production guests included Andy C and Anthony Miles under one of their many aliases, Desired State, Hopa And Bones, and perceived rivals, Omni Trio. The new tracks included 'Ignorance', a massively complex rhythmic collage, and 'Artificial Intelligence', quiet jungle complete with classical string section. Bradshaw died of multiple sclerosis in 1997. Morrow teamed up with former **Tygers Of Pan Tang** guitarist Neil Shepherd in the newly rechristened Foul Play Productions, who released *Field Of Action* in late 1999.

● ALBUMS: *Suspected* (Moving Shadow 1995) ★★★★, as Foul Play Productions *Field Of Action* (Partisan 1999) ★★★.

Found Free

Formed in Philadelphia, Pennsylvania, USA, during the 70s, contemporary Christian group Found Free comprised Keith Lancaster (vocals), David Michael Ed (keyboards/vocals), Catherine MacCallum (vocals), Bish Alverson (drums), Jack Faulkner (bass), Wayne Farley (guitar) and Rebecca Ed (vocals). The group began in the early 70s and concentrated on a musical platform that drew on elements of blues, jazz and rock. They soon established a performance itinerary that included church social meetings, colleges and community concerts. Eventually these led to the group being discovered by Jim Van Hook, senior vice-president of the Benson Company, who served as producer on *Closer Than Ever*, their debut release for Greentree Records. However, the reception afforded it by the more puritanical gospel sources was not particularly positive, and the group has subsequently disappeared.

● ALBUMS: *Closer Than Ever* (Greentree 1978) ★★.

Foundation (reggae)

A roots reggae vocal trio, styled after classic acts like **Culture** and **Burning Spear**, Foundation formed in 1977 around lead singer Errol 'Keith' Douglas in the St Ann's area of Jamaica's north coast. Douglas' chief claim to fame prior to Foundation was as the writer of **Dennis Brown**'s 'Jah Can Do It'. Douglas had recorded it himself for producer **Joe Gibbs** on a fame-hunting excursion to Kingston, but Gibbs had, instead, got Brown to re-voice the track. Douglas returned to the north coast for a rethink and formed Foundation with Emilio 'Father' Smiley (ex-Revealers) and Euston 'Ipal' Thomas. The trio wrote and practised for months, but by the time they had arrived at the yard of producer **Jack Ruby**, who had overseen Burning Spear's classic **Marcus Garvey**, he was winding down his recording activities. He did, however, promise that 'when the time was right' he would take them into the studio, and Ruby kept that promise almost a decade later when he signed them to **Island Records** for their debut set, *Flames*, coproduced and somewhat overwhelmed by the guitar of Steven 'Cat' Coore of **Third World**. The group appeared on **Sly And Robbie**'s 1988 Rhythm Killers tour before releasing a much-improved second set, 1989's *Heart Feel It*. However,

just after its completion producer Ruby died of a heart attack, and Foundation fell silent once more.

● ALBUMS: *Flames* (Island 1988) ★★, *Heart Feel It* (Mango/Island 1989) ★★★, *One Shirt* (Island Jamaica 1997) ★★★.

Foundation (rock)

One of the few male singing duos working in the contemporary pop idiom, Sweden's Per Strandberg (vocals) and Lars Mertanen (vocals/guitar) took their initial influence from artists such as **Johnny Cash**, **Roxy Music** and the **Velvet Underground**. Most critical comparisons, however, have cited a detectable similarity to the work of the **Walker Brothers**. Before electing to work together, both Mertanen and Strandberg had performed in a number of Swedish bands during the 80s—including the Gary Cooper Combo and Iguana Foundation. While studying at the Arts Academy in Madrid, Spain, Mertanen was also a member of the briefly successful Decima Victima. Their career together as Foundation began strongly with the release of three acclaimed singles—'Dumb Generation', 'Next In Line' and 'Back To You'—each of which carried a social message beyond Strandberg's soulful voice and Mertanen's accomplished guitar playing.

Foundations

Formed in January 1967, the Foundations were discovered by London record dealer Barry Class as they rehearsed in the Butterfly, a club situated in a basement below his office. He introduced the group to songwriters **Tony Macaulay** and John Macleod, whose composition 'Baby, Now That I've Found You' became the group's debut release. An engaging slice of commercial pop/soul, the single soared to the top of the UK charts and by February 1968 had reached number 9 in the USA, with global sales eventually exceeding three million. The group's multiracial line-up included Clem Curtis (b. 28 November 1940, Trinidad, West Indies; vocals), Alan Warner (b. 21 April 1947, London, England; guitar), Tony Gomez (b. 13 December 1948, Colombo, Sri Lanka; organ), Pat Burke (b. 9 October 1937, Jamaica, West Indies; tenor saxophone flute), Mike Elliot (b. 6 August 1929, Jamaica, West Indies; tenor saxophone), Eric Allandale (b. 4 March 1936, Dominica, West Indies, d. September 2001; trombone), Peter Macbeth (b. 2 February 1943, London, England; bass) and Tim Harris (b. 14 January 1948, London, England; drums). Allandale was a former member of the **Terry Lightfoot** and **Alex Welsh** jazz bands, while Elliot had backed Colin Hicks, brother of British rock 'n' roll singer **Tommy Steele**. This mixture of youth and experience drew much contemporary comment.

The Foundations scored a second multimillionseller in 1968 with 'Build Me Up Buttercup'. Written by Macaulay in partnership with **Manfred Mann**'s **Michael D'Abo**, this compulsive song reached number 2 in Britain before topping the US chart for two weeks. The group enjoyed further success with several similarly styled releases, including 'Back On My Feet Again' and 'Any Old Time' (both 1968), but their momentum faltered when Curtis embarked on an ill-starred solo career. He was replaced by Colin Young (b. 12 September 1944, Barbados, West Indies), but the departure of Elliot signalled internal dissatisfaction. 'In The Bad Bad Old Days' (1969) returned the group to the UK Top 10, but that year's minor hit, 'Born To Live And Born To Die', was their last chart entry. The septet split up in 1970 when the rhythm section broke away to form the progressive group Pluto. A completely new line-up later resurrected the Foundations' name with little success.

● ALBUMS: *From The Foundations* (Pye 1967) ★★, *Rocking The Foundations* (Pye 1968) ★★, *Digging The Foundations* (Pye 1969) ★★.

● COMPILATIONS: *Back To The Beat* (PRT 1983) ★★, *The Best Of The Foundations* (PRT 1987) ★★★, *Foundations Greatest Hits* (Knight 1990) ★★★, *Strong Foundations: The Singles And More* (Music Club 1997) ★★★★, *Baby Now That I've Found You* (Sequel 1999) ★★★, *Greatest Hits* (BMG 2003) ★★★, *Build Me Up Buttercup* (Sanctuary 2004) ★★★.

● FILMS: *The Cool Ones* (1967).

Fountain, Pete

b. 3 July 1930, New Orleans, Louisiana, USA. Taking up the clarinet as a small boy, Fountain was sufficiently adept to play and record before he was out of his teens. In the early 50s he worked with various bands in his home-town, including the Basin Street Six. In 1954 he formed his own small band and for the next couple of years played with this group and with the **Dukes Of Dixieland**. In the later years of the decade he appeared as featured soloist on **Lawrence Welk**'s networked show. Regular performances with **Al Hirt** ensured that he remained in demand, both in New Orleans and in the vastly different atmosphere of Las Vegas. Fountain's ability transcends the formulaic limitations of some post-revival Dixieland. Although he has long been musically associated with this area of jazz, his consummate skills might more accurately place him in the mainstream. Nevertheless, he has chosen to remain in a field which has proved to be enormously popular and commercially successful and has thus, inevitably, met with critical displeasure and disregard.

● ALBUMS: with Basin Street Six *Dixieland Jazz Concert* (Circle 1951) ★★★, with Dukes Of Dixieland *At The Jazz Band Ball* (Vik 1957) ★★★★, *Lawrence Welk Presents Pete Fountain* (Coral 1957) ★★★, *Music From Dixie* (Coral 1961) ★★★, *South Rampart Street Parade* (Coral 1963) ★★★★, with Bob Havens *Standing Room Only* (Coral 1965) ★★★, shared with Al Hirt *Super Jazz 1* (Monument 1976) ★★★★, *Alive In New Orleans* (First American 1978) ★★★, *Live At The Ryman* 1963 recording (Sacramento 1988) ★★, *High Society* (Bluebird 1992) ★★★, *Swingin' Blues* (Start 1992) ★★★, *At Piper's Opera House* (Jazzology 1993) ★★★, *New Orleans All-Stars* (Tradition/Rykodisc 1997) ★★★★, with the New Lawrence Welk Orchestra *Big Band Blues* (Ranwood 2001) ★★★.

● COMPILATIONS: *The Very Best Of Pete Fountain* (BCI 1998) ★★★, *The Best Of Dixieland* (Verve 2001) ★★★★.

Fountains Of Wayne

The idiosyncratic pop duo Adam Schlesinger (b. New Jersey, USA) and Chris Collingwood (b. Pennsylvania, USA) first met on the roof of their college dorm in Williamstown, Massachusetts, in the mid-80s. The idea to collaborate came after Collingwood showed Schlesinger the chords to an **R.E.M.** song. They were members of a succession of college bands, including Wooly Mammoth, Are You My Mother? and the esoterically named Three Men When Stood Side By Side Have A Wingspan Of Over 12 Feet. However, when

college ended Collingwood concentrated on writing one-act plays, while his partner took a number of temporary positions. They eventually reunited in Boston, but after signing a recording contract as the Wallflowers they abandoned their claim to that name (they actually sold the rights to the name to another **Wallflowers**, featuring **Bob Dylan**'s son Jakob). The proposed record never appeared. Despite problems over freedom of contract that dogged them for three years, and their geographical separation (Collingwood was now living in New York), the pair continued to play the occasional gig under the name Pinwheel, then worked together as **Ivy**. By the time they finally found the time to record new songs together, Schlesinger had become co-owner of Scratchie Records with D'Arcy Wretzky and James Iha of **Smashing Pumpkins**. Taking their new recording moniker from the name of a New Jersey gift shop, the result was 1996's self-titled collection, featuring 12 brittle songs that were occasionally arch about pop music history but still affectionate towards it: 'When we came across some total cliché, we'd immediately leap right into it. If there was a bit of the melody that sounded like the **Beach Boys** or **Cheap Trick**, or a guitar riff that sounded like **Blue Öyster Cult**, we immediately put it in.' Little wonder the duo had adopted the mocking self-description 'the grunge **Everly Brothers**'. The first single to be extracted from the album, the irritatingly catchy 'Radiation Vibe', reached the UK Top 40. The band also achieved a flurry of publicity when their song 'That Thing You Do!' was included in the Tom Hanks movie of the same name and led to them being nominated for an Oscar. By the time Fountains Of Wayne began their European tour of 1997 they had expanded their line-up to include Brian Young of the **Posies** on drums and former Belltower guitarist Jody Porter. *Utopia Parkway*, another collection of note perfect power pop classics, was released in 1999. Similarly entertaining was 2003's beautiful *Welcome Interstate Managers*, featuring the sublime 'Fire Island' and the US Top 40 hit 'Stacy's Mom'. Even the double album of b-sides and outtakes *Out-Of-State-Plates* contained enough gems to put many major indie pop bands to shame. Fountains Of Wayne are a glorious secret awaiting mass market discovery.

● ALBUMS: *Fountains Of Wayne* (Scratchie/Atlantic 1996) ★★★★, *Utopia Parkway* (Atlantic 1999) ★★★★★, *Welcome Interstate Managers* (S-Curve/Virgin 2003) ★★★★.

● COMPILATIONS: *Out-Of State-Plates* (Virgin 2005) ★★★.

Four Aces

A close-harmony vocal group of the pre-rock 'n' roll era, the quartet was founded in Pennsylvania, USA, in 1949 by baritone lead singer Al Alberts (b. Chester, Pennsylvania, USA). With Dave Mahoney, Lou Silvestri and Sol Vocare, he recorded a single on the local Victoria label in 1951. 'Sin (Not A Sin)' sold a million copies, and the Four Aces were signed to **Decca Records**. Alberts and Martin Gold co-wrote 'Tell Me Why', which began a string of hit singles during the mid-50s. Among them were the 1952 revival of **Hoagy Carmichael** and **Frank Loesser**'s 1938 song 'Heart And Soul', 'Stranger In Paradise' (from the stage musical *Kismet*), 'Mister Sandman' (1954), 'Heart' and 'Melody Of Love' (1955). The group's only number 1 record was the Oscar-winning 'Love Is A Many-Splendored Thing', the title song from the 1955 movie starring Jennifer Jones and William Holden. The Four Aces also recorded versions of the theme from *Three Coins In The Fountain* and 'The World Outside' from the movie *Suicide Squadron*. In 1956 the group suffered a double blow as Alberts left to follow a solo career and rock 'n' roll arrived. The Four Aces tried various strategies to survive, including covering a **Pat Boone** song 'Friendly Persuasion (Thee I Love)' and jumping on the calypso and rock bandwagons with 'Bahama Mama' and 'Rock And Roll Rhapsody'. However, few of these records were even minor hits, and by the end of the 50s the Four Aces had disappeared from view. Alberts did little better, although 'Willingly' (1958) was only a minor success.

● ALBUMS: *The Four Aces* 10-inch album (Decca 1952) ★★★★, *The Mood For Love* (Decca 1955) ★★★, *Merry Christmas* (Decca 1956) ★★★, *Sentimental Souvenirs* (Decca 1956) ★★★, *Heart And Soul* (Decca 1957) ★★★, *She Sees All The Hollywood Hits* (Decca 1957) ★★★, *Written On The Wind* film soundtrack (Decca 1957) ★★, *Shuffling Along* (Decca 1957) ★★, *Hits From Hollywood* (Decca 1958) ★★★, *The Swingin' Aces* (Decca 1959) ★★, *Hits From Broadway* (Decca 1959) ★★, *Beyond The Blue Horizon* (Decca 1959) ★★.

● COMPILATIONS: *The Golden Hits Of The Four Aces* (Decca 1960) ★★★★, *Record Oldies* (United Artists 1963) ★★★★, *The Best Of The Four Aces* (Spectrum 2001) ★★★.

● FILMS: *The Big Beat* (1957).

4AD Records

Few independent record labels can boast as distinctive a roster as 4AD, both aesthetically and musically. The label was formed in early 1980 by Ivo Watts-Russell and Peter Kent (who were both then working at **Beggars Banquet Records**) reputedly after hearing a demo from new act **Modern English**. At first, the label was called Axis for the initial clutch of singles by the Fast Set, the Bearz, Shox and most importantly, **Bauhaus**, but this was changed to avoid confusion with a similarly named company, and 4AD was born. A loan of £2,000 from Beggars Banquet ensured that 4AD got off the ground, signing **Modern English**, In Camera, Mass, Dance Chapter and Rema Rema among others. Kent soon left to set up Situation 2, working heavily with Bauhaus who shortly graduated to Beggars Banquet. 4AD, however, steered away from their parent company, witnessing a one-off single for the then-unknown **The The** (and later **Matt Johnson**'s solo album) plus several uncompromising recordings from Australian outfit the **Birthday Party** and providing a home for ex-**Wire** personnel **Bruce Gilbert**, Graham Lewis/Cupol and **Colin Newman**.

From 1981–82 new acts as eclectic as Sort Col, the Past Seven Days, My Captains, **Dif Juz** and the Happy Family appeared alongside solo works from ex-Bauhaus individuals David Jay and **Daniel Ash/Tones On Tail** and a collaboration between **Lydia Lunch** and the Birthday Party's Rowland S. Howard. More significantly, Watts-Russell stumbled upon the **Cocteau Twins**, who were to prove the act that, aside from emerging as the label's major artists, crystallized the ethereal nature often associated with 4AD product, aided later by the oblique yet attractive sleeve designs from Vaughn Oliver's 23 Envelope art studio. There was also **Colourbox**, another 4AD mainstay who embodied the label's experimental approach to recording and the studio as well as the more sinister **Xmal Deutschland**.

Watts-Russell teamed with the Cocteau Twins among others for his own project in 1983, **This Mortal Coil**, which enjoyed both critical and commercial support. Apart from **Dead Can Dance**, **Xymox**, Richenel and the **Wolfgang Press**, the mid-80s saw few signings as 4AD concentrated on their existing roster. The late 80s, on the other hand, signalled a slight reappraisal, with the departure of Colourbox and the signing of new American acts **Throwing Muses**, Boston exports the **Pixies** and New York's **Ultra Vivid Scene**. The influential but often-ignored **AR Kane** also arrived for a brief time, which spawned a one-off project with members of Colourbox, **M.A.R.R.S**' 'Pump Up The Volume'. A UK number 1 hit, this pivotal single was perhaps the first successful mesh of white rock and rhythm, paving the way for a commercial and artistic revolution in both British dance and independent music.

Then came the two-pronged attack of guitar bands **Lush** and the **Pale Saints** to see in the new decade, as the Pixies made serious commercial headway. When the Pixies dissolved it was to much wringing of hands in the music press, but 4AD soon picked up **Frank Black** as a solo artist (though he would eventually be dropped after two albums). Greater consolation came with the commercial approbation of Throwing Muses spin-off **Belly**, which was just as well, as the quintessential 4AD group, the Cocteau Twins, had now moved on to a major. 4AD moved its operational base to California when Watts-Russell relocated to Los Angeles in the mid-90s and continued to discover exciting new talent including **Gus Gus**, **Kristin Hersh** and **Mojave 3**. Treading a tightrope between financial well being and artistic purity, 4AD has spotlighted an impressive yet diverse roster since its inception and continues to excel in bringing idiosyncratic music into the commercial mainstream.

● COMPILATIONS: *Lonely Is An Eyesore* (4AD 1987) ★★★★, *Anakin* (4AD 1998) ★★★, *1980 Forward: 25 Years Of 4AD* (4AD 2005) ★★★★.

Four Blazes

The most famous line-up of this group from Chicago, Illinois, USA, was Tommy Braden (d. 1957; lead vocals/bass), William 'Shorty' Hill (vocals/guitar), Floyd McDaniels (vocals/guitar) and Paul Lindsley 'Jelly' Holt (vocals, drums). The Four Blazes became hitmakers in the early 50s with a mélange of jive, ballad and jazz sounds that combined vocal harmony with their own instrumental support. This type of group was common in the 40s, when acts such as **Cats And The Fiddle** and **Five Red Caps** held sway, and the Four Blazes were one of the last of this breed to have R&B hits. The group was formed in 1940 by Holt, who recruited Hill, McDaniels and bass player Prentice Butler, and they soon became perennials in Chicago clubs. They became the Five Blazes when they added pianist and lead vocalist Ernie Harper in 1946. They first recorded for Aristocrat in 1947 but were unable to garner more than a few local plays for their records. In 1950, after Butler died and Harper left the group, Holt recruited Tennessee bass player Tommy Braden, who became the new lead singer of the renamed Four Blazes. In 1952 they signed with United and immediately achieved a number 1 R&B hit in 1952 with the Braden-composed 'Mary Jo'. Tenor saxophonist **Eddie Chamblee** was prominently featured on the record and in effect became a part of the group both while touring and recording. 'Mary Jo' was followed with two more charting records, 'Please Send Her Back To Me' (number 7 R&B) and 'Perfect Woman' (number 5 R&B), both from 1953. Another record that received strong regional sales was 'My Hat's On The Side Of My Head' (1953). Braden left the group in late 1954, and neither he nor the group could return to the charts. Holt recruited new members and continued to play Chicago clubs as the Five Blazes until disbanding the group in 1957. Braden died in 1957.

● COMPILATIONS: *Swingin' & Singin'* six tracks, remainder by the Dozier Boy (P-Vine 1982) ★★★, *Mary Jo* (Delmark 1998) ★★★★.

Four Brothers

(see **Herman, Woody**)

Four Buddies

The Four Buddies, from Baltimore, Maryland, USA, were one of the best representatives of the smooth, deep-sounding vocal harmony style that was popular in the early 50s. The group members were Leon Harrison (lead/first tenor), Gregory Carroll (second tenor), Bert Palmer (baritone) and Tommy Smith (bass). The group was discovered and signed by **Savoy Records** in 1951 and managed by Friz Pollard (the famed All-American football star from Brown in 1915). They first recorded as the Metronomes with **Johnny Otis** on Savoy. Then as the Four Buddies they had one R&B hit, 'I Will Wait' (number 2 R&B), in 1951, but other outstanding songs included 'My Summer's Gone' and 'Don't Leave Me Now'. The group toured extensively from Las Vegas to the chitlin' circuit theatres of the **Apollo** and the Howard. When the Four Buddies' contract at Savoy expired in 1953, the group broke up. Gregory joined the **Orioles** a year later, but Harrison formed a new group, the Buddies, which included second tenor Luther Dixon (who later produced and wrote for **Scepter** and **Wand**), baritone Roger Wainwright and bass Danny Ferguson. During 1954 the Buddies recorded for Glory and as the Barons for **Decca**, but without any chart success.

Four Coins

Formed in Canonsburg, Pennsylvania, USA, in 1952, the vocal harmony group the Four Coins consisted of George Mantalis, James Gregorakis and brothers George and Michael Mahramas. Originally the quartet were horn players in an orchestra with **Bobby Vinton**, who was an unknown at the time. At the end of 1952 the foursome began harmonizing together and in January 1953 appeared on an 'amateur hour' radio programme, which they won. They left Vinton in 1953 and began a residency at a Pittsburgh club called the Blue Ridge Inn, naming themselves the Four Keys. They recorded their first singles in November 1953 for Corona Records, which led to a contract with Epic Records, a branch of the larger **Columbia Records**. Taking their cue from another quartet, the **Four Aces**, the group changed its name to the Four Coins. The group's first Epic single, 'We'll Be Married (In The Church In The Wildwood)', sold well but it was not until 1957 that they recorded their biggest hit, 'Shangri-La', which reached number 11 in the US charts and earned a gold record. The group had charted seven times by 1959. In 1960 they changed labels to **MGM Records** and continued to record for Jubilee Records, **Vee Jay Records** and Roulette Records, undergoing personnel changes along the way. They disbanded in 1970.

● ALBUMS: *The Four Coins* (Epic 1955) ★★★★, *The Four Coins In Shangri-La* (Epic 1958) ★★, *Greek Songs By The Four Coins* (1961) ★★★, *Greek Songs Mama Never Taught Me* (1964) ★★.

● FILMS: *Jamboree* aka *Disc Jockey Jamboree* (1957).

Four Esquires

Bill Courtney (lead singer) and backing vocalists Walter Gold, Robert Golden and Frank Mahoney were students at the University of Boston, Massachusetts, USA, in the early 50s who harmonized for their own amusement to whatever instrumental accompaniment they could muster. Though popular locally, they waited until they were sufficiently schooled before becoming professional entertainers. After **London Records** signed them in March 1956, 'Look Homeward Angel' was a turntable hit, but it was eclipsed by **Johnnie Ray**'s version. Their workmanlike 'Love Me Forever' (augmented with a female session vocalist's obligato), was overshadowed by a US cover version by **Eydie Gorme** and one in Britain by **Marion Ryan**. Nevertheless, it clawed into each country's Top 30 and, unhindered by competition, so did 1958's 'Hideaway' in the USA. While able to fill moderate-sized auditoriums and becoming a reliable support act in bigger venues, the Esquires clocked up no further chart entries and had disbanded by the early 60s.

Four-Evers

The Four-Evers formed in Brooklyn, New York, USA, in the early 60s and consisted of Joe Di Benedetto (lead), John Cipriani (first tenor), Steve Tudanger (second tenor) and Nick Zagami (baritone). Their debut came in 1962 with 'I'll Be Seeing You', which saw them signed to **Columbia Records** at an average collective age of just 15. Although this received a strong local reception, it was not until the song was covered by the **Duprees** the following year that it became a chart hit. By 1963 the Four Evers had moved to Smash Records, a subsidiary operation run by **Mercury Records**, for whom they recorded 'It's Love' in September. However, a better reaction was afforded to its follow-up, 'Please Be Mine' (aka 'Be My Girl'), written by Bob Gaudio, which reached number 75 in the *Billboard* national charts. Joining **Leslie Gore** and **Bobby Rydell** on tours of the US and Canada, the Four-Evers also backed Eddie Rambeau and Vinnie Monte on record. However, when their last single for Smash '(Doo Bee Dum) Say I Love You' flopped and their remaining outings for three successive labels fared poorly, they dissolved in 1968. Tudanger and Di Benedetto formed a new group, Playhouse, to back recordings made with producer Jeff Barry. In this guise they performed uncredited behind a number of hits including those ascribed to the **Archies, Andy Kim** and **Robin McNamara**. By the time they broke up in 1970, Playhouse had also recorded two singles on their own account for Barry's Steel Records. Afterwards Di Benedetto joined New York's Joe Casey Orchestra.

Four Fellows

Formed in Brooklyn, New York, USA, the group consisted of Jimmy McGowan, Larry Banks, Davy Jones and Teddy Williams. McGowan and Williams began their careers in the late 40s when they were a part of a gospel and jubilee group, the Starlight Toppers. That unit broke up around 1951, but in 1953 McGowan and Williams joined Banks and Jones to form the Four Fellows. The group's debut for Derby went unnoticed, and they next signed with Glory Records. They recorded a fine record, 'I Wish I Didn't Love You', but it, too, went unnoticed. The Four Fellows' third record was a song that Banks had written while serving in the Korean War, 'Soldier Boy' (not be confused with the **Shirelles'** later hit of the same title), and it finally reached number 4 R&B in 1955. The following year, after the group recorded the fine ballad 'Darling You', Jones left and joined the **Rays**. He was replaced by Jimmy Mobley. The Four Fellows never returned to the charts and broke up in 1957. Banks later wrote the hit 'Go Now', which was first recorded by his wife, Bessie Banks, and became a hit for the **Moody Blues** in 1964. McGowan wrote and published his memoirs in 1983 under the title *Here Today! Here To Stay!*

Four Freshmen

Formed at Arthur Jordan Conservatory of Music in Indianapolis, Indiana, USA, in 1948, the Four Freshmen were a groundbreaking vocal group who influenced the **Hi-Lo's**, the **Beach Boys**, **Manhattan Transfer** and countless other close-harmony outfits. The group originally consisted of lead vocalist Bob Flanigan (b. 22 August 1926, Greencastle, Indiana, USA), his cousins Ross Barbour (b. 31 December 1928, Columbus, Indiana, USA) and Don Barbour (b. 19 April 1927, Columbus, Indiana, USA, d. 5 October 1961) and Hal Kratzsch (b. 6 October 1925, Warsaw, Indiana, USA, d. 18 November 1970). Prior to the formation of the Four Freshmen, the Barbour brothers and Kratzsch, along with lead singer Marvin Pruitt, had been in a barbershop quartet called Hal's Harmonizers, each member playing an instrument. The same line-up formed a more jazz-orientated second group, called the Toppers, in 1948. Pruitt left that same year, at which point Flanigan returned from Florida, where he had spent the summer. Inspired by **Mel Tormé**'s Mel-Tones, the new group, renamed the Four Freshmen, was discovered in September 1949 by **Woody Herman**.

In 1950 **Stan Kenton** saw the quartet in concert in Dayton, Ohio, and arranged for them to audition for **Capitol Records**, who signed them. Their first hit single came in 1952, 'It's A Blue World', which reached number 30 in the USA. Spring 1953 saw a personnel change when Kratzsch left, replaced by Ken Errair (b. 23 January 1930, Detroit, Michigan, USA, d. 14 June 1968). Errair also departed in 1955, replaced by Ken Albers (b. 10 December 1924, Pitman, New Jersey, USA). By that time the group had logged two more Top 40 hits, 'It Happened Once Before' and 'Mood Indigo'. Three final chart singles were issued in 1955-56, including the number 17 'Graduation Day', later covered by the Beach Boys. The group had seven album hits, including the Top 10 *Four Freshmen And 5 Trombones* in 1956 and *4 Freshmen And 5 Trumpets* the following year. Further personnel changes marked the group's career. Don Barbour left in 1960, replaced by Bill Comstock (who left in 1972). Ross Barbour stayed on until 1977 and Ken Albers until 1982. Flanigan remained with the group into the early 90s. Don Barbour was killed in a car crash in 1961, Kratzsch died of cancer in 1970, and Errair died in a plane crash in 1968.

Flanigan continues to act as manager and agent for the present day line-up, Brian Eichenberger (b. 16 May 1976), Curtis Calderon, Bob Ferreira and Vince Johnson (b. 3 September 1970), who are able to reproduce the original sound. They won the *DownBeat* readers poll in 2000 for Best Vocal Group, over 50 years since they were formed.

● ALBUMS: *Voices In Modern* (Capitol 1955) ★★★★, *Four Freshmen And 5 Trombones* (Capitol 1956) ★★★★, *Freshmen Favorites* (Capitol 1956) ★★★, *4 Freshmen And 5 Trumpets* (Capitol 1957) ★★★, *Four Freshmen And Five Saxes* (Capitol 1957) ★★★, *Voices In Latin* (Capitol 1958) ★★, *The Four Freshmen In Person* (Capitol 1958) ★★★, *Voices In Love* (Capitol 1958) ★★★, *Freshmen Favorites Vol. 2* (Capitol 1959) ★★★, *Love Lost* (Capitol 1959) ★★, *The Four Freshmen And Five Guitars* (Capitol 1960) ★★, *Voices And Brass* (Capitol 1960) ★★, *Road Show* (Capitol 1960) ★★★, *First Affair* (Capitol 1960) ★★, *Freshmen Year* (Capitol 1961) ★★, *Voices In Fun* (Capitol 1961) ★★, *Stars In Our Eyes* (Capitol 1962) ★★, *Got That Feelin'* (Capitol 1963) ★★, *More With 5 Trombones* (Capitol 1964) ★★★, *Time Slips Away* (Capitol 1964) ★★★, *Four Freshmen Live At Butler University With Stan Kenton And His Orchestra* double album (Creative World 1986) ★★★, *Angel Eyes* (Viper's Nest 1995) ★★★, *Day By Day* 1962 recording (Hindsight 1995) ★★★, *It's A Blue World* 1958 live recording (Viper's Nest 1995) ★★★, *Easy Street* (Aero Space 1997) ★★★, *Golden Anniversary Celebration* (Collector's Choice 1998) ★★★★, *Still Fresh* (Pat's Gold 1999) ★★★, *Live In The New Millennium* (Pat's Gold 2002) ★★★, *In Session* (Four Freshmen 2005) ★★.

Solo: Hal Kratzsch *Thanks To You By Hal Kratzsch* (Capitol 1955) ★★★. Ken Errair *Solo Session* (Capitol 1957) ★★★. Don Barbour *The Solo Voice Of Don Barbour* (Capitol 1961) ★★★.

● COMPILATIONS: *The Best Of The Four Freshmen* (Capitol 1962) ★★★★, *The EP Collection* (See For Miles 2000) ★★★★.

● FURTHER READING: *Now You Know: The Four Freshmen*, Ross Barbour.

4 Hero

Publicity shy London, England–based duo Dego MacFarlane and Mark 'Mac' Clair first emerged at the height of the late 80s **acid house** explosion. Together they established the Dollis Hill–based **Reinforced Records**, which became the foremost UK outlet for hardcore **techno** (at that time often referred to as dark **hardcore**). Their releases for Reinforced included 1991's devastating 'Mr Kirk's Nightmare', which provided a thematic bridge between hardcore and the embryonic **jungle**/breakbeat scene. Alongside **Goldie**, who joined Reinforced in the early 90s, 4 Hero became innovative members of a new aristocracy in the **dance music** community, though unlike Goldie, the duo eschewed publicity. As well as 4 Hero, the duo released singles as Manix, Tom&Jerry (not the **Simon And Garfunkel** duo), Jacob (whose *Optical Stairway* EP was inspired by the writings of Nostradamus), Clair's Nu Era project and MacFarlane's solo project Tek 9. The second 4 Hero long-player, *Parallel Universe*, was considered by many to be the first album to showcase the full potential of drum 'n' bass music. Its themes included science-fiction television programmes and science fact (with references to author Stephen Hawking). It was followed by a release credited to Tek 9 and remix and production work for **Nicolette**, **DJ Krush** and **Courtney Pine**. As 4 Hero, collaborations with **Josh Wink** and **Juan Atkins** preceded *Two Pages*, which was attacked in some quarters for its perceived pretension and interminable two-hour length. A remix version was hastily released the following year. The duo's busy work schedule meant that a new 4 Hero album was not ready for release until autumn 2001.

● ALBUMS: *In Rough Territory* (Reinforced 1991) ★★★, *Parallel Universe* (Reinforced 1994) ★★★★, *Two Pages* (Talkin' Loud 1998) ★★★, *Two Pages Reinterpretations* remix album (Talkin' Loud 1999) ★★★, *Creating Patterns* (Talkin' Loud 2001) ★★★.

● COMPILATIONS: *Life:Styles* (Harmless 2003) ★★, *The Remix Album* (Raw Canvas 2004) ★★★.

Four Horsemen

This UK heavy metal/rock 'n' roll outfit was formed in 1991 by former **Cult** bass player Haggis, who in a previous life had been Kid Chaos of **Zodiac Mindwarp And The Love Reaction**, although his parents have always known him as Mark Manning. Recruiting Frank C. Starr (vocals), Ken 'Dimwit' Montgomery (drums), Dave Lizmi (guitar) and Ben Pape (bass), they negotiated a contract with **Rick Rubin**'s Def American label (with whom the band's leader had worked during his stint with the Cult). With Haggis on rhythm guitar, their music drew heavily from **AC/DC**, the **Black Crowes** and the **Georgia Satellites**, though most critics seemed unable to see past their Cult affiliations. Their debut album, *Nobody Said It Was Easy*, was a powerful collection of heavy-duty rockers based on loud riffs and infectious chorus lines. Like Haggis' former employers, they exaggerated every cliché in the book, yet this approach did not groan under the same weight of lofty ideals and was consequently much more fun. Manning was last sighted in 1994 promoting his book of illustrations, *A Bible Of Dreams*, in conjunction with **Bill Drummond** of the **KLF**. *Gettin' Pretty Good At Barely Gettin' By* featured Randy Cooke (drums) and Pharoah (bass) in place of Pape and Montgomery. While the album was being mastered, Starr crashed his motorcycle in Los Angeles, leaving him in a coma.

● ALBUMS: *Nobody Said It Was Easy* (Def American 1991) ★★★, *Gettin' Pretty Good At Barely Gettin' By* (Magnetic Air 1996) ★★.

400 Blows

Coming together in 1981 in Croydon, London, this versatile ensemble combined funk, reggae, African music and disco. Their obvious influences, in addition to various ethnic styles, included **23 Skidoo** and **Throbbing Gristle**. The debut release was 'Beat The Devil', much in the vein of **Cabaret Voltaire**, which attracted the attention of Illuminated Records. The band is basically the creation of Edward Beer, who dismissed original collaborator Scott Fraser after the single. The two Anthonys, Thorpe and Lea, were then roped in, although Beer continued to maintain artistic control. Early controversy surrounded the title of their debut album, *If I Kissed Her, I'd Have To Kill Her First*, which prompted the question of whether they liked women. 'Oh, maybe sexually I like them, but I don't like having them around that much. They just get on my nerves', was Beer's reply. A minor hit came with 'Movin'', an update of the old **Brass Construction** number, at which point he had been joined by female vocalist Lee. By the late 80s and early 90s they were turning to the beat of **acid house**, releasing singles such as 'Champion Sound' on Warrior Records. Thorpe would go on to significant solo success as the **Moody Boyz**, also remixing for the **KLF**.

● ALBUMS: *If I Kissed Her, I'd Have To Kill Her First* (Illuminated 1985) ★★★, *The Good Clean English Fist* (Dojo 1986) ★★, *Look* (Illuminated 1986) ★★, *Yesterday, Today, Tomorrow, Forever* (Concrete 1989) ★★, *New Lords On The Block* (Concrete 1989) ★★.

Four Jacks And A Jill

Somewhat uninspired and simplistic, this 1942 musical film follows the misfortunes of a small dance band when they are urged into hiring a gangster's girlfriend as their singer. The film was directed by Jack Hively from Monte Brice's screenplay, which was based on John Twist's original story. That said, the plot does bear a marked resemblance to a 1936 Lily Pons film, *That Girl From Paris*. Here, **Ray Bolger** stars as band leader Nifty Sullivan, and not at all surprisingly, there are some good dance sequences, including one in which he portrays a tap-dancing boxer. Other members of Nifty's little band are Steve Sarto (**Desi Arnaz**), The Noodle (Jack Durant) and Happy McScud (**Eddie Foy Jnr.**). Also in the cast are June Havoc (Opal), Fritz Feld (Mr. Hoople), and Henry Daniell (Bobo). Costarring with Bolger is Anne Shirley (Nina Novak, the singer). In black and white and with a running time of 68 minutes, the film includes some songs by Mort Greene and **Harry Revel**. Overall, though, it does seem to be an unfortunate waste of some good talent.

Four Jewels

(see **Jewels**)

Four Just Men

Dee Christopholos (b. Dimitrious Christopholos, Liverpool, England) originally fronted the Huyton band Dee Fenton And The Silhouettes. When the line-up settled to Christopholos, John Kelman (lead guitar), Peter Turner (rhythm guitar), Harry Bear (bass) and Larry King (drums), they dropped Bear, put Turner on bass and became the Four Just Men. The Four Just Men, sometimes known as Just Four Men, moved en masse to Stockport and so were based in Manchester. They had other bass players (Keith Shepherd, Barrie Ashall) and another lead guitarist, Lally Stott. Stott joined **Denny Seyton And The Sabres** and wrote 'Chirpy Chirpy Cheep Cheep'. For a time, the Four Just Men also backed Pete Maclaine. They recorded two singles for **Parlophone Records**, 'Things Will Never Be Same'/'That's My Baby' (as the Four Just Men) and 'There's Not One Thing'/'Don't Come Any Closer' (as Just Four Men). The group became the underrated but significant psychedelic band, **Wimple Winch**, but Kelman left the band and reconstituted the Four Just Men with a new line-up, now based in Runcorn. Arthur Davies was the new drummer, and the vocalist was first Frank Garland and then Peter Hackett, the bass player Mal Hoyland and then Colin Owen. Many of the musicians connected to the band have remained in the business, but Frank Garland moved to the Isle of Skye and became a shepherd.

Four Knights

The singing of Gene Alford was framed by the backing harmonies of Oscar Broadway, Clarence Dixon and John Wallace (who also strummed guitar). From regular performances in the late 40s on radio stations local to their native Charlotte, North Carolina, USA, the Knights graduated to television, providing musical interludes on nationally broadcast situation comedies starring Arthur Godfrey and Red Skelton. This exposure aided the combo's procurement of a **Capitol** contract and much airplay for their debut single, 1951's 'It's No Sin', on which Broadway's bass grumblings were conspicuous. In 1953 they reached the national hit parade with 'Oh Happy Day'—lush with orchestral accompaniment—and the following year came up with the million-selling 'I Get So Lonely', a clever up-tempo reworking of a hillbilly ballad. After 'O Falling Star' slipped from the charts, the quartet teamed up with **Nat 'King' Cole** for a 1956 smash with 'That's All There Is To That'—and so it was for the Four Knights, who never had another hit.

● ALBUMS: *Spotlight Songs* (Capitol 1953/6) ★★★, *The Four Knights* (Coral 1959) ★★★, *Million $ Baby* (Coral 1960) ★★★.

Four Lads

The line-up comprised Frank Busseri (b. Toronto, Canada; baritone), Bernard Toorish (b. Toronto, Canada; second tenor), James Arnold (b. Toronto, Canada; first tenor) and Connie Codarini (b. Toronto, Canada; bass). A versatile vocal quartet, popular in US clubs and theatres and on television and records, especially during the 50s. The Lads formed their group while attending St. Michael's Choir School in Toronto. Aided by 'Dad' Wilson, a member of the **Golden Gate Quartet**, the Lads played a tryout engagement at Le Ruban Bleu in New York, stayed for some 30 weeks, and then toured extensively. They were signed by **Columbia Records** as a background group and in 1951 accompanied **Johnnie Ray** on his first big hit, 'Cry', which sold over two million copies. Their first solo success was in 1952 with 'Mocking Bird', followed by 'He Who Has Love', 'Down By The Riverside', 'Istanbul (Not Constantinople)', 'Gilly Gilly Ossenfeffer Katzenellen Bogen By The Sea' and 'Skokiaan', a South African song. In 1955 they had one of their biggest hits with 'Moments To Remember', written by Robert Allen and Al Stillman.

The songwriters also provided the Lads with several other successful singles such as 'No, Not Much', 'Who Needs You', 'Enchanted Island' and 'There's Only One Of You'. Allen and Stillman also contributed to **Johnny Mathis**' early success with numbers such as 'Chances Are' and 'It's Not For Me To Say'. Other Four Lads' US Top 20 entries, through 1958, included 'The Bus Stop Song (A Paper Of Pins)', 'A House With Love In It', 'Put A Light In The Window' and 'Standing On The Corner', from **Frank Loesser**'s Broadway show *The Most Happy Fella*. In 1957 the group recorded the album *The Four Lads Sing Frank Loesser*, which featured medleys from three of his successful scores, **Where's Charley?**, **Hans Christian Andersen** and **Guys And Dolls**. Other successful albums were their US Top 20 entry, *On The Sunny Side*, with the **Claude Thornhill** Orchestra, *Breezin' Along*, conducted by Ray Ellis and *Four On The Aisle*, a collection of extended medleys from the musical shows **Annie Get Your Gun**, **Babes In Arms** and **Kiss Me, Kate**. A modified version of the group continued to work in the following decades, with Arnold and Busseri performing with two new members. Toorish was to be found singing with the Vince Mastro Quartet and later became an insurance underwriter. He reactivated the Four Lads following their induction into the Juno Awards Hall Of Fame in 1984 and continues to lead the group (of which he is the only remaining original member) on the oldies circuit.

● ALBUMS: *Stage Show* 10-inch album (Columbia 1954) ★★★, *On The Sunny Side* (Columbia 1956) ★★★★, *The Stingiest Man In Town* film soundtrack (Columbia 1956) ★★, *The Four Lads With Frankie Laine* (Columbia 1956) ★★★, *The Four Lads Sing Frank Loesser* (Columbia 1957) ★★★, *Breezin' Along* (Columbia 1959) ★★★★, *Four On The Aisle* (Columbia 1959) ★★★, *The Four Lads Swing Along* (Columbia 1959) ★★★, *High Spirits!* (Columbia 1959) ★★, *Love Affair* (Columbia 1960) ★★★, *Everything Goes* (Columbia 1960) ★★★, *Dixieland Doin's* (Columbia 1961) ★★★★, *Hits Of The 60's* (Columbia 1962) ★★★, *Oh, Happy Day* (Columbia 1963) ★★★, *This Year's Top Movie Hits* (Columbia 1964) ★★★, *Songs Of World War I* (Columbia 1964) ★★.

● COMPILATIONS: *The Four Lads' Greatest Hits* (Columbia 1958) ★★★★, *Twelve Hits* (Columbia 1961) ★★★★.

Four Lovers

Under the name the Variatones, this New Jersey, USA, quartet originally encompassed country, pop and rockabilly in their repertoire. Comprising Francis Castelluccio (aka **Frankie Valli**, who had already recorded solo as Frankie Valley), Tommy DeVito, Nick DeVito and Hank Majewski, they formed in 1955 and played the local club circuit before attracting the attention of **RCA Records**. By the time they recorded for their new employers in April 1956, they had switched names to the Four Lovers and changed their style to a firm R&B direction. Two potent singles emerged as the result of these sessions, 'You're The Apple Of My Eye' and 'Honey Love'. The former release made the *Billboard* charts at number 62 and resulted in an appearance on Ed Sullivan's television show. Sadly, their next three releases for RCA, 'Jambalaya (On The Bayou)', 'Happy Am I' and 'Shake A Hand', failed to match their debut's impact. They switched to Epic Records in 1957 but attracted little interest. A change of direction was required—this coincided with the replacement of Nick DeVito by Charlie Calello and with a change of name, giving their lead vocalist improved status in its label credits, which now read Frankie Valle And The Romans. Eventually success did come their way, but not until the Four Lovers were reborn as Valli's backing band, the Four Seasons (with only Tommy DeVito surviving the transition).

● ALBUMS: *The Four Lovers* (RCA 1957) ★★★.

Four Men And A Dog

Widely acclaimed for bringing freshness and vitality back to traditional Irish music, Four Men And A Dog's debut album in 1991, the aptly titled *Barking Mad*, was a spectacular distillation of the new and the old, earning comparisons to the **Bothy Band** at their peak. It became *Folk Roots* magazine's Album Of The Year, despite being recorded in rushed circumstances and at minimal expense. Including everything from jigs and reels to probably the first ever Irish folk rap song, it entranced almost all who heard it. It featured three musicians who subsequently left the band, Dónal Murphy (b. 1970, Birmingham, West Midlands, England), Brian McGrath and vocalist Mick Daly, and by 1993 the line-up had changed radically to include original member Gino Lupari (bodhrán) plus Cathal Hayden (fiddle), Conor Keane (accordion) and Gerry O'Connor (banjo). The occasional services of noted guitarist Arty McGlynn (ex-**Clancy Brothers**, **Planxty Patrick Street**) were also made a permanent feature of the band (he had produced their debut). Fiddler Hayden had previously recorded a solo album, as had Keane, a former member of Arcady, while O'Connor was drawn from the ranks of Skylark.

Four Men And A Dog classify their sound as 'traditional music with balls', and few who encounter their lives shows—host to scenes of unabashed merriment and wild dancing—would disagree with that description. As Lupari stated: 'Our music is basically dance music, it shouldn't be analysed too close, it shouldn't be studied and listened to in silence. We play music to get a buzz off it, it's free and spontaneous and that's what keeps it fresh and alive.' To this end they categorically refuse to rehearse. However, the reception afforded their second album, 1993's *Shifting Gravel*, was not as generous. Some critics took exception to the central presence of newly acquired pop/rock singer-songwriter Kevin Doherty, whose stylistic departures overshadowed some of the original Celtic gusto of the debut. His input was more restrained on 1995's *Doctor A's Secret Remedies*, however, and his songwriting was consequently much improved. In place of the stream-of-consciousness lyrics that had dominated the 1993 release, Doherty now added structure to build narrative stories much more befitting of his musical backing.

The disappointing *Long Roads* brought an end to this period of Four Men And A Dog's career. They officially disbanded in 1997 to concentrate on solo projects, although various members got back together on an ad hoc basis to play the occasional concert. Hayden, Lupari, Doherty and Gerry O'Connor resurrected the band on a more permanent basis in the new millennium, reuniting with former members Dónal Murphy and Arty McGlynn and accordion player Maírtín O'Connor to record the well-received *Maybe Tonight*.

● ALBUMS: *Barking Mad* (Topic/Green Linnet 1991) ★★★★, *Shifting Gravel* (Topic/Green Linnet 1993) ★★★★, *Doctor A's Secret Remedies* (Transatlantic 1995) ★★★, *Long Roads* (Transatlantic 1996) ★★, *Maybe Tonight* (Hook Music 2002) ★★★.

Four Musketeers, The

Over the years, Alexander Dumas' famous story of *The Three Musketeers* has turned up in many forms on stage, television and at least five films. This comedy musical, which opened at the Theatre Royal, Drury Lane in London on 5 December 1967, gave the highly experienced English writer, Michael Pertwee, the opportunity to turn the legend upside down. In Pertwee's book, the dashing and fearless D'Artagnan (**Harry Secombe**) is turned into 'Neddy' D'Artagna—a country bumpkin, an accident-prone figure whose bravest deeds are accomplished purely by chance. His compatriots, portrayed here as womanizing sots, were obviously recruited from some of the UK's top low-brow comedy talent and included Porthos (Jeremy Lloyd), Athos (Glyn Owen) and Aramis (John Junkin), with Kenneth Connor as King Louis XIII. In complete contrast, Elizabeth Larner, whose thrilling voice had last been heard in the West End when she played Guinevere in **Camelot** (1964), was this time cast as Milady. Obviously, the whole affair was an attempt to repeat the success of **Pickwick** four years earlier, but **Laurie Johnson** and **Herbert Kretzmer**'s score did not provide Secombe with anything nearly as powerful as 'If I Ruled the World', although its pleasant score did contain songs such as 'A Little Bit Of Glory', 'Think Big', 'What Love Can Do', 'Masquerade',

'There Comes A Time', 'Nobody's Changing Places With Me', 'Strike While The Iron Is Hot', 'If You Are Looking For A Girl', 'Got A Lot Of Love To Give', 'Give Me A Man's Life' and 'There's A New Face In The Old Town'. The critics did not like it much, and despite a decent run of over a year, a total of 462 performances, *The Four Musketeers* is reported to have lost much of its investment. Herbert Kretzmer, the journalist and lyricist, had his greatest success 20 years later with **Les Misérables**.

4 Non Blondes

San Francisco quartet who formed in 1989, making a slow rise through the traditional round of bar shows and club dates, going on to win a Best Unsigned Band award and then a prestigious support date to **Primus**. In 1993 their commercial arrival corresponded to that of fellow San Franciscans the **Spin Doctors**, achieving a surprise UK number 2 single ('What's Up') and a Top 10 debut album, *Bigger, Better, Faster, More!*, produced by **Prince** associate David Tickle. Selling half a million copies in the USA where it was originally released in 1992, it also topped charts in Germany and Sweden. The band comprised the strong visual and almost hectoring vocal presence of **Linda Perry** alongside Christa Hillhouse (bass), Roger Rocha (guitar) and Dawn Richardson (drums). Rocha, the grandson of abstract expressionist Clyfford Still and an art school veteran, stepped in to replace original incumbent Shanna Hall during sessions for the debut album. Richardson, a trained percussionist with a degree from California State University and several years' experience in jazz and salsa bands, replaced Wanda Day shortly before preproduction. Hillhouse and Perry began the band together, having to cancel their first ever rehearsal on 7 October 1989 when an earthquake hit the Bay Area. Hillhouse had first spotted Perry playing an acoustic set, and the latter's songs quickly became the dominant force within 4 Non Blondes, including 'Spaceman', the follow-up to 'What's Up'. However, suspicions were raised in the press that 4 Non Blondes represented a corporate chart raid, providing designer grunge for the post-**Nirvana** and **Lemonheads** (to whose label, Interscope/**Atlantic Records**, they signed) generation. Support slots to Prince and **Neil Young** did little to dispel these assumptions, and Perry broke up the band to pursue a solo career and work as a songwriter (most notably, contributing several tracks to US singer **Pink**'s hit album *M!ssundazstood* and providing **Christina Aguilera** with her transatlantic hit single 'Beautiful'). However, there was an undeniable infectious simplicity to 'What's Up' that indelibly marked it as one of the records of 1993.

● ALBUMS: *Bigger, Better, Faster, More!* (Interscope 1993) ★★★.

411

This UK R&B quartet comprises vocalists Carolyn Owlett (b. England), Suzie Furlonger (b. Dumfries, Scotland), Tisha Martin (b. Jamaica), and Tanya Boniface (b. Surrey, England). The 411 can trace its formation back to when Martin and Boniface met while singing backing vocals for UK soul vocalist **Lemar**. They were encouraged to assemble their own group by a representative of Sony Records, and with the addition of Owlett and Furlonger, 411 was formed at the start of 2003. The quartet's name was chosen from rap slang and out of respect to **Mary J. Blige**'s urban classic, *What's The 411?* The group wrote the majority of the material on their debut album themselves, with US star **Ashanti** contributing one track, 'No Excuses'. Rapper **Ghostface Killah** guested on the UK Top 5 hit 'On My Knees', which managed to introduce a storyline about domestic violence into the upper regions of the charts in the summer of 2004. The follow-up, 'Dumb', was also a UK Top 5 hit and preceded the release of *Between The Sheets* in November.

● ALBUMS: *Between The Sheets* (Sony 2004) ★★★.

Four Pennies

This Blackburn, Lancaster beat group comprised Lionel Morton (14 August 1942, Blackburn, Lancashire, England; vocals/rhythm guitar), Fritz Fryer (b. David Roderick Carnie Fryer, 6 December 1944, Oldham, England; lead guitar), Mike Wilsh (b. 21 July 1945, Stoke-on-Trent, England; bass) and Alan Buck (b. 7 April 1943, Brierfield, Lancashire, England; drums). They scored a notable UK number 1 hit in 1964 with 'Juliet'—a Morton-penned ballad that was originally the b-side of the less immediate 'Tell Me Girl', which had a stark simplicity that enhanced its plaintive qualities. The quartet enjoyed three further Top 20 entries with 'I Found Out The Hard Way', 'Black Girl' (both 1964) and 'Until It's Time For You To Go' (1965) but were unable to sustain a long career. Fryer, having briefly fronted a new act, Fritz, Mike and Mo, later became a successful record producer, while Morton, who married actress Julia Foster, made frequent appearances in children's television programmes.

● ALBUMS: *2 Sides Of The 4 Pennies* (Philips 1964) ★★★, *Mixed Bag* (Philips 1966) ★★★.

● COMPILATIONS: *Juliet* (Wing 1967) ★★★.

Four Preps

Formed in the early 50s in Hollywood, California, USA, the Four Preps were a vocal group consisting of Bruce Belland, Glen Larson, Marvin Inabnett and Ed Cobb (d. 1999, Honolulu, Hawaii, USA). Recording for **Capitol Records**, they placed 13 singles in the US charts between 1956 and 1964, 2 of which made the Top 5 in 1958. The quartet began singing together during their high-school years, influenced by the **Mills Brothers**, **Four Aces** and **Four Freshmen** acts. Impressed by a demo tape the group recorded, Mel Shauer, manager of **Les Paul** And **Mary Ford**, took the group under his wing and arranged a recording contract with Capitol. Their first session, in late 1956, yielded 'Dreamy Eyes', which was a minor hit, but the follow-up, '26 Miles (Santa Catalina)', written by Belland and Larson years earlier, reached number 2, and their next single, 'Big Man', made number 3. Subsequent singles failed to reach the US Top 10 although the group did achieve a Top 10 album, *Four Preps On Campus*, in 1961 during the height of the folk music revival in the USA. The group's final charting single, 1964's 'A Letter To The **Beatles**', parodied Beatlemania but was allegedly withdrawn from distribution by Capitol upon the request of the Beatles' management. The group continued until 1967. Cobb went on to join the group **Piltdown Men** and later to produce such records as the **Standells**' 'Dirty Water'; he also wrote 'Tainted Love', a hit for **Soft Cell** in 1982. In 1988 the Four Preps were back on the road, with two of the original members, Belland and Cobb, joined by David Somerville, former lead singer of the **Diamonds** and Jim Pike, founder of the **Lettermen**.

● ALBUMS: *The Four Preps* (Capitol 1958) ★★★★, *The Things We Did Last Summer* (Capitol 1958) ★★★★,

Dancing And Dreaming (Capitol 1959) ★★★, *Early In The Morning* (Capitol 1960) ★★, *Those Good Old Memories* (Capitol 1960) ★★★, *Four Preps On Campus* (Capitol 1961) ★★★, *Campus Encore* (Capitol 1962) ★★★, *Campus Confidential* (Capitol 1963) ★★, *Songs For A Campus Party* (Capitol 1963) ★★, *How To Succeed In Love!* (Capitol 1964) ★★.

● COMPILATIONS: *Best Of The Four Preps* (Capitol 1967) ★★★★, *Capitol Collectors Series* (Capitol 1989) ★★★★.

4 Runner

The 90s US vocal country group 4 Runner take their name from a type of Toyota four-wheel-drive estate car that also inspired the title of their song 'A Heart With 4 Wheel Drive'. The group consists of Craig Morris (lead vocal), Billy Crittenden (baritone), Lee Hilliard (tenor) and Jim Chapman (bass). Morris has toured with **Marie Osmond** and **Dobie Gray** and has written songs for **Ray Charles**, **Reba McEntire** and the **Oak Ridge Boys**. Crittenden sang in **Tanya Tucker**'s band for five years and co-wrote **Diamond Rio**'s 'Love A Little Stronger'. Hilliard worked with **Loretta Lynn** for nine years. Their experience shows in their witty debut single, 'Cain's Blood', with its excellent four-part harmonies, which made the US country charts.

A few weeks prior to their follow-up album being released, Polydor's parent company A&M Nashville closed their Nashville branch and left the band without a record label. The 4 Runner members continued throughout the 90s with individual music projects. In the early 00s Chapman left the line-up to concentrate on illustrating children's books. The remaining three vocalists issued a new album on Fresh Records in 2003.

● ALBUMS: *4 Runner* (Polydor 1995) ★★★, *One For The Ages* (A&M 1996) ★★★, *Getaway Car* (Fresh 2003) ★★★.

Four Seasons

This highly acclaimed New Jersey, USA, vocal group first came together in the mid-50s with a line-up comprising vocalists **Frankie Valli** (b. Francis Castelluccio, 3 May 1937, Newark, New Jersey, USA), brothers Nick and Tommy DeVito (b. 19 June 1936, Bellville, New Jersey, USA) and Hank Majewski. Initially known as the Variatones, then the **Four Lovers**, they enjoyed a minor US hit in 1956 with 'You're The Apple Of My Eye', composed by **Otis Blackwell**. After being dropped by **RCA Records**, they recorded a single for Epic, following which Valli departed in 1958. As a soloist he released 'I Go Ape', composed by singer **Bob Crewe**. Meanwhile, the Four Lovers released several records under pseudonymous names, during which Nick DeVito and Majewski departed to be replaced by Nick Massi (b. Nicholas Macioci, 19 September 1935, Newark, New Jersey, USA, d. 24 December 2000, Newark, New Jersey, USA) and Bob Gaudio (b. 17 December 1942, Bronx, New York, USA), a former member of the **Royal Teens**. After combining with Crewe and Gaudio, the group evolved into the Four Seasons, recording the single 'Bermuda'/'Spanish Lace' for the End label before signing with **Vee Jay Records**.

There, they released 'Sherry', which reached number 1 in the USA in September 1962. A brilliant example of falsetto, harmony pop, the track established the group as one of America's most popular. Two months later, they were back at the top with the powerful 'Big Girls Don't Cry' and achieved the same feat the following March with the equally powerful

'Walk Like A Man'. All these hits were underpinned by lustrous, soaring harmonies and thick up-front production, which gave the Seasons a sound that was totally unique in pop at that time. Their international fame continued throughout 1964 when they met fierce competition from the **Beatles**. A sign of their standing was evinced by Vee Jay's release of a battle of the bands album featuring the Seasons and the Beatles. Significantly, when the Fab Four held four of the Top 5 positions in the *Billboard* chart during early 1964, the Four Seasons represented the solitary competition with 'Dawn (Go Away)' at number 3. The sublime 'Rag Doll' brought them back to the top in the summer of 1964. Nick Massi left the group the following year and was replaced by Charles Calello and then Joe Long. It was during this period that they playfully released a version of **Bob Dylan**'s 'Don't Think Twice, It's All Right' under the pseudonym the **Wonder Who?**

Valli, meanwhile, was continuing to enjoy solo hits including the US number 2 single 'Can't Take My Eyes Off You'. By the end of the 60s, the group reflected the changing times by attempting to establish themselves as a more serious act with *Genuine Imitation Life Gazette*. The album was poorly received, however, and following its release Gaudio replaced Crewe as producer. When Tommy DeVito left in 1970, the lucrative Four Seasons back catalogue and rights to the group name rested with Valli and Gaudio. A brief tie-up with **Berry Gordy**'s **Motown Records** label saw the release of *Chameleon*, which despite favourable reviews sold poorly. Meanwhile, Valli was receiving unexpected success in the UK thanks to a **northern soul** dancefloor revival of 'You're Ready Now', which reached number 11 in 1971.

Throughout the early 70s, membership of the Four Seasons was erratic, and Gaudio retired from performing to concentrate on producing. Despite impending deafness, Valli was back at number 1 in 1975 with 'My Eyes Adored You'. With an old track from *Chameleon*, 'The Night', adding to the glory and the latest group line-up reaching the US Top 3 with 'Who Loves You', it was evident that the Four Seasons were as popular as ever. Immense success followed as the group became part of the disco boom sweeping America. The nostalgic 'December 1963 (Oh What A Night)' was a formidable transatlantic number 1 in 1976, but the following year, Valli left the group to concentrate on his solo career. While he again hit number 1 in the USA with the **Barry Gibb** movie theme, *Grease*, the Four Seasons continued with drummer Gerry Polci taking on lead vocals. Valli returned to the group for a double album recorded live at Madison Square Garden. A team-up with the **Beach Boys** on the single 'East Meets West' in 1984 was followed by a studio album, *Streetfighter*, which featured Valli. In 1990 the group was inducted into the **Rock And Roll Hall Of Fame**. Still going strong, Valli and the Four Seasons have become an institution whose illustrious history spans several musical eras, from the barber shop harmonies of the 50s to the disco beat of the 70s and beyond. It is however the timeless hit singles of the 60s to which the group are indelibly linked.

● ALBUMS: *Sherry And 11 Others* (Vee Jay 1962) ★★★★, *Ain't That A Shame And 11 Others* (Vee Jay 1963) ★★★, *The 4 Seasons Greetings* (Vee Jay 1963) ★★★, *Big Girls Don't Cry* (Vee Jay 1963) ★★★, *Folk-Nanny* (Vee Jay 1963) ★★★, *Born To Wander* (Philips 1964) ★★★, *Dawn And 11 Other Great Songs* (Philips 1964) ★★★★, *Stay And Other Great Hits* (Vee Jay 1964) ★★★, *Rag Doll* (Philips 1964) ★★★★, *We Love Girls* (Vee Jay 1965) ★★★, *The Four Seasons Entertain You* (Philips 1965) ★★★, *Recorded Live On Stage* (Vee Jay 1965) ★★, *The Four Seasons Sing Big Hits By Bacharach, David And Dylan* (Philips 1965) ★★, *Working My Way Back To You* (Philips 1966) ★★★, *Lookin' Back* (Philips 1966) ★★★, *Christmas Album* (Philips 1967) ★★★, *Genuine Imitation Life Gazette* (Philips 1969) ★★★, *Edizione D'Oro* (Philips 1969) ★★★★, *Chameleon* (Mowest 1972) ★★★, *Who Loves You* (Warners 1976) ★★★, *Helicon* (Warners 1977) ★★★, *Reunited Live* (Sweet Thunder 1981) ★★, *Streetfighter* (Curb 1985) ★★★, *Hope/Glory* (Curb 1992) ★★★.

● COMPILATIONS: *Golden Hits Of The Four Seasons* (Vee Jay 1963) ★★★★, *More Golden Hits By The Four Seasons* (Vee Jay 1964) ★★★★, *Gold Vault Of Hits* (Philips 1965) ★★★★, *Second Vault Of Golden Hits* (Philips 1967) ★★★★, *Seasoned Hits* (Fontana 1968) ★★★★, *The Big Ones* (Philips 1971) ★★★★, *The Four Seasons Story* (Private Stock 1976) ★★★★, *Greatest Hits* (K-Tel 1976) ★★★, *The Collection* (Telstar 1988) ★★★★, *Anthology* (Rhino 1988) ★★★★, *Rarities Volume 1* (Rhino 1990) ★★★, *Rarities Volume 2* (Rhino 1990) ★★★, *The Very Best Of Frankie Valli And The Four Seasons* (PolyGram 1992) ★★★★, *In Season: Frankie Valli And The Four Seasons Anthology* (Rhino 2001) ★★★★, *Off Season: Criminally Ignored Sides From Frankie Valli & The 4 Seasons* (Rhino 2001) ★★★★, *The Definitive Frankie Valli & The Four Seasons* (Warners 2001) ★★★★.

● FILMS: *Beach Ball* (1965).

4 Skins

As their name suggests, this London, England, band comprised four skinheads who specialized in vitriolic three-chord 'yob-rock'. Their membership was fluid, including no less than four lead singers, with only Hoxton Tom (bass) still resident between their first and second albums. Taking their musical brief from outfits such as **Sham 69**, the **Angelic Upstarts** and the **Cockney Rejects**, they were a third generation punk band heavily associated with the Oi! Movement, alongside fellow travellers the Business. With a blatantly patriotic image, the band attracted National Front supporters to their live shows, which occasionally erupted into full-scale riots. Lyrically they expounded on racism, police brutality and corrupt governments. However, musically they were not so adventurous, being rigidly formularized and unable to develop from their simplistic origins (basic punk spiced by the odd foray into skinhead's 'other' music, ska). From a creative standpoint, the band had ground to a halt by 1983. Their fanbase continued to contract, and they soon faded into oblivion, although re-releases and compilations have reminded many of their enduring street popularity.

● ALBUMS: *The Good, The Bad And The 4 Skins* (Secret 1982) ★★, *A Fistful Of 4 Skins* (Syndicate 1983) ★★, *From Chaos To 1984* (Syndicate 1984) ★★.

● COMPILATIONS: *The Wonderful World Of The 4 Skins* (Link 1987) ★★★, *A Few 4 Skins More Vol. 1* (Link 1987) ★★, *A Few 4 Skins More Vol. 2* (Link 1987) ★★, *Live And Loud!* (Link 1989) ★★, *Clockwork Skinhead* (Harry May 1999) ★★★, *Singles & Rarities* (Captain Oi 1999) ★★★, *The Secret Life Of The 4 Skins* (Captain Oi! 2002) ★★★.

Four Tet

b. Kieran Hebden, England. Hebden decided to experiment with electronic music while taking a break from his involvement with acclaimed post-rockers **Fridge**. He began releasing solo material under the moniker Four Tet in 1997, a period during which Fridge were in the middle of a prolific burst of recording activity. His first two Four Tet singles, 'Thirtysixtwentyfive' and 'Misnomer', were both awarded Single Of The Week by the *New Musical Express*. His wildly inventive 1999 debut, *Dialogue*, mixed instrumental jazz with a bizarre range of samples and sounded completely different from his work with Fridge. The album was well received and became the Output label's bestselling release. In 2000 Hebden hooked up with Stefan Betke to record the *Pole v Four Tet* EP for release on the Leaf label. The following year he launched his own label, Text Records, and journeyed to Toronto, Canada, to collaborate with **Manitoba**'s Dan Snaith. Hebden's second long-player, *Pause*, was released in May 2001 by Domino Records. The album's extensive use of folk samples was noteworthy and prompted comparison with other so-called 'folktronica' artists, including Manitoba, **Boards Of Canada Savath And Savalas** and **Greg Davis**. The superb *Rounds*, released in summer 2003, honed the folktronica style to something close to perfection and was nominated by many critics in their end of year 'best of' polls. Following the release of a limited edition live album and a mix collection in 2004, Hebden returned to the studio to complete work on *Everything Ecstatic*. Released in May 2005, the album shifted away from the folktronica style into an unsettling mix of Krautrock and free jazz. In addition to his solo work, Hebden has DJed at diverse venues including London's Fabric and remixed tracks for artists such as **Aphex Twin**, **David Holmes**, **Cinematic Orchestra** and **His Name Is Alive**.

● ALBUMS: *Dialogue* (Output 1999) ★★★★, *Pause* (Domino 2001) ★★★, *Rounds* (Domino 2003) ★★★★, *Live In Copenhagen 30th March 2004* (Domino 2004) ★★★, *Everything Ecstatic* (Domino 2005) ★★★.

● COMPILATIONS: *LateNightTales* (Azuli 2004) ★★★.

● DVD/VIDEOS: *Everything Ecstatic* (Domino 2005).

430 West Records

One of the pre-eminent labels to host the much admired second wave Detroit **techno** sound of the early 90s, 430 West was formed in 1990 by brothers Lawrence, Lenny and Lynell Burden. The inspiration for the label came from their first release together as Octave One on **Derrick May**'s **Transmat Records**. 'I Believe', recorded with Antony Shakir, became an instant agenda-setter with its tightly marshalled rhythms and harmonies, sung by Lisa Newberry. The Burden brothers elected to form 430 West Records thereafter, taking the label's name from its address at 430 West Eight Mile Road in Detroit. Its first release was another Octave One project, the *Octivation* EP, recorded with a budget of $500. The label grew rapidly, with its discography encompassing ground-breaking releases by artists such as **Eddie 'Flashin'' Fowlkes**, **Terrence Parker** and others. These producers were attracted to the group's low-key ethos. Distributed by Mike Banks' enterprising Submerge distribution company, the label has been largely responsible for keeping Detroit at the forefront of contemporary **dance music**. As well as hosting pivotal releases by artists such as Sight Beyond Sight ('Good Stuff', 'No More Tears'), Tokyo Gospel Renegades ('Tokyo Soul') and Unknown Force's self-titled EP, the brothers have also launched a subsidiary **electro** label, Direct Beat (Will Webb, **Aux 88**, etc.). Octave One have also continued to record with

the label and were most recently heard on the *Foundation* and *Point Blank* EPs.

Four Tops

Levi Stubbs (b. 6 June 1936, Detroit, Michigan, USA), Renaldo 'Obie' Benson (b. 14 June 1936, Detroit, Michigan, USA, d. 1 July 2005, Detroit, Michigan, USA), Lawrence Payton (b. 2 June 1938, Detroit, Michigan, USA, d. 10 June 1997, USA) and Abdul 'Duke' Fakir (b. 26 December 1935, Detroit, Michigan, USA) first sang together at a party in Detroit in 1954. Calling themselves the Four Aims, they began performing at supper clubs in the city, with a repertoire of jazz songs and standards. In 1956 they changed their name to the Four Tops to avoid confusion with the popular singing group the **Ames Brothers** and recorded a one-off single ('Kiss Me Baby') for the R&B label **Chess Records**. Further unsuccessful recordings appeared on Red Top, **Columbia Records** and Riverside between 1958 and 1962 before the Four Tops were signed to the **Motown Records** jazz subsidiary Workshop in 1963. Motown boss **Berry Gordy** elected not to release their initial album, *Breaking Through*, in 1964 and suggested that they record with the label's **Holland/Dozier/Holland** writing and production team. The initial release from this liaison was 'Baby I Need Your Lovin'', which showcased the group's strong harmonies and the gruff, soulful lead vocals of Levi Stubbs; it reached the US Top 20. The following year, another Holland/Dozier/Holland song, 'I Can't Help Myself (Sugar Pie, Honey Bunch)', topped the charts and established the Four Tops as one of Motown's most successful groups. Holland/Dozier/Holland continued to write and produce for the Four Tops until 1967. The peak of this collaboration was 'Reach Out, I'll Be There', a transatlantic hit in 1966. This represented the pinnacle of the traditional Motown style, bringing an almost symphonic arrangement to an R&B love song; producer **Phil Spector** described the record as 'black [**Bob**] **Dylan**'. Other major hits such as 'It's The Same Old Song' and 'Bernadette' were not as ambitious, although they are still regarded as Motown classics today.

In 1967 the Four Tops began to widen their appeal with soul-tinged versions of pop hits, such as the **Left Banke**'s 'Walk Away Renee' and **Tim Hardin**'s 'If I Were A Carpenter'. The departure of Holland, Dozier and Holland from Motown later that year brought a temporary halt to the group's progress, and it was only in 1970, under the aegis of producer/writers like **Frank Wilson** and **Smokey Robinson**, that the Four Tops regained their hit status with a revival of the **Tommy Edwards** hit 'It's All In The Game' and the socially aware ballad 'Still Water (Love)'. That same year, they teamed up with the **Supremes** for the first of three albums of collaborations. Another revival, **Richard Harris**' hit 'MacArthur Park', brought them success in 1971, while Renaldo Benson also co-wrote **Marvin Gaye**'s hit single 'What's Going On'.

After working with the **Moody Blues** on 'A Simple Game' in 1972, the Four Tops elected to leave Motown when the corporation relocated its head office from Detroit to California. They signed a contract with **Dunhill Records** and immediately restored their chart success with records that marked a return to their mid-60s style, notably the theme song to the 'blaxploitation' movie *Shaft In Africa*, 'Are You Man Enough'. Subsequent releases were less dynamic, and for the remainder of the 70s the Four Tops enjoyed only sporadic chart success, although they continued touring and performing their Motown hits. After two years of inactivity at the end of the decade, they joined Casablanca Records and immediately secured a number 1 soul hit with 'When She Was My Girl', which revived their familiar style. Subsequent releases in a similar vein also charted in Britain and America. In 1983 the group performed a storming medley 'duel' of their 60s hits with the **Temptations** during the Motown 25th Anniversary television special. They re-signed to the label for the aptly titled *Back Where I Belong*, one side of which was produced by Holland/Dozier/Holland. However, disappointing sales and disputes about the group's musical direction led them to leave Motown once again for **Arista Records**, where they found immediate success in 1988 with the singles 'Indestructible' and 'Loco In Acapulco', the latter taken from the soundtrack to the movie *Buster*. Two years later the group was inducted into the **Rock And Roll Hall Of Fame**.

The Four Tops retained a constant line-up from their inception up until Payton's death in June 1997. He was replaced on tour by former Temptations vocalist Theo Peoples who subsequently took over lead vocal duties as Levi Stubbs fell ill, with Ronnie McNeir also drafted into the line-up. The group's immaculate choreography and harmonies ensured them ongoing success as a live act, notably in the UK and Europe, where they have always been held in higher regard than in their homeland. Benson succumbed to lung cancer in July 2005 and was replaced by Roquel Payton, the son of Lawrence Payton.

● ALBUMS: *Four Tops* (Motown 1965) ★★★, *No. 2* (Motown 1965) ★★★★, *On Top* (Motown 1966) ★★★★, *Live!* (Motown 1966) ★★★★, *On Broadway* (Motown 1967) ★★★, *Reach Out* (Motown 1967) ★★★★, *Yesterday's Dreams* (Motown 1968) ★★★, *Now!* (Motown 1969) ★★★, *Soul Spin* (Motown 1969) ★★★, *Still Waters Run Deep* (Motown 1970) ★★★, *Changing Times* (Motown 1970) ★★★, with the Supremes *The Magnificent Seven* (Motown 1970) ★★★★, with the Supremes *The Return Of The Magnificent Seven* (Motown 1971) ★★, with the Supremes *Dynamite* (Motown 1972) ★★★, *Nature Planned It* (Motown 1972) ★★★, *Keeper Of The Castle* (Dunhill 1972) ★★★, *Shaft In Africa* film soundtrack (Dunhill 1973) ★★, *Main Street People* (Dunhill 1973) ★★, *Meeting Of The Minds* (Dunhill 1974) ★★, *Live And In Concert* (Dunhill 1974) ★★, *Night Lights Harmony* (ABC 1975) ★★, *Catfish* (ABC 1976) ★★, *The Show Must Go On* (ABC 1977) ★★, *At The Top* (MCA 1978) ★★, *Tonight!* (Casablanca 1981) ★★, *One More Mountain* (Casablanca 1982) ★★, *Back Where I Belong* (Motown 1983) ★★, *Magic* (Motown 1985) ★★, *Hot Nights* (Motown 1986) ★★, *Indestructible* (Arista 1988) ★★★, *Christmas Here With You* (Motown 1995) ★★.

● COMPILATIONS: *Greatest Hits* (Motown 1967) ★★★★★, *Greatest Hits, Volume 2* (Motown 1971) ★★★★, *Story* (Motown 1973) ★★★★, *Anthology* (Motown 1974) ★★★★★, *Best Of The Four Tops* (K-Tel 1982) ★★★, *Collection: Four Tops* (Castle 1992) ★★★, *Early Classics* (Spectrum 1996) ★★★, *The Best Of The ABC Years 1972-77* (Music Club 1998) ★★★, *The Ultimate Collection* (Motown 1998) ★★★★, *Breaking Through* (Motown 1999) ★★★, *The Best Of The Four Tops: The Millennium Collection* (Polydor 1999) ★★★★, *Fourever* 4-CD box set (Hip-O 2001) ★★★★, *Keepers Of The Castle: Their Best 1972-1978* (MCA 2002) ★★, *50th Anniversary Anthology* (Hip-O 2004) ★★★★, *The Best Of Volume 2: The Millennium Collection* (Motown 2005) ★★★.

Four Tunes

The Four Tunes, like many African-American groups of the 40s and early 50s, were a pop rather than a R&B ensemble. The group had its origin in the **Brown Dots** and was formed by Ivory 'Deek' Watson (b. 18 July 1909, Mounds, Illinois, USA, d. 4 November 1969, Washington, DC, USA) after he first fell out with the rest of the **Ink Spots** in November 1944. The other members of the original Brown Dots line-up were Pat Best (b. William Best, 6 June 1923, Wilmington, North Carolina, USA, d. 14 October 2004, Roseville, California, USA; baritone), Jimmy Gordon (bass) and Joe King (first tenor), although the latter was quickly replaced by Jimmy Nabbie (b. USA, d. September 1992). While still with the Brown Dots, Best, Gordon and Nabbie left Watson and joined with second tenor Danny Owens in 1946 to record on the Manor label as the Sentimentalists, changing their name shortly afterwards to the Four Tunes. As the Sentimentalists they backed **Savannah Churchill** on her bestselling 1947 R&B chart-topper 'I Want To Be Loved (But Only By You)'. The following year, and now known as the Four Tunes, the quartet backed Churchill on the Top 20 R&B hits 'Time Out For Tears' (number 10) and 'I Want To Cry' (number 14). After a two year spell on **RCA-Victor Records**, during which time their former label Manor/Arco continued to release Four Tunes material, the quartet moved to the Jubilee label and enjoyed two big hits with a cover version of **Irving Berlin**'s 'Marie' (number 2 R&B, number 13 pop) from 1953 and Pat Best's 'I Understand Just How You Feel' (number 7 R&B, number 6 pop) from 1954. The Four Tunes continued recording for Jubilee until 1957, with further releases appearing on smaller labels such as Crosby and Robin's Nest (as the Four Tunes And One). Their musical legacy was remembered in 1961 when the **G-Clefs** had a big pop hit with 'I Understand Just How You Feel' and in 1965 when the **Bachelors** had success with 'Marie'.

The original line-up of the Four Tunes sundered in 1963 when Jimmy Nabbie and Danny Owens were replaced by Billy Wells and Gaines Steele, while Frank Dawes (tenor/piano) was brought in as a utility singer in the mid-60s. This line-up, with the addition of drummer Chuck Hampton, recorded an album for the Ara label in 1969 under the Tunes moniker. The group kept going throughout subsequent decades, although Wells left in the 80s for medical reasons and was replaced by Andre Williams, who in turn made way for Rufus McKay. Pat Best and Jimmy Gordon finally wound the group up in the late 90s.

● ALBUMS: *12 X 4* (Jubilee 1957) ★★★, as The Tunes *I've Been Waiting* (Ara 1969) ★★.

● COMPILATIONS: *The Complete Jubilee Sessions* (Sequel 1992) ★★★.

Four Vagabonds

A vocal group formed in St. Louis, Missouri, USA. In the wake of the success of the **Mills Brothers**, a number of African-American groups emerged who specialized in harmonized pop songs flavoured by imitation horn sounds, and the Four Vagabonds were one of the most outstanding. Unlike the Mills Brothers, however, the group throughout its career was not primarily a recording group but instead radio performers. For most of their career they were based in

Chicago and consisted of lead John Jordan, tenor Robert O'Neal, baritone Narval Taborn and bass and guitarist Ray 'Happy Pappy' Grant Jnr. They formed the group at Vashon High in 1933 and soon began singing on St. Louis radio stations. In 1936 they moved to Chicago and became regulars on the popular radio show *Don McNeal's Breakfast Club*, on which for the next decade they sang pop tunes and spirituals. Radio exposure for the group expanded rapidly in the years that followed, and they appeared on programmes such as *Club Matinee*, hosted by Durwood Kirby and Gary Moore, ABC's *Tin Pan Alley*, the *Curt Massey Show*, the *Chesterfield Supper Club* with **Perry Como** and a programme with Danny Thomas. The Four Vagabonds first recorded in 1941. Their one hit was 'It Can't Be Wrong' (number 3 R&B) from 1943. The group made its last record in 1949 and broke up in 1952.
● COMPILATIONS: *Yesterday's Memories* (Relic 1988) ★★★.

Four Voices

Formed in the USA during the mid-50s, the Four Voices were Allan Chase (tenor), Sal Mayo (tenor), Bill McBride (baritone) and Frank Fosta (bass baritone). The group appeared on the *Arthur Godfrey* television programme and were seen by **Columbia Records**' A&R executive **Mitch Miller**, who signed them in 1955. The quartet placed one single, 'Lovely One', in the Top 20 in 1956 and a second at number 50. They then had an uneventful five years, but by the early 60s Chase had left with the others trying to carry on for another year before resigning themselves to anonymity. They recorded no albums.

4 Yn Y Bar

This Welsh folk group includes Iwan Roberts (b. 24 October 1953, Carmarthen, Dyfed, South Wales; mandolin/mandola), Tudur Huws Jones (b. 29 October 1955, Bangor, Gwynedd, North Wales; banjo, mandolin, whistle, bouzouki), Tudur Morgan (b. 8 May 1958, Bangor, Gwynedd, North Wales; guitar, bass, vocals) and Huw Roberts (b. 1 September 1957, Bangor, Gwynedd, North Wales; fiddle/vocals). Fiercely nationalistic, they make a point of using only Welsh traditional and contemporary songs and tunes in their repertoire. They first performed in 1983 and followed up with the release of *Byth Adra* (*We're Never At Home*), on **Sain Records**. *Byth Adra* features 'Nos Galan', a traditional Welsh tune which the Americans 'borrowed' and turned into 'Deck The Halls'. The independent Christmas release, *Seren Nadolig*, was followed by a tour of Scotland in April 1986 and the group's second Sain release, *Newid Cynefin*, in October of the same year. In 1987, on St David's Day, the group appeared at London's Royal Albert Hall, and their second independent production *Ffiwsio*, saw them experimenting with bluegrass and reggae. In 1988 Morgan produced the first solo release by **Plethyn**'s Linda Healy, with all of the members of 4 Yn Y Bar playing on some of the tracks. In 1989 the group was invited to play at the Orkney Islands Folk Festival in May, and in November the same year the group recorded their first television special. Since then, 4 Yn Y Bar have given up live performances, but Tudur Morgan released *Branwen* in November 1991, an album based on an Irish, Welsh mythological character and containing mostly original material. 4 Yn Y Bar also released a new album, *Stryd America* (America Street), on St David's Day (1 March) 1992.

● ALBUMS: *Byth Adra* (Sain 1984) ★★★, *Seren Nadolig* (1985) ★★, *Newid Cynefin* (Sain 1986) ★★★★, *Ffiwsio* (1987) ★★★, *Stryd America* (1992) ★★★.
Solo: Tudur Morgan *Branwen* (1991) ★★★.

Fourmost

Originally known as the Blue Jays, then the Four Jays, then the Four Mosts, this Mersey beat group comprised Brian O'Hara (b. 12 March 1942, Liverpool, England, d. 27 June 1999, Liverpool, England; lead guitar/vocals), Mike Millward (b. 9 May 1942, Bromborough, Cheshire, England, d. March 1966; rhythm guitar/vocals), Billy Hatton (b. 9 June 1941, Liverpool England; bass) and Dave Lovelady (b. 16 October 1942, Liverpool, England; drums) and achieved momentary fame under the management wing of **Brian Epstein**. The unit had already been part of the boom of beat music in Liverpool and played the famous Cavern Club in 1961 long before the **Beatles** had made their debut. After being auditioned by **George Martin** they were signed to **Parlophone Records**, the same label as the Beatles. Two commercial **John Lennon** and **Paul McCartney** songs, 'Hello Little Girl' and 'I'm In Love', served as their initial a-sides, but the unflinchingly chirpy 'A Little Lovin'' became the quartet's biggest hit on reaching number 6 in April 1964.

An archetypal Mersey beat group, the Fourmost's later releases veered from **Motown Records** with an excellent version of the **Four Tops**' 'Baby I Need Your Lovin'' to the music hall humour of **George Formby** ('Aunt Maggie's Remedy'), and their unswerving 'showbusiness' professionalism was deemed anachronistic in the wake of the R&B boom. Millward developed leukemia and recovered from chemotherapy, but he then died in March 1966. Some reports stated that he died of throat cancer. This tragedy undermined the group's confidence, and despite McCartney's continued patronage—he produced their 1969 rendition of 'Rosetta'—the Fourmost were later consigned to the cabaret circuit and variety engagements. The Fourmost were one of the better outfits to come from the Mersey beat era. Their vocal prowess was powerful, and their instrumental delivery always crisp and punchy. Brian O'Hara continued the name until the early 80s before moving onto become a second-hand car dealer. He committed suicide in 1999.
● ALBUMS: *First And Fourmost* (Parlophone 1965) ★★★.
● COMPILATIONS: *The Most Of The Fourmost* (Parlophone 1982) ★★★.
● FILMS: *Pop Gear* (1964), *Ferry Cross The Mersey* (1964).

Fournier, Vernel

b. Vernel Anthony Fournier, 30 July 1928, New Orleans, Louisiana, USA, d. 4 November 2000, Jackson, Mississippi, USA. Fournier began studying drumming while a very young child. At the age of 10 he played in a marching band, and during his years at school studied with Sidney Montague. In the mid-40s he studied at Alabama State College playing drums not only in a band with fellow students but also with visiting musicians both in Alabama and back home in New Orleans where he worked with artists such as Adam Cato and **Harold Dejan**. By 1946, when he moved to Chicago, he was already proficient as a Dixieland and as a bop drummer although his first important engagement was with King Kolax's R&B band. He also played with Tom Archia, **Paul Bascomb** and **Teddy Wilson**. During the early 50s Fournier accompanied numerous important jazzmen while working with the house band at the Bee Hive Club, and he also appeared with some of them on record; these artists included **Lorez Alexandria**, **Gene Ammons**, **Stan Getz**, **Wardell Gray**, **J.J. Johnson–Kai Winding**, **Howard McGhee**, **Norman Simmons**, **Sonny Stitt**, **Ben Webster** and **Lester Young**.

In 1957 Fournier began the engagement that was to bring him lasting fame, as drummer with the **Ahmad Jamal** trio. During the next five years the trio, the third member of which was **Israel Crosby**, was mainly resident at Chicago's Pershing Lounge. The group achieved considerable critical and commercial success, making several recordings for **Chess Records**, including the classic *But Not For Me/Ahmad Jamal At The Pershing*, which was in the *Billboard* charts for more than two years. From Jamal, Fournier moved to another high profile job, this time with **George Shearing**. After two years with Shearing, he rejoined Jamal for another spell, then worked with **Nancy Wilson** before leading his own small group in Chicago where he also played with Larry Novak.

Conversion to Islam in 1975 brought a change of name, to Amir Rushdan. In New York at the start of the 80s, he worked with instrumentalists such as **Barry Harris**, **John Lewis** and **Clifford Jordan** and with singers **Billy Eckstine** and **Joe Williams**. Once again, he also led his own trio and became a well-known and respected teacher at various establishments, including the New School and the Mannes College of Music, and he was also involved with Harris at the pianist's Jazz Cultural Theatre. A stroke in 1994 left Fournier unable to continue with his playing career but did not inhibit his teaching. Towards the end of the 90s he left New York for Mississippi where he lived out his final years. Fournier's playing style, subtle and fluid, was of enormous importance to the success of the Jamal group, and it is evident from all of his recorded work that understatement, sensitive accompaniment and a gently loping swing were inherent characteristics.

Fourplay

A group who have earned consistent critical praise for their blend of pop and contemporary jazz, Fourplay comprise **Bob James** (b. 25 December 1939, Marshall, Missouri, USA; keyboards), **Lee Ritenour** (b. 1 November 1953, Los Angeles, California, USA; guitar), Nathan East (bass) and **Harvey Mason** (b. 22 February 1947, Atlantic City, New Jersey, USA; drums). Since forming in the early 90s they have worked with a number of prominent R&B singers—including **El DeBarge** and **Chaka Khan**. Their self-titled debut album spent 31 weeks at number 1 on *Billboard*'s Contemporary Jazz Albums chart. Their second collection, *Between The Sheets*, also reached number 1 on the chart. *Elixir* featured a succession of typically smooth instrumentals and sung numbers. The styles echoed developments in pop music (particularly R&B) as well as jazz. As James told *Billboard* magazine, 'Those references to older styles are there in our roots, our training and our respect for what went before'. The album included a guest appearance from **Phil Collins** with his own composition, 'Why Can't I Wait Till Morning'. The first single taken from the album, 'The Closer I Get To You', was an update of the **Roberta Flack** and **Donny Hathaway** duet, newly reinterpreted by **Patti Austin** and **Peabo Bryson**.

New guitarist **Larry Carlton** (b. 2 March 1948, Torrance, California, USA) was brought in to replace Ritenour following the release of *Elixir* and made his recording debut

on 1998's *4*. The seasonal *Snowbound* featured traditional and modern holiday songs, all played in the quartet's increasingly slick style. They attempted to break out of the mould with 2002's *Heartfelt*, jamming in the studio and assembling the best part through Pro Tools editing.

● ALBUMS: *Fourplay* (Warners 1991) ★★★★, *Between The Sheets* (Warners 1993) ★★★, *Elixir* (Warners 1995) ★★★, *4* (Warners 1998) ★★, *Snowbound* (Warners 1999) ★★, *Yes, Please!* (Warners 2000) ★★, *Heartfelt* (Bluebird 2002) ★★★, *Journey* (Bluebird 2004) ★★★.

● COMPILATIONS: *The Best Of Fourplay* (Warners 1997) ★★★.

14 Iced Bears

Few bands epitomized the mid-80s 'shambling' pop music scene in Britain more succinctly than Brighton's 14 Iced Bears. Formed in 1985 by Rob Sekula (b. 12 December 1963, Camberwell, Surrey, England), Alan White and Nick Emery, the band quickly became embroiled in an alternative network peppered with anoraks, cheap fanzines and guitar-based songs for which the word 'amateur' could have been invented. With more line-up changes than record releases, 14 Iced Bears' history is almost as shambolic as their music. They released their first single on ex–**Television Personalities** Mark Flunder's Frank label. Alan White soon departed to form Pleasure Splinters, to be replaced by Dominic Minques and guitarist Kevin Canham (b. 10 October 1964, Aldershot, Hampshire, England). Nick Roughley (b. West Riding, Yorkshire, England) joined for the band's second single in 1987 before leaving to form Blow Up. Steve Ormsby and Bill Cox briefly replaced Minques and Emery before 1988 when 14 Iced Bears—then consisting of Sekula, Kevin Canham, Will Taylor (b. 23 August 1968, Brighton, Sussex, England; bass) and Graham Durrant (b. 10 October 1963, Camberwell, Surrey, England; drums)—finally began making an album for the Essex-based Thunderball Records. After suffering from the curse of 'shambling', *14 Iced Bears* demonstrated an admirable progression towards heavier, more psychedelic territories and benefitted from a scattering of warmly surprised responses from the UK music press. Fittingly, this line-up remained stable until 1991 when Tim White (b. 30 March 1967, Essex, England) replaced Taylor, who had moved over to Blow Up, and 14 Iced Bears recorded their second 60s-tinged album, *Wonder*. Soon afterwards, an extra chapter was added to the Bears' story when White made way for Rob Colley (b. 27 June 1963, Brighton, Sussex, England), formerly in Whirl, but the band split up soon afterwards.

● ALBUMS: *14 Iced Bears* (Thunderball 1988) ★★, *Wonder* (Borderline 1991) ★★★.

● COMPILATIONS: *Let The Breeze Open Our Hearts* (Overground 1999) ★★★, *In The Beginning* (Slumberland 2001) ★★★.

Fourth World

The conception of Brazil's most famous percussionist, **Airto Moreira** (b. 5 August 1941, Itaiopolis, Brazil), best known as a side man to jazz legends **Chick Corea** and **Miles Davis**, Fourth World were formed in the late 80s as his return to the traditional sounds of his youth in Curitiba, Parana State, Brazil. Before moving to the USA in 1968 he had played with a number of bossa nova groups, including the Sambalanco Trio and Quarteto Novo. Fourth World additionally includes his partner, singer **Flora Purim** (b. 6 March 1942, Rio de

Janeiro, Brazil), José Neto (guitar) and Gary Meek (keyboards, flute, saxophone), occasionally supplemented by the central duo's daughter, Diana Moreira. Their live activities were limited somewhat by Neto's main occupation, as **Harry Belafonte**'s musical director, but in August 1992 they travelled to England to play five weeks of engagements at **Ronnie Scott**'s clubs in London and Birmingham. These sessions provided the recordings issued on their self-titled debut album of 1992, the first of a number of inspired worldbeat sessions to see the light of day during the 90s.

● ALBUMS: *Fourth World* (B&W 1992) ★★★, *Live At Ronnie Scott's* (Ronnie Scott's Jazz House 1992) ★★★, *Live In South Africa* 1993 recording (B&W 1996) ★★★, *Encounters Of The Fourth World* (B&W 1995) ★★★★, *Last Journey* (M.E.L.T. 2000 1998) ★★★, *Return Journey* remix album (Electric Melt 1999) ★★★.

Fowler, Kevin

b. Amarillo, Texas, USA. Guitarist and singer-songwriter Kevin Fowler began his musical career playing in rock bands before launching a solo career as a honky-tonk country artist, in the process returning to the style of music he had first fallen in love with as a youngster. Growing up in West Texas, he dabbled with the drums and piano before settling on the guitar as his chosen instrument. He studied the guitar in Los Angeles before relocating to Austin, Texas, where he played with the hard rock outfit **Dangerous Toys** in the latter days of their career. Fowler then spent a brief period pursuing a southern rock style with his own band Thunderfoot before realizing that he wanted to return to his country roots. By the late 90s, Fowler and his new band were beginning to make waves on the Austin bar circuit with their rousing update on the honky-tonk style. His self-released debut, *Beer, Bait And Ammo*, was a big local hit, with Texans taking the sentiments of the title track to their hearts. Two further releases on his own Tin Roof label, *One For The Road* (2000) and *High On The Hog* (2002), established Fowler's status as a gritty chronicler of everyday Texan life. Following the release of a live set from Billy Bob's in Texas, Fowler attempted to break into a bigger market with his new studio album, *Loose, Loud & Crazy*, his first national release.

● ALBUMS: *Beer, Bait And Ammo* (Tin Roof 2000) ★★★★, *One For The Road* (Tin Roof 2000) ★★★, *High On The Hog* (Tin Roof 2002) ★★★, *Live At Billy Bob's Texas* (Smith Music Group 2002) ★★★, *Loose, Loud & Crazy* (Equity Music Group 2004) ★★★.

Fowler, Wally

b. Wallace Fowler, 15 February 1917, near Adairsville, Georgia, USA, d. 3 June 1994, Hollow Lake, near Nashville, Tennessee, USA. His father was the cotton king of Bartow County until the Depression left him broken both in health and financially. Fowler once worked in a florist's to support the family and began singing in the Harmony Quartet. In 1936 he became lead singer with the John Daniel Quartet, whose repertoire varied from gospel to variety songs, and moved to Lubbock, Texas. He began to write songs and first sang his popular 'I'm Sending You Red Roses' (a number 2 hit for **Jimmy Wakely** in 1944) in Dallas. In 1940 the quartet relocated to Nashville, where they played on WSM and the *Grand Ole Opry*. In 1944 Fowler formed his own group, the Georgia Clodhoppers, which included **Chet Atkins** on lead guitar, to work on WNOX Knoxville. They became regulars

on the *Mid-day Merry Go Round* and before long Fowler also formed his Harmony Quartet. Among many appearances, the quartet began to sing in weekly concerts for children at nearby Oak Ridge, Tennessee, which led to Fowler renaming the group the Oak Ridge Quartet. He moved to Nashville, and from 1946-50 became a regular part of the *Prince Albert Show* on the *Grand Ole Opry*. After **Red Foley** continually introduced them as 'Wally Fowler And His **Oak Ridge Boys**', the name became permanent, and the quartet became one of the country's most popular gospel groups. Fowler left them in 1952, but in 1970, after many personnel changes, the group turned to country music and have since registered many chart hits and won many awards. Apart from his activities with the quartet, Fowler became involved in promotional work and songwriting (**Eddy Arnold** enjoyed Top 5 country hits with 'That's How Much I Love You' and 'I Couldn't Believe It Was True'). In 1948 he organized his first *All-Night Singing* in Nashville, an event that proved so popular it led to many more in other towns. During his long career, Fowler often helped others, including the young **Patsy Cline**. He recorded for several labels, but in later years, he went into semi-retirement and tended to avoid publicity, although he continued to promote some gospel and variety shows in North Carolina. He also surprisingly gained a minor country chart hit, 'Lo And Behold', in 1984, singing with his Tennessee Valley Boys. He was elected to the *Gospel Music Hall Of Fame* in 1988. Fowler drowned on a fishing trip with his son-in-law in 1994 when he was found face down in a lake. A doctor believed he may have fallen in after suffering a heart attack.

● ALBUMS: *Call Of The Cross* (Decca 1960) ★★★, with the Oak Ridge Quartet *Gospel Song Festival* (King 1960) ★★, *Wally Fowler's All Nite Singing Gospel Concert* (Starday 1960) ★★, *More Wally Fowler All Nite Singing Gospel Concert* (Starday 1964) ★★, *Victory Through Jesus* (Pickwick/Hilltop 1965) ★★★, *Gospel Sing* (Vocalion 1967) ★★★, *Pure Country Gospel* (1976) ★★★, *A Tribute To Elvis Presley* (Dove 1977) ★★, *You Will Reap* (Pickwick 1978) ★★★, *A Tribute To Mother* (Nashwood 1984) ★★★.

Fowley, Kim

b. 21 July 1942, Manila, the Philippines. A prodigious talent, Fowley's role as a producer, songwriter, recording artist and catalyst proved important to 60s and 70s pop. He recorded with drummer **Sandy Nelson** during the late 50s and later worked with several short-lived hit groups including the **Paradons** ('Diamonds And Pearls') and the **Innocents** ('Honest I Do'). Durable success came from his collaborations with school friends **Gary S. Paxton** and **Skip Battin**, who performed as **Skip And Flip**. Fowley produced 'Cherry Pie' (1960), their US Top 20 entry and, with Paxton, created the **Hollywood Argyles** whose novelty smash, 'Alley Oop' (1960) topped the US charts. The pair were also responsible for shaping **Paul Revere And The Raiders**' debut hit, 'Like Long Hair', and in 1962 they assembled the **Rivingtons**, whose gloriously nonsensical single 'Papa-Oom-Mow-Mow' was a minor success. That same year Fowley produced 'Nut Rocker' for **B. Bumble And The Stingers**, which was a hit on both sides of the Atlantic and a UK number 1. In 1964 Fowley undertook promotional work for singer **P.J. Proby** and the following year began embracing the Los Angeles counter-culture through his association with scene guru Vito and **Frank Zappa**'s nascent **Mothers Of Invention**.

Fowley came to Britain on several occasions. The **Rockin' Berries** recorded 'Poor Man's Son' at his suggestion, he composed 'Portobello Road' with **Cat Stevens**, and he produced sessions for **Deep Feeling** (which included **Dave Mason** and **Jim Capaldi**, later of **Traffic**), the **Farinas** (who evolved into **Family**), the **Belfast Gypsies** and the **Soft Machine**. Fowley also recorded in his own right, completing a cover version of the **Napoleon XIV** hit 'They're Coming To Take Me Away, Ha-Haaa!' and 'The Trip', a hypnotic paean to underground predilections. He became closely associated with flower power, recording *Love Is Alive And Well* in 1967. This debut album was the first of a prolific output that, although of undoubted interest and merit, failed to match the artist's intuitive grasp of current trends for other acts. He produced material for the **Seeds**, **A.B. Skhy**, **Warren Zevon** and **Gene Vincent** while maintaining his links with Europe through Finnish progressive act Wigwam.

Skip Battin joined the **Byrds** in 1970 and several collaborations with Fowley became a part of the band's late period repertoire, although longtime fans baulked at such ill-fitting material as 'Citizen Kane' and 'America's Great National Pastime'. Battin's first solo album, *Skip*, consisted of songs written with Fowley, while their partnership continued when the bass player joined the **New Riders Of The Purple Sage**. Fowley's role as a pop Svengali continued unabated, and in the mid-70s he was responsible for piecing together the **Runaways**, an all-female group whose average age was 16. They quickly outgrew the initial hype and abandoned their mentor, who in turn formed a new vehicle, Venus And The Razorblades.

The advent of punk provided scope for further exploitation, but as the 80s progressed Fowley's once-sure touch seemed to desert him. He remains a cult name, however, and as such can still release challenging records. The 1995 album *Let The Madness In* was idiosyncratic and unfunny, while 1998's *The Trip Of A Lifetime* saw Fowley branching out into a club-orientated direction.

● ALBUMS: *Love Is Alive And Well* (Tower 1967) ★★★, *Born To Be Wild* (Imperial 1968) ★★, *Outrageous* (Imperial 1968) ★★★, *Good Clean Fun* (Imperial 1969) ★★, *The Day The Earth Stood Still* (MNW 1970) ★★, *I'm Bad* (Capitol 1972) ★★, *International Heroes* (Capitol 1973) ★★, *Visions Of The Future* (Capitol 1974) ★★, *Animal God Of The Street* (Capitol 1975) ★★★, *Living In The Streets* (Sonet 1978) ★★, *Sunset Boulevard* (PVC 1978) ★★, *Snake Document Masquerade* (Antilles 1979) ★★, *Hollywood Confidential* (GNP 1980) ★★, *Frankenstein & Monster Band* (Sonet 1984) ★★, *Hotel Insomnia* (Maria 1993) ★★, *White Negroes In Deutschland* (Marilyn 1994) ★★, *Bad News From The Underworld* (Marilyn 1994) ★★, with Ben Vaughn *Kings Of Saturday Night* (Sector Two 1995) ★★, *Let The Madness In* (Receiver 1995) ★, *Mondo Hollywood: The Phantom Juxebox Collection* (Rev-Ola 1996) ★★, *Hidden Agenda* (Receiver 1997) ★★, *The Trip Of A Lifetime* (Resurgence 1998) ★★, *Sex Cars & God* (Koch 1999) ★★★, *Fantasy World* (Shoeshine 2003) ★★, as Sand featuring Roy Swedeen *The West Is Best* (Zip 2003) ★★★.

● COMPILATIONS: *Legendary Dog Duke Sessions* (BFD 1979) ★★, *Underground Animal* (Dionysuc/Bacchus Archives 1999) ★★★, *Impossible But True: The Kim Fowley Story* (Ace 2003) ★★★★.

● FURTHER READING: *California Confidential! A Small Taste Of California Dreamin' & California Schemin' In Conversation With Kim Fowley*, Stephen J. McPartland.

● FILMS: *Mayor Of The Sunset Strip* (2003), *Edgeplay* (2004).

Fowlkes, Charlie

b. 16 February 1916, New York City, USA, d. 9 February 1980, Dallas, Texas, USA. Although able to play a variety of instruments, Fowlkes appeared to recognize early on in life that he was destined to be an unsung section musician. He adopted the baritone saxophone as his chosen instrument, and spells with **Tiny Bradshaw** and **Lionel Hampton** beginning in 1938 kept him busy for a decade. In the late 40s he was in **Arnett Cobb**'s small band, and then, in 1951, he became one of the most reliable members of the **Count Basie** band, remaining there until 1969. Six years later he was back in the band, which was where he remained until his death in 1980.

Fowlkes, Curtis

b. 19 March 1950, New York City, USA. A strikingly gifted trombone player, Fowlkes did not become a full-time musician until 1977 when he joined **Ernie Wilkins**' Jazzmobile educational project. He worked with several musicians and bands active in the contemporary jazz scene of the 80s and 90s, notably **Henry Threadgill**, **Bill Frisell**, the **Lounge Lizards** and the **Jazz Passengers**, of which group he was a cofounder. Unabashedly forward thinking in his playing and composing, Fowlkes has a style that artlessly blends dramatically surging blowing with subtly lyrical introspection. Although his work suggests influences by stylistically diverse trombonists such as **Grachan Moncur III** and **J.J. Johnson**, Fowlkes has a distinctive sound that is all his own. At the start of the new century he was leading his group, Catfish Corner, to a rising tide of praise. Aided and abetted by his penchant for writing music in unusual time signatures, Fowlkes' was certainly making an impressive mark.

● ALBUMS: with Catfish Corner *Reflect* (Knitting Factory 1999) ★★★.

Fowlkes, Eddie 'Flashin''

b. 24 December 1962, Detroit, Michigan, USA. One of the less celebrated **techno** artists from the ever fertile Detroit region, Fowlkes began making mix tapes at the age of 14. His first booking as a DJ came in 1981 at a campus party. In the early 80s he built up his record collection and began to secure a reputation for both his live appearances at the Music Institute and his mix tapes. His nickname 'Flashin'' came from his early prowess as a scratch and mix DJ. Fowlkes was a friend of many of the Detroit giants, DJing alongside **Derrick May** and **Juan Atkins** in the early 80s. He recorded his debut, 1986's 'Goodbye Kiss', on Atkins' **Metroplex** imprint and also released singles on the labels **KMS Records**, **430 West Records** ('Inequality') and Play It Again Sam. His style, which blended in elements of deep **house** music and soul, was dubbed 'black technosoul' by Fowlkes himself. In the 90s he began to build his recording profile, working with labels including Jump Street, **React Music** and Tresor Records. Among the best of these releases were 'Turn Me Out', produced by **Graeme Park**. Throughout the 90s he performed regularly at Detroit's The Alley club and in 1991 relocated to Berlin to record *Serious Techno Vol. 1*, featuring his brand of tough but soulful techno. As he reasoned, 'most Euro techno has no feeling because the makers haven't got the history'. He also recorded for **Infonet Records**, Back To Basics, Peacefrog as well as issuing a third album, *Black Technosoul*, for Tresor. During the late 90s he issued material on the City Boy, Dance Pool and Azuli labels.

● ALBUMS: *Serious Techno Vol. 1* (Tresor 1991) ★★★★, *The Birth Of Technosoul* (Tresor/Pow Wow 1993) ★★★★, *Deep Detroit Techno-Soul Volume 1* (Tresor/Pow Wow 1993) ★★★, *Black Technosoul* (Tresor 1996) ★★★.

Fox

This UK band was formed in the mid-70s and comprised Noosha Fox (lead vocals), Herbie Armstrong (guitar/vocals, ex-duo partner to Rod Demick), **Kenny Young** (guitar/vocals), Jim Gannon (guitar/vocals, ex-**Black Widow**), plus session musicians Pete Solley (keyboards/vocals), Jim Frank (drums) and Gary Taylor (bass). They scored three UK hits on the GTO label with 'Only You Can' (number 3, 1975), 'Imagine Me, Imagine You' (number 15, 1975) and 'S-S-S-Single Bed' (number 4, 1976)—a run of hits that earned Fox a UK Top 10 album. Despite the band's musical credentials, their popularity centred mainly around the sexily voiced Fox, who later left the band in 1977 to pursue a solo career. The only notable profit for Fox from this move, however, was the achievement of a UK Top 40 single, 'Georgina Bailey'. The band soldiered on for one more album, *Blue Hotel*, which flopped, resulting in them splitting soon afterwards. Armstrong and Young went on to form the briefly successful **Yellow Dog** in 1977. Armstrong later engaged in solo performances and worked with **Van Morrison** from 1978–82, appearing on *Wavelength, Into The Music, Common One* and *Beautiful Vision*. Not to be confused with the late 60s UK psych band of the same name.

● ALBUMS: *Fox* (GTO 1975) ★★★★, *Tales Of Illusion* (GTO 1975) ★★, *Blue Hotel* (GTO 1977) ★★.

● COMPILATIONS: *The Very Best Of Fox* (The Hit Label 1999) ★★★.

Fox, Curley, And Texas Ruby

b. Arnim LeRoy Fox, 9 November 1910, Graysville, Tennessee, USA, d. 10 November 1995, Graysville, Tennessee, USA. At the age of 13, Fox, the son of a fiddler, was already touring with a medicine show before joining the **Roane County Ramblers**, with whom he made his first recordings in 1929. In the early 30s, he played with the **Carolina Tar Heels**, and in 1932 with his own band, the Tennessee Firecrackers, he was a popular performer on WSB Atlanta. In 1935 he recorded some **Decca** recordings with the **Shelton Brothers**, including his noted instrumental, 'Listen To the Mocking Bird' (complete with special fiddle-made bird effects) and his vocal 'Curley's New Talking Blues'. In 1937 Fox teamed up with Texas Ruby (b. Ruby Owens, 4 June 1908, Wise County, Texas, USA, d. 29 March 1963, Nashville, Tennessee, USA). She was the sister of **Tex Owens** (the writer of 'Cattle Call') and had played on many radio stations, including the *Iowa Barn Dance Frolics* and appeared on the **Grand Ole Opry** in 1934 with **Zeke Clements**. Fox and Owens (often working with the Shelton Brothers) toured the South, where they appeared on numerous stations and where Fox won a great many fiddle contests. They were married in 1939 and became firm favourites on the *Opry*, where, along with **Rod Brasfield**, they were stars of the Purina segment. During the 40s, they

recorded for **Columbia** and **King Records**, and between 1948 and 1955, they were regulars on a KPRC Houston television show but then returned to the *Opry* and also made further recordings for Starday.

Their close partnership was ended in 1963 when Texas Ruby was killed by a fire that destroyed their trailer home. Fox was devastated and effectively retired from the business; although from the mid-70s, he was, on occasions, persuaded to make special appearances at some bluegrass festivals, he never recovered from his loss. He is rated by experts to have been perhaps the greatest showman of all the early country fiddlers. Texas Ruby initially billed herself as Radio's Original Yodeling Cowgirl, but she was an outstanding vocalist. Equally at home with country ballads or blues songs, she was an undoubted influence on other female singers including **Patsy Cline** and **Loretta Lynn**.

● ALBUMS: *Curley Fox & Texas Ruby* (Starday 1962) ★★★, *Travellin' Blues* (Harmony 1963) ★★★, *Favorite Songs Of Texas Ruby* (1963) ★★★.

● COMPILATIONS: *Curley Fox, Champion Fiddler Volumes 1 & 2* (Rural Rhythm 1972) ★★★★.

Fox, Norm, And The Rob-Roys

A rock 'n' roll vocal group from Manhattan, New York City, USA, who had one hit song, 'Tell Me Why' (1957). Members came from Dewitt Clinton High School and were Norm Fox (lead tenor), Bobby Troutman (tenor), Andre Lilly (second tenor), Bobby Thierer (baritone) and Buzz Halfan (bass). The group surprisingly recorded on a Houston, Texas, imprint, Backbeat, a subsidiary of **Don Robey**'s Duke label. A follow-up, 'Dance Girl Dance', met with no success upon its release in 1958. One more recording for Hammer (later on **Capitol**) in 1959, 'Pizza Pie', likewise failed to find an audience, and the group not long after broke up. In the late 80s, Fox and Thierer re-formed the Rob-Roys with three new members and recorded some a cappella sides for the Starlight label.

Fox, Roy

b. 25 October 1901, Denver, Colorado, USA, d. 20 March 1982, Twickenham, England. Raised in Hollywood, Fox played the cornet in local bands at the age of 16 and was later with **Abe Lyman** before joining **Art Hickman** with whom he made his first records. Fronting his own band at Hollywood's Cafe Montmartre led to a job as musical director with Fox Films and an offer to form a seven-piece American band to play at the Café de Paris in London for eight weeks, where he was billed as the 'Whispering Cornetist'. After that engagement Fox formed an all-British band to record for **Decca Records**, and in May 1931 it opened at the new Monseigneur Restaurant in Piccadilly. The impressive personnel included **Lew Stone** as pianist, arranger, **Nat Gonella**, Joe Ferrie, Billy Amstell, Sid Buckman and vocalist **Al Bowlly**. The band became extremely popular mostly through their regular Wednesday night BBC broadcasts.

Late in 1931 Stone took over as leader when Fox went to Switzerland to recuperate from illness. When Fox returned in 1932 he formed a new band to play at the Café Anglais, the Kit Kat Club, the Café De Paris and on extensive theatre tours. In 1934 he filled the gap left by Al Bowlly by engaging the 'British **Bing Crosby**', **Denny Dennis**, and later sponsored a national contest to find a girl singer for the band. The winner was 13-year-old Mary McDevitt, who sang under the name

Little Mary Lee. In 1938, beset by ill health, Fox disbanded and moved to Australia and at the outset of World War II was not allowed back into Britain. He spent the war years mostly playing New York clubs before returning to Britain in 1946 and a vastly different entertainment scene. His 1947 theatre tour was a financial disaster. In the 50s he went bankrupt and gave up band leading to run a small entertainment agency.

At his peak Fox was one of the most popular band leaders of the 30s, remembered particularly for his theme, 'Whispering', the recording complete with his own spoken introduction. Credit should also be given to the work of his star vocalists, Al Bowlly on 'Thank Your Father' and 'You Forgot Your Gloves' and Denny Dennis with 'June In January', 'Everything I Have Is Yours' and 'Roses In December'. Roy Fox died in 1982 in the Brinsworth Home for Retired Variety Artists in Twickenham, England, where he had been a resident for several years.

● COMPILATIONS: *At Monseigneur Restaurant, Piccadilly* (1964) ★★★, *Roy Fox And His Orchestra 1936–38* (1975) ★★★, *Roy Fox And His Orchestra With Vocal Refrain* (1979) ★★★, *Strictly Instrumental* (1980) ★★★, *This Is Roy Fox* (1980) ★★★, *The Golden Age Of Roy Fox* (1985) ★★★, *Invitation To Dance* (1986) ★★★★, *I'll String Along* (1987) ★★★, *Rise And Shine* (1988) ★★★, *Ten Cents A Dance* (1988) ★★★.
● FURTHER READING: *Hollywood, Mayfair And All That Jazz*, Roy Fox.

Fox, Samantha

b. 15 April 1966, London, England. While studying for her O-level examinations, 16-year-old Fox was 'discovered' by the *Sun* newspaper and promoted as a topless model. Before long she became something of a British institution, and a recording career beckoned. Her debut single in 1986, 'Touch Me', elicited almost universally favourable reviews with critics registering surprise at her strong vocal performance. After the disc charted at number 3, she followed up with the sultry 'Do Ya, Do Ya (Wanna Please Me)', which also hit the UK Top 10. Further major British hits followed with 'Hold On Tight', 'Nothing's Gonna Stop Me Now' and 'I Surrender'. Having proven that former newspaper models can be hit artists, Fox defied all expectations by exporting her talents to the USA, where she enjoyed even greater chart success with three Top 10 hits including 'Naughty Girls', recorded with **Full Force**. Her albums were uneven but displayed her range to some effect, most notably on the **acid house**–inspired 'Love House', which was also an UK hit.

Overexposure and increasing media prejudice finally persuaded her to relocate to America, but despite her strong visual appeal, particularly to the **MTV** audience, further hits were not forthcoming, and Fox attempted to launch an acting and television career. In January 1996 she was banned from singing at a charity concert in Calcutta, India, owing to police fears she might cause a riot.

● ALBUMS: *Touch Me* (Jive 1986) ★★★, *Samantha Fox* (Jive 1987) ★★, *I Wanna Have Some Fun* (Jive 1989) ★★, *Just One Night* (Jive 1991) ★★, *21st Century Fox* (Ichiban 1998) ★★.
● COMPILATIONS: *Greatest Hits* (Jive 1992) ★★★, *Hot Tracks: The Best Of Samantha Fox* (BMG 2000) ★★★.
● FILMS: *Rock Dancer* (1994), *The Beautiful Game* aka *The Match* (1999).

Foxton, Bruce

b. 1 September 1955, Woking, Surrey, England. Following the breakup of the **Jam**, guitarist Foxton set out on a predictably difficult solo career. During the summer of 1983, he enjoyed UK Top 30 success with 'Freak'. His strong, straightforward pop, with often distinct Jam overtones, was generally well produced, with 'This Is The Way' proving particularly effective. In 1984 Foxton released *Touch Sensitive*, which featured all-original compositions and another solid production. While deserving of chart success, Foxton's work was, not surprisingly, compared unfavourably with that of the Jam, and consequently, his solo career failed to ignite.
● ALBUMS: *Touch Sensitive* (Arista 1984) ★★★.
● FURTHER READING: *Our Story*, Bruce Foxton and Rick Buckler with Alex Ogg.

Foxworthy, Jeff

b. 6 September 1958, Hapeville, Georgia, USA. Foxworthy is a highly successful comedian and writer who has appeared on country radio and released a string of platinum-selling albums. He walked out of a successful job at IBM to become a stand-up comedian, developing his famous catchphrase 'You might be a redneck if . . .', an example being, 'You might be a redneck if you lost a tooth opening a beer can.' The southern states have taken Foxworthy to heart and appreciate that his humour is affectionate. He collaborated with **Little Texas** for 'Party All Night' and makes a guest appearance in **Alan Jackson**'s video for 'I'm In Love With You Honey And I Don't Even Know Your Name'. Foxworthy's US television series ran for two successful seasons, he hosts a weekly country countdown show, and his spin-off merchandising remains big business. His albums have now sold over 15 million copies in the USA, and his books are a permanent feature on the bestsellers list.
● ALBUMS: *The Redneck Test Vol 11* (Laughing Hyena 1994) ★★, *You Might Be A Redneck If . . .* (Warners 1994) ★★★, *Games Rednecks Play* (Warners 1995) ★★★, *The Redneck Test Vol 43* (Laughing Hyena 1995) ★★, *The Original 1989 recording* (Laughing Hyena 1995) ★★, *Sold Out 1989 recording* (Laughing Hyena 1995) ★★, *Live 1989 recording* (Laughing Hyena 1996) ★★, *Crank It Up: The Music Album* (Warners 1996) ★★★, *Totally Committed* (Warners 1998) ★★★, *Big Funny* (DreamWorks 2000) ★★★, *Have Your Loved Ones Spayed Or Neutered* (Warners 2004) ★★★.
● COMPILATIONS: *The Ultimate Jeff Foxworthy Gift Collection* (Warners 1996) ★★★, *Greatest Bits* (Warners 1999) ★★★, *The Best Of Jeff Foxworthy: Double Wide, Single Minded* (Warners 2003) ★★★.
● DVD/VIDEOS: *Totally Committed* (HBO 1998), *The Best Of Jeff Foxworthy: Double Wide, Single Minded* (Rhino Home Video 2003).
● FURTHER READING: *You Might Be A Redneck If . . .*, Jeff Foxworthy and David Boyd. *Red Ain't Dead: 150 More Ways To Tell If You're A Redneck*, Jeff Foxworthy. *Hick Is Chic . . . A Guide To Etiquette For The (Grossly) Unsophisticated*, Jeff Foxworthy and David Boyd. *Check Your Neck: More Of You Might Be A Redneck If . . .*, Jeff Foxworthy and David Boyd. *You're Not A Kid Anymore . . .*, Jeff Foxworthy and David Boyd. *Games Rednecks Play*, Jeff Foxworthy and Vic Henley. *Redneck Classic: The Best Of Jeff Foxworthy*, Jeff Foxworthy and David Boyd. *Those People: Humorous Drawings*, Jeff Foxworthy. *No Shirt, No Shoes . . . No Problem!*, Jeff Foxworthy. *The Foxworthy Down-Home Cookbook: No*

Argula, No Paté . . . No Problem!, 'Big' Jim Foxworthy and Jeff Foxworthy. *The Final Helping Of You Might Be A Redneck If . . .*, Jeff Foxworthy and David Boyd.

Foxx, Inez And Charlie

Inez Foxx (b. 9 September 1942, Greensboro, North Carolina, USA) and Charlie Foxx (b. 29 October 1939, Greensboro, North Carolina, USA, d. 18 September 1998, Mobile, Alabama, USA). A brother and sister duo, Inez was a former member of the Gospel Tide Chorus. Her first solo single, 'A Feeling', was issued on **Brunswick Records**, credited to 'Inez Johnston'. Charlie was, meanwhile, a budding songwriter, and his reworking of a nursery rhyme, 'Mockingbird', became their first single together. Released on **Sue Records**' subsidiary Symbol, it was a US Top 10 hit in 1963, although it was not until 1969 that the song charted in the UK Top 40. Their immediate releases followed the same contrived pattern, but later recordings for Musicor/Dynamo, in particular 'I Stand Accused', were more adventurous. However, their final hit together, '(1-2-3-4-5-6-7) Count The Days' (1967), was modelled closely on that early style. Solo again, Inez continued to record for Dynamo before signing with **Stax Records** in 1972. Although apparently uncomfortable with their recording methods, the results, including the *Inez Foxx In Memphis* album, were excellent.

● ALBUMS: *Mockingbird* (Sue 1963) ★★★, *Inez And Charlie Foxx* (Sue 1964) ★★★, *Come By Here* (Musicor/Dynamo 1965) ★★★.
Solo: Inez Foxx *Inez Foxx In Memphis* (Volt 1972) ★★★★, *At Memphis And More* (Ace 1990) ★★★. Charlie Foxx *Foxx/Hill* (Foxx/Hill 1982) ★★★.

● COMPILATIONS: *The Best Of Charlie And Inez Foxx* (Stateside 1986) ★★★, *Count The Days* (Charly 1995) ★★★, *Greatest Hits* (Musicor/Dynamo 1996) ★★★★, *The Dynamic Duo* (Kent 2001) ★★★, *Mockingbird—Phase 1: The Complete Sue Recordings* (Connoisseur 2001) ★★★★.

Foxx, Jamie

b. Eric Bishop, 13 December 1967, Terrell, Texas, USA. Actor, comedian and R&B singer Jamie Foxx overcame a difficult upbringing to become one of the most prominent American performers of his generation. Adopted by his grandparents shortly after his birth, Eric Bishop endured a troubled adolescence to win a scholarship to study classical piano at the prestigious Juilliard School in New York. He finished his musical studies at the United States International University in San Diego. In 1989 he began performing stand-up at comedy clubs, in the process dropping his birth name and adopting the stage moniker Jamie Foxx. His success on the comedy circuit led to television roles in the popular series *In Living Color* and *Roc*. In 1992 he made his film debut in *Toys* and two years later launched an early attempt at a music career with the flop album *Peep This*. In 1996 he landed his own series, *The Jamie Foxx Show*, which proved successful enough to run for over 5 years and 100 episodes. His first starring role came in the 1999 American football-based movie *Any Given Sunday*, and further prominent roles followed in *Bait* (2000) and *Ali* (2001). During this period he kept his hand in with the music business, collaborating with artists including **Adina Howard** and **Gladys Knight** and appearing on the *Any Given Sunday* soundtrack.

Foxx's breakthrough year was 2004. He received an Oscar nomination for Best Supporting Actor in *Collateral*, but the critical acclaim for this performance was dwarfed later in the year by the success of his portrayal of **Ray Charles** in *Ray*. To prepare for the role Foxx spent pre-production time with the legendary singer, and the result was a striking performance in which he captured every nuance of Charles' inimitable style. He was rewarded with an Oscar for Best Actor, only the third black male actor to win the award.

During 2004 Foxx also relaunched his music career. He appeared alongside **Kanye West** on rapper **Twista**'s US chart-topping 'Slow Jamz'. The following year he appeared on West's 'Gold Digger' singing the Ray Charles–sampling hookline. 'Gold Digger' stayed at the top of the US singles chart for an impressive 10 weeks. Released at the end of 2005, Foxx's follow-up *Unpredictable* reached the top of the US charts in its second week of release. This solid modern R&B collection included guest appearances from the **Game**, **Ludacris**, **Common**, **Mary J. Blige**, **Snoop Dogg**, Twista and West. Foxx was also nominated for a Grammy Award for Best Male Vocal Performance for his version of **Luther Vandross**' 'Creepin'', from the J Records tribute album *So Amazing: An All Star Tribute To Luther Vandross*.

● ALBUMS: *Peep This* (Fox 1994) ★★, *Unpredictable* (J 2005) ★★★.
● FILMS: *Toys* (1992), *The Truth About Cats & Dogs* (1996), *The Great White Hype* (1996), *Booty Call* (1997), *The Players Club* (1998), *Held Up* (1999), *Any Given Sunday* (1999), *Bait* (2000), *Date From Hell* (2001), *Ali* (2001), *Shade* (2003), *Breakin' All The Rules* (2004), *Collateral* (2004), *Ray* (2004), *Stealth* (2005), *Jarhead* (2005).

Foxx, John

b. Dennis Leigh, Chorley, Lancashire, England. Foxx moved to London in 1974 where he became a key instigator in the rise of the UK electro pop scene. He was a founder member of **Ultravox**, with whom he wrote, sang and dabbled in synthetic noises. **Gary Numan** cited Foxx as his main influence, which was some consolation for the fact that Numan was having hits when Ultravox were dropped by **Island Records** in 1978. They subsequently regrouped, without Foxx but with new singer **Midge Ure**, and enjoyed great success during the 80s with a string of synth-pop singles. Foxx went solo in 1979 and formed his own label Metal Beat, distributed by **Virgin Records**. The infectious 'Underpass' began a short string of minor Top 40 UK hits that included further electronic pop classics 'No-One Driving', 'Burning Car' and 'Europe After The Rain'. The stark, minimalist *Metamatic* has since been hailed as a pioneering influence on the UK's **dance music** scene.

Foxx's appearances on the singles and album charts ended in the mid-80s, since which time he has balanced work as a graphic designer with his ongoing musical explorations, which included a foray into the dance scene with Nation XII. He resurfaced in the late 90s, releasing several albums on his own Metamatic label. The lush, atmospheric *Cathedral Oceans* had originally been recorded in the mid-80s, too early to reap the benefits of the **ambient house** explosion of the early 90s. *Shifting City*, a 1997 collaboration with Louis Gordon, was a largely successful fusion of Foxx's early 80s sound with modern electronica.

● ALBUMS: *Metamatic* (Metal Beat 1980) ★★★★, *The Garden* (Virgin 1981) ★★★, *The Golden Section* (Virgin

1983) ★★★, *In Mysterious Ways* (Virgin 1985) ★★★, *Cathedral Oceans* (Metamatic 1997) ★★★, with Louis Gordon *Shifting City* (Metamatic 1997) ★★★, *Exotour 97* mini-album (Metamatic 1997) ★★★, *Subterranean Omni-delic Exotour* (Metamatic 1998) ★★★, with Gordon *The Pleasures Of Electricity* (Metamatic 2002) ★★★, with Gordon *Crash And Burn* (Metamatic 2003) ★★★, with Harold Budd *Translucence/Drift Music* (Edsel 2004) ★★.

● COMPILATIONS: *Assembly* (Virgin 1992) ★★★★, *Modern Art: The Best Of John Foxx* (Music Club 2001) ★★★★.

Foy Willing And The Riders Of The Purple Sage
(see **Willing, Foy, And The Riders Of The Purple Sage**)

Foy, Eddie

b. Edwin Fitzgerald, 9 March 1856, New York City, USA, d. 16 February 1928, Kansas City, Missouri, USA. Born into a family of Irish immigrants, at the age of six Foy began singing and dancing in an effort to help to support his family after the death of his father. At first performing in the streets and in saloons, he moved on to the vaudeville circuit and by the end of the century had reached Broadway. He played in musical comedies including *The Strollers* (1901), *Mr. Blue-beard* (1903), *Piff! Paff! Pouf!!* (1904), *The Earl And The Girl* (1907), *The Orchid* (1907), *Mr. Hamlet Of Broadway* (1908), *Up And Down Broadway* (1910) and *Over The River* (1912). With his third wife, Foy had 11 children, seven of them surviving and eventually going on stage with him as Eddie Foy And The Seven Little Foys. This act began in 1910 and proved to be a smash hit wherever they played on their nationwide tours. In 1923 the act broke up, and Foy returned to being a solo performer, appearing successfully on Broadway and on tour. Two of his sons remained in showbusiness, Brian Foy as a film director and producer, **Eddie Foy Jnr.** as singer, dancer and comedian. Foy never retired and was still on the road when he died.

● FILMS: *Actors' Fund Field Day* (1910), *A Favorite Fool* (1915), *Yankee Doodle In Berlin* aka *The Kaiser's Last Squeal* (1919).

Foy, Eddie, Jnr.

b. Edwin Fitzgerald Jnr., 4 February 1905, New Rochelle, New York, USA, d. 15 July 1983, Woodland Hills, Los Angeles, California, USA. Foy's showbusiness career began at age five as a member of the vaudeville troupe run by his father, **Eddie Foy**. Their act, Eddie Foy And The Seven Little Foys, was a huge success and toured extensively. Following the breakup of the act in 1923, Foy (Jnr.) began a solo career. In 1929 he was in **Florenz Ziegfeld**'s *Show Girl* (1929), proving that he had what it took to survive alone. He then spent several years alternating between stage and screen performances. On film, he played small roles in numerous low-budget productions including *Queen Of The Night Clubs* (1929), which was directed by his brother, Brian Foy, *Leathernecking* (1930) and **Broadway Through A Keyhole** (1933). In *Frontier Marshal* (1939) and *Lillian Russell* (1940) he portrayed his father, as he did in 1942's **Yankee Doodle Dandy**. Similar fare continued through the 40s and 50s with *Dixie* (1943), *Wilson* (again as his father), *And The Angels Sing* (both 1944), *The Farmer Takes A Wife* (1953) and *Lucky Me* (1954).

Meanwhile, on stage Foy had a starring role in **Jerome Kern**'s **The Cat And The Fiddle** (1931) and was in a very successful revival of **Victor Herbert**'s **The Red Mill** (1945). He was in **The Pajama Game**, appearing in both the stage (1954) and screen versions (1957). He played a leading role in the unsuccessful stage production *Rumple* (1957), had a brief but telling part in the film **Bells Are Ringing** (1960) and the following year was back on Broadway for *Donnybrook!* (1961), another show that failed at the box office, and appeared in the film *Gidget Goes Hawaiian*. In 1968 he had a leading role in **Dudley Moore**'s movie *30 Is A Dangerous Age, Cynthia*. Foy continued working through the 70s, appearing on the big and small screens in many and varied roles. He also appeared on stage although after *Donnybrook!* there were no more Broadway shows. An engaging personality and showbiz to his bones, Foy brought a whiff of vaudeville nostalgia to new generations of theatregoers and film fans.

● FILMS: *A Favorite Fool* (1915), *Queen Of The Night Clubs* (1929), *The Heart Breaker* (1930), *Leathernecking* (1930), *Broadway Through A Keyhole* (1933), *Myrt And Marge* (1933), *Moulin Rouge* (1934), *Mrs. Barnacle Bill* (1934), *Roamin' Vandals* (1934), *A Duke For A Day* (1934), *Maid In Hollywood* (1934), *Benny From Panama* (1934), *I'll Be Suing You* (1934), *Lucky Beginners* (1935), *George Hall And His Orchestra* (1936), *Star For A Night* (1936), *College Holiday* (1936), *Turn Off The Moon* (1937), *The Prisoner Of Swing* (1938), *Secret Service Of The Air* (1939), *Women In The Wind* (1939), *Code Of The Secret Service* (1939), *Frontier Marshal* (1939), *Cowboy Quarterback* (1939), *Smashing The Money Ring* aka *Queer Money* (1939), *Alex In Wonderland* (1940), *Lillian Russell* (1940), *Murder In The Air* (1940), *A Fugitive From Justice* (1940), *Scatterbrain* (1940), *The Texas Rangers Ride Again* (1940), *The Case Of The Black Parrot* (1941), *Rookies On Parade* aka *Jamboree* (1941), *Country Fair* (1941), *Puddin' Head* aka *Judy Goes To Town* (1941), *Four Jacks And A Jill* (1942), *Yokel Boy* aka *Hitting The Headlines* (1942), *Yankee Doodle Dandy* (1942), *Powder Town* (1942), *Moonlight Masquerade* (1942), *Joan Of Ozark* aka *The Queen Of Spies* (1942), *Dixie Dugan* (1943), *Dixie* (1943), *And The Angels Sing* (1944), *Fun Time* (1944), *Wilson* (1944), *Dance, Dunce, Dance* (1945), *Foy Meets Girl* (1950), *Wedding Yells* (1951), *Honeychile* (1951), *The Farmer Takes A Wife* (1953), *Lucky Me* (1954), *The Pajama Game* (1957), *Bells Are Ringing* (1960), *Gidget Goes Hawaiian* (1961), *Gidget Goes To Rome* (1963), *30 Is A Dangerous Age, Cynthia* (1968), *Won Ton Ton, The Dog Who Saved Hollywood* (1976).

FPI Project

Principally Damon Rochefort (b. c.1965, Cardiff, Wales), a former law student, and Sharon Dee Clarke (b. c.1965), a part-time actor with bit parts in several television soap operas. They scored an instant hit in late 1989, early 1990 when 'Going Back To My Roots' gatecrashed the UK Top 10. It was available in two formats, the first with a Paulo Dini vocal, the second version by Clarke. Following further singles 'Risky' and 'Everybody (All Over The World)', the two protagonists would go on to enjoy further chart success as **Nomad**. However, Rochefort continued to use the FPI banner on occasion, such as the 1992 *Paradise* EP.

Fragile State

This UK-based chill-out unit is the partnership of two friends, Neil Cowley and Ben Mynott. Both experienced musicians, keyboard player Cowley has produced tracks for EastWest Connection and for the acclaimed San Francisco soulful **house** label, Naked Music, and toured as a keyboard player with **Zero 7**. Mynott is also a journalist for *Blues And Soul* magazine and compiler of jazz compilation albums for UK radio station Jazz FM and soulful house mixes for the Bar De Lune label. After a successful single, 'Nocturnal Beats', in October 2002, the duo released *The Facts And The Dreams*, a musically rich album, combining complimentary elements of hip-hop, jazz and classical music, that attracted plaudits from many observers. The title is a reference to an obscure 20s book on German architecture, a theme continued on the album's artwork design featuring architectural drawings.

In demand as remixers on the lucrative chill-out scene, Cowley and Mynott managed to find the time to compile a strong mix collection of their own, *Just Got Home*. The duo released the follow-up proper to their acclaimed debut in early 2004.

● ALBUMS: *The Facts And The Dreams* (Bar De Lune 2002) ★★★★, *Voices From The Dust Bowl* (Bar De Lune 2004) ★★★.

● COMPILATIONS: *Just Got Home* (Just Got Home 2003) ★★★.

Fragma

This European **dance music** act comprises brothers Marco and Dirk Duderstadt and Ramon Zenker. The Duderstadt brothers have been DJing successfully in Europe since the mid-90s, and Fragma arose out of a desire to produce their own material. Zenker found success in 1989 with Honesty 69's 'French Kiss', then as one half of the **Hardfloor** duo that brought **acid house** to prominence during the next decade. The three co-wrote and produced the hit 'Toca Me', whose laid-back guitar sounds were an integral part of the European **trance** upsurge in the summer of 1999. A chance bootleg showed that this instrumental track snugly fitted the vocals of Coco's **house** anthem 'I Need A Miracle'. The resulting 'Toca's Miracle', now a great pop song, was snapped up by **Positiva Records** and raced to the top of several charts throughout Europe in early 2000. Eva, the first of various Fragma vocalists, sang Coco's vocal line. Maria Rubia then sang on the follow-up 'Everytime You Need Me', a catchy pop song and Top 10 European success. The classically trained Damae appeared on the outfit's third hit, 'You Are Alive', and the majority of *Toca*. Released in early 2001, the album promoted Fragma's trance sensibilities.

● ALBUMS: *Toca* (Positiva 2001) ★★★.

Frahm, Joel

b. 1970, Racine, Wisconsin, USA. As a child Frahm studied piano and also played bassoon, but while in eighth grade at the Stephen Bull Fine Arts School where he had tuition from music teacher Gary Mollenkopf, he began playing tenor saxophone. In 1985 he moved with his family to West Hartford, Connecticut, where, as a student at William H. Hall High School, he came under the wing of Bill Stanley, founder of the school jazz band. It was here that Frahm also encountered fellow students with an interest in jazz. One was a drummer named Bill Dobrow, the other was pianist **Brad Mehldau**. Frahm and Mehldau formed what was to become a long-lasting and productive musical relationship. They teamed up for a weekly engagement at a local club, a portent of much to come. While playing in the high school jazz band, Frahm also augmented his musical knowledge by listening to records by artists such as **Art Blakey**, **Freddie Hubbard**,

Horace Silver and **Miles Davis**, paying particular attention to saxophonists **Wayne Shorter**, **Bob Berg** and **Charlie Parker**.

After leaving high school in 1988, Frahm attended Rutgers University for a year before transferring to the Manhattan School of Music, and following graduation with a bachelor of arts degree in jazz performance, he entered **Betty Carter**'s Jazz Ahead workshop. Thereafter, he played with **Maynard Ferguson** and **Larry Goldings** and was also a member of Mehldau's early 90s quartet with bass player **Dwayne Burno** and drummer Greg Hutchinson. In 1996 Frahm, who also plays soprano saxophone, reached the semifinal of the **Thelonious Monk** competition. After a 1998 duo fundraiser concert with Mehldau, on behalf of their old high school, the pair recorded in this format including 2004's *Don't Explain*. In the early 00s, Frahm toured and recorded with **Jane Monheit**, appearing on *Taking A Chance On Love*. In October 2004 Frahm was back again at his high school, this time with his quartet, for another benefit concert, this time on behalf of Gifts of Music, a nonprofit community group that collaborates with Hartt School of Music to provide local students with music lessons. Not only does Frahm have full command of the instruments he plays, he is inventive and adventurous in his playing. The verve and enthusiasm he has for his music is thoroughly communicated to fellow musicians and audiences alike.

● ALBUMS: *Sorry, No Decaf* (Palmetto 1998) ★★★★, *The Navigator* (Palmetto 2000) ★★★, with Brad Mehldau *Don't Explain* (Palmetto 2004) ★★★.

Frame, Roddy

b. 29 January 1964, East Kilbride, Scotland. Frame was one of the most gifted songwriters to emerge on the UK post-punk scene. His band **Aztec Camera** was formed in 1980, and before long Frame was being championed by the UK music press as an outstanding talent. The exceptionally strong debut album, **High Land, Hard Rain**, resulted in a major label contract with the global **WEA Records** label. Frame and Aztec Camera reached a commercial zenith with their third album, *Love*, which included the memorable soul-influenced UK Top 5 hit 'Somewhere In My Heart'. Later albums embraced new musical styles but sacrificed sales in the process.

Aztec Camera disintegrated following the release of 1995's *Frestonia*, with Frame opting to work on his next project under his own name. Released in September 1998 on Andy McDonald's Independiente Records label, *The North Star* marked a return to the singer-songwriter style of Aztec Camera's debut. A beguiling mix of ballads ('Hymn To Grace', 'Autumn Flower') and guitar pop ('Reason For Living', 'Back To The One'), the album was a critical success but failed to break into the UK Top 50. The belated follow-up, *Surf*, featured 11 acoustic performances and was released by **Cooking Vinyl Records** in August 2002.

● ALBUMS: *The North Star* (Independiente 1998) ★★★★, *Surf* (Cooking Vinyl 2002) ★★★.

Frames

Fronted by singer-songwriter and guitarist Glen Hansard (b. 21 April 1970, Dublin, Eire), this highly acclaimed Irish band was formed in Dublin at the end of the 80s, making their debut live appearance at a festival in the west of Ireland in September 1990. At the same time, Hansard also appeared in Alan Parker's film adaptation of the Roddy Doyle novel *The Commitments*, a lucrative enough experience at the time, but a connection that has proven wearisome over the years. The original line-up featured Hansard, David Odlum (b. 14 January 1970, Dublin, Eire; guitar), Colm Mac Con Iomaire (b. 18 May 1971, Dublin, Eire; violin/electronics), John Carney (bass), Paul Brennan (drums) and Noreen O'Donnell (vocals). The other members supported Hansard through the negativity of media queries (specifically in relation to *The Commitments*), although Hansard himself shrugged off criticisms by ensuring that the Frames quickly became one of the most talked about live attractions in Ireland.

The Frames' 1992 debut for **Island Records** was lost in the label's subsequent housecleaning, and the band went about fulfilling live commitments with new bass player Graham Downey. Vocalist Noreen O'Donnell left during recording sessions for a second album, but such was the strength of the new songs that **ZTT Records** signed the band. Yet at this time, the Frames were undergoing an evolutionary process which witnessed major creative changes: the **Pixies**–meets–**Nick Drake** sound of their earlier years was slowly transforming into a style of US post-rock, with influences from acts such as **Slint**, **Tortoise**, **Pavement** and **Will Oldham** making their presence felt. The Frames mindset was getting stranger but was no less incendiary, and the new material on *Fitzcarraldo* reflected their evolution, being simultaneously direct but sonically askew.

Further line-up changes during this period saw Joe Doyle (b. 8 May 1977, Dublin, Eire; bass/vocals) and Dave Hingerty (b. 4 March 1968, Dublin, Eire; drums) replacing Downey and Brennan respectively. This line-up completed 1999's *Dance The Devil . . .*, which featured the moving **Jeff Buckley** tribute 'Neath The Beeches'. They recorded 2001's *For The Birds* in Kerry, Eire, with Craig Ward from **dEUS** and in Chicago with **Steve Albini**. The choice of producers was reflected in a less commercially orientated approach to songwriting, allowing the band to explore the subtleties and nuances that had too often been buried in their previous work.

Despite further plaudits for the Frames, Odlum announced he was departing the band to concentrate on production work. He was replaced by Simon Goode and then Rob Bochnik as the band took stock with two live releases, *Breadcrumb Trail* (recorded in the Czech Republic) and *Set List*. Their new studio album *Burn The Maps* was recorded in France with the help of former band member Odlum. The Frames remain one of Ireland's best kept secrets.

● ALBUMS: *Another Love Song* (Island 1992) ★★★, *Fitzcarraldo* (ZTT/Elektra 1996) ★★★, *Dance The Devil . . .* (ZTT/Universal 1999) ★★★★, *For The Birds* (Plateau/Overcoat 2001) ★★★★, *Breadcrumb Trail* (Plateau/Indies 2002) ★★★, *Set List* (Plateau/Anti 2003) ★★★, *The Roads Outgrown* mini-album (Overcoat 2003) ★★★, *Burn The Maps* (Plateau/Anti 2004) ★★★.

Frampton, Peter

b. 22 April 1950, Beckenham, Kent, England. The former 'Face of 1968', with his pin-up good looks as part of the 60s pop group the **Herd**, Frampton grew his hair longer and joined **Humble Pie**. His solo career debuted with *Wind Of Change* in 1971, although he immediately set about forming another band, Frampton's Camel, to carry out US concert dates. This formidable unit consisted of Mike Kellie (b. 24 March 1947, Birmingham, England; drums), Rick Wills (bass) and Mickey Gallagher (keyboards), all seasoned players from **Spooky Tooth**, **Cochise** and **Bell And Arc**, respectively.

Frampton in 1975 was a great success in the USA, while in the UK he was commercially ignored. The following year a double set recorded at Winterland in San Francisco, *Frampton Comes Alive!*, scaled the US chart and stayed on top for a total of 10 weeks, in four visits during a record-breaking two-year stay. It also reached number 6 in the UK album chart. The record became the biggest-selling live album in history and to date has sold over 15 million copies. Quite why the record was so successful has perplexed many rock critics.

Like **Jeff Beck**, Frampton perfected the voice tube effect and used this gimmick on 'Show Me The Way', a US number 6 hit in February 1976 (this single was also Frampton's only UK Top 10 entry). The follow-up, *I'm In You*, sold in vast quantities, although compared to the former it was a flop, selling a modest 'several million'. The title-track climbed to number 2 in the US singles chart in May 1977. Again Frampton found little critical acclaim, but his records were selling in vast quantities. He continued to reach younger audiences with aplomb. In 1978 he suffered a near fatal car crash, although his fans were able to see him in the previously filmed *Sgt Pepper's Lonely Hearts Club Band*. Frampton played Billy Shears alongside the **Bee Gees** in the **Robert Stigwood** extravaganza that was a commercial and critical disaster.

When he returned in 1979 with *Where I Should Be*, his star was dwindling. The album garnered favourable reviews, but it was his last successful record. Even the short-haired image for *Breaking All The Rules* failed, with only America, his loyal base, nudging it into the Top 50. Following *The Art Of Control* Frampton 'disappeared' until 1986, when he was signed to **Virgin Records** and released the synthesizer-laced *Premonition*. He returned to session work thereafter. Later on in the decade Frampton was found playing guitar with his former schoolfriend **David Bowie** on his 1987 release *Never Let Me Down*. In 1991 he was allegedly making plans to re-form **Humble Pie** with **Steve Marriott**, but a week after their meeting in New York, Marriott tragically died in a fire at his Essex home. Frampton diverted his interest to the other great success of his career by releasing *Frampton Comes Alive II*. In 2000 Frampton served as a musical consultant on Cameron Crowe's 70s rock biopic, *Almost Famous*.

● ALBUMS: *Wind Of Change* (A&M 1972) ★★★, *Frampton's Camel* (A&M 1973) ★★★, *Somethin's Happening* (A&M 1974) ★★, *Frampton* (A&M 1975) ★★, *Frampton Comes Alive!* (A&M 1976) ★★★★, *I'm In You* (A&M 1977) ★★, *Where I Should Be* (A&M 1979) ★★, *Breaking All The Rules* (A&M 1981) ★★, *The Art Of Control* (A&M 1982) ★★, *Premonition* (Atlantic 1986) ★, *When All The Pieces Fit* (Atlantic 1989) ★★, *Peter Frampton* (Relativity 1994) ★★★, *Acoustics* (Relativity 1994) ★★★, *Frampton Comes Alive II* (El Dorado/I.R.S. 1995) ★★, *Live In Detroit* (CMC 2000) ★★★, *Now* (Framptone 2003) ★★★.

● COMPILATIONS: *Peter Frampton's Greatest Hits* (A&M 1987) ★★★★, *Shine On: A Collection* (A&M 1992) ★★★★, *The Very Best Of Peter Frampton* (A&M 1998) ★★★, *Anthology: The History Of Peter Frampton* (Universal 2001) ★★★★, *The Best Of Peter Frampton: The Millennium Collection* (A&M 2003) ★★★★.

● DVD/VIDEOS: *Frampton Comes Alive II* (El Dorado/I.R.S. 1995), *Live In Detroit* (Image Entertainment 2000).

● FURTHER READING: *Frampton!: An Unauthorized Biography*, Susan Katz. *Peter Frampton*, Marsha Daly. *Peter Frampton: A Photo Biography*, Irene Adler.
● FILMS: *Son Of Dracula* aka *Young Dracula* (1974), *Sgt. Pepper's Lonely Hearts Club Band* (1978), *Almost Famous* (2000).

France, Martin

b. 29 February 1964, Rainham, Kent, England. Growing up in Manchester, France began playing drums at an early age and before entering his teens was in an organ-led trio backing singers appearing at local clubs. Leaving school at 16, he became a professional musician and after moving to London joined other rising young players in **Loose Tubes**. That early 80s spell with the outfit brought him into contact with many like-minded musicians, notably **Django Bates** and **Iain Ballamy**. Subsequently, France was with Bates in First House, recording for **ECM Records** and also appearing on Bates' 1997 recording *Quiet Nights*. These musical relationships continued through the decades, and among many sometimes inter-related groups with which he played were Delightful Precipice, Human Chain and Perfect Houseplants. France was in several bands led by Ballamy and also played with **Billy Jenkins**, **Mark Lockheart** and **Julian Argüelles**. In the early 00s, both Bates and Ballamy played in France's band, Live, a remarkably eclectic group, using electronic, programmed and sampled sounds as well freely improvised music, especially in drum 'n' bass mode. In the latter he teamed with bass player Tim Harries, creating a richly textured parade of sounds. France and Harries also linked up with guitarist **John Parricelli** to perform an experimental repertoire.

Among many other jazz musicians with whom France has played are **Arild Anderson**, **Mike Gibbs**, **Lee Konitz**, **Maria Schneider**, **Steve Swallow** and **Bugge Wesseltoft**. Together with **John Taylor** and **Dave Holland**, he also played in a quartet led by **Kenny Wheeler** on a Scandinavian tour, accompanying singer Sidsel Endresen. He has toured internationally for many years, appearing in some 40 countries. In addition to jazz dates, France has worked extensively in film and television studios and multimedia and cross-genre sessions. These have included working with the London Sinfonietta, the BBC Welsh Symphony Orchestra, in the Netherlands with the ASKO Ensemble and in Germany with the NDR Radio Orchestra. In addition to his crowded performing schedule, France is also active as a teacher, including working at London's Trinity College of Music and the Royal Academy of Music. A thoroughly schooled drummer, adept in many musical styles, in his playing France can be subtly discreet while displaying a richly interesting and sometimes experimental percussion palette.
● ALBUMS: *Spin Marvel* (Babel/F-ire 2005) ★★★.

Francis, Cleve

b. 22 April 1945, Jennings, Louisiana, USA. The eldest of six children, Francis had childhood ambitions to play the guitar and sing country music. He gained his first experience towards his ambition by singing and playing gospel music in the local church choir. After completing his college education, he attended medical school, where he qualified as a cardiologist. After relocating to Washington, DC, he worked at his qualified profession during the day and gradually built a reputation as a singer by performing in local clubs in the evenings. He eventually attracted attention when his album *Lovelight* was released in the USA by Playback, whose distribution arrangement with the Cottage label also saw it released in the UK. A video of the title track attracted attention on CMT and TNN and led to him joining **Liberty Records**, where he then had the distinction of being, at the time, the only black country singer signed to a major label. What was more distinctive, however, was his being signed to Liberty at the relatively advanced age of 48 and his decision to put on hold his medical career. His first album release for Liberty saw him gain three minor country chart entries, 'You Do My Heart Good', 'How Can I Hold You' and a re-recording of 'Lovelight'. 'Walkin', the title track of his follow-up album, also gained minor chart success in 1993. However, his refined vocals and especially the more MOR material and musical backings that he has been given by his producers seem unlikely to endear him to traditionally minded country fans. Francis returned to his medical profession later in the 90s.
● ALBUMS: *Lovelight* (Playback 1991, released in UK on Cottage 1992) ★★★, *Tourist In Paradise* (Liberty 1992) ★★★★, *Walkin'* (Liberty 1993) ★★★, *You've Got Me Now* (Liberty 1994) ★★★.

Francis, Connie

b. Concetta Rosa Maria Franconero, 12 December 1938, Newark, New Jersey, USA. A popular singer of tearful ballads and jaunty up-tempo numbers, Francis was one of the most successful female artists of the 50s and 60s. She began playing the accordion at the age of four and was singing and playing professionally when she was 11. After winning an *Arthur Godfrey Talent Show*, she changed her name, at Godfrey's suggestion. Signed for **MGM Records** in 1955, her first record was a German import, 'Freddy', which was also recorded by **Eartha Kitt** and **Stan Kenton**. 'Majesty Of Love', her 10th release, a duet with **Marvin Rainwater**, was her first US chart entry. In 1957 she was persuaded by her father, against her will, to record one of his favourites, the 1923 song 'Who's Sorry Now', by **Harry Ruby**, **Bert Kalmar** and Ted Snyder. It went to number 4 in the US charts and number 1 in the UK and was the first of a string of hits through to 1962. These included reworkings of more oldies, such as 'My Happiness', 'Among My Souvenirs' and 'Together'.

Among her more jaunty, upbeat songs were 'Stupid Cupid' (another UK number 1 coupled with 'Carolina Moon') and 'Where The Boys Are' by the new songwriting team of **Neil Sedaka** and Howard Greenfield. Her other US Top 10 entries included 'Lipstick On Your Collar', 'Frankie', 'Mama', 'Everybody's Somebody's Fool' (her first US number 1), 'My Mind Has A Heart Of Its Own' (another US number 1), 'Many Tears Ago', 'Breakin' In A Brand New Broken Heart', 'When The Boy In Your Arms (Is The Boy In Your Heart)', 'Don't Break The Heart That Loves You' (US number 1), 'Second Hand Love' and 'Vacation'. Francis made her film debut in 1960 with *Where The Boys Are* and followed it with similar 'frothy' comedy musicals such as *Follow The Boys* (1963), *Looking For Love* (1964) and *When The Boys Meet The Girls* (1965). Outdated by the 60s beat boom, she worked in nightclubs in the late 60s and did much charity work for UNICEF and similar organizations besides entertaining US troops in Vietnam. She also extended her repertoire and kept her options open by recording albums in several languages, including French, Spanish and Japanese, and one entitled

Connie Francis Sings Great Jewish Favorites. Late 70s issues included more country music selections.

In 1974 she was the victim of a rape in her motel room after performing at the Westbury Theatre, outside New York. She later sued the motel for negligence and was reputedly awarded damages of over 3 million. For several years afterwards she did not perform in public and underwent psychiatric treatment for long periods. She returned to the Westbury in 1981, to an enthusiastic reception, and resumed performing in the USA and abroad, including appearances at the London Palladium in 1989 and in Las Vegas in the same year, where she received a standing ovation after a mature performance ranging from her opening number, 'Let Me Try Again', to the climactic 'If I Never Sing Another Song'. While at the Palladium, her speech became slurred, and she was suspected of being drunk. In 1991 she had trouble speaking on a US television show and, a year later, collapsed at a show in New Jersey. She was diagnosed as suffering from 'a complex illness' and of 'having been toxic for 18 years'. After drastically reducing her daily lithium intake, in 1993 she signed a new recording contract with Sony, buoyed up by the fact that her 1959 hit, 'Lipstick On Your Collar', was climbing high in the UK charts, triggered by its use as the title track of playwright Dennis Potter's television drama.

● ALBUMS: *Who's Sorry Now?* (MGM 1958) ★★★★, *The Exciting Connie Francis* (MGM 1959) ★★★★, *My Thanks To You* (MGM 1959) ★★★★, *Christmas In My Heart* (MGM 1959) ★★★, *Italian Favorites* (MGM 1960) ★★★, *More Italian Favorites* (MGM 1960) ★★★, *Rock 'N' Roll Million Sellers* (MGM 1960) ★★★, *Country And Western Golden Hits* (MGM 1960) ★★, *Spanish And Latin American Favorites* (MGM 1960) ★★★, *Connie Francis At The Copa* (MGM 1961) ★★, *Connie Francis Sings Great Jewish Favorites* (MGM 1961) ★★, *Songs To A Swingin' Band* (MGM 1961) ★★, *Never On Sunday And Other Title Songs From Motion Pictures* (MGM 1961) ★★★, *Folk Song Favorites* (MGM 1961) ★★★, *Do The Twist* (MGM 1962) ★★★, *Second Hand Love And Other Hits* (MGM 1962) ★★★, *Country Music Connie Style* (MGM 1962) ★★★, *Modern Italian Hits* (MGM 1963) ★★★, *Follow The Boys* film soundtrack (MGM 1963) ★★★, *German Favorites* (MGM 1963) ★★, *Award Winning Motion Picture Hits* (MGM 1963) ★★, *Great American Waltzes* (MGM 1963) ★★★, *In The Summer Of His Years* (MGM 1964) ★★★, *Looking For Love* film soundtrack (MGM 1964) ★★, with Hank Williams Jnr. *Great Country Favorites* (MGM 1964) ★★, *A New Kind Of Connie* (MGM 1964) ★★★, *Connie Francis Sings For Mama* (MGM 1965) ★★★, *When The Boys Meet The Girls* film soundtrack (MGM 1965) ★★★, *Movie Greats Of The Sixties* (MGM 1966) ★★★, *Live At The Sahara In Las Vegas* (MGM 1966) ★★, *Love Italian Style* (MGM 1967) ★★★, *Happiness* (MGM 1967) ★★, *My Heart Cries For You* (MGM 1967) ★★★, *Hawaii Connie* (MGM 1968) ★★, *Connie And Clyde* (MGM 1968) ★★, *Connie Sings Bacharach And David* (MGM 1968) ★★★, *The Wedding Cake* (MGM 1969) ★★★, *Connie Francis Sings Great Country Hits, Volume Two* (MGM 1973) ★★, *Sings The Big Band Hits* (MGM 1977) ★★, *I'm Me Again—Silver Anniversary Album* (MGM 1981) ★★★, *Connie Francis And Peter Kraus, Volumes 1 & 2* (MGM 1984) ★★★, *Country Store* (MGM 1988) ★★, *Live At Trump's Castle* (Click 1996) ★★★.

● COMPILATIONS: *Connie's Greatest Hits* (MGM 1960) ★★★★, *More Greatest Hits* (MGM 1961) ★★★★, *Mala Femmena And Connie's Big Hits From Italy* (MGM 1963) ★★★, *The Very Best Of Connie Francis* (MGM 1963) ★★★★, *The All Time International Hits* (MGM 1965) ★★★★, *20 All Time Greats* (Polydor 1977) ★★★★, *Connie Francis In Deutschland* 8-LP box set (Bear Family 1988) ★★★★, *The Very Best Of Connie Francis* (Polydor 1988) ★★★, *The Singles Collection* (PolyGram 1993) ★★★, *White Sox, Pink Lipstick . . . And Stupid Cupid* 5-CD box set (Bear Family 1993) ★★★★, *Souvenirs* 4-CD box set (Polydor/Chronicles 1996) ★★★★, *On Guard With Connie Francis* (Jazz Band 1996) ★★★, *Where The Boys Are: Connie Francis In Hollywood* (Rhino/Turner 1997) ★★★, *Kissin' And Twistin': Going Where The Boys Are* 5-CD box set (Bear Family 1997) ★★★, *The Best Of Connie Francis: The Millennium Collection* (Polydor 1999) ★★★★, *The Ultimate EP Collection* (See For Miles 2002) ★★★★.

● DVD/VIDEOS: *The Legend Live* (Prism Video 1990).

● FURTHER READING: *Who's Sorry Now?*, Connie Francis.

● FILMS: *Jamboree* aka *Disc Jockey Jamboree* (1957), *Where The Boys Are* (1960), *Follow The Boys* (1963), *Looking For Love* (1964), *When The Boys Meet The Girls* (1965).

Francis, David 'Panama'

b. 21 December 1918, Miami, Florida, USA, d. 12 November 2001, Orlando, Florida, USA. Francis began to play drums at the age of eight and made his first professional club appearance when he was 13 years old. Twelve months later he was on tour and in 1934 became a member of **George Kelly**'s band. By the time he was in his late teens he was resident in New York, where he quickly found work with **Tab Smith** and **Roy Eldridge**. In 1940 he joined **Lucky Millinder**'s big band, remaining there until 1945. Millinder's band was very popular at Harlem's Savoy Ballroom, and Francis was a significant factor in that popularity. He then briefly led his own band, which toured the South but met with only limited success. In 1947 he was hired by **Cab Calloway** for a five-year stint. Subsequently Francis worked in radio and was regularly on call as a recording session musician, backing artists such as **John Lee Hooker**, **Eubie Blake**, **Ella Fitzgerald**, **Ray Charles** and **Mahalia Jackson**.

Francis' long absence from the jazz scene ended in the late 70s, when he returned to play with **Lionel Hampton**'s all-star big band and, most importantly, to lead his own nine-piece band, the Savoy Sultans (named after Al Cooper's **Savoy Sultans** he had played opposite three decades earlier). The new Sultans included Francis Williams, **Norris Turney** and Francis' old boss, George Kelly. A highly accomplished drummer with an exemplary technique, Francis played with a loosely flowing swing that benefited any band of which he was a member.

● ALBUMS: *Latin American Dixieland* (MGM 1955) ★★★, *Exploding Drums* (Epic 1959) ★★★★, *Tough Talk* (20th Century Fox 1963) ★★★, *Gettin' In The Groove* (Black & Blue 1979) ★★★, *Jimmy Witherspoon With Panama Francis' Savoy Sultans* (Black & Blue 1979) ★★★★, *Grooving* (Stash 1982) ★★★, *Everything Swings* (Stash 1984) ★★★, *Panama Francis All-Stars 1949* recording (Collectables 1994) ★★★.

● COMPILATIONS: *Get Up And Dance* (Stash 1988) ★★★.

Francis, Joe

b. New Jersey, USA. Francis began singing professionally in 1982 while still a student, working in fringe theatre and nightclubs. He also sang on cruise liners, including the *QE2*. In 1983 he was personally recommended by **John Bunch** for the featured vocalist spot with the New **Glenn Miller** Orchestra. He toured extensively with the band for three years, then went out as a single. He also studied music and has worked with coaches Vera Mazel and Maria Farmworth. Since 1986 Francis has continued with solo work apart from a brief spell as solo singer with the New Pied Pipers. He customarily works with writer-producer Ken Barnes and arranger Pete Moore. In the mid-90s Francis sang for the UK-based Sinatra Music Society and also performed at Buckingham Palace in a benefit concert for the Not Forgotten Association. Singing in the **Frank Sinatra** tradition and working with a repertoire culled from the Great American Song Book, Francis has established a good reputation as a sensitive interpreter of popular music.

Francis, Panama

(see **Francis, David 'Panama'**)

Francis, Winston

b. 1948, Kingston, Jamaica, West Indies. Francis attended school in Jamaica and began an apprenticeship in the printing trade before relocating to Miami, Florida, USA, at the age of 16. In Miami he attended a music school where his teacher, the impresario, writer and performer Chuck Bird, likened his vocals to those of **Nat 'King' Cole**. Bird arranged a performance at the Fountain Blue Hotel in Miami in 1965 with the **Jackie Gleason** Orchestra, witnessed by noted US politician Spiro Agnew. Francis began his career in earnest, performing with Carlos Malcolm alongside **Derrick Harriott** and **Boris Gardiner**, touring the USA and Caribbean. His recording career began at **Studio One** where he made a number of classic **rocksteady** hits, including a version of **Joe South**'s 'Games People Play' and the captivating 'Reggae And Cry', while in combination with **Alton Ellis** he covered **Junior Walker**'s 'What Does It Take'. He had also recorded with producer **Joe Gibbs** as part of the Mellowtones, noted for their hit 'Feel Good'. In 1971 he relocated to the UK to promote his version of the **Mamas And The Papas**' 'California Dreaming', which was chosen as record of the week for two consecutive weeks on national radio. The b-side, 'Too Experienced', featured falsetto backing vocals from **Bob Marley** and **Bunny Wailer**. In 1972 Francis began touring the club circuit and recorded sessions for **EMI Records**, including 'Follow Your Star' and a version of 'Blue Moon'. Throughout the 70s he recorded a number of sessions in the UK, including a remake of 'California Dreaming' with **Danny Ray**. Between 1980 and 1986 he took a sabbatical from the music business and worked as a youth leader and social worker. He was coaxed back into the recording studio in 1987 when he sang backing vocals for the **Melodians** and performed for Trevor Star and the Skaticians, with whom he still sings. In 1993 Francis was approached by **Dennis Bovell** to record as a soul performer under the pseudonym of King Cool for the compilation *Jamaican Soul*. He became a prominent performer in France when his interpretation of **Ben E. King**'s 'Stand By Me' was released as a single, selling in excess of 90,000 copies. Although a celebrity in Europe he remained in relative obscurity in the UK, remembered predominantly

as a Studio One veteran. His European success resulted in collaborations with **Sly And Robbie**, albeit playing soul tunes for his King Cool album debut. In the 90s Francis was asked by **Linton Kwesi Johnson** to provide the vocals for a rocksteady revival project under the direction of the distinguished reggae guitarist **John Kpiaye**. Francis toured Europe and the USA performing rocksteady classics, including a notable performance at the Sierra Nevada Reggae Festival in San Francisco. The project led to a compilation of Jamaican classics, *Sweet Rock Steady*. The cover featured a photograph of the young Francis that originally appeared on the Studio One various artists compilation *Reggae In The Grass*, released in the late 60s.

● ALBUMS: *Mr Fix It* (Studio One 1970) ★★★★, as King Cool *His Majesty Requests* (BMG France 1993) ★★, *Sweet Rock Steady* (LKJ 1997) ★★★, *Feel Good All Over* (Jetstar 2005) ★★★.

● COMPILATIONS: *California Dreaming/Mr Fix It* (Sprint Music 1998) ★★★★.

Francisco, Don

b. Decatur, Georgia, USA. Born and raised in a seminary campus, gospel singer Don Francisco attended church regularly in his childhood. His full conversion to born again Christianity took place in 1974, after which he began to write his own praise songs. His first album, *Brother Of The Sun*, followed for NewPax Records in 1975. However, neither this nor the subsequent *Forgiven* managed to create much of an impression beyond the southern states gospel community. He was noticeably more quiet in the 80s but was once again making the *Billboard* chart in 2004.

● ALBUMS: *Brother Of The Sun* (NewPax 1975) ★★★★, *Forgiven* (NewPax 1977) ★★★, *Mi Homenaje Gigante A La Musica Nortena* (Univision 2004) ★★★★.

● DVD/VIDEOS: *Mi Homenaje Gigante A La Musica Nortena* (Univision 2004).

Franco

b. L'Okanga La Ndju Pene Luambo Makiada, 9 September 1939, Sona Bata, Zaire, d. 15 October 1989, Kinshasa, Zaire. Probably the greatest and most influential figure in the pantheon of contemporary African music, Franco's achievements up until his premature death in 1989 were impressive. He recorded some 180 albums, created a rhythm—rumba odemba—that became a permanent part of Zairean music and, through his band **OK Jazz**, showcased many of Zaire's top musicians, from **Sam Mangwana** to **Dalienst**, Youlou Mabial, **Wuta May**, **Mose Fan Fan** and Michelino. His organization was equally vast; three record labels—Edipop, Visa 80 and Choc—and, in the mid-80s, three separate bands—one, OK Jazz, in Belgium and two in Zaire. He was born in a small village 78 kilometres from the Zairean capital, Kinshasa. His father wanted him to be a doctor, but Franco had other ideas. Armed with a homemade tin-can guitar and folk song repertoire, he played around the markets in Kinshasa before joining an acoustic group Bikunda.

In 1950 Bikunda became **Watam**. It featured two guitarists, Franco and Paul Ebongo Dewayon, and a rhythm section playing traditional percussion. Loningisa, a local record company, kept an eye on the group, and three years later Watam recorded 'Bolingo Na Ngai Na Beatrice', the first of four hit singles. In 1956 OK Jazz, a 10-piece band that would later more than double in size, was born. OK meant two things: Orchestre Kinois, Kinois being a citizen of Kinshasa; OK were also the initials of an early sponsor, Omar Kashama, who ran a bar called Chez Cassien OK Bar. At this time, Zairean music was deeply influenced by Latin-American styles—bolero, cha-cha and rumba. In 1960 Franco's love affair with a woman called Majos inspired a set of classic love songs and a rumba style that would form the basis of his later, extended lyric satires. While **Kalle** and his young singer **Tabu Ley** developed new dances and styles, Franco stuck with the rumba and developed his own, faster variant, which he named rumba odemba.

Later he added new dance rhythms, and incorporated much of Zairean folk song into his approach, but rumba odemba remained the foundation of his music. Franco's lyrics made as much impact as his rhythms: his earthy vocals and love of street wisdom and gossip created memorable songs and defined a new style that looked not to Belgium or Latin America but back to Zaire itself. With his big, gruff, conversational voice, Franco sang about everyday issues in tones that seemed to boom from the back of a Kinshasa taxi rather than the tonsils of a lovesick rumba star. As if to point up the contrast, he surrounded himself with backing singers whose fruity tones conjured up the energy and gusto of a barber shop close-harmony quintet. Much of this early output is still available on a series of albums titled *Authenticite*. Of his mid-period work, the double-album *20th Anniversaire* (1976), also still on catalogue, is a particularly fine example. By the late 70s Franco was able to fill dancehalls anywhere in Africa, and in 1978 he proved it by undertaking a 10-month tour of the continent with OK Jazz, which had now grown to a 23-piece orchestra: four horns, four guitars, bass, percussion and a chorus of backup vocalists. It is this line-up that recorded the magnificent 1980 double-album *24th Anniversaire*.

Franco's output was prodigious and his lyric themes many and varied. He sang about love—usually when it went wrong; related street gossip, current events and political issues. When President Mobutu decided to change the name of the country to Zaire in 1973 and to rename all the country's main towns and provinces, Franco toured the country explaining the changes. During general elections, he threw his weight behind Mobutu. And when things went sour, he would pick up what people were saying—complaints about the economy perhaps—and work them into songs. He created a position for himself that was unique: a man of the people, a folk musician who was also a confidant of the president. As such, he had a licence to sing about issues that most Zaireans only dared whisper about. He made a thinly veiled attack on government corruption in 'Lettre A Monsieur Le Directeur General' on the 1983 album *Choc Choc Choc* (recorded with Tabu Ley) for instance, and struck a similarly universal note in 1987 with the album *Attention Na SIDA*, a warning about AIDS. (It was AIDS which killed Franco in 1989 and also several members of OK Jazz.) Franco was not, however, immune from government sanctions.

He was imprisoned twice, once in the 60s for recording an indecent lyric and once when a minor official took offence over a criticism he made of Mobutu in a lyric and jailed him on a trumped-up motoring charge. On the latter occasion, Mobutu himself ordered Franco's release, imprisoning the official in his place. Franco's songs about women and love were on an epic scale. On the 1984 album *Chez Rythmes Et*

Musiques De Paris, the extraordinary track '12,600 Lettres A Franco' finds him taking on the role of an agony uncle to the constant stream of women who would write to him asking for advice about their marriages and relationships. On the title track to 1985's *Mario* he attacks the common Zairean practice of rich, older women taking on a younger gigolo. For all the humour of his lyrics, he gave good advice, and his fans paid heed to it. His lyrics contained frequent references to other singers, and during his time he quarrelled with a number of artists; both Tabu Ley and Kwamy were attacked in song. At other times he lent his name to commercial products: 'Azda' advertised Volkswagen cars in 1973; 'Fabrice' promoted a Belgian-based Zairean tailor in 1984; 'FC 105' praised Gabon's national football team in 1985.

Usually far too busy recording and performing for his followers at home or for expatriate Zaireans in Belgium and France, in the mid-80s Franco made some attempt to latch onto the growing UK and USA market for African music. In 1983 he toured the USA and played a stunning London concert. It was a route he intended to pursue until he fell ill in 1987 and was forced to limit his activities. In 1978 Franco was decorated by President Mobutu for his contribution to the development of Zaire's musical heritage. In 1980 he received the highest accolade the state could bestow when Mobutu dubbed him Le Grand Maitre of Zairean music.

● ALBUMS: *Authenticite, Volumes 1–4* (African Sonodisc) ★★★, *Les Grands Success Africaines* (African Sonodisc 1972) ★★★★, *10th Anniversaire 1965—1975* (African Sonodisc 1975) ★★★★, *20th Anniversaire* (African Sun Music 1976) ★★★★, *Na Loba Loba Panda* (African Sun Music 1977) ★★★, *African Party* (African Sun Music 1977) ★★★, *Africain Danses* (African Sun Music 1979) ★★★, *24th Anniversaire* (FRAN 1980) ★★★, *Mandola* (Edipop 1981) ★★★★, *A Paris* (M 1981) ★★★, with Sam Mangwana *Co-Operation* (Edipop 1982) ★★★, *Chez Fabrice A Bruxelles* (Edipop 1983) ★★, with Tabu Ley *Choc Choc Choc* (Choc Choc Choc 1983) ★★, *L'Evenement* (1983) ★★★, *Chez Rythmes Et Musique De Paris* (Genidia 1984) ★★★, *Mario* (Choc Choc Choc 1985) ★★★, *A Nairobi* (Edipop 1986) ★★★★, *Bois Noir* (Rhythmes Et Musique 1986) ★★★★, *Originalité* (RetroAfric 1986) ★★★, *Attention Na SIDA* (African Sun Music 1987) ★★★.

● COMPILATIONS: *20ème Anniversaire Volumes 1 & 2* (Sonodisc 1989) ★★★★, *Testament Ya Bowule* (Sonodisc 1990) ★★★★, *Kita Mata Bloque* (Sonodisc 1990) ★★★, *J'ai Peur* (Sonodisc 1990) ★★★, *Eperduement* (Sonodisc 1990) ★★★, *Mario & La Résponse de Mario* (Sonodisc 1993) ★★★, *The Rough Guide To Franco* (World Music Network 2001) ★★★★.

● FURTHER READING: *Congo Colossus: The Life And Legacy Of Franco And OK Jazz*, Graeme Ewens.

François, Claude

b. 4 February 1942, Suez, Egypt, d. 11 March 1978. François inherited musical skills from his parents who, with worsening political antagonism in the East, returned him to France where, on leaving school, he drummed in a Monte Carlo jazz combo before ambition drove him to Paris where, demonstrating the **twist**, mashed potato and similar dance crazes in the Caramel Club, he was noticed by record company talent scouts. **Steve Lawrence**'s 'Girls Girls Girls' was, in 1961, the first of many swift translations of US hits for home consumers by François. His strategy was best exemplified by a version of 'If I Had A Hammer', in the shops a mere week after **Trini Lopez**'s 1963 original. More idiosyncratic smashes included 'Marche Tout Troit' and an up-tempo revival of **Noël Coward**'s 'Poor Little Rich Girl'. Adored as 'Clo-Clo' by teenagers, Francois next addressed himself to their parents with a greater proportion of largely self-composed ballads such as 'J'Y Pense Et Puis J'Oublie', 'J'Attendrai' and 'Qu'Est-Ce Que Tu Deviens'. Although 1976's 'Tears On The Telephone' inched into Britain's Top 40, his deepest penetration into markets beyond French regions had been by proxy with the reflective 'Comme d'Habitude'—written with Jacques Revaux and Gilles Thibault—which, with English lyrics by **Paul Anka**, was covered (as 'My Way') by artists as diverse as **Frank Sinatra** and the **Sex Pistols**. While this syndication enabled Francois to purchase a mansion near Fontainebleau, his private life was marred by divorce and maladies that included chronic insomnia. His death (by electrocution) on 11 March 1978 was mourned in microcosm as passionately as that of **Elvis Presley**—another of the many who recorded 'My Way'.

● ALBUMS: *Tourneé Été 71 Live* (Arcade 1971) ★★★, *Le Lundi Au Soleil* (Sony 1972) ★★★, *Je Viens Diner Ce Soir* (Sony 1972) ★★★, *Chanson Populaire* (Sony 1973) ★★★, *Le Mal Aimé* (Sony 1974) ★★★, *Pour Les Jeunes De 8 A 88 Ans* (Carrère 1976) ★★★, *Le Vagabond* (Carrère 1976) ★★★, *Je Vais A Rio* (Carrère 1977) ★★★, *Magnolias For Ever* (Carrère 1978) ★★★.

● COMPILATIONS: *Hommages* (PolyGram 1993) ★★★, *Le Monde Extraordinaire De Claude François* (PolyGram 1996) ★★★, *En Vrai* (Sony 1996) ★★★, *Les Concerts Inédits De Musicorama* (Arcade 1998) ★★★, *Eloise—65/69* (PolyGram 1998) ★★★, *Danse Ma Vie (Remix)* (Carrère 1998) ★★★, *Bernadette—68/75* (PolyGram 1998) ★★★.

Frank And Walters

This indie pop trio from Cork, Ireland, took their unusual name from two tramps who inhabited a nearby village. Comprising Paul Linehan (vocals/bass), Niall Linehan (guitar) and Ashley Keating (drums), they attracted immediate press attention through a debut EP released in April 1991 on the homely Setanta label, the songwriting on which was highly unassuming in its parochial good humour. 'Michael', for instance, concerned the band's best friend who was the star of the town via his expensive car, until he crashed it and reverted to the use of a bicycle. Paul Linehan's tender lyrics emphasized the cathartic nature of this bodyblow in a manner heavily reminiscent of the slow passage of time and wisdom in rural Ireland. Two Single Of The Week awards later, 'Fashion Crisis Hits New York' proved another instant favourite: 'Fashion Crisis hits New York/I saw a blind man/He was eating his fork/He said that's what you had/To do to be cool,/You eat your cutlery instead of your food'. This was enough to ensure **Go! Discs** would step in to shepherd future releases, as the band took up residence at a YMCA in Wimbledon. A third EP, led off by the typically infectious 'Happy Busman', was piloted by **Edwyn Collins**. However, the resulting debut album failed to fulfil critical expectations for journalists primed on the band's superior early material (which was largely rehashed to less immediate effect). 'This Is Not A Song' and a reissued 'Fashion Crisis Hits New York' offered chart hits via bigger promotion and production, with the reworked album track 'After All' narrowly failing to reach the UK Top 10.

Afterwards, the band retreated to Cork in an attempt to recover from the 'too much too early' syndrome that, as some critics were already suggesting, had robbed them of their native charm. By the time the more earnest *Grand Parade* was released in 1997, however, the fickle world of pop had moved on. An extended sojourn in the USA inspired the lush, melancholic songs on 1999's *Beauty Becomes More Than Life*. This album and the following year's electro pop influenced *Glass* did much to restore the band's critical standing. The trio took a break from the music scene between 2002 and 2005, during which time Niall Linehan opted to leave the band. Paul Linhean and Ashley Keating continued with new guitarist Kevin Pedreschi, returning to the live circuit and releasing the rarities compilation *Souvenirs*.

● ALBUMS: *Trains, Boats And Planes* (Go! Discs 1992) ★★★, *Grand Parade* (Setanta 1997) ★★★, *Beauty Becomes More Than Life* (Setanta 1999) ★★★★, *Glass* (Setanta 2000) ★★★.

● COMPILATIONS: *The Frank And Walters* (Setanta 1991) ★★★, *The Best Of The Frank And Walters* (Setanta 2002) ★★★★, *Souvenirs* (Fifa 2005) ★★★.

Frank Chickens

Japan's ebullient Frank Chickens were formed by Kazuko Hohki (b. 1952, Tokyo, Japan; vocals) and Kazumi Taguchi (later replaced by Atsuko Kamura). The duo met in London in 1978 while working with the Japanese-American Toy Theatre. The JATT would perform extracts from classic fiction using toy figurines, mechanical robots and 'Godzilla' models as the central characters to the play. This bizarre concept was given publicity by BBC Radio 1 producer **John Walters**' *Walters' Week*. The Frank Chickens achieved something of a cult hit with 'Blue Canary' in 1985, which received strong airplay from disc jockey **John Peel** (whose producer was Walters). As well as depicting a socio-comic view of the modern Japanese woman in Western society, the Frank Chickens also tackled the subject of the Western male's perception of Japanese women in general, as in 'Yellow Toast'. Their best-known number, however, remained the proto-feminist 'We Are Ninja' ('We Are Ninja/Not Geisha'). Kazuko was, to some degree, also instrumental in popularizing the phenomenon of karaoke (amateur singing to backing tapes) to English culture by way of the Channel 4 television programme *The Karaoke Klub*. The Frank Chickens have continued to perform on the London fringe theatre and cabaret club circuit into the 90s.

● ALBUMS: *We Are Frank Chickens* (Kaz 1984) ★★★, *Get Chickenised* (Flying Lecords 1987) ★★★, *Club Monkey* (Flying Lecords 1988) ★★★, *Do The Karaoke* (Flying Lecords 1989) ★★★, *Underfloor World* (Toy's Factory 1996) ★★.

● COMPILATIONS: *The Best Of Frank Chickens* (Kaz 1987) ★★★.

Frank, J.L.

b. Joseph Lee Frank, 15 April 1900, Rossal, Limestone County, Alabama, USA, d. 4 May 1952. Orphaned at seven, he grew up in Tennessee and as a youth worked as a coal miner and a hotel bellboy. In 1923 he relocated to Chicago and after his marriage in 1925, he and his wife, Marie, became involved in artist management. Between 1928 and 1935, he was involved with WLS *Roundup*, and in 1929 he became manager of **Gene Autry** and **Smiley Burnette**. Between 1935 and 1939, he worked from Louisville, Kentucky, but, believing that Nashville, was to become an important venue for country music, he opened an office there. His ability to promote country shows and organize tours for artists soon made him a popular and important figure in Music City. He was prominent in helping many artists, especially **Pee Wee King** (his son-in-law), **Roy Acuff**, **Eddy Arnold**, **Hank Williams**, **Hank Snow**, **Minnie Pearl** and **Ernest Tubb**, and managed numerous others. His association with a major theatre chain enabled country artists to be booked into venues that previously had been unavailable to the genre. Frank's ability to promote the artists also helped to promote the image of the *Grand Ole Opry*, and he was instrumental in helping many to actual membership of the *Opry*, particularly Roy Acuff. He also wrote a few country songs, including 'Sundown And Sorrow' and 'Chapel On The Hill'. However, he was no vocalist, he did not play any instrument, nor could he read music. On 4 May 1952 he died of a major throat infection while on a trip to Dallas to promote a show. In 1967 J.L. 'Joe' Frank was inducted into the **Country Music Hall Of Fame**. His plaque reads: 'Pioneer promoter of Country & Western Shows. His method of combining broadcasting and personal appearances moved country entertainers from rural schoolhouses into city auditoriums and coliseums. The unselfish, compassionate man was one of the industry's most loved members'.

Frank, Jackson C.

b. Jackson Carey Frank, 1943, Buffalo, New York, USA, d. 3 March 1999, Great Barrington, Massachusetts, USA. Singer-songwriter Frank made a strong impression in the mid-60s folk scene with songs such as 'Blues Run The Game'. This was contained on his 1965 debut, recorded in London with production from **Paul Simon** and guitar support from **Al Stewart**. Like Simon and Shawn Phillips, he was one of several American folk performers who temporarily resided in Britain during this period. Frank's life thus far had already been a troubled one. At the age of 11 he had been badly burned in a fire at his school in Cheektowago, Buffalo, his life only saved when classmates patted snow on his burning back (18 other children died). The reason for his journey to England was the belated arrival of his large compensation cheque (over $100,000), which he intended to invest in a brand new Jaguar car.

He wrote 'Blues Run The Game', his very first song despite experience in several rock 'n' roll bands, while aboard the *Queen Elizabeth* cruise ship *en route*. However, after the success of his debut album he became something of a recluse, although he was continually celebrated by other artists of the period. **John Renbourn** included a cover of 'Blues Run The Game' on his *So Clear* album, while **Sandy Denny** wrote a song about him as well as interpreting his compositions both as a solo artist and when she was a member of **Fairport Convention**. **Roy Harper**, too, celebrated him in song ('My Friend'). When he returned to England in 1968 he joined Fairport on tour but was unable to pick up the impetus of his career. As Stewart recalled, 'He started doing songs that were completely impenetrable, they were basically about psychological angst played at full volume with lots of thrashing.' Disillusioned, Frank returned to America to edit a local paper, but his marriage to an English fashion model

broke up, and his baby son died of cystic fibrosis. Frank suffered a nervous breakdown and entered hospital.

In 1984 he travelled to New York in order to set up a meeting with his old friend Paul Simon, but he fell to begging in the streets, his mind by now blurred by medicinal drug use. Interned in institution after institution, he was diagnosed as a paranoid schizophrenic, which Frank justly refuted, putting these 'lost years' down to the trauma caused by the death of his child. It was only in the 90s and through the efforts of record collector Jim Abbott that the artist was traced. Abbott found him new accommodation in Woodstock, but not before Frank had been the victim of a point-blank shooting that left him blind in his left eye. Dishevelled and overweight (due to a parathyroid malfunction resulting from his original injuries in the fire), he began to write songs again. One of the most tragic lives in the history of popular music ended in March 1999.

● ALBUMS: *Jackson C. Frank* (Columbia 1965) ★★★.
● COMPILATIONS: *Blues Run The Game* (Castle 2003) ★★★.

Franke And The Knockouts

This New Jersey soft rock quartet were fronted by Franke Previte from New Brunswick, New Jersey, USA. They originally included Billy Elworthy (guitar), Blake Levinsohn (keyboards), Leigh Foxx (bass) and Claude LeHenaff (drums). Singer-songwriter Previte, who had previously sung with the Oxford Watch Band and a heavy metal act Bull Angus, formed the band in 1980. They joined Millennium Records in 1981 and within 12 months had notched up three US Top 40 singles and two Top 50 albums. Their biggest hit single was a song written by Previte and Elworthy, 'Sweetheart', a Top 10 hit in 1981. The hits dried up and the band, who experienced several personnel changes including the recruiting of future **Bon Jovi** drummer Tico Torres, recorded on MCA in 1984 but split up in the mid-80s. Previte, however, went on to co-write tracks on the 11 million-selling, transatlantic chart-topping soundtrack *Dirty Dancing*, including the big hit singles 'All By Myself' by **Eric Carmen** and '(I've Had) The Time Of My Life' by **Bill Medley** and **Jennifer Warnes**.

● ALBUMS: *Franke & The Knockouts* (Millennium 1981) ★★★, *Below The Belt* (Millennium 1982) ★★★, *Makin' The Point* (MCA 1984) ★★.
● COMPILATIONS: *Sweet Heart Collection* (Razor & Tie 1999) ★★★.

Franke, Bob

b. Robert J. Franke, 1947, Hamtramck, Michigan, USA. Singer and songwriter Franke began his career in 1965, while still a student at the University of Michigan. One of the first people to perform at the famous Ark Coffeehouse in Ann Arbor, Michigan, he graduated in English literature from university and moved to New England. Well respected by other musicians in the field, Franke has appeared at coffeehouses, colleges, festivals, and a whole variety of venues in over half the states in the USA. In 1990 he was nominated Outstanding Folk Act by the Boston Music Awards. In addition to performing, he has run workshops in songwriting and guitar as well as lecturing on the blues at Boston University's College of Basic Studies. Franke is also an extremely versatile instrumentalist, accompanying himself on 12-string guitar, banjo, pennywhistle and lap steel guitar. As a writer, his songs have been covered by such talents as **June Tabor, John McCutcheon**, Claudia Schmidt and numerous others. In August 1990 he wrote a set of songs for a ballet, commissioned by the Dance Company of San Francisco, entitled *The Velveteen Rabbit*. He has also composed two cantatas as well as a number of hymns for the Church of St. Andrew in Marblehead, Massachusetts. *In This Night* was named number 1 album of 1991 by Boston radio station WUMB-FM and was further nominated by the Boston Music Awards as Outstanding Folk Album of 1992. Despite appearances at the prestigious Philadelphia and Kerrville Folk Festivals, he deserves to be a more widely acknowledged figure.

● ALBUMS: *Love Can't Be Bitter All The Time* (Fretless 1976) ★★★, *One Evening In Chicago* (Great Divide 1983) ★★, *For Real* (Flying Fish 1986) ★★★★, *Brief Histories* (Flying Fish 1989) ★★★★, *In This Night* (Flying Fish 1991) ★★★, *The Heart Of The Flower* (Rounder 1995) ★★★.

● FURTHER READING: *The Songs Of Bob Franke*, Bob Franke.

Frankie And Johnny

The first of three **Elvis Presley** films released in 1966, *Frankie And Johnny* boasted a plot loosely based on the traditional jazz song of the same name. Presley plays a gambler aboard a Mississippi paddleboat, down on his luck. He changes girlfriends hoping this will change his fortunes. The feature is better than the rest of that year's output, although the soundtrack material leaves a lot to be desired. A medley of 'Down By The Riverside' and 'When The Saints Go Marching In' was an obvious sop to the New Orleans setting, while 'Petunia, The Gardener's Daughter' was another in a line of notoriously terrible songs that marred the singer's movies. The title track was issued as single, but its comparatively low chart placing in the US and UK showed the public was weary of Presley's formula-based output.

Frankie

b. George Franklin Jackson III, *c.*1978, Washington, DC, USA. A young R&B talent sponsored by producer/mentor Chucki Thompson, Frankie recorded his debut album for Thompson's Epic Records subsidized imprint Chucklife in 1997. Fashioned by Thompson as a return to a classic soul crooning style, it featured an all-star cast including **Faith Evans** (singing on the duet 'Think Of You') and hit R&B band **112**. The latter group also wrote material for the set, as did fellow guest star **Mary J. Blige** ('All I Do'). Frankie had originally met Thompson at the age of 14 through mutual acquaintance Notch Howell of **Born Jamericans**. The album was the result of a five-year apprenticeship, during which Jackson would frequently 'tag along' at Thompson's recording sessions, and was promoted with the single, 'If I Had You'.

● ALBUMS: *My Heart Belongs To You* (Chucklife Productions/Epic 1997) ★★★.

Frankie Goes To Hollywood

Formed in the summer of 1980, this Liverpool, England–based outfit comprised former **Big In Japan** vocalist **Holly Johnson** (b. William Johnson, 19 February 1960, Khartoum, Sudan) backed by Paul Rutherford (b. 8 December 1959, Liverpool, England; vocals), Nasher Nash (b. Brian Nash, 20 May 1963; guitar), Mark O'Toole (b. 6 January 1964,

Liverpool, England; bass) and Peter 'Ped' Gill (b. 8 March 1964, Liverpool, England; drums). It was a further two years before they started to make any real headway with television appearances and a recording contract with Trevor Horn's **ZTT Records.** Their debut single, 'Relax', produced by Horn, was a pyrotechnic production and superb dance track with a suitably suggestive lyric that led to a BBC radio and television ban in Britain. Paradoxically, the censorship produced even greater public interest in the single, which topped the UK charts for five weeks from January 1984, selling close to two million copies in the process. The promotion behind Frankie Goes To Hollywood, engineered by former music journalist Paul Morley, was both clever and inventive, utilizing marketing techniques such as single word slogans and the production of bestselling T-shirts that offered the enigmatic message 'Frankie Says . . .' The band's peculiar image of Liverpool laddishness coupled with the unabashed homosexuality of vocalists Johnson and Rutherford merely added to their curiosity value and sensationalism while also providing them with a distinctive identity that their detractors seriously underestimated.

The follow-up to 'Relax' was the even more astonishing 'Two Tribes'. A spectacular production built round a throbbing, infectiously original riff, it showed off Johnson's distinctive vocal style to striking effect. Like all the band's singles, the record was available in various 7-inch and 12-inch remixed formats with superb packaging and artwork. The power of the single lay not merely in its appropriately epic production but the topicality of its lyric, which dealt with the escalation of nuclear arms and the prospect of global annihilation. In order to reinforce the harrowing theme, the band included a chilling voice over from actor Patrick Allen taken from government papers on the dissemination of information to the public in the event of nuclear war. Allen's Orwellian instructions on how to avoid fall out while disposing of dogs, grandparents and other loved ones gave the disc a frightening authenticity that perfectly captured the mood of the time. Johnson's closing lines of the song, borrowed from an unnamed literary source, provided a neat rhetorical conclusion: 'Are we living in a land where sex and horror are the new gods?' The six-minute plus version of 'Two Tribes' was played in its entirety on UK lunch time radio shows and duly entered the chart at number 1, remaining in the premier position for an incredible nine weeks during the summer of 1984 while the revitalized 'Relax' nestled alongside its successor at number 2. A **Godley And Creme** promotional film of 'Two Tribes', which featured caricatures of US president Reagan and Soviet leader Mr Chernenko wrestling, was rightly acclaimed as one of the best videos of the period and contributed strongly to the Frankie Goes To Hollywood package.

Having dominated the upper echelons of the chart like no other artist since the **Beatles**, the pressure to produce an album for the Christmas market was immense. *Welcome To The Pleasure Dome* finally emerged as a double with a number of cover versions including interesting readings of **Bruce Springsteen**'s 'Born To Run', **Dionne Warwick**'s 'Do You Know The Way To San Jose?' and **Gerry And The Pacemakers**' 'Ferry Across The Mersey'. Like all the band's recordings, the sound was epic and glorious and the reviews proclaimed the album an undoubted hit, though some commentators felt its irresistible charm might prove ephemeral. 1984 ended with a necessary change of style as the band enjoyed their third number 1 hit with the moving festive ballad 'The Power Of Love'. Thus they joined Gerry And The Pacemakers as only the second act in UK pop history to see their first three singles reach the top. History repeated itself the following year when, like Gerry And The Pacemakers, Frankie Goes To Hollywood saw their fourth single ('Welcome To The Pleasure Dome') stall at number 2.

Thereafter, Frankie Goes To Hollywood was never again to attain the ascendancy that it had enjoyed during the golden year of 1984. A sabbatical spent in Eire for tax purposes meant that the band's comeback in 1986 had to be emphatic. Having failed to conquer America during the same period, merely increased the pressure. Critics had long been claiming that they were little more than puppets in the hands of a talented producer despite the fact that they sang, played and even wrote their own material. The grand return with 'Rage Hard' (the title borrowed from Dylan Thomas) won them a number 4 UK hit, but that seemed decidedly anticlimactic. The second album, *Liverpool*, cost a small fortune but lacked the charm and vibrancy of its predecessor. Within a year Johnson and Rutherford had quit, effectively spelling the end of the band, although the remaining three attempted to continue with new vocalist Grant Boult. Johnson prevented them using the Frankie Goes To Hollywood name, and attempts to record as the Lads came to nothing. Johnson himself went on to enjoy UK Top 5 solo hits with 'Love Train' and 'Americanos' and a chart-topping debut album, *Blast*. He announced he was HIV positive in 1993 and shortly afterwards published his autobiography, *A Bone In My Flute*. A second album appeared on his own Pleasuredome label at the end of the decade, but Johnson now spends most of his time working as an exhibited oil painter.

The story of Frankie Goes To Hollywood charts a remarkable rise and fall, with the band managing to cram a decade of sales, creativity and controversy into less than 24 months. In many ways, their fate was the perfect pop parable of the 80s. For a band that was so symptomatic of their age, it was appropriate that the Frankie Goes To Hollywood saga should end not in the recording studio but in the High Court. In a battle royal between Johnson and his former record company ZTT in early 1988, the artist not only won his artistic freedom but substantial damages which were to have vast implications for the UK music business as a whole.

● ALBUMS: *Welcome To The Pleasure Dome* (ZTT 1984) ★★★★, *Liverpool* (ZTT 1986) ★★.

● COMPILATIONS: *Bang! The Greatest Hits Of Frankie Goes To Hollywood* (ZTT 1993) ★★★★, *Maximum Joy* (ZTT 2000) ★★★, *Twelve Inches* (ZTT 2001) ★★★.

● DVD/VIDEOS: *Shoot!: The Greatest Hits* (ZTT 1993), *Hard On* (ZTT 2000).

● FURTHER READING: *Give It Loads: The Story Of Frankie Goes To Hollywood*, Bruno Hizer. *Frankie Say: The Rise Of Frankie Goes To Hollywood*, Danny Jackson. *A Bone In My Flute*, Holly Johnson.

Frankie J

b. Francisco Javier Bautista Jnr., 14 December 1980, Tijuana, Baja California, Mexico. Debonair R&B singer Frankie J relocated with his family to San Diego, California, at the age of two. Raised on a diet of traditional Mexican music and American rap and soul, the young Francisco Bautista began singing while still at school and was talented and devoted

enough to secure a minor recording contract with a Canadian label. Signed as a solo Latin freestyle artist at the age of 15, he recorded several singles before obtaining a more substantial contract with **Jellybean**'s label Hola Recordings. Problems with the label meant a projected album was scrapped, and in 1999 Frankie J left to join the Latin pop act Los Kumbia Kings. In his three years with the A.B. Quintanilla-led group he enjoyed his first taste of the limelight, singing on hit singles and multiplatinum selling albums, receiving Grammy nominations and performing in front of huge crowds.

In 2003 Frankie J left Los Kumbia Kings to relaunch his solo career. He signed a solo recording contract with **Columbia Records** and recorded his debut, *What's A Man To Do?* Marking a transition to a smooth urban soul sound, the album featured the singer's breakthrough mainstream hit, 'Don't Wanna Try', which soared into the upper regions of the US pop charts later in the year. A Spanish-language version of the album entitled *Frankie J* followed later in the year. By now firmly established as a mainstream R&B artist, Frankie J returned to the upper regions of the US pop charts at the start of 2005 with the single 'Obsession (No Es Amor)'. The track featured rapper **Baby Bash**, with whom Frankie J had previously collaborated on the US hit 'Suga Suga'. Released shortly afterwards, Frankie J's new album *The One* also reached the US Top 5.

● ALBUMS: *What's A Man To Do?* (Columbia 2003) ★★★, *Frankie J* (Columbia 2003) ★★★, *The One* (Columbia 2005) ★★★.

Frankie Lymon And The Teenagers
(see **Lymon, Frankie, And The Teenagers**)

Franklin, Aretha

b. 25 March 1942, Memphis, Tennessee, USA. Aretha Franklin's music is steeped in the traditions of the church. Her father, **Rev. C.L. Franklin**, was a Baptist preacher who, once he had moved his family to Detroit, became famous throughout black America for his fiery sermons and magnetic public appearances. He knew the major gospel stars **Mahalia Jackson** and **Clara Ward**, who in turn gave his daughter valuable tutelage, along with two other sisters Erma and Carolyn. At the age of 12, Aretha was promoted from the choir to become a featured soloist. Two years later she began recording for JVB and Checker. Between 1956 and 1960, her output consisted solely of devotional material, but the secular success of **Sam Cooke** encouraged a change of emphasis. Franklin auditioned for **John Hammond Jnr.**, who signed her to **Columbia Records**. Sadly, the company was indecisive on how best to showcase her remarkable talent. They tried blues, cocktail jazz, standards, pop songs and contemporary soul hits, each of which wasted the singer's natural improvisational instincts. There were some occasional bright spots—'Runnin' Out Of Fools' (1964) and 'Cry Like A Baby' (1966)—but in both cases content succeeded over style.

After a dozen albums, a disillusioned Franklin joined **Atlantic Records** in 1966, where the magnificent 'I Never Loved A Man (The Way I Loved You)', recorded in January 1967 in New York, declared her liberation. An album was scheduled to be made in **Muscle Shoals**, but Franklin's husband Ted White had an argument with the owner of Fame Studios, **Rick Hall**. At short notice **Jerry Wexler** flew the musicians to New York.

The single soared into the US Top 10 and, coupled with the expressive 'Do Right Woman—Do Right Man', only the backing track of which was recorded in Alabama, it announced the arrival of a major artist. The releases that followed—'Respect', 'Baby I Love You', '(You Make Me Feel Like) A Natural Woman', 'Chain Of Fools' and '(Sweet Sweet Baby) Since You've Been Gone'—many of which featured the Fame rhythm section 'borrowed' by Wexler for sessions in New York, confirmed her authority and claim to being the 'Queen Of Soul'. The conditions and atmosphere created by Wexler and the outstanding musicians gave Franklin such confidence that her voice gained amazing power and control. Despite Franklin's professional success, her personal life grew confused. Her relationship with husband and manager White disintegrated, and while excellent singles such as 'Think' still appeared, others betrayed a discernible lethargy. She followed 'Think' with a sublime cover version of **Hal David** and **Burt Bacharach**'s 'I Say A Little Prayer', giving power and authority to simple yet delightful lyrics: 'The moment I wake up, before I put on my make-up, I say a little prayer for you'. Following a slight dip in her fortunes during the late 60s, she had regained her powers in 1970 as 'Call Me', 'Spirit In The Dark' and 'Don't Play That Song' ably testified. *Aretha Live At Fillmore West* (1971), meanwhile, restated her in-concert power. The following year, another live appearance resulted in *Amazing Grace*, a double gospel set recorded with James Cleveland and the Southern California Community Choir. Its passion encapsulated her career to date. Franklin continued to record strong material throughout the early 70s and enjoyed three R&B chart-toppers, 'Angel', 'Until You Come Back To Me (That's What I'm Gonna Do)' and 'I'm In Love'. Sadly, the rest of the decade was marred by recordings that were at best predictable, at worst dull. It was never the fault of Franklin's voice, merely that the material was often poor and indifferent. Her cameo role in the movie **The Blues Brothers**, however, rekindled her flagging career. Franklin moved to **Arista Records** in 1980, and she immediately regained a commercial momentum with 'United Together' and two confident albums, *Aretha* and *Love All The Hurt Away*. 'Jump To It' and 'Get It Right', both written and produced by **Luther Vandross**, and *Who's Zoomin' Who?* continued her rejuvenation. From the album, produced by **Narada Michael Walden**, Franklin had hit singles with 'Freeway Of Love', 'Another Night' and the superb title track. In the mid-80s, she made the charts again, in company with **Annie Lennox** ('Sisters Are Doin' It For Themselves') and **George Michael** ('I Knew You Were Waiting [For Me]'), which went to number 1 in the USA and UK in 1987. Though by now lacking the instinct of her classic Atlantic recordings, Franklin's 'return to gospel' *One Lord One Faith One Baptism* proved she was still a commanding singer. *Through The Storm*, from 1989, contained more powerful duets, this time with **Elton John** on the title track, **James Brown** ('Gimme Some Lovin'', remixed by Prince for 12-inch) and **Whitney Houston** ('It Isn't, It Wasn't, It Ain't Never Gonna Be'). The album also included a remake of her 1968 US Top 10 title, 'Think'.

Franklin's first album of the 90s, *What You See Is What You Sweat*, was criticized for its cornucopia of different styles: a couple of tracks by Burt Bacharach and **Carole Bayer Sager**; a collaboration with Luther Vandross; a fairly thin title ballad; and the highlight, 'Everyday People', a mainstream disco number, written by **Sly Stone** and brilliantly produced by Narada Michael Walden. Another lengthy hiatus ensued before the release of 1998's impressive *A Rose Is Still A Rose*, on which Franklin co-opted the songwriting and production talents of the cream of contemporary urban music. She reconfirmed her creative renaissance with the follow-up *So Damn Happy*. Released in 2003, it is unquestionably one of the best albums of Franklin's career.

Franklin possesses an astonishing voice that has often been wasted on a poor choice of material, but she is rightfully heralded as the Queen of Soul, even though that reputation was gained in the 60s. There are certain musical notes that can be played on a saxophone that are chilling; similarly, there are sounds above the twelfth fret on a guitar that are orgasmic—Aretha Franklin is better than any instrument, as she can hit notes that do not exist in instrumental terms. Her vocal range and depth is truly remarkable. The superlative 4-CD box set *Queen Of Soul*, highlighting the best of her Atlantic recordings, confirmed her position as one of the greatest voices, if not *the* greatest, in recording history.

● ALBUMS: *Aretha* (Columbia 1961) ★★, *The Electrifying Aretha Franklin* (Columbia 1962) ★★, *The Tender, The Moving, The Swinging Aretha Franklin* (Columbia 1962) ★★, *Laughing On The Outside* (Columbia 1963) ★★, *Unforgettable* (Columbia 1964) ★★, *Songs Of Faith* (Checker 1964) ★★, *Runnin' Out Of Fools* (Columbia 1964) ★★, *Yeah!!!* (Columbia 1965) ★★, *Soul Sister* (Columbia 1966) ★★★, *Take It Like You Give It* (Columbia 1967) ★★★, *I Never Loved A Man The Way That I Love You* (Atlantic 1967) ★★★★★, *Aretha Arrives* (Atlantic 1967) ★★★★, *Take A Look* early recordings (Columbia 1967) ★★★, *Aretha: Lady Soul* (Atlantic 1968) ★★★★★, *Aretha Now* (Atlantic 1968) ★★★★★, *Aretha In Paris* (Atlantic 1968) ★★, *Soul '69* (Atlantic 1969) ★★★★, *Today I Sing The Blues* (Columbia 1969) ★★★, *Soft And Beautiful* (Columbia 1969) ★★★, *This Girl's In Love With You* (Atlantic 1970) ★★★, *Spirit In The Dark* (Atlantic 1970) ★★★, *Aretha Live At Fillmore West* (Atlantic 1971) ★★★★, *Young, Gifted And Black* (Atlantic 1972) ★★★, *Amazing Grace* (Atlantic 1972) ★★★★, *Hey Now Hey (The Other Side Of The Sky)* (Atlantic 1973) ★★, *Let Me Into Your Life* (Atlantic 1974) ★★★★, *With Everything I Feel In Me* (Atlantic 1974) ★★★, *You* (Atlantic 1975) ★★, *Sparkle* film soundtrack (Atlantic 1976) ★★, *Sweet Passion* (Atlantic 1977) ★★, *Almighty Fire* (Atlantic 1978) ★★, *La Diva* (Atlantic 1979) ★★, *Aretha* (Arista 1980) ★★★, *Love All The Hurt Away* (Arista 1981) ★★, *Jump To It* (Arista 1982) ★★, *Get It Right* (Arista 1983) ★★, *Who's Zoomin' Who?* (Arista 1985) ★★★, *Aretha* (Arista 1986) ★★★, *One Lord, One Faith, One Baptism* (Arista 1987) ★★★, *Through The Storm* (Arista 1989) ★★, *What You See Is What You Sweat* (Arista 1991) ★★, *A Rose Is Still A Rose* (Arista 1998) ★★★, with Mariah Carey, Celine Dion, Gloria Estefan, Shania Twain *Divas Live* (Epic 1998) ★★, *So Damn Happy* (Arista 2003) ★★★★.

● COMPILATIONS: *Aretha Franklin's Greatest Hits* Columbia recordings 1961–66 (Columbia 1967) ★★★, *Aretha's Gold* (Atlantic 1969) ★★★★, *Aretha's Greatest Hits* (Atlantic 1971) ★★★★, *In The Beginning/The World Of Aretha Franklin 1960–1967* (Columbia 1972) ★★★, *The Great Aretha Franklin: The First 12 Sides* (Columbia 1973) ★★★, *Ten Years Of Gold* (Atlantic 1976) ★★★★, *Legendary Queen Of Soul* (Columbia 1983) ★★★★, *Aretha's Jazz* (Atlantic 1984) ★★★, *Aretha Sings The Blues*

(Columbia 1985) ★★★, *The Collection* (Castle 1986) ★★★★, *Never Grow Old* (Chess 1987) ★★★★, *20 Greatest Hits* (Warners 1987) ★★★★, *Aretha Franklin's Greatest Hits 1960–1965* (Columbia 1987) ★★★★, *Queen Of Soul: The Atlantic Recordings* 4-CD box set (Rhino/Atlantic 1992) ★★★★★, *Aretha's Jazz* (Atlantic 1993) ★★★, *Greatest Hits 1980–1994* (Arista 1994) ★★★, *Love Songs* (Rhino/Atlantic 1997) ★★★, *This Is Jazz* (Columbia Legacy 1998) ★★★, *Greatest Hits* (Global/Warners 1998) ★★★★, *Amazing Grace: The Complete Recordings* (Rhino 1999) ★★★★, *Aretha's Best* (Rhino 2001) ★★★★, *Respect: The Very Best Of Aretha Franklin* (Warners 2002) ★★★★, *The Queen in Waiting: The Columbia Years* (Columbia 2002) ★★★, *The Tender, The Moving, The Swinging/Soft And Beautiful* (Columbia 2004) ★★★, with King Curtis *Live At Fillmore West: Don't Fight The Feeling* 4-CD box set (Rhino 2005) ★★★.

● DVD/VIDEOS: *Queen Of Soul* (Music Club 1988), *Live At Park West* (PVE 1995), with Mariah Carey, Celine Dion, Gloria Estefan, Shania Twain *Divas Live* (Sony Music Video 1998).

● FURTHER READING: *Aretha Franklin*, Mark Bego. *Aretha: From These Roots*, Aretha Franklin and David Ritz.

● FILMS: *The Blues Brothers* (1980).

Franklin, C.L., Rev.

b. Clarence LaVaughn Franklin, 22 January 1915, Sunflower County, Mississippi, USA, d. 24 July 1984. Although his own career was eclipsed by that of his daughter, **Aretha Franklin**, the Rev. C.L. Franklin was a popular religious recording artist in his own right. Franklin began singing in church at the age of 12 and began preaching two years later. He attended college and gained a ministerial degree, preaching in Mississippi, New York and Tennessee before being named pastor of the New Bethel Baptist Church in Detroit, Michigan, USA, in 1946. He began recording 78s featuring his sermons for the J-V-B label in 1953, some of which were leased to **Chess Records** for more widespread distribution. He recorded over a dozen singles for the label. Each summer, daughter Aretha would accompany her father on the road, where he participated in gospel revues; much of her exposure to the gospel singing style came during those tours. In the 60s the Rev. Franklin became active in the civil rights movement and helped organize the 1963 March on Washington, at which Dr. Martin Luther King delivered his famous 'I Have A Dream' speech. Also the father of **Erma Franklin** and **Carolyn Franklin**, the Rev. Franklin was shot by burglars entering his home in 1979. He lapsed into a coma from which he never recovered.

Franklin, Carolyn

b. 13 May 1944, Memphis, Tennessee, USA, d. 25 April 1988, Bloomfield Hills, Detroit, Michigan, USA. The younger sister of **Aretha** and **Erma Franklin**, Carolyn was born while her pastor father **Rev. C.L. Franklin** was in charge of the New Salem Baptist Church in Memphis. Subsequently, the family moved to Buffalo in New York State and then to Detroit, where she and her sisters and two brothers grew up. From an early age, Carolyn played the piano, sang, and wrote her own music and lyrics. She recorded some demos in a 'late-night supper-club' style for **Lloyd Price**'s Double L label around 1963/4, and these were released in 1970 on a UK Joy album, *The First Time I Cried*. It included Carolyn's early 60s

version of 'Don't Catch The Dog's Bone', which her sister Erma later recorded for Shout. Backing Aretha on her early recordings, alongside Erma and cousin Brenda Bryant (later Corbett), introduced Carolyn to 'big time' secular music, and her own solo recording career did not take off properly until after the early peak of Aretha's post-**Columbia** success with **Atlantic** between 1967 and 1969 and Erma's somewhat secondary success for **Bert Berns'** Shout label during the same period. Her first two albums, *Baby Dynamite* (1969) and *Chain Reaction* (1970), were both produced by Jimmy Radcliffe. Neither album included a hit single, although they contained two songs, 'All I Want To Be Is Your Woman' and 'It's True I'm Gonna Miss You', that became minor R&B hits. Franklin's 1973 album *I'd Rather Be Lonely* was named after a Radcliffe song, and he started out as the album's producer but died later in the year. He was still credited as coproducer of Franklin's final solo album, *If You Want Me*, due to its inclusion of some earlier material. As well as singing backup, Carolyn wrote several songs for Aretha, including 'Baby Baby Baby', 'Without Love', 'Sing It Again—Say It Again', 'I Was Made For You', 'Ain't No Way', 'Save Me', 'As Long As You Are There' and the big hit, 'Angel'. In 1980, along with Brenda Corbett and Margaret Branch, she was seen backing her sister during the 'Think' sequence in the successful cult film **The Blues Brothers**, and in 1987, with Erma and Brenda, she supported Aretha's second 'return to gospel' album, *One Lord, One Faith, One Baptism*, recorded at the Franklin family's New Bethel Baptist Church. The same year, in a very different venture, Carolyn sang backing vocals on British singer Paul King's album *Joy*, produced by her close friend **Dan Hartman**. By this time, Carolyn had cancer but doggedly pursued her desire to obtain a college degree in entertainment law, which she received some 10 days before she died at Aretha's Bloomfield Hills home in April 1988.

● ALBUMS: *Baby Dynamite* (Shout 1969) ★★★, *Chain Reaction* (Shout 1970) ★★★, *I'd Rather Be Lonely* (1973) ★★★, *If You Want Me* (RCA 1976) ★★★.

● COMPILATIONS: *The First Time I Cried* (1970) ★★★.

Franklin, Chevelle

b. 1976, Spanish Town, Jamaica, West Indies. Franklin came from a large family and left school at an early age. She demonstrated her singing skills whenever the opportunity arose, and was eventually noticed by **Winston Riley**, who recorded her performing a cover version of **Janet Jackson**'s 'Let's Wait A While'. Franklin's initial recording did not make a significant impression on the reggae charts, but her determination led to an association with **Brian And Tony Gold**, and the result was a Jamaican number 1 hit with 'Here I Am'. It was through Brian and Tony that Franklin teamed up with **Home T** and Clifton 'Specialist' Dillon, where her international reputation grew. In 1992 Franklin was asked to record **Deborahe Glasgow**'s 'Champion Lover', which was covered by **Shabba Ranks** as 'Mr Loverman'. Shabba's success led to a major label signing and a decision to rerecord versions of his earlier hits. Franklin was drafted in for the challenging task of emulating Glasgow's fine vocals, which, despite the predictable opposition, she accomplished. The song was released in 1992 but found success two years later upon its rerelease, when it featured in the film *Deep Cover*. A year later, Franklin released 'Ooh Ah', through **Buju Banton**'s Cell Block 321 label. Franklin continues to record both as a soloist and in combination; she performed with **Spragga Benz** on his

'A1 Lover', with Daddy Lizard on 'Wait Until Tonight' and with **Lady G** on a series of classic songs, including 'Love And Hate', 'Thank You' and 'The Real Slam'. Her solo hits include 'Heart Of Mine', 'Wanna Be Down', 'Bending Knees' and the semi-autobiographical 'Mama Are You Proud'.

● ALBUMS: *Serious Girl* (Blue Moon 1996) ★★★, *Joy* (Main Street Music 2001) ★★★.

Franklin, Erma

b. 13 March 1938, Shelby, Mississippi, USA, d. 7 September 2002, Detroit, Michigan, USA. The older sister of **Aretha Franklin** and **Carolyn Franklin**, this excellent singer's career was overshadowed by her illustrious sibling. Erma's most celebrated moment came in 1967 with 'Piece Of My Heart', an intense uptown soul ballad co-written, produced and released by **Bert Berns** of Shout Records. The song was adopted by **Janis Joplin**, but Franklin's own progress faltered with the collapse of the Shout label after Berns' untimely death. Although she did secure a minor 1969 hit with 'Gotta Find Me A Lover (24 Hours A Day)' for **Brunswick Records**, her later work failed to match that early promise. From the early 70s much of her time was spent working for Boysville, a child care charity in Detroit. In 1992 Levi Strauss Jeans chose 'Piece Of My Heart' for one of their television advertisements, and in predictable fashion it scaled the charts and gave Franklin her true moment of (belated) glory. Franklin died of throat cancer in September 2002.

● ALBUMS: *Her Name Is Erma* (Epic 1962) ★★★, *Soul Sister* (Brunswick 1969) ★★★.

● COMPILATIONS: *Piece Of My Heart—The Best Of* (Epic 1992) ★★★, *Golden Classics* (Collectables 1993) ★★★.

Franklin, Guitar Pete

b. Edward Lamonte Franklin, 16 January 1928, Indianapolis, Indiana, USA, d. 31 July 1975, Indianapolis, Indiana, USA. His mother wrote many songs for her lodger **Leroy Carr**, and Franklin's interest in music developed early, beginning with piano, on which he was as adept as on guitar. His guitar playing was influenced by local musicians Scrapper Blackwell and Jesse Ellery (who recorded as accompanist to **Jack 'Champion' Dupree**), but he could change his playing completely to fit with an amplified Chicago ensemble. As a pianist, Franklin was, not surprisingly, indebted to Leroy Carr, but on both instruments he was an original and remarkably accomplished musician who was not recorded to the extent his talent merited.

● ALBUMS: *Guitar Pete's Blues* (Bluesville 1963) ★★★★, *Windy City Blues* (1975) ★★★, *Indianapolis Jump* (1977) ★★★.

Franklin, Kirk

b. 26 January 1970, Fort Worth, Texas, USA. A meteoric success story in gospel music, a genre more usually associated with the longevity of its artists, Franklin made a huge impact with his 1994 debut. A fixture at the top of the US Contemporary Christian and Gospel charts, and the first platinum-selling gospel album, it featured powerful performances from the 17-piece 'Family' of musicians and singers, many of whom were drawn from Franklin's home-town of Fort Worth, Texas. Franklin was raised by his aunt as a strict Baptist, and he was leading the Mt. Rose Baptist Church choir by the time he was 11. Despite a troubled and rebellious teenage period, by his early twenties Franklin was writing

material for gospel greats including Rev. Milton Biggham, Daryl Coley, **Yolanda Adams** and **Rev. John P. Kee**. The success of his debut saw the Family booked to appear on syndicated USA television programme *The Arsenio Hall Show*, while contemporary artists as diverse as **Ice Cube** and **R. Kelly** paid public respect to their craft. Subsequent albums have established Franklin and his bands (God's Property and Nu Nation) as probably contemporary gospel's biggest and most commercially successful star and have featured guest appearances from artists including Kelly, **Bono** and **Mary J. Blige**.

● ALBUMS: *Kirk Franklin And The Family* (Gospo Centric 1994) ★★★, *Kirk Franklin & The Family Christmas* (Chordant 1995) ★★★, *Whatcha Lookin' 4* (Gospo Centric 1995) ★★★, *God's Property From Kirk Franklin's New Nation* (B-Rite/Interscope 1997) ★★★★, *The Nu Nation Project* (Gospo Centric/Interscope 1998) ★★★, *The Rebirth Of Kirk Franklin* (Gospo Centric 2002) ★★★★, *Hero* (Fo Yo Soul/Gospo Centric 2005) ★★★.

● DVD/VIDEOS: *Whatcha Lookin' 4* (Gospo Centric 1996), *The Nu Nation Tour* (Interscope 1999), *Video Revolution: The Kirk Franklin Collection* (Interscope 2002).

● FURTHER READING: *Church Boy*, Kirk Franklin.

Franklin, Rex, And Noelene

Rex Franklin (b. 25 September 1935, Hawkes Bay, New Zealand) was attracted to country music as a boy from hearing the recordings of **Tex Morton** and **Buddy Williams** and American stars **Wilf Carter** and **Hank Snow**, which had been released in New Zealand. After leaving school, he worked on a remote farm and bought his first guitar with his first wages. In September 1953 he made his first public appearance in a talent show, and soon after, he formed the Ruahine Ramblers with two fellow contestants. They made their debut in January 1954, singing to the crowd waiting the arrival of Queen Elizabeth during her New Zealand visit. They played regularly on 2ZA Palmerston North, toured locally, and in May 1954 Franklin met his future wife, Noelene Anderson (b. 22 January 1936, Fielding, New Zealand). The Ramblers played on several other stations including 2YZ Napier and 2XA Wanganui, and in January 1955 they recorded seven sides for the Tanza label. Franklin and Noelene began singing together and calling themselves the Sun Valley Trail Singers, they toured both North and South Island. In September 1956, they recorded four sides for Tanza Records, and their first 78rpm release, 'Would You Mind'/'I Wonder Where You Are Tonight', proved popular. They were married on 17 November 1956 and toured with their Western Variety Show.

Between 1959 and 1962, they made recordings for Viking Records, which led to albums and several EPs including *The Shearer's Jamboree* (1959), *Serenading In The Evening* (1960) both as the Sun Valley Trail Singers, *Drover's Dream* (1962), *Fraulein* (1963) *Western Round Up Volume Five* (1963). In 1963 Franklin also recorded with his band, the Prairie Pals. In 1966 their bestselling *A Country Singalong* was released. The following year they relocated to Palmerston North, where Franklin began his popular *Country Round Up Show* on 2ZA. This later moved to Nelson, South Island, on 2ZN, where he was regularly joined on air by touring artists that included his idol Hank Snow. The show lasted until 1976, and during this time they made further recordings for Viking and Franklin and also recorded two albums for **Philips Records**. Later Franklin hosted a popular weekly talent show. In the late 70s, they worked the club and hotel circuits sometimes with drummer Bruce Lauchlan as a trio calling themselves Wildwood.

During his long career Rex had Australian chart hits and in the mid-60s surprisingly had Top 20 success in the Netherlands with his recordings of 'Shackles And Chains' and 'Mansion On The Hill'. He has written several songs with 'On The Takapau Plains' being the most popular, but he has never classed himself a great songwriter. In 1988 the Franklin's were presented with the New Zealand Country Music Pioneer Award. Their daughter Lorraine sings and, owing to her father's tuition, has became a fine guitarist. They are still active on the New Zealand/Australian country scene. They recorded two cassette albums for sales on tour, and in 1997 they released a CD album *Trip To Paradise*, which contains some of their very best recordings. In 1999 **Bear Family Records** released two CDs by the Franklins that contained many of their early recordings plus several previously unreleased tracks.

● ALBUMS: as Sun Valley Trail Singers *1000 Miles Out Yonder* (Viking 1960) ★★★, *Hillbilly Hit Parade* (Viking 1961) ★★★, *Westerns* (Viking 1962) ★★★, *Rex Franklin & His Prairie Pals* (Viking 1963) ★★★★, *The Good Old Days* (Viking 1964) ★★★, *A Country Singalong* (Viking 1966) ★★★★, *Another Country Singalong* (Viking 1969) ★★★, *Rex Franklin—Country Gold* (Philips 1970) ★★★, *Rex Franklin—Redback On The Toilet Seat* (Philips 1971) ★★★, *Out Behind The Barn* cassette (No Label) ★★★, *Trip To Paradise* i cassette (No Label) ★★★, *Trip To Paradise* ii (No Label 1999) ★★★★.

● COMPILATIONS: *Upon The Outlaw Trail* 1962–65 recordings (Bear Family 1999) ★★★, *A Real New Zealand Cowboy Song* 1956–62 recordings (Bear Family 1999) ★★★.

Franklin, Rodney

b. 16 September 1958, Berkeley, California, USA, Rodney Franklin was something of a child prodigy, taking piano lessons at the age of 6 at the Washington Elementary School. Upon graduation he worked extensively with **John Handy** in San Francisco and subsequently toured with **Bill Summers**, **Freddie Hubbard** and **Marlena Shaw**. In 1978 he signed with **Columbia Records** and recorded his debut album for the label, *In The Center*, a jazz fusion workout that was not released in the UK. His second album, *You'll Never Know*, redressed the balance. Aided by the hit single 'The Groove', which sparked a popular dance craze (dancers had to 'freeze' in time with the track's breaks), Rodney hit the Top 10 of the singles charts and saw *You'll Never Know* rise in the album listings. Although subsequent Columbia releases never came anywhere near repeating the extraordinary success of *You'll Never Know*, they did establish Franklin as a considerable name in the fusion market, particularly with *Marathon*. In 1988 he switched labels to BMG, recording *Diamond Inside You*, which featured lead vocals by **Jennifer Holliday** on the single 'Gotta Give It Up'. Subsequent releases have failed to restore Franklin to his previous commercial position, but he remains a respected keyboard player and fusion artist.

● ALBUMS: *In The Center* (Columbia 1978) ★★★, *You'll Never Know* (Columbia 1980) ★★★★, *Rodney Franklin* (Columbia 1980) ★★★, *Endless Flight* (Columbia 1981) ★★★, *Learning To Love* (Columbia 1982) ★★, *Marathon* (Columbia 1984) ★★★★, *Sky Dance* (Columbia 1985)

★★★, *It Takes Two* (Columbia 1986) ★★★, *Street Language* (Columbia 1986) ★★★, *Diamond Inside Of You* (BMG 1988) ★★★, *Love Dancin* (Nova 1992) ★★★.

● COMPILATIONS: *The Best Of Rodney Franklin* (Columbia 1998) ★★★.

Franks, Michael

b. 18 September 1944, La Jolla, California, USA. As a young teenager, Franks began singing to his own guitar accompaniment. He drew his eclectic repertoire from a broad field including folk music and aspects of the blues. He also began composing in the blues idiom, performing his own work and also hearing it picked up by other musicians. By the 70s Franks had become a well-known teacher and composer. His songs have been recorded by **Mark Murphy**, **Carmen McRae** and others. In the mid-70s he made a number of well-received records with jazzmen such as **Kenny Barron** and **Ron Carter** and appeared with the original line-up of the popular **Yellowjackets**. Franks sings with a huskily intimate sound, interpreting lyrics with feeling and imparting a smooth swing to all his performances.

● ALBUMS: *Michael Franks* (Brut 1973) ★★★, *The Art Of Tea* (Reprise 1976) ★★★, *Sleeping Gypsy* (Warners 1977) ★★★★, *Burchfield Nines* (Warners 1978) ★★★, *Tiger In The Rain* (Warners 1979) ★★★, *One Bad Habit* (Warners 1980) ★★★, with Crossfire *Live* (Warners Australia 1980) ★★, *Objects Of Desire* (Warners 1982) ★★, *Passionfruit* (Warners 1983) ★★★, *Skin Dive* (Warners 1985) ★★, *The Camera Never Lies* (Warners 1987) ★★★, *Blue Pacific* (Reprise 1990) ★★★, *Dragonfly Summer* (Reprise 1993) ★★★, *Abandoned Garden* (Warners 1995) ★★★, *Barefoot On The Beach* (Windham Hill 1999) ★★★, *Watching The Snow* (Sleeping Gypsy 2003) ★★.

● COMPILATIONS: *Indispensable* (Warners 1988) ★★★, *The Best Of Michael Franks: A Backward Glance* (Warners 1998) ★★★, *The Michael Franks Anthology: The Art Of Love* (Rhino 2003) ★★★★.

Franks, Tillman

b. 29 September 1920, Stamps, Arkansas, USA. In 1922 the family relocated to Shreveport, where his father worked on the Louisiana Railroad. Franks had aspirations to play baseball for a career, but after hearing **Roy Acuff** singing 'Would You Care', he decided that a country music career was the thing for him. His father swapped some rabbits for an old guitar, and he taught himself to play. In his teens, he played with Buddy Attaway and **Claude King** as the Rainbow Boys. (They were inspired by the **Shelton Brothers** who, as the Sunshine Boys, were a popular act on KWKH Louisiana). During World War II, he served with the US Army in the Pacific theatre and played bass fiddle on Voice of America radio broadcasts with folk singer **Pete Seeger** and also played with **Gene Autry**. After the war, Franks returned to Shreveport where he became friendly with a young **Webb Pierce** then struggling to make his name. He played bass with Pierce's Southern Valley Boys and appeared on some of Pierce's early recordings listed at times as Radar Franks. Some of the Pacemaker recordings of Pierce's vocals were even listed as by Tillman Franks And The Rainbow Valley Boys.

Franks became a booking agent and, as such, later claimed to be instrumental in bringing both **Hank Williams** and **Elvis Presley** to **The Louisiana Hayride**. He soon managed several acts including Pierce, **Slim Whitman** and the **Bailes Brothers**, and at one time, he worked for the Shreveport Police Department. (He once relocated to Dallas where he worked as a car salesman although he could not drive a car.) He soon returned to Shreveport, where he attended radio school and also began Shreveport's first guitar school. Among his pupils were **Jerry Kennedy** and **Merle Kilgore**. In 1952 a disagreement saw Franks and Pierce part company, when the singer moved to the *Grand Ole Opry* in Nashville. Apart from working as a booking agent, Franks presented a radio show, worked with **Billy Walker** and **Jimmy C. Newman** and managed the **Carlisles** with whom he worked briefly in Nashville. He never liked Nashville and returned to Shreveport where he managed Jimmy And Johnny (Jimmy Lee Fautheree and **Country Johnny Mathis**). In 1955 he became the manager of **Johnny Horton**, whom he knew from their *Louisiana Hayride* appearances. By careful management, he resurrected Horton's career to that of star status. He carefully selected songs and arranged recordings. On 5 November 1960 Franks was a passenger, with guitarist Tommy (Gerald) Tomlinson, in a car driven by Horton, when they were hit by a drunken driver near Milano, Texas. Horton died, Franks, who at the time was recovering from surgery, suffered head injuries, and Tomlinson suffered bad crushing of the left leg that necessitated amputation a few months later.

When he recovered Franks returned to management and worked with various artists including Claude King and **David Houston**. He remained in Shreveport, a city he described as 'the country soul of the world', where he became known as 'the man who knew everybody who was anybody in the country field' and continued to be involved in many aspects of the music industry. He has been described as the Honky Tonk Manager and is deeply respected for his vast knowledge of the country music scene. Over the years he wrote or co-wrote several hit songs including 'Sink The Bismarck', 'The Comancheros', 'Wolverton Mountain' and 'When It's Springtime In Alaska'. He had little success as a recording artist himself gaining only two *Billboard* chart entries namely 'Tadpole' (1963) as Tillman Franks And The Cedar Grove Three and 'When The World's On Fire' (1964) as the Tillman Franks Singers, both recorded on Starday and both reaching number 30. Franks never slowed down, and at the age of 80, he wrote his autobiography.
● ALBUMS: *The Tillman Franks Singers* (Pickwick/Hilltop 1965) ★★★.
● FURTHER READING: *I Was There When It Happened*, Tillman Franks with Robert Gentry.

Franti, Michael

(see **Disposable Heroes Of Hiphoprisy**; **Spearhead**)

Frantic Elevators

This Manchester, England–based punk/pop unit is notable for starting the musical career of Mick Hucknall (b. 8 June 1960, Denton, Greater Manchester, England). Together with his school chum Neil Moss (guitar), Kevin Williams (drums) and Brian Turner (bass), he released a number of interesting but undistinguished singles during 1979 and the early 80s. Their debut single, comprising the tracks 'Voice In The Dark', 'Passion' and 'Every Day I Die', was an independent production of 2,000 copies. A planned second release failed to materialize, and the white label pressings are now much sought after. Three further singles were eventually

released, including a version of Hucknall's modern classic 'Holding Back The Years'. Hucknall folded the Frantic Elevators in 1983 to pursue his plans for a white soul band, which became **Simply Red**. Various members gigged as the Elevators for a brief while. When listening to the Frantic Elevators material, it is hard to place Hucknall the vocalist, in punk staccato, against the smooth pop stylist he became in Simply Red. Interesting but primitive.
● COMPILATIONS: *Singles* mini-album (Essential 2000) ★★.

Franz Ferdinand

One of the most intriguing UK guitar bands to emerge in the early years of the twenty-first century, Franz Ferdinand derive their name from an Austro-Hungarian royal whose assassination proved to be the catalyst for the World War I (via a racehorse named Archduke Ferdinand that the band had seen on the television). The Glasgow, Scotland–based quartet, Alex Kapranos (b. Alexander Paul Kapranos, 20 March 1972, Gloucestershire, England; vocals/guitar, ex-Karelia), Nick McCarthy (b. Nicholas Augustine McCarthy, 13 December 1974, Blackpool, England; guitar, keyboards, vocals), Bob Hardy (b. Robert Byron Hardy, 16 August 1980, Bradford, West Yorkshire, England; bass) and Paul Thomson (b. Paul Robert Thompson, 15 September 1977, Edinburgh, Scotland; drums), coalesced through the Glasgow School of Art where Hardy studied painting and Thomson was employed as a life model. Although their stated desire to usurp the significance of their namesake seemed fairly implausible, the band's intent was nevertheless admirable. Drawing overt inspiration from early 80s punk funk artists such as **Gang Of Four** and **James White**, mixed with a liberal dose of early **Roxy Music** and **Sparks**, the band operated to a principal of 'cutting away excess crap' and forbidding the presence of solos and 'clutter' in their songs. From this ethos, the band created a music that was terse, concise and, for the most part, genuinely enthralling. Echoing the **Chic**-worshipping post-punk band **Josef K**, the quartet's wired and angular guitar pop was shot through with the impulse of disco and nervy tension of funk. Although they rejected the tag of 'artiness', Franz Ferdinand's sharp attire and pithy lyrics nevertheless suggested inventiveness, dexterity and smartness (in more than one sense) that was not evident in most of their peers.

Even before the release of 2004's self-titled debut album, Franz Ferdinand's history had acquired the status of near myth. The band reportedly came together after two of the members were involved in an altercation over a bottle of vodka. They played their first gig in a bedroom-cum-art show in front of 80 girls and hosted shows/mixed art events on the seventh floor of a disused art deco warehouse dubbed the Chateau. Nicely, given their rapid ascent to the pages of the UK's tabloids and broadsheets, the band held a healthy disdain for celebrity culture in the twentieth/twenty-first century: 'So I'm on BBC2 now / Telling Terry Wogan how I made it / But what I made isn't clear', sang Kapranos on the track 'Matinee'. What initially appeared to be a boast of 'I am the new Scottish gentry' on 'Shopping For Blood', was suffixed by the line 'Anglicised vowels, sub-London thoughts' and was apparently (sarcastically) directed at those in Glasgow who simply aped their peers in London. Although signed to independent label Domino Records (partly, it transpires, because the label head cooked for them rather than taking them out for a flash meal), Franz Ferdinand's second single, 'Take Me Out', reached the Top 3 in the UK singles chart, showing the band could take their edgy, kinetic pop into the mainstream. Further reward followed in September when *Franz Ferdinand* was awarded the prestigious Mercury Music Prize.

By the end of 2004, Franz Ferdinand was playing arena-sized shows and making inroads into the American market, completing their remarkable rise from humble origins to mainstream acceptance. The band spent most of 2005 working in their Scottish studio on the follow-up to their debut album. The first release to emerge from the sessions was the upbeat stomper 'Do You Want To', a UK Top 5 single in September. The attendant *You Could Have It So Much Better* debuted at the top of the UK album chart the following month.

● ALBUMS: *Franz Ferdinand* (Domino 2004) ★★★★, *You Could Have It So Much Better* (Domino 2005) ★★★.
● DVD/VIDEOS: *Franz Ferdinand* (Domino 2005).

Franz, Johnny

b. John Charles Franz, 23 February 1922, London, England, d. 29 January 1977, London, England. An extremely successful and highly regarded pianist, and A&R producer for **Philips Records** in the UK. Franz began to study the piano when he was 13, and 2 years later, he joined the music publishers Francis, Day and Hunter. In parallel with his day job, Franz worked in the evenings with artists such as **Jack Jackson**, George Elrick and Nat Allen. He also served as accompanist to harmonica soloist Ronald Chesney on the latter's radio series. In 1940 Franz played the piano for the band singer Bernard Hunter's first stage appearance at Collins Music Hall and, by the late 40s, had established a reputation as one of the leading accompanists in Britain, working with **Adelaide Hall**, Benny Lee and visiting American star **Vivian Blaine**. One of his most enduring associations was with **Anne Shelton**, and they were part of an entertainment 'package' that was flown on a round trip of 1,500 miles to play 3 dates in the American zone of Nurembourg, West Germany, in 1950. Ironically, not long afterwards, Franz was a passenger in a Rapide small aircraft that up-ended on a runway in Jersey, and he was reluctant ever to fly again. In 1954, after spending 17 years with Francis, Day and Hunter, while also discovering and coaching new talent, Franz was appointed the A&R Manager of Philips Records in 1954. His previous background meant that he was ideally suited to the job. He was able to select the right kind of material for his roster of artists, routine them, and explain to the musical arrangers precisely the sound that he wanted to hear on the finished records. Blessed with perfect pitch, he could also spot a clinker in the string section from the other side of the control room. In the late 50s Franz was responsible for the output of some of the most successful artists in the UK, such as **Frankie Vaughan**, Shirley Bassey, Harry Secombe, the **Beverley Sisters**, the **Kaye Sisters**, **Robert Earl**, **Ronnie Carroll**, **Susan Maughan**, **Julie Rogers** and, of course, Anne Shelton. It was his idea, when recording Shelton's 1956 chart-topper 'Lay Down Your Arms', to add the sound of martial marching feet by having one of the studio staff shuffle about in a sand tray. In complete contrast, he worked with the risqué American cabaret star Ruth Wallis and also produced the sophisticated *Mel Tormé Meets The British*, which was arranged by **Wally Stott**, one of Franz's key conductor-arrangers along with Ivor Raymonde and

Peter Knight. In the late 50s, **Marty Wilde** was at the forefront of Philips' assault on the charts, as Franz adapted to the radical musical changes that were happening all around him. Early in the 60s he nurtured the vocal instrumental group the **Springfields**, from which emerged one of the decade's superstars, **Dusty Springfield**, with a string of hits that included the million-sellers 'I Only Want To Be With You' (written by her musical director, Ivor Raymonde, with Mike Hawker) and 'You Don't Have To Say You Love Me'. The **Four Pennies** were another successful Franz act around that time, with their UK number 1 'Juliet'; so too were the **Walker Brothers**, who introduced the pop world to another 60s icon, **Scott Walker**. The sound that Franz created for Walker Brothers hits such as 'Make It Easy On Yourself', 'My Ship Is Coming In' and 'The Sun Ain't Gonna Shine Any More', is sometimes called 'Phil Spectorish'. This had shades of truth, although the two producers were very different in appearance and style: Franz could easily have been mistaken for a bank manager—albeit one who chain-smoked and devoured copious amounts of tea. As well as producing Scott Walker's chart hits 'Jackie', 'Joanna' and 'Lights Of Cincinnati', Franz's influence was also apparent on *Sings Songs From His T.V. Series*, which, with show numbers such as 'I Have Dreamed', 'The Song Is You' and 'If She Walked Into My Life', showed Walker to be a romantic balladeer of the old school. In a way, it was the 'old pals' act' that brought much of the best commercial material Franz's way. His contacts in the music publishing business, such as Cyril Shane, ensured that Philips were offered many potential hit songs, some of them from abroad. Springfield's 'I Only Want To Be With You' came to London from the 1965 San Remo Song Festival, and in 1973, Franz placed 'Welcome Home' ('Vivre'), a French number with an English lyric by Bryan Blackburn, with *Opportunity Knocks* winners **Peters And Lee**. It gave them a UK number 1, and they hit the top spot again in the same year with *We Can Make It*, the first of their four Top 10 albums in the 70s. Among the most fondly remembered television and recording performers of the decade, the duo was a part of the final flourish in the life of a man who has been called 'the last of the great pro's'. Johnny Franz died in 1977 at the age of 55, in a Chelsea hospital.

Fraser-Simson, Harold

b. 15 August 1872, London, England, d. 19 January 1944, Dalcross Castle, Inverness, Scotland. Educated at Charterhouse and Cambridge, Fraser-Simson worked in commerce while attempting to launch a songwriting career. Among early songs that met with moderate success are 'I Sent My Love Two Roses', 'The Raindrop And The Rose', 'Falmouth Town' and 'The Old Land'. His first London musical, *Bonita* (1911), ran for 46 performances. With *The Maid Of The Mountains*, on which he collaborated with lyricist **Harry Graham**, Fraser-Simson's career blossomed. Starring **José Collins**, the show tried out in Manchester before opening in the West End in February 1917 for a run of 1,352 performances. Later came revivals, a film version in 1932, and a staging on Broadway. Ironically, three of the four best-loved songs from this show are not Fraser-Simson's work but additional songs written by **James W. Tate**, Clifford Harris and Arthur Valentine: 'My Life Is Love', 'A Paradise For Two' and 'A Bachelor Gay Am I'. Of the popular four, only 'Love Will Find A Way' is by Graham and Fraser-Simson. His next show, *A Southern Maid*, opened in Manchester in 1917 but then toured the provinces until *The Maid Of The Mountains* closed in 1920 and Collins was free to star in London. Fraser-Simson's other shows included *Our Peg* (1919, with Graham and Collins), *Missy Jo* (1921, Graham), *Head Over Heels* (1923, Graham and **Adrian Ross**), *Our Nell* (1924, with **Ivor Novello**), *The Street Singer* (1924, with **Percy Greenbank**) and *Betty In Mayfair* (1925, with Graham).

From here on, Fraser-Simson left musical comedies, composing a ballet, *Venetian Wedding* (1926), and incidental music for *The Nightingale And The Rose* (1927) and *Toad Of Toad Hall* (1929). On the latter, he collaborated with A.A. Milne who had adapted the show from Kenneth Grahame's classic children's book, *The Wind In The Willows*. Having found his métier, Fraser-Simson next wrote musical settings for Milne's children's poems, *When We Were Very Young*. So popular were these that he followed them with Milne's *Now We Are Six*, *Winnie The Pooh* and *The House At Pooh Corner*. In total, the Milne material resulted in 67 songs, among which are, memorably, 'Christopher Robin Is Saying His Prayers' and 'They're Changing Guard At Buckingham Palace'. Fraser-Simson also composed music for other poems, publishing collections entitled *Teddy Bear And Other Songs* and *Alice In Wonderland*.

Fraser, Andy

b. 7 August 1952, London, England. Fraser was a founder member and bass player of the late 60s and early 70s UK blues, rock group **Free**. He worked as a teenager for **John Mayall**. Fraser broke from Free on two occasions, first in 1971, going on to form Toby with guitarist Adrian Fisher (later to join **Sparks**) and drummer Stan Speake. The re-formation of Free early in 1972 was short-lived, for Fraser quit in July that same year. He teamed up with **Chris Spedding** to form Sharks, recording two albums for **Island Records**. With the folding of Sharks and after a brief period with **Frankie Miller** and Henry McCullough, Fraser created the Andy Fraser Band with Nick Judd (keyboards) and Kim Turner (drums), recording two albums for Island in 1975. Having retired from playing, Fraser still enjoys the benefits of regular royalty cheques from his most productive period with Free.

● ALBUMS: as the Andy Fraser Band *The Andy Fraser Band* (Island 1975) ★★★, *In Your Eyes* (Island 1975) ★★, *Fine Fine Line* (Island 1984) ★★.

Fraser, Dean

b. *c.*1955, Kingston, Jamaica, West Indies. Fraser's rich, fulsome tenor tone has helped to make him the foremost Jamaican reggae saxophonist. He first appeared on the Jamaican music scene in the mid-70s when the importance of brass in reggae bands was starting to fade. He began by playing clarinet with the National Volunteer Programme in Jonestown, where he met Ronald 'Nambo' Robinson and Junior 'Chico' Chinn, a trombonist and trumpeter. Together they would become the most well-known brass section in Jamaica during the 80s. To begin with, they played jazz and R&B standards at old people's homes, but Fraser left to join Sonny Bradshaw's band, which played mainly jazz arrangements and provided an opportunity for young musicians to learn about the music business. Fraser first recorded with Lloyd 'Gitsy' Willis in 1975, and in 1977 he joined the We The People Band, led by **Lloyd Parks**, the singer, producer and bass player. The band recorded several successful records for

Joe Gibbs and gained a high profile backing **Dennis Brown**. In 1978 Gibbs produced Fraser's first album, *Black Horn Man*. **Donovan Germain** produced *Revolutionary Dream* in 1980. Some of Fraser's early singles included versions of vocal records, delivered in a smooth, delicate tone similar to that of **Slim Smith**. As Youth Sax, he regularly backed **Sly And Robbie** on world tours and in the studio and also played with **Gregory Isaacs**. He performed an emotionally charged version of **Bob Marley**'s 'Redemption Song' at the 1981 Reggae Sunsplash (the first since Marley's death), which unusually put Fraser centre stage and led to Mango commissioning *Pumping Air*. Demand for Fraser's playing ironically increased as computerized music began to infiltrate reggae in the mid-80s, and his saxophone playing added a human touch to numerous **digital** rhythms. He had a surprise hit in 1987 with 'Girlfriend' for Dennis Star, and this prompted him to rejuvenate his singing voice on *Sings And Blows* and *Dancehall Sax* for Star, which provided him with further Jamaican hits. **Gussie Clarke** increasingly used Fraser's talents from 1988 onwards, initially as a session player on Clarke's one-rhythm albums, then as a vital part of the production team, arranging and playing on work by artists such as **Cocoa Tea**, Gregory Isaacs, Dennis Brown and **Freddie McGregor**. He still takes this role for producers Carlton Hines and **Philip 'Fatis' Burrell**. Fraser is part of a saxophone tradition leading back to musicians such as **Tommy McCook** and **Roland Alphonso**. An older Jamaican community will always have a fondness for his records. He was awarded the Musgrave Medal by the Jamaican government in 1993 for his musical achievements.

● ALBUMS: *Black Horn Man* (1978) ★★★, *Revolutionary Dream* (1980) ★★★, *A Touch Of Sax*, *Revolutionary Sounds* (1982) ★★★, *Pure Horn* (1983) ★★★, with Willie Lindo *Double Dynamite* (1983) ★★★, *Pumping Air* (Mango/Island 1984) ★★★, *Big Bad Sax* (Super Power 1988) ★★, *Sings And Blows* (Greensleeves 1988) ★★★★, *Dancehall Sax* (Greensleeves 1988) ★★★, *Raw Sax* (Greensleeves 1989) ★★★, *Call On Dean* (1991) ★★★, *Moonlight* (Greensleeves 1991) ★★★, *Taking Chances* (1993) ★★★, *Dean Plays Bob* (1994) ★★★, *Dean Plays Bob Volume 2* (1996) ★★★, *Jesus Loves Me* (1997) ★★★, *Big Up* (Island 1997) ★★★★.

Fraser, Norma

b. Norma Fraser, St. Andrew, Jamaica, West Indies. Fraser's initial recording was a duet with **Lord Creator** recorded in 1961. The debut release from the session, 'We Will Be Lovers'/'Come On Pretty Baby', topped the Jamaican chart and maintained a significant profile throughout the year. In 1963 the song was released in the UK through **Island Records** where it proved a hit among the West Indian community. Her success led to sessions at **Studio One** performing alongside **Bob Marley** And The Wailers, **Ken Boothe**, the **Skatalites** and **Delroy Wilson** to name a few. A series of solo hits, with **Coxsone Dodd** producing, ensued including 'Heartaches', 'Respect', 'Time' and 'Come By Here'. The latter song has the distinction of being released as the a-side to the Wailers' 'I Stand Predominate'. She was later employed as the resident vocalist at the prestigious *Club 35* in Montego Bay and also provided vocals for a number of Jamaican bands including the **Roland Alphonso** Trio, the Sheikhs and the Cavaliers. Fraser additionally performed on the north coast of Jamaica, including notable appearances at the Playboy Club, the Silver

Seas Hotel, the Arawak Hotel and the Sheraton. She was also enrolled to support a number of visiting soul performers including the legendary **Sam Cooke** and **Chuck Jackson**. Following a number of low key releases she released a cover version of **P.P. Arnold**'s 'The First Cut Is The Deepest', which was greeted with critical acclaim when released in the UK. The single resulted in Fraser being voted the best Female Newcomer in 1967. She maintained her profile with the release of the accusative 'Telling Me Lies', coupled with the **Viceroys**' classic 'Shake Up'. The song failed to emulate its predecessor, which led to a temporary state of anonymity. Fraser later enjoyed a modicum of success with 'Heartbreak Hotel'. She migrated to the USA in 1970 and soon found work as a featured performer at a benefit gig that demonstrated solidarity with the US congresswoman Bella Abzug. While based there she maintained a low profile, although she performed as lead vocalist for a number of obscure bands. In the early 90s her reputation blossomed when she toured Colorado and Texas, performing as the opening act in support of **Yellowman** and **Inner Circle** on their respective US tours.

● ALBUMS: *Norma Fraser—Hot Again* (Indie 1994) ★★★.

Fraternity Of Man

This US outfit was formed in Los Angeles, California, USA, in 1967 when Elliot Ingber (guitar, ex-**Mothers Of Invention**) joined forces with three members of struggling aspirants the **Factory**: Warren Klein (guitar/sitar), Martin Kibbee (bass) and Richard Hayward (drums). Lawrence 'Stash' Wagner (lead vocals/guitar) completed the line-up featured on *Fraternity Of Man*, a musically disparate selection ranging from melodic flower-power ('Wispy Paisley Skies') to rhetorical politics ('Just Doin' Our Job'). The album also featured a version of **Frank Zappa**'s 'Oh No I Don't Believe It' but is best recalled for the 'dopers' anthem 'Don't Bogart Me', later immortalized in the movie *Easy Rider*. The blues-influenced *Get It On* lacked the charm of its predecessor but featured contributions from pianist Bill Payne and former Factory guitarist Lowell George, both of whom resurfaced, with Hayward, in **Little Feat**. Ingber was also involved with the last-named act during its embryonic stages but left to join **Captain Beefheart**, where he was rechristened Winged Eel Fingerling. In later years he emerged as a member of the Mothers' offshoot, Grandmothers.

● ALBUMS: *Fraternity Of Man* (ABC 1968) ★★★, *Get It On* (Dot 1969) ★★.

Frazier Chorus

Originally a four-piece band from Brighton, Sussex, England, this mid-80s pop outfit, originally under the name Plop!, set out with the grand ambition of being the antithesis of **Wham!** Singer and keyboard player Tim Freeman's songs were circulated on a demo tape, and he and the rest of the band, Michele Allardyce (percussion), Kate Holmes (flute) and Chris Taplin (clarinet), were signed to **4AD Records** under the name Frazier Chorus, a name taken from the back of a 50s US baseball jacket. With their unusual instrumental line-up, which lent an almost synth-pop/pastoral feel, their 4AD debut, 'Sloppy Heart' (1987), did not fit easily with the harder edge towards which the label was moving. As a consequence, the band soon switched to **Virgin Records**. In 1989 they released their debut album, *Sue*, which featured orchestral arrangements from **David Bedford** and contributions from

Tim Sanders (tenor saxophone), Roddy Lorimer (trumpet, flügelhorn) and Simon Clarke (piccolo, saxophones). Minor UK hits with 'Dream Kitchen' and 'Typical' promised much, but none reached the Top 50. A reissue of 'Sloppy Heart' featured a laconic version of the **Sex Pistols**' 'Anarchy In The UK' on its b-side.

Allardyce left acrimoniously during the recording of Frazier Chorus' second album (with the **Lightning Seeds**' Ian Broudie on production), leaving the band as a trio. Allardyce, whose orientation was geared towards **dance music**, would continue to work as a journalist for disc jockey magazine *Jocks*. Freeman had previously collaborated on the 4AD house project **This Mortal Coil**. Further minor Frazier Chorus hits included the **Paul Oakenfold** remixes of 'Cloud 8' and 'Nothing'. The disappointing performance of 1991's 'Walking On Air' confirmed that Frazier Chorus' cult appeal had apparently peaked, but the band pressed on regardless. Freeman's muse had not deserted him, and their final album, 1995's *Wide Awake*, included further strong songwriting in songs such as 'If The Weather Was Up To Me'. Holmes later recorded for **Creation Records** before working with two electronic duos—Technique with Xan Tyler and **Client** with Sarah Blackwood. She is now married to **Alan McGee**.

● ALBUMS: *Sue* (Virgin 1989) ★★★, *Ray* (Virgin 1991) ★★, *Wide Awake* (Pinkerton 1995) ★★★.

Frazier, Calvin

b. 16 February 1915, Osceola, Arkansas, USA, d. 23 September 1972, Detroit, Michigan, USA. The Frazier family was large, musical and deeply religious; father Van played fiddle, guitar and banjo, mother Bell played bass, and Lonnie, Rebecca and Johnny all played guitar and mandolin, as did Calvin. By 1922, they lived in South Hobart Place in Memphis, along with cousin **Johnny Shines**. Nine years later, Shines linked up with Calvin and Johnny and played for handouts on the Memphis streets. During the early 30s, Calvin also worked with **Robert Johnson** and **James 'Peck' Curtis**. In April 1935 Frazier was involved in a shooting incident that forced him to leave town, in company with Johnson and Shines. The trio fled to Canada and found work in religious broadcasting, playing on *The Elder Moten Hour*. Shortly after returning to Detroit, Shines and Johnson moved on, but Frazier stayed, teaming up with guitarist Sampson Pittman. They were recorded in October 1938 for the Library of Congress by **Alan Lomax**, Frazier revealing a guitar style whose boogie patterns and falsetto vocals echoed Johnson's. During the 40s, he played with **Big Maceo**, **Baby Boy Warren** and **Eddie Kirkland** but did not record again until 1952 for Savoy, with pianist T.J. Fowler's band. He also played on sessions by Baby Boy Warren and **Washboard Willie**. He recorded infrequently during the 50s; 'Lilly Mae', first recorded for the Library of Congress, and 'Have Blues, Must Travel' were recorded for **Fortune** and JVB, the latter also issued by **Checker**.

● ALBUMS: *I'm In The Highway Man* (1980) ★★★.

Frazier, Dallas

b. 27 October 1939, Spiro, Oklahoma, USA. Frazier wrote realistically about his family's move to Bakersfield in his song 'California Cottonfields', which was recorded by **Merle Haggard**. In his teens, he won a talent contest sponsored by **Ferlin Husky** and became part of his roadshow, with Husky subsequently recording 'Timber, I'm Falling'. However, Frazier's first success as a songwriter was with a novelty

about a cartoon caveman, 'Alley-Oop'. This 1960 record by a studio band, the **Hollywood Argyles**, which included Frazier himself, was a US number 1, and the song was also covered by Dante And The Evergreens, the **Beach Boys**, **Brian Poole And The Tremeloes**, the **Bonzo Dog Doo-Dah Band** and the Dynasores. Frazier wrote several songs in the same vein, notably 'Mohair Sam', a hit for **Charlie Rich**, and 'Elvira', a minor US pop hit for Frazier himself in 1966. Frazier's writing displays versatility, and his songs include 'There Goes My Everything' (**Jack Greene**, **Engelbert Humperdinck**, **Elvis Presley**), 'The Son Of Hickory Holler's Tramp' (**O.C. Smith**), 'Beneath Still Waters' (**Emmylou Harris**), 'If My Heart Had Windows' (**George Jones**) and 'Fourteen Carat Mind' (**Gene Watson**). He wrote four US country number 1 hits for **Charley Pride** with A.L. 'Doodle' Owens ('All I Have To Offer You [Is Me]', '[I'm So] Afraid Of Losing You Again', 'I Can't Believe That You've Stopped Loving Me', 'Then Who Am I'). Although he has a fine voice, Frazier has only had moderate success as a performer, notably with 'Everybody Ought To Sing A Song', 'Sunshine Of My World' and 'The Birthmark Henry Thompson Talked About'. In addition to his own albums, both George Jones and **Connie Smith** have recorded albums of his songs. Smith's *If It Ain't Love* includes three duets with him. Although he has been involved with the ministry since 1976, many of his older songs have become successful. He was inducted into the Nashville Songwriters Hall of Fame in 1976. In 1981 the **Oak Ridge Boys** won a gold disc for their version of 'Elvira'.
● ALBUMS: *Elvira* (Capitol 1966) ★★★★, *Tell It Like It Is* (Capitol 1967) ★★★, *Singin' My Songs* (RCA Victor 1970) ★★★, *My Baby Packed Up My Mind And Left Me* (RCA Victor 1971) ★★★.

Frazier, Josiah 'Cié'

b. 23 February 1904, New Orleans, Louisiana, USA. Taught to play drums by Louis Cottrell Snr., Frazier played in several New Orleans bands in the early and mid-20s including those led by **Papa Celestin** and Sidney Desvigne. Working in music only part time during the 30s and the war years, Frazier worked extensively from the mid-40s, mostly in New Orleans, with bands such as that led by **Percy Humphrey** at Manny's Tavern as well as with **Kid Howard**. In 1962 Frazier became the regular drummer for the Eureka Brass Band. Later in his career, Frazier toured Europe and the UK. In a class close to that of **Zutty Singleton**, Frazier's springy beat and exemplary time keeping made him one of the best of the New Orleans drummers.

Frazier, Philip

b. Philip Fraser, c.1958, Kingston, Jamaica, West Indies. In 1975 Frazier improvised songs in Greenwich Town alongside his colleague **Earl Zero**. Earl had enjoyed previous hits produced by **Al Campbell** and **Tommy Cowan** and urged Frazier to pursue a recording career. The Freedom Sounds collective, founded by Bertram Brown, produced Frazier's debut, 'This Time Won't Be Like The Last Time'. His career went into overdrive with the releases of 'Breaking Up', 'Come Ethiopians', 'Single Man', '2000 Years' and 'Sentimental Feelings', a double a-side backed with **Prince Allah**'s 'Sun Is Shining'. Freedom Sounds was an ambitious project, designed to promote forthright dealings in the industry, and it enrolled top-class performers including Earl Zero, **Michael Prophet**, Sammy Dread, Prince Allah, **Rod Taylor** and

the **Soul Syndicate**. Frazier's career enjoyed a boost when he recorded a version of 'Never Let Go' as a tribute to his neighbouring companion **Slim Smith**. His success continued with 'Ain't No Sunshine', 'Mr Wicked Man', 'Blood Of The Saint' and a tribute to his R&B idols, 'Special Request To The Manhattans'. By 1978 his reputation had extended to Europe and the USA, resulting in an international tour. While in Britain he linked up with the Silver Camel Sound System based at the 100 Club in London's Oxford Street. Like their Jamaican counterparts, the sound diversified into distribution and began releasing a number of roots hits. The label secured the release of Frazier's 'Blood Of The Saint' and a rare compilation, *Loving You*, before it dissolved. The label's demise prompted Frazier's return to Jamaica, recording with **Henry 'Junjo' Lawes** and Barry Clarke. The hits continued, including 'Please Stay' and 'When I Run Out', which both featured heavily on **U-Roy**'s Stur Gav Sound System and resulted in Frazier becoming a cult hero. By the mid-80s he was working with Bunny Gemini and **Triston Palma**. His solo hits included 'Send Us Back Home', 'Sad And Blue' and 'Don't Ring My Doorbell'. Throughout the late 80s and early 90s he surfaced with sporadic hits, including a version of the **Uniques**' 'Watch This Sound', a variation of the **Four Tops**' hit 'If I Was A Carpenter' and 'Coming On Strong', and in 1995 he released 'It's Magic' over the **Wailers**' 'Hypocrites' rhythm.
● ALBUMS: *Come Ethiopians* (Freedom Sounds 1976) ★★★, *Loving You* (Silver Camel 1978) ★★★, with Earl Zero, Prince Allah *Ethiopian Kings* (Love Child 1981) ★★★★, with Triston Palma *I & I In Inity* (Black Solidarity 1985) ★★★.

Freak Of Nature

Following the breakup of **White Lion**, frontman Mike Tramp assembled Freak Of Nature with guitarist Kenny Korade, former White Lion bass player Jerry Best, drummer Johnny Haro and ex-VVSI/**House Of Lords** guitarist Dennis Chick, a replacement for original member Oliver Steffenson. Away from record company pressures, the band developed a strong collection of melodic rock songs with a distinctly harder edge than White Lion, with Tramp concentrating on introspective, personal lyrics, again in contrast to the simpler themes of his previous group. '92' dealt with a traumatic year in Tramp's personal and professional life, while 'Rescue Me' tackled the difficult subject of his brother's addiction problems. While acquiring recording contracts for Europe and Japan, Freak Of Nature had trouble finding a contract for the USA owing to their unwillingness to compromise. However, they were prepared to be patient and to let their music and growing live reputation break the band. A lengthy touring schedule, taking in the USA, Japan and Europe, from May 1993 made the band many friends and served to reinforce the idea of Freak Of Nature as a band rather than a Tramp solo project. Late 1994 saw the introduction of new guitarist Marcus Mand in place of Kenny Korade.
● ALBUMS: *Freak Of Nature* (Music For Nations 1993) ★★★, *Gathering Of Freaks* (Music For Nations 1994) ★★, *Outcasts* (Dream Catcher 1998) ★★★.

Freakwater

Formed in Louisville, Kentucky, USA, the original idea behind Freakwater arose from informal country jams improvised in a basement by Janet Beveridge Bean (b. 10 February 1964, Bartow, Florida, USA), who is also drummer for **Eleventh Dream Day**, and Catherine Irwin (b. 4 March 1962, New Haven, Connecticut, USA). When Bean moved to Chicago, they kept their songwriting partnership alive by singing to each other over the telephone. Bean's stay in Chicago was beneficial, however, as it was here she met bass player Dave Gay. It was at this point the trio (augmented by guitar player Bob Egan and other musicians as necessary) began to record for the first time. Early critical comparisons to the **Carter Family** ensued, with the central duo's songwriting evoking a similar sense of innocence, albeit in a much more contemporary vein. As the **New Musical Express** wrote, 'Despite their straight-ahead approach to heartache folkisms and bourbon blues, Freakwater's gorgeous songs share the indie-led, country cliché-shaking agenda.' This view was confirmed by the fact that early in their career they released a cover version of **Black Sabbath**'s 'War Pigs'. Freakwater's fourth recording, 1995's *Old Paint*, was again produced by Brad Wood and witnessed their expressive voices addressing familiar subjects such as love, regret and drinking. Cover versions included **Woody Guthrie**'s 'Little Black Train' and **Loudon Wainwright III**'s 'Out Of This World'. 1998's *Springtime* concentrated on original material, but the album's seamless flow was indicative of Bean and Irwin's ability to create new folk and country classics. The follow-up *End Time*, featuring entirely self-composed material, fleshed out Freakwater's sound with strings and percussion.

Bean's split from husband and fellow Eleventh Dream Day member Rick Rizzo in 1999 coincided with a hiatus in Freakwater activities. Bean took a job at a Chicago law firm and began working with a new band, the Concertina Wire. Irwin, meanwhile, released her solo debut *Cut Yourself A Switch*. The central duo reunited with Dave Gay in 2004 and revived the Freakwater moniker, releasing *Thinking Of You* the following year.

● ALBUMS: *Freakwater* (Amoeba 1989) ★★★, *Dancing Underwater* (Amoeba 1991) ★★★, *Feels Like The Third Time* (Thrill Jockey 1993) ★★★, *Old Paint* (Thrill Jockey 1995) ★★★★, *Springtime* (Thrill Jockey 1998) ★★★★, *End Time* (Thrill Jockey 1999) ★★★★, *Thinking Of You* (Thrill Jockey 2005) ★★★.
Solo: Catherine Irwin *Cut Yourself A Switch* (Thrill Jockey 2002) ★★★.

Freaky Realistic

Based in Peckham, London, this 90s group was founded by Justin Anderson, whose cockney leer was the focal point for much of their press. He sang alongside Texan rapper Michael Lord and female Japanese vocalist Aki Omori. Four singles, 'Something New', 'Cosmic Love Vibes', 'Leonard Nimoy' and 'Koochie Ryder', all featured on their debut album before Lord quit the band in the summer of 1993.
● ALBUMS: *Frealism* (Polydor 1993) ★★★.

Freberg, Stan

b. Stanley Victor Freberg, 7 August 1926, Los Angeles, California, USA. Stan Freberg was a satirist who experienced great popularity during the early 50s in the USA. Freberg pioneered the style of satire and parody later used on such television programmes as *Saturday Night Live*. He performed on radio and television acted, wrote books as well as his own comedy material, worked in advertising and was even an accomplished puppeteer. Freberg grew up the son of a Baptist minister in Pasadena, California. His first showbusiness experience was at the age of 11 as an assistant to his uncle, a magician. Freberg became enthralled with the radio during his youth. As well as performing, he wrote and produced student shows and became his high school's speech champion, going on to win a national competition. He was awarded a drama scholarship but turned it down to work with Mel Blanc, who provided the voices of Warner Brothers cartoon characters such as Bugs Bunny and Porky Pig. Freberg provided voice-overs for other characters.

In the mid-40s he appeared on radio for the first time and soon became a regular on such programmes as the *Jack Benny* Show and on the Armed Forces Radio Network. He spent two years in the army and then joined a small orchestra, Red Fox And His Musical Hounds, as comedian, guitarist. He and actor Daws Butler (later the voice of Yogi Bear and Huckleberry Hound) then wrote and performed for the cartoon show *Time For Beany*, an Emmy-winning programme that served as inspiration to *Muppets* creator Jim Henson. In 1951 Freberg signed to **Capitol Records** and recorded 'John And Marsha', a spoof of soap operas in which the only lyrics were the two names of the title, repeated dramatically throughout the record. The record became a US hit and was followed by parodies of **Cole Porter**'s 'I've Got You Under My Skin', **Johnnie Ray**'s 'Cry' and others. In 1953 Freberg scored a number 1 record with 'St. George And The Dragonet', a parody of the *Dragnet* television series.

As the rock 'n' roll era began in 1954 Freberg lampooned such hits as 'Sh-Boom' and 'The Great Pretender', with orchestration by **Billy May**, who remains Freberg's arranger, conductor in the 90s. In 1956 Freberg took on **Elvis Presley**'s 'Heartbreak Hotel' and British skiffle artist **Lonnie Donegan**'s 'Rock Island Line', while the following year found him satirizing **Harry Belafonte**'s 'Banana Boat Day-O'. Other Freberg targets were **Lawrence Welk**, **Mitch Miller** and the television medium itself. In 1957 Freberg was given his own 17-week radio programme, some of which was collected on the Grammy-winning album *The Best Of The Stan Freberg Shows*. Freberg's 1958 single 'Green Chritma' brilliantly attacked the commercialization of Christmas and was subsequently banned by many radio stations. His final chart hit, 1960's 'The Old Payola Roll Blues (Side 1)' was another controversial release. Freberg continued to release albums throughout the 60s, his most successful being 1961's *Stan Freberg Presents The United States Of America*. He is active as an advertising writer in the 90s and still lends his voice to advertisement and voice-overs and the occasional cartoon, such as the CBS television animation anthology *Toon Night* (1991).

● ALBUMS: *Comedy Caravan* (1956) ★★★★, *A Child's Garden Of Freberg* (Capitol 1957) ★★★★, *The Best Of The Stan Freberg Show* (Capitol 1958) ★★★★, *Stan Freberg With The Original Cast* (Capitol 1959) ★★★, *Presents The United States Of America* (Capitol 1961) ★★★★, *Face The Funnies* (Capitol 1962) ★★★, *Madison Avenue Werewolf* (Capitol 1962) ★★★★, *Mickey Mouse's Birthday Party* (Capitol 1963) ★★★, *Underground Show #1* (Capitol 1966) ★★★.
● COMPILATIONS: *The Best Of Stan Freberg* (Capitol 1964) ★★★★, *The Capitol Years* (Capitol 1989) ★★★★, *Capitol Collectors Series* (Capitol 1990) ★★★★, *The Tip Of The Freberg: The Stan Freberg Collection 1951–1998* 4-CD box set (Rhino 1999) ★★★.

● FURTHER READING: *It Only Hurts When I Laugh*, Stan Freberg

Fred Everything

b. Frédéric Blais, Hull, Quebec, Canada. Based in Montreal, **deep house** DJ/producer Fred Everything first made an impact on the European **dance music** scene when he played an impressive and memorable set at 1997's In The City festival in Glasgow, Scotland. His remix of **Derrick Carter**'s 'Life Is Like A Circle' in 1999 also brought him to the attention of the dance music industry and record buyers. Since then, he has gone on to remix tracks for labels including 20:20 Vision, Om, Mantis, Shaboom, Grand Royal, Stereo Deluxe, Turbo and Bombay. Fred Everything's DJing style is firmly in the deep house genre but draws influences from disco, funk and soul. He has appeared at many UK club nights including Fabric, Basics, SubClub, Tribal Funktion, Moog and Bugged Out. His non-mix debut, 2000's *Under The Sun*, was a success with critics and the public. Working with studio partner, Mark Bell, he also records on the Shaboom label as Bell And Everything and Fred Everything And The Jazz Twit. He has remixed artists such as KemeticJust, **Random Factor**, AtJazz, Joeski, **Bran Van 3000** and **Roy Davis Jnr.**'s classic track 'Watch Them Come'.

● ALBUMS: *Under The Sun* (20:20 Vision 2000) ★★★★.
● COMPILATIONS: *Disconnection* (Inmix 1999) ★★★, *DJ Set 01* (Intonation 2000) ★★★, *From The Deep: Remixes By Fred Everything1998–2001* (Bombay 2001) ★★★.

Fred, John, And His Playboy Band

John Fred (b. John Fred Gourrier, 8 May 1941, Baton Rouge, Louisiana, USA, d. 15 April 2005, New Orleans, Louisiana, USA) was a 6-foot, 5-inch, blue-eyed soul singer who originally formed John Fred And The Playboys in 1956. This unit made their first record ('Shirley') two years later with **Fats Domino**'s backing group. During the early 60s various versions of the Playboys recorded for small independent record labels such as Jewel and N-Joy and eventually became known as John Fred And His Playboy Band. It was not until the end of 1967 that success finally came with the international hit, 'Judy In Disguise (With Glasses)'. An amusing satire on the **Beatles**' 'Lucy In The Sky With Diamonds', the single beat off a rival version by **Amboy Dukes**. Unfortunately this meant the Playboy Band were unfairly perceived as a novelty group, when in fact they were a tight, well organized and long-serving unit. Fred's blue-eyed soul vocals were most evident on *Agnes English*, which included a rasping version of 'She Shot A Hole In My Soul'. By the end of the 60s the band had split up, with Fred going on to record with a new group and work as a producer for RCS in Baton Rouge.

● ALBUMS: *John Fred And His Playboys* (Paula 1965) ★★★, *34:40 Of John Fred And His Playboys* (Paula 1966) ★★★, *Agnes English* aka *Judy In Disguise* (Paula 1967) ★★★, *Permanently Stated* (Paula 1968) ★★★, *Love My Soul* (Universal City 1969) ★★★.
● COMPILATIONS: *With Glasses: The Very Best Of John Fred And His Playboy Band* (Westside 2001) ★★★★.

Freda'

Comprising Uno Svenningsson (vocals), Arne Johansson (guitar) and Mats Johansson (drums; no relation), Swedish trio Freda' possess a distinctive musical character empha- sized by Svenningsson's somewhat shrill singing. Influenced by vocalists such as **Shane MacGowan** and **Tom Waits**, Freda' nevertheless provide a more upbeat rock/pop model than might be envisaged. Indeed, Freda' have endured frequent comparisons with **U2** because of their dense, multitextured sound. Like U2, Freda' have also suffered from being perceived as 'Christian rockers'. Specifically, they were awarded a Swedish Grammy as Best Religious Artists in the mid-80s. Their refusal to accept the award resulted in its subsequent abolition from the awards ceremony. Albums such as *Tusen Eldar* (A Thousand Fires), *Undan För Undan* (Little By Little) and *Alla Behöver* (Everybody Needs) have consecutively refined and expanded on their U2 influence, gradually producing greater commercial rewards as Freda' grow into a virile commercial domestic alternative to imported 'conscious rock'. While *Tusen Eldar* achieved gold status, their second and third albums each achieved platinum status.

● ALBUMS: *Tusen Eldar* (Record Station 1988) ★★★, *Undan För Undan* (Record Station 1990) ★★★, *Alla Behöver* (Record Station 1993) ★★★.

Freddie And The Dreamers

This Manchester, England–based 60s beat group, comprising Freddie Garrity (b. 14 November 1940, Manchester, England; vocals), Roy Crewsdon (b. 29 May 1941; guitar), Derek Quinn (b. 24 May 1942; guitar), Pete Birrell (b. 9 May 1941; bass) and Bernie Dwyer (b. 11 September 1940, Manchester, England d. 4 December 2002; drums), was briefly renowned for its mixture of beat music and comedy. Garrity formed the group in 1959, and it remained semiprofessional until passing a BBC audition in 1963. Although their debut, 'If You Gotta Make A Fool Of Somebody', was an R&B favourite (**James Ray** and **Maxine Brown**), subsequent releases were tailored to the quintet's effervescent insouciant image. 'I'm Telling You Now' and 'You Were Made For Me' also reached the UK Top 3, establishing the group at the height of the beat boom. Although Garrity displayed his songwriting skill with strong ballads such as 'Send A Letter To Me', his work was not used for a-side recordings. Further hits followed in 1964 with 'Over You', 'I Love You Baby', 'Just For You' and the seasonal favourite 'I Understand'.

The group's appeal declined in the UK, but early in 1965, they made a startling breakthrough in America where 'I'm Telling You Now' topped the charts. American audiences were entranced by Garrity's zany stage antics (which resulted in frequent twisted ankles) and eagerly demanded the name of his unusual dance routine. 'It's called the Freddie', he innocently replied. A US Top 20 hit rapidly followed with 'Do The Freddie'. Although the group appeared in a couple of movies, *Just For You* and *Cuckoo Patrol*, their main audience was in pantomime and cabaret. They broke up at the end of the decade, but Garrity and Birtles remained together in the children's show *Little Big Time*. Garrity revived the group during the mid-70s, with new personnel, for revival concerts at home and abroad. By the late 80s Garrity was attempting to establish an acting career, but has since returned to the cabaret circuit with a new line-up of the Dreamers.

● ALBUMS: *Freddie And The Dreamers* (Columbia 1963) ★★★, *You Were Made For Me* (Columbia 1964) ★★★, *Freddie And The Dreamers* (Mercury 1965) ★★★, *Sing-Along Party* (Columbia 1965) ★★, *Do The Freddie* (Mercury 1965) ★★, *Seaside Swingers* aka *Everyday's A Holiday* film

soundtrack (Mercury 1965) ★★, *Frantic Freddie* (Mercury 1965) ★★, *Freddie And The Dreamers In Disneyland* (Columbia 1966) ★, *Fun Lovin' Freddie* (Mercury 1966) ★★, *King Freddie And His Dreaming Knights* (Columbia 1967) ★★, *Oliver In The Underworld* (Starline 1970) ★★.
● COMPILATIONS: *The Best Of Freddie And The Dreamers* (EMI 1982) ★★★, *The Hits Of Freddie And The Dreamers* (EMI 1988) ★★★, *The Best Of Freddie And The Dreamers: The Definitive Collection* (EMI 1992) ★★★, *The Very Best Of Freddie And The Dreamers* (MFP 2001) ★★★, *As Bs & EPs* (EMI Gold 2004) ★★★.
● FILMS: *What A Crazy World* (1963), *Cuckoo Patrol* (1965).

Freddie Bell And The Bellboys
(see **Bell, Freddie, And The Bellboys**)

Freddie Foxxx
MC whose career has seen more highs and lows than most. By the age of 13 he had built his reputation as a talented freestyler in Westbury, Long Island, New York. He recorded a debut album in 1989, produced by **Eric B**, which promptly sank without trace. He was left to lick his wounds as the hip-hop populace forgot his name. However, a resurgence in his fortunes was kickstarted by collaborations with **KRS-One** ('Ruff Ruff'), then **Naughty By Nature** ('Hot Potato') before he was signed to **Queen Latifah**'s Epic subsidiary Flavor Unit. It was his third record deal. His first release for his new home was 'So Tough'. This boasted his sharply observed lyrics about the ghetto, 'We went from African kings / To Martin Luther King / Now they wanna make us all Rodney Kings'. He also produced videos that reminded would-be gangstas about the realities of prison life and helped found Dream House, a Brooklyn charity that helps local youths out of the negative downward spiral of poverty and homelessness.
● ALBUMS: *Freddie Foxxx Is Here* (1989) ★★★, *Crazy Like A Foxxx* (Flavor Unit/Epic 1994) ★★★.

Fredette, Carol
b. Bronx, New York City, USA. Fredette's father, an amateur pianist, encouraged her interest in singing from a very early age. At the age of seven she began studying piano, and although her first inclination was towards classical music, her older siblings drew her attention towards the popular singing of **Frank Sinatra** and to jazz artists such as **Chet Baker** and **Stan Kenton**. She began singing professionally when she was 18 and worked with big bands including those led by **Larry Elgart** and **Neal Hefti**. Over the years, she has worked with many noted jazz musicians, among them **Eddie Gomez**, **Ronnie Cuber**, **Hank Jones**, **Ron Carter** and **Al Cohn**. She was also heard by **Stan Getz**, who observed of her, 'She's as good as they come.' Another musician she encountered was pianist **Steve Kuhn** with whom she formed a long-lasting musical partnership that, by the end of the 90s, had endured for more than three decades.

Although based in and usually working in her home-town, appearing with great success at prestigious venues such as Fat Tuesdays, Michael's Pub and The Blue Note, Fredette has also travelled to Europe and elsewhere. In South America, her penchant for Brazilian music has proved to be very popular. Fredette's voice is rich and smooth, and she brings subtle dynamics to her extremely varied repertoire, imparting to the music an acute sense of the composers' intentions. Her handling of song lyrics is exceptionally good, and with

perfect diction she delivers carefully nuanced interpretations with wit, sophistication and a jazz artist's sense of phrasing.
● ALBUMS: with Steve Kuhn *In The Shadows* (Owl 1990) ★★★, *Everything I Need: Carol Fredette Sings Dave Frishberg And Bob Dorough* (Brownstone 1999) ★★★.

Fredriksson, Marie
(see **Roxette**)

Free
Formed in the midst of 1968's British blues boom, Free originally comprised **Paul Rodgers** (b. 17 December 1949, Middlesbrough, Cleveland, England; vocals), **Paul Kossoff** (b. 14 September 1950, Hampstead, London, England, d. 19 March 1976; guitar), **Andy Fraser** (b. 7 August 1952, London, England; bass) and Simon Kirke (b. 28 July 1949, Shrewsbury, Shropshire, England; drums). Despite their comparative youth, the individual musicians were seasoned performers, particularly Fraser, a former member of **John Mayall**'s Bluesbreakers. Kossoff and Kirke had backed **Champion Jack Dupree** as part of **Black Cat Bones**.

Free received early encouragement from **Alexis Korner**, but having completed an excellent, earthy debut album, 1968's *Tons Of Sobs*, the band began honing a more individual style with their second set. The injection of powerful original songs, including 'I'll Be Creeping', showed a maturing talent, while Rodgers' expressive voice and Kossoff's stinging guitar enhanced a growing reputation. The quartet's stylish blues rock reached its commercial peak on 1970's *Fire And Water*. This confident collection featured moving ballads—'Heavy Load', 'Oh I Wept'—and compulsive, up-tempo material, the standard-bearer of which was 'All Right Now'. An edited version of this soulful composition reached number 2 in the UK and number 4 in the USA in 1970, since which time the song has become one of pop's most enduring performances, making periodic reappearances in the singles chart.

Free's fourth album, *Highway*, revealed a more mellow perspective, highlighted by an increased use of piano at the expense of Kossoff's guitar. This was the result, in part, of friction within the band, a situation exacerbated when 'The Stealer' failed to emulate its predecessor's success. Free broke up in May 1971, paradoxically in the wake of another hit single, 'My Brother Jake' (UK number 4), but regrouped in January the following year when spin-off projects faltered, although Kossoff and Kirke's amalgamation (**Kossoff, Kirke, Tetsu And Rabbit**) proved fruitful. A sixth album, 1972's *At Last*, offered some of the unit's erstwhile fire and included another UK Top 20 entry, 'Little Bit Of Love'.

Kossoff's increasing ill health and Fraser's departure for the Sharks undermined any new-found confidence. A hastily convened line-up consisting of Rodgers, Kirke, **John 'Rabbit' Bundrick** (b. 21 November 1948, Houston, Texas, USA; keyboards) and Tetsu Yamauchi (b. 21 October 1946, Fukuokoa, Japan; bass) undertook a Japanese tour, but although the guitarist rejoined the quartet for several UK dates, his contribution to Free's final album, *Heartbreaker*, was muted. Kossoff embarked on a solo career in October 1972, and Wendel Richardson from **Osibisa** replaced him on a temporary basis. Despite a final Top 10 single, 'Wishing Well', in January 1973 Free had ceased to function by July of that year. Rodgers and Kirke subsequently formed **Bad Company**, while Yamauchi joined the **Faces**. Free represented all that was good with British rock in an era that was developing faster than sound. By mixing elements of blues, metal and melodic pop they carved a small niche that is destined to last.

● ALBUMS: *Tons Of Sobs* (Island 1968) ★★★, *Free* (Island 1969) ★★★, *Fire And Water* (Island 1970) ★★★★, *Highway* (Island 1970) ★★★, *Live* (Island 1971) ★★, *At Last* (Island 1972) ★★, *Heartbreaker* (Island 1973) ★★.

● COMPILATIONS: *The Free Story* (Island 1974) ★★★★, *Completely Free* (Island 1982) ★★★, *All Right Now* (Island 1991) ★★★, *Molton Gold: The Anthology* (Island 1993) ★★★★, *Walk In My Shadow: An Introduction To Free* (Island 1998) ★★★★, *Songs Of Yesterday* 5-CD box set (Island 2000) ★★★, *The Best Of Free: The Millennium Collection* (A&M 2002) ★★★★, *Chronicles* (Island 2005) ★★★★.

● DVD/VIDEOS: *Free* (Island Visual Arts 1989).

● FURTHER READING: *Heavy Load: Free*, David Clayton and Todd K. Smith.

Free As Air

Julian Slade and Dorothy Reynolds' follow-up to their 1954 mega-hit *Salad Days* opened at London's Savoy Theatre on 6 June 1957—at a time when *Salad Days*, itself, had nearly another three years to run. This musical play was set on the island of Terhou, a location the authors had based on Sark, one of the Channel Islands situated off the north coast of France. A somewhat philosophical piece, it told the story of the beautiful and wealthy Geraldine Melford (Gillian Lewis), who escapes from the press (and a persistent and unwelcome lover) and settles on this isolated island where she finally finds true happiness with one of the residents, Albert Posthumous (John Trevor). Along the way (and in line with the play's 'back-to-nature approach') she also foils the attempts of the sophisticated Jack Amersham (Gerald Harper) and the hard-nosed newspaper reporter (Josephine Tewson) to bring 'progress and civilization' to the island. Also in the cast were Michael Aldridge, who played the Lord Paul Posthumous, Dorothy Reynolds, Patricia Bredin and Leonard Rossiter, who became a household name in British television situation comedies such as *Rising Damp* and *The Fall And Rise Of Reginald Perrin*. As usual, Julian Slade and Dorothy Reynolds came up with a delightful and elegant score, the highlight of which was probably the charming 'Let The Grass Grow', sung by Michael Aldridge with two of the islanders, played by Roy Godfrey and Howard Goorney. The other songs included 'I'm Up Early', 'I've Got My Feet On The Ground', 'A Man From the Mainland', 'Nothing But Sea And Sky', 'Free As Air', 'The Girl From London', 'I'd Like To Be Like You', 'We're Holding Hands' and 'Terhou'. *Free As Air* closed on 7 June 1958 after a run of 417 performances, proving that there was still a place in the theatre for the homegrown product, despite the current popularity of imported American shows such as *My Fair Lady*, *Bells Are Ringing*, *Where's Charley?*—and in December 1958—*West Side Story*.

Free Association

Originally conceived by DJ/producer **David Holmes** (b. 14 February 1969, Belfast, Northern Ireland) as a means of performing his own studio creations live, the Free Association rapidly mutated into a recording entity in their own right. The group first surfaced as a predominantly instrumental collaboration between Holmes and programmer Steve Hilton on the former's 2002 mix album, *Come Get It I Got It*.

The Free Association's early atmospheric idents appeared alongside the DJ's mix of 60s and 70s funk and R&B from luminaries such as **Muddy Waters**, **Johnny Otis**, Betty Adams and the Peter Thomas Soundtrack Orchestra. For the Free Association's self-titled debut album, the band was extended to include sometime **Beta Band** collaborator Sean Reveron and Petra Jean Phillipson, a singer whose voice recalled that of **Billie Holiday**. Ironically, however, the Free Association's fried funk seemed oddly prosaic in comparison to Holmes' solo albums. Hilton is one half of 13 Amp project Children and notably worked alongside producer **David Arnold** as a programmer and cocomposer on the soundtrack to the James Bond movie *Die Another Day*.

● ALBUMS: *The Free Association* (13 Amp 2002) ★★★.

● COMPILATIONS: as David Holmes Introducing Free Association *Come Get It I Got It* (13 Amp 2002) ★★★.

Free I

b. Jeff Samuel Dixon, 31 March 1946, Davyton, Manchester, Jamaica, West Indies, d. 11 September 1987. In 1964 Dixon began working as a radio broadcaster on JBC where he built a strong following on his show, playing both local and American hits. His recording debut was at Studio One with **Coxsone Dodd** where he performed with **Marcia Griffiths** on 'Words' and released the solo hits 'Tickle Me' and 'The Rock'. A myriad of recordings followed under various guises as Soul Sam, Bigger D and Free I. With Treasure Isle he performed over **John Holt**'s 'I'll Be Lonely' and as JD The Rock for 'Superbad'. By the late 60s Free I found work in the USA broadcasting the sounds of Jamaica to a new audience. He was a staunch advocate of black pride, which was clearly evident in his transmissions. While in America, he combined his radio career with a successful foray into artist management. As with many Jamaicans, the homeland beckoned and by the early 80s he had returned to JBC to pursue his promotional work. He formed an allegiance with **Peter Tosh** and was invited to be the road manager on the singer's 1987 US tour. On 11 September of that year, Free I and his wife Joy were at Tosh's house when an armed robbery took place. Alongside Free I were Tosh, Carlton 'Santa' Davis, Joy Dixon, Marlene Tosh, Doc Brown and Michael. All were robbed and Tosh, Brown and, three days after the felony, Free I joined the number of fatalities as a result of the shooting. After the tragic incident, Free I was nominated for a citation as a broadcaster in the Jamaican Music Hall Of Fame.

Free Kitten

Founded in New York by **Sonic Youth** bass player Kim Gordon and former **Pussy Galore** guitarist Julie Cafritz, Free Kitten announced their arrival with a series of singles, including a version of **X-Ray Spex**'s 'Oh Bondage, Up Yours'. These were later collected on *Free Kitten*. The duo's brand of angry, 'post-punk' music was more forcibly unveiled on *Call Now*, a six-track set issued on Sonic Youth's Ecstatic Peace label. Elements of both musicians' antecedents were present, notably on the extended 'Falling Backwards'. Buoyed by the addition of Mark Ibold (bass) and Yoshimi (drums, trumpet, harmonica), Free Kitten undertook a UK tour to promote *Nice Ass*, on which the experimental nature of the group's music was placed within a more disciplined, rock-based structure. *Sentimental Education* was equally diverse, with the title track proving to be particularly challenging listening.

● ALBUMS: *Call Now* (Ecstatic Peace 1992) ★★★, *Unboxed* (Wiija 1994) ★★★, *Nice Ass* (Wiija 1995) ★★★, *Sentimental Education* (Wiija 1997) ★★★.
● COMPILATIONS: *Free Kitten* (Wiija 1994) ★★★.

Free Movement

Formed in Los Angeles, California, USA, in 1970, Free Movement made the **Billboard** Top 5 in the US with 'I've Found Someone On My Own'. The group was a sextet, some of whom had gospel singing experience, including Josephine Brown, Godoy Colbert, Cheryl Conley, Jennifer Gates, Adrian Jefferson and Claude Jefferson. The group made a demo record and was signed by **Decca Records** in 1971. The debut single took six months to climb the charts, eventually reaching number 5. Ironically, by the time the record was a hit, the group had left Decca and signed with **Columbia Records**, where they released an album and two singles.
● ALBUMS: *I've Found Someone On My Own* (Columbia 1972) ★★.

Free Music Production

FMP has been flying the flag for uncompromising free jazz and improvisation since 1969, when a musicians' collective comprising **Peter Brötzmann**, **Alexander von Schlippenbach**, **Peter Kowald** and Jost Gebers founded the company as both a record label and concert agency. Gebers was then still active as a bass player, but serious illness put paid to his performing career, and he became FMP's administrator, producer and finally its conscience. As they would say in Hollywood, Jost Gebers *is* FMP. He has produced over 300 albums for the label and recorded virtually every minute of the twice-yearly festivals that FMP organizes in Berlin. The recordings add up to a massive archive of European improvisation, a treasure trove for musicologists of the future. FMP's original plan, to document the growth of a strictly German free jazz, was modified as the musicians formed alliances with players of other nationalities. In the early years the main dialogues were with the British and Dutch free camps. Meanwhile, the music has become truly international, and one of FMP's major achievements has been the bringing together of European players with their American counterparts, including some of the black music trailblazers who initiated free jazz, **Cecil Taylor**, **Sunny Murray**, **Andrew Cyrille**, **Rashied Ali** and **Frank Wright**.
A festival organised around Taylor, juxtaposing the master pianist with the cream of Europe's improvisers, resulted in an 11-CD boxed set, *Cecil Taylor In Berlin '88*, which was showered in awards and nominated as the release of the year in jazz magazines throughout the world. (What makes this achievement particularly remarkable is that just a few years earlier FMP had been hit by financial crisis which almost destroyed them.) Until 1991, all FMP albums were recorded live, whether in concert or in the FMP studio, and reflected the natural ebb and flow of 'the living music' in its raw (sometimes very raw) state. **Evan Parker**'s *Process And Reality* departed from this tradition by using studio technology as another improvisational tool and multitracking the soprano saxophone. The striking results pointed to fresh possibilities for free music production.

Freed, Alan

b. 15 December 1922, Johnstown, Pennsylvania, USA, d. 20 January 1965, Palm Springs, California, USA. Freed was one of several key individuals who helped to create the audience for rock 'n' roll. As an influential disc jockey, he made enemies among the music business establishment by championing the cause of black artists, but his career ended tragically when he was found to be guilty of payola in 1962. The son of European immigrants, he played trombone in a high school band named the Sultans Of Swing. After US Army service, he secured his first radio job in 1946, playing classical records. He moved on to Akron, Ohio, to play contemporary pop material and in 1951 joined WJW Cleveland. There Freed hosted a show sponsored by local record store owner Leo Mintz, consisting of R&B originals rather than white pop cover versions. Entitled *Moondog's Rock 'N' Roll Party*, the show attracted large audiences of white teenagers who swamped a 1952 concert by the **Moonglows**, a group Freed had discovered and signed to his own short-lived Champagne label.
A near riot at the Moondog Coronation Ball the same year resulted in pressure from the local authorities, and Freed moved to New York and WINS in 1953. He was stopped from using the Moondog title after litigation with the blind Manhattan street musician **Moondog** (Louis Hardin). Still a champion of black artists such as **Chuck Berry** and **Fats Domino**, Freed hosted major live shows at the Paramount Theatre and in 1956–58 appeared in the movies *Rock Around The Clock*, *Rock Rock Rock*, *Don't Knock The Rock* and *Go Johnny Go*. However, with the rise of **Bill Haley**, **Elvis Presley** and **Pat Boone** (whose cover versions he frequently ignored), Freed's power as a disc jockey was weakened. In particular, he became a target of opponents of rock 'n' roll such as **Columbia Records**' A&R chief **Mitch Miller**, and when Freed refused to play Columbia releases he was fired by WINS. He then joined WABC and hosted a televised *Dance Party* show on WNEW-TV based on **Dick Clark**'s *American Bandstand*. Freed's arrest on a charge of inciting a riot at a Boston concert left him ill prepared to deal with the accusations of payola levelled by a congressional investigation in 1959. It emerged that independent labels had offered cash or publishing rights to Freed in return for the airplay they were denied by the prejudices of other radio stations. In 1962 Freed was found guilty of bribery, and this was followed by charges of tax evasion. He died of uremic poisoning in January 1965.
● ALBUMS: *The Big Beat* 10-inch album (MGM 1956) ★★★, *Alan Freed's Rock 'N Roll Dance Party, Volume 1* (Coral 1956) ★★★, *Alan Freed's Rock 'N Roll Dance Party, Volume 2* (Coral 1956) ★★★, *Go Go Go—Alan Freed's TV Record Hop* (Coral 1957) ★★★, *Rock Around The Block* (Coral 1958) ★★★, *Alan Freed Presents The King's Henchmen* (Coral 1958) ★★★, *The Alan Freed Rock & Roll Show* (Brunswick 1959) ★★★, *Alan Freed's Memory Lane* (End 1962) ★★.
● FURTHER READING: *Big Beat Heat: Alan Freed And The Early Years Of Rock 'N' Roll*, John A. Jackson.
● FILMS: *Rock Around The Clock* (1956), *Don't Knock The Rock* (1956), *Rock Rock Rock* (1956), *Mister Rock And Roll* (1957), *Go Johnny Go* (1958).

Freed, Arthur

b. Arthur Grossman, 9 September 1894, Charleston, South Carolina, USA, d. 12 April 1973, Los Angeles, California, USA. A distinguished film producer and lyricist, Freed was instrumental in elevating MGM Studios to its position as the king of the film school. His first job was as a demonstrator in a Chicago music shop where he met Minnie Marx, mother of the **Marx Brothers**. With her encouragement he quit his job and joined her sons' show as a singer. He later teamed up with **Gus Edwards** as a musical act in vaudeville. During this period he wrote many songs with different collaborators and had his first big success in 1923 with 'I Cried For You', written with **Gus Arnheim** and **Abe Lyman**. By the end of the 20s Freed was in Hollywood where he contributed the score to *The Broadway Melody* (1929) and *The Hollywood Revue Of 1929* amongst others. Throughout the 30s he continued to write songs for films such as *Montana Moon, Lord Byron Of Broadway, Those Three French Girls*, **The Big Broadcast**, *The Barbarian*, **Going Hollywood**, *Sadie McKee, Student Tour, A Night At The Opera, Broadway Melody Of 1936*, **San Francisco**, *Broadway Melody Of 1938* and **Babes In Arms**. As well as being a hit for all concerned, including its stars, **Judy Garland** and **Mickey Rooney**, the latter picture was significant in that it marked the beginning of Arthur Freed's second career, that of a producer.

During the next two decades the legendary Freed Unit produced most of MGM's outstanding musicals, including **The Wizard Of Oz, Strike Up The Band**, *Lady Be Good*, **Cabin In the Sky, Meet Me In St. Louis, The Ziegfeld Follies, The Pirate, The Barkleys Of Broadway, Easter Parade, Take Me Out To The Ball Game, Words And Music, Annie Get Your Gun, On The Town, An American In Paris** (1951 Oscar for Best Film), **Show Boat, Singin' In The Rain, The Band Wagon, Brigadoon, Kismet, Silk Stockings** and **Gigi** (1958 Oscar for Best Film). During his long stay at MGM, Freed's closest associate was musical arranger and songwriter **Roger Edens**. However, his chief composing partner was **Nacio Herb Brown**, with whom he wrote 'After Sundown', 'Alone', 'The Boy Friend,' 'Broadway Rhythm', 'You Were Meant For Me', 'The Wedding Of The Painted Doll', 'The Broadway Melody', 'Singin' In The Rain', 'Should I?', 'Temptation', 'Fit As A Fiddle', 'Pagan Love Song', 'Alone', 'I Got A Feelin' You're Foolin', 'You Are My Lucky Star', ' Lovely Lady', 'Good Morning', 'All I Do Is Dream Of You' and many others. These were all written for various films before Freed devoted himself to producing, although several of their most popular numbers were reprised in *Singin' In The Rain*, (1951), including the title song which was originally introduced in *Hollywood Revue Of 1929*. For *Singin' In The Rain,* Freed and Brown wrote a new song, 'Make 'Em Laugh', which **Donald O'Connor** immediately made his own. Freed's other collaborators included **Al Hoffman**, **Harry Warren** and **Burton Lane**. For a number of years in the 60s Freed was president of the American Academy of Motion Picture Arts and Sciences, from whom he received the Irving Thalberg Award in 1951 and a further award in 1967 'for distinguished service to the Academy and the production of six top-rated Awards telecasts'.

Arthur Freed's brother, Ralph Freed (b. 1 May 1907, Vancouver, Canada, d. 13 February 1973, California, USA), was also a lyricist and contributed songs, written mainly with composers Burton Lane and **Sammy Fain**, to several movies during the 30s and 40s. These included *Champagne Waltz* (1937), *College Holiday, Double Or Nothing, Swing High, Swing Low, Cocoanut Grove, She Married A Cop*, **Babes On Broadway, Ziegfeld Girl, Du Barry Was A Lady, Thousands Cheer**, *Thrill Of Romance, No Leave, No Love,*

Two Sisters From Boston and **Ziegfeld Follies** (1946). One of his numbers, 'The Worry Song' (with Fain), was featured in the renowned live, action sequence in **Anchors Aweigh** in which **Gene Kelly** danced with Jerry the cartoon mouse. His other songs included 'How About You?', 'You Leave Me Breathless', 'Love Lies', 'Smarty', 'Little Dutch Mill', 'Hawaiian War Chant' and 'Who Walks In When I Walk Out?'.

● FURTHER READING: *The Movies' Greatest Musicals—Produced In Hollywood USA By The Freed Unit*, Hugh Fordin.

Freed, Ralph
(see **Freed, Arthur**)

Freedley, Vinton
(see **Aarons, Alex A.**)

Freedom (70s)
This UK rock act was formed in 1967 by two former members of **Procol Harum**, Bobby Harrison (b. 22 June 1939, East Ham, London, England; drums/vocals) and Ray Royer (b. 8 October 1945, the Pinewoods, Essex, England; guitar), with Steve Shirley (bass/vocals) and Mike Lease (keyboards). Together, they recorded a little-known soundtrack album to the Dino De Laurentiis–associated movie *Black On White (Nero Su Bianco)*. The second line-up of the band, featuring Harrison, Steve Jolly (guitar), Peter Dennis (vocals, bass, keyboards), Walt Monaghan and ex–Washington DCs and the Fabulous Telstars' guitarist Roger Saunders (b. 9 March 1947, Essex, England, d. 2000; guitar, piano, vocals), was a highly respected power unit who made an impact with concert audiences during late 60s British blues boom. The ever-restless Harrison sealed the band's fate when he decided to make a solo album. Ironically, 1970's *Funkest* eclipsed all of Freedom's efforts in total sales. The band finally petered out in 1972, following which Harrison formed **Snafu**.

● ALBUMS: *Nero Su Bianco* film soundtrack (Atlantic 1969) ★★, *At Last* (Metronome 1970) ★★★, *Freedom* (Probe 1970) ★★★, *Through The Years* (Cotillion 1971) ★★, *Freedom Is More Than A Word* (Vertigo 1972) ★★.

Freedom (90s)
Comprising Mark Dean (vocals) and Andy Jack (keyboards), this Dublin, Eire, duo originally called themselves Blue Boy and then Raw during their 'heavy metal phase'. By the time they had become Freedom they had attuned their style to a slick teen pop presentation which saw them signed by **Parlophone Records**. However, their debut single, the innocuous 'Obsession', failed to chart when released in November 1990, and their brief flirtation with teenage pop magazines such as *Smash Hits* never blossomed into a lasting relationship.

Freedom Of Speech
Comprising Luke Losey, Mickey Mann and Stika, UK group Freedom Of Speech are proponents of what has come to be known in dance clubs of the mid-90s as 'darkside', a style of **techno** that attacks the conscious and subconscious with images culled from horror books, nursery rhymes and Kafka-esque noises. The trio met on the **Shamen**'s Synergy tour in 1987, and each member has subsequently made a sizeable contribution to the evolution of **dance music**. Losey prepared lights for stage shows from the **KLF** and **Curve**, Mann coproduced an album with **Orbital** and continued to

organize warehouse parties, often in conjunction with the Mutoid Waste Company. The trio came together as part of the Midi Circus tour and made their debut with 'Surveillance', which appeared on **Planet Dog**'s *Feed Your Head* compilation. There was a big brother theme to back it up, the single built on samples of surveillance workers. They also released 'X-Beats', which preceded their debut album. 'We're into the kind of paranoia and bleakness of emotions which **Joy Division** used to put across', they noted. The 'negative vibes for the future of the world' syndrome was informed in part by a visit to Russia when supporting the Shamen on tour.

● ALBUMS: *Art Of The State* (1994) ★★★.

Freeez

This British funk group was led by John Rocca (b. 23 September 1960, London, England), and included Peter Maas (bass), Andy Stennet (keyboards) and Paul Morgan (drums). Rocca, a former van salesman for the dance music specialist shop Disc Empire, formed the group in 1978. They released their first single, 'Keep In Touch', on their own Pink Rythm (sic) label (one of the first British acts to form their own label), and it narrowly missed the UK Top 40 in 1980 when picked up by Calibre. After moving to **Beggars Banquet Records** in 1981, they hit the UK Top 10 with 'Southern Freeze', which included vocals by Ingrid Mansfield-Allman (b. London, England). The album of the same name reached the Top 20. The group expanded to a seven piece with the addition of Gordon Sullivan, George Whitmore, and new vocalist Alison Gordon. Later reduced to the basic duo of Rocca and Maas, they had their biggest success in 1983 with 'I.O.U.', written and produced in the USA by **Arthur Baker** with mixing assistance from **Jellybean**. In 1985, Rocca and Stennet recorded as Pink Rhythm while Freeez continued with Maas, Morgan, Billy Crichton and Louis Smith and recorded on Siren in 1986. As a solo artist Rocca had a US dance number 1 with 'I Want To Be Real' in 1987; the same year a remix of Freeez's 'I.O.U.' on Citybeat made the UK Top 30. Rocca later recorded on Who'd She Coo and Cobra (where he re-recorded 'Southern Freeze') and reappeared in 1991 as Midi Rain on the Vinyl Solution label.

● ALBUMS: *Southern Freeze* (Beggars Banquet 1981) ★★★, *Gonna Get You* (Beggars Banquet 1983) ★★★.

Freeform

b. Simon Pyke, 1977, Swindon, Wiltshire, England. The Brighton-based Pyke has released his experimental electronic music on several of the genre's leading labels, including **Warp Records**, **Ninja Tune Records**, Language, Skam, Worm Interface, Leaf, and Law And Auder. In his own terms, he describes his productions as 'junk-funk' and 'super-acoustic'.

Pyke's passion for electronic music formed when he received a toy Casio sampler for his twelfth birthday and began making beats from household sounds. He also assembled a makeshift studio from equipment he collected from car boot sales. At 17 he started to assail the record store Ambient Soho with a deluge of cassettes of his own recordings. In 1995 Pyke made his debut with *Elastic Speakers* on the Ambient Soho's in-house record label, Worm Interface. In the same year, he released *The Free EP*, which was later sampled by **Howie B.** for his production of a **U2** single. He also made his debut live appearance with **Autechre** at a pub

in north London before going on to support the acclaimed **techno** act on a 30-date tour around the UK and Eire. *Heterarchy*, a limited edition CD again on Worm Interface, saw Pyke exploring the more abstract elements of his music. *Pattern Tub* was released in 1998 and presented Pyke's vision of a 'super-acoustic' sound and incorporated vocals and flute. *Me Shape* appeared the following year and, according to Pyke, was 'created for, between, and after live sets'. In the same year, he began studying for a degree in sound engineering and released the well-received *Green Park*.

The turning point for Pyke and Freeform came in 2001. He toured Vietnam and China, collecting ambient sounds or 'found sounds' on a Mini-Disc player. These formed the backbone of his acclaimed *Audiotourism, Original Music: Vietnam And China*, which was released on the Belgian label Quatermass. Highly praised by the critics, it was followed by a remix album that included reworkings by **Bill Laswell**, Autechre and others. After relocating to Brighton in 2002, Pyke established his own label, Freefarm and released *Human* on Skam. The following year's *Condensed* collected some his most successful recordings.

● ALBUMS: *Elastic Speakers* (Worm Interface 1995) ★★★, *Heterarchy* (Worm Interface 1996) ★★★★, *Pattern Tub* (Headphone 1998) ★★★★, *Me Shape* (Sprawl 1999) ★★★, *Green Park* (Sub Rosa 1999) ★★★, *Audiotourism, Original Music: Vietnam And China* (Quatermass 2001) ★★★, *Human* (Skam 2002) ★★★.

● COMPILATIONS: *Audiotourism: Reinterpretations* (Quatermass 2002) ★★★, *Late Surfaces: 1990–2000* (Freefarm 2002) ★★★, *Condensed* (Nonplace 2003) ★★★★.

Freeland, Adam

b. 7 August 1973, Welwyn Garden City, England. Like James Lavelle of **Mo' Wax Records**, Freeland rose to prominence as a **dance music** *wünderkind*, becoming a highly successful, DJ, remixer, club promoter and record label boss while still in his early twenties. Originally a **deep house** DJ, Freeland became known for seamlessly blending hip-hop and **electro** into his sets. He pioneered 'nu-school breaks'—break beats with an eclectic range of influences including **techno**, drum 'n' bass and world music. Although DJing on the London club scene from 1992, his first mix compilation, *Coastal Breaks*, was not released until 1996. A double CD comprising 32 tracks, it received high praise from the critics and raised Freeland's profile, enabling him to tour in the UK and the USA. He won the admiration of many respected UK DJs such as **Carl Cox**, **Sasha**, the **Chemical Brothers** and **Andy Weatherall**. He supported Cox on several dates of his F.A.C.T. 2 world tour.

In 1997 he ran a successful night, 'Friction', in Soho, London, with DJ friends **Rennie Pilgrem** and **Tayo**. In that year, he also released a single with his friend Kevin Beber, 'Number 43 With Steamed Rice Please' under the name Tsunami One. The popularity of the track in the clubs led to remix work for the **Orb**, **DeeJay Punk-Roc**, Headrillaz and **Orbital**. Freeland began 1998 by touring Australia with **DJ Krush**, **Pressure Drop** and **José Padilla**. *Coastal Breaks 2* was released and was a critical and commercial success. Further mix albums on the Marine Parade label preceded a surprise move by the DJ, which saw him forming his own band, Freeland, and performing a series of excellent live shows. The band's debut album, *Now & Them*, was released in September 2003.

● ALBUMS: with Freeland *Now & Them* (Marine Parade 2003) ★★★.

● COMPILATIONS: *Coastal Breaks* (Avex 1996) ★★★★, *Coastal Breaks 2* (React 1998) ★★★★, *Tectonics* (Marine Parade 2000) ★★★, *On Tour* (Marine Parade 2001) ★★★, *Fabriclive.16* (Fabric 2004) ★★★, *Back To Mine* (DMC 2005) ★★★.

Freelon, Nnenna

b. Nnenna Chinyere Freelon, 28 July 1954, Cambridge, Massachusetts, USA. Although Freelon had displayed an interest in singing from an early age, she first graduated from Simmons College, then had a career in social services in Durham, North Carolina. She also raised three children before being encouraged to consider a career in music. She studied with **Yusef Lateef**, developing her singing through listening to horn players. For several years she had a regular working band with Bill Anschell (piano), John Brown (bass) and Woody Williams (drums). Her breakthrough followed an informal session at the start of the 90s in which she sat in with **Ellis Marsalis**. Her recording debut came in 1992 and attracted some attention although there were some critical misgivings over perceived similarities to **Sarah Vaughan**'s singing style. Her second album was more favourably received, and by her third even the most recalcitrant observers were forced to admit that hers was an exceptional talent that had at last found its own voice.

For her repertoire, Freelon's draws not only upon jazz but also pop and folk origins, transmuting even the latter forms into her own distinctive conception of jazz. A change of labels in early 1996 found Freelon making a much more personal mark than before and her second Concord Jazz set, 1998's *Maiden Voyage*, displayed her interest in the role of women in music and in society in general. In 2000 Freelon made her acting debut in *What Women Want* and released her first self-produced set, *Soulcall. Tales Of Wonder* in 2002 was her own tribute to the songs of one of her idols, **Stevie Wonder**. Some indication of the regard in which she is held in the jazz community can be gained from the musicians who have joined her for gigs and recording sessions. Among these artists are Mike Abene, **Kenny Barron**, **Joe Beck**, **Herbie Hancock**, **Christian McBride**, **Bob Mintzer**, **Lewis Nash** and **Kirk Whalum**. Freelon's voice is rich in emotional qualities, and she employs a full-bodied sound. Nevertheless, when the music demands, she ably finds a measure cool yet sensual detachment that is especially persuasive on ballads.

● ALBUMS: *Nnenna Freelon* (Columbia 1992) ★★★, *Heritage* (Columbia 1993) ★★★★, *Listen* (Columbia 1994) ★★★, *Shaking Free* (Concord Jazz 1996) ★★★★, *Maiden Voyage* (Concord Jazz 1998) ★★★★, *Soulcall* (Concord Jazz 2000) ★★★★, *Tales Of Wonder* (Concord Jazz 2002) ★★★, *Live* (Concord Jazz 2003) ★★, *Blueprint Of A Lady* (Concord Jazz 2005) ★★★.

● FILMS: *What Women Want* (2000).

Freeman, Alan

b. 6 July 1927, Australia. One of the most familiar personalities of UK radio, the disc jockey Alan 'Fluff' Freeman arrived on British shores in 1957 for a holiday. Previously he had been employed as an announcer on Melbourne's 3KZ station. His earlier ambitions had been to follow his operatic idols into singing, but when he discovered his baritone was not of sufficient quality to make that a realistic career choice, he opted for a job with which he could combine radio and music. Indeed, his early 50s radio shows in Australia combined the roles of presenter, reader of commercials and impassioned crooner of various *ad hoc* selections. Unimpressed at first by existing British radio, he opted instead for a position at **Radio Luxembourg**, where he was posted as a summer relief disc jockey. By 1961 he had transferred to the BBC Light Programme with his *Records Around Five* show, introducing his signature tune, 'At The Sign Of The Swinging Cymbal'. During September of the same year he introduced *Pick Of The Pops*, initially as part of a Saturday evening show entitled *Trad Tavern*, before the slot became a permanent show the following year. Freeman presented this well-loved programme until 1972.

An inveterate champion of hard rock and heavy metal, he quickly attracted a following who liked their presenters unpretentious. He eventually resigned from BBC Radio 1 (as it had become during his time with the corporation) in 1978, to the horror of many of those listeners. Within 12 months, however, he had transferred to London's Capital Radio frequency, enjoying further popularity through his Saturday morning *Pick Of The Pops Take Two* slot. In the meantime, Freeman had become a fixture of British television screens via appearances on **Top Of The Pops** and his own show, *All Systems Freeman*. In 1986 he had a small role in the film **Absolute Beginners**. In January 1989 Freeman returned to Radio 1, broadcasting on Sunday afternoons until the end of 1992. When *Pick Of The Pops* finally ended with 30 years service behind it, the BBC commemorated the occasion with a special 'Fluff day'. Moving to Virgin Radio in 1996 he was honoured by his colleagues with the Music Industry Trusts award. Following a brief return to the BBC in the late 90s Freeman's health began to let him down, and he voluntarily handed over the *Pick Of The Pops* mantle when he was forced to enter a nursing home. Freeman is one of the legends of UK radio, with a rich and unforgettable voice.

Freeman, Bobby

b. 13 June 1940, San Francisco, California, USA. Freeman is generally recognized as his home city's first rock 'n' roll star by virtue of 'Do You Want To Dance'. This 1958 smash hit was later immortalized by the **Beach Boys** and **Cliff Richard**. The singer enjoyed further success in 1964 with 'C'mon And Swim', a dance-craze novelty song produced and co-written by **Sly Stone**. Freeman later elected to pursue his singing career at a local topless club, but later appearances at the annual San Francisco Bay Area Music ('Bammy') awards showed him an able performer.

● ALBUMS: *Do You Wanna Dance?* (Jubilee 1958) ★★, *Twist With Bobby Freeman* (Jubilee 1962) ★★, *C'mon And S-W-I-M* (Autumn 1964) ★★, *The Lovable Style Of Bobby Freeman* (King 1965) ★★, *Get In The Swim With Bobby Freeman* (Josie 1965) ★★.

● COMPILATIONS: *The Best Of Bobby Freeman* (Sequel 1992) ★★★.

Freeman, Bud

b. Lawrence Freeman, 3 April 1906, Chicago, Illinois, USA, d. 15 March 1991, Chicago, Illinois, USA. Freeman's early career found him in company with **Jimmy McPartland**, **Frank Teschemacher** and other members of the Austin High School Gang. Having set out playing the C-melody saxophone, Freeman switched to tenor in 1925 and quickly established a reputation on that instrument as one of the few genuine rivals to **Coleman Hawkins**. Through the late 20s and early 30s he worked in numerous bands, recording extensively and consolidating his reputation. He gravitated into big bands, playing with **Joe Haymes**, **Ray Noble**, **Paul Whiteman**, **Tommy Dorsey**, **Benny Goodman** and others, but he preferred a different kind of jazz and in 1939 formed his own Summa Cum Laude Orchestra, which delighted audiences in New York during its brief life. From 1940 Freeman played in various bands, led his own short-lived big band, and by the middle of the decade had settled into leading a small group at **Eddie Condon**'s New York club. For the rest of his career Freeman played as a freelance, sometimes leading, sometimes as sideman, touring the USA and Europe. A confirmed Anglophile, he lived in London in the 70s and even managed to 'look' British. In 1980, Freeman returned to live in his native Chicago, but by the end of the decade his health had failed. By the start of the decade he was almost blind, hospitalized and frail, and he died early in 1991.

Freeman's masterly solo on his 1933 recording of 'The Eel' displayed his qualities to the full. In later years some detractors remarked that he spent the rest of his career repeating that solo. While it is true that his playing style did not subsequently alter very much, such adverse criticism failed to recognize that like his great but very different contemporary Coleman Hawkins, Freeman had achieved such a pinnacle of excellence that wholesale change was pointless. In fact, Freeman's later recordings show him to have an inventive mind that, allied to a fluent delivery, make all his work a delight to the ear.

● ALBUMS: *Wolverine Jazz* 10-inch album (Decca 1950) ★★★, *Comes Jazz* 10-inch album (Columbia 1950) ★★★, *Nice And Easy* (Bethlehem 1955) ★★★, *Chicago—Austin High School Jazz In Hi-Fi* (RCA Victor 1957) ★★★, *Bud Freeman & His Summa Cum Laude Trio* (Dot 1959) ★★★, *Midnight Session* (Dot 1960) ★★★, *The Bud Freeman All-Stars Featuring Shorty Baker* (Swingville 1960) ★★★★, *Something To Remember You By* (Black Lion 1962) ★★★, *Chicago* (Black Lion 1962) ★★★, *Two Guitars And A Horn* (Stash 1962) ★★★, *Something Tender—Bud Freeman And Two Guitars* (United Artists 1963) ★★★, with Cliff Leeman *The Joy Of Sax* (Chiaroscuro 1974) ★★★, *The Compleat Bud Freeman* (Monmouth 1970) ★★★★, *Superbud* (77 1974) ★★★, *Song Of The Tenor* (Philips 1975) ★★★, with Buddy Tate *Two Beautiful* (Circle 1976) ★★★★, with Bucky Pizzarelli *Bucky And Bud* (Flying Dutchman 1977) ★★★, *Last Night When We Were Young* (Black & Blue 1978) ★★★, *The Real Bud Freeman* (Principally Jazz 1984) ★★★, *Keep Smilin' At Trouble* (Affinity 1987) ★★★, *California Session* 1982 recording (Jazzology 1997) ★★★.

● COMPILATIONS: *Chicago Styled, Vol. 1* 1935–40 recordings (Swaggie) ★★★★, *Chicagoans In New York* 1935–40 recordings (Dawn Club) ★★★★, *1928–1938* (Classics) ★★★★, *1939–1940* (Classics) ★★★, *1945–1946* (Classics) ★★★, *See What The Boys In The Back Room Will Have* 1940 recordings (IAJRC) ★★★★, *Swingin' With The Eel* (ASV/Living Era 1998) ★★★, *All Star Swing Sessions* (Prestige 2004) ★★★★.

● FURTHER READING: *Crazeology: The Autobiography Of A Chicago Jazzman*, Bud Freeman with Robert Wolf. *You Don't Look Like A Musician*, Bud Freeman. *If You Know Of A Better Life, Please Tell Me*, Bud Freeman.

Freeman, Chico

b. Earl Lavon Freeman Jnr., 17 July 1949, Chicago, Illinois, USA. Freeman started out playing trumpet but while at university switched to tenor saxophone, the instrument played by his father **Von Freeman**. After university, where he studied music education, he played in R&B bands before changing direction and working with **Muhal Richard Abrams** and the Association for the Advancement of Creative Musicians (**AACM**). In the mid-to late 70s he continued his studies, meanwhile working with many leading contemporary jazz artists, including **Elvin Jones, Sun Ra** and **Don Pullen**. In the early 80s he recorded *Freeman & Freeman* with his father, toured as leader of his own small group, and also appeared with **Wynton Marsalis, Cecil McBee, Jack DeJohnette** and others. Interestingly, Freeman's striking playing style blends the post-Coltrane tradition of long angular lines with the rougher-toned urgency of his R&B schooling into a sound that is identifiably his own. The 1979 set *Spirit Sensitive* is one of the finest collections of ballads by a modern tenor player, but by the late 80s Freeman was devoting most of his time to his fusion band Brainstorm. He was also a member of the occasional supergroup, the Leaders, alongside alto saxophonist **Arthur Blythe**, trumpeter **Lester Bowie**, pianist **Kirk Lightsey**, drummer **Famoudou Don Moye** and bass player McBee.

● ALBUMS: *Morning Prayer* (India Navigation 1976) ★★★, *Beyond The Rain* (Contemporary 1977) ★★★★, *Chico* (India Navigation 1977) ★★★, *Kings Of Mali* (India Navigation 1978) ★★★, *The Outside Within* (India 1978) ★★★, *Spirit Sensitive* (India Navigation 1979) ★★★★, *No Time Left* (Black Saint 1979) ★★★★, *Peaceful Heart, Gentle Spirit* (Contemporary 1980) ★★★, with Von Freeman *Freeman & Freeman* (India Navigation 1981) ★★, *Destiny's Dance* (Contemporary 1981) ★★★★, *Tradition In Transition* (Elektra 1982) ★★, *Tangents* (Elektra 1984) ★★★, *The Search* (India Navigation 1984) ★★★, *Groovin' Late* (Castle 1986) ★★★, *The Pied Piper* (Blackhawk 1986) ★★★★, with the Leaders *Mudfoot* (Black Hawk 1986) ★★★, with the Leaders *Out Here Like This* (Black Saint 1987) ★★★, *Live At Ronnie Scott's* (Hendring 1987) ★★, *You'll Know When You Get There* (Black Saint 1988) ★★★, *Tales Of Ellington* (Blackhawk 1988) ★★★, with the Leaders *Unforseen Blessings* (Black Saint 1989) ★★★, *Luminous* (Jazz House 1989) ★★★, *Up And Down* (Black Saint 1990) ★★★, *The Mystical Dreamer* (In And Out 1990) ★★★, with Brainstorm *Sweet Explosion* (In And Out 1990) ★★★, *Threshold* (In And Out 1993) ★★★, *The Unspoken Word* (Jazz House 1994) ★★★★, *Focus* (Contemporary 1995) ★★★★, *Still Sensitive* (India Navigation 1996) ★★★★, *The Emissary* (Clarity 1997) ★★★, with Von Freeman *Von Freeman's 75th Birthday Celebration: Live At The Blue Note* (Half Note 1999) ★★★, with Guataca *Oh, By The Way . . .* (Challenge 2002) ★★★.

Freeman, Ernie

b. 16 August 1922, Cleveland, Ohio, USA, d. 16 May 1981. A noted pianist, arranger and producer, Freeman enjoyed a series of minor hits during the late 50s and early 60s. His chart entries included 'Dumplins' (1957) and 'Indian Love Call' (1959), but his biggest success came with a cover version of **Bill Justis**' smash 'Raunchy'. Although the original reached the US Top 3, Freeman's interpretation peaked at number 12. He recorded as **B. Bumble And The Stingers** on all of this act's releases, bar 'Nut Rocker', before embarking on a successful session career. Freeman appeared on material by **Frank Sinatra**, **Dean Martin** and **Connie Francis** and later became musical director with the **Reprise Records** label, a post he held for 10 years. Freeman retired during the 70s and died as the result of a heart attack.

● ALBUMS: *Ernie Freeman Plays Irving Berlin* (Imperial 1957) ★★, *Jivin' Around* (Imperial 1957) ★★★, *Ernie Freeman Plays: Dreaming With Freeman* (Imperial 1958) ★★★, *Dark At The Top Of The Stairs* (Imperial 1959) ★★★, *Twistin' Time* (Imperial 1960) ★★★, *The Stripper* (Imperial 1962) ★★, *Limbo Dance Party* (Liberty 1963) ★★, *Comin' Home, Baby* (Liberty 1963) ★★★, *Ernie Freeman Hit Maker* (Dunhill 1968) ★★.

● COMPILATIONS: *Raunchy: Ernie Freeman And His Combo* (Ace 1997) ★★★★.

Freeman, George

b. 10 April 1927, Chicago, Illinois, USA. Based in Chicago throughout his career, guitarist Freeman has a much lower profile than other family members. During the late 40s, he played in the house band at Chicago's Pershing Hotel alongside his brothers, drummer Eldridge 'Bruz' Freeman and saxophonist **Von Freeman**. There, he accompanied visiting jazzmen such as **Lester Young** and **Charlie Parker**, appearing with the latter on the rare, and poorly recorded, *One Night In Chicago*. In 1950, together with his brothers and **Ahmad Jamal**, he formed a quartet, Jamal later being replaced by **Andrew Hill**. Thereafter, Freeman's profile was low, and perhaps from choice, he played only occasionally in Chicago clubs and from time to time made records. Among leaders with whom he recorded are **Gene 'Jug' Ammons** and **Richard 'Groove' Holmes**. In the late 70s Freeman recorded with **Johnny Griffin**, playing on the outstanding 1978 session that produced *Bush Dance*.

Despite his avoidance of the limelight, Freeman has many faithful fans in Chicago, and his records, some of which appear on the specialist label Southport Records, prove that he has the talent to appeal to a much wider audience. His playing is adorned by touches of R&B and funk from the 50s atmosphere in which he came through. Brother Von appeared on his sought after *Franticdiagnosis,* as did **Charles Earland**. Although Freeman's style and sound carry echoes of the trail-blazing swing to bop transition of **Charlie Christian**, there is about his best work a distinctive tongue-in-cheek quirkiness. **Chico Freeman** is his nephew.

● ALBUMS: *Birth Sign* (Delmark 1969) ★★★, *New Improved Funk* (Groove Merchant 1973) ★★★★, *Man & Woman* (Groove Merchant 1974) ★★★, *Franticdiagnosis* (Bamboo 1976) ★★★★, *All In The Game* (LRC 1977) ★★★, *Rebellion* (Southport 1995) ★★★, *George Burns!* (Southport 1999) ★★★, *At Long Last George* (Savant 2001) ★★★.

Freeman, Louis

b. 2 December 1893, Glasgow, Scotland, d. 9 March 1994, Glasgow, Scotland. A classically trained jazz pianist of the dance band era, Freeman's spirit was rarely contained by location or age, and up until his death at the age of 100 he would regularly employ a nurse and ambulance to conduct him to venues that were otherwise inaccessible. The progeny of the Jewish exodus from Russia following the tsarist pogroms, Freeman entered the musical arena by winning the Royal Scottish Academy Of Music's Bechstein Gold Medal in 1912. Later he became the proprietor of a musical instrument shop in Glasgow's Renfield Street, where his basement was a meeting ground for local jazzers investigating the newest US imports from artists like **Red Nichols** and the **Dorsey Brothers**. Local musicians like Alan Ferguson, **Billy Munn** and Issy Duman were among the regular members of the congregation, the owner having already journeyed to the USA, where he played vaudeville and met **Al Jolson**. In addition to his own Glasgow-based band, Freeman also acted as musical director for the Walter Donaldson Shipping Company, booking artists for their cruises (including **Tommy McQuater** and **George Chisholm**). He continued to be a respected member of the Scottish musical community up to his death.

Freeman, Porky

b. Quilla Hugh Freeman, 29 June 1916, near Vera Cruz, Missouri, USA. The Freeman's, who eked a living from a small farm, were a musical family, and Quilla began playing piano, fife, ocarina and harmonica as a young child. In 1928 he added banjo and trumpet and played in the school band, soon adding fiddle, mandolin and, his main instrument, guitar to the list. In 1931 he dropped out of school and hoboed around for a time before forming a quartet that played on a Jefferson City station. In 1933 he returned home and became a member of a trio, Raul Hatfield And His Ava Wildcats, on KGBX Springfield, Missouri, where he made his first recordings. After again deciding to return home to complete his education, he performed locally. In 1937 he worked on KWTO Springfield sometimes as member of the Brownlow Boys and sometimes with Otie and **Sue Thompson**, who gave him the nickname of Porky. He later played guitar and trumpet with Doc James and toured with the Weaver Brothers before playing with **Bill Boyd** and **Roy Newman** in Fort Worth, Texas.

In 1942 he returned to KGBX Springfield, where he became a regular on the Slim Wilson Show before playing with Bill Nicholls in Los Angeles. During this time he had become one of the first musicians to feature boogie woogie style guitar music, and in 1943 he recorded 'Porky's Boogie Woogie On The Strings' for the Morris Lee label, which became the first country boogie instrumental. It proved popular, and in 1944 he was given a contract with ARA, where he recorded as the Porky Freeman Trio. He played on **Jack Guthrie**'s hit recording of 'Oklahoma Hills' and his reputation saw him play and tour with numerous top acts including the **Sons Of The Pioneers**, **Spade Cooley**, **Hank Penny**, **Jimmy Wakely**, **Stuart Hamblen** and many others. He was also much in demand as a session musician. In September 1945 the Porky Freeman Trio, which comprised **Merle Travis**, Tommy Sergeant and Alan Barker, recorded two versions of 'Boogie Woogie Boy'. Freeman played lead guitar, and Travis added the vocal. The first take was released on ARA and the second with a variation on the lyrics later on 4 Star Records. That Porky was used as lead guitarist when Travis was on the recordings emphasizes the instrumental brilliance of Freeman.

Throughout the 50s, 60s and 70s, he played and/or recorded with many popular acts in the Los Angeles area. Freeman, who retired to make his home in West Hollywood, continued to perform locally into the late 80s. In 1987 the German Cattle label released an album of 21 of Freeman's 40s recordings, including a version of the instrumental that started his recording career. The recordings with Travis were included in a 5-CD set of Merle Travis' work by **Bear Family Records** in 1994.

● COMPILATIONS: *The Guitar Boogie That Startled The World—Porky Freeman 1944–49 recordings* (Cattle 1987) ★★★.

Freeman, Russ (guitar)

b. Russell Donald Freeman, 11 February 1960, Nashville, Tennessee, USA. Freeman began playing guitar early in life. After attending Cal Arts and UCLA he worked for a while as a studio musician. He made a rather obscure recording debut in 1985 but two years later was engaged for another recording session for which an all-star group was assembled. This band, which originally included **Kenny G.** and **David Benoit**, Freeman named the **Rippingtons**. This recording proved to be very popular with radio stations and the younger generation of jazz fans, filling as it did the jazz pop crossover niche with considerable flair. Encouraged by the sales of *Moonlighting*, Freeman formed a regular band using the same generic name and began touring and recording, mostly for **GRP Records**. In 1996 Freeman joined with record producer Andi Howard to form Peak Records, which enjoys an operational association with **Windham Hill Records**. Throughout the existence of the Rippingtons, most of the band's repertoire has been composed by Freeman, effectively drawing upon jazz, pop and Latin concepts to create a smooth, radio-friendly jazz style. His solo recordings have adhered to the same formula. He reunited in 2004 to tour and record again with Benoit.

● ALBUMS: *Nocturnal Playground* (Brainchild 1985) ★★, with David Benoit *The Benoit/Freeman Project* (GRP 1993) ★★★, *Holiday* (GRP 1995) ★★★, with Craig Chaquico *From The Redwoods To The Rockies* (Windham Hill 1998) ★★★, *Drive* (Peak 2002) ★★★, with Benoit *Benoit/Freeman Project 2* (Peak 2004) ★★★.

Freeman, Russ (piano)

b. Russell Donald Freeman, 28 May 1926, Chicago, Illinois, USA, d. 27 June 2002, Las Vegas, Nevada, USA. Emerging onto the west coast jazz scene in the late 40s, Freeman's piano style was typically bop orientated. He played with many important west coast musicians during the next few years including **Art Pepper**, **Shorty Rogers**, **Chet Baker** and **Shelly Manne**. He collaborated extensively with Manne during the second half of the 50s but also accompanied important figures from other areas of jazz, among them **Benny Goodman**. As a child Freeman had studied classical music, and his range and technical accomplishment allowed him to work in diverse fields of music such as film and television. In common with a growing number of musicians he also formed his own music publishing company thus giving him greater control over his own compositions. Within the jazz world Freeman's bop credentials were overlaid with an ability to accommodate other concepts. His work outside jazz somewhat overshadowed his reputation with the wider audience, but his early recordings, especially those with Manne, revealed him to have been an important contributor to a particularly creative period in the modern jazz movement.

● ALBUMS: *The Russ Freeman Trio* 10-inch album (Pacific Jazz 1953) ★★★★, *Chet Baker Quartet Featuring Russ Freeman* 10-inch album (Pacific Jazz 1953) ★★★, *Quartet: Russ Freeman/Chet Baker* (Pacific Jazz 1956) ★★★★, *Trio: Russ Freeman/Richard Twardzik* (Pacific Jazz 1956) ★★★.

● COMPILATIONS: with Chet Baker *A Grand Encounter* (Giant Steps 2004) ★★★★.

Freeman, Stan

b. 3 April 1920, Waterbury, Connecticut, USA, d. 13 January 2001, Los Angeles, California, USA. Freeman studied classical piano, graduating from the University of Hartford in 1942 with a music degree. During World War II he was in **Glenn Miller**'s army band and was later with the Miller band under **Tex Beneke**. From the mid-40s he recorded with Beneke, **Carl Kress** and **Jerry Jerome** and and in bands accompanying **Lee Wiley**, **Ella Fitzgerald** and **Anita O'Day**. He played with **Charlie 'Bird' Parker**, appearing on a session with strings in 1949. In the 50s Freeman was a studio player, appearing in orchestras accompanying **Johnny Hartman**, **Sarah Vaughan** and others. He made memorable harpsichord contributions to **Rosemary Clooney**'s 'Come On-A My House' and **Percy Faith**'s 'Delicado'. In 1951 he recorded with **Artie Shaw**'s revived Gramercy Five and **Benny Goodman**'s *King Of Jazz*. With fellow pianist Cy Walter he cohosted a weekly radio show, *Piano Playhouse*. His often anonymous studio work continued through the 50s and 60s, interspersed with solo nightclub appearances.

From early in his nightclub career, Freeman had peppered music with comedy, and in the late 70s he provided additional material for the shows of Mary Tyler Moore and **Carol Burnett**. With the latter, he won an Emmy for composing a **Fred Astaire** parody, 'Hi-Hat'. He wrote *At Wit's End*, a tribute to **Oscar Levant**, and the score for *I Had A Ball*, a 1965 Broadway musical. Periodically, he wrote arrangements for cabaret performers, including **Marlene Dietrich** and **Michael Feinstein**. Towards the end of the 60s he played on **Bobby Hackett**'s *A Time For Love* and early in the 70s was with fellow 'piano aces' **Dick Hyman**, **Ralph Sutton** and Lee Evans, both albums for Enoch Light's Project Records. Freeman's own dates usually catered to the popular audience. Occasionally, he would sing engagingly, as he did on a 1985 album for Audiophile Records.

● ALBUMS: *Piano Moods* 10-inch album (Columbia 1950) ★★★, *Come On-a Stan's House: Stan Freeman At The Harpsichord* 10-inch album (Columbia 1951) ★★★, *At The Blue Angel* (Epic 1956) ★★★, *Swings 'The Music Man'* (Columbia 1958) ★★★, *Plays 30 All-Time Hits* (Harmony 1959) ★★★, *Oh Captain!* (Columbia 1960) ★★★, *Stan Freeman's Piano Sweethearts* (Columbia) ★★★★, with Cy Walter *Manhattan* (Epic) ★★★, *Piano Moods* (Columbia) ★★★, *Everybody's Twistin'* (Columbia) ★★★, *Fascination* (Project 3) ★★★, *Not A Care In The World* (Audiophile 1985) ★★★, *The Music Of Scandinavia* (Sony 1992) ★★★.

Freeman, Von

b. Earl Lavon Freeman Snr., 3 October 1922, Chicago, Illinois, USA. Freeman played 'C' melody saxophone as a child, later switching to tenor. In the early 40s he played with several bands including, most notably, that of **Horace Henderson**. Late in the decade he was briefly with **Sun Ra** and then settled into a residency at a Chicago hotel in a band which included his brothers Buzz on drums and George on guitar. Other members of the band included at different times

Ahmad Jamal and **Muhal Richard Abrams**. The band accompanied many visiting jazzmen, notably **Charlie Parker** and **Lester Young**. In the 60s Freeman toured with a variety of artists, including several blues singers. From the 70s onwards he was again leading a jazz group, sometimes in harness with his son, **Chico Freeman**, with whom he recorded the album *Freeman & Freeman*. In the 80s and beyond he has recorded with Ed Petersen, **Teddy Edwards, Clifford Jordan, Willis Jackson** and **Frank Catalano** and was still active as a solo artist in the new millennium. Freeman's playing style combines the toughness of the Chicago blues scene with a plangent swing and fluent improvisation; his ballad playing is especially engaging.

● ALBUMS: *Doin' It Right Now* (Atlantic 1972) ★★★, *Have No Fear* (Nessa 1975) ★★★, *Serenade And Blues* (Nessa 1975) ★★★, *Young And Foolish* (Daybreak 1977) ★★★★, with Chico Freeman *Freeman & Freeman* (India Navigation 1981) ★★★, *Walkin' Tuff!* (Southport 1989) ★★★, *Lester Leaps In* (SteepleChase 1992) ★★★★, with Teddy Edwards, Buck Hill *Tenor Conclave* (Timeless 1992) ★★★, *Never Let Me Go* (SteepleChase 1994) ★★★★, *Dedicated To You* (SteepleChase 1995) ★★★, with Fire *Fire With Von Freeman* (Southport 1996) ★★★, with Ed Petersen *Von & Ed* (Delmark 1999) ★★★, with Chico Freeman *Von Freeman's 75th Birthday Celebration: Live At The Blue Note* (Half Note 1999) ★★★, with Frank Catalano *You Talkin' To Me?!* (Delmark 2000) ★★★★, with Brad Goode, Joan Hickey, Sherman Davis, Michael Raynor *Inside Chicago Vol. 1* (SteepleChase 2001) ★★★, with Goode, Hickey, Davis, Raynor *Inside Chicago Vol. 2* (SteepleChase 2001) ★★★, *Live At The Dakota* (Premonition 2001) ★★★, *The Improvisor* (Premonition 2002) ★★★, with Brad Goode, Paul McKee, Ron Perrillo, Stewart Miller, Bob Rummage *Inside Chicago Vol. 3* (SteepleChase 2002) ★★★★, with Goode, McKee, Perrillo, Miller, Rummage *Inside Chicago Vol. 4* (SteepleChase 2003) ★★★, *The Great Divide* (Premonition 2004) ★★.

Freescha

As if to deliberately demarcate their torpid, supine and near devotional recordings, Freescha named their beguiling 2002 release *Slower Than Church Music*. Formed by San Francisco California, USA–based duo Nick Huntington and Michael McGroarty, Freescha's deliberately paced electronic dirges and de-tuned laments most readily recall the nostalgic electronica of Scotland's **Boards Of Canada**. Including tracks named after soft-bodied invertebrate ('Mollusk') as well as an elegy to sacred music ('Church Music'), the appositely named *Slower Than Church Music* juxtaposed retarded hip-hop beats with plaintive childlike synthesizer lines, electronic whirs and pretty piano pieces to create an album with a similar emotive and nightmarish charge to Boards Of Canada's *Music Has The Right To Children*. Like Boards Of Canada, Freescha seem to (occasionally) deploy voices for their subliminal impact and their power of suggestion rather than their literal meaning: when voices do appear, they are mutated, sluggish and indistinct. Though *Slower Than Church Music* was released via Norwich, England–based label Shingle Street, Huntington and McGroarty run their own imprint, Attack Nine, releasing music by Drexon Field and Freescha themselves, including their debut *Kids Fill The Floor*.

● ALBUMS: *Kids Fill The Floor* (Attack Nine 2001) ★★★, *Slower Than Church Music* (Shingle Street 2002) ★★★★.

Freestyle Fellowship

From South Central Los Angeles, USA, 90s rap band Freestyle Fellowship were named after their rhyming abilities and dextrous word play. Comparisons to **De La Soul** and the **Dream Warriors** frustrated them, but the impressive thing about the group, as revealed on singles like 'Hot Potato', with its samples from **Dizzy Gillespie** and **Kool And The Gang**, was the dizzy speed of their delivery and appetite for innovation. The group comprised Mikah Nine, Mtulazaji (Peace), Self Jupiter, Aceyalone and DJ Kiilu, who grew from the Los Angeles Good Life Cafe collective. Mikah Nine had formerly recorded with Carmet Carter and the **Wailers**. However, the most important music in the Freestyle Fellowship cocktail was undoubtedly jazz, whose experimental edge was reflected in their lyrics.

● ALBUMS: *To Whom It May Concern* (Sun Music 1991) ★★, *Inner City Griots* (Island 1993) ★★★.

Freestylers

This hip-hop/rock crossover band comprises Matt Cantor, Aston Harvey and Andrew Galea and was formed in London in 1996. All three were involved in the UK's **dance music** scene in the late-80s. Harvey had written the 1990 break beat classic 'Don't Hold Back' as the Blapps! Posse and had worked with the **Rebel MC** and **Definition Of Sound**. The band's name came from their first sample, 'Don't Stop the Rock', and they released their first single 'Drop The Boom (AK-48)' on their own label, Scratch City Records, in 1996. Using the vocoder, the track was old school **electro** and became an underground club classic. In late 1996, they released *The Freestyle EP* and had a chart hit and *Top Of The Pops* television appearance with 'B-Boy Stance', featuring the vocalist **Tenor Fly**. Following this, they completed various remix projects, including those for **Audioweb**, **Afrika Bambaataa** and the **Jungle Brothers**. They also mixed the **Ministry Of Sound**'s **big beat** compilation *FSUK 2* and played an 'Essential Mix' for the UK's BBC Radio 1. They also made live appearances on the European festival circuit, including the **Glastonbury Festival**. Their debut, *We Rock Hard,* was released in 1998 to a positive critical reception. The same year the trio won the UK's *Muzik* magazine's award for Best Band.

● ALBUMS: *We Rock Hard* (Mammoth 1999) ★★★.
● COMPILATIONS: *FSUK 2* (MOS 1998) ★★★.

Freeway

b. Arturo Molina Jnr., Philadelphia, Pennsylvania, USA. As part of **Jay-Z**'s Roc-A-Fella stable of artists, Freeway hit the upper reaches of the US charts in 2003 with his tough, streetwise rap. Growing up in the northern section of Philadelphia, Pennsylvania, USA, Freeway turned to hustling on the streets early on, at one point serving a six-month jail sentence for possession of illegal narcotics with intent to deliver. Upon his release, Freeway opted to pursue rap more seriously, as his unique and unpredictable rhyming style caught the attention of Jay-Z, who in turn signed the rapper. It was also around the same time of singer **Aaliyah**'s tragic plane crash, and according to Freeway, she was on her way to work with the rapper in Miami to work on a remix together. Despite the tragedy, Freeway shifted his focus onto his debut,

Philadelphia Freeway, which was issued in 2003. The album spawned the hit singles 'Flipside' and 'What We Do'.

● ALBUMS: *Philadelphia Freeway* (Roc-A-Fella 2003) ★★★.

Frehley, Ace

b. Paul Daniel Frehley, 27 April 1951, Bronx, New York City, USA. Ace Frehley rose to fame as the lead guitarist for premier US hard rock band **Kiss** during its prime years. Often nicknamed 'Space Ace' or 'The Spaceman' by fans, Frehley released his first, self-titled solo album in September 1978, with albums by the other three members of Kiss also recorded simultaneously. Released on Casablanca Records, the album, which found the guitarist attempting more diverse musical styles than he was allowed to follow within the context of Kiss, reached the US Top 30 and spawned a number 13 single, the **Russ Ballard**-penned 'New York Groove'.

Frehley left Kiss in December 1982 following a near-fatal car accident and attempted to free himself of a drug habit over the next four years. He formed his own band **Frehley's Comet** in 1987, with whom he recorded three studio albums, the last of which was issued as his second solo album. Frehley rejoined Kiss on their successful reunion tour in 1996, but left again at the start of the new millennium. He has since concentrated on acting work.

● ALBUMS: *Ace Frehley* (Casablanca 1978) ★★★, *Trouble Walkin'* (Megaforce 1989) ★★.

● COMPILATIONS: *12 Picks* (Megaforce/Steamhammer 1997) ★★, *Loaded Deck* (Megaforce 1998) ★★.

● DVD/VIDEOS: *Ace Vision: Volume 1* (Rock Soldiers Fan Club 1994).

● FURTHER READING: *Into The Void . . . With Ace Frehley*, Wendy Moore.

● FILMS: *Remedy* (2005).

Frehley's Comet

Following drug and alcohol-related problems, US guitarist **Ace Frehley** (b. Paul Daniel Frehley, 27 April 1951, Bronx, New York City, USA) left hugely successful hard rock band **Kiss** in December 1982. After a four-year period of rehabilitation, he began writing again, signing to the Megaforce label in 1987. He had already made tentative steps back at the end of 1984, launching Frehley's Comet with John Regan (bass), Anton Fig (drums), Richie Scarlet (guitar/vocals) and Arthur Stead (keyboards). The new line-up of the band that began gigging at the end of 1986 featured Frehley, Regan, Fig and Tod Howarth (ex-**707**; vocals, keyboards, guitar). With an emphasis on Americanized hard rock with a commercial edge, their self-titled debut album was given a favourable reception from critics and Kiss fans alike. In time, Tod Howarth's creative input began to change the band's sound, pushing them in a more lightweight AOR direction. This was clearly illustrated on 1988's *Second Sighting*. Frehley, concerned that this new direction might alienate his loyal fanbase, relieved Tod Howarth of vocal duties on *Trouble Walkin'* (issued as an Ace Frehley solo album), drafting in original guitarist Richie Scarlet as a replacement. This album was a backward step musically in an attempt to appeal to the same market as Kiss, even employing that band's drummer, **Peter Criss**, as guest vocalist and covering Paul Stanley's (Kiss guitarist) 'Hide Your Heart'. The rest of the band became

frustrated by Frehley's controlling interest and left halfway through the tour to support the album.

Frehley carried on working with a new band, but his career had hit rock bottom before he resurfaced with Kiss on their reunion tour in 1996. He stayed with the band until the start of the new millennium, following which he embarked on an acting career.

● ALBUMS: *Frehley's Comet* (Megaforce 1987) ★★★, *Live +1* (Megaforce 1988) ★★, *Second Sighting* (Megaforce 1988) ★★★.

● DVD/VIDEOS: *Live . . . +4* (Atlantic Video 1988).

French Kicks

This US east coast quartet draw equally from the **Kinks**' sense of melody and the **Pixies**' jagged art rock. Nick Stumpf (vocals/drums) formed the band with Matt Stinchcomb (vocals/guitar), Josh Wise (keyboards) and Jamie Krents (bass). Stumpf and Stinchcomb had been friends and bandmates from their school days in Washington, DC, even attending the same Ohio college together and relocating to Brooklyn, New York, to pursue their rock 'n' roll dreams. Joining them in their move was Krents, and they met Alabama, Georgia native Wise shortly after settling into their new home-town. After several months of rehearsing and writing demo material, the French Kicks quickly made a name for themselves on the New York live scene. Two EPs followed, 1999's *French Kicks* and 2001's *Young Lawyer*, the latter of which was supported by a UK tour that saw the arrival of Lawrence Stumpf as the band's new bass player. With demand for an album rising among their quickly increasing following, the French Kicks delivered the 11-track *One Time Bells* in 2002. Two years later the band had changed direction with a more AOR sounding release.

● ALBUMS: *One Time Bells* (Star Time 2002) ★★★, *The Trial Of The Century* (Star Time 2004) ★★★.

Frente!

Hailing from Melbourne, Australia, Frente! (which means 'forehead' and 'front' in Spanish) was formed in 1991 by Angie Hart (vocals), Simon Austin (guitar), Tim O'Connor (bass) and Mark Picton (drums). Specializing in a disarming blend of simple guitar and piano compositions, accompanied by tape loops and the occasional sample, the quartet attracted immediate attention with their self-financed *Whirled* EP. Their debut album was originally issued in Australia in 1992, but by the time it gained an international release two years later a number of new tracks had been added, the most notable of which was a cover version of **New Order**'s 'Bizarre Love Triangle'. The album was promoted on tours with the **Beautiful South** and **Crowded House** and attracted press support throughout Europe as well as Australasia.

In February 1995 tracks from *Marvin The Album* were remixed for the EP *Ordinary Angels* by the **Black Crowes/Primal Scream** producer George Drakoulias, as Frente! searched for mainstream international acceptance. By this point the original rhythm section had been replaced by Bill McDonald (bass) and Alistair Barden (drums), and the band had lost the exclamation mark from their name. Frente's second album *Shape* was well received by the music press, although commercial success was still lacking, and the quartet sundered soon after its release. Hart relocated to Los Angeles and formed Splendid with her husband Jesse Tobias. She reunited with Austin in 2004, reviving the Frente name with help from Bill McDonald and drummer Peter Luscombe. They released the EP *Try To Think Less* on the Australian label Popboomerang Records.

● ALBUMS: *Marvin The Album* (Mushroom/Mammoth 1992) ★★★, *Shape* (Mammoth 1996) ★★★.

Frenzal Rhomb

Formed in Sydney, Australia, Frenzal Rhomb once notoriously claimed to be 'the punkest band in the world'. Led by singer Jay Whalley, famed for his purple dreadlocks and high-energy performances, the group built its reputation as part of Sydney's burgeoning anarcho-punk/skateboarding culture of the early 90s. Following the edicts of their US 'skatecore' peers, the group have come to prominence despite refusing to compromise their aims and objectives. They still decline to appear at any shows boasting corporate sponsorship and have released two albums on their own Shagpile Records despite offers from major labels. Members of the group are also active in environmental politics, fanzine culture and counterculture art. As the group's work began to attract international attention, their records were distributed by independents such as Real Cool (Japan) and Fat Wreck Chords (USA).

● ALBUMS: *Coughing Up A Storm* (Shagpile/Shock 1995) ★★★, *Not So Tough Now* (Shagpile/Shock 1996) ★★★.

Freq Nasty

b. Darin McFadyen, 15 November 1969, Fiji. Raised in New Zealand, Freq Nasty is, despite his exotic origins, signed to the UK's influential independent Botchit & Scarper. The label is a purveyor of 'nu-school breaks'—experimental, abstract **electro** as practised by artists such as **Adam Freeland**, Soul Of Man, **Tayo** and **Rennie Pilgrem**. Indeed, his single 'Funky As . . .' was released on Freeland's label, Marine Parade. His tough, electronic rhythms are punctuated with obscure, kitsch samples of film dialogue and synthesised squelches and bleeps. Occasionally, he uses the vocal skills of rappers such as Phoebe One and the drum 'n' bass MC Skibadee. His debut single for Botchit & Scarper, 'Boomin' Back Atcha', became popular with more underground DJs. His next single 'Underglass' also made an impact on dancefloors and in the music press and established his trademark sound of 'acid' sounds underpinned by fierce breakbeats and powerful bass. 'Freq-A-Zoid', his third single, was a surprise. Alluding to **Kraftwerk**, **Daft Punk** and **Les Rythmes Digitales**, it was an unusual slice of 'tech-funk' that proved to work equally well on **techno**, **house** and hip-hop dancefloors. Freq Nasty, and his studio partner Blim, have remixed Sousounde's 'Metisse' and **Steve Reich**'s 'Desert Music'. McFadyen is also an in-demand DJ, playing all over the world and at the seminal Big Beat Boutique (**Norman Cook**'s home club) at its venue, London's Scala. His debut *Freq's Geeks & Mutilations* received ecstatic praise from the UK music press, won over by the album's refreshing experimentation and undeniable funkiness.

● ALBUMS: *Freq's Geeks & Mutilations* (Botchit & Scarper 1999) ★★★★, *Bring Me The Head Of Freq Nasty* (Skint 2003) ★★★.

● COMPILATIONS: *Y4K: Next Level Breaks* (Distinctive 2002) ★★★★.

Fresh Fruit Records

After **ESP**, Amsterdam's most important, slightly more underground **dance music** label. The location of the enterprise, run by Rene 'DJ Zki' and Gaston Dobre, is a bedroom in Gaston's mother's house. From here emerged records by the Goodmen (the debut 'Give It Up', which brought them mainstream chart success), Klatsch ('God Save The Queer') or Rene Et Gaston ('Contes De Fees'), which are the three names the duo employ. They also use these names for their remixing activities, i.e., the Goodmen's work on Ricky Rouge's 'Strange Love'. The label started in November 1991, before which they had both already been active in the dance scene. Rene's string of Euro **house** credits included SiL and World Series Of Life ('Spread Love'), while Gaston operated as Trancesetters, Virtual Reality, Jark Prongo, Con-Am, Jamshed and 41 Days. Working together Gaston adopts responsibility for keyboards and computers, while Rene, with 15 years DJing work behind him, furnishes ideas. Their mode of operation involves a week-long bedroom routine, with sampling a key but invisible component: 'We use records for sampling . . . we build a song around the sample, then we take the sample away'. 'Father In The Bathroom', the title-track to the Goodmen's debut album, was in fact a sample of exactly that; Gaston's father cleaning the bathroom. Other names used by the duo include South Street Player.

● ALBUMS: as the Goodmen *Father In The Bathroom* (Fresh Fruit 1994) ★★★.

Fresh Gordon

Fresh Gordon was a popular early DJ in Los Angeles, California, USA, who rose to prominence as the hip-hop message spread from the Bronx in New York to America's west coast. His infamous early bootleg 12-inch, 'Feelin' James', combined samples of **James Brown**'s 'Funky Drummer' and 'Sex Machine' long before Brown had become such a popular staple of rap samplers as well as **Aretha Franklin**'s 'Rock Steady'. The record was finally given an official release when **Tommy Boy Records** issued it in 1987, in a slightly diluted format because of the complexities of sample clearance. By this time Fresh Gordon had long since disappeared into obscurity.

Fresh Maggots

A duo of Mick Burgoyne (guitar, tambourine, violin) and Leigh Dolphin (acoustic guitar), Fresh Maggots was formed in Nuneaton, Warwickshire, England, at the beginning of the 70s. Though they only issued two records, the 1971 single 'Car Song' and an attendant self-titled debut album, critics were impressed by the warmth and immediacy of the duo's confident folk rock style. Unlike many of their peers, they were attracted to themes divorced from the fantastical concerns of the period, preferring to write poignant songs such as 'Dole Song' and 'Everyone's Gone To War'. The album was never followed up as the duo went their separate ways.

● ALBUMS: *Fresh Maggots* (RCA 1971) ★★★.

Fresh, Doug E.
(see **Doug E. Fresh**)

Fresh, Freddy

b. Frederick Schmidt, New York City, USA. Fresh is a leading hip-hop/**big beat** producer, remixer and DJ who has released over 100 records since his first in 1988, encompassing other electronic styles such as **house, trance** and **techno**. Based in Minneapolis, Fresh has his own imprints, Butterbeat, Analog Records, Boriqua and Socket. He has DJed all over the world, working alongside **Jeff Mills**, **Roy Davis Jnr.**, **Frankie Bones** and **Fatboy Slim** (with whom he is friends) and other **Skint Records** artists. Fatboy Slim sampled Fresh's voice from an answerphone message, saying, 'Fatboy Slim is fucking in heaven', and used it on his album *You've Come A Long Way, Baby*. Growing up, Fresh had jobs as a pizza delivery boy and etching trophy plates for his father before pursuing his interests in **electro**, hip-hop and electronic music. He discovered analogue sounds when his wife took him to the Bronx in 1984, and he became obsessed with the **dance music** street culture of the time and producers such as **Shep Pettibone** and **François Kevorkian**. Fresh began to collect **mix tapes** by DJs such as Jeff Mills and Frankie Bones and records by a range of diverse artists from Jonzun Crew, Newcleus to **Bill Withers** and **Cat Stevens**.

His first studio experience was with the famous **Boogie Down Productions**, where he mixed a b-side. He then began to amass a sizeable collection of analogue synthesizers and other equipment and began experimenting with his own sounds. His fondness for analogue equipment is evident in the sound of his productions—lo-fi and mixed live. Fresh released his debut singles on **Nu Groove Records** before establishing his Analog label in 1992. In 1995 Fresh signed a contract with the German techno label **Harthouse Records**. He has released many acclaimed singles and has found his popularity growing with the resurgence of interest in old school hip-hop and electro, particularly in Europe and the UK, where he is a frequent visitor, playing DJ sets at major clubs and festivals, including the **Glastonbury Festival** and Creamfields. He has also DJed at the UK's **Cream**, **Ministry Of Sound** and at **Norman Cook**'s Big Beat Boutique, the club that gave the musical style its name. Fresh has also broadcast many DJ mixes on UK regional and national radio, including an 'Essential Mix' on BBC Radio 1 FM. In 1999 Fresh released the singles 'Badder Badder Schwing' (which reached the UK Top 40) and 'What It Is'. *The Last True Family Man* received excellent reviews. Fresh also supported the **Jungle Brothers** on tour during summer 1999.

● ALBUMS: *Analog Space Funk* (Analog 1996) ★★★, *Accidentally Classic* (Harthouse 1997) ★★★, *The Last True Family Man* (Harthouse Eye Q 1999) ★★★★, *Music For Swingers* (Shelter 2001) ★★★★.
● FURTHER READING: *Freddy Fresh Presents The Rap Records*, Freddy Fresh.

Freshies

The seeds of this UK pop group were sown in 1971 when Chris Sievey and his brother hitched a lift to London and staged a sit-in at the **Beatles' Apple Records** headquarters—eventually going on to record a session. Subsequently Sievey recorded numerous demos that were sent to record companies, resulting in an avalanche of rejection slips he later published as a small book. Another book was dedicated to **Virgin Records** rejections alone. His own label Razz was formed in 1974, releasing a variety of singles, videos and over 60 cassettes. In the meantime, Sievey attempted to form his own band under the title the Freshies. Among a stream of musicians who collaborated were Martin Jackson (later **Magazine** and **Swing Out Sister**) and Billy Duffy (later the **Cult**). The most consistent line-up, however, was Barry Spencer (guitar), Rick Sarko (bass, ex–Ed Banger And The Nosebleeds) and Mike Doherty (drums, ex-Smirks), the line-up operating between 1980 and 1982. After several small pressings on Razz, Sievey finally hit the charts with 'I'm In Love With The Girl On The Manchester Virgin Megastore Checkout Desk' when it was rereleased by MCA in 1981. Two other curious but enduring singles were also released on the major, the ambiguous antiwar ode 'Wrap Up The Rockets' and the paean to record collecting 'I Can't Get (Boing Boing) Bouncing Babies By The **Teardrop Explodes**'. However, after a solitary single on **Stiff Records** the band split. Sievey, ever the optimist, went on to a similarly bizarre solo career alongside appearances as his alter ego Frank Sidebottom. Incredibly for a band with literally hundreds of songs behind them, the Freshies never released an official album.

● ALBUMS: *Junkfuel* (Polydor 1994) ★★★.
● COMPILATIONS: *The Very Very Best Of . . . Some Long And Short Titles* (Cherry Red 1996) ★★★.

Freshmen

Formed in Northern Ireland in 1962, this highly respected showband comprised Barney McKeon (vocals), Damien McIlroy (lead guitar), Billy Brown (piano/saxophone), Maurice Henry (saxophone), Terry McGahey (bass guitar), Sean Mahon (trombone) and Davy McKnight (drums). After losing McKeon early on, they recruited Limerick singer Tommy Drennan (later Tommy Dean) in 1963, who was in turn replaced by baritone Derek McMenamin. It was this line-up that first recorded in 1964 under the pseudonym Six Of One. The following year, as Dean And The Freshmen, they issued the Drennan-composed 'I Stand Alone'. It was not until late 1965, however, that they finally infiltrated the Irish charts with a cover of Johnny And Charly's 'La Yenka'. Unlike many showbands, the Freshmen spent heavily on musical equipment and were known throughout Ireland for their superb vocal harmonies. Their 1967 Christmas hit, 'Papa-Oom-Mow-Mow', reached the Irish Top 10, as did 'Just To See You Smile' and 'Halfway To Where'. What was most extraordinary about the Freshmen, however, was their live sound and ability to master the intricate harmonies of their mentors the **Beach Boys**. They enjoyed chart success with a version of 'The Little Old Lady From Pasadena' (retitled 'Go Granny Go') and even included an ambitious version of 'Good Vibrations' in their live act. The Freshmen survived the showband scourge of the early 70s and found Irish chart success in 1976 with 'And God Created Woman'. Meanwhile, original Freshman Billy Brown released successful chart covers of 'The Leaving Of Liverpool' and 'Cinderella'. By the end of the decade, however, they disbanded, the victims of changing times and tastes.

● COMPILATIONS: *When Summer Comes: The Pye Anthology* (Castle 2001) ★★★.

Fresu, Paolo

b. 10 February 1961, Berchidda, Sardinia, Italy. An accomplished trumpet and flügelhorn player, Fresu was self-taught and grew up playing the band music of his native island. He discovered jazz in 1980 but had to move to the mainland to practise the new-found craft. He gained a degree after studying the trumpet formally at Cagliari Conservatoire, and also attended the music faculty at Bologna. Into the early 80s and onwards, he taught at various music schools, contributed to magazines and wrote for theatres and orchestras as well as leading an excellent jazz quintet. The foundations for his own quintet were laid as a result of meeting like-minded musicians at the 1982 Sienna Jazz seminar, and the band was finally formed in late 1984. It went on to become the most fêted of the 80s Italian new wave (La Nuova Onda), with Fresu winning numerous prizes and polls. He and his band (including the excellent saxophonist Tino Tracanna) are primarily inspired by the classic **Miles Davis** quintets of the 50s and 60s and play with considerable panache and conviction. Notable releases include *Ostinato* (1985), *Mamût: Music For A Mime* (1987) and *Ballads* (1992). In addition to his quintet and sextet, Fresu has worked in a duo with bass player Furio Di Castri (later a trio with the addition of pianist Antonello Salis). He has also worked with **Franco D'Andrea, Dave Holland, Lee Konitz, Nguyên Lê, Albert Mangelsdorff, Michael Nyman, Tony Oxley, Evan Parker, Enrico Rava, Paul Rutherford, John Taylor, Kenny Wheeler** and many other jazz artists.

● ALBUMS: with Norma Winstone, Kenny Wheeler, John Taylor, Paolo Damiani, Tony Oxley *Live At Roccella Jonica* (Ismez Polis 1984) ★★★, *Ostinato* (Splasch 1985) ★★★★, *Inner Voices* (Splasch 1986) ★★★, *Mamût: Music For A Mime* (Splasch 1987) ★★★★, *Qvarto* (Splasch 1988) ★★, *Live In Montpellier* (Splasch 1990) ★★★, *Ossi Di Seppia* (Splasch 1991) ★★★, *Ballads* (Splasch 1992) ★★★★, *Live* (Blue Jazz 1992) ★★★, *Ensalada Mistica* (Splasch 1994) ★★★★, *6x30* (Onyx 1996) ★★★, *Wanderlust* (RCA-Victor 1997) ★★★★, *Mèlos* (RCA 2000) ★★★, *Here Be Changes Made* (Musica Jazz 2002) ★★★, *Montreal Diary A: Enrico Rava, Paolo Fresu, Stefano Bollani, Enzo Pietropaolo, Roberto Gatto Play Miles Davis* (Label Bleu 2002) ★★★★, *Scores!* (Cam Jazz 2003) ★★★.

● COMPILATIONS: *Berchidda: The Italian Years* (Arco Iris 1999) ★★★★.

Fretwell, Stephen

b. 10 November 1981, Scunthorpe, Lincolnshire, England. Singer-songwriter Fretwell enjoyed a surge of media interest at the end of 2004 following the release of his debut *Magpie* and a number of support slots for the bestselling band **Keane**. Fretwell moved to Manchester to study at Salford University but decided to launch a full-time music career instead of completing his degree. Having begun writing songs at an early age, he quickly found his niche as a singer-songwriter, establishing himself on the Manchester live circuit and performing a support slot for semi-famous local band **Elbow**. His debut recording *8 Songs* was released on 10-inch vinyl in 2002 in a limited edition run of 1,000 copies. Recorded on budget equipment by Fretwell and his friend Jay Sikora, the material on the mini-album transcended its lo-fi origins through the strength of Fretwell's songwriting and performance. Stand-outs 'Lost Without You' and the bittersweet love song 'Emilie' wove delicate folk and jazz textures into the basic acoustic format. The follow-ups, the *Something's Got To Give* EP and the mini-album *The Lines*, were released in 2003 by the Tape Recordings label on both CD and vinyl. Both releases featured a more band-orientated approach, with Fretwell and Sikora joined by additional musicians Jonny Lexus, Matt Watson and Dave Urmston.

Fretwell then signed a major label recording contract with the **Polydor Records** imprint Fiction, recording his album debut at Abbey Road in the company of the same musicians who had performed on *The Lines*. The production on 2004's *Magpie*, which included a number of tracks from the earlier releases, struck a delicate balance between the stripped-down approach of his debut and the layered sound of the follow-up. The album included a new version of 'Emilie' (now spelt 'Emily') that was released as a single the following year.

● ALBUMS: *8 Songs* mini-album (Northern Ambition 2002) ★★★★, *The Lines* mini-album (Tape Recordings 2003) ★★★, *Magpie* (Fiction/Polydor 2004) ★★★★.

Freur

Minor UK indie pop band which is most notable for featuring Carl (later Karl) Hyde (b. 1961, Bewdley, West Midlands, England) and Rick Smith (b. 1959, Wales), who would go on to release some of the most seminal **dance music** of the 90s as **Underworld**. Hyde and Smith originally worked together in the early 80s as the Screen Gemz, having met while at college in Cardiff, Wales. They formed Freur with guitarist Alfie Thomas. Their name was actually written as a hieroglyphic squiggle, to the amusement and bemusement of writers and chart compilers everywhere. 'Freur' was the phonetic pronunciation. They expanded their line-up with drummer Bryn Burrows (ex-Fabulous Poodles) and keyboard player/video guru John Warwicker. The quintet signed to **CBS Records** in 1983 and enjoyed a minor UK chart success with 'Doot Doot'. Its popularity was made all the more unlikely by the fact that their record company had issued the original demo version rather than the recording the band had made with Conny Plank and **Holger Czukay** in Cologne. The record was also a big hit throughout Europe and topped the Italian charts. A second album *Get Us Out Of Here* was withheld from release in the UK by CBS, after which Warwicker was replaced by Baz Allen. The quintet re-emerged in 1988 with a different recording contract and a new name, Underworld.

● ALBUMS: *Doot Doot* (CBS 1983) ★★★, *Get Us Out Of Here* (CBS 1985) ★★.

Frey, Glenn

b. 6 November 1948, Detroit, Michigan, USA. Frey's early career was forged as singer, guitarist in a number of local attractions, including the Mushrooms and Subterraneans. He appeared on several sessions by the **Bob Seger** System, singing back-up on 'Ramblin' Gamblin' Man', a 1968 hit, before moving to Los Angeles. Here Frey formed **Longbranch Pennywhistle** with **J.D. Souther**, but this harmony duo floundered on record label intransigence, and in 1972 the now-disengaged musician opted for singer **Linda Ronstadt**'s backing group. Frey then joined fellow band members **Bernie Leadon, Don Henley** and **Randy Meisner** in the **Eagles**, which grew from humble country rock origins into one of America's most successful attractions. Frey co-wrote many of the unit's best-known songs, including 'Take It Easy', 'Lyin' Eyes', 'Take It To The Limit' and 'Hotel California', while his distinctive vocal formed the ideal counterpoint to that of Henley.

The Eagles broke up in 1980 amid rancorous professional and personal circumstances. A new-found partnership with songwriter Jack Tempchin formed the basis of Frey's solo debut, *No Fun Aloud*, which achieved gold status and spawned US hits in 'I Found Somebody' and 'The One You Love'. In 1984 he wrote and performed 'The Heat Is On', the hit theme to the highly successful movie *Beverly Hills Cop*, before resuming his association with Tempchin for *The Allnighter*. The following year Frey reached number 2 in the US charts with 'You Belong To The City', a song culled from the soundtrack of *Miami Vice*. He subsequently took an acting role in this popular television crime series and in 1988 completed *Soul Searchin'*, the third in a series of slick, professional AOR-styled albums. Frey was a key member of the highly successful Eagles reunion in 1994. During their financially lucrative *Hell Freezes Over* tour in 1995 he was taken seriously ill and received surgery for a stomach complaint. The following year he made a guest appearance in the Don Johnson television series, *Nash Bridges*, and acted in the Tom Cruise movie *Jerry Maguire*.

● ALBUMS: *No Fun Aloud* (Asylum 1982) ★★, *The Allnighter* (MCA 1984) ★★★, *Soul Searchin'* (MCA 1988) ★★, *Strange Weather* (MCA 1992) ★★, *Live* (MCA 1993) ★★.

● COMPILATIONS: *Solo Collection* (MCA 1995) ★★★, *The Best Of Glenn Frey: The Millennium Collection* (MCA 2000) ★★★.

● FILMS: *Let's Get Harry* aka *The Rescue* (1986), *Jerry Maguire* (1996).

Fricke, Janie

b. Jane Frickie, 19 December 1947, on the family farm near South Whitney, Indiana, USA. Fricke, who adopted the spelling in 1986 to avoid mispronunciation, has sung in public since the age of 10. Her father was a guitarist and her mother a piano teacher and organist. Fricke sang jingles to pay her university fees and then moved to Los Angeles to find work as a session singer. As this was not productive, she moved to Nashville and joined the Lea Jane Singers, often recording three sessions a day, five days a week. Fricke has added background vocals to thousands of records, mostly country, including ones by **Crystal Gayle** ('I'll Get Over You'), **Ronnie Milsap** ('[I'm A] Stand By My Woman Man'), **Elvis Presley** ('My Way'), **Tanya Tucker** ('Here's Some Love') and **Conway Twitty** ('I'd Love To Lay You Down'). Fricke's uncredited contribution on **Johnny Duncan**'s 'Jo And The Cowboy' led to several other records with Duncan. The disc jockeys and public alike were curious about the mystery voice on his country hits 'Stranger', 'Thinkin' Of A Rendezvous' and 'It Couldn't Have Been Any Better', and she was finally given equal billing on 'Come A Little Bit Closer'. This led to considerable interest in her first solo recordings, and she had US country hits with 'What're You Doing Tonight?' and a revival of 'Please Help Me, I'm Falling'. At first, she was reluctant to tour because she found herself in continuing demand as a session singer. She joined **Vern Gosdin** for 'Till The End' and 'Mother Country Music' and **Charlie Rich** for a US country number 1, 'On My Knees'. In 1982 Fricke had her first solo US country number 1 with 'Don't Worry 'Bout Me, Baby', co-written by 60s hitmaker **Bruce Channel** and featuring **Ricky Skaggs**' harmony vocals. **Johnny Rodriguez**'s road manager, Randy Jackson, proposed to Fricke on a radio phone-in show and later married her and became her manager. Fricke, who toured with **Alabama**, had a US country number 1 with a similarly styled, high-

energy performance, 'He's A Heartache (Looking For A Place To Happen)' (1983). It was taken from *It Ain't Easy*, which she made with her own Heart City Band and which was produced by **Bob Montgomery**. 'It Ain't Easy Bein' Easy' (1982) and 'Tell Me A Lie' (1983) were other US country number 1s from the same album. She joined **Merle Haggard** for another number 1, 'A Place To Fall Apart' (1985), which was based on a letter he had written about his ex-wife, **Leona Williams**, and Fricke's other duet partners include **George Jones** ('All I Want To Do In Life'), **Ray Charles** ('Who Cares?'), **Tommy Cash** ('The Cowboy And The Lady') and **Larry Gatlin** ('From Time To Time'). Her *Black And White* album was more blues-based, while *Labor Of Love* was produced by Chris Waters and included an ingenious song he had written with his sister, **Holly Dunn**, 'Love Is One Of Those Words', as well as **Steve Earle**'s 'My Old Friend The Blues'. She recorded albums for Intersound and Branson Entertainment in the 90s, reverting to the original spelling of her surname.

● ALBUMS: *Singer Of Songs* (Columbia 1978) ★★★, *Love Notes* (Columbia 1979) ★★★, with Johnny Duncan *Nice 'N' Easy* (Columbia 1979) ★★, *From The Heart* (Columbia 1980) ★★★, *I'll Need Someone To Hold Me When I Cry* (Columbia 1981) ★★★, *Sleeping With Your Memory* (Columbia 1981) ★★★, *It Ain't Easy* (Columbia 1982) ★★★, *Love Lies* (Columbia 1983) ★★★, *The First Word In Memory Is Me* (Columbia 1984) ★★★, *Somebody Else's Fire* (Columbia 1985) ★★, *Black And White* (Columbia 1986) ★★★★, *After Midnight* (Columbia 1987) ★★★, *Saddle The Wind* (Columbia 1988) ★★★, *Labor Of Love* (Columbia 1989) ★★★, *Janie Fricke* (Intersound 1990) ★★★, *Crossroads* (Branson 1992) ★★★, *Now & Then* (Branson 1993) ★★★, *Bouncin' Back* (JMF 1999) ★★★★, *Tributes To My Heroes* (JMF 2004) ★★.

● COMPILATIONS: *Greatest Hits* (Columbia 1982) ★★★, *The Very Best Of Janie Fricke* (Columbia 1986) ★★★★, *17 Greatest Hits* (Columbia 1986) ★★★, *Country Store: Janie Fricke* (Country Store 1988) ★★★.

Frida

b. Anni-Frid Synni Lyngstad, 15 November 1945, Björkåsen, Narvik, Norway. Frida attempted to revive her career as a solo singer after the break-up of **Abba** in 1981, having already released two Swedish-language albums in the early 70s prior to her membership of the group. She was the first of the group to make an English-language solo album, 1982's *Something's Going On*, which was produced by **Phil Collins**. Somewhat downbeat in tone (many thought it reflected the recent breakdown of the separate marriages of both Frida and Collins) it included songs by **Per Gessle**, later of **Roxette**. The most successful track, 'I Know There's Something Going On' reached the US Top 20 and was written by **Russ Ballard** who also composed the first solo hit for another ex-Abba soloist **Agnetha Fältskog**. 'To Turn The Stone' was also successful in Europe. The following year, Frida's duet with **B.A. Robertson**, 'Time', was a minor British hit, but her second solo album made little impact on either side of the Atlantic, although the title track was a hit across Europe. She waited another 12 years before releasing a new album, the Swedish-language *Djupa Andetag*.

● ALBUMS: *Frida* (EMI 1971) ★★, *Ensam* (Polar 1975) ★★★, *Something's Going On* (Polar 1982) ★★★, *Shine* (Polar 1984) ★★, *Djupa Andetag* (Anderson 1996) ★★★.

● COMPILATIONS: *Anni-Frid Lyngstad* (EMI 1971) ★★, *På Egen Hand* (EMI 1991) ★★★, *Tre Kvart Från Nu* (EMI 1993) ★★, shared with Agnetha *The Voice Of Abba* (Spectrum 1994) ★★★, *1967–1972* (EMI 1997) ★★★, *The Mixes* (Newmusic 1998) ★★, *Svenska Popfavoriter* (Polar/PolyGram 1998) ★★, *The Collection* (EMI 2001) ★★★, *Frida* 4-CD/1 DVD box set (Universal 2005) ★★★.
● FURTHER READING: *Abbamania Volume 2: The Solo Years*, Peter Bingham and Bernadette Dolan.

Friday, Gavin

b. Fionan Hanvey, 8 October 1959, Dublin, Eire. Friday was founder of the **Virgin Prunes** and spent the late 80s and early 90s moving away from the discordant art expression that dominated the Prunes' turbulent but vivid career. Following their demise he took a break to concentrate on painting and open a cabaret nightclub (The Blue Jesus, a pun on **Marlene Dietrich**'s 'Blue Angel' nightclub in the movie *Touch Of Evil*), though he did also record a 12-inch single version of the **Rolling Stones**' 'You Can't Always Get What You Want' with friend Simon Carmody. The launch of a solo career proper was largely inspired through the efforts of his friend **Agnes Bernelle**, who years earlier had introduced him to the pre-war Germany of **Edith Piaf**, **Jacques Brel**, **Bertolt Brecht** and **Kurt Weill**. The Berlin vaudeville circuit of the 30s and 40s thus inspired both The Blue Jesus and *Each Man Kills The Thing He Loves*, produced by Hal Willner with skilled accompaniment from drummer Michael Blair, bass player Fernando Saunders and guitarist **Marc Ribot**. A densely crafted and moralistic take on the beauty and decadence of the period, measuring pathos with humour, it proved an instant critical success. *Adam 'N' Eve* was more playful, with Friday parodying himself on the self-eulogizing 'King Of Trash', while elsewhere he was evidently still the maverick: 'It's egotistical and outrageous, but this record is the world according to me. It's saying no, no, no to everyone who just toes the line.' Tracks such as 'Fun And Entertainment' were delivered in an impenetrable, working-class Dublin accent. Later in the 90s he moved into film work, writing three tracks with Bono of **U2** and long-time collaborator Maurice Roycroft (aka The Man Seezer) for the soundtrack to *In The Name Of The Father* and scoring Robert Altman's *Short Cuts*, though his attitude to this new art form was typically acidic: 'I generally dislike rock 'n' rollers getting involved in the music on a film. When you get to a very emotional part in the movie and you hear Phil Collins' voice you start getting the puke bag out.' *Shag Tobacco* was coproduced with Seezer and Tim Simenon of **Bomb The Bass** and reflected some of the shifts in the mid-90s music scene. However, the cover version of **Marc Bolan**'s 'The Slider' was one concession to an earlier period, while songs such as 'Dolls' and 'Little Black Dress' both alluded to Friday's camp cabaret fixations. Two more Australian film soundtracks followed, *The Passion Of Darkly Noon* and *Angel Baby*, before a radically altered, spoken-word version of *Shag Tobacco* was released early in 1996. The same year, Friday and Seezer's 'Angel' was featured on the soundtrack of *Romeo And Juliet*. In 1998 Friday and Seezer composed a full score for Jim Sheridan's *The Boxer*.
● ALBUMS: as Gavin Friday And The Man Seezer *Each Man Kills The Thing He Loves* (Island 1990) ★★★, *Adam 'N' Eve* (Island 1992) ★★, *Shag Tobacco* (Island 1995) ★★★, *The Boxer* film soundtrack (MCA 1998) ★★★.

● FURTHER READING: *Gavin Friday: The Light And The Dark*, Caroline Van Oosten De Boer. *Peter & The Wolf*, Gavin Friday & The Friday-Seezer Ensemble.

Fridge

This post-rock experimental trio originally formed in 1995, while all three members (guitarist Kieran Hebden, bass player Adem Ilhan and drummer Sam Jeffers) were still attending school in Putney, London, England. While balancing school studies with jam sessions that mixed styles such as jazz, rock, funk, electronica and dub, the trio recorded a demo, which they passed along to renowned hip-hop producer the Underdog (aka **Trevor Jackson**) upon a chance meeting at a local record store. It did not take long for Jackson to appreciate the demo, as he signed them immediately to his Output Recordings label. Fridge's 1997 debut recording, *Ceefax*, was issued while all three members were still teenagers. College was put on hold in order to pursue music full-time, resulting in further releases such as 1998's *Semaphore* and *Sevens And Twelves* (the latter of which is an 18-track compilation). For 1999's *EPH*, Fridge had relocated to the Go! Beat label, while its members made time for outside projects (Hebden's being the most successful, the electronic outfit **Four Tet**). The members reunited in 2001 for the release of Fridge's new studio album, *Happiness*. Following its release, Hebden returned to Four Tet and recorded the acclaimed *Rounds*. Ilhan, meanwhile, released an album under his **Adem** moniker.
● ALBUMS: *Ceefax* (Output 1997) ★★★, *Semaphore* (Output 1998) ★★★★, *EPH* (Go! Beat 1999) ★★★★, *Happiness* (Temporary Residence/Brainwashed 2001) ★★★★.
● COMPILATIONS: *Sevens & Twelves* (Output 1998) ★★★.

Fried, Fred

b. 2 December 1948, New York City, USA. Listening to records from early childhood, Fried liked many kinds of music, including rock 'n' roll and Broadway show tunes. From the age of 12, he played clarinet in junior high school bands and orchestras. In his teens he attended New York's High School Of Performing Arts as a drama major but went on to Boston University to study English with the intention of becoming a writer. While there, however, he began playing guitar and was soon obsessed with the instrument. He began serious guitar studies, eventually being turned towards jazz through hearing on record **Kenny Burrell** and **Wes Montgomery**. Among other guitarists whose recorded work influenced him are **George Benson**, **Lenny Breau**, **George Van Eps**, **Jim Hall** and **Pat Martino**. Fried also listened extensively to jazz pianists, a major influence being **Bill Evans**.
After graduating from college, Fried moved to Los Angeles where he studied with Van Eps, an experience that not only influenced his style but also directed him towards the seven-string guitar. Back in New York, Fried joined the Judd Woldin Trio for a four-year engagement at the Windows On The World at the World Trade Center. He also played as a soloist and as small group leader at the Rockefeller Center's Rainbow Room, Gregory's, Birdland and at the Weill Recital Hall at Carnegie Hall. Among the many artists from the worlds of jazz and pop with whom Fried has appeared are **Greg Abate**, **Perry Como**, **Barbara Cook**, **Billy Drummond**,

Steve LaSpina, Jay Leonhart, Marty Napoleon, Helen O'Connell, Art Pepper, Derek Smith and Harvie Swartz. He is also a member of the trio Threeba, which includes tuba player Sam Pilafian of the Empire Brass Quintet.

In addition to gigging as sideman, soloist and leader, Fried is also very active as a teacher. A masterly improviser, with a pianistic approach to the guitar, Fried has a highly distinctive playing style. He is thoroughly committed to jazz guitar, and with every appearance his work advances the genre.

● ALBUMS: with Steve LaSpina, Gary Johnson *Crystalline* (Rush/City Hall 1996) ★★★, with LaSpina, Johnson *Out Of My Dreams* (Ballet Tree 1996) ★★★, with Bob Nieske, Matt Gordy *Cloud 3* (Ballet Tree 1996) ★★★★, *Nobody Else But Me* (Ballet Tree 1998) ★★★★, with Mitch Seidman, Harvie Swartz *This Over That* (Jardis 1998) ★★★, with LaSpina, Billy Drummond *Infantry Of Leaves* (Ballet Tree 2001) ★★★, with LaSpina, Drummond *When Winter Comes* (Ballet Tree 2003) ★★★.

Friedhofer, Hugo Wilhelm

b. 3 May 1901, San Francisco, California, USA, d. 17 May 1981. After an early career as a painter, Friedhofer turned to another branch of the arts, taking up the cello and studying composition under Domenico Brescia. He wrote music to accompany silent films and in 1929 went to Hollywood to arrange and direct music for the new sound films. When procedures changed and composers were hired to write specifically for films, Friedhofer was well-suited for a new role and was called upon to orchestrate the music for *Keep Your Sunny Side Up*. He later orchestrated music composed by acclaimed and much better-known people such as **Erich Wolfgang Korngold**, **Max Steiner** and **Franz Waxman**. The films on which he worked for these composers are numerous and his contribution to their success undoubted, if undervalued. As a film composer in his own right, Friedhofer's first complete score was for the 1938 film *The Adventures Of Marco Polo*. He also composed for films such as *Brewster's Millions*, *Joan Of Arc*, *Body And Soul*, *No Man Of Her Own*, *Hondo*, *Vera Cruz*, *Young Lions* and *The Best Years Of Our Lives* (for which he won an Oscar) and *One-Eyed Jacks*—just a few of a very long list. Greatly admired by fellow musicians as diverse as Paul Glass and **John Lewis**, Friedhofer remained almost unknown to the world outside the music business. **Gene Lees**, a longtime friend, wrote movingly of him in his book *Singers And The Song*.

● FURTHER READING: *The Art Of Film Music (Special Emphasis On Hugo Friedhofer, Alex North, David Raksin & Leonard Rosenman)*, George Burt. *Singers And The Song*, Gene Lees.

Friedman, Burnt

(see **Friedmann, Bernd**).

Friedman, Dean

b. 1955, Paramus, New Jersey, USA. This US singer-songwriter found instant success on both sides of the Atlantic with a mixture of sentimental ballads and pleasant tunes about romance. He had a US Top 30 hit with 'Ariel', which made ripples in Europe, but his 1978 single 'Lucky Stars' (a duet with Denise Marsa) reached the Top 3 position in the UK and made him a household name. A lack of promotion and sporadic record releases led to declining sales (due

mainly to problems at the Lifesong label), although 'Lydia' gave him his last notable chart hit, reaching the UK Top 40. Friedman briefly recorded for the Epic label, releasing *Rumpled Romeo* in 1981, but the album's single 'McDonald's Girl' was officially banned by the BBC for naming the fast food restaurant in its chorus. Throughout the 80s he released occasional singles on minor labels. One track, 'The Lakelands', was included on a compilation album which sold a quarter of a million units. Friedman reappeared in 1990 writing and performing the soundtrack to a low-budget British horror film, *I Bought A Vampire Motorcycle*. In the 80s and 90s Friedman became heavily involved in virtual reality software and video game design with his successful company InVideo Systems. He also invented a range of musical instruments for children. His first studio release in over 15 years was 1998's laboured double-CD, *Songs For Grownups*. The 2002 follow-up *The Treehouse Journals* was financed entirely by the artist's fans. Friedman has also self-released a number of children's albums and DVDs.

● ALBUMS: *Dean Friedman* (Lifesong 1977) ★★, *Well, Well, Said The Rocking Chair* (Lifesong 1978) ★★★, *Rumpled Romeo* (Epic 1981) ★★, *Songs For Grownups* (Eagle/Real Life 1998) ★★, *The Treehouse Journals* (Dean Friedman/Real Life 2002) ★★, *Squirrels In The Attic: Comedy Songs For Adults* (Dean Friedman 2005) ★★★.

● COMPILATIONS: *Very Best Of Dean Friedman* (Music Club 1991) ★★★.

● DVD/VIDEOS: *In Concert: Edinburgh Fringe* (Dean Friedman), *Dean's Silly Song Sing-Along: Edinburgh Fringe* (Dean Friedman).

Friedman, Kinky

b. Richard Friedman, 31 October 1944, Rio Duckworth, Palestine, Texas, USA. Friedman, a Jew in Texas, remarks: 'Cowboys and Jews have a common bond. They are the only two groups to wear their hats indoors and attach a certain importance to it.' Friedman, whose father was a university lecturer, first recorded as part of the surfing band King Arthur And The Carrots in 1966. One of the Carrots, Jeff Shelby, became Little Jewford Shelby in Friedman's band the Texas Jewboys, the name satirizing **Bob Wills**' Texas Playboys. Chuck Glaser of the **Glaser Brothers** took him to Nashville for his first album, 1973's *Sold American*. The title song combined the qualities of **Ralph McTell**'s 'Streets Of London' with **Phil Ochs**' 'Chords Of Fame' and has been recorded by **Glen Campbell** and Tompall Glaser, the latter version being coproduced by Friedman. His Jewish upbringing and culture was reinforced in songs such as 'We Refuse The Right To Refuse Service To You' and 'Ride 'Em Jewboy'. Friedman's single 'Carryin' The Torch', an offbeat look at the Statue of Liberty, was produced by **Waylon Jennings**.

Friedman's self-titled second album was a patchy mixture of blasphemy and ballads and included a good-natured romp produced by **Willie Nelson**, 'They Ain't Makin' Jews Like Jesus Anymore'. A hoarse recording of 'Sold American', recorded as part of **Bob Dylan**'s Rolling Thunder Revue, was included on *Lasso From El Paso*. **Buck Owens**, who published 'Okie From Muskogee', refused to allow the album to be called Asshole From El Paso. 'Ol' Ben Lucas', about nose-picking, features **Eric Clapton**'s guitar-picking, while 'Men's Room, L.A.' is about a shortage of toilet paper and features **Ringo Starr** as Christ wanting to use the toilet.

Friedman's own career never shone as brightly as the 3-D portrait of Christ he had at his home, and in 1977 he dropped his touring band and went solo. He also improved his diction so that his insults could be understood. He sang the title song of the movie *Skating On Thin Ice,* and he was murdered in his acting role in *Easter Sunday,* a reel starring Dorothy Malone and Ruth Buzzi. Friedman is also a perceptive writer, writing on country music for **Rolling Stone,** and his novel *Greenwich Killing Time* is about a country singer turned detective. Friedman briefly returned to performing to promote this anthology, although his live sets merely reprised his old material. In recent years he has become a successful writer of crime novels, and he tries to write a new novel each year. Friedman says his autobiography will be printed backwards, like old Jewish texts. He also intends to write a mystery in which one of Willie Nelson's ex-wives is out to kill him—and has the full co-operation of the participants for this! On his promotional tours for his books, he goes 'singing the song that made me infamous and reading from the books that made me respectable'.

● ALBUMS: *Sold American* (Vanguard 1973) ★★★★, *Kinky Friedman* (ABC 1974) ★★★, *Lasso From El Paso* (Epic 1976) ★★★, *Under The Double Ego* (Sunrise 1983) ★★, *Old Testaments And New Revelations* (Fruit Of The Tune 1992) ★★★, *From One Great American To Another* (Fruit Of The Tune 1995) ★★★, with Little Jewford *Classic Snatches From Europe* (Sphincter 2003) ★★★, with Billy Joe Shaver *Live From Down Under* (Sphincter 2003) ★★.

● COMPILATIONS: various artists *Pearls In The Snow: The Songs Of Kinky Friedman* (Kinkajou 1998) ★★★.

● DVD/VIDEOS: *Proud To Be An A**hole From El Paso* (Kultur Video 2003).

● FURTHER READING: *Greenwich Killing Time,* Kinky Friedman. *A Case Of Lone Star,* Kinky Friedman. *When The Cat's Away,* Kinky Friedman. *Frequent Flyer,* Kinky Friedman. *Musical Chairs,* Kinky Friedman. *The Kinky Friedman Crime Club.* Kinky Friedman. *Elvis, Jesus And Coca Cola,* Kinky Friedman. *More Kinky Friedman,* Kinky Friedman. *Armadillos And Old Lace,* Kinky Friedman. *God Bless John Wayne,* Kinky Friedman. *Roadkill,* Kinky Friedman.

Friedman, Maria

b. 1960, Switzerland. An actress, musician, singer and dancer with a penchant for the works of **Stephen Sondheim,** Friedman was born into a musical family. Her mother, Claire, is a concert pianist and composer, and her late Russian-Jewish father Leonard Friedman was an accomplished violinist who founded the Scottish Chamber Orchestra and Scottish Opera. The family moved to Germany when she was three on her father's appointment as Leader of the Bremen Philharmonic Orchestra. Shortly afterwards, the marriage broke up, and Friedman was subsequently brought up in England. Early training as a cellist was abandoned because 'I quickly realised I didn't have the discipline required', but her musical ability was never in question, and after training at the Arts Educational School, Friedman joined Sonnet, an all-girl trio that backed Vernon Nesbeth, founder of the **Southlanders** vocal group, on a European tour. On her return to England, she played the chorus role of Doris in **Cameron Mackintosh's** 1980 revival of **Oklahoma!** at the Palace Theatre (the programme misspelled her name as Freedman) and subsequently took over the leading part of

Ado Annie in the same show. During the remainder of the 80s, she was in London productions such as **Blondel** (Aldwych), *Small Expectations* (Queen Elizabeth Hall), *By George It's Gershwin* (Purcell Rooms), *Spin Of The Wheel* (Comedy), *April In Paris* (Ambassadors) and **Blues In The Night** (Piccadilly). In the latter show she played the Girl With A Date, more than holding her own in the heady company of Debby Bishop and Carol Woods. Another very important role was that of Hayyah in *Ghetto* (Royal National Theatre 1989), Joseph Sobol's unforgettable play about a theatre created by Jewish inhabitants of the Vilna, Lithuania, ghetto during the Holocaust. Friedman first met Stephen Sondheim after singing his 'Broadway Baby' at a charity concert at the Theatre Royal, Drury Lane, and he subsequently cast her as Dot/Marie in **Sunday In The Park With George** (1990). This was followed by a Leicester Haymarket revival of the composer's *Merrily We Roll Along* (1992). Her big break came when she was seen providing 'a little light entertainment' at her father's annual international music festival in the Hebrides called *Mendelssohn On Mull,* by Caro Newling, the administrator of London's Donmar Warehouse Theatre. Newling booked her to appear at the venue for three Sunday performances in February–March 1994. Her one-woman show, *Maria Friedman By Special Arrangement,* for which she was supported by a group of handpicked musicians playing brand new arrangements, sent hardened critics into the realms of ecstasy. Her eclectic programme was topped and tailed by Sondheim's 'Our Time' and 'Marry Me A Little' and included two songs from *Ghetto,* 'In The Sky' and 'Springtime'. The show won the 1995 Best Entertainment **Laurence Olivier Award,** and she encored with *Maria Friedman By Extra Special Arrangement,* which played the Whitehall Theatre for a limited season. In 1997 there was another Olivier Award, this time for Best Actress In A Musical, in recognition of her outstanding performance as the disfigured Fosca, opposite **Michael Ball,** in the London premiere of Sondheim and James Lapine's *Passion.* A year later, she was back at the National's Lyttleton Theatre as Liza Elliot in the first London production of the **Ira Gershwin–Kurt Weill–Moss Hart** 1941 musical **Lady In The Dark.** After that, she moved on to something quite different, taking over the 'murderous' role of Roxie Hart in the West End hit production of **Chicago** (1998). As a concert performer Friedman has sung at most of the major venues in the UK and also appeared frequently on television. On the small screen she is probably best known for her portrayal of social worker Trish Baynes in the top-rated television hospital series *Casualty* but has also featured in other shows such as *Me And The Girls, Blues In The Night, Red Dwarf, Black Daisies For The Bride, Shakers, The Ancient Mariner* and *Frank Stubbs Promotes.*

● ALBUMS: *Maria Friedman* (Carlton Sounds 1996) ★★★, as well as studio and stage cast recordings.

Friedman, Marty

b. 8 December 1962, Washington, DC, USA. This technically brilliant guitarist has a long and impressive pedigree. Stints with Vixen, **Hawaii** and **Cacophony** helped to formulate and define his characteristic quick-fire style before he embarked on a solo career. *Dragon's Kiss* was an impressive instrumental debut, combining heavy-duty riffs and intricate solos with Far Eastern influences and undertones. Friedman later went on to produce speed-metallers **Apocrypha** before commencing work on a second solo project. This was put on hold after he accepted an invitation to join **Megadeth** in February 1990, though it did finally emerge three years later. By *Introduction*, the guitarist had moved on to a spacious, new age technique, on a set more expansive in tone that anything he had previously recorded in the rock field.

● ALBUMS: *Dragon's Kiss* (Roadrunner 1988) ★★★, *Scenes* (Roadrunner 1993) ★★, *Introduction* (Roadrunner 1994) ★★, *The Obsessions* (Metal Blade 1996) ★★★.

Friedmann, Bernd

b. 1965, Kassel, Germany. Friedmann is one of the more intriguing figures operating in electronic music. He has listed German progressive rock, **Gary Numan**, **Iron Maiden** and **Tangerine Dream** as early influences. However, his life seems to have been irrevocably changed by childhood experiments with a cassette player, and he has previously quoted Andy Warhol's maxim: 'The acquisition of my tape recorder really finished whatever emotional life I might have had. But I was glad to see it go.'

Friedmann named his own label Nonplace, as a metaphor for where he sees himself in the music industry. The concept behind the label, he says, is to mess around with genres. Claiming that 'identity is the enemy because I don't want to get stuck in a certain style', the Cologne-based artist has scattered his personality through a series of aliases and alter-egos. He has released music as Gummibox, Some More Crime, Drome, Nonplace Urban Field, Flanger, the Nu Dub Players, Burnt Friedman and even—though he claims to dislike it when artists use their own name—Bernd Friedmann. The musician, however, refuses to define or pigeonhole any of his monikers. Rather, he says this multiplex of identities is an inevitable consequence of the invention of a concept for each of his releases, with each new idea necessitating a new label. Alongside his multitude of identities (he also records with **Atom Heart** as Flanger), Friedmann creates his own curious fictions and elaborately constructed biographies. The Nu Dub Players release *Just Landed* was supposedly a live album recorded in a South American club; in truth it took Friedmann almost three years to complete it in a studio. Though the methodology may often be esoteric (he has sampled the sound of a ballerina cracking her back and played live using five MiniDisc players) and his intent often quirky (1996's *Leisure Zones* was created because he wanted to record something he could fall asleep to and included the recommendation that it be played at a volume 'approximating the throb of traffic'), Friedmann's recordings are often beguiling and always fascinating.

● ALBUMS: as Some More Crime *Ohnmacht* (ZZO 1990) ★★★, as Some More Crime *Code Opera* (ZZO 1991) ★★★, as Drome *Anachronism* (Silent 1992) ★★★, as Nonplace Urban Field *Nonplace Urban Field* (Incoming! 1993) ★★★, as Some More Crime *Another Domestic Drama In Suburban Hell* (ZZO 1993) ★★★, as Drome *The Final Corporate Colonisation Of The Unconscious* (Ninja Tune 1994) ★★★, as Nonplace Urban Field *Nuf Said* (Incoming! 1994) ★★★, as Drome *Dromed* (Kiff SM 1995) ★★★, as Nonplace Urban Field *Raum Für Notizen* (Incoming! 1995) ★★★★, as Some More Crime *Fuzzy Sets* (ZZO 1995) ★★★, as Bernd Friedmann *Leisure Zones* (Ash International 1996) ★★★, as Nonplace Urban Field *Golden Star* (Incoming! 1996) ★★★★, as Burnt Friedman *Con Ritmo* (Nonplace 2000) ★★★, as Burnt Friedman And The Nu

Dub Players *Just Landed* (Scape 2000) ★★★, as Burnt Friedman *Plays Love Songs* (Nonplace 2001) ★★★, as Burnt Friedman with Jaki Liebezeit *Secret Rhythms* (Nonplace 2002) ★★★, as Burnt Friedman And The Nu Dub Players *Can't Cool* (Nonplace 2003) ★★★.

Friend And Lover

With the 1968 flower power movement at full bloom, how could an optimistic song like 'Reach Out Of The Darkness', by a group called Friend And Lover, possibly fail? Friend And Lover were a married couple, Jim Post (b. 28 October 1939, Houston, Texas, USA) and Cathy (b. Cathy Conn, Chicago, Illinois, USA), who met in 1964 at a Canadian state fair. Jim had performed with a folk group called the Rum Runners, while Cathy had sung and danced. Inspired by a New York love-in, Jim Post wrote the duo's only hit, revolving around the uplifting advice 'reach out of the darkness and you might find a friend'. Recorded in Nashville, (with **Ray Stevens** and **Joe South** on the session) and released on **Verve** Forecast, the single made the US Top 10 in 1968. Although the pair recorded other singles and an album, the act *and* the marriage broke up. Post went on to record solo albums for such labels as Flying Fish and **Fantasy Records**.

● ALBUMS: *Reach Out Of The Darkness* (Verve 1968) ★★★.

Friend, Cliff

b. 1 October 1893, Cincinnati, Ohio, USA, d. 27 June 1974, Las Vegas, Nevada, USA. A prolific songwriter from the early 20s through to the late 40s, Friend studied the piano from the age of 10 and attended the Cincinnati College and Conservatory. He worked in vaudeville with performers such as **Buddy De Silva** and **Harry Richman** and also visited England where he played in various music halls. Friend was also a test pilot for a time at the well-known Wright Field. Encouraged by **Al Jolson**, during the 20s he wrote numerous songs, several of which were used in Broadway revues and shows, such as *Piggy*, **Whoopee!** and *George White's Scandals* of 1929. These included 'Lovesick Blues' (1922, with **Irving Mills**), which was revived 40 years later by Australian yodeller **Frank Ifield**, whose version went to number 1 in the UK, 'Mama Loves Papa, Papa Loves Mama', 'June Night', 'There's Yes, Yes In Your Eyes', 'Where The Lazy Daisies Grow', 'Chili Bom Bom', 'I Wanna Go Where You Go, Do What You Do, Then I'll Be Happy', 'Let It Rain, Let It Pour', 'It's Easy To Say Hello', 'Oh, Baby', 'Give Me A Night In June', 'Hello Bluebird', 'I'm Telling The Birds, I'm Telling The Bees', 'Oh! If I Only Had You', 'So Will I', 'It Goes Like This (That Funny Melody)', 'My Blackbirds Are Bluebirds Now', 'There's Something Spanish In Your Eyes'. With the coming of talking pictures in the late 20s, Friend spent much of the following decade writing the occasional number for a string of generally undistinguished movies such as *Lucky Boy*, *Let's Go Places*, *The Golden Calf*, *Fox Movietone Follies Of 1930*, *Palmy Days*, *Crooner*, *Many Happy Returns*, *Down To Their Last Yacht*, *George White's 1935 Scandals*, *Millions In The Air*, *Happy-Go-Lucky* and *Ice Follies Of 1939*. The films themselves may have been modest, but there were a good many immensely popular songs among Friend's mixture of ballads, comedy and novelty songs, which included 'Let's Go Places', 'My Honey Said Yes Yes', 'There's Nothing Else To Do In Ma-La-Ka-Mo-Ka-Lu But Love', 'You Belong To Me', 'I Got Shoes, You Got Shoesies', 'It's Time To Say

Goodnight', 'You Tell Her-I Stutter', 'South American Joe', 'The Broken Record', 'Wah-Hoo', 'Wake Up And Sing', 'When My Dream Boat Comes Home', 'The Merry-Go-Round Broke Down', 'You Can't Stop Me From Dreaming', 'I Must See Annie Tonight' and 'Concert In The Park'. Friend wrote those last five numbers with his principal collaborator Dave Franklin (b. 28 September 1895, New York, USA, d. 3 February 1970, Los Angeles, California, USA). Among the many other composer/lyricists with whom Friend worked throughout his career were Abel Baer, **Walter Donaldson**, **Lew Brown**, Sidney Clare, **Gus Kahn**, **Irving Caesar**, **Jimmy Monaco**, **Billy Rose**, **Charles Tobias**, Boyd Bunch, Katharine Phillips, George Olsen, **Joseph Meyer**, **Jack Yellen** and **Carmen Lombardo**. With the last, Friend wrote 'The Sweetest Music This Side Of Heaven', which Carmen's brother, **Guy Lombardo**, adopted as his band's theme. The tune also became identified with the popular British band led by **Maurice Winnick**. Friend's output declined during the 40s, although in 1940 **Bing Crosby** took his 'Trade Winds' (written with Charles Tobias) to number 1 in the US, and during the years of World War II, he contributed the optimistic 'We Did It Before (And We Can Do It Again)' as well as 'Don't Sweetheart Me', 'Gonna Build A Big Fence Around Texas' and 'Time Waits For No One', which featured in *Shine On, Harvest Moon*, the 1944 biopic of top entertainers Nora Bayes and Jack Norworth. In 1952 Paramount's *Somebody Loves Me*, which purported to tell the life story of vaudevillians **Blossom Seeley** and **Benny Fields**, used Friend's 'June Night', and more than 10 years later, one of his 1927 numbers, 'Hello Bluebird', was sung by **Judy Garland** in her last film, *I Could Go On Singing* (1963).

Friends Again

This Glasgow, Scotland–based indie pop band, featuring **James Grant** (lead guitar/vocals), Chris Thomson (vocals/rhythm guitar), Neil Cunningham (bass), Stuart Kerr (drums/vocals), and Paul McGeechan (keyboards), emerged in 1982. They released their independently financed debut single, 'Honey At The Core', the following year. It was followed by two further singles on Moonboot Records, 'Sunkissed' and 'State Of The Art'. However, when the band signed to **Mercury Records**, they not only rereleased 'Honey At The Core' but also issued the lavish *Friends Again* EP. This elaborate package included new versions of the previous two singles plus the affecting, delicately orchestrated lead track 'Lullaby No. 2', which nevertheless concealed typically sombre lyrical matter from Thomson ('Everyone's the same, they've got deep dark hearts'). However, debut album *Trapped And Unwrapped* failed to showcase the band adequately, with a combination of producers diluting their sound. With its lack of sales Grant departed in 1984, conscious of requiring his own songwriting platform, though at first he linked with **Hipsway**. Friends Again imploded in his absence, with Thomson going on to work under the title the **Bathers**. Grant would eventually forge **Love And Money** from the ashes of Friends Again, using the services of McGeechan, Kerr and, temporarily, Cunningham. Kerr would later join **Texas**.

● ALBUMS: *Trapped And Unwrapped* (Mercury 1984) ★★★.

Friends Of Distinction

The band was formed in 1968 by Floyd Butler (b. 5 June 1941, San Diego, California, USA, d. 29 April 1990), Harry Elston (b. 4 November 1938, Dallas, Texas, USA), Jessica Cleaves (b. 10 December 1948, Los Angeles, California, USA) and Barbara Jean Love (b. 24 July 1941, Los Angeles, California, USA). This smooth vocal quartet began working together in the **Ray Charles**' revue. Stylistically similar to the **Fifth Dimension**, the Friends scored a million-selling hit with a vocal version of **Hugh Masekela**'s 'Grazing In The Grass' (1969). Two further releases, 'Going In Circles' and 'Love Or Let Me Be Lonely', were also substantial hits before their sweet-harmony, MOR soul established them as an attraction on the cabaret circuit.

● ALBUMS: *Grazin'* (RCA 1969) ★★★, *Highly Distinct* (RCA 1969) ★★★, *Real Friends* (RCA 1970) ★★, *Whatever* (RCA 1970) ★★, *Friends And People* (RCA 1971) ★★, *Friends And People* (RCA 1971) ★★★, *Love Can Make It Easier* (RCA 1973) ★★.

● COMPILATIONS: *Friends Of Distinction's Greatest Hits* (RCA 1973) ★★★, *Golden Classics* (Collectables 1989) ★★★, *The Best Of The Friends Of Distinction* (RCA 1996) ★★★.

Friesen, David

b. 6 May 1942, Tacoma, Washington, USA. As a child, Friesen played ukulele, accordion and guitar, working as a semi-professional on the latter instrument at the age of 16. Three years later, while serving with the US Army in Europe, he began playing bass. In France, he sat in with musicians such as **Johnny Griffin** and **Art Taylor** and in Denmark with drummer Dick Berk, and he also encountered **Ted Curson**. Back home in the northwestern corner of the USA, he played with established artists such as **John Handy**, **Marian McPartland** and **Joe Henderson** and also with contemporaries **Larry Coryell** and **Randy Brecker**. In the 70s he toured Europe with **Billy Harper**, and this was followed by engagements, in some cases including recording sessions, with **George Adams**, **Mose Allison**, **Kenny Drew**, **Stan Getz**, **Dexter Gordon**, **Dannie Richmond** and **Sam Rivers**. He attracted considerable attention while touring with Curson, in whose group he was extensively featured, including an appearance at the 1977 **Monterey Jazz Festival**. Among other musicians with whom he played during this and later periods were **Duke Jordan**, **Paul Horn**, with whom he toured the then Soviet Union in 1983, **Paul McCandless**, **Chick Corea**, **Tom Harrell** and **Mal Waldron**, playing with the latter in duo and in a trio with drummer Eddie Moore for some five years in the mid-80s.

In the 90s, still based in the northwest but constantly touring worldwide, Friesen continued to attract admirers, and his many recordings as leader and/or co-leader have been very well received by fans and critics alike. Among the artists with whom he has shared recording credits are **Denny Zeitlin**, guitarist John Stowell, **Bob Moses**, **Bud Shank**, Uwe Kropinski, Larry Koonse, **Joe LaBarbera**, **Airto Moreira** and Randy Porter, often teaming up in duos. He has also shown a liking for unconventional formats, including a quartet using bass, tenor saxophone, flügelhorn and drums. Regular companions in his popular trio during this decade were pianist Randy Porter and drummer Alan Jones.

Always eager to experiment and extend the range of possibilities for his instrument yet always decidedly accessible in his sometimes visionary instrumental voicings, Friesen regularly performs on unusual variations of the bass; he has, for example, used an amplified instrument with a standard fretboard and a cutaway solid body. He has also used a digital delay device to allow him to sustain and repeat lines and has developed new fingering techniques. He is especially adept in the upper register of the bass, often producing a sound that is remarkably akin to that of a guitar. He is similarly imaginative in his repertoire, drawing not only from the jazz heritage but also from ethnic music of other continents. Some of his music reflects his deep religious beliefs, which, too, are drawn from various origins. He has also boldly performed solo concerts, and in the recent past his recorded solo work has been of a particularly high standard.

● ALBUMS: *Color Pool* (Muse 1975) ★★★, *Star Dance* (Inner City 1976) ★★★, *Waterfall Rainbow* (Inner City 1977) ★★★, *Through The Listening Glass* (Inner City 1978) ★★★, *Other Mansions* (Inner City 1979), with Paul Horn *Heart To Heart* (Golden Flute 1980) ★★★, *Paths Beyond Tracing* (SteepleChase 1980) ★★★, *In Concert* (Vanguard 1981) ★★★, *Storyteller* (Muse 1981) ★★★, with Hozan Yamamoto *Hozan, Friesen Plus 1* (Next Wave 1982) ★★, *Amber Skies* (Palo Alto/Quicksilver 1983) ★★★, *Sentimental 'Round Christmas* (Choice Cuts 1983) ★★★, with Mal Waldron *Encounters* (Muse 1984) ★★★, with Waldron *Dedication* (Soul Note 1985) ★★★, *Gonna Plant Me Some Seeds* (Grass Root 1986) ★★★, *Jonah's Journey* (Sound World 1987) ★★★, *Born Of Water* (Ark/Meadow Lark 1987) ★★★, *To Hear The World In A Grain Of Sand* (Soul Note 1987) ★★★, *Inner Voices* (Global Pacific 1987) ★★★, *Dancing With The Bass* (ITM 1988) ★★★, with Denny Zeitlin *In Concert* (ITM Pacific 1988) ★★, *Three To Get Ready* (ITM Pacific 1988) ★★★, *Friends Of Miles Smiles* (Seven Stix 1988) ★★★, *Portland Jazz, Volume 1* (Pillar Productions 1989) ★★★, *Returning* (Burnside 1989) ★★★, *Two For The Show* (ITM Pacific 1989) ★★, *Upon The Swing* (Shamrock 1989) ★★★, *Other Times, Other Places* (Global Pacific 1989) ★★★, *Departure* (Global Pacific 1990) ★★★, *Four To Go* (ITM Pacific 1990) ★★★, *Castles And Flags* (Shamrock 1990) ★★★, *Long Trip Home* (ITM Pacific 1991) ★★, *Ageless Pathways* (Global Pacific 1991) ★★★, *From Worldbeat To Bluenote* (Shamrock 1992) ★★★, *The Spirit Of Christmas* (Burnside 1992) ★★, *Facing The Wind* (Power Bros 1992) ★★★, with Joe Henderson *Voices* 70s recording (West Wind 1993) ★★, *Like Drops In The Ocean* (ITM Pacific 1993) ★★★, *Global Voyage* (Global Pacific 1994) ★★★, *Still Waters* (Shamrock 1994) ★★★, *Tomorrow's Dreams* (Shamrock 1994) ★★★, *Remembering The Moment* 1987 recording (Soul Note 1994) ★★★, *One, Two, Three/1. 2. 3* (Burnside 1994) ★★★, with Zeitlin *Concord Duo Series, Volume 8* (Concord Jazz 1995) ★★★, with Zeitlin *Live At The Jazz Bakery* (Intuition 1995) ★★★, *Made In Berlin* (ITM 1996) ★★★, *The Name Of A Woman* (Intuition 1997) ★★★, *Ancient Kings* 1994 recording (Shamrock 1998) ★★★, *With You In Mind* (Summit 1998) ★★★, *Two For the Show* (ITM 1999) ★★★★, *Three To Get Ready* 1994 live recording (Summit 2001) ★★★★, *The Name Of A Women* (Intuition 2002) ★★★★, with Jeff Gardner *Grace* (Khaeon 2002) ★★, *Midnight Mood: Live In Stockholm* (Intuition 2005) ★★★.

Frigo, Johnny

b. 27 December 1916, Chicago, Illinois, USA. Frigo began playing violin while still a small child, taking lessons and quickly becoming proficient. In high school, however, he took up both tuba and string bass and gradually settled on the latter instrument. He played bass with several bands in Chicago in the late 30s, including the Four Californians, and then, in 1942, he joined the band led by Chico Marx, one of the four Marx Brothers. With Marx he occasionally played violin and also sang in a vocal quartet, as did new arrival **Mel Tormé**. Also in Marx's band at this time was **Barney Kessel**. During World War II, Frigo served in the US Coastguard, playing in a band that also included **Al Haig** and **Kai Winding**. After the war, Frigo played bass in **Jimmy Dorsey**'s band where two of his rhythm section colleagues were **Herb Ellis** and pianist Lou Carter. Together, these three formed the popular instrumental trio, Soft Winds. They also collaborated on writing 'I Told Ya I Love Ya, Now Get Out' and 'Detour Ahead', the latter song subsequently becoming a staple in the repertoire of many jazz singers. In 1952 Soft Winds broke up, and thereafter Frigo was active mainly as a studio musician in Chicago, playing bass on countless commercial sessions. However, he did occasionally play again on violin, one gig being as a strolling player in the restaurant of the Regency Hyatt Hotel in Chicago. Also in the 50s he made his first own-name recording for **Mercury Records**, on which **Ray Brown** appeared, as did Ellis. Frigo also worked in a duo with pianist Dick Marx (not a relation of the Marx Brothers).

After three decades, Frigo emerged into the jazz spotlight again. Frigo had encountered **Monty Alexander** when the pianist was playing at a Chicago hotel not far from one where Frigo had another strolling violin gig. Frigo sat in with Brown, Ellis and Alexander and was invited to California to play violin on their *Triple Treat II* and *Triple Treat III*. When these Concord Records albums were released in 1987 Frigo, now in his seventies, was suddenly in demand, appearing on Johnny Carson's *The Tonight Show*. Frigo went on to play in numerous small groups. This re-emergence in the 80s also brought recording sessions, including a session with Ellis and a 1988 own-name set that truly launched not only his revitalized career but also the Chesky Records label. Frigo also made overseas tours, and along with the records, this brought the accompanying realization of the jazz audience that he was a jazz violin player of distinction and great merit. Among his recording sessions are several with singers, including **Holly Cole**, **Meredith D'Ambrosio** and **Helen Merrill**. Frigo continued to play regularly through the 90s, telling *Jazz Journal International*'s Stan Woolley in a 1998 interview, when he was in his mid-eighties, 'I still live in Chicago and play every Monday night with a pianist by the name of Joe Vito. . . . The rest of the week I play private affairs and at the weekends I have started doing lots of festivals. It's a whole new thing and I feel like a kid with a new toy.'

● ALBUMS: *I Love John Frigo, He Swings* (Mercury 1957) ★★★, with Monty Alexander, Ray Brown, Herb Ellis *Triple Treat II* (Concord Jazz 1987) ★★★, with Brown, Ellis *Triple Treat III* (Concord Jazz 1987) ★★★, *Live From Studio A In New York City* (Chesky 1988) ★★★, *Debut Of A Legend* (Chesky 1994) ★★★★, *Then And Now: The Soft Winds, 1946-1996* (Chiaroscuro 1997) ★★★, *Live At The 1997 Floating Jazz Festival* (Chiaroscuro 1999) ★★★, *Renaissance Man* 1985 recording (Arbors 2001) ★★★, *DNA Exposed!* (Arbors 2001) ★★★.

● COMPILATIONS: *Collected Works* (Luv N Haight 2002) ★★★.

Frijid Pink

Kelly Green (vocals/harmonica), Gary Ray Thompson (guitar), Thomas Beaudry (bass), Larry Zelanka (keyboards) and Rick Stevens (drums) emerged from the hard rock circuit in Detroit, USA. In 1970 they scored a surprise transatlantic hit with their powerhouse interpretation of 'The House Of The Rising Sun', based on the **Animals'** highly original arrangement but to which they added a searing, guitar-strewn approach, reminiscent of contemporaries the **MC5** and **Stooges**. The single reached number 7 in the US and number 4 in the UK, but the group's subsequent chart entries, 'Sing A Song For Freedom' and 'Heartbreak Hotel' (both 1971), were confined to the lower regions of the US chart. It confirmed a suspicion that the song, rather than the group, was responsible for that first flush of success. By the time of their final album in 1975 for **Fantasy Records** only Stevens remained from the original line-up.

● ALBUMS: *Frijid Pink* (Parrot 1970) ★★, *Defrosted* (Parrot 1970) ★★, *Earth Omen* (1972) ★★, *All Pink Inside* (Fantasy 1975) ★★.

● COMPILATIONS: *Hibernated* 3-CD set (Arkarna 2003) ★★★.

Frikyiwa

(see **Galliano, Frederic**)

Friml, Rudolph

b. 8 December 1879, Prague, Bohemia, d. 12 November 1972, Hollywood, California, USA. An important composer who helped to perpetuate the romantic operetta-style of musical that was so popular in America at the turn of the century. After studying at Prague University, Friml toured Europe and America as a concert pianist and settled in the US in 1906. As a composer his first opportunity came when he took over from **Victor Herbert** on the score for *The Firefly* (1912), from which came 'Giannina Mia' and 'Sympathy'. His collaborator for that show was **Otto Harbach**, and the two men worked together on a further nine productions. Throughout his career Friml's other lyricists and librettists included **P.G. Wodehouse**, Herbert Reynolds, Harold Atteridge, Rida Johnson Young, **Oscar Hammerstein II**, Brian Hooker, Clifford Grey, Dailey Paskman, Edward Clark, Chisholm Cushing and Rowland Leigh. He composed the music for some of the most popular songs of the time in a list of shows that includes *High Jinks* ('The Bubble'; 'Love's Own Kiss'; 'Not Now But Later'), *The Peasant Girl* ('Love Is Like A Butterfly'; 'Listen, Dear'; 'And The Dream Came True'), *Katinka* ('Allah's Holiday'; 'I Want To Marry A Male Quartet'; 'Katinka'), *You're In Love* ('I'm Only Dreaming'; 'You're In Love'), *Glorianna* ('My Climbing Rose'; 'Toodle-oo'), *Sometime* ('Sometime'; 'Keep On Smiling') *Tumble Inn* ('Snuggle And Dream'; 'I've Told My Love'), *The Little Whopper* ('You'll Dream And I'll Dream'; ''Round The Corner'), *June Love* ('June Love'; 'The Flapper And The Vamp'; 'Don't Keep Calling Me Dearie'), *Ziegfeld Follies Of 1921* ('Bring Back My Blushing Rose'; 'Every Time I Hear The Band Play'), *The Blue Kitten* ('When I Waltz With You'; 'Cutie'; 'Blue Kitten Blues'), *Cinders* ('Belle Of The Bronx'; 'I'm Simply Mad About The Boys'), **Rose-Marie** ('Rose-Marie'; 'Indian Love Call'; 'Totem Tom-Tom'; 'Song Of The Mounties'), **The Vagabond King** ('Only A Rose'; 'Song Of The Vagabonds'; 'Some Day'), *The Wild Rose* ('Brown Eyes'; 'One Golden Hour'), *No Foolin'* ('Wasn't It Nice?'; 'Florida,

The Moon And You'), *The Three Musketeers* ('March Of The Musketeers'; 'Ma Belle'; 'Queen Of My Heart'; 'Heart Of Mine'), *The White Eagle* ('Gather The Rose'; 'Give Me One Hour'), *Luana* ('My Bird of Paradise'; 'Aloha') and *Music Hath Charms* (1934) ('My Heart Is Yours'; 'Sweet Fool'). In the lavish 1935 film version of Friml's first show, *The Firefly*, **Allan Jones** had a big hit with 'The Donkey Serenade', which was adapted from Friml's composition 'Chansonette', a piece he had originally written for the *Ziegfeld Follies Of 1923*. Some of his other shows were filmed, and he also wrote the music for the 1947 movie *Northwest Outpost*. Friml's last two shows, *Luana* and *Music Hath Charms*, only ran for some 20-odd performances each, and he appeared unable or unwilling to adapt his music to the ever-growing American style of musical comedy, although he remained active in his later years and appeared frequently on US television.

Fripp, Robert

b. 16 May 1946, Wimbourne, Dorset, England. Guitarist, composer and producer, Fripp began his diverse career in the small but flourishing circuit centred on Bournemouth, Dorset. He subsequently joined the League Of Gentlemen, a London-based outfit renowned for backing visiting American singers, and later founded Giles, Giles And Fripp, with brothers Pete and Mike Giles. This eccentric trio completed one album, *The Cheerful Insanity of Giles, Giles And Fripp*, in 1968 before evolving into **King Crimson**, the progressive act though which the artist forged his reputation. Between 1969 and 1974, Fripp led several contrasting versions of this constantly challenging ensemble, during which time he also enjoyed an artistically fruitful collaboration with **Brian Eno**. *No Pussyfooting* (1973) and *Evening Star* (1975) were among the era's leading *avant garde* recordings, the former of which introduced the tape loop and layered guitar technique known as 'Frippertronics', which later became an artistic trademark. During this period Fripp also produced several experimental jazz releases, notably by Centipede, and having disbanded King Crimson at a time 'all English bands in that genre should have ceased to exist', Fripp retired from music altogether. He re-emerged in 1977, contributing several excellent passages to **David Bowie**'s *Heroes*, before playing on and producing **Peter Gabriel**'s second album. Fripp provided a similar role on **Daryl Hall**'s *Sacred Songs* before completing *Exposure*, on which the artist acknowledged the concurrent punk movement. Simpler and more incisive than previous work, its energetic purpose contrasted the measured, sculpted approach of King Crimson, whom Fripp nonetheless surprisingly reconstituted in 1981. Three well-received albums followed, during which time the guitarist pursued a parallel, more personal path leading an ensemble bearing another resurrected name, the League Of Gentlemen. Both units were disbanded later in the decade, and Fripp subsequently performed and gave tutorials under a 'League Of Crafty Guitarists' banner and recorded with former **Police** member **Andy Summers** and **David Sylvian**.

Now married to singer and actress **Toyah**, this highly talented individual has doggedly followed an uncompromising path, resulting in some highly individual, provocative music. He constantly seeks new and interesting musical ventures, including the various ProjeKct albums with latter-day King Crimson members **Adrian Belew**, **Bill Bruford**, Tony Levin, Pat Mastelotto and Trey Gunn and cofounded the Discipline

Global Mobile label. He also reconvened King Crimson in the mid-90s.

● ALBUMS: as Giles, Giles And Fripp *The Cheerful Insanity Of Giles, Giles And Fripp* (Deram 1968) ★★★, with Brian Eno *No Pussyfooting* (Island/Antilles 1973) ★★★, with Eno *Evening Star* (Island/Antilles 1975) ★★★, *Exposure* (Polydor 1979) ★★★★, *God Save The Queen/Under Heavy Manners* (EG/Polydor 1980) ★★, *Robert Fripp/The League Of Gentlemen* (Editions EG 1981) ★★★, *Let The Power Fall* (Editions EG 1981) ★★★, with Andy Summers *I Advance Masked* (A&M 1982) ★★★★, with Andy Summers *Bewitched* (A&M 1984) ★★★, with The League Of Gentlemen *God Save The King* (Editions EG 1985) ★★★, with Toyah *The Lady Or The Tiger* (Editions EG 1986) ★★★, with The League Of Crafty Guitarists *Live!* (Editions EG 1986) ★★★, *Network* (Editions 1987) ★★★, with The League Of Crafty Guitarists *Get Crafty I* (Guitar Craft Services 1988) ★★★, with The League Of Crafty Guitarists *Live II* (Guitar Craft Services 1990) ★★★, with The League Of Crafty Guitarists *Show Of Hands* (Editions EG 1991) ★★★, with David Sylvian *The First Day* (Virgin 1993) ★★★, as the Robert Fripp String Quintet *The Bridge Between* (Discipline/DGM 1993) ★★★, with David Sylvian *Damage* (Virgin 1994) ★★★, *1999: Soundscapes—Live In Argentina* (DGM 1994) ★★★, *A Blessing Of Tears: 1995 Soundscapes Volume Two—Live In California* (DGM 1995) ★★★, with The League Of Crafty Guitarists *Intergalactic Boogie Express: Live In Europe 1991* (DGM 1995) ★★★, *Radiophonics: 1995 Soundscapes Volume 1—Live In Argentina* (DGM 1996) ★★★, with The League Of Gentlemen *Thrang Thrang Gozinbulx: Official Bootleg Live In 1980* (DGM 1996) ★★★, *That Which Passes: 1995 Soundscapes—Live Volume 3* (DGM 1996) ★★★, *November Suite: Live At Green Park Station* (DGM 1997) ★★, *The Gates Of Paradise* (DGM 1997) ★★★, with Trey Gunn, Bill Rieflin *The Repercussions Of Angelic Behaviour* (First World 1999) ★★★, with Jeffrey Fayman *A Temple In The Clouds* (Projekt 2000) ★★★, with Eno *The Equatorial Stars* (Opal 2004) ★★★.

● COMPILATIONS: *The Essential Fripp And Eno* (Venture 1993) ★★★★.

● DVD/VIDEOS: *Live In Japan* (Discipline 1994), with David Sylvian *Live In Japan* (VAP 1995).

● FURTHER READING: *Robert Fripp: From King Crimson To Guitar Craft*, Eric Tamm.

Frisco Kid

b. Stephen Wray, Western Kingston, Jamaica, West Indies. Wray began to emulate leading DJs while still at school and was eventually given a chance on the microphone at smaller dances. While working in a garage in Kingston, a chance meeting with the owner of the Exodus Nuclear **sound system** led to his performing as the Paro Kid. He became the resident DJ for Exodus and subsequently went to **King Jammy**'s studio to record some specials, changing his name to Frisco Kid. As his career developed, he recorded 'Dance Again' at **Donovan Germain**'s Penthouse studio. Frisco Kid's career prospects looked promising as a result of this release, but after the initial fervour died down, no further recordings surfaced. He returned to recording specials for the sound, and it was at Black Scorpio in 1993 that his recording career took an upward turn. Confusion over studio time led Frisco Kid and DJ **Terror Fabulous** back to Penthouse, where he recorded 'Big Speech'. His second break led to a number of

hits, including 'Wakey News', 'Yuh And Yuh Man', 'Tribulation', 'Yuh A Boom', 'Step Up In Life' and 'Gal A Di Clothes'. His notoriety led to an appearance at the 1995 Reggae Sunsplash festival where he captivated the crowds with an exceptional performance. His success led to an alliance with Patrick Roberts, who enrolled Frisco Kid as part of the Shocking Vibes crew. The crew embarked on an international tour featuring **Little Kirk**, **Silver Cat**, **Tanto Metro**, **Snagga Puss** and **Beenie Man**; the tour represented the debut performances in Europe for Silver Cat and Frisco Kid. The shows received rave receptions from both the critics and audiences alike. In 1996 Frisco Kid joined **Buju Banton**'s label, the newly formed Cell Block 321. The enterprise was designed to promote new talent and Frisco Kid's career advanced with the release of the phenomenal 'Video Light'. His success continued with 'If Looks' and the multi-combination hit 'Matey Anthem', alongside **Mega Banton**, **Spragga Benz**, **Mad Cobra**, **General Degree**, Gringo and **Johnny P**. Many of his hits were featured on the excellent debut album, *Finally*.

● ALBUMS: *Finally* (VP 1999) ★★★★.

Frisell, Bill

b. William Richard Frisell, 18 March 1951, Baltimore, Maryland, USA. Frisell is acknowledged as one of the most influential and exciting jazz guitarists to emerge in the latter half of the 20th century. Collaborating with artists from the world of pop, country, world and classical music has, in addition, brought his unique style to a much wider audience than many of his contemporaries.

Frisell, whose father was a tuba and string-bass player, was raised in Denver, Colorado. He began playing clarinet, then saxophone, finally settling on guitar. He also plays banjo, ukulele and bass. He majored in music at North Colorado University (1969–71) and in 1977 was awarded a diploma in arranging and composition from **Berklee College Of Music** as well as winning the Harris Stanton guitar award. He took lessons from **Jim Hall**, **Johnny Smith** and **Dale Bruning** and cited his favourite players as Hall, **Wes Montgomery** and **Jimi Hendrix**. In the late 70s he began to experiment with a quasi-microtonal style, developing an ambient sound that allowed him to diversify from his bebop roots. At the start of the following decade he signed to **ECM Records**, recording a number of solo albums and collaborating freely with many of the label's artists. During this period he played with many major contemporary jazz figures, including **Eberhard Weber**, **Mike Gibbs**, **Jan Garbarek**, **Charlie Haden**, **Carla Bley**, **Julius Hemphill**, **Gunter Hampel** and **John Scofield**.

Since the late 80s, the Seattle-based Frisell has collaborated with a startling number of artists from a diverse range of musical genres, including **Ronald Shannon Jackson** and bass player Melvin Gibbs as Power Tools, **John Zorn**'s harmolodic hardcore indulgence **Naked City**, the News For Lulu bebop trio with Zorn and **George Lewis**, the **Paul Bley** Quartet featuring **John Surman** and **Paul Motian** and Motian's trio with Frisell and **Joe Lovano**. Frisell's solo work found a wider audience with the release of 1993's *Have A Little Faith* together with a lengthy (by his standards) tour. Ever-changing, in typical jazz musician style, just as he had established a first class trio (with Kermit Driscoll and **Joey Baron**), in 1995 he abandoned the idea for a drummerless unit of trombone, trumpet, guitar and violin. This quartet (featuring Ron Miles, **Curtis Fowlkes** and Eyvind Kang) released a superb album for the Nonesuch label in 1996. By the mid-90s, Frisell was so in-demand that he was working on several projects at the same time, including collaborations with drummers **Ginger Baker** and **Michael Shrieve** and singer-songwriter **Elvis Costello**. He also composed two albums of soundtracks for the silent films of Buster Keaton and in 1997 decamped to Nashville, to record a country-influenced album with the aid of dobro player **Jerry Douglas**, bass player **Viktor Krauss** and members of **Alison Krauss**' band Union Station. Frisell continued to experiment with roots music on the late 90s albums, *Gone, Just Like A Train* and *Good Dog, Happy Man*. At the start of the new millennium, he released his first truly 'solo' album, *Ghost Town*, playing all the instruments (guitar, bass, banjo) and contributing looped samples. Trumpeter Ron Miles and steel guitarist Greg Leisz contributed beautifully understated support to the follow-up *Blues Dream*. Frisell returned to the country vibe of *Nashville* with 2002's *The Willies*, teaming up with Danny Barnes (the **Bad Livers**) and bass player Keith Lowe on a collection of largely traditional material. He cast his net wider for the superlative follow-up *The Intercontinentals*, blending his investigation of Americana with folk music from other continents. He was supported in this venture by regular collaborators Jenny Scheinman (violin) and Greg Leisz (steel guitar) as well as Brazilian guitarist **Vinicius Cantuária**, Malian percussionist/vocalist Sidiki Camara and Greek-Macedonian vocalist/oud player Christos Govetas. During the same period, Frisell collaborated with Jenny Scheinman (violin), Eyvind Kang (viola) and Hank Roberts (cello) on music to accompany a book of paintings by Gerhard Richter.

In 2004 Frisell broke with regular producer Lee Townsend to record *Unspeakable* with the more maverick talents of Hal Willner. The album eschewed Americana and instead took inspiration from classic US soul, utilizing a string section and Tony Scherr (bass) and Kenny Wollesen (drums) from **Sex Mob** to great effect on what proved to be Frisell's most upbeat recording for some time.

Frisell's style makes use of electronics to produce long sustained notes with lots of vibrato and legato lines, possibly a legacy of his training as a reed player. He is equally convincing whether stitching feedback howls into the midst of violent Naked City melees or playing gentle country-influenced solo tunes, post-modern bottleneck blues or lop-sided melancholic ballads. Much of his most recent work shows him riding a peak of creativity. With the likes of John Scofield and **Pat Metheny** he is currently one of the world's leading all-round jazz guitarists.

● ALBUMS: *In Line* (ECM 1983) ★★★, with Tim Berne *... Theoretically* (Empire 1984) ★★★, *Rambler* (ECM 1985) ★★★, with Vernon Reid *Smash & Scatteration* (Rykodisc 1985) ★★★, with Power Tools *Strange Meeting* (Antilles 1987) ★★★, *Lookout For Hope* (ECM 1988) ★★★, with John Zorn, George Lewis *News For Lulu* (hatART 1988) ★★★, *Before We Were Born* (Elektra/Musician 1989) ★★★★, *Is That You?* (Elektra/Musician 1989) ★★★, *Where In The World?* (Elektra 1991) ★★★, with Zorn, Lewis *More News For Lulu* 1989 recording (hatART 1992) ★★★, *Have A Little Faith* (Nonesuch 1993) ★★★★, *This Land* (Nonesuch 1993) ★★★, with Ginger Baker, Charlie Haden *Going Back Home* (Atlantic 1994) ★★★, *The High Sign/One Week (Music For The Films Of Buster Keaton)* (Nonesuch 1994) ★★★, *Go West (Music For The Films Of Buster*

Keaton) (Nonesuch 1994) ★★★, with Kermit Driscoll, Joey Baron *Live* (Gramavision 1995) ★★★, with Elvis Costello *Deep Dead Blue Live 25 June 95* (Nonesuch 1995) ★★★, with Victor Bruce Godsey, Brian Ales *American Blood/Safety In Numbers* (Intuition 1995) ★★★, *Quartet* (Nonesuch 1996) ★★★★, with Baker, Haden *Falling Off The Roof* (Atlantic 1996) ★★★★, with Dave Holland, Lee Konitz, Kenny Wheeler *Angel Song* (ECM 1997) ★★★★, *Nashville* (Nonesuch 1997) ★★★★, *Gone, Just Like A Train* (Nonesuch 1997) ★★★, with Fred Hersch *Songs We Know* (Nonesuch 1998) ★★★, *Good Dog, Happy Man* (Nonesuch 1999) ★★★★, *Ghost Town* (Nonesuch 2000) ★★★★, *Blues Dream* (Nonesuch 2001) ★★★★, with Dave Holland, Elvin Jones *Bill Frisell With Dave Holland And Elvin Jones* (Nonesuch 2001) ★★★, *The Willies* (Nonesuch 2002) ★★★, *Richter 858* (Label 2002) ★★★, *The Intercontinentals* (Nonesuch 2003) ★★★★, *Petra Haden And Bill Frisell* (True North 2003) ★★★, *Unspeakable* (Nonesuch 2004) ★★★★, with Paul Motian, Joe Lovano *I Have The Room Above Her* (ECM 2005) ★★★, *East/West* (Nonesuch 2005) ★★★, with Petra Haden *Petra Haden And Bill Frisell* (Rykodisc 2005) ★★★.

● COMPILATIONS: *Works* (ECM 1988) ★★★★, *A Collection* (WEA 2000) ★★★★, *Selected Recordings* (ECM 2002) ★★★★.

● DVD/VIDEOS: *The Guitar Artistry Of Bill Frisell* (Rittor Music).

Frishberg, Dave

b. David L. Frishberg, 23 March 1933, St. Paul, Minnesota, USA. Frishberg learned to play piano as a child, at one point horrifying his teacher by arranging a Mozart test-piece as a conga. After studying journalism at the University of Minnesota, he spent two years in the US Air Force before he decided to take the plunge and try to earn his living playing piano in New York City. During the 60s, musically his formative decade, he played in bands led by jazz musicians such as **Bobby Hackett**, **Al Cohn**, **Zoot Sims**, **Ben Webster**, **Roy Eldridge** and **Gene Krupa**. He also accompanied many singers, including **Carmen McRae**, **Dick Haymes**, **Susannah McCorkle**, **Anita O'Day**, **Irene Kral** and **Jimmy Rushing**, often creating stylish arrangements that presented the singer in a new light (for example, Rushing's 1971 set, *The You And Me That Used To Be*). During this period, Frishberg was busily writing songs, which were performed by O'Day, **Blossom Dearie**, **Al Jarreau**, **Cleo Laine** and others, while he was gradually summoning up the nerve to perform them himself in public. In 1971 he moved to Los Angeles, where he worked in film and television studios, spent a long stint with **Herb Alpert**, played occasionally in the big band of **Bill Berry** and began performing a cabaret-style act that combined superb jazz piano playing with highly sophisticated, witty songs delivered in an eccentric vocal style.

Although his piano playing is of a very high order, ranging from bebop through mainstream and back to romping stride, it is as a composer and lyricist that Frishberg has made his greatest and probably most lasting mark on music. His songs, which tell contemporary tales and fables, concern themselves with seemingly mundane topics, such as lawyers, ('My Attorney Bernie'), long-forgotten brands of beer ('White Castle'), love's deceits ('Blizzard Of Lies') and heroes of baseball and jazz ('Van Lingle Mungo' and 'Dear Bix'). His wittily ironic lyric writing combines devilish ingenuity with a childlike innocence and an appreciation of life's better but fleeting moments, as in the song 'Here's To Yesterday', which contains the line 'tomorrow wasn't built to last.'

In the 80s Frishberg, now resident in Portland, Oregon, continued to play on the west coast but also regularly appeared in clubs and at festivals across the USA and in the UK. During the following decade and into the new millennium, Frishberg continued touring and recording, concentrating more on his piano playing but still writing songs which eloquently prove that, for all fears to the contrary, they still do write songs like that anymore.

● ALBUMS: *Oklahoma Toad* (CTI 1968) ★★★, *Solo And Trio* (Seeds 1975) ★★★, *Getting Some Fun Out Of Life* (Concord Jazz 1977) ★★★★, *You're A Lucky Guy* (Concord Jazz 1978) ★★★★, *The Dave Frishberg Songbook, Vol. 1* (Omnisound 1981) ★★★★, *The Dave Frishberg Songbook, Vol. 2* (Omnisound 1981) ★★★, *Live At Vine Street* (Fantasy 1984) ★★★★, *Can't Take You Nowhere* (Fantasy 1986) ★★★★, *Let's Eat Home* (Concord Jazz 1989) ★★★, *Where You At?* (Bloomdido 1991) ★★★, *Double Play* (Arbors 1992) ★★★, *Quality Time* (Sterling 1993) ★★★, with Rebecca Kilgore *Not A Care In The World* (Arbors 1997) ★★★, *By Himself: Arbors Piano Series, Volume 3* (Arbors 1998) ★★★★, with Kilgore *The Starlit Hour* (Arbors 2001) ★★★, *Do You Miss New York? Live At Jazz At Lincoln Center* (Arbors 2003) ★★★.

● COMPILATIONS: *Classics* (Concord Jazz 1981) ★★★★, *Lookin' Good* (Concord Jazz 2001) ★★★★.

Frith, Fred

b. 17 February 1949, Heathfield, East Sussex, England. One of the leading *avant garde* guitarists in contemporary music, Frith played violin and piano as a child before falling in love with the guitar. In 1968 he cofounded the left-field rock group **Henry Cow** and in 1974 recorded an innovative album of electric guitar improvisations, *Guitar Solos*. After Henry Cow's demise in the late 70s, he worked with several ex-members in the Art Bears (releasing *Hopes And Fears*, *Winter Songs* and *The World As It Is Today*). During the 80s Frith was based mostly in New York City, where he guested with **Material** (*Memory Serves*) and played in the groups Skeleton Crew (*Learn To Talk* and *The Country Of Blinds*), Massacre (*Killing Time*) and **Naked City**. He also recorded two superb albums (*Live, Love, Larf & Loaf* and *Invisible Means*) with fellow guitarists **Henry Kaiser**, Jim French and **Richard Thompson**.

At the end of the decade, Frith began to branch out, writing music for films, theatre and dance projects while continuing to play with his own groups, Keep The Dog and the Fred Frith Guitar Quartet. His own prolific solo output, meanwhile, continued to showcase a quirky blend of guitar experimentation, free jazz, hard rock, fold music and improvisation. Long-time collaborators **John Zorn**, Larry Ochs, Miya Masaoka, Chris Cutler, **Tom Cora**, Bob Ostertag, Ikue Mori and **Zeena Parkins** frequently join him. Frith has worked as a session guitarist on records by innumerable artists (including **Brian Eno**, **Robert Wyatt**, the **Golden Palominos**, Gavin Bryars, his own recent unit Maybe Monday and the **Residents**); has played total improvisation with **Lol Coxhill**, Phil Minton, **Hans Reichel** and many others; and has had several of his compositions recorded by the **ROVA Saxophone Quartet** (*Long On Logic*). He continues to hold improvising workshops throughout the world and in 1995

moved to Germany before becoming composer-in-residence at L'Ecole Nationale de Musique in Villeurbanne, France. In 1997 he relocated to America to become composer-in-residence at Mills College, Oakland, California. Two years later he became professor of composition at the college.

● ALBUMS: *Guitar Solos* (Caroline 1974) ★★★, with Henry Kaiser *With Friends Like These* (Metalanguage 1979) ★★★, *Gravity* (Ralph 1980) ★★★, *Speechless* (Ralph 1981) ★★★, *Live In Japan* (Recommended 1982) ★★★, with Phil Minton, Bob Ostertag *Voice Of America* (Rift 1982) ★★★, with Totsuzen Danball *Live At Loft Shinjuku Tokyo Japan 23 July '81* (Floor 1983) ★★★, *Cheap At Half The Price* (Ralph 1983) ★★★, with Chris Cutler *Live In Prague And Washington* (Re 1983) ★★★, with Lol Coxhill *French Gigs* (AAA 1983) ★★★, with Kaiser *Who Needs Enemies?* (Metalanguage 1983) ★★★, with Rene Lussier *Nous Autres* (Victo 1987) ★★★, with Kaiser, John French, Richard Thompson *Live, Love, Larf & Loaf* (Rhino/Demon 1987) ★★★★, *The Technology Of Tears* (RecRec/SST 1988) ★★★★, *The Top Of His Head* film soundtrack (Crammed Discs 1989) ★★★, with French, Kaiser, Thompson *Invisible Means* (Windham Hill/Demon 1990) ★★★, *Step Across The Border* film soundtrack (RecRec/East Side Digital 1990) ★★★, with Ferdinand Richard *Dropera* (RecRec 1991) ★★★, with Tim Hodginkson *Live Improvisations* (Woof/Megaphone 1992) ★★★, with Francois-Michel Pesenti *Helter Skelter* (RecRec 1993) ★★★, *Quartets* 1992 recordings (RecRec 1994) ★★★, with Marc Ribot *Subsonic 1: Sound Of A Distant Episode* (Sub Rosa/Subsonic 1994) ★★★★, with Cutler *Live In Trondheim, Berlin, Limoges* (ReR 1994) ★★★, with John Zorn *Art Of Memory* (Incus 1995) ★★★, *Middle Of The Moment* (RecRec 1995) ★★★, with Kato Hideki, Ikue Mori *Death Ambient* (Tzadik 1995) ★★★★, with Karin Scholl, Daniel Erismann, Lucas N. Niggli, Hans Koch, Peter Kowald *Nil* (Unit 1995) ★★★, *Allies* (RecRec 1996) ★★★, *Eye To Ear* (Tzadik 1997) ★★★, *Ayaya Moses* (Ambiances Magnetiques 1997) ★★★, with Jean-Pierre Drouet *Improvisations* (Transes Europeennes 1997) ★★★, with Noel Akchote *Reel* (Rectangle 1997) ★★★, *The Previous Evening* (ReR Megacorp 1997) ★★★, with Tom Cora *Etymology* 1995 recordings (Rarefaction 1997) ★★★, with Percy Howard, Charles Hayward, Bill Laswell *Meridiem* (Materiali Sonori 1998) ★★★, *Upbeat* (Ambiances Magnetiques 1999) ★★★, *Traffic Continues* (Winter & Winter 2000) ★★★, with Cutler *2 Gentlemen In Verona* (ReR Megacorp 2000) ★★★★, with J.P. Drouet, Louis Sclavis *I Dream Of You Jumping* (Victo 2001) ★★★, *Clearing* (Tzadik 2001) ★★★★, with Maybe Monday *Digital Wildlife* (Winter & Winter 2002) ★★, with Rova Saxophone Quartet *Freedom In Fragments* (Tzadik 2002) ★★★, with Anne Bourne, John Oswald *Dearness* (Spool 2002) ★★★, *Accidental* (ReR Megacorp 2002) ★★, with Jean Derome, Pierre Tanguay, Myles Boisen *All Is Bright, But It Is Not Day* (Ambiances Magnéticques 2002) ★★★, with Keep The Dog *That House We Lived In* (Fred 2003) ★★★, *Rivers And Tides (Working With Time)* (Winter & WInter 2003) ★★★, *Middle Of The Moment* (RER 2004) ★★★, *Eleventh Hour* (Winter & Winter 2005) ★★.

● COMPILATIONS: with Henry Kaiser *With Enemies Like These, Who Needs Friends?* (SST 1987) ★★★★, *Live In Moscow, Prague And Washington* 1979, 1989 live recordings (ReR 1990) ★★★, *Guitar Solos* (RecRec/East Side Digital

1994) ★★★★, with Kaiser *Friends & Enemies* (Cuneiform 1999) ★★★★, *Stone, Brick, Glass, Wood, Wire (Graphic Scores 1986–1996)* (I Dischi Di Angelica 1999) ★★★, *Prints: Snapshots, Postcards, Messages And Miniatures 1987–2001* (ReR 2002) ★★★★.

Frizzell, David

b. 26 September 1941, El Dorado, Arkansas, USA. In the mid-50s, David hitchhiked to California to join and tour with his older brother **Lefty Frizzell**. He recorded some unsuccessful country rockabilly tracks for **Columbia Records** in 1958 and served in the US Army during the early 60s. After his discharge, he made further recordings for various labels and gained a Top 40 US country chart hit in 1970, after returning to Columbia, with 'I Just Can't Help Believing'. He worked for a time in the 70s for **Buck Owens** on his networked *Ranch Show* television programme, managed a nightclub and had minor hits on Cartwheel, **Capitol Records** and RSO. He first worked at the club with **Shelly West** (the daughter of singer **Dottie West**), who was at the time married to his younger brother Allen Frizzell (b. 1951). Allen was for a time Dottie West's lead guitarist and frontman. He had three minor country hits in the 80s in his own right but became more involved with the business side of the industry than with performing. In 1978 the two brothers and Shelly West toured extensively. David and Shelly had a US country number 1 in 1981 with 'You're The Reason God Made Oklahoma', which featured in the Clint Eastwood movie *Any Which Way You Can*. They had made a demo recording of the song some considerable time before, but it had been turned down by record companies until chosen by Eastwood for the movie. Further country Top 10 hits followed including 'A Texas State Of Mind' and 'I Just Came Here To Dance'. He also had a popular solo recording, 'Lefty', a tribute to his brother, that also featured **Merle Haggard**. In 1982 he had a US country number 1 with 'I'm Gonna Hire A Wino To Decorate Our Home', followed by a number 5 hit with 'Lost My Baby Blues'. Another duet recording with Shelly West called 'Please Surrender' was used by Eastwood in his movie *Honkytonk Man*. Further solo hits include 'Where Are You Spending Your Nights These Days', 'A Million Light Beers Ago' and a further Top 20 duet with 'It's A Be Together Night'. A talented and capable singer, although by no means the equal of his legendary brother, even if at times there is a slight vocal resemblance.

● ALBUMS: *The Family's Fine But This One's All Mine* (Warners 1982) ★★★, *On My Own Again* (Viva 1983) ★★★, *Solo* (1984) ★★★, *David Sings Lefty Frizzell* (1987) ★★★, *My Life Is Just A Bridge* (1993) ★★★; with Shelly West *Carrying On The Family Names* (Warners 1981) ★★★, *Our Best To You* (Viva 1982) ★★★, *In Session* (Viva 1983) ★★★, *Golden Duets* (Viva 1984) ★★★★, *David Frizzell 2001* (Nashville America 2001) ★★, *Confidentially* (Nashville America 2005) ★★★.

Frizzell, Lefty

b. William Orville Frizzell, 31 March 1928, Corsicana, Navarro County, Texas, USA, d. 19 July 1975, Nashville, Tennessee, USA. The eldest of eight children of an itinerant oilfield worker, Frizzell was raised mainly in El Dorado, Arkansas, but also lived in sundry places in Texas and Oklahoma. Greatly influenced by his parents' old 78s of **Jimmie Rodgers**, he sang as a young boy, and when aged 12, he had a regular

spot on KELD El Dorado. Two years later he was performing at local dances at Greenville and further exposure on other radio stations followed as the family moved around. At the age of 16, he was playing the honky tonks and clubs in places such as Waco and Dallas and grew into a tough character himself, performing the music of Jimmie Rodgers, plus some of his own songs. Some accounts suggest that it was at this time that he became known as Lefty after fighting in a Golden Gloves boxing match, but this appears to have been later publicity hype by **Columbia Records**. Both his father and his wife steadfastly denied the story, maintaining that Lefty actually gained the nickname when he beat the school bully during his schooldays. It is further claimed that it was a schoolfriend and guitarist called Gene Whitworth who first called him Lefty (he was actually always known as Sonny to his family).

In 1945 he married, and his wife Alice became the inspiration for several of his songs over the 30 years the marriage lasted. More and more frequently, his drinking landed him in trouble with the authorities, and he was inspired to write his famous song 'I Love You A Thousand Ways' while spending a night in a Texas country jail. He made his first recordings for Columbia in 1950 and had immediate success when 'If You've Got The Money, I've Got The Time' and 'I Love You A Thousand Ways' both became US country number 1 hits. He became close friends with **Hank Williams**, who suggested Frizzell should join the *Grand Ole Opry*. Frizzell replied, 'Look, I got the number-one song, the number-two song, the number-seven song, the number-eight song on the charts and you tell me I need to join the *Opry*'. Williams thought for a while and commented, 'Darned if you ain't got a hell of an argument'. The following year he had seven Top 10 entries, which included three more number 1 hits, 'I Want To Be With You Always' (which also gained Top 30 status in the US pop charts), 'Always Late (With Your Kisses)' and 'Give Me More More More (Of Your Kisses)'. Further Top 10s followed, and as **Merle Haggard** later sang in his song 'The Way It Was in '51', 'Hank and Lefty crowded every jukebox'. In 1952 Frizzell did join the *Grand Ole Opry* but left after a few months, stating that he did not like it.

In 1953 Frizzell moved from Beaumont, Texas, to Los Angeles, where he became a regular on *Town Hall Party*. He had by now become accepted as a national entertainer, and he recorded regularly, although the hits became less frequent. His hard-drinking lifestyle was partly to blame, and certainly he and Williams suffered similar troubles. Charles Wolfe quotes Frizzell as once saying: 'All Hank thought about was writing. He did record a number he wrote because I was having trouble with my better half, called 'I'm Sorry for You, My Friend'.' Some time later, the friendship between the two men was damaged when Frizzell refused to allow Williams to record 'What Am I Gonna Do With All This Love I Have For You', Frizzell intending to record it himself, although, for some reason, he never did so.

Lefty Frizzell became upset about material not being released by Columbia, and in 1954 he broke up his band and stopped writing songs; tired of the way he had been exploited, his behaviour became more unpredictable. He was joined in California by his brother **David Frizzell**, and for a time they toured together. Eventually he charted again with his version of **Marty Robbins**' 'Cigarettes And Coffee Blues', and in 1959 he enjoyed a number 6 US country hit with 'The Long Black

Veil'. The *Town Hall Party* had closed in 1960, and late in 1961 Frizzell decided to move to Nashville. He played bookings wherever he could and made further recordings, achieving minor hits that included 'Don't Let Her See Me Cry'. His career received a welcome boost in 1964 when 'Saginaw, Michigan' became a country number 1 and also entered the US pop charts. This song must rate as one of country music's finest ballads, and Frizzell's version has rightly become a standard and worthy of a place in any collection. Twelve more chart entries followed between 1964 and 1972, but only 'She's Gone Gone Gone' reached the Top 20. In the late 60s, he became despondent that Columbia was not releasing his material; the label issued some albums but released few singles that were potential chart hits.

In 1968 he even recorded with **June Stearns** as Agnes And Orville, but concerned at the lack of promotion of his own material, his drinking worsened. In 1972, after 22 years with the label, he left Columbia and joined **ABC Records**. The change seemed to work wonders—he set about recording material for albums, resumed playing concerts all over the USA and appeared on network television. He charted with such songs as 'I Can't Get Over You To Change My Life', 'I Never Go Around Mirrors' and 'Railroad Lady', and his album releases proved very popular. His superb song 'That's The Way Love Goes' (his own recording was only issued as a b-side) became a US country number 1 for **Johnny Rodriguez** in 1974 and Merle Haggard in 1984. Frizzell developed high blood pressure but refused to take medication to treat the condition since he thought the medicine would interfere with his alcohol consumption. Even in the depths of his drinking, he remained humorous, which led writer Bob Oermann to describe him as 'a loveable, punch-drunk, boozy, puddin'-headed, bear-like kind of a guy who never really got along with Nashville or the *Opry*'. He spent much time between concerts fishing at his home just outside Nashville. He was 47 (although he looked older) and, aside from the blood pressure, seemed to be in reasonable health. It therefore came as a surprise to most when, on the morning of 19 July 1975, he suffered a massive stroke and died later that evening of the resulting haemorrhage.

Lefty Frizzell was a great songwriter and one of the best stylists that the world of country music has ever seen. His singing was distinctive, with a unique style of pronunciation and a laid-back delivery and gentle vibrato that may have appeared lazy but was in fact part of a carefully designed pattern that he alone mastered. The bending of words as emphasized in 'Alway-yayys Lay-yate' (Always Late) and similar songs led to him being described as a genius for phrasing. John Pugh once described his singing as 'a compelling, ethereal, transcendent vocal quality that has produced some of the most hauntingly beautiful sounds ever to emanate from a pair of human vocal chords'. His influence is evident on later performers such as Merle Haggard, **John Anderson**, **Stoney Edwards**, **Randy Travis** and **George Strait**, who, although not perhaps intentionally trying to imitate their mentor, are readily identifiable as students of Frizzell. Since his death many artists have recorded tribute songs, while some have even recorded complete albums, including **Willie Nelson** (*To Lefty From Willie*) and brother David Frizzell (*David Sings Lefty*). Lefty Frizzell was elected to the Nashville Songwriters' Association International Hall Of Fame in 1972 and inducted into the **Country Music Hall Of Fame** in 1982.

● ALBUMS: *The Songs Of Jimmie Rodgers* 10-inch album (Columbia 1951) ★★★★, *Listen To Lefty* 10-inch album (Columbia 1952) ★★★★, shared with Carl Smith and Marty Robbins *Carl, Lefty & Marty* (Columbia 1956) ★★★★, *The One And Only Lefty Frizzell* (Columbia 1959) ★★★★, *Lefty Frizzell Sings The Songs Of Jimmie Rodgers* (Harmony 1960) ★★★★, *Saginaw, Michigan* (Columbia 1964) ★★★, *The Sad Side Of Love* (Columbia 1965) ★★★, *Lefty Frizzell's Country Favorites* (Harmony 1966) ★★★, *Lefty Frizzell Puttin' On* (Columbia 1967) ★★★, *Mom And Dad's Waltz (& Other Great Country Hits)* (Harmony 1967) ★★★, *Signed Sealed And Delivered* (Columbia 1968) ★★★, *The Legendary Lefty Frizzell* aka *Lefty* (ABC 1973) ★★★, *The Legend Lives On* (Columbia 1983) ★★★, *The Legendary Last Sessions* (MCA 1986) ★★★ *Lefty Goes To Nashville* (Rounder 1988) ★★★.

● COMPILATIONS: *Lefty Frizzell's Greatest Hits* (Columbia 1966) ★★★★, *Remembering . . . The Greatest Hits Of Lefty Frizzell* (Columbia 1975) ★★★, *The ABC Collection* (ABC 1977) ★★★★, *Treasures Untold: The Early Recordings Of Lefty* (Rounder 1980) ★★★, *Lefty Frizzell* (Columbia Historic Edition 1982) ★★★, *American Originals* (Columbia 1990) ★★★, *The Best Of Lefty Frizzell* (Rhino 1991) ★★★★, *His Life—His Music* 14-LP box set (Bear Family 1984) ★★★★ reissued as *Life's Like Poetry* 12-CD box set (Bear Family 1992) ★★★★, *That's The Way Love Goes: The Final Recordings Of Lefty Frizzell* (Varèse Sarabande 1997) ★★★, *Look What Thoughts Will Do: The Essential, 1950–1963* (Columbia 1997) ★★★★, *Shine, Shave, Shower (It's Saturday Night)* (Proper 2004) ★★★★.

● FURTHER READING: *Lefty Frizzell His Life—His Music*, Charles Wolfe. *The Honky Tonk Life Of Country Music's Greatest Singer*, Daniel Cooper.

Froeba, Frank

b. August 1907, New Orleans, Louisiana, USA, d. 16 February 1981, Miami, Florida, USA. Froeba was a jazz pianist and composer who played with many bands. He turned professional at the age of 15, working as a pianist in clubs and as a theatre organist before leading his own band in Atlantic City, New Jersey. He then played with **Enoch Light**, **Irving Aaronson** and **Will Osborne** during the early 30s and appeared with **Benny Goodman** in 1934/5 on his *Let's Dance* US radio show. Major hits with his own band included 'The Music Goes Round And Round' and 'The Organ Grinder's Swing' in 1936. He then spent the rest of the 30s as part of the **Farley And Riley** band and the Milt Herth Quartet before embarking on a solo career once more, recording in ragtime and honky tonk style during the 40s and 50s. During the late 50s he worked mainly in the Miami area, leading a variety of ensembles. His best known composition 'Jumpin' Jive', written with **Cab Calloway** and Jack Palmer, was revived in 1981 by **Joe Jackson** as the title track of a album featuring music from the 40s.

● ALBUMS: *Back Room Piano* 10-inch album (Decca 1950) ★★★, *Old Time Piano* 10-inch album (Decca 1950) ★★★, *Boys In The Backroom* 10-inch album (Varsity 1950) ★★★.

Froggatt, Raymond

b. Raymond William Froggatt, 13 November 1941, Birmingham, West Midlands, England. Froggatt had a traumatic childhood, with his father dying when he was young and his missing schooling because of tuberculosis. Froggatt joined the Birmingham scene in the mid-60s, and his group, the Monopoly, was signed to **Polydor Records**. Their first single, 'House Of Lords', was written by the **Bee Gees**, and at Polydor's request, he used the stage name of Steve Newman—a cross between Steve McQueen and Paul Newman—but he soon reverted back to his own name. As part of the band the Raymond Froggatt, he recorded 'Red Balloon', explaining: 'I spent some time in Paris and there's a game in which children hold balloons on strings and weave in and out of them. If you get to the end of the balloons, you marry the farmer's daughter.' Dave Clark heard Froggatt's version, covered it with the **Dave Clark Five**, and reached number 7 in the UK chart. Although Froggatt's 'Big Ship' was rejected for **Lulu** in the *Eurovision Song Contest*, it became a Top 10 hit for **Cliff Richard**, who recorded several more of his songs. Other compositions include 'Rachel's Comin' Home' (**Joan Baez**), 'Only The Memories' (**Gladys Knight And The Pips**) and 'Everybody's Losin'' (**Leon Russell**). The track 'Louise' included a concertina solo from an 82-year-old busker.

In the mid-70s, Froggatt, with guidance from promoter **Mervyn Conn**, switched to country and made a popular easy listening album, *Southern Fried Frog*, in Nashville, with top producer **Larry Butler**. This helped establish him as the UK's top country artist and for a time, at every live performance, fans would hold up toy frogs and sway with their 'Froggie' scarves. His rough-hewn features, shades, white dinner jacket and torn jeans made him a distinctive figure, and he has even been accepted in Warsaw ('I was not allowed to do 'Teach Me Pa' as the authorities thought it was subversive'). 'Don't Let Me Cry Again' was an airplay hit on BBC Radio 2 in 1983, and he recorded 'Maybe The Angels' in aid of leukaemia research. Hartley Cain has long provided lead guitar for Froggatt, who says of his own playing: 'I'm worse now than I was after a few lessons. It helps with my writing because I'm not restricted to certain chord sequences. Some of my songs sound clever but really it's a total lack of knowledge.' He is also one of the few musicians to be granted the Freedom of the City of Birmingham. Froggatt published his entertaining autobiography in 1992.

● ALBUMS: *The Voice And Writing Of Raymond Froggatt* (Polydor 1968) ★★, *Bleach* (Bell 1972) ★★★, *Rogues And Thieves* (Darbilt/Reprise 1974) ★★, *Southern Fried Frog* (Jet 1978) ★★★★, *Conversations* (Jet 1979) ★★★, *Stay With Me* (Merco 1980) ★★★, *Sooner Or Later* (1982) ★★★, *Why* (Happy Face 1984) ★★★, *Raymond Froggatt* (1986) ★★★, *Live At Birmingham Odeon* (1987) ★★, *Is It Rollin' Bob* (1988) ★★★, *Tour '89* (1989) ★★, *Songs From A Minstrel* (1992) ★★★, *Here's To Everyone* (Red Balloon 1993) ★★★, *Someday* (Red Balloon 1995) ★★★, *Moonshine* (Mooncrest 1997) ★★.

● COMPILATIONS: Collection (Red Balloon 1996), *As Cold As A Landlord's Heart: The Jet Years* (Castle 2003) ★★★, *The Voice And Writing Of Raymond Froggatt* (Repertoire 2004) ★★★.

● DVD/VIDEOS: *Froggie At The Symphony Hall Sept 04* 2-CD set (Red Balloon 2004).

● FURTHER READING: *Raymond Who?*, Raymond Froggatt.

Frogmorton

A refreshing UK folk rock band whose members wrote their own, characteristic material and distinguished themselves in

the 70s by having no fiddle and not relying on any juiced up jigs to create an atmosphere.

● ALBUMS: *At Last* (1976) ★★★.

Frogs

With a sound that is best described as a cross between **Captain Beefheart** and lo-fi indie rock, the Frogs became one of the most name-checked bands by established 90s alt rockers such as **Nirvana**, **Pearl Jam**, **Beck** and **Smashing Pumpkins**, although they remain in a ghetto of obscurity. Several different members have passed through the band's ranks since their formation during the early 80s, but through all Milwaukee, Wisconsin, USA–based brothers Dennis and Jimmy Flemion (who play drums and guitar, respectively) have been present. A series of home recordings and local live shows followed, which featured Jimmy develop a gimmick that remains with him, sporting larger-than-life 'monster wings'. The band's self-titled and self-issued debut followed in 1988. A year later, the band issued the pro-gay underground classic *It's Only Right And Natural*.

Surprisingly, nothing was heard from the Frogs on record for several years afterwards, although they received much press attention when the aforementioned bands began praising them. Pearl Jam issued a split single ('Immortality'/'Rearviewmirror'), the Smashing Pumpkins included a Frogs 'profile' on their *Vieuphoria* home video, while **Beck** sampled them on his hit single 'Where It's At'. Beginning in the late 90s, the Flemion brothers began issuing albums on a more regular basis, including 1999's *Bananimals* and 2001's *Hopscotch Lollipop Sunday Surprise*. The 1996 release, *My Daughter The Broad*, compiled highlights from a series of cassettes distributed to the band's fans during the early 90s, while the controversial *Racially Yours* finally gained a release in 2000 after being kept in limbo since the recording sessions seven years earlier.

● ALBUMS: *The Frogs* (Frogs 1988) ★★★, *It's Only Right And Natural* (Homestead 1989) ★★★★, *Bananimals* (Four Alarm 1999) ★★★, *Racially Yours* 1993 recording (Four Alarm 2000) ★★★, *Hopscotch Lollipop Sunday Surprise* (Scratchie 2001) ★★★.

● COMPILATIONS: *My Daughter The Broad* (Matador 1996) ★★★★.

Frohman, Charles

b. 17 June 1860, Sandusky, Ohio, USA, d. 7 May 1915, Atlantic Ocean. Intent on a life in the theatre, Frohman took many menial backstage jobs as he learned his trade. He was still only in his mid-twenties when he staged his first production and was soon chalking up successes, among them being the New York premiere of Oscar Wilde's *The Importance of Being Earnest* (1895). Throughout the last decade of the old century and the first of the new, Frohman was responsible for bringing to the stage many musical comedies. These he produced in the USA and in the UK, sometimes taking Broadway shows to London's West End, sometimes reversing this traffic. Among Frohman's productions in these years were *The Shop Girl* (1894), J.M. Barrie's **Peter Pan** (1899, New York/1901, London), **Madame Sherry** (1903, London), *A Waltz Dream* (1908), *The Dollar Princess*, **The Arcadians** (both 1909), *The Sunshine Girl* and **The Girl From Utah** (both 1913). Included in the latter was **Jerome Kern**'s timeless standard 'They Didn't Believe Me'. In 1915 Frohman was aboard the S.S. *Lusitania* when the ship was torpedoed off the coast of Ireland. Reputedly, before the ship went down, he quoted a line from *Peter Pan*: 'To die would be an awfully big adventure.'

From A Jack To A King

With a title borrowed from **Ned Miller**'s 1963 hit record, *From A Jack To A King* opened in London's West End on 20 July 1992 at the Ambassador's Theatre, following a run at the tiny Boulevard Theatre in Soho. Bob Carlton's rock 'n' roll musical spoof of Shakespeare's *Macbeth* followed his tremendous success in 1989 with **Return To The Forbidden Planet**, a rock version of *The Tempest*. In this show, Eric Glamis (Matthew Devitt) is a stand-in drummer for the Coronets, a band run by Duke Box (Christian Roberts). He aspires to replace the megastar lead singer Terry King (an arrogant **Elvis Presley** impersonation by Robert Dallas). Goaded by his lover, Queenie (Allison Harding), Glasmis tinkers with the King's motorbike ('Is this a spanner I see before me?') with fatal results. He gets the gig, though, and experiences (temporary) glory but subsequent disillusionment. Large extracts, and sometimes complete speeches and scenes, are extracted from not only *Macbeth* but other works by the Bard, such as *Hamlet* and *Romeo And Juliet*. These are absorbed into the story, which is punctuated with lots of classic songs such as 'Shakin' All Over', 'You've Lost That Lovin' Feelin'', 'Keep On Running', 'Leader Of The Pack', 'Stepping Stone'. Unfortunately for Carlton, the show arrived in London at a time when audiences were already being saturated with the old songs in shows such as **Good Rockin' Tonite**, **Buddy**, **The Cotton Club**, **Five Guys Named Moe**—and his own **Return To The Forbidden Planet**—and this may well have been the reason why *From A Jack To A King* was unable to stay around for longer than 202 performances. A 'cabaret-style' revival was presented at the Studio Theatre in the London suburb of Wimbledon in 1994.

Froman, Jane

b. 10 November 1911, St. Louis, Missouri, USA, d. 22 April 1980. Raised in Columbia, Missouri, where her mother was head of music at the Christian College, Froman showed early musical promise. Educated at the college and later at the University of Missouri and the Cincinnati Conservatory of Music, she began singing professionally while still in her teens. She was heard by **Paul Whiteman**, who placed her under contract. Froman made her Broadway debut in the **Ziegfeld Follies** of 1934 and introduced **E.Y. 'Yip' Harburg** and **Vernon Duke**'s 'Suddenly' and 'What Is There To Say?' with Everett Marshall. In the same year she had her first hit record with 'I Only Have Eyes For You'. Later in the decade and into the early 40s she made a name as a leading nightclub performer and was also a popular draw on the radio.

In 1943 she was on her way to Europe to sing for US servicemen when the aircraft in which she was travelling crashed at sea. Although severely injured, she was one of 15 survivors of the accident. Subsequently, she underwent numerous operations, but despite pain and lasting disabilities, she returned to performing. Indeed, she rehearsed her return to the stage, in *Artists And Models* (1944), while still convalescing. In the 50s she had further record success with 'I'll Walk Alone', 'Wish You Were Here', 'I Believe' and 'Robe Of Cavalry'. She continued to tour and recorded the soundtrack for a Hollywood biopic of her life, **With A Song In My Heart** (1952), in which Susan Hayward mimed to her

singing. Froman also appeared on television, but by 1962 she had finally decided to retire. With her distinctive, deep voice, Froman was one of the most popular singers on the New York scene and on the radio in the 30s. Her undoubted courage and determination made her comeback during the 40s especially noteworthy.

● ALBUMS: *With A Song In My Heart* (1956) ★★★, *Faith* (1958) ★★★.

● FURTHER READING: *Jane Froman: Missouri's First Lady Of Song*, Ilene Stone.

Fromholz, Steven

b. 8 June 1945, Temple, Texas, USA. Fromholz's father worked for the Ford Motor Company, and the family travelled around the country. At the age of 18, he met **Michael Martin Murphey** at North Texas State University, and they formed the Dallas County Jug Band and then the Michael Murphey Trio. Fromholz became half of Frummox with Dan McCrimmon, and their poor-selling 1969 album *Here To There* is prized by collectors. The duo split in 1971, and Fromholz and his wife ran a restaurant in Gold Hill, Colorado. **Stephen Stills** invited him to join **Manassas** on the road, but Fromholz left after six months because 'I'd had too much cocaine and was sick.' He dedicated a single he recorded for **Michael Nesmith**'s Countryside label, 'Sweet Janey', to his wife, but the album he made for Nesmith, *How Long Is The Road To Kentucky?*, was never released. **Willie Nelson** had a US country hit with Fromholz's song 'I'd Have To Be Crazy' and featured him on his live album, *The Sound In Your Mind*. Fromholz's **Capitol Records** debut, *A Rumor In My Own Time*, released in 1976 and featuring Nelson, **Doug Dillard** and **John Sebastian**, is a fine example of outlaw country. He was not suited to the easy listening arrangements on 1977's *Frolicking In The Myth*, although the album contained good material. He did, however, sound fine next to Peter Fonda on the soundtrack of the movie *Outlaw Blues*. He recorded an album for Nelson's Lone Star label, *Jus' Playin' Along*, which included his tribute to Hondo Crouch.

Fromholz has continued to record for his own Felicity Records label, in addition to recording the wonderfully titled *The Old Fart In The Mirror* for Jerry Jeff's Tried & True label. He has also appeared on stage and screen in a number of roles and coauthored *Bosque County, Texas*, a play based on his most famous song, 'Texas Trilogy'. His songs have been recorded by such artists as **Hoyt Axton**, **John Denver**, **Lyle Lovett** and **Jerry Jeff Walker**.

● ALBUMS: *A Rumor In My Own Time* (Capitol 1976) ★★★★, *Frolicking In The Myth* (Capitol 1977) ★★★, *Jus' Playin' Along* (Lone Star 1978) ★★★★, *Fromholz Live!* (Felicity 1979) ★★, *Love Songs* (Felicity 1986) ★★★, with the Almost Brothers *Everybody's Goin' On The Road* (Felicity 1991) ★★★, *The Old Fart In The Mirror* (Tried & True 1995) ★★★, *A Guest In Your Heart* (Felicity 2001) ★★★, *Live At Anderson Fair* (Felicity 2001) ★★★, *Cow Jazz* (Felicity 2003) ★★★.

● COMPILATIONS: *Come On Down To Texas For A While: The Anthology 1969–1991* (Raven 2001) ★★★.

Front Line Assembly

Despite helping to create the industrial rock genre and being cited as an important influence by many, when similarly styled units began infiltrating the mainstream during the early 90s, for reasons unknown, Front Line Assembly never truly managed to make the transition. The band originally came together during 1985 in Vancouver, Canada, when former **Skinny Puppy** member Bill Leeb aka Wilhelm Schroeder decided to give it a go on his own. Almost immediately, Leeb issued two cassette-only releases, *Nerve War* and *Total Terror*, that were reissued years later (with bonus tracks) under the titles *Total Terror I* and *Total Terror II*. Synth player Michael Balch was present on the early recordings, and two years later Leeb enlisted Rhys Fulber into Front Line Assembly, resulting in a long and fruitful artistic relationship. The band began churning out releases at a rapid-fire pace for a variety of labels. It was not until the band signed American distribution, **Wax Trax! Records**, that Front Line Assembly began carving their niche—metallic **techno** with an unmistakable dance groove. Late 80s/early 90s releases such as *Gashed Senses & Crossfire* and *Caustic Grip* (the first without Balch) made the band a true industrial force, and as they moved further into the decade, Front Line Assembly's sound took a more decidedly heavier turn. Their union with the Third Mind, label resulted in the release of one of the duo's finest recordings, *Tactical Neural Implant*, before moving to the heavy metal imprint Roadrunner Records.

Despite what seemed like a nonstop recording and touring schedule with Front Line Assembly, both Fulber and Leeb found the time to launch numerous off-shoot projects, including **Delerium**, Intermix, Noise Unit, Synaesthesia, Cyberaktif (with Skinny Puppy's cEVIN Key) and Will among others. In the late 90s Fulber left Front Line Assembly (to concentrate more on producing and remixing other artists), and Chris Peterson took his place. As evidenced by the first few Leeb/Peterson works, *Implode* and *Epitaph*, the trademark Front Line Assembly sound remained very much intact.

● ALBUMS: *Nerve War* (Own Label 1986) ★★, *Total Terror* (Own Label 1986) ★★, *The Initial Command* (KK 1986) ★★★, *State Of Mind* (Dossier 1987) ★★★, *Corrosion* (Third Mind/Wax Trax! 1988) ★★★, *Gashed Senses & Crossfire* (Third Mind/Wax Trax! 1989) ★★★★, *Caustic Grip* (Third Mind/Wax Trax! 1990) ★★★, *Tactical Neural Implant* (Third Mind 1992) ★★★★, *Millennium* (Roadrunner 1994) ★★★, *Hard Wired* (Off Beat 1995) ★★★, *Live Wired* (Off Beat 1996) ★★★, *Flavour Of The Weak* (Off Beat 1997) ★★★, *Implode* (Metropolis 1999) ★★★, *Epitaph* (Metropolis 2001) ★★★.

● COMPILATIONS: *Convergence* aka *Corroded Disorder* (Wax Trax! 1988) ★★, *Total Terror I* (Dossier 1993) ★★, *Total Terror II* (Dossier 1993) ★★, *Reclamation: Singles + Rarities* (Roadrunner 1997) ★★★, *Cryogenic Studios FLA + Sideprojects* (Cleopatra 1998) ★★, *Re-Wind* (Off Beat 1998) ★★, *Monument* (Roadrunner 1998) ★★★, *FourFit Singles 90–92* (Zoth Ommog 1998) ★★★, *Explosion Singles 95–98* (Off Beat 1999) ★★★★, *Cryogenic Studios 2 FLA + Sideprojects* (Cleopatra 2000) ★★.

● DVD/VIDEOS: *Live Wired Video* (Metropolis 2000).

Front (1)

Comprising Keith Angelino (vocals/guitar), Steven Mark (keyboards), Sean Healy (bass) and Chris Cavill (drums), US hard rock band the Front formed in the early 80s. Their sound was heavily derivative of the **Cheap Trick** school of unhinged hard rock, combining youthful angst with often irreverent lyrics. However, their self-titled 1982 debut album failed to provide evidence of the sort of musical sophistication which could mark them apart from other Cheap Trick imitators such as **New England**. With independent distribution it failed to make a dent in the mainstream marketplace, and the group sundered before a follow-up collection could be considered.

● ALBUMS: *The Front* (Arockolypse 1982) ★★.

Front (2)

A second US hard rock group to emerge in the 80s under the name the Front, this incarnation comprised Michael Anthony Franano (vocals), Mike Greene (guitar), Bobby Franano (keyboards), Randy Jordan (bass) and Shane (drums). Unlike their namesakes, they specialized in material heavily influenced by the **Doors**—Michael Anthony Franano's vocals earning him a reputation as a Jim Morrison sound-alike, while his brother's dense keyboard patterns recalled Ray Manzarek's contribution to the same band. Despite a major label recording contract with **Columbia Records**, the band proved unable to break into the mainstream.

● ALBUMS: *The Front* (Columbia 1989) ★★★.

Front 242

A duo of Patrick Codenys (b. 16 November 1958, Brussels, Belgium; composition, computers, synthesizers, guitars, vocals) and Daniel Bressanutti (b. 27 August 1954, Brussels, Belgium; programming/samples), Front 242 earned their long-standing reputation within the industrial/*avant garde* community via a largely compelling series of experimental exercises in sound. Originally, Front 242 comprised Codenys alone, for the 1982 single 'Principles', then became a trio with Jean-Luc De Meyer and Bressanutti. These early releases were more in tune with the elementary synth-pop of artists such as **Depeche Mode**, and it was not until after the release of *Geography* that they appeared live. A fourth member, Geoff Bellingham, was added for this purpose, although he was later replaced by ex-roadie and concurrent **Revolting Cocks** member Richard 23. Front 242's journey through the 80s gradually saw them becoming a more distinctive unit, however, with politically motivated samples filtering through the repetition. On the back of an impressive reputation for live events and visuals, they were launched out of cult status by the success of *Official Version*. This introduced the intemperate, militaristic rhythms that would become a signature as well as a diversity enshrined by nods to disco and pop in other tracks. It was not until the advent of *Tyranny For You* that the ingredients were significantly rearranged once more, this time to instil a darker overtone to proceedings (the album emerged at the same time as the Gulf War and proclamations of a New World Order). Influenced by the German antirock movement (**Can**, **Neu!**, **Faust**), cinema and architecture, the duo (following De Meyer's departure in 1995) continue to run the Art & Strategy design company and record label. New studio material surfaced in 2003.

● ALBUMS: *Geography* (RRE 1982) ★★, *No Comment* mini-album (Wax Trax! 1985) ★★★, *Official Version* (Wax Trax! 1987) ★★★★, *Front By Front* (Wax Trax! 1988) ★★★, *Tyranny (for You)* (RRE/Epic 1991) ★★★, *Live Target* (Guzzi 1993) ★★★, *06:21:03:11 Up Evil* (RRE/Epic 1993) ★★★, *05:22:09:12 Off* (RRE/Epic 1993) ★★★,

Mut@ge Mix@ge (RPE 1995) ★★★, *Re-Boot: Live '98* (Metropolis 1998) ★★★, *Headhunter 2000 remixes* (Metropolis 1998) ★★★, *Pulse* (Metropolis 2003) ★★★.
● COMPILATIONS: *Backcatalogue* (Wax Trax! 1987) ★★★, *Geography 1981–1983* (RRECD 1992) ★★★, *No Comment 1984–1985* (RRECD 1992) ★★★, *Back Catalogue 1981–1985* (RRECD 1992) ★★★, *Official Version 1986–1987* (RRECD 1992) ★★★, *Front By Front 1988–1989* (RRECD 1992) ★★★.

Frost (rap)

b. Arturo Molina Jnr., 31 May 1964, Los Angeles, California, USA. This Mexican-descended rapper was raised on military bases in Guam and Germany but spent most of his youth in East Los Angeles, where he began writing his first rhymes in 1982. He was initially inducted into the ranks of break-dance crew Uncle Jam's Army, as west coast rap began to accommodate the innovations of the Bronx. He released a number of 12-inch singles during this period as well as competing in 'backyard parties'. His breakthrough came in 1989 with 'La Raza', a single typically demonstrating 'Chicano pride'. A major force in the establishment of Latin hip-hop, Frost (then working as Kid Frost) brought together several other Hispanic rappers for the **Latin Alliance** project in 1991. This came shortly after the release of his 1990 debut solo set, another important signpost in the development of Latin rap. His blend of Chicano social observation and break beats provided him with a considerable audience outside of his own social bracket. He subsequently signed to **Virgin Records**, for whom he continued to deploy the intelligence to sample not only from funk's back catalogue but also that of the salsa tradition of his own people. However, he received scant commercial recognition for his efforts.
In 1995 Frost dropped the prefix Kid ('the kid's a man now') and became **Eazy-E**'s final signing to **Ruthless Records**. An album, *Smile Now, Die Later*, and single, 'East Side Rendezvous', placed him firmly 'back on the block', as one reviewer observed. Frost recorded one further album for the Ruthless, label before returning to independent label status and appears to have missed out on the Hispanic rap boom of the late 90s.
● ALBUMS: as Kid Frost *Hispanic Causing Panic* (Virgin 1990) ★★★, as Kid Frost *East Side Story* (Virgin 1992) ★★★★, *Smile Now, Die Later* (Ruthless/Relativity 1995) ★★★, *When Hell. A Freezes Over* (Ruthless/Relativity 1997) ★★★, *That Was Then, This Is Now Vol. I* (Celeb-Entertainment 1999) ★★★, *That Was Then, This Is Now Vol. II* (Celeb-Entertainment 2000) ★★★.
● COMPILATIONS: *Greatest Joints* (Thump 2001) ★★★.

Frost (rock)

Formed in Flint-Saginaw, Michigan, USA, Frost revolved around the talents of guitarist, songwriter, producer Dick Wagner. During the mid-60s he led the Bossmen, regional contemporaries of **? And The Mysterians** and **Terry Knight** And The Pack. The Bossmen held sway at Saginaw's leading club, Daniel's Den, and completed six singles for local labels including Dicto Records, Soft Records and Lucky Eleven Records. These included the **Searchers**-like 'Here's Congratulations' and the **Beatles**-influenced 'Help Me Baby'. The Bossmen were later billed as Dick Wagner And The Frosts. As such they completed two singles, 'Bad Girl' and 'Little

Girl', before Wagner formed Frost with Don Hartman, Gerdy Garris and Bob Riggs in 1969. Frost secured a recording contract with **Vanguard Records** and the excellent *Frost Music* followed. The group's hard rock style was especially popular in Detroit, Michigan, USA, and Frost resettled there in 1970. *Rock'n'Roll Music*, which included a remake of 'Help Me Baby', lacked the incision of its predecessor, and by the time *Through The Eyes Of Love* appeared, it was clear Frost had lost their initial impetus. Wagner dissolved the group in 1972. In 1973 he played guitar on **Lou Reed**'s *Berlin* and later toured with Reed. Wagner's distinctive style can be heard on *Rock'n'Roll Animal* and *Lou Reed Live*.
● ALBUMS: *Frost Music* (Vanguard 1970) ★★★, *Rock'n'-Roll Music* (Vanguard 1971) ★★, *Through The Eyes Of Love* (Vanguard 1972) ★★.
● COMPILATIONS: *The Best Of The Frost* (Vanguard 2003) ★★★.

Frost, Frank

b. 15 April 1936, Auvergne, Arkansas, USA, d. 12 October 1999, Helena, Arkansas, USA. Frost's skills encompassed keyboards and guitar, but like many other blues artists, he started with the harmonica. After moving to St. Louis, as a teenager, he took up playing with **Sonny Boy 'Rice Miller' Williamson** in the mid-50s, appearing regularly with him on the famous radio show *King Biscuit Time*. He also teamed up with **Robert Nighthawk** and his son Sam Carr before relocating to the South. In 1962 he recorded for **Sam Phillips** as part of the Nighthawks trio, featuring Carr on drums and guitarist **'Big' Jack Johnson**. One single and an album, *Hey Boss Man!*, resulted, featuring a very tough and raw, but tight, down-home blues sound, unusual on record at this time. A similar sound emerged from his next sessions in Nashville, in 1966, produced by **Scotty Moore**, which produced three fine singles and, later, an album on Jewel Records. 'My Back Scratcher', Frost's take on **Slim Harpo**'s 'Baby Scratch My Back', was even a minor R&B hit. Subsequently, Frost went back to mainly local performing in the juke joints around his home area in the Mississippi Delta, basing himself at Eddie Mae's Café in Helena, Arkansas. He also continued to make records and tour with Carr and Johnson, releasing 1979's *Rockin' The Juke Joint Down* as the Jelly Roll Kings. Frost undertook some highly acclaimed appearances in Europe and, following his appearance in the 1986 movie *Crossroads*, recorded several well-received solo albums before his death in October 1999.
● ALBUMS: with the Nighthawks *Hey Boss Man!* (Phillips 1962) ★★★★, *Frank Frost* reissued as *Jelly Roll Blues* (Jewel 1974) ★★★, *Midnight Prowler* (Earwig 1988) ★★★, *Deep Blues* (Appaloosa 1993) ★★★, with Sam Carr *Keep Yourself Together* (Evidence 1996) ★★★, with Carr *The Jelly Roll Kings* (HMG 1999) ★★★, *Live In Lucerne* 1998 recording (ROAD 2004) ★★★.
● COMPILATIONS: *Ride With Your Daddy Tonight* (Charly 1985) ★★★, *Jelly Roll King* (Charly 1990) ★★★, *Big Boss Man: The Very Best Of Frank Frost* (Collectables 1999) ★★★★.
● FILMS: *Crossroads* (1986).

Frumious Bandersnatch

This highly promising quintet was based in Berkeley, California, USA, in the late 60s. They completed an album for **Fantasy Records** that was never issued, and consequently, their sole recorded legacy lies in a privately pressed EP. The group—Jimmy Warner (solo guitar/vocals), David Denny (b. 5 February 1948, Berkeley, California, USA; lead guitar/vocals), Bob Winkelman (rhythm guitar/vocals), Ross Vallory (b. 2 February 1949, San Francisco, California, USA; bass/vocals) and Jackson King (drums/vocals)—were highly accomplished musicians and the opening track, 'Hearts To Cry', offered some exciting, *de rigueur* acid-rock. Denny was later replaced by George Tickner, but the band subsequently folded in the face of corporate disinterest. Winkelman, Warner, King and Vallory all appeared at various times as members of the **Steve Miller** Band. Vallory then found greater success with Tickner as members of **Journey**.

● COMPILATIONS: *A Young Man's Song* (Big Beat 1996) ★★.

Fruscella, Tony

b. 4 February 1927, Orangeburg, New Jersey, USA, d. 14 August 1969, New York City, USA. Raised in an orphanage until the age of 14, Fruscella started playing trumpet the following year. Largely self-taught, he did later study under Jerome Canudie. While serving in the US Army in 1945, he played trumpet in an army band. On his release, he played professionally with various bands, including that led by alto saxophonist Chuck Maure. In 1950 he worked with **Lester Young**, following this with spells with trumpeter Don Joseph, **Brew Moore**, **Charlie Parker**, **Gerry Mulligan** and Young again, and in 1955 he had an eight-month engagement with **Stan Getz**. That same year, he made his own name debut for **Atlantic Records**. Although the result was very well received by critics and public alike, Fruscella's career was soon severely damaged by his drug addiction. From the end of the 50s, he played occasionally with Joseph, but he was unable to achieve anything of consequence.

Fruscella's cool playing style, undemonstrative and intro-spective, allied as it was to a sometimes thin, veiled sound, is often likened to that of **Chet Baker**, whose lifestyle bore similar self-imposed and ultimately tragic hallmarks. Never-theless, although the stylistic similarities are valid, neither trumpeter appears to have been knowingly influenced by the other. Indeed, as Harvey Pekar has suggested, writing in *JazzTimes*, their similarities most likely stem from having both been influenced by Young. In any event, similarities notwithstanding, their playing is readily distinguishable, Fruscella displaying a particular liking for the lower register of the instrument and was somewhat more interesting improviser. To his few own name studio sides have been added some live date sessions. All of these and his recordings with musicians such as Moore, Maures, Parker, Getz, **Allen Eager**, **Danny Bank**, **Herb Geller**, **Red Mitchell** and **Gene DiNovi** offer tantalizing hints of what might have been.

● ALBUMS: *Tony Fruscella* (Atlantic 1955) ★★★★, *A Night At The Open Door* 1948/1953 recordings (Jazz Factory 1992) ★★★, *Tony's Blues* 1952/1955 recordings (Cool & Blue 1992) ★★★, *Debut* 1948/1953 recordings (Spotlite 1998) ★★★, with Brew Moore *Fru 'N Brew* 1953 recording (Spotlite 1998) ★★★, *Pernod* 1948/1955 recordings (Jazz Factory 1999) ★★★.

● COMPILATIONS: *The Complete Recordings* 1948–59 recordings (Jazz Factory 1999) ★★★.

Frusciante, John

b. 5 March 1970, New York City, USA. US guitarist and singer-songwriter Frusciante is best known for his work with the **Red Hot Chili Peppers**, earning both commercial success and critical plaudits during two separate stints with the Los Angeles based rock band. Despite his commitments to the Red Hot Chili Peppers and some well-documented personal problems, Frusciante has also maintained a busy schedule as a solo recording artist.

Frusciante was raised in California, and after mastering the guitar at an early age, the precocious musical talent dropped out of college to devote himself to music, joining a number of LA-based bands before being recruited by the Red Hot Chili Peppers to replace their recently deceased guitarist Hillel Slovak. Frusciante made his debut on the band's 1989 breakthrough album *Mother's Milk*. His fluid guitar playing was instrumental to the success of both this album and its successor, *Blood Sugar Sex Magik*, but increasing fame fell heavy on Frusciante's shoulders, and he announced his departure in May 1992 while the band was touring Japan. The guitarist descended into a drug-induced stupor for the next two years, rousing himself briefly to oversee the release of his solo debut *Niandra LaDes & Usually Just A T-Shirt*. This set actually comprised two separate albums, both recorded on basic four-track home set-ups at various stages in the early 90s, with *Niandra LaDes* comprising singer-songwriter fare and *Usually Just A T-Shirt* focusing on quirky psychedelic instrumentals. Disturbing reports began to emerge about Frusciante's health during this period, and although a second album was released, the inclusion of several tracks recorded in the late 80s on *Smile From The Streets You Hold* indicated all was not well. The collection provided media vultures with further evidence of Frusciante's personal decline although his innate musical talent shone through on a number of the more interesting tracks.

By this point Frusciante seemed oblivious to his waning musical reputation, declaring himself more interested in painting and writing stories and scripts. In 1997, shortly after the release of *Smile From The Streets You Hold*, friends persuaded Frusciante to clean up his act and kick the hard drugs, a decision he would later admit was responsible for saving his life. More encouraging news emerged when the newly drug-free Frusciante was reported to be working with his former bandmates in the Red Hot Chili Peppers, who had recently lost the services of their guitarist **Dave Navarro**. The union became a permanent one, and Frusciante helped the band record their 1999 comeback album, *Californication*. This superb collection resurrected the Red Hot Chili Peppers' career (dwarfing sales of their previous albums) and re-established Frusciante as one, of the leading guitarists of his generation. The 2002 follow-up, *By The Way*, confirmed the Red Hot Chili Peppers' creative rebirth and was another huge commercial success, confirming their position as one of the biggest bands in the world.

While the Red Hot Chili Peppers were recording *By The Way*, Frusciante was also completing work on a new solo release. Released in 2001, *To Record Only Water For Ten Days* eschewed the haphazard recording style of his earlier work in favour of a more crafted approach. Despite lacking the quirky, nonlinear bursts of experimental genius to be found on his 90s recordings, enough of Frusciante's eccentric songwriting vision carried over to produce on of the year's most endearing releases. The 21-track downloadable-only

From The Sounds Inside was also made available. Frusciante's second release for **Warner Brothers Records**, *Shadows Collide With People*, was released at the start of 2004. The album was recorded with Frusciante's regular collaborator, Josh Klinghoffer of Bicycle Thief. Their interest in electronic experimentation, which bubbled away throughout *Shadows Collide With People*, found further expression on a series of independent releases by the duo that appeared at regular intervals at the tail end of the year. Only *A Sphere In The Heart Of Silence* was credited to both Frusciante and Klinghoffer, while the *Automatic Writing* album was recorded with Joe Lally of **Fugazi** and released under the Ataxia moniker.

● ALBUMS: *Niandra LaDes & Usually Just A T-Shirt* (American 1994) ★★★, *Smile From The Streets You Hold* (Birdman 1997) ★★★, *To Record Only Water For Ten Days* (Warners 2001) ★★★★, *Shadows Collide With People* (Warners 2004) ★★★★, *The Will To Death* (Record Collection 2004) ★★★, *Inside Of Emptiness* (Record Collection 2004) ★★★, with Josh Klinghoffer *A Sphere In The Heart Of Silence* (Record Collection 2004) ★★★, *Curtains* (Record Collection 2004) ★★★.

Fruup

Vince McCusker (guitar, vocals) was the mainstay of this 70s outfit from Belfast, Northern Ireland. With Steve Houston (keyboards/vocals), Peter Farrelly (bass/vocals) and Martin Foye (drums), he recorded a debut album for Dawn Records, which defined the pomp-rock style with vaguely mystical overtones that sustained Fruup on a five-year career around the European college circuit. During exploratory sessions for 1974's *Seven Secrets*, Houston was replaced by John Mason, and Ian McDonald played saxophone on the following year's *Modern Masquerades*. Although respected as a competent act, the group was unable to climb to higher rungs on the progressive rock ladder before punk's levelling blow. Obliged to drastically reduce engagement fees, the inevitable cracks appeared, and by 1978 Fruup was no more.

● ALBUMS: *Future Legends* (Dawn 1973) ★★★★, *Prince Of Heaven's Eyes* (Dawn 1974) ★★★, *Seven Secrets* (Dawn 1974) ★★, *Modern Masquerades* (Dawn 1975) ★★★.

● COMPILATIONS: *Songs For A Thought* (1992) ★★★, *It's All Up Now: Anthology* (Castle 2004) ★★★.

Fryer, Robert

b. 18 November 1920, Washington, DC, USA, d. 28 May 2000, Los Angeles, California, USA. Fryer worked for some years as casting director for the New York stage before turning to production. His first Broadway show was a musical version of **A Tree Grows In Brooklyn** (1951), and he followed this with the very successful **Wonderful Town** (1953). Through the 50s and 60s, in collaboration with his business partner Lawrence Carr, he was responsible for many shows, mostly musical comedies, a high proportion of which were very successful. Among these shows were *By The Beautiful Sea* (1954), *Shangri-la* (1956), **Redhead** (1959, winner of a **Tony Award**), *Saratoga* (1959), *Hot Spot* (1963, which starred **Judy Holliday**), and in 1966 **Sweet Charity** and **Jerry Herman**'s **Mame**, both of which were hugely successful, the latter earning a Tony award for **Bea Arthur** in a costarring role. Although he was not done with Broadway, Fryer produced a number of films, including *The Boston Strangler* (1968) and *The Prime Of Miss Jean Brodie* (1969). He also produced the

screen version of *Mame* (1974), starring **Lucille Ball**. This production completed a circle because one of his earlier non-musical stage productions had been *Auntie Mame* from which the musicals were derived. The film version of *Mame* was met with critical disapproval and audience indifference, but on Fryer's return to Broadway in the late 70s, he proved that he had not lost his touch. These years found him involved in the production of *Chicago* (1975), **On The Twentieth Century** (1978) and **Sweeney Todd** (1979). He began the 80s inauspiciously with poorly received productions of **Merrily We Roll Along** (1981) and *A Doll's Life* (1982), but then, as artistic director at the Ahmanson Theatre in Los Angeles, he coproduced *Noises Off* (1983) and *Benefactors* (1985).

Fu Manchu

Formed in Orange County, California, USA, by Scott Hill (vocals/guitar), Ruben Romano (drums), Brad Davis (bass) and Eddie Glass (lead guitar). Their debut EP was released in 1990, establishing their headily psychedelic, groove-orientated approach. While many compared them to **Kyuss**, Fu Manchu preferred to make cryptic references to pharmaceuticals and produce cover images that tied them to older generations of rock bands. *In Search Of . . .* , for example, featured a woman in flares preparing to start an illegal drag race, while the album's title derived from a lacklustre science-fiction programme of the 70s. Suitably, Hill has never spent much time perfecting his lyrics, instead using his voice as a fifth instrument to complement the band's dense, rhythmic passages. Glass and Romano both left in October 1996, later resurfacing in Nebula. They were replaced by Brant Bjork (ex-**Kyuss**) and Bob Balch, respectively. Fu Manchu's subsequent releases, 1997's *The Action Is Go* and 1999's *King Of The Road*, catapulted the band into the mainstream.

● ALBUMS: *No One Rides For Free* (Mammoth 1994) ★★★, *Daredevil* (Mammoth 1995) ★★, *In Search Of . . .* (Mammoth 1996) ★★, *The Action Is Go* (Mammoth 1998) ★★★, *King Of The Road* (Mammoth 1999) ★★★, *California Crossing* (Mammoth 2002) ★★★, *Go For It . . . Live!* (Steamhammer 2003) ★★.

● COMPILATIONS: *Return To Earth 91—93* (Elastic 1998) ★★.

Fu-Schnickens

Brooklyn, New York, rap trio who comprise Poc Fu (Prophet Overseeing Creativity), Chip Fu (Creative Harmony:Intertwine Perfection) and Moc (Manifest Culture) Fu. Not content with wearing ludicrous Oriental costumes, the band also claim to have descended on the world of rap via a mythical fireball. The Fu part of their names and the band's moniker indicates 'For Unity', while 'Schnickens' is a wholly invented term signifying 'coalition'. Raised in East Flatbush in Brooklyn, the trio was discovered at the Carwash club, a specialist showcase event. Soon after Phil Pabon took over their affairs as manager and began to set up dates for the group all over New York. They finally earned their break with an appearance in February 1991 at the 1st Annual Rap Conference, at Howard University in Washington, DC. An A&R representative from Jive saw and liked their performance, and asked them to submit a tape. They received a contract in return. Famed for their onstage humour and high-speed delivery (including perfectly executed backward raps), they opened their account for their new employers with the dancehall-flavoured 'Ring The Alarm!', the warmth and humour of which typified the contents of their well-received debut album.

● ALBUMS: *Don't Take It Personal* (Jive 1992) ★★★.

Fucking Champs

Originating from Berkeley, California, USA, the Fucking Champs combine all of their varied influences—everything from **Fugazi** to **Iron Maiden**—to create an original and highly unpredictable style. The trio (guitarists Josh Smith and Tim Green and drummer/guitarist Tim Soete) came together in 1995, with Green having previously made a name for himself as a member of **Nation Of Ulysses**. Originally called simply the Champs, the band issued two independent singles before discovering there was a 50s instrumental rock group (best known for the song 'Tequila') that already owned the name. To get around judicial ramifications, the trio changed the spelling of their name to the code-like C4AM95, and in 1997 issued the double album, *III* (the reason for the album's title reflected the band's brash confidence, especially when Smith was quoted as saying 'We wanted to skip right to *Led Zeppelin III*, to get to *Physical Graffiti* sooner'). Soon after the album's release, the trio decided on another plan on how to fix their 'moniker problem'. Remembering how several 80s era metal bands often used a certain obscene word on T-shirts, the band soon became known as the Fucking Champs. Signed to the Chicago indie label Drag City, the Fucking Champs decided to stick with the number system for their album titles, issuing the acclaimed *IV* and *V* in 2000 and 2002 respectively.

● ALBUMS: as C4AM95 *III* (Frenetic 1997) ★★★★, *IV* (Drag City 2000) ★★★, *V* (Drag City 2002) ★★★.

Fudge Tunnel

UK noise operatives Fudge Tunnel were formed in 1989 by 18-year-old vocalist, guitarist and songwriter Alex Newport when he moved to Nottingham. He quickly sought out sympathizers in the shape of Dave Ryley (bass) and Adrian Parkin (drums). Their first ever release, 1990's *Sex Mammoth* EP, was immediately chosen as Single Of The Week in the *New Musical Express*. Six months later came *The Sweet Sound Of Excess* EP, then touring commitments with **Silverfish** and **Godflesh**. In 1991 they gained a permanent home at Earache Records, which culminated in the release of their debut album, which arrived with the self-explanatory title of *Hate Songs In E Minor*. This immensely caustic epistle was released in May 1991 after initial copies, controversially featuring a drawing of a decapitation taken from the John Minnery book *How To Kill*, were confiscated by Nottingham vice police. The acclaim eventually accrued in metal and indie magazines by the Colin Richardson–produced disc was huge, however, with barely a word of dissent and plenty more that earmarked Fudge Tunnel as the ultimate in brutal music. A commercially successful EP, *Teeth* (UK indie chart number 4—a major landmark for such extreme music), preceded the release of a second album, *Creep Diets*. Despite continued progress, the band was unhappily bracketed with the emerging Seattle 'grunge' sound (which they actually predated) and some of the momentum waned. As well as time spent touring, in 1993 Newport worked with Max Cavalera (**Sepultura**) on the **Nailbomb** project. Fudge Tunnel then reconvened at Sawmill Studios in Cornwall for their third album. *The Complicated Futility Of Ignorance* saw the grunge comparisons finally dropped as the group processed a further increase in their already massively violent sound.

● ALBUMS: *Hate Songs In E Minor* (Earache 1991) ★★★, *Fudge Cake* comprises *Sex Mammoth* and *The Sweet Sound Of Excess* EPs (Pigboy/Vinyl Solution 1992) ★★, *Creep Diets* (Earache 1993) ★★★, *The Complicated Futility Of Ignorance* (Earache 1994) ★★★.

● COMPILATIONS: *In A Word* 1990–93 recordings (Earache 1995) ★★★.

Fuel

Originally featuring engaging singer Brett Scallions (b. 21 December 1971, USA), Carl Bell (b. 9 January 1967, Kenton, Tennessee, USA; guitar) and Jeff Abercrombie (b. 8 January 1969, Kenton, Tennessee, USA; bass), post-grunge band Fuel came to prominence in the mid-90s by developing a fraternal relationship with their local audience: 'We don't want fans, we want friends', they pointed out. Based in Harrisburg, Philadelphia, USA, the band was formed in 1989 by Bell, Abercrombie and Scallions, with other members passing through including Jody Abbott (drums) and Erik Avakian (keyboards). The band established a strong fanbase along the eastern seaboard through an arduous touring schedule, culminating in the release of a self-financed debut album in 1994. The follow-up *Porcelain* eventually sold more than 10,000 copies. As a result the band, by now featuring new drummer Kevin Miller (b. 6 September 1962, USA), signed a contract with Sony Records subsidiary 550, recording their debut *Sunburst* early in 1998. Taken from it, the single 'Shimmer' became a minor hit, featuring in **Billboard**'s Top 10 modern rock tracks listing for several consecutive weeks and climbed to number 42 on the Hot 100. Before the release of a follow-up single, 'Bittersweet', the band took time out to contribute a song, 'Walk The Sky', to the soundtrack of *Godzilla*. The band's second major label album, 2000's *Something Like Human*, despite demonstrating precious little musical progress, was another highly melodic collection of modern alternative rock. The single 'Hemorrhage (In My Hands)' was a major hit on US rock radio and helped boost sales of the album. The follow-up *Natural Selection* lacked a similar stand-out track and as a result was largely overlooked by fickle rock fans. Miller left the band in 2004.

● ALBUMS: *Fuel* mini-album (Own Label 1994) ★★, *Porcelain* mini-album (Own Label 1997) ★★★, *Sunburn* (550/Sony 1998) ★★★, *Something Like Human* (550/Sony 2000) ★★★, *Natural Selection* (550/Sony 2003) ★★.

● COMPILATIONS: *The Best Of Fuel* (550/Sony 2005) ★★★★.

Fugain, Michel

b. 12 May 1942, Grenoble, France. Rather than following his father into the medical profession, Fugain decided instead to pursue a career in films. Within two years, he had become an assistant producer, but as a self-taught guitarist who sang semi-professionally, he also rose from Parisian clubland to supporting **Eddy Mitchell** at the city's Olympia auditorium in 1966. After enthralling the audiences there, this handsome young man's potential as a recording artist was obliquely realized when the French public preferred 'Prend Ta Guitare Chante Avec Moi', the audience participation number that was the b-side of his debut single, 'Un Pas Devant L'Autre'. Its success initiated Fugain's reign as a national pop idol, but he would not duplicate this feat to any great extent in English-language territories.

Fugazi

The thinking person's modern hardcore band and vocalist/guitarist Ian MacKaye's most permanent institution since his **Minor Threat** days. More so than **Henry Rollins** and, probably, **Jello Biafra**, Fugazi continued and expanded on the arguments of their antecedents, keeping down album and door prices, shunning mainstream press interviews, and maintaining a commitment to all-age shows. They were also among the first to object publicly to the ridiculous macho ritual of slam-dancing: 'We're about challenging crowds, confronting ourselves and them with new ideas and if I was a teenager now, I would not be doing a dance that's been going on for ten years'.

It is a shame that Fugazi's press seems to focus unerringly on MacKaye's Minor Threat connections, as the contribution from his co-lyricist Guy Picciotto (vocals/guitar, ex–Rites Of Spring) deserves to be ranked above that of supporting cast. His more abstract, less direct communiqués blend well with his partner's realism. The other members of the band, which was formed in 1987, are Brendan Canty (drums) and Joe Lally (bass), and together the quartet has forged one of the most consistent and challenging discographies within the US underground. Although they have concentrated primarily on touring rather than studio efforts, each of their albums has gone on to sell more than 100,000 copies, produced entirely independently within their own Dischord Records framework. In a rare mainstream music press interview in 1995, MacKaye continued to decry those who would use the guise of punk rock to record for major corporations, commenting on the success of **Green Day** and **Offspring** by stating: 'They'll be forgotten, 'cos they're the fucking Ugly Kid Joe's of the 90s'. Fugazi's own record of the time, *Red Medicine*, proved just as abrasive and disciplined an exercise as usual. In 1999 the band was filmed by Jem Cohen for the documentary *Instrument*. The attendant soundtrack album featured several unreleased studio tracks and outtakes. Following the release of one further studio album (*The Argument*) in 2001 the band was put on temporary hiatus, during which MacKaye concentrated on Dischord and his side project, the Evens. In 2004 fans of Fugazi were rewarded for their patience by the release of the first 20 CDs from the band's extensive live library.

● ALBUMS: *Repeater* (Dischord 1990) ★★★★, *Steady Diet Of Nothing* (Dischord 1991) ★★★, *In On The Killtaker* (Dischord 1993) ★★★, *Red Medicine* (Dischord 1995) ★★★, *End Hits* (Dischord 1998) ★★★, *Instrument Soundtrack* (Dischord 1999) ★★, *The Argument* (Dischord 2001) ★★★.
● COMPILATIONS: *13 Songs* (Dischord 1990) ★★★★.
● DVD/VIDEOS: *Instrument* (Dischord 1999).

Fugees

New York, USA–based crew comprising **Wyclef Jean** (b. Nelust Wyclef Jean, 17 October 1972, Haiti), his cousin **Pras** (b. Samuel Prakazrel Michel, 19 October 1972) and **Lauryn Hill** (b. 25 May 1975, South Orange, New Jersey, USA) who became the most successful crossover rap outfit of the 90s with 1996's bestselling **The Score**. Originally signed to Ruffhouse Records in 1992 as the Tranzlator Crew, their new name was a shortened version of Refugees (inspired by

Wyclef and Pras' Haitian backgrounds). The Fugees' style combines dry, cushioning beats with clever, rhythmic wordplay. All three members rap over acoustic guitars as well as more upbeat numbers informed by **dub** and reggae, both modes in which they excel. The sound was not exactly unfamiliar, and the title of their 1994 debut album, *Blunted On Reality*, seemed to suggest they were coming from a similar direction to **Cypress Hill** and **Digable Planets**. All three members professed to be nonusers, however, indicating that the album title signified their belief that they did not need to smoke the weed to induce a state of heightened perception and relaxation. Similarly, the lyrical concerns on the album were somewhat different, as might be expected of a crew where the majority of members also attended university courses. Some of their targets included America's perception of Haitians as 'Boat People' (Pras stated his intention to return to Haiti, using profits from his music to help build schools and decent roads on the island) and their own mixed gender status.

The magnificent follow-up, *The Score*, was one of the musical highlights of 1996 and proved accessible enough to bring their soulful jazz-rap to a wider market. 'Ready Or Not' and reworkings of 'Killing Me Softly' (**Roberta Flack**) and 'No Woman No Cry' (**Bob Marley**) were all international hit singles, and the album achieved multiplatinum worldwide success. Hill's pregnancy meant the trio was largely inactive during 1997, with Wyclef Jean taking the time to release a solo album. Pras and Hill also embarked on solo careers, with the latter's 1998 debut **The Miseducation Of Lauryn Hill** enjoying huge critical and commercial success. The three Fugees reunited in 2005.

● ALBUMS: as Fugees Tranzlator Crew *Blunted On Reality* (Ruffhouse/Columbia 1994) ★★, *The Score* (Ruffhouse/Columbia 1996) ★★★★★, *Bootleg Versions* (Columbia 1996) ★★★, *The Complete Score* (Columbia 2001) ★★★★★.
● COMPILATIONS: *Greatest Hits* (Columbia 2003) ★★★★.
● DVD/VIDEOS: *The Score* (SMV 1996).
● FURTHER READING: *Fugees: The Unofficial Book*, Chris Roberts.

Fugs

Formed in 1964 in the USA, the Fugs combined the bohemian poetry of New York's Lower East Side with an engaging musical naïvety and the shock tactic of outrage. Writers **Ed Sanders** (b. 17 August 1939, Kansas City, Missouri, USA), **Tuli Kupferberg** (b. 28 September 1922, USA, although other dates have been claimed) and Ken Weaver made their recording debut on the **Folkways Records** subsidiary Broadside, which viewed the unit's work as 'ballads of contemporary protest'. The set included poetry by William Blake alongside the irreverent Weaver offerings 'Slum Goddess' and 'I Couldn't Get High', while the original trio was supported by several musicians, including Peter Stampfel and Steve Weber from fellow cultural dissidents the **Holy Modal Rounders**. The Fugs subsequently signed a new recording contract with ESP Records, a notorious outlet for the *avant garde*. A projected second collection was withheld when the company deemed it 'too obscene', and a feverish rock album, entitled *The Fugs*, was issued instead. This excellent collection featured Kupferberg's satirical 'Kill For Peace' and the almost lyrical 'Morning, Morning'. The disputed second album was then released as *Virgin Fugs*, with the track line-up featuring the classic Kupferberg songs 'CIA Man' and 'Coca Cola Douche'.

In 1967 the Fugs switched outlets to **Atlantic Records** but after finishing an album were unceremoniously dumped by the label. After relocating to **Reprise Records** the band was shot back into the media spotlight in October 1967 when Sanders and Kupferberg performed an exorcism of the Pentagon during a peace march in Washington, DC. Although *Tenderness Junction* featured a more proficient backing group, including Danny Kootch (guitar) and Charles Larkey (bass), the subject matter—hippie politics and sex—remained as before. *It Crawled Into My Hand, Honest*, released the following year, was another idiomatic record, but subsequent releases undermined the balance between literary and carnal pursuits, erring in favour of the latter. The Fugs disbanded to avoid the dangers of self-parody and also because they were worn out by constant harassment from the police and the FBI.

Sanders continued his musical pursuits with two country-influenced selections and in 1971 published an acclaimed book, *The Family*, about the hippie-cult leader Charles Manson. He also wrote several books of poetry and short stories during this period and branched out into inventing and constructing musical instruments. Kupferberg continued to perform with his group Revolting Theater but became better known for his work as a political cartoonist. Ken Weaver, meanwhile, returned to college and also published a book, *Texas Crude*.

Sanders and Kupferberg resumed live work as the Fugs in 1984, joined by Steve Taylor (guitar/vocals), Coby Batty (percussion) and Mark Kramer (bass). With the replacement of the latter by multi-instrumentalist Scott Petito, this line-up continued to perform and record throughout the rest of the decade and beyond. Contemporary releases, issued through the French New Rose and Danish Olufsen labels, invoked a world-consciousness portrayed in the unit's earlier political work, and they retained the same idealistic optimism. During the 90s Sanders and Kupferberg retrieved the rights to their ESP recordings. The material was then licensed to **Ace Records** on the recommendation of the **Grateful Dead**. Subsequent repackages were augmented by archive photographs and previously unissued recordings.

Sanders and Kupferberg were incensed by the overt commercialism behind plans for an anniversary **Woodstock Festival** in 1994 and set up their own rival event tagged the 'Real Woodstock Festival'. The results were issued on a double CD in 1995, but the duo's satire and humour was now sounding dated. Nevertheless, they continued to balance outside pursuits (Sanders' ongoing literary career and Kupferberg's work as a political cartoonist) with an admirable commitment to the Fugs. The 2003 release *The Fugs Final CD (Part 1)* was warmly received by the American media, with the band's mix of idealism and satirical humour providing a beacon of hope in uncertain times.

● ALBUMS: *The Village Fugs* aka *The Fugs First Album* (Broadside/Folkways 1965) ★★★★, *The Fugs* (ESP 1966) ★★★★, *Virgin Fugs* (ESP 1966) ★★★★, *Tenderness Junction* (Reprise 1967) ★★★, *It Crawled Into My Hand, Honest* (Reprise 1968) ★★★, *Golden Filth: Live At The Fillmore East* (Reprise 1969) ★★★★, *The Belle Of Avenue A* (Reprise 1969) ★★, *No More Slavery* (Olufsen/New Rose 1986) ★★★, *Star Peace* (Olufsen/New Rose 1987) ★★, *The Real Woodstock Festival* (Fugs 1995) ★★, *The Fugs Final CD (Part 1)* (Artemis 2003) ★★★.

● COMPILATIONS: *The Fugs 4, Rounders Score* (ESP 1975) ★★★, *Refuse To Be Burnt Out: Live In The 1960s* (Olufsen/New Rose 1984) ★★, *Songs From A Portable Forest* (Gazelle 1990) ★★, *Live From The 60s* (Fugs 1994) ★★, *Electromagnetic Forest: The Reprise Recordings* (Rhino Handmade 2001) ★★★★, *Greatest Hits: The Olufsen Years* (Olufsen 2002) ★★★.

● FILMS: *Chappaqua* (1966).

Fuji

The musical term fuji was originally taken from the Japanese mountain of the same name by originator Sikiru **Barrister** simply because of the 'sound of the word'. It described a Nigerian variant of traditional musics, were and apala. The first fuji groups existed in the late 60s, but none achieved more than local success until an explosion of interest in the late 80s caused by the rise of stars such as Ayinla **Kollington**, **Wasiu Barrister** and his namesake, Sikiru Barrister. Unlike the more sophisticated guitar styles of **juju**, fuji concentrates on rhythmic passages that are built on the traditional use of Yoruba percussion. With an absence of stringed instruments, fuji's melodic content is provided by declamatory singing, similar to the wailing tradition of Arabic or Muslim music. Indeed, fuji's rise is often linked with the Yoruba community's shift from Christianity to Islam. Kollington and both Barristers each enjoyed enormous popularity at the close of the 80s. This period, akin to juju's creative boom at the beginning of the decade, was marked by the search for constant innovation and reinvention. Each successive album added new textures or sounds in an attempt to out-manoeuvre the competition. The reason for the music's popularity was evident in the furious dancing it aroused throughout Nigeria, especially among the young. By the 90s the triumvirate of major fuji stars were beginning to encroach on international markets, enjoying sustained success throughout Europe.

Fujii, Satoko

b. 9 October 1958, Tokyo, Japan. Fujii began playing piano at the age of four, studying classical music until she was 20. Concurrently in this period, she also spent three years studying violin. In 1978 she abandoned the piano for a year to conduct practical studies into the origins of music. She then returned to the piano and developed her improvisational abilities under the guidance of Koji Taku, a classical pianist turned jazzman, and then, importantly, with jazz pianist Fumio Itabashi. Among early influences were **John Coltrane**'s *A Love Supreme*, and she has expressed her admiration for the piano playing of Itabashi, **Bill Evans** and **Abdullah Ibrahim**. In 1984 she met her future husband, trumpeter Natsuki Tamura. A year later, she was playing piano in a big band in a Tokyo nightclub when she decided to return to studying, this time entering **Berklee College Of Music** where her teachers included **Herb Pomeroy**, and she also studied privately with **Jerry Bergonzi**. Fujii graduated from Berklee in 1987 and returned to Japan to play at jazz clubs in Tokyo and Yokohama and also to teach at the Yamaha Popular Music School. There followed seven years as a television and recording studio musician, and she also worked with several Japanese groups and with **Joseph Jarman** and **Douglas Ewart**.

In 1993 Fujii returned to the USA, again on a scholarship. This time it was to the New England Conservatory of Music where her tutors included **George Russell**, **Cecil McBee**, **Joe Maneri** and **Paul Bley**, and she made her first recording with the latter. After graduation in 1996, she began playing and recording in earnest, averaging two albums a year thereafter. Her 1996 solo *Indication* was highly praised as was the following year's duo set, *How Many?*, on which she was partnered with Tamura. The year after that, she displayed the range of her interests and skills with two albums, a trio set with bass player **Mark Dresser** and drummer Jim Black (*Looking Out Of The Window*) and a set with a big band (*South Wind*). Fujii's interest in music for large ensembles led to her forming two such groups, one in Japan (the Satoko Fujii Orchestra East) and one in the USA (the Satoko Fujii Orchestra West). These two bands were interestingly presented on *Double Take*, a double album with one CD by each band. In striking contrast were *April Shower*, with violinist Mark Feldman, and *Vulcan*, which plunged headlong into the complex melding of avant rock and free jazz. All of these albums received great critical acclaim, although, necessarily, from very different areas of the music press.

With great virtuosity, Fujii ranges widely in her music, absorbing and synthesizing not only jazz and latter-day classical music but also traditional Japanese folk forms. Here, simplicity and melodic minimalism; there, dense and highly sophisticated complexities. In addition to her own various bands, she is also a member of her husband's quartet, along with guitarist Takayuki Kato and drummer Koji Shibata. In this group, she plays synthesizer, not piano. Among the many musicians with whom Fujii has worked are alto saxophonist **Oscar Noriega**, tenor saxophonist **Ellery Eskelin**, trumpeters **Herb Robertson** and **Steven Bernstein** and drummer Aaron Alexander. Although generally content to confine her geographical range to her homeland and to the northeastern corner of the USA, in the early 00s she and her husband toured nationally and also worked in Germany with the NDR big band. A strikingly gifted musician, with the technical skills needed to bring her imaginative concepts to fruition, Fujii is clearly a talent to watch as some areas of jazz develop more and more into worldwide boundary-free musical forms.

● ALBUMS: with Paul Bley *Something About Water* (Libra 1996) ★★★, *Indication* (Libra 1996) ★★★★, *Looking Out Of The Window* (Nippon Crown 1997) ★★★, with Natsuki Tamura *How Many?* (Leo Lab 1997) ★★★, *South Wind* (Leo Lab 1997) ★★★, *Past Life* (Libra 1999) ★★★, *Kitsune-bi* (Tzadik 1999) ★★★, *Jo* (Buzz 1999) ★★★, *Toward, To West* (Enja 2000) ★★★, *Double Take* (Ewe 2000) ★★★, *April Shower* (Ewe 2001) ★★★, *Vulcan* (Libra 2001) ★★★, *Junction* (Ewe 2001) ★★★, with Tamura *Clouds* (Libra 2001) ★★★, *Bell The Cat!* (Tokuma 2002) ★★★, *Minerva* (Jazzprint 2002) ★★★, *Toh-Kichi* (Victo 2002) ★★★, *The Future Of The Past* (Enja 2003) ★★★, *Hada Hada* (Libra 2003) ★★★.

Fuld, Leo

b. 1912, Amsterdam, Netherlands, d. 1997, Amsterdam, Netherlands. Known as the last performer of Yiddish popular ballads, singer-songwriter Fuld was born into a family of eight children. His remarkable voice was discovered when he attended the Amsterdam Jewish Seminary, and he travelled all over the country to serve as cantor for Jewish congregations on the Sabbath. When he was 18 he performed for the BBC in London, and in 1938 starred on Broadway in New York. One of his first hits was called 'Where Can I Go', and he also enjoyed great success throughout the world with 'My Yiddishe Momma', 'Dos Pintele Yid', 'Mein Shtetele' and many more. He is said to have sold 30 million records worldwide. Shortly after his country was occupied by the Nazis, Fuld left for America and for 10 years was the owner of the Sahbra, an Israeli nightclub and restaurant in New York. During the war most members of his family were killed in the concentration camps. Later in his life he returned to Amsterdam and just a few months before his death performed with the Algerian rock group Railand, recording *The Legend*. Critics raved about the album, saying: 'Never before has Yiddish music sounded so oriental. It is so refreshing after decades of being earnest and very serious about the lost heritage of Yiddish music.'

● ALBUMS: *The Legend* (Music And Words 1997) ★★★★.

● FILMS: *The International Singing Star Leo Fuld* (1993), *Fuld In Railand* (1997).

Fulford, Tommy

b. 1912, USA, d. 16 December 1956. Fulford played piano with various **territory bands** in the Midwest in the early 30s, and then, after a short spell with Blanche Calloway, he went to New York where he played with **Snub Mosley** before joining the **Chick Webb** band. This was in 1936, and he remained more or less continuously with the band until 1942, by which time it was under the nominal leadership of **Ella Fitzgerald**. Fulford then began a solo career, working in clubs and restaurants until the mid-50s when he was a member of **Tony Parenti**'s Dixieland-style band. Fulford was a very good section player, fully a master of the difficult art of being pianist in a big band. His discreet work in this context when accompanying Fitzgerald is particularly noteworthy.

Fulks, Robbie

b. 25 March 1963, York, Pennsylvania, USA. Fulks is the best of the many artists to emerge from Chicago's mid-90s alt country community, which centred on the city's homegrown Bloodshot Records. Like fellow Bloodshot artists the **Old 97's** and the **Waco Brothers**, Fulks works primarily in the country milieu but is also comfortable with rock, pop and jazz idioms. He attended Columbia University briefly in the early 80s. While there he performed regularly in New York folk venues Gerde's Folk City and the Speakeasy. He soon relocated to Chicago, and quickly built a local following. By 1987 his reputation for flat-picking was such that area bluegrass mainstays Special Consensus invited him to join them. Fulks stayed with the band for four years, appearing on their 1989 Grammy-nominated album *Hole In My Heart* and touring regularly. He then left the band to join the cast of the award-winning play *Woody Guthrie's American Song*. Exhausted from years of constant touring, Fulks returned to Chicago to refocus on songwriting and performing locally. In 1993 he signed a music publishing contract in Nashville, but the city was unready for Fulks' defiantly original music. Fulks later immortalized his experiences in Music City with 'Fuck This Town'. In 1994 his 'Cigarette State' appeared on the first Bloodshot anthology, and a year after that, 'She Took A Lot Of Pills And Died' was featured on Bloodshot's second compilation. A full-length album, *Country Love Songs*, followed in 1996. The record, featuring members of the Skeletons and pedal steel guitarist Tom Brumley (formerly of **Buck Owens**' Buckaroos), was an underground success, leading to the release of *South Mouth* and a subsequent contract with **Geffen Records**. On his major label debut *Let's Kill Saturday Night*, Fulks abandoned the 'strictly country' formula he had adhered to with Bloodshot, instead indulging both his tastes and considerable talents for rock, pop and thrash. Released in an era when hip-hop and divas dominated the charts, the record never had a legitimate chance for widespread commercial success. By 1999 Fulks was back on his own, licensing a compilation of b-sides and other rarities to Bloodshot under the title *The Very Best Of Robbie Fulks* followed by some new material in 2001. In 2004 he produced the tribute album *Touch My Heart: A Tribute To Johnny Paycheck*.

● ALBUMS: *Country Love Songs* (Bloodshot 1996) ★★★★, *South Mouth* (Bloodshot 1997) ★★★★, *Let's Kill Saturday Night* (Geffen 1998) ★★★, *13 Hillbilly Giants* (Boondoggle 2001) ★★★, *Couples In Trouble* (Boondoggle 2001) ★★★, *Georgia Hard* (Yep Roc 2005) ★★★.

● COMPILATIONS: *The Very Best Of Robbie Fulks* (Bloodshot 1999) ★★★.

Full Force

This six-piece rap ensemble from Brooklyn, New York, USA, comprises the three George brothers, Brian 'B-Fine', Paul Anthony and 'Bowlegged' Lou, plus cousins 'Baby' Gerry Charles, Junior 'Shy Shy' Clark and Curt 'TT' Bedeau. In addition to their three hit albums (all placed in the lower reaches of the **Billboard** Top 200), the sextet also provided production, arranging and writing duties for protégés **Lisa Lisa And Cult Jam** as well as **U.T.F.O.**, Cheryl 'Pepsi' Riley and even **James Brown**. Full Force's debut album saw their anthropology rewarded with friends like Lisa Lisa, U.T.F.O., **Howie Tee** and the **Real Roxanne** dropping in. B-Fine would also help ex-U.T.F.O. man **Doctor Ice** write songs for his debut album. They also found time to appear in *Krush Groove*, *House Party 1* and *2* and form their own independent label, Homegrown Records. The first signing to their new empire was rap group Scream. A more dubious honour was also being the only rap group ever to be lent vocal assistance by **Samantha Fox** (on *Smoove*). A serious car accident threatened their future for some time as two members were out of action. They returned to full strength in 1997 and finally released a new album in 2001.

● ALBUMS: *Full Force* (Columbia 1985) ★★, *Full Force Get Busy 1 Time!* (Columbia 1986) ★★★★, *Guess Who's Comin' To The Crib?* (Columbia 1987) ★★★, *Smoove* (Columbia 1989) ★★, *Don't Sleep* (Columbia 1994) ★★★, *Sugar On Top* (Calibre 1995) ★★, *Still Standing* (TVT 2001) ★★★.

● COMPILATIONS: *Ahead Of Their Time: Greatest Hits* (Thump 2001) ★★★.

Fuller, Blind Boy
(see **Blind Boy Fuller**)

Fuller, Bobby

b. 22 October 1943, Baytown, Texas, USA, d. 18 July 1966, Los Angeles, California, USA. An inventive and compulsive musician, Bobby Fuller made his recording debut in 1961. 'You're In Love' was the first of several outings for local independent labels, but the artist's development was more apparent on the many demos completed in his home-based studio. Fuller later moved to Los Angeles where his group, the Bobby Fuller Four—Randy Fuller (bass), Jim Reese (rhythm guitar) and DeWayne Quirico (drums)—became a leading attraction, infusing **Buddy Holly**–styled rockabilly with the emergent British beat. Their early releases were regional hits; nevertheless, in January 1966 the group reached the US Top 10 with an ebullient reading of the **Crickets**' 'I Fought The Law'. This pop classic, later memorably covered by UK punk rockers **Clash**, was followed up by a Top 30 hit, 'Love's Made A Fool Of You'. The singer's stature now seemed assured, but on 18 July that same year any hope for a bright future was cut short when Fuller's badly beaten body was discovered in a parked car in Los Angeles. His death was attributed to asphyxia through the forced inhalation of gasoline, but further investigations as to the perpetrators of this deed remain unresolved.

● ALBUMS: *KRLA King Of The Wheels* (Mustang 1965) ★★★, *I Fought The Law* aka *Memorial Album* (Mustang 1966) ★★★, *Live Again* (Eva 1984) ★★.

● COMPILATIONS: *The Best Of The Bobby Fuller Four* (Rhino 1981) ★★★★, *The Bobby Fuller Tapes, Volume 1* (Voxx 1983) ★★★, *Bobby Fuller Tapes Volume 2* (Voxx 1984) ★★, *The Bobby Fuller Instrumental Album* (Rockhouse 1985) ★★, *Never To Be Forgotten* 3-CD box set (Mustang 1998) ★★★, *I Fought The Law* (Rhino 2004) ★★★.

Fuller, Curtis

b. 15 December 1934, Detroit, Michigan, USA. Fuller began studying trombone in his teens, eventually playing in a band during his military service in the early 50s. As the leader of the band was **Cannonball Adderley**, it was not surprising that, following his discharge, Fuller quickly turned to jazz. At first he worked in his home-town, playing with **Kenny Burrell**, **Yusef Lateef** and others, but then he moved to New York, where he worked with **Dizzy Gillespie**, **Hampton Hawes**, **John Coltrane** and **Miles Davis**, led his own small bands and was a founder member of the Jazztet with **Art Farmer** and **Benny Golson**. In the early 60s he was a member of **Art Blakey**'s **Jazz Messengers**, touring extensively with this band and also with Gillespie. In the 70s Fuller gradually incorporated jazz rock concepts into his repertoire and worked with musicians such as **Stanley Clarke**. In the mid-to late 70s he was with **Count Basie**, **Kai Winding**, **Lionel Hampton**, **Cedar Walton**, **Red Garland** and **Sal Nistico** and also continued to lead his own groups. In the 80s his musical associates included Golson again, and he also played in a re-formed Jazztet and in the Timeless All Stars band. In 1993 he reunited with the four surviving members of his 1959 quintet (Golson, pianist **Tommy Flanagan** and drummer Al Harewood, with bass player **Ray Drummond** standing in for the deceased **Jimmy Garrison**), to record the excellent *BLUES-ette Part II*. A major post-bop stylist on trombone, Fuller's technical facility on the instrument allows him great freedom to develop his inventive lines.

● ALBUMS: *New Trombone* (Prestige 1957) ★★★, *Jazz . . . It's Magic* (Regent 1957) ★★★, *The Opener* (Blue Note 1957) ★★★★, *Bone & Bari* (Blue Note 1957) ★★★★, *Curtis Fuller, Volume 3* (Blue Note 1958) ★★★, *Sliding Easy* (United Artists 1959) ★★★★, *BLUES-ette* (Savoy Jazz 1959) ★★★★, *The Curtis Fuller Jazztet With Benny Golson* (Savoy Jazz 1959) ★★★★, *Imagination* (Savoy Jazz 1959)

★★★, with Art Farmer, Benny Golson *Meet The Jazztet* (Argo 1960) ★★★, *Images Of Curtis Fuller* (Savoy Jazz 1960) ★★★, *Boss Of The Soul Stream Trombone* (Warwick 1961) ★★★, *The Magnificent Trombone Of Curtis Fuller* (Epic 1961) ★★★, *South American Cookin'* (Epic 1961) ★★★, *Soul Trombone* (Impulse! 1962) ★★★, *Cabin In The Sky* (Impulse! 1962) ★★★, *Jazz Conference Abroad* (Smash 1962) ★★★, *Curtis Fuller With Red Garland* 1957 recording (New Jazz 1962) ★★★★, *Curtis Fuller And Hampton Hawes With French Horns* 1957 recording (Status 1965) ★★★, *Crankin'* (MRL 1973) ★★★, *Smokin'* (Mainstream 1974) ★★★, *Fire And Filigree* (Beehive 1978) ★★, with Timeless All Stars *It's Timeless* (Timeless 1982) ★★, with Farmer, Golson *Back To The City* (Contemporary 1986) ★★★, *Four On The Outside* 1978 recording (Timeless 1986) ★★★, *Curtis Fuller Meets Roma Jazz Trio* (Timeless 1988) ★★★, *BLUES-ette Part II* (Savoy Jazz 1993) ★★★★, *Up Jumped Spring* (Delmark 2004) ★★★, *Keep It Simple* (Savant 2005) ★★.

● COMPILATIONS: *The Complete Blue Note/UA Curtis Fuller Sessions* 5-LP/3-CD box set (Mosaic 1996) ★★★★.

Fuller, Gil

b. Walter Gilbert Fuller, 14 April 1920, Los Angeles, California, USA. Although he started out in the early 40s writing for orthodox swing-era big bands such as **Charlie Barnet**'s, Fuller's true métier was revealed in 1942 when he began an association with **Dizzy Gillespie**. In 1944 they were together in the **Billy Eckstine** band and continued their working relationship when Gillespie formed his 1946 bebop big band. Gillespie's interest in Latin American music was complemented by Fuller, who had previously written for **Tito Puente**, and his arrangements included 'Manteca'. Despite the importance of his work with Gillespie, Fuller's interest had waned by the end of the 40s. Although he wrote occasionally for Gillespie and **Stan Kenton** in the 50s and 60s, a new career, in engineering, occupied his time.

● ALBUMS: *Gil Fuller And The Monterey Jazz Festival Orchestra With Dizzy Gillespie* (Pacific Jazz 1965) ★★★, *Night Flight* (Pacific Jazz 1966) ★★★.

Fuller, Jane

b. Jane Elizabeth Fuller, San Francisco, California, USA. As a small child Fuller was encouraged to follow a musical path by her family and studied piano from the age of nine, but two years later she 'fell in love with the guitar and stuck with it ever since'. Several years of intensive study, both privately and in college, culminated in her earning two degrees: in theatre from the American Academy of Dramatic Arts and in literature at the University of California, Santa Cruz. She played bass and sang in a high school rock band and also performed in music theatre and was a member of college choral groups. She began performing jazz standards in small ensembles at clubs, in coffeehouses and on casual gigs. Performing throughout the 90s, mainly in Southern California, Fuller has appeared as a solo act, accompanying herself on guitar, and also with various jazz ensembles. Her independently produced debut CD received positive reviews and widened her audience. Two of her original songs from this CD were picked up for use on television shows. Fuller's repertoire, which reflects her varied musical interests, includes languorous ballads like 'Black Coffee' alongside lithe swingers such as 'No Moon At All' and 'Route 66' as well as standards like 'All Of Me'. Interested in and adept at Latin, rock, jazz, blues and classical music, she has also developed songwriting skills and her lyrics are filled with wit and charm. Fuller sings in a lightly floating manner and interprets lyrics with care and intelligence.

● ALBUMS: *You're Coming Back Again* (Jane Fuller Music 2003) ★★★.

Fuller, Jesse 'Lone Cat'

b. 12 March 1896, Jonesboro, Georgia, USA, d. 29 January 1976, Oakland, California, USA. A veteran of tent shows, Fuller fashioned himself a unique one-man band of six-string bass (played with his right foot), a combination of kazoo, harmonica and microphone fixed to a harness around his neck, a hi-hat cymbal (played with the left foot) and a 12-string guitar. Fuller was also known for preceding many of his songs with a spoken intro. He came to fame in the late 50s as a result of appearances on US television, where he followed **Ramblin' Jack Elliot**'s lionization via his recording of 'San Francisco Bay Blues'. In the 50s he made three albums of original and traditional material and by the mid-60s became a darling of the 'coffeehouse circuit' after **Bob Dylan** cited him as one of his influences. Similar success followed in the UK resulting from **Donovan**'s performance of 'San Francisco Bay Blues' on UK Independent Television's **Ready, Steady, Go!** music show in 1965. Although Fuller's output was meagre, his influence has been considerable. **Eric Clapton** provoked renewed interest with an excellent version of 'San Francisco Bay Blues' on his *MTV Unplugged* album in 1992. Original Blues Classics have reissued his albums on CD with the original covers. Although often repetitive his originality is irresistible.

● ALBUMS: *Workin' On The Railroad* 10-inch album (World Songs 1954) ★★★, *Frisco Bound* (Cavalier 1955/58) ★★★★, *Jazz, Folk Songs, Spirituals & Blues* (Good Time Jazz 1958) ★★★★, *The Lone Cat* (Good Time Jazz 1961) ★★★★, *San Francisco Bay Blues* (Folklore 1964) ★★★★, *Favorites* (Stateside 1965) ★★★★, *Move On Down The Line* (Topic 1965) ★★★.

Fuller, Johnny

b. 20 April 1929, Edwards, Mississippi, USA. Major Fuller moved his family west to Vallejo, California, in 1935, possibly drawn by work in the shipyards. Johnny was a largely self-taught musician and played guitar, his first interest being C&W music, particularly the songs of **Ernest Tubb** and **Gene Autry**. At the age of 15, he was singing in church, later forming the Teenage Gospel Singers, who became the Golden West Gospel Singers. In about 1948 he made solo gospel records for Jackson and for several years performed every Sunday on stations KWBR in Oakland and KRE in Berkeley. In the early 50s, he learned piano and organ and played blues in a style reminiscent of **Charles Brown** but with less sophistication. This was evident on his first record, 'Train, Train Blues', for **Bob Geddins**' Rhythm label. Subsequent sessions were sold to Flair and Hollywood. His tribute, 'Johnny Ace's Last Letter', leased to Aladdin, became his first success and put him on the package tour circuit for several years. His 1956 single for **Imperial**, 'Don't Slam That Door', was later covered by **Snooks Eaglin.** Later records for Irma and **Specialty** strayed into rock 'n' roll and rockabilly. He spent much of the 60s outside music, returning to the clubs of Oakland and Richmond at the end of the decade. In 1973 he recorded an album, released in Australia, combining new material with older songs such as 'Fools Paradise', 'Bad Luck Overtook Me' and 'Strange Land' with a band that also featured **Philip Walker**. Further club and festival work continued through the 70s, since which time nothing further has been reported.

● ALBUMS: *Fuller's Blues* (Diving Duck 1974/1988) ★★★.

Fuller, Simon

b. Brighton, England. Pop Svengali Fuller is most famous for guiding the **Spice Girls** to commercial success in the 90s and for cocreating the reality television show *Pop Idol* in the new millennium.

Fuller's first job in the music business was as a talent scout for Chrysalis Music, where he bought the UK rights to **Madonna**'s first hit, 'Holiday'. He set up his own management company in 1985 and enjoyed immediate success with **Paul Hardcastle**'s anti-Vietnam war song '19', a million-selling UK chart-topper. Fuller went on to name his company 19 Entertainment Limited after the hit song. The company continued to grow at a steady rate during the latter part of the decade and into the early 90s, with clients including former **Eurythmics** lead singer **Annie Lennox**. In May 1995 Fuller took over management of the Spice Girls, a quintet of aspiring female pop stars. Under his wing the group went on to dominate the UK charts for the next three years and also enjoy major US success. During this period Fuller also managed the soccer players David Beckham and Steve McManaman. The former had married Victoria Adams of the Spice Girls. Fuller parted company with the Spice Girls in 1997 amid allegations of financial mismanagement, but his role in their success became readily apparent when they disbanded shortly afterwards. He then took over the reins of Spice Girls members **Emma Bunton** and Victoria Beckham's solo careers. His own attempt to launch a girl group with the 21st Century Girls was an abject failure, however. He enjoyed more success with the mixed gender group **S Club 7**, overseeing a string of UK chart-toppers and spawning the spin-off groups S Club Juniors and S Club 8.

In 2001 Fuller and BMG A&R executive **Simon Cowell** created the reality television show *Pop Idol*. The series was a huge ratings success and spawned the equally successful US version, *American Idol*, and a host of other international spin-offs. Part of the deal with the show was that Fuller and 19 Management would control the management rights of the finalists, leading to lucrative contracts with the singers **Will Young**, **Kelly Clarkson**, **Clay Aiken** and **Fantasia**. In March 2005 Fuller sold 19 Entertainment to CKX Inc. in a contract worth a reputed $192 million. He is also involved in the online downloading venture I Love Music.

Fulson, Lowell

b. 31 March 1921, Tulsa, Oklahoma, USA, d. 6 March 1999, Los Angeles, California, USA. Blues guitarist Lowell Fulson (whose surname was often mistakenly misspelled Fulsom) recorded steadily from 1946 onwards and performed regularly on the US and European club circuits into the 90s. One of the founding fathers of west coast blues, Fulson blended the rural blues of his home state with the modern sounds of urban California. Fulson was raised in Atoka, close to the Texas border, and began his career performing with string bands and backing country blues vocalist **Alger 'Texas' Alexander** in the late 30s. During World War II he was stationed in Oakland, California, where he met record producer **Bob Geddins**. Following his discharge from the US Navy, Fulson recorded for several labels under the direction of Geddins, including Big Town, Down Town, Gilt Edge and Trilon. His first hit came in 1950 on the Swing Time label when he reworked **Memphis Slim**'s 'Nobody Loves Me' into 'Every Day I Have The Blues'. At that time his 12-piece orchestra included a young **Ray Charles** on piano and tenor saxophonist **Stanley Turrentine**.

Fulson recorded for Aladdin Records in 1953 and then switched to **Checker Records**, a subsidiary of **Chess Records**, the following year. His first side for that company, 'Reconsider Baby', was later covered by **Elvis Presley** and became a blues standard. Fulson stayed with Checker Records into the early 60s and then moved to Kent Records, who changed the spelling of his name. Now recording in a more contemporary and commercial soul-blues vein, Fulson's biggest hits for Kent were 'Black Nights' in 1965 and 'Tramp' a year later. The latter song, co-written with **Jimmy McCracklin**, was later a duet hit for **Otis Redding** and **Carla Thomas**. In 1968 Fulson signed with Jewel Records and then recorded for a succession of small labels including Crazy Cajun and Granite. He reappeared on the international circuit in the mid-80s, his sound and voice seemingly undiminished by the passing years. By the early 90s his early work often appeared on reissues, while much of his new material was only released on minor labels, such as France's Blue Phoenix Records. However, in 1993 the artist received five **W.C. Handy** Awards and was inducted into the Blues Hall Of Fame, both for himself and his song 'Reconsider Baby'. He continued working up until 1997. An excellent remastered and expanded version of *I've Got The Blues* was released in 2001.

● ALBUMS: *In A Heavy Bag* (Jewel 1965) ★★★★, *I've Got The Blues* (Jewel 1965) ★★★★, *Lowell Fulson* (Kent 1965) ★★★★, *Soul* (Kent 1966) ★★★★, *Tramp* (Kent 1967) ★★★, *Lowell Fulson Now!* (Kent 1969) ★★★, *Let's Go Get Stoned* (United Artists 1971) ★★★, *The Ol' Blues Singer* (Jet 1976) ★★★, *Lovemaker* (Big Town 1978) ★★★, *Think Twice Before You Speak* (JSP 1984) ★★★, *Blue Days, Black Nights* (Ace 1986) ★★★, *I Don't Know My Mind* (Bear Family 1987) ★★★, *Baby Won't You Jump With Me* (Crown Prince 1988) ★★★, *Hold On* (Bullseye 1993) ★★★, *Them Update Blues* (Bullseye 1995) ★★★, *Blue Shadows* 1981 recording (Stony Plain 1998) ★★★.

● COMPILATIONS: *Man Of Motion* (Charly 1981) ★★★, *Everyday I Have The Blues* (Night Train 1984) ★★★★, *Lowell Fulson 1946–57* (Blues Boy 1987) ★★★, *San Francisco Blues* (Black Lion 1993) ★★★, *Reconsider Baby* (Charly 1993) ★★★, *Sinner's Prayer* (Night Train 1996) ★★★★, *The Complete Chess Masters* (MCA/Chess 1998) ★★★★, *The Crazy Cajun Recordings* (Crazy Cajun 1998) ★★★, *I've Got The Blues (. . . And Then Some!): The Jewel Recordings 1969–71* (Westside 2001) ★★★, *The Final Kent Years* (Ace 2002) ★★★, *Trying To Find My Baby* (Complete Blues 2004) ★★★, *1948–1949* (Classics 2005) ★★★.

Fun Boy Three

When the **Specials** topped the UK charts in June 1981 with the spellbinding 'Ghost Town', few would have guessed that three of their members would depart immediately to form an offshoot group. By October, **Terry Hall** (b. 19 March 1959,

Coventry, England; vocals), Neville Staple(s) (vocals/drums) and Lynval Golding (b. 24 July 1951, Coventry, England; guitar) had launched the Fun Boy Three. Their UK Top 20 debut single was the extraordinary 'The Lunatics (Have Taken Over The Asylum)', a haunting protest against political conservatism, made all the more effective by Hall's deadpan, languid vocal. The single effectively established the trio as both original and innovative commentators, whose work compared favourably with that of their mother group, the Specials. For their follow-up, the Fun Boy Three teamed-up with the then unknown **Bananarama** for a hit revival of band leader **Jimmie Lunceford**'s 'It Ain't What You Do, It's The Way That You Do It'. The Bananarama connection continued when the Fun Boy Three appeared on their hit 'Really Saying Something (He Was Really Sayin' Somethin')'. The girl trio also sang on several tracks of their mentors' self-titled debut album.

By 1982 the Fun Boy Three were proving themselves adept at writing political songs and reviving classic songs, which they moulded into their own distinctive style. Hall's lazy vocal on **George Gershwin**'s 'Summertime' was a typical example of this and provided another Top 20 hit. The wonderfully cynical comment on teenage love and pregnancy 'Tunnel Of Love' and the Top 10 hit 'Our Lips Are Sealed' proved the trio's last major statements. Following a second album, they split during 1983, with Hall going on to form the **Colour Field** and work as a solo artist.

● ALBUMS: *Fun Boy Three* (Chrysalis 1982) ★★★, *Waiting* (Chrysalis 1983) ★★★.

● COMPILATIONS: *Really Saying Something: The Best Of Fun Boy Three* (Chrysalis 1997) ★★★★.

Fun-Da-Mental

An Asian world dance band, the original Fun-Da-Mental formed in Bradford, Yorkshire, in August 1991, specifically to play at the Notting Hill Carnival of that year. Though all of the initial quartet were born in Pakistan or India, they had each grown up in northern English cities. The initial line-up was Propa-Ghandi (b. Aki Nawaz; aka Haq Quereshi), DJ Obeyo, Bad-Sha Lallaman and Man Tharoo Goldfinger (b. Inder Matharu; also of **Transglobal Underground**). Their debut single was 'Janaam—The Message', which immediately brought them to the attention of the national music press, particularly the dance magazines. After a cassette-only release, they followed up with 'Gandhi's Revenge' before 'Sister India', initially recorded for a live **John Peel** Radio 1 session. On the back of such exposure they looked certain to be on the verge of a significant breakthrough—when they themselves broke in two in late 1993, during a video shoot in Pakistan. Industry conjecture suggested rows over royalty payments and allocations, as rappers Goldfinger and Bad-Sha Lallaman left to team up with DJ Obeyo (b. Khaled Malik) and attempted to take the name with them. Eventually they became Det-Ri-Mental. Fun-Da-Mental carried on, now comprising Propa-Ghandi, MCs Mushtaq and Hot Dog Dennis, Amir Ali (lyrics), Inder Matharu (percussion), Dave 'D' Watts (aka Impi-D; samples) and Count Dubulah (bass/guitar).

Their first release following the departures was 'Countryman' in November 1993. Fun-Da-Mental's leader remained Propa-Ghandi, formerly a member of gothic bands Southern Death Cult and Getting The Fear, and who is also responsible for **Nation Records**. They joined with **Pop Will Eat Itself** for the

'Ich Bin Ein Auslander' antiracism tirade. Another controversial single followed in 1994, 'Dog Tribe', which began with a recorded answerphone message left at the offices of Youth Against Racism by a member of sinister far-right group, Combat 18. Fun-Da-Mental themselves have been targeted by the likes of the British National Party—who were forced to apologize after printing their picture in one of their magazines with the caption 'a gang of Asian thugs'. Fun-Da-Mental also became one of the first bands to visit the post-apartheid South Africa, which left a lasting impression on them, prior to the release of their debut album. This, the title adapted from Black Panther Bobby Seale, included remixes of 'Wrath Of The Black Man' and 'Countryman', guest appearances by Neil Sparkes of Transglobal Underground, poet Subi Shah and ex–**Collapsed Lung** singer Nihal. On subsequent albums the band has relentlessly pursued their political ideals, while their music has shown an increasing interest in traditional Asian styles. To this end, they have toured with traditional qawwali singers and appeared at the 1997 Tanz&FolkFest in Rudolstadt. In 1999 they released the superbly titled remix set *Why America Will Go To Hell*. The album also included several new tracks.

● ALBUMS: *Seize The Time* (Beggars Banquet 1994) ★★★★, *With Intent To Pervert The Cause Of Injustice!* (Nation 1995) ★★★, *Erotic Terrorism* (Nation 1998) ★★★, *There Shall Be Love!* (Nation 2001) ★★★.

● COMPILATIONS: *Why America Will Go To Hell* (Nation 1999) ★★★★.

Fun Factory

A cosmopolitan 90s pop/dance group from Hamburg, Germany, Fun Factory comprise singer Marie-Annett (b. France), backing singer Smooth T. (b. Italy), dancer Steve (b. Germany) and rapper Rod D. (b. USA). Since their inception in the early 90s and with the substantive help of producer Bulow Aris, they have successfully achieved a string of pop hits including 'Groove Me', 'Take Your Chance', 'Close To You' and 'Pain'. Though these have failed to cross over to either the USA or UK, such singles have enjoyed enormous success in mainland European countries including France, Holland, Sweden, and Germany. Promoting their debut album, *Non Stop!*, Rod D. described their appeal thus: 'The main thing is that it grooves, kicks and beeps, and that people have a good time.'

● ALBUMS: *Non Stop!* (Edel 1995) ★★★.

● COMPILATIONS: *All Their Best* (Edel 1997) ★★★.

Fun In Acapulco

Elvis Presley's second film of 1963 featured the singer as a former trapeze artist, who, following an accident to his partner, is now afraid of heights. He decamps to Acapulco, ultimately conquering this phobia with a high-dive from the coastal rock. Ursula Andress, thrust into the public eye following her role in the first James Bond feature *Dr. No*, costarred in this slice of light entertainment. The soundtrack provided 11 songs, including the much-maligned '(There's) No Room To Rhumba In A Sports Car'. It is a terrible composition, but several other tracks, notably 'The Bullfighter Was A Lady' and 'El Toro', were equally poor. *Fun In Acapulco* contained the obligatory spin-off single, but the relatively low chart placings gained by 'Bossa Nova Baby' (number 8 US, number 13 UK) suggested Presley's audience was beginning to tire of substandard material.

Paradoxically, the course he had embarked upon exacerbated the problem. 1963 was the first year in which the singer did not complete a regular studio album, and in deference to his film schedule, Presley began to overdub vocals on to pre-existing backing tracks, rather than record them with his backing group. He completed his contributions to the songs on *Fun In Acapulco* in one day.

Fun Lovin' Criminals

This US hip-hop/funk crossover outfit was formed in New York City in 1993 by Huey Morgan (b. 8 August 1968, USA; vocals/guitar), Steve Borovini (drums/programming) and Fast (b. Brian Leiser; bass, keyboards, harmonica). Assimilating a variety of local music influences—predominantly hip-hop but also funk, rock and blues—as well as cult cinema references, in October 1995 the trio released the four track *Original Soundtrack For Hi-Fi Living* on Silver Spotlight Records. With samples drawn from movies such as *Pulp Fiction* as well as records by obscure British gothic band **Tones On Tail** and lyrical narratives describing New York's criminal underclass, they soon drew comparisons to the **Beastie Boys** as well as other urban east coast hip-hop crews such as **Lordz Of Brooklyn** and **Young Black Teenagers**. In common with both those outfits, Fun Lovin' Criminals initially struggled to establish a singular identity outside of the Beastie Boys comparisons. The excellent *Come Find Yourself* (1996) and a string of single releases (including 'Fun Lovin' Criminal', 'Scooby Snacks' and 'King Of New York') did secure strong airplay, particularly in the UK where the album reached the Top 10. They also received a series of rave reviews for their concert appearances. *100% Colombian* downplayed the hip-hop rhythms in favour of a soulful vibe, characterised by the **Barry White** tribute single, 'Love Unlimited', which debuted at number 18 in August 1998. The album entered the UK charts at number 3 a month later, but failed to break through in their homeland where they continue to be ignored.

Borovini was subsequently replaced in the line-up by Maxwell 'Mackie' Jayson. 1999's b-side compilation *Mimosa* collected together the band's lounge style cover versions of their own and other artist's material. Their first album of the new millennium *Loco* saw the new look trio pursuing the funk/soul vibe to great effect, and slipping in a slinky cover version of **Eric B And Rakim**'s 'Microphone Fiend'. It proved to be the Fun Lovin' Criminals' last major label release, however, with subsequent albums *Welcome To Poppy's* (2003) and *Livin' In The City* (2005) appearing through Sanctuary Records.

● ALBUMS: *Come Find Yourself* (EMI/Chrysalis 1996) ★★★★, *100% Colombian* (Virgin/Chrysalis 1998) ★★★★, *Loco* (Chrysalis 2001) ★★★, *Welcome To Poppy's* (Sanctuary 2003) ★★, *Livin' in The City* (Sanctuary 2005) ★★★.

● COMPILATIONS: *Mimosa* (Chrysalis 1999) ★★★, *Bag Of Hits* (Chrysalis 2002) ★★★★, *Scooby Snacks: The Collection* (EMI 2003) ★★★, *A's, B's And Rarities* (Chrysalis 2004) ★★★.

● DVD/VIDEOS: *Love Ya Back: A Video Collection* (Chrysalis 2001).

Funderburgh, Anson

b. 15 November 1954, Plano, Texas, USA. Funderburgh played blues guitar with several local bands and in 1981 recorded with the **Fabulous Thunderbirds**. He later formed his own band, the Rockets, and signed to blues revivalist label Black Top in 1984. Funderburgh's guitar pyrotechnics made the group a favourite at blues festivals, where they often performed with veteran harmonica player **Sammy Myers** (b. 19 February 1936, Laurel, Mississippi, USA). Myers also featured on Funderburgh's studio releases, and in 1997 the partnership celebrated their tenth anniversary together. This is an unlikely partnership, primarily because of the considerable age difference. In addition to their working relationship, they are close friends. As Funderburgh stated to Art Tipaldi, 'We've both slung ourselves around to where we really compliment one another without whittling away at who we both are'.

● ALBUMS: with the Rockets *Talk To You By Hand* (Black Top 1981) ★★★, with the Rockets *She Knocks Me Out* (Black Top 1985) ★★★, with Sam Myers *My Love Is Here To Stay* (Black Top 1986) ★★★, with the Rockets featuring Sam Myers *Sins* (Black Top 1987) ★★★, with the Rockets featuring Sam Myers *Rack 'Em Up* (Black Top 1989) ★★★, with the Rockets featuring Sam Myers *Tell Me What I Want To Hear* (Black Top 1991) ★★★, with the Rockets featuring Sam Myers *Live At The Grand Emporium* (Black Top 1995) ★★★, with Sam Myers *That's What They Want* (Black Top 1997) ★★★, with Debbie Davies, Otis Grand *Grand Union* (Blueside 1998) ★★★, with the Rockets featuring Sam Myers *Change In My Pocket* (Bullseye Blues 1999) ★★★★, with the Rockets *Which Way Is Texas?* (Bullseye Blues 2003) ★★★.

● COMPILATIONS: with the Rockets *Thru The Years: A Retrospective* (Black Top 1992) ★★★★.

Fundis, Garth

b. 20 September 1949, Lawrence, Kansas, USA. The country music producer Garth Fundis was raised in Kansas but went to Nashville, in 1971, where he was employed by the studio owner **Jack Clement**. He sang harmony on 'Amanda' by **Don Williams**, for whom he also worked as recording engineer until Williams elevated him to coproducer for records such as 'Tulsa Time' and 'Lay Down Beside Me'. Since then, he has made a succession of big-selling records with Williams, often finding him the songs to record. He has also produced **Keith Whitley** and gave him the song 'Don't Close Your Eyes' and thereby relaunched his career. Fundis also produced 'When You Say Nothing At All' and was mixing Whitley's next album when he heard of his death. He discovered **Trisha Yearwood** singing backing vocals for **Pat Alger** and produced her first hit, 'She's In Love With The Boy'. He has also had some success producing **Ty England**.

Fungus

Similar in style to **Fairport Convention** and **Steeleye Span**, the founder members of Fungus were Fred Piek (guitar/vocals), Sido Martens (guitars), Kees Maat (piano) and Koos Pakvis were joined later Louis Debij (drums). They mixed Dutch and British material, although *Lief Ende Leid*, their finest album, is devoted to the traditional music of their homeland—a thorough exercise in folk rock. After Martens had left to pursue a solo career, he released *Land And Water*, and developed a style similar to **Richard Thompson**. In 1977 Fungus released the impressive, ironically titled, *Mushrooms*, devoted to English songs and tunes. In the following year, Debij and the lead guitarist Arie Graff departed, leaving the remaining trio, Piek, Pakvis and Rens Van Der Zalm to recorded their final album acoustically before disbanding in 1980. Fungus is seen as having served as an example to other Dutch musicians on the local folk scene, and a small group of bands followed in their footsteps. Piek went on to a solo career, while the remainder of Fungus' personnel formed a comedy band, The Amazing Strompwa Fels. A Fungus reunion took place in October 1984.

● ALBUMS: *Fungus* (1974) ★★★, *Lief Ende Leid* (1975) ★★, *Van Keil Naar Vlaring* (1976) ★★★, *Mushrooms* (1977) ★★★, *De Kaarten Zign Geschud* (1979) ★★★.

Funicello, Annette

(see **Annette**)

Funk Brothers

For many the greatest group of session musicians to ever grace a recording studio, the Funk Brothers played on more number 1 singles than any other band in history, racking up more hits than the **Beatles**, the **Beach Boys**, **Elvis Presley** and the **Rolling Stones** combined. Sadly, their status as sidemen for **Berry Gordy**'s **Motown Records** operation largely consigned these unsung pioneers to the dusty corners of the annals of popular music, although a 2002 documentary *Standing In The Shadows Of Motown* went some way to redressing the balance.

The dozen or so players who featured in the Funk Brothers were drawn from the local jazz and blues clubs. The personnel included guitarists Robert White (b. 19 November 1936, Billmyre, Pennsylvania, USA, d. 1994, Los Angeles, California, USA), Joe Messina (b. 1928, Detroit, Michigan, USA) and Eddie Willis (b. 1936, Grenada, Mississippi, USA), bass players **James Jamerson** (b. James Lee Jamerson, 29 January 1936, Charleston, South Carolina, USA, d. 2 August 1983, Los Angeles, California, USA) and Bob Babbitt (b. Robert Kreinar, Pittsburgh, Pennsylvania, USA), drummers Benny 'Papa Zita' Benjamin (b. William Benjamin, 25 July 1925, Birmingham, Alabama, USA, d. 20 April 1969, USA), Richard 'Pistol' Allen (b. 12 August 1932, Memphis, Tennessee, USA, d. 30 June 2002, Royal Oak, Michigan, USA) and Uriel Jones (b. 1934, Detroit, Michigan, USA), percussionists Jack Ashford (b. 1934, Philadelphia, Pennsylvania, USA) and Eddie 'Bongo' Brown (b. 1932, Clarksdale, Mississippi, USA, d. 28 December 1984, Los Angeles, California, USA) and keyboard players Joe Hunter (b. Joseph Hunter, 19 November 1927, Jackson, Tennessee, USA), **Earl Van Dyke** (b. 8 July 1930, Detroit, Michigan, USA, d. 18 September 1992, Detroit, Michigan, USA) and Johnny Griffith (b. 10 July 1936, Detroit, Michigan, USA, d. 10 November 2002, Detroit, Michigan, USA). Joe Hunter was the original band leader, a position he relinquished in 1964 to Earl Van Dyke.

Based at Hitsville USA, the Motown recording studios in Detroit, Michigan, the Funk Brothers worked with all the leading stars of America's premier black music label, a role call including such giants as the **Miracles**, the **Temptations**, **Marvin Gaye**, **Stevie Wonder** and the **Supremes**. Sequestered in the tiny Studio A (the 'Snakepit'), the musicians spent all day recording the instrumental backing for releases by Motown artists, who they rarely ever saw because vocals were added at different sessions. Paid at the rate of $10 a song, the Funk Brothers were given no credit on album covers (save Gaye's 1971 masterpiece **What's Going On**) and rarely toured with the big stars. Nevertheless, they were instrumental in fashioning the trademark Motown sound, a fact the astute Gordy realized by keeping most of the musicians under contract for the period between 1959 and 1972 when the company was based in Detroit.

When Motown relocated from Detroit to Los Angeles, the Funk Brothers were left behind by the now waning company. Several members found work on the local club circuit while others gave up music and settled into an altogether different routine of day jobs and raising families. The revival of the Funk Brothers began in the 80s when Allan Slutsky aka Dr. Licks wrote a book about the recently deceased James Jamerson. Slutsky's work helped elevate the unsung musician to the status his extraordinary bass work deserved (he was later posthumously inducted into the **Rock And Roll Hall Of Fame**). A project about the rest of the session crew was a natural follow-up, and Slutsky began work on the documentary *Standing In The Shadows Of Motown* in the 90s. The surviving Funk Brothers (casualties included Jamerson, Van Dyke, Brown and White; original drummer Benjamin had suffered a fatal stroke in 1969) reunited at the insistence of Slutsky to shoot new footage for the documentary, with guest vocalists including **Joan Osborne**, **Ben Harper** and **Chaka Khan**. The film was finally completed in 2002 and was released the same year to rapturous applause, winning the Best Film Of The Year Award (nonfiction) from the National Society of Film Critics.

The reunited Funk Brothers embarked on a US tour with guest vocalists including Osborne, **Bootsy Collins** and **Maxi Priest**. The soundtrack from the film later won two Grammy Awards for Best Compilation Soundtrack Album and Best Traditional R&B Vocal Performance (for a cover version of 'What's Going On' with Chaka Khan). Sadly, in the ensuing period two further members of the Funk Brothers passed away, keyboard player Johnny Griffith and drummer Richard 'Pistol' Allen. Even sadder, after all the various members had been through, was the announcement at the start of 2005 that the Funk Brothers had split into two camps due to personal and legal reasons.

● COMPILATIONS: *Standing In The Shadows Of Motown* (Motown 2003) ★★★★, *The Best Of The Funk Brothers: The Millennium Collection* (Motown 2004) ★★★★.

● DVD/VIDEOS: *Standing In The Shadows Of Motown* (Motown 2003).

● FURTHER READING: *Standing In The Shadows Of Motown: The Life And Music Of Legendary Bassist James Jamerson*, Allan Slutsky. *Motown: The View From The Bottom*, Jack Ashford with Charlene Ashford.

● FILMS: *Standing In The Shadows Of Motown* (2002).

Funk Masters

A collection of UK funk musicians (sometimes including members of **Gonzalez**), vocalists and rapper Bo Kool, masterminded by reggae radio disc jockey Tony Williams. Williams, who was then heard regularly on Radio London, produced several records under this name, including 'Love Money' in 1982, one of the earliest UK rap tracks. It came out on his own Tania label, and created some interest on the US dance scene. The act's only chart success came in June 1983 with 'It's Over', a Tony Williams song that made UK number 8 on his Master Funk label. The hit introduced the public to the voice of **Juliet Roberts** (b. 1962, London, England), who had started in reggae band Black Jade. Roberts was working in the USA when the record charted and had to be substituted for all promotion work. She later recorded many singles for Bluebird Records and sang with **Courtney Pine**'s **Jazz Warriors** as well as **Working Week**. She also later helped to host the UK version of television's *Soul Train*.

Funkadelic

George Clinton (b. 22 July 1940, Kannapolis, North Carolina, USA) established this inventive, experimental group out of the 1969 line-up of his doo-wop vocal outfit the **Parliaments** Raymond Davis (b. 29 March 1940, Sumter, South Carolina, USA, d. 5 July 2005, New Brunswick, USA), Grady Thomas (b. 5 January 1941, Newark, New Jersey, USA), Calvin Simon (b. 22 May 1942, Beckley, West Virginia, USA), Clarence 'Fuzzy' Haskins (b. 8 June 1941, Elkhorn, West Virginia, USA), plus the backing group Bernard Worrell (b. 19 April 1944, Long Beach, New Jersey, USA; keyboards), Billy 'Bass' Nelson (b. William Nelson Jnr., 28 January 1951, Plainfield, New Jersey, USA; bass), Eddie Hazel (b. 10 April 1950, Brooklyn, New York City, USA, d. 23 December 1992; lead guitar), Lucius 'Tawl' Ross (b. 5 October 1948, Wagram, North Carolina, USA; rhythm guitar) and Ramon 'Tiki' Fulwood (b. 23 May 1944, Philadelphia, Pennsylvania, USA, d. 29 November 1979; drums), when contractual problems prevented the use of their original name. Band leader Clinton seized the opportunity to reconstruct his music and the result laced hard funk with a heady dose of psychedelia, hence the name Funkadelic (originally suggested by Nelson). Primarily viewed as an album-orientated vehicle, the group's instinctive grasp of such contrasting styles nonetheless crossed over into their singles. Although few managed to enter the R&B Top 30, Funkadelic consistently reached the chart's lower placings. Bass sensation **Bootsy Collins** (b. William Collins, 26 October 1951, Cincinnati, Ohio, USA) was added to the line-up for the recording of 1972's *America Eats Its Young*, while teenage guitar player Michael Hampton joined up for the group's major label debut, *Hardcore Jollies*.

The compulsive 'One Nation Under A Groove' provided the group with their first million-seller. By this point the distinction between Funkadelic and Clinton's other major act, **Parliament**, was becoming increasingly blurred. The former secured another major hit in 1979 with '(Not Just) Knee Deep'. Several offshoot projects, Bootsy's Rubber Band, Parlet and the Brides Of Funkenstein, also emanated from within the burgeoning corporation, but a protracted contractual wrangle with Warners ended with legal action. Three long-time associates, Clarence Haskins, Calvin Simon and Grady Thomas, then broke away, taking the Funkadelic name with them. Despite an early R&B hit 'Connections And Disconnections', they were unable to maintain their own direction, and the group later dissolved. In 1993 the band was favourably reappraised and courted by the soul and **dance music** cognoscenti. Now recording as the P-Funk All Stars, Clinton's 1996 album *The Awesome Power Of A Fully Operational Mothership* was a superb blend of the Funkadelic and Parliament sounds.

● ALBUMS: *Funkadelic* (Westbound 1970) ★★★, *Free Your Mind . . . And Your Ass Will Follow* (Westbound 1970) ★★★, *Maggot Brain* (Westbound 1971) ★★★★, *America Eats Its Young* (Westbound 1972) ★★★★, *Cosmic Slop* (Westbound 1973) ★★★, *Standing On The Verge Of Getting It On* (Westbound 1974) ★★★, *Let's Take It To The Stage* (Westbound 1975) ★★★★, *Hardcore Jollies* (Warners 1976) ★★★, *One Nation Under A Groove* (Warners 1978) ★★★★★, *Uncle Jam Wants You* (Warners 1979) ★★★, *Connections And Disconnections* (LAX 1981) ★★, *The Electric Spanking Of War Babies* (Warners 1981) ★★★★, *Live: Meadowbrook, Rochester, Michigan 12th September 1971* (Westbound 1996) ★★★.

● COMPILATIONS: *Funkadelic's Greatest Hits* (Westbound 1975) ★★★, *Tales Of Kidd Funkadelic* (Westbound 1976) ★★★, *The Best Of The Early Years—Volume One* (Westbound 1977) ★★★★, *Music For Your Mother* (Westbound 1993) ★★★★, *The Best Of Funkadelic 1976–1981* (Charly 1994) ★★★★, *Parliament-Funkadelic Live 1976–1993* 4-CD box set (Sequel 1994) ★★★, *Funkadelic's Finest* (Westbound 1997) ★★★★, *The Complete Recordings 1976–81* (Charly 2000) ★★★, *The Original Cosmic Funk Crew* (Metro 2000) ★★★, *Motor City Madness: The Ultimate Funkadelic Compilation* (Westbound 2003) ★★★★, *Under A Groove* (Charly 2004) ★★★, *The Whole Funk And Nothing But The Funk: Definitive Funkadelic 1976–1981* (Union Square 2005) ★★★.

Funkdoobiest

One of the hardest working crews in hip-hop, mid-90s rap group Funkdoobiest comprise Son Doobie, DJ Ralph M the Mexican and Tomahawk Funk (aka T-Bone). From Los Angeles, USA, they are managed by Happy Walters, who also looks after **Cypress Hill** and **House Of Pain**. Prior to their establishment as a band Ralph M had worked on the now defunct Los Angeles radio station KDAY, at only 13 years of age, going on to DJ for **Kid Frost**. Funkdoobiest's debut single was the incessant 'Bow Wow Wow', which instantly launched them into the hearts of a nation of B-boys. Typically, their debut album was a reinstatement of old school principles, as Son Doobie eulogized in interviews: 'I'm an old skool supremacist. I'm a hip-hop inspector, I'm a fundamentalist, to me hip-hop is a religion. You know it can't be trivialised'. The title-track of their second album was released as a single and as well as a **Little Richard** sample featured a guest first verse from Cypress Hill's B-Real. Unfortunately it proved to be the best segment on the single, which was in turn the best track on the album. Ralph M has gone on to produce tracks for both House Of Pain and **Mellow Man Ace**. Funkdoobiest are certainly not the most politically correct of rappers. Many of their lyrics are vividly pro-pornography, Son Doobie's alter ego being the 'Porno King'. At least their commitment to rap's history is as staunch as their fondness for exposed flesh.

● ALBUMS: *Which Doobie U B* (Immortal 1993) ★★★, *Wopbabuloop* (Immortal 1993) ★★★, *Brothas Doobie* (Epic 1995) ★★★.

Funki Porcini

b. James Bradell, Oxfordshire, England. Bradell left England at the age of 19 and moved to California, later settling in Italy to run a multimedia business. While there he began recording for **Ninja Tune Records** as 9 Lazy 9, releasing two singles and the albums *Paradise Blown* and *Electric Lazyland* (both 1994) on which he combined hip-hop and funk breakbeats with jazz-influenced sounds. He later assumed the name Funki Porcini and returned to England, where he continued his association with Ninja Tune. His single 'Long Road/Poseathon' was released at the beginning of 1995 and was followed by the album *Hed Phone Sex* in May; the latter was described as 'a trip around a bedlam-addled musical sex asylum' and 'a lush voyeuristic fantasy'. 'Long Road' presents a chilled hip-hop groove, melodic dub bass, tinkling piano, sleazy saxophone, sampled voice and various other sounds, to create a lush, abstract texture. 'Big Pink Inflatable' (1995) and *Love, Pussycats & Carwrecks* (1996) pursued Funky Porcini's themes of sex, pornography and voyeurism. Tracks such as 'River Of Smack' move away from the hip-hop and drum 'n' bass rhythms of most of the album, creating a dark, psychedelic dirge, underpinned by double bass and shuffling percussion. Funki Porcini has subsequently balanced a busy remixing schedule with his own prolific output, which has included *The Ultimately Empty Million Pounds*, the *Zombie EP* and *Fast Asleep*. A new 9 Lazy 9 recording, *Sweet Jones*, surfaced in 2003.

● ALBUMS: *Hed Phone Sex* (Ninja Tune 1995) ★★★★, *Love, Pussycats & Carwrecks* (Ninja Tune 1996) ★★★, *The Ultimately Empty Million Pounds* (Ninja Tune 1999) ★★★★, *Fast Asleep* (Ninja Tune 2002) ★★★.

Funkmaster Flex

b. Aston Taylor, Bronx, New York City, USA. One of New York's most prominent hip-hop DJs thanks to his appearances on the Hot 97FM show, the number 1-rated rap outlet in Chicago and Los Angeles, where it is syndicated. Flex has also turned his skills to production and remix work for other artists as well as making his own recordings. He started in hip-hop as a disc jockey for the band Deuces Wild before securing his first radio slots for Chuck Chillout at Kiss FM in 1987. He went on to play the Manhattan club circuit until the end of the decade, having already served his apprenticeship on block parties in the early 80s. Together with his 'Flip Squad', which started as a partnership with Big Kap but expanded to include DJ Enuff, DJ Boodakhan, DJ Riz, Frankie Cutlass and **Biz Markie**, he has gone on to become a prominent remixer.

His own recording career began with 'Dope On Plastic', for **Bobby Konders**' label Massive B. It was followed by 'Six Million Ways To Die' and 'C'Mon Baby' for **Nervous Records**' subsidiary Wreck Records. His debut mix set followed in 1995, comprising 'old school jams' as well as the artist's own creations. 'Every Day & Every Night', sung by R&B singer Yvette Michell, was released as a single. Flex subsequently broadcast in the UK as cohost of Tim Westwood's regular link-ups for the Radio 1 *Rap Show*. Further instalments of his mix series continued to successfully capture the atmosphere of the unofficial mix tapes sold widely on the streets of New York. His 1999 'debut' featured an astonishing role call of big name MCs past and present, including a live recording of the ill-fated **2Pac** and the **Notorious B.I.G.** from 1993.

● ALBUMS: with Big Kap *The Tunnel* (Def Jam 1999) ★★★★.

● COMPILATIONS: *The Mix Tape Volume 1: 60 Minutes Of Funk* (Loud/RCA 1995) ★★★★, *The Mix Tape Volume II: 60 Minutes Of Funk* (Loud/RCA 1997) ★★★, *The Mix Tape Volume III: 60 Minutes Of Funk, The Final Chapter* (Loud/RCA 1998) ★★★★, *60 Minutes Of Funk: Volume IV The Mix Tape* (Loud/RCA 2000) ★★★★, *60 Minutes Of Funk: Volume V* (Loud 2002) ★★★.

Funkstörung

Employing acute attention to detail, Funkstörung excavate electronica's prettiest of melodies and merge these with flickering, debilitated beats to create some of the early twenty-first century's most evocative and resonant music. The Munich, Germany–based duo assemble sonic glitches, crackles of static and curt electronic clicks with the painstaking precision of the fetishist to create oft-brutal, oft-lovely recordings. Tellingly, they derive their name from the German for 'radio interference', and their logo is an abstracted version of Deutsche Telekom's warning sign for the phenomenon. Michael Fakesch (b. 8 March 1975, Rosenheim, Germany) and Chris De Luca (b. 11 May 1974, Kolbermoor, Germany) are probably best known for their radical redesign of **Björk**'s 'All Is Full Of Love', which re-invigorated the final track of 1997's *Homogenic* with glacial rhythms and a scattering of astringent beats. Their own recordings for the Chocolate Industries, Fat Cat, Skam, Compost and their own Musik Aus Strom record labels are equally compelling.

The duo's first album length release, 1999's *Additional Productions*, was an archive compilation of their best remixes/re-interpretations that demonstrated the Fakesch/de Luca aesthetic as applied to other people's music (Björk, **Finitribe**). With reconstructions of tracks by East Flatbush Project and the **Wu-Tang Clan**, Funkstörung notably traced the common threads shared between electronica and hip-hop. The release also showcased the duo's new-found desire to experiment with the human voice: words are warped, accelerated, slowed-down and manipulated against rapid, staccato beats. Fakesch also released the solo *Marion* at the close of 1999. Compiling new and previously released tracks, *Marion* was less overtly melodic than Funkstörung's collaborative recordings, foregrounding Fakesch's hyper-detailed rhythms. The duo's first collection of new tracks, *Appetite For Disctruction*, was released the following April to ecstatic reviews.

Following the release of the 2001 remix collection *Viceversa*, little was heard of Funkstörung over the next few years. De Luca recorded with Peabird (b. Dominik Gilbert Marcel) under the **Chris De Luca And Peabird** moniker before reuniting with Fakesch to record 2004's disappointing *Disconnected*. The album featured collaborations with **Lamb**'s Louise Rhodes and **Massive Attack** associate Sara Jay.

● ALBUMS: *Appetite For Disctruction* (!K7 2000) ★★★★, *Disconnected* (!K7 2004) ★★★, *The Return To The Acid Planet* (!K7 2005) ★★★.

● COMPILATIONS: *Additional Productions* (!K7 1999) ★★★★, *Viceversa* (!K7 2001) ★★★.

Funky Four (Plus One More)

The Funky Four's background is an interesting one, with Lil' Rodney Cee having been part of the street-jivers the Magnificent Seven between 1977 and 1978. The Funky Four were founded when KK Rockwell and DJ Breakout, adding first Keith Keith and then female MC Sha Rock. Rahiem (b. Guy Todd Williams) joined, then departed to take up an engagement with **Grandmaster Flash**. Keith Keith also left. With the addition of Lil' Rodney Cee then **Jazzy Jeff**, they became the Funky Four. None of the crew were older than 17 when they signed with **Enjoy Records**, opening that imprint's account (in rap terms) with 'Rappin' And Rockin' The House'. This utilized the **Cheryl Lynn** break 'Gotta To Be Real', over which a 16-minute rap commentary was placed. The drums were programmed by Pumpkin, probably rap's first production hero, and it was an impressive overall introduction. Shortly afterwards they switched to **Sugarhill Records**, adding the Plus or + One More suffix. In addition to this cast **DJ Mark The 45 King** would act as Breakout's 'record boy', locating and passing records up to the decks as his DJ requested them. They made their debut for Sugarhill with 'That's The Joint', a song arranged by jazz-funk organist **Clifton 'Jiggs' Chase**. Their performances at Bronx house parties included full-blown dance routines, a rare precursor to the vibrant live hip-hop of **Stetsasonic**. After a clash album with the **Cash Crew**, their career petered out somewhat, though Jazzy Jeff would go on to a brief solo career with **Jive Records**. Lil' Rodney Cee and KK Rockwell would go on to be partners in fellow underachievers, Double Trouble.

Funky Fresh Few

UK hip-hop crew formed in Blackpool, Lancashire, in the mid-80s by James Folks, Damon Savage and graffiti artist Timeone. Their first musical excursions were doing pause-button mix tapes and in Timeone's case decorating some of the dreary buildings in and around Blackpool. On one of their frequent trips to Manchester (the nearest place to buy good rap music) they met Mark Rae (of **Rae And Christian**) at Fat City, Manchester, one of the best hip-hop stores around. Rae was in the process of setting up Grand Central Records and released the Funky Fresh Fews' debut EP *Slow For Focus* in 1996. The trio had one more release, 'Through These Veins', on Grand Central featuring **Jeru The Damaja**'s friend Afu Ra in 1997 before starting to drift apart. Rather than completely dissolve, they lost Savage, who was replaced by another Blackpool MC Glenn Reynolds, who had already released a material under the guise of OSC.

In 2002 the new look trio had pieced together enough equipment to have a little studio set-up, enabling the music to flow at a much faster rate. Funky Fresh Few's 2002 debut, *Stealing* attracted some quality US MCs in the form of Craig G (who wrote the rhymes for **Eminem**'s *8 Mile*) and newcomers Jimmy Grand and Dirk Diggla. However, the stars of the show were the guest UK MCs in the form of Wig, who shone on '24.7' and the superb Sage on 'Never Simple' and 'Sageblaze'. This accomplished debut confirmed the growing reputation of UK rap as a musical force to be taken seriously.

● ALBUMS: *Stealing* (Grand Central 2002) ★★★★.

Funky Green Dogs

(see **Murk**)

Funky Poets

Presenting one of the more positive images of young black men in the ghetto, mid-90s US rap group the Funky Poets are a four-piece whose intelligent lyrical trickery is defiantly old school yet whose outlook has been unquestionably informed by the Afrocentricity noises of the **Jungle Brothers** and **De La Soul**. The group is made up of brothers Paul and Ray Frazier and their cousins Christian Jordon and Gene Johnson. Together they broke through on the hit single 'Born In The Ghetto', on which they recounted the urban tale of a young sister learning that she is pregnant at the age of 14. The narrative was turned round, making the situation a positive, with the central character emerging renewed, defiant and proud. 'We're just telling young black people that there is hope, despite the negative things they face everyday living in neighbourhoods that resemble war zones'. Their lyrics are sharply focused to this end, notably on the self-explanatory 'Message To A Funky Poet' poem, which contains couplets relaying the black inner-city experience in its many shades, from crack-dealing to barbecues and fountains gushing from fire hydrants.

● ALBUMS: *True To Life* (Epic 1993) ★★★.

Funny Face (film musical)

George and **Ira Gershwin**'s 1927 Broadway hit *Funny Face* took 30 years to travel from New York to Hollywood, but the wait was well worthwhile. Screenwriter Leonard Gershe discarded the original story entirely and adapted the plot from his own unproduced musical *Wedding Day*. Five songs survived the trip—and so did **Fred Astaire**, who had costarred with his sister **Adele Astaire** in *Funny Face* in both New York and London. In this new scenario, Fred played a fashion photographer who transforms a shy, intellectual Greenwich Village librarian (**Audrey Hepburn**) into a cover girl for a sophisticated magazine. She agrees to go with him to Paris for the photo-shoot so that she can meet her intellectual mentor, who is portrayed in the film as a Jean-Paul Sartre figure, the founder of the then popular existentialist movement. However, he and his philosophies are soon forgotten shortly after the elegant Astaire takes her in his arms and the magical music begins.

Although Astaire was in his late fifties, the years seemed to fall away as he re-created the wonderful numbers from 30 years earlier, such as 'Funny Face', ''S Wonderful', 'He Loves And She Loves', and 'Let's Kiss And Make Up'. Hepburn, too, was charming on 'How Long Has This Been Going On?', which had been written for the original show but was cut before the New York opening night. **Kay Thompson** gave an outstanding performance as the magazine editor with lots of pizzazz and duetted with Astaire on another Gershwin song, 'Clap Yo' Hands', which had been used previously in the musical *Oh, Kay!* (1926). Leonard Gershe and **Roger Edens** contributed 'Bonjour Paris', 'On How To Be Lovely' and 'Think Pink', which was the opening number in what is generally regarded as a visually gorgeous movie. Much of the credit for that aspect of the production was owing to fashion photographer Richard Avedon's work as visual consultant. Ray June photographed the film in Technicolor and VistaVision. *Funny Face* was originally conceived by the **Arthur Freed** Unit at MGM, who, for various reasons, decided not to proceed with it themselves and sold it to Paramount, along with the services of MGM stalwarts such as Edens, Gershe, director **Stanley Donen**, dance director Eugene Loring, and music arranger **Adolph Deutsch**. In 1992 *Funny Face* was released on laserdisc with its colour enhanced and featuring a slightly 'letterboxed' format.

Funny Face (stage musical)

When producers Alex A. Aarons and **Vincent Freedley** built the Alvin Theatre in New York, they each gave the project just a small part of their names ('Al' and 'Vin') but a great deal of their money. Some of that money had been earned from **George** and **Ira Gershwin**'s shows such as *Oh, Kay!*, *Tip-Toes* and *Lady, Be Good*, and now there was more to be made from *Funny Face*, the Gershwins' latest offering and the first presentation at their new theatre on 2 November 1927. The show's title had originally been *Smarty*, but a change of name was only one of a series of measures that were taken when the production was clearly in trouble during its pre-Broadway tryout. Robert Benchley, the renowned American humorist and co-writer of the book with **Fred Thompson**, was replaced by Paul Gerard Smith; several songs were dropped and five more added; and **Victor Moore**, who, for 20 years, had been one of Broadway and Hollywood's much-loved bumbling clowns, joined the party. Moore plays one of the two comic burglars caught up in a story of mistakes and mayhem. Frankie Wynne (**Adele Astaire**) is the ward of the autocratic Jimmie Reeve (**Fred Astaire**). She persuades her aviator boyfriend, Peter Thurston (Allen Kearns), to retrieve an incriminating diary that belongs to her from Jimmie's wall safe, but the silly boy comes away with a bracelet instead. This act of carelessness on his part sets off a mad chase that takes the assembled cast to exotic locations such as Lake Wapatog, New Jersey, and then on to the Paymore Hotel and the Two-Million Dollar Pier, Atlantic City. Fred and his sister, Adele, were together again with another Gershwin score, following their great success in 1924 with **Lady, Be Good!** The songs were right out of the composers' top drawer—one all-time standard, 'S Wonderful'—and other great numbers such as the lovely ballad 'He Loves And She Loves', 'Let's Kiss And Make Up', 'Tell The Doc' (an hilarious lampoon of psychiatrists), 'High Hat' (along with the white tie and tails, it became Astaire's trademark in many Hollywood movies), 'My One And Only', the engaging 'Funny Face' and 'The Babbitt And The Bromide', which Astaire later sung with **Gene Kelly** when they met for the first time on film in **Ziegfeld Follies** (1945). *Funny Face* was a tremendous success and ran for 250 performances in New York. It played for two weeks longer than that in London, where the Astaires were very popular, especially with British royalty. They were joined in the West End production by Sydney Howard and **Leslie Henson**. The 1957 film version, which had a different story but retained some of the songs, and borrowed others from different Gershwin shows, starred Fred Astaire (Adele had retired long since) with Audrey Hepburn and **Kay Thompson**. The story was overhauled yet again in 1983, when a projected Broadway revival of *Funny Face* underwent such drastic changes, that, although, as with the film, it had some of the original numbers, it turned out to be essentially a quite different show, and the title was changed to *My One And Only*. It starred Twiggy and **Tommy Tune** and ran for 767 performances.

Funny Girl (film musical)

Youth and experience were celebrated by the Academy Awards committee in April 1969, when **Barbra Streisand** and Katharine Hepburn tied for the best actress Oscar. It was Hepburn's third award, for her 36th film, while Streisand was making her movie debut in what proved to the role of a lifetime as comedienne **Fanny Brice**, the most famous star of the **Ziegfeld Follies**. Streisand had already enjoyed much success on Broadway and in London with this saga of Fanny's onstage triumphs and her turbulent marriage to compulsive gambler Nicky Arnstein (Omar Sharif). Kay Medford, who was in the original Broadway cast, re-created her fine and funny performance as Fanny's typically Jewish mother, and some of the other parts went to Walter Pidgeon (as **Florenz Ziegfeld**), Anne Francis, Ma Questel, Lee Allen, Tommy Rall and Gerald Mohr. Three of Brice's genuine hit songs, 'My Man' (Channing Pollock–Maurice Yvain), 'I'd Rather Be Blue Over You (Than Be Happy With Somebody Else)' (**Billy Rose**–**Fred Fisher**) and 'Second Hand Rose' (Grant Clarke–James F. Hanley), were added to what remained of **Jule Styne** and **Bob Merrill**'s splendid stage score and some additional songs they wrote especially for the film. Streisand's big emotional numbers, such as 'People', 'His Love Makes Me Beautiful' and 'Don't Rain On My Parade', were all retained, and the rest of the songs, including several comedy items that fitted the 'funny girl' like a glove, were 'I'm The Greatest Star' (Streisand), 'If A Girl Isn't Pretty' (Streisand-Medford-Questel), 'Roller Skate Rag' (Streisand), 'You Are Woman, I Am Man' (Streisand-Sharif), 'Sadie, Sadie' (Streisand), 'The Swan' (orchestral ballet parody) and 'Funny Girl' (Streisand). Styne and Merrill wrote at least one more title song, a lively, up-tempo number that Streisand released on record but was not included in the film. Isobel Lennart, adapted her own witty stage libretto for the screenplay, and Herbert Ross designed the often hilarious choreography. He is also said to have collaborated with director William Wyler on some of the film's spectacular sequences, including the 'Don't Rain On My Parade' number that Streisand performed while tearing around on various modes of transport, ending up on a tugboat in New York harbour. *Funny Girl* was photographed by Harry Stradling in Technicolor and Panavision and released by Columbia in 1968. According to *Variety*, it went on to become the 10th highest-grossing film of the decade.

Streisand starred in the 1975 sequel, *Funny Lady*, in which Fanny marries producer Billy Rose (James Caan) but is still unable to find enduring happiness. **John Kander** and **Fred Ebb** provided most of the songs, including the appealing 'How Lucky Can You Get?', 'Isn't It Better?', 'Blind Date', 'Let's Hear It For Me' and 'So Long, Honey Lamb', and there were also several oldies such as 'More Than You Know' (Billy Rose–Edward Eliscu–**Vincent Youmans**), 'I Found A Million-Dollar Baby (In A Five-And-Ten-Cent Store)' (Rose–**Mort Dixon**–**Harry Warren**), and 'Great Day' (Rose-Eliscu-Youmans). Roddy McDowall, **Ben Vereen** and Carole Wells were also in the cast, along with Omar Sharif, who made a brief appearance as Fanny's ex-husband who passes briefly through her life again. The screenplay was by Jay Presson Allen and Arnold Shulman, and Herbert Ross was present again, this time as choreographer-director.

Funny Girl (stage musical)

The story goes that agent and producer Ray Stark had the idea that the life of his mother-in-law, the legendary *Ziegfeld Follies* comedienne, actress and singer **Fanny Brice**, would be a great subject for a film. That was before she died in 1951. Several screenplays and prospective leading ladies (including **Mary Martin**, Anne Bancroft, **Eydie Gorme** and **Carol Burnett**) later, *Funny Girl* opened on Broadway at the Winter Garden Theatre on 26 March 1964. Isobel Lennart adapted her draft screenplay for the stage, while regular trips by composer **Jule Styne** to a Greenwich Village club called the Bon Soir resolved the leading lady problem and gave Broadway an outstanding new star—**Barbra Streisand**. She had attracted some interest in *I Can Get It For You Wholesale* two years before, but this time she was carrying a major musical on those 22-year-old shoulders. Lennart's book has Fanny sitting in her Follies dressing room, looking back over the years to when, as an awkward, plain-looking teenager, she gets a job at Keeney's Music Hall with the aid of dance director Eddie Ryan (Danny Meehan) and gambler Nick

Arnstein (**Sydney Chaplin**). That pleases her mom, Mrs. Brice (Kay Medford), and mom's three-cent poker-playing cronies, who include Mrs. Strakosh (Jean Stapleton), back in 'Henry Street' on New York's East Side. They are even more delighted when Fanny joins the famous *Ziegfeld Follies*. Once there, she constantly tries the patience of the Big Boss, **Florenz Ziegfeld (Reginald DeKoven)**, especially when she leaves to marry and have a baby with the suave and totally gorgeous Arnstein. However, due to Nick's cash flow problem (he speculates on the wrong oil well) she is soon forced to return to the theatre, and then Arnstein's financial antics eventually land him in jail. Back to the present, and as Fanny sits and reflects, Nick, having served his sentence, returns to see her again. This time though, Fanny has had enough. She stands firm, and they part, presumably for ever. The perfect opportunity for a reprise of the Act I finalé number, 'Don't Rain On My Parade'. Jule Styne and **Bob Merrill**'s score was full of funny, disarming and often poignant songs, including Nick's seduction piece, 'You Are Woman' (Fanny: 'Well, a bit of dinner never hurt / But guess who is gonna be dessert'), the 'Henry Street' mob's soft-shoe shuffle to 'Who Taught Her Everything?' ('She sings like a bird, yes indeed / But who used to stand there and feed her the seed'), Fanny's paean to domesticity, 'Sadie, Sadie' ('The honeymoon was such delight / That we got married that same night'), her aching request for Nick to stay, 'Who Are You Now?' ('Are you someone better for my love?') as well as 'If A Girl Isn't Pretty', 'I'm The Greatest Star', 'Cornet Man', 'His Love Makes Me Beautiful', 'I Want To Be Seen With You Tonight', 'Henry Street', 'Find Yourself A Man', 'Rat-Tat-Tat-Tat' and 'The Music That Makes Me Dance'. Streisand's recording of the immensely compelling 'People' reached the US Top 10 and won a Grammy for best vocal performance. Another Grammy went to the Original Cast album, consolation perhaps for the show's inability to convert even one of its eight **Tony Awards** nominations. *Funny Girl* was choreographed by **Carol Haney**, and three directors, **Bob Fosse**, Garson Kanin and **Jerome Robbins**, were used on the trip to Broadway, with the last two getting programme credit. Costumes were by Irene Sharaff, and **Ralph Burns** was responsible for the terrific orchestrations, including an overture which is a mini-show in itself. The New York production ran for a satisfying 1,348 performances, and when Streisand left for London, she was succeeded by Mimi Hines. Streisand's triumph at London's Prince of Wales Theatre in 1966, with Michael Craig (Arnstein), Kay Medford (Mrs. Brice), Lee Allen (Eddie), Stella Moray (Mrs. Strakosh) and Ronald Leigh-Hunt (Ziegfeld), was confined to 112 performances after the star informed the producers that she was pregnant. Since then, regional stagings have proliferated, especially in the USA, and it appeared that Broadway audiences would finally see a major revival before a 1996 production starring **Debbie Gibson** closed on the road. The 1968 film version starred Streisand and Omar Sharif as Arnstein.

Funny Lady
(see *Funny Girl*)

Funny Thing Happened On The Way To The Forum, A

Stephen Sondheim's third Broadway show and the first for which he wrote the music as well as the lyrics. It opened at the Alvin Theatre in New York on 8 May 1962 and was still there over two years later. The book, by **Burt Shevelove** and **Larry Gelbart**, was freely adapted from all 21 of the comedies by the Roman playwright Plautus. Set 'in a street in Rome, on a day in spring, two hundred years before the Christian era', the show has been described variously as 'a funny vaudeville farce . . . a bawdy farcical musical . . . an old-fashioned musical burlesque' and 'a riot of risqué patter'. The Prologus (the slave Pseudolus, played by **Zero Mostel**) addresses the audience and welcomes them with 'Comedy Tonight' ('Something appealing / Something appalling / Something for everyone / A comedy tonight!'). There follows a joyous, fast-moving romp, involving an old man, Senex (David Burns) and his wife Domina (Ruth Kobart), their son Hero (Brian Davies), their slave Hysterium (**Jack Gilford**), another old man, Erronius (Raymond Walburn), a buyer and seller of courtesans, Marcus Lycus (John Carradine), a warrior, Miles Gloriosus (Ronald Holgate) and a virgin, Philia (Preshy Marker). Mostel, in his role as Pseudolus, slave to Hero, updates the audience regularly when he is not trying to help the other characters out of various embarrassing situations. Sondheim punctuated the action with songs such as 'Everybody Ought To Have A Maid', 'Bring Me My Bride', 'That'll Show Him', 'Love I Hear', 'Lovely', 'Free', 'I'm Calm', 'Pretty Little Picture' and 'Impossible'.

The show ran for 964 performances and scooped the **Tony Awards**, winning for best musical, book, actor (Mostel), supporting actor (David Burns), director (**George Abbott**) and producer (**Harold Prince**). The 1963 London production, which stayed at the Strand Theatre for 762 performances, starred Frankie Howerd as Pseudolus and a band of renowned British low-farce comedians, including Kenneth Connor, 'Monsewer' Eddie Gray, Robertson Hare and Jon Pertwee. Howerd reprised his role in the 1986 West End revival that was directed by Larry Gelbart. His co-librettist Burt Shevelove staged the show when Broadway audiences saw it for the second time in 1972. **Phil Silvers**, who had been the original choice for Pseudolus in 1962, appeared in the revival until he had a stroke and it was forced to close. The production won Tony Awards for Silvers and supporting actor Larry Blyden. When he recovered, Silvers took the show to the UK provinces at a time when his popularity rating was high due to reruns of the *Sergeant Bilko* television show. In 1991, in an effort to reduce costs but still revive some favourite Broadway musicals, a scaled-down production of *A Funny Thing Happened On The Way To The Forum* was presented at the Church of the Heavenly Rest by the New York Theatre Company. Five years later *Forum* was back on Broadway for a run of 715 performances. 'One of the great actors of the American theatre', Nathan Lane, headed a cast that also included Mark Linn-Baker (Hysterium), Ernie Sabella (Marcus Lycus), Lewis J. Stadlen (Senex), Jessica Boevers (Philia), Mary Testa (Domina), Cris Groenendaal (Miles Gloriosus) and Jim Stanex (Hero). Lane, won a Tony Award for his outstanding performance and was succeeded—somewhat controversially—by popular film actress Whoopi Goldberg. Among the cast of the 1999 production at the Open Air Theatre, Regent's Park, in London, were Roy Hudd (Prologus/Pseudolus), Michael Tudor Barnes (Senex), Rhashan Stone (Hero), Gavin Muir (Hysterium), Peter Forbes (Lycus), Claire Carrie (Philia) and Susie Blake (Domina).

The 1966 film version starred Zero Mostel, Phil Silvers, **Jack Gilford** and Buster Keaton.

Fuqua, Harvey

b. 27 July 1929, Louisville, Kentucky, USA. Alternate lead and founder of the famed vocal group the **Moonglows**, Fuqua began moving towards A&R and production work in 1959 while still singing with the group. In 1960 he disbanded the Moonglows and moved to Detroit, to work with Gwen Gordy, **Berry Gordy**'s sister, at her Anna label. The following year, he and Gwen Gordy, soon to be husband and wife, formed the Harvey and Tri-Phi, labels. They had only moderate success with the labels but managed to sign some top talents, including the **Detroit Spinners**, **Shorty Long**, **Johnny Bristol**, and **Junior Walker And The All Stars**. In 1963 Fuqua closed down the labels and joined Berry Gordy's growing **Motown Records** operation as writer, producer and promotion man, bringing with him several of the Harvey and Tri-Phi acts to the company.

Fuqua was responsible for Motown's Artist Development section, which groomed Motown acts in their stage performances and public behaviour. In 1970 Fuqua left Motown and formed his own production company. He drew talent from both Louisville and Detroit to form a staple of artists—the Niteliters, New Birth and Love, Peace & Happiness. The Niteliters were a funk instrumental group, New Birth was the Niteliters with a vocal ensemble and Love, Peace & Happiness a vocal spin-off from New Birth. In 1971 he placed these artists with **RCA Records** and enjoyed hits with all three. New Birth, which lasted the longest, remained on the charts to 1979. In the late 70s Fuqua established a production company in San Francisco and produced disco hits for **Sylvester** for **Fantasy Records**. In the early 80s he produced most of **Marvin Gaye**'s **Columbia Records** material
● FILMS: *Go Johnny Go* (1958).

Furay, Richie

b. 9 May 1944, Yellow Springs, Ohio, USA. Originally a member of the **Au Go-Go Singers**, Furay first came to prominence as the crystal clear vocalist acting as a foil between the voices of **Stephen Stills**' soulful blues and **Neil Young**'s Canadian folk rock in the seminal **Buffalo Springfield** during 1967. The short-lived Springfield fragmented, and out of the ashes came **Poco**, one of the leaders of the country rock movement. Much of Furay's best work appeared during his time as leader of Poco, with notably impressive contributions to *A Good Feelin' To Know* and *Crazy Eyes*. His subsequent departure was mainly out of frustration of seeing Poco unable to break out of the second division, while bands like the **Eagles** reaped massive fame and fortune by mining the same seam.

A lucrative recording contract with **David Geffen** saw the formation of the **Souther Hillman Furay Band** in 1974. Touted as a country rock super group, they were unable to live up to expectations, and after two average albums they resumed their respective solo careers with varying degrees of success. Furay's solo debut, 1976's *I've Got A Reason*, was a credible but laid-back album. Billed as the Richie Furay Band, the record was an autobiographical journey with 'Look At The Sun' and the title track as the strongest songs. A new line-up supported him on 1978's *Dance A Little Light*, a lesser album marred by lethargy. *I Still Have Dreams*, however, was a marked improvement, benefitting from the seasoned talents of musicians such as Dan Dugmore, Leland Sklar, Craig Doerge and the steady drumming of Russell Kunkel. Further vocal enhancements were added by **J.D. Souther**, Timothy B.

Schmit, **Randy Meisner** and Craig Fuller. Ironically, the two stand-out songs were written by band member Billy Batstone, who contributed the title track and the tear-jerking ballad 'I Was A Fool'.

Furay then began to devote his life to the church. The content of 1982's *Seasons Of Change* clearly showed this direction. He retired from music many years, appearing on a latter-day Poco album and adding the occasional vocal backing to other albums. In 1989, now a full-time pastor in Colorado, he joined with his original Poco colleagues for the excellent reunion album *Legacy*. Furay's shining voice was once again leading the only band with whom he has ever sounded in total control. After leaving Poco for a second time Furay returned to the church, although he did record another religious album, *In My Father's House*, in 1997.
● ALBUMS: *I've Got A Reason* (Asylum 1976) ★★★★, *Dance A Little Light* (Asylum 1978) ★★, *I Still Have Dreams* (Asylum 1979) ★★★, *Seasons Of Change* (Myrrh 1982) ★★, *In My Father's House* (Calvary Chapel 1997) ★★.

Furber, Douglas

b. 13 May 1885, London, England, d. 20 February 1961, London, England. After appearing successfully in shows in London, in 1924 Furber appeared on Broadway in **André Charlot**'s *Revue Of 1924*. The following year he was again involved with a Charlot revue, writing several of the sketches and also lyrics for two songs, 'The Fox Has Left Its Lair' and 'Follow Master Cook'. In 1937 **Me And My Girl**, for which Furber wrote the book in collaboration with L. Arthur Rose, opened at London's Victoria Palace. Starring **Lupino Lane**, the show ran for 1,646 performances. The songs for the show, music by **Noel Gay** with lyrics by Furber and Rose, included the endearingly melodic 'Me And My Girl' as well as 'Thinking Of No One But Me', 'I Would If I Could' and 'Take It On The Chin'. Although the title song remained popular for decades, it was another song that entered the national consciousness and became a veritable anthem for Londoners in general and Cockneys in particular 'The Lambeth Walk'. Apart from a three-week hiccup at the outbreak of war, the show ran on until June 1940 and then enjoyed revivals in 1941, 1946 and 1949. A film version, entitled *The Lambeth Walk* (1940), starred Lane, Sally Gray and **Seymour Hicks**.

A 1985 revival in London, with the original book revised by Stephen Fry and the score extended with other songs by Gay and starring Robert Lindsay and Emma Thompson, won Olivier Awards during its phenomenal eight-year run. In 1986 the show also opened at Broadway's Marquis Theatre where it ran for more than three years. The book was nominated for **Tony Award**s as Best Book Of A Musical and Best Original Score, and it won the Drama Desk Award for Outstanding Book.

Fureys

This musical family group from Ballyfermont, Dublin, Eire, originally featured George Furey (b. 11 June 1951, Dublin, Eire; vocals, guitar, accordion, mandola, autoharp, whistles), Finbar Furey (b. 28 September 1946, Dublin, Eire; vocals, uillean pipes, banjo, whistles, flute), Eddie Furey (b. 23 December 1944, Dublin, Eire; guitar, mandola, mandolin, harmonica, fiddle, bodhrán, vocals) and Paul Furey (b. 6 May 1948, Dublin, Eire; accordion, melodeon, concertina, whistles, bones, spoons, vocals). During the 60s Finbar and Eddie Furey had performed as a duo, playing clubs and doing radio work. Despite the offer of a recording contract, they turned it down and went to Scotland to play. Having established a reputation for themselves, they later signed to Transatlantic Records and joined the **Clancy Brothers** on the latter group's American tour in 1969. In 1972 the duo toured most of Europe, but while they were away, Paul and George had formed a group called the Buskers, with Davy Arthur (b. 24 September 1954, Edinburgh, Scotland; multi-instrumentalist/vocals). This group was involved in a road crash, bringing Finbar and Eddie back home, where they formed Tam Linn with Davey and Paul and played the **Cambridge Folk Festival**. George later joined the line-up, and they became the Fureys And Davey Arthur. The following year, 1981, the group, credited as the Fureys And Davy Arthur, reached the UK Top 20 with 'When You Were Sweet Sixteen'. By contrast, the album, having the same title, only just made the Top 100 in the UK during 1982. A follow-up single, 'I Will Love You (Every Time When We Are Gone)', failed to make the Top 50. *Golden Days*, released on K-Tel, made the UK Top 20 in 1984, selling in excess of 250,000 copies, while *At The End Of A Perfect Day*, also on K-Tel, made the UK Top 40 in 1985.

Numerous compilations abound, but *The Sound Of The Fureys And Davey Arthur*, on **PolyGram Records**, was released only in Ireland. *Golden Days* and *At The End Of A Perfect Day* were repackaged, in 1991, as *The Very Best Of The Fureys And Davy Arthur*. The group has successfully followed the middle-of-the-road folk musical path by producing melodic and popular music. Folk purists argue that this detracts from 'real' folk music, while their supporters say that the group has encouraged people to listen to folk music. Either way, their concerts are popular worldwide, and while not a hugely successful chart act domestically, their records still sell extremely well. Towards the end of 1993, Davy Arthur left the group and formed Davy Arthur And Co.

● ALBUMS: *When You Were Sweet Sixteen* (Castle Classics 1982) ★★★, *Steal Away* (Ritz 1983) ★★★, *In Concert* (Ritz 1984) ★★★, *Golden Days* (K-Tel 1984) ★★★★, *At The End Of A Perfect Day* (K-Tel 1985) ★★★, *The First Leaves Of Autumn* (Ritz 1986) ★★★, *The Scattering* (BMG/Ariola 1989) ★★★.

● COMPILATIONS: *The Sound Of The Fureys And Davey Arthur* (PolyGram Ireland 1981) ★★★, *The Fureys Finest* (Telstar 1987) ★★★★, *The Fureys Collection* (Castle Communications 1989) ★★★★, *The Very Best Of The Fureys And Davy Arthur* (Music Club 1991) ★★★★, *Winds Of Change* (Ritz 1992) ★★★, *The Essential Fureys* (Erin 2001) ★★★★.

Furlong, Michael

b. USA. Formerly the vocalist with Wild Dogs, hard rock singer-songwriter Michael Furlong recorded two well-received solo albums in the 80s. Both *Head On Rock 'n' Roll* and *Breakaway* were well-orchestrated, highly melodic examples of contemporary AOR, with many critics citing **Boston** as the closest musical comparison. This was partially due to the fact that, similarly, Furlong's work remains primarily a studio rather than a live concoction. Since 1987 he has moved away from solo work to employment as a session singer and songwriter.

● ALBUMS: *Head On Rock 'N' Roll* (Roadrunner 1984) ★★★, *Breakaway* (Music For Nations 1987) ★★★.

Furniture

Led by James Irvin (b. 20 July 1959, Chiswick, London, England; vocals), UK guitar band Furniture originally formed in 1981 with the intention of marrying the influences of 'the **Undertones** and **Chic**'. With their line-up completed by Tim Whelan (b. 15 September 1958, London, England; guitar) and Hamilton Lee (b. 7 September 1958, London, England; drums), they released their debut single, 'Shaking Story', on their own The Guy From Paraguay label. Afterwards they were joined by Sally Still (b. 5 February 1964, London, England; bass) and Maya Gilder (b. 25 April 1964, Poonak, India; keyboards) and recorded a debut mini-album for independent label Survival Records in September 1983. Reaction was almost nonexistent, and the group considered an early exit before **Stiff Records** heard one of the new songs they had written, 'Brilliant Mind', and signed them. Released as a single, this evocative, understated song reached number 21 in the UK charts in May 1986. Stiff, however, collapsed after the release of only one further single, 'Love Your Shoes' (itself a new version of a 1985 Premonition single). **ZTT Records** acquired the Stiff catalogue, and Furniture spent the next two years attempting to free themselves from their contract. They finally achieved this in 1989 via a new contract with **Arista Records**, but their chart stature had long since declined. Arista released an album, *Food Sex And Paranoia*, but sacked almost half of its A&R department (including the team that had signed Furniture) immediately afterwards. Underexposed and overlooked, the album that should have resurrected their career managed only 5,000 sales.

Irvin broke up the group after a farewell performance at the 1990 Reading Festival before recording his debut solo album (attributed to Because) in 1991. He became Reviews Editor at **Melody Maker** magazine, then Features Editor at **Mojo** magazine before going completely freelance. His former colleagues, Lee and Whelan, enjoyed notable success as members of **Transglobal Underground**. Gilder joined the BBC.

● ALBUMS: *When The Boom Was On* mini-album (Premonition 1983) ★★★, *The Wrong People* (Stiff 1986) ★★★, *Food Sex And Paranoia* (Arista 1990) ★★★.

Solo: Jim Irvin as Because *Mad, Scared, Dumb And Gorgeous* (Haven 1991) ★★★.

● COMPILATIONS: *The Lovemongers* (Survival 1986) ★★★, *She Gets Out The Scrapbook—The Best Of Furniture* (Survival 1991) ★★★.

Furtado, Nelly

b. 2 December 1978, Victoria, British Columbia, Canada. One of the most intriguing singer-songwriters to emerge in the new millennium, Furtado's music embraces enough styles to defy easy categorisation. This first generation Canadian was raised in British Columbia by her parents, who were originally from the Portuguese archipelago Azores. As a teenager she learned to play ukulele, trombone and guitar while embracing a range of musical genres, from urban R&B and hip-hop to rock, Latin and world music. Moving to Toronto in the late 90s to work, she performed at night as one-half of the hip-hop duo Nelstar and as a solo freestyler. She recorded a demo with two fans, Gerald Eaton and Brian West of fellow Canadians the **Philosopher Kings**, which eventually led to a major label contract with DreamWorks Records.

After making her live debut proper on select dates of the 1999 **Lilith Fair** tour, Furtado released her debut *Whoa, Nelly!* in October 2000. Rooted in contemporary urban sounds, Furtado's songwriting embraced folk, trip-hop, bossa nova, and reggae in a post-modern stew that was inevitably reminiscent of **Beck**'s work. The one downside was some rather clichéd teen-chick lyrics, with one of the worst culprits the poppy hit single 'I'm Like A Bird'. The album was a notable commercial success on both sides of the Atlantic and established Furtado as one of music's brightest new stars. The length of time she spent recording a follow-up album suggested that Furtado would not be bowing down to commercial demands, which was confirmed by the release of 2003's ambitious *Folklore*.

● ALBUMS: *Whoa, Nelly!* (DreamWorks 2000) ★★★, *Folklore* (DreamWorks 2003) ★★★.

Further Seems Forever

Originating from Pompano Beach, Florida, USA, most of this Christian-leaning emo band's members previously resided in other local bands, most notably the hardcore outfit Strongarm, Josh Colbert (guitar), Chad Neptune (bass), and Steve Kleisath (drums). To many, Further Seems Forever is best known for being one of the first bands of **Dashboard Confessional** leader Chris Carrabba. Although influenced early on by the usual suspects (**Fugazi** and **Jawbox**), Further Seems Forever draws from other less likely influences, including classic rockers such as **Pink Floyd**, **Led Zeppelin** and the **Beatles** among others. With Carrabba on vocals and second guitarist Nick Dominguez in the line-up, the band made their debut in 1999 on the fourth instalment of the Emo Diaries series, *An Ocean Of Doubt*, which was followed by a split EP alongside Recess Theory, *From The 27th State*. Further Seems Forever then signed a recording contract with the independent label Tooth & Nail and released their debut, *The Moon Is Down*. One of the more notable releases on the burgeoning emo scene, the album proved to be the final Further Seems Forever release to feature Carrabba who left the band to concentrate on Dashboard Confessional. Former **Affinity** vocalist Jason Gleason made his debut on a cover version of **Weezer**'s 'Say It Ain't So' for a tribute album, while new guitarist Derick Cordoba replaced Dominguez on 2003's *How To Start A Fire*.

● ALBUMS: *The Moon Is Down* (Tooth & Nail 2001) ★★★, *How To Start A Fire* (Tooth & Nail 2003) ★★★.

Fury, Billy

b. Ronald Wycherley, 17 April 1940, Dingle, Liverpool, England, d. 28 January 1983, London, England. An impromptu audition in a Birkenhead dressing room resulted in Wycherley joining **Larry Parnes**' management stable. The entrepreneur provided the suitably enigmatic stage name and added the aspirant to the bill of a current package tour. Fury enjoyed a UK Top 20 hit with his debut single 'Maybe Tomorrow' in 1959 and the following year completed **The Sound Of Fury**, which consisted entirely of the artist's own songs. Probably Britain's finest example of the rockabilly genre, it owed much of its authenticity to sterling support from guitarist **Joe Brown**, while the Four Jays provided backing vocals. However, Fury found his greatest success with a series of dramatic ballads that, in suggesting a vulnerability, enhanced the singer's undoubted sex appeal. His stylish good looks complemented a vocal prowess

blossoming in 1961 with a cover version of **Tony Orlando**'s 'Halfway To Paradise'. This superior single, arranged and scored by Ivor Raymonde, established a pattern that provided Fury with 16 further UK Top 30 hits, including 'Jealousy' (1961), 'I'd Never Find Another You' (1961), 'Last Night Was Made For Love' (1962), 'Once Upon A Dream' (1962), 'Like I've Never Been Gone' (1963), 'When Will You Say I Love You' (1963), 'In Summer' (1963), 'It's Only Make Believe' (1964) and 'In Thoughts Of You' (1965). Fury also completed two exploitative pop movies, *Play It Cool* (1962) and *I've Gotta Horse* (1965), and remained one of Britain's leading in-concert attractions throughout the early 60s. Supported initially by the **Tornados**, then the Gamblers, the singer showed a wider repertoire live than his label would allow on record.

Bedevilled by ill health and overtaken by changing musical fashions, Fury's final hit came in 1965 with 'Give Me Your Word'. The following year he left **Decca Records** for **Parlophone Records**, debuting with a **Peter And Gordon** song, 'Hurtin' Is Lovin'. Subsequent recordings included **David Bowie**'s 'Silly Boy Blue', the **Bee Gees**' 'One Minute Woman' (both 1968) and **Carole King**'s 'Why Are You Leaving' (1970), but the singer was unable to regain his erstwhile success. In 1971 he underwent open-heart surgery but recovered to record 'Will The Real Man Stand Up' on his own Fury label and played the part of Stormy Tempest in the film *That'll Be The Day* (1973). A second major operation in 1976 forced Fury to retire again, but he re-emerged at the end of the decade with new recordings of his best-known songs and several live and television appearances. In 1981 Fury struck a new contract with **Polydor Records**, but his health was rapidly deteriorating, and on 28 January 1983 he succumbed to a fatal heart attack. Unlike many of his pre-**Beatles** contemporaries, the artist's reputation has grown over the years, and Billy Fury is now rightly regarded as one of the finest rock 'n' roll singers Britain ever produced, even though the material he recorded often never matched the quality of his voice.

● ALBUMS: *The Sound Of Fury* 10-inch album (Decca 1960) ★★★★, *Billy Fury* (Ace Of Clubs 1960) ★★★, *Halfway To Paradise* (Ace Of Clubs 1961) ★★★, *Billy* (Decca 1963) ★★★, with the Tornados *We Want Billy!* (Decca 1963) ★★, *I've Gotta Horse* film soundtrack (Decca 1965) ★★, *The One And Only* (Polydor 1983) ★★★, *Last Concert* 1982 recording (Ozit 2002) ★★, *The Sound Of Fury Demos* (Earmark 2005) ★★★.

● COMPILATIONS: *Best Of Billy Fury* (Ace Of Clubs 1967) ★★★★, *The World Of Billy Fury* (Decca 1972) ★★★★, *The Billy Fury Story* (Decca 1977) ★★★, *The World Of Billy Fury, Volume 2* (Decca 1980) ★★★, *The Missing Years 1967–1980* (Red Bus 1983) ★★★, *The Billy Fury Hit Parade* (Rock Echoes 1983) ★★★, *The Other Side Of Fury* (See For Miles 1984) ★★★★, *Loving You* (Magnum Force 1984) ★★★, *Stick 'N' Stones* (Magnum Force 1985) ★★★, *The EP Collection* (See For Miles 1985) ★★★★, *The Collection* (Castle 1987) ★★★, *The Best Of Billy Fury* (K-Tel 1988) ★★★, *The Sound Of Fury + 10* (Decca 1988) ★★★, *Am I Blue?* (Decca 1993) ★★★, *The 40th Anniversary Anthology* (Deram 1998) ★★★★, *Wondrous Place: The Billy Fury Collection* (K-Tel 1999) ★★★, *Love Songs* (Decca 2002) ★★★, *Rarities And Teenage Jottings* (Ozit 2004) ★★, *The Rocker* (Decca 2005) ★★★.

● FILMS: *Play It Cool* (1962), *I've Gotta Horse* aka *Wonderful Day* (1965), *That'll Be The Day* (1973).

Fuse

Signed to Epic Records in the early 70s, Fuse was the early home to later **Cheap Trick** members Rick Nielsen (b. 22 December 1946, Rockford, Illinois, USA; vocals/guitar), Tom Petersson (b. Tom Peterson, 9 May 1950, Rockford, Illinois, USA; bass/vocals) and Bun E. Carlos (b. Brad Carlson, 12 June 1951, Rockford, Illinois, USA; drums). Together with Joe Sunderberg (vocals), Craig Myers (guitar) and drummer Chip Greenman, whom Carlos would later replace, they made their debut as Fuse with a self-titled collection in 1972. Less irreverent and amusing than the style with which Cheap Trick would become identified, it failed to chart but remains an interesting footnote in the development of one of America's most enduring rock bands.
● ALBUMS: *Fuse* (Epic 1972) ★★★.

Future Bible Heroes

To have been the driving force behind four bands or collectives is quite a mean feat, considering they have all received critical acclaim. This is the achievement of US musician **Stephin Merritt**, the creative mastermind behind the **Magnetic Fields**, the **6ths**, the Gothic Archies and the Future Bible Heroes. Merritt seems to be a fascination, indeed an obsession to music journalists because of his delight in giving multilayered answers to even the simplest of questions. With this and the fact that he has produced some of the most inventive and intelligent music of the 90s and new millennium, it just adds fuel to his abstract fire. This playful intelligence was to the fore on Future Bible Heroes' 1997 debut, *Memories Of Love*, which featured a cryptic lyric sheet that required the purchaser to solve a number of puzzles to decipher the words. The album's sublime fusion of acoustic instruments and electronics was co-credited to Christopher Ewen, Merritt's writing partner and an innovative arranger who pushes the boundaries of electronic pop to their limits. Merritt shared vocal duties with Claudia Gonson, a singer with an off-the-cuff delivery reminiscent of early **Kirsty MacColl**.
Merritt, Ewen and Gonson reunited in 2002 to record a new Future Bible Heroes album, *Eternal Youth*. This angst-ridden, funny and thought provoking album managed to eclipse its illustrious predecessor, offering up a dizzying array of musical and lyrical ideas.
● ALBUMS: *Memories Of Love* (Slow River/Circus 1997) ★★★, *Eternal Youth* (Instinct/Circus 2002) ★★★★.

Future Kings Of Spain

Formed in Dublin, Eire, the indie rock band Future Kings Of Spain comprises Joey Wilson (vocals/guitar), Anton Hegarty (bass) and Bryan McMahon (drums). The trio holed themselves away for most of 2000, with the sole purpose of improving their playing and songs. Their first gig occurred later that year, when they opened for J. Mascis (ex–**Dinosaur Jr**), at Dublin's Temple Bar Music Centre during December. Things happened quickly for the band soon after, as members of another Dublin-based rock band Ten Speed Racer brought the Kings to the attention of their label, London's Red Flag Records. After an ongoing period of recording demos and a contract being finalized, the Future Kings Of Spain finally signed with Red Flag. Further gigs ensued (including a week of inaugural US dates in Los Angeles), before they released their hard rocking debut single, 'A Place For Everything And Everything In Its Place',

in late 2002. The Future Kings Of Spain briefly relocated to New York to record their self-titled debut album with renowned indie producer Ted Niceley overseeing the sessions. Before the album was released, two singles were issued in early 2003, 'Face I Know' and 'Your Starlight', that were supported by European dates opening for **Idlewild**, **Biffy Clyro** and **Cosmic Rough Riders** as well as several headlining shows on their own. In August 2003 the highly anticipated, *Future Kings Of Spain* was released.
● ALBUMS: *Future Kings Of Spain* (Red Flag 2003) ★★★.

Future Pilot AKA

Future Pilot AKA is a project spearheaded by Sushil K. Dade (b 15 July 1966, Scotland). Dade's background lies in late 80s/early 90s indie pop, playing bass for the **Soup Dragons** and **BMX Bandits**. His own recording career is far removed from his previous work, however, ranging from improvisational electronica to folk and spirituals. As well as his bass contributions, Dade can boast collaborations with **Two Lone Swordsmen**, **Kim Fowley** and Brix Smith, the fruits of which were issued on EP prior to a collective release in 1999 on Sulfur Records. A collection of mostly instrumental cuts, *Vs A Galaxy Of Sound* explored innovative textures, melodies and rhythms, sustaining a high quality over two CDs. By the time of this release, Dade was working on a first album proper, his obsession with water reflected in the title. *Tiny Waves, Mighty Sea* blended traditional Indian chants and spirituals with a pop-based, guitar-led sound. Dade featured in a number of guises, playing guitars and bass, producing, singing and even providing the album's photography. The lengthy meditation 'Om Namah Shivaya' that appeared towards the close was played during the birth of his first child and featured Stuart Murdoch on vocals. Other guests on the album included members of a number of Scottish bands, including **Teenage Fanclub**, **Belle And Sebastian**, the **Delgados** and the **Pastels**, making for a highly intriguing and listenable 40 minutes.
● ALBUMS: *Vs A Galaxy Of Sound* (Sulfur 1999) ★★★★, *Tiny Waves, Mighty Sea* (Geographic 2001) ★★★, *Salute Your Soul* (Geographic 2004) ★★★.

Future Sound Of London

Offered to **dance music** punters as the 'intelligent way out of blind-alley hardcore', Future Sound Of London emerged in the 90s, the brainchild of Garry Cobain (b. Bedford, England) and Brian Dougans (b. Glasgow, Scotland). They met at college in Manchester in 1985, but Cobain soon left in order to set up his own studio under an Enterprise Allowance scheme. Both went on to earn their spurs in the Manchester **house** scene, Dougans completing 1988's groundbreaking Top 20 hit (as Humanoid) with 'Stakker Humanoid', after it had been adopted by the BBC as the theme tune to a 'youth' television programme. Their other projects together spawned Semi Real ('People Livin' Today'), Yage, Metropolis (the industrial *Metropolis* EP), Art Science Technology, Mental Cube (the ambient 'So This Is Love'), Candese, Intelligent Communication and Smart Systems. However, as Future Sound Of London they enjoyed a major crossover success with 'Papua New Guinea', an enticing, beautifully orchestrated piece. Both 'Papua New Guinea' and 'Metropolis' can be found on *Accelerator*, a seamless collection of rhythmic tracks.

Under the name Amorphous Androgynous the pair recorded *Tales Of Ephidrina*, which used imaginative samples from sources as diverse as **Peter Gabriel**'s soundtrack to *The Last Temptation Of Christ* and the alien's voice from *Predator*. Back under the FSOL banner, the duo released the excellent 'Cascade' in October 1993, a 30-minute workout taken from their second album, *Lifeforms*, which combined break beats with rumbling bass and heavy atmospherics. Unfortunately, the album was, at times, disappointing. On several of the pieces, they had the potential to allow an interesting groove to develop into a full-blown track, as with the 'Cascade' single. However, they were all too willing to allow the vibe to deconstruct to basic, although well-produced, chill-out fodder. Having already expressed their desire to break into other media, throughout 1994 the Future Sound Of London experimented with live broadcasts from their own north London studio, via ISDN telephone links to various national and international radio stations, inviting listeners to view accompanying video graphics on their home computers. They released a collection of these tracks on an (originally limited release) album, simply titled *ISDN*. Taken from various live radio broadcasts and electronic café sessions, *ISDN* proved to be an engaging and involving departure from their previous full-length work. In 1996 they released *Dead Cities*, which offered fresh sounds, ranging from the furiously harsh 'Herd Killing', to the pure choral piece, 'Everyone In The World Is Doing Something Without Me'. The duo was forced to take a lengthy hiatus during the late 90s due to Cobain's ill health before resuming recording sessions in the new millennium. Their first release was an album featuring new versions of 'Papua New Guinea'. A new album under the Amorphous Androgynous moniker was released in 2002.

● ALBUMS: *Accelerator* (Jumpin' & Pumpin' 1992) ★★★★, as Amorphous Androgynous *Tales Of Ephidrina* (Virgin/Astralwerks 1993) ★★★★, *Lifeforms* (Virgin/Astralwerks 1994) ★★★, *ISDN* (Virgin/Astralwerks 1994) ★★★, *Dead Cities* (Virgin/Astralwerks 1996) ★★★, *Papua New Guinea Translations* (Jumpin' & Pumpin' 2001) ★★★, as Amorphous Androgynous *The Isness* (FSOL/Hypnotic 2002) ★★★★, as Amorphous Androgynous *The Mellow Hippo Disco Show* (Random 2003) ★★★, as Amorphous Androgynous *The Isness & The Otherness* (FSOL/Hypnotic 2003) ★★★★.

Futureheads

Formed in 2000, this UK indie rock quartet can trace its origins to a government-funded youth project in their native Sunderlan,. Guitarist Barry Hyde was employed at the project as a tutor and through his work met up with fellow guitarist Ross Millard (b. Sunderland, Tyne & Wear, England) and drummer Pete Brewis. The trio formed the Futureheads with bass player David 'Jaff' Craig, taking their name from a **Flaming Lips** album. After performing a number of local gigs and recording a limited edition demo tape, Barry's younger brother Dave Hyde was brought in to the line-up to replace the otherwise occupied Brewis. The new look quartet continued to rehearse at all hours and play whenever possible before setting off on a character-defining European tour. On their return they completed a self-released 7-inch single before recording two EPs for Fantastic Plastic. The material on these releases, *1,2,3—Nul* and *First Day*, demonstrated the quartet's sound working knowledge of

the back catalogue of UK post-punk pioneers such as **XTC** and **Gang Of Four**, but it was their frenetic live shows that caught the attention of the record labels. A recording contract with the **Sire Records** imprint 679 Recordings followed. Ex–Gang Of Four member Andy Gill produced a number of the tracks on the Futureheads' self-titled debut album, which was released to generally positive reviews in summer 2004. A witty cover of the **Kate Bush** track 'Hounds Of Love' reached the UK Top 10 the following February.

● ALBUMS: *The Futureheads* (679 2004) ★★★.

Fuzzbox

(see **We've Got A Fuzzbox And We're Gonna Use It**)

Fuzztones

Obsessed with the psychedelic punk sound of the late 60s, the Fuzztones emerged from New York in the mid-80s. The group consisted of Rudi Protrudi (vocals/guitar, ex–Tina Peel and Devil Dogs), Deb O'Nair (organ, also ex–Tina Peel), Elan Portnoy (guitar), Michael Jay (bass) and Michael Phillips (drums, ex-Polyrock). They had formed during 1980 after the breakup of Tina Peel (who released the *Extra Kicks* cassette in 1980) and spent their formative years gigging around the east coast of the USA. The Fuzztones' first UK release was a live album, *Leave Your Mind At Home*, on the Midnight Music label in 1984, which combined brash garage guitar riffs with a definite nod to the **Cramps**. *Lysergic Emanations* on the independent ABC label was less forthright and delved further into acid rock, although the singles 'She's Wicked' (1985) and 'Bad News Travels Fast' (1986) were all-out slabs of loud, raunchy guitar rock. All was quiet in their wake as the Fuzztones returned to the States for a while. Protrudi put together the Jaymen to record low-quality instrumental music before resurfacing with an all-new Fuzztones in 1988 and releasing 'Nine Months Later' on Music Maniac. However, the label folded after *Creatures That Time Forgot* (featuring the original line-up) early in 1989, and the band transferred to Situation 2. 'Hurt On Hold' accompanied the band's second album of that year, *In Heat*. 'Action Speaks Louder Than Words' continued the staple diet of garage trash in 1990, but by then the Fuzztones' formula seemed to be wearing thin, and they have since kept a low profile.

● ALBUMS: *Leave Your Mind At Home—Live* (Midnight 1984) ★★, *Lysergic Emanations* (ABC 1984) ★★★, *Live In Europe* (Music Maniac 1987) ★★, *Creatures That Time Forgot* (Music Maniac 1989) ★★★, *In Heat* (Beggars Banquet/RCA 1989) ★.
Solo: Link Protrudi And The Jaymen *Drive It Home* (Music Maniac 1987) ★★, *Missing Links* mini-album (Skyclad 1989) ★★.

Fuzzy

Indie pop quartet from Boston, USA, formed by Hilken Mancini (vocals), Chris Tappin (vocals/guitar), Winston Braman (bass) and David Ryan (also **Lemonheads**; drums). The band was formed by Mancini and Tappin when they worked in a record shop; the two discovered that they had similar tastes in music and shared a lack of success with bands and boyfriends. Braman introduced himself to Mancini at a party, and the trio set about booking themselves into the Lemonheads' rehearsal studios, whereupon Ryan decided he would like to join the band. However, he disappeared before their first show, which was performed with a stand-in drummer known as Tom The Monk. Despite a catastrophic performance, **Soul Asylum**'s Dave Pirner was impressed by their potential and encouraged the band, and Ryan returned after finishing touring commitments with the Lemonheads. The well-regarded single, 'Flashlight' spearheaded Fuzzy's self-titled 1994 debut, though touring was complicated by Ryan's sporadic availability. The major label follow-up *Electric Juices* proved to be an excellent album, combining an imaginative choice of material including **Brian Wilson**'s neglected gem of innocence 'Girl Don't Tell Me', given the irresistible Fuzzy treatment. Other strong tracks included 'Throw Me A Bone' and 'Miss The Mark'. The band lost their major label contract shortly afterwards. Their third album was recorded without the absent Ryan and was released by the independent Catapult label in 1999.

● ALBUMS: *Fuzzy* (Seed 1994) ★★★, *Electric Juices* (Tag/ Atlantic 1996) ★★★★, *Hurray For Everything* (Catapult 1999) ★★★.

Fuzzy Duck

Their name taken from the popular linguistic inversion of the time (Fuzzy Duck—Duzz 'E Fuck?), this early 70s UK progressive rock quartet featured Paul Francis (drums), Mick Hawksworth (bass), Roy Sharland (organ) and Garth Watt-Roy (guitar/vocals). Prior to the group's formation Hawksworth had played with **Andromeda** and Five Day Week Straw People, while Sharland had been a member of Spice and worked with **Arthur Brown**. Watt-Roy had been a member of **Greatest Show On Earth**. Fuzzy Duck recorded one self-titled album for Mam Records and two singles, 'Double Time Woman' and 'Big Brass Band', for the same label. The album, which was musically if not lyrically impressive, was issued in a limited pressing of 500 copies, the cover depicting a duck wearing an 'Afro hairstyle'. A popular item among collectors of progressive rock, it was eventually rereleased in 1993 on Repertoire Records.

● ALBUMS: *Fuzzy Duck* (Mam 1971) ★★★.

G

G.B.H.

Formerly known as Charged G.B.H. (truncating the name by the release of 1986's *Oh No It's G.B.H. Again! EP*), the band formed just as the initial impetus of the punk movement was petering out in 1980, counting the **Exploited** and **Discharge** among their peers. Comprising Cal (b. Colin Abrahall; vocals), Jock Blyth (guitar), Ross (bass) and Wilf (drums), they adopted a violent and aggressive image (G.B.H., of course, standing for 'grievous bodily harm'), sporting multi-coloured mohican haircuts and *de rigeur* studded and chained leathers. Musically, they combined influences such as the **Ramones** and **Venom** into a hard-core metallic barrage of testosterone-led frustration. With 'smash-the-system' sloganeering in place of lyrics, they were an uncompromising and extreme musical outfit during the early 80s, and exerted some influence on the thrash and hardcore movements that followed. While musically they could be exciting, any enjoyment was downgraded by the poverty of intellect behind the lyrics (notable examples being the anti-feminist tract 'Womb With A View', from *City Baby's Revenge*, or 'Limpwristed', from *Midnight Madness And Beyond*). Furthermore, their success was always limited by an inability to progress musically. Kai replaced Wilf on drums in 1989, as the band veered away from regimented hardcore towards speed metal. This trend continued with the arrival of new bass player Anthony Morgan. Even the mohicans had disappeared on their tour to promote *From Here To Reality*, which the **New Musical Express** kindly reviewed as having 'no redeeming features whatsoever'.

● ALBUMS: *Leather, Bristles, Studs And Acne* mini-album (Clay 1981) ★★, *City Baby Attacked By Rats* (Clay 1982) ★★★, *Live At City Garden* (Clay 1982) ★★, *City Baby's Revenge* (Clay 1983) ★★★, *Midnight Madness And Beyond* (Rough Justice 1986) ★★★, *No Need To Panic!* (Rough Justice 1987) ★★, *A Fridge Too Far* (Rough Justice 1989) ★★, *From Here To Reality* (Music For Nations 1990) ★★, *Church Of The Truly Warped* (Rough Justice 1993) ★★, *Punk Junkies* (We Bite 1996) ★★.

● COMPILATIONS: *Leather, Bristles, No Survivors And Sick Boys* (Clay 1982) ★★★, *The Clay Years 81-84* (Clay 1986) ★★★, *Diplomatic Immunity* (Clay 1990) ★★, *The Punk Singles 1981-84* (Castle 2001) ★★★, *Dead On Arrival—Anthology* (Castle 2004) ★★★.

● DVD/VIDEOS: *Live At The Ace Brixton* (Jettisoundz 1983), *A Video Too Far* (Video For Nations 1989), *Kawasaki Live* (Visionary 1993).

G-Clefs

This US doo-wop-styled vocal group comprised brothers Teddy, Chris, Timmy and Arnold Scott and friend Ray Gibson, all from Roxbury, Massachusetts, USA. The quintet, who began singing gospel, were spotted by Pilgrim Records' Jack Gould and in 1956 their first release, 'Ka-Ding-Dong' (on which **Freddy Cannon** is reputed to have played guitar), reached the R&B Juke Box Top 10 and the US Top 40 pop chart. It probably would have been a bigger hit but for cover versions by two name acts, the **Diamonds** and **Hilltoppers**. Following another release on Pilgrim and two on Paris they decided to put their singing careers on ice and finish their schooling. After the youngest member Arnold left school in 1960 they re-formed and, with help from Gould, joined Terrace Records. Their first release, a version of the **Four Tunes**' song 'I Understand' cleverly combined with the chorus of 'Auld Lang Syne', gave them their only US Top 10 entry and five months later (around New Year) their sole UK Top 20 hit. The follow-up 'A Girl Has To Know' charted, but later releases including ones on Loma, Regina and Veep brought them no further success. **Freddie And The Dreamers** had a UK Top 5 hit with a version of their arrangement of 'I Understand' in 1964.

G. Dep

b. Travell Coleman, Harlem, New York City, USA. Closely affiliated to **Sean 'Puffy' Combs** aka P. Diddy and his Bad Boy Entertainment label, G. Dep aka the Deputy rose to prominence in the new millennium alongside another Combs protégé, **Black Rob**. Signed to Bad Boy in the late 90s, Dep honed his rapping style by appearing on several of the label's releases, including Black Rob's 1999 debut and P Diddy's *The Saga Continues . . .* (most notably the hit 'Let's Get It'). Dep released his solo debut, *Child Of The Ghetto*, in November 2001. Backed by the usual Bad Boy production crew, the album failed to raise his profile above that of reliable sideman despite reworking three tracks from *The Saga Continues . . . .* The stand-out track, 'I Am', benefited greatly from the contribution of veterans **Rakim** and **Kool G Rap**.

● ALBUMS: *Child Of The Ghetto* (Bad Boy 2001) ★★.

G-Force

G-Force was the brainchild of ex–**Skid Row**, **Colosseum** II, and **Thin Lizzy** guitarist **Gary Moore** (b. 4 April 1952, Belfast, Northern Ireland). After leaving Lizzy shortly after playing on the band's *Black Rose* in 1979, Moore headed for Los Angeles with the intention of forming a new group there. He teamed up with some reputable local musicians and, not wishing at that time to be known as the Gary Moore Band, they chose to travel under the moniker G-Force. Joining Moore in this project were Tony Newton (vocals), Willie Dee (ex-Pipedream; bass) and Mark Nauseef (drums). The band played some low-key gigs in and around the Los Angeles area and signed to Jet Records, for whom they released their debut album in 1980. A slice of melodic hard rock with definite commercial prospects, it nevertheless flopped. The band folded soon after its release, with Moore resuming his solo career.

● ALBUMS: *G-Force* (Jet 1980) ★★★.

G.G.F.H.

G.G.F.H. (an acronym for Global Genocide Forget Heaven) comprised two Californians, Brian J. Walls and Ghost. Highly media-literate and pessimistic, G.G.F.H.'s music paints a picture of pain, ignorance and perversity with a palette of harsh electronic music, robotic vocals and sampled dialogue. Their main obsession, however, is the way in which a paranoid establishment creates sensationalist panics to feed to the television-addicted populace. *Eclipse*, their first full album, concentrated on the media panic around Satanism, with audio samples from talk shows and cheap films as its backdrop. The second album, *Disease*, dropped the Satanic theme in favour of the more generic territory of serial murder, sexual violence and urban alienation. A lighter, more electronic, though no less disturbing, tone for *Disease* replaced the grinding hum of Eclipse. The grim *Halloween EP*, released in a limited edition in 1991, was re-released in an extended form as their third full album, comprising demo material recorded between 1986 and 1989.

● ALBUMS: *Eclipse* (Dreamtime 1991) ★★, *Disease* (Dreamtime 1993) ★★★, *Halloween* (Dreamtime 1994) ★★.

G.I. Blues

Art imitated life in this 1960 feature, **Elvis Presley**'s first film since completing military service. His manager, **Colonel Tom Parker** had skilfully manipulated the singer's career during his absence. What better way of announcing Presley's return than with a film romanticizing his period of induction? Elvis portrayed a guitar-playing gunner in the US Army, stationed in West Germany, who woos a cabaret dancer, played by Juliet Prowse, as a bet, before predictably falling in love with her. Considerable publicity was generated by a rumoured off-screen affair, all of which fuelled further interest in the film. *G.I. Blues* remains one of Presley's most popular and enduring features, although purists murmured disquiet when he sang 'Wooden Heart' to a puppet. That particular song—based on a German composition 'Muss I Den'—became a UK chart-topping single when culled from the film's soundtrack. The *G.I. Blues* album also reached number 1 in its respective UK chart and remained on the listing for over a year. The joint success of the film and music confirmed that indeed Elvis was back.

G Love And Special Sauce

Formed by Philadelphia native G Love (b. Garrett Dutton III, 3 October 1972, Philadelphia, Pennsylvania, USA), this trio consciously recalls the pre-pop blues world alongside scat lyrics from the jazz tradition and hip-hop beats. G Love met his partners, Jeffrey 'Houseman' Clemens (drums) and Jimmy 'Jazz' Prescott (bass) in Boston, Massachusetts, USA, in 1992, after failing to earn a decent living busking in his native city. The intent was simple but unusual, as Clemens recalls: 'G Love writes great songs and each of us brings the spirit of the blues to the music.' They met while Prescott was running a jam session at the Tam O Shanter bar, playing their debut performance there on 18 February 1993. Their debut album was the first to be released on Sony Music's newly reactivated **OKeh Records** label, and the first ever by a white act in the label's history. Though taking critics by surprise, it received almost universal praise for its uninhibited approach, using acoustic instruments to propel a unique, unreconstructed blues sound. For their second album the trio relocated to New Orleans from their Boston base, and their attempts to capture something of the 'soul' of the city resulted in another acclaimed release. The key lay in their approach, never so reverent that the city's musical ghosts haunted it, with Dutton choosing instead to write in raw, scratchy but undeniably attractive movements.

After falling out with Clemens and Prescott, Dutton began recording 1997's *Yeah, It's That Easy* with members of the All Fellas Band, Philly Cartel and King's Court. The three musicians reconciled during the recording process, however, and members of all the bands eventually showed up on the finished product. The trio format was restored for proper on 1999's *Philadelphonic*. The album was named after the term used by Dutton to encapsulate their eclectic sound, and featured hip-hop beats provided by producer T-Ray. Following one further release for OKeh/Sony, the trio signed a new recording contract with **Jack Johnson**'s Brushfire Records. They made their debut for the label in 2004 with *The Hustle*.

● ALBUMS: *G Love And Special Sauce* (OKeh 1994) ★★★★, *Coast To Coast Motel* (OKeh 1995) ★★★★, *Yeah, It's That Easy* (OKeh 1997) ★★★, *Philadelphonic* (OKeh 1999) ★★★★, *Electric Mile* (OKeh 2001) ★★★, *The Hustle* (Brushfire 2004) ★★★.

● COMPILATIONS: *The Best Of G Love And Special Sauce* (Sony 2002) ★★★★.

G.Q.

This quartet formed in New York City, USA and comprised Keith 'Sabu' Crier (who subsequently changed his name and enjoyed solo success as **Keith Sweat**, on bass/vocals), Emmanuel Rahiem LeBlanc (guitar/lead vocals), Paul Service (drums/vocals) and Herb Lane (keyboards/vocals). Crier and LeBlanc had previously worked as Sabu And The Survivors, Sons Of Darkness and Third Chance before linking up with Lane and drummer Kenny Banks as the Rhythm Makers and signing with Vigor (part of the De-Lite label). Their one album, *Soul On Your Side*, attracted considerable import interest in the UK, owing to the hypnotic 'Zone' in 1976. Following the departure of Banks, Paul Service was drafted in as replacement and the group became G.Q. (which stood for Good Quality) upon the suggestion of their manager, Tony Lopez. They played one of their tapes to producer Beau Ray Fleming, and he in turn invited Larkin Arnold, Senior Vice-President of **Arista Records**, to audition the group in a South Bronx basement. One cut in particular from their audition stood out; 'Disco Nights (Rock Freak)', which they were made to play several times. Two weeks later G.Q. were in the studio recording their debut album for the company. The single peaked at number 12 on the US Top 100 (and number 42 in the UK), earning a gold disc and propelling their debut album to gold status. Their second album spawned another hit single in 'Standing Ovation', after which Paul Service left, and the group continued as a trio for their final album for Arista. They recorded one final single, 'You Are The One For Me', for the independent Stadium label and then disbanded permanently following Crier's decision to pursue a solo career.

● ALBUMS: *Disco Nights* (Arista 1979) ★★★, *GQ Two* (Arista 1980) ★★★, *Face To Face* (Arista 1981) ★★.

● COMPILATIONS: *Disco Nights* (Camden 1999) ★★★.

G-Unit

Owing to the extraordinary success of his official solo debut, *Get Rich Or Die Tryin'*, it was only a matter of time before US rapper **50 Cent** (b. Curtis Jackson, 6 July 1975, Queens, New York City, USA) launched his own collective, G-Unit. While many new fans assumed it was a freshly assembled outfit, it turns out that G-Unit's history stretched back before 50 Cent's hit debut, with a line-up that included longtime friends **Tony Yayo** (b. Marvin Bernard, 31 March 1978, Queens, New York City, USA) and **Lloyd Banks** (b. Chris Lloyd, 30 April 1982, Queens, New York City, USA). Following his near-fatal shooting in mid-2000, 50 Cent sought to rebuild his career, and one of the first matters of business was setting up G-Unit. In the early years of the twenty-first century, the crew released a series of mixtapes featuring the DJs Whookid and Cutmaster C. After the blockbuster success of *Get Rich Or Die Tryin'* (which set a record in the USA for most copies sold of a single album in its first week of release), G-Unit was promptly signed to their own record contract as well. Yayo was sentenced to prison during December 2002 after being arrested for an outstanding warrant and was replaced by **Young Buck** (b. Memphis, Tennessee, USA) for the recording of G-Unit's debut release, 2003's *Beg For Mercy*. The album featured input by a variety of acclaimed producers, including **Dr. Dre**, **Eminem**, **Hi-Tek**, and 7th EMP. With the music world still in the grips of 50 Cent mania, the album quickly scaled the charts globally upon its November 2003 release. Shortly afterwards, Yayo was welcomed back into the G-Unit ranks, upon his release in January 2004, but returned to jail immediately after handing a forged passport to his parole officer. Free for a second time a few months later, he enjoyed commercial success in his own right the following year with the solo album *Thoughts Of A Predicate Felon*.

● ALBUMS: *Beg For Mercy* (Interscope 2003) ★★★.

G-Wiz, Gary

b. North Carolina, USA. A white hip-hop producer, who moved to Freeport, New York, at the age of six. Musically inclined parents, who owned a nightclub and booked acts like the **Coasters** and **Drifters**, were an early influence. Teaching himself first drums then computer programming, he sat in on the decks behind two rappers as part of New York rap group 516. In 1985 he met Chuck D of **Public Enemy** for the first time, and the two struck up a friendship, as G-Wiz was invited to work alongside Eric Sadler and Keith Schocklee as part of the **Bomb Squad**. When Schocklee formed his S.O.U.L. label, G-Wiz brought him their first act, **Young Black Teenagers**, whom he would go on to produce and manage. His own production credits had begun with Public Enemy's *Apocalypse '91: The Enemy Strikes Black*, and 'Can't Truss It'. He would subsequently work with **Run-DMC** ('Oooh Watcha Gonna Do', '3 In The Head'). Further work with Public Enemy followed on *Greatest Misses*, while Aaron Hall's 'Don't Be Afraid', for the *Juice* film soundtrack, gave him a hit record. His remix client base has branched out beyond the hip-hop frontier, including work for **Janet Jackson**, **Bel Biv Devoe**, **Peter Gabriel**, **Lisa Stansfield**, **Anthrax**, **Helmut** and **Sinéad O'Connor**.

G/Z/R

Ostensibly a solo vehicle for Geezer Butler (b. Terry Butler, 17 July 1949, Birmingham, England), this project allowed the bass player to 'blow off some steam' at events taking place with his parent band **Black Sabbath** during the mid-90s. The resulting album, *Plastic Planet*, included the scathing 'Giving Up The Ghost'. Lines such as 'You bastardised my intellect/ Castrated our conviction' left critics in no doubt as to what Butler thought of **Tony Iommi**'s handling of Black Sabbath affairs. The rest of the album made much less of an impact, with Butler's attempted accommodation of new metal styles frequently falling flat. He had first conceived the idea of a solo album in 1985 but 'couldn't find a singer'. It took him a full decade to realize his ambition with the addition of Burton C. Bell of **Fear Factory**, with Pedro Howse (guitar) and Deen Castronovo (drums) completing the line-up. A second album, *Black Science*, was released in 1997 under the Geezer moniker. New member Clark Brown handled vocals, while Howse and Castronovo were again in attendance. Butler's renewed commitment to Black Sabbath in the new millennium put his solo career on temporary hiatus, before he reunited with Brown, Howse and Castronovo in 2005 to record the new G/Z/R album, *Ohmwork*.

● ALBUMS: *Plastic Planet* (TVT 1995) ★★★, as Geezer *Black Science* (TVT 1997) ★★★, *Ohmwork* (Sanctuary 2005) ★★★.

G., Bobby

b. Robert Gubby, 23 August 1953, Epsom, Surrey, England. UK vocalist with 1981 Eurovision Song Contest winners **Bucks Fizz**. His solo debut, 'Big Deal', was specially recorded for the BBC as the theme tune to the acclaimed UK television drama series starring Ray Brooks. The single entered the charts on three occasions but never reached a high position. Following its release he continued working with his original hit-making band.

G., Gilly

b. Birmingham, West Midlands, England. The debut album of this harsh-voiced rapper from Birmingham, England, combined the geographically strong tradition of reggae with funk and soul samples. The most effective track on 1992's *Brothers Of The Jungle Zone* was 'Push It Along', which employed the widely imitated 'shuffling' drum pattern from **Massive Attack**'s 'Daydreaming'. Although lyrically astute, the rest of the album's tracks, especially 'State Of Self-Decline', were too obviously redolent of west coast gangsta rappers such as **Ice-T** and **Ice Cube**. In the light of poor sales MCA Records chose not to renew Gilly G.'s contract.

● ALBUMS: *Brothers Of The Jungle Zone* (MCA 1992) ★★.

G., Gina

Having moved to Melbourne, Australia, in 1987, this female vocalist began work as a DJ in that city's dance clubs. Eventually, she joined the influential **dance music** outfit, Bass Culture. Signed to **Mushroom Records**, the group reached the Australian Top 40 with their first single in 1992, which was written and sung by Gina herself. Later she moved to the UK, where she became involved in several projects before recording 'Ooh Aah . . . Just A Little Bit'. A trite, Euro-pop dance song, it was entered in the Great British Song Contest (a preliminary round preceding the Eurovision Song Contest), and progressed to the final four of the competition before becoming the official British entry. Written by Simon Tauber and Motiv8's Steve Rodway (previously responsible for remixing **Pulp**'s 'Disco 2000' and 'Common People', as well as their own hits 'Searching For The Golden Eye' and 'Break The Chain'), it was released on **Warner Brothers Records**' dance subsidiary, Eternal, in March 1996 and raced to the top of the UK charts. It also became the first Eurovision song contest entry to be voted Single Of The Week by **Melody Maker**. Two more irritatingly catchy singles, 'I Belong To You' and 'Fresh!', made it into the UK Top 10 before the singer's brief moment in the spotlight was over.

● ALBUMS: *Fresh* (Eternal/WEA 1997) ★★★.

G., Kenny

b. Kenneth Gorelick, 6 July 1956, Seattle, Washington, USA. Gorelick learned saxophone as a child and toured Europe in 1974 with the Franklin High School band. Two years later he played with **Barry White**'s **Love Unlimited Orchestra** in Seattle before entering the University of Washington to study accounting. Gorelick first recorded with local funk band Cold, Bold And Together and also backed many leading artists on their Seattle shows. After graduation, he joined the **Jeff Lorber** Fusion, recording with the jazz rock band for **Arista Records**, the label that in 1981 signed him to a solo contract. Produced by Preston Glass and **Narada Michael Walden**, *Duotones* was a major success and it included 'Songbird', a US Top 5 hit in 1987. Like much of his other work, it featured a flawless, melodic alto saxophone solo. By now, Kenny G. was in demand to play solos on albums by such singers as **Whitney Houston**, **Natalie Cole** and **Aretha Franklin**. Among the guest artists on *Silhouette* was **Smokey Robinson** who sang 'We've Saved The Best For Last'. Like its predecessor, the album sold over three million copies worldwide.

Kenny G.'s extraordinary success continued into the 90s. In 1992, he collaborated with **Michael Bolton**'s on the US Top 20 hit 'Missing You Now', and released the multi-platinum *Breathless*. He was also acknowledged as fellow musician President Clinton's favourite saxophonist. *Miracles: The Holiday Album* rocketed to the top of the US pop charts, reigniting interest in *Breathless*, which by the mid-90s had sold over 11 million copies in the USA alone and had remained at the top of the *Billboard* jazz chart for well over 18 months. It was finally toppled in October 1996 after an incredible run. The rude interloper to this was *The Moment*, the new album from . . . Kenny G. He changed tack for the subsequent *Classics In The Key Of G*, a collection of jazz standards, which still managed to sound like all his other recordings.

In January 2000, Kenny G. enjoyed a US Top 10 single with his version of 'Auld Lang Syne'. A badly chosen career move that year was to sample **Louis Armstrong**'s 'What A Wonderful World' and to solo alongside it. Jazz guitarist **Pat Metheny**, not normally known for abusive language and outbursts of anger, was moved to offer his thoughts on the matter via his own website. Part of his tirade included a description of Kenny G.'s 'lame-ass, jive, pseudo bluesy, out-of-tune, noodling, wimped out, fucked up playing'. The crossover into pop is felt to be too strong by most jazz critics, as the type of music he plays is very structured and contrived. Popular music has at least given rise to the 'great crossover debate'. Arguments aside; Kenny G. is a phenomenon, he sells albums in rock group proportions and his popularity is consistent.

● ALBUMS: *Kenny G* (Arista 1982) ★★★, *G Force* (Arista 1983) ★★★, with G Force *Gravity* (Arista 1985) ★★★, *Duotones* (Arista 1986) ★★★, *Silhouette* (Arista 1988) ★★★, *Kenny G Live* (Arista 1989) ★★, *Breathless* (Arista 1992) ★★★★, *Miracles: The Holiday Album.* (Arista 1994) ★★, *The Moment* (Arista 1996) ★★★, *Classics In The Key Of G* (Arista 1999) ★★★, *Faith: A Holiday Album* (Arista 1999) ★★★, *Paradise* (Arista 2002) ★★★, *Wishes* (Arista 2002) ★★, *At Last . . . The Duets Albums* (Arista 2004) ★★.

● COMPILATIONS: *Greatest Hits* (Arista 1997) ★★★, *Songbird: The Ultimate Collection* (BMG 2004) ★★★.

G., Warren

b. Warren Griffin III, 10 November 1970, Long Beach, California, USA. Griffin's parents relocated to Long Beach from Tennessee and Oklahoma before he was born. Half-brother to **Dr. Dre**, he was raised in a staunchly Christian tradition and, despite affiliations with gangsta rap, he maintained his allegiance to 'Jesus' at the top of his list of dedications on his debut album. It was Dre's World Class Wreckin' Cru that inspired him to follow a musical path. He first began rapping and producing while working at the local VIP record store. Later he helped form Dre's Dogg Pound collective, with **Nate Dogg** and his best friend, **Snoop Doggy Dogg**. The trio also worked together as part of **213**.

Warren G.'s role in the development of west coast rap was crucial—he is credited with having introduced Snoop Doggy Dogg to Dre (a meeting recalled in his debut album's 'Do You See'). Having subsequently produced a track for **M.C. Breed** ('Gotta Get Mine'), and appeared on both *The Chronic* and *Doggy Style*, he then wrote, produced and guested on Mista Grimm's 'Indo Smoke' and **2Pac**'s 'Definition Of A Thug'. 'Indo Smoke' appeared in the movie *Poetic Justice*, while 'Definition Of A Thug' was included on the soundtrack album *Above The Rim*, which hit the number 1 spot on the US R&B album, charts. Griffin's own debut as Warren G., 'Regulate', a duet with Nate Dogg, was the keynote to that album's success. Built around a sample of **Michael McDonald**'s 'I Keep Forgettin' (Every Time You're Near)', which his father had played constantly when he was a child, it also became his first US Top 5 single. The attendant *Regulate* immediately achieved triple-platinum status, and confirmed the accessibility of his approach. He also departed from rap norms with his employment of live musicians.

Following a US tour with **R. Kelly** and **Heavy D**, Warren G. concentrated on producing the debut of his protégés, Da Twinz, who were part of the collective involved with *Regulate*. In 1996, he scored further international success with 'What's Love Got To Do With It', a hit single from the soundtrack to *Super Cop*, which topped the German charts and reached UK number 2. His disappointing second album, *Take A Look Over Your Shoulder (Reality)*, was released as part of a new contract with **Def Jam Records** in 1997. The album incorporated cover versions of **Bob Marley**'s 'I Shot The Sheriff' (a UK number 2 hit) and the **Isley Brothers**' 'Smokin' Me Out' (with a chorus sung by Ronald Isley). 1999's *I Want It All* featured a stellar cast list of guest MCs, including **Snoop Dogg**, **Mack 10** and **Kurupt**, but both this release and the follow-up *The Return Of The Regulator* ultimately disappointed. Warren G. subsequently lost his major label recording contract with Universal Records. His first independent release, 2005's *In The Mid-Nite Hour*, indicated a welcome return to form.

● ALBUMS: *Regulate . . . G Funk Era* (Violator/Def Jam 1994) ★★★★, *Take A Look Over Your Shoulder (Reality)* (G Funk/Def Jam 1997) ★★★, *I Want It All* (G Funk 1999) ★★★, *The Return Of The Regulator* (Universal 2001) ★★, *In The Mid-Nite Hour* (Hawino/Lightyear 2005) ★★★.

● FILMS: *The Show* (1995), *The Wizard Of Oz* (1998), *Speedway Junky* (1999).

Gabinelli, Gerald

b. USA, d. 27 January 1995, Summit, New Jersey, USA. The New York–based engineer, producer and songwriter Gerald Gabinelli began his career with Bob Clearmountain at Media Sound Studios and Ton Bongiovi at the Power Station. He subsequently spent much of his career as chief engineer at OD Studios before becoming staff engineer at Media Sound, The Hit Factory and Sound Works. His notable credits include one for producing, engineering and co-writing the lyrics to 'Superstar' by **Lydia Murdock**. He also engineered platinum albums by **Joan Jett And The Blackhearts** (*I Love Rock 'N' Roll*) and **Steely Dan** (*Gaucho*). He has also worked on albums by **Cameo**, **James Brown**, **Barry Manilow**, **Harry Belafonte**, **Gloria Gaynor**, **Liza Minnelli**, **Humble Pie**, **Kiss**, and provided live sound for concerts by **Cyndi Lauper** and **Tina Turner**, and worked on Broadway cast albums for *Beatlemania* and *Annie*.

Gabler, Milt

b. 20 May 1911, New York City, USA, d. 20 July 2001, New York City, USA. In 1926 Gabler's father opened a store, the Commodore Music Shop, at 144 East 42nd Street in New York City. When Gabler took over its operation he sold sporting goods and novelties as sidelines to the main trade, which was in sheet music, records and radio. To buy anything there, however, a customer had to like jazz: all day long Gabler played jazz records on a wind-up phonograph and soon the shop became the in-place for jazz fans to gather. In the late 30s and early 40s the habitués included several noted journalists and academics who wrote on jazz, among them Marshall Stearns, Wilder and **John Hammond Jnr**. Gabler's first big steps in serving the needs of jazz fans came when he persuaded several major record companies to reissue sought-after but out-of-print records even though he had to guarantee orders far in excess of likely sales. The next logical step was to make his own records, for which he hired the services of another Commodore regular, **Eddie Condon**. Additionally, Gabler and Condon launched weekly jam sessions at Jimmy Ryan's, a leading 52nd Street nightspot, and Gabler later opened a branch of his store across the street from Ryan's.

Among the many artists recorded by Gabler for his Commodore label was **Billie Holiday**, who in 1939 made four tracks that became classics: 'Yesterdays', 'I Gotta Right To Sing The Blues', 'Fine And Mellow' and the sombre 'Strange Fruit'. Gabler and associate Jack Crystal were responsible for assembling a series of long-playing records featuring the pick of the Commodore recordings, including sessions by Holiday, **Lester Young**, **Pee Wee Russell**, **Don Byas**, **Jelly Roll Morton**, **Wild Bill Davison**, **Eddie Heywood**. Gabler became head of A&R at **Decca Records** in 1943 and worked with **Ella Fitzgerald**. Gabler wound up Commodore following Crystal's death in 1963, but later leased the masters to a

succession of labels, including Mainstream, **Atlantic Records**, Columbia Special Products, Mosaic (who released three mammoth box sets in 1988), and **GRP Records**. *DownBeat* bestowed him with their Lifetime Achievement award in 2001.

● COMPILATIONS: *The Commodore Story* (Commodore 1997) ★★★★★.

Gabriel, Juan

b. Alberto Aguilera Valadés, 7 January 1950, Parácuaro, Michoacán, Mexico. Valadés was raised by his mother following the death of his father before his birth. He attended boarding school in Ciudad Juárez, Chihuahua, but left to work as a craftsman at the age of 13. Already a budding songwriter, he began his performing career on local television using the moniker Adán Luna. He subsequently performed in local nightclubs under this name, before securing a recording contract with **RCA Records** in 1971, a partnership that has already lasted over 25 years. Changing his name to Juan Gabriel, he gradually established himself as one of Mexico's leading songwriters, penning mariachi hits for leading Latin artists including Estela Nuñez, Angélica María, and Enriqueta Jiménez. As well as recording his own material, he made his screen debut in 1975 in the movie *Nobleza Ranchera*. His work an arranger, producer and songwriter throughout the subsequent decades brought him into contact with the leading Latin artists of the day, including Rocio Dúrcal and Isabel Pantoja, although he refused to record any new material between 1986 and 1994 owing to a copyright dispute with BMG. He was awarded the **ASCAP** Songwriter Of The Year Award in 1995. His gigantic contribution to Latin American music was honoured in 1996 when he was inducted into the *Billboard* Latin Hall of Fame. On the same year's tribute album, *Las Tres Señoras*, he persuaded three female giants of Mexican music, Lucha Villa, **Lola Beltrán**, and Amalia Mendoza, to perform together for the first time. His solo concerts remain sell outs all over Mexico and the USA, and he has sold over 30 million records worldwide.

● ALBUMS: *El Alma Joven* (RCA Victor) ★★★, *Juan Gabriel* (RCA Victor) ★★★, *El Alma Joven Vol II* (RCA Victor) ★★★, *Con El Mariachi Vargas De Tecatitlan* (RCA Victor) ★★★, *10 Éxitos* (RCA Victor 1975) ★★★, *A Mi Guitarra . . .* (RCA Victor) ★★★, *10 De Los Grandes De Juan Gabriel* (RCA Victor) ★★★, *Juan Gabriel Con Mariachi Vol. II* (RCA Victor) ★★★, *Te Llegará Mi Olvido* (RCA Victor) ★★★, *Siempre En Mi Mente* (RCA Victor) ★★★, *Espectacular!* (RCA Victor) ★★★, *Mis Ojos Tristes* (RCA Victor) ★★★, *Recuerdos* (RCA Victor 1980) ★★★, *Con Tu Amor* (RCA Victor 1981) ★★★, *Cosas De Enamorados* (RCA Victor 1982) ★★★, *Todo* (RCA Victor 1983) ★★★, *Recuerdos II* (RCA Victor 1984) ★★★, *Pensamientos* (RCA Victor 1986) ★★★, *Gracias Por Esperar* (BMG 1994) ★★★, *El México Que Se Nos Fue* (BMG 1995) ★★★, *Juan Gabriel Con La Banda El Recodo* (BMG 1998) ★★★, *Por Mi Orgullo* (BMG 1998) ★★★, *Todo Está Bien* (BMG 1999) ★★★★, *Querida* (BMG 2000) ★★★, *Por Los Siglos* (BMG 2001) ★★★, *Innocente De Tí* (BMG 2003) ★★★.

● COMPILATIONS: *25 Aniversario* (BMG 1996) ★★★, *25 Aniversario 1971–1996* 5-CD box set (BMG 1996) ★★★.

● FILMS: *Nobleza Ranchera* (1975), *El Noa Noa* (1980), *Es Mi Vida* (1980).

Gabriel, Peter

b. 13 February 1950, Cobham, Surrey, England. After seven years fronting **Genesis**, Gabriel tired of the extensive touring and band format and went solo in 1975. Until the release of 1983's *Plays Live*, his solo albums for **Charisma Records** were all called *Peter Gabriel*. His 1977 debut included the track 'Solsbury Hill', a metaphorical account of his split from Genesis, which made the Top 20 in the UK. The album charted in the UK Top 10 and the **Billboard** Top 40 and Gabriel began his solo touring career in the USA, expressing a nervousness of facing his home country audiences. Unlike his earlier extravagant, theatrical presentations, he favoured minimalism and often played shows in a plain boiler suit. **Robert Fripp** was brought in as producer for the second album, which made the UK Top 10. The album contained chiefly introspective, experimental music, but healthy sales figures were encouraging. However, **Atlantic Records** refused to distribute his third album in the USA, claiming its maudlin nature would mean 'commercial suicide'. **Mercury Records** stepped in and with **Steve Lillywhite**'s disciplined production the striking collection was far from the flop Atlantic feared, narrowly failing to break into the Top 20 (the album topped the UK chart). 'Games Without Frontiers' was a UK Top 5 hit and the track 'Biko', about the murdered South African activist Stephen Biko, became an anti-racist anthem.

Continuing his deliberated approach, Gabriel's fourth album, given the full title of *Peter Gabriel (Security)*, was not released until 1982 and appeared to be hinting at a more accessible approach, tempering the third album's dense electronic production values with African and Latin rhythms. **Geffen Records** distributed the album in the USA, and a German-language edition was also released. In 1985, Gabriel composed the haunting soundtrack to the Alan Parker movie, *Birdy*. The journey to complete commercial acceptance was finished in 1986 with his **Virgin Records** debut *So*. The album contained the hit single 'Sledgehammer' (US number 1/UK number 4), which was supported by a pioneering, award-winning video featuring puppetry and animation. He was celebrated as an artist whose work was popular without being compromised. A duet with **Kate Bush**, 'Don't Give Up', also lifted from *So*, became a UK Top 10 hit in November 1986.

Throughout the 80s, Gabriel dedicated much of his time to absorbing world music and in 1982 inaugurated the WOMAD (World Of Music And Dance) Festival. He also became heavily involved in Amnesty International and recorded with Senegalese star **Youssou N'Dour**. The pair toured the USA under the banner of 'Conspiracy Of Hope' and raised money for Amnesty. He invited musicians from all over the world to record at his luxurious self-built Real World studios in Bath and incorporated many non-Western ideas into his own music. In 1989, Gabriel was commissioned to write the score for Martin Scorsese's *The Last Temptation Of Christ*. **Virgin Records**, now the owners of the Charisma back-catalogue, released a greatest hits collection in 1990, *Shaking The Tree: Sixteen Golden Greats*. The title track was written by Gabriel with N'Dour and was included originally on N'Dour's album, *The Lion*. Although 1992's *Us* fell short of the high standard set by *So*, it put Gabriel back in the public eye with a series of outstandingly creative videos for singles such as 'Steam' (a UK number 10 hit), 'Digging In The Dirt', and 'Kiss That Frog'.

In 1999, Gabriel was commissioned to contribute music and act as musical director for the Millennium Dome show in London. The soundtrack was released the following year on the *Ovo* album. Gabriel's next project was the soundtrack to the Australian film *The Rabbit-Proof Fence*, released in June 2002. His brand new studio album, *Up*, the followed three months later to mixed reviews and disappointing sales in the UK. Gabriel enjoyed more success with OD2, the music download service he co-founded in 2000, which was sold to US digital media firm Loudeye in June 2004 for $38.2m (£20.9m).

● ALBUMS: *Peter Gabriel* (Charisma/Atco 1977) ★★★, *Peter Gabriel* (Charisma/Atlantic 1978) ★★★★, *Peter Gabriel* (Charisma/Mercury 1980) ★★★★, *Peter Gabriel* aka *Security* (Charisma/Geffen 1982) ★★★★★, *Plays Live* (Charisma/Geffen 1983) ★★, *Birdy* film soundtrack (Charisma/Geffen 1985) ★★, *So* (Virgin/Geffen 1986) ★★★★, *Passion: Music For The Last Temptation Of Christ* film soundtrack (Virgin/Geffen 1989) ★★, *Us* (Real World/Geffen 1992) ★★★, *Secret World—Live* (Real World 1994) ★★★, *Ovo* (Real World 2000) ★★★, *Long Walk Home: Music From The Rabbit-Proof Fence* film soundtrack (Real World 2002) ★★, *Up* (Charisma/Geffen 2002) ★★★.

● COMPILATIONS: *Shaking The Tree: Sixteen Golden Greats* (Virgin/Geffen 1990) ★★★★, *Hit* (Real World/EMI 2003) ★★★★.

● DVD/VIDEOS: *Point Of View (Live In Athens)* (Virgin Vision 1989), *The Desert And Her Daughters* (Hendring Music Video 1990), *CV* (Virgin Vision 1991), *All About Us* (Real World 1993), *Secret World Live* (Real World 1994), *Computer Animation: Vol. 2.0* (Real World 1994), *Growing Up Live* (Real World/EMI 2003), *Play: The Videos* (Warner Music Vision 2004), *Still Growing Up: Live & Unwrapped* (Warner Music Vision 2005).

● FURTHER READING: *Peter Gabriel: An Authorized Biography*, Spenser Bright. *In His Own Words*, Mick St. Michael.

Gabrielle

b. Louise Gabrielle Bobb, 16 April 1970, London, England. The corporate record industry's new soul diva of the 90s, Gabrielle earned a high commercial profile via a series of perfectly realized, expertly pitched releases. Visually distinguished by a black eye patch when she first appeared, the singer made a dramatic entrance with her UK chart-topping debut single, 'Dreams', in summer 1993. The song also entered the US Top 30 later in the year. Equally accessible was the UK Top 10 follow-up, 'Going Nowhere'. The album that followed was assembled by seven different producers, including the Boilerhouse (Andy Cox and David Steele of the **Fine Young Cannibals**) and Steve Jervier (famed for his work with **Take That**). She was fêted at various awards ceremonies, and became such a celebrity that she was invited to appear at the Armani fashion show in Milan.

During the break between her albums, the singer gave birth to a child. Ten of the tracks on the heavily anticipated *Gabrielle* were written by Andy Dean and Ben Wolff, and they shared the production with Foster And McElroy. The **Motown Records** pastiche 'Give Me A Little More Time' was a Top 5 UK hit in the spring of 1996. Further singles were less successful, before 'If You Ever', a collaboration with boy band **East 17**, reached number 2 in November. Her third collection, *Rise*, benefited from the production skills of

Johnny Dollar (**Massive Attack**), and was premiered by the UK hit single 'Sunshine'. The title track, built around a hypnotic sample from **Bob Dylan**'s 'Knockin' On Heaven's Door', provided Gabrielle with her second UK chart-topper in February 2000. 'Out Of Reach', another Top 10 hit taken from the singer's 'greatest hits' set, benefited from extensive exposure on the *Bridget Jones' Diary* soundtrack.

Following another three-year hiatus, Gabrielle returned on a new label (**Island Records**) and with a more AOR-orientated sound on the summer 2004 release, *Play To Win*.

● ALBUMS: *Find Your Way* (Go! Beat 1994) ★★★, *Gabrielle* (Go! Beat 1996) ★★★, *Rise* (Go! Beat 1999) ★★★★, *Play To Win* (Island 2004) ★★★.

● COMPILATIONS: *Dreams Can Come True: Greatest Hits Vol. 1* (Go! Beat 2001) ★★★★.

Gadd, Steve

b. Stephen K. Gadd, 4 September 1945, Rochester, New York, USA. Gadd was taught the drums by an uncle from the age of three: he enjoyed Sousa marches and worked with a drum corps. He spent two years at Manhattan's School of Music before going on to Eastman College in Rochester after which he was drafted into the army and spent three years in an army band. His first professional work was with **Chuck Mangione** before he joined **Chick Corea**'s **Return To Forever** in 1975. Corea described him as bringing 'orchestral and compositional thinking to the drum kit while at the same time having a great imagination and a great ability to swing'.

Gadd worked extensively in the New York studios from the early 70s onwards and was able to provide the perfect accompaniment for a diverse series of sessions. He developed his own style of linear drumming in which no two drums are sounded at the same time. He played for many artists from **Charles Mingus** via **George Benson** to **Paul Simon**, with whom he toured in 1991, directing the large group of percussionists on the Rhythm Of The Saints tour. So ubiquitous did he become that it was his sound that was sampled for the earlier drum machines. In 1976, he played in the influential funk band **Stuff** along with other session musicians such as **Eric Gale** and **Richard Tee**. Throughout the 80s and 90s Gadd continued with a busy studio schedule but also played in the straight jazz Manhattan Jazz Quintet.

● ALBUMS: *Gaddabout* (King 1984) ★★★, *The Gadd Gang* (CBS/Sony 1986) ★★★, with the Gadd Gang *Here & Now* (Epic/Sony 1988) ★★★, with the Gadd Gang *Live At The Bottom Line* 1988 recording (Epic/Sony 1994) ★★★.

Gaddy, Bob

b. 4 February 1924, Vivian, West Virginia, USA. Gaddy took a childhood interest in the piano from watching his minister, Clayton Jones, playing in church. Gospel music remained his musical focus until he was drafted into the army in 1943. Transferred to the San Francisco area, he frequented the local clubs and bars, encouraged by his friends to play the latest boogie hits. Demobbed in 1946, he made his way to New York, where he met **Brownie McGhee** and sat in with his band, the Three B's. Soon afterwards, he and McGhee formed the Mighty Houserockers and played a four-year residency at Billy's Tavern, a New Jersey nightclub. Through McGhee, Gaddy made records for Jackson, Jax, **Dot Records** and Harlem, before signing with Old Town in 1955. Over the next five years, records such as 'Operator', 'Paper Lady' and 'Woe, Woe Is Me' achieved success principally in the New York

area, but were popular enough for him to tour the Midwest and the south. Other tracks from his nine singles tended to be minimally disguised rewrites of more popular songs by artists such as **Chuck Willis** and **Ray Charles**. As the 50s ended, Gaddy formed a new partnership with guitarist Larry Dale that lasted until the 70s. When rediscovered in 1986, he was working as a cook in a Madison Avenue restaurant.

● ALBUMS: *Rip'n'Run* (Ace 1986) ★★★, *Bob Gaddy And Friends* (Moonshine 1986), *Harlem Hit Parade* (Ace 1987) ★★★, *Harlem Blues Operator* (Ace 1993) ★★★, *Old Town Blues Volume 1 Downtown Sides* (Ace 1993) ★★★.

Gael Linn Records

Loosely translating as 'the Irish within us', Gael Linn is an organization established by Cork University graduate Riobard McGoirin to promote Irish language and music, song and literature. Its range of activities originally included film, music and the Slogadh—a youth festival of music and Irish handicrafts. McGoirin's first concern was to promote native Irish newsreels, broadcast in Gaelic, to replace the imported Pathé versions from the UK. These were followed by a series of feature films including *Mise Eire* in 1959, with a semi-orchestral score by Sean O'Riada, whom McGoirin had originally met at Cork University. The company's recorded output began in 1957 with a series of 78s, combining instrumental music on one side of the record and a cappella Irish ballads (sean-nós) on the flip. Featured artists included uillean pipers Willie Clancy and Tommy Rock as well as the singers Joe Heaney and Mâire Ni Dhonncha. O'Riada, through his association with Ceoltoiri Chusallan ('the musicians of old Dublin') also pioneered a series of albums documenting artists such as piper **Paddy Moloney**, concertina and fiddle player John Kelly, accordionist Sonny Brogan and others. In turn he encouraged a succession of musicians who have made Irish traditional music the global phenomenon it is today, allowing it to grow from its roots in dance band music to a living, thriving art form. O'Riada died in 1971, but **Planxty**, **Boys Of The Lough** and the **Bothy Band**, giants of Irish music who all recorded for Gael Linn, readily acknowledged their debt to his endeavours.

By the 80s Gael Linn had released material by **Clannad**, Paddy Keenan and practically every other Irish artist of note. Others to have worked for the label and endorsed its ethos include **Mary Black** (with General Humbert 2), **Dolores Keane** and **De Danaan**. The label has also documented the *Fleadh Ceoil* and *Clones Fleadh Ceoil* with various artist compilations, as well as capturing Irish music's most natural setting—the session. Few singles were ever released (save a handful from the likes of Peter Browne and Mac Murrough), but by the early 00s the label had built up a substantial back catalogue. Despite being a full-time concern, it has never sacrificed its firm commitment to the Irish language and its musical practitioners.

Gaff, Billy

A colourful member of the UK music business, Gaff guided the careers of **Rod Stewart** and **John Mellencamp**. He entered the industry as a member of **Robert Stigwood**'s staff in the early 60s, becoming a manager with the **Herd** in 1967. Three years later, Gaff took on the career of Stewart, who had recently left the **Faces**. He set up Stewart's solo recording contracts with **Mercury Records** and in 1975 with Gaff's own Riva label. Riva had less success with Gaff discoveries Phil

Thornalley and the Lewis Sisters. In 1977, he signed Mellencamp to Riva, publicizing the US artist with a major advertising campaign in the London area. During the 70s and early 80s, Gaff was also involved with the careers of **Long John Baldry**, **Status Quo**, **Air Supply** and **Rory Gallagher**. In 1986, Gaff became majority shareholder of London's famous Marquee club, moving it to a new site in Charing Cross Road.

Gaffney, Chris

b. Vienna, Austria. Although not born in the USA, the 90s country singer and accordion player Chris Gaffney was raised in Arizona and southern California and spent 10 years working in Los Angeles shipyards. He has been performing since the 60s and his music has evolved into a honky tonk mixture of Cajun, Tex-Mex, rock 'n' roll and western swing. His songs are full of stories, characters and unusual scenarios, such as the fear of a gangland reprisal in 'The Gardens' and the drunken soldier remembering his lost friend in Vietnam. Gaffney sings with a rough, world-weary voice and plays guitar and accordion. His band is called the Cold Hard Facts and he is assisted on record by musicians such as **Dave Alvin** and **Jim Lauderdale**. On 1995's *Loser's Paradise* he duetted with **Lucinda Williams** on a cover version of the **Intruders**' 'Cowboys To Girls'.

In 2005, Gaffney teamed up with Dave Gonzalez of the **Paladins** to form the **Hacienda Brothers**. The duo released a **Dan Penn**-produced, self-titled album the same year on Koch Nashville Records.

● ALBUMS: *Road To Indio* (Cactus Club 1986) ★★★, *Chris Gaffney And The Cold Hard Facts* (ROM 1990) ★★★, *Mi Vida Loca* (HighTone 1992) ★★★, *Man Of Somebody's Dreams* (Country 1994), *Loser's Paradise* (HighTone 1995) ★★★★, *Live And Then Some* (Tres Pescadores 1999) ★★★.

Gage, Mark

b. USA. From Rochester, New York, Gage can genuinely point to a life-long commitment to his art. 'I've been possessed by music ever since I was a very little kid. I was collecting 45s when I was four or five years old. I had boxes for them, and I would go off to my Grandma's house and just play records the whole time I was there. So, in a sense, even at that age I was a DJ'. However, until the early 90s he subsisted entirely on wages from waiting tables. Two cult 12-inch successes, the *Cusp* EP and Vapourspace's 'Gravitational Arch Of 10', both for **Plus 8 Records**, changed that. 'Gravitational Arch Of 10', was, in fact, a misprint. The title was meant to have read 'Arch Of Lo', but a mix up at the pressing plant ensured that it passed into **techno** folklore under a slightly different title. He went on to tour as Vapourspace, which is also the name of his studio, and was quickly signed up to a multi-album recording contract with **ffrr Records**, gaining rave reviews from a US tour with the **Aphex Twin**, **Moby** and **Orbital**.

● ALBUMS: as Vapourspace *Themes From Vapourspace* (Internal 1994) ★★★.

Gage, Yvonne

b. 1959, Chicago, USA. When aged only 14 Gage joined the Soulettes, with whom she stayed until she was 21. During this period they changed their name to First Love and then Love, subsequently recording an album for Chycago International Music in 1980. However, by then Gage had departed to join the backing singers for Captain Sky. She made her solo debut with 'Garden Of Eve' in 1981 on **Atlantic Records** to little reaction. Gage then sang with new wave group **Ministry**, appearing in shows with **Madness**, **Police** and **Culture Club**. After singing a commercial for Ultra-Curl, she recorded her first album *Virginity* on CIM/Epic which, like Captain Sky's records, was produced by Don Burnside. Billed as the unofficial answer to **Michael Jackson**'s 'Thriller', the album track, 'Doin' It In A Haunted House' made the bottom of the US R&B chart and reached the UK Top 50 in June 1984. Simultaneously, another of her singles 'Lover Of My Dreams' was also doing well in the UK clubs. However, despite this encouraging start Gage never visited the charts again. She reappeared in the UK in 1990 on Trax Records but with no further success.

● ALBUMS: *Virginity* (CIM/Epic 1984) ★★.

Gahan, Dave

b. 9 May 1962, Epping, Essex, England. In a surprise move, both of the main protagonists in UK rock act **Depeche Mode** chose 2003 as the year to launch their solo careers. Gahan, the vocal foil to main songwriter **Martin Gore**, had been the very public face of Depeche Mode during the peak of their popularity in the 80s and 90s. Relocating from England to America in the early 90s, Gahan adopted a grunge look shockingly at odds with the clean cut, short-haired young man who helmed Depeche Mode's classic run of electro pop hits in the mid- to late 80s. More disturbingly, Gahan lost himself to heroin addiction and during the lowest point of his life attempted suicide. He began to get his life back together at the end of the 90s, kicking his drug habit and reuniting with Depeche Mode to record the highly successful albums *Ultra* (1997) and *Exciter* (2001).

During a lull in band activities, Gahan began work on his solo debut with multi-instrumentalist Knox Chandler. The two men teamed up with producer Ken Thomas and recorded *Paper Monsters* over a period of several months, concocting a heady brew of bluesy rock and electronica similar in approach to late period Depeche Mode. Gahan's lyrics were of particular note, dealing with his personal demons in the frank and hard-hitting manner suggested by song titles such as 'Dirty Sticky Floors' and 'Bottle Living'.

● ALBUMS: *Paper Monsters* (Mute 2003) ★★★.
● DVD/VIDEOS: *Live Monsters* (Mute Films 2004).

Gaillard, Slim

b. Bulee Gaillard, 4 January 1916, Detroit, Michigan, USA, d. 26 February 1991, London, England. Other sources including Gaillard himself have claimed he was born on 1 January 1916 in Santa Clara, Cuba. Gaillard led an adventurous childhood. On one occasion, while travelling on board a ship on which his father was steward, he was left behind in Crete when the ship sailed. His adventures became more exciting every time he recounted his tales and include stints as professional boxer, mortician and truck driver for bootleggers. Originally based in Detroit, Gaillard entered vaudeville in the early 30s with an act during which he played the guitar while tap-dancing. Later in the decade he moved to New York and formed a duo with bass player **Slam Stewart** in which Gaillard mostly played guitar and sang. Much of their repertoire was original material with lyrics conceived in Gaillard's personal version of the currently popular 'jive talk', which on his lips developed extraordinary surrealist overtones. Gaillard's language, which he named 'Vout' or 'Vout Oreenie', helped the duo achieve a number of hit records, including 'Flat Foot Floogie'. Their success led to a long-running radio series and an appearance in the film *Hellzapoppin*. In 1943 Stewart was inducted for military service and was replaced by Bam Brown.

Now based in Los Angeles, Gaillard continued to write songs, often in collaboration with Brown, and had another big hit with 'Cement Mixer (Put-ti Put-ti)'. With Brown he co-authored a remarkable extended work, 'Opera In Vout', which premiered in Los Angeles in 1946. (In fact, it was not an opera and not much of it was in vout!) Another huge hit was 'Down By The Station', a song which, uniquely for a jazz artist, entered the catalogue of classic children's nursery rhymes. Contrastingly, he also recorded with bebop musicians, including **Charlie Parker** and **Dizzy Gillespie** (*Slim's Jam*). In the late 40s he continued his eccentric entertaining, which included such intriguing routines as playing piano with his hands upside-down. Not surprisingly, given his manner of performance and his private language, some people never quite understood Gaillard and one radio station banned his record 'Yep Roc Heresy', declaring it to be degenerate; in fact, the lyric was merely a recitation of the menu from an Armenian restaurant.

In the late 50s and for several years thereafter, Gaillard worked mostly outside music but gradually returned to prominence by way of acting roles, (including a part in the US television series *Roots*), festival appearances with Stewart and, in the 80s, numerous television and stage shows in the UK, where he became resident in 1983. His tall, loping figure, invariably topped by a big grin and a rakish white beret, became a familiar sight in London's jazz-land. In 1989 he starred in a four-part UK BBC television series, *The World Of Slim Gaillard*. In addition to his singing and guitar playing, Gaillard also played piano, vibraphone and tenor saxophone.

● ALBUMS: with Meade Lux Lewis *Boogie Woogie At The Philharmonic* 10-inch album (Mercury 1951) ★★★, *Mish Mash* 10-inch album (Clef 1953) ★★★, *Opera In Vout* 10-inch album (Disc 1953) ★★★, *Slim Gaillard And His Musical Aggregation Wherever They May Be* aka *Slim Gaillard Cavorts* (Norgran 1954), with Dizzy Gillespie *Gaillard And Gillespie* (Ultraphonic 1958) ★★★, *Slim Gaillard Rides Again* (Dot 1959) ★★★★, *Anytime, Anyplace, Anywhere* (Hep 1982) ★★★, *Live At Billy Berg's: The Voutest!* 1946 recording (Hep 1983) ★★★.

● COMPILATIONS: tribute album *The Legendary McVouty* (Hep 1993) ★★★, *Slim Gaillard 1946* (Classics 1998) ★★★, with Slam Stewart *Complete Columbia Master Takes* (Definitive 2002) ★★★, *Laughing In Rhythm* 4-CD set (Proper 2003) ★★★.

● FILMS: *Hellzapoppin* (1941), *Sweetheart Of Sigma Chi* (1946), *Stairway For A Star* (1947), *O'Voutie O'Rooney* (1947), *Go, Man Go!* (1954), *Too Late Blues* (1961), *The Curious Female* (1969), *Absolute Beginners* (1986), *Sky Bandits* (1986).

Gaines, Charlie

b. 8 August 1900, Philadelphia, Pennsylvania, USA. He played trumpet with several east coast **territory bands** in the years between the ending of World War I and 1921, when he settled in New York. He remained there throughout the 20s, playing and sometimes recording with **Fess Johnson**, **Wilbur Sweatman**, **Fats Waller**, **Clarence Williams** and several singers including **Edith Wilson**. In the early 30s Gaines was in bands

led by **Louis Armstrong** and Williams again, but mostly played in his home town. He stayed in Philadelphia, leading groups of all sizes from trios to big bands, for the next 40 years. An undistinguished soloist, Gaines was a solid journeyman trumpeter, reliable and with a good accompanist's ear.

Gaines, Chris
(see **Brooks, Garth**)

Gaines, Earl

b. 19 August 1935, Decater, Alabama, USA. Gaines is one of the finest examples of the southern style of deep soul that draws heavily from gospel singing, so much so that the music is almost identical to gospel music, but with secular lyrics. Gaines moved with his family to Nashville, Tennessee, in 1951. He first gained fame as the vocalist with Louis Brooks And His Hi-Toppers, and it is Gaines' voice that is heard on the group's lone hit single, 'It's Love Baby (24 Hours A Day)' (number 2 R&B, 1955), released on **Excello Records**. Gaines achieved success under his own name in 1966 on HBR with 'The Best Of Luck To You' (number 28 R&B), and in 1973 on Sound Stage 7 with 'Hymn Number 5' (number 36 R&B), a remake of Mighty Hamilton's hit from 1966. In 1995, after a long break from the music business, Gaines made the first album of his career, *I Believe In Your Love*, for Appaloosa. Recorded in Nashville by producer Fred James, it showed that Gaines had not lost any of his vocal prowess. Less successful was another James-produced CD, *Tennessee RnB*, in 1997, on which Gaines joined with two other legends, **Clifford Curry** and **Roscoe Shelton**, to form a trio, the Excello Legends. A live Excello Legends set was then followed by the superlative *Everything's Gonna Be Alright*. Gaines continued recording and performing into the new millennium.

● ALBUMS: *I Believe In Your Love* (Appaloosa 1995) ★★★, as the Excello Legends *Tennessee RnB* (Repete 1997) ★★, as the Excello Legends *Tennessee R&B Live!* (Appaloosa 1997) ★★★, *Everything's Gonna Be Alright* (Black Top 1998) ★★★★, *The Different Feelings Of Blues & Soul* (Blue Fye 2005) ★★★.

● COMPILATIONS: *24 Hours A Day* (Black Magic 1999) ★★★★, *Lovin' Blues: The Starday King Years 1967–1973* (WestSide 1999) ★★★★, *The Lost Soul Tapes* (Aim 2006) ★★★.

Gaines, Grady

b. 14 May 1934, Waskom, Texas, USA. By the time his family moved to Houston, the 12-year-old Gaines was already intent upon following **Louis Jordan**'s example by becoming a saxophonist. He took lessons and at the E.L. Smith Junior High School, he met **Calvin Owens**, a student music teacher at the time. While in senior high school, he met **Little Richard** at the Club Matinee and played with his band, the Tempo Toppers. Gaines worked on studio sessions for Duke/Peacock until 1955, when Little Richard asked him to join his touring band. The association lasted for three years, during which time they recorded 'Keep A Knockin'' and appeared in *Don't Knock The Rock*, *The Girl Can't Help It* and *Mister Rock And Roll*. When Little Richard renounced rock 'n' roll in favour of religion in 1958, Gaines and the band named themselves the Upsetters and hired **Dee Clark** to be their singer. They also worked and recorded with **Little Willie**

John and **Sam Cooke**, appearing on the latter's 'Twistin' The Night Away'. During the 70s, Gaines worked with **Joe Tex**, **'Little' Johnny Taylor**, **Curtis Mayfield** and **Millie Jackson**. He left the music business in 1980 but made a comeback five years later that resulted in a contract with Black Top. His records call on the services of veterans such as Carol Fran and Clarence Hollimon, Teddy Reynolds and Lloyd Lambert, as well as featuring his regular vocalist, Big Robert Smith.
● ALBUMS: *Full Gain* (Black Top 1987) ★★★, *Gulf Coast Blues Vol. 1* (Black Top 1990) ★★★, *Black Top Blues-A-Rama Vol. 4* (Black Top 1990) ★★★, *Horn Of Plenty* (Black Top 1992) ★★★.

Gaines, Jeffrey

b. Harrisburg, Pennsylvania, USA. Singer Jeffrey Gaines specializes in gentle romantic songs that centre around his smooth, crooning voice. Gaines' musical interest was sparked at a young age, owing largely in part to his parents' collection of soul records, but it was his discovery of **Ziggy Stardust**-era **David Bowie** that truly sealed his fate, leading to his participation in local bands. After relocating to Philadelphia after graduation, Gaines' talents were recognized by **Chrysalis Records**, who signed the singer to a recording contract during the early 90s. A pair of under-appreciated soul rock albums soon followed, 1992's *Jeffrey Gaines* and 1994's *Somewhat Slightly Dazed*, before the label dropped him. **Rykodisc Records** issued Gaines' third release, 1998's *Galore*, an album that featured input by members of his idol David Bowie's then current backing band, Reeves Gabrels (guitar), Gail Ann Dorsey (bass), and Zachary Alford (drums). Switching labels once more (this time to Artemis), Gaines issued two further albums during the early twenty-first century, 2001's *Always Be* and 2003's *Toward The Sun*, the former of which included a popular reading of **Peter Gabriel**'s 'In Your Eyes', which crossed over to the US Adult charts.
● ALBUMS: *Jeffrey Gaines* (Chrysalis 1992) ★★★, *Somewhat Slightly Dazed* (Chrysalis 1994) ★★, *Galore* (Rykodisc 1995) ★★★, *Always Be* (Artemis 2001) ★★★, *Toward The Sun* (Artemis 2003) ★★★.

Gaines, Reg E.

b. USA. Based in Los Angeles, California, this US hip-hop artist has laboured hard to escape critical comparisons with **Gil Scott-Heron**, though that artist has also been a useful advocate. Gaines shared the bill with Scott-Heron at his first concerts for several years, at the Troubadour club in Los Angeles in 1994. The title of Gaines' debut album of the same year for **Mercury Records**, *Please Don't Take My Air Jordans*, gave notice of his sense of humour and cynicism at the preoccupation of modern rap with the trappings of fiscal success. The album, which sold particularly well in the UK, combined such rich humour with Gaines' deeply held philosophical convictions, narrated in thoughtful spiels that combined lyricism with a deep-seated realism forged by his own experiences of urban ghettos. Gaines subsequently toured as part of **MTV**'s 'Free Your Mind' spoken-word tour, alongside Maggie Estep and John S. Hall of **King Missile**, before the release of his second album, *Sweeper Don't Clean My Street*. Cited by *Mojo* reviewer Lloyd Bradley as 'blues for the new millennium', it was another critical triumph.

● ALBUMS: *Please Don't Take My Air Jordans* (Mercury 1994) ★★★★, *Sweeper Don't Clean My Street* (Mercury 1995) ★★★.

Gaines, Roy

b. 12 August 1934, Houston, Texas, USA. The brother of **Grady Gaines**, Roy became interested in the electric guitar at an early age and began fraternizing with other local young blues guitarists such as Clarence Hollimon and **Johnny Copeland**. Gaines made his debut with an obscure release on the Miami-based Chart label before coming to the attention of local Houston band leader and head of Duke Records' house band, Bill Harvey. Gaines was featured with Harvey's band on various releases by **Big Mama Thornton** and **Bobby Bland** in 1955 for the Duke and Peacock labels, before being enticed away by an impressed **Chuck Willis**. After moving to New York City, Gaines recorded with Willis for **Atlantic Records** as well as signing to **RCA-Victor Records**' Groove subsidiary under his own name. This resulted in two releases in 1956. The following year he signed to DeLuxe, returned to Victor in 1958 and experienced a lean decade in the 60s with only two releases on the small Del-Fi and Uni labels. In the 70s, Gaines was again in demand, both for public appearances and as guitarist with the celebrated **Crusaders**. In 1981, Red Lightnin Records interrupted his busy touring schedule and recorded a fine album, *Gainelining*, which underlined Gaines' four decades of musical influence. Solo outings in subsequent decades included an excellent tribute to one of his heroes, **T-Bone Walker**.
● ALBUMS: *Gainelining* (Red Lightnin 1981) ★★★★, *Bluesman For Life* (JSP 1998) ★★★, *I Got The T-Bone Walker Blues* (Groove Note 1999) ★★★★, *New Frontier Lover* (Severn 2000) ★★★, *In The House* (CrossCut 2003) ★★★★.

Gainsbourg, Serge

b. Lucien Ginsburg, 2 April 1928, Paris, France, d. 2 March 1991, Paris, France. Gainsbourg was a frustrated painter who eked out a living as a bar pianist before joining the band hired for the musical *Milord L'Arsouville* starring Michèle Arnaud. Eventually given a reluctant singing role, his stage fright was interpreted by the audience as part of the act. His subsequent self-penned hit parade successes included 'Le Poinçonneur Des Lilas', 'La Chanson De Prévert' (an homage to the renowned French poet) and 'La Javanaise' but, an unlikely looking pop star with his heavy-lidded homeliness, he preferred to compose for others. More prestigious than his soundtrack work and songs for Régine, Valérie Lagrange and Dominique Walter were those commissioned by such as **Juliette Gréco**, **France Gall**, **Sacha Distel**, **Johnny Hallyday**, **Claude Francois** and also English language vocalists, **Petula Clark** and **Dionne Warwick**. 'Je T'Aime . . . Moi Non Plus' was written for Brigitte Bardot, with whom Gainsbourg was having an affair, but her management were unwilling to risk releasing a record that famously simulated the sounds of sexual congress.
Instead, Gainsbourg recorded it himself as an album track with English actress **Jane Birkin**, the 'constant companion' he had met on the set of the movie *Slogan*. Issued as a single in 1969, publicity earned via a BBC ban caused its abrupt deletion by **Fontana Records** but, unworried by moral opprobrium, other labels seized the opportunity to take up the slack as it swept to number 1 all over Europe and hovered

around the middle of the US Hot 100. It would enjoy a further few weeks in the UK Top 40 when reissued in 1974. Other Gainsbourg records were confined to home charts, with his pop genius managing to encompass subjects as diverse and shocking as Nazi death camps, incest, underage sex, farting and cabbages. The 1979 reggae outing *Aux Armes Et Caetera* earned particular notoriety for its Jamaican reworking of 'La Marseillaise'. The artist's occasional outrages on Gallic chat-shows, including one memorable live moment where he asked **Whitney Houston** if she would sleep with him, were thought newsworthy in those areas that remembered his erotic duet. The whole of France went into mourning when Gainsbourg, one of the country's national sons, suffered a fatal heart attack in March 1991. His work as a singer, songwriter, composer, actor, novelist, artist, photographer and screenwriter continues to influence.

● ALBUMS: *Du Chant À La Une!* 10-inch album (Philips 1958) ★★★, *No. 2* 10-inch album (Philips 1959) ★★★, *L'Étonnant Serge Gainsbourg* 10-inch album (Philips 1961) ★★★, *No. 4* 10-inch album (Philips 1962) ★★★, *Gainsbourg Confidentiel* (Philips 1964) ★★★, *Gainsbourg Percussions* (Philips 1964) ★★★, *Anna* film soundtrack (Philips 1967) ★★★, with Brigitte Bardot *Bonnie And Clyde* (Fontana 1968) ★★★, *Initials B.B.* (Philips 1968) ★★★, *Mister Freedom* film soundtrack (Barclay 1969) ★★★, with Jane Birkin *Jane Birkin/Serge Gainsbourg* (Fontana 1969) ★★★, *Cannabis* film soundtrack (Philips 1970) ★★★, *Histoire De Melody Nelson* (Philips 1971) ★★★★, *Vu De L'Extérieur* (Philips 1973) ★★★, *Rock Around The Bunker* (Philips 1975) ★★★, *L'Homme À Tête De Chou* (Philips 1976) ★★★★, *Je T'Aime . . . Moi Non Plus* film soundtrack (Philips 1976) ★★, *Madame Claude* film soundtrack (Philips 1977) ★★★, *Aux Armes Et Caetera* (Philips 1979) ★★★, *Enregistrement Public Au Théâtre Le Palace* (Philips 1980) ★★★, *Je Vous Aime* film soundtrack (Philips 1980) ★★★, *Mauvaises Nouvelles Des Étoiles* (Philips 1981) ★★★, *Love On The Beat* (Philips 1984) ★★★, *Live* (Philips 1986) ★★★, *Tenue De Soirée* film soundtrack (Apache/WEA 1986) ★★★, *You're Under Arrest* (Philips 1987) ★★★, *Le Zénith De Gainsbourg* (Philips 1989) ★★★.

● COMPILATIONS: *De Gainsbourg À Gainsbarre* 3-CD set (Philips 1989) ★★★, *De Gainsbourg À Gainsbarre* 9-CD box set (Philips 1989) ★★★, *Chansons Et Musiques De Film* (Hortensia 1990) ★★★, *Master Serie: Vol. 1* (Philips 1991) ★★★★, *Master Serie: Vol. 2* (Philips 1991) ★★★, *Master Serie: Vol. 3* (Philips 1991) ★★★, *Initials SG* (Mercury 2003) ★★★★★.

● DVD/VIDEOS: *D'Autres Nouvelles Des Etoiles* (Universal Music 2005).

● FURTHER READING: *Evguénie Sokolov*, Serge Gainsbourg. *Gainsbourg*, Micheline de Pierrefeu, Jean-Claude Maillard. *Gainsbourg Sans Filtre*, Marie-Dominique Lelièvre. *Gainsbourg Ou La Provocation Permanante*, Yves Salgues. *Gainsbourg: Le Livre Du Souvenir*, Bernard Pascuito. *Gainsbourg*, Gilles Verlant. *Gainsbourg Et Caetera*, Isabelle Salmon, Gilles Verlant. *Dernières Nouvelles Des Étoiles: L'Intégrale*, Serge Gainsbourg. *Serge Gainsbourg: View From The Exterior*, Allan Clayson. *Serge Gainsbourg: A Fistful Of Gitanes*, Sylvie Simmons.

● FILMS: *Voulez-Vous Danser Avec Moi?* aka *Come Dance With Me* (1959), *La Rivolta Degli Schiavi* aka *The Revolt Of The Slaves* (1961), *La Furia Di Ercole* aka *The Fury Of Hercules* (1961), *L'Inconnue De Hong Kong* (1963), *Le Jardinier D'Argenteuil* (1965), *Anna* (1965), *Estouffade À La Caraibe* aka *The Looters* (1966), *Vivre La Nuit* (1967), *Toutes Folles De Lui* (1967), *Le Pacha* (1967), *L'Inconnu De Shandigor* (1967), *Ce Sacré Grand-Père* aka *The Marriage Came Tumbling Down* (1967), *Paris N'Existe Pas* (1968), *Erotissimo* (1968), *Mister Freedom* (1969), *Slogan* (1969), *Les Chemins De Katmandou* aka *The Road To Katmandu* (1969), *Cannabis* aka *The Mafia Wants Your Blood* (1969), *Romance Of A Horsethief* (1971), *19 Djevojaka i Mornar* (1971), *Trop Jolies Pour Être Honnêtes* aka *Too Pretty To Be Honest* (1972), *Le Sex Shop* (1973), *La Morte Negli Occhi Del Gatto* aka *Seven Deaths In The Cat's Eye* (1973), *Sérieux Comme Le Plaisir* aka *Serious As Pleasure* (1974), *Je Vous Aime* aka *I Love You All* (1980), *Le Grand Pardon* (1981), *Charlotte For Ever* (1986).

Gaither, Bill (blues)

Gaither's first issued recordings were made in 1935. This session included an unissued tribute to **Leroy Carr**, who had died the same year, and Gaither, billed on many of his records as 'Leroy's Buddy', recorded a 'Life Of Leroy Carr' as late as 1940. Gaither's guitar playing was, not surprisingly, much in the manner of Carr's partner **Scrapper Blackwell**, while his regular pianist Honey Hill imitated Carr. Gaither's light, wistful voice continues the imitative process, as do his bittersweet lyrics, which sometimes contain interesting topical material. Evidently popular with contemporary black record buyers, and more of an original than his avowed indebtedness to his inspirations might suggest, Gaither nevertheless lacks both the musical variety and the poetic depth of Carr and Blackwell.

● COMPILATIONS: *Leroy's Buddy 1935–1941* (Magpie 1987) ★★★, *Leroy's Buddy 1936–1939* (Neovox 1990) ★★★.

Gaither, Bill (gospel)

b. 28 March 1936, Alexandria, Indiana, USA. One of the heavyweights behind the re-emergence of US gospel as a viable commercial force in contemporary music, Gaither's list of credits includes spells as a presenter, disc jockey and record/video compiler. In the latter respect he was responsible for the 'Gaither Gospel Series' of audio and video archive releases of the 90s, featuring several nearly forgotten southern gospel greats such as the Blackwoods and the **Speer Family**. He has also recorded prolifically with his wife Gloria as the Gaither Vocal Band and with the Bill Gaither Trio, which included his brother **Danny Gaither** (b. 20 November 1938, Alexandria, Indiana, USA, d. 6 April 2001, Indianapolis, Indiana, USA) and sister Mary Ann.

● ALBUMS: with Bill Gaither Trio *A Praise Gathering* (Starsong 1992) ★★★, with Gaither Vocal Band *Southern Classics, Vol. I* (Benson 1993) ★★★, with Gaither Vocal Band *Testify* (Spring House 1995) ★★★, *Reunion* (Starsong 1995) ★★★, *All Day Singin' With Dinner On The Ground* (Chordant 1995) ★★★, with Gaither Vocal Band *Southern Classics, Vol. 2* (Chordant 1996) ★★★, *Sing Your Blues Away* (Chordant 1996) ★★★, *Homecoming Texas Style* (Spring House 1996) ★★★, *Moments To Remember* (Chordant 1996) ★★★, *Ryman Gospel Reunion* (Chordant 1996) ★★★, *Joy To The World* (Chordant 1997) ★★★, *Joy In The Camp* (Chordant 1997) ★★★, *Atlanta Homecoming: All Day Singing At The Dome, Vol. I* live (Chordant 1998) ★★★, with Gaither Vocal Band *Still The Greatest Story Ever Told* (Chordant 1998) ★★★, *Down By The Tabernacle*

(Spring House 1998) ★★★, *Favorite Hymns Of The Homecoming Friends* (Spring House 1999) ★★★, with Bill Gaither Trio *Hymn Classics* (Word 1999) ★★★, with Gaither Vocal Band *God Is Good* (Spring House 1999) ★★★, *Mountain Homecoming* (Spring House 1999) ★★★, *Kennedy Center Homecoming* live (Spring House 1999) ★★★, with Gaither Vocal Band *I Do Believe* (Spring House 2000) ★★★, *Christmas In The Country* (Spring House 2000) ★★★, *Bill Gaither Trio, Vols. 1–4* (Benson 2000) ★★★, *Christmas: A Time For Joy* (Spring House 2001) ★★★, *Let Freedom Ring: Live From Carnegie Hall* (Spring House 2002) ★★★, with Gaither Vocal Band *Everything Good* (Spring House 2002) ★★★, *Freedom Band* (Spring House 2002) ★★★, *God Bless America* (Spring House 2002) ★★★, *Heaven* (Spring House 2003) ★★★, with Gaither Vocal Band *A Cappella* (Spring House 2003) ★★★.

● COMPILATIONS: *Classic Moments From The Gaither Vocal Band, Vols. I & II* (Benson 2000) ★★★, *Gaither Vocal Band & The Bill Gaither Trio* 2-CD set (Madacy Christian 2001) ★★★, *Best Of The Gaither Vocal Band* (Spring House 2004) ★★★.

● DVD/VIDEOS: *I'll Meet You On The Mountain* (Spring House Video 1999), *Mountain Homecoming* (Spring House Video 1999), *Memphis Homecoming* (Spring House Video 2000), *Bill Gaither's All Time Favorite Homecoming Songs And Performances, Vol. 1 & 2* (Gaither Music Video 2004), *A Tribute To Howard & Vestal Goodman* (Gaither Music Video 2004), *A Tribute To Jake Hess* (Gaither Music Video 2004), *Journey To The Sky* (Spring House Video 2004), *Passin' The Faith Along* (Spring House Video 2004), *Church In The Wildwood* (Gaither Music Video 2004), *Hymns* (Gaither Music Video 2004), *Israel Homecoming* (Gaither Music Video 2005), *A Tribute To George Younce* (Spring House Video 2005).

● FURTHER READING: *Because He Lives: The Stories And Inspiration Behind The Songs*, Gloria Gaither.

Gaither, Danny

b. 20 November 1938, Alexandria, Virginia, USA, d. 6 April 2001, Indianapolis, Indiana, USA. Gospel singer Danny Gaither began singing for communal audiences at the age of three—his mother accompanying him on the piano. Eventually he was joined by brother **Bill Gaither**, as well as his cousin, until that relation was replaced by sister Mary Ann. The trio, still accompanied by their mother, toured and played widely until each attended college. When they resumed the group in 1970 as a full-time touring ensemble, the Bill Gaither Trio rose to become one of gospel music's most famous groups. However, in 1977 Danny left the group in order to record solo. He made his debut with *Singing To The World* for Impact Records in 1977. For his third collection, *Sing A Song Of Love*, he began work with producer Joe Huffman of Nashville company Benson (who own Impact). At this time he also convened his own backing group, and set out on the type of rigorous touring schedule that had been such a large part of the Bill Gaither Trio's activities. He died after a five-year battle with lymphoma.

● ALBUMS: *Singing To The World* (Impact 1977) ★★★, *It Is Well With My Soul* (Impact 1977) ★★★, *Sing A Song Of Love* (Impact 1978) ★★★★, *Sweet And High* (Impact 1979) ★★★.

Galactic

Despite being responsible for such funky sounds, Galactic's founding members, Jeff Raines (guitar) and Robert Mercurio (bass), were originally in Washington DC, USA–based punk bands. It was only after relocating to New Orleans, Louisiana, that the duo began playing the funk and soul inflected sounds closely associated with the area (the **Meters**, the **Neville Brothers**, **Dr. John**). Rounding out the line-up soon after were Rich Vogel (organ), Ben Ellman and Jason Mingeldorff (saxophone), Stanton Moore (drums), and Theryl 'The Houseman' de'Clouet (vocals). It did not take long for them to gain a local following, which soon spread to include the jam band crowd, as well.

A recording contract with the Capricorn label followed, as did 1996's reissue of *Coolin' Off* (originally issued as an independent release) and 1998's *Crazyhorse Mongoose*. Although both recordings failed to trouble the charts, they did touch off a strong cult following that became further solidified owing to the band's incessant touring. Similarly styled releases followed, including 2000's *Late For The Future* and the band's first official in-concert set, 2001's *We Love 'Em Tonight: Live At Tipitina's*, before Galactic decided to experiment with their sound. Incorporating elements of hip-hop and electronic music into their already rich sound, the band unveiled *Ruckus* during late 2003. Earlier the same year, a 15-track career overview, *Vintage Reserve*, appeared. As if their recording/touring schedule was not busy enough, the members of Galactic also guested on a large list of recordings by other artists, in addition to solo releases by de'Clouet (2001's *The Houseman Cometh!*) and Moore (1998's *All Kooked Out!* and 2001's *Flyin' The Koop*).

● ALBUMS: *Coolin' Off* (Capricorn 1996) ★★★, *Crazyhorse Mongoose* (Capricorn 1998) ★★★, *Late For The Future* (Capricorn 2000) ★★★, *We Love 'Em Tonight: Live At Tipitina's* (Volcano 2001) ★★★★, *Ruckus* (Sanctuary 2003) ★★★★.

● COMPILATIONS: *Vintage Reserve* (Volcano 2003) ★★★★.

Galactic Cowboys

This US metallic art-rock quartet was formed in 1990 by vocalist Ben Huggins and guitarist Dane Sonnier. With the addition of bass player Monty Colvin and drummer Alan Doss, they specialized in complex and densely melodic song structures that typically exceeded the six-minute mark. Combining elements of **King's X**, **Metallica** and **Neil Young** with state-of-the-art technology, they produced one of 1991's most impressive debut albums. Defying simple categorization, they surprised the listener with what initially seemed the *ad hoc* juxtaposition of incompatible styles. Somehow, the strange fusion worked, manic thrashing giving way to harmonica solos, which in turn were followed by four-part vocal harmonies. The Galactic Cowboys' flair for innovation was further confirmed by 1993's *Space In Your Face*, a second chapter in what promises to be an intriguing career. Following their departure from MCA, they signed to the specialist label Metal Blade and produced a highly commercial album, *Machine Fish*. Sonnier was replaced by Wally Farkas.

● ALBUMS: *Galactic Cowboys* (MCA 1991) ★★★★, *Space In Your Face* (MCA 1993) ★★★, *Machine Fish* (Metal Blade 1996) ★★★, *The Horse That Bud Bought* (Metal Blade 1997) ★★★.

Galas, Diamanda

b. 29 August 1955, San Diego, California, USA. A confrontational writer whose glass-shattering, pristine vocals are derived from the Schrei (shriek) opera of German expressionism where 'sounds become corporal and movements aural'. On stage this is achieved with the aid of four microphones and a system of delays and echoes. Galas is a classically trained Greek American who released her debut *The Litanies Of Satan* on Y Records in 1982, before moving on to **Mute Records**. Her self-titled 1984 album is typical, comprising two 'endless plays of pain'. 'Panoptikon' deals with Jeremy Bentham's harrowing prison regime, while 'Song From The Blood Of Those Murdered' is dedicated to the Greek women killed by the Junta between 1967 and 1974. *The Divine Punishment, Saint Of The Pit* and *You Must Be Certain Of The Devil* comprise the *Masque Of The Red Death* trilogy, written in response to her brother's death from AIDS. Galas has since produced a series of albums dominated by her remarkable banshee-like delivery, rooted more in performance art than any notions of popular music.

● ALBUMS: *The Litanies Of Satan* (Y 1982) ★★★, *Diamanda Galas* (Metalanguage 1984) ★★★★, *The Divine Punishment* (Mute 1986) ★★★, *Saint Of The Pit* (Mute 1986) ★★★, *You Must Be Certain Of The Devil* (Mute 1988) ★★★, *Plague Mass* (Mute 1991) ★★★, *The Singer* (Mute 1992) ★★★, *Vena Cava* (Mute 1993) ★★★, with John Paul Jones *The Sporting Life* (Mute 1994) ★★★, *Schrei X* (Mute 1996) ★★★, *Schrei X Live* (Mute 1996) ★★★, *Malediction And Prayer* (Mute 1998) ★★★, *La Serpenta Canta* (Mute 2003) ★★★, *Defixiones, Will And Testament* (Mute 2003) ★★★.

● COMPILATIONS: *Masque Of The Red Death* (Mute 1988) ★★★.

● DVD/VIDEOS: *The Litanies Of Satan* (Target Video), *Judgement Day* (Mute Film/Atavistic Video).

Galaxie 500

Ex-Harvard College alumni Dean Wareham (b. New Zealand; guitar/vocals), Naomi Yang (bass/vocals) and Damon Krukowski (drums) formed this group (named after an American car) in Boston, Massachusetts, USA. Having released one track, 'Obvious', on a flexi-disc given away with the magazine *Chemical Imbalance*, they moved to New York. Maverick producer **Kramer** allowed the trio's brittle amateurism to flourish on *Today*, wherein Wareham's plaintive voice and scratchy guitar work inspired comparisons with the **Velvet Underground** and **Jonathan Richman**. A version of the latter's 'Don't Let Our Youth Go To Waste' was featured on this engaging set that inspired **Rough Trade Records** to sign the band. *On Fire* continued their established *métier*, and a growing self-confidence imbued the songs with resonance and atmosphere. *This Is Our Music* provided a greater emphasis on light and shade, sacrificing some of Yang's silky bass lines for traditional dynamism. A cover version of **Yoko Ono**'s 'Listen, The Snow Is Falling' proved captivating, but the set lacked the warmth of its predecessors.

Rumours of internal disaffection proved true when Wareham left in 1991. He subsequently formed the enthralling Luna 2, later known simply as **Luna**. His former Galaxie 500 partners continued as Pierre Etoile, issuing a self-titled EP in August, then simply **Damon And Naomi**. After releasing a 1992 album (*More Sad Hits*), Yang and Krukowski collaborated with Kate

Biggar of Crystallised Movements as Magic Hour. The duo released another album with Kramer, 1995's *The Wondrous World Of . . .*, before concentrating on their publishing company Exact Change. In 1996, they issued a box set containing the entire recorded output of Galaxie 500, and returned to the studio two years later with the self-produced *Playback Singers*.

● ALBUMS: *Today* (Aurora 1989) ★★, *On Fire* (Rough Trade 1989) ★★★, *This Is Our Music* (Rough Trade 1990) ★★★, *Copenhagen* 1990 live recording (Rykodisc 1997) ★★★.

● COMPILATIONS: *1987–1991* 4-CD box set (Rykodisc 1996) ★★★, *The Portable Galaxie 500* (Rykodisc 1998) ★★★, *Uncollected* (Rykodisc 2004) ★★★, *Peel Sessions* (20/20/20 2005) ★★★.

● DVD/VIDEOS: *Don't Let Our Youth Go To Waste: 1987–1991* (Plexifilm 2004).

Galbán, Manuel

b. 1931, Gibara, Cuba. Galbán's father and two brothers played guitar and tres (an adapted guitar), and as a small child he picked up the rudiments by watching and listening. Before he was 10 years old he had also begun to play piano. In mid-1944, a band was formed in his home village. This was the Orquesta Villa Blanca, and its personnel included Galbán and three of his brothers. At first he played guitar but later also played piano with the band. Early in 1963, Galbán joined the recently formed doo-wop group **Los Zafiros** and for 10 years was their musical director, guitarist, pianist and arranger. After many years of productive work in music, Galbán retired but following the success of **The Buena Vista Social Club** (1997), he appeared on several albums made by other participants in that film, among them **Ibrahim Ferrer**, with whom he also toured, **Orlando 'Cachaíto' López, Eliades Ochoa** and **Omara Portuondo**; he also appeared on *Calle Segundo* by **Compay Segundo**. This resumed activity led to a musical association with **Ry Cooder** that resulted in *Mambo Sinuendo*, which won the 2004 Grammy Award for Best Pop instrumental album. A highly rhythmic guitarist who plays with the fire and dash expected of a leading exponent of Cuban music, Galbán has also made a significant contribution to keeping alive and relevant the music of Cuba's vibrant past.

● ALBUMS: with Ry Cooder *Mambo Sinuendo* (Perro Verde/Nonesuch 2003) ★★★★.

Galbreath, Frank

b. 2 September 1913, Roberson County, North Carolina, USA, d. November 1971. Galbreath began playing trumpet as a young teenager, working in bands in Washington, DC. During the next few years he gained experience playing in bands in the south-eastern states and along the east coast until, in the early 30s, he visited Chicago and New York. During the rest of the decade he played in bands led by **Fletcher Henderson, Jelly Roll Morton, Lucky Millinder, Louis Armstrong** and many others, mostly in New York. After military service during World War II, Galbreath played in the bands of **Willie Bryant, Tab Smith, Sy Oliver** and others, then in 1948 rejoined Millinder, this time for over three years, and then was with **Snub Mosley** for a USO tour that brought him to the UK and Europe. Between tours he also led his own band and accompanied musicians such as **Benny Goodman**, and backed singers including **Ray Charles, Fats**

Domino and **Sammy Davis Jnr.** During the mid-60s he was resident in Atlantic City, continuing to play until a year or so before his death. Not renowned as a soloist, Galbreath provided able backing to many more gifted musicians and was also a strong ensemble voice in the bands with which he played.

Gale, Eric

b. 20 September 1938, Brooklyn, New York City, USA, d. 25 May 1994, Baja California, Mexico. Gale studied chemistry at Niagara University. He took up the double bass when he was 12 years old and also played tenor saxophone, trombone and tuba before he chose the guitar. The basis of his style was formed on the 50s and 60s R&B circuit. He was with the **Drifters**, **Jackie Wilson**, the **Flamingos** and **Maxine Brown**, before playing in the 60s with **King Curtis**, **Jimmy Smith**, **David 'Fathead' Newman**, **Mongo Santamaría** and **Aretha Franklin**. In the early 70s Gale became the house guitarist with **Creed Taylor**'s new **CTI Records** label and worked with **Stanley Turrentine**'s band. He took four years off on his Ohio farm and went to Jamaica where he assimilated the reggae style. On his return to New York in 1976 he was a founder of the influential funk band **Stuff** along with artists including **Steve Gadd**, **Cornell Dupree** and **Richard Tee**. They played regularly at Mikell's in Manhattan with only minimal rehearsal. In the early 90s he performed as a regular band member in several US television shows. Gale thought like a frontline musician and played like a saxophonist.

● ALBUMS: *Forecast* (Kudu 1975) ★★★, *Ginseng Woman* (Columbia 1976) ★★★, *Multiplication* (Columbia 1978) ★★★, *Part Of You* (Columbia 1979) ★★★, *Touch Of Silk* (Columbia 1980) ★★, *Blue Horizon* (Elektra 1981) ★★★, *Island Breeze* (Elektra 1982) ★★, *In A Jazz Tradition* (EmArcy 1987) ★★★.

● COMPILATIONS: *The Best Of Eric Gale* (Columbia 1980) ★★★.

Galeforce

US rock band Galeforce took their name from the surnames of the brothers who gave them their creative thrust—Len Gale (vocals/drums) and Ken Gale (guitar). Together with Sneaky Pete (guitar), Bobby Lyle (keyboards) and Charlie Souza (bass), they made their debut with a self-titled collection for **Fantasy Records** in 1978. The group's tough, high-spirited blues rock style earned immediate comparisons to **Bad Company**, though Len Gale's place behind the drum kit limited his ambitions to emulate **Paul Rodgers**. Nevertheless, *Gale Force* remains an impressive achievement, despite its commercial misfortune.

● ALBUMS: *Gale Force* (Fantasy 1978) ★★★.

Gall, France

b. Isabelle Gall, 9 October 1947, Paris, France. Gall's grandfather, Daniel Berthier, was a choirmaster and her father, Roger Gall, a composer whose output included songs such as 'La Mamma' for **Charles Aznavour**, 'A Bientot Nous Deux' for Hugues Auffray—and the litany 'Sacre Charlemagne', his flaxen-haired daughter's first hit-parade entry. She would owe continued record success to **Serge Gainsbourg**, a family friend who wrote the typically suggestive 'Poupée De Cire, Poupée De Son' and 'Les Sucettes' for her 'little girl' mezzo soprano. Her singing career was stabilized by a victory (under the Luxembourg banner) in 1965's

Eurovision Song Contest singing the former. Gall's other Gallic chartbusters include 'N'Écoute Pas Les Idoles', 'Attends Ou Va T'En', 'L'Amérique' and 'La Petite', the latter a coy duet with Maurice Biraud, but she was ultimately more successful on the German market. Her later records diversified into cloying soft pop and disco, and included collaborations with **Elton John** (1980's 'Les Aveux') and her husband **Michel Berger**.

● ALBUMS: *Sacre Charlemagne* 10-inch album (Philips 1965) ★★★, *France Gall* (Philips 1965) ★★★, *Baby Pop* (Philips 1966) ★★★, *1968* (Philips 1968) ★★, *Die Grossen Erfolge* (Decca 1968) ★★★, *France Gall* (Atlantic 1975) ★★★, *Dancing Disco* (Atlantic 1977) ★★, *Paris, France* (WEA 1980) ★★, *Tout Pour La Musique* (WEA 1981) ★★, *Débranche!* (WEA 1984) ★★, *Au Zénith* (WEA 1984) ★★, *Babacar* (WEA/Apache 1987) ★★★, *Le Tour De France '88* (WEA/Apache 1988) ★★, with Michel Berger *Double Jeu* (WEA/Apache 1992) ★★★, *Simple Je: Débranchée À Bercy 93* (WEA/Apache 1993) ★★, *Simple Je: Rébranchée À Bercy 93* (WEA/Apache 1994) ★★, *Concert Public* (WEA/Apache 1996) ★★★, *France* (WEA 1996) ★★★, *Concert Acoustique* (WEA/Apache 1997) ★★★.

● COMPILATIONS: *France Gall* (Apache 1988) ★★★, *Les Années Musique* (WEA 1990) ★★★, *Poupée De Son* 4-CD set (Polydor 1992) ★★★, *Les Plus Belles Chansons De France Gall* (WEA 1994) ★★★, *Master Série* (Bar 2000) ★★★.

Gallagher And Lyle

Benny Gallagher (vocals/guitar) and Graham Lyle (vocals/guitar) were both born in Largs, Ayrshire, Scotland. Having sung with several nascent beat groups, they began a songwriting career with 'Mr. Heartbreak's Here Instead', a 1964 single for Dean Ford And The Gaylords. The duo later moved to London where they joined the Apple label as in-house composers. One of their songs, 'International', was recorded by **Mary Hopkin**. In 1969 the pair joined **McGuinness Flint**, for whom they wrote two successful singles, 'When I'm Dead And Gone' (1970) and 'Malt And Barley Blues' (1971), before leaving the group for an independent career. Several well-crafted, if low-key, albums followed, which showcased the duo's flair for folk-styled melody, but it was not until 1976 that they enjoyed a commercial breakthrough. *Breakaway* spawned two major hits in 'I Wanna Stay With You' and 'Heart On My Sleeve', both of which reached number 6 in the UK. Further recognition of their compositional talents was endorsed by **Art Garfunkel** taking a cover version of the album's title track into the US Top 40, but the act was curiously unable to sustain its newfound profile. Gallagher and Lyle parted following the release of *Lonesome No More* in order to pursue different projects. Graham Lyle later found a new partner, Terry Britten, with whom he composed 'What's Love Got To Do With It' and 'Just Good Friends' which were recorded, respectively, by **Tina Turner** and **Michael Jackson**. Both have continued successful careers as songwriters.

● ALBUMS: *Gallagher And Lyle* (A&M 1972) ★★, *Willie And The Lap Dog* (A&M 1973) ★★, *Seeds* (A&M 1973) ★★, *The Last Cowboy* (A&M 1974) ★★★, *Breakaway* (A&M 1976) ★★★, *Love On The Airwaves* (A&M 1977) ★★, *Showdown* (A&M 1978) ★★, *Gone Crazy* (A&M 1979) ★★, *Lonesome No More* (Mercury 1979) ★★, *Live In Concert* (Strange Fruit 1999) ★★.

● COMPILATIONS: *The Best Of Gallagher And Lyle* (A&M 1980) ★★★, *Heart On My Sleeve* (A&M 1991) ★★★, *The Best Of Gallagher And Lyle* (Spectrum 1998) ★★★.

Gallagher And Shean

Gallagher (b. Edward Gallagher, 1873, San Francisco, California, USA, d. 28 May 1929, Astoria, New York City, USA) and Shean (b. Alfred Schoenberg, 12 May 1868, Dornum, Germany, d. 12 August 1949, New York City, USA, were a popular vaudeville double act of the 20s, and appeared notably in some of the spectacular shows of **Florenz Ziegfeld**. Many of the shows in which Shean appeared were on Broadway and include the short-lived *The Fisher Maiden* (1903) and *The Rose Maid* (1912), in which he teamed up with Gallagher. Two years on from this, the pair fell out and split up their act. Shean's sister, Minnie Marx, mother of the **Marx Brothers**, brought them together again in 1920. They were hired by Ziegfeld but the **Shubert Brothers** brought legal action against them, claiming that their act was 'unique and irreplaceable', a claim which Gallagher and Shean refuted, insisting instead that they were merely mediocre.

Regardless of their (presumably tongue-in-cheek) counter-claim they became hugely popular on Broadway, notably in *Ziegfeld Follies* of 1922, in which they introduced their hit song, 'Mister Gallagher And Mister Shean'. In passing, according to a Mark Hellinger newspaper piece in 1926, that song was written by Brian Foy, son of **Eddie Foy**, for which he was remunerated with the gift of a cigarette case. For a purple patch that lasted about five years, the team retained their popularity; one of their verbal exchanges could be heard in everyday conversations: 'Positively, Mr Gallagher. Absolutely, Mr Shean.' By 1926, however, the act had broken up again and Gallagher was throwing wild parties and drinking heavily. In time, the parties stopped but the drinking did not; Gallagher lived a few more years as a recluse, broke but supported by his first wife, whom he had earlier abandoned, and cared for by a manservant he could not afford to pay. After his former partner's death, Shean appeared in mostly short-lived plays such as *The Prince Of Pilsen* and *Light Wines And Beer* (both 1930), *Music In The Air* (1932), *Father Malachy's Miracle* (1937), *Popsy* (1941), *Meet A Body* (1944) and *Doctor Social*, which had only a three-day run in October 1948.

Gallagher, Benny
(see **Gallagher And Lyle**)

Gallagher, Ed
(see **Gallagher And Shean**)

Gallagher, Helen

b. 19 July 1926, New York City, USA. Gallagher started out as a dancer, appearing in the chorus of *Seven Lively Arts* (1944), her first time on Broadway. In a similar capacity she appeared in *Billion Dollar Baby* (1945) and then had a bigger role, this time an acting one, in **High Button Shoes** (1947). She was again in the ensemble for **Brigadoon** (1947), but soon thereafter began to improve her standing with audiences thanks to playing in *Touch And Go* (1949) in New York and the following year in the London production. Her roles in the early 50s included Poupette in *Make A Wish* (1951) and Gladys in the 1952 revival of **Pal Joey**. For the

latter she received a **Tony Award** as Best Featured Actress In A Musical. Gallagher played the lead in *Hazel Flagg* (1953), but the show was a failure. She made appearances in revivals of **The Pajama Game** (1954), **Finian's Rainbow** (1955) and *Brigadoon* (1957). This was followed by a leading role in *Portofino* (1958), but this was another flop and retirement followed.

Gallagher came back in 1966 for **Sweet Charity** and although she was in the same year's **Mame**, good roles usually eluded her, witness an appearance as Bessie Legg in the 1970 flop *Cry For Us All*. In the following year, however, Gallagher was back on top as Lucille in a revival of **No, No, Nanette**. The show was a big hit, as was Gallagher, who won another Tony award. She was involved in a performance of *Much Ado About Nothing* that ran in the winter of 1972/3. Gallagher was among several leading ladies of Broadway who appeared at Brothers And Sisters, a New York nightclub on West 46th Street, in 1974, although as James Gavin reports in his book, *Intimate Nights*, she did not endear herself to the audience by refusing to sing any of the songs for which she was known, declaring that she had forgotten them and that to relearn them would have been boring. In 1978 she was responsible for the choreography in *The American Dance Machine*. On into the 80s and beyond, Gallagher took acting roles in television soaps, and played in off-Broadway musicals.

● FILMS: *Strangers When We Meet* (1960), *Roseland* (1977), *Neptune's Rocking Horse* (1997).

Gallagher, Rory

b. 2 March 1948, Ballyshannon, Co. Donegal, Eire, d. 14 June 1995, London, England. Having served his musical apprenticeship in the Fontana and Impact Showbands, Gallagher put together the original **Taste** in 1965. This exciting blues-based rock trio rose from regional obscurity to the verge of international fame, but broke up acrimoniously five years later. Gallagher was by then a guitar hero and embarked on a solo voyage supported by Gerry McAvoy (bass) and Wilgar Campbell (drums). He introduced an unpretentious approach, which marked a career that deftly retained all the purpose of the blues without erring on the side of excessive reverence. Gallagher's early influences were **Lonnie Donegan**, **Woody Guthrie**, **Chuck Berry** and **Muddy Waters**, and he strayed very little from those paths. The artist's refreshing blues guitar work, which featured his confident bottleneck playing, was always of interest, and by 1972 Gallagher was a major live attraction. Campbell was replaced by Rod De'ath following the release of *Live In Europe*, while Lou Martin was added on keyboards.

This line-up remained constant for the next six years and was responsible for Gallagher's major commercial triumphs, *Blueprint* and *Irish Tour*. De'ath and Martin left the group in 1978. Former **Sensational Alex Harvey Band** drummer Ted McKenna joined the ever-present McAvoy but was in turn replaced by Brendan O'Neill. Former **Nine Below Zero** member and blues harmonica virtuoso Mark Feltham became a full-time 'guest', as Gallagher quietly continued with his career.

Shunning the glitzy aspect of the music business, Gallagher toured America over 30 times in addition to touring the globe twice. His record sales reached several millions and he retained a fiercely loyal following. He had several opportunities to record with his heroes, such as Donegan, Waters,

Jerry Lee Lewis and Albert King, and his love for his homeland resulted in contributions to the work of the Fureys, Davy Spillane and Joe O'Donnell. Gallagher retained his perennial love for the blues, his original Stratocaster guitar (now badly battered) and the respect of many for his uncompromising approach. Shy and without any enemies, he died following complications after a liver transplant in 1995. Since his death most of his back catalogue has been remastered and this has led to the obligatory reappraisal. He sang with great heart and could play his Stratocaster like a familiar demon, with both sounding effortlessly natural. He was, like many others, under-appreciated during his lifetime.

● ALBUMS: *Rory Gallagher* (Polydor 1971) ★★★, *Deuce* (Polydor 1971) ★★★★, *Live! In Europe* (Polydor 1972) ★★★, *Blueprint* (Polydor 1973) ★★★★, *Tattoo* (Polydor 1973) ★★★★, *Irish Tour 74* (Polydor 1974) ★★★★, *Saint . . . And Sinner* (Polydor 1975) ★★★, *Against The Grain* (Chrysalis 1975) ★★★★, *Calling-Card* (Chrysalis 1976) ★★★★, *Photo Finish* (Chrysalis 1978) ★★★, *Top Priority* (Chrysalis 1978) ★★★, *Stage Struck* (Chrysalis 1980) ★★★, *Jinx* (Chrysalis 1982) ★★★, *Defender* (Demon 1987) ★★, *Fresh Evidence* (Castle 1990) ★★, *BBC Sessions* (RCA 1999) ★★★★.

● COMPILATIONS: *The Best Years* (Polydor 1973) ★★★, *In The Beginning* (Emerald 1974) ★★★, *The Story So Far* (Polydor 1976) ★★★, *Best Of Rory Gallagher And Taste* (Razor 1988) ★★★★, *Edged In Blue* (Demon 1992) ★★★, *A Blue Day For The Blues* (I.R.S. 1995) ★★★, *Let's Go To Work* 4-CD box set (Capo/RCA 2001) ★★★★, *Wheels Within Wheels* (Capo/RCA 2003) ★★★★, *Meeting With The G-Man* (BMG 2004) ★★★, *Big Guns: The Very Best Of Rory Gallagher* (BMG 2005) ★★★★.

● DVD/VIDEOS: *Live In Cork* (Castle Hendring Video 1989), *Messin' With The Kid: Live At The Cork Opera House* (BMG 1999), *At Rockpalast* (Studio Hamburg 2004).

● FURTHER READING: *Rory Gallagher*, Jean Noel Coghe.

Galliano

This sprawling UK outfit enjoyed a fruitful period in the spotlight at the height of acid jazz's popularity in the late 80s and early 90s. The band was formed by new-age rapper and jazz poet Rob Gallagher (b. 1966, England), who was originally inspired by a school visit to see Linton Kwesi Johnson and subsequently retraced rap's origins to the Last Poets. When he left school Gallagher began broadcasting on pirate radio and made appearances on the underground poetry circuit. The most important of these dates was at Gilles Peterson's Babylon club in Charing Cross, London. There he enthusiastically partook of the resident rare groove/jazz sounds, and incorporated these as his musical backing. He released his first record, 'Frederick Lies Still', a tribute to Curtis Mayfield and Last Poets' Jalal Nuridin, with Peterson, but his first vinyl as Galliano was to be 'Welcome To The Story'. Galliano became an intrinsic component in the rise of Acid Jazz Records, building a fruitful relationship with producer Chris Bangs.

When Peterson was headhunted by Phonogram Records to set up the similarly inclined Talkin' Loud Records label, Galliano was his first signing. Although his solo work had thus far been successful, he elected to extend his live and studio performances by adding musicians and collaborators. Vocalist Constantine Weir (who had sung with S'Express' and managed the 70s funk club The Shack) and percussionist

Brother Spry (b. Crispin Robinson; formerly a professional skateboarder and an experienced session musician) became official members of Galliano, and Jalal Nuridin made occasional appearances. Aided by former Style Council member Mick Talbot, this line-up completed Galliano's 1991 debut. The excellent follow-up, *A Joyful Noise Unto The Creator*, featured the minor hit singles 'Skunk Funk' and 'Prince Of Peace'. Galliano extended their cult reputation by touring incessantly throughout the world, thrilling crowds with their inspirational live shows.

By this point, the line-up boasted Gallagher, Talbot, Brother Spry, Valerie Étienne (vocals), Ernie McKone (bass), Crispin Taylor (drums), Mark Vandergucht (guitar), Brother Constantine (vocals), and Daddy Smith (vibe controller). The 1994 UK Top 20 single, 'Long Time Gone', based on the David Crosby song, was the band's first release in over two years. The subsequent album *The Plot Thickens* was acclaimed, despite mainstream critics who had only just noticed the band somewhat cumbersomely describing their sound as an acid jazz/funk/urban alternative. The album was to prove their commercial highpoint, however, as acid jazz's popularity waned and returned to the small clubs and clique status from whence it had risen. Following the release of a fourth album and a live set, the various members have concentrated on solo projects. Of particular note are Gallagher's recordings under the Earl Zinger moniker.

● ALBUMS: *In Pursuit Of The 13th Note* (Talkin' Loud 1991) ★★★, *A Joyful Noise Unto The Creator* (Talkin' Loud 1992) ★★★★, *What Colour Our Flag* US only (Talkin' Loud/ PolyGram 1994) ★★★, *The Plot Thickens* (Talkin' Loud 1994) ★★★★, *4* (Talkin' Loud 1996) ★★★, *Live At The Liquid Rooms* (Talkin' Loud 1997) ★★★.

Galliano, Frederic

b. 23 December 1969, Grenoble, France. The DJ, producer and remixer Galliano blends West African roots sounds with the styles of contemporary dance music. He played drums and keyboards in a jazz group for three years and then started to work as a DJ. He first heard African music listening to late-night shows on French State radio and was drawn to the rootsy, traditional style of artists such as Oumou Sangaré. Galliano initially began remixing African music in order to supply himself with modern dance-friendly African tunes to play in his DJ set. Founding his own Frikyiwa (pronounced Freaky Wah) label, he released a series of 12-inch singles containing tracks by West African artists. The tracks were collected from the vaults of the highly respected Paris-based world music label Cobalt and remixed by various dub, house and drum 'n' bass DJs. The first Frikyiwa release featured Neba Solo with one side produced by Galliano and the other by Jeff Sharel. However on subsequent releases Galliano acted only as artistic director, choosing the track and the remixer. In spite of this, Frikyiwa has developed a strongly identifiable sound, in which both the traditional African elements and the electronic dance beats are strong and uncompromised. *Frikyiwa Collection 1* is a compilation of nine of the tracks that originally appeared on 12-inch single, including excellent remixes of tracks by Nahaw Doumbia and Lobi Traoré. It was followed by a second volume of remixes.

● COMPILATIONS: *Frikyiwa Collection 1* (Frikyiwa 2000) ★★★★, *Frikyiwa Collection 2* (Frikyiwa 2000) ★★★.

Galliards
(see Hall, Robin, And Jimmie MacGregor; Rosselson, Leon)

Gallinger, Karen
b. Venice, California, USA. A powerful singer with a commanding style and a richly expressive voice with a husky undertone, she remains little known outside the west coast environs in which she mostly works. In a branch of music that was inundated with new singers at the beginning of the new century, it is hard to forecast her future, but, given the breaks, she has the ability to carve a successful career. Her second and third albums, the latter a vocal tribute to **Bill Evans**, received favourable reviews.
● ALBUMS: *Live At The Jazz Bakery* (Sea Breeze 1994) ★★★, *My Foolish Heart* (Sea Breeze 1999) ★★★, *Remembering Bill Evans: A Vocal Tribute* (Sea Breeze 2000) ★★★★.

Gallion, Bob
b. 22 April 1929, Ashland, Kentucky, USA, d. 20 August 1999. Gallion began his career as a guitarist in the late 40s. He played in various clubs and honky tonks until 1952, when he became the vocalist with **Stoney Cooper And Wilma Lee**'s band. He appeared with their Clinch Mountain Clan at various venues, including the WWVA *Wheeling Jamboree* in West Virginia. In the mid-50s, when offered a recording contract with **MGM Records**, he decided to pursue a solo career. Singing mainly honky tonk country and occasional rockabilly tracks, he worked on the *Louisiana Hayride* at Shreveport but eventually relocated to Nashville, guested on the *Grand Ole Opry* and worked tours with other singers. He gained his first chart successes in 1958/9 with 'That's What I Tell My Heart' and 'You Take The Table And I'll Take The Chairs'. In 1960, after joining **Acuff-Rose Music**, he moved to the Hickory label and immediately scored a Top 10 with 'Loving You Was Worth This Broken Heart' and followed up with two Top 20 hits 'One Way Street' and 'Sweethearts Again'. In 1962, he gained his biggest chart hit, a number 5, with 'Wall To Wall Love'. He gradually turned more and more towards disc jockey work and after moving his centre of operations to Georgia, he spent six years on WGUN Atlanta. He recorded for **United Artists Records** in 1968, gaining his last solo chart entry with 'Pick A Little Happy Song'. He also decided to return to the *Wheeling Jamboree*, where he became a featured artist until 1983. During this time, he often toured with Patti Powell. They recorded together, registered a minor hit with 'Love By Appointment' in 1973 and later made an album for Starday. Gallion gradually phased out most of his performing and instead headed Bob Gallion Productions, a booking agency that operated in Wheeling but dealt with tours for many acts as well as those playing the *Jamboree*.
● ALBUMS: *Bob Gallion And Patti Powell—Together And Alone* (B&P 1975) ★★★, *Bob Gallion & Patti Powell—Greatest Hits* (Starday-Gusto 1978) ★★★★.
● COMPILATIONS: *Out Of A Honky Tonk* (Bear Family 2000) ★★★★.

Gallivan, Joe
b. Joseph John Gallivan, 8 September 1937, Rochester, New York, USA. Gallivan played drums professionally in Miami, Florida, gigging with **Art Mooney** and **Charlie Spivak**, while studying music at the University of Miami. Later, he played at local clubs backing visitors such as **Dizzy Gillespie** and **Dakota Staton**. In Boston in the late 50s, Gallivan made his recording debut in a band including **Bill Berry**, and played with the Modern Jazz Orchestra alongside **Kenny Drew**. In New York City in 1961, he and **Donald Byrd** co-led a band that at various times included **Pepper Adams**, **Eddie Bert**, **Eric Dolphy**, **Don Ellis**, **Herbie Hancock** and **Jimmy Knepper**. In Miami the following year, he began a decades-long collaboration with multi-reed player Charles Austin. An early advocate of electronics, Gallivan tested the Minimoog and Moog drum for inventor **Robert Moog**. In the late 60s, Gallivan was with the New Rhythm And Blues Quartet and an all-electronic big band, A Train Of Thought. In 1969, again in New York City, he created improvisational film scores before joining **Larry Young** and guitar player Nicholas for an extended engagement in the pioneering fusion group Love Cry Want.

In the mid-70s, Gallivan moved to Europe, touring and recording with **Elton Dean**, **Keith Tippett** and Hugh Hopper. From the late 70s and through the following decade, Gallivan toured internationally and appeared, often on record, with Dean, **Kenny Wheeler**, **John Scofield**, **Miroslov Vitous**, **Kenny Kirkland**, Austin, **Butch Morris** and **Albert Mangelsdorff**. Additionally, he led and co-led several bands, among them Intercontinental Express. In 1984, he settled in London, England, which where he organized an *avant garde* big band, Soldiers Of The Road, which at various times featured Dean, **Evan Parker**, **Claude Deppa** and **Guy Barker**. This group, which played chiefly in London, broadcast for the BBC.

At the end of the 80s, Gallivan again relocated, this time to Hawaii, and continued touring and recording, now on his own label, No-Budget Records. Other bands he continued to lead or co-lead include a duo with pianist Brian Cuomo, sometimes joined by singer Jackie Ryan, the electronic trio Powerfield, and the multi-national sextet Ektal Ensemble, co-led by Marti Perramon and based in Barcelona, Spain. A strikingly gifted improviser, Gallivan is also a prolific composer having written music for jazz ensembles of all sizes as well as for films and television.
● ALBUMS: with Charles Austin *At Last* (Man Made) ★★★, with Hugh Hopper, Elton Dean, Keith Tippett *Cruel But Fair* (Compendium 1977) ★★★, with Austin *Mindscapes* (Spitball 1977) ★★★, with Austin *Expressions To The Winds* (Spitball 1977) ★★★, with Dean, Kenny Wheeler *The Cheque Is In The Mail* (Ogun 1977) ★★★, with Austin *Peace On Earth* (Compendium) ★★★, with Austin, Roy Babbington *Home From Home* (Ogun 1978) ★★★, with Hopper, Dean, Tippett *Mercy Dash* (Atmosphere 1978) ★★★, with Austin, Jean Schwartz *And Around* (Colin) ★★★, with Austin *Miami* (Atmosphere) ★★★, with Austin, Ryo Kawasaki, Clive Stevens, Peter Ponzol *The New Orchestra* (Hannibal) ★★★, with Soldiers Of The Road *Mysterious Planet* (Hannibal) ★★★★, with Ponzol, Abbey Rader *Prism* (Vinyl 1986) ★★★, with Soldiers Of The Road *Innocence* (Cadence 1991) ★★★★, with Dean, Brian Cuomo *The Origin Of Man* (No-Budget 1996) ★★★, with Nicholas, Larry Young *Love Cry Want* 1972 recording (No-Budget 1997) ★★★★, with Cuomo, Jackie Ryan *Surrender* (No-Budget 1997) ★★★, with Austin *Timeless* (No-Budget) ★★★, *Wiretapper* i (No-Budget 1998) ★★★, *Wiretapper* ii (No-Budget 1999) ★★★, with Powerfield *Electronic/ Electric/Electronic* (Paratactile 1999) ★★★★, *Night Vision* (No-Budget 2000) ★★★, *Orchestral Meditations* (No-Budget 2000) ★★★.

Gallon Drunk

High-energy rock 'n' roll band that emerged as contenders for the vacant **Birthday Party** throne in the early 90s. The band's line-up was James Johnston (vocals, guitar, organ), Mike Delanian (bass)—both of whom were at school together, Max Decharne (drums, also keyboard player with the Earls Of Suave) and Joe Byfield (maracas), the latter having spent a brief period with **My Bloody Valentine**. Formed early in 1990 and based in north London, original drummer Nick Combe was soon jettisoned. They quickly garnered plaudits from the music press, the **New Musical Express** describing them as 'a synthesis of quite disparate elements, from Memphis soul slew to primal rockabilly'. Others noted a similarity to the more raucous Birthday Party/**Nick Cave** recordings.

After releasing singles on their manager's own Massive label, Gallon Drunk moved on to Clawfist, where their debut album was released in 1992. Given their high press profile, this proved to be a little lacklustre, with strong songs smothered by a flat production. *From The Heart Of Town* was much closer to the mark, with Johnston's lyrics given a strong empathy by the band's voodoo rhythms and dry musicianship (including the contribution of new Gallon Drunk horn player **Terry Edwards**). Johnston's vignettes included some startling depictions of the grubbier elements of life in the capital, populated by characters of the grim majesty of 'Jake On The Make' and the tramp in 'Arlington Road'. Johnston played with the **Bad Seeds**, and then collaborated with Edwards on *Dora Saurez*, a spoken-word album, with crime writer Derek Raymond. The band returned in 1996 with new members Ian Watson (guitar/trumpet), Andy Dewar (percussion) and Ian White (drums), proving to be as raucous and menacing as ever. Despite Johnston's subsequent claim that the band was finished, and that he was embarking on a solo career under the name JJ Stone, they returned in October 1999 with a new EP, *Blood Is Red*, and the soundtrack to Nicholas Traindafyllidis' *Black Milk*. A new studio album appeared three years later.

● ALBUMS: *You, The Night And The Music* (Clawfist 1992) ★★, *From The Heart Of Town* (Clawfist 1993) ★★★, *In The Long Still Night* (City Slang 1996) ★★★, *Fire Music* (City Slang 1996) ★★★, *Black Milk* film soundtrack (FM 2000) ★★★, *Fire Music* (Sweet Nothing 2002) ★★★.
● COMPILATIONS: *Tonite . . . The Singles Bar* (Clawfist 1991) ★★, *Bear Me Away* (Sweet Nothing 2002) ★★★.
● DVD/VIDEOS: *One For The Ladies* (Cherry Red 2005).

Galloway, Jim

b. James Galloway, 28 July 1936, Kilwinning, Scotland. After working in Glasgow while still a teenager, Galloway, a clarinettist and saxophonist, emigrated in the mid-60s to Canada, where he became well known as a sideman, leader of the Metro Stompers, accompanist to visiting American jazz stars and radio personality. Success at the 1976 **Montreux Jazz Festival** with a band that included **Jay McShann** and **Buddy Tate** led to worldwide recognition for this dedicated musician. Rooted in the mainstream, Galloway's playing of the many instruments on which he performs betrays his admiration for **Sidney Bechet**, **Edmond Hall** and **Coleman Hawkins** among others. A major work, 'Hot And Suite', was given its first performance at the 1985 Edinburgh Arts Festival.

● ALBUMS: *Metro Stompers* (Sackville 1973) ★★★, *Three's Company* (Sackville 1973) ★★★, *Bojangles* (Hep Jazz 1978) ★★, *Thou Swell* (Sackville 1981) ★★★, with Jay McShann *Jim And Jay's Christmas* (Sackville 1992) ★★★, *Kansas City Nights* (Sackville 1993) ★★★, with Ed Polcer *At The Ball* (Jazzology 1998) ★★★, *Echos Of Swing* (Cornerstone 2004) ★★★.

Galper, Hal

b. Harold Galper, 18 April 1938, Salem, Massachusetts, USA. Galper was taught classical piano as a boy but turned to jazz and studied at the **Berklee College Of Music** between 1955 and 1958. He was taught privately by **Jaki Byard** and **Herb Pomeroy**. He moved to Boston in 1959 and played with Herb Pomeroy's big band. Then he worked with **Sam Rivers**, **Tony Williams**, **Chet Baker**, **Stan Getz**, **Randy** and **Michael Brecker**, **Bobby Hutcherson** and **Attila Zoller**. His harmonically sophisticated playing made him a masterful accompanist to vocalists **Joe Williams**, **Anita O'Day** and **Chris Connor**. He played with the **Cannonball Adderley** Quintet between 1973 and 1975 but is said not to have enjoyed playing the electric piano. In 1981 he joined **Phil Woods'** Quintet, with whom he played throughout the 80s. Although he is a distinctive stylist in his own right, Galper has expressed his admiration for **Bud Powell**, 'I've always tried to emulate Bud's dryness in my trio. His presentation was so dry, so unadorned, like a dry martini.' In the late 90s Galper could be heard playing with musicians such as **Tim Hagans** and **Jerry Bergonzi**, although his recorded output was never as extensive as might have been the case had he not preferred live performances. As he stated, 'Recording's for documentation. I like playing for an audience.'

● ALBUMS: *Inner Journey* (Mainstream 1973) ★★, *Reach Out* (SteepleChase 1976) ★★, *Now Hear This* (Enja 1977) ★★, *Speak With A Single Voice* (Enja 1978) ★★★★, *Children Of The Night* (Double Time 1978), *Redux 1978* (Concord Jazz 1978) ★★★, *Ivory Forest* (Enja 1981) ★★, *Dreamsville* (Enja 1987) ★★★, *Portrait* (Concord Jazz 1989) ★★★, *Invitation To A Concert* (Concord Jazz 1990) ★★★, *Live At Maybeck Hall* (Concord Jazz 1991) ★★, *Tippin'* (Concord Jazz 1994) ★★, with Jerry Bergonzi *Rebop* (Enja 1996) ★★★, *Live At Vartan Jazz* (Vartan Jazz 1997) ★★★, *Fugue State* (Blue Chip 1998) ★★★, *At Café Des Copains* 1990 live recording (Philology 1998) ★★★, with Jeff Johnson *Maybeck Duets* 1996 recording (Philology 1998) ★★★, *Let's Call This That* (Double Time 1999) ★★★.

Galway, James

b. 8 December 1939, Belfast, Northern Ireland. The future president of the British Flute Society inherited his woodwind skills from his paternal grandfather. Progressing from mouth organ and penny whistle, Galway earned victories in all three classes of the Irish Flute Championships at the age of 10, leading to a place in the Belfast Youth Orchestra and his first BBC broadcasts. A brief spell as a trainee piano tuner preceded scholarships at London's Guildhall School of Music and then the Paris Conservatoire—where he supplemented his grant by busking on city subways. From the rank-and-file at Sadlers Wells, he rose to become principal flautist with the Berlin Philharmonic in 1969. Six years later, manager Michael Emerson suggested he go solo. While averaging 120 concerts per annum, his award-winning recordings of Mozart and Vivaldi paralleled a more financially rewarding venture into pop in the late 70s that culminated with three hit albums and, also in 1978, an international smash with an arrangement of **John Denver**'s 'Annie's Song'. As well as two more bestselling albums, Galway has written his autobiography, recorded an album (*Sometimes We Touch*) with **Cleo Laine** and two with the **Chieftains**, and undertaken world tours to full houses.

● ALBUMS: *The Magic Flute Of James Galway* (RCA 1978) ★★★, *The Man With The Golden Flute* (RCA 1978) ★★, *James Galway Plays The Songs For Annie* (RCA 1978) ★★, *Songs Of The Seashore* (Solar 1979) ★★, with Cleo Laine *Sometimes When We Touch* (RCA Victor 1980) ★★★, *Songs Of The Southern Cross* (RCA 1981) ★★, with Henry Mancini *In The Pink* (RCA 1984) ★★★, *The Wayward Wind* (RCA Victor 1984) ★★, *Christmas Carol* (RCA Victor 1986) ★★, *James Galway And The Chieftains In Ireland* (RCA 1987) ★★★, *The Celtic Connection: James Galway And The Chieftains* (RCA 1990) ★★★★, with Phil Coulter *Legends* (RCA 1997) ★★★, with Coulter *Winter's Crossing* (RCA 1998) ★★★.

● COMPILATIONS: *The James Galway Collection* (Telstar 1982) ★★★, *The James Galway Collection Volume 2* (Telstar 1986) ★★★, *Masterpieces: The Essential Flute Of James Galway* (RCA 1993) ★★★.

● FURTHER READING: *James Galway*, James Galway. *James Galway's Music In Time*, William Mann.

Gama, Victor

b. Angola. Often recalling the work of American minimalist composer **Steve Reich**, Gama's fascinating and beautiful music is inspired by the belief that as a consequence of migration and nomadism, traditional African instruments have had to adapt throughout history while simultaneously retaining their traditional sound and identity.

Born in Angola of Portuguese origin, Gama developed an interest in the traditional instruments of his birthplace, which led to him learning the kissange (or thumb piano) and the hungo (a musical bow) alongside studying the 12-string guitar. In the early 90s, having completed an engineering degree in electronics and communications and having worked in the area of digital signal processing, he began constructing his Pangeia Instrumentos, a range of contemporary instruments designed and built from traditional materials including wood, metal and found objects. Frequently sculptural, beautiful and strange, these instruments juxtapose the modern and the ancient and, as if to stress the importance of dialogue and sharing, can often be played by two people at the same time. These self-made instruments include one inspired by a kalimba. Although the kalimba is traditionally made from a board box or calabash, Gama constructed his own from a discarded Angolan soldier's helmet. Such actions add an extra potency to Gama's already moving music and imply a further political context to his sonic creations.

Gama is part of PangeiArt, a trans-national non-profit cultural association of musicians, artists, academics and people, that produces cultural exchange projects based on creative processes in Africa, South America and the Caribbean countries. In both group and solo contexts, Gama has presented his music and exhibited his instruments and sound installations internationally and he has made extensive field recordings for several projects in Angola, Cuba, Colombia, South Africa, Namibia and Brazil. Gama's *Pangeia*

Instrumentos was licensed by PangeiArt for release in the UK via **Rephlex Records**, the label co-run by Richard D. James aka the **Aphex Twin**. Unusually for the label, the recording eschewed electronic interventions but nevertheless *Pangeia Instrumentos* sat comfortably alongside releases by label luminaries such as **Leila**, Pierre Bastien and James himself. Late in 2003, an exhibition of Gama's instruments in London was opened by ambient DJ sets from Rephlex artists.

● ALBUMS: *Sounds Of Amnesia* (Susette Boe 1998) ★★★, *Pangeia Instrumentos* (PangeiArt 2000) ★★★★, *Oceanites Erraticus* (PangeiArt 2001) ★★★.

● COMPILATIONS: *Odantalan* (PangeiArt 2002) ★★★.

Gambale, Frank

b. 22 December 1958, Canberra, Australia. A virtuoso guitarist nicknamed 'The Thunder From Down Under', Gambale, after making his name with fusion keyboard legend **Chick Corea**'s popular Elektric Band, is most commonly associated with America's west coast fusion/studio scene. In Australia he began his career concentrating on the pop field, singing and playing guitar in vocal-orientated bands. He became involved in Hollywood's celebrated Guitar Institute of Technology in 1982, when he moved to the US, first enrolling as a student and finally staying on as a teacher, before joining Chick Corea's group in 1986. He stayed with the outfit for seven years, soloing infrequently but blinding other guitarists with his advanced technical facility during the band's stunningly fast and intricate ensemble passages.

When Corea formed his concurrent Akoustic Band, Gambale had more time on his hands to pursue his solo career, and work with other projects, including drummer **Steve Smith**'s highly regarded fusion quartet Vital Information. Gambale (and the virtuoso rhythm section of bass player **John Pattitucci** and drummer **Dave Weckl**) left the Elektric Band in 1993, and concentrated on recording a series of albums on the JVC label. *Thinking Out Loud* was a change of direction, with his guitar lines being replaced by smooth chords not unlike **Barney Kessel** or **Jim Hall**. He also records with GHS (**Stuart Hamm** and **Steve Smith**). A guitarist with perhaps more technique than he knows what to do with, Gambale plays with a rock sensibility, firing blistering, aggressive lines and more recently reverting to his old interests in singing.

● ALBUMS: *Brave New Guitar* (Legato 1986) ★★★, *Present For The Future* (Legato 1987) ★★★, *Thunder From Down Under* (JVC 1989) ★★★, *The Great Explorers* (JVC 1990) ★★★★, *Note Worker* (JVC 1991) ★★★, *Passages* (JVC 1994) ★★★, *Thinking Out Loud* (JVC 1995) ★★★, with Stuart Hamm, Steve Smith *Show Me What You Can Do* (Tone Center 1998) ★★★★, *Coming To Your Senses* (Favored Nations 2000) ★★★, with Hamm, Smith *The Light Beyond* (Tone Center 2000) ★★★, with Maurizio Colonna *Imagery Suite* (Wombat 2000) ★★★, *Resident Aliens — Live Bootlegs* (Wombat 2001) ★★★, *Absolutely Live — In Poland* (Wombat 2002) ★★★, with Hamm, Smith *GHS3* (Tone Center 2003) ★★★, *Raison D'Etre* (Wombat 2004) ★★★★.

● COMPILATIONS: *The Best Of Frank Gambale* (JVC 1999) ★★★★.

Gamble And Huff

This exceptional songwriting and production team first met while working on 'The 81', a 1964 single by **Candy And The**

Kisses. Leon Huff (b. 1942, Camden, New Jersey, USA), an established session musician, played piano on the recording, while the songwriter Kenny Gamble (b. 11 August 1943, Philadelphia, Pennsylvania, USA) was also a member of the Romeos, a Philadelphia group Huff would later join. The duo achieved a US Top 10 hit in 1967, producing 'Expressway To Your Heart' for the **Soul Survivors**. However, their work with the **Intruders** ('(Love Is Like A) Baseball Game') gave a better indication of subsequent developments. The homely lyrics, tightened rhythm and sweetening strings, so prevalent on the team's later recordings, were already present on these 1968 recordings. Gamble and Huff productions also provided hits for **Archie Bell And The Drells** ('I Can't Stop Dancing'), **Jerry Butler** ('Only The Strong Survive') and, later, **Wilson Pickett** ('Don't Let The Green Grass Fool You'). Having disbanded their Excel and Gamble outlets, the duo formed a third label, Neptune, where they pieced together an impressive roster of acts, many of whom were retained when its successor, **Philadelphia International Records**, was founded in 1971.

This definitive company was responsible for many of the decade's finest soul singles, including 'If You Don't Know Me By Now' (**Harold Melvin And The Blue Notes**), 'Backstabbers' (the **O'Jays**) and 'Me And Mrs Jones' (**Billy Paul**). Gamble and Huff had, by now, defined their art. Their music formed a natural stepping-stone between Tamla/**Motown Records** and disco, but this pre-eminent position was undermined by a 1975 payola scandal that accused the label of offering bribes in return for airplay. Although the charges against Huff were dismissed, Gamble was fined $2,500. By coincidence or not, the pair's work suffered following the indictment. Their records became increasingly formula-bound, imitative of a now-passing golden era, but lacking flair and innovation. Their last consistent commercial success came with **Teddy Pendergrass**, but the singer's horrific car accident forestalled his career. **McFadden And Whitehead**'s 1979 single, 'Ain't No Stoppin' Us Now', was a proud promulgation, but the Philly-soul sound was unable to adapt to the new decade. Nonetheless, Gamble and Huff remain one of the most important, and successful, writing/production teams to emerge from black music.

Gamblers

Formed in Newcastle, England, the Gamblers comprised Jim Crawford (lead guitar), Tony Damond (rhythm guitar/trumpet), Alan George (keyboards), Ken Brady (saxophone), Alan Sanderson (bass) and Andy Mac (drums). They sprang to fame momentarily in 1963 upon replacing the **Tornadoes** as singer **Billy Fury**'s backing group. Their reward was a recording contract with **Decca Records**, debuting with a version of the **Miracles**' 'You Really Got A Hold On Me'. The Gamblers' spell with Fury complete, they returned to Newcastle to hold a residency at the Majestic Ballroom. In 1964 'It's So Nice' reached the lower reaches of the UK Top 30, but it was not until 1964 that the Gamblers recorded again. Their version of 'Find Out What's Happening' was issued in competition with the **Downliners Sect**. It made no commercial impression, and the group was dropped after releasing 'Dr. Goldfoot' in 1966. The Gamblers completed a strong version of 'Cry Me A River' for **Parlophone Records** in 1967, after which they retreated into the north of England's ballroom/club circuit.

● FILMS: *I've Gotta Horse* (1965) ★★.

Game

A beat group that was victim to endless line-up changes, the Game originally formed in Mitcham, Surrey, England, in 1964, the first line-up comprising Tony Bird (guitar/vocals), Terry Boyes (vocals), Allen Janaway (bass), Jim Nelson (drums) and Terry Spencer (lead guitar). Both Spencer and Janaway had previously played together in the Secrets, from whose ranks future Game member Terry Brown would later be drawn. At their outset the group worked as support act to popular comedian/singer **Kenny Lynch** before signing to the Original Sound Productions management agency—formed by local songwriters Lesley Blake, Alan Gowing (who wrote much of their music) and the aforementioned Terry Brown. The group's first single, 'Gotta Keep On Moving Baby', was released on **Pye Records** in 1965 but achieved no chart success. By the advent of its follow-up, 1966's 'Gonna Get me Someone', the group had moved to **Decca Records** and recruited Ray Charlesly as vocalist in place of Boyes. Promoted as a 'mod' single in the wake of the **Who**'s popularity, it again failed. The Game moved on once more to **Parlophone Records**, and Charlesly now left, as did Nelson, with Terry Brown taking over on drums and Bird adopting lead vocal duties. The group then recorded their best single, 'The Addicted Man', a pulsating R&B track with hints of psychedelia. However, when it was voted a 'miss' on television show **Juke Box Jury**, Parlophone withdrew it from retail outlets. The Game instead rush-released 'It's Shocking What They Call Me', recorded in a single day. Remarkably the song, which was their most psychedelic offering to date, betrayed no signs of its hasty construction, but it too missed the charts. The group then broke up, Spencer and Decker, the bass player in the group's final line-up, joined Oak Records group Lavender Grove. They then joined Grail, who recorded a **Rod Stewart**-produced album for German label Metronome. In the 90s the Game re-formed around Bird, Brown, Janaway and Spencer. In 1995 they released their first single for over 25 years, appropriately titled 'Still On The Game'.

● DVD/VIDEOS: *The Documentary* (Interscope 2005).

Game Theory

Based in Sacramento, California, USA, rock band Game Theory comprised Scott Miller (b. 1960, Sacramento, California, USA; guitar/vocals/synthesizer, ex–Alternate Learning), Nancy Becker (keyboards), Fred Juhos (bass/vocals) and Michael Irwin (drums), making its recording debut in 1981. Although loosely associated with the Los Angeles Paisley Underground movement (Miller was previously a member of Alternate Learning, with Joe Becker of True West and **Thin White Rope**), the quartet's progress was determined by their guitarist's infatuation with classic US pop and melody, rather then musical fashion. The best example of their early muse, following a scene-setting, competent debut, is *Dead Center*, which compiles the EPs *Pointed Accounts Of People You Know* and *Distortion*. The latter tracks were co-produced by Michael Quercio of **Three O'Clock**, which cemented their ties to the Paisley scene. Matters improved further with *Real Nighttime*, wherein a cover version of **Big Star**'s 'You Can't Have Me' stands shoulder-to-shoulder with Miller's increasingly adventurous lyrical scenarios. Though his occasional co-writer Juhos had departed before its release (along with the rest of the founding members), *The Big Shot Chronicles* continued to demonstrate Game Theory's excellence in power pop construction. Miller's fusion of 60s and 80s styles was expertly captured on *Lolita Nations*, another fruitful partnership with **R.E.M./dB's** producer Mitch Easter (their relationship having begun with *Real Nighttime*), and *2 Steps From The Middle Ages*, which placed his band on a pop/rock pantheon with the equally accomplished and underrated **Shoes**. Both titles saw a new five-piece line-up, with the addition of Donnette Thayer (guitar; ex-**Veil** (US)), Shelley LaFreniere (keyboards), Gui Gassuan (bass), and Gil Ray (drums).

After their failure to break through with *2 Steps From The Middle Ages*, the line-up fluctuated once more, with Quercio joining full-time on bass, Jozef Becker (ex–Thin White Rope) on percussion and Ray switching to guitar and keyboards. Thayer, meanwhile, moved on to Hex. Miller's creation thus survived several personnel changes, including the leader's own temporary defection, without losing its sense of direction. Persistent though they were, Game Theory finally called it a day in 1990. Miller would go on to form a new vehicle for his undervalued talents, **Loud Family**.

● ALBUMS: *Blaze Of Glory* (Rational 1981) ★★, *Real Nighttime* (Rational 1985) ★★★, *The Big Shot Chronicles* (Rational 1986) ★★★, *Lolita Nation* (Rational 1987) ★★★★, *2 Steps From The Middle Ages* (Enigma 1988) ★★★.

● COMPILATIONS: *Dead Center* (Lolita 1984) ★★★, *Tinker To Evers To Chance* (Enigma 1989) ★★★★, *Distortion Of Glory* (Alias 1993) ★★★.

Game, The

b. Jayceon Taylor, 27 November 1979, Compton, California, USA. This west coast gangsta rapper rose to fame in 2004 on the strength of his association with **Dr. Dre** and **50 Cent**. Taylor was raised in a foster home in Compton and, like many young men from his neighbourhood, followed a path into crime and dealing. His redemption came when he decided to take up rapping after a near fatal shooting in October 2001. A quick learner, Taylor renamed himself The Game (after a childhood nickname bestowed upon him by his grandmother) and immersed himself in classic gangsta rap from the 80s and 90s. His demo came to the attention of veteran rapper **JT The Bigga Figga**, who worked with the up-and-coming artist on a planned album project. Before anything could be released, however, The Game had been offered a new recording contract with Dr. Dre's Aftermath/G-Unit label. The JT The Bigga Figga sessions were subsequently released on *Untold Story* in October 2004, much to the annoyance of Aftermath and The Game. At the same time The Game's official debut single, 'How We Do', featuring G-Unit's star-turn 50 Cent, began storming up the US charts. With all the hype by now surrounding The Game it was no surprise when his Aftermath debut, *The Documentary*, topped the US charts in January 2005.

● ALBUMS: *Untold Story* (Get Low 2004) ★★, *The Documentary* (Aftermath/G-Unit 2005) ★★★.

Gamley, Douglas

b. 13 September 1924, Melbourne, Australia. Composer, pianist, musical director and arranger—Douglas Gamley has played an important part in the musical scene of Britain and Australia since the early 50s. Initially he specialized in film work, and he acknowledges the valuable guidance he received from **Robert Farnon**, who assisted him on several projects. More recently he has concentrated on concert work, especially with the Melbourne-based Australian 'Pops' Orchestra, which he frequently conducts. He also had a spell (from 1976 onwards) as assistant musical director for the Vancouver Opera. Like many composers working in films, Gamley spent much of his time collaborating with other composers, often not receiving any screen credit. It is not uncommon for major writers to hire 'assistants' who often score the majority of the music in the film. In this capacity Gamley has worked with **Richard Addinsell**, John Hollingsworth, Bruce Montgomery (who did the early *Carry On* films), Kenneth V. Jones, **Miklos Rozsa** (Gamley orchestrated half of *El Cid*) and **Henry Mancini**. His list of scores is impressive: *Jumping For Joy*—orchestrator for **Larry Adler** (1955), *One Wish Too Many* (1956), *High Flight*—with Kenneth V. Jones, title march by **Eric Coates** (1957), *The Prince And The Showgirl*—orchestrator for Richard Addinsell (1957), *The Admirable Crichton*—dances by Richard Addinsell (1957), *Fire Down Below*—with Kenneth V. Jones (1957), *Gideon's Day*—also known as *Gideon Of Scotland Yard* (1958), *A Tale Of Two Cities*—orchestrator for Richard Addinsell (1958), *Cry From The Streets*—orchestrator for Larry Adler (1958), *Another Time, Another Place* (1958), *Tom Thumb*—dance sequences by Ken Jones (1958), *Beyond This Place* aka *Web Of Evidence* (1959), *The Rough And The Smooth* aka *Portrait Of A Sinner* (1959), *Tarzan's Greatest Adventure* (1959), *The Ugly Duckling* (1959), *City Of The Dead*—with Kenneth V. Jones (1960), *Foxhole In Cairo*—period music by Ken Jones (1960), *Light Up The Sky* (1960), *Watch It Sailor* (1960), *Carry On Cruising*—theme and two cues by Bruce Montgomery (1961), *Macbeth*—orchestrator for Richard Addinsell (1961), *The Roman Spring Of Mrs Stone*—orchestrator for Richard Addinsell (1961), *The Canadians* (1961), *The War Lover*—orchestrator for Richard Addinsell (1962), *Charade*—orchestrator for Henry Mancini (1964), *A Shot In The Dark*—orchestrator for Henry Mancini (1964), *The Return Of Mr. Moto* (1965), *Rotten To The Core*—musical director (score by Michael Dress) (1966), *The Family Way*—musical director (score **Paul McCartney**) (1966), *The Deadly Affair*—musical director (score **Quincy Jones**) (1966), *Arabesque*—orchestrator for Henry Mancini (1966), *Two For The Road*—orchestrator for Henry Mancini (1966), *Girl On A Motorcycle*—musical director (score **Les Reed**) (1968), *Spring And Port Wine* (1970), *Sunday Bloody Sunday*—with **Ron Geesin** (1971), *Tales From The Crypt* (1972), *Asylum* (1972), *And Now The Screaming Starts* (1972), *Vault Of Horror* (1973), *The Beast Must Die* (1974), *The Little Prince*—musical director (score **Alan Jay Lerner** and **Frederick Loewe**) (1974), *Return Of The Pink Panther*—orchestrator for Henry Mancini (1974), *The Land That Time Forgot* (1974), *From Beyond The Grave* (1974), *Madhouse*—also known as *The Return Of Dr. Death* (1974), *The Monster Club* (1975), *Enigma* with Marc Wilkinson (1983). Douglas Gamley's own compositions include 'London Bridge March', 'Souvenir de Granada' and 'Prater Fest'. As a pianist he has recorded an album of Robert Farnon compositions (Delyse Envoy 1960). By far his most extensive work in the recording studios has been numerous titles arranged and conducted for *Reader's Digest*, including some under the pseudonym Eric Hammerstein.

Gamma

After the failure of his solo album, Colorado-born guitarist **Ronnie Montrose** reunited with former **Montrose** members Jim Alcivar (keyboards) and Alan Fitzgerald (bass) and, with the addition of Davey Patison on vocals and Skip Gallette on drums, formed Gamma in 1979. Following the release of a debut album, the line-up changed, with another ex-Montrose member, Denny Carmassi, taking over drumming duties, and newcomer Glen Letsch on bass. This new line-up recorded *Gamma 2*—a much stronger album, which spawned a hit single in 'Voyager' and a successful tour of America and Europe. Alcivar left soon afterwards to be replaced by Mitchell Froom (ex-**Bruzer**). Despite being a fine synthesizer player in his own right, his input led to keyboard saturation on the third album, relegating Montrose's perennially excellent guitar-playing to secondary status. Gamma then toured with **Foreigner** in 1983 but failed to record again as Montrose attempted to re-form the band of his name with original vocalist **Sammy Hagar**. Davey Pattison later surfaced with **Robin Trower**, and Montrose, never fulfilling his wish, returned to a solo career.
● ALBUMS: *Gamma* (Elektra 1979) ★★, *Gamma 2* (Elektra 1980) ★★★★, *Gamma 3* (Elektra 1982) ★★★, *Concert Classics* 1979 recording (Ranch Life 1998) ★★.

Gamma Ray

After leaving **Helloween**, the band he founded, in 1989, guitarist Kai Hansen (b. 17 January 1963, Hamburg, Germany) teamed up with ex–Tyran Pace vocalist Ralf Scheepers. The intention was to record an album of existing material that had been deemed unsuitable for Hansen's previous band. Joining them for this proposed project were Uwe Wessel (bass), Mathias Burchadt (drums) and a host of guest musicians, including guitarist Dirk Schlächter (b. 15 February 1966, Bad Nauheim, Germany). Signing to Noise Records they entered the Horus Sound Studios in Germany with producer Tommy Newton. The resulting recordings were released under the Gamma Ray moniker as *Heading For Tomorrow* in 1990. The album was an excellent blend of powerful melodic heavy metal, with song structures reminiscent of **Queen**.

Having proved a favourite with press and public alike, Hansen began to realize the band's potential and decided to form a working unit out of the musicians who had played on the project to tour in support of the album. The fully assembled Gamma Ray comprised Scheepers (vocals), Hansen (guitar/vocals), Schlächter (guitar), Wessel (bass) and Uli Kusch (drums). They toured extensively throughout Europe and Japan, where they gained a substantial following, and, as a stopgap between albums, released an EP of new material, *Heaven Can Wait*. Come the next album, *Sigh No More*, Gamma Ray were in fine form; extensive touring had disciplined them into a tight, cohesive unit. Though heavier than its predecessor the album boasted high-quality heavy metal with melody and power, serving as a more than worthy encore to their impressive debut.

Wessel and Kusch were subsequently replaced by Jan Rubach and Thomas Nack respectively. Scheepers' final recording as vocalist, 1993's *Insanity And Genius*, was a more muted affair. Hansen took over vocals for *Land Of The Free*, an album that revealed little in the way of progression, relying heavily on his virtuoso guitar to provide texture for the lacklustre songwriting. 1997's *Somewhere Out In Space*

featured new members Henjo Richter (b. 24 November 1963, Hamburg, Germany; guitar/keyboards) and Dan Zimmerman (b. 30 October 1966, Nurnberg, Germany; drums), with Schlächter reverting to bass. This line-up remained constant into the new millennium, during which they released a number of new albums, including 2000's *Blast From The Past*. This double disc featured new tracks alongside reworkings of material from their extensive back catalogue.
● ALBUMS: *Heading For Tomorrow* (Noise 1990) ★★★, *Sigh No More* (Noise 1991) ★★★, *Insanity And Genius* (Noise 1993) ★★, *Land Of The Free* (Noise 1995) ★★, *Alive '95* (Noise 1996) ★★, *Somewhere Out In Space* (Noise 1997) ★★, *The Karaoke Album* (Noise 1997) ★★, *Power Plant* (Noise 1999) ★★★, *Blast From The Past* (Noise 2000) ★★★, *No World Order* (Noise 2001) ★★★, *Skeletons In The Closet* (Metal-Is 2003) ★★★.
● DVD/VIDEOS: *Heading For The East* (Noise 1991), *Lust For Live* (Noise 1994).

Ganafoul

Prior to the breakthrough of **Trust** and Telephone, rated among the best hard rock bands working in France were Ganafoul. Comprising Jack Bon (vocals/guitar), Jean Yves Astier (bass/vocals) and Yves Rotacher (drums), their music relied on the type of 12-bar blues boogie patented by **Status Quo**. However, their execution of similar material was altogether tougher, drawing equally on the nascent punk tradition for their rhythmic attack. After their 1977 debut, a cheaply produced and packaged but still incendiary collection entitled *Side 3*, Rotacher was replaced on drums by Bernard Antoine, who provided more percussive versatility. Subsequent albums for Crypto Records continued to follow the group's *oeuvre* of stylistically delimited but brutally played hard rock, which found a ready audience on France's late-70s club circuit.
● ALBUMS: *Side 3* (Crypto 1977) ★★★, *Full Speed Ahead* (Crypto 1978) ★★★★, *Live* (Crypto 1979) ★★, *Saturday Night* (Crypto 1980) ★★★, *T'As Failli Crever* (Crypto 1981) ★★★.

Gandee, Al

b. Albert Gandee, 1900, USA, d. 3 June 1944, Cincinnati, Ohio, USA. A competent trombonist, Gandee's brief hour of fame resulted from a spell with the **Wolverines**, with whom he recorded in 1924. He chose to earn his living in later years outside of music although he continued to play in bands in Cincinnati until his death in an automobile accident.

Ganelin Trio

When originally formed in 1971 this Soviet trio consisted of Vyacheslav Ganelin (b. Kraskov, USSR; keyboards, flute, percussion, guitar), **Vladimir Chekasin** (b. Sverdlovsk; reeds, trombone, violin, percussion, voice), and Vladimir Tarasov (b. Archangelsk, USSR; drums, percussion). Although firmly based on composition, a recording or concert performance by the trio is a rich mix of Slavonic folk, free jazz, contemporary classical music and parodies of all three traditions. Their first album, *Con Anima*, was recorded in the USSR in 1976, but the Soviet state record label, Melodiya, was highly dilatory about issuing their recordings. Leo Feigin's London-based **Leo Records** took on the task, though his first releases, of tapes smuggled out of the USSR, were issued with a disclaimer that the musicians bore no responsibility for their music's appearance on record. In the 80s the trio began to play outside the Soviet Union and Eastern bloc, scoring a great success at the 1980 West Berlin Jazz Festival, then visiting Italy in 1981, and the UK on a Contemporary Music Network tour in 1984, where they met with a mixed reception from jazz critics and musicians. Ganelin emigrated to Israel in 1987, where he formed a new trio, exhibiting a more severe style of music on two albums, with Victor Fonarev (bass/percussion) and Mika Markovich (drums/percussion). Tarasov and Chekasin continued to work together.

● ALBUMS: *Con Anima* 1976 recording (Leo 1980) ★★★, *Live In East Germany* aka *Catalogue* (Leo 1980) ★★★★, *Con Fuoco* 1978-80 recordings (Leo 1981) ★★★★, *Concerto Grosso* 1978 recordings (Leo 1982) ★★★, *Poi Segue* (Melodja 1982) ★★★★, *Ancora De Capo Part I* 1980 recording (Leo 1982) ★★★★, *Ancora De Capo Part 2* 1980 recording (Leo 1982) ★★★, *New Wine* (Leo 1983) ★★★, *Strictly For Our Friends* 1978 recording (Leo 1984) ★★★★, *Vide* (Leo 1984) ★★★, *Baltic Triangle* 1981 recording (Leo 1985) ★★★, *Con Affetto* (Leo 1985) ★★★, *Non Troppo* 1980-83 recording (hatART 1985) ★★★, *Ttaango . . . In Nickelsdorf* (Leo 1986) ★★★, *Great Concerts Of New Jazz Vol. 1* (Leo 1987) ★★★, *Poco A Poco* 1978 recording (Leo 1988) ★★★★, *Jerusalem February Cantabile* (Leo 1989) ★★★★, *Opuses* (Leo 1990) ★★★.

● FURTHER READING: *Russian Jazz New Identity*, Leo Feigin (ed.).

Gang Green

This quartet from Boston, Massachusetts, USA, specializing in a fusion of hardcore and thrash, was put together by guitarist/vocalist Chris Doherty. Although originally formed in 1982 by Doherty, Mike Dean and Bill Manley, it was a completely different 1985 incarnation that secured a contract with Taang! Records (Doherty had spent some of the intervening period with Jerry's Kids). After numerous line-up changes, a degree of stability was achieved for *You Got It*, with Doherty, plus Brian Betzger (drums), Fritz Erickson (guitar; replacing Chuck Stilphen), and Joe Gittleman (bass), the latter eventually replaced by ex-**D.R.I.** member Josh Pappe. Extolling the virtues of alcohol and skateboarding, and ridiculing the P.M.R.C. at every opportunity, their music was fast, aggressive and occasionally abusive. One career highlight was the mini-album *I81B4U*, where the band's irreverent sense of fun put 'two fingers up' at **Van Halen**'s *OU812*. They also released one record as a skateboard-shaped picture disc. Although they were unable to progress on the songwriting front, their sound, nevertheless, grew louder and more impressive as time wore on, particularly on 1989's *Older . . . Budweiser*, which took their obsession with the eponymous beer to excessive lengths. *Can't Live Without It* was a very loud live album. Following an extended hiatus, Doherty revived Gang Green in the mid-90s and recorded a new studio album, *Another Case Of Brewtality*.

● ALBUMS: *Another Wasted Night* (Taang! 1986) ★★★, *You Got It* (Roadracer 1987) ★★★, *I81B4U* mini-album (Roadracer 1988) ★★★, *Older . . . Budweiser* (Emergo 1989) ★★★, *Can't Live Without It* (Emergo 1990) ★★, *Another Case Of Brewtality* (Taang! 1997) ★★★, *Preschool* (Taang! 1997) ★★.

● COMPILATIONS: *King Of Bands* (Roadracer 1991) ★★★, *The Taang Years* (Rhythm Vicar 2002) ★★★.

Gang Of Four

UK post-punk band formed in Leeds, Yorkshire, in 1977, and named after the radical Chinese group that rose to power during that country's Cultural Revolution. The Gang Of Four—Jon King (b. 8 June 1955, London, England; vocals/melodica), Andy Gill (b. 1 January 1956, Manchester, England; guitar/vocals), Dave Allen (b. 23 December 1955, Kendal, Cumbria, England; bass) and Hugo Burnham (b. 25 March 1956, London, England; drums)—made their debut on Fast Product the following year with *Damaged Goods*. This uncompromising three-track EP ('Damaged Goods'/'Love Like Anthrax'/'Armalite Rifle') introduced the band's strident approach, wherein Burnham's pounding, compulsive drumming and Gill's staccato, stuttering guitar work, reminiscent of **Wilko Johnson** from **Dr. Feelgood**, framed their overtly political lyrics. The quartet maintained this direction on their 1979 debut album *Entertainment!*, while introducing the interest in funk music that marked future recordings. Its most impressive track, 'At Home He's A Tourist', was issued as a single, but encountered censorship problems over its pre-AIDS reference to prophylactics ('rubbers').

Following the release of *Solid Gold*, internal strife resulted in Allen's departure, later to join **Shriekback**, in July 1981. He was replaced by Sara Lee, formerly of **Jane Aire And The Belvederes**, as the band pursued a fuller, more expansive sound. *Songs Of The Free* featured the tongue-in-cheek single 'I Love A Man In Uniform', which seemed destined for chart success until disappearing from radio playlists in the wake of the Falklands conflict. Burnham was fired in 1983, and a three-piece line-up completed *Hard* with sundry session musicians. This disappointing release made little difference to a band unable to satisfy now-divergent audiences, and they split up the following year.

Following several rather inconclusive projects, King and Gill exhumed the Gang Of Four name in 1990. The reunion was marked by *Mall* for **Polydor Records**, which justified the decision to resume their career with a set of typically bracing, still politically motivated songs. However, it did little to revive their commercial fortunes, and was never released in the UK. Gill and King subsequently worked on movie soundtracks, one of which, *Delinquent*, formed the basis of the energetic 1995 release *Shrinkwrapped*, on which the duo was joined by **Curve** members Dean Garcia and Steve Monti. The furious rhythms and dark musical scenarios of earlier years made a welcome return, while the lyrics continued to paint the agents of capitalism as the enemy (notably on 'Lord Of The Anthill'). Gill and King played some rare live dates to a rapturous reception, but shortly afterwards the latter announced he was retiring from the music business. Gill teamed up with Burnham and Allen in 1998 to compile the excellent *100 Flowers Bloom* compilation.

The original line-up of the Gang Of Four announced they were re-forming to play a string of UK dates in January 2005. They were celebrated in the music press for their influence on the contemporary wave of art-punk bands led by **Franz Ferdinand**, **Bloc Party** and **Radio 4**. A new studio album, featuring re-recordings of selections from the band's back catalogue, followed later in the year.

● ALBUMS: *Entertainment!* (EMI/Warners 1979) ★★★★★, *Solid Gold* (EMI/Warners 1981) ★★★, *Songs Of The Free* (EMI/Warners 1982) ★★★, *Hard* (EMI/Warners 1983) ★★, *At The Palace* (Mercury/Phonogram

1984) ★★, *Mall* (Polydor 1991) ★★★, *Shrinkwrapped* (When! 1995) ★★★, *Return The Gift* (V2 2005) ★★★.
● COMPILATIONS: *The Peel Sessions* (Strange Fruit 1990) ★★★, *A Brief History Of The Twentieth Century* (EMI/ Warners 1990) ★★★★, *100 Flowers Bloom* (Rhino 1998) ★★★★.

Gang Starr

Arguably hip-hop's most literate, challenging act on both musical and lyrical fronts, Gang Starr comprises Guru Keith E (b. Keith Elam, 18 July 1966, Roxbury, Massachusetts, USA; vocals/lyrics) and **DJ Premier** (b. Chris Martin, 3 May 1969, Brooklyn, New York City, USA; music). Guru (Gifted Unlimited Rhymes Universal) was born the son of a Boston municipal and superior court judge, but moved to Brooklyn following graduation with a degree in business administration from Atlanta's Morehouse College. He had previously worked as a counsellor in a maximum detention home in Boston, an experience that would inform many of his lyrics. Gang Starr was in existence before DJ Premier joined, originally also comprising fellow rapper Damo D-Ski and DJ Wanna Be Down. Their early labours are recalled on cuts like 'The Lesson' and 'Bust A Move', both of which were produced by **DJ Mark The 45 King**. However, they were at that time still Boston-based, and in the end opted to pursue more geographically convenient projects.

Premier, meanwhile, had relocated to Texas to attend college, but left demos of his work with various labels before his departure. In Texas, he put together the Inner City Posse, who finally saw their demo get some attention. Premier was offered a recording contract with **Wild Pitch Records**, but only on the condition that he lose his original rapper. The label put him in touch with Guru instead, who had chanced upon one of Premier's demo tapes in their offices, and a marriage made in hip-hop heaven was born. However, Premier had to return to college in Texas, and so the duo's liaison took place largely over the phone, and by sending each other tapes. The fruits of their labour were unveiled on 1989's debut album, *No More Mr. Nice Guy*, completed in 10 days while Premier was on vacation. 'Manifest', taken from the album, picked up airplay on *Yo! MTV Raps*, and caught the attention of film director Spike Lee. In the process of completing his new movie, *Mo Better Blues*, Lee was greatly impressed by album track 'Jazz Thing', and asked his musical director, **Branford Marsalis**, to track Gang Starr down. Marsalis urged the duo to cut a recording of Lotis Eli's poem about the history of jazz to a hip-hop rhythm, for inclusion on the movie's sound-track. The song they eventually came up with would see release as 'Jazz Thing'. Not only one of rap's most crucial moments, 'Jazz Thing' also gave Gang Starr a manifesto for their subsequent career. Credited with popularizing jazz-rap, they took the form to its logical conclusion with *Step In The Arena*, before retreating to hardcore pastures for *Daily Operation*.

Both Guru and Premier have striven to be seen as individuals outside of the Gang Starr hallmark. A joint collaboration with the **Dream Warriors** on 'I've Lost My Ignorance' aside, each has increased their profile with solo projects. Premier has produced widely for **KRS-One**, **Fu-Schnickens**, **Big Daddy Kane** and **Heavy D** among many others, while Guru set up the winning **Jazzmatazz** situation. The latter comprised his distinctive rap style with the best of modern freeform jazz. An interesting departure considering that Premier has always used samples rather than live instruments, though since *Daily Operation* he has been forced to credit and clear them. Though such forays encouraged speculation that Gang Starr was about to split, the duo belied the critics with a storming return on *Hard To Earn*. Back to their freestyle, flowing best, it was the second outing for the posse of rappers that Guru had formed into the Gang Starr Foundation: **Jeru The Damaja**, Big Shug (who was a collaborator with Guru in his early days in Boston), Little Dap and Felachi The Nutcracker.

After a prolonged absence they returned to the scene in 1998 with the inventive *Moment Of Truth*. The following year's compilation set provided a comprehensive overview of one of hip-hop's most consistently excellent teams. Guru and Premier then put Gang Starr on extended hiatus to concentrate on a number of solo projects. It was something of a pleasant surprise when the duo returned in 2003 with a new Gang Starr album, *The Ownerz*.
● ALBUMS: *No More Mr. Nice Guy* (Wild Pitch 1989) ★★★, *Step In The Arena* (Chrysalis 1990) ★★★★, *Daily Operation* (Chrysalis 1992) ★★, *Hard To Earn* (Chrysalis 1994) ★★★, *Moment Of Truth* (Cooltempo 1998) ★★★, *The Ownerz* (Virgin 2003) ★★★.
● COMPILATIONS: *Full Clip: A Decade Of Gang Starr* (Noo Trybe/Virgin 1999) ★★★★.

Gang's All Here, The

Although **Alice Faye**, **Carmen Miranda**, Phil Baker and **Benny Goodman** And His Orchestra were top-billed in this 1943 20th Century-Fox release, the real star, by general consent, was director-choreographer **Busby Berkeley**. Taking full advantage of Edward Cronjager's photography and the Technicolor process, early in the film Berkeley created the famous 'The Lady In The Tutti-Frutti Hat' sequence, during which dozens of girls manipulating gigantic bananas dance around Carmen Miranda, who is topped by her basket of fruit *chapeau*. Later on, Alice Faye joins a group of snazzily dressed children in the spectacular finale based on 'The Polka Dot Polka', in which Berkely added a display of pink and other delicately coloured discs and fluorescent rings to his trade-mark kaleidoscopic patterns. In between those two quite stunning set pieces, there was a slight story by Walter Bullock that involved a US Army sergeant (James Ellison) who finds it impossible to resist a nightclub singer (Faye), especially when she sings **Harry Warren** and **Leo Robin**'s tearful 'No Love, No Nothin'' and 'A Journey To A Star': millions of real-life American (and British) servicemen and civilians knew exactly how he felt. As for the rest, the slim and sassy **Charlotte Greenwood**'s high-kicks were well up to her usual standard, clarinettist Benny Goodman's vocals on 'Minnie's In The Money' and 'Paducah' (with Miranda) were not in the least offensive, and Miranda combined with Baker (and others) for the lively 'You Discover You're In New York'. Among a strong supporting cast were the always amusing Edward Everett Horton, Sheila Ryan, Eugene Pallette, Tony DeMarco, and Dave Willock. Two future movie favourites, Jeanne Crain and June Haver, also made brief appearances. The film was known as *The Girls He Left Behind* in the UK.

Gangsta Pat

b. Patrick Hall, Memphis, Tennessee, USA. Gangsta Pat is the son of Willie Hall, who had played with R&B greats like **Isaac Hayes**, and continues his family's musical traditions by playing all the instruments on his releases. He is also responsible for their writing, composition and production. He quickly rose to prominence with his 1990 debut album and single (the introductory 'I Am The Gangsta'). Both became hot items in the southwest of America, while a second set for Wrap Records spawned hit singles in 'Gangsta Boogie' and 'Stay Away From Cali'. The video for the former was particularly well received, capitalized on the then vogueish hip-hop dance craze of the same name. The rapper switched to independent labels during the mid-90s, releasing the introspective *Deadly Verses* (1995) and *Homicidal Lifestyle* (1997). He has maintained an underground following into the new millennium.

● ALBUMS: *#1 Suspect* (Atlantic 1990) ★★★, *All About Comin' Up* (Wrap/Ichiban 1993) ★★★★, *Sex, Money & Murder* (Wrap/Ichiban 1994) ★★★, *Deadly Verses* (Navarre 1995) ★★★, *Homicidal Lifestyle* (Power 1997) ★★★, *The Story Of My Life* (Redrum 1997) ★★, *Gangsta Pat And Da Street Muthafuckas* (Hitman 1998) ★★, *Tear Yo Club Down* (Redrum 1999) ★★★, *Show Ya Grill* (Redrum 2000) ★★, *Return Of The #1 Suspect* (Redrum 2001) ★★★, *Da Dro* (Redrum 2004) ★★★.

Ganja Kru

One of the collectives at the forefront of UK **jungle** in 1997, Ganja Kru is a collaboration between the pseudonymous trio of Pascal, DJ Zinc and leader DJ Hype. Releases such as 1996's 'Super Sharp Shooter' 12-inch (which sampled **LL Cool J**), the following year's *New Frontiers* EP, and 1999's *Fu-k The Millennium* EP, helped to establish a reputation for intelligent but unrelenting drum 'n' bass. With a major label contract with **RCA Records** (through its Parousia Records dependent), the trio was also made responsible for running the Frontline and Tru Playaz independent labels. The latter brought artists including **DJ Swift** and MC Fats to vinyl. Before Ganja Kru's breakthrough, all three DJs could boast of a significant past on the UK club scene.

● COMPILATIONS: *Presents Dark Light* (Obsessive 2002) ★★★.

Ganley, Allan

b. 11 March 1931, Tolworth, Surrey, England. A self-taught drummer, in the early 50s Ganley played in the dance band led by Bert **Ambrose**. In 1953 he came to prominence as a member of **John Dankworth**'s band, then the most popular modern jazz group in the UK. Also in the 50s, he worked with pianist Derek Smith, **Dizzy Reece**, clarinettist Vic Ash, **Ronnie Scott** and several visiting American musicians. Towards the end of the decade he was co-leader with **Ronnie Ross** of a small group known as the Jazzmakers. In the early 60s Ganley was often with **Tubby Hayes**, playing with his small groups and the occasionally assembled big band. As house drummer at Scott's club he played with numerous leading American jazzmen, including **Dizzy Gillespie**, **Stan Getz**, **Jim Hall**, **Freddie Hubbard** and **Rahsaan Roland Kirk**. In the early 70s he took time out to study at **Berklee College Of Music**, then returned to the UK to form and lead a big band, which he maintained sporadically for the next 10 years. Throughout the 70s and 80s Ganley could be seen and heard on countless broadcasts and recording sessions, playing with jazz musicians of all styles, effortlessly slipping from traditional to post-bop to big band to mainstream, all the while swinging with great subtlety. In the 90s Ganley was as active as ever, playing club and festival dates throughout the

UK with occasional overseas trips. The self-effacing nature of his playing has made him a perfect accompanist for pianists as different as **Teddy Wilson** and **Al Haig** and for singers from **Carol Kidd** to **Blossom Dearie**. Although less well known for his work as an arranger, Ganley has provided charts for many leading British jazzmen as well as for the BBC Radio Big Band, thus enhancing the enormous yet understated contribution he has made to the British jazz scene over the years.

● ALBUMS: with Tony Coe, John Horler, Dave Horler, Malcolm Creese *Blue Jersey* (Audio-B 1995) ★★★.

Gant, Cecil

b. 4 April 1913, Nashville, Tennessee, USA, d. 4 February 1951, Nashville, Tennessee, USA. Usually regarded as a blues singer and pianist, Gant's crooning style had a significantly wider appeal, somewhat in the manner of **Nat 'King' Cole** and **Billy Eckstine**. After playing clubs in the Nashville area in the late 30s, he joined the US Army and sang at a major War Bond Rally in Los Angeles. Signed to the Gilt-Edge label he had an enormous hit in 1945 with 'I Wonder', which he wrote with Raymond Leveen; the label credit read 'Private Cecil Gant'. Dressed in Army khaki, and billed as 'The GI Sing-sation', he toured extensively, playing to large, enthusiastic black and white audiences. After the war he appeared at clubs in Los Angeles and elsewhere, and recorded for several labels, including **King Records**, Bullet, Four Star, Downbeat/Swingtime and **Imperial Records**. For **Decca Records** (1950–51), he cut several precursors to **Bill Haley**, such as 'Rock Little Baby' and 'We're Gonna Rock', but was never able achieve anything to match the engaging 'I Wonder'. He died of pneumonia at the comparatively early age of 37.

● COMPILATIONS: *Cecil Boogie* (Flyright 1976) ★★★, *Rock Little Baby* (Flyright 1976) ★★★, *Killer Diller Boogie* (Magpie 1979) ★★★, *Rock This Boogie* (Krazy Kat 1983) ★★★, *Cecil Gant* (Krazy Kat 1990) ★★★.

Ganxsta Rid And The Otha Side

One of the least appetizing and gifted of the new breed of west coast rap collectives, Ganxsta Rid and his backing group, the Otha Side, made their debut in 1996 with *Occupation Hazardous*. The album was released in the UK on the predominantly hard rock–based Music For Nations label. The only other rap group to have made much of an impression on that label were fellow Los Angeles group **Boo-Yaa Tribe**, leading many critics to suspect that the groups were one and the same. It was later confirmed that Ganxsta Rid And The Otha Side were indeed an attempt by the Tribe to adopt a new persona and pick up on some of the commercial possibilities granted by the breakthrough of **Dr. Dre**'s G-funk style. It was an attempt that failed miserably.

● ALBUMS: *Occupation Hazardous* (Music For Nations 1996) ★★★.

Ganzie, Terry

b. Vandorne Johnson, Hanover, Jamaica, West Indies. Terry 'The Outlaw' Ganzie is often considered as the DJ who, alongside **Buju Banton**, rejuvenated **Donovan Germain**'s profile in the **dancehall**. Following on from his crossover success with **Audrey Hall** and **Freddie McGregor**, Germain's winning formula was sustained when he recruited Ganzie, **Wayne Wonder** and Banton in the early 90s. The crew often recorded in combination and when Banton signed with **Mercury**

Records Ganzie and Rebel joined him on a superb interpretation of **Little Roy**'s 'Tribal War'. Emerging from Banton's shadow Ganzie proved he was more than just a sidekick with the release of a series of hit singles notably, 'Showdown' and 'Heavy Like Lead', the latter of which lent its title to his best album. The release was considered by many to be badly timed, as Banton's international recognition resulted in less attention being paid to Ganzie's debut. Undeterred by the international indifference, Ganzie maintained a high profile in Jamaica with the 1995 hits, 'Outlaw From The Past', 'Who Is It' and the chart-topping 'Fly Away Home'. With the trend for crews in the mid-90s Ganzie, inspired by his earlier hit, recruited a group of young performers to join the Outlaw crew that included newcomers Ritchie Melody, Rapper Richie and Wayne Sample. The crew enjoyed a successful run in the dancehall, while Ganzie continued releasing his solo work. In 1996, he released the favoured 'Hey, Hello, Hi', 'Praise Jahoviah', 'Once Bitten' and 'Waan Go Home'. Ganzie continues to release dancehall hits, enjoying chart success in 2000 with 'Wicked And Hot', 'Can't Dictate' and 'Free'.

● ALBUMS: *Team Up* (VP 1992) ★★★, *Heavy Like Lead* (Profile 1993) ★★★, *Outlaw Nuff Reward* (VP 1993) ★★★★, *Loose And Running* (Intruder 1998) ★★★, *Heavy Like Lead* (Penthouse 1995) ★★★.

Gap Band

This influential US funk/soul outfit was formed in 1967 by three brothers, **Charlie Wilson** (b. Charles Wilson, Tulsa, Oklahoma, USA; vocals/keyboards), Ronnie Wilson (trumpet/keyboards) and Robert Wilson (bass/vocals). They took their name from the initials of three streets, Greenwood, Archer and Pine, in their home town of Tulsa, Oklahoma. Initially known as the Greenwood, Archer And Pine Street Band, the brothers were joined on stage by up to 10 other musicians, although their early recordings featured the slimmed down line-up of the Wilsons, James Macon (guitar), Tommy Lokey (horns) and Chris Clayton (horns). The group placed a couple of hits in the lower regions of the US R&B chart in 1977 before the departure of Macon, Lokey and Clayton. Studio musicians John Black (keyboards), Greg Phillinganes (keyboards), Glenn Nightingale (guitar) and Raymond Calhoun (drums) were then brought in to support the Wilsons.

A major label recording contract with **Mercury Records** helped raise the Gap Band's profile to a national level, and in the space of a year the group hit the R&B Top 10 with 'Shake', 'Steppin' (Out)' and 'I Don't Believe You Want To Get Up And Dance'. The last release is better known by its subtitle, 'Oops, Up Side Your Head' and this infectious dance-based song also reached the UK Top 10 in 1980. The Gap Band continued to score substantial US R&B hits; 'Burn Rubber (Why You Wanna Hurt Me)' (1980), 'Early In The Morning' and 'Outstanding' (both 1982), all topped that particular chart, while 'Yearning For Love' (1981), 'You Dropped A Bomb On Me' (1982), 'Party Train' (1983), 'Beep A Freak' (1984), 'I Found My Baby' (1985), 'Going In Circles' and 'Big Fun' (both 1986) all reached the R&B Top 10. The latter was also a UK Top 5 hit. Two years later they recorded the theme song to the movie *I'm Gonna Git You Sucka*, a pastiche of 70s 'blaxploitation' movies. Written by **Norman Whitfield**, the song was mixed by **Frankie Knuckles**, and as such confirmed the Gap Band's unerring ability to adapt to current musical fashions.

The Gap Band returned to the top of the R&B charts in 1989 with 'All Of My Love', but despite this success their commercial momentum had slowed considerably. Charlie Wilson was by now a prominent session vocalist, and during a break in Gap Band activities at the start of the 90s released his debut solo album. The brothers reunited in 1994 and resumed touring and recording. Charlie Wilson has continued to record as a solo artist in addition to working with the Gap Band.

● ALBUMS: *Magician's Holiday* (Shelter 1974) ★★, *Momma's Boys* (Shelter 1974) ★★, *The Gap Band* i (Tattoo 1976) ★★★, *The Gap Band* ii (Mercury 1977) ★★★, *II* (Mercury 1979) ★★★, *III* (Mercury 1980) ★★★★, *IV* (Total Experience 1982) ★★★★, *V: Jammin'* (Total Experience 1983) ★★★, *VI* (Total Experience 1984) ★★★, *VII* (Total Experience 1986) ★★★, *VIII* (Total Experience 1987) ★★, *Straight From The Heart* (Total Experience 1988) ★★, *Round Trip* (Capitol 1989) ★★★, *Testimony* (Rhino 1994) ★★, *Ain't Nothin' But A Party!* (Raging Bull 1997) ★★, *Live & Well* (Intersound 1996) ★★, *Gotta Get Up* (EMI 1997), *Y2K: Funkin' 'Till 2000 Comz* (Mercury/Eagle 1999) ★★, *Love At Your Fingatips* (Ark 21 2001) ★.

● COMPILATIONS: *Gap Gold: Best Of The Gap Band* (Mercury 1985) ★★★★, *The 12" Collection* (Mercury 1986) ★★★, *Greatest Hits* (Spectrum 1998) ★★★, *The Best Of Gap Band: The Millennium Collection* (Mercury 2000) ★★★, *Ultimate Collection* (Hip-O 2001) ★★★★, *Gap Band '80s* (Varèse Sarabande 2003) ★★★, *Greatest Hits* (Collectables 2004) ★★.

Garage

Like its sibling style, **house**, garage takes its name from a US nightclub. Whereas house is named after Chicago's The Warehouse, it was New York's The Paradise Garage that gave its name to this reinvention of disco music. It was the DJ **Larry Levan** who helped develop this more soulful, more vocal form of **dance music**, blending influences from disco, funk and gospel, rather than the slightly tougher electronic feel of house. Following the dance music 'explosion' in the mid-80s and the huge popularity of Chicago-based house, it was New York that took the torch, with DJ-producers such as **Todd Terry**, **Tony Humphries**, **David Morales**, Kerri Chandler and **Masters At Work** leading the way. The scene was spurred on by support and interest from the burgeoning UK club scene — with clubs such as the **Ministry Of Sound** flying in DJs such as Humphries and Masters At Work. **Danny Rampling**'s clubs 'Pure Sexy' and 'Glam' also placed an emphasis on US garage. This interest also boosted a raft of US garage labels such as **Strictly Rhythm Records**, King Street, **Nervous Records**, Perfect Pair, Freeze and Streetside. In the tradition of the disco diva the tracks were frequently led by powerful female vocals, regularly featuring the talents of singers such as **Ultra Naté**, Dajae, Jocelyn Brown and **Loleatta Holloway** among many others. Garage has remained popular in the UK, where DJ-producers such as **Joey Negro**, **Farley And Heller**, **Graeme Park**, **Ashley Beedle** and **C.J. Mackintosh** have continued to play and produce it. A sub-genre named 'speed garage' by a label-hungry media developed in the mid-90s, adding basslines, raps and vocals from drum 'n' bass, ragga and R&B to the US blueprint.

A more refined style of UK garage gained a high media profile in the late 90s and early 00s, popularized by London-based DJ-producers such as **Tuff Jam**, the **Artful Dodger** and the **Dreem Teem**. This revitalized London scene gave rise to numerous pirate radio stations, mix compilations and a migrating summer scene in Ayia Napa, Cyprus. Somewhat reminiscent of the dance scene in **Ibiza**, the Ayia Napa garage scene was even documented in a weekly television programme, *Fantasy Island*, on the UK's Channel Four. By the end of 2000, however, the scene had begun to fragment, with the original DJs reacting testily to the gimmicky 'breakbeat garage' style of younger crews such as **Oxide And Neutrino** and DJ Dee Kline.

● FURTHER READING: *My Life And The Paradise Garage: Keep On Dancin'*, Mel Cheren and Gabriel Rotello.

Garbage

This US-based rock band, founded in 1993, was immediately heralded in the press as a producers' supergroup. In addition to several other notable bands (**Smashing Pumpkins**, **U2**), Butch Vig (b. 2 August 1957, Viroqua, Wisconsin, USA) had previously produced **Nirvana**'s influential *Nevermind*. He formed Garbage with the help of his long-standing remixing partners Steve Marker (b. 16 March 1959, Minneapolis, Minnesota, USA) and Duke Erikson (b. 15 January 1953, Nebraska, USA), with whom he had been involved in the bands Spooner and Firetown. To this core trio was added singer Shirley Manson (b. 26 August 1966, Edinburgh, Scotland), recruited after the members saw her fronting her former unit, Angel Fish, on a video shown on **MTV** (she had previously sung with the unheralded **Goodbye Mr Mackenzie**). Garbage's debut single, 'Vow', issued in a metal sleeve, was widely acclaimed, as was the follow-up, 'Subhuman'. Both borrowed from various traditions, notably punk, glam rock and art rock, with Vig commenting: 'We want to use all these different elements like techno, punk and noise, ambient, jazz and rock, and mix them all up around a pop song.' This eclecticism was further explored on their 1995 self-titled debut album, a dark collection of songs with the main emotions being fear, lust and envy. Symptomatic of these concerns was 'Only Happy When It Rains', which reached the US and UK charts when issued as a single. Further UK chart entries came with a remix of 'Milk' (featuring **Tricky** as guest vocalist) and 'Stupid Girl', a US Top 30/UK Top 5 success.

Garbage's unexpected global success (especially in America) delayed the recording of their follow-up as they committed themselves to a relentless touring schedule. In the interim, the *Romeo & Juliet* soundtrack song '#1 Crush' reached the US Top 30. When *Version 2.0* finally appeared in 1998 the band gained further praise for their compelling blend of slick electronic pop featuring Manson's emotive vocals. The album topped the UK charts in May 1998 and generated the hit singles 'Push It', 'I Think I'm Paranoid', 'Special', 'When I Grow Up' and 'You Look So Fine'.

In 1999, Garbage was commissioned to write the theme tune to the new James Bond movie, *The World Is Not Enough*, giving the band another UK Top 20 hit. Their third album, 2001's *Beautifulgarbage*, lacked the stand-out singles from the earlier releases but was nevertheless another highly impressive collection. The album's commercial failure prompted a lengthy hiatus during which the various members concentrated on other matters. They returned to

the studio in 2004 to complete an album for new label **Geffen Records**. While hardly breaking any new ground, *Bleed Like Me* was a slick, impeccably performed and produced collection of modern rock songs. In September 2005 the band announced they would be taking an extended hiatus after completing their Australian tour.

● ALBUMS: *Garbage* (Almo Sounds/Mushroom 1995) ★★★★, *Version 2.0* (Almo Sounds/Mushroom 1998) ★★★, *Beautifulgarbage* (Interscope/Mushroom 2001) ★★★★, *Bleed Like Me* (Geffen 2005) ★★★.

● DVD/VIDEOS: *Video* (Almo Sounds/Mushroom 1996).

Garbarek, Jan

b. 4 March 1947, Norway. Inspired by hearing **John Coltrane** on the radio in 1961, Garbarek taught himself to play tenor saxophone (subsequently adding soprano and bass saxophone). In 1962 he won an amateur competition, which resulted in his first professional work, and he was soon leading a group with **Jon Christensen**, **Terje Rypdal** and **Arild Andersen**. In 1968 he was the Norwegian representative at the European Broadcasting Union festival, and the recordings of this (notably an impressive version of Coltrane's 'Naima') brought him to wider notice when they were transmitted throughout Europe. Subsequently his style has become more severe, sometimes almost bleak, although there is a restrained warmth to his sound. Garbarek's playing is representative of the kind of music associated with **Manfred Eicher**'s **ECM Records** and of a characteristically Scandinavian strand of jazz, melodic and atmospheric, which has little overt emotionalism but does not lack intensity. Garbarek's writing and playing display considerable concern with tone and texture and appear to have exerted some influence on **Tommy Smith** and post-sabbatical **Charles Lloyd** (with whom he has shared colleagues Christensen, **Keith Jarrett** and Palle Danielsson) as well as a variety of European players such as Joakim Milder and Alberto Nacci.

In the mid-70s Garbarek worked in Jarrett's 'Belonging' band with Christensen and Danielsson, recording the much-praised *Belonging* and *My Song*, and also played with **Ralph Towner** on *Solstice* and *Sounds And Shadows*. In the 80s his own groups featured **Eberhard Weber**, **Bill Frisell** and **John Abercrombie** among others. His tours in the late 80s with a band including the remarkable percussionist **Nana Vasconcelos** were highly acclaimed and inspired many other musicians and bands to essay the juxtaposition of glacially imposing saxophone lines with exotic, tropical rhythm. Garbarek has also worked with **Don Cherry**, **Chick Corea**, **David Torn** and with **George Russell** during Russell's residency in Scandinavia in the late 60s—an association that resulted in a fine series of recordings featuring the young Garbarek, notably *Othello Ballet Suite*, *Trip To Prillarguri* and *Electronic Sonata For Souls Loved By Nature* (though none was released until the 80s). Garbarek has also shown an increasing interest in folk and ethnic musics that has not only coloured his own playing but led to him recording with **Ravi Shankar** on the 1984 *Song For Everyone* and producing an ECM album for the Norwegian folk singer Agnes Buen Gårnas, 1991's *Rosensfole*. For *Ragas & Sagas* (1993), Garbarek collaborated with the Pakistani classical singer, **Usted Fateh Ali Khan** and a trio of musicians playing tabla and sarangi, a 39-string violin. Garbarek's melodic solos effectively complemented the traditional Pakistani instrumental sounds. In the same year, Garbarek's *Twelve Moons* concentrated once again on the Scandinavian folk melodies he is continually exploring. The album's emphatic rhythmic 'feel' was due in no small part to the presence of drummer Manu Katché and bass player **Eberhard Weber**.

Rather surprisingly, given his avoidance of gallery-pleasing pyrotechnics, Garbarek has steadily acquired a public following equal to his huge critical reputation. His collaboration with the Hilliard Ensemble, *Officium*, became a surprise hit on both the jazz and classical charts, although the album managed to offend as many old fans as it attracted new ones. Observers of the UK Top 75 album chart in the spring of 1996 would not have been as shocked as would a jazz fan, but horror upon horror, Garbarek's *Visible World* became a hit. The highly accessible nature of the opening tracks such as 'Red Wind', 'The Creek' and the folk-inspired 'The Survivor' aided its wider appeal. World music followers would also have found a great rapport with the 12-minute mantra 'Evening Land', featuring some wonderful vocals from **Marie Boine**. Following 1998's acclaimed *Rites*, Garbarek collaborated with the Hilliard Ensemble on the following year's *Mnemosyne*. A lengthy wait followed before Garbarek returned to the studio to record *In Praise Of Dreams* with his new trio, featuring Armenian-American classical violinist Kim Kashkashian and drummer Manu Katché.

● ALBUMS: *Esoteric Circle* (Freedom 1969) ★★★, *Afric Pepperbird* (ECM 1971) ★★★, with Bobo Stenson, Terje Rypdal, Arild Andersen, Jon Christensen *Sart* (ECM 1971) ★★★, with Arild Andersen, Edward Vesala *Triptykon* (ECM 1972) ★★★, with Art Lande *Red Lanta* (ECM 1974) ★★★, with Bobo Stenson *Witchi-Tai-To* (ECM 1973) ★★★, with Stenson *Dansere* (ECM 1975) ★★★, *Dis* (ECM 1977) ★★★★, *Places* (ECM 1978) ★★★★, *Photo With Blue Sky* (ECM 1979) ★★★, with Kjell Johnsen *Aftenland* (ECM 1980) ★★★, with Haden, Gismonti *Folksongs* (ECM 1981) ★★★★, *Eventyr* (ECM 1981) ★★★, *Paths, Prints* (ECM 1982) ★★★, *Wayfarer* (ECM 1983) ★★★, *It's OK To Listen To The Gray Voice* (ECM 1985) ★★★★★, *All Those Born With Wings* (ECM 1986) ★★★, *Legend Of The Seven Dreams* (ECM 1988) ★★★, *I Took Up The Runes* (ECM 1990) ★★★★, with Peter Erskine, Miroslav Vitous *Star* (ECM 1991) ★★★, with Agnes Buen Gårnas *Rosensfole* (ECM 1991) ★★★, with Nusrat Fateh Ali Khan and Musicians From Pakistan *Ragas & Sagas* (ECM 1992) ★★★, *Twelve Moons* (ECM 1993) ★★★★, with Vitous *Atmos* (ECM 1993) ★★★, *Madar* (ECM 1993) ★★★, with the Hilliard Ensemble *Officium* (ECM New Series 1994) ★★★, *Visible World* (ECM 1996) ★★★★, *Rites* (ECM 1998) ★★★★, with the Hilliard Ensemble *Mnemosyne* (ECM New Series 1999) ★★★, *In Praise Of Dreams* (ECM 2004) ★★★.

● COMPILATIONS: *Works* (ECM 1984) ★★★, *Selected Recordings* (ECM 2002) ★★★★.

Garber, Jan

b. 5 November 1897, Morristown, Pennsylvania, USA, d. 5 October 1977, Shreveport, Louisiana, USA. Known as 'The Idol of the Air Lanes', Garber led both sweet and swing bands, although he is generally remembered as a creator of saccharine sounds. He attended the University of North Carolina and later became a violinist with the Philadelphia Symphony Orchestra. After military service in World War I he formed a band with pianist **Milt Davis** and during the early 20s founded his own band, which performed much of the

then popular 'hot' jazz style. When **Guy Lombardo**'s Royal Canadians began making the headlines in the late 20's, Garber took over **Freddie Large**'s Orchestra, yet another Canadian sweet band, and headed down the Lombardo path to success, offering syrupy saxophones, muted brass and a few comedy routines in an effort to win friends and influence radio stations. The band became a popular attraction, gaining a coveted spot on the Burns And Allen radio series. In 1942 Garber did a backflip once again and headed into the world of swing, employing Gray Rains to write some fine arrangements, with vocals being provided by Liz Tilton, sister of **Martha Tilton**, and her male counterpart **Bob Davis**. Not even an appearance in the film *Here Comes Elmer*, which also featured **Nat 'King' Cole**, gained Garber's new sound a substantial following. It was no surprise then when, four years later, he reverted to the sweet format once more in 1945. In 1949 the Garber band was back on film in *Make Believe Ballroom* alongside **Charlie Barnet** and **Jimmy Dorsey**. They also had two hit records that year with 'You're Breaking My Heart' and 'Jealous Heart'. As the big band era faded, Garber continued to record, but by the 60s was only working occasionally mainly on the west coast.

● COMPILATIONS: *Jan Garber And Orchestra Play 22 Big Band Recordings* (Hindsight 1984) ★★★★, *Uncollected Jan Garber And His Orchestra* 1939–41 recordings (Hindsight 1985) ★★★, *Jan Garber 1939/41* (Hindsight 1988) ★★★, *Original Live Radio Broadcasts* (Hindsight 1988) ★★★.

Garbutt, Vin

b. Vincent Paul Garbutt, 20 November 1947, South Bank, Middlesbrough, Cleveland, England. Having served a six-year apprenticeship with ICI, Garbutt decided to go to Europe in 1969. While there he managed to earn his living by singing and playing in bars. When he returned to England, he continued performing in a full-time capacity as a singer-songwriter, guitarist and whistle player. Garbutt has a distinctive voice and commands a huge following on the folk circuit, both at home and abroad. His albums have been well received, but many feel that live performances show Garbutt at his best. His combination of jigs and hornpipes, played on tin whistle, are backed by songs of strong insight. One example of this is 'The Chemical Workers Song', from the 1975 recording *The Young Tin Whistle Pest*, written by Ron Angel. The 1983 album *Little Innocents* caused considerable comment on release due to its uncompromising stance on abortion. All royalties from the sale of the album were directed to a number of pro-Life charities.

The 1990 release *When The Tide Turns* remains Garbutt's bestselling album. The recording featured a number of notable musicians from outside the folk arena. A video by Home Roots Music, *The South Banker Show*, was released in 1992 featuring Garbutt singing and telling stories. During the same period Garbutt began recording for his own Home Roots Music label. The all-new *Word Of Mouth*, released in 1999, marked his 30 years in the business. After recovering from major heart surgery at the start of 2005, Garbutt embarked on the recording of his new album, *Persona . . . Grata*.

● ALBUMS: *The Valley Of Tees* (Trailer 1972) ★★★, *The Young Tin Whistle Pest* (Topic 1975) ★★★★, *King Gooden* (Topic 1976) ★★, *Eston California* (Topic 1977) ★★★, *Tossin' A Wobbler* (Topic 1978) ★★★, *Little Innocents* (Topic 1983) ★★★, *Shy Tot Pommy—Live* (Celtic Music

1985) ★★★, *When The Tide Turns* (Celtic Music 1990) ★★★★, *The Bypass Syndrome* (Home Roots Music 1991) ★★★, *The South Banker Show* (Home Roots 1992) ★★★, *Bandalised* (Home Roots Music 1994) ★★★, *Plugged* (Home Roots Music 1996) ★★★, *Word Of Mouth* (Home Roots Music 1999) ★★★, *Persona . . . Grata* (Home Roots Music 2005) ★★★.

● DVD/VIDEOS: *The South Banker Show* (Home Roots Music 1992).

Garcia, Andy

b. *c.*1953, Bricktown, New Jersey, USA, d. 19 November 2002, California, USA. Interested in singing from early childhood, Garcia learned his chosen trade, and gained a substantial following, working in hotels and clubs in towns and cities in Florida, Illinois, Colorado, and many other states before making his name in New York City. Among the many clubs he played in the city were Kelly's, Gypsy's, Club Manhattan, Upstairs At Greene Street, Don't Tell Mama, and The Triad. Garcia won the 1988 *Backstage* magazine Bistro Award as Outstanding Vocalist and in the same year the Manhattan Association of Cabaret and Clubs (MAC) Award for his cabaret debut. In 1997, he appeared in the acclaimed *Miracle On 35th Street* benefit for the Manhattan Center for Living. Despite the high quality of other acts, including **Betty Buckley**, **Baby Jane Dexter**, and **Liza Minnelli**, Garcia's performance proved to be a highlight. Garcia sang in an emotionally charged manner; unusually for a cabaret artist, his powerful lyric tenor voice was of operatic quality. For several years he suffered from brain cancer but fought bravely and successfully against the disease. The cause of his early death was given as kidney failure resulting from late-diagnosed diabetes.

Garcia, Jerry

b. 1 August 1942, San Francisco, California, USA, d. 9 August 1995, Forest Knolls, California, USA. The mercurial guitarist of the **Grateful Dead** was able to simultaneously play with two or three other conglomerations without it affecting his career as leader of one of rock music's legendary bands. For four decades Garcia was a leading light on the west coast musical scene—he was credited on **Jefferson Airplane**'s *Surrealistic Pillow* as 'musical and spiritual adviser' and known locally as 'Captain Trips'. In addition to his session work with the Airplane, he worked with **David Crosby**, **Paul Kantner**, **Jefferson Starship**, **New Riders Of The Purple Sage** and **Crosby, Stills, Nash And Young** as well as various spin-offs involving David Nelson, **John Kahn**, **David Grisman**, **Peter Rowan**, **Merl Saunders** and Howard Wales (ex-**A.B. Skhy**). Garcia was equally at home on banjo and pedal-steel guitar, and had the ability to play two entirely different styles of music without a hint of musical overlap (rock 'n' roll/blues and country/bluegrass). His flowing manner was all the more remarkable given that the third finger of his right hand was missing, owing to an accident as a child. Jerry and his older brother Tiff were both chopping wood with axes, Jerry kept putting his finger on the block and removing it just in time before Tiff chopped the wood. He was a split second too late and Tiff accidentally chopped the finger.

Garcia was known and loved as a true hippie who never 'sold out'. Following his heroin addiction and much publicized near-death in 1986, Garcia philosophically stated, 'I'm 45 years old, I'm ready for anything, I didn't even plan on living this long, so all this shit is add-on stuff.' He continued touring and recording, with the Dead, David Grisman, and with his own versions of the Jerry Garcia Band, until shortly before his death from a heart attack during a stay at the Serenity Knolls treatment centre, near his home in Marin County, California (see Grateful Dead entry). Years of drug abuse, heavy smoking and a bad diet (he loved hot dogs) contributed to his decline. This should not overshadow the love and affection he commanded, and his major significance as a dedicated musician, singer and songwriter. Garcia had an incredibly wide musical palette. He could play with anybody at anytime, almost anywhere, and retained the remarkable ability to play any style or genre. The posthumous release *The Pizza Tapes* demonstrates this; it is a spontaneous recording full of the sheer joy of being able to play with other musicians in an informal atmosphere. His was a rare genius.

● ALBUMS: *Hooteroll* (Douglas 1971) ★★, *Garcia* (Warners 1972) ★★★★, with Merl Saunders, John Kahn, Bill Vitt *Live At The Keystone* (Fantasy 1973) ★★★, *Garcia (Compliments)* (Round 1974) ★★★, *Reflections* (Reflections 1976) ★★, *Cats Under The Stars* (Arista 1978) ★★★★, *Run For The Roses* (Arista 1982) ★★★, with Saunders, Kahn, Vitt *Keystone Encores, Volume 1* 1973 recording (Fantasy 1988) ★★, with Saunders, Kahn, Vitt *Keystone Encores, Volume 2* 1973 recording (Fantasy 1988) ★★, as the Jerry Garcia Acoustic Band *Almost Acoustic* (Grateful Dead 1989) ★★★, *Jerry Garcia Band* (Arista 1991) ★★★★, with David Grisman *Garcia/Grisman* (Acoustic Disc 1991) ★★★★, with Grisman *Not For Kids Only* (Acoustic Disc 1993) ★★★, with Grisman *Shady Grove* (Acoustic 1996) ★★★, *How Sweet It Is* (Grateful Dead Records 1997) ★★★, with Grisman *So What* (Acoustic Disc 1998) ★★★, with Grisman, Tony Rice *The Pizza Tapes* (Acoustic Disc 2000) ★★★★, with Grisman *Been All Around This World* (Acoustic Disc 2004) ★★★, *After Midnight Kean College, 2/28/80* (Rhino 2004) ★★★, *Theatre 1839, San Francisco* 1977 recording (Jerry Garcia Estate 2004) ★★★.

● COMPILATIONS: *Shining Star* (Arista 2001) ★★★, *All Good Things: Jerry Garcia Studio Sessions* 6-CD box set (Rhino 2004) ★★★, *Ladder To The Stars: Garcia Plays Dylan* (Rhino 2005) ★★★, *Collection Vol. 1: Legion Of Mary* (Rhino 2005) ★★★.

● DVD/VIDEOS: with David Grisman *Grateful Dawg* (Columbia Tristar 2003), *Jerry Garcia Band Live At Shoreline* (Rhino 2005).

● FURTHER READING: *Garcia: A Signpost To A New Space*, Charles Reich and Jann Wenner. *Grateful Dead: The Music Never Stopped*, Blair Jackson. *Captain Trips: A Biography Of Jerry Garcia*, Sandy Troy. *Living With The Dead*, Rock Scully with David Dalton. *Sweet Chaos: The Grateful Dead's American Adventure*, Carol Brightman. *Garcia*, Editors of Rolling Stone. *Dark Star: An Oral Biography Of Jerry Garcia*, Robert Greenfield. *Garcia: An American Life*, Blair Jackson.

Gardiner, Boris

b. 13 January 1946, Kingston, Jamaica, West Indies. Boris Gardiner, bass player, vocalist and musical director, has never been one of reggae's most celebrated names, but he has remained a permanent fixture in the music and has three major UK chart hits to his credit. His bass-playing skills first emerged in the late 60s, and the bands he graced included **Byron Lee**'s Dragonaires, the **Aggrovators**, Crystalites and many more. His first brush with chart success was 'Elizabethan Reggae', recorded for Lee, which hit number 14 in January 1970. Gardiner toured the UK in support of his hit, which, at first, was incorrectly credited to its producer. His debut album, again produced by Lee, was released the same year. In its wake, Gardiner immersed himself in session work, regularly playing as part of the **Now Generation** band, and he later became a member of **Lee Perry**'s **Upsetters**, following Carlton and **Aston 'Family-man' Barrett**'s defection to the **Wailers**. His solid, incisive basslines were seldom prominent, yet always effective. In the 80s, as reggae was on the cusp of the digital era, an age likely to put paid to the careers of bass players, Gardiner's mellow, soulful voice came to the fore on a MOR reggae ballad, 'I Want To Wake Up With You', which hit number 1 in the UK charts. Gardiner, who had been intermittently dogged by illness throughout the 80s, was finally receiving his due. His follow-up, 'You're Everything To Me', went to number 11, and the seasonal 'The Meaning Of Christmas' also scraped the charts.

● ALBUMS: *Reggae Happening* (Duke 1970) ★★★★, *I Want To Wake Up With You* (Revue 1986) ★★★, *Everything To Me* (Revue 1986) ★★, *Its Nice To Be With You* (K&K 1986) ★★★, *Soulful Experience* (Dynamic 1988) ★★★, *Let's Take A Holiday* (WKS 1989) ★★★.

● COMPILATIONS: *Classic Tracks* (Counterpoint 1988) ★★★, *Reggae Happening* (Jamaican Gold 1994) ★★★★.

Gardner, Dave

b. 11 June 1926, Jackson, Tennessee, USA. Vocalist 'Brother' Dave Gardner first hit the US charts in 1957 with a rendition of 'White Silver Sands', which climbed into the Top 30. He achieved no UK success; in fact the only single released was 'Hop Along Rock' on **Brunswick Records** in 1958. From 1960–63 he charted in with four comedy albums under the name 'Brother Dave', including *Rejoice, Dear Hearts!* and *Kick Thy Own Self*, which both made the US Top 5 in 1960.

● ALBUMS: *Rejoice, Dear Hearts!* (RCA Victor 1960) ★★★, *Kick Thy Own Self* (RCA Victor 1960) ★★, *Ain't That Weird* (RCA Victor 1961) ★★, *Did You Ever* (RCA Victor 1962) ★★★, *All Seriousness Aside* (RCA Victor 1963) ★★★, *It Don't Make No Difference* (1963) ★★★.

Gare, Lou

b. Leslie Arthur Gare 16 June 1939, Rugby, Warwickshire, England. A unique tenor saxophonist, deriving some elements of his playing from **Sonny Rollins**, Gare was a member of the early **Mike Westbrook** Band. He, Keith Rowe (guitar) and Lawrence Sheaff (cello/clarinet) found themselves increasingly at odds with the rest of the unit and inevitably split away. After moving to London, Gare, Rowe, and drummer **Eddie Prévost** founded **AMM**. Gare's improvising typified the AMM approach, not least in his use of passages of silence, and the underpinning melodic logic of even his most abstract solos is so compelling that he gives a potent impression of phrases continuing, understood but unheard, through the gaps he leaves. During much of the 70s AMM comprised only Gare and Prévost, but Gare left the band and went to live in Exeter, Devon. For a while he led a free jazz trio but, although he occasionally plays with Prévost and others, including bass player Marcio Mattos, he has virtually given up public performing.

Garfunkel, Art

b. Arthur Garfunkel, 5 November 1941, Forest Hills, New York City, USA. The possessor of one of the most pitch-perfect voices in popular music has had a sparse recording career since the initial demise of **Simon And Garfunkel** in 1970. The break-up of one of the most successful post-war singing duos was due in part to Garfunkel's desire to go into acting, and **Paul Simon**'s understandable resentment that his non-songwriting partner took the glory on his compositions like 'Bridge Over Troubled Water'. While Simon had the songs, Garfunkel possessed *the* voice. The split would be revisited in 'The Breakup', included on Garfunkel's 1993 oddities collection, *Up 'Til Now*, though by this time the two parties had made their peace.

In terms of personal history, Garfunkel can lay claim to a masters degree in mathematics, and the fact that he completed a mission to walk all the way across the USA, in 100-mile increments (commemorated by the 1997 live release *Across America*). His solo recording career actually started while he was singing with Simon as the duo **Tom And Jerry**. Two solo singles were released in 1961 under the name of Artie Garr, 'Private World'/'Forgive Me' and 'Beat Love'/'Dream Alone'. In the late 70s and early 80s, Garfunkel's acting career landed him substantial parts in *Catch-22*, *Carnal Knowledge*, *Bad Timing* and *Good To Go*. During this time his recorded output, although sporadic, was of a consistently high quality. His 1973 debut *Angel Clare* contained the beautiful 'All I Know', which was a US Top 10 hit. In the UK two of his records made the top spot, a luscious 'I Only Have Eyes For You' and the **Mike Batt** theme for *Watership Down*, 'Bright Eyes'. In 1978 '(What A) Wonderful World' featured the additional voices of **James Taylor** and Paul Simon, fuelling rumours of a reunion. The track appeared on *Watermark*, which otherwise featured Garfunkel tackling an album's worth of **Jimmy Webb** classics. Garfunkel and Simon appeared together occasionally both on television and on record, but it was not until October 1981 that the historic Central Park concert occurred. The duo struggled through a world tour, opening up old wounds, until once again they parted company. Garfunkel resumed his solo career, the best moments of which remained largely attributable to the songwriting of Jimmy Webb (notably on 1981's *Scissors Cut* and 1986's delightful seasonal album *The Animals' Christmas*, recorded with **Amy Grant**). In the autumn of 1993, he reunited with Paul Simon to complete 21 sell-out dates in New York. A further reunion took place in 2003. The previous year Garfunkel had recorded an album with Maia Sharp (daughter of songwriter Randy Sharp) and Buddy Mondlock.

● ALBUMS: *Angel Clare* (Columbia 1973) ★★★, *Breakaway* (Columbia 1975) ★★★★, *Watermark* (Columbia 1977) ★★★★, *Fate For Breakfast* (Columbia 1979) ★★, *Scissors Cut* (Watermark 1981) ★★★, with Amy Grant *The Animals' Christmas* (Columbia 1986) ★★★★, *Lefty* (Columbia 1988) ★★, *Across America* (Virgin 1997) ★★★, *Songs From A Parent To A Child* (Sony Wonder 1997) ★★, with Maia Sharp, Buddy Mondlock *Everything Waits To Be Noticed* (EMI Manhattan 2002) ★★★.

● COMPILATIONS: *The Art Garfunkel Album* (CBS 1984) ★★★, *Garfunkel: Best Of* (Columbia 1990) ★★★★, *Up 'Til Now* (Columbia 1993) ★★.

● FURTHER READING: *Still Water: Prose Poems*, Art Garfunkel.

● FILMS: *Monterey Pop* (1968), *Catch-22* (1970), *Carnal Knowledge* (1971), *Bad Timing* (1980), *Good To Go* aka *Short Fuse* (1986), *Boxing Helena* (1993), *54* (1998), *Longshot* aka *Jack Of All Trades* (2000).

Garland, Ed 'Montudie'

b. Edward Bertrand Garland, 9 January 1885, New Orleans, Louisiana, USA, d. 22 January 1980, Los Angeles, California, USA. As a child, Garland played drums and brass bass, often working in marching bands in his home town. Among the early jazz stars with whom he claims to have played were **Buddy Bolden** (1904), **Freddie Keppard** (1906), and **Kid Ory** (1910). By 1914 he was based in Chicago, from where he toured the black vaudeville circuit, but was on hand in 1921 to help form a band, led by **King Oliver**, to play a residency at the city's newly opened Royal Garden. When the Oliver band toured California, Garland, by now playing string bass, stayed behind in Los Angeles, working frequently with Ory. In 1927 he formed his own group in Los Angeles, which lasted for a number of years. Late in 1940 he assembled a band to be led by **Jelly Roll Morton** for a recording date, but Morton was gravely ill and died before the session could take place.

In 1944 Garland was a member of a band assembled by Orson Welles for a series of radio programmes. The Mercury Theatre All Stars included **Jimmy Noone**, who died on the morning of the third broadcast, and an impromptu performance of 'Blues For Jimmy' featured a bowed bass solo by Garland, which thereafter became a permanent part of his repertoire. In 1944 Garland, was reunited with Ory and remained with him for the next decade, their relationship ending when a misunderstanding led to a fist-fight at the Hangover club in San Francisco. From 1955 Garland freelanced with **Andy Blakeney**, **Earl 'Fatha' Hines**, **Turk Murphy** and others. In 1971 he returned to his birthplace for the first time in over half a century to play at the 4th New Orleans Jazz Festival. From 1973 Garland played at several festivals and toured the USA and Europe with **Barry Martyn**'s Legends Of Jazz band. Despite failing sight and hearing, and general frailty, Garland toured until September 1977, when he was hospitalized in Germany. Back home in Los Angeles he retired, at the age of 92, but still played with the Legends Of Jazz whenever they came to town. Although he often played his instrument in the traditional 'slapping' manner, Garland had a notably light touch but he favoured using the bow, thus adding variety to his always rhythmic support.

Garland, Hank

b. Walter Louis Garland, 11 November 1930, Cowpens, South Carolina, USA, d. 27 December 2004, Orange Park, Florida, USA. A professional electric guitarist at the age of 15, Garland played on *The Grand Ole Opry* with **Paul Howard** for several weeks, before Howard found out he was violating the state's child labour laws and reluctantly sent the talented youngster home. Garland returned on his sixteenth birthday to Nashville, where he quickly became one of the most popular and respected session guitarists and played on recordings by countless artists. In 1950, he made his first solo recordings for **Decca Records**, even including a few vocals, which clearly failed to match his instrumental talent. His recording of 'Sugarfoot Rag' not only inspired his nickname ('Sugarfoot'), it also firmly established him in Nashville. During the 50s, he recorded for Decca and **Dot Records**, being remembered for versions of 'E-String Rag' and 'Guitar Shuffle', and also

worked with **Chet Atkins**. In the late 50s, Garland's playing was a prominent part of the coming of the Nashville Sound and his work extended to rockabilly and recording with **Elvis Presley**, **Roy Orbison** and the **Everly Brothers**. In 1959, it was Garland who played the lead on **Jim Reeves**' recording of 'He'll Have To Go' and later on **Patsy Cline**'s 'I Fall To Pieces'. Garland also became respected in other genres of music, particularly jazz, which he had always loved. He appeared at the 1960 **Newport Jazz Festival** and made jazz recordings with **Gary Burton** (vibes), **Joe Morello** (drums) and Joe Benjamin (bass), most notably the superb 1961 set *Jazz Winds From A New Direction*.

On 8 September 1961, a serious car crash near Springfield, Tennessee, left him in a coma for some weeks and although he slowly recovered, the crash permanently affected his co-ordination. Considerable practice saw him managing to play a few bars but he could never remember what he was playing and his professional career ended. He left Nashville in 1963 and lived for a time in Milwaukee, but moved to South Carolina after his wife's death in a car crash. It seems that in 1962, he was so respected by his fellow musicians that they often added his name to Musician Union forms indicating he should be paid for playing on sessions. In later years he resided in Jacksonville, Florida, with his brother. Garland, who passed away in December 2004, greatly influenced a whole new generation of guitarists including **Willie Nelson** and **Albert Lee**.

● ALBUMS: *Velvet Guitar: The Guitar Artistry Of Hank Garland* (Columbia Harmony 1960) ★★★, *Jazz Winds From A New Direction* (Columbia 1961) ★★★★, *The Unforgettable Guitar Of Hank Garland* (RCA 1962) ★★★.
● COMPILATIONS: *Hank Garland & His Sugar Footers* (Bear Family 1992) ★★★★, *Move! The Guitar Artistry Of Hank Garland* (Euphoria 2001) ★★★★.

Garland, Joe

b. Joseph Copeland Garland, 15 August 1903, Norfolk, Virginia, USA, d. 21 April 1977, Teaneck, New Jersey, USA. After studying formally and playing clarinet and saxophones in concert bands, Garland moved into dance band and jazz work under **Elmer Snowden**, Leon Abbey, **Jelly Roll Morton**, the **Mills Blue Rhythm Band**, **Lucky Millinder** and **Duke Ellington**. In the late 30s and through most of the 40s he freelanced with various bands, including two spells as a member of **Louis Armstrong**'s big band, where his skilled musicianship made him invaluable. In due course he became musical director of the band, a position he also held with **Earl Hines** in the late 40s. In the early 50s Garland ended his full-time involvement in music, turning instead to what became a very successful career in photography. Highly respected by fellow musicians, Garland is best remembered today for two of his compositions: 'Leap Frog', which was recorded by Armstrong in 1941, and became the theme tune of **Les Brown** And His Band Of Renown, while 'In The Mood' was **Joe Loss**' theme and a hit record for **Glenn Miller**.

Garland, Judy

b. Frances Ethel Gumm, 10 June 1922, Grand Rapids, Minnesota, USA, d. 22 June 1969, Chelsea, London, England. The Gumms were a theatrical family. Parents Frank and Ethel had appeared in vaudeville as Jack and Virginia Lee, and later, with the addition of their first two daughters, Mary Jane and Virginia, they appeared locally as 'The Four

Gumms'. 'Baby Frances' joined the troupe when she was just over two years of age, and it was quickly apparent that with her arrival, even at that early age, the Gumm family had outgrown their locale. The family moved to Los Angeles, where all three girls were enrolled in a dance school. When Frank Gumm bought a run-down theatre in Lancaster, a desert town north of Los Angeles, the family moved again. Domestic problems beset the Gumm family throughout this period and Frances' life was further disrupted by Ethel Gumm's determined belief in her youngest daughter's showbusiness potential. The act had become the Gumm Sisters, although Baby Frances was clearly the one audiences wanted to see and hear. In 1933 Ethel Gumm returned to Los Angeles, taking the girls with her. Frances was again enrolled in a theatrical school.

A visit to Chicago was an important step for the girls, with the youngest once more attracting the most attention; here too, at the urging of comedian George Jessell, they changed their name to the Garland Sisters. On their return to Los Angeles in 1934 the sisters played a successful engagement at Grauman's Chinese Theater in Hollywood. Soon afterwards, Frances was personally auditioned by Louis B. Mayer, head of MGM. Deeply impressed by what he saw and heard, Mayer signed the girl before she had even taken a screen test. With another adjustment to her name, Frances became Judy Garland. She made her first notable film appearance in **Every Sunday** (1936), a short musical film that also featured **Deanna Durbin**. Her first major impact on audiences came with her third film, **Broadway Melody** Of 1938, in which she sang 'Dear Mr Gable' (to a photograph of Clark Gable), segueing into 'You Made Me Love You'. She was then teamed with MGM's established child star **Mickey Rooney**, a partnership that brought a succession of popular films in the 'Andy Hardy' series. By now, everyone at MGM knew that they had a star on their hands. This fact was triumphantly confirmed with her appearance in **The Wizard Of Oz** (1939), in which she sang 'Over The Rainbow', the song with which she would subsequently always be associated. Unfortunately, this period of frenzied activity came at a time when she was still developing physically.

Like many young teenagers, Garland tended to put on weight, which was something film makers could not tolerate. Undoubtedly, they did not want a podgy celebrity, and continuity considerations could not allow their star to change appearance during the course of the film. Regardless of the reason, she was prescribed some drugs for weight control, others to ensure she was bright and perky for the long hours of shooting, and still more to bring her down at the end of the day so that she could sleep. This was long before the side effects of amphetamines (which she took to suppress her appetite) were understood, and no one at the time was aware that the pills she was consuming in such huge quantities were highly addictive. Added to the growing girl's problems were emotional difficulties that had begun during her parents' stormy relationship and were exacerbated by the pressures of her new life. In 1941, against the wishes and advice of her mother and the studio, she married **David Rose** and soon afterwards became pregnant, but was persuaded by her mother and Mayer to have an abortion. With her personal life already on a downward spiral, Garland's successful film career conversely took a further upswing. In 1942 she appeared in **For Me And My Gal**, then made *Presenting Lily Mars*, **Thousands Cheer**, **Girl Crazy** (all 1943), **Meet Me In St. Louis** (1944), **The Harvey Girls**, **Ziegfeld Follies** and **Till The Clouds Roll By** (all 1946). Garland's popularity extended beyond films into radio and records, but her private life was still in disarray.

In 1945 Garland divorced Rose and married **Vincente Minnelli**, who had directed her in *Meet Me In St Louis*. In 1946 her daughter, **Liza Minnelli**, was born. The late 40s brought more film successes with **The Pirate, Easter Parade, Words And Music** (all 1948) and *In The Good Old Summertime* (1949). Although Garland's career appeared to be in splendid shape, in 1950 her private life was fast deteriorating. Pills, alcohol and severe emotional disturbances led to her failing to appear before the cameras on several occasions and resulted in the ending of her contract with MGM. In 1951 her marriage to Minnelli also dissolved and she attempted suicide. Her subsequent marriage to Sid Luft and his handling of her career brought an upturn both emotionally and professionally. She made a trip to Europe, appearing at the London Palladium to great acclaim. On her return to the USA she played the Palace Theater in New York for a hugely successful 19-week run. Her film career resumed with a dramatic/singing role in **A Star Is Born** (1954), for which she was nominated for an Oscar. By the late 50s, her problems had returned, and in some cases, had worsened. She suffered nervous and emotional breakdowns, and made further suicide attempts. A straight dramatic role in *Judgement At Nuremberg* (1961), for which she was again nominated for an Oscar, enhanced her reputation. However, her marriage was in trouble, although she and Luft made repeated attempts to hold it together (they had two children, Lorna and Joey).

Despite the personal traumas and the professional ups and downs, Garland achieved another huge success with a personal appearance at New York's Carnegie Hall on 23 April 1961, the subsequent album of the concert winning five Grammy Awards. A 1963 television series was disappointing and, despite another good film performance in a dramatic role in *A Child Is Waiting*, and a fair dramatic/singing appearance in **I Could Go On Singing** (both 1963), her career remained plagued with inconsistencies. The marriage with Luft ended in divorce, as did a subsequent marriage. Remarried again in 1969, Garland attempted a comeback in a season at London's Talk Of The Town nightclub, but suffered the indignity of having bread sticks and other objects thrown at her when she turned up late for some performances. On 22 June 1969 she was found dead, apparently from an accidental overdose of sleeping pills. She was at her best in such films as *Meet Me In St. Louis* and *The Wizard Of Oz* and on stage for the superb Carnegie Hall concert, and had she done nothing else, she would have earned a substantial reputation as a major singing star. To her powerful singing voice she added great emotional depths, which came not only through artifice but from the often cruel reality of her life. When the catalogue of personal tragedies was added to Garland's performing talent she became something else, a cult figure, and a showbusiness legend. She was a figure that only Hollywood could have created and yet, had she been a character in a melodrama, no one would have believed such a life was possible.

● ALBUMS: *Sings* (MGM 1951) ★★★, *Judy At The Palace* (Decca 1951) ★★★, *If You Feel Like Singing Sing* (MGM 1955) ★★★, *Judy Garland's Greatest Performances* (Decca 1955) ★★★, *Miss Show Business* (Capitol 1955) ★★★, *With The MGM Orchestra* (MGM 1956) ★★★, *Judy* (Capitol

1956) ★★★, *Alone* (Capitol 1957) ★★★, *In Love* (Capitol 1958) ★★★, *Garland At The Grove* (Capitol 1959) ★★★, with John Ireland *The Letter* (Capitol 1959) ★★★, *Judy! That's Entertainment* (Capitol 1960) ★★★, *Judy At Carnegie Hall* (Capitol 1961) ★★★★★, *The Star Years* (MGM 1961) ★★★, *The Magic Of Judy Garland* (Decca 1961) ★★★, *The Hollywood Years* (MGM 1962) ★★★, *The Garland Touch* (Capitol 1962) ★★★, *Our Love Letter* (Capitol 1963) ★★★, *Just For Openers* (Capitol 1964) ★★★, with Liza Minnelli *'Live' At The London Palladium* (Capitol 1965) ★★★★, *At Home At The Palace* (ABC 1967) ★★★, *The Last Concert 20-7-68* (Paragon 1984) ★★★, *Live! 1962* recording (Capitol 1989) ★★★, *Get Happy* (Recall 2002) ★★.

● COMPILATIONS: *The Very Best Of Judy Garland* (MGM 1962) ★★★, *The Hits Of Judy Garland* (Capitol 1963) ★★★★, *The Best Of Judy Garland* (Decca 1964) ★★★, *The Judy Garland DeLuxe Set* 3-LP box set (Capitol 1957) ★★★★, *The ABC Years* (ABC 1976) ★★★, *The Young Judy Garland 1938–42* (MCA 1983) ★★★, *Golden Greats* (MCA 1985) ★★★, *Collection* (Castle 1986) ★★★, *The Capitol Years* (Capitol 1989) ★★★★, *Great MGM Stars* (MGM 1991) ★★★, *The One And Only* 3-CD box set (Capitol 1991) ★★★, *On Radio: 1936–44, Volume One* (Vintage Jazz Classics 1993) ★★★, *The Complete Decca Masters (Plus)* 4-CD box set (MCA 1994) ★★★★, *Child Of Hollywood* (CDS 1994) ★★★, *Collectors' Gems From The M-G-M Films* (R2 1997) ★★★, *The Best Of Judy Garland* (Half Moon 1998) ★★★, *Over The Rainbow: The Very Best Of Judy Garland* (MCA 2001) ★★★★.

● DVD/VIDEOS: *Best Of Judy Garland* (World Of Video 1988), *In Concert* (RCA/Columbia 1988).

● FURTHER READING: *Mickey Rooney And Judy Garland: And How They Got Into The Movies*, Edward I. Gruskin. *Judy: The Films And Career Of Judy Garland*, Joe Morella and Edward Epstein. *The Other Side Of The Rainbow: With Judy Garland On The Dawn Patrol*, Mel Tormé. *Weep No More, My Lady: An Intimate Biography Of Judy Garland*, Mickey Deans. *Judy With Love*, Lorna Smith. *Judy*, Gerold Frank. *Rainbow: The Stormy Life Of Judy Garland*, Christopher Finch. *Judy Garland: A Mortgaged Life*, Anne Edwards. *Little Girl Lost: The Life And Hard Times Of Judy Garland*, Al DiOrio. *The Young Judy*, David Dahl and Barry Kehoe. *Judy & Liza*, James Spada and Karen Swenson. *Judy: Portrait Of An American Legend*, Thomas J. Watson and Bill Chapman. *The Complete Judy Garland*, Emily R. Coleman. *Rainbow's End: The Judy Garland Show*, Coyne Steven Sanders. *Judy Garland*, David Shipman. *Me And My Shadows: Living With The Legacy Of Judy Garland*, Lorna Luft. *Judy Garland: Beyond The Rainbow*, Sheridan Morley and Ruth Leon.

● FILMS: *The Big Revue* aka *Starlet Revue* (1929), *Pigskin Parade* aka *Harmony Parade* (1936), *Every Sunday* (1936), *Broadway Melody Of 1938* (1937), *Thoroughbreds Don't Cry* (1937), *Love Finds Andy Hardy* (1938), *Everybody Sing* (1938), *Listen, Darling* (1938), *The Wizard Of Oz* (1939), *Babes In Arms* (1939), *Andy Hardy Meets Debutante* (1940), *Strike Up The Band* (1940), *Little Nellie Kelly* (1940), *If I Forgot About You* (1940), *Life Begins For Andy Hardy* (1941), *Ziegfeld Girl* (1941), *Babes On Broadway* (1941), *For Me And My Gal* (1942), *We Must Have Music* (1942), *Thousands Cheer* (1943), *Presenting Lily Mars* (1943), *Girl Crazy* aka *When The Girls Meet The Boys* (1943), *Meet Me In St. Louis* (1944), *The Clock*

aka *Under The Clock* (1945), *Ziegfeld Follies* (1946), *The Harvey Girls* (1946), *Till The Clouds Roll By* (1947), *Easter Parade* (1948), *Words And Music* (1948), *The Pirate* (1948), *In The Good Old Summertime* (1949), *Moments In Music* (1950), *Summer Stock* (1950), *A Star Is Born* (1954), *Pepe* (1960), *Judgement At Nuremberg* (1961), *Gay Purr-ee* voice only (1962), *A Child Is Waiting* (1963), *I Could Go On Singing* (1963).

Garland, Red

b. William M. Garland, 13 May 1923, Dallas, Texas, USA, d. 23 April 1984, Dallas, Texas, USA. Garland turned to the piano in his late teens, having earlier studied and played reed instruments. Although initially inspired by mainstream artists, he moved into bebop in the late 40s, accompanying **Charlie Parker**, **Fats Navarro** and others while still playing regularly with musicians such as **Coleman Hawkins** and **Ben Webster**. In 1955 he joined **Miles Davis**, remaining a member of the quintet until 1958. For the next 10 years he led his own trio, which recorded extensively, but drifted into obscurity after 1968 when he settled in Texas. Towards the end of the following decade he returned to the national and international jazz scene. As a soloist Garland was often lyrical if not especially commanding; but he made an important contribution to the powerful rhythm section (with **Paul Chambers** and **Philly Joe Jones**) of one of Davis' best bands, where his sophisticated technique, use of harmonic substitutions and block-chording set standards for many contemporary and later bop bands.

● ALBUMS: *A Garland Of Red* (Prestige 1956) ★★★, *The P.C. Blues* (Prestige 1957) ★★★, *Groovy/Red Garland Revisited* (Prestige 1957) ★★★★, *All Mornin' Long* (Prestige 1957) ★★★, *Soul Junction* (Prestige 1957) ★★★★, *High Pressure* (Prestige 1957) ★★★, featuring John Coltrane *Dig It!* (Prestige 1957) ★★★★, *It's A Blue World* (Prestige 1958) ★★★, *Manteca* (Prestige 1958) ★★★, *Rediscovered Masters* (Prestige 1958) ★★★, *Rojo* (Prestige 1958) ★★★, *All Kinds Of Weather* (Prestige 1958) ★★★, *Red In Bluesville* (Prestige 1959) ★★★, *At The Prelude: The Red Garland Trio iii* (Prestige 1959) ★★, *The Red Garland Trio With Eddie 'Lockjaw' Davis* (Moodsville 1959) ★★★, *Coleman Hawkins Plus The Red Garland Trio* (Swingville 1960) ★★★, *Red Alone* (Moodsville 1960) ★★★, *Alone With The Blues* (Moodsville 1960) ★★★, *Hallello-y'all* (Prestige 1960) ★★, *Bright And Breezy* (Jazzland 1961) ★★, *The Nearness Of You* (Jazzland 1961) ★★★, *High Pressure* (Prestige 1961) ★★★★, *Solar* (Jazzland 1962) ★★★, *Red's Good Groove* (Jazzland 1962) ★★, *When There Are Grey Skies* (Prestige 1962) ★★★★, *Curtis Fuller With Red Garland 1957* recording (New Jazz 1962) ★★★, *Can't See For Lookin'* (Prestige 1963) ★★★★, *Li'l Darlin'* (New Jazz 1963) ★★★★, *High Pressure* (New Jazz 1963) ★★, *Live!* (New Jazz 1963) ★★★, *Soul Burnin'* (Prestige 1964) ★★★, *Red Garland Revisited* (Prestige 1969) ★★, *Auf Wiedersehen* (MPS 1971) ★★★, *The Quota* (MPS 1971) ★★★, *Crossings* (Galaxy 1977) ★★★, *Red Alert* (Galaxy 1977) ★★★★, *Feelin' Red* (Muse 1978) ★★★, *I Left My Heart* (Muse 1978) ★★★, *Equinox* (Galaxy 1978) ★★★, *Stepping Out* (Galaxy 1979) ★★, *Strike Up The Band* (Galaxy 1979) ★★, *Wee Small Hours* (Galaxy 1980) ★★★, *Misty Red* (Timeless 1982) ★★★.

● COMPILATIONS: *Red's Blues 1956–62* recordings (Prestige 1999) ★★★.

Garland, Terry

b. 1953, Johnson City, Tennessee, USA. Although interested in blues, Garland spent the first 20 years of his professional career playing guitar in a variety of bar and showbands, performing popular chart-based rock 'n' roll and latterly, R&B. Tiring of this rigorous life, he took to playing acoustic blues in clubs around the southern states. The 90s rehabilitation of the dobro in the blues idiom saw Terry Garland become the latest in a long line of solo artists, including **John Hammond** and **Keb' Mo'**, to employ the instrument. As a Tennessee child of the 50s Garland naturally picked out the blues of **Howlin' Wolf** and **Lightnin' Hopkins** as his inspiration. By the 60s he had begun to play in a series of local R&B groups, but a major turning point came when he opened a show for **Leon Russell**—his first solo performance. He subsequently began to write his own songs, adding them to his existing canon of traditional country and delta blues numbers. Encouraged by friends, he prepared an album that was subsequently rejected by every blues-orientated American label. Instead, interest came from the New York–based First Warning, and *Trouble In Mind* was recorded with the assistance of Nighthawks harmonica player Mark Wenner. On this 1991 set, Garland performed songs by **Mississippi Fred McDowell**, **Bukka White**, **Skip James** and others with confidence, with only an occasional penchant for excess. The album featured two of his own songs alongside a selection of 'one-take' versions of blues classics from **Willie Dixon**, **Jimmy Reed** and the more contemporaneous **Johnny Winter**. *Edge Of The Valley* relied on a more polished production and sophisticated instrumentation but was also well received. Garland signed to Demon Records in 1996 to record his third collection, *The One To Blame*. Including **Robert Johnson**'s 'Phonograph Blues', the gospel standard 'A Closer Walk With Thee' and **Jerry Lee Lewis**' 'It'll Be Me', it displayed the same powerful conviction as its predecessors, but showed the artist's smoky, curdled vocals in their best light to date.

● ALBUMS: *Trouble In Mind* (First Warning 1991) ★★★, *Edge Of The Valley* (First Warning 1992) ★★★, *The One To Blame* (Demon 1996) ★★★★, *Out Where The Blue Begins* (Planetary 2002) ★★★.

Garland, Tim

b. 19 October 1966, Ilford, Essex, England. Growing up in a musical environment, Garland first studied classical music composition, meanwhile also listening to recorded jazz. While still in his early teens, he played professionally and was profoundly influenced by a chance encounter with saxophonist **Tony Coe**. Nevertheless, he did not turn purposefully to reed instruments as a means of expressing his musical thought until he was 20. In those intervening years, Garland listened to and was influenced by several of the musicians recording for **ECM Records**, among them **Keith Jarrett**, **Jan Garbarek**, **Pat Metheny** and **Eberhard Weber**. He found in the approach of these artists—and indeed that of the label itself—intriguing echoes of the classical music of his formative years. While studying at the Guildhall School of Music, he was encouraged to learn to play an instrument to professional standards in order to better develop his abilities as a composer. He thus began an intensive and fast learning curve on the tenor saxophone. At this point, he was heavily influenced by **Joe Lovano** and also by **Kenny Wheeler** and **John Taylor**. In 1990, he formed the folk jazz group **Lammas** with guitarist/composer Don Paterson, eventually recording five albums. During the 10-year life of Lammas, Garland also worked with other musicians in other contexts, including **Jason Rebello** and drummer Jeremy Stacey.

Towards the end of the decade, Garland joined **Chick Corea**'s Origin. Encouraged by Corea, he recorded for the pianist's own label. This was *Made By Walking*, on which Garland presents a suite commissioned by the 1999 London Jazz Festival and which is performed by musicians such as **Gerard Presencer**, Avishai Cohen, **Geoff Keezer** and **Joe Locke**. Arising from this session, Garland formed his Storms/Nocturnes Trio with Keezer and Locke, meanwhile continuing touring extensively with Origin and he also found the time, and the energy, to form yet another group, the Dean Street Underground Orchestra. Conceived for a one-off gig at London's Pizza Express, the band stayed together, albeit with changing personnel, for a UK tour and appearances in New York. The band was recorded live on *Soho Story*. Adding to Garland's busy schedule, he joined **Bill Bruford**'s Earthworks as both composer and performer, worked in a **John Dankworth** big band, and formed the Acoustic Triangle trio, this latter group artfully blending jazz and classical music. In 2003, he formed a new quintet for a recording session with **Paul Bollenback** (guitar), **John Patitucci** (bass) and Gary Novak (drums). Also in the early 00s, Garland was appointed composer-in-residence at Newcastle University's International Centre for Music Studies. In addition to tenor saxophone, Garland also plays soprano saxophone and the bass clarinet. By 2004 Garland had become a leading and potentially highly influential musician on the contemporary UK jazz scene.

● ALBUMS: *Tales From The South* (EFZ 1995) ★★★, *Enter The Fire* (Linn 1997) ★★★, *Made By Walking* (Stretch/Universal/MCA 2000) ★★★★, with Dean Street Underground Orchestra *Soho Story* (Dean Street 2001) ★★★, with Geoff Keezer, Joe Locke *Storms/Nocturnes* (Sirocco Jazz 2001) ★★★, *Playing To The Moon* (Ronnie Scott's Jazz House 2002) ★★★, with Keezer, Locke *Rising Tide* (Sirocco Jazz 2003) ★★★, *Change Of Season* (Sirocco Jazz 2004) ★★★.

Garlow, Clarence

b. 27 February 1911, Welsh, Louisiana, USA, d. 24 July 1986, Beaumont, Texas, USA. Brought up in the black community in south Louisiana and east Texas, Garlow, aka Bon Ton, became proficient on both guitar and accordion. On the former, his principal influence was **T-Bone Walker**, and the smooth, jazzy Walker sound can be heard on many of his records, particularly those of the late 40s and early 50s, which appeared on locally distributed record labels such as Macy's, Lyric and Feature. Other records show a more rocking R&B tendency, in particular the classic pairing of 'Route 90' and 'Crawfishin'' on a single for Flair Records. Later, there was a fine zydeco pairing on Folk Star Records, but while recording for **Jay Miller** he moved towards the swamp blues sound. Garlow retired from playing in the early 60s, but worked for some years as a postman and a disc jockey in Beaumont, Texas.

● COMPILATIONS: *Bon Ton Roola* (Flyright 1986) ★★★.

Garner, Erroll

b. Erroll Louis Garner, 15 June 1921, Pittsburgh, Pennsylvania, USA, d. 2 January 1977, Los Angeles, California, USA. A self-taught pianist, Garner played on the radio at the age of 10 and within a few more years was playing professionally in his home town. Among the bands with which he played during this period were those led by Leroy Brown and, reputedly, **Fate Marable**. In 1944 Garner moved to New York and began working in nightclubs, including the Rendezvous and the Melody Bar. He became a popular and successful performer in these establishments, but also enjoyed playing at the more jazz-orientated venues along 52nd Street, such as Tonde-layo's and the Three Deuces. For a short time, he worked in a trio led by **Slam Stewart**, but soon formed his own trio.

For the rest of his life, with only occasional exceptions, Garner worked as leader of a trio or as a soloist. Throughout the 50s, 60s and early 70s, he toured the USA, playing prestigious club and hotel engagements, appearing at festivals and on radio and television. He also visited Europe and the UK, where he appeared on television, and in 1962 he had an album in the UK charts. During these years, Garner recorded numerous albums, some of them, such as the classic **Concert By The Sea**, becoming virtual fixtures in the catalogue. Although Garner taught himself to play, he never learned to read music, yet he contrived to create several jazz tunes, including one, 'Misty', that became a standard when **Johnny Burke** added a lyric. Slight echoes of the full sound of **Earl 'Fatha' Hines** occasionally appear in Garner's playing, as do touches that suggest he had absorbed the work of the stride piano players, yet throughout the bulk of his vast output, Garner remains unique. Playing consistently to a very high standard, he developed certain characteristics that bear few resemblances to other pianists. Notably, these include a plangent left-hand, block-chorded pulse, a dancing pattern of seemingly random ideas played with the right hand in chords or single notes, and playful introductions, which appear as independent miniature compositions, only to sweep suddenly, with apparent spontaneity and complete logic, into an entirely different song.

Sumptuously romantic on ballads, and fleet and daring on up-tempo swingers, Garner's range was wide. Nicknamed 'The Elf', more, perhaps, for his diminutive stature than for the impish good humour of those introductions, Garner was the first jazz pianist since **Fats Waller** to appeal to the non-jazz audience, and the first jazzman ever to achieve popular acclaim from this audience without recourse to singing or clowning. **Dudley Moore** acknowledges much of his style to Garner, and 'swinging 60s piano jazz' owes a massive debt to him. Stylistically, Garner is in a category of which he is, so far, the only true member. Since his death in January 1977, there has been no sign that any other pianist other than **Keith Jarrett** is following his independent path in jazz.

● ALBUMS: *Free Piano Improvisations Recorded By Baron Timme Rosenkrantz At One Of His Famous Gaslight Jazz Sessions* aka *Early Erroll* (Dial 1949) ★★★, *Piano Moods* (Columbia 1950) ★★, *Rhapsody* (Atlantic 1950) ★★, *Volume 1* (Dial 1950) ★★★, *Playing Piano Solos, Volume 1* (Savoy Jazz 1950) ★★★, *Playing Piano Solos, Volume 2* (Savoy Jazz 1950) ★★★, *Playing Piano Solos, Volume 3* (Savoy Jazz 1950) ★★★, *Playing Piano Solos, Volume 4* (Savoy Jazz 1951) ★★★, *Gone With Garner* (Mercury 1951) ★★★, *Gems* (Columbia 1951) ★★, *At The Piano* (Mercury 1951) ★★★, *At The Piano* (Atlantic 1951) ★★★, *Passport To Fame* (Atlantic 1952) ★★★, *Solo Flight* (Columbia 1952) ★★★, *Piano Solos Volume 2* (Atlantic 1952) ★★★, *Overture To Dawn Volume 1* (Blue Note 1952) ★★★★, *Overture To Dawn Volume 2* (Blue Note 1952) ★★★★, *Piano Stylist* aka *Piano Variations* (King 1952) ★★★,

Separate Keyboards (Savoy Jazz) ★★, *Long Ago And Far Away* (Columbia) ★★★, *At The Piano* (Savoy Jazz 1953) ★★★, *At The Piano* (Columbia 1953) ★★★, *Overture To Dawn Volume 3* (Blue Note 1953) ★★★, *Overture To Dawn Volume 4* (Blue Note 1953) ★★★, *Overture To Dawn Volume 5* (Blue Note 1953) ★★★, *Plays For Dancing* (Columbia 1953) ★★★, *Body And Soul* (Columbia 1953) ★★★★, *Mambo Moves Garner* (Mercury 1954) ★★, *Solitaire* (Mercury 1954) ★★★, *Garnering* (EmArcy 1954) ★★★★, *Contrasts* (EmArcy 1954) ★★★, *Afternoon Of An Elf* (Mercury 1955) ★★, *Garnerland* (Columbia 1955) ★★★, *Penthouse Serenade* (Savoy Jazz 1955) ★★★, *Serenade To Laura* (Savoy Jazz 1955) ★★★, *Gone Garner Gonest* (Columbia 1955) ★★★, *Erroll!* (EmArcy 1956) ★★★★, *The Greatest Garner* (Atlantic 1956) ★★★★, *He's Here! He's Gone! He's Garner* (Columbia 1956) ★★★, *Concert By The Sea* (Columbia 1956) ★★★★★, with Art Tatum *Giants Of The Piano* (Roost 1956) ★★★, *Most Happy Piano* (Columbia 1957) ★★★, *Other Voices* (Columbia 1957) ★★, *Soliloquy* (Columbia 1957) ★★★, *Erroll Garner* (Ron-lette 1958) ★★★, *Encores In Hi-Fi* (Columbia 1958) ★★★, *Paris Impressions* (Columbia 1958) ★★★★, *Paris Impressions Volume 2* (Columbia 1958) ★★★★, *Perpetual Motion* (Atlantic 1959) ★★★, *The One And Only Erroll Garner* (Columbia 1960) ★★★, *Swinging Solos* (Columbia 1960) ★★★, *Dreamstreet* (ABC-Paramount 1961) ★★★, *The Provocative Erroll Garner* (Columbia 1961) ★★★★, *Closeup In Swing* (ABC-Paramount 1961) ★★★, *Informal Piano Improvisations* (Baronet 1962) ★★★, *Misty* (Mercury 1962) ★★★★, *One World Concert* (Reprise 1963) ★★★, *Seeing Is Believing* (Mercury 1964) ★★★, *Now Playing* (MGM 1966) ★★★, *Campus Concert* (MGM 1966) ★★★, *That's My Kick* (MGM 1967) ★★★, *Up In Erroll's Room* (MPS 1968) ★★★, *Feeling Is Believing* (Mercury 1969) ★★★, *Gemini* (MPS 1971) ★★★, *Magician* (London 1974) ★★★.

● COMPILATIONS: *Historical First Recordings* (Jazz Anthology) ★★★★, *The Elf* (Savoy) ★★★, *Gemini* (Decca 1978) ★★★, *The Great Garner* (Atlantic 1979) ★★★, *Complete Savoy Sessions Volume 1* 1945–49 recordings (RCA 1986) ★★★, *Complete Savoy Sessions Volume 2* 1949 recordings (RCA 1986) ★★★, *Jazz Portraits* (Jazz Portraits 1993) ★★★, *Dreamstreet/One World Concert* (Telarc 1996) ★★★★, *Gershwin & Kern/Magician* (Telarc 1996) ★★★, *That's My Kick/Gemini* (Telarc 1996) ★★★, *A Night At The Movies/Up In Erroll's Room* (Telarc 1996) ★★★, *Erroll Garner* 6-CD box set (Telarc 1999) ★★★★, *The Complete Savoy Master Takes* (Savoy Jazz 1999) ★★★, *Erroll Garner On Dial: The Complete Sessions 1946–48* recordings (Spotlite 1999) ★★★, *Memories Of You 1945–47* recordings (Memoir 1999) ★★★★, *Enjoys Rodgers And Porter* (Ocium 2003) ★★★.

● FURTHER READING: *Erroll Garner: The Most Happy Piano*, James M. Doran.

Garner, Larry

b. 8 July 1952, New Orleans, Louisiana, USA. Unlike many of his contemporaries, Garner draws upon a natural talent for storytelling and music making that differentiates him from those who attempt to find a personal synthesis of prevailing styles and influences. Raised in the Baton Rouge area, Garner learned guitar from his uncle, George Lathers. By the age of 11, he was playing with a gospel group, the Stars Of Joy, broadcasting on WXOK in Zachary, Louisiana. Four years later, he joined his cousin in the Twisters, an R&B band that played in various Baton Rouge clubs, including the Black Cat Lounge and the Jackson Club. Garner served with the army in Korea, playing at every base to which he was sent. On his return, he abandoned music for 10 years to raise a family and work at a local chemical plant. In 1983, he began to sit in on open nights at Tabby's Blues Box, owned by self-styled 'King of Swamp Blues', **Tabby Thomas**. Two years later Garner formed his own band and rapidly gained a reputation for performing his own songs. One, 'Dog House Blues', gained him a **B.B. King** Lucille Award in 1988. Two years later, he released his own cassette of original material, which led to the recording of his first proper album, *Double Dues*. By the time *Too Blues* was released, he had become a regular at festivals throughout the UK and Europe. A brief move to Verve/Gitanes and the opportunity to utilize a larger budget and guest musicians has not changed his pragmatic approach to music making. In the late 90s he settled with the European label Ruf.

● ALBUMS: *Catch The Feeling* cassette (Own Label 1990) ★★, *Chemical City Shakedown* (Sidetrack 1991) ★★, *Double Dues* (JSP 1991) ★★★, *Too Blues* (JSP 1993) ★★★★, *You Need To Live A Little* (Verve/Gitanes 1995) ★★★, *Baton Rouge* (Verve 1996) ★★★, *Standing Room Only* (Ruf 1998) ★★★, *Once Upon The Blues* (Ruf 2000) ★★★, *Embarrassment To The Blues?* (Ruf 2002) ★★.

Garner, Sue

b. Cave Spring, Georgia, USA. Originating from the same town as **R.E.M.** and the **B-52's** (Athens, Georgia, USA), indie rock veteran Garner specializes as a solo artist in a rootsy brand of the singer-songwriter style. Getting her start with the obscure early 80s new wave outfit Vietnam, Garner relocated to New York City when the band split up. Since then, Garner has been a member of several different outfits, including the country-based the Last Round Up and the Shams, as well as the more punk orientated Fish And Roses and Run On (the latter two of which she founded with her husband, Rick Brown). Additionally, Garner also completed homemade demos of solo tunes, and in 1998, one such tape landed her a recording contract with the indie Thrill Jockey label. Garner's solo debut, 1998's *To Run More Smoothly*, was written almost entirely on her own, while the 2000 outing, *Still*, saw Garner collaborate with Brown. Her third album release, *Shadyside*, featured songs credited solely to Garner and collaborations with others (chiefly former Shams bandmate Fay Hart), and was recorded by former **Dwight Yoakam** bass player J.D. Foster.

● ALBUMS: *To Run More Smoothly* (Thrill Jockey 1998) ★★★, with Rick Brown *Still* (Thrill Jockey 2000) ★★★, *Shadyside* (Thrill Jockey 2002) ★★★.

Garnet Mimms And The Enchanters

(see **Mimms, Garnet, And The Enchanters**)

Garnett, Carlos

b. 1 December 1938, Red Tank, Canal Zone, Panama. Garnett began teaching himself to play the tenor saxophone in his mid-teens, playing with musicians who were in the US military and were stationed nearby. In the early 60s, Garnett moved to New York City, where he mostly played in rock bands, although the modern jazz influence of **John Coltrane**

was never very far away. In the late 80s, Garnett joined **Freddie Hubbard**'s band, making his recording debut with the trumpeter. He then spent time with **Art Blakey** and **Charles Mingus** before forming his own group, Universal Black Force, in which he drew upon jazz, rock, funk and Panamanian music.

After folding this band, during the 70s Garnett played with **Miles Davis**, **Andrew Hill** and **Brother Jack McDuff**, then was with **Norman Simmons** for almost three years before re-forming Universal Black Force and also leading a quartet at various New York clubs. In addition to tenor, Garnett also plays soprano and baritone saxophones, being self-taught on these instruments too. His earlier recordings show the sometimes untamed fusing of the manifold influences upon Garnett; by the new millennium he was very much in control of his music and vividly demonstrated that he is among the best of the post-Coltrane saxophonists of his generation.

● ALBUMS: *Black Love* (Muse 1974) ★★★, *Journey To Enlightenment* (Muse 1974) ★★★★, *Let This Melody Ring On* (Muse 1975) ★★★, *Cosmos Nucleus* (Muse 1976) ★★★, *The New Love* (Muse 1977) ★★★, *Resurgence* (Muse 1996) ★★★, *Fuego En Mi Alma (Fire In My Soul)* (HighNote 1996) ★★★★, *Under Nubian Skies* (HighNote 1997) ★★★★, *Moon Shadow* (Savant 2001) ★★★.

● COMPILATIONS: *Fire* 70s Muse recordings (32 Jazz 1996) ★★★★.

Garnett, Gale

b. 17 July 1942, Auckland, New Zealand. Garnett moved with her parents to the USA in 1951. Garnett's 'We'll Sing In The Sunshine' was a US number 4 hit and a product of the folk music boom of the early 60s. It probably achieved pop success because of its cheerful and innocent young teen sound. Garnett began her career as an actress, appearing in many stage productions and numerous television shows, including *Hawaiian Eye*, *77 Sunset Strip*, and *Bonanza*. She wrote songs as a hobby, but in 1963 **RCA-Victor Records**, impressed with her voice and songs, including 'We'll Sing In The Sunshine', signed her up. In the UK, 'We'll Sing In The Sunshine' was covered with moderate success by the UK band the **Lancastrians** in 1964. Garnett was not able to sustain her career with more hits, getting only 'Lovin' Place' (US number 54) on the charts in 1965. By the late 60s Garnett, influenced by the hippie counter-cultural movement, embraced psychedelia, singing about rainbows, magic wands, and other enchantments. But she could no longer sell records, and retired from the music business in the early 70s.

● ALBUMS: *My Kind Of Folk Songs* (RCA Victor 1964) ★★★, *Lovin' Place* (RCA Victor 1965) ★★★★, *The Many Faces Of Gale Garnett* (RCA Victor 1965) ★★★, *Variety Is The Spice Of Gale Garnett* (RCA Victor 1966) ★★★, *New Adventures* (RCA Victor 1966) ★★★, *Flying And Rainbows And Love* (RCA Victor 1967) ★★, *An Audience With The King Of Wands* (Columbia 1968) ★★, *Sausalito Heliport* (Columbia 1969) ★★★.

● COMPILATIONS: *We'll Sing In The Sunshine* (Collectables 1997) ★★★.

Garnier, Laurent

b. 1 February 1966, Boulogne sur Seine, near Paris, France. Influential European DJ figurehead Garnier enjoyed a previous life as a restaurant manager, then footman at the

French Embassy (where he claims to have served UK dignitaries like the Queen, Princess Diana and Margaret Thatcher). Regarded as France's finest **techno** DJ, Garnier, who started behind the decks at Manchester, England's **Haçienda** in October 1987, insists that his musical spectrum is much wider. Although he has been a powerful advocate of all things Detroit for some time, he also had a hand in the establishment of the European hard **trance** movement. A typical evening sees him mixing standbys from Rhythim Is Rhythim (**Derrick May**) and **Joe Smooth** ('Promised Land') against classic Salsoul and disco records (typically **Donna Summer**'s 'I Feel Love'), in addition to the hottest new underground sounds.

Garnier's reputation was built up by a punishing schedule, performing five nights a week at up to four different countries within Europe. He also inaugurated a club in Paris called Wake Up, whose free-ranging music policy was reflected on the 'Wake Up' remix of **Moby**'s 'Hymn'. The latter was just one such remixing project, which has brought him to the forefront of **dance music**. So too his label, FNAC, which, together with Eric Morand (his PR) pioneered French dance music. It has been superseded by a new imprint, F Communications. However, before they bowed out of their involvement with FNAC, they put together a compilation, *La Collection*, which was extraordinarily well received by dance critics and pundits. Many of the acts featured followed Garnier and Morand to their new label.

Garnier has released several challenging long-players, while his singles output includes the club favourites 'Acid Eiffel' and 'Crispy Bacon'. Ironically, he is most associated with the novelty item 'Flat Beat' by **Mr Oizo**. The single, a UK chart-topper in March 1999, gained cult status when it was used as a soundtrack to a series of Levi's television advertisements. In the new millennium, Garnier began to experiment with a live show that eschewed samplers and sequencers in favour of real musicians and dancers.

● ALBUMS: *Shot In The Dark* (F Communications 1994) ★★★★, *RawWorks* (F Communications 1996) ★★★, *30* (F Communications 1997) ★★★, *Unreasonable Behaviour* (F Communications/Mute 2000) ★★★★, *The Cloud Making Machine* (PIAS/Mute 2005) ★★★.

● COMPILATIONS: *Laboratoire Mix* (F Communications 1995) ★★★, *Raw Works* (Never 1996) ★★★, *Early Works* (Arcade 1998) ★★★, *X-Mix 2: Destination Planet Dream* (!K7 1998) ★★★★, *Excess Luggage* (F Communications 2003) ★★★, *Life:Styles* (Harmless 2004) ★★★.

● DVD/VIDEOS: *Unreasonable Live* (Vital Distribution 2002).

Garon, Jesse, And The Desperadoes

This Edinburgh-based act emerged in 1986. Initially viewed as an informal venture—its founding line-up was largely drawn from members of another group, Rote Kopelle—the Desperadoes nonetheless established themselves as the leading exponents of the city's 'shambling' scene, alongside the more fêted **Shop Assistants**. Fran Schoppler (vocals) Andrew Tully (guitar/vocals), Angus McPake (bass) and Marguerita Vazquez Ponte (drums) provided the core of a unit that made its debut with the melodic 'Splashing Along', a single sympathetically produced by ex–**Jesus And Mary Chain** bass player Douglas Hart. The Desperadoes' deft blend of charm and melancholia was captured on a series of excellent singles, including 'The Rain Fell Down' and 'And If

The Sky Should Fall', although their lone album, *Nixon*, revealed a more forthright perspective. The Desperadoes split up at the end of the decade, unable to fully exploit their substantial early promise.

● ALBUMS: *Nixon* (Avalanche 1989) ★★★.

● COMPILATIONS: *A Cabinet Of Curiosities* (Velocity 1988) ★★★.

Garrett, Betty

b. 23 May 1919, St. Joseph, Missouri, USA. After winning a scholarship to a New York theatre company, Garrett enjoyed some success on the stage. She was an accomplished dancer, working with the celebrated Martha Graham troupe, and she also sang in clubs and hotel lounges. She made her Broadway debut in 1942 in the revue *Let Freedom Ring*, and had supporting roles in other stage shows such as *Something For The Boys*, *Jackpot*, and *Laffing Room Only*. After starring in *Call Me Mister* (1946) in which she introduced **Harold Rome**'s 'South America, Take It Away', she was signed to a film contract. In the late 40s she sang and danced with immense zest and vitality in popular movie musicals such as *Big City*, *Words And Music*, *Take Me Out To The Ball Game*, *On The Town*, and *Neptune's Daughter*.

After retiring to have children Garrett attempted a come-back, but her husband, Larry Parks, who had starred in two bio-pics about **Al Jolson**, had been blacklisted for refusing to testify before the House Un-American Activities Committee, and her career, too, was severely damaged. Later, Garrett and Parks developed a nightclub act and, later still, they worked in repertory theatres. She made one more film musical in the 50s, *My Sister Eileen*, but was reluctant to be parted from Parks and dropped out of that area of show business. She did appear on television, however, with roles in the long-running comedy *All In The Family*, and *Laverne And Shirley* (1976). In the 80s she toured with Sheree North and **Gale Storm** in the comedy *Breaking Up The Act*, and returned to Broadway in the short-lived stage adaptation of the hit film musical *Meet Me In St. Louis*. In 1990 her one-woman show, *Betty Garrett And Other Songs*, was acclaimed at the Ballroom in New York, and in the early 90s she presented her cabaret act, which included Broadway and Hollywood songs old and new—plus a little **Jacques Brel**—at London's Pizza On The Park.

● FURTHER READING: *Betty Garrett And Other Songs: A Life On Stage And Screen*, Betty Garrett and Ron Rapoport.

Garrett, Bobby

b. 22 March 1935, Dallas, Texas, USA, d. 24 April 1999, Tyler, Texas, USA. Garrett played steel guitar and is closely associated with **Hank Thompson**. He composed 'Rose City Chimes' in 1958; this latter-day classic can be heard on Thompson's 1962 album, *Live At The Cherokee Frontier Days Rodeo In Wyoming*. Garrett also worked with **Jim Reeves**, **Ernest Tubb**, **George Jones**, **Bob Wills**, **George Morgan** and **Ray Price**. He became known as 'the King of Thumb Style' and was elected to the Steel Guitar Hall of Fame in 1995. Shortly before his death, Garrett worked with Thompson on his acclaimed comeback release, *Hank Thompson And Friends*.

Garrett, Donald Rafael

b. 28 February 1932, El Dorado, Arkansas, USA, d. 14 August 1989. An immensely gifted multi-instrumentalist, playing bass and several reed instruments, notably the bass clarinet,

Garrett made a great impression on the hard bop scene in Chicago and elsewhere in the early and mid-60s. He played and occasionally recorded with artists such as **Muhal Richard Abrams**, **John Coltrane** and **Archie Shepp**. During the 70s he toured internationally and also led his own band, the Sea Ensemble, in which he was joined by his wife, Zusaan Fasteau. Garrett's ability to play a wide variety of instruments, including several ethnic wind instruments, brought an intriguingly textured atmosphere to his performances.

● ALBUMS: with the Sea Ensemble *We Move Together* (ESP 1976) ★★★★, with Craig Harris, Joseph Jarman, Famoudou Don Moye *Earth Passage-Density* (Black Saint 1981) ★★★.

Garrett, Kenny

b. 9 October 1960, Detroit, Michigan, USA. It would be fair to say that Kenny Garrett was the main musical force in **Miles Davis**' final band, and perhaps the last truly special young musician to emerge from the Davis hot house. As the great trumpeter played less and less, he relied more and more on his sideman to fill in the gaps, and be ready to step in quickly and build something accomplished into the gaps. Garrett proved himself an incredible alto saxophone powerhouse — an intense and complex improviser with an astonishing energy and drive. Starting early at the age of 17 with a saxophone spot in **Mercer Ellington**'s revived Ellington Orchestra, Garrett earned a complete musical education, in a series of perhaps surprisingly mainstream bands, considering his edgy and experimental, funky style. **Mel Lewis**' group (a traditional route for young and aspiring jazzers) followed, and a spell with veteran vibes and piano man **Lionel Hampton** followed that. His first recording as a leader came in 1984, and it was an assured affair, featuring the brilliant **Woody Shaw** on trumpet and a young, as yet unknown, **Mulgrew Miller** at the piano.

In the following years Garrett became involved in the **Blue Note Records** label's Out Of The Blue project, recording with the band in 1986, before continuing his extensive jazz education with a stint in **Art Blakey**'s prestigious **Jazz Messengers**. A year later, in 1987, Garrett joined Miles Davis for what would be the biggest boost for his career. Garrett was given all the room he needed, and excelled in his ability to build long, escalating solos out of simple riffs and grooves, using exotic scales and sophisticated inner chord changes as the basis for an individualistic 'outside' approach. Since Davis' death, Garrett has continued to record under his own name, with variable degrees of success, as well as working on a huge array of projects by such notable leaders as **Dizzy Gillespie**, **Donald Byrd** and **Freddie Hubbard**. Recommended listening must include *African Exchange Student*, featuring his regular rhythm section of the time, with pianist Mulgrew Miller, bass player Charnett Moffett and drummer Tony Reedus, as well as occasional appearances by **Ron Carter** and **Elvin Jones**. The record provides a fine example of Garrett's edgy and acidic style, on compositions that range from the **Louis Armstrong** anthem 'Mack The Knife' to Garrett's own raucous title track.

● ALBUMS: *Introducing Kenny Garrett* (Criss Cross 1984) ★★★, *The Eternal Triangle* (Blue Note 1987) ★★, *Garrett 5* (Paddle Wheel 1988) ★★★, *Prisoner Of Love* (Atlantic 1989) ★★★, *African Exchange Student* (Atlantic 1990) ★★★★, *Black Hope* (Warners 1992) ★★★★, *Trilogy* (Warners 1995) ★★★, *Pursuance: The Music Of John Coltrane* (Warners 1996) ★★★★, *Songbook* (Warners 1997) ★★★★, *Simply Said* (Warners 1999) ★★★, *Happy People* (Warners 2002) ★★★, *Standard Of Language* (Warners 2003) ★★★.

Garrett, Leif

b. Leif Per Garrett, 8 November 1961, Hollywood, California, USA. Garrett had been acting since the age of five, but it was as a teenager that he made his commercial breakthrough as a highly photogenic bubblegum pop singer. After signing a recording contract with **Atlantic Records** he hit the US Top 20 with a remake of the **Beach Boys**' 'Surfin' USA', in 1977. His US chart career continued with updates of **Dion**'s 'Runaround Sue' and 'The Wanderer' and **Paul Anka**'s 'Put Your Head On My Shoulder'. Garrett moved to the Scotti Brothers label in 1978 and achieved his biggest hit, 'I Was Made For Dancin'', a Top 10 smash in both the US and UK in 1979.

Garrett was by now at the peak of his fame, with his blond good looks making him a natural adornment to the walls of many a teenage pop fan. He was also instrumental in promoting the skateboard craze in the mid to late 70s in the UK. Disaster struck three days before his 18th birthday when he drove his Porsche off the road while high on drugs. His passenger, Roland Winkler, was crippled for life. A few more albums appeared at the start of the 80s before Garrett attempted to resurrect his acting career. His personal life descended into a mess of addictions for much of the following decade. Since then he has avoided the spotlight and now prefers yoga and meditation to heroin.

● ALBUMS: *Leif Garrett* (Atlantic 1977) ★★, *Feel The Need* (Scotti Brothers 1978) ★★, *Same Goes For You* (Scotti Brothers 1979) ★, *Can't Explain* (Scotti Brothers 1980) ★★, *My Movie Of You* (Scotti Brothers 1981) ★.
● COMPILATIONS: *The Leif Garrett Collection* (Volcano 1998) ★★★.
● FILMS: *Walking Tall* (1973), *Macon County Line* (1974), *Devil Times Five* (1974), *Walking Tall Part II* aka *Legend Of The Lawman* (1975), *Diamante Lobo* (1976), *Kid Vengeance* aka *Take Another Hard Ride* (1977), *Final Chapter—Walking Tall* aka *The Man In The Back Seat* (1977), *Skateboard* (1978), *Sgt. Pepper's Lonely Hearts Club Band* (1978), *Longshot* (1981), *The Outsiders* (1983), *Thunder Alley* (1985), *Shaker Run* (1985), *Delta Fever* aka *Summer Fever* (1987), *Party Line* (1988), *The Banker* (1989), *The Spirit Of '76* (1990), *Dominion* (1995), *The Whispering* (1996), *The Next Tenant* (1998), *The Art Of A Bullet* (1999), *Dickie Roberts: Former Child Star* (2003).

Garrett, Robert 'Bud'

b. 1916, Free Hill, Tennessee, USA. A jack of all trades when not playing music, Garrett has resided for most of his life in Free Hill, an isolated community founded by freed slaves around 1830. He recorded a splendid electric blues single for **Excello Records** in 1962, and played occasional festivals from the 80s, by which time he was the only performer in Free Hill of the live music that had been otherwise supplanted by disco and cable television. His music included a few originals, which often employed a talking blues structure, but consisted largely of blues standards by the likes of **Little Milton** and **T-Bone Walker**, and country music by artists such as **Don Williams** and **Merle Haggard**, adapted to blues formats.

Garrett, Siedah

b. 1963, Los Angeles, California, USA. Despite only having issued two solo albums by the early twenty-first century (that were released 15 years apart), vocalist Garrett is a well known name in the music industry, not so much as a recording artist, but for her talent of producing albums and writing hit songs for some of pop's biggest names. As a protégée of **Quincy Jones**, Garrett was signed to Jones' Qwest record label early on, and either duetted with or sang lead on recordings by renowned names such as **Tom Browne**, **Dennis Edwards**, **Sergio Mendes**, the **Pointer Sisters**, the **Commodores**, and **Michael Jackson**. Jones recognized Garrett's songwriting talents, which resulted in the singer turning tunesmith for **Aretha Franklin**, **Paula Abdul**, and **Natalie Cole**, but it was Garrett's songwriting for Michael Jackson that would bring her the most acclaim, as she co-wrote the massive worldwide hit 'Man In The Mirror'. Garrett subsequently appeared on stage as part of Jackson's concert tours, especially the one in support of *Dangerous*, that saw her join Jackson each night for a duet of 'I Just Can't Stop Loving You'.

Garrett attempted to launch a solo career during the late 80s, with the release of 1988's *Kiss Of Life*, which despite spawning two club hits ('Do You Want It Right Now' and 'K.I.S.S.I.N.G.'), failed to break through commercially. Garrett returned to her 'hired gun' status for other artists before accepting an invitation to join the **Brand New Heavies** for 1997's *Shelter*. Despite favourable reviews, the album did not perform well and Garrett left the band in 1998. She continued to write songs for others, including the Irish folk pop act the **Corrs**, and by the early twenty-first century had relocated to England, where she began focusing on relaunching her solo career. She signed to the Omtown Music label and issued *Siedah* in 2003.

● ALBUMS: *Kiss Of Life* (Warners 1988) ★★★, *Siedah* (Omtown Music 2003) ★★★.

Garrett, Snuff

b. Thomas Garrett, Dallas, Texas, USA. Producer Garrett was largely responsible for the rise of the Los Angeles-based **Liberty Records** label. In 1960 he astutely transformed **Johnny Burnette** from rockabilly singer to pop crooner, and while purists baulked at this new direction, both 'Dreamin'' and 'You're Sixteen' enjoyed sales in excess of one million. Garrett then began a fruitful partnership with **Bobby Vee** and, drawing material from **Don Kirshner**'s Aldon publishing house, produced a series of polished, highly commercial singles, including 'Take Good Care Of My Baby' and 'Run To Him' (both 1961). He also embarked on a concurrent recording career and, as Tommy Garrett, was responsible for several MOR albums. The artist subsequently supervised releases by **Gary Lewis And The Playboys**, many of which were arranged by the prolific session player **Leon Russell**, who joined Garrett at the newly formed Viva label during the mid-60s. Although not prolific, the venture did release the cult favourite *A Trip Down Sunset Strip* by the Leathercoated Minds, an *ad hoc* group that included **J.J. Cale**. Garrett later retired from music, but emerged the following decade to work with **Sonny And Cher** before resuming his low profile.

● ALBUMS: *50 Guitars Of Tommy Garrett Go South Of The Border Volume 1* (Liberty 1961) ★★★, *Evergreens Of Broadway* (Liberty 1961) ★★★, *Fifty Guitars Visit Hawaii* (Liberty 1962) ★★★, *Maria Elena* (Liberty 1963) ★★★, *Fifty Guitars Go Italiano* (Liberty 1964) ★★★, *Bordertown*

Bandito (Liberty) ★★★, *Fifty Guitars In Love* (Liberty 1966) ★★★, *More Fifty Guitars In Love* (Liberty 1967) ★★★, *Return To Paradise* (Liberty) ★★★, *Love Songs From South Of The Border* (Liberty) ★★★, *Viva Mexico!* (Liberty) ★★★, *Fifty Guitars Go South Of The Border, Volume 2* (Liberty) ★★★.

● COMPILATIONS: *The Best Of Fifty Guitars* (Liberty 1969) ★★★, *The Fifty Guitars Of Tommy Garrett* (United Artists 1984) ★★★.

Garrick Gaieties, The

Sub-titled 'A Bubbling Satirical Musical Revue Of Plays, Problems and Persons', the first of three editions of this satirical revue was presented by the Theatre Guild Junior Players, a group of young Theatre Guild actors, for two Sunday performances on 17 May 1925, in an effort to raise money for their new theatre on 52nd Street in New York. The production aroused such interest that it began a commercial run at the Garrick Theatre on 8 June that year. It was an irreverent mix of sketches and songs that lampooned the musical theatre in general, and the Theatre Guild in particular (a kind of early **Forbidden Broadway**, perhaps?). The show gave the young songwriters **Richard Rodgers** and **Lorenz Hart** their first big Broadway opportunity, and they came through with several outstanding numbers such as 'April Fool', 'Sentimental Me', 'On With The Dance', 'Old Fashioned Girl' (lyric by Edith Meiser), 'Do You Love Me? (I Wonder)', 'Black And Blue', and 'Manhattan', a song that was first popularized by **Ben Selvin** and **Paul Whiteman**, and eventually became a much-loved standard.

That first show ran for 211 performances, and a second edition opened a year later, again at the Garrick Theatre, on 10 May 1926. Once more, the score was by Rodgers and Hart, and included 'Keys To Heaven', 'Back To Nature', 'Say It With Flowers', 'It May Rain', 'What's The Use Of Talking?', 'A Little Souvenir', and an operetta spoof 'The Rose Of Arizona'. The show's big hit was 'Mountain Greenery', which became such a success on record for **Mel Tormé**, and turned up in the 1948 Rodgers and Hart biopic *Words And Music*, where it was sung by **Perry Como** and Allyn Ann McLerie. The third, and final version of the *The Garrick Gaieties* was presented at the Guild Theatre in 1930, with songs by a variety of composers and lyricists. Several of the numbers had music by **Vernon Duke**, including 'I Am Only Human After All' (lyric by **Ira Gershwin** and Harburg), 'Too, Too Divine' (**E.Y. 'Yip' Harburg** and Duke), and 'Ankle Up The Altar With Me (Harburg and Richard Myers). Also in the score was 'Triple Sec', a 'progressive opera' by the *avant garde* composer **Marc Blitzstein**, and 'Out Of Breath And Scared To Death Of You' by **Johnny Mercer** and Everett Miller, which is said to be Mercer's first published song. Some of the cast who were in the first *Gaieties* and still there at the end included Sterling Holloway, Edith Meiser, James Norris, Hidegarde Halliday, and Philip Loeb, who also directed. Lee Strasberg, who was later Artistic Director of the Actors Studio Theatre, was in one of the shows, as was **Libby Holman**. Two talented newcomers in the third show were Ray Heatherton and the actress-comedienne Imogen Coca, and the future Hollywood star, **Rosalind Russell**, made her Broadway debut when the 1930 edition returned briefly to Broadway in October of that same year.

Garrick, David

b. 1946, Liverpool, England. Opera-trained Garrick began his career at the famed **Cavern** club, where he performed as a member of the Dions, before moving to London on securing a recording contract with the Piccadilly label as a solo artist. Two unsuccessful singles were released before the singer scored a UK Top 30 hit with 'Lady Jane', originally recorded by the **Rolling Stones**, in June 1966. Garrick enjoyed a second chart entry with 'Dear Mrs Applebee', a boyish performance redolent of **Herman's Hermits**, which sold a million copies in Germany. Despite sharing management with the **Kinks** and enjoying a front page advertisement for 'I Found A Love', further chart success proved elusive.

● ALBUMS: *A Boy Called David* (Piccadilly 1966) ★★★, *Don't Go Out Into The Rain Sugar* (Piccadilly 1968) ★★.
● COMPILATIONS: *The Pye Anthology* (Sequel 1998) ★★★.

Garrick, Michael

b. 30 May 1933, Enfield, Middlesex, England. Largely self-taught as a pianist and composer, Garrick led bands during the 50s and was active in the 'poetry and jazz' movement. In the mid-60s he worked with the band co-led by **Don Rendell** and **Ian Carr** and also fronted his own small group, which often featured the outstanding saxophonist **Joe Harriott**. A prolific composer, in the late 60s Garrick's writing reflected his beliefs and 'Jazz Praises' was performed at St Paul's Cathedral in London. 'Judas Kiss' was a two-hour setting of Christ's passion drawn from four gospels. In keeping with the mood of works such as this, Garrick also played the pipe organ.

In the 70s Garrick advanced his own musical knowledge by studying at **Berklee College Of Music** in the USA and subsequently taught extensively in the UK. In the late 70s he formed a trio with **Phil Lee** and **Norma Winstone**. The following decades saw Garrick active with small and large bands, notably those led by **Chris Hunter** and **Dave Green**, and his own sextet and big band. Throughout this time Garrick has maintained his interest in jazz education, holding teaching posts at the Royal Academy of Music and Trinity College of Music in London, and forming his own Jazz Academy Vacation Courses in 1989.

Garrick's extensive list of jazz-choral works and suites include: 'Mr Smith's Apocalypse' (for sextet, speakers and chorus), 'Four Ritual Dances' (for jazz quintet and speaker), 'Five Songs Of Resurrection' (for jazz quintet and speaker), 'The Stirring' (for sextet and chorus), and 'Zodiac Of Angels' (for symphony orchestra, jazz soloists, solo singers and chorus). His jazz orchestra, formed in 1985, has performed pieces including 'Hardy Country', 'The Royal Box', 'Rhapsody For Violin And Jazz Orchestra' (written for his son Christian), and 'Song Of Gladness And Farewell' (a sonata written for Princess Diana).

● ALBUMS: *Kronos* (Hep 1959) ★★★, *Poetry And Jazz In Concert* (Argo 1963) ★★★★, *October Woman* (Argo 1964) ★★★, *Moonscape* (Airborne 1964) ★★★, *Promises* (Argo 1965) ★★★, *Before Night/Day* (Argo 1966) ★★★, *Black Marigolds* (Argo 1966) ★★★, *Jazz Praises At St Paul's* (Airborne 1968) ★★★★, *Poetry And Jazz* (Argo 1969) ★★, *The Heart Is A Lotus* (Argo 1970) ★★★, *Mr Smith's Apocalypse* (Argo 1971) ★★★, *Cold Mountain* (Argo 1972) ★★★, *Home Stretch Blues* (Argo 1972) ★★★, *Troppo* (Argo 1973) ★★★, *You've Changed* (Hep Jazz 1978) ★★★,

A Lady In Waiting (Jazz Academy 1993) ★★★★, *Meteors Close At Hand* (Jazz Academy 1994) ★★★, *Parting Is Such* (Jazz Academy 1995) ★★★★, *For Love Of Duke . . . And Ronnie* (Jazz Academy 1997) ★★★★, *Down On Your Knees* (Jazz Academy 1999) ★★★, *Peter Pan Jazz Dance Suite* (Jazz Academy 2003) ★★★.

Garrison, Jimmy

b. 3 March 1934, Miami, Florida, USA, d. 7 April 1976, New York, USA. Garrison began playing bass in Philadelphia, where he grew up, moving to New York in the late 50s with **Philly Joe Jones**. By 1961 he was deeply involved with the free jazz movement, and played with **Ornette Coleman** at New York's Five Spot. **John Coltrane** sitting in with the group, was so impressed by Garrison that he invited the bass player to join his own quartet, so beginning a five-year association in which Garrison proved 'the pivot' (to quote **McCoy Tyner**) of the pre-eminent modern jazz group of the era, thanks to his dynamic and forceful musical personality. In 1963 he took time out to co-lead a sextet session, *Illumination!*, with his Coltrane rhythm-section partner, **Elvin Jones**. After leaving Coltrane in 1966 he led his own group, played with the bands of **Hampton Hawes**, **Archie Shepp** and Elvin Jones and recorded, again with Coleman, 1968's *New York Is Now!* and *Love Call* supplementing a previous vinyl meeting on *Ornette On Tenor* (1961).

Despite his career-long involvement with the *avant garde*, Garrison retained a traditional view of the role the bass should have in jazz; and although a gifted soloist, he chose to concentrate upon his instrument's rhythmic function, seeing that as the foundation of good group jazz. In the 70s Garrison taught, played with **Alice Coltrane** and also returned for a further spell with Elvin Jones but was troubled with ill health. He died of lung cancer in April 1976.

Gary Clail And The On U Sound System
(see **Clail, Gary, And The On U Sound System**)

Gary Lewis And The Playboys
(see **Lewis, Gary, And The Playboys**)

Gary O
(see **Aerial**)

Gary Puckett And The Union Gap
(see **Puckett, Gary, And The Union Gap**)

Garzone, George

b. 23 September 1950, Boston, Massachusetts, USA. A popular and highly respected tenor saxophonist, Garzone has spent a large part of his working life as a jazz educator in the Boston area. After attending music college in Boston, Garzone formed a long running trio, the Fringe, in 1972. Highlighting Garzone's adventurous tenor, the Fringe developed into one of Boston's most respected and adored groups. Away from the spotlight, Garzone built a career mentoring future jazz prodigies, including **Billy Hart**, **Eddie Henderson** and **Dave Liebman**, at the **Berklee College Of Music** and New England Conservatory. He has also recorded and toured with a diverse range of artists, including **Jack DeJohnette**, **Joe Lovano**, **John Patitucci** and **Danilo Pérez**. Garzone was signed to NYC Records in 1995, debuting with *Alone*, a smooth **Stan Getz** homage. The follow-up, *Four's And Two's*, was a more characteristically edgy set that successfully paired Garzone with fellow tenor Lovano. In the late 90s Garzone relocated to New York, although he still teaches and plays in Boston. He still works with the Fringe, alongside drummer and founder member Bob Gullotti and bass player John Lockwood.

● ALBUMS: *Alone* (NYC 1995) ★★★, with Joe Lovano *Four's And Two's* (NYC 1996) ★★★, *Moodiology* (NYC 1999) ★★★, *The Fringe In New York* (NYC 2000) ★★★.

Gas
(see **Voigt, Wolfgang**)

Gas Giants
This US trio was formed by ex–**Gin Blossoms** members Robin Wilson (b. 12 July 1965; vocals), Phillip Rhodes (b. 26 May 1969, USA; drums) and Daniel Henzerling (guitar). Originally known as the Pharaohs, their debut album was recorded while both Wilson and Rhodes were still under contract to **A&M Records**, but was shelved owing to the record label's ongoing problems. They eventually signed a recording contract with the Internet-based Atomic Pop, releasing the album in October 1999. *From Beyond The Back Burner*, recorded with producer John Hampton in Arizona, featured a harder edge than the country rock sound of the Gin Blossoms. This was ably illustrated on tracks such as the debut single 'Quitter' and 'I Hope My Kids Like Marilyn Manson'. The band broke up in summer 2001.

● ALBUMS: *From Beyond The Back Burner* (Atomic Pop 1999) ★★★.

Gas Mark 5
This group formed following the demise of the UK folk dance band **Flowers And Frolics**. The initial line-up featured Dan Quinn (b. 11 October 1949, Grimsby, South Humberside, England; melodeon), Nick Havell (b. Nicholas George Havell, 7 January 1951, Stratford, London, England; bass trombone/piano), Trevor Bennett (b. 4 August 1945, Grantham, Lincolnshire, England; tenor and alto trombones, wind synthesizer, keyboards), Rob Gifford (b. 1 March 1955, Wanstead, London, England; drums/percussion) and Chris Taylor (mouth organs,melodeon,guitar) and got together in 1985. Taylor had formerly been with the **Oyster Band**. Quinn left in November 1989, and his place was taken by Terry Mann (b. 6 October 1963, Barking, London, England; guitar,soprano saxophone,melodeons,bass,wind synthesizer). The final line-up, between 1993 and 1996, featured Bennett, Gifford, Taylor, Michael Davidson (bass/guitar) and Dave Blackmore (saxophone/keyboards). Regularly seen at folk festivals, and essentially a dance band, the group drew their material from both the British Isles and elsewhere, unlike their predecessors, Flowers And Frolics, who specialized in English country dance.

● ALBUMS: *In The Kitchen* cassette (Regular 1987) ★★★, *Gas Mark 5* (Festival 1989) ★★★★, *Jump!* (Regular 1991) ★★★, *Guizers* (Regular 1993) ★★.

Gaskin
UK **New Wave Of British Heavy Metal** group Gaskin were led by namesake Paul Gaskin (vocals, guitar, keyboards) with Stef Prokopczuk (bass) and Dave Norman (drums). Formed in Scunthorpe, south Humberside, England, they secured a strong following in the north-east and Midlands club circuit, areas eternally receptive to unpretentious hard rock. Paul Gaskin's singing earned the group comparisons to **Rush**, though in truth his songwriting was closer in conception to NWOBHM peers such as **Tygers Of Pan Tang** or **Def Leppard**. The group recorded two disciplined, well-executed albums for Rondolet Records in the early 80s before disbanding. With Rondolet primarily a punk label, Gaskin felt out of place and with no new offers forthcoming they had broken up permanently by 1984. Prokopczuk formed the short-lived **Ace Lane**.

● ALBUMS: *End Of The World* (Rondolet 1981) ★★★, *No Way Out* (Rondolet 1982) ★★★.

Gaskin, Barbara
(see **Spirogyra; Stewart, Dave, And Barbara Gaskin**)

Gaskin, Leonard
b. 25 August 1920, New York City, USA. Gaskin first entered jazz at the deep end, playing bass in the regular rhythm section at Clark Monroe's Uptown House, where bebop was forged in the early 40s. Among the musicians Gaskin backed there were **Charlie Parker** and **Dizzy Gillespie**. Despite his involvement with bebop, Gaskin was also in demand by mainstream jazz artists and played with such diverse groups as those led by **Eddie South** and **Erroll Garner**. In 1953 he recorded with **Miles Davis** and in 1956 joined the traditional line-up led by **Eddie Condon**. Throughout the 60s and beyond, Gaskin's versatility ensured him a successful career in the studios, from where he regularly emerged to play with many musicians including **David 'Panama' Francis** and **Oliver Jackson**. He also became a sought-after teacher.

● ALBUMS: *A Dixieland Sound Spectacular/At The Jazz Band Ball* (Swingville 1961) ★★★★, *At The Darktown Strutters Ball* (Swingville 1962) ★★★★, *Dixieland Hits* (Swingville 1962) ★★★.

Gaslini, Giorgio
b. 22 October 1929, Milan, Italy. Gaslini learned the piano as a child and started performing when he was 13 years old, appearing with his own trio at the Florence Jazz Festival in 1947. He studied at the Milan Conservatory before a career in which he has been equally at home in jazz and classical music. He would like to bring these various skills together in what he describes as 'total music'. He composed and played the music for Antonioni's film *La Notte* (1960) and wrote a jazz opera *Colloquio Con Malcolm X* (1970). He was friends with **Eric Dolphy** and worked with artists including **Don Cherry, Gato Barbieri, Max Roach** and **Roswell Rudd** as well as performing as a solo pianist and with his own groups. He has been involved in music education both directly as a teacher and by taking his quartet into less usual venues like factories and hospitals.

● ALBUMS: *Nuovi Sentimenti/New Feelings* (La Voce Del Padrone 1966) ★★★, *Grido* (Durium 1968) ★★★, *Colloquio Con Malcolm X* (PDU 1974) ★★★★, *Fabbrica Occupata* (Produttoriassociati 1974) ★★★, with Roswell Rudd *Sharing* (Dischi Della Quercia 1978) ★★★, *Free Actions* (Dischi Della Querchia 1977) ★★★, *Gaslini Plays Monk* (Soul Note 1980) ★★★, with Anthony Braxton *Four Pieces* (Dischi Della Querchia 1981) ★★★★, *Schumann Reflections* (Soul Note 1984) ★★★, *Multiple* (Soul Note 1991) ★★★★, *Ayler's Wings* (Soul Note 1991) ★★★★, *Lampi* (Soul Note 1994) ★★★, *Jelly's Back In Town*

(DDQ 1997) ★★★, *Mister O: A Jazz Opera* (Soul Note 1997) ★★, *Ballets* (Soul Note 1999) ★★★, *Gasilini Plays Sun Ra* (Soul Note 2005) ★★★.

Gass

One of the less-renowned groups to emerge from London's late 60s and early 70s club/soul circuit, Gass completed several raw-edged singles for the **Parlophone** label before embarking on a more progressive direction. The original line-up—Bob Tench (b. 24 March 1941; vocals/bass), Alan Roskams (b. 18 March 1941; lead guitar), Frank Clark (b. 26 January 1942; organ), Humphrey Okan (b. 18 March 1938; saxophone), **Lol Coxhill** (b. 19 July 1932; saxophone), Errol McLean (b. 24 March 1941; congas) and Godfrey McClean (b. 24 March 1941; drums)—gradually broke apart, although Tench and McClean were present on the unit's sole album. Its rhythmic pulse, reminiscent in places of **Santana**, was enhanced by a cameo appearance by guitarist **Peter Green**, but the set was not a commercial success. A year after the release of the album the band appeared in Jack Good's musical *Catch My Soul*. The line-up of the band had Derek Austin on organ and piano. The band also performed on the soundtrack album for the show and was produced by Peter Knight Jnr. (the son of the highly respected composer and arranger). Tench joined the **Jeff Beck** Group when Gass broke up, while early saxophonist Coxhill pursued a maverick career with **Delivery**, **Kevin Ayers** and a host of experimental ensembles.

● ALBUMS: *Ju Ju* (Polydor 1970) ★★★.

Gastr Del Sol

Gastr Del Sol is the creation of **David Grubbs** (b. Louisville, Kentucky, USA; guitar, piano, vocals), a former member of the Louisville-based hardcore outfit **Squirrel Bait**. When that influential band split up in 1987, Grubbs formed Bastro and recorded for Homestead Records three albums that gradually moved away from the noise-rock squall of Squirrel Bait towards *avant garde* experimentalism, although he continued to satisfy his rock instincts as guitarist for **Bitch Magnet**. Grubbs first used the Gastr Del Sol moniker for 1991's *The Serpentine Similar* EP, recorded with bass player Bundy K. Brown and drummer John McEntire from Bastro. Eschewing conventional rock melody altogether, the EP's exploratory tone set the tone for future Gastr Del Sol releases. The '20 Songs Less' single introduced an important new member to the line-up, guitarist/composer/tape manipulator and *avant garde* hero, **Jim O'Rourke**. Brown left before the esoteric *Crookt, Crackt, Or Fly*, recorded like all subsequent Gastr Del Sol releases, by Grubbs and O'Rourke and a loose collective of guest musicians. Their EPs and albums focused on the interplay of Grubbs and O'Rourke's acoustic guitars, reminiscent at times of the plangent tones of **John Fahey**, although there was the occasional rock workout in a nod to Grubbs' hardcore past. O'Rourke's subtle tape work and Grubbs' impressionistic lyrics were vital elements in the creation of unconventional tonal patterns.

Moving further away from the mainstream, 1995's *The Harp Factory On Lake Street* EP, released on the Table Of The Elements label, comprised a single extended piece of music for a small orchestra. Grubbs released his abstract solo work, *Banana Cabbage, Potato Lettuce, Onion Orange*, on the same label. *Upgrade & Afterlife* saw Grubbs and O'Rourke making a few concessions to the mainstream in terms of melody and

structure, and emerging with their most accessible and likeable album. O'Rourke left in July 1997, although he featured alongside fellow electronic genius Markus Popp on *Camoufleur*, a deceptively complex release that radiated a Zen-like aura of calming restraint. With Gastr Del Sol seemingly laid to rest, Grubbs has subsequently concentrated on solo work and his continued involvement with the **Red Crayola**.

● ALBUMS: *The Serpentine Similar* (TeenBeat 1993) ★★★, *Crookt, Crackt, Or Fly* (Drag City 1994) ★★★, *Upgrade & Afterlife* (Drag City 1996) ★★★★, *Camoufleur* (Drag City 1998) ★★★★.

Gatecrasher

In only a few years, Gatecrasher became one of the most important, popular and influential clubs on the UK and European **dance music** scene. Famous for its outrageously flamboyant and notoriously 'up for it' crowds and the uncompromisingly 'full on' **trance** sound of its music. Gatecrasher can certainly be ranked alongside **Cream**, **Renaissance** and the **Ministry Of Sound** as being one of the UK's most successful and trend-setting clubs.

Gatecrasher was started by UK DJ Scott Bond with partner, Simon Raine and, after a number of informal parties began its life at Sheffield's the Arches in 1994. Gatecrasher moved in 1997 to the Republic, a former iron and steel works that was converted into a nightclub venue by architect Charles Baker. The club purchased the Republic in 1998 and, later that year, undertook a major refurbishment and improvement of sound, lighting and facilities. Gatecrasher's groundbreaking musical policy is the result of experimenting with less well-known DJ talent, which it 'imports' from continental Europe and elsewhere. Germany's **Paul Van Dyk** first found popularity in the UK by being invited to play at the club and the same can be said for fellow German, DJ **Taucher**, Dutchman **DJ Tiësto** and Israel's Jez and Choopie. The approach that the club seems to take is if the quality and style of the music fit the unique Gatecrasher atmosphere, then whether or not it is played by a big name DJ is of no consequence. Other innovations are the five- and six-hour sets played by DJs such as **Sasha** and Paul-Van Dyk, an information point within the club and a travel service from other UK cities. The club has also released several very successful compilations through the Sony dance subsidiary, INCredible.

Gatecrasher's millennium gig featured over 15 hours worth of classic tracks played by some of the finest names in contemporary dance music, including the **Chemical Brothers**, **Paul Oakenfold**, **Sasha**, **Judge Jules**, Paul Van Dyk, **'Tall' Paul Newman**, **Sonique**, Scott Bond and Matt Hardwick. In 2002, the club announced it was cutting back from weekly nights in its home-town to monthly openings.

● COMPILATIONS: *Gold* (INCredible 1998) ★★★★, *Red* (INCredible 1999) ★★★★, *Wet* (INCredible 1999) ★★★★, *Disco-Tech* (INCredible 1999) ★★★★, *Global Soundsystem* (INCredible 2000) ★★★★, *National Anthems* (INCredible 2000) ★★★, *Discotech Generation* (INCredible 2001) ★★★★, *Digital* (Gatecrasher 2001) ★★★.

Gateley, Jimmy

b. James David Gateley, 1 May 1931, Springfield, Missouri, USA, d. 17 March 1985. Gateley learned to play fiddle and first appeared with a local band on KGBX Springfield in 1951. After a spell with the Red River Rustlers in Jamestown, North Dakota, he became a member of Dusty Owen's Rodeo Boys on *Wheeling Jamboree* on WWVA Wheeling, West Virginia. He returned to Springfield in 1954, where, until 1963, he worked on radio and television with **Red Foley** on *Ozark Jubilee* and *Jubilee USA*. In 1963, he started a long association with **Bill Anderson**, for whom he played fiddle, sang, acted as frontman and was also featured on many of Anderson's recordings. He became a regular on the *Grand Ole Opry* with Anderson and also in a double act with **Harold Morrison**. He made his first solo recordings for Cullman in 1959 but later recorded for several labels, including Starday, **Decca Records**, **Columbia Records**, Chart, Sapphire, B.T. and Constoga. He failed to achieve a chart hit with his own recordings but his talents as a songwriter led to some of his songs becoming hits when recorded by others. These include 'Alla My Love' (a number 5 in 1962 for **Webb Pierce**) and 'The Minute You're Gone' (a number 9 in 1963 for **Sonny James**). He co-wrote 'Bright Lights And Country Music' with Bill Anderson, whose recording of the song reached number 11 in 1965. He appeared in the films *The Road To Nashville* and *Las Vegas Hillbillies*. He became a deacon of his local Madison, Tennessee church and in the 70s he became more inclined towards gospel music. In the early 80s, he released an album of gospel songs, and a further one, *My Kind Of Country*, was distributed by his local church after his death.

● ALBUMS: *Jimmy Gateley* (Constoga 1979) ★★★, *The Dreamer* (Sapphire 1979) ★★, *Lookin' Up* (B.T. 1982) ★★★.

Gately, Stephen

b. Stephen Patrick David Gately, 17 March 1976, Dublin, Eire. After lead singer **Ronan Keating**, Gately was the most prominent member of the highly successful Irish pop group, **Boyzone**. It was somewhat inevitable, therefore, that he would follow Keating by branching out into solo projects during a lull in Boyzone's activities after the release of 1999's greatest hits set, *By Request*. In June, shortly after the release of *By Request*, Gately pre-empted the UK tabloid press by making a dignified public declaration of his homosexuality. He kept in the spotlight by recording a cover version of the **Art Garfunkel** hit 'Bright Eyes' for the new animated version of *Watership Down*, for which he also provided the voice of Blackavar. The following June, Gately released his solo debut, *New Beginning*. Despite featuring the sumptuous UK Top 5 hit title track, this was a disappointingly bland collection with Gately apparently lacking the conviction to stray too far from the teen ballad blueprint mined so successfully by Boyzone.

Gately's stuttering solo career and the seemingly terminal demise of Boyzone saw the singer attempting to branch out into other areas. His most notable achievement was landing the title role in *Joseph And The Amazing Technicolor Dreamcoat*, making his West End debut in February 2003. The following September he debuted as the Child Catcher in the London production of *Chitty Chitty Bang Bang*.

● ALBUMS: *New Beginning* (Polydor 2000) ★★.

Gates, David

b. 11 December 1940, Tulsa, Oklahoma, USA. Having played in a home-town high school band alongside **Leon Russell**, Gates followed his former colleague to Los Angeles. He initially pursued a career as a rockabilly singer, recording a series of locally issued singles including 'Swinging Baby Doll' (1958), which featured Russell on piano, and 'My Baby's Gone Away' (1961). He later switched to studio work, and appearances on sessions for **Duane Eddy** and **Pat Boone** preceded a fruitful period in the budding 'girl-group' genre. Gates produced and/or composed a string of excellent releases, notably **Merry Clayton**'s 'Usher Boy', the **Murmaids**' 'Popsicles And Icicles', Dorothy Berry's 'You're So Fine' (all 1963), **Shelly Fabares**' 'He Don't Love Me' and **Connie Stevens**' 'A Girl Never Knows' (both 1964).

Having founded, then closed, the short-lived Planetary label in 1966, Gates switched his attentions to the emergent west coast group scene. He produced material for **Captain Beefheart** and the Gants, while work with a harmony act, the Pleasure Fair in 1968, led to the formation of **Bread**. For three years Gates led this highly popular attraction, composing many of their best-known songs including 'Make It With You', 'If', 'Baby I'm-A Want You' and 'Everything I Own'. He began a solo career in 1973, but despite two albums of a similar high quality, the artist failed to sustain this level of success. A short-lived Bread reunion was equally ill-starred, suggesting that Gates' brand of soft, melodic pop was now out of fashion. He did enjoy a US Top 20 hit in 1978 with 'Goodbye Girl' but ensuing releases were less well received. He continues to write and produce at his recording studio on his California ranch.

● ALBUMS: *First Album* (Elektra 1973) ★★, *Never Let Her Go* (Elektra 1975) ★★★, *Goodbye Girl* (Elektra 1978) ★★★, *Songbook* (Elektra 1979) ★★, *Falling In Love Again* (Elektra 1980) ★★, *Take Me Now* (Arista 1981) ★★, *Love Is Always Seventeen* (Discovery 1994) ★★.

● COMPILATIONS: as David Gates & Bread *Essentials* (Elektra 1996) ★★★★, *The David Gates Songbook: A Lifetime Of Music* (Warners 2002) ★★★.

Gates, Gareth

b. 12 July 1984, Bradford, West Yorkshire, England. The story of this UK singer's rise to fame in the new millennium embraces both the mass popularity of the 'reality TV' concept and the slick machinations involved in the creation of pre-packaged pop music. Gates made his debut on the UK's television screens in October 2001 as one of the final 50 contestants on the UK entertainment programme *Pop Idol*. The series offered a new slant on the highly successful *Popstars* format by offering a record contract to the winner of a multi-staged talent contest, to be aired over several months on the ITV1 channel. A-level student Gates endeared himself to young and old alike with his spiky hair, boyish looks, and the fact that he overcame a slight speech defect when he sang, but contrary to the public's expectations he lost out in the February 2002 final to middle-class graduate **Will Young**.

Over the course of the next few months, Gates rewrote the *Pop Idol* script by signing his own major label recording contract and slugging it out at the top of the UK pop charts with Young. His anaemic cover version of the **Righteous Brothers**' classic ballad 'Unchained Melody' achieved advance sales of 1.3 million prior to topping the UK charts in March. Gates was also featured on the bestselling *Pop Idol: The Big Band Album*, on which the 10 finalists from the show performed cover versions of material from the Rat Pack era. By now the UK charts were awash with former *Pop Idol* and

Popstars contestants, paying testament to the greed of the major record companies and the willingness of the UK public to purchase anything associated with the shows. Gates proved his enduring popularity when he returned to the top of the charts in July with his second single, 'Anyone Of Us (Stupid Mistake)'. In September, he duetted with Young on a pedestrian cover version of the **Beatles**' 'The Long And Winding Road', backed with **Elvis Presley**'s 'Suspicious Minds'. His solo album, *What My Heart Wants To Say*, was released the following month, peaking at number 2 in the album charts and going on to achieve double platinum sales. Gates' status as the best loved of the reality TV pop stars was confirmed in March 2003, when his workmanlike but pointless cover version of **Norman Greenbaum**'s 'Spirit In The Sky', recorded with members of the television comedy show, *The Kumars At Number 42*, in aid of the Red Nose Day charity, topped the UK charts.

● ALBUMS: *What My Heart Wants To Say* (RCA 2002) ★, *Go Your Own Way* (RCA 2003) ★.

● DVD/VIDEOS: *Live* (Warner Music Vision 2003).

● FURTHER READING: *Right From The Start*, Gareth Gates & Sian Solanas. *Talking Point*, Gareth Gates & Gavin Reeve.

Gates, Giacomo

b. Connecticut, USA. Gates listened to classical and big band music from his very early years. He studied tap dancing, then guitar before starting to sing. He played guitar and sang during his teenage years and was heavily influenced by jazz singer **Eddie Jefferson**. After college, he worked on construction sites in Alaska but meanwhile performed at a music festival and attended master classes in Fairbanks, Alaska. There, farsighted faculty members urged him to move to where he could work as a singer. In 1989, he returned to Connecticut and became deeply involved in the local jazz scene. In 2001 and again in 2002, he was voted Talent Deserving Wider Recognition in *DownBeat*.

Gates' revelatory recording debut, 1995's *Blue Skies*, attracted commercial and critical attention. Included on it was a lyric by Gates to a composition by **Thelonious Monk** and a solo by **Charlie Rouse**. The 1998 follow-up also included Gates' lyrics to jazz solos, including **Chet Baker**'s 'But Not For Me', **Lee Morgan**'s 'Speedball' as well as performances of **Dizzy Gillespie**'s 'Night In Tunisia' and a version of Monk's 'Epistrophy'. Among musicians with whom Gates has worked and sometimes recorded are **Randy Brecker**, **Richie Cole**, Harold Danko, **Lou Donaldson**, **Jon Faddis**, **David Hazeltine**, **Vic Juris**, Eddie Landsberg, **Jerome Richardson**, **Jim Rotondi**, and **Hilton Ruiz**. In addition to performing, Gates is also deeply involved in education, conducting jazz singing clinics and workshops at universities and schools of music, in particular teaching at Wesleyan University and the Hartford Conservatory of Music. A deep voice and a commanding style and presence, have helped make Gates a popular figure on the contemporary jazz singing scene. Always inventive, he intelligently interprets lyrics and scats with flair, additionally imitating musical instruments, including bass, flute, and trombone.

● ALBUMS: *Blue Skies* (DMP 1995) ★★★★, *Fly Rite* (Sharp Nine 1998) ★★★★, *Centerpiece* (Origin 2004) ★★★.

Gateway

An occasional jazz trio featuring the immense talents of **John Abercrombie**, (b. 16 December 1944, Portchester, New York, USA; guitar), **Dave Holland** (b. 1 October 1946, Wolverhampton, Staffordshire, England; bass) and **Jack DeJohnette** (b. 9 August 1942, Chicago, Illinois, USA; drums). They have recorded four excellent albums over the past three decades. It is a testament to their strength as musicians that they can reunite sporadically, and immediately ignite the same spark.

● ALBUMS: *Gateway* (ECM 1975) ★★★★, *Gateway 2* (ECM 1978) ★★, *Homecoming* (ECM 1995) ★★★, *In The Moment* (ECM 1996) ★★★★.

Gateway Singers

Like many groups formed during the popular commercial folk explosion of the late 50s, the Gateway Singers had a relatively short life. The line-up comprised Jerry Walter (vocals/banjo), Elmerlee Thomas (vocals), Lou Gottlieb (b. 10 October 1923, Los Angeles, California, USA, d. 11 July 1996, Sebastopol, California, USA; bass) and Travis Edmondson (guitar). Following a path started by others, such as the **Almanac Singers** and the **Weavers**, they became one of the better-known US groups in the field at the time. Gottlieb left the group in 1959, after the group's two releases on **Decca Records**, and was replaced by Ernie Sheldon as lead guitar player. The group split up in 1961, at the height of the folk boom. For a time, the Gateway Trio, comprising Milt Chapman (bass/vocals), Betty Mann (guitar/vocals), and original founder Jerry Walter, continued performing. After releasing albums for **Capitol Records**, the trio broke up.

● ALBUMS: *The Gateway Singers At The Hungry i* (Decca 1956) ★★★, *The Gateway Singers In Hi-Fi* (Decca 1958) ★★★★, *The Gateway Singers On The Lot* (Warners 1959) ★★★, *Wagons West* (Warners 1960) ★★★, *Down In The Valley* (MGM 1961) ★★★, *Hootenanny* (MGM 1963) ★★★.

Gathering

No death metal band has evolved so much as the Gathering, whose early recordings were formed of the aggressive riffs and custard-gargling vocals that typify the genre, but who have since become a pleasantly mellow indie rock outfit, regularly charting in Europe and with more in common with **Deacon Blue** than **Deicide**.

The band was formed in 1989 by René Rutten (b. 2 July 1972, Nijmegen, Netherlands; guitar), Jelmer Wiersma (guitar), Hugo Prinsen Geerligs (b. 16 December 1973, Oss, Netherlands; bass), Frank Boeijen (b. 4 December 1973, Berghem, Netherlands; keyboards), Hans Rutten (b. 3 June 1969, Nijmegen, Netherlands; drums) and leather-throated vocalist Bart Smits. They debuted in 1992 with a well-crafted doom/death metal album, *Always*. Smits departed, but his replacement, Niels Duffhues, did not last long. It was the recruitment of female singer Anneke van Giersbergen (b. 8 March 1973, Sint Michielsgestel, Netherlands) that was the turning-point for the Gathering. Her soaring vocals and profound lyrics lent the band's sound a much needed emotional edge and their third album, *Mandylion*, received rave reviews. Its appeal also lay in the sympathetic production by Waldemar Sorychta and its almost psychedelic atmosphere.

Since *Mandylion* the Gathering's progress has seemed inexorable, with each successive album more fêted than the last, although Wiersma left following the recording of 1997's *Nighttime Birds*. In 2000 *If_Then_Else* charted in several countries, supported by the band's successful slots at the

Dynamo and Pink Pop festivals. Marjolein Kooijman replaced Geerligs following the release of 2004's *Sleepy Buildings: A Semi Acoustic Evening*. The only fly in the ointment has been the appearance of a weak rarities collection from the early days, which showed just how far the Gathering has progressed rather than encouraging any nostalgia.

● ALBUMS: *Always* (Foundation 2000 1992) ★★, *Almost A Dance* (Foundation 2000 1993) ★★★, *Mandylion* (Century Media 1995) ★★★★, *Nighttime Birds* (Century Media 1997) ★★★, *How To Measure A Planet?* (Century Media 1998) ★★★, *Superheat* (Century Media 2000) ★★★, *If_Then_Else* (Century Media 2000) ★★★★, *Souvenirs* (Psychonaut 2003) ★★★, *Sleepy Buildings: A Semi Acoustic Evening* (Century Media 2004) ★★★.

● COMPILATIONS: *Downfall: The Early Years* (Hammerheart 2001) ★★.

Gathering Field

This Pittsburgh, Pennsylvania, USA rock group was originally put together informally by vocalist Bill Deasy and guitarist Dave Brown in 1994. They released their debut album the following year, and were encouraged to see it top the local charts. Deasy already boasted a long history in local rock groups, later commenting that 'I'd been writing songs for years, but they didn't really have the depth of the things I've done in the past year.' He was speaking to *Billboard* magazine in 1996, on the advent of the group's major label debut for **Atlantic Records**, *Lost In America* (a re-recorded version of the earlier independent debut). The title-track of this set was inspired by Deasy's reading of author Jack Kerouac, while songs such as 'Middle Road' and 'Bound To Be' could have easily been taken from the beat poet's canon. The most frequent critical comparison proved to be **Hootie And The Blowfish**, a similarly earnest, artisan-like rock band formed outside of America's east and west coast musical hothouses.

● ALBUMS: *Lost In America* (Mudpuppy 1995) ★★★, *Lost In America* (Atlantic 1996) ★★★.

Gatlin, Larry, And The Gatlin Brothers Band

Larry (b. Larry Wayne Gatlin, 2 May 1948, Seminole, but raised in nearby Odessa, Texas, USA) and his brothers, Steve (b. 4 April 1951, Olney, Texas, USA) and Rudy (b. 20 August 1952, Olney, Texas, USA), were encouraged in their fledgling talent by their father, an oil driller, and with their younger sister LaDonna (b. 18 August 1954, Abilene, Texas, USA), they sang at church functions, appeared on television and made an album. They worked together for several years until Larry enrolled at the University of Houston. In 1971, he was a temporary replacement in the **Imperials** gospel group, and then **Dottie West** recorded his songs 'Once You Were Mine' and 'You're The Other Half Of Me', and he moved to Nashville. **Johnny Cash** performed 'The Last Supper' and 'Help Me' in his documentary film *The Gospel Road*, and also sang with **Kris Kristofferson** on his *Jesus Was A Capricorn*. At Kristofferson's insistence, he was signed to Monument Records, and two singles were released simultaneously— the solo 'My Mind's Gone To Memphis' and the Gatlins' 'Come On In', which featured Steve, Rudy and LaDonna. In October 1973 Gatlin had his first US country hit with 'Sweet Becky Walker', which was followed by a personal collection

of beautifully sung love songs, *The Pilgrim*, with liner notes by Johnny Cash.

Further successes followed with 'Bigger They Are, The Harder They Fall' (later recorded by **Elvis Presley**, who also sang 'Help Me') and 'Delta Dirt'. Larry produced **Johnny Duncan**'s 'Jo And The Cowboy' and 'Third Rate Romance', and Steve, Rudy and LaDonna joined him as part of **Tammy Wynette**'s roadshow (Wynette, incidentally, recorded one of the quirkiest of Gatlin's compositions, 'Brown Paper Bag'). Wynette's autobiography recounts how her affair with Rudy created friction between him and Larry. After leaving the show, LaDonna married Tim Johnson and they worked as travelling evangelists. The Gatlin brothers, with Larry singing lead, Steve bass and Rudy tenor, had a US country Top 10 hit with 'Broken Lady', which won a Grammy as the Best Country Song of 1976. Larry recalls, 'the Eagles were very hot at the time with a lot of harmony and some real pretty acoustic guitars, so I decided to write something that had our voices up front without a lot of other things going on. That was 'Broken Lady' and it set the style for the Gatlin Brothers from then on.' The Gatlin brothers had success with 'Statues Without Hearts', 'I Don't Wanna Cry' (the title line followed a chance remark to an American disc jockey), 'Love Is Just A Game' (Larry later said: 'I wrote that for **Neil Diamond** but then realized that he didn't need another hit record, and I did!'), and 'I Just Wish You Were Someone I Love' (his first US country number 1).

Their first single for US **Columbia Records**, 'All The Gold In California', was another country number 1, but many US radio stations banned 'The Midnight Choir' as sacrilegious. Their success tailed off when Larry's songs stopped being so distinctive, and, with much reluctance, he agreed to perform songs by outside writers. *Houston To Denver* was one of their best albums but, ironically, the number 1 country single, 'Houston (Means I'm One Day Closer To You)', was Larry's own song. For some years, Larry had been an embarrassment to those who knew him, even causing songwriter **Roger Bowling** to include a snide reference to the Gatlins in 'Coward Of The County'. For example, Larry refused to sign autographs after shows—a cardinal sin for a country performer—saying, 'It's unfair to step off a stage after I've been singing my butt off and be met with 200 people sticking pencils in my face.' From 1979–84 Larry Gatlin had spent an estimated $500,000 on cocaine, but, to the relief of his friends, he eventually underwent treatment. Once cured, he joined Nancy Reagan's 'Just Say No' anti-drug campaign. The *Smile* album included 'Indian Summer', co-written with **Barry Gibb** and featuring a tender-voiced **Roy Orbison**. Larry said, 'I think I have proven I can write great songs because those who are acknowledged as having written great songs say so.' The group disbanded in 1991, but still performed regularly at their theatre in Branson, Missouri. In 1993 Larry took the lead in the Broadway musical *The Will Rogers Follies*. The group signed to the Branson Entertainment label the same year, releasing the tribute album *Moments To Remember*.

● ALBUMS: by the Gatlin Quartet *The Old Country Church* (Sword & Shield 1961) ★★, by Larry Gatlin *The Pilgrim* (Monument 1973) ★★★★, *Rain-Rainbow* (Monument 1974) ★★★, by Larry Gatlin With Family And Friends *Larry Gatlin With Family And Friends* (Monument 1976) ★★★, by Larry Gatlin With Brothers And Friends *High Time* (Monument 1976) ★★★, *Broken Lady* (Monument

1976) ★★★, *Love Is Just A Game* (Monument 1977) ★★★, *Oh! Brother* (Monument 1978) ★★★, by Gatlin Brothers Band *Straight Ahead* (Columbia 1979) ★★★, *Help Yourself* (Columbia 1980) ★★★, *Not Guilty* (Columbia 1981) ★★★, *Sure Feels Like Love* (Columbia 1982) ★★★, *A Gatlin Family Christmas* (Columbia 1983) ★★, *Houston To Denver* (Columbia 1984) ★★★, *Smile* (Columbia 1986) ★★★, *Partners* (Columbia 1987) ★★★, *Pure 'N' Simple* (Columbia 1989) ★★★, *Cookin' Up A Storm* (Columbia 1990) ★★★, *Adios* (Liberty 1991) ★★★, *Moments To Remember* (Branson 1993) ★★★, *Cool Water* (Branson 1994) ★★, *Sing Their Family Gospel Favorites* (Dualtone 2004) ★★★.

● COMPILATIONS: *Greatest Hits* (Columbia 1978) ★★★, *Greatest Hits, Volume 2* (Columbia 1983) ★★★, *17 Greatest Hits* (Columbia 1985) ★★★, *Biggest Hits* (Columbia 1988) ★★★, *Best Of The Gatlins: All The Gold In California* (Columbia/Legacy 1996) ★★★★, *16 Biggest Hits* (Columbia/Legacy 2000) ★★★.

● FURTHER READING: *All The Gold In California And Other People, Places & Things: The Man, His Music, And The Faith That Saved His Life*, Larry Gatlin with Jeff Lenburg.

Gattis, Keith

b. 26 May 1971, Austin, Texas, USA. This country singer-songwriter began to develop his ambitions in the music industry when in his mid-teens he purchased a second-hand guitar and an instruction book. Almost immediately, he formed a local country band and played impromptu concerts in the vicinity. In testament to his agricultural roots, he then founded a group with fellow members of the Future Farmers Of America. This group won a major national talent contest and performed in front of over 25,000 as headline act at the FFA Nationals in Kansas City. Gattis then pursued a degree in Performing Arts Technology, while developing his songwriting. This course allowed him access to the school studio, where he spent much of his time. Eventually he moved to Nashville to take a job at a steel guitar shop. By night he played 'hole in the wall dives and honky tonks', and this brought him to the attention of local legends **Ernest Tubbs** and **Johnny Paycheck**. A demo tape was eventually passed to producer Norro Wilson via Jim Dowell, then manager of **Sammy Kershaw**. Wilson secured a contract with **RCA Records**, for whom Gattis recorded his *The Real Deal* debut in 1996. A traditional, somewhat conservative country record, its commercial fortunes improved when the attendant debut single, 'Little Drops Of My Heart', became a minor hit.

● ALBUMS: *The Real Deal* (RCA 1996) ★★★.

Gatton, Danny

b. 4 September 1945, Washington DC, USA, d. 20 October 1994, Newburg, Maryland, USA. Guitarist and songwriter Danny Gatton first picked up a guitar at the age of nine. Inspired by guitarist **Charlie Christian** and **Bob Wills**' Texas Playboys, Gatton soon developed a unique individual style. Much of this was due to his customization of a standard **Les Paul** guitar into what he termed the 'Les Paulveriser'. He enhanced this sound by making home recordings using two reel-to-reel tapes that produced an echo effect when one machine was played slightly out of synchronization with the other. Through his thirties and forties he played regularly in Washington to an audience who appreciated his unique take on jazz, bluegrass and rockabilly, issuing a series of

exclusively mail-order albums that gradually expanded his audience. Eventually, one of these, *Unfinished Business*, provoked enough critical feedback to prompt **Elektra Records** into offering him a recording contract. However, despite further strong reviews, neither *88 Elmira St.* (1991) nor *Cruisin' Deuces* (1993) succeeded commercially. Gatton collaborated with jazz musician **Joey DeFrancesco** on his *Relentless* project but, depressed by the loss of his contract with Elektra, he committed suicide in 1994.

● ALBUMS: *American Music* (NRG 1975) ★★★, *Redneck Jazz* (NRG 1978) ★★★, *Unfinished Business* (NRG 1987) ★★★★, *88 Elmira St.* (Elektra 1991) ★★★★, *Cruisin' Deuces* (Elektra 1993) ★★★, with Joey DeFrancesco *Relentless* (Big Mo 1994) ★★★, with Robert Gordon *Live: The Humbler* (NRG 1996) ★★★, *In Concert 9/9/94* (Big Mo 1997) ★★★.

● COMPILATIONS: *Portraits* (Big Mo 1998) ★★, *Untouchable* (NRG 1998) ★★★, *Hot Rod Guitar: The Danny Gatton Anthology* (Rhino 1999) ★★★★.

● FURTHER READING: *Unfinished Business: The Life & Times Of Danny Gatton*, Ralph Heibutzki.

Gaughan, Dick

b. Richard Peter Gaughan, 17 May 1948, Rutherglen, South Lanarkshire, Scotland. A veteran of Scotland's thriving folk circuit, Gaughan rose to national prominence in the 70s as a member of the **Boys Of The Lough**. From there, he became a founder member of **Five Hand Reel**, an electric folk group that enjoyed considerable critical acclaim. Gaughan left them in 1978 following the release of their third album, *Earl O' Moray*, having already embarked on a concurrent solo career. His early releases, *No More Forever* and *Kist O' Gold*, concentrated on traditional material, while *Coppers And Brass* showcased guitar interpretations of Scottish and Irish dance music. However, it was the release of 1981's *Handful Of Earth* that established Gaughan as a major force in contemporary folk. This politically charged album included the beautifully vitriolic 'Worker's Song' and 'The World Turned Upside Down' while at the same time scotched notions of nationalism with the reconciliatory 'Both Sides The Tweed'. This exceptional set is rightly regarded as a landmark in British traditional music, but its ever-restless creator surprised many commentators with 1983's *A Different Kind Of Love Song*, which included a cover version of **Joe South**'s 60s protest song, 'Games People Play'. Gaughan was part of the folk 'supergroup' **Clan Alba** in the mid-90s, alongside veteran artists Mary MacMaster, Brian McNeill, Fred Morrison, Patsy Seddon, Davy Steele, Mike Travis and Dave Tulloch. He made a return to solo work with 1996's *Sail On*, a typically inspired album featuring a superb cover version of the **Rolling Stones**' 'Ruby Tuesday'. Gaughan has enjoyed a fervent popularity both at home and abroad while continuing to pursue his uncompromising, idiosyncratic musical path. Gaughan calls himself a 'hard-nosed Communist' and is a passionate lover and supporter of Scotland, while not tolerating any anti-English feeling. Both his playing and singing come from the heart and by the new millennium he was being lauded as arguably Scotland's greatest living troubadour.

● ALBUMS: *No More Forever* (Trailer 1972) ★★, *Coppers And Brass* (Topic 1977) ★★, *Kist O' Gold* (Trailer 1977) ★★★, with Dave Burland, Tony Capstick *Songs Of Ewan MacColl* (Rubber 1978) ★★★, *Gaughan* (Topic 1978)

★★★, *Handful Of Earth* (Topic 1981) ★★★★★, with Andy Irvine *Parallel Lines* (Folk Freak 1982) ★★★, *A Different Kind Of Love Song* (Celtic 1983) ★★★, with Ken Hyder *Fanfare For Tomorrow* (Impetus 1985) ★★★, *Live In Edinburgh* (Celtic 1985) ★★★, *True And Bold* (Stuc 1986) ★★★, *Call It Freedom* (Celtic 1988) ★★★, *Sail On* (Greentrax 1996) ★★★, *Redwood Cathedral* (Greentrax 1998) ★★★, *Outlaws & Dreamers* (Greentrax 2001) ★★★.
● COMPILATIONS: *Prentice Piece* (Greentrax 2002) ★★★★, *The Definitive Collection* (Highpoint 2006) ★★★.

Gauthier, Mary

b. Thibodaux, Louisiana, USA. This New England–based alt country singer-songwriter has plenty of autobiographical material on which to draw from. After dropping out of high school at the age of 15, Gauthier stole the family car and landed in detox barely a year later and spent her eighteenth birthday in a Kansas City jail. She began to turn her life around in her early twenties, studying philosophy at Louisiana State University and then attending the Cambridge School of Culinary Arts. Her remarkable transformation was complete when Gauthier opened her Dixie Kitchen restaurant in Boston. While running this successful business, Gauthier began attending songwriting workshops and in the late 90s, she launched a performing career with an album named after her restaurant. Drawing on both folk and country tradition, Gauthier ploughed a furrow similar to fellow US singer-songwriters **John Prine** and **Steve Earle**. Her lyrics made ample reference to Gauthier's colourful past and the motley assortment of characters passing in and out of her life, with the aching pain of 'Goddamn HIV' and the hard-edged nostalgia of 'Mama Louisianna' earning particular praise. Gauthier came to wider attention with the release of her second album, the wonderfully titled *Drag Queens In Limousines*. A more fully realized work than her debut, the album focused on the hopes and thwarted desires of a group of outcasts and misfits, while never losing sight of the essential humanity that exists in even these social rejects. Gauthier's third album, 2002's *Filth & Fire*, boasted a fuller production sound courtesy of **Lucinda Williams** associate Gurf Morlix. The bigger budget spurred on Gauthier to compose some of her most affecting songs to date, notably 'Camelot Motel' and 'The Sun Fades The Color Of Everything'.
● ALBUMS: *Dixie Kitchen* (R.G. 1997) ★★★, *Drag Queens In Limousines* (Groove House 1999) ★★★★, *Filth & Fire* (Signature/Munich 2002) ★★★★, *Mercy Now* (Lost Highway 2005) ★★★.

Gaxton, William

b. Arturo Antonio Gaxiola, 2 December 1893, San Francisco, California, USA, d. 12 February 1963, New York City, USA. Appearances in amateur productions led to a desire to pursue a theatrical career. Gaxton performed as a singer in vaudeville for some years, interrupted by World War I, during which he was in the US Navy. In 1922 he made his first Broadway appearance, in **Irving Berlin**'s *Music Box Revue*, and over the next few years developed his singing and stagecraft. His breakthrough came when he took a starring role in **Richard Rodgers** and **Lorenz Hart**'s *A Connecticut Yankee* (1927). In this show, Gaxton sang what was to become an enduring standard, 'Thou Swell', and in

the process began to secure his lasting stage fame. In 1929 he consolidated his standing, this time in **Cole Porter**'s *Fifty Million Frenchmen*, singing another standard-to-be, 'You Do Something To Me'. In the early 30s he was in successive **George** and **Ira Gershwin** musical comedies, *Of Thee I Sing* (1931) and *Let 'Em Eat Cake* (1933), then went into Porter's *Anything Goes* (1934). In all three of these shows, Gaxton's elegant sophistication was contrasted with **Victor Moore**'s bumbling comedic stage presence, while in the Porter show he had two more hit songs, a solo, 'All Through The Night', and a duet, 'You're The Top', with co-star, **Ethel Merman**. Later in the 30s, Gaxton extended his popularity through the American adaptation, by composer-lyricist **Irving Caesar**, of Robert Stolz's *White Horse Inn* (1936), which bore the touch of many other composing and lyric-writing hands. In this show, Gaxton played Leopold, the head waiter who is secretly in love with aristocratic Katerina Vogelhuber, played by **Kitty Carlisle**. Gaxton was in Porter's *Leave It To Me!* (1938, which also featured Moore), *Louisiana Purchase* (1940), and *Hollywood Pinafore* (1945). During the early 40s Gaxton made a handful of musical films, among them *Best Foot Forward* (1943, opposite **Lucille Ball**), and *Billy Rose's Diamond Horseshoe* (1945, with **Dick Haymes**, **Betty Grable** and **Phil Silvers**), but despite the merits of the films Gaxton's commanding stage presence did not adapt well to the screen. He returned to stage with *Nelly Bly* (1946), but the show flopped and shortly thereafter Gaxton retired.
● FILMS: *It's The Old Army Game* (1926), *Stepping Along* (1926), *Fifty Million Frenchmen* (1931), *Ladies Not Allowed* (1932), *Their Big Moment* aka *Afterwards* (1934), *Something To Shout About* (1943), *Best Foot Forward* (1943), *The Heat's On* aka *Tropicana* (1943), *Diamond Horseshoe* (1945).

Gay Dad

The brainchild of a music journalist, this UK band arrived on the back of a wave of hype generated by a music press desperate to promote them as the new saviours of indie music. After floating around the fringes of the music scene for several years, Gay Dad eventually became a reality in 1997, with a line-up comprising Cliff Jones (guitar/vocals), James Risebero (keyboards), Nigel Hoyle (bass) and Nicholas 'Baz' Crowe (drummer). Jones was a marginally successful journalist who had been published in magazines including *The Face* and *Mojo*. Hoyle was a medical student, Crowe worked in publishing, and Risebero was a trained architect. The quartet recorded demos at Raezor Studios, including a song called 'To Earth With Love'. Although originally intended to win the band some live dates, the demo soon attracted keen record company interest. The band signed to **London Records** in December 1997 after an A&R scramble. Adding guitarist Charley Stone they embarked on a low-key tour with **Superstar** in early 1998. Afterwards, the band began recording sessions at The Dairy studio in Brixton with producers/engineers Gary Langan (ex-**Art Of Noise**) and Chris Hughes (ex-**Adam And The Ants**). A re-recorded 'To Earth With Love' was released on the back of tremendous press hype, with the band's name and their logo (road sign posters depicting a white man against a blue background) skilfully exploiting the zeitgeist. The single debuted at UK number 10 in January 1999, but poor live shows initiated the predictable critical backlash. The follow-up single 'Joy' stalled outside the Top 20 in May, while *Leisurenoise* entered the charts at number 14. The album was a surprisingly effective pastiche of 70s musical styles, from the driving glam rock of their debut single to the power pop of 'Pathfinder' and 'Different Kind Of Blue'. The band, now reduced to a trio with the departure of Risebero, were released by London the following November. They bounced back in some style with September 2001's *Transmission*.

● ALBUMS: *Leisurenoise* (London 1999) ★★★, *Transmission* (B-Unique/Thirsty Ear 2001) ★★★.

Gay Divorce

Opening at New York's Ethel Barrymore Theatre on 29 November 1932, this show was **Fred Astaire**'s first stage musical without his sister, Adele (she retired after **The Band Wagon** in 1931)—and Astaire's own final Broadway appearance before leaving for Hollywood to star in some 30 musical films. Music and lyrics were provided by **Cole Porter**, and the book was written by Kenneth Webb and Samuel Hoffenstein from Dwight Taylor's adaptation of an unproduced play, *An Adorable Adventure*, by J. Hartley Manners. It seems that Mimi Pratt (Claire Luce) wants to divorce her husband. Guy Holden (Fred Astaire), a British novelist who loves Mimi, is mistaken for Toneti (Erik Rhodes), the professional co-respondent Mimi has hired in an effort to shake herself loose. That kind of story can use a great score, and Porter came up with one of his best. Comedienne **Luella Gear** had the amusing 'I Still Love The Red, White And Blue' and 'Mister And Missus Fitch'; Erik Rhodes sang 'How's Your Romance?' ('Does he or not love you an awful lot?/Cold, tepid, warm, or hot/How's your romance?'); **Eric Blore**, who played an immaculate waiter in the show (and later made a career in films, usually as a butler), enquired 'What Will Become Of Our England?' ('When the Prince of Wales finds a wife'); Astaire crooned the haunting 'After You, Who?' ('I could search years but who else could change my tears/Into laughter after you?') and joined Claire Luce in 'I've Got You On My Mind' ('You're not wild enough/You're not gay enough/You don't let me lead you astray enough') and one of Porter's most potent love songs, 'Night And Day'. The composer claimed the music for the latter number was inspired by a call to worship that he had heard in Morocco. Initially, the show had an indifferent response, but the exposure of some of the songs, especially 'Night And Day', soon boosted audiences. The number became a nation-wide hit through recordings by Astaire himself (With **Leo Reisman**'s Orchestra), **Eddy Duchin**, **Charlie Barnet**, **Frank Sinatra**, and **Bing Crosby**. *Gay Divorce* played 248 performances on Broadway, and another 180 in London in 1933, where Astaire, Luce, Rhodes, and Blore recreated their roles. It was revived briefly off-Broadway in 1960. Over 30 years later, in 1993, the show was presented in concert by John McGlinn at Carnegie Hall's Weill Recital Hall complete with the original orchestrations by Hans Spialek and **Robert Russell Bennett**. The 1934 film version, called **The Gay Divorcee**, starred Astaire and **Ginger Rogers**, but the only song retained from the original score was 'Night And Day'.

Gay Divorcee, The

It was not just the title that was changed when **Cole Porter**'s 1932 hit Broadway show, **The Gay Divorce**, was transferred to the screen two years later. The title itself was not seen to be fit for wider consumption in America, and only one song, the incomparable 'Night And Day', survived from the smart and sophisticated stage score. Fortunately, **Fred Astaire** also

made the trip from New York to Hollywood, and the screenplay, by George Marion Jnr., Dorothy Yost and Edward Kaufman, remained reasonably true to the original book. After the plot, which was set in an English seaside town and involved Guy Holden (Astaire) being mistaken for the professional co-respondent hired by Mimi Glossop (**Ginger Rogers**) in an effort to facilitate her divorce, had got under way, delighted audiences were able to sit back and enjoy the sublime dancing of Astaire and Rogers in their first starring role together. 'Night And Day' would dominate any film musical, especially when it accompanied dancing of this style and grace, The Gay Divorcee was no exception, but there were several other engaging numbers by a variety of composers, including 'A Needle In A Haystack' (Con Conrad–Herb Magidson), and two by **Mack Gordon** and **Harry Revel**—'Don't Let It Bother You' and 'Let's K-nock K-nees'. The latter was punched out with a great deal of zest by **Betty Grable**, whose 'pin-up' image during the 40s necessitated her own legs being insured for many thousands of dollars. 'Night And Day' may have been the film's major romantic moment, but *The Gay Divorcee* is probably best-remembered for another song, 'The Continental' (Conrad-Magidson), which was introduced by Fred and Ginger in a spectacular 17-minute sequence, and went on to become all the rage of dance floors everywhere. It also has the distinction of being the first song to win an Academy Award. Meanwhile, back to the plot. As for the details of the prospective divorce, a character by the name of Rodolfo Tonetti (Erik Rhodes) turned out to be the real co-respondent, and the rest of the cast was made up of always reliable and amusing supporting players such as Edward Everett Horton and Alice Brady. Dave Gould and **Hermes Pan** were responsible for the innovative choreography, and the film, which was released by RKO, was directed by Mark Sandrich. In view of the film's title change, which was apparently demanded by the US censor, it is interesting that the UK equivalent had no such problems, and both the original British cinema and subsequent video release bear the title: *The Gay Divorce*.

Gay Rosalinda

Produced in London's West End in 1945, this show was based upon Johann Strauss II's operetta *Die Fledermaus* (1874), as had been a 1911 revival entitled *Nightbirds*, staged at London's Lyric Theatre and the 1942 Broadway show, *Rosalinda*. With the 1911 libretto by Gladys Unger and lyrics by Arthur Anderson, *Gay Rosalinda* opened at the Palace Theatre on 8 March 1945 and enjoyed a moderately successful run. While the plot was typical of operetta, with its trite tale of mistaken identities and secret love, the sweeping romanticism of Strauss' music that had enraptured audiences for generations was expectedly effective. There have been countless revivals of the show in its original form, including a production that opened at the London Coliseum on 16 April 1959 and starred John Heddle Nash, Victoria Elliott, Alexander Young, Marion Studholme and Rowland Jones. It has also been staged under titles such as *Champagne, Sec*, *The Merry Countess* and *A Wonderful Night*.

In 1955, the Michael Powell and Emeric Pressburger film, *Oh . . . Rosalinda!!* was based upon the same source material but uncomfortably updated the setting to Cold War Vienna. The film starred Anthony Quayle, Ludmilla Tcherina, Anton

Walbrook and Anneliese Rothenberger, with Richard Marner, Michael Redgrave, Mel Ferrer and Dennis Price also in the cast. Although Quayle, Rothenberger and Redgrave sang their roles, some of the soundtrack singing was dubbed: Walter Berry (for Walbrook), Sari Barabas (Tcherina), Dennis Dowling (Ferrer), and Alexander Young (Price). New lyrics for this version were by Dennis Arundell.

Gay, Al

b. 25 February 1928, London, England. After formal studies in clarinet and saxophones at the Guildhall School of Music, Gay worked in various dance bands during the mid- and late 40s. In 1953 he joined the **Freddy Randall** band and, after leaving three years later, he remained strongly connected with the traditional jazz scene, playing with bands led by **Joe Daniels**, **Harry Gold** and **Bob Wallis**. In the early 60s Gay became a member of **Alex Welsh**'s band, where he remained for almost five years, returning in 1977 for a further six years. In between these stints, and on into the 80s, Gay freelanced, working in radio and as accompanist to numerous visiting jazz artists. In the late 80s and 90s Gay could be heard leading his own band and also playing with groups such as the Pizza Express All Stars. A sound mainstream performer, Gay's work on tenor saxophone is particularly pleasing.

Gay, Connie B.

b. Connie Barriot Gay, 22 August 1914, Lizard Lick, North Carolina, USA, d. 3 December 1989. After local education, Gay attended the State University and graduated in 1935. He first worked as a salesman in Washington DC, but in the early 40s, his interest in radio led to his joining the Department of Agriculture and becoming involved with its *National Farm And Home Hour*. In 1946, he became the presenter of *Town And Country*, a one-hour country music show on WARL Arlington, Virginia, working only for a percentage of the advertising monies, but he was shrewd enough to register 'Town And Country' as a trademark. Listener reaction soon saw the show increased to three hours and renamed *Gay Time*. In 1947, after promoting two major sell-out country shows starring **Eddy Arnold**, Gay moved more towards promotional work. His friendship with **Jim Denny**, a fellow promoter but also the manager of the **Grand Ole Opry**, led to Gay promoting *Opry* acts and quickly establishing himself as a major promoter. His shows gained network coverage on radio and television and he was never short of promotional gimmicks. He arranged train tours to Nashville, river cruises on the Potomac, country concerts starring the major acts at many prestigious 'intown' venues and even Special Service Road Shows, which toured to US bases overseas. In the late 50s, an alcohol problem ended his marriage and saw him disappear for a time when he entered Alcoholics Anonymous.

In 1961, he remarried and with his wife's financial help, he relaunched his promotional activities. He promoted major radio and television shows, including *Town And Country Jamboree*, *Town And Country Time* and *Country Style*. His investments at one time made him the owner of nine radio stations. He was involved in the discovery of **Patsy Cline** and promoting **Roy Clark** and **Jimmy Dean** to major stardom. In 1960, after failing to become the Governor of the Virgin Islands, he relocated to McLean, Virginia. He was inducted into the **Country Music Hall Of Fame** in 1980. His plaque notes that he was an advisor to five Presidents and states: 'His

pioneer use of the term country music and registered trademark 'Town And Country' were instrumental in bringing country music 'uptown''. He has served as founding President of the Country Music Association and President of the Country Music Foundation'. Gay died of cancer, at his home in McLean, in 1989.

Gay, Noel

b. Richard Moxon Armitage, 3 March 1898, Wakefield, Yorkshire, England, d. 3 March 1954, London England. A prolific composer and lyricist, Gay was responsible for many of the most popular and memorable songs in the UK during the 30s and 40s. A child prodigy, he was educated at Wakefield Cathedral School, and often deputized for the Cathedral organist. In 1913 he moved to London to study at the Royal College of Music, and later became the director of music and organist at St. Anne's Church in Soho. After four years studying for his MA and B.Mus. at Christ's Church College, Cambridge, he seemed destined for a career in a university or cathedral. However, while at Cambridge he became interested in the world of musical comedy, and started to write songs. After contributing to the revue *Stop Press*, he was commissioned to write the complete score for the *Charlot Show Of 1926*. He was also the principal composer for *Clowns In Clover*, which starred **Jack Hulbert** and **Cicely Courtneidge**, and ran for over 500 performances. Around this time he took the name of Noel Gay for his popular work to avoid embarrassment to the church authorities.

In 1930, Gay, with Harry Graham, wrote his most successful song to date, 'The King's Horses', which was sung in another Charlot revue, *Folly To Be Wise*. He then collaborated with lyricist Desmond Carter for the score of his first musical show, *Hold My Hand* (1931). Starring **Jessie Matthews**, **Sonnie Hale** and **Stanley Lupino**, the songs included 'Pied Piper', 'What's In A Kiss', 'Hold My Hand' and 'Turn On The Music'. During the 30s Gay wrote complete, or contributed to, scores for popular shows such as *She Couldn't Say No*, *That's A Pretty Thing*, *Jack O'Diamonds*, *Love Laughs!*, *O-Kay For Sound* (one of the early Crazy Gang music hall–type revues at the London Palladium, in which **Bud Flanagan** sang Gay's 'The Fleet's In Port Again'), *Wild Oats* and *Me And My Girl* (1937). The latter show, with a book and lyrics by L. Arthur Rose, and starring **Lupino Lane** in the central role of Bill Sibson, ran for over 1,600 performances and featured 'The Lambeth Walk', which became an enormously popular sequence dance craze—so popular, in fact, that when the show was filmed in 1939, it was re-titled *The Lambeth Walk*. In the same year, with Ralph Butler, Gay gave Bud Flanagan the big song, 'Run, Rabbit, Run', in another Crazy Gang revue, *The Little Dog Laughed*.

During the 40s, Gay wrote for several shows with lyrics mostly by Frank Eyton, including *Lights Up* ('Let The People Sing', 'Only A Glass Of Champagne' and 'You've Done Something To My Heart'), *Present Arms*, *La-Di-Di-Di-Da*', *The Love Racket*, **Meet Me Victoria**, *Sweetheart Mine* and *Bob's Your Uncle* (1948). His songs for films included 'All For A Shilling A Day' and 'There's Something About A Soldier', sung by Courtneidge in *Me And Marlborough* (1935); 'Leaning On A Lamp Post' introduced by comedian **George Formby** in *Feather Your Nest*; 'Who's Been Polishing The Sun', sung by Jack Hulbert in *The Camels Are Coming*; 'I Don't Want To Go to Bed' (Stanley Lupino in *Sleepless Nights*) and 'All Over The Place' (*Sailors Three*). Gay also composed 'Tondeleyo', the first song to be synchronized into a British talking picture (*White Cargo*). His other songs included 'Round The Marble Arch', 'All For The Love Of A Lady', 'I Took My Harp To A Party' (a hit for **Gracie Fields**), 'Let's Have A Tiddley At The Milk Bar', 'Red, White And Blue', 'Love Makes The World Go Round', 'The Moon Remembered, But You Forgot', 'The Girl Who Loves A Soldier', 'The Birthday Of The Little Princess', 'Are We Downhearted?—No!', 'Hey Little Hen', 'Happy Days Happy Months', 'I'll Always Love You', 'Just A Little Fond Affection', 'When Alice Blue Gown Met Little Boy Blue', 'I Was Much Better Off In The Army' and 'My Thanks To You' (co-written with **Norman Newell**).

Gay's other collaborators included Archie Gottler, Clifford Grey, Dion Titheradge, Donavan Parsons and Ian Grant. In the early 50s Gay wrote very little, just a few songs such as 'I Was Much Better Off In The Army' and 'You Smile At Everyone But Me'. He had been going deaf for some years, and had to wear a hearing aid. After his death in March 1954, his publishing company, Noel Gay Music, which he had formed in 1938, published one more song, 'Love Me Now'. His son, Richard Armitage (b. 12 August 1928, Wakefield, England, d. 17 November 1986), a successful impresario and agent, took over the company, and extended and developed the organization into one of the biggest television and representational agencies in Europe. His clients included David Frost, Rowan Atkinson, Esther Rantzen, **Russ Conway**, Russell Harty, Jonathan Miller, John Cleese, the **King's Singers** and many more. The publishing side had several hit copyrights, including the **Scaffold**'s 'Thank U Very Much'. After mounting several minor productions, Armitage revived his father's most popular show, *Me And My Girl*, in London in February 1985. With the versatile actor Robert Lindsay as Sibson, a revised book, and two other Gay hits, 'The Sun Has Got His Hat On' and 'Leaning On A Lamp Post' interpolated into the score, the new production was an immediate success. It closed in 1993 following a stay of eight years. Around the same time, *Radio Times*, a new show featuring Noel Gay's music, enjoyed a brief West End run. Opening on Broadway in 1986, *Me And My Girl* ran for over 1,500 performances, New York's biggest hit for years. Armitage died just three months after the show's Broadway debut.

Gaye Bykers On Acid

This UK rock band employed an image that combined traditional biker attire with elements of psychedelia and hippie camp. They were led by the colourful figure of Mary Millington, aka Mary Mary (b. Ian Garfield Hoxley; vocals), alongside Kevin Hyde (drums), Robber (b. Ian Michael Reynolds; bass) and Tony Horsfall (b. Richard Anthony Horsfall; guitar). They were later complemented by disc jockey William Samuel Ronald Monroe ('Rocket Ronnie'). Mary Mary, who had once come second in Leicester's Alternative Miss Universe competition, was often to be seen in platform shoes and dresses, which fuelled the critics' confusion with regard to the band's name and gender orientation. Their debut album, *Drill Your Own Hole*, required purchasers to do just that, as the record was initially issued without a hole in its centre. After leaving **Virgin Records**, they set up their own label, Naked Brain, quite conceivably because nobody else would have them. Subsequent to the band's demise, Hyde instigated a new band, GROWTH, with Jeff (ex-Janitors), Horsfall teamed up with

Brad Bradbury in Camp Collision, Reynolds worked as a DJ, and Rocket Ronnie went on to collaborate with the **Grid**'s Richard Norris and run the drum 'n' bass label Warm Interface. Mary Mary joined ex-members of **Killing Joke**, **Ministry** and **Public Image Limited** in the multi-member outfit Pigface. The 90s brought a more permanent home for his talents with **Hyperhead**, a band he formed with Karl Leiker (ex-Luxuria; Bugblot), and breakbeat dance outfit **Apollo 440**.

● ALBUMS: *Drill Your Own Hole* (Virgin 1987) ★★★, *Stewed To The Gills* (Virgin 1989) ★★★, *GrooveDiveSoapDish* (Bleed 1989) ★★★, *Cancer Planet Mission* (Naked Brain 1990) ★★, as PFX *Pernicious Nonsense* (Naked Brain 1991) ★★, *From The Tomb Of The Near Legendary* (Receiver 1993) ★★.

● DVD/VIDEOS: *Drill Your Own Hole* (Virgin Vision 1987).

Gaye, Marvin

b. Marvin Pentz Gay Jnr., 2 April 1939, Washington, DC, USA, d. 1 April 1984, Los Angeles, California, USA. Gaye was named after his father, a minister in the Apostolic Church. The spiritual influence of his early years played a formative role in his musical career, particularly from the 70s onwards, when his songwriting shifted back and forth between secular and religious topics. He abandoned a place in his father's church choir to team up with **Don Covay** and **Billy Stewart** in the R&B vocal group the **Rainbows**. In 1957, he joined the Marquees, who recorded for **Chess Records** under the guidance of **Bo Diddley**. The following year the group was taken under the wing of producer and singer **Harvey Fuqua**, who used them to re-form his doo-wop outfit the **Moonglows**. When Fuqua moved to Detroit in 1960, Gay went with him: Fuqua soon joined forces with **Berry Gordy** at **Motown Records**, and Gay became a session drummer and vocalist for the label.

In 1961, the singer married Gordy's sister, Anna, and was offered a solo recording contract. His first release for Tamla Motown was '(I'm Afraid) The Masquerade Is Over', released under his birth name Marvin Gay. Renamed Marvin Gaye he initially began as a jazz balladeer, but in 1962 he was persuaded to record R&B, and notched up his first hit single with the confident 'Stubborn Kind Of Fellow', a Top 10 R&B hit. This record set the style for the next three years, as Gaye enjoyed hits with a series of joyous, dance-flavoured songs that cast him as a smooth, macho, Don Juan figure. He also continued to work behind the scenes at Motown, co-writing **Martha And The Vandellas**' hit 'Dancing In The Street', and playing drums on several early recordings by Little **Stevie Wonder**. In 1965, Gaye dropped the call-and-response vocal arrangements of his earlier hits and began to record in a more sophisticated style. The striking 'How Sweet It Is (To Be Loved By You)' epitomized his new direction, and it was followed by two successive R&B number 1 hits, 'I'll Be Doggone' and 'Ain't That Peculiar'. His status as Motown's bestselling male vocalist left him free to pursue more esoteric avenues on his albums, which in 1965 included a tribute to the late **Nat 'King' Cole** and a misguided collection of Broadway standards.

To capitalize on his image as a ladies' man, Motown teamed Gaye with their leading female vocalist, **Mary Wells**, for some romantic duets. When Wells left Motown in 1964, Gaye recorded with **Kim Weston** until 1967, when she was succeeded by **Tammi Terrell**. The Gaye/Terrell partnership represented the apogee of the soul duet, as their voices blended sensually on a string of hits written specifically for the duo by **Ashford And Simpson**. Terrell developed a brain tumour in 1968, and collapsed onstage in Gaye's arms. Records continued to be issued under the duo's name, although Simpson allegedly took Terrell's place on some recordings. Through the mid-60s, Gaye allowed his duet recordings to take precedence over his solo work, but in 1968 he issued the epochal 'I Heard It Through The Grapevine' (written by Whitfield/Strong), a song originally released on Motown by **Gladys Knight And The Pips**, although Gaye's version had actually been recorded first. With its tense, ominous rhythm arrangement, and Gaye's typically fluent and emotional vocal, the record represented a landmark in Motown's history—not least because it became the label's biggest-selling record to date. Gaye followed up with another number 1 R&B hit, 'Too Busy Thinking 'Bout My Baby', but his career was derailed by the insidious illness and eventual death of Terrell in March 1970.

Devastated by the loss of his close friend and partner, Gaye spent most of 1970 in seclusion. The following year, he emerged with a set of recordings that Motown at first refused to release, but which eventually formed his most successful solo album. On 'What's Going On', a number 1 hit in 1971, and its two chart-topping follow-ups, 'Mercy Mercy Me (The Ecology)' and 'Inner City Blues', Gaye combined his spiritual beliefs with his increasing concern about poverty, discrimination and political corruption in American society. To match the shift in subject matter, Gaye evolved a new musical style that influenced a generation of black performers. Built on a heavily percussive base, Gaye's arrangements mingled jazz and classical influences into his soul roots, creating a fluid instrumental backdrop for his sensual, almost despairing vocals. The three singles were all contained on **What's Going On**, a conceptual masterpiece on which every track contributed to the spiritual yearning suggested by its title. After making a sly comment on the 1972 US presidential election campaign with the single 'You're The Man', Gaye composed the soundtrack to the 'blaxploitation' thriller **Trouble Man**. His primarily instrumental score highlighted his interest in jazz, while the title song provided him with another hit single.

Gaye's next project saw him shifting his attention from the spiritual to the sexual with **Let's Get It On**, which included a quote from T.S. Eliot on the sleeve and devoted itself to the art of talking a woman into bed. Its explicit sexuality marked a sea-change in Gaye's career; as he began to use cocaine more and more regularly, he became obsessed with his personal life, and rarely let the outside world figure in his work. Paradoxically, he continued to let Motown market him in a traditional fashion by agreeing to collaborate with **Diana Ross** on a sensuous album of duets in 1973—although the two singers allegedly did not actually meet during the recording of the project. The break-up of his marriage to Anna Gordy in 1975 delayed work on his next album. **I Want You** was merely a pleasant reworking of the *Let's Get It On* set, albeit cast in slightly more contemporary mode. The title track was another number 1 hit on the soul charts, however, as was his 1977 disco extravaganza, 'Got To Give It Up'.

Drug problems and tax demands interrupted Gaye's career, and in 1978 he fled the US mainland to Hawaii in a vain attempt to salvage his second marriage. He devoted the next year to the **Here, My Dear** double album, which provided a bitter commentary on his relationship with his first wife. Its title was ironic: he had been ordered to give all royalties from the project to Anna as part of their divorce settlement. With this catharsis behind him, Gaye began work on an album to be called *Lover Man*, but he cancelled its release after the lukewarm sales of its initial single, the sharply self-mocking 'Ego Tripping Out', which he had presented as a duet between the warring sides of his nature. In 1980, under increasing pressure from the Internal Revenue Service, Gaye moved to London, England where he began work on an ambitious concept album, *In My Lifetime*. When it emerged in 1981, Gaye accused Motown of remixing and editing the album without his consent, of removing a vital question mark from the title, and of parodying his original cover artwork. The relationship between artist and record company had been shattered, and Gaye left Motown for **Columbia Records**.

Persistent reports of Gaye's erratic personal conduct and reliance on cocaine fuelled pessimism about his future career, but he relocated to the incongruous surroundings of Ostend, Belgium and re-emerged in 1982 with a startling single, 'Sexual Healing', which combined his passionate soul vocals with a contemporary electro-disco backing. The subsequent album, **Midnight Love**, offered no equal surprises, but the success of the single seemed to herald a new era in Gaye's music. He returned to the USA, where he took up residence at his parents' home. The intensity of his cocaine addiction made it impossible for him to work on another album, and he fell into a prolonged bout of depression. He repeatedly announced his wish to commit suicide in the early weeks of 1984, and his abrupt shifts of mood brought him into heated conflict with his father, rekindling animosity that had festered since Gaye's adolescence. On 1 April 1984, another violent disagreement provoked Marvin Gay Snr. to shoot his son dead, a tawdry end to the life of one of soul music's premier performers.

Motown and Columbia collaborated to produce two albums based on Gaye's unfinished recordings. *Dream Of A Lifetime* mixed spiritual ballads from the early 70s with sexually explicit funk songs from a decade later, while *Romantically Yours* offered a travesty of Gaye's original intentions in 1979 to record an album of big band ballads. Although Gaye's weighty canon is often reduced to a quartet of 'I Heard It Through The Grapevine', 'Sexual Healing', *What's Going On* and *Let's Get It On*, his entire recorded output signifies the development of black music from raw rhythm and blues, through sophisticated soul to the political awareness of the early 70s, and the increased concentration on personal and sexual politics thereafter. Gaye's remarkable vocal range and fluency remains a touchstone for all subsequent soul vocalists, and his lover man stance has been frequently copied as well as parodied.

● ALBUMS: *The Soulful Moods Of Marvin Gaye* (Tamla 1961) ★★★, *That Stubborn Kind Of Fella* (Tamla 1963) ★★★★, *Recorded Live: On Stage* (Tamla 1964) ★★★, *When I'm Alone I Cry* (Tamla 1964) ★★★, with Mary Wells *Together* (Motown 1964) ★★★, *Hello Broadway This Is Marvin* (Tamla 1965) ★★, *How Sweet It Is To Be Loved By You* (Tamla 1965) ★★★, *A Tribute To The Great Nat King Cole* (Tamla 1965) ★★★, *Moods Of Marvin Gaye* (Tamla 1966) ★★★, with Kim Weston *Take Two* (Tamla 1966) ★★★, with Tammi Terrell *United* (Tamla 1967) ★★★, *In The Groove* (Tamla 1968) ★★★, with Terrell *You're All I Need* (Tamla 1968) ★★★, with Terrell, Weston, Mary Wells

Marvin Gaye And His Girls (Tamla 1969) ★★★, with Terrell *Easy* (Tamla 1969) ★★★, *M.P.G.* (Tamla 1969) ★★★, *That's The Way Love Is* (Tamla 1970) ★★★, *What's Going On* (Tamla 1971) ★★★★★, *Trouble Man* film soundtrack (Tamla 1972) ★★★, *Let's Get It On* (Tamla 1973) ★★★★★, with Diana Ross *Diana And Marvin* (Motown 1973) ★★★, *Live!* (Tamla 1974) ★★, *I Want You* (Tamla 1976) ★★★★, *Live At The London Palladium* (Tamla 1977) ★★★, *Here, My Dear* (Tamla 1978) ★★★★, *In Our Lifetime* (Tamla 1981) ★★★, *Midnight Love* (Columbia 1982) ★★★★, *Romantically Yours* (Columbia 1985) ★★★, *The Last Concert Tour* (Giant 1991) ★★, *Vulnerable* (Motown 1997) ★★★, *Midnight Love & The Sexual Healing Sessions* (Columbia/Legacy 1998) ★★★, *The Final Concert* 1983 recording (Capitol 2000) ★★★, *What's Going On: Deluxe Edition* (Motown/Chronicles 2002) ★★★★★, *Let's Get It On: Deluxe Edition* (Motown/Chronicles 2002) ★★★★★, *I Want You: Deluxe Edition* (Motown/Chronicles 2003) ★★★★, *North American Tour* (Universe 2003) ★, *Live In Montreux 1980* (Eagle 2004) ★★.

● COMPILATIONS: *Marvin Gaye's Greatest Hits* (Tamla 1964) ★★★★, *Marvin Gaye's Greatest Hits Vol. 2* (Tamla 1967) ★★★, with Tammi Terrell *Marvin Gaye & Tammi Terrell: Greatest Hits* (Tamla 1970) ★★★, *Super Hits* (Tamla 1970) ★★★, *Anthology* (Motown 1974) ★★★, *Marvin Gaye's Greatest Hits* (Tamla 1976) ★★★★, *Every Great Motown Hit Of Marvin Gaye* (Motown 1983) ★★★★, *Dream Of A Lifetime* (Columbia 1985) ★★★, *Motown Remembers Marvin Gaye* (Tamla 1986) ★★★, *18 Greatest Hits* (Motown 1988) ★★★★, *Love Songs* (Telstar 1990) ★★★★, *The Marvin Gaye Collection* 4-CD box set (Tamla/Motown 1990) ★★★★★, *Seek And You Shall Find: More Of The Best (1963–1981)* (Rhino 1993) ★★★, *Love Starved Heart* (Motown 1994) ★★★, *The Master: 1961–1984* 4-CD box set (Motown 1995) ★★★★, *Early Classics* (Spectrum 1996) ★★★, *The Love Songs* (Motown 2000) ★★★★, with Terrell *The Complete Duets* (Motown 2001) ★★★★, *The Master 1961–1984* (Universal 2004) ★★★★, *Got To Give It Up: The Funk Collection* (Spectrum 2004) ★★★.

● DVD/VIDEOS: *Behind The Music* (Eagle Vision 2002), *Live In Montreux 1980* (Eagle Vision 2002), *What's Going On: The Life And Death Of Marvin Gaye* (Eagle Vision 2005).

● FURTHER READING: *Divided Soul: The Life Of Marvin Gaye*, David Ritz. *I Heard It Through The Grapevine: Marvin Gaye, The Biography*, Sharon Davis. *Trouble Man: The Life And Death Of Marvin Gaye*, Steve Turner. *What's Going On And The Last Days Of The Motown Sound*, Ben Edmunds. *Marvin Gaye, My Brother*, Frankie Gaye with Fred E. Basten. *Mercy, Mercy Me: The Art, Loves And Demons Of Marvin Gaye*, Michael Eric Dyson.

Gayfeet Records

(see **Pottinger, Sonia**)

Gaylads

A vocal trio comprising **Delano Stewart** (b. 5 January 1947, Kingston, Jamaica, West Indies), **B.B. Seaton** (b. 3 September 1944, Kingston, Jamaica, West Indies), and Maurice Roberts (b. 2 July 1945, Kingston, Jamaica, West Indies). Together they began recording during the **ska** period but came to prominence during the **rocksteady** era in the mid- to late 60s. It is probable that at any other time and in any other

place, their names would be highly revered, but such was the strength of the competition for three-part harmony vocal groups in Jamaica during the 60s that they are seldom remembered outside of reggae's cognoscenti. Most of their finest ska and rocksteady material was recorded for **Coxsone Dodd**'s Studio One organization (where they also recorded in the calypso style), and the best of it is collected on two classic albums, *Soul Beat* and *The Best Of The Gaylads*, with Seaton writing most of their material. As with most other Dodd singers, their talents were used extensively for harmony work for other Studio One artists such as **Slim Smith** and **Peter Tosh**. They also recorded some beautiful rocksteady sides for WIRL—'Joy In The Morning' is one of their most enduring and much versioned songs—and 'ABC Rocksteady' and 'It's Hard To Confess', for **Sonia Pottinger**'s Gayfeet label, are two all-time classics of the genre. Stewart and Seaton pursued solo careers in the 70s with varying degrees of success. Their legacy is a proud one, the Gaylads' name gracing some of the most beautiful three-part harmonies ever recorded.

● ALBUMS: *Sunshine Is Golden* (Studio One 1967) ★★★, *Soul Beat* (Studio One 1969) ★★★.

● COMPILATIONS: *The Best Of* (Studio One 1992) ★★★★, *After Studio One* (Metronome 1992) ★★★, *Over The Rainbow's End* (Trojan 1995) ★★★.

Gayle, Charles

b. 28 February 1939, Buffalo, New York, USA. While working in industry, Gayle studied piano in his spare time. Eventually taking up the tenor saxophone, he became involved in the New York, *avant garde* movement of the 60s. At the end of the decade he was back in his home town but returned to New York, where for the next decade he often scuffled for work, sometimes playing in obscure venues and even in the subway. He worked briefly with **Sunny Murray** and in 1984 was heard by **Peter Kowald** who, recognizing a fellow free improvising spirit, invited him to visit Europe. During the late 80s and early 90s, Gayle played in various US and European locations, and also made records under his own name and in a trio with **William Parker** and **Rashied Ali**. A forceful, dramatic player in the ferocious sound-and-fury tradition of New York's loft scene, Gayle is also very effective when he plays bass clarinet. He has continued to play piano occasionally, albeit less successfully than when he appears on reed instruments. His multi-instrumental abilities were displayed on *Unto I Am*, on which he plays all three of his regular instruments together with the drums.

Gayle's playing, which initially is somewhat reminiscent of **Albert Ayler**'s, is forceful and demanding of listener and performer alike as it proceeds with relentless intensity. With repeated hearings, however, the impressions of Ayler recede, revealing Gayle to be an endlessly inventive improviser who is very much his own man. Nevertheless, a newcomer to Gayle's work might well find it useful to test the waters with the relative orthodoxy of *Ancient Of Days* rather than dive right in to the storm-tossed oceans of sound that suffuse most of his work.

● ALBUMS: *Always Born* (Silkheart 1988) ★★★, *Homeless* (Silkheart 1988) ★★★, *Spirits Before* (Silkheart 1988) ★★★, with William Parker, Rashied Ali *Touchin' On Trane* (FMP 1991) ★★★★, *Repent* (Knitting Factory 1992) ★★★★, *Berlin Movement From Future Years* (FMP 1993) ★★★, *Abiding Variations* (FMP 1993) ★★★, *More Live*

At KF (Knitting Factory 1993) ★★★, *Raining Fire* (Silkheart 1993) ★★★, *Translation* (Silkheart 1993) ★★★, *Consecration* (Black Saint 1993) ★★★, *Kingdom Come* (Knitting Factory 1994) ★★★, *Unto I Am* (Victo 1995) ★★★, *Testaments* (Knitting Factory 1996) ★★★, *Delivered* (2.13.61 1997) ★★★★, *Solo In Japan* (PSF 1997) ★★★, *Ancient Of Days* (Knitting Factory 1999) ★★★★, *Jazz Solo Piano* (Knitting Factory 2000) ★★, *Precious Soul* (FMP 2001) ★★★, *Shout!* (Clean Feed 2005) ★★★★.

Gayle, Crystal

b. Brenda Gail Webb, 9 January 1951, Paintsville, Kentucky, USA. Gayle was the last of eight children born to Ted and Clara Webb. Her sister, the country singer **Loretta Lynn**, had her own story told in the movie *The Coal Miner's Daughter*. By the time Gayle was born, her father had lung disease, and he died when she was eight. When Gayle was four, the family moved to Wabash, Indiana, where her mother worked in a nursing home. Clara Webb, who was musical, encouraged Gayle to sing at family gatherings and church socials. Unlike Lynn, her influences came from the **Beatles** and **Peter, Paul And Mary**. In the late 60s, after graduation, she signed with her sister's recording label, **Decca Records**. As the label already had **Brenda Lee**, a change of name was needed and, when they drove past a sign for Krystal hamburgers, Lynn said, 'That's your name. Crystals are bright and shiny, like you.' At first, she was managed by Lynn's husband, Mooney, and she was part of her stage show. She established herself with regular appearances on **Jim Ed Brown**'s television show *The Country Place*. Lynn wrote some of her first records ('Sparklin' Look Of Love', 'Mama, It's Different This Time') and therein lay the problem—Crystal Gayle sounded like Loretta Lynn.

Gayle first entered the US country charts in 1970 with the Top 30 hit, 'I've Cried (The Blue Right Out Of My Eyes)', which was followed by 'Everybody Oughta Cry' and 'I Hope You're Havin' Better Luck Than Me'. There was nothing original about the records and Gayle, wanting a say in what she recorded, left the label. She joined **United Artists Records** and was teamed with producer **Allen Reynolds**, who was having success with **Don Williams**. Her first records had the easy-going charm of Williams' records, but her 1974 Top 10 country hit, 'Wrong Road Again', hinted at the dynamics in her voice. Reynolds, who wrote the song, did not have enough time to devote to composing but nurtured several songwriters (including **Richard Leigh** and **Bob McDill**) who supplied Gayle with excellent songs. Gayle also had a Top 30 country hit with 'Beyond You', co-written with her lawyer/manager/husband Vassilios 'Bill' Gatzimos. Gayle returned to the country Top 10 with the title song from *Somebody Loves You*, and followed it with her first number 1 country single, 'I'll Get Over You', written by Leigh. In 1976, Gayle was voted Female Vocalist of the Year by the Academy of Country Music, but Reynolds knew there was a bigger market than merely country fans for her records. He seized the opportunity when Leigh wrote the jazz-tinged ballad 'Don't It Make My Brown Eyes Blue', although United Artists had reservations. 'They thought it was a mistake', said Reynolds. 'It was gimmickless, straight ahead, soulful and classy, but that's all it takes.' The public found 'Don't It Make My Brown Eyes Blue' irresistible and in 1977 it went to number 2 in the US pop charts and reached number 5 in the UK. It also won Grammy awards for the Best Female Country

Vocal Performance and for the Best Country Song. The album on which it appeared, *We Must Believe In Magic*, became the first album by a female country artist to sell over a million copies.

Gayle, who was Female Vocalist of the Year for both the Academy of Country Music and the **Country Music Association**, said, 'There is no rivalry between me and Loretta and if there is, it is on a friendly basis. I know that Loretta voted for me at the CMA awards in Nashville.' In 1979, she became the first US country artist to perform in China. Although petite in stature, her stage act is mesmerizing. She stands with her back to the audience, who watch her luxurious hair sway back and forth. Gayle grows her hair to three inches off the floor: 'If it's on the ground, I find I step on it on stage. When you've hair like this, you cannot plan anything other than washing your hair and doing your concert.' Her fifth album, again produced by Reynolds, *When I Dream*, included the credit, 'Suggestions: Crystal'. It was a lavish production with 50 musicians being credited, including such established Nashville names as **Pig Robbins**, **Lloyd Green**, **Bob Moore** and Kenny Malone. The title track, a torch ballad, brought out the best in Gayle's voice. The British writer **Roger Cook**, who had settled in Nashville, gave her a soulful ballad touching on the paranoia some lovers feel, 'Talking In Your Sleep'. Released as a single, it reached number 11 in the UK and number 18 in the USA, as well topping the US country chart. Another popular single was 'Why Have You Left The One You Left Me For?', which also topped the country charts. In 1979, Gayle released her final album for United Artists, ironically called *We Should Be Together*. It included two more country hits with the ballads 'Your Kisses Will' and 'Your Old Cold Shoulder'. In an impressive chart run, Gayle had enjoyed 6 chart-topping country singles during her time with United Artists, with 'You Never Miss A Real Good Thing (Till He Says Goodbye)' (1976) and 'Ready For The Times To Get Better' (1978) completing the list. She also hosted two prime time television specials, the *Crystal Gayle Special* and *Crystal*.

In 1980, Gayle joined **Columbia Records** and enjoyed a US Top 20 pop hit with 'Half The Way'. Gayle had three country chart-toppers for Columbia, 'It's Like We Never Said Goodbye', 'If You Ever Change Your Mind', and 'Too Many Lovers'. She recorded an excellent version of **Neil Sedaka**'s 'The Other Side Of Me' and surprised many fans by reviving an early country record, **Jimmie Rodgers**' 'Miss The Mississippi And You'. In 1982, she moved to **Elektra Records** and worked on the soundtrack of the Francis Ford Coppola movie, *One From The Heart*, with **Tom Waits**. The same year's duet with **Eddie Rabbitt** ('You And I') topped the country chart and broke into the pop Top 10. Her string of country hits for Elektra/**Warner Brothers Records** included eight chart-topping singles; ''Til I Gain Control Again' (1982), 'Our Love Is On The Faultline', 'Baby, What About You', 'The Sound Of Goodbye' (all 1983), 'Turning Away' (1984), 'Makin' Up For Lost Time (The Dallas Lovers' Song)' (1985), a revival of **Johnnie Ray**'s 'Cry', and 'Straight To The Heart' (both 1986). She also recorded a duet album with **Gary Morris**, which included the theme song from the television soap opera *Another World*, in which Gayle made several guest appearances. Despite joining **Capitol Records** at the turn of the decade, Gayle's commercial profile has declined in recent years. *Ain't Gonna Worry* reunited her with Reynolds, while Buzz Stone produced 1992's *Three Good Reasons*, a heartening return to her country roots. In the latter part of the decade, Gayle recorded two inspirational albums and a collection of **Hoagy Carmichael** songs, and began the new millennium with her first-ever album for children. In 2005 she moved to singing songbook standards.

● ALBUMS: *Crystal Gayle* (United Artists 1975) ★★★, *Somebody Loves You* (United Artists 1975) ★★★, *Crystal* (United Artists 1976) ★★★, *We Must Believe In Magic* (United Artists 1977) ★★★, *When I Dream* (United Artists 1978) ★★★★, *I've Cried The Blue Right Out Of My Eyes* (MCA 1978) ★★★, *We Should Be Together* (United Artists 1979) ★★★, *Miss The Mississippi* (Columbia 1979) ★★★★, *A Woman's Heart* (Columbia 1980) ★★★★, *These Days* (Columbia 1980) ★★★, *Hollywood, Tennessee* (Columbia 1981) ★★★, *True Love* (Elektra 1982) ★★★★, with Tom Waits *One From The Heart* film soundtrack (Columbia 1982) ★★★★, *Cage The Songbird* (Warners 1983) ★★★, *Nobody Wants To Be Alone* (Warners 1985) ★★★, *Straight To The Heart* (Warners 1986) ★★★, *A Crystal Christmas* (Warners 1986) ★★, with Gary Morris *What If We Fall In Love* (Warners 1987) ★★, *I Love Country* (Columbia 1987) ★★, *Nobody's Angel* (Warners 1988) ★★★, *Ain't Gonna Worry* (Capitol 1990) ★★★, *Three Good Reasons* (Liberty 1992) ★★★★, *Someday* (Intersound 1995) ★★★, *Joy And Inspiration* aka *He Is Beautiful!* (Intersound 1997) ★★★, *Crystal Gayle Sings The Heart & Soul Of Hoagy Carmichael* (Intersound 1999) ★★★, *In My Arms* (Madacy 2000) ★★, *All My Tomorrows* (Southpaw 2005) ★★★.

● COMPILATIONS: *Classic Crystal* (United Artists 1979) ★★★, *Favorites* (United Artists 1980) ★★★, *Crystal Gayle's Greatest Hits* (Columbia 1983) ★★★★, *The Best Of Crystal Gayle* (Warners 1987) ★★★, *All-Time Greatest Hits* (Curb 1990) ★★★, *Best Always* (Branson 1993) ★★★, *Super Hits* (Sony 1998) ★★★.

Gayle, Michelle

b. 2 February 1971, London, England. Immediately recognizable to fans of pop culture through her role as Hattie Tavernier in BBC Television soap opera *EastEnders* (1990–1993), Gayle's crossover to the music charts in the mid-90s was one of the most viable amid a slew of sorry cash-ins: 'I wasn't even going to do *EastEnders*. I was going to turn it down because I just wanted to focus on music. I was in a band, Amorphous, at the time and basically agreed to play Hattie to help make some money to pay for demos and equipment for the group.' She had started writing songs at the age of 13, following advice from her music teacher, by which time she had already appeared in another BBC Television programme, *Grange Hill*. Certainly, her attempts to convince the press that her real calling had always been music were backed up by a voice with impressive range and control, best demonstrated on the UK hit singles 'Looking Up' (number 11) and 'Sweetness' (number 4). She was taken under the wing of Dennis Ingoldsby, who helped to procure a series of suitable musical compositions for her chart forays, over which Gayle would customize lyrics. Although the selection of material on her debut was certainly limited, the best of it was undoubtedly first-class pop soul. Its reward was gold status in the UK charts, as Gayle became a major star via widespread UK touring in support of **Eternal**. She enjoyed further UK hit singles in 1995 with 'Freedom' (number 16), 'Happy Just To Be With You' (number 11). Her second album was premiered by the excellent 'Do You Know', which reached UK number 6 in February 1997. The title track was also a Top 20 hit.

Gayle recorded a third album for **EMI Records** but record company politics meant it was never released. She then appeared on stage in London's West End in *Beauty And The Beast* (as Belle) before taking a career break to raise her son with soccer player Mark Bright. She returned to the nation's television screens in 2003 in the reality television series *Reborn In The USA* (finishing as runner-up to Tony Hadley). She also acted in the UK television dramas *Doctors*, *Holby City* and *Family Affairs*.

● ALBUMS: *Michelle Gayle* (RCA 1994) ★★★, *Sensational* (RCA 1997) ★★★.

Gayle, Otis

b. Kingston, Jamaica, West Indies. Gayle began his musical career as a vocalist with **Byron Lee And The Dragonaires**. The singer performed with the group on the international circuit and in 1967 settled in Canada. While he continued to perform as part of the Dragonaires, Gayle also recorded a series of solo hits, notably a cover version of the **Detroit Spinners'** 'I'll Be Around' for **Coxsone Dodd** at Studio One in Jamaica. As a soloist Gayle released a series of local hits and in 1983 he was awarded a Juno. The award has since been acknowledged as a particularly notable achievement, as Gayle was one of the first black artists to be recognized by the prestigious panel of adjudicators. His hit, 'Heaven Must Have Sent You', was accredited as the Best Reggae Song at the awards, which resulted in the singer maintaining a high profile on the Canadian reggae circuit. In spite of his successful solo career Gayle continued to tour with the Dragonaires, where he performed a unique blend of soca and reggae primarily in North America. The singer has also supported artists such as **Barry White**, **Joe Tex** and **Jackie Mittoo**. By the start of the millennium Gayle had built a solid reputation as a 'big people's singer' with favoured tracks such as, 'Follow Your Dreams', 'Give A Little More Love' and 'He Is My Friend'. His legendary status as one of the music's pioneers was finally acknowledged when in 2001 the revival label Soul Jazz released *Studio One Soul*, featuring Gayle's interpretation of 'I'll Be Around'.

Gaynair, Bogey

b. Wilton Gaynair, 11 January 1927, Kingston, Jamaica, West Indies, d. 13 February 1995, Germany. Early in his career Gaynair played tenor saxophone in bands in his homeland. In the mid-50s he moved to Europe and into jazz. He played with **Dizzy Reece** in London, then became resident in Germany, where he extended his musical understanding through the study of composition and arranging, and also played with many important German musicians as well as visiting jazz stars from the USA and UK. With **Ellsworth 'Shake' Keane** he was a member of **Kurt Edelhagen**'s orchestra, and he was co-founder of Third Eye, which included **Kenny Wheeler** and **Alan Skidmore**.

A fluent improviser in the hard-bop mould, Gaynair continued to perform into the early 80s, but in 1983, while playing with **Peter Herbolzheimer**, he suffered a stroke. Although much of his career was spent outside the international spotlight, Gaynair built a small but dedicated body of critical approval, including several long-time advocates such as jazz writer Val Wilmer. Gaynair played with a full-throated sound yet retained a melodic approach to his interpretations. If there were sometimes hints of **John Coltrane** in his playing, these were comfortably subordinated to his personal conceptions of his music.

● ALBUMS: *Blue Bogey* (Tempo/Jasmine 1959) ★★★, with Horace Parlan *One For Wilton* (Ego 1980) ★★★★, *Third Eye Live!* (View 1982) ★★★, *Alpharian* 1982 recording (Konnex 1991) ★★★.

Gaynor, Gloria

b. Gloria Fowles, 7 September 1949, Newark, New Jersey, USA. The 'Queen Of The Discotheques' spent several years struggling on the east coast circuit prior to finding success. A 1965 single, produced by **Johnny Nash**, preceded her spell as a member of the Soul Satisfiers. Gaynor was discovered singing in a Manhattan nightclub by her future manager, Jay Ellis. He teamed with producers Tony Bongiovia and Meco Monardo to create an unswerving disco backbeat that propelled such exemplary Gaynor performances as 1974's 'Never Can Say Goodbye' (US number 9/UK number 2) and 'Reach Out, I'll Be There' (1975). Her crowning achievement followed in 1979 when 'I Will Survive' topped both the UK and US charts. This emotional, almost defiant performance, later adapted as a gay movement anthem, rose above the increasingly mechanical settings her producers were fashioning for the disco market. 'I Am What I Am', another song with militant implications, was a UK Top 20 hit in 1983, but the singer was too closely tied to a now dying form, and her later career suffered as a result. She bounced back in the new millennium with the club favourites 'Last Night' and 'Just Keep Thinkin' About You', and a brand new studio album. 'I Will Survive' has been re-released successfully several times, and Gaynor continues to perform her old disco classics alongside gospel material to fans around the world.

● ALBUMS: *Never Can Say Goodbye* (MGM 1975) ★★★★, *Experience Gloria Gaynor* (MGM 1975) ★★★, *I've Got You* (Polydor 1976) ★★, *Glorious* (Polydor 1977) ★★, *Park Avenue Sound* (Polydor 1978) ★★★, *I Have A Right* (Polydor 1979) ★★★, *Love Tracks* (Polydor 1979) ★★★, *Stories* (Polydor 1980) ★★, *I Kinda Like Me* (Polydor 1981) ★★, *Gloria Gaynor* (Polydor 1983) ★★★, *I Am Gloria Gaynor* (Chrysalis 1984) ★★, *The Power Of Gloria Gaynor* (Stylus 1986) ★★, *I Will Survive* (PolyGram 1990) ★★, *Just Keep Thinking About You* (Logic 2001) ★★★, *I Wish You Love* (Logic 2002) ★★★.

● COMPILATIONS: *Greatest Hits* (Polydor 1982) ★★★★, *The Collection* (Castle 1992) ★★★, *I Will Survive: The Anthology* (Polydor 1998) ★★★, *The Best Of Gloria Gaynor* (Pegasus 1999) ★★★, *The Best Of Gloria Gaynor: The Millennium Collection* (Polydor 2000) ★★★★.

● FURTHER READING: *I Will Survive*, Gloria Gaynor.

Gaynor, Janet

b. Laura Gainor, 6 October 1906, Philadelphia, Pennsylvania, USA, d. 14 September 1984, Palm Springs, California, USA. Determined on a career in films, Gaynor found work as an extra in Hollywood, played in some Hal Roach comedies, and in 1926 was signed by Fox. A WAMPAS Baby Star of 1926 (selected by the Western Association of Motion Picture Advertisers), she made several films from 1926–29, notably *Seventh Heaven* and *Sunrise* (both 1927 and both silent) and *Street Angel* (1928, part-talkie). For these films collectively she was awarded the first Academy Award as Best Actress.

Gaynor quickly gained in popularity, becoming Hollywood's leading box-office favourite. Leaving Fox, she continued to be successful, making for David O. Selznick *A Star Is Born* (1937), the least flamboyant if non-musical version of this tale, for which she was nominated for an Academy Award. Also for Selznick, she made *The Young In Heart* (1938), another all-round success. In 1939 she married for the second time and retired from films. In the late 50s she was occasionally on radio and television and appeared in one film, *Bernadine* (1957), which starred **Pat Boone**. Some of Gaynor's time was spent painting and in 1976 an exhibition of her work was given in New York. In the early 50s and again in the 70s she presented Academy Awards and in 1978 was herself recipient of a special award. On Broadway in 1980 she and Keith McDermott played the co-leads in the play *Harold And Maude*. After 21 previews in January and early February, the play opened on 7 February, only to close two days and four performances later. In 1981 she took a role in an episode of television's *The Love Boat* but otherwise lived in retirement. Her death was attributed to severe injuries sustained in a road accident two years earlier.

● FURTHER READING: *Janet Gaynor: A Bio-Bibliography*, Connie Billips.

Gaynor, Mitzi

b. Francesca Mitzi Gerber, 4 September 1930, Chicago, Illinois. USA. This vivacious and extremely talented actress, singer and dancer, reputedly of Hungarian descent, graced several good movie musicals in the 50s, and is probably best remembered as the girl who tried to 'wash that man (Rossano Brazzi) right out of her hair' in **South Pacific** (1958). After taking ballet lessons from an early age, Gaynor danced with the Los Angeles Civic Light Opera while in her early teens, and made a strong impression with **Betty Grable** and **Dan Dailey** in her first movie, *My Blue Heaven* (1950). This was followed by one or two straight parts, and a few musicals such as *Golden Girl*, *Bloodhounds Of Broadway*, *Down Among The Sheltering Palms* and *The 'I Don't Care' Girl* (1953), which were not as satisfying. The situation improved as the 50s progressed and she had excellent roles in **There's No Business Like Show Business**, **Anything Goes**, *The Birds And The Bees*, **The Joker Is Wild** and *Les Girls* (1957). She was good, too, in *South Pacific*, but although it remains, to date, the fourth highest-grossing screen musical of the period in the USA, she was reportedly personally disaffected with the experience. Her particular genre of film musicals was becoming extinct, and, like so many others, she worked more often in television and had her own top-rated specials during the 60s. She also toured in stage musical revivals, and, as an accomplished actress, continued to play the occasional comic or dramatic movie role.

Gaynor also built up a polished and highly regarded concert and cabaret act. As recently as 1987 she was acclaimed for her nightclub performances, which included a section devoted to **Irving Berlin** and **Fred Astaire**, a satirical version of **Harry Von Tilzer** and Arthur Lamb's nineteenth century song 'A Bird In A Gilded Cage', and a rousing singalong 'God Bless America' finale. Two years later she embarked on an 11-month, 36-city tour of the USA in a revival of **Cole Porter**'s 1934 show *Anything Goes*, the first time in her long career that she had been on the road in a book musical. The *Daily News*, commenting on a New York performance of hers in the late 90s, wrote: 'She is what showbusiness is all about.'

● ALBUMS: *Mitzi* (Verve 1959) ★★★, *Sings The Lyrics Of Ira Gershwin* (Verve 1959) ★★★, and soundtrack recordings.
● FILMS: *My Blue Heaven* (1950), *Take Care Of My Little Girl* (1951), *Golden Girl* (1951), *Bloodhounds Of Broadway* (1952), *We're Not Married!* (1952), *The 'I Don't Care' Girl* (1953), *Down Among The Sheltering Palms* (1953), *Three Young Texans* (1954), *There's No Business Like Show Business* (1954), *Birds And The Bees* (1956), *Anything Goes* (1956), *The Joker Is Wild* (1957), *Les Girls* (1957), *South Pacific* (1958), *Happy Anniversary* (1959), *Surprise Package* (1960), *For Love Or Money* (1963).

Gay's The Word

A light musical comedy that turned out to be the last production involving **Ivor Novello**, one of the London musical theatre's favourite sons; he died less than a month after *Gay's The Word* opened at the Saville Theatre on 16 February 1951. Novello provided the music and libretto, and Alan Melville wrote the sharp, witty lyrics for a show that, in some ways lampooned the composer's previous extravagantly staged operetta-style shows. This was particularly evident in 'Ruritania', the opening number for the chorus, with lines such as 'Since Oklahoma!/We've been in a coma'. **Jack Hulbert** directed the piece, and his wife, **Cicely Courtneidge** took the lead as Gay Daventry, a 'star actress in charge of a drama school'. Her young pupils included the lovely Linda (Lizbeth Webb) with her boyfriend, Peter Lynton (Thorley Walters). The school was located in an English seaside town with lots of sea and sand, plus plenty of rocky cliffs, which gave Courtneidge a chance to be 'bossy', and the author an ideal excuse for a sub-plot involving smugglers and their midnight shenanigans. Courtneidge was her usually ebullient self. Even at the age of 57 she had lost none of the energy and enthusiasm for which she was renowned. Novello and Melville summed it up perfectly in 'Vitality', which she delivered with such style, along with another song that, being a seasoned trouper, could well have been her life-long creed, 'It's Bound To Be Right On The Night' ('Over cold pork, pink blancmange and unripe Stilton/You've rather a nasty supper with Jack Hylton'). The rest of the score included the songs 'Gaiety Glad', 'Bees Are Buzzin'', 'Finder, Please Return', 'On Such A Night As This', 'A Matter Of Minutes', and 'Guards Are On Parade'.

It was fitting, considering Novello's previous contributions to the London theatre, that he should go out with a big hit; *Gay's The Word* ran for 504 performances. It proved to be Cicely Courtneidge's last musical comedy in the West End (she still continued to appear in other kinds of productions) until 1964 and her appearance as Mme. Arcati in **High Spirits**, a musical adaptation of **Noël Coward**'s *Blithe Spirit*.

Gayten, Paul

b. 29 January 1920, New Orleans, Louisiana, USA, d. 29 March 1991. This R&B band leader and producer began his professional career when he formed a combo in the late 30s. Gayten made his first sides for the New Jersey–based Deluxe label in 1947 and immediately had a US R&B hit with '(You Don't Love Me) True' (number 5). The follow-up, 'Since I Fell For You' (number 3, 1947), featured vocalist Annie Laurie, who would lead on many other Gayten hits, including 'Cuttin' Out' (number 6, 1949) and 'I'll Never Be Free'

(number 4, 1950). Another chart record, 'Goodnight Irene' (number 6, 1950), featured the Coleman Brothers ensemble on vocals. By 1949 Gayten had expanded his combo into a nine-piece orchestra and switched to the Regal label. Besides his own hits on the label, he backed and produced Larry Darnell on a spate of hits. He moved to **OKeh Records** in 1951. In 1954 Gayten moved to **Chess Records**, and began production and A&R work in New Orleans for the company, producing records on various New Orleans artists, namely **Clarence 'Frogman' Henry**, **Sugar Boy Crawford**, **TV Slim** and **Bobby Charles**, as well as for himself. His most successful records were a revival of 'The Music Goes Round And Round' (1956) and the instrumental 'Nervous Boogie' (1957). In 1960 he moved to Los Angeles to open a Chess office there. Gayten left Chess in 1968 and retired from the music business in 1978. *Creole Gal* is a retrospective of Gayten's late 40s and early 50s material and the 1989 album is a retrospective of his Chess years.
● COMPILATIONS: *Creole Gal* (Route 66 1978) ★★★, *Chess King Of New Orleans* (Chess 1989) ★★★, with Annie Laurie *Regal Records In New Orleans* (Ace 1992) ★★★.

Gear, Luella

b. 5 September 1897, New York City, USA, d. 3 April 1980, New York City, USA. Among Gear's earliest Broadway appearances was the musical *Love O' Mike* (1917), book by Thomas Sydney, music by **Jerome Kern**, lyrics by **Harry B. Smith**. She was in a comedy, *The Gold Diggers* (1919), and a farce, *A Bachelor Night* (1921), before appearing in *Elsie* at the Vanderbilt Theatre (1923). Although this show closed after only 40 performances it had interesting credits: book by Charles W. Bell, music and lyrics by **Noble Sissle**, **Eubie Blake**, Monte Carlo and Alma M. Sanders. Gear then went into **Poppy**, starring **W.C. Fields**, book and lyrics by Dorothy Donnelly, music by Stephen Jones and Arthur Samuels. Next came *Queen High* (1926), book by Laurence Schwab and **Buddy De Sylva**, music by Lewis E. Gensler with lyrics by De Sylva, plus additional songs by **James Hanley**. Gear followed this with a flop musical, *The Optimists* (1928) and barely any more successful was *Ups-A Daisy* (1928), with book and lyrics by **Clifford Grey** and Robert A. Simon, music by Gensler. A hit followed for Gear when she appeared in **Gay Divorce** (1932), starring **Fred Astaire** and **Claire Luce** and which ran for 248 performances.

In the mid-30s Gear was in the revue **Life Begins At 8:40** (1934), **On Your Toes** (1936), and *Love In My Fashion* (1937). In 1939 she was in *Streets Of Paris*, which had a 274-performance run at the Broadhurst Theatre. With music by **Jimmy McHugh**, lyrics by **Al Dubin** with **Harold Rome**, and vocal arrangements by **Hugh Martin**, the show featured **Abbott And Costello**, Bobby Clark, **Carmen Miranda** and **Gower Champion**. In the 40s Gear was in the troubled musical *Crazy With The Heat* (1941), which opened and closed in four days, then reopened two weeks later with a different producer, **Ed Sullivan**, only to close again after a total of 92 performances. Then came a play, *Pie In The Sky* (1942), and the musicals *Count Me In* (1942) and *My Romance* (1948). The latter had music by **Sigmund Romberg**, book and lyrics by Rowland Leigh, with Gear singing 'Little Emmaline'. The following decade found Gear mostly in non-musical productions, including *To Be Continued* (1952), *Sabrina Fair* (1953) and *Four Winds* (1957).

● FILMS: *Adam And Eva* (1923), *The Poor Fish* (1933), *Carefree* (1938), *The Perfect Marriage* (1947), *Jigsaw* aka *Gun Moll* (1949), *Phffft!* (1954).

Gebers, Jost
(see **Free Music Production**)

Gebert, Bobby
b. John Robert Gebert, 1 April 1944, Adelaide, Australia. Gebert was classically trained on piano and studied at the London College of Music before returning to Australia. In his teens he led jazz groups in Melbourne, Adelaide and also at the El Rocco Jazz Club, Sydney. He played with the best jazz musicians and forged a reputation as a progressive pianist and composer. In April 1961 Gebert made his recording debut with his trio, recording three originals. He also became a popular accompanist working with local musicians and many international visitors. He broadened his versatility by working in television, film and in the theatre and became musical director for *Hair* and assistant director for *Jesus Christ Superstar*. Possessing endless musical curiosity, Gebert continued his education in America, studying with Walter Davis Jnr. and working with eminent jazz musicians, **Art Pepper**, **Freddie Hubbard** and **Milt Jackson**.
In the 90s Gebert occasionally led a successful trio and was involved in jazz education. The pop singer Delilah employed Gebert as her musical director, as did **Renée Geyer** and her Australian tour band. He also played piano in the **Dale Barlow** Quartet. Although Gebert recorded with other artists including **Bernie McGann** (*Kindred Spirits*) and Andrew Speight (*Now's The Time*) it was not until 1994, at the age of 50, that Gebert recorded his first album under his own name. *The Sculptor* was highly regarded and comprised originals and standards. The cohesiveness of the trio with Jonathon Zwartz (bass), Andrew Dickeson (drums), and the leader's, deft, delicate and imaginative piano playing, resulted in the album winning an ARIA award in 1995. Gebert has taken no short cuts in reaching his stature as one of the leading jazz musicians in Australia, equally gifted with talent and integrity.
● ALBUMS: *The Sculptor* (ABC Music 1994) ★★★★.

Geddes Axe
Far from having anything to do with a tribute to **Rush**'s bass player, UK rock band Martin Wilson and Andrew Barrot took their name from a school book titled *Geddex Axe 1921–1922*. Coming together in 1980 with Andy Millard (vocals), Dave Clayton (drums) and Mick Peace (bass), the band decided to follow in the footsteps of fellow Sheffield citizens **Def Leppard** and record a self-financed EP. Entitled *Return Of The Gods*, it failed to generate the public interest that Def Leppard had aroused. After one further single, 'Sharpen Your Wits', the band underwent a major personnel change, with Barrot joining **Baby Tuckoo** (and later **Chrome Molly**), and Millard and Clayton quitting, being replaced with Nick Brown, Tony Rose and John Burke, respectively. A revamped live set included the progressive 'Valley Of The Kings' (sadly unrecorded) and cover versions of **Kiss** songs. The Bullet label picked up the band and released an improved 12-inch single, 'Escape From New York', but it failed to gain any ground for them, and by 1983 they had again broken up.

Geddins, Bob
b. 1913, Marlin, Texas, USA, d. 16 February 1991, Oakland, California, USA. A black entrepreneur, Geddins operated a series of labels from the late 40s, recording blues and gospel in the Bay Area. Lacking capital and distribution, he had to lease his recordings to larger labels; if a hit resulted, the artists were lured away. In this way, Geddins lost **Lowell Fulson**, **Jimmy McCracklin**, **Roy Hawkins**, **Ray Agee** and **Koko Taylor**. Among other hits, Geddins composed **Johnny Ace**'s 'Last Letter' and 'Haunted House' for **Johnny Fuller** (the latter was also a hit for **Gene Simmons** and the **Compton Brothers**). Geddins also wrote the classic 'My Time After Awhile', and reworked a pre-war **Curtis Jones** song into 'Tin Pan Alley'. Geddins was a prime mover behind the Oakland blues scene of the 40s and 50s, but his business abilities were not the equal of his composing and producing talents.

Gee Street Records
Established at the end of 1987 by managing director Jon Baker, who had lived in New York in the early 80s, gaining his roots in black music, hip-hop and **electro**. He returned to London but tired quickly of music industry machinations within the majors and elected to set up a separate entity. He enrolled his co-conspirator DJ Richie Rich as his partner and Gee Street was born. The label began with the 'Scam 1 & 2' record, but soon built up an eclectic dance/rap roster, gaining a distribution deal through **Rough Trade**. They immediately set up a sister office in New York to allow them to gauge and exploit both markets, their first US signing being the **Jungle Brothers**. The label also licensed material from US labels like Warlock and Idlers. However, the most succesful act would prove to be the **Stereo MC's** and their Ultimatum remix arm (Birch and 'The Head' having played a prominent role in establishing Gee Street studio). Other early acts included **Outlaw Posse** and Boonsquawk. Rich, who also recorded for the label, went on to found Happy Family Records in 1992 and become a video jockey for MTV. He split with Baker when **Island Records** bought out Gee Street, but agreed to offer their artists his remix skills. Simon Quance took over as label manager, while the label also grew an extra tentacle with the Gee-Zone subsidiary.

Gee, George
b. 31 March 1960, New York City, USA. Of Chinese and American parentage, Gee took an early interest in music and although he liked R&B and rock 'n' roll, he found a special affinity with big band music of the 30s and 40s. While still attending high school, Gee played bass in the school's jazz band. In his first year at Carnegie Mellon University in Pittsburgh, Pennsylvania, he began broadcasting as a disc jockey on the college radio station, basing and naming his show after Martin Block's 30s *Make-Believe Ballroom* radio programme. An opportunity to interview **Count Basie** and to hear the band live led to his decision to form a big band, which he named the Make-Believe Ballroom Orchestra. Playing mostly college and society dance dates, the band was popular in and around Pittsburgh, and on graduating and his return to New York City in 1989 Gee formed a similar band but instead of fellow college students he now hired experienced New York jazz and session musicians. This new version of the Make-Believe Ballroom Orchestra attracted attention and dates.

In 1998, Gee formed another band, a 10-piece group, the Jump, Jive And Wailers, that benefited from the current interest in **New Swing**. The two bands continued to thrive in the early 00s, and among engagements the big band has played are the annual New York Swing Dance Society (1987–2002), American Swing Dance Championships, NYC (1994–1997), the Boston Swing Dance Network (1994–2001), and the American Lindyhop Championships (1995, 1998–9). Gee has also appeared at the Mellon Jazz Festival, Pittsburgh (1985–1989), the 1995 JVC Jazz Festival in New York, and in 2001 at the Zurich Arts Festival and the Greater Connecticut Jazz Festival. The band has also played in Tokyo. Among musicians who have played in Gee's bands are trombonist **Eddie Bert**, guitarist Joe Cohn, saxophonist **Michael Hashim** and trumpeter Walt Szymanski. In addition to performing, Gee has lectured at the New School University, and conducts clinics and master classes.

● ALBUMS: with the Make-Believe Ballroom Orchestra *Swingin' Away* (Zort Music 1999) ★★★, with the Make-Believe Ballroom Orchestra *Swingin' Live!* (Swing 46) ★★★, with the Jump, Jive And Wailers *Buddha Boogie* (Swing 46 1999) ★★★, *Swingin' At Swing City Zurich* (Zort Music 2001) ★★★, *Settin' The Pace: The Music Of Frank Foster* (GJazz 2004) ★★★.

Gee, Jonathan

b. London, England. After an early classical training between the ages of five and nine, Gee lost interest in the piano during his teens. But it was during his time at Sheffield University that he developed his love of modern jazz, and began to practise the piano again. On his return to London he attended the jazz course at the Guildhall School of Music for a short time, but soon left, disenchanted with the system of jazz education. Since then Gee has quickly earned himself a reputation on the British jazz scene. Leading a trio with **Wayne Batchelor** and Winston Clifford, he won the 1991 *Wire* Best Newcomer Award. During the rest of the decade he played regularly with saxophonist Ed Jones, and toured the world with his trio, featuring Steve Rose (bass) and Winston Clifford (drums).

● ALBUMS: *Blah, Blah, Blah, Etc., Etc.* cassette (Own Label 1988) ★★★, *Closer To* (ASC 1997) ★★★★, *Your Shining Heart* (ASC 1998) ★★★★, with Damon Brown *Good Cop Bad Cop* (33 2001) ★★★, *Chez Auguste* (Jazz House 2001) ★★★, *Wishbone* (33 2003) ★★★, with Danilo Gallo, Alessandro Minetto *Cream Of Mandarins* (Artesuono 2004) ★★★.

Geesin, Ron

b. Ayrshire, Scotland. One of Britain's leading *avant garde* composers and performers, Geesin began his recording career in 1962 as a member of a jazz band, the Original Downtown Syncopators. Having released a self-titled solo EP of piano rolls, he left the group in 1965, initially to record soundtracks for television commercials. With the ensuing revenue Geesin built a studio in his flat and took a one-man show around the emergent 'underground' clubs. His radical first album, *A Raise Of Eyebrows*, was an experimental sound collage, blending unusual vocal and instrumental effects with synthesiser and banjo. It proved highly influential on Britain's progressive rock scene. **Pink Floyd** adapted several of his ideas for the studio segments of 1969's *Ummagumma* and Geesin collaborated with the band on the following

year's **Atom Heart Mother**. His spell within their circle was more fully realized on the film soundtrack *Music From The Body*, on which he collaborated with bass player **Roger Waters**. In 1971, he arranged and produced *Song For The Gentle Man* for **Bridget St. John**, and shortly afterwards supported **Genesis**. Such work introduced Geesin to a much wider audience, but his own releases (on his Ron Geesin label) proved too uncompromising for the public at large. He pursues a parallel career, composing music for corporate training films, as well as radio and television productions. A skilled studio technician, Geesin has also been involved in the remastering of blues recordings for the specialist Flyright label.

● ALBUMS: *A Raise Of Eyebrows* (Transatlantic 1967) ★★★★, with Roger Waters *Music From The Body* film soundtrack (Harvest 1970) ★★★, *Electrosound* (KPM 1972) ★★, *As He Stands* (Ron Geesin 1973) ★★★, *Electrosound Vol. 2* (KPM 1975) ★★, *Patruns* (Ron Geesin 1975) ★★★, *Right Through* (Ron Geesin 1978) ★★★, *Atmospheres* (KPM 1979) ★★★, *Magnificent Machines* (Themes International 1988) ★★★, *Funny Frown* (Headscope 1981) ★★★, *BlueFuse* (Headscope 1993) ★★★.

● COMPILATIONS: *Hystery* (Cherry Red 1994) ★★★★, *Land Of Mist* (Cleopatra 1995) ★★★★, *Right Through And Beyond* (Headscope 2003) ★★★★.

Geezinslaw Brothers

Based in Austin, Texas, USA, this novelty country music duo comprises Sam Aldred (b. 5 May 1934) and DeWayne 'Son' Smith. Very much in the vein of **Homer And Jethro**, they recorded 'Chubby (Please Take Your Love To Town)' and the alternative 'Ruby, Don't Take Your Love To Town'. They recorded some duets with **Willie Nelson**. In the 90s and working as just the Geezinslaws, they had moderate success with 'Help, I'm White And I Can't Get Down', which was co-written with fiddle player Clinton Gregory.

● ALBUMS: *The Kooky World Of The Geezinslaw Brothers* (Columbia 1963) ★★★, *Can You Believe* (Capitol 1966) ★★★, *My Dirty, Lowdown, Rotten, Cotton-Pickin' Little Darlin'* (Capitol 1967) ★★★, *Chubby (Please Take Your Love To Town)* (Capitol 1968) ★★★, *The Geezinslaws Are Alive And Well* (Capitol 1969) ★★★, *If You Think I'm Crazy* (Lone Star 1979) ★★, *The Geezinslaws* (Step One 1989) ★★★, *World Tour* (Step One 1990) ★★★, *Feelin' Good, Gittin' Up, Gittin' Down* (Step One 1992) ★★, *I Wish I Had A Job To Shove* (Step One 1994) ★★★.

Geffen Records

Founded in 1980 by **David Geffen** (b. David Lawrence Geffen, 21 February 1943, Brooklyn, New York, USA) with financial backing from **WEA Records**, Geffen became a major player in the rock and heavy metal area before being sold to MCA in 1990. To start with, Geffen relied on established artists such as **Elton John** and **Donna Summer**, but the first mega-hit was *Double Fantasy*, the last album recorded by **John Lennon** with **Yoko Ono**. Seeming to specialize in revitalizing the careers of veteran performers, the Geffen label produced hits for **Cher**, **Aerosmith** and **Whitesnake** from the mid-80s. The company also added **Don Henley**, **Jimmy Page**, **Joni Mitchell**, and **Peter Gabriel** to its roster. The most important of the younger generation of rock artists signed by Geffen was **Guns N'Roses**, whose **Appetite For Destruction** sold over 16 million albums worldwide. Other new artists included **Nelson** and **Edie**

Brickell And The New Bohemians. By 1990, Geffen was the third largest pop label in the US market and MCA (later Universal Music Group) paid $540,000,000 to acquire it. David Geffen remained chairperson, with Ed Rosenblatt president of both Geffen and DGC, a label devoted to new artists. In 1994, David Geffen founded the multi-media company Dream-Works with Steven Spielberg and Jeffrey Katzenberg, and left Geffen the following year. In 1998 the label was merged into Interscope Records, while DGC ceased operations. After a number of years Jordan Schur was appointed as president of Geffen Records in October 1999 with a mission to once again make their roster of artists as important as it was when the company was formed. In 2003, MCA and DreamWorks were absorbed into the flourishing Geffen imprint.

● FURTHER READING: *David Geffen: A Biography Of New Hollywood*, Tom King.

Geffen, David

b. David Lawrence Geffen, 21 February 1943, Brooklyn, New York City, USA. Geffen became one of the richest individuals in rock through his activities as manager, label owner and film producer. After failing to complete his studies at the University Of Texas, Geffen got his start in showbusiness in 1963 with a job at CBS Television in Los Angeles, before moving to the mailroom of the William Morris Agency. In 1968, after establishing himself as one of the company leading agents, he become the manager of **Laura Nyro**, helping her sign to **Columbia Records** after he had befriended **Clive Davis**. Next Geffen formed a company with Elliott Roberts, to manage **Crosby, Stills And Nash**, **Joni Mitchell** (her song 'Free Man In Paris' was about Geffen), **Jackson Browne**, **Linda Ronstadt** and others. In 1970, he founded his first label, **Asylum Records**, signing Mitchell and the **Eagles**. Two years later it was sold to **WEA Records** for $7,000,000 although Geffen stayed on as chairperson. During this time he had a lengthy relationship with **Cher**, at one stage they were close to being married. He was promoted to chief of Elektra/Asylum in 1973, signing **Bob Dylan** for a brief stay at the label. He became vice-chairman of Warner Brothers Pictures two years later, but was fired by chairman Ted Ashley a year later.

Cancer of the bladder forced Geffen to leave the music business for several years but he returned in 1980 with another new label, **Geffen Records**, whose initial roster included **John Lennon** and **Elton John**. The following year he also started Geffen Films, with distribution by Warner Brothers. Among his movies productions were *Risky Business* and **Little Shop Of Horrors** while on Broadway he backed *Cats* and *Dreamgirls*. In 1986, Geffen Records enjoyed huge international success with **Peter Gabriel**'s *So*, and signed **Guns N'Roses** and **Nirvana**. In 1990, Geffen sold his label to MCA for $540 million in stock and when MCA itself was bought by Japanese company Matsushita he made over $700 million. At MCA, he remained chairman of Geffen Records and introduced a new label, DGC. In 1994, he founded the multi-media company DreamWorks with Steven Spielberg and Jeffrey Katzenberg. Geffen has been shown to be a ruthless businessman, sometime forsaking friendships over business. Much of this is revealed in Tom King's compelling biography. What is not in dispute is that he is probably the most successful person the music business has ever known, both commercially, and certainly financially.

● FURTHER READING: *The Hit Men*, Frederic Dannen. *The Operator: David Geffen Builds, Buys, And Sells The New Hollywood*, Tom King.

Geggy Tah

American duo Geggy Tah comprised Greg Kurstin and Tommy Jordan, who in the late 80s were in a band called Cocu. Later the duo scored several 'docu-poems' for the film director David Lynch, examples of which won both first and second place at the Houston International Film Festival. Luka Bop Records (headed by **David Byrne**) signed them after three hours of unmarked music arrived in their offices. As Byrne said: 'They sound like nothing I've ever heard before.' Their debut contained fourteen tracks, ranging in tone from flippancy to earnest songwriting craft. Using samples and unusual instrumentation, it was recorded at Jordan's own studio in Pomona, California, USA. Instruments such as steel drums, bass, piano, harmonica, melodica, trumpets, 'bottles, bags and throats' were all employed to produce hypnotic structures such as 'Last Word (The One For Her)' and a tribute, conducted with the aid of yodelling, to the group's home town—'L.A. Lujah'. Jordan's sister, Amy, provided additional vocals on the haunting 'The Ghost O P. Sluff'.

● ALBUMS: *Grand Opening* (Luka Bop/Warners 1994) ★★★, *Sacred Cow: Tornados And Terriers* (Luka Bop 1996) ★★★.

Geils, J., Band

Formed in Boston, Massachusetts, USA in 1969, the group—J. Geils (b. Jerome Geils, 20 February, 1946, New York City, USA; guitar), **Peter Wolf** (b. 7 March 1947, New York City, USA; vocals), Magic Dick (b. Richard Salwitz, 13 May 1945, New London, Connecticut, USA; harmonica), Seth Justman (b. 27 January 1951, Washington, DC, USA; keyboards), Danny Klein (b. 13 May 1946, New York City, USA; bass) and Stephan Jo Bladd (b. 31 July 1942, Boston, Massachusetts; drums)—was originally known as the J. Geils Blues Band. Their first two albums established a tough, raw R&B that encouraged comparisons with **Butterfield Blues Band**. Versions of songs by **Albert Collins**, **Otis Rush** and **John Lee Hooker** showed an undoubted flair, and with Wolf as an extrovert frontman, they quickly became a popular live attraction. 1973's *Bloodshot*, a gold US album, introduced the band to a wider audience, but at the same time suggested a tardiness, which marred subsequent releases. The major exception was 1977's *Monkey Island* where Wolf, Geils and Magic Dick reclaimed the fire and excitement enlivening those first two albums.

The band moved from **Atlantic Records** to **EMI Records** at the end of the 70s and secured a massive international hit in 1982 with the leering 'Centrefold'. Now divorced from its blues roots, the J. Geils Band was unsure of its direction, a factor emphasized in 1984 when Wolf departed for a solo career, midway through a recording session. The group completed a final album, *You're Gettin' Even, While I'm Gettin' Old*, without him. Geils and Magic Dick reunited during the early 90s to form the blues outfit, Bluestime. In 2004, Geils recorded with guitarist **Duke Robillard**.

● ALBUMS: *J. Geils Band* (Atlantic 1971) ★★★, *The Morning After* (Atlantic 1971) ★★★, *Live—Full House* (Atlantic 1972) ★★★, *Bloodshot* (Atlantic 1973) ★★★, *Ladies Invited* (Atlantic 1973) ★★★, *Nightmares . . . And*

Other Tales From The Vinyl Jungle (Atlantic 1974) ★★, *Hotline* (Atlantic 1975) ★★, *Live—Blow Your Face Out* (Atlantic 1976) ★★★, *Monkey Island* (Atlantic 1977) ★★★, *Sanctuary* (Atlantic 1978) ★★★, *Love Stinks* (EMI 1980) ★★★, *Freeze Frame* (EMI 1981) ★★★, *Showtime!* (EMI 1982) ★★★, *You're Gettin' Even, While I'm Gettin' Old* (EMI 1984) ★★, with Duke Robillard, Gerry Beaudon *New Guitar Summit* (Stony Plain 2004) ★★★.

● COMPILATIONS: *The Best Of The J. Geils Band* (Atlantic 1979) ★★★, *Houseparty: The J. Geils Band Anthology* (Rhino 1992) ★★★, *Masters Of Rock* (EMI 2002) ★★.

Gelato, Ray

b. Ray Keith Irwin, 25 October 1961, London, England. As a child, Ray Irwin heard music from the record collection of his father, an American soldier stationed in Britain. The music included **Frank Sinatra**, **Sammy Davis Jnr.** and swing bands of the 40s, as well as 50s rock 'n' roll and R&B, with the bands led by **Louis Jordan** and **Louis Prima** proving to be especially influential. In the latter's case, Irwin was drawn to the leader's singing and to the tenor saxophone playing of Sam Butera. In 1979, Irwin began studying the tenor saxophone and the following year was sufficiently proficient to play professionally with the Dynamite Band, a group that was influenced by **Bill Haley**.

In 1982, Gelato teamed up as a duo with French guitarist Patrice Serapiglia, who called himself Maurice Chevalier, and they named their band the Chevalier Brothers. Among the pioneers of the revival of interest in London in R&B and the jump bands of the 40s and 50s, the band expanded to a five-piece. After winning a talent contest at London's Camden Palace, the band toured extensively in the UK and Europe. At this time, the band included Gelato (tenor saxophone/vocals), Chevalier (guitar), Clark Kent (bass), John Piper (d. 2000; drums), and Roger Beaujolais (vibraphone). Only the drummer used his real name. It was at Chevalier's urging that Gelato not only adopted the name by which he has been known ever since, but also began singing regularly. Quickly established on the London scene, the band's international fame spread through appearances at the **Montreux International Jazz Festival**, the North Sea Jazz Festival, and a tour of Japan. Shortly after this, Chevalier left to be replaced by pianist Marc Adelman, and then Beaujolais left the band to start a solo career.

In 1988 the Chevalier Brothers folded, and Gelato formed his own band, a seven-piece group, which he named the Giants Of Jive. Kent and Piper remained, and soon Adelman too came on board. The band's enormous popularity in Italy was responsible for a 1992 Carnegie Hall engagement, which was for an Italian television special. Ray Gelato And The Giants Of Jive folded in 1994, and the leader promptly established a new group, the Ray Gelato Giants. The new band retained some of the original quirkiness and all of its dynamic stage presence, but the material moved closer to the middle of the road, drawing its repertoire from the music popularized by artists such as **Nat 'King' Cole**, **Duke Ellington**, **Dean Martin** and Sinatra. Nevertheless, Gelato's singing continued to show allegiance to Prima and his tenor saxophone playing to Butera. More jazz festival engagements followed, including Umbria, Montreal, Molde, Marciac and San Sebastian. There were also tours of the USA and Italy, where Gelato's popularity was unabated. In 2001 the band opened for

Robbie Williams and his *Swing When You're Winning* concert at London's Royal Albert Hall and the following year played at **Paul McCartney**'s wedding. Gelato has also played at private parties hosted by the rich and famous, not least Queen Elizabeth II. Having previously made several hugely popular appearances at the Umbria Jazz Festival in Italy, the band returned there in 2003.

By the early 00s, Gelato's band included Danny Marsden (trumpet), Richard Busiakiewicz (piano; who has worked with Gelato since 1994), Alex Garnett (saxophones; with Gelato in this band since 1996 and also in the occasionally formed Tough Tenors group), Andy Rogers (trombone), Tom Gordon (drums), and Kent (bass; who is also Gelato's business partner). Gelato has been hugely successful, finding a niche and retaining his dominance in it through hard work, good musicianship and a flair for showmanship.

● ALBUMS: *Ray Gelato's Giants Of Jive* (Blue Horizon 1990) ★★★, *Gelato All' Italiano* (Durium 1997) ★★★, *Gelato Espresso* (Durium 1997) ★★★, *The Full Flavour* 1996 recording (Honest 1998) ★★★, *The Men From Uncle* (Dynosupreme 1998) ★★★, *Gelato Dal Vivo: Live In Italy* (Double Scoop 2000) ★★★, *The Ice Cream Man* (Double Scoop 2002) ★★★★, *Smokin'* (Double Scoop 2003) ★★★, *Ray Gelato* (2Blue 2004) ★★★.

● FILMS: *Scandal* (1989), *Enigma* (2001).

Gelb, Howe

b. Pennsylvania, USA. This singer-songwriter has been pursuing his often wayward muse from his base in Tucson, Arizona for over three decades. The main outlet for his work has been **Giant Sand**, whose 'desert rock' sound, with its mix of country, rock, and beatnik lyricism, is often cited as a key influence on many of the roots-orientated bands to emerge during the alternative country resurgence of the mid-90s. Gelb has always been keen to disassociate himself from any labels, however, and although his work began to crossover to a wider audience during the mid-90s he has resolutely refused to stray from his unique musical path.

Gelb's first serious musical venture, the Giant Sandworms, was formed in 1980 with **Rainer**. An unsuccessful stint in New York City was followed by a return to Tucson, where Gelb put together both Giant Sand and the **Band Of Blacky Ranchette**. Various personnel continued to come and go, including Gelb's then wife Paula Jean Brown, before a stable line-up comprising Gelb, John Convertino and Joey Burns recorded a string of superb albums in the early 90s. All three members subsequently worked with **Lisa Germano** on the OP8 project, while Convertino and Burns formed the side project Spoke, followed by Friends Of Dean Martinez and, most successfully, **Calexico**. Gelb overcame the death of his close friend Rainer in 1997 to record the solo set *Hisser*, his debut album proper following two previous low-key releases. It was followed by the excellent Giant Sand release *Chore Of Enchantment*, an album that Gelb had been working on at the time of Rainer's death. His second solo collection, *Confluence*, was released in 2001. The same year's *Lull Some Piano* comprised an album of piano ballads, a typically left-field move from Gelb. He subsequently parted company with long-term collaborators Burns and Convertino and relocated to his Danish wife's home town of Aarhus. Gelb recorded the majority of his 2003 solo set *The Listener* in Denmark, and also teamed up with local musicians to record the following year's Giant Sand album, *Is All Over . . . The Map*.

● ALBUMS: *Incidental Music* cassette (Left For Dead 1983) ★★★, *Dreaded Brown Recluse* (Restless/Houses In Motion 1991) ★★★, as Howe *Hisser* (V2 1998) ★★★, *Down Home* (Ow Om 1998) ★★★, *Down Home 2000* (Ow Om 2000) ★★★, as Howe *Confluence* (Thrill Jockey/Loose 2001) ★★★★, *Lull Some Piano* (Thrill Jockey 2001) ★★★, *Down Home 2002* (Ow Om 2002) ★★★, *The Listener* (Thrill Jockey 2003) ★★★, *Ogle Some Piano* (Ow Om 2004) ★★, *Down Home 2004: Year Of The Monkey* (Ow Om 2004) ★★★, *'Sno Angel Like You* (Thrill Jockey 2006) ★★★.
● DVD/VIDEOS: *The Listener's Coffee Companion* (Ow Om 2004).

Gelbart, Larry

b. Larry Simon Gelbart, 25 February 1928, Chicago, Illinois, USA. A pre-eminent screenwriter, librettist, director and producer, Gelbart moved as a child with his family to California. His father was a barber, and used to cut the famous comedian Danny Thomas' hair. When Gelbart was 16, he went to work for Thomas, writing jokes, and then moved on to other top radio comics such as **Bob Hope** and **Eddie Cantor**. Hope took Gelbart into television, where he met **Burt Shevelove**, and in 1958 the two of them set about the task of working through all 21 of the surviving comedies by the Roman playwright, Plautus. Together with composer **Stephen Sondheim**, they took four years writing and re-writing what became *A Funny Thing Happened On The Way To The Forum*. The show opened on Broadway in May 1962, and ran for 964 performances. Gelbart and Shevelove both won **Tony Awards**. Gelbart went to London in 1963 for the West End opening, and stayed for nine years. He wrote for Marty Feldman, and provided the screenplays for a number of movies, many of them uncredited.

Back in the USA, Gelbart started work on turning the 1970 film *M*A*S*H* into a television series. He won Emmys for his contributions—writing many of the almost 100 episodes 1972–83, as well as directing and serving as executive producer on the series. Gelbart made his stage debut as a director with a UK revival of '*Forum*', which transferred from the Chichester Festival to the West End in 1986. Three years later, *City Of Angels*, an ingenious and hilarious private eye spoof of a musical, for which Gelbart wrote the book (and won his third Tony), opened on Broadway. It was a stinging satire on Hollywood, and the indignities that screenwriters suffer in 'the ego-fuelled jungle warfare that rages on the West Coast', in particular, Gelbart's experience on the film *Tootsie*, the story of a 'resting' actor who masquerades as a woman in order to get a job in a television soap opera. Of its star, Dustin Hoffman, Gelbart was quoted thus: 'Never argue with a man who is shorter than his Oscar.' A legend in the business, renowned for his skill and wit, apart from his two big hits, '*Forum*' and *City Of Angels*, Gelbart's credits have included *Sly Fox*, *Mastergate*, *Jump*, and *Power Failure*. He has not emerged unscathed. In 1961, after experiencing immense difficulties getting *The Conquering Hero*, a show based on Preston Sturges' sentimental comedy movie *Hail The Conquering Hero*, into New York for its eight-performance run, he is reported to have said somewhat wearily, 'If Hitler is still alive, I hope he's out of town with a musical.'
● FURTHER READING: *The Classically American Comedy Of Larry Gelbart*, Jay Malarcher.

Geldof, Bob

b. Robert Frederick Zenon Geldof, 5 October 1951, Dún Laoghaire, Co. Dublin, Eire. Geldof initially entered the music scene as a journalist on Canada's premier underground rock journal *Georgia Straight*. Further experience with the **New Musical Express** and **Melody Maker** sharpened his prose and upon returning to Dublin, he formed the band Nightlife Thugs, which subsequently evolved into the **Boomtown Rats**, one of the first acts to emerge during the punk/new wave explosion of 1976/77.

After a series of hits, including two UK number 1 singles, the band fell from favour, but Geldof was about to emerge unexpectedly as one of the most well known pop personalities of his era. He had always had an acerbic wit and provided excellent interviews with an energy and enthusiasm that matched any of his articulate rivals. After starring in the film of **Pink Floyd**'s *The Wall*, he turned his attention to the dreadful famine that was plaguing Ethiopia in 1984. Shocked by the horrific pictures that he saw on television, Geldof organized the celebrated **Band Aid** aggregation for the charity record, which he co-wrote with **Midge Ure**, 'Do They Know It's Christmas?' The single sold in excess of three million copies and thanks to Geldof's foresight in gaining financial control of every aspect of the record's production, manufacture and distribution, famine relief received over 96 pence of the £1.35 retail price. The record inspired 1985's mammoth **Live Aid** extravaganza, in which Geldof herded together rock's elite to play before a worldwide television audience of over 1,000,000,000.

Geldof continued to help with the administration of Band Aid, which effectively put his singing career on hold for a couple of years. After receiving a knighthood in June 1986 and publishing his autobiography, he recorded the solo album *Deep In The Heart Of Nowhere*, which spawned the minor hit 'This Is The World Calling'. Unfortunately, Geldof's celebrity status seemed to have worked against him in the fashion-conscious pop world, a fact that he freely admitted. His second album, 1990's *The Vegetarians Of Love*, was recorded in a mere five days and proved a hit with critics and fans alike. Complete with folk and Cajun flavourings and an irreverent stab at apathy in the hit single 'The Great Song Of Indifference', the album brought some hope that Geldof might be able to continue his recording career, despite the perennial publicity that associates his name almost exclusively with Live Aid.

A further album was poorly received, and the singer's attention began to be diverted by other interests. By now he had established himself as a highly astute businessman with his co-ownership of the television production house Planet 24, which began life as Planet Pictures back in the mid-80s. The company broke into the big time by launching the pioneering early morning television series *The Big Breakfast* in 1992. Geldof was once again in the headlines in late 1994, although this time not by his choosing. His marriage to television presenter/writer Paula Yates had seemingly broken up following her affair with Michael Hutchence of **INXS**. Throughout the whole tawdry media exposure Geldof remained calm and kept his dignity.

In the late 90s, Geldof moved into new media, founding the online travel agency site deckchair.com and the mobile portal WapWorld. He also held a major share in the online music retailer clickmusic.com, prior to its financial problems. Geldof returned to the music scene in September 2001 with his first new recording in over eight years. A raw and brutally frank album dealing in unflinching detail with the recent emotional upheavals of Geldof's personal life, *Sex, Age & Death* was in marked contrast to his previous studio set, the relatively upbeat *The Happy Club*.

It is, however, for both Live Aid and the 2005 'follow-up' **Live 8** that Sir Bob Geldof is rightly applauded. He has carried off both events with a winning formula of enthusiasm and bullish passion. He is articulate and highly motivated, and nobody has done more for world causes from within the world of popular music than he has. Whatever his limitations as a musician Geldof is unquestionably one of the all-time 'great' figures in an industry often tainted as shallow and irresponsible.

● ALBUMS: *Deep In The Heart Of Nowhere* (Mercury/Atlantic 1986) ★★★, *The Vegetarians Of Love* (Mercury/Atlantic 1990) ★★★, *The Happy Club* (Vertigo 1992) ★★, *Sex, Age & Death* (Eagle 2001) ★★★.
● COMPILATIONS: *Loudmouth: The Best Of The Boomtown Rats And Bob Geldof* (Vertigo 1994) ★★★, *Great Songs Of Indifference: The Best Of Bob Geldof & The Boomtown Rats* (Columbia 1997) ★★★, *Under The Influence* (DMC 2004) ★★★, *Great Songs Of Indifference: The Anthology 1986–2001* (Mercury 2005) ★★★.
● DVD/VIDEOS: *Geldof In Africa* (Warner Vision International 2005).
● FURTHER READING: *Is That It?*, Bob Geldof. *Bob Geldof*, Charlotte Gray. *Paula, Michael & Bob: Everything You Know Is Wrong*, Gerry Agar. *Geldof In Africa*, Bob Geldof.
● FILMS: *The Wall* (1982), *Diana & Me* (1997), *Spice World* (1997).

Geldray, Max

b. Max Leon van Gelder, 12 February 1916, Amsterdam, the Netherlands, d. 2 October 2004, Palm Springs, California, USA. Geldray was born into a musical family and is reputed to be one of the first jazz harmonica players in Europe. His mother was a classically trained pianist, and the young Geldray inherited his father's ability to play an instrument by ear. He bought his first harmonica when he was aged 16, and taught himself to play it. Influenced by hearing jazz greats such as **Louis Armstrong** on the radio, Geldray formed his own eight-piece group, which soon evolved into a quartet, the Hollander Boys. They were spotted by the English comedian and impresario Tom Moss, and travelled to the UK, where they toured the variety theatres. On his return to Holland Geldray went solo, and played at the Boeuf sur la Toit Club in Brussels, and with the Johnny Fresco Band in Ostend. It was there that he met the French band leader Ray Ventura, who took him to Paris in the late 30s. Geldray was billed as the 'special attraction' with Ventura's orchestra, which was considered to be one of the top bands in Europe, and he became something of a celebrity, often jamming with the legendary jazz guitarist **Django Reinhardt**.

Just after the outbreak of World War II, Geldray fled to Britain and joined the Princess Irene Brigade. He also did numerous broadcasts for the BBC, and appeared in a special Royal Command Performance at Windsor Castle to celebrate Princess Elizabeth's 16th birthday. In 1945 he rejoined Ray Ventura in Paris for a time, and then returned to Britain and subsequently provided the musical interludes (and, as 'the world's worst actor', spoke a few lines) in the radio series that started out as *Crazy People*, but was soon retitled *The Goon*

Show, starring Spike Milligan, **Harry Secombe**, Peter Sellers and (initially) Michael Bentine. Geldray (nicknamed 'Conk') and his harmonica were ever-present in more than 200 episodes of the series from 1951 until the series ended in 1960. In the early 60s, after working in Australia and on cruise ships, Geldray moved to the USA and put his music career on the backburner to work as a clothing salesman, but was reunited with his former colleagues in *The Last Goon Show Of All* in 1972. On returning to America, he again took work outside the music business before eventually retiring to Palm Springs, California, emerging only to play the occasional gig. In later years Geldray did extensive voluntary work for the local Stroke Centre and the Betty Ford Centre for drugs, and alcohol rehabilitation.

● ALBUMS: *Goon With The Wind* (Parlophone) ★★★.
● FURTHER READING: *Goon With The Wind*, Max Geldray with John R. Vance.

Geller, Herb

b. 2 November 1928, Los Angeles, California, USA. Geller's first major engagement on alto saxophone was with **Joe Venuti** in the mid-40s. By the end of the decade he was in New York City, USA, playing in **Claude Thornhill**'s big band and early in the 50s he was performing with **Billy May**. In the mid-50s Geller worked with several leading west coast musicians, including **Chet Baker**, **Shelly Manne**, **Maynard Ferguson**, **Shorty Rogers** and **Bill Holman**. He was also co-leader of a small group with his wife, pianist Lorraine Walsh. After her sudden death in 1958 Geller worked with **Benny Goodman** and **Louie Bellson**, spent some time in South America and toured Europe, where he decided to settle. In 1962 he was in Berlin, playing in radio orchestras and running a nightclub. He later moved to Hamburg, where he again worked in radio and in several big bands, in between times playing and recording with his own small groups. A striking bebop player in the **Charlie Parker** mould, Geller chose a pattern of work that has limited his exposure to international audiences.

● ALBUMS: *Herb Geller Plays* (EmArcy 1954) ★★★, *Herb Geller Sextette* (EmArcy 1955) ★★★★, *The Gellers* (EmArcy 1955) ★★★, *Fire In The West* (Jubilee 1957) ★★, *Stax Of Sax* (Jubilee 1958) ★★★, *Gypsy* (Atco 1959) ★★★, *Herb Geller Alto Saxophone* (Josie 1963) ★★★, *An American In Hamburg* (Nova 1975) ★★★, *Rhyme To Reason* (Discovery 1978) ★★★, *Hot House* (Circle 1984) ★★★, *Birdland Stomp* (Enja 1986) ★★★, *A Jazz Songbook Meeting* (Enja 1989) ★★★, *West Coast Scene* (Vogue 1989) ★★★★, *The Herb Geller Quartet* (VSOP 1994) ★★★★, with Jan Lundgren *Stockholm Get-Together!* (Fresh Sound 1994) ★★★, *Playing Jazz* (Fresh Sound 1995) ★★★, *I'll Be Back* (Hep 1996) ★★★, *You're Looking At Me* (Fresh Sound 1997) ★★★, *Plays The Al Cohn Songbook* (Hep 1998) ★★★, *I'll Be Back!* (Hep 1998) ★★★, with Brian Kellock *Hollywood Portraits* (Hep 2000) ★★★, *To Benny And Johnny With Love From Herb* (Hep 2002) ★★★.

Gem

Formed in Cleveland, Ohio, USA, Gem originally featured Doug Gillard (guitar, ex–Death Of Samantha, also a member of Cobra Verde), Scott Pickering (drums, ex-**Prisonshake**), Chris Burgess (bass, ex-Prisonshake) and Tim Tobias (guitar, ex–Four Coyotes). The idea for the group came after an impromptu jam session in 1992. Gillard had written songs for the Cleveland compilation *Hotel Cleveland*, and used this line-up as a means of road-testing the songs, eventually electing to put the group on a permanent footing as Gem. Burgess was then replaced by Jeff Curtis of My Dad Is Dead. Influenced by groups such as **Pere Ubu** and **Wire**, Gillard confessed: 'we're not the youngest of the young whippers-nappers, things come out in the music that are more traditional.' Gem recorded its debut single, 'Suburban Girl'/'Drool', for Carcrashh Records, owned by the senior editor of Cleveland's *Alternative Press* magazine, Jason Pettigrew. Their second single, 'Your Heroes Hate You', was described by *Billboard* as a 'brilliant detonation of post-modern rockabilly', setting the agenda for the group's long-playing Restless Records debut, *Hexed*.

● ALBUMS: *Hexed* (Restless 1995) ★★★.

Gems

Formed in Chicago in 1961 and originally known as the Lovettes, the group comprised Raynard Miner, Vandine Harris, Theresa Washum, Dorothy Hucklebee and Jessica Collins. Students at Marshall High School on Chicago's West Side, the Lovettes progressed from amateur talent contests to a contract with **Chess Records**. A sixth member, Bertha Watts, was added in 1962. The group recorded two singles as the Lovettes, 'The Crush' and 'Hands Off', before becoming the Gems. Under this name they would issue a further six singles, of which 'I Can't Help Myself' was arguably the best. By that time (1964), Bertha Watts had dropped out again and Vandine Harris had been replaced by **Minnie Riperton**. The group was used as backing singers on sessions by the **Dells**, **Billy Stewart** and **Etta James**. Miner was, meanwhile, developing a songwriting talent and he collaborated on 'Rescue Me' (**Fontella Bass**), 'We're Gonna Make It' (**Little Milton**) and 'Higher And Higher' (**Jackie Wilson**). Following the Gems' final single, 'Happy New Love', Riperton issued a solo single in 1966 under the name of Andrea Davis, while the other group members became back-up singers for several Chess recording artists. A regrouped Gems was formed in 1967. Now called the Starlets, Riperton, Washum, Jessica Edmund and Dorothy Martin released two singles for Chess before breaking up for good. Riperton then joined **Rotary Connection** before achieving fame as a solo artist under her own name in the mid-70s. Miner later wrote material for Invictus/Hot Wax label acts **Chairmen Of The Board**, **Honey Cone**, **Freda Payne** and **Flaming Ember**. In 1974 he wrote and produced 'Shortage' for Coda, which included Martin and Edmund from the Starlets.

Gene

Foppish UK aesthetes Gene formed in the summer of 1993, quickly melding a waspish chemistry from the base components of Steve Mason (b. England; guitar), Martin Rossiter (b. England; vocals), Kevin Miles (b. England; bass) and Matt James (b. England; drums). Mason and James were formerly together in Spin. Writing songs together and honing their live profile, their influences were culled from **Paul Weller**, the **Small Faces** and, most obviously, the **Smiths**. Their debut release, the double a-side 'For The Dead'/'Child's Body', released on the fledgling Costermonger label in May 1994, set out a distinct musical agenda. Single Of The Week and Month awards followed from *New Musical Express* and *Select* magazines, with the limited 1,994 pressing selling out within two days after it was play-listed by BBC Radio 1. A

strong reaction was also gained as support to **Pulp** at London's Forum, where Rossiter's stage presence illuminated Gene's performance. August brought a second single, this time promoted as a 'triple a-side', featuring 'Be My Light, Be My Guide', 'This Is Not My Crime' and 'I Can't Help Myself'. Gaining pole position in the UK independent poll, and reaching number 54 in the UK charts proper, the band set out on their first headlining UK tour.

Following further positive press, the band signed a major label recording contract with **Polydor Records**. A third single, 'Sleep Well Tonight', followed an appearance at the Reading Festival, and the band also played mainland Europe for the first time with **Elastica** and **Oasis**. *Select*'s description of the single, 'ace crooning and rock and roll iridescence', came closest to cornering Gene's appeal. It saw them break the UK Top 40, as they featured highly in various end-of-year polls for brightest newcomers. The release of 'Haunted By You' in February 1995 prefigured a debut album proper, produced by Phil Vinall. With less direct, even nebulous material sandwiching the energy of the singles, there was much for critics to reflect on. Eschewing the self-consciously fey approach of **Suede**, the uncouth voyeurism of Pulp or the 'new lad' abrasiveness of Oasis, Rossiter's songs were dominated instead by a wholly unromantic cast of characters inhabiting a down-at-heel, broken world with little hope of redemption.

The 1996 release *To See The Lights* compiled b-sides and live recordings, acting as a stop-gap for the accomplished *Drawn To The Deep End*, released in early 1997, with the band displaying a greater musical diversity to back-up Rossiter's lyrical dramas. *Revelations* was another occasionally inspired collection, although critics bemoaned the fact that Gene still seemed unable to successfully translate their excellent live sound onto record. The band was released from its Polydor contract at the end of the year. The following summer they recorded a live album at Hollywood's legendary Troubadour club. Their new studio set, *Libertine*, was released in October 2001. Three years later the band decided to call it a day, playing their final gig at the London Astoria on 16 December 2004.

● ALBUMS: *Olympian* (Costermonger 1995) ★★★★, *Drawn To The Deep End* (Polydor 1997) ★★★, *Revelations* (Polydor 1999) ★★★, *Rising From Sunset* (Contra 2000) ★★★, *Libertine* (Contra/iMUSIC 2001) ★★★.
● COMPILATIONS: *To See The Lights* (Costermonger 1996) ★★★, *As Good As It Gets: The Best Of* (Polydor 2001) ★★★.
● DVD/VIDEOS: *Rising For Sunset* (Snapper 2003), *Live* (ILC 2004).

Gene And Debbe

Gene Thomas (b. 28 December 1938, Palestine, Texas, USA) was already a hit-maker in his own right before teaming up with Debbe Neville in 1967. Thomas had logged two chart hits: 1961's 'Sometime' and 1964's 'Baby's Gone', both country ballads. He met Neville when he was a staff songwriter for **Acuff-Rose Music** in Nashville. Their first single, on TRX Records, 'Go With Me', was a minor hit but 'Playboy' the following year made it to the US Top 20. After one last collaboration, 'Lovin' Season', the duo split up, Thomas returned to his writing job and Neville disappeared from the pop music scene.

Gene Krupa Story, The

This film, made in 1959, is another jazz biopic that misses its target by a mile. **Sal Mineo** portrays **Gene Krupa** as a sulky rebel, quite unlike the real-life drummer. Despite other shortcomings, Mineo convincingly played on-screen drums to Krupa's ghosted backing, and, to his credit, the actor later acknowledged the film's mediocrity. On the strength of this telling of Krupa's tale, no one could have imagined that he was a heart-throb idol of millions and one of the greatest showbiz attractions of his era; but then, any film on Krupa that manages to omit **Benny Goodman** is more than a little short on veracity. Shot in black and white, the film was directed by Don Weis. Musically, there are low and high points. Among the former is a scrappy jam session with **Red Nichols**; the best of the latter is a wonderful version of 'Memories Of You' sung by **Anita O'Day. Shelly Manne** appears as Dave Tough (he also played the late drummer in **The Five Pennies**). Krupa's return to the stage after a drug bust that put him in jail and cost him his highly popular band is quite well represented, with Tommy Pederson playing the role of **Tommy Dorsey**, who hired Krupa in 1944. In 1989 a projected remake was abandoned when a leading Hollywood star, interested in the role of Krupa, had to bow out to meet other obligations. (Alternative title: *Drum Crazy*).

Gene Loves Jezebel

Identical twins Jay (John) and Mike Aston, ostensibly Gene Loves Jezebel, enjoyed cult appeal, largely within the UK gothic rock community, but achieved greater success in America. The pair grew up in the South Wales town of Porthcawl, together with guitarist Ian Hudson. After moving to London, they made their debut in late 1981 supporting the **Higsons**. A recording contract with Situation 2 resulted in 'Shavin' My Neck' (a collection of demos) the following May. The dense, experimental sound was matched by live performances, featuring bass player Julianne Regan and drummer Dick Hawkins, where they mixed almost tribal rhythms with furious guitar work. Hawkins was replaced by a succession of drummers, including John Murphy (ex-**Associates; SPK**) and Steve Goulding, while Regan left to front **All About Eve**. Her space was filled by Hudson, allowing Albio De Luca (later of Furyo) to operate as guitarist in time for 'Screaming (For Emmalene)' in 1983.

Following Luca and Goulding's departure, Hudson reverted to guitar and Hawkins/Murphy offered a two-pronged drum attack. Murphy then left before a third single, the strong commercial sound of 'Bruises' (1983). Hot on its heels came their powerful debut album, *Promise*, promoted by a **John Peel** BBC radio session. A trip to the USA in 1984 to work with **John Cale** ensued, before returning for two quick-fire singles, 'Influenza (Relapse)' and 'Shame (Whole Heart Howl)'. Marshall then left, Mike Aston briefly switching from rhythm guitar to play bass, before Peter Rizzo was recruited. Ex–**Spear Of Destiny** drummer Chris Bell arrived in place of Hawkins, but it was a year before 'The Cow' hit the UK independent charts, preceding *Immigrant* in June 1985. After 'Desire' in November, the band left for a further North American tour, a traumatic time that led to Hudson's departure, ex–**Generation X** guitarist James Stevenson taking his place. The band skirted the Top 75 with 'Sweetest Thing' and *Discover* (which included a free live album), while 'Heartache' hinted at a passing interest in **dance music**. They subsequently concentrated their efforts on the US market.

However, all was not well in their camp, and Mike Aston left the band in mid-1989.

In 1993 Gene Loves Jezebel, now comprising Jay Aston, Rizzo, Stevenson and Robert Adam, released the ill-fated *Heavenly Bodies*. The band subsequently ground to a halt, with the various members moving on to different projects. The Astons reunited with Stevenson, Bell and Rizzo to record new material for a 1995 compilation set, before re-forming Gene Loves Jezebel on a more permanent basis in the late 90s.

● ALBUMS: *Promise* (Situation 2 1983) ★★★, *Immigrant* (Beggars Banquet 1985) ★★★, *Discover* (Beggars Banquet 1986) ★★★, *The House Of Dolls* (Beggars Banquet 1987) ★★, *Kiss Of Life* (Beggars Banquet 1990) ★★, *Heavenly Bodies* (Savage/Arista 1993) ★★★, *VII* (Robison 1999) ★★★, *Love Lies Bleeding* (Robison 1999) ★★★, *Live In The Voodoo City* (Triple X 1999) ★★, *Giving Up The Ghost* (Triple X 2001) ★★, *Live At Nottingham* (Perris 2002) ★★.

● COMPILATIONS: *Some Of The Best Of Gene Loves Jezebel: From The Mouths Of Babes* (Avalanche 1995) ★★★, *Voodoo Dollies: The Best Of Gene Loves Jezebel* (Beggars Banquet 1999) ★★★.

General B

b. David Parkes, 1972, Kingston, Jamaica, West Indies. Parkes was raised in the notorious ghetto areas of Seaview, Waterhouse, Rose Lane and Waltham Park and was inspired by **General Trees** to chat in the **dancehall**. It was through his connection with Trees that he became known as General and later added the B as he was considered the baby of the sound who was distinguished by his 'turbine whine'. In 1994, General B joined forces with **Ghost** and Roundhead in the **Monster Shack Crew**. Although considered one of the crew, General B's songwriting skills enabled him to maintain a high profile individually with hit tunes such as, 'God Heart' (a duet with Jason Sweetness), 'Nicky', 'Bad Inna New Clothes' and 'Scream' (his biggest solo hit). In the late 90s, General B recorded on sessions in New York, USA, that resulted in the hip-hop release, 'If Me Did Know'. At the start of the millennium he recorded in sessions for the second Monster Shack Crew album and with Roundhead released 'True Lover'. A series of hits followed including dancehall favourites 'Shock Him Up', 'Jump', 'N-Vious', 'Ah Me Dis' and 'When We Roll'. By the end of 2000, General B established his solo career with the hardcore **ragga** anthem, 'The Business', and he is widely considered as the man who inspired younger DJs to serve their apprenticeship as a part of a crew.

General Degree

(see **Degree**)

General Echo

d. 1980. Jamaican DJ Echo (aka Ranking Slackness) was one of the first to challenge the predominantly 'cultural' approach of the majority of mid- to late-70s DJs, and his influence on the new generation of DJs who made it in the 80s (in particular the UK MC school) was profound. He was one of the first DJs to be heard and fully appreciated on **yard tapes**, as he tore up Jamaica on his own Echo Tone Hi Fi set, and his preference for 'slack' or risqué lyrics, in particular his timing and tone of voice, was very popular and widely imitated. Echo felt no compunction about stopping the music altogether, if the vibes were right, in order to tell a joke or two—a facet that endeared him even more to his followers. His version of **Winston Riley**'s 'Stalag' rhythm—'Arleen'—was a number 1 hit in Jamaica, and the future was looking very bright for Echo until he was shot dead by the police in Kingston in 1980, along with Flux and Big John (both from his **sound system**), in an incident that has never been fully explained.

● ALBUMS: as Ranking Slackness *The Slackest LP* (Techniques 1979) ★★, *12-Inches Of Pleasure* (Greensleeves 1980) ★★★.

General Kane

US group fronted by Mitch McDowell (b. 1954, San Bernadino, California, USA, d. January 1992). McDowell took the professional name General Kane (formerly General Caine) in tribute to an officer who had supported his artistic ambitions when he was at military school. After leaving that institution, he formed the group Booty People with several future members of **War**, before assembling an eight-piece rap group and signing with Groove Time Records in 1978. Two albums for the label preceded a move to Tabu Records. A slimmed-down version of the group signed a recording contract with **Motown Records** in the mid-80s. Their debut single for the label, 'Crack Killed Applejack', was an uncompromising reflection of drug addiction on the inner city streets, and reached number 12 in the black music charts despite being barred from airplay. Subsequent releases mellowed General Kane's approach, without losing their commitment to the basic rap sound of the late 80s—though the group's album *Wide Open* did include a romantic ballad, 'Close Your Eyes', which featured vocals from two of the group's less prominent members, Cheryl McDowell and Danny Macon. Mitch McDowell was murdered in January 1992. General Kane's catalogue remained in print through the efforts of their former producer, Grover Wimberly III, who runs his own label, King Bee Records.

● ALBUMS: *General Caine* (Groove Time 1978) ★★★, *Get Down Attack* (Groove Time 1981) ★★★★, *Girls* (Tabu 1982) ★★, *Dangerous* (Tabu 1984) ★★★, *In Full Chill* (Motown 1986) ★★★, *Wide Open* (Motown 1987) ★★★.

General Levy

b. Paul Levy, 1971, Park Royal, London, England. As **ragga** music finally made it into the mainstream in 1993 with **Chaka Demus And Pliers**, **Shaggy**, **Shabba Ranks** and others storming the UK national charts, it was left to just one home-grown DJ to fly the flag for British ragga music. A north London youth, Levy began his career DJing as General Levy, working his way through Vigilante, Java and Robbo Ranx's Tipatone **sound systems**. His first release was for Robbo's Muzik Street label in 1988, and 'New Cockatoo' proved to be something quite different, as Levy's freshness, youth and enthusiasm poured out of every groove. His next move was to south London, where **Fashion Records**' resident engineer, Gussie P, released his debut album, *Double Trouble*, on which he shared the honours with Jamaican superstar DJ **Capleton**. The format (already tried and trusted) highlighted both Levy's and Capleton's different styles and approaches, spanning Jamaican and UK traditions. Levy's popularity was boosted by numerous 'specials' for sound systems and he finally came to the public's attention in a big way with

'Original Length & Strength' on Fashion Records. His next trio of releases for Fashion, 'Heat', 'Breeze' and 'The Wig' established him as *the* British DJ. His lyrics ranged from serious culture to risqué 'slackness', with barely a pause for breath. His live shows had to be experienced to be believed, as he exploded all over the stage, arms and legs flailing to the accompaniment of non-stop, infectious, raucous rhyming. His branching out with Justice Records for some hip-hop-based recordings further broadened his appeal, and the late-1992 long-playing release for Fashion of *The Wickeder General* was an immediate runaway success. His burgeoning talent and personality was soon spotted by the majors (especially with all the frantic interest in ragga in the spring of 1993), and **ffrr Records** clinched the big contract. They retitled, repackaged and repromoted *The Wickeder General* as *Wickedness Increase* and the strength of the added tracks ensured healthy sales—even to the reggae market, where his fans had already purchased the original pressing.

● ALBUMS: with Capleton *Double Trouble* (Gussie P. 1991) ★★★, *The Wickeder General* (Fashion 1992) ★★★★, *Wickedness Increase* (ffrr/London 1993) ★★★★, with Top Cat *Rumble In The Jungle* (Glamma 1995) ★★★★, *New Breed* (Trojan 2002) ★★★.

General Public

When the Birmingham, England–based **Beat** disbanded, the band's two vocalists, Dave Wakeling and Ranking Roger, formed General Public with ex-**Specials** bass player Horace Panter, Stoker (drums), Micky Billingham (keyboards) and Kevin White (guitar), plus veteran saxophonist Saxa. A self-titled debut single on **Virgin Records** combined a strong pop sound with an underlying dance feel and brushed the UK charts. 'Tenderness', in October, fared better in the USA (on I.R.S. Records), coinciding with a fine debut album, . . . *All The Rage*. Without a British hit, the band's blend of musical influences, characterized by Roger's all-round skills, was largely ignored. General Public tried again in 1986 with *Hand To Mouth*, but, though they aimed at the singles market with 'Faults And All', the world seemed oblivious and the band disappeared. Ranking Roger surfaced in a revitalized International Beat, before a new album finally appeared in 1995, with the line-up comprising Wakeling, Ranking Roger, Michael Railton (vocals/keyboards), Norman Jones (vocals/percussion), Wayne Lothian (bass), and Dan Chase (drums). Produced by **Jerry Harrison**, the album sounded fresh and energetic. In addition to invigorating originals such as 'It Must Be Tough' and 'Rainy Days', there was an interesting ska/reggae version of **Van Morrison**'s 'Warm Love'.

● ALBUMS: . . . *All The Rage* (Virgin/I.R.S. 1984) ★★★, *Hand To Mouth* (Virgin/I.R.S. 1986) ★★★, *Rub It Better* (Epic 1995) ★★★.

● COMPILATIONS: *Classic Masters* (Capitol 2002) ★★★.

General Saint

(see **Clint Eastwood And General Saint**)

General T.K.

b. Trevor Keith Williams, Manchester, Jamaica, West Indies. Williams began writing lyrics in the parish of Mandeville in his childhood, drawing inspiration from **Johnny Ringo**. The leading Gemini Hi Power DJ encouraged Williams to perform on the **sound system**s, and Williams embarked on a career adopting the T.K. moniker. His early experience in the dancehall was with the country sound, Wisdom, followed by a spell with Lightning High Power from Spanish Town. His popularity on the sound resulted in his recording debut 'Nah Money Nah Run', which was released in 1986 through the production team of Dennis and Junie Star. A number of hits followed with **King Jammy** and **Bobby Digital**, purveyors of the prevalent Waterhouse sound. The DJ maintained a high profile in Jamaica, although it was not until 1992 that he gained international acclaim, in spite of two successful Canadian tours. His big break came with **Captain Sinbad**, who released 'Fanciness'. The tune was a version of the then popular 'Heart Attack' rhythm, a reworking of **Burning Spear**'s 'He Prayed'. General T.K.'s distinctive gravely delivery, with rough-edged lyrics, is reminiscent of **Dirtsman**, with whom he frequently clashed in the dancehall. The hits continued to flow, notably 'God Alone', 'Main Point', 'Poisonous Dettol' and 'I Spy', an answer to **Simpleton**'s 'Eye Nah See'. Simpleton's original version was a barrage of risqué lyricism, while Williams' interpretation has since become a **dancehall** anthem. By 1993 General T.K. revoiced 'I Spy', with debutant producer Adrian Genus. The song again proved a hit and led to his album debut featuring the vitriolic 'Screwface', the culturally inclined 'Preach The Gospel' and 'Matie A Mad' (a tune he had previously voiced with E.J. Robinson). He also recorded with **Johnny Osbourne** ('Street Knowledge', 'Coke And Crack', 'Money Is A Thing' and 'Coop A Broke Down'). He continued working with Captain Sinbad, being featured on *Ragga Clash Volume Two* as well as enjoying hits with **Henry 'Junjo' Lawes**, including the hilarious 'Donkey Meat', a lewd tune inspired by Major Mackerel.

● ALBUMS: *I'm Wicked* (Imp 1992) ★★, *Original Poisonous* (Pre 1992) ★★★, *I Spy* (Greensleeves 1993) ★★★★.

General Trees

b. Anthony Edwards, *c*.1955, Kingston, Jamaica, West Indies. As General Trees, Edwards was one of the most popular DJs of the 80s who is widely regarded as the best Jamaican speed rapper. The 'fast style' is commonly accepted as arriving in Jamaica from the UK, through London-born **Phillip Papa Levi**. General Trees' debut, 'Mi God Mi King', topped the chart on the island and inspired a number of Jamaican DJs to emulate his approach. He adopted the fast style and demonstrated his skill to producer **Maurice Johnson** who promptly recorded the DJ's debut. His inaugural chart success 'Boasy Boy', led to a series of hits including 'Heel And Toe', 'Monkey And Ape', 'Ghost Rider' and 'Crucifixion', although his magnum opus was the anecdotal 'Mini Bus'. The song has since proved his best-known hit and led to an award in 1986 as the Song Of The Year from the Jamaican Broadcasting Corporation. The award improved his profile, and General Trees was soon recording with a variety of producers in Jamaica. He enjoyed a successful career locally with his both timely and topical lyrics alongside his legendary high-energy performances in the **dancehall**. A series of hits ensued including 'Gone A Negril' and 'Calling All Higglers' as well as a 'clash album', *Battle Of The Generals*, which featured versions of 'Lambada' and 'Think Twice'. The DJ also enjoyed combination hits such as 'Coke Pipe' with Fancy Black and 'Nightmare' with **Little John**. In the early 90s General Trees returned to recording at the Black Scorpio studio with Johnson, who continued to manage his career. General Trees was unable to repeat his early accomplishments although he enjoyed a modicum of success with 'Eye Nah See', 'Great Jamaican Jockeys' and 'Goodie Goodie'.

● ALBUMS: *Ghost Rider* (Sunset 1985) ★★, *The Younger Horseman* (Sunset 1985) ★★★, *Nuff Respect* (Shanachie 1987) ★★★★, with General Degree *Battle Of The Generals* (King Dragon 1987) ★★★, with Yellowman *A Reggae Calypso Encounter* (Rohit 1987) ★★, *Ragga Ragga Raggamuffin* (JA 1988) ★★★, *Everything So So* (World 1990) ★★★.

Generation X

This UK outfit emerged during the punk explosion of 1976. **Billy Idol** (b. William Michael Albert Broad, 30 November 1955, Stanmore, Middlesex, England; vocals) had previously worked with Tony James (bass/vocals) in the short-lived Chelsea. With Bob Andrews (guitar/vocals) and John Towe (drums), Generation X made their performing debut in London during December 1976. By the following May, Towe was replaced on drums by Mark Laff, while record companies sought their hand. Eventually they signed with **Chrysalis Records**. The group soon arrived in the lower regions of the UK chart with 'Your Generation' and 'Ready Steady Go'. The latter, strange for a punk group, was an affectionate tribute to the 60s, full of references to **Bob Dylan**, the **Beatles**, the **Rolling Stones** and Cathy McGowan (the legendary presenter of the UK music programme *Ready, Steady, Go!*). Following 'Friday's Angels' in June 1979, former **Clash** drummer Terry Chimes stepped in for Laff. The group lasted until 1981, but soon came to be regarded as a rock band in punk garb. Their biggest commercial success was with the 1979 single 'King Rocker', which reached number 11 in the UK. Idol later went on to solo stardom, departed drummer John Towe reappeared in the **Adverts**, and Terry Chimes rejoined the Clash, while Tony James reinvented himself in **Sigue Sigue Sputnik**.

● ALBUMS: *Generation X* (Chrysalis 1978) ★★★, *Valley Of The Dolls* (Chrysalis 1979) ★★, as Gen X *Kiss Me Deadly* (Chrysalis 1981) ★★.

● COMPILATIONS: *Best Of Generation X* (Chrysalis 1985) ★★★, *The Original Generation X* (MBC 1987) ★★★, *Generation X Live* (MBC 1987) ★★, *Perfect Hits (1975–81)* (Chrysalis 1991) ★★★, *Live At The Paris Theatre '78 & '81* (EMI 1999) ★★★, *Radio 1 Sessions* (Strange Fruit 2002) ★★★, *One Hundred Punks: BBC Live In Concert* (Strange Fruit 2003) ★★★, *Anthology* 3-CD set (EMI 2003) ★★★.

Genesis

This leading UK rock band first came together at the public school Charterhouse. **Peter Gabriel** (b. 13 February 1950, Cobham, Surrey, England; vocals), Tony Banks (b. 27 March 1951, East Heathly, Sussex, England; keyboards) and Chris Stewart (drums) were in an ensemble named the Garden Wall, and joined forces with Anthony Philips (guitar/vocals) and **Mike Rutherford** (b. 2 October 1950; bass,guitar,vocals), who were in a rival group, the Anon. In January 1967, the student musicians sent a demonstration tape to another Charterhouse alumnus, **Jonathan King**, then at **Decca Records**. King financed further recordings and christened the band Genesis. They recorded one single, 'The Silent Sun' in 1968, but it was not until the following year that their debut album, *From Genesis To Revelation*, was issued. Its lack of success left them without a label until the enterprising **Tony**

Stratton-Smith signed them to his recently formed **Charisma Records** in 1970. The band had already lost three drummers from their line-up before finding the perfect candidate that August. **Phil Collins** (b. 31 January 1951, London, England) had already worked with a professional group, **Flaming Youth**, and his involvement would later prove crucial in helping Genesis achieve international success.

The already recorded *Trespass* was issued in October 1970 but sold poorly. Further line-up changes ensued with the arrival of new guitarist **Steve Hackett** (b. 12 February 1950, London, England). The band was known for their highly theatrical stage act and costumes, but this did not help record sales. When the 1971 album *Nursery Cryme* also failed commercially, the band was again in danger of being dropped from their label. Success on the continent brought renewed faith, which was vindicated with the release of *Foxtrot*. The album reached the UK Top 20 and included the epic live favourite 'Supper's Ready'. Over the next two-and-a-half years, Genesis increased their profile with the bestselling albums **Selling England By The Pound** and **The Lamb Lies Down On Broadway**.

Having reached a new peak, however, their prospects were completely undermined by the shock departure of singer Gabriel in May 1975. Many commentators understandably wrote Genesis off at this point, particularly when it was announced that the new singer was to be their drummer Collins. The streamlined quartet proved remarkably resilient, however, and the succeeding albums **A Trick Of The Tail** and *Wind And Wuthering* were well received. In the summer of 1977, Hackett left to pursue a solo career, after which Genesis carried on as a trio, backed by various short-term employees. Amazingly, the band appeared to grow in popularity with the successive departure of each key member. During 1978, they received their first gold disc for the appropriately titled *And Then There Were Three* and two years later enjoyed a chart-topping album with **Duke**. With various solo excursions underway, Genesis still managed to sustain its identity as a working group and reached new levels of popularity with hits in the USA. By late 1981, they were in the US Top 10 with *Abacab* and could rightly claim to be one of the most popular rock acts in the world. Helped by Collins' high profile as a soloist, they enjoyed their biggest UK singles hit with 'Mama' and followed with 'Thats All' and 'Illegal Alien'. In America, they scored a number 1 single in 1986 with 'Invisible Touch', while the following four singles all made the US Top 5. Both *Genesis* and **Invisible Touch** topped the UK charts, while the latter also reached number 1 in the USA.

By the mid-80s, the group format was not sufficient to contain all their various projects, and Collins pursued a parallel solo career, while Rutherford formed the hit act **Mike And The Mechanics**. In 1991, the trio reconvened to record and issue *We Can't Dance*. Although this was their first album in over five years, it immediately topped the charts throughout the world, confirming their status as one of the world's leading dinosaur bands. Collins decided that his solo career and relocation to Switzerland had put too much pressure on trying to maintain his role in the band and he officially resigned. Although either of Mike's Mechanics, **Paul Carrack** or Paul Young would have fitted the bill perfectly, his replacement was Ray Wilson, the former lead singer of **Stiltskin**. He was heard on *Calling All Stations* released in August 1997, which proved to be the final

Genesis recording as Rutherford and Banks also elected to call it a day.

● ALBUMS: *From Genesis To Revelation* (Decca 1969) ★, *Trespass* (Charisma 1970) ★★, *Nursery Cryme* (Charisma 1971) ★★★, *Foxtrot* (Charisma 1972) ★★★, *Genesis Live* (Charisma 1973) ★★, *Selling England By The Pound* (Charisma 1973) ★★★, *The Lamb Lies Down On Broadway* (Charisma 1974) ★★★★, *A Trick Of The Tail* (Charisma 1976) ★★★, *Wind And Wuthering* (Charisma 1977) ★★★, *Seconds Out* (Charisma 1977) ★★, *And Then There Were Three* (Charisma 1978) ★★★, *Duke* (Charisma 1980) ★★★★, *Abacab* (Charisma 1981) ★★★, *3 Sides Live* (Charisma 1982) ★★, *Genesis* (Charisma 1983) ★★★, *Invisible Touch* (Charisma 1986) ★★★, *We Can't Dance* (Virgin 1991) ★★★, *The Way We Walk—Volume 1: The Shorts* (Virgin 1992) ★★, *Live The Way We Walk—Volume 2: The Longs* (Virgin 1993) ★★, *Calling All Stations* (Virgin 1997) ★★.

● COMPILATIONS: *Archive 1967–75* 4-CD box set (Virgin 1998) ★★★★, *Turn It On Again . . . The Hits* (Virgin 1999) ★★★★, *Archive #2 1976–1992* 3-CD box set (Virgin 2000) ★★★★, *Platinum Collection* (Virgin 2004) ★★★★.

● DVD/VIDEOS: *Three Sides Live* (Virgin 1986), *Live: The Mama Tour* (Virgin 1986), *Visible Touch* (Virgin 1987), *Genesis 2* (Virgin 1988), *Genesis 1* (Virgin 1988), *Invisible Touch Tour* (Virgin 1989), *Genesis: A History 1967–1991* (Virgin 1991), *Live: The Way We Walk* (Virgin 1993), *Songbook* (Eagle Vision 2001), *Live At Wembley Stadium* (Virgin 2003), *Inside Genesis: 1975–1980* (Classic Rock Legends 2004), *The Video Show* (Virgin 2004).

● FURTHER READING: *Genesis: The Evolution Of A Rock Band*, Armando Gallo. *Genesis Lyrics*, Kim Poor. *Genesis: Turn It On Again*, Steve Clarke. *Genesis: A Biography*, Dave Bowler and Brian Dray. *Opening The Musical Box*, Alan Hewitt. *Genesis: Inside & Out*, Robin Platts. *Turn It On Again: Peter Gabriel, Phil Collins & Genesis*, Dave Thompson.

Geneva

Formed in Aberdeen, Scotland, in 1993, Geneva comprises former *Sunday Post* journalist Andrew Montgomery (vocals), former marine biologist Steven Dora (guitar) and ex-students Douglas Caskie (drums), Keith Graham (bass) and Stuart Evans (guitar). It was several years into the band's existence before the members decided to take their music seriously. Once they did, however, the rewards were instantaneous. They signed a recording contract with Nude Records in December 1995, after their progress had been noted in London. They then came to the attention of the UK press through support tours with labelmates **Suede**. Montgomery's highly affecting vocals, by turns vulnerable and stoic, became the subject of heightened media interest, and critical comparisons to **Tim Buckley**. A series of singles followed, bringing the band to the periphery of the British charts. *Further*, released early in 1997, was cited by many reviewers as one of the best British debut albums of the 90s. Andrew Mueller in *The Independent* was just one of those impressed by its marriage of Scottish pop craft and expressionistic songwriting: 'They are . . . fluent in the peculiarly haunting dialect of Scottish pop, that strange and lovely language of luxurious, exuberant, redemptive melancholy that characterizes acts as disparate as **Aztec Camera**, the **Associates**, **Teenage Fanclub**, **Jesus And Mary Chain** and the

Blue Nile'. The last-named band provides the most opportune reference point, the Blue Nile sharing Geneva's devotion to aural aesthetics and texture. The band enlisted the heavyweight help of producer **Howie B** for the eagerly anticipated follow-up, *Weather Underground*.

● ALBUMS: *Further* (Nude 1997) ★★★★, *Weather Underground* (Nude 2000) ★★★.

Genevieve

Genevieve was a pseudonym for model Sue Hunt, who briefly launched her UK pop career on **CBS Records** in 1966 with the minor hit 'Once'. Managed by the chart hyper Harvey Freed (alias Brian Lane), she briefly received some press when it was announced that she had become engaged to the notorious **Screaming Lord Sutch**. The fictional story ended with Freed banning the engagement and Genevieve having to choose between love for Sutch and love for her career. No further hits were forthcoming, although she did make a cameo film appearance in *Casino Royale*.

Genies

From Long Beach, Long Island, New York, USA, the Genies comprised Roy Hammond (lead and tenor), Bill Gains (second tenor), Alexander 'Buddy' Faison (baritone) and Fred Jones (bass). Claude Johnson was added on lead shortly after the group's formation in 1956. Shad Records released 'Who's That Knockin'' in June 1958. Its eventual placing at number 71 in the **Billboard** charts (March 1959) failed adequately to reflect its enormous east coast popularity. Bill Gains eloped to Canada during a week of performances at the **Apollo** Theatre supporting the **Channels** and the **Cadillacs**, which forced the remaining members to improvise parts of their act to cover the vacated second tenor role. The theme of their debut was then reprised with 'No More Knockin'' for Hollywood Records in 1959. However, three singles for Warwick Records during 1960 and 1961, 'There Goes The Train', 'Just Like The Bluebird' and 'Crazy Feeling', failed to impress, and in truth the band members had long since gone their separate ways. Johnson enjoyed subsequent success as part of a duo with Roland Trone as **Don And Juan**. Their 'What's Your Name' single reached number 7 in the **Billboard** charts in February 1962, but they, too, were unable to build on their initial singles success.

Genitorturers

During the early 90s, sexual fetish trappings—such as rubber and leather garb and increasingly extravagant body piercings—became fashionable. It was no surprise, therefore, that a band surfaced who used elaborate sado-masochistic imagery as the basis for their act. The band in question was the Genitorturers, a Florida, USA, alternative rock band that was discovered by I.R.S. Records when they were looking for acts for a film featuring rock bands with spectacular stage shows. The film project was abandoned, but the Genitorturers secured a recording contract and recorded 1993's sadist debut, *120 Days Of Genitorture*.

The founder, vocalist and core of the band, Gen, is a statuesque dominatrix who is not only a professional body piercer but was previously employed as a transplant co-ordinator in a local hospital. She became a persuasive spokesperson for the new piercing ethos, which presented sado-masochism as not only a sexual but also a spiritual and tribal practice. This translates into an unforgettable stage show, featuring everything from whips and chains, to live nipple and genital piercing. Inevitably, the Genitorturers' striking visual aspects rather eclipse their music, which is a somewhat pedestrian blend of power metal and hardcore punk, combined with a few modern touches such as sampled dialogue. Gen's vocals are gruff and assertive, and the whole package is reminiscent of the **Plasmatics**, the punk posse of another blonde rock sex queen, Wendy 'O' Williams. Another regular in the Genitorturers line-up, Gen's husband, ex-**Morbid Angel** bass player David Vincent, who goes under the pseudonym Evil-D. Chains (b. Chuck Lenihan) played guitar with the band between 1995 and 2003, while Racci Shay was the drummer between 1997 and 2001. They were replaced by Bizz and Angel respectively.

● ALBUMS: *120 Days Of Genitorture* (EMD/I.R.S. 1993) ★★★, *Sin City* (Cleopatra/SPV 1998) ★★, *Machine Love* (Cleopatra 2000) ★★★, *X Sin City* (Zain/Big MF 2000) ★★.

● DVD/VIDEOS: *The Society Of Genitorture* (G-Spot Films 1997).

Genius

b. Gary Grice, 22 August 1966, Staten Island, New York City, USA. The Genius (aka GZA) is one of the many talents who comprise the **Wu-Tang Clan**, the chess-playing, martial arts hip-hop crew whose members include **Raekwon**, **Method Man**, **Ol' Dirty Bastard** and **RZA**, among others. The roots of the Wu-Tang Clan lay in All In Together Now, formed by Genius with his cousins RZA and Ol' Dirty Bastard. Like the majority of his compatriots he is a native of New York's Staten Island district. In common with RZA, the Genius had already recorded as a solo artist for **Cold Chillin' Records** before becoming part of the collective. However, when the Clan as a whole signed with BMG Records, provision for each member to work solo was enshrined in the contract, and the Genius used the opportunity to link with his third record company, **Geffen Records**.

The Genius' *Liquid Swords* closely mirrored the sound of the Wu-Tang Clan, built around a musical backing of stripped-down beats, with samples culled from martial arts movies and movie dialogue. This came as little surprise given that RZA, the production mastermind behind both the collective Wu-Tang Clan and several associated solo releases, was again involved in *Liquid Swords*. Lyrically, Genius continued to concentrate on down-at-heel scenarios concerning blue-collar crime and drug smuggling, epitomized by the chilling true story tale of 'Killah Hills 10304'. Following the Wu-Tang Clan's disappointing second album, 1997's *Wu-Tang Forever*, Genius began work on *Beneath The Surface*. Released in June 1999, album tracks such as 'Publicity' and 'Victim' served as a timely reminder of Genius' striking lyrical talent.

● ALBUMS: *Words From The Genius* (Cold Chillin' 1991) ★★★, *Liquid Swords* (Geffen 1995) ★★★★, *Beneath The Surface* (MCA 1999) ★★★, *Legend Of The Liquid Sword* (MCA 2002) ★★★.

● FILMS: *Wu-Tang* (1998), *Coffee And Cigarettes* (2003).

Gennaro, Peter

b. 23 November 1919, Metairie, Louisiana, USA, d. 28 September 2000, New York City, USA. A talented dancer, Gennaro performed in the chorus for several Broadway shows of the late 40s and early 50s, among them *Make Mine Manhattan*, *Kiss Me, Kate* (both 1948), *Guys*

And Dolls (1950), **The Pajama Game** (1954), and **Bells Are Ringing** (1956), having features in the latter two. By this time he had begun to establish his credentials as a choreographer and in this capacity worked on *Seventh Heaven* (1955), but it was as co-choreographer with **Jerome Robbins** on **West Side Story** (1957) that he really broke through. The verve and vitality of the dancing in *West Side Story* was reflected in Gennaro's choreography for **Fiorello!** (1959) and **The Unsinkable Molly Brown** (1960); the routines from the latter being reprised in the 1964 film version. Over the years, Gennaro was also responsible for many of the routines performed by the Radio City Music Hall Rockettes.

In the 60s and early 70s, Gennaro worked on some lesser musicals, including *Mr. President* (1962), *Bajour* (1964) and *Jimmy* (1973). Also in 1973 he worked on **Irene** with **Debbie Reynolds**, who had starred in the film version of *The Unsinkable Molly Brown*, with Gennaro's choreography being singled out for special praise. Later in the 70s, Gennaro's notices were even better owing to his work on **Annie** (1977). That year he also worked on an unsuccessful revival of **Little Me**. Other late 70s and early 80s shows included **Bar Mitzvah Boy** (1978) in London, *Carmelina* (1979), **Singin' In The Rain** (1983), which was also in London, and the 1989 New York revival of **The Threepenny Opera**, which proved to be his last Broadway show.

● FILMS: *The Pajama Game* (1957).

Gentle Giant

Formed in 1969 by the Shulman brothers; Derek (b. 11 February 1947, Glasgow, Scotland; vocals, guitar, bass), Ray (b. 3 December 1949, Portsmouth, Hampshire, England; vocals,bass,violin) and Phil (b. 27 August 1937, Glasgow, Scotland; saxophone), on the collapse of their previous group, **Simon Dupree And The Big Sound**. Kerry Minnear (b. 2 January 1948, Shaftesbury, Dorset, England; keyboards/vocals), Gary Green (b. 20 November 1950, Muswell Hill, London, England; guitar/vocals) and Martin Smith (drums) completed the first Gentle Giant line-up, which eschewed the pop/soul leanings of its predecessor for an experimental, progressive style reminiscent of **Yes** and **King Crimson**. The sextet was signed to the renowned **Vertigo Records** in 1970 and, teamed with producer **Tony Visconti**, completed a debut album that offered all the hallmarks of their subsequent recordings. This ambitious set blended hard rock and classics with an adventurous use of complex chord changes that, if not commercially successful, indicated a quest for both excellence and originality. Although deemed pretentious by many commentators, there was no denying the ambition and individuality this release introduced.

Smith left the line-up following *Acquiring The Taste*, but although his replacement, Malcolm Mortimore, appeared on *Three Friends*, a motorcycle accident forced the newcomer's departure. John 'Pugwash' Weathers (b. 2 February 1947, Carmarthen, Glamorganshire, Wales), veteran of **Eyes Of Blue**, **Graham Bond** and **Piblokto!**, joined Gentle Giant for *Octopus*, arguably their best-known release. However, an attendant tour ended with the departure of Phil, who retired from music altogether. The group then switched outlets to WWA, but encountered problems in America when *In A Glass House* was deemed too uncommercial for release there. *The Power And The Glory* proved less daunting and in turn engendered a new recording contract with **Chrysalis Records**. The ensuing *Free Hand* became Gentle Giant's bestselling UK

album, but this ascendancy faltered when *In'terview* invoked the experimental style of earlier releases. A double set, *Playing The Fool*, confirmed the quintet's in-concert dexterity, but subsequent albums unsuccessfully courted an AOR audience. *Civilian* was a conscious attempt at regaining former glories, but the departure of Minnear, by this point the band's musical director, signalled their demise. Gentle Giant split up in 1980 and several former members have pursued low-key careers. Ray Shulman has become a highly successful producer, working with such diverse acts as the **Sugarcubes**, the **Sundays** and **Ian McCulloch**. Brother Derek moved to New York to become director of A&R at **PolyGram Records**.

● ALBUMS: *Gentle Giant* (Vertigo 1970) ★★★, *Acquiring The Taste* (Vertigo 1971) ★★★, *Three Friends* (Vertigo 1972) ★★★, *Octopus* (Vertigo 1973) ★★, *In A Glass House* (WWA 1973) ★★, *The Power And The Glory* (WWA 1974) ★★, *Free Hand* (Chrysalis 1975) ★★★, *In'terview* (Chrysalis 1976) ★★★, *The Official 'Live' Gentle Giant (Playing The Fool)* (Chrysalis 1977) ★★★, *The Missing Piece* (Chrysalis 1977) ★★, *Giant For A Day* (Chrysalis 1978) ★★, *Civilian* (Chrysalis 1980) ★★, *Live-Playing The Fool* (Essential 1989) ★★, *Live On The King Biscuit Flower Hour* recorded 1975 (King Biscuit Flower Hour 1998) ★★★, *In A Palesport House* 1973 live recording (Glasshouse 2001) ★★, *1975 Santa Monica* (Glasshouse 2005) ★★.

● COMPILATIONS: *Giant Steps (The First Five Years)* (Vertigo 1975) ★★★, *Pretentious (For The Sake Of It)* (Vertigo 1977) ★★, *Greatest Hits* (Vertigo 1981) ★★★, *In Concert* (Windsong 1995) ★★, *Out Of The Woods: The BBC Sessions* (Band Of Joy 1996) ★★, *Out Of The Fire: The BBC Concerts* 1973, 1978 recordings (Hux 1998) ★★, *Totally Out Of The Woods: The BBC Sessions* (Hux 2000) ★★, *Way Of Life* (Snapper 2003) ★★, *Scraping The Barrel* 4-CD box set (Alucard 2005) ★★★.

Gentle Soul

Based in Los Angeles, California, USA, this act revolved around former folk-singing duo Pamela Polland and Rick Stanley. Polland had been active in the city's mid-60s acoustic circuit and was briefly a member of a trio completed by **Ry Cooder** and **Taj Mahal**. The latter pair subsequently formed the **Rising Sons**, who recorded one of Polland's compositions, 'Tulsa County'. This memorable country rock song was later covered by **Jesse Davis** and the **Byrds**. Stanley (guitar/vocals), a native of Boston, Massachusetts, performed as a solo act before joining Polland. They took the name Gentle Soul upon the arrival of Riley Wyldflower (rhythm guitar) and Sandy Konikoff (drums). The quartet secured a recording contract with **Columbia Records** in 1967, making their debut with 'Tell Me Love', a marvellous slice of flower-power styled folk rock. They produced the same sound on *Gentle Soul*, an album now seen as an excellent example of Californian 60s pop. Polland subsequently embarked on a solo career, releasing *Pamela Polland* in 1969, while Koikoff later played with **Joe Cocker**.

● ALBUMS: *Gentle Soul* (Columbia 1968) ★★★★.

Gentle Waves

The late 90s saw a few members of the Scottish indie outfit **Belle And Sebastian** launch side-projects, with cellist Isobel Campbell forming Gentle Waves. Campbell handled a wider variety of instruments with Gentle Waves, but enlisted most of her long-time Belle And Sebastian bandmates to lend a hand with the recording of her debut under the Gentle Waves moniker, *Green Fields Of Foreverland*. Instead of signing a contract and then recording an album, Campbell and her friends recorded *Green Fields Of Foreverland* first (over a mere seven days during 1998), before linking up with the Jeepster label, who issued the album a year later. Instead of taking a significant musical detour away from Belle And Sebastian, Gentle Waves proved to be quite similar in style to her full-time band. After a supporting tour wrapped up in the middle of 1999 (with various members of Belle And Sebastian joining Campbell on stage), Campbell went directly back into the studio to work on Gentle Waves' second album, *Swangsong For You*. She finally left Belle And Sebastian in 2002, and made her solo debut the following year with the underwhelming *Amorino*.

● ALBUMS: *Green Fields Of Foreverland* (Jeepster 1999) ★★★★, *Swangsong For You* (Jeepster 2000) ★★★.

Gentle, Johnny

b. John Askew, 1941, Liverpool, England. Askew was a merchant seaman who sang as a semi-professional before he was spotted and rechristened by the celebrated 50s svengali, **Larry Parnes**. Beginning with 1959's 'Boys And Girls Were Meant For Each Other' on **Philips Records**, this square-jawed hunk's singles all missed the UK chart, but he was often seen on British television pop series such as *Oh Boy* and *Drumbeat* and was, therefore, guaranteed a period of well-paid one-nighters. His backing groups for these included fellow Merseysiders the **Beatles** and Cass And The Cassanovas with entertainments that embraced mutually familiar rock 'n' roll standards and the simpler sides of Gentle's singles, such as the self-penned 'Wendy'. Without a recording contract in 1963, Gentle replaced **Gordon Mills** in the **Viscounts** before retiring from showbusiness by the mid-60s.

Gentlemen Marry Brunettes

(see *Gentlemen Prefer Blondes*)

Gentlemen Prefer Blondes (film musical)

Carol Channing really started something in 1949 when she created the role of diamond-loving Lorelei Lee in the hit Broadway musical *Gentlemen Prefer Blondes*. Ever since then—even into the early 90s—actresses all over the world have endeavoured to purvey the right mixture of sexiness and vulnerability that was Lorelei, and one of them who achieved it, in this 1953 screen version, was **Marilyn Monroe**. The concept started with Anita Loos' novel, which she turned into a stage show with the help of Joseph Fields. Charles Lederer's screenplay followed the same familiar path: thoroughly modern 20s girls Lorelei and her best friend, Dorothy Shaw (**Jane Russell**), travel to Paris with the intention of improving Lorelei's finances and Dorothy's marriage prospects. After causing a certain amount of havoc among the city's male population, they return to New York having accomplished their aims (and celebrate with a double wedding). The supporting cast was exceptionally fine, and included Charles Coburn, Tommy Noonan, Elliot Reid, Taylor Holmes, Norma Varden, Steven Geray, the seven-year-old 'frog-voiced' George Winslow, and the 20-year-old George (*West Side Story*) Chakiris. Only three of **Jule Styne** and **Leo Robin**'s songs survived from the original show: the

delicious 'Diamonds Are A Girl's Best Friend' (Monroe), 'A Little Girl From Little Rock'—or rather, 'Two Little Girls From Little Rock' (Monroe-Russell)—and 'Bye, Bye Baby'. **Hoagy Carmichael** and **Harold Adamson** contributed two more: 'Ain't There Anyone Here For Love?', Jane Russell's touching plea to a gymnasium full of muscular males, and the reflective 'When Love Goes Wrong' (Monroe-Russell). The whole affair was a delight, with both Monroe and Russell, who were essentially very different in style, giving marvellous performances. **Jack Cole** designed the spirited choreography, and the director was Howard Hawks. Sol C. Seigel produced the film in Technicolor for 20th Century Fox. A sequel, *Gentlemen Marry Brunettes*, was released in 1955. Jeanne Crain replaced Marilyn Monroe and played Jane Russell's sister in a lacklustre, pale shadow of the original, which, apart from the title song by Herbert Spencer and Earle Hagen, featured a score comprising old standards.

Gentlemen Prefer Blondes (stage musical)

This show opened at the Ziegfeld Theatre in New York on 8 December 1949, but the story immediately transported audiences back to the roaring 20s. Working on the basis that 'there's gold in them thar tycoons', Lorelei Lee (**Carol Channing**), has got herself engaged to Gus Esmond (Jack McCauley), who has made a fortune out of buttons. At midnight, she bids him a tearful farewell on the dockside (He: 'I'll be in my room alone every post meridian'/She: 'And I'll be with my diary and that book by Mr. Gideon') as she sails with her best chum, Dorothy Shaw (Yvonne Adair), on the Ile de France. When she hits Paris, her pursuit of a lifestyle to which she would dearly like to become accustomed, involves a zipper tycoon, Josephus Gage (George S. Irving), and sundry other potential gold-mines, such as Sir Francis Beekman (Rex Evans), as she takes in most of the glamorous sights of the city. As befits 'A Little Girl From Little Rock', she eventually returns home to marry her Mr. Esmond, and Dorothy also finds her happiness in America, with Philadelphian Henry Spofford (Eric Brotherson). The book, by Anita Loos and Joseph Fields, from Anita Loos' novel was charming and funny. Channing had appeared on Broadway the year before in the revue *Lend An Ear*, but *Gentleman Prefer Blondes* rocketed her to stardom in the space of just a few weeks. The score, by **Jule Styne** (music) and **Leo Robin** (lyrics), was full of good songs. As well as the tender 'Bye, Bye Baby' (with McCauley), 'It's Delightful Down In Chile' (with Evans), and two numbers with the ensemble, 'Homesick Blues' and 'Gentlemen Prefer Blondes', Channing also had 'I'm Just A Little Girl From Little Rock' and the marvellous 'Diamonds Are A Girl's Best Friend' ('He's your guy when stocks go high/But beware when they start to descend/It's then that those louses go back to their spouses/Diamonds are a girl's best friend'). The rest of the songs included 'I Love What I'm Doing', 'Just A Kiss Apart', 'You Say You Care', 'I'm A'Tingle, I'm Aglow', 'Mamie Is Mimi', and 'It's High Time'. The show was a great success and ran on Broadway for 740 performances.

A film version of *Gentlemen Prefer Blondes* with extra songs by **Hoagy Carmichael** and **Harold Adamson**, and starring **Marilyn Monroe** and Jane Russell, was released in 1953, and there was a sequel, *Gentlemen Marry Brunettes*, two years later. For some reason, the show was not presented in London until 1962 when **Dora Bryan** played Lorelei during a run of 223 performances. In 1974, Carol Channing starred on

Broadway in the musical, *Lorelei*, which was sub-titled 'Gentlemen Still Prefer Blondes', retained some of the best features of the 1949 original, and incorporated a prologue and an epilogue in which Lorelei appeared as an older woman. The revised book was by Kenny Solms and Gail Parent, and Jule Styne contributed some new songs with lyrics by **Betty Comden** and **Adolph Green**. The show enjoyed a run of 320 performances. In April 1995, a revival of the original *Gentlemen Prefer Blondes*, presented by Tony Randall's National Actors Theater in association with the Goodspeed Opera House, opened on Broadway. It starred cabaret singer **K.T. Sullivan** (Lorelei), Karen Prunzik (Dorothy), Allen Fitzpatrick (Gus), Henry (George Dvorsky), Jamie Ross (Josephus), and David Ponting (Sir Francis). As usual, the score was juggled around quite a bit, and there was one interpolation, the lovely 'A Ride On A Rainbow' which Styne and Robin wrote for a 1957 NBC musical of *Ruggles Of Red Gap*. It later received a memorable treatment on *Lena Horne At The Sands*. London audiences saw Lorelei and her pals again at the Open Air Theatre, Regent's Park in 1998. The gold-digging, not-so-dumb flapper was played by Sara Crowe, with Debby Bishop as Dorothy ('giving a master class in laid-back teasing raunchiness'), and Clive Rowe (Gus).

Gentry, Bobbie

b. Roberta Lee Streeter, 27 July 1944, Chickasaw County, Mississippi, USA. Gentry, of Portuguese descent, was raised on a poverty-stricken farm in Greenwood, Mississippi, and was interested in music from an early age. She wrote her first song at the age of seven ('My Dog Sergeant Is A Good Dog') and learned piano—black keys only!—guitar, banjo and vibes. By her teens, she was performing regularly and took her stage name from the movie *Ruby Gentry*. After studying both philosophy and music, she was signed to **Capitol Records** and recorded 'Mississippi Delta' for an a-side. To her own guitar accompaniment, Gentry recorded for the b-side one of her own songs, 'Ode To Billie Joe', in 30 minutes. Violins and cellos were added, the song was reduced from its original seven minutes, and, as a result of disc jockeys' reactions, it became a-side. Despite competition from **Lee Hazlewood**, Gentry's version topped the US charts for four weeks and reached number 13 in the UK. Capitol's truncated version added to the song's mystery: what did Billie Joe and his girlfriend throw off the Tallahatchie Bridge and why did Billie Joe commit suicide? The song's main thrust, however, was the callousness of the girl's family regarding the event, and it can be twinned with **Jeannie C. Riley**'s subsequent story song, 'Harper Valley PTA'.

Gentry became a regular headliner in Las Vegas and she married Bill Harrah, the manager of the Desert Inn Hotel (Gentry's second marriage, in 1978, was to singer-songwriter **Jim Stafford**). Gentry made an easy listening album with **Glen Campbell**, which included successful revivals of the **Everly Brothers** hits 'Let It Be Me' (US Top 40) and 'All I Have To Do Is Dream' (US Top 30/UK number 3). Gentry, with good looks similar to Priscilla Presley, was given her own UK television series, *The Bobbie Gentry Show*, which helped her to top the charts in 1969 with the **Burt Bacharach** and **Hal David** song from *Promises, Promises*, 'I'll Never Fall In Love Again'. The 1976 movie *Ode To Billy Joe* [*sic*], starred Robby Benson and Glynnis O'Connor, and had Billy Joe throw his girlfriend's rag doll over the bridge and commit suicide

because of a homosexual affair. Gentry herself retired from performing to devote time to her business interests.

● ALBUMS: *Ode To Billie Joe* (Capitol 1967) ★★★, *Delta Sweetie* (Columbia 1968) ★★★, *Bobbie Gentry And Glen Campbell* (Capitol 1968) ★★★, *Touch 'Em With Love* (Capitol 1969) ★★★, *I'll Never Fall In Love Again* (Capitol 1970) ★★★, *Fancy* (Capitol 1970) ★★, *Patchwork* (Capitol 1971) ★★★, *Sittin' Pretty/Tobacco Road* (Capitol 1971) ★★.

● COMPILATIONS: *Bobby Gentry's Greatest* (Capitol 1969) ★★★, *Greatest Hits* (Curb 1990) ★★★, *The Best Of* (Music For Pleasure 1994) ★★★, *Ode To Bobbie Gentry: The Capitol Years* (Capitol 2000) ★★★, *An American Quilt 1967–1974* (Raven 2003) ★★★, *Chickasaw County Child* (Shout! Factory 2004) ★★★.

Gentry, Chuck

b. Charles T. Gentry, 14 December 1911, Belgrade, Nebraska, USA, d. 1988. Starting out on clarinet, Gentry later mastered most of the saxophone family, specializing on the baritone. He began playing professionally in his mid-20s and in 1939 joined **Vido Musso**'s big band, which soon folded; by the following year both Gentry and his former boss were working for **Harry James**. A year later the two men were still together, but this time with **Benny Goodman**. After a spell with **Jimmy Dorsey**, Gentry was drafted into the army and, following basic training, was transferred to the unit of musicians being assembled by **Glenn Miller**, where he remained until 1944. Once discharged, Gentry joined **Artie Shaw** and then returned for a second period with Goodman. By the late 40s, with most of the name big bands folding, Gentry was turning to studio work in Hollywood, which is where he spent most of the remainder of his career. He made numerous recordings in orchestras, backing artists such as **June Christy** and **Nancy Wilson** and performing with various leaders, including **Louis Armstrong**, **Pete Rugolo**, **Woody Herman** and **Benny Carter**. Occasionally he emerged from the studios to play dates with, for example, **Stan Kenton**'s Los Angeles Neophonic Orchestra and with **Bob Crosby** at Disneyland.

Gentrys

Formed in 1963 in Memphis, Tennessee, USA, the Gentrys forged their early reputation playing high school dances. The group—Larry Raspberry (vocals/guitar), Bruce Bowles (vocals), Jimmy Hart (vocals), Bobby Fisher (tenor saxophone, piano, guitar), Jimmy Johnson (trumpet/organ), Pat Neal (bass) and Larry Wall (drums)—later won the city's 'Battle Of The Bands' contest and within months had secured a recording contract with the independent Youngstown label. Their first release, 'Sometimes', was coupled with the infectious 'Keep On Dancing', an R&B track that attracted more interest than the a-side. The major label **MGM Records** picked up the national distribution rights to the single, resulting in the single reaching number 4 in the US charts, subsequently selling in excess of one million copies. The song was later covered by the **Bay City Rollers**, giving them their first chart hit in 1971. The Gentrys were unable to repeat their early success, but remained a popular live attraction throughout America's southern states. After the break-up of the group in 1970, Jimmy Hart resuscitated the Gentrys' name by forming a new line-up with Steve Speer (bass), Dave Beaver (keyboards), Jimmy Tarbutton (guitar) and Mike

Gardner (drums). This incarnation achieved some success with minor placings in the singles chart. Late-period member Rick Allen resurfaced in the **Box Tops**, while Raspberry later embarked on a solo career, leading a new group, the High-Steppers.

● ALBUMS: *Keep On Dancing* (MGM 1965) ★★★, *Time* (MGM 1966) ★★★, *The Gentrys* (Sun 1970) ★★.
● COMPILATIONS: *Gentrys* (MGM 1966) ★★★.
● FILMS: *It's A Bikini World* (1967).

Geordie

From the north-east of England, Brian Johnson (b. 5 October 1947, Newcastle, England; vocals), Victor Malcolm (guitar), Tom Hill (bass) and Brian Gibson (drums) started life as a poor man's **Slade**, originally calling themselves USA before adopting the more appropriate Geordie. Their unconsciously professional style was based on the pop end of the hard rock spectrum, with a stage act that included an audience participation opus, the dialectal 'Geordie's Lost His Liggy', which involved Johnson hoisting Malcolm onto his shoulders. After one single for **Regal Zonophone Records**, 'Don't Do That', scraped the hit parade, they were signed by **EMI Records**, whose faith was justified when 'All Because Of You', from 1973's *Hope You Like It*, reached the UK Top 20. Two lesser entries—'Can You Do It' and 'Electric Lady'—followed, and the group's albums sold steadily. Geordie's power as a concert attraction outlasted this chart run, and when the going became difficult in the watershed year of 1976–77, the quartet signed off with *Save The World*—a consolidation rather than development of their derivative music. They were remembered not for their hits, but as the *alma mater* of Johnson who, after a lean period in which he was heard in a vacuum cleaner commercial, replaced the late Bon Scott in **AC/DC**. His former bandmates reunited in 1982 to record *No Sweat*, before changing their name to Powerhouse.

● ALBUMS: *Hope You Like It* (EMI 1973) ★★★, *Don't Be Fooled By The Name* (EMI 1974) ★★★, *Save The World* (EMI 1976) ★★★, *No Sweat* (Neat 1982) ★★★.
● COMPILATIONS: *Featuring Brian Johnson* (Red Bus 1981) ★★, *The Singles Collection* (7T's 2001) ★★★.

George M!

A celebratory musical about the life of the multi-talented **George M. Cohan** (singer-dancer-author-director and more) detailing his early days in vaudeville, through his ups and downs, to his final Broadway triumph when he portrayed President Franklin D. Roosevelt in *I'd Rather Be Right* in 1937. With a book by Michael Stewart, and John and Fran Pascal, *George M!* opened at the Palace Theatre in New York on 10 April 1968. After his triumph as the MC in *Cabaret* two years earlier, **Joel Grey** strutted his stuff somewhat in the manner of Cohan, but did not go for a precise impersonation as **James Cagney** did in the 1942 film, *Yankee Doodle Dandy*. Most of the songs associated with the master showman—all the flag-waving favourites—were included, many of which he wrote himself, such as 'Yankee Doodle Dandy', 'So Long, Mary', 'Forty-Five Minutes From Broadway', 'Harrigan', 'Over There', 'Mary's A Grand Old Name', 'You're A Grand Old Flag', and 'Give My Regards To Broadway'. The show also featured the future Broadway star, **Bernadette Peters**, in the relatively minor role of Cohan's sister. She made a sufficiently strong impression to be awarded a Theatre

World Citation for her performance. These compilation shows are not everyone's idea of what the musical theatre should be all about, but they can be entertaining, and this one, which ran for 427 performances—over a year—was cited by a US critic as 'The one flicker of light in a drab Broadway season.'

George White's Scandals
(see **White, George**)

George, Barbara

b. 16 August 1942, New Orleans, Louisiana, USA. Barbara George is best remembered for her 1961 R&B number 1 hit 'I Know (You Don't Love Me No More)', released on the small AFO (All For One) label. George was discovered by **Jessie Hill**, another New Orleans R&B artist, himself known for the hit 'Ooh Poo Pah Doo'. Hill brought George to AFO, where label head **Harold Battiste** at first did not see much potential in the girl. They recorded 'I Know' in spite of this, and it was heard by Sue Records owner Juggy Murray, who agreed to distribute the record. 'I Know' not only reached the top of the R&B chart, but was an enormous success in the US pop charts. George was unable to follow her hit with any other significant records, however, and by the end of the 60s she had retired from music, although she made a brief return in the early 80s.

● ALBUMS: *I Know (You Don't Love Me Anymore)* (AFO 1962) ★★★.

George, Fatty

b. Franz Georg Pressler, 24 April 1927, Vienna, Austria, d. 29 March 1982. In his early teens he began playing alto saxophone, later studying this and clarinet formally. At 20 George played bop, working in Austria and Germany, often leading his own band, continuing into the mid-50s when he opened a jazz club in Vienna. Among the sidemen in his bands was **Joe Zawinul**, who played in the Two Sounds band, a group that enjoyed a varied repertoire including bop and traditional jazz. He continued to run clubs in Vienna but spent part of the mid-60s playing in Berlin. He led bands regularly on radio and television in Austria. A gifted and hugely enthusiastic character, George moved smoothly between different styles of jazz, usually playing clarinet in traditional and mainstream swing-based settings and alto in more contemporary mode. On both instruments he revealed a smooth lyricism and was always harmonically interesting.

● ALBUMS: *Fatty 69* (Preiser 1969) ★★★.
● COMPILATIONS: *The Complete Fatty George* (Rst 1996) ★★★.

George, Karl

b. Karl Curtis George, 26 April 1913, St. Louis, Missouri, USA. Among George's early engagements was one in the early 30s, when he played trumpet with **McKinney's Cotton Pickers**. He also worked with the **Jeter-Pillars** territory band, then, in 1939, joined the highly musical if unfortunately short-lived **Teddy Wilson** orchestra. After a spell with **Lionel Hampton**'s first big band he served in the military during World War II. Immediately following the war, he played with several big bands on the west coast, including **Stan Kenton** and **Benny Carter**, and also played with small groups on recording sessions, including one led by **Lucky Thompson**. He occasionally formed bands for club and recording sessions, often employing first-rate sidemen such as **J.J. Johnson** and **Buddy Tate**. By the 50s poor health had driven him into retirement in his home town. Usually restricted to section work, George could play interesting solo lines, as he demonstrated with the Wilson band, often displaying a liking for the kind of linear, single-note solo adopted by **Harry Edison**. His truncated career severely limited the opportunities for him to develop.

George, Lowell
(see **Little Feat**)

George, Robin
The style of UK-born guitarist/producer Robin George, despite his geographical origins, is pure US AOR. George began his career with his band Life, who released one single, 'Too Late'. The line-up also included Dave Holland (later of **Judas Priest**) and Mark Stanway (later of **Magnum**). He then played guitar in the Byron Band, fronted by one-time **Uriah Heep** vocalist David Byron. His fine guitar work can be heard to good effect on their debut album, *On The Rocks* (Creole Records), in 1981, though after a year with them he left to pursue a solo career. He first signed to **Arista Records** in 1983, cementing the relationship with the release of a single, 'Go Down Fighting', the melodic guitar work of which quickly brought attention and a reputation as the UK's answer to **Billy Squier**. Despite this, Arista dropped him, and he went on to work in a production capacity with Heavy Metal Records, helping various acts including **Wrathchild** (UK). In 1984 **Bronze Records** signed him, and the release of 'Heartline' preceded his first full album, *Dangerous Music*—both releases were noted for their pristine production and the bass work of Pino Pallidino (**Paul Young** Band). Despite the good auspices, 'Heartline' remained his only real success and was reissued in 1985, again selling well. He remained in production until 1990 when he formed a partnership with ex–**Diamond Head** vocalist Sean Harris in **Notorious**. This was an ill-fated project that advanced neither career, and they soon parted. George has since returned to the mixing desk.
- ALBUMS: *Dangerous Music* (Bronze 1984) ★★★.
- DVD/VIDEOS: *Dangerous Music* (Bronze 1985).

George, Sophia
b. Jamaica, West Indies. In 1985 the reggae media were printing laudatory articles about a pre-release from Jamaica produced by Sangie Davis, entitled 'Girlie Girlie'. The song was a tale about a philandering juvenile manipulating the opposite sex. By December, the record was released in the UK and crossed over into the pop chart, peaking at number 7. George's appearance on the UK chart show *Top Of The Pops* was commended because she actually performed the song live. While in the UK she embarked on a tour, where her performances included a cover version of **Dire Straits'** 'Walk Of Life'. In 1986 her follow-up, 'Lazy Body', originally a hit for **Echo Minott**, made a minor impression in the pop charts and proved a favourable hit within the reggae market. The single was released as a double a-side with the carefully crafted 'Can't Live Without You', which demonstrated her fine vocals. In 1987 George recorded 'Final Decision' with producer Willie Lindo, a warning to domineering males emulating the dancehall style of her debut. Other notable recordings included 'Aint No Meaning' with DJ **Charlie Chaplin**, 'It Burn Me Belly' and 'Maga Dog', loosely based around

the **Peter Tosh** classic. Between her extensive touring, which included the 1989 Reggae Sunsplash Festival and supporting **Yellowman** on his 1990 US concerts, George returned to the recording studio with producer **HomeT** and the Two Friends crew to cut *For Everyone*. George continued to record for the Pow Wow label during the 90s without ever coming close to matching the impact of her greatest hit.
- ALBUMS: *Fresh* (Winner 1987) ★★, *For Everyone* (Pow Wow 1989) ★★★, *Stepping Out* (Pow Wow 1994) ★★.
- COMPILATIONS: *Girlie Girlie: The Best Of Sophia George* (Trojan 2004) ★★★.

Georgia Crackers
A close harmony singing group sometimes also referred to as the Newman Brothers. It originally comprised Hank (b. Henry J. Newman, 3 April 1905, d. July 1978, Cochran, Georgia, USA; guitar, string bass, vocals), Slim (b. Marion Alonzo Newman, 18 June 1910, d. 1 October 1982, Cochran, Georgia, USA; guitar/vocals) and Bob (b. Robert Newman, 16 October 1915, d. 8 October 1979, Cochran, Georgia, USA; songwriter, string bass, guitar, vocals). Hank worked first as a solo singer on WCOC Meridian, Mississippi, before joining KWKH Shreveport. After being joined by brother Slim and singing mainly popular ballads, they toured and worked on radio in several places, including WRDW Augusta and WTAM Cleveland, where they replaced **Gid Tanner**, when he decided to return to Georgia. In 1931, they settled in Columbus, Ohio, where they found sponsors for their daily programme on WAIU. (The station later changed to WHKC and eventually WTVN). Their popularity soon saw them appearing on several other stations in different states including WROW Atlanta, WBT Charlotte, WWVA Wheeling, and Reading, Pennsylvania. In 1934, at Charlotte, they recorded for **Vocalion Records**, the records being released as Hank And Slim. In 1935, Bob, who also wrote many of their songs, began playing bass with his brothers. Soon after, other musicians saw the act become a band. Some others to play with the brothers during the late 30s include fiddlers **Shorty Long**, Clarence 'Curly' Herdman (1918–1968) and Winnie Waters, guitarist Jerry Langston and Hawaiian and Spanish guitarist Harold Snyder. Dressed in cowboy clothes, playing mainly in a western swing style and singing in the style of the **Sons Of The Pioneers**, they became known as the Georgia Crackers. In 1940, the band comprised the three Newmans, Waters and Snyder and were featured on WHKC Columbus and the Mutual Network radio. In 1941, they disbanded when Slim and Bob were drafted for military service. Hank moved to California, where he became the manager of film actor **Smiley Burnette** (He also played a small part in *Red River Valley*).
After the war, the brothers and Johnny Spies (accordion) re-formed the band. In the late 40s, they spent time in California, where they appeared as a band in several of Charles Starrett's (Durango Kid) B-Westerns. Their films included *The Fighting Frontiersman* (1946), *South Of The Chisholm Trail* (1947), *Desert Vigilante* (1949) and *Old Trail*. They also presented a regular evening show on KXLA Pasadena. They recorded for **RCA Victor Records** in 1947 and 1949, and Slim also recorded four solo sides for Black And White Records with a group billed as Cactus Andy And The Texas Dandies (actually **Tex Williams'** band). Between 1950 and 1958, they were joined by Allan Myers (lead guitar), and were resident in Columbus, where, sometimes including

singer Janie Swetman, they broadcast a daily programme on WHKC that was carried by the Mutual And National Broadcast Networks. They also established The G Bar C Ranch, a country music park near Columbus, where they presented shows. They toured in the state and recorded numerous transcription disks, which enabled them to meet their radio commitments during the time they were touring. In the late 50s, Bob also made more than 20 solo recordings for King. (Some were reissued on *Hangover Boogie*, a 1984 release by the German **Bear Family Records** label).

He continued to write songs but, in 1958, his health deteriorated and he relocated to the warmer climate of Arizona, where he worked as a disc jockey on, and later became programme controller of, KHAT Phoenix. (Bob died in 1979.) In 1958, they made their final recordings for Robin, and after Bob's departure, they disbanded. In the late 60s, they briefly reunited to record an album for Hank's G Bar C label, which sold locally. In the early 70s, the brothers re-formed to make special reunion shows including appearing with **Ernest Tubb**. Hank and Slim remained in Columbus until their deaths, after which their wives continued to run the restaurant at 2882 Johnstown Road in Columbus that they had opened in 1954. The restaurant became a place of special interest for country music fans. It should also be mentioned that the Georgia Crackers were one of the few southern country acts to play most of their successful years in the north.

● COMPILATIONS: *The Georgia Crackers* 40s radio recordings (Jewel 1972) ★★★★.

Georgia Satellites

This rock quartet was formed as the Hellhounds in 1980 in Atlanta, USA, when **Dan Baird** (b. Daniel John Baird, 12 December 1953, San Diego, California, USA; vocals) and Rick Richards (guitar) started jamming together inspired by the **Rolling Stones**, the **Kinks** and the **Pretty Things**. Rick Price (bass) and Mauro Magellan (drums) completed the band. Magellan was the only one of the four not to originate in the Deep South, hailing from Miami. After a small-budget independent EP, they signed to **Elektra Records**. Their debut album rose to number 5 in the US charts in 1987, thanks to the Top 5 success of the inspired single 'Keep Your Hands To Yourself'. They followed up with two cover versions; the Woods' 'Battleship Chains' and Chan Romero's 'Hippy Hippy Shake' (featured on the soundtrack of the Tom Cruise movie *Cocktail*). One of their heroes, **Ian McLagan** of the **Small Faces**, later joined them for *In The Land Of Salvation And Sin*, following which Baird left to start a solo career. The rest of the band went their separate ways shortly afterwards, although Richards and Price re-formed the Georgia Satellites in 1996, recruiting Billy Pitts (drums) and Joey Huffman (keyboards) to help record *Shaken Not Stirred*. Richards and Price continue to play together as the Hellhounds in addition to their commitments to the Georgia Satellites.

● ALBUMS: *Keep The Faith* mini-album (Making Waves 1985) ★★★, *Georgia Satellites* (Elektra 1986) ★★★★, *Open All Night* (Elektra 1988) ★★★, *In The Land Of Salvation And Sin* (Elektra 1989) ★★★, *Shaken Not Stirred* (CMC/3NM 1997) ★★.

● COMPILATIONS: *Let It Rock* (Elektra 1993) ★★★★, *Greatest & Latest* (Disky 2001) ★★★, *The Essentials* (Rhino 2002) ★★★★.

Georgia Tom

(see **Dorsey, Thomas A.**)

Georgio

b. Georgio Allentini, 1966, San Francisco, USA. Georgio launched his musical career in Los Angeles in 1986, when he began working as a disc jockey. He then financed the recording and release of his debut single, 'Sexappeal'. This track was picked up for release by **Motown Records**, and became a national hit, followed by a US Top 10 black music smash, 'Tina Cherry'. Both releases emphasized his debt to the music of **Prince**, whose sexual outrageousness is imitated by Georgio. This stance was maintained for later singles, 'Lover's Lane' and 'Bedrock', which also reached the US charts.

● ALBUMS: *Georgio* (Motown 1987) ★★.

Geraldine Fibbers

Carla Bozulich and her band, the Geraldine Fibbers, were frequently cited as natural inheritors of **X**'s crown, through their animation of the disillusionment and moral abandonment of contemporary Los Angeles. However, where X hinted at discordant country rock as the appropriate metaphor for the death of the old west, Geraldine Fibbers embraced this medium with less reservation. Prior to forming the band, which comprised William Tutton (bass), Kevin Fitzgerald (drums) and **Nels Cline** (guitar), who replaced Daniel Keenan in 1996 (violin player Jessy Greene also left the band in 1997), Bozulich had been the centrepiece of controversial industrial punk outfit Ethyl Meatplow. Geraldine Fibbers' debut album, *Lost Somewhere Between The Earth And My Home*, continued the theme of punk isolationism but combined it with a musical platform featuring double bass, fiddle and drums. This blend of country roots proved an excellent platform for Bozulich's feisty lyrics, especially on the more self-conscious material such as 'Dragon Lady' and 'The French Song'. The follow-up *Butch* received strong reviews, focusing again on Bozulich's twisted vision. The album also contained a brave cover version of **Can**'s 'Yoo Doo Right'.

After the demise of Geraldine Fibbers, Bozulich embarked on a predictably erratic solo career. In 2003, she recorded a spellbinding interpretation of **Willie Nelson**'s classic *Red Headed Stranger* album, even persuading the veteran country artist to play guitar on three tracks.

● ALBUMS: *Lost Somewhere Between The Earth And My Home* (Virgin 1996) ★★★, *Butch* (Virgin 1997) ★★★★.

● COMPILATIONS: *What Part Of Get Thee Gone Don't You Understand?* (Sympathy For The Record Industry 1997) ★★★.

Geraldo

b. Gerald Walcan Bright, 10 August 1904, London, England, d. 4 May 1974, Vevey, Switzerland. A child prodigy, Geraldo played piano and organ, and studied at the Royal Academy of Music in London. After leading several small groups he formed his own Light Orchestra under the name of Gerald Bright and played a five-year residency at the Hotel Majestic, St Anne's-on-Sea making his first broadcast from there. He disbanded the orchestra at the peak of its success, and toured South America to study authentic Latin-American rhythms. On his return to London in 1930 he changed his name to Geraldo, took his flamboyantly garbed Gaucho Tango

Orchestra into the Savoy Hotel and stayed there for 10 years, reputedly making over 2,000 broadcasts. Throughout his career he was extremely popular on BBC radio. His theme song, 'Hello, Again', heralded such shows as *Geraldo's Guest House, Romance In Rhythm, Milestones Of Melody, Dancing Through The Music Shop, Band Box*, and many more. He also recorded prolifically, at first for **Decca Records**, and then for an assortment of labels including **Parlophone Records**.

Soon after the orchestra's appearance in the Royal Command Performance of 1933, Geraldo changed his image and formed a conventional dance orchestra, Geraldo and His Sweet Music. At the outbreak of World War II he was appointed Supervisor of Bands for ENSA, and toured Europe, the Middle East and North Africa with his own orchestra. The 40s are generally considered to be the period in which he led his best orchestras, and are remembered on *50 Hits Of The Naughty 40s*, a double album released on Pickwick Records in the UK. All the selections are claimed to be private recordings made for Geraldo, and owned by his widow, Manja. During most of the 40s and the early 50s Geraldo's orchestra was the most prominent in the UK. The music also became somewhat jazzier, due perhaps to the inclusion in the orchestra of musicians such as **Harry Hayes**, George Evans, and **Leslie 'Jiver' Hutchinson**. In the late 30s Geraldo launched his *Sunday Night Swing Club* sessions at London's St Martin's Theatre, and in the early 40s played a 'swing' concert at London's Stoll Theatre to an enthusiastic audience of some 3,000. He made several records in the style of US big bands of the era. After the war Geraldo, besides leading his own orchestra, became engaged in band management, particularly in supplying ensembles to perform on the big Cunard ocean liners. These groups were nicknamed 'Geraldo's Navy', and included many young UK jazz musicians, eager to get to the USA and taste the exciting sounds emanating from the clubs on New York's 52nd Street. Geraldo's was the first band to play on UK's infant television service after the war, and later, after he had retired from band leading in the mid-50s, he became musical director for Scottish Television. He kept his name in the public eye by occasionally assembling a group of musicians and playing concerts in a nostalgic style, which was attracting audiences as late as 1970 at London's Royal Festival Hall.

Over the years, most of the UK's top musicians played with Geraldo's orchestra, including Andy McDevitt, **Ivor Mairants**, Nat Temple, George Evans, Harry Roche, **Ted Heath**, Max Goldberg, Alfie Noakes, Freddie Clayton, Joe Ferrie, Dougie Robinson and many others. His popular vocalists included Dorothy Carless, **Johnny Green**, Doreen Villiers, Carol Carr, **Jill Day**, **Rosemary Squires**, **Dick James**, Denny Vaughan, Bob Dale, and even, for a brief while in the early days, **Al Bowlly**. Geraldo died from a heart attack while on holiday in Switzerland. In 1993 a new Geraldo Orchestra, directed by trombonist Chris Dean, toured the UK provinces. One of the stars of the original band, drummer **Eric Delaney**, was featured prominently, along with vocalist Eleanor Keenan and Russell Stone.

● COMPILATIONS: *Geraldo And His Orchestra* (World 1974) ★★★, *Hello Again . . . Again* (Transatlantic 1976) ★★★, *50 Hits Of The Naughty 40s* (Pickwick 1977) ★★★, *Gerry's Music Shop* (Decca 1980) ★★★, *Heart And Soul* (HMV 1983) ★★★, with the Gaucho Tango Orchestra *Jealousy* (Parlophone 1983) ★★★, *The Golden Age Of Geraldo* (EMI 1986) ★★★★, *The Man And His Music* (EMI 1992) ★★★, *The Dance Band Years* (Pulse 1997) ★★★.

Gerard, Danyel

b. 7 March 1939, Paris, France. Gerard spent much of his childhood in South America but he was a Parisian student when taken under the wing of Lucien Morisse, a Gallic equivalent of UK svengali **Larry Parnes**. Gerard's debut single, a 1958 adaptation (in French) of the nursery rhyme 'Billy Boy', can be cited as the country's first original attempt at rock 'n' roll. Its singer's continued commercial prosperity was stifled by national service in Great Kubylie. During this two-year absence, he was overtaken by **Johnny Hallyday**, Eddy Mitchell and other newer icons. Demobbed, he regained lost ground with 'La Leçon De Twist' and a translation of **Pat Boone**'s 'Speedy Gonzales'. The adoration of his female fans might have palled when he became engaged to chanteuse Christine LeBail, as his subsequent cover version of **Ben E. King**'s 'I (Who Have Nothing)' followed by 'Il Pleut Dans Ma Maison' and 'D'Accord D'Accord' were only moderate hits. Nevertheless, self-managed by that point, he ploughed back his earnings into a lucrative production company, and forged a second career as a songwriter, with **Marie LaForet**'s 'Les Vendanges De L'Amour' and Herve Villand's 'Mourir Ou Vivre' being among his successes.

Gerardo

b. Gerardo Mejía III, 16 April 1965, Guayaquil, Ecuador. This Latin rapper based his career in Los Angeles following his move to Glendale, California, USA, at the age of 12. From the outset of his career Gerardo has specialized in both Spanish and English rhymes, though it is his athleticism in jumping between the two languages that has most distinguished him. In 1985 he won two separate televised street-dance competitions, leading to roles in the movies *Colors*, playing a gang leader, and *Can't Buy Me Love*. He would enjoy his first major crossover success for Interscope Records in April 1990, with 'Rico Suave' making number 7 in the US charts. 'We Want The Funk' was also successful. His debut album, released the following year, included an appearance by 'rap grandfather' **George Clinton**. The title of this collection, *Mo' Ritmo*, translates as 'more rhythm'. Notorious for taking the stage bare-chested and with his zip undone to tantalize his female followers, Gerardo enjoyed a short period of popularity as an **MTV** star but ultimately enjoyed more fame on the Latin dance scene. He latterly became head of A&R at Interscope's Dance division, and was instrumental in signing new artists such as **Enrique Iglesias** and **Bubba Sparxxx**. He returned to the studio in the new millennium to record *Fame, Sex Y Dinero*.

● ALBUMS: *Mo' Ritmo* (Interscope 1991) ★★★★, *Dos* (Interscope 1992) ★★★, *Asi Es* (EMI 1994) ★★, *Derrumbe* (EMI 1995) ★★★, *Fame, Sex Y Dinero* (Thump 2002) ★★★.

● FILMS: *Hot Moves* (1985), *Winners Take All* (1986), *Can't Buy Me Love* aka *Boy Rents Girl* (1987), *Colors* (1988), *Sundown: The Vampire In Retreat* (1989), *Sheer Bliss* (2001).

Geremia, Paul

b. 21 April 1944, Providence, Rhode Island, USA. Like his contemporary **Roy Book Binder**, Geremia has spent a long and fruitful career out of the spotlight, playing the college circuit, small clubs and folk festivals. He was initially influenced by folk artists and took up the harmonica before learning the guitar. Attending the 1964 **Newport Folk Festival**, he saw bluesmen such as **Sleepy John Estes, Mississippi John Hurt, Skip James** and **Robert Pete Williams**, and as a result took up blues-playing as a full-time career. While being particularly known for the authenticity of his Piedmont guitar techniques, Geremia has a comprehensive knowledge of most regional styles. His albums, mostly for smaller specialist labels, have appeared infrequently since 1968 and serve to illustrate his skill. In the 90s and into the new millennium he was more prolific, and his recent recordings are excellent examples of folk-blues played with modern recording technique and experience.

● ALBUMS: *Just Enough* (Folkways 1968) ★★★, *Paul Geremia* (Sire 1971) ★★★, *Hard Life Rockin' Chair* (Adelphi 1973) ★★★, *I Really Don't Mind Livin'* (Flying Fish 1983) ★★★, *My Kinda Place* (Flying Fish 1987) ★★★, *Gamblin' Woman Blues* (Red House 1993) ★★★, *Self-Portrait In Blues* (Shamrock 1995) ★★★, *Live From Uncle Sam's Backyard* (Red House 1997) ★★★★, *The Devil's Music* (Red House 2000) ★★★★, *Love, Murder & Mosquitos* (Red House 2004) ★★★.

Germain, Donovan

b. 7 March 1952. A producer whose involvement in 80s and 90s reggae music helped to define and popularize the format, Germain started in the business with a record shop in New York, and he began producing his own work in 1972. From the outset his style was characterized by its dignified, musical approach, and Germain soon proved that he could make **lovers rock** as adeptly as 'roots' records—his 'Mr Boss Man' with Cultural Roots was a huge underground hit in 1980. He made the UK national Top 20 in 1986 with **Audrey Hall**'s 'One Dance Won't Do'. Strangely enough, the song was an answer version to **Beres Hammond**'s 'What One Dance Can Do', which was not a hit outside of the reggae sphere. He had many more hits throughout the 80s, including Hall's follow-up single 'Smile'. However, everything came together towards the end of the decade when he opened his own Penthouse Studio on Slipe Road in Kingston Jamaica, West Indies, in 1987.

The quality and feel of the studio ensured that it was in constant demand for outside sessions and many classic recordings were recorded on the premises under the auspices of Germain and **Dave 'Rude Boy' Kelly**. It retains its position as one of the top Kingston studios, no mean feat in the hectic competition that abounds in this particular field. Penthouse's clean, sophisticated sound and production work has ensured the popularity of the music with a much wider audience. Germain is a modest man who always prefers to let his music do the talking. A keen student of reggae, his involvement has always been imbued with a sense of, and sympathy for, the music's history and traditions. Now recognized as one of the very top reggae producers, he has proved himself many times over, and there are few who would begrudge him the accolade. The discography lists just a small selection of the man's prolific output. All the releases demonstrate the clean, crisp sound that has become a byword for Penthouse productions, and Germain's ability to draw the best from both vocalists and DJs.

German, Edward

b. German Edward Jones, 17 February 1862, Whitchurch, Shropshire, England, d. 11 November 1936, London, England.

Greatly admired by Sir Arthur Sullivan, German carried on the tradition of British light music, paving the way for the likes of Haydn Wood and **Eric Coates**. His first important score was for a production of Shakespeare's *Richard III* in 1889. His work was noted by Henry Irving, who asked German to compose for *Henry VIII*, which he was putting on at London's Lyceum Theatre. When the production opened in 1892 German's work was highly praised, and his 'Morris Dance', 'Shepherds' Dance' and 'Torch Dance' have remained popular ever since. The same year saw his 'Gipsy Suite', followed by further success with an 1895 production of *Romeo And Juliet*, then 'Nell Gwyn' (1900), 'Merrie England' (1902), and 'Tom Jones' (1907). His two most popular songs were 'Glorious Devon' and 'The Yeomen Of England'. He was plagued with ill health, and the rest of his life was marked with occasional new works, and the advent of radio brought fresh recognition and knighthood in 1928. German was honoured in 1934 with the award of the prestigious Gold Medal of the Royal Philharmonic Society.

● ALBUMS: *British Light Music—Edward German* (Marco Polo 1992) ★★★★, *Orchestral Music* (Marco Polo 1995) ★★★★.

Germano, Lisa

b. USA. This Mishawaka, Indiana, USA native folk rocker and multi-instrumentalist first started playing piano aged seven, alongside her six other siblings, each of whom was forced to play an instrument until they were 18. Afterwards, she went on to become violinist with **John Mellencamp** and **Bob Seger**, also working as a session musician for **Billy Joel**, **Simple Minds** and **Iggy Pop**. Her 1991 debut album arrived on her own label, Major Bill, but suffered from inadequate production and distribution. Her second album was released by **Capitol Records**, and on it she added feedback, samples and tape loops to the diet of guitar and violin. It was presented in a radically different form to UK audiences by **4AD Records**, whose Ivo Watts Russell also remixed a five-track mini-album sampler, *Inconsiderate Bitch*, in January 1994. This was Germano at her most effective, with stunning arrangements of her multi-instrumental skills, including effects-driven guitar, synthesizer, piano, violin and mandolin. *Geek The Girl*, as Germano wrote in her sleeve notes, was 'the story of a girl who is confused about how to be sexual and cool in the world'. Harrowing and committed, songs such as ' . . . A Psychopath' revealed artistic positioning somewhere between **PJ Harvey** and **Tori Amos**, though Germano failed to reap a similar level of commercial reward. An excellent remix of 'Love Sick' by the **Underdog** was released in late 1997. Germano also collaborated with **Giant Sand** on their OP8 project *Slush* the same year, before completing work on the solo *Slide*.

A lengthy absence from the music scene due to her battle with alcoholism was broken by the release of her first album of the new millennium, 2003's harrowing, semi-autobiographical *Lullaby For Liquid Pig*.

● ALBUMS: *On The Way Down From The Moon Palace* (Major Bill 1991) ★★★, *Happiness* (Capitol/4AD 1993) ★★★★, *Inconsiderate Bitch* mini-album (4AD 1994) ★★★, *Geek The Girl* (4AD 1994) ★★★★, *Excerpts From A Love Circus* (4AD 1996) ★★★★, with OP8 *Slush* (V2 1997) ★★, *Slide* (4AD 1998) ★★★, *Lullaby For Liquid Pig* (Ineffable/iMusic 2003) ★★★.

Germs

This Los Angeles, California, USA–based punk band was formed in April 1977. The original members were Darby Crash (b. Jan Paul Beahm, 26 September 1958, USA, d. 7 December 1980, USA; vocals), Pat Smear (b. 5 August 1959; guitar), Lorna Doom (bass) and **Belinda Carlisle** (b. Belinda Kerzcheski, 17 August 1958, Hollywood, California, USA; drums), later of the **Go-Go's**. Carlisle soon left and was replaced by a succession of percussionists, including future **X** drummer D.J. Bonebrake and Don Bolles of 45 Grave. The band's first single, 'Forming', was issued on What? Records in 1977 and is considered by some to be the first example of the post-punk 'hardcore' genre, later popularized by bands such as **Black Flag** and the **Dead Kennedys**. Their next single was issued on Slash Records, which in 1979 released the band's only proper album, *GI*. The Germs disbanded in early 1980 but re-formed later that year. A week after their first reunion concert, however, singer Crash died of a heroin overdose. Smear later worked with **Nirvana** and the **Foo Fighters**.

The catalyst to a thousand US punk bands, though few modelled themselves on Crash's legendary self-destructive nature, the Germs were fated only ever to offer a musical flashpoint rather than a career blueprint. A tribute album was issued in 1996 featuring **White Zombie**, **Courtney Love**, the **Melvins**, **Mudhoney** and others. In September 2005, the surviving members of the Germs announced they would be playing a number of live dates with actor Shane West assuming the lead singer role.

● ALBUMS: *GI* (Slash 1979) ★★★, *Germicide: Recorded Live At The Whisky, June 1977* (ROIR 1982) ★★, *Rock N' Rule* 1979 recording (XES 1986) ★★.

● COMPILATIONS: *What We Do Is Secret* (Slash 1981) ★★, *Let The Circle Be Unbroken* (Gasatanka 1985) ★★, *Lion's Share* (Ghost O' Darb 1985) ★★, *MIA* (Slash 1994) ★★, *The Complete Anthology* (Slash/Rhino 2001) ★★★.

● FURTHER READING: *Lexicon Devil: The Fast Times And Short Life Of Darby Crash And The Germs*, Brenan Mullen with Don Bolles and Adam Parfrey.

Geronimo Black

Geronimo Black was formed in the USA in 1970 by Jimmy Carl Black (drums/vocals) and Bunk Gardner (saxophone/flute), two ex-members of the **Mothers Of Invention**. Former **Love** saxophonist Tjay Cantrelli, Denny Walley (guitar), Andy Cahan (keyboards) and Tom Leavey (bass) completed the line-up. Eschewing the more adventurous side of their previous group, Black and Gardner played a raunchy rock style infused with a sense of humour. Geronimo Black split up in 1973, after which Walley joined **Frank Zappa** while Cahan switched to **Flo And Eddie**. The band was briefly re-formed for *Welcome Back*, but the two former Mothers Of Invention found more widespread acclaim in the Grandmothers, which they formed with other refugees from Frank Zappa.

● ALBUMS: *Geronimo Black* (UNI 1971) ★★★, *Welcome Back* (Helios 1981) ★★.

Gerrard, Alice

b. 8 July 1934, Seattle, Washington, USA. Gerrard grew up in California and while still at college in the late 50s she became greatly attracted to old-time and bluegrass music. She learned to play guitar and banjo and began writing her own material early in her career. At college, she had met (and married) Jeremy Foster (a friend and former classmate of **Mike Seeger**) and together they organized the Green County Stump Jumpers. In the early 60s, she met **Hazel Dickens**, and the two formed a partnership that saw them write songs about various aspects of life, as well as performing together at numerous folk festivals all over the south. In their work both together and apart, Dickens and Gerrard have done much to influence countless traditional music fans as well as pioneering the role of women in bluegrass.

In 1972, for some time, they joined with Mike Seeger (whom Gerrard had married in 1970), **Tracy Schwarz** and Lamar Greer to perform as the **Strange Creek Singers**. After their partnership ended amicably, Gerrard continued her career and worked various venues, sometimes with her husband. In the late 70s, along with Jeanie McLerie and Irene Herrmann, she formed the Harmony Sisters. They later recorded two albums for **Flying Fish Records**. She has also worked with and in some cases recorded with other artists including **Peter Rowan** and the **Red Clay Ramblers**.

Like her friend Dickens, she continued to appear at festivals and around the bluegrass/folk music circuit. In the 80s, she relocated to Durham, North Carolina, USA, where she founded and edited a music magazine called *The Old Time Herald* and also worked with a group called the Herald Angels. In 1994, using mainly her own material, she made further recordings for the Copper Creek label. During the same year Gerrard joined forces with multi-instrumentalist Tom Sauber and fiddle player Brad Leftwich to form Tom, Brad And Alice. The unit continue to record and perform traditional American music into the new millennium.

● ALBUMS: with Hazel Dickens *Who's That Knocking & Other Bluegrass Music* (Folkways 1965) ★★★, with Mike Seeger *Mike And Alice Seeger In Concert* (1970) ★★★, with Dickens *Won't You Come And Sing For Me* (Folkways 1973) ★★★, with Seeger *Alice And Mike* (Greenhays 1980) ★★★, with the Harmony Sisters *Harmony Pie* (Flying Fish 1982) ★★★, *Second Helping* (Flying Fish 1984) ★★★, *Pieces Of My Heart* (Copper Creek 1994) ★★★, *Calling Me Home: Songs Of Love & Loss* (Copper Creek 2004) ★★★.

● COMPILATIONS: with Dickens *Hazel & Alice* (Rounder 1973) ★★★, with Dickens *Hazel Dickens & Alice Gerrard* (Rounder 1976) ★★★.

Gerrard, Denny

b. Denver Gerrard. Gerrard was a founder member of pop duo the **Warm Sounds**, who enjoyed a UK hit in 1967 with 'Birds And Bees'. When the duo split up Gerrard embarked on a brief career as a producer, notably with progressive act **High Tide**. Members of this exceptional unit supported Gerrard on *Sinister Morning*, issued on the budget-line Nova Records. Although of occasional interest, the set is ultimately disappointing, as High Tide's contributions are rather muted and the singer's material is often insubstantial. Gerrard ceased recording following its release.

● ALBUMS: *Sinister Morning* (Deram Nova 1970) ★★.

Gerry And The Pacemakers

Gerry Marsden (b. Gerard Marsden, 24 September 1942, Liverpool, Lancashire, guitar/vocals), Freddie Marsden (b. 23 October 1940, Liverpool, Lancashire, drums) and John 'Les' Chadwick (b. 11 May 1943, Liverpool, Lancashire, bass) formed the original Pacemakers in 1959. Two years later they were joined by Les Maguire (b. 27 December 1941, Wallasey, Cheshire, piano) and, having completed highly successful spells in German beat clubs, became the second group signed to **Brian Epstein**'s management stable. The effervescent 'How Do You Do It', rejected as unsuitable by the **Beatles**, gave the more pliant Pacemakers a number 1 hit. Further chart-toppers 'I Like It' and 'You'll Never Walk Alone' (both 1963) followed in quick succession, earning the group the distinction of becoming the first act to have their first three releases reach number 1. The latter song, taken from the musical *Carousel*, was later adopted as the anthem of Liverpool Football Club.

Although the group's sole UK album revealed a penchant for R&B, their singles often emphasized Gerry Marsden's cheeky persona. The exceptions included two excellent in-house compositions 'Don't Let The Sun Catch You Crying' (1964) and 'Ferry Cross The Mersey' (1965), the theme song to the Pacemakers' starring film. A follow-up release, 'I'll Be There', was the quartet's final Top 20 entry and in 1967 Gerry embarked on a solo career. He remained a popular figure in television and on the cabaret circuit, but regained the national spotlight in 1985 following the Bradford City Football Club fire tragedy, when a charity recording, credited to the **Crowd** and featuring an all-star cast, took a new version of 'You'll Never Walk Alone' to the top of the UK chart for the second time. Another re-recording of an earlier hit for charity, 'Ferry Cross The Mersey', this time for the victims of the Hillsborough crowd disaster, involving supporters of Liverpool FC in 1989, reached number 1. Marsden is still very active gigging with various versions of the Pacemakers.

● ALBUMS: *How Do You Like It* (Columbia 1963) ★★★★, *Don't Let The Sun Catch You Crying* US only (Laurie 1964) ★★★, *Second Album* US only (Laurie 1964) ★★★, *I'll Be There* US only (Laurie 1964) ★★★, *Ferry Cross The Mersey* film soundtrack (Columbia/United Artists 1965) ★★★★, *Girl On A Swing* (Laurie 1966) ★★★, *20 Year Anniversary Album* (Deb 1982) ★★.
Solo: Gerry Marsden *Much Missed Man* (Ozit 2001) ★.
● COMPILATIONS: *Gerry And The Pacemakers' Greatest Hits* (Laurie 1965) ★★★★, *The Best Of Gerry And The Pacemakers* (Capitol 1977) ★★★★, *The Very Best Of Gerry And The Pacemakers* (MFP 1984) ★★★★, *Hit Singles Album* (EMI 1986) ★★★★, *The EP Collection* (See For Miles 1987) ★★★★, *The Singles Plus* (EMI 1987) ★★★★, *All The Hits Of Gerry And The Pacemakers* (Razor & Tie 1995) ★★★★, *As Bs & EPs* (EMI Gold 2004) ★★★★.
● DVD/VIDEOS: *In Concert* (Legend 1990).
● FURTHER READING: *I'll Never Walk Alone*, Gerry Marsden with Ray Coleman.
● FILMS: *Ferry Cross The Mersey* (1965).

Gershwin, George

b. 26 September 1898, New York City, USA, d. 11 June 1937, Beverly Hills, California, USA. One of the select group of all-time great American composers, as a youngster George Gershwin was a poor student, happy to spend his days playing in the streets. He eventually took up the piano when the family bought an instrument for his older brother, **Ira Gershwin**. He quickly showed enormous enthusiasm for music, taking lessons and studying harmony and theory. His taste was eclectic: he listened to classical music and to the popular music of the day, in particular the music of black Americans, which

was then gaining a widespread appeal. After becoming a professional musician in 1912, he played the piano at holiday resorts in upstate New York, and worked as a song plugger for the renowned Remick Music Company. He continued with his studies and began to write music. His first songs were undistinguished, but attracted the attention of important figures such as **Sophie Tucker**, **Harry Von Tilzer** and **Sigmund Romberg**. Some of his early compositions were influenced by ragtime—'Rialto Ripples' (1916, with Will Donaldson) was one such example—and he also continued to gain a reputation as a performer. In 1917 he was hired as a rehearsal pianist for the **Jerome Kern/Victor Herbert** Broadway show *Miss 1917*, and his own compositions continued to flow, some with lyrics by his brother Ira, and others by **Irving Caesar**.

It was a collaboration in 1919 with Caesar that gave Gershwin his first hit: 'Swanee' had originally been played by the popular **Arthur Pryor** band, but it was only when **Al Jolson** sang it in the musical *Sinbad* that it became a success. Also in 1919, George Gershwin collaborated with Arthur J. Jackson and **Buddy De Sylva** on his first complete Broadway score, for *La, La Lucille*. In the early 20s, he wrote the exquisite ballad 'The Man I Love', with Ira, and contributed to revues such as *George White's Scandals* of 1922 ('I'll Build A Stairway To Paradise' lyric: Buddy De Sylva and Ira Gershwin), *George White's Scandals* of 1924 ('Somebody Loves Me' lyric: De Sylva and Ballard MacDonald) and the London musical *Primrose* (lyrics mostly by Ira Gershwin and Desmond Carter). Band leader **Paul Whiteman** commissioned George to write an extended piece that was to be classical in structure but that would use the jazz idiom, in complete contrast to his work for the musical theatre. The result was 'Rhapsody In Blue', arranged by **Ferde Grofé**, and first performed by Whiteman at the Aeolian Hall in New York in 1924, with the composer at the piano.

In the same year, George and Ira were back on Broadway with the hit musical *Lady, Be Good!* ('Fascinating Rhythm', 'The 'Half Of It, Dearie' Blues', title song), which was followed throughout the decade by several other delightful productions, including *Tip Toes* ('Sweet And Low-Down', 'That Certain Feeling'), *Oh, Kay!* (with Sigmund Romberg and **P.G. Wodehouse**, 'Clap Yo' Hands', 'Dear Little Girl', 'Do-Do-Do', 'Maybe', 'Someone To Watch Over Me'), *Funny Face*, with **Fred Astaire** and his sister Adele ('He Loves And She Loves', ''S Wonderful', title song), *Rosalie* ('How Long Has This Been Going On?', 'Oh Gee! Oh Joy!'), *Treasure Girl* ('Feeling I'm Falling'), and *Show Girl* ('Liza (All The Clouds Will Roll Away)', 1929). During this period the brothers each worked with other collaborators. The Gershwins' success was maintained in the early 30s with *Strike Up The Band* ('I've Got A Crush On You', 'Soon', title song) and the magnificent *Girl Crazy*, which starred **Ethel Merman** ('I Got Rhythm', 'But Not For Me', 'Embraceable You', 'Bidin' My Time', 'Boy! What Love Has Done To Me', 'But Not For Me'). In the pit band for *Girl Crazy* were up-and-coming musicians such as **Benny Goodman**, **Glenn Miller** and **Gene Krupa**. The Pulitzer Prize–winning *Of Thee I Sing* ('Love Is Sweeping The Country', 'Who Cares', title song) was another hit, but the Gershwins' next two Broadway shows, *Pardon My English!* and *Let 'Em Eat Cake*, were flops. After the success of 'Rhapsody In Blue', George Gershwin had again written music in classical form with 'Concert In F' (1925), the tone poem 'An American In Paris' (1928) and his 'Second Rhapsody' (1930).

In 1935, his folk opera **Porgy And Bess** (lyrics by Ira Gershwin and DuBose Heyward) opened in Boston, Massachusetts and despite early critical disapproval and audience indifference it became one of his most performed works. The score included such memorable songs as 'It Ain't Necessarily So', 'Bess, You Is My Woman', 'I Loves You Porgy', 'I Got Plenty O' Nuttin'' (Ira Gershwin, in his book *Lyrics On Several Occasions*, refers to this song as 'I've Got Plenty O' Nuthin'), 'There's A Boat Dat's Leavin' Soon For New York', and the immortal 'Summertime'. In 1936, the Gershwin brothers returned to Hollywood, after visiting a few years earlier with only modest results. Now they entered into a new phase of creativity, writing the score for the Fred Astaire/ **Ginger Rogers** musical **Shall We Dance** ('They All Laughed', 'Let's Call The Whole Thing Off', 'They Can't Take That Away From Me'), and **A Damsel In Distress** ('Nice Work If You Can Get It', 'Stiff Upper Lip', 'Things Are Looking Up', 'A Foggy Day'), in which Astaire was teamed with the English actress, Joan Fontaine.

It was while he was working on the next film, *The Goldwyn Follies*, that George Gershwin was taken ill. He died of a brain tumour in June 1937. Despite the severity of his illness, Gershwin's songs for the film, which included 'Love Walked In', 'I Was Doing All Right', 'I Love To Rhyme', 'Just Another Rhumba', and the beautiful 'Love Is Here To Stay' were among his best work. In 1947, some hitherto unpublished songs, such as 'For You, For Me, Forevermore', 'Aren't You Kind Of Glad We Did?', and 'Changing My Tune', were used in the **Betty Grable/Dick Haymes** movie **The Shocking Miss Pilgrim**, and other Gershwin numbers were heard on the screen in **The Barkleys Of Broadway** (1949) and **An American In Paris** (1951), as well as in the film adaptations of *Girl Crazy*, *Funny Face*, and *Porgy And Bess*. Although his life span was relatively short, Gershwin's work was not merely extensive but also imperishable. Hardly any of his songs have dated, and they are performed frequently more than 50 years after his death. As with so many of his contemporaries, Gershwin's popular songs adapted to the latest musical developments, in particular incorporating concepts from the jazz world, and, not surprisingly, his work is especially popular among jazz instrumentalists.

Another accomplished exponent of the best of Gershwin was pianist **Oscar Levant**, a valued lifelong friend of the composer. It is, however, with singers that the full glory of Gershwin's music emerges, and he remains a key and influential figure in the story of American popular song. In 1992, many of his most enduring numbers were showcased in two contrasting productions: the intimate New York revue *'S Wonderful, 'S Marvelous, 'S Gershwin!*, and the big budget Broadway musical, **Crazy For You**, which was 'very loosely based' on the Gershwins' 1930 show *Girl Crazy*. In 1993, a West End production of *Crazy For You* opened to rave notices, and looked set for a long residency. In 1994, Elektra Nonesuch released a unique CD entitled *Gershwin Plays Gershwin*, which contained transcribed piano rolls made by the composer between 1916 and 1927. Among the tracks were his earliest versions of immortal melodies such as 'Swanee', 'That Certain Feeling', 'An American In Paris', and 'Rhapsody In Blue'.

After Ira's centennial celebrations in 1996, it was George's turn two years later. One of the highlights was *George Gershwin At 100*, a concert at Carnegie Hall, with the San Francisco Symphony Orchestra conducted by Michael Tilson

Thomas, and starring Audra McDonald, Brian Stokes Mitchell, and Frederica Von Stade. Another proved to be Hope Clarke's new ballet based on *Porgy And Bess*, which premiered at Lincoln Center. The Library of Congress also paid tribute to George and Ira by dedicating a room to them. It is dominated by George's grand piano and Ira's portable typewriter. In addition, the team now have a star on the Hollywood Walk of Fame. In Britain, *S'Wonderful: A Celebration Of George Gershwin*, was presented at the London Palladium, and—a rare honour—George was made Composer Of The Week on BBC Radio 3. The BBC also broadcast a concert version of the 1931 Broadway musical, *Of Thee I Sing*.

● COMPILATIONS: *Gershwin Plays Gershwin* (Elektra Nonesuch 1994) ★★★, *I Got Rhythm: The Music Of George Gershwin* 4-CD box set (Koch 1995) ★★★★, *George & Ira Gershwin In Hollywood* (Rhino/Turner 1997) ★★★, *Gershwin And Grofé* (Pearl GEM 1998) ★★★, *The Essential* (Sony Classical 2003) ★★★★.

● FURTHER READING: *Gershwin*, Edward Jablonski. *The Memory Of All That: The Life Of George Gershwin*, Joan Peyser. *A Journey To Greatness*, David Ewen. *Gershwin*, Robert Payne. *The Gershwins*, Robert Kimball and Alfred E. Simon. *Gershwin*, Isaac Goldberg. *George Gershwin*, Alan Kendall. *Rhapsody In Blue*, George Gershwin. *Fascinating Rhythm: The Collaborations Of George & Ira Gershwin*, Deena Rosenberg. *A Gershwin Companion: A Critical Inventory & Discography 1916–1984*, Walter Rimler. *George Gershwin*, Merle Armitage. *George Gershwin: Man And Legend*, Merle Armstrong. *George Gershwin*, René Chalupt. *George Gershwin*, Christian Longolius. *George Gershwin*, Mario Pasi. *The Life Of George Gershwin*, Robert Rushmore. *George Gershwin*, Andre Gauthier. *George Gershwin: A Selective Bibliography And Discography*, Charles Schwartz. *Gershwin: His Life And Music*, Charles Schwartz. *The Gershwin Years: George And Ira*, Edward Jablonski and Lawrence D. Stewart. *George Gershwin*, Rodney Greenberg. *George Gershwin: A New Biography*, William G. Hyland.

Gershwin, Ira

b. 6 December 1896, New York City, USA, d. 17 August 1983, Beverly Hills, California, USA. A consummate lyricist, whose career spanned some 40 years, like his younger brother **George Gershwin**, Ira was an indifferent student, but became fascinated by popular music, and particularly the lyrics of songs. He began writing seriously in 1917, sometimes using the pseudonym 'Arthur Francis', and had a number of minor successes, including the score for the stage show, *Two Little Girls In Blue* (music by **Vincent Youmans**). In the 20s and 30s he was closely associated with his brother, collaborating on numerous Broadway shows such as *Primrose* (with Desmond Carter), *Tell Me More!* (with **Buddy De Sylva**), *Tip Toes*, **Lady, Be Good!**, **Oh, Kay!**, **Funny Face**, *Rosalie*, *Treasure Girl*, *Show Girl* (with **Gus Kahn**), **Strike Up The Band**, *Girl Crazy*, *Pardon My English*, *Let 'Em Eat Cake*, and **Porgy And Bess**. From those productions came some of the perennial standards of American popular song.

Despite the brothers' prolific output, which resulted in hits such as 'That Certain Feeling', 'Someone To Watch Over Me', 'Do-Do-Do', 'S Wonderful', 'How Long Has This Been Going On?', 'I've Got A Crush On You', 'I Got Rhythm', 'But Not For Me', 'It Ain't Necessarily So', 'Embraceable You', and so many more, Ira Gershwin found time to write lyrics for other composers. Among these collaborations were 'Cheerful Little Earful' (from the stage show *Sweet And Low*, with **Billy Rose** and **Harry Warren**), 'Let's Take A Walk Around The Block', 'You're A Builder-Upper', 'Fun To Be Fooled', and 'What Can You Say In A Love Song?' (from the revue *Life Begins At 8:40*, with **Harold Arlen** and **E.Y. 'Yip' Harburg**), and 'I Can't Get Started', 'He Hasn't A Thing Except Me', and 'Island In The West Indies' (from the revue *Ziegfeld Follies* of 1936, with **Vernon Duke**). In 1931, the brothers collaborated on the score for the Broadway show, *Of Thee I Sing*, which became the first musical to be awarded a Pulitzer Prize for Drama.

Just before George died in 1937 from a brain tumour, he worked with Ira on the movies *A Damsel In Distress* ('A Foggy Day', 'Nice Work If You Can Get It'), *Shall We Dance* ('Let's Call The Whole Thing Off', 'They All Laughed', 'They Can't Take That Away From Me'), and *The Goldwyn Follies* ('Love Is Here To Stay', 'Love Walked In'). Ira finished the score for the latter film with Vernon Duke, and in the years immediately following his brother's early death, wrote very little. When he eventually resumed work, he teamed with **Kurt Weill** on the Broadway musicals *Lady In The Dark* (1941), which starred **Gertrude Lawrence**, with **Danny Kaye** ('My Ship', 'Jenny', 'This Is New', 'Tchaikovsky'), and *The Firebrand Of Florence* (1945), and worked on other stage shows with Aaron Copland (*North Star*, 1945) and **Arthur Schwartz** (*Park Avenue*, 1946). He also wrote the lyrics for several films, among them the outstanding scores for *Cover Girl*, with **Gene Kelly** ('Long Ago And Far Away', 'Make Way For Tomorrow', 'The Show Must Go On', 'Put Me To The Test', with **Jerome Kern**), *A Star Is Born* with **Judy Garland** (the unforgettable 'The Man That Got Away', 'Gotta Have Me Go With You', 'It's A New World, with **Harold Arlen**), and *The Barkleys of Broadway*, starring **Fred Astaire** and **Ginger Rogers** ('My One And Only Highland Fling', 'Shoes With Wings On', 'You'd Be Hard To Replace', with **Harry Warren**). Several of George and Ira Gershwin's stage shows were adapted for the screen, and a collection of their old numbers formed the score for the multi Oscar-winning *An American In Paris* (1951). In 1959, Ira published a delightful collection of his wonderfully witty and colloquial lyrics, entitled *Lyrics On Several Occasions*. He retired in the following year, occasionally working on lyrics of past successes when they needed refining or updating for revivals of the most popular Gershwin shows. Ten years after his death in 1983, some of his most popular lyrics were still being relished in the New York and London productions of *Crazy For You*, a re-hash of the Gershwins' 1930 hit, *Girl Crazy*.

There was a full house in December 1996 when a gala concert was held at Carnegie Hall to celebrate the centennial of Ira's birth. Stars such as a leading Gershwin authority **Michael Feinstein**, Debbie Gravitte, **Vic Damone**, **Rosemary Clooney**, and **Maureen McGovern** were there, as was **Burton Lane**, Ira's only living collaborator. Lorna Luft led an all-star cast in the British tribute, *Who Could Ask For Anything More!*, at London's Royal Albert Hall.

● COMPILATIONS: *George & Ira Gershwin In Hollywood* (Rhino/Turner 1997) ★★★.

● FURTHER READING: *Lyrics On Several Occasions*, Ira Gershwin. *The Gershwins*, R. Kimball and A. Simon. *The Complete Lyrics Of Ira Gershwin*, R. Kimball (ed.). *Fascinating Rhythm: Collaboration Of George And Ira Gershwin*, Deena Rosenberg. *The Art Of The Lyricist*, Philip Furia. *The Gershwin Years: George And Ira*, Edward Jablonski and Lawrence D. Stewart.

Gescom

Gescom is an abridged version of Gestalt Communications, although all those involved remain evasive about the exact meaning of this. With an obsession with sound, an unusual ear for melody and a wayward sense of malfunction, Gescom continue to create some stunning music. Their **Warp Records** 12-inch 'Keynell' merits particular mention as an apex of electronica. The exact identities of Gescom's ever mutating personnel have been deliberately obscured, but the project is generally considered to be an alter ego for **Autechre**'s Sean Booth and Rob Brown with various friends and collaborators. Autechre themselves have described Gescom as 'us not being us—it might not even be us on [any particular] record' and additional input on existing Gescom recordings has been attributed to Darrell Fitton (aka **Bola**), Rob Hall, the elusively named Daniel 72 and Andy Maddocks. Maddocks is known to be a former flatmate of Booth and Brown and runs Manchester's idiosyncratic Skam Records. The introduction of additional personnel is presumably intended to disrupt the core duo's normal working methods and, more importantly, to be fun. The fluctuating format of Gescom allows for releases across a variety of labels (Clear, Futro, JVC, Leaf, MYSLB, Skam, Source, Warp, Worm Interface) and for esoteric projects such as the *MiniDisc* album. Reportedly the first independent release solely on the format, the recording features tracks specifically created to utilize MiniDisc's functions, brief 'song' fragments to be 'looped' and 'shuffled' as well as more complete tracks. Perversely, given the release of the album on this supposedly hi-fidelity format, Gescom often recall damaged electronic equipment, with glitches of static and distorted 'bits' forming the basis of their music.

● ALBUMS: *MiniDisc* (OR 1998) ★★★★.

Gessle, Per

(see **Roxette**)

Get Set VOP

This mid-90s US rap duo comprised brothers Infinite Kundalini and Kwabena The Triumphant, or Mark and Scott Batson as their mother knew them. Raised in the Bushwick sector of Brooklyn, New York, the group was first spotted while playing support for Maverick recording artist Me'Shell during the Washington Area Music Association's 1990 convention. Leotis Clyburn of **Polydor Records** was in attendance, but lost touch until two years later, when he saw their name under the live listings. The first result of a long-term recording contract was the single, 'Pretty Brown Babies (Pro Seed)', and live dates with **Jazzamatazz**, with whom they were frequently compared thanks to their mellow, jazzy groove.

● ALBUMS: *Voice Of The Projects* (Polydor 1993) ★★★.

Get Up Kids

This Kansas City, Missouri, USA–based outfit was formed in October 1994 by Matthew Pryor (b. USA; vocals/guitar), Jim Suptic (b. 14 October 1977, Milford, Delaware, USA; vocals/ guitar), Robbie Pope (b. USA; bass) and Nathan Shay (drums). Their unusual name is taken from a song by Pryor's former band Secular Theme, 'Suburban Get Up Kids'. Shay was replaced by Ryan Pope (b. USA) shortly after the release of the band's debut 7-inch single, 'Shorty'/'The Breathing Method'. Several independently released singles followed before the band affiliated themselves with the Doghouse Records label. They released their long-playing debut, *Four Minute Mile*, in September 1997, and set off on a non-stop tour of the USA and Europe supporting fellow emo (emotional hardcore) bands the **Promise Ring** and **Braid**. A projected major label recording contract with Mojo Records fell through, so March 1999's *Red Letter Day* EP was released by Doghouse instead. The EP was the first release to feature new keyboard player, James DeWees (b. 1976, USA). In April the band inaugurated their own Heroes And Villians label and signed a distribution deal with Vagrant Records. The excellent *Something To Write Home About* saw the band moving towards a more commercial punk pop sound. Pryor also records with alt pop outfit **New Amsterdams**.

● ALBUMS: *Four Minute Mile* (Doghouse 1997) ★★★, *Something To Write Home About* (Heroes And Villians/ Vagrant 1999) ★★★★, *On A Wire* (Heroes And Villians/ Vagrant 2002) ★★★, *Guilt Show* (Vagrant 2004) ★★★.

● COMPILATIONS: *Eudora* (Heroes And Villians/Vagrant 2000) ★★★.

Geto Boys

Houston, Texas, USA–based gangsta rap crew led by the notorious **Bushwick Bill** (b. Richard Shaw, 8 December 1966, Jamaica), alongside **Scarface** (b. Brad Jordan, 9 November 1969, Houston, Texas, USA), **Willie D.** (b. William Dennis, 1 November 1966, Houston, Texas, USA) and DJ Ready Red (b. Collins Lyaseth). The latter had left the crew by early 1991. In fact the Geto Boys had originally started as the Ghetto Boys with a completely different line-up in 1988, featuring Slim Jukebox, DJ Ready Red and Prince Johnny C, with Bushwick a dancer. When Johnny C and Jukebox quit (Jukebox was subsequently jailed for murder) former **Rap-A-Lot Records** solo artists Scarface and Willie D. were added by the record company. It was this line-up that made the headlines. In 1990, **Geffen Records** refused to distribute their second album *Grip It! On That Other Level*, following the controversy over some of its lyrics (which included allusions to necrophilia). A revamped version of the album with a number of new tracks and some re-recordings appeared the following year as *The Geto Boys*, distributed this time by Def American Records. The crew returned to Rap-A-Lot, but shortly afterwards Bushwick Bill forced his girlfriend to shoot him after threatening their baby (he lost an eye). Their next album *We Can't Be Stopped* was bedecked with a picture of him being pushed through a hospital by his two pals after the incident. A fair introduction into the world of the Geto Boys, characterized by thoroughly nasty, sensationalist tales, which made their work difficult to evaluate objectively. Some of the most vile sequences of words ever used in popular music appeared on their albums, glorying in rape, mutilation and violence. Though at first appearance a cocktail of pure hatred, hidden beneath their more self-serving statements were tiny vignettes filled with persuasive detail—'Life In The Fast Lane' (on *Grip It! On That Other Level* and *The Geto Boys*), and 'Mind Playing Tricks On Me' (on *We Can't Be Stopped*) being the best examples. Certainly though, the defence of 'reporting from the front-line' would seem to be more honourable in their case than many others, bearing in mind Bushwick Bill's aforementioned partial blinding, and the alarmingly high gun profile of the deep south.

The Geto Boys went on to concentrate more on their solo careers, following internal friction (Bushwick and Willie D. at several points refusing to appear on stage at the same time), and Willie D. was replaced by Big Mike on 1993's *Till Death Us Do Part*. Bushwick, Willie D. and Scarface were reunited for 1996's *The Resurrection*. In a further upheaval, Bushwick Bill was replaced by DMG on the follow-up, *Da Good, Da Bad & Da Ugly*. The original members eventually made up and put their disappointing solo careers behind them to record the surprisingly effective comeback album, *The Foundation*. Released at the start of 2005, the album provided the trio with an unlikely Top 20 hit.

● ALBUMS: *Making Trouble* (Rap-A-Lot 1988) ★★, *Grip It! On That Other Level* (Rap-A-Lot 1989) ★★★, *The Geto Boys* (Rap-A-Lot/Def American 1990) ★★★★, *We Can't Be Stopped* (Rap-A-Lot/Priority 1991) ★★★, *Till Death Us Do Part* (Rap-A-Lot 1993) ★★, *The Resurrection* (Rap-A-Lot/ Noo Trybe 1996) ★★★, *Da Good, Da Bad & Da Ugly* (Rap-A-Lot 1998) ★★, *The Foundation* (Rap-A-Lot/Asylum 2005) ★★★.

● COMPILATIONS: *Uncut Dope: Geto Boys Best* (Rap-A-Lot 1992) ★★★.

Getz, Stan

b. 2 February 1927, Philadelphia, Pennsylvania, USA, d. 6 June 1991, Malibu, California, USA. Getz played several reed instruments as a child, especially the alto saxophone, but he finally chose the tenor saxophone and by the age of 15 was playing professionally. Within a year he had made his first records, playing with **Jack Teagarden**, who became, technically at least, Getz's guardian so that the youngster could go on the road with the band. The following year Getz worked with **Stan Kenton**, then with the bands of **Jimmy Dorsey** and **Benny Goodman**. Although he had already attracted attention in jazz circles during these tenures and through record sessions under his own name, it was as a member of **Woody Herman**'s 'Four Brothers' band in 1947 that he became an internationally recognized name. He was with Herman for about two years and then, during the 50s, he began leading a small group on a semi-regular basis. Spells with Kenton and **Jazz At The Philharmonic** were followed by an uncertain period as Getz sought, successfully, to throw off drug addiction.

In the late 50s and early 60s Getz spent some time in Europe, being resident for a while in Copenhagen, Denmark. Back in the USA in the early 60s he made a milestone album, *Focus*, and worked with **Charlie Byrd**, developing an interest in Brazilian and other Latin American musical forms. As a result Getz made a number of Latin records that proved to be very popular, among them 'The Girl From Ipanema', featuring singer **Astrud Gilberto**, which helped to launch the bossa nova craze. Throughout the 60s and 70s Getz led small groups, whose line-ups often featured up-and-coming musicians such as **Gary Burton**, **Chick Corea**, **Jimmy Raney**, **Al Haig**, **Steve Swallow**, **Airto Moreira** and **JoAnne Brackeen**. Nevertheless his activity in these years was sporadic. His earlier popular success and the control he exercised over his career, including production of his own recording sessions, allowed him to work as and when he wanted. In the 80s he became more active again; in addition to playing clubs, concerts and festivals around the world he was also artist-in-residence at Stanford University. He recorded with among others **Everything But The Girl**. This late period saw a new surge in popularity, which sadly coincided with gradual awareness that he was suffering a terminal illness: he died of cancer in June 1991.

One of the most highly regarded tenor saxophonists in jazz history, Getz's early recording career was highlighted by his work with Herman. His playing on several records, notably 'Early Autumn', a part of **Ralph Burns**' 'Summer Sequence' suite, displays to great effect the featherweight and almost vibrato-free tone that hints at the admiration he had for the work of **Lester Young**. Getz followed the success of this recording with a string of fine albums with his own small groups, notably those he made with Haig and Raney, in the process influencing a generation of tenor saxophonists who aspired to his coolly elegant style. The remarkable *Focus* album, a suite composed and arranged by **Eddie Sauter** for jazz players and a string quartet, and the bossa nova recordings, which included the single, 'Desafinado', were other features of his first period. The smoothness of Getz's sound, the delicate floating effect he created, proved immensely popular with the fringe audience and led some observers to conclude that his was a detached and introspective style. In fact, during this period he had made a conscious attempt to subdue the emotional content of his playing, in order to fit in with current commercial vogues. Beneath the surface calm there was a burning, emotional quality that flared only occasionally.

By the mid-60s Getz had become bored with the style he had adopted and entered a new period of brief experimentation with electronics, followed by the gradual development of a new and deeply soulful ballad style. Although he was still playing with a delicately floating sound, his rich melodic sense was given much freer rein. Towards the end of his life, when he knew he was slowly dying of cancer, Getz entered a third and in some respects even more fulfilling phase of his career. Despite, or perhaps because of, the state of his health, the emotional content of his work began to burn with a romantic fire, a glorious outpouring of which is heard on his *Anniversary* and *Serenity* albums. In retrospect it was possible to see that this romanticism had always been there, even if, at various times, it had been deliberately suppressed to accord with the musical spirit of the times. No one could doubt the emotional thrust of his late work. His sound was still smooth, but now that quality was more obviously a surface patina beneath which surged a fierce desire to communicate with his audience. He succeeded in doing so, and thus helped to make those years when his life waned as his music waxed a period not of sadness but one of grateful joy for his many admirers.

● ALBUMS: *Stan Getz And The Tenor Sax Stars* (New Jazz 1950) ★★★, *Volume 2* (New Jazz 1950) ★★★★, *Stan Getz–Lee Konitz* (Prestige 1951) ★★★★, *In Retrospect* (Dale 1951) ★★★, with Billie Holiday *Billie And Stan* (Dale 1951) ★★★, *New Sounds In Modern Music* (Savoy Jazz 1951) ★★★, *Jazz At Storyville* (Roost 1952) ★★★★, *Jazz At Storyville Volume 2* (Roost 1953) ★★★★, *Plays* (Clef 1953) ★★★, *The Artistry Of Stan Getz* (Clef 1953) ★★★, *Jazz At Storyville Volume 3* (Roost 1953) ★★★★, *Chamber Music* (Roost 1953) ★★★, *Stan Plays Getz* (Verve 1954) ★★★, *Split Kick* (Roost 1954) ★★★, *The Dizzy Gillespie–Stan Getz Sextet #1* 10-inch album (Norgran 1954) ★★★★, *The Dizzy Gillespie–Stan Getz Sextet #2* 10-inch album (Norgran 1954) ★★★★, *Interpretations By The Stan Getz Quintet Volume 1*

(Norgran 1954) ★★★★, *Interpretations By The Stan Getz Quintet Volume 2* (Norgran 1954) ★★★★, *Interpretations By The Stan Getz Quintet Volume 3* (Norgran 1955) ★★★★, *At The Shrine Auditorium* (Verve 1955) ★★★, *West Coast Jazz* (Norgran 1955) ★★★★, with Dizzy Gillespie *Diz And Getz* (Verve 1955) ★★★★, *Stan Getz* (American Record Society 1955) ★★★, *Groovin' High* (Modern 1956) ★★★, *Stan Getz's Most Famous* (Jazztone 1956) ★★★, *The Sound* (Metronome 1956) ★★★, *Stan Getz & J.J. Johnson At The Opera House* (Verve 1958) ★★★★, with Gerry Mulligan *Getz Meets Mulligan In Hi-Fi* (Verve 1958) ★★★★, *Stan Getz And The Oscar Peterson Trio* (Verve 1958) ★★★★, *At The Opera House* (Verve 1958) ★★★, *The Steamer* (Verve 1959) ★★★, *Award Winner* (Verve 1959) ★★★, *The Soft Swing* (Verve 1959) ★★★, *Imported From Europe* (Verve 1959) ★★★, *Stan Getz Quintet* (Verve 1960) ★★★, *At Large* (Verve 1960) ★★★, *Cool Velvet: Stan Getz With Strings* (Verve 1960) ★★★★, *Rhythms* (Blue Ribbon 1961) ★★★, *Plays* (Verve 1961) ★★★, *More West Coast Jazz With Stan Getz* (Verve 1961) ★★★, *And The Cool Sounds* (Verve 1961) ★★★, *In Stockholm* (Verve 1961) ★★★, with Chet Baker *Stan Meets Chet* (Verve 1961) ★★★, *Focus* (Verve 1962) ★★★★, with Charlie Byrd *Jazz Samba* (Verve 1962) ★★★★★, with Byrd *Jazz Samba Encore* (Verve 1963) ★★★, *Moonlight In Vermont* (Roost 1963) ★★★★, *Modern World* (Roost 1963) ★★★, *Reflections* (Verve 1963) ★★★, *Getz Age* (Roost 1963) ★★★, with João Gilberto *Getz/Gilberto* (Verve 1963) ★★★★, *Big Band Bossa Nova* (Verve 1963) ★★★★, with Gilberto *Getz/Gilberto 2* (Verve 1964) ★★★, *The Melodic Stan Getz* (Metro 1965) ★★★, *Getz Au Go Go* (Verve 1965) ★★★★, *Stan Getz And Bill Evans* (Verve 1965) ★★★★, *A Song After Sundown* (RCA Victor 1966) ★★★, *Stan Getz With Guest Laurindo Almeida* (Verve 1966) ★★★, *Eloquence* (Verve 1966) ★★★, *Another Time Another Place* (Verve 1966) ★★★, *Plays Blues* (Verve 1966) ★★★, *Sweet Rain* (Verve 1967) ★★★, *Preservation* (Prestige 1967) ★★★, *Voices* (Verve 1967) ★★★, *What The World Needs Now* (Verve 1968) ★★, *Marrakesh Express* (MGM 1969) ★★, *Didn't We* (Verve 1969) ★★★★, *Dynasty* (Verve 1971) ★★★, *Captain Marvel* (Columbia 1972) ★★, *Best Of Two Worlds* (Columbia 1975) ★★★, *The Master* (Columbia 1976) ★★, with Jimmy Rowles *The Peacocks* (Columbia 1977) ★★★, *Live At Montmartre* (SteepleChase 1977) ★★★, *Another World* (Columbia 1978) ★★★, *Children Of The World* (Columbia 1980) ★★, *The Dolphin* (Concord Jazz 1981) ★★★, *Spring Is Here* (Concord Jazz 1982) ★★, *Pure Getz* (Concord Jazz 1982) ★★★, with Albert Dailey *Poetry* (Elektra 1983) ★★★, *Line For Lyons* (Sonet 1983) ★★★, *The Stockholm Concert* (Sonet 1983) ★★★, *Anniversary* (EmArcy 1987) ★★★, *Serenity* (EmArcy 1987) ★★★★, with James Moody *Tenor Contrasts* (Esquire 1988) ★★★, *Apasionado* (A&M 1989) ★★★, with Abbey Lincoln *You Gotta Pay The Band* (Verve 1992) ★★★, with Kenny Barron *People Time* (Phonogram 1992) ★★★★, *Nobody Else But Me* (Verve 1994) ★★★, *Blue Skies* (Concord Jazz 1996) ★★★★, *Stan Getz Quartet Live In Paris 1982* recording (Dreyfus 1996) ★★★, with Bill Evans *But Beautiful 1974* recordings (Milestone 1996) ★★★, *Yours And Mine: Live At The Glasgow International Jazz Festival 1989* (Concord Jazz 1997) ★★★, *Soul Eyes 1989* recording (Concord Jazz 1998) ★★★, *Lover Man 1974* recording (Moon 1998) ★★, *Autumn Leaves 1980* recording (West

Wind 1998) ★★, with Chet Baker *Quintessence Vol. 1* 1983 recording (Concord Jazz 1999) ★★, *Quintessence Vol. 2* 1983 recording (Concord Jazz 1999) ★★★, *My Foolish Heart* 1975 recording (Label M 2000) ★★, *The Final Concert Recording* (Eagle Jazz 2002) ★★★, *Bossas And Ballads: The Lost Sessions* (Verve 2004) ★★★.

● COMPILATIONS: *The Greatest Of Stan Getz* (Roost 1963) ★★★, *The Stan Getz Years* (Roost 1964) ★★★, *The Best Of Stan Getz* (Verve 1967) ★★★, *You, The Night And Music* (Jazz Door 1991) ★★★, *The Roost Years* (Roulette 1991) ★★★, *New Collection* (Sony 1993) ★★★, *Early Stan* (Original Jazz Classics 1993) ★★★, *The Rare Dawn Sessions* (Biograph 1995) ★★★, *A Life In Jazz: A Musical Biography* (Verve 1996) ★★★, *Best Of The West Coast Sessions* 3-CD box set (Verve 1997) ★★★, *The Complete Roost Recordings* 3-CD box set (Roost/Blue Note 1997) ★★★★, *Sax Moods—The Very Best Of Stan Getz* (Verve 1998) ★★★★, *Autour De Minuit* 60s recordings (Gitanes 1998) ★★★, *The Golden Years 1952-1958 Volume 1* (Moon 1998) ★★★★, *The Golden Years 1958-1961 Volume 2* (Moon 1998) ★★★★, *The Bossa Nova Years 1962-64* (Verve 2000) ★★★★, *Getz For Lovers* (Verve 2002) ★★★, *The Complete Savoy Recordings* (Savoy Jazz 2002) ★★★★, *The Definitive Stan Getz* (Verve/Blue Note 2002) ★★★★, *The Sound* (Snapper 2003) ★★.

● DVD/VIDEOS: *Warm Valley* (K-Jazz 1994).

● FURTHER READING: *The Stan Getz Discography*, Anne Astrup. *Stan Getz*, Richard Palmer. *Stan Getz: An Appreciation Of His Recorded Work*, Ron Kirkpatrick. *Stan Getz: A Life In Jazz*, Donald Maggin.

Geva, Tamara

b. 17 March 1907, St. Petersburg, Russia, d. 9 December 1997, New York City, USA. After training for the ballet, Geva appeared as a classical dancer and then began appearing in musical comedies, often dancing interpolated classical sequences. She had married choreographer **George Balanchine**, although their marriage ended in 1926. An early appearance in the USA was in *Chauve-Souris* (1927). She was in **Whoopee!** (1928), the **Eddie Cantor** vehicle that ran the New Amsterdam Theatre on Broadway for 407 performances. Also in the show, which had music by **Walter Donaldson** and lyrics by **Gus Kahn**, were Agnes Ayres and **Buddy Ebsen**. Her next Broadway musical show was *Three's A Crowd* (1930), which was produced by Max Gordon. With music by **Arthur Schwartz** and lyrics by **Howard Dietz**, who also wrote the book, the show ran for 272 performances. The cast included **Fred Allen** and **Clifton Webb**.

Other shows of the 30s were the revue *Flying Colors* (1932), the dramas *A Divine Drudge* (1933) and *The Red Cat* (1934) and the musical *Alma Mater* (1935), in which she danced a ballet sequence. In 1936 she was in **Richard Rodgers** and **Lorenz Hart**'s *On Your Toes*, which ran for 315 performances. Produced by **Dwight Deere Wiman**, the show starred **Ray Bolger** and also featured **Monty Woolley**. Geva danced the 'Princess Zenobia' and the 'Slaughter On Tenth Avenue' ballets, with choreography by Balanchine. In the 50s, Geva returned to Broadway with roles in the plays *Pride's Crossing* (1950) and *Misalliance* (1953).

● FURTHER READING: *Split Seconds: A Remembrance By Tamara Geva*, Tamara Geva.

● FILMS: *Ein Sommernachtstraum* aka *Wood Love* (1925), *Der Hahn Im Korb* (1925), *Die Freudlose Gasse* aka *The Joyless Street* (1925), *Die Unberührte Frau* (1925), *Gräfin Plättmamsell* (1926), *Night Club* (1929), *Zwischen Vierzehn Und Siebzehn—Sexualnot Der Jugend* (1929), *The Girl Habit* (1931), *Their Big Moment* aka *Afterwards* (1934), *Manhattan Merry-Go-Round* aka *Manhattan Music Box* (1937), *Orchestra Wives* (1942), *Night Plane From Chungking* (1943), *The Gay Intruders* (1948), *Cartas De Amor De Una Monja* (1978), *Frevel* aka *Mischief* (1984).

Geyer, Renée

b. 11 September 1953, Melbourne, Australia. Geyer is one of Australia's most established rock and soul vocalists, having recorded over 15 albums since the early 70s. She first came to notice as vocalist on jazz rock band Sun's 1972 album. Next came a more lauded combo, Mother Earth, who also provided backing for her first solo album, which consisted mostly of cover versions. She charted with 'It's A Man's Man's Man's World'. The band Sanctuary, composed of seasoned rock and session players, became her regular backing band, also writing songs for her. The mid-70s provided several hit singles and successful albums and also established her as Australia's premier female soul vocalist. In 1976 she went to the USA for the first time, and over the next decade split her time between the USA and Australia, steadily releasing records and playing live with self-titled bands put together from the cream of Australia's musicians for the duration of the tour. By the mid-80s Geyer was ensconced in Los Angeles, writing and doing session work. An album with Easy Pieces was recorded in 1988 but sunk rapidly. Unfortunately, as yet she has not been able to demonstrate her talent to the international market, but she remains an icon in her native Australia.

● ALBUMS: *Renée Geyer* (RCA 1973) ★★★, *It's A Man's Man's World* (RCA 1974) ★★★, *Ready To Deal* (RCA 1975) ★★★, *Really Really Love You* (RCA 1976) ★★★, *Moving Along* (RCA 1977) ★★★★, *Winner* (RCA 1978) ★★, *Blues Licence* (RCA 1979) ★★★★, *So Lucky* (Mushroom 1981) ★★, *Renée Live* (Mushroom 1983) ★★, *Faves* (Mushroom 1984) ★★★, *Sing To Me* (WEA 1985) ★★★, *Live At The Basement* (ABC 1986) ★★★, *Easy Pieces* (A&M 1988) ★★★, *Difficult Woman* (Larrikin 1994) ★★★, *Sweet Life* (Mushroom 1999) ★★★, *Tenderland* (ABC 2003) ★★★, *Tonight* (ABC 2005) ★★★.

● COMPILATIONS: *At Her Very Best* (RCA 1977) ★★★★, *The Best Of Renée Geyer: 1973-1998* (Mushroom 1998) ★★★★, *The Great* (Rajon 2001) ★★★.

Ghanaba, Kofi

(see **Warren, Guy**)

Ghazal

World music fusionists Ghazal comprises Kayhan Kalhor (b. Tehran, Iran; kamancheh or spike fiddle) and Shujaat Khan (b. India; sitar/vocals). They first collaborated in 1996, and a recording contract soon followed with world music specialists Shanachie Records. Their three albums in the late 90s blended traditional and classical influences, with all including contributions from Shri Swapan Chaudhuri (tabla). The group, who have successfully toured America, prefer to extemporize rather than stick to preconceived musical patterns — their natural spontaneity is evidenced by the fact that their most commercially visible album, *Moon Rise Over*

The Silk Road, was recorded in just two days. The group's reflective, pastoral sound found a ready audience in America for its 'relaxing' qualities — although it would be foolish to deny the complexity of performances that underpin Ghazal's work. Both Kalhor and Khan are now based in America, although on opposite coasts.

● ALBUMS: *Lost Songs Of The Silk Road* (Shanachie 1997) ★★★, *As Night Falls On The Silk Road* (Shanachie 1998) ★★★★, *Moon Rise Over The Silk Road* (Shanachie 2000) ★★★, *The Rain* (ECM 2003) ★★★.

Ghetto Mafia

An Atlanta, Georgia, USA–based crew, the Ghetto Mafia are, as their name implies, a hardcore rap outfit, relentlessly exploring the life cycle of the young, alienated black man. The group is fronted by the twin rapping talents of Nino and Wicked. The lead-off single for their 1994 debut album, 'Everday Thang In The Hood', introduced guest vocals by **MC Breed**, who also produced the album. These were nothing if not controversial songs—'Mr President' talking about not only assassinating the president, but wiping out his whole family for good measure. The group has carried on recording into the late 90s and the new millennium.

● ALBUMS: *Draw The Line* (Funk Town 1994) ★★, *Straight From The Dec* (Down South 1997) ★★, *On Da Ground* (Rap Artist 1998) ★★★, *Presents Wicked & The Hood Show* (ITD 2004) ★★, *Da Return Of . . .* (Down South 2005) ★★.

● COMPILATIONS: *Greatest Hits* (ITD 2003) ★★★.

Ghost Dance

If ever a supergroup were created to fulfil the demands of the enormous 'goth' fraternity in Britain during the mid-80s then, on paper at least, Ghost Dance fitted the bill. Formed in 1985 by Gary Marx (guitar), from **Sisters Of Mercy**, and Anne Marie (vocals), previously with **Skeletal Family**, the duo recruited Etch (bass) from the Citron Girls and added 'Pandora' the drum machine. Throughout 1986, Ghost Dance attracted a ready-made audience with their brand of brooding rock, utilizing extra guitarists Steve Smith and Paul Southern from **Red Lorry Yellow Lorry** and swiftly releasing three independent singles that became highly collectable items. At the close of the year Richard Steel joined on guitar and John Grant replaced the drum machine. Their commercial position fortified by 'A Word To The Wise' entering the Top 100 of the UK chart, and a sell-out nationwide tour, Ghost Dance signed to **Chrysalis Records** and struggled to lose the 'gothic' tag. Unfortunately, while recording their debut album, various band members started to drift apart, and the 'Celebrate' single, a further attempt to broaden the band's musical horizons, merely served to alienate Ghost Dance's die-hard fans. Perplexed by their protégés' evolution, the label dropped the band halfway through an ironically successful European tour with the **Ramones**, encouraging the personal ructions to come to the fore and subsequently causing Ghost Dance to split at the beginning of 1990. Anne Marie embarked upon an unsuccessful solo career, Etch played guitar with the **Mission** and **Loud**, while Gary Marx concentrated on collaborating with local musicians.

● ALBUMS: *Stop The World* (Chrysalis 1989) ★★.
● COMPILATIONS: *Gathering Dust* (Chrysalis 1988) ★★.

Ghost (reggae)

b. Carlton Hylton, 1974, Kingston, Jamaica, West Indies. Hylton began his career while in his teens when he performed on various **sound systems**. He first came to prominence in 1993 when he recorded with producer **Clifton 'Specialist' Dillon.** Dillon enrolled Hylton, who performed as Ghost, to sing in combination with another newcomer, the raspy DJ **Culture**. The singjay style of Ghost combined with Culture's **ragga** rapping was widely considered as being testament to the evolution of the **digital** reggae sound. A notable track from these sessions was the braggadocio 'Gal Pickney', featured on the ragga showcase *Strictly Dancehall*. His solo career was established, and he released a series of hits. Notable **dancehall** anthems included 'Arms Of Love', 'Program For Your Body', 'Mix Up Situation', 'It's All Coming Back', 'Roses Are Red', 'Say It Loud' and the duet with **Tony Curtis**, 'Whine'. Hylton continued to maintain a high profile in the dancehall, and in 1996 his career was further enhanced when he joined the **Monster Shack Crew** alongside the DJs Roundhead and **General B**. Although part of a crew, Hylton continued to record sporadic solo hits including the favoured 'Body Guard'. The song proved a dancehall smash and was later re-recorded in combination with the Monster Shack Crew. Initially the crew released 'Monster World' followed by 'Wanna Mek Noise', a classic hit riding the prevalent 'Medina' rhythm. The increasing popularity of the crew in Jamaica and subsequently the world resulted in Hylton receiving international acclaim following the release of *Monster Party*, produced by Colin 'Fatta' Waters. The release included the re-recording of his hit, 'Body Guard' alongside notable tracks including 'Flava', 'Dem Time Deh' and 'Weed Is Life'. The crew continued to record in combination and individually, which led to Hylton's chart success with the haunting 'What Have You Done'. The song demonstrated his unique style and signalled his emergence as a serious contender for the singjay crown. His new-found affluence resulted in a move to St. Andrew, where he was falsely accused of being in possession of firearms. The case was thrown out of court, and the action resulted in favourable publicity for the performer.

● ALBUMS: *Slowly* (White Label 1996) ★★★★, *Love You* (Music Ambassadors 2000) ★★★, *Under The Moonlight* (Musical Ambassador 2002) ★★★.

Ghost (rock)

The Ghost was formed by Paul Eastment (vocals; ex–**Velvett Fogg**), Terry Guy (keyboards), Daniel MacGuire (bass) and Charlie Grima (drums) in Birmingham, Midlands, England, in the late 60s. The band began to play at local clubs with a sound that owed as much to blues as to pop and rock. However, they made little impression until recruiting a female singer and acoustic guitarist, Shirley Kent. Kent had previously recorded two tracks for a charity/agit prop EP, *The Master Singers And Shirley Kent Sing For Charec 77* for Keele University Records. They began writing songs together and released their debut single, 'When You're Dead', for Gemini Records in 1969. The song, which clearly betrayed the west coast psychedelic rock influence of the **Byrds** and **Jefferson Airplane**, failed to hit the charts. A second single, 'I've Got To Get To Know You', and the band's debut album, *When You're Dead—One Second*, followed a year later. On album the distinction between Kent's songwriting style—close in execution to **Sandy Denny**'s work with **Fairport**

Convention—and her male colleagues' more macho blues rock convictions, became readily apparent. Perhaps because of this schism, sales were disappointing. Kent later pursued a solo career under the name Virginia Tree, though Eastment and Guy from Ghost featured on some of the tracks. After Kent's defection the remaining members of the band persevered under the new name Resurrection but failed to record. Their sole album was re-released by Bam Caruso Records in 1987 under a slightly altered title.

● ALBUMS: *When You're Dead—One Second* reissued as *For One Second* (Gemini 1970) ★★★.

Ghost Goes Gear, The

The manager of a successful pop group sets out to finance his stately home by organizing a festival. *The Ghost Goes Gear* proved as trite as its plot and failed completely to take account of trailblazing British pop films **A Hard Day's Night** or **Catch Us If You Can**. This 1966 film was a throw-back to the era of **Summer Holiday**, despite the starring presence of the **Spencer Davis Group**, one of the period's most exciting, innovative groups. Their compulsive singles included 'Keep On Running' and 'Gimme Some Lovin'', but *The Ghost Goes Gear* was a woeful waste of their talent, a feature compounded by the inclusion of **Acker Bilk**'s Paramount Jazzmen and the **Lorne Gibson** Trio. The producers' aim to turn an ailing project into 'all-round' family entertainment simply worsened the film. Cameo appearances by **Dave Berry** and the **St. Louis Union** lightened the gloom momentarily, but the positive aspects of *The Ghost Goes Gear* are far outweighed by the bad. The film gained only limited screening upon release despite the appeal of its leading lights.

Ghost, Amanda

b. London, England. This singer-songwriter of Spanish and Indian descent was raised in north London, and made a notable impression in 2000 with her debut *Ghost Stories*. Ghost first began performing while studying at the London College of Fashion, creating a favourable impression on the city's tight-knit club scene. She formed a songwriting and performing partnership with Ian Dench (ex-**EMF**), remixer Lucas Barton and keyboard player Sacha Skarbek, and signed a worldwide recording contract with **Warner Brothers Records**. Although *Ghost Stories* opens with the strident industrial leanings of 'Filthy Mind', the downbeat lyrics and mix of folk-based melodies and club beats on the following tracks place Ghost firmly in **Beth Orton** territory.

● ALBUMS: *Ghost Stories* (Warners 2000) ★★★.

Ghostface Killah

b. Dennis Coles, 9 May 1970, New York City, USA. Raised in the Staten Island district of New York City, Ghostface Killah was an original member of the **Wu-Tang Clan** crew. On early appearances his face was hidden behind a stocking mask, although no explanation was ever given for his anonymity. Ghostface Killah's voice was the first to be heard on their acclaimed 1993 debut, **Enter The Wu-Tang (36 Chambers)**. Minus the mask, he made his mark in Wu-Tang Clan lore with a major contribution to **Raekwon**'s hard hitting *Only Built 4 Cuban Linx . . .*, adopting the Tony Starks moniker on the album cover. Further appearances on the *Sunset Park* and *Don't Be A Menace To South Central While You're Drinking Your Juice In The Hood* soundtracks, prefigured the

release of his debut album in November 1996. *Ironman* was the first release on producer **RZA**'s Razor Sharp Records imprint. Featuring major contributions from new Wu-Tang Clan rapper **Cappadonna** and Raekwon (the three appeared on the album cover together), *Ironman* was one of the Wu-Tang family's most acclaimed releases. Featuring a more soul-orientated production than other Wu-Tang releases, the album included the highly successful duet with **Mary J. Blige** on 'All That I Got Is You'. *Ironman* proved to be the most commercially successful Wu-Tang Clan product until the release of the following year's *Wu-Tang Forever*, debuting at number 2 on the **Billboard** album chart.

Further work with various members of the Wu-Tang Clan preceded the release of Ghostface Killah's eagerly anticipated second album. *Supreme Clientele* was an excellent companion to the rapper's debut and confirmed his reputation as one of the most artistically and commercially viable solo members of the Wu-Tang Clan. The hastily recorded follow-up *Bulletproof Wallets* was a marked disappointment, however, and ushered in a period of doubt and falling sales for all member of the Wu-Tang circle.

After completing work on a new Clan album and promoting a solo compilation, Ghostface Killah began casting around for a new solo recording contract. He signed on with **Def Jam Records** and returned to the studio to record a new album. Released under the Ghostface moniker in April 2004, *The Pretty Toney Album* saw the rapper sharpening up his act and getting his solo career back on track.

● ALBUMS: *Ironman* (Razor Sharp/Epic 1996) ★★★★, *Supreme Clientele* (Razor Sharp/Epic 2000) ★★★★, *Bulletproof Wallets* (Starks Enterprise/Epic 2001) ★★★, as Ghostface *The Pretty Toney Album* (Def Jam 2004) ★★★, as Ghostface *Raw Footage* (Fastlife 2005) ★★★, *Fishscale* (Def Jam 2006) ★★★.

● COMPILATIONS: *Shaolin's Finest* (Epic 2003) ★★★★.

Ghostwriters

An Australian garage rock band, the Ghostwriters is a side project for **Hoodoo Gurus** bass player Rick Grossman and **Midnight Oil** drummer Rob Hirst. However, nothing about the group was known in 1991, when they released their first, self-titled album for **Virgin Records**. Instead, the participants kept their identities secret. In fact, Grossman and Hirst had been friends for over 20 years and had always intended to work together on such a project. Eventually they admitted to their involvement, but it was a full five years before the advent of a second Ghostwriters album. As Grossman told **Billboard** magazine after its release: 'I love being in the Gurus, and I know Rob loves being in the Oils, but after you've been on the road for six months, it becomes a bit of a grind, and to collaborate with Ghostwriters is refreshing.' *Second Skin* was also released in the USA, via a new recording contract with **Mercury Records**.

● ALBUMS: *Ghostwriters* (Virgin 1991) ★★★, *Second Skin* (Mercury 1996) ★★★.

Giant

Originating from Nashville, USA, Giant developed in the mid-80s when seasoned session guitarist **Dann Huff** (b. 15 November 1960, Nashville, Tennessee, USA) met with keyboard player **Alan Pasqua** on various projects, notably **Whitesnake**'s *1987* album. However, it was not until 1988 that

Giant evolved into a fully fledged unit, with Huff's younger brother, David, joining as drummer and Mike Brignardello on bass (the Huff brothers had formerly been in partnership as part of Christian rockers White Heart). By this time, Dann Huff had taken on lead vocal duties after an unsuccessful search for a suitable singer. Candidates for the job had included the highly successful songwriter and backing vocalist, **Tom Kelly**. Giant signed to **A&M Records** in 1988 and released their debut album, *Last Of The Runaways*, in the USA in 1989, a potent brew of hard rock, strong on melody and presentation. It included the Top 10 hit single, 'I'll See You In My Dreams'. The success of the album and single in the USA and impressive sales on import in the UK prompted A&M to give *Last Of The Runaways* a European release in 1990, to a moderate degree of success. This was followed by a series of highly acclaimed club dates around the UK. In 1991, Huff, Pasque and Brignardello played together on **Amy Grant**'s *Heart In Motion*, and prepared material for a new album. However, *Time To Burn* did not feature Pasqua, and though it was again critically lauded, soon after its release Epic, to whom Giant had transferred, dropped the band.

● ALBUMS: *Last Of The Runaways* (A&M 1989) ★★★★, *Time To Burn* (Epic 1992) ★★★.

Giant Sand

Formed by singer-songwriter **Howe Gelb** (vocals, guitar, bass, keyboards) in his home-town of Tucson, Arizona, USA, in 1980 with **Rainer** (b. Rainer Ptacek, 7 June 1951, East Berlin, Germany, d. 12 November 1997, Tucson, Arizona, USA; guitar) and Billy Sed (drums). This line-up recorded a four-track EP as Giant Sandworms on a local label before departing for New York, where Sed's drug escapades forced a return to Arizona. They were joined by David Seger (bass) for a further EP, before he left to join **Naked Prey**. His replacement was Scott Gerber. Shortly afterwards the band's name was changed to Giant Sand (the original name had unintentional connotations with the wildlife in Frank Herbert's science fiction novel *Dune*), with Gelb firing all personnel except Gerber in the process. Ptacek, though, reappeared in Gelb's countrified alter ego group, the **Band Of Blacky Ranchette**. Tom Larkins, who played concurrently with Naked Prey, joined as drummer, and together they recorded 1985's *Valley Of Rain* with guest pianist Chris Cavacas from **Green On Red**. Gelb's girlfriend Paula Jean Brown then joined on bass and guitar but after recording 1986's *Ballad Of A Thin Line Man*, Gerber left to join the Sidewinders, eventually moving on to Los Cruzos with former Giant Sandworms drummer Sed. A variety of personnel has populated later Giant Sand recordings, including Neil Harry (pedal steel guitar), John Convertino (drums), Joey Burns (guitar/bass), and Mark Walton (bass, ex-**Dream Syndicate**). The most stable line-up, featuring Gelb, Burns and Convertino, was in place from 1990 into the new millennium, before the latter duo elected to concentrate on their own project, **Calexico**.

Giant Sand's early stark sound (often described as 'desert rock', and a noted influence on the alternative country movement) evolved into a crisp mix of swing, country, rock, and beatnik lyricism. It remains tempered, as ever, by Gelb's evocative, arid imagery. The members of Giant Sand teamed up with **Lisa Germano** in 1997 for the strangely evocative *Slush*, recorded under the name OP8. Gelb put Giant Sand on hold to work on his second solo album, 1999's *Hisser*, before

returning to the band format the following year with the wonderful *Chore Of Enchantment*. 2002's *Cover Magazine* featured cover versions of material by artists including **Black Sabbath**, **Johnny Cash**, **Nick Cave** and **Bob Dylan**. The follow-up *Is All Over . . . The Map* featured an international Giant Sand line-up, with Gelb joined by Anders Pedersen (guitar), Thøger T. Lund (bass), and Peter Dombernowsky (drums), reflecting his new base in Denmark.

● ALBUMS: *Valley Of Rain* (Enigma 1985) ★★★, *Ballad Of A Thin Line Man* (Zippo 1986) ★★★, *Storm* (What Goes On 1988) ★★★, *The Love Songs LP* (Homestead 1988) ★★★, *Long Stem Rant* (Homestead 1989) ★★★, *Swerve* (Amazing Black Sand 1990) ★★★, *Ramp* (Amazing Black Sand 1992) ★★★, *Center Of The Universe* (Restless 1992) ★★★, *Purge And Slouch* (Restless 1993) ★★★, *Stromausfall* (Return To Sender 1993) ★★★, *Glum* (Imago 1994) ★★★, *Backyard Barbeque Broadcast* (Koch 1995) ★★★, as OP8 *Slush* (V2 1997) ★★★, *Chore Of Enchantment* (Thrill Jockey/Loose 2000) ★★★★, *Cover Magazine* (Thrill Jockey/Loose 2002) ★★★, *Is All Over . . . The Map* (Thrill Jockey/Loose 2004) ★★★.

● COMPILATIONS: *Giant Songs: The Best Of Giant Sand* (Demon 1989) ★★★, *Giant Sandwich* (Homestead 1989) ★★★, *Giant Songs Two: The Best Of Giant Sand Volume 2* (Demon 1995) ★★★, *Selections Circa 1990–2000* (Vinyl Junkie/Loose 2001) ★★★★.

Gibb, Andy

b. 5 March 1958, Manchester, England, d. 10 March 1988, Oxford, England. Following the international success of his three elder brothers in the **Bee Gees**, Andy appeared as a star in his own right in 1977. Emerging at the beginning of the disco boom, he scored three consecutive US number 1 hits with his first three chart entries. 'I Just Want To Be Your Everything', '(Love Is) Thicker Than Water' and 'Shadow Dancing' made him one of the most commercially successful recording artists of his era and for a time he even eclipsed his illustrious brothers in popularity. Six further hits followed, including a collaboration with **Olivia Newton-John** ('I Can't Help It') before Gibb moved into television work. The pressure of living with the reputation of his superstar brothers, coupled with immense wealth and a hedonistic bent, brought personal problems, and he became alarmingly reliant upon cocaine. Within months of his brothers' autumnal and highly successful reunion in the late 80s, tragedy struck when the 30-year-old singer died of an inflammatory heart virus at his home. It was the end of a career that had brought spectacular success in a remarkably short period.

● ALBUMS: *Flowing Rivers* (RSO 1977) ★★, *Shadow Dancing* (RSO 1978) ★★, *After Dark* (RSO 1980) ★★.

● COMPILATIONS: *Andy Gibb's Greatest Hits* (RSO 1981) ★★.

Gibb, Barry

b. 1 September 1946, Douglas, Isle Of Man, British Isles. Gibb first came to prominence as a member of the **Bee Gees** in 1967. Generally regarded as the best looking of the brood, he proved surprisingly reluctant to branch out into any serious solo ventures of his own. When the group fell out in the late 60s and **Robin Gibb** briefly pursed a solo career, Barry preferred to keep the Bee Gees name in conjunction with brother Maurice. A one-off single, 'I'll Kiss Your Memory', was issued in 1970 but it was poorly promoted and did not distract Barry from the group venture. Although the remarkable success of the Bee Gees was enough to keep most artists in full-time work, Gibb decided to extend his work load in the late 70s. He contributed vocals to Samantha Sang's US hit 'Emotion' and this encouraged a series of duets with major artists. A highly successful collaboration with **Barbra Streisand** resulted in the smash hit 'Guilty' and this was followed by an equally attractive duet with **Dionne Warwick** on the ballad 'Heartbreaker'. Toward the end of 1984 Gibb finally released his debut solo album *Now Voyager*, which spawned the hit 'Shine Shine'. While preparing for the Bee Gees return in the late 80s, he found time to release a novelty disc 'We Are The Bunburys' under the group pseudonym the Bunburys. An accomplished producer and superb harmony singer, Gibb's multifarious talents and hit-making abilities extend far beyond his more famous work as a member of the Bee Gees.

● ALBUMS: *Now Voyager* (Polydor 1984) ★★★, *Hawks* (Polydor 1988) ★★.

Gibb, Robin

b. 22 December 1949, Douglas, Isle Of Man, British Isles. Gibb had already achieved considerable success in the chart-topping **Bee Gees** when, following a disagreement with his brothers, he elected to go solo. With his distinctive nasal delivery, he initially outdid his fraternal rivals by reaching number 2 in the UK charts in 1969 with 'Saved By The Bell'. When the follow-up, 'One Million Years', failed to chart, however, it was clear that Gibb's continued success was by no means assured. He scraped into the UK charts again in early 1970 with 'August October' but soon afterwards reunited with his brothers and curtailed his solo adventures. It was not until as late as 1978 that he entered the US charts in his own right, courtesy of 'Oh! Darling' from the soundtrack of the movie ***Sgt Pepper's Lonely Hearts Club Band***. Six years later Robin Gibb the soloist enjoyed another isolated success with 'Boys Do Fall In Love', taken from his third solo album *Secret Agent*. Although he has continued to record solo albums, Gibb's most memorable material has been in conjunction with the Bee Gees, and his vocal identity remains one of the most familiar in all pop. The release of *Magnet* in 2003 cruelly coincided with the death of his brother Maurice.

● ALBUMS: *Robin's Reign* (Polydor 1970) ★★★, *How Old Are You?* (Polydor 1983) ★★★, *Secret Agent* (Polydor 1984) ★★★, *Walls Have Eyes* (Polydor 1985) ★★★, *Magnet* (SPV 2003) ★★, with the Neue Philharmonie Franfurt Orchestra *Live* (Eagle 2005) ★★★.

● DVD/VIDEOS: with the Neue Philharmonie Franfurt Orchestra *Live* (Eagle 2005).

Gibbons, Carroll

b. Richard Carroll Gibbons, 4 January 1903, Clinton, Massachusetts, USA, d. 10 May 1954, London, England. Gibbons studied classical piano at the New England Conservatory in Boston and became interested in dance music while at college. In 1924 he went to London with singer **Rudy Vallee** and worked in the Berkeley Hotel's resident group, the Boston Orchestra. He led his own band, the Sylvians, at the Savoy Hotel in 1926 and a year later took over the leadership of the celebrated Savoy Orpheans from Debroy Somers. After a German tour in 1928, the Orpheans

disbanded and Gibbons went to **HMV Records** as director of light music. He assembled their house band, the New Mayfair Dance Orchestra, before leaving in 1929 to become musical director for British and Dominion Films. Back in the USA he worked for MGM films and, with **Harry Warren** and **Richard Rodgers**, provided music for **Billy Rose**'s 1930 Broadway revue *Crazy Quilt*, starring **Fanny Brice**.

In 1931 Gibbons returned to London as co-director with Howard Jacobs, of the New Savoy Orpheans, eventually becoming sole leader. He broadcast frequently from the hotel, sometimes with 'The Boy Friends', a small group drawn from within the main band. At the outbreak of World War II he was on holiday in the USA but returned to the UK and formed a touring band before again residing at the Savoy, eventually becoming director of entertainment there in 1950, a position he held until his death in May 1954. Gibbons' individual piano style and quiet, almost shy, personality made him very popular on UK radio. Records such as 'Room 504', 'A Nightingale Sang In Berkeley Square', 'Home', and 'These Foolish Things', were all big hits in the USA. He also made a series of solo piano records entitled 'Carroll Calls The Tunes'. His personnel included musicians Howard Jacobs, Paul Fenhoulet, Joe Brannelly, Laurie Payne, Max Goldberg and **George Melachrino**, who also sang with the band along with other vocalists such as **Ann Lenner**, Dorothy Stedeford and Brian Lawrence. Gibbons' best known compositions are probably 'Garden In The Rain' and his theme tune 'On The Air'. He also contributed music to several West End shows including *Leslie Henson's Gaieties*, *Big Boy*, *Open Your Eyes* and *Sylvia*.

● COMPILATIONS: *Carroll Gibbons Story 1925-1946* (1972) ★★★, *Hartley's Jam Broadcasts 1934-35* (1980) ★★★, *Body And Soul* (1982) ★★★, with Ray Noble *The New Mayfair Dance Orchestra—Harmony Heaven 1928-1930* (1983) ★★★, *The Golden Age Of Carroll Gibbons* (1985) ★★★, *Dancing In The Dark* (1986) ★★★, *Carroll Recalls The Tunes* (1986) ★★★, *On The Air—Hartley's Jam Broadcasts 1943-45* (1986) ★★★, *Brighter Than The Sun* (1986) ★★★, *I Saw Stars* (1987) ★★★, *Too Marvellous For Words* (1988) ★★★, *Music Maestro Please* (1989) ★★★, with the Savoy Hotel Orpheans *Time Was* (1994) ★★★, *On The Air* (1994) ★★★.

Gibbons, Steve

b. Birmingham, England. Gibbons was the quintessential product of the English beat group era, with a powerful vocal style and a quiverful of imaginative and intelligent composi-tions. He started in 1958 as the vocalist with the Dominettes. After several changes of line-up this became the **Uglys** in 1962. With **Dave Pegg** (later of **Fairport Convention**) on bass the group recorded unsuccessfully for **Pye Records** and later for **MGM Records**. In 1969, the Uglys split and Gibbons joined ex–**Moody Blues** member **Denny Laine** and Trevor Burton, formerly of the **Move**, in **Balls**, an abortive attempt by ex-Move manager **Tony Secunda** to create a Brum 'supergroup'. With the aid of session guitarists **Albert Lee** and **Chris Spedding**, Balls made *Short Stories* for Secunda's Wizzard label before disbanding in 1971. Gibbons next briefly joined the **Idle Race**, which evolved into the Steve Gibbons Band, which has continued with line-up changes to this day. The early line-up included Burton (bass), Dave Carroll and Bob Wilson on guitars and Bob Lamb (drums). Their debut album appeared on **Roger Daltrey**'s Goldhawk label in 1976, and the

following year Gibbons had a Top 20 hit with **Chuck Berry**'s 'Tulane', from the Kenny Laguna–produced *Caught In The Act*. Soon afterwards Lamb quit the band to concentrate on running his own studio, where he produced the early work of another local band, **UB40**. In the early 80s the Steve Gibbons Band recorded two albums for **RCA Records** with Gibbons maintaining his imaginative and witty approach to co-songwriting, as the titles 'Biggles Flys Undone', 'B.S.A.' and 'Somebody Stole My Synthesiser' suggest. Burton left the band around this time. Though no longer a commercial proposition, Gibbons has remained a popular live performer, especially in the Birmingham area. Studio albums continue to appear on an infrequent basis on small UK labels.
● ALBUMS: *Any Road Up* (Goldhawk/MCA 1976) ★★★, *Rollin' On* (Polydor/MCA 1977) ★★★, *Caught In The Act* (Polydor/MCA 1977) ★★★, *Down In The Bunker* (Polydor 1978) ★★★★, *Street Parade* (RCA/Polydor 1980) ★★★, *Saints And Sinners* (RCA 1981) ★★★, *On The Loose* (Magnum Force 1986) ★★★, *Maintaining Radio Silence* (Episode 1988) ★★★, *Ridin' Out The Dark* (SPV 1990) ★★★, *Birmingham To Memphis* (Linn 1993) ★★★★, *Stained Glass* (Havic 1996) ★★★, *Live At The Robin '98* (Reckless 1998) ★★, *The Dylan Project* (Woodworm 1998) ★★★.
● COMPILATIONS: *The Best Of Steve Gibbons Band: Get Up And Dance* (Polydor 1980) ★★★.

Gibbons, Walter

b. 2 April 1954, New York City, USA, d. 23 September 1994, Long Island, New York, USA. Gibbons is often cited as the first 'remixer'. It was he who transformed Double Exposure's 'Ten Percent' from a three-minute album track into a nine-minute dancefloor epic and subsequently the first commercially available 12-inch single in 1975. Gibbons moved away from disco's emphasis on orchestration towards percussion, and developed contemporary mixing techniques with his DJing at clubs such as New York's Galaxy 21, Fantasia and Buttermilk Bottom, Philadelphia's Second Storey and the Monastery in Seattle. It was his DJing skills that influenced the respected producer **François Kevorkian**—whose live drumming accompanied Gibbons' sets. Gibbons not only advanced the skills of the DJ but also developed the art of 'remixing', adding **dub**-inspired effects to early disco records, often transforming them from mediocre **dance music** tracks into epic-sounding disco anthems for labels such as Salsoul, West End and Gold Mind. He also worked with artists such as **Loleatta Holloway** (remixing her 'Hit And Run' and 'Catch Me On The Rebound') and the Salsoul Orchestra ('Nice 'N' Nasty').
At the peak of his popularity, Gibbons rejected the decadence of disco to become a born-again Christian, even refusing to play records with a sexual content. However, in 1984, he released a 12-inch single, 'Set It Off' by Strafe, on his own independent Jus' Born label that had a massive impact on the emergent Chicago **house** scene. The record was a sensation at Levan's Garage in New York City and spawned covers by C. Sharpe and Masquerade and a 'response' single in the form of Number 1's 'Set It Off (Party Rock)'. The track determined the tone for much of the house music that followed, with its seductive vocal refrain repeated over sparse and atmospheric beats. 'Set It Off' did just that, becoming massively popular in Chicago's nascent house clubs, where it was played by **Frankie Knuckles** and **Farley Jackmaster Funk**, and by the

city's influential radio DJs. Gibbons also completed remix work on two tracks by **Arthur Russell** in 1986— Indian Ocean's 'Tree House'/'School Bell' on **Sleeping Bag Records**— before leaving the music business.

Gibbs, Georgia

b. Freda Gibbons, 17 August 1920, Worcester, Massachusetts, USA. Gibbs has been unfairly maligned by rock critics for building her career in the 50s by covering R&B hits of **LaVern Baker** and **Etta James**. In reality, she was a genuinely talented pop vocalist, whose jazz-tinged approach reflected years of experience in the big band era, a period when there was no stigma attached to cover versions. Her big break in showbusiness came in 1936, when she joined the Hudson-DeLange Orchestra, recording for **Brunswick Records**. That led to a radio career in 1937, including *Your Hit Parade*. There were also recording stints with the bands of Frankie Trumbauer (1940), **Artie Shaw** (1942) and **Tommy Dorsey** (1944).
On the *Jimmy Durante Camel Caravan* radio show 1943–47, Gibbs received her trademark nickname when host Garry Moore dubbed her 'Her Nibs, Miss Gibbs'. Gibbs first entered the charts in 1950 with a cover version of Eileen Barton's 'If I Knew You Were Comin' I'd've Baked A Cake' (number 5 pop), and had her first number 1 hit with 'Kiss Of Fire', a vocal version of the 30s tango instrumental 'El Choclo'. After gaining another hit with 'Seven Lonely Days' (number 5 pop 1953), Gibbs achieved notoriety in 1955 when she hit with two note-for-note cover versions of R&B tunes—'Tweedle Dee' (US pop number 2) by Baker and 'Dance With Me, Henry' (US pop number 1) by James. 'Kiss Me Another' (US pop number 30) and 'Tra La La' (US pop number 24) kept her in the public eye in 1956, but not for long. Her last chart record was 'The Hula Hoop Song' (US pop Top 40, 1958), which tried to ride the success of the silly toy fad. In the UK, Gibb's chart success was minuscule, constituting two one-week appearances by 'Tweedle Dee' and 'Kiss Me Another', respectively.
● ALBUMS: *Ballin' The Jack* 10-inch album (Coral 1951) ★★★★, *Georgia Gibbs Sings Oldies* 10-inch album (Mercury 1953) ★★★★, *The Man That Got Away* 10-inch album (Mercury 1954) ★★★, *Music And Memories* (Mercury 1956) ★★★, *Song Favorites* (Mercury 1956) ★★★, *Swingin' With Her Nibs* (Mercury 1956) ★★★, *Her Nibs* (Coral 1957) ★★★, *Something's Gotta Give* (1964) ★★★★, *Call Me* (1966). ★★★.
● COMPILATIONS: *Georgia Gibbs' Greatest Hits* (1963) ★★★★, *Her Nibs Miss Georgia Gibbs* (1994) ★★★★.

Gibbs, Joe

b. Joel Gibson, 1945, Montego Bay, Jamaica, West Indies. Gibbs started in the music business selling records in his television repair shop situated in Beeston Street, Kingston. In 1966, he moved into record production, releasing his material on the Jogib, Amalgamated and Pressure Beat labels in Jamaica. He found instant success with **Roy Shirley**'s 'Hold Them', one of the earliest records to introduce the new **rocksteady** beat, issued on the Doctor Bird label in the UK. By 1968 his productions were being released in the UK on Amalgamated, a subsidiary of **Trojan Records** set up exclusively for that purpose. The early issues were in the rocksteady format including 'Just Like A River' and 'Seeing Is Knowing' by **Stranger** (**Cole**) And Gladdy (Gladstone

Anderson), and 'El Casino Royale' by guitarist **Lynn Tait**. Later came reggae sides by the **Versatiles**, who included **Junior Byles** in their number, **Errol Dunkley**, the **Royals**, the Reggae Boys, **Ken Parker**, the Immortals, the **Slickers**, **Jimmy London**, Ernest Wilson, Keith Blake (aka **Prince Allah**, also a member of the Leaders with Milton Henry), the Soulmates, and **Nicky Thomas**, whose 'Love Of The Common People' reached number 9 in the UK pop charts during July 1970.

Other local hits came via the **Pioneers**, who recorded extensively for Gibbs before defecting to the **Leslie Kong** camp. Their hits included 'Give Me A Little Loving', 'Long Shot', 'Jackpot', 'Catch The Beat', and 'Mama Look Deh'. Many of these were written and produced by **Lee Perry**, who cut his own records, 'The Upsetter' and 'Kimble', for Gibbs before leaving to set up his own label. The parting was not exactly amicable, Perry's first self-production, 'People Funny Boy', being a vitriolic attack on Gibbs, who responded on record with the identical-sounding 'People Grudgeful'. Once Perry had departed, Gibbs enlisted **Winston 'Niney' Holness** to perform similar duties. With Holness at the helm, working the board alongside **Errol Thompson** at Randy's, Gibbs' label entered into the nascent **dub/version** boom with instrumental sides such as 'Nevada Joe' and its version, 'Straight To The Head', and 'Franco Nero' by Joe Gibbs And The Destroyers. Other popular instrumentals such as 'Hi-Jacked' and 'Movements' were credited to the Joe Gibbs All Stars. In 1969, he installed a two-track studio at the back of his newly established Joe Gibbs Record Mart in West Parade, later moving to North Parade, and began producing successful records such as 'Jack Of My Trade' by veteran DJ **Sir Lord Comic**, 'Them A Fi Get A Beatin'', 'Maga Dog' and 'Arise Black Man' by **Peter Tosh**, the first cut of 'Money In My Pocket' by **Dennis Brown**, and its DJ version 'A So We Stay' by **Big Youth**, 'Warricka Hill' by the Versatiles, and 'Pretty Girl' by **Delroy Wilson**. These appeared on a variety of labels in Jamaica and, primarily, on the Pressure Beat imprint through Trojan in the UK.

Gibbs also released several albums including *Best Of Dennis Brown*, *Heptones & Friends Vols. 1 & 2* and two of the earliest dub albums, the elusive *Dub Serial* and the first chapter of his classic *African Dub* series, both mixed by Thompson. By 1975 Gibbs had opened his own 16-track studio and pressing plant in Retirement Crescent, Kingston Jamaica. With Thompson installed at the controls, the hits soon flowed from artists such as Leo Graham, Sylford Walker ('Burn Babylon'), **Junior Byles** ('Heart And Soul'), **Dillinger** ('Production Plan'), George Washington ('Rockers No Crackers'), Dhaima ('Inna Jah Children'), **Earl Sixteen** ('Malcolm X'), Ruddy Thomas ('Every Day Is A Holiday'), **Gregory Isaacs** ('Babylon Too Rough'), Jah Berry aka **Prince Hammer** ('Dreadlocks Thing'), Naggo 'Dolphin' Morris ('Su Su Pon Rasta'), **Trinity** (*Three Piece Suit*), **Prince Far I** (*Under Heavy Manners*), and a brace of **Revolutionaries**-style instrumentals by Joe Gibbs And The Professionals. This was his studio band, incorporating the talents of **Lloyd Parks**, **Sly And Robbie**, **Bingi Bunny** and Bopeep on keyboards, **Cool Sticky** and Ruddy Thomas on percussion, and a horn section comprising Bobby Ellis, **Tommy McCook**, Herman Marquis and Vin Gordon.

Two further instalments of the *African Dub* series also emerged, with the notorious *Chapter 3*, which benefited (or suffered, depending on your point of view) from a particularly over-the-top mix from Thompson and Gibbs, achieving great popularity among the UK's punk adherents

in 1977. These records appeared on a variety of Gibbs-affiliated labels, including Joe Gibbs, Town & Country, Errol T, Reflections and Heavy Duty. The late 70s/early 80s were a fruitful time for Gibbs, with two of his acts, **Culture** and Dennis Brown, breaking internationally. Gibbs gained two more UK chart entries, with teenage female DJ duo **Althea And Donna**'s novelty 'Up Town Top Ranking' in 1977 and Dennis Brown's re-recording of 'Money In My Pocket' in 1979. Gibbs also produced popular sides by **Eek A Mouse** ('Virgin Girl'), **Kojak And Liza** ('Sky Juice'), and **Junior Murvin** ('Cool Out Son'). This activity continued on into the 80s, when, after moving to Miami, he temporarily ceased his operations following a lawsuit over copyright. He sold his old studio to **Bunny Lee**, but continues to lease and reissue his old material.

● COMPILATIONS: as Joe Gibbs And Friends *The Reggae Train 1968–1971* (Heartbeat 1988) ★★★, as Joe Gibbs And Errol Thompson *The Mighty Two* (Heartbeat 1990) ★★★, with various artists *Get On Up! Joe Gibbs Rocksteady 1967–1968* (Trojan 1998) ★★★★, with various artists *Joe Gibbs Mood: The Amalgamated Label 1968–1971* (Trojan 1998) ★★★★, with various artists *Uptown Top Ranking: Joe Gibbs Reggae Productions 1970–1978* (Trojan 1998) ★★★★, with various artists *Love Of The Common People: Anthology 1967 To 1979* (Trojan 2001) ★★★★, as Joe Gibbs & The Professionals *No Bones For The Dogs* (Pressure Sounds 2002) ★★★★, with various artists *Joe Gibbs Productions: Roots, Culture, DJs And The Birth Of Dancehall* (Soul Jazz 2003) ★★★★.

Gibbs, Mike

b. Michael Clement Irving Gibbs, 25 September 1937, Harare, Zimbabwe. One of the most individual and original composers and arrangers, Gibbs has said that he began to concentrate on writing because performing solos terrified him. He studied piano between the ages of seven and 13, then took up trombone when he was 17. He moved to Boston, Massachusetts, in 1959 to study at the **Berklee College Of Music** (where he played and recorded with the college band organized by **Herb Pomeroy**) and Boston Conservatory. He also took up a scholarship at the Lenox School of Jazz in 1961, where he studied with **Gunther Schuller**, **George Russell** and **J.J. Johnson**. He graduated from Berklee in 1962 and the conservatory in 1963. That same year he obtained another scholarship, this time at Tanglewood, where he studied with classical composers Xenakis, Copland, Foss and Schuller again.

After this he returned to Southern Rhodesia (Zimbabwe), then in 1965 he settled in England, playing trombone for **Graham Collier** and **John Dankworth**, working in pit orchestras for pantomimes and musicals, and subsequently recording a series of highly acclaimed and influential albums featuring many of the most prominent British-based players who were beginning to flirt with jazz/rock; (**Kenny Wheeler**, **Henry Lowther**, **Chris Pyne**, **Harry Beckett**, **Alan Skidmore**, **Chris Spedding**, **Roy Babbington**, **John Marshall**, **Ray Warleigh** and **Frank Ricotti**. His concert at London's Rainbow Theatre in 1974 was significant in that it was the first time for some decades that the Musicians Union permitted Americans to play with British musicians other than as featured soloists with local rhythm sections. This came about through Gibbs' long association with **Gary Burton**, whose quartet integrated with Gibbs' big band for this gig. Gibbs and Burton had studied and worked together at Berklee, and Burton had been the first to record Gibbs' arrangements in 1963. He returned to Berklee as a tutor and composer-in-residence from 1974–83. In 1983 he resigned from the school to freelance as an arranger and producer, and worked with **Michael Mantler**, **Joni Mitchell**, **Pat Metheny**, **John McLaughlin**, **Whitney Houston**, **Peter Gabriel** and **Sister Sledge** among many others.

In 1988 Gibbs made an own-name comeback with *Big Music* (composing and arranging all tracks as well as playing piano and trombone), and in 1991 toured with featured guitarist **John Scofield**, and appeared on Scofield's *Grace Under Pressure* in 1992. He was among the first writers to convincingly incorporate rock elements into orchestral jazz, and shared with one of his major influences, **Gil Evans**, the ability to organically integrate carefully arranged and scored frameworks with the most 'outside' improvisations. Gibbs is both a meticulous arranger and a frugal composer. Everything he delivers is carefully thought through and not a note is wasted. The list of albums below excludes those on which he only arranged or scored other people's music.

● ALBUMS: *Michael Gibbs* (Deram 1970) ★★★, *Tanglewood 63* (Deram 1971) ★★★★, *Just Ahead* (Polydor 1972) ★★★, with Gary Burton *In The Public Interest* (Polydor 1974) ★★★, *The Only Chrome Waterfall Orchestra* (Ah-Um 1976) ★★★★, *Big Music* (Virgin 1988) ★★★★, *By The Way* (Ah-Um 1994) ★★★, *Nonsequence* (Provocateur 2001) ★★★★.

Gibbs, Terri

b. 15 June 1954, Augusta, Georgia, USA. Gibbs was born blind and has been playing the piano since she was three. She listened to a wide repertoire of music and, even though she is regarded as a country singer, there are many other influences, notably **Ray Charles**. Gibbs sang gospel in her early teens and formed her own band, Sound Dimension. Meeting **Chet Atkins**, she was encouraged to become a professional performer. In 1975, she started a long residency at the Augusta Steak And Ale Restaurant, playing 50 songs a night. Her appearance had impressed an MCA executive, while her demo tapes had been noticed by producer/songwriter Ed Penney. Her debut single for MCA, the country soul of 'Somebody's Knockin', reached number 13 on the US pop charts. Subsequently, she only had country hits, which included 'Rich Man', 'Mis'ry River', 'Somedays It Rains All Day Long' and 'Anybody Else's Heart But Mine', but, despite her talent, she did not emerge as a major country star. In 1984, she recorded a duet, 'Slow Burning Fire', with **George Jones**. She turned to gospel music in 1986, signing with the Word label, and enjoyed three Top 5 singles on the Christian charts in 1988. She has since retired from the music business.

● ALBUMS: *Somebody's Knockin'* (MCA 1981) ★★★, *I'm A Lady* (MCA 1981) ★★★, *Some Days It Rains All Night* (MCA 1982) ★★★, *Over Easy* (MCA 1983) ★★★, *Hiding From Love* (MCA 1984) ★★★, *Old Friends* (MCA 1985) ★★★, *Turn Around* (Word 1987) ★★★, *Great Day* (Morning Gate 1990) ★★★, *Comfort The People* (Word 1991) ★★★.

● COMPILATIONS: *Best Of . . .* (Varèse Sarabande 1996) ★★★★.

Gibbs, Terry

b. Julius Gubenko, 13 October 1924, New York City, USA. After all-round study of percussion, Gibbs briefly played drums professionally before and during military service.

After discharge he concentrated on vibraphone, working with leaders such as **Tommy Dorsey**, **Chubby Jackson** and **Buddy Rich**. At the end of the 40s he achieved international prominence thanks to a two-year spell with **Woody Herman** followed by a brief period as a member of **Benny Goodman**'s sextet. In the early 50s he also formed a big band and worked on television with **Mel Tormé**. Based in California towards the end of the decade, he re-formed a big band, which he led at the prestigious **Monterey Jazz Festival** in 1961. Gibbs' big bands became a notable annual event in Los Angeles, featuring many well-known players who clearly enjoyed taking time out from the studios to play jazz. In the early 80s Gibbs teamed up with **Buddy De Franco** for a highly acclaimed album, the first of several the duo recorded. Gibbs' vibraphone style reflects the hard-driving **Lionel Hampton** tradition, but with slightly boppish overtones. Gibbs' playing always swings and with a big band in full cry behind him, he creates some of the most exciting sounds in jazz.

● ALBUMS: *Terry Gibbs Quartet* 10-inch album (Brunswick 1954) ★★★, *Terry* (Brunswick 1954) ★★★, *Terry Gibbs* (EmArcy 1955) ★★★, *Vibes On Velvet* (EmArcy 1956) ★★★, *Mallets A-Plenty* (EmArcy 1956) ★★★, *Swingin' Terry Gibbs* (EmArcy 1956) ★★★, *More Vibes On Velvet* (EmArcy 1956) ★★★, *A Jazz Band Ball* aka *Vibrations* (Mode/Interlude 1957) ★★★★, with Bill Harris *The Ex-Hermanites* reissued as *Woodchoppers' Ball* (Mode/Premier 1957) ★★★★, *Terry Plays The Duke* (EmArcy 1958) ★★★, *Steve Allen's All Stars* (EmArcy 1958) ★★★, *Launching A New Sound In Music* (Mercury 1959) ★★★, *Swing Is Here!* (Verve 1960) ★★★, *The Exciting Terry Gibbs Big Band* (Verve 1960) ★★★, *Music From Cole Porter's Can Can* (Verve 1960) ★★, *Main Stem* (Contemporary 1961) ★★★, *That Swing Thing* (Verve 1962) ★★★, *Straight Ahead* (Verve 1962) ★★★, *Explosion* (Mercury 1962), *Jewish Melodies In Jazztime* (Mercury 1963) ★★★, *Hootenanny My Way* reissued as *It's Time We Met* (Time 1963) ★★★, *El Nutto* (Limelight 1964) ★★★, *Take It From Me* (Impulse! 1964) ★★★, *Latino* (Roost 1965) ★★★, *Reza* (Dot 1966) ★★★, *Bobstacle Course* (Xanadu 1974) ★★★, *Live At The Lord* (Jazz A La 1978) ★★★, *Smoke 'Em Up* (Jazz A La 1978) ★★★, with Buddy De Franco *Jazz Party: First Time Together* (Palo Alto 1981) ★★★, *The Latin Connection* (Contemporary 1986) ★★, *Dream Band* 1959 recording (Contemporary 1986) ★★★, *Dream Band Volume Two: The Sandown Sessions* 1959 recording (Contemporary 1987) ★★★, with De Franco *Chicago Fire* (Contemporary 1987) ★★★★, *Holiday For Swing* (Contemporary 1988) ★★★, *Air Mail Special* 1981 recording (Contemporary 1988) ★★★★, *Dream Band Volume 3: Flying Home* 1959 recording (Contemporary 1988) ★★★, *Dream Band Volume Four: Main Stem* 1959 recording (Contemporary 1990) ★★★, *Dream Band Volume 5: The Big Cat* 1959 recording (Contemporary 1991) ★★★, *Memories Of You* (Contemporary 1992) ★★★, *Kings Of Swing* (Contemporary 1993) ★★★★, *Hollywood Swing* 1978 recording (TRG 1999) ★★★, with DeFranco *Terry Gibbs & Buddy De Franco Play Steve Allen* (Contemporary 1999) ★★★★, *Dream Band Volume 6: One More Time* 1959 recording (Contemporary 2002) ★★★★, *From Me To You: A Tribute To Lionel Hampton* (Mack Avenue 2003) ★★★, *52nd & Broadway: Songs Of The Bebop Era* (Mack Avenue 2004) ★★★.

● FURTHER READING: *Good Vibes: A Life In Jazz*, Terry Gibbs with Cary Ginell.

Gibby

b. Leebert Morrison, c.1959, Clarendon, Jamaica, West Indies. Morrison, known as Gibby, initially played lead guitar with the Solid Foundation band. His experience with the group led to him playing lead guitar for a number of reggae stars, including **Jimmy Cliff**, **Peter Tosh**, **Dennis Brown**, **Gregory Isaacs**, **Bunny Wailer** and dub poet **Mutaburaka**. Other prestigious performances include sessions with Earl 'Chinna' Smith's High Times band and with **Dean Fraser**'s 809 band through to the 90s. Following the demise of the 809 band, Morrison performed his debut as a solo guitarist in Kingston at a theme night promoting rock music. He performed a heavy metal interpretation of the **Troggs**' 60s hit, 'Wild Thing', inspired by his guitar hero, **Jimi Hendrix**. Although his performance was well received, heavy guitar sounds were not prevalent in Jamaica; nevertheless, Peter Blake of Kingston Muzik was sufficiently inspired to sign him. Morrison ambitiously embarked on a mission to introduce this style to the **dancehall** and enrolled Junior 'Big Bird' Baille (drums), Lyndon 'Ace Bass' Webb (bass guitar) and Andrew 'Simmo' Simpson (guitar) to perform as Gibby. The band embarked on sessions for *Electric Avenue*, which showcased their unique style and the versatility of the reggae veteran Ruddy Thomas, who engineered the project. In 1997 Morrison performed at MIDEM in Cannes, France, illustrating the diversity of Jamaican music. Although his endeavours have been lauded by the media, the dancehall audience generally remains impervious to Gibby's unprecedented sound.

● ALBUMS: *Electric Avenue* (Kingston Muzik 1997) ★★★.

Gibson/Miller Band

Dave Gibson (b. 1 October 1956, El Dorado, Arkansas, USA) was a folk musician in Chicago in the 70s, although he grew up influenced by the music of **Hank Williams**, **Eddy Arnold** and **Elvis Presley**. He moved to Nashville, as a singer-songwriter in 1982. Several of his songs have been recorded by well-known artists, such as 'Jukebox In My Mind' (**Alabama**) and 'Ships That Don't Come In' (**Joe Diffie**). The Gibson/Miller Band were formed in 1990 when Doug Johnson, the vice president/producer at Epic Records, introduced Gibson to Blue Miller (b. 15 July 1952, Detroit, Michigan, USA), who had worked with **Bob Seger** and **Isaac Hayes**, and who at the time had no interest in country music. Johnson filled out their sound with bass player Bryan Grassmeyer (b. 6 June 1954, Nebraska, USA, ex-**Vince Gill**, **Suzy Bogguss**), steel guitarist Mike Daly (b. 11 June 1955, Cleveland, Ohio, USA) and ex-**Sweethearts Of The Rodeo** drummer Steve Grossman (b. 3 April 1962, West Islip, New York, USA). *Where There's Smoke* was well received and the singles 'Big Heart' and 'High Rollin'' were US country chart hits. *Red, White And Blue Collar* includes a cover version of **Waylon Jennings**' and **Willie Nelson**'s 'Mammas, Don't Let Your Babies Grow Up To Be Cowboys'.

● ALBUMS: *Where There's Smoke* (Epic 1993) ★★★, *Red, White And Blue Collar* (Epic 1994) ★★★.

Gibson, Bob

b. 16 November 1931, New York City, USA. Although commercial success proved illusive, Gibson was one of folk music's most influential figures. His songs were recorded by the **Kingston Trio** and **Peter, Paul And Mary** and he was responsible for launching and/or furthering the careers of Bob Camp, **Judy Collins** and **Joan Baez**. Having recorded his debut single, 'I'm Never To Marry', in 1956, Gibson embarked on a series of excellent albums including *Offbeat Folksongs* and *Carnegie Concert*. Indifferent to marketplace pressure, his novelty collection, *Ski Songs*, was issued at the height of the hootenanny boom, while *Yes I See*, arguably the nadir of his recording career, appeared as **Bob Dylan** began to attract peer group acclaim. These disappointing releases were followed by a duet with Bob (Hamilton) Camp, *At The Gate Of Horn*, paradoxically one of American folk's definitive works. Gibson was absent from music for much of the 60s, but he re-emerged early in the 70s with a melodic album that featured **Roger McGuinn**, Spanky McFarland and **Cyrus Faryar**. This respected artist has since pursued a more public path. During the 80s he toured with **Tom Paxton** and was a frequent performer at international folk festivals.

● ALBUMS: *Folksongs Of Ohio* (Stateside 1956) ★★★, *Offbeat Folksongs* (Riverside 1956) ★★★, *I Come For To Sing* (Riverside 1957) ★★★★, *Carnegie Concert* (Riverside 1957) ★★★★, *There's A Meeting Here Tonight* (Riverside 1959) ★★★, *Ski Songs* (Elektra 1959) ★★★, *Yes I See* (Elektra 1961) ★★★, with Bob 'Hamilton' Camp *At The Gate Of Horn* (1961) ★★, *Hootenanny At Carnegie* (Riverside 1963) ★★★★, *Where I'm Bound* (Elektra 1963) ★★★, *Bob Gibson* (70s) ★★★, *Funky In The Country* (1974) ★★, with Camp *Homemade Music* (1978) ★★★.

Gibson, Clifford

b. 17 April 1901, Louisville, Kentucky, USA, d. 21 December 1963, St. Louis, Missouri, USA. The bulk of Gibson's recordings (20 titles) were made in 1929, by which time he was one of the most respected blues guitarists in St. Louis. Influenced by **Lonnie Johnson**, Gibson had a similar clear diction and a penchant for original, moralizing lyrics. His guitar work, characterized by extended treble runs, was outstanding: clean, precise, inventive, and at times astonishingly fast. Away from the studios, he worked as a street musician, assisted by a performing dog. He recorded (in a small band format) as Grandpappy Gibson for Bobbin in 1960.

● COMPILATIONS: *Beat You Doing It* (Yazoo 1988) ★★★.

Gibson, Debbie

b. Deborah Ann Gibson, 31 August 1970, Brooklyn, New York, USA. This pop singer generated massive sales in the late 80s, particularly in her homeland. Following training in piano and early songwriting ventures, Gibson was signed to the management of Doug Breithart by the time she was 13 years old. The following three years saw her apprenticeship in recording studios as she produced and wrote over 100 original compositions, mostly in her own multi-track home studio. Before leaving school, she had signed to **Atlantic Records** and was only turned down for the lead role in a US production of **Les Misérables** when the producers discovered her age. By the end of 1987, she emerged alongside a rash of female teenage singers in the US charts, hitting number 4 twice with 'Only In My Dreams' and 'Shake Your Love'. Her songwriting status and production involvement on *Out Of The Blue* was duly noted by critics. When 'Foolish Beat' topped the charts in 1988, she became the youngest artist to have written, produced and performed a US number 1 single. 'Lost In Your Eyes', a sentimental ballad replaced the high-energy pop of previous singles, and topped the US charts once more after the disappointing 'Staying Together'. The equivalent accolade in the album chart would be hers for five weeks with *Electric Youth*, co-produced, as was her debut, by Fred Zarr. However, a batch of subsequent singles, including the album's title track, 'No More Rhyme' and 'We Could Be Together' fared progressively worse in the US charts. The sales of the third album *Anything Is Possible* proved similarly disappointing, despite the appearance of Freddie Jackson and **Lamont Dozier** in the studio.

In 1991, Gibson finally got to appear in *Les Misérables*, playing the part of Eponine in the Broadway production. She continued in the theatre after releasing 1993's *Body Mind Soul*, appearing as Sandy in the London, England production of **Grease**. She switched to the character of Betty Rizzo in the National Touring Company Of Grease, which performed throughout the USA from October 1995 to March 1996. Further acting roles have included stints in productions of **Funny Girl**, **Beauty And The Beast**, **Gypsy** and **Cinderella**. Her recording career has largely taken a back seat to her theatre work, and has moved away from the dance pop of her teen years to a more considered AOR style. Gibson made the headlines in March 2005 when she posed naked for *Playboy* magazine.

● ALBUMS: *Out Of The Blue* (Atlantic 1987) ★★★★, *Electric Youth* (Atlantic 1989) ★★★, *Anything Is Possible* (Atlantic 1990) ★★, *Body Mind Soul* (Atlantic 1993) ★★, *Think With Your Heart* (EMI 1995) ★★★, *Deborah* (Espiritu 1997) ★★★, *M.Y.O.B.* (Golden Egg 2001) ★★★, *Colored Lights* (Fynsworth Alley 2003) ★★★.
● COMPILATIONS: *Greatest Hits* (Atlantic 1996) ★★★.
● DVD/VIDEOS: *Live: Out Of The Blue* (Atlantic Video 1989), *Smart Pack* (Atlantic Video 1990), *Live Around The World* (Atlantic Video 1990).

Gibson, Don

b. 3 April 1928, Shelby, North Carolina, USA, d. 17 November 2003, Nashville, Tennessee, USA. If loneliness meant world acclaim, then Gibson, with his catalogue of songs about despair and heartbreak, should have been a superstar. Considering himself 'a songwriter who sings rather than a singer who writes songs', Gibson is best remembered as the author of three standards: 'Sweet Dreams', 'Oh Lonesome Me', and 'I Can't Stop Loving You'.

Gibson learned the guitar from an early age and started performing while still at school in North Carolina. He worked some years around the clubs in Knoxville and built up a reputation as local radio. His first records were made as part of the Sons Of The Soil for **Mercury Records** in 1949. His first recorded composition was 'Why Am I So Lonely?'. Gibson recorded for **RCA Records**, **Columbia Records** and **MGM Records** (where he recorded the rockabilly 'I Ain't A-Studyin' You, Baby' in 1957), but with little chart success. However, **Faron Young** took his forlorn ballad 'Sweet Dreams' to number 2 in the US country charts in 1956. The song has since been associated with **Patsy Cline** and also recorded by **Emmylou Harris**, **Don Everly**, **Roy Buchanan**, **Reba McIntyre** and **Elvis Costello**.

In 1958 'I Can't Stop Loving You' was a US country success for **Kitty Wells** and then, in 1962, a transatlantic number 1

pop hit for **Ray Charles**. In 1991, the song was revived by **Van Morrison** with the **Chieftains**. 'I Can't Stop Loving You' was also one side of the hit single (US number 7 pop, number 1 country) that marked Gibson's return to RCA in 1958. The other side, 'Oh Lonesome Me', which Gibson had originally intended for **George Jones**, is also a much-recorded country classic. Gibson actually sings 'Ole lonesome me', but a clerk misheard his vocal. **Chet Atkins**' skilful productions appealed to both pop and country fans, and this single was followed by 'Blue Blue Day' (number 20 pop/number 1 country), 'Give Myself A Party', 'Don't Tell Me Your Troubles', 'Just One Time' and his own version of 'Sweet Dreams'. In 1961 Gibson made his UK chart debut with 'Sea Of Heartbreak', which was followed by the similar-sounding 'Lonesome Number One'. The sadness of his songs matched **Roy Orbison**'s, who recorded an album *Sings Don Gibson* in 1967 and had a hit single with 'Too Soon To Know'. Gibson's own bleak *King Of Country Soul*, which includes some country standards, is highly regarded.

Gibson lost his impetus in the mid-60s through alcohol and drug dependency, but he recorded successful duets with both **Dottie West** and **Sue Thompson**. He had a US country number 1 with 'Woman (Sensuous Woman)' in 1972, and **Ronnie Milsap** took his '(I'd Be) A Legend In My Time' to the top of the country charts two years later. Further hits with 'One Day At A Time' and 'Bring Back Your Love To Me' marked the end of Gibson's chart success, but he continued performing throughout subsequent decades. He was voted into the Nashville Songwriters Hall Of Fame in 1973, and the **Country Music Hall Of Fame** in 2001.

● ALBUMS: *Oh Lonesome Me* (RCA Victor 1958) ★★★★, *Songs By Don Gibson* (Lion 1958) ★★, *No One Stands Alone* (RCA Victor 1959) ★★★, *That Gibson Boy* (RCA Victor 1959) ★★★, *Look Who's Blue* i (RCA Victor 1960) ★★★, *Sweet Dreams* (RCA Victor 1960) ★★★★, *Girls, Guitars And Gibson* (RCA Victor 1961) ★★★★, *Some Favorites Of Mine* (RCA Victor 1962) ★★★, *I Wrote A Song* (RCA Victor 1963) ★★★, *God Walks These Hills* (RCA Victor 1964) ★★, *Too Much Hurt* (RCA Victor 1965) ★★★, *Don Gibson* (RCA Victor 1965) ★★★, *The Fabulous Don Gibson* (RCA Victor 1965) ★★★, *A Million Blue Tears* (RCA Victor 1965) ★★★, *Hurtin' Inside* (RCA Victor 1966) ★★★, *With Spanish Guitars* (RCA Victor 1966) ★★, *Great Country Songs* (RCA Victor 1966) ★★★★, *All My Love* (RCA Victor 1967) ★★★, *The King Of Country Soul* (RCA Victor 1968) ★★★, *More Country Soul* (RCA Victor 1968) ★★★, *I Love You So Much It Hurts* (RCA Victor 1968) ★★★, *My God Is Real* (RCA Victor 1969) ★★, with Dottie West *Dottie And Don* (RCA Victor 1969) ★★★, *Sings All-Time Country Gold* (RCA Victor 1969) ★★★, *Hits—The Don Gibson Way* (RCA Victor 1970) ★★★, *A Perfect Mountain* (Hickory 1970) ★★★, *Hank Williams As Sung By Don Gibson* (Hickory 1971) ★★★, *Country Green* (Hickory 1972) ★★★, *Woman (Sensuous Woman)* (Hickory 1972) ★★★, *Sample Kisses* (Hickory 1972) ★★★, *Am I That Easy To Forget?* (Hickory 1973) ★★★, *Touch The Morning/ That's What I'll Do* (Hickory 1973) ★★★, with Sue Thompson *Warm Love* (Hickory 1973) ★★★, *Just Call Me Lonesome* (Hickory 1973) ★★★, *Snap Your Fingers* (Hickory 1974) ★★★, *Bring Back Your Love To Me* (Hickory 1974) ★★★, *Just One Time* (Hickory 1974) ★★★, *I'm The Loneliest Man/There She Goes I Wish Her Well* (Hickory 1975) ★★★, with Thompson *Oh How Love*

Changes (Hickory 1975) ★★★, Don't Stop Loving Me (Hickory 1975) ★★★, I'm All Wrapped Up In You (Hickory 1976) ★★★, If You Ever Get To Houston (Look Me Down) (Hickory 1977) ★★★, Starting All Over Again (Hickory 1978) ★★★, Look Who's Blue ii (Hickory 1978) ★★★.
● COMPILATIONS: 20 Of The Best (RCA 1982) ★★★, Rockin' Rollin' Gibson, Volume 1 (Bear Family 1984) ★★★★, Rockin' Rollin' Gibson, Volume 2 (Bear Family 1984) ★★★★, Collector's Series (RCA 1985) ★★, Don Gibson And Los Indios Tabajaras (Bear Family 1986) ★★, The Early Days (Bear Family 1986) ★★, Collection: Don Gibson (Castle 1987) ★★★, A Legend In His Time (Bear Family 1988) ★★★, All Time Greatest Hits (RCA 1990) ★★★★, The Singer: The Songwriter, 1949–60 (Bear Family 1991) ★★★, The Singer: The Songwriter 1961–66 4-CD box set (Bear Family 1993) ★★★★, The Singer: The Songwriter 1966–69 4-CD box set (Bear Family 2004) ★★★★, Anthology (BMG 2004) ★★★★.
● FURTHER READING: Don Gibson: A Legend In His Own Time, Richard Weize and Charles K. Wolfe.

Gibson, Harry 'The Hipster'

b. Harry Raab, 1914, New York City, USA, d. May 1991, California, USA. Gibson's first job was playing piano in a band that included future jazz musicians such as **Flip Phillips** and **Billy Bauer**. At this time he was working under his real name, but later changed it when he formed a double act with singer Ruth Gibson. In the 40s he enjoyed a brief period of fame when he caught to perfection the attitudes, language and mannerisms of a generation of zoot-suited, streetwise hipsters. Much of Gibson's nightclub act was built around his own compositions, which included gems such as 'Who Put the Benzedrine In Mrs Murphy's Ovaltine?' and 'Zoot Gibson Rides Again'. Gibson's lyrics, and the patter with which he surrounded his songs, made a marked impression upon a succeeding generation of stand-up comedians; his peers included **Lord Buckley** and Lenny Bruce. Gibson's troubled lifestyle was akin to that of Bruce and another friend and musical associate, **Charlie Parker**.
Gibson was reputed to be instrumental in persuading Billy Berg to bring Parker and **Dizzy Gillespie** to Los Angeles for their ground-breaking engagement in 1945. Despite a frenetic life, which included periods of incarceration for drug offences, and several marriages, Gibson managed to avoid the limelight. Indeed, few jazz reference books mention him, and perhaps the longest magazine article on him came in the form of Mark Gardner's obituary in Jazz Journal International. For all his other-worldliness, Gibson's anarchic humour had much to say that was relevant. His music, especially his piano playing, despite its boppish overtones, was firmly rooted in the older traditions of his early idols such as **Fats Waller** and **Erroll Garner**. During his later years Gibson worked sporadically, fronting a band in the 70s that included his sons in its ranks.
● ALBUMS: Harry The Hipster Digs Christmas (Viper's Nest 1974) ★★.
● COMPILATIONS: Boogie Woogie In Blue 40s recordings (Musicraft 1988) ★★★, Everybody's Crazy But Me 40s recordings (Progressive 1988) ★★★★, Who Put The Benzedrine In Mrs Murphy's Ovaltine? (Delmark 1996) ★★★★.
● DVD/VIDEOS: Boogie In Blue (Rhapsody Films 1992).

Gibson, Lacy

b. 1 May 1936, Salisbury, North Carolina, USA. Gibson's family settled in Chicago in 1949, and he quickly became involved in the city's blues scene, receiving tips on blues guitar playing from musicians such as **Muddy Waters** and **T-Bone Walker**. Besides working with innumerable blues artists, he was also involved in the jazz scene. He recorded with **Buddy Guy** in 1963 and worked on many sessions. Gibson had two singles of his own on the Repeto label, and had material released on albums by the Alligator, Red Lightnin', El Saturn, and Black Magic labels. He is a strong vocalist and very talented blues guitarist who seems to be equally at home in small west-side Chicago bars or European concert halls.
● ALBUMS: four tracks only Living Chicago Blues Volume Five (1980) ★★★★, Switchy Titchy (Black Magic 1983) ★★★, Crying For My Baby (Delmark 1996) ★★.

Gibson, Lee

b. 5 March 1950, Watford, Hertfordshire, England. Gibson began her show business career as a singer and dancer, performing in many of the top nightspots in London's West End. These included the Talk Of The Town, where she headlined and was heard by a BBC radio producer who booked her for her first jazz broadcast. During succeeding years she made over 1,000 broadcasts for the BBC and toured with several big bands, including those led by **Syd Lawrence** and **Don Lusher** and the BBC Radio Big Band. Her parallel career as a session singer extended into films and television, and she also appeared at seven Royal Command Variety Shows. She was a member of the folk rock group Chorale, recording a self-titled album for **Arista Records** in 1980, and the single, 'Riu Riu', which charted in several European countries.
Meanwhile, Gibson extended her reputation as a solo singer throughout Europe, performing at concerts and on radio and television with leading orchestras. In Finland she sang with the UMO Jazz Orchestra, in Denmark with the Danish Radio Big Band, directed by **Thad Jones**, in the Netherlands with the Skymasters and the Metropole Orchestra, recording 1998's Night Songs with the latter, and in Germany with the WDR Orchestra and the **Francy Boland** Band, conducted by **Lalo Schifrin**. She also sang the music of **Andrew Lloyd Webber** with the Royal Philharmonic Orchestra at a Royal Gala concert in London. Her jazz festival performances have included Munich, Sydney, Montreux, Birmingham, Cork and Grimsby, appearing at the latter with **Michael Brecker**. Gibson sings with elegant charm, her interpretations of lyrics being eloquent and understanding. Adjusting to the needs of the material and the nature of the performance, she can deliver the popular repertoire with warmth and enormous confidence while her jazz work is suffused with an intense yet subtle sense of swing.
● ALBUMS: You Can See Forever (Digital Six 1994) ★★★, The Nearness Of You (Zephyr 1996) ★★★, The Magic Of Gershwin (Merlin Audio 1997) ★★★★, Night Songs (Koch 1998) ★★★, with Fat Chops Big Band The Frim Fram Sauce (Choice Music 1999) ★★★, Songs Of Time And Place (Spotlite 2002) ★★★, Linger Awhile (Spotlite 2003) ★★★.

Gibson, Lorne

b. Eric Brown, 20 August 1940, Edinburgh, Scotland, d. 12 May 2003, London, England. At the age of 17, Gibson, who was working in a cafe, developed an interest in country music when a customer played him a **Hank Williams** EP. He said, 'The songs were simple and easy to play and sing. It was several years before I realized how good they were.' In the early 60s, rock 'n' roll impresario **Larry Parnes** wanted to promote Gibson, who took his stage name from the make of guitar, as 'sweet rock'. Instead, Gibson signed with Tommy Sanderson, who went on to manage the **Hollies** and **Lulu**. The BBC Light Programme was looking for a British country performer, so he formed the Lorne Gibson Trio, the most regular members being Steve Vaughan (guitar) and Vic Arnold (bass).

As well as regular sessions on *East Beat*, his own radio series *Side By Side,* series featured various musical guests, including the **Beatles**, who had just released their first records; Gibson later guested on their series *Pop Go The Beatles!* Although Gibson did not have chart hits, cover versions of **Jimmy Dean**'s 'Little Black Book' and **Freddie Hart**'s 'Some Do, Some Don't' for **Decca** sold 60,000 apiece. Gibson never made an album for Decca, saying, 'They wouldn't let me. If I'd made an album it could only have been on my own terms. They didn't want me doing country and had me listed as a calypso singer.' Gibson sang the theme of the Peter Sellers comedy film *Heavens Above!,* and played the ghost in the pop film *The Ghost Goes Gear*. Gibson was only filmed from one side as an accident had necessitated several stitches on the other side of his face.

Over a period of months, 'Red Roses For A Blue Lady' sold a respectable 175,000, but did not reach the charts. He said, 'I never expected to have a hit. I discovered early on that country music fans don't buy British records. They didn't then and, to a great extent, they still don't.' Gibson maintained his repertoire—'Devil Woman', 'Eighteen Yellow Roses', the tongue-twisting 'The Auctioneer' and an off-beat **Jack Clement** song, 'You've Got The Cleanest Mind In The Whole Wide World ('Cause You Change It Every Minute)'. An album he recorded in 1978, *For The Life Of A Song*, has never been released. He was, however, featured on the 1974 album based on the BBC Radio 2 series *Up Country*.

● FILMS: *The Ghost Goes Gear* (1966).

Gibson, Orville H.

b. 1856, Chatauay, New York, USA. Together with **Leo Fender**, Orville Gibson's name is carried on the most famous of all electric guitars. The company was founded in Kalamazoo in 1903 and shortly afterwards became established as a market leader with a series of beautiful arch-top acoustic guitars that found immediate favour. The O Style was their flagship, which later was replaced by the equally revered L4 and L5. These guitars, although unamplified, projected a loud sound that was clearly heard in large bands. Their range of acoustic flat top instruments was also a success with the famous J series producing a number of models second only to **Martin** guitars. The range included the inexpensive J45, the J160E (regularly used by **John Lennon** and **George Harrison** in the mid-60s), the Hummingbird, the Dove and the beautiful, big and booming J200. Although dozens of famous country, rock and folk artists have used Gibson Jumbos (including **Elvis Presley**), no act has become more inextricably linked than the **Everly Brothers**, with their trademark black guitars. Gibson manufactured a special model carrying their name between 1962 and 1973.

The company entered the electric-acoustic market in the late 40s, producing instruments favoured by jazz players such as **Joe Pass**. The mellow tone of the ES175, ES5 and the ES350 is still acclaimed and used. They electrified the L5 in 1951 and moved into the rock 'n' roll world with the 400CES during the late 50s and introduced the thin line jazz-style Byrdland around the same time. The now legendary ES335 started production in 1958. It combined a harder solid guitar sound within a slim line hollow body. The instrument has continued to be a consistent favourite with pure rock and blues guitarists as it minimizes feedback. **B.B. King** has endorsed the guitar and has his own specially made gold-plated model known as 'Lucille'. Following the success of the solid body Fender guitar, Gibson worked with Les Paul to produce what is now one of the most famous guitars of all time. This unusually small, solid bodied, single cutaway instrument is deceptively heavy, yet has been the undisputed joint leader with the Fender Stratocaster for rock guitarists since the late 60s. The Gibson Les Paul range includes the Gold Top, the Special, the Junior, the Deluxe, the Standard, and the Custom. Another successful variation was the double cutaway SG series. Additionally, Gibson has produced some unusually shaped electric guitars with varying degrees of success the most notable being the Explorer, the Firebird and the Flying V, but it is with the 'industry standard' Les Paul that Gibson will continue to become a household name.

● FURTHER READING: *Gibson's Fabulous Flat-Top Guitars*, Eldon Whitford, David Vinopal & Dan Erlewine *Gibson Guitars: 100 Years Of An American Icon*, Walter Carter.

Gibson, Wayne, And The Dynamic Sounds

Originally known as the Tornadoes, this short-lived British group was formed by bass player Ray Rogers. Completed by Wayne Gibson (vocals), Mike Todd (lead guitar), Peter Cook (organ) and Larry Cole (drums) this early line-up achieved fame as the resident backing band on BBC television's *Beat Room* show. They enjoyed a minor hit with 'Kelly' in 1964, but Gibson was later groomed for an ill-starred solo career. In 1966 he completed a version of 'Under My Thumb', a track from the **Rolling Stones**' *Aftermath* album, but his reading was roundly condemned by **Mick Jagger**. However the singer's energized interpretation was later adopted by the **northern soul** fraternity, and it became a belated hit in 1974 when it reached number 17 in the UK charts.

● FILMS: *It's All Over Town* (1964).

Gidea Park

(see **Baker, Adrian**)

Gifford, Gene

b. Harold Eugene Gifford, 31 May 1908, Americus, Georgia, USA, d. 12 November 1970, Memphis, Tennessee, USA. Gifford began arranging music while still in high school and in the mid- to late 20s played banjo and guitar with several **territory bands**. In 1929, he was with **Jean Goldkette**'s Orange Blossoms band, which metamorphosed into the **Casa Loma Orchestra**. It was here that Gifford's arranging talent proved to be invaluable; indeed, it might well be cited as the principal reason for the band's great success. His arranging style for the band appears to owe something to that of **John Nesbitt** (**Gunther Schuller** offers compelling musical evidence to this effect in his book, *The Swing Era*); however, there is no doubt that Gifford set a pattern for numerous swing-era arrangers who followed him.

During the early 30s the Casa Loma band set standards by which hot dance bands were measured and laid the foundation for the coming era's commercial popularity. Although there was a slightly stiff approach in Gifford's arranging, he provided challenging, technically complex and difficult charts within which Casa Loma soloists could carve their brief moments in the spotlight. It is, however, the riff-based ensemble sound that most testifies to Gifford's ability to render the free-flowing drive of many black bands of the pre-swing period into formal arrangements accessible to many. When later bands built upon Gifford's concepts through their own arrangers, many were able to inject more swing and a greater freedom; nevertheless, his contribution to the period and to much of what followed in big band music during future decades is enormous.

In 1939 Gifford left the Casa Loma band, thereafter working in radio and writing charts for other bands. In the 50s he worked in radio as an engineer and consultant. His last years were spent teaching in Memphis. Although it might be argued with reason that Gifford's work was constrained, and there are signs that long before he quit Casa Loma his ideas were drying up, the Casa Loma band, thanks to his charts, set standards by which later, better-known, if not always more technically accomplished, bands are judged.

Gift

Formed in Portland, Oregon, USA, in 1994 by former **Poison Idea** leader Jerry A. (b. Jerry Lang, USA; guitar/vocals), alongside his wife, May May Del Castro (bass/vocals, ex-Destroy All Blonds) and Sam Henry (drums, ex-**Wipers**). Poison Idea had built a reputation as the most fearsome, brutal studio and performance band of their era, but the Gift allowed Jerry A. to indulge himself in more accessible pop punk (bizarrely, including both a **Bauhaus** and a **Tones On Tail** cover version). The band's shows were just as frenetic and violent, however, with the intention being to keep the group on the road on a semi-permanent basis. They did find the time to record a well-received debut album in 1994, though it was only given worldwide release a year later. Jerry A later rejoined Poison Idea for their abortive reunion in 1998.

● ALBUMS: *Multum In Parvo* (Tim/Kerr 1994) ★★★.

Gifted

The Gifted are a religiously motivated hip-hop trio from London, England, led by rapper Prince Gilbert Okyere. He had originally released a debut solo EP on his own GBR Recordings label, which introduced his advocacy of Christian 'street ministry'. A debut album followed, credited to the Gifted and provocatively titled *Transformation Of The Mind*. Much of the interest surrounding its release could be attributed to the unusual presence of Christian imagery in a rap community now dominated by Muslim principles. Despite the record's unorthodoxy within its own genre, there was little else about *Transformation Of The Mind* to distinguish the Gifted from other under-achieving UK rap acts of the period.

● ALBUMS: *Transformation Of The Mind* (GBR 1994) ★★.

Gigi (film musical)

The golden era of MGM film musicals was drawing to a close when this most delightful of films was released in 1958. The original story, by the French novelist Colette, had previously been adapted into a non-musical film in 1948 starring Daniele Delormé and Gaby Morlay, and a play that was subsequently performed in New York and London. **Alan Jay Lerner**'s screenplay for this musical treatment was set in Paris at the turn of the century and tells of the young, strong-willed Gigi (**Leslie Caron**), who is being brought up by her grandmother, Mamita (**Hermione Gingold**), and her great-aunt Alicia (Isabel Jeans) to be a courtesan, but breaks with that family tradition—and actually marries her suitor, Gaston Lachailles (Louis Jourdan). Watching over this somewhat shocking situation is Honoré Lachailles (**Maurice Chevalier**), Gaston's grandfather and a good friend of Mamita. He is also a gentleman with much experience in the delights of romance, and, therefore, is appalled when Gaston, his well-heeled grandson, who, permanently surrounded by lovely ladies and all the other good things in life, suddenly declares that 'It's A Bore'.

This was just one of Alan Jay Lerner and **Frederick Loewe**'s memorable songs that were so skilfully integrated into the charming story. Other highlights included Chevalier's 'Thank Heaven For Little Girls' ('Those little eyes so helpless and appealing/One day will flash, and send you crashing through the ceiling'), 'The Parisians' (Caron), 'Waltz At Maxim's' (Jourdan), 'The Night They Invented Champagne' (Caron-Jourdan-Mamita), 'Say A Prayer For Me Tonight' (Caron), 'I'm Glad I'm Not Young Anymore' (Chevalier) and 'Gigi (Gaston's Soliloquy)' (Jourdan). For many, the most endearing moment came when Honoré and Mamita reminisced about old times with 'I Remember It Well' (He: 'You wore a gown of gold.' She: 'I was all in blue.' He: 'Am I getting old?' She: 'Oh, no—not you.'). Vincente Minnelli directed the film, which was mostly shot on location in Paris, and the producer was **Arthur Freed**. It was magnificently photographed in Metrocolor and CinemaScope by Joseph Ruttenberg, and he won one of the picture's Academy Awards, along with those for Cecil Beaton's sumptuous Costumes and Best Picture, Director, Writer (Lerner), Art Direction–Set Direction (William A. Horning and Preston Ames; Henry Grace and Keogh Gleason), Film Editing (Adrienne Fazan), Best Song ('Gigi') and Scoring Of A Musical Picture (**André Previn**). At the same awards ceremony Maurice Chevalier received a special Oscar 'for his contributions to the world of entertainment for more than half a century'. *Gigi* was one of the Top 10 highest-grossing films of the 50s in the USA, but subsequent stage productions did not appeal. The 1973 Broadway production starring **Alfred Drake**, Agnes Moorhead, **Maria Karnilova** and **Daniel Massey** only ran for three months, and West End audiences saw *Gigi* for seven months in 1985–86.

GiGi (world)

b. Ejigayehu Shibabaw, 1974, Ethiopia. The multi-octave voice of New York–based Ethiopian singer GiGi has been dubbed a 'Gift of God' in her home country. Ironically, however, although Shibabaw grew up singing in the Ethiopian Church (and was given voice lessons by a local priest), this practice was not strictly permitted for women. Prompted by such repression, at the age of 18 Shibabaw absconded from her home in the coffee-farming area of northern Ethiopia to Kenya, where she was allowed to sing. When she returned to Ethiopia in 1996 she joined the Ethiopian National Theatre and worked in a musical trio with Fantahun Shewankochew and Wores Egziabher, touring around Africa and even visiting France. At the age of 24, Shibabaw relocated to the USA, where she recorded her solo debut, *One Ethiopia*. However, it was the singer's self-titled 2001 collection that propelled her to international attention. Dubbed (and perhaps overstated as) 'the best, and most important, Ethiopian album in decades', *GiGi* was produced by world music mastermind **Bill Laswell** and featured an illustrious inventory of guests including **Herbie Hancock**, **Wayne Shorter**, **Henry Threadgill**, **Pharoah Sanders**, **Nicky Skopelitis**, percussionist Aiyb Dieng and New York-based electronic musician Karsh Kale. On the release, GiGi derived lyrical inspiration from 'scripture, the ancient Ethiopian church and the beauty of the Ethiopian civilisation' and musical influence from the celebrations of Genna, where men and women would assemble for feasting, zefen (songs) and chifera (group dancing). In 2003, Laswell returned to the original multi-track masters to forge a new version of *GiGi*, rethinking the entire album and creating a complete reconstruction, *Illuminated Audio*.

● ALBUMS: *One Ethiopia* (Barkhanns 2000) ★★★, *GiGi* (Palm Pictures 2001) ★★★★, *Illuminated Audio* (Palm Pictures 2003) ★★★.

Gigolo Aunts

Formed in 1986 in Boston, Massachusetts, USA, the Gigolo Aunts originally comprised Dave Gibbs (vocals/rhythm guitar), brothers Phil (lead guitar) and Steve Hurley (bass) and Paul Brouwer (drums), who had played together since 1981, initially as a band entitled Sniper. This name was soon jettisoned for Marauder, then Rosetta Stone (since they did not know a band of the same name already existed). When they finally became the Gigolo Aunts (from a **Syd Barrett** song), there was little immediate fanfare, despite a developing ability to write inviting guitar pop songs in the tradition of **Big Star**. In fact the band remained practically unknown until Gibbs journeyed to the UK in 1992 to play guest guitar with **Velvet Crush**, where he met **Creation Records**' boss **Alan McGee** and swapped anecdotes with the similarly inclined **Teenage Fanclub**. The Gigolo Aunts signed to Fire Records in the UK shortly thereafter. Their live reputation grew on the back of a formidable array of cover versions amassed over their 14 years together (ranging from **Duran Duran**'s 'Rio' to **Foreigner**'s 'Hot Blooded' and the **Vapors**' 'Turning Japanese'). Having once opened for a **Beastie Boys** covers band, there was little left to faze them. They released the UK-only *Gigolo Aunts* and *Gun* EPs, before the California-based Alias label issued the six-track *Full On Bloom*, which included a cover version of the **BMX Bandits**' 'Serious Drugs'.

The 1994 long-player *Flippin' Out*, actually the band's third, was a marvellous summary of progress so far, with top notch playing and execution. It led to Gibbs and Phil Hurley being invited to join the re-formed Big Star, an offer they had to decline due to European touring commitments. In 1995, the band's composition 'Where I Find My Heaven' appeared on the soundtrack to the hit movie *Dumb And Dumber*, and also as the theme to BBC Television sitcom *Game On*, belatedly providing the Gigolo Aunts with a UK Top 30 hit. The same year saw a tour-weary Brouwer replaced on drums by Fred Eltringham. Phil Hurley was later replaced by new guitarist Jon Skibic, while the band took a hiatus from recording. They returned in 1999 on **Counting Crows** singer Adam Duritz's new label with the charming *Minor Chords And*

Major Themes. After a further hiatus the delightfully retro *Pacific Ocean Blues* arrived in 2002, but the band elected to call it a day not long afterwards. Gibbs went on to record as Kid Lightning.

● ALBUMS: *Everybody Happy* (Coyote 1988) ★★, *Tales From The Vinegar Side* (Impossible 1990) ★★★, *Flippin' Out* (Summerville/Fire/RCA 1994) ★★★, *Minor Chords And Major Themes* (E Pluribus Unum 1999) ★★★, *Pacific Ocean Blues* (Bittersweet/Q 2002) ★★★.

● COMPILATIONS: *Where I Find My Heaven: The Singles Album* (Fire 1998) ★★★★, *The One Before The Last* (Bittersweet 2000) ★★★.

Gil, Gilberto

b. Gilberto Passos Gil Moreira, 29 June 1942, Salvador, Brazil. Singer-songwriter Gil—also a competent accordionist, guitarist, drummer and trumpeter—joined his first group, the Desafinados, in the mid-50s, and by the start of the 60s was making a living composing jingles for television commercials. Along with **Caetano Veloso**, Gil was one of the leading lights of the tropicalismo cultural music movement, which stirred up a heady and controversial brew of native genres and modern rock instrumentation. Gil recorded his self-titled debut album in 1966, but he did not enjoy his first single hit until 1969's 'Aquele Abraco'. Popular with young Brazilians, the oblique lyrics of tropicalismo artists criticized the military regime that had held power in Brazil since 1964's coup, but in 1971 the music's figureheads, Gil and Veloso, were forced into temporary exile in the UK. Gil returned in 1972, and the same year's *Expresso 2222* produced two hit singles with 'Back In Bahia' and 'Oriente'. In 1974 he teamed up with **Jorge Ben** for the album *Gil And Jorge*. A prolific recording and performing artist throughout the 70s and 80s, Gil signed an international recording contract with the **WEA Records** group of labels in 1978, achieving two UK and US successes with *Nightingale* and *Realce*. His biggest crossover success to date was 1982's 'Palco', eased into dancefloor acceptance with its **Earth, Wind And Fire** inspired arrangement. Gil also became actively involved in Brazilian politics as a member of the Green Party, and in 2002 accepted an offer to become the country's culture minister in President Luiz Inacio Lula de Silva's new government.

● ALBUMS: *Gilberto Gil* (Philips 1966) ★★★★, with Caetano Veloso *Barra 69* (Philips 1972) ★★★★, *Expresso 2222* (Philips 1972) ★★★★, with Veloso, Gal Costa *Temporada De Verão: Ao Vivo Na Bahia* (Philips 1974) ★★★, with Jorge Ben *Gil E Jorge* (Philips 1975) ★★★★, *Refazenda* (WEA 1975) ★★★, with Veloso, Costa, Maria Bethânia *Doces Bárbaros* (Philips 1976) ★★★, *Refavela* (WEA 1977) ★★★, *Gil In Montreux* (WEA 1978) ★★★★, *Nightingale* (WEA 1979) ★★★, *Realce* (WEA 1979) ★★★, with João Gilberto, Bethânia *Brasil* (WEA 1981) ★★★, *Luar (A Gente Precisa Ver O Luar)* (WEA 1981) ★★★★, *Um Banda Um* (WEA 1982) ★★★, *Extra* (WEA 1983) ★★★, *Raça Humana* (WEA 1984) ★★★★, *Gilberto A Bahia* (WEA 1985) ★★★, *Parabolic* (WEA 1992) ★★★, *Oriente—Live In Tokyo* (Westwind 1993) ★★, with Veloso *Tropicália 2* (PolyGram 1993) ★★★★, *Acoustic* (Atlantic 1994) ★★★, *Quanta* (Warner Brazil 1997) ★★★, *Quanta Live* (Atlantic 1998) ★★, *O Sol De Oslo* (Pau Brasil 1998) ★★★, *Gilberto Gil & Milton Nascimento* (Warners 2000) ★★★★, *Music From The Film; Me, You Them* (Atlantic 2001) ★★★, *São João Vivo* (Warners 2001) ★★★, *Kaya*

N'Gan Daya (Warners 2002) ★★, *Eletracústico* (Warners 2005) ★★★.

● COMPILATIONS: *Personalidade* (PolyGram Brazil 1982) ★★★★, *Mestres Da MFB* (WEA 1996) ★★★★, *Mestres Da MFB, Vol. 2* (WEA 1996) ★★★★, *The Definitive Gilberto Gil: Bossa, Samba And Pop* (Warners 2002) ★★★★, *The Early Years* (Wrasse 2004) ★★★★.

● DVD/VIDEOS: *Eletracústico* (Warner Music Vision 2005).

Gilbert, Bruce

b. 18 May 1946, Watford, Hertfordshire, England. Gilbert forged a reputation as a purveyor of challenging music as guitarist/vocalist and composer with **Wire**. When this acclaimed art-punk quartet broke up in 1980, he joined group bass player Graham Lewis in Dome, a unit that continued its predecessor's *avant garde* inclinations. The duo also worked as P'o and Duet Emmo, the latter of which marked a collaboration with **Mute** label boss Daniel Miller. Although Wire reunited in 1984, Gilbert embarked on a concurrent solo career with *This Way*, the enthralling nature of which was maintained on the artist's second set, *The Shivering Man*. Both albums confirmed his position as an innovative musician. *Ab Ovo* was ultimately too challenging to move his career forward beyond his loyal fanbase. Wire re-formed for a second time in 1999, playing acclaimed live shows and returning to the studio to record new material.

● ALBUMS: *This Way* (Mute 1984) ★★★, *The Shivering Man* (Mute 1986) ★★★, *Insiding* (Mute 1991) ★★, *Ab Ovo* (Mute 1996) ★★★.

Gilbert, Jim

b. 2 August 1950, Baltimore, Maryland, USA. The son of a preacher (the Rev. Jack Gilbert), gospel singer Jim Gilbert regularly tours nationally and internationally to promote what he calls his 'musical ministry'. As an adolescent he majored in vocal music through a scholarship at Western Maryland College, before transferring to Oral Roberts University. There, in the late 60s, he was asked to participate in the founding of the institution's Living Sound weekend ministry. The Living Sound was a concept that spawned four touring groups, and Gilbert was at various times responsible for vocals, keyboards, arranging, composing and musical direction. He has featured on several of the Living Sound albums, while in 1978 he released his first solo effort for Light Records. His debut, *I Love You With The Love Of The Lord*, was successful in the contemporary Christian charts, while the title-track was recorded by several other artists, and has reputedly been translated into at least six different languages. Nothing he has done subsequently has lived up to that song's enduring stature.

● ALBUMS: *I Love You With The Love Of The Lord* (Light 1978) ★★★.

Gilberto, Astrud

b. Astrud Weinert, 30 March 1940, Bahia, Brazil. Gilberto's career began by accident in March 1963 during a recording session featuring her husband, guitarist **João Gilberto**, and saxophonist **Stan Getz**. A projected track, 'The Girl From Ipanema', required a singer conversant with English and although strictly a non-professional, Astrud was coaxed into performing the soft, *sang-froid* vocal. Her contribution was considered relatively unimportant—early pressings of the resultant *Stan Getz/João Gilberto* did not credit the singer—

even when the track was issued as a single the following year. 'The Girl From Ipanema' eventually reached the US Top 5 and UK Top 20, garnering sales in excess of one million and forever binding the artist to the subject of the song. Astrud later toured with Getz; their collaboration was chronicled on *Getz A-Go-Go*, but she later pursued an independent career, bringing her distinctive, if limited, style to a variety of material, including standards, Brazilian samba/bossa nova and contemporary songs from **Tim Hardin**, **Jimmy Webb** and the **Doors**. Gilberto was the subject of renewed attention when 'The Girl From Ipanema' re-entered the UK charts in 1984 as a result of the UK bossa nova/jazz revival perpetrated by artists such as **Everything But The Girl**, **Matt Bianco**, the **Style Council**, **Weekend** and **Sade**.

● ALBUMS: *The Astrud Gilberto Album* (Verve 1965) ★★★★, *The Shadow Of Your Smile* (Verve 1965) ★★★, *Look To The Rainbow* (Verve 1965) ★★★, *A Certain Smile, A Certain Sadness* (Verve 1966) ★★★, *Beach Samba* (Verve 1967) ★★★★, *Windy* (Verve 1968) ★★, *I Haven't Got Anything Better To Do* (Verve 1969) ★★★, *September 17 1969* (Verve 1969) ★★, *Astrud Gilberto With Stanley Turrentine* (Columbia 1971) ★★★, *Astrud Gilberto Plus James Last* Orchestra (Verve 1987) ★★★.

● COMPILATIONS: *Once Upon A Summertime* (Verve 1971) ★★★, *That Girl From Ipanema* (Verve 1977) ★★★★, *The Best Of Astrud Gilberto* (Verve 1982) ★★★★, *The Essential Astrud Gilberto* (Verve 1984) ★★★★, *Compact Jazz* (Verve 1987) ★★★★, *Talkin' Verve* (Verve 1998) ★★★, *Astrud Gilberto's Finest Hour* (Verve 2001) ★★★.

Gilberto, Bebel

b. Isobel Gilberto, 1967, New York City, USA. Gilberto's provenance almost suggests that she was destined to produce music that has been judged 'the epitome of cool' and 'gorgeously seductive'. Gilberto is the progeny of a fêted Brazilian chanteuse, Miúcha Gilberto, and the guitarist **João Gilberto** (who is credited with inventing bossa nova alongside **Antonio Carlos Jobim**). Having been surrounded by beautiful sounds from an early age, Bebel made her recording debut at the age of seven on an album by her mother, whom she joined onstage at Carnegie Hall two years later. Bebel released her own eponymous debut EP in 1986 but despite collaborations with artists such as **David Byrne** and **Deee-Lite**'s Towa Tei (she appeared on the latter's 'Technova' single and the albums *Future Listening!* and *Sound Museum*), Gilberto did not release a solo album until the start of the new century. This extended gestation period is alluded to in the title of *Tanto Tempo*, which translates as 'So Long'. The collection of subtle electronics and unhurried Brazilian rhythms was, for the most part, recorded in Brazil with the producer **Suba**. Tragically, Suba died in a house fire before the album was released, reportedly after returning to the burning building to rescue recordings.

Echoing *Tanto Tempo*'s juxtaposition of the traditional and the contemporary, the album mixed old songs (**Baden Powell** and **Vinícius De Morães**' 'Samba Da Bênção', **Marcos Valle**'s 'So Nice (Summer Samba)', and **Chico Buarque**'s 'Samba E Amor') with new compositions. Collaborators on the album included **Amon Tobin**, **Carlinhos Brown**, **Smoke City**, the **Thievery Corporation**, **Celso Fonseca**, and Mario Caldato Jnr. *Tanto Tempo* was reissued the following year alongside an album's worth of remixes by artists such as **Derrick Carter**, **4 Hero**, **Rae And Christian**, **King Britt**, and **Layo And Bushwacka!** Prior to the release of her album Gilberto apparently performed jingles for McDonald's in New York, a vocation that seems incongruous with her subtle, sophisticated recordings. Curiously, *Tanto Tempo* has been reported as former US president Bill Clinton's favourite album.

For her next project Gilberto teamed up with a number of producers, including Marius de Vries, in an attempt to replicate the success of her work with Suba. Released in summer 2004, *Bebel Gilberto* was a more downbeat collection than *Tanto Tempo* and lacked the experimental edge that Suba brought to the earlier album.

● ALBUMS: *Tanto Tempo* (Ziriguiboom/Six Degrees 2000) ★★★★, *Tanto Tempo Remixes* (Ziriguiboom/Six Degrees 2003) ★★★, *Bebel Gilberto* (Six Degrees/EastWest 2004) ★★★.

Gilberto, João

b. 10 June 1931, Juazeiro, Brazil. The Gilberto name is utterly synonymous with bossa nova: the light, melodic, samba-based musical hybrid that swept America and the rest of the world in the mid-60s. Guitarist/vocalist/composer João Gilberto grew up interested in Brazilian samba, absorbing the traditional rhythms and melodies, but became seduced by jazz—the other ingredient in the bossa recipe—listening to radio stations playing American music. During the early 50s he settled in Rio De Janeiro, where the colourful cultural mix was already inspiring the brilliant guitarist/composer **Antonio Carlos Jobim**, with whom he soon began to collaborate. Recording toward the end of the decade, Gilberto's tune 'Bim Bom' met with considerable success, and the pair established the bossa nova sound locally; but it was not until American guitarist **Charlie Byrd** picked up on the craze and, with soft-toned saxophone genius **Stan Getz**, brought it to the USA, that the bossa nova era and Gilberto's stardom really began. Getz and Byrd's *Jazz Samba*, recorded in 1962, featured compositions by both Jobim and Gilberto, and put bossa nova squarely on the map; but it was the 1963 classic, *Getz/Gilberto*, that made the Gilberto name. The album featured both Jobim and Gilberto, and gave a receptive American audience the first taste of João's sophisticated, romantic whisper, Portuguese lyrics and mellow guitar accompaniment. The surprise hit came courtesy of João's first wife **Astrud Gilberto**, singing the now ubiquitous 'The Girl From Ipanema'—soon a feature of every American jukebox.

The bossa nova as popular American music was just a craze, but the delicate and sophisticated sound that was João Gilberto's has been absorbed into the jazz mainstream, along with a number of his and Jobim's much-loved compositions. Recommended listening from the 60s must include the original *Getz/Gilberto* album, and a live date from Carnegie Hall, recorded toward the end of 1964 when the music was at its peak of popularity. Issued as *Getz/Gilberto 2*, the album includes a series of performances by Getz with his own quartet featuring vibraphonist **Gary Burton**, some mellow, quiet tracks by Gilberto's trio, and a series of performances featuring everyone together, and Astrud Gilberto making a guest appearance to sing, among other things, the hit record of the year, 'The Girl From Ipanema'.

● ALBUMS: *Chega De Saudade* (Odeon Brasil 1959) ★★★, *O Amor, O Sorriso E A Flor* (Odeon Brasil 1960) ★★★, *João Gilberto* (Odeon Brasil 1961) ★★★, *Brazil's Brilliant João Gilberto* (Capitol 1961) ★★★, *The Warm World Of João*

Gilberto (Atlantic 1963) ★★★, with Stan Getz *Getz/Gilberto* (Verve 1963) ★★★★, *Getz/Gilberto 2* (Verve 1964) ★★, *João Gilberto* live (Polydor Brasil 1973) ★★★★, with Getz *Best Of Two Worlds* (Columbia 1976) ★★★, *Amoroso* (WEA Brasil 1977) ★★★, *João Gilberto Prado Pereira De Oliveira* (WEA Brasil 1980) ★★★, with Caetano Veloso, Gilberto Gil, Maria Bethânia *Brasil* (Warners 1981) ★★★, *Meditacao* (EMI Brasil 1985) ★★★, *João* (PolyGram 1991) ★★, *Ela E' Carioca* (Orfeon 1994) ★★★, *Ao Vivo — Eu Sei Que Vou Te Amar* (Epic Brasil 1994) ★★★, *João Voz E Violão* (Mercury 1999) ★★★, *In Tokyo* (Verve 2004) ★★★★.

● COMPILATIONS: *O Mito* (EMI Brasil 1988) ★★★★, *Personalidade* (PolyGram Brasil 1990) ★★, *Millennium* (PolyGram 1998) ★★★★.

Gilder, Nick

b. 21 December 1951, London, England. Gilder is best known for the 1978 hit 'Hot Child In The City', which reached number 1 in the US. Gilder moved to Vancouver, Canada, at the age of 10 and after leaving high school formed a band called Rasputin. This band eventually became known as Sweeney Todd, and they charted in the US with their 1976 single 'Roxy Roller'. With band member Jim McCulloch, Gilder relocated to Los Angeles and signed as a solo artist to **Chrysalis Records**. Shortly afterwards, the band recorded another version of 'Roxy Roller', featuring a young **Bryan Adams** on vocals, which broke into the US chart nine positions below the Gilder-sung version. 'Hot Child In The City' was his first and greatest success, followed by two lesser chart singles, 'Here Comes The Night' and 'Rock Me'. Gilder also placed two albums on the chart, *City Nights* and *Frequency*, but he was unable to repeat his success after the end of the 70s, despite further albums for Casablanca Records and **RCA Records**. He continued to write material for other artists and contribute to soundtracks before returning to Vancouver in 1994. Gilder has released two albums worth of new material, 1997's *Stairways* and 1999's *Longtime Coming*, with his new band.

● ALBUMS: *You Know Who You Are* (Chrysalis 1977) ★★, *City Nights* (Chrysalis 1978) ★★★, *Frequency* (Chrysalis 1979) ★★, *Rock America* (Casablanca 1980) ★★, *Body Talk Muzik* (Casablanca 1981) ★★, *Nick Gilder* (RCA 1985) ★★, *Stairways* (Spinner 1997) ★★★, *Longtime Coming* (Page/Oasis 1999) ★★★.

Gilford, Jack

b. Jacob Gellman, 25 July 1907, New York City, USA, d. 2 June 1990, New York City, USA. Born and raised in a tough section of the city, Gilford had a Romanian-born mother who reputedly supported her family as a bootlegger. In the 30s he worked as a comedian at vaudeville theatres and in New York clubs. Hired by Barney Josephson for his new and racially integrated club, Café Society, Gilford appeared on opening night, 18 December 1938, sharing the bill with boogie woogie pianists **Albert Ammons** and **Meade 'Lux' Lewis** and singer **Billie Holiday**. From the early 40s, he appeared on Broadway, usually in revues including *Meet The People* (1940), *Alive And Kicking* (1950), *The World Of Sholom Aleichem* (1953) and *Once Over Lightly* (1955). He had also made a few appearances in films, including *Hey, Rookie*, *The Reckless Age* (both 1944) and *Main Street To Broadway* (1953). His career suffered a blow in 1956, when he and his wife, actress Madeline Lee, were blacklisted for their political beliefs by the House Un-American Activities Committee. While was hampered his ability to make films, he was able to continue his stage and club work. He appeared in *Once Upon A Mattress* (1959) and played in **Stephen Sondheim**'s *A Funny Thing Happened On The Way To The Forum* (1962), in which **Zero Mostel**, an old friend, also appeared.

In the 60s, Gilford resumed working in films, repeating his role in the screen version of *A Funny Thing Happened On The Way To The Forum* (1966). He played on Broadway in **John Kander** and **Fred Ebb**'s *Cabaret* (1966), had film roles in *Enter Laughing* and *Who's Minding The Mint?* (both 1969), and early in the 70s played in the Broadway revival of *No, No, Nanette* (1971); Through this decade and the next he was mainly active in films, including *Catch-22* (1970); *They Might Be Giants* (1971); *Save The Tiger* (1973), for which he was nominated unsuccessfully for an Oscar as Best Supporting Actor; *Harry And Walter Go To New York* (1976); *Cocoon* (1985) and *Cocoon: The Return* (1988). In 1983 he interrupted his film career for a Broadway revival of *The World Of Sholom Aleichem*. American television audiences knew him for occasional roles in situation comedies and in commercials for Cracker Jack candied corn. Together with his wife and Mostel and his wife, Kate, he wrote a book, *170 Years Of Show Business*.

● FURTHER READING: *170 Years Of Showbusiness*, Kate Mostel and Madeline Gilford with Jack Gilford and Zero Mostel.

● FILMS: *Hey, Rookie* (1944), *Reckless Age* (1944), *Main Street To Broadway* (1953), *The Daydreamer* (1966), *Mister Buddwing* aka *Woman Without A Face* (1966), *A Funny Thing Happened On The Way To The Forum* (1966), *Enter Laughing* (1967), *Who's Minding The Mint?* (1967), *The Incident* (1967), *Catch-22* (1970), *They Might Be Giants* (1971), *Save The Tiger* (1973), *Tubby The Tuba* voice only (1976), *Max* (1976), *Harry And Walter Go To New York* (1976), *The Doonesbury Special* voice only (1977), *Cheaper To Keep Her* (1980), *Wholly Moses!* (1980), *Caveman* (1981), *Anna To The Infinite Power* (1983), *Cocoon* (1985), *Arthur 2: On The Rocks* (1988), *Cocoon: The Return* (1988).

Gilgames J

Comprising Frank Van Stijn (vocals), Henry Van Santen (guitar), Gerry Den Hartog (guitar), Jan Vos (bass) and Hans Laponder (drums), Dutch heavy metal band Gilgames J made their debut in 1982 with a track on the compilation album *Metal Clogs*. Two years later they followed it with their debut album for the same label, *Take One*. Self-evidently influenced by other mainland European bands such as the **Scorpions** and **Gamma**, their forceful but uninspiring melodic hard rock failed to build an audience beyond the Netherlands, and there was no follow-up.

● ALBUMS: *Take One* (Rave On 1984) ★★.

Gilkyson, Eliza

b. 1950, Hollywood, California, USA. Singer-songwriter Eliza Gilkyson has enjoyed a long if not always fruitful career, although by the start of the new millennium she had begun to reap some much deserved critical and commercial acclaim.

Gilkyson is from a musical family, with her late father, the noted performer and songwriter Terry Gilkyson enjoying a US Top 5 hit in 1957 with an adaptation of the Bahamian folk song 'Marianne', in addition to writing the classic 'Green-

fields' and Disney's *The Jungle Book* favourite 'The Bare Necessities'. Her brother Tony, meanwhile, appeared with the mid-80s line-up of rock band **X**. After singing on film soundtracks in her early years the budding singer-songwriter relocated to New Mexico in her late teens, a base from which she continued to operate until the late 70s. She made her debut in 1969 with the singer-songwriter album *Eliza* but her recording career struggled to take flight. Another album, *Love From The Heart*, appeared at the end of the 70s, credited to Lisa Gilkyson and far removed from her folk roots. The belated follow-up, 1986's *Pilgrims*, proved unexpectedly popular with new age fans with its dreamlike fusion of folk and pop styles, but the tag was one Gilkyson subsequently disowned. Nevertheless, she pursued a similar style on 1988's *Legends Of Rainmaker* and then spent several years touring and recording with Swiss harpist and new age star **Andreas Vollenweider**.

Back in the USA at the start of the 90s, Gilkyson began the next stage of her career with the 1992 release *Through The Looking Glass*. This album paid tribute to her folk roots while also exploring genres as diverse as gospel and R&B. The introspective follow-ups, *Undressed* and *Beyond Redemption Road*, were informed by an unsettled period in Gilkyson's personal life, including a divorce from her husband (and manager) of almost 14 years. In 1999, she released *Misfits*, a collection of previously unissued recordings from the last decade, on her own Realiza label. Gilkyson secured a more permanent home on the Red House imprint at the start of the new millennium, making her debut for the label in 2000 with *Hard Times In Babylon*. This beautiful album was informed by the recent death of Gilkyson's father and another troubled period in her personal life, although the final track 'Sanctuary' offered a cautious note of hope.

Gilkyson then collaborated with fellow singer-songwriters **Iain Matthews** and Ad Vanderveen on *More Than A Song*, before resuming her solo career in 2002 with another collection of mature, reflective folk rock, *Lost And Found*. Her 2004 release, *Land Of Milk And Honey*, featured Gilkyson performing the newly discovered **Woody Guthrie** song 'Peace Call' with guests **Mary-Chapin Carpenter**, **Iris DeMent** and **Patty Griffin**.

● ALBUMS: *Eliza* (Mont Clare 1969) ★★★, as Lisa Gilkyson *Love From The Heart* (Helios 1979) ★★, *Pilgrims* (Gold Castle 1986) ★★★, *Legends Of Rainmaker* (Gold Castle 1988) ★★, *Through The Looking Glass* (Private 1992) ★★★, *Undressed* (Realiza 1994) ★★★, *Beyond Redemption Road* (MTI SilverWave 1996) ★★★, *Hard Times In Babylon* (Red House 2000) ★★★★, with Iain Matthews, Ad Vanderveen *More Than A Song* (Perfect Pitch 2001) ★★★, *Lost And Found* (Red House 2002) ★★★★, *Land Of Milk And Honey* (Red House 2004) ★★★.

● COMPILATIONS: *Misfits* (Realiza 1999) ★★★★.

Gill, Johnny

b. 22 May 1966, Washington, DC, USA. Gill's expertly delivered soul vocal chords have been working since an early age. At the age of seven, he was singing with his three brothers in the gospel quartet the Wings Of Faith. His debut album was recorded when he was only 16. Following his meeting and subsequent recording with **Stacy Lattisaw** (*Perfect Combination*), she proffered his rough demo to **Ahmet Ertegun** at **Atlantic Records**, resulting in 1985's *Chemistry*. Although Gill failed to dent the charts he had built a considerable reputation with his voice, and replaced **Bobby Brown** in **New Edition** towards the end of their heyday, singing on their comeback hit 'If It Isn't Love' in 1988. He reinvented himself once again, following a similar pattern: working with Lattisaw, followed by another self-titled solo album, this time on **Motown Records**. The mix was favourable, having been produced by **Jimmy Jam And Terry Lewis** and **L.A. And Babyface**. The album was a major success and established him as a potential modern R&B giant, spawning a number of US hits including 'Rub You The Right Way', 'My My My' and 'Fairweather Friend'. Further success came as a featured vocalist with **Shanice** ('Silent Prayer') and **Shabba Ranks** ('Slow And Sexy'). 'This Floor' kept Gill's profile alive in 1993, together with *Provocative*, but it was not until 1996 that a new solo album was released. In 1997 Gill joined with **Gerald LeVert** and **Keith Sweat** for the 'soul supergroup' **LSG**.

● ALBUMS: *Johnny Gill* (Cotillion 1983) ★★, with Stacy Lattisaw *Perfect Combination* (Cotillion 1984) ★★, *Chemistry* (Atlantic 1985) ★★★, *Johnny Gill* (Motown 1990) ★★★★, *Provocative* (Motown 1993) ★★★, *Let's Get The Mood Right* (Motown 1996) ★★★.

● COMPILATIONS: *Favorites* (Motown 1997) ★★★★, *Ultimate Collection* (Hip-O 2002) ★★★★.

Gill, Vince

b. Vincent Grant Gill, 12 April 1957, Norman, Oklahoma, USA. Gill's father, a lawyer who played in a part-time country band, encouraged his son to have a career in country music. While still at school, Gill joined the bluegrass group Mountain Smoke. He moved to Louisville in 1975 and joined **Bluegrass Alliance** before demonstrating his vocal, guitar, banjo and fiddle talents on the **Pure Prairie League**'s albums *Can't Hold Back*, *Firin' Up* and *Something In The Night*. In the early 80s, Gill moved on to **Rodney Crowell**'s backing group, the Cherry Bombs, and recorded an album with **David Grisman** before inaugurating his solo recording career with a six-track mini-album for **RCA Records**, *Turn Me Loose*. His 1985 hit duet with **Rosanne Cash**, 'If It Weren't For Him', was later withdrawn due to contractual difficulties. Gill also continued to work prolifically as a session musician and songwriter, working with artists including Cash, **Emmylou Harris**, **Dire Straits**, and **Patty Loveless**. The latter repaid the compliment by duetting with Gill on 'When I Call Your Name', which was named Single Of The Year by the **Country Music Association** in 1990.

Gill's career took off at MCA Records, and in 1991 he enjoyed several US Top 10 country chart hits with 'Pocket Full Of Gold', 'Liza Jane' and 'Look At Us' and was voted the Male Vocalist Of The Year at the 1991 Country Music Association's Annual Awards Show. In 1992, Gill went one better when he not only picked up the Male Vocalist Of The Year award but also the award for Song Of The Year with 'Look At Us', a song he co-wrote with **Max Barnes**. In 1992, additions to his chart successes included 'I Still Believe In You' (number 1) and 'Take Your Memory With You' (number 2), and he received a further three CMA Awards. Gill later revealed he had turned down the offer to join Dire Straits for their 1992 world tour, preferring to concentrate on his own career. Among performers and public alike, Gill is now established as one of the most successful figures in country music, and has won more CMA Awards than any other artist. The excellent *When Love Finds You* included a tribute to his brother and **KeithWhitley**, 'Go Rest High On That Mountain', with harmonies from **Patty Loveless** and Ricky Skaggs.

Gill has mainly concentrated on romantic ballads, although he proved he could turn his hand to soul music when he duetted with **Gladys Knight** on 'Ain't Nothing Like The Real Thing' (although, at the time, Knight was not even sure who he was). His duet with **Dolly Parton** on her incredibly successful 'I Will Always Love You' was a US country hit in 1995, after they performed it at the CMA awards. Gill also proved he has a long future in the limelight by being an excellent host at the awards ceremony. *High Lonesome Sound* explored several styles of American music, with varying degrees of success. *The Key* returned him to the heart of the mainstream, gathering a number of major awards and reaching the *Billboard* Top 20. His 17-year marriage to Janis Oliver of the **Sweethearts Of The Rodeo** ended in divorce in the late 90s, and in March 2000 he wed singer **Amy Grant**. His new album, *Let's Make Sure We Kiss Goodbye*, followed a month later. The follow-up *Next Big Thing* was an important album that saw Gill restating his musical credentials.

● ALBUMS: with David Grisman, Herb Pedersen, Jim Buchanan, Emory Gordy *Here Today* (Rounder 1982) ★★★, *Turn Me Loose* mini-album (RCA 1984) ★★, *The Things That Matter* (RCA 1985) ★★★, *The Way Back Home* (RCA 1987) ★★★, *When I Call Your Name* (MCA 1989) ★★★, *Pocket Full Of Gold* (MCA 1991) ★★★, *I Still Believe In You* (MCA 1992) ★★★★, *Let There Be Peace On Earth* (MCA 1993) ★★, *When Love Finds You* (MCA 1994) ★★★★, *High Lonesome Sound* (MCA 1996) ★★★, *The Key* (MCA 1998) ★★★★, with Patrick Williams And His Orchestra *Breath Of Heaven: A Christmas Collection* (MCA 1998) ★★, *Let's Make Sure We Kiss Goodbye* (MCA 2000) ★★, *Next Big Thing* (MCA 2003) ★★★.

● COMPILATIONS: *The Best Of Vince Gill* (MCA 1989) ★★★, *I Never Knew Lonely* (RCA 1992) ★★★, *The Essential Vince Gill* (RCA 1995) ★★★★, *Souvenirs* (MCA 1995) ★★★★, *Super Hits* (RCA 1996) ★★★, *Vintage Gill* (RCA 1997) ★★★.

● DVD/VIDEOS: *I Still Believe In You* (MCA Music Video 1993).

● FURTHER READING: *For The Music: The Vince Gill Story*, Jo Sgammato.

Gillan, Ian

b. 19 August 1945, Hounslow, Middlesex, England. Heavily influenced by **Elvis Presley**, vocalist Gillan formed his first band at the age of 16. In 1962 he was invited to join local semi-professional R&B band the Javelins, who eventually disbanded in March 1964. Gillan next formed the Hickies, but abandoned the project to join established soul band Wainwright's Gentlemen. He quickly became unhappy with this group and readily accepted an invitation to join the fully professional outfit **Episode Six**, in May 1965. A succession of tours and singles failed to produce any domestic chart placings, however, and by early 1969 the band was beginning to disintegrate. In August of the same year, Gillan and Roger Glover were recruited to join **Deep Purple**, forming the legendary 'Mk II' line-up with **Ritchie Blackmore**, Jon Lord and Ian Paice. Deep Purple gradually established themselves as a major rock band, helped by their dynamic live show and an aggressive sound, characterized by a mix of long instrumentals and Gillan's powerful vocals. The latter part of 1972 saw Deep Purple, acknowledged as the biggest-selling rock band in the world, enter the *Guinness Book Of Records* as the loudest pop group of their day.

Their status was consolidated with the release of the live album **Made In Japan**. In August 1972 Gillan decided to leave the band, but was persuaded to remain with them until June 1973. By the time of his last show with Deep Purple on 28 June, he had already purchased the De Lane Lea studio in London, and it was on this venture that he concentrated after leaving the band, forming Kingsway Studios. He recorded a solo album in 1974 for the Purple label, to whom he was still signed, but it was rejected as being too radical a musical departure, and has never been released. After a brief attempt to launch Ian Gillan's Shand Grenade, which included Glover, in late 1975, it was the Ian Gillan Band that began recording *Child In Time* in the first days of 1976. The line-up was Gillan, Ray Fenwick (guitar), Mike Moran (keyboards), Mark Nauseef (drums; ex-**Elf**) and John Gustafson (bass). This first album was much lighter in tone than Deep Purple, but included some excellent songs. The next two albums, now with **Colin Towns** on keyboards, demonstrated a notable jazz rock influence, particularly on *Clear Air Turbulence*, which was also distinguished by its striking Chris Foss–designed cover. None of these albums was particularly successful commercially, and after a disappointing tour in spring 1978, Gillan disbanded the group.

Within just a few months of dissolving the Ian Gillan Band, he was back in the studio with a new outfit, inspired by a Towns song, 'Fighting Man'. New members Liam Genocky (drums), Steve Byrd (guitar) and John McCoy (bass) joined Ian Gillan and Towns to record *Gillan* in summer 1978. The lack of a record contract meant that this excellent album was never released in the UK, although several of the tracks did appear on the next album, *Mr. Universe*, recorded early in 1979 with Pete Barnacle on drums. The title track was based on a song of the same name that Ian Gillan had recorded with Episode Six. The album as a whole marked the return of the imposing frontman to solid rock music. In so doing, this collection was instrumental in developing the **New Wave Of British Heavy Metal**, a label even more applicable to Gillan's subsequent album, *Glory Road*. Now with **Bernie Torme** on guitar and former Episode Six drummer Mick Underwood, Gillan produced one of his finest albums, the first copies of which contained a second, free album, *For Gillan Fans Only*. After the slightly disappointing *Future Shock*, Torme left to be replaced by guitarist Janick Gers of **White Spirit**, who featured on *Double Trouble*, a double album comprising one studio and one live album, recorded mainly at the 1981 Reading Rock Festival, at which the band appeared for the third consecutive year, a testimony to their popularity. Summer 1982 saw the release of *Magic*, another album of quality, although sadly also the group's last.

After many years of speculation and rumour, a Deep Purple re-formation seemed imminent, and Gillan wound up his band amid a certain amount of acrimony and uncertainty, early in 1983. Finding that he had ended Gillan somewhat prematurely, he joined **Black Sabbath**, a move he claims he was motivated by financial necessity. Artistically, the time he spent with this band is deplored by both Gillan and Sabbath fans. After one album and a tour with Sabbath, the much discussed Deep Purple reunion took off, and Gillan had his opportunity to escape. After 11 years apart, and all with successful, if turbulent careers during that time, the essential question remained as to whether the various band members would be able to co-operate. A successful tour and a sell-out British concert at the 1985 Knebworth Festival seemed to suggest the reunion had worked, but by the time of the next album, *House Of The Blue Light*, it was clear that the latent tensions within the band were beginning to reappear. Between Deep Purple tours, and adding to the speculation about a break-up, Gillan and Glover recorded an album together; a curious but thoroughly enjoyable collection of material, it seemed to fulfil a need in both musicians to escape from the confines of the parent band.

The 1988/9 Deep Purple tour revealed the true extent of the rift between the members, and Gillan's departure was formally announced in May 1989. The collaboration had been effectively finished since January, when Gillan was informed not to attend rehearsals for the next album. Gillan's response was to perform a short tour as his alter ego, Garth Rockett, in spring 1989, before recording vocals for the Rock Aid Armenia version of 'Smoke On The Water', in July. By the end of 1989 Gillan had assembled a band to record a solo album, which he financed himself to escape record company pressures, and recorded under his own name to avoid the politics of group decisions. The line-up featured Steve Morris (guitar), from the Garth Rockett tour, Chris Glen (bass) and Ted McKenna (drums), both formerly of the **Michael Schenker Group**, Tommy Eyre (keyboards), Mick O'Donoghue (ex–Grand Prix; rhythm guitar) and Dave Lloyd (ex-**Nutz**, **Rage** and 2am; backing vocals/percussion). The album, *Naked Thunder*, released in July 1990, was labelled middle-of-the-road by some critics, while Gillan himself described it as 'hard rock with a funky blues feel.'

After touring in support of it, Gillan returned to the studio to prepare a second solo album. Now formulating a highly productive partnership with Steve Morris, he recruited Brett Bloomfield (bass) and Leonard Haze (ex-**Y&T**; drums) and produced an excellent album as a four-piece rock band, blending straightforward music with Gillan's often bizarre sense of humour and offbeat lyrics. *Toolbox* was released in October 1991 to critical acclaim. Gillan rejoined Deep Purple in 1992, undertaking new recording sessions with the band and touring, before yet again quitting. However, the career decision taken in 1994 was indeed a strange one, seeing him reunited with his very first band, the Javelins, for a moribund collection of 60s cover versions. His third solo album, *Dreamcatcher*, was a poor attempt at a more acoustic style. However, Gillan's durability alone makes him a central player in the British rock tradition, despite occasional lapses.

● ALBUMS: with Ian Gillan Band *Child In Time* (Oyster 1976) ★★★, with Ian Gillan Band *Clear Air Turbulence* (Island 1977) ★★, with Ian Gillan Band *Scarabus* (Scarabus 1977) ★★, with Ian Gillan Band *I.G.B. Live At The Budokan* (Island 1978) ★★, with Gillan *Gillan* (Eastworld 1978) ★★, with Gillan *Mr. Universe* (Acrobat 1979) ★★, *Glory Road* (Virgin 1980) ★★★★, with Gillan *Future Shock* (Virgin 1981) ★★★, with Gillan *Double Trouble* (Virgin 1982) ★★★, with Gillan *Magic* (Virgin 1982) ★★★, with Gillan *Live At The Budokan* (Virgin 1983) ★★, with Gillan *What I Did On My Vacation* (Virgin 1986) ★★, with Gillan *Live At Reading 1980* (Raw Fruit 1990) ★★, as Garth Rockett *Story Of* (Rock Hard 1990) ★★★, *Naked Thunder* (EastWest 1990) ★★★, *Toolbox* (EastWest 1991) ★★★, with the Javelins *Raving . . . With The Javelins* (RPM 1994) ★★, *Dreamcatcher* (Carambi 1997) ★★, with Gillan *Dead Of Night: The BBC Tapes Volume 1 1979* (RPM 1998) ★★, with

Ian Gillan Band *Live At The Rainbow* 1977 recording (Angel Air 1998) ★★, with Gillan *Unchain Your Brain: The BBC Tapes Volume 2 1980* (RPM 1998) ★★, *Live Yubin Chokin Hall, Hiroshima 1977* (Angel Air 2001) ★, with Gillan *Live Tokyo 23rd October 1978, Shinjuku Koseinenkin Hall* (Angel Air 2001) ★★, *On The Rocks* 1981 recording (Angel Air 2002) ★★, *Live Wembley 17th December 1982* (Angel Air 2004) ★★.

● COMPILATIONS: with Episode Six *Put Yourself In My Place* (PRT 1987) ★★, with Gillan/Glover *Accidentally On Purpose* (Virgin 1988) ★★, *Trouble: The Best Of* (Virgin 1991) ★★★, *The Japanese Album* (EastWest 1993) ★★★, *The Gillan Tapes Volume 2* (Angel Air 1999) ★★, *Rarities 1975–1977* (Angel Air 2003) ★★★.

● DVD/VIDEOS: *Gillan Live At The Rainbow 1978* (Spectrum 1988), *Ian Gillan Band* (Spectrum 1990), as Garth Rockett And The Moonshiners *Live* (Fotodisk 1990), *Ian Gillan Live* (Castle 1992).

● FURTHER READING: *Child In Time: The Life Story Of The Singer From Deep Purple*, Ian Gillan with David Cohen.

Gillespie, Dana

b. 30 March 1949, Woking, Surrey, England. A former British water-skiing champion at the age of 15, Gillespie embarked on a singing career during the folk boom of the mid-60s. She befriended **Donovan**, who played guitar on her 1965 single, 'Donna Donna', but was later drawn towards acting with roles in the 1968 Hammer film *The Lost Continent* and the stage musical *Liz*. **Dick Rowe**, the **Decca Records** A&R man who turned down the **Beatles**, allegedly said to her, 'It doesn't really matter if you can sing or not, you've got a great pair of tits'. However, Gillespie subsequently proved her worth throughout her incredibly varied career. Gillespie's 1968 album, *Box Of Surprises*, presaged spells in *Catch My Soul* and *Jesus Christ Superstar*, and she was then signed to Tony DeFries' Mainman management stable, which also included **David Bowie**. She was saddled with an overtly sexual image, dressed as a scantily clad, basque-wearing vamp on *Weren't Born A Man*, and as a male sailor scanning soft-core pornography (of herself) on *Ain't Gonna Play No Second Fiddle*, but this approach detracted from any musical content the sets had to offer.

In later years Gillespie has continued to perform throughout Europe and the USA with the Dana Gillespie Blues Band, whose line-up has included Dave Rowberry (piano, ex-**Animals**), Ed Deane (guitar), Charlie Hart and Adrian Stout (bass), Chris Hunt (drums) and Mike Paice (saxophone, harmonica). She has also released Bhaja based music under the pseudonym Third Man, recording in Sanskrit. By the end of the 90s Gillespie had won numerous blues magazine polls as best female vocalist, making a nonsense of Dick Rowe's original judgement.

● ALBUMS: *Foolish Seasons* (London 1967) ★★, *Box Of Surprises* (Decca 1968) ★★, *Weren't Born A Man* (RCA 1973) ★★★★, *Ain't Gonna Play No Second Fiddle* (RCA 1974) ★★, with the Mojo Blues Band *And The Rockin' Boogie Flu* (Bellaphon 1981) ★★★, *Blue Job* (Ace 1982) ★★★, *Solid Romance* (Bellaphon 1984) ★★, *Below The Belt* (Ace 1985) ★★★, *It Belongs To Me* (Bellaphon 1985) ★★★, with the Mojo Blues Band *I'm A Woman (The Blues Line)* (Bellaphon 1986) ★★★, *Hot News* (GIG 1987) ★★★, *Sweet Meat* (Ace 1989) ★★★, *Amor* (GIG 1990) ★★★, *Blues It Up* (Ace 1990) ★★★, *Where Blue Begins* (GIG/

Ariola 1991) ★★★, with Joachim Palden *Boogie Woogie Nights* (Wolf 1991) ★★★, with Palden *Big Boy* (Wolf 1992) ★★★, *Methods Of Release* (Bellaphon 1993) ★★, *Andy Warhol* (Trident 1994) ★★, *Blue One* (Wolf 1994) ★★★, *Hot Stuff* (Ace 1995) ★★★, *Have I Got Blues For You!* (Wolf 1996) ★★★★, with Big Jay McNeely *Cherry Pie* (Big J 1997) ★★★, *Back To The Blues* (Wolf 1998) ★★★, *Experienced* (Ace 2001) ★★★★, *Staying Power* (Ace 2003) ★★★.

● FILMS: *Secrets Of A Windmill Girl* (1966), *The Lost Continent* (1968), *Mahler* (1974), *The People That Time Forgot* (1977), *The Hound Of The Baskervilles* (1978), *Bad Timing* (1980), *Scrubbers* (1983), *Bones* (1984), *Strapless* (1989), *Sunday Pursuit* (1990).

Gillespie, Dizzy

b. John Birks Gillespie, 21 October 1917, Cheraw, South Carolina, USA, d. 6 January 1993, Englewood, New Jersey, USA. Born into a large family, Gillespie began playing trombone at the age of 12 and a year or so later took up the trumpet. Largely self-taught, he won a musical scholarship but preferred playing music to formal study. In 1935 he quit university and went to live in Philadelphia, where he began playing in local bands. It was during this period that he acquired the nickname by which he was to become universally known. The name Dizzy resulted from his zestful behaviour and was actually bestowed by a fellow trumpeter, Fats Palmer, whose life Gillespie saved when Palmer was overcome by fumes in a gas-filled room during a tour with the Frankie Fairfax band. Gillespie's startling technical facility attracted a great deal of attention, and in 1937 he went to New York to try out for the **Lucky Millinder** band. He did not get the job but stayed in town and soon afterwards was hired for a European tour by **Teddy Hill**, in whose band he succeeded his idol, **Roy Eldridge**.

Back in the USA in 1939, Gillespie played in various New York bands before returning to Hill, where he was joined by drummer **Kenny Clarke**, in whom he found a kindred spirit, who was similarly tired of big band conventions. When Hill folded his band to become booking manager for Minton's Playhouse in New York, he gave free rein to young musicians eager to experiment and among the regulars were Clarke, **Thelonious Monk**, **Joe Guy** and, a little later, Gillespie. In the meantime, Gillespie had joined the **Cab Calloway** Band, which was then riding high in popular esteem. While with Calloway, Gillespie began to experiment with phrasing that was out of character with what was until this time accepted jazz trumpet parlance. He also appeared on a **Lionel Hampton** record date, playing a solo on a tune entitled 'Hot Mallets' that many observers believe to be the first recorded example of what would later be called bebop. The following year, 1940, Gillespie met **Charlie Parker** in Kansas City, during a tour with the Calloway band, and established musical rapport with the man with whom he was to change the face and sound of jazz. In 1941 Gillespie was fired by Calloway following some on-stage high jinks that ended with Gillespie and his boss embroiled in a minor fracas.

Gillespie returned to New York, where he worked with numerous musicians, including **Benny Carter**, Millinder, **Charlie Barnet** and **Earl Hines**, in whose band he again met Parker and also singer **Billy Eckstine**. Gillespie had begun to hang out, after hours, at Minton's and also at Clark Monroe's Uptown House. He led his own small band for club and record sessions, both appealing to a small, specialized, but growing, audience. Among his influential recordings of the period were 'Salt Peanuts' and 'Hot House'. In 1944 Gillespie joined the big band Eckstine had just formed: originally intended as a backing group for Eckstine's new career as a solo singer, the outfit quickly became a forcing house for big band bebop. Apart from Gillespie, the sidemen Eckstine hired at various times included **Gene Ammons, Sonny Stitt, Wardell Gray, Dexter Gordon, Fats Navarro, Howard McGhee** and **Miles Davis**. Subsequently, Gillespie formed his own big band, which enjoyed only limited commercial success but which was, musically, an early peaking of the concept of big band bebop. He also began playing and recording regularly with Parker in a quintet that the two men co-led.

During this period Gillespie was constantly in excellent musical company, playing with most of the major voices in bop and many of those swing-era veterans who tried, with varying levels of success, to adapt to the new music. In the big band, Gillespie had employed at one time or another during its two separate periods of existence **James Moody, Cecil Payne, Benny Bailey, Al McKibbon, Willie Cook, Big Nick Nicholas, John Lewis, Milt Jackson, Ray Brown** and Clarke. In his small groups he recorded with **Don Byas, Al Haig** and others, but it was in the band he co-led with Parker that Gillespie did his most influential work. The other members of the quintet varied, but initially included Haig, **Curley Russell** and **'Big' Sid Catlett** and, later, Haig, Jackson, Brown and **Stan Levey**. These small bands brought Gillespie to the fascinated attention of countless musicians; from their performances evolved the establishment of bop as a valid form of jazz, with its necessary renewal of a music that had begun to fall prey to the inroads of blandness, sanitization and formulaic repetitiveness that accompanied the commercial successes of the swing era. Gillespie was feverishly active as a composer too. And, despite his youth he was fast becoming an *eminence grise* to beboppers. Aided by his stable private life and a disdain for the addictive stimulants increasingly favoured by a small but well-publicized coterie of bebop musicians, he was the epitome of the successful businessman. That he combined such qualities with those of musical explorer and adventurer made him one of the more dominant figures in jazz. Moreover, in his work with **Chano Pozo** (who joined Gillespie's orchestra in 1947) and later **Machito** he was one of the pioneers of US-based Latin jazz. Most important of all, his personal demeanour helped bop rise above the prevailing tide of contemptuous ignorance that, in those days, often passed for critical comment.

Gillespie's busy career continued into the 50s; he recorded with **J.J. Johnson, John Coltrane**, Jackson, **Art Blakey, Wynton Kelly** and others. Many of his record sessions of this period were on his own label, Dee Gee Records. With his big band folded, Gillespie toured Europe, returning to New York in 1952 to find that his record company was on the skids. He was already undergoing some difficulties as he adjusted his playing style to accommodate new ideas and the shift from large to small band. In 1953, during a party for his wife, the members of a two-man knockabout act fell on his trumpet. The instrument was badly bent, but when Gillespie tried to play it he found that, miraculously, he preferred it that way. The upward 45-degree angle of the bell allowed him to hear the notes he was playing sooner than before. In addition he found that when he was playing from a chart, and therefore was looking down, the horn was pointing outwards towards microphone or audience. He liked all these unexpected

benefits and within a few weeks had arranged to have a trumpet especially constructed to incorporate them. By the end of 1953 the temporary hiatus in Gillespie's career was over. A concert in Toronto in this year featured Gillespie and Parker with **Bud Powell, Charles Mingus** and **Max Roach** in a group that was billed, and in some quarters received, as *The Quintet Of The Year*. Although all five musicians did better things at other times, collectively it was an exciting and frequently excellent session. Significantly, it was an occasion that displayed the virility of bop at a time when, elsewhere, its fire was being gently doused into something more palatable for the masses. Gillespie then began working with **Norman Granz**'s **Jazz At The Philharmonic** and he also began a long series of recording sessions for Granz, in which he was teamed with a rich and frequently rewarding mixture of musicians. In 1956 Gillespie's standing in jazz circles was such that Adam Clayton Powell Jnr. recommended him to President Dwight D. Eisenhower as the ideal man to lead an orchestra on a State Department–sponsored goodwill tour of Africa, the Middle East and Asia. The tour was a great success, even if Gillespie proved unwilling to play up its propagandist element, and soon after his return to the USA he was invited to make another tour, this time to South America. The all-star band assembled for these tours was maintained for a while and was also recorded by Granz.

By the end of the 50s Gillespie was again leading a small group and had embarked upon a ceaseless round of club, concert, festival and recording sessions that continued for the next three decades. He continued to work on prestigious projects, which included, in the early 70s, a tour with an all-star group featuring Blakey, Monk, Stitt, McKibbon and **Kai Winding**. Throughout the 70s and during the 80s he was the recipient of many awards, and his earlier status as an absurdly young *eminence grise* was succeeded by his later role as an elder statesman of jazz even though when the 70s began, he was still only in his early fifties. By the middle of the 70s Gillespie was once again at a point in his career where a downturn seemed rather more likely than a further climb. In the event, it was another trumpet player who gave him the nudge he needed. **Jon Faddis** had come into Gillespie's life as an eager fan, but in 1977 was teamed with his idol on a record session at the **Montreux International Jazz Festival**, where their planned performance was abruptly altered when the scheduled rhythm section ended up in the wrong country. Hastily assembling a substitute team of Milt Jackson, Ray Brown, **Monty Alexander** and drummer Jimmie Smith, the two trumpeters played a highly successful set, which was recorded by Norman Granz. Subsequently, Gillespie and Faddis often played together, making a great deal of memorable music, with the veteran seemingly sparked into new life.

In the early 80s Gillespie recorded for television in the USA as part of the *Jazz America* project, appeared in London with a new quintet featuring **Paquito D'Rivera**, and played at the Nice, Knebworth and Kool festivals in duets with, respectively, such varied artists as **Art Farmer, Chico Freeman** and Art Blakey. He showed himself eager to experiment, although sometimes, as with his less-than-wonderful teaming with **Stevie Wonder**, his judgement was somewhat awry. In 1987 he celebrated his 70th birthday and found himself again leading a big band, which had no shortage of engagements and some excellent players, including Faddis and **Sam Rivers**. He was also fêted during the JVC Festival at the Saratoga Springs

Performing Arts Center, where he brilliantly matched horns with Faddis and new pretender, **Wynton Marsalis**. He was not always in the spotlight, however. One night in Los Angeles he went into a club where **Bill Berry**'s LA Big Band was working and sat in, happily playing fourth trumpet. As the 90s began Gillespie was still performing, usually occupying centre stage, but also happy to sit and reminisce with old friends and new, to sit in with other musicians, and to live life pretty much the way he had done for more than half a century. It was a shock to the music world on 6 January 1993 when it was announced that he was no longer with us; perhaps we had selfishly thought that Gillespie was immortal.

In the history of the development of jazz trumpet, Gillespie's place ranked second only to that of **Louis Armstrong**. In the history of jazz as a whole he was firmly in the small group of major innovators who reshaped the music in a manner so profound that everything that follows has to be measured by reference, conscious or not, to their achievements. Just as Armstrong had created a new trumpet style that affected players of all instruments in the two decades following his emergence in Chicago in 1922, so did Gillespie, in 1940, redirect trumpet players and all other jazz musicians along new and undefined paths. He also reaffirmed the trumpet's vital role in jazz after a decade (the 30s) in which the saxophone had begun its inexorable rise to prominence as the instrument for change. In a wider context Gillespie's steadying hand did much to ensure that bop would survive beyond the impractical, errant genius of Parker. In much of Gillespie's earlier playing the dazzling speed of his execution frequently gave an impression of a purely technical bravura, but as time passed it became clear that there was no lack of ideas or real emotion in his playing. Throughout his career, Gillespie rarely failed to find fresh thoughts; and, beneath the spectacular high note flourishes, the raw excitement and the exuberant vitality, there was a depth of feeling akin to that of the most romantic balladeers. He earned and will forever retain his place as one of the true giants of jazz. Without his presence, the music would have been not only different but much less than it had become.

● ALBUMS: *Modern Trumpets* (Dial 1950) ★★★★, *Dizzy Gillespie Plays/Johnny Richards Conducts* 10-inch album (Discovery 1950) ★★★, *Dizzy Gillespie* aka *School Days* (Dee Gee 1952) ★★★, *Dizzy Gillespie Volume 1* 10-inch album (Atlantic 1952) ★★★★, *Dizzy Gillespie Volume 2* 10-inch album (Atlantic 1952) ★★★★, *Pleyel Concert 1953* (Vogue 1953) ★★★, *Horn Of Plenty* 10-inch album (Blue Note 1953) ★★★★, *Dizzy Gillespie With Charlie Christian* 10-inch album (Esoteric 1953) ★★★★★, *Dizzy Gillespie With Strings* (Clef 1953) ★★★, *Dizzy In Paris* 10-inch album (Contemporary 1953) ★★★★, *Dizzy Over Paris* aka *Concert In Paris* (Roost 1953) ★★★★, *Dizzy Gillespie Orchestra* 10-inch album (Allegro 1954) ★★★, *Dizzy Gillespie And His Original Big Band* 10-inch album (Gene Norman 1954) ★★★, *Dizzier And Dizzier* (RCA Victor 1954) ★★★, *The Dizzy Gillespie–Stan Getz Sextet #1* 10-inch album (Norgran 1954) ★★★★, *The Dizzy Gillespie–Stan Getz Sextet #2* 10-inch album (Norgran 1954) ★★★★, *Afro* (Norgran 1954) ★★★, *Dizzy Gillespie Plays* 10-inch album (Allegro 1954) ★★★, *Dizzy And Strings* aka *Diz Big Band* (Norgran 1955) ★★★, with Stan Getz *Diz And Getz* (Verve 1955) ★★★★, with Roy Eldridge *Roy And Diz* (Clef 1955) ★★★★, with Eldridge *Roy And Diz, Volume 2* (Clef 1955) ★★★★, *Dizzy Gillespie* (Allegro 1955) ★★★, *Groovin' High* (Savoy Jazz 1955) ★★★, with Jimmy McPartland *Hot Vs. Cool* (MGM 1955) ★★★★, *Dizzy Gillespie And His Orchestra* aka *Jazz Recital* (Norgran 1956) ★★★, *Dizzy Gillespie* (American Recording Society 1956) ★★★, *Big Band Jazz* (American Recording Society 1956) ★★★, with Eldridge *Trumpet Battle* (Clef 1956) ★★★, with Eldridge *The Trumpet Kings* (Clef 1956) ★★★, *The Champ* (Savoy Jazz 1956) ★★★, *The New Continent* (Limelight 1956) ★★★, *For Musicians Only* (Verve 1956) ★★★, *World Statesman* (Norgran 1956) ★★★, *Dizzy At Home And Abroad* (Atlantic 1957) ★★★★, *The Dizzy Gillespie Story* (Savoy Jazz 1957) ★★★, *Dizzy In Greece* (Verve 1957) ★★★, *Manteca* (Verve 1958) ★★★, *Dizzy Gillespie And Stuff Smith* (Verve 1958) ★★★★, with Slim Gaillard *Gaillard And Gillespie* (Ultraphonic 1958) ★★★, with Harry 'Sweets' Edison, Eldridge *Tour De Force* (Verve 1958) ★★★, *Birk's Works* (Verve 1958) ★★★★, *At Newport* (Verve 1958) ★★★★, *Dizzy Gillespie And Count Basie At Newport* (Verve 1958) ★★★★, with Sonny Rollins, Sonny Stitt *Duets* aka *Dizzy, Rollins & Stitt* (Verve 1958) ★★★★, with Charlie Parker *Diz 'N' Bird In Concert* (Roost 1959) ★★★★, *The Ebullient Mr. Gillespie* (Verve 1959) ★★★, *Have Trumpet, Will Excite!* (Verve 1959) ★★★★, *The Greatest Trumpet Of Them All* (Verve 1959) ★★★, *A Portrait Of Duke Ellington* (Verve 1960) ★★★★, *Gillespiana: The Carnegie Hall Concert* (Verve 1960) ★★★★, with Count Basie *First Time! The Count Meets The Duke* (Columbia 1961) ★★★★, *An Electrifying Evening With The Dizzy Gillespie Quintet* (Verve 1961) ★★★★, *Perceptions* (Verve 1961) ★★★, *Jazz Recital* (Verve 1961) ★★★, with Miles Davis, Fats Navarro *Trumpet Giants* (New Jazz 1962) ★★★★, *Jazz On The French Riviera* (Philips 1962) ★★★, *Dateline Europe* (Reprise 1963) ★★★, *New Wave!* (Philips 1963) ★★★, *Something Old, Something New* (Philips 1963) ★★★, *Dizzy Goes Hollywood* (Philips 1964) ★★★, *Dizzy Gillespie And The Double Six Of Paris* (Philips 1964) ★★★★, *The Cool World* film soundtrack (Philips 1964) ★★★, *Jambo Caribe* (Limelight 1964) ★★★, *The New Continent* (Limelight 1965) ★★★, *The Essential Dizzy Gillespie* (Verve 1964) ★★★, *Angel City* (Moon 1965) ★★★, *Gil Fuller And The Monterey Jazz Festival Orchestra With Dizzy Gillespie* (Pacific Jazz 1965) ★★★, with Eldridge *Soul Mates* (Verve 1966) ★★★★, *A Night In Tunisia* (Verve 1966) ★★★★, *Swing Low, Sweet Cadillac* (Impulse! 1967) ★★★, *Reunion Big Band* (MPS 1968) ★★★★, *Live At The Village Vanguard* (Solid State 1969) ★★★★, *My Way* (Solid State 1969) ★★, *Cornacopia* (Solid State 1969) ★★★, *The Real Thing* (Perception 1970) ★★, *Giants* (Perception 1970) ★★★, *Portrait Of Jenny* (Perception 1970) ★★, *Dizzy Gillespie And The Dwike Mitchell–Willie Ruff Duo* (Mainstream 1971) ★★★, *Giants Of Jazz* (Atlantic 1973) ★★★★, *The Giant* (Accord 1973) ★★★, *Dizzy Gillespie's Big Four* (Pablo 1974) ★★★★, with Machito *Afro-Cuban Jazz Moods* (Pablo 1975) ★★★★, with Eldridge *Jazz Maturity . . . Where It's Coming From* (Pablo 1975) ★★★, with Eldridge *The Trumpet Kings At Montreux '75* (Pablo 1975) ★★★★, *Dizzy's Party* (Pablo 1976) ★★★, *Free Ride* (Pablo 1977) ★★★, with Count Basie *The Gifted Ones* (Pablo 1977) ★★★, *Montreux '77* (Pablo 1977) ★★★, *Trumpet Summit Meets Oscar Peterson Big Four* (Pablo 1980) ★★★, with Mongo Santamaria, Toots Thielemans *Summertime* (Pablo 1980) ★★, *Musician-Composer-Raconteur* (Pablo 1981) ★★, with Arturo Sandoval *To A Finland Station* (Pablo

1982) ★★★, *New Faces* (GRP 1984) ★★★, *Arturo Sandoval And His Group With Dizzy Gillespie* (Egrem 1985) ★★★, *Closer To The Source* (Atlantic 1985) ★★, *Dizzy Gillespie Meets Phil Woods Quintet* (Timeless 1987) ★★★, *Live At The Royal Festival Hall* (Enja 1990) ★★★, *Symphony Sessions* (Pro Arte 1990) ★★, with Max Roach *Max & Dizzy—Paris 1989* (A&M 1990) ★★★, *The Winter In Lisbon* film soundtrack (Milan 1990) ★★★, *To Diz With Love: Diamond Jubilee Recordings* (Telarc 1992) ★★★, *To Bird With Love: Live At The Blue Note* (Telarc 1992) ★★★, *Bird Songs: The Final Recordings* 1991 recording (Telarc 1997) ★★★, the Dizzy Gillespie Alumni All-Stars *Dizzy's 80th Birthday Party!* (Shanachie 1998) ★★★, *On The Sunny Side Of The Street* 1953 recording (Moon 1998) ★★★, *Angel City* 1965 recording (Moon 1998) ★★, *Tour De Force* 1969 recording (Moon 1998) ★★, with Sonny Stitt *Diz Meets Stitt* 1974 recording (Moon 1998) ★★★, *Dizzy In South America Vol. 1* 1956 recordings (Red Anchor 1998) ★★★★, *Dizzy In South America Vol. 2* 1956 recordings (Consolidated Artists 2000) ★★★.

● COMPILATIONS: *Shaw Nuff* 1945-46 recordings (Musicraft) ★★★★, *One Bass Hit* 1946 recordings (Musicraft) ★★★★★, with Dwike Mitchell, Willie Ruff *Enduring Magic* 1970-85 recordings (Black Hawk) ★★★★, *Dizzy Gillespie 1946-1949* (RCA 1983) ★★★★, *Dee Gee Days* 1951-52 recordings (Savoy Jazz 1985) ★★★, *Dizzy's Diamonds: The Best Of The Verve Years* 1950-64 recordings (Verve 1993) ★★★★, *Birk's Works: Verve Big Band Sessions* 1956-57 recordings (Verve 1993) ★★★★, *Dizzy Songs* (Vogue 1993) ★★★★, *The Complete RCA Victor Recordings* 1937-49 recordings (RCA 1996) ★★★★★, *Dizzier And Dizzier* 1946-49 recordings (RCA 1997) ★★★, *Talkin' Verve* (Verve 1997) ★★★, *Jivin' In Be Bop* 1947 recordings (Moon 1998) ★★★, *Good Bait* 40s recordings (Moon 1998) ★★★, *1945-6* (Classics 1998) ★★★, *1947-1949* (Classics 2000) ★★★★, *Ken Burns Jazz: The Definitive Dizzy Gillespie* (Verve 2001) ★★★★, *Matrix: The Perception Sessions* (Castle 2001) ★★★★, *The Dizzy Gillespie Story 1939-1950* 4-CD box set (Proper 2001) ★★★★, *Odyssey 1945-1952* 3-CD set (Savoy Jazz 2002) ★★★★, *Matrix* (Castle Music 2003) ★★, *The Early Years 1937-1951* (Allegro 2004) ★★.

● DVD/VIDEOS: *A Night In Chicago* (View Video 1995), *Ralph J. Gleason's Jazz Casual: Dizzy Gillespie* (Rhino 2000).

● FURTHER READING: *Dizzy: To Be Or Not To Bop*, Dizzy Gillespie and Al Fraser. *Dizzy Gillespie: His Life And Times*, Barry McRae. *Dizzy Gillespie*, M James. *The Trumpets Of Dizzy Gillespie, 1937-1943*, Jan Evensmo. *Dizzy Gillespie And The Be-Bop Revolution*, Raymond Horricks. *Waiting for Dizzy*, Gene Lees. *Dizzy: John Birks Gillespie In His 75th Year*, Lee Tanner (ed.). *Groovin' High: The Life Of Dizzy Gillespie*, Alyn Shipton. *Dizzy Gillespie: The Bebop Years 1937-1952*, Ken Vail. *Dizzy, The Life And Times Of John Birks Gillespie*, Donald L. Maggin.

Gillett, Charlie

b. 20 February 1942, Morecambe, Lancashire, England. Gillett has been successively a historian of rock 'n' roll, an influential disc jockey and head of an independent record label. While studying for a master's degree in New York in 1966, Gillett researched the history of rock 'n' roll to 1964, publishing his work as *The Sound Of The City* (1970). With its careful delineation of 'five styles of rock 'n' roll' and its acknowledgement of the role of independently owned labels, the book remains the best summary of rock's development. A second edition, published in 1983, took the story up to 1971. During the late 60s Gillett was a columnist for London music paper *Record Mirror* and was a guiding light on early UK rock magazines *Creem* and *Let It Rock*. He co-edited the *Rock File* series of annuals with Simon Frith from 1972-78 and in 1974 he published *Making Tracks*, a study of **Atlantic Records**. In 1972, Gillett began broadcasting on BBC Radio London, giving opportunities to artists such as **Dire Straits**, **Elvis Costello** and **Graham Parker**. Each had tracks on *Honky Tonk Demos*, an album of material from Gillett's Sunday morning show. The album was issued in 1982 on Oval, a label Gillett had set up in 1974 to pursue an eclectic path, issuing cajun (Johnny Allan), jazz (**Helen Shapiro**) and left-field rock (Local Heroes). Oval also managed **Kilburn And The High Roads** (featuring **Ian Dury**) and published hits by **Lene Lovich** and **Paul Hardcastle**. In the 80s Gillett became a champion of African music as a club DJ, through radio shows on Capital and GLR and by releasing albums by **George Darko** and **Jali Musa Jawara** on Oval. Never a supporter of progressive rock or punk, he saw in African music many of the same qualities that American black music had embodied in the golden age of the 50s. After a period of hiatus, Oval was reactivated in 1991 under a new contract with EastWest Records. Among its first releases was an album by **Jah Wobble**'s Invaders Of The Heart. Into the new millennium Gillett remained a prominent figure in the championing of new music from around the globe.

Gilley, Mickey

b. 9 March 1936, Natchez, Louisiana, USA, but raised in Ferriday, Louisiana. Gilley is a cousin to **Jerry Lee Lewis** and the evangelist Jimmy Swaggart. He grew up with his cousins and his mother, a waitress, who saved her money to buy him a piano when he was 12 years old. Gilley left Louisiana when he was 17 and started working in bars in Houston. His first record was 'Tell Me Why' for the aptly named Minor label in 1953. He had regional success in 1959 with 'Is It Wrong?', with **Kenny Rogers** on bass. In 1964 he started a record label, Astro, in Houston and again did well locally with 'Lonely Wine'. In 1968 he signed with Louisiana's Paula label and had short-lived success with 'Now I Can Live Again'. He was heard at the Des Nesadel club in Houston by Sherwood Cryer, a local businessman. Cryer was impressed with Gilley's performance and invited him to his club, Shelley's, in Pasadena, Texas, with a view to establishing a partnership.

In 1971, the club reopened as Gilley's, and through regular exposure on television, became very popular. Gilley himself was a resident performer and, to please a jukebox operator, he recorded **Harlan Howard**'s 'She Called Me Baby' for his Astro label. The Houston disc jockeys preferred the b-side, a revival of **George Morgan**'s country hit 'Room Full Of Roses'. In 1974, *Playboy* magazine, which had its own label, reissued it nationally and 'Room Full Of Roses' was a number 1 US country hit and also made the Top 50 of the pop charts. Continuing with his country 'flower power', he followed it with another chart-topping revival, 'I Overlooked An Orchid'. His success on the US country charts was soon outstripping his cousin's as he had number 1 records with revivals ('City Lights', 'Window Up Above', 'Bring It On Home To Me') and with new songs ('Don't The Girls All Get

Prettier At Closing Time', 'She's Pulling Me Back Again'). Gilley also made the US country Top 10 with 'Overnight Sensation', a duet with Playmate-turned-country-singer Barbi Benton. However, most of his records, for the good or the worse, were strongly influenced by Jerry Lee Lewis and were made quickly and cheaply.

After Gilley signed with Epic Records, the producer Jim Ed Norman was determined to take him out of Lewis' shadow and have him spend more time on his records. His revival of 'True Love Ways' was a US number 1 country hit in 1980 and was followed by 'Stand By Me', which he sang in *Urban Cowboy*, a movie starring **John Travolta**—and a mechanical bull—and set in Gilley's. Gilley's was so successful that it had been extended to take 3,500 customers and Cryer, having the patent on the mechanical bull, made a fortune by selling them to other clubs. 'Stand By Me' made number 22 on the US pop charts, and **Johnny Lee**, the band leader at Gilley's, also did well with 'Lookin' For Love'. Gilley continued his run of country number 1s with revivals of 'You Don't Know Me' and 'Talk To Me', and 'That's All That Matters', 'A Headache Tomorrow (Or A Heartache Tonight)', 'Lonely Nights', 'Put Your Dreams Away', 'Fool For Your Love' and the 1983 duet with **Charly McClain**, 'Paradise Tonight'. In 1987 he split acrimoniously with Cryer, which resulted in the closure of Gilley's club. After a legal action, Gilley was awarded $17 million, which included considerable back-royalties on T-shirt sales alone.

No longer confined to the club, Gilley has toured extensively, but has not tried to build a UK following. He also opened a theatre in Branson, Missouri in the 90s. Surprisingly, Gilley has only ever had three singles released in the UK ('Room Full Of Roses', 'Stand By Me' and 'You Don't Know Me'). Gilley mentions Jerry Lee Lewis in his stage show, also performing 'Great Balls Of Fire', and is keen to record an album with his cousin. He says, 'I've always given Jerry Lee credit for being the best talent in the family. He created that piano style and it rubbed off on me.' Gilley underwent major surgery in 2003.

● ALBUMS: *Lonely Wine* (Astro 1964) ★★, *Down The Line* (Paula 1967) ★★★, *Room Full Of Roses* (Playboy 1974) ★★★, *City Lights* (Playboy 1974) ★★, *Mickey's Movin' On* (Playboy 1975) ★★★, *Overnight Sensation* (Playboy 1975) ★★★, *Gilley's Smokin'* (Playboy 1976) ★★★★, *First Class* (Playboy 1977) ★★★, *Mickey Gilley Live At Gilley's* (Epic 1978) ★★★, *Mickey Gilley* (Paula 1978) ★★★, *Flyin' High* (Playboy 1978) ★★★, *The Songs We Made Love To* (Epic 1979) ★★★, *That's All That Matters To Me* (Epic 1980) ★★★★, *You Don't Know Me* (Epic 1981) ★★★, *Christmas At Gilley's* (Epic 1981) ★★, *Put Your Dreams Away* (Epic 1982) ★★★, *Fool For Your Love* (Epic 1983) ★★★, *You've Really Got A Hold On Me* (Epic 1983) ★★★, with Charly McClain *It Takes Believers* (Epic 1984) ★★, *Too Good To Stop Now* (Epic 1984) ★★★, *Live! At Gilley's* (Epic 1985) ★★★, *I Feel Good (About Lovin' You)* (Epic 1985) ★★, *One And Only* (Epic 1986) ★★★, *Chasing Rainbows* (Airborne 1988) ★★★.

● COMPILATIONS: *Mickey Gilley At His Best* (Paula 1974) ★★★, *Gilley's Greatest Hits Vol. 1* (Playboy 1976) ★★★★, *Greatest Hits, Vol. II* (Playboy 1977) ★★★, *Encore* (Epic 1980) ★★★, *Biggest Hits* (Epic 1982) ★★★, *20 Golden Songs* (Astan 1984) ★★★, *Ten Years Of Hits* (Epic 1984) ★★★, *Back To Basics* (Epic 1987) ★★★, *The Crazy Cajun Recordings* (Crazy Cajun 1998) ★★★.

Gillum, Jazz

b. William McKinley Gillum, 11 September 1904, Indianola, Mississippi, USA, d. 29 March 1966, Chicago, Illinois, USA. Gillum had a difficult childhood, starting with the deaths of his parents during his infancy. He was made to live with his uncle, a deacon and apparently also a bully. This harrowing period was rendered bearable only by the boy's interest in music, and he quickly learned to play the organ and the harmonica. Gillum ran away at the age of seven and found work in fields and stores, augmenting his income by playing harmonica on street corners until 1923, when he travelled north to Chicago to attempt a career in the music business. He formed a long association with **Big Bill Broonzy** and started his recording career with him in 1934. The blues harmonica came into its own in 1937, when **John Lee 'Sonny Boy' Williamson** began his immensely successful career. Although second only to Williamson in popularity, Gillum was nowhere near as inventive a musician or as exciting a singer. His strength lay in his ability as a songwriter. Nevertheless, his work as a performer and sideman was much in demand throughout the 30s and 40s, when he was a stalwart of the **Bluebird Records** and **Victor Records** labels. In 1961 he recorded an album for **Folkways Records** but participated only marginally in the 'blues boom' before he was shot dead during an argument in 1966. Despite his limitations, at his best Gillum recorded some satisfactory performances and was popular both with his black audience and white collectors.

● ALBUMS: *You Got To Reap What You Sow* (1970) ★★★.
● COMPILATIONS: *Jazz Gillum* (Travellin' Man 1986) ★★★, *Best Of Blues 1935-46* (Best Of Blues 1988) ★★★.

Gilman, Billy

b. William Wendell Gilman, 24 May 1988, Westerly, Rhode Island, USA. The youngest artist ever to have a US hit country single, Gilman's precocious talent rivals that of pop singer **Aaron Carter**, classical soprano **Charlotte Church**, and rapper **Lil Bow Wow**. He began singing at the age of seven, made his first public appearance a year later, and was soon playing regular opening slots at country fairs. Gilman was signed by Epic Nashville after they heard the demo tape he recorded with Ray Benson of veteran swing act **Asleep At The Wheel**. *One Voice*, recorded with writer/producers David Malloy, **Don Cook** and Blake Chancey, demonstrates Gilman's undoubted natural ability, but like Carter his talent is restricted by his producers' selection of songs. This is fine on the aforementioned hit 'One Voice', a heartfelt examination of violence in American schools, but other selections include strained cover versions of adult-orientated material and simple pop fare like 'Little Bitty Pretty One' and 'I Think She Likes Me'. The album was a phenomenal sales success, however, quickly achieving platinum status. A perfunctory seasonal album, including an awkward duet with Church on 'Sleigh Ride', followed in December. *Dare To Dream*, released in May 2001, was hampered by poor song selection.

● ALBUMS: *One Voice* (Epic 2000) ★★★, *Classic Christmas* (Epic 2000) ★★, *Dare To Dream* (Epic 2001) ★★, *Music Through Heartsongs: Songs Based On The Poems Of Mattie J.T. Stepanek* (Epic 2003) ★★★.

Gilmer, Jimmy, And The Fireballs

(see **Fireballs**)

Gilmore, Boyd

b. 12 June 1910, Belzoni, Mississippi, USA, d. 23 December 1976, Fresno, California, USA. A guitarist, although seemingly not recorded as such, and an exuberant singer, Gilmore recorded for Modern in 1952 with **Ike Turner** on piano and James Scott Jnr. on guitar; Scott was an early victim of recording technology when an introduction and guitar break by **Elmore James** were spliced into 'Rambling On My Mind' The following year, Gilmore recorded for **Sun Records**, backed by **Earl Hooker**'s band, but the results were not issued until later. Gilmore performed in delta juke joints for a while, also playing in St. Louis and Pine Bluff, Arkansas, before settling in California for the remainder of his life.
● COMPILATIONS: *Memphis & The Delta* (1969) ★★★, *Mississippi Blues* (1972) ★★★, *Sun Records The Blues Years* (1985) ★★★.

Gilmore, Jimmie Dale

b. 6 May 1945, Amarillo, Texas, USA. Gilmore is one of the many singer-songwriters to emerge from Lubbock; he says, 'People used to ask us why there is so much music in Lubbock and we'd say that maybe it was the UFOs that came through in the early 50s. There was a famous sighting that was known as the Lubbock Lights.' Apart from such extraterrestrial help, Gilmore acknowledges the three common influences for American singer-songwriters: **Hank Williams**, **Elvis Presley** and **Bob Dylan**. His father Brian Gilmore played in an old-time country band, and Gilmore learned fiddle, trombone and guitar. He began to perform around coffeehouses in Lubbock and one of his earliest compositions was 'Treat Me Like A Saturday Night'. **Joe Ely** gave him a **Townes Van Zandt** record, which changed his life: 'It was a revelation to me because I heard both worlds, folk and country, in the same place.' Gilmore, Ely and **Butch Hancock** worked in different combinations until all three came together in the **Flatlanders**, which was formed in 1970. The acoustic band also featured Steve Wesson's musical saw, and fanciful commentators have likened its sound to the Lubbock wind. The Flatlanders took their name from the landscape and they played bars around Austin and Lubbock. Gilmore's nasal whine was as flat as that landscape, but it was suited to his laid-back, evocative songwriting. Under the name of Jimmie Dale, they released a single of Gilmore's 'Dallas', with its oft-quoted first line, 'Did you ever see Dallas from a DC-9 at night?'. Another key song was Gilmore's 'Tonight I Think I'm Gonna Go Downtown', but the album they made in 1972 was not released until 1980. The Flatlanders was over within a year but it is fondly remembered by all the members.
Following the demise of the Flatlanders, Gilmore spent much of his time in Denver studying philosophy and only occasionally playing music. He returned to Austin at the start of the 80s and was prompted to begin playing regularly after Ely covered several of his songs on record. Gilmore launched his solo career at the end of the 80s. His two albums for HighTone, *Fair And Square* and *Jimmie Dale Gilmore*, exhibited strong country roots and included some superb Butch Hancock songs ('Red Chevrolet', 'Just A Wave, Not The Water'). The two men later recorded together. Gilmore subsequently joined **Elektra Records**' American Explorer series, excelling himself on his 1991 recording *After Awhile*. Following the lesser *Spinning Around The Sun*, 1996's *Braver Newer World* moved Gilmore away from his country-based music into what he described as 'west Texas psychedelic blues rockabilly'.
In 1998, Gilmore teamed up with Ely and Hancock to record 'South Wind Of Summer' for the soundtrack to Robert Redford's 1998 film adaptation of *The Horse Whisperer*. His 2000 solo release *One Endless Night* largely featured songs by artists such as **John Hiatt** ('Your Love Is My Rest'), the **Grateful Dead** ('Ripple'), **Townes Van Zandt** ('No Lonesome Tune'), **Jesse Winchester** ('Defying Gravity'), and a surprising reading of 'Mack The Knife' alongside two by Hancock. Gilmore, Ely and Hancock then embarked on a more serious Flatlanders reunion, touring and recording the new studio albums *Now Again* (2002) and *Wheels Of Fortune* (2004). Gilmore's new solo album, the 2005 cover versions set *Come On Back*, was recorded in tribute to the guitarist's late father.
● ALBUMS: *Fair And Square* (HighTone 1988) ★★★, *Jimmie Dale Gilmore* (HighTone 1989) ★★★★, with Butch Hancock *Two Roads—Live In Australia* (Virgin Australia 1990) ★★★, *After Awhile* (Elektra 1991) ★★★★, *Spinning Around The Sun* (Elektra 1993) ★★★, *Braver Newer World* (Elektra 1996) ★★★★, *One Endless Night* (Windchanger/Rounder 2000) ★★★★, *Come On Back* (Rounder 2005) ★★★.
● COMPILATIONS: *Don't Look For A Heartache* (HighTone 2004) ★★★★.

Gilmore, John

b. 28 September 1931, Summit, Mississippi, USA, d. 20 August 1995, Philadelphia, Pennsylvania, USA. Growing up in Chicago, Gilmore became fascinated by the sound of the tenor saxophone. He was given a clarinet, which he learned to play, graduating to the saxophone. Between 1948 and 1952 he was in the air force, and played clarinet, and started on tenor saxophone while stationed in San Antonio, Texas. After leaving the air force he worked for the US postal service for a while, then decided to take a chance on earning a living as a musician. When the Harlem Globetrotters toured America in 1952, music was supplied by pianist **Earl 'Fatha' Hines** with Gilmore in the band, playing tenor saxophone. In 1953 he joined **Sun Ra**, then leading a trio, an association that was to last many decades, interrupted only by a short spell in **Art Blakey**'s **Jazz Messengers** (1964–65), when he replaced **Wayne Shorter**. Outside of his work with Sun Ra, Gilmore has recorded with **McCoy Tyner**, **Dizzy Reece**, **Pete LaRoca**, **Elmo Hope**, **Paul Bley** (on *Turns*) and with his old Chicago school-friend, pianist **Andrew Hill**, on two superb mid-60s **Blue Note Records** sessions, *Andrew* and *Compulsion*. Nevertheless the vast bulk of his music for over three decades was with Sun Ra.
Despite spending so many years in one band, Gilmore was never in danger of falling into routine. Sun Ra's musical philosophy was such that his band's repertoire was in almost constant flux. He made occasional forays outside the band, once with **Miles Davis**, although this project was aborted owing to the trumpet player's financial and personal problems, and toured Japan with **Art Blakey**. Such brief encounters aside, Gilmore's career is inextricably linked to Sun Ra and after the leader's death he struggled to keep the band together under his own leadership despite being in poor health. If Gilmore had not devoted his playing career to Sun Ra's music he would probably be regarded as a much more important tenor player in jazz than has been the case. It is perhaps on Sun Ra's rare small group recordings, such

as *New Steps*, that Gilmore is given the space he needs to really stretch out. In addition to tenor saxophone and bass clarinet, he sometimes played percussion with the Arkestra (and was featured as a percussionist on *My Brother The Wind*) and also sang in an enthusiastic, gravelly voice—his speciality being 'East Of The Sun, West Of The Moon'. A forceful and dynamic player, Gilmore frequently drew high praise from other musicians. **John Coltrane** was emphatic, declaring: 'I listened to John Gilmore kind of closely before I made *Chasin' The Trane* . . . Some of the things on there are a direct influence of listening to this cat.' Gilmore died of emphysema in 1995.

● ALBUMS: with Clifford Jordan *Blowing In From Chicago* (Blue Note 1957) ★★★, *Dizzy Reece/John Gilmore* (Futura 1970) ★★.

Gilmore, Marque

b. USA. A highly accomplished drummer immersed in ethnic musicology, in 1993 Gilmore formed and has since performed regularly with the band Live Drum & Bass. Billed as the first live jungle/drum 'n' bass ensemble, the band performs music that combines live interactive MIDI-electronics and DJs, and became very popular in both London and New York, where Gilmore was a founding member of NYC Black Rock Coalition. His group, the Drum-FM Interactive Tribalistic Session, was launched in 1994. Among artists with whom Gilmore has performed is Malian keyboard player and singer Cheick Tidiane Seck. From 1998 Gilmore toured during the next two years with composer and multi-instrumentalist **Nitin Sawhney**. In the spring of 1999, Gilmore received the New Music Commission Grant from the UK Arts Council, and his and Seck's resulting 'Millennium Migration' was premiered at London's Hackney Empire. In 2000, he toured the UK as support for **Sting**. Starting in 2000 Gilmore benefited from a three-year fixed-term funding grant allowing him to further develop his musical concepts. In May 2001, Gilmore and Seck shared the bill at London's Barbican Centre with the Arts Ensemble Of Chicago. That same year, he toured Europe and India and made a five-city tour of China. Among other musicians with whom Gilmore has worked are concert pianist Katia Labeque and jazz pianist **Gonzalo Rubalcaba**.

● ALBUMS: *Project 23* (Dorado 1997) ★★★.

Gilmore, Thea

b. 25 November 1979, Banbury, Oxfordshire, England. This UK singer-songwriter presents a distinctly English take on the angst-rock blueprint of American artists such as **Ani DiFranco** and **Alanis Morissette**. Gilmore was brought up in Oxford, where she listened to classic rock records and began to write short stories and poetry. By her mid-teens Gilmore had begun composing and performing her own songs, and was first noticed during a work experience placement at **Fairport Convention**'s Woodworm Studios. At the age of 16 she recorded an album for the independent Beautiful Jo label. A single 'Instead Of The Saints' was released before Gilmore, demonstrating a precocious distrust of the record industry, broke away to set up her own Shameless Records label. *Burning Dorothy* was released to general acclaim in November 1998, revealing a songwriter of rare passion and intent. *The Lipstick Conspiracies* benefited from a distribution contract with Naim, while retaining the edgy production sound (courtesy of Nigel Stonier) and venomous polemic of

her debut. Gilmore went from strength to strength on *Rules For Jokers*, a more acoustic-orientated album that nevertheless possessed a bite and snap missing from the work of the majority of her contemporaries. *Songs From The Gutter*, which was initially only made available for purchase through Gilmore's website, collected a batch of previously unissued material that confirmed her burgeoning reputation as one of the UK's most promising singer-songwriters.

● ALBUMS: *Burning Dorothy* (Shameless 1998) ★★★, *The Lipstick Conspiracies* (Shameless/Naim 2000) ★★★★, *Rules For Jokers* (Shameless/Compass 2001) ★★★★, *Songs From The Gutter* (Flying Sparks 2002) ★★★, *Avalanche* (Hungry Dog 2003) ★★★, *Loft Music* (Compass 2004) ★★★.

Gilmour, David

b. 6 March 1946, Cambridge, England. The solo career of **Pink Floyd**'s lead guitarist started in 1978 with a self-titled debut album. The material was recorded during a perilously long Pink Floyd hiatus and amid rumours of a break-up. The album was well-received and made a respectable showing in the UK and US charts. A second collection, the lesser *About Face*, arrived in 1984 after the official and acrimonious split of the band. During that year Gilmour was very active; he performed at the **Live Aid** concert with **Bryan Ferry**, and was later to play a major role in the recording of the singer's 1987 collection *Bête Noire*. He also performed on **Grace Jones**' bestselling *Slave To The Rhythm*. In 1987, Gilmour reunited with Nick Mason and decided to use the Pink Floyd title. As Rick Wright had also been hired it seemed legitimate, until **Roger Waters** objected. Gilmour has been involved in a subtle war of words with Waters ever since. Waters at present has lost title to the name (he does not want to use it anyway) and Gilmour now leads the band when they choose to record and tour.

Gilmour's confidence both as a writer and as a performer has notably grown in stature, and in the new millennium he began performing a stripped-down, largely acoustic show that was at the opposite end of the spectrum to Pink Floyd's grandiose concerts. In May 2003 he sold one of his London houses and donated the nearly £4 million pound profit to a local housing project. The same November, Gilmour was awarded a CBE for philanthropy and for services to music. On 2 July 2005, Gilmour performed with Pink Floyd (including Waters) at the **Live 8** concert in Hyde Park, London. Rumours of a Pink Floyd reunion were later roundly scotched by the guitarist. Gilmour's third solo album, *On An Island*, debuted at the top of the UK charts in March 2006 and also reached the US Top 10. The lyrics to the songs were written by Gilmour's wife Polly Samson.

● ALBUMS: *David Gilmour* (Harvest/Columbia 1978) ★★★, *About Face* (Harvest/Columbia 1984) ★★, *On An Island* (EMI 2006) ★★★.

● DVD/VIDEOS: *In Concert* (Capitol 2002).

Giltrap, Gordon

b. 6 April 1948, East Peckham, Tonbridge, Kent, England. A renowned and innovative guitarist, Giltrap came through the early days of the UK folk revival, and established himself in rock music circles. His first guitar was a present, at the age of 12, from his mother. Leaving school aged 15, he wanted to pursue a career in art, but had insufficient qualifications, so spent time working on building sites. As his interest and ability developed, he started playing regularly at Les Cousins, in London's Greek Street. There he met a number of singers and musicians who later became household names in the folk and blues world. Names such as **Bert Jansch**, **John Renbourn**, **John Martyn** and **Al Stewart** were just a few such notables. Although still only semi-professional, Giltrap signed a recording contract with Transatlantic Records and released *Gordon Giltrap* and *Portrait*. He also appeared on the 1970 debut album by folk rock/progressive outfit **Accolade**. Playing the college, folk club and university circuit, and establishing a growing following, Giltrap had begun to write mainly instrumental pieces by the 70s.

This change of direction led to *Visionary*, an album based on the work of William Blake, the eighteenth-century English artist and poet. By now Giltrap was receiving favourable reviews for his style blending classical and rock music, and this led to him being commissioned to write for a number of special events. 'Heartsong', from *Perilous Journey*, just failed to broach the Top 20 in the British singles charts in 1978. The tune, a Giltrap composition, was later used by BBC Television, as the theme tune to the *Holiday* programme during the 80s. The album from which it came reached the Top 30 in the British charts, while the following year, 1979, 'Fear Of The Dark' narrowly failed to make the Top 50 singles chart. In 1979, he composed, for London's Capital Radio, an orchestral piece to commemorate 'Operation Drake', a two-year round-the-world scientific expedition following in the footsteps of Sir Francis Drake. This resulted in the premiere, in 1980, of 'The Eye Of The Wind Rhapsody' with the London Philharmonic Orchestra, conducted by Vernon Handley.

Many of Giltrap's other compositions have been used for UK television work, on programmes such as ITV's *Wish You Were Here*, *The Open University*, and, in 1985, the television drama *Hold The Back Page*, and other subsequent television films. Giltrap now tours regularly with **Ric Sanders** in addition to solo work, and has also duetted with John Renbourn, and Juan Martin. *The Best Of Gordon Giltrap: All The Hits Plus More*, includes a previously unreleased track, 'Catwalk Blues', which was recorded live at Oxford Polytechnic. As well as performing, recording and owning a guitar shop Giltrap is a regular contributor to *Guitarist* magazine and has written a book on the history of Hofner guitars. He received widespread publicity for his collaboration with **Cliff Richard** on the 1995 stage musical *Heathcliff*, leading to a new record contract with **K-Tel Records**, for whom he recorded *Troubadour*. Giltrap is an outstanding guitarist, recognized by many as being one of the leading players in the UK.

● ALBUMS: *Gordon Giltrap* (Transatlantic 1968) ★★★, *Portrait* (Transatlantic 1969) ★★★, *A Testament Of Time* (MCA 1971) ★★★, *Giltrap* (Philips 1973) ★★★, *Visionary* (Electric 1976) ★★★★, *Perilous Journey* (Electric 1977) ★★★★, *Fear Of The Dark* (Electric 1978) ★★★, *Performance* (K-Tel 1980) ★★★, *The Peacock Party* (PVK 1981) ★★★, *Live* (Cube 1981) ★★, *Airwaves* (PVK 1982) ★★★, *Elegy* (Modern 1987) ★★, *A Midnight Clear* (Modern 1987) ★★★, with Ric Sanders *One To One* (Nico Polo 1989) ★★★, *Guitarist* (Music Maker 1990) ★★★, with Martin Taylor *A Matter Of Time* (Prestige 1991) ★★★, *The Solo Album* (Prestige 1992) ★★★, *On A Summer's Night—Gordon Giltrap Live* (Music Maker 1992) ★★★, *Music For The Small Screen* (Munchkin 1995) ★★★, *Live At*

The BBC (Windsong 1995) ★★★, with the Nottinghamshire Education String Orchestra *The Brotherhood Suite* (Munchkin 1995) ★★★, *Troubadour* (K-Tel 1998) ★★★.
● COMPILATIONS: *The Early Days* (Allegro 1978) ★★★, *The Platinum Collection* (Cube 1981) ★★★, *The Best Of Gordon Giltrap: All The Hits Plus More* (Prestige 1991) ★★★, *The River Sessions* (River 2004) ★★★.

Giltrap, Joe

b. 4 July 1943, Leixlip, County Kildare, Eire. Before taking up music in 1966, singer Giltrap had been a keen soccer and Gaelic footballer. He started singing with a local group, the Rye Folk, before joining top recording folk band the Broadsiders. He then left them to join a new country band, the Cotton Mill Boys, for a brief period in 1969, before rejoining the Broadsiders. By 1972 all the chopping and changing had become an irritant, and Giltrap went solo. As Jason Cord he recorded a single, 'Keeps Right On A Hurtin'', for **Polydor Records**, moving to London later the same year. Eschewing music for a year, he formed the duo Irish Mist in 1973, along with fiddle player Malcolm Rogers. The combination of Southern Irish Catholic and Northern Irish Protestant sharing a common love of folk music was noted by Rob Dickens at **Warner Brothers Records**, who signed the duo, producing their first album in 1974. Owing to the prevailing political climate at the time, it was not released by Warner Brothers. Instead, Giltrap and Rogers released *Rosin The Bow* independently on SRT. This album is now a collector's item. The duo split in the late 70s, with Giltrap forming his own group, Zozimus (named after an old Dublin street singer), in 1977. They made only two albums before Irish Mist re-formed in 1980. The two toured Britain and Europe, appearing on radio and television in a number of countries. In 1984 Irish Mist recorded two tracks for the Ronco label Irish compilation, *Green Velvet*. The album reached number 6 in the UK charts, and made the Top 10 again, a year later, on re-release. This earned the duo a gold disc. The follow-up, *More Green Velvet*, for which the duo recorded one track, earned a silver disc. After a number of recordings either as Irish Mist or in a solo capacity, Giltrap took over the running of the now prestigious London music venue, The Weavers, in 1987. After spending a good deal of time promoting live acoustic music in London, Giltrap, who had put his own career on hold, felt the urge to record and perform again. Recording as either the Joe Giltrap Band or as a duo with Joe Palmer, the live work culminated in his first solo release for many years. In 1993 *Where There's Life* was released. Apart from his own guitar, banjo, bodhran and vocal work, Giltrap recruited a number of guest musicians for the album.

● ALBUMS: with the Broadsiders *The Broadsiders* (Bullseye 1970) ★★★, with Irish Mist *Rosin The Bow* (SRT 1974) ★★★, with Zozimus *As Zozimus Says* (Loco 1977) ★★, with Zozimus *Follow Me Up To Carlow* (Loco 1978) ★★, *Second Time 'Round* (Loco 1982) ★★★, *Solo* (Loco 1986) ★★★, *Rocky Road To Dublin* (Etude 1986) ★★★, with Joe Palmer *A Place In Your Heart* (Etude 1987) ★★★, *Where There's Life* (Minidoka 1993) ★★★.

Gimble, Johnny

b. 30 May 1926, near Tyler, Texas, USA. The fifth of six brothers, Gimble grew up in a musical environment, and each of his brothers played a stringed instrument. By the age of 12, having already learned both fiddle and mandolin, he was playing with four of his brothers at local dances and made his first radio appearances while still at school. He left home when he was 17 and found work playing fiddle and banjo with the Shelton Brothers and also with **Jimmie Davis** on KWKH Shreveport. In 1949, he joined **Bob Wills**' Texas Playboys (for the first time) and moved with Wills from Oklahoma to Dallas, when he opened the Bob Wills Ranch House. Around 1951, he left full-time work with Wills but later played with him on other occasions. Gimble continued to play local venues and did session work with several artists including **Marty Robbins** and **Lefty Frizzell**, but in 1955, seeking some work with security, he became a barber and moved to Waco. During the 60s, he returned to a full-time musical career. He realized that he could find a lot of work as a session musician and relocated with his family to Nashville. Here his talents were much in demand and he worked with many top artists including **Merle Haggard**, who used him, as an ex–Texas Playboy, on his tribute album to Bob Wills. Apart from his countless session recordings with others, he recorded in his own right and worked with the popular First Nashville Jesus Band. He moved to Austin in the late 70s but still continued with some session work in Nashville. He has toured with many artists including **Willie Nelson**, has been featured on the popular *Hee-Haw* and *Austin City Limits* television series and has made several appearances at the Wembley Festival in London. He is equally at home with western-swing, country, blues or jazz music and during his career he has won many awards in recognition of his outstanding fiddle-playing.

● ALBUMS: *Fiddlin' Around* (Capitol 1974) ★★★, *Honky Tonk Hits* (1976) ★★★, *Texas Dance Party* (Lone Star 1975) ★★★★, with the Texas Swing Pioneers *Still Swingin'* (CMH 1976) ★★★, *Honky Tonk Hurtin' Songs* (1981) ★★, *More Texas Dance Hall Favorites* (1981) ★★★, *I Saw The Light* (1981) ★★★, with Joe Barnhill's Nashville Sound Company *Swingin' The Standards* (1981) ★★★, *My Kinda Music* (1984) ★★★, *Still Fiddlin' Around* (MCA 1988) ★★★.

● COMPILATIONS: *Texas Fiddle Connection* (CMH 1981) ★★★.

Gimme Shelter

Released in 1970, *Gimme Shelter* was directed by brothers David and Albert Maysles, renowned for their work as documentary film makers. Their skills and experience brought a chilling intensity to a project initially viewed as a commemoration of the **Rolling Stones** 1969 tour of the USA. The tour ended with the ill-fated Altamont Concert, which exposed the dark side of the 60s counter-culture dream when Hells Angels, employed as stewards, murdered a member of the audience. The film's focus was changed irrevocably. *Gimme Shelter* provides lighter moments, including a pulsating recording session at the **Muscle Shoals** studio, but a sense of foreboding sweeps the entire proceedings. Other acts featured include the **Flying Burrito Brothers** and **Jefferson Airplane** (whose lead singer, **Marty Balin,** was knocked unconscious by the Hells Angels), but the power of *Gimme Shelter* rests in its uncompromising documentation of one of rock music's most tragic episodes.

Gin Blossoms

'A big slice of American cheese' was how the singer of this American country rock band once described their sound.

Favoured sons of **MTV**, they had earlier attracted a fierce local following after formation in Tempe, Arizona, USA, in 1987. Their original line-up comprised Doug Hopkins (b. Douglas Hopkins, 11 April 1961, USA, d. 5 December 1993, Tempe, Arizona, USA; guitar), Bill Leen (b. 1 March 1962; bass), Jesse Valenzuela (b. 22 May 1962; guitar/vocals), Richard Taylor (rhythm guitar/vocals) and Chris McCann (drums). Robin Wilson (b. 12 July 1965) and Daniel Henzerling were brought in the following year to replace Taylor and McCann respectively. The classic Gin Blossoms finally fell into place when Wilson was promoted to lead singer, Valenzuela switched to rhythm guitar and vocals, and Phillip Rhodes (b. 26 May 1969) replaced Henzerling.

The band's debut, *Dusted*, was released in 1989 on vinyl and cassette. The musical backdrop and Wilson's vocals brought critical comparisons to **R.E.M.** and the **Byrds**. Comparisons that found fruition on the major hit single, 'Hey Jealousy', and 1992's accompanying major label debut, *New Miserable Experience*. However, soon after, tragedy struck the band. After struggling for years against depression and alcoholism, chief songwriter Hopkins' behaviour had became so unstable that it was necessary to eject him from the band. His departure came in April 1992, soon after recording sessions for the album were completed. A bitter wrangle ensued, with the band reportedly forcing him to sign over half his publishing royalties in return for a one-off payment of $15,000 owed to him. As 'Hey Jealousy' and 'Found Out About You', two excellent songs he had written for the Gin Blossoms, became major hits, his personal problems increased. On 3 December 1993 he left a detox unit in Phoenix, Arizona, and shot himself two days later. Hopkins had been replaced as lead guitarist by Scott Johnson (b. 11 October 1962), but of more concern was how the Gin Blossoms would replace him as a songwriter. Although both Wilson ('Allison Road') and Valenzuela ('Mrs Rita') had written songs on the band's debut, critics were in no doubt as to the identity of the author of the more compelling tracks. **Marshall Crenshaw** was recruited as co-writer on "Til I Hear It From You', the hit single from the predictably weaker *Congratulations I'm Sorry*. The band eventually split up in spring 1997, with Wilson and Rhodes going on to form the **Gas Giants**.

● ALBUMS: *Dusted* (San Jacinto 1989) ★★★, *New Miserable Experience* (A&M 1992) ★★★★★, *Congratulations I'm Sorry* (A&M 1996) ★★★.

● COMPILATIONS: *Outside Looking In: The Best Of The Gin Blossoms* (A&M 1999) ★★★★.

Gingold, Hermione

b. Hermione Ferdinanda Gingold, 9 December 1897, London, England, d. 24 May 1987, New York City, USA. Starting out in the theatre at age 11, Gingold became popular in London's West End and on Broadway in New York, owing in the main to appearances in revues and her engagingly eccentric manner. She made her first film appearance in 1932, uncredited, and played minor roles in a few more films through the late 30s and into the early 40s. More minor roles came in 50s films until her brief though memorable appearance as Madame Alvarez in the film musical *Gigi* (1958). Therein, she sang the trio, 'The Night They Invented Champagne' (with **Leslie Caron** and Louis Jourdan), and the duet, 'I Remember It Well' (with **Maurice Chevalier**). She was also in the comedy *Bell, Book And Candle* (1958) and the suspenseful drama *The Naked Edge* (1961). Gingold also appeared in two more film musicals, these based upon successful Broadway shows: the well-made **The Music Man** (1962), in the role of Eulalie Mackechnie Shinn, and the best-forgotten screen version of *A Little Night Music* (1977). Her last film appearance was in *Garbo Talks* (1984).

Back in the 50s, Gingold appeared on BBC radio in *Home At Eight* (1952). A segment within this show, entitled 'Mrs Doom's Diary', was a bizarre blending of *Mrs Dale's Diary* and Charles Addams' sinister family, in which Gingold and Alfred Marks would weekly share the exchange: 'Tea, Edmond?' 'Yes, Drusilla.' 'Millock?'. Gingold was also on television in the UK and the USA. Her UK appearances included the satirical show, *Before The Fringe* (1967). In the USA she made numerous guest appearances on *Toast Of The Town* in the 50s and *The Merv Griffin Show* in the 60s, as well as in drama series such as *Ironside* (1970), *Banyon* (1971), *Trapper John, M.D.* (1981) and *Hotel* (1983). Her Broadway appearances included the 1953 revue, *John Murray Anderson's Almanac*, *First Impressions*, *From A To Z* (both 1959), **Milk And Honey** (1961), *Oh Dad, Poor Dad, Mama's Hung You In The Closet And I'm Feeling So Sad* (1963), **A Little Night Music** (1973) and *Side By Side By Sondheim* (1977).

● FURTHER READING: *How To Grow Old Disgracefully*, Hermione Gingold and Eyre Anne Clements.

● FILMS: *Dance Pretty Lady* (1932), *Someone At The Door* (1936), *Merry Comes To Town* aka *Merry Comes To Stay* (1937), *Meet Mr. Penny* (1938), *The Butler's Dilemma* (1943), *The Pickwick Papers* (1952), *Cosh Boy* aka *The Slasher* (1952), *Our Girl Friday* aka *The Adventures Of Sadie* (1954), *Around The World In Eighty Days* (1956), *Gigi* (1958), *Bell, Book And Candle* (1958), *The Naked Edge* (1961), *The Music Man* (1962), *Gay Purr-ee* voice only (1962), *The World Of Henry Orient* (1964), *I'd Rather Be Rich* (1964), *Harvey Middleman, Fireman* (1965), *The Itch* voice only (1965), *Promise Her Anything* (1965), *Munster, Go Home* (1966), *Rocket To The Moon* (1967), *The Special London Bridge Special* (1972), *Tubby The Tuba* voice only (1976), *A Little Night Music* (1977), *Garbo Talks* (1984).

Ginsberg, Allen

b. 3 June 1926, New Jersey, USA, d. 5 April 1997, New York City, USA. One of the most prominent poets of the 20th century, Ginsberg also recorded several singles and albums, some including unaccompanied readings of his poetry, others featuring his writings set to music. Ginsberg originally aligned with the 'beat' movement of the 50s and 60s. He befriended and worked with many musicians through the years, among them **Bob Dylan**, the **Grateful Dead**, the **Clash**, **John Lennon**, **Leonard Cohen**, **Phil Ochs**, the **Fugs**, **Pete Seeger** and **Phil Spector**. He was a member of Dylan's 1975 Rolling Thunder Revue touring company.

● ALBUMS: *Howl And Other Poems* (Fantasy 1959) ★★★★, *Ginsberg's Thing* (Douglas 1969) ★★★, *Songs Of Innocence And Experience* (MGM 1970) ★★★, *First Blues: A.G. On Harmonium* (Smithsonian/Folkways 1981) ★★★, *Made-Up In Texas* (Paris 1986) ★★★, *The Lion For Real* (Mouth Almighty/Mercury 1989) ★★★.

● COMPILATIONS: *First Blues: Songs: 1975–81* (John Hammond 1983) ★★★, *Holy Soul Jelly Roll: Poems And Songs 1948-1993* 4-CD box set (Rhino 1994) ★★★.

● FURTHER READING: *The Beat Hotel: Ginsberg, Burroughs & Corso In Paris, 1957—1963*, Barry Miles.

Ginuwine

b. Elgin Baylor Lumpkin, 15 October 1970 (1975 is also cited), Washington, DC, USA. Talented R&B performer Ginuwine began his musical apprenticeship at the age of 12, performing at parties and (illegally) at bars with his friends in the neighbourhood outfit, Finesse Five. From this he progressed to a solo act, which was initially built around impersonations of his childhood idol, **Michael Jackson**. Working on his education at the same time, he graduated from Princes Georges Community College with a paralegal degree. He met rookie producer **Timbaland** in New York, and the two recorded the unusual, synthesizer-infused R&B effort 'The Pony' together. The song attracted strong interest, and at the age of 21 Ginuwine chose to sign with the New York–based Sony subsidiary 550 Music. He enjoyed immediate success with the release of 'Pony', which reached number 1 on **Billboard**'s R&B chart, and number 6 on the Hot 100 chart. As a result his debut album, written and recorded with Timbaland, was assured of mainstream media attention, and reached number 45 on the album chart. To promote the set, Ginuwine set out on a national tour supporting **Aaliyah**, **Dru Hill**, **Mary J. Blige** and **Bone Thugs-N-Harmony**. A string of crossover hit singles followed, including 'Tell Me Do U Wanna', 'I'll Do Anything/I'm Sorry' and 'Only When U R Lonely'. On the strength of his work with the singer, Timbaland went on to become one of the main forces in late 90s R&B.

Ginuwine made his acting debut in November 1998, appearing in the CBS series *Martial Law*. Another standout Timbaland track, March 1999's 'What's So Different' (which reached UK number 10), provided him with his strongest single to date. The US Top 10 album *100% Ginuwine* was another showcase for his classy vocal skills and Timbaland's inventive production, featuring the huge radio hit 'So Anxious'. During the following two years, Ginuwine balanced shooting his movie debut with the recording of a new album, *The Life*. The single 'Differences' was a major US pop hit. In 2002 he made his big-screen debut in the basketball comedy *Juwanna Mann*. Both *The Senior* (2003) and *Back II Da Basics* (2005) were classy, mature collections that focused on ballads and mid-tempo songs.

● ALBUMS: *Ginuwine: The Bachelor* (550 Music/Epic 1997) ★★★★, *100% Ginuwine* (550 Music/Epic 1999) ★★★★, *The Life* (Epic 2001) ★★★, *The Senior* (Epic 2003) ★★★, *Back II Da Basics* (Epic 2005) ★★★.

● DVD/VIDEOS: *The Videos* (Sony 2003).

● FILMS: *Juwanna Mann* (2002), *Honey* (2003).

Gipsy Kings

These popular flamenco artists initially formed as an offshoot of the family group Los Reyes (the Kings), who in the 70s and 80s were led by father José Reyes, together with sons Nicólas and Andre Reyes. They enjoyed significant domestic success in Spain, though contrary to popular belief their origins lay on the other side of the French border. In 1982, Nicólas and Andre Reyes teamed up with Chico Bouchikhi when he married into the family. The Gipsy Kings were formed when they joined with three cousins from the Baliardo family (Diego, Tonino and Paci), each member singing and playing guitar with Nicólas Reyes as their lead vocalist.

As the Gipsy Kings the band attempted to reach a worldwide market for the first time, initially earning their reputation by playing to film stars and royalty at France's St. Tropez holiday resort. They made their worldwide debut with a self-titled album for **Elektra Records** in 1988, by which time several collections had already been released in Spain and mainland Europe. As before, the music blended elements of the Nueva Andalucia flamenco style, with the inclusion of percussive foot stamps, handclaps and vocals drawn from Arabic music. In addition to their trademark multi-guitar sound, they also added other components, including drums, bass, percussion and synthesizers. This effort to broaden their appeal resulted in a massive international break-through, including number 1 status in the Canadian and Australian charts, with *Gipsy Kings* peaking at number 16 in the UK. The ensuing *Mosaique*, though marginally less successful, saw the group incorporate elements of jazz (collaborating with **Rubén Blades**) and 50s/60s pop.

In the early 90s, the personnel shuffled, and the Gipsy Kings began to lose much of the momentum they had built up in the previous decade, despite the release of a live album in 1993. *Cantos De Amor* reversed the trend, becoming a major success for them in 1998. The follow-up *Somos Gitanos* was another slick, highly commercial effort, but long-time fans of the Gipsy Kings were more encouraged by 2004's *Roots*. Recorded in a farmhouse in the south of France, the album returned the Gipsy Kings quite literally to their roots, with the production sheen of their hit albums largely dispensed with in favour of a rollicking, down-home atmosphere.

● ALBUMS: *Luna De Fuego* (Philips 1983) ★★★, *Allegria* (Elektra 1986) ★★★, *Gipsy Kings* (Elektra 1988) ★★★, *Mosaique* (Elektra 1989) ★★★, *Love & Liberty* (Elektra 1993) ★★, *Tierra Gitana* (Atlantic 1996) ★★, *Compas* (Atlantic 1997) ★★★★, *Cantos De Amor* (Nonesuch 1998) ★★★★, *Somos Gitanos* (Nonesuch 2001) ★★★, *Roots* (Nonesuch 2004) ★★★★.

● COMPILATIONS: *The Best Of The Gipsy Kings* (Elektra 1995) ★★★, *¡Volare! The Very Best Of The Gipsy Kings* (Columbia 1999) ★★★★.

● FURTHER READING: *Root: The Gipsy Kings And Their Journey*, Lucien Clergue.

Gipsy Princess, The
(see **Gypsy Princess, The**)

Girard, Adele

b. 1913, USA, d. 7 September 1993, Denver, Colorado, USA. By choosing the harp as her instrument, Girard severely damaged her chances of being taking seriously when she began playing jazz. Nevertheless, she persevered, working in bands such as Harry Sosnick's before coming to wider attention as a member of **Joe Marsala**'s band at 52nd Street's Hickory House in 1938. That same year Girard and Marsala married and continued to play together during the next decade. After Marsala retired from regular performing, Girard continued her career, now as a solo act, also singing and playing piano. She worked in clubs, hotels and casinos in Los Angeles and surrounding areas, especially the popular resorts, and in the 70s appeared briefly in London with the Festival Theatre USC. By dint of her delightful melodic approach, a subtle sense of swing, allied to her perfect pitch, she became an able member of some good small jazz groups

and qualified as one of the two or three—of an admittedly small number—best harpists in jazz.

● ALBUMS: *The Bobby Gordon Quartet Featuring Adele Girard Marsala* (Arbors 1992) ★★★, with Bobby Gordon *Don't Let It End* (Arbors 1992) ★★★★.

Girard, Chuck

b. USA. Girard is a founder member of Love Song, a rock group who experienced a similar 'spiritual transformation' to Girard himself. Having spent several years in rock 'n' roll groups, Girard became a born again Christian after joining the Calvary Chapel in Costa Mesa, California. The result was a softening of the group's sound to a more acoustic, message-based formula, and the launch of Girard's own solo career. Three albums followed for Good News Records in the mid-to late 70s, though none of these captured the gospel community's imagination in quite the same way as the work of Love Song had.

● ALBUMS: *Chuck Girard* (Good News 1975) ★★★, *Glow In The Dark* (Good News 1977) ★★★, *Written On The Wind* (Good News 1979) ★★★.

Girl

A band very much ahead of their time, Girl's lipstick and glam image, portrayed on the cover of their debut, *Sheer Greed*, was quite a shock to the traditional UK heavy metal community during the rise of the **New Wave Of British Heavy Metal**, despite the existence of more outrageous glam bands in the preceding decade. Recorded with a line-up of Philip Lewis (vocals), Phil Collen (b. 8 December 1957, Hackney, London, England; guitar), brothers Gerry (guitar) and Simon Laffy (bass) and Dave Gaynor (drums), *Sheer Greed* was an impressive slice of sleazy hard rock, but was overshadowed by the band's image and by publicity surrounding Lewis' relationship with actress Britt Ekland. Although they were a capable live act, and were given great exposure by support slots on major UK tours with the **Pat Travers Band** and **UFO** (twice), they failed to capture the public's imagination. *Wasted Youth*, with Pete Barnacle taking over on drums, paled beside the debut, and the band, dispirited, dissolved as Collen was invited to join **Def Leppard**. A third, currently unreleased album, exists on tape. Lewis later became frontman for **L.A. Guns**, with whom he re-recorded 'Hollywood Tease', the opening track on *Sheer Greed*, and the success of this band, along with the likes of **Poison** and **Guns N'Roses**, suggests that Girl may have met a better fate had they appeared only a few years later. Receiver Records reissued both albums in 1999. Two live albums followed on the same label in 2001.

● ALBUMS: *Sheer Greed* (Jet 1980) ★★★, *Wasted Youth* (Jet 1982) ★★, *Live At The Marquee* (Receiver 2001) ★★, *Live At The Exposition Hall, Osaka, Japan* (Receiver 2001) ★★★.

Girl Called Eddy, A
(see **A Girl Called Eddy**)

Girl Can't Help It, The

Perhaps the finest film of the rock 'n' roll era, this 1956 outing has much to recommend it. In a plot liberally borrowed from **Judy Holliday**'s *Born Yesterday*, struggling agent Tom Ewell is charged by mobster Edmund O'Brien to further the career of his girlfriend (Jayne Mansfield). Risqué (for 1956) references to the latter's physical attributes aside—a running gag throughout—the film is fired by comedy veteran Frank Tashlin's script and direction which, for once, matches the pace and rhythm of the musical interludes. **Gene Vincent** contributes a memorable 'The Girl Can't Help It', the fledgling talent of **Eddie Cochran** is heard on 'Twenty Flight Rock' and **Fats Domino** adds a superb 'Blue Monday'. However, the star is undoubtedly **Little Richard**, who tears through the title song, 'She's Got It' and 'Ready Teddy'. *The Girl Can't Help It* not only showcased such acts without condescension, it was the first rock 'n' roll film shot in colour. However, the film's strength does not solely rest on these pivotal figures. Tom Ewell is superb as the long-suffering agent, and his hallucinations about a former client immortalized **Julie London**'s 'Cry Me A River'. Edmund O'Brien relished his rare excursion into comedy and the gangster-inspired composition he sang, 'Rock Around The Rock Pile', acted as a thinly veiled sideswipe at exploitative releases made to cash in on fads. Few films embraced rock 'n' roll with similar understanding and respect.

Girl Crazy (film musical)
(see *Babes In Arms* (film musical))

Girl Crazy (stage musical)
The American Depression was biting hard, but Broadway itself was remarkably buoyant when *Girl Crazy* opened at the Alvin Theatre on 14 October 1930. The show's producers, Alex A. Aarons and Vincent Freedley, wanted Bert Lahr as their chief laughter-maker, but they had rather carelessly loaned him out to **George White** for *Flying Home!*, and could not get him back in time. So they signed the singing comedy team of Willie and Eugene Howard instead, although only Willie appeared in the show. In **Guy Bolton** and John McGowan's contemporary tale of cowboy life, Willie plays the role of Gieber Goldfarb, a taxi driver who is hired by a wealthy New Yorker to transport his philandering son, Danny Churchill (Allan Kearns), 3000 miles to Custerville, a town that has not had a female resident in 50 years. Danny soon changes that situation by turning the family lodge into Buzzards, a dude ranch with imported New York showgirls and a gambling saloon that is managed by Slick Fothergill (William Kent) and his wife Kate (**Ethel Merman**). Danny himself falls for the local postmistress, Molly Gray (**Ginger Rogers**), and Goldfarb gives up driving taxis and becomes the town's sheriff (Custerville gets through two of those a week). It was the first time that Ethel Merman had been seen and heard (!) on Broadway, and she excelled with 'Boy! What Love Has Done To Me!', and the smoochy 'Sam And Delilah', which was followed almost immediately by the ebullient 'I Got Rhythm'—just three of the outstanding numbers in this marvellous score by **George** and **Ira Gershwin**. Naturally enough, Kearns and Rogers shared the big romantic ballad, 'Embraceable You' and the getting-to-know-you 'Could You Use Me?'. Rogers also had 'Cactus Time In Arizona' and the wistful 'But Not For Me'. The rest of the songs included 'The Lonesome Cowboy', 'Bronco Busters', Geiber's campaign song, 'Goldfarb! That's I'm!', 'Land Of The Gay Caballero', and 'Treat Me Rough'.
Another of the show's most endearing numbers, 'Bidin' My Time', was sung at various moments throughout the show by a quartet of cowboys played by the Foursome. That sequence was recreated in the film, *The Glenn Miller Story*, when

James Stewart, as Miller, was supposed to be playing in the pit orchestra for *Girl Crazy*. Unlike many of Hollywood's inaccurate representations of Broadway musicals, this one was true. Miller did play in the orchestra, along with **Benny Goodman** and **Gene Krupa**, in what was an augmented version of **Red Nichols**' dance band. Nichols also had big record hits with 'I Got Rhythm' and 'Embraceable You'. With those songs, a bright, colourful production, and its famous curtain line: 'Go on—marry him Molly. It's 11:15 now!', *Girl Crazy* seemed to be set for a long run, but when Willy Howard and Ethel Merman left for the 1931 edition of *George White's Scandals*, it closed after 272 performances. Three film adaptations were made: an early talkie version in 1932, the definitive version with **Judy Garland** and **Mickey Rooney** in 1943, and a 1965 re-hash, *When The Boys Meet The Girls*, starring **Connie Francis**, Harve Presnell, **Herman's Hermits**, **Louis Armstrong**, and **Liberace**. More than 60 years later, on 24 February 1992, a 'revamp' of the show, entitled *Crazy For You*, conceived by Mike Ockrent and Ken Ludwig, opened on Broadway and became a smash-hit, winning the **Tony Award** for best musical. It repeated its success in London during the following year. In 1991, a CD recording of *Girl Crazy* was released complete with the original orchestrations by **Robert Russell Bennett**, and starring Lorna Luft, David Carroll, Judy Blazer, and Frank Gorshin.

Girl Friend, The
One of **Richard Rodgers** and **Lorenz Hart**'s earliest shows, *The Girl Friend* opened at the Vanderbilt Theatre in New York on 17 March 1926. After their success with *Dearest Enemy*, the young songwriters teamed again with librettist Herbert Fields for this story of a six-day cycle race in which the apparent long-shot for the title is nobbled by unscrupulous punters, which was a vehicle for the husband and wife dance team Eva Puck and Sammy White. They introduced Rodgers and Hart's Charleston-styled title song ('Isn't she cute?/Isn't she sweet?/An eyeful you'd die full/Of pleasure to meet/In my funny fashion/I'm cursed with a passion/For the girl friend!'), and one of the composers' loveliest ballads, 'The Blue Room' ('We will thrive on/Keep alive on/Just nothing but kisses/With Mister and Missus/On little blue chairs'). Eva Puck also had the amusing 'The Damsel Who Done All The Dirt' ('The greatest of heroes/Would now rank as zeros/If not for the hem of a skirt'), and the rest of the score included 'Good Fellow Mine', 'Why Do I?', 'Hey, Hey', 'The Simple Life', 'Goodbye, Lenny', and 'Creole Crooning Song'. After initially poor audiences, the show picked up and ran for a creditable 301 performances. A different production with a new book, but still called *The Girl Friend*, opened in London on 8 September 1927. It contained several Rodgers and Hart numbers, including the title song, 'The Blue Room, 'What's The Use Of Talking?', and 'Mountain Greenery', and ran for 421 performances.

Girl From Utah, The
Even with its sub-title, 'The Acme Of Musical Comedy', this show would not be of any particular interest except that it contains a certain song. That song was not present when *The Girl From Utah* opened in London at the Adelphi Theatre on 18 October 1913 where it played for 195 performances. It was added, along with a few others, when the show was presented nearly a year later in New York. The score for the original West End production was written by Sidney Jones and Paul

Rubens (music) and **Adrian Ross**, **Percy Greenbank** and Rubens (lyrics). It included songs such as 'D'You Follow Me?', 'Una', 'Call Right Here', 'The Girl From Utah', 'Kissing Time', 'At The Bottom Of Brixton Hill', 'The Music Of Love', and 'When We Meet A Mormon'. The last two titles give a good clue as to the location and the subject of the piece. James T. Tanner's book was set in England, and dealt with Una Trance (Ina Claire), an American girl who flees to London in an attempt to avoid being added to a Mormon's wedding list—for wives. Although he pursues her to Europe, she is rescued from a meandering existence with the Mormon by a handsome local hoofer Sandy Blair (Joseph Coyne).

When *The Girl From Utah* transferred to the Knickerbocker Theatre on Broadway in August 1914, producer **Charles Frohman** gave it the American touch, and commissioned some interpolations from an up-and-coming young composer named **Jerome Kern**, and here is where that special song comes in. Following its introduction in this show by David Brian (Sandy), 'They'll Never Believe Me', with a lyric by Herbert Reynolds, became one of the most enduring standards in the history of popular music. Aside from numerous recordings by some of the world's leading singers, it was featured in two London musicals, *Tonight's The Night* (1915) and *Oh! What A Lovely War* (1963, also the 1969 film), and in films such as the Jerome Kern biopic *Till The Clouds Roll By* (1946, sung by **Kathryn Grayson**), and *That Midnight Kiss* (1949, **Mario Lanza**). Kern's other songs for the US version of *The Girl From Utah*, with lyrics by **Harry B. Smith**, were all of a very high standard, and included 'You Can Never Tell', 'Same Sort Of Girl', 'The Land Of Let's Pretend', 'Alice In Wonderland', 'We'll Take Care Of You' (The Little Refugees)', and the vivacious 'Why Don't They Dance The Polka?'. The rest of the New York cast included **Julia Sanderson** as Una and Joseph Cawthorn in the role of the Mormon. *The Girl From Utah*, which ran for 120 performances on Broadway, was an early example of the move, spearheaded by Kern, to create a modern American musical that would eventually replace the imported European operettas.

Girl Happy

One of the poorest **Elvis Presley** films, this 1965 feature portrayed the singer as a pop star charged with chaperoning a group of girl students while on holiday. **Shelley Fabares**, creator of the sublime 'Johnny Angel', co-starred alongside **Bing Crosby**'s son, Gary. Presley's lack of interest in the project stretched to the material he was required to sing on the attendant soundtrack. The title song, 'Do Not Disturb' and 'Do The Clam' may have been of comparative interest; each paled into insignificance when set beside recordings from the singer's halcyon era. He found little to inspire his talent on the remaining selections; boredom is very palpable in his voice.

Girl Thing

The rise and fall of this manufactured female vocal group offered a damning indictment of the state of the UK pop market at the start of the new millennium. Michelle Claire Barber (b. 5 January 1979, Blackpool, Lancashire, England), Linsay Sarah Martin (b. 2 April 1981, Manchester, England), Anika Bostelaar (b. 5 June 1981, Etten-Leur, Netherlands), Nicola Jane Stuart (b. 4 July 1979, Bradford, West Yorkshire, England) and Jodi Albert (b. 22 July 1983, Chingford,

London, England) were recruited by ex–**Spice Girls** manager and **S Club 7** creator **Simon Fuller** through an advertisement in *The Stage*. Despite misgivings from many sectors of the industry, a recording contract with BMG Records followed at the end of 1999. Everything seemed to be going to plan with the UK Top 10 success of the following year's debut single 'Last One Standing', but the relative failure of 'Girls On Top' and the group's self-titled album proved fatal in a notoriously fickle marketplace. Despite building up a substantial fanbase in Australia and the Far East, the writing was on the wall for the quintet when 'Pure And Simple', a track featured on *Girl Thing*, was axed as their third UK single and instead passed on to television pop sensations **Hear'Say**. BMG dropped Girl Thing in March 2001, barely a week before Hear'Say broke several UK sales records in the process of debuting at number 1 on the singles chart.

● ALBUMS: *Girl Thing* (RCA 2000) ★★.

Girls Against Boys

Evocative US alternative rock band Girls Against Boys formed originally in Washington, DC, in 1990, but soon relocated to New York. A quartet of Scott McCloud (vocals/guitar), Alexis Fleisig (drums), Eli Janney (bass/keyboards) and Johnny Temple (bass), had all formerly been part of Dischord Records recording artists Soul Side (Janney was that unit's sound engineer). Having recorded two albums together, they broke up at the end of the 80s before Janney and McCloud elected to continue working together. This collaboration soon evolved to encompass their former Soul Side bandmates in time for their debut *Nineties Vs. Eighties* EP. A debut album, also for Adult Swim Records, followed, before the band moved to Chicago independent Touch & Go Records. Following the release of 'Bulletproof Cupid', they recorded *Venus Luxure No. 1 Baby* for the label in 1993.

By now the band's sound had been clearly established, with McCloud's insular, melancholy lyrics driven by a distinctive double-bass sound. *Cruise Yourself* (1997) was another acclaimed release, with songs such as '(I) Don't Get A Place' earning particular praise. Again, the band's sound remained somehow foreboding, but McCloud's narratives were maturing rapidly, and by this time Girls Against Boys had become popular fixtures on the US alternative rock scene (despite several snipes from puritanical hardcore fans who had formerly supported the band in their original incarnation as Soul Side). *House Of GVSB* refined previous musical currents and was just as disquieting an aural experience, with outstanding songs such as 'Vera Cruz' and 'Click Click' twisting sexual themes into startling new shapes. McCloud, ironically, was widely cited as the US underground's latest pin-up—despite the barbed nature of most of his lyrics. The band made their major label debut with 1998's disappointingly pedestrian *Freak*on*ica*. During this time, McCloud and Temple were also recording with their side project **New Wet Kojak**, but returned to Girls Against Boys to fashion their excellent comeback album, *You Can't Fight What You Can't See*.

● ALBUMS: *Tropic Of Scorpio* (Adult Swim 1992) ★★★, *Venus Luxure No. 1 Baby* (Touch & Go 1993) ★★★★, *Cruise Yourself* (Touch & Go 1994) ★★★, *House Of GVSB* (Touch & Go 1996) ★★★, *Freak*on*ica* (Geffen 1998) ★★, *You Can't Fight What You Can't See* (Jade Tree 2002) ★★★★.

Girls Aloud

Buoyed by the runaway success of the reality television show *Popstars*, the UK's ITV1 channel launched *Popstars: The Rivals* in 2002. The show adopted a new twist on the *Popstars* theme, picking opposing boy and girl bands to battle it out in the UK charts, with pop svengalis Louis Walsh and Pete Waterman in charge of managing the girls and boys respectively, and ex-**Spice Girls** singer **Geri Halliwell** brought in to lend 'expert' advice. The show, after a shaky start, began to attract larger audiences in the latter stages of transmission, leading to the final selection of the two groups in November 2002. The winning females were announced as Cheryl Tweedy (b. 30 June 1983, Newcastle, England), Kimberley Walsh (b. 20 November 1981, Bradford, England), Nadine Coyle (b. 15 June 1985, Derry, Northern Ireland), Nicola Roberts (b. 5 October 1985, Stanford, England), and Sarah Harding (b. 17 November 1981, Manchester, England). Adopting the moniker Girls Aloud, the quintet was launched into a nakedly commercial race for the Christmas number 1 position with their boy band rivals, One True Voice. Girls Aloud triumphed when the double a-side, 'Sound Of The Underground'/'Stay Another Day', topped the charts. The single's hypnotic beat and sinuous vocals made a pleasant change from the usual manufactured pop fare, although their insipid cover of the **East 17** song on the flip side was more in keeping with the quality of One True Voice's offering, 'Sacred Voice'/'After You're Gone'. The quintet suffered a setback the following March when a prospective *Popstars* tour was cancelled owing to poor ticket sales, but they bounced back in May with the number 2, 'No Good Advice', and the Top 10 album, *Sound Of The Underground*. In marked contrast to their pre-packaged predecessors **Hear'-Say**, the album was a surprisingly adept collection of electro pop with 'Love Bomb' and 'Stop' repeating the formula of the two singles to great effect.

Girls Aloud enjoyed further UK Top 5 hits in 2003 and 2004 with 'Life Got Cold', 'Jump' (a cover version of the **Pointer Sisters** classic), 'The Show' and 'Love Machine'. Their cover version of the **Pretenders**' 'I'll Stand By You', commissioned by the Children In Need charity, topped the UK charts in December 2004. The group's second album, *What Will The Neighbours Say?*, also received a surprising number of positive reviews. A lot of the credit was directed towards Brian Higgins' **Xenomania** production and songwriting team, however, rather than the slick vocal performance of their charges. Girls Aloud's run of chart successes continued into 2005 with 'Wake Me Up' reaching the UK Top 5. 'Long Hot Summer', the thrilling 'Biology' and the Christmas single 'See The Day' were all taken from the group's third album, *Chemistry*.

● ALBUMS: *Sound Of The Underground* (Polydor 2003) ★★★, *What Will The Neighbours Say?* (Polydor 2004) ★★★, *Chemistry* (Polydor 2005) ★★★.

● DVD/VIDEOS: *Girls On Film* (Universal 2005), *What Will The Neighbours Say? Live In Concert* (Universal 2005).

Girls At Our Best!

Girls At Our Best! were formed in Leeds, Yorkshire, England, in 1979, originally calling themselves S.O.S., then the Butterflies. Led by Judy 'Jo' Evans (vocals), the rest of the band included James 'Jez' Alan (guitar), Gerard 'Terry' Swift (bass) and Chris Oldroyd (drums). Their first release was April 1980's 'Getting Nowhere Fast', a memorable post-punk bubblegum pop song later recorded by the **Wedding Present**. Their second single, 'Politics', was released on **Rough Trade Records** in November, after which Darren Carl Harper became the new drummer, with Oldroyd joining Music For Pleasure. Harper stayed for just one single, June 1981's 'Go For Gold', before being replaced by Rod Johnson. Both drummers were featured on the subsequent debut album, *Pleasure*, alongside guests including Dave Fisher (piano), Alan Wakeman (clarinet) and **Thomas Dolby** (synthesizer). Evans returned the compliment by singing on Dolby's 1982 album, *The Golden Age Of The Wireless*. Despite the good reviews it received, not least from long-term supporter **John Peel**, the group only released two further singles, the anthemic 'Fast Boyfriends' and 'Heaven'. The group broke up in 1982, Alan joining first Sexbeat then the Tall Boys before tackling a career in musical instrument-making. Swift became a plumber and Harper a computer repairer. Interest in the group was revived in 1987 when **Strange Fruit Records** released the group's 1981 session. This included their memorable 'deadly medley' of all four sides of their first two singles, 'Getting Beautiful Warm Gold Fast From Nowhere'. It prompted Peel to remark that Girls At Our Best! were 'one of the few bands that made the early part of the 80s bearable'. Despite renewed interest, Evans resisted approaches to re-form the band.

● ALBUMS: *Pleasure* (Happy Birthday 1981) ★★★.

Girls! Girls! Girls!

The first signs of a decline in the quality of films starring **Elvis Presley** could be seen in this 1962 feature. The plot involved the singer's wish to buy a boat, an ambition he finances by performing in nightclubs and fishing for tuna. This noticeably slight premise lacked the spark of **King Creole** or the solid light-heartedness of **GI Blues**, offering little for the star to engage with. More worrying still was the quality of the songs contained in the soundtrack. *Girls! Girls! Girls!* may well have reached the upper echelons of the UK and US album charts, but few could imagine that its content, notably 'Song Of The Shrimp', 'We're Coming In Loaded' and 'Thanks To The Rolling Sea', bore serious comparison with previous recordings. Parsimonious to the end, **RCA** omitted three tracks featured in the film, but included the concurrent hit, 'Return To Sender', which topped the UK charts and reached number 2 in the US. Singles inspired interest in the film, which in turn generated an album release. A promotional Presley jigsaw had been established, irrespective of the merits of the pieces.

Girls Next Door

In 1982, the Nashville record producer Tommy West, formerly of **Cashman And West**, asked session singer Doris King (b. 13 February 1957, Nashville, Tennessee, USA) to find three other females for a harmony group that could blend country with soul and big band music. King recruited Cindy Nixon (b. 3 August 1958, Nashville, Tennessee, USA), Tammy Stephens (b. 13 April 1961, Arlington, Texas, USA) and Diane Williams (b. 9 August 1959, Hahn, AFB, Germany), and they originally called themselves Belle. Changing their name to the Girls Next Door, they had moderate success on the US country charts, including a Top 10 entry with a revival of 'Slow Boat To China'. After moving to **Atlantic Records** in 1989 they released one more album before disbanding in 1991.

● ALBUMS: *Girls Next Door* (MTM 1986) ★★, *What A Girl Next Door Can Do* (MTM 1987) ★★, *How 'Bout Us* (Atlantic 1989) ★★.

Girls Of The Golden West

Mildred Fern Good (b. 11 April 1913, Mount Carmel, Illinois, USA, d. 2 May 1993) and Dorothy Laverne Good (b. 11 December 1915, Mount Carmel, Illinois, USA, d. 12 November 1967, Hamilton, Ohio, USA). During the 30s, when duets were extremely popular, the Good Sisters were the most famous of the female duet singers. The Good family were of German extraction (originally being named Goad), and their father had at times been a schoolteacher, a farmer and storekeeper before moving to East St. Louis, where he worked in a factory. Their mother played guitar and taught the young Dorothy the essentials, and the girls made their radio debut as Mildred and Dorothy Goad on KMOX St. Louis around 1930. They soon became Millie and Dolly Good, but a smart agent dressed them in cowboy outfits with fringed skirts, announced that they came from Muleshoe, Texas, and billed them somewhat imaginatively as the Girls Of The Golden West. They were to maintain the erroneous Texas connection for the whole of their career. Using only Dolly's simple guitar accompaniment and drawing heavily on western-type songs, they developed a pleasant style, with Dolly singing lead vocals and Millie providing the harmony. They had both learned to yodel as children and their ability to do so in harmony made them almost unique in their field. Around 1931, they moved to WLS Chicago, where they joined the *National Barn Dance* and in July 1933, they made their first recordings for **RCA-Victor**. They made further recordings in 1934 and 1935 and in 1937 moved to WLW Cincinnati, appearing first on the *Renfro Valley Barn Dance* and then in 1939, they became stars of the *Boone County Jamboree* and *Midwestern Hayride*. They made their final Victor recordings in Chicago in 1938, which brought their recorded output to 64 tracks. During the 30s and 40s, they were a very popular act and toured extensively throughout the Midwest and parts of the south. They remained in Cincinnati until 1949 when, except for the occasional appearance in the 50s, they nominally retired. In 1963, they recorded for Bluebonnet and Dolly did some solo work. One of their popular songs was 'Silver Moon On The Golden Gate', which they found amusing since neither had ever seen the noted bridge or even been to San Francisco.

● COMPILATIONS: *Girls Of The Golden West Volumes 1-6* (1965) ★★★★, *The Girls Of The Golden West (Selected Recordings)* (1980) ★★★★, *Songs Of The West* (1981) ★★★★, *Roll Along Prairie Moon* (British Archive Of Country Music 2005) ★★★★.

Girls On The Beach, The

Taking its cue from a succession of 'quickie' films emanating from the American International Pictures company, *The Girls On The Beach* tied a flimsy plot to a series of pop act cameos. In this 1965 feature, girl students wishing to raise funds decide to organize a concert, which they mistakenly believe will feature the **Beatles**. Fortunately other performers step into the breech, including the **Crickets**, who offer a version of 'La Bamba', and **Lesley Gore**. The latter sings three numbers, 'Leave Me Alone', 'It's Got To Be You' and 'I Don't Wanna Be A Loser', the last of which was a minor US hit the previous year. Topping the bill are the **Beach Boys** with 'Little Honda', 'The Lonely Sea' and the title song itself. Prolific surf and drag music producer/composer **Gary Usher** was responsible for the bulk of the soundtrack score, but the appeal of the 'beach' genre was waning by the time this film was released. The **Byrds**' 'Mr. Tambourine Man', also issued in 1965, signalled the rise of an altogether different Californian sub-culture.

Girlschool

This all-female heavy metal band had its origins in Painted Lady, founded by teenagers Enid Williams (bass/vocals) and Kim McAuliffe (b. 13 April 1959; guitar/vocals). The remaining members of Painted Lady went on to form Tour De Force. After Kelly Johnson (guitar/vocals) and Denise Dufort (drums) had joined in 1978 the name became Girlschool and the independently produced single 'Take It All Away', for City Records, led to a tour with **Motörhead**. As a direct result of Lemmy's sponsorship of the band, in 1980 they signed to the Bronze label, for whom Vic Maile produced the first two albums. There was a minor hit with a revival of **Adrian Gurvitz**'s 'Race With The Devil', a 1968 success for **Gun**, before the band combined with Motörhead to reach the UK Top 10 as **Headgirl** with an EP entitled *St Valentine's Day Massacre*. The lead track was a frenetic version of **Johnny Kidd**'s 'Please Don't Touch'.

Girlschool had smaller hits later in 1981 with 'Hit And Run' and 'C'mon Let's Go', but soon afterwards a bored Williams was replaced by former **Killjoys** bass player Gill Weston-Jones (introduced to the band by Lemmy). Williams went on to form melodic rockers Framed, record two singles with **Sham 69**'s Dave Parsons, and work on sessions with disco producer Biddu, before joining Moho Pack. Later she also sang, variously, country and opera (appearing in Fay Weldon's *The Small Green Space* and her own opera, *The Waterfall*) and taught performance and vocal skills. Girlschool, meanwhile, persevered, with **Slade**'s Noddy Holder and Jim Lea producing the glam-influenced *Play Dirty*, which found the band opting for a more mainstream rock sound. In 1984, Johnson left for an unsuccessful solo career (later abandoning music and taking up sign language to work with the deaf) and Girlschool added guitarist Cris Bonacci, and keyboard player and singer Jackie aka Jacqui Bodimead from **Canis Major**. The new line-up recorded an album for **Mercury Records** before Bodimead became the next member to leave. The band switched visual style towards a more glam rock look as they recorded 'I'm The Leader Of The Gang (I Am)' with **Gary Glitter**. After the departure of Weston in 1987, ex–**Rock Goddess** bass player Tracey Lamb was enlisted to help record *Take A Bite*. Girlschool split following a Russian tour supporting **Black Sabbath**.

McAuliffe left to work with punk singer Beki Bondage and present the cable show *Raw Power*, and later formed Strangegirls with **Toyah**, Dufort and Williams. In 1992, Girlschool reunited with the addition of ex-**Flatmates** bass player Jackie Carrera. The new line-up recorded a self-titled album for Progressive Records. Three years later Kelly Johnson returned for a series of European dates before being replaced by another original member, Enid Williams. Several live albums were released during the 90s, featuring additional guitarist Jackie Chambers and various original members. McAuliffe, Dufort, Chambers and Williams recorded 2002's new studio album, with additional input from Johnson and Lamb.

● ALBUMS: *Demolition* (Bronze 1980) ★★, *Hit 'N' Run* (Bronze 1981) ★★★, *Screaming Blue Murder* (Bronze 1982) ★★★, *Play Dirty* (Bronze 1983) ★★★, *Running Wild* (Mercury 1985) ★★, *Nightmare At Maple Cross* (GWR 1986) ★★★, *Take A Bite* (GWR 1988) ★★, *Girlschool* (Progressive 1992) ★★, *Live On The King Biscuit Flower Hour 1984* recording (Strange Fruit 1997) ★★, *Race With The Devil: Live 1982* (Receiver 1998) ★★, *Live* (Communiqué 1998) ★★, *21st Anniversary: Not That Innocent* (Communiqué 2002) ★★.

● COMPILATIONS: *Race With The Devil* (Raw Power 1986) ★★★, *Cheers You Lot* (Razor 1989) ★★, *Collection* (Castle 1991) ★★★, *From The Vaults* (Sequel 1994) ★★, *Demolition* (Sanctuary 2004) ★★★, *Hit 'N' Run* (Sanctuary 2004) ★★★.

● DVD/VIDEOS: *Play Dirty Live* (Bronze 1984), *Bronze Rocks* (Bronze 1985).

Giscombe, Junior

b. Norman Giscombe, 10 November 1961, England. Known simply as Junior, this young performer promised much in his early years when he achieved a UK Top 10 hit with 'Mama Used To Say' (picking up a Grammy award). The follow-up, 'Too Late', was his last Top 20 hit in the UK. The tag he was given as 'the future of UK soul' hung heavily around him, and his career ended up being handled by a variety of labels from **Mercury Records** and **London Records** to MCA. Each one found difficulty, despite good reviews, in breaking Giscombe. He did make a brief return to the UK Top 10 in April 1987 when he duetted with **Kim Wilde** on 'Another Step Closer To You'. He became involved with the formation of Red Wedge in 1986 with **Billy Bragg**, **Jimmy Somerville** and **Paul Weller**. During the 90s, he recorded as Junior Giscombe.

● ALBUMS: *JI* (Mercury 1982) ★★★, *Inside Lookin' Out* (Mercury 1983) ★★★, *Acquired Taste* (London 1986) ★★★, *Sophisticated Street* (MCA 1988) ★★, *Stand Strong* (MCA 1990) ★★★, *Renewal* (MCA 1992) ★★.

● COMPILATIONS: *The Best Of Junior* (Mercury 1995) ★★★.

Gismonti, Egberto

b. 5 December 1947, Carmo, Rio de Janeiro, Brazil. Gismonti had a classical musical education starting to play the piano when he was six years old. He went to Paris in the 60s to study orchestration and analysis with Nadia Boulanger and composition with the *avant garde* composer Barraqué. On his return to Brazil in 1966 he became interested in choro, which he has described as a kind of popular Brazilian funk. Gismonti successfully blends African-Brazilian forms with jazz in his compositions. He taught himself the guitar and was at first influenced by **Baden Powell** and Deno. His influences during the early 70s were as wide ranging as **Django Reinhardt** and **Jimi Hendrix**.

In 1973 Gismonti changed to the 8-string guitar which allowed him a greater variety of chord voicings, more flexible bass lines and drones: in 1981 he moved on to the 10-string guitar on which the extra strings extended the bass. His performances on either piano or guitar are always exhilarating and tuneful. He toured the USA in 1976 with **Airto Moreira** and **Flora Purim** and in 1978/9 with **Nana Vasconcelos**. Gismonti's compositional and playing styles were influenced by his study in 1976 of the music of Xingu Indians. He described the resulting album as 'a walk through the jungle'.

His evocative writing and playing has been used in at least 11 film scores. He has recorded regularly with members of the **ECM Records** label, **Jan Garbarek**, **Collin Walcott**, **Ralph Towner** and **Charlie Haden**, and was the orchestrator on Vasconcelos' *Suadedos* with the Stuttgart RSO.

● ALBUMS: *Danca Das Cabeças* (ECM 1976) ★★★★, *Sol Do Meia Dia* (ECM 1977) ★★★, with Charlie Haden, Jan Garbarek *Magico* (ECM 1980) ★★, with Garbarek *Folk Songs* (ECM 1979) ★★★★, *Circense* (Cameo 1980) ★★★, *Duas Vozes* (ECM 1985) ★★★, *Solo* (ECM 1985) ★★★★, *Danca Dos Escarvos* (ECM 1989) ★★★, *Arvore* (Cameo 1991) ★★★, *Kuarup* (Cameo 1991) ★★★, *Infancia* (ECM 1991) ★★★, *Academia De Dancas* (Cameo 1992) ★★★, *Trem Caipira* (Cameo 1992) ★★★, *Amazonia* (Cameo 1993) ★★★, *No Caipira* (Cameo 1993) ★★★, *ZigZag* (ECM 1996) ★★★, with the Lithuanian Symphony Orchestra *Meeting Point* (ECM 1997) ★★★, *Sanfona* (ECM 2000) ★★★, with Haden *In Montreal* (ECM 2001) ★★★.

● COMPILATIONS: *Works* (ECM 1983) ★★★★.

Gisselle

b. Gisselle Ortiz Cáceres, 28 March 1969, New York City, USA. Of Puerto Rican heritage, merengue vocalist Gisselle was raised in New York City, where she excelled as a teenage dancer. Her dancing career led her to performances on stage and television before she launched herself as a vocalist with the merengue group Kaviar. In 1991 she moved on to Punto G, with whom she enjoyed a couple of years of great fame, both in America and her spiritual homeland of Puerto Rico. Cáceres was talent-spotted by BMG Records while singing with Punto G, leading to a solo recording contract with the label. Her 1995 self-titled debut album was a durable hit on the Latin pop market, going on to achieve platinum sales status owing in no small part to the success of the singles 'Perfume De Mujer En Tu Camisa' and 'Pesadilla'. Follow-up albums, including *A Que Vuelve* (1996) and *Atada* (1998) and the Sergio Vargas collaboration *Juntos*, maintained the singer's popularity, but it was not until 2000's Grammy-nominated *Voy A Enamorarte* that Gisselle broke through into the North American market. The album introduced a range of ballads and bachatas to the singer's merengue repertoire, a ploy repeated to lesser effect on the following year's *8*. Nevertheless, this album and subsequent releases have helped spread the singer's music to a wider audience.

● ALBUMS: *Gisselle* (RCA 1995) ★★★, *A Que Vuelve* (RCA 1996) ★★★, *Quiero Estar Contigo* (RCA 1997) ★★★, with Sergio Vargas *Juntos* (RCA 1998) ★★★, *Atada* (RCA 1998) ★★★, *Voy A Enamorarte* (RCA 2000) ★★★★, *8* (RCA 2001) ★★★, *En Alma, Cuerpo Y Corazon* (RCA 2002) ★★★, *Contra La Marea* (Universal Latino 2004) ★★★.

● COMPILATIONS: *Lo Mejor De* (RCA 1999) ★★★★, *Merengue & Ritmo* (RCA 2003) ★★★.

Gist

(see **Young Marble Giants**)

Gitte

b. Gitte Haenning, 29 July 1946, Copenhagen, Denmark. Intended for a showbusiness career from birth, this vocalist's first single—a duet with her songwriting father—was issued in 1954, and she began recording as a soloist for Germany's

Electrola-Columbia label in 1960—though she would sometimes team up with Rex Gildo, a teenage star less prominent in the West German and Scandinavian hit parades. Gitte's fame touched its apogee in 1963, when she won the televised German Song Festival with 'Ich Will Einen Cowboy Als Mann (I Want To Marry A Cowboy)' (composed by Nils Nobach and Rudy von den Dovenmuhle). This was ensconced at number 1 in the national chart for nearly two months, selling over a million copies by 1965.

Giuffre, Jimmy

b. James Peter Giuffre, 26 April 1921, Dallas, Texas, USA. A graduate of the North Texas College in 1942, Giuffre entered the US Army, where he gained professional band experience playing saxophones and clarinet. On his discharge he played in a succession of big bands, including those led by **Buddy Rich**, **Jimmy Dorsey**, **Boyd Raeburn** and **Woody Herman**. It was with Herman that Giuffre gained most attention, both as a member of the saxophone section and as the composer of 'Four Brothers', which gave that particular Herman band its tag. After leaving Herman he worked on the west coast, playing mostly in small groups, and also began to teach. He formed a trio that included **Jim Hall** and, later, **Bob Brookmeyer** plus various bass players. Giuffre appeared at the 1958 **Newport Jazz Festival** and in the filmed record of the event, *Jazz On A Summer's Day* (1960), playing his own composition 'The Train And The River'. He made numerous records, including sessions with **Lee Konitz** for which he wrote beautiful and inventive arrangements, the **Modern Jazz Quartet** (*At Music Inn*) and **Anita O'Day**, for whom he devised elegant and deceptively simple charts (*Cool Heat*). Giuffre also began to explore the world of composition, writing both film scores (*Music Man*) and neo-classical third-stream pieces, such as 'Pharoah' and 'Suspensions', both recorded by **Gunther Schuller**.

In the 60s Giuffre became involved in free jazz, leading a trio in which he was accompanied by **Paul Bley** and **Steve Swallow**. The trio's recordings became increasingly abstract, culminating in *Free Fall*, a collection of duos and trios interspersed by totally improvised tracks on solo clarinet. *Free Fall* was deleted within a few months of release and then, in Giuffre's words, 'the doors closed'—his unique mixture of quiet, free and drummerless music proved so threatening to 'jazz' prejudices, it was nearly a decade before he was able to record again. In the 70s he was still moving with the times, introducing eastern and African sounds into his work. Later, inspired by **Weather Report**, he introduced electric bass and keyboards into his quartet, recording three albums for Italy's **Black Saint Records** label (*Dragonfly*, *Quasar*, *Liquid Dancers*). He also recorded a duo album with André Jaume, *Eiffel* (one of the quietest records ever made!) and in 1989 was reunited with Bley and Swallow for two sessions released by the French Owl label. In 1990, Giuffre, his frail appearance proving deceptive, was in fine musical form at the South Bank Jazz Festival in Grimsby, England, where he premiered a new work, 'Timeless', commissioned by the festival organizers.

Giuffre's playing of many of the lesser-known members of the saxophone family, and especially the bass clarinet (*The Jimmy Giuffre Clarinet*), have helped to give his work unusual and frequently sombre shadings. Throughout his career, he has been an important and visionary member of

the *avant garde*, yet his playing has always been filled with coolly reflective tonal qualities that prove most attractive.

● ALBUMS: *Jimmy Guiffre* (Capitol 1954) ★★★, *Tangents In Jazz* (Capitol 1955) ★★★, *The Jimmy Giuffre Clarinet* (Atlantic 1956) ★★★★, *The Jimmy Giuffre 3* (Atlantic 1957) ★★★★★, *Music Man* (Atlantic 1958) ★★★, *Trav'lin' Light* (Atlantic 1958) ★★★, *Princess* (Fini 1958) ★★★, *Four Brothers Sound* (Atlantic 1958) ★★★, *Seven Pieces* (Verve 1959) ★★★, *Herb Ellis Meets Jimmy Giuffre* (Verve 1959) ★★★★, *Lee Konitz Meets Jimmy Giuffre* (Verve 1959) ★★★★, *Cool Heat—Anita O'Day Sings Jimmy Giuffre Arrangements* (Verve 1959) ★★★★, *The Easy Way* (Verve 1959) ★★★★, *Ad Lib* (Verve 1960) ★★★, *Western Suite* (Atlantic 1960) ★★★, *The Jimmy Giuffre Quartet In Person* (Verve 1961) ★★★, *Piece For Clarinet And String Orchestra* (Verve 1961) ★★★, *Fusion* (Verve 1961) ★★★★, *Thesis* (Verve 1961) ★★★★, *Free Fall* (Columbia 1963) ★★★★, *Music For People, Birds, Butterflies And Mosquitos* (Choice 1972) ★★★, *River Chant/Mosquito Dance* (Choice 1975) ★★★, with Paul Bley, Bill Connors *Quiet Song* (Improvising Artists 1975) ★★★, *Tenors West* (GNP 1978) ★★★, with Bley, Connors, Konitz *IAI Festival* (Improvising Artists 1978) ★★★★, *Tangents In Jazz* (Affinity 1981) ★★★, *Dragonfly* (Black Saint 1983) ★★★★, *Quasar* (Black Saint 1985) ★★★, *Liquid Dancers* (Black Saint 1989) ★★★, with André Jaume *Eiffel* (CELP 1989) ★★★, with Bley, Steve Swallow *The Diary Of A Trio: Saturday* (Owl 1990) ★★★★, with Bley, Swallow *The Diary Of A Trio: Sunday* (Owl 1990) ★★★, with Joe McPhee *River Station* (CELP 1991) ★★★, *Fly Away Little Bird* (Owl 1992) ★★★, *Emphasis, Stuttgart 1961* (hatART 1993) ★★★, *Flight, Bremen 1961* (hatART 1993) ★★★, *The Train And The River 1975* recording (Candid 1996) ★★★, with Bley, Swallow *Conversations With A Goose* (Soul Note 1996) ★★★★, with Jaume *Momentum: Willisau 1988* (hatOLOGY 1998) ★★★.

● COMPILATIONS: featuring Ralph Burns, Lee Konitz, Bill Russo *Lee Konitz Meets Jimmy Giuffre* (Verve 1997) ★★★★, *The Complete Capitol & Atlantic Recordings Of Jimmy Giuffre* 6-CD/10-LP box set (Mosaic 1998) ★★★★.

● FILMS: *Jazz On A Summer's Day* (1960).

Giuffria

This US band was formed in 1981 by Greg Giuffria (keyboards) when his previous band, **Angel**, split up. His first step was to secure a good rhythm section comprising Chuck Wright (bass) and Alan Krigger (drums), and David Glen Eisley (vocals). Rough Cutt guitarist Craig Goldy joined after his former group disintegrated. In 1984 Giuffria's self-titled debut album, released on MCA, demonstrated a melodic rock band that sounded symphonic in places and could have been mistaken for Angel on some tracks. Greg Giuffria referred to their music as 'cinema rock'. After the promotional tour for the album, Goldy left to join Driver and, subsequently, **Ronnie James Dio**, while Wright returned to session work. They were replaced by Lanny Cordola (guitar) and David Sikes (bass). As a result of these personnel changes, the follow-up album, *Silk And Steel*, was not released until August 1986. This was very much a continuation of their first album—it did not sell in anything like sufficient quantities, and in 1987 MCA dropped the group. Giuffria, Cordola, Wright, Ken Mary (drums) and David Glen Eisley attempted to start again. They gained some support from **Gene Simmons** of **Kiss**, who had just set up his own record label. However, Simmons insisted that the name be changed to **House Of Lords**, and that James Christian should replace Eisley on vocals.

● ALBUMS: *Giuffria* (MCA 1984) ★★, *Silk And Steel* (MCA 1986) ★★.

Gizmos

Formed in Bloomington, Indiana, USA, in 1976, the Gizmos revolved around several contributors to the alternative broadsheet fanzine *Gulcher*. They were initially led by vocalist 'Krazy' Ken Highland, but he left the 'group' to serve time in the US Marines. The Gizmos issued four EPs, *The Gizmos* (1976), *Amerika First* (1977), *Gizmos World Tour* and *Never Mind The Sex Pistols Here's The Gizmos* (both 1978). Their music was a curious mixture of 70s-styled rock and smirking, locker-room humour, as evinced in titles such as 'Pumping To Playboy' and 'Gimme Back My Foreskin'. The results were largely non-entertaining and the already-thin premise wore out very quickly. They folded in 1980, having contributed material to *Hoosier Hysteria*, which they shared with another Bloomington act, Dow Jones And The Industrials. Vocalist and guitarist Dale Lawrence, who wrote much of the Gizmos' later work, then formed Crawlspace, while Eddie Flowers joined the **Vulgar Boatmen**. In 1987 Highland reignited his recording career with the Kenne Highland Clan And The Exploding Pidgins, a 60s-influenced garage band, who released a self-titled debut that year on the Stanton Park label.

● ALBUMS: with Dow Jones And The Industrials *Hoosier Hysteria* (Gulcher 1980) ★★★.

Gjerstad, Frode

b. 24 March 1948, Stavanger, Norway. Gjerstad began playing tenor saxophone but was less than satisfied with the kind of jazz he played and heard. In the late 60s he was heavily influenced by hearing on record **Ornette Coleman**, **Jimmy Lyons** and **Albert Ayler**, finding their music more suited to his taste. In 1971 he moved to Sweden to study economics, returning to Norway in 1975. He began working with contemporary Scandinavian musicians and from the 80s onwards widened his appeal to musicians from other parts of the world, in particular **John Stevens**, a significant influence and someone through whom the saxophonist gained entrance to the important UK and European improvised music scenes and was introduced to practitioners such as **Derek Bailey**, **Billy Bang**, **Borah Bergman** and **Evan Parker**. Gjerstad worked with Stevens in the longstanding group **Detail**, initially started as a trio in 1981 with keyboard player Eivin One Pedersen. Various bass players subsequently played with Gjerstad and Stevens, while cornet player **Bobby Bradford** fleshed out the line-up in the mid-80s. Detail carried on playing until the death of Stevens in 1994. Gjerstad acknowledged his debt to Stevens with 2000's *The Blessing Light: For John Stevens*.

In the mid-80s Gjerstad's tenor saxophone and mouthpiece were stolen while on tour and unable to find a satisfactory replacement, he switched to alto saxophone. In 1997, he was voted Norway's Jazz Musician Of The Year. The prize allowed him to tour with musicians of his choice; he chose bass player **William Parker** and drummer **Hamid Drake**. The trio toured Scandinavia, recorded two CDs, and later toured North America. In January 2000, Gjerstad played with a trio that reunited him with Parker and Drake, eliciting consider-

able acclaim. In 2002, the regular bass player and drummer in his trio were Oyvind Storesund and Paal Nilssen-Love. In 1981, Gjerstad had formed his own record label Circulasione Totale (named after his main band), at first producing only cassettes but gradually building not only an impressive catalogue but also the respect and trust of the musicians he has recorded and who include **Bobby Bradford**, **Peter Brötzmann**, Kent Carter, **Barry Guy**, Eivin One Pedersen, **Paul Rutherford** and Stevens.

● ALBUMS: with John Stevens *Sunshine* (Impetus 1984) ★★★, with Circulasione Totale Orchestra *Accent* (Odin 1987) ★★★, with Circulasione Totale Orchestra *Enten Eller* (Circulasione Totale 1992) ★★★, with Stevens, Derek Bailey *Hello Goodbye 1992* (Emanem 1992) ★★★, *Last Detail: Live At The Café Sting* (Cadence 1994) ★★★, with Circulasione Totale Orchestra *Recycling Grieg* (Circulasione Totale 1995) ★★★, with Rashid Bakr, William Parker *Seeing New York From The Ear* (Cadence 1996) ★★★, with Parker, Hamid Drake *Remember To Forget* (Cadence 1997) ★★★, with Nick Stephens *North Atlantic Drift* (Falçata-Galia 1997) ★★★, *Through The Woods* (CIMP 1997) ★★★★, *Ikosa Mura* (Cadence 1997) ★★★★, with Parker, Drake *Ultima* (Cadence 1997) ★★★, with Circulasione Totale Orchestra *Borealis* (Cadence 1998) ★★★★, with Peter Brötzmann *Invisible Touch* (Cadence 1998) ★★★, *Ism* (Circulasione Totale 1998) ★★★, with Steve Hubback *Demystify* (FMR 1999) ★★★, *Last First* (Falçata-Galia 1999) ★★★, *The Blessing Light: For John Stevens* (Cadence 2000) ★★★, with Terje Isungset *Shadows And Lights* (FMR 2001) ★★★, *Sharp Knives Cut Deeper* (Splasc(h) 2001) ★★★, with Bailey *Nearly A D* (Emanem 2002) ★★★, *St. Louis* (FMR 2002) ★★★, with Borah Bergman *Rivers In Time* (FMR 2002) ★★★, with John Edwards, Mark Sanders *The Welsh Chapel* (Cadence 2002) ★★★★, with Lasse Marhaug *TOU* (FMR 2002) ★★★, with Marhaug *Red Edge* (Breathmint 2002) ★★★, with Brötzmann *Soria Moria* (FMR 2003) ★★★, with Paul Hession *May Day* (FMR 2003) ★★★, with Kevin Norton *No Definitive* (FMR 2004) ★★★.

Glad

Formed in Sacramento, California, USA, in 1970, Glad comprised Tom Phillips (guitar/vocals), Ron Flogel (guitar/vocals), Timothy B. Schmit (bass/vocals) and George Hullin (drums/vocals). All of the group, bar Hullin, were originally members of Tim, Tom And Ron. Upon the drummer's arrival they became the Contenders, before adopting a new name, the New Breed, in 1965. As the New Breed they recorded a series of excellent punk/garage singles, notably 'Want Ad Reader'. The quartet was later known as Never Mind, and changed their name again to Glad when they secured a contract with **ABC Records**. The ensuing album is a fine showcase for tight, four-part harmonies and country-influenced rock. Schmit left to join **Poco** just prior to the album's release. He was replaced by Andy Samuel and the new line-up established themselves as **Redwing**.

● ALBUMS: *Glad* (ABC 1970) ★★.

Gladden, Eddie

b. 6 December 1937, Newark, New Jersey, USA, d. 30 September 2003, Newark, New Jersey, USA. As a small child, Gladden demonstrated a precocious interest in drumming, hammering away at the furniture until his mother bought him a set of drums. He attended Newark's Arts High School, majoring in music, and was soon active in various local bands. His influences included **Art Blakey** and **Max Roach**, as well as New Jersey–based drummers Buddy Mack and Bobby Thomas. Among the musicians with whom he worked while he was in his early twenties were trumpeters **Johnny Coles** and **Woody Shaw**, saxophonists Conrad Lester and Buddy Terry, and organists **Freddie Roach** and **Larry Young**. In 1972 he toured with **James Moody** then worked with several jazz groups, including those led by **Richie Cole**, **Kenny Dorham**, **Jimmy McGriff**, **Cecil Payne**, **Shirley Scott**, and **Horace Silver**. His most important hiring was the decade-long spell he spent with **Dexter Gordon**. He joined Gordon's quartet in 1977 and played on many international tours and several recording sessions, thus spreading audience awareness of his drumming skills. Gladden suffered a stroke in 1988, bringing his association with Gordon to an end. Later, diabetes still further curtailed his playing. During the 90s, Gladden played occasionally but rarely strayed far outside his home town. In 1995, he played on *This One's For Ja* with **'Big' John Patton**. A few months before his death, he took part in a photographic session, Great Day In Jersey, organized by the *Newark Star-Ledger*. Among other musicians with whom he played and recorded during his career were **Chet Baker**, **George Cables**, **Kirk Lightsey**, **Jimmy Raney**, **John Stubblefield** and Mickey Tucker.

A forceful drummer with impeccable time, Gladden was a player much valued by his associates, including bass player **Rufus Reid**, who for a while played alongside him in Gordon's band: 'He was easy to play with, but you had to be able to play or he'd run over you.'

Gladiators

Formed in Jamaica in the mid-60s, the group originally comprised Albert Griffiths (b. 1 January 1947, St. Elizabeth, Jamaica, West Indies; vocals/guitar), **Clinton Fearon** (b. 16 January 1951, St. Andrew, Jamaica, West Indies; vocals/guitar) and David Webber (b. *c.*1948, Kingston, Jamaica, West Indies; vocals). Griffiths adopted the group's name after a workmate suggested it. Their earliest recordings include 'The Train Is Coming Back' (1968) for Leeward Robinson, 'You Were To Be' (*c.*1969) for **Duke Reid** and 'Hello Carol' (1969) for **Coxsone Dodd**. During 1970, Webber was replaced by Dallimore Sutherland (bass/vocals). The group's focus became more roots-orientated, and good examples of this approach include two fine songs they recorded for **Lloyd Daley** in 1971, 'Rock A Man Soul' and 'Freedom Train'. Throughout the early 70s they recorded a stunning body of work for Dodd, including 'A Prayer To Thee', 'Bongo Red', 'Jah Jah Go Before Us', 'Roots Natty' and 'Serious Thing'. In 1976, they signed to **Virgin Records**. Their first album, *Trenchtown Mix-up*, was a strong collection of new songs and remakes, and this was followed by *Proverbial Reggae* and *Naturality*. Between 1977 and 1978, further singles appeared from **Studio One**, including 'Mr Baldwin' and 'Peace'. In 1979, Dodd finally released a collection of their singles as *Presenting The Gladiators*. Meanwhile, their Virgin contract concluded with *Sweet So Till* and *The Gladiators*, the latter being a misjudged crossover attempt. Further albums have all been consistent, although failing to reach the heights of their earlier recordings.

● ALBUMS: *Trenchtown Mix-up* (Virgin 1976) ★★★, *Proverbial Reggae* (Front Line 1978) ★★★★, *Naturality*

(Front Line 1979) ★★★, *Sweet So Till* (Front Line 1980) ★★★, *The Gladiators* (Virgin 1980) ★★, *Symbol Of Reality* (1982) ★★★, *Serious Thing* (Night Hawk 1984) ★★, *Country Living* (Heartbeat 1985) ★★★, *In Store For You* (1988) ★★★, *On The Right Track* (1989) ★★★, *Dreadlocks The Time Is Now* (Front Line 1990) ★★★, *Valley Of Decision* (1991) ★★, *A True Rastaman* (1993) ★★★, *Something A Gwaan* (XIII Bis 2000) ★★★.

● COMPILATIONS: *Presenting The Gladiators 1969–78* recordings (Studio One 1979) ★★★★, *Vital Selection* (Virgin 1987) ★★★★, *Bongo Red: The Gladiators Featuring Albert Griffiths At Studio One* (Heartbeat 1998) ★★★★, *Dreadlocks: The Time Is Now* (Virgin 2004) ★★★★.

Gladys Knight And The Pips
(see Knight, Gladys, And The Pips)

Glahe, Will

b. Elberfeld, Germany, 12 February 1902, d. 21 November 1989. This European accordionist–band leader, in conjunction with his Musette Orchestra, had a big hit in the USA in 1939 with 'Beer Barrel Polka'. The song was based on an original Czechoslovakian melody, 'Skoda Lasky' ('Lost Love'), by Jaromir Vejvoda and Wladimir Timm, with an English lyric by Lew Brown. It sold over a million copies for Glahe, who followed it in the USA with other hits such as 'Hot Pretzels', 'W.P.A. Polka', 'Woodpecker', 'Bartender Polka' and 'You Can't Be True, Dear'. It was almost 10 years before Glahe, with his orchestra and chorus, made the US charts again, with 'Liechtensteiner Polka' in 1957. The number also had some success in the UK, along with 'The Crazy Otto Rag', which was credited to 'Will Glahe and his Sunshine Quintet'.

● ALBUMS: *In Bavaria* (Decca 1979) ★★★, *Golden Will Glahe Album* (Teldec 1986) ★★★.

Glam Metal Detectives

Conceived by Peter Richardson (of television show *The Comic Strip Presents* fame), the Glam Metal Detectives launched one of the first 'synergized' multi-media assaults of the mid-90s. A seven-part comedy series, which began its run on UK television on 23 February 1995, the plot concerned a million-selling rock band who as well as performing worldwide, also found time to solve simple crimes (generally perpetrated by their arch enemy, Royston Brulcade). Described in some quarters as 'Scooby Doo with guitars', it assumed the same sort of stupidity in rock bands familiar to viewers of **Spinal Tap** or **Bad News**. The unfortunate actors/musicians recruited to work on the project were: Gary Beadle (ex–Seventh Wonder), Mark Caven, Phil Cornwell, Doon Mackichan, Sara Stockbridge and session guitarist George Yiascumi. Released just four days after the first programme aired, their debut single, 'Everybody's Up', was backed by a suitably atrocious version of the **Osmonds**' 'Crazy Horses'. An album conducted with a similar absence of merit followed it.

● ALBUMS: *The Glam Metal Detectives* (ZTT 1995) ★★.

Glamma Kid

b. Iyael Constable, 14 March 1978, Hackney, London, England. Constable began his quest for stardom in his formative years by imitating **Michael Jackson**'s dance steps and emulating his singing style. He attended acting classes at the Anna Shears Drama School, where he secured a role on the television series *Corners*. In addition to pursuing his quest to be an all-round entertainer, he joined the Air Training Corps and in two years climbed to the rank of corporal. In 1989, he entered a talent competition and was pipped at the winning post by a DJ; this influenced his subsequent change of direction. In the next competition, he switched from dancing to performing as a DJ and came away with first prize. His success led to the formation of his own Glamma Guard **sound system**, playing in local blues and house parties in and around London. The system disbanded in 1994 with the members branching out in different musical directions.

In the autumn of 1994, Constable, performing as Glamma Kid, met up with **Mafia And Fluxy**, who both managed his career and produced his debut, 'Fashion Magazine'. The song led to a number of sessions, and Glamma Kid became regarded as the UK's answer to **Bounty Killer**. He provided the DJ lyrics to a number of hits including 'Moschino', 'Girls Terminus', 'Nation Of Girls' and the anti-cocaine anthem, 'Outertain'. He was also notable for comments regarding the unhealthy obsession of some musicians with the gangster image, leading to the release of 'Eastwood Clint', where he warned against guns: 'Bwoy you could a bad like a Eastwood Clint—but you tink bad man gun fire flint'. He was also in demand for recording in a combination style, notably alongside **Sylvia Tella**, **Peter Hunningale**, **Nerious Joseph** and Robbie Valentine. In January 1997, he joined forces with Mafia And Fluxy, Hunningale and Joseph as part of the reggae supergroup Passion, for 'Share Your Love', which crossed over into the lower end of the UK pop chart. Glamma Kid was offered and accepted the role of supporting act to his Jamaican counterpart Bounty Killer on his 1997 UK tour, and continued working on his debut album for **WEA Records**. He enjoyed huge crossover success in 1999 with two UK Top 10 hits; 'Taboo', a collaboration with R&B singer **Shola Ama**, and 'Why'.

● ALBUMS: *Kidology* (WEA 2000) ★★★.

Glamorous Hooligan

Comprising Dean Cavanagh, Enzo Annechianni and Martin Diver, and based in Bradford, Yorkshire, England, Glamorous Hooligan took their name from the members' past experiences 'running with a local football firm'. Their breakthrough release came with 1994's *Wasted Youth Club Classics*, a collision of breakbeats with disparate samples and trip-hop inspired 'otherness'. Part of the record's ethos was a rebuttal of the way the modern club scene had evolved, and the expensive ticket prices charged by name DJs. The bleak but realistic mood of the album was further explored with the release of the attendant 10-inch single, 'Stone Island Estate'. Cavanagh also works as an underground music journalist, scriptwriter and a club promoter.

● ALBUMS: *Wasted Youth Club Classics* (Delancey 1994) ★★★, *Naked City Soundtrax* (Arthrob 1998) ★★★.

Glamorous Night (film musical)

When **Ivor Novello**'s hit show opened at the Drury Lane Theatre in London in 1935, critics were quick to compare its story of the king who is so infatuated with a gypsy girl that he is willing to give up his throne, with a similar state of affairs between the king of Rumania and Mme. Lupesco. Two years later, when this film version was released by the

Associated British Picture Corporation, a situation much nearer home—the abdication of King Edward owing to his relationship with the American Mrs. Simpson—was still very fresh in the British people's minds. **Mary Ellis** recreated her stage role as the fiery gypsy, and Otto Kruger gave a fine performance as the weak and confused king. Barry Mackay, in the role originally played by Ivor Novello, was suitably macho as the young Englishman who saves the Romany girl's life, and the villainy and comedy aspects were handled by Victor Jory and Finlay Currie respectively. Other roles went to Trefor Jones, Antony Holles, Maire O'Neill, Charles Carson and Felix Aylmer. Most of Ivor Novello and Christopher Hassall's lovely stage score survived, including four of the most popular pieces, 'Shine Through My Dreams', 'Fold Your Wings', 'When A Gypsy Played', and 'Glamorous Night'. The screenplay was adapted from Novello's original play by Dudley Leslie, Hugh Brooke, and William Freshman. Fritz Arno Wagner photographed this lavish and good-looking production, which was directed by Brian Desmond Hurst.

Glamorous Night (stage musical)

In his first great stage musical hit, which opened at London's Theatre Royal, Drury Lane on 2 May 1935, **Ivor Novello** discovered a way of setting before British audiences of the 30s a home-grown version of the highly-popular Viennese operettas of the late nineteenth century. Filling the stage with beautifully costumed elegant ladies, and with some deliberately heart-tugging music, Novello concocted a fairy-tale world to which audiences flocked consistently. The hugely improbable plot concerned the inventor of a television system (Novello) who is paid handsomely by the head of radio to disappear and take his invention with him. He goes to the Ruritanian-style land of Krasnia, meets the gypsy princess Militza (**Mary Ellis**), who is about to marry the Krasnian king (Barry Jones), saves her life, falls in love, is almost killed, then gives up his love for the greater good of Krasnia. Also cast were Lyn Harding, Clifford Heatherley, Bettie Bucknelle, Trefor Jones, and **Elisabeth Welch**. The appropriately operetta-style score included 'Fold Your Wings', 'Shine Through My Dreams', 'When The Gypsy Played', 'Far Away In Shanty Town', 'Glamorous Night', 'Royal Wedding', 'Singing Waltz', and 'Her Majesty Militza'. Christopher Hassall wrote the lyrics, and composer Novello found himself with a show that looked as though it would run forever. In fact, the management of the theatre closed it after only 243 performances because of a prior commitment to stage a Christmas pantomime. However, after touring for a while, *Glamorous Night* reopened at the London Coliseum for a brief run in 1936, and subsequently became an enduring part of regional theatre repertoires the length and breadth of the land. A 1937 film version starred Mary Ellis, Barry Mackay and Otto Kruger.

Glaser Brothers
(see **Tompall And The Glaser Brothers**)

Glaser, Jim

b. James Wilson Glaser, 16 December 1937, Spalding, Nebraska, USA. The youngest member of the famed country group **Tompall And The Glaser Brothers**, tenor vocalist Jim Glaser also enjoyed notable success as a solo artist during the early 80s.

The Glaser brothers, Jim, Tompall and Chuck, were raised in rural Nebraska and first began singing together as teenagers. Their recording career took off in the mid-60s with a string of country hits for **MGM Records**, but by 1973 the trio had split up to concentrate on their solo careers. Jim Glaser had already enjoyed a number of minor hits for **RCA Records** in the late 60s, including 'God Help You Woman', 'Please Take Me Back' and 'I'm Not Through Loving You'. He stayed with MGM after the family group split-up, but his singles during this period failed to make much of an impact on the country charts, with his only Top 50 hit coming in 1975 with 'Woman Woman', a Glaser original which had previously been taken into the pop charts by **Gary Puckett**. A move to MCA Records failed to generate any notable chart action, and in 1979 Glaser rejoined Tompall and Chuck in the family group, touring to great acclaim and enjoying a string of hits including 1981's number 2 single 'Lovin' Her Was Easier (Than Anything I'll Ever Do Again)'.

Glaser relaunched his solo career in 1983, recording for the independent Noble Vision Records label and finally replicating the success of Tompall And The Glaser Brothers. His first single for the label, 'When You're Not A Lady', stayed on the country charts for over 30 weeks between 1982 and 1983, peaking at the number 16 position. Further hits followed with 'You Got Me Running', 'The Man In The Mirror' and 'If I Could Only Dance With You', before 'You're Gettin' To Me' soared to the top of the *Billboard* chart in summer 1984. The follow-up 'Let Me Down Easy' and the attendant *The Man In The Mirror* also reached the US Top 20. Glaser's return to the MCA label was less successful, with only 1985's 'In Another Minute' reaching the Top 30.

After parting company with MCA in 1986, Glaser remained a popular touring attraction before deciding to retire from the music business in 1990. He set up a computer graphics business that later expanded to include website design and database consultancy. Glaser returned to performing in 1997 as the opening act for **Slim Whitman** and also worked as a session vocalist. *Me And My Dream*, his first new album in almost 20 years, was released in 2004.

● ALBUMS: *The Man In The Mirror* (Noble Vision 1983) ★★★★, *Past The Point Of No Return* (MCA 1985) ★★★, *Everybody Knows I'm Yours* (MCA 1986) ★★★, *Me And My Dream* (Solitaire 2004) ★★★.
● COMPILATIONS: *The Very Best Of Jim Glaser* (Country Store 1985) ★★★.

Glaser, Tompall
(see **Tompall And The Glaser Brothers**)

Glasgow, Deborahe
b. 1965, d. 25 January 1994. Glasgow's career began at the tender age of 12 when she first worked with the Mad Professor. Under the name Debbie G. she released 'Falling In Love' for his **Ariwa Records**, which anticipated her powerful **lovers rock** style. She subsequently apprenticed herself to the London **sound system** circuit, mixing with the likes of **Tippa Irie** and **Phillip Papa Levi**, gaining a reputation for knowing her own mind and music. After meeting London producer Patrick Donegan, she signed to UK Bubblers, a **Greensleeves Records**' subsidiary, making her debut for the label with 'You're My Sugar'. It became her first entry in the reggae charts. Other hits followed, including 'Knight In Shining Armour', 'Don't Stay Away' and 'When Somebody Loves You Back', a lovers rock standard. Later she travelled to Jamaica to work with **Gussie Clarke**, and these sessions would produce the best work of her tragically short life. A self-titled album emerged, which was strengthened by the presence of **Shabba Ranks** and the inclusion of the singles 'Champion Lover' and 'Don't Test Me'. Later, Shabba's version of 'Champion Lover', retitled 'Mr Loverman', became a huge international hit. After this career peak, Glasgow kept her distance from the music business, concentrating instead on bringing up her family in Wandsworth, London. However, she did collaborate with General Lee on the tracks 'Weak' and 'Knocking The Boots'. Shortly afterwards, she was diagnosed as having cancer of the lymph gland, and died of a brain haemorrhage in January 1994.
● ALBUMS: *Deborahe Glasgow* (Greensleeves 1989) ★★★.

Glasper, Robert
b. 1978, Texas, USA. Raised in Houston, Texas, Glasper took an early interest in music and began playing piano under the approving eye of his mother who played piano for the local church. She also led a small band that played jazz and blues. By the age of 12, Glasper had begun playing piano in that same church and developed not only his playing skills but also a thorough understanding of the emotional roots of gospel, blues and jazz. His piano playing developed during his school years, a school friend was future R&B singer **Bilal**, and he later attended Houston's High School for the Performing Arts. There, he met drummer Damon Reid, with whom he built a mutually beneficial musical association. After graduation, Glasper went to New York, where he studied at New School University in Manhattan. During his time there, he had occasional opportunities to play with musicians such as **Kenny Garrett**, **Russell Malone** and **Christian McBride**. Remaining in the city, Glasper later found work in various settings, playing engagements and sometimes recording with bands led by trumpeters **Terence Blanchard**, **Roy Hargrove**, **Nicholas Payton** and **Jeremy Pelt** and with singers **Carmen Lundy** and **Carly Simon**. He played and recorded with bass player Robert Hurst's trio, a group of which Reid was also a member, and with guitarist **Mark Whitfield**.

For Glasper's 2004 debut album, he brought in Hurst and Reid, this giving the recording a secure base from which to develop a pleasing set. Although rooted in the jazz piano tradition of musicians such as **Herbie Hancock** and **Chick Corea**, Glasper brings to his playing elements of the hip-hop and alternative rock music that surrounded him as a child. He continued to work with Bilal, thus adding yet another layer. The manner in which Glasper has developed a broad repertoire that appeals to a wider audience than is usual for a jazz pianist of his generation made him a potentially high profile artist and he attracted the attention of **Blue Note Records**. Signed by the label in 2005, Glasper took the opportunity of his second album to put on display his composing skills. On this set, with the piano-bass-drums format expanded on occasion by Bilal and tenor saxophonist **Mark Turner**, Glasper ranged through the many styles that form his musical background.
● ALBUMS: *Mood* (Fresh Sound New Talent 2004) ★★★, *Canvas* (Blue Note 2005) ★★★★.

Glass House
Tyrone 'Ty' Hunter (b. 14 July 1940, USA, d. 24 February 1981), **Scherrie Payne** (b. 14 November 1944, Detroit,

Michigan, USA), Larry Mitchell, Pearl Jones and Eric Dunham made up this Detroit-based group. Hunter's prolific career had begun in the Voice Masters, after which he followed a solid, if unspectacular, solo path. Pearl Jones, meanwhile, was a back-up singer for several acts, including **Billy Stewart** and **Mitch Ryder**. Glass House secured a US R&B hit in 1969 with 'Crumbs Off The Table', but despite minor hits between 1970 and 1972 on **Invictus Records**, Payne's concurrent solo releases accelerated their demise. Scherrie, sister of singer Freda, joined the **Supremes** in 1975 and stayed there for two years. She later returned to the R&B chart in 1987 with 'Incredible' (a duet with Phillip Ingram) and 'Testify'. Hunter had, meanwhile, replaced C.P. Spencer in the **Originals** but died of lung cancer, almost forgotten, in February 1981.

● ALBUMS: *Inside The Glass House* (Invictus 1971) ★★★, *Thanks, I Needed That* (Invictus 1972) ★★★.

● COMPILATIONS: *Crumbs Off The Table (The Invictus Sessions)* (Sequel 1999) ★★★.

Glass Menagerie

After moving from their native Lancashire to seek commercial success in London, England, this psych pop quartet released a series of singles for **Pye Records** and **Polydor Records** without ever completing an album. Comprising Bill Atkinson (drums), John Medley (bass), Alan Kendall (guitar) and Lou Stonebridge (vocals/harmonica), the group made their debut in 1968 with the typically floral 'She's A Rainbow'. Two further singles followed for Pye in the same year, 'You Don't Have To Be So Nice' and 'Frederick Jordan', but neither reached the charts. Transferring to Polydor in 1969, 'Have You Forgotten Who You Are' and 'Do My Thing Myself' failed to rectify their commercial misfortune. By now the group had adopted a heavier, progressive rock styled sound, which might have been better sampled on a full album release. However, despite the existence of an album acetate, Polydor declined to release it officially and the group broke up. Kendall subsequently joined **Toe Fat**, while Stonebridge worked with Paladin and **McGuinness Flint**.

Glass, Philip

b. 31 January 1937, Chicago, Illinois, USA. Glass was educated at the University of Chicago and the Juilliard School of Music before going to Paris to study with Nadia Boulanger between 1963 and 1965. By this time he knew that 'playing second fiddle to Stockhausen didn't seem like a lot of fun. . . . There didn't seem to be any need to write any more of that kind of music. The only thing to do was to start somewhere else . . .'. He did not know where that point was until he was hired to work on an **Ornette Coleman** film score. He did not want to change the music, so **Ravi Shankar** was asked to write additional material, which Glass orchestrated. As he struggled with the problem of writing this music down, Glass came to see that there was another way that music could be organized. It could be structured by rhythm. Instead of dividing the music up as he had been trying to do to write it down, the Indian musicians added to rhythmic phrases and let the music expand. With Ravi Shankar he had now also worked with a composer who was a performer. Glass travelled to North Africa and Asia before returning to New York in 1967, where he studied with the tabla player Alla Rakha.

In 1968 Glass formed the ensemble he needed to perform the music he was now writing. This was the period of the purest minimalism with extending and contracting rhythmic figures in a stable diatonic framework performed at the kind of volume more often associated with rock music. Glass later described it as music which 'must be listened to as a pure sound event, an act without any dramatic structure.' It did not stay in that abstract world of pure sound for very long. In 1975 he had no record contract and began work with Robert Wilson on *Einstein On The Beach*, which turned out to be the first of three operas on 'historical figures who changed the course of world events through the wisdom and strength of their inner vision'. *Einstein On The Beach* was premiered in Europe and reached the Metropolitan on 21 November 1976. He was signed by **CBS Records** in 1982 and produced the successful *Glassworks*. In 1970 he had been joined by Kurt Munkacsi, sound designer, mixer and engineer and the two explored all the potential studios and new technology on offer. The operas were produced in the studio first so that others could work with them, and their final recordings were enhanced by the capabilities of the studio: 'We don't hang a mike in front of an orchestra. . . . Almost every section is extended electronically.'

Although Glass' music has stayed close to the method he established in the early 70s, from *Einstein On The Beach* onwards the harmony has been richer and he has been willing to explore orchestral colour because 'the most important thing is that the music provides an emotional framework or context. It literally tells you what to feel about what you're seeing.' Much of his work since has been either for the stage or for film. This includes the two operas *Satyagraha* (1980) and *Ahknaten* (1984) and two visually striking films with Godfrey Reggio—*Koyaanisqatsi* (1983) and *Powaqqatsi* (1988). In the late 80s and early 90s Glass also wrote film scores for *The Thin Blue Line*, *Hamburger Hill*, *Candyman*, and *Compassion In Exile: The Life Of The 14th Dalai Lama*. Most recently, he co-operated with **Brian Eno** on an reappraisal of the latter's **Low** project for **David Bowie** and repeated the formula with *Heroes* in 1997. At the start of 1998 he gained an Oscar nomination for the score of Martin Scorcese's *Kundun*. In 1999, he created a new musical score for the 1931 screen version of *Dracula*, which was performed by the **Kronos Quartet**. His opera *White Raven* opened in New York in 2001.

● ALBUMS: *Two Pages* (Folkways 1974) ★★★, *Music In 12 Parts 1 & 2* (Cardine 1976) ★★★, *Solo Music* (Shandar 1978) ★★★★, *Einstein On The Beach* (Columbia 1979) ★★★, *Glassworks* (Columbia 1982) ★★★★, *Koyaanisqatsi* film soundtrack (Island 1983) ★★★★, *Mishima* (Nonesuch 1985), *Songs From Liquid Days* (Columbia 1986) ★★★, *Powaqqatsi* film soundtrack (Nonesuch 1988) ★★, *North Star* (Virgin 1988) ★★★, *The Photographer* (CBS 1988) ★★, *1000 Airplanes On The Roof* (Venture 1989) ★★★, *Solo Piano* (Venture 1989) ★★★★, with Ravi Shankar *Passages* (Private Music 1990) ★★★, *Low* (Philips 1993) ★★★, *Hydrogen Jukebox* (1994) ★★★, *Heroes* (Point 1997) ★★★★, *Kundun* (Nonesuch 1998) ★★★, with Robert Wilson *The Civil Wars: A Tree Is Best Measured When It Is Down Act V—The Rome Section* (Nonesuch 1999) ★★★, with the Kronos Quartet *Dracula* film soundtrack (Nonesuch 1999) ★★★, *The Hours* film soundtrack (Nonesuch 2002) ★★★★, *Etudes For Piano Vol. 1* (Orange Mountain 2003) ★★★.

● COMPILATIONS: *Philip On Film* 5-CD box set (Nonesuch 2001) ★★★★.
● FURTHER READING: *Glass: A Biography Of Philip Glass*, Robert Maycock. *Talking Music*, William Duckworth.

Glasser, Don

b. August 1920, d. 26 April 2004. Don Glasser formed his first dance band orchestra in Derry, Pennsylvania, USA, in 1938. Previously he had played alongside **Jerry Grey**, **Ray Pearl** and **Art Kassel**. With vocalists including Lois Costello (Glasser's wife) and Roger Lopez, the band soon relocated to Chicago, which served as a base for their touring activities in the Midwest. Their longest engagement was one of 26 weeks at the Vogue Hotel in Chicago, by which time Glasser's 'Music Smooth As Glass' had become an enormous local hit. Other recordings, issued on Stephanie and Cha Cha Records, included 'Hey, Pretty Legs', 'I Saw Both Ends Of A Rainbow' and the orchestra's theme tune, 'You Call It Madness, I Call It Love'. Engagements at the Roseland (New York) and Willowbrook (Chicago) spread their popularity, with a style of sweet big-band music often compared to **Jan Garber**. Glasser remained active despite the big-band decline and toured the one-nighter Midwest circuit into the late 70s. From 1997 Glasser suffered a series of strokes, but during his incapacity his wife took over the leadership of the band and continued to do so after his death in 2004.

Glassjaw

A nu metal band discovered by the producer **Ross Robinson** (who had acted as midwife to the genre in the mid-90s), Glassjaw was formed by Daryl Palumbo (b. 10 February 1979, Long Island, New York, USA; vocals), Kris Baldwin (guitar), Todd Weinstock (b. 5 November 1978, Queens, New York City, USA; guitar/vocals), Ariel Telford (bass) and Justin Beck (b. 17 December 1979, Long Island, New York, USA; drums). Long Island residents Palumbo and Beck took their first steps towards music making in 1995. The singer, who was afflicted with the intestinal disorder Crohn's disease, wrote lyrics that reflected a certain obvious angst and fitted well with the enraged riffs created by Beck (who switched from drums and bass to guitar). A rounded sound developed and the band was soon demoing and playing live. Robinson's interest ensured that industry attention was soon focused on Glassjaw and a contract was signed with Roadrunner Records, with whom Robinson's I Am label was in partnership at the time.

The line-up on Glassjaw's 2001 debut album comprised Palumbo, Beck, Weinstock, Manuel Carrero (bass) and veteran Sam Siegler (drums). *Everything You Ever Wanted To Know About Silence* was released amid hopes that it might represent the face of future rock. The band, joined by new drummer Larry Gorman (b. 9 May 1972, Queens, New York City, USA), also went down very well with international audiences on tours with **Soulfly** and others. A dispute with Roadrunner put the band's future in doubt, before they were bought out by Robinson and signed a new contract with **Warner Brothers Records**. Their second album, *Worship And Tribute*, was released in September 2002. In 2004, Palumbo collaborated with **Dan 'The Automator' Nakamura** on the bizarre Head Automatica project.
● ALBUMS: *Everything You Ever Wanted To Know About Silence* (Roadrunner 2001) ★★★, *Worship And Tribute* (Warners 2002) ★★★.

Glastonbury Festival

The Glastonbury Festival, one of the most prestigious and distinctive occasions on the UK's music calendar, was started in 1970 by the dairy farmer **Michael Eavis** (b. 17 October 1935, England) on his own land at Worthy Farm, in the Vale of Avalon. Inspired by watching **Led Zeppelin** and **Frank Zappa** at the Bath Blues Festival of that year, the first Glastonbury Fayre took place a few weeks later (19–20 September). **T. Rex** were the headline act before an audience of 1,500, with the £1 admission fee including free milk from Eavis' farm. After 1971's follow-up event with **David Bowie** and **Fairport Convention** the festival was not held again until 1979's Year Of The Child Benefit Concert (an impromptu 'free' mini-festival took place the year before, attended by travellers from Stonehenge).

In the 80s and 90s Glastonbury (known as the Glastonbury Festival from the 1981 event onwards) grew in size and prestige, often signing major artists who shared the festival's idealism and commitment to good causes at a fraction of their normal fees. The event (usually running over three days from Friday to Sunday) was inspired by the 60s idealism of Eavis' youth, and 10 per cent of Glastonbury's gross receipts are always passed on to charity. Each year there are displays of cabaret, film, theatre and environmental activism (notably the Campaign For Nuclear Disarmament), as well as a musical doctrine that encompasses folk, jazz, classical and world music as well as the headline rock bands. However, not all the artists concerned have necessarily advocated the same radicalism, as Eavis recalled in his introduction to the 1986 festival programme: 'There are still some old hands that whinge on about it being too political. Some of them even covered the CND symbol over the stage with a sun one year.' No festival was held in 1988 because of a decision to let the fields lie fallow and review the increasing security problems. In 1990, the event changed its name to the Glastonbury Festival for Contemporary Performing Arts, but a confrontation between security teams and travellers soured the atmosphere. As a result no festival was held the following year. In 1992, donations were made to Greenpeace and Oxfam for the first time, and crooner **Tom Jones** became the first of the festival's 'unusual' headliners. Two years later, the famous Pyramid stage burned down two weeks before the festival started. The same year, a wind turbine was used to generate power to the main stage. Sadly, the festival's first death was also recorded when a man was found dead from a drug overdose. Continuing to grow in popularity, in 1995 Glastonbury sold its entire 80,000 allocation within one week of tickets going on sale. That year's festival celebrated 25 years since the first Glastonbury, and accordingly a live compilation of artists recorded at the show accompanied it (sadly few selections were in any way representative of the festival's past, with current headline bands such as **Oasis**, **Blur** and **Radiohead** dominating the tracklisting).

Eavis took the decision not to hold a 1996 festival as he needed a rest and more time to devote to his farming activities. The 1997 event came close to being a disaster as artists and organizers struggled to keep the audience amused amidst a deluge of mud and rain. A number of acts had to be cancelled due to safety restrictions. In 1998, the rains came again. Reports of bands being stuck in the mud and bad organization were rife, but Eavis defended himself in the *NME* against a barrage of complaints. **Robbie Williams** was one of the highlights, managing to bring a smile to the wet faces. In 1999, the sun shone, but the event's ongoing security problems led to the early cancellation of the following year's festival. By 2002, a £1 million security fence had been installed around the entire perimeter of the 800-acre site. Despite grumbles about the 'corporatization' of the festival, the fence effectively solved the security problems that had plagued Glastonbury since the late 80s. The ongoing popularity of the festival was not diminished, with that year's allocation of tickets selling out two months in advance. In recent years parts of the festival have been filmed for broadcast, starting in 1994 with Channel 4 and taken over by the BBC in the new millennium. This has helped further the importance of Glastonbury as an outlet for left-field bands and as a melting pot for alternative lifestyles.

● COMPILATIONS: *Glastonbury 25th Anniversary—A Celebration* (Chrysalis 1995) ★★★.

● DVD/VIDEOS: *Glastonbury Anthems: The Best Of Glastonbury 1994–2004* (EMI 2005).

● FURTHER READING: *Glastonbury: The Festival*, Ron Reid & Liam Bailey. *Glastonbury: Festival Tales*, Crispin Aubrey & John Shearlaw.

Glazer, Tom

b. 3 September 1914, Philadelphia, Pennsylvania, USA, d. 21 February 2003, Philadelphia, Pennsylvania, USA. Glazer's major claim to fame as an artist was as the instigator behind the 1963 novelty record 'On Top Of Spaghetti'. Sung to the tune of **Burl Ives** favourite 'On Top Of Old Smoky', the parody featured a chorus of children (the Do-Re-Mi Children's Chorus) offering such lines as 'On top of spaghetti, all covered with cheese.' Glazer had sung in choirs as a child, and after three years at New York's City College, he began making his living in music, playing bass and tuba in jazz and military outfits. He became a folk singer in the 40s, specializing in children's music, and hosted his own radio programme between 1945 and 1947. Along with contemporaries **Woody Guthrie** and **Josh White**, Glazer was responsible for helping establish folk music as a national phenomenon in the 40s. In 1957, he wrote the score for the film *A Face In The Crowd*. Recording for the Young People's Records label in the 50s, he sold large quantities of his folk songs. During the 50s he also wrote lyrics and music for others; among the songs he was involved with were 'More' (**Kai Winding**) and 'Melody Of Love' (**Billy Vaughn**). Glazer's spaghetti song reached number 14 in the summer of 1963, after which he failed to chart again.

● ALBUMS: with Richard Dyer-Bennett *Olden Ballads* (Mercury 1955) ★★★, *The Tom Glazer Concert For And With Children* (Washington 1959) ★★★, *On Top Of Spaghetti* (Kapp 1963) ★★★.

Gleason, Jackie

b. Herbert John Gleason, 26 February 1916, Brooklyn, New York City, USA, d. 24 June 1987, Fort Lauderdale, Florida, USA. Gleason was primarily a comedian, starring on stage, screen and television, but he also recorded a number of albums in the 50s and 60s. He established his persona with early films such as *Orchestra Wives* (1942) and several appearances on Broadway (*Artists And Models*, *Follow The Girls* and *Along Fifth Avenue*). However, stardom came with the dawn of the 50s. The formative television series *The Life Of Riley* led to *Cavalcade Of Stars* in 1949, from which Gleason, alongside Art Carney, launched a series of sketches

and basic comedy routines. He then fronted a variety/new talent CBS programme *Stageshow* before **Tommy Dorsey** and **Jimmy Dorsey** took over. The programme was notable for introducing **Elvis Presley** to a television audience. The enormously popular television show *The Honeymooners* followed in 1955, before a series of films leading into the 60s. Notable among these were *The Hustler* (1961), alongside Paul Newman, for which Gleason was nominated for an Oscar as Best Supporting Actor, and *Requiem For A Heavyweight*, the first major play by *The Twilight Zone*'s creator Rod Serling. Gleason also appeared as Buford T. Justice, a law officer prone to mishap in the Burt Reynolds vehicle *Smokey And The Bandit* in 1977. By this time his recording career had largely ended. He had previously written the score for *Gigot* (1962), and his own television theme, 'Melancholy Serenade'. In addition there were several 'mood music' albums on **Capitol Records**, which represented his most successful material, and a projected ballet. A string of Top 10 US albums between 1956 and 1957 featured **Bobby Hackett** and **Pee Wee Erwin** in his studio orchestras.

● ALBUMS: *Music For Lovers Only* (Capitol 1952/53) ★★★, *Lover's Rhapsody* 10-inch album (Capitol 1953) ★★★, *Music To Make You Misty* (Capitol 1954) ★★★★, *Tawny* (Capitol 1954) ★★, *And Awaaay We Go!* TV soundtrack (Capitol 1954/55) ★★, *Music Martinis And Memories* (Capitol 1954) ★★★, *Music To Remember Her* (Capitol 1955) ★★, *Lonesome Echo* (Capitol 1955) ★★★★, *Romantic Jazz* (Capitol 1955) ★★★, *Music To Change Her Mind* (Capitol 1956) ★★★, *Night Winds* (Capitol 1956) ★★★★, *Merry Christmas* (Capitol 1956) ★★, *Music For The Love Hours* (Capitol 1957) ★★★★, *Velvet Brass* (Capitol 1957) ★★★★, *Jackie Gleason Presents 'Oooo!'* (Capitol 1957) ★★★, *The Torch With The Blue Flame* (Capitol 1958) ★★★, *Riff Jazz* (Capitol 1958) ★★★, *Take Me Along* film soundtrack (RCA Victor 1959) ★★★, *Aphrodisia* (Capitol 1960) ★★★, *The Gentle Touch* (Capitol 1961) ★★★, *Gigot* film soundtrack (Capitol 1962) ★★★, *Movie Themes—For Lovers Only* (Capitol 1963) ★★, *Today's Romantic Hits: For Lovers Only* (Capitol 1963) ★★, *Today's Romantic Hits: For Lovers Only, Volume 2* (Capitol 1964) ★★, *Silk 'N' Brass* (Capitol 1966) ★★★, *How Sweet It Is For Lovers* (Capitol 1966) ★★★, *A Taste Of Brass For Lovers Only* (Capitol 1967) ★★.

● COMPILATIONS: *Close-Up* (Capitol 1969) ★★★, *The Romantic Moods Of . . .* (Capitol 1997) ★★★.

● FURTHER READING: *The Great One: The Life And Legend Of Jackie Gleason*, William A. Henry III. *Jackie Gleason: An Intimate Portrait Of The Great One*, W.J. Weatherby. *How Sweet It Is: The Jackie Gleason Story*, James Bacon.

● FILMS: *The Hustler* (1961), *Blood Money* (1962), *Gigot* (1962), *Requiem For A Heavyweight* (1963), *Soldier In The Rain* (1964), *Skidoo* (1968), *How To Commit Marriage* (1969), *Don't Drink The Water* (1969), *Smokey And The Bandit* (1977).

Glencoe

Based in London, England, Glencoe was formed in 1971 by two ex-members of Forevermore; Mick Travis (guitar/vocals) and Stewart Francis (drums). Graham Maitland (d. 1997; keyboards/vocals), who had previously played with Francis in the 60s act Hopscotch, and Norman Watt-Roy (bass; ex–**Greatest Show On Earth**) completed the early line-up. In 1972

Travis was replaced by John Turnbull (ex–**Skip Bifferty** and **Bell And Arc**). Glencoe then became a highly popular live attraction, renowned for thoughtful, melodic, unpretentious rock music. *Glencoe* fully captured their talents, but sadly *The Spirit Of Glencoe* was a marked disappointment. The group split up in 1974. Francis joined Sharks, while Maitland moved to the USA where he pursued a songwriting career. Watt-Roy and Turnbull formed Loving Awareness with Mickey Gallagher and Charley Charles, a group that in 1977 became the Blockheads, backing group to **Ian Dury**.

● ALBUMS: *Glencoe* (Columbia 1972) ★★★, *The Spirit Of Glencoe* (Columbia 1973) ★★.

Glenn And Chris

In 1987 Glenn Hoddle (b. 27 October 1957, Hayes Middlesex, England; vocals) and Chris Waddle (b. 14 December 1960, Heworth, England; vocals) were two of the highest paid football stars in England. They had represented their country in the sport and regularly turned out for the First Division football club, Tottenham Hotspur. Both decided to take time off from the football pitch by recording 'Diamond Lights', which against the odds managed to reach the UK Top 20 in 1987. To cash in on the surprise success the duo quickly recorded and released a follow up, 'It's Goodbye', but this time the record failed to sell, and they wisely returned to their day jobs.

Glenn Miller Story, The

Competently directed by Anthony Mann, and featuring a fine James Stewart performance as Miller (portrayed as much more warm-hearted than the real man), this 1953 biopic does not pass up any opportunity for a cliché. Miller's search for a 'new sound' is hounded to death (scratch any ex-sideman of Miller and one would hear a different version of how he achieved it), but the storyline omits the obvious, if dull, solution that it was all a matter of a workmanlike arranger sticking to his trade. The cross-country slogs on a tour of one-night shows are well presented, and the studio-assembled band accurately recreates Miller's music. Stewart copes well with his on-screen trombone miming, and off-screen, **Joe Yukl** (and possibly **Murray McEachern**) provides the sound. Miller's disappearance, just before Christmas 1944, is tied into a mythical 'gift' to his wife of an arrangement of her favourite tune, 'Little Brown Jug'. In fact, Miller's hit recording of this tune came some years before his death, but in this way, the film can end without a dry eye in the house. In a jazz club sequence, the 1953 edition of the **Louis Armstrong** All Stars, including **Barney Bigard**, **William 'Cozy' Cole** and **Trummy Young**, teams up with a handful of 30s swing stars, including **Gene Krupa** and **Babe Russin**, to knock spots off 'Basin Street Blues'.

Glenn, Garry

b. Detroit, Michigan, USA. Glenn is the brother of the gospel singer Beverly Glenn, with whom he toured as a teenager. He subsequently submitted songs to various soul acts, the **Dramatics** being the first to record his work. In the early 80s he worked as an arranger and keyboard player for Al Hudson And The Soul Partners, and wrote material for **Earth, Wind And Fire**. His major breakthrough came when **Anita Baker** recorded his song 'Caught Up In The Rapture' and invited him to play keyboards with her touring band in 1984/5. He then performed a similar role for **Billy Ocean**, before quitting

live work to produce an album for **Freddie Jackson** in 1986. That same year, he was signed to **Motown Records** after contributing a song to the *Police Academy IV* soundtrack. He scored immediate success as a solo artist with 'Do You Have To Go' in 1987, which showcased his falsetto vocals. A follow-up hit, 'Feels Good To Feel Good', matched him with Sheila Hutchinson of the **Emotions**.

● ALBUMS: *Feels Good To Feel Good* (Motown 1987) ★★★.

Glenn, Lloyd

b. 21 November 1909, San Antonio, Texas, USA, d. 23 May 1985, Los Angeles, California, USA. Glenn's economic, propulsive technique helped to establish the west coast blues piano style. Having been taught ragtime by his father and uncle, he worked with a number of **territory bands**, including the Royal Aces and Boots And His Buddies, while in his teens. He first recorded as a member of Don Albert's band for **Vocalion Records** in 1936. Five years later, he moved to Los Angeles, where he worked the club circuit and became a session musician, most notably on **T-Bone Walker**'s 'Call It Stormy Monday'. He made his first records for **Imperial Records** in December 1947 and the following year for RPM. He worked with **Edgar Hayes**' Stardusters, and when the band's Exclusive recordings were bought by Swing Time in 1949, he was taken on as the label's A&R man. There, he formed a long-term relationship with **Lowell Fulson** and had hits of his own with 'Old Time Shuffle' and 'Chica Boo'. He stayed with Fulson when the latter moved to Checker and secured his own contract with Aladdin, having a minor hit with 'Southbound Special'. A 1960 **Chess Records** session remained unissued until individual titles appeared on a pair of compilation albums. Glenn rarely travelled far from Los Angeles, but did visit Europe in 1982 and recorded in Stockholm and in Paris with **Clarence 'Gatemouth' Brown**. *Blue Ivories* also contained a number of his Swing Time and Aladdin recordings.

● ALBUMS: with Clarence 'Gatemouth' Brown *Heat Wave* (Black & Blue 1982) ★★★, *Blue Ivories* (Stockholm 1985) ★★★, *After Hours* (Pathe Marconi 1986) ★★★, *Honky Tonk* (Night Train 1991) ★★★, *Chica Boo* (Night Train 1995) ★★★.

● COMPILATIONS: *Wrinkles* (Chess 1989) ★★★, *Chess Blues* (Chess 1992) ★★★.

Glenn, Tyree

b. Evans Tyree Glenn, 23 November 1912, Corsicana, Texas, USA, d. 18 May 1974, Englewood, New Jersey, USA. After working in his home state on vibraphone and principally trombone, Glenn moved to the Washington, DC, area in the early 30s and by 1936 was in Los Angeles playing with the **Charlie Echols** band. He also worked with **Eddie Barefield**, **Benny Carter** and **Lionel Hampton** and in the band **Eddie Mallory** directed to accompany his wife, **Ethel Waters**. In 1939 Glenn was briefly with Carter again before joining **Cab Calloway**, with whom he remained until 1946. He next played with **Don Redman** and **Duke Ellington**, where he skilfully essayed the **Joe 'Tricky Sam' Nanton** trombone role, but by 1952 had turned his attention to studio work. During the next decade he occasionally acted and periodically led his own small groups, sometimes with **Shorty Baker**, and in 1965 joined **Louis Armstrong**'s All Stars. After three years he again formed his own small band, but later made short return visits to Armstrong and, in the summer of 1971, to Ellington. From then until shortly before his death, in May 1974, Glenn led his own band.

A gifted musician, Glenn was an important member of any band in which he played, especially the fine big band of Cab Calloway. Too often for a man with his talent, he appeared content to take a back seat as, for example, when he was in company with Armstrong. When he did solo (other than on the Tricky Sam repertoire) he showed himself to be a robust and inventive player. An occasional composer, he wrote 'Sultry Serenade', which was recorded by Ellington and **Erroll Garner** (under the title 'How Could You Do A Thing Like That to Me'). Glenn's two sons are musicians, Tyree Jnr. plays tenor saxophone, Roger plays vibraphone and flute.

● ALBUMS: *Tyree Glenn And His Embers All Stars And Orchestra* (Roulette 1957) ★★★, *At The Roundhouse* (Roulette 1958) ★★, *With Strings* i (Roulette 1960) ★★, *With Strings* ii (Roulette 1960) ★★★, *At The London House* (Roulette 1961) ★★★, *Tyree Glenn With Sy Oliver And His Orchestra* (Roulette 1962) ★★★, with Louis Armstrong *Louis* (Mercury 1966) ★★★★.

Glinn, Lillian

b. *c.*1902, near Dallas, Texas, USA. Glinn's career as a blues-singing recording artist and vaudeville performer was brief but successful. She was the protégée of **Hattie Burleson**, a Texas blues singer who first heard Glinn sing in a Dallas church. Although religious, Glinn allowed herself to pursue the worldly course that led to R.T. Ashford securing her a recording contract with **Columbia Records** in 1927. During the following two years she recorded 22 titles for that label. Her blues were notable for their apposite lyrics sung in a warm, mature manner. She was still young when she gave up her career to return to the 'other world' of the church, and when interviewed by Paul Oliver in 1970 she was reluctant to recall her long-gone temporal fame.

● COMPILATIONS: *Lillian Glinn: Columbia Blues Issues* (VJM 1987) ★★★.

Glitter Band

Formed as a backing group for UK pop singer **Gary Glitter**, the Glitter Band also enjoyed a period of fame in their own right. The group's line-up originally comprised John Springate (bass/vocals), Tony Leonard (drums), Gerry Shephard (b. 28 December 1951, d. 6 May 2003, England; guitar/vocals), Pete Phipps (b. 5 August 1951, England: drums/keyboards), John Rossall (saxophone/trombone) and Harvey Ellison (saxophone). Their gimmick and distinctive musical punch lay in the employment of two drummers. At the height of the glitter fad they secured a series of Top 10 UK hits, including 'Angel Face', 'Just For You', 'Let's Get Together Again', 'Goodbye My Love', 'The Tears I Cried', and 'People Like You And People Like Me'. They signed a new recording contract with **CBS Records** and changed their name to the G-Band in 1977, but split up later in the year. They reunited in 1981 in order to tour with their former mentor, and various line-ups of the Glitter Band have continued to work as a live unit ever since. Main songwriter Shephard succumbed to cancer in May 2003.

● ALBUMS: *Hey!* (Bell 1974) ★★, *Rock 'N' Roll Dudes* (Bell 1975) ★★, *Listen To The Band* (Bell 1975) ★★, *Paris Match* (CBS 1977) ★★, *Live At The Marquee* (Quest 1986) ★.

● COMPILATIONS: *Greatest Hits* (Bell 1976) ★★★, *People Like You, People Like Me* (MFP 1977) ★★, *The Collection* (Grab It 1990) ★★★, *The Best Of The Glitter Band* (Repertoire 1998) ★★★, *Solid Silver: The Ultimate Glitter Band Volume 1* (Edsel 1998) ★★★, *The Bell Singles Collection* (7T's 2000) ★★★.

Glitter, Gary

b. Paul Francis Gadd, 8 May 1944, Banbury, Oxfordshire, England. The elder statesman of the 70s UK glam rock scene, Glitter began his career in a skiffle group, Paul Russell And The Rebels. He then became Paul Raven, under which name he recorded an unsuccessful debut for **Decca Records**, 'Alone In The Night', in 1960. His cover of 'Tower Of Strength' lost out to **Frankie Vaughan**'s UK chart-topper, after which he spent increasingly long periods abroad, particularly in Germany. During the late 60s, having been signed to MCA Records by his former orchestral backing leader and MCA head **Mike Leander**, he attempted to revitalize his career under the names Paul Raven and Monday, the latter of which was used for a cover version of the **Beatles**' 'Here Comes The Sun', which flopped.

In 1971, seemingly in the autumn of his career, Gadd relaunched himself as Gary Glitter, complete with thigh-high boots and a silver costume. His debut for **Bell Records**, 'Rock And Roll Part 2' unexpectedly reached number 2 in the UK and climbed into the US Top 10. Although he failed to establish himself in America, his career in the UK traversed the early 70s, stretching up until the punk explosion of 1977. Among his many UK hits were three number 1 singles, 'I'm The Leader Of The Gang (I Am!)', 'I Love You Love Me Love' and 'Always Yours', and Top 5 placings for 'I Didn't Know I Loved You (Till I Saw You Rock And Roll)', 'Do You Wanna Touch Me? (Oh Yeah!)', 'Hello! Hello! I'm Back Again', 'Remember Me This Way', and 'Oh Yes! You're Beautiful'. His backing musicians, the aptly named **Glitter Band**, also enjoyed hits of their own at the height of Glitter's popularity. An accidental drug overdose and bankruptcy each threatened to end his career, but he survived and continued to play regular concerts in the UK.

In later years the now sober figure of Glitter was courted favourably by the media and became a minor legend, even returning to the UK Top 10 in 1984 with 'Another Rock And Roll Christmas'. In 1988 he was back at the top of the UK charts when the **Timelords**' 'Doctoring The Tardis', which featured a prominent sample of 'Rock And Roll', reached number 1. The commercial longevity of his back catalogue, a bestselling autobiography, a London stage show, and a highly praised role in the *Quadrophenia* revival kept Glitter's name alive during the late 80s and early to mid-90s.

In a disturbing development the singer was arrested in November 1997 over allegations of harbouring child pornography on his computer. He was charged the following year, and in November 1999 was found guilty and sentenced to four months in prison. He resorted to living overseas because his unpopularity with the UK press had made him a hunted man. The occasional single and album continued to leak out during this time. In November 2005, Glitter was arrested in Vietnam and convicted of sexually abusing two girls, aged 10 and 11 respectively. On 3 March 2006 he was sentenced to three years in prison after being found guilty of obscene acts with the girls.

● ALBUMS: *Glitter* (Bell 1972) ★★, *Touch Me* (Bell 1973) ★★, *Remember Me This Way* (Bell 1974) ★★★, *Always Yours* (MFP 1975) ★★, *GG* (Bell 1975) ★★, *I Love You Love* (Hallmark 1977) ★★★, *Silver Star* (Arista 1978) ★★, *The Leader* (GTO 1980) ★★, *Boys Will Be Boys* (Arista 1984) ★, *Leader II* (Attitude 1991) ★, *On* (MachMain 2001) ★.

● COMPILATIONS: *Greatest Hits* (Bell 1976) ★★★, *Gary Glitter's Golden Greats* (GTO 1977) ★★★, *The Leader* (GTO 1980) ★★, *Gary Glitter's Gangshow* (Castle 1989) ★★, *Rock And Roll: Greatest Hits* (Rhino 1990) ★★★, *Many Happy Returns: The Hits* (EMI 1992) ★★★, *The Glam Years: Part 1* (Repertoire 1995) ★★★.

● DVD/VIDEOS: *Gary Glitter's Gangshow* (Hendring Video 1989), *Story* (Channel 5 1990), *Rock'n'Roll's Greatest Show: Gary Glitter Live* (PMI 1993).

● FURTHER READING: *The Gary Glitter Story*, George Tremlett. *Leader: The Autobiography Of Gary Glitter*, Gary Glitter with Lloyd Bradley.

● FILMS: *Remember Me This Way* (1974), *Spice World* (1997).

Glitterbox

Comprising vocalist Jonny Green, guitarist/vocalist Michael Heseltine and drummer Mark Servas, the three members of Glitterbox originally met while attending college lectures in Norwich, Norfolk, England. In the early 90s they moved to London and shared a flat. With the addition of bass player Tony Holland, they played their first gig together in early 1994. At this stage operating under the name She, they began touring as a fully functioning unit a year later. Demos were produced and, the band claimed, interested parties from American record companies flew over on Concorde to try to sign the band. They elected to join **Atlantic Records** subsidiary Radar before starting on sessions for their debut album. However, it was then the group encountered the first of a series of problems. A female R&B band signed to **Death Row Records**, also entitled She, threatened to sue them if they did not change their name. The quartet thus became Glitterbox 'because glitter rhymes with shitter'. Green was then struck down by a serious throat virus. *Tired & Tangled* eventually emerged in 1998, two years after it was originally recorded. The acknowledged influences at work here included **Flaming Lips** and **Afghan Whigs**, two groups with a similar 'off-kilter' attitude to hard rock music.

● ALBUMS: *Tied & Tangled* (Radar/Atlantic 1998) ★★★.

Global Communication
(see **Middleton, Tom**)

Global Underground

The respected and internationally successful (60% of its sales are outside the UK) Global Underground is a series released on the Boxed independent **dance music** record label. It is the brainchild of two self-confessed 'chancers' from Newcastle upon Tyne, England: Andy Horsefield and James Todd. The pair started selling their own mix tapes before hitting on the idea of recording the sets of well-known DJs in a 'live' context—that is, in the actual clubs themselves, at various events around the world and therefore trying to capture something of the spirit of the night in the recording. Referring to themselves as the 'Fat Lads', the label bosses Horsefield and Todd take the unique step of travelling with

the DJs to the various locations around the world and making the recording of the mix an event in itself.

The first release in 1996 featured a performance by **Tony De Vit** in Tel Aviv. The themed mix compilation albums are usually stylishly packaged with a 'travelogue', detailing in words and photographs the entourage's antics and the events of the trip. The series initially concentrated on the progressive house genre, featuring big-name DJs such as **Sasha**, **Paul Oakenfold** and **John Digweed**, but the company also has vinyl-based single imprints such as Quad, Coded and Halogen that specialize in other niches of progressive house, **trance** and **techno**. Their Nu Breed imprint, as the name suggests, champions skilled and respected DJs, such as **Steve Lawler**, **Sander Kleinenberg**, **Anthony Pappa** and Lee Burridge, who may not have the same level of fame as other superstar DJs but who nevertheless have very large followings.

Global Underground's releases are distinguished from more commercial mix compilations because of their tasteful and sumptuous packaging but more importantly by their authentic representation of the DJs' sets and therefore the selection of more underground and left-field tracks. The label has somewhat disappointingly departed from its original manifesto of 'live' recordings of DJs sets by recording mixes in a studio and using a disclaimer on the albums' liner notes. Nevertheless, the Global Underground name remains associated with credible dance music for grown-up clubbers. It also deserves praise for taking an international approach to the club scene, including places such as Prague, Oslo, Moscow, Buenos Aires, Romania, and Shanghai on its tours; for bringing less well-known DJs and recording artists to the public's attention, and for the care that goes into the packaging of its releases. In May 2000, the UK's Channel Four broadcast a television documentary, *Getting Away With It*, that told the story of the label's rise and depicted Todd and Horsefield's champagne lifestyle—flying to exotic locations, partying in the world's most glamorous clubs with world-famous DJs. Also in 2000, Global Underground released its first DVD.

Global Village Trucking Company

One of several groups to emerge from London's alternative scene of the early 70s, the Global Village Trucking Company came to national prominence in 1973. The quintet—Jon Owen (guitar/vocals), Jimmy Lascelles (keyboards), Mike Medora (harmonica/guitar/vocals), John McKenzie (bass) and Simon Stewart (drums)—were featured on the 'benefit' release, *Greasy Truckers Live At Dingwalls*. Three years later the band was augmented by Peter Kitley (guitar), Jim Cuomo (saxophone), Jeremy Lacalles (percussion) and vocalists Caromay Dixon and Monica Garelts for the *Global Village Trucking Company*. This album, issued on the **Virgin Records** subsidiary, Caroline, reflected the free spirit the collective brought to their music, but it was not a commercial success. The group slipped from the limelight upon the advent of punk.

● ALBUMS: *Greasy Truckers Live At Dingwalls* (Greasy Truckers 1973) ★★, *Global Village Trucking Company* (Caroline 1976) ★★.

Globe Unity Orchestra

This important European orchestra was formed in 1966 by the German free jazz pianist **Alexander Von Schlippenbach**, initially to perform his composition 'Globe Unity' in Berlin.

Until the mid-70s the orchestra worked principally in West Germany, performing at the key festivals of improvised music, such as the Total Music Meeting, the Workshop Freie Musik in Berlin and the Free Jazz Workshop in Wuppertal. Since then it has toured worldwide, playing festivals throughout Europe, the Far East and India. Alongside Schlippenbach, regulars in its distinguished line-up include Germans **Peter Brötzmann, Gerd Dudek, Paul Lovens, Albert Mangelsdorff** and **Manfred Schoof**; Britons **Derek Bailey, Evan Parker** and **Paul Rutherford**; Canadian **Kenny Wheeler** and Luxembourgian Michel Pilz. Although the orchestra has its roots in the 60s free jazz tradition, its improvisations sometimes echo earlier styles of jazz as well as contemporary classical music.

● ALBUMS: *Globe Unity* (Saba 1966) ★★★★, *Live In Wuppertal* (FMP 1973) ★★★, *Der Alte Mann Bricht . . . Sein Schweigen* (FMP 1974) ★★★, *Evidence—Vol. 1* (FMP 1976) ★★★, *Into The Valley—Vol. 2* (FMP 1976) ★★★★, *Pearls* 1975 recording (FMP 1977) ★★★★, *Jahrmart/Local Fair* (Po Torch 1977) ★★★, *Improvisations* (Japo 1978) ★★★, *Hamburg '74* (FMP 1979) ★★★, *Compositions* (Japo 1979) ★★★, *Intergalatic Blow* (Japo/ECM 1983) ★★★, *20th Anniversary* 1986 recording (FMP 1993) ★★★★, *2002* (Intakt 2003) ★★★.

● COMPILATIONS: *Rumbling* (FMP 1991) ★★★★.

Gloria Estefan And Miami Sound Machine
(see **Estefan, Gloria, And Miami Sound Machine**)

Gloria Record

This Austin, Texas, USA–based indie rock band was formed in 1997 by Chris Simpson (guitar/vocals) and Jeremy Gomez (bass). The duo had previously been bandmates in the highly regarded emo (emotional hardcore) group **Mineral**, who disbanded shortly after completing work on their second album, *EndSerenading*. With the addition of Brian Hubbard (guitar) and Matt Hammon (drums), the Gloria Record made their recording debut in 1998 with the independently released, 'Grace, The Snow Is Here'. A well-received self-titled EP was then recorded before Ben Houtman (keyboards) was added to the line-up. Houtman's synth work helped flesh out the band's sound and marked a notable progression from Simpson and Gomez's work with Mineral, with the band's more organic approach earning comparisons to both **Seam**'s 'slowcore' sound and **Radiohead**'s epic productions. A succession of personnel changes saw Hammon replaced by Jeremy Tappero and then Brian Malone, with the latter making his debut on the *A Lull In Traffic* EP, on which the debt to Radiohead became even more apparent. The quintet took two years to complete work on their first album, which was recorded sporadically without the financial backing of a label. A recording contract was eventually signed with the Arena Rock label, and *Start Here* was released in summer 2002.

● ALBUMS: *Start Here* (Arena Rock/Rykodisc 2002) ★★★.

Glory Bell's Band

From Sweden, Glory Bell's Band was led by Glory North (vocals), a consummate live performer of considerable local reputation. Together with Miguel Santana (guitar), Franco Santuione (guitar), Marks Anderson (guitar, keyboards), Bob Anderson (bass) and Peter Udd (drums), the band made its debut in 1982 with *Dressed In Black*, a solid collection of hard rock songs distinguished by the presence of three fluent guitarists. Early reviews compared the group to **Judas Priest**. Three years later a follow-up collection was released, but *Century Rendezvous* failed to break the group outside of Scandinavia. No further recordings have been issued.

● ALBUMS: *Dressed In Black* (SOS 1982) ★★★, *Century Rendezvous* (SOS 1985) ★★.

Glosson, Lonnie

b. 14 February 1908, Judsonia, White County, Arkansas, USA, d. 2 March 2001, Arkansas, USA. One of country music's greatest harmonica players but also a talented guitarist. His mother, Cora, taught him to play the harmonica as a child and in 1926, he made his radio debut on the KMOX station in St. Louis. He hoboed his way around for the next four years playing and singing at numerous venues, before he became a cast member of WLS Chicago's **National Barn Dance** in 1930. After a few years, he moved to the WWVA **Wheeling Jamboree**, until his wanderlust saw him move to another station, a practice he continued throughout the 30s. In the early 40s, he was at WHAS Louisville, where he worked with **Molly O'Day** on the *Early Morning Frolic*. When she moved to Wheeling, he spent some time starring on the *Renfro Valley Barn Dance*, and worked with the **Lilly Brothers** and **Fiddling Burk Barbour** in the Smiling Mountain Boys, before rejoining O'Day in Knoxville, Tennessee. In 1947, she made the first recording of Glosson's sacred song 'Matthew 24'. Glosson had written the song, which predicted the second coming, in the mid-30s and had sung it himself on various stations. O'Day and her husband Lynn Davis' noted duet recording of Glosson's 'Don't Forget The Family Prayer' also became very popular with their fans. Glosson also sometimes appeared with his brother and sister, Buck and Esther, who were also entertainers. In 1948, Glosson began a long association with fellow harmonica player **Wayne Raney**, which generated the country chart-topper 'Why Don't You Haul Off And Love Me'. They presented radio programmes together that sold harmonicas and tuition books. It has been estimated that, from the late 40s through to the mid-50s, several million harmonicas were sold through this radio advertising. After 1956, Glosson mainly confined his performing to special matinee shows in schools all over the south and Midwest, a practice he continued into the 80s. He incorporated words of wisdom of the dangers of drink and drugs and generally proved popular not only with his audiences but also with the education authorities. Glosson made his first solo recordings for ARC in 1932, which included his noted 'Lonnie's Fox Chase' and the bluesy styled recitation 'Arkansas Hard Luck'. He also recorded for **Mercury Records** (1949) and **Decca Records** (1950) and later in the 50s he recorded instrumentals and vocals on the Acme label, including the semi-talkie 'The Old Dutchman's Prayer'. He also played on some of Raney's **King Records** recordings. In the 70s, he made further recordings on Raney's Rimrock label, and in 1980, the two old friends reunited to record an album.

● ALBUMS: *The Living Legend* (Rimrock) ★★★, *The Blues Harp Man* (Rimrock) ★★★★, with Wayne Raney *All Harmonica* (Old Homestead 1982) ★★★★.

Glove

The Glove was essentially a one-off project for UK guitarist/ vocalist Robert Smith of the **Cure** and bass player/multi-

instrumentalist Steve Severin of **Siouxsie And The Banshees**, with singer/dancer Jeanette Landray. Heavily influenced by 60s cult imagery and psychedelia, the Glove (the name taken from the film *Yellow Submarine*) recorded two singles, 'Like An Animal' (a minor hit) and 'Punish Me With Kisses', and a distinctive album, *Blue Sunshine*, issued on the Banshees' Wonderland label in August 1983. Although the material's multi-layered sound was endearing, the Glove was plainly a self-indulgent exercise for Severin and Smith (who was also a Banshee at that time), and had an enduring influence on both parties. The Banshees, in particular, later injected a strong late 60s feel into their music, not least with a cover version of the **Beatles**' 'Dear Prudence'. The Glove, meanwhile, were destined to become a historical curio, although demand was strong enough to warrant a reissue of *Blue Sunshine* in 1990.
● ALBUMS: *Blue Sunshine* (Wonderland 1983) ★★★.

Glover, Dana

b. Rocky Mount, North Carolina, USA. Singer-songwriter and ex-model Glover grew up in small town North Carolina, learning to play the piano and saxophone at an early age. She left her rural upbringing far behind at the age of 16, relocating to New York City to work as a model. Two years later she decided to leave modelling and the city behind, relocating to Nashville and then Los Angeles to pursue a music career. With her good looks and impressive vocal ability Glover was not short of offers from record companies, opting to sign a major label contract with DreamWorks Records. While she was recording her debut album she contributed material to the soundtracks for *Shrek* ('It Is You (I Have Loved)' and *The Wedding Planner* ('Plan On Forever'). *Testimony* was released in October 2002 but failed to make much of a commercial impact. Glover's bluesy vocals were undoubtedly impressive but tended to be buried beneath the slick musical and vocal accompaniment.
● ALBUMS: *Testimony* (DreamWorks 2002) ★★★.

Glover, Dave, Band

Northern Ireland trumpeter Dave Glover first came to prominence during the late 40s playing dixieland in Belfast. His orchestral and big-band seasons included a 'show' routine, which helped spawn the showband phenomenon, which subsequently spread southwards to Eire. Glover's first showband line-up included Big Joe Clarke (vocals), Andy Wilson (trombone), Harry Mitchel (keyboards), Gerry Rice (saxophone), Harry 'Trixie' Hamilton (bass), Alex Burns (guitar) and David Martin (drums). By 1963, most of the above line-up departed to form the **Witnesses**, while Glover found fresh musicians. Two promising vocalists, Muriel Day and Mike Munroe were backed by Jim Gunner (guitar), Jim McDermot (saxophone), Johnny Anderson (trombone), Jackie Flavelle (bass) and Desmond McCarathy (drums). The new line-up enjoyed a modicum of success, most notably when Day represented Ireland in the 1969 Eurovision Song Contest, with the chart-topping 'Wages Of Love'. Glover's presence on the Northern Ireland dance scene was much missed when he subsequently emigrated to Canada.

Glover, Roger

b. 30 November 1945, Brecon, Wales. Bass player Glover's professional musical career began when his group, the Madisons, amalgamated with fellow aspirants the Lightnings to form **Episode Six**. This popular act released nine singles

between 1966 and 1969, but eclectic interests—including harmony pop, MOR and progressive rock–styled instrumentals—engendered a commercial impasse. Frustrated, both Glover and vocalist **Ian Gillan** then accepted an offer to join **Deep Purple**, where they enjoyed considerable international acclaim. However, clashes with guitarist **Ritchie Blackmore** led to Glover's sacking in 1973, although he remained nominal head of A&R at Purple Records, the group's custom-created label. Glover later embarked on a successful career in production with **Nazareth**, **Status Quo**, **Judas Priest** and **Rory Gallagher**. In 1974 Glover was commissioned to write the music to *The Butterfly Ball*, which in turn inspired a book, illustrated by Alan Aldridge, and film. The album featured the services of **David Coverdale**, **Glenn Hughes** and **Ronnie James Dio**. He recorded a solo album, *Elements*, which again boasted the assistance of vocalist Dio, but Glover surprised several commentators in 1979 by rejoining Blackmore in **Rainbow**. Any lingering animosity was further undermined in 1984, when both musicians were active in a rekindled Deep Purple, which, although unable to recreate the halcyon days of the early 70s, proved to be a much-in-demand live attraction. Glover released a new solo album in 2002.
● ALBUMS: *The Butterfly Ball* (Purple 1975) ★★★, *Elements* (Polydor 1978) ★★, *Mask* (Polydor 1984) ★★, with Ian Gillan *Accidentally On Purpose* (Virgin 1988) ★★★, *Snapshot* (Eagle 2002) ★★★.

Gloworm

Crossover **dance music** act fronted by Sedric Johnson (b. Alabama, USA). The leader of the 100-strong Long Beach Choir, he was spotted at a soul revue by Englishman Will Mount, who was on the lookout for a singer. After an impromptu performance Mount, who together with producer/remixer Rollo formed the musician team behind Gloworm, was won over. They anchored Johnson's gospel-inspired vocals to a club beat to produce records like 'I Lift My Cup' and 'Carry Me Home', both based on traditional songs. The result was reviewed as spiritual hard **house**, and widely admired. 'I Lift My Cup', on **Pulse 8 Records**, broke into the UK Top 20 in February 1993. 'Carry Me Home', on Go! Beat, had even more crossover success, reaching number 9 the following May.

Gnac

b. Mark Tranmer, Beverley, Yorkshire, England. Gnac (pronounced 'neeyak') is the alter ego of former catalogue model Mark Tranmer. He derives his recording name from the Italo Calvino short story *Moon And Gnac* and creates music that could happily soundtrack the mirthful adventures of a farcical Italian anti-hero. Tranmer has cited the influence of **Michel Legrand**, **Plaid**, **Harold Budd** and **Michael Nyman** upon his music while, tellingly, Gnac's first release, 'Sofia' (alongside a duo of other Gnac tracks, on the compilation *An Evening In The Company Of The Vespertine*) was dedicated to **Durutti Column** guitarist Vini Reilly, for whom Tranmer seems to hold particular affection. Synthesizing the sounds of harpsichords, piano and xylophones via a cheap keyboard and expensive effects, Gnac seems to create music at the mid-point between contemporary chamber music and incidental music from television serials. Gnac has released a series of singles on micro-indies Acetone, Amberley, Earworm, Liquefaction Empire, Fuzzy

Box and Kooky. Following 1999's *Friend Sleeping* (a beguiling album for Salford-based independent Vespertine) and *Sevens* (a singles collection on Rocket Girl), Gnac released *Biscuit Barrel Fashion* on **Alan McGee**'s Poptones label. Endearingly, Tranmer inverted the expected meta-rock 'n' roll aesthetics associated with previous McGee signings such as **Primal Scream** and **Oasis**: the musician completed a doctorate in social statistics alongside recording his quirky instrumental creations. Foregrounding his interest in the visual arts, Gnac has collaborated with art illuminati such as Vanessa Beecroft and Miltos Manetas. Tranmer also creates perfectly poised, pretty melancholia as one-half of the **Montgolfier Brothers**.

● ALBUMS: *Friend Sleeping* (Vespertine 1999) ★★★, *Biscuit Barrel Fashion* (Poptones 2001) ★★★.
● COMPILATIONS: *Sevens* (Rocket Girl 1999) ★★★.

Go-Betweens

Critical favourites formed in late 1977 in Brisbane, Australia, by **Robert Forster** (b. 29 June 1957, Brisbane, Queensland, Australia; guitar/vocals) and **Grant McLennan** (b. 12 February 1958, Rockhampton, Queensland, Australia; bass,guitar, vocals). These two songwriters were influenced by **Bob Dylan**, the **Velvet Underground**, the **Monkees** and the then-burgeoning New York no wave scene involving **Television**, **Talking Heads** and **Patti Smith**. Although sharing the same subject matter in trouble-torn love songs, melancholy and desolation, Forster and McLennan's very different compositional styles fully complemented each other.

The Go-Betweens first recorded as a trio on the Able label with the Numbers' drummer Dennis Cantwell. McLennan took on bass playing duties for 'Lee Remick'/'Karen' (1978) and 'People Say'/'Don't Let Him Come Back' (1979). By the time of the latter release, the line-up included drummer Tim Mustafa (b. Temucin Mustafa, Cyprus), while Malcolm Kelly of the Godots guested on organ. At the invitation of **Postcard Records** boss Alan Horne, Forster and McLennan came to Britain to record a single, 'I Need Two Heads'/'Stop Before You Say It' (featuring **Orange Juice** drummer Steven Daly). After this visit, Forster and McLennan returned to Australia, where, after a brief experiment with a line-up featuring Clare McKenna (drums) and David Tyrer (guitar), they recruited ex-Zero drummer Lindy Morrison (b. Belinda Morrison, 2 November 1951, Australia) to complete the classic early Go-Betweens line-up. They relocated to Melbourne and recorded *Send Me A Lullaby* for the independent label Missing Link. This roughly hewn but still charming set was heard by Geoff Travis at **Rough Trade Records** in London, who picked it up for distribution in the UK. Travis proposed that the Go-Betweens return to England, sign a recording contract and settle in London, which the band accepted. *Before Hollywood* garnered favourable reviews, prompting many to predict a rosy future for the Go-Betweens. The highlight of this set was McLennan's evocative 'Cattle And Cane', one of the Go-Betweens' most enduring tracks (later covered by the **Wedding Present**).

The problem of finding a permanent bass player was solved with the enrolment of Brisbane associate Robert Vickers (b. 25 November 1959, Australia) in the post, thus enabling McLennan to concentrate on guitar and giving the band a fuller sound. The move to a major label, **Sire Records**, brought expectations of a 'big breakthrough' in terms of sales, but for all the critical acclaim heaped upon *Spring Hill Fair*, success still eluded the Go-Betweens. The break with Sire left the band almost on the brink of returning to Australia. The intervention of **Beggars Banquet Records** led them to a relationship that allowed the band to develop at their own pace. *Liberty Belle And The Black Diamond Express* presented what was by far their best album to date. The successful use of violins and oboes led to the introduction of a fifth member, Amanda Brown (b. 17 November 1965, Australia; violin,oboe,guitar,keyboards), adding an extra dimension and smoother texture to the band's sound. With *Tallulah* in 1987, the Go-Betweens made their best showing so far in the UK album chart, peaking at number 91. The album was a bit too polished for some of the band's fans, although it did contain one of their finest songs in McLennan's 'Bye Bye Pride'. That same year, Robert Vickers left to reside in New York and was replaced by John Willsteed (b. 13 February 1957, Australia). Prior to the release of *16 Lovers Lane* in 1988, the single 'Streets Of Your Town', an upbeat pop song with a dark lyric tackling the subject of wife-battering, was given generous UK airplay. However, once again, the single failed to make any impact on the charts despite being lavished with praise from the music press. The album only managed to peak at UK number 81, a hugely disappointing setback for the band.

After touring with the set, with Michael Armiger replacing Willsteed on bass, Forster and McLennan dissolved the Go-Betweens in December 1989. Remaining with Beggars Banquet they both released solo albums that proved that neither artist was lost without the other, while McLennan released an album with fellow antipodean **Steve Kilbey**, from the **Church**, under the title **Jack Frost**. Lindy Morrison and Amanda Brown, meanwhile, had formed Cleopatra Wong, who went on to release two EPs (1992's *Egg* and the following year's *Cleopatra's Lament*).

When McLennan joined Forster onstage in 1991, subsequent rumours of a Go-Betweens reunion were strengthened by a Forster/McLennan support slot with **Lloyd Cole** in Toronto that same year. However, both artists continued to release solo records at regular intervals throughout the 90s, although critical acclaim was not matched by commercial success. In 1997, McLennan and Forster re-formed for special live dates, and two years later played a series of shows to promote the release of two compilations (one of which, *78 'Til 79: The Lost Album*, featured the Go-Betweens' Able Label releases and a number of early tracks recorded in Forster's bedroom). In the new millennium, Forster and McLennan teamed up with members of **Sleater-Kinney** and regular associate Adele Pickvance (bass) to record the new Go-Betweens set, *The Friends Of Rachel Worth*. Forster's 'He Lives My Life', in particular, was easily the equal of any of his songs from the previous decade. The second coming of the Go-Betweens picked up steam with 2003's *Bright Yellow Bright Orange*, which was recorded in Melbourne with Pickvance and another musician who had regularly played with Forster and McLennan during the 90s, drummer Glenn Thompson. The set was even better than its predecessor, and was not at all overshadowed by the concurrent expanded re-releases of the band's classic 80s albums.

In June 2004, Forster and McLennan played a spellbinding set at the Barbican in London, completing the second half of the concert with a string quartet drawn from the players originally featured on *Liberty Belle And The Black Diamond Express*. They then completed the recording of another studio album with Pickvance and Thompson. Released in April 2005, *Oceans Apart* received even greater praise than the first two albums by the 'new' Go-Betweens.

● ALBUMS: *Send Me A Lullaby* (Missing Link/Rough Trade 1981) ★★★, *Before Hollywood* (Rough Trade 1983) ★★★★, *Spring Hill Fair* (Sire 1984) ★★★★, *Liberty Belle And The Black Diamond Express* (Beggars Banquet 1986) ★★★★★, *Tallulah* (Beggars Banquet 1987) ★★★, *16 Lovers Lane* (Beggars Banquet/Capitol 1988) ★★★★, *The Friends Of Rachel Worth* (Circus/Jetset 2000) ★★★★, *Bright Yellow Bright Orange* (Circus/Jetset 2003) ★★★★, *Oceans Apart* (Lomax/Yep Roc 2005) ★★★★.

● COMPILATIONS: *Metals And Shells* (PVC 1985) ★★★, *Very Quick On The Eye = Brisbane, 1981* (Man Made 1986) ★★, *1978–1990* (Beggars Banquet/Capitol 1990) ★★★★, *78 'Til 79: The Lost Album* (Tag 5/Jetset 1999) ★★★, *Bellavista Terrace: Best Of The Go-Betweens* (Beggars Banquet 1999) ★★★★.

● DVD/VIDEOS: *Video Singles* (Beggars Banquet 1990), *That Way* (Visionary 1993), *That Striped Sunlight Sound* (Tuition 2006).

● FURTHER READING: *The Go-Betweens*, David Nichols.

Go! Discs

Small but perfectly formed record label founded by managing director Andy McDonald in 1983 with a loan of £1,500. By the following year the label had found additional finance with a worldwide licensing agreement through **Chrysalis Records**. The highest profile early name attached to the label would be **Billy Bragg**, but it was the **Housemartins** who made the commercial breakthrough. Their 'Happy Hour' made the number 3 slot in 1986 and was followed by the Christmas number 1, 'Caravan Of Love'. **PolyGram Records** took out a minority stake in the company in the following year, by which point their most successful act were on the verge of transmuting into the **Beautiful South**. *Welcome To The Beautiful South* duly emerged in 1989 as the label's first million-selling release. By the turn of the decade the same band's 'A Little Time' had gone to number 1, as had **Beats International** with 'Dub Be Good To Me'—a strong Housemartins connection being maintained, as that group was headed by former drummer Norman Cook. A rare talent was unearthed with the discovery of the **La's**, while Go! Discs anticipated future trends by launching a dance subsidiary, Go! Beat (headed by Ferdy Hamilton). However, 1991 brought the first major setbacks. With bands such as Father Father, Southernaires and Sound Systemme failing to recoup the label's promotion of them, and the recession biting, by the following year McDonald had been forced to dismiss five staff. This was merely a temporary blip, and one straightened by the arrival of a revitalized **Paul Weller**. The **Frank And Walters** failed to sell in nearly the quantities envisaged, but this was compensated for by a number 1 single from **Gabrielle**. Weller's second album for the label, **Wild Wood**, was nominated for the Mercury Music Prize in 1994, before the multi-platinum Beautiful South compilation *Carry On Up The Charts* became Go! Discs' first number 1 album. Arguably just as significant was the arrival of the critically drooled-over **Portishead**. New arrivals in 1995 included **Drugstore**, British hip-hop act the Muddie Funksters, while Go! Beat's roster boasted Gabrielle and **Gloworm. John Martyn** was signed in 1996. During a flurry of activity in the summer of 1996, founder McDonald walked out and then resigned

following PolyGram's purchase of his 51% equity. In a statement McDonald attacked PolyGram and insisted that he had been forced out. He subsequently formed a new label, Independiente.

Go-Go's

This all-female band, originally called the Misfits, was formed in California, USA, in 1978 by **Belinda Carlisle** (b. 17 August 1958, Hollywood, California, USA; lead vocals) and **Jane Wiedlin** (b. 20 May 1958, Oconomowoc, Wisconsin, USA; rhythm guitar/vocals). They were joined by Charlotte Caffey (b. 21 October 1953, Santa Monica, California, USA; lead guitar/keyboards), Elissa Bello (drums) and Margot Olaverra (bass). Inspired by the new wave scene, the Go-Go's performed bright, infectious harmony pop songs and were initially signed to the UK independent label **Stiff Records** and to Miles Copeland's I.R.S. Records in the USA, where they would enjoy practically all their success. By the time of the release of debut album *Beauty And The Beat*, Olaverra was replaced by Kathy Valentine (b. 7 January 1959; ex-Textone) and Bello by Gina Schock (b. 31 August 1957). Produced by Rob Freeman and **Richard Gottehrer**, who had earlier worked with a long line of female singers in the 60s, the sprightly pop qualities of *Beauty And The Beat* drew comparisons with **Blondie**, with whom Gottehrer and Freeman had also worked. The album, which stayed at the US number 1 spot for 6 weeks in 1981, included 'Our Lips Are Sealed' (US Top 20), which was co-written by Wiedlin with Terry Hall of the **Fun Boy Three**, and 'We Got The Beat', which gave the band a US number 2 hit the following year. The second album provided a further US Top 10 hit with the title track, but the band was by now showing signs of burnout. Despite their 'safe' image, it later transpired that the Go-Go's were more than able to give the average all-male outfit a run for their money when it came to on-the-road excesses, which eventually took their toll. *Talk Show* reached the US Top 20, as did the most successful single culled from the set, 'Head Over Heels' (1984).

With the break-up of the band in 1985, Belinda Carlisle subsequently pursued a successful solo career with assistance from Charlotte Caffey, who, for a time, appeared in her backing group. Caffey later formed the Graces with **Meredith Brooks** and Gia Campbell and recorded for **A&M Records**, releasing *Perfect View* in 1989, before moving into soundtrack work (*Clueless*). Schock formed the short-lived House Of Shock, releasing a self-titled album for **Capitol Records** in 1988. As well as recording as a solo artist, Wiedlin attempted to break into acting with a few minor movie roles. Galvanized by her, the Go-Go's re-formed briefly in 1990 for a benefit for the anti-fur trade organization PETA (People for the Ethical Treatment of Animals).

A fuller reunion took place in 1994 for well-paid shows in Las Vegas, prompted by which I.R.S. issued *Return To The Valley Of The Go-Go's*, a compilation of the band's best-known moments with the addition of two new tracks. Carlisle and Wiedlin then resumed their solo careers, while Valentine and Schock formed the Delphines. Another reunion took place in summer 2000 for a US tour alongside the **B-52's**, with a new album released in May 2001.

● ALBUMS: *Beauty And The Beat* (I.R.S. 1981) ★★★, *Vacation* (I.R.S. 1982) ★★★, *Talk Show* (I.R.S. 1984) ★★, *God Bless The Go-Go's* (Go-Go's/Beyond 2001) ★★★.

● COMPILATIONS: *Go-Go's Greatest* (I.R.S. 1990) ★★★, *Return To The Valley Of The Go-Go's* (I.R.S. 1995) ★★★, *Go-Go's Collection* (A&M 2000) ★★★.

Go Into Your Dance

The only film in which **Al Jolson** and his wife, **Ruby Keeler**, starred together was released by Warner Brothers in 1935. Al plays a woman-chasing entertainer on the loose in Chicago, hanging around clubs such as La Cucaracha (complete with sombrero and Mexican shawl), before Keeler is persuaded by a mutual friend to look after him. After surviving being framed for a murder he probably is not even capable (mostly too drunk) of committing, he and Keeler celebrate the happy ending in their own nightspot. The songs, by **Harry Warren** and **Al Dubin**, included a smart little floor-show number for Keeler called 'A Good Old-Fashioned Cocktail', and there were several attractive items for Jolson such as 'She's A Latin From Manhattan', 'Mammy, I'll Sing About You', and 'Go Into Your Dance'. He also strutted with Keeler in the film's high spot, a spectacular production number constructed around the spirited 'About A Quarter To Nine', in which, after a brief and slightly incongruous segue into 'Way Down Upon The Swanee River', the faces of Jolson and the male chorus turn black, while their top hats become white. It was almost as if the film was being shown in negative, except that Keeler's face and costume remained white all the time. Torch singer **Helen Morgan**, who was to make such an impact as Julie in the film of *Show Boat* in 1936, also brought a touch of class to *Go Into Your Dance* with a lovely version of 'The Little Things You Used To Do'. Earl Baldwin wrote the screenplay, Bobby Connolly created the lively and enterprising choreography, and the film was directed by Archie Mayo.

Go, Johnny, Go!

Disc jockey **Alan Freed**, who reputedly coined the phrase 'rock 'n' roll', took part in several 50s genre films, including *Rock Around The Clock* and *Rock Rock Rock*. He assumed the lead role in this 1958 feature, playing to type as a DJ searching for singer Johnny Melody, whose demo recordings proved highly popular with Freed's audience. **Chuck Berry** also enjoys a (brief) acting part, but is clearly more comfortable performing the title song, plus 'Little Queenie' and 'Memphis, Tennessee', the last of which became a UK Top 10 entry five years later. Rising star **Richie Valens** contributes 'Ooh My Head' in what would be his only film appearance, while other notable cameos include the **Flamingos**' 'Jump Children', **Eddie Cochran**'s 'Teenage Heaven', **Jackie Wilson**'s 'You'd Better Know It' and **Harvey Fuqua**'s 'Don't Be Afraid To Love Me'. New Orleans-based singer **Jimmy Clanton**, who played Melody, provides four songs for the soundtrack, including 'My Own True Love', a US Top 40 entry in 1959. The film did not propel Clanton to stardom, although the singer did enjoy several subsequent hit singles, including 'Go Jimmy Go' (clearly based on his starring feature) and 'Venus In Blue Jeans'.

Go West

Peter Cox (b. 17 November 1955, London, England; vocals) and Richard Drummie (b. 20 March 1959, England; guitar, keyboard, vocals) were a songwriting partnership before forming Go West in 1982. The publishers, ATV Music, had teamed them up to write with artists such as **Peter Frampton** and **David Grant**. **Chrysalis Records** signed the duo and the result was a string of quality pop rock hits in 1985 with, 'We Close Our Eyes', 'Call Me', 'Don't Look Down' and a successful debut album. Sylvester Stallone heard the latter and liked it, and they wrote 'One Way Street' for the *Rocky IV* soundtrack. The songs were well crafted, well-arranged and well-produced and they used a regular session crew of talented and innovative players. Cox's voice was strong and distinctive and the **Godley And Creme** video for 'We Close Our Eyes' was extremely inventive. *Indian Summer* came after a lengthy gap and they demonstrated that they had developed and matured since they were first viewed as pop pin-ups. It contained the transatlantic hit 'King Of Wishful Thinking'. Following the album's release, Cox and Drummie elected to disband Go West and concentrate on solo projects.

● ALBUMS: *Go West* (Chrysalis 1985) ★★★, *Bangs And Crashes* (Chrysalis 1985) ★★, *Dancing On The Couch* (Chrysalis 1987) ★★, *Indian Summer* (Chrysalis 1992) ★★★.
● COMPILATIONS: *Aces And Kings: The Best Of Go West* (Chrysalis 1993) ★★★, *Greatest Hits* (EMI 1999) ★★★.
● DVD/VIDEOS: *Aces And Kings: The Best Of The Videos* (Chrysalis 1993).

Goanna

Formed in 1976 in the Australian provincial port city of Geelong, Victoria by Shane Howard. With a line-up that has fluctuated over years, the most notable members to have played alongside Howard have been his sister Marcia Howard (vocals), Rose Bygrave (keyboards/vocals), Ross Hunnaford (guitar), Russell Smith (trumpet), Venetta Fields (bass), Mick O'Connor and Sam See (guitar)—the latter was also a member of the **Flying Circus**. Goanna played many venues along the Victoria state coast, using the popular west coast mix of harmonies and acoustic guitar–orientated sound. It was not until a move to Melbourne, Australian, in 1980 that the band began to widen its audience with Howard's probing lyrics and songwriting. After an obscure, self-financed mini-album in 1979, the band released its commercial debut in 1982 for **WEA Records** and the second single from the album, 'Solid Rock' propelled the band into national stardom overnight. The single revealed the band's social conscience, exploring, as it did, the Australian white population's poor treatment of the Aborigines. While no subsequent singles repeated the success of 'Solid Rock', Goanna's second album was more cohesive, yet, unfortunately, was overlooked by critics and public alike. The band, right from the start had an enormous turnover of musicians and Howard's attempts at controlling his involvement in the music scene by incorporating everyone involved into a communal arrangement left a large, cumbersome entourage that sapped the band's finances. Howard, tiring of this scene, left the band in 1986 to play casually at folk festivals. It was not until after travelling throughout the country that he released two solo albums—the first not achieving much attention, but the second, *Back To The Track* (1989) holding more promise. Rose Bygrave also recorded a solo album. The Howards and Bygrave reunited at the end of the 90s to tour and record a new album.

● ALBUMS: *Spirit Of Place* (WEA 1982) ★★, *Oceana* (WEA 1984) ★★★, *Spirit Returns* (Aus 1998) ★★★.

Goats

This Philadelphia, USA rap trio comprised Oa Tiekato, Madd and Swayzack. From early in their career they made a conscious decision to play live (without DAT, often rapping freestyle) whenever possible, and earned immediate notoriety by playing at a celebration of Columbus' discovery of America—educating their audience about the degradation native Americans consequently suffered. They were snapped up by **Columbia Records**' subsidiary **Ruffhouse Records** on the basis of their first, four-track demo. Their 1993 debut was a joy, with alter-egos Chickenlittle and his kid brother Hangerhead acting as tour guides through the strange world of 90s America. Their political targets included Dan Quayle, while 'Drive By Bumper Cars' parodied hardcore rap. Their puns were incisive, sometimes almost funny: ('Hey Mr Columbus! You took all my money/No I didn't kid, I discovered it'). Singles such as 'Do The Digs Dug?' again returned to the rights of the oppressed, singling out the imprisoned community leader Leonard Peltier as 'Our Mandela'. However, their UK appearances in 1993 without founder member Tiekato fuelled rumours of a split, which were confirmed on the advent of their less-politicized second album, on which Swayzack took the lead.

● ALBUMS: *Tricks Of The Shade* (Ruffhouse/Columbia 1993) ★★★★, *No Goats, No Glory* (Ruffhouse/Columbia 1994) ★★★.

Goatsnake

This US band was formed in 1996 by Southern Lord label boss Greg Anderson (guitar, ex–**Burning Witch**), with the line-up completed by two former **Obsessed** members, Guy Pinhas (bass) and Greg Rogers (drums). After initial jams together the trio wanted to add a melodic vocalist to complement their ultra-heavy doom metal sound, eventually selecting Pete Stahl (ex-Wool). Goatsnake's initial output comprised two 1998 limited edition singles, 'IV' (on Prosthetic Records) and 'Man Of Light' (on Warpburner). Their full-length debut *I* featured production contributions from the **Melvins**' Buzz Osborne. While maintaining a retro, hard rocking feel, the album drew heavily on the sombre atmosphere and down tuned riffage of the members' former bands, but was still consistently in check with late-90s metal. Following this release Goatsnake toured around Europe, putting in an impressive performance at Holland's Dynamo Festival, with the indisposed Pinhas replaced by Scott Reeder. The former then left the band a short time later owing to personal differences. His replacement was low-end specialist, G. Stuart Dahlquist (ex–Burning Witch). Two EPs, *Dog Days* (on Southern Lord) and a split release with Burning Witch (on HydraHead), followed. 2000's *Flower Of Disease* extended Goatsnake's move towards southern-fried doom leanings, further refining their bludgeoning style. Goatsnake disbanded in 2002 but was revived the following year by Stahl and Anderson. Joined by Scott Reeder and drummer JR they finished recording sessions for a new, five-track EP, *Trampled Under Hoof*.

● ALBUMS: *I* (Man's Ruin/Rise Above 1999) ★★★, *Flower Of Disease* (Man's Ruin/Rise Above 2000) ★★★.

God Dethroned

An intensely satanic black metal band from the Netherlands, the first incarnation of God Dethroned were formed in 1991 by Henri Sattler (vocals/guitar), Marco Arends (bass), Ard De Weerd (drums) and Oscar Carre (guitar), but lasted only long enough for one demo, 1992's *The Christhunt*, to be produced. Although a certain degree of underground popularity was achieved, Sattler dissolved the band and recorded with a thrash outfit, Ministry Of Terror, which released *Fall Of Life* in 1994 and toured with **Impaled Nazarene**. While on the road Sattler was surprised at the number of fans who asked him about God Dethroned, and on his return decided to resurrect his old act with new members Jens (guitar), Beef (bass) and Roel (drums). After demoing new material, the band was rapidly signed to Metal Blade and released *The Grand Grimoire* in 1997. After a tour with **Six Feet Under** confirmed their renewed popularity among European audiences, *The Christhunt* was reissued and festival slots with **Cannibal Corpse**, **Immortal**, **Marduk**, **Obituary** and **Angel Corpse** followed. Subsequent albums have seen Sattler's virulent message remain on the boundaries of black and thrash metal.

● ALBUMS: *The Christhunt* (Shark 1992) ★★★, *The Grand Grimoire* (Metal Blade 1997) ★★★, *Bloody Blasphemy* (Metal Blade 1999) ★★★, *Ravenous* (Metal Blade 2000) ★★★, *Into The Lungs Of Hell* (Metal Blade 2003) ★★★.

God Machine

Capable of producing work of the most devilish intensity, American-bred but UK-based band God Machine briefly sparked in the 90s before they were overtaken by tragic events. Melding **Black Sabbath**–styled riffs with more detached, free-form passages, the band engendered a strong critical reaction throughout their brief existence.

Comprising Robin Proper-Sheppard (vocals/guitar), Jimmy Fernandez (d. 23 May 1994; bass) and Ronald Austin (drums), they formed in January 1990 when all three, who had been friends at high school, elected to move from San Diego, California, to England to form a band. Without money or equipment, they soon found themselves hungry and homeless, until they broke into a disused apartment in Camden, north London, and furnished it with items stolen from an abandoned pub. They then found jobs (illegally) selling fruit at the nearby market, saving the money to buy instruments. Six months elapsed before they had enough to make the necessary purchases, and a further six months while they learned to play them. They soon amassed a significant following in British indie circles reared on the imported sounds of **Sonic Youth** and **Big Black**, though when they elected to return to America, their illegal immigrant status meant they first had to stowaway on a ferry from England to Ireland. On the back of a series of well-received EPs for Fiction Records the band toured the UK with **My Bloody Valentine** and announced their first album, *Scenes From The Second Storey*. A powerful, almost tribalistic assault on the senses, its brutal aesthetic was the key to its impact.

Not content with their travels thus far, the trio journeyed to Prague to record a follow-up set. However, in May 1994, one day after its completion, Fernandez became ill. On 23 May he died from a cancerous brain tumour, aged 28. As Sheppard declared: 'The only thing I was really beginning to identify with was our music, and now our music has essentially ceased to exist, or the band identity has ceased to exist.' *Last Laugh In A Place Of Dying* thus became an epitaph to both Fernandez and the God Machine. Proper-Sheppard later recorded acoustic material as **Sophia** and inaugurated his own Flower Shop Recordings label.

● ALBUMS: *Scenes From The Second Storey* (Fiction 1993) ★★★, *Last Laugh In A Place Of Dying* (Fiction 1995) ★★★.

Godard, Vic, And The Subway Sect

Godard, of Mortlake, London, England, put his band together during 1976, centring it on the friends with whom he used to attend **Sex Pistols** gigs. Subway Sect made their live debut on 20 September 1976 at the 100 Club, featuring Godard (vocals), Paul Myers (bass), Robert Miller (guitar), and Paul Smith (drums). Their name came from brief flirtations with busking upon their inauguration. Rehearsing in the **Clash**'s studio, a series of short sets followed around the capital, featuring embryonic songwriting prowess to add to the abrasiveness they learned at the hands of the Sex Pistols. They opened for the Clash at Harlesdon and subsequently joined them for their White Riot tour. Mark Laff had replaced Smith, but he too was lured away (to **Generation X**) before they set out on their first European trek. Bob Ward was the Subway Sect's new drummer when they released their April 1978 debut 'Nobody's Scared'. However, a major split followed, leaving Ward and Godard to recruit John Britain (guitar), Colin Scott (bass) and Steve Atkinson (keyboards) in the summer of 1978. 'Ambition' was a trailblazing single, but afterwards the band fell into inactivity before reviving in 1980 with another new line-up with definite New Romantic leanings. This time the band featured Rob Marche (b. 13 October 1962, Bristol, England; guitar), Dave Collard (b. 17 January 1961, Bristol, England; keyboards), Chris Bostock (b. 23 November 1962, Bristol, England; bass) and Sean McLusky (b. 5 May 1961, Bristol, England; drums). *Songs For Sale* presented a collection of slick, swing-style songs with Godard adopting a cocktail lounge, crooner image. Supports with the Clash and **Buzzcocks** had transformed into guest spots on the **Altered Images** tour, and Godard's new backing band departed to find commercial success with **JoBoxers**. *T.R.O.U.B.L.E.* (1986), a collection of jazz songs, was recorded with **Working Week**, but a bad mix sunk the album.

Disillusioned, Godard retired from the music scene to work as a postman until, in 1992, the death of **Johnny Thunders** inspired him to show some interest in music again, and he began experimenting in his home recording studio. With support from **Edwyn Collins** and ex-**Sex Pistols** drummer Paul Cook, Godard subsequently released solo albums until a Subway Sect rebirth in 2002 with the eclectic *Sansend*.

● ALBUMS: *What's The Matter Boy?* (Oddball 1980) ★★, *Songs For Sale* (London 1982) ★★★, as Vic Godard *T.R.O.U.B.L.E.* (Upside 1986) ★★, as Vic Godard *The End Of The Surrey People* (Overground 1993) ★★★, as Vic Godard *Long Term Side Effect* (Tugboat 1998) ★★★, *Sansend* (Motion 2002) ★★★.

● COMPILATIONS: *A Retrospective (1977–81)* (Rough Trade 1984) ★★★, *Twenty Odd Years: The Story Of* (Motion 1999) ★★★, *Singles Anthology* (Motion 2005) ★★★★.

Godding, Brian

b. 19 August 1945, Wales. Godding is a self-taught guitarist who started his professional career in the rock bands **Blossom Toes** and **B.B. Blunder** before **John McLaughlin**'s *Extrapolation* 'opened the door to jazz'. He played with **Magma** and **Dick Morrissey** before performing with **Keith Tippett**'s band Centipede in the early 70s. Since then he has played

with many British musicians but has worked most regularly with **Mike Westbrook**, who describes him as 'one of the truly great guitarists'. His playing reflects his own eclectic taste in guitarists, which ranges from John McLaughlin right through to **Jeff Beck** and **Jimi Hendrix**. He also wrote material with UK singer-songwriter **Kevin Coyne**.

● ALBUMS: *Slaughter On Shaftesbury Avenue* 1981–86 recordings (Reckless 1988) ★★★.

Goddo

Hard rock band Goddo were formed in Canada in the late 70s after bass player and vocalist Greg Godovitz had left his previous employers, the briefly successful pop band Fludd. Together with Gino Scarpelli (guitar) and Doug Inglis (drums), Goddo allowed him to indulge his twin passions—one for dynamic, gritty rock music and the other for articulate but esoteric lyrics. The group's irreverent sense of humour was celebrated in their album titles as well as lyrics, and each of their three albums for **Polydor Records** in the late 70s impressed with their musical adventurousness. By the 80s the group had switched to **Attic Records**, but neither *Pretty Bad Boys* nor the live set, *Live, Best Seat In The House*, managed to secure mainstream success. This was a great pity, as Godovitz remains one of Canada's unsung talents, a genuine maverick in the contemporary recording industry.

● ALBUMS: *Goddo* (Polydor 1977) ★★★, *Who Cares* (Polydor 1978) ★★★, *An Act Of Goddo* (Polydor 1979) ★★, *Pretty Bad Boys* (Attic 1981) ★★, *Live, Best Seat In The House* (Attic 1981) ★★.

Godfathers

A tough, R&B-fired rock band, the Godfathers centred on brothers Peter and Chris Coyne (b. London, England). The group's beginnings were in the south London punk quartet Sid Presley Experience (the Coynes on vocals and bass, plus Del Bartle—guitar, and Kevin Murphy—drums) who released two singles in 1984 and toured with **Billy Bragg** on the 'Jobs For Youth' tour. They split in 1985 and Bartle and Murphy toured as the New Sid Presley Experience before recruiting Mad Dog Lucas and forming the Unholy Trinity. The Coyne brothers also retained the Sid Presley moniker for a while but having recruited Mike Gibson (b. London, England; guitar), Kris Dollimore (b. Isle Of Sheppey, Kent, England; guitar) and George Mazur (b. Bradford, Yorkshire, England; drums), they became the Godfathers. 'Lonely Man' was released on their own Corporate Image label in 1985 and *Hit By Hit* came out the following year, collecting together their first three singles with other tracks. In 1986 came the first of their regular St Valentine's Day gigs in London, which would take place at such venues as the London Dungeon as well as more conventional halls. With their reputation growing they were signed to the American arm of the Epic Records organization, who released their best-known work—*Birth, School, Work, Death*. Kris Dollimore left in 1989 (he would later work with **Johnny Thunders** and join the **Damned** and then **Del Amitri**) and was replaced in January 1990 by Chris Burrows. Burrows had previously worked with many bands including the Presidents Of Explosion, which had also included former Sid Presley drummer Kevin Murphy. The band toured constantly, particularly in Europe, and released *Unreal World* in 1991. However, by this time much of their impetus had been lost, and despite a staunchly resilient fanbase, they had become static. The band was dropped by Epic; matters got worse when Gibson and Mazur left in 1992. The Coyne brothers persevered on the German label, Intercord. Backed by various musicians they have since released *Orange* and *Afterlife*.

● ALBUMS: *Hit By Hit* (Corporate Image 1986) ★★★, *Birth, School, Work, Death* (Epic 1988) ★★★, *More Songs About Love And Hate* (Epic 1989) ★★, *Unreal World* (Epic 1991) ★★★, *Dope, Rock 'N' Roll, And Fu**ing In The Streets* (Corporate Image 1992) ★★★, *Orange* (Intercord 1993) ★★, *Afterlife* (Intercord 1996) ★★.

● COMPILATIONS: *Birth, School, Work, Death: The Best Of The Godfathers* (Sony 1996) ★★★.

Godflesh

The Godflesh partnership was inaugurated by Justin Broadrick (guitar/vocals) and G. Christian Green (bass) in 1988, when the former left the venerated (by UK radio presenter **John Peel**, at least) hardcore industrial trio, Head Of David. Green had formerly served time in industrialists Fall Of Because, and Godflesh were completed by the addition of a drum machine. A self-titled EP was released on the Swordfish label before moving to the more permanent home of Earache Records. By the advent of their debut album, the band had expanded temporarily to include guitarist Paul Neville (also ex–Fall Of Because). With strong critical reaction, they toured with **Loop** and as part of the Earache Grindcrusher USA package, alongside **Napalm Death**. Broadrick had actually appeared with the latter as guitarist on side one of the legendary *Scum* album. In 1991, there were three limited-edition 12-inches (including one for the **Sub Pop Records** empire), which were eventually collected together as the *Slavestate* mini-album. With Neville opting to concentrate on his own project, Cabel Regime, Robert Hampson of **Loop** stepped in for additional guitar duties on the band's excellently reviewed *Pure*. He would choose to stay at home, however, as the duo embarked on a promotional European tour. In 1993, Broadrick branched out by providing guitar tracks for labelmates **Scorn** (on their *Vae Solis* debut), and he also produced a 'biomechanical' remix of **Pantera**'s 'Walk'. This 'biomechanical' method is described by Green as involving: 'stripping them (the tracks) down and reconstructing them from scratch with different drum patterns, different vocal lines etc.'

Meanwhile, Godflesh's first own-name project in nearly two years, the *Merciless* EP, resurrected an eight-year-old Fall Of Because song. October 1994 saw the introduction of a major new work, *Selfless*, a stunningly direct and brutal album from a band whose quality threshold has hardly wavered since their inception. *Songs Of Love And Hate* was challenging and provocative and one of their finest albums. Drummer Mantia left to join **Primus** in August 1996. Broadrick's involvement in side-projects Final and **Techno Animal** meant fans had to wait three years before the release of the new Godflesh album, *Us And Them*. The album's seamless fusion of metal and electronics received great acclaim, which was just reward for Broadrick and Green's pioneering work in the field.

● ALBUMS: *Godflesh* mini-album (Swordfish 1988) ★★★, *Streetcleaner* (Earache 1989) ★★★, *Slavestate* mini-album (Earache 1990) ★★★, *Pure* (Earache 1992) ★★★, *Selfless* (Earache 1994) ★★★, *Songs Of Love And Hate* (Earache 1996) ★★★, *Love And Hate In Dub* remix album (Earache 1997) ★★★, *Us And Them* (Earache 1999) ★★★★,

Hymns (Koch/Music For Nations 2001) ★★★, *Messiah* mini-album (Relapse 2003) ★★★.

● COMPILATIONS: *In All Languages* (Earache 2001) ★★★.

● DVD/VIDEOS: *In All Languages* (Earache 2001).

Godhead

A gothic, **Marilyn Manson**–influenced industrial band from Washington, DC, USA, comprising Jason Miller (vocals/guitar), The Method (bass), Mike Miller (guitar) and James O'Connor (drums), Godhead formed in 1995 and built a local fanbase supporting bands such as **GWAR**, **Christian Death** and the **Genitorturers**. It was a long struggle: in the absence of major-label interest, the band released three independent albums: *Godhead* (1995), *Nothingness* (1996) and *Power Tool Stigmata* (1998). Godhead's unusual appearance (Miller sports a shaved scalp and covers his head with white corpse-paint, for example) and eclectic mix of influences (**David Bowie** is a prime inspiration) finally led them to Marilyn Manson, who signed them to his Posthuman label. *2000 Years Of Human Error* was executive-produced by Manson and produced by Danny Saber, with assistance by Bowie's touring guitarist Reeves Gabrels. Its stand-out track was a cover version of the **Beatles**' 'Eleanor Rigby', which saw some chart success in 2001.

● ALBUMS: *Godhead* (Sonic 1995) ★★★, *Nothingness* (Sol 3 1996) ★★, *Power Tool Stigmata* (Sol 3 1998) ★★★, *2000 Years Of Human Error* (Posthuman 2001) ★★★, *Evolver* (Reality 2003) ★★★.

Godley And Creme

This highly talented duo began recording together in 1976, having already enjoyed an illustrious career in British pop. Kevin Godley (b. 7 October 1945, Manchester, England; vocals/drums) and Lol Creme (b. 19 September 1947, Manchester, England; vocals/guitar) had previously been involved with such groups as the **Mockingbirds**, **Hotlegs** and, most crucially, **10cc**. After leaving the latter in 1976, they intended to abandon mainstream pop in favour of a more elaborate project. The result was a staggeringly overblown triple album *Consequences*, whose concept was nothing less than 'The Story Of Man's Last Defence Against An Irate Nature'. The work was lampooned in the music press, as was the duo's invention of a new musical instrument the 'Gizmo' gadget, which had been used on the album. As their frustrated manager **Harvey Lisberg** sagely noted: 'They turned their back on huge success. They were brilliant, innovative— and what did they do? A triple album that goes on forever and became a disaster'. An edited version of the work was later issued but also failed to sell.

The duo reverted to a more accessible approach for albums such as *L* and *Freeze Frame* and 1981's UK Top 10 hit 'Under My Thumb', a ghost story in song. Although they enjoyed two more singles hits with 'Wedding Bells' and 'Cry', it was as video makers that they found their greatest success. Their video for 'Cry' won many awards and is a classic of the genre, with the monochrome film superimposing a series of gradually changing faces. **Visage**, **Duran Duran**, **Toyah**, the **Police** and **Herbie Hancock** were some of the artists that used their services. Then, in 1984, they took the rock video form to new heights with their work with **Frankie Goes To Hollywood**. Godley And Creme are regarded as arguably the best in their field having pushed rock videos into a highly creative and competitive new market. Creme joined the **Art Of Noise** in the late 90s.

● ALBUMS: *Consequences* (Mercury 1977) ★★, *L* (Mercury 1978) ★★★, *Freeze Frame* (Polydor 1979) ★★★, *Ismism* (Polydor 1981) ★★★, *Birds Of Prey* (Polydor 1983) ★★, *The History Mix Volume 1* (Polydor 1985) ★★★★, *Goodbye Blue Sky* (Polydor 1988) ★★.

● COMPILATIONS: *The Changing Face Of 10cc And Godley And Creme* (Polydor 1987) ★★★, *Images* (Polydor 1993) ★★★.

● DVD/VIDEOS: *Changing Faces—The Very Best Of 10cc And Godley And Creme* (PolyGram Music Video 1988), *Cry* (PolyGram Music Video 1988), *Mondo Video* (Virgin 1989).

Gods

Formed in 1965 in Hatfield, England, the first incarnation of the Gods comprised **Mick Taylor** (b. Michael Kevin Taylor, 17 January 1948, Welwyn Garden City, Hertfordshire, England; guitar), **Ken Hensley** (keyboards/vocals), John Glascock (b. 1951, London, England, d. 17 November 1979; bass/vocals) and Brian Glascock (drums). They remained active until 1967, but broke up when Taylor joined **John Mayall**'s Bluesbreakers. Within months Hensley had reconstituted the band around Joe Konas (guitar/vocals), Paul Newton (bass) and Lee Kerslake (drums). **Greg Lake** (b. 10 November 1948, Bournemouth, Dorset, England) then replaced Newton, but the newcomer left to help found **King Crimson** in 1968. John Glascock returned to the fold as the Gods secured a recording contract with **Columbia Records**. *Genesis* was an ambitious concept album, brimming with late-60s naïve pretension, but it was not a commercial success. The Gods did create a minor stir with their reading of the **Beatles**' 'Hey Bulldog', but they disbanded in February 1969. *To Samuel A Son* was issued posthumously when various ex-members had achieved a higher profile elsewhere. Hensley, Kerslake and both Glascock brothers were all members of **Toe Fat**, before Hensley, Kerslake and Paul Newton found fame at various different points in **Uriah Heep**.

● ALBUMS: *Genesis* (Columbia 1968) ★★★, *To Samuel A Son* (Columbia 1970) ★★, *Gods* (Harvest 1976) ★★.

● COMPILATIONS: *The Gods: Featuring Ken Hensley* (Harvest Heritage 1976) ★★★.

Gods Little Monkeys

Based in York, England, this indie group played a mixture of rock and folk. The founder members were Jo Swiss (vocals), Jon Townend (vocals/guitar), Dave Allen (drums), and Martin Appleby (bass), with the addition of various keyboard players. Initially named Malcolm's Mother, their own Eggs Will Walk label issued an excellent 12-inch EP in 1986, on which they reworked the traditional 'Cruel Mother'. When Appleby departed, the band recruited Dave Wall. Capturing the atmosphere of 80s urban bleakness, with Townend's oblique, witty political comments, they recorded an album for Special Delivery, and two more noise-folk releases for the modernist label **Cooking Vinyl Record**s. After *Lip*, which was remixed against their wishes, they disbanded. Townend and Swiss retained the band's name, and continued to search for a US label.

● ALBUMS: *Breakfast In Bedlam* (Special Delivery 1987) ★★★, *New Maps Of Hell* (Cooking Vinyl 1989) ★★★, *Lip* (Cooking Vinyl 1991) ★★.

Godsmack

This US heavy rock band revolves around the diminutive figure of Sully Erna, a self-confessed witch from Boston, Massachusetts, USA. Erna had played drums with local Boston band Strip Mind before taking a yearlong break from music. He formed Godsmack (named after an **Alice In Chains** song) in 1995 with Robbie Merrill (bass), Tommy Stewart (drums) and Lee Richards (guitar). The latter pair only lasted a few months, and were replaced by Tony Rombolo (guitar) and Joe Darko (drums). The new line-up, with Erna playing drums, recorded a self-titled album in 1996 on a budget of $2500 and sold it through local retail chain Newbury Comics. Local radio station WAAF picked up the track 'Keep Away' for heavy rotation, and the band also came to the attention of ex-**Extreme** drummer Paul Geary, who signed them to his management company PGE. The album's stand-out track, 'Whatever', became a big local hit, and, with their fortunes rising, original drummer Stewart rejoined the band in mid-1997.

The new line-up signed a recording contract with Republic Records in July 1998. The heavily remixed album (also released under the title *All Wound Up*) became a surprise hit, selling over a million copies in America, helped immeasurably by the band's appearance at the US Ozzfest and their subsequent support slot on **Black Sabbath**'s reunion tour. Reaction to the album was mixed, with some critics accusing the band of straying too close to the sound of Alice In Chains and **Metallica** to be considered truly original. A wry sense of timing saw the band's second album arrive on Halloween 2000. In hardly deviating from the sound of the debut, *Awake* did not exactly endear the band to their critics, although it was snapped up by their substantial fanbase. *Faceless* was even more successful, debuting at number 1 on the US mainstream album chart in April 2003. The following year's *The Other Side* EP featured three new songs and acoustic versions of some of the band's best-known songs.

● ALBUMS: *Godsmack* aka *All Wound Up* (Republic/Universal 1997) ★★★, *Awake* (Republic/Universal 2000) ★★★, *Faceless* (Republic/Universal 2003) ★★★★, *The Other Side* mini-album (Republic/Universal 2004) ★★★.

● DVD/VIDEOS: *Live* (Aviva International 2001), *Smack This!* (Republic/Universal 2002), *Changes* (Rounder/Universal 2004).

Godspeed You Black Emperor!

Disenfranchised Canadian outsiders Godspeed You Black Emperor! appropriate their lengthy moniker from a Japanese motorbike gang, probably via Mitsuo Yanagimachi's documentary *Buraku Empororu*. The collective was formed in Montreal, Quebec, in 1994 by Efrim Menuck (guitar), Roger Tellier-Craig (guitar), Bruce Caudron (drums), Aidan Girt (drums), Mauro Pezzente (bass), Thierry Amar (bass), Norsola Johnson (cello), Sophie Trudeau (violin), and David Bryant (guitar, tapes). That year's *All Lights Fucked On The Hairy Amp Drooling* was a cassette-only release, with a print run of just 33 copies and, notably featured track titles such as 'Revisionist Alternatif Wound To The Haircut Hit Head' and 'Perfumed Pink Corpses From The Lips of Ms Dion'. Portentous by more than one definition, the collective creates romantically pessimistic music that is pretentiously weighty and full of unspecifiable significance.

Finding the world we live in 'lost, violent and obscene', they explore eschatological concerns through atmospheric, apocalyptic rock. Importantly, their music is under-pinned with political intent (although they claim to encompass disparate opinions and standpoints). Unusually for such a politically motivated band, Godspeed You Black Emperor! forge lyric-free music. Rather, they frame their compositions with field recordings and tape manipulation to create ad hoc narratives: on 'Blaise Bailey Finnegan III' (from the *Slow Riot For New Zero Kanada* EP), an increasingly agitated invective reads 'I don't like the way the country's ran, don't you know? The American government, they're sneaky, they're very deceitful, they're liars, they're cheats, they rip-offs'. A repeated, manipulated folk sample at the close of 'Providence' (from *F#A#∞*) asks simply 'Where are we going?'

These monologues foreground the collective's latent anger and despair, although whether such rants are intended to be taken as documentary or opinion is unclear. They are astute enough to find contradiction in **Radiohead**'s anti-corporate politics while signed to a subsidiary of **EMI Records** and, equally, highlight their own short-comings in their decision to create music rather than pursue more direct political action: 'I think there are forces of evil in this world', Menuck has stated in esoteric music magazine *The Wire*. 'I think that global capitalism is just one inch away from being everywhere. I think that now is not the time to be frittering away playing in a silly-assed post-rock band.' That said, permutations of the collective also create music under a number of different identities including A Silver Mt. Zion, 1-Speed Bike, Exhaust and Fly Pan Am.

● ALBUMS: *All Lights Fucked On The Hairy Amp Drooling* (Own Label 1994) ★★★, *F#A#∞* (Constellation/Kranky 1997) ★★★★, *Slow Riot For New Zero Kanada* mini-album (Constellation/Kranky 1999) ★★★, *Lift Your Skinny Fists Like Antennas To Heaven* (Constellation/Kranky 2000) ★★★, as Godspeed You! Black Emperor *Yanqui U.X.O.* (Constellation 2002) ★★★.

Godspell

One of the first of the rock-type religious musicals that began to emerge in the 70s, *Godspell* opened off-Broadway at the Cherry Lane Theatre in New York on 17 May 1971. It had a book, by John-Michael Tebelak, that was based on the Gospel according to St Matthew, and music and lyrics by newcomer **Stephen Schwartz**. The cast included Stephen Nathan (Jesus) and David Haskell (Judas), and the score contained songs such as 'All Good Gifts', 'Save The People', 'Prepare Ye The Way Of The Lord', 'Light Of The Best', and 'Day By Day', a number that epitomizes this style of production, and which became an enormous US hit in a version by the Broadway original cast. After 2,124 performances, the show moved to a main house, the Broadhurst Theatre, for a further 527. The cast of the London production, which stayed at Wyndham's Theatre for nearly three years, included **Julie Covington**, **David Essex**, **Marti Webb**, and the future movie heartthrob Jeremy Irons. A 1993 revival at the Barbican Hall in London, which starred the actress and singer Gemma Craven, was not helped by the fact that 'Andy Crane, the blond and denimed children's television personality signed up to play Jesus, is strikingly uncharismatic and bland—this resurrection is not good news'. Also in 1993, Los Angeles saw *Godspell—Now!*, a contemporary reinterpretation of the original show, based around the riots in that city in April 1992.

Godz

Originating from Cleveland, Ohio, USA, the Godz were a heavy metal band with a strong 'biker' image. Formed in 1977, they featured vocalist/bass player Eric Moore, guitarist Mark Chatfield, drummer Glen Cataline and guitarist/keyboard player Bob Hill. Their first album, produced by **Grand Funk**'s Don Brewer, was an intensely powerful barrage with raw, gutsy vocals filtered through its core, which remains something of a metal minor-classic. *Nothing Is Sacred* was self-produced and featured Cataline on vocals, the most obvious contributory factor to the disappointment it brought on almost every level. The band split soon after the album's release. In 1985 Moore and Chatfield resurrected the name and a new partnership was forged with former **Outlaws** guitarist Freddy Salem and drummer Kevin Valentine. *I'll Get You Rockin'* materialized, but met with a lacklustre reception. In 1987 most of the album was remixed and re-recorded, with three new tracks added and re-released as *Mongolians*. However hard they have tried, the Godz have never recaptured the energy and excitement generated by their debut.

● ALBUMS: *The Godz* (Millenium 1978) ★★★★, *Nothing Is Sacred* (Millenium 1979) ★★, *I'll Get You Rockin'* (Heavy Metal 1985) ★★, *Mongolians* (Grudge 1987) ★★.

Goedert, Ron

b. USA. Before embarking on a solo career Goedert had previously led White Witch. His new group, which featured Jerry Runyman on guitar, Riff West on bass and Jack West on drums, in addition to his own singing and keyboard playing, continued his fixation with 60s west coast counterculture. The cover of *Breaking All The Rules* depicted Goedert in huge flared trousers, matching the esotericism of the lyrical contents. Similar to **Hawkwind** in its employment of far-flung themes, it failed to cultivate a similar niche audience.

● ALBUMS: *Breaking All The Rules* (Polydor 1980) ★★.

Goetz, E. Ray

b. 12 June 1886, Buffalo, New York, USA, d. 12 June 1954 Greenwich, Connecticut, USA. Also billed as Ray Goetz, he was active as a songwriter on Broadway in the 10s and as a producer in the 20s. Some of his songs were included in *Ziegfeld Follies Of 1907*, *The Gay White Way* and *Two Islands* (all 1907), *The Prince Of Bohemia* and *A Matinee Idol* (both 1910), *The Hen-Pecks* and *The Never Homes* (both 1911), *Hokey-Pokey/Bunty*, *Bulls And Strings* and *Hanky Panky* (all 1912). In addition to lyrics, Goetz also wrote the music and sometimes the libretto for shows such as *Roly Poly/Without The Law* and *The Sun Dodgers* (both 1912), *All Aboard* and *The Pleasure Seekers* (both 1913), *Hands Up* (1915), *Step This Way* (1916), *Hitchy-Koo* and *Words And Music* (both 1917), both of which he also produced as he did *Follow The Girl* (1918), *As You Were* (1920, which starred **Irene Bordoni**, to whom he was married for a time), and *The French Doll* (1922). He contributed lyrics to songs for **George White's Scandals** of 1922 and 1923. He produced *Little Miss Bluebeard* (1924), *Naughty Cinderella* and *Mozart* (both 1926), *Paris* (1928), also composing the music, *The Lady Of The Orchids* (1928, also libretto), **Fifty Million Frenchmen** (1929, which was **Cole Porter**'s first big hit show) and *The New Yorkers* (1930), the latter based upon a story of his. Among his many songs were 'Do I Love You?' (with Henri

Christiné), 'Yaka Hula Hickey Dula' (**Joe Young**–Pete Wendling), and best known of all, 'For Me And My Gal' (**Edgar Leslie**–George W. Mayer). Used in numerous shows and films, this song also provided the title for the 1942 film *For Me And My Gal* (UK title: *For Me And My Girl*), wherein it was sung by **Judy Garland** and **Gene Kelly**.

Goffin/King

(see **Goffin, Gerry**; **King, Carole**)

Goffin, Gerry

b. 11 February 1939, New York City, USA. Goffin was a chemistry major at New York's Queens College when he met fellow student **Carole King**. Both harboured songwriting ambitions and pooled resources when the former's lyrical gifts gelled with the latter's musical talent. The now-married couple were introduced to publisher **Don Kirshner** in 1960 following the release of 'Oh! Neil', King's answer disc to **Neil Sedaka**'s 'Oh! Carol'. They joined the staff of the magnate's Aldon company, where their early compositions included 'Will You Still Love Me Tomorrow?' (the **Shirelles**), 'Take Good Care Of My Baby' (**Bobby Vee**), 'Go Away Little Girl' (**Steve Lawrence**) and 'Up On The Roof' (the **Drifters**). Goffin also enjoyed success with Jack Keller and **Barry Mann**, but the compositions he produced with his wife ultimately proved the most memorable. Together they wrote 'The Loco-Motion' (**Little Eva**), 'One Fine Day' (the **Chiffons**), 'I'm Into Something Good' (**Earl-Jean/Herman's Hermits**), 'Just Once In My Life' (the **Righteous Brothers**) and 'Oh No Not My Baby' (**Maxine Brown/Manfred Mann**), and as the 60s developed so Goffin's lyrics developed from the mundane to the meaningful.

'Don't Bring Me Down', a 1966 hit for the **Animals**, established a personal perspective, while the images evoked in **Aretha Franklin**'s 'A Natural Woman'—'when my soul was in the lost and found, you came along to claim it'—verged on the poetic. His ability to assume a feminine perspective emphasized a now incontrovertible skill, consolidated in the introspection of 'Goin' Back' (**Dusty Springfield**/the **Byrds**) and the anti-suburbia protest of 'Pleasant Valley Sunday' (the **Monkees**). However, pressure both professional and personal undermined the couple's relationship and their marriage ended in 1967. Whereas King forged a second successful career during the 70s singer-songwriter boom, Goffin enjoyed a less public profile. Bereft of a melodious partner and out of place in an era where musicians both composed and performed, he remained in the public eye due to the enduring popularity of his early compositions. **Blood, Sweat And Tears** recorded 'Hi De Hi', **Grand Funk Railroad** covered 'The Loco-Motion', while his ex-wife later paid tribute to their partnership with *Pearls*, a selection of their 60s collaborations. During the 70s Goffin worked as a producer for several artists, including **Diana Ross**. He did record a solo album, *It Ain't Exactly Entertainment*, in 1973, but it failed to emulate the popularity of his former partner. Goffin's contribution to popular music is considerable and many of former hits are now classics. Always literate and melodic, his work remains timeless. He had a second attempt at fame as a recording artist in 1996.

● ALBUMS: *It Ain't Exactly Entertainment* (Adelphi 1973) ★★, *Back Room Blood* (Adelphi 1996) ★★.

● COMPILATIONS: *The Goffin And King Songbook* various artists interpretations of Goffin And King compositions (Columbia 1989) ★★★.

Gogmagog

This group was formed in 1985 in London, England, by **Jonathan King**, who wanted to create some sort of heavy-metal theatre. At first he attracted the interest of **Cozy Powell** and **John Entwistle**, but they elected to concentrate on other projects. The line-up was eventually finalized as Paul Dianno (ex-**Iron Maiden**; vocals), Clive Burr (ex-Iron Maiden; drums), Pete Willis (ex-Def Leppard; guitar), Janick Gers (ex-**White Spirit**; guitar) and Neil Murray (ex-**Whitesnake**; bass), a line-up that saw Gogmagog christened a **New Wave Of British Heavy Metal** 'supergroup'. To test critical reaction, King put Gogmagog in a studio to record three songs that he had written with **Russ Ballard**. With these tracks in hand, King visited various major record companies to see if there was any support, and all showed a genuine interest in the project. The only stumbling block was King's insistence on a substantial advance, which saw him universally rejected. The project subsequently disintegrated, and the members of Gogmagog went their separate ways. After the group's demise, a three-track single appeared on Music For Nations subsidiary Food For Thought, entitled 'I Will Be There'. The group's music was in contradiction to the heavy metal tag it was given, being closer to pop, with only a slight nod towards the musicians' rock roots.

Goines, Victor

b. 6 August 1961, New Orleans, Louisiana, USA. Studying clarinet from the age of eight, Goines began adding various members of the saxophone family to his instrumental arsenal while attending high school. In 1980 he studied clarinet and saxophones at Loyola University, graduating in 1984. Shortly before graduation, he had become interested in jazz and sought tuition from **Ellis Marsalis**, who soon inducted him into his working quartet. In 1987 Goines extended his studies, this time at Virginia Commonwealth University. While there, he occupied any spare time by playing in New York with artists such as **Lionel Hampton**, **Bobby Watson**, **Jack McDuff** and singer **Ruth Brown**, and he also played in the orchestra for the Broadway show *Black And Blue*. Back in his home town in 1991, he attracted considerable attention with award- and competition-winning performances and soon thereafter made his first solo album. As a performer, he toured with **Wynton Marsalis** in 1993/4, and worked with **Marcus Roberts**, **Terence Blanchard**, the Lincoln Center Jazz Orchestra and the Smithsonian Jazz Masterworks Orchestra, playing clarinet, alto, tenor and baritone saxophones.

Goines' recording credits include appearances on sessions with Ellis and Wynton Marsalis (including the latter's *Blood On The Fields*), Roberts, the LCJO, **Donald Harrison** and Damon Short, and with singers Brown, **Germaine Bazzle** and **Irma Thomas**. He has also played on scores for films and television and on numerous music videos, including those by **Linda Ronstadt** and **Aaron Neville**, **Dianne Reeves**, **Bobby McFerrin** and **Chick Corea**, and Wynton Marsalis. From his early days as a professional musician, Goines was interested in pursuing a career as a jazz educator and worked at the universities of Xavier, Loyola and New Orleans. He has conducted workshops and clinics in New Orleans and at Cornell University among many venues. Late in 2000, he was appointed Director of Juilliard Jazz Studies, a new collaborative venture by the Juilliard School and Jazz at Lincoln Center.

● ALBUMS: *Genesis* (AFO 1991) ★★★, *Joe's Blues* (Rosemary Joseph 1998) ★★★★, *To Those We Love So Dearly* (Rosemary Joseph 1999) ★★★.

Going Hollywood

Bing Crosby was on temporary loan from Paramount for this 1933 MGM release, which teamed him with Marion Davies, who, despite being a talented actress, is best-known for her friendship with millionaire newspaper tycoon William Randolph Hearst. Screenwriter Donald Ogden Stewart's slight story concerns a young teacher (Davies), who follows her crooning idol (Crosby) to Hollywood, and masquerades as a maid before playing a starring role in Bing's latest movie (and his subsequent personal life) when his leading lady (Fifi D'Orsay) hits the bottle. Generously built comedienne Patsy Kelly, who had enjoyed success in Broadway revues, made a big impression in her screen debut, and the cast also included Stuart Erwin, Bobby Watson, Ned Sparks and Sterling Holloway. **Nacio Herb Brown** and **Arthur Freed** wrote songs, and one of them, the powerful 'Temptation', became popular for Crosby at the time of the picture's release, and was revived by **Perry Como** some 10 years later. The other songs included the spirited 'Going Hollywood', 'Beautiful Girl', 'After Sundown', 'Our Big Love Scene', and 'We'll Make Hay While The Sun Shines' which became a record hit for Crosby and was also popular with the British dance bands of the period, particularly Billy Merrin And His Commanders. *Going Hollywood* was directed by Raoul Walsh and the choreographer was **Albertina Rasch**. Bing Crosby did not appear in another film for MGM until **High Society** in 1956.

Going My Way

This enormously successful light-comedy musical was released by Paramount in 1944. It starred **Bing Crosby** as Father Chuck O'Malley, a young priest whose attempts to introduce order to the run-down St. Dominick's Church in a tough area of New York, bring him into conflict with the crotchety long-time incumbent, Father Fitzgibbon (Barry Fitzgerald). Frank Butler and Frank Cavett's screenplay (from an original story by producer-director Leo McCarey) was warm and tender, without being maudlin, but there was not a dry eye in the house when, towards the end, the two men resolve their differences and Father Fitzgibbon is reunited with his aged mother (Adeline DeWalt Reynolds). Crosby and Fitzgerald were splendid together, and the admirable supporting cast included Risë Stevens, Jean Heather, Frank McHugh, Gene Lockhart, William Frawley, Carl Switzer, Stanley Clements, James Brown, and the Robert Mitchell Boys' Choir. **Jimmy Van Heusen** and **Johnny Burke** wrote three of the songs: 'The Day After Forever' (Crosby-Heather), 'Going My Way' (Crosby-Stevens), and the lively 'Swinging On A Star', which Crosby performed in beguiling style at the piano, surrounded by a group of youngsters. He also gave a memorable reading of the lovely 1914 ballad 'Too-Ra-Loo-Ra-Loo-Ral' (J.R. Shannon). The rest of the score comprised 'Silent Night' (Franz Gruber), 'Ave Maria' (Schubert), and 'Haberna' (Bizet). Not only was *Going My Way* one of the top money-spinners of the decade, it also scooped the Oscars for 1944, winning for best picture, actor (Crosby), supporting actor (Fitzgerald), director (McCarey), original story (McCarey), and song ('Swinging On A Star'). Bing Crosby reprised his role of Father O'Malley in *The Bells Of St. Mary's*, which was released by RKO in 1945. This time he was called upon to win over Sister Benedict (Ingrid Bergman) at the local Catholic school, but luckily still found the time to sing 'Aren't You Glad You're You?' (Van Heusen-Burke). *The Bells Of St. Mary's* was even more successful at the box-office than *Going My Way*.

Going Steady

This 1979 Israeli film was a successor to **Lemon Popsicle**. Taking its cue from 50s revival films such as **American Graffiti** and **Grease**, *Going Steady* revolved around the antics of high-school students. However, the film failed to re-create the atmosphere of the times, a feature compounded by a series of anachronisms. The equally expansive soundtrack included material by **Jerry Lee Lewis**, **Brian Hyland**, **Bobby Darin** and **Chubby Checker**, as well as **Debbie Reynolds**. Her hit song 'Tammy' inspired the name given to the central character in this largely forgettable film.

Goins Brothers

A brother bluegrass act formed in 1953 by Melvin (b. Melvin Glen Goins, 30 December 1933, Bramwell, West Virginia, USA; guitar, bass fiddle, vocals, comedy) and his brother Ray (b. Ray Elwood Goins, 3 January 1936, Bramwell, West Virginia, USA; banjo, vocals). The Goins came from a musical family and grew up influenced by the major bluegrass acts that played in their locality. In the late 40s, Melvin was a member of the **Lonesome Pine Fiddlers** and in 1951, he was joined in the band by his 15-year-old brother. In 1952, they played on **RCA Victor** recordings with the Fiddlers but the following year, when the Fiddlers moved to Detroit, they formed a trio with fiddler Ralph Meadows. About 1954, the Fiddlers returned to West Virginia and the brothers made further recordings and worked at different venues, including WLSI Pikeville, Kentucky, with them, until 1955. For some years they toured on their own before rejoining the Fiddlers in 1961. They stayed until 1964, during which time they made Starday recordings with the band and played regularly on television with them in Bristol, Virginia. Ray left the music in 1964 and Melvin worked with other bluegrass artists, including **Hylo Brown** and notably with the **Stanley Brothers**, where he sang lead vocals, played guitar and also did comedy as Big Wilbur. When Ray returned to the music, they formed the Goins Brothers band and started a long period of playing bluegrass festivals, some of which Melvin promoted, that continued into the 90s. Their younger brother Conley later became their bass player and at times, Melvin's wife, Willa and her three sisters, billed as the Woodettes, sang harmony gospel numbers with them. The Goins Brothers also appeared at schools and colleges and from the mid-70s, they presented a weekly television show on WKYH-TV at Hazard, Kentucky. Melvin and two other band members, performing as the Shedhouse Trio, sang cowboy and comedy songs as part of their regular show. They first recorded for Rem in 1969 but later recorded albums for Jalyn, Jessup, Rebel and Old Homestead. In the late 80s, they recorded for Vetco and have issued their own cassette recordings, including one recorded live at the University of Chicago Folk Festival.

Ray retired in the late 90s, but Melvin continued recording and performing with his new band, Windy Mountain. In 1999, they released *Bluegrass Blues* on the Hay Holler label.
● ALBUMS: *Bluegrass Hits: Old And New* (Rem 1969) ★★★, *Bluegrass Country* (Jalyn 1970) ★★, *In The Head Of The Holler* (Jessup 1973) ★★★, *A Tribute To The Lonesome Pine Fiddlers* (Jessup 1973) ★★★★, *God Bless Her She's My Mother* (Jessup 1974) ★★, *The Goins Brothers* (Rebel 1976) ★★★, *On The Way Home* (Rebel 1977) ★★★, *Take This Hammer* (Rebel 1977) ★★★, *Wandering Soul* (Rebel 1980) ★★★, *At Their Best* (Old Homestead 1981) ★★★★, *Second Edition: Most Requested Hymns* (Old Homestead 1981) ★★, *Sweet Sunny South* (Old Homestead 1986) ★★★.

Goins, Herbie

Goins, like **Geno Washington**, was a former US serviceman who remained in the UK when his military service ended. In 1963 he joined **Alexis Korner**'s Blues Incorporated and was featured vocalist on several of this seminal band's releases, including *Red Hot From Alex* and *At The Cavern*. In 1965 he left to lead Herbie Goins And The Night Timers, which became a highly popular attraction in London's clubs. The group was signed to **Parlophone Records**, for whom they recorded several excellent dance-orientated soul singles, including 'The Music Played On' (1965), 'Number One In Your Heart' and 'Incredible Miss Brown' (both 1966). In 1967 the Night Timers recorded their only album. *Number One In Your Heart* is an exciting set, with swinging versions of such club standards as 'Pucker Up Buttercup', 'Knock On Wood' and 'Look At Granny Run, Run', but it was deemed anachronistic when compared with the contemporary psychedelic trends. The group broke up in 1968.
● ALBUMS: *Number One In Your Heart* (Parlophone 1967) ★★★.

Golbey, Brian

b. Brian James Golbey, 5 February 1939, Pyecombe, Sussex, England. Golbey inherited a love of early American country music from his father, who had already taught him to play harmonica and melodeon by the time he was given a guitar for his eleventh birthday. He was soon playing along with **Jimmie Rodgers** recordings and, in 1953, he earned his first money singing 'Little Joe The Wrangler' at a Coronation celebration party. He next learned to play a fiddle that his grandfather had brought back from France in World War I and began to entertain during National Service in the army. He played clubs during the folk revival of the early 60s and around 1965, he helped to start what was probably one of the first country music clubs in the UK. In 1966, he turned professional and made his recording debut playing fiddle on **Paul Jones'** first solo album. In 1967, he teamed up with banjoist Pete Stanley. They toured, made radio and television appearances and, during 1969/70, played residencies in Florence and Rome. In 1970, Golbey became a solo act on the emerging British country music scene and made his own first recordings. He also made his first visit to America, appearing in Nashville as the British representative on the International Show and on the *Midnight Jamboree*. He also appeared on the noted *Wheeling Jamboree* and the *Renfro Valley Barn Dance*. He toured the UK with **Patsy Montana** and **Mac Wiseman**, and in 1972, won the *Billboard/Record Mirror* award as Top UK Solo Performer and the Male Vocalist of the Year

award from the British Country Music Association. A further trip to America followed. In 1975, he and Allan Taylor formed the folk-orientated band Cajun Moon, but various problems and differences of opinion arose, and after recording a single album, the band broke up. In 1977, Golbey again began to work partly with Stanley and until the mid-80s, when for personal reasons he decided to reduce travelling commitments, they toured on a regular basis to Switzerland, Germany, Norway, Belgium, Holland and France (Golbey and Stanley maintain their friendship and still appear on occasions together). Golbey married Sandra Youngman in 1969; the marriage produced two sons, James (b. 1971) and David (b. 1973), but ended in divorce. He married Sandi Stubbs in 1980 and they have a son Daniel (b. 1985). Over the years, Golbey has done voice-overs for radio and television commercials and also appeared in a film, *The American Way* (although he stresses it is through no fault of his own that the film sank without trace). He has played in locations ranging from the Shetland Islands to Lands End and Berne to Belfast and in venues that vary from small school halls to the Albert Hall and from pubs to the Palladium. Working as a session musician, he has played on countless recordings but fondly remembers contributing 'Widdicombe Fair' and 'My Darling Clementine' for a mid-80s nursery rhyme album by Tim Hart (of **Steeleye Span**) & Friends. Apart from his albums, other Golbey recordings appear on various compilation albums. In 1993, the BCMA (GB) honoured him with an award for his long and continuing service to country music. A pioneer of British country music and a knowledgeable expert on early country music artists, he regularly contributes to the UK magazine *Country Music People*.
● ALBUMS: *The Old And The New* (Lucky 1970) ★★★, *Virginia Waters* (Phoenix 1972) ★★★, *Silver Haired Daddy Of Mine* (Avenue 1973) ★★★★, *Moments* (Emerald Gem 1974) ★★★, *Cajun Moon* (Chrysalis 1976) ★★★, *The London Tapes* (Waterfall 1977) ★★, with Pete Stanley *When The Dealing Is Done* (Waterfront 1979) ★★★, with Nick Strutt *Last Train South* (Waterfront 1983) ★★★, *Dew On The Purple Sage Tonight* (Swamp Opera 1999) ★★★★.

Gold Chains

b. Topher LaFata, Reading, Pennsylvania, USA. Gold Chains is a serial collaborator who has worked with electronic wizards **Kid 606** and **Kit Clayton** to create booty-quaking music for crowded house parties. The San Francisco–based producer/rapper forges a weird and wonderful hybrid of experimental musics. Although his first release, for the Orthlorng Musork label, proclaimed Gold Chains as 'the number one face in hip-hop', LaFata admits he actually perceives himself in a lineage of art-punk bands and electronic artists. He claims his preferred listening as German **techno** and music that is dark and relaxing. Showing admirable dedication to the Gold Chains cause, LaFata claims to care almost exclusively about 'beats, girls and clubs'. Although he has been self-described as 'the bedroom commander, the King of Love' Gold Chains has also stated that he eschews the extravagances of diamond rings and silk sheets in favour of spending his hard-earned dollars on DAT tapes, Moogs, ARP synthesizers and Roland 808s. Presumably intentionally, Gold Chain's boasts and gloats are often close to absurd and/or comedic—'Mountains of coke up in the VIP/Miles of gold ropes just hanging round me' he raps on 'Mountains Of Coke'—but there are genuinely exciting things going on in his distillation of hip-hop, techno, ghetto tech and rock 'n' roll. Gold Chains has released music via PIAS, Kit Clayton and Suzanne Constable's Orthlorng Musork, Kid 606's Tigerbeat6, and **Adult**'s Ersatz Audio label. Intriguingly, the rapper is reported to have a degree in Cognitive Neuroscience.

● ALBUMS: *Young Miss America* (PIAS 2003) ★★★★, with Sue Cie *When The World Was Our Friend* (Kitty-Yo 2004) ★★★.

Gold Diggers Of Broadway

This film, the first in a series of popular backstage musicals produced by Warner Brothers in the early days of sound, was released in 1929. It was adapted from Avery Hopwood's 1919 play *The Gold Diggers*, which the studio originally filmed as a silent in 1923. Robert Lord's charming and amusing screenplay was all about a trio of chorus girls played by Winnie Lightner, Nancy Welford and Anne Pennington, whose feminine charms break down all social barriers in their quest for well-heeled husbands. **Al Dubin** and **Joe Burke**'s tuneful score contained two enduring numbers, 'Painting The Clouds With Sunshine' and 'Tip Toe Through The Tulips', which were introduced by Nick Lucas, a singer with an appealing, easy-going style. He had enormous record hits with both of them. The rest of the songs included 'What Will I Do Without You?', 'And They Still Fall In Love', 'Go To Bed', 'In A Kitchenette', 'Song Of The Gold Diggers', and 'Mechanical Man'. Also in the cast were Conway Tearle, Lilyan Tashman, William Blakewell, and Helen Foster. The lively dance sequences were staged by Larry Ceballos, and the director was Roy Del Ruth. It was filmed in two-colour Technicolor, a process which, at times, could be surprisingly effective. Even as early as this in the evolvement of movie musicals, different studios were beginning to specialize in their own particular aspects of the genre: Paramount had their operettas with **Maurice Chevalier** and **Jeanette MacDonald**, MGM pioneered revue-type features, RKO were to enjoy tremendous success with the **Fred Astaire** and **Ginger Rogers** dance diversions, and Warners soon led the way (with MGM in hot pursuit) in memorable backstage sagas such as **42nd Street** and **Footlight Parade** and others in the same vein:
Gold Diggers Of 1933. **Dick Powell** and **Ruby Keeler**, who had made such a favourable impression in the aforementioned *42nd Street*, were reunited for this film, whose screenplay, by Erwin Gelsey, James Seymour, David Boehm and Ben Markson, was again based on that Avery Hopwood play. **Harry Warren** and Al Dubin's songs provided the inspiration for choreographer **Busby Berkeley**'s memorable production numbers, complete with his trademark 'top shots': 'We're In The Money', in which Ginger Rogers, her fellow chorus girls, and the stage on which they are performing, are completely clad in various-sized models of silver dollars (an ironic touch considering America was still in the midst of its worst Depression); 'Shadow Waltz', and a spectacular array of white-wigged girls in double-hooped dresses 'playing' neon-edged violins; and 'Pettin' In The Park', a risqué sequence, during which several apparently nude female forms are tantalizingly silhouetted behind flimsy roller blinds. When the blinds are raised the girls emerge dressed in *metal* costumes, and the scene ends with Dick Powell hard at work with a can opener! The most poignant sequence, though, is 'Remember My Forgotten Man', a powerful portrait of post–World War I disillusionment with the

American Dream, which culminates in three sets of armed soldiers marching over a curved bridge set, while, in the foreground, **Joan Blondell** sings the heart-rending lyric. All in all, with its persistent emphasis on the scarcity of money, the picture was as much a social document as a lively and entertaining musical. Also among the cast were Warren William, Aline MacMahon, Guy Kibbee, Ned Sparks, Sterling Holloway, and Dennis O'Keefe. Mervyn LeRoy directed, and this edition, and the rest of the series, was shot in more conventional black and white.
Gold Diggers Of 1935. Busby Berkeley served as director as well as choreographer, and this picture is mainly remembered for his creation of one of the most outstanding sequences in movie musical history based on the Oscar-winning song 'Lullaby Of Broadway'. It begins as dawn breaks, and ends 24 hours later. The spectacular climax comes when Dick Powell and Wini Shaw, a couple of good-time pleasure seekers, are seated high up in a nightclub looking down on a sensational orgy of power tap dancing, after which the girl falls to her death from a window. Another memorable number is 'The Words Are In My Heart', during which more than 50 girls seated at white pianos are slickly manoeuvred around in time with the music—by very small men, if you look closely enough. Harry Warren and Al Dubin also contributed the appealing 'I'm Going Shopping With You'. Manuel Seff and Peter Milne's slight screenplay (adapted from a story by Robert Lord and Peter Milne), concerns the efforts of the wealthy set to put on a lavish musical show at a country house (makes a change from a barn). Also involved were Adolph Menjou, Frank McHugh, Gloria Stuart, Glenda Farrell, Alice Brady, Joseph Cawthorn, Hugh Herbert, Grant Mitchell, and Virginia Grey.
Gold Diggers Of 1937. Dick Powell's last '*Gold Diggers*' outing found him cast as an insurance salesman who sells a $1 million life-insurance policy to a Broadway producer (**Victor Moore**) and ends up starring in the (still healthy) impresario's lavish show. Yet again Busby Berkeley came up with some marvellous production numbers including 'Let's Put Our Heads Together' (**Harold Arlen–E.Y. 'Yip' Harburg**) with its bevy of girls on rocking chairs, and the razzamatazz finalé, 'All's Fair In Love And War' (Warren-Dubin), in which Joan Blondell puts a kind of all-girl military band, some 70 strong, through their paces, predating the 'Seventy-Six Trombones' sequence in **The Music Man** by some 25 years. Powell also introduced the delightful 'With Plenty Of Money And You' (Warren-Dubin), and the score was completed by 'Life Insurance Song', 'Speaking Of The Weather', and 'Hush Ma Mouth' (Arlen-Harburg). Also cast were Glenda Farrell, Lee Dixon, Osgood Perkins, and Rosalind Marquis. Warren Duff wrote the screenplay and the director was Lloyd Bacon.
Gold Diggers In Paris (1938). **Rudy Vallee** takes a three-girl dance act to Europe, where they are mistaken for a classical troupe—with the inevitable complications. Earl Baldwin and Warren Duff's slight story was just an excuse for more of Berkeley's ingenious ideas based around such numbers as 'I Wanna Go Back To Bali', 'The Latin Quarter', 'Put That Down In Writing', and 'A Stranger In Paree' (all Warren-Dubin), and 'Day Dreaming All Night Long', 'Waltz Of The Flowers' and 'My Adventure' (Warren-Mercer). Rosemary Lane was Vallee's love interest, and supporting the couple were Hugh Herbert, Allen Jenkins, and Gloria Dickson. the film was released as *Gay Imposters* in the UK and Ray Enright directed, but the *Gold Diggers* concept was worn out.

However, it resurfaced again in *Painting The Clouds With Sunshine* (1951). Named after one of the hit songs in the original 1929 film, it was loosely based on Avery Hopwood's story, only this time the girls (Virginia Mayo, Virginia Gibson and Lucille Norman) are sisters, and Las Vegas is the base for the male chase. Most of the songs were old standards, and the creaky screenplay was by Harry Clark, Roland Kibbee, and Peter Milne. **Gene Nelson**, **Dennis Morgan**, S.Z. Sakall, Tom Conway, and Wallace Ford tried their best to put some life in it, as did choreographer LeRoy Prince and director David Butler. It was photographed in Technicolor by William Jacobs, and, like the rest of what is regarded as an historic series, produced by Warner brothers.

Gold, Andrew

b. 2 August 1951, Burbank, California, USA. This accomplished guitarist/vocalist/keyboard player was the son of two notable musicians. His father, **Ernest Gold**, composed several film scores, including *Exodus*, while his mother, **Marni Nixon**, provided the off-screen singing voice for actors Audrey Hepburn and Natalie Wood in *My Fair Lady* and *West Side Story*, respectively. Andrew Gold first drew attention as a member of Los Angeles–based acts, The Fraternal Order Of The All, **Bryndle** and the Rangers. Both groups also featured guitarist Kenny Edwards, formerly of the **Stone Poneys**, and the pair subsequently pursued their careers as part of **Linda Ronstadt**'s backing group. Gold's skills as a musician and arranger contributed greatly to several of her releases, including *Prisoner In Disguise* and *Hasten Down The Wind*, while sessions for **Carly Simon**, **Art Garfunkel** and **Loudon Wainwright** were also undertaken. Gold completed his solo debut in 1975 and the following year he enjoyed a transatlantic hit with 'Lonely Boy'. A follow-up single, 'Never Let Her Slip Away', reached number 5 in the UK, while other chart entries included 'How Can This Be Love' and 'Thank You For Being A Friend'. However the artist was unable to circumvent an increasingly sterile sound and was dropped by his label in the wake of the disappointing *Whirlwind*. Gold continued to tour with Ronstadt as part of her back-up band before forming **Wax** with **Graham Gouldman** in 1986. In 1992 **Undercover** had a UK number 5 hit with a club version of 'Never Let Her Slip Away'. Gold concentrated on Nashville session work in the 90s, and wrote **Wynonna**'s number 1 US country hit 'I Saw The Light'. *The Spence Manor Suite* was his first full-blown country album.

● ALBUMS: *Andrew Gold* (Asylum 1975) ★★★, *What's Wrong With This Picture?* (Asylum 1976) ★★, *All This And Heaven Too* (Asylum 1978) ★★★, *Whirlwind* (Asylum 1979) ★★, *Since 1951* (Pony Canyon 1996) ★★★, *Halloween Howls* (Music For Little People 1996) ★★, as The Fraternal Order Of The All *Greetings From Planet Love* (J-Bird/Dome 1997) ★★★, *The Spence Manor Suite* (Dome 2000) ★★★, *Intermission* (Quarkbrain 2002) ★★★.

● COMPILATIONS: *Thank You For Being A Friend: The Best Of Andrew Gold* (Rhino 1997) ★★★, *Leftovers* (Quarkbrain 1998) ★★.

Gold, Brian And Tony

During a trip to Jamaica, Anthony Anderson (b. 1968, Birmingham, West Midlands, England) entered a variety of talent shows on the island, frequently appearing on the same bill as Brian Thompson (b. 1967, Kingston, Jamaica, West Indies), and they eventually formed an illustrious partner-ship. They decided to perform together as Brian And Tony Gold and with the demise of vocal groups were in the fortunate position of being regarded as *the* unrivalled vocal duo in Jamaica. They embarked on recording sessions for **King Jammy**, Mickey Bennett, **Donovan Germain**, **Philip 'Fatis' Burrell** and **Dave 'Rude Boy' Kelly**. Although the duo was primarily considered to be session singers, they released the occasional hit, including the haunting, anti-apartheid 'Can You', in 1992. The song showcased their distinctive style, which inspired **Sly And Robbie** to enrol the singers to perform with DJ **Red Dragon** on 'Compliments On Your Kiss'. The relaxed rhythm and smooth singing, combined with the laid-back DJ, was destined to cross over. The formula proved successful, and the single reached number 2 in the UK pop chart in 1994. Following their commercial success, the duo returned to Jamaica, where they recorded a series of notable songs including 'If Loving Was A Crime' with **Buju Banton**, who later released the favoured 'Searching For The Light' on his own Cell Block 321 label. The duo continue to release sporadic hits, including 'Girls Can't Do', 'All I Want', 'Free At Last', 'Ram Dance', 'Bulls Eye', and the popular combination hits 'Private Property' (with **Shabba Ranks**), 'Saturday Night At The Movies' (with **Lady Saw**), 'S.L.A.' (with **Junior Tucker**) and 'You Give Me Your Love' (with **Shaggy**).

● ALBUMS: *Green Light* (Pow Wow 1993) ★★, *Bulls Eye* (VP 1995) ★★★.

Gold, Ernest

b. Ernst Golder, 13 July 1921, Vienna, Austria, d. 17 March 1999, Santa Monica, California, USA. A composer, conductor and arranger for movies from the 40s through to the 80s, Gold was a child prodigy and wrote a full-length opera when he was only 13. After studying at the State Academy of Music in Vienna, he fled with his family to the USA in 1938, when the Nazis gained control of Austria. A year later his first symphony was performed by the NBC Orchestra. After writing a few popular songs such as 'Practice Makes Perfect' (with Don Roberts), which became popular on record for both **Bob Chester** and Al Lavelin in 1940, Gold moved to Hollywood in 1945, where he worked with George Antheil and began writing scores for a series of small budget films. These included *The Girl Of The Limberlost* (1945), *Smooth As Silk* (1946), *The Falcon's Alibi* (1946), *G.I. War Brides* (1947), *Lighthouse* (1947), *Wyoming* (1947), *Exposed* (1947), *Old Los Angeles* (1948), *Unknown World* (1951), *Jennifer* (1953), *Man Crazy* (1953), *Karamoja* (1954), *The Other Woman* (1954) and *The Naked Street* (1955). His breakthrough came when he was commissioned by director Stanley Kramer to conduct and/or orchestrate several movies, including two **Frank Sinatra** dramas, *Not As A Stranger* (1955) and *The Pride And The Passion* (1957). He also worked on **Matty Malneck**'s score for the acclaimed Billy Wilder picture *Witness For The Prosecution* (1957). Further Kramer projects followed, and Gold composed the scores for his *The Defiant Ones* (1958), *Inherit The Wind* (1960), *Judgement At Nuremberg* (1961), *Pressure Point* (1962), *A Child Is Waiting* (1963), and *Ship Of Fools* (1965). His scores for *On The Beach* (1959), *The Secret Of Santa Vittoria* (1969), and *It's A Mad, Mad, Mad, Mad World* (1963), were nominated for Oscars, with the latter also being nominated for best title song (written with **Mack David**). Gold won the Academy Award and two Grammys for his music to Otto Preminger's epic *Exodus* (1960), and there were hit instrumental versions of the main theme by **Ferrante And**

Teicher, Mantovani, and **Eddie Harris. Pat Boone** wrote a lyric for the re-titled 'Exodus Song'. Gold's other film music included *Unidentified Flying Objects* (1956), *Edge Of Hell* (1956), *Running Target* (1956), *Affair In Havana* (1957), *Man On The Prowl* (1957), *Too Much, Too Soon* (1958), *Wink Of An Eye* (1958), *Tarzan's Fight For Life* (1958), *The Screaming Skull* (1958), *The Battle Of The Coral Sea* (1958), *The Young Philadelphians* (1960), *A Fever In The Blood* (1961), *The Last Sunset* (1961), *The Wild McCullochs* (1975), *Fun With Dick And Jane* (1977), *Cross Of Iron* (1977), *Good Luck, Miss Wyckoff* (1979), *The Runner Stumbles* (1979), *Tom Horn* (1980), *Safari 3000* (1982). He also conducted and/or orchestrated *Unknown World* (1951), *Sirocco* (1951), *Jennifer* (1953), and *Daughter Of Horror* (1955), as well as composing the music for television projects such as *Footsteps* (1972), *The Small Miracle* (1973), *Betrayal* (1974), *Letters From Frank* (1979), *Marciano* (1979), *Wallenberg: A Hero's Story* (1985), *Dreams Of Gold: The Mel Fisher Story* (1986), and *Gore Vidal's Lincoln* (mini-series) (1988).

In parallel with his Hollywood career, Gold continued to write classical music, and served as the musical director of the Santa Barbara Symphony Orchestra and was founder and principal conductor of the Los Angeles Senior Citizens Orchestra. Gold's foray into the world of musical theatre was not successful, and his *I'm Solomon* closed after seven performances on Broadway in April 1968. His score for that show utilized folk music themes in an appealing way, a practice that he had previously used in some of his film work. Gold's chief collaborators were Robert Sour, Don McCray, Anne Croswell, and Jeanette Keller. His first wife was singer **Marni Nixon**, known particularly for dubbing the screen voices of Audrey Hepburn, Deborah Kerr, and Natalie Wood.

Gold, Graham

b. 5 July 1954, Ealing, London, England. Gold, who has been a DJ for over 25 years, has a reputation as one of the hardest working DJs in the UK. He broadcasts on Fridays and Mondays on London's Kiss 100 FM, DJs all over the world, promotes his own club nights and runs his own label, Good:As with business partner Giles Sawney. In the UK's *DJ* magazine readers' poll of the Top 100 DJs In The World, he was voted number 22. Gold is managed by **Judge Jules**' management company, Serious Artist Management. Originally, Gold was a soul DJ and played at the popular Caister Soul Weekends in the UK before presenting various radio shows, including one on London's Capital Radio. During the 80s, he broadcast on several **pirate radio** stations and wrote for the UK magazine *Blues And Soul*. His musical style is now more orientated towards **trance** and energetic, uplifting **house**. He has played at most of the major clubs and events in the south of England and has been a resident at 'Peach' at the Camden Palace for more than five years. He has also DJed in the antipodes, South Africa, Tel Aviv, Canada, USA and the Balearic Islands, visiting **Ibiza** several times during the summer clubbing season. He has mixed many **dance music** compilations and had two mix albums in the UK Top 10 simultaneously in 1997—*Kiss Mix 97* and *Club Cuts Volume 2*. He has remixed the work of artists such as Jez And Choopie, 666, Berri, Spirito, Ambrosia, Happy Nation, 2HD (aka **Ferry Corsten**) and **Carl Cox**. Always a crowd-pleasing DJ, Gold is also well liked within the music industry.

● COMPILATIONS: *DJs In The Box* (Urban Collective 1995) ★★★, *Kiss Mix* (PolyGram TV 1996) ★★★, *Worth Its

Weight In Gold (Bullion 1997) ★★★, *Club Cuts Volume 2* (Telstar TV 1997) ★★★, *Kiss Mix 97* (PolyGram TV 1997) ★★★, *Club Connect* (Future Sound & Vision 1998) ★★★, *Kiss Mix 98* (PolyGram TV) ★★★, *Graham Gold: Delicious* (Logic/BMG 1999) ★★★★.

Gold, Harry

b. Harry Goldberg, 26 February 1907, Dundrum, Dublin, Eire, d. 13 November 2005. Gold grew up in London from the age of four. He studied music and learned to play several reed instruments, starting his professional career on alto saxophone. Later, he settled on the uncommon bass saxophone as his primary instrument. His earliest engagement was with another young musician struggling to form his first band, **Joe Loss**. Gold also led a small dance band that included in its ranks the young guitarist **Ivor Mairants**. During the 20s and 30s Gold played in several top British dance bands including those led by Jack Padbury, **Roy Fox**, **Geraldo**, Bert Firman and **Oscar Rabin**.

It was during his stint with Rabin that Gold emerged as leader of a band-within-the-band; that was known as Harry Gold's Pieces Of Eight and became the basis of his own popular group. Playing a form of highly polished dixieland, the little band worked successfully during the late 40s, making its major breakthrough with an appearance at the 1947 Jazz Jamboree. Among his sidemen at one time or another were **Norrie Paramor**, **Bert Weedon** and **Geoff Love**. The band retained its popularity during the trad jazz boom of the early 50s, even though it was never really a part of the movement.

In 1956 Gold handed over leadership of the band to his brother, Laurie Gold, intending to concentrate on composing and arranging. However, he continued to play through the 60s and 70s, often obscurely or anonymously as a busy session musician and arranger. In the mid-70s, soon after an appearance as a member of the New Paul Whiteman Orchestra, Gold re-formed his Pieces Of Eight. He continued to lead the band, still playing its own smoothed-out but very musicianly brand of jazz, into the 80s. Gold disdainfully ignored the fact that he was 80 years old in 1987 and continued playing into the next decade. In 1991, the Pieces Of Eight broke up in some acrimony, but Gold played on, guesting with many bands throughout the UK, and appearing regularly at the Yorkshire Grey in London. He published his autobiography in 2000 and was still performing shortly before his death in November 2005.

Gold's playing of the bass saxophone was remarkably deft, and the sonority of the instrument added immeasurably to the sound of any band in which he played. Gold also performed in other areas of music, appearing with the Liverpool Philharmonic under **André Kostelanetz** in 1946 and under Charles Groves a quarter-century later. He also composed 'Rhapsody In Green: An Irish Rhapsody'.

● ALBUMS: *Harry Gold And His Pieces Of Eight* (Lake 1960) ★★★★, *Octagonal Gold* (Lake 1980) ★★★★, *Bouncing Back* (Lake 1988) ★★★, *Live In Leipzig* (Lake 2000) ★★★.

● FURTHER READING: *Gold, Doubloons & Pieces Of Eight*, Harry Gold.

Goldberg, Barry

b. 1941, Chicago, Illinois, USA. Goldberg was one of several white aspirants frequenting Chicago's blues clubs during the early 60s. He befriended guitarist **Michael Bloomfield** prior to forming the Goldberg-Miller Blues Band with itinerant Texan **Steve Miller**. Goldberg assumed the group's leadership on his partner's departure, and the resultant album is a fine example of pop-influenced R&B. An accomplished keyboard player, Goldberg was part of the back-up band supporting **Bob Dylan** on his controversial appearance at 1965's Newport Folk Festival. Sessions supporting **Mitch Ryder** preceded a brief spell with **Chicago Loop** before Goldberg joined the **Electric Flag**. The artist resumed his own career in 1968 with the Barry Goldberg Reunion. Several erratic albums followed including *Two Jews Blues*, which featured contributions from Bloomfield and **Duane Allman**, and a collaboration with **Neil Merryweather** and **Charlie Musselwhite**, *Ivar Avenue Reunion*. Goldberg also continued his session work and produced albums for Musselwhite and the **Rockets**, but has been unable to translate his status as a sideman into a coherent solo path.

● ALBUMS: *Blowing My Mind* (Epic 1966) ★★★, *The Barry Goldberg Reunion* (Buddah 1968) ★★★, with Mike Bloomfield *Two Jews Blues* (Buddah 1969) ★★, *Barry Goldberg And Friends* (Record Man 1969) ★★, *Streetman* (Buddah 1970) ★★★, with Neil Merryweather, Charlie Musselwhite *Ivar Avenue Reunion* (RCA 1970) ★★★, *Blasts From My Past* (Buddah 1971) ★★★, *Barry Goldberg* (Record Man 1974) ★★, *Barry Goldberg And Friends Recorded Live* (Buddah 1976) ★★★.

● COMPILATIONS: *Goldberg-Miller Blues Band: 1965–66 Blowing My Mind Plus* (Acadia 2003) ★★★.

Goldberg, Stu

b. Stuart Wayne Goldberg, 10 July 1954, Malden, Massachusetts, USA. Goldberg played the piano from the age of 10 and took up the organ a couple of years later but continued to study classical music. At the age of 16 he played with **Ray Brown**'s Quartet at the **Monterey Jazz Festival**. In 1974 he studied jazz at the University of Utah before moving to Los Angeles, and joining the **Mahavishnu Orchestra**. He plays in the necessary virtuoso manner and is much influenced by the generation of keyboard players, which includes **Herbie Hancock** and **Joe Zawinul**. When he left the Mahavishnu Orchestra he played with **Miroslav Vitous**, **Al DiMeola** and **Freddie Hubbard** before joining **Alphonze Mouzon** between 1976 and 1977. In 1978 he came to Europe as a soloist, recording for the Saba and Pausa labels. Goldberg relocated in the 80s to Los Angeles, where he worked with a number of leading Hollywood composers. He has since concentrated on writing his own scores for film and television, while still recording the occasional session as leader.

● ALBUMS: *Solos, Duos, Trios* (Saba 1979) ★★★, *Variations By Goldberg* (Pausa 1982) ★★★, *Fancy Glance* (Inakustik 1988) ★★★, *Going Home* (Rhombus 2001) ★★★★, *Dedication* (Dedication 2002) ★★★.

Golden Apple, The

Following its enthusiastic reception at the off-Broadway Phoenix Theatre, New York City, USA, in March 1954, *The Golden Apple* was rapidly moved uptown to the Alvin Theatre, where it reopened on 20 April. Based on Homer's *Iliad* and *The Odyssey*, **John Latouche** (book and lyrics) and **Jerome Moross** (music) transported those epic tales to the state of Washington in the early part of the 20th century. The story concerns the consternation caused in the town of

Angel's Roost when a travelling salesman named Paris (Jonathan Lucas) arrives unannounced in a balloon, and takes Helen (Kaye Ballard), the impressionable wife of old Sheriff Menelaus (Dean Michener), off to Rhododendron by-the-sea (not entirely against her will). For some reason, the intrepid Ulysses (Stephen Douglass), who has just returned from the Spanish-American War, leaves his wife Penelope (Priscilla Gillette), and sets off to retrieve the errant Helen. After a decade of excitement and adventure—during which time he engages successfully in fisticuffs with Paris—Ulysses is finally reunited with his incredibly patient spouse. As for the songs—which carried the story almost on their own— Kaye Ballard's languid reading of 'Lazy Afternoon' was one of the high points of a delicious score that is treasured in recordings by stage musical buffs the world over. The other numbers, a mixture of witty spoofs and appealing ballads, included 'Goona-Goona', 'It's The Going Home Together', 'Come Along, Boys', 'Doomed, Doomed Doomed', 'My Picture In The Papers', 'Store-Bought Suit', 'Helen Is Always Willing', 'My Love Is On the Way' and 'Scylla And Charybdis'. This 'brilliant, innovative theatre experience', which was just pipped for a Tony Award by **The Pajama Game**, but which won the New York Drama Critics Award for best musical, closed after only 127 performances. It was revived off-Broadway in 1962 (112 performances), and is regarded as something of a musical theatre legend.

● FURTHER READING: *The Golden Apple: A Musical In Two Parts*, John Latouche and Jerome Moross.

Golden Boy (dance)

b. Stefan Altenburger, Switzerland. Altenburger has released electronic and **techno** tracks under a variety of pseudonyms, and as Klettermax he released an album of techno tracks on Source Records in 1998. Shortly after this, he was impressed with the DJing of the Geneva-based singer **Miss Kittin**, whom he encountered at a Berlin club in 1999, mixing **New Order**'s 'Blue Monday' into one of his Klettermax recordings. Altenburger collaborated with her on his 2002 debut, *Or*, which first appeared on the German label Ladomat before being released in the USA on the hip Emperor Norton record, home to the acclaimed **Felix Da Housecat**. *Or* saw Altenburger and Miss Kittin developing their trademark sound of thumping beats and slick synthetics providing the backdrop for Kittin's oddball lyrics, sung deadpan and sometimes using a vocoder for added 'futuristic' effect. A beguiling combination, the album captured the glamour and kitsch of the European club scene. The UK dance label Illustrious licensed the duo's 'Rippin' Kittin'' and released it as a single in August 2002. Taking as its lyrical theme a woman contemplating committing murder (or possibly suicide), it featured lines such as: 'Mommy, can I go out and kill tonight?' and 'Please, I want to steal the kitchen knife and feel, feel like taking a life'. It was an international club hit and was even featured in US magazine **Rolling Stone**'s Top 10 Dance Songs of 2002. Altenburger has also received considerable recognition for his art and design work, for which he has won prizes in his native Switzerland.

● ALBUMS: with Miss Kittin *Or* (Emperor Norton 2002) ★★★★.

Golden Boy (stage musical)

Frank Sinatra is said to have tried to discourage **Sammy Davis Jnr.**, a fellow-member of the infamous 60s 'Clan', from continually submitting himself to the discipline of an eight-shows-a-week stint in a Broadway musical. Davis, a major star in nightclubs and on records, had made his debut on the 'great white way' in **Mr. Wonderful** in 1956, and, 12 years later, he ignored Sinatra's advice and opened in *Golden Boy* at the Majestic Theatre on 20 October 1964. Clifford Odets died a few months after he began to adapt his well-known play for this Broadway musical, and the work was finished by his friend, William Gibson. In a neat twist of both name and colour, the writers changed the name of the leading character, a boxer, from an Italian-American named Joe Bonaparte, to a Negro-American named Joe Wellington. Davis was impressive as the young fighter, who is determined to get out, get rich, and make it to the top. One of the oustanding features of the production was Donald McKayle's innovative and exciting choreography, particularly in the opening scene, which simulated a high-energy workout, and a marvellously conceived fight sequence.

The score, by **Charles Strouse** (music) and **Lee Adams** (lyrics), received a mixed press. There was one show-stopper, 'Don't Forget 127th Street', in which Wellington berates his young fans, telling them to be proud of their Harlem roots. Davis also had a couple of telling ballads, 'Night Song' and 'I Want To Be With You', and the rest of the score included 'Workout', 'Everything's Great', 'Gimme Some', 'Lorna's Here', 'This Is The Life', 'While The City Sleeps', 'Golden Boy', 'Colourful', 'No More', and 'The Fight'. Also in the cast were Kenneth Tobey, who played Tom Moody, the fighter's manager; Paula Wayne in the role of Lorna Moon, a lady who shares her favours with both of them, and **Billy Daniels** as Eddie Satin. Davis was credited with being the main reason that *Golden Boy* played for well over a year in New York, a total of 569 performances, but West End audiences were not so impressed, and the London Palladium production folded after nearly four months. A 25th anniversary edition of the show, with a new book by Leslie Lee, reworked music and lyrics, and starring Obba Babatunde, played venues such as Miami's Coconut Grove Playhouse and the Candlewood Playhouse in New Fairfield, Connecticut, in the late 80s–early 90s.

● FURTHER READING: *Golden Boy: The Book Of The Musical*, Clifford Odets and William Gibson.

Golden Carillo

New York, USA, rock duo Annie Golden and **Frank Carillo** can both boast of distinguished pasts in various rock genres. Guitarist, singer and songwriter Carillo had previously contributed to three major **Peter Frampton** albums, *Winds Of Change*, *Frampton's Camel* and *Something Happening*, plus two solo collections, *Rings Around The Moon* and *Street Of Dreams* for **Atlantic Records**. A prolific songwriter, his credits also include songs for **Joan Jett**'s platinum set, *Up Your Alley*, and the film soundtracks *Heartbreak Hotel* and *Prelude To A Kiss*. Vocalist, actor and songwriter Annie Golden previously fronted **Capitol Records**' recording artists the **Shirts** during the late 70s. They enjoyed one hit single in Europe, 'Hang Up The Phone', before Golden took up a Broadway acting career in productions of *Leader Of The Pack*, *Dinner At Eight*, *Ah Wilderness* and Steven Sondheim's *Assassins*. She also made brief television appearances in *Cheers* and *Miami Vice*, having previously taken a role in the movie *Hair*. Golden and Carillo hooked up during the 90s,

going on to release an album, *Toxic Emotion*, for Silenz Records in 1995, before setting out on a tour of Europe.
● ALBUMS: *Toxic Emotion* (Silenz 1995) ★★★.

Golden Dawn

This US group was formed in Austin, Texas, in 1967, when ex-Fugitives vocalist George Kinney joined high-school friends Tom Ramsey (guitar), Jimmy Bird (guitar), Bill Hallman (bass) and Bobby Rector (drums). Having taken their name from the Aleister Crowley book, *The Sect Of The Golden Dawn*, the quintet secured a recording contract with International Artists through the aegis of the **Thirteenth Floor Elevators**, whose guitarist, **Roky Erickson**, was also a former member of the Fugitives. *Power Plant* is regarded as one of the finest psychedelic albums to emerge from Texas, adeptly combining hooklines and experimentation, with the pulsating 'Starvation' an undoubted highlight. Promotion, however, was distinctly low-key and Golden Dawn split up soon after a brief period based in California. Kinney and Banks later published Erickson's poetry book, *Openers*, which in turn aided the latter's release from Rusk State Hospital.
● ALBUMS: *Power Plant* (Sarah 1968) ★★★★.

Golden Disc, The

Titled *The In-Between Age* for the USA, *The Golden Disc* starred ill-fated British rock 'n' roll star **Terry Dene**. This **Jack Good** discovery was briefly touted as a bona fide star, although none of his three UK chart entries actually reached the Top 10. A former record packer, Dene briefly enjoyed the limelight upon joining the army, but praise turned to derision when the singer was discharged following a nervous breakdown. The fiancée who 'would wait for him' promptly broke off their engagement and his recording career was left in tatters. He later joined the Salvation Army. Real-life events were certainly more interesting than the plot of this 1957 film, in which the owners of a café turn it into an expresso bar before founding a record label to showcase the acts performing there. With skiffle the fad of the moment, acts including **Nancy Whiskey** and Sonny Stewart And The Skiffle Kings featured in the cast alongside the disc jockey David Jacobs, crooner **Dennis Lotis** and the exceptional **Phil Seamen** Jazz Group. Other performers included future impresario Terry Kennedy, Sheila Buxton and Murray Campbell. *The Golden Disc* is not an auspicious feature, but the film serves as a timely reminder of Terry Dene's all too brief pop ascendancy.

Golden Earring

Formed in the Hague, Netherlands, in 1961, by George Kooymans (b. 11 March 1948, the Hague, Netherlands; guitar/vocals) and Rinus Gerritsen (b. 9 August 1946, the Hague, Netherlands; bass/vocals) along with Hans Van Herwerden (guitar) and Fred Van Der Hilst (drums). The group, initially known as the Golden Earrings, subsequently underwent several changes before they secured a Dutch Top 10 hit with their debut release, 'Please Go' (1965). By this point Kooymans and Gerritsen had been joined by Frans Krassenburg (vocals), Peter De Ronde (guitar) and Jaap Eggermont (drums) and the revitalized line-up became one of the most popular 'nederbeat' attractions. Barry Hay (b. 16 August 1948, Fyzabad, India; lead vocals, flute, saxophone, guitar) replaced Krassenburg in 1966, while De Ronde also left the group as they embraced a more radical direction. The group's first Dutch number 1 hit, 'Dong-Dong-Di-Ki-Di-Gi-Dong', came in 1968 and saw them branching out from their homeland to other European countries as well as a successful tour of the USA. Eggermont left the group to become a producer and was eventually supplanted by Cesar Zuiderwijk (b. 18 July 1948, the Hague, Netherlands) in 1969 as Golden Earring began courting an international audience with their compulsive *Eight Miles High*, which featured an extended version of the famous **Byrds** song.

After years of experimenting with various music styles, they settled for a straight, hard rock sound and in 1972 Golden Earring were invited to support the **Who** on a European tour. They were subsequently signed to Track Records and the following year had a Dutch number 1/UK Top 10 hit with 'Radar Love', which subsequently found its way into the US Top 20 in 1974. Despite this, they were curiously unable to secure overseas success, which was not helped by a consistently unstable line-up. Robert Jan Stips augmented the quartet between 1974 and 1976 and on his departure Eelco Gelling joined as supplementary guitarist. By the end of the decade, however, the group had reverted to its basic line-up of Kooymans, Gerritsen, Hay and Zuiderwijk, who continued to forge an imaginative brand of rock, and their reputation as a top European live act was reinforced by *Second Live*. With the release of *Cut* in 1982, Golden Earring earned themselves a US Top 10 hit with 'Twilight Zone'. This was followed by a triumphant tour of the USA and Canada, where further chart success was secured with 'Lady Smiles'. With various members able to indulge themselves in solo projects, Golden Earring have deservedly earned themselves respect throughout Europe and America as the Netherlands' longest surviving and successful rock group.

● ALBUMS: *Just Ear-rings* (Polydor 1965) ★★★, *Winter Harvest* (Polydor/Capitol 1966) ★★★, *Miracle Mirror* (Polydor/Capitol 1968) ★★★, *On The Double* (Polydor 1969) ★★★, *Eight Miles High* (Polydor 1969) ★★★, *Golden Earring (Wall Of Dolls)* (Polydor 1970) ★★★, *Seven Tears* (Polydor 1971) ★★★, *Together* (Polydor 1972) ★★★, *Moontan* (Polydor/MCA 1974) ★★★, *Switch* (Polydor 1975) ★★★, *To The Hilt* (Polydor 1976) ★★★, *Contraband* (Polydor 1976) ★★★, *Mad Love* (Polydor 1977) ★★★, *Live* (Polydor 1977) ★★★, *Grab It For A Second* (Polydor 1978) ★★★, *No Promises . . . No Debts* (Polydor 1979) ★★★, *Prisoner Of The Night* (Polydor 1980) ★★★, *2nd Live* (Polydor 1981) ★★★, *Cut* (21 1982) ★★★, *N.E.W.S. (North East West South)* (21 1984) ★★★, *Something Heavy Going Down—Live From The Twilight Zone* (21 1984) ★★★, *The Hole* (21 1986) ★★★, *Keeper Of The Flame* (Jaws 1989) ★★★, *Bloody Buccaneers* (Columbia 1991) ★★★, *The Naked Truth* (Columbia 1992) ★★★, *Face It* (Columbia 1994) ★★★, *Love Sweat* (Columbia 1995) ★★, *Naked II* (Arcade 1997) ★★★, *Paradise In Distress* (Arcade 1999) ★★, *Last Blast Of The Century* (Arcade 2000) ★★.

Solo: George Kooymans *Jojo* (Polydor 1972) ★★, *Solo* (Ring 1987) ★★. Barry Hay *Only Parrots, Frogs And Angels* (Polydor 1972) ★★★, *Victory Of Bad Taste* (Ring 1987) ★★. Rinus Gerritsen and Michel Van Dijk *Gerritsen En Van Dijk* (Atlantic 1979) ★★. Cesar Zuiderwijk as Labyrinth *Labyrinth* (21 1985) ★★.

● COMPILATIONS: *Hits Van De Golden Earrings* (Polydor 1967) ★★★, *Greatest Hits* (Polydor 1968) ★★★★, *Golden Earring Box* 5-LP box set (Polydor 1970) ★★★★, *Greatest Hits Volume 2* (Polydor 1970) ★★★, *Superstarshine Vol. 1* (Polydor 1972) ★★★, *The Best Of Golden Earring* (Polydor 1974) ★★★, *The Best Ten Years: Twenty Hits* (Arcade 1975) ★★★, *Fabulous Golden Earring* (Polydor 1976) ★★★, *Greatest Hits Volume 3* (Polydor 1981) ★★★★, *Just Golden Earrings* (Polydor 1990) ★★★, *The Complete Singles Collection 1 1965–1974* (Arcade 1992) ★★★★, *The Complete Singles Collection 1975–1991* (Arcade 1992) ★★★★.

● DVD/VIDEOS: *Clips* (Red Bullet 1984), *Live From The Twilight Zone* (RCA 1984), *Video EP* (Sony 1984), *Twilight Zone* (Musicvision 1991), *The Naked Truth (Acoustic Live)* (Columbia 1991), *Making Face It* (Sony Music Video 1995), *Last Blast Of The Century* (Arcade 2000), *Golden Earring At Rockpalast* (Wienerworld 2005).

Golden Gate Quartet

This four-piece vocal group, originally titled Golden Gate Jubilee Quartet, started singing together in the mid-30s at the Booker T. Washington High School in Norfolk, Virginia, USA. The group comprised Willie Johnson (baritone), Henry Owens (first tenor), Orlandus Wilson (b. *c.*1917, d. 1998, Paris, France; bass) and William Langford (second tenor). Influenced by the sound of jazz and by the **Mills Brothers**, their live reputation quickly grew. In 1937 they signed to the **Victor Records** subsidiary **Bluebird Records**, and recorded several singles (often in one take), including 'Go Where I Send Thee' and 'When The Saints Go Marching In'. After Claude Riddick replaced Langford as second tenor the band moved to New York, where they recorded with the folk singer **Lead Belly** in June 1940. Although predominantly gospel-orientated at first, the group branched out into pop and jazz with singles including 'Stormy Weather' and 'My Prayer'. They also played at President Franklin D. Roosevelt's inauguration ceremony, the first of a series of performances at the White House. In 1941 the group moved to **OKeh Records**, and enjoyed some success with a version of 'Comin' In On A Wing And A Prayer' in 1943. Wilson and Johnson saw service in the war, and Alton Bradley and Cliff Givens stepped in as replacements until 1946 (Givens then joined the **Ink Spots**). In 1948 they featured in the RKO musical *A Song Is Born* alongside **Benny Goodman** and **Louis Armstrong**. Other films to feature the group included *Star Spangled Rhythm*, *Hollywood Canteen* and *Hit Parade Of 1943*. Johnson left to become lead with the Jubilaires, and was replaced by Orville Brooks. Their output slowed down during the 50s, when they were joined by Caleb J.C. Ginyard of the Dixiaires, as they attempted, largely unsuccessfully, to adapt their sound to prevailing R&B trends. In 1959 they uprooted to France, with the promise of a two-year residency at the Casino de Paris. Only Wilson and Riddick remained as original members in the 70s, joined by Calvin Williams (second tenor) and Paul Brembly (baritone).

● COMPILATIONS: *35 Historic Recordings 1937-39* recordings (RCA 1983) ★★★, *Negro Spirituals* (Happy Bird 1983) ★★★, *Jubilee* (Ibach 1984) ★★★, *The Number 1's* (Ibach 1984) ★★★, *Spirituals* (EMI 1986) ★★★, *Historical Recordings From The 40s And 50s* (Columbia 1990) ★★★★, *Complete Recorded Works 1937-39* (Document 1996) ★★★, *Radio Transcriptions 1941-44* (Document 1997) ★★★.

Golden Palominos

This unorthodox rock act's profile has been much enhanced by the glittering array of celebrities who have contributed to their work. They are led by drummer Anton Fier (b. 20 June 1956, Cleveland, Ohio, USA), who gave birth to the Golden Palominos in 1981. Prior to this he had spent time in the ranks of experimental bands **Lounge Lizards**, the **Feelies** and **Pere Ubu**. The band's albums have seen guest appearances by John Lydon (the **Sex Pistols, PiL**), Michael Stipe (**R.E.M.**), **Arto Lindsay**, **Bill Laswell**, **John Zorn**, **Daniel Ponce**, **Richard Thompson**, **T-Bone Burnett**, **Jack Bruce** and **Syd Straw**, among others. The other core members of the band have included **Nicky Skopelitis** (guitar), Robert Kidney (guitar, vocals) and Amanda Kramer (vocals).

Both Thompson and Stipe made their bow with the Golden Palominos on 1985's *Visions Of Excess*, along with **Henry Kaiser** and Lydon. The maverick talents employed on the follow-up *Blast Of Silence* included **Peter Blegvad** and **Don Dixon**, though it failed to match the impact of the first two albums—an obvious example of the sum not being as great as the parts. *Drunk With Passion* featured Stipe on 'Alive And Living Now', while **Bob Mould** provided vocals on the excellent 'Dying From The Inside Out'. For *This Is How It Feels* in 1993, Fier avoided the super-session framework, recruiting instead singer **Lori Carson**, who added both warmth and sexuality to that and the subsequent *Pure*. Mainstays Skopelitis and Laswell were additionally joined by the guitar of **Bootsy Collins**.

The Golden Palominos more recent work has also seen Fier adopted by the **techno** cognoscenti of Britain, where he believes the most innovative modern music is being made. This has led to remixes of the band's work from **Bandulu** and **Psychick Warriors Of Gaia** appearing in UK clubs. *Dead Inside* was largely the work of Fier, Knox Chandler (guitar) and Nicole Blackman (vocals).

● ALBUMS: *The Golden Palominos* (OAO/Celluloid 1983) ★★★★, *Visions Of Excess* (Celluloid 1985) ★★★★, *Blast Of Silence* (Celluloid 1986) ★★★, *A Dead Horse* (Celluloid 1989) ★★★, *Drunk With Passion* (Nation/Charisma 1991) ★★★★, *This Is How It Feels* (Restless 1993) ★★★, *Pure* (Restless 1994) ★★★, *Dead Inside* (Restless 1996) ★★★.
● COMPILATIONS: *A History (1982–1985)* (Metrotone/Restless 1992) ★★★★, *A History (1986–1989)* (Metrotone/Restless 1992) ★★★, *The Best Of The Golden Palominos 1983–1989* (Music Club 1997) ★★★, *Surrealistic Surfer* (Dressed To Kill 2001) ★★★, *Run Pony Run: An Essential Collection* (Varèse Sarabande 2002) ★★★★.

Golden Smog

A side project for members of **Soul Asylum**, the **Jayhawks**, Run Westy Run, **Wilco** and the **Honeydogs**, the indie band Golden Smog kept the real names of those involved a closely guarded secret on the release of their debut album in 1996. However, the pseudonyms David Spear, Michael Macklyn, Raymond Virginia, Scott Summitt, Jarret Decatur-Lane and Leonardson Saratoga were deliberate clues—each including the actual middle name and part of the address of those involved. The songwriting credits, however, betrayed at least some of those involved—Kraig Johnson (Run Westy Run), Gary Louris and Marc Perlman (Jayhawks), Jeff Tweedy (Wilco) and Dan Murphy (Soul Asylum). The band first appeared in 1992 with the release of an EP, *On Golden Pond*, which featured **Chris Mars** of the **Replacements** on drums (he

was subsequently replaced by Noah Levy of the Honeydogs). Golden Smog's debut album was recorded in the autumn of 1994, the first occasion on which the band's various other activities allowed it. Recorded in just five days, *Down By The Old Mainstream* captured the band ethic: 'Once every six months we would learn a bunch of covers and play. It would be sloppy and fun. Then one day, we looked at what we had and said, "This is a really good band . . . Let's do it".' Keen to dismiss accusations of Golden Smog being a 'joke' band, **Rykodisc Records** released a pre-emptive single, 'Redheaded Stepchild', prior to the album's release in January 1996. It was followed by a tour in February and March. Former **Big Star** drummer Jody Stephens appeared on the follow-up, *Weird Tales*.
● ALBUMS: *Down By The Old Mainstream* (Rykodisc 1996) ★★★, *Weird Tales* (Rykodisc 1998) ★★★★.

Goldfinger

Goldfinger sprang from a new wave of ska punk bands formed in California, USA, in the wake of **Green Day** and the **Offspring**'s international breakthrough. Based in Los Angeles, Goldfinger blend elements of ska and punk (*à la* **Rancid** and **Reel Big Fish**) with emocore (as pioneered by Guy Piccoloto's pre-**Fugazi** group, Rites Of Spring). The band was formed in 1994 by John Feldmann (guitar/vocals), Darrin Pfeiffer (drums) and Simon Williams (bass), with Charlie Paulson (guitar) joining shortly afterwards. In keeping with the traditions of the west coast punk scene (as opposed to its east coast and UK counterparts), the quartet remained wary of any 'radical punk' tag: 'Punk was about being different, about being against the establishment. We're on the Warped Tour. We're on **MTV**. How fucking against the establishment can we possibly be?'. It took Goldfinger some time to break through, however. **Rick Rubin** of American Records was among many who turned down their demo tape, stating that they were too close in sound to Green Day. Eventually, they signed with Mojo Records. Instead of political subjects, Feldmann's lyrics focused on the time-honoured frustrations of boy-girl relationships—he pointed out that: 'I write what I know. Relationships affect me like the IRA probably affects Bono.' He also confessed that one particular girl provided the inspiration for much of Goldfinger's 1996 debut album; 'Only A Day' was about 'Wishing I could be with her', and the radio hit 'Here In Your Bedroom' about spending time with her.

Williams was replaced by Kelly Lemieux after the recording of the 1997 follow-up, *Hang-Ups*. Despite their punishing live schedule, the quartet also found the time to record the celebratory cover versions mini-album, *Darrin's Coconut Ass: Live From Omaha*. The studio set *Stomping Ground* and the live *Foot In Mouth* were eagerly snapped up by the band's loyal fanbase, but failed to reach a wider audience (understandable with the latter, as it was a limited edition release). Paulson was subsequently replaced by Brian Arthur (ex-Unloco). The new look quartet pursued a broader music palette with 2002's *Open Your Eyes* in the hope of reaching a wider market. They signed to Maverick Records for the release of 2005's *Disconnection Notice*. Feldmann is also an in-demand producer and engineer, working on albums by **Good Charlotte**, the **Used** and **Story Of The Year**.
● ALBUMS: *Goldfinger* (Mojo 1996) ★★★, *Hang-Ups* (Mojo 1997) ★★★, *Darrin's Coconut Ass: Live From Omaha* mini-album (Mojo 1999) ★★★, *Stomping Ground* (Mojo

2000) ★★, *Foot In Mouth* (Goldfinger 2001) ★★★, *Open Your Eyes* (Mojo/Jive 2002) ★★★, *Disconnection Notice* (Maverick 2005) ★★★.
● DVD/VIDEOS: *Live At The House Of Blues* (Kung Fu 2004).

Goldfrapp

b. Alison Goldfrapp, Enfield, Middlesex, England. While studying for a degree in fine art at Middlesex University in the early 90s, Goldfrapp found her vocation in music and provided vocals on *Maxinquaye*, the award-winning debut of the UK trip-hop artist, **Tricky**. She also toured with him and worked with another acclaimed UK **dance music** act, **Orbital** before pursuing a solo career. She came into contact with the UK soundtrack composer, Will Gregory in the late 90s and the pair found a shared interest in various kinds of music such as 60s French pop and Weimar Republic cabaret as well as movie soundtracks and electronica. Recorded over a five-month period in the remote Wiltshire countryside in late 1999, her debut, *Felt Mountain*, appeared to much acclaim in September 2000. The album's dramatic, emotional sound combined *avant garde* production and electronics with traditional musical values.
After being nominated for the 2001 Mercury Music Prize, Goldfrapp and Gregory elected to pursue a completely different direction on their second album. The upbeat glam rock of 2003's *Black Cherry* found greater favour with the record buying public, generating the UK hit singles 'Train', 'Strict Machine' and 'Twist'. The duo's third album *Supernature* was released at the end of August 2005, and spawned further UK hits with the singles 'Ooh La La', 'Number 1' and 'Ride A White Horse'.
● ALBUMS: *Felt Mountain* (Mute 2000) ★★★★, *Black Cherry* (Mute 2003) ★★★★, *Supernature* (Mute 2005) ★★★.
● DVD/VIDEOS: *Wonderful Electric: Live In London* (Mute 2004).

Goldie (70s)

(see **Ravan, Genya**)

Goldie (90s)

b. Clifford Price, 28 December 1985, Wolverhampton, Staffordshire, England. A distinctive visual as well as aural presence, graffiti artist, **hardcore**, **jungle** and drum 'n' bass innovator Goldie is distinguished by the gold-inlaid front teeth from which many assume he takes his name. In fact, Goldie is an abbreviation of 'Goldilocks', a nickname he earned from his gold-dreadlocked hip-hop days. Though he jealously guards his true identity, his origins can be fixed in Wolverhampton, England, where he was born to a Scottish mother and a Jamaican father. In his youth he travelled to Miami and New York but returned to subsidize his musical activities as a (somewhat unsuccessful) mugger. Possibly his most famous graffiti illustration was his 'Change The World' mural at Queens Park Rangers' Loftus Road football ground in London. Later his paintings, which had once been the main source of his criminal record, were sold for over £3,000 each. Goldie's early musical experiences were most notably conducted as part of the Metalheads collective (later **Metal-headz**) on hardcore imprint **Reinforced Records**. He had previously recorded a white label EP under the name Ajax Project and then 'Killer Muffin' as a solo artist. The

Metalheads' *Angel* EP was a major breakthrough for 'intelligent hardcore', and when offshoots of hardcore (an extreme hybrid of **techno**) mixed with reggae and evolved into jungle in 1993/4, Goldie found himself at the centre of the new movement. However, he had little time for **General Levy**, and other artists he saw as 'bandwagon jumpers'. His own 'Inner City Life' single maximized the possibilities of the drum 'n' bass sound of jungle, using them as a framework for melodious vocals (courtesy of Diane Charlemagne) and other musical innovations. Similarly, the sounds contained on *Timeless*, the first jungle album released on a major label and to find mainstream approval, eschewed any notion of observing **dance music** convention. He admitted to influences as diverse as the **Stranglers** (notably **Jean Jacques Burnel**'s bass), **10cc** and hip-hop behind this multi-layered recording. His compatriots in the project were **Moving Shadow Records**' boss Rob Playford, jungle artist Dillinja, keyboard player Justina Curtis and singers Diane Charlemagne and Lorna Harris, plus jazz musicians **Cleveland Watkiss** and **Steve Wil-liamson**. This array of talent ensured a multi-dimensional sound, underpinned by breakbeats and rolling cycles of rhythm. The press had finally found a figurehead for the previously anonymous jungle movement, a role Goldie subsequently lived up to in sometimes reckless style. The uneven 1998 set *Saturnz Return* was, for all its failings, jungle's most ambitious album to date, and boasted guest appearances from **David Bowie**, **KRS-One**, Noel Gallagher, Dillinja, Charlemagne and Virus Records' co-owner Optical (Matt Quinn). The DJ now balances club work with a burgeoning acting career, which has included appearances in *The World Is Not Enough*, *Snatch* and the UK soap opera, *EastEnders*. He also appeared in the reality television show *Big Brother*.
● ALBUMS: *Timeless* (Ffrr 1995) ★★★★, *Saturnz Return* (Ffrr 1998) ★★★.
● COMPILATIONS: *INCredible Sound Of Drum 'N' Bass* (INCredible 1999) ★★★, *Goldie.co.uk* (Trust The DJ/Mixed 2001) ★★★.
● DVD/VIDEOS: *Talkin' Headz: The Metalheadz Documentary* (Manga Video 1998).
● FURTHER READING: *Nine Lives*, Goldie with Paul Gorman.
● FILMS: *Everybody Loves Sunshine* aka *B.U.S.T.E.D.* (1999), *The Ninth Gate* (1999), *The World Is Not Enough* (1999), *Snatch* (2000), *The Price Of Air* (2000), *The Case* (2002).

Goldie And The Gingerbreads

Formed in Brooklyn, New York City, USA, in 1963, Goldie And The Gingerbreads made their debut at the city's famed Peppermint Lounge. They were discovered by British outfit the **Animals** who, impressed by the quartet's musical abilities, suggested they move to the UK. **Goldie** (b. Genyusha Zelkowitz, 19 April 1945, Lodz, Poland; vocals), Carol MacDonald (b. Wilmington, Delaware, USA; guitar), Margo Crocitto aka Margo Lewis (b. Brooklyn, New York City, USA; organ) and Ginger Bianco (b. Long Island, New York, USA; drums) arrived in London in November 1964, and their debut single was issued the following year in the wake of successful appearances at the Crazy Elephant and Flamingo clubs. Animals keyboard player **Alan Price** produced the excellent 'Can't You Hear My Heart Beat?', a UK Top 30 entry, but two further singles failed to achieve similar success. The group toured with the **Rolling Stones** and **Kinks**, but despite their undoubted dexterity—Crocitto made several session appearances—they were unfairly perceived as a novelty. The quartet split up in October 1965, when Goldie embarked on a solo career, but the remaining trio maintained contact and they continued to record upon returning to New York, releasing 'Song To The Moon'/'Walking In Different Circles' in 1967. They later re-emerged during the 70s as part of Isis, an all-female group. Goldie found greater fame during the same decade as **Genya Ravan**.

● FURTHER READING: *Lollilop Lounge: Memoirs Of A Rock And Roll Refugee*, Genya Ravan.

Goldie Lookin Chain

Welsh hip-hop collective Goldie Lookin Chain is either a novelty band with one joke (and arguably a two-decade-old joke, at that), or satirists of hip-hop and contemporary society, finding humour in the gulf between the band's own aesthetics and the bling more commonly associated with rap music. Dressing like early 80s shopping centre breakdancers, the collective—Eggsy (aka Mr Love Eggs), Dwayne 'Xain' Zedong, Adam Hussain, Mike Balls (aka Hardest Man In Soccer Violence), Two Hats, Billy Webb (aka Tim Westcountry), Mystikal and The Maggot—appropriate a genre that fetishizes black American culture and transpose it to Newport, Wales.

After releasing a series of home-made CD-Rs, Goldie Lookin Chain debuted for **Atlantic Records** in 2004 with *Greatest Hits*, apparently because the **Queen** album of the same name 'did very well so we thought we'd have a go'. *Greatest Hits* found currency in a variety of subjects including, Mecca bingo halls, Victoria Beckham, and 'medium value' McDonalds meals. The single 'Guns Don't Kill People, Rappers Do' mocked government hysteria over hip-hop while referencing Zammo from children's school-based UK television series *Grange Hill*. 'Half Man, Half Machine' referenced 80s computers including ZX Spectrums, Commodores, BBC Micros and Speak 'N' Spell machines in a tale of dressing up as a (silver foil–covered) automaton and nipping down to the newsagent, while faux boy-band ballad and Christmas single 'You Knows I Love You' rhymed **Milli Vanilli** with Caerphilly and sought resonance from lines like 'I see you walking on the way home from work/Your Tesco tunic really drives me berserk'. Over the course of an album, however, it became apparent that once past the humour of their utter incongruousness, Goldie Lookin Chain really were not hugely funny. As *The Guardian* newspaper problematically recognized, 'When GLC name-drop murdered **Boogie Down Productions** producer Scott LaRock while interpolating a song by BDP's **KRS-One**, they prove that they know and (presumably) love hip-hop, yet their whole schtick panders to the outdated prejudices of listeners who don't and that's what makes this album rotten.'

Goldie Lookin Chain notably caused a minor furore when they performed at Cardiff's Millennium Stadium before the World Cup qualifying match between England and Wales: the group was criticized by the Welsh Football Association after dedicating 'Your Missus Is A Nutter' (the first single from second album *Safe As F**k*) to Victoria Beckham.

● ALBUMS: *Greatest Hits* (UK) *Straight Outta Newport* (USA) (Atlantic/Record Collection 2004) ★★★, *Safe As F**k* (Atlantic 2005) ★★.

Goldie, Don

b. Donald Elliott Goldfield, 5 February 1930, Newark, New Jersey, USA, d. 19 November 1995, Miami, Florida, USA. Goldie was raised in a highly musical family. His mother was Claire St. Claire, concert pianist, composer and teacher (**George Gershwin** was a pupil), and his father was Harry 'Goldie' Goldfield, who played trumpet and acted as assistant conductor with **Paul Whiteman**. Following in his father's wake, he took up the trumpet and early in his career played with country blues bands. He also worked in the society dance band of **Lester Lanin** before moving into jazz, where his principal influences were **Louis Armstrong**, **Bunny Berigan** and **Billy Butterfield**. A four-year engagement with **Jack Teagarden** starting in 1959 brought him most attention in the jazz world, although, over the years, he also played and sometimes recorded with bands led by **Ralph Burns**, **Neal Hefti**, **Earl 'Fatha' Hines**, **Gene Krupa**, **Joe Mooney** and **Buddy Rich**. Unlike his spell with Teagarden, Goldie's appearances with these bands were relatively anonymous. With Teagarden, he made some excellent recordings, including performances from the 1958 **Newport Jazz Festival**, reissued in a compilation by Phontastic Records, *The Legendary Jack Teagarden*, from 1960/1, on Roulette Records, and the exceptional *Think Well Of Me*, a 1962 recording reissued by **Verve Records** in 1999.

During the 70s, Goldie played in studio bands assembled by **Jackie Gleason** for his popular *Music For Lovers* albums. Goldie later settled in Miami, Florida, where he played regularly, often leading his own small bands, notably Jazz Express. During his time in Florida he also made numerous albums, mostly for Jazz Forum Records, on which he was joined by local resident musicians such as **Sonny Dunham**, alto saxophonist Carl Perkel, pianist Jack Keller and drummer Red Hawley. Few if any of these late albums appear to have been transferred to CD, and the same fate seems to have befallen some own name sets he made for Argo Records several years earlier, factors that have contributed towards the lack of latter-day attention paid to his work.

Goldie's playing was an intriguing mix of dixieland, mainstream and bop. His playing was always assured and filled with displays of his quite remarkable technical mastery. He also enjoyed singing in a rather good imitation of Armstrong. Unfortunately, the Armstrong impersonations, allied to his penchant for triple-tonguing and a sometimes flamboyant playing style, met with disapproval from hardcore jazz fans, who failed to discern that the man behind these occasional commercial displays was a consummate musician. Mostly, he employed his ample technique in the development of the cascading ideas that flowed from his inventive mind. In the course of his career, Goldie acquired a dedicated if small and localized following and since his death in 1995 he has remained well remembered by musicians such as Florida band leader Gary Lawrence, who maintains a Don Goldie website. In addition to performing, Goldie also operated a music agency and invented a 'Muffler' trumpet mute. After a long and debilitating fight against illness, Goldie ended his own life.

● ALBUMS: *Brilliant* (Argo 1960) ★★★, *Trumpet Caliente* (Argo 1962) ★★★, *Trumpet Exodus* (Verve 1962) ★★★, *The Immortal Cole Porter* (Jazz Forum 70s) ★★★, *The Best Of Cole Porter* (Jazz Forum 70s) ★★★, *The Best Of Burt Bacharach* (Jazz Forum 70s) ★★, *The Best Of George And*

Ira Gershwin (Jazz Forum 70s) ★★★, *The Best Of Jerome Kern* (Jazz Forum 70s) ★★★, *The Best Of Lerner And Loewe* (Jazz Forum 70s) ★★★, *Mixed Bag* (Jazz Forum 70s) ★★★, *The Best Of Rodgers & Hammerstein* (Jazz Forum 70s) ★★★, *The Best Of Irving Berlin* (Jazz Forum 70s) ★★★, *The Best Of Jimmy McHugh* (Jazz Forum 1977) ★★, *The Dixie Factory* (Jazz Forum 80s) ★★★, *Bourbon Street Parade* (Jazz Forum 80s) ★★★, *Sound Off* (Jazz Forum 80s) ★★, *The Best Of Jimmy Van Heusen* (Jazz Forum 80s) ★★★, *Washington & Lee Swing* (Jazz Forum 80s) ★★★, *The Best Of Richard Rodgers, Vol. 2* (Jazz Forum 80s) ★★★, *All That Jazz* (Jazz Forum 80s) ★★★, *Baby Face* (Jazz Forum 80s) ★★★, *Reflections* (Jazz Forum 80s) ★★★, *Dangerous Jazz Band* (Jazzology 1982) ★★★, *Jazz Express* (Jazzology 80s) ★★★, *The 24-Karat Trumpet Of Don Goldie* (Hurrah 80s) ★★★.

Goldilocks

This show, which opened at the Lunt Fontanne Theatre in New York on 11 October 1958, afforded Broadway audiences their only opportunity to hear the music of **Leroy Anderson**, who was better known as a composer of light, engaging, and some times humorous works, such as 'Blue Tango', 'Sleigh Ride', 'Forgotten Dreams', and 'The Typewriter'. Anderson's lyricists for *Goldilocks* were John Ford and Walter and Jean Kerr. The husband-and-wife team also wrote the book, which was set in 1913, and was essentially a sometimes hilarious spoof on the silent-movie business. As the curtain rises, an actress Maggie Harris (**Elaine Stritch**, in one of her typically 'acerbic' roles), is about to give up the theatre and marry the millionaire George Randolph Brown (**Russell Nype**). Enter film producer-director Max Grady (**Don Ameche**) to remind her that she is, in fact, contracted to appear in his movie, *Frontier Woman*, which is about to begin shooting. Max tricks Maggie into filming enough footage for several movies, and, although they admit their feelings for each other, she fully intends to marry George. However, when the unexpected happens, and snow begins falls on the site of Max's latest movie—an Egyptian epic which is being shot in downstate California (in April)—she takes that as a sign that she should do something equally unconventional—so she marries Max instead. Jilted George has to make do with Lois (Pat Stanley), but both Stanley and Nype were consoled by receiving real-life **Tony Awards** for their performances. 'Never mind the story—the score's the thing,' has been said so many times, and this was yet another of them. The songs were indeed both charming and amusing. Stritch was beautifully served with 'Give The Little Lady', 'Whose Been Sitting In My Chair?', 'The Beast In You', 'I Never Know When', and 'Save A Kiss' (with Nype), and an 'abusive' duet with Ameche, 'No One'll Ever Love You' ('Like you do'). Ameche displayed an impressive singing voice in 'There Never Was A Woman', and the insistent, disbelieving 'I Can't Be In Love' (with the accent very much on the 'can't'), and the rest of the score included 'Lazy Moon', 'Lady In Waiting', 'Shall I Take My Heart And Go?' (Nype), 'Bad Companions', 'Two Years In The Making', and 'Heart Of Stone'. The Broadway veteran choreographer, **Agnes De Mille**, was acclaimed for her staging of both songs and dances, and she had a great time with the comic 'Pussy Foot'. It all added up to another of those fondly remembered flops. A run of 161 performances equalled a reported financial loss in the region of $360,000 dollars—and an Original Cast album to treasure.

Goldings, Larry

b. Lawrence Sam Goldings, 28 August 1968, Boston, Massachusetts, USA. Known primarily for his organ playing, Goldings began at the age of seven on the piano. His father, a lawyer, was a classical music enthusiast and the sound of this music took hold of the young Goldings' interest. He also developed a keen ear by listening to popular songs from the radio and learning the harmonies. At the age of 12, Goldings attended music camp in Sweden, Maine, where he studied with his first important jazz instructor, Dave Cozzolongo, who taught him about the work of **Bud Powell**, **Art Tatum** and **Oscar Peterson**. In his high-school years, Goldings played in school bands and local rock 'n' roll groups. He also attended a high-school jazz programme at the Eastman School of Music in Rochester, New York. At this time he was very influenced by the works of **Dave McKenna**, **Bill Evans** and **Wynton Kelly**, along with the groups of **Miles Davis** and **John Coltrane**. He was helped in his development by some influential teachers, including **Ran Blake** at the New England Conservatory of Music, Peter Cassino and even **Keith Jarrett**, on occasion.

When he graduated from high school in 1986, Goldings moved to New York City and attended the music programme of the New School for Social Research, where he studied with **Fred Hersch** and **Jaki Byard**. Goldings also led the school's weekly jam sessions, where he was heard by the great pianist **Sir Roland Hanna**, who invited Goldings to accompany him to an annual jazz gathering in Copenhagen, Denmark. There, Goldings performed for many great jazz artists, such as **Hank Jones**, **Tommy Flanagan** and **Sarah Vaughan**. After participating in a masterclass at the New School conducted by vocalist **Jon Hendricks**, Goldings gained his first professional experience working with the singer on a trip to Paris, France. Hendricks eventually employed the pianist for more than a year.

In New York, Goldings began leading his own groups and jam sessions at clubs such as Augie's and The Village Gate, with other young musicians including **Leon Parker**. It was Parker who suggested that Goldings should begin to play the organ. Later, he was heard by the saxophonist **Maceo Parker**, who asked him to join his band. Goldings established his own organ trio with his first release, *Intimacy Of The Blues* (1991). He was soon performing and recording with artists including **Jim Hall**, Christopher Hollyday and **John Scofield**. As an organist, Goldings has followed the path of masters such as **Jimmy Smith**, **Melvyn Rhyne**, **Shirley Scott** and **Lonnie Smith**, whom he cites as his favourite. Subsequent releases with the trio—Peter Bernstein on guitar and **Bill Stewart** on drums—included *Light Blue* (1992) and *Caminhos Cruzados* (1994), a collection of Brazilian jazz. Goldings began to show the funkier side of his organ music with the release of *Whatever It Takes* (1995) and *Big Stuff* (1996). These included compositions by **Ray Charles**, **Stevie Wonder** and **Sly Stone** and allowed Goldings to express some of his pop music leanings. On his next release, *Awareness* (1997), Goldings was finally able to feature his piano work, with Larry Grenadier (bass) and former Bill Evans trio member **Paul Motian** (drums).

Goldings is an extremely versatile performer and a very prolific composer of jazz, pop and folk music. He performed as a member of **James Taylor**'s touring band in 2002. With an eye towards the future, Goldings has become involved in writing music for films, and maintains a desire to experiment with new and developing technologies that will allow him to communicate with as large an audience as possible.

● ALBUMS: *Intimacy Of The Blues* (Verve 1991) ★★★★, *Light Blue* (Minor Music 1992) ★★★, *Caminhos Cruzados* (Novus 1994) ★★★★, *Whatever It Takes* (Warners 1995) ★★★, *Big Stuff* (Warners 1996) ★★★★, *Awareness* (Warners 1997) ★★★, *Moonbird* (Palmetto 1999) ★★★★, with Bob Ward *Voodoo Dogs* (Palmetto 2000) ★★, *As One* (Palmetto 2001) ★★★, *Sweet Science* (Palmetto 2002) ★★★.

Goldkette, Jean

b. 18 March 1899, Valenciennes, France, d. 24 May 1962, Santa Barbara, California, USA. A child prodigy, Goldkette toured as a concert pianist, spending several years in Greece and Russia and was still only 12 years old when he settled in America. Equipped with an astute business brain, Goldkette was soon working as a dance band pianist and joined the organization headed by Chicago's Edgar Benson. As director of one of the several Benson Orchestras, Goldkette expanded his knowledge of the band circuit to the point where he decided to set up his own business. He established an organization similar to Benson's and later acquired a building in Detroit, which he turned into the Graystone Ballroom. With a recording contract for **Victor Records**, Goldkette soon had more work than he could handle with one band and once again followed Benson's example by forming additional bands, each labelled as a 'Jean Goldkette Orchestra'.

Throughout the late 20s Goldkette's bands were home to several white jazz stars, including **Bix Beiderbecke**, **Frank Trumbauer**, **Joe Venuti** and **Tommy Dorsey** and **Jimmy Dorsey**, and several important early big band arrangers, notably **Bill Challis** and **Bill Rank**. At the end of 1927, after a hugely successful engagement at the Roseland Ballroom in New York, the jazz nucleus of Goldkette's number one orchestra left to join **Paul Whiteman**. In the 30s Goldkette concentrated his energies on operating his many dancehalls and the 20-plus bands that bore his name (in none of which he ever played). Although the bands became of less importance, Jean Goldkette orchestras were still performing into the 50s. Later in his life, Goldkette returned to his first love, classical piano music. He died in March 1962, thus missing the nostalgia boom from which he would doubtless have benefited.

● ALBUMS: *Jean Goldkette And His Orchestra* (Victor 1959) ★★★★.
● COMPILATIONS: *Victor Recordings (1924–1928)* (Victor 2002) ★★★★.

Goldman, Albert

Specifically within the field of rock biography, but also in the wider context of rock and pop itself, there are few more controversial characters than Albert Goldman (b. 1927, d. 29 March 1994). Consigned by his critics to the status of assassin, Goldman's thorough explorations of characters such as **John Lennon** and **Elvis Presley** (in addition to comedian **Lenny Bruce**), often merely intensified the stubbornly held opinions of fans who viewed his research as if it were property violation. Goldman's ethos of debunking popular myths and reconstructing historical data had been an early conviction. His PhD thesis from the 50s saw him denouncing Thomas De Quincey as a plagiarist. He remained a peripheral university lecturer in popular culture at Columbia and freelance columnist on pop music for *Life* Magazine (essays collected together in *Freakshow*) for much

of his professional life. The release of his *Elvis* text in 1981 duly earned the outrage of the King's fan community (its tone was described by Greil Marcus, famously, as 'cultural genocide'). He spared no blushes, revealing in this, and his subsequent *The Lives Of Lennon* opus, the inevitable dehumanizing process of such massive success. **Yoko Ono** would ascribe reading the book on her husband as tantamount to enduring '800 punches'. While there may have been some self-satisfied delight in soiling these icons, Goldman maintained until his death (when due to fly to Britain for a television appearance on the *Late Show*) that he was maintaining a tradition of biography that stretched back to Lyton Strachey.

● FURTHER READING: *Freakshow: The Rocksoulbluesjazz-sickjewblackhumorsexpoppsych* (1975), *Elvis* (1981), *The Lives Of John Lennon* (1988).

Goldman, James

b. 30 June 1927, Chicago, Illinois, USA, d. 28 October 1998, New York City, USA. A writer of stage plays and screenplays, an early play by Goldman was *Blood, Sweat And Stanley Poole* (1961), co-written with his younger brother, **William Goldman**. A musical play that reached Broadway was *A Family Affair* (1962), which had a 65-performance run at the Billy Rose Theatre. Set in contemporary Chicago, the show's book was by Goldman with music by **John Kander** and lyrics by William Goldman. Directed by **Harold Prince** with choreography by John Butler, the show had a very large cast, which on opening night was headed by Shelley Berman (Alfie Nathan), Eileen Heckart (Tilly Siegal), Morris Carnovsky (Morris Siegal), Rita Gardner (Sally Nathan), Larry Kert (Gerry Siegal), and Bibi Osterwald (Miss Lumpe). Goldman's first big success in both theatre and films came with *The Lion In Winter*, which was staged in 1966 and filmed in 1968. The screen version brought him an Academy Award for Best Screenplay.

Other screenplays were for *They Might Be Giants* (which was based upon his stage play) and *Nicholas And Alexandra* (both 1971), *Robin And Marian* (1976) and *White Nights* (1985, which starred dancers Mikhail Baryshnikov and Gregory Hines). His musical credits were enhanced with **Follies**, which was staged on Broadway, opening 4 April 1971 and running until 1 July 1972. With music and lyrics by **Stephen Sondheim**, the show achieved its 522 performances despite initially mixed reviews. Goldman appeared on stage in *Sondheim: A Musical Tribute*, a special one-night performance on 11 March 1973. After his death, *The Lion In Winter* was revived for a short run between 11 March and 30 May 1999, and there have been several revivals of *Follies*.

Goldman, William

b. 12 August 1931, Highland Park, Chicago, Illinois, USA. Goldman is a prolific writer of books, plays and films. He collaborated with his older brother, **James Goldman**, on the 1961 stage play *Blood, Sweat And Stanley Poole* (1961). He also wrote lyrics to **John Kander**'s music for his brother's *A Family Affair* (1962), a musical play staged on Broadway where it ran for 65 performances. Goldman is primarily known, however, for his screenplays, which include *Butch Cassidy And The Sundance Kid* (1969) and *All The President's Men* (1976), for both of which he won Oscars. He also wrote the screenplay for *Marathon Man* (1976), which was based upon his own novel. Goldman's other novels include *The*

Temple Of Gold, Your Turn To Curtsy, My Turn To Bow, Soldier In The Rain, Boys And Girls Together, No Way To Treat A Lady, The Thing It Is . . ., Father's Day, The Princess Bride, Magic: A Novel, Tinsel: A Novel, Control, The Silent Gondoliers, The Color Of Light, Heat, Brothers and a book for children, *Wigger*. His other titles include works on his craft, *The Season: A Candid Look At Broadway, The Story Of 'A Bridge Too Far', Wait Till Next Year, Hype And Glory, Four Screenplays, Five Screenplays, The Big Picture: Who Killed Hollywood? And Other Essays*, and his memoirs 1983's *Adventures In The Screen Trade: A Personal View Of Hollywood And Screenwriting* and 2000's *Which Lie Did I Tell? (More Adventures In The Screen Trade)*. Goldman is also noted as Hollywood script doctor, work for which he sometimes goes uncredited.

● FURTHER READING: *Adventures In The Screen Trade: A Personal View Of Hollywood And Screenwriting*, William Goldman. *Which Lie Did I Tell? (More Adventures In The Screen Trade)*, William Goldman.

Goldner, George

b. 1919, near Turtle Bay, Manhattan, USA, d. 15 April 1970. Goldner's long association with New York music circles began in the early 50s. Although initially employed at Tico, a label specializing in Latin music, he switched to R&B in 1953 with the formation of Rama. Its roster included vocal groups the **Crows** and Harptones, establishing a pattern for Goldner's subsequent outlets, Gee, Gone/End and Roulette. Drawing on New York's profligate street-corner harmony acts, the entrepreneur launched the careers of **Frankie Lymon And The Teenagers**, **Little Anthony And The Imperials** and the **Chantels**, but subsequently sold his interests in each of the companies. Goldner re-emerged in 1964, partnering songwriters/producers **Jerry Leiber** and **Mike Stoller** in **Red Bird Records**. The label enjoyed a highly successful initial period with hits by the **Dixie Cups**, **Jelly Beans** and **Shangri-Las**, and Goldner later bought out his partners when they tired of administrative roles. Despite a promotional acumen, he was unable to maintain the outlet's position and it folded in 1966. In keeping with many contemporaries faced with a new generation of self-sufficient acts, Goldner was unable to exert the same influence in pop's post-**Beatles** history and later dropped out of music altogether.

Goldsboro, Bobby

b. 18 January 1941, Marianna, Florida, USA. Goldsboro first came to prominence as a guitarist in **Roy Orbison**'s touring band in 1960. His major chart breakthrough as a solo singer for the **United Artists Records** label occurred in 1964 with the self-penned US Top 10 hit 'See The Funny Little Clown'. During the mid-60s, he also enjoyed minor US hits with such compositions as 'Whenever He Holds You', 'Little Things' (a UK hit for **Dave Berry**), 'Voodoo Woman', 'It's Too Late' and 'Blue Autumn'. His international status was assured in 1968 with the elegiacal 'Honey', a **Bobby Russell** composition, perfectly suited to Goldsboro's urbane, but anguished, vocal style. The song dominated the US number 1 position for five weeks and was arguably the most unlucky single never to reach number 1 in the UK, twice reaching the number 2 slot, in 1968 and 1975. Goldsboro enjoyed further hits in the early 70s, most notably 'Watching Scotty Grow' and the risqué 'Summer (The First Time)'. In the mid-70s he hosted the syndicated variety series, *The Bobby Goldsboro Show*, but by

1975 the hits had dried up. In an attempt to extend his appeal, Goldsboro subsequently turned to the country market, forming the House Of Gold Music publishing firm. In the mid-80s he inaugurated a successful career in children's entertainment, writing and producing stories and animated specials, including the highly successful *The Swamp Critters Of Lost Lagoon*.

● ALBUMS: *The Bobby Goldsboro Album* (United Artists 1964) ★★★, *I Can't Stop Loving You* (United Artists 1964) ★★, *Little Things* (United Artists 1965) ★★, *Broomstick Cowboy* (United Artists 1965) ★★, *It's Too Late* (United Artists 1966) ★★, *Blue Autumn* (United Artists 1966) ★★★, *The Romantic, Wacky, Soulful, Rockin', Country, Bobby Goldsboro* (United Artists 1967) ★★★, with Del Reeves *Our Way Of Life* (United Artists 1967) ★★★, *Honey* (United Artists 1968) ★★★, *Word Pictures—Autumn Of My Life* (United Artists 1968) ★★★, *Today* (United Artists 1969) ★★★, *Muddy Mississippi Line* (United Artists 1970) ★★★, *We Gotta Start Lovin'* (United Artists 1970) ★★★, *Come Back Home* (United Artists 1971) ★★, *California Wine* (United Artists 1972) ★★★, *Brand New Kind Of Love* (United Artists 1973) ★★, *Summer (The First Time)* (United Artists 1973) ★★★, *10th Anniversary Album* (United Artists 1974) ★★, *Through The Eyes Of A Man* (United Artists 1975) ★★★, *A Butterfly For Bucky* (United Artists 1976) ★★, *Goldsboro* (Epic 1977) ★★, *Bobby Goldsboro* (Curb 1980) ★★, *Round Up Saloon* (Curb 1982) ★★, *Honey* (Ariola 1990) ★★, *Happy Holidays From Bobby Goldsboro* (La Rana 1999) ★★, *The Greatest Hits Collection* (La Rana 1999) ★★.

● COMPILATIONS: *Solid Goldsboro: Bobby Goldsboro's Greatest Hits* (United Artists 1967) ★★★, *Hello Summertime* (United Artists 1974) ★★★, *Bobby Goldsboro's Greatest Hits* (United Artists 1978) ★★★★, *Best Of Bobby Goldsboro* (MFP 1983) ★★★★, *The Very Best Of Bobby Goldsboro* (C5 1988) ★★★★, *All Time Greatest Hits* (Curb 1990) ★★★, *22 Greatest Hits* (Remember 1995) ★★★, *Honey: The Best Of Bobby Goldsboro* (Collectables 1996) ★★★, *Hello Summertime: The Very Best Of Bobby Goldsboro* (EMI 1999) ★★★, *Absolutely The Best* (Fuel 2000 2003) ★★★★.

Goldsmith, Jerry

b. Jerrald Goldsmith, 10 February 1929, Los Angeles, California, USA, d. 21 July 2004, Beverly Hills, California, USA. A prolific composer for films and television, from the late 50s through to the new millennium. Besides studying music at the University of South Carolina (under Hungarian composer Miklos Rozsa), Goldsmith also took lessons in office practice and secured a job as a clerk/typist with CBS Television, before moving to the company's music department in Los Angeles in 1950. During the 50s, first as a staffer, and then as a freelancer, he wrote theme music for popular television series such as *Gunsmoke, Have Gun Will Travel, Perry Mason, The Twilight Zone, Dr. Kildare, The Man From U.N.C.L.E.*, and several more.

In the late 50s, Goldsmith started to compose for movies such as *Black Patch* and *City Of Fear* and, through the good auspices of film composer **Alfred Newman**, he came to prominence with his score for *Lonely Are The Brave* (1962). It was the start of a career in which he composed the music for over 150 films, ranging from westerns such as *Rio Conchos, Bandolero!* and a re-make of *Stagecoach* to the 'shockers', *The Omen*, *Damien: Omen II*, *The Final Conflict*, *Poltergeist* and *Psycho II*. He worked on several films with his favourite director, Franklin J. Schaffner, including *The Stripper*, *Planet Of The Apes*, *Patton*, *Papillon*, *Islands In The Stream* and *The Boys From Brazil*.

During the 60s it was estimated that Goldsmith was averaging about six films a year. These included *The Spiral Road*, *Lilies Of The Field*, *The Prize*, *Seven Days In May*, *To Trap A Spy*, *The Satan Bug*, *In Harm's Way*, *Von Ryan's Express*, *A Patch Of Blue*, *Our Man Flint*, *The Trouble With Angels*, *The Blue Max*, *The Sand Pebbles*, *In Like Flint*, *The Flim-Flam Man* aka *One Born Every Minute*, *The Detective* and *Justine*. Throughout the 70s, 80s and into the new millennium, Goldsmith was still one of the busiest film composers around, contributing to movies such as *Tora! Tora! Tora!*, *The Mephisto Waltz*, *Chinatown*, *Logan's Run*, *MacArthur*, *Capricorn One*, *Alien*, *Star Trek: The Motion Picture*, *Outland*, *Raggedy Man*, *First Blood*, *Under Fire*, *Gremlins*, *Rambo: First Blood Part II*, *King Solomon's Mines*, *Hoosiers* aka *Best Shot*, *Extreme Prejudice*, *Innerspace*, *Rambo III*, *Star Trek V: The Final Frontier*, *Total Recall*, *Gremlins 2: The New Batch*, *The Russia House*, *Sleeping With The Enemy*, *Basic Instinct*, *Love Field*, *Forever Young*, *Matinee*, *The Vanishing*, *Malice*, *Angie*, *Bad Girls*, *The Shadow*, *The River Wild*, *I.Q.*, *First Knight*, *City Hall*, *Fierce Creatures*, *L.A. Confidential*, *Mulan*, *Small Soliders*, *Hollow Man*, *The Sum Of All Fears*, and *Star Trek: Nemesis*. By this stage, more than 15 of his scores had been nominated for an Academy Award, but only *The Omen* (1976) received an Oscar. In addition to composing, Goldsmith conducted orchestras such as the San Diego Symphony and Britain's Royal Philharmonic, playing his music in concert halls around the world. He died of cancer in July 2004. His son Joel Goldsmith is also a composer for films

● COMPILATIONS: *40 Years* 4-CD set (Silva Screen 2005) ★★★★.

Goldwax Records

A label founded in 1964 in Memphis, Tennessee, USA, that recorded some of the classic deep soul sounds of the south. It was founded by a pharmacist, Rudolph 'Doc' Russell, and an air conditioner salesman, Quinton Clauch. Clauch was the experienced half of the team, having supervised some recording sessions at **Sun Records** and then become a co-founder of Hi Records. Goldwax's most notable artists were **James Carr**, **Spencer Wiggins**, and the **Ovations**, a vocal group whose leader sounded like **Sam Cooke**. The label briefly had **O.V. Wright**, who recorded the song 'That's How Strong My Love Is' before **Otis Redding** covered it and brought it acclaim. The company closed its doors in 1969. Clauch revived the label in 1991, recording a few acts, notably, **Ruby Andrews**, **Gwen McCrae** and James Carr.

● COMPILATIONS: *The Goldwax Story Volume 1* (Kent 2001) ★★★★, *The Goldwax Story Volume 2* (Kent 2004) ★★★.

Goldwyn, Samuel

b. Schmuel Gelbfisz, 17 or 27 August 1882, Warsaw, Poland, d. 31 January 1974, Los Angeles, California, USA. Emigrating alone to England, Gelbfisz worked as a labourer before going to America to work as a glove maker. He was still only 13 years old. In 1910, he now called himself Samuel Goldfish and was a glove salesman, and married to Blanche Lasky. He

joined her brother Jesse L. Lasky and Cecil B. De Mille to form the Jesse L. Lasky Feature Play Company. Their first film, *The Squaw Man* (1914), was a huge success. Goldfish was bought out after a 1916 merger with a company owned by Adolph Zukor. Teaming up with others, who included Edgar Selwyn, a new company was named from the first syllable of Goldfish and the last of Selwyn. In 1918 Goldfish legally changed his name to Goldwyn. The company struggled and Goldwyn left, but it retained his name and in 1924 merged with Metro Pictures and Louis B. Mayer Productions to form Metro-Goldwyn-Mayer (MGM). Meanwhile, in 1923, he had formed Samuel Goldwyn Productions. Among films Goldwyn produced were *Ben-Hur* (1925), *Dodsworth* (1936), *Stella Dallas* (1937), *Wuthering Heights* (1939), *The Westerner* (1940), *The Little Foxes* (1941), and *The Best Years Of Our Lives* (1946), which won six Oscars including Best Picture. Among the screen musicals Goldwyn produced are **Whoopee!** (1930, from **William McGuire**'s musical play in turn derived from **Owen Davis**' play and starring **Eddie Cantor**), **Roman Scandals** (1933, another Cantor vehicle), *The Goldwyn Follies* (1938, an unsuccessful attempt at a **Florenz Ziegfeld**-style musical, featuring Kenny Baker, **Vera Zorina** and the **Ritz Brothers**), and **Ball Of Fire** (1942, starring Barbara Stanwyck and Gary Cooper, with **Gene Krupa** and his band). In 1944 came **Up In Arms**, the first of several starring **Danny Kaye**, of which others were **Wonder Man** (1945), **The Kid From Brooklyn** (1946), **A Song Is Born** (1948), a remake of *Ball Of Fire* (featuring several noted names from the jazz world, including **Louis Armstrong**, **Lionel Hampton** and **Tommy Dorsey**), and *Hans Christian Andersen* (1952). His biggest musicals were **Guys And Dolls** (1955), which was based upon the successful Broadway show, and **Porgy And Bess** (1959), which was Goldwyn's last film. After his death, his son, Samuel Goldwyn Jnr. (b. 7 September 1926), continued to develop the company in areas of film production and distribution, television and home video.

● FURTHER READING: *Samuel Goldwyn: Movie Mogul*, Jeremy Barnes. *Samuel Goldwyn: The Producer And His Films*, Richard Griffith. *Samuel Goldwyn Presents*, Alvin H. Marill.

Golia, Vinny

b. 1 March 1946, New York City, USA. Vinny Golia has the unique distinction of having appeared on **Blue Note Records** and **ECM Records** albums before he had learned to play an instrument! He did it as an artist: it is his painting on the cover of **Chick Corea**'s *The Song Of Singing*, his drawing that adorns the sleeve of **Dave Holland**'s *Music For Two Basses*. Golia graduated with a degree in fine art in 1969 and moved, by chance, into the apartment block where Corea, Holland and **Dave Liebman** were all living. He began to attend their concerts, drawing the musicians as they played and later turning the sketches into large, abstract canvasses. With the money he received for the *The Song Of Singing* sleeve he bought a soprano saxophone and, after taking lessons from Liebman and **Anthony Braxton** (also an influence on his later composing), spent the next few years teaching himself to play. Then, rather than invite musicians to 'play' his paintings (as happened at one event he staged with **Circle**), Golia started to play them himself, before deciding he could cut out the painting and simply play.

In 1973 Golia moved to Los Angeles and in 1977 started his own label, Nine Winds, which provided an outlet for a new generation of west coast musicians, including **Wayne Peet** (piano), Ken Filiano (bass), **Alex Cline** (percussion), **Nels Cline** (guitar) and John Rapson (trombone). Golia's own recordings include solo, duo, trio and small-group albums (*No Reverse* and *Goin' Ahead* are outstanding) as well as big band releases—*Compositions For Large Ensemble, Facts Of Their Own Lives, Pilgrimage To Obscurity, Decenium Dans Axlan, Tutto Contare*—which feature guests such as **Bobby Bradford**, **John Carter** and **Tim Berne**. Golia also kept practising: he now plays over 20 instruments, all self-taught—they include nearly all of the saxophone, clarinet and flute families plus piccolo, bassoon and various non-Western pieces such as conch, sho, hotchiku, shakuhachi and khee. Though he mostly leads his own groups, he has toured and/ or recorded as a sideman with Berne, Braxton, **George Gruntz** and several of his west coast colleagues. In addition to his jazz activities, Golia's love of chamber music has prompted him to work with various classical players and to record a set of improvised duets with bass maestro Bertram Turetzky.

● ALBUMS: *Spirits In Fellowship* (Nine Winds 1978) ★★, *Openhearted* (Nine Winds 1979) ★★★, *In The Right Order . . .* (Nine Winds 1980) ★★, *Solo* (Nine Winds 1980) ★★★, *Slice Of Life* (Nine Winds 1981) ★★★, *The Gift Of Fury* (Nine Winds 1981) ★★★, with Wayne Peet *No Reverse* (Nine Winds 1984) ★★★★, *Compositions For Large Ensemble* 1982 recording (Nine Winds 1985) ★★★, *Goin' Ahead* (Nine Winds 1985) ★★★★, *Facts Of Their Own Lives* 1984 recording (Nine Winds 1987) ★★, *Out For Blood* (Nine Winds 1989) ★★★, *Pilgrimage To Obscurity* 1985 recording (Nine Winds 1990) ★★★★, *Worldwide & Portable* 1986 recording (Nine Winds 1990) ★★★, with Bertram Turetzky *Intersections* 1986 recording (Nine Winds 1991) ★★★, *Regards From Norma Desmond* 1986 recording (Fresh Sound 1992) ★★★★, *Commemoration* (Nine Winds 1993) ★★★★, *Decennium Dans Axlan* (Nine Winds 1993) ★★★★, *Collaboration* (Nine Winds 1995) ★★★, with Ken Filiano, Joëlle Léandre *Haunting The Spirits Inside Them . . .* (Music And Arts 1996) ★★★★, *Against The Grain* 1993 recording (Nine Winds 1996) ★★★, with Paul Smoker *Halloween '96* (CIMP 1996) ★★★, *Nations Of Laws* (Nine Winds 1997) ★★★★, *The Art Of Negotiation* (CIMP 1997) ★★, with Bertram Turetzky *11 Reasons To Begin* (Music And Arts 1997) ★★, with Smoker *Halloween, The Sequel* (Nine Winds 1998) ★★★, with Turetzky, Barre Phillips *Trignition* (Nine Winds 1998) ★★★, *Tutto Contare* (Nine Winds 1998) ★★★, *Large Ensemble—Portland 1996* (Nine Winds 1998) ★★★, with Wadada Leo Smith, Turetzky *Prataksis* (Nine Winds 1998) ★★★★, with Ed Harkins, Turetzky *Glossarium* (Nine Winds 1998) ★★★, with Steve Adams *Circular Logic* (Nine Winds 1999) ★★★★, with Susan Allen *Duets* (Nine Winds 1999) ★★, *Lineage* (Nine Winds 1999) ★★★, *The Other Bridge (Oakland 1999)* (Nine Winds 2000) ★★★, *Clarinet* (Meniscus 2001) ★★★, *Feeding Frenzy* (Nine Winds 2002) ★★★, *Music For Electronics & Woodwinds* (Nine Winds 2002) ★★★, *Music For Woodwinds & String Quartet* (Nine Winds 2002) ★★★.

Golightly, Holly

b. England. Singer-songwriter and guitarist Holly Golightly (she insists it is her real name) has always been a fan of classic Britpop from the 60s British Invasion era, as evidenced by her work as a member of **Billy Childish**'s spin-off group Thee Headcoatees, and as a solo recording artist. While with Thee Headcoatees, Golightly was present for underground favourites such as 1992's *Have Love, Will Travel* and 1994's *Girlsville*. She launched her own solo career while still a member of the band, making her debut in 1995 with *The Good Things*. Straight away, the artist showed that she was looking to break free of the usual three-chord garage rock of Thee Headcoatees, mixing in blues rock and folk compositions alongside the expected styles. Golightly has since issued solo recordings at an average of a new album per year, including stand-out releases such as the 1996 all-covers set *Laugh It Up!* (featuring songs by **Willie Dixon**, **Ray Davies**, **Mudhoney** and the Soul Sisters, among others), plus notable collaborations with Childish (1999's *In Blood*) and Dan Melchoir (2001's *Desperate Little Town*). Golightly has promoted these releases with several world tours, including supporting the **White Stripes** on numerous occasions. As a result, Golightly befriended the US duo and contributed some guest vocals on the closing track from their hit 2003 album, *Elephant* (titled 'It's True That We Love One Another', the track was actually recorded a year and a half earlier). Golightly subsequently worked with another US band, the Greenhornes (members from which feature in her live shows), before returning to her solo career with 2003's *Truly She Is None Other*.

● ALBUMS: *The Good Things* 10-inch album (Damaged Goods 1995) ★★★, *The Main Attraction* (Teenage Kicks 1996) ★★★★, *Laugh It Up!* aka *Laugh It All Up!* (Vinyl Japan 1996) ★★★★, *Painted On* (Sympathy For The Record Industry 1997) ★★★, *Up The Empire* (Sympathy For The Record Industry 1998) ★★★, *Serial Girlfriend* (Damaged Goods 1998) ★★★★, with Billy Childish *In Blood* (Wabana 1999) ★★★★, *God Don't Like It* (Damaged Goods 2000) ★★★, with Dan Melchior *Desperate Little Town* (Sympathy For The Record Industry 2001) ★★★, *Truly She Is None Other* (Damaged Goods 2003) ★★★, *Down Gina's At 3* (Sympathy For The Record Industry 2004) ★★★, *Slowly But Surely* (Damaged Goods 2004) ★★★.
● COMPILATIONS: *Singles Round-Up* (Damaged Goods 2001) ★★★, *My First Holly Golightly Album* (Damaged Goods 2005) ★★★★.

Golla, George

b. 10 May 1935, Chorzów, Poland. While still in his teens Golla immigrated to Australia, where his guitar playing attracted considerable attention. Late in the 50s he teamed up with **Don Burrows**, playing throughout Australia and also travelling worldwide gaining plaudits from critics and audiences alike. He also appeared on record with Burrows, on his acclaimed Sydney Opera House album, and with **Stéphane Grappelli** on *Steph' 'N' Us*. In the 90s he was still very active and took part in an acclaimed **Martin Taylor** set of duets, *Two's Company*.

Golliwogs

Formed in El Cerrito, California, USA, this accomplished quartet—**John Fogerty** (b. 28 May 1945, Berkeley, California, USA; guitar/vocals), **Tom Fogerty** (b. 9 November 1941, Berkeley, California, USA, d. 6 September 1990, Scottsdale, Arizona, USA; guitar/vocals), Stu Cook (b. 25 April 1945, Oakland, California, USA; bass) and Doug Clifford (b. 24 April 1945, Palo Alto, California, USA; drums)—were initially known as the **Blue Velvets**, but took the Golliwogs name as a precondition to their recording contract with **Fantasy Records**. The group was never happy with the appellation, or the blond wigs they were sometimes required to wear, but between 1964 and 1967 they completed a series of excellent singles. Tom Fogerty dominated early releases, but by 1966 his younger brother was wresting control of the group. 'Walk On The Water' and 'Fight Fire' showed the unit developing a defined, original sound. Having turned fully professional in December 1967, they evolved into **Creedence Clearwater Revival**.

● COMPILATIONS: *The Golliwogs* (Fantasy 1975) ★★★.

Golowin, Albert
(see **Gulda, Friedrich**)

Golson, Benny
b. 25 January 1929, Philadelphia, Pennsylvania, USA. After receiving tuition on the piano as a child, Golson began playing tenor saxophone professionally in 1951 in **Bullmoose Jackson**'s R&B band. It was here that he first met **Tadd Dameron**, who had a great influence upon his writing. In the early and mid-50s he played in bands led by Dameron, **Lionel Hampton** and **Earl Bostic**, then worked for **Dizzy Gillespie**, playing in and arranging for the 1956–58 big band. Next, Golson became a member of **Art Blakey**'s **Jazz Messengers**, for whom he composed several tunes. He later formed bands with **Curtis Fuller** and **Art Farmer** (the Jazztet), then went into the studios, writing for films and television but making occasional appearances on record sessions and on jazz stages around the world. In the late 70s he returned to regular live work and toured Europe with a reunited Jazztet in 1982. The following year he recorded an acclaimed tribute album to his old Philadelphia jamming partner, **John Coltrane**.

Golson's playing, which followed the melodic progression of late swing-era stylists such as **Lucky Thompson** and **Don Byas**, was always effective. He remains best known, however, for his writing, and some of his compositions have become latter-day jazz standards: 'Blues March', 'Killer Joe', 'Whisper Not' and 'I Remember Clifford'.

● ALBUMS: *Benny Golson's New York Scene* (Contemporary 1958) ★★★★, *The Modern Touch Of Benny Golson* aka *Reunion* (Riverside/Jazzland 1958) ★★★★, *The Other Side Of Benny Golson* (Riverside 1958) ★★★, *Benny Golson And The Philadelphians* (United Artists 1959) ★★★, *The Curtis Fuller Jazztet With Benny Golson* (Savoy Jazz 1959) ★★★, *Gone With Golson* (New Jazz 1959) ★★★★, *Groovin' With Golson* (New Jazz 1959) ★★★, with Art Farmer, Curtis Fuller *Meet The Jazztet* (Argo 1960) ★★★, *Gettin' With It* (New Jazz 1960) ★★★, with Farmer *Big City Sounds* (Argo 1961) ★★★, with Farmer *The Jazztet And John Lewis* (Argo 1961) ★★★, with Farmer *The Jazztet At Birdhouse* (Argo 1961) ★★★★, *Take A Number From 1 To 10* (Argo 1961) ★★★, with Farmer *Here And Now* (Mercury 1962) ★★★, with Farmer *Another Git Together* (Mercury 1962) ★★★, *Pop + Jazz = Swing* (Audio Fidelity 1962) ★★★, with Rahsaan Roland Kirk *Roland Kirk Meets The Benny Golson Orchestra* (Mercury 1963) ★★★, *Free: Benny Golson Quartet* (Argo 1963) ★★★, *Just Jazz!* (Audio Fidelity 1963) ★★★, *Turning Point* (Mercury 1963) ★★★, *Stockholm Sojourn* (Prestige 1965) ★★★, *Turn In, Turn On To The Hippest Commercials Of The Sixties* (Verve 1967) ★★, *Killer Joe* (Columbia 1977) ★★, *California Message* (Baystate 1980) ★★★, *One More Mem'ry* (Timeless 1982)

★★★, *Time Speaks* (Timeless 1983) ★★★, *This Is For You, John* (Timeless 1984) ★★★, with Farmer *The Jazztet: Moment To Moment* (Soul Note 1983) ★★★, with Farmer, Fuller *Back To The City* (Contemporary 1986) ★★★, *In Paris* 1958 recordings (Disques Swing 1987) ★★★★, with Freddie Hubbard *Stardust* (Denon 1988) ★★★★, *Live* (Dreyfus 1990) ★★★, *Domingo* (Dreyfus 1992) ★★★★, *I Remember Miles* (Evidence 1993) ★★★★, *California Message* (Timeless 1995) ★★★, *Up Jumped Benny* (Arkadia 1996) ★★★, *Three Little Words* 1965 recordings (Jazz House 1997) ★★★, *Remembering Clifford* (Milestone 1998) ★★★, *Free* (Chess 1998) ★★★★, *Tenor Legacy* (Arkadia Jazz 1999) ★★★, *That's Funky* (Arkadia Jazz 2000) ★★★, *One Day, Forever* (Arkadia Jazz 2001) ★★★★, *Terminal 1* (Concord Jazz 2004) ★★★.

Golub, Jeff
b. 15 April 1955, Akron, Ohio, USA. Golub was already an accomplished guitarist when he attended Boston's **Berklee College Of Music**. At the end of the 70s he settled in New York City, where he was invited to join **Billy Squier**'s band. In addition to several albums, this engagement also resulted in three world tours. Aside from his work with Squier, Golub was also in demand as a session player and sideman, and he supported artists such as **Tina Turner**, **Vanessa Williams** and **Rod Stewart**. Golub worked with Stewart for eight years but in 1988 made his solo record debut, *Unspoken Words*. He left Stewart's band in 1994 and formed his own contemporary jazz group, Avenue Blue. The following year, Golub toured with pianist **Bob James**, appearing on the Grammy-nominated *Joined At The Hip* with James and **Kirk Whalum**. After three acclaimed albums with Avenue Blue for Bluemoon Records, Golub returned to his solo career with *Out Of The Blue*, on which he blended progressive blues-inflected instrumentals with engagingly soulful ballads of which the single, 'The Velvet Touch', proved to be especially attractive. A later move to **GRP Records** found his eclecticism in full flow as he drew upon many aspects of popular music while simultaneously revealing an awareness of the 'less is more' characteristic of many jazzmen of earlier generations. Golub's fluid playing, ranging from the gracefully limpid to the fiercely storming, is ably complemented by his imaginative musical concepts. These qualities have allowed him to move from his rock and blues roots into the contemporary jazz scene with considerable authority and élan.

● ALBUMS: *Unspoken Words* (Gaia 1988) ★★★, *Avenue Blue* (Bluemoon 1994) ★★★, with Avenue Blue *Naked City* (Bluemoon 1996) ★★★, with Avenue Blue *Nightlife* (Bluemoon 1997) ★★★, *Out Of The Blue* (Atlantic 1999) ★★★, *Dangerous Curves* (GRP 2000) ★★★★, *Do It Again* (GRP 2002) ★★★, *Soul Sessions* (GRP 2003) ★★★, *Temptation* (Narada 2005) ★★.

Gomelsky, Giorgio
b. 28 February 1934, Georgia, formerly USSR. Exiled to Switzerland and educated in Italy, Gomelsky later settled in Britain, where he became a leading figure of London's jazz scene during the 50s. He organized the first Richmond Jazz Festival and was later responsible for bringing bluesman **Sonny Boy 'Rice Miller' Williamson** to Europe. Giorgio's first club was the Piccadilly, but in 1963 he established the famed Crawdaddy Club in Richmond's Station Hotel, which quickly

became one of the country's leading venues for rhythm and blues. The **Rolling Stones** enjoyed a successful residency there prior to recording and Gomelsky initially acted as the group's manager before being supplanted by **Andrew Loog Oldham**. However, the impresario fared better with their successors, the **Yardbirds**, whom he guided and produced between 1964 and 1966. Gomelsky subsequently managed the **T-Bones** and the **Steampacket** before founding the Marmalade label in 1967. He enjoyed a modicum of success with **Blossom Toes**, before securing international hits with protégés **Julie Driscoll** and **Brian Auger And The Trinity**. The company, however, proved short-lived, and Giorgio subsequently left England for Paris, where he established an alternative music circuit for radical groups **Magma**, whom he also managed, and **Gong**. Gomelsky also enjoyed a fruitful relationship with BYG Records, who issued several albums culled from tapes he had recorded during the 60s. Having founded a new label, Utopia, in 1975, he then moved to New York, where he continues to supervise releases drawn from his considerable archive.

Gomez

This UK rock band was originally formed by four school friends from Southport, Ian Ball (guitar, harmonica, vocals), Tom Gray (guitar, keyboards, vocals), Olly Peacock (drums/ percussion) and Paul Blackburn (bass). Ball and Peacock's musical background included a period spent on the local metal circuit in heavy rock band Severed. Ball met Ben Ottewell (b. Matlock Bath, Derbyshire, England) while studying at Sheffield University, inviting the fledgling vocalist to join the band. Briefly known as Gomez, Kill, Kill The Vortex, the band began recording four-track demo tapes in a Southport garage. They attracted immediate interest when tapes from these sessions were posted to record labels, triggering a frenzied A&R scramble for their signatures. With Stephen Fellows (ex-**Comsat Angels**) in position as their manager, the band signed to **Virgin Records** subsidiary Hut. Gomez toured with **Embrace** in late 1997 and spent time in a 16-track studio polishing off their raw demos. Their debut single, '78 Stone Wobble', was released in March 1998, and was followed a month later by **Bring It On**. Acclaimed by critics on both sides of the Atlantic, the album drew comparisons to a diverse range of American artists including **Tim Buckley**, **Tom Waits**, **Al Green**, **Marvin Gaye** and **Jimi Hendrix**. Ottewell's raw, bluesy vocals added a further touch of authenticity to the band's stylized fusion of various forms of American roots music, with the songs often struggling to rise above their influences and establish an identity of their own. One of the stand-out tracks, 'Get Myself Arrested', was released as a single in May 1998. *Bring It On* won the UK's Mercury Music Prize in September the same year, boosting sales past gold and pushing the album to a UK chart high of number 11. The following month the band completed a US tour opening for **Eagle-Eye Cherry**, and continued working on recording sessions for their next album. A new single, 'Bring It On' (not featured on their debut), was released in June 1999. *Liquid Skin* was a remarkably mature collection from a band under pressure to produce a worthy follow-up to their acclaimed debut. Both *In Our Gun* (2002) and *Split The Difference* (2004) satisfied Gomez's loyal following but were unable to expand their music into wider territory.

● ALBUMS: *Bring It On* (Hut 1998) ★★★, *Liquid Skin* (Hut 1999) ★★★★, *In Our Gun* (Hut 2002) ★★★, *Split*

The Difference (Hut 2004) ★★★, *Out West* (Independiente 2005) ★★.
● COMPILATIONS: *Abandoned Shopping Trolley Hotline* (Hut 2000) ★★★.

Gomez, Eddie

b. Edgar Gomez, 4 November 1944, San Juan, Texas, USA. Gomez moved to New York City as a child and took up the bass when he was 12 years old. He was at the High School of Music and Art before going on to the Juilliard School of Music where he studied with Frederick Zimmerman. He played with **Marshall Brown**'s International Youth Band and then in the early 60s with **Gary McFarland**, **Jim Hall**, **Paul Bley**, **Jeremy Steig** and **Gerry Mulligan** before joining **Bill Evans**, with whom he stayed for 10 years (1966-77). He needed his musically agile mind and technical dexterity in that trio, with which he often played melodically in the upper register of the bass. During the early 80s he played in the band **Steps Ahead**, which **Mike Mainieri** (vibes) kept together after a group of New York session musicians made an acclaimed tour of Japan. He has successfully played this fusion music on the amplified double bass rather than moving to bass guitar. Gomez continued as a very much in-demand musician through the 80s playing and recording with **Jack DeJohnette**, **Hank Jones** and **JoAnne Brackeen** among others. In the 90s he recorded with **Chick Corea**.
● ALBUMS: *Down Stretch* (Black Hawk 1976) ★★★, *Gomez* (Denon 1985) ★★, *Mezgo* (Epic 1986) ★★, *Down Stretch* (Blackhawk 1987) ★★★, *Power Play* (Epic 1988) ★★★, *Streetsmart* (Epic 1990) ★★★, *Live In Moscow* (B&W 1992) ★★★, *Next Future* (GRP 1993) ★★★, with Bill Bruford, Ralph Towner *If Summer Had Its Ghosts* (Discipline 1997) ★★, *Dedication* (Evidence 1999) ★★★, with Mark Kramer *Jazz Fiddler On The Roof* (Twinz 2005) ★★.

Gomez, Roy

b. 27 February 1953, Casablanca, Morocco. Gomez appears regularly in guitarist magazines the world over—a testament to an enduring talent and virtuoso technique that has seen him play on countless sessions for a myriad of rock, jazz and blues artists. He has thus far released only one solo album, 1980's *Volume* for **CBS Records**. Despite his obvious technical ability and the fluency of his guitar playing, it proved an unhappy transition to self-composition that attracted lukewarm reviews. Since then he has concentrated exclusively on collaborative work. His trio recording with Bill Campbell (drums) and Mike McGuirk in 2002 was much better received.
● ALBUMS: *Volume* (CBS 1980) ★★★, *Robert Gomez Trio* (Basement Front 2002) ★★★★.

Gómez, Tito

(see **Niche, Grupo**; **Lucca, Papu**; **Nati**; **Barretto, Ray**)

Gomm, Ian

b. 17 March 1947, Chiswick, London, England. Former **Brinsley Schwarz** guitarist, Gomm went into semi-retirement from the music business after the break-up of the band in 1975. After a period working in studio production at **United Artists Records** with Martin Rushent, Gomm put together a solo album with the assistance of **Herbie Flowers** (bass; also of **Sky**), Barry De Sousa (drums) and Chris Parren (keyboards).

Although completely out of step with the then-current fashion of punk, the album revived memories of the golden era of pub rock in enough people to entice Gomm for a short spell back on the road. An unexpected bonus in the shape of US Top 20 single with 'Hold On' in 1979 gave optimistic portents for the future, but all efforts for a successful follow-up failed. Gomm's brief flush of stardom faded after the release of his second album, and despite continuing to issue albums into the new millennium, big time success still eludes Gomm.

● ALBUMS: *Summer Holiday* (UK) *Gomm With The Wind* (US) (Albion/Stiff 1978) ★★★★, *What A Blow* (Albion/Stiff 1980) ★★★, *The Village Voice* (Albion 1983) ★★, *What Makes A Man A Man?* aka *Images* (Decal 1986) ★★★, *Crazy For You* (MSI 1997) ★★, *Rock 'N' Roll Heart* (Gommsongs 2002) ★★★, *24 Hour Service* 1979 recording (Hux 2002) ★★★.

● COMPILATIONS: *Come On Ian Gomm* (Line 1997) ★★★.

Gompie

Dutch band Gompie was created by Dureco Records' head Rob Peters and veteran guitarist/singer Peter Koelewijn and a team of session musicians in 1995. Their debut release, 'Who The X Is Alice?', was an offbeat (and lewd) response to **Smokie**'s enduring 1976 single, 'Living Next Door To Alice'. Peters struck a distribution deal for the Benelux nations with Artur Prait of RPC Entertainment, resulting in the single staying at number 1 in the Netherlands charts for four weeks. A full-length album followed.

● ALBUMS: *Who The X Is Gompie?* (RPC/Dureco 1995) ★★.

Gone To Earth

Formed in Manchester, England, this 80s group of thrash folksters cut several rumbling singles (predominantly for Liverpool indie label Probe) and changed members constantly. One regular was fiddler and **Christy Moore** fan Dave Clarke, who wrote songs about Salford and drinking profusely.

● ALBUMS: *Vegetarian Bullfighter* (Probe Plus 1987) ★★★.

Gonella, Nat

b. Nathaniel Charles Gonella, 7 March 1908, Islington, London, England. d. 6 August 1998, Gosport, Hampshire, England. A trumpeter, vocalist, and band leader, Gonella was a major pioneer of British jazz, and one of its best-loved personalities. After learning to play the cornet and read music while at school, Gonella worked in the tailoring trade and as an errand-boy before buying his own cornet in 1923. A year later he switched to trumpet when joining Archie Pitt's Busby Boys in the **Gracie Fields** revue, *A Week's Pleasure*. During the four years that he was touring with that show and its successor, *Safety First*, Gonella began his lifelong love affair with jazz via records such as 'Wild Man Blues' and 'Cushion Foot Stomp'. These featured the musician who was to influence him most, **Louis Armstrong**. After leaving the Busby Boys, Gonella played in dance bands led by Bob Dryden and Archie Alexander, before being hired by **Billy Cotton** in 1930. The Cotton band's broadcasts from the ritzy Ciro's Club in London provided a wider audience for this

sensational up-and-coming young musician who played trumpet and sang in the Armstrong style. In the same year he began recording, and appeared on Cotton sides such as 'That Rhythm Man', 'Bessie Couldn't Help It' and 'The New Tiger Rag'.

In 1931, Cotton was naturally incensed when his complete brass section, Gonella, Sid Buckman and Joe Ferrie, defected overnight to the Monseigneur Band, which was fronted by one of the most successful band leaders of the 30s, **Roy Fox**. One of the Monseigneur Restaurant's frequent patrons was the Prince of Wales, and he was especially keen on a Gonella speciality, 'Georgia On My Mind'. **Hoagy Carmichael** and Stuart Gorrell's memorable number became the musician's lifelong theme, and the title of his 1985 biography. Gonella's recording of the tune with the Fox band was made early in 1932, shortly after his highly individual version of the Negro spiritual, 'Oh! Monah!'. The latter number was adopted by Fox's pianist and arranger **Lew Stone**, who took over the Monseigneur band, still featuring Gonella, when Fox moved to the Café Anglais. Gonella continued to record with various ensembles and cut a few titles such as 'Rockin' Chair' and 'That's My Home' under the pseudonym Eddie Hines. On 14 September 1932, he made 'I Can't Believe That You're In Love With Me'/'I Heard', the first record to have 'Nat Gonella and his Trumpet' on the label. A few months earlier, Gonella had met his idol for the first time, when Louis Armstrong played two weeks at the London Palladium. In later years, after they had finished their evening work, they often jammed in the early morning at clubs such as The Nest and Bag O' Nails. After working in the Netherlands with **Ray Noble** in 1933, in the summer of 1934, Gonella toured Variety theatres with Stone, and was featured with the Georgians, a five-piece band within a band. He also topped the bill at the Holborn Empire with violinist-singer Brian Lawrence and the Quaglino Quartette. In November 1934, Nat Gonella And His Georgians (Albert Torrence and George Evans (alto saxophones), **Don Barrigo** (tenor saxophone), Harold Hood (piano), Arthur Baker (guitar), Will Hemmings (string bass) and Bob Dryden (drums)) cut several sides for **Parlophone Records**, including 'Moon Glow', 'Don't Let Your Love Go Wrong' and two 'Fox Trot Medleys' containing songs such as 'Dinah', 'Troublesome Trumpet' and 'Georgia On My Mind'. When Nat Gonella And His Georgians—'Britain's Hottest Quintette'—finally undertook their first theatre tour in April 1935, they shrewdly mixed jazz with strong elements of comedy and crowd-pleasing numbers such as 'Tiger Rag'. In the late 30s, Gonella recorded prolifically—on one occasion accompanying **George Formby** on 'Doh-De-Oh-Do'—and packed theatres with shows such as *South American Joe*, which featured xylophone player Teddy Brown and singer Phyllis Robins. Another triumph came in 1938, with a summer season at Blackpool with *King Revel*, which co-starred Sandy Powell and Norman Evans. After a brief but successful spell in New York early in 1939, Gonella formed a larger band, the New Georgians, but with the advent of World War II, he was called up in the army, and served in the Pioneer Corps and Royal Tank Regiment in North Africa.

After the war, with musical tastes changing rapidly, his 13-piece outfit was quickly reduced to a quartet, and Gonella eventually went out on his own, playing holiday camps and Variety theatres. In spite of the late 50s-early 60s trad-jazz boom, bookings slumped, and he was reduced to working in a bookmaker's office for a time. Encouraged by the response to his *Salute To Satchmo* album, Gonella formed his Georgia Jazz Band, which, ironically, made its debut at the **Cavern Club** in Liverpool in 1960. With an appearance as the subject of television's *This Is Your Life*, his comeback gathered pace for a time, and he issued *The Nat Gonella Story*. However, later in the decade he was working solo once more, and on one of his last recording sessions he played the role of Fagin in the Society label's version of **Lionel Bart**'s hit musical, **Oliver!** In the early 70s he returned to the Netherlands, and while there, he recorded 'Oh! Monah!', which reached the Top 5 in the Dutch hit parade. His subsequent retirement to Gosport in Hampshire was interrupted by occasional appearances at the local jazz club, sometimes in company with his long-time friend, supporter and fellow trumpeter, **Digby Fairweather**, along with ex-Georgians such as **Tiny Winters**, Jim Shepherd and Pat Smuts.

In the 80s there was a renewed interest in the man and his music. Fairweather embarked on a concert tour with *A Tribute To Nat Gonella*, and several collections of his work were re-released on album. In September 1994, the Gosport Borough Council named an area in the town after him: Nat Gonella Square (although one jazz-loving councillor observed that it was illogical to place the two words, 'Gonella' and 'Square' in the same sentence). Three years later, fans of contemporary music were privileged to hear just a very brief example of vintage Gonella, when computer wizard Jyoti Mishra 'sampled' part of his trumpet introduction to the 1932 Lew Stone disc, 'My Woman', and used it on his UK chart-topper, 'Your Woman', issued under the name of **White Town**. Just a week before he celebrated his 90th birthday, Gonella joined Digby Fairweather and other friends at the Pizza on the Park in London. Although he had put down the horn a long time ago, the years rolled back as this splendid, innovative musician delighted the audience with 'Shine', 'St. James Infirmary', 'When You're Smiling', and of course, 'Georgia On My Mind'.

● ALBUMS: *Runnin' Wild* (Columbia 1958) ★★★, *Salute To Satchmo* (Columbia 1959) ★★★, *The Nat Gonella Story* (Columbia 1961) ★★★★, *Nat Gonella And His Trumpet* (Ace Of Clubs 1967) ★★★, *When You're Smiling* (Decca 1970) ★★★★, *The Music Goes 'Round And 'Round* (Decca 1975) ★★★★, *My Favourite Things* (Decca 1975) ★★★, *Wishing You A Swinging Christmas* (CNR 1975) ★★.

● COMPILATIONS: *Nat Gonella Story* (Note 1978) ★★★, *Georgia On My Mind* 1931-46 recordings (Decca Recollections 1980) ★★★★, *Mister Rhythm Man* 1934-35 recordings (EMI Retrospective 1984) ★★★, *Golden Age Of Nat Gonella* (Golden Age 1985) ★★★, *Nat Gonella Scrapbook* (Joy 1985) ★★★, *Naturally Gonella* 1935 recordings (Happy Days 1986) ★★★, *How'm I Doin'?* 1936 recordings (Old Bean 1987) ★★★, *Crazy Valves* 1934-37 recordings (Living Era 1988) ★★★★, *Running Wild* (Harlequin 1988) ★★★, *Yeah Man* 1935-37 recordings (Harlequin 1988) ★★★, *Nat Gonella Volume One* 1934-35 recordings (Neovox 1990) ★★★★, *Nat Gonella Volume Two* 1932-35 recordings (Neovox 1990) ★★★, *Hold Tight* (Memoir 1991) ★★★, *The Cream Of Nat Gonella* (Flapper 1991) ★★★★, *Nat Gonella: The Dance Band Years* 2-CD set (Pulse 1998) ★★★, *Georgia On My Mind* 1931-41 recordings (ASV 1998) ★★★.

● FURTHER READING: *Modern Style Of Trumpet Playing*, Nat Gonella. *Georgia On My Mind: The Nat Gonella Story*, Ron Brown with Cyril Brown.

● FILMS: *Pity The Poor Rich* (1935), *Sing As You Swing* (1937).

Gong

Although not officially applied to a group until 1971, the name Gong had already appeared on several projects undertaken by guitarist Daevid Allen, a founder member of the **Soft Machine**. After relocating to Paris, Allen recorded two idiosyncratic albums before establishing this anarchic, experimental ensemble. Gilli Smyth aka Shanti Yoni (vocals), Didier Malherbe aka Bloomdido Bad De Grasse (saxophone/flute), Christian Tritsch aka The Submarine Captain (bass) and Pip Pyle (drums) had assisted Allen on his solo collection *Banana Moon* (1971), but Gong assumed a more permanent air when the musicians moved into a communal farmhouse in Sens, near Fontainbleu, France. Lauri Allen replaced Pyle as the group completed two exceptional albums, *Continental Circus* and *Camembert Electrique*. Musically, these sets expanded on the quirky, *avant garde* nature of the original Soft Machine, while the flights of fancy undertaken by their leader, involving science fiction, mysticism and 'pot-head pixies', emphasized their hippie-based surrealism. Subsequent releases included an ambitious 'Radio Gnome Invisible' trilogy; *Flying Teapot*, *Angel's Egg* and *You*.

This period of the Gong story saw the band reach the peak of their commercial success with stunning, colourful live performances, plus the roles of newcomers **Steve Hillage** (guitar), Mike Howlett (bass) and Tim Blake (synthesizer) emphasized the group's long-ignored, adept musicianship. During this period however, Allen had became estranged from his creation, with Hillage becoming increasingly perceived as the group leader, resulting in the guitarist leaving the group in July 1975. Gong subsequently abandoned his original, experimental vision in favour of a tamer style. Within months Hillage, who had enjoyed great success with his solo album, *Fish Rising*, had begun a solo career, leaving Pierre Moerlen, prodigal drummer since 1973, in control of an increasingly tepid, jazz rock direction. Mike Howlett left soon after to pursue a successful career in studio production and was replaced by Hanny Rowe. The guitarist role was filled by **Allan Holdsworth** (ex-**Nucleus**, **Tempest**). After a period of inaction in the early 80s the Gong name was used in performances alongside anarchic space/jazz rock group Here And Now, before being swallowed whole by the latter. In doing so, it returned to its roots appearing at free festivals, new age and neo-hippie gatherings. Often billed with various appendages to the name, by the late 80s and 90s Gong was once more under the control of its original leader.

● ALBUMS: *Magick Brother, Mystic Sister* (BYG 1969) ★★, *Continental Circus* (Philips 1971) ★★★, *Camembert Electrique* (BYG 1971) ★★★★, *Radio Gnome Invisible Part 1: The Flying Teapot* (Virgin 1973) ★★★★, *Radio Gnome Invisible Part 2: Angel's Egg* (Virgin 1973) ★★★, *You* (Virgin 1974) ★★★, *Shamal* (Virgin 1975) ★★★, *Gazeuse!* (UK) *Expresso 1* (US) (Virgin 1976) ★★, *Gong Est Mort—Vive Gong* (Tapioca 1977) ★★, *Expresso 2* (Virgin 1978) ★★, *Downwind* (Arista 1979) ★★, *Time Is The Key* (Arista 1979) ★★, *Pierre Moerlen's Gong, Live* (Arista 1980) ★★, *Leave It Open* (Arista 1981) ★★, *Breakthrough* (Arc/Eulenspiegel 1986) ★★, *Second Wind* (Line 1988) ★★, *Floating Anarchy* (Decal 1990) ★★, *Live Au Bataclan 1973* (Mantra 1990) ★★★, *Live At Sheffield 1974* (Mantra 1990)

★★★, *25th Birthday Party* (Voiceprint 1995) ★★, *The Peel Sessions* (Strange Fruit 1995) ★★★, *Shapeshifter +* (Viceroy 1997) ★★, *You—Remixed* (Gliss 1997) ★★, *Zero To Infinity* (Snapper 2000) ★★★, *From Here To Eternitea* (Snapper 2002) ★★★, *Acid Motherhood* (Voiceprint 2004) ★★.

Solo: Tim Blake *The Tide Of The Century* (Blueprint 2000) ★★★.

● COMPILATIONS: *Gong Live Etc.* (Virgin 1977) ★★, *A Wingful Of Eyes* (Virgin 1987) ★★★, *The Mystery And The History Of The Planet G**g* (Demi-Monde 1989) ★★★, *The Best Of Gong* (Nectar Masters 1995) ★★★, *The Best Of Gong* (Reactive Masters 1998) ★★★, *Family Jewels* (Gas 1998) ★★★, *The World Of . . .* (Charly 2003) ★★★.

● DVD/VIDEOS: *Maison* (Voiceprint 1993), *High Above The Subterrania Club 2000* (Snapper 2002).

Gonks Go Beat

Inspired by the plot from the AIP film, *Pajama Party*, this 1965 feature offered a wafer-thin premise whereby a space-travelling alien versed in the wonder of pop attempts to placate rivalry between Beatland and Balladisle. This is achieved through an unlikely combination of acts, most of which were culled from the **Decca Records** roster. Although the bulk of the acts were undistinguished—precocious child stars Elaine and Derek were set beside second-string beat groups the Long And The Short and Trolls—the film did include otherwise unavailable recordings by chart acts the **Nashville Teens** and **Lulu** And The Luvvers. The latter featured future **Stone The Crows** and **Robin Trower** member Jimmy Dewar on bass. A brief cameo appearance as an extra soldier from **Cream** lyricist and poet **Pete Brown** is also spotted. However, the highlight of *Gonks Go Beat* was unquestionably an appearance by the **Graham Bond Organization**, one of the finest—and most influential—60s groups. Vocalist/keyboard player Bond was herein joined by **Jack Bruce** and **Ginger Baker**, both later of Cream, and future **Colosseum** saxophonist, **Dick Heckstall-Smith**. Their contribution, 'Harmonica', was shot in a studio bedecked in tropical style, but the ill-fitting setting did not undermine the quartet's charismatic power. It did nothing to salvage the film's commercial prospects and an attendant soundtrack album enjoyed negligible success. Another in a line of British 'quickie' pop films, *Gonks Go Beat* does at least boast one highly memorable sequence. The long deleted soundtrack album released on Decca currently fetches huge prices at auction.

Gonsalves, Paul

b. 12 July 1920, Boston, Massachusetts, USA, d. 15 May 1974, London, England. Gonsalves' first professional engagement in Boston was on tenor saxophone with the **Sabby Lewis** band, in which he played both before and after his military service during World War II. On leaving Lewis he played with **Count Basie** (1946–49), was briefly with **Dizzy Gillespie** and then joined **Duke Ellington** in 1950. Gonsalves remained with Ellington for the rest of his life, his occasional absences from the band resulting from his addiction to alcohol and narcotics. Like many other would-be Ellingtonian tenor players, Gonsalves began by learning **Ben Webster**'s 'Cotton-tail' solo note for note, but quickly established his own distinctive style. The circumstance that made Gonsalves' reputation was his appearance with Ellington at the 1956 **Newport Jazz Festival**, when his storming, 27-chorus bridge

between the opening and closing sections of 'Diminuendo And Crescendo In Blue' helped to focus media attention on the band and provided the basis of Ellington's 'comeback'. Thereafter, Gonsalves was obliged to play extended gallery-pleasing, up-tempo solos every night, a fact that over-shadowed his enormous affinity with ballads.

Gonsalves' relaxed and thoughtful approach to tunes displayed a love for melody and an ability to develop long, clean and logical solo lines. His rhapsodic playing on Ellington performances such as 'Happy Reunion', 'Chelsea Bridge', 'Solitude' and 'Mount Harissa' from the *Far East Suite* all testify to his vulnerable, often tender sound. His playing on records made outside the Ellington aegis is usually of a similarly reflective nature. A 1970 album with **Ray Nance**, *Just A-Sittin' And A-Rockin'*, is a good example, including a marvellous performance of 'Don't Blame Me'. Gonsalves surpassed even this on *Love Calls*, his 1967 album of duets with **Eddie 'Lockjaw' Davis**, where he delivers what might well be the definitive version of this song. In such performances, the quality of the playing perhaps reflect the man himself: Gonsalves was a sensitive yet fragile human being. He succumbed to drug addiction and alcohol dependence early in life and his career was afterwards dogged by these twin perils. When he died in London, in May 1974, his employer for close on a quarter of a century was himself too ill to be told. Ellington died a few days later and the bodies of both men, and that of **Tyree Glenn**, lay together in the same New York funeral home.

● ALBUMS: *Gettin' Together* (Jazzland 1960) ★★★★, *Rare Paul Gonsalves Sextet In Europe* (Jazz Connoisseur 1963) ★★★, *Tell It The Way It Is!* (Jasmine 1963) ★★★, *Salt And Pepper* (Impulse! 1963) ★★★★, *Cleopatra—Feelin' Jazzy* (Jasmine 1963) ★★★, *Jazz Till Midnight* (Storyville 1967) ★★★, *Encuentro* (Fresh Sound 1968) ★★★, *Humming Bird* (Deram 1969) ★★★, with Ray Nance *Just A-Sittin' And A-Rockin'* (Black Lion 1970) ★★★, *Meets Earl Hines* (Black Lion 1970) ★★★, with Roy Eldridge *The Mexican Bandit Meets The Pittsburgh Pirate* (Fantasy 1973) ★★★★, with C-Jam All Stars *Diminuendo, Crescendo And Blues* 1958 recording (RCA Victor 2000) ★★★.

Gonzales

b. Jason Beck. Raised in Canada, Beck learned to play the piano at an early age and later studied at Concordia University. After finishing his studies he played with the Toronto-based alt rock band Son, who released two albums in the mid-90s. After the band's final album was rejected by **Warner Brothers Records**, Beck relocated to Berlin where he invented Chilly Gonzales, a medallion-wearing MC and the 'only one-eyed Jewish rapper in Berlin.' He allegedly created his bizarre cut-and-paste electronica and pastiche hip-hop from a squat in a disused television station in East Berlin, Germany. His excellent solo debut, 2000's *Gonzales Uber Alles*, was released on the trendy German label Kitty-Yo. The album revelled in a sense of fun, with Gonzales attacking everyone from **Cole Porter** to **Leonard Cohen** and castigating **techno** snobs for not writing melodies. *The Entertainist* and *Presidential Suite* delved further into Beck's bag of tricks, running the gamut from perverse rap to squelchy funk. He was joined on the latter by his sometime duettist, **Peaches**. Following one more album as MC Gonzales, Beck unceremoniously retired his rap persona and moved to Paris,

France, to work with fellow Canadian **Feist** and chanteuse **Jane Birkin**. He returned to his first love with an album of piano pieces released through Universal Jazz.

● ALBUMS: *Gonzales Uber Alles* (Kitty-Yo 2000) ★★★★, *The Entertainist* (Kitty-Yo 2001) ★★, *Presidential Suite* (Kitty-Yo 2002) ★★★, *Z* (Kitty-Yo 2003) ★★★, *Solo Piano* (No Format/Universal Jazz 2004) ★★★.

Gonzales, Babs

b. Lee Brown, 27 October 1919, Newark, New Jersey, USA, d. 23 January 1980, Newark, New Jersey, USA. After working as a vocalist with a number of bands, including those led by **Charlie Barnet** and **Lionel Hampton**, Gonzales teamed up with **Tadd Dameron** and **Rudy Williams**. Their trio, Three Bips And A Bop, was successful in clubs and on record with a Gonzales composition, 'Oop-Pop-A-Da' being sufficiently popular to encourage a later and much more successful recording by **Dizzy Gillespie**. One of the few vocalists to take comfortably to bebop, Gonzales was also one of the most able of scat singers. He incorporated hip and humorous monologues into his act and was active in promoting jazz. When employment was scarce, he sought work outside music and was once chauffeur to film star Errol Flynn. A frequently surreal performer, Gonzales overcame deficiencies of poor pitch and a rough-edged voice thanks to excellent timing and a good sense of harmony. In the mid-50s he worked with, and also managed, **James Moody**. Gonzales continued working in the 60s and 70s although he never regained his earlier popularity. He published two volumes of memoirs, in 1967 and 1975, and died in 1980.

● ALBUMS: *Voila!* (Hope 1958) ★★★, *Tales Of Manhattan* (Jaro 1959) ★★★, *Sunday's At Small's Paradise* (Dauntless 1963) ★★★, *The Expubident World Of Babs Gonzales* (Expubidence 1968) ★★★, *The Ghettosburg Address* (Expubidence 1970) ★★★.

Gonzalez

Gonzalez were a very loose UK-based group of some 15 to 30 itinerants (many of whom also played in **Georgie Fame**'s Blue Flames), who assembled in England during 1971 to play a blend of funky soul music. The key members were keyboard player Roy Davies (also in the **Butts Band** with ex-**Doors** Robbie Krieger and John Densmore), Mick Eve (former saxophone player with Herbie Goins' Night-Timers and Georgie Fame's Blue Flames), Chris Mercer (former saxophone player with **John Mayall**, **Keef Hartley** and **Juicy Lucy**), Steve Gregory (former saxophone player with Tony Colton's Crawdaddies, **Geno Washington**'s Ram Jam Band and Riff Raff), Gordon Hunte (ex-guitar with **Johnny Nash**), Lisle Harpe (ex-bass with the Night-Timers, Juicy Lucy and **Stealers Wheel**) and Rosko Gee (later to play bass with **Traffic**). They released a self-titled album in 1974, but it was not a great success. In 1977, however, with the line-up standing at Davies, Hunte, Eve, Mercer, plus Ron Carthy (trumpet), Geoffrey 'Bud' Beadle (saxophone), Colin Jacas (trombone), Alan Sharp, Godfrey McLean, and Bobby 'John' Stigmac (percussion), John Giblin (bass), Richard Bailey and Preston Heyman (drums), and Lenny Zakatek (vocals), they recorded the Gloria Jones–penned 'I Haven't Stopped Dancing Yet' for **EMI Records**' soul label Sidewalk. It was not issued until 1979, when it gave the band a surprise hit. The follow-up, 'Ain't No Way To Treat A Lady', flopped. They later recorded for PRT and by the mid-80s were on the Tooti Fruiti label. Having

undergone many more personnel changes, the band finally disintegrated in 1986 after the death of founding member Roy Davies.

● ALBUMS: *Gonzalez* (1974) ★★, *Shipwrecked* (Capitol 1979) ★★★.

Gonzalez, Celina

b. 1928, Jovellanos, Matanzas Province, Cuba. Gonzalez is recognized both in her own country and abroad as the 'Queen of Musica Campesina' or Cuban country music, though it is impossible to mistake her sound for that of the North American equivalent. Musica Campesina depends instead on Latin melodies (played on guitar and tres), African percussion and restrained salsa. She describes her music thus: 'The true folklore of Cuba. Even though I now incorporate modern elements, it still remains firmly rooted in the Campesina tradition.' Occasionally using full brass backing but more often simply accompanied by guitar and drums, Gonzalez draws on the traditional Spanish verse form adopted by local country workers. She grew up in the small town of Jovellanos, to the east of Havana, where sugar plantations and strong rural traditions continue to incorporate African religious worship (Gonzalez follows the Afro religion, Santeria) and musical elements imported by the plantation slaves. At the age of 16, having moved to Santiago de Cuba, she first met Reutilio Dominguez, her singing partner and husband until his death in 1971. They performed together regularly on a programme for Saurito Radio, denouncing the government and lifting the spirits of the populace (she is an unreconstructed supporter of the Cuban revolution). Her early songs were largely religious, the first and most famous dedicated to her patron saint, Santa Barbara. In the early 50s she toured the Caribbean and also played in New York with **Beny Moré**, but Cuba's isolation meant she rarely ventured abroad again until the 80s. Her massive popularity in Cuba was later translated into sales in Latin America, particularly Venezuela and Colombia. When her husband died in the 70s she was joined by her son, Reutilio Junior, as her new singing partner, adding a full backing band known as Campo Alegre. She continues to perform widely on television and radio, hosting her own daily show on Radio Taino, but in Cuba recording opportunities have proved more elusive, though her recordings for the Egrem Records label in the 80s discovered new audiences in the west when recompiled by World Circuit Records in the UK and Qbadisc in the USA.

● ALBUMS: *Fiesta Guajira* (World Circuit 1993) ★★★★, *La Rica Cosecha* (Tumi 1996) ★★★.

● COMPILATIONS: *This Is Cuba: The Queen Of Cuban Folk* (Columbia 2000) ★★★★.

Gonzalez, Dennis

b. 15 August 1954, Abilene, Texas, USA. Born into a Mexican American family, Gonzalez grew up in Mercedes, Texas, studied French, journalism and music at various institutions and is an accomplished visual artist, linguist, teacher, writer and disc jockey as well as an internationally acclaimed trumpeter, composer and record-producer. In 1976 he settled in Dallas and two years later founded DAAGNIM (the Dallas Association for Avant Garde and Neo Impressionistic Music), setting up the similarly titled record label in 1979. His first album, *Air Light (Sleep Sailor)*, was recorded in his living room and had him playing a dozen or so instruments—at the time there were few local musicians sympathetic to his music! Later, with the help of reedsman **John Purcell**, he began to establish an impressive catalogue of work on Daagnim and in 1986 also started to record for the Swedish label Silkheart, releasing three albums of his own music and playing on three more by **Charles Brackeen**. Of these, it was his own *Stefan* and *Namesake* that really established his talent internationally. Gonzalez has worked hard to link the Dallas new music scene with like-minded communities in other areas of the USA. In particular, he has contacts with Austin, New Orleans, Los Angeles and Jackson, Mississippi, as well as with some of Chicago's **AACM** members—as a result his recordings feature a wide array of musicians (including Brackeen, Alvin Fielder, **Ahmed Abdullah**, **Douglas Ewart**, **Malachi Favors** and **Kidd Jordan**) in exotically named ensembles such as New Dallasorleanssippi. He has also worked in the UK, playing and recording with **Keith Tippett**, **Elton Dean**, **Louis Moholo** and Marcio Mattos (*Catechism*), while two new albums from Berlin's Konnex label have him in the company of **Andrew Cyrille**, **Alex Cline**, **Carlos Ward** and **Paul Rogers** among others.

A flowing, lyrical trumpeter, fond of wide intervals, Gonzalez in his music sometimes shows Latin and South African influences but more often draws on the hymns of his Baptist Church upbringing: one hymn in particular, 'Holy Manna', has appeared in different guises on several of his albums. 'I found it to be a perfect link between heaven and earth, a tribute to spiritual strength,' Gonzalez has said, explaining his belief in the spiritual roots of all art. 'We are a creation, and in order to stay alive you must keep creating'.

● ALBUMS: *Air Light (Sleep Sailor)* (Daagnim 1979) ★★★, *Music From Ancient Texts* (Daagnim 1981) ★★★, *Kukkia* (Daagnim 1981) ★★, *Stars/Air/Stripes* (Daagnim 1982) ★★, *Witness* (Daagnim 1983) ★★★, *Stefan* (Silkheart 1986) ★★★★, *Namesake* (Silkheart 1987) ★★★, *Catechism* (Daagnim 1987) ★★★, *Debenge-Debenge* (Silkheart 1989) ★★★★, *The Earth And The Heart* (Konnex 1991) ★★★, *Hymn For The Perfect Heart Of A Pearl* (Konnex 1991) ★★★, *The River Is Deep* (Enja 1991) ★★★, *Earth Dance* (Sunnyside 1991) ★★★, *Obatala* (Enja 1992) ★★★, *The Desert Wind* (Silkheart 1992) ★★★, *Welcome To Us* (GOWI 1993) ★★★, with Yells At Eels *Home* (Daagnim 2001) ★★★.

González, Jerry

b. 5 June 1949, New York City, USA. Multi-instrumentalist González and his Fort Apache Band are one of the most exciting Latin jazz ensembles to emerge in the 90s, fusing the rhythms of **Cal Tjader**, **Tito Puente** and **Eddie Palmieri** with a fiery bebop horn section, with González featuring on trumpet and percussion. He started off playing congas in a Latin jazz quintet alongside his bass-playing younger brother Andy, and attended the New York High School Of Music And Art and the New York City College Of Music. He joined **Dizzy Gillespie**'s band as a percussionist, and then played with Palmieri for four years, during which he was able to nurture his interest in Afro-Cuban rhythms. Gonzáles left Palmieri to form the influential progressive salsa band **Libre** with his brother and timbales player Manny Oquendo.

González continued to develop his jazz and rumba fusion experiments with a series of informal basement sessions at his mother's house in the Bronx, attended by a stellar cast of musicians including **Kenny Dorham**, **Woody Shaw**, **Alfredo De La Fé**, **Alfredo Rodriguez**, Eddie Martínez and Wilfredo Velez. These sessions resulted in two all-star albums by the influential Grupo Folklorico y Experimental Nuevayorquino. In 1979 González was given the opportunity to transfer his fusion experiments to vinyl when he was signed to the American Clavé label as a solo artist by producer **Kip Hanrahan**. He made his solo debut with the notable *Ya Yo Me Curé* in 1980, backed by sidemen including trombonist **Steve Turré**, tenor saxophonist Mario Rivera, pianist **Hilton Ruiz** and singer Frankie Rodriguez on a mixture of Afro-Cuban originals and jazz standards by **Wayne Shorter**, **Duke Ellington** and **Thelonious Monk** (a remarkable reading of 'Evidence'). A European tour followed, with González's ensemble hastily named the Fort Apache Band (taken from the 1981 movie *Fort Apache, The Bronx*). González made his recording debut with the Fort Apache Band on *The River Is Deep*, which was recorded at the Berlin Jazz Festival in November 1982.

González left Libre at the end of the 80s to devote his energies to band leading. In 1989, he released *Obatalá* and *Rumba Para Monk*. On the latter album, an Afro-Cuban Monk tribute, González scaled his band down to a quintet comprising his brother, pianist **Larry Willis**, percussionist Steve Berrios and tenor Carter Jefferson. In November 1990, the Fort Apache Band made their UK debut with an outstanding concert at London's Empire Ballroom. With the addition of alto saxophonist Joe Ford, González's sextet recorded two more acclaimed albums on the Sunnyside label. Jefferson died in 1993 and was replaced by the experienced **John Stubblefield**. The current line-up of the band has released several albums, on Milestone Records, that have helped firmly establish them at the forefront of Latin jazz.

● ALBUMS: *Ya Yo Me Curé* (American Clavé 1980) ★★★, *The River Is Deep* (Enja 1983) ★★★★, *Obatalá* (Enja 1989) ★★★★, *Rumba Para Monk* (Sunnyside 1989) ★★★★, *Earthdance* (Sunnyside 1991) ★★★★, *Moliendo Café* (Sunnyside) ★★★, *Crossroads* (Milestone 1994) ★★★★, *Pensativo* (Milestone 1995) ★★★, *Fire Dance* (Milestone 1996) ★★★★, *Jerry Gonzalez Y Los Piratos Del Flamenco* (Lola 2004) ★★★.

González, José

b. 1978, Gothenburg, Sweden. This Swedish singer-songwriter and guitarist creates music of ephemeral beauty and timeless simplicity. González's Latin-American name is a result of being born in Sweden to Argentinian parents. He was first heard in his homeland with a series of EP releases at the start of the new millennium, before releasing his debut album *Veneer* in 2003. González's immaculate guitar picking was reminiscent of **Alex De Grassi** and **Michael Hedges**, and his gentle vocals earned comparisons to the introspective style of UK folk icons **Bert Jansch** and **Nick Drake**, although his brooding lyrics were more akin to the work of the late **Elliott Smith**. Despite or because of the intimate nature of his music, González began to attract a lot of press interest and his music spread to a wider audience when the song 'Crosses' was used in the finale of the second season of the American television drama *The O.C.* His atmospheric version of Swedish electronica duo the Knife's 'Heartbeats' was then used in a memorable commercial for Sony BRAVIA (the one with the coloured balls bouncing down a San Francisco street). The interest generated by the song led to *Veneer* being re-released in Europe and North America in 2005.

● ALBUMS: *Veneer* (Imperial/Peacefrog 2003) ★★★.

Gonzaléz, Junior
(see **Harlow, Larry**)

Gonzalez, Kenny 'Dope'
(see **Bucketheads; Masters At Work**)

Gonzaléz, Rubén
b. 26 September 1919, Santa Clara, Cuba, d. 8 December 2003, Havana, Cuba. Gonzaléz became a full-time musician in 1941 having studied medicine and classical piano (he had planned to be a doctor by day and musician by night). During the 40s, while playing piano with **Arsenio Rodríguez** and the Orquesta De La Hermanes, he helped to shape the sound of modern Cuban music, incorporating jazz influences and developing the mambo. In the 50s he travelled to Panama and Argentina, where he played with local tango musicians, subsequently returning to Havana to play in cabaret bands. He joined the band of Enrique Jorrin (the creator of the cha-cha-cha) in the early 60s, and stayed for 25 years until Jorrin's death. Following a brief and unsuccessful attempt to lead the band himself, Gonzaléz retired from music completely.

In 1996, Gonzaléz was invited out of retirement by Juan de Marcos González of **Sierra Maestra** to participate in a two-week recording session involving the cream of three generations of Cuban musicians and guest guitarist **Ry Cooder**. Gonzaléz took every opportunity to play in the studio and was a key participant in both the albums planned for the session (the **Afro-Cuban All Stars**' *A Toda Cuba Le Gusta* and **Buena Vista Social Club**'s *Buena Vista Social Club*). His playing impressed Cooder, Juan de Marcos González and co-producer Nick Gold to such an extent that time was also found to record *Introducing . . . Rubén González*, his debut as a band leader. Recorded live over two days, with a small group of specially chosen musicians playing a collection of Cuban standards, some of the album is as stately and graceful as would be expected from a veteran. However, at other times he played with a ferocious attack and improvisational inventiveness, going some way towards justifying Cooder's description of González as 'the greatest piano soloist I have ever heard in my life. He's like a Cuban cross between **Thelonious Monk** and Felix the Cat'.

González made the most of his unexpected second chance, embarking on world concert tours and recording a second album, *Chanchullo*, in 2000. The two solo albums notched up sales in excess of a million, but by now the pianist's health had begun to fail with lung and kidney ailments and cerebral sclerosis curtailing his live appearances. His final live appearance was in Mexico in 2002.

● ALBUMS: *Introducing . . . Rubén González* (World Circuit/Nonesuch 1997) ★★★★, *Chanchullo* (World Circuit/Nonesuch 2000) ★★★.

● COMPILATIONS: *Momentos* (Escondida 2005) ★★★.

Goo Goo Dolls
This US rock band, formed in Buffalo, New York, in 1986, originally comprised Robby Takac (b. 30 September 1964, USA; bass/vocals), Johnny Rzeznik (b. John Rzeznik, 5 December 1965, Buffalo, New York, USA; guitar/vocals) and George Tutuska (drums). Taking their name from an advertisement in a magazine, the band's first two albums were compared to **Cheap Trick** and the **Replacements**. They started doing unlikely cover versions on the second of these, 1989's *Jed*, when the professional crooner Lance Diamond sang guest vocals on a cover version of **Creedence Clearwater Revival**'s 'Down On The Corner'. He also sang on a version of **Prince**'s 'I Could Never Take The Place Of Your Man' on 1990's *Hold Me Up*. Both albums featured unpretentious pop punk songwriting, and the band was now being celebrated by a growing number of fans in the media. Their commercial breakthrough came with 1995's hit single 'Name' and *A Boy Named Goo*, which was produced by **Pere Ubu**, **Hüsker Dü** and **Sugar** accomplice Lou Giordano.

The Goo Goo Dolls' career showed signs of stalling in the mid-90s following litigation with their record company **Warner Brothers Records** and the departure of Tutuska following the recording of *A Boy Named Goo*. Mike Malinin (b. 10 October 1967, USA) replaced him and the band was saved by the anthemic 'Iris', which became a huge radio hit after featuring on the soundtrack of the Nicolas Cage movie, *City Of Angels*. Having built up a strong following on the back of that single, the new album *Dizzy Up The Girl* climbed to number 15 on the *Billboard* 200 album chart in late 1998. 'Slide' hit the US Top 10 the following January, as the album continued its march to multi-platinum status. To put out a 'best of' album in 2001 seemed just a little premature, however. *Gutterflower*, the long-awaited follow-up to *Dizzy Up The Girl*, was released in spring 2002. The band enjoyed further hits with the singles 'Here Is Gone', 'Big Machine' and 'Sympathy'. A live CD/DVD package was released in 2004, which included a notable cover version of the **Supertramp** hit 'Give A Little Bit'.

● ALBUMS: *Goo Goo Dolls* (Celluloid/Mercenary 1987) ★★, *Jed* (Enigma/Death 1989) ★★, *Hold Me Up* (Metal Blade 1990) ★★★, *Superstar Car Wash* (Metal Blade/Warners 1993) ★★★, *A Boy Named Goo* (Metal Blade/Warners 1995) ★★★★, *Dizzy Up The Girl* (Warners 1998) ★★★★★, *Gutterflower* (Warners 2002) ★★★, *Live In Buffalo July 4th 2004* (Warners 2004) ★★★, *Let Love In* (Warners 2006) ★★★.

● COMPILATIONS: *What I Learned About Ego, Opinion, Art & Commerce (1987–2000)* (Warners 2001) ★★★.

● DVD/VIDEOS: *Live In Buffalo July 4th 2004* (Warners 2004).

Goober Patrol
From Norwich, East Anglia, England, Goober Patrol will doubtless never achieve more than a fleeting mention when the early 90s punk guitar scene is assessed, but they released several competent, engaging records that justify their inclusion in such a history. Comprising Simon Sandall (vocals/guitar), Tim Snelson (guitar), Stuart Sandall (vocals/drums) and Tom Blyth (bass), their sound was closely modelled on the **Mega City Four/Senseless Things** axis, though their lyrics opt for irreverence in place of profundity. There was also an obvious debt to the US punk bands of the late 80s, a fact made obvious by their choice of a name derived from slang for 'hillbilly'. Maintaining an attitude of playing 'anywhere, any time', Goober Patrol supported a number of imported American bands including **Green Day**, Samiam and **No FX**, in addition to the stylistically similar British band **Snuff**. Their recording career began with numerous 7-inch

records on a variety of labels and *Truck Off*, their debut album released on German label Lost & Found Records. Later dismissed by the band for its inept production and unfocused performances, it nevertheless identified their as yet unfulfilled search for urgent melodies. The same label then released *Dutch Ovens!*—the title a reference to 'farting under the duvet'—which sold out its print run of 4,000 copies, and was later re-released on Them's Good Records. In the gap before 1995's *Vacation*, the group continued to tour widely, including US dates alongside Rich Kids On LSD and Mr T Experience. Although claims that Goober Patrol represented 'Britain's ready-made answer to Green Day' seemed hopelessly optimistic, the band earned their modicum of celebrity through genuine endeavour rather than press favouritism.

● ALBUMS: *Truck Off* (Lost & Found 1991) ★★, *Dutch Ovens!* (Lost & Found 1992) ★★★, *Vacation* (Them's Good 1995) ★★★, *Extended Vacation* (Them's Good 1997) ★★, *The Unbearable Lightness Of Being Drunk* (Them's Good 1998) ★★, *Songs That Were Too Shit For Fat* (Them's Good) ★★.

Good Boy Records

Mark Auerbach and Steve Travell's London, England–based operation. The company was formed in December 1992. Auerbach and Travell were already well-known in dance circles for their work as **Bump** (whose 'I'm Rushin'' graced the label). They set up their own studio, and elected to start Good Boy because they were giving away too many of their own ideas on remixes for other people. A 'Classy New York style' was the stated intention, based on the duo's admiration for the **Strictly Rhythm Records** empire. Distributed through the **Network Records** umbrella, they certainly started well with releases like Wax Factor's 'Only Love'.

Good Charlotte

Punk pop became a lucrative commodity in the late 90s, as countless skaters decided to put down their boards and pick up instruments in the hope of enjoying the commercial success achieved by bands such as **Green Day** and **Blink-182**. The Waldorf, Maryland, USA–based quintet, Good Charlotte, is just one of a countless stream of similarly styled bands, using the same chord patterns and vocal inflections. The band's leaders are twin brothers, vocalist Joel and guitarist Benji Madden (b. 11 March 1979, USA), who began writing songs together at the age of 16. Influenced by bands such as **Rancid** and Green Day, the duo cut a demo tape, and upon their high school graduation in 1997, relocated to Berkeley, California, to try to follow in the footsteps of their heroes Green Day. Things did not exactly work out that way, and the twins returned to Maryland and completed Good Charlotte's line-up by enlisting Billy (b. William Martin, 15 June 1981; guitar), Paul Thomas (b. 5 October 1980; bass) and Aaron (drums).

In 2000, Good Charlotte signed with Epic Records, and the same year, issued a self-titled debut album. The band supported the release by touring steadily throughout the remainder of 2000 and for much of 2001, during which time they opened shows for **MxPx** and travelled as part of the Warped Tour, while Benji and Joel regularly hosted the **MTV** show, *All Things Rock*. Aaron left the band prior to the recording of Good Charlotte's second album, *The Young And The Hopeless*, which featured session drummer Josh Freese.

The singles 'Lifestyles Of The Rich And Famous' and 'The Anthem' became staples on the MTV and VH1 channels. The band's third album debuted in the US Top 5 in October 2004.

● ALBUMS: *Good Charlotte* (Epic 2000) ★★★, *The Young And The Hopeless* (Epic 2002) ★★★★, *The Chronicles Of Life And Death* (Daylight/Epic 2004) ★★★.

● DVD/VIDEOS: *Video Collection* (Epic Music Video 2003), *Live At Brixton Academy* (Daylight/Epic Music Video 2004).

Good Life

While they are often tagged as emo (emotional hardcore), the slow moving, roots music that the Omaha, Nebraska, USA-based outfit the Good Life composes could serve as the perfect soundtrack for a dreary, rainy Sunday. The band contains several members, but it is widely understood that the Good Life's leader is **Cursive** lead singer and guitarist, Tim Kasher. Specializing in sparse songs that contain unmistakable roots rock elements (with lyrics that often chronicle life's disappointments), the Good Life started out as a Kasher solo project, as evidenced by the 2000 debut, *Novena On A Nocturn*, that featured a non-permanent band backing him up. Soon after however, Kasher opted to assemble a permanent line-up to function as a real 'band,' as Jiha Lee (keyboards), Roger Lewis (drums), Landon Hedges (guitar/bass), and Ryan Fox (multi-instruments) were all enlisted into the Good Life. The quintet debuted in 2002 on *Black Out*, their first release for new label Saddle Creek. For the album, Kasher shifted the band towards a more experimental and rich sound, as drum machines, synthesizers, saxophone, cello, and accordion were added to their musical palette.

● ALBUMS: *Novena On A Nocturn* (Better Looking 2000) ★★★★, *Black Out* (Saddle Creek 2002) ★★★.

Good Looking Records

This label was set up in 1991 by the DJ **LTJ Bukem** and helped to pioneer and develop drum 'n' bass. After four of Bukem's own singles, including 'A Demon's Theme' (1991) and 'Music' (1993), Good Looking began to release material by other artists, including Aquarius, **Blame**, Intense, **Peshay** and PFM. Following the success of the club Speed in central London, in 1995 Good Looking began promoting Bukem's touring club Logical Progression, which featured the label's artists and was accompanied by a series of albums of the same name; it has since completed trips to Germany, Japan and America as well as several tours of the UK including nights at the **Ministry Of Sound** and **Cream**. One side of each *Logical Progression* album featured material, generally by Good Looking artists, selected by Bukem. The first two also included mixed sides, by Bukem and Blame respectively, while the third contained a recording of Bukem DJing with the nine-piece drum 'n' bass band Intense at Brixton Academy. In 1995, Tony Fordham joined as a business partner and helped to develop the label into an umbrella for a number of subsidiaries, including Looking Good, Nexus, Ascendant Grooves, Diverse, 720° and Cookin'. Much of the sound associated with Good Looking revolves around high tempos and busy drums contrasted with slow-moving dubby bass and impressionistic chords and patterns. Other releases include the *Earth* compilations and the *Progression Sessions* albums. The label has also developed a range of clothing and merchandise.

Good News (film musical)

Twenty years after it became a smash-hit Broadway musical, **Good News** came to the screen in 1947 courtesy of MGM. It was one of songwriters' **De Sylva, Brown And Henderson**'s 'fad' musicals—and the fad this time was US football. Star player Tommy Marlowe (**Peter Lawford**) might not be able to play for Tait College in the big game because he has been neglecting his studies and concentrating on having fun and games with Pat McClellan (Pat Marshall). However, after Connie Lane (**June Allyson**) has helped him to swot, Tommy wins the game and Connie as well. Classy singer **Mel Tormé** was in the admirable supporting cast, along with **Joan McCracken**, Donald MacBride, Ray McDonald, Robert Strickland, Tommy Dugan, Clinton Sundberg, and Loren Tindall. The lively and hugely enjoyable 'Varsity Drag' and 'Good News' were two of the songs retained from the original stage production in a score that included 'He's A Ladies Man', 'Lucky In Love', 'The Best Things In Life Are Free', 'Just Imagine' (all De Sylva, Brown And Henderson), 'The French Lesson' (**Roger Edens-Kay Thompson**), and 'Pass That Peace Pipe' (Edens-**Ralph Blane-Hugh Martin**), which accompanied just one of the entertaining and energetic dance numbers staged by Robert Alton and **Charles Walters**. The latter was also making his debut as a director. **Betty Comden** and **Adolph Green**'s screenplay (their first) was adapted from De Sylva and Laurence Schwab's Broadway libretto, and the film was produced by **Arthur Freed**. A previous version of *Good News* had been made in 1930 as an early talkie. It starred Bessie Love, Stanley Smith, Gus Shy and Mary Lawlor, and used more songs from the stage show than this 1947 version did.

Good News (stage musical)

The first, and probably the best of **De Sylva, Brown And Henderson**'s 'fad' musicals that were so popular in the 20s, opened at the 46th Street Theatre in New York on 15 August 1927. College football was the craze in question this time, and, in the book by Laurence Schwab and De Sylva, Tom Marlow (John Price Jones) is in a quandary: he may not be allowed to continue to shine as the incandescent star of the Tait College football team if he fails his astronomy exam. What to do? Enter Connie Lane (Mary Lawlor), who is pretty, and pretty intelligent, too. She guides Tom through the galaxies so that he can play in the big match. Naturally, because this is musical comedy, they find that they have other interests in common, one of which is singing the show's big love songs, 'Just Imagine', 'Lucky In Love', and 'The Best Things In Life Are Free', while the breezy title song, and what must surely rank as the Roaring 20s liveliest and most engaging Charleston-styled number, 'Varsity Drag', is performed with great style and panache by Zelma O'Neal. The rest of the score included 'He's A Ladies Man' and 'A Girl Of The Pi Beta Phi'. *Good News!* was sub-titled 'The Collegiate Musical', and, just to emphasize the point, before the show started the George Olsen Orchestra, dressed in appropriate college uniforms, marched down the aisles of the auditorium shouting football slogans on their way to the orchestra pit. The high-spirited and exuberant production, which ran for 551 performances in New York, and a further 132 in London, was the epitome of that happy-go-lucky, razzle-dazzle era, with its flappers and bootleg gin, which would sadly plummet all too soon into the Depression. Some of the show's songs were destined to live on for many years,

especially 'The Best Things In Life Are Free', which, although it was omitted from the 1930 film version of *Good News*, was included in the 1947 remake, and became the title of the 1956 De Sylva, Brown And Henderson biopic, starring **Gordon MacRae**, Ernest Borgnine, **Dan Dailey**, and Sheree North. In 1974, the show resurfaced on Broadway, starring **Alice Faye** and **Gene Nelson**—but did not stay around for long.

Good Rats

This US group was formed while the members were at college in 1964 by Peppi and Mickey Marchello, both from Long Island, New York, USA. Their debut was a mixture of rock 'n' roll and progressive rock. A succession of poor-selling albums coupled with regular changes of record labels hampered their commercial prospects. They broke up for three years during 1969-72. By the time of their fourth and best album—*From Rats To Riches*—(which was later issued on Radar in the UK), the line-up was the gruff-voiced Peppi, Mickey (guitar), John 'the Cat' Gatto (guitar), Lenny Kotke (bass) and Joe Franco (drums). This album was recorded on Long Island in late 1977 with **Flo And Eddie** (Mark Volman and Howard Kaylan) producing. Although their place in the market has never been clear the Good Rats are essentially a good old-fashioned, basic US rock 'n' roll band. Peppi Marchello is now joined in the line-up by his two sons, Stefan (drums) and Gene (guitar).

● ALBUMS: *The Good Rats* (Kapp 1968) ★★★, *Tasty* (Rat City 1974) ★★, *Rat City In Blue* (Rat City 1976) ★★, *From Rats To Riches* (Passport/Radar 1978) ★★★, *Rats The Way You Like It—Live* (Passport 1978) ★★, *Birth Comes To Us All* (Passport 1978) ★★, *Live At Last* (Rat City 1980) ★★, *Great American Music* (Great American/Passport 1981) ★★, *Cover Of Night* (Now & Then/Frontier 2000) ★★.

● COMPILATIONS: *Tasty Seconds* (Uncle Rat Music 1997) ★★★.

Good Rockin' Charles

b. Charles Edwards, 4 March 1933, Pratt City, Alabama, USA, d. 18 May 1989, Chicago, Illinois, USA. One of the journeyman musicians of the Chicago blues scene, Charles Edwards was engaged to play harmonica on a **Jimmy Rogers** session in the 50s, but failed to appear; an attempt by **Eli Toscano** to record him failed for similar reasons, and it was not until 1975 that he recorded an album. This, and a trip to Europe, revealed him to be, if not an innovative performer, then an outgoing and entertaining one, and a harmonica player of considerable authority, influenced by both **Sonny Boy 'Rice Miller'** and **John Lee 'Sonny Boy' Williamson**.

● ALBUMS: *Good Rockin' Charles* (Rooster 1976) ★★★.

Good Rockin' Tonite

There was plenty of that when this show opened at the Strand Theatre in London on 28 January 1992. It was devised by **Jack Good**, the influential producer who gave British television its earliest—and many still say best—pop music programmes, such as *6.5 Special* and *Oh Boy!* Some of the early beneficiaries of his ingenuity were there on the show's opening night—rock 'n' roll survivors such as **Cliff Richard**, **Lonnie Donegan**, **Joe Brown**, **Marty Wilde**, and **Jess Conrad**. Brilliantly staged by Good and Ian Kellgran, the story, which was only loosely based on Good's life, was really an excuse to celebrate some 60 of those seminal numbers from the 50s and early 60s, in the onstage company of **Tommy Steele**

(David Howarth), **Gene Vincent** (Michael Dimitri), Cliff Richard (Tim Whitnall), **Eddie Cochrane**, the **Vernon Girls** and more. There was also an 'uncanny' impression of **Billy Fury** by Gavin Stanley, and a 'creepy' one of the agent **Larry Parnes** by David Howarth (again). Good himself, engagingly played by Philip Bird, 'stumbles amusingly through an obsessive relationship with music, and a stormy one with his wife (Anna-Juliana Claire) and the BBC's Head of Light Entertainment, played hilariously by James Compton'. After the show transferred to the Prince Of Wales Theatre in July, the jiving in the aisles (literally) continued until November, when the show closed after a rock 'n' rolling 327 performances.

Good Sons

This UK band was one of the finest acts to emerge from the country's alt country scene, releasing a string of critically praised but commercially doomed albums during the mid- to late 90s. Taking their name from a **Nick Cave** album, the Good Sons was formed in 1992 by singer-songwriter **Michael Weston King** (ex-**Gary Hall** And The Stormkeepers), Phil Abram (guitar), Sean McFetridge (bass; ex-Gary Hall And The Stormkeepers), and Ben Jackson (drums). In 1995, they signed a recording contract with the German Glitterhouse label and released their debut, *Singing The Glory Down*. The album featured a guest appearance from US singer-songwriter **Townes Van Zandt** on the track 'Riding The Range'. A series of headlining live shows confirmed the favourable reception afforded the album, and the band appeared as support to a number of their leading influences, including **Joe Ely** and **Blue Rodeo**. The more acoustic-orientated *The Kings Highway* paid homage to the years spent playing folk clubs by main songwriter King. In marked contrast, *Wines, Lines And Valentines* rocked out in a manner reminiscent of their US compatriots the **Jayhawks** and **Wilco**. The album was repackaged and retitled *Angels In The End* for US release through Watermelon Records.

A number of incidents then derailed the band's career, with guitarist Abram relocating to Turin and a bus accident ruining their equipment and leaving King in hospital. More damaging still, Watermelon collapsed into financial ruin leaving the band's nascent US career in tatters. King opted to put the band on hiatus and record his solo debut, *God Shaped Hole*, a brooding, acoustic set in marked contrast to the effervescent surge of the Good Sons' finest work.

The band reconvened in 2000 to complete a short UK tour and begin recording sessions for their fourth album, *Happiness*. Despite receiving the usual excellent reviews, the commercial failure of the album prompted a more permanent break-up. King resumed his solo career with a live album and the studio set, *A Decent Man*.

● ALBUMS: *Singing The Glory Down* (Glitterhouse 1995) ★★★★, *The Kings Highway* (Glitterhouse 1996) ★★★, *Wines, Lines And Valentines* (UK) *Angels In The End* (USA) (Glitterhouse 1997) ★★★★, *Happiness* (Floating World 2001) ★★★★.

● COMPILATIONS: *Cosmic Fireworks: The Best Of The Good Sons* (Phantasmagoria 2004) ★★★★.

Good Times

There was a moment during 1965 when it seemed **Sonny And Cher** could do little wrong. Singles together, singles apart and archive recordings scaled the US and UK charts with impunity, aurally blending **Phil Spector** with folk rock. Visually the pair extolled mutual love and bohemian imagery but their popularity was short-lived. By the time *Good Times* was released in 1966, their star was already waning, although re-invention has allowed **Cher**'s career to prosper. She harboured acting ambitions before becoming a singer and thus this project provided a particularly welcome opportunity. During the film the couple imagine all the movies they could have made, creating genuinely amusing scenes from this unlikely premise. Their international bestseller, 'I Got You Babe', is among the nine songs in a film that has been too quickly overlooked. Despite this, however, few would have predicted this was Cher's first step towards winning a Best Actress Oscar.

Good, Jack

b. 7 August 1931, Greenford, Middlesex, England, This founder of British pop television was president of Oxford University Drama Society and then a stand-up comedian before enrolling on a BBC training course. His final test film was centred on Freddie Mills. The late boxer was also an interlocutor on 1957's *6.5 Special*, a BBC magazine programme for teenagers produced by Good and Josephine Douglas. While he became evangelical about rock 'n' roll, Good's staid superiors obliged him to balance the pop with comedy sketches, string quartets and features on sport and hobbies. He was fired for flaunting Corporation dictates by presenting a stage version of the show. Snapped up by ITV, he broke ground with *Oh Boy!* which introduced **Cliff Richard**, **Marty Wilde** and other homegrown rockers to the nation. So swiftly did its atmospheric parade of idols—mostly male—pass before the cameras that the screaming studio audience, urged on by Good, scarcely had pause to draw breath. While overseeing the less exciting *Boy Meets Girls* (1959) and *Wham!* (1960), Good branched out into publishing and record production, such as **Billy Fury**'s *The Sound Of Fury*. In 1962 Good was in North America, where he worked intermittently as an actor. His self-financed pilot programme, *Young America Swings The World*, fell on stony ground, but, after **Brian Epstein** commissioned him for 1964's *Around The Beatles*, he superintended the nationally broadcast pop showcase *Shindig!* which, as well as making 'discoveries' such as the **Righteous Brothers** and **Sonny And Cher**, represented a media breakthrough for diverse black artists from **Howlin' Wolf** to the **Chambers Brothers**—and held its own in a ratings war against *The Beverly Hillbillies* on a main rival channel. Leaving *Shindig!* to fend for itself, Good's most interesting career tangent of the late 60s was *Catch My Soul*, a rock adaptation in a Los Angeles theatre of Shakespeare's *Othello* with **Jerry Lee Lewis** as Iago. For a season in London, **P.J. Proby** assumed the Lewis role with Good himself as the Moor. Back in the USA, he ticked over with one-shot television specials concerning, among others, **Andy Williams**, the **Monkees** and 1970's Emmy Award-winning classical/pop hybrid of **Ray Charles**, **Jethro Tull**, the **Nice** and the LA Philharmonic.

On an extended visit to England from his Santa Fe, home in the late 70s, Good put on *Elvis*, a biographical musical starring, initially, Proby and **Shakin' Stevens** before daring an updated reconstruction of *Oh Boy!* (later transferred to television) at the same London West End theatre. By the 80s, income from the inspired Good's less frequent television and stage ventures underwrote another vocational episode—as a painter. In the 90s it was reported that Good was training to become a monk, but, while he was contemplating it, he travelled to London to oversee the West End launch of his own autobiographical musical, *Good Rockin' Tonite*, which had them dancing in the aisles—just like the old days. He subsequently took up residence in an adobe chapel in New Mexico.

Good, Matthew, Band

One of Canada's leading alternative rock bands of the 90s, the Matthew Good Band was based around the central figure of singer-songwriter Matthew Good (b. 29 June 1971, Burnaby, British Columbia, Canada). He started his music career as part of an acoustic folk outfit touring the Canadian circuit. This line-up recorded a five-song demo before Good returned to Vancouver and formed a rock band with Geoff Lloyd (bass) and Charlie Quintana (drums). The latter was soon replaced by Ian Browne (b. 12 November 1973, New Westminster, British Columbia, Canada), and Dave Genn (b. 2 March 1969, White Rock, British Columbia, Canada) was added on guitar and keyboards. The new line-up of the Matthew Good Band recorded and independently released 1995's *Last Of The Ghetto Astronauts*. The album gained airplay on local alternative stations and eventually sold in excess of 20,000 copies, leading to a recording contract with the US label Private Music. The band recorded the *Raygun* EP for the label, but owing to record company machinations were released from their contract. They recorded their second album, *Underdogs*, independently at Greenhouse Studios in Burnaby, British Columbia. A distribution contract with **A&M Records** and extensive radio play of the singles 'Everything Is Automatic' and 'Apparitions' confirmed the band's popularity, however, and the album went on to achieve platinum sales. In 1998, Rich Priske (b. 29 August 1969) replaced Lloyd on bass. The band's third collection, *Beautiful Midnight*, was released by Universal Records the following September, and swiftly topped the Canadian charts. The creation of The Audio Of Being was a fraught affair, with Genn leaving during the recording and Good undergoing difficult throat surgery. Following the album's release Good pulled the plug on the band and embarked on a career as a solo artist. He made his debut in 2003 with the album *Avalanche*.

● ALBUMS: *Last Of The Ghetto Astronauts* (Independent Release 1995) ★★★, *Underdogs* (Darktown/A&M 1997) ★★★, *Beautiful Midnight* (Universal 1999) ★★★★, *The Audio Of Being* (Universal 2001) ★★★.
Solo: Matthew Good *Avalanche* (Universal 2003) ★★★, *White Light Rock & Roll Review* (Universal 2004) ★★★.
● COMPILATIONS: *In A Coma 1995–2005* (Universal 2005) ★★★★.

Goodacre, Tony

b. 3 February 1938, Leeds, England. With up to 300 shows a year, Tony Goodacre has been among the hardest-working British country musicians. In his adolescence, Goodacre acted, sang and played piano but, realizing the advantages of being able to entertain on demand, he switched to guitar. He formed the Tigers Skiffle Group while in the Royal Air Force, and conversations with American servicemen inspired his passion for country music. He borrowed dozens of rare American country records and set about learning the songs. In September 1956, Goodacre secured his first professional engagement singing country music. He had a day job in Leeds during the late 50s and 60s but he worked clubs and pubs in the evenings. In 1969 he began working regularly with steel guitarist Arthur Layfield, and they became the nucleus for a new group, Goodacre Country. Economics are such that Goodacre now usually works solo but he still occasionally teams up with Layfield as well as several seasoned musicians, many of whom have played on his albums.

Ever since 1975, when he included eight original songs on *Grandma's Feather Bed*, Goodacre has championed the cause of British country songwriters. *Written In Britain* was totally that, and among the songwriters he has featured are Terry McKenna, Geoff Ashford, Sammy King and Stewart Ross. **George Hamilton IV**, president of his fan club, encouraged Goodacre to play in Nashville, which culminated in appearances at the **Grand Ole Opry** in 1977. The following year he returned to Nashville to record *Mr Country Music*, and his tours have encompassed the USA, Australasia and Europe. In 1980, along with his wife Sylvia, Goodacre formed his own Sylvantone label, which has released albums by other British acts, some of which received his management guidance. His albums—and videos—are sold at personal appearances where his most popular songs include 'Old Shep', 'The Country Hall Of Fame' and 'The Old Rugged Cross', as well as several of the original songs he has recorded over the years.

● ALBUMS: *Roaming 'Round In Nashville* (Outlet 1974) ★★★, *Grandma's Feather Bed* (Outlet 1975) ★★★, *Thanks To The Hanks* (Outlet 1976) ★★★, *Written In Britain* (Outlet 1977) ★★★★, *Mr. Country Music* (Outlet 1978) ★★, *You've Made My Life Complete* (Outlet 1979) ★★★, *Recorded Live In Ilkley* (Sylvantone 1980) ★★, *25th Anniversary* (Sylvantone 1981) ★★★, *Red Roses* (Sylvantone 1984) ★★★, *Country Favourites* (Sylvantone 1988) ★★, *Something Special* (Sylvantone 1989) ★★★, *40th Anniversary Album* (Sylvantone 1996) ★★★, *Livin' On Lovin'* (Sylvantone 1998) ★★★, with Steve Isherwood *The Millennium Project* (Sylvantone 2001) ★★★, *More Favourite Tracks* (Sylantone 2002) ★★★, *Sings The Songs Of Geoff Ashford* (Sylvantone 2003) ★★★, with Isherwood *Snow Covered* (Sylvantone 2004) ★★★.
● COMPILATIONS: *The Tony Goodacre Collection* (Sylvantone 1986) ★★★, *Favourite Tracks From The 1970's* (Sylvantone 2000) ★★★, *Favourite Tracks From The 1980's* (Sylvantone 2000) ★★★.

Goodbye Girl, The

By the time this musical blew into New York's Marquis Theatre from Chicago on 4 March 1993, it had lost its original director (Gene Saks) and opening number. Rather appropriately for Saks, who was replaced by 73-year-old veteran stager **Michael Kidd**, the discarded number was called 'I'm Outta Here'. These changes did nothing to dampen the climate of anticipation for what some out-of-town critics regarded as 'a sure-fire winner . . . the funniest new musical for years'. The production certainly had some good things going for it, notably a score by composer **Marvin (*A Chorus Line*) Hamlisch** and lyricist David (*City Of Angels*) Zippel, as well as a cast headed by Broadway favourite **Bernadette Peters** and Hollywood and television funny man Martin Short. Best of all (in theory), the book was written by **Neil Simon**, the most popular playwright of his time. He adapted it from his 1977 romantic film comedy of the same name, starring the one-time Mrs. Simon, Marsha Mason, and the Oscar-winning Richard Dreyfus. Set in New York City, the story concerns Paula (Peters), a struggling single mother, who is eventually attracted to an unemployed émigré Chicago actor Elliot (Short), after she is forced to share an apartment with him. In his pursuit of Paula, Elliot finds an ally in her daughter, Lucy (Tammy Minoff), extolling his virtues as a prospective father with the vocally impressive 'I Can Play This Part'. The domestic situation is frequently enlivened—and enhanced—by the rhythm-and-blues rantings of landlady Mrs. Crosby (Carol Woods).

Making his Broadway musical theatre debut, Short attracted all the best notices, and proved a charismatic, assured performer, especially in the gay 'Richard Interred' sequence, where he is forced by a manic stage director (John Christopher-Jones), to play Richard III as 'a man playing a woman playing a man' rather than a homosexual. Although some critics felt that she was upstaged by Short, the never-less-than-superb Peters had her moments—including one scene in which she danced in a pile of French fries for the sake of a television show—with three big solos and various duets in among the rest of the score, which comprised 'This Is As Good As It Gets', 'No More', 'A Beat Behind', 'My Rules', 'Good News, Bad News', 'Footsteps', 'How Can I Win?', 'Too Good To Be Bad', '2 Good 2 B Bad', 'Who Would've Thought?', 'Paula (An Improvised Love Song)', 'Jump For Joy', and 'What A Guy'. Musical staging was by Graciela Daniele, and **Billy Byers** and Torrie Zito were responsible for the lively orchestrations. Despite its earlier promise, *The Goodbye Girl* was immediately faced with a batch of negative reviews, which criticized particularly its slim storyline, old-fashioned style, and unimaginative staging. The writing (and closing notice) was on the wall, and, after failing to convert any of its five **Tony Award** nominations for best musical, actor (Short), actress (Peters), director, and choreography (Daniele), it was withdrawn in August after 188 performances. The original cast album differed in several respects from the score performed on stage, with the new opening number for Broadway, 'This Is As Good As It Gets', going the same way as its predecessor, 'I'm Outta Here'.

The show was the third unsuccessful attempt—along with **Nick And Nora** and **My Favorite Year**—to convert well-known films into stage musicals in the early 90s. Having been jilted in New York, *The Goodbye Girl* subsequently went back to her Chicago roots early in 1994, when a production starring Kathy Santen and James FitzGerald, directed by Joe Leonardo and David Zippel, played at Marriot's Lincolnshire Theatre. Three years later, West End audiences and critics rejected a new version of the show starring Gary Wilmot and Ann Crumb, which closed after only two months. Hamlisch wrote seven new songs, 'I'll Take The Sky', 'Body Talk', 'Get A Life', 'Am I Who I Think I Am?'/'Are You Who You Think You Are?', 'If You Break Their Hearts', 'Do You Want To Be In My Movie?' and 'the Future Isn't What It Used To Be', with lyricist **Don Black**. Fortunately, two of the three Zippel numbers to be retained were first act highlights, 'Elliot Garfield Grant' and 'Good News, Bad News'.

Goodbye Mr. Mackenzie

One of Scotland's highly tipped 80s pop exports, Goodbye Mr. Mackenzie combined the emotive songwriting style of fellow Scots **Deacon Blue** or **Del Amitri**, with inspiring guitar work by 'Big' John Duncan. They formed in Edinburgh in 1986 and additionally featured Martin Metcalfe (vocals/guitar), Rona Scobie (keyboards/vocals) and Shirley Manson (b. 26 August 1966, Edinburgh, Scotland; keyboards/vocals), Chuck Parker (bass) and Derek Kelly (drums). A debut single, 'The Rattler', appeared on the Precious Organisation label (also home to **Wet Wet Wet**'s first releases) in September 1986 and attracted a degree of attention, earning them supportive press and several radio sessions. Jimmy Anderson was brought in on guitar, allowing Metcalfe to concentrate on singing, and Neil Baldwin replaced Parker in time for a second single—this time on the Claude label. In February 1988 they signed to **EMI Records**, and shortly afterwards Fin Wilson took over bass duties, while Big John Duncan (from the Blood Uncles and, before that, the **Exploited**) replaced Anderson, thus forming the best-known and most successful line-up. Their often anthemic sound, embellished with a touch of melodrama, drew upon such influences as **David Bowie**, the **Doors**' Jim Morrison and **Bruce Springsteen**. Their first UK national chart appearance came with 'Goodbye Mr. Mackenzie' in the summer of 1988, and a year later, 'The Rattler' (re-recorded) finally made an impact on the charts, reaching the Top 40. This followed the release of their debut, *Good Deeds And Dirty Rags*, and later, *Fish Heads And Tails*, both housed on **Capitol Records**. However, a second studio album for Capitol, *Hammer And Tongs*, went unissued, until it was unearthed by new home Radioactive (a subsidiary of MCA Records) in 1991. It did little to revive fortunes. Duncan would later go on to guest with **Nirvana** on various touring engagements, where he acted as their guitar roadie (he was rumoured to be joining the band at one point). Manson later found huge success as lead singer with **Garbage**.

● ALBUMS: *Good Deeds And Dirty Rags* (Capitol 1989) ★★★, *Hammer And Tongs* (Radioactive/MCA 1991) ★★★, *Live: On The Day Of Storms* (Radioactive 1993) ★★, *Five* (Radioactive 1993) ★★★.
● COMPILATIONS: *Fish Heads And Tails* mini-album (Capitol 1989) ★★.

Goode, Coleridge

b. Coleridge George Emerson Goode, 29 November 1914, St. Andrew, Jamaica, West Indies. While studying at Glasgow University, Goode began playing violin, later switching to bass. He first played professionally in 1942 and was soon working in clubs, on radio and records with noted European and UK artists such as **Johnny Claes**, **Stéphane Grappelli**, **Django Reinhardt** and **George Shearing**. In the early 40s he performed with **Eric Winstone**'s showband and in 1944 became a member of **Leslie 'Jiver' Hutchinson**'s all-black band, among the first of its kind in the UK. Later in the 40s he joined **Ray Ellington** and a decade later was a member of **Joe Harriott**'s free-form quintet. In the 60s Goode was involved with **Michael Garrick** and also led his own groups, which, like Harriott's, experimented with the fusion of Indian music and jazz. In the mid-70s Goode teamed up with pianist Iggy Quayle, an association that persisted for over two decades.
● FURTHER READING: *Bass Lines: A Life In Jazz*, Coleridge Goode and Roger Cotterrell.

Goodfellaz

A modern R&B act formed in Los Angeles, California, USA, in the mid-90s, Goodfellaz comprises DeLouie Avant, Angel

Vasquez and Ray Vencier. Prior to signing to **A&M Records** subsidiary Avatar, the trio 'shopped' for a record contract with a collection of demo tracks that were considered sufficiently strong to comprise their debut album. After securing a contract, Family Stand founders Jeff Smith and Peter Lord were enrolled as producers for this self-titled project. Justifying their appeal to the press in an already-crowded market for vocal R&B, Vasquez told **Billboard** magazine: 'It's our distinct vocals that sets us apart from other guy groups. Ray has a really big voice, mine has a lighter, falsetto tone to it, and Louie has a really soulful feel. When you hear our tracks, you can pick each of us out easily.' The album was promoted with the release of a single, 'Sugar Honey Ice Tea', which secured heavy rotation on R&B-themed television and radio stations.

● ALBUMS: *Goodfellaz* (Avatar/A&M 1997) ★★★.

Goodhand-Tait, Philip

b. 3 January 1945, Hull, England. This singing pianist is best known for his work as a composer for **Love Affair** who recorded his 'Gone Are the Songs Of Yesterday' as the b-side of 'Everlasting Love', their 1968 UK chart-topper. Goodhand-Tait numbers became the main track on future hits—notably 'A Day Without Love' that was included in the **Sex Pistols** early repertoire. Although he seemed an obvious choice, Goodhand-Tait was considered too old to apply for the post when Love Affair's singer resigned in 1969. Nevertheless, he resumed writing for Love Affair after their ill-advised bid to 'go progressive'. His own outfit, the Stormsville Shakers, had been hitless despite a prestigious stint backing **Larry Williams** in Europe, and a **Parlophone** contract for 'You Can't Take Love' and other singles. Neither did he fare any better in the 70s as an alternative to **Elton John**—despite the promotion of 1973's *Philip Goodhand-Tait* (on **DJM Records**) on a UK tour supporting **Lou Reed**. After moving to **Chrysalis Records** in 1975, he was recording for the humbler Gundog label by the 80s.

● ALBUMS: *Rehearsal* (DJM 1971) ★★, *I Think I'll Write A Song* (DJM 1971) ★★★, *Songfall* (DJM 1972) ★★★, *Philip Goodhand-Tait* (DJM 1973) ★★★, *Jingle Jangle Man* (DJM 1975) ★★★, *Oceans Away* (Chrysalis 1976) ★★, *Teaching An Old Dog New Tricks* (Chrysalis 1977) ★★★, *Good Old Phil's* (Gundog 1980) ★★.

Goodie Mob

One of the first and most successful groups to emerge from the Dirty South hip-hop scene from the USA, Goodie Mob helped break the west coast–east coast axis dominating rap music in the mid-90s. Formed in Atlanta, Georgia, by **Cee-Lo** (b. Thomas Callaway, 30 May 1974, Atlanta, Georgia, USA), Khujo (b. Willie Knighton, 13 March 1972), T-Mo (b. Robert Barnett, 2 February 1972) and Big Gipp (b. Cameron Gipp, 28 April 1973), Goodie Mob debuted in 1995 with the excellent *Soul Food*. Collaborating with inspired production team **Organized Noize** and employing live instrumentation in the studio, the quartet retreated from the prevalent gangsta rap ethic to explore a series of moral and social concerns particular to the ghettos of their home state. Heralded alongside **Outkast** as the leaders of the new Dirty South movement, the quartet returned in 1998 with another fine album, *Still Standing*, on which their socially conscious brand of hip-hop reached a creative peak. Their third release *World Party* was a more commercial offering, but its sales

were completely overshadowed the following year by Out-kast's bestselling *Stankonia*. Members of both crews went on to collaborate in the **Dungeon Family** project.

Cee-Lo left Goodie Mob to launch his solo career in 2002 with the erratically entertaining *Cee-Lo Green And His Perfect Imperfections*. The same June, Khujo was involved in a serious car accident in Atlanta and lost his right leg below the kneecap. The cover of Goodie Mob's next studio set, *One Monkey Don't Stop No Show*, featured a monkey in a tuxedo lining up alongside the band members on the album cover, a less than subtle reference to the departed Cee-Lo.

● ALBUMS: *Soul Food* (LaFace 1995) ★★★★, *Still Standing* (LaFace 1998) ★★★★, *World Party* (LaFace 1999) ★★★, *One Monkey Don't Stop No Show* (Koch 2004) ★★★.

● COMPILATIONS: *Dirty South Classics* (Arista 2003) ★★★★.

Goodies

One of the few British television comedy acts to put together a consistent run of hit records, the Goodies comprised Bill Oddie (b. 7 July 1941, Rochdale, Lancashire, England), Graeme Garden (b. 18 February 1943, Aberdeen, Scotland) and Tim Brooke-Taylor (b. 17 July 1940, Buxton, Derbyshire, England). All three were educated at Cambridge University and were involved in the Footlights Revue in the early 60s, although not all at the same time. Oddie and Brooke-Taylor then joined the Cambridge Circus Show (with John Cleese) and toured worldwide. They then moved on to the BBC radio show *I'm Sorry I'll Read That Again* where they were eventually joined by Graeme Garden (who replaced Graham Chapman). Brooke-Taylor also spent time in the theatre and made films before starting to work in television on programmes such as *At Last The 1948 Show*. Oddie wrote and performed for programmes like *That Was The Week That Was* and *Twice A Fortnight* before meeting up with Brooke-Taylor again, and Garden (now a qualified doctor after medical training at Kings College Hospital, London) in the comedy programme *Broaden Your Mind*. Oddie, a prolific songwriter, also entered the recording world with three singles on **Parlophone Records** including a passable stab at pop with 'Nothing Better To Do' (a lament about Mods And Rockers fighting). The three teamed up for their own comedy show, which was originally to have been called *Narrow Your Mind* but was eventually broadcast as *The Goodies* starting on the BBC on 8 November 1970. Several series were broadcast throughout the 70s, and a number of spin-offs including several UK hit singles were created including 'The In Betweenies', 'The Funky Gibbon', and 'Black Pudding Bertha (The Queen Of Northern Soul)', the first two of which both made the UK Top 10.

In 1980 they left the BBC for Independent Television but the Goodies soon went their separate ways. Oddie, a keen ornithologist, has written several books on the subject and appears regularly on television in this guise or in general factual programmes. He also hosted a jazz programme (another of his passions) on radio. Garden works in radio quizzes and game shows but has also used his medical background to present some light-hearted health and fitness programmes. Brooke-Taylor has worked successfully in television situation comedies.

● ALBUMS: *Goodies Sing Songs* (Decca 1973) ★★, *The New Goodies LP* (Bradley's 1975) ★★, *Nothing To Do With Us*

(Island 1976) ★★, *The Goodies' Beastly Record* (EMI 1978) ★★.

● COMPILATIONS: *The World Of The Goodies* (EMI 1975) ★★★, *The Goodies' Greatest* (Bradley's 1976) ★★★, *Funky Gibbon: The Best Of The Goodies* (Castle Pie 2000) ★★★.

Gooding, Cuba

b. 27 April 1944, New York City, USA. Gooding began his professional musical career in 1971, when he was chosen to replace the late Donald McPherson in the **Main Ingredient**. His easy, soulful vocals fitted in immediately with the group's cabaret-based style, and the first release by the new line-up, 'Everybody Plays The Fool', was a major hit in the USA. Gooding was showcased on 10 further chart entries, before electing to begin a solo career at **Motown Records** in 1978. The ambitiously titled *The First Cuba Gooding Album* suggested that his solo work might rival the popularity of the Main Ingredient, but the poor reception of *Love Dancer* and his subsequent singles blighted this promise. Motown dropped Gooding in 1983. He subsequently reunited with his former colleagues in the Main Ingredient. His son is rapper and actor Cuba Gooding Jnr., who won an Academy Award in 1997 for his role in the movie *Jerry Maguire*. Gooding left the Main Ingredient in 1999 to concentrate on his acting and solo career.

● ALBUMS: *The First Cuba Gooding Album* (Motown 1978) ★★★, *Love Dancer* (Motown 1979) ★★.

● FILMS: *Children Of The Struggle* (1999), *Gedo* aka *Fatal Blade* (2000).

Goodman, Benny

b. Benjamin David Goodman, 30 May 1909, Chicago, Illinois, USA, d. 20 June 1986, New York City, USA. Born into a large, impoverished family of immigrants, Goodman experienced hard times while growing up. Encouraged by his father to learn a musical instrument, Goodman and two of his brothers took lessons; as the youngest and smallest he learned to play the clarinet. These early studies took place at the Kehelah Jacob Synagogue and later at Hull House, a settlement house founded by reformer Jane Addams. From the start, Goodman displayed an exceptional talent and he received personal tuition from James Sylvester and then the renowned classicist Franz Schoepp (who also taught **Buster Bailey** around the same time). Before he was in his teens, Goodman had begun performing in public and was soon playing in bands with such emerging jazz artists as **Jimmy McPartland**, **Frank Teschemacher** and **Dave Tough**. Goodman's precocious talent allowed him to become a member of the American Federation of Musicians at the age of 14, and that same year he played with **Bix Beiderbecke**. By his mid-teens Goodman was already established as a leading musician, working on numerous engagements with many bands to the detriment of his formal education. In 1925 he was heard by **Gil Rodin**, who was then with the popular band led by **Ben Pollack**. Goodman was hired by Pollack, then working in California, and the following year made a triumphal return to Chicago as featured soloist with the band. Goodman remained with Pollack until 1929, when he became a much-in-demand session musician in New York, making many hundreds of record and radio sessions. Keenly ambitious and already a determined perfectionist, Goodman continued to develop his craft until he was perhaps the most skilled clarinet player in the country, even if he was virtually unknown to the general public.

During the late 20s and early 30s Goodman played in bands led by **Red Nichols**, **Ben Selvin**, **Ted Lewis**, **Sam Lanin** and others, sometimes for club, dance hall and theatre engagements and often on record sessions. In 1934 his ambitions led him to form a large dance band which was successful in being hired for a residency at **Billy Rose**'s Music Hall. After a few months, this date collapsed when Rose was replaced by someone who did not like the band, but Goodman persisted and late that same year was successful in gaining one of three places for dance bands on a regular radio show broadcast by NBC. The show, entitled *Let's Dance*, ran for about six months. By this time Goodman was using arrangements by leading writers of the day such as **Fletcher Henderson** and **Spud Murphy** and including in his band musicians such as **Bunny Berigan**, trombonists Red Ballard and Jack Lacey, saxophonists **Toots Mondello** and **Hymie Schertzer**, and in the rhythm section **George Van Eps** and **Frank Froeba**, who were quickly replaced by Allan Reuss and **Jess Stacy**. Goodman's brother, Harry, was on bass, and the drummer was **Stan King**, who was soon replaced by the more urgent and exciting **Gene Krupa**. The band's singer was **Helen Ward**, one of the most popular band singers of the day. When the *Let's Dance* show ended, Goodman took the band on a nationwide tour.

Prompted in part by producer **John Hammond Jnr.** and also by his desire for the band to develop, Goodman made many changes to the personnel, something he would continue to do throughout his career as a big band leader, and by the time the tour reached Los Angeles, in August 1935, the band was in extremely good form. Despite the success of the radio show and the band's records, the tour had met with mixed fortunes and some outright failures. However, business picked up on the west coast, and on 21 August 1935 the band played a dance at the Palomar Ballroom in Los Angeles. They created a sensation and the massive success that night at the Palomar is generally credited as the time and place where the showbusiness phenomenon that became known as the 'swing era' was born.

After an extended engagement at the Palomar the band headed back east, stopping over in Chicago for another extended run, this time at the Joseph Urban Room at the Congress Hotel. Earlier, Goodman had made some trio recordings using Krupa and pianist **Teddy Wilson**. The records sold well and he was encouraged by Helen Oakley, later Helen Oakley Dance, to feature Wilson in the trio at the hotel. Goodman eventually was persuaded that featuring a racially mixed group in this manner was not a recipe for disaster and when the occasion passed unremarked, except for musical plaudits, he soon afterwards employed Wilson as a regular member of the featured trio. In 1936 he added **Lionel Hampton** to form the Benny Goodman Quartet and while this was not the first integrated group in jazz it was by far the one with the highest profile. Goodman's big band continued to attract huge and enthusiastic audiences. In the band now were leading swing-era players such as **Harry James**, **Ziggy Elman**, **Chris Griffin**, **Vernon Brown**, **Babe Russin** and **Arthur Rollini**.

Goodman had an especially successful date at the Paramount Theatre in New York, beginning on 3 March 1937, and his records continued to sell very well. On 16 January 1938, the band played a concert at Carnegie Hall, sealing its success and Goodman's reputation as the 'King of Swing.' Soon after the Carnegie Hall date the band's personnel underwent significant changes. Krupa left to form his own band, soon followed by Wilson and James. Goodman found replacements and carried on as before although, inevitably, the band sounded different. In the early 40s he had a particularly interesting personnel, which included **Cootie Williams, 'Big' Sid Catlett, Georgie Auld** and, in the small group (which was now a septet although labelled as the Benny Goodman Sextet), **Charlie Christian**. Other Goodman musicians of this period included **Jimmy Maxwell** and **Mel Powell**, while his singer, who had followed Ward, **Martha Tilton** and **Helen Forrest**, was **Peggy Lee**. With occasional fallow periods, which usually coincided with the persistent back trouble with which he was plagued, Goodman continued to the end of the 40s, dabbling with bop by way of a small group that featured musicians such as Doug Mettome, **Åke 'Stan' Hasselgård, Wardell Gray** and, fleetingly, **Fats Navarro** and with big bands that included Mettome, Gray, **Stan Getz, Don Lamond** and **Jimmy Rowles**.

Goodman soon ended his flirtation with bop, but the release, in 1953, of a long-playing album made from acetates cut during the 1938 Carnegie Hall concert and forgotten during the intervening years revitalized interest in him and his career. He re-formed a band for a concert tour that brought together many of the old gang; but a decision to enhance the tour's chances of success by also featuring **Louis Armstrong** and his All Stars was an error. The two stars clashed at rehearsals and during the out-of-town warm-up concert. By the time the package was ready for opening at Carnegie Hall, Goodman was in hospital, whether for a genuine illness, or because of a sudden attack of diplomacy, no one is quite sure. In 1955 he recorded the soundtrack for a feature film, *The Benny Goodman Story*, and a soundtrack album was also released that featured Wilson, Hampton, Krupa, James, Getz and other former sidemen.

During the rest of the 50s and in succeeding decades, Goodman made many appearances with small groups and with occasional big bands, but his days as a leader of a regular big band were over. Even as a small group leader, his bands tended to be one-off only affairs, although he did regularly associate with musicians for whom he had high regard, among them **Ruby Braff** and **Urbie Green**. In Europe he led a big band for an appearance at the 1958 World's Fair in Brussels and in 1962 took a band to the USSR for a visit sponsored by the US State Department. Later, he fronted other big bands, including two formed from British musicians for concert tours in 1969 and again in 1970. From the late 60s he began appearing at regular reunions of the quartet with Wilson, Hampton and Krupa. These reunions, along with club and television sessions, occasional tours to Europe and the Far East, occupied the 70s. This decade also saw, on 16 January 1978, a Carnegie Hall date that attempted to recreate the magic of his first appearance there, 30 years before. Goodman continued to record and play concert and other dates into the early 80s. In the last few years of his life and ensconced in his apartment on west 44th, Manhattan he lived quietly and is well remembered with great affection by the local community.

From the earliest days of his career Goodman was marked out as a hot clarinettist. Although he had an early regard for **Ted Lewis**, it was the playing of such musicians as Teschemacher and **Jimmy Noone** that most influenced him. By the start of the 30s, however, Goodman was very much his own man, playing in a highly distinctive style and beginning to influence other clarinettists. His dazzling technique, allied to his delight in playing hot jazz, made him one of the most exciting players of his day. Without question, he was the most technically proficient of all musicians regularly playing jazz clarinet. On the many records he made during this period Goodman almost always soloed, yet he rarely made an error, even on unused takes. During the swing era, despite the rising popularity of **Artie Shaw** and a handful of others, Goodman retained his popularity, even though his jazz style became noticeably less hot as the decade progressed. His dabblings with bop were never fully convincing, although in his playing of the 40s and later there are signs that he was aware of the changes being wrought in jazz. There are also fleeting stylistic nods towards **Lester Young**, whose playing he clearly admired.

From the late 30s Goodman had become steadily more interested in classical music and periodically appeared and recorded in this context, often performing pieces that he had specially commissioned. The classical pursuits led him to adopt a different embouchure thus altering the sound of all his playing, and further attenuating the gap some felt had arisen between the current Goodman style and the hot jazz playing of his youth. As a musician Goodman was a perfectionist, practising every day until the end of his life (in his biography of Goodman, James Lincoln Collier reports that, at the time of his death, the clarinettist, alone at home, appeared to have been playing a Brahms Sonata). As with so many perfectionists, Goodman expected his employees to adhere to his own high standards. Many were similarly dedicated musicians, but they were also individualistic, and in some cases had egos that matched his own. Inevitably, there were many clashes; over the years a succession of Goodman stories have emerged that suggest that he was a man who was totally preoccupied with his music to the exclusion of almost everything else including social niceties. Goodman's achievements in this particular field of American popular music are virtually matchless. He rose from poverty to become a millionaire before he was 30 years old, a real rags-to-riches story. He was, for a while, the best-known and most popular musician in the USA. And if the title King of Swing rankled with many musicians and was clearly inappropriate when his work is compared with that of such peers as Armstrong and **Duke Ellington**, Goodman's band of the late 30s was a hard-driving outfit that contrasted sharply with many other white bands of the period and at its best was usually their superior. The trio and quartet brought to small group jazz a sophistication rarely heard before, and seldom matched since; but which nevertheless included much hot music, especially from the leader. It was, perhaps, in the sextet, with Christian, Williams, Auld and others that Goodman made his greatest contribution to jazz. All the tracks recorded by this group before Christian's untimely death are classics of the form. His encouragement of musicians like Christian, Wilson and Hampton not only helped Goodman to promote important careers in jazz but also did much to break down racial taboos in showbusiness and American society. The fact that he was never an innovator means Goodman was not a great jazzman in the sense that Armstrong, Ellington, **Charlie Parker** and others were. Nevertheless, he was a major figure in jazz and played an important role in the history of twentieth-century popular music.

● ALBUMS: *Benny Goodman And Peggy Lee* 10-inch album (Columbia 1949) ★★★, *Dance Parade* 10-inch album (Columbia 1949) ★★★, *Goodman Sextet Session* 10-inch album (Columbia 1949) ★★★★, *Let's Hear The Melody* 10-inch album (Columbia 1950) ★★★, *Dance Parade Vol. 2* 10-inch album (Columbia 1950) ★★★★, *Carnegie Hall Jazz Concert* 10-inch album (Columbia 1950) ★★★★, *King Of Swing* 6-LP box set (Columbia 1950) ★★★★, with Jack Teagarden *Goodman & Teagarden* 10-inch album (Jazz Panorama 1951) ★★★★, *Benny Goodman* (RCA Victor 1951) ★★★, *Plays For The Fletcher Henderson Fund* (Tax 1951) ★★★, *1937-38 Jazz Concert No 2* (Columbia 1952) ★★★, *Easy Does It* (Capitol 1952) ★★★, *Immortal Performances* (RCA Victor 1952) ★★★★, *The Benny Goodman Trio* (Capitol 1952) ★★★★, *The Benny Goodman Band* (Capitol 1953) ★★★, *The Golden Era: Combos* (Columbia 1953) ★★★★, *The Goodman Touch* (Capitol 1953) ★★★★, *The Golden Era: Bands* (Columbia 1953) ★★★★, *Presents Eddie Sauter Arrangements* (Columbia 1954) ★★★★, *Benny Goodman 1937-1939* (RCA Victor 1954) ★★★★★, *Small Combo 1947* (Capitol 1954) ★★★★, *Benny Goodman 1927-1934* (Brunswick 1954) ★★★★, *Benny Goodman Featuring Jack Teagarden* 10-inch album (Jolly Rogers 1954) ★★★★, *The Golden Age Of Benny Goodman* (RCA Victor 1955) ★★★★, *The Benny Goodman Story* (Coral 1955) ★★★★, *The Great Benny Goodman* (Columbia 1956) ★★★, *Trio, Quartet, Quintet* (RCA Victor 1956) ★★★★, *The Vintage Benny Goodman* (Columbia 1956) ★★★★, *This Is Benny Goodman* (RCA Victor 1956) ★★★★, *In Brussels Vol. 1* (Columbia 1958) ★★★★, *Mostly Sextets* (Capitol 1958) ★★★, *In Brussels Vol. 2* (Columbia 1958) ★★★★, *The Superlative Goodman* (Verve 1958) ★★★, *Happy Session* (Columbia 1959) ★★★, *Swings Again* (Columbia 1960) ★★★, *The Kingdom Of Swing* (RCA Victor 1960) ★★★, *Swing Swing Swing* (RCA Camden 1960) ★★★, *In Moscow* (RCA Victor 1962) ★★★, *Hello Benny* (Capitol 1964) ★★★, with Lionel Hampton, Gene Krupa, Teddy Wilson *Together Again!* (RCA Victor 1964) ★★★, *The Essential Benny Goodman* (Verve 1964) ★★★, *Made In Japan* (Capitol 1964) ★★★★, *B.G. The Small Groups* (RCA Victor 1965) ★★★, *London Date* (Philips 1969) ★★★★, *Today* (Decca 1970) ★★★, *Live In Stockholm* (Decca 1970) ★★★, *On Stage With Benny Goodman And His Sextet* (Decca 1972) ★★★★, *Seven Come Eleven* (CBS 1975) ★★★, *The King* (Century 1978) ★★★, *Carnegie Hall Reunion Concert* (Decca 1978) ★★★, *King Of Swing* (East World 1980) ★★★★, *In Stockholm 1959* (Phontastic 1988) ★★★, *Breakfast Ball* 1934 recording (Decca 1988) ★★★, *The Famous 1938 Carnegie Hall Jazz Concert* (Columbia/Legacy 1998) ★★★★★.

● COMPILATIONS: *The Hits Of Benny Goodman* (Capitol 1961) ★★★, *Benny Goodman's Greatest Hits* (Columbia 1966) ★★★, *BG With Ben Pollack* 1926-31 recordings (Sunbeam 1980) ★★★, *The Rare BG* (Sunbeam) ★★★, *The Formative Years* (Sunbeam) ★★★★, *Benny Goodman's Boys* 1928-29 recordings (Sunbeam 1980) ★★★, *The Hotsy Totsy Gang With Benny Goodman* (Sunbeam) ★★★, *Benny Goodman On The Side* (Sunbeam) ★★★, *Red Nichols Featuring Benny Goodman* (Sunbeam) ★★★, *Ben Selvin And His Orchestra Featuring Benny Goodman Vol. 1, 2, 3* (Sunbeam) ★★★, *Benny Goodman In A Melotone Manner* (Sunbeam) ★★★, *Ted Lewis And His Band Featuring Benny Goodman* (Sunbeam) ★★★, *Benny Good-man Accompanies The Girls* (Sunbeam) ★★★, *Benny Goodman: The Early Years* (Sunbeam) ★★★★, *BG With Chick Bullock And Steve Washington* (Sunbeam 1933) ★★★, *BG With Adrian Rollini And His Orchestra* (Sunbeam) ★★★, *The 'Let's Dance' Broadcasts Vols. 1-3* 1934-35 recordings (Sunbeam 1982) ★★★★, *The Alternate Goodman Vols. 1-9* (Nostalgia 1982) ★★★★, *The Rhythm Makers Vols. 1, 2, 3* 1935 recordings (Sunbeam 1982) ★★★★, *The Indispensable Benny Goodman Vols. 1/2* 1935-36 recordings (RCA Victor 1984) ★★★★, *The Complete Small Combinations Vols. 1/2* 1935-37 recordings (RCA Victor 1984) ★★★★, *The Indispensable Benny Goodman Vols. 3/4* 1936-37 recordings (RCA Victor 1984) ★★★★, *BG—The Camel Caravan Vols. 1 & 2* 1937 recordings (Sunbeam 1984) ★★★, *Benny Goodman At The Manhattan Room Vols. 1-11* 1937 recordings (Sunbeam 1985) ★★★, *Benny Goodman Trio And Quartet Live* (Sunbeam) ★★★★, *The Complete Small Combinations Vols. 3/4* 1937-39 recordings (RCA Victor 1985) ★★★★, *Benny Goodman On V-Disc* (Sunbeam) ★★★★, *The Forgotten Year* 1943 transcriptions (Swing Treasury 1980) ★★★, *Permanent Goodman Vols. 1 & 2* 20s recordings (Phontastic) ★★★, *Camel Caravan Broadcasts Vols. 1-3* 1939 recordings (Phontastic) ★★★, *Alternate Takes Vols. 1-12* 1939-40 recordings (Phontastic) ★★★, *Different Version Vols. 1-5* 1940-45 recordings (Phontastic 80s) ★★★, *Dance & Swing* 1945-46 recordings (Phontastic) ★★★, *Benny Goodman On The Fitch Bandwagon* (Sunbeam) ★★★, *Benny Goodman Featuring Jess Stacy* (Sunbeam) ★★★, *Live 1945 Broadcasts* (Sunbeam) ★★★, *Benny Goodman* (Flapper 1991) ★★★, *The Birth Of Swing 1935-36* (Bluebird 1992) ★★★★, *King Of Swing (1935-5)* (Giants Of Jazz 1992) ★★★★, *Air Checks 1937-1938* (Sony 1993) ★★★, *Swing Sessions* 1946 recording (Hindsight 1996) ★★★★, *The Complete RCA Victor Small Group Recordings* 3-CD box set (BMG/RCA Victor 1997) ★★★, *Benny Rides Again* 1940-47 recordings (Vocalion 1999) ★★★, *1939* (Classics 1999) ★★★, *The Breakdown Sessions Vol. 1* 1944 recordings (Slipped Disc 1999) ★★★, *The Radio Years 1940-41, Vol. 1* (Jazz Unlimited 1999) ★★★, *The Complete Capitol Trios 1947-54* recordings (Capitol 2000) ★★★, *Complete RCA Victor Small Group Master Takes 1935-39* recordings (Definitive Records 2000) ★★★★, with Helen Forrest *The Original Recordings Of The 40s* (Columbia 2001) ★★★★.

● FURTHER READING: *The Kingdom Of Swing*, Benny Goodman and Irving Kolodin. *Benny Goodman: Listen To His Legacy*, D. Russell Connor. *Benny Goodman And The Swing Era*, James Lincoln Collier. *Swing, Swing, Swing: The Life And Times Of Benny Goodman*, Ross Firestone. *BG On The Record: A Bio-Discography Of Benny Goodman*, D. Russell Connor and W. Hicks Warren. *Benny, King Of Swing*, Benny Goodman. *Benny Goodman*, Bruce Crowther.

Goodman, Dickie

b. 19 April 1934, Hewlett, New York, USA, d. 10 November 1989, South Carolina, USA. Richard 'Dickie' Goodman, along with Bill Buchanan (b. 1935), was known as the pioneer of the so-called 'break-in' record, a recording technique that involved weaving short snippets of hit recordings into a narrative story, usually in the form of a news report. The duo's first hit was 'The Flying Saucer (Parts 1 & 2)' on Luniverse Records in 1956. The record told of a visit to earth by aliens from space who explained their reasons for landing on earth to reporters with bits of rock 'n' roll hits by **Little Richard**, the **Platters** and others. Buchanan and Goodman charted three further times before Buchanan retired from the music industry. Goodman continued the concept on solo records on numerous labels and continued to score chart records with it into the late 70s. His biggest solo hit was the 1975 'Mr. Jaws', a take-off on the film *Jaws*. Goodman shot himself in November 1989.

● ALBUMS: *The Many Heads Of Dickie Goodman* (Rori 1962) ★★★, *My Son The Joke* (Comet 1964) ★★★, *The Original Flying Saucers* (IX Chains 1973) ★★, *Mr. Jaws (And Other Fables By Dickie Goodman)* (Cash 1975) ★★.

● COMPILATIONS: *Dickie Goodman's Greatest Hits* (Rhino 1983) ★★★★, *Greatest Fables* (Hot Productions 1997) ★★★, *The King Of Novelty: Greatest Fables Volume 2* (Hot Productions 1998) ★★★.

Goodman, Steve

b. 25 July 1948, Chicago, Illinois, USA, d. 20 September 1984, Seattle, Washington, USA. An engaging singer-songwriter from Chicago, Steve Goodman was a favourite with critics, although his albums rarely achieved the commercial success that reviews suggested they deserved.

Goodman's first appearance on record came in 1970 on *Gathering At The Earl Of Old Town*, an album featuring guest appearances by artists who regularly performed at a Chicago folk club, the Earl Of Old Town, which was run by an enthusiast named Earl Pionke. Released initially on Dunwich Records and later by Mountain Railroad, the album included three tracks by Goodman, 'Eight Ball', 'Chicago Bust Rag' (written by Greg Hildebrand) and his classic train song, 'City Of New Orleans'. By 1972, Goodman's talent had been spotted by **Kris Kristofferson**, who recommended him to **Paul Anka**. Anka, who was an admirer of Kris Kristofferson, convinced **Buddah Records** (the label to which Anka was signed at the time) to sign Goodman, while Goodman in turn recommended his friend and fellow singer-songwriter **John Prine** to both Anka and Kristofferson, resulting in **Atlantic Records** signing Prine.

Unfortunately for Goodman, Prine's career took off and he remained a cult figure. He made two excellent albums for Buddah; *Steve Goodman* (which was produced by Kristofferson) included his two best-known songs in commercial terms, 'You Never Even Called Me By My Name', which was **David Allan Coe**'s breakthrough country hit in 1975, and 'City Of New Orleans', a 1972 US Top 20 hit for **Arlo Guthrie** that was also covered by dozens of artists. Recorded in Nashville, the album featured many **Area Code 615** musicians including **Charlie McCoy** and Kenny Buttrey. It was followed by *Somebody Else's Troubles* (produced by Arif Mardin), which featured musicians including **David Bromberg**, **Bob Dylan** (under the alias Robert Milkwood Thomas) and members of the **Rascals**.

Although his work had failed thus far to chart, Goodman quickly secured a new recording contract with **Asylum Records**, a label that specialized in notable singer-songwriters. While his next two self-produced albums, *Jessie's Jig & Other Favorites* (1975) and *Words We Can Dance To* (1976), were minor US hits, 1977's *Say It In Private* (produced by **Joel Dorn** and including a cover version of 'Two Lovers', the **Mary Wells** classic written by **Smokey Robinson**), 1979's *High And*

Outside and 1980's *Hot Spot* failed to chart, and Goodman's days on major labels ended at this point.

By this time, Goodman, who had been suffering from leukaemia since the early 70s, was often unwell, but by 1983, he had formed his own record label, Red Pajamas, with the help of his (and Prine's) manager, Al Bunetta. The first album to be released on the label was a live collection covering 10 years of performances by Goodman. *Artistic Hair*'s sleeve pictured him as almost bald, due to the chemotherapy he was receiving in a bid to cure his illness. Soon afterwards came *Affordable Art*, which also included some live tracks and at least one out-take from an Asylum album, and with John Prine guesting. Goodman's final album, *Santa Ana Winds*, on which **Emmylou Harris** and Kris Kristofferson guested, included two songs he co-wrote with Jim Ibbotson and Jeff Hanna of the **Nitty Gritty Dirt Band**, 'Face On The Cutting Room Floor' and 'Queen Of The Road', but in September 1984, he died from kidney and liver failure following a bone marrow transplant operation.

In 1985, Red Pajamas Records released a double album *Tribute To Steve Goodman*, on which many paid their musical respects to their late friend, including Prine, Bromberg, Guthrie, **Bonnie Raitt**, **John Hartford**, **Richie Havens** and the Nitty Gritty Dirt Band. It is highly likely that the largely excellent catalogue of this notable performer will be re-evaluated in the future—while he cannot be aware of the posthumous praise he has received, few would regard it as less than well deserved.

● ALBUMS: *Gathering At The Earl Of Old Town* (Dunwich 1970) ★★★, *Steve Goodman* (Buddah 1972) ★★★★, *Somebody Else's Troubles* (Buddah 1973) ★★★, *Jessie's Jig & Other Favorites* (Asylum 1975) ★★★★, *Words We Can Dance To* (Asylum 1976) ★★★★, *Say It In Private* (Asylum 1977) ★★★, *High And Outside* (Asylum 1979) ★★★, *Hot Spot* (Asylum 1980) ★★★, *Artistic Hair* (Red Pajamas 1983) ★★★, *Affordable Art* (Red Pajamas 1983) ★★★, *Santa Ana Winds* (Red Pajamas 1984) ★★★, *Unfinished Business* (Red Pajamas 1986) ★★★, *The Easter Tapes* 1978 recordings (Red Pajamas 1996) ★★★, *Live Wire* (Red Pajamas 2000) ★★★.

● COMPILATIONS: *The Essential . . . Steve Goodman* (Buddah 1976) ★★★, *The Best Of The Asylum Years: Volume One* (Red Pajamas 1988) ★★★, *The Best Of The Asylum Years: Volume Two* (Red Pajamas 1989) ★★★, *No Big Surprise: The Steve Goodman Anthology* (Red Pajamas 1994) ★★★★.

● DVD/VIDEOS: *Live From Austin City Limits . . . And More!* (Red Pajamas 2004).

Goodness

Comprising Danny Newcomb (vocals/guitar), Carrie Akre (vocals), Chris Friel (drums), Garth Reeves (guitar/vocals) and Fiia McGann (bass, vocals, cello), Goodness was formed by old friends on the Seattle, Washington, USA, music scene. Akre was formerly with Hammerbox, and had also worked with Best Kissers In The World and the **Wedding Present**. Both Newcomb and Friel were former members of Shadow, a group that also featured Mike McCready, later of **Pearl Jam**. McGann also ran the concurrent musical project, Miracle Baby. The members chose the name Goodness, as Akre believed it embodied more positive, familial qualities than she had experienced with Hammerbox. She also stressed the musical differences: 'That band was a lot harder and guitar-orientated. This is more vocal-orientated and more poppy and more satisfying because I get to do what's closer to me—and discover myself as a musician.' Goodness made their debut in 1995 with a self-titled collection that featured several strong Akre/Newcomb collaborations, such as 'Smoking' and 'Sincerely Yours'. Produced by Seattle scene veteran John Goodmanson, it was originally released in September on local independent label Y Records, but the new **Atlantic Records** subsidiary Lava re-released it with a bonus track, 'Electricity', taken from the *Schoolhouse Rock Rocks* tribute to the educational cartoon series. The re-release was promoted by an opening spot for **Oasis** at their New York Paramount show. A second album appeared on Epic in 1998, and a third on the independent Good-Ink label a year later, before Akre launched her solo career in 2000 with *Home*. Goodness reunited in 2004 for a series of live shows, later documented on CD by the Kufala Recordings label.

● ALBUMS: *Goodness* (Y/Lava 1995) ★★★★, *Anthem* (Epic 1998) ★★★, *These Days* (Good-Ink 1999) ★★★, *Live Seattle 8/7/2004* (Kufala 2005) ★★★, *Live Tacoma, WA 6/19/04* (Kufala 2005) ★★★.

● COMPILATIONS: *1995–1998* (Fundamental 2004) ★★★.

Goodnight Vienna

After a brief foray to Hollywood in 1930 to co-star with **Jeanette MacDonald** in **Ernst Lubitsch**'s *Monte Carlo*, **Jack Buchanan** returned to England for this popular film, which was released by the British Dominions company two years later. Set in Vienna in 1914, it concerns a bachelor gay, Captain Maximilian Schlettoff (Buchanan), who falls in love with Viki (**Anna Neagle**), a pretty young assistant in a flower shop. On the night they are due to elope the gallant Captain is ordered to leave for the war front immediately, and the note he sends to Viki is never delivered. She is distraught when she receives a letter from Maximilian's father (Clive Currie) telling her that his son has entered into an arranged marriage with Countess Helga (Joyce Bland). After the war has ended, the Captain returns to Vienna in reduced financial circumstances and gets a job in a shoe shop where one of his first customers is Viki—now a famous opera star. She is initially aloof, but eventually, according to the film's publicity handout at the time, 'they meet again in a charming café set amidst flowering trees, where in the old days they had laughed and sung with carefree joyousness, and their favourite song re-unites them.' All four of the songs in the film, 'Just Heaven', 'Living In Clover', 'Marching Song', and 'Goodnight Vienna', were the work of **Eric Maschwitz** and George Posford, who also adapted the screenplay from the original radio play. Buchanan gave his usual engaging performance, and Neagle, who had come to prominence only the year before in Buchanan's musical comedy *Stand Up And Sing*, was delightful and obviously a star in the making. Gina Malo as Frieda, headed a supporting cast, which included William Kendall, Herbert Carrick, Gibb McLaughlin, Clifford Heatherley, O.B. Clarence, Aubrey Fitzgerald, Peggy Cartwright, and Muriel Aked. The producer-director was **Herbert Wilcox**. For its release in the USA the film was re-titled *Magic Night*.

Goodrem, Delta

b. 9 November 1984, Sydney, Australia. One of the more impressive musical talents to emerge from the world of daytime television, Australian singer-songwriter Goodrem had already signed with a major label record company before she landed a choice role in the popular soap opera, *Neighbours*. The aspiring performer was playing piano by the age of eight and began writing material soon afterwards. She signed a recording contract with Sony Music Australia at the age of 15, and launched her solo recording career in November 2001 with 'I Don't Care'. The record stalled at number 64 in the Australian charts, necessitating a rethink from the starlet and her record company. Goodrem landed the role of aspiring singer Nina Tucker in *Neighbours* and joined the cast in July 2002. Four months later, she relaunched her recording career with the self-written piano ballad, 'Born To Try'. The single was a huge success, topping the Australian charts and also reaching the UK Top 5 (*Neighbours* enjoys strong viewing figures in England). Her debut album, *Innocent Eyes*, was equally successful, staying on the top of the Australian charts for over four months and spawning another chart-topping single, 'Lost Without You'. In July 2003, Goodrem was forced to face up to an even greater challenge when she was diagnosed with early-stage Hodgkin's disease.

● ALBUMS: *Innocent Eyes* (Sony 2003) ★★★.

● DVD/VIDEOS: *Innocent Eyes* (Sony 2003).

Goodrick, Mick

b. 9 June 1945, Sharon, Pennsylvania, USA. Along with many young people of his generation, Goodrick began playing guitar before entering his teens. Nevertheless, his musical interests lay in less predictable directions than those offered by contemporaneous pop, and he attended summer camp operated under the auspices of **Stan Kenton**. Goodrick studied at **Berklee College Of Music**, staying on as a tutor after graduating in 1967. In the 70s he played with numerous jazz artists of very different persuasions, among them **Woody Herman**, **Alan Broadbent**, **Pat Metheny**, **Jack DeJohnette**, **Joe Williams** and **John Surman**. In particular, he had a fruitful and important three-year musical relationship with **Gary Burton** that began in 1973.

A well-schooled technician and an inventive soloist, Goodrick ably adapts to the stylistic needs of fellow musicians. In suitably stimulating company, such as that he encountered in **Charlie Haden**'s Liberation Orchestra in the mid-80s, his interplay is fluid and both supports and encourages the work of his colleagues. Goodrick has continued a distinguished career in teaching, including a period at the New England Conservatory, and this has contributed to a much lower profile with audiences than his performing talent deserves.

● ALBUMS: *In Pas(s)ing* (ECM 1978) ★★★★, *Biorhythms* (CMP 1990) ★★, with Joe Diorio *Rare Birds* (Ram 1993) ★★★, *Sunscreams* (Ram 1993) ★★★, with Dave Liebman, Wolfgang Muthspiel *In The Same Breath* (CMP 1996) ★★★.

Goodwin, Henry

b. Henry Clay Goodwin, 2 January 1910, Columbia, South Carolina, USA, d. 2 July 1979, New York City, USA. While still a young teenager Goodwin played several instruments with sufficient ability to secure a place in a band **Claude Hopkins** took to Europe. Back in the USA he played with several bands, mostly in New York, during the late 20s, by now playing the trumpet. In the early 30s he was in Europe again, this time with the **Lucky Millinder** band. On his return to the USA he worked with many bands including those of **Cab Calloway** and **Sidney Bechet**, then visited Scandinavia with a band that included **Edgar Hayes** and was led by **Kenny Clarke**. In the mid-40s he played with **Cecil Scott**, **Art Hodes**, **Mezz Mezzrow** and **Bob Wilber**. The 50s found Goodwin playing with **Earl 'Fatha' Hines** and many other band leaders, usually in bands specializing in the more traditional areas of jazz. An inventive soloist with a penchant for the effects created by plunger mute, he was a stalwart of the dixieland revival without ever becoming bogged down in the repetitiveness that afflicted many of his colleagues.

Goodwin, Myles

When Canadian hard rockers **April Wine** disintegrated in 1985, lead vocalist Goodwin embarked on a solo career. He immediately divorced himself from the style to which he was accustomed. Forsaking his blues rock roots, he concentrated on MOR pop/rock with understated guitar and lightweight harmonies. Utilizing the services of session musicians, he recorded a self-titled debut on the **Atlantic** label in 1988. This failed to win a new audience, and at the same time alienated his former fanbase. The album sank without trace, and little has been heard of him since.
● ALBUMS: *Myles Goodwin* (Atlantic 1988) ★★.

Goodwin, Ron

b. Ronald Alfred Goodwin, 17 February 1925, Plymouth, Devon, England, d. 8 January 2003, Brimpton Common, Berkshire, England. An important composer, conductor and arranger, from an early age Goodwin was deeply interested in all things musical, but began his working life outside the business. Eventually, he took a job as a music copier with music publishers Campbell Connelly. He also studied trumpet and arranging at the Guildhall School of Music in London, and played trumpet professionally with **Harry Gold** and wrote arrangements for the bands of **Ted Heath** and **Geraldo**. Employed by the short-lived Polygon label and then **Parlophone Records**, Goodwin made several records under the name of Ron Goodwin And His Concert Orchestra, in addition to arranging and conducting the backing music for singers, including **Petula Clark** and **Jimmy Young**. Goodwin also composed music in the classical form, including his 'Drake 400 Concert Suite' and 'New Zealand Suite', and wrote several television advertising jingles, including Ricicles ('I like Ricicles: they're twicicle as nicicles') and Mr Sheen ('Mr Sheen shines umpteen things clean').

Despite his other achievements, it is as a writer for films that Goodwin made his greatest impact. After first writing for documentaries, from the 60s through to the 80s he composed the scores—and generally served as the musical director—for numerous feature films, including *Whirlpool, The Witness, I'm All Right Jack, In The Nick, Village Of The Damned, The Trials Of Oscar Wilde, The Man With The Green Carnation, The Man At The Carleton Tower, The Clue Of The New Pin, Partners In Crime, Invasion Quartet*, a series of 'Miss Marple' films starring Margaret Rutherford (*Murder, She Said, Murder At The Gallop, Murder Most Foul* and *Murder Ahoy*), *The Day Of The Triffids, Follow The Boys, Of Human Bondage, Children Of The Damned, 633 Squadron, A Home Of Your Own, Those Magnificent Men In Their Flying Machines, Operation Crossbow, The Alphabet Murders, That Riviera Touch, The Trap* (used as the theme for the London Marathon), **Mrs Brown, You've Got A Lovely Daughter**,

Where Eagles Dare, Battle Of Britain, The Executioner, Frenzy, One Of Our Dinosaurs Is Missing, Escape From The Dark, Ride A Wild Pony, Candleshoe, Force 10 From Navarone, The Spaceman And King Arthur, Clash Of Loyalties, and *Valhalla*. In the 70s, Goodwin became in-house composer for all **Walt Disney**'s British productions, and produced a popular series of easy listening albums. Goodwin won several **Ivor Novello** Awards, including the Entertainment Music Award in 1972, and a Lifetime Achievement Award in 1994. In the 70s, Goodwin made concert tours of the UK with an orchestra performing his own film scores. He continued to broadcast on radio, and worked extensively in Canada.
● ALBUMS: *Film Favourites* (Parlophone 1954) ★★★★, *Music To Set You Dreaming* (Parlophone 1956) ★★★, *Out Of This World* (Parlophone 1958) ★★★★, *Adventure And Excitement/Music For An Arabian Night* (Parlophone 1958) ★★★, *Decline And Fall . . . Of A Birdwatcher* film soundtrack (Stateside 1968) ★★, *Monte Carlo Or Bust* film soundtrack (Paramount 1969) ★★★, *Legend Of The Glass Mountain* (Studio 2 1970) ★★★, *Spellbound* (Studio 2 1973) ★★★, *Elizabethan Serenade* (MFP 1975) ★★★, *I'll See You In My Dreams* (Studio 2 1976) ★★★, *Escape From The Dark* film soundtrack (EMI 1976) ★★, *Rhythm And Romance* (Studio 2 1977) ★★★, with the New Zealand Symphony Orchestra *Going Places* (Studio 2 1978) ★★★, *Christmas Wonderland* (One-Up 1978) ★★★, with the Bournemouth Symphony Orchestra *Ron Goodwin And The Bournemouth Symphony Orchestra* (Chandos 1980) ★★★, *Drake 400 Concert Suite* (Chandos 1980) ★★★, *Sounds Superb* (MFP 1981) ★★★, with the Royal Philharmonic Orchestra *Projections* (EMI 1983) ★★★, *Fire And Romance* (EMI 1984) ★★★, with the New Zealand Symphony Orchestra *New Zealand Suite* (Columbia 1984) ★★★, *Ron Goodwin Plays Bacharach And David* (Ideal 1984) ★★★, *The Love Album* (MFP 1985) ★★★, with the Bournemouth Symphony Orchestra *My Kind Of Music* (Chandos 1989) ★★★.
● COMPILATIONS: *This Is Ron Goodwin* (EMI 1973) ★★★, *Very Best Of Ron Goodwin* (Studio 2 1977) ★★★, *First 25 Years* (Studio 2 1978) ★★★★.

Goofy

b. Chad Simpson, 1 June 1974, Kingston, Jamaica, West Indies. Simpson grew up within the reggae industry and drew help as well as inspiration in his burgeoning career from the likes of **Big Youth**, **Yellowman**, **Beenie Man**, **Bounty Killer** and **General Degree**. In 1996, he recorded the chart-topping 'Fudgie', which also featured **Lady Saw** and **Hawkeye** on the 12-inch disco mix. A hit in Jamaica and the US, it led to a series of singles including 'Don't Talk', 'How You Bless' and 'Dog Bark'. Goofy's association with **Danny Browne**'s Main Street Crew led to him recording in combination with **Red Rat**, initially on 'Big Man Little Yute' for Studio 2000, which topped the reggae charts worldwide. The duo followed their success with 'Cruise'. The Main Street Crew made their UK debut at the 1997 Notting Hill Carnival in London, featuring the trio of Red Rat, Goofy and Hawkeye. Scheduled to appear on both the Radio One and Kiss FM stages, the trio's arrival caused a crushing surge towards the stage, an incident grossly exaggerated in the national press. Goofy continued to produce hits, including 'Brush Yu Teeth' and 'Bad Man Fearless'. Several of his hit singles were included on his debut set, *I Don't Give A Damn!!*

● ALBUMS: *I Don't Give A Damn!!* (Main Street 1999) ★★★.

Goombay Dance Band

This Germany-based theatrical band was in a similar vein to the more successful **Boney M.** They were led by Olivier Bendt, and included his wife Alicia and children Danny and Yasmin plus Dorothy Hellings, Wendy Doorsen and Mario Slijngaard. Olivier is by profession a fire-eater who learned his trade in St. Lucia, West Indies. By 1980, the Goombay Dance Band was one of the most successful acts in Germany, and entered the UK charts with '7 Tears'. Originally recorded in 1980, it was only released in the UK in 1982 and, after many previous flops, its success was something of a surprise. It eventually went all the way to number 1, only the second UK chart-topper by a German act following **Kraftwerk**'s 'The Model'. The follow up 'Sun Of Jamaica' fared less well and the band returned to Germany to continue their domestic success. However, occasional singles still received a UK release, such as 1986's 'A Typical Jamaican Mess'.
● ALBUMS: *Seven Tears* (Epic 1982) ★★.

Goons

Mutating from Britain's radio show *Crazy People* in 1951, the high summer of the BBC Home Service's *Goon Show* was reflected in UK hit parade entries in 1956 for its spin-off double a-sides, 'I'm Walking Backwards For Christmas'/'Bluebottle Blues' and 'Bloodnok's Rock 'N' Roll'/'Ying Tong Song'—which encapsulated the offbeat humour, topical parodies and musical interludes (under the baton of band leader **Ray Ellington**) of the radio series starring Spike Milligan (b. 16 April 1918, Ahmednagar, India, d. 27 February 2002, Rye, East Sussex, England), Peter Sellers (b. Richard Henry Sellers, 8 September 1925, Southsea, Hampshire, England, d. 24 July 1980, London, England), **Harry Secombe** (b. Harold Donald Secombe, 8 September 1921, Swansea, West Glamorgan, Wales, d. 11 April 2001, Guildford, Surrey, England) and, briefly, Michael Bentine (b. 26 January 1922, Watford, Hertfordshire, England, d. 26 November 1996, England). As well as ushering in the strata of English comedy that culminated in the late 60s with *Monty Python's Flying Circus*, aspects of the Goons became apparent in the stylistic determination of the **Scaffold**, the **Bonzo Dog Doo-Dah Band** and, less directly, the **Beatles**—particularly in their first two films and in **John Lennon**'s literary output. In reciprocation, a cod-Shakespearian recitation of 'A Hard Day's Night' was among Sellers' solo successes. However, Secombe—whose chart career began before that of the Goons—enjoyed greater success with sonorous ballads, almost topping the British list in 1967 with 'This Is My Song'. Nevertheless, Secombe's next—and last—Top 10 entry came six years later with a reissue of the Goons' 'Ying Tong Song', shortly after the troupe's one-off radio and television reunion recorded during the BBC's 50th anniversary celebrations.
● ALBUMS: *The Best Of The Goon Shows* (Parlophone 1959) ★★★★, *The Best Of The Goon Shows Volume 2* (Parlophone 1960) ★★★★, *The Last Goon Show Of All* (BBC 1972) ★★★, there are also many BBC spoken word cassettes of *The Goon Show*.

Gopher, Alex

b. Alex Latrobe, Versailles, France. A central figure on the booming mid-90s Parisian **house** scene, Gopher is a former member of indie rock band Orange, a band he formed with the members of **Air**, Nicolas Godin and Jean-Benoit Dunckel. His unusual pseudonym is taken from a character in the US television series, *The Loveboat*. Gopher was also a producer for the extremely influential Paris-based **dance music** labels, Source and Solid, home to the acclaimed Parisian producer, **Etienne De Crécy**. In 1996, Gopher contributed two tracks to De Crécy's highly praised *Super Discount* compilation of French lounge-house tracks. His funky sound has been compared to the quirky, slightly kitsch 'filtered disco' style of **Cassius** and **Dimitri From Paris**. Gopher claims influences such as **Herbie Hancock, Stevie Wonder, Sly And The Family Stone** and **George Clinton**, and his 1998 debut, *You, My Baby & I*, featured the P-funk vocalist, Michael 'Clip' Payne singing on several tracks. Payne also co-wrote two tracks with Gopher. Dunckel, Gopher's long-standing friend and associate, also contributed vocals and keyboards. While using the most advanced studio technology favoured by US house and hip-hop producers, Gopher's preferred instrument is the Fender-Rhodes keyboard, which he describes as 'a more soulful instrument than any I know.' Although not a concept album, the central theme of *You, My Baby & I* was indeed children and parenthood. The track '06 10 98' was named after the birth date of his son. Another, 'The Child', samples **Billie Holiday**'s 'God Bless The Child'. Gopher remains one of the leading exponents of a stylish French sound, funky, dancefloor-friendly and musically sophisticated.
● ALBUMS: *You, My Baby & I* (Gee Street/V2 1998) ★★★★.
● COMPILATIONS: with Demon *Alex Gopher And Demon Presents Wuz* (V2 2002) ★★★.

Gopthal, Lee

b. 1 March 1939, Constant Spring, Kingston, Jamaica, West Indies, d. 29 August 1997. Gopthal is regarded as a pioneer in promoting Jamaican music. He moved in 1952 to the UK where he qualified as an accountant, and by the early 60s was representing producer **Leslie Kong** in the UK. Initially, Gopthal was involved in providing records for the West Indian population through his primary venture, Pyramid Records. By the early 60s **Chris Blackwell** had arrived in the UK and joined forces with Gopthal, who distributed Black Swan and **Island Records** pressings under the Beat And Commercial banner. The association led to the inauguration of the Muzik City chain, which sold Jamaican music within the Afro-Caribbean community. The shops were opened in and around London and included the legendary Desmond's Hip City in Brixton. In 1967 Gopthal's Pyramid label released **Desmond Dekker**'s 'The Israelites', which topped the UK charts two years after its release and is acknowledged as the first reggae tune to conquer the US charts. Gopthal and Blackwell co-founded **Trojan Records** in 1967, releasing Jamaican hits and allocating labels to represent the growing number of producers, including **Lee Perry, Joe Gibbs, Duke Reid, Clancy Eccles** and, for a brief period, **Coxsone Dodd**. Gopthal also worked with UK-based performers, including **Dandy Livingstone**, whose production of Tony Tribe's version of **Neil Diamond**'s 'Red Red Wine' gave the company its first reggae hit on the UK chart. Following his label's early chart success Gopthal also enjoyed mainstream hits with 'The Liquidator', by **Harry J.**'s Allstars, 'Long Shot Kick De Bucket' by the **Pioneers**, 'Wonderful World, Beautiful People' by

Jimmy Cliff, and the double a-side, 'Return Of Django'/'Dollar In The Teeth', by the **Upsetters**. The hits continued in abundance following the departure of Blackwell, who decided to concentrate on the lucrative rock market, although the **Wailers** later emerged as the label's most significant asset. By 1974, with increasing financial problems, Trojan were unable to compete with the major record companies, and the label was eventually sold to Saga Records. Gopthal maintained a low profile within the music industry until the late 70s when he decided to pursue a career in commerce.

Gordi

The pre-eminent hard rock group of Yugoslavia in the early 80s, Gordi comprised Zlatko Manojlovic (guitar/vocals), Slobodan Surdlan (bass/vocals) and Gedomir Petrovic (drums). Heavily influenced by British rock music, the sound they offered on their 1981 debut album, *Pakleni Trio*, was close in conception to that of **Black Sabbath** or **Motör- head**—albeit without the originality of songwriting. A follow-up collection released the following year, *Kraljica Smrti*, was just as brutal, and managed to secure a cult audience outside of central Europe. Sadly, the group found it difficult to gain work permits to tour outside of the Balkans, and this hampered their original impetus.

● ALBUMS: *Pakleni Trio* (LSY 1981) ★★, *Kraljica Smrti* (Jugoton 1982) ★★.

Gordon, Alan
(see **Bonner And Gordon**)

Gordon, Archie 'Stomp'

Singer and pianist Gordon led a fine jump quintet throughout the 50s that included Billy Brooks on trumpet and 'Little' Hiawatha Edmundson on tenor saxophone. Beginning with **Decca Records**' 48000 R&B series in 1952, with which the band recorded the insulting 'Damp Rag', the Gordon band recorded excellent tracks for **Mercury Records** in 1953—including an uproarious celebration of the then recent Kinsey Sex Report in 'What's Her Whimsey Dr Kinsey?'—and later recorded for **Chess Records** and Savoy in the mid-50s.

Gordon, Barry

b. 21 December 1948, Brookline, Massachusetts, USA. A precocious Barry Gordon found himself at the number 6 position in the US charts at the age of seven with a novelty song, 'Nuttin' For Christmas'. His first television appearance came at the age of three, followed by numerous other guest slots on programmes hosted by stars such as **Jackie Gleason**. **MGM Records** signed Gordon to sing the 'Christmas Song', written by Sid Tepper and Roy Bennett, which quickly reached the Top 10. Within weeks cover versions were released by such artists as **Stan Freberg**, **Homer And Jethro**, **Fontane Sisters** and Joe Ward, who reached number 20 with his version. Gordon placed only one other single in the charts, another novelty tune called 'Rock Around Mother Goose', in 1956. He went on to act on television and the stage and was still active in those areas in the mid-80s.

Gordon, Bobby

b. Robert Cameron Gordon, 29 June 1941, Hartford, Connecticut, USA. Raised in Manhasset, New York, at an early age Gordon was introduced to the music of **Eddie Con-** don, **Bobby Hackett** and **Pee Wee Russell** by attending jazz concerts and nightclubs with his tutor, **Joe Marsala**. He had begun taking lessons on clarinet at the age of 12, played in his high school band, and started his professional career at the age of 16, playing for high school dances and private parties. He also performed three times on the *Ted Mack Amateur Hour* on television. More importantly, perhaps, and certainly formatively, he sat in with many jazz musicians, including not only his mentor Marsala and Marsala's wife **Adele Girard**, but also **Ernie Caceres**, **Sonny Dunham** and **Billy Butterfield**. He had continued his musical education with studies at the **Berklee College Of Music** and his breakthrough came when, in 1964, he was the most programmed artist on radio and also performed on **Steve Allen**'s television show.

By the mid-60s Gordon had established his name in the traditional jazz scene, performing with many distinguished players from an earlier generation, among them **Muggsy Spanier**, **Wild Bill Davison**, **Georg Brunis** and **Marty Marsala**. He also worked with **Leon Redbone**, touring with him for 20 years, appearing a number of times on the Johnny Carson Show and surviving a plane crash. Later, he was a founder member of **Marty Grosz**'s Orphan Newsboys and in the 90s and at the start of the following decade was regularly leading his own bands for national and international tours and for record sessions. He has appeared at numerous festivals, playing with his own groups and also in those led by Grosz and others, including **Jim Cullum** with whom he appeared on PBS in *The Chicago Clarinetists*. Influenced early in his career by Marsala and Russell, Gordon's playing on clarinet shows a rare understanding of the roots of his music that underpins his remarkable technical expertise. He plays in a warm, melodic manner that imbues ballads with great depths, while everything that he does is enhanced by his apparently effortlessness swing. As an accompanist he is clearly a listener, while his solo work ably demonstrates a fertile imagination and excellent improvising skills.

● ALBUMS: *Old South, New Sounds* (Dot 1961) ★★★, *Warm & Sentimental* (Decca 1962) ★★★, *Young Man's Fancy* (Decca 1963) ★★★, *The Lamp Is Low* (Decca 1965) ★★★, *Bobby Gordon* (American Jazz 1974) ★★★, *Bobby Gordon, Keith Ingham & Hal Smith Trio* (Jump 1990) ★★★, *The Bobby Gordon Quartet Featuring Adele Girard Marsala* (Arbors 1992) ★★★, with Adele Girard Marsala *Don't Let It End* (Arbors 1992) ★★★★, with Ingham, Smith *Music From The Mauve Decade* (Sackville 1993) ★★★★, *Music Of Pee Wee Russell* (Arbors 1993) ★★★, *Swing And Other Things* (Arbors 1997) ★★★, *Bobby Gordon Plays Bing: A Tribute To Bing Crosby* (Arbors 1997) ★★★★, with Dave McKenna *Clarinet Blue* (Arbors 1999) ★★★, *Bobby Gordon Trio* (Jazz Connoisseur 2001) ★★★.

Gordon, Claude

b. 5 April 1916, Helena, Montana, USA, d. 1996. Claude Gordon's dance band orchestra came to prominence in 1959 when the American Federation Of Musicians, faced with the advances of rock 'n' roll, attempted to institute a big band revival. They organized a series of regional heats to find the 'best new band' of the day, with a national final at New York's Roseland Ballroom. The overall winner was Claude Gordon, whose 13-piece group (plus singer Darts Alexander) had formed a few years previously in Los Angeles, California. Having been active in the Hollywood music scene for several years, Gordon's main experience was drawn from his time as a staff musician for **CBS Records**. A talented trumpet player, he had also taught that instrument and the accordion at the Los Angeles Conservatory of Music. In the 40s he had tasted the dance band touring experience by working with artists including **Matty Malneck**, **Ronnie Kemper** and **Frankie Masters**. The reward for winning the competition was a new suite of instruments, a recording contract with Alma Records, a network television opening, and a coast to coast tour. The organizers also arranged for the group to be managed by Frank Motte, who had previously guided the careers of both **Benny Goodman** and **Harry James**, while **Billy May** was taken on as arranger. Despite all these good auspices, the Claude Gordon Orchestra found itself unable to prosper in the face of music industry and public apathy towards dance bands in the 60s. Eventually Gordon returned to teaching music full-time, although the band was occasionally reunited for one-off dates in California.

Gordon, Curtis

b. Edward Curtis Gordon, 27 July 1928, Moultrie, Georgia, USA, d. 2 May 2004, Moultrie, Georgia, USA. A dedicated traditionalist, Gordon began playing guitar and singing as a child. His country music leaning was strongly towards the western swing of **Bob Wills** and he also admired **Ernest Tubb**. As a teenager and still in school, he played on local radio and also played in Mississippi bands including Pee Wee Mills And The Twilight Cowboys. He led his own band for a while, playing mainly in Georgia, which is where he was heard and signed to a recording date with **RCA Victor Records**. This was in the early 50s, and during the next few years, which saw him move over to **Mercury Records**, Gordon's material became increasingly orientated towards rock 'n' roll while maintaining the western swing ambience of his earlier work. He was also writing and recording his own songs, most of which admirably blended the disparate elements of his musical make-up.

By the late 50s Gordon had a strong localized following for his live appearances and, now with Dollie Records, enjoyed moderate record sales. Clearly, Gordon's career had failed to take off in the way that had happened with a near contemporary, **Elvis Presley**. He continued performing for a while but then opened a club in Georgia, the running of which gradually consumed most of his time and energy. In the late 80s some of his records were re-released and attracted attention, mainly in Europe, and he came out of retirement to perform again for fans old and new. Always interesting and often exhilarating, if unfocused, Gordon's recordings clearly demonstrate considerable if sadly unrealized potential for greatness.

● COMPILATIONS: *Play The Music Louder* (Bear Family 1998) ★★★.

Gordon, Dexter

b. 27 February 1923, Los Angeles, California, USA, d. 25 April 1990, Philadelphia, Pennsylvania, USA. Gordon began his musical career studying clarinet; by his mid-teens he had switched to tenor saxophone, on which instrument he played with **Lionel Hampton** in 1940. He stayed with Hampton for a little over two years, recording with the band and gaining in stature so that no less an artist than **Coleman Hawkins** could nominate him, in 1941, as one of his favourite tenor players. Gordon then worked with **Lee Young**, his own small group, **Fletcher Henderson**, **Louis Armstrong** and **Billy Eckstine**. By late 1944 Gordon had absorbed many of the new developments in jazz and his exposure to numerous eager beboppers in the Eckstine band soon won him over completely. In the next few years he played frequently on both the east and west coasts, comfortably ignoring the artificial but effective dividing line in the bop of the early 50s. Among his playing partners of this period was **Wardell Gray**, with whom he made several important and much-imitated records.

During the rest of the 50s Gordon's career was disrupted by his addiction to narcotics, but by the 60s he was off drugs and playing better than ever. Throughout the 60s and into the 70s he toured extensively, becoming especially popular in Europe, where he mostly resided. He returned to the USA in 1976 and continued to record, attracting considerable attention with his mature yet evolving style. His personal life was then in some disarray due to a second broken marriage and a drink problem. He reached a turning point in 1986 when he secured an acting role in a feature film. He had previously dabbled with acting in the early 60s, but the leading role in a major film was a very different matter. He rose to the challenge and the film, *'Round Midnight*, was widely considered an artistic and commercial success with Gordon being nominated for an Academy Award for his portrayal of an alcoholic saxophonist.

One of the outstanding tenor saxophonists in jazz, Gordon's early influences gave him a deeply felt appreciation of swing. Although he was rightly regarded as a major figure in bop, his playing always displayed his awareness of the swing-era cadences. In his up-tempo performances, especially in his duets and duels with Gray, there is a thrusting aggression to his playing. On ballads he could be tough or tender, able to enhance any tune through his unique combination of experience and inspiration. His recordings stand as eloquent testimony to a man who influenced many musicians. Perhaps because he was not at his best in his later years (one drummer who worked with him then described the experience as 'a crash course in playing slow'), Gordon was largely ignored by record companies during the 80s, recording only the soundtrack album for *'Round Midnight* between 1982 and his death in 1990. However, in 1985 **Blue Note Records**, for whom he had made many of his finest records in the 60s, did release the double *Nights At The Keystone*, comprising live recordings from 1978–79, and later added more material from the same sessions to make up a three-volume CD set with the same title, which was reissued in 1990.

● ALBUMS: *Dexter Gordon Quintet* (Dial 1950) ★★★★, *All Star Series* (Savoy Jazz 1951) ★★★★, *New Trends In Modern Jazz Vol. 3* (Savoy Jazz 1952) ★★★★, *Daddy Plays The Horn* (Bethlehem 1955) ★★★, *Dexter Blows Hot And Cool* (Dootone 1956) ★★★, with Howard McGhee *The Chase* (Jazztone 1956) ★★★, *The Resurgence Of Dexter Gordon* (Jazzland 1960) ★★★, *Doin' Alright* (Blue Note 1961) ★★★★, *Dexter Calling* (Blue Note 1961) ★★★★, *Go* (Blue Note 1962) ★★★★, *A Swingin' Affair* (Blue Note 1962) ★★★★, *Cry Me A River* (SteepleChase 1962) ★★, *Our Man In Paris* (Blue Note 1963) ★★★★★, *One Flight Up* (Blue Note 1964) ★★★★, *Cheese Cake* (SteepleChase 1964) ★★, *King Neptune* (SteepleChase 1964) ★★★, *I Want More* (SteepleChase 1964) ★★★, *It's You Or No One* (SteepleChase 1964) ★★, *Billie's Bounce* (SteepleChase 1964) ★★, *Love For Sale* (SteepleChase 1964) ★★, *Clubhouse* (Blue Note 1965) ★★★, *Gettin' Around* (Blue

Note 1965) ★★★★, with Booker Ervin *Settin' The Pace* (Prestige 1967) ★★★, *The Montmartre Collection* (Black Lion 1967) ★★★, *Take The 'A' Train* (Black Lion 1967) ★★, *Both Sides Of Midnight* (Black Lion 1967) ★★★, *Body And Soul* (Black Lion 1967) ★★, *Live At The Amsterdam Paradiso* (Affinity 1969) ★★★, with Slide Hampton *A Day In Copenhagen* (MPS 1969) ★★★, *The Tower Of Power/ More Power* (Prestige 1969) ★★★, with Karin Krog *Some Other Spring* (Polydor 1970) ★★★★, with Gene Ammons *The Chase!* (Prestige 1970) ★★★, *At Montreux* (Prestige 1970) ★★★, *The Panther!* (Prestige 1970) ★★, with Jackie McLean *The Meeting* (SteepleChase 1973) ★★★, *Blues A La Suisse* (Prestige 1973) ★★★, with McLean *The Source* (SteepleChase 1974) ★★★, *The Apartment* (SteepleChase 1974) ★★, *Bouncin' With Dex* (SteepleChase 1975) ★★★, *Stable Mable* (SteepleChase 1975) ★★★, *Homecoming* (Columbia 1976) ★★★, *Lullaby For A Monster* (SteepleChase 1977) ★★, *Biting The Apple* (SteepleChase 1977) ★★★, *Sophisticated Giant* (Columbia 1977) ★★★, *More Than You Know* (SteepleChase 1977) ★★, *Something Different* (SteepleChase 1977) ★★★, *Midnight Dream* (West Wind 1977) ★★★, *Nights At The Keystone Vol. 1–3* (Blue Note 1979) ★★★, *Gotham City* (Columbia 1981) ★★★, *American Classic* (Elektra Musician 1982) ★★★, *'Round Midnight: Soundtrack* (Columbia 1986) ★★★, *The Other Side Of Round Midnight* (Blue Note 1986) ★★★, *A Gordon Cantata* 1978 recording (West Wind 1993) ★★★, *Live At Carnegie Hall: Complete* (Columbia/Legacy 1998) ★★★★, *The Squirrel* 1967 live recording (Blue Note 1998) ★★★, *In A Soulful Mood* 1955, 1962–69 recordings (Music Club 1999) ★★★, *The Jumpin' Blues* (Prestige 1970) ★★, *Those Were The Days* 1971 recording (Moon 1999) ★★, with Ben Webster *Baden 1972* (TCB 1999) ★★★, *L.T.D.* 1969 recording (Prestige 2001) ★★, *The Rainbow People* 1974 recording (SteepleChase 2002) ★★★, *XXL: Live At The Left Bank* 1969 recording (Prestige 2003) ★★★, *Our Man In Amsterdam* (Fuel 2000 2003) ★★★.

● COMPILATIONS: *Dexter Rides Again* 1945–47 recordings (Savoy Jazz 1958) ★★★, *Best Of Dexter Gordon: The Blue Note Years* (Blue Note 1988) ★★★★, *Ballads* (Blue Note 1992) ★★★★, *The Complete Blue Note Sixties Sessions* 6-CD box set (Blue Note 1996) ★★★★, *The Art Of The Ballad* 1969–73 recordings (Prestige 1998) ★★★★, with Wardell Gray *Citizens Bop* 40s recordings (Black Lion 1998), *In A Soulful Mood* (Music Club 1999) ★★★, *Settin' The Pace* 1945–47 recordings (Savoy Jazz 1999) ★★★★, *Happy Birthday* (Storyville 2003) ★★★★, *The Classic Blue Note Recordings* (Blue Note 2003) ★★★★, *The Complete Trio & Quartet Studio Recordings* (SteepleChase 2003) ★★★, *Bopland* 3-CD set (Savoy 2004) ★★★, *The Complete Prestige Recordings* 11-CD box set (Fantasy 2004) ★★★★.

● DVD/VIDEOS: *The Dexter Gordon Quartet* (Rhapsody 1995), *More Than You Know* (Academy Video 1998).

● FURTHER READING: *Long Tall Dexter*, Stan Britt.

● FILMS: *Unchained* (1955), *Stopforbud* voice only (1963), *Jag Älskar, Du Älskar* (1968), *'Round Midnight* (1986), *Awakenings* (1990).

Gordon, Jimmie

Blues artist Gordon was based in St. Louis, Missouri, USA, and was billed on one record as **'Peetie Wheatstraw's** brother'; on another, 'Black Gal', he appeared as 'Joe Bullum', an attempt by **Decca Records** to pass him off as **Joe**

Pullum. Like 'Black Gal', many of his recordings were covers of then-popular blues. Gordon was a slightly anonymous figure, and has excited little attention from researchers. Nevertheless, his records are often worthwhile, for he combines the ingratiating approach of **Bumble Bee Slim** with some of Wheatstraw's forcefulness, and was often backed by enjoyable small jazz bands. He was also a more than competent pianist, although he seldom played on his own records.

● COMPILATIONS: *Mississippi Murder* (Document 1987) ★★★, *Jimmie Gordon* (Blues Document 1989) ★★★.

Gordon, Joe

b. Joseph Henry Gordon, 15 May 1928, Boston, Massachusetts, USA, d. 4 November 1963, Santa Monica, California, USA. After taking formal tuition on trumpet, Gordon began playing jazz professionally in the late 40s. In addition to leading his own small group in and around his home town, he also gained experience through the early 50s sitting in with visiting musicians and playing in several well-known bands. He subsequently worked with top-flight artists such as **Georgie Auld**, **Lionel Hampton**, **Charlie 'Bird' Parker** and **Art Blakey**, appearing on the latter's *The Jazz Messengers Featuring Art Blakey*. In the middle of the decade he toured and recorded with **Dizzy Gillespie**, and also recorded with **Horace Silver** and the **Herb Pomeroy** big band. After moving to Los Angeles towards the end of the 50s, Gordon again played in important company, recording with **Benny Carter** and **Shelly Manne**, appearing with the latter on 1960's *The Proper Time*. A fierce and dynamic hard bop trumpeter, Gordon's abilities were barely stretched by the time of his early death.

● ALBUMS: *Introducing Joe Gordon* (EmArcy 1955) ★★★, *Lookin' Good!* (Contemporary 1961) ★★★★.

Gordon, John

b. 30 May 1939, USA. Gordon began playing trombone as a child and later studied formally at the Juilliard School Of Music in New York. He played professionally with various bands including several in the blues idiom and was also with **Buddy Johnson**. When he was 22 he joined **Lionel Hampton** where he remained for a year, then returned to his studies. For seven years he was with R&B star **Lloyd Price**, whose musical director at the time was **Slide Hampton**. In 1962 he began a 20-year stint in Broadway pit bands, appearing also on many recordings on **Motown Records**. He found time for jazz engagements during this period, including spells with **Clark Terry**, **Count Basie**, **Howard McGhee**, **Frank Foster** and Lionel Hampton. He was a founder member of Trombones Incorporated (later known as Trombones Unlimited) and he also worked with **Al Grey**'s Trombone Summit. In the early 90s he played in bands led by **Illinois Jacquet** and he also toured and recorded with a trombone trio alongside Slide Hampton and Joshua Roseman. At this time Gordon was also an occasional member of **Nancie Banks**' big band and of a trio, which included **Curtis Fuller**. An extremely gifted technician, Gordon plays with drive and enthusiasm and his work with other trombonists has helped improve the instrument's following in the post-bop era after some years of neglect as a front-line jazz voice.

● ALBUMS: *Step By Step* (Bellaphon 1976) ★★★, *Live In Concert* (Mons 1995) ★★★.

Gordon, Mack

b. Morris Gittler, 21 June 1904, Warsaw, Poland, d. 1 March 1959, New York, USA. A prolific lyricist, mainly for movie songs during the 30s and 40s, Gordon was taken to the USA at an early age, and grew up in the Brooklyn area of New York. He toured with minstrel shows as a boy soprano, and later became a singer-comedian in vaudeville, before starting to write songs in the late 20s. His 'Aintcha', with music by Max Rich, was featured in the 1929 movie *Painted Heels*, and he also contributed to *The Song Of Love* and *Swing High* (1930). In the same year he teamed with **Harold Adamson** and **Vincent Youmans** for 'Time On My Hands', which was performed by **Marilyn Miller** and Paul Gregory in the Broadway revue *Smiles*.

In 1931, Gordon began a collaboration with composer **Harry Revel** that lasted until 1939. Initially they contributed songs to stage shows such as the **Ziegfeld Follies** Of 1931 ('Help Yourself To Happiness' and 'Cigarettes, Cigars') and *Everybody's Welcome* ('All Wrapped Up In You') but, from 1933 onwards, they wrote mainly for the movies—over 30 of them. These included **Broadway Through A Keyhole**, starring **Russ Columbo** and Constance Cummings, and featuring 'Doin' The Uptown Lowdown'; *Shoot The Works* ('With My Eyes Wide Open I'm Dreaming'); *Sitting Pretty* ('Did You Ever See A Dream Walking?'); *We're Not Dressing*, with **Bing Crosby** and Carole Lombard ('May I?', 'Love Thy Neighbour' and 'She Reminds Me Of You'); **The Gay Divorcée**, ('Don't Let It Bother You', sung by **Fred Astaire**); *College Rhythm* ('Stay As Sweet As You Are'); *Love In Bloom* ('Here Comes Cookie' and 'My Heart Is An Open Book'); *Two For Tonight*, with Crosby and Joan Bennett ('Without A Word Of Warning' and 'From The Top Of Your Head'); *Collegiate* ('I Feel Like A Feather In The Breeze' and 'You Hit The Spot'); **Stowaway** starring **Shirley Temple**, **Alice Faye** and Robert Young ('Goodnight My Love' and 'One Never Knows, Does One?'); **Wake Up And Live** ('Never In A Million Years' and 'There's A Lull In My Life'); *You Can't Have Everything* (title song); *Love Finds Andy Hardy*, with **Judy Garland** and **Mickey Rooney** ('What Do You Know About Love?' and 'Meet The Beat Of My Heart'); *Thanks For Everything* (title song) and *My Lucky Star* ('I've Got A Date With A Dream').

In 1940 Gordon teamed up with **Harry Warren**, fresh from his Warner Brothers triumphs with **Al Dubin**. During the next 10 years they wrote some of America's most memorable popular songs, for films such as **Down Argentine Way** (title song and 'Two Dreams Met'); **Tin Pan Alley** ('You Say The Sweetest Things, Baby'); **That Night In Rio** ('Chica Chica Boom Chic', 'Boa Noite' and 'I, Yi, Yi, Yi, Yi (I Like You Very Much)'); **The Great American Broadcast** ('Where You Are' and 'Long Ago Last Night') and *Weekend In Havana* ('When I Love, I Love' and 'Tropical Magic'). They featured some of the biggest stars of the day, including Alice Faye, **John Payne**, **Carmen Miranda**, **Betty Grable**, **Don Ameche**, the **Nicholas Brothers**, and many more. In 1941/2, Gordon and Warren contributed perhaps their best known songs to **Sun Valley Serenade** and **Orchestra Wives**, starring the enormously popular **Glenn Miller** And His Orchestra. They included 'I Know Why', 'Chattanooga Choo Choo', 'It Happened In Sun Valley', 'The Kiss Polka', 'At Last', 'I Got A Girl In Kalamazoo' and 'People Like You And Me'. Miller's million-selling record of 'Chattanooga Choo Choo' was the first to be awarded a gold disc. Gordon and Warren continued throughout the 40s, with films such as *Iceland*

('There Will Never Be Another You'); *Sweet Rosie O'Grady* ('My Heart Tells Me' and 'The Wishing Waltz'); **Hello, Frisco, Hello** ('You'll Never Know', the Academy Award-winning song of 1943); **Billy Rose's Diamond Horseshoe**, with **Dick Haymes** ('I Wish I Knew' and 'The More I See You'); and **Summer Stock**, with Judy Garland ('If You Feel Like Singing, Sing').

Even during the period of almost 20 years with Revel and Warren, Gordon found the time to collaborate with several other composers on songs such as 'Mamselle' (with Edmund Goulding); 'Time Alone Will Tell', 'I Can't Begin To Tell You' (with **Jimmy V. Monaco**); 'Somewhere In The Night', 'You Make Me Feel So Young', 'You Do', 'Baby, Won't You Say You Love Me?' and 'A Lady Loves To Love' (with **Joseph Myrow**). His last film score, with Myrow, was for *Bundle Of Joy* (1956), starring **Eddie Fisher** and **Debbie Reynolds**. Among Gordon's other collaborators were **Ray Henderson**, **Jimmy Van Heusen**, Max Rich, **Maurice Abrahams**, Ted Snyder, Abner Silver and George Weist.

Gordon, Michael

b. London England. When Gordon was four years old his family moved to Jamaica, where he was raised in the Parish of St. Mary. He returned in his teens to the UK, where he completed his education in Battersea, south London. On leaving school Gordon joined forces with Lorenzo Hall, Ian Austin, Leroy Graham and Martin Christie in the studio band the Private I's. The group enjoyed a modicum of success, but they accomplished greater recognition when they evolved into the **Investigators**.

In 1986, a year after the Investigators disbanded, Gordon embarked on a solo career and signed to **Fashion Records** in the UK. His debut, 'Magic Feeling', was a commercial success, and led to the release of the equally popular, 'Love Is In The Air'. In 1988, Gordon did not renew his contract with Fashion, although his debut album *Feelings Of Love* went to the top of the reggae charts. The singer's independent stance led to the formation of his own Sweet Freedom label. In 1990, an album of the Investigators greatest hits was released on **Jet Star**. As a result of the compilation's success Gordon re-formed the Investigators with Tony Christie, Colin Burton and the original line-up aside from Ian Austin. The revitalized group embarked on a tour of Europe and the UK for 18 months before Gordon returned to concentrate on his solo career. The singer maintained his profile in the reggae chart with hits such as, 'Twenty Four Hours', 'Angel Eyes', and 'Amazing Love' (a duet with Paulette Tajah), while producer **Mikey Simpson** released 2001's sublime *Changing Circles*.

● ALBUMS: *Feelings Of Love* (Fashion 1988) ★★★, *Changing Circles* (MCS 2001) ★★★★.

Gordon, Robert

b. 1947, Washington, DC, USA. Gordon was briefly a leading light during the 70s rediscovery of pop's roots. His own preferences for rockabilly and soul became apparent on stage when, after moving to New York City in 1970, he began singing with various groups including Tuff Darts, with whom he was heard among other acts on a concert album from the celebrated **CBGB's** club. As a solo artist, he was produced by **Richard Gottehrer** and signed to Private Stock. On a 1977 album with **Link Wray**, the ghost of the 50s faced the spirit of the 70s in state-of-the-art workouts of old chestnuts such as

'Summertime Blues', **Frankie Ford**'s 'Sea Cruise' and the tie-in single, 'Red Hot'. Hopes of a hit via **Bruce Springsteen**'s 'Fire', the single from *Fresh Fish Special*, were dashed by a cover version from the better-known **Pointer Sisters** but, transferring to **RCA Records**, Gordon tried again with help from Gottehrer, **Chris Spedding** and the cream of Nashville session players on *Rock Billy Boogie*, which contained 'The Catman', a self-penned tribute to **Gene Vincent**. A promotional tour of North America and Europe stoked up much revivalist fervour, and guaranteed a fair hearing for 1980's *Bad Boy*, highlighted by arrangements of **Conway Twitty**'s 'It's Only Make Believe' and **Joe Brown**'s 'A Picture Of You'. However, most consumers favoured the original sounds to Gordon's remakes and stylized homages—though few quarrelled over his integrity and taste. He recorded one more album for RCA in 1981 before returning to independent status.

● ALBUMS: with Link Wray *Robert Gordon With Link Wray* (Private Stock 1977) ★★★, with Link Wray *Fresh Fish Special* (Private Stock 1978) ★★★, *Rock Billy Boogie* (RCA 1979) ★★, *Bad Boy* (RCA 1980) ★★, *Are You Gonna Be The One* (RCA 1981) ★★, *Live At Lone Star* (New Rose 1989) ★★, *Greetings From New York City* (New Rose 1991) ★★, *King Biscuit Flower Hour* 1979 recording (King Biscuit 1996) ★★, *Satisfied Mind* (Jungle/Koch 2004) ★★★.

● COMPILATIONS: *Too Fast To Live, Too Young To Die* (One Way 1982) ★★★, *Is Red Hot* (Bear Family 1989) ★★★, *Black Slacks* (Bear Family 1990) ★★★, *Red Hot 1977–1981* (Razor & Tie 1995) ★★★, *The Robert Gordon Story* (One Way 1997) ★★★, *Lost Album Plus* (Bear Family 1998) ★★, *Hits You Remember Live* (Madacy 2001) ★★.

Gordon, Rosco

b. 10 April 1928, Memphis, Tennessee, USA, d. 11 July 2002, Queens, New York City, USA. A self-taught boogie-woogie styled pianist with no acknowledged influences other than a presumed awareness of the work of **Amos Milburn** and **Little Willie Littlefield**. Gordon was part of the Beale Streeters group in the late 40s, alongside **Johnny Ace**, **B.B. King** and later, **Bobby Bland**. **Ike Turner**, then a freelance producer and talent scout, recognized the potential of Gordon's powerful singing and recorded him for **Modern Records**. Gordon was still a teenager when he first recorded at **Sam Phillips**' Memphis Recording Service in January 1951. Phillips sold masters to both **Chess Records** in Chicago and RPM in Los Angeles, and thus, Gordon's 'Booted' appeared on both labels, a possible factor in its becoming the number 1 R&B hit in the spring of 1952. The follow-up, 'No More Doggin'', was another Top 5 R&B hit and typified what became known as 'Rosco's Rhythm', a loping boogie shuffle rhythm that predated and perhaps influenced Jamaican ska and blue-heat music. Gordon signed to Phillips' own **Sun Records** label in 1955, recording a regional hit, 'The Chicken', which led to his appearance in the movie *Rock Baby, Rock It* two years later. Moving to New York, he formed the duo Rosco And Barbara, making singles for Old Town. Many tracks recorded during this time remained unissued until the 70s and 80s.

Gordon's most well-known song reached number 2 in the R&B charts and was recorded in 1960 for the Chicago-based label **Vee Jay Records**. With its catchy saxophone-driven riff, 'Just A Little Bit' captured the imaginations of British R&B groups as well as black record buyers. A cover version by Merseybeat band the **Undertakers** was a minor hit in 1964. Further records for **ABC Records**, Old Town, Jomada, Rae-Cox

and Calla made little impression and in 1970, Gordon created his own label, Bab-Roc, issuing records by himself and his wife Barbara. An album of new compositions plus remakes of his hits was recorded for Organic Productions in 1971 but never released. A brief visit to England in 1982 brought an onstage reunion with B.B. King at London's 100 Club. At that time he was financing recordings from his own cleaning business. *Memphis, Tennessee*, a newly recorded batch of songs with musical support from **Duke Robillard**, appeared in 2000. It is a great pity that Gordon left it so long to deliver a new album of such quality, and unfortunately he passed away two years later.

● ALBUMS: *Memphis, Tennessee* (Stony Plain 2000) ★★★★, *No Dark In America* (Dualtone 2005) ★★★.

● COMPILATIONS: *The Legendary Sun Performers: Rosco Gordon* (Charly 1977) ★★★, *Best Of Rosco Gordon Volume 1* (Ace 1980) ★★★★, *Keep On Doggin'* (Mr R&B 1982) ★★★, *The Memphis Masters* (Ace 1982) ★★★, *Rosco Rocks Again* (JSP 1983) ★★★, *Lets Get High* (Charly 1990) ★★★★, *Just A Little Bit* (Vee-Jay 1993) ★★★★, *Rosco's Rhythm* (Charly 1997) ★★★, *Bootin': The Best Of The RPM Years* (Ace 1998) ★★★★, *The Very Best Of Rosco Gordon: Just A Little Bit* (Collectables 2001) ★★★★, *I'm Gonna Shake It* (Varèse Sarabande 2002) ★★★★, *Roscoe's Rhythm* (Charly 2004) ★★★★, *No More Doggin'* (Proper 2005) ★★★.

● FILMS: *Rock Baby, Rock It* (1957).

Gordon, Wycliffe

b. 29 May 1967, Waynesboro, Georgia, USA. Gordon was born into a musical family, his father, Lucius Gordon, being a classical pianist and teacher, and a lover of the blues. At first, he played piano but also learned to play clarinet, bassoon, bass, drums and tuba, before choosing the trombone at the age of 12. By this time the family had moved to Augusta, where all six Gordon children were displaying musical abilities. As a young teenager, he played in the Georgia All-State Concert And Jazz Band and also in McDonalds All-American High School Marching Band And Jazz Band. He attended A&M University at Tallahassee, Florida, where, during his sophomore year, 1987, he attended a master class conducted by **Wynton Marsalis**. He played with several high-school bands and in the late 80s played professionally with **Marcus Roberts** and others before joining Marsalis' band in June 1989. Gordon also played with several noted jazz artists, including **Dizzy Gillespie**, **Al Grey**, **Slide Hampton**, **Joe Henderson**, **Lionel Hampton** and **Shirley Horn**. His spell with Marsalis attracted worldwide attention and from 1990 he also became associated with the Lincoln Center Jazz Orchestra. During 1991, Gordon endured and overcame orthodontic problems, continuing to play during what was a very difficult and physically demanding period.

Gordon, who plays with a rich and burnished sound, is capable of robustly rollicking performances and those of passionate intensity. He has also composed several interesting and well-crafted pieces. In 2000, he was acknowledged as Best Trombonist in the Jazz Journalists Association's Jazz Awards, and Trombone Talent Deserving Wider Recognition in the *DownBeat* Critics Poll. Also in 2000, he was commissioned to write a new score for the classic silent of black cinema, Oscar Micheaux's *Body And Soul*. In addition to performing and writing, Gordon is also engaged in jazz education and in 2001 was an associate professor at Michigan State University.

Although Gordon has expressed his great admiration for a number of trombonists of earlier generations, including **Lawrence Brown**, **Vic Dickenson**, **Dicky Wells**, **J.J. Johnson** and **Frank Rosolino**, he has declared that it was not a trombonist, but **Louis Armstrong**, who was his greatest musical influence. Although he is very much a musician of his day and is forward thinking in his approach to jazz, in all that he does Gordon demonstrates a deep interest in the traditions of the music he so clearly loves.

● ALBUMS: with Ron Westray *Bone Structure* (Atlantic 1996) ★★★, *Slidin' Home* (Nagel-Heyer 1999) ★★★★, *The Gospel Truth* (Criss Cross 2000) ★★★, *The Search* (Nagel-Heyer 2000) ★★★, *What You Dealin' With* (Criss Cross 2001) ★★★★, with Eric Reed *We* (Nagel-Heyer 2002) ★★★, *United Soul Experience* (Criss Cross 2002) ★★★, *The Joyride* (Nagel-Heyer 2003) ★★★★, *Dig It* (Criss Cross 2003) ★★★, with the Garden City Gospel Choir *Dig It* (Criss Cross 2004) ★★, with the Garden City Gospel Choir *In The Cross* (Criss Cross 2005) ★★.

Gordy, Berry

b. Berry Gordy Jnr., 28 November 1929, Detroit, Michigan, USA. Gordy took his first tentative steps into the music business in 1955, when he opened a jazz record store in Detroit. When it folded, he returned to the automobile assembly lines until he met the manager of young R&B singer **Jackie Wilson**. Gordy wrote Wilson's first major hit, the novelty and now classic 'Reet Petite', and joined the singer's entourage, composing four further chart successes over the next two years. In 1958, Gordy set himself up as an independent producer, working with young unknowns such as the **Miracles**, **Marv Johnson** and **Eddie Holland**. That year he formed the Jobete Music company to handle songs by himself and his associates. At the suggestion of the Miracles' vocalist **Smokey Robinson**, Gordy went a stage further in 1959 by launching his own record company, Tamla Records. This was merely the first of a succession of labels gathered under his **Motown Records** umbrella, which rapidly became one of America's most important independent concerns.

Gordy masterminded Motown from the outside, choosing the artist-roster, writing and producing many of the early releases, and chairing weekly meetings that determined every aspect of the company's artistic direction. Having co-produced and co-written Motown's first major hit, the Miracles' 'Shop Around' in 1960, Gordy was also responsible for hits such as 'Do You Love Me' and 'Shake Sherry' by the **Contours**, 'Fingertips (Part 2)' by **Stevie Wonder**, 'Try It Baby' by **Marvin Gaye** and 'Shotgun' by **Junior Walker And The All Stars**. As Motown's influence and reputation grew, Gordy groomed a school of producers and writers to create the style that he dubbed 'The Sound of Young America'. Gradually his own artistic input lessened, although he continued to collaborate on **Supremes** hits such as 'Love Child' and 'No Matter What Sign You Are' until the end of the decade. His time was primarily devoted to increasing Motown's market share, and to dealing with a series of bitter clashes between artists and company, which threatened to halt the label's progress by the early 70s. Anxious to secure new power bases, Gordy shifted Motown's main offices from Detroit to California, and inaugurated a new films division with the highly acclaimed *Lady Sings The Blues*. This movie on the life of **Billie Holiday** starred former Supreme **Diana Ross**, with whom Gordy had long been rumoured to be enjoying a romantic liaison. Their relationship was part of the company's backbone, and her eventual decision to leave Motown in the early 80s was read as an indicator of the label's declining fortunes.

Having lost many of its major creative talents, Motown subsisted through the 70s and early 80s on the backs of several unique individuals, notably Stevie Wonder and **Lionel Richie**. Gordy was no longer finding significant new talent, however. Ironically, one of his company's most successful newcomers of the 80s was his own son, **Rockwell**. Gordy's personal career has long since been synonymous with the fortunes of his company, and he surprised the industry when he sold Motown Records to MCA in 1988—just weeks after he had been inducted into the **Rock And Roll Hall of Fame** in recognition of his pioneering talents as a major songwriter, impresario and executive. In the 90s, new label head Andre Harrell attempted to reassert the label as a leading force in black music, achieving notable success with acts such as **Johnny Gill**, **Boyz II Men** and **Queen Latifah**. In 1997 Gordy sold 50% of his Jobete music publishing to EMI. This catalogue of the golden age of Motown contains many of the finest songs of the era, and was unquestionably worth the purchase price of $135 million.

● FURTHER READING: *Movin' Up*, Berry Gordy. *To Be Loved: The Music, The Magic, The Memories Of Motown* Berry Gordy. *Where Did Our Love Go?*, Nelson George.

Gordy, Emory, Jnr.

b. 25 December 1944, Atlanta, Georgia, USA. Gordy was first noted as the bass player for **Elvis Presley**'s 70s band. At the same time he was playing with **Gram Parsons** and after Parsons' death, he became a member of **Emmylou Harris**' Hot Band. He was a session musician on many country rock albums, notably by **Eric Andersen**, the **Bellamy Brothers**, **Jonathan Edwards**, the **Flying Burrito Brothers**, **Chris Hillman**, **Albert Lee**, **Lyle Lovett**, **Mickey Newbury** and **Ricky Skaggs**. He also played on several **Billy Joel** albums. When he turned to record production, he had four US country number 1s with **Earl Thomas Conley**—'What She Is (Is A Woman In Love)', 'We Believe In Happy Endings' (a duet with Emmylou Harris), 'What'd I Say' and 'Love Out Loud'. He also produced the Bellamy Brothers including 'Old Hippie' and 'Kids Of The Baby Boom'. In the mid-90s he tried to re-establish **Alabama** as a major chart act. Gordy is married to **Patty Loveless** and, naturally, produces her records.

● ALBUMS: with David Grisman, Vince Gill, Herb Pedersen, Jim Buchanan *Here Today* (Rounder 1982) ★★★.

Gore, Charlie

b. Charles Mansfield Gore, 4 October 1930, Chapmanville, West Virginia, USA, d. 30 June 1984. He learned guitar and fiddle as a boy and played WLOG Logan during World War II while still at school. After completing his education, he worked on WSAZ Huntington and WRFD Worthington, before he eventually arrived at WLW Cincinnati in 1951. For several years, he was a star on the popular *Midwestern Hayride* and also appeared on the NBC-TV network. His charm and popularity on the television won him the nickname of The Handsome Guy From West Virginia. In 1956, he relocated to Indiana and appeared on radio and television in Indianapolis and Queen City until 1959. He then returned to Logan, where he worked as a disc jockey and later became involved with local politics. Between 1952 and 1956, he recorded over 30 sides for **King Records**, including two duets with **Ruby Wright**. He gained local success with 'If God Can Forgive You, So Can I' but registered no actual *Billboard* chart entries. In the 60s, he made further recordings for his own Blank label. He later returned to Ohio and made occasional appearances at local venues around the Cincinnati area before retiring to Fairfield, where he died in 1984. Gore never gained the one big hit that would have given him national stardom. In the early 90s, a German label released an album containing some of the King recordings.

● ALBUMS: *The Country Gentleman* (Audio Lab 1959) ★★★.

● COMPILATIONS: *The Handsome Guy From West Virginia* 50s recordings (CowgirlBoy 1992) ★★★★.

Gore, Lesley

b. Lesley Goldstein, 2 May 1946, New York City, USA, and raised in Tenafly, New Jersey. Having secured a recording contract with **Mercury Records** on the basis of a privately financed demonstration disc, Gore enjoyed a sensational debut when 'It's My Party' topped the US chart in May 1963, reached number 9 in the UK and grossed sales in excess of one million. This tale of adolescent trauma has retained its timeless appeal—the singer's birthday celebrations are irrevocably marred on losing boyfriend Johnny to Judy— and it remains one of the era's most memorable releases. The vengeful follow-up, 'Judy's Turn To Cry', reached US number 5 and earned another gold disc, but successive releases, including 'She's A Fool' (US number 5); 'You Don't Own Me' (US number 2), a powerful call for independence; 'That's The Way Boys Are' (US number 12) and 'Maybe I Know' (US number 14), confirmed that the singer was not simply a novelty act. Gore made several appearances in teen-orientated movies including *The Girls On The Beach* and *Ski Party*, and television shows including *Batman*, but her career was marred by periods of inactivity.

After a few singles on the Crew label Gore re-emerged in 1972 with *Someplace Else Now*, released on **Motown Records**' MoWest subsidiary. Three years later she was briefly reunited with producer/songwriter **Quincy Jones**, who had produced her early Mercury recordings, on the exceptional **A&M Records** single, 'Immortality'. Gore established herself as a songwriter of note with her contribution to the *Fame* soundtrack, earning an Oscar nomination for 'Out Here On My Own', which was co-written with her songwriter brother Michael. Her own recordings have subsequently been few and far between, with an album for the short-lived 51 West label in 1981, a single five years later on the Manhattan label, and a new album in 2005 for the Engine Company label. She has continued to tour to packed audiences on the cabaret circuit, while her acting career includes highlights such as 1999's appearance on Broadway in *Smokey Joe's Cafe*.

Despite the frailty exhibited on her debut single, Lesley Gore is now viewed by commentators as an early champion of women's rights, despite the fact that the songs that made her famous were penned by a male writing team.

● ALBUMS: *I'll Cry If I Want To* (Mercury 1963) ★★★★, *Sings Of Mixed-Up Hearts* (Mercury 1963) ★★★★, *Boys, Boys, Boys* (Mercury 1964) ★★★, *Girl Talk* (Mercury 1964) ★★★, *My Town, My Guy & Me* (Mercury 1965) ★★★,

Sings All About Love aka *Love Love Love* (Mercury 1966) ★★★, *California Nights* (Mercury 1967) ★★, *Someplace Else Now* (MoWest 1972) ★★, *Love Me By Name* (A&M 1976) ★★★, *The Canvas Can Do Miracles* (51 West 1982) ★★★, *Ever Since* (Engine Company 2005) ★★★.

● COMPILATIONS: *The Golden Hits Of Lesley Gore* (Mercury 1965) ★★★★, *Golden Hits Vol. 2* (Mercury 1968) ★★★, *The Sound Of Young Love* (Wing 1969) ★★★, *The Lesley Gore Anthology* (Rhino 1986) ★★★, *It's My Party* (Mercury 1991) ★★★, *Start The Party Again* (Raven 1993) ★★★, *It's My Party!* 5-CD box set (Bear Family 1994) ★★★, *It's My Party: The Mercury Anthology* (PolyGram 1996) ★★★, *Sunshine, Lollipops & Rainbows: The Best Of Lesley Gore* (Rhino 1998) ★★★★, *The Essential Collection* (Spectrum 1999) ★★★.

● FILMS: *The T.A.M.I. Show* (1964), *Ski Party* (1965), *The Girls On The Beach* aka *Summer Of '64* (1965),

Gore, Martin

b. 23 July 1961, Basildon, Essex, England. Gore has spent most of his music career as the keyboard player and main songwriter with the highly successful **Depeche Mode**, happily surrendering the spotlight to the band's more flamboyant frontman **Dave Gahan**. Gore was one of the original founding members of Depeche Mode with **Vince Clarke** and Andy Fletcher, and following the departure of Clarke he took over the songwriting duties. Lyrically, Gore introduced sado-masochism ('Master And Servant'), capitalism ('Everything Counts'), and religious fetishism ('Personal Jesus') into the UK charts, but wrapped his dark impulses in highly commercial melodies. Gore's first solo venture was the *Counterfeit* EP, released in 1989 during a hiatus in band activities. Somewhat surprisingly, the songwriter chose to tackle six cover versions by a range of artists including **Sparks** and the **Comsat Angels**. Gore's sweet tenor voice failed to raise the level of interest on a downbeat and musically tentative collection. He then returned to songwriting duties with Depeche Mode, who by the middle of the following decade had established themselves as one of the UK's most successful imports on the American market. Following a period of retrenchment necessitated by Gahan's personal problems, the band enjoyed further success with *Ultra* (1997) and *Exciter* (2001). Two years after the release of the latter, Gore chose to expand on the idea of his earlier EP and record a whole album of cover versions. Released a month before Gahan's solo debut, *Counterfeit2* tackled material by the **Velvet Underground**, **David Essex** and **Nick Cave** among others, in addition to a take on the traditional 'In My Time Of Dying'.

● ALBUMS: as Martin L. Gore *Counterfeit2* (Mute/Reprise 2003) ★★★.

Gorefest

Formed in 1989, Dutch band Gorefest managed to carve a niche for themselves in an increasingly overcrowded death metal genre, making their debut on the underground demo scene with two tapes, *Tangled In Gore* and *Horrors In A Retarded Mind*. After *Mindloss*, they secured a contract with Nuclear Blast Records and released *False*. Gorefest's material was morbidly metaphysical, and at their best they managed to combine melodic and inventive riffs with an abrasive edge. A popular live band, they released a recording of their performance at 1993's Dynamo Open Air Festival as *The Eindhoven Insanity*, which some argue was the first-ever live death-metal album. The 1994 studio album *Erase* represented their most confident outing, and featured the line up of Jan-Chris De Koeijer (vocals/bass), Frank Harthoorn (rhythm guitar), Boudewijn Bonebakker (guitar) and Ed Warby (drums).

● ALBUMS: *Mindloss* (F2000 1991) ★★, *False* (Nuclear Blast/Relapse 1992) ★★★, *The Eindhoven Insanity* (Nuclear Blast/Relapse 1993) ★★, *Erase* (Nuclear Blast/Relapse 1994) ★★★★, *Soul Survivor* (Nucear Blast 1996) ★★, *Chapter 13* (SPV 1997) ★★★.

Gorgoroth

A proficient Norwegian black metal band, Gorgoroth was formed in 1992 and took their name from J.R.R. Tolkien's book *The Lord Of The Rings*. Although personnel changes have been frequent, the core of the band has always been the guitarist Infernus, with expert assistance from various players on the ever-overlapping black metal scene. Samoth of **Emperor** played bass on the band's 1994 debut, *Pentagram*. The other musicians were drummer Goat and the oddly named vocalist Hat. The follow-up *Antichrist* was recorded by Infernus, Hat, new singer Pest and **Satyricon** drummer Frost (b. Kjetil Haraldstad). Aeternus bass player Ares, Pest and the late Borknagar drummer Grim (b. Erik Brodreskift, 23 December 1969, Norway, d. 4 October 1999) featured on 1997's *Under The Sign Of Hell*. Nuclear Blast then signed a long-term recording contract with Gorgoroth, reissuing the Malicious albums and releasing *Destroyer*, which was recorded with guitarist Tormentor, singer Gaahl, the returning Frost, second drummer Vrolok, Ares and second bass player T-Reaper, and synth player Daimonion. The band's second album for Nuclear Blast, 2000's *Incipit Satan*, featured Infernus, Tormentor, Gaahl, bass player King ovHell and drummer Sersjant Erichsen, and continued the band's obsession with raw, unsophisticated black metal.

● ALBUMS: *Pentagram* (Embassy 1994) ★★★, *Antichrist* (Malicious 1996) ★★★, *Under The Sign Of Hell* (Malicious 1997) ★★, *Destroyer* (Malicious 1998) ★★★, *Incipit Satan* (Nuclear Blast 2000) ★★★, *Twilight Of The Idols* (Nuclear Blast 2003) ★★★.

Gorguts

This Quebec, Canada–based death metal band, formed by Luc Lemay (vocals/guitar), Sylvain Marcoux (guitar), Eric Giguere (bass) and Stephane Provencher (drums), promised great things on their 1990 debut, *Considered Dead*, which featured guest spots from the **Death** guitarist James Murphy and **Cannibal Corpse** vocalist Chris Barnes. The Roadrunner Records label had signed the band on the strength of the impressive *And Then Comes Lividity* demo of 1990. However, *The Erosion Of Sanity* failed to make an impact in the midst of the black metal explosion of 1993 and band and label parted ways. Gorguts then fell silent for five years, and many fans assumed that they had parted ways permanently, but singer Lemay returned in 1998 with a new line-up (guitarist Steve Hurdle, bass player Steve Cloutier and drummer Patrick Robert), a new recording contract with the Olympic label and *Obscura*, which lived up to its title by exploring progressive, almost *avant garde* areas to an uncertain response. The 2001 follow-up *From Wisdom To Hate*, featuring new guitarist Daniel Mongrain and new drummer Steve MacDonald (d. October 2002), was similarly difficult. This popular Canadian act finally called it a day in 2005,

having never recovered from MacDonald's suicide three years previously.

● ALBUMS: *Considered Dead* (Roadrunner 1990) ★★★, *The Erosion Of Sanity* (Roadrunner 1993) ★★, *Obscura* (Olympic 1998) ★★★, *From Wisdom To Hate* (Olympic 2001) ★★★.

● COMPILATIONS: *. . . And Then Comes Lividity: Demo Anthology* (Galy 2003) ★★★.

Gories

Comprising three Detroit, Michigan, USA, natives—Mick Collins (b. 18 December 1965), Dan Kroha (b. 30 May 1965; guitar) and Margaret Ann 'Peg' O'Neill (b. 29 July 1967; drums)—lo-fi garage rock group the Gories formed in 1986, taking their name from a mock band featured on the popular 60s era television series, *Gidget*. Despite having little experience playing their respective instruments at the time, the trio hooked up with producer Len Puch during summer 1987 to record some songs at Garageland Studios, many of which would go on to become 'standards' for the band—'Hey, Hey, We're The Gories', 'Thunderbird ESQ' and 'Sister Ann', among others. The band's first appearance on record occurred in 1987, when the bass-less trio was included on the compilation *It Came From The Garage II!* (issued via Puch's own label, Wanghead With Lips). The Gories' debut, *House Rockin'*, followed two years later, and once more, was produced by Puch and issued via his label.

The trio broke up for a short spell soon afterwards, but when **Alex Chilton** offered to produce their next album for them, the Gories reassembled, resulting in the release of 1990's *I Know You Fine, But How You Doin'* (recorded in Chilton's home town of Memphis, Tennessee). Several singles ensued, which included covers by **Bo Diddley** ('You Don't Love Me' for **Sub Pop Records**) and **Spinal Tap** ('Give Me Some Money'), as well as an inaugural visit to Europe in May 1992. Later the same year, the Gories issued what would turn out to be their final release, the appropriately titled *Outta Here*, before disbanding. All former Gories members have since turned up elsewhere, O'Neill in the Darkest Hours, Kroha in the **Demolition Doll Rods**, and Collins in the **Dirtbombs**, in addition to countless other projects.

● ALBUMS: *House Rockin'* (Wanghead With Lips 1989) ★★★, *I Know You Fine, But How You Doin'* (New Rose 1990) ★★★, *Outta Here* (Crypt 1992) ★★★.

Gorilla Biscuits

Perhaps the quintessential band of the New York City, USA–based hardcore punk scene of the late 80s, Gorilla Biscuits became highly influential in the space of just one album and EP. Originally comprising Arthur Smilios (bass), Anthony 'Civ' Civocelli (vocals), Walter Schreifels (guitar) and Token Entry member Ernie Parada (drums), the band's initial demo was recorded while most of the members were still in high school, and still learning their instruments. Despite this, it was an immediate underground hit, and the band soon graduated to playing all-ages matinee shows at the infamous **CBGB's** alongside Warzone, **Youth Of Today**, Bold, **Sick Of It All** and Underdog. After contributing a track for the *New York City Hardcore: The Way It Is* compilation, the band (now including drummer Luke) recorded their 1988 eponymous debut for Connecticut hardcore label Revelation Records. Conveying the dynamism of the band's live shows, it was immediately much sought after and although rough around the edges was noticeably more accessible and better crafted than many of their contemporaries' efforts.

Expanding to a five-piece with the addition of second guitarist Alex Brown, the band began work on *Start Today*. Produced by Don Fury and partly funded by compensation Revelation boss Jordan Cooper received for a car accident, it became one of the fledgling label's biggest-ever sellers and a landmark release for the hardcore scene. Opening with a trumpet fanfare and including a harmonica solo on the title track, it was also something of a departure from the norm. Civocelli articulated intelligent lyrics about friendship, vegetarianism and of course 'the scene' over frantically paced hardcore workouts that rose above the standard verse/chorus/mosh-part that was customary at that time. Sporadic US dates and two European tours (the second with replacement drummer Sam Siegler) followed, but by 1992 the band was all but finished. After making one of the most complete hardcore records ever, they simply had nothing more to prove. Chief songwriter Schreifels went on to form the equally well regarded **Quicksand**, while Civocelli, Siegler and Smilios formed **CIV**.

● ALBUMS: *Gorilla Biscuits* mini-album (Revelation 1988) ★★★, *Start Today* (Revelation 1989) ★★★★.

Gorilla

Formed in Derby, Derbyshire, England, in the mid-90s, experimental hard rock band Gorilla was formed when the **Beyond**'s two albums failed to achieve either strong critical support or healthy sales. John Whitby (vocals), Andy Gatford (guitar), Jim Kersey (bass) and Neil Cooper (drums) added violinist Andy Lingard to complete the new line-up, making their debut in May 1995 with a four-track EP, *Extended Play*, on Embryo Records. A raw self-production, it saw the group receive excellent reviews, although it also marked the departure of Kersey, who had tired of living on the breadline in a fringe rock band.

Gorillas

Originally known as the Hammersmith Gorillas, this English trio played their own brand of punk meets rhythm and blues meets heavy rock. Initially riding on the back of the punk movement, they built up a loyal fanbase and released a string of excellent singles during the mid-to late 70s, including 'You Really Got Me' (a cover version of the **Kinks** classic), 'Gatecrasher', 'It's My Life' and 'She's My Gal'. Band leader Jesse Hector (vocals/ guitar), ably supported by Alan Butler (bass) and Gary Anderson (drums), was influenced by several dead 'stars'. These included **Elvis Presley**, **Eddie Cochran**, **Buddy Holly**, Brian Jones, **Marc Bolan** and **Jimi Hendrix**. The extravagantly side-burned singer was a noted self-publicist, whose passionate belief in the importance of the Gorillas as the 'future of rock music' was taken in surprisingly good humour by the UK music press. Several of the tracks on the Gorillas' album were delivered in the musical style of Hector's heroes, most notably a superb cover version of Hendrix's 'Foxy Lady' and the Marc Bolan–influenced 'Going Fishing'. After a lengthy absence, Hector was to be found working the London live circuit in 1992 with his group the Sound.

● ALBUMS: *Message To The World* (Chiswick 1978) ★★★.

Gorillaz

A unique phenomenon, Gorillaz is best described as a multi-national virtual hip-hop group comprising the fictional characters 2D (vocals/keyboards), Murdoc (bass), Russel (drums) and Noodle (guitar). The prominent brains behind the formation of the outfit were **Blur**'s lead singer Damon Albarn, producer **Dan 'The Automator' Nakamura**, and the cartoonist Jamie Hewlett, creator of the cult *Tank Girl*. The Gorillaz' refreshing take on hip-hop and electronica was a revelation. After November 2000's debut *Tomorrow Comes Today* EP, the real breakthrough came with the following year's UK Top 5 hit, 'Clint Eastwood'. Equally sinister and humorous, the song's lasting imprint proved to be Albarn's carefree 'sunshine in a bag' vocal hook. A fine remix by **Ed Case** introduced the song to lovers of UK garage and also crossed over to the US charts. The catchy '19/2000' was equally successful, and like its predecessor featured a high quality video which benefited greatly from Hewlett's input. Gorillaz made great use of the Internet to promote their fictional crew, with their homepage offering a wealth of animated trickery. Their self-titled debut album encompassed a broad spectrum of musical influences, with lo-fi, hip-hop, dub and punk the most prominent, with the **Buena Vista Social Club**'s veteran Cuban singer **Ibrahim Ferrer** guesting on 'Latin Simone'. Other contributors included rapper **Del Tha Funkee Homosapien**, **Kid Koala**, Miho Hatori of **Cibo Matto**, and Chris Frantz and Tina Weymouth of **Tom Tom Club**. The group mastered the problem of live performances by remaining hidden behind a screen, ensuring that they stayed part of the animated scenery.

Despite the enormous worldwide success of the album, notably in the USA, the Gorillaz were put on hiatus after the release of a b-sides compilation and a remix album in 2002. Albarn reconvened the project at the end of 2004 after fulfilling a number of solo and Blur commitments. Although Hewlett returned to provide animations, infamous 'mash-up' DJ **Danger Mouse** took the place of Nakamura as producer. Collaborators on the long-awaited *Demon Days* included **De La Soul**, **Deborah Harry**, **Martina Topley-Bird** and Shaun Ryder. Released in spring 2005, the album spawned the hits 'Feel Good Inc.', 'Dare' (featuring a memorable cameo from Ryder) and 'Dirty Harry', and broke into both the US and UK Top 10. Albarn launched a series of spectacular live shows in November 2005 at Manchester's Opera House, featuring cartoon projections, guest artists and backing from over 80 musicians.

● ALBUMS: *Gorillaz* (Parlophone/Virgin 2001) ★★★, *Demon Days* (Parlophone/Virgin 2005) ★★★★.

● COMPILATIONS: *G Sides* (Parlophone/Virgin 2002) ★★★, as Space Monkeyz Vs. Gorillaz *Laika Come Home* remix album (Astralwerks 2002) ★★★.

● DVD/VIDEOS: *Phase One: Celebrity Take Down* (Virgin 2002), *Demon Days: Live At The Manchester Opera House* (EMI 2006).

Gorka, John

b. New Jersey, USA. Singer-songwriter Gorka, who possesses a rich and emotive baritone, honed his craft in America's north-eastern folk scene of the early 80s before recording a succession of acclaimed albums. Influenced by **Tom Paxton**, **Richard Thompson** and **Tom Waits**, among others, his musical career began in 1986 when he was attending Moravian College in Bethlehem, with the intention of studying history and philosophy. A small coffee-house folk scene had sprung up at a nearby venue called Godfrey

Daniels, and Gorka graduated from open-mic spots to leading a group, the Razzy Dazzy Spasm Band. However, he packed his guitar and took his songs out to the wider world, playing throughout north-east America, then travelling to Texas, where he won the Kerrville Folk Festival's New Folk Award in 1984. His debut album, *I Know*, was released on Red House Records in 1987, and featured the best of his early songwriting, including 'Blues Palace', 'Downtown Tonight', and 'Down In The Milltown'. Afterwards, he would enjoy a more stable relationship with High Street/**Windham Hill Records**. The ensuing albums explored a multi-faceted talent, with earnest vocals bedecking Gorka's dry wit and sharp observations and character sketches.

By the advent of *Temporary Road* in 1993, the artist found increased exposure, touring with **Mary-Chapin Carpenter** and **Nanci Griffith**. Meanwhile, a single drawn from the album, 'When She Kisses Me', was voted the CMT Best Independent Video Of The Year. For *Out Of The Valley* Gorka relocated from Bethlehem to Nashville, teaming up with producer/guitarist **John Jennings**. Together they recruited an all-star cast to accompany the singer, including Mary-Chapin Carpenter, **Kathy Mattea**, **Leo Kottke** and Dave Mattacks. Gorka also drew on the rich musical environment that surrounded him in the studio, using a guitar once owned by **Buddy Holly**, the piano with which **Carole King** had recorded ***Tapestry*** and a mixing board that had been used for sessions with **Elvis Presley** and **Roy Orbison**. This time the songs were less personally defined, using a third-person mechanism to allow the artist to explore his characters, giving them individual motivation and colour.

Following a final album for High Street, Gorka relocated to Minnesota, married and became a parent. He returned to the Red House label in 1998 to release the acclaimed *After Yesterday*. Gorka's creative roll showed no sign of coming to an end on the follow-up *The Company You Keep*, which included the wry baby-boomer sketch 'People My Age' and the Republican-baiting 'Oh Abraham'.

● ALBUMS: *I Know* (Red House 1987) ★★★★, *Land Of The Bottom Line* (Windham Hill 1990) ★★★★, *Jack's Crows* (High Street 1992) ★★★, *Temporary Road* (High Street 1993) ★★★, *Out Of The Valley* (High Street 1994) ★★★★, *Between Five And Seven* (High Street 1996) ★★★, *After Yesterday* (Red House 1998) ★★★★, *The Company You Keep* (Red House 2001) ★★★★, *Old Futures Gone* (Red House 2003) ★★★.

● DVD/VIDEOS: *Good Noise* (High Street 1994).

Gorky Park

Comprising Nikolai Naskov (vocals), Alex Belov (guitar), Jan Janewkow (guitar), Alexander Minkov (bass) and Sascha Lvov (drums), Russian hard rock band Gorky Park formed in the late 80s. They rose to international prominence at the 1989 Moscow Music And Peace Festival, where they shared a stage with **Mötley Crüe**, **Bon Jovi** and **Ozzy Osbourne**. Those artists were sufficiently impressed by Gorky Park's powerful stage show to spread news of them to the west, eventually resulting in a US release for their self-titled 1989 album. However, once the novelty of a Russian hard rock band had worn off, Gorky Park faced critical and commercial resistance to their unspectacular hard rock presentation.

● ALBUMS: *Gorky Park* (PolyGram 1989) ★★.

Gorky's Zygotic Mynci

One of the most idiosyncratic bands to emerge from the Welsh indie scene of the mid-90s, Gorky's Zygotic Mynci followed **Super Furry Animals** in getting Welsh language music onto mainstream radio. The band was formed in Carmarthen by school friends Euros Childs (vocals/keyboards), Richard James (bass) and John Lawrence (guitar), later joined by Euros Rowlands (drums) and Megan Childs (violin). After recording demo tapes in their bedrooms (later released on the *Patio* CD), the band was signed to the Gwynedd-based independent label Ankst, and released a 10-inch mini-album, *Patio*, in 1992. Commenting on the songs written in their native language, Euros Childs later stated: 'we used to sing mainly in Welsh just because we didn't really expect to be heard outside Wales'. Touring gave a curious press an opportunity to review the band, whose quasi-medieval music was matched by their retro-hippy garb, leading to inevitable comparisons with the **Incredible String Band**.

Their debut album *Tatay* contained predominantly Welsh-language songs, but it was the cover version of **Robert Wyatt**'s 'O, Caroline', and a track called 'Kevin Ayers', that revealed the source of the band's love of experimental whimsy. The catchy single 'Miss Trudy' gained them more critical praise and a wider audience, while 1995's *Bwyd Time* proved to be a more accessible record than the debut. Now touring as headliners in their own right, it was no surprise when the band secured a major recording contract with **Fontana Records**. *Barafundle* was released in 1997 to unanimous critical praise, a beautiful and haunting blend of psychedelic pop music and quirky, original lyrics. The ever-productive Gorky's then released the non-album single 'Young Girls And Happy Endings'. *Gorky 5* was a less accessible, harder-edged album, juxtaposing the **Velvet Underground** inspired single 'Sweet Johnny' with the melodic beauty of 'Tidal Wave' and 'Only The Sea Makes Sense'.

The band departed from Fontana's books shortly afterwards, and founder member Lawrence left the following June. Typically unfazed the remaining quartet bounced back on the Mantra label with the excellent albums *Spanish Dance Troupe* (1999) and *How I Long To Feel That Summer In My Heart* (2001). Another change of label followed for 2003's *Sleep:Holiday*, but unfortunately their Sanctuary Records debut was one of the band's least inspiring offerings. With Gorky's Zygotic Mynci on temporary hiatus, Euros Childs made his solo bow in late 2005 with the single 'Donkey Island'.

● ALBUMS: *Patio* mini-album (Ankst 1992) ★★★, *Tatay* (Ankst 1994) ★★★, *Bwyd Time* (Ankst 1995) ★★★, *Barafundle* (Fontana 1997) ★★★★★, *Gorky 5* (Fontana 1998) ★★★, *Spanish Dance Troupe* (Mantra/Beggars Banquet 1999) ★★★★, *The Blue Trees* mini-album (Mantra/Beggars Banquet 2000) ★★★★, *How I Long To Feel That Summer In My Heart* (Mantra/Beggars Banquet 2001) ★★★, *Sleep:Holiday* (Sanctuary 2003) ★★. Solo: Euros Childs *Chops* (Wichita 2006) ★★★.

● COMPILATIONS: *Patio* (Ankst 1995) ★★★, *Introducing Gorky's Zygotic Mynci* US only (PolyGram 1996) ★★★, *20: EPs And Singles 1994–1996* (Castle 2003) ★★★.

Gorme, Eydie

b. Edith Gorme, 16 August 1931, New York City, USA the youngest of three children. Gorme's parents were of

Turkish and Spanish origin, and since Spanish was the family language, she grew up speaking it fluently. At the age of three she made her radio debut, singing in a children's programme from a department store. While at the William Howard Taft High School in the Bronx, Gorme was voted 'the prettiest, peppiest cheerleader', starred in the school musicals and sang with her friend Ken Greengrass' band at the weekends. On leaving school, she worked as a Spanish interpreter with the Theatrical Supply Export Company before deciding to concentrate on a singing career with Greengrass as her manager. Her first break came in 1950, when she successfully auditioned for band leader **Tommy Tucker** and toured with him for two months. When that tour ended she spent a year with **Tex Beneke** before going out on her own, appearing in nightclubs and on radio and television.

After being turned down several times by Arthur Godfrey's talent scouts ('the fourth time I tried, they locked the office door when they saw me coming up the stairs'), Gorme signed for **Coral Records** in 1952. Her singles included 'Frenesi', 'I've Gotta Crow', 'Tea For Two' and 'Fini', which entered the US Top 20. She also hosted her own radio show, *Cita Con Eydie* (*A Date With Eydie*), which was transmitted to Spanish-speaking countries via the *Voice Of America*. In September 1953, she became a permanent member of **Steve Allen**'s top-rated *Tonight* show, on which she sang, and wrote and performed sketches with another regular, **Steve Lawrence**. They also introduced Allen's composition 'This Could Be The Start Of Something (Big)', which became associated with them as their singing partnership blossomed into romance. Lawrence was the son of Eastern European parents and had sung in the choir at his cantor father's synagogue. Lawrence *did* make it onto the *Arthur Godfrey Talent Show*, in 1952, and had made an impression with his version of **Tony Martin**'s hit 'Domino'.

An important and influential figure in both Gorme and Lawrence's recording careers was conductor, arranger and producer **Don Costa**. In February 1956, Gorme deputized at short notice for **Billy Daniels** at New York's Copacabana nightclub, and was so well received that she returned in July to headline with her own show. In January 1957, she made her Broadway debut in the *Jerry Lewis Stage Show* at the Palace Theatre, and in December, Gorme and Lawrence were married in Las Vegas. Gorme's success in the US singles chart up to this period had included 'Too Close For Comfort', 'Mama, Teach Me To Dance' (both 1956), 'Love Me Forever' (1957) and the number 11 hit 'You Need Hands' (1958).

During the summer of 1958 the couple starred in their own weekly one-hour musical variety television show, as a replacement for Steve Allen. Shortly afterwards, Lawrence was inducted into the US Army for two years. Gorme embarked on a country-wide nightclub tour until 1960, when she was reunited with Lawrence at the Copacabana and the Coconut Grove, Los Angeles, and the Sands and Sahara Hotels in Las Vegas. In 1960 they won a Grammy Award for *We Got Us*, their first complete duet album, which was followed by several others, including *Two On The Aisle*, a set of Broadway show numbers, and *At The Movies*. In the singles chart, the couple's most successful joint efforts included 'I Want To Stay Here' (1963) and 'I Can't Stop Talking About You' (1964). Eydie received a Grammy Award for Best Popular Female Vocalist for her version of 'If He Walked Into My Life', from **Jerry Herman**'s musical *Mame*.

In 1968, the couple appeared on Broadway in *Golden Rainbow*, a musical adaptation of Arnold Schulman's play *A Hole In the Head*, with words and music by Walter Marks. One of the songs, 'I've Gotta Be Me', became the title of a Lawrence album, and also became a regular part of **Sammy Davis Jnr.**'s repertoire. In 1969, Gorme and Lawrence recorded their first musical, *What It Was, Was Love*, written for them by **Gordon Jenkins**.

During the 70s and 80s, the couple continued to record and appear regularly on television. Several of their 'specials', commemorating the music of composers such as **Cole Porter** and **George** and **Ira Gershwin**, won awards; *Steve And Eydie Celebrate Irving Berlin* gained a record-breaking seven Emmys. In 1987, they were in a television production of *Alice In Wonderland*, written by Steve Allen, playing the parts of Tweedledum and Tweedledee. In 1989, they released *Alone Together*, on their own GL label. It was for their live performances, however, that they received the most applause. During the 80s, they appeared at venues such as Carnegie Hall in 1981 and 1983, the Universal Amphitheatre, in Los Angeles, Harrah's, Tahoe, and the 1,400-seater Bally's at Las Vegas. Their skilful blend of classy songs (or, as they put it, 'no punk, no funk, no rock, no schlock'), coupled with a brand of humour that has been honed for over 30 years, make them one of the few consistently successful acts of their kind in the world. In 1991, they saw quite a lot of that world, when they joined **Frank Sinatra** on his year long *Diamond Jubilee Tour*, to commemorate his 75th birthday.

● ALBUMS: *Delight* (Coral 1957) ★★, *Eydie Gorme* (ABC-Paramount 1957) ★★★, *Eydie Swings The Blues* (ABC-Paramount 1957) ★★★★, *Eydie Gorme Vamps The Roaring '20s* (ABC-Paramount 1958) ★★★★, *Eydie In Love . . .* (ABC-Paramount 1958) ★★★★, *Love Is A Season* (ABC-Paramount 1958) ★★★, *Eydie Sings Showstoppers* (ABC-Paramount 1959) ★★★★, *Eydie Gorme On Stage* (ABC-Paramount 1959) ★★★★, *Eydie Gorme In Dixieland* (ABC-Paramount 1960) ★★, *Come Sing With Me* (United Artists 1961) ★★★, *I Feel So Spanish* (United Artists 1962) ★★★, *Blame It On The Bossa Nova* (Columbia 1963) ★★★★, *Let The Good Times Roll* (Columbia 1963) ★★★, *Gorme Country Style* (Columbia 1964) ★, *Amor* (Columbia 1964) ★★★, *More Amor* (Columbia 1965) ★★, *Don't Go To Strangers* (Columbia 1966) ★★★, with the Trio Los Panchos *Navidad Means Christmas* (Columbia 1966) ★★, *Softly, As I Love You* (Columbia 1967) ★★★, *Tonight I'll Say A Prayer* (RCA 1970) ★★★, *Tomame O Dejame* (President 1985) ★★★, *Come In From The Rain* (President 1985) ★★★, *Sings/Canta* (Sound 1987) ★★★.

With Steve Lawrence *We Got Us* (ABC-Paramount 1960) ★★★★, *Steve And Eydie Sing The Golden Hits* (ABC-Paramount 1960) ★★★, *Cozy* (United Artists 1961) ★★★, *Two On The Aisle* (United Artists 1963) ★★★, *Our Best To You* (ABC-Paramount 1964) ★★★, *Together On Broadway* (Columbia 1967) ★★★, *What It Was, Was Love* (RCA 1969) ★★★, *Real True Lovin'* (RCA 1969) ★★★, *Tonight I'll Say A Prayer* (RCA 1970) ★★★, *We Can Make It Together* (Ember 1975) ★★★, *Our Love Is Here To Stay* (United Artists 1977) ★★★, *I Still Believe In Love* (President 1985) ★★★, *Alone Together* (GL 1989) ★★★, *Since I Fell For You* (GL 1993) ★★★.

● COMPILATIONS: *The Very Best Of Eydie Gorme* (ABC-Paramount 1961) ★★★, *Eydie Gorme's Greatest Hits* (Columbia 1967) ★★★.

With Steve Lawrence *The Very Best Of Eydie And Steve* (United Artists 1962) ★★★, *The Golden Hits Of Eydie And Steve* (United Artists 1962) ★★★, *The Best Of Steve And Eydie* (Columbia 1977) ★★★, *20 Golden Performances* (Columbia 1977) ★★★.

Gosdin, Vern

b. 5 August 1934, Woodland, Alabama, USA. Gosdin's first steps in carrying out his wish to be a country singer-songwriter came in the early 50s, when as a result of singing with his two brothers in the local church, they became regulars as the Gosdin Family on WVOK Birmingham. In 1953, he moved to Atlanta where he sold ice cream and in 1956 to Chicago where he ran a country music nightclub. During this time he worked hard to develop his singing and writing, and also became a talented instrumentalist on guitar, banjo and mandolin. In 1960, he moved to California, where he joined his brother Rex (b. 1938, d. 23 May 1983), first in a bluegrass group called the Golden State Boys and then as members of **Chris Hillman**'s bluegrass band the Hillmen. When Hillman moved on to rock as a founder member of the **Byrds**, Gosdin also worked as a session musician while continuing to perform bluegrass with Rex. He recorded for several labels with no real success, and in 1966, recorded an album with **Gene Clark** (*Gene Clark With The Gosdin Brothers*), who had recently left the Byrds. In 1967, the brothers finally achieved a US country chart hit with 'Hangin' On', but lacking any follow-up success, Gosdin soon returned to Atlanta and opened a glass and mirror shop, singing only in his spare time. His song, 'Someone To Turn To', was recorded by the Byrds at the instigation of guitarist **Clarence White**.

In 1976, Gosdin returned to recording, charting a version of 'Hangin' On' and enjoying Top 10 hits with 'Yesterday's Gone (both of which featured backing vocals by **Emmylou Harris**) and 'Till The End'. He left his sons to run the business and with Rex returned to touring and concerts. Between 1978 and 1988, he registered 27 more US country chart hits, including number 1s with 'I Can Tell By The Way You Dance (You're Gonna Love Me Tonight)' and 'Set 'Em Up Joe'. In 1979 and 1980, his brother Rex had three minor chart entries, the biggest being a duet with **Tommy Jennings** on 'Just Give Me What You Think Is Fair'. Rex died in May 1983 at the age of 45, some two weeks before his recording of 'That Old Time Feelin'' entered the charts.

Gosdin continues to record and perform although he was hospitalized in 1995 with a stroke, and was dropped by **Columbia Records**. He resurfaced on BTM Records with 1998's *The Voice*. He is a rare performer in that his solid country voice and heartbreaking songs are somewhat alien to much of Nashville's modern music scene. Like **George Jones**, he appears to improve with age. Even **Tammy Wynette** once said, 'If anybody sounded like Jones other than Jones without really trying to, it is Vern Gosdin.'

● ALBUMS: as the Gosdin Brothers *The Sounds Of Goodbye* (Bakersfield International/Capitol 1967) ★★★, *Till The End* (Elektra 1977) ★★★★, *Never My Love* (Elektra 1978) ★★★, *You've Got Somebody* (Elektra 1979) ★★★, *Passion* (Ovation 1981) ★★★, *If You're Gonna Do Me Wrong, (Do It Right)* (Compleat 1983) ★★★, *Today My World Slipped Away* (Compleat 1983) ★★★, *Dream Lady* (Compleat 1984) ★★★, *There Is A Season* (Compleat 1984) ★★★, *If Jesus Comes Tomorrow* (Compleat 1984) ★★★, *Time Stood Still*

(Compleat 1985) ★★★, *Chiseled In Stone* (Columbia 1988) ★★★★, *Alone* (Columbia 1989) ★★★, *Rough Around The Edges: A.M.I. Sessions* (RCA 1989) ★★, *10 Years Of Hits—Newly Recorded* (Columbia 1990) ★★★, *Out Of My Heart* (Columbia 1991) ★★★, *Nickels And Dimes And Love* (Columbia 1993) ★★★, *24 Karat Heartache* (American Harvest 1997) ★★★, *The Voice* (BTM 1998) ★★★★, *Back In The Swing Of Things* (Goldrhyme 2004) ★★★.

● COMPILATIONS: *The Best Of Vern Gosdin* (Columbia 1989) ★★★★, *Super Hits* (Columbia 1994) ★★★, *Warning: Contains Country Music (The Great Ballads Of Vern Gosdin)* (American Harvest 1997) ★★★★, *The Truly Great Hits Of Vern Gosdin* (VGM 2004) ★★★.

Gospel Fish

b. Everald Thomas, Spanish Town, Jamaica, West Indies. The sensitivity and maturity of Gospel Fish's lyrics distinguish him from many of his peers. He was brought up in Thompson Pen, where his Rasta father taught him hand drums. DJ Jimmy Crazy named him Gospel Fish after hearing him sing in the local church choir. They duetted on 1987's 'Neighbourhood Cousin', which Gospel, then working as a security guard, produced himself. 'Walk An' Wine', 'Ruff An' Tuff' and 'Cash Ready' followed, but it was over a year before he had his first two hits, 'Golden Rule' and 'Bandy Leg'. Dennis Star, his producer, brought him to the UK in 1988 for his first performances outside Jamaica. Before then, he had regularly appeared on the Happy Tone, Nite Flight, Lightning and Leo Taurus **sound systems**, inspired by DJs such as **Lieutenant Stitchie**, **Tony Rebel** and Professor Nuts. He began voicing for **Captain Sinbad**, **Fashion Records** and Gussie P, who all helped him gain exposure to a wider audience. He moved away from 'slack' themes to more cultural topics with tracks such as 'Wickedest Thing In Life', 'You Must Be Fool' and 'Too Much Gun Talk'. During 1991/2, he recorded for Soljie, Top Rank, Bee Cat and Taxi. He recorded a confrontational 'burial' tune called 'Brush Dem', which became his biggest hit thus far. He made a guest appearance on the **Aswad/Yazz** collaboration 'Hold On' while in the UK in 1993, and also recorded for both Fashion and Sinbad, sometimes in combination, as with **John McLean** on *Romantic Ragga*.

● ALBUMS: various *Romantic Ragga* (Sinbad 1993) ★★★★.

Gospel Seed

This contemporary US Christian music project was inaugurated in 1974 by two experienced gospel performers, Michael Moore and Gary Luttrell. Taking the name Gospel Seed, the duo began to tour throughout the country, playing acoustic pop and gospel in coffee houses, schools and prisons. They were soon booked to appear on a succession of television shows, including *The 700 Club* and *The PTL Club*. Employing autoharp in addition to acoustic guitar, the group's compositions relied heavily on the smooth harmonies the duo had perfected by the late 70s. Most of the group's lyrics were profoundly evangelical—as Moore told one magazine 'Our message in songs is geared to exhort and challenge Christians, as well as to show unbelievers their need for a saviour.' Consequently their debut album for Myrrh Records, *Growing*, was uneasy listening for anybody not already totally committed to Christian music.

● ALBUMS: *Growing* (Myrrh 1977) ★★★.

Gossip

Following the highly successful example of the **White Stripes**, a number of bass-less garage rock outfits emerged at the dawn of the twenty-first century, including the trio Gossip. Beth Ditto (vocals), Nathan Howdeshell (guitar), and Kathy Mendonca (drums) originated from Searcy, Arkansas, USA, before relocating to Olympia, Washington. The trio was soon up and running, issuing a self-titled four-song EP in 1999 and undaunted to publicize their pro-gay stance (as evidenced in their lyrics). Soon after, the trio signed a recording contract with the Kill Rock Stars label, and issued their debut, *That's Not What I Heard*, in 2000. A six-track EP, *Arkansas Heat*, followed two years later before the band got to work on their second album. Recorded in Seattle under the watchful eye of John Goodmanson, the sessions marked the first time that the Gossip had recorded in a true studio. The resulting release, 2003's *Movement*, showed that working in this environment did not hinder the trio's trademark raging rock.

● ALBUMS: *That's Not What I Heard* (Kill Rock Stars 2000) ★★★★, *Movement* (Kill Rock Stars 2003) ★★★, *Undead In NYC* (Dim Mak 2003) ★★★, *Standing In The Way Of Control* (Kill Rock Stars 2006) ★★★.

Gota And The Low Dog

London, England–based jazz funk group Gota And The Low Dog are led by Japanese drummer and multi-instrumentalist Gota Yashiki. A veteran of sessions with **Simply Red**, **Sinéad O'Connor** and **Soul II Soul**, he formed the band, originally called Gota And The Heart Of Gold, with Warren Dowd (vocals), Kenji Jammer (guitar) and Yolanda Charles (bass). *Somethin' To Think About*, their 1994 debut album, featured a pleasant blend of funk and soul influences, with a high quality of musicianship throughout. *Live Wired Electro* drew its aesthetic from the 70s/80s electro hybrid of hip-hop, with several instrumentals and disorientating free-form jazz sketches similar to the more experimental work of **Herbie Hancock**. It included the single 'Hey Bulldog', a rare cover version of the **Beatles**' song from the film *Yellow Submarine*. Yashiki released his solo debut in 1997.

● ALBUMS: *Somethin' To Think About* (RPL 1994) ★★★, *Live Wired Electro* (RPL 1995) ★★★, as Gota *It's So Different Here* (Instinct 1997) ★★★.

Gotan Project

A Paris, France–based trio comprising Philippe Cohen Solal (b. 1962, France; DJ/producer), Christophe Mueller (b. 1968, France; producer) and Eduardo Makaroff (b. 1955; guitar). They formed in the late 90s, united by their interest in combining contemporary electronic sounds with more traditional and acoustic ones. Their tracks have featured on compilations such as **Gilles Peterson**'s *Worldwide* and the Buddha Bar series, based on the music played in the famous Parisian club. They are signed to **XL Recordings**, the respected **dance music** imprint of **Beggars Banquet Records**. Solal and Mueller had worked independently as soundtrack musicians with directors such as Lars Von Trier, Didier Le Pecheur and Yolande Zauberman, and released records as the Boys From Brazil and Stereo Action Unlimited. Makaroff was well known in France and Argentina as an accomplished guitarist on the tango scene. The trio create their unusual sound by combining production influenced by **house**, **dub** and hip-hop with the sounds of numerous talented Argentinean tango musicians, who were exiled in France as a result of the dictatorial regime of the 70s. The sound of bandonion (a type of accordion) with violin and traditional vocal sounds made a remarkable hybrid. Three 10-inch single releases on their own ¡;Ya Basta! Records received ecstatic press reactions and support from a range of producers and DJs. The track 'Triptico' became a firm favourite among the more leftfield DJs on the UK circuit, and the band was embraced by commentators from the worlds of jazz, chillout, dance and tango.

● ALBUMS: *La Revancha Del Tango* (XL 2001) ★★★★.
● COMPILATIONS: *Inspiración-Espiración* (XL 2004) ★★★.
● DVD/VIDEOS: *La Revancha Del Tango Live* (Ya Basta! 2005).

Gottehrer, Richard

b. New York City, USA. Gottehrer's career as a songwriter and producer stretched from the **Brill Building** era of the 60s to rock in the 90s. He is probably the only direct connection between **Pat Boone** and punk. As a teenager, he played piano and wrote songs, making his first record as Richie And The Playboys. While studying law at college he released 'The Twistle by Troy And The T-Birds (1961) before meeting fellow writers Bob Feldman and Jerry Goldstein. The trio formed a prolific partnership, providing songs for **Freddie Cannon** and Pat Boone ('Ten Lonely Guys') before their first hit came with 'My Boyfriend's Back' by the **Angels**, a 1963 number 1 in the USA. Over the next three years Feldman, Gottehrer and Goldstein wrote and produced over 100 singles, some on their own Stork label. The trio also performed and recorded as the **Strangeloves**. In 1966, Goldstein moved to the west coast, becoming the producer of **War** and Gottehrer joined forces with Seymour Stein to set up **Sire Records**. There he produced work by **Martha Velez** and the **Climax Blues Band**. Leaving Sire in 1975, he became involved with the growing New York punk scene around **CBGB's** club, eventually producing early albums by **Blondie**, **Richard Hell** and **Robert Gordon**. During the 80s, Gottehrer continued to be active as an independent producer, working on albums by acts including **Joan Armatrading**, the **Go-Go's**, the **Yachts**, **Holly And The Italians**, **Marshall Crenshaw** and the **Colour Field**.

Gotti, Irv

b. Irvin Domingo Lorenzo Jnr., New York City, USA. Renowned hip-hop figures such as **Dr. Dre** and **Sean 'Puffy' Combs** showed that rap artists could do much more than just perform on the mic, as they produced others and scouted talent, among countless other business endeavours, and inadvertently paved the way for future rap entrepreneurs such as Irv Gotti.

Hailing from New York City, Gotti got his start in hip-hop as a producer in the mid-90s, teaming up with Mic Geronimo on his 1995 release *The Natural*. In the late 90s he worked on some of the era's most acclaimed rap releases, including **Jay-Z**'s *Reasonable Doubt*, **DMX**'s *It's Dark And Hell Is Hot*, and **Ja Rule**'s *Venni Vetti Vecci*. Gotti's hot streak continued, as he worked on further releases by DMX and Ja Rule, as well as **Ol' Dirty Bastard** and **Foxy Brown**, before he was rewarded with his own label imprint, Murder Inc., distributed via **Def Jam Records**. Gotti attempted to start the label off with a bang, as he issued the compilation, *Irv Gotti Presents: The Murderers* in 2000. Disappointingly, the album failed to light up the charts, but Gotti continued to pump out the hits for others, including releases by **Fat Joe, Eve, Ruff Ryders**, and even non-rap artists such as **Toni Braxton** and **Jennifer Lopez**.

Gotti broke through into the superstar league with his promotion of female vocalist **Ashanti**, who enjoyed a series of huge international hits at the start of 2002 in duets with Ja Rule ('Always On Time'), Fat Joe ('What's Luv?'), and her own single 'Foolish'. The same year Gotti issued two more compilation discs, *Irv Gotti Presents: The Inc* and *Irv Gotti Presents: The Remixes*. Just as Gotti's Murder Inc. empire seemed indestructible, its future was suddenly thrust into doubt in early 2003, when US Federal investigators searched the company's New York offices (owing to an alleged financial link between Gotti and New York drug kingpin Kenneth McGriff). Sales of much-hyped albums by Ja Rule and Ashanti failed to match their predecessors, and a number of incidents involving fellow New York rapper **50 Cent** helped further muddy Murder Inc.'s name. In response, the beleaguered Gotti announced the label was changing its name to The Inc.

● COMPILATIONS: *Presents: The Murderers* (Def Jam 2000) ★★, *Presents: The Inc.* (Def Jam 2002) ★★★, *Presents: The Remixes* (Def Jam 2002) ★★★.

Gottlieb, Danny

b. Daniel Richard Gottlieb, 18 April 1953, New York City, USA. Gottlieb studied percussion intensively, as a pupil of **Mel Lewis** and **Joe Morello** while still at school, and later at university. His professional career began while he was at the University of Miami, when he played with musicians such as **Pat Metheny, Paul Bley** and **Jaco Pastorius**. This was in the early 70s, and although whenever possible he worked in jazz, he also played in rock bands. In the middle of the decade he became a member of **Gary Burton**'s quartet, recording 1976's *Passengers*, subsequently joining a band formed by fellow sideman Metheny. He remained with Metheny into the early 80s, recording albums such as *American Garage*. By the time he left, the group's popularity had helped establish Gottlieb's name around the world. Simultaneously he had begun a musical association with **Mark Egan**, a founder member of Metheny's group, and with him he formed a band named **Elements**. Overlapping his work with Egan he played with **John McLaughlin**, and **Al Di Meola** (*Soaring Through A Dream*).

A strikingly eclectic player, Gottlieb has consistently worked in harmony with a wide range of performers, including **Gil Evans, Stan Getz, Sting**, the **Blues Brothers, Ahmad Jamal** and, in a late 90s recording session, **John Abercrombie**. A fleet and subtle drummer, Gottlieb is a very supportive player, ably finding appropriate backing for the many and diverse musicians with whom he works. In addition to teaching and organizing clinics, he has also appeared in instructional videos.

● ALBUMS: *Aquamarine* (Atlantic 1987) ★★★, *Whirlwind* (Atlantic 1989) ★★★, *Brooklyn Blues* (Big World 1991) ★★★.

Gottschalk, Norbert

b. Germany. Although known as a jazz singer, Gottschalk is also an accomplished instrumentalist, playing guitar and trumpet. Among instrumentalists with whom Gottschalk has worked are saxophonist Peter Weniger, keyboard player Matthias Bröde, guitarist Rolf Marx, bass players Stefan Rademacher and Bernd Zinsius and drummers Peter Baumgärtner and Wolfgang Ekholt. He has also performed and recorded very successfully in duo with guitarist Frank Haunschild. With Haunschild, Gottschalk has attracted wide and favourable attention on the German jazz scene of the early 00s. Their joint repertoire is an intriguing blend of jazz, folk, pop and Latin. Gottschalk sings in a vigorous fluid tenor on up-tempo songs while finding a delicate intimacy for ballads. He draws his personal repertoire primarily from jazz and popular standards.

● ALBUMS: *Light, Weight, Sight* (Dr. Jazz 1988) ★★★, *Two Sessions* (Dr. Jazz 1993) ★★★, with Frank Haunschild *The Art Of A Duo: Favorite Songs* (Mons 1997) ★★★, with Haunschild *Bridges* (Acoustic Music 2001) ★★★, with Haunschild *Better Days* (Acoustic Music 2003) ★★★.

Goudie, Frank

b. 13 September 1899, Youngsville, Louisiana, USA, d. 9 January 1964, San Francisco, California, USA. Frank 'Big Boy' Goudie grew up in New Orleans, where he first played cornet and piano before switching to reed instruments, principally the tenor saxophone. He worked with numerous bands in the city, including **Papa Celestin**'s, before touring extensively in the south-western states. In 1925 he left for Europe, where he remained for several years, playing in bands led by touring Americans who included showman-drummer **Louis Mitchell, Sam Wooding, Noble Sissle, Bill Coleman** and **Willie Lewis**. Upon the outbreak of World War II, Goudie left Europe for South America but was back in 1946. During the next few years he lived and worked in France, Germany and Switzerland, and renewed his association with Coleman. In 1957 he finally returned to America, settling in San Francisco where he worked outside music but continued to play in local clubs, especially when jazz stars visited the city. A solid, work-manlike performer, Goudie's 30 years in voluntary exile from the USA made him a marginal figure in jazz. Nevertheless, his long domicile in Europe meant that he was influential in widening the appeal of jazz in many countries.

● ALBUMS: *Frank 'Big Boy' Goudie With Amos White* (American Music 1994) ★★★.

Goudreau, Barry

b. 29 November 1951, Boston, Massachusetts, USA. The original guitarist with **Boston**, Goudreau launched his solo career in 1980 following the release of that group's *Don't Look Back*. Much of the impetus behind his self-titled debut collection, which also included contributions from Boston colleagues Brad Delp and Sib Hashian, arose from Goudreau's frustration with Scholz's laborious studio methodology. *Barry Goudreau* reached number 88 in the *Billboard* album charts, an admirable feat for a debut album but a poor performance given the fact that both Boston's previous releases had topped the US charts. After its release he chose not to return to Boston but launched Orion The Hunter instead, joined by singer Fran Cosmo and Delp. They achieved a little success with their self-titled debut album in 1984, but thereafter Goudreau became embroiled in legal proceedings with his former Boston colleague Scholz. In 1991 he regrouped with Delp, Tim Archibald, Brian Mayes and Dave Stefanelli as Return To Zero, releasing a self-titled album the following year.

● ALBUMS: *Barry Goudreau* (Portrait 1980) ★★★.

Gould, Morton

b. 10 December 1913, Richmond Hill, New York, USA, d. 21 February 1996, Orlando, Florida, USA. Gould was one of the most important figures in American music of the twentieth century. His composition 'Pavane' (from his 'American Symphonette No. 2') has become a light-music standard. By the age of 21 he was conducting and arranging a weekly series of orchestral radio shows, which allowed him to introduce many of his lighter works to a wider public. Equally at home in the popular and classical fields, his compositions included 'American Salute', 'Latin-American Symphonette', 'Spirituals For Orchestra', 'Interplay For Piano And Orchestra', 'Tap Dance Concerto', 'Dance Variations For Two Pianos And Orchestra', 'Jekyll And Hyde Variations', plus five symphonies and numerous works for symphonic band. Among many special commissions were 'Fall River Legend', 'Inventions For Four Pianos And Wind Orchestra', 'Declaration', 'St Lawrence Suite', 'Festive Music', 'Venice', 'Columbia', 'Soundings', 'Cheers' (commissioned by the Boston Symphony for Arthur Fiedler's 50th anniversary), 'Burchfield Gallery', 'Celebration '81', 'Housewarming', 'Cello Suite', 'Concerto Concertante', 'Centennial Symphony For Band' and 'Troubador Music For Four Guitars'. Gould's musical scores for Broadway included *Billion Dollar Baby* (1945) and *Arms And The Girl* (1950). For the cinema he scored *Delightfully Dangerous*, *Cinerama Holiday* and *Windjammer*. Ballets included **Jerome Robbins**' *Interplay*, **Agnes De Mille**'s *Fall River Legend*, **George Balanchine**'s *Clarinade* and Eliot Field's *Santa Fe Saga* and *Halftime*.

Gould's television work included a *CBS World War 1* documentary series, *F. Scott Fitzgerald In Hollywood* for ABC, the four-part mini-series *Holocaust* (1978) and a role as musical host for the National Educational Network series *The World Of Music With Morton Gould*. His list of recordings is extensive, and he received many Grammy nominations. In 1966 his RCA Red Seal recording of Charles Ives with the Chicago Symphony won the NARAS Grammy Award as the best classical recording of the year. In lighter vein, Gould's mood albums by his own orchestra from the 40s and 50s are collector's items. He also recorded with the London Symphony, London Philharmonic, the American Symphony Orchestra and the Louisville Orchestra. Gould travelled widely in the USA and throughout the world as a guest conductor, and was the recipient of numerous awards from fellow musicians. In March 1986 he became president of the American Society of Composers, Authors and Publishers (**ASCAP**), holding the post until 1994. Much of his music featured a strong patriotic American flavour, partly explaining why his own compositions were not better known outside the USA. In 1995, at the age of 81, Morton Gould won his first Pulitzer Prize in music for his work 'Stringmusic'. He died suddenly at a hotel in Orlando, Florida, while attending the Disney Institute as artist-in-residence.

● ALBUMS: *After Dark* (Columbia 1949) ★★★, *South Of The Border* (Columbia) ★★★, *Rhapsodies For Piano And Orchestra* (Columbia) ★★★, *Soft Lights And Sweet Music* (Columbia) ★★★, *Strike Up The Band* (Columbia) ★★★, *Christmas Music For Orchestra* (Columbia) ★★★, *Interplay For Piano And Orchestra—Music Of Morton Gould* (Columbia) ★★★, *Family Album/Tap Dance Concerts* (Columbia) ★★★, *Manhattan Moods* (Columbia) ★★★, *Victor Herbert Serenades* (Columbia) ★★★, *Symphonic Serenade* (Columbia) ★★★, *Starlight Serenade* (Columbia) ★★★, *Music At Midnight* (Columbia) ★★★, *Morton Gould Showcase* (Columbia) ★★★, *Music Of Morton Gould* (Columbia) ★★★, *Curtain Time* (Columbia 1951) ★★★, *Morton Gould Programme* (Columbia 1951) ★★★, *The Months (Tchaikovsky)* (Columbia) ★★★, *Movie Time* (Columbia) ★★★, *Memories* (Columbia) ★★★, *Wagon Wheels* (Columbia) ★★★, *Famous Operettas* (Columbia) ★★★, *Oklahoma! And Carousel Suites* (RCA 1955) ★★★, *An American In Paris/Porgy And Bess Suite* (RCA 1956) ★★★, *Music For Summertime* (RCA 1956) ★★★, *Where's The Melody* (RCA 1958) ★★★, *Moon, Wind And Stars* (RCA 1958) ★★★, *World's Best Loved Waltzes* (RCA) ★★★, *Pendagrass* (Columbia) ★★★, *High-Fi Band Concert* (Columbia) ★★★, *Brass And Percussion* (RCA) ★★★, *Blues In The Night* (RCA 1957) ★★★, *Temptation* (RCA 1957) ★★★, *Batons And Bows* (RCA 1958) ★★★, *Coffee Time* (RCA 1958) ★★★, *Jungle Drums* (RCA 1960) ★★★, *Doubling In Brass* (RCA 1961) ★★★, *Beyond The Blue Horizon* (RCA 1961) ★★★, *Kern And Porter Favorites* (RCA 1961) ★★★, *Sousa Forever!* (RCA 1961) ★★★, *Love Walked In* (RCA 1961) ★★★, *Moonlight Sonata* (RCA 1961) ★★★, *Goodnight Sweetheart* (RCA 1962) ★★★, *Finlandia* (RCA 1963) ★★★, *More Jungle Drums* (RCA 1964) ★★★, *Spirituals For Strings* (RCA 1965) ★★★, *World War I* (RCA 1965) ★★★, *Spirituals For Orchestra* (RCA 1965) ★★★, *Latin Lush And Lovely* (RCA 1966) ★★★, *Two Worlds Of Kurt Weill* (RCA 1966) ★★★, *Charles Ives Orchestra Set No. 2* (RCA 1967) ★★★, *Morton Gould Makes The Scene* (RCA 1967) ★★★, with Larry Adler *Discovery* (RCA 1969) ★★★★, *Musical Christmas Tree* (RCA 1969) ★★★, *Holocaust* (RCA 1978) ★★★, *Gould Conducts Gould* (RCA 1978) ★★★, *The Louisville Orchestra First Edition Series: Morton Gould* (Albany 1988) ★★★.

Gould, Tony

b. Anthony James Gould, 2 February 1940, Melbourne, Victoria, Australia. After playing piano semi-professionally Gould began attracting notice on the Australian jazz scene in the early 60s, and later in the decade became linked with **Brian Brown**. Soon after this Gould entered a period during which he extended his studies, taught, engaged in lecture tours and, while retaining his interest in jazz, also performed with symphony orchestras and chamber music ensembles. In the mid-70s, he returned to the jazz audience's attention to take a significant role as performer and composer. Throughout his career, Gould's contribution to Australian jazz, especially to the stylistic cutting edge, has been invaluable.

● ALBUMS: *Gould Plays Gould* (Move 1978) ★★★, *Best Of Friends* (Move 1984) ★★★.

Goulder, Dave

b. John David Goulder, 29 June 1939, Greenwich, London, England. Gouder was initially influenced by the steam songs from the American railroad tradition, and composers such as **Ewan MacColl** and Ralph Vaughan Williams. After a variety of jobs, Goulder started working for the railways in 1954, and a year or so later formed a group with workmates playing and singing in working men's clubs in the north of England. He left the railway in 1961 and moved to Scotland to live and spent the next 10 years running hostels for mountaineers, while occasionally playing folk clubs to supplement his income. Still writing songs, Goulder turned to dry stone walling for a living, where he achieved a master craftsman certificate. His surroundings provided inspiration for songs and poems, an interest in nature started by his father, who had been a travelling farm worker for the War Agricultural Department. It was not until Goulder's first tour of the USA, with Gordon Bok, that he began writing seriously again, producing *The Man Who Put The Engine In The Chip Shop*, and a retrospective book of songs, *January Man*. 'January Man' is probably Goulder's most famous song, having been covered by countless performers. His lifelong passion for anything concerning railways continues, even to the extent of including the actual sounds of locomotives and engines on *The Man Who Put The Engine In The Chip Shop*.

● ALBUMS: *January Man* i (Argo 1969) ★★★★, with Liz Dyer *The Raven And The Crow* (Argo 1971) ★★★, *Requiem For Steam—The Railway Songs Of Dave Goulder* (Tangent Big Ben 1971) ★★★★, with Miriam Backhouse, Irvine Hunt, Brian Miller *Fortuna* (Sweet Folk All 1976) ★★★, *January Man* ii (1986) ★★★, *The Man Who Put The Engine In The Chip Shop* (Fellside 1989) ★★, *Stone, Steam And Starlings* (Harbourtown 1991) ★★★.

Gouldman, Graham

b. 10 May 1946, Manchester, England. Gouldman began his recording career with the Whirlwinds, before forming the **Mockingbirds** with drummer Kevin Godley. One of Gouldman's compositions, 'For Your Love', was scheduled as the new band's first single, but when their label rejected it the song was passed on to the **Yardbirds**. Their version topped the charts and this fruitful songwriter/client relationship continued with 'Heart Full Of Soul' and 'Evil Hearted You'. Gouldman also penned a series of exemplary British pop hits for the **Hollies** ('Look Through Any Window', 'Bus Stop'), **Herman's Hermits** ('No Milk Today'), **Wayne Fontana** ('Pamela Pamela') and **Jeff Beck** ('Tallyman'), but paradoxically the Mockingbirds failed to find a similar commercial success.

Gouldman began a solo career with 'Stop Or Honey I'll Be Gone' (1966), but was again unable to make an impact as a performer. An album blending versions of old and new songs, *The Graham Gouldman Thing*, was only issued in the USA at the time but it served as the spur to a brief period domiciled in New York City working under the auspices of producers Jerry Kasenetz and Jeff Katz. He joined the late period **Mindbenders**, where he collaborated with guitarist **Eric Stewart**. An unreleased album for **Giorgio Gomelsky**'s Marmalade label brought Gouldman into contact with ex-Mockingbird Kevin Godley and talented instrumentalist Lol Creme. Their studio experiments created the hit group **Hotlegs**, which soon evolved into **10cc**, one of the most consistent hit acts of the 70s. Gouldman remained a member throughout the band's history, but re-embraced outside interests at the end of the decade. He scored the cartoon film *Animalympics* and later enjoyed a minor hit with 'Sunburn'. He produced albums by the **Ramones** and **Gilbert O'Sullivan** and in 1986 formed **Wax** with **Andrew Gold**. He was part of the brief 10cc reunion in the 90s, before striking up a writing partnership with singer-songwriter **Kirsty MacColl**. Gouldman released his second solo album, *And Another Thing . . .*, in 2000.

● ALBUMS: *The Graham Gouldman Thing* (RCA Victor 1968) ★★★, *Animalympics* film soundtrack (Mercury 1980) ★, *And Another Thing . . .* (For Your Love 2000) ★★★.

Goulet, Robert

b. 26 November 1933, Lawrence, Massachusetts, USA. An actor and singer, Goulet made his first professional appearance in 1951 with the Edmonton Summer Pops. He also played in *Thunder Rock* and *Visit To A Small Planet*. After appearing in Canadian productions of **South Pacific**, **Finian's Rainbow**, and **Gentlemen Prefer Blondes**, he moved to the USA, and made his Broadway debut in 1960, when he played Sir Lancelot in the musical **Camelot**, introducing the poignant 'If Ever I Would Leave You'. He also began launching his singing career during this time, and appeared on the **Ed Sullivan** television variety programme as well as others of that kind. Goulet signed with **Columbia Records** in 1962 and had his first chart entry with 'What Kind Of Fool Am I?' from the musical **Stop The World—I Want To Get Off**. He won the Grammy Award for Best New Artist in 1962, and his greatest singles success came in 1965 with the operatic 'My Love Forgive Me (Amore, Scusami)'. By then he had already proven that his strength was in album sales, as was often the case with middle of the road performers at that time. His 1962 Columbia debut, *Always You*, had charted, but it was the following year's *Sincerely Yours . . .* and 1964's *My Love Forgive Me* that became Goulet's top-performing albums. In 1968, he returned to the Broadway musical theatre in **The Happy Time**, and won a **Tony Award** for his portrayal of the French-Canadian man-about-the-world Uncle Jacques. In the 70s and 80s he toured in several musical revivals and appeared extensively in concerts, cabaret's (with his wife **Carol Lawrence**) and on his own television series. In 1993, after taking a new production of *Camelot* around the USA (in which, more than 30 years on, he played King Arthur instead of Lancelot), Goulet took the show to New York, where it was greeted without enthusiasm. The same year he was diagnosed with prostate cancer.

● ALBUMS: *Always You* (Columbia 1962) ★★★, *Two Of Us* (Columbia 1962) ★★★, *Sincerely Yours . . .* (Columbia 1963) ★★★★, *The Wonderful World Of Love* (Columbia 1963) ★★★, *Robert Goulet In Person* (Columbia 1963) ★★★, *Manhattan Tower/The Man Who Loves Manhattan* (Columbia 1964) ★★★, *Without You* (Columbia 1964) ★★★, *My Love Forgive Me* (Columbia 1964) ★★★★, *Begin To Love* (Columbia 1965) ★★★, *Summer Sounds* (Columbia 1965) ★★★, *Robert Goulet On Broadway* (Columbia 1965) ★★★, *Traveling On* (Columbia 1966) ★★★, *I Remember You* (Columbia 1966) ★★★, *Robert Goulet On Broadway, Volume 2* (Columbia 1967) ★★★, *Woman, Woman* (Columbia 1968) ★★★★, *Hollywood Mon Amour—Great Love Songs From The Movies* (Columbia 1968) ★★★, *Both Sides Now* (Columbia 1969) ★★, *Souvenir D'Italie* (Columbia 1969) ★★★, *Greatest Hits* (Columbia 1969) ★★★★, *I Wish You Love* (Columbia 1970) ★★, *Close To You* (Columbia 1992) ★★.

● COMPILATIONS: *The Best Of Robert Goulet* (Atlantic 1990) ★★★, *Golden Classics Edition* (Collectables 1997) ★★★.

Gourds

Originating from Austin, Texas, USA, the Gourds' distinctive alternative country sound marries influences as diverse as **Lynyrd Skynyrd**, **David Bowie** and **Charlie Daniels**. The band was formed in the mid-90s by singer/guitarist Kevin Russell (b. Beaumont, Texas, USA), a veteran of outfits including the

Picket Line Coyotes, whom he once described as a cross between **Hüsker Dü** and **Hank Williams**. They released three albums, *Fashion Dogs*, *Upholstery Van Songs* and *We Shall Annex The Sudetenland*, in the late 80s and early 90s, the latter pair being self-released cassettes. Among Russell's colleagues in Picket Line Coyotes was Robert Bernard, whose younger brother Claude later became a founder member of the Gourds. The Picket Line Coyotes broke up in 1991, shortly after another future Gourds member, Jimmy Smith, had joined them.

For two years following the break-up Russell played open mic sessions, preparing two unreleased solo albums. After returning to Austin, he and Smith formed Grackles, alongside Ron Byrd (with whom Russell had collaborated on his solo work) and drummer Claude Bernard. When the Grackles fell through, Smith and Bernard formed the Old Government duo, before linking up with Russell once again. With Bernard having switched to accordion, the trio needed a drummer, and recruited Welshman Charlie Llewellin. The quartet took the name Gourds and made their debut at Another Cup Of Coffee in 1994. A year later they recorded their debut album for European label Munich Records, *Dem's Good Beeble*, at Laurel's Ranch in Comfort, Texas. They played some 200 shows around America and Europe to promote the record in the ensuing 12 months. After being approached at the 1997 MIDEM conference in France, Mike Stewart (who had helped arrange their original recording contract) negotiated a new recording contract with Austin's Watermelon Records for the band, resulting in second album *Stadium Blitzer*. After its release Llewellin left the band to be replaced by Keith Langford. Prior to delivery of a third album in 1999, Watermelon also issued an EP (*Gogitchyershinebox*, titled after a line in the movie *Goodfellas*) containing the band's cover versions of Bowie's 'Ziggy Stardust' and, even more surprising, **Snoop Doggy Dogg**'s 'Gin & Juice'.

The Gourds' recording contract with Watermelon fell through following the release of *Ghosts Of Hallelujah*. They relocated to the **Sugar Hill Records** label and welcomed occasional collaborator Max Johnston (ex-**Wilco**) into the line-up. The excellent *Bolsa De Agua* matched the band's debut album for its sheer eclecticism. The 2001 release *Shinebox* expanded the old *Gogitchyershinebox* EP with new cover versions, including an inspired take on **Nils Lofgren**'s 'Everybody's Missing The Sun'. Their final recording for Sugar Hill, *Cow Fish Fowl Or Pig*, was followed by a soundtrack for Mike Woolf's quirky documentary *Growin' A Beard*. The quintet demonstrated that they had lost none of their enthusiasm on the new studio album, *Blood Of The Ram*, released on the independent Eleven Thirty label at the end of 2004.

● ALBUMS: *Dem's Good Beeble* (Munich 1997) ★★★★, *Stadium Blitzer* (Watermelon 1998) ★★★, *Ghosts Of Hallelujah* (Watermelon 1999) ★★★, *Bolsa De Agua* (Sugar Hill/Munich 2000) ★★★★, *Shinebox* (Sugar Hill/Munich 2001) ★★★, *Cow Fish Fowl Or Pig* (Sugar Hill/Munich 2002) ★★★, *Growin' A Beard* film soundtrack (Aspyr Media 2003) ★★★, *Blood Of The Ram* (Eleven Thirty 2004) ★★★, *Heavy Ornamentals* (Eleven Thirty 2006) ★★★.

Gouryella
(see **Corsten, Ferry**)

Gov't Mule

Modern-day southern rockers Gov't Mule started as merely a side-project for latter-day **Allman Brothers Band** members **Warren Haynes** (b. 6 April 1960, Asheville, North Carolina, USA; guitar/vocals) and Douglas Allen Woody (b. 1956, USA, d. 26 August 2000, Queens, New York City, USA; bass), but soon took on a life all its own. Haynes and Woody had been part of the Allman Brothers circle for several years by 1994, when the duo jammed with drummer Matt Abts (b. 30 September 1953, Oklahoma, USA) at a Los Angeles club after a local Allman Brothers Band gig in May of that year. The trio remained in contact and continued to play when their busy schedules allowed it, as its members began to take the new project more seriously with each successive jam session. At first, Haynes and Woody attempted to keep Gov't Mule going along with their Allman Brothers Band duties, resulting in albums such as 1995's self-titled debut and 1996's *Live At Roseland Ballroom*. By April 1997, Haynes and Woody had both handed in their resignation to the Allmans and were now free to focus on Gov't Mule full-time. Unlike their work with the Allmans, Gov't Mule's music crossed over into hard rock territory at times. The trio signed on with Capricorn Records, and issued two albums during the late 90s. *Dose* and yet another live set, 1999's *Live With A Little Help From Our Friends*, which featured contributions from members of the **Black Crowes**. Gov't Mule's fifth release, *Life Before Insanity*, was issued in early 2000, but just a few months after its release Woody was found dead in a New York City hotel room. Haynes and Abts opted to carry on, and for 2001's *The Deep End: Volume 1*, enlisted an impressive roster of renowned rock bass players to take Woody's place, including **Jack Bruce**, **Larry Graham**, **Roger Glover**, **John Entwistle**, **Mike Watt**, the **Red Hot Chili Peppers**' Flea, and **Phish**'s Mike Gordon. Gordon filmed the album's recording sessions, which were included as part of the documentary, *On The Banks*. In 2002, *The Deep End: Volume 2* was issued, and like its predecessor, included a wide variety of acclaimed bass players lending a hand. Andy Hess became the full-time bass player and the band completed their 2004 album with a stable line-up.

● ALBUMS: *Gov't Mule* (Relativity 1995) ★★★★, *Live At Roseland Ballroom* (Foundation 1996) ★★★, *Live With A Little Help From Our Friends* (Capricorn 1998) ★★★, *Dose* (Capricorn 1998) ★★★, *Life Before Insanity* (Capricorn 2000) ★★★, *The Deep End: Volume 1* (ATO 2001) ★★★, *The Deep End: Volume 2* (ATO 2002) ★★★, *The Deepest End* (ATO 2003) ★★★, *Déja Voodoo* (ATO 2004) ★★★.

● DVD/VIDEOS: *Rising Low* (ATO Video 2002).

Gowans, Brad

b. Arthur Bradford Gowans, 3 December 1903, Billerica, Massachusetts, USA, d. 8 September 1954, Los Angeles, California, USA. A child prodigy on a wide range of brass and reed instruments, Gowans first played professionally in the early and mid-20s, happily switching back and forth between instruments. Among the bands with which he played were those led by **Joe Venuti**, **Mal Hallett**, **Jimmy Durante** and **Red Nichols**. After a spell outside music he joined **Bobby Hackett** in 1936 and during the next few years worked with **Joe Marsala**, **Bud Freeman**, **Ray McKinley**, **Art Hodes** and **Eddie Condon**. After World War II he played with **Max Kaminsky**, **Jimmy Dorsey** and **Nappy Lamare**, again using a variety of instruments but notably the valve-trombone. Apart from his extraordinary instrumental command, Gowans was also a good arranger, supplying charts in a range of styles for McKinley's big band, for Freeman's small group and for singer **Lee Wiley**.

● ALBUMS: *Brad Gowans* (Victor 1954) ★★★.

Gowen, Alan

b. 19 August 1947, London, England, d. 17 May 1981, London, England. Gowen began his professional career playing keyboards in rock and post-bop jazz groups, where his musical colleagues included Roger Odell and Phil Miller. At the start of the 70s he joined Assagai, this band spinning off from the Afro-rock group **Osibisa**. When Assagai folded, Gowen and the band's percussionist, Jamie Muir, and bass player Laurie Baker formed Sunship, in which guitarist **Allan Holdsworth** also played for a while. Sunship was short-lived, and Gowen then played in three bands for which he was a driving and organizing force: Gilgamesh, **National Health** and Soft Heap. Among the musicians who were involved in early versions of Gilgamesh were drummer Mike Travis, guitarists **Phil Lee** and Rick Morcombe, bass players **Jeff Clyne** and Neil Murray and saxophonist Alan Wakeman. Experimental gigs with Gilgamesh and **Hatfield And The North**, playing arrangements by Gowen, led to the formation of National Health, a band co-led by Gowen and fellow keyboard player, from Hatfield And The North, **Dave Stewart**. National Health played several engagements and also broadcast for BBC Radio. Meanwhile, Gowen had maintained Gilgamesh's separate existence, and in 1975 the band was signed to the Caroline subdivision of **Virgin Records**. By 1977 Gowen was fronting a revised version of Gilgamesh, along with Lee, Murray, later replaced by Hugh Hopper, and drummer **Trevor Tomkins** (ex-**Nucleus**). The new band, again playing largely Gowen scores, had a more overtly jazz ambience than had Hatfield And The North and the earlier Gilgamesh.

Constantly seeking new forums for his musical ideas, Gowen had become immersed in a new quartet, Soft Heap, in which he was teamed with **Elton Dean**, Hopper and Pip Pyle. In 1978, as the band prepared to set out on a tour of France, Pyle, committed to gigs with National Health, dropped out and was replaced by Dave Sheen. For the tour and an album, the name of the band was changed to Soft Head. The following year, Gowen replaced Stewart in National Health in time to make tours of Europe and the USA, although the band folded soon thereafter. During their French tour, Gowen had made some duo recordings with Hopper, and the pair now repeated the concept with *Two Rainbows Daily*. With the addition of drummer Nigel Morris, Gowen and Hopper, gave a solitary live performance in Bracknell. Within days of this appearance Gowen was diagnosed with leukaemia. Given only a few months to live, he composed his musical epitaph, 'Before A Word Is Said', recording it during late April/early May 1981 with Miller, Richard Sinclair and Tomkins. Two weeks later, Gowen died. Later, the discovery of previously unrecorded and/or re-arranged music prompted the formation of a version of National Health and a benefit gig and recording session, *D.S. Al Coda*, featuring Miller, Stewart, John Greaves and Pyle, along with guests Dean, Jimmy Hastings and Sinclair. This musical swan song was also performed during the 1983 Edinburgh Festival. A very good player and a strikingly talented composer, Gowen's tragically foreshortened career robbed rock of a potential giant.

● ALBUMS: with Hugh Hopper *Two Rainbows Daily* (Red/Europa 1980) ★★★, with Phil Miller, Richard Sinclair, Trevor Tomkins *Before A Word Is Said* (Europa 1981) ★★★, with Hopper *Improvisations* 1978, 1980 recordings (Blueprint 1997) ★★★.

Goya Dress

This short-lived Scottish alt rock band from the mid- to late 90s was led by vocalist, guitarist, pianist Astrid Williamson. Raised in Shetland, Williamson was influenced by a wide variety of music growing up and she began penning her own songs at an early age. This led to her attendance at a Glasgow music college during the early 90s, before relocating to London, England in 1994. Shortly after her move, Williamson began looking to play with a band, which led to the formation of Goya Dress. Joined by bass player and guitarist Terry de Castro and drummer Simon Pearson, the trio was signed to a recording contract with Nude Records (best known as the home of **Suede**). Four EPs, *Bedroom Cinema*, *Ruby*, *Glorious*, and *Crush*, followed during a one-year period—1995/6, before Goya Dress released their debut, *Rooms*. Unfortunately, the album got lost in the shuffle, resulting in discouragement and the trio splitting up shortly thereafter. After Goya Dress' dissolution, Williamson launched a solo career, issuing her debut solo recording in 1998, *Boy For You*. De Castro and Pearson joined David Gedge in his new venture, **Cinerama**.

● ALBUMS: *Rooms* (Nude 1996) ★★★.

Goykovich, Dusko

b. Dusan Gojkovic, 14 October 1931, Jajce, Yugoslavia. After completing his formal studies at the Academy of Music in Belgrade, Goykovich played trumpet and flügelhorn in various dance bands and radio orchestras in Europe, including those of Max Greger and **Kurt Edelhagen**. In the late 50s he travelled to the USA, played at the **Newport Jazz Festival** and then pursued his studies at **Berklee College Of Music**. Thereafter, like many Berklee alumni, he entered the bands of **Maynard Ferguson** and **Woody Herman**. Back in Europe he played in the small group led by **Sal Nistico** and then joined the **Clarke-Boland Big Band**, where he remained for five years until 1973. In the 70s Goykovich's associates included **Slide Hampton** and Alvin Queen. He also worked extensively in radio and education in Europe. A fine post-bop trumpeter, Goykovich's style derives from early **Miles Davis**, but the inclusion of traditional melodies from his homeland in his playing makes him a distinctive soloist. In the 90s Goykovich toured European venues, both as a soloist and in tandem with Italian alto saxophonist **Gianni Basso**.

● ALBUMS: *Swinging Macedonia* (Enja 1966) ★★★, *After Hours* (Enja 1971) ★★★, *A Day In Holland* (Nova 1983) ★★, *Celebration* (DIW 1987) ★★★, *Soul Connection* (Enja 1994) ★★★★, *Bebop City* (Enja 1995) ★★★, *Balkan Blue* 1992/1994 recordings (Enja 1997) ★★★, *In My Dreams* (Enja 2000) ★★★, *Trumpets And Rhythm Unit* (Cosmic Sounds 2002) ★★★.

Gozzo, Conrad

b. 6 February 1922, New Britain, Connecticut, USA, d. 8 October 1964, Burbank, California, USA. Gozzo's first notable appearance was in 1938 as a member of the trumpet section of the polished **Isham Jones** band. In the early 40s he played with several big bands of the swing era, including those led by **Red Norvo**, **Claude Thornhill** and **Benny Goodman**. While serving in the US Navy during World War II he played in the band led by **Artie Shaw**. After the war he returned to Goodman, played with **Woody Herman**, **Boyd Raeburn** and others, then settled in Los Angeles, where he was active in the studios. During the 50s he made many record sessions, some under his own name and others with leaders such as Herman, **Ray Anthony**, **Shorty Rogers**, **Stan Kenton**, **Billy May**, **Cy Touff**, **Glen Gray**'s **Casa Loma Orchestra** and Goodman. Although he was a good soloist, Gozzo's greatest contribution to big band music lay in his talent as a lead trumpeter.

● ALBUMS: *The Great Goz* (RCA Victor 1955) ★★★★.

Grab Grab The Haddock
(see **Marine Girls**)

Grab Me A Gondola

In the 50s, many years before film actresses such as **Barbra Streisand** and **Bette Midler** had their own production companies, the major studios called their young ladies 'starlets', and required them to flaunt their assets at annual film festivals around the world. One of Britain's leading glamour girls was **Diana Dors**, and she and her mink bikini were a common sight at the cinematic celebrations that took place at various venues such as the Venice Film Festival. The lady, and the location, provided the inspiration for this highly successful musical, which was written by **Julian More**, and opened at the Lyric theatre in London on 26 December 1956. Tom Wilson (**Denis Quilley**) is a showbiz reporter, and has gone to Venice to interview Virginia Jones (Joan Heal), who is a very 'hot property'. Tom's girlfriend, Margaret Kyle (Jane Wenham), finds it difficult to believe that his interest in Virginia is exclusively professional, and is flattered when the unctuous Prince Luigi Bourbon Corielli (Guido Lorraine) suggests that they sip champagne together. However, Tom is just not the cheating kind, and anyway, Virginia needs the Prince to finance her Shakespearean ambitions ('Cravin' For The Avon'), so everyone else is paired-off accordingly. Julian More, together with the composer James Gilbert, contributed a delightful score, which included Heal's amusing introductory number, 'That's My Biography', and then she, and the rest of the cast, had a ball with numbers such as 'Plain In Love', 'The Motor Car Is Treacherous', 'Bid Him A Fond Goodbye', 'Star Quality', 'Man, Not A Mouse', 'Lonely In A Crowd', 'Jimmy's Bar', 'Chianti', 'What Are The Facts?', 'Rig 'O The Day', 'When I Find That Girl', and 'Rockin' At The Cannon Ball'. Heal, a veteran of the London revue scene, was outstanding, and, generally, the show had a first-rate cast. *Grab Me A Gondola* was light, bright, bubbly stuff—a perfect antidote to the current American musical invasion—an enormous hit that eventually ran for 673 performances, and provided Julian More with his first West End success—*Expresso Bongo*, *Irma La Douce* and *Songbook* were all still a few years away.

Grable, Betty

b. Ruth Elizabeth Grable, 18 December 1916, St. Louis Missouri, USA, d. 2 July 1973, Santa Monica, California, USA. An actress, singer and dancer in movie musicals of the 30s, 40s and early 50s. A beautiful blonde with a peaches-and-cream complexion, during World War II the famous picture of her wearing a white bathing suit displaying her shapely legs (which were reportedly insured for a million dollars) and

looking over her right shoulder, was pinned up on servicemen's lockers the world over. Encouraged by her mother, Grable began to take singing and dancing lessons while she was still very young, and she was part of the chorus in musical films such as *Let's Go Places*, *New Movietone Follies Of 1930*, and *Whoopee!* while still in her early teens. During the 30s, sometimes under the name of Frances Dean, she played roles of varying importance (but never starring ones) in a several comedies such as *Hold 'Em Jail* and *The Nitwits*, and musicals, which included *Palmy Days*, **The Kid From Spain**, *Student Tour*, **The Gay Divorcee**, *Old Man Rhythm*, *Collegiate*, **Follow The Fleet**, *Pigskin Parade*, *This Way Please*, *College Swing*, *Give Me A Sailor* and *Million Dollar Legs* (1939). Also in 1939 she had a good role in the Broadway musical *Du Barry Was A Lady*, in which she introduced **Cole Porter**'s famous song of 'social scandal', 'Well, Did You Evah?', with **Charles Walters**. In 1937 Grable had married former child star Jackie Coogan, and their divorce in 1940 coincided with her elevation to star status when she signed for 20th-Century Fox. After co-starring with **Don Ameche** in **Down Argentine Way**, she worked with several other handsome leading men of the day, such as **John Payne**, Victor Mature, **Dan Dailey**, George Montgomery, Cesar Romero, Robert Cummings, and **Dick Haymes** in a string of mostly entertaining and tuneful musicals such as *Tin Pan Alley*, **Moon Over Miami**, *Footlight Serenade*, *Song Of The Islands*, *Springtime In The Rockies*, **Coney Island**, *Sweet Rosie O'Grady*, *Four Jills In A Jeep*, **Pin Up Girl**, *Billy Rose's Diamond Horseshoe*, *The Dolly Sisters*, **The Shocking Miss Pilgrim**, *Mother Wore Tights*, *That Lady In Ermine*, *When My Baby Smiles At Me*, *The Beautiful Blonde From Bashful Bend*, *Wabash Avenue*, *My Blue Heaven*, *Call Me Mister*, *Meet Me After The Show*, *The Farmer Takes A Wife* and *Three For The Show* (1955). Several of those were set at the turn of the century, and, by the late 50s, Grable's kind of movie musical was itself a period piece. She played nightclubs, appeared on television, and also worked with her husband, band leader **Harry James**, before they divorced in 1964. In 1967 she took over the leading role from **Carol Channing** in the Broadway production of **Hello, Dolly!**, and subsequently headed a road tour of the show. In 1969 she travelled to London and appeared briefly in the spectacular flop American musical, *Belle Starr*, at the Palace Theatre. On her return to the US, she continued to work on television and in provincial theatre until her death from cancer at the age of only 56. In 1997 came the treat that fans had been waiting for—a collection of 48 original Grable songs from soundtracks dating back to 1930.

● ALBUMS: *The Pin-Up Girl* 2-CD set (Jasmine 1997) ★★★.

● FURTHER READING: *Betty Grable: The Reluctant Movie Queen*, Doug Warren. *Betty Grable: A Bio-Bibliography*, Larry Billman. *Pin-Up: The Tragedy Of Betty Grable*, Spero Pastos. *Betty Grable: The Girl With The Million Dollar Legs*, Tom McGee.

● FILMS: *Whoopee* (1930), *New Movietone Follies Of 1930* (1930), *Let's Go Places* (1930), *Palmy Days* (1931), *Kiki* (1931), *Hold 'Em Jail* (1932), *Probation* (1932), *Child Of Manhattan* (1932), *The Kid From Spain* (1932), *The Greeks Had A Word For Them* (1932), *What Price Innocence* (1933), *Cavalcade* (1933), *The Gay Divorcee* (1934), *Student Tour* (1934), *Collegiate* (1935), *Old Man Rhythm* (1935), *The Nitwits* (1935), *Don't Turn 'Em Loose* (1936), *Pigskin Parade* (1936), *Follow The Fleet* (1936), *Thrill Of A Lifetime* (1937), *This Way*

Please (1937), *Campus Confessions* (1938), *Give Me A Sailor* (1938), *College Swing* (1938), *The Day The Bookies Wept* (1939), *Million Dollar Legs* (1939), *Man About Town* (1939), *Tin Pan Alley* (1940), *Down Argentine Way* (1940), *I Wake Up Screaming* (1941), *A Yank In The RAF* (1941), *Moon Over Miami* (1941), *Springtime In The Rockies* (1942), *Song Of The Islands* (1942), *Footlight Serenade* (1942), *Sweet Rosie O'Grady* (1943), *Coney Island* (1943), *Pin Up Girl* (1944), *Four Jills In A Jeep* (1944), *The Dolly Sisters* (1945), *Billy Rose's Diamond Horseshoe* (1945), *Mother Wore Tights* (1947), *The Shocking Miss Pilgrim* (1947), *When My Baby Smiles At Me* (1948), *That Lady In Ermine* (1948), *The Beautiful Blonde From Bashful Bend* (1949), *My Blue Heaven* (1950), *Wabash Avenue* (1950), *Meet Me After The Show* (1951), *Call Me Mister* (1951), *How To Marry A Millionaire* (1953), *The Farmer Takes A Wife* (1953), *Three For The Show* (1954), *How To Be Very Very Popular* (1955).

Grace Of My Heart

A tribute to the female songwriters of the 60s, particularly the early life of **Carole King**, who with husband **Gerry Goffin** turned out classic hits such as 'Will You Love Me Tomorrow', 'The Loco-Motion', and 'Take Good Care Of My Baby'. In this film, Illeana Douglas plays the King character, Philadelphia-born steel heiress Edna Buxton, who changes her name to Denise Waverly when she starts work in New York's legendary **Brill Building**. She and husband Howard Caszatt (Eric Stolz) write a string of hits for girl groups, before he cheats on her. From then on, Denise has a torrid time, involved with radio DJ John Murray (Bruce Davison), the **Brian Wilson**-like destructive genius of a record producer Jay Phillips (Matt Dillon), teen idol and closet lesbian Kelly Porter (Bridget Fonda), and publisher-manager Joel Millner (John Turturro), her mentor. Like Carole King with her **Tapestry**, in the early 70s Denise finally gets to record her own multi-million-selling album, *Grace Of My Heart*. Allison Anders (*Gas, Food Lodging, Mi Vida Loca*) wrote and directed this picture, and apparently it was her idea to ask writers from then and from now to come up with songs that evoked those fabulous 60s sounds. It resulted in a fascinating mix—**Burt Bacharach**, **Elvis Costello**, **Los Lobos**, **Carol Bayer Sager**, Larry Klein, **Dave Stewart**, and even Gerry Goffin himself. Stand-out tracks included 'God Give Me Strength' (Bacharach-Costello), 'My Secret Love' (Klein–David Baerwald–**Leslie Gore**), 'Born To Love That Boy' (Klein-Geffen), and 'Turn Around' (Mike Johnson). Illeana Douglas' singing voice was dubbed by Kristen Vigard. Keith Young was the choreographer, executive producer Martin Scorsese, and *Grace Of My Heart* was a 1996 release produced by Universal Records.

Grace, Teddy

b. Stella Gloria Crowson, 26 June 1905, Arcadia, Louisiana, USA, d. 4 January 1992, La Mirada, California, USA. Born into a middle-class white family in the deep south, Grace studied piano and guitar as a child but was fascinated by the black music that pervaded the region. While she was still a young teenager her parents died, and she lived for a while in Virginia before returning to Louisiana, where she met and, at 19, married a local businessman named Grace (she had been nicknamed 'Teddy' from childhood). With her husband, she settled in Montgomery, Alabama, and became a member of the local country club set. One night in 1931, at a club dinner party, she responded to a 'dare' by going up to the microphone to sing with the band. The result electrified the audience and within a very short space of time she was broadcasting over local radio stations, appearing at clubs and in theatres. Owing to radio remotes she was heard widely and in 1933 was hired by **Al Katz** and eventually went with him to New York. There, in 1934, she was signed to sing with **Mal Hallett**, one of the most popular of the second-string dance bands of the pre–swing era years.

Teaming up with Hallett, Grace worked extensively along the east coast. Her travelling conflicted with her husband's plans, and they were divorced. Nevertheless, during 1935 the hard grind of endless one-night stands became too much for her and she left Hallett and remarried. Two years later she returned to Hallett and began her recording career with him for **Decca Records**. The company also recorded her under her own name, including a session with **Jack Teagarden** during which some serious drinking took place and the trombonist eventually passed out. As she left the studio, Grace remarked to pianist **Billy Kyle**, 'When that Indian wakes up tell him he's a helluva musician but he can't drink worth a damn'. Surprisingly given Decca's attitude towards jazz and blues at the time, she also made a set of 10 blues songs. These were issued as an album of 78s, *Blues Sung By Teddy Grace*, and were very well received and led many listeners to think that she was black. In September 1940 Grace also recorded with **Bob Crosby**'s band and with **Bud Freeman**'s Cumma Sum Lauda Orchestra. During the session she told Freeman that she was disillusioned with the music business in general and with Decca in particular and that she was quitting. When the USA entered World War II Grace, who was again divorced, joined the WACs and worked hard as a recruiter, organizing shows and touring extensively.

In 1944 Grace was taken ill, lost her voice and was hospitalized. It was six months before her voice returned and when it did it was in such a state that, regardless of personal choice, she was unable to sing again. In 1946 she left the army, remarried and moved to the west coast and a secretarial job. In 1991, by now living in a nursing home, she was tracked down by journalist David W. McCain. The subsequent article resulted in mail from fans who thought that she was already dead. McCain's article and the response to it came only just in time to assure the singer that she was not forgotten. Grace's voice was used expressively on ballads, which she sang with poise and care. When singing the blues she could be effectively growly. She was a noteworthy singer even if, owing to her unusual career, she was too often overlooked.

● COMPILATIONS: *1937–1940* (Timeless 1996) ★★★★, *Turn On That Red Hot Heat* (Hep 1997) ★★★.

Gracie, Charlie

b. Charles Anthony Graci, 14 May 1936, Philadelphia, Pennsylvania, USA. When guitarist and songwriter Charlie Gracie recorded the original version of the rock 'n' roll song 'Butterfly' in 1957, he faced stiff competition from **Andy Williams**' cover version. Gracie's **Elvis Presley**-like vocal took the song to number 5 in the US charts and Top 20 in the UK, but Williams' charted higher, number 1 in the UK and USA. They both sold over a million copies. He started out appearing as a teenager on **Paul Whiteman**'s top-rated American television show. Gracie's subsequent singles were styled to suit his voice, including the ballads 'Fabulous' and 'Wanderin' Eyes', both Top 10 smashes in the UK in the same year. For many years he has been a legend rather than a performing artist. Often controversial, he has changed record labels countless times and still regularly performs in the USA and Europe. In the UK he has a fiercely loyal following, probably owing to the fact that he was the first ever rock 'n' roller to tour the UK in the 50s.

● ALBUMS: *The Cameo Parkway Sessions* (London 1978) ★★★, *Charlie Gracie's Early Recordings* (Revival 1979) ★★★, *Rockin' Philadelphia* (Magnum Force 1982) ★★★, *Amazing Gracie* (Charly 1982) ★★★, *Live At The Stockton Globe 1957* (Rollercoaster 1983) ★★, *Boogie Boogie Blues And Other Rarities* (Revival 1990) ★★.

● COMPILATIONS: *Best Of Charlie Gracie* (Revival 1988) ★★★, *It's Fabulous* (Stomper Time 1995) ★★★, *It's Fabulous It's Charlie Gracie* (Cotton Town Jubilee 1995) ★★★.

● FILMS: *Jamboree* aka *Disc Jockey Jamboree* (1957).

Gracin, Josh

b. 18 October 1980, Westland, Michigan, USA. Country pop vocalist Gracin came to prominence in summer 2003 during the second series of the US reality television series **American Idol**, when his chiselled good looks and MOR leanings helped propel him into the final stages of the competition. Gracin's gentle take on pop standards such as **Billy Joel**'s 'Piano Man' and **Rascal Flatts**' 'I'm Movin' On' were not enough to challenge the vocal pyrotechnics of eventual winner **Ruben Studdard**. Gracin, a serving lance corporal in the US Marines, was obliged to pull out of the subsequent *American Idol* tour because of his army commitments. Nevertheless, he attracted the attention of Rascal Flatts' producer Marty Williams, who helped the singer land a recording contract with the Lyric Street label. Gracin made his debut for the label at the start of 2004 with 'I Want To Live', followed by a self-titled debut album later in the year.

● ALBUMS: *Josh Gracin* (Lyric Street/Hollywood 2004) ★★★.

Gracious

British progressive act Gracious—Alan Cowderoy (guitar/vocals), Paul Davis (guitar/vocals), Martin Kitcat (keyboards/vocals), Tim Wheatley (bass) and Robert Lipson (bass)—made its recording debut in 1968 with 'Once In A Windy Day', issued by **Polydor Records**. A second single, 'Beautiful', followed in 1969, when Gracious supported the **Who** on a national UK tour. In 1970 the group was signed by the feted **Vertigo Records**, for which they completed *Gracious!*, a bold synthesis of classic and symphonic influences, progressive hard rock and judicious use of the mellotron. 'Fugue In 'D' Minor' is representative of their mock-baroque ambitions. Davis then sang on the film soundtrack of *Jesus Christ Superstar*, before rejoining his colleagues for *This Is . . . Gracious!!* This equally ambitious set was issued on a budget-price label, which undermined the group's music and confidence, and Gracious disbanded soon after its release. Alan Cowderoy subsequently worked behind the scenes at **Stiff Records**.

● ALBUMS: *Gracious!* (Vertigo 1970) ★★★, *This Is . . . Gracious!!* (Phillips International 1972) ★★★.

Graduate

At the start of the 80s a five-piece band from Bath, Avon, England, released four singles and a **Tony Hatch**–produced album for the Precision label. Graduate featured guitarist Roland Orzabal De La Quintana (b. 22 August 1961, Portsmouth, Hampshire, England)—who was of Basque Spanish descent, Curt Smith (b. 24 June 1961, Bath, Avon, England; bass), John Baker (b. 2 April 1961, Bath, Avon, England; guitar), Steve Buck (keyboards) and Andy Marsden (drums). They had started out as Smith's school band and evolved into Graduate around 1979. Of their four singles, only 'Elvis Should Play Ska' attracted much attention, but the band did receive some coverage in the pop press of the time. Orzabal and Smith decided to split from the rest of the band and initially they formed Neon with Rob Fisher (later of **Climie Fisher**) before dropping down to a duo and finding worldwide success as **Tears For Fears**.

● ALBUMS: *Acting My Age* (Precision 1980) ★★.
● COMPILATIONS: *Acting My Age* (Castle 2001) ★★.

Graduate, The

One of the biggest grossing films of 1968—and one that has proved enduringly popular—*The Graduate* launched Dustin Hoffman's acting career. He plays the part of the graduate, Benjamin Braddock, unsure about his future. He is seduced by his father's business partner's wife, Mrs. Robinson, memorably played by Anne Bancroft, before falling in love and eloping with Bancroft's screen daughter (Katherine Ross). A mild comment on US middle-class values, *The Graduate*'s strengths are derived from Hoffman's portrayal of Braddock, suitably lost and decisive when the need arose. The film's charm was enhanced by a soundtrack featuring **Simon And Garfunkel**. Although the duo had enjoyed chart success with 'Homeward Bound' and 'Sound Of Silence', they were not a household name prior to this film. The latter song enhanced one of the film's most poignant scenes, a feature shared with 'Scarborough Fair' and 'April Come She Will'. The album reached number 3 in the UK charts, while the duo's recording of 'Mrs. Robinson' broached the UK Top 5. Indeed, such was the attendant popularity an EP comprising the aforementioned four songs peaked at number 9 in the singles chart early the following year. Simon And Garfunkel were no longer viewed as an alternative act; their next album, **Bridge Over Troubled Water** effortlessly topped the UK chart and remained on the list for 303 weeks.

Graettinger, Bob

b. 31 October 1923, Ontario, Canada, d. 12 March 1957, Los Angeles, California, USA. Early in his professional career, Graettinger composed fairly orthodox material for the bands of **Benny Carter**, **Alvino Rey** and others; but in the late 40s he became associated with **Stan Kenton**, where his work began to explore new areas. He took a principle adopted by **Duke Ellington**, that of writing each part with a specific musician in mind, to extremes, creating music that was not only difficult to play but in which each part was independent of any other. He travelled with the Kenton band, listening to each musician in turn until he knew exactly what their individual capabilities were. His unusual approach to writing extended to the form his arrangements took on paper; he used colours and symbols to indicate the sound he wanted the musicians to achieve. His major works for Kenton were the suites 'City Of Glass' and 'This Modern World', both of which anticipated the atonality later explored by freeform jazz musicians.

Graham Central Station

Formed in San Francisco in late 1972 by **Larry Graham** (b. 14 August 1946, Beaumont, Texas, USA), erstwhile bass player in **Sly And The Family Stone**. The core of the group—David Vega (lead guitar), Hershall Kennedy (keyboards), Willie Sparks and Patrice Banks (both drums)—comprised former members of Hot Chocolate (USA), a local band Graham was producing, while a second keyboard player, Robert Sam, was drafted in from **Billy Preston**'s touring ensemble. Musically, Graham Central Station emulated the rhythmic funk of Sly And The Family Stone, but lacked their perception. Renowned as one of the era's flashiest live attractions, the group's shows included light panels programmed to oscillate in time to their pulsating sound. Although their initial albums enjoyed critical and commercial success, later releases failed to capitalize on this in-concert popularity and in 1980 Graham embarked on a solo career. At the end of the 90s he was once again using the original moniker as a whole new audience discovered Graham's brand of dance/funk.

● ALBUMS: *Graham Central Station* (Warners 1974) ★★★, *Release Yourself* (Warners 1974) ★★★, *Ain't No 'Bout-A-Doubt It* (Warners 1975) ★★★, *Mirror* (Warners 1976) ★★★, *Now Do U Wanta Dance* (Warners 1977) ★★★. As Larry Graham & Graham Central Station *My Radio Sure Sounds Good To Me* (Warners 1978) ★★★, *Star Walk* (Warners 1979) ★★.

● COMPILATIONS: *The Jam: The Larry Graham & Graham Central Station Anthology* (Rhino 2001) ★★★★.

Graham, Bill

b. Wolfgang Wolodia Grajonca, 8 January 1931, Berlin, Germany, d. 25 October 1991, Concord, California, USA. Born into a Russian-Jewish family, Graham arrived in New York during 1941, a refugee from Nazi persecution. After earning a degree in business administration, he moved to the west coast. By 1965 he was managing the San Francisco Mime Troupe, organizing the requisite benefit gigs to keep the revue afloat. Such work brought him into contact with the nascent rock fraternity, and Graham began promoting concerts at the city's Fillmore Auditorium. The venue became the leading showcase for the 'San Francisco Sound', exemplified by **Jefferson Airplane**, **Quicksilver Messenger Service**, the **Grateful Dead** and **Big Brother And The Holding Company**. Graham, in turn, became a leading impresario, and by 1968 had bought the larger Carousel Ballroom, renaming it the Fillmore West. Within weeks he had opened a corresponding Fillmore East in a vacant cinema on New York's Second Avenue. As a hard-headed entrepreneur, Graham often came into conflict with the free-loading hippie idealism inherent in running a music venue. Yet Graham often confounded his critics by contributing to local organizations in the form of benefits. In addition, the presentation of concerts at his venues paved the way for future promoters by way of introducing light shows, showing films between acts, free apples and taking a personal interest in the musicians giving a professional performance. He was also instrumental in efforts to integrate black artists on billings, so introducing many musicians to a predominantly white audience. These artists included **B.B. King**, **Leon Thomas**, **Raahsan Roland Kirk**, **Miles Davis**, **Muddy Waters** and **Ravi Shankar**.

By the end of 1971, Graham had closed down both halls and was determined to retire from a business for which he was losing respect. The final performances at the Fillmore West were captured on the film and accompanying album box set, *Fillmore—The Last Days* (1972). The sabbatical was brief, and during the next decade he was involved in national tours by **Bob Dylan** and **Crosby, Stills, Nash And Young**, as well as major one-off events. Such work culminated on 13 July 1985, when Graham organized the American segment of the **Live Aid** concert for famine relief. A controversial and outspoken character, he also pursued a successful career in management, guiding, at different times, the paths of Jefferson Airplane, **Santana**, **Van Morrison** and Dylan. Graham's tragic death in a helicopter crash occurred while returning from a **Huey Lewis And The News** concert he had promoted in South County, California. It robbed the rock music business of one its most legendary characters and greatest promoters. Members of the Grateful Dead, Santana and Quicksilver Messenger Service attended his funeral service, all of whom offered musical tributes.

● FURTHER READING: *Bill Graham Presents My Life Inside Rock And Out*, Bill Graham and Robert Greenfield.

Graham, Chick, And The Coasters

After **Billy J. Kramer** split with his first group, the Coasters, in January 1963, the Liverpool band resolved to continue with a new front man. Their manager, Ted Knibbs, found 14-year-old Graham Jennings (b. 7 June 1948, Liverpool, England), who had been performing with a children's road show, and renamed him Chick Graham. They were signed to **Decca Records** but had the misfortune to record a feeble **Gordon Mills** song for their first single, 'I Know'. 'When you think of all his subsequent wealth, it is amazing that he was pleading with us to record his song,' says Graham. They would have been better off turning him down but the record does contain unusual simulated guitar effects. Their second single, 'A Little You', also by Mills was later a hit for **Freddie And The Dreamers**. The group disbanded in 1965, disappointed that they had not had any success. Chick Graham went into mental nursing: 'I never had the music business in my blood. I was 16 and I wanted to do something else.'

Graham, Davey

b. 22 November 1940, Leicester, England, of Scottish and Guyanese parents. An influential guitarist in British folk circles, Graham's itinerant travels throughout Europe and North Africa resulted in a cosmopolitan and unorthodox repertoire. By the early 60s he was a fixture of the London fraternity and his 1961 recording with **Alexis Korner**, *3/4 A.D.*, showcased his exceptional talent. The EP included the much-fêted 'Angi' (later spelt 'Anji'), an evocative instrumental that **Paul Simon** and **Bert Jansch** later covered using Graham's innovative DADGAD guitar tuning. The 1964 album *Folk, Blues & Beyond . . .* showcased Graham's eclectic talent, with material drawn from **Charles Mingus**, **Lead Belly**, **Bob Dylan** and **Blind Willie Johnson**. The expressive instrumental, 'Maajun (A Taste Of Tangier)', emphasized the modal element of Graham's playing, and although he was never more than adequate as a singer his inspired guitar work was a revelation. The follow-up *Folk Roots, New Routes* was an unlikely collaboration with traditional vocalist **Shirley Collins**, and while the latter's purity was sometimes at odds with

Graham's earthier approach, the album is rightly lauded as a milestone in British folk music.

Graham maintained his idiosyncratic style throughout the 60s, experimenting with western and eastern musical styles, but although the respect of his peers was assured, commercial success proved elusive. At the end of the decade he began recording with the American singer Holly Gwinn, who later became his wife. Drug problems and ill health undermined the artist's progress, but he later re-emerged in the late 70s with the private pressing *All That Moody* and two excellent albums for the specialist Kicking Mule outlet. During his latter years, Graham has resided in west Scotland, where he has taught guitar, while continuing to perform on the folk club circuit, often performing on double bills with Bert Jansch, and demonstrating his credentials as one of Britain's finest folk blues guitarists.

● ALBUMS: *The Guitar Player* (Golden Guinea 1963) ★★★, *Folk, Blues & Beyond . . .* (Decca 1964) ★★★★, with Shirley Collins *Folk Roots, New Routes* (Decca 1965) ★★★, *Midnight Man* (Decca 1966) ★★★, *Large As Life And Twice As Natural* (Decca/London 1968) ★★★, *Hat* (Decca 1969) ★★★, *Holly Kaleidoscope* (Decca 1970) ★★★, with Holly *Godington Boundry* (President 1970) ★★, *All That Moody* (Eron 1976) ★★★, *The Complete Guitarist* (Kicking Mule 1978) ★★★, *Dance For Two People* (Kicking Mule 1979) ★★★, *Playing In Traffic* (Crack Probe 1993) ★★★, *After Hours At Hull University* 1967 recording (Rollercoaster 1997) ★★★.

● COMPILATIONS: *Folk, Blues And All Points In Between* (See For Miles 1985) ★★★★, *The Guitar Player . . . Plus* (See For Miles 1992) ★★★★, *Fire In The Soul* (Topic 1999) ★★★.

Graham, Jaki

b. Birmingham, England. This UK soul artist sang at school before taking a secretarial position. In the evenings she continued her singing in a band called Ferrari with David 'Dee' Harris (later of **Fashion**) before moving on to the Medium Wave band. She was spotted there by Rian Freshwater, who managed **David Grant** (ex-**Linx**) and singer/producer Derek Bramble, formerly of **Heatwave**, who became her producer and songwriter. She signed to **EMI Records**, who released her debut 45 'What's The Name Of Your Game' (1984). Her first chart appearance came via a duet with production stablemate David Grant on 'Could It Be I'm Falling In Love' in 1985. She followed that success with the solo hits 'Round And Round' and 'Heaven Knows', before another Grant duet, 'Mated' (written by **Todd Rundgren**). The second album provided a trio of hits; 'Set Me Free', 'Breaking Away', and 'Step Right Up'. Her only notable UK chart entry since then has been 1994's Top 50 hit, 'Ain't Nobody'. She remains hugely popular on the Japanese market, although her studio albums are now only available in her native England on import.

● ALBUMS: *Heaven Knows* (EMI 1985) ★★★, *Breaking Away* (EMI 1986) ★★★, *From Now On* (EMI 1989) ★★, *Real Life* (BMG 1995) ★★★, *Don't Keep Me Waiting* (WEA 1997) ★★★, *My Life* (Phantom 1998) ★★★.

● DVD/VIDEOS: *Set Free* (PMI 1986).

Graham, Kenny

b. Kenneth Thomas Skingle, 19 July 1924, London, England, d. 17 February 1997. Graham first played professionally at the age of 15, making his debut on alto saxophone with the Nottingham-based Rube Sunshine band. He later moved to London to join Billy Smith at the Cricklewood Palais but used his spare time to good effect by touring London clubs, where he met and played with well-known British jazzmen such as **Jack Parnell** and **Nat Gonella**. He spent some time with **Johnny Claes'** Claepigeons, a band that included drummer **Carlo Krahmer** (who later founded **Esquire Records**). After military service during World War II he worked with a variety of bands, including **Ambrose** and Macari And His Dutch Serenaders and was by that point usually heard on tenor saxophone.

In April 1950 Graham introduced his own band, the Afro-Cubists, who successfully fused bebop with Latin and Caribbean rhythms. The band was home to pianist Ralph Dollimore and at one time, a five-man saxophone section that included **Derek Humble** and **Joe Temperley**. The band folded in 1958, and thereafter Graham concentrated on arranging, his charts being played and recorded by jazz artists as diverse as **Ted Heath** and **Humphrey Lyttelton**. Graham proved especially adept at building interesting arrangements upon unusual tonal effects, a good example being his 'Moondog Suite', which developed the ethereal sounds of Louis Hardin aka **Moondog**, the legendary blind street musician who was recorded on the streets of New York in the early 50s. In the 80s Graham was still writing, and the incorporation of synthesizers and other electronic instruments into his work showed that he had lost none of the enthusiasm for new sounds that had marked his early career. In the 80s he had to supplement his income by taking on extra work, and in his last years he was a warden at an apartment block.

● ALBUMS: *Mango Walk* (Esquire 1953) ★★★★, *Caribbean Suite/Afro Kadabra* (Esquire 1953) ★★, *Moondog And Suncat Suites* (MGM 1956) ★★★, *Kenny Graham And His Orchestra* (MGM 1957) ★★★.

Graham, Larry

b. 14 August 1946, Beaumont, Texas, USA. Graham moved to Oakland, California, while still a child and by his late teens had established a proficiency on several instruments. A member of **Sly And The Family Stone** between 1967 and 1972, he left to form **Graham Central Station**, one of the era's most popular funk bands. In 1980, he embarked on a solo career, which opened successfully with 'One In A Million You', a US Top 10 hit. The singer enjoyed R&B hits with 'When We Get Married' (1980) and 'Just Be My Lady' (1981), while his last chart entry was 'If You Need My Love Tonight', a 1987 duet with **Aretha Franklin**. At the end of the 90s, Graham revived the Graham Central Station moniker for a new studio album.

● ALBUMS: *One In A Million You* (Warners 1980) ★★★, *Just Be My Lady* (Warners 1981) ★★★, *Sooner Or Later* (Warners 1982) ★★, *Victory* (Warners 1983) ★★, *Fired Up* (Warners 1985) ★★★.

● COMPILATIONS: *The Jam: The Larry Graham & Graham Central Station Anthology* (Rhino 2001) ★★★★.

Graham, Len

b. 20 December 1944, Glenarm, County Antrim, Northern Ireland. Traditional singer who combines his strong vocal talents with a thorough knowledge of indigenous Irish folk music and tradition. His rich recording history has also given many songs to other high profile artists. **Altan**,

Battlefield Band, Boys Of The Lough, Cherish The Ladies, Chieftains, De Dannan, Dick Gaughan, Andy Irvine, Delores Keane and the **Voice Squad** are among those who have learned songs from him. Graham came from a musical family, with early recollections of hearth singing sessions, and 78-RPM records from **Delia Murphy** and **Richard Hayward** on the gramophone. In 1964 he met Cathal McConnell at the Fleadh Cheoil na hÉireann in Clones, Monaghan. Their friendship would prove a long-standing one, while McConnell joined up with Boys Of The Lough, with whom Graham would often perform. In 1971 he won the All-Ireland senior traditional singers competition at Fleadh Cheoil hÉireann in Listowel, County Kerry.

Graham's recording career, meanwhile, would begin in 1975 with *Chaste Muses, Bards & Sages*, the first of two duet albums with **Joe Holmes**. The second, *After Dawning*, was completed in 1978, just two weeks before Holmes' death. In-between came Graham's first solo effort, *Wind & Water*. Before his second solo outing, *Do Me Justice* (a number 1 Irish folk album), he appeared on Boys From The Lough's 1989 album, *Regrouped*. After his third solo set, *Ye Lovers All*, he helped form Skylark in 1986. This group, comprising Graham, Gerry O'Connor (fiddle), Garry O'Briain (mandocello, guitar, keyboards) and, since 1989, Mairtin O'Connor (button accordion) recorded several albums together, and toured widely. Outside of these activities Graham also produced a book with cassettes concerning his field collection of early northern Irish singers and musicians. This won him the Sean O'Boyle Cultural Traditions Award in recognition of his work in Ireland as a collector and singer. He has also worked with his wife, sean-nós singer Pádraigin Ní Uallacháin, on an album of children's songs, and with storyteller/singer John Campbell. As Ciarán Carson has declared of Graham: 'By definition, any traditional singer is obliged to the past; but he assimilates the songs in the here-and-now, and re-makes them in his own voice, continually . . . I have heard Len praised for the 'spontaneity' of his voice; but there is no spontaneity without recollection. To be here, you must have been there, and Len has, many times'.

● ALBUMS: with Joe Holmes: *Chaste Muses, Bards & Sages* (Free Reed 1975) ★★★, *Wind & Water* (Topic 1976) ★★★, *Do Me Justice* (Claddagh 1983) ★★★★, *Ye Lovers All* (Claddagh 1985) ★★, with Holmes *After Dawning* (Topic 1978) ★★, with Cathal McConnell: *For The Sake Of Old Decency* (Sage Arts 1993) ★★★, with John Campbell *Ebb & Flow* (Label) ★★★, with Campbell *Two For The Road* (Label) ★★★, with Garry O'Briain, Pádraigin Ní Uallacháin *When I Was Young* (Gael Linn 1999) ★★★.

● COMPILATIONS: *The One Tradition* (Label) ★★★★.

Graham, Max

b. 1971, Canada. A DJ/producer, Graham rose to prominence on the **trance/progressive house** scene, owing in part to acclaim from peers such as **Paul Oakenfold, Timo Maas** and **Nick Warren** and to several well-received 12-inch singles on the Scottish label Hope Recordings. Taking to the decks at the age of 15, Graham experimented with numerous styles of **dance music** before being inspired by the 'epic' or progressive house sound of the early 90s. Excited by the music of **Underworld, BT, Sasha** and Oakenfold, Graham persevered in evangelizing a style of music that was relatively unpopular in his native Canada. His DJing style of melodic, string-laden trance juxtaposed with harder **techno**-based tracks, heard to

best effect on the club favourites 'Airtight' and 'Backdraft', has now secured him an international following, and he has a monthly residency at the UK's high-profile mega-club, **Gatecrasher**. He tours extensively as a DJ, regularly playing at large clubs and festivals. In 2001, he mixed the fourth instalment in Kinetic Records' Transport series.

● COMPILATIONS: *Transport 4* (Kinetic 2001) ★★★★.

Graham, Sandy

b. Sandra Gardell Graham, Santa Barbara, California, USA. Sandy's father, David Garland Graham, played clarinet and saxophones, and this musical home environment saw Sandy begin singing at a very early age. She learned from her father and also in high school, in Portland, Oregon, where she appeared in dramatic productions. At 16, Graham won a talent show, appearing on television as a result, and three years later, in Los Angeles, played her first nightclub engagement. She gained experience at jam sessions in Los Angeles and in 1975 began singing in television studios, mostly providing source music (background music to dramatic scenes in which the singer might appear on- or off-screen). During these years she continued to sing in nightclubs. Among artists with whom Graham has worked are **Dizzy Gillespie, Sir Roland Hanna, Mundell Lowe, Lalo Schifrin, Blue Mitchell, David 'Fathead' Newman, Jimmy Rowles** and **Clark Terry**. She has sung with several California-based big bands, including those led by **Bill Berry, Frank Capp** and **Gerald Wilson**, and has also sung with Stacy Rowles and the Jazz Birds. In 1991, she toured Europe with the Duke Ellington All Stars, a band that included **Rolf Ericson, Norris Turney, Jimmy Woode** and **Britt Woodman**.

Graham's early vocal influences were wide ranging, and she drew different things from different singers: '**Billie Holiday** for feeling, **Sarah Vaughan** for tone quality and control, **Lena Horne** for stage presence and storytelling ability, **Rosemary Clooney** for diction and beautiful round tone.' Despite, or perhaps because of, these manifold influences, Graham was never an imitator. Instead, she developed her own distinctive singing style and sound. Instantly identifiable, her voice has a gorgeously honeyed texture, which she uses with fluid grace on ballads and with airy swing on mid- and up-tempo songs. Always, in Graham's performances, there is an understated but highly propulsive sense of swing. For all her great talent, Graham has not been well served by recording companies. She recorded her first album in 1991 and found time to work with students at Jefferson High School of Performing Arts, her alma mater, and the University of Southern California. That first CD received three Grammy nominations: Best New Artist, Best Jazz Vocalist, Best New Composition (**Teri Thornton**'s 'Wishing Well'). It was almost a decade before a second CD appeared. This later set was seized upon by critics and received numerous well-deserved accolades.

● ALBUMS: *Sandy Graham* (Muse 1991) ★★★, *Comes Love* (Jazz Link Enterprises 2000) ★★★★.

Graham, Tammy

b. Tammy Wynette Graham, c.1968, Little Rock, Arkansas, USA. Named by her parents after **Tammy Wynette**, this country singer began to make some progress towards a similar level of name recognition in the mid-90s. Graham spent much of her youth as a child singer, before spending several years as one of the most successful acts at Caesar's

Palace in Las Vegas. She had begun singing at the age of three, going on to teach herself piano. By the time she was 10 she was opening shows for **Jerry Lee Lewis**, moving to Nashville a year later. Although her demos failed to secure a contract, she continued to sing semi-professionally, working with gospel singer **Wally Fowler** and serving as support act to **Faron Young** and **Danny Davis**. When she became a teenager she elected to go on the road with a group for the first time: 'Me and my momma and daddy in the front seat and my three musicians in the back seat of a Lincoln Continental, pulling a U-Haul trailer. We went all over, from Florida to Mexico.' She began performing in Las Vegas casinos at the age of 17. Thus began her record-breaking seven-year, three shows a night, six nights a week residence at Caesar's Palace. She returned to Nashville only after one of these performances had been observed by **Joe Diffie**'s manager, Danny Morrison. He introduced her to Tim DuBois, who signed her to Career Records after travelling to Las Vegas to see her play. Paired with producer **Barry Beckett** she made her long-playing debut in 1996. This self-titled collection utilized some of 'Music Row's' best writers, including Mark D. Snaders, Bob DiPiero and **Bob McDill**.

● ALBUMS: *Tammy Graham* (Career 1996) ★★★.

Grain

There is, according to his record label, very little anyone knows or is allowed to know about Grain, beyond that the moniker is a project name for maverick producer Arthur Smith. As Grain, Smith has released a series of 12-inch singles for the Brighton, England–based label FatCat. Each of the discs and all of the tracks were untitled, and the EPs were packaged with the barest of information, usually just the artist name and catalogue number. Nevertheless, Grain's funky, percussive **dance music** (although minimal) is far from faceless. His EPs contain both blistering floor friendly vocal tracks as well as disorientating **Basic Channel**–style **techno**. Curiously, Grain augments his ultra-cool, perfectly poised music with occasional wind-up/prank phone calls. On *12Fat016*, for example, Smith called a local radio station claiming to be 'Graham from Redhill', with a dog called 'Ralphy who can actually play the piano'. Despite Grain's obscured biography, it is widely believed (but not officially confirmed) that he also records as Santos Rogriguez, notably releasing the *Road To Rio* EP on the Cosmic ID label. Both this latter alter ego and Grain were featured on **Richie Hawtin**'s 1999 *Decks, EFX & 909* compilation. Smith is also one half of Mr. Smith And Professor Ludlow, a duo that previously released a track ('I Hope You Like Mice') painstakingly constructed from **Rolf Harris** samples.

Grainer, Ron

b. 11 August 1922, Queensland, Australia, d. 22 February 1981, Sussex, England. A highly successful musical director, and composer for television, films and theatre, Grainer trained as a musician in Australia before moving to England in 1952 with the intention of working as a pianist and writing classical music. Instead, at first he became part of a knockabout variety act, the Allen Brothers And June, touring the UK music halls, and staying in touch with music by being hit on the head every night by the lid of a grand piano! Later in the 50s, he served as musical director for London's West End musical comedy, *Zuleika*, and spent some time as a rehearsal pianist for television, which led to his contributing

music for a few plays. His big break came when he wrote the theme music for the highly popular BBC detective series, *Maigret*. This won him an **Ivor Novello** Award in 1961, and he also received 'Ivors' for his themes for *Steptoe And Son* (1962) and the satirical *Not So Much A Programme, More A Way Of Life*, in collaboration with writer-director Ned Sherrin and his oft-time partner Caryl Brahms. Grainer's other television music included, *Comedy Playhouse*, *Dr Who* (on which he pioneered the use of electronic music in the medium as Ray Cathode), *Panorama*, *Five O'Clock Club*, *That Was The Week That Was*, *Oliver Twist*, *Boy Meets Girl*, *The Flying Swan*, *Man In A Suitcase*, *The Prisoner*, *Thief*, *For The Love Of Ada*, *Paul Temple*, *South Riding*, *Kim The Detective*, *Edward And Mrs Simpson*, *Malice Aforethought*, *Rebecca* and *Tales Of The Unexpected*.

Grainer's enormous success in television led to continuous film work during the 60s and 70s. His film scores included *A Kind Of Loving* (1962), *The Moonspinners* (1964), *Night Must Fall* (1964), *The Caretaker* (1964), *Nothing But The Best* (1964), *Station Six-Sahara* (1964), *To Sir With Love* (1967), *Only When I Larf* (1968), *The Assassination Bureau* (1969), *Before Winter Comes* (1969), *Hoffman* (1970), *In Search Of Gregory* (1970), *The Omega Man* (1971), *Cat And Mouse* (1974), *I Don't Want To Be Born* (1975) and *The Bawdy Adventures Of Tom Jones* (1976). For the stage, Grainer contributed some songs for the pasticcio, **Cindy-Ella, Or I Gotta Shoe** in 1962, a Sherrin/Brahms all-black production of the traditional English pantomime *Cinderella*. Two years later, he wrote the music, with Ronald Millar's lyrics, for **Robert And Elizabeth**, a musical adaptation of *The Barretts Of Wimpole Street*, by Rudolph Besier. It was a great success, running for over 900 performances in the West End, and winning another Ivor Novello Award in 1964, for The Year's Outstanding Score Of A Stage Musical. Grainer's other music for the London theatre included *On The Level*, also with Millar, a tale of contemporary education, which featured an amusing number entitled 'Thermodynamically Yours'; *Sing A Rude Song*, a musical biography of legendary British Music Hall star, Marie Lloyd and *Nickleby And Me*, a musical play-within-a-play about the famous Dickens character. Grainer's orchestral albums, mainly of film and television music, included *Tales Of The Unexpected*, which contained the insinuating, 'I've Danced With The Man', sung by Jenny Wren over the titles of *Edward And Mrs. Simpson*; and 'A Touch Of Velvet, A Sting Of Brass', which was a minor chart hit in 1978 for Ron Grainer And His Orchestra.

● ALBUMS: *'Maigret Theme' And Other Themes From BBC Television Series* (early 60s) ★★★★, *To Sir With Love* soundtrack (Fontana 1967) ★★★★, *Edward And Mrs. Simpson* television soundtrack (1978) ★★★, *Tales Of The Unexpected And Other Themes* (1980) ★★★★, *Dr. Who And Other Classic Ron Grainer Themes* (Play It Again 1994) ★★★★.

● COMPILATIONS: *The A–Z Of British TV Themes—The Ron Grainer Years* (Play It Again 1997) ★★★★.

Grainger, Gary

b. *c.*1955, Baltimore, Maryland, USA. Grainger began playing bass with his older brother, drummer Gregory Grainger. In the late 70s the pair joined Pockets, recording for **Columbia Records**, and toured extensively with a package headlined by **Earth, Wind And Fire**. He first attracted wide attention in the late 80s, playing electric bass with **John Scofield** on tour and

on several recording sessions, including two late 80s Gramavision albums, *Blue Matter* and *Loud Jazz*. After leaving Scofield he teamed up with the band's drummer, **Dennis Chambers**, forming the funk band, Graffiti. He has also recorded with Carl Filipiak and Haakon Graf. In the late 90s he began working with his brother in a fusion band, designed to display the highly empathetic nature of their musical relationship as well as Grainger's composing skills.
● ALBUMS: *Phase I* (GBM 1997) ★★★.

Grainger, Richard

b. 21 May 1949, Middlesbrough, Cleveland, England. Grainger first played in folk clubs in Teesside at 17 years of age, accompanying himself on guitar. Having worked with several groups, including the Teesside Fettlers, Grainger has written a number of songs that have become well known on the folk circuit. His songs reflect many of the social problems that have beset the north-east of England. Based in Whitby, North Yorkshire, he travels the UK regularly, working at folk clubs and festivals alike, combining musical talent and dry north-east humour. His recording debut in 1984 was well received, and he continues to produce quality songs. *Herbs On The Heart* contained a number of Grainger originals, including 'Whitby Whaler'. As a contemporary songwriter, Richard still has a strong feel for traditional song, and this is evident on 'Teeside And Yorkshire'. 'Give Me A Job', from 1989's *Darklands* deals with the problem of unemployment, especially prevalent in his region.
● ALBUMS: *Herbs On The Heart* (Fellside 1984) ★★★, *Darklands* (Label 1989) ★★★★, with Dick Miles *Home Routes* (Label 1990) ★★★, *Thunderwood* (Folksound 1994) ★★★, *Town In Time* (Klondike 1999), *Wings Of Angels* (Klondike 2002) ★★★, with Sir David Attenborough *Eye Of The Wind* (Klondike 2003) ★★★, *On Heather & Clarty Moor* (Klondike 2004) ★★★★.

Gramm, Lou

b. Lou Grammatico, 2 May 1950, Rochester, New York, USA. Vocalist Lou Gramm possesses one of the great hard rock voices, and rose from small beginnings with late 60s group Poor Heart and **Black Sheep** to fame and fortune with **Foreigner**. After the enormous success of *Agent Provocateur*, however, Gramm's desire for more upbeat, guitar-based songs led him to write solo material with bass playing friend Bruce Turgon. His 1987 release *Ready Or Not* was a satisfying solo debut, proving that Gramm could produce classy AOR material without Foreigner cohort Mick Jones, and produced a surprise hit in 'Midnight Blue'. Gramm returned to Foreigner for *Inside Information*, but solo success had only increased the tension between Jones and the vocalist, and a split was inevitable. Gramm and Turgon worked together again on 1989's *Long Hard Look*, producing another US hit in 'Just Between You And Me', and Gramm's departure from Foreigner was confirmed as he embarked on a solo US tour, with Jones drafting in former Wild Horses (USA) vocalist Johnny Edwards for *Unusual Heat*, which ironically returned to the harder style that Gramm had been missing.
Gramm subsequently put together the ill-fated **Shadow King** with Turgon, drummer Kevin Valentine and ex-**Dio/Whitesnake** guitarist Vivian Campbell. The band barely lasted beyond their first album and live show before Campbell left to replace the late Steve Clark in **Def Leppard** and Valentine joined **Cinderella**. However, Gramm and Jones eventually put

their differences behind them, and the vocalist rejoined Foreigner in 1992, taking Turgon along with him. The band's 1994 album *Mr. Moonlight* was not as successful as previous releases, although they continued to be a strong live draw. In 1997, Gramm was successfully treated for a brain tumour before Foreigner reconvened briefly two years later. A more substantial reunion took place in 2002 for the band's 25th anniversary tour, but the following year Gramm announced he was resuming his solo career.
● ALBUMS: *Ready Or Not* (Atlantic 1987) ★★★, *Long Hard Look* (Atlantic 1989) ★★.
● COMPILATIONS: *A Foreigner In His Own Land: Rare Vintage 1970 Recordings* (Collectables 1993) ★★.

Grammer, Billy

b. William Wayne Grammer, 28 August 1925, Benton, Illinois, USA. Grammer was a coalminer's son and one of 13 children. His father played the fiddle, and by the time he was in his teens, Grammer was playing guitar, mandolin and banjo at local dances. After a spell in the forces, he started in C&W radio on WRAL in Arlington, Virginia, in 1947, but established his reputation as a session guitarist in Washington. He played lead guitar for several country performers—**Hawkshaw Hawkins**, **Grandpa Jones**, **T. Texas Tyler**—and he worked with **Jimmy Dean** on his television series from 1955–59. Grammer first recorded as a solo performer in 1949, but in 1959, had a vocal success with the million-selling 'Gotta Travel On', a nineteenth-century British melody that had previously been revived by the **Weavers**. Grammer's pop success was short-lived as the excellent double-sided 'Bonaparte's Retreat'/'The Kissing Tree' barely made the US Top 50. He had a country hit with 'I Wanna Go Home' in 1963, which **Bobby Bare** reworked as 'Detroit City'. He joined the **Grand Ole Opry** and became a session guitarist. His first model of the Grammer Flat-Top Guitar, which he now manufactures, is in the **Country Music Hall Of Fame**.
● ALBUMS: *Travellin' On* (Monument 1959) ★★★, *Gospel Guitar* (Decca 1962) ★★, *Billy Grammer Sings Gotta Travel On* (Decca 1964) ★★★, *Country Gospel Favourites* (Decca 1964) ★★, *Country Guitar* (Decca 1965) ★★★, *Sunday Guitar* (Epic 1967) ★★, *Country Favourites* (Vocalion 1968) ★★★, *Billy Grammer Plays* (Stoneway 1975) ★★★, *Christmas Guitars* (Classic Christmas 1977) ★★.

Granahan, Gerry

b. 17 June 1939, Pittston, Pennsylvania, USA. Granahan was associated with the 50s groups Dicky Doo And The Don'ts and the **Fireflies** and also recorded under his own name. Granahan started out as a disc jockey in his home-town before switching to a music career. At the age of 17 he began recording demos for **Elvis Presley** at the latter's Gladys Music firm. He recorded an unreleased single under the name Jerry Grant in 1957. The following year he co-wrote a song called 'No Chemise, Please' and recorded it under his name for Sunbeam Records; it reached number 23 in the summer of 1958. That same year Granahan also reached the US charts as a member of the Fireflies, who just missed the Top 20 with the ballad 'You Were Mine', on Ribbon Records, and led Dicky Doo And The Don'ts, a quintet that charted five times on Swan Records, first and most notably with 'Click Clack', a novelty rock 'n' roll song Granahan co-wrote with Dave Alldred, ex-drummer of **Jimmy Bowen** and the Rhythm

Orchids. In later years Granahan became a producer for such artists as **Shirley Ellis**, **Linda Scott**, the **Dave Clark Five**, **Jay And The Americans**, **Patty Duke** and **Farrante And Teicher**, and ran his own Caprice label, whose roster at one time included Linda Scott, the **Angels**, **James Ray** and **Santo And Johnny** (the latter actually signed to the related Canadian-American label). In the early 90s he began running his own GPG Studios based in Warwick, Rhode Island.

● ALBUMS: *Gerry Granahan's King-Sized Hits Volumes 1 & 2*. (Caprice) ★★★.

Granata, Rocco

b. 16 August 1938, Figline Vigliaturo, Italy. After relocating to Germany this singing songwriter was also a capable guitarist and accordionist. Equally convincing with romantic ballads and racier material, he was contracted by Germany's Electrola label, who were most optimistic about the longevity of his chart career, but his only major success was with 1960's 'Marina', a highlight of his stage act, which, as well as selling a million in Germany, also spent several weeks in the USA Top 40.

Grand Drive

Brothers Danny (vocals/guitar) and Julian Wilson (vocals/keyboards) were born in Australia, brought up in Sutton, Surry, England, and raised on a musical diet of classic American rock. They met Ed Balch (bass) at school in London, and after a short spell in a band named Soul Green the trio teamed up with Paul Wigens (drums) to form Grand Drive in 1995. The band was named after a road in Raynes Park, west London, although their title conjures up images far more in keeping with their exquisite take on US country rock. It took two years for the band, now a quartet, to find an outlet for the *Tell It Like It Is* EP, which was finally released in November 1997 by the independent Vaclav Records label. The *On A Good Day* EP followed before they signed a new contract with Loose Records. *Road Music*, a beguiling collection of up-tempo roots rock material largely drawn from the EPs, and the band's heartfelt live shows helped confirm Grand Drive's burgeoning reputation. The lush harmonies and adventurous arrangements of tracks such as 'Wheels' and 'A Ladder To The Stars' on the follow-up, *True Love And High Adventures*, saw the Wilson's songwriting rising to new creative heights.

The band was subsequently signed to BMG Records, making their debut for the label in 2002 with the exquisite country soul collection *See The Morning In*. Another quality recording, *The Lights In This Town Are Too Many To Count*, followed in 2004. During this period Danny Wilson also recorded his solo debut, *The Famous Mad Mile*, which was eventually released in 2005 on the Fargo label.

● ALBUMS: *Road Music* (Loose 1999) ★★★, *True Love And High Adventure* (Loose 2000) ★★★★, *See The Morning In* (Gravity/BMG 2002) ★★★★, *The Lights In This Town Are Too Many To Count* (Gravity/BMG 2004) ★★★.

Solo: Danny George Wilson *The Famous Mad Mile* (Fargo 2005) ★★★.

● COMPILATIONS: *Grand Drive* (RCA Victor 2003) ★★★★, *Being Alive: Loose Wheels & Latchkeys 2000-2005* (BMG 2005) ★★★.

Grand Funk Railroad

Formed in 1968, Grand Funk Railroad was the first American heavy rock 'power trio' to achieve massive fame, while alienating another large segment of the rock audience and critics at the same time. The group was a spin-off of **Terry Knight** And The Pack, a popular soul rock group in the Michigan area in the mid-60s, and originally comprised guitarist Mark Farner (b. 29 September 1948, Flint, Michigan, USA), bass player Mel Schacher (b. 3 April 1951, Owosso, Michigan, USA) and drummer Don Brewer (b. 3 September 1948, Flint, Michigan, USA). Farner and Brewer had both been members of the Pack, while Brewer had also belonged to the Jazz Masters. Following a single release on the small Lucky Eleven label, 'I (Who Have Nothin)', which reached number 46 in the US chart, the Pack were joined by Schacher, formerly of **? And The Mysterians**. At this point Knight stopped performing to become the band's manager, renaming it Grand Funk Railroad (the name was taken from the Michigan landmark the Grand Trunk Railroad). The new trio signed with **Capitol Records** in 1969 and immediately began making its name by performing at several large pop festivals. Their first singles reached the charts but Grand Funk soon proved its real strength in the album market. *On Time* reached number 27 in 1969, followed by the number 11 *Grand Funk* in 1970. By the summer of that year they had become a major concert attraction, and their albums routinely reached the Top 10 for the next four years. Of those, 1973's *We're An American Band* was the biggest seller, reaching number 2.

Grand Funk Railroad's huge success is often attributed to the public relations expertise of manager Knight. In 1970, for example, Knight reportedly paid $100,000 for a huge billboard in New York City's Times Square to promote the band's *Closer To Home*, which subsequently became their first Top 10 album, reaching number 6 and spawning the FM radio-staple title track. That promotional campaign back-fired with the press, however, which dismissed the band's efforts despite spiralling success with the public. In June 1971, for example, Grand Funk Railroad became only the second band (after the **Beatles**) to sell out New York's Shea Stadium. Their recordings sold in greater quantity even though many radio stations ignored their releases. 1970's *Live Album* reached number 5 and included another concert and radio favourite in Farner's 'Mean Mistreater'. The next year saw the release of *Survival* and *E Pluribus Funk*, the latter most notable for its round album cover.

In 1972 the band fired Knight, resulting in a series of lawsuits involving millions of dollars (they hired John Eastman, father of Linda McCartney, as their new manager). In 1973 the band shortened its name officially to Grand Funk, and added a fourth member, keyboard player Craig Frost (b. 20 April 1948, Flint, Michigan, USA). Now produced by **Todd Rundgren**, they finally broke into the singles market, reaching number 1 with the album title track 'We're An American Band', a celebration of their times on the road. In 1974 a major revision of **Little Eva**'s 'The Loco-Motion' also reached the top (the first time in US chart history that a cover version of a song that had previously reached number 1 also attained that position). In 1975, with their popularity considerably diminished, the band reverted to its original name of Grand Funk Railroad. The following year they signed with MCA Records and recorded *Good Singin', Good Playin'*, produced by **Frank Zappa**. When it failed to reach the Top 50, Farner left for a solo career. The others stayed together, adding guitarist Billy Elworthy and changing their name to Flint, a unit who failed to find commercial success with their solitary album.

Grand Funk, this time comprising Farner, Brewer and bass player Dennis Bellinger, re-formed for two years in 1981–83 and recorded *Grand Funk Lives* and *What's Funk?* for the Full Moon label. Failing to recapture former glories, they split again. Farner returned to his solo career, before joining **Adrenalin**. Brewer and Frost joined **Bob Seger**'s Silver Bullet Band. The band reunited for a benefit for Bosnian orphans in 1997. Farner continues to perform the Grand Funk catalogue all over the world as a solo artist.

● ALBUMS: *On Time* (Capitol 1969) ★★★, *Grand Funk* (Capitol 1970) ★★★★, *Closer To Home* (Capitol 1970) ★★★, *Live* (Capitol 1970) ★★, *Survival* (Capitol 1971) ★★, *E Pluribus Funk* (Capitol 1971) ★★★, *Phoenix* (Capitol 1972) ★★★, *We're An American Band* (Capitol 1973) ★★★, *Shinin' On* (Capitol 1974) ★★, *All The Girls In The World Beware!!!* (Capitol 1974) ★★, *Caught In The Act* (MCA 1975) ★★, *Good Singin', Good Playin'* (MCA 1976) ★★★, *Grand Funk Lives* (Full Moon 1981) ★★, *What's Funk?* (Full Moon 1983) ★★, *Live: The 1971 Tour* (Capitol 2002) ★★.

● COMPILATIONS: *Mark, Don & Mel 1969–71* (Capitol 1972) ★★, *Grand Funk Hits* (Capitol 1976) ★★★, *The Best Of Grand Funk Railroad* (Capitol 1990) ★★★, *More Of The Best Of Grand Funk Railroad* (Capitol 1991) ★★, *The Collection* (Castle 1992) ★★★, *Classic Masters* (Capitol 2002) ★★★.

● FURTHER READING: *An American Band: The Story Of Grand Funk Railroad*, Billy James. *From Grand Funk To Grace: The Authorized Biography Of Mark Farner*, Kristopher Englehardt.

Grand Hotel

An impressive stage production, with music and lyrics by **Robert Wright** and **George Forrest** (additional numbers by Maury Yeston) and a book by Luther Davis based on the novel by Vicki Baum and the classic 1932 film that starred Greta Garbo, John Barrymore, Joan Crawford and several other well-known Hollywood names. *Grand Hotel* opened at the Martin Beck Theatre in New York on 12 October 1989. The show had begun its life under the title of *At The Grand* in 1958, but on that occasion it failed to reach Broadway. Now set in a ritzy Berlin hotel in 1928 when Germany was already on the brink of Nazism, the main characters in this heavily plotted story whirl through the revolving doors: there is Elizaveta Grushinskaya (Liliane Montevecchi), the ageing Russian ballerina; Felix von Gaigern (David Carroll), the impoverished romantic German nobleman; Otto Kringelein (Michael Jeter), a Jewish bookkeeper dying of cancer and blowing his life savings on a few days of high living and Flaemmchen (Jane Krakowski), the pregnant typist who is desperate to take up a career in Hollywood. However, the real star of the piece was **Tommy Tune**, whose fluid direction and razzle dazzle choreography made this the most visually exciting musical that Broadway had seen for many a year. The songs came in for some severe criticism, although there were several appealing numbers among the score, which included 'As It Should Be', 'Some Have, Some Have Not', 'At The Grand Hotel', 'And Life Goes On', 'Fire And Ice', 'I Want To Go To Hollywood', 'Everybody's Doing It', 'Who Couldn't

Dance With You?', 'Love Can't Happen', 'I Waltz Alone', 'Roses At The Station', 'Bolero' (brilliantly danced adagio-style by Yvonne Marceau and Pierre Dulaine) and 'How Can I Tell Her?'. One of the highspots towards the end of the piece (there was no interval) came when the bookkeeper Kringelein and the Baron Gaigern link arms and kick up their heels in the exuberant 'We'll Take A Glass Together'. After transferring to the Gershwin Theatre early in 1992 to make way for a revival of **Guys And Dolls**, *Grand Hotel* continued its run for 1,018 performances, before closing in May of that year. The show was showered with awards, including five Tonys, for costumes, lighting, and featured actor (Michael Jeter). Most of the kudos went to Tommy Tune, who won two **Tony Awards** and several others honours, including a couple of Astaire awards for his brilliant direction and choreography. The London production of *Grand Hotel* opened at the refurbished 2,000-seater Dominion Theatre but, despite initially good reviews, never really took off and closed after three months with losses estimated at around £2 million. The original cast album was not issued until more than two and half years after the show opened. Most of the original principals recreated their roles, but a notably exception was David Carroll who played the Baron. He died of AIDS in March 1992, and, as a tribute, the CD contains a live recording of his version of one of the show's most attractive ballads, 'Love Can't Happen'.

Grand Mal

Even though Ziggy Stardust committed suicide, his spirit lives on in the New York City, USA–based quintet, Grand Mal. Although they sound remarkably like the first wave of glam rock (**David Bowie** and **Mott The Hoople** being two obvious reference points), the band's streamlined look is not (all members could pass for 'hip' record store clerks). Grand Mal's roots reach back to the early/mid-90s alt rock outfit, St. Johnny, led by vocalist/guitarist Bill Whitten. When St. Johnny split up in 1995 after three unappreciated albums, Whitten formed Grand Mal shortly thereafter. The band was originally thought to be a Whitten solo vehicle because the vast majority of compositions on their first few releases (1996's *Grand Mal* EP, 1997's *Pleasure Is No Fun*, and 1999's *Maledictions*) were credited solely to Whitten, in addition to constant line-up fluctuation. Among the musicians joining Whitten and guitarist John DeVries were backing vocalist Carmen Quiñones, keyboard players Jonathon Toubin and Nathan Brown, bass players Steve Borgerding and Chris Isom and drummer Parker Kindred. Employing renowned alt rock producer David Fridmann (who has worked with **Mercury Rev**, the **Flaming Lips**, **Mogwai** and **Sparklehorse**, among others), Grand Mal issued their third album, *Bad Timing*, in 2003. Prior to the album's release, DeVries was replaced by Aaron Romanello.

● ALBUMS: *Pleasure Is No Fun* (Number Six 1997) ★★★, *Maledictions* (Slash 1999) ★★★, *Bad Timing* (Arena Rock 2003) ★★★★.

Grand Ole Opry
(see **Hay, George D.**)

Grand Popo Football Club

Grand Popo Football Club is Ariel Wizman (b. Morocco) and Nicolas Errera (b. France), a DJ/book-loving television presenter/chat show host and a producer/classically trained pianist who studied at the National Conservatory in Paris, respectively. The duo apparently adopted their unusual moniker after Wizman visited the West African village of Grand Popo to film a television programme and decided that the community was missing a football club. After studying piano, composition, and electronic music, Errera became involved in theatre and successfully directed short films (winning the Clemant Ferrant prize for his *Going To Dieppe Without Seeing The Sea*) as well as becoming half of pop duo 2 Source. Wizman, meanwhile, DJed at Colombian parties in Paris. He became renowned for his show on Radio Nova that mixed easy listening, soundtracks, and electronic music. When the show transferred to television, Wizman brought in guests as disparate as Johnny Rotten and German philosophers: fortuitously, his guests also included 2 Source, an invite that rekindled Wizman and Errera's previous friendship. Grand Popo FC's first recording appeared on the *Source Lab 3* compilation in 1996, but they did not release their debut, *Shampoo Victims*, until 2000 (the album was re-released two years later).

Together the duo creates Gallic pop that seems to revere and revile the music of peers such as **Daft Punk**, **Air**, and **Cassius** in equal measure. They dubbed a song that sounded curiously like the former 'One More Song On The Market' while 'Nothing To Say In A House Song' railed against the duo's perceived vacuousness in **house** music by (vacuously) repeating the title over and over. *Shampoo Victims* also included a duo of collaborations with friends/heroes **Sparks**. Russell and Ron Mael provide both lyrics and vocals on the album's best tracks 'La Nuit Est Là' and 'Yo Quinero Mas Dinero'. As if to accentuate this fondness for 70s/80s pop, the duo also sampled **Giorgio Moroder**'s 'Love Fever' on 'Each Finger Has An Attitude'. Nevertheless, *Shampoo Victims* seemed curiously slight and never as clever as Wizman and Errera probably imagined.

● ALBUMS: *Shampoo Victims* (Atmospheriques/BMG 2000) ★★★.

Grand Prix

Ranked alongside **Magnum** as the UK's most accomplished pomp rock/AOR group, Grand Prix originally comprised Bernie Shaw (vocals), Phil Lanzon (keyboards), Michael O'Donoghue (guitar), Ralph Hood (bass) and Andy Beirne (drums, ex–**Dirty Tricks**). After an excellent self-titled debut collection for **RCA Records** in 1980, which highlighted the band's melodic strengths and structured songwriting, Shaw left to join **Praying Mantis** (and later **Stratus**). He was replaced by Robin McAuley, who settled into the role for two further albums. *There For None To See* was an excellent platform for his abilities, but proved to be Grand Prix's final album for RCA. One further album emerged, 1983's *Samurai*, released on **Chrysalis Records**, but by the early months of 1984 the band had broken up permanently. McAuley subsequently joined the McAuley Shenker Group (aka **MSG**), while his former band's three records became highly esteemed collector's items among fans of British AOR.

● ALBUMS: *Grand Prix* (RCA 1980) ★★★★, *There For None To See* (RCA 1982) ★★★★, *Samurai* (Chrysalis 1983) ★★.

Grand Puba

b. Maxwell Dixon, 4 March 1966, New Rochelle, New York, USA. A founder member of **Brand Nubian**, and before that

Masters Of Ceremony, Puba left the former following their acclaimed 1990 set, *One For All*. He kicked off his solo career with a track, 'Fat Rat', on the *Strictly Business* soundtrack. When his debut album was unveiled, the smooth reggae backing was subjugated by Puba's by now familiar lyrical subject matter. Born the son of a 5% Nation Islamic father, Puba's raps reinstated that doctrine just as forcefully as he had done with Brand Nubian, but it was generally a more playful set. It included a guest appearance from **Mary J. Blige**. He later appeared on **Fat Joe**'s *Represent* album, performing on 'Watch The Sound'. His second solo outing, released in 1995, was a less forceful set. Puba rejoined Brand Nubian for their 1998 comeback set, *Foundation*.

● ALBUMS: *Reel To Reel* (Elektra 1992) ★★★, *2000* (Elektra 1995) ★★★, *Understand This* (Koch 2001) ★★★.

Grand, Otis

b. Fred Bishti, 14 February 1950, Beirut, Lebanon. Grand has spent most of his life in the USA, although he lived in France for a few years. He began playing guitar at the age of 13, citing his influences as **B.B. King**, **T-Bone Walker**, **Otis Rush** and **Johnny Otis**, and he has played with many San Francisco Bay area blues artists. Otis Grand And The Dance Kings created a sensation when they burst onto the British blues scene in the late 80s, enhanced on the first album (a **W.C. Handy** award nomination) by the presence of **Joe Louis Walker**. The second album includes guests **Jimmy Nelson**, **Pee Wee Ellis**, and Walker again. A great live attraction, Grand was voted UK Blues Guitarist Of The Year in 1990 and continued to appear in annual polls throughout the 90s due to his constant touring schedule. He now resides in Croydon, Surrey, gateway to the blues!

● ALBUMS: *Always Hot* (Special Delivery 1988) ★★★, *He Knows The Blues* (Volt 1991) ★★★, with Phillip Walker *Big Blues From Texas* (JSP 1992) ★★★, with Joe Houston *The Return Of Honk* (JSP 1994) ★★, *Nothing Else Matters* (Sequel 1994) ★★★, *Perfume And Grime* (Sequel 1996) ★★★, with Debbie Davies, Anson Funderburgh *Grand Union* (Blueside 1998) ★★★, with Joe Louis Walker *Guitar Brothers* (JSP 2002) ★★★.

● COMPILATIONS: *The Blues Sessions 1990–1994* (JSP 1997) ★★★★, *In Grand Style: The Otis Grand Anthology* (Castle 2002) ★★★★.

Grandaddy

Based in songwriter Jason Lytle's home town of Modesto, California, USA, Grandaddy's lo-fi slacker rock insidiously worked its way into the heart of the alternative music press during the late 90s. Lytle was a former skateboarder whose employment record boasted a spell in a hazardous waste treatment plant. Around 1992, he formed Grandaddy with Kevin Garcia (bass) and Aaron Burtch (drums). The band spent several uneventful years putting together demo tapes recorded in Lytle's home studio, and playing bars and coffee shops in Modesto. Jim Fairchild (guitar) and Tim Dryden (keyboards) swelled the band's ranks for 1995's seven-track cassette debut, *A Pretty Mess By This One Band*. A haphazard mix of lo-fi and college rock, the band only managed to rise above the sum of their influences on the standout track 'Taster'. The record attracted enough attention, however, for the band to be able to record a full-length album. 1997's *Under The Western Freeway* was another home-produced recording. Fleshing out their lo-fi production with some odd sound effects, songs such as the single 'Summer Here Kids' and 'A.M. 180' built around simple but winning melodies, at odds with Lytle's relentlessly downbeat lyrics.

V2 Records reissued Grandaddy's debut album in 1998. Their first major label recording *The Sophtware Slump* benefited from the increased production budget available to the band, and was roundly hailed in the press as one of 2000's finest rock releases. Lyrics about alcoholic androids, lost pilots and miners, and the impersonal nature of the high-tech world, prompted flattering comparisons to **Radiohead**'s late 90s masterpiece **OK Computer**. The follow-up *Sumday* pursued the same themes but was an oddly flat-sounding collection, lacking the musical urgency of its predecessor and paling in comparison to contemporary work by the similarly styled **Flaming Lips**. A mini-album was released in 2005, but at the start of the following year Lytle announced that the band was splitting up.

● ALBUMS: *A Pretty Mess By This One Band* mini-album (Will 1995) ★★, *Under The Western Freeway* (Will 1997) ★★★★, *The Sophtware Slump* (V2 2000) ★★★★★, *Sumday* (V2 2003) ★★★, *Excerpts From The Diary Of Todd Zilla* mini-album (V2 2005) ★★★.

● COMPILATIONS: *The Broken Down Comforter Collection* (Big Cat 1999) ★★★, *Concrete Dunes* (Lakeshore 2002) ★★★, *Below The Radio* (Ultra 2004) ★★★.

Grandaddy IU

b. USA. Cool, ascerbic US hip-hop artist, briefly active in the early 90s, who only let himself down by indulging in cheap sexual innuendo, often followed by graphic descriptions of his conquests. Which detracted enormously from the spare, jazzy tones that carried his best rhymes with a feathery touch.

● ALBUMS: *Grandaddy IU* (Cold Chillin' 1990) ★★★, *Lead Pipe* (Cold Chillin' 1994) ★★.

Granderson, John Lee

b. 11 April 1913, Ellendale, Tennessee, USA, d. 22 August 1979, Chicago, Illinois, USA. Granderson left home when he was in his teens, moving to Chicago, Illinois, in 1928. Although not a professional musician, he did work with **John Lee 'Sonny Boy' Williamson**, among others. He turned to music full-time in the 60s and was featured as sideman and leader on many anthologies, although he never made a full album in his own right. Granderson sang and played guitar close to the style of the Memphis musicians of his youth. He stopped performing in public in 1975 and died of cancer in 1979.

● ALBUMS: *Hard Luck John* 1962–1966 recordings (Testament 1998) ★★.

● COMPILATIONS: with Johnny Young, Carl Martin, John Wrencher *The Chicago String Band* (Testament 1994) ★★★.

Grandmaster Flash

b. Joseph Saddler, 1 January 1958, Barbados, West Indies, but raised in the Bronx, New York City, USA. This pivotal force in early rap music grew up in the South Bronx, studying at Samuel Gompers Vocational Technical High School, spending his leisure time attending DJ parties thrown by early movers such as Grandmaster/**DJ Flowers**, MaBoya and **DJ Pete Jones**. The latter took him under his wing, and Flash intended to combine Jones' timing on the decks with the sort of records that **Kool Herc** was spinning. Hence in the early 70s

Saddler set about discovering the way to segue records smoothly together, highlighting the 'break'—the point in a record where the drum rhythm is isolated or accentuated—and repeating it. With admirable fortitude, Saddler spent upwards of a year in his apartment on 167th Street experimenting. The basis of his technique was to adapt Herc's approach, using two turntables each spinning the same record. He would then interrupt the flow of the disc offering the basic rhythm by overlaying the 'break', repeating the process by switching channels on the mixer, as necessary. The complexity and speed of the operation (the second desk would have to be rotated backwards to the beginning of the 'break' section) earned him the nickname Flash when he brought the style to his public, owing to the rapid hand movements. However, attention grabbing though this was, the style had not yet quite gelled into what Flash required. He decided, instead, to invite a vocalist to share the stage with him. He worked in this respect with first **Lovebug Starski** then Keith Wiggins. Wiggins would eventually come to be known as Cowboy within Grandmaster Flash's Furious Five, in the process becoming one of the first 'MCs', delivering rhymes to accompany Flash's turntable wizardry. Flash continued in the block/park party vein for a considerable time, often illegally by hooking up his sound system to an intercepted mains cable until the police arrived. One person, at least, saw some commercial potential in his abilities, however. Ray Chandler stepped up and invited Flash to allow him to promote him, and charge an entrance fee (previous hip-hop events had always been free). Initially incredulous at the thought that anyone would actually pay to see them, Flash nevertheless accepted.

Flash put together a strong line-up of local talent to support him: Grandmaster **Melle Mel** (b. Melvin Glover, New York City, USA) and his brother Kid Creole (b. Nathaniel Glover) joining Cowboy, this line-up initially titled Grandmaster Flash And The 3MCs. Two further rappers, **Duke Bootee** (b. Ed Fletcher) and **Kurtis Blow** subsequently joined, but were eventually replaced by Rahiem (b. Guy Todd Williams; ex-**Funky Four**) and Scorpio (b. Eddie Morris, aka Mr Ness). The Zulu Tribe was also inaugurated, with the express purpose of acting as security at live events: with Flash popularizing the rap format, rival MCs sprang up to take their mentor and each other on. These head to heads often had the result of garnering the participants equipment as prize money. A crew who were not popular could expect to see their turntables and **sound system** rehabilitated for their troubles. Just as Jamaican sound system owners like **Duke Reid** and **Coxsone Dodd** had done in the 60s, Flash, Kool Herc and Afrika Bambaataa would hide their records from prying eyes to stop their 'sound' being pirated. Similarly, record labels were removed to avoid identifying marks.

The Furious Five, meanwhile, made their debut proper on 2 September 1976. Shortly afterwards they released their first record, 'Super Rappin'', for **Enjoy Records**. Although hugely popular within the hip-hop fraternity, it failed to make commercial inroads, and Flash tried again with 'We Rap Mellow' (as the Younger Generation on Brass). However, it would be Joe Robinson Jnr. of **Sugarhill Records** who finally bought out their Enjoy contract. He had seen the Grandmaster in action at Disco Fever, 'hip-hop's first home', which had opened in the Bronx in 1978. His wife, Sylvia, wrote and produced their subsequent record, a relationship that kicked off with 'Freedom'. On the back of a major tour, certainly the first in rap's embryonic history, the single sold well, going on to earn a gold disc. The follow-up 'Birthday Party' was totally eclipsed by 'The Adventures Of Grandmaster Flash On The Wheels Of Steel', the first rap record to use samples, and a musical *tour de force*, dramatically showcasing the Flash quickmixing and scratching skills. Memorable enough, it too was overshadowed when Sugarhill brought the band in to record one of Robinson's most memorable compositions (written in tandem with Bootee): 'The Message'. The single, with its daunting, apocalyptic rumblings, significantly expanded not just rap but black music's boundaries, though the Furious Five had been less convinced of its worth when it was first offered to them in demo form. In just over a month the record achieved platinum sales. In the wake of the record's success Flash enquired of his Sugarhill bosses why no money was forthcoming. When he did not receive satisfactory explanation, he elected to split, taking Kid Creole and Rahiem with him, signing to **Elektra Records**. The others, headed by Melle Mel, would continue as **Melle Mel And The Furious 5**, scoring nearly instantly with another classic, 'White Lines (Don't Do It)'. Bearing in mind the subject matter of Mel's flush of success, it was deeply ironic that Flash had now become a freebase cocaine addict.

In the 80s Flash's name largely retreated into the mists of rap folklore until he was reunited with his Furious Five in 1987 for a **Paul Simon**, hosted charity concert in New York, and talk of a reunion in 1994 eventually led to the real thing. Back with the Furious Five he hosted New York's WQHT Hot 97 show, 'Mic Checka', spinning discs while prospective rappers rang up to try to pitch their freestyle rhymes down the telephone. Unfortunately, the reunion would not include Cowboy, who died on 8 September 1989 after a slow descent into crack addiction. Flash also helped out on **Terminator X**'s *Super Bad* set, which brought together many of the old school legends. In January 2002, he released an acclaimed mix album recreating the sounds of his legendary mid-70s block parties.

● ALBUMS: as Grandmaster Flash And The Furious Five *The Message* (Sugarhill 1982) ★★★★, as Grandmaster Flash And The Furious Five *Greatest Messages* (Sugarhill 1983) ★★★, as Grandmaster Flash And The Furious Five *On The Strength* (Elektra 1988) ★★, *They Said It Couldn't Be Done* (Elektra 1985) ★★, *The Source* (Elektra 1986) ★★, *Ba-Dop-Boom-Bang* (Elektra 1987) ★★★.

● COMPILATIONS: as Grandmaster Flash And The Furious Five/Grandmaster Melle Mel *Greatest Hits* (Sugarhill 1989) ★★★★, *The Best Of . . .* (Rhino 1994) ★★★★, *The Greatest Mixes* (Deepbeats 1998) ★★★, *Adventures On The Wheels Of Steel* 3-CD set (Sequel 1999) ★★★, *The Official Adventures Of Grandmaster Flash* (Strut 2002) ★★★★, *Best Of* (Sanctuary 2005) ★★★★.

Grandmaster Slice

b. *c.*1967, South Boston, Virginia, USA. 90s US rap artist Slice began to flex his rapping skills at the age of 11, going on to DJ and dance for a group titled Ebony Express by his teenage years. He subsequently formed his own combo, playing at parties in and outside of his home town, taking his talents seriously enough to record his first demo tapes. It was while attending Halifax County Senior High School that Slice hooked up with Scratchmaster Chuck T. (b. Charles Fulp), who became his road manager and DJ. They had known of

each other's rapping interests, having previously gone head to head in an after-school talent show. Together they released a debut album on independent distributor Selecto Hits Records, which was subsequently picked up by **Jive Records**. They had been suitably impressed by one of the album cuts, 'Thinking Of You', a slow-climbing hit throughout the US.

● ALBUMS: *The Electric Slice (Shall We Dance)* (Selecto Hits/Jive 1991) ★★★.

Grandmixer DST

b. Derek Howells, 23 August 1960, New York City, USA. Born and raised in the south Bronx area—the tough spawning ground of many of the finest first-generation hip-hop artists—scratch DJ DST was a member of **Afrika Bambaataa**'s street gang/sound system crew the Zulu Nation, before quitting to carve out a solo career in 1982 with the single 'Grandmixer Cuts It Up' on French label Celluloid, backed by the Infinity Rappers (KC Roc and Shahiem). With a formidable underground reputation behind him, he achieved an international breakthrough in 1983 as the scratcher on **Herbie Hancock**'s 'Rockit', and was prominently featured on other tracks from Hancock's album *Future Shock* the same year. It was the first collaboration between jazz and hip-hop, until then seen as mutually exclusive forms. In 1984, he enjoyed an international dancefloor hit with his own single, 'Crazy Cuts'. He raised his profile further with a series of collaborations with avant-funk/jazz producer **Bill Laswell**, producer of *Future Shock* and 'Rockit', appearing on a wide range of Laswell-produced tracks by Deadline, **Manu Dibango**, **Foday Musa Suso** and **Material**. A supremely talented, musical scratcher, DST's star faded in the late 80s as new generations of DJs replaced him in hip-hop's notoriously short-shelf-life marketplace. (DST derived his tag from the New York garment district's Delancey Street, where the young DJ was often to be found in the late 70s adding to his collection of fashion wear.)

● ALBUMS: *Crazy Cuts* (Celluloid 1984) ★★★.

Grandquist, Nancy

b. California, USA. The wife of a Christian minister, gospel singer Nancy Grandquist spent much of her earlier life in church, where her dynamic vocals proved popular in a myriad of choirs. Influenced primarily by **Mahalia Jackson** and the black gospel singers, she took her first piano lessons at the age of four. As a teenager she enrolled at the Christian Life Center in Stockton, California, USA, where bible classes were a prominent component of academic life. There she met her minister husband Richard, and began to look for a recording contract. NewPax Records signed her, resulting in the release of her *Somebody Special* debut set in the 70s. Although this received considerable acclaim within the gospel community, it failed to promote Grandquist as a major artist.

● ALBUMS: *Somebody Special* (NewPax 1977) ★★★★.

Granelli, Jerry

b. Gerald John Granelli, 30 December 1940, San Francisco, California, USA. Granelli began playing drums as a small child, later studying formally and taking tuition from **Joe Morello**. In the early and mid-60s he played with many musicians including **Vince Guaraldi**, **Denny Zeitlin**, **Jon Hendricks**, **Earl 'Fatha' Hines**, **Mose Allison**, **Ornette Coleman** and **Jimmy Witherspoon**. This eclectic mix helped contribute to

Granelli's questing musical style, which continued into the next decade, a time which found him forming his own bands, including Visions, and also teaching, first in Denver and then in Seattle. In the 70s he retired from the jazz scene for several years, co-founding the Naropa Institute in Boulder, Colorado, with **Collin Walcott** and **Allen Ginsberg**. Returning to jazz he toured internationally, with **Gary Peacock** and **Ralph Towner** among others, and also recorded with singer **Jay Clayton**. Later, Granelli settled in Germany while still finding time to teach in Halifax, Nova Scotia. He also began recording as a leader, using up-and-coming young German musicians as well as established international stars such as **Jane Ira Bloom**, **Robben Ford**, **Bill Frisell** and **Julian Priester**.

Perhaps as a result of the eclectic nature of his earlier years as a sideman, Granelli's records intriguingly and effectively blend aspects of hard bop, free jazz, blues, jazz rock fusion, R&B and jazz funk. In his bands Granelli is very much an ensemble player, adding colour, texture and atmosphere as well as providing a time base that can be fluid without ever losing contact with the reality of the music being performed by his colleagues. At the end of the 90s he began playing with UFB, alongside guitarists Kai Brückner and Christian Kögel and bass player Andreas Walter. Additionally he worked with his own unit Mr Lucky.

● ALBUMS: with Jay Clayton *Sound Songs* (JMT 1985) ★★★, *Koputai* (ITM 1989) ★★, *Forces Of Flight* (ITM 1990) ★★, *A Song I Thought I Heard Buddy Sing* (Evidence 1992) ★★★, *Another Place* (Intuition 1994) ★★★, with UFB *News From The Street* (Intuition 1995) ★★★, with UFB *Broken Circle* (Intuition 1996) ★★★, with Badlands *Enter, A Dragon* (Songlines 1998) ★★★★, with Badlands *Crowd Theory* (Songlines 1999) ★★★, with Badlands *Enter A Dragon* (Songlines 1999) ★★, with Jeff Reilly *Iron Sky* (Love Slave 2001) ★★★, with Jamie Saft *The Only Juan* (Love Slave 2002) ★★★, *The V16 Project* (Songlines 2003) ★★★, with Mr Lucky *Gigantic* (Love Slave 2004) ★★, *Sandhills Reunion* (Songlines 2005) ★★★★.

Graney, Dave

b. Mount Gambier, near Melbourne, Australia. Dave Graney first worked as a professional musician in the late 70s with Adelaide, Australia, band the Sputniks. With Graney disguising himself under the pseudonym Dave Munroe, the band recorded one single, 'Second Chance', but they were best known for mingling cover versions of material by **Wire** and **Wilson Pickett** in a chaotic, drunken live set. In the 80s, he joined the Moodists—an acclaimed psychedelic rock/pop band who recorded one album for **Creation Records** with his involvement. He subsequently became a labelmate of the pre-success **Pulp** and **Teenage Fanclub** by signing to Fire Records and releasing material with his own band. That outfit was alternatively named Dave Graney With The Coral Snakes (for the debut *At His Stone Beach* EP) and Dave Graney With The White Buffaloes (for the frontier-fixated 1989 album *My Life On The Plains*). However, despite critical approbation the sales response was subdued, and in the early 90s Graney returned to Australia and set up his own label, ID Records. Following the issue of the live *The Lure Of The Tropics*, Graney then began work on *Night Of The Wolverine* with a reshuffled Coral Snakes—his wife Clare Moore on drums, Robin Casinader on organ/piano, Gordy Blair on bass and Rod Hayward on guitar. Having always been a critical favourite, the results were seized upon by the Australian

media as evidence of the return of a great songwriter. As the Australian listings magazine, *Time Off*, commented: 'It was almost a relief when Dave Graney arrived. All of a sudden, Australia had a new icon of musical sophistication, an artist to match the McCombs (the **Triffids**) and McLennans (the **Go-Betweens**). He'd always promised to do so, but it wasn't until this year's wonderful *Night Of The Wolverine* that it became a reality.' The contents of the album, which also received a five star review in *Rolling Stone*, swelled with the usual Graney touchstones, including cinema, adolescent yearning and loss, and self-deprecating humour. *The Soft 'N' Sexy Sound* was a strong follow-up, although by now Graney's music was moving noticeably towards the mainstream. Following one more album Graney disbanded the Coral Snakes in 1997. His new outfit, the Dave Graney Show, released their self-titled debut in 1998.

● ALBUMS: with the White Buffaloes *My Life On The Plains* (Fire/ID 1989) ★★★, with the Coral Snakes *I Was The Hunter And I Was The Prey* (Fire 1992) ★★★, with the Coral Snakes *The Lure Of The Tropics* (Torn & Frayed 1992) ★★★, with the Coral Snakes *Night Of The Wolverine* (ID/This Way Up 1993) ★★★★, with the Coral Snakes *You Wanna Be There But You Don't Wanna Travel* (ID 1994) ★★★, with the Coral Snakes *The Soft 'N' Sexy Sound* (ID/This Way Up 1995) ★★★, with the Coral Snakes *The Devil Drives* (Mercury 1997) ★★★, with the Dave Graney Show *The Dave Graney Show* (Festival 1998) ★★★, with the Dave Graney Show *Kiss Tomorrow Goodbye* (Festival/Cooking Vinyl 2000) ★★★.

● COMPILATIONS: with the Coral Snakes *The Baddest* (Universal 1999) ★★★★.

● FURTHER READING: *It Is Written Baby*, Dave Graney.

Granmax

Comprising Nick Christopher (vocals), Steve Myers (guitar), Tim McCorkle (bass) and Louis McCorkle (drums), US rock band Granmax were powerfully animated by rhythm siblings, the McCorkle brothers. Otherwise there was little immediately distinctive about their two late-70s albums for Panama Records, though some claim their style to be antecedent to much of the late 70s west coast hard rock sound. Certainly there are elements of innovation at play on both *A Night Alive* and *Kiss Heaven Goodbye*, though the poor production standards hardly help these rise to the surface.

● ALBUMS: *A Night Alive* (Panama 1976) ★★, *Kiss Heaven Goodbye* (Panama 1978) ★★.

Grant Lee Buffalo

This Los Angeles, California, USA–based band was formed by **Grant-Lee Phillips** (b. 1 September 1963, Stockton, California, USA; vocals/12-string guitar), Paul Kimble (b. 24 September 1960, Freeport, Illinois, USA; bass/keyboards) and Joey Peters (b. 9 April 1965, New York, USA; drums). Phillips grew up in California the son of a minister and the grandson of a southern gospel singer grandmother, before enrolling in film school. Grant Lee Buffalo began to evolve in 1989, when Phillips joined Peters and Kimble in Shiva Burlesque, but despite attracting critical acclaim they soon realized that the band's impetus was stalling. The trio became the only ones arriving for rehearsals, and sacked the other two members to concentrate on a new band. Mouth Of Rasputin, Rex Mundi, Soft Wolf Tread and Machine Elves were all rejected as names. The band chose Grant Lee Buffalo after their singer's Christian names, and the image of a buffalo to symbolize all 'that had gone wrong in this country' (it had previously been employed by Phillips for a set of solo country standards he had sung before his former band King Of The World came onstage). Their influences were 'the music of America from the 30s to the 60s that's based on story-telling and improvisation, blues, jazz or country'.

By the autumn of 1991 the band had recorded 11 songs in Kimble's home studio, a tape of which was passed to **Bob Mould**, who released 'Fuzzy' as a 7-inch on his Singles Only Label (SOL). A month later they had earned a contract with **Slash Records**, primarily because the band felt an affinity with several other acts on the label (**X**, **Los Lobos**, **Violent Femmes**). A debut album was recorded in two weeks in San Francisco, with Kimble again producing. The songs attacked modern America's complacency and pursuit of material wealth, harking back to a golden age of American optimism. Phillips' acute observation and lyrical poignancy, which earned comparisons to **Neil Young** and **Mike Scott** (the **Waterboys**), was steeped in a grainy, cinematic sweep that saw the set lauded by Michael Stipe of **R.E.M.** as '1993's finest album, hands down'. 'America Snoring', released as a single in both the USA and UK, symbolized the faithless, faceless climate of the USA so despised by the author, and was written as a response to the Los Angeles riots. A companion piece, 'Stars N' Stripes', was Phillips' evocative homage to **Elvis Presley**'s Vegas period, and offered another passionate chapter in his thematic dissection of modern Americana.

The follow-up album *Mighty Joe Moon* proved more restrained, with its anger at the vulgarity of characters and situations tempered by greater texture and guile. The keynote spirituality implicit in earlier recordings was maintained by 'Rock Of Ages', one of the few dramatic gestures on offer. The band progressed further with the more vocally orientated *Copperopolis*, which broke away from the traditional rock band format by introducing pedal steel guitar (Greg Leisz), bass clarinet (Ralph Carney) and violin (Bob Fergo). Kimble left the band prior to the release of their final album *Jubilee*, which featured guest appearances from Michael Stipe, **Robyn Hitchcock** and **Eels** frontman E. Phillips (as Grant-Lee Phillips) subsequently released a series of excellent solo albums, including *Ladies' Love Oracle*, *Mobilize* and *Virginia Creeper*.

● ALBUMS: *Fuzzy* (Slash 1993) ★★★★, *Mighty Joe Moon* (Slash 1994) ★★★★★, *Copperopolis* (Slash 1996) ★★★, *Jubilee* (Slash 1998) ★★★.

● COMPILATIONS: *Storm Hymnal: Gems From The Vault Of Grant Lee Buffalo* (London 2001) ★★★★.

Grant, Amy

b. 25 November 1960, Augusta, Georgia, USA. A huge influence on the development of modern gospel music, Grant's perennially youthful but always convincing vocal has imbued her many recordings with a purity of spirit and performance that can be awe-inspiring. Songs such as 'Angels', 'Raining On The Inside' and 'Find A Way', scattered through a consistently high-quality recording career, have endeared her to her massive contemporary and gospel audience as well as critics. Though originally a primarily religious performer, her material also blends in rhythms derived from modern R&B and soul, while her lyrics contemplate subjects outside of the average gospel singer's

repertoire. However, when secular subjects are tackled, there is an abiding spirituality to Grant's treatment of them that ensures her position as a gospel singer despite her R&B success: 'The point of my songs is never singer-focused. It's experience focused. When I go in the studio, I'm taking my experience as a wife and a mother with me.'

Though earlier albums had flirted with pop, rock, soul and country, and Grant enjoyed a US number 1 single as far back as 1986, duetting with **Peter Cetera** on 'The Next Time I Fall', Grant's first truly secular release arrived in 1991 with *Heart In Motion*. Featuring the US number 1/UK number 2 single 'Baby Baby', this move into the contemporary pop world was rewarded with platinum sales, the album spending 52 consecutive weeks on the US *Billboard* chart. Subsequent singles carried on Grant's commercial renaissance, with 'Every Heartbeat' (number 2), 'That's What Love Is For' (number 7) and 'Good For Me' (number 8) all breaking into the US Top 10 in 1991–92. Long-term collaborators **Keith Thomas** and **Michael Omartian** were again in place for the follow-up, *House Of Love*. Boosted by a strong duet with **Vince Gill** on the title track and the presence of another hit single, 'Lucky One', this collection also included a cover version of the **Joni Mitchell** standard 'Big Yellow Taxi'.

Grant took a giant leap in credibility with *Behind The Eyes* in 1997. This was an album of much greater depth that dispelled the perception of her as merely a vacuous pop diva. In March 2000, Grant married Vince Gill. In the new millennium, Grant began to gravitate back towards inspirational material, releasing two collections of old-time hymns and religious songs (2002's *Legacy: Hymns & Faith* and 2005's *Rock Of Ages . . . Hymns & Faith*). In between these two releases Grant completed the pop album, *Simple Things*.

● ALBUMS: *My Father's Eyes* (Myrrh/Reunion 1979) ★★★, *Never Alone* (Myrrh/Reunion 1980) ★★★, *In Concert* (Myrrh/Reunion 1981) ★★★★, *In Concert Volume Two* (Myrrh/Reunion 1981) ★★★, *Age To Age* (Myrrh/Reunion 1982) ★★★, *Straight Ahead* (A&M 1984) ★★★★, *Unguarded* (A&M 1985) ★★★, with Art Garfunkel *The Animals' Christmas* (Columbia 1986) ★★★★, *A Christmas Album* (Myrrh/Reunion 1988) ★★★, *Lead Me On* (A&M 1988) ★★★, *Heart In Motion* (A&M 1991) ★★★, *Home For Christmas* (A&M 1992) ★★★, *House Of Love* (A&M 1994) ★★★, *Behind The Eyes* (A&M 1997) ★★★★, *A Christmas To Remember* (A&M 1999) ★★★, *Legacy: Hymns & Faith* (A&M 2002) ★★★★, *Simple Things* (A&M 2003) ★★★, *Rock Of Ages . . . Hymns & Faith* (Word/Curb 2005) ★★★.

● COMPILATIONS: *The Collection* (Myrrh/Reunion 1986) ★★★★, *Her Great Inspirational Songs* (BMG Heritage/RCA 2002) ★★★, *Greatest Hits 1986–2004* (A&M 2004) ★★★★.

● DVD/VIDEOS: *Building The House Of Love* (A&M 1994).

Grant, Bill
(see **Bell, Delia, And Bill Grant**)

Grant, Cary

b. Archibald Alexander Leach, 18 January 1904, Horfield, Bristol, Gloucestershire, England, d. 29 November 1986, Davenport, Iowa, USA. As a child, Leach joined a troupe of itinerant entertainers and was still in his teens when they travelled to the USA, where he struggled in vaudeville while doing menial day work. In 1923 he returned to the UK, graduating to minor roles in musical comedies before returning to New York to play in *Golden Dawn* (1927). After this he was in other Broadway productions, including *Boom Boom*, *A Wonderful Night* (both 1929) and *Nikki* (1931). Signed with the Paramount Picture Corporation, he played supporting roles in several films in 1932, including *Blonde Venus* (starring **Marlene Dietrich**), and a non-musical version of *Madame Butterfly* (playing Lt. Pinkerton to Sylvia Sidney's Butterfly). By 1933 he had moved swiftly up the cast list, co-starring with **Mae West**, at her request, in *She Done Him Wrong* and *I'm No Angel*. In the first of this pair Grant was recipient of one of the most famous lines in films: 'Why don't you come up sometime 'n see me?'.

Moving from Paramount to work for both RKO and Columbia in the late 30s, Grant made a string of critically praised and still-popular screwball comedies, including *Topper* (co-starring with Constance Bennett), *The Awful Truth* (with **Irene Dunne**) (both 1937), *Bringing Up Baby* (1938, with Katharine Hepburn), and *His Girl Friday* (1940, with **Rosalind Russell**). In the 40s, he was in the farce *Arsenic And Old Lace* (1944), the musical biopic **Night And Day** (playing the role of songwriter **Cole Porter**) and the drama *Notorious* (both 1946), and the comedies *Mr. Blandings Builds His Dream House* (1948) and *I Was A Male War Bride* (1949). Through the 50s and into the 60s he made comedies and dramas with equal aplomb, including Alfred Hitchcock's *To Catch A Thief* (1955), *Indiscreet* (1958), Hitchcock's *North By Northwest* (1959), *That Touch Of Mink* (1962, with **Doris Day**) and *Charade* (1963). Although he aged very well, Grant made his final film in 1966, *Walk Don't Run*, retiring from films to work as a director of various international companies, including Fabergé and Western Airlines, as well as the film company MGM. In 1970, he received a special Academy Award for his Lifetime Achievement In Films, having been unsuccessfully nominated as Best Actor for both *Penny Serenade* (1941) and *None But The Lonely Heart* (1944).

● FURTHER READING: *Cary Grant: A Biography*, Marc Eliot. *Cary Grant: A Bio-Bibliography*, Beverley Bare Buehrer. *The Private Cary Grant*, William Currie McIntosh and William D. Weaver. *An Affair To Remember: My Life With Cary Grant*, Maureen Donaldson and William Royce. *Cary Grant: The Lonely Heart*, Charles Higham and Roy Moseley. *Cary Grant: A Touch Of Elegance*, Warren G. Harris. *Cary Grant*, Lane Harris. *Haunted Idol: The Story Of The Real Cary Grant*, Geoffrey Wansell. *The Life And Loves Of Cary Grant*, Lee Guthrie. *Not This Time, Cary Grant!: And Other Stories About Hollywood*, Shirley Eder. *Cary Grant: A Class Apart*, Graham McCann. *The Man Who Knew Cary Grant*, Jonathan Schwartz. *Cary Grant: A Celebration*, Richard Schickel. *Cary Grant: His Movies And His Life*, Pamela Trescott. *Cary Grant: The Light Touch*, Lionel Godfrey. *The Films Of Cary Grant*, Donald Deschner. *Evenings With Cary Grant: Recollections In His Own Words And By Those Who Knew Him*, Nancy Nelson.

Grant, Coot, And Sox Wilson

Coot Grant (b. Leola B. Pettigrew, 17 June 1893, Birmingham, Alabama, USA, d. date unknown) and Wesley Wilson (b. 1 October 1893, Jacksonville, Florida, USA, d. 10 October 1958, Cape May Court House, New Jersey, USA). Pettigrew used various names including Patsy Hunter but was usually called Coot, for Cutie. She worked in vaudeville as a dancer from early childhood, touring the USA and appearing overseas, including visits to Europe and South Africa in the years before World War I. From around 1905 she sometimes worked with Wilson, a pianist and organist, who also used different names including Kid Wilson, Pigmeat Pete, Jenkins, Socks and Sox Wilson. Around 1912 they married and thereafter worked mostly as a team, usually as Grant And Wilson but occasionally using other combinations of their multiple names, such as Hunter And Jenkins. Additionally, from time to time, each worked alone: Grant recorded serious blues numbers under her own name, some in the company of the celebrated guitarist **Blind Blake** (1926) and others with the **Sidney Bechet/Mezz Mezzrow** quintet (1946), while Wilson duetted with Harry McDaniels (as Pigmeat Pete And Catjuice Charlie). They appeared and recorded with leading bands of the day, including **Fletcher Henderson**'s, and also with groups such as the **Mezz Mezzrow–Sidney Bechet** Quintet. The duo also played in musical comedies, vaudeville, travelling shows and revues, including one with **Louis Armstrong**.

As important as their performing was their songwriting, which produced over 400 numbers, including 'Gimme A Pigfoot', and the other three songs recorded at **Bessie Smith**'s last session. In 1933 they appeared in the film *Emperor Jones*, which starred **Paul Robeson**, but the 30s were generally not very successful years for the pair. They reappeared briefly in the late 40s, recording and writing for Mezz Mezzrow's King Jazz label. In 1949 Wilson's health was such that they worked less as a team, while Grant kept going a little longer. After Wilson's death, nothing more was heard about Grant, and her date of death remains unknown. An engaging duo with an effective line in vaudeville and popular material, they were very popular artists of their day.

● COMPILATIONS: *Complete Recorded Works In Chronological Order Volume 1: 1925–1928* (Document 1998) ★★★, *Complete Recorded Works In Chronological Order Volume 2: 1928–1931* (Document 1998) ★★★, *Complete Recorded Works In Chronological Order Volume 3: 1931–1938* (Document 1998) ★★★.

Grant, Darrell

b. Darrell Lemont Grant, 30 May 1962, Pittsburgh, Pennsylvania, USA. Grant was raised in Denver, Colorado, and from an early age studied classical and jazz piano. As a youth he toured jazz festivals with the Pearl Street Jazz Band and at 17 took up a scholarship at the Eastman School of Music, where he was awarded a BM in piano performance. He also attended the University of Miami before moving to New York, where he played with noted musicians including **Woody Shaw**, **Junior Cook** and **Charlie Persip**, and was also involved with the **M-Base** project. In 1986, his band, Current Events, had a brief recording contract with a major label and in 1988 he joined **Betty Carter**, becoming one of a succession of fine pianists whose talents were honed in the diva's service. In addition to touring with Carter, he also worked with **Tony Williams**, **Donald Byrd**, **Roy Haynes** and **Chico Freeman**. He also played with **Greg Osby**, appearing on 1993's *3-D Lifestyles*. Grant moved from the action of the New York jazz scene in 1997 to become professor of music in Portland, Oregon, before relocating to Toronto, Canada.

A strikingly gifted pianist and composer, through his commitment and passion Grant evokes memories of **Horace Silver** although he is indisputably a thoroughly original performer. In common with many jazz performers, Grant has learned the lesson that theirs is an art scorned by the media. In his case, rather than resign himself to it, he has actively publicized his own engagements resulting in a growing audience base.

● ALBUMS: *Current Events* (Verve 1986) ★★★, *Black Art* (Criss Cross 1994) ★★★, *The New Bop* (Criss Cross 1996) ★★★★, *Twilight Stories* (32 Jazz 1998) ★★★, *Smokin' Java* (Lair Hill 2000) ★★★.

Grant, David

b. 8 August 1956, Kingston, Jamaica, West Indies. By the time everyone realized that **Linx** was not the spearhead of a new UK soul movement, singer David Grant had swapped his glasses and moustache for a sweatband and aerobics gear and gone solo. Suddenly he was Britain's answer to **Michael Jackson**. He could dance, he was pretty and his voice was high, and 'Stop And Go', 'Watching You Watching Me' and 'Love Will Find A Way' all made the UK Top 30 in 1983. His songwriting partnership with Derek Bramble developed, resulting in the Steve Levine–produced self-titled album. More memorable, however, were his duets with **Jaki Graham** in 1985, on the **Spinners**' 'Could It Be I'm Falling In Love' and **Todd Rundgren**'s 'Mated'. 'Hopes And Dreams' was an altogether weightier offering, with contributions from **Aswad** and **Go West**, but it just made the Top 100. Grant penned further hits for Gavin Christopher, **Cheryl Lynn** and **Hot Chocolate**. He maintained a loyal club following for a time, where his energetic 'soul' music was highly popular. In the 90s he was active in session work, acting and television.

● ALBUMS: *David Grant* (Chrysalis 1983) ★★★, *Hopes And Dreams* (Chrysalis 1985) ★★, *Change* (Polydor 1987) ★★, *Anxious Edge* (4th & Broadway 1990) ★★.

● COMPILATIONS: *The Best Of David Grant And Linx* (Chrysalis 1993) ★★★.

Grant, Della

b. Georgia, USA. Grant's early influences include gospel and soul music, which, when combined with her love of reggae, produce exceptional results. She began singing at the age of six and came from a family of talented musicians. Although not Jamaican-born, her feel for the music and her faultless phrasing led to assumptions that she had grown up there. She linked up with the **Twinkle Brothers** and married Ralston Grant, who occasionally provided lead vocals on the group's classics, including 'Barabus', 'Gone Already', 'Jahoviah' and 'Free Us'. While remaining part of the Twinkle Brothers, Ralston concurrently led Grant's backing band, the Pace-setters. He accompanied her on her hectic touring schedule, which included Reggae Sunsplash and The White River Reggae Bash, while internationally she wowed the crowds at Reggae On The River in Vancouver, The 10th Annual Sunsplash in the Grand Rapids, and numerous **Bob Marley** Day Festivals. As part of the Twinkle Showcase she toured Poland and appeared at the UK's Essential Festival Roots Day. She is a prominent force in the album chart but has also enjoyed successful singles, including a version of **Chaka Khan**'s 'Sweet Thing' (a Jamaican hit) and the equally popular 'Black Rose'. Outstanding album tracks include 'I'm A Rastawoman', 'Calling Mama Africa', 'The Lord's Prayer' and a version of 'Swing Low, Sweet Chariot'. She maintains a high profile, touring alongside such luminaries as **Bunny Wailer**, **Buju Banton**, **Charlie Chaplin**, **Luciano**, **Sister Carol**, **Rita Marley**, **Mutabaruka**, **Capleton**, **Josie Wales** and **Burning Spear**.

● ALBUMS: *Arrival* (Twinkle 1993) ★★★★, *Rootically Yours* (Twinkle 1993) ★★, *Listen* (Twinkle 1994) ★★★, *Ruff 'N' Ready* (Twinkles 1994) ★★★, *Black Rose* (Twinkle 1995) ★★★, *Dawta Of The Dust* (Twinkle 1996) ★★, *In Fine Style* (Twinkle 1998) ★★★, *Give Jah The Glory* (Twinkle 2002) ★★.

Grant, Earl

b. 20 January 1933, Oklahoma City, Oklahoma, USA, d. 10 June 1970. Earl Grant was an easy-listening pianist/organist and singer who was popular in the late 50s and early 60s. Grant played trumpet and drums in addition to piano, and studied at four music schools, after which he taught music himself, and then began performing in nightclubs while stationed in Texas during his army service. Grant signed to **Decca Records** in 1958 and reached number 7 in the US charts with his first single, 'The End', which received airplay on 'beautiful music' stations in the USA. His first album, *Ebb Tide*, released in 1961, was also a number 7 entry. He placed five further singles in the US charts and six more albums (of over 20 released on Decca) through 1968. Grant appeared in a number of films as well. He died in a car accident in Lordsburg, New Mexico, USA.

● ALBUMS: *The Magic Of Earl Grant* (Decca 1960) ★★★, *Ebb Tide* (Decca 1961) ★★★★, *The End* (Decca 1961) ★★★, *Earl After Dark* (Decca 1961) ★★, *Beyond The Reef And Other Instrumental Favorites* (Decca 1962) ★★★★, *At Basin Street East* (Decca 1962) ★★★, *Midnight Sun* (Decca 1963) ★★★, *Fly Me To The Moon* (Decca 1963) ★★★, *Just For A Thrill* (Decca 1964) ★★★, *Just One More Time* (Decca 1965) ★★, *Spotlight On* (Decca 1965) ★★★, *Tradewinds* (Decca 1965) ★★★, *Stand By Me* (Decca 1965) ★★, *Sings And Plays Songs Made Famous By Nat 'King' Cole* (Decca 1966) ★★★, *Bali Ha'i* (Decca 1966) ★★, *Gently Swingin'* (Decca 1968) ★★★, *Spanish Eyes* (Decca 1968) ★★, *Time For Us* (Decca 1969) ★★★, *Earl Grant* (Decca 1970) ★★.

● COMPILATIONS: *Greatest Hits* (Decca 1967) ★★★★.

Grant, Eddy

b. Edmond Montague Grant, 5 March 1948, Plaisance, Guyana, West Indies. Grant moved to England in 1960. Over the next few years, he wrote a number of ska songs, some of which have become classics, including the suggestive hit for **Prince Buster**, 'Rough Rider'. During the late 60s he enjoyed pop success as part of the **Equals**, with 'Baby Come Back' topping the UK singles chart. Grant was 24 years old, with several further Equals hits to his credit, when he left the band to form his own production company. After producing other acts, he made his own debut in 1977 with *Message Man*. It was certainly a solo effort: not only did he sing and play every note, but it was recorded in his own studio, the Coach House, and released on his own label, Ice Records. Grant had developed his own sound—part reggae, part funk, with strong musical motifs and strong melodies—producing pop with credibility. More than 10 years after the Equals' first hit, 'Living On The Front Line' (1979) was a UK number 11 hit, and the now dreadlocked Grant had found himself a whole new audience. 'Do You Feel My Love' and 'Can't Get Enough Of You' kept him in the UK Top 20.

In 1982, Grant moved his home and studio to Barbados, signed Ice Records to **RCA Records**, and achieved a memorable UK number 1 hit with 'I Don't Wanna Dance'. The following year 'Electric Avenue' reached number 2 on both sides of the Atlantic, and the parent album *Killer On The Rampage* proved his biggest seller. The huge hits eluded him for four years until he stormed back in January 1988 with 'Gimme Hope Jo'anna', as if he had never been away. The dressing of the anti-apartheid message in the apparent simplicity of a pop song was typically inspired. In recent years, Grant has continued recording and writing quality material, but has concentrated his efforts on building a successful music publishing company and record label in Barbados. A dance remix of 'Electric Avenue' was a huge club hit in 2001.

● ALBUMS: *Message Man* (Ice 1977) ★★★, *Walking On Sunshine* (Ice 1979) ★★★, *Love In Exile* (Ice 1980) ★★★, *Can't Get Enough* (Ice 1981) ★★★, *Live At Notting Hill* (Ice 1981) ★★, *Paintings Of The Soul* (Ice 1982) ★★★, *Killer On The Rampage* (Ice/RCA 1982) ★★★, *Can't Get Enough* (Ice/RCA 1983) ★★★, *Going For Broke* (Ice/RCA 1984) ★★, *Born Tuff* (Ice 1987) ★★, *File Under Rock* (Parlophone 1988) ★★★, *Paintings Of The Soul* (Ice 1992) ★★★, *Hearts And Diamonds* (Ice 1999) ★★★.

● COMPILATIONS: *All The Hits: The Killer At His Best* (K-Tel 1984) ★★, *Hits* (Starr 1988) ★★, *Walking On Sunshine (The Best Of Eddy Grant)* (Parlophone 1989) ★★★, *Greatest Hits Collection* (Ice/Castle 1999) ★★★★, *Hits From The Frontline* (Music Club 1999) ★★★, *The Greatest Hits* (Ice/EastWest 2001) ★★★★.

● DVD/VIDEOS: *Live In London* (PMI 1986), *Walking On Sunshine* (PMI 1989).

Grant, Gogi

b. Myrtle Audrey Arinsberg, 20 September 1924, Philadelphia, Pennsylvania, USA. Pop vocalist Grant was apparently named after a New York restaurant called Gogi's La Rue, which was frequented by Dave Kapp, head of A&R at **RCA Records**. She had previously recorded, without success, as Audrey Brown and Audrey Grant, but as Gogi Grant she hit the US Top 10 in 1955 with the ballad 'Suddenly There's A Valley'. Her biggest hit came a year later with a sad ballad about lost love, 'The Wayward Wind', which shot to number 1 in the USA and reached the Top 10 in the UK. After signing to RCA Victor she was heavily marketed as an easy-listening singer. She provided all the vocals for actress Ann Blyth's portrayal of 1920s torch singer **Helen Morgan** in the 1957 biopic *The Helen Morgan Story*.

● ALBUMS: *Suddenly There's Gogi Grant* (Era 1956) ★★★, *The Helen Morgan Story* film soundtrack (RCA Victor 1957) ★★★, *Welcome To My Heart* (RCA Victor 1958) ★★★, *Torch Time* (RCA Victor 1959) ★★, *Kiss Me Kate* (RCA Victor 1959) ★★, *Granted . . . It's Gogi* (RCA Victor 1960) ★★, *If You Want To Get To Heaven, Shout* (Liberty 1960) ★★, *The Wayward Wind* (Era 1960) ★★★.

● COMPILATIONS: *Her Very Best* (Varèse Sarabande 2002) ★★★.

● FILMS: *The Big Beat* (1957).

Grant, James

b. 8 October 1964, Scotland. Formerly the guitarist/vocalist with acclaimed indie pop band **Love And Money**, and prior to that a member of **Friends Again**, singer-songwriter James

Grant launched a solo recording career in the mid-90s. He was introduced to producer Donald Shaw when he worked on **Capercaillie** vocalist Karen Matheson's debut solo album, *The Dreaming Sea*. The two teamed up again on Grant's 1998 debut *Sawdust In My Veins*, an unusual title that was actually lifted from a line in the classic movie *The Greatest Show On Earth*. The album explored a more acoustic-based direction than Grant's earlier work with Love And Money, with Grant's rich baritone, fluid guitar work and melancholic lyrics in stark contrast to the pop funk sound pursued by that band. Grant and Shaw then collaborated on a soundtrack for the film *Transitions*, for which Grant edited and read a selection of modern Scottish poetry. This approach later informed Grant's 2002 release *I Shot The Albatross* with works by poets such as Helen Adams, W.H. Auden, Charles Bukowski, e.e. cummings and Edwin Muir set to music. This project was preceded by Grant's second studio album, *My Thrawn Glory*, one of 2001's finest but sadly overlooked UK releases. The title track and 'Religion', in particular, were prime examples of a remarkable songwriting talent. Grant's career reached a mature peak with the 2004 release, *Holy Love*, his first for Sanctuary Records. Featuring support from long-term collaborators Shaw, Matheson, and Monica Queen, the stripped-down production brought the intimate details of Grant's songwriting into focus, making *Holy Love* truly an album that repaid repeat listening.

● ALBUMS: *Sawdust In My Veins* (Survival 1998) ★★★, *My Thrawn Glory* (Vertical 2001) ★★★★, *I Shot The Albatross* (Vertical 2002) ★★★, *Holy Love* (Sanctuary 2004) ★★★★.

Grant, Julie

b. Vivian Foreman, 12 July 1946, Blackpool, Lancashire, England. A product of early 60s vintage UK pop, Grant found some success with a string of singles for **Pye Records**. Her half-beehive hairstyle and angular eye make-up was seen regularly on package tours and UK television. **Tony Hatch** signed Grant to the Pye label and guided her career for a number of years. Her manager was Eric Easton, who briefly managed the **Rolling Stones**, with whom she shared the bill on their first major package tour. Her 1962 cover version of the **Drifters**' 'Up On The Roof' made the UK hit parade but was overtaken by **Kenny Lynch**'s version. Nevertheless, she bounced back with 'Count On Me', reaching number 24—her highest (and penultimate) chart placing. However, after 1964's 'Come To Me', a tempestuous ballad that was frequently played on the BBC Light Programme, and, consequently made its way to the edge of the Top 30, Grant's fortunes on record declined. She relocated to the USA in 1967 after joining a Spanish group, the Zaras. She was romantically linked to the lead singer and the couple married a few years later. She continued performing during the 70s and is now involved in music business management with her present husband, David Connelly.

● COMPILATIONS: *Come To Me: The Pye Anthology* (Castle 2004) ★★★.

Grant, Norman

(see **Twinkle Brothers**)

Grant, Peter

b. 5 April 1935, London, England, d. 21 November 1995. Best known as the heavyweight manager of UK rock group **Led**

Zeppelin, Grant began his career as a wrestler (Count Bruno Alessio of Milan). He also enjoyed spells as an actor, deputizing for Robert Morley and appearing among many others in the UK television series *Dixon Of Dock Green* and the *Benny Hill Show*. Grant learned his trade in the pop business from the notorious **Don Arden**, then went on to manage his own acts, sharing an office for many years with **Mickie Most**. His first discoveries, the Flintstones and the She Trinity, were unsuccessful, but the **New Vaudeville Band** did a little better. Having already worked with **Jimmy Page** as a busy session musician, he was then approached by manager **Simon Napier-Bell** with a view to overseeing the career of the fragmenting **Yardbirds**. This eventually resulted in the formation and management of Led Zeppelin. Under Grant's tutelage they became one of the biggest-selling albums bands in the world. Grant's speciality was the American tour, from which he gained his charges enormous amounts of money. During his heyday, Grant was one of the fiercest and most feared entrepreneurs in the rock business, a reputation that often worked to Led Zeppelin's advantage.

During the 70s, Grant co-managed other acts, including **Bad Company** and **Maggie Bell**, who appeared on Led Zeppelin's Swansong label along with the **Pretty Things**, which was also co-owned by Grant. However, the label failed to establish an identity beyond Led Zeppelin. Grant, like many others, fell victim to the excesses that were associated with Led Zeppelin at their most decadent, and following the break-up of his marriage he spent most of the 80s in relative retirement at his huge 15th-century manor house in Sussex and later in a humble apartment in Eastborne. During this time he suffered heart problems, although in the mid-90s he was to be seen at music business functions. He died following a heart attack at his home in 1995.

Grant's gangster image and success should not cloud his immense qualities as a human being. Throughout the heady years of touring he always put the welfare of his own family and children high on his list. He was similarly protective and loyal to his artists, especially Led Zeppelin. He became much more than merely a manager, and was the first of this type of svengali.

● FURTHER READING: *Peter Grant: The Man Who Led Zeppelin*, Chris Welch.

Granz, Norman

b. 6 August 1918, Los Angeles, California, USA, d. 22 November 2001, Geneva, Switzerland. A lifelong love of jazz led to Granz's early involvement in music as both film maker and concert promoter. Together with photographer Gjon Mili, he made *Jammin' The Blues* (1944), still regarded as one of the best jazz short films ever made. Granz also promoted jazz sessions at Los Angeles clubs, insisting upon desegregated audiences. In 1944 he staged a jazz concert at the Philharmonic Auditorium in Los Angeles, an event whose title was shortened to fit the available advertising space. The abbreviated version, **Jazz At The Philharmonic**, or JATP, became synonymous with concert-hall jam sessions featuring the very best jazz talent. A few of the saxophonists who played at JATP in its formative years were **Lester Young**, **Coleman Hawkins**, **Charlie Parker**, **Benny Carter**, **Charlie Ventura**, **Illinois Jacquet**, **Willie Smith** and **Flip Phillips**.

Granz insisted on desegregated audiences and first-class travel and hotel accommodation—things of which jazz musicians, especially those who were black, had previously

only dreamed. From the start, Granz recorded his concerts and eventually began releasing them, often on labels he owned or controlled, among them Clef, Norgran, **Verve Records** and Pablo. On recording sessions, Granz arranged for the return to the studios of several musicians who had been neglected by the major record companies. Among those whose careers were resuscitated was **Art Tatum**, whom Granz recorded with a wide range of musical partners and also in an extensive series of solo albums. Granz became personal manager for some of the artists he promoted, notably **Ella Fitzgerald**, with whom he recorded the remarkable 'Song Book' sequence of albums, and **Oscar Peterson**. Granz was also responsible for recording much of **Billie Holiday**'s later work. He received the *DownBeat* lifetime achievement award in 1989.

In appraising Granz's remarkable career it is astonishing to wade through the cavalcade of names he not only knew well but with whom he formed productive working partnerships. The back catalogue of Verve Records alone is a testament to his greatness and undiminished enthusiasm for popular music.

● FURTHER READING: *The White Moses Of Black Jazz*, Dempsey J. Travis.

Grapefruit

Formed in Britain during 1967, Grapefruit was originally comprised of three former members of harmony group Tony Rivers And The Castaways—John Perry (b. 16 July 1949, London, England; lead guitar/vocals), Pete Sweetenham (b. 24 April 1949, London, England; rhythm guitar/vocals) and Geoff Sweetenham (b. 8 March 1948, London, England; drums)—and songwriter George Alexander (b. 28 December 1946; Glasgow, Scotland; bass/vocals). The quartet, named by **John Lennon** (after the title of a book written by **Yoko Ono**), was the first act signed to the **Beatles**' Apple publishing company, whose faith was confirmed when Grapefruit's debut single, 'Dear Delilah', became a UK Top 30 hit. Alexander's penchant for high-quality British pop was matched by **Terry Melcher**'s sympathetic production, but despite several equally excellent follow-up releases, the group's only other chart entry was 'C'mon Marianne', originally recorded by the **Four Seasons**. By 1969 Mick Fowler (keyboards) had been added to the line-up, while Geoff Sweetenham was later replaced by Bobby Ware. *Deep Water* revealed an unsatisfactory soul/rock perspective and Alexander subsequently dissolved the band. He joined former **Easybeats** members George Young and Harry Vanda (Young and Alexander were brothers) for a variety of projects issued under different names. The Grapefruit appellation was briefly revived in 1971 for 'Universal Party', a melodic pop song redolent of the act's initial releases, although it failed to make a similar impact on the singles chart.

● ALBUMS: *Around Grapefruit* (Dunhill 1968) ★★★, *Deep Water* (RCA Victor 1969) ★★.

Grappelli, Stéphane

b. 26 January 1908, Paris, France, d. 1 December 1997, Paris, France. After learning to play keyboard instruments, Grappelli took up the violin, later studying it formally. In the mid-20s he played in dance bands in Paris, gradually turning more to jazz. In the early 30s he met **Django Reinhardt** and with him formed the Quintette du Hot Club de France. Until this point in his career Grappelli had been playing piano and violin, but now concentrated on the latter instrument. Performances and especially records by the QHCF alerted the jazz world to the arrival of both an intriguing new sound and, in Reinhardt, the first authentic non-American genius of jazz. In these years Grappelli was still learning, and his early popularity was largely a result of that of his collaborator. Shortly before the outbreak of World War II Grappelli settled in London, where he played with **George Shearing**. In the post-war years he worked briefly with Reinhardt again but spent the late 40s and 50s playing to diminishing audiences across Europe.

In the 60s Grappelli enjoyed a revival of popularity, making records with other violinists such as **Stuff Smith** and **Joe Venuti**. In the early 70s he appeared on UK television performing duets with classical violinist Yehudi Menuhin, and the records they made together sold well. However, Grappelli's real breakthrough to the big time had come when, at the urging of **Diz Disley**, he made appearances at the 1973 UK **Cambridge Folk Festival** (accompanied by Disley and **Denny Wright**). Grappelli was a sensation. For the rest of the decade, throughout the 80s and into the early 90s he was on a non-stop tour of the world, playing the most prestigious venues in the UK, Europe, the USA and the Far East. In January 1994, he celebrated his 86th birthday in concert with **Stanley Black** at London's Barbican Hall.

Grappelli made records with several backing groups, played duets with **Gary Burton**, **Earl Hines**, **Martial Solal**, **Jean-Luc Ponty** and many other leading jazzmen. He also ventured into other areas of music and, in addition to the duets with Menuhin, he recorded with the western swing fiddler, **Vassar Clements**. At ease with a repertoire based upon his early career successes, Grappelli's flowing style steadily matured over the years and the occasional uncertainties of his early work with Reinhardt are long forgotten. Perhaps at odd moments in his later years he seemed to be coasting, yet some of his recorded performances are very good while several of those from the mid- and late 70s are among the most distinguished in the history of jazz violin. Of particular merit are *Parisian Thoroughfare*, recorded with the rhythm section of **Roland Hanna**, **George Mraz** and **Mel Lewis**, and a set recorded at the Queen Elizabeth Hall in London in 1973 when he was backed by Disley and **Len Skeat**. Grappelli's late flowering prompted appreciation of the old tradition of jazz violin playing. His death at the end of 1997 left a gap in music that is unlikely to ever be filled, and probably never to be bettered.

● ALBUMS: *Improvisations* (EmArcy 1957) ★★★, with Stuff Smith *Violins No End* (Verve 1957) ★★★, *Feeling + Finesse = Jazz* (Atlantic 1962) ★★★, with Svend Asmussen *Two Of A Kind* (Storyville 1965) ★★★★, with Asmussen, Smith, Jean-Luc Ponty *Violin Summit* (MPS 1966) ★★★★, *I Remember Django* (Black Lion 1969) ★★★★, with Joe Venuti *Venupelli Blues* (Charly 1969) ★★★★, *Afternoon In Paris* (MPS 1971) ★★★, *Recorded Live At The Queen Elizabeth Hall, London* (Pye 1971) ★★★★, *Satin Doll* (Vanguard 1972) ★★★, *I Got Rhythm* (Black Lion 1973) ★★★★, *Just One Of Those Things* (Angel 1973) ★★★, *Stéphane Grappelli & Jean-Luc Ponty* (Musidisc France 1973) ★★★★, *Live In London* (Black Lion 1973) ★★★★, with Earl Hines *Giants* (Black Lion 1974) ★★★, with Baden Powell *La Grande Réunion* (Imagem 1974) ★★★★, *Violinspiration* (Pausa 1975), with George Shearing *The Reunion* (MPS 1976) ★★★, *Steph' 'N' Us* (Cherry Pie

1977) ★★★, *Live At Carnegie Hall* (Doctor Jazz 1978) ★★★★, with Larry Coryell, Niels-Henning Ørsted Pedersen *Young Django* (MPS 1979) ★★★, *Tivoli Gardens, Copenhagen, Denmark* (Pablo 1979) ★★★, *We've Got The World On A String* (IA 1980) ★★★★, *At The Winery* (Concord Jazz 1980) ★★★★, with David Grisman *Live* (Warners 1981) ★★★★, *Vintage 1981* (Concord Jazz 1981) ★★★, *Stephanova* (Concord Jazz 1983) ★★★, with Teresa Brewer *On The Road Again* (Doctor Jazz 1984) ★★★, with Vassar Clements *Together At Last* (Flying Fish 1985) ★★★, with Helen Merrill, Gordon Beck, Steve Lacy *Music Makers* (Owl 1986) ★★★, *Plays Jerome Kern* (GRP 1987) ★★★, *In Tokyo* (Denon 1990) ★★★, *Piano My Other Love* (Columbia 1990) ★★★, with Michel Petrucciani *Flamingo* (Dreyfus 1996) ★★★★, *Live At The Blue Note* (Telarc 1996) ★★★, *Limehouse Blues* 1969 recording (Black Lion 1998) ★★★, *Live In Toronto* 1986 recording (Justin Time 1999) ★★★, *Live In San Francisco* 1982 (Storyville 1999) ★★★, *Live At The Cambridge Folk Festival* 1983 recording (Strange Fruit 2000) ★★★.

● COMPILATIONS: *1935–1940* (Classics) ★★★★, *1941–1943* (Classics) ★★★★, *Parisian Thoroughfare* (Delta 1973) ★★★★, *Verve Jazz Masters* (Verve 1994) ★★★★, *Is Jazz* (Music Club 1999) ★★★, *Vintage Grappelli* (Concord Jazz 2001) ★★★★, *Collection* (Castle 2002) ★★★, *Timeless* (Savoy Jazz 2003) ★★★★.

● FURTHER READING: *Stéphane Grappelli*, Geoffrey Smith. *Stéphane Grappelli, Or, The Violin With Wings*, Raymond Horricks.

Grascals

Accomplished bluegrass outfit the Grascals is the recording outlet for six experienced session players; Jamie Johnson (b. Indiana, USA; guitar/vocals), Danny Roberts (b. Kentucky, USA; mandolin), David Talbot (b. Canada; banjo/vocals), Jimmy Mattingly (b. Kentucky, USA; fiddle), Terry Smith (bass) and Terry Eldredge (b. Indiana, USA; vocals). Between them the sextet can boast experience performing with artists including **Bill Monroe**, **Jimmy Martin**, **Lonzo And Oscar** and **Wilma Lee Cooper**. Eldredge, Smith and Mattingly also played together on stage with the **Osborne Brothers**, while Talbot and Eldredge spent several years with Larry Cordle And Lonesome Standard Time. Most of the members also worked together in the Sidemen, playing every week on a Tuesday night at the Station Inn in Nashville. The six musicians came together as the Grascals in summer 2004 and were signed by **Rounder Records** on the strength of their demo recording. Shortly afterwards the sextet was recruited to back **Dolly Parton** on her 2004 tour. Their duet with Parton on a bluegrass version of the **Elvis Presley** hit 'Viva Las Vegas' shot into the upper regions of the country singles listings and also broke into the pop charts later in the year. The sextet made their debut on the *Grand Ole Opry* shortly before the release of their self-titled debut in February 2005. The album featured original material by Johnson and Talbot alongside rousing interpretations of standards including 'My Saro Jane', 'Sally Goodin', and 'Sweet By And By'.

● ALBUMS: *The Grascals* (Rounder 2005) ★★★★.

Grass Roots

Although several Californian acts claimed this sobriquet, including the embryonic **Love**, it was appropriated by songwriters **P.F. Sloan** and **Steve Barri**, who employed the name pseudonymously on several folk rock performances. When 'Where Were You When I Needed You?' reached the US Top 30 in 1966, the need for a permanent line-up arose, and the duo enticed Warren Entner (b. 7 July 1944, Boston, Massachusetts, USA; vocals/guitar), Creed Bratton (b. 8 February 1943, Sacramento, California, USA; guitar), Rob Grill (b. 30 November 1944, Los Angeles, California, USA; vocals/bass) and Rick Coonce (b. Erik Michael Coonce, 1 August 1947, Los Angeles, California, USA; drums) to adopt the Grass Roots name. The new unit enjoyed immediate success with 'Let's Live For Today', a remake of an Italian hit. This distanced the quartet from their mentors, but although Sloan's input decreased dramatically, Barri retained his role as producer. The Grass Roots then became one of America's leading commercial attractions with a series of confident, if undemanding, performances, including 'Midnight Confessions' (1968), 'Bella Linda' (1968), 'I'd Wait A Million Years' (1969) and 'Sooner Or Later' (1971). Later incarnations of the band, led by Rob Grill, enjoyed continuing popularity in the following decades, although the verve of their early work has largely evaporated.

● ALBUMS: *Where Were You When I Needed You* (Dunhill 1966) ★★★, *Let's Live For Today* (Dunhill 1967) ★★★, *Feelings* (Dunhill 1968) ★★★, *Lovin' Things* (Dunhill 1969) ★★★, *Leaving It All Behind* (Dunhill 1969) ★★★, *Move Along* (Dunhill 1972) ★★, *A Lotta' Mileage* (Dunhill 1973) ★★, *Symphonic Hits* (Purple Pyramid 2001) ★★★.

● COMPILATIONS: *Golden Grass (Their Greatest Hits)* (Dunhill 1968) ★★★, *More Golden Grass* (Dunhill 1970) ★★, *Their Sixteen Greatest Hits* (Dunhill 1974) ★★★, *Anthology 1965-1975* (Rhino 1991) ★★★★, *All-Time Greatest Hits* (MCA 1996) ★★★, *The Best Of The Grass Roots: The Millennium Collection* (MCA 2001) ★★★★.

Grass-Show

The horticultural nature of this quintet's name reflects their formation—Peter Agren and Erik Kinell met when they were both employed as gardeners by the city council of Falun, Sweden. Most of the time that could have been wasted in cutting back hydrangeas, however, was more creatively spent in listening to Agren's collection of **Beatles** and **XTC** tapes and playing air guitar on garden implements. After relocation to Stockholm and a succession of songwriting spells, EMI Sweden saw some potential in the pair's quirky harmonies and a proper band was formed, with the addition of Robert Gehring (guitar), Andrew Dry (bass) and Mattius Moberg (drums). The band's Scandinavian debut came to the attention of **Food Records** boss Andy Ross, who moved them into a communal flat in west London and secured them support slots with **Kula Shaker** and **Silver Sun**. The relocation was an appropriate move, as Grass-Show have always shown more affinity for the sounds of British new wave than the so-called 'Swedepop' of their compatriots. As if to highlight this, their debut album included a cover version of **Ace Of Base**'s 'All That She Wants', neatly dismembered in the style of a young **Elvis Costello**.

● ALBUMS: *Something Smells Good In Stinkville* (Food 1997) ★★★.

Grassi, Lou

b. 21 January 1947, Summit, New Jersey, USA. Grassi began playing drums at the age of 15. In the mid-60s, he served in the military, during which time he played in the 328th US Army Band meanwhile studying at the Navy School of Music at Norfolk, Virginia. Upon his discharge in 1968, Grassi, who had been developing an interest in free jazz and improvised music, decided to pursue this form and in the early 70s he worked with the Innermost Society, a mixed-media group that included singer **Sheila Jordan** and bass player **Jimmy Garrison**. He continued with his studies, attaining a Bachelor of Arts degree in music from Jersey City State College. His tutor there was Nick Cerrato and others who helped develop his percussion skills included Tony Inzalaco, Sam Ulano, and in particular **Beaver Harris**, whom he met in 1973. His work with the latter was aided by the award in 1974 of a National Endowment of the Arts Fellowship. In addition to all of this, Grassi was studying arranging with **Marshall Brown**.

From the late 70s, Grassi moved away from his *avant garde* leanings, working in a remarkably varied range of musical settings, including appearing, often on record, with **Marshall Allen**, **Billy Bang**, **Borah Bergman**, **Charles Gayle**, **Vinny Golia**, **Urbie Green**, **Gunter Hampel**, **Johnny Hartman**, Phillip Johnston, **Perry Robinson**, **Roswell Rudd**, **John Tchicai** and **Mark Whitecage**, among many. In 1980, he formed his own quintet, playing a highly eclectic repertoire that drew upon many areas of jazz. In addition to playing throughout the USA and Canada, Grassi has played in Germany, Portugal and France, and in 1984 he was sponsored by the US Department of Defence for a tour of Central America leading a traditional jazz band, the Dixie Peppers. In 1985-87 he toured the USA with ragtime pianist Max Morath. It was during a 1989 tour of dixieland festivals in north and central Europe, with the Syncopatin' Seven, a band led by Warren Vaché Snr., that Grassi encountered the German keyboard player Andreas Böttcher, in whom he found a kindred free music spirit. From 1992 onwards, the pair began playing regular concerts and making records.

By 1994, and the start of his association with the New York group formed by **William Parker** and Patricia Nicholson Parker, the Improviser's Collective, Grassi had begun his return to the *avant garde* and this time it was as a prime mover, something that was highlighted by his very well received live concert recording released as *PoGressions*, and with the Lou Grassi PoBand, which plays a fierily exuberant yet cogent form of free jazz. The PoBand has been joined for records by artists such as John Tchicai (*ComPOsed*), Marshall Allen (*PoZest*), and **Joseph Jarman** (*Joy Of Being*). Grassi's own groups include a zesty sextet and the highly stimulating Neo Neo band. Best known is the Nu Band, of which he is co-leader with trumpeter **Roy Campbell** and has included Whitecage and bass player Joe Fonda. He has also appeared as co-leader of other groups, including the Implicate Order, with Ursel Schlicht (a band that includes trombonist Steve Swell and bass player Ken Filiano), Large Music (with trumpeter **Paul Smoker**, tenor saxophonist **Bob Magnuson** and Filiano), and a duo with trombonist Günter Heinz. Additionally, he has recorded with alto saxophonist **Rob Brown**, guitarist Bruce Eisenbeil, saxophonist William Gagliardi, pianist Burton Greene, trumpeter Matt Lavelle, and Swell.

In addition to his jazz work, Grassi also plays in musical theatre groups and has composed music for modern dance ensembles. Among these have been associations with the Daniel Nagrin Workgroup in 1971, the Dance Department at Brockport State University in 1973, and at New Jersey City University since 1979. Among choreographers with whom he has worked as composer are Richard Bull, Bill T. Jones, Lois Welk, Paul Wilson and Arnie Zane.

● ALBUMS: with the Dixie Peppers *Hot And Sweet* cassette (Elgee 1984) ★★, with Andreas Böttcher *Free Improvisation* cassette (Bridge 1992) ★★, with Böttcher *Noises From An Open Window* (Bridge 1994) ★★★, *PoGressions* (Cadence 1995) ★★★★, with the Saxtet *Quick Wits* (Cadence 1996) ★★★, with Rob Brown *Scratching The Surface* (CIMP 1997) ★★★, with the Po'Band *Mo' Po* (CIMP 1997) ★★★★, with Bob Magnuson *Creative Catalysts* (CIMP 1997) ★★★, with Tom Varner, Ron Horton, Tomas Ulrich *Neo Neo* (CIMP 1999) ★★★, *The Implicate Order: At Seixal* (Clean Feed 2000) ★★★, with the PoBand, Marshall Allen *PoZest* (CIMP 2000) ★★★, with Paul Smoker, Bob Magnuson, Ken Filiano *Large Music 1* (CIMP 2000) ★★★, with Smoker, Magnuson, Filiano *Large Music 2* (CIMP 2001) ★★★, with the PoBand, Joseph Jarman *Joy Of Being* (CIMP 2001) ★★★★, with Günter Heinz *Live In Wuppertal* (Alea 2001) ★★★, *The Nu Band Live At The Bop Shop* (Clean Feed 2001) ★★★, with the PoBand, John Tchicai *ComPOsed* (CIMP 2002) ★★★★, with David Wertman, Charlie Kohlhase *NorthCountry Pie* (CIMP 2002) ★★★, with Tchicai, Pierre Dørge *Hope Is Bright Green Up North* (CIMP 2003) ★★★, *Avanti Galoppi* (CIMP 2004) ★★★.

Grasso, Francis
(see **Mancuso, David**)

Grateful Dead

The enigmatic, erratic and mercurial (cliché, but absolutely true) Grateful Dead evolved from Mother McCree's Uptown Jug Champions to become the Warlocks in 1965. A number of conflicting reasons for the choice of name have arisen over the years. The most popular one is that the name was chosen from a randomly opened copy of the *Oxford Companion To Classical Music* (others say a Funk & Wagnells dictionary and **Phil Lesh** cites the *Britannica World Language Dictionary*) the juxtaposition of words evidently immediately appealing to Garcia and his chums, who at the time were somewhat chemically stimulated on DMT. The theory that it came from the *Egyptian Book Of The Dead* has been denied by each member of the band. The original line-up comprised **Jerry Garcia** (b. Jerome John Garcia, 1 August 1942, San Francisco, California, USA, d. 9 August 1995, Forest Knolls, California, USA; lead guitar), **Bob Weir** (b. Robert Hall, 16 October 1947, San Francisco, California, USA; rhythm guitar), Phil Lesh (b. Philip Chapman, 15 March 1940, Berkeley, California, USA; bass), Ron 'Pigpen' McKernan (b. 8 September 1945, San Bruno, California, USA. d. 8 March 1973; keyboards) and Bill Kreutzmann (b. 7 April 1946, Palo Alto, California, USA; drums). The Grateful Dead have been synonymous with the San Francisco/Acid Rock scene since its inception in 1965, when they took part in Ken Kesey's Acid Tests. Stanley Owsley manufactured the then legal LSD and plied the band and their friends with copious amounts. This hallucinogenic opus was duly recorded onto tape over a six-month period, and documented in Tom Wolfe's book *The Electric Kool-Aid Acid Test*. Wolfe stated that 'They were not to be psychedelic dabblers, painting pretty pictures, but true explorers.'

Their music, which started out as straightforward rock, blues and R&B, germinated into a hybrid of styles, but has the distinction of being long, wandering and improvisational. By the time their first album was released in 1967 they were already a huge local cult band. *Grateful Dead* sounds raw in the light of 90s record production, but it was a brave, early attempt to capture a live concert sound on a studio album. 'Cold Rain And Snow' and 'The Golden Road To Unlimited Devotion' are short compositions that could have been successful pop singles, had Warner Brothers known how to market the band. The follow-up **Anthem Of The Sun** was much more satisfying. On this alleged 'live' record, 17 different concerts and four different live studios were used. The non-stop suite of ambitious segments with tantalizing titles such as 'The Faster We Go, The Rounder We Get' and 'Quadlibet For Tenderfeet' was an artistic success. Their innovative and colourful album covers were among the finest examples of San Franciscan art, utilizing the talents of Kelley Mouse Studios (Alton Kelley and Stanley Mouse). The third album contained structured songs and was not as inaccessible as the palindrome title **Aoxomoxoa** suggested. Hints of a mellowing Grateful Dead surfaced on 'China Cat Sunflower' and the sublime 'Mountains Of The Moon', complete with medieval-sounding harpsichord. It was with this album that their lyrics came under close scrutiny as being something special. In particular those by additional member **Robert Hunter** (b. 23 June 1941, Arroyo Grande, California, USA), who wrote mysterious tales of intrigue.

In concert, the band was playing longer and longer sets, sometimes lasting six hours with only as many songs. Their legion of fans, now known as 'Deadheads' relished the possibility of a marathon concert. It was never ascertained who imbibed more psychedelic chemicals, the audience or the band. Nevertheless, the sounds produced sometimes took them to breathtaking heights of musical achievement. The interplay between Garcia's shrill, flowing solos and Lesh's meandering bass lines complemented the adventurous jazzy chords of Weir's rhythm guitar. The band had now added a second drummer, **Mickey Hart** (b. 11 September 1943, New York, USA), and a second keyboard player, Tom Constanten, to accompany the unstable McKernan, who had, by now, a severe drinking problem. It was this line-up that produced the seminal double album **Live/Dead** in 1970. Their peak of improvisation is best demonstrated on the track 'Dark Star'. During its 23 minutes of recorded life, the music simmers, builds and explodes four times, each with a crescendo of superb playing from Garcia and his colleagues. For many, this one song was the epitome of what the band was all about.

On the two following records **Workingman's Dead** and **American Beauty**, a strong **Crosby, Stills And Nash** harmony influence prevailed. The short, country-feel songs brought Garcia's pedal steel guitar to the fore (he had recently guested on **Crosby, Stills, Nash And Young**'s *Déjà Vu*). Uplifting songs such as 'Uncle John's Band', 'Ripple' and 'Till The Morning Come' were shared with powerful yet sentimental ballads such as 'Attics Of My Life', 'Brokendown Palace' and 'High Time'. These two outstanding albums were like sister and brother, and broke the band to a much wider audience. Paradoxically, the 'Dead' reverted to releasing live sets by issuing a second, self-titled double album (originally to be named *Skullfuck*), closely followed by the triple, *Europe '72*. After years of ill health through alcohol abuse, McKernan died in 1973. He was replaced by Keith Godchaux from **Dave Mason**'s band, who, together with his wife Donna on vocals, compensated for the tragic loss of Pigpen. *Wake Of The*

Flood in 1973 showed a delicate jazz influence and proved to be their most commercially successful album to date. With this and subsequent studio albums the band produced a more mellow sound. It was not until *Terrapin Station* in 1977 that their gradual move towards beautiful lethargy was averted. Producer Keith Olsen expertly introduced a fuller, more orchestrated sound, and forced them to be more musically disciplined in the studio.

As a touring band the Grateful Dead continued to prosper, but their studio albums began to lose direction. For the funky but disappointing *Shakedown Street* they enlisted **Little Feat**'s **Lowell George** as producer. Although they had been with the band for some years, Keith and Donna Godchaux had never truly fitted in. Donna often had trouble with her vocal pitch, resulting in some excruciating performances, while Keith began to use hard drugs. They were asked to leave at the end of 1979 and on 21 July 1980, Keith was killed in a car crash. *Go To Heaven* (1980) with new keyboard player Brent Mydland betrayed a hint of disco pop. The album sleeve showed the band posing in white suits which prompted 'Deadheads' to demand: 'Have they gone soft?' Ironically, it was this disappointing record that spawned their first, albeit minor, success in the US singles chart with 'Alabama Getaway'. All of the band had seriously experimented with drugs for many years and, unlike many of their contemporaries, had survived. Garcia, however, succumbed to heroin addiction in 1982. This retrospectively explained his somnolent playing and gradual decline as a guitarist over recent years, together with his often weak and shaky vocals. By the mid-80s, the band had become amorphous but still commanded a massive following. Garcia eventually collapsed and came close to death when he went into a diabetic coma in 1986.

The joy and relief of his survival showed in their first studio album in seven years, **In The Dark**. It was a stunning return to form, resulting in a worldwide hit single 'Touch Of Grey', with Garcia singing his long-time co-songwriter Robert Hunter's simplistic yet honest lyric: 'Oh well a touch of grey, kinda suits you anyway, that's all I've got to say, it's alright'. The band joined in for a joyous repeated chorus of 'I will survive' followed by 'We will survive'. They were even persuaded to make a video and the resulting exposure on **MTV** introduced them to a whole new generation of younger fans. The laconic Garcia humorously stated that he was 'appalled' to find they had a smash hit on their hands. Garcia attempted to get fit and to shake off years of drug abuse. While *Built To Last* (1989) was a dull affair, they continued to play to vast audiences. They have since received the accolade of being the largest grossing band in musical history. In August 1990 Mydland died from a lethal combination of cocaine and morphine. Remarkably, this was the third keyboard player to die in the band. Mydland's temporary replacement was **Bruce Hornsby** until Vince Welnick was recruited full-time. In 1990, the band's live album catalogue was increased with the release of the erratic *Without A Net* and the poor *Dylan And The Dead*.

The transcendental Grateful Dead have endured, throughout the many difficult stages in their long career. Their progress was again halted when Garcia became seriously ill with a lung infection. After a long spell in hospital Garcia returned, this time promising to listen to doctors' advice. They continued to tour throughout 1993 and 1994, after which they began to record a new studio album. However, on 9 August 1995, Garcia suffered a fatal heart attack, ironically while staying in Serenity Knolls, a drug treatment centre in Marin County. It was alleged he was found curled on his bed clutching an apple with a smile on his face. The reaction from the world press was surprisingly significant: Garcia would have had a wry grin at having finally achieved this kind of respectability all over the planet. The press were largely in agreement, concurring that a major talent in the world of music had passed on (either that or all the news editors on daily newspapers were all 40-something ex-hippies). In the USA the reaction was comparable to the death of President Kennedy, Martin Luther King, **Elvis Presley** and **John Lennon**. Within hours over 10,000 postings were made on the Internet, an all-night vigil took place in San Francisco and the president of the USA Bill Clinton gave him high praise and called him a genius. The mayor of San Francisco called for flags to be flown at half-mast and, appropriately, flew a tie dyed flag from city hall. **Bob Dylan** said that there was no way to measure his greatness or magnitude.

Garcia's high standing in the USA is undisputed, but it is hoped that he will be remembered elsewhere in the world not just as the man who played the familiar opening pedal steel guitar solo on Crosby, Stills And Nash's 'Teach Your Children'. Garcia was a giant who remained hip, humorous, philosophical, humble and credible right up to his untimely death. At a press conference in December 1995 the remaining band members announced that they would bury the band name along with Garcia. With no financial worries, the remaining members embarked on a number of solo projects to see them into the 21st century, which is precisely where many of their fans believed that they always belonged. In 1998, Lesh was hospitalized with hepatitis, which briefly curtailed his activity with Bob Weir in their new project, the Other Ones. In February 2003, Weir, Lesh, Hart and Kreutzmann announced they would be touring once again, this time as the Dead, in respect of Garcia. Guest musicians joining them have included **Joan Osborne** (vocals), Rob Barraco (keyboards/vocals), and **Warren Haynes** (guitar/vocals).

The Grateful Dead felt all the emotions of rock, folk, soul, R&B, blues and country music, and they played it always from the heart. The resulting sound was a hybrid that was unique to them. Sometimes they were ragged and occasionally they were lacklustre, but mostly they were outstanding in their ability to interact and improvise. Love or hate, black or white, it is impossible to be indifferent about the Grateful Dead's music. Quite simply, you either get it or you don't.

● ALBUMS: *The Grateful Dead* (Warners 1967) ★★★, *Anthem Of The Sun* (Warners 1968) ★★★★★, *Aoxomoxoa* (Warners 1969) ★★★★, *Live/Dead* (Warners 1970) ★★★★★, *Workingman's Dead* (Warners 1970) ★★★★★, *Vintage Dead* (Sunflower 1970) ★, *American Beauty* (Warners 1970) ★★★★★, *Historic Dead* (Sunflower 1971) ★, *Grateful Dead aka Skullfuck* (Warners 1971) ★★★★, *Europe '72* (Warners 1972) ★★★, *History Of The Grateful Dead, Vol. 1 (Bear's Choice)* (Warners 1973) ★★★, *Wake Of The Flood* (Grateful Dead 1973) ★★★★, *From The Mars Hotel* (Grateful Dead 1974) ★★★★, *Blues For Allah* (Grateful Dead 1975) ★★, *Steal Your Face* (Grateful Dead 1976) ★★, *Terrapin Station* (Arista 1977) ★★★★, *Shakedown Street* (Arista 1978) ★★, *Go To Heaven* (Arista 1980) ★, *Reckoning* (Arista 1981) ★★★, *Dead Set* (Arista 1981)

★★, *In The Dark* (Arista 1987) ★★★★, *Built To Last* (Arista 1989) ★★, with Bob Dylan *Dylan And The Dead* (Columbia 1990) ★, *Without A Net* (Arista 1990) ★★, *One From The Vault* (Grateful Dead 1991) ★★★, *Infrared Roses* (Grateful Dead 1991) ★★, *Two From The Vault* (Grateful Dead 1992) ★★★, *Dick's Picks, Volume One: Tampa, Florida, December 19 1973* (Grateful Dead 1993) ★★★, *Dick's Picks, Volume Two: Columbus, Ohio, October 31, 1971* (Grateful Dead 1995) ★★★, *Hundred Year Hall* (Arista 1995) ★★★★, *Dick's Picks, Volume Three: Pembroke Pines, Florida, May 22 1977* (Grateful Dead 1995) ★★★, *Dick's Picks, Volume Four: Fillmore East, New York, 13/14 February 1970* (Grateful Dead 1996) ★★★★, *Dick's Picks, Volume Five: Oakland Auditorium Arena, California, December 26 1979* (Grateful Dead 1996) ★★★, *Dozin' At The Knick* (Grateful Dead/Arista 1996) ★★★★, *Dick's Picks, Volume Six: Hartford Civic Center, October 14 1983* (Grateful Dead 1996) ★★★★, *Dick's Picks, Volume Seven: Alexandra Palace, London, England, September 1974* (Grateful Dead 1997) ★★, *Dick's Picks, Volume Eight: Harpur College, Binghamton, NY, May 2 1970* (Grateful Dead 1997) ★★★, *Fallout From The Phil Zone* (Grateful Dead/Arista 1997) ★★★★, *Dick's Picks, Volume Nine: Madison Square Garden, September 16 1990* 3-CD set (Grateful Dead 1997) ★★★, *Fillmore East 2-11-69* (Grateful Dead 1997) ★★★★, *Dick's Picks, Volume Ten: Winterland Arena, December 29 1977* (Grateful Dead 1998) ★★★★, *Dick's Picks, Volume Eleven: Stanley Theater, Jersey City, September 27 1972* (Grateful Dead 1998) ★★★, *Dick's Picks, Volume Twelve: Providence Civic, June 26 1974, Boston Garden, June 28 1974* (Grateful Dead 1998) ★★★, *Trouble Ahead, Trouble Behind: The Dead Live In Concert 1971* (Pinnacle 1999) ★★, *Dick's Picks, Volume Thirteen: Nassau Coliseum, New York, May 6 1981* (Grateful Dead 1999) ★★★★, *Dick's Picks, Volume Fourteen: Boston Music Hall, 30 November & 2 December 1973* (Grateful Dead 1999) ★★★★, *Dick's Picks, Volume Fifteen: Englishtown, New Jersey, September 3 1977* (Grateful Dead 1999) ★★★, *Dick's Picks, Volume Sixteen: Fillmore Auditorium, San Francisco, November 8 1969* (Grateful Dead 2000) ★★★, *Dick's Picks, Volume Seventeen: Boston Garden, September 25 1991* (Grateful Dead 2000) ★★★★, *View From The Vault Soundtrack 1990* live recording (Grateful Dead 2000) ★★★, *Dick's Picks, Volume Eighteen: Dane County Coliseum, February 3 1978, Uni-Dome, University Of North Iowa, February 5 1978* (Grateful Dead 2000) ★★★, *Ladies And Gentlemen . . . Fillmore East: New York City, April 1971* 4-CD set (Arista 2000) ★★★★, *Dick's Picks, Volume Nineteen: Fairgrounds Arena, Oklahoma City, OK, October 19 1973* (Grateful Dead 2000) ★★★, *Dick's Picks, Volume Twenty 1976 Capital Centre, Landover, Maryland, 25 September 1976/Onondaga County War Memorial, Syracuse, New York, 28 September 1976* (Grateful Dead 2001) ★★★, *Dick's Picks, Volume Twenty-One: Richmond Coliseum, Richmond, Vancouver, 1 November 1985* (Grateful Dead 2001) ★★★, *Dick's Picks, Volume Twenty-Two: Kings Beach Bowl, Kings Beach, Lake Tahoe, 23/24 February 1968* (Grateful Dead 2001) ★★★★, *View From The Vault II Soundtrack 1990/1991* live recordings (Grateful Dead 2001) ★★★, *Nightfall Of Diamonds* (Arista 2001) ★★★★, *Dick's Picks, Volume Twenty-Three: Baltimore Civic Center, September 17 1972* (Grateful Dead 2001) ★★★, *Steppin' Out With The Grateful Dead: England '72* 4-CD set (Grateful Dead 2002) ★★★, *Dick's Picks, Volume Twenty-Four: Cow Palace Daly City CA, 23 March 1974* (Grateful Dead 2002) ★★★, *Dick's Picks, Volume Twenty-Five: New Haven CT 10 May 1978, Springfield, MA, 11 May 1978* (Grateful Dead 2002) ★★★, *Dick's Picks 26: Electric Theatre, Chicago, Il, April 26 1969/Labor Temple, Minneapolis, MN, April 27 1969* (Grateful Dead 2002) ★★★, *Go To Nassau 1980* recording (Grateful Dead 2002) ★★★, *Dick's Picks 27: Oakland Coliseum Arena, Oakland, CA, December 16 1992* 3-CD set (Grateful Dead 2003) ★★, *Dick's Picks 28: Salt Palace, Salt Lake City, UT, February 28 1973/Pershing Municipal Auditorium, Lincoln, NE, February 26 1973* 4-CD set (Grateful Dead 2003) ★★★, *Dick's Picks 29: Fox Theatre, Atlanta, GA, May 19 1977/Lakeland Civic Center, Lakeland, Fl, May 21 1977* 6-CD set (Grateful Dead 2003) ★★★, *New Year's Eve: The Closing Of Winterland—December 31, 1978* 4-CD set (Grateful Dead/Rhino 2003) ★★★, *Dick's Picks 30: Academy Of Music, New York City, March 25 & 28 1972* 4-CD set (Grateful Dead 2004) ★★, *Dick's Picks 31: 8/4–5/74 Philadelphia Civic Center, Philadelphia, PA, 8/6/74 Roosevelt Stadium, Jersey City, NJ* 4-CD set (Grateful Dead 2004) ★★★★, *Rockin' The Rhein* 3-CD set (Grateful Dead/Rhino 2004) ★★★★, *Dick's Picks 32: 8/7/82 Alpine Valley Music Theatre, East Troy, WI* 2-CD set (Grateful Dead 2004) ★★★, *Dick's Picks 33: 10/9 & 10/76 Oakland Coliseum Stadium, Oakland, CA* 4-CD set (Grateful Dead 2004) ★★★, *The Grateful Dead Movie Soundtrack* 5-CD set (Rhino 2005) ★★★★, *Dick's Picks 34: 11/5/77 Community War Memorial, Rochester, NY* 3-CD set (Grateful Dead 2005) ★★★, *Fillmore West 1969: The Complete Recordings* 10-CD box set (Grateful Dead 2005) ★★★, *Truckin' Up To Buffalo, July 4 1989* (Grateful Dead 2005) ★★★.

● COMPILATIONS: *The Best Of: Skeletons From The Closet* (Warners 1974) ★★★★, *What A Long Strange Trip It's Been: The Best Of The Grateful Dead* (Warners 1977) ★★★★, *The Arista Years* (Arista 1996) ★★★, *So Many Roads (1965–1995)* 5-CD box set (Grateful Dead/Arista 1999) ★★★★★, *The Golden Road (1965–1973)* 12-CD box set (Rhino 2001) ★★★★★, *Postcards Of The Hanging: Grateful Dead Perform The Songs Of Bob Dylan* (Grateful Dead/Arista 2002) ★★★, *Birth Of The Dead* (Rhino 2003) ★★★, *The Very Best Of The Grateful Dead* (Warners 2003) ★★★★, *Beyond Description (1973–1989)* 12-CD box set (Rhino 2004) ★★★.

● DVD/VIDEOS: *In Concert* (RCA Video 1984), *So Far* (Virgin Vision 1988), *The Grateful Dead Movie* (Palace Premiere 1990), *Infrared Sightings* (Trigon 1995), *Dead Ahead* (Monterey 1995), *Backstage Pass: Access All Areas* (Pearson 1995), *Ticket To New Year's* (Monterey Home Video 1996), *Tie Died: Rock 'N' Roll's Most Dedicated Fans* (BMG Video 1996), *Downhill From Here* (Monterey 1997), *Anthem To Beauty* (Rhino Home Video 1998), *View From The Vault II* (Monterey Home Video 2001), *The Closing Of Winterland* (Rhino 2003), *The Grateful Dead Movie* (Grateful Dead 2004).

● FURTHER READING: *The Dead Book: A Social History Of The Grateful Dead*, Hank Harrison. *The Grateful Dead*, Hank Harrison. *Grateful Dead: The Official Book Of The Deadheads*, Paul Grushkin, Jonas Grushkin and Cynthia Bassett. *History Of The Grateful Dead*, William Ruhlmann. *Built To Last: Twenty-Five Years Of The Grateful Dead*, Jamie Jensen. *Drumming At The Edge Of Magic*, Mickey Hart. *Grateful Dead Family Album*, Jerilyn Lee Brandelius. *Sunshine Daydreams: Grateful Dead Journal*, Herb Greene. *Aesthetics*

Of The Grateful Dead, David Womack. *One More Saturday Night: Reflections With The Grateful Dead*, Sandy Troy. *Drumming At the Edge Of Magic*, Mickey Hart and Jay Stevens. *Planet Drum*, Mickey Hart and Fredric Lieberman. *Book Of The Dead: Celebrating 25 Years With The Grateful Dead*, Herb Greene. *Conversations With The Grateful Dead*, David Gans. *Story Of The Grateful Dead*, Adrian Hall. *Dead Base IX: Complete Guide To Grateful Dead Song Lists*, Nixon and Scot Dolgushkin. *Living With The Dead*, Rock Scully with David Dalton. *A Box Of Rain: Collected Lyrics Of Robert Hunter 1965–1993*, Robert Hunter. *Dead To The Core: A Grateful Dead Almanack*, Eric F. Wybenga. *The Music Never Stopped*, Blair Jackson. *Captain Trips: A Biography Of Jerry Garcia*, Sandy Troy. *Sweet Chaos: The Grateful Dead's American Adventure*, Carol Brightman. *Dark Star: An Oral Biography Of Jerry Garcia*, Robert Greenfield. *What A Long Strange Trip: The Stories Behind Every Grateful Dead Song 1965–1995*, Stephen Peters. *Garcia: An American Life*, Blair Jackson. *A Long Strange Trip: The Inside History Of The Grateful Dead*, Dennis McNally. *The Illustrated Trip*, Grateful Dead Productions. *Searching For The Sound*, Phil Lesh.

Grauso, Joe

b. 1897, New York City, USA, d. 11 June 1952. Grauso first played drums professionally while still a teenager, taking all manner of jobs in travelling shows and circuses. He also played in theatre pit bands, playing jazz gigs in-between times. After a period of poor health he returned to work in the early 40s, leading his own band and also playing with a number of jazzmen including **Art Hodes**, **Eddie Condon** and **Miff Mole**. He spent some time with the **Muggsy Spanier** band and also played drums with **Billy Butterfield**. A workmanlike drummer, as befits one who learned his trade in brass bands, Grauso supplied a solid foundation for the bands in which he played, although he perhaps lacked the finesse to provide the lift needed for exceptional jazz performances.

Grave

One of Scandinavia's heaviest death metal bands, this Swedish band started life as Corpse in 1986. Jorgen Sandstrom (vocals/guitar), Ola Lindgren (guitar), Jonas Torndal (bass) and Jensa Paulsson (drums) made several demo recordings under their new name before attracting the attention of the Century Media label, which issued the phenomenally brutal *Into The Grave* in 1991. Tours in Europe and the USA saw a fanbase grow, but led to the departure of Torndal. Sandstrom switched to bass and the remaining trio consolidated their reputation with 1992's *You'll Never See . . . .* An EP of rare Grave tracks, *. . . And Here I Die . . . Satisfied*, was recorded in 1993 and marked the end of the band's first (and best) phase. *Soulless* and *Hating Life* were cleaner, more technical albums and appealed to followers of the late-90s trend towards melodic death metal that had seen many rawer bands forced to evolve. Lindgren took over vocals on the latter as Sandstrom had left to join **Entombed**, which may explain its less visceral feel. After the release of a live album the band fell silent for some time before, in 1999, Lindgren and Paulsson reunited with Torndal (now on guitar) and recruited new bass player Frederik Isaksson.

● ALBUMS: *Into The Grave* (Century Media 1991) ★★★★, *You'll Never See . . .* (Century Media 1992) ★★★★, *Soulless* (Century Media 1994) ★★★, *Hating Life* (Century Media 1996) ★★★, *Extremely Rotten Live* (Century Media 1997) ★★★, *Back From The Grave* (Century Media 2003) ★★★.

Grave Digger

Originally comprising Chris Boltendahl (b. 2 January 1962, Gladbeck, Germany; vocals), Peter Masson (guitar), Willi Lackmann (bass) and Albert Eckardt (drums), German heavy metal unit Grave Digger has suffered from numerous personnel shifts during their career. Formed in 1980, they released their debut six-track demo shortly thereafter, but then broke up before any official releases could be planned. However, offered a contract in 1983 by Noise Records, the band re-formed to record a fiery rock track for inclusion on the German *Rock From Hell* sampler compilation, and led to sessions for a debut album. Several European tours were arranged, and by the mid-80s the band had established a strong live reputation in mainland Europe. C.F. Brank replaced Lackmann on 1986's *War Games*, following which the band recruited new guitarist Uwe Lulis and changed their name to Digger for the hard rocking *Stronger Than Ever*. The name change was to little avail and as Noise Records concentrated on developing new acts the band called it a day. Boltendahl resurrected Grave Digger in the early 90s, with Lulis (guitar), Tomi Göttlich (bass) and Jörg Michael (drums) joining him on *The Reaper*. Frank Ulrich replaced Michael on *Heart Of Darkness*, before in turn vacating the drum stool to Stefan Arnold (b. 29 August 1965, Rüsselsheim, Germany) for 1997's *Tunes Of War*. Jens Becker (b. 24 May 1965, Germany) replaced Göttlich on *Knights Of The Cross*, while H.P. Katzenburg (b. Köln, Germany; keyboards) made his debut on the follow-up *Excalibur*. New guitar player Manni Schmidt (b. Manfred Albert Schmidt, 27 November 1964, Andernach, Germany) joined Boltendahl, Becker, Arnold and Katzenburg in 2000. The band has continued to record studio albums into the new millennium but their sound is now significantly dated.

● ALBUMS: *Heavy Metal Breakdown* (Noise 1984) ★★★, *Witch Hunter* (Noise 1985) ★★★, *War Games* (Noise 1986) ★★★, as Digger *Stronger Than Ever* (Noise 1986) ★★★, *The Reaper* (Gun 1993) ★★, *Heart Of Darkness* (Gun 1995) ★★, *Tunes Of War* (Gun 1996) ★★, *Knights Of The Cross* (Gun 1998) ★, *Excalibur* (Gun 1999) ★, *The Grave Digger* (Nuclear Blast 2001) ★★.

● COMPILATIONS: *Best Of The Eighties* (Noise 1994) ★★★.

Gravediggaz

This New York, USA–based hip-hop 'supergroup' was formed by ex-**Stetsasonic** personnel **Prince Paul** (b. Paul Huston, USA) and Fruitkwan, renamed the Undertaker and the Gatekeeper respectively, plus Poetic the Grym Reaper aka Too Poetic (b. Anthony Berkeley, 1966, New York City, USA, d. 15 July 2001, Los Angeles, California, USA) and **RZA** the Rzarector. Poetic was formerly a member of the Grimm Brothers, while RZA was the production genius behind Staten Island's **Wu-Tang Clan**. Prince Paul started the group after his Doo Dew label collapsed, needing a new venture to express his frustration. He had originally contacted his fellow band members with the intention of putting together a compilation album. The outfit's debut single was 'Diary Of A Madman', which premiered their gothic/horror style, and utilized loops donated by producer RNS (famed for his work on **Shyheim**'s debut set). They toured in the USA with the Wu-Tang Clan, while Prince Paul went back to production work for **Soul II Soul** (having already recorded the groundbreaking *3 Feet High And Rising* with them) and **Living Colour**. Further work such as the *Nowhere To Run, Nowhere To Hide* EP and the *6 Feet Deep* set embossed a growing reputation for their horror-core hip-hop. By 1995, they were also considered by many to be the nearest US approximation of the UK's trip-hop scene. This impression was cemented by a collaboration with **Tricky** on *The Hell* EP, which entered the UK Top 40. The Wu-Tang production crew worked on *The Pick, The Sickle And The Shovel*, leaving RZA free to concentrate on his rhymes. Poetic died of colon cancer in July 2001, shortly after completing work on a third Gravediggaz album.

● ALBUMS: *6 Feet Deep* (Gee Street 1994) ★★, *The Pick, The Sickle And The Shovel* (Gee Street 1997) ★★★★, *Nightmare In A-Minor* (Echo 2001) ★★★.

Gravenhurst

UK neo-folk act Gravenhurst is the creation of the Bristol-based musician and songwriter Nick Talbot. Adopting the name of a song on US alt rock band Pullman's *Turnstyles And Junkpiles*, Talbot's variation on folk music notably takes in influences such as **Hüsker Dü** and **My Bloody Valentine**. Talbot has said his voice is so weak he has to 'coo' like the latter band's Bilinda Butcher. Talbot moved to Bristol in 1990, apparently drawn to the town after hearing records by **Flying Saucer Attack** and **Third Eye Foundation**. He played with the cult Bristol band Assembly Communications before founding the Silent Age Records label. Silent Age released Gravenhurst's 2002 debut *Internal Travels* as well as works by Mole Harness and War Against Sleep, before Gravenhurst's second album *Flashlight Seasons* was (perhaps unexpectedly) licensed by electronica label **Warp Records**. Tellingly, Talbot has admitted to being obsessed with horror movies because 'I'm interested in violence'. Nevertheless, Gravenhurst generally eschew overt violence in their music with Talbot even being compared to **Nick Drake**—a comparison the Gravenhurst vocalist vehemently rejects, suggesting Drake was 'disgustingly timid'. Lines such as 'I understand anger/I know what it is for' ('Tunnels' from *Flashlight Seasons*), 'You can't rely on those you turn to/They turn against you' ('Bluebeard' from *Flashlight Seasons*), and 'I've seen bad things in bad places' ('Song From Under The Arches' from 2005's *Fires In Distant Buildings*) are typical, and Gravenhurst has also covered Hüsker Dü's 'rape fantasy' 'Diane'. Gravenhurst notably appeared on the soundtrack album to *Dead Man's Shoes* (Warp), though their contribution ('The Diver') did not apparently appear in the film itself. Talbot additionally performs in 'horrortronica' outfit Bronnt Industries Kapital.

● ALBUMS: *Internal Travels* (Silent Age 2002) ★★★, *Flashlight Seasons* (Silent Age/Warp 2003) ★★★★, *Black Holes In The Sand* mini-album (Warp 2004) ★★★, *Fires In Distant Buildings* (Warp 2005) ★★★.

Gravenites, Nick

b. Chicago, Illinois, USA. Gravenites grew up on Chicago's south side. He entered university in 1956 and was immediately drawn to its bohemian circle. Having discovered several blues nightclubs, including Frader's Jukebox Lounge, Gravenites joined a loosely knit group of white aficionados, which included **Charlie Musselwhite**, **Mike**

Bloomfield and **Paul Butterfield**. The last-named recorded a Gravenites composition, 'Born In Chicago', on his band's debut album, but it was with Bloomfield that the artist forged a fruitful partnership. In 1967 they formed the short-lived **Electric Flag** and, having settled in San Francisco, the duo became an integral part of the Bay Area live circuit. *Live At Bill Graham's Fillmore West* captured part of one informal appearance while other tracks, recorded at the same show, formed the basis for Gravenites' solo debut *My Labors*. In addition to Gravenites' effortless blues vocals the set also featured some inspired playing from Bloomfield.

Gravenites also produced the debut album from **Quicksilver Messenger Service**. The group later recorded several of his compositions, notably 'Joseph's Coat', which Gravenites later took to **Big Brother And The Holding Company** during his tenure in the band. **Janis Joplin**, their former lead singer, meanwhile, completed an impassioned reading of his 'Work Me Lord' on *Kozmic Blues*. The artist wrote and performed part of the soundtrack of *Steelyard Blues* (1973), and remained an active figure during the 70s and 80s, fronting Nick Gravenites Blues, Monday Night Live (with **Huey Lewis**), as well as several projects with former Quicksilver guitarist **John Cipollina**. Gravenites remains a highly respected figure, particularly in Europe, where he has toured extensively. Andrew Lauder's Evangeline label reissued *My Labors* with extra tracks from the *Fillmore* album in 2002.

● ALBUMS: *My Labors* (Columbia 1969) ★★★★, *Blue Star* (Line 1980) ★★★, *Junkyard In Malibu* (Line 1981) ★★★, with John Cipollina *Monkey Medicine* (Big Beat 1982) ★★★, with Animal Mind *Kill My Brain* (2Burn1 1999) ★★★.

Graves, Josh

b. Burkett K. Graves, 27 September 1925, Tellico Springs, Tennessee, USA. One of the greatest of all dobro players and probably the first to have played the instrument in bluegrass music. Historian Bill C. Malone summarized Graves' abilities as follows: 'Graves perfected a rolling syncopated style that enabled him to play galloping breakdowns as well as slow love songs or ballads'. He was attracted to the dobro as a child on hearing **Cliff Carlisle** play on **Jimmie Rodgers'** recordings, and he later met Carlisle, who gave him help and encouragement. He was also influenced in his early career by the dobro playing of **Pete Kirby** (Bashful Brother Oswald). He learned not only dobro but also guitar and bass, and in 1942, he made his professional debut with the Pierce Brothers. After then playing with **Esco Hankins** in Knoxville, he played with **Molly O'Day** and **Mac Wiseman**, before joining **Stoney Cooper And Wilma Lee** on the WWVA **Wheeling Jamboree**. In 1957, he moved with them to the **Grand Ole Opry**, where he first met **Flatt And Scruggs**. He soon became a permanent member of their Foggy Mountain Boys, initially playing bass, but soon changing to dobro. He was impressed by Scruggs' brilliant three-fingered style of banjo playing which, with Scruggs' help, he soon adapted to the dobro. When Flatt And Scruggs split in 1969, he became a member of Flatt's Nashville Grass until 1971, when he joined the Earl Scruggs Revue until 1974. During the 60s and early 70s, he played on albums by both Flatt and Scruggs and as a session musician, he played albums by other artists including **Steve Young** and **Kris Kristofferson**.

In 1974, Graves left Scruggs to work as a session musician and to make solo appearances. He recorded his debut, *Alone*

At Last, for Epic Records and also appeared on releases by **Charlie McCoy**, **Boots Randolph** and **James Talley**. In 1975, he recorded a duet album with Jake Tullock as Uncle Jake And Uncle Josh (he had created Uncle Josh as an alter-ego comic character that he portrayed on stage, and he was friendly with Tullock from his days with Flatt And Scruggs). During the late 70s, he recorded with Bobby Smith and as one of **Joe Maphis**' Super Picker Pals while also recording solo albums for CMH. In the 80s, Graves, **Mike Auldridge** and **Jerry Douglas** produced *Dobro Summit*, an educational video, and he also played as a member of the Masters with **Eddie Adcock**, **Kenny Baker** and Jesse McReynolds. In 1988, he recorded an album with his son Billy Troy (guitar). In the 90s and 00s, Graves was still in demand for session work and was regularly making appearances on various radio and television shows.

● ALBUMS: with Kenny Baker *Something Different* (Puritan 1972) ★★, with Baker *Something Different* (Puritan 1972) ★★, with Graves Bucktime (Puritan 1973) ★★, *Alone At Last* (Epic 1974), *Uncle Josh & His Dobro* (Cottontown) ★★★, with Jake Tullock *Just Joshing* (Cottontown Jubilee 1975) ★★, with Bobby Smith *Sweet Sunny South* (CMH 1976) ★★★, *Bobby Smith & Josh Graves* (Vetco 1976) ★★★, *Same Old Blues* (CMH 1978) ★★★, with Smith *Smokin' Bluegrass* (CMH 1978) ★★★, with Vassar Clements *Sing Away The Pain* (CMH 1979) ★★★, *Josh Graves & Friends* 1962–63 recordings (Cowboy Carl 1979) ★★, *Playing It Simple* (Vetco 1980) ★★★, *King Of The Dobro* (CMH 1980) ★★★, with Red Taylor *Living Legends* (Old Homestead 1984) ★★★, with Baker *Flying South* (Ridge Runner 1986) ★★★, with Baker *Bluegrass Instrumentals* Swiss release (Montana 1988) ★★★, with Billy Troy *Dad The Dobro Man* (CMH 1988) ★★★, *The Real Josh* (Amber 1988) ★★★, with Baker *The Puritan Sessions* (Rebel 1989) ★★★, *Sultan Of Slide* (OMS 2001) ★★★.

Graves, Milford

b. 20 August 1941, New York City, USA. Born into a musical environment (his uncle and grandfather encouraged and coached his interest in music) Graves was playing drums at the age of three, though he had no formal teaching until he was 17. He took up congas when he was eight years old and led his own percussion ensemble and, later, workshops, while at school. He subsequently studied with George Stone in Boston and learned tabla techniques from Washantha Singh. Between 1959 and 1962 he played with dance and Latin bands around New York. He heard and was impressed by **Elvin Jones** with **John Coltrane**'s group in 1961 and in 1963 decided to concentrate on his own ideas rather than stay with commercial gigs. His first recordings were all on the ESP label and included appearances with the New York Art Quartet (with **John Tchicai**, **Archie Shepp** and Lewis Warrell), pianists Lowell Davidson and **Paul Bley** (*Barrage*), saxophonist **Giuseppi Logan** and his own *Percussion Duo* with Sunny Morgan. In 1965 he and **Don Pullen** set up their own SRP label, later releasing three duo albums and in 1969 Graves began a long association with **Andrew Cyrille**, with whom he recorded *Dialogue Of The Drums* in 1974.

Back in 1965 Graves began researching into the medical and psychological uses of music. He was also involved in the Storefront Museum, a community arts project in his home area of Jamaica, in the borough of Queens, New York City. An important figure in the 60s free jazz movement, he made an impression on a wider audience with two appearances at the 1973 Newport in New York Jazz Festival, but within two years he was forced to earn his living from teaching rather than performing. He has worked or recorded with **Albert Ayler**, **Sonny Sharrock** (*Black Woman*), **Miriam Makeba**, the **Jazz Composer's Orchestra Association**, and in a percussion trio with Cyrille and **Rashied Ali** and in a percussion quartet, Pieces Of Time, with Cyrille, **Don Moye** and **Kenny Clarke** (later **Philly Joe Jones**). Many of the musicians he worked with in the early and mid-60s have credited him with being the first drummer to provide the combination of looseness and rhythmic propulsion that the new music needed.

● ALBUMS: with Sunny Morgan *Percussion Duo* (ESP 1964) ★★★, *Milford Graves Percussion Ensemble* (ESP 1966) ★★★, with Don Pullen *Graves-Pullen Duo* (Pullen-Graves 1967) ★★★, with Pullen *Nommo* (SRP 1967) ★★, *The Giuseppi Logan Quartet* (ESP 1964) ★★, with Andrew Cyrille *Dialogue Of The Drums* (ISP 1974) ★★★, with David Murray *Real Deal* (DIW 1992) ★★★★, *Grand Unification* (Tzadik 1998) ★★★, *Stories* (Tzadik 2000) ★★★★.

Gravine, Anita

b. 11 April 1946, Carbondale, Pennsylvania, USA. Both Gravine's parents played musical instruments, while her brother became a studio trombonist. From the mid-60s Gravine studied singing, and also piano theory, in New York. She sang with **Larry Elgart**'s orchestra and also with bands led by **Urbie Green** and **Buddy Morrow** among several. Freelancing in New York, she worked with several noted jazz musicians, including **Chick Corea**, **Roy Eldridge** and **Hank Jones**. For a spell starting in the late 70s she lived in Europe but by the mid-80s was back in New York, where she recorded her first album. Her second outing as leader won her great critical acclaim, although her third was shelved for a number of years. Also during the mid-80s, she began a parallel career as a teacher of jazz singing. In the 90s Gravine was active in video and film production and after a long gap returned to recording in 1998, reuniting for the occasion with pianist-arranger Mike Abene, who had worked on her first two albums. A stylish singer with a delightfully understated sense of swing, the path chosen by Gravine for her career has led to her being far less well known that an artist of her quality deserves.

● ALBUMS: *Dream Dancing* (Progressive 1983) ★★★★, *I Always Knew* (Stash 1985) ★★★★, *Welcome To My Dream* 1986 recording (Jazz Alliance 1993) ★★, *Lights! Camera! Passion! Jazz And The Italian Cinema* (Soul Note 1999) ★★★.

Gravity Kills

Modern-day St. Louis, USA, the cradle of the blues, seems an unlikely place to start a band firmly in the **Nine Inch Nails** style of industrial metal; yet Gravity Kills' genesis was as unusual as the unlikely setting from which they emerged. The roots of the band can be traced back to late 1995, when the unit of Matt Dudenhoeffer (guitar), Douglas Firley (keyboards), Kurt Kerns (bass/drums) and Kern's cousin Jeff Scheel (vocals) decided they wanted one of their tracks to be included on the local radio station compilation album. They produced 'Guilty' in six frantic hours and beat the radio station deadline by half an hour. The single showed an incredible degree of songwriting awareness and boasted a danceable, hypnotic rhythm. Suddenly Gravity Kills were an ongoing concern.

On the back of this success, the band supported the **Sex Pistols** in the USA while material was finished for their first self-titled album. Their frenetic and compelling live performances were soon experienced in Europe as they began a bout of touring. One of their main assets was the presence of a keyboard player not permanently rooted behind banks of hi-tech equipment. Firley's simple stage set-up comprised industrial-strength tripods built to take his weight, allowing him to become a breathtaking gymnastic blur without missing a beat. To match the bleakness of their first single, the album boasted tracks of tense and dramatic electro-metal, which lent itself easily to cinematic interpretation. 'Guilty' was featured in the movie *Seven*, while the qualities of the other tracks attracted directors as diverse as Rocky Morton (creator of Max Headroom) and Peter Christopher-son (**Rage Against The Machine** video director), to provide visual accompaniment to the brooding tales. A perfunctory remix set was released in 1997, and was followed by the band's lacklustre new studio album *Perversion*.

The quartet, stung by media criticism, left TVT shortly afterwards. They continued to tour while searching for a more suitable outlet for their work, eventually settling on independent label Sanctuary Records. *Superstarved*, released in March 2002, rediscovered the passion and commitment of the band's debut and was warmly received by their loyal fans.

● ALBUMS: *Gravity Kills* (TVT 1996) ★★★, *Perversion* (TVT 1998) ★★, *Superstarved* (Sanctuary 2002) ★★★.

● COMPILATIONS: *Manipulated* (TVT 1997) ★★.

Gravy Train

Typifying the excesses that have frequently been denounced in their genre, UK progressive rock band Gravy Train recorded a series of albums for **Vertigo Records** and Dawn Records in the early 70s bedecked in grandiose, conceptual artwork. The group's core members were Norman Barrett (vocals/guitar), Barry Davenport (drums), J.D. Hughes (woodwind,keyboards,vocals) and Les Williams (bass/vocals). Their first, self-titled 1970 album was dominated by Hughes' flute melodies, which earned the group initial comparisons to **Jethro Tull**, as well as extended rock riffs. One of the songs, 'Tribute To Syd', was an obvious salute to the genius of **Syd Barrett**. The follow-up collection, which sold poorly, was *Ballad Of A Peaceful Man*. Despite its relative lack of success, many critics considered it to be far superior to the group's debut, with its complex arrangements, strong musical values and disciplined vocals attracting particular praise. Though the band continued to draw crowds on their extensive UK touring schedule, Vertigo became frustrated with their lack of record sales, leading to a move to Dawn. *Second Birth* is considered by most to be a disappointing effort, lacking the focus and drive of its predecessor. For their final album, 1974's *Staircase To The Day*, the group experimented with Greek folk and classical signatures (notably on the Bach-inspired title-track), while Roger Dean supplied the cover artwork. The group utilized a wide variety of collaborators for this album, including Russell Cordwell (drums), Jim Frank (drums), George Lynon (guitar), Pete Solley (synthesizer) and Mary Zinovieff (synthesizer/violin). Original drummer Davenport had now left, and the rest of the band elected to close their career after further moderate sales.

● ALBUMS: *Gravy Train* (Vertigo 1970) ★★★, *Ballad Of A Peaceful Man* (Vertigo 1971) ★★★, *Second Birth* (Dawn 1973) ★★, *Staircase To The Day* (Dawn 1974) ★★★.

Gray, Arvella

b. Walter Dixon, 28 January 1906, Somerville, Texas, USA, d. 7 September 1980, Chicago, Illinois, USA. Brought up in farm work, Gray left home early and travelled, eventually moving north. In 1930, he lost his sight and two fingers of his left hand in a fight, and took to making music for a living. He played blues, with a rudimentary bottleneck guitar style, on the streets of Chicago for many years, and became well known for his regular appearances at the Maxwell Street outdoor market and other locations around the city. He attracted the attention of younger blues fans and, in the 60s and 70s, appeared in concerts, festivals and even a couple of short films. His repertoire was limited, but he made a number of records, including some singles, which he sold on the streets.

● ALBUMS: *The Singing Drifter* (Birch 1972) ★★★.

Gray, Barry

b. 1925, Blackburn, Lancashire, England, d. 26 April 1984, Guernsey, Channel Islands, Britain. A true 'backroom boy' of the music business, Gray's name will be familiar to television viewers who read the credits. His distinctive scores were an important ingredient in the huge success of shows such as *Thunderbirds* and *Stingray*. Gray's professional music career started with London publishers B. Feldman & Co., where he gained much experience arranging for large and small orchestras in variety theatres. He also worked pre-war for the commercial station Radio Normandy, before war service with the RAF took him to India, Africa and Burma. Back home he relaunched his career as a freelance, writing lyrics and music for radio shows, performers, films and publishers. His works were performed by singers such as **Eartha Kitt** and **Hoagy Carmichael**, and in 1949 he began a 10-year period as arranger and accompanist to **Vera Lynn**. In 1956 he began his long association with producer of puppet films Gerry Anderson. The first television series was *Twizzle*, to be followed by *Torchy The Battery Boy*, *Four Feather Falls*, *Supercar*, *Fireball XL5*, *Stingray*, *Thunderbirds*, *Captain Scarlet And The Mysterons*, *Joe 90*, *U.F.O.*, and *Space 1999*. His feature films (sometimes supplying special effects for the named composer) included *Dr. Who And The Daleks* (1965), *Farenheit 451* (1966), *Island Of Terror* (1966), *Daleks: Invasion Earth 2150 AD* (1966), *Thunderbirds Are Go* (1967), *Thunderbird Six* (1968) and *Doppelganger* (1969). On 27 October 1979 he conducted the National Philharmonic Orchestra in a suite of his own scores as part of 'Filmharmonic 1979' at London's Royal Albert Hall. Gray's best remembered theme is his 'Thunderbirds March'.

Gray, Billy

b. 29 December 1924, Paris, Texas, USA, d. 27 March 1975. Gray bought himself a second-hand guitar and was singing on local radio at 15. In 1943, he formed a band and had his own show on KPLT Paris until 1946. He then toured with his band playing theatres and dance halls in Louisiana and Texas until 1950. During one tour, he became very friendly with **Hank Thompson** and, soon after, he accepted Thompson's offer to lead his Brazos Valley Boys. The two men also formed two music publishing companies, Texoma Music and

Brazos Valley Publishing and also began writing songs together. In the 50s, Thompson gained Top 20 hits with several of them including 'Waiting In The Lobby Of Your Heart', 'The New Wears Off Too Fast', 'Yesterday's Girl', 'Breakin' The Rules' and 'A Fooler, A Faker'. During this time, Gray also met **Wanda Jackson**, who sang on occasions with Thompson's band, and was instrumental in persuading **Decca Records** to sign her as a country singer. In 1954, their duet recording, 'You Can't Have My Love', became a number 8 hit—her first but Gray's only chart entry. After some years he left Thompson to form his own band, the Western Oakies. They recorded a 10-inch album for Decca's Dance-O-Rama series and proved popular playing various dance venues, but the expense of keeping a large band on the road eventually proved too much for him. In 1964, he disbanded and returned to leading Thompson's band for some time. Afterwards, he played with several groups and appeared regularly on the televised syndicated *Music Country Style*. In the 60s, he also appeared with **Ray Price** and recorded a solo album on the Longhorn label. In the early 70s, he began to suffer heart problems and died while undergoing a heart operation at the age of 50.

● ALBUMS: *Dance-O-Rama* (Decca 1955) ★★★, *Billy Gray* (Longhorn 1965) ★★.

Gray, Claude

b. 26 January 1932, Henderson, Texas, USA. During his schooldays, he showed more interest in music than sports and, learning to play the guitar, he began to perform locally. By the late 50s, he was playing venues over a wide area, for a time he worked as a disc jockey on WDAL Meridian, Mississippi, and made his first recordings for **Decca Records**. However, it was in 1960, on the 'D' label (a subsidiary of **Mercury Records**), that he gained his first US country chart hit, when his recording of **Willie Nelson**'s 'Family Bible' peaked at number 10. This success led to him being moved to the major label and in 1961, he enjoyed major Top 5 hits with 'I'll Just Have Another Cup Of Coffee (Then I'll Go)' and **Roger Miller**'s song 'My Ears Should Burn (When Fools Are Talked About)'. In 1966, after further Mercury successes, he recorded for **Columbia Records** and charted with 'Mean Old Woman', before returning to Decca. He formed the Graymen, which became a very popular touring band all over the USA, being especially popular on the nightclub circuit around Las Vegas. In the late 60s he had eight chart entries, including Top 20 hits with 'I Never Had The One I Wanted' and the truck-driving song 'How Fast Them Trucks Can Go'. He left Decca in 1971 but achieved a few small hits on the Million and Granny labels. In 1982 he had a minor hit with a duet recording with **Norma Jean** of 'Let's Go All The Way' (a 1964 solo hit for Norma Jean). Known as 'The Tall Texan' (for obvious reasons), Gray is much better as a live performer, it is said, than as a recording artist. This perhaps accounts for his inability to maintain chart hits. He is still active, his last chart entry having been a minor hit with **Neil Diamond**'s 'Sweet Caroline' in 1986.

● ALBUMS: *Songs Of Broken Love Affairs* (Mercury 1962) ★★★, with the Melody Singers *Country Goes To Town* (Mercury 1962) ★★★, *Claude Gray Sings* (Decca 1967) ★★★, *Treasure Of Love* (Hilltop 1967) ★★, *The Easy Way Of Claude Gray* (Decca 1968) ★★, *Presenting Claude Gray* (Million 1972) ★★★, *Great Country Roads* (Sunrise 1997) ★★★.

● COMPILATIONS: *The Best Of Claude Gray Volume One* (Sunrise 2000) ★★★★.

Gray, David

b. 13 June 1968, Manchester, England, but raised in the Welsh fishing village of Solva. Gray first aspired to being a rock performer after watching 2-Tone bands on television. He formed a punkish outfit at school, cranking out rock classics at double speed, then began writing songs when he was 17. **Polydor Records** A&R man Rob Holden heard a demo while recuperating from a motorcycle crash and was sufficiently convinced to quit his job and become Gray's manager. Pegged as a 'crop-headed Welsh troubadour' with 'a chip on both shoulders', Gray's early material was in fact as sensitive as it was angry, and the manic energy communicated with his acoustic guitar thrash set him apart from the folkies. He enjoyed an initial breakthrough in Ireland with 'Shine', taken from 1993's debut *A Century Ends*. A number of tours as support to singer-songwriters (**Maria McKee**, **Kirsty MacColl**, **Shawn Colvin**) brought him early exposure in America, and a one-off support with **Joan Baez** led to her praising 'the best lyrics since the young **Bob Dylan**'.

Although acknowledging a debt to Dylan, whose music had influenced him from the age of 13, Gray tempered his spirit of folksy protest with a 90s street-level sensibility. This attitude brought comparisons with **Mark Eitzel** of **American Music Club**, but also appeared destined to consign Gray to the same perennial cult status as Eitzel. The singer's 1998 collection *White Ladder* was recorded in his bedroom on a four-track, and several of the tracks featured heavily in the film *This Year's Love*. The album became a bestseller in Ireland and, backed by the might of EastWest Records, belatedly broke into the UK Top 10 the following year on the back of the Top 5 single, 'Babylon'. The record's success prompted a resurgence in the singer-songwriter format, with the UK's **New Musical Express** dubbing the trend the 'new acoustic movement'. The album finally topped the UK charts in August 2001, almost three years after its initial release.

Gray's eagerly awaited new studio album *A New Day At Midnight* was finally released in November 2002, and duly swept to the top of the UK charts. The album rarely departed from the successful formula established by its predecessor, although the lack of memorable melodies ultimately marked it down as a less compelling release, a fact borne out by long-term sales figures. Gray clearly put a lot of effort into 2005's *Life In Slow Motion*, an album that reclaimed his credibility after the overplayed 'Babylon' had threatened to become his albatross.

● ALBUMS: *A Century Ends* (Hut 1993) ★★★, *Flesh* (Hut 1994) ★★★, *Sell, Sell, Sell* (EMI/Nettwerk 1996) ★★★★, *White Ladder* (IHT/EastWest/ATO 1998) ★★★★, *A New Day At Midnight* (IHT/EastWest 2002) ★★, *Life In Slow Motion* (IHT/EastWest 2005) ★★★★.

● COMPILATIONS: *Lost Songs 95–98* (IHT/RCA 2000) ★★★, *The EP's 92–94* (Hut/Caroline 2001) ★★★.

● DVD/VIDEOS: *Live* (Warner Music Vision 2000).

● FURTHER READING: *David Gray: A Biography*, Michael Heatley.

● FILMS: *This Year's Love* (1999).

Gray, Dobie

b. 26 July 1940, Simonton, Texas, USA. Gray moved from Texas to California in the early 60s, where he began recording for local labels. His seventh single 'Look At Me' was a minor hit for the Cordak label in January 1963. The compulsive, if boastful, single 'The 'In' Crowd' (written by Billy Page) was his major breakthrough in 1965, spending several months in the **Billboard** pop charts and peaking at number 13. It was followed by 'See You At The 'Go Go'', which featured leading session players **Hal Blaine**, **Carol Kaye** and Larry Knechtal as backing musicians. It was eight years before the singer secured another chart entry. In the intervening period, Gray worked as an actor, appearing in productions of **Hair** and the controversial play The Beard. He also contributed to the soundtracks for the movies Out Of Sight, Uptown Saturday Night and The Commitment.

In the early 70s Gray sang several lead vocals for a hard rock group, Pollution; they recorded two albums for the Prophecy label that were well received but were commercial failures. He also recorded several demos for songwriter **Paul Williams**, whose brother Mentor, a producer, was responsible for relaunching Dobie's singing career. The superbly crafted 'Drift Away' (a US Top 5 hit in February 1973), provided an artistic and commercial success that the singer followed with further examples of progressive southern rock/soul, including Tom Jans' oft-covered 'Loving Arms'. Relocating to Nashville, Tennessee, to concentrate on his songwriting, Gray remained a popular concert draw throughout the world, including South Africa, where he played to integrated audiences in defiance of the apartheid government. Minor chart successes for the Capricorn and Infinity labels followed in the late 70s, after which Gray remained quiet for several years. He resurfaced on Capitol/EMI America, recording with Nashville producer Harold Shedd and enjoyed country chart hits with 'That's One To Grow On', 'The Dark Side Of Town' and 'From Where I Stand'. He also made several appearances at **Charlie Daniels**' hugely popular Volunteer Jam concerts. Gray's songs have been performed by artists of the calibre of **Ray Charles**, **Johnny Mathis**, **Julio Iglesias**, **Nina Simone**, **Tammy Wynette** and **Charly Pride**. He returned to the studio in the mid-90s, releasing The Diamond Cuts, which featured reworkings of his old classics alongside new material.

● ALBUMS: Look! (Stripe 1963) ★★★, Sings For 'In' Crowders That Go 'Go Go' (Charger 1965) ★★★, Drift Away (Decca 1973) ★★★, Loving Arms (MCA 1974) ★★★, Hey Dixie (MCA 1974) ★★★, New Ray Of Sunshine (Capricorn 1975) ★★, Let Go (Capricorn 1977) ★★, Midnight Diamond (Infinity 1978) ★★★, Dobie Gray (Infinity 1979) ★★★, From Where I Stand (Capitol/EMI America 1986) ★★★★, Love's Talkin' (Capitol/EMI America 1987) ★★★, The Diamond Cuts (Dobie Gray 1997) ★★★.

● COMPILATIONS: Best Of Dobie Gray (MCA 1973) ★★★★, Drift Away: His Very Best (Razor & Tie 1996) ★★★★, The Soulful Sound Of (Half Moon 1998) ★★★, Out On The Floor With The In Crowd (Music Club 1999) ★★★.

Gray, Dolores

b. 7 June 1924, Chicago, Illinois, USA, d. 26 June 2002, Manhattan, New York City, USA. A dynamic, full-blooded singer, early in her career Gray sang on radio with Milton Berle and **Rudy Vallee**. Making her Broadway debut in **Cole Porter**'s Seven Lively Arts (1944), she went on to appear in Are You With It? and Sweet Bye And Bye in 1946, and was then chosen by **Richard Rodgers** and **Oscar Hammerstein II** for the lead in their London production of **Annie Get Your Gun**.

That historic opening night in 1947, on her 23rd birthday, she took London by storm with a performance that almost matched **Ethel Merman**'s triumph in the role on Broadway. She was back there herself in 1951 with Two On The Aisle, and followed this two years later with Carnival In Flanders, for which she won a **Tony Award** as the outstanding actress in a musical. MGM signed her for **It's Always Fair Weather** (1955), in which she shared the spotlight with **Gene Kelly**, **Dan Dailey**, **Michael Kidd** and **Cyd Charisse**, and excelled with her vibrant versions of 'Music Is Better Than Words' and 'Thanks A Lot But No Thanks'. She was rewarded with a starring role in **Kismet**, followed by The Opposite Sex in 1956, but because film musicals were on the wane, MGM had only the comedy Designing Woman to offer, and she returned to Broadway in Destry Rides Again.

Gray worked steadily in television and clubs and made singles for **Capitol Records** showing that she was no mere stage belter but a sensitive interpreter of standards. Apart from the splendid Warm Brandy, she was heard only on soundtrack and Original Cast albums. After taking over from **Angela Lansbury** in the 1973 London production of **Gypsy**, in 1987 she returned to the West End in the role of Carlotta Campion, singing that memorable anthem, 'I'm Still Here', in **Stephen Sondheim**'s **Follies**. Gray died from a heart attack in New York City in June 2002.

● ALBUMS: Warm Brandy (Capitol 1957) ★★★★.

● FILMS: Lady For A Night (1941), Mr. Skeffingon (1944), It's Always Fair Weather (1955), Kismet (1955), The Opposite Sex (1956), Designing Women (1957).

Gray, Glen

b. Glen Gray Knoblaugh, 7 June 1906, Roanoke, Illinois, USA, d. 23 August 1963, Plymouth, Massachusetts, USA. Educated at Illinois Westleyan College, Gray played the saxophone with one of the **Jean Goldkette** outfits, the Orange Blossom Band. In 1928 the group played the Casa Loma hotel in Toronto, which later folded, and adopted the name **Casa Loma Orchestra** for its gigs around the Detroit area. Gray was the president and leader when the co-operative band was formed in 1929; it was headed by Henry Biagini, then by violinist Mel Jenssen, who remained its leader for several years. The band recorded for **Brunswick Records** in the early 30s with **Gene Gifford** shaping the band's arrangements and style. A fine swing unit with catchy riffs and attractive ballads, the Casa Loma orchestra gained a spot on the Camel Caravan radio show during 1934–36 and was later signed for **Burns And Allen**'s show. Glen Gray was elected leader by popular vote in 1937 until his retirement in 1950; he and the Casa Loma appeared in such movies as Time Out For Rhythm (1941) and Gals, Inc (1943). During the mid-50s he began recording a series of extremely successful albums for **Capitol Records**, recreating the sounds of the Casa Loma and other bands of the swing era. He was still engaged on this project when he became a victim of cancer in 1963.

Highly regarded by pundits and swing fans alike, the Casa Loma orchestra had a large number of bestselling records on Brunswick and **Decca**, including 'Blue Moon', 'When I Grow Too Old To Dream', 'Smoke Rings' (the Casa Loma theme), 'Heaven Can Wait', 'My Heart Tells Me', 'It's The Talk Of The Town', 'Sophisticated Lady', 'Out In The Cold Again', 'Fare Thee Well, Annabelle', 'My Shining Hour' and 'Sunrise Serenade', which featured its composer **Frankie Carle** on piano. Many of them had romantic vocals by **Kenny Sargent**.

The band also recorded powerful instrumentals such as 'Blue Jazz', 'White Jazz', 'Black Jazz' and 'No Name Jive'.

● ALBUMS: *Hoagy Carmichael Songs* 10-inch album (Decca 1950) ★★★★, *Glen Gray Souvenirs* 10-inch album (Decca 1950) ★★★, *Musical Smoke Rings* 10-inch album (Decca 1950) ★★★, *No Name Jive* 10-inch album (Decca 1952) ★★★, *Casa Loma In Hi Fi!* (Capitol 1956) ★★★, *The Great Recordings Of Glen Gray* (Harmony 1957) ★★★, *Sounds Of The Great Bands!* (Capitol 1959) ★★★, with Jonah Jones *Jonah Jones/Glen Gray* (Capitol 1961) ★★★, *Themes Of The Great Bands* (Capitol 1963) ★★, *Today's Best* (Capitol 1963) ★★.

● COMPILATIONS: *Glen Gray And The Casa Loma Orchestra 1943–46* (London-American 1979) ★★★★, *Solo Spotlight* (Capitol 1986) ★★★, *Casa Loma Stomp (1929–30)* (Hep Jazz 1986) ★★★, *Glen Gray And The Casa Loma Orchestra 1939–40* (Hindsight 1988) ★★★★, *Glen Gray And The Casa Loma Orchestra 1943–46* (Hindsight 1988) ★★★★, *Glen Gray And The Casa Loma Orchestra* (Columbia 1990) ★★★.

Gray, Henry

b. 19 January 1925, Kenner, Louisiana, USA. Having grown up in rural Louisiana, where he taught himself piano at an early age, Gray moved to Chicago in the 40s. He soon built a solid reputation as a band pianist in the city's blues clubs, and as accompanist on records by artists such as **Junior Wells** and **Billy Boy Arnold**. His own recordings in the early 50s featured strong, rocking blues, but they remained unissued for many years. Following a long period with the **Howlin' Wolf** band, he moved back to Louisiana in 1969. He has continued to work in music, including stints at **Tabby Thomas'** Blues Box club, and has made several fine records, most notably singles on **Jay Miller**'s Blues Unlimited label and Sunland, and an album recorded during a European tour in 1977. His recorded work in the 90s was patchy even when bolstered by the likes of Kid Ramos and **Bob Margolin**. In 2001 he was recording as Henry Gray And The Cats.

● ALBUMS: *They Call Me Little Henry* (Label 1977) ★★★★, *Lucky Man* (Blind Pig 1988) ★★★, with Clarence Edwards and Short Fuse *Thibodeaux's Cafe* (Sidetrack 1995) ★★, *Don't Start That Stuff* (Sidetrack 1996) ★★★, *Plays Chicago Blues* (HighTone 2001) ★★, *Watch Yourself* (Lucky Cat 2001) ★★★.

● COMPILATIONS: *The Blues Of Henry Gray & Cousin Joe* (Storyville 2004) ★★★.

Gray, Jerry

b. 3 July 1915, East Boston, Massachusetts, USA, d. 10 August 1976, Dallas, Texas, USA. As a child Gray first studied violin and later composing and arranging. At the age of 12 he played in the Boston Junior Symphony Orchestra. In the mid-30s he was hired by **Artie Shaw**, for whom he wrote several charts, including 'Any Old Time', which featured **Billie Holiday**, 'What Is This Thing Called Love?' and 'Begin The Beguine', one of Shaw's most popular recordings. In 1939 he left Shaw for the **Glenn Miller** band, where he was responsible for writing and arranging several major successes, including 'String Of Pearls' and 'Pennsylvania 6–5000'. Gray remained with Miller throughout World War II, continuing to run the band after Miller's death.

In the late 40s and early 50s Gray worked in Hollywood, freelancing in the studios, where one of the films on which he worked was *The Glenn Miller Story* (1954). He also led his own band on radio and had a successful record with 'Sound Off'. In the early 60s he turned to full-time studio work and continued to form bands for special engagements. He wrote the arrangement for **Vic Damone**'s hit, 'I Have But One Heart'. Gray's career continued in much the same fashion in the 70s, following his relocation to Dallas, Texas. Despite his early work with Shaw, once Gray began his association with Miller he settled into the style of writing associated with that band and rarely varied the formula thereafter.

● ALBUMS: *Dance To The Music Of Gray* 10-inch album (Decca 1950) ★★★, *A Tribute To Glen Miller* 10-inch album (Decca 1951) ★★★, *Dance Time* 10-inch album (Decca 1952) ★★★, *Jerry Gray & His Orchestra* (Decca 1955) ★★★, *At The Hollywood Palladium* (Liberty 1957) ★★★, *Hi Fi Shades Of Grey* (Liberty 1958) ★★★, *Singin' & Swingin'* (Warners 1962) ★★★.

● COMPILATIONS: *The Uncollected Jerry Gray* (Hindsight) ★★★, *Re-Stringing The Pearls: 1949–1951 Recordings* (Jazz Band 2002) ★★★.

Gray, Macy

b. Natalie McIntyre, 9 September 1970, Canton, Ohio, USA. Downplaying the hype surrounding her as the saviour of soul music, Gray often repeated the story about how she was afraid to speak as a child because other kids would tease her about her voice. That voice, an amazing hybrid of **Billie Holiday** and **Tina Turner** refreshingly free from the modern clichés of the R&B diva and the rap gangstress, entranced critics and music fans alike when her debut album was released in autumn 1999.

Gray, who received several years formal piano training, was raised on a classic soul diet of **Stevie Wonder** and **Aretha Franklin**, but was also drawn to hip-hop in the early 80s. She later moved to Los Angeles to enrol in a screen-writing programme at the USC Film School. Here she was cajoled into singing on demo sessions, and began creating a stir at live appearances fronting a covers band. She set up her own after hours club, the We Ours, in Hollywood, where an open microphone policy allowed her to demo her own material in front of friends. Gray signed to Epic Records in April 1998, and set about recording an album with producer Andrew Slater. The cast of musicians included her songwriting partners Darryl Swann and Jeremy Ruzumna, Arik Marshall (guitar, ex-**Red Hot Chili Peppers**), and the highly experienced session musicians Blackbird McKnight (guitar, ex-**Funkadelic**) and Lenny Castro (percussion, ex-**Tower Of Power**). *On How Life Is* proved to be a melodic fusion of classic soul, urban R&B and hip-hop beats rounded off by Gray's earthy rasp. Stand-out tracks included the excellent singles 'Do Something' and 'I Try', and the dramatic 'Sex-o-matic Venus Freak' and 'Caligula'. The album was particularly well received in the UK; glowing reviews and word-of-mouth approval helping it climb steadily up the charts (eventually reaching number 6 in October). 'I Try' also stayed in the lower reaches of the Top 10 for several weeks. The track finally broke Gray in the US the following year, climbing into the Top 5 in May.

After working with **Fatboy Slim**, the **Black Eyed Peas** and **Slick Rick**, and making her debut as an actress in the Denzel Washington police drama *Training Day*, Gray returned to the studio in 2001 to record *The ID* with **Rick Rubin**. This experimental work confused her newly acquired fanbase and sold poorly, leading to suggestions that she was a one-hit wonder. The follow-up attempted to redress the balance, including pleasant pop material such as 'When I See You' and 'She Ain't Right For You'. Gray's incredible voice sets her apart from many of her contemporaries. A greatest hits package in 2004 seemed to be a little premature.

● ALBUMS: *On How Life Is* (Epic 1999) ★★★★, *The ID* (Epic 2001) ★★★, *The Trouble With Being Myself* (Epic 2003) ★★.

● COMPILATIONS: *The Very Best Of Macy Gray* (Epic 2004) ★★★★.

● FILMS: *Training Day* (2001), *Spider-Man* (2002), *Scary Movie 3* (2003).

Gray, Mark

b. 24 October 1952, Vicksburg, Mississippi, USA. Singer-songwriter Gray first played piano at the age of 12 and headed his own gospel group at 19. He joined the **Oak Ridge Boys** as a writer with their publishing company, also becoming the keyboard player with their road band. Later he became a member of pop-country band **Exile** and was lead vocalist on two of their albums, *Don't Leave Me This Way* (1980) and *Heart And Soul* (1981). In the early 80s, three of his songs were US country number 1s, 'Take Me Down' and 'The Closer You Get', both for **Alabama** and 'It Ain't Easy Bein' Easy' for **Janie Frickie**. He signed with **Columbia Records** in 1983 and between 1983 and 1988, he registered 11 US country chart successes, including solo Top 10 hits with 'If The Magic Is Gone' and 'Please Be Love', but his highest chart entry came with his 1985 duet recording with **Tammy Wynette** of 'Sometimes When We Touch'. He had two minor duet hits in 1988 with Bobbi Lace, but has not achieved a solo hit since 1986.

● ALBUMS: *Magic* (Columbia 1984) ★★★, *This Ol' Piano* (Columbia 1984) ★★★, *That Feeling Inside* (Columbia 1986) ★★★.

Gray, Otto, And His Oklahoma Cowboys

Around 1923, a group of musicians in Stillwater, Oklahoma, began playing as the Billy McGinty Cowboy Band. William McGinty, an old-time cowboy who had ridden with Roosevelt's Rough Riders, formed the band to preserve the music of the Old West and hired Otto Gray (b. 2 March 1884, Ponca, on the Ponca Indian Reservation, in Indian Territory, Oklahoma, USA, d. 8 November 1967) as the band's manager. Little is known of Gray's early years but at the time McGinty hired him, he was a successful rancher. An adept promoter, he soon found the band work, only to discover that the original members would not tour.

A talented fiddle player, Gray formed his own Oklahoma Cowboys, which included his wife (Mommie) as the featured vocalist and his son Owen, by recruiting genuine cowboy musicians working on Oklahoma ranches. They first broadcast in 1924 on KFRU Bristow, but later played on KVOO Tulsa and KFJF Oklahoma City and went on to play countless radio stations all over the USA. With shrewd organization, Gray assembled a show that featured, in addition to the music, himself and Mommie doing trick roping and whip cracking, a trained dog and speciality musical items. He publicized the show by advertising in national magazines such as *Billboard*, sending publicity men ahead to forthcoming venues and by using booking agencies in Chicago and New York to co-ordinate the band's appearances on various entertainment circuits. At one time their show was carried by over 100 radio stations. Very likely the first touring cowboy stage show to perform genuine cowboy songs, they were also probably the first-ever group to use custom-made cars to transport them on tour. Gray's personal vehicle, a $20,000 Cadillac, was even equipped for radio transmissions.

By the time Gray finally disbanded the group (and disappeared into obscurity) in 1936, he had inspired other country groups to dress as cowboys, he had popularized 'western' music and he may even have been a candidate for the title of the first singing cowboy. It is probable that Gray's Cowboys were an inspiration to **Bob Wills**, who moved to Tulsa to organize his Texas Playboys. Gray was the first western star to have his photograph on the cover of *Billboard* magazine. Two of his Cowboys, **Zeke Clements** and 'Whitey' Ford (**Duke Of Paducah**), went on to successful solo careers.

Gray, Owen

b. 5 July 1939, Jamaica, West Indies. Gray's singing won him a local talent contest at the age of nine, and three years later he began to appear in public, playing drums, guitar and keyboards. In 1960 he became one of the first artists produced by **Chris Blackwell**, later the owner of **Island Records**. His first single, 'Please Let Me Go', with its easy shuffle rhythm and hard **Ernest Ranglin** guitar solo adding to the singer's appeal, was a number 1 hit in Jamaica. Gray's voice, light but with a cutting edge, won him favour throughout the decade; he turned his hand to R&B ('Let Me Go Free', based on **Professor Longhair**'s 'Tipitina'), ska ('Millie Girl') and ballads ('Far Love') before emigrating to Britain. He maintained a prodigious output, following the trends of ska, **rocksteady** and reggae, scoring a big seller with 'Cupid' (1968) and recording one of the steamiest soul dances ever issued in England in 'Help Me' (1966). By the late 70s he was no longer in the forefront of British black music, and a 1982 attempt at 'Sexual Healing' was less than successful. He now lives in Miami, where he still finds an audience for his extensive oldies repertoire.

● ALBUMS: *Cupid* (1969) ★★★, *Fire And Bullets* (Trojan 1977) ★★★★, *Dreams Of Owen Gray* (Trojan 1978) ★★★★, *Forward On The Scene* (Third World 1978) ★★★, with Pluggy Satchmo *Battle Of The Giants Round 1* (Vista Sounds 1983) ★★★, with Delroy Wilson *Oldies But Goldies* (Vista Sounds 1983) ★★★, with Max Romeo *Owen Gray Meets Max Romeo* (Culture Press 1984) ★★★, *Little Girl* (Vista Sounds 1984) ★★★, *Owen Gray Sings Bob Marley* (Sarge 1984) ★★, *Room At The Top* (World Enterprise 1986) ★★, *Watch This Sound* (Sky Note 1986) ★★, *Stand By Me* (Hitbound 1986) ★★, *Instant Rapport* (Bushranger 1989) ★★★, *Ready Willing And Able* (Park Heights 1989) ★★★.

● COMPILATIONS: *Hit After Hit Vols. 1, 2 & 3* (Carib Gems 1980, Vista Sounds 1983) ★★★★, *Shook, Shimmy & Shake: The Anthology* (Trojan 2004) ★★★★.

Gray, Wardell

b. 13 February 1921, Oklahoma City, Oklahoma, USA, d. 25 May 1955, Las Vegas, Nevada, USA. Growing up in Detroit, Gray first played clarinet before switching to tenor saxophone and joining the **Earl 'Fatha' Hines** band in 1943. After two years he relocated to the west coast, where he became prominent among local beboppers, notably **Dexter**

Gordon, with whom he played at Central Avenue clubs such as The Bird In The Basket. Gray made some successful recordings with Gordon, among them 'The Chase' and 'The Hunt', and also composed a number of tunes himself, including 'Twisted', which, with lyrics added, became popular with vocalese singers. In the late 40s and early 50s Gray worked with **Benny Carter**, **Billy Eckstine** and **Count Basie**, and was a member of **Benny Goodman**'s short-lived bebop big band, where he elicited a rare compliment from Goodman, who never really liked bebop: 'If Wardell Gray plays bop then it's great because he's wonderful.' He also played in a Goodman small group alongside **Stan Hasselgård**. Gray's tone was soft and he played light, flowing lines that reflected the influence **Lester Young** had upon him. Gray died on 25 May 1955 in circumstances that have never been fully resolved: his body was found in the Nevada Desert, his neck broken. The official report gave the cause of death as a drug overdose, though there was no autopsy, and rumours persisted that Gray had been murdered—either for failing to pay gambling debts or simply as a random victim of racial violence.

● ALBUMS: *Tenor Sax* 10-inch album (Prestige 1951) ★★★★, *Jazz Concert* 10-inch album (Prestige 1952) ★★★, *Wardell Gray's Los Angeles Stars* 10-inch album (Prestige 1953) ★★★, *Way Out Wardell* (Modern 1956) ★★★★, with Dexter Gordon *The Chase And Steeplechase* 10-inch album (Decca 1952) ★★★★, *Live At The Haig 1952* (Fresh Sound 1952) ★★, *One For Prez* 1946 recordings (Black Lion 1989) ★★★, *How High The Moon* 1953 recordings (Moon 1998) ★★★.

● COMPILATIONS: *Volume 1: 1944–1946* (Masters Of Jazz 1999) ★★★, *Volume 2: 1946* (Masters Of Jazz 1999) ★★★, *Volume 3: 1946–1947* (Masters Of Jazz 1999) ★★★, *Volume 4: 1947* (Masters Of Jazz 2000) ★★★, *Complete Sunset & New Jazz Masters* (Jazz Factory 2000) ★★★★, *Small Combos: 1946–1949* (Epm Musique 2001) ★★★★, *1946–1950* (Classics 2002) ★★★, *The Wardell Gray Story* 4-CD box set (Proper 2003) ★★★★.

Grayson, G.B.

b. Gilliam Banmon Grayson, 11 November 1887, Grayson, Ashe County, Tennessee, USA, d. 16 August 1930. Grayson was raised in Laurel Bloomery, Johnson County. Although blinded as a child, he learned the fiddle and began singing. When the family moved to Tennessee, he took to busking. Eventually, he teamed up with **Clarence Tom Ashley** and Doc Walsh and forged a reputation in Virginia, Tennessee and North Carolina. He met **Henry Whitter**, who made the original recording of 'The Wreck Of The Old '97', and recorded with him in 1927. In 1929 they made the first-ever recording of 'Tom Dooley' (shortly after the Civil War, Grayson's uncle had been involved in the capture of suspected murderer Tom Dula). Grayson died in a car crash near Damascus, Virginia, in August 1930, leaving a wife and six children. Today he is accepted as an important pioneer of country music and fiddle-playing, and is generally considered a superior vocalist to Whitter, having even sung lead on several records under Whitter's name.

● COMPILATIONS: *Grayson And Whitter, 1927–1930* (Old Homestead 1976) ★★★, *Going Down The Highway* 1927–29 recordings (Davis Unlimited 1976) ★★★, *The Recordings Of Grayson & Whitter* (County 1999) ★★★★.

Grayson, Hal

b. 1908, USA, d. 1959, Hollywood, Los Angeles, California, USA. Purveyors of 'sweet' big band dance sounds, society group the Hal Grayson Orchestra formed in 1932 in California, USA. Grayson was backed by sidemen who at one time included a young **Stan Kenton**, with vocalists **Betty Grable**, **Martha Tilton** and **Shirley Ross**. As well as weddings and functions the group embarked on major tours of the time's most popular ballroom venues, including the Jantzen Beach Hotel in Portland, the St. Francis and Ambassador Hotels in California and the Avalan Hotel in Catalinia. During their 12-year existence, which ended in 1944, they also secured dates at the Waldorf-Astoria in New York and appeared in a handful of Warner Brothers movies. After the end of the band Grayson remained active in the music industry in a variety of roles, but never returned to band leading. He suffered a nervous breakdown in the early 50s, and was hospitalised at the Camarillo State Hospital until 1958.

Grayson, Jack

b. Jack Lebsock, Sterling, Colorado, USA. Singing from an early age, Lebsock appeared on shows with top artists, including **Johnny Cash**. However, he found little success and turning to songwriting, becoming a staff writer for **Dot Records** during the 70s. He co-wrote 'Bless Your Heart' (with **Freddie Hart**) and wrote 'Super Kind Of Woman', both of which became number 1 country hits for Hart in 1972 and 1973, respectively. He also wrote 'The First Time', a number 2 for Hart in 1975. He made his own chart debut as a recording artist on **Capitol Records** in 1973 when, as Jack Lebsock, he had a minor hit with 'For Lovers Only'. After a further minor hit the following year, he changed his name (in tribute to his mother); in 1979 and 1980, he recorded for Churchill and Hitbound, achieving four minor chart hits as Blackjack Jack Grayson. He next recorded for Koala (this time as Jack Grayson and Blackjack), gaining a Top 20 hit with his version of 'When A Man Loves A Woman' (a number 1 pop hit in 1966 for **Percy Sledge**). In the early 80s, he recorded for Joe-Wes and his last chart entry, 'Lean On Me' (another former pop number 1, recorded by **Bill Withers** in 1972), was on AMI in 1984.

● ALBUMS: *Jack Grayson Sings* (Joe-Wes 1982) ★★★.

Grayson, Kathryn

b. Zelma Kathryn Hedrick, 9 February 1922, Winston-Salem, North Carolina, USA. An actress and singer with a spectacular soprano voice and a charming and ingenuous personality, who was popular in MGM musicals in the 40s and 50s. She is said to have been discovered while singing on **Eddie Cantor**'s radio show in the late 30s, and made her film debut in 1941 with **Mickey Rooney** in *Andy Hardy's Private Secretary*. After being teamed with the comedy duo **Abbott And Costello** in *Rio Rita* (1942), during the rest of the 40s and in the 50s she co-starred with major stars such as **Frank Sinatra**, **Mario Lanza** and **Howard Keel** in a string of musicals that included *Seven Sweethearts*, **Thousands Cheer**, **Two Sisters From Boston**, **Ziegfeld Follies**, **Till The Clouds Roll By**, **It Happened In Brooklyn**, *The Toast Of New Orleans*, **Show Boat**, *Lovely To Look At*, **The Desert Song**, **Kiss Me Kate** and **The Vagabond King** (1956). In *So This Is Love* (1953), she portrayed opera singer **Grace Moore**, and in some of her other films, she again played characters attempting to audition for maestros, such as José Iturbi, with the intention of making a career as a classical singer. As the golden age of movie musicals drew to a close in the late 50s, Grayson played concerts and clubs for a time, and subsequently toured in revivals of well-known stage musicals.

● ALBUMS: *Kathryn Grayson* 10-inch album (MGM 1952) ★★★, *Kathryn Grayson Sings* (MGM 1956) ★★★, *Kathryn Grayson* (Lion 1959) ★★★, and film soundtracks.
● COMPILATIONS: *20 Golden Favorites* (Bulldog 1984) ★★★.

Grean, Charles

b. 1 October 1913, New York City, USA, d. 20 December 2003, New York City, USA. As a child Grean played violin and then went to study bass at Wesleyan College in Connecticut. His first musical engagement came as a member of the Catskill Mountains. By the mid-30s he was regularly appearing on cruise ship revues, including spells with the Marine Synchopaters and the Caribbean Collegiates. Afterwards he moved to Nashville, and became a member of legendary A&R executive **Steve Sholes**' team at **RCA-Victor Records** from 1947 onwards, assessing songs for Sholes' consideration and helping produce the final masters. As well as playing bass on a number of sessions, Grean also helped fledgling artists with arrangements. Among the many artists who benefited from his wisdom in the late 40s and 50s were Texas Jim Robertson, **Wilf Carter**, **Sons Of The Pioneers** and many others. He also co-wrote a number of successful songs, particularly for **Eddy Arnold**—'Something Old, Something New' (1951) and 'Eddy's Song' (1953). He also penned an answer song to **Jim Reeves**' enduring romantic country hit 'He'll Have To Go', entitled 'He'll Have To Stay' (recorded by **Jeanne Black** in 1960). However, his biggest hit came outside the country field with the novelty song 'The Thing', which **Phil Harris** took to the top of the charts in 1950. He also recorded albums with *Star Trek*'s Dr. Spock, Leonard Nimoy, and recorded theme music for the horror show *Dark Shadows*.

After leaving Victor in 1952, Grean joined with Joe Csida to form Csida-Grean Associations, managing acts including Betty Johnson and **Bobby Darin**. However, he continued to collaborate with both Sholes and Eddy Arnold. He eventually married Betty Johnson (also of gospel act the Johnson Family) in the late 50s and ended his relationship with Csida-Grean. Afterwards his influence waned, although he continued to work sporadically in country music, with employment on the *Jimmy Dean Show* in the 50s and as touring conductor to Eddy Arnold in the 80s.

Grease (film musical)

Released in 1978 and adapted from a stage play, this endearingly simple musical became one of the decade's most spectacular successes. Set in a high school during the early 60s, the plot recalled those of the **Annette/Frankie Avalon** 'beach' movies. Stars **John Travolta** and **Olivia Newton-John** meet during the summer break, but their affair seems doomed when the former plays up to his 'tough-guy' image, fearful of the admonishment of fellow gang members. Naturally, the pair are together at the end and only the occasional sexual innuendo—and co-star Stockard Channing's pregnancy—indicate the film is a product of a later decade. What elevated *Grease* from mere formula was Travolta, then riding on the crest of success from *Saturday Night Fever*, and a succession of memorable songs. He

paired with Newton-John on 'You're The One That I Want' and 'Summer Nights', which together topped the UK singles chart in 1978 for a total of 16 weeks. Travolta's solo release, 'Sandy', reached number 2, a position equalled by Newton-John with 'Hopelessly Devoted To You'. Meanwhile, the soundtrack album spent 13 consecutive weeks at the top of the album charts, and climbed high again in 1998 when *Grease* was re-released worldwide. A reminder of its phenomenal success 20 years previously.
● FURTHER READING: *Grease: The Fotonovel*, Bronte Woodward (ed.). *Grease*, Ron De Christoforo.

Grease (stage musical)

After starting its life as a five-hour amateur production in Chicago in 1971, *Grease* opened in New York, off-Broadway, at the Eden Theatre in February 1972. Following a surprisingly enthusiastic reaction there, it moved to the Broadhurst Theatre on Broadway on 7 June. The book, music and lyrics, by Jim Jacobs (b. 7 October 1942, Chicago, Illinois, USA) and Warren Casey (b. 2 April 1935, Yonkers, New York City, USA, d. 8 November 1988), transported excited audiences (but not unimpressed theatre critics) back to the rock 'n' roll days of the 50s, when bored, sexually frustrated teenagers went around in gangs with names like 'Pink Ladies' and 'Burger Palace Boys'. At a reunion of the class of 1959, the assembled group relive the time when Danny Zuko (Barry Bostwick) and Sandy Dumbrowski (Carol Demas) met up again at Rydell High School after an innocent summer romance. At first they seemed to be incompatible—him with his tough, macho image—and her so prim and proper and virginal—quite unlike the seemingly hard-bitten Betty Rizzo (Adrienne Barbeau). However, by the end of the piece, it was Sandy (some years before the advent of women's lib) who changed her attitude and donned the leather jacket and tight pants—along with the rest of the uniform of a 'greaser''s steady girl friend. The satirical and highly entertaining score contained plenty of affectionate digs at the period ('Look at me, I'm Sandra Dee/ Lousy with virginity'), and other numbers such as 'Summer Nights', 'Freddie, My Love', 'Beauty School Dropout', 'We Go Together', 'Greased Lightnin'', 'There Are Worse Things That I Could Do', 'Mooning', and 'It's Raining On Prom Night'. *Grease* stayed on Broadway for 3,388 performances, closing in February 1980.

The first London production, in 1973, ran for 236 performances, and starred the then unknown Richard Gere as Danny. **Elaine Paige** was also in the company as an understudy, and eventually took over the role of Sandy. The show was revived in the West End in 1979, and again, in 1993, when **Paul Nicholas**, who had succeeded Richard Gere in the original 1973 London production, collaborated with the impresario **Robert Stigwood**, to present a radically revised version. It starred the Australian soap actor, **Craig McLachlan** and the popular US singer **Debbie Gibson**, and incorporated several songs that were written by **Barry Gibb**, John Farrar, Louis St. Louis, and Scott Simon for the 1978 smash-hit *Grease* movie, such as 'Hopelessly Devoted To You', 'You're The One That I Want', 'Grease', and 'Sandy'. On-screen, Danny and Sandy were played by **John Travolta** and **Olivia Newton-John**.

The 1994 Broadway revival, directed and choreographed by Jeff Calhoun, and starring Rosie O'Donnell (Rizzo), Susan Wood (Sandy), Ricky Paull Goldin (Danny) and Marcia

Lewis (Miss Lynch), did not use the film songs, but interpolated the old **Skyliners**' hit, 'Since I Don't Have You'. During its 1,501-performance run, which ended in January 1998, producers Fran and Barry Weissler made a practice of introducing stars from various areas of showbusiness into the leading roles. Brooke Shields, **Sheena Easton** and **Debby Boone** all took turns as Sandy, **Jon Secada** served as Danny, and ex-**Monkees** Davy Jones and Mickey Dolenz played Vince Fontaine, while JoAnn Worley and Sally Struthers were among those to lecture as Miss Lynch. Teen Angel, the cameo character who, along with Frenchy and the rest of the company gives out with 'Beauty School Dropout', tempted **Chubby Checker** and **Darlene Love** onto the brightly coloured Grease sets. Some of those involved in the David Gilmore–directed long-running West End show included Shane Richie, Ian Kelsey, Luke Goss (ex-Bros), **Sonia**, Samantha Janus, Marissa Dunlop (Sandy), Sally Ann Triplett and Linzi Hately (Rizzo). In the spring of 1998, an Italian production opened in Rome, and an 'arena spectacular' Grease tour of Australia starred Craig McLachlan (Danny), **Danni Minogue** (Rizzo), Jane Scali (Sandy) and Australia's original 'Phantom', Anthony Warlow, as Teen Angel.

Grease Band

The Grease Band was formed in 1966 to back singer **Joe Cocker** but the original line-up—Frank Myles (guitar), Vernon Nash (piano), Chris Stainton (bass) and Dave Demmott (drums)—underwent several changes over the ensuing years. **Henry McCullough** (b. Portstewart, Eire; guitar), Alan Spenner (bass) and Bruce Rowland (bass) joined Stainton in the band's best-known incarnation, but this unit split from Cocker in 1970 at the end of an arduous American tour. Spenner, Rowlands and McCullough were then joined by guitarist Neil Hubbard, as the Grease Band embarked on an independent career. The band's brand of blues rock was perfectly captured on their debut album and they enjoyed a reputation as an exciting live attraction. Stainton remained an associate member, although **Mick Weaver**, aka Wynder K. Frog, subsequently augmented the line-up. John 'Pugwash' Weathers came in for the defecting Rowlands, but the band broke up in December 1971 when McCullough joined **Wings**. *Amazing Grease* culled together unreleased recordings of the band.
● ALBUMS: *The Grease Band* (Shelter 1971) ★★★.
● COMPILATIONS: *Amazing Grease* (Shelter 1975) ★★.

Greasy Bear

This group from Manchester, England, comprised Chris 'C.P.' Lee, Ian Wilson (vocals/12-string guitar), Steve Whalley (guitars/vocals), John Gibson (bass/vocals) and Bruce Mitchell (drums). Emerging out of the hedonistic late-60s Manchester, Greasy Bear never achieved the success they deserved, even though many counted them among the finest British exponents of a loose jamming country rock style. Lee and Wilson teamed up first; slowly the line-up emerged as the two vocalists/12-string players added drums; bass, later, and the stunning lead guitarist Whalley last of all. Despite their growing live reputation, they ran into problems in the studio with their producer and with their record contract. The tensions eventually forced Lee out. Later concerts and demos continued to demonstrate their ability, but they disbanded in the 70s. Lee and Mitchell achieved notoriety in

Alberto Y Lost Trios Paranoias, Wilson joined **Sad Cafe** and Whalley began a solo career.

Great American Broadcast, The

Even before this film was released by 20th Century-Fox in 1941, the American public's fascination with radio had already spawned several entertaining musicals—and **Alice Faye** had favoured more than one of them with her presence. Here she is again—this time playing a singer whose involvement with radio pioneers Jack Oakie and **John Payne**, along with businessman Cesar Romero, eventually leads her to stardom. Also cast were Mary Beth Hughes, William Pawley, Lucien Littlefield, Eula Morgan, and guest artists, the **Ink Spots**, the **Nicholas Brothers**, and the Wiere Brothers. **Mack Gordon** and **Harry Warren** wrote most of the songs, which included 'Where You Are', 'I Take To You', 'The Great American Broadcast', 'Long Ago Last Night', 'It's All In A Lifetime' and 'I've Got A Bone To Pick With You'. They were joined by the Ink Spots' theme song 'If I Didn't Care' (Jack Lawrence), 'Give My Regards To Broadway' (**George M. Cohan**) and 'Alabamy Bound' (**Buddy De Sylva**–Bud Green–**Ray Henderson**). Don Ettlinger, Edwin Blum, Robert Ellis and Helen Logan provided an entertaining and sometimes witty screenplay, and the director was Archie Mayo.

Great Awakening

This little-known band made a brief impression in 1969 with an outstanding instrumental version of 'Amazing Grace', long before **Judy Collins** popularized the song. The mantra-like fuzz guitar added a spiritual quality that was missing from later versions. So little was known of the group that they were often referred to as Amazing Grace, and the song as 'The Great Awakening'! For years it was thought that the man responsible was guitarist David Cohen from **Country Joe And The Fish**; others suggested it was by members of the **Band**. Later it was discovered that it was a different David Cohen, helped out by Joe Osborn (bass) and Jimmy Gordon (drums). The latter Cohen has worked as session guitarist for **Bobby Darin**, **Tim Hardin** and **Frank Sinatra**.

Great Big Radio Show, The

One of the most entertaining musical comedies to emerge in the UK during the 90s, this show won a special prize at the **Vivian Ellis** Awards in 1989. It was subsequently workshopped at the Festival of New Musicals at Buxton Opera House three years later, before having its premiere in 1993 at the Watermill Theatre, Newbury, in England. It was optioned for the West End by one of Britain's leading producers, **Harold Fielding**, but ill health prevented him from moving forward. The project lost momentum until it resurfaced at London's Bridewell Theatre in May 1997. Philip Glassborow and Nick McIvor's book is set in 1933, on a Saturday night when America's favourite radio variety show is about to go on the air coast to coast. However, producer Bernie Bernstein (Peter Goodwright) has a problem. Only seven minutes to the red light, and Gloria Pilbeam, the golden-voiced 'Songstress of the Airwaves' ('a top recording star who enjoys all kind of sports') has not arrived at the NBS (National Broadcasting System) 'Studio of the Stars'. What is more, Alfred H. Zannenberg (Brian Greene), the show's sponsor, and inventor/proprietor of Nourishvite, the famous nerve tonic and all-round pick-me-up, is due any moment. Orchestra leader Blue Woodword (David Staller) retires to the cafeteria for a shot of caffeine, and hears waitress Freckles Murray (Danielle Carson) singing happily as she works. Great voice, but surely she cannot save the show? Oh yes she can, even though she has picked up the wrong 'violin' case at her previous nightclub job, and is therefore being pursued by two gangsters, Big Louie Rosenbaum (Howard Attfield) and Two-Gun Shapiro (Nick Burnell), who want their machine gun back. They turn out to be a couple of vaudeville hoofers anyway. By curtain time everything is sorted out. Blue and Freckles are harmonizing happily, while Alfred H. ('the meal in a spoon') Zannenberg has discovered that the slinky Olga (Elizabeth Counsell) is his long-lost childhood sweetheart.

Counsell had one of the best songs in the show, 'I Felt Myself Falling', but there was much else to enjoy in Glassborow's score, which affectionately recalled a much loved era, and included 'Unmistakably', 'She Ain't Here Yet!', 'Surprises', 'What Can I Do For You?', 'Radio In My Mind', 'No Matter What', 'Where Have I Seen You Before?', 'Pretty As A Picture', 'Suddenly I'm Singing', 'You Came By', 'Nourishvite', 'You Take My Breath Away', 'Then I Bumped Into You', 'The Balalaika', 'Tomorrow Is Another Day' and 'Me And My Stradivarius'. Also joining in the ('Radio') fun were Jerry Palmer (Richard Brightiff), Polly March (Myrtle Gray), Gavin Faulkner-Hackett (Flash Harry), and Carl Patrick (Stanley Wintergreen). The arrangements and dance music were by David Rhind-Tutt, and this 'fast-moving and delightful pastiche, with its agonising puns, hilarious commercials, and fine performances', was directed and choreographed by Angela Hardcastle.

Great Caruso, The

This lavishly produced biopic of the celebrated Italian opera singer was released by MGM in 1951. **Mario Lanza**, making his third screen appearance, was the perfect choice to play the lead in a screenplay by Sonia Levian and William Ludwig that, in certain areas of Caruso's life, was somewhat economical with the truth. For instance, the existence of one of his wives was totally ignored in the haste to condense drastically his rise to fame, and to feature as much music on the screen as possible. It was all rather false, and even the hit song that emerged from the film, 'The Loveliest Night Of The Year', was not actually associated with Caruso, being a Mexican instrumental piece, 'Over The Waves' (Juventino Rosas), adapted by **Irving Aaronson** and lyricist **Paul Francis Webster**. As for the remainder of the musical fare, it was a collection of songs and operatic excerpts that included 'Last Rose Of Summer' (Thomas Moore–Richard Alfred Milliken), 'Sextet' (Donizetti), 'La Donna E Mobile' (Verdi), 'Celeste Aida' (Verdi), 'Ave Maria' (Bach–Charles Gounod), 'Sweethearts' (**Victor Herbert**–Robert B. Smith), 'Vesti La Guibba' (Leoncavallo) and 'M'Appari' (Flotow). Anne Blyth played Dorothy Benjamin, Caruso's wife, and among the rest of the cast were Dorothy Kirsten, Jarmila Novotna, Richard Hageman, Eduard Franz, Carl Benton, Ludwig Donath, Ian Wolfe and Mae Clarke.

Joseph Ruttenbergs' Technicolor photography enhanced the whole spectacular affair, which was produced by Joe Pasternak and directed by Richard Thorpe. Musical directors **Johnny Green** and Peter Herman Adler were nominated for Oscars, and Douglas Shearer won one for sound recording. *The Great Caruso* grossed over $4.5 million in North America (a great deal of money in those days), and proved to be the most popular of Mario Lanza's brief film career (he made only seven films).

Great Guitars
(see **Byrd, Charlie**; **Ellis, Herb**; **Kessel, Barney**)

Great Hussar, The
(see *Balalaika*)

Great Plains

A US country rock group led by vocalist Jack Sundrud, Great Plains originally made their debut in 1991 with 'A Picture Of You'. Two further singles for **Columbia Records**, 'Faster Gun' and 'Iola', followed a year later, but immediately afterwards changes at their record company enforced a sabbatical from recording and touring. As a result, guitarist Russ Pahl left to find session work and drummer Michael Young decided to spend more time on his business affairs, restoring vintage cars. The group's fourth founding member, bass player Danny Dadmun-Bixby, toured with **Mary Chapin Carpenter**, while Sundrud spent much of the period writing new songs, one of which, 'Cain's Blood', was recorded by 4Runner. Eventually Great Plains were reconvened when Sundrud and Dadmun-Bixby met multi-instrumentalist Lex Browning. The trio then signed with Magnatone Records, the label headed by long-time friend Brent Maher. Maher also produced the album *Homeland*, which featured the excellent single 'Dancing With The Wind'.

● ALBUMS: *Great Plains* (Columbia 1991) ★★★, *Homeland* (Magnatone 1996) ★★★.

Great Rock'n'Roll Swindle, The

By the time this film was released in 1979, its progenitors the **Sex Pistols** had disintegrated owing chiefly to disagreements between group vocalist John Lydon (aka Johnny Rotten) and manager **Malcolm McLaren**. *The Great Rock'n'Roll Swindle* took the latter's philosophical line, offering his blueprint on methods of how to manipulate the music industry, based on Situationist rhetoric. Different scenes reflect McLaren's pointers for success, drawn on notorious vistas during the Sex Pistols' career. These include the group's appearance on Bill Grundy's show, the loss of contracts with **EMI Records** and **A&M Records** while retaining fiscal advances, and the anti-establishment attitude of punk. The film features footage of the Rotten line-up as well as several subsequent incarnations, notably the brief liaison with great train robber Ronnie Biggs. Staged sequences and animation are also included. Edward Tudor-Pole is the featured vocalist on 'Who Killed Bambi', a title briefly mooted for the film during the period McLaren declared it would be directed by controversial exploitation figure Russ Meyer. Long-time McLaren associate Julien Temple subsequently took charge, but the presence of pornography star Mary Millington in the final print provided a lingering link to that early notion. The absence of Rotten allowed bass player **Sid Vicious** to assume centre stage. He sang two rock 'n' roll classics first recorded by **Eddie Cochran**, 'Somethin' Else' and 'C'mon Everybody', but his most memorable contribution was a rendition of 'My Way'. Having begun the song in balladeer fashion, Vicious deconstructs it into a punk-attitude *tour-de-force*. The accompanying visual images, filmed at the Paris Olympia, close with the singer shooting members of the audience before proffering a 'V' sign. Such recordings were at the core of a soundtrack album that reached number 7 in the UK chart. *The Great Rock'n'Roll Swindle* contained other hit singles, including 'Silly Thing', but chief interest in its content lies in archive recordings drawn from the group's early incarnation. Neither a documentary nor fiction, the film is a tribute to McLaren's manifesto. As such, it provides an entertaining insight into one of pop's most mercurial characters.

Great Society

The Great Society was formed in August 1965 by **Grace Slick** (b. Grace Barnett Wing, 30 October 1939, Evanston, Illinois, USA; vocals, piano, recorder, guitar), her husband Jerry (drums) and his brother Darby Slick (lead guitar). David Minor (rhythm guitar) and Bard DuPont (bass) completed the line-up, having replaced Bill and Jean Piersol, although DuPont was replaced by Peter van Gelder, who also doubled on saxophone. One of the first San Franciscan rock groups, the quintet was active for 13 months, during which they issued one single, 'Someone To Love' (later known as 'Somebody To Love') on **Tom Donahue**'s Autumn Records/Northbeach label. This intriguing Darby Slick composition achieved fame when it was adopted by **Jefferson Airplane**, the group Grace joined in October 1966. The Great Society broke up on her departure, but two live collections, released solely in the wake of the singer's subsequent fame, show a group of rare imagination. The first album features 'White Rabbit', another composition Grace introduced to her new-found companions, which is preceded by a lengthy instrumental passage performed in a raga style that typified the Great Society's approach to many of their songs. Indeed, on the dissolution of the group, Darby Slick, Vandergelder and Minor went to study music in India, while Jerry was briefly a member of Final Solution before returning to film work.

● ALBUMS: *Conspicuous Only In Its Absence* (Columbia 1968) ★★★, *How It Was* (Columbia 1968) ★★.
● COMPILATIONS: *Live At The Matrix* (Sundazed 1989) ★★, *Born To Be Burned* (Sundazed 1996) ★★★.
● FURTHER READING: *The Jefferson Airplane And The San Francisco Sound*, Ralph J. Gleeson. *Grace Slick—The Biography*, Barbara Rowe. *Don't You Want Somebody To Love*, Darby Slick.

Great Waltz, The

In a Broadway season that was dominated by the all-American, smart and sophisticated **Anything Goes**, one of the most spectacular and elaborate stage productions of the 30s, *The Great Waltz*, opened at New York's huge Center Theatre in the Rockefeller Centre on 22 September 1934. A gigantic undertaking—almost 200 performers appeared onstage, including an orchestra of some 50 musicians—the show was based on a London production of the operetta, *Waltzes In Vienna*, and had music and lyrics by Johann Strauss Jnr. and Desmond Carter. The book, by **Moss Hart**, details the struggles between the younger Strauss (Guy Robertson), and his father, Johann Strauss Snr. (H. Reeves-Smith), which eventually results in the latter relinquishing his position—and his baton—to his son. The score contained several attractive numbers such as 'Like A Star In The Sky', 'Danube So Blue', 'Love Will Find You', and 'While You Love Me'. Audience and critical reactions were mixed, but the show ran for a creditable 298 performances and was revived briefly in 1935. A different

version of the *The Great Waltz* opened at London's Drury Lane Theatre in 1970. It had music by both Strauss Snr. and Jnr, with **Robert Wright** and **George Forrest**'s lyrics, and a book by Jerome Chodorov that was based on a story by Moss Hart and Milton Lazarus. This production ran for more than 600 performances.

Great White

This Los Angeles, California, USA–based heavy metal band was formed (as Dante Fox) in 1981 by Jack Russell (b. 5 December 1960, Montebello, California, USA; vocals), Mark Kendall (b. 29 April 1957, Loma Linda, California, USA; guitar), Lorne Black (bass) and Gary Holland (drums). Changing their name to Great White, they adopted a no-frills approach from the start, relying on the music—earthy, honest blues rock delivered with stunning precision—rather than gimmicks. The band attracted the attention of **EMI Records** with their self-financed mini-album, *Out Of The Night*, produced by their friend **Don Dokken**. Unfortunately, the momentum was not maintained, and their EMI debut was erratic and sold poorly, and the band was subsequently dropped. Far from disillusioned, they funded the recording of *Shot In The Dark* out of their own pockets, which eventually opened the door to a new contract with **Capitol Records**. Lorne Black and Gary Holland had already broken rank by this stage and were replaced by Tony Montana and Audie Desbrow (b. 17 May 1957, Los Angeles, California, USA), respectively. Michael Lardie (b. 8 September 1958, Anchorage, Alaska, USA) was also added on keyboards to expand the line-up to a five-piece and add an extra dimension to the band's sound. Enjoying the benefits of a larger budget, *Once Bitten . . .* received considerable critical acclaim with its more melodic, accessible sound. Sales of the album went on to pass the million mark. *Recovery . . . Live* paid homage to their roots, being an inspired selection of blues-styled cover versions from the **Who**, **Led Zeppelin**, **Humble Pie** and **Jimi Hendrix**. *. . . Twice Shy* and *Hooked* consolidated their success with further platinum awards.

Montana was replaced in 1992 by Dave Spitz, who was in turn replaced by Teddy Cook. The band parted company with Capitol following the release of a compilation set, and signed a new recording contract with Zoo Entertainment. *Sail Away*, the first album to feature Cook, was influenced by UK writer Julian Barnes' novel *The History Of The World In Ten And A Half Chapters*. The band continued to release new studio albums, albeit with diminishing returns, although they remained a popular live attraction. New bass player Sean McNabb (b. 24 September 1965, South Bend, Indiana, USA) featured on 1999's *Can't Get There From Here*. Desbrow left in 2000 and was replaced by Derrick Pontier. Ty Longley (b. 4 September 1974, Sharon, Pennsylvania, USA, d. 20 February 2003) replaced founder member Kendall the same year.

Tragedy struck Great White and many of their fans on 20 February 2003, when a fire broke out at the band's concert in West Warwick, Rhode Island. Guitarist Longley was among the 100 people who lost their lives.

● ALBUMS: *Out Of The Night* mini-album (Aegan 1982) ★★★, *Great White* (EMI 1984) ★★, *Shot In The Dark* (Capitol 1986) ★★★, *Once Bitten . . .* (Capitol 1987) ★★★★, *Recovery: Live!* (Enigma 1987) ★★, *Twice Shy* (Capitol 1989) ★★★, *Live In London* (Capitol 1990) ★★, *Hooked* (Capitol 1991) ★★★★, *Psycho City* (Capitol 1992)

★★★, *Sail Away* (Zoo 1994) ★★★, *Stage* (Zoo 1996) ★★, *Let It Rock* (Imago 1996) ★★, *Gallery* (Axe Killer 1999) ★★, *Great Zeppelin: A Tribute To Led Zeppelin* (Deadline 1999) ★★, *Can't Get There From Here* (Portrait 1999) ★★, *Latest & Greatest* (Portrait 2000) ★★★, *Final Cuts* aka *Recover* (Axe Killer/Cleopatra 2002) ★★.

● COMPILATIONS: *The Best Of Great White 1986–1992* (Capitol 1993) ★★★, *The Gold Collection* (EMI 1997) ★★★, *Rock Me: Best Of Great White* (Disky 1997) ★★★, *The Best Of Great White* (Capitol 2000) ★★★, *Greatest Hits* (Capitol 2001) ★★★★.

Great Ziegfeld, The

This vastly overblown, but breathtakingly opulent biopic of America's master showman, **Florenz Ziegfeld**, was produced for MGM by Hunt Stromberg in 1936. William Powell played the leading role, and William Anthony Macguire's screenplay, conveniently omitting the subject's reported excesses and philandering, concentrated on his undoubted charm, and unrivalled fervour and skill in the art of discovering a host of talented artists, before presenting them in the most lavish of settings, which displayed those talents to the full. The most impressive—and extravagant—scene involves an enormous fluted spiral structure which is surrounded by an imposing staircase. **Dennis Morgan** (dubbed by **Allan Jones**) sings 'A Pretty Girl Is Like A Melody', which segues into various classical excerpts as dozens of singers, dancers, and 'musicians', dressed in a variety of costumes ranging from white tie and tails, to bewigged Regency-style, 'perform' musical excerpts from the classics. As the sequence draws to a close, Virginia Bruce, as the Spirit of the *Follies*, appears high up on top of the set. Morgan resumes his song, and a circular curtain descends, shrouding everything and everybody, and somehow forms itself precisely on to the spiral surface. An extraordinary experience, and something that has to be seen to be believed. In complete contrast, the other most remarked-on sequence in the film comes when Luise Rainer, as Ziegfeld's first wife, **Anna Held**, makes a frenzied telephone call to her husband after discovering that he has married Billy Burke (played here by Myrna Loy). However, the film was mostly a feast of lavish spectacle and music featuring some memorable songs, including 'It's Delightful To Be Married' (Vincent Sotto–Anna Held), 'A Circus Must Be Different In A Ziegfeld Show' (Con Conrad–Herb Magidson), 'Shine On Harvest Moon' (Jack Norworth–Nora Bayes), 'Won't You Come And Play With Me' (Held), 'If You Knew Susie' (**Buddy De Sylva–Joseph Meyer**); and 'She's A Ziegfeld Follies Girl', 'You Gotta Pull Strings', 'Queen Of The Jungle' and 'You Never Looked So Beautiful' (all **Walter Donaldson–Harold Adamson**). **Fanny Brice**, the biggest star to emerge from the real-life *Ziegfeld Follies*, sang 'Yiddle On Your Fiddle' (**Irving Berlin**) and part of another of her all-time favourites, 'My Man' (Maurice Yvain–Channing Pollack) Also among the starry cast were **Ray Bolger**, Frank Morgan, Reginald Owen, Nat Pendleton, Herman Bing, Raymond Walburn, Ernest Cossart, Joseph Cawthorn, Virginia Grey, Buddy Doyle, Jean Chatburn, and Robert Greig. The credit for the film's splendid photography went to Oliver T. Marsh, Ray June, and George Folsey, and the dance sequences were staged by Seymour Felix. The director was Robert Z. Leonard. *The Great Ziegfeld* won Academy Awards for best picture and actress (Luise Rainer). William Powell played Florenz Ziegfeld again in the 1946 film *Ziegfeld Follies*.

Greatest Show On Earth (rock)

This London-based octet—Ozzie Lane (vocals), Garth Watt-Roy (guitar/vocals), Mick Deacon (keyboards), Ian Aitcheson (saxophone), Tex Philpotts (saxophone), Dick Hanson (trumpet), Norman Watt-Roy (bass) and Ron Prudence (drums)—was formed in 1968 as a soul band. New Orleans-born Lane later returned to America leaving his erstwhile colleagues to forge a more progressive direction with new singer Colin Horton-Jennings. The group completed two albums that displayed a strong compositional skill as well as an imaginative use of brass. They enjoyed a brief popularity in Europe following the success of the single, 'Real Cool World', but the Greatest Show On Earth found little favour at home and broke up in 1971. Norman Watt-Roy then formed **Glencoe**, and later became a member of **Ian Dury**'s Block-heads.

● ALBUMS: *Horizons* (Harvest 1970) ★★★, *The Going's Easy* (Harvest 1970) ★★, *The Greatest Show On Earth* (Harvest 1975) ★★★.

Greatest Show On Earth, The (film musical)

Tracing the fortunes and misfortunes of a touring circus, and the lives and loves of some of its star performers, this 1952 film was directed by Cecil B. De Mille in the spectacular manner that was his trademark. The central plot has manager/ringmaster Brad Braden (Charlton Heston) hiring trapeze artist The Great Sebastian (Cornel Wilde) who thus ousts Holly (**Betty Hutton**) from her starring role. As the pair of aerialists seek to outdo one another high above the sawdust, down in the ring other stories unfold, notably that of the on-the-run clown, Buttons (James Stewart). Also in the cast are **Dorothy Lamour**, Gloria Grahame, Henry Wilcoxon (who also co-produced with De Mille), Lyle Bettger and Lawrence Tierney. Appearing as themselves are Emmett Kelly, Cucciola, Antoinette Concello, John Ringling North and Tuffy Genders. Filmed in Technicolor and running two and a half hours, the film won an Oscar for the Best Picture. Disappointingly, the film's view of circus life was cliché-ridden; the most memorable scene comes not in the sawdust ring but is a spectacular train wreck. The film's excellent score was by **Victor Young** with Hutton and Lamour performing the songs. As the latter sings 'Lovely Luawanna Lady', a cutaway shows her co-stars from their 'Road' movies, **Bing Crosby** and **Bob Hope** in the audience.

Greaves, R.B.

b. Ronald Bertram Aloysius Greaves III, 28 November 1944, Georgetown, British Guyana. This singer, half North American Indian, made his greatest impact with the 1969 single, 'Take A Letter Maria'. A nephew of **Sam Cooke**, Greaves had built a career both in the Caribbean and in the UK, where he performed as Sonny Childs with his group the TNTs. His biggest hit had been recorded by both **Tom Jones** and **Stevie Wonder** before the author recorded it himself at the insistence of **Atlantic Records** president **Ahmet Ertegun**, who produced it. The ska-flavoured soul song peaked at number 2 in the US charts in late 1969. Greaves recorded a series of cover records as follow-ups, including **Burt Bacharach** and **Hal David**'s '(There's) Always Something There To Remind Me', **James Taylor**'s 'Fire And Rain' and **Procol Harum**'s 'Whiter Shade Of Pale'. All charted, as did his self-titled 1970 album. Greaves left the label in the 70s when Ertegun could no longer spare time to work with him directly. He recorded briefly for **MGM Records** and then turned to country music without much commercial success.

● ALBUMS: *Greaves* (Atco 1969) ★★★, *R.B. Greaves* (Atco 1970) ★★★.

Grebenshikov, Boris

b. 1953, Russia. With the advent of *perestroika*, singer and songwriter Grebenshikov became the first Russian rock artist to record and perform in the West. At school in Leningrad (St. Petersburg), he translated western songs and performed them with a beat group. In 1972 he formed Aquarium, which became the most famous of Russian rock groups. Among its members were Sasha Titov (bass), Seva Gakkel (cello) and Diusha Romanov. Grebenshikov's early writing method was to adapt foreign material to the Russian language. Thus **Bob Dylan**'s 'Knockin' On Heaven's Door' became 'Knocking On The Doors Of Grass', and **George Harrison** was honoured in 'In The Temple Of Radjah Krishnu' and a **David Bowie** tune became 'Song Of The Silent Days'. Aquarium also had hippie and reggae phases in its musical evolution. By the mid-80s, however, Grebenshikov had achieved a personal voice, best heard on his biggest Russian hit, 'This Train's On Fire' (1988). In the same year, he was signed by **CBS Records** and travelled to the UK and the USA to record an album with **David A. Stewart** of the **Eurythmics**. Grebenshikov returned to St. Petersburg in 1989 and rejoined Aquarium. His decision to record in the West was fiercely attacked in songs by rival Russian bands Alissa and Brigada S.

● ALBUMS: *Radio Silence* (CBS 1989) ★★★.

● COMPILATIONS: *Russian Songwriter: A Collection From Boris Grebenshikov* (Naxos 2003) ★★★.

Grech, Ric

b. Richard Roman Grech, 1 November 1946, Bordeaux, France, d. 16 March 1990, Leicester, England. Bass player Ric (sometimes Rick) Grech embraced professional music in 1965, when he joined Leicester-based outfit, the **Farinas** (also using the names X-Citers and Roaring Sixties), which later evolved into **Family**. Prior to that he had played with the Leicester City Youth Orchestra. By doubling on violin, Grech added considerable texture to an already inventive, exciting attraction but abandoned them in rancorous circumstances during an American tour. Grech then joined **Blind Faith**, where an understanding forged with **Steve Winwood** continued with spells in **Airforce** (1970) and **Traffic** (1970–71) and on many other albums as a session player with Winwood. He found time during this hectic period to produce **Rosetta Hightower** and carry out sessions with the **Faces** and **Fairport Convention**. After leaving Traffic in December 1971 Grech was later a member of the **Crickets**, alongside guitarist **Albert Lee**, and he also appeared on a session basis for **Jim Capaldi**, **Vivian Stanshall**, **Chuck Berry**, **Muddy Waters**, Gordon Jackson, **Graham Bond** and **Streetwalkers**, the latter featuring former Family colleagues **Roger Chapman** and John Whitney. Grech then moved to the USA, where an association with **Gram Parsons** resulted in his composing 'Kiss The Children' and 'Las Vegas' and co-producing *G.P.* with the singer. Grech then performed at **Eric Clapton**'s famous Rainbow Concert and briefly joined **KGB** with **Mike Bloomfield** and Ray Kennedy. On his return to the UK he formed a country rock band Square Dance Machine, but drug problems increasingly undermined his career. Years of sustained substance abuse took their toll on his liver and he died in March 1990.

Grech was a musician who was able to embrace many styles and play them all with conviction. The combination of violin and bass was in itself interesting, but to be musically at home with country, jazz, blues, folk, soul and rock, was a remarkable achievement.

● COMPILATIONS: *The Last Five Years* (RSO 1973) ★★★.

Greco, Buddy

b. Armando Greco, 14 August 1926, Philadelphia, Pennsylvania, USA. Greco is a singer and pianist known for his swinging, ultra-hip interpretations of classy songs. The son of a music critic who had his own radio show on station WPEN, Buddy himself appeared on WPEN at the age of five, initially making his mark as a singer and actor. Later on, like his two brothers, he studied to become a pianist, practising and playing at the Philadelphia Settlement House, a 10-block complex of recreational and hobby facilities, where so many of the city's youthful musicians congregated. Greco led his own trio during 1944–49, and recorded a major hit version of Carmen Lombardo's 'Ooh! Look-A-There, Ain't She Pretty?', though the singer received only $32 for recording the single. Heard by **Benny Goodman** while playing at Philadelphia's Club 13, he was offered a job by the band leader and subsequently became pianist-vocalist-arranger with the Goodman orchestra, appearing with Goodman's sextet at the London Palladium in 1949, embarking on several tours with the band and his vocals gracing such Goodman sides as 'It Isn't Fair', 'Don't Worry 'Bout Me', 'The Land of Oo-Bla-Dee' and 'Brother Bill'.

By 1951 Greco had become a solo act once more, gaining a regular spot on the *Broadway Open House* television show and providing **Coral Records** with a hit single in 'I Ran All The Way Home'. He also won many lucrative nightclub engagements, one of which provided the bestselling album *Buddy Greco At Mister Kelly's*, a superb document of his appearances at the Chicago club in 1955. Greco's biggest hit was still to come, a non-stop, grab-at-the-lyrics version of **Richard Rodgers** and **Lorenz Hart**'s 'The Lady Is A Tramp', cut for Epic Records in 1960. This track sold over a million copies worldwide and gave the singer his first UK chart entry. During the late 60s and 70s Greco became increasingly associated with the British showbusiness scene, playing dates at London's Talk Of The Town, appearing on the Royal Command Performance and recording an instrumental album with the London Symphony Orchestra. This well-travelled and appreciated performer claims to have played every major club in the world on at least two occasions, and was still touring round some of them again in the late 80s. In the early 90s he re-established himself in Britain with some well-received cabaret appearances at London's Café Royal.

● ALBUMS: *At Mr. Kelly's* (Coral 1956) ★★★, *Broadway Melodies* (Kapp 1956) ★★★, *My Buddy* (Epic 1959) ★★★, *Songs For Swinging Losers* (Columbia 1960) ★★★, *Buddy's Back In Town* (Columbia 1961) ★★★, *I Like It Swinging* (Columbia 1961) ★★★, *Let's Love* (Columbia 1962) ★★★, *Buddy And Soul* (Columbia 1963) ★★★, *Buddy's Back In Town* (Columbia 1963) ★★★, *Sings For Intimate Moments* (Columbia 1963) ★★★, *Soft And Gentle* (Columbia 1963) ★★★, *One More Time* (Columbia 1964) ★★★, *On Stage* (Columbia 1964) ★★★, *Modern Sounds Of Hank Williams* (Columbia 1965) ★★, *I Love A Piano* (Columbia 1966)

★★★, *Let The Sunshine In* (Wand 1970) ★★, *Live At Pullen's Talk Of North, April 1974* (Pye 1974) ★★★, *For Once In My Life* (Bulldog 1982) ★★★, *Moving On (It's Magic)* (Prestige 1990) ★★★, *Route 66* (Capitol 1994) ★★★, *MacArthur Park* (Candid 1996) ★★, *Live Buddy Greco* (Dolphin 1998) ★★, *Jazz Grooves* (Candid 1999) ★★★, *Swing In The Key Of BG* (Houston Party 2003) ★★★.

● COMPILATIONS: *Golden Hour Presents Buddy Greco* (Golden Hour 1978) ★★★, *Greatest Hits* (Columbia 1984) ★★★, *Talkin' Verve* (Verve 2001) ★★★.

Gréco, Juliette

b. 7 February 1927, Montpelier, France. An actress and inimitable singer of the *chanson*, Gréco was born the daughter of a police chief and a mother who became a Resistance worker in 1939. After spending some time in prison during the Occupation when she was 15, Gréco took acting lessons, and began to dress in men's black clothing—heavy overcoats and trousers, with polo neck sweaters—and cut her hair in a fringe. In the mid-40s she became a leading member of the philosopher Jean-Paul Sartre's intellectual Existentialist movement, which flourished in cafés such as Le Boeuf Sur Le Toit and Café Flore on Paris' Left Bank. Sartre encouraged her to sing, and with her slightly raw-edged voice, attractive appearance and impressive stage presence, she soon became immensely popular in the world of cabaret. Among her most memorable—and usually sad—songs are Hubert Giraud and Jean Drejec's 'Sous Le Ciel De Paris' ('Under Paris Skies'), **Jacques Brel**'s 'J'arrive' and 'Je Suis Bien', along with several written by Joseph Kosma and Jacques Prevert, including 'Les Feuilles Mortes', which, with an English lyric by **Johnny Mercer**, became the wistful 'Autumn Leaves'.

After appearing in a few French films from 1949 onwards, in the late 50s Gréco embarked on a brief Hollywood career sponsored by Darryl F. Zanuck, starring in *The Sun Also Rises*, *Roots Of Heaven*, *Crack In The Mirror* and *The Big Gamble*. Afterwards, she returned to her *chansons*, and has continued to sing ever since. Her popularity in Britain has waned since the 50s, but she did perform in London in 1989 for the first time in 10 years. In the previous year, she married her musical director and accompanist Gérard Jouannest. Her previous husbands, Philippe Lemaire and Michel Piccoli, were both actors.

● ALBUMS: *Juliette Gréco* (Philips 1954) ★★★, *Gréco* (Philips 1957) ★★, *Les Grandes Chansons* (Philips 1961) ★★★★, *Juliette Gréco Showcase* (Philips 1962) ★★★, *La Femme* (Philips 1968) ★★, *Juliette Gréco* (French Decca 1972) ★★★, *Je Vous Attends* (French Decca 1974) ★★, *Le Disque D'Or* (Phonogram 1974) ★★, *Un Jour D'ete Et Quelques Nuits* (Label 1999) ★★★.

● COMPILATIONS: *Greatest Hits* (Impact 1977) ★★★.

● FILMS: *Au Royaume Des Cieux* (1949), *Orpheus* (1950), *The Green Glove* (1952), *Quand Tu Liras Cette Lettre* (1953), *Paris Does Strange Things* (1956), *The Sun Also Rises* (1957), *Bonjour Tristesse* (1958), *Naked Earth* (1958), *Roots Of Heaven* (1959), *Whirlpool* (1959), *Crack In The Mirror* (1960), *The Big Gamble* (1961), *Where The Truth Lies* (1962), *Uncle Tom's Cabin* (1965), *The Night Of The Generals* (1967).

Greedies

This UK-based trio featured **Thin Lizzy**'s **Phil Lynott** (b. 20 August 1951, Dublin, Eire, d. 4 January 1986; vocals/bass), the **Sex Pistols**' Steve Jones (b. 3 September 1955, London, England; guitar) and Paul Cook (b. 20 July 1956, London, England; drums). They amalgamated in December 1979 as the Greedies for a one-off UK hit, a frantic version of 'We Wish You A Merry Christmas' titled 'A Merry Jingle', which peaked at number 28 in the first week of January 1980. Later on in the year Jones and Cook, recording as the **Professionals**, narrowly missed the UK Top 40 with '1-2-3'. Lynott died aged 34, from liver, kidney and heart failure and pneumonia following a drug overdose.

Green Apple Quick Step

Led by vocalist Tyler Willman, alongside Mari Anne Braeden (bass/vocals), Dana Turner (guitar) and drummer Jeff Reading, Seattle's Green Apple Quick Step underwent a difficult germination. The rock band's debut was critically well received but not promoted by their record label (at that time the label, Medicine Records, was backed by Reprise Records), a problem doubled by the failure of the band to secure mainstream airplay. When their tour van was stolen midway through touring in support of the debut, a reappraisal was called for. This resulted in the band moving over to Medicine/Giant Records, and a second album was co-produced by Nick DiDia and **Pearl Jam**'s Stone Gossard, with whom the band share management (Gossard also allowed the band to use his home studio facility free). This second collection included 'Dizzy', featured on the soundtrack to *The Basketball Diaries* film. For *New Disaster* in 1998, the band changed direction and adopted a more 'indie pop' style. They added a further guitarist Dan Kempthorne that year.

● ALBUMS: *Wonderful Virus* (Medicine/Reprise 1993) ★★★, *Reloaded* (Medicine/Giant 1995) ★★★, *New Disaster* (Columbia 1998) ★★★.

Green Bullfrog

A one-off 'concept' band who recorded a single album for **Decca Records** in 1971 while 'off-duty' from their day jobs as members of **Deep Purple**, Green Bullfrog comprised **Roger Glover** (bass), **Ian Gillan** (vocals), Jon Lord (keyboards), Ian Paice (drums) and **Ritchie Blackmore** (guitar). Although the album's sleeve did not list musicians in its credits, few were in any doubt as to whom the participants were—Blackmore's distinctive guitar playing giving the game away to the critics. Comprising a series of unappetizing studio jams, it later transpired that the record was issued only to fulfil contractual ties.

● ALBUMS: *Green Bullfrog* (Decca 1971) ★★.

Green Day

With alternative rock music going overground in the early 90s, few acts were better positioned to exploit the commercial possibilities than Green Day—Billie Joe Armstrong (b. 17 February 1972, California, USA; vocals/guitar), Mike Dirnt (b. 4 May 1972, California, USA; bass/vocals) and Tre Cool (b. Frank Edwin Wright III, 9 December 1972, Germany; drums/vocals). Armstrong and Dirnt had been playing together since the age of 11 in the refinery town of Rodeo, California, performing in various garage bands. Tre Cool had been in a band called the Lookouts who broke up in 1990, but their final EP, *IV*, featured Billie Joe Armstrong playing guitar and singing backing vocals on three tracks. Armstrong and Dirnt had already formed Sweet Children with ex-Isocracy drummer John Kiffmeyer, releasing an EP in 1987. The new trio's debut release came on Livermore's Lookout! Records in 1989, the *1,000 Hours* EP. However, two weeks before release the band informed Livermore that they had changed their name to Green Day, inspired by their fondness for marijuana and by the fact that another local band, Sweet Baby Jesus, had just changed their name to Sweet Baby and signed with Slash/**Warner Brothers Records**. Green Day's debut album, *39/Smooth*, recorded in a single day, comprised 10 pop punk tracks. A limited edition EP (*Slappy*) for Lookout! followed. Kiffmeyer booked their first national tour, but afterwards left the band to concentrate on college (his only subsequent musical activity came in the Ne'er Do Wells). Cool was asked to fill in, and immediately wrote the comedic 'Dominated Love Slave' for 1992's *Kerplunk!*, where the 60s pop quotient was reduced in favour of a synthesis of 70s British punk bands the **Jam** and **Stiff Little Fingers**. It sold over 50,000 records through word of mouth and underground media support

Green Day decided to take the plunge and move to a major label, signing to Warner Brothers subsidiary **Reprise Records**, despite bigger offers from elsewhere. A&R man Rob Cavallo was also recruited as producer for their third album. Released in 1994, *Dookie* gradually stalked the charts going on to sell over nine million copies in the USA. The album tracks 'Long View', 'Basket Case', 'Welcome To Paradise', 'When I Come Around' and 'She', in addition to the soundtrack cut 'J.A.R. (Jason Andrew Relva)', received extensive airplay on rock radio and **MTV**. The band's arduous touring schedule was the chief reason for their rise, and was topped off by appearances on the 1994 **Lollapalooza** package and the revived **Woodstock** event. The other main factor was the estimable quality of their songwriting. As Dirnt said: 'We just figured out a formula and Billie Joe writes real good songs, that's all.'

With *Dookie* being so successful, it came as no surprise when Green Day was nominated in no less than four Grammy categories. In 1995, it was confirmed that they had sold over 10 million albums worldwide, a stunning achievement for a band remaining faithful to a basic punk pop framework. *Insomniac* (1995) and *Nimrod* (1997) confirmed their popularity, with the band's fans seemingly unfazed by the weakness of the songs compared to the material on *Dookie*. The tracks 'Geek Stink Breath', 'Brain Stew'/'Jaded', 'Hitchin' A Ride' and 'Good Riddance (Time Of Your Life)' received extensive airplay. Their fourth major label release, October 2000's *Warning*, was a hugely enjoyable power pop album that, contrary to the band's defiant claims, owed little to their punk roots.

After remaining quiet for a couple of years, the members of Green Day returned to the studio to begin work on a new album. Eschewing the frat boy lyrics that had a tendency to dominate the band's earlier work, songwriter Armstrong took stock of the prevailing political climate to construct a remarkably mature concept album. The band's faith in their audience was repaid when *American Idiot* debuted at the top of the *Billboard* 200 in September 2004. They also enjoyed a US Top 5 hit single with the album's stand-out track, 'Boulevard Of Broken Dreams'.

● ALBUMS: *39/Smooth* (Lookout! 1990) ★★★, *Kerplunk!* (Lookout! 1992) ★★★, *Dookie* (Reprise 1994) ★★★★★, *Insomniac* (Reprise 1995) ★★, *Nimrod* (Reprise 1997) ★★★, *Warning* (Reprise 2000) ★★★, *American Idiot* (Reprise 2004) ★★★★, *Bullet In A Bible* (Reprise 2005) ★★★.

● COMPILATIONS: *1,039/Smoothed Out Slappy Hours* (Lookout! 1991) ★★, *International Superhits!* (Warners 2001) ★★★★, *Shenanigans* (Reprise 2002) ★★★.

● DVD/VIDEOS: *International Supervideos!* (Warner Music Vision 2001), *Bullet In A Bible* (Reprise 2005).

● FURTHER READING: *Green Day: American Idiots & The New Punk Explosion*, Ben Myers.

Green Jelly

Described as 'this year's musical lowpoint' by **Rolling Stone** magazine in 1993, Green Jello ended that same year being forced to change their name to Green Jelly, in order to avoid a lawsuit from General Foods. Initially conceived as a 'video' band, they rose to fame largely through this medium. Their breakthrough hit certainly boasted excellent animation, but little musical substance, allied as it was to a psychedelic heavy metal version of the popular nursery rhyme, 'Three Little Pigs'. Like their follow-up, a cover version of the **Sex Pistols**' 'Anarchy In The UK', it was an exercise of limited merit.

● ALBUMS: *Cereal Killer* (Zoo/BMG 1993) ★★★, *333* (Zoo/BMG 1994) ★.

Green Linnet Records

Green Linnet was established in 1976 by the former executive director of America's World Affairs Centre, Wendy Newton (b. New York City, USA). She gave up that campaigning role (for various humanitarian causes) through exhaustion and moved to Ireland to recuperate. However, once there she immediately stumbled upon Tommy Peoples playing in a pub in Ennistymon, thus instigating her obsession with documenting and re-releasing traditional Irish music. Sourcing every traditional record she could find, particularly those of the **Chieftains**, she flew back to America to continue the chase. Eventually she found a regular session at the Bunratty pub in the Bronx, New York, which she made her home for the next year and a half. Prompted by the suggestion of a friend, she decided the only way to adequately rationalize her conversion to Irish music was to record and release it herself. Newton acquired Green Linnet, which had previously been established by the same friend to release cassettes of **Seamus Ennis**, in 1976. Her first signing was Mick Moloney, and through him subsequent artists including **Eileen Ivers** followed. Still looking on the label as a hobby rather than business or career, Newton's first major coup was in recording the band Irish Tradition. The roster of artists to appear have subsequently included many of the greats of both contemporary and traditional Irish music— including **Altan**, **Patrick Street**, the **Tannahill Weavers**, Hugh Gillespie, James Keane, **Rosalie Sorrels**, **Wolfstone**, **Relativity**, **Niamh Parsons** and **Capercaillie**. There have been setbacks in Green Linnet's ascendancy, however, not least when their pressing plant burned down in 1985 without insurance. The label's success has led to the launch of a world music subsidiary, Xenophile, and well-equipped offices in Danbury, Connecticut. As Newton stated to *Folk Roots* magazine in 1996 while celebrating the label's 20th anniversary, 'Record companies have a lousy reputation for being greedy and having no integrity or taste and I believe they have that reputation because they've earned it . . . We've always tried to be fair and behave with integrity.' Few if any of the numerous musicians to have worked with Newton have been forced to qualify that statement.

● COMPILATIONS: *The Twentieth Anniversary Collection* (Green Linnet 1996) ★★★★, *Joyful Noise: Celtic Favorites From Green Linnet* (Green Linnet 1998) ★★★★, *Song Of The Green Linnet* (Green Linnet 2000) ★★★, *25 Years Of Celtic Music* (Green Linnet 2001) ★★★★.

Green Nuns Of The Revolution

The Green Nuns was initially formed in 1994 when Matt Coldrick and Sev Burden were sharing a flat. Coldrick was working as a session guitarist and composing soundtracks for natural history films, while Burden was a psychedelic trance DJ. Together they made their first recording, 'The Whirling Dervish', which was produced by Pete Smith (**The Hypnotist**) and released on Triumph Records, before Burden left the country to travel. In the meantime, Burden had introduced Coldrick to the sound engineer Dick Trevor, who had been on the techno/trance scene since the days of Castle Morton. Having established their Blaglands Studios, Coldrick and Trevor released a series of recordings that began with 'Cor/Conflict' (**TIP Records** 1995) and included 'Atomic Armadillo' (on **Flying Rhino**'s compilation *Boyd In The Void*). Radio exposure from such DJs as **Danny Rampling**, **Annie Nightingale** and **John Peel** broadcast their sound around the UK before the Green Nuns played a number of live shows, including the Brixton Academy, the Trinity Centre in Bristol and the Liberty Science Centre in New York. While performing on a session for soul singer **Gabrielle**, Coldrick met the keyboard player Neil Cowley (who has also played with the **Brand New Heavies**), who soon joined the group to work on new tracks for a debut album. Released in October 1997, *Rock Bitch Mafia* featured more of the band's muscular psychedelic trance. Straightahead rockers such as 'Cor' and 'Rock Bitch' feature chunky sledgehammer riffs, while 'Octofunk' has more quirky, funky melodies and 'Klunk' includes fragments of cartoon noise. The group also produced a number of excellent remixes for other artists, notably **Prana** ('Scarab') and Tufaan ('Tufaan').

● ALBUMS: *Rock Bitch Mafia* (Flying Rhino 1997) ★★★.

Green On Red

Formed as the Serfers in Tucson, Arizona, USA, in 1979, this influential rock band initially featured Dan Stuart (guitar/vocals), Jack Waterson (bass), Van Christian (drums) and Sean Nagore (keyboards). Christian and Nagore were replaced by Alex MacNicol (d. 2004) and Chris Cacavas respectively for the first EP, *Two Bibles*, released under their new name. Green On Red attracted attention as part of the 60s-influenced 'paisley underground' alongside the **Rain Parade** and the **Dream Syndicate**. However, their sound owed more to **Neil Young** and country/blues traditions, an influence that became more apparent when **Chuck Prophet** IV joined on lead guitar in 1984, making his debut on the following year's excellent full-length *Gas Food Lodging*. Sophisticated arrangements on their major label debuts, 1985's *No Free Lunch* EP and 1987's *The Killer Inside Me*, the latter the first to feature new drummer Keith Mitchell, saw Green On Red pushing for mainstream recognition, but shortly afterwards frontman Stuart had a nervous breakdown on stage in Athens, Greece.

Waterson and Cacavas left to pursue solo careers, while the remaining duo, Prophet and Stuart, forged ahead, using session musicians for 1989's well-received comeback *Here Come The Snakes*. Both members also operated outside the confines of Green On Red, most notably Stuart's involvement on *Danny And Dusty*, featuring Steve Wynn and members of the **Long Ryders**. In 1991, Prophet and Stuart re-emerged with a new Green On Red collection, *Scapegoats*, recorded in Nashville with the help of producer **Al Kooper** on keyboards. Following one further Green On Red release, they elected to concentrate on solo work, with Prophet's career taking off in 1993 with the well-received *Balinese Dancer*. Stuart relocated to Spain, where he settled for a quiet life away from the music business. The original line-up, minus the recently deceased MacNicol, reconvened in January 2006 to play a live show at the Astoria, London. The band had been due to play at the venue back in 1987 before Stuart's breakdown in Athens.

● ALBUMS: *Green On Red* mini-album (Down There 1982) ★★★, *Gravity Talks* (Slash 1983) ★★★, *Gas Food Lodging* (Enigma/Zippo 1985) ★★★★★, *The Killer Inside Me* (Mercury 1987) ★★★★, *Here Come The Snakes* (China/Ariole 1989) ★★★★, *Live At The Town And Country Club* 10-inch album (China 1989) ★★, *This Time Around* (China 1989) ★★★, *Scapegoats* (China 1991) ★★★, *Too Much Fun* (China 1992) ★★★.

● COMPILATIONS: *The Best Of Green On Red* (China 1989) ★★★★, *The Little Things In Life* (Music Club 1991) ★★★, *What Were We Thinking?* (Normal 1997) ★★★.

Green Pajamas

The inspired creation of multi-instrumentalists **Jeff Kelly** and Joe Ross, this cult Seattle, Washington, USA–based psychedelic pop outfit was formed in 1983 when the two protagonists met at a party. Influenced by the Los Angeles 'paisley underground' scene, the duo recorded the *Summer Of Lust* cassette in Ross' attic on a basic four-track machine with occasional help from drummers Karl Wilhelm and Joe Bauer. The cassette was released on Tom Dyer's local Green Monkey label (an abridged version of the album was later released on vinyl by the UK label Ubik Records). The extremely limited private pressing *Happy Halloween* followed later in the year. Ross and Kelly were joined by Wilhelm and singer-songwriter Steven Lawrence on 1986's 7-inch single 'Kim The Waitress' (later a minor hit for **Material Issue**), following which Ross temporarily left the band. The Green Pajama's debut album proper, *Book Of Hours*, was recorded by Kelly, Wilhelm and keyboard player Bruce Haedt on an eight-track in Dyer's basement studio.

Two solo projects, Kelly's *Coffee In Nepal* and Haedt's *Miss Lyons Looking Sideways*, preceded the return of Joe Ross on 1989's 'Sister Anne' single. The following year's *Ghosts Of Love* featured Kelly, Ross and Wilhelm and a sprawling cast of supporting musicians, but despite the excellence of the material the Green Pajamas remained strictly a cult act. A number of Kelly solo recordings appeared in the early 90s, including his first CD release *Ash Wednesday Rain*. He continued to work with Ross and Wilhelm in the Goblin Market, before reviving the Green Pajamas for the 1994 single, 'Song For Christina'.

The band's overseas popularity was confirmed when they signed to the Australian Camera Obscura label in the late 90s. Kelly, Ross and Wilhelm were joined by another singer-songwriter, Eric Lichter for the recording of 1997's *Strung*

Behind The Sun. A two-year period of intense productivity saw the release of the *Strung Out* EP and *All Clues Lead To Meagan's Bed*, while the band's singles back catalogue was compiled on Get Hip's *Indian Winter* collection. Long-time friend and collaborator Laura Weller (guitar/vocals) was added to the line-up on 1999's *Seven Fathoms Down And Falling*. The *In A Glass Darkly* EP, released in 2001 on the Hidden Agenda label, was inspired by the writings of J.S. Le Fanu.

● ALBUMS: *Summer Of Lust* cassette (Green Monkey 1984) ★★★, *Happy Halloween* cassette (Private 1984) ★★★★, *Book Of Hours* (Green Monkey 1987) ★★★, *November* cassette (Green Monkey 1988) ★★★, *Ghosts Of Love* (Green Monkey/Bomp 1990) ★★★★, *Strung Behind The Sun* (Camera Obscura 1997) ★★★★, *Strung Out* mini-album (Camera Obscura 1997) ★★★, *All Clues Lead To Meagan's Bed* (Camera Obscura 1998) ★★★★, *Seven Fathoms Down And Falling* (Woronzow/Rubric 1999) ★★★★, *The Caro-lers' Song* (Hidden Agenda 2001) ★★★, *This Is Where We Disappear* (Woronzow/Rubric 2002) ★★★, *Lust Never Sleeps* 1996 live recording (Endgame 2003) ★★★, *Northern Gothic* (Camera Obscura 2003) ★★★, *21st Century Seance* (Hidden Agenda 2005) ★★★.

● COMPILATIONS: *Indian Winter: A Collection Of Singles And Unreleased Songs Recorded 1985—1996* (Get Hip 1997) ★★★.

Green River

Seattle, USA band Green River may go down in history as the first 'grunge' band, and were certainly the first to release a record on the **Sub Pop Records** label. The band was formed in 1984 with Jeff Ament (ex-Deranged Diction) on bass, drummer Alex Shumway, guitarist and vocalist Mark Arm and former Mr Epp guitarist Steve Turner. The line-up was expanded with the addition of ex-Ducky Boys/March Of Crimes guitarist Stone Gossard, and they began to air their wares on the local north west scene. By 1985 they had appeared alongside the **Melvins** on the *Deep Six* compilation album on the C/Z label, released a six-song EP, *Come On Down*, for Homestead, and were playing the same clubs as another local band, **Soundgarden**. Both bands came to the attention of Sub Pop owner Bruce Pavitt, who decided to expand his cassette-based fanzine into a full record label and worked with them in producing the 12-inch EP *Dry As A Bone*, which was released in June 1987. Turner left soon afterwards and was replaced by another Deranged Diction member, Bruce Fairweather. In May 1988 they released the mini-album *Rehab Doll* (cassette and CD versions added *Dry As A Bone*), but the band was already falling apart due to musical differences between Arm and Ament, which led to them splitting in June. Arm joined Turner with ex-Melvins bass player Matt Lukin and drummer Dan Peters to form **Mudhoney**. Ament, Gossard and Fairweather regrouped with ex-Malfunkshun vocalist Andrew Wood and drummer Regan Hagar and formed Lords Of The Wasteland, who quickly evolved into **Mother Love Bone**. After the death of Wood in March 1990, that band fractured, with Gossard and Ament forming the hugely successful **Pearl Jam**. Green River thus became an important footnote in the development of the 90s' strongest rock movement, although their light was reignited temporarily on 30 November 1993 at the Aladdin Hotel in Las Vegas, when Pearl Jam ended their live set early to make way for a one-off re-formation of Green River, with Gossard,

Arm, Turner and Ament joined by Chuck Treece (bass player from **Urge Overkill**) playing drums.

● ALBUMS: *Rehab Doll* mini-album (Sub Pop 1988) ★★★.

Green Velvet

b. Curtis Alan Jones, 26 April 1967, Chicago, Illinois, USA. Whereas **Cajmere** is the name associated with his **house** productions, Green Velvet is Jones' green-haired **techno** incarnation. Jones became interested in club culture while studying a degree in chemical engineering at the University of Illinois. After graduating in 1991, he pursued his musical interests as both a DJ and producer. Establishing his own label, Cajual/Relief, he released his own infectious, humorous singles such as 'Preacherman', 'Answering Machine', 'The Stalker' and 'Flash' (released in the UK on the Open label) as well as those by DJ Sneak, Glenn Underground, Paul Johnson, Gemini, Tim Harper and Boo Williams. His debut as Green Velvet, *Constant Chaos* demonstrated Jones' fondness for both house and techno and drew inspiration from both the sinister disco of **Grace Jones** and the eccentricity of P-Funk. *The Nineties* compiled the best of his singles.

● ALBUMS: *Constant Chaos* (Music Man 1999) ★★★, *Whatever* (Music Man/Relief 2001) ★★★.

● COMPILATIONS: *The Nineties* (Music Man 1999) ★★★.

Green, Adam

b. 28 May 1981, Mount Kisco, New York, USA. Green began exorcising his songs onto four-track tape at the age of 12, eventually forming anti-folk favourites the **Moldy Peaches** (with, allegedly, one-time baby-sitter Kimya Dawson), for whom he would regularly appear on stage dressed in a Robin Hood costume. Although unreleased until 2002, Green's self-titled debut album (aka *Garfield*, in a version released with extra tracks) was actually recorded prior to the Moldy Peaches first album. The album took its emotional resonance from mildly abstract (and often amusing) songs that picked over the detritus of a childhood that Green has said was less than idyllic. This sense of loss for childhood was accentuated by songs that seemed to scan like nursery rhymes. Green's first 'proper' studio album, *Friends Of Mine*, backed Green's curious outsider songs with succinct, lush string arrange-ments orchestrated by cellist Jane Scarpantoni, a sometime collaborator of **Lou Reed**. Although aligned with anti-folk musicians, Green took overt inspiration from artists such as **Frank Sinatra** and **Chet Baker**. Oddly, the album included a paean to over-emotive American singer **Jessica Simpson** which asked: 'Jessica Simpson/Where has your love gone?/ It's not in your music, no' ('Jessica').

● ALBUMS: *Adam Green* (Rough Trade 2002) ★★★, *Garfield* (Rough Trade 2002) ★★★, *Friends Of Mine* (Rough Trade 2003) ★★★★, *Gemstones* (Rough Trade 2005) ★★★.

Green, Adolph

(see **Comden, Betty**)

Green, Al

b. Al Greene, 13 April 1946, Forrest City, Arkansas, USA. Having served his musical apprenticeship in the Greene Brothers, a fraternal gospel quartet, this urbane singer made his first recordings in 1960. Four years later he helped form the Creations with Curtis Rogers and Palmer Jones. These two companions subsequently wrote and produced 'Back Up Train', a simple, effective ballad and a 1967 R&B hit for his new group, Al Greene And The Soul Mates. Similar releases fared less well, prompting Greene's decision to work solo (as Al Green).

In 1969, Green shared a bill with band leader **Willie Mitchell**, who took the singer to **Hi Records**. The combination of a crack house band, Mitchell's tight production and Green's silky, sensuous voice, resulted in some of soul's definitive moments. The combination took a little time to gel, but with the release of 'I Can't Get Next To You' (1970), they were clearly on course. Previously a hit for the **Temptations**, this slower, blues-like interpretation established an early pattern. However, the success of 'Tired Of Being Alone' (1971), a Green original, introduced a smoother perspective. A US number 11 and a UK number 4, it was followed by 'Let's Stay Together' (1971), 'I'm Still In Love With You' (1972), 'Call Me (Come Back Home)', 'Here I Am (Come And Take Me)' (both 1973), each of which increased Green's stature as a major artist.

The singer's personal life, however, was rocked in October 1974. Following an argument, his girlfriend, Mary Woodson, burst in while the singer was taking a bath and poured boiling grits over his back. She then shot herself dead. Although he occasionally recorded gospel material, a scarred and shaken Green vowed to devote more time to God. His singles, meanwhile, remained popular, 'L-O-V-E (Love)' and 'Full Of Fire' were both R&B chart toppers in 1975, but his work grew increasingly predictable and lacked the passion of his earlier records. The solution was drastic. The partnership with Mitchell was dissolved and Green opened his own recording studio, American Music. The first single was the majestic 'Belle' (a US R&B Top 10 hit), although the accompanying album was a departure from his commercial formula and something of a 'critics favourite', as were the later Hi collections. The failure of further singles suggested that the problem was more than simply a tired working relationship. In 1979 Green fell from a Cincinnati stage, which he took as a further religious sign. *The Lord Will Make A Way* was the first of several gospel-only recordings, which included a 1985 reunion with Mitchell for *He Is The Light*. Green continued to record sacred material throughout the rest of the decade. His album, *Precious Lord*, won a Grammy for Best Gospel Album in 1982. A practising minister, he nonetheless reached the UK singles chart in 1989 with the distinctly secular 'Put A Little Love In Your Heart'. *Don't Look Back*, released in 1993, was a sparkling return to recording new R&B/soul material, and some critics rated it as high as albums such as *Let's Stay Together*. The US release was delayed for over two years, until *Your Heart's In Good Hands* was issued, containing eight tracks from *Don't Look Back*. In the ensuing period, Green was inducted into the **Rock And Roll Hall Of Fame**. Green's first album of the new millennium, the 2003 secular recording *I Can't Stop*, saw him teaming up with Mitchell and many of the original Hi session musicians for the first time in years. The album was released on the famous jazz label **Blue Note Records**. The duo kept their revived partnership going on another fine collection for Blue Note, *Everything's OK*.

Green's 70s albums, *Gets Next To You*, **Let's Stay Together**, *I'm Still In Love With You*, *Call Me* and *Explores Your Mind*, are particularly recommended. *Greatest Hits* and *Take Me To The River (Greatest Hits Volume 2)* offer the simplest overview, with the former being reissued on CD in an expanded form with 15 tracks. *Truth 'N' Time* (1978) best represents the post-Mitchell, pre-gospel recordings.

● ALBUMS: *Green Is Blues* (Hi 1970) ★★★, *Gets Next To You* (Hi 1971) ★★★★, *Let's Stay Together* (Hi 1972) ★★★★★, *Al Green* (Bell 1972) ★★★, *I'm Still In Love With You* (Hi 1972) ★★★★, *Call Me* (Hi 1973) ★★★★, *Livin' For You* (Hi 1973) ★★★★, *Explores Your Mind* (Hi 1974) ★★★★★, *Is Love* (Hi 1975) ★★★, *Full Of Fire* (Hi 1976) ★★★, *Have A Good Time* (Hi 1976) ★★★, *The Belle Album* (Hi 1977) ★★★★, *Truth 'N' Time* (Hi 1978) ★★★★, *The Lord Will Make A Way* (Myrrh 1980) ★★★, *Higher Plane* (Myrrh 1981) ★★★, *Tokyo Live* (Hi 1981) ★★★★, *Precious Lord* (Myrhh 1982) ★★★★, *I'll Rise Again* (Myrrh 1983) ★★★, *Christmas* (A&M 1983) ★★, *Trust In God* (Myrrh 1984) ★★★, *He Is The Light* (A&M 1985) ★★★, *Going Away* (A&M 1986) ★★★, *White Christmas* (Hi 1986) ★★, *Soul Survivor* (A&M 1987) ★★★, *I Get Joy* (A&M 1989) ★★, *Love Is Reality* (Word 1992) ★★, *Don't Look Back* (RCA 1993) ★★★, *Your Heart's In Good Hands* (MCA 1995) ★★★, *On Fire In Tokyo* (Xenon 1998) ★★★, *I Can't Stop* (Blue Note 2003) ★★★★, as the Reverend Al Green *Everything's OK* (Blue Note 2005) ★★★★.

● COMPILATIONS: *Greatest Hits* (Hi 1975) ★★★★★, *Greatest Hits, Volume 2* (Hi 1977) ★★★★, *The Cream Of Al Green* (Hi 1980) ★★★★, *Spotlight On Al Green* (PRT 1981) ★★★★, *Take Me To The River (Greatest Hits Volume 2)* (Hi 1987) ★★★★, *Hi-Life: The Best Of Al Green* (K-Tel 1988) ★★★, *Love Ritual: Rare & Previously Unreleased 1968-1976* (Hi 1989) ★★★★, *You Say It!* (Hi 1990) ★★★, *Christmas Cheers* nine tracks plus 12 by Ace Cannon (Hi 1991) ★★, *One In A Million* (Word/Epic 1991) ★★★★, *The Flipside Of Al Green* (Hi 1993) ★★★, *Hi And Mighty: The Story Of Al Green (1969–78)* (Edsel 1998) ★★★★, *True Love: A Collection* (Music Club 1999) ★★★★, *Greatest Gospel Hits* (Right Stuff 2000) ★★★★, *The Hi Singles As And Bs* (Hi 2000) ★★★★, *Listen: The Rarities* (Hi 2000) ★★★, *Testify: The Best Of The A&M Years* (A&M 2001) ★★★, *Love & Happiness* (Hi 2001) ★★★, *The Love Song Collection* (Hi/The Right Stuff 2003) ★★★, *Unchained Melodies* (Hi 2003) ★★★, *The Immortal Soul Of Al Green* 4-CD box set (The Right Stuff 2003) ★★★★, *Shades Of Al Green* (Hi 2004) ★★★.

● DVD/VIDEOS: *Gospel According To Al Green* (Hendring Music Video 1990), *Everything's Gonna Be Alright: Filmed Live At The Celebrity Theatre* (Xenon Pictures 2004).

● FURTHER READING: *Take Me To The River*, Al Green with Davin Seay.

Green, Bennie

b. 16 April 1923, Chicago, Illinois, USA, d. 23 March 1977, San Diego, California, USA. After playing locally for a while during his teenage years, trombonist Green joined the bebop-orientated **Earl 'Fatha' Hines** band in 1942. He continued to be associated with Hines until the early 50s, his spells with the band being interrupted by military service and periods working with **Charlie Ventura**, the band co-led by **Gene Ammons** and **Sonny Stitt** and the small groups he led himself. In the late 60s he was briefly with **Duke Ellington**, then settled in Las Vegas, where he worked in various hotel and casino house bands. Green's playing ranged widely, encompassing the swing-era style prominent during his formative years; he was one of only a few trombonists to adapt comfortably to bebop, and he also played R&B.

● ALBUMS: with J.J. Johnson, Kai Winding *Jazz Workshop, Vol. 1* 10-inch album (Debut 1953) ★★★, with Johnson, Winding *Jazz Workshop, Vol. 2* 10-inch album (Debut 1953) ★★★, with Paul Quinchette *Blow Your Horn* (Decca 1955) ★★★, *Blows His Horn* 10-inch album (Prestige 1955) ★★★★, *Bennie Green & Art Farmer* (Prestige 1956) ★★★★, with Johnson, Winding *Trombone By Three* (Prestige 1956) ★★★★, *J.J. Johnson, Kai Winding, Bennie Green* (Prestige 1956) ★★★★, *Walking Down* (Prestige 1956) ★★★★, *Back On The Scene* (Blue Note 1958) ★★★, *Soul Stirrin'* (Blue Note 1958) ★★★★, *Walkin' And Talkin'* (Blue Note 1959) ★★★★, *The Swingin'est* (Vee Jay 1960) ★★★, *Bennie Green* (Time 1960) ★★★, *Bennie Green Swings The Blues* (Enrica 1960) ★★★, *Catwalk* (Bethlehem 1961) ★★★, *Glidin' Along* (Jazzland 1961) ★★★, *Futura* (RCA Victor 1961) ★★★.

● COMPILATIONS: *Mosaic Select* (Mosaic 2003) ★★★★.

Green, Benny

b. 4 April 1963, New York City, USA. An exciting and hard-swinging pianist in the **Bud Powell** mould, Benny Green ranks alongside **Mulgrew Miller** and **Donald Brown**, as one of a number of talented hard-bop keyboard stars to have graduated from **Art Blakey**'s **Jazz Messengers** training ground during America's hard-bop revival of the 80s, leading bands and establishing his own voice towards the end of the decade. A student of classical piano from the age of seven, Green developed a taste for jazz through the influence of his tenor saxophone–playing father, and was keen enough as a child to start borrowing records and imitating the bebop sounds of the 40s and 50s. He played in school bands, until his keen ear and obvious commitment brought him to the attention of singer Fay Carroll, with whom he got his first real taste of a working jazz band—learning invaluable lessons about accompaniment and the blues, and gaining his first chance to play in a trio context as a way of opening the set. Still in his teens, he filled the piano chair in a quintet co-led by trumpeter **Eddie Henderson** and saxophonist Hadley Caliman, and a 12-piece led by bass player **Chuck Israels**.

On finishing high school, Green moved to the west coast and freelanced around the San Francisco Bay area, gaining experience working as a sideman. It was with his return to New York in the spring of 1982 that Green's career took a swift upward turn, benefiting from studies with **Walter Bishop Jnr.** and joining **Betty Carter**'s band in April 1983—the beginning of a four-year stint of performing, recording and learning with jazz's most respected vocalist. The piano chair in Art Blakey's prestigious Jazz Messengers followed, and then, in 1989, a year with the **Freddie Hubbard** Quintet. By 1990, Green had already led a couple of blowing sessions on the Criss Cross label, but it was with his **Blue Note Records** debut (*Lineage*) that Green really came of age, earning international respect and a reputation as one of the label's most exciting new stars. Since 1991 he has been touring with his regular, finely tuned trio comprising bass player **Christian McBride** and drummer **Carl Allen**. He teamed up with legendary pianist **Oscar Peterson** for 1998's masterly *Oscar And Benny* and in 2000 featured McBride extensively on *Naturally*. In 2002 he formed a loose duo with guitarist **Russell Malone**.

● ALBUMS: *Prelude* (Criss Cross 1988) ★★★★, *In This Direction* (Criss Cross 1989) ★★★★, *Lineage* (Blue Note 1990) ★★★★, *Greens* (Blue Note 1991) ★★★★, *Testifyin'! The Benny Green Trio Live At The Village Vanguard* (Blue Note 1992) ★★★★, *That's Right!* (Blue Note 1993) ★★★★, *The Place To Be* (Blue Note 1994) ★★★, with Mark Murphy *Dim The Lights* 1995 recording (Millennium 1997) ★★★★, *Kaleidoscope* (Blue Note 1997) ★★★, with Oscar Peterson *Oscar And Benny* (Telarc 1998) ★★★★, *These Are Soulful Days* (Blue Note 1999) ★★★, *Naturally* (Telarc 2000) ★★★★, *Green's Blues* (Telarc 2001) ★★★, with Russell Malone *Jazz At The Bistro* (Telarc 2003) ★★★★, with Malone *Bluebird* (Telarc 2004) ★★★★.

Green, Bunky

b. 23 April 1935, Milwaukee, Wisconsin, USA. Alto saxophonist Green was raised in Milwaukee, where he played with local pianist Billy Wallace. A spell in New York gave him his first big break when he was hired by **Charles Mingus** as a replacement for **Jackie McLean**. His brief spell with the eccentric bass player made a deep impression, Mingus' sparing use of notation and his belief that there was no such thing as a wrong note having a lasting influence on Green's own style. After playing with Mingus, Green moved to Chicago, where he appeared with several prominent players including **Sonny Stitt**, **Louie Bellson**, **Andrew Hill**, **Yusef Lateef** and **Ira Sullivan**, and recorded as leader for the Cadet and Argo labels.

Despite being touted as a future star, Green gradually withdrew from the public eye to develop a career as a leading jazz educator. He taught at Chicago State University from 1972–89, and in the 90s took up the directorship of the jazz studies programme at the University of North Florida in Jacksonville. He has also served as president of the International Association of Jazz Educators. As a result of his educational activities Green has only released a few selective sessions since the mid-60s, including a superb spell on **Vanguard Records**, which culminated in 1979's *Places We've Never Been*. Backed by an all-star group including trumpeter **Randy Brecker**, pianist **Albert Dailey**, bass player **Eddie Gomez** and drummer **Freddie Waits**, this recording highlighted Green's free movement in and out of chord changes, an original technique that played a significant part in shaping the style of **Steve Coleman** and other **M-Base** players in the following decade. Green's 1989 session, *Healing The Pain*, is a melodic and deeply moving recording commemorating the death of his parents.

● ALBUMS: *My Baby* (Vee Jay 1960) ★★★, *Testifyin' Time* (Argo 1965) ★★★, *Playin' For Keeps* (Cadet 1966) ★★★, *The Latinization Of Bunky Green* (Cadet 1967) ★★★, *Transformations* (Vanguard 1977) ★★★★, *Visions* (Vanguard 1978) ★★★, *Places We've Never Been* (Vanguard 1979) ★★★★, *In Love Again* (Mark 1987) ★★★, *Healing The Pain* (Delos 1989) ★★★★.

Green, Charlie

b. c.1900, Omaha, Nebraska, USA, d. February 1936, New York City, USA. After working tent shows in the early 20s, trombonist Charlie 'Big' Green joined **Fletcher Henderson** in 1924. He drifted in and out of the band over the next few years, in between times playing in the outfits of **Benny Carter** and **Chick Webb**. In the mid- and late 20s he played on numerous recording sessions, including those led by **Louis**

Armstrong, **Fats Waller**, **James P. Johnson**, **Zutty Singleton**, **Don Redman**, **Jimmie Noone** and the Empress of the Blues, **Bessie Smith**. On some of his records Green's playing sounds basic but he was in fact a gifted melodic player with a delightful tone and wide-ranging ability who sometimes chose to play within fairly narrow limits. He was an exceptional accompanist and was especially sensitive when working with singers. His performances with Smith include 'Work House Blues', 'House Rent Blues', 'Trombone Cholly' and 'Shipwreck Blues', all classics, with the last title being a particularly fine example of his understanding of the singer's needs. Green died in New York in February 1936 when, on returning home from an engagement, he found he could not gain access to his home, fell asleep on the doorstep, and froze to death.

Green, Clarence

b. 15 March 1929, Galveston, Texas, USA. A self-taught blues piano player, Clarence 'Candy' Green performed on radio and in the numerous clubs of Galveston, a naval town known as the 'Playground Of The South'. His first record was 'Green's Bounce', made in Houston for Eddie's in 1948. His brother Cal Green was a guitarist who also recorded. Clarence recorded 'Hard Headed Woman' (Peacock) before starting army service in 1951. Returning to Texas two years later, he remained a familiar figure in local clubs throughout the 50s, sometimes recording as Galveston Green and working with **Clarence 'Gatemouth' Brown**. In 1966 he recorded 'I Saw You Last Night' for Duke Records.

Green, Dave

b. 5 March 1942, London, England. Surprisingly for a bass player of such skill and prestige, Green is self-taught. His first important engagement as a professional musician was with the **Don Rendell–Ian Carr** band, which he joined in the early 60s. By the end of the decade he had established himself as a major figure, having worked with musicians as diverse as **Stan Tracey** and **Humphrey Lyttelton**. He also played and recorded with many front-rank visiting Americans, who counted themselves fortunate in having his solidity and flair behind them. For a while in the early 80s he led his own group, Fingers, which featured **Lol Coxhill**, **Bruce Turner** and **Michael Garrick**. Throughout the 80s and into the following decades, Green remained at the forefront of British jazz, working with **Peter King**, **Didier Lockwood**, **Spike Robinson** and a host of other British and visiting jazzmen. A superb timekeeper and exceptional soloist, Green is the essence of the international jazz musician.

Green, Freddie

b. Frederick William Greene, 31 March 1911, Charleston, South Carolina, USA, d. 1 March 1987, Las Vegas, Nevada, USA. A self-taught musician who began on banjo, Green became known around New York jazz clubs in the early 30s. By 1936 he had switched to guitar and was recommended by **John Hammond** to **Count Basie**, who was looking for a replacement guitarist in his band. Green was hired in 1937 and became a member of the famous All-American Rhythm Section (with Basie, **Walter Page** and **Jo Jones**). He remained there until 1950, when the big band folded and Basie organized a sextet. Unwilling to be left out of the band Green returned, uninvited. He was thus on hand when Basie re-formed his big band and was still resident when Basie died in 1984.

A meticulous timekeeper, Green's presence helped ensure the superb swing of the Basie band from its freewheeling Kansas City sound of the late 30s and 40s through to the metronomic accuracy of the 50s and after. On some recordings by the band, Green's contribution is virtually inaudible, but everyone who played with him insisted that his discreet beat was one of the principal factors in ensuring the band's propulsive swing. After Jones' departure Green was seldom happy with his replacements and reputedly kept a long stick by his chair with which to poke any drummer (especially **Sonny Payne**) who strayed off the beat. After Basie's death Green continued to work, making records with, among others, **Manhattan Transfer**.

● ALBUMS: *Natural Rhythm* (RCA Victor 1955) ★★★, *Mr Rhythm* (RCA Victor 1956) ★★, with Herb Ellis *Rhythm Willie* (Concord Jazz 1975) ★★★.
● COMPILATIONS: *King Of Rhythm Session* 50s recordings (Giants Of Jazz 1999) ★★★.

Green, Garland

b. 24 June 1942, Dunleath, Mississippi, USA. Green used his most distinctive of baritones, plaintive with a blues feel, to create a marvellous body of typical Chicago-style uptown soul during the late 60s and early 70s. He came to Chicago in 1958, and found work in a corn starch factory while singing on weekends in local clubs. He was discovered by **Jo Armstead** in 1967, who was intrigued by the 'pleading quality' of his voice, which was in the same vein as fellow Chicagoan **Tyrone Davis**, Green was quickly put into a recording studio. He first made a mark with the beautiful 'Girl I Need You', with a Chicago-style mid-tempo approach, but it failed to chart. Fame came with the later 'Jealous Kind Of Fellow', which went to number 5 R&B and number 20 pop in 1969. 'Plain And Simple Girl' (US R&B number 17, 1971) was his next most successful release, but he continued to produce top-quality songs, such as 'Let The Good Times Roll' (US R&B number 65, 1974) and 'Bumpin' And Stompin'' (US R&B number 72, 1975), despite modest chart success. Green moved to Los Angeles in 1979 and had one more minor chart record in 1983 with 'Tryin' To Hold On' (US R&B number 6), a remake of an earlier **Lamont Dozier** hit. An excellent compilation of his best work was recently issued using the same title as his debut album.

● ALBUMS: *Jealous Kind Of Fellow* (Gamma 1969) ★★★, *Love Is What We Came Here For* (Uni 1977) ★★★, *Garland Green* (Revue 1983) ★★★.
● COMPILATIONS: *Jealous Kind Of Fellow* (Varèse 1996) ★★★★.

Green, Grant

b. 6 June 1935, St Louis, Missouri, USA, d. 31 January 1979, New York City, USA. Heavily influenced by **Charlie Christian**, guitarist Green first played professionally with tenor saxophonist **Jimmy Forrest** and made his recording debut on organist **Brother Jack McDuff**'s classic 1960 session, *The Honeydripper*. Although noted particularly for his work in organ-guitar-drum trios in the 50s, throughout his career Green was associated with post-bop musicians and in the 60s he recorded for **Blue Note Records** with **Stanley Turrentine**, Hank Mobley, **McCoy Tyner**, **Herbie Hancock** and others. The flowing, single-line solos characteristic of Christian's early experiments in bebop were evident in much of Green's work. At home in several areas of jazz, he had a particularly strong affinity with the blues, while one album, *Feelin' The Spirit*, features gospel music. Nevertheless, he was essentially modern in his approach to music. Drug addiction severely limited Green's career in the 70s, and he died in 1979. Since his death much of his catalogue remains in print as his star continues to rise. Green is now seen as one of the most talented and underrated guitarists of his era. Rarely has smoky laid-back late-night guitar ever been played to greater effect. Green managed to turn the volume down to minimal, and still be heard clearly. His son Grant Green Jnr. is also a jazz guitarist, playing in a similar style. His daughter-in-law has attempted to redress the critical balance with a fine biography, *Grant Green: Rediscovering The Forgotten Genius Of Jazz Guitar*.

● ALBUMS: *Grant's First Stand* (Blue Note 1961) ★★★, *Reaching Out* (Black Lion 1961) ★★★, *Green Street* (Blue Note 1961) ★★★★, *Sunday Mornin'* (Blue Note 1961) ★★★★, *Grantstand* (Blue Note 1961) ★★★★★, *Remembering* (Blue Note 1961) ★★★, *Gooden's Corner* (Blue Note 1961) ★★★, *Nigeria* (Blue Note 1962) ★★★, *Oleo* (Blue Note 1962) ★★★★, *The Latin Bit* (Blue Note 1962) ★★★, *Goin' West* (Blue Note 1962) ★★★, *Feelin' The Spirit* (Blue Note 1962) ★★★★★, *Born To Be Blue* (Blue Note 1962) ★★★★★, *Am I Blue?* (Blue Note 1963) ★★★, *Idle Moments* (Blue Note 1963) ★★★★, *Talkin' About!* (Blue Note 1964) ★★★★, *Matador* (Blue Note 1964) ★★★★, *Street Of Dreams* (Blue Note 1964) ★★★, *I Want To Hold Your Hand* (Blue Note 1965) ★★★, *His Majesty King Funk* (Verve 1965) ★★★, *Iron City* (Muse 1967) ★★★, *All The Gin Is Gone* (Delmark 1967) ★★★, *Black Forrest* (Delmark 1967) ★★★, *Carryin' On* (Blue Note 1969) ★★★, *Green Is Beautiful* (Blue Note 1970) ★★★, *Alive!* (Blue Note 1970) ★★, *Visions* (Blue Note 1971) ★★★, *Shades Of Green* (Blue Note 1971) ★★★, *The Final Comedown* film soundtrack (Blue Note 1972) ★★, *Live At The Lighthouse* (Blue Note 1972) ★★★, *The Main Attraction* (Kudu 1976) ★★★, *Solid* 1964 recording (Blue Note 1979) ★★★★, *Last Session* (Atlantic 1987) ★★, *Standards* 1961 recording (Blue Note 1998) ★★★.

● COMPILATIONS: with Sonny Clark *The Complete Blue Note Recordings With Sonny Clark* 4-CD box set (Mosaic 1991) ★★★★, *Best Of Grant Green* (Blue Note 1993) ★★★, with Clark *The Complete Quartets With Sonny Clark* (Blue Note 1997) ★★★★, *Jazz Profile 1961–1965* recordings (Blue Note 1998) ★★★★, *Ballads* (Blue Note 2002) ★★★★, *Retrospective 1961–66* 4-CD box set (Blue Note 2002) ★★★★.

● FURTHER READING: *Grant Green: Rediscovering The Forgotten Genius Of Jazz Guitar*, Sharony Andrews Green.

Green, Jack

b. England. Known to UK rock and pop fans through his involvement with the **Pretty Things**, Green relocated to Canada to build his solo career. Though now regularly consigned to the 'where are they now?' columns in the country of his birth, a sequence of albums for **RCA Records** in Canada have produced a cult following in that territory. *Humanesque*, which featured **Ritchie Blackmore** of **Rainbow** on one track, and *Essential Logic* are two collections that married melodious pop hooks with Green's own rock guitar licks. *Latest Game* saw him move to FM/Revolver, but distribution of the record in the UK failed to excite much

critical interest despite Green's reputation and stature in Canada.

● ALBUMS: *Humanesque* (RCA Canada 1980) ★★★, *Essential Logic* (RCA Canada 1981) ★★★, *Latest Game* (FM/Revolver 1987) ★★.

Green, Johnny

b. 10 October 1908, New York City, USA, d. 15 May 1989, Beverly Hills, California, USA. Fascinated by music from childhood, Green studied piano from the age of five. By the time he entered his teens he had mastered orchestration, and throughout his years at Harvard University he greatly advanced his knowledge and understanding of all aspects of musical theory. While at Harvard he led a band that made records. During one vacation he was hired by **Guy Lombardo** as an arranger. Green's first song, 'Coquette', was written in collaboration with Lombardo's brother, Carmen, and **Gus Kahn**. After graduating from Harvard, Green worked on Wall Street but continued his musical studies, eventually making the decision in 1928 to concentrate on music for his livelihood. For the next few years he arranged music for films, working in the east coast studios of Paramount. With different lyricists he wrote several songs during the 30s, including 'I'm Yours' (lyrics by **E.Y. 'Yip' Harburg**), 'Hello, My Lover, Goodbye' (Edward Heyman), 'Out Of Nowhere' (Heyman), 'I Wanna Be Loved' (Heyman and **Billy Rose**), 'Rain, Rain, Go Away' (Heyman and **Mack David**), 'I Cover The Waterfront' (Heyman) and the massively successful 'Body And Soul' (Heyman, Frank Eyton and Robert Sour). 'Body And Soul' was introduced by **Libby Holman** in the 1930 revue **Three's A Crowd**. Also during the 30s, Green led a dance band, appearing regularly on radio, and also worked on Broadway as musical director for shows. In 1942 he moved to Hollywood, where he began writing scores for motion pictures. He was nominated for an Oscar for *Fiesta* (1947), his music including passages from Aaron Copland's 'El Salón México'. He won an Oscar the following year for his scoring of **Easter Parade**. During the 50s Green was general music director at **MGM**, working either directly or indirectly on many of the best musicals of the period. He won a second Oscar for his arrangements for **An American In Paris** (1951) and a third for his work on *The Merry Wives Of Windsor* (1953). He continued to write songs, including 'The Song Of Raintree County' (lyric by **Paul Francis Webster**). In the 60s he received two more Oscars for his work on **West Side Story** (1960) and **Oliver!** (1968). Green's musical range was such that he frequently appeared as guest conductor of symphony orchestras, notably the Los Angeles Philharmonic, with which he worked regularly for many years. He was the recipient of many honours and awards, and in the late 70s was artist-in-residence at Harvard.

Green, Keith

b. Brooklyn, New York City, USA, d. July 1982. Green was born into a religious and musical family and started to sing and play the ukulele at the age of three. He graduated to piano by the age of six, and wrote his first songs as an eight-year-old. His songwriting matured rapidly. At the age of 11 he became the youngest ever member of **ASCAP** (American Society Of Composers, Authors And Publishers) after negotiating a recording contract with **Decca Records**. He travelled extensively during this time, though his performances were still at secular venues. By the early 70s he had

become a born again Christian, appearing on television shows such as **Barry McGuire**'s *Anyone But Jesus*, spreading the word at church congregations throughout California. By this time Green and wife Melody had become staff writers for **CBS Records**/April Blackwood Music, writing for numerous recording artists, both Christian and secular. With Melody he founded the Last Days Ministries, urging the Christian community to 'purge itself' of biblical impurity. His own solo recording career began in the mid-70s with *For Him Who Has Ears To Hear* for Sparrow Records. Further albums followed, mixing contemporary Christian protest songs with historical church tracts drawing on the literature of nineteenth-century Evangelism. However, at the height of his success he died in a plane crash.
● ALBUMS: *For Him Who Has Ears To Hear* (Sparrow 1975) ★★★★, *No Compromise* (Sparrow 1977) ★★★.
● COMPILATIONS: *The Ministry Years Vol. 1* (Sparrow 1987) ★★★★, *The Ministry Years Vol. 2* (Sparrow 1988) ★★★.

Green, L.C.

b. 23 October 1921, Minter City, Mississippi, USA, d. 24 August 1985, Pontiac, Michigan, USA. Vocally and for his repertoire, L.C. Greene, whose records were issued without the final 'e' to his name, was indebted to **John Lee 'Sonny Boy' Williamson**. His amplified guitar playing is clearly Mississippi Delta–derived, but probably owes something to the popularity of fellow Detroit blues singer **John Lee Hooker**. Greene recorded in the early 50s (often with his cousin Walter Mitchell on harmonica) for **Joe Von Battle**'s shoestring operation, which leased a few sides to **Dot Records**, but he never matched the fortunes of Hooker, whom he equalled in guitar talent and power, although not in songwriting ability.
● COMPILATIONS: *Detroit Blues Guitar Killers!* (1977) ★★★.

Green, Lil

b. 22 December 1919, Mississippi, USA, d. 14 April 1954. Growing up in Chicago, Green began to sing in clubs in the mid-30s. By the end of the decade she was appearing regularly at some of the city's best-known nightspots, and was recording with artists such as **'Big' Bill Broonzy**, who wrote several songs for her, including 'Country Boy Blues' and 'My Mellow Man'. Green composed some well-known songs herself, among them 'Romance In The Dark', later covered by **Mary Ann McCall**, **Jeri Southern** and **Billie Holiday**. In the early 40s she toured with **Tiny Bradshaw** and **Luis Russell** but never really broke away from the black theatre circuit and those areas of the record business that catered specifically for black audiences. The limitations this placed upon her career were severe, even in the case of one of Green's most popular recordings, **Joe McCoy**'s 'Why Don't You Do Right?'. The record was heard by **Peggy Lee**, who was then with **Benny Goodman** And His Orchestra. Their cover version was an enormous hit, thus further shading Green's fortunes. Although signed by **Atlantic Records** in 1951, she was in poor health and died in 1954.
● COMPILATIONS: *Romance In The Dark* 1940–46 recordings (RCA 1971) ★★★.

Green, Lilly

b. Lilly Crozier, 13 September 1951, Renfrew, Ontario, Canada. As a young child Green began singing in a gospel duo with her sister. Both performed frequently at church congregations as well as local television shows. At age 15 she took her first guitar lessons, subsequently launching a solo career as a contemporary Christian singer-songwriter. She moved to Michigan, USA, to seek further musical tuition, before embarking on a tour of Scandinavia with the Solid Rock Foundation. She moved on to California in 1972 but she remained an active member of evangelical church communities. She married Kelly Green in the mid-70s, joining the Shekinah Fellowship of which he was the Minister of Music. She calls her music a 'kind of soul contemporary', exemplified by songs such as 'God, A Woman And A Man', a song written for her husband that she sang at their wedding. She began her recording career for Myrrh Records with *Especially For You* in the mid-70s, an album that enjoyed considerable acclaim in gospel circles.
● ALBUMS: *Especially For You* (Myrrh 1975) ★★★★, *I Am Blessed* (Myrrh 1977) ★★★.

Green, Lloyd

b. Lloyd L. Green, 4 October 1937, Mississippi, USA. Green's family moved to Mobile, Alabama, when he was four years old, and he was raised there. He learned Hawaiian string guitar from the age of seven and graduated to steel guitar. He was playing professionally by the time he was 10, and recalls, 'I played in clubs a couple of nights a week with a rhythm guitarist called Emmanuel Abates, who was also a yo-yo champion. He wasn't a very good guitarist and eventually he went back to his yo-yos.' Green studied psychology at the University of Southern Mississippi, but he left at the age of 19 to seek fame in Nashville. In December 1956 he joined **Faron Young**'s road band and stayed for 18 months. During that time, he played steel guitar on his first session, **George Jones**' 'Too Much Water Runs Under The Bridge'. He returned to Mobile and later came back to Nashville as a shoe salesman. When he told one customer that he could not afford $75 to renew his union card, she renewed it for him—she was the widow of the publisher **Fred Rose**.
The first successful session on which Green played was **Warner Mack**'s 'The Bridge Washed Out' in 1965. For the next 15 years, 'the steelworker' averaged 400 sessions a year, which included 'It's Four In The Morning' (Faron Young), 'Easy Lovin'' (**Freddie Hart**) and the **Byrds**' seminal country rock album, *Sweetheart Of The Rodeo*. He says, '**Bob Dylan** had hinted and flirted with the steel guitar before the Byrds, but he'd only let **Pete Drake** colour the songs very lightly. 'You Ain't Goin' Nowhere' took a whole day to record, which was a whole new revolution for me. I was used to sessions that were highly organized and where everyone was clock-watching.' He also played on **Paul McCartney**'s 'Sally G' but turned down a US tour because he did not want to lose work in Nashville.
Green made several solo records, mostly easy-listening country music, although his technique is skilfully demonstrated on 'I Can See Clearly Now'. He popularized the blocking technique, used by **Jimmy Day** in the 50s, whereby the palm of the picking hand is used to mute the strings in order to lose the ringing effect. Green, who was not a solo attraction in the USA, made successful appearances at the Wembley Country Music Festival and his 1979 three-week UK tour with **Billie Jo Spears** was the longest he had been away from Nashville since 1964. He also worked in the UK with his fellow session musicians **Charlie McCoy** and **Pig**

Robbins. He says, 'It's laughable when I read of Nashville session men getting together after hours and having a jam session. We play enough music in the studio. We'd rather get drunk and have a good time.'

● ALBUMS: *Big Steel Guitar* (Time 1964) ★★★, *Day For Decision* (Little Darlin' 1966) ★★★, *Mr. Nashville Sound* (Chart 1968) ★★★, *Cool Steel Man* (Chart 1968) ★★★, *Green Country* (Little Darlin' 1969) ★★★, *Moody River* (Chart 1969) ★★★, *Lloyd Green And His Steel Guitar* (Prize 1971) ★★★, *Shades Of Steel* (Monument 1973) ★★★, *Steel Rides* (Monument 1976) ★★★, *Ten Shades Of Green* (Mid-Land 1976) ★★★, *Stainless Steel Lloyd's Of Nashville* (Mid-Land 1980) ★★★, *Green Velvet* (President 1982) ★★★, *Reflections* (Hitsound 1991) ★★★.

● COMPILATIONS: *Master Of The Steel Strings: The Little Darlin' Sound Of Lloyd Green* (Koch 2004) ★★★.

Green, Pat

b. San Antonio, Texas, USA. This **Willie Nelson**-inspired country singer-songwriter was a self-made star in his home state of Texas prior to winning a major label recording contract at the start of the new millennium. Raised in Waco, Texas, Green was inspired to take up music by his actor father. He began performing his own material on stage while in college at Texas Tech in Lubbock, and by the mid-90s had built up enough of a following to launch his recording career. *Dancehall Dreamer*, on Green's Greenhorse label, was the first of several independent releases that established the singer as one of the biggest draws on the Texas dancehall circuit, regularly performing in front of thousands of fans. The major labels inevitably took an interest in Green, leading to a contract with Republic/Universal Records. His Universal debut, 2001's *Three Days*, included a guest appearance from Green's hero, Willie Nelson, on the stand-out track 'Threadbare Gypsy Soul'. Green also performs regularly with fellow Texas-based singer-songwriter, **Cory Morrow**. Green continues to perform for most of the year building a strong core of fans (in 2004 he performed over 200 gigs).

● ALBUMS: *Dancehall Dreamer* (Greenhorse 1995) ★★★, *George's Bar* (Greenhorse 1997) ★★★, *Here We Go* (Greenhorse 1998) ★★★, *Live At Billy Bob's Texas* (Smith Music Group 1999) ★★★★, *Carry On* (Greenhorse 2000) ★★★, with Cory Morrow *Songs We Wish We'd Written* (Write On 2001) ★★★, *Three Days* (Universal 2001) ★★★, *Wave On Wave* (Republic 2003) ★★★★, *Lucky Ones* (Republic 2004) ★★★.

Green, Peter

b. Peter Allen Greenbaum, 29 October 1946, Bethnal Green, London, England. Having served an apprenticeship in various semi-professional groups, including the Muskrats and the Tridents, Peter Green became one of several guitarists who joined **John Mayall**'s Bluesbreakers as a temporary substitute for **Eric Clapton** during the latter's late-1965 sabbatical. When Mayall's preferred choice returned to the fold, Green joined **Peter Bardens** (organ), Dave Ambrose (bass) and Mick Fleetwood (drums) in a short-lived club band, the Peter B's Looners. The quartet completed one single for **Columbia Records**: 'If You Wanna Be Happy'/'Jodrell Blues' in February 1966. The b-side, an instrumental, showcased Green's already distinctive style. The entire unit subsequently formed the instrumental core to the **Shotgun**

Express, backing singers **Rod Stewart** and **Beryl Marsden**, but the guitarist found this role too restrictive and left after a matter of weeks. Green rejoined Mayall in July 1966 when Clapton left to form **Cream**.

Over the next 12 months Green made several telling contributions to the Bluesbreakers' recordings, most notably on their third album, *A Hard Road*. This powerful release featured two of the guitarist's compositions, of which 'The Supernatural', a riveting instrumental, anticipated the style he would forge later in the decade. The seeds of Green's own band were sown during several sessions without Mayall and a Bluesbreakers 'solo' single, 'Curly', was released in March 1967. Two months later Green left to form his own band with drummer Mick Fleetwood. The two musicians added a second guitarist, Jeremy Spencer, to form **Fleetwood Mac**, whose line-up was eventually completed by another former Mayall sideman, **John McVie**. Fleetwood Mac became one of the most popular acts of the era, developing blues-based origins into an exciting, experimental unit. Green's personality, however, grew increasingly unstable, and he became estranged from his colleagues. 'Pete should never have taken acid,' Fleetwood later recalled. 'He was charming, amusing, just a wonderful person (but) off he went and never came back.'

Green has followed an erratic course since leaving the band in May 1970. His solo debut, *The End Of The Game*, was a perplexing collection, comprising six instrumentals, all of which were little more than jams. An atmospheric single, 'Heavy Heart', followed in June 1971, while a collaboration with Nigel Watson, 'Beasts Of Burden', was issued the following year. Green also made sporadic session appearances but following a cameo role on Fleetwood Mac's *Penguin*, the guitarist dropped out of music altogether. The mid-70s proved particularly harrowing; this tormented individual was committed to two mental institutions in the wake of his unsettled behaviour. Green returned to active recording in 1979 with *In The Skies*, a light but optimistic collection that showed traces of his erstwhile fire and included a version of 'A Fool No More', first recorded by Fleetwood Mac. A second album, *Little Dreamer*, offered a more blues-based perspective, while two further releases attempted to consolidate the artist's position.

In 1982, Green, now reverting to Greenbaum, began touring with a band named Kolors, but the results were unsatisfactory. A hastily concocted album, comprising out-takes and unfinished demos, was issued, but a collaboration with former **Mungo Jerry** singer Ray Dorset aside, this once-skilful musician again abandoned music. Nicknamed the 'Wizard' by local children, Green lived a hermit-like existence, shunning any links with his past. Rumours frequently circulated about his return to the music business, but most were instigated by tabloid journalists pining for his reappearance. In 1995, **Gary Moore** recorded an album of Peter Green tracks, *Blues For Greeny*.

In 1996, rumours were confirmed that Green was becoming active again. He had purchased a guitar, was keen to play some old blues material, showed up onstage at a Gary Moore gig and best of all played live in May 1996. In August he played with the Splinter Group, **Cozy Powell** (b. Colin Flooks, 29 December 1947, Cirencester, Gloucestershire, England, d. 5 April 1998, Bristol, England; drums), Nigel Watson (guitar/vocals) and Neil Murray (bass) at the Guildford Blues Festival. Although shaky on some numbers, he excelled on two familiar **Freddie King** songs, 'The Stumble' and 'Going Down'. His new manager at that time Stuart Taylor stated about Green's future, back in music; 'I am cautiously optimistic.' Watson has also been an ever present and important figure in Green's climb back. An album from the Splinter group was released in June 1997, and although flawed, it demonstrated Green's commitment to regaining the crown he never sought in the first place—as the UK's finest, ever white blues guitarist. He then released *The Robert Johnson Songbook*, his first full studio album in almost two decades. Further albums followed, demonstrating clearly that Green and his Splinter Group are serious about their music, and in particular Green's rediscovery of his pure blues roots. The recent line-up comprises Green, Watson, Roger Cotton (keyboards), Pete Stroud (bass) and Larry Tolfree (drums). While Green may no longer be a prolific guitar player or songwriter, his voice now has a fantastic smoky tone, beautifully aged and pleading. The way back is slow, but most definitely in the right direction.

● ALBUMS: *The End Of The Game* (Reprise 1970) ★★, *In The Skies* (PVK 1979) ★★★, *Little Dreamer* (PVK 1980) ★★★, *Whatcha Gonna Do* (PVK 1981) ★★, *Blue Guitar* (Creole 1981) ★★, *White Sky* (Headline 1982) ★★, *Kolors* (Headline 1983) ★★, *Legend* (Creole 1988) ★★, *Peter Green Splinter Group* (Red Snapper 1997) ★★, with Nigel Watson *The Robert Johnson Songbook* (Artisan/Snapper 1998) ★★★, with the Splinter Group *Soho Session* (Artisan/Snapper 1999) ★★★, with the Splinter Group *Destiny Road* (Artisan/Snapper 1999) ★★★★, with the Splinter Group *Hot Foot Powder* (Artisan/Snapper 2000) ★★★, with the Splinter Group *Time Traders* (Eagle/Blue Storm 2001) ★★★, with the Splinter Group *Blues Don't Change* (Eagle 2002) ★★, with the Splinter Group *Reaching The Cold 100* (Eagle 2002) ★★★.

● COMPILATIONS: *Backtrackin'* (Backtrackin' 1990) ★★★, *The Best Of Peter Green 1977–1981* (Music Collection 1996) ★★★, *Me And The Devil* box set (Snapper 2001) ★★★, *The Best Of Peter Green Splinter Group* (Snapper 2002) ★★★★, *Man Of The World: The Anthology 1968–1988* (Sanctuary 2004) ★★★.

● DVD/VIDEOS: *An Evening With Peter Green Splinter Group In Concert* (Eagle Vision 2003).

● FURTHER READING: *Peter Green: The Biography* (updated as *Peter Green: Founder Of Fleetwood Mac*), Martin Celmins.

Green, Philip

b. 1911, England, d. 1983, Dublin, Eire. Although not a big 'name' as far as the public is concerned, Green was one of the most prolific 'backroom-boys' in the British music business. He is believed to have created more original compositions than any other writer, and he scored over 150 British films. His radio credits included the theme for BBC's *Meet The Huggets* ('Horse Feathers') and among the countless television shows that used his music were BBC's *Picture Page* ('Shopping Centre'), ITV's early filmed drama *Ghost Squad* and ATV's *The Golden Shot*. Green's first recording for **EMI Records** was in 1933, and from 1935–39 he was closely associated with commercial radio, at times up to 17 shows a week. During the war he was responsible for numerous successful BBC series such as *Salute To Rhythm, Band Call, Cuban Caballeros* and *Music Society Of Lower Basin Street*. He assisted **Gracie Fields**' revival after the war (her big hits

'Now Is The Hour' and 'Pedro The Fisherman' were recorded under his musical direction). Green also composed under the names Don Felipe, Louise Duke and Jose Belmonte. Some of his memorable works included his 'Cuban Suite', 'La Maja De Goya', 'Ecstasy—Tango', 'White Orchids', 'Follow Me Around', 'Romance' (from the film *The Magic Bow*), 'Two Mexican Pictures', 'Sensation For Strings', 'Mandolins In The Moonlight', 'Silhouette' and 'Pan American Panorama'.

In the cinema Green's main scores included *Saints And Sinners* (1946), *Man On The Run* (1949), *Ha'penny Breeze* (1950), *Young Wives Tale* (1951), *Isn't Life Wonderful* (1952), *Park Plaza 605* (1953), *Conflict Of Wings*—US title *Fuss Over Feathers* (1954), *One Good Turn* (1954), *John And Julie* (1955), *The March Hare* (1956), *Carry On Admiral*—US title *The Ship Was Loaded* (1957), *Sea Fury* (1958), *The Square Peg* (1958), *Violent Playground* (1958), *The Golden Disc*—US title *The In-Between Age* (1958), *Operation Amsterdam* (1959), *Sapphire* (1959), *Make Mine Mink* (1960), *The League Of Gentlemen* (1960), *The Singer Not The Song* (1961), *Victim* (1961), *Tiara Tahiti* (1962), *A Stitch In Time* (1963), *Masquerade* (1964), *The Intelligence Men*—US title *Spylarks* (1965), and *The Yellow Hat* (1967). His themes for *John And Julie* and *The March Hare* won **Ivor Novello** Awards, and he became resident musical director of the Rank Organisation. He also wrote many short pieces for publishers' libraries (Chappell, Francis Day & Hunter, Paxton, Photoplay etc.) especially for radio, film and television use. Green's hundreds of commercial recordings included hit selections, various novelty and jazz numbers, countless accompaniments for popular singers plus special recordings for **Decca Records**' wartime *Music While You Work* series and a series of MGM 78s for the American market.

● ALBUMS: *Rhythm On Reeds* (Decca) ★★, *Moments In Mayfair* (EMI-Columbia) ★★★, *Follow The Sun* (EMI-Columbia) ★★★, *Pan-American Panorama* (EMI-Columbia) ★★★, *Wings Of Song* (Top Rank) ★★, *Music Of Rodgers And Hammerstein* (RCA) ★★★, *Jerome Kern* (RCA) ★★★, *Irving Berlin* (RCA) ★★★★, *Rodgers & Hart* (RCA) ★★★, *Great Opera And Ballet Themes* (RCA) ★★★.

Green, Pork Chops

b. Leothus Green. Biographical detail is scant for this remarkable blues pianist and is largely based on the memories of **Roosevelt Sykes** and **Little Brother Montgomery**. It is likely that Green originated from Mississippi, but he made his name working in St. Louis, Missouri. He is believed to have died around 1944. His recordings spanned the years 1929–37 and show him to have been a distinctive and versatile performer who deserves greater recognition than he has received to date. His most significant role was in influencing Sykes, for whom he acted as a blues catalyst to some degree. Green also taught Sykes to play Montgomery's most famous and difficult composition, known as 'The Forty-fours'.

Green, Urbie

b. Urban Clifford Green, 8 August 1926, Mobile, Alabama, USA. Trombonist Green's first major engagement was with **Gene Krupa** in the late 40s; from there he joined the **Woody Herman** band. In the early 50s he appeared on **Buck Clayton**'s celebrated Jam Session recordings. He then joined **Benny Goodman**, occasionally leading the band when Goodman was unwell. In the 60s and thereafter, Green freelanced; played in the studios; made numerous records, some of which were under his own name; gigged with **Count Basie** and led the reconstituted **Tommy Dorsey** orchestra. A masterly performer, especially in the upper register, Green has throughout his career consistently demonstrated that it is possible to blend deep jazz feeling with a seemingly perfect technique.

● ALBUMS: *Urbie Green Septet* 10-inch album (Blue Note 1954) ★★★, *Urbie Green And His Band* 10-inch album (Vanguard 1954) ★★★, *A Cool Yuletide* 10-inch album (X 1954) ★★★, *East Coast Jazz/6* (Bethlehem 1955) ★★★★, *Blues And Other Shades Of Green* (ABC-Paramount 1956) ★★★★, *Best Of The New Broadway Show Hits* (RCA Victor 1957) ★★★, *All About Urbie Green* (ABC-Paramount 1956) ★★★, *Let's Face The Music And Dance* (RCA Victor 1958) ★★★, *The Persuasive Trombone Of Urbie Green* (Command 1960) ★★★, *The Persuasive Trombone Of Urbie Green Volume 2* (Command 1962) ★★, *And His 6-Tet* (Command 1963) ★★, *21 Trombones* (Project 3 1968) ★★★★, *21 Trombones Volume 2* (Project 3 1968) ★★★, *Green Power* (Project 3 1970) ★★★, *Bein' Green* (Project 3 1972) ★★★, *The Fox* (CTI 1976) ★★, *Senor Blues* (CTI 1977) ★★★★, *Live At Rick's Café Americain* (1978) ★★, *The Message* (Fresh Sound 1988) ★★★, *Sea Jam Blues* 1995 recording (Chiaroscuro 1998) ★★★.

Green, Vivian

b. 1979, Philadelphia, Pennsylvania, USA. This versatile singer benefited from the rise in popularity of the neo-soul movement around the new millennium, releasing her debut album in 2002. Green developed an early appreciation of music through her mother, who would often sing songs to her. At the age of eight, Green began playing piano, and within a span of five years, began writing her own compositions and performing as part of a group called Younique. By 15, Green was sending out demos of her original songs and writing for other artists, in addition to performing old time standards alongside a big band. While still a teenager, Green began singing back-up for renowned acts such as **Boyz II Men** and **Jill Scott**, which resulted in a recording contract of her own in November 2001, with Sony Records. Instead of having a wide variety of songs already written to select from, Green opted to write the majority of her subsequent debut album from scratch. *A Love Story*, which was released in November 2002, spawned the popular single 'Emotional Rollercoaster'.

● ALBUMS: *A Love Story* (Sony 2002) ★★★, *Vivian* (Columbia 2005) ★★★.

Greenaway, Roger

(see **Blue Mink; Cook And Greenaway; David And Jonathan**)

Greenbank, Percy

b. 24 January 1878, London, England, d. 9 December 1968, Rickmansworth, Hertfordshire, England. Like his older brother, Harry Greenbank, Percy worked first as a journalist before entering the theatre as a songwriter. At the behest of **George Edwardes**, when Harry died he began writing lyrics for songs for interpolation into musical comedies the impresario produced at his theatres, including the Gaiety and Daly's. Among composers and other lyricists with whom Greenbank collaborated were **Ivan Caryll**, Lilian Eldée, **Harry Graham**, **Seymour Hicks**, Frederick Lonsdale, **Lionel Monckton**, **Adrian Ross**, **Paul Rubens**, Howard Talbot, **Fred Thompson** and **Hadyn Wood**.

The first of the shows was *The Messenger Boy* (1900), writing the lyric for the title song, and he added new material to the previous year's *San Toy*, on which his brother had worked, notably 'Somebody' and 'All I Want Is A Little Bit Of Fun'. Through the next two decades he collaborated on songs included in *The Toreador* and *The Gay Cadets* (both 1901), **A Country Girl** and *Three Little Maids* (both 1902), *My Lady Molly*, *The Orchid* and *The Earl And The Girl* (all 1903), *The Blue Moon*, *The Cingalee*, *Véronique* and *Lady Madcap* (all 1904), *The Little Michus* (with Greenbank writing English lyrics for the original *Les P'tites Michu*) and *The Spring Chicken* (both 1905), *The Girl Behind The Counter*, *See See*, *The New Aladdin* and *Two Naughty Boys* (all 1906), *The Three Kisses* (1907), *The Belle Of Brittany* (1908), **Our Miss Gibbs** and *A Persian Princess* (both 1909), **The Quaker Girl** (1910), *The Mousmé* (1911), *Princess Caprice*, *Autumn Manoeuvres* and *The Dancing Mistress* (all 1912), **The Girl From Utah** (1913), *The Cinema Star*, *After The Girl* and *Tonight's The Night* (all 1914, the latter in New York), *Tina* (1915), *Houp-La!* (1916) and *The Boy* (1917). In the years following the end of World War I, Greenbank's contributions continued although for fewer productions: *The Girl For The Boy*, *The Kiss Call* (both 1919), *My Nieces* (1921), *The Little Duchess* (1922), **The Street Singer** (1924), and *Yvonne* (1926), for which he wrote the English libretto based upon the original German production. That show, his last important work, had music and lyrics by Jean Gilbert and **Vernon Duke**. Although he continued to work on occasional projects, from the early 30s Greenbank was effectively in retirement from the theatre.

Greenbaum, Norman

b. 20 November 1942, Malden, Massachusetts, USA. Greenbaum first tasted minor US chart fame as the founder of Los Angeles jug band Dr. West's Medicine Show And Junk Band, who achieved a minor hit with the novelty 'The Eggplant That Ate Chicago'. After the break-up of the group in 1967, Greenbaum effectively retired from the music business to run a dairy farm in Petaluma, California (he later recorded 'Milk Cow Blues'). In 1970, however, one of his recordings, 'Spirit In The Sky' (inspired by a **Porter Wagoner** song), unexpectedly scaled the US charts, finally reaching number 3 and later hitting the top in the UK. It was a startling single of its era, highlighted by a memorable fuzz guitar riff and some spirited backing vocals and handclaps. Although Greenbaum was teased out of retirement to record a couple of albums, he remained the quintessential one-hit-wonder chart-topper. Since 1981, he has worked as a short-order chef in Santa Rosa, California. In 1986, 16 years after his finest moment, the British group **Doctor And The Medics** revived 'Spirit In The Sky', which hit number 1 in the UK for the second occasion. In the 90s, the song was prominently used in the Tom Hanks' movie *Apollo 13*, leading to the release of a new compilation album. Although in poor health, Greenbaum has also started to write new material. In 2003, UK crooner **Gareth Gates** once again took the song to the top of the charts as part of the charity appeal Comic Relief.

● ALBUMS: *Spirit In The Sky* (Reprise 1970) ★★, *Back Home Again* (Reprise 1971) ★, *Petaluma* (Reprise 1972) ★★.

● COMPILATIONS: *Spirit In The Sky: The Best Of Norman Greenbaum* (Varèse Sarabande 1996) ★★★, with Dr. West's Medicine Show And Junk Band *Euphoria! The Best Of* (Sundazed 1999) ★★.

Greenberg, Florence

b. 1914, New York City, USA, d. 2 November 1995. A record company executive who founded one of the most significant independent labels in the recording industry, **Scepter Records**, Greenberg was responsible for the success of a host of popular recording stars during the 60s and 70s, notably the **Shirelles**, **Chuck Jackson**, **Maxine Brown**, **Dionne Warwick**, **Tommy Hunt**, **Isley Brothers** and **B.J. Thomas**. Scepter operated from 1958–77, primarily through the imprints Scepter and **Wand** (begun in 1961).

Greenberg began her career in music peddling songs by local songwriters to Tin Pan Alley publishers in New York City. She was 44 years old when she entered the record business, after hearing her daughter, in 1957, raving about the performance of the girl group the Shirelles, who were classmates at Passiac High. She formed Tiara Records to record the group on what became their first hit, 'I Met Him On A Sunday'. **Decca Records** subsequently picked up the Shirelles' contract, but after they released them in 1958, Greenberg signed the group again and founded Scepter. A few months later, in 1959, the company moved across the river to Manhattan, and eventually occupied an entire floor at 1650 Broadway. In addition to the recording talent, Greenberg attracted the likes of producer Luther Dixon and songwriter **Burt Bacharach**. The company became so successful that Greenberg was offered $6 million for Scepter by Gulf & Western in 1965. She rejected the offer in what she retrospectively called 'the biggest mistake' of her career. During the 70s the majors took much of the record business from the independents, and one by one, Greenberg lost the artists that had made the company successful. She lost everything when Scepter collapsed in 1977, and never established another label.

Greenbriar Boys

Formed in New York City, USA, in 1958, the Greenbriar Boys were one of the leading exponents of urban bluegrass. The original line-up comprised John Herald (b. John Whittier Sirabian, 6 September 1939, New York City, New York, USA, d. 18 July 2005, West Hurley, USA; guitar/vocals), Bob Yellin (b. 10 June 1936, New York City, New York, USA; banjo, tenor vocals) and Eric Weissberg (banjo, mandolin, dobro, fiddle), but in 1959 the latter was replaced by Paul Prestopino and then **Ralph Rinzler** (b. 20 July 1934, New York, USA; mandolin, baritone vocals). The following year the group won the top award at the annual Union Grove Fiddlers' Convention, while Yellin secured the first of several hits as a solo artist. The Greenbriar Boys completed several excellent albums for the **Vanguard Records** label and became a highly popular attraction on the club, concert and festival circuits. Individually the members appeared as session musicians for, among others, **Ramblin' Jack Elliott**, **Joan Baez** and **Patrick Sky**. The trio was later augmented by vocalist Dian Edmondson; this reshaped unit recorded a lone release for **Elektra Records**. The group then underwent a radical change. Edmondson dropped out of the line-up, while Rinzler left for an administrative post with the Newport Folk Festival committee. Herald and Yellin added Frank Wakefield (b.

26 June 1934, Emory Gap, Tennessee, USA; mandolin) and Jim Buchanan (fiddle), but the Greenbriars' impetus was waning and the group was officially disbanded in 1967. They have occasionally reunited.

● ALBUMS: *The Greenbriar Boys* (Vanguard 1962) ★★★★, *Ragged But Right!* (Vanguard 1964) ★★★, *Dian And The Greenbriar Boys* (Elektra 1964) ★★★, *Better Late Than Never* (Vanguard 1966) ★★★.

● COMPILATIONS: *The Best Of John Herald And The Greenbriar Boys* (Vanguard 1972) ★★★★, *Best Of The Vanguard Years* (Vanguard 2002) ★★★★.

Greene, Jack

b. Jack Henry Greene, 7 January 1930, Maryville, Tennessee, USA. Greene took guitar lessons when he was eight years old, then added drumming to his abilities. Moving to Atlanta in the late 40s, he became part of the Cherokee Trio with Lem Bryant and Speedy Price. He then became a member of the Rhythm Ranch Boys and was a popular radio entertainer on *Georgia Jublilee* on WTJH. Greene's career was interrupted for military service in Korea, but he returned to Atlanta and joined the Peachtree Cowboys, also working as a salesperson and construction worker. In 1962, he joined **Ernest Tubb** And The Texas Troubadours as a drummer and occasional vocalist. He was featured on *Presents The Texas Troubadours*, and his performance on 'The Last Letter' led to solo recordings. Starting in 1965 with 'Ever Since My Baby Went Away', Greene had a succession of country hits, including number 1s with 'There Goes My Everything', 'All The Time', 'You Are My Treasure', 'Until My Dreams Come True' and 'Statue Of A Fool'. He did not leave Tubb's band until 1967, and only then because Tubb tired of hearing calls for the drummer to sing.

In 1969, Greene had a further hit with **Hank Cochran**'s song 'I Wish I Didn't Have To Miss You', on which he was partnered by Cochran's wife, **Jeannie Seely**. She became part of his road show and they continued to record together. Capitalizing on the popularity of outlaw country, they changed the name of their band from the Jolly Greene Giants to the Renegades, but they stayed with middle-of-the-road country music. Although his last chart entry was with 'If It's Love (Then Bet It All)' in 1984, Greene, who joined the **Grand Ole Opry** in 1967, is still a regular performer.

● ALBUMS: *There Goes My Everything* (Decca 1966) ★★★, *All The Time* (Decca 1967) ★★★, *What Locks The Door* (Decca 1967) ★★★, *You Are My Treasure* (Decca 1968) ★★★, *Love Takes Care Of Me* (Decca 1968) ★★★, *I Am Not Alone* (Decca 1968) ★★★, *Until My Dreams Come True* (Decca 1969) ★★★, *Statue Of A Fool* (Decca 1969) ★★, *Back In The Arms Of Love* (Decca 1969) ★★, with Jeannie Seely *Jack Greene/Jeannie Seely* (Decca 1970) ★★★, *Lord Is That Me* (Decca 1970) ★★★, *There's A Whole Lot About A Woman A Man Don't Know* (Decca 1971) ★★★, *Greene Country* (Decca 1971) ★★★, with Seely *Two For The Show* (Decca 1972) ★★, *Last Letter* (Vocalion 1972) ★★, *Love Stories* (Coral 1973) ★★, *I Never Had It So Good* (Hilltop 1976) ★★★, with Seely *At The Grand Ole Opry* (Pinnacle 1978) ★★★, *Yours For The Taking* (Frontline 1980) ★★, *Sings His Best* (Step One 1986) ★★, *He Is My Everything* (Step One 1991) ★★, *Highway To The Sky* (Step One 1995) ★★, *Lost Love* (Own Label 2000) ★★★, *Green Christmas* (Own Label 2003) ★★★.

● COMPILATIONS: *Greatest Hits* (Decca 1970) ★★★★, with Jeannie Seely *Greatest Hits* (Gusto 1982) ★★★★, *20 Greatest Hits* (Deluxe 1994) ★★★, *The Jolly Green Giant* (Edsel 1997) ★★★★, *20 All Time Greatest Hits* (TeeVee 2003) ★★★, *The Best Of: Statue Of A Fool* (K-Tel 2005) ★★★.

Greene, Jimmy

b. 1975, Bloomfield, Connecticut, USA. Encouraged by his father, an amateur saxophonist and songwriter, Greene acquired his first instrument, an alto saxophone, at the age of six. He studied formally while still in junior high school and quickly developed a passion for jazz. In 1990, he was introduced to **Jackie McLean**, then director of the jazz programme at Hartt College of Music. He also drew a great deal from working with McLean's community school, the Artists' Collective. On graduating from high school, Greene attended Hartt, where he proved to be an excellent student, displaying a prodigious ability to assimilate knowledge. He also switched to tenor saxophone. In 1996, shortly before completing his studies at Hartt, Greene was runner-up in a Thelonious Monk Institute competition. Moving to New York, he played with various leaders, including Omer Avital, **Kenny Barron**, **Avishai Cohen**, **Eddie Henderson**, Jason Lindner, **Claudio Roditi**, with whom he made his recording debut on *Double Standards*, **TanaReid**, **Horace Silver** and the New Jazz Composers Octet. Among musicians recruited by Greene for his own recording sessions are trumpeter Darren Barrett, bass player **Dwayne Burno** and, fellow students with McLean, trombonist **Steve Davis** and drummer Eric McPherson.

Greene, who also plays soprano saxophone and flute, and composes many of the pieces he performs, is a gifted instrumentalist with a pleasing light tone. His dexterity and imagination on up-tempo numbers is impressive, but so too is the manner in which he finds deeply satisfying lyrical undertones to ballads. Although the influence of McLean is pervasive, it is as an educator and role model rather than as someone to imitate. Indeed, by the start of the new millennium, Greene's playing was starting to display his own character and as he matures he seems likely to become, in his turn, a distinctive improviser and composer.

● ALBUMS: *Brand New World* (RCA Victor 1999) ★★★, *Introducing Jimmy Greene* 1997 recording (Criss Cross 2000) ★★★, *Forever* (Criss Cross 2004) ★★.

Greene, Richard

b. 9 November 1942, Beverly Hills, California, USA. This virtuoso fiddle player began his career in 1962 in a duo called the Orange Coast Ramblers with Ken Frankel on mandolin. They broke up in 1963 when Frankel joined **Jerry Garcia** and **Robert Hunter** in the Hart Valley Drifters. Greene joined the Dry City Scat Band with **David Lindley**, **Chris Darrow** (both of whom were later in **Kaleidoscope**), Steve Cahill and Pete Maldem. Greene was with them until 1965, playing on their privately pressed EP and on the **Elektra Records** compilation *String Band Project*. After this, Greene was briefly a member of the **Greenbriar Boys** and between March 1966 and March 1967 served in **Bill Monroe**'s Bluegrass Boys; he is featured on the **Decca Records** album *Blue Grass Time*. Greene joined **Red Allen** And The Kentuckians before switching to the **Jim Kweskin Jug Band** in time for *Garden Of Joy*.

In 1968 Greene joined the **Blues Project** and played a pivotal role in revitalizing their career. Having moved from the east coast to west, the group took a new name, **Seatrain**, and with the addition of **Peter Rowan** (ex-Bill Monroe; **Earth Opera**), they played a well-regarded fusion of rock and traditional styles. In 1971 Greene and Rowan formed an offshoot project, **Muleskinner**, with **David Grisman**, **Clarence White** and **Bill Keith**, and together they recorded an album that was issued following White's premature death. After the break-up of Seatrain in 1973, Greene formed Richard Greene And Zone with Randy Resnick (guitar, ex-**Pure Food And Drug Act**), Larry Taylor (bass, ex-Pure Food And Drug Act), Ken Collier (drums) and Richard Martin (vocals). They recorded a disappointing album, after which Greene was involved with several traditional acts, notably **Old And In The Way**, the Great American String Band and **Country Gazette**. In 1985 he founded the innovative Greene String Quartet, who over the course of three albums fused jazz, folk, rock and chamber music to great effect. He has also recorded with his all-instrumental Americana band the Grass Is Greener, in addition to releasing several solo albums. Greene received a Grammy Award in 1997 for his work on the **Bill Monroe** tribute album, *True Life Blues*.

● ALBUMS: *Richard Greene And Zone* (Warners 1973) ★★★, *Duets* (Rounder 1978) ★★★, *Ramblin'* (Rounder 1980) ★★★, *Peter Rowan, Richard Greene And The Red-Hot Pickers* (Nippon Columbia 1980) ★★★★, *Blue Rondo* (Sierra 1982) ★★★, with the Greene String Quartet *Molly On The Shore* (Hannibal 1988) ★★★★, with the Greene String Quartet *The String Machine* (Virgin 1991) ★★★★, *The Greene Fiddler* (Sierra 1995) ★★★, with the Grass Is Greener *Wolves A' Howlin'* (Rebel 1996) ★★★, with the Grass Is Greener *Sales Tax Toddle* (Rebel 1997) ★★★, with Beryl Marriott *Hands Across The Pond: Haunting, Evocative Melodies From The British-American Tradition* (Richard Greene 2001) ★★★.

Greene, Tony

b. Anthony Greene, March 1957, Kingston, Jamaica, West Indies. Greene's earliest involvement in music came at the renowned Alpha Boys School in Jamaica, whose alumni included the **Skatalites**' horn section (featuring **Don Drummond**, **Tommy McCook** and **Roland Alphonso**). Greene initially played the clarinet, although on joining the Jamaican Military Band he switched to playing the saxophone. His playing skills led to a scholarship in the UK at the Royal Academy Of Music from 1975–77. During the late 70s Greene returned to Jamaica, where he played on sessions for the **Roots Radics** and joined Sonny Bradshaw's Band, followed by a spell with **Lloyd Parks**' We The People Band. In this respect, his career duplicated that of the distinguished saxophonist **Dean Fraser**, who had also performed with both bands. However, by the mid-80s their careers diverged, as Fraser continued to perform over the emerging **digital** reggae beat, while Greene accompanied visiting R&B acts. He performed alongside **Gladys Knight**, **Lou Rawls** and **Aretha Franklin** on the island, which led to Greene being employed as a saxophonist on the international circuit. In the 90s Greene returned to his roots with the release of *Sax Man*. Although instrumental albums rarely enjoy the commercial success of their vocal counterparts, Greene's work led to further solo recording sessions. His releases proved especially popular in North America, although reggae purists considered his work too jazzy. Greene's follow-up featured vocal contributions from **Tanya Stephens**, and samples from **Beenie Man**, **Bounty**

Killer and **Capleton**. In addition to releasing his own work Greene established the Sax Man label with the aim of promoting local talent.

● ALBUMS: *Mean Greene* (Gone Clear 1997) ★★★, *Square From Cuba* (Sax Man 1998) ★★★.

Greensill, Mike

b. Michael Robert Greensill, 5 September 1946, Trowbridge, Wiltshire, England. Growing up in a small English village that had an outstanding church choir and choirmaster, Greensill gained an excellent musical foundation. At the age of 13 he discovered **Louis Armstrong** and **Jelly Roll Morton** and he began playing clarinet. For most of the 60s, he gained experience playing in the currently popular trad jazz bands. In 1968 he went to Leeds College of Music, where for four years he studied with trumpeter **Dickie Hawdon**, tenor saxophonist Red Price and others, gradually changing from clarinet to piano. During this time, he took all the local gigs he could find, playing many kinds of music. After his early exposure to Armstrong and Morton, other important influences were pianists **Earl 'Fatha' Hines**, **Thelonious Monk**, **Jimmy Rowles**, **Ellis Larkins**, and **Wynton Kelly**. Following graduation from Leeds, Greensill lived for four years in Hong Kong, working as staff arranger at **EMI Records** and as accompanist to many visiting American jazz artists. In 1977, he moved to San Francisco, where in 1981 he met and later married singer **Wesla Whitfield**. As Whitfield's musical director he toured extensively and made 15 CDs between 1986 and 2005. In the early 00s, he was also resident piano player on *West Coast Live*, a live radio show on NPR.

In addition to his role as accompanist, Greensill is in demand as an arranger, writing not only for his own trio and the small groups that usually accompany his wife, but also for big bands and symphony orchestras, the latter including the Boston Pops, the San Francisco Symphony and the Sacramento Symphony. Among musicians with whom Greensill has worked over the years are **Junior Cook**, **Scott Hamilton**, **Joe Henderson**, **James Moody**, **Cecil Payne**, **Charlie Rouse**, **Bud Shank**, and bass player John Wiitala and drummer **Donald Bailey**, the latter pair joining Greensill on a live date recorded at the Plush Room in San Francisco. Among many prestigious venues at which he has performed are Carnegie Hall, the Lincoln Center and the White House, during the Clinton administration. Less often on display are Greensill's skills as piano soloist, but when he is heard in this role, as on his own name releases, his interpretative and improvisational gifts are clearly evident.

● ALBUMS: *San Francisco Piano Jazz* (Myoho 1988) ★★★, with Noel Jewkes *American Lullaby* (Myoho 1991) ★★★, *Live At The Plush Room* (Pismo 2003) ★★★.

Greenslade

Formed in 1972 by ex-**Colosseum** members **Dave Greenslade** (b. 18 January 1943, Woking, Surrey, England; keyboards) and Tony Reeves (b. 18 April 1943, London, England). The line-up was completed by ex-**Episode Six** and **Alan Bown** Set member Dave Lawson (keyboards/vocals) and Andrew McCulloch (drums). Their four well-received albums all proved to be moderately successful—the strong emphasis on keyboard sounds with a hint of classical roots was perfect for the progressive rock market of the early 70s. Their distinctive album covers were illustrated and calligraphed by Roger Dean. **Dave Clempson**, another ex-Colosseum member, joined

them for *Spyglass Guest*, and alongside new recruit, violinist Graham Smith, the organ-dominated sound became less prominent. Reeves departed and returned for the second time to his main interest as record producer, where he became a highly respected figure. Six months after their last album Greenslade dismantled the band as managerial and legal problems continued. He embroiled himself in television music scores, where he has found great success. His solo *Cactus Choir* in 1976 sold only moderately. Greenslade re-formed briefly in 1977 with yet another ex-Colosseum member, **Jon Hiseman**, who together with Tony Reeves and Mick Rodgers, lasted only one tour. Their intricate and occasionally brilliant music was out of step with the burgeoning punk scene.

● ALBUMS: *Greenslade* (Warners 1973) ★★★, *Bedside Manners Are Extra* (Warners 1973) ★★★, *Spyglass Guest* (Warners 1974) ★★★, *Time And Tide* (Warners 1975) ★★★, *Live* 1973/75 recording (Mystic 1999) ★★.

Greenslade, Dave

b. 18 January 1943, Woking, Surrey, England. Former member of **Colosseum** and founder of the progressive jazz/rock group, **Greenslade**. In 1979 he collaborated with fantasy artist/writer Patrick Woodroffe in an lavish and expensive concept double album, *The Pentateuch Of The Cosmogony*. Released at the 'wrong' end of the 70s, it was doomed to failure, yet in recent times it has achieved a notoriety as a valued artefact among collectors. Throughout the 80s and into the 90s, he has carved out a successful career composing theme music for British film and television.

● ALBUMS: *Cactus Choir* (Warners 1976) ★★, *The Pentateuch Of The Cosmogony* (EMI 1979) ★★, *Terry Pratchett's From The Discworld* (Virgin 1994) ★★★.

Greensleeves Records

Despite its humble origins as a record shop in West Ealing, London, in November 1975, Greensleeves continues to thrive in the keenly contested environs of the reggae marketplace. The label was started in 1977 when the shop moved to new premises in Shepherd's Bush. The first two releases were Reggae Regular's 'Where Is Jah' and **Dr. Alimantado**'s 'Born For A Purpose'. The latter artist also offered them their first long-player, the *Best Dressed Chicken In Town* compilation. Tony McDermott's distinctive artwork soon established Greensleeves' visual image and identity. The label further consolidated its name with the emergence of **dancehall**, licensing much of **Henry 'Junjo' Lawes**' catalogue for domestic release. Others included **Scientist**, **Channel One**'s technical guru, and Prince (later **King**) **Jammy**'s productions, notably his early works with **Black Uhuru**. The UK side were equally productive with their Bubblers label, peaking commercially with **Tippa Irie**'s UK Top 30 hit, 'Hello Darling', in 1986. Other notable successes on the domestic front included **Clint Eastwood And General Saint**. The mid-80s saw impressive repackagings of Jamaican standards (**Hugh Mundell, Burning Spear, Yabby You**) as well as major new works from **Eek A Mouse, Josey Wales, Junior Reid** and **Yellowman**. Their profile was enhanced further via the UK release of two groundbreaking singles: **Wayne Smith**'s 'Under Me Sleng Teng', which kickstarted the **digital** revolution, and **Gregory Isaacs**' 'Rumours', the bestselling reggae record of 1988, and an important staging post in the development of **ragga**. A new wave of artists had their records released in the UK by

Greensleeves: **Shabba Ranks**, **Cocoa Tea** and **Papa San** among them. The English **lovers rock** scene was represented by **Deborahe Glasgow**, while the company scored a bestseller when they picked up **Shaggy**'s 'Oh Carolina'. They also market several other independent labels, notably **Jah Shaka**'s idiosyncratic roster. The company, which later moved to Isleworth, launched its Ragga Ragga Ragga series in the mid-90s, showcasing the work of the new generation of dancehall acts including **Bounty Killer**, **Sizzla**, **Mr. Vegas**, **Buccaneer**, **Elephant Man**, **Goofy** and **Beenie Man**. The latter enjoyed a UK Top 10 hit in 1998 with 'Who Am I'.

Greenthal, Stanley

b. Stanley Scott Greenthal, 16 April 1949, New York City, USA. Greenthal's family came from England around the time of the Mayflower. His father's family originate from Alsace Lorraine; this combination probably explains his passion for the various musical styles emanating from those areas. Receiving his first guitar at the age of 14, he moved west at the age of 17. He studied English Literature at the University of Colorado, achieving a BA. By now he was married, but two years later his wife died, and the title track of *Songs For The Journey* was written about the experience. The album includes two exceptional instrumentals, 'January/After Midnight Polkas' and 'Still Untitled'. As well as Stanley on guitar and mandocello the album includes such respected musicians as **Kevin Burke**, of **Patrick Street** (fiddle), and Michaél Ó Dhomhnaill, of the **Bothy Band** and Relativity, who also produced the album. In the early 70s, Greenthal was living in southern England, and listened to Irish music a great deal. He also spent time travelling round Scotland, Ireland, Greece and Brittany, and absorbed the many musical influences inherent in the different cultures. *All Roads* continues the Celtic and Balkan themes in the music. Greenthal has played both coasts of the USA, and has performed with **Robin Williamson**.
● ALBUMS: *Songs For The Journey* (Madrona Ring 1986) ★★★, *All Roads* (Madrona Ring 1990) ★★★, *Turning Towards You* (Madrona Ring 2001) ★★★.

Greentrax Records

Greentrax is the result of the vision of one man, former Scottish police inspector Ian Green (b. Forres, Edinburgh, Scotland), a fan of traditional music for over 40 years. Green grew up in a musical family, his father a Scottish piper, but concentrated on his police career until the mid-60s, when he saw an edition of the *Hootenanny* show on television. His enthusiasm rekindled, he organized his first concert for the police social club. This led to the weekly Fuzzfolk club, which ran for over 10 years under his guidance, and then the Edinburgh Folk Club. He documented developments on the scene through his *Sandy Bell's Broadsheet* publication, and also became a prominent member of the Traditional Music and Song Association. While running the Edinburgh Folk Club he became involved in acquiring records for his members, an occupation which eventually led to his starting Discount Folk Records as a mail-order service. After retiring from the police in the mid-70s he concentrated on this thriving business but also continued to be a fixture at local folk gatherings. His first involvement with the production of music had come when he made a cassette recording of the floor singers at the Fuzzfolk club, and then a benefit for *Sandy Bell's Broadsheet*, which included material from **Aly**

Bain and **Dick Gaughan**. The first three Greentrax releases featured another of the contributors to that compilation, the **McCalmans** (*Peace And Plenty*), fiddler Ian Hardie (*A Breath Of Fresh Air*) and songwriter Ian MacDonald (*Beneath Still Waters*). The initial intention was for three releases per year, but as the fame of Greentrax spread, boosted by its proprietor's reputation for honesty and fair play with his artists, the release schedule escalated. By the 90s a weighty catalogue had been amassed, with some of the highlights including Cathie-Ann McPhee, **Niamh Parsons**, **Heather Heywood**, Archie Fisher, Billy Jackson, Brian MacDonald, Brian McNeill, Black Eyed Biddy, Ceolbeg and Robin Laing. An album drawn from the Scottish television series hosted by Aly Bain became Green's biggest seller so far, attaining platinum status in Scotland. This success enabled him to launch a subsidiary label, Tangent Records, for archive releases, with several projects part-funded by the Scottish Arts Council.
● COMPILATIONS: *The Music & Song Of Greentrax: The Best Of Scottish Music* (Greentrax 1996) ★★★★, *Folkal Point: Edinburgh—Traditional Music From A New Generation* (Greentrax 1998) ★★★.

Greenway, Brian

b. 1 October 1951, Canada. When Canadian heavy metal band **April Wine** broke up in 1988 following singer **Myles Goodwin**'s decision to embark on a solo project, his move predicted the future course of former colleague Brian Greenway's career. In reality, Greenway simply did not have the songwriting skills to make it on his own—the vocals on *Serious Business*, his debut album for **Atlantic Records** in 1988, were laboured and unconvincing, despite the obvious skill of his guitar playing. It proved to be a one-off experiment before Greenway and Goodwin reunited in a re-formed April Wine at the turn of the 90s.
● ALBUMS: *Serious Business* (Atlantic 1988) ★★.

Greenwich Village Follies

The first of these revues, which were similar to, but less lavish than, the **Ziegfeld Follies**, opened at the Greenwich Village Theatre on 15 July 1919. All of the eight editions, through to 1928, played on Broadway, and were presented by the Bohemians Inc. (Al Jones and Morris Green). Most of them were directed by **John Murray Anderson**, who also contributed sketches and lyrics. The show's satirical targets included most aspects of the Greenwich Village district and its uninhibited, arty inhabitants. The first edition, which ran for 232 performances—the most successful of all—was subtitled 'A Revusical Comedy Of New York's Latin Quarter', and had songs by A. Baldwin Sloane, Arthur Swanstrom and John Murray Anderson, which included 'My Marionette', 'I'm Ashamed To Look The Moon In The Face', 'My Little Javanese', and 'Message Of the Cameo'. An additional number was **Irving Berlin**'s 'I'll See You In C-U-B-A'. Subsequent editions continued to arrive with the occasional appealing song such as Dorothy Terris and Julian Robeldo's 'Three O'Clock In The Morning' (1921), 'Georgette' (1922) by **Lew Brown** and **Ray Henderson** (of **De Sylva, Brown And Henderson**), and **Cole Porter**'s gorgeous 'I'm In Love Again' (1924), but, generally speaking, the music department was not this particular *Follies*' strongest point. However, a great many talented entertainers graced its various productions, including Bobby Edwards, Bessie McCoy, Cecil Cunningham,

Ted Lewis And His Orchestra, James Watts, Rex Story, Grace La Rue, **Benny Fields**, Bobby Watson, **Frank Crumit**, **Howard Marsh**, **Joe E. Browne**, Sammy White and Eva Puck, **Vincent Lopez** And His Orchestra, **Bert Savoy** and Jay Brennan, and Florence Moore.

Greenwich, Ellie

b. 23 October 1940, Brooklyn, New York City, USA. Greenwich's singing career began in 1958 with 'Cha-Cha-Charming', released under the name Ellie Gaye. Two years later she met budding songwriter **Jeff Barry**, and, following a release as Ellie Gee And The Jets, the couple formed the **Raindrops** in 1963. The group enjoyed a US Top 20 hit with 'The Kind Of Boy You Can't Forget', but increased demand on the now-married duo's compositional skills led to the band's demise. Having abandoned respective partnerships with Toni Powers and Art Resnick, Greenwich and Barry enjoyed a sustained period of success with a series of notable compositions, including 'Do Wah Diddy Diddy' (the **Exciters/Manfred Mann**), 'I Wanna Love Him So Bad' (the **Jelly Beans**) and 'Hanky Panky' (**Tommy James And The Shondells**). Collaborations with **Phil Spector** generated hits for the **Crystals** ('Da Doo Ron Ron' and 'Then He Kissed Me'), the **Ronettes** ('Be My Baby' and 'Baby, I Love You') and **Ike And Tina Turner** ('River Deep—Mountain High') while work with **Shadow Morton** reaped commercial success for the **Shangri-Las**, notably 'Leader Of The Pack'. Ellie also rekindled her solo career with 'You Don't Know', but her divorce from Barry in 1965 put an intolerable strain on their working relationship. Together they produced **Neil Diamond**'s early recordings, but in 1967 she severed their partnership and made an exclusive songwriting contract with Unart Music. *Ellie Greenwich Composes, Produces, Sings* combined original songs with current favourites, but was a commercial failure, while her subsequent Pineywood Productions company was similarly ill-starred in the wake of changing musical tastes. 'I couldn't understand what (acid rock) was all about', she later stated, and instead switched to writing jingles. She re-emerged during the singer-songwriter boom with *Let It Be Written, Let It Be Sung*, but this excellent album failed to rekindle her career when stage fright blighted an attendant tour. Ellie remained in seclusion for most of the ensuing decade but re-emerged in the 80s as a performer in the acclaimed biographical revue *Leader Of The Pack*. A new generation of acts, including **Nona Hendryx**, **Cyndi Lauper** and **Ellen Foley**, recorded her songs, insuring Greenwich's position as one of pop's finest composers.

● ALBUMS: *Ellie Greenwich Composes, Produces And Sings* (United Artists 1968) ★★★, *Let It Be Written, Let It Be Sung* (Verve 1973) ★★★.

● COMPILATIONS: *I Can Hear Music: The Ellie Greenwich Collection* (Razor & Tie 1999) ★★★.

Greenwich, Sonny

b. Herbert Lawrence Greenidge, 1 January 1936, Hamilton, Ontario, Canada. Greenwich began playing guitar in R&B groups but turned to jazz after working with a number of visiting American musicians. He moved to the USA, playing in bands of his own, as co-leader, and also as a sideman. This was during the 60s, when his musical associates included **Miles Davis**. He also played with **John Handy**, appearing with him at the *Spirituals To Swing* anniversary concert at Carnegie Hall in 1967. Shortly after this he led his own

quartet at the Village Vanguard. From the 70s onwards, Greenwich's appearances on the US jazz scene became sporadic, although he frequently performed in Canada and continued to make records and festival appearances. These activities continued through succeeding decades and included dates with **Kenny Wheeler**, and a 1994 engagement at the Montreal Jazz Festival, where an encounter with **Paul Bley** resulted in a studio session.

By the early 90s, Greenwich was turning ever more towards composing, many of the resulting works appearing on a succession of well-received albums. On some of his 90s recordings he was accompanied by his own band, Meantime. Greenwich's playing draws interestingly from many areas of popular music, and from time to time also includes musical elements from other cultures, including Latin American. Forward thinking, and frequently displaying a penchant for out-of-tempo pieces, Greenwich has made an important contribution to Canada's position as a producer of fine jazz musicians.

● ALBUMS: *The Old Man And The Child* (CBC 1969) ★★★, *Sun Song* (CBC 1974) ★★★, *Evol-ution: Love's Reverse* (PM 1978) ★★★, *Sonny Greenwich* (Justin Time 1986) ★★★, *Bird Of Paradise* (Justin Time 1987) ★★★★, *Live At Sweet Basil* (Justin Time 1988) ★★, with Paul Bley *Outside In* (Justin Time 1994) ★★★, *Standard Idioms* (Kleo 1994) ★★★, *Hymn To The Earth* (Kleo 1995) ★★★, *Welcome: Mother Earth* (Justin Time 1995) ★★★, *Spirit In The Air* (Kleo 1996) ★★★, with Kenny Wheeler *Live At The Montreal Bistro* (Justin Time 1997) ★★★, *Days Gone By* 1979 recording (Sackville 2000) ★★★, *Fragments Of A Memory* (Cornerstone 2002) ★★★, *Special Angel* (Cbc 2003) ★★★.

Greenwillow

A whimsical, fantasy piece, with music and lyrics by **Frank Loesser**, and a book by Loesser and Lesser Samuels, *Greenwillow* opened on Broadway at the Alvin Theatre on 8 March 1960. Based on B.J. Chute's novel, it was set in a mythical American village, and told the story of Gideon Briggs (Anthony Perkins) and his reluctance to marry his sweetheart, Dorrie (Ellen McCown), because he is afraid that he may have inherited the family trait—wanderlust—and so may up and leave her. Loesser's songs were tender and charming, and have continued to be admired. They included 'The Music Of Home', 'Summertime Love', 'A Day Borrowed From Heaven', 'Gideon Briggs, I Love You', 'Walking Away Whistling', and 'Faraway Boy'. Anthony Perkins, making his Broadway musical debut, had the reflective 'Never Will I Marry', which attained some popularity. The whole affair was far removed from another of Perkin's projects in 1960, Alfred Hitchcock's terrifying film *Psycho*, in which he gave a performance that will always be remembered. The folksy, thoughtful *Greenwillow* just did not appeal to New York theatre audiences at a time when the entertainment world in general was on the brink of the brash, swinging 60s, and it closed after only 95 performances. By then, Loesser was in the throes of a far different proposition: his 1961 blockbuster, **How To Succeed In Business Without Really Trying**, lasted for 1,417 performances.

Greenwood, Charlotte

b. 25 June 1890, Philadelphia, Pennsylvania, USA, d. 18 January 1978, Beverly Hills, California, USA. A tall, slender and immensely likeable musical comedy and film actress who graced several musical pictures in the 40s with her spunky and eccentric style and amazingly loose-jointed high-kick. Greenwood first came to notice on Broadway in *The Passing Show Of 1913*, and in the following year made such an impression with her 'flat-footed' kicks and 'splits' in *Pretty Miss Smith*, particularly in one number, 'Long, Lean, Lanky Letty', that producer Oliver Morosco re-titled the show *Long-Legged Letty*. The Letty character kept Greenwood in occasional employment during the next few years via *So Long, Letty* (1916), *Linger Longer Letty* (1919), and *Letty Pepper* (1922), and there were subsequent film versions. Greenwood also appeared in several Broadway revues in the 20s, but by then she had also established herself in silent movies. In the 30s she easily made the transition into talkies, mostly with comedies, but also in occasional musicals such as *Flying High* (1931) and the **Eddie Cantor** vehicle *Palmy Days* (1932). In 1940 she co-starred with **Shirley Temple** and Jack Oakie in *Young People*, and during the rest of the decade made effective and highly entertaining contributions to a number of 20th Century–Fox musicals including *Down Argentine Way*, *Tall, Dark And Handsome*, *Moon Over Miami*, *Springtime In The Rockies*, *The Gang's All Here*, *Wake Up And Dream*, and *Oh, You Beautiful Doll* (1949). She also had her own US networked radio show in the 40s. In 1950 Greenwood returned to Broadway (high-kicks and all) in **Cole Porter**'s musical *Out Of This World*, and stopped the show every night with the plaintive (but hilarious) 'Nobody's Chasing Me' ('Nobody wants to own me/And I object/Nobody wants to 'phone me/Even collect'). Three years later she showed **Esther Williams** a few aquatic tricks in *Dangerous When Wet*, and in 1957 made her last screen appearance as Aunt Eller in *Oklahoma!* According to the obituary in *Variety* following her sudden death at the age of 87, the part had originally been written for her by **Oscar Hammerstein II**, in the historic 1943 Broadway production. For some reason she had been unable to accept it then.

● FURTHER READING: *Never Too Tall*, Charlotte Greenwood.

Greenwood, Lee

b. Melvin Lee Greenwood, 27 October 1942, Southgate, California, USA. Because of his parents' divorce, Greenwood was brought up by his grandparents in Sacramento, California, but he inherited their musical talent (his mother played piano and his father woodwind). In his teens, he played in various bands in Sacramento and Los Angeles and was even part of a dixieland jazz band at Disneyland. He played saxophone for country star **Del Reeves** and then formed his own band, Apollo, which found work in Las Vegas in 1962. He turned down an opportunity to join the **Young Rascals** and for many years he was arranging and playing music for bands in casinos (and working as a blackjack dealer by day). The environment narrowed his vocal range and he developed a husky-voiced approach to ballads similar to **Kenny Rogers**.

In 1979, Greenwood's career took a major step forward when he was heard by Larry McFaden of **Mel Tillis**' band, who became his manager. His first MCA single, 'It Turns Me Inside Out', was a US Top 20 country hit in 1981. This was followed by several other hits including two number 1s, 'Somebody's Gonna Love You' and 'Going, Going, Gone'. His

songs were also recorded by several other performers including Kenny Rogers who found success with 'A Love Song'. In 1984 he recorded an album with **Barbara Mandrell** and they made the US country charts with 'To Me' and he recorded his own patriotic song, 'God Bless The USA', which won the **Country Music Association**'s Song Of The Year. His other number 1 country singles are 'Dixie Road', 'I Don't Mind The Thorns (If You're The Rose)', 'Don't Underestimate My Love For You', 'Hearts Aren't Made To Break (They're Made To Love)', and the sensual 'Mornin' Ride'. He has won numerous country awards and a Grammy for Best Vocal Performance, and is known as the original performer of 'The Wind Beneath My Wings'.

Greenwood switched labels to **Capitol Records**, but this was not enough to stop the decline of his career during the 90s. He subsequently concentrated on performing at his own theatre in Sevierville, Tennessee, while continuing to release the occasional album of new material. 'God Bless The USA' enjoyed a chart revival in the wake of the terrorist attacks in America on 11 September 2001.

● ALBUMS: *Inside Out* (MCA 1982) ★★★, *Somebody's Gonna Love You* (MCA 1983) ★★, *You've Got A Good Love Coming* (MCA 1984) ★★★, with Barbara Mandrell *Meant For Each Other* (MCA 1984) ★★★, *Streamline* (MCA 1985) ★★★, *Christmas To Christmas* (MCA 1985) ★★, *Love Will Find It's Way To You* (MCA 1986) ★★★★, *If There's Any Justice* (MCA 1987) ★★★, *This Is My Country* (MCA 1988) ★★★, *If Only For One Night* (MCA 1989) ★★★, *Holdin' A Good Hand* (Capitol 1990) ★★★, *A Perfect 10* (Capitol 1991) ★★, *American Patriot* (Liberty 1992) ★★★, *Totally Devoted To You* (Arrival 1995) ★★, *Super Hits* (Epic 1996) ★★, *Wounded Heart* (Kardina 1998) ★★, *Same River, Different Bridge* (FreeFalls 2000) ★★★, *Have Yourself A Merry Little Christmas* (FreeFalls 2001) ★★.

● COMPILATIONS: *Greatest Hits* (MCA 1985) ★★★★, *Greatest Hits Volume Two* (MCA 1988) ★★★, *Best Of Lee Greenwood* (Curb 1992) ★★★, *The Best Of Lee Greenwood* (Liberty 1993) ★★★, *God Bless The USA: Best Of Lee Greenwood* (Curb 1996) ★★★, *The Best Of Lee Greenwood: The Wind Beneath My Wings* (Half Moon 1998) ★★★, *The Best Of Lee Greenwood: The Millennium Collection* (MCA 2002) ★★★★, *Inspirational Songs Featuring 'God Bless The USA'* (Curb 2002) ★★★.

Greer, 'Big' John

b. John Marshall Greer, 21 November 1923, Hot Springs, Arkansas, USA, d. 12 May 1972. Greer, who performed both as a vocalist and a tenor saxophonist, is a perfect representative of the flowering of the saxophone in the post–World War II era as an R&B instrument. He first made his mark in the music business leading his own quintet in 1948 and made some favourably received recordings. In late 1948 he joined the **Lucky Millinder** Band, with whom he recorded as both a vocalist and sax soloist, but in April 1949 he was again making solo recordings for the **RCA Records** label. Over the following years he had releases both as a member of the Millinder band and as a solo artist. 'Got You On My Mind' from 1952 was his only national R&B hit. RCA released him from his contract in 1955, and after a short stay at **King Records** in 1956, he never made another recording.

● COMPILATIONS: *R&B In New York City* (Official 1988) ★★★, *Rockin' With Big John* (Bear Family 1992) ★★★.

Greer, Jim

b. James Marvin Greer, 3 September 1942, West Liberty, Logan County, Ohio, USA. Greer was attracted to country music by his sisters, Bonnie and Valeda, who, as the Greer Sisters, sang on several stations in the 50s, including the *Renfro Valley Barn Dance*, on WLW Cincinnati. After learning banjo, guitar and mandolin, he played with them, until Bonnie tired of the travelling and they disbanded. Greer then formed his Mac-O-Chee Valley Folks, which featured himself on banjo, sister Valeda (guitar), Bob McPherson (guitar, mandolin), Dalton Burroughs (bass), Valeda's husband John Wentz (dobro) and later added Aaron Hicks or Herb Collins (fiddle). They played bluegrass and traditional music, plus a few numbers written by McPherson, as a semi-professional group appearing at various local shows or bluegrass festivals. Between 1965 and 1969, they also played weekly on *Jamboree USA* at WWVA Wheeling, West Virginia. They made their first recordings in the early 60s for Rite and Starday, but later recorded albums for Uncle Jim O'Neal's popular Rural Rhythm label, before returning to Rite's Golden Shield subsidiary for a gospel album. In the mid-70s, the band found themselves faced with a common problem for semi-professional bands. Faced with more work than they could handle on a part-time basis, they had to choose between going fully professional or disbanding. Since all members had full-time occupations that they were hesitant to give up, they reluctantly decided on the latter. Greer concentrated on running his West Liberty clothing store and apart from occasional local appearances has remained inactive. Collins has since died but the remainder of the band stayed in their beloved Mac-O-Chee Valley area.
● ALBUMS: *Bluegrass In Ohio* (Rite 1963) ★★★★, *Log Cabin Songs* (Rural Rhythm 1965) ★★★, *Memories In Song* (Rural Rhythm 1966) ★★★, *Stars Of The WWVA Jamboree* (Rural Rhythm 1966) ★★★, *Country Favorites* (Rural Rhythm 1967) ★★★, *Gospel Singing Time* (Golden Shield 1970) ★★.

Greer, Sonny

b. William Alexander Greer, 13 December 1895, Long Branch, New Jersey, USA, d. 23 March 1982, New York City, USA. After playing in New Jersey, drummer Greer appeared in 1919 in Washington, DC, where he encountered a local musician named **Duke Ellington**. In the early 20s the two men worked together in New York City, where Greer became a permanent member of the Ellington entourage. One of Duke's closest acquaintances, Greer was a subtle player who occasionally erred on the side of casualness. His timekeeping was supported initially by guitarist **Freddie Guy** and later by bass player **Jimmy Blanton**. Visually, Greer was spectacular, surrounding himself with an astonishing array of percussion instruments, including bells, gongs, timpani and xylophone. During his time with Ellington, Greer rarely went outside the band, although he did play on **Lionel Hampton**'s famous Victor recording sessions. A smooth-talking, sharp-dressing, pool-hustler, Greer's on-stage behaviour gradually deteriorated through his inability to control his drinking. In 1951 Ellington finally asked him to leave, and thereafter Greer freelanced, recording with other ex-Ellingtonians such as **Johnny Hodges** and **Tyree Glenn** and with **Henry 'Red' Allen** and **J.C. Higginbotham**. Despite his failings as a drummer, in retrospect it is possible to see and hear that Greer was the ideal Ellington drummer for the 30s and 40s. In the late 60s

and 70s Greer led his own groups, usually a trio, appearing in concerts celebrating Ellington and proving that he was never more at ease than when playing his old boss' music.

Greger, Max

b. 2 April 1926, Munich, Germany. After studying classical music, Greger turned to dance band work for a living. Having trained on piano and clarinet, he added accordion and tenor saxophone and in the late 40s was regularly leading his own small bands. In the mid-50s he had bigger bands, adopting a musical style that catered for popular tastes. During this period he worked with visiting American musicians, either as a sideman or leading an accompanying orchestra. He toured Europe with his band and visited Russia. In 1963 he formed a large ensemble that he led for the next two decades, appearing frequently on German radio and television and making over a hundred albums. From time to time he had expatriate Americans in his band, among them **Benny Bailey**. A good all-round instrumentalist, Greger's main contribution to popular music in Europe has been the high standard of musicianship he has demanded from members of his orchestra. If he did not break new boundaries, he certainly set standards of excellence in performance that measure up to those set anywhere else in the world.
● ALBUMS: *European Jazz Sounds* (Brunswick 1963) ★★★, *Maximum* (Polydor 1965) ★★★.

Gregg, Ricky Lynn

b. 22 August 1961, Longview, Texas, USA. The 90s country singer/guitarist Ricky Lynn Gregg is of Native American descent. He formed two rock groups, the Ricky Lynn Project and Head East, and with them opened for **Huey Lewis And The News** and **Heart**. He then switched direction to honky tonk country and formed the band Cherokee Thunder, with whom he played clubs in Dallas. He reached the US country charts with a revival of **Mel Street**'s 'If I Had A Cheatin' Heart'. Little was heard of the singer after he was dropped by his record company. He reappeared in 2001 with a credible album co-produced by **Barry Beckett**.
● ALBUMS: *Ricky Lynn Gregg* (Liberty 1993) ★★★, *Get A Little Closer* (Liberty 1994) ★★★, *Careful What You Wish For* (RMG 2001) ★★★.

Gregory, John

b. John Gregori, 12 October 1928, London, England. A band leader, arranger and composer, Gregory learned to play the violin when he was seven, and studied under Albert Campoli. He made his first public appearance with the instrument when he was nine, and in his teens played a variety of instruments with his father, Frank Gregori And His Band, at London's Normandy Hotel. During the 50s he worked as an arranger for Eddie Kassner's Music Publishing Company, and in 1957 arranged and accompanied UK singer **Russ Hamilton** on his two-sided hit, 'We Will Make Love'/ 'Rainbow', which made the UK and US Top 5. He also backed many other top artists, such as **Matt Monro**, **Cleo Laine** and **Nana Mouskouri**. In 1960 he launched a very successful series of more than 20 big band Latin-American style albums under the pseudonym of the Chaquito Orchestra. Two of these, *This Chaquito* and *Thriller Themes* entered the UK album charts. He has made many albums under his own name, including those with his Cascading

Strings, which were especially popular in Japan. Gregory has also written for films and television, and continues to broadcast extensively, particularly with the BBC Radio Orchestra. His composition, 'Introduction And Air To A Stained Glass Window', won an **Ivor Novello** Award in 1976 for 'The Best Instrumental Work'.

● ALBUMS: with the Chaquito Orchestra *Oooh . . .It's That Chaquito Again* (1960) ★★, *This Chaquito* (1968) ★★★, *Thriller Themes* (1972) ★★★; with the Johnny Gregory Orchestra *TV Western Themes* (1961) ★★★, *Carols In Wonderland* (1962) ★★, *TV Thriller Themes* (1962) ★★★, *French Polish* (1962) ★★★, *The Detectives* (1977) ★★★, *The Dynamic Sound Of John Gregory* (1990) ★★★; with his Cascading Strings *I Write The Songs* (1984) ★★★.

Gregory, Steve

b. 1945, London, England. Gregory embarked on a musical course playing clarinet in the St. Paul's school orchestra, and while at the school he also learned to play the guitar and piano. In 1963 he was offered a place in the Guildhall School of Music, but rejected the proposal. In 1964 he played with the **Alan Price** band, which led to session work with a number of top 60s bands. He played on sessions for **'Screamin' Jay' Hawkins**, **Geno Washington**, **Chicken Shack**, **Georgie Fame**, and on **Fleetwood Mac**'s *Mr Wonderful* as well as the **Rolling Stones**' 'Honky Tonk Women'. In the 70s, in addition to performing alongside Fame, Gregory found work supporting **Fela Kuti**, **Linda Lewis**, **Gonzalez**, **Ginger Baker**'s **Airforce** and, oddly, **Rocky Sharpe And The Replays**. The 80s saw work with **Steel Pulse**, **Maxi Priest**, the Inspirational Choir, **Amazulu**, **Freddie King** and **China Crisis**. Gregory also has the distinction of having provided the infectious saxophone melody on **George Michael**'s 'Careless Whisper'. Other notable solo performances were featured on **Alison Moyet**'s interpretation of 'That Ole Devil Called Love', **Chris Rea**'s 'Fool' and **Queen**'s 'One Year Of Love'. In the 90s Gregory performed in **Dennis Bovell**'s Dub Band, contributing his playing skills to **Linton Kwesi Johnson**'s classic *Tings And Times*. Gregory also toured with **Wet Wet Wet**, **Van Morrison** and a host of other celebrated performers. His association with Dennis Bovell led to Gregory's debut, *Bushfire*, an acid-jazz-reggae fusion. The album featured original compositions by Linton Kwesi Johnson, Dennis Bovell and Gregory, and also featured the playing skills of **John Kpiaye**, Georgie Fame, John Deacon and Kuma Harada. In 1998 he was a featured artist on the LKJ 20th Anniversary show alongside Jean 'Binta' Breeze, Winston Francis and the Dub Band.

● ALBUMS: *Bushfire* (LKJ Records 1997) ★★★.

Gregson And Collister

Comprising **Clive Gregson** (b. 4 January 1955, Ashton-Under-Lyne, Manchester, England; guitar, keyboards, vocals), and **Christine Collister** (b. 28 December 1961, Douglas, Isle Of Man; guitar, percussion, vocals), this UK act was one of the most notable duos working in folk music. Gregson was already known as the writer and prominent frontman of the band **Any Trouble**, with whom he recorded five albums before turning solo. He released *Strange Persuasions* in 1985, and then became a member of the **Richard Thompson** Band. In addition, he acquired the role of producer on albums by such artists as the **Oyster Band**, Stephen Fearing and **Keith Hancock**. Another solo album was released in 1990, *Welcome To The Workhouse*, comprising material that had hitherto

been unreleased. Collister had made a living singing and playing guitar in Italian bars, and as a session singer for Piccadilly Radio in Manchester. She was discovered performing in a local club by Gregson and this led to her place in the Richard Thompson Band, and subsequent position in the duo with Gregson himself. Collister also provided backing vocals for **Loudon Wainwright III** and Mark Germino. Her warm sensuous vocals were instantly recognizable as the soundtrack to the BBC television series *The Life And Loves Of A She Devil*.

Gregson's lyrical ability and harmonies, together with Collister's unmistakable vocal style produced a number of critically acclaimed albums of note. The duo toured extensively throughout the UK, USA and Canada, and also played in Japan and Europe. In 1990, the duo completed their first tour of Australia. In March 1992, they announced the start of a farewell tour. Later that year following the tour, Collister worked with Barb Jungr (of **Jungr And Parker**) and Heather Joyce in a part-time unit, the Jailbirds. Both Gregson and Collister continue to work and perform but no longer together. Collister toured with Richard Thompson in the mid-90s, and Gregson worked with **Boo Hewerdine** in addition to releasing his own solo records.

● ALBUMS: *Home And Away* (Eleventh Hour 1986) ★★★, *Mischief* (Special Delivery 1987) ★★★, *A Change In The Weather* (Special Delivery 1989) ★★★★, *Love Is A Strange Hotel* (Special Delivery 1990) ★★★, *The Last Word* (Special Delivery 1992) ★★★★.

Gregson, Clive

b. 4 January 1955, Ashton-Under-Lyne, Manchester, England. This highly respected singer-songwriter started his career as a member of **Any Trouble** before he embarked on an acclaimed partnership with **Christine Collister**. They announced a parting of the ways after seven years of performing and recording together. Gregson then performed with **Richard Thompson** and worked as a record producer. Throughout this time he continued to write and record subtly powerful songs, as highlighted on 1990's *Welcome To The Workhouse*, with the pathos of Thompson and the humour of **Billy Bragg**. Gregson has also worked and toured with **Boo Hewerdine**, **Eddi Reader** and **Plainsong**. Gregson continues to release credible solo albums and, like Thompson, is hugely talented, totally underrated and, likely to remain a cult item only for those lucky enough to be aware of his fine catalogue of songs.

● ALBUMS: *Strange Persuasions* (Demon 1985) ★★★, *Welcome To The Workhouse* (Special Delivery 1990) ★★★★, *Carousel Of Noise* (Gregsongs 1994) ★★★, *People & Places* (Compass/Demon 1995) ★★★, *I Love This Town* (Compass 1996) ★★★, *Clive Gregson* (Demon 1996) ★★★, *Happy Hour* (Fellside 1999) ★★★, *Comfort And Joy* (Fellside 2001) ★★★, *Long Story Short* (Fellside 2004) ★★★.

Greig, Charlotte

b. Malta. This Wales-based singer-songwriter, harmonium player and occasional journalist has earned critical praise for her modernist take on traditional English music, fashioning a gothic indie folk sound that owes as much to cult German singer **Nico** as it does to revivalists such as **Shirley Collins** and **June Tabor**.

Raised in Somerset, England, Greig spent some time in France as a teenager before moving to London and immersing herself in the capital's nascent hip-hop scene. Despite joining the rap outfit Streetsounds, Greig also retained her love for the folk music she first heard as a child and while still in London she began performing with the Folk City Sisters. Greig moved in the mid-90s to Cardiff, Wales, where she set up a home studio with the intention of pursuing a career as a solo artist. The minimalist sound of her 1998 debut, *Night Visiting Songs*, was built around the eerie moan of Greig's Indian harmonium and dulcimer, and a primitive drum machine, with her plaintive vocals complementing the instrumentation perfectly. Her stunning take on the traditional 'Gathering Rushes' settled down alongside impressive originals including 'Vine Leaves' and 'Bury Me'.

Phil Moxham of defunct UK indie band **Young Marble Giants** offered musical assistance on Greig's follow-up, *Down In The Valley*. The album repeated the formula of her debut, mixing often startling interpretations of traditional material with Greig originals. The song cycle, *At Llangennith*, opted for a less gloomy approach, with Julian Hayman's guitar proving a bright foil to Greig's keyboard work. The album even included some folk surf songs and a cover version of Eugene Wilde's 80s pop soul hit, 'Gotta Get You Home Tonight'. Her fourth album, 2003's *Winter Woods*, marked a return to the gothic atmosphere of *Night Visiting Songs* but was also her most refined recording yet. The album attracted a string of positive reviews from the mainstream press. Greig also co-hosts the monthly acoustic club alt.Cardiff and contributes to the UK music magazine *Mojo*.

● ALBUMS: *Night Visiting Songs* (Harmonium 1998) ★★★, *Down In The Valley* (Harmonium 1999) ★★★, *At Llangennith* (Harmonium 2001) ★★★★, *Winter Woods* (Harmonium 2003) ★★★★, *Quite Silent* (Harmonium 2005) ★★★.

Greig, Stan

b. Stanley Mackay Greig, 12 August 1930, Edinburgh, Scotland. A gifted pianist and competent drummer, Greig began playing in his home-town, where his school friends and fellow musicians included **Al Fairweather** and **Sandy Brown**. He played both piano and drums with Brown in the mid to late 40s and by the mid-50s was established on the London jazz scene, working mostly in traditional jazz groups. Until the late 60s he primarily played drums but thereafter was heard more often on piano, the instrument with which he found his true, distinctive voice. Once again he stayed mostly in the traditional repertoire but also formed and led the London Jazz Big Band, in which Fairweather also played. In the late 80s he was with **Humphrey Lyttelton**, with whom he had first played in the mid-50s. A solid, blues-based pianist, Greig is an exceptionally interesting soloist and as a band member knows few equals in his field.

Rhythmically forceful, perhaps as a result of his drumming, he enhances every rhythm section in which he works.
● ALBUMS: *Blues Every Time* (Calligraph 1985) ★★★.
● COMPILATIONS: *Boogie Woogie 1971/1997 recordings* (Lake 1999) ★★★.

Gren

A trio of Brett White (vocals/guitar), Marcus Gonzales (bass) and Possum (drums), Gren formed in Los Angeles, California, USA, in the spring of 1994. Two of the songs featured on their first four-track demo cassette were then included on I.R.S. Records' *Six Sided Single* compilation, a series that highlights unsigned talent. IRS duly offered the group a contract, resulting in the release of *French Fries Optional* in 1995. Produced by Tim O'Heir (**Sebadoh**, **Belly**, **Dinosaur Jr**) at Fort Apache Studios, it was promoted by a support slot on the **Ramones**' US tour of that year. The record's youthful bluster and catchy pop punk sound prompted immediate comparisons with **Green Day** and **Rancid**.
● ALBUMS: *French Fries Optional* (I.R.S. 1995) ★★★.

Grenadine

One of several bands signed to the Simple Machines label (through vocalist/guitarist Mark Robinson's own label, TeenBeat), Grenadine formed in Washington, DC, USA, in the early 90s. Previously, **Jenny Toomey** (guitar/vocals) had played in several local bands including Geek, My New Boyfriend, and the short-lived acoustic duo Choke and labelmates **Tsunami**. Robinson's previous bands included **Unrest**, while he also concurrently played in **Air Miami**. Rob Christiansen formerly played both guitar and trombone in **Eggs**. Grenadine offered the trio an outlet for their fixation with pre-war dancehall music, jitterbugs and vaudeville. Their arrival saw them bracketed with UK bands such as **Stereolab** currently espousing the 'easy listening' or 'lounge' tradition, although there was some evidence that Grenadine's commitment to such source music was more authentic than many of their peers (they also, accordingly, wore the required ball-gowns/dinner jackets). They made their debut in 1992 with the 'Trilogy' 7-inch, which was followed by a full-length album for **Kramer**'s **Shimmy-Disc** label in 1993. Two further singles, 'Don't Forget The Halo' and 'Christiansen', preceded the release of 1994's *Nopalitos*. Songs on this collection such as 'Mexico Big Sky' and 'What On Earth Has Happened To Today's Youth' were firmly tongue-in-cheek. The critical reaction, perhaps unsurprisingly, was outright confusion. Afterwards, Robinson concentrated on the increasingly successful activities of Air Miami, while Toomey returned to Tsunami and also collaborated with Dan Littleton and Trey Many in Liquorice.
● ALBUMS: *Goya* (Simple Machines/TeenBeat/Shimmy-Disc 1993) ★★★, *Nopalitos* (Simple Machine/TeenBeat 1994) ★★.